A2 ALTITUDE CORRECTION TABLES 10°-90°—SUN, STARS, PLANETS

SUN

OCT.—MAR.

App. Alt.	Lower Limb	Upper Limb
° ′	′	′
9 33	+10·8	−21·5
9 45	+10·9	−21·4
9 56	+11·0	−21·3
10 08	+11·1	−21·2
10 20	+11·2	−21·1
10 33	+11·3	−21·0
10 46	+11·4	−20·9
11 00	+11·5	−20·8
11 15	+11·6	−20·7
11 30	+11·7	−20·6
11 45	+11·8	−20·5
12 01	+11·9	−20·4
12 18	+12·0	−20·3
12 36	+12·1	−20·2
12 54	+12·2	−20·1
13 14	+12·3	−20·0
13 34	+12·4	−19·9
13 55	+12·5	−19·8
14 17	+12·6	−19·7
14 41	+12·7	−19·6
15 05	+12·8	−19·5
15 31	+12·9	−19·4
15 59	+13·0	−19·3
16 27	+13·1	−19·2
16 58	+13·2	−19·1
17 30	+13·3	−19·0
18 05	+13·4	−18·9
18 41	+13·5	−18·8
19 20	+13·6	−18·7
20 02	+13·7	−18·6
20 46	+13·8	−18·5
21 34	+13·9	−18·4
22 25	+14·0	−18·3
23 20	+14·1	−18·2
24 20	+14·2	−18·1
25 24	+14·3	−18·0
26 34	+14·4	−17·9
27 50	+14·5	−17·8
29 13	+14·6	−17·7
30 44	+14·7	−17·6
32 24	+14·8	−17·5
34 15	+14·9	−17·4
36 17	+15·0	−17·3
38 34	+15·1	−17·2
41 06	+15·2	−17·1
43 56	+15·3	−17·0
47 07	+15·4	−16·9
50 43	+15·5	−16·8
54 46	+15·6	−16·7
59 21	+15·7	−16·6
64 28	+15·8	−16·5
70 10	+15·9	−16·4
76 24	+16·0	−16·3
83 05	+16·1	−16·2
90 00		

APR.—SEPT.

App. Alt.	Lower Limb	Upper Limb
° ′	′	′
9 39	+10·6	−21·2
9 50	+10·7	−21·1
10 02	+10·8	−21·0
10 14	+10·9	−20·9
10 27	+11·0	−20·8
10 40	+11·1	−20·7
10 53	+11·2	−20·6
11 07	+11·3	−20·5
11 22	+11·4	−20·4
11 37	+11·5	−20·3
11 53	+11·6	−20·2
12 10	+11·7	−20·1
12 27	+11·8	−20·0
12 45	+11·9	−19·9
13 04	+12·0	−19·8
13 24	+12·1	−19·7
13 44	+12·2	−19·6
14 06	+12·3	−19·5
14 29	+12·4	−19·4
14 53	+12·5	−19·3
15 18	+12·6	−19·2
15 45	+12·7	−19·1
16 13	+12·8	−19·0
16 43	+12·9	−18·9
17 14	+13·0	−18·8
17 47	+13·1	−18·7
18 23	+13·2	−18·6
19 00	+13·3	−18·5
19 41	+13·4	−18·4
20 24	+13·5	−18·3
21 10	+13·6	−18·2
21 59	+13·7	−18·1
22 52	+13·8	−18·0
23 49	+13·9	−17·9
24 51	+14·0	−17·8
25 58	+14·1	−17·7
27 11	+14·2	−17·6
28 31	+14·3	−17·5
29 58	+14·4	−17·4
31 33	+14·5	−17·3
33 18	+14·6	−17·2
35 15	+14·7	−17·1
37 24	+14·8	−17·0
39 48	+14·9	−16·9
42 28	+15·0	−16·8
45 29	+15·1	−16·7
48 52	+15·2	−16·6
52 41	+15·3	−16·5
56 59	+15·4	−16·4
61 50	+15·5	−16·3
67 15	+15·6	−16·2
73 14	+15·7	−16·1
79 42	+15·8	−16·0
86 31	+15·9	−15·9
90 00		

STARS AND PLANETS

App Alt.	Corrⁿ
° ′	′
9 55	−5·3
10 07	−5·2
10 20	−5·1
10 32	−5·0
10 46	−4·9
10 59	−4·8
11 14	−4·7
11 29	−4·6
11 44	−4·5
12 00	−4·4
12 17	−4·3
12 35	−4·2
12 53	−4·1
13 12	−4·0
13 32	−3·9
13 53	−3·8
14 16	−3·7
14 39	−3·6
15 03	−3·5
15 29	−3·4
15 56	−3·3
16 25	−3·2
16 55	−3·1
17 27	−3·0
18 01	−2·9
18 37	−2·8
19 16	−2·7
19 56	−2·6
20 40	−2·5
21 27	−2·4
22 17	−2·3
23 11	−2·2
24 09	−2·1
25 12	−2·0
26 20	−1·9
27 34	−1·8
28 54	−1·7
30 22	−1·6
31 58	−1·5
33 43	−1·4
35 38	−1·3
37 45	−1·2
40 06	−1·1
42 42	−1·0
45 34	−0·9
48 45	−0·8
52 16	−0·7
56 09	−0·6
60 26	−0·5
65 06	−0·4
70 09	−0·3
75 32	−0·2
81 12	−0·1
87 03	0·0
90 00	

App. Alt. / Additional Corrⁿ

2016

VENUS

Jan. 1–Dec. 3

°	′
0	+0·1
60	

Dec. 4–Dec. 31

°	′
0	+0·2
41	+0·1
76	

MARS

Jan. 1–Mar. 11
Sept. 16–Dec. 31

°	′
0	+0·1
60	

Mar. 12–Apr. 30
July 5–Sept. 15

°	′
0	+0·2
41	+0·1
76	

May 1–July 4

°	′
0	+0·3
34	+0·2
60	+0·1
80	

DIP

Ht. of Eye (m)	Corrⁿ (′)	Ht. of Eye (ft.)
2·4	−2·8	8·0
2·6	−2·9	8·6
2·8	−3·0	9·2
3·0	−3·1	9·8
3·2	−3·2	10·5
3·4	−3·3	11·2
3·6	−3·4	11·9
3·8	−3·5	12·6
4·0	−3·6	13·3
4·3	−3·7	14·1
4·5	−3·8	14·9
4·7	−3·9	15·7
5·0	−4·0	16·5
5·2	−4·1	17·4
5·5	−4·2	18·3
5·8	−4·3	19·1
6·1	−4·4	20·1
6·3	−4·5	21·0
6·6	−4·6	22·0
6·9	−4·7	22·9
7·2	−4·8	23·9
7·5	−4·9	24·9
7·9	−5·0	26·0
8·2	−5·1	27·1
8·5	−5·2	28·1
8·8	−5·3	29·2
9·2	−5·4	30·4
9·5	−5·5	31·5
9·9	−5·6	32·7
10·3	−5·7	33·9
10·6	−5·8	35·1
11·0	−5·9	36·3
11·4	−6·0	37·6
11·8	−6·1	38·9
12·2	−6·2	40·1
12·6	−6·3	41·5
13·0	−6·4	42·8
13·4	−6·5	44·2
13·8	−6·6	45·5
14·2	−6·7	46·9
14·7	−6·8	48·4
15·1	−6·9	49·8
15·5	−7·0	51·3
16·0	−7·1	52·8
16·5	−7·2	54·3
16·9	−7·3	55·8
17·4	−7·4	57·4
17·9	−7·5	58·9
18·4	−7·6	60·5
18·8	−7·7	62·1
19·3	−7·8	63·8
19·8	−7·9	65·4
20·4	−8·0	67·1
20·9	−8·1	68·8
21·4		70·5

Ht. of Eye	Corrⁿ
m	′
1·0	− 1·8
1·5	− 2·2
2·0	− 2·5
2·5	− 2·8
3·0	− 3·0
See table ←	
m	′
20	− 7·9
22	− 8·3
24	− 8·6
26	− 9·0
28	− 9·3
30	− 9·6
32	−10·0
34	−10·3
36	−10·6
38	−10·8
40	−11·1
42	−11·4
44	−11·7
46	−11·9
48	−12·2
ft.	′
2	− 1·4
4	− 1·9
6	− 2·4
8	− 2·7
10	− 3·1
See table ←	
ft.	′
70	− 8·1
75	− 8·4
80	− 8·7
85	− 8·9
90	− 9·2
95	− 9·5
100	− 9·7
105	− 9·9
110	−10·2
115	−10·4
120	−10·6
125	−10·8
130	−11·1
135	−11·3
140	−11·5
145	−11·7
150	−11·9
155	−12·1

App. Alt. = Apparent altitude = Sextant altitude corrected for index error and dip.

ALTITUDE CORRECTION TABLES 0°-10°—SUN, STARS, PLANETS A3

App. Alt.	OCT.—MAR. SUN Lower Limb	OCT.—MAR. SUN Upper Limb	APR.—SEPT. SUN Lower Limb	APR.—SEPT. SUN Upper Limb	STARS PLANETS
° ′	′	′	′	′	′
0 00	−17·5	−49·8	−17·8	−49·6	−33·8
0 03	16·9	49·2	17·2	49·0	33·2
0 06	16·3	48·6	16·6	48·4	32·6
0 09	15·7	48·0	16·0	47·8	32·0
0 12	15·2	47·5	15·4	47·2	31·5
0 15	14·6	46·9	14·8	46·6	30·9
0 18	−14·1	−46·4	−14·3	−46·1	−30·4
0 21	13·5	45·8	13·8	45·6	29·8
0 24	13·0	45·3	13·3	45·1	29·3
0 27	12·5	44·8	12·8	44·6	28·8
0 30	12·0	44·3	12·3	44·1	28·3
0 33	11·6	43·9	11·8	43·6	27·9
0 36	−11·1	−43·4	−11·3	−43·1	−27·4
0 39	10·6	42·9	10·9	42·7	26·9
0 42	10·2	42·5	10·5	42·3	26·5
0 45	9·8	42·1	10·0	41·8	26·1
0 48	9·4	41·7	9·6	41·4	25·7
0 51	9·0	41·3	9·2	41·0	25·3
0 54	− 8·6	−40·9	− 8·8	−40·6	−24·9
0 57	8·2	40·5	8·4	40·2	24·5
1 00	7·8	40·1	8·0	39·8	24·1
1 03	7·4	39·7	7·7	39·5	23·7
1 06	7·1	39·4	7·3	39·1	23·4
1 09	6·7	39·0	7·0	38·8	23·0
1 12	− 6·4	−38·7	− 6·6	−38·4	−22·7
1 15	6·0	38·3	6·3	38·1	22·3
1 18	5·7	38·0	6·0	37·8	22·0
1 21	5·4	37·7	5·7	37·5	21·7
1 24	5·1	37·4	5·3	37·1	21·4
1 27	4·8	37·1	5·0	36·8	21·1
1 30	− 4·5	−36·8	− 4·7	−36·5	−20·8
1 35	4·0	36·3	4·3	36·1	20·3
1 40	3·6	35·9	3·8	35·6	19·9
1 45	3·1	35·4	3·4	35·2	19·4
1 50	2·7	35·0	2·9	34·7	19·0
1 55	2·3	34·6	2·5	34·3	18·6
2 00	− 1·9	−34·2	− 2·1	−33·9	−18·2
2 05	1·5	33·8	1·7	33·5	17·8
2 10	1·1	33·4	1·4	33·2	17·4
2 15	0·8	33·1	1·0	32·8	17·1
2 20	0·4	32·7	0·7	32·5	16·7
2 25	− 0·1	32·4	− 0·3	32·1	16·4
2 30	+ 0·2	−32·1	0·0	−31·8	−16·1
2 35	0·5	31·8	+ 0·3	31·5	15·8
2 40	0·8	31·5	0·6	31·2	15·4
2 45	1·1	31·2	0·9	30·9	15·2
2 50	1·4	30·9	1·2	30·6	14·9
2 55	1·7	30·6	1·4	30·4	14·6
3 00	+ 2·0	−30·3	+ 1·7	−30·1	−14·3
3 05	2·2	30·1	2·0	29·8	14·1
3 10	2·5	29·8	2·2	29·6	13·8
3 15	2·7	29·6	2·5	29·3	13·6
3 20	2·9	29·4	2·7	29·1	13·4
3 25	3·2	29·1	2·9	28·9	13·1
3 30	+ 3·4	−28·9	+ 3·1	−28·7	−12·9

App. Alt.	OCT.—MAR. SUN Lower Limb	OCT.—MAR. SUN Upper Limb	APR.—SEPT. SUN Lower Limb	APR.—SEPT. SUN Upper Limb	STARS PLANETS
° ′	′	′	′	′	′
3 30	+ 3·4	−28·9	+ 3·1	−28·7	−12·9
3 35	3·6	28·7	3·3	28·5	12·7
3 40	3·8	28·5	3·6	28·2	12·5
3 45	4·0	28·3	3·8	28·0	12·3
3 50	4·2	28·1	4·0	27·8	12·1
3 55	4·4	27·9	4·1	27·7	11·9
4 00	+ 4·6	−27·7	+ 4·3	−27·5	−11·7
4 05	4·8	27·5	4·5	27·3	11·5
4 10	4·9	27·4	4·7	27·1	11·4
4 15	5·1	27·2	4·9	26·9	11·2
4 20	5·3	27·0	5·0	26·8	11·0
4 25	5·4	26·9	5·2	26·6	10·9
4 30	+ 5·6	−26·7	+ 5·3	−26·5	−10·7
4 35	5·7	26·6	5·5	26·3	10·6
4 40	5·9	26·4	5·6	26·2	10·4
4 45	6·0	26·3	5·8	26·0	10·3
4 50	6·2	26·1	5·9	25·9	10·1
4 55	6·3	26·0	6·1	25·7	10·0
5 00	+ 6·4	−25·9	+ 6·2	−25·6	− 9·8
5 05	6·6	25·7	6·3	25·5	9·7
5 10	6·7	25·6	6·5	25·3	9·6
5 15	6·8	25·5	6·6	25·2	9·5
5 20	7·0	25·3	6·7	25·1	9·3
5 25	7·1	25·2	6·8	25·0	9·2
5 30	+ 7·2	−25·1	+ 6·9	−24·9	− 9·1
5 35	7·3	25·0	7·1	24·7	9·0
5 40	7·4	24·9	7·2	24·6	8·9
5 45	7·5	24·8	7·3	24·5	8·8
5 50	7·6	24·7	7·4	24·4	8·7
5 55	7·7	24·6	7·5	24·3	8·6
6 00	+ 7·8	−24·5	+ 7·6	−24·2	− 8·5
6 10	8·0	24·3	7·8	24·0	8·3
6 20	8·2	24·1	8·0	23·8	8·1
6 30	8·4	23·9	8·2	23·6	7·9
6 40	8·6	23·7	8·3	23·5	7·7
6 50	8·7	23·6	8·5	23·3	7·6
7 00	+ 8·9	−23·4	+ 8·7	−23·1	− 7·4
7 10	9·1	23·2	8·8	23·0	7·2
7 20	9·2	23·1	9·0	22·8	7·1
7 30	9·3	23·0	9·1	22·7	6·9
7 40	9·5	22·8	9·2	22·6	6·8
7 50	9·6	22·7	9·4	22·4	6·7
8 00	+ 9·7	−22·6	+ 9·5	−22·3	− 6·6
8 10	9·9	22·4	9·6	22·2	6·4
8 20	10·0	22·3	9·7	22·1	6·3
8 30	10·1	22·2	9·9	21·9	6·2
8 40	10·2	22·1	10·0	21·8	6·1
8 50	10·3	22·0	10·1	21·7	6·0
9 00	+10·4	−21·9	+10·2	−21·6	− 5·9
9 10	10·5	21·8	10·3	21·5	5·8
9 20	10·6	21·7	10·4	21·4	5·7
9 30	10·7	21·6	10·5	21·3	5·6
9 40	10·8	21·5	10·6	21·2	5·5
9 50	10·9	21·4	10·6	21·2	5·4
10 00	+11·0	−21·3	+10·7	−21·1	− 5·3

Additional corrections for temperature and pressure are given on the following page.

For bubble sextant observations ignore dip and use the star corrections for Sun, planets and stars.

ALTITUDE CORRECTION TABLES—ADDITIONAL CORRECTIONS

ADDITIONAL REFRACTION CORRECTIONS FOR NON-STANDARD CONDITIONS

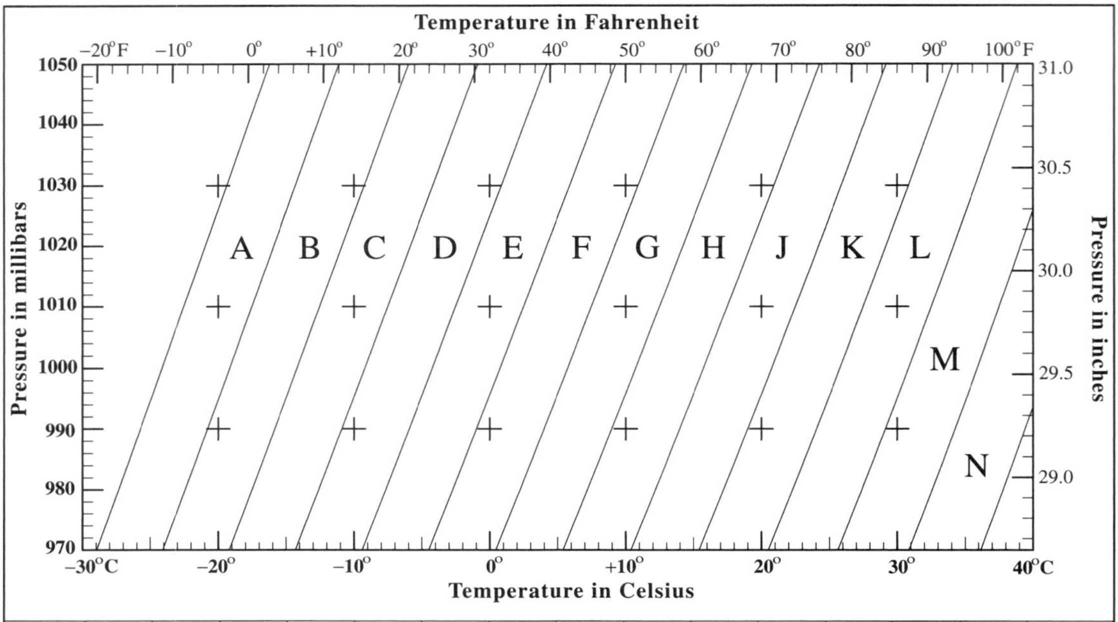

Temperature in Fahrenheit

−20°F −10° 0° +10° 20° 30° 40° 50° 60° 70° 80° 90° 100°F

Pressure in millibars: 1050 1040 1030 1020 1010 1000 990 980 970

Pressure in inches: 31.0 30.5 30.0 29.5 29.0

A B C D E F G H J K L M N

−30°C −20° −10° 0° +10° 20° 30° 40°C

Temperature in Celsius

App. Alt.	A	B	C	D	E	F	G	H	J	K	L	M	N	P	App. Alt.
° ′	′	′	′	′	′	′	′	′	′	′	′	′	′	′	° ′
00 00	−7·3	−5·9	−4·6	−3·4	−2·2	−1·1	0·0	+1·0	+2·0	+3·0	+4·0	+4·9	+5·9	+6·9	**00 00**
00 30	5·5	4·5	3·5	2·6	1·7	0·8	0·0	0·8	1·6	2·3	3·1	3·8	4·5	5·3	**00 30**
01 00	4·4	3·5	2·8	2·0	1·3	0·7	0·0	0·6	1·2	1·8	2·4	3·0	3·6	4·2	**01 00**
01 30	3·5	2·9	2·2	1·7	1·1	0·5	0·0	0·5	1·0	1·5	2·0	2·5	2·9	3·4	**01 30**
02 00	2·9	2·4	1·9	1·4	0·9	0·4	0·0	0·4	0·8	1·3	1·7	2·0	2·4	2·8	**02 00**
02 30	−2·5	−2·0	−1·6	−1·2	−0·8	−0·4	0·0	+0·4	+0·7	+1·1	+1·4	+1·7	+2·1	+2·4	**02 30**
03 00	2·1	1·7	1·4	1·0	0·7	0·3	0·0	0·3	0·6	0·9	1·2	1·5	1·8	2·1	**03 00**
03 30	1·9	1·5	1·2	0·9	0·6	0·3	0·0	0·3	0·5	0·8	1·1	1·3	1·6	1·8	**03 30**
04 00	1·6	1·3	1·1	0·8	0·5	0·3	0·0	0·2	0·5	0·7	0·9	1·2	1·4	1·6	**04 00**
04 30	1·5	1·2	0·9	0·7	0·5	0·2	0·0	0·2	0·4	0·6	0·8	1·0	1·3	1·5	**04 30**
05 00	−1·3	−1·1	−0·9	−0·6	−0·4	−0·2	0·0	+0·2	+0·4	+0·6	+0·8	+0·9	+1·1	+1·3	**05 00**
06	1·1	0·9	0·7	0·5	0·3	0·2	0·0	0·2	0·3	0·5	0·6	0·8	0·9	1·1	**06**
07	1·0	0·8	0·6	0·5	0·3	0·1	0·0	0·1	0·3	0·4	0·5	0·7	0·8	0·9	**07**
08	0·8	0·7	0·5	0·4	0·3	0·1	0·0	0·1	0·2	0·4	0·5	0·6	0·7	0·8	**08**
09	0·7	0·6	0·5	0·4	0·2	0·1	0·0	0·1	0·2	0·3	0·4	0·5	0·6	0·7	**09**
10 00	−0·7	−0·5	−0·4	−0·3	−0·2	−0·1	0·0	+0·1	+0·2	+0·3	+0·4	+0·5	+0·6	+0·7	**10 00**
12	0·6	0·5	0·4	0·3	0·2	0·1	0·0	0·1	0·2	0·2	0·3	0·4	0·5	0·5	**12**
14	0·5	0·4	0·3	0·2	0·1	0·1	0·0	0·1	0·1	0·2	0·3	0·3	0·4	0·5	**14**
16	0·4	0·3	0·3	0·2	0·1	0·1	0·0	0·1	0·1	0·2	0·2	0·3	0·3	0·4	**16**
18	0·4	0·3	0·2	0·2	0·1	−0·1	0·0	+0·1	0·1	0·2	0·2	0·3	0·3	0·4	**18**
20 00	−0·3	−0·3	−0·2	−0·2	−0·1	0·0	0·0	0·0	+0·1	+0·1	+0·2	+0·2	+0·3	+0·3	**20 00**
25	0·3	0·2	0·2	0·1	0·1	0·0	0·0	0·0	0·1	0·1	0·1	0·2	0·2	0·2	**25**
30	0·2	0·2	0·1	0·1	0·1	0·0	0·0	0·0	+0·1	0·1	0·1	0·1	0·2	0·2	**30**
35	0·2	0·1	0·1	0·1	−0·1	0·0	0·0	0·0	0·0	0·1	0·1	0·1	0·1	0·2	**35**
40	0·1	0·1	0·1	−0·1	0·0	0·0	0·0	0·0	0·0	+0·1	0·1	0·1	0·1	0·1	**40**
50 00	−0·1	−0·1	−0·1	0·0	0·0	0·0	0·0	0·0	0·0	0·0	+0·1	+0·1	+0·1	+0·1	**50 00**

The graph is entered with arguments temperature and pressure to find a zone letter; using as arguments this zone letter and apparent altitude (sextant altitude corrected for index error and dip), a correction is taken from the table. This correction is to be applied to the sextant altitude in addition to the corrections for standard conditions (for the Sun, stars and planets from page A2-A3 and for the Moon from pages xxxiv and xxxv).

2016
Nautical Almanac
COMMERCIAL EDITION

PUBLISHED BY:

Paradise Cay Publications, Inc.
Post Office Box 29
Arcata, CA 95518-0029
Tel: 1-707-822-9063
Fax: 1-707-822-9163
www.paracay.com

ISBN: 978-1-937196-33-2

Printed and distributed with permission by Paradise Cay Publications, Inc.

NOTE

Every care is taken to prevent errors in the production of this publication. As a final precaution it is recommended that the sequence of pages in this copy be examined on receipt. If faulty, it should be returned for replacement.

PREFACE

The first three sections of this book are a complete and accurate duplication from *The Nautical Almanac* produced jointly by Her Majesty's Nautical Almanac Office, United Kingdom Hydrographic Office, Admiralty Way, Taunton, Somerset, TA1 2DN, United Kingdom and the Nautical Almanac Office of the US Naval Observatory.

We gratefully acknowledge the United Kingdom Hydrographic Office and the United States Naval Observatory for permission to use the material contained in the almanac sections of this publication.

The 2016 Nautical Almanac
Commercial Edition

RELIGIOUS CALENDARS

Epiphany	Jan. 6	Low Sunday	Apr. 3
Septuagesima Sunday	Jan. 24	Rogation Sunday	May 1
Quinquagesima Sunday	Feb. 7	Ascension Day—Holy Thursday	May 5
Ash Wednesday	Feb. 10	Whit Sunday—Pentecost	May 15
Quadragesima Sunday	Feb. 14	Trinity Sunday	May 22
Palm Sunday	Mar. 20	Corpus Christi	May 26
Good Friday	Mar. 25	First Sunday in Advent	Nov. 27
Easter Day	Mar. 27	Christmas Day (Sunday)	Dec. 25
First Day of Passover (Pesach)	Apr. 23	Day of Atonement (Yom Kippur)	Oct. 12
Feast of Weeks (Shavuot)	June 12	First day of Tabernacles (Succoth)	Oct. 17
Jewish New Year 5777 (Rosh Hashanah)	Oct. 3		
Ramadân, First day of (tabular)	June 7	Islamic New Year (1438)	Oct. 3

The Jewish and Islamic dates above are tabular dates, which begin at sunset on the previous evening and end at sunset on the date tabulated. In practice, the dates of Islamic fasts and festivals are determined by an actual sighting of the appropriate new moon.

CIVIL CALENDAR—UNITED KINGDOM

Accession of Queen Elizabeth II	Feb. 6	Birthday of Prince Philip, Duke of Edinburgh	June 10
St David (Wales)	Mar. 1	The Queen's Official Birthday†	June 11
Commonwealth Day	Mar. 14	Remembrance Sunday	Nov. 13
St Patrick (Ireland)	Mar. 17	Birthday of the Prince of Wales	Nov. 14
Birthday of Queen Elizabeth II	Apr. 21	St Andrew (Scotland)	Nov. 30
St George (England)	Apr. 23		
Coronation Day	June 2		

PUBLIC HOLIDAYS

England and Wales—Jan. 1†, Mar. 25, Mar. 28, May 2†, May 30, Aug. 29, Dec. 26, Dec. 27

Northern Ireland—Jan. 1†, Mar. 17, Mar. 25, Mar. 28, May 2†, May 30, July 12†, Aug. 29, Dec. 26, Dec. 27

Scotland—Jan. 1, Jan. 4†, Mar. 25, May 2, May 30†, Aug. 1, Dec. 26†, Dec. 27

CIVIL CALENDAR—UNITED STATES OF AMERICA

New Year's Day	Jan. 1	Labor Day	Sept. 5
Martin Luther King's Birthday	Jan. 18	Columbus Day	Oct. 10
Washington's Birthday	Feb. 15	General Election Day	Nov. 8
Memorial Day	May 30	Veterans Day	Nov. 11
Independence Day	July 4	Thanksgiving Day	Nov. 24

†Dates subject to confirmation

PHASES OF THE MOON

New Moon	d h m	First Quarter	d h m	Full Moon	d h m	Last Quarter	d h m
						Jan.	2 05 30
Jan.	10 01 31	Jan.	16 23 26	Jan.	24 01 46	Feb.	1 03 28
Feb.	8 14 39	Feb.	15 07 46	Feb.	22 18 20	Mar.	1 23 11
Mar.	9 01 54	Mar.	15 17 03	Mar.	23 12 01	Mar.	31 15 17
Apr.	7 11 24	Apr.	14 03 59	Apr.	22 05 24	Apr.	30 03 29
May	6 19 30	May	13 17 02	May	21 21 14	May	29 12 12
June	5 03 00	June	12 08 10	June	20 11 02	June	27 18 19
July	4 11 01	July	12 00 52	July	19 22 57	July	26 23 00
Aug.	2 20 45	Aug.	10 18 21	Aug.	18 09 27	Aug.	25 03 41
Sept.	1 09 03	Sept.	9 11 49	Sept.	16 19 05	Sept.	23 09 56
Oct.	1 00 11	Oct.	9 04 33	Oct.	16 04 23	Oct.	22 19 14
Oct.	30 17 38	Nov.	7 19 51	Nov.	14 13 52	Nov.	21 08 33
Nov.	29 12 18	Dec.	7 09 03	Dec.	14 00 06	Dec.	21 01 56
Dec.	29 06 53						

DAYS OF THE WEEK AND DAYS OF THE YEAR

	JAN.		FEB.		MAR.		APR.		MAY		JUNE		JULY		AUG.		SEPT.		OCT.		NOV.		DEC.	
Day	Wk	Yr	Wk	Yr	Wk	Yr	Wk	Yr	Wk	Yr	Wk	Yr	Wk	Yr	Wk	Yr	Wk	Yr	Wk	Yr	Wk	Yr	Wk	Yr
1	F.	1	M.	32	Tu.	61	F.	92	Su.	122	W.	153	F.	183	M.	214	Th.	245	Sa.	275	Tu.	306	Th.	336
2	Sa.	2	Tu.	33	W.	62	Sa.	93	M.	123	Th.	154	Sa.	184	Tu.	215	F.	246	Su.	276	W.	307	F.	337
3	Su.	3	W.	34	Th.	63	Su.	94	Tu.	124	F.	155	Su.	185	W.	216	Sa.	247	M.	277	Th.	308	Sa.	338
4	M.	4	Th.	35	F.	64	M.	95	W.	125	Sa.	156	M.	186	Th.	217	Su.	248	Tu.	278	F.	309	Su.	339
5	Tu.	5	F.	36	Sa.	65	Tu.	96	Th.	126	Su.	157	Tu.	187	F.	218	M.	249	W.	279	Sa.	310	M.	340
6	W.	6	Sa.	37	Su.	66	W.	97	F.	127	M.	158	W.	188	Sa.	219	Tu.	250	Th.	280	Su.	311	Tu.	341
7	Th.	7	Su.	38	M.	67	Th.	98	Sa.	128	Tu.	159	Th.	189	Su.	220	W.	251	F.	281	M.	312	W.	342
8	F.	8	M.	39	Tu.	68	F.	99	Su.	129	W.	160	F.	190	M.	221	Th.	252	Sa.	282	Tu.	313	Th.	343
9	Sa.	9	Tu.	40	W.	69	Sa.	100	M.	130	Th.	161	Sa.	191	Tu.	222	F.	253	Su.	283	W.	314	F.	344
10	Su.	10	W.	41	Th.	70	Su.	101	Tu.	131	F.	162	Su.	192	W.	223	Sa.	254	M.	284	Th.	315	Sa.	345
11	M.	11	Th.	42	F.	71	M.	102	W.	132	Sa.	163	M.	193	Th.	224	Su.	255	Tu.	285	F.	316	Su.	346
12	Tu.	12	F.	43	Sa.	72	Tu.	103	Th.	133	Su.	164	Tu.	194	F.	225	M.	256	W.	286	Sa.	317	M.	347
13	W.	13	Sa.	44	Su.	73	W.	104	F.	134	M.	165	W.	195	Sa.	226	Tu.	257	Th.	287	Su.	318	Tu.	348
14	Th.	14	Su.	45	M.	74	Th.	105	Sa.	135	Tu.	166	Th.	196	Su.	227	W.	258	F.	288	M.	319	W.	349
15	F.	15	M.	46	Tu.	75	F.	106	Su.	136	W.	167	F.	197	M.	228	Th.	259	Sa.	289	Tu.	320	Th.	350
16	Sa.	16	Tu.	47	W.	76	Sa.	107	M.	137	Th.	168	Sa.	198	Tu.	229	F.	260	Su.	290	W.	321	F.	351
17	Su.	17	W.	48	Th.	77	Su.	108	Tu.	138	F.	169	Su.	199	W.	230	Sa.	261	M.	291	Th.	322	Sa.	352
18	M.	18	Th.	49	F.	78	M.	109	W.	139	Sa.	170	M.	200	Th.	231	Su.	262	Tu.	292	F.	323	Su.	353
19	Tu.	19	F.	50	Sa.	79	Tu.	110	Th.	140	Su.	171	Tu.	201	F.	232	M.	263	W.	293	Sa.	324	M.	354
20	W.	20	Sa.	51	Su.	80	W.	111	F.	141	M.	172	W.	202	Sa.	233	Tu.	264	Th.	294	Su.	325	Tu.	355
21	Th.	21	Su.	52	M.	81	Th.	112	Sa.	142	Tu.	173	Th.	203	Su.	234	W.	265	F.	295	M.	326	W.	356
22	F.	22	M.	53	Tu.	82	F.	113	Su.	143	W.	174	F.	204	M.	235	Th.	266	Sa.	296	Tu.	327	Th.	357
23	Sa.	23	Tu.	54	W.	83	Sa.	114	M.	144	Th.	175	Sa.	205	Tu.	236	F.	267	Su.	297	W.	328	F.	358
24	Su.	24	W.	55	Th.	84	Su.	115	Tu.	145	F.	176	Su.	206	W.	237	Sa.	268	M.	298	Th.	329	Sa.	359
25	M.	25	Th.	56	F.	85	M.	116	W.	146	Sa.	177	M.	207	Th.	238	Su.	269	Tu.	299	F.	330	Su.	360
26	Tu.	26	F.	57	Sa.	86	Tu.	117	Th.	147	Su.	178	Tu.	208	F.	239	M.	270	W.	300	Sa.	331	M.	361
27	W.	27	Sa.	58	Su.	87	W.	118	F.	148	M.	179	W.	209	Sa.	240	Tu.	271	Th.	301	Su.	332	Tu.	362
28	Th.	28	Su.	59	M.	88	Th.	119	Sa.	149	Tu.	180	Th.	210	Su.	241	W.	272	F.	302	M.	333	W.	363
29	F.	29	M.	60	Tu.	89	F.	120	Su.	150	W.	181	F.	211	M.	242	Th.	273	Sa.	303	Tu.	334	Th.	364
30	Sa.	30			W.	90	Sa.	121	M.	151	Th.	182	Sa.	212	Tu.	243	F.	274	Su.	304	W.	335	F.	365
31	Su.	31			Th.	91			Tu.	152			Su.	213	W.	244			M.	305			Sa.	366

ECLIPSES

There are two eclipses of the Sun.

1. *A total eclipse of the Sun,* March 8-9. See map on page 6. The eclipse begins on March 8 at 23^h 19^m and ends at 04^h 35^m on March 9; the total phase begins on March 9 at 00^h 17^m and ends at 03^h 38^m on March 9. The maximum duration of totality is 4^m 14^s.

2. *An annular eclipse of the Sun,* September 1. See map on page 7. The eclipse begins at 06^h 13^m and ends at 12^h 01^m; the annular phase begins at 07^h 19^m and ends at 10^h 54^m. The maximum duration of annularity is 3^m 00^s.

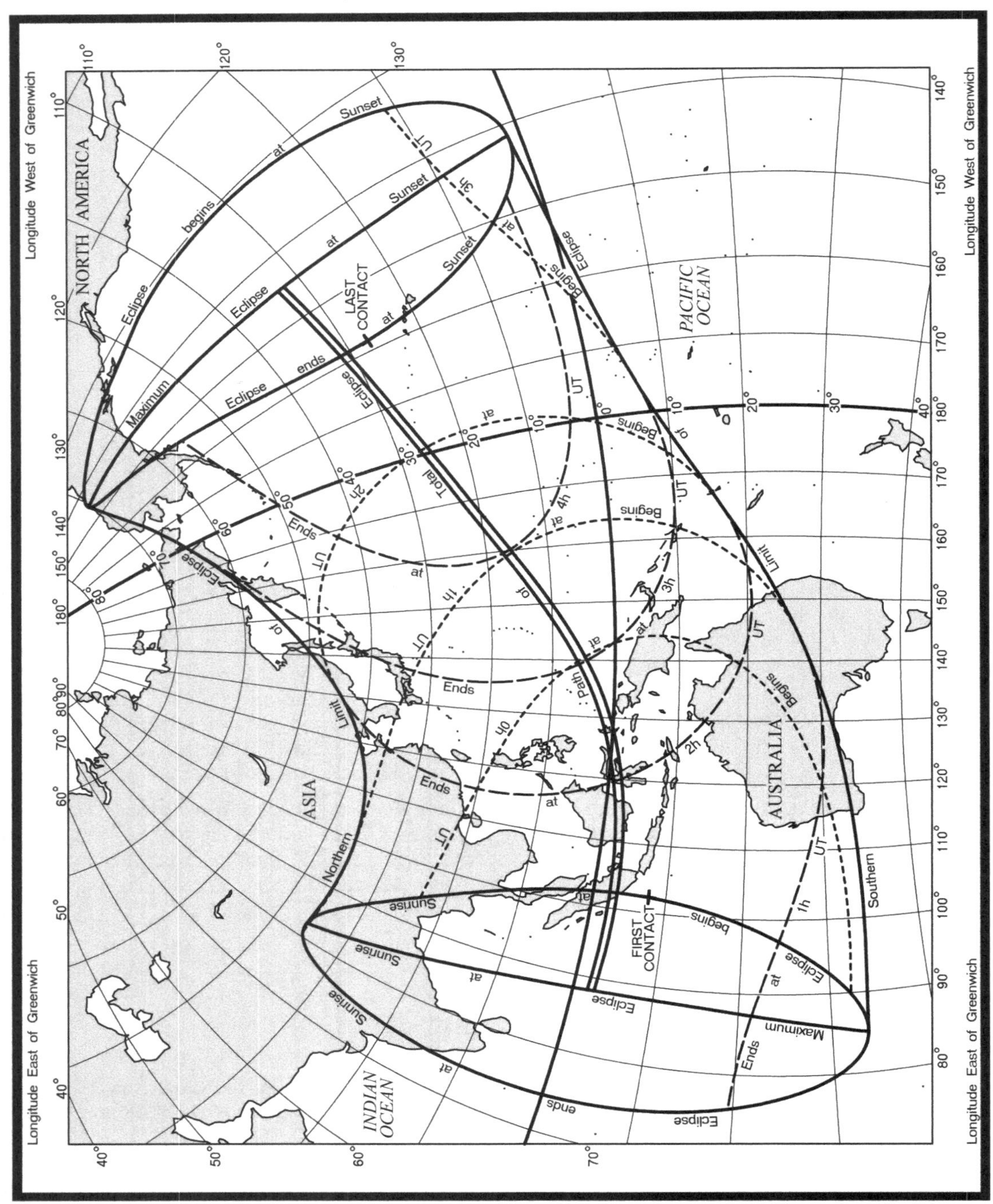

SOLAR ECLIPSE DIAGRAMS

The principal features shown on the above diagrams are: the paths of total and annular eclipses; the northern and southern limits of partial eclipse; the sunrise and sunset curves; dashed lines which show the times of beginning and end of partial eclipse at hourly intervals.

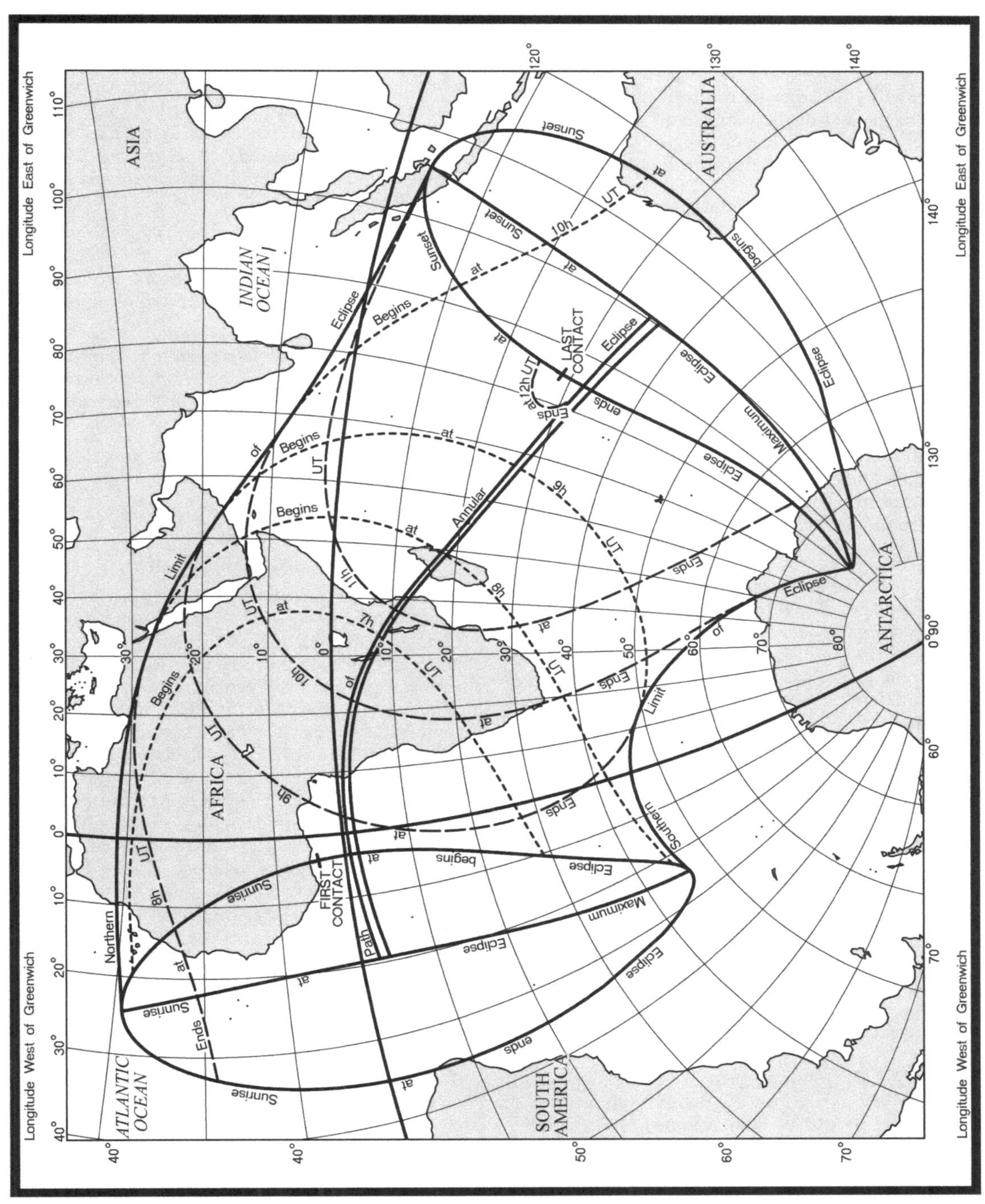

SOLAR ECLIPSE DIAGRAMS

Further details of the paths and times of central eclipse are given in *The Astronomical Almanac.*

VISIBILITY OF PLANETS

VENUS is a brilliant object in the morning sky from the beginning of the year until the end of April after which it becomes too close to the Sun for observation. From mid-July it reappears in the evening sky where it stays until the end of the year. Venus is in conjunction with Mercury on July 16 and August 27, with Jupiter on August 27 and with Saturn on Jan. 9 and Oct. 30.

MARS rises shortly after midnight at the beginning of the year in Virgo. It moves into Libra in mid-January, Scorpius from mid-March and into Ophiuchus from early April returning to Scorpius at the beginning of May. The westward elongation gradually increases until opposition on May 22, when it can be seen throughout the night. The planet enters Libra in late May, Scorpius in early August, Ophiuchus in the second half of August (passing 1°·8 N. of *Antares* on August 24), back into Scorpius in late August and once again into Ophiuchus in early September. From early September until the end of the year it can only be seen in the evening sky, moving into Sagittarius in the second half of September, Capricornus in early November and into Aquarius from mid-December. Mars is in conjunction with Saturn on August 25.

JUPITER can be seen from the beginning of the year until early March for more than half the night in Leo. It is at opposition on March 8 when it can be seen throughout the night. By early June it can be seen only in the evening sky, passing into Virgo in early August. From mid-Sept. it becomes too close to the Sun for observation until in the second week of Oct. when it reappears in the morning sky. Jupiter is in conjunction with Venus on August 27 and with Mercury on Oct. 11.

SATURN rises before sunrise at the beginning of the year in Ophiuchus, in which constellation it remains throughout the year, and can only be seen in the morning sky until early March. Its westward elongation gradually increases until it is at oppsition on June 3, when it can be seen throughout the night. From late August until late November it can only be seen in the evening sky and then becomes too close to the Sun for observation until late December, when it reappears in the morning sky. Saturn is in conjunction with Venus on January 9 and October 30 and with Mars on August 25.

MERCURY can only be seen low in the east before sunrise, or low in the west after sunset (about the time of beginning or end of civil twilight). It is visible in the mornings between the following approximate dates: January 20 (+2·2) to March 14 (−1·0), May 19 (+3·1) to June 30 (−1·5) and September 20 (+2·0) to October 15 (−1·2); the planet is brighter at the end of each period. It is visible in the evenings between the following approximate dates: January 1 (−0·4) to January 9 (+1·8), April 1 (−1·5) to April 30 (+2·7), July 15 (−1·2) to September 6 (+2·6) and November 13 (−0·7) to December 23 (+1·6); the planet is brighter at the beginning of each period. The figures in parentheses are the magnitudes.

PLANET DIAGRAM

General Description. The diagram on the opposite page shows, in graphical form for any date during the year, the local mean time of meridian passage of the Sun, of the five planets Mercury, Venus, Mars, Jupiter, and Saturn, and of each 30° of SHA; intermediate lines corresponding to particular stars, may be drawn in by the user if desired. It is intended to provide a general picture of the availability of planets and stars for observation.

On each side of the line marking the time of meridian passage of the Sun a band, 45^{m} wide, is shaded to indicate that planets and most stars crossing the meridian within 45^{m} of the Sun are too close to the Sun for observation.

Method of use and interpretation. For any date the diagram provides immediately the local mean times of meridian passage of the Sun, planets and stars, and thus the following information:

(a) whether a planet or star is too close to the Sun for observation;

(b) some indication of its position in the sky, especially during twilight;

(c) the proximity of other planets.

When the meridian passage of an outer planet occurs at midnight, the body is in opposition to the Sun and is visible all night; a planet may then be observable during both morning and evening twilights. As the time of meridian passage decreases, the body eventually ceases to be observable in the morning, but its altitude above the eastern horizon at sunset gradually increases; this continues until the body is on the meridian during evening twilight. From then onwards the body is observable above the western horizon and its altitude at sunset gradually decreases; eventually the body becomes too close to the Sun for observation. When the body again becomes visible it is seen low in the east during morning twilight; its altitude at sunrise increases until meridian passage occurs during morning twilight. Then, as the time of meridian passage decreases to 0^{h}, the body is observable in the west during morning twilight with a gradually decreasing altitude, until it once again reaches opposition.

DO NOT CONFUSE

Venus with Saturn in the first half of January and again in late October to early November, with Mercury in mid-February and again in mid-July and with Jupiter in late August to the start of September; on all occasions Venus is the brighter object.

Jupiter with Mercury in the second half of August and again in mid-October; on both occasions Jupiter is the brighter object.

Saturn with Mars in late August when Mars is the brighter object, and with Mercury in mid-November when Mercury is the brighter object.

LOCAL MEAN TIME OF MERIDIAN PASSAGE

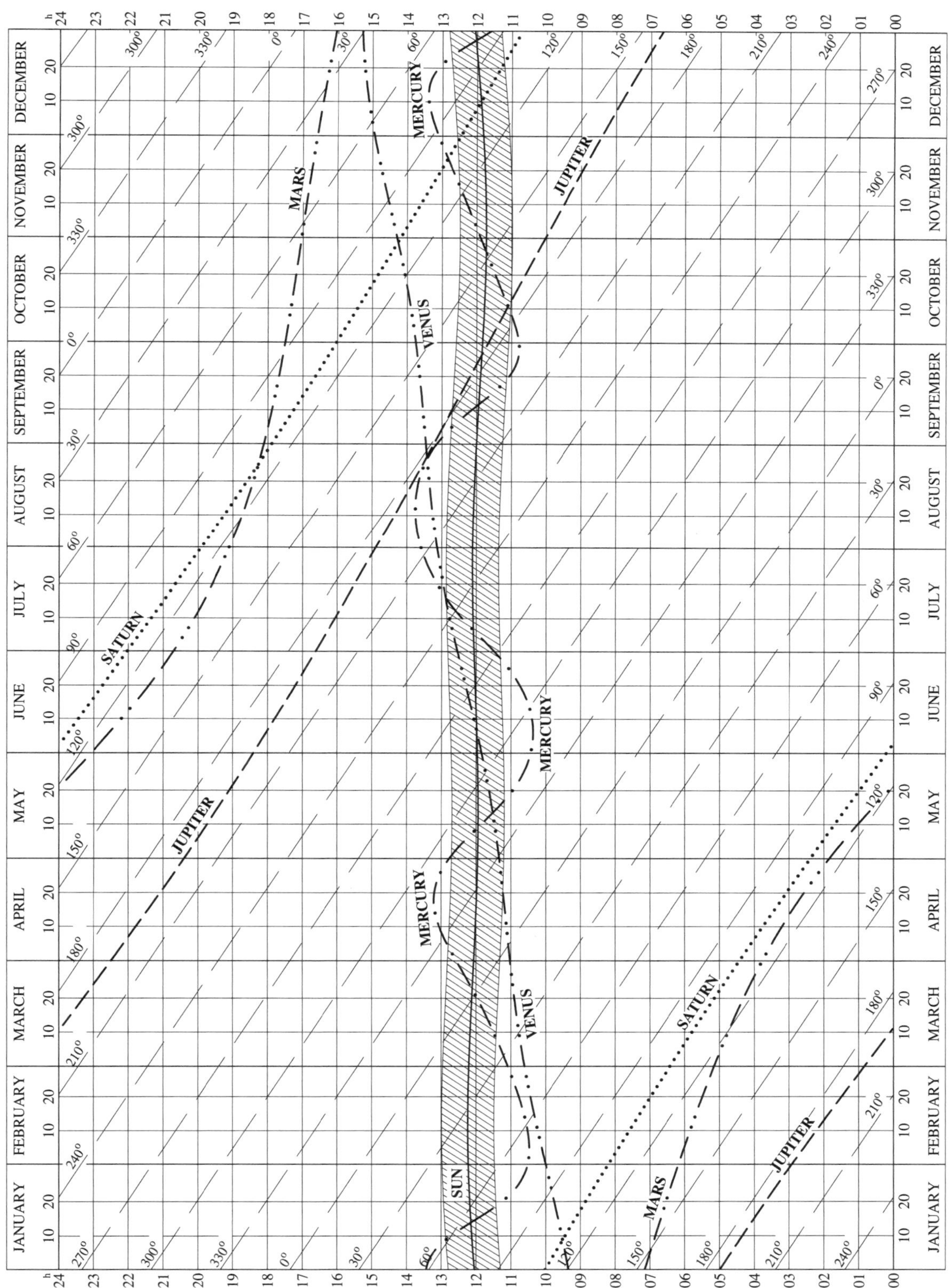

LOCAL MEAN TIME OF MERIDIAN PASSAGE

2016 JANUARY 1, 2, 3 (FRI., SAT., SUN.)

d	h	ARIES GHA	VENUS −4·0 GHA	VENUS Dec	MARS +1·2 GHA	MARS Dec	JUPITER −2·2 GHA	JUPITER Dec	SATURN +0·5 GHA	SATURN Dec
		° ′	° ′	° ′	° ′	° ′	° ′	° ′	° ′	° ′
1 FRIDAY	00	100 05.4	219 42.2	S18 36.9	253 00.9	S 9 33.5	285 53.1	N 3 51.3	210 16.0	S20 29.6
	01	115 07.9	234 41.6	37.6	268 02.1	34.0	300 55.5	51.3	225 18.2	29.6
	02	130 10.4	249 40.9	38.3	283 03.2	34.5	315 57.9	51.3	240 20.4	29.7
	03	145 12.8	264 40.3	38.9	298 04.4	35.0	331 00.3	51.3	255 22.6	29.7
	04	160 15.3	279 39.6	39.6	313 05.5	35.5	346 02.7	51.3	270 24.7	29.7
	05	175 17.8	294 38.9	40.3	328 06.7	36.0	1 05.1	51.3	285 26.9	29.8
	06	190 20.2	309 38.3	S18 40.9	343 07.8	S 9 36.5	16 07.5	N 3 51.3	300 29.1	S20 29.8
	07	205 22.7	324 37.6	41.6	358 09.0	37.0	31 10.0	51.3	315 31.3	29.8
	08	220 25.2	339 37.0	42.2	13 10.1	37.5	46 12.4	51.2	330 33.4	29.9
	09	235 27.6	354 36.3	42.9	28 11.3	37.9	61 14.8	51.2	345 35.6	29.9
	10	250 30.1	9 35.6	43.6	43 12.4	38.4	76 17.2	51.2	0 37.8	30.0
	11	265 32.6	24 35.0	44.2	58 13.6	38.9	91 19.6	51.2	15 40.0	30.0
	12	280 35.0	39 34.3	S18 44.9	73 14.7	S 9 39.4	106 22.0	N 3 51.2	30 42.1	S20 30.0
	13	295 37.5	54 33.6	45.5	88 15.8	39.9	121 24.4	51.2	45 44.3	30.1
	14	310 39.9	69 33.0	46.2	103 17.0	40.4	136 26.8	51.2	60 46.5	30.1
	15	325 42.4	84 32.3	46.9	118 18.1	40.9	151 29.2	51.2	75 48.7	30.1
	16	340 44.9	99 31.6	47.5	133 19.3	41.4	166 31.6	51.2	90 50.9	30.2
	17	355 47.3	114 31.0	48.2	148 20.4	41.9	181 34.1	51.2	105 53.0	30.2
	18	10 49.8	129 30.3	S18 48.8	163 21.6	S 9 42.4	196 36.5	N 3 51.1	120 55.2	S20 30.2
	19	25 52.3	144 29.6	49.5	178 22.7	42.8	211 38.9	51.1	135 57.4	30.3
	20	40 54.7	159 29.0	50.1	193 23.9	43.3	226 41.3	51.1	150 59.6	30.3
	21	55 57.2	174 28.3	50.8	208 25.0	43.8	241 43.7	51.1	166 01.7	30.4
	22	70 59.7	189 27.6	51.4	223 26.2	44.3	256 46.1	51.1	181 03.9	30.4
	23	86 02.1	204 27.0	52.1	238 27.3	44.8	271 48.5	51.1	196 06.1	30.4
2 SATURDAY	00	101 04.6	219 26.3	S18 52.7	253 28.5	S 9 45.3	286 50.9	N 3 51.1	211 08.3	S20 30.5
	01	116 07.0	234 25.6	53.4	268 29.6	45.8	301 53.4	51.1	226 10.5	30.5
	02	131 09.5	249 25.0	54.0	283 30.8	46.3	316 55.8	51.1	241 12.6	30.5
	03	146 12.0	264 24.3	54.7	298 31.9	46.7	331 58.2	51.1	256 14.8	30.6
	04	161 14.4	279 23.6	55.3	313 33.1	47.2	347 00.6	51.1	271 17.0	30.6
	05	176 16.9	294 22.9	55.9	328 34.2	47.7	2 03.0	51.0	286 19.2	30.6
	06	191 19.4	309 22.3	S18 56.6	343 35.4	S 9 48.2	17 05.4	N 3 51.0	301 21.3	S20 30.7
	07	206 21.8	324 21.6	57.2	358 36.5	48.7	32 07.8	51.0	316 23.5	30.7
	08	221 24.3	339 20.9	57.9	13 37.7	49.2	47 10.3	51.0	331 25.7	30.7
	09	236 26.8	354 20.2	58.5	28 38.8	49.7	62 12.7	51.0	346 27.9	30.8
	10	251 29.2	9 19.6	59.1	43 40.0	50.2	77 15.1	51.0	1 30.1	30.8
	11	266 31.7	24 18.9	18 59.8	58 41.1	50.6	92 17.5	51.0	16 32.2	30.9
	12	281 34.2	39 18.2	S19 00.4	73 42.3	S 9 51.1	107 19.9	N 3 51.0	31 34.4	S20 30.9
	13	296 36.6	54 17.5	01.1	88 43.4	51.6	122 22.3	51.0	46 36.6	30.9
	14	311 39.1	69 16.9	01.7	103 44.6	52.1	137 24.8	51.0	61 38.8	31.0
	15	326 41.5	84 16.2	02.3	118 45.7	52.6	152 27.2	51.0	76 41.0	31.0
	16	341 44.0	99 15.5	03.0	133 46.9	53.1	167 29.6	51.0	91 43.1	31.0
	17	356 46.5	114 14.8	03.6	148 48.0	53.6	182 32.0	51.0	106 45.3	31.1
	18	11 48.9	129 14.1	S19 04.2	163 49.2	S 9 54.0	197 34.4	N 3 50.9	121 47.5	S20 31.1
	19	26 51.4	144 13.5	04.9	178 50.3	54.5	212 36.9	50.9	136 49.7	31.1
	20	41 53.9	159 12.8	05.5	193 51.4	55.0	227 39.3	50.9	151 51.8	31.2
	21	56 56.3	174 12.1	06.1	208 52.6	55.5	242 41.7	50.9	166 54.0	31.2
	22	71 58.8	189 11.4	06.8	223 53.7	56.0	257 44.1	50.9	181 56.2	31.2
	23	87 01.3	204 10.7	07.4	238 54.9	56.5	272 46.5	50.9	196 58.4	31.3
3 SUNDAY	00	102 03.7	219 10.1	S19 08.0	253 56.0	S 9 56.9	287 49.0	N 3 50.9	212 00.6	S20 31.3
	01	117 06.2	234 09.4	08.6	268 57.2	57.4	302 51.4	50.9	227 02.7	31.4
	02	132 08.7	249 08.7	09.3	283 58.3	57.9	317 53.8	50.9	242 04.9	31.4
	03	147 11.1	264 08.0	09.9	298 59.5	58.4	332 56.2	50.9	257 07.1	31.4
	04	162 13.6	279 07.3	10.5	314 00.6	58.9	347 58.6	50.9	272 09.3	31.5
	05	177 16.0	294 06.6	11.1	329 01.8	59.4	3 01.1	50.9	287 11.5	31.5
	06	192 18.5	309 06.0	S19 11.8	344 02.9	S 9 59.9	18 03.5	N 3 50.9	302 13.6	S20 31.5
	07	207 21.0	324 05.3	12.4	359 04.1	10 00.3	33 05.9	50.9	317 15.8	31.6
	08	222 23.4	339 04.6	13.0	14 05.3	00.8	48 08.3	50.9	332 18.0	31.6
	09	237 25.9	354 03.9	13.6	29 06.4	01.3	63 10.8	50.9	347 20.2	31.6
	10	252 28.4	9 03.2	14.2	44 07.6	01.8	78 13.2	50.9	2 22.4	31.7
	11	267 30.8	24 02.5	14.9	59 08.7	02.3	93 15.6	50.9	17 24.5	31.7
	12	282 33.3	39 01.8	S19 15.5	74 09.9	S10 02.7	108 18.0	N 3 50.9	32 26.7	S20 31.7
	13	297 35.8	54 01.1	16.1	89 11.0	03.2	123 20.5	50.8	47 28.9	31.8
	14	312 38.2	69 00.5	16.7	104 12.2	03.7	138 22.9	50.8	62 31.1	31.8
	15	327 40.7	83 59.8	17.3	119 13.3	04.2	153 25.3	50.8	77 33.3	31.8
	16	342 43.1	98 59.1	17.9	134 14.5	04.7	168 27.7	50.8	92 35.4	31.9
	17	357 45.6	113 58.4	18.6	149 15.6	05.2	183 30.2	50.8	107 37.6	31.9
	18	12 48.1	128 57.7	S19 19.2	164 16.8	S10 05.6	198 32.6	N 3 50.8	122 39.8	S20 31.9
	19	27 50.5	143 57.0	19.8	179 17.9	06.1	213 35.0	50.8	137 42.0	32.0
	20	42 53.0	158 56.3	20.4	194 19.1	06.6	228 37.4	50.8	152 44.2	32.0
	21	57 55.5	173 55.6	21.0	209 20.2	07.1	243 39.9	50.8	167 46.4	32.1
	22	72 57.9	188 54.9	21.6	224 21.4	07.6	258 42.3	50.8	182 48.5	32.1
	23	88 00.4	203 54.2	22.2	239 22.5	08.0	273 44.7	50.8	197 50.7	32.1
Mer. Pass.		h m 17 12.9	v −0.7	d 0.6	v 1.1	d 0.5	v 2.4	d 0.0	v 2.2	d 0.0

STARS

Name	SHA	Dec
	° ′	° ′
Acamar	315 16.8	S40 14.8
Achernar	335 25.5	S57 09.7
Acrux	173 07.1	S63 10.9
Adhara	255 10.8	S28 59.9
Aldebaran	290 47.1	N16 32.3
Alioth	166 19.3	N55 52.1
Alkaid	152 57.8	N49 13.8
Al Na'ir	27 42.0	S46 53.1
Alnilam	275 44.3	S 1 11.8
Alphard	217 54.1	S 8 43.8
Alphecca	126 09.8	N26 39.7
Alpheratz	357 41.7	N29 10.9
Altair	62 06.9	N 8 54.8
Ankaa	353 14.1	S42 13.4
Antares	112 24.4	S26 27.8
Arcturus	145 54.3	N19 05.9
Atria	107 25.2	S69 03.0
Avior	234 16.6	S59 33.7
Bellatrix	278 29.8	N 6 21.6
Betelgeuse	270 59.1	N 7 24.3
Canopus	263 54.8	S52 42.5
Capella	280 31.4	N46 00.7
Deneb	49 30.7	N45 20.5
Denebola	182 31.9	N14 28.8
Diphda	348 54.2	S17 54.1
Dubhe	193 49.5	N61 39.5
Elnath	278 10.1	N28 37.0
Eltanin	90 45.9	N51 29.3
Enif	33 45.7	N 9 57.0
Fomalhaut	15 22.3	S29 32.4
Gacrux	171 58.8	S57 11.9
Gienah	175 50.5	S17 37.7
Hadar	148 45.5	S60 26.6
Hamal	327 58.6	N23 32.3
Kaus Aust.	83 41.9	S34 22.4
Kochab	137 21.0	N74 05.2
Markab	13 36.7	N15 17.6
Menkar	314 13.0	N 4 09.0
Menkent	148 05.6	S36 26.6
Miaplacidus	221 38.3	S69 46.9
Mirfak	308 37.4	N49 55.1
Nunki	75 56.6	S26 16.4
Peacock	53 17.2	S56 41.0
Pollux	243 25.3	N27 59.0
Procyon	244 57.6	N 5 10.8
Rasalhague	96 05.2	N12 33.1
Regulus	207 41.5	N11 53.2
Rigel	281 10.1	S 8 11.3
Rigil Kent.	139 49.6	S60 53.6
Sabik	102 10.9	S15 44.4
Schedar	349 38.4	N56 37.7
Shaula	96 20.0	S37 06.6
Sirius	258 31.8	S16 44.5
Spica	158 29.5	S11 14.6
Suhail	222 50.7	S43 29.8
Vega	80 38.2	N38 48.1
Zuben'ubi	137 03.7	S16 06.3

	SHA	Mer. Pass.
	° ′	h m
Venus	118 21.7	9 23
Mars	152 23.9	7 06
Jupiter	185 46.4	4 52
Saturn	110 03.7	9 54

2016 JANUARY 1, 2, 3 (FRI., SAT., SUN.)

UT		SUN		MOON				
		GHA	Dec	GHA	*v*	Dec	*d*	HP
d	h	° ′	° ′	° ′	′	° ′	′	′
1	00	179 13.7	S23 03.5	283 03.3	15.1	N 1 27.6	9.4	54.4
	01	194 13.4	03.4	297 37.4	15.2	1 18.2	9.4	54.4
	02	209 13.2	03.2	312 11.6	15.2	1 08.8	9.3	54.4
	03	224 12.9	. . 03.0	326 45.8	15.2	0 59.5	9.4	54.4
	04	239 12.6	02.8	341 20.0	15.3	0 50.1	9.4	54.4
	05	254 12.3	02.6	355 54.3	15.2	0 40.7	9.4	54.4
	06	269 12.0	S23 02.4	10 28.5	15.3	N 0 31.3	9.4	54.4
	07	284 11.7	02.2	25 02.8	15.2	0 21.9	9.3	54.4
	08	299 11.4	02.0	39 37.0	15.3	0 12.6	9.4	54.4
F	09	314 11.1	. . 01.8	54 11.3	15.3	N 0 03.2	9.4	54.3
R	10	329 10.8	01.6	68 45.6	15.3	S 0 06.2	9.3	54.3
I	11	344 10.5	01.4	83 19.9	15.3	0 15.5	9.4	54.3
D	12	359 10.2	S23 01.2	97 54.2	15.3	S 0 24.9	9.4	54.3
A	13	14 09.9	01.0	112 28.5	15.3	0 34.3	9.3	54.3
Y	14	29 09.6	00.8	127 02.8	15.3	0 43.6	9.3	54.3
	15	44 09.3	. . 00.6	141 37.1	15.3	0 52.9	9.4	54.3
	16	59 09.0	00.4	156 11.4	15.4	1 02.3	9.3	54.3
	17	74 08.7	00.2	170 45.8	15.3	1 11.6	9.3	54.3
	18	89 08.4	S23 00.0	185 20.1	15.3	S 1 20.9	9.4	54.3
	19	104 08.1	22 59.8	199 54.4	15.4	1 30.3	9.3	54.3
	20	119 07.8	59.6	214 28.8	15.3	1 39.6	9.3	54.3
	21	134 07.5	. . 59.4	229 03.1	15.4	1 48.9	9.3	54.3
	22	149 07.2	59.2	243 37.5	15.3	1 58.2	9.3	54.3
	23	164 06.9	58.9	258 11.8	15.3	2 07.5	9.2	54.3
2	00	179 06.7	S22 58.7	272 46.1	15.4	S 2 16.7	9.3	54.3
	01	194 06.4	58.5	287 20.5	15.3	2 26.0	9.2	54.3
	02	209 06.1	58.3	301 54.8	15.3	2 35.2	9.3	54.3
	03	224 05.8	. . 58.1	316 29.1	15.3	2 44.5	9.2	54.3
	04	239 05.5	57.9	331 03.4	15.4	2 53.7	9.2	54.2
	05	254 05.2	57.7	345 37.8	15.3	3 02.9	9.2	54.2
	06	269 04.9	S22 57.5	0 12.1	15.3	S 3 12.1	9.2	54.2
	07	284 04.6	57.2	14 46.4	15.3	3 21.3	9.2	54.2
S	08	299 04.3	57.0	29 20.7	15.3	3 30.5	9.2	54.2
A	09	314 04.0	. . 56.8	43 55.0	15.3	3 39.7	9.1	54.2
T	10	329 03.7	56.6	58 29.3	15.2	3 48.8	9.1	54.2
U	11	344 03.4	56.4	73 03.5	15.3	3 57.9	9.2	54.2
R	12	359 03.1	S22 56.2	87 37.8	15.2	S 4 07.1	9.1	54.2
D	13	14 02.8	55.9	102 12.0	15.3	4 16.2	9.0	54.2
A	14	29 02.5	55.7	116 46.3	15.2	4 25.2	9.1	54.2
Y	15	44 02.3	. . 55.5	131 20.5	15.2	4 34.3	9.0	54.2
	16	59 02.0	55.3	145 54.7	15.2	4 43.3	9.1	54.2
	17	74 01.7	55.0	160 28.9	15.2	4 52.4	9.0	54.2
	18	89 01.4	S22 54.8	175 03.1	15.2	S 5 01.4	9.0	54.2
	19	104 01.1	54.6	189 37.3	15.1	5 10.4	8.9	54.2
	20	119 00.8	54.4	204 11.4	15.2	5 19.3	9.0	54.2
	21	134 00.5	. . 54.1	218 45.6	15.1	5 28.3	8.9	54.3
	22	149 00.2	53.9	233 19.7	15.1	5 37.2	8.9	54.3
	23	163 59.9	53.7	247 53.8	15.1	5 46.1	8.9	54.3
3	00	178 59.6	S22 53.5	262 27.9	15.0	S 5 55.0	8.9	54.3
	01	193 59.3	53.2	277 01.9	15.1	6 03.9	8.8	54.3
	02	208 59.1	53.0	291 36.0	15.0	6 12.7	8.8	54.3
	03	223 58.8	. . 52.8	306 10.0	15.0	6 21.5	8.8	54.3
	04	238 58.5	52.5	320 44.0	15.0	6 30.3	8.8	54.3
	05	253 58.2	52.3	335 18.0	14.9	6 39.1	8.7	54.3
	06	268 57.9	S22 52.1	349 51.9	15.0	S 6 47.8	8.7	54.3
	07	283 57.6	51.8	4 25.9	14.9	6 56.5	8.7	54.3
	08	298 57.3	51.6	18 59.8	14.8	7 05.2	8.7	54.3
S	09	313 57.0	. . 51.4	33 33.6	14.9	7 13.9	8.6	54.3
U	10	328 56.7	51.1	48 07.5	14.8	7 22.5	8.6	54.3
N	11	343 56.4	50.9	62 41.3	14.8	7 31.1	8.6	54.3
D	12	358 56.2	S22 50.7	77 15.1	14.8	S 7 39.7	8.6	54.3
A	13	13 55.9	50.4	91 48.9	14.7	7 48.3	8.5	54.3
Y	14	28 55.6	50.2	106 22.6	14.7	7 56.8	8.5	54.3
	15	43 55.3	. . 49.9	120 56.3	14.7	8 05.3	8.4	54.4
	16	58 55.0	49.7	135 30.0	14.7	8 13.7	8.5	54.4
	17	73 54.7	49.4	150 03.7	14.6	8 22.2	8.4	54.4
	18	88 54.4	S22 49.2	164 37.3	14.6	S 8 30.6	8.3	54.4
	19	103 54.1	49.0	179 10.9	14.5	8 38.9	8.4	54.4
	20	118 53.8	48.7	193 44.4	14.5	8 47.3	8.3	54.4
	21	133 53.6	. . 48.5	208 17.9	14.5	8 55.6	8.2	54.4
	22	148 53.3	48.2	222 51.4	14.5	9 03.8	8.3	54.4
	23	163 53.0	48.0	237 24.9	14.4	S 9 12.1	8.2	54.4
		SD 16.3	*d* 0.2	SD 14.8		14.8		14.8

Lat.	Twilight		Sunrise	Moonrise			
	Naut.	Civil		1	2	3	4
°	h m	h m	h m	h m	h m	h m	h m
N 72	08 23	10 41	■	24 19	00 19	01 53	03 28
N 70	08 05	09 49	■	24 16	00 16	01 43	03 12
68	07 49	09 16	■	24 13	00 13	01 36	02 59
66	07 37	08 53	10 27	24 11	00 11	01 30	02 49
64	07 26	08 34	09 49	24 09	00 09	01 24	02 40
62	07 17	08 18	09 22	24 07	00 07	01 20	02 32
60	07 09	08 05	09 02	24 06	00 06	01 16	02 26
N 58	07 02	07 54	08 45	24 04	00 04	01 12	02 20
56	06 55	07 44	08 31	24 03	00 03	01 09	02 15
54	06 50	07 35	08 19	24 02	00 02	01 06	02 11
52	06 44	07 28	08 08	24 01	00 01	01 04	02 07
50	06 39	07 20	07 58	24 00	00 00	01 02	02 03
45	06 28	07 05	07 38	23 59	24 57	00 57	01 55
N 40	06 18	06 52	07 22	23 57	24 53	00 53	01 48
35	06 08	06 40	07 08	23 56	24 49	00 49	01 43
30	06 00	06 30	06 56	23 54	24 46	00 46	01 38
20	05 44	06 11	06 35	23 52	24 40	00 40	01 29
N 10	05 28	05 54	06 17	23 51	24 36	00 36	01 22
0	05 11	05 38	06 00	23 49	24 31	00 31	01 15
S 10	04 53	05 20	05 43	23 47	24 27	00 27	01 08
20	04 31	05 00	05 24	23 46	24 22	00 22	01 00
30	04 02	04 35	05 03	23 44	24 17	00 17	00 52
35	03 44	04 20	04 50	23 43	24 14	00 14	00 47
40	03 21	04 03	04 35	23 41	24 11	00 11	00 42
45	02 52	03 41	04 18	23 40	24 07	00 07	00 36
S 50	02 08	03 12	03 56	23 38	24 02	00 02	00 28
52	01 42	02 57	03 45	23 37	24 00	00 00	00 25
54	01 02	02 40	03 33	23 37	23 58	24 21	00 21
56	////	02 19	03 19	23 36	23 55	24 17	00 17
58	////	01 51	03 03	23 35	23 53	24 12	00 12
S 60	////	01 07	02 44	23 34	23 49	24 07	00 07

Lat.	Sunset	Twilight		Moonset			
		Civil	Naut.	1	2	3	4
°	h m	h m	h m	h m	h m	h m	h m
N 72	■	13 27	15 45	11 22	11 17	11 12	11 06
N 70	■	14 19	16 03	11 23	11 23	11 23	11 24
68	■	14 52	16 18	11 23	11 27	11 32	11 38
66	13 41	15 15	16 31	11 24	11 31	11 40	11 50
64	14 19	15 34	16 41	11 24	11 34	11 46	11 59
62	14 45	15 49	16 51	11 24	11 37	11 51	12 08
60	15 06	16 02	16 59	11 24	11 40	11 56	12 15
N 58	15 23	16 14	17 06	11 25	11 42	12 01	12 21
56	15 37	16 24	17 12	11 25	11 44	12 04	12 27
54	15 49	16 32	17 18	11 25	11 46	12 08	12 32
52	16 00	16 40	17 24	11 25	11 48	12 11	12 36
50	16 09	16 47	17 29	11 25	11 49	12 14	12 41
45	16 29	17 03	17 40	11 26	11 52	12 20	12 50
N 40	16 46	17 16	17 50	11 26	11 55	12 25	12 57
35	17 00	17 28	17 59	11 26	11 57	12 30	13 04
30	17 12	17 38	18 08	11 26	12 00	12 34	13 09
20	17 32	17 56	18 24	11 27	12 03	12 40	13 19
N 10	17 50	18 13	18 40	11 27	12 06	12 46	13 28
0	18 08	18 30	18 56	11 27	12 09	12 52	13 36
S 10	18 25	18 48	19 15	11 27	12 12	12 58	13 44
20	18 43	19 08	19 37	11 28	12 16	13 04	13 53
30	19 05	19 32	20 05	11 28	12 19	13 11	14 03
35	19 17	19 47	20 23	11 28	12 21	13 15	14 09
40	19 32	20 05	20 46	11 28	12 24	13 19	14 15
45	19 50	20 27	21 15	11 28	12 27	13 25	14 23
S 50	20 11	20 55	21 59	11 29	12 30	13 31	14 32
52	20 22	21 10	22 24	11 29	12 31	13 34	14 37
54	20 34	21 27	23 03	11 29	12 33	13 37	14 41
56	20 48	21 48	////	11 29	12 35	13 41	14 47
58	21 04	22 16	////	11 29	12 37	13 45	14 53
S 60	21 23	22 58	////	11 29	12 39	13 49	14 59

Day	SUN			MOON			
	Eqn. of Time		Mer. Pass.	Mer. Pass.		Age	Phase
	00^h	12^h		Upper	Lower		
d	m s	m s	h m	h m	h m	d %	
1	03 04	03 19	12 03	05 17	17 38	21 57	
2	03 33	03 47	12 04	05 59	18 20	22 48	◑
3	04 01	04 15	12 04	06 42	19 03	23 38	

UT	ARIES	VENUS −4·0		MARS +1·2		JUPITER −2·2		SATURN +0·5	
d h	GHA ° ′	GHA ° ′	Dec ° ′	GHA ° ′	Dec ° ′	GHA ° ′	Dec ° ′	GHA ° ′	Dec ° ′
4 00 (MONDAY)	103 02.9	218 53.5	S19 22.8	254 23.7	S10 08.5	288 47.2	N 3 50.8	212 52.9	S20 32.2
01	118 05.3	233 52.8	23.4	269 24.8	09.0	303 49.6	50.8	227 55.1	32.2
02	133 07.8	248 52.1	24.0	284 26.0	09.5	318 52.0	50.8	242 57.3	32.2
03	148 10.3	263 51.4	. . 24.6	299 27.1	. . 10.0	333 54.4	. . 50.8	257 59.4	. . 32.3
04	163 12.7	278 50.7	25.2	314 28.3	10.5	348 56.9	50.8	273 01.6	32.3
05	178 15.2	293 50.1	25.8	329 29.4	10.9	3 59.3	50.8	288 03.8	32.3
06	193 17.6	308 49.4	S19 26.5	344 30.6	S10 11.4	19 01.7	N 3 50.8	303 06.0	S20 32.4
07	208 20.1	323 48.7	27.1	359 31.7	11.9	34 04.2	50.8	318 08.2	32.4
08	223 22.6	338 48.0	27.7	14 32.9	12.4	49 06.6	50.8	333 10.3	32.4
09	238 25.0	353 47.3	. . 28.3	29 34.0	. . 12.9	64 09.0	. . 50.8	348 12.5	. . 32.5
10	253 27.5	8 46.6	28.9	44 35.2	13.3	79 11.5	50.8	3 14.7	32.5
11	268 30.0	23 45.9	29.4	59 36.3	13.8	94 13.9	50.8	18 16.9	32.5
12	283 32.4	38 45.2	S19 30.0	74 37.5	S10 14.3	109 16.3	N 3 50.8	33 19.1	S20 32.6
13	298 34.9	53 44.5	30.6	89 38.6	14.8	124 18.7	50.8	48 21.3	32.6
14	313 37.4	68 43.8	31.2	104 39.8	15.2	139 21.2	50.8	63 23.4	32.6
15	328 39.8	83 43.1	. . 31.8	119 41.0	. . 15.7	154 23.6	. . 50.8	78 25.6	. . 32.7
16	343 42.3	98 42.4	32.4	134 42.1	16.2	169 26.0	50.8	93 27.8	32.7
17	358 44.8	113 41.7	33.0	149 43.3	16.7	184 28.5	50.8	108 30.0	32.7
18	13 47.2	128 40.9	S19 33.6	164 44.4	S10 17.2	199 30.9	N 3 50.8	123 32.2	S20 32.8
19	28 49.7	143 40.2	34.2	179 45.6	17.6	214 33.3	50.8	138 34.4	32.8
20	43 52.1	158 39.5	34.8	194 46.7	18.1	229 35.8	50.8	153 36.5	32.9
21	58 54.6	173 38.8	. . 35.4	209 47.9	. . 18.6	244 38.2	. . 50.8	168 38.7	. . 32.9
22	73 57.1	188 38.1	36.0	224 49.0	19.1	259 40.6	50.8	183 40.9	32.9
23	88 59.5	203 37.4	36.6	239 50.2	19.6	274 43.1	50.8	198 43.1	33.0
5 00 (TUESDAY)	104 02.0	218 36.7	S19 37.1	254 51.3	S10 20.0	289 45.5	N 3 50.8	213 45.3	S20 33.0
01	119 04.5	233 36.0	37.7	269 52.5	20.5	304 48.0	50.8	228 47.4	33.0
02	134 06.9	248 35.3	38.3	284 53.6	21.0	319 50.4	50.8	243 49.6	33.1
03	149 09.4	263 34.6	. . 38.9	299 54.8	. . 21.5	334 52.8	. . 50.8	258 51.8	. . 33.1
04	164 11.9	278 33.9	39.5	314 55.9	21.9	349 55.3	50.8	273 54.0	33.1
05	179 14.3	293 33.2	40.1	329 57.1	22.4	4 57.7	50.8	288 56.2	33.2
06	194 16.8	308 32.5	S19 40.6	344 58.3	S10 22.9	20 00.1	N 3 50.8	303 58.4	S20 33.2
07	209 19.2	323 31.8	41.2	359 59.4	23.4	35 02.6	50.8	319 00.5	33.2
08	224 21.7	338 31.1	41.8	15 00.6	23.8	50 05.0	50.8	334 02.7	33.3
09	239 24.2	353 30.3	. . 42.4	30 01.7	. . 24.3	65 07.5	. . 50.8	349 04.9	. . 33.3
10	254 26.6	8 29.6	43.0	45 02.9	24.8	80 09.9	50.8	4 07.1	33.3
11	269 29.1	23 28.9	43.5	60 04.0	25.3	95 12.3	50.8	19 09.3	33.4
12	284 31.6	38 28.2	S19 44.1	75 05.2	S10 25.7	110 14.8	N 3 50.8	34 11.5	S20 33.4
13	299 34.0	53 27.5	44.7	90 06.3	26.2	125 17.2	50.8	49 13.6	33.4
14	314 36.5	68 26.8	45.3	105 07.5	26.7	140 19.7	50.8	64 15.8	33.5
15	329 39.0	83 26.1	. . 45.8	120 08.6	. . 27.2	155 22.1	. . 50.8	79 18.0	. . 33.5
16	344 41.4	98 25.4	46.4	135 09.8	27.6	170 24.5	50.8	94 20.2	33.5
17	359 43.9	113 24.6	47.0	150 11.0	28.1	185 27.0	50.8	109 22.4	33.6
18	14 46.4	128 23.9	S19 47.5	165 12.1	S10 28.6	200 29.4	N 3 50.8	124 24.6	S20 33.6
19	29 48.8	143 23.2	48.1	180 13.3	29.1	215 31.9	50.8	139 26.8	33.6
20	44 51.3	158 22.5	48.7	195 14.4	29.5	230 34.3	50.8	154 28.9	33.7
21	59 53.7	173 21.8	. . 49.2	210 15.6	. . 30.0	245 36.7	. . 50.8	169 31.1	. . 33.7
22	74 56.2	188 21.1	49.8	225 16.7	30.5	260 39.2	50.8	184 33.3	33.7
23	89 58.7	203 20.3	50.4	240 17.9	31.0	275 41.6	50.8	199 35.5	33.8
6 00 (WEDNESDAY)	105 01.1	218 19.6	S19 50.9	255 19.0	S10 31.4	290 44.1	N 3 50.8	214 37.7	S20 33.8
01	120 03.6	233 18.9	51.5	270 20.2	31.9	305 46.5	50.8	229 39.9	33.8
02	135 06.1	248 18.2	52.1	285 21.4	32.4	320 49.0	50.8	244 42.0	33.9
03	150 08.5	263 17.5	. . 52.6	300 22.5	. . 32.9	335 51.4	. . 50.9	259 44.2	. . 33.9
04	165 11.0	278 16.7	53.2	315 23.7	33.3	350 53.8	50.9	274 46.4	33.9
05	180 13.5	293 16.0	53.8	330 24.8	33.8	5 56.3	50.9	289 48.6	34.0
06	195 15.9	308 15.3	S19 54.3	345 26.0	S10 34.3	20 58.7	N 3 50.9	304 50.8	S20 34.0
07	210 18.4	323 14.6	54.9	0 27.1	34.8	36 01.2	50.9	319 53.0	34.0
08	225 20.9	338 13.9	55.4	15 28.3	35.2	51 03.6	50.9	334 55.2	34.1
09	240 23.3	353 13.1	. . 56.0	30 29.4	. . 35.7	66 06.1	. . 50.9	349 57.3	. . 34.1
10	255 25.8	8 12.4	56.5	45 30.6	36.2	81 08.5	50.9	4 59.5	34.1
11	270 28.2	23 11.7	57.1	60 31.8	36.6	96 11.0	50.9	20 01.7	34.2
12	285 30.7	38 11.0	S19 57.7	75 32.9	S10 37.1	111 13.4	N 3 50.9	35 03.9	S20 34.2
13	300 33.2	53 10.3	58.2	90 34.1	37.6	126 15.9	50.9	50 06.1	34.2
14	315 35.6	68 09.5	58.8	105 35.2	38.1	141 18.3	50.9	65 08.3	34.3
15	330 38.1	83 08.8	. . 59.3	120 36.4	. . 38.5	156 20.8	. . 50.9	80 10.5	. . 34.3
16	345 40.6	98 08.1	19 59.9	135 37.5	39.0	171 23.2	50.9	95 12.6	34.3
17	0 43.0	113 07.4	20 00.4	150 38.7	39.5	186 25.6	50.9	110 14.8	34.4
18	15 45.5	128 06.6	S20 01.0	165 39.9	S10 39.9	201 28.1	N 3 50.9	125 17.0	S20 34.4
19	30 48.0	143 05.9	01.5	180 41.0	40.4	216 30.5	50.9	140 19.2	34.4
20	45 50.4	158 05.2	02.1	195 42.2	40.9	231 33.0	50.9	155 21.4	34.5
21	60 52.9	173 04.4	. . 02.6	210 43.3	. . 41.4	246 35.4	. . 50.9	170 23.6	. . 34.5
22	75 55.4	188 03.7	03.1	225 44.5	41.8	261 37.9	51.0	185 25.8	34.5
23	90 57.8	203 03.0	03.7	240 45.6	42.3	276 40.3	51.0	200 27.9	34.6
Mer. Pass.	h m 17 01.1	*v* −0.7	*d* 0.6	*v* 1.2	*d* 0.5	*v* 2.4	*d* 0.0	*v* 2.2	*d* 0.0

STARS

Name	SHA ° ′	Dec ° ′
Acamar	315 16.8	S40 14.8
Achernar	335 25.5	S57 09.7
Acrux	173 07.1	S63 11.0
Adhara	255 10.8	S28 59.9
Aldebaran	290 47.1	N16 32.3
Alioth	166 19.3	N55 52.1
Alkaid	152 57.8	N49 13.8
Al Na'ir	27 42.0	S46 53.1
Alnilam	275 44.3	S 1 11.8
Alphard	217 54.1	S 8 43.8
Alphecca	126 09.8	N26 39.7
Alpheratz	357 41.7	N29 10.8
Altair	62 06.9	N 8 54.8
Ankaa	353 14.1	S42 13.4
Antares	112 24.4	S26 27.8
Arcturus	145 54.3	N19 05.9
Atria	107 25.1	S69 03.0
Avior	234 16.6	S59 33.7
Bellatrix	278 29.8	N 6 21.6
Betelgeuse	270 59.1	N 7 24.3
Canopus	263 54.8	S52 42.5
Capella	280 31.4	N46 00.7
Deneb	49 30.7	N45 20.5
Denebola	182 31.8	N14 28.8
Diphda	348 54.2	S17 54.1
Dubhe	193 49.4	N61 39.5
Elnath	278 10.1	N28 37.0
Eltanin	90 45.9	N51 29.3
Enif	33 45.7	N 9 57.0
Fomalhaut	15 22.3	S29 32.4
Gacrux	171 58.8	S57 11.9
Gienah	175 50.4	S17 37.8
Hadar	148 45.5	S60 26.6
Hamal	327 58.6	N23 32.3
Kaus Aust.	83 41.9	S34 22.4
Kochab	137 20.9	N74 05.2
Markab	13 36.7	N15 17.6
Menkar	314 13.0	N 4 09.0
Menkent	148 05.6	S36 26.6
Miaplacidus	221 38.3	S69 46.9
Mirfak	308 37.5	N49 55.1
Nunki	75 56.6	S26 16.4
Peacock	53 17.2	S56 40.9
Pollux	243 25.3	N27 59.0
Procyon	244 57.6	N 5 10.8
Rasalhague	96 05.2	N12 33.1
Regulus	207 41.5	N11 53.1
Rigel	281 10.1	S 8 11.3
Rigil Kent.	139 49.5	S60 53.6
Sabik	102 10.9	S15 44.4
Schedar	349 38.4	N56 37.7
Shaula	96 20.0	S37 06.6
Sirius	258 31.8	S16 44.5
Spica	158 29.5	S11 14.6
Suhail	222 50.7	S43 29.9
Vega	80 38.2	N38 48.1
Zuben'ubi	137 03.7	S16 06.3

	SHA ° ′	Mer. Pass. h m
Venus	114 34.7	9 26
Mars	150 49.3	7 00
Jupiter	185 43.5	4 40
Saturn	109 43.3	9 44

Day	UT d h	SUN GHA ° ′	SUN Dec ° ′	MOON GHA ° ′	MOON v ′	MOON Dec ° ′	MOON d ′	MOON HP ′
MONDAY	4 00	178 52.7	S22 47.7	251 58.3	14.4	S 9 20.3	8.1	54.4
	01	193 52.4	47.5	266 31.7	14.3	9 28.4	8.2	54.4
	02	208 52.1	47.2	281 05.0	14.3	9 36.6	8.0	54.5
	03	223 51.8	. . 47.0	295 38.3	14.3	9 44.6	8.1	54.5
	04	238 51.6	46.7	310 11.6	14.2	9 52.7	8.0	54.5
	05	253 51.3	46.5	324 44.8	14.2	10 00.7	8.0	54.5
	06	268 51.0	S22 46.2	339 18.0	14.2	S10 08.7	7.9	54.5
	07	283 50.7	46.0	353 51.2	14.1	10 16.6	7.9	54.5
	08	298 50.4	45.7	8 24.3	14.0	10 24.5	7.9	54.5
	09	313 50.1	. . 45.5	22 57.3	14.1	10 32.4	7.8	54.5
	10	328 49.8	45.2	37 30.4	14.0	10 40.2	7.8	54.6
	11	343 49.5	45.0	52 03.4	13.9	10 48.0	7.7	54.6
	12	358 49.3	S22 44.7	66 36.3	13.9	S10 55.7	7.7	54.6
	13	13 49.0	44.4	81 09.2	13.9	11 03.4	7.6	54.6
	14	28 48.7	44.2	95 42.1	13.8	11 11.0	7.6	54.6
	15	43 48.4	. . 43.9	110 14.9	13.8	11 18.6	7.6	54.6
	16	58 48.1	43.7	124 47.7	13.7	11 26.2	7.5	54.6
	17	73 47.8	43.4	139 20.4	13.7	11 33.7	7.5	54.7
	18	88 47.6	S22 43.1	153 53.1	13.6	S11 41.2	7.4	54.7
	19	103 47.3	42.9	168 25.7	13.6	11 48.6	7.4	54.7
	20	118 47.0	42.6	182 58.3	13.5	11 56.0	7.3	54.7
	21	133 46.7	. . 42.3	197 30.8	13.5	12 03.3	7.3	54.7
	22	148 46.4	42.1	212 03.3	13.5	12 10.6	7.2	54.7
	23	163 46.1	41.8	226 35.8	13.4	12 17.8	7.2	54.8
TUESDAY	5 00	178 45.9	S22 41.5	241 08.2	13.3	S12 25.0	7.1	54.8
	01	193 45.6	41.3	255 40.5	13.3	12 32.1	7.1	54.8
	02	208 45.3	41.0	270 12.8	13.3	12 39.2	7.0	54.8
	03	223 45.0	. . 40.7	284 45.1	13.2	12 46.2	7.0	54.8
	04	238 44.7	40.5	299 17.3	13.1	12 53.2	7.0	54.8
	05	253 44.4	40.2	313 49.4	13.1	13 00.2	6.8	54.9
	06	268 44.2	S22 39.9	328 21.5	13.1	S13 07.0	6.8	54.9
	07	283 43.9	39.7	342 53.6	13.0	13 13.8	6.8	54.9
	08	298 43.6	39.4	357 25.6	12.9	13 20.6	6.7	54.9
	09	313 43.3	. . 39.1	11 57.5	12.9	13 27.3	6.7	54.9
	10	328 43.0	38.8	26 29.4	12.8	13 34.0	6.6	55.0
	11	343 42.8	38.6	41 01.2	12.8	13 40.6	6.5	55.0
	12	358 42.5	S22 38.3	55 33.0	12.8	S13 47.1	6.5	55.0
	13	13 42.2	38.0	70 04.8	12.6	13 53.6	6.4	55.0
	14	28 41.9	37.7	84 36.4	12.7	14 00.0	6.4	55.0
	15	43 41.6	. . 37.5	99 08.1	12.5	14 06.4	6.3	55.1
	16	58 41.3	37.2	113 39.6	12.6	14 12.7	6.2	55.1
	17	73 41.1	36.9	128 11.2	12.4	14 18.9	6.2	55.1
	18	88 40.8	S22 36.6	142 42.6	12.4	S14 25.1	6.1	55.1
	19	103 40.5	36.3	157 14.0	12.4	14 31.2	6.1	55.1
	20	118 40.2	36.1	171 45.4	12.3	14 37.3	6.0	55.2
	21	133 39.9	. . 35.8	186 16.7	12.2	14 43.3	5.9	55.2
	22	148 39.7	35.5	200 47.9	12.2	14 49.2	5.9	55.2
	23	163 39.4	35.2	215 19.1	12.1	14 55.1	5.8	55.2
WEDNESDAY	6 00	178 39.1	S22 34.9	229 50.2	12.1	S15 00.9	5.7	55.3
	01	193 38.8	34.6	244 21.3	12.0	15 06.6	5.6	55.3
	02	208 38.6	34.3	258 52.3	12.0	15 12.2	5.6	55.3
	03	223 38.3	. . 34.1	273 23.3	11.9	15 17.8	5.6	55.3
	04	238 38.0	33.8	287 54.2	11.8	15 23.4	5.4	55.3
	05	253 37.7	33.5	302 25.0	11.8	15 28.8	5.4	55.4
	06	268 37.4	S22 33.2	316 55.8	11.7	S15 34.2	5.4	55.4
	07	283 37.2	32.9	331 26.5	11.7	15 39.6	5.2	55.4
	08	298 36.9	32.6	345 57.2	11.6	15 44.8	5.2	55.4
	09	313 36.6	. . 32.3	0 27.8	11.6	15 50.0	5.1	55.5
	10	328 36.3	32.0	14 58.4	11.5	15 55.1	5.0	55.5
	11	343 36.1	31.7	29 28.9	11.4	16 00.1	5.0	55.5
	12	358 35.8	S22 31.4	43 59.3	11.4	S16 05.1	4.9	55.5
	13	13 35.5	31.1	58 29.7	11.4	16 10.0	4.8	55.6
	14	28 35.2	30.8	73 00.1	11.2	16 14.8	4.7	55.6
	15	43 34.9	. . 30.5	87 30.3	11.2	16 19.5	4.7	55.6
	16	58 34.7	30.2	102 00.5	11.2	16 24.2	4.5	55.6
	17	73 34.4	30.0	116 30.7	11.1	16 28.7	4.5	55.7
	18	88 34.1	S22 29.7	131 00.8	11.0	S16 33.2	4.5	55.7
	19	103 33.8	29.4	145 30.8	11.0	16 37.7	4.3	55.7
	20	118 33.6	29.1	160 00.8	11.0	16 42.0	4.3	55.7
	21	133 33.3	. . 28.7	174 30.8	10.8	16 46.3	4.2	55.8
	22	148 33.0	28.4	189 00.6	10.9	16 50.5	4.1	55.8
	23	163 32.7	28.1	203 30.5	10.7	S16 54.6	4.0	55.8
		SD 16.3	*d* 0.3	SD 14.9		15.0		15.1

Lat. °	Twilight Naut. h m	Twilight Civil h m	Sunrise h m	Moonrise 4 h m	Moonrise 5 h m	Moonrise 6 h m	Moonrise 7 h m
N 72	08 20	10 31	■	03 28	05 08	06 55	08 58
N 70	08 02	09 44	■	03 12	04 43	06 15	07 45
68	07 47	09 13	11 33	02 59	04 23	05 48	07 08
66	07 35	08 50	10 21	02 49	04 08	05 27	06 42
64	07 25	08 32	09 45	02 40	03 56	05 10	06 22
62	07 16	08 17	09 20	02 32	03 45	04 57	06 06
60	07 08	08 04	09 00	02 26	03 36	04 45	05 52
N 58	07 01	07 53	08 44	02 20	03 28	04 35	05 40
56	06 55	07 43	08 30	02 15	03 21	04 27	05 30
54	06 49	07 35	08 18	02 11	03 15	04 19	05 21
52	06 44	07 27	08 07	02 07	03 10	04 12	05 13
50	06 39	07 20	07 58	02 03	03 05	04 06	05 06
45	06 28	07 05	07 38	01 55	02 54	03 53	04 51
N 40	06 18	06 52	07 22	01 48	02 45	03 42	04 39
35	06 09	06 41	07 08	01 43	02 37	03 32	04 28
30	06 01	06 30	06 57	01 38	02 30	03 24	04 19
20	05 45	06 12	06 36	01 29	02 19	03 10	04 03
N 10	05 29	05 56	06 18	01 22	02 09	02 58	03 49
0	05 13	05 39	06 01	01 15	02 00	02 46	03 36
S 10	04 55	05 22	05 44	01 08	01 50	02 35	03 23
20	04 33	05 02	05 26	01 00	01 40	02 23	03 09
30	04 05	04 38	05 05	00 52	01 29	02 09	02 53
35	03 47	04 23	04 52	00 47	01 23	02 01	02 44
40	03 24	04 05	04 38	00 42	01 15	01 52	02 34
45	02 55	03 44	04 21	00 36	01 07	01 42	02 22
S 50	02 13	03 15	03 59	00 28	00 56	01 29	02 07
52	01 48	03 01	03 49	00 25	00 52	01 23	02 00
54	01 11	02 44	03 37	00 21	00 46	01 16	01 52
56	////	02 24	03 24	00 17	00 41	01 09	01 44
58	////	01 57	03 08	00 12	00 34	01 01	01 34
S 60	////	01 17	02 49	00 07	00 27	00 52	01 23

Lat. °	Sunset h m	Twilight Civil h m	Twilight Naut. h m	Moonset 4 h m	Moonset 5 h m	Moonset 6 h m	Moonset 7 h m
N 72	■	13 39	15 51	11 06	11 00	10 51	10 32
N 70	■	14 27	16 09	11 24	11 27	11 32	11 45
68	12 38	14 58	16 23	11 38	11 47	12 00	12 23
66	13 50	15 21	16 35	11 50	12 03	12 21	12 49
64	14 25	15 39	16 46	11 59	12 16	12 39	13 10
62	14 51	15 54	16 55	12 08	12 27	12 53	13 26
60	15 11	16 07	17 02	12 15	12 37	13 05	13 40
N 58	15 27	16 17	17 09	12 21	12 45	13 15	13 52
56	15 41	16 27	17 16	12 27	12 53	13 24	14 02
54	15 53	16 36	17 21	12 32	12 59	13 32	14 11
52	16 03	16 43	17 27	12 36	13 05	13 39	14 19
50	16 13	16 51	17 32	12 41	13 11	13 46	14 27
45	16 32	17 06	17 43	12 50	13 22	14 00	14 42
N 40	16 48	17 19	17 53	12 57	13 32	14 11	14 55
35	17 02	17 30	18 01	13 04	13 40	14 21	15 06
30	17 14	17 40	18 10	13 09	13 48	14 30	15 16
20	17 34	17 58	18 25	13 19	14 00	14 45	15 32
N 10	17 52	18 15	18 41	13 28	14 11	14 58	15 47
0	18 09	18 31	18 57	13 36	14 22	15 10	16 00
S 10	18 26	18 49	19 16	13 44	14 32	15 22	16 14
20	18 44	19 08	19 37	13 53	14 43	15 35	16 28
30	19 05	19 32	20 05	14 03	14 56	15 50	16 45
35	19 18	19 47	20 23	14 09	15 04	15 59	16 54
40	19 32	20 05	20 45	14 15	15 12	16 09	17 05
45	19 49	20 26	21 14	14 23	15 22	16 21	17 18
S 50	20 11	20 54	21 57	14 32	15 34	16 35	17 34
52	20 21	21 08	22 21	14 37	15 39	16 41	17 41
54	20 33	21 25	22 57	14 41	15 46	16 49	17 49
56	20 46	21 45	////	14 47	15 52	16 57	17 59
58	21 02	22 12	////	14 53	16 00	17 06	18 09
S 60	21 20	22 50	////	14 59	16 09	17 17	18 21

Day d	SUN Eqn. of Time 00^h m s	SUN Eqn. of Time 12^h m s	SUN Mer. Pass. h m	MOON Mer. Pass. Upper h m	MOON Mer. Pass. Lower h m	MOON Age d	MOON %	MOON Phase
4	04 29	04 42	12 05	07 25	19 48	24	29	
5	04 56	05 10	12 05	08 11	20 34	25	21	
6	05 23	05 36	12 06	08 58	21 23	26	14	

Day	UT d h	ARIES GHA	VENUS −4·0 GHA	VENUS Dec	MARS +1·2 GHA	MARS Dec	JUPITER −2·2 GHA	JUPITER Dec	SATURN +0·5 GHA	SATURN Dec
		° ′	° ′	° ′	° ′	° ′	° ′	° ′	° ′	° ′
THURSDAY	7 00	106 00.3	218 02.3	S20 04.2	255 46.8	S10 42.8	291 42.8	N 3 51.0	215 30.1	S20 34.6
	01	121 02.7	233 01.5	04.8	270 48.0	43.2	306 45.2	51.0	230 32.3	34.6
	02	136 05.2	248 00.8	05.3	285 49.1	43.7	321 47.7	51.0	245 34.5	34.7
	03	151 07.7	263 00.1	. . 05.9	300 50.3	. . 44.2	336 50.1	. . 51.0	260 36.7	. . 34.7
	04	166 10.1	277 59.3	06.4	315 51.4	44.7	351 52.6	51.0	275 38.9	34.7
	05	181 12.6	292 58.6	06.9	330 52.6	45.1	6 55.1	51.0	290 41.1	34.8
	06	196 15.1	307 57.9	S20 07.5	345 53.7	S10 45.6	21 57.5	N 3 51.0	305 43.3	S20 34.8
	07	211 17.5	322 57.1	08.0	0 54.9	46.1	37 00.0	51.0	320 45.4	34.8
	08	226 20.0	337 56.4	08.5	15 56.1	46.5	52 02.4	51.0	335 47.6	34.9
	09	241 22.5	352 55.7	. . 09.1	30 57.2	. . 47.0	67 04.9	. . 51.0	350 49.8	. . 34.9
	10	256 24.9	7 54.9	09.6	45 58.4	47.5	82 07.3	51.0	5 52.0	34.9
	11	271 27.4	22 54.2	10.1	60 59.5	47.9	97 09.8	51.1	20 54.2	35.0
	12	286 29.8	37 53.5	S20 10.7	76 00.7	S10 48.4	112 12.2	N 3 51.1	35 56.4	S20 35.0
	13	301 32.3	52 52.7	11.2	91 01.9	48.9	127 14.7	51.1	50 58.6	35.0
	14	316 34.8	67 52.0	11.7	106 03.0	49.3	142 17.1	51.1	66 00.8	35.1
	15	331 37.2	82 51.3	. . 12.3	121 04.2	. . 49.8	157 19.6	. . 51.1	81 02.9	. . 35.1
	16	346 39.7	97 50.5	12.8	136 05.3	50.3	172 22.0	51.1	96 05.1	35.1
	17	1 42.2	112 49.8	13.3	151 06.5	50.7	187 24.5	51.1	111 07.3	35.2
	18	16 44.6	127 49.1	S20 13.9	166 07.7	S10 51.2	202 27.0	N 3 51.1	126 09.5	S20 35.2
	19	31 47.1	142 48.3	14.4	181 08.8	51.7	217 29.4	51.1	141 11.7	35.2
	20	46 49.6	157 47.6	14.9	196 10.0	52.1	232 31.9	51.1	156 13.9	35.3
	21	61 52.0	172 46.8	. . 15.4	211 11.1	. . 52.6	247 34.3	. . 51.1	171 16.1	. . 35.3
	22	76 54.5	187 46.1	15.9	226 12.3	53.1	262 36.8	51.2	186 18.3	35.3
	23	91 57.0	202 45.4	16.5	241 13.4	53.5	277 39.2	51.2	201 20.4	35.4
FRIDAY	8 00	106 59.4	217 44.6	S20 17.0	256 14.6	S10 54.0	292 41.7	N 3 51.2	216 22.6	S20 35.4
	01	122 01.9	232 43.9	17.5	271 15.8	54.5	307 44.2	51.2	231 24.8	35.4
	02	137 04.3	247 43.1	18.0	286 16.9	54.9	322 46.6	51.2	246 27.0	35.5
	03	152 06.8	262 42.4	. . 18.5	301 18.1	. . 55.4	337 49.1	. . 51.2	261 29.2	. . 35.5
	04	167 09.3	277 41.7	19.1	316 19.2	55.9	352 51.5	51.2	276 31.4	35.5
	05	182 11.7	292 40.9	19.6	331 20.4	56.3	7 54.0	51.2	291 33.6	35.6
	06	197 14.2	307 40.2	S20 20.1	346 21.6	S10 56.8	22 56.5	N 3 51.2	306 35.8	S20 35.6
	07	212 16.7	322 39.4	20.6	1 22.7	57.3	37 58.9	51.2	321 38.0	35.6
	08	227 19.1	337 38.7	21.1	16 23.9	57.7	53 01.4	51.3	336 40.1	35.7
	09	242 21.6	352 38.0	. . 21.6	31 25.0	. . 58.2	68 03.8	. . 51.3	351 42.3	. . 35.7
	10	257 24.1	7 37.2	22.1	46 26.2	58.7	83 06.3	51.3	6 44.5	35.7
	11	272 26.5	22 36.5	22.7	61 27.4	59.1	98 08.8	51.3	21 46.7	35.8
	12	287 29.0	37 35.7	S20 23.2	76 28.5	S10 59.6	113 11.2	N 3 51.3	36 48.9	S20 35.8
	13	302 31.5	52 35.0	23.7	91 29.7	11 00.1	128 13.7	51.3	51 51.1	35.8
	14	317 33.9	67 34.2	24.2	106 30.9	00.5	143 16.1	51.3	66 53.3	35.9
	15	332 36.4	82 33.5	. . 24.7	121 32.0	. . 01.0	158 18.6	. . 51.3	81 55.5	. . 35.9
	16	347 38.8	97 32.7	25.2	136 33.2	01.5	173 21.1	51.3	96 57.7	35.9
	17	2 41.3	112 32.0	25.7	151 34.3	01.9	188 23.5	51.4	111 59.8	36.0
	18	17 43.8	127 31.2	S20 26.2	166 35.5	S11 02.4	203 26.0	N 3 51.4	127 02.0	S20 36.0
	19	32 46.2	142 30.5	26.7	181 36.7	02.8	218 28.5	51.4	142 04.2	36.0
	20	47 48.7	157 29.7	27.2	196 37.8	03.3	233 30.9	51.4	157 06.4	36.1
	21	62 51.2	172 29.0	. . 27.7	211 39.0	. . 03.8	248 33.4	. . 51.4	172 08.6	. . 36.1
	22	77 53.6	187 28.2	28.2	226 40.1	04.2	263 35.9	51.4	187 10.8	36.1
	23	92 56.1	202 27.5	28.7	241 41.3	04.7	278 38.3	51.4	202 13.0	36.2
SATURDAY	9 00	107 58.6	217 26.7	S20 29.2	256 42.5	S11 05.2	293 40.8	N 3 51.5	217 15.2	S20 36.2
	01	123 01.0	232 26.0	29.7	271 43.6	05.6	308 43.2	51.5	232 17.4	36.2
	02	138 03.5	247 25.2	30.2	286 44.8	06.1	323 45.7	51.5	247 19.6	36.3
	03	153 06.0	262 24.5	. . 30.7	301 46.0	. . 06.6	338 48.2	. . 51.5	262 21.7	. . 36.3
	04	168 08.4	277 23.7	31.2	316 47.1	07.0	353 50.6	51.5	277 23.9	36.3
	05	183 10.9	292 23.0	31.7	331 48.3	07.5	8 53.1	51.5	292 26.1	36.4
	06	198 13.3	307 22.2	S20 32.2	346 49.4	S11 07.9	23 55.6	N 3 51.5	307 28.3	S20 36.4
	07	213 15.8	322 21.5	32.7	1 50.6	08.4	38 58.1	51.5	322 30.5	36.4
	08	228 18.3	337 20.7	33.2	16 51.8	08.9	54 00.5	51.6	337 32.7	36.4
	09	243 20.7	352 20.0	. . 33.6	31 52.9	. . 09.3	69 03.0	. . 51.6	352 34.9	. . 36.5
	10	258 23.2	7 19.2	34.1	46 54.1	09.8	84 05.5	51.6	7 37.1	36.5
	11	273 25.7	22 18.5	34.6	61 55.3	10.2	99 07.9	51.6	22 39.3	36.5
	12	288 28.1	37 17.7	S20 35.1	76 56.4	S11 10.7	114 10.4	N 3 51.6	37 41.5	S20 36.6
	13	303 30.6	52 16.9	35.6	91 57.6	11.2	129 12.9	51.6	52 43.7	36.6
	14	318 33.1	67 16.2	36.1	106 58.7	11.6	144 15.3	51.7	67 45.9	36.6
	15	333 35.5	82 15.4	. . 36.6	121 59.9	. . 12.1	159 17.8	. . 51.7	82 48.0	. . 36.7
	16	348 38.0	97 14.7	37.0	137 01.1	12.5	174 20.3	51.7	97 50.2	36.7
	17	3 40.5	112 13.9	37.5	152 02.2	13.0	189 22.7	51.7	112 52.4	36.7
	18	18 42.9	127 13.2	S20 38.0	167 03.4	S11 13.5	204 25.2	N 3 51.7	127 54.6	S20 36.8
	19	33 45.4	142 12.4	38.5	182 04.6	13.9	219 27.7	51.7	142 56.8	36.8
	20	48 47.8	157 11.6	39.0	197 05.7	14.4	234 30.2	51.7	157 59.0	36.8
	21	63 50.3	172 10.9	. . 39.4	212 06.9	. . 14.8	249 32.6	. . 51.8	173 01.2	. . 36.9
	22	78 52.8	187 10.1	39.9	227 08.1	15.3	264 35.1	51.8	188 03.4	36.9
	23	93 55.2	202 09.4	40.4	242 09.2	15.8	279 37.6	51.8	203 05.6	36.9
	Mer. Pass.	h m 16 49.3	v −0.7	d 0.5	v 1.2	d 0.5	v 2.5	d 0.0	v 2.2	d 0.0

STARS Name	SHA	Dec
	° ′	° ′
Acamar	315 16.9	S40 14.8
Achernar	335 25.5	S57 09.7
Acrux	173 07.0	S63 11.0
Adhara	255 10.8	S28 59.9
Aldebaran	290 47.1	N16 32.3
Alioth	166 19.3	N55 52.1
Alkaid	152 57.7	N49 13.8
Al Na'ir	27 42.0	S46 53.1
Alnilam	275 44.3	S 1 11.8
Alphard	217 54.1	S 8 43.8
Alphecca	126 09.8	N26 39.7
Alpheratz	357 41.7	N29 10.8
Altair	62 06.9	N 8 54.8
Ankaa	353 14.1	S42 13.4
Antares	112 24.4	S26 27.8
Arcturus	145 54.3	N19 05.9
Atria	107 25.1	S69 03.0
Avior	234 16.6	S59 33.7
Bellatrix	278 29.8	N 6 21.6
Betelgeuse	270 59.1	N 7 24.3
Canopus	263 54.8	S52 42.5
Capella	280 31.4	N46 00.7
Deneb	49 30.7	N45 20.5
Denebola	182 31.8	N14 28.8
Diphda	348 54.2	S17 54.1
Dubhe	193 49.4	N61 39.5
Elnath	278 10.1	N28 37.0
Eltanin	90 45.9	N51 29.3
Enif	33 45.7	N 9 57.0
Fomalhaut	15 22.3	S29 32.4
Gacrux	171 58.7	S57 11.9
Gienah	175 50.4	S17 37.8
Hadar	148 45.4	S60 26.6
Hamal	327 58.6	N23 32.3
Kaus Aust.	83 41.9	S34 22.4
Kochab	137 20.9	N74 05.2
Markab	13 36.7	N15 17.6
Menkar	314 13.1	N 4 09.0
Menkent	148 05.6	S36 26.6
Miaplacidus	221 38.3	S69 46.9
Mirfak	308 37.5	N49 55.1
Nunki	75 56.6	S26 16.4
Peacock	53 17.2	S56 40.9
Pollux	243 25.3	N27 59.0
Procyon	244 57.6	N 5 10.8
Rasalhague	96 05.2	N12 33.1
Regulus	207 41.4	N11 53.1
Rigel	281 10.1	S 8 11.3
Rigil Kent.	139 49.5	S60 53.6
Sabik	102 10.8	S15 44.4
Schedar	349 38.4	N56 37.7
Shaula	96 19.9	S37 06.6
Sirius	258 31.8	S16 44.6
Spica	158 29.4	S11 14.6
Suhail	222 50.7	S43 29.9
Vega	80 38.2	N38 48.1
Zuben'ubi	137 03.6	S16 06.3

	SHA	Mer. Pass.
	° ′	h m
Venus	110 45.2	9 29
Mars	149 15.2	6 54
Jupiter	185 42.3	4 28
Saturn	109 23.2	9 33

UT	SUN GHA	SUN Dec	MOON GHA	*v*	MOON Dec	*d*	HP
d h	° ′	° ′	° ′	′	° ′	′	′
7 00 (THURSDAY)	178 32.5	S22 27.8	218 00.2	10.7	S16 58.6	3.9	55.8
01	193 32.2	27.5	232 29.9	10.7	17 02.5	3.9	55.9
02	208 31.9	27.2	246 59.6	10.6	17 06.4	3.7	55.9
03	223 31.7	. . 26.9	261 29.2	10.5	17 10.1	3.7	55.9
04	238 31.4	26.6	275 58.7	10.5	17 13.8	3.6	55.9
05	253 31.1	26.3	290 28.2	10.4	17 17.4	3.6	56.0
06	268 30.8	S22 26.0	304 57.6	10.4	S17 21.0	3.4	56.0
07	283 30.6	25.7	319 27.0	10.3	17 24.4	3.3	56.0
08	298 30.3	25.4	333 56.3	10.3	17 27.7	3.3	56.0
09	313 30.0	. . 25.1	348 25.6	10.2	17 31.0	3.1	56.1
10	328 29.7	24.8	2 54.8	10.1	17 34.1	3.1	56.1
11	343 29.5	24.4	17 23.9	10.1	17 37.2	3.0	56.1
12	358 29.2	S22 24.1	31 53.0	10.1	S17 40.2	2.9	56.2
13	13 28.9	23.8	46 22.1	10.0	17 43.1	2.8	56.2
14	28 28.7	23.5	60 51.1	9.9	17 45.9	2.7	56.2
15	43 28.4	. . 23.2	75 20.0	9.9	17 48.6	2.6	56.2
16	58 28.1	22.9	89 48.9	9.8	17 51.2	2.6	56.3
17	73 27.8	22.6	104 17.7	9.8	17 53.8	2.4	56.3
18	88 27.6	S22 22.2	118 46.5	9.8	S17 56.2	2.3	56.3
19	103 27.3	21.9	133 15.3	9.7	17 58.5	2.3	56.3
20	118 27.0	21.6	147 44.0	9.6	18 00.8	2.1	56.4
21	133 26.8	. . 21.3	162 12.6	9.6	18 02.9	2.1	56.4
22	148 26.5	21.0	176 41.2	9.5	18 05.0	2.0	56.4
23	163 26.2	20.6	191 09.7	9.5	18 07.0	1.8	56.5
8 00 (FRIDAY)	178 25.9	S22 20.3	205 38.2	9.5	S18 08.8	1.8	56.5
01	193 25.7	20.0	220 06.7	9.4	18 10.6	1.6	56.5
02	208 25.4	19.7	234 35.1	9.3	18 12.2	1.6	56.5
03	223 25.1	. . 19.3	249 03.4	9.4	18 13.8	1.5	56.6
04	238 24.9	19.0	263 31.8	9.2	18 15.3	1.4	56.6
05	253 24.6	18.7	278 00.0	9.2	18 16.7	1.2	56.6
06	268 24.3	S22 18.4	292 28.2	9.2	S18 17.9	1.2	56.6
07	283 24.1	18.0	306 56.4	9.1	18 19.1	1.1	56.7
08	298 23.8	17.7	321 24.5	9.1	18 20.2	0.9	56.7
09	313 23.5	. . 17.4	335 52.6	9.1	18 21.1	0.9	56.7
10	328 23.3	17.1	350 20.7	9.0	18 22.0	0.8	56.8
11	343 23.0	16.7	4 48.7	9.0	18 22.8	0.7	56.8
12	358 22.7	S22 16.4	19 16.7	8.9	S18 23.5	0.5	56.8
13	13 22.5	16.1	33 44.6	8.9	18 24.0	0.5	56.8
14	28 22.2	15.7	48 12.5	8.8	18 24.5	0.3	56.9
15	43 21.9	. . 15.4	62 40.3	8.9	18 24.8	0.3	56.9
16	58 21.7	15.1	77 08.2	8.7	18 25.1	0.1	56.9
17	73 21.4	14.7	91 35.9	8.8	18 25.2	0.1	57.0
18	88 21.1	S22 14.4	106 03.7	8.7	S18 25.3	0.1	57.0
19	103 20.9	14.1	120 31.4	8.7	18 25.2	0.2	57.0
20	118 20.6	13.7	134 59.1	8.6	18 25.0	0.2	57.0
21	133 20.3	. . 13.4	149 26.7	8.6	18 24.8	0.4	57.1
22	148 20.1	13.0	163 54.3	8.6	18 24.4	0.5	57.1
23	163 19.8	12.7	178 21.9	8.5	18 23.9	0.6	57.1
9 00 (SATURDAY)	178 19.5	S22 12.4	192 49.4	8.5	S18 23.3	0.7	57.1
01	193 19.3	12.0	207 16.9	8.5	18 22.6	0.8	57.2
02	208 19.0	11.7	221 44.4	8.5	18 21.8	0.9	57.2
03	223 18.8	. . 11.3	236 11.9	8.4	18 20.9	1.0	57.2
04	238 18.5	11.0	250 39.3	8.4	18 19.9	1.1	57.3
05	253 18.2	10.6	265 06.7	8.4	18 18.8	1.3	57.3
06	268 18.0	S22 10.3	279 34.1	8.3	S18 17.5	1.3	57.3
07	283 17.7	10.0	294 01.4	8.3	18 16.2	1.4	57.3
08	298 17.4	09.6	308 28.7	8.3	18 14.8	1.6	57.4
09	313 17.2	. . 09.3	322 56.0	8.3	18 13.2	1.7	57.4
10	328 16.9	08.9	337 23.3	8.3	18 11.5	1.7	57.4
11	343 16.7	08.6	351 50.6	8.2	18 09.8	1.9	57.4
12	358 16.4	S22 08.2	6 17.8	8.2	S18 07.9	2.0	57.5
13	13 16.1	07.9	20 45.0	8.2	18 05.9	2.1	57.5
14	28 15.9	07.5	35 12.2	8.2	18 03.8	2.2	57.5
15	43 15.6	. . 07.2	49 39.4	8.2	18 01.6	2.3	57.5
16	58 15.4	06.8	64 06.6	8.1	17 59.3	2.4	57.6
17	73 15.1	06.5	78 33.7	8.1	17 56.9	2.6	57.6
18	88 14.8	S22 06.1	93 00.8	8.2	S17 54.3	2.6	57.6
19	103 14.6	05.7	107 28.0	8.1	17 51.7	2.7	57.6
20	118 14.3	05.4	121 55.1	8.0	17 49.0	2.9	57.7
21	133 14.1	. . 05.0	136 22.1	8.1	17 46.1	3.0	57.7
22	148 13.8	04.7	150 49.2	8.1	17 43.1	3.0	57.7
23	163 13.5	04.3	165 16.3	8.0	S17 40.1	3.2	57.7
	SD 16.3	*d* 0.3	SD 15.3		15.5		15.7

Lat.	Twilight Naut.	Twilight Civil	Sunrise	Moonrise 7	Moonrise 8	Moonrise 9	Moonrise 10
°	h m	h m	h m	h m	h m	h m	h m
N 72	08 16	10 21	■	08 58	■	■	11 08
N 70	07 58	09 37	■	07 45	09 03	09 52	10 15
68	07 44	09 08	11 12	07 08	08 18	09 09	09 42
66	07 33	08 46	10 14	06 42	07 48	08 40	09 17
64	07 23	08 29	09 41	06 22	07 26	08 18	08 58
62	07 14	08 15	09 16	06 06	07 08	08 01	08 43
60	07 07	08 02	08 57	05 52	06 53	07 46	08 30
N 58	07 00	07 52	08 42	05 40	06 41	07 34	08 19
56	06 54	07 42	08 28	05 30	06 30	07 23	08 09
54	06 48	07 34	08 16	05 21	06 20	07 14	08 00
52	06 43	07 26	08 06	05 13	06 12	07 05	07 52
50	06 38	07 19	07 57	05 06	06 04	06 57	07 45
45	06 28	07 04	07 38	04 51	05 48	06 41	07 30
N 40	06 18	06 52	07 22	04 39	05 34	06 28	07 18
35	06 09	06 41	07 09	04 28	05 23	06 17	07 08
30	06 01	06 31	06 57	04 19	05 13	06 07	06 58
20	05 46	06 13	06 37	04 03	04 56	05 50	06 42
N 10	05 30	05 57	06 19	03 49	04 41	05 35	06 28
0	05 14	05 40	06 03	03 36	04 27	05 21	06 15
S 10	04 56	05 23	05 46	03 23	04 14	05 07	06 02
20	04 35	05 04	05 28	03 09	03 59	04 52	05 49
30	04 07	04 40	05 07	02 53	03 42	04 35	05 33
35	03 50	04 26	04 55	02 44	03 32	04 25	05 23
40	03 28	04 08	04 41	02 34	03 21	04 14	05 13
45	02 59	03 47	04 24	02 22	03 08	04 01	05 00
S 50	02 18	03 20	04 03	02 07	02 52	03 45	04 45
52	01 54	03 06	03 53	02 00	02 44	03 37	04 38
54	01 21	02 49	03 41	01 52	02 36	03 29	04 30
56	////	02 30	03 28	01 44	02 27	03 19	04 21
58	////	02 04	03 13	01 34	02 16	03 09	04 11
S 60	////	01 28	02 54	01 23	02 04	02 56	04 00

Lat.	Sunset	Twilight Civil	Twilight Naut.	Moonset 7	Moonset 8	Moonset 9	Moonset 10
°	h m	h m	h m	h m	h m	h m	h m
N 72	■	13 53	15 58	10 32	■	■	13 57
N 70	■	14 36	16 15	11 45	12 16	13 19	14 50
68	13 01	15 05	16 29	12 23	13 01	14 01	15 23
66	14 00	15 27	16 41	12 49	13 31	14 30	15 46
64	14 33	15 44	16 50	13 10	13 53	14 52	16 05
62	14 57	15 59	16 59	13 26	14 11	15 09	16 20
60	15 16	16 11	17 06	13 40	14 26	15 24	16 33
N 58	15 32	16 22	17 13	13 52	14 39	15 36	16 44
56	15 45	16 31	17 19	14 02	14 50	15 47	16 53
54	15 57	16 39	17 25	14 11	14 59	15 56	17 02
52	16 07	16 47	17 30	14 19	15 08	16 05	17 09
50	16 16	16 54	17 35	14 27	15 15	16 12	17 16
45	16 36	17 09	17 46	14 42	15 32	16 28	17 30
N 40	16 51	17 21	17 55	14 55	15 45	16 41	17 42
35	17 05	17 32	18 04	15 06	15 57	16 52	17 52
30	17 16	17 42	18 12	15 16	16 07	17 02	18 01
20	17 36	18 00	18 27	15 32	16 24	17 19	18 16
N 10	17 54	18 16	18 42	15 47	16 39	17 33	18 29
0	18 10	18 33	18 59	16 00	16 53	17 47	18 42
S 10	18 27	18 50	19 16	16 14	17 07	18 00	18 54
20	18 45	19 09	19 38	16 28	17 22	18 15	19 07
30	19 05	19 33	20 05	16 45	17 39	18 31	19 22
35	19 18	19 47	20 23	16 54	17 49	18 41	19 30
40	19 32	20 04	20 45	17 05	18 00	18 52	19 40
45	19 49	20 25	21 13	17 18	18 13	19 05	19 51
S 50	20 10	20 53	21 54	17 34	18 29	19 20	20 05
52	20 20	21 06	22 17	17 41	18 37	19 27	20 12
54	20 31	21 23	22 50	17 49	18 46	19 36	20 19
56	20 44	21 42	////	17 59	18 55	19 45	20 27
58	20 59	22 07	////	18 09	19 06	19 55	20 35
S 60	21 17	22 42	////	18 21	19 18	20 06	20 46

Day	SUN Eqn. of Time 00^h	SUN Eqn. of Time 12^h	SUN Mer. Pass.	MOON Mer. Pass. Upper	MOON Mer. Pass. Lower	MOON Age	MOON Phase
d	m s	m s	h m	h m	h m	d %	
7	05 50	06 03	12 06	09 48	22 14	27 7	●
8	06 16	06 29	12 06	10 40	23 07	28 3	
9	06 41	06 54	12 07	11 34	24 01	29 1	

UT	ARIES	VENUS −4·0		MARS +1·1		JUPITER −2·2		SATURN +0·5	
d h	GHA ° ′	GHA ° ′	Dec ° ′	GHA ° ′	Dec ° ′	GHA ° ′	Dec ° ′	GHA ° ′	Dec ° ′
10 00 (SUNDAY)	108 57.7	217 08.6	S20 40.9	257 10.4	S11 16.2	294 40.0	N 3 51.8	218 07.8	S20 37.0
01	124 00.2	232 07.8	41.3	272 11.5	16.7	309 42.5	51.8	233 10.0	37.0
02	139 02.6	247 07.1	41.8	287 12.7	17.1	324 45.0	51.8	248 12.2	37.0
03	154 05.1	262 06.3	. . 42.3	302 13.9	. . 17.6	339 47.5	. . 51.9	263 14.3	. . 37.1
04	169 07.6	277 05.6	42.8	317 15.0	18.1	354 49.9	51.9	278 16.5	37.1
05	184 10.0	292 04.8	43.2	332 16.2	18.5	9 52.4	51.9	293 18.7	37.1
06	199 12.5	307 04.0	S20 43.7	347 17.4	S11 19.0	24 54.9	N 3 51.9	308 20.9	S20 37.2
07	214 15.0	322 03.3	44.2	2 18.5	19.4	39 57.4	51.9	323 23.1	37.2
08	229 17.4	337 02.5	44.6	17 19.7	19.9	54 59.8	51.9	338 25.3	37.2
09	244 19.9	352 01.7	. . 45.1	32 20.9	. . 20.3	70 02.3	. . 52.0	353 27.5	. . 37.2
10	259 22.3	7 01.0	45.6	47 22.0	20.8	85 04.8	52.0	8 29.7	37.3
11	274 24.8	22 00.2	46.0	62 23.2	21.3	100 07.3	52.0	23 31.9	37.3
12	289 27.3	36 59.4	S20 46.5	77 24.4	S11 21.7	115 09.7	N 3 52.0	38 34.1	S20 37.3
13	304 29.7	51 58.7	47.0	92 25.5	22.2	130 12.2	52.0	53 36.3	37.4
14	319 32.2	66 57.9	47.4	107 26.7	22.6	145 14.7	52.1	68 38.5	37.4
15	334 34.7	81 57.1	. . 47.9	122 27.9	. . 23.1	160 17.2	. . 52.1	83 40.7	. . 37.4
16	349 37.1	96 56.4	48.3	137 29.0	23.5	175 19.7	52.1	98 42.9	37.5
17	4 39.6	111 55.6	48.8	152 30.2	24.0	190 22.1	52.1	113 45.1	37.5
18	19 42.1	126 54.8	S20 49.2	167 31.4	S11 24.5	205 24.6	N 3 52.1	128 47.2	S20 37.5
19	34 44.5	141 54.1	49.7	182 32.5	24.9	220 27.1	52.1	143 49.4	37.6
20	49 47.0	156 53.3	50.2	197 33.7	25.4	235 29.6	52.2	158 51.6	37.6
21	64 49.4	171 52.5	. . 50.6	212 34.9	. . 25.8	250 32.0	. . 52.2	173 53.8	. . 37.6
22	79 51.9	186 51.8	51.1	227 36.0	26.3	265 34.5	52.2	188 56.0	37.7
23	94 54.4	201 51.0	51.5	242 37.2	26.7	280 37.0	52.2	203 58.2	37.7
11 00 (MONDAY)	109 56.8	216 50.2	S20 52.0	257 38.4	S11 27.2	295 39.5	N 3 52.2	219 00.4	S20 37.7
01	124 59.3	231 49.5	52.4	272 39.5	27.6	310 42.0	52.3	234 02.6	37.7
02	140 01.8	246 48.7	52.9	287 40.7	28.1	325 44.5	52.3	249 04.8	37.8
03	155 04.2	261 47.9	. . 53.3	302 41.9	. . 28.6	340 46.9	. . 52.3	264 07.0	. . 37.8
04	170 06.7	276 47.1	53.8	317 43.0	29.0	355 49.4	52.3	279 09.2	37.8
05	185 09.2	291 46.4	54.2	332 44.2	29.5	10 51.9	52.3	294 11.4	37.9
06	200 11.6	306 45.6	S20 54.7	347 45.4	S11 29.9	25 54.4	N 3 52.4	309 13.6	S20 37.9
07	215 14.1	321 44.8	55.1	2 46.5	30.4	40 56.9	52.4	324 15.8	37.9
08	230 16.6	336 44.0	55.5	17 47.7	30.8	55 59.3	52.4	339 18.0	38.0
09	245 19.0	351 43.3	. . 56.0	32 48.9	. . 31.3	71 01.8	. . 52.4	354 20.2	. . 38.0
10	260 21.5	6 42.5	56.4	47 50.0	31.7	86 04.3	52.4	9 22.4	38.0
11	275 23.9	21 41.7	56.9	62 51.2	32.2	101 06.8	52.5	24 24.6	38.1
12	290 26.4	36 41.0	S20 57.3	77 52.4	S11 32.6	116 09.3	N 3 52.5	39 26.8	S20 38.1
13	305 28.9	51 40.2	57.7	92 53.5	33.1	131 11.8	52.5	54 29.0	38.1
14	320 31.3	66 39.4	58.2	107 54.7	33.6	146 14.2	52.5	69 31.1	38.2
15	335 33.8	81 38.6	. . 58.6	122 55.9	. . 34.0	161 16.7	. . 52.6	84 33.3	. . 38.2
16	350 36.3	96 37.8	59.1	137 57.0	34.5	176 19.2	52.6	99 35.5	38.2
17	5 38.7	111 37.1	59.5	152 58.2	34.9	191 21.7	52.6	114 37.7	38.2
18	20 41.2	126 36.3	S20 59.9	167 59.4	S11 35.4	206 24.2	N 3 52.6	129 39.9	S20 38.3
19	35 43.7	141 35.5	21 00.4	183 00.5	35.8	221 26.7	52.6	144 42.1	38.3
20	50 46.1	156 34.7	00.8	198 01.7	36.3	236 29.2	52.7	159 44.3	38.3
21	65 48.6	171 34.0	. . 01.2	213 02.9	. . 36.7	251 31.6	. . 52.7	174 46.5	. . 38.4
22	80 51.1	186 33.2	01.6	228 04.0	37.2	266 34.1	52.7	189 48.7	38.4
23	95 53.5	201 32.4	02.1	243 05.2	37.6	281 36.6	52.7	204 50.9	38.4
12 00 (TUESDAY)	110 56.0	216 31.6	S21 02.5	258 06.4	S11 38.1	296 39.1	N 3 52.8	219 53.1	S20 38.5
01	125 58.4	231 30.8	02.9	273 07.6	38.5	311 41.6	52.8	234 55.3	38.5
02	141 00.9	246 30.1	03.4	288 08.7	39.0	326 44.1	52.8	249 57.5	38.5
03	156 03.4	261 29.3	. . 03.8	303 09.9	. . 39.4	341 46.6	. . 52.8	264 59.7	. . 38.6
04	171 05.8	276 28.5	04.2	318 11.1	39.9	356 49.1	52.8	280 01.9	38.6
05	186 08.3	291 27.7	04.6	333 12.2	40.3	11 51.6	52.9	295 04.1	38.6
06	201 10.8	306 26.9	S21 05.0	348 13.4	S11 40.8	26 54.0	N 3 52.9	310 06.3	S20 38.6
07	216 13.2	321 26.2	05.5	3 14.6	41.2	41 56.5	52.9	325 08.5	38.7
08	231 15.7	336 25.4	05.9	18 15.7	41.7	56 59.0	52.9	340 10.7	38.7
09	246 18.2	351 24.6	. . 06.3	33 16.9	. . 42.1	72 01.5	. . 53.0	355 12.9	. . 38.7
10	261 20.6	6 23.8	06.7	48 18.1	42.6	87 04.0	53.0	10 15.1	38.8
11	276 23.1	21 23.0	07.1	63 19.3	43.0	102 06.5	53.0	25 17.3	38.8
12	291 25.6	36 22.2	S21 07.5	78 20.4	S11 43.5	117 09.0	N 3 53.0	40 19.5	S20 38.8
13	306 28.0	51 21.4	08.0	93 21.6	43.9	132 11.5	53.1	55 21.7	38.9
14	321 30.5	66 20.7	08.4	108 22.8	44.4	147 14.0	53.1	70 23.9	38.9
15	336 32.9	81 19.9	. . 08.8	123 23.9	. . 44.8	162 16.5	. . 53.1	85 26.1	. . 38.9
16	351 35.4	96 19.1	09.2	138 25.1	45.3	177 19.0	53.1	100 28.3	39.0
17	6 37.9	111 18.3	09.6	153 26.3	45.7	192 21.5	53.2	115 30.5	39.0
18	21 40.3	126 17.5	S21 10.0	168 27.4	S11 46.2	207 23.9	N 3 53.2	130 32.7	S20 39.0
19	36 42.8	141 16.7	10.4	183 28.6	46.6	222 26.4	53.2	145 34.9	39.0
20	51 45.3	156 15.9	10.8	198 29.8	47.1	237 28.9	53.2	160 37.1	39.1
21	66 47.7	171 15.2	. . 11.2	213 31.0	. . 47.5	252 31.4	. . 53.3	175 39.3	. . 39.1
22	81 50.2	186 14.4	11.6	228 32.1	48.0	267 33.9	53.3	190 41.5	39.1
23	96 52.7	201 13.6	12.0	243 33.3	48.4	282 36.4	53.3	205 43.7	39.2
Mer. Pass.	h m 16 37.5	*v* −0.8	*d* 0.4	*v* 1.2	*d* 0.5	*v* 2.5	*d* 0.0	*v* 2.2	*d* 0.0

STARS

Name	SHA ° ′	Dec ° ′
Acamar	315 16.9	S40 14.8
Achernar	335 25.5	S57 09.7
Acrux	173 07.0	S63 11.0
Adhara	255 10.7	S28 59.9
Aldebaran	290 47.1	N16 32.3
Alioth	166 19.2	N55 52.1
Alkaid	152 57.7	N49 13.8
Al Na'ir	27 42.0	S46 53.1
Alnilam	275 44.3	S 1 11.8
Alphard	217 54.1	S 8 43.8
Alphecca	126 09.8	N26 39.7
Alpheratz	357 41.7	N29 10.8
Altair	62 06.9	N 8 54.8
Ankaa	353 14.1	S42 13.4
Antares	112 24.4	S26 27.8
Arcturus	145 54.3	N19 05.9
Atria	107 25.0	S69 03.0
Avior	234 16.6	S59 33.8
Bellatrix	278 29.8	N 6 21.6
Betelgeuse	270 59.1	N 7 24.3
Canopus	263 54.8	S52 42.5
Capella	280 31.4	N46 00.7
Deneb	49 30.7	N45 20.5
Denebola	182 31.8	N14 28.8
Diphda	348 54.2	S17 54.1
Dubhe	193 49.3	N61 39.5
Elnath	278 10.1	N28 37.0
Eltanin	90 45.8	N51 29.3
Enif	33 45.7	N 9 57.0
Fomalhaut	15 22.3	S29 32.4
Gacrux	171 58.7	S57 11.9
Gienah	175 50.4	S17 37.8
Hadar	148 45.4	S60 26.6
Hamal	327 58.7	N23 32.3
Kaus Aust.	83 41.9	S34 22.4
Kochab	137 20.8	N74 05.2
Markab	13 36.8	N15 17.6
Menkar	314 13.1	N 4 09.0
Menkent	148 05.5	S36 26.6
Miaplacidus	221 38.3	S69 47.0
Mirfak	308 37.5	N49 55.1
Nunki	75 56.5	S26 16.4
Peacock	53 17.2	S56 40.9
Pollux	243 25.2	N27 59.0
Procyon	244 57.6	N 5 10.8
Rasalhague	96 05.1	N12 33.0
Regulus	207 41.4	N11 53.1
Rigel	281 10.1	S 8 11.3
Rigil Kent.	139 49.4	S60 53.6
Sabik	102 10.8	S15 44.4
Schedar	349 38.5	N56 37.7
Shaula	96 19.9	S37 06.6
Sirius	258 31.8	S16 44.6
Spica	158 29.4	S11 14.6
Suhail	222 50.7	S43 29.9
Vega	80 38.2	N38 48.0
Zuben'ubi	137 03.6	S16 06.3

	SHA ° ′	Mer. Pass. h m
Venus	106 53.4	9 33
Mars	147 41.5	6 49
Jupiter	185 42.6	4 17
Saturn	109 03.6	9 23

Day	UT (d h)	SUN GHA (° ′)	SUN Dec (° ′)	MOON GHA (° ′)	*v* (′)	MOON Dec (° ′)	*d* (′)	HP (′)
10 SUNDAY	00	178 13.3	S22 04.0	179 43.3	8.1	S17 36.9	3.3	57.8
	01	193 13.0	03.6	194 10.4	8.0	17 33.6	3.4	57.8
	02	208 12.8	03.2	208 37.4	8.0	17 30.2	3.5	57.8
	03	223 12.5	. . 02.9	223 04.4	8.1	17 26.7	3.6	57.8
	04	238 12.2	02.5	237 31.5	8.0	17 23.1	3.7	57.9
	05	253 12.0	02.2	251 58.5	8.0	17 19.4	3.8	57.9
	06	268 11.7	S22 01.8	266 25.5	8.0	S17 15.6	3.9	57.9
	07	283 11.5	01.4	280 52.5	8.0	17 11.7	4.1	57.9
	08	298 11.2	01.1	295 19.5	8.0	17 07.6	4.1	58.0
	09	313 11.0	. . 00.7	309 46.5	8.0	17 03.5	4.3	58.0
	10	328 10.7	00.3	324 13.5	8.0	16 59.2	4.3	58.0
	11	343 10.4	22 00.0	338 40.5	8.0	16 54.9	4.5	58.0
	12	358 10.2	S21 59.6	353 07.5	8.0	S16 50.4	4.5	58.1
	13	13 09.9	59.2	7 34.5	7.9	16 45.9	4.7	58.1
	14	28 09.7	58.9	22 01.4	8.0	16 41.2	4.7	58.1
	15	43 09.4	. . 58.5	36 28.4	8.0	16 36.5	4.9	58.1
	16	58 09.2	58.1	50 55.4	8.0	16 31.6	5.0	58.2
	17	73 08.9	57.8	65 22.4	8.1	16 26.6	5.1	58.2
	18	88 08.7	S21 57.4	79 49.5	8.0	S16 21.5	5.1	58.2
	19	103 08.4	57.0	94 16.5	8.0	16 16.4	5.3	58.2
	20	118 08.2	56.6	108 43.5	8.0	16 11.1	5.4	58.2
	21	133 07.9	. . 56.3	123 10.5	8.0	16 05.7	5.5	58.3
	22	148 07.6	55.9	137 37.5	8.1	16 00.2	5.6	58.3
	23	163 07.4	55.5	152 04.6	8.0	15 54.6	5.6	58.3
11 MONDAY	00	178 07.1	S21 55.1	166 31.6	8.1	S15 49.0	5.8	58.3
	01	193 06.9	54.8	180 58.7	8.1	15 43.2	5.9	58.3
	02	208 06.6	54.4	195 25.8	8.0	15 37.3	6.0	58.4
	03	223 06.4	. . 54.0	209 52.8	8.1	15 31.3	6.1	58.4
	04	238 06.1	53.6	224 19.9	8.1	15 25.2	6.1	58.4
	05	253 05.9	53.2	238 47.0	8.1	15 19.1	6.3	58.4
	06	268 05.6	S21 52.9	253 14.1	8.2	S15 12.8	6.4	58.4
	07	283 05.4	52.5	267 41.3	8.1	15 06.4	6.4	58.5
	08	298 05.1	52.1	282 08.4	8.2	15 00.0	6.6	58.5
	09	313 04.9	. . 51.7	296 35.6	8.1	14 53.4	6.6	58.5
	10	328 04.6	51.3	311 02.7	8.2	14 46.8	6.7	58.5
	11	343 04.4	50.9	325 29.9	8.2	14 40.1	6.9	58.5
	12	358 04.1	S21 50.6	339 57.1	8.2	S14 33.2	6.9	58.6
	13	13 03.9	50.2	354 24.3	8.2	14 26.3	7.0	58.6
	14	28 03.6	49.8	8 51.5	8.3	14 19.3	7.1	58.6
	15	43 03.4	. . 49.4	23 18.8	8.3	14 12.2	7.2	58.6
	16	58 03.1	49.0	37 46.1	8.2	14 05.0	7.3	58.6
	17	73 02.9	48.6	52 13.3	8.3	13 57.7	7.4	58.7
	18	88 02.6	S21 48.2	66 40.6	8.4	S13 50.3	7.4	58.7
	19	103 02.4	47.8	81 08.0	8.3	13 42.9	7.6	58.7
	20	118 02.1	47.4	95 35.3	8.4	13 35.3	7.6	58.7
	21	133 01.9	. . 47.1	110 02.7	8.3	13 27.7	7.7	58.7
	22	148 01.6	46.7	124 30.0	8.4	13 20.0	7.8	58.7
	23	163 01.4	46.3	138 57.4	8.5	13 12.2	7.9	58.8
12 TUESDAY	00	178 01.1	S21 45.9	153 24.9	8.4	S13 04.3	7.9	58.8
	01	193 00.9	45.5	167 52.3	8.5	12 56.4	8.1	58.8
	02	208 00.7	45.1	182 19.8	8.4	12 48.3	8.1	58.8
	03	223 00.4	. . 44.7	196 47.2	8.5	12 40.2	8.2	58.8
	04	238 00.2	44.3	211 14.7	8.6	12 32.0	8.3	58.8
	05	252 59.9	43.9	225 42.3	8.5	12 23.7	8.3	58.8
	06	267 59.7	S21 43.5	240 09.8	8.6	S12 15.4	8.5	58.9
	07	282 59.4	43.1	254 37.4	8.6	12 06.9	8.5	58.9
	08	297 59.2	42.7	269 05.0	8.6	11 58.4	8.6	58.9
	09	312 58.9	. . 42.3	283 32.6	8.6	11 49.8	8.6	58.9
	10	327 58.7	41.9	298 00.2	8.7	11 41.2	8.8	58.9
	11	342 58.5	41.5	312 27.9	8.7	11 32.4	8.8	58.9
	12	357 58.2	S21 41.1	326 55.6	8.7	S11 23.6	8.8	58.9
	13	12 58.0	40.7	341 23.3	8.7	11 14.8	9.0	59.0
	14	27 57.7	40.3	355 51.0	8.7	11 05.8	9.0	59.0
	15	42 57.5	. . 39.9	10 18.7	8.8	10 56.8	9.1	59.0
	16	57 57.2	39.5	24 46.5	8.8	10 47.7	9.1	59.0
	17	72 57.0	39.1	39 14.3	8.8	10 38.6	9.2	59.0
	18	87 56.8	S21 38.7	53 42.1	8.9	S10 29.4	9.3	59.0
	19	102 56.5	38.3	68 10.0	8.8	10 20.1	9.4	59.0
	20	117 56.3	37.8	82 37.8	8.9	10 10.7	9.4	59.0
	21	132 56.0	. . 37.4	97 05.7	8.9	10 01.3	9.4	59.0
	22	147 55.8	37.0	111 33.6	9.0	9 51.9	9.6	59.1
	23	162 55.5	36.6	126 01.6	8.9	S 9 42.3	9.6	59.1
		SD 16.3	*d* 0.4	SD 15.8		16.0		16.1

Lat.	Twilight Naut. (h m)	Twilight Civil (h m)	Sunrise (h m)	Moonrise 10 (h m)	Moonrise 11 (h m)	Moonrise 12 (h m)	Moonrise 13 (h m)
N 72	08 10	10 09	■	11 08	10 56	10 48	10 42
N 70	07 54	09 30	■	10 15	10 24	10 29	10 31
68	07 41	09 03	10 55	09 42	10 01	10 13	10 21
66	07 30	08 42	10 06	09 17	09 43	10 00	10 14
64	07 20	08 26	09 35	08 58	09 28	09 50	10 07
62	07 12	08 12	09 12	08 43	09 15	09 41	10 01
60	07 05	08 00	08 54	08 30	09 05	09 33	09 56
N 58	06 58	07 49	08 39	08 19	08 55	09 26	09 52
56	06 53	07 40	08 26	08 09	08 47	09 20	09 48
54	06 47	07 32	08 15	08 00	08 40	09 14	09 44
52	06 42	07 25	08 05	07 52	08 34	09 09	09 41
50	06 37	07 18	07 56	07 45	08 28	09 05	09 38
45	06 27	07 04	07 37	07 30	08 15	08 55	09 31
N 40	06 18	06 51	07 21	07 18	08 04	08 47	09 26
35	06 09	06 41	07 08	07 08	07 55	08 40	09 21
30	06 01	06 31	06 57	06 58	07 47	08 34	09 17
20	05 46	06 14	06 37	06 42	07 34	08 23	09 10
N 10	05 32	05 58	06 20	06 28	07 22	08 13	09 04
0	05 16	05 42	06 04	06 15	07 10	08 04	08 58
S 10	04 58	05 25	05 48	06 02	06 59	07 56	08 52
20	04 37	05 06	05 30	05 49	06 47	07 46	08 45
30	04 10	04 43	05 10	05 33	06 33	07 35	08 38
35	03 53	04 29	04 58	05 23	06 25	07 29	08 34
40	03 31	04 12	04 44	05 13	06 16	07 22	08 29
45	03 04	03 51	04 27	05 00	06 05	07 13	08 24
S 50	02 24	03 24	04 07	04 45	05 52	07 03	08 17
52	02 02	03 11	03 57	04 38	05 46	06 59	08 14
54	01 31	02 55	03 46	04 30	05 39	06 54	08 11
56	00 25	02 36	03 33	04 21	05 32	06 48	08 07
58	////	02 12	03 18	04 11	05 23	06 41	08 03
S 60	////	01 39	03 01	04 00	05 14	06 34	07 58

Lat.	Sunset (h m)	Twilight Civil (h m)	Twilight Naut. (h m)	Moonset 10 (h m)	Moonset 11 (h m)	Moonset 12 (h m)	Moonset 13 (h m)
N 72	■	14 07	16 06	13 57	16 04	18 04	20 01
N 70	■	14 46	16 22	14 50	16 35	18 22	20 10
68	13 21	15 13	16 35	15 23	16 57	18 37	20 18
66	14 10	15 34	16 46	15 46	17 14	18 48	20 24
64	14 41	15 50	16 56	16 05	17 29	18 58	20 30
62	15 04	16 04	17 04	16 20	17 40	19 06	20 34
60	15 22	16 16	17 11	16 33	17 50	19 13	20 38
N 58	15 37	16 26	17 17	16 44	17 59	19 19	20 42
56	15 50	16 35	17 23	16 53	18 07	19 25	20 45
54	16 01	16 44	17 29	17 02	18 14	19 30	20 48
52	16 11	16 51	17 34	17 09	18 20	19 34	20 50
50	16 20	16 58	17 38	17 16	18 25	19 38	20 52
45	16 39	17 12	17 49	17 30	18 37	19 47	20 57
N 40	16 54	17 24	17 58	17 42	18 47	19 54	21 02
35	17 07	17 35	18 06	17 52	18 55	20 00	21 05
30	17 19	17 45	18 14	18 01	19 02	20 05	21 08
20	17 38	18 02	18 29	18 16	19 15	20 14	21 14
N 10	17 55	18 18	18 44	18 29	19 26	20 22	21 18
0	18 11	18 34	19 00	18 42	19 36	20 30	21 23
S 10	18 28	18 50	19 17	18 54	19 46	20 37	21 27
20	18 45	19 09	19 38	19 07	19 57	20 45	21 32
30	19 06	19 32	20 05	19 22	20 09	20 54	21 37
35	19 17	19 47	20 22	19 30	20 16	20 59	21 40
40	19 31	20 03	20 43	19 40	20 24	21 05	21 43
45	19 48	20 24	21 11	19 51	20 34	21 12	21 47
S 50	20 08	20 50	21 50	20 05	20 45	21 20	21 51
52	20 18	21 04	22 12	20 12	20 50	21 23	21 53
54	20 29	21 19	22 42	20 19	20 56	21 27	21 56
56	20 41	21 38	23 40	20 27	21 02	21 32	21 58
58	20 56	22 02	////	20 35	21 09	21 37	22 01
S 60	21 13	22 34	////	20 46	21 17	21 42	22 04

Day	SUN Eqn. of Time 00^h (m s)	SUN Eqn. of Time 12^h (m s)	SUN Mer. Pass. (h m)	MOON Mer. Pass. Upper (h m)	MOON Mer. Pass. Lower (h m)	MOON Age (d)	MOON Phase (%)
10	07 06	07 19	12 07	12 29	00 01	00	0 ●
11	07 31	07 43	12 08	13 23	00 56	01	3
12	07 55	08 07	12 08	14 17	01 50	02	7

UT d	UT h	ARIES GHA	VENUS −4·0 GHA	VENUS Dec	MARS +1·1 GHA	MARS Dec	JUPITER −2·3 GHA	JUPITER Dec	SATURN +0·5 GHA	SATURN Dec
d	h	° ′	° ′	° ′	° ′	° ′	° ′	° ′	° ′	° ′
13	00	111 55.1	216 12.8	S21 12.5	258 34.5	S11 48.9	297 38.9	N 3 53.3	220 45.9	S20 39.2
	01	126 57.6	231 12.0	12.9	273 35.6	49.3	312 41.4	53.4	235 48.1	39.2
	02	142 00.0	246 11.2	13.3	288 36.8	49.7	327 43.9	53.4	250 50.3	39.3
	03	157 02.5	261 10.4	. . 13.7	303 38.0	. . 50.2	342 46.4	. . 53.4	265 52.4	. . 39.3
	04	172 05.0	276 09.6	14.1	318 39.2	50.6	357 48.9	53.4	280 54.6	39.3
	05	187 07.4	291 08.8	14.5	333 40.3	51.1	12 51.4	53.5	295 56.8	39.3
W	06	202 09.9	306 08.1	S21 14.8	348 41.5	S11 51.5	27 53.9	N 3 53.5	310 59.0	S20 39.4
E	07	217 12.4	321 07.3	15.2	3 42.7	52.0	42 56.4	53.5	326 01.2	39.4
D	08	232 14.8	336 06.5	15.6	18 43.9	52.4	57 58.9	53.6	341 03.4	39.4
N	09	247 17.3	351 05.7	. . 16.0	33 45.0	. . 52.9	73 01.4	. . 53.6	356 05.6	. . 39.5
E	10	262 19.8	6 04.9	16.4	48 46.2	53.3	88 03.9	53.6	11 07.8	39.5
S	11	277 22.2	21 04.1	16.8	63 47.4	53.8	103 06.4	53.6	26 10.0	39.5
D	12	292 24.7	36 03.3	S21 17.2	78 48.5	S11 54.2	118 08.9	N 3 53.7	41 12.2	S20 39.6
A	13	307 27.2	51 02.5	17.6	93 49.7	54.7	133 11.4	53.7	56 14.4	39.6
Y	14	322 29.6	66 01.7	18.0	108 50.9	55.1	148 13.9	53.7	71 16.6	39.6
	15	337 32.1	81 00.9	. . 18.4	123 52.1	. . 55.5	163 16.4	. . 53.7	86 18.8	. . 39.6
	16	352 34.5	96 00.1	18.8	138 53.2	56.0	178 18.9	53.8	101 21.0	39.7
	17	7 37.0	110 59.3	19.1	153 54.4	56.4	193 21.4	53.8	116 23.2	39.7
	18	22 39.5	125 58.5	S21 19.5	168 55.6	S11 56.9	208 23.9	N 3 53.8	131 25.4	S20 39.7
	19	37 41.9	140 57.7	19.9	183 56.8	57.3	223 26.4	53.9	146 27.6	39.8
	20	52 44.4	155 56.9	20.3	198 57.9	57.8	238 28.9	53.9	161 29.8	39.8
	21	67 46.9	170 56.1	. . 20.7	213 59.1	. . 58.2	253 31.4	. . 53.9	176 32.0	. . 39.8
	22	82 49.3	185 55.3	21.1	229 00.3	58.7	268 33.9	53.9	191 34.2	39.9
	23	97 51.8	200 54.5	21.4	244 01.5	59.1	283 36.4	54.0	206 36.4	39.9
14	00	112 54.3	215 53.8	S21 21.8	259 02.6	S11 59.5	298 38.9	N 3 54.0	221 38.7	S20 39.9
	01	127 56.7	230 53.0	22.2	274 03.8	12 00.0	313 41.4	54.0	236 40.9	39.9
	02	142 59.2	245 52.2	22.6	289 05.0	00.4	328 43.9	54.1	251 43.1	40.0
	03	158 01.7	260 51.4	. . 22.9	304 06.1	. . 00.9	343 46.4	. . 54.1	266 45.3	. . 40.0
	04	173 04.1	275 50.6	23.3	319 07.3	01.3	358 48.9	54.1	281 47.5	40.0
	05	188 06.6	290 49.8	23.7	334 08.5	01.8	13 51.4	54.2	296 49.7	40.1
	06	203 09.0	305 49.0	S21 24.1	349 09.7	S12 02.2	28 53.9	N 3 54.2	311 51.9	S20 40.1
	07	218 11.5	320 48.2	24.4	4 10.8	02.6	43 56.4	54.2	326 54.1	40.1
T	08	233 14.0	335 47.4	24.8	19 12.0	03.1	58 58.9	54.2	341 56.3	40.2
H	09	248 16.4	350 46.6	. . 25.2	34 13.2	. . 03.5	74 01.4	. . 54.3	356 58.5	. . 40.2
U	10	263 18.9	5 45.8	25.5	49 14.4	04.0	89 03.9	54.3	12 00.7	40.2
R	11	278 21.4	20 45.0	25.9	64 15.6	04.4	104 06.4	54.3	27 02.9	40.2
S	12	293 23.8	35 44.2	S21 26.3	79 16.7	S12 04.9	119 08.9	N 3 54.4	42 05.1	S20 40.3
D	13	308 26.3	50 43.4	26.6	94 17.9	05.3	134 11.5	54.4	57 07.3	40.3
A	14	323 28.8	65 42.6	27.0	109 19.1	05.7	149 14.0	54.4	72 09.5	40.3
Y	15	338 31.2	80 41.7	. . 27.4	124 20.3	. . 06.2	164 16.5	. . 54.5	87 11.7	. . 40.4
	16	353 33.7	95 40.9	27.7	139 21.4	06.6	179 19.0	54.5	102 13.9	40.4
	17	8 36.1	110 40.1	28.1	154 22.6	07.1	194 21.5	54.5	117 16.1	40.4
	18	23 38.6	125 39.3	S21 28.4	169 23.8	S12 07.5	209 24.0	N 3 54.6	132 18.3	S20 40.4
	19	38 41.1	140 38.5	28.8	184 25.0	07.9	224 26.5	54.6	147 20.5	40.5
	20	53 43.5	155 37.7	29.2	199 26.1	08.4	239 29.0	54.6	162 22.7	40.5
	21	68 46.0	170 36.9	. . 29.5	214 27.3	. . 08.8	254 31.5	. . 54.6	177 24.9	. . 40.5
	22	83 48.5	185 36.1	29.9	229 28.5	09.3	269 34.0	54.7	192 27.1	40.6
	23	98 50.9	200 35.3	30.2	244 29.7	09.7	284 36.5	54.7	207 29.3	40.6
15	00	113 53.4	215 34.5	S21 30.6	259 30.8	S12 10.1	299 39.0	N 3 54.7	222 31.5	S20 40.6
	01	128 55.9	230 33.7	30.9	274 32.0	10.6	314 41.6	54.8	237 33.7	40.6
	02	143 58.3	245 32.9	31.3	289 33.2	11.0	329 44.1	54.8	252 35.9	40.7
	03	159 00.8	260 32.1	. . 31.6	304 34.4	. . 11.5	344 46.6	. . 54.8	267 38.1	. . 40.7
	04	174 03.3	275 31.3	32.0	319 35.6	11.9	359 49.1	54.9	282 40.3	40.7
	05	189 05.7	290 30.5	32.3	334 36.7	12.3	14 51.6	54.9	297 42.5	40.8
	06	204 08.2	305 29.7	S21 32.7	349 37.9	S12 12.8	29 54.1	N 3 54.9	312 44.7	S20 40.8
	07	219 10.6	320 28.9	33.0	4 39.1	13.2	44 56.6	55.0	327 46.9	40.8
	08	234 13.1	335 28.1	33.4	19 40.3	13.7	59 59.1	55.0	342 49.1	40.9
F	09	249 15.6	350 27.2	. . 33.7	34 41.4	. . 14.1	75 01.7	. . 55.0	357 51.3	. . 40.9
R	10	264 18.0	5 26.4	34.1	49 42.6	14.5	90 04.2	55.1	12 53.5	40.9
I	11	279 20.5	20 25.6	34.4	64 43.8	15.0	105 06.7	55.1	27 55.7	40.9
D	12	294 23.0	35 24.8	S21 34.7	79 45.0	S12 15.4	120 09.2	N 3 55.1	42 57.9	S20 41.0
A	13	309 25.4	50 24.0	35.1	94 46.2	15.8	135 11.7	55.2	58 00.2	41.0
Y	14	324 27.9	65 23.2	35.4	109 47.3	16.3	150 14.2	55.2	73 02.4	41.0
	15	339 30.4	80 22.4	. . 35.7	124 48.5	. . 16.7	165 16.7	. . 55.2	88 04.6	. . 41.1
	16	354 32.8	95 21.6	36.1	139 49.7	17.1	180 19.3	55.3	103 06.8	41.1
	17	9 35.3	110 20.8	36.4	154 50.9	17.6	195 21.8	55.3	118 09.0	41.1
	18	24 37.7	125 20.0	S21 36.8	169 52.0	S12 18.0	210 24.3	N 3 55.3	133 11.2	S20 41.1
	19	39 40.2	140 19.1	37.1	184 53.2	18.5	225 26.8	55.4	148 13.4	41.2
	20	54 42.7	155 18.3	37.4	199 54.4	18.9	240 29.3	55.4	163 15.6	41.2
	21	69 45.1	170 17.5	. . 37.8	214 55.6	. . 19.3	255 31.8	. . 55.5	178 17.8	. . 41.2
	22	84 47.6	185 16.7	38.1	229 56.8	19.8	270 34.3	55.5	193 20.0	41.3
	23	99 50.1	200 15.9	38.4	244 57.9	20.2	285 36.9	55.5	208 22.2	41.3
Mer. Pass.		h m 16 25.7	*v* −0.8	*d* 0.4	*v* 1.2	*d* 0.4	*v* 2.5	*d* 0.0	*v* 2.2	*d* 0.0

STARS

Name	SHA	Dec
	° ′	° ′
Acamar	315 16.9	S40 14.8
Achernar	335 25.6	S57 09.7
Acrux	173 06.9	S63 11.0
Adhara	255 10.7	S28 59.9
Aldebaran	290 47.1	N16 32.3
Alioth	166 19.2	N55 52.1
Alkaid	152 57.7	N49 13.8
Al Na'ir	27 42.0	S46 53.1
Alnilam	275 44.3	S 1 11.8
Alphard	217 54.1	S 8 43.9
Alphecca	126 09.7	N26 39.6
Alpheratz	357 41.8	N29 10.8
Altair	62 06.9	N 8 54.8
Ankaa	353 14.2	S42 13.4
Antares	112 24.4	S26 27.8
Arcturus	145 54.2	N19 05.9
Atria	107 25.0	S69 03.0
Avior	234 16.6	S59 33.8
Bellatrix	278 29.8	N 6 21.6
Betelgeuse	270 59.1	N 7 24.3
Canopus	263 54.8	S52 42.6
Capella	280 31.4	N46 00.7
Deneb	49 30.7	N45 20.5
Denebola	182 31.8	N14 28.8
Diphda	348 54.2	S17 54.1
Dubhe	193 49.3	N61 39.5
Elnath	278 10.1	N28 37.0
Eltanin	90 45.8	N51 29.3
Enif	33 45.7	N 9 57.0
Fomalhaut	15 22.3	S29 32.4
Gacrux	171 58.6	S57 11.9
Gienah	175 50.4	S17 37.8
Hadar	148 45.4	S60 26.6
Hamal	327 58.7	N23 32.2
Kaus Aust.	83 41.9	S34 22.4
Kochab	137 20.7	N74 05.2
Markab	13 36.8	N15 17.6
Menkar	314 13.1	N 4 09.0
Menkent	148 05.5	S36 26.6
Miaplacidus	221 38.2	S69 47.0
Mirfak	308 37.5	N49 55.1
Nunki	75 56.5	S26 16.4
Peacock	53 17.2	S56 40.9
Pollux	243 25.2	N27 59.0
Procyon	244 57.6	N 5 10.8
Rasalhague	96 05.1	N12 33.0
Regulus	207 41.4	N11 53.1
Rigel	281 10.1	S 8 11.3
Rigil Kent.	139 49.4	S60 53.6
Sabik	102 10.8	S15 44.5
Schedar	349 38.5	N56 37.7
Shaula	96 19.9	S37 06.6
Sirius	258 31.8	S16 44.6
Spica	158 29.4	S11 14.6
Suhail	222 50.7	S43 29.9
Vega	80 38.2	N38 48.0
Zuben'ubi	137 03.6	S16 06.3

	SHA	Mer. Pass.
	° ′	h m
Venus	102 59.5	9 37
Mars	146 08.4	6 43
Jupiter	185 44.6	4 05
Saturn	108 44.4	9 12

UT d h	SUN GHA ° ′	SUN Dec ° ′	MOON GHA ° ′	v ′	MOON Dec ° ′	d ′	HP ′
13 00	177 55.3	S21 36.2	140 29.5	9.0	S 9 32.7	9.6	59.1
01	192 55.1	35.8	154 57.5	9.0	9 23.1	9.7	59.1
02	207 54.8	35.4	169 25.5	9.1	9 13.4	9.8	59.1
03	222 54.6	. . 35.0	183 53.6	9.0	9 03.6	9.8	59.1
04	237 54.3	34.5	198 21.6	9.1	8 53.8	9.9	59.1
05	252 54.1	34.1	212 49.7	9.1	8 43.9	9.9	59.1
06	267 53.9	S21 33.7	227 17.8	9.1	S 8 34.0	10.0	59.1
W 07	282 53.6	33.3	241 45.9	9.1	8 24.0	10.0	59.1
E 08	297 53.4	32.9	256 14.0	9.2	8 14.0	10.1	59.2
D 09	312 53.2	. . 32.5	270 42.2	9.2	8 03.9	10.1	59.2
N 10	327 52.9	32.0	285 10.4	9.2	7 53.8	10.2	59.2
E 11	342 52.7	31.6	299 38.6	9.2	7 43.6	10.2	59.2
S 12	357 52.4	S21 31.2	314 06.8	9.3	S 7 33.4	10.3	59.2
D 13	12 52.2	30.8	328 35.1	9.2	7 23.1	10.3	59.2
A 14	27 52.0	30.4	343 03.3	9.3	7 12.8	10.4	59.2
Y 15	42 51.7	. . 29.9	357 31.6	9.3	7 02.4	10.4	59.2
16	57 51.5	29.5	11 59.9	9.3	6 52.0	10.4	59.2
17	72 51.3	29.1	26 28.2	9.4	6 41.6	10.5	59.2
18	87 51.0	S21 28.7	40 56.6	9.4	S 6 31.1	10.6	59.2
19	102 50.8	28.2	55 25.0	9.3	6 20.5	10.5	59.2
20	117 50.6	27.8	69 53.3	9.4	6 10.0	10.6	59.2
21	132 50.3	. . 27.4	84 21.7	9.5	5 59.4	10.7	59.2
22	147 50.1	27.0	98 50.2	9.4	5 48.7	10.6	59.3
23	162 49.9	26.5	113 18.6	9.5	5 38.1	10.7	59.3
14 00	177 49.6	S21 26.1	127 47.1	9.4	S 5 27.4	10.8	59.3
01	192 49.4	25.7	142 15.5	9.5	5 16.6	10.7	59.3
02	207 49.2	25.2	156 44.0	9.5	5 05.9	10.8	59.3
03	222 48.9	. . 24.8	171 12.5	9.6	4 55.1	10.9	59.3
04	237 48.7	24.4	185 41.1	9.5	4 44.2	10.8	59.3
05	252 48.5	24.0	200 09.6	9.6	4 33.4	10.9	59.3
06	267 48.2	S21 23.5	214 38.2	9.5	S 4 22.5	10.9	59.3
T 07	282 48.0	23.1	229 06.7	9.6	4 11.6	10.9	59.3
H 08	297 47.8	22.6	243 35.3	9.6	4 00.7	11.0	59.3
U 09	312 47.5	. . 22.2	258 03.9	9.6	3 49.7	11.0	59.3
R 10	327 47.3	21.8	272 32.5	9.6	3 38.7	11.0	59.3
S 11	342 47.1	21.3	287 01.1	9.7	3 27.7	11.0	59.3
D 12	357 46.8	S21 20.9	301 29.8	9.6	S 3 16.7	11.0	59.3
A 13	12 46.6	20.5	315 58.4	9.7	3 05.7	11.1	59.3
Y 14	27 46.4	20.0	330 27.1	9.6	2 54.6	11.1	59.3
15	42 46.2	. . 19.6	344 55.7	9.7	2 43.5	11.1	59.3
16	57 45.9	19.1	359 24.4	9.7	2 32.4	11.1	59.3
17	72 45.7	18.7	13 53.1	9.7	2 21.3	11.1	59.3
18	87 45.5	S21 18.3	28 21.8	9.7	S 2 10.2	11.1	59.3
19	102 45.2	17.8	42 50.5	9.7	1 59.1	11.2	59.3
20	117 45.0	17.4	57 19.2	9.7	1 47.9	11.1	59.3
21	132 44.8	. . 16.9	71 47.9	9.8	1 36.8	11.2	59.3
22	147 44.6	16.5	86 16.7	9.7	1 25.6	11.1	59.3
23	162 44.3	16.0	100 45.4	9.7	1 14.5	11.2	59.3
15 00	177 44.1	S21 15.6	115 14.1	9.8	S 1 03.3	11.2	59.3
01	192 43.9	15.2	129 42.9	9.7	0 52.1	11.2	59.3
02	207 43.7	14.7	144 11.6	9.8	0 40.9	11.2	59.3
03	222 43.4	. . 14.3	158 40.4	9.8	0 29.7	11.1	59.3
04	237 43.2	13.8	173 09.2	9.7	0 18.6	11.2	59.3
05	252 43.0	13.4	187 37.9	9.8	S 0 07.4	11.2	59.3
06	267 42.8	S21 12.9	202 06.7	9.8	N 0 03.8	11.2	59.3
07	282 42.5	12.5	216 35.5	9.7	0 15.0	11.2	59.3
08	297 42.3	12.0	231 04.2	9.8	0 26.2	11.2	59.3
F 09	312 42.1	. . 11.6	245 33.0	9.8	0 37.4	11.2	59.3
R 10	327 41.9	11.1	260 01.8	9.8	0 48.6	11.1	59.3
I 11	342 41.6	10.6	274 30.6	9.7	0 59.7	11.2	59.3
D 12	357 41.4	S21 10.2	288 59.3	9.8	N 1 10.9	11.1	59.3
A 13	12 41.2	09.7	303 28.1	9.8	1 22.0	11.2	59.3
Y 14	27 41.0	09.3	317 56.9	9.7	1 33.2	11.1	59.3
15	42 40.7	. . 08.8	332 25.6	9.8	1 44.3	11.2	59.3
16	57 40.5	08.4	346 54.4	9.8	1 55.5	11.1	59.3
17	72 40.3	07.9	1 23.2	9.7	2 06.6	11.1	59.3
18	87 40.1	S21 07.4	15 51.9	9.8	N 2 17.7	11.0	59.3
19	102 39.9	07.0	30 20.7	9.7	2 28.7	11.1	59.3
20	117 39.6	06.5	44 49.4	9.8	2 39.8	11.1	59.3
21	132 39.4	. . 06.1	59 18.2	9.7	2 50.9	11.0	59.3
22	147 39.2	05.6	73 46.9	9.7	3 01.9	11.0	59.3
23	162 39.0	05.1	88 15.6	9.8	N 3 12.9	11.0	59.3
	SD 16.3	*d* 0.4	SD 16.1		16.2		16.2

Lat. °	Twilight Naut. h m	Twilight Civil h m	Sunrise h m	Moonrise 13 h m	Moonrise 14 h m	Moonrise 15 h m	Moonrise 16 h m
N 72	08 04	09 58	▬	10 42	10 37	10 32	10 27
N 70	07 49	09 22	▬	10 31	10 32	10 33	10 34
68	07 36	08 57	10 40	10 21	10 28	10 34	10 40
66	07 26	08 37	09 57	10 14	10 24	10 34	10 45
64	07 17	08 21	09 29	10 07	10 21	10 35	10 49
62	07 09	08 08	09 07	10 01	10 19	10 35	10 52
60	07 02	07 57	08 50	09 56	10 17	10 36	10 56
N 58	06 56	07 47	08 35	09 52	10 15	10 36	10 58
56	06 51	07 38	08 23	09 48	10 13	10 37	11 01
54	06 45	07 30	08 12	09 44	10 11	10 37	11 03
52	06 41	07 23	08 02	09 41	10 10	10 37	11 05
50	06 36	07 17	07 54	09 38	10 08	10 38	11 07
45	06 26	07 03	07 36	09 31	10 05	10 38	11 12
N 40	06 17	06 51	07 21	09 26	10 03	10 39	11 15
35	06 09	06 40	07 08	09 21	10 01	10 39	11 18
30	06 02	06 31	06 57	09 17	09 59	10 40	11 21
20	05 47	06 14	06 38	09 10	09 56	10 41	11 26
N 10	05 32	05 58	06 21	09 04	09 53	10 41	11 30
0	05 17	05 43	06 05	08 58	09 50	10 42	11 34
S 10	05 00	05 27	05 49	08 52	09 47	10 43	11 38
20	04 39	05 08	05 32	08 45	09 45	10 43	11 42
30	04 13	04 45	05 12	08 38	09 41	10 44	11 47
35	03 56	04 32	05 00	08 34	09 39	10 45	11 50
40	03 35	04 15	04 47	08 29	09 37	10 45	11 53
45	03 08	03 55	04 31	08 24	09 35	10 46	11 57
S 50	02 30	03 29	04 11	08 17	09 32	10 47	12 02
52	02 09	03 16	04 01	08 14	09 31	10 47	12 04
54	01 41	03 01	03 51	08 11	09 29	10 48	12 06
56	00 53	02 43	03 39	08 07	09 28	10 48	12 09
58	////	02 20	03 24	08 03	09 26	10 49	12 12
S 60	////	01 50	03 08	07 58	09 24	10 49	12 15

Lat. °	Sunset h m	Twilight Civil h m	Twilight Naut. h m	Moonset 13 h m	Moonset 14 h m	Moonset 15 h m	Moonset 16 h m
N 72	▬	14 21	16 15	20 01	21 55	23 48	25 42
N 70	▬	14 56	16 30	20 10	21 57	23 44	25 30
68	13 38	15 22	16 42	20 18	21 59	23 40	25 21
66	14 21	15 41	16 52	20 24	22 01	23 37	25 12
64	14 49	15 57	17 01	20 30	22 02	23 34	25 06
62	15 11	16 10	17 09	20 34	22 03	23 32	25 00
60	15 28	16 22	17 16	20 38	22 04	23 30	24 55
N 58	15 43	16 31	17 22	20 42	22 05	23 28	24 51
56	15 55	16 40	17 28	20 45	22 06	23 26	24 47
54	16 06	16 48	17 33	20 48	22 06	23 25	24 43
52	16 16	16 55	17 38	20 50	22 07	23 24	24 40
50	16 24	17 01	17 42	20 52	22 07	23 22	24 37
45	16 43	17 15	17 52	20 57	22 09	23 20	24 31
N 40	16 57	17 27	18 01	21 02	22 10	23 18	24 26
35	17 10	17 38	18 09	21 05	22 11	23 16	24 21
30	17 21	17 47	18 16	21 08	22 11	23 14	24 17
20	17 40	18 04	18 31	21 14	22 13	23 11	24 10
N 10	17 57	18 19	18 45	21 18	22 14	23 09	24 04
0	18 13	18 35	19 01	21 23	22 15	23 07	23 59
S 10	18 28	18 51	19 18	21 27	22 16	23 04	23 53
20	18 45	19 10	19 38	21 32	22 17	23 02	23 47
30	19 05	19 32	20 04	21 37	22 18	22 59	23 40
35	19 17	19 46	20 21	21 40	22 19	22 57	23 36
40	19 30	20 02	20 42	21 43	22 19	22 55	23 32
45	19 46	20 22	21 08	21 47	22 20	22 53	23 27
S 50	20 06	20 48	21 46	21 51	22 21	22 50	23 21
52	20 15	21 01	22 07	21 53	22 22	22 49	23 18
54	20 26	21 16	22 34	21 56	22 22	22 48	23 15
56	20 38	21 33	23 19	21 58	22 23	22 47	23 11
58	20 52	21 55	////	22 01	22 23	22 45	23 08
S 60	21 09	22 25	////	22 04	22 24	22 43	23 03

Day	SUN Eqn. of Time 00^h	SUN Eqn. of Time 12^h	SUN Mer. Pass.	MOON Mer. Pass. Upper	MOON Mer. Pass. Lower	MOON Age	MOON Phase
d	m s	m s	h m	h m	h m	d	%
13	08 18	08 30	12 08	15 10	02 44	03	14
14	08 41	08 52	12 09	16 02	03 36	04	23
15	09 03	09 14	12 09	16 54	04 28	05	34

Day	UT (d h)	ARIES GHA	VENUS −4·0 GHA	VENUS Dec	MARS +1·0 GHA	MARS Dec	JUPITER −2·3 GHA	JUPITER Dec	SATURN +0·5 GHA	SATURN Dec
		° ′	° ′	° ′	° ′	° ′	° ′	° ′	° ′	° ′
SATURDAY	16 00	114 52.5	215 15.1	S21 38.7	259 59.1	S12 20.6	300 39.4	N 3 55.6	223 24.4	S20 41.3
	01	129 55.0	230 14.3	39.1	275 00.3	21.1	315 41.9	55.6	238 26.6	41.3
	02	144 57.5	245 13.5	39.4	290 01.5	21.5	330 44.4	55.6	253 28.8	41.4
	03	159 59.9	260 12.6	39.7	305 02.7	21.9	345 46.9	55.7	268 31.0	41.4
	04	175 02.4	275 11.8	40.0	320 03.8	22.4	0 49.5	55.7	283 33.2	41.4
	05	190 04.9	290 11.0	40.4	335 05.0	22.8	15 52.0	55.7	298 35.4	41.5
	06	205 07.3	305 10.2	S21 40.7	350 06.2	S12 23.2	30 54.5	N 3 55.8	313 37.6	S20 41.5
	07	220 09.8	320 09.4	41.0	5 07.4	23.7	45 57.0	55.8	328 39.9	41.5
	08	235 12.2	335 08.6	41.3	20 08.6	24.1	60 59.5	55.8	343 42.1	41.5
	09	250 14.7	350 07.7	41.6	35 09.7	24.6	76 02.1	55.9	358 44.3	41.6
	10	265 17.2	5 06.9	42.0	50 10.9	25.0	91 04.6	55.9	13 46.5	41.6
	11	280 19.6	20 06.1	42.3	65 12.1	25.4	106 07.1	56.0	28 48.7	41.6
	12	295 22.1	35 05.3	S21 42.6	80 13.3	S12 25.9	121 09.6	N 3 56.0	43 50.9	S20 41.7
	13	310 24.6	50 04.5	42.9	95 14.5	26.3	136 12.1	56.0	58 53.1	41.7
	14	325 27.0	65 03.7	43.2	110 15.7	26.7	151 14.7	56.1	73 55.3	41.7
	15	340 29.5	80 02.8	43.5	125 16.8	27.2	166 17.2	56.1	88 57.5	41.7
	16	355 32.0	95 02.0	43.8	140 18.0	27.6	181 19.7	56.1	103 59.7	41.8
	17	10 34.4	110 01.2	44.1	155 19.2	28.0	196 22.2	56.2	119 01.9	41.8
	18	25 36.9	125 00.4	S21 44.5	170 20.4	S12 28.4	211 24.7	N 3 56.2	134 04.1	S20 41.8
	19	40 39.4	139 59.6	44.8	185 21.6	28.9	226 27.3	56.3	149 06.3	41.9
	20	55 41.8	154 58.7	45.1	200 22.7	29.3	241 29.8	56.3	164 08.5	41.9
	21	70 44.3	169 57.9	45.4	215 23.9	29.7	256 32.3	56.3	179 10.7	41.9
	22	85 46.7	184 57.1	45.7	230 25.1	30.2	271 34.8	56.4	194 13.0	41.9
	23	100 49.2	199 56.3	46.0	245 26.3	30.6	286 37.4	56.4	209 15.2	42.0
SUNDAY	17 00	115 51.7	214 55.5	S21 46.3	260 27.5	S12 31.0	301 39.9	N 3 56.4	224 17.4	S20 42.0
	01	130 54.1	229 54.6	46.6	275 28.7	31.5	316 42.4	56.5	239 19.6	42.0
	02	145 56.6	244 53.8	46.9	290 29.8	31.9	331 44.9	56.5	254 21.8	42.0
	03	160 59.1	259 53.0	47.2	305 31.0	32.3	346 47.5	56.6	269 24.0	42.1
	04	176 01.5	274 52.2	47.5	320 32.2	32.8	1 50.0	56.6	284 26.2	42.1
	05	191 04.0	289 51.4	47.8	335 33.4	33.2	16 52.5	56.6	299 28.4	42.1
	06	206 06.5	304 50.5	S21 48.1	350 34.6	S12 33.6	31 55.0	N 3 56.7	314 30.6	S20 42.2
	07	221 08.9	319 49.7	48.4	5 35.8	34.1	46 57.6	56.7	329 32.8	42.2
	08	236 11.4	334 48.9	48.7	20 36.9	34.5	62 00.1	56.8	344 35.0	42.2
	09	251 13.8	349 48.1	49.0	35 38.1	34.9	77 02.6	56.8	359 37.2	42.2
	10	266 16.3	4 47.2	49.2	50 39.3	35.3	92 05.2	56.8	14 39.5	42.3
	11	281 18.8	19 46.4	49.5	65 40.5	35.8	107 07.7	56.9	29 41.7	42.3
	12	296 21.2	34 45.6	S21 49.8	80 41.7	S12 36.2	122 10.2	N 3 56.9	44 43.9	S20 42.3
	13	311 23.7	49 44.8	50.1	95 42.9	36.6	137 12.7	57.0	59 46.1	42.4
	14	326 26.2	64 44.0	50.4	110 44.0	37.1	152 15.3	57.0	74 48.3	42.4
	15	341 28.6	79 43.1	50.7	125 45.2	37.5	167 17.8	57.0	89 50.5	42.4
	16	356 31.1	94 42.3	51.0	140 46.4	37.9	182 20.3	57.1	104 52.7	42.4
	17	11 33.6	109 41.5	51.3	155 47.6	38.4	197 22.9	57.1	119 54.9	42.5
	18	26 36.0	124 40.6	S21 51.5	170 48.8	S12 38.8	212 25.4	N 3 57.2	134 57.1	S20 42.5
	19	41 38.5	139 39.8	51.8	185 50.0	39.2	227 27.9	57.2	149 59.3	42.5
	20	56 41.0	154 39.0	52.1	200 51.1	39.6	242 30.5	57.2	165 01.6	42.6
	21	71 43.4	169 38.2	52.4	215 52.3	40.1	257 33.0	57.3	180 03.8	42.6
	22	86 45.9	184 37.3	52.7	230 53.5	40.5	272 35.5	57.3	195 06.0	42.6
	23	101 48.3	199 36.5	52.9	245 54.7	40.9	287 38.0	57.4	210 08.2	42.6
MONDAY	18 00	116 50.8	214 35.7	S21 53.2	260 55.9	S12 41.3	302 40.6	N 3 57.4	225 10.4	S20 42.7
	01	131 53.3	229 34.9	53.5	275 57.1	41.8	317 43.1	57.4	240 12.6	42.7
	02	146 55.7	244 34.0	53.8	290 58.3	42.2	332 45.6	57.5	255 14.8	42.7
	03	161 58.2	259 33.2	54.0	305 59.4	42.6	347 48.2	57.5	270 17.0	42.7
	04	177 00.7	274 32.4	54.3	321 00.6	43.1	2 50.7	57.6	285 19.2	42.8
	05	192 03.1	289 31.5	54.6	336 01.8	43.5	17 53.2	57.6	300 21.4	42.8
	06	207 05.6	304 30.7	S21 54.8	351 03.0	S12 43.9	32 55.8	N 3 57.7	315 23.7	S20 42.8
	07	222 08.1	319 29.9	55.1	6 04.2	44.3	47 58.3	57.7	330 25.9	42.9
	08	237 10.5	334 29.1	55.4	21 05.4	44.8	63 00.8	57.7	345 28.1	42.9
	09	252 13.0	349 28.2	55.6	36 06.6	45.2	78 03.4	57.8	0 30.3	42.9
	10	267 15.5	4 27.4	55.9	51 07.7	45.6	93 05.9	57.8	15 32.5	42.9
	11	282 17.9	19 26.6	56.2	66 08.9	46.0	108 08.5	57.9	30 34.7	43.0
	12	297 20.4	34 25.7	S21 56.4	81 10.1	S12 46.5	123 11.0	N 3 57.9	45 36.9	S20 43.0
	13	312 22.8	49 24.9	56.7	96 11.3	46.9	138 13.5	58.0	60 39.1	43.0
	14	327 25.3	64 24.1	57.0	111 12.5	47.3	153 16.1	58.0	75 41.4	43.0
	15	342 27.8	79 23.2	57.2	126 13.7	47.7	168 18.6	58.0	90 43.6	43.1
	16	357 30.2	94 22.4	57.5	141 14.9	48.2	183 21.1	58.1	105 45.8	43.1
	17	12 32.7	109 21.6	57.7	156 16.1	48.6	198 23.7	58.1	120 48.0	43.1
	18	27 35.2	124 20.7	S21 58.0	171 17.2	S12 49.0	213 26.2	N 3 58.2	135 50.2	S20 43.2
	19	42 37.6	139 19.9	58.2	186 18.4	49.4	228 28.7	58.2	150 52.4	43.2
	20	57 40.1	154 19.1	58.5	201 19.6	49.9	243 31.3	58.3	165 54.6	43.2
	21	72 42.6	169 18.3	58.8	216 20.8	50.3	258 33.8	58.3	180 56.8	43.2
	22	87 45.0	184 17.4	59.0	231 22.0	50.7	273 36.4	58.4	195 59.0	43.3
	23	102 47.5	199 16.6	59.3	246 23.2	51.1	288 38.9	58.4	211 01.3	43.3
	Mer. Pass. (h m)	16 13.9	v −0.8	d 0.3	v 1.2	d 0.4	v 2.5	d 0.0	v 2.2	d 0.0

STARS

Name	SHA	Dec
	° ′	° ′
Acamar	315 16.9	S40 14.8
Achernar	335 25.6	S57 09.7
Acrux	173 06.9	S63 11.0
Adhara	255 10.7	S28 59.9
Aldebaran	290 47.1	N16 32.3
Alioth	166 19.2	N55 52.1
Alkaid	152 57.6	N49 13.8
Al Na'ir	27 42.0	S46 53.1
Alnilam	275 44.3	S 1 11.8
Alphard	217 54.0	S 8 43.9
Alphecca	126 09.7	N26 39.6
Alpheratz	357 41.8	N29 10.8
Altair	62 06.9	N 8 54.8
Ankaa	353 14.2	S42 13.4
Antares	112 24.3	S26 27.8
Arcturus	145 54.2	N19 05.9
Atria	107 25.0	S69 02.9
Avior	234 16.6	S59 33.8
Bellatrix	278 29.8	N 6 21.6
Betelgeuse	270 59.1	N 7 24.3
Canopus	263 54.8	S52 42.6
Capella	280 31.4	N46 00.7
Deneb	49 30.7	N45 20.4
Denebola	182 31.7	N14 28.8
Diphda	348 54.2	S17 54.1
Dubhe	193 49.3	N61 39.6
Elnath	278 10.1	N28 37.0
Eltanin	90 45.8	N51 29.3
Enif	33 45.7	N 9 57.0
Fomalhaut	15 22.3	S29 32.4
Gacrux	171 58.6	S57 11.9
Gienah	175 50.3	S17 37.8
Hadar	148 45.3	S60 26.6
Hamal	327 58.7	N23 32.2
Kaus Aust.	83 41.9	S34 22.4
Kochab	137 20.7	N74 05.2
Markab	13 36.8	N15 17.6
Menkar	314 13.1	N 4 09.0
Menkent	148 05.5	S36 26.7
Miaplacidus	221 38.2	S69 47.0
Mirfak	308 37.5	N49 55.1
Nunki	75 56.5	S26 16.4
Peacock	53 17.2	S56 40.9
Pollux	243 25.2	N27 59.0
Procyon	244 57.6	N 5 10.8
Rasalhague	96 05.1	N12 33.0
Regulus	207 41.4	N11 53.1
Rigel	281 10.1	S 8 11.3
Rigil Kent.	139 49.4	S60 53.6
Sabik	102 10.8	S15 44.5
Schedar	349 38.5	N56 37.7
Shaula	96 19.9	S37 06.6
Sirius	258 31.8	S16 44.6
Spica	158 29.4	S11 14.6
Suhail	222 50.7	S43 29.9
Vega	80 38.2	N38 48.0
Zuben'ubi	137 03.6	S16 06.3

	SHA	Mer. Pass.
	° ′	h m
Venus	99 03.8	9 41
Mars	144 35.8	6 38
Jupiter	185 48.2	3 53
Saturn	108 25.7	9 02

	UT	SUN GHA	SUN Dec	MOON GHA	*v*	MOON Dec	*d*	HP
	d h	° ′	° ′	° ′	′	° ′	′	′
	16 00	177 38.8	S21 04.7	102 44.4	9.7	N 3 23.9	11.0	59.3
	01	192 38.5	04.2	117 13.1	9.7	3 34.9	10.9	59.3
	02	207 38.3	03.8	131 41.8	9.7	3 45.8	11.0	59.3
	03	222 38.1	. . 03.3	146 10.5	9.7	3 56.8	10.9	59.3
	04	237 37.9	02.8	160 39.2	9.6	4 07.7	10.8	59.3
	05	252 37.7	02.4	175 07.8	9.7	4 18.5	10.9	59.3
	06	267 37.4	S21 01.9	189 36.5	9.7	N 4 29.4	10.8	59.3
S	07	282 37.2	01.4	204 05.2	9.6	4 40.2	10.8	59.3
A	08	297 37.0	01.0	218 33.8	9.6	4 51.0	10.8	59.3
T	09	312 36.8	. . 00.5	233 02.4	9.7	5 01.8	10.7	59.2
U	10	327 36.6	21 00.0	247 31.1	9.6	5 12.5	10.7	59.2
R	11	342 36.4	20 59.5	261 59.7	9.6	5 23.2	10.7	59.2
D	12	357 36.1	S20 59.1	276 28.3	9.6	N 5 33.9	10.6	59.2
A	13	12 35.9	58.6	290 56.9	9.5	5 44.5	10.6	59.2
Y	14	27 35.7	58.1	305 25.4	9.6	5 55.1	10.5	59.2
	15	42 35.5	. . 57.7	319 54.0	9.5	6 05.6	10.6	59.2
	16	57 35.3	57.2	334 22.5	9.5	6 16.2	10.5	59.2
	17	72 35.1	56.7	348 51.0	9.5	6 26.7	10.4	59.2
	18	87 34.9	S20 56.2	3 19.5	9.5	N 6 37.1	10.4	59.2
	19	102 34.6	55.8	17 48.0	9.5	6 47.5	10.4	59.2
	20	117 34.4	55.3	32 16.5	9.4	6 57.9	10.3	59.2
	21	132 34.2	. . 54.8	46 44.9	9.4	7 08.2	10.3	59.2
	22	147 34.0	54.3	61 13.3	9.5	7 18.5	10.2	59.2
	23	162 33.8	53.8	75 41.8	9.4	7 28.7	10.2	59.2
	17 00	177 33.6	S20 53.4	90 10.2	9.3	N 7 38.9	10.1	59.2
	01	192 33.4	52.9	104 38.5	9.4	7 49.0	10.1	59.2
	02	207 33.2	52.4	119 06.9	9.3	7 59.1	10.1	59.2
	03	222 32.9	. . 51.9	133 35.2	9.3	8 09.2	9.9	59.1
	04	237 32.7	51.4	148 03.5	9.3	8 19.1	10.0	59.1
	05	252 32.5	51.0	162 31.8	9.3	8 29.1	9.9	59.1
	06	267 32.3	S20 50.5	177 00.1	9.2	N 8 39.0	9.8	59.1
	07	282 32.1	50.0	191 28.3	9.3	8 48.8	9.8	59.1
	08	297 31.9	49.5	205 56.6	9.2	8 58.6	9.7	59.1
S	09	312 31.7	. . 49.0	220 24.8	9.1	9 08.3	9.7	59.1
U	10	327 31.5	48.5	234 52.9	9.2	9 18.0	9.6	59.1
N	11	342 31.3	48.0	249 21.1	9.1	9 27.6	9.6	59.1
D	12	357 31.1	S20 47.6	263 49.2	9.1	N 9 37.2	9.5	59.1
A	13	12 30.8	47.1	278 17.3	9.1	9 46.7	9.4	59.1
Y	14	27 30.6	46.6	292 45.4	9.1	9 56.1	9.4	59.1
	15	42 30.4	. . 46.1	307 13.5	9.0	10 05.5	9.3	59.1
	16	57 30.2	45.6	321 41.5	9.0	10 14.8	9.3	59.0
	17	72 30.0	45.1	336 09.5	9.0	10 24.1	9.1	59.0
	18	87 29.8	S20 44.6	350 37.5	9.0	N10 33.2	9.2	59.0
	19	102 29.6	44.1	5 05.5	8.9	10 42.4	9.0	59.0
	20	117 29.4	43.6	19 33.4	8.9	10 51.4	9.0	59.0
	21	132 29.2	. . 43.1	34 01.3	8.9	11 00.4	9.0	59.0
	22	147 29.0	42.6	48 29.2	8.9	11 09.4	8.8	59.0
	23	162 28.8	42.1	62 57.1	8.8	11 18.2	8.8	59.0
	18 00	177 28.6	S20 41.6	77 24.9	8.8	N11 27.0	8.7	59.0
	01	192 28.4	41.1	91 52.7	8.8	11 35.7	8.7	59.0
	02	207 28.2	40.7	106 20.5	8.7	11 44.4	8.5	59.0
	03	222 28.0	. . 40.2	120 48.2	8.8	11 52.9	8.5	58.9
	04	237 27.8	39.7	135 16.0	8.7	12 01.4	8.5	58.9
	05	252 27.6	39.2	149 43.7	8.6	12 09.9	8.3	58.9
	06	267 27.4	S20 38.7	164 11.3	8.7	N12 18.2	8.3	58.9
	07	282 27.2	38.2	178 39.0	8.6	12 26.5	8.2	58.9
	08	297 27.0	37.7	193 06.6	8.6	12 34.7	8.1	58.9
M	09	312 26.8	. . 37.2	207 34.2	8.6	12 42.8	8.1	58.9
O	10	327 26.5	36.6	222 01.8	8.5	12 50.9	7.9	58.9
N	11	342 26.3	36.1	236 29.3	8.5	12 58.8	7.9	58.9
D	12	357 26.1	S20 35.6	250 56.8	8.5	N13 06.7	7.8	58.9
A	13	12 25.9	35.1	265 24.3	8.5	13 14.5	7.7	58.8
Y	14	27 25.7	34.6	279 51.8	8.4	13 22.2	7.7	58.8
	15	42 25.5	. . 34.1	294 19.2	8.4	13 29.9	7.5	58.8
	16	57 25.3	33.6	308 46.6	8.4	13 37.4	7.5	58.8
	17	72 25.1	33.1	323 14.0	8.4	13 44.9	7.4	58.8
	18	87 24.9	S20 32.6	337 41.4	8.3	N13 52.3	7.3	58.8
	19	102 24.8	32.1	352 08.7	8.3	13 59.6	7.2	58.8
	20	117 24.6	31.6	6 36.0	8.3	14 06.8	7.2	58.8
	21	132 24.4	. . 31.1	21 03.3	8.2	14 14.0	7.0	58.8
	22	147 24.2	30.6	35 30.5	8.3	14 21.0	7.0	58.8
	23	162 24.0	30.0	49 57.8	8.2	N14 28.0	6.8	58.7
		SD 16.3	*d* 0.5	SD 16.1		16.1		16.0

Lat.	Twilight Naut.	Twilight Civil	Sunrise	Moonrise 16	Moonrise 17	Moonrise 18	Moonrise 19
°	h m	h m	h m	h m	h m	h m	h m
N 72	07 57	09 45	■	10 27	10 22	10 16	10 10
N 70	07 43	09 13	11 55	10 34	10 36	10 39	10 46
68	07 31	08 50	10 26	10 40	10 47	10 57	11 12
66	07 22	08 31	09 48	10 45	10 56	11 11	11 32
64	07 13	08 16	09 22	10 49	11 04	11 23	11 48
62	07 06	08 04	09 02	10 52	11 11	11 33	12 01
60	06 59	07 53	08 45	10 56	11 17	11 42	12 13
N 58	06 53	07 44	08 31	10 58	11 22	11 50	12 23
56	06 48	07 35	08 20	11 01	11 27	11 56	12 31
54	06 43	07 28	08 09	11 03	11 31	12 03	12 39
52	06 39	07 21	08 00	11 05	11 35	12 08	12 46
50	06 35	07 15	07 52	11 07	11 39	12 13	12 52
45	06 25	07 01	07 34	11 12	11 46	12 24	13 06
N 40	06 16	06 50	07 19	11 15	11 53	12 33	13 17
35	06 09	06 40	07 07	11 18	11 58	12 41	13 26
30	06 01	06 31	06 56	11 21	12 03	12 47	13 35
20	05 47	06 14	06 38	11 26	12 12	12 59	13 49
N 10	05 33	05 59	06 22	11 30	12 19	13 10	14 02
0	05 18	05 44	06 06	11 34	12 26	13 20	14 14
S 10	05 02	05 28	05 51	11 38	12 33	13 30	14 26
20	04 42	05 10	05 34	11 42	12 41	13 40	14 39
30	04 16	04 48	05 15	11 47	12 50	13 52	14 54
35	04 00	04 35	05 03	11 50	12 55	14 00	15 03
40	03 39	04 19	04 50	11 53	13 01	14 08	15 13
45	03 13	03 59	04 35	11 57	13 08	14 17	15 24
S 50	02 37	03 34	04 16	12 02	13 16	14 29	15 39
52	02 17	03 22	04 06	12 04	13 20	14 34	15 45
54	01 51	03 07	03 56	12 06	13 24	14 40	15 53
56	01 12	02 50	03 44	12 09	13 29	14 47	16 01
58	////	02 29	03 31	12 12	13 34	14 54	16 10
S 60	////	02 01	03 15	12 15	13 40	15 02	16 21

Lat.	Sunset	Twilight Civil	Twilight Naut.	Moonset 16	Moonset 17	Moonset 18	Moonset 19
°	h m	h m	h m	h m	h m	h m	h m
N 72	■	14 35	16 24	25 42	01 42	03 39	05 38
N 70	12 26	15 07	16 38	25 30	01 30	03 17	05 03
68	13 55	15 31	16 49	25 21	01 21	03 00	04 38
66	14 32	15 49	16 59	25 12	01 12	02 47	04 19
64	14 58	16 04	17 07	25 06	01 06	02 36	04 03
62	15 19	16 17	17 15	25 00	01 00	02 27	03 50
60	15 35	16 27	17 21	24 55	00 55	02 19	03 39
N 58	15 49	16 37	17 27	24 51	00 51	02 12	03 30
56	16 01	16 45	17 32	24 47	00 47	02 06	03 22
54	16 11	16 53	17 37	24 43	00 43	02 00	03 15
52	16 20	16 59	17 42	24 40	00 40	01 55	03 08
50	16 29	17 06	17 46	24 37	00 37	01 51	03 02
45	16 46	17 19	17 55	24 31	00 31	01 41	02 49
N 40	17 01	17 30	18 04	24 26	00 26	01 33	02 39
35	17 13	17 40	18 11	24 21	00 21	01 26	02 30
30	17 24	17 49	18 19	24 17	00 17	01 20	02 22
20	17 42	18 06	18 33	24 10	00 10	01 09	02 08
N 10	17 58	18 21	18 47	24 04	00 04	01 00	01 57
0	18 14	18 36	19 01	23 59	24 52	00 52	01 46
S 10	18 29	18 52	19 18	23 53	24 43	00 43	01 35
20	18 46	19 10	19 38	23 47	24 34	00 34	01 23
30	19 05	19 31	20 04	23 40	24 23	00 23	01 09
35	19 16	19 45	20 20	23 36	24 17	00 17	01 02
40	19 29	20 00	20 40	23 32	24 11	00 11	00 53
45	19 44	20 20	21 05	23 27	24 03	00 03	00 42
S 50	20 04	20 45	21 41	23 21	23 53	24 30	00 30
52	20 13	20 57	22 01	23 18	23 49	24 24	00 24
54	20 23	21 11	22 26	23 15	23 44	24 18	00 18
56	20 34	21 28	23 03	23 11	23 39	24 11	00 11
58	20 48	21 49	////	23 08	23 33	24 03	00 03
S 60	21 03	22 16	////	23 03	23 26	23 54	24 28

Day	SUN Eqn. of Time 00^h	SUN Eqn. of Time 12^h	SUN Mer. Pass.	MOON Mer. Pass. Upper	MOON Mer. Pass. Lower	MOON Age	MOON Phase
d	m s	m s	h m	h m	h m	d %	
16	09 25	09 35	12 10	17 46	05 20	06 45	
17	09 45	09 55	12 10	18 39	06 12	07 56	◐
18	10 05	10 15	12 10	19 33	07 06	08 67	

	UT	ARIES	VENUS −4·0		MARS +1·0		JUPITER −2·3		SATURN +0·5	
		GHA	GHA	Dec	GHA	Dec	GHA	Dec	GHA	Dec
	d h	° ′	° ′	° ′	° ′	° ′	° ′	° ′	° ′	° ′
	19 00	117 49.9	214 15.7	S21 59.5	261 24.4	S12 51.6	303 41.4	N 3 58.4	226 03.5	S20 43.3
	01	132 52.4	229 14.9	21 59.8	276 25.6	52.0	318 44.0	58.5	241 05.7	43.3
	02	147 54.9	244 14.1	22 00.0	291 26.7	52.4	333 46.5	58.5	256 07.9	43.4
	03	162 57.3	259 13.2	. . 00.3	306 27.9	. . 52.8	348 49.1	. . 58.6	271 10.1	. . 43.4
	04	177 59.8	274 12.4	00.5	321 29.1	53.2	3 51.6	58.6	286 12.3	43.4
	05	193 02.3	289 11.6	00.7	336 30.3	53.7	18 54.1	58.7	301 14.5	43.5
	06	208 04.7	304 10.7	S22 01.0	351 31.5	S12 54.1	33 56.7	N 3 58.7	316 16.8	S20 43.5
	07	223 07.2	319 09.9	01.2	6 32.7	54.5	48 59.2	58.8	331 19.0	43.5
T	08	238 09.7	334 09.1	01.5	21 33.9	54.9	64 01.8	58.8	346 21.2	43.5
U	09	253 12.1	349 08.2	. . 01.7	36 35.1	. . 55.4	79 04.3	. . 58.9	1 23.4	. . 43.6
E	10	268 14.6	4 07.4	01.9	51 36.3	55.8	94 06.9	58.9	16 25.6	43.6
	11	283 17.1	19 06.6	02.2	66 37.5	56.2	109 09.4	58.9	31 27.8	43.6
S	12	298 19.5	34 05.7	S22 02.4	81 38.6	S12 56.6	124 11.9	N 3 59.0	46 30.0	S20 43.6
D	13	313 22.0	49 04.9	02.7	96 39.8	57.0	139 14.5	59.0	61 32.3	43.7
A	14	328 24.4	64 04.1	02.9	111 41.0	57.5	154 17.0	59.1	76 34.5	43.7
Y	15	343 26.9	79 03.2	. . 03.1	126 42.2	. . 57.9	169 19.6	. . 59.1	91 36.7	. . 43.7
	16	358 29.4	94 02.4	03.4	141 43.4	58.3	184 22.1	59.2	106 38.9	43.7
	17	13 31.8	109 01.5	03.6	156 44.6	58.7	199 24.7	59.2	121 41.1	43.8
	18	28 34.3	124 00.7	S22 03.8	171 45.8	S12 59.1	214 27.2	N 3 59.3	136 43.3	S20 43.8
	19	43 36.8	138 59.9	04.0	186 47.0	12 59.6	229 29.7	59.3	151 45.5	43.8
	20	58 39.2	153 59.0	04.3	201 48.2	13 00.0	244 32.3	59.4	166 47.8	43.9
	21	73 41.7	168 58.2	. . 04.5	216 49.4	. . 00.4	259 34.8	. . 59.4	181 50.0	. . 43.9
	22	88 44.2	183 57.3	04.7	231 50.5	00.8	274 37.4	59.5	196 52.2	43.9
	23	103 46.6	198 56.5	05.0	246 51.7	01.2	289 39.9	59.5	211 54.4	43.9
	20 00	118 49.1	213 55.7	S22 05.2	261 52.9	S13 01.7	304 42.5	N 3 59.6	226 56.6	S20 44.0
	01	133 51.6	228 54.8	05.4	276 54.1	02.1	319 45.0	59.6	241 58.8	44.0
	02	148 54.0	243 54.0	05.6	291 55.3	02.5	334 47.6	59.6	257 01.0	44.0
	03	163 56.5	258 53.1	. . 05.8	306 56.5	. . 02.9	349 50.1	. . 59.7	272 03.3	. . 44.0
	04	178 58.9	273 52.3	06.1	321 57.7	03.3	4 52.7	59.7	287 05.5	44.1
	05	194 01.4	288 51.5	06.3	336 58.9	03.8	19 55.2	59.8	302 07.7	44.1
	06	209 03.9	303 50.6	S22 06.5	352 00.1	S13 04.2	34 57.8	N 3 59.8	317 09.9	S20 44.1
W	07	224 06.3	318 49.8	06.7	7 01.3	04.6	50 00.3	59.9	332 12.1	44.1
E	08	239 08.8	333 48.9	06.9	22 02.5	05.0	65 02.9	3 59.9	347 14.3	44.2
D	09	254 11.3	348 48.1	. . 07.1	37 03.7	. . 05.4	80 05.4	4 00.0	2 16.6	. . 44.2
N	10	269 13.7	3 47.3	07.3	52 04.8	05.8	95 08.0	00.0	17 18.8	44.2
E	11	284 16.2	18 46.4	07.6	67 06.0	06.3	110 10.5	00.1	32 21.0	44.2
S	12	299 18.7	33 45.6	S22 07.8	82 07.2	S13 06.7	125 13.1	N 4 00.1	47 23.2	S20 44.3
D	13	314 21.1	48 44.7	08.0	97 08.4	07.1	140 15.6	00.2	62 25.4	44.3
A	14	329 23.6	63 43.9	08.2	112 09.6	07.5	155 18.2	00.2	77 27.6	44.3
Y	15	344 26.1	78 43.0	. . 08.4	127 10.8	. . 07.9	170 20.7	. . 00.3	92 29.9	. . 44.4
	16	359 28.5	93 42.2	08.6	142 12.0	08.4	185 23.3	00.3	107 32.1	44.4
	17	14 31.0	108 41.4	08.8	157 13.2	08.8	200 25.8	00.4	122 34.3	44.4
	18	29 33.4	123 40.5	S22 09.0	172 14.4	S13 09.2	215 28.4	N 4 00.4	137 36.5	S20 44.4
	19	44 35.9	138 39.7	09.2	187 15.6	09.6	230 30.9	00.5	152 38.7	44.5
	20	59 38.4	153 38.8	09.4	202 16.8	10.0	245 33.5	00.5	167 40.9	44.5
	21	74 40.8	168 38.0	. . 09.6	217 18.0	. . 10.4	260 36.0	. . 00.6	182 43.2	. . 44.5
	22	89 43.3	183 37.1	09.8	232 19.2	10.8	275 38.6	00.6	197 45.4	44.5
	23	104 45.8	198 36.3	10.0	247 20.4	11.3	290 41.1	00.7	212 47.6	44.6
	21 00	119 48.2	213 35.4	S22 10.2	262 21.6	S13 11.7	305 43.7	N 4 00.7	227 49.8	S20 44.6
	01	134 50.7	228 34.6	10.4	277 22.8	12.1	320 46.2	00.8	242 52.0	44.6
	02	149 53.2	243 33.8	10.6	292 23.9	12.5	335 48.8	00.8	257 54.2	44.6
	03	164 55.6	258 32.9	. . 10.8	307 25.1	. . 12.9	350 51.3	. . 00.9	272 56.5	. . 44.7
	04	179 58.1	273 32.1	11.0	322 26.3	13.3	5 53.9	00.9	287 58.7	44.7
	05	195 00.6	288 31.2	11.2	337 27.5	13.8	20 56.5	01.0	303 00.9	44.7
	06	210 03.0	303 30.4	S22 11.4	352 28.7	S13 14.2	35 59.0	N 4 01.0	318 03.1	S20 44.7
	07	225 05.5	318 29.5	11.5	7 29.9	14.6	51 01.6	01.1	333 05.3	44.8
T	08	240 07.9	333 28.7	11.7	22 31.1	15.0	66 04.1	01.1	348 07.6	44.8
H	09	255 10.4	348 27.8	. . 11.9	37 32.3	. . 15.4	81 06.7	. . 01.2	3 09.8	. . 44.8
U	10	270 12.9	3 27.0	12.1	52 33.5	15.8	96 09.2	01.2	18 12.0	44.8
R	11	285 15.3	18 26.1	12.3	67 34.7	16.2	111 11.8	01.3	33 14.2	44.9
S	12	300 17.8	33 25.3	S22 12.5	82 35.9	S13 16.6	126 14.4	N 4 01.4	48 16.4	S20 44.9
D	13	315 20.3	48 24.4	12.7	97 37.1	17.1	141 16.9	01.4	63 18.7	44.9
A	14	330 22.7	63 23.6	12.8	112 38.3	17.5	156 19.5	01.5	78 20.9	44.9
Y	15	345 25.2	78 22.7	. . 13.0	127 39.5	. . 17.9	171 22.0	. . 01.5	93 23.1	. . 45.0
	16	0 27.7	93 21.9	13.2	142 40.7	18.3	186 24.6	01.6	108 25.3	45.0
	17	15 30.1	108 21.0	13.4	157 41.9	18.7	201 27.1	01.6	123 27.5	45.0
	18	30 32.6	123 20.2	S22 13.6	172 43.1	S13 19.1	216 29.7	N 4 01.7	138 29.8	S20 45.1
	19	45 35.0	138 19.3	13.7	187 44.3	19.5	231 32.3	01.7	153 32.0	45.1
	20	60 37.5	153 18.5	13.9	202 45.5	19.9	246 34.8	01.8	168 34.2	45.1
	21	75 40.0	168 17.6	. . 14.1	217 46.7	. . 20.4	261 37.4	. . 01.8	183 36.4	. . 45.1
	22	90 42.4	183 16.8	14.2	232 47.9	20.8	276 39.9	01.9	198 38.6	45.2
	23	105 44.9	198 15.9	14.4	247 49.1	21.2	291 42.5	01.9	213 40.9	45.2
		h m								
	Mer. Pass.	16 02.1	*v* −0.8	*d* 0.2	*v* 1.2	*d* 0.4	*v* 2.6	*d* 0.0	*v* 2.2	*d* 0.0

STARS		
Name	SHA	Dec
	° ′	° ′
Acamar	315 16.9	S40 14.8
Achernar	335 25.6	S57 09.7
Acrux	173 06.8	S63 11.0
Adhara	255 10.7	S28 59.9
Aldebaran	290 47.1	N16 32.3
Alioth	166 19.1	N55 52.1
Alkaid	152 57.6	N49 13.8
Al Na'ir	27 42.0	S46 53.1
Alnilam	275 44.3	S 1 11.8
Alphard	217 54.0	S 8 43.9
Alphecca	126 09.7	N26 39.6
Alpheratz	357 41.8	N29 10.8
Altair	62 06.8	N 8 54.8
Ankaa	353 14.2	S42 13.4
Antares	112 24.3	S26 27.8
Arcturus	145 54.2	N19 05.9
Atria	107 24.9	S69 02.9
Avior	234 16.5	S59 33.8
Bellatrix	278 29.8	N 6 21.6
Betelgeuse	270 59.1	N 7 24.3
Canopus	263 54.8	S52 42.6
Capella	280 31.4	N46 00.7
Deneb	49 30.7	N45 20.4
Denebola	182 31.7	N14 28.8
Diphda	348 54.2	S17 54.1
Dubhe	193 49.2	N61 39.6
Elnath	278 10.1	N28 37.1
Eltanin	90 45.8	N51 29.2
Enif	33 45.7	N 9 57.0
Fomalhaut	15 22.3	S29 32.4
Gacrux	171 58.6	S57 11.9
Gienah	175 50.3	S17 37.8
Hadar	148 45.3	S60 26.6
Hamal	327 58.7	N23 32.2
Kaus Aust.	83 41.9	S34 22.4
Kochab	137 20.6	N74 05.2
Markab	13 36.8	N15 17.5
Menkar	314 13.1	N 4 08.9
Menkent	148 05.5	S36 26.7
Miaplacidus	221 38.2	S69 47.0
Mirfak	308 37.5	N49 55.1
Nunki	75 56.5	S26 16.4
Peacock	53 17.2	S56 40.9
Pollux	243 25.2	N27 59.0
Procyon	244 57.6	N 5 10.8
Rasalhague	96 05.1	N12 33.0
Regulus	207 41.4	N11 53.1
Rigel	281 10.1	S 8 11.3
Rigil Kent.	139 49.3	S60 53.6
Sabik	102 10.8	S15 44.5
Schedar	349 38.5	N56 37.7
Shaula	96 19.9	S37 06.6
Sirius	258 31.8	S16 44.6
Spica	158 29.3	S11 14.6
Suhail	222 50.6	S43 30.0
Vega	80 38.2	N38 48.0
Zuben'ubi	137 03.5	S16 06.3

	SHA	Mer. Pass.
	° ′	h m
Venus	95 06.6	9 45
Mars	143 03.8	6 32
Jupiter	185 53.4	3 41
Saturn	108 07.5	8 51

UT		SUN GHA	SUN Dec	MOON GHA	*v*	MOON Dec	*d*	HP
d h		° ′	° ′	° ′	′	° ′	′	′
19 00	TUESDAY	177 23.8	S20 29.5	64 25.0	8.1	N14 34.8	6.8	58.7
01		192 23.6	29.0	78 52.1	8.2	14 41.6	6.7	58.7
02		207 23.4	28.5	93 19.3	8.1	14 48.3	6.6	58.7
03		222 23.2	. . 28.0	107 46.4	8.1	14 54.9	6.5	58.7
04		237 23.0	27.5	122 13.5	8.1	15 01.4	6.4	58.7
05		252 22.8	27.0	136 40.6	8.1	15 07.8	6.3	58.7
06		267 22.6	S20 26.4	151 07.7	8.0	N15 14.1	6.2	58.7
07		282 22.4	25.9	165 34.7	8.0	15 20.3	6.1	58.6
08		297 22.2	25.4	180 01.7	8.0	15 26.4	6.0	58.6
09		312 22.0	. . 24.9	194 28.7	8.0	15 32.4	6.0	58.6
10		327 21.8	24.4	208 55.7	8.0	15 38.4	5.8	58.6
11		342 21.6	23.9	223 22.7	7.9	15 44.2	5.7	58.6
12		357 21.4	S20 23.3	237 49.6	7.9	N15 49.9	5.7	58.6
13		12 21.2	22.8	252 16.5	7.9	15 55.6	5.5	58.6
14		27 21.0	22.3	266 43.4	7.9	16 01.1	5.4	58.6
15		42 20.8	. . 21.8	281 10.3	7.8	16 06.5	5.4	58.5
16		57 20.7	21.2	295 37.1	7.8	16 11.9	5.2	58.5
17		72 20.5	20.7	310 03.9	7.9	16 17.1	5.2	58.5
18		87 20.3	S20 20.2	324 30.8	7.8	N16 22.3	5.0	58.5
19		102 20.1	19.7	338 57.6	7.7	16 27.3	4.9	58.5
20		117 19.9	19.1	353 24.3	7.8	16 32.2	4.9	58.5
21		132 19.7	. . 18.6	7 51.1	7.8	16 37.1	4.7	58.5
22		147 19.5	18.1	22 17.9	7.7	16 41.8	4.6	58.4
23		162 19.3	17.6	36 44.6	7.7	16 46.4	4.5	58.4
20 00	WEDNESDAY	177 19.1	S20 17.0	51 11.3	7.7	N16 50.9	4.4	58.4
01		192 18.9	16.5	65 38.0	7.7	16 55.3	4.3	58.4
02		207 18.8	16.0	80 04.7	7.7	16 59.6	4.2	58.4
03		222 18.6	. . 15.5	94 31.4	7.7	17 03.8	4.1	58.4
04		237 18.4	14.9	108 58.1	7.6	17 07.9	4.0	58.4
05		252 18.2	14.4	123 24.7	7.7	17 11.9	3.9	58.3
06		267 18.0	S20 13.9	137 51.4	7.6	N17 15.8	3.8	58.3
07		282 17.8	13.3	152 18.0	7.7	17 19.6	3.7	58.3
08		297 17.6	12.8	166 44.7	7.6	17 23.3	3.5	58.3
09		312 17.4	. . 12.3	181 11.3	7.6	17 26.8	3.5	58.3
10		327 17.3	11.7	195 37.9	7.6	17 30.3	3.3	58.3
11		342 17.1	11.2	210 04.5	7.6	17 33.6	3.2	58.3
12		357 16.9	S20 10.6	224 31.1	7.6	N17 36.8	3.2	58.2
13		12 16.7	10.1	238 57.7	7.6	17 40.0	3.0	58.2
14		27 16.5	09.6	253 24.3	7.6	17 43.0	2.9	58.2
15		42 16.3	. . 09.0	267 50.9	7.6	17 45.9	2.8	58.2
16		57 16.1	08.5	282 17.5	7.6	17 48.7	2.7	58.2
17		72 16.0	08.0	296 44.1	7.6	17 51.4	2.6	58.2
18		87 15.8	S20 07.4	311 10.7	7.6	N17 54.0	2.4	58.1
19		102 15.6	06.9	325 37.3	7.6	17 56.4	2.4	58.1
20		117 15.4	06.3	340 03.9	7.6	17 58.8	2.2	58.1
21		132 15.2	. . 05.8	354 30.5	7.6	18 01.0	2.2	58.1
22		147 15.1	05.3	8 57.1	7.6	18 03.2	2.0	58.1
23		162 14.9	04.7	23 23.7	7.6	18 05.2	1.9	58.1
21 00	THURSDAY	177 14.7	S20 04.2	37 50.3	7.6	N18 07.1	1.8	58.0
01		192 14.5	03.6	52 16.9	7.6	18 08.9	1.7	58.0
02		207 14.3	03.1	66 43.5	7.6	18 10.6	1.6	58.0
03		222 14.1	. . 02.5	81 10.1	7.6	18 12.2	1.4	58.0
04		237 14.0	02.0	95 36.7	7.7	18 13.6	1.4	58.0
05		252 13.8	01.4	110 03.4	7.6	18 15.0	1.2	58.0
06		267 13.6	S20 00.9	124 30.0	7.7	N18 16.2	1.2	57.9
07		282 13.4	20 00.3	138 56.7	7.6	18 17.4	1.0	57.9
08		297 13.3	19 59.8	153 23.3	7.7	18 18.4	0.9	57.9
09		312 13.1	. . 59.2	167 50.0	7.7	18 19.3	0.8	57.9
10		327 12.9	58.7	182 16.7	7.7	18 20.1	0.7	57.9
11		342 12.7	58.1	196 43.4	7.7	18 20.8	0.6	57.9
12		357 12.5	S19 57.6	211 10.1	7.8	N18 21.4	0.4	57.8
13		12 12.4	57.0	225 36.9	7.7	18 21.8	0.4	57.8
14		27 12.2	56.5	240 03.6	7.8	18 22.2	0.2	57.8
15		42 12.0	. . 55.9	254 30.4	7.8	18 22.4	0.2	57.8
16		57 11.8	55.4	268 57.2	7.8	18 22.6	0.0	57.8
17		72 11.7	54.8	283 24.0	7.9	18 22.6	0.1	57.7
18		87 11.5	S19 54.3	297 50.9	7.8	N18 22.5	0.2	57.7
19		102 11.3	53.7	312 17.7	7.9	18 22.3	0.3	57.7
20		117 11.1	53.1	326 44.6	7.9	18 22.0	0.4	57.7
21		132 11.0	. . 52.6	341 11.5	7.9	18 21.6	0.5	57.7
22		147 10.8	52.0	355 38.4	8.0	18 21.1	0.7	57.7
23		162 10.6	51.5	10 05.4	8.0	N18 20.4	0.7	57.6
		SD 16.3	*d* 0.5	SD 16.0		15.9		15.8

Lat.	Twilight Naut.	Twilight Civil	Sunrise	Moonrise 19	Moonrise 20	Moonrise 21	Moonrise 22
°	h m	h m	h m	h m	h m	h m	h m
N 72	07 49	09 33	■	10 10	10 01	□	11 05
N 70	07 36	09 04	11 10	10 46	11 02	11 36	12 40
68	07 25	08 42	10 12	11 12	11 37	12 18	13 19
66	07 16	08 25	09 39	11 32	12 02	12 46	13 47
64	07 09	08 11	09 15	11 48	12 22	13 08	14 08
62	07 02	07 59	08 56	12 01	12 38	13 25	14 25
60	06 56	07 49	08 40	12 13	12 51	13 40	14 39
N 58	06 50	07 40	08 27	12 23	13 03	13 52	14 51
56	06 45	07 32	08 16	12 31	13 13	14 03	15 01
54	06 41	07 25	08 06	12 39	13 22	14 12	15 10
52	06 36	07 18	07 57	12 46	13 30	14 21	15 18
50	06 32	07 12	07 49	12 52	13 37	14 28	15 26
45	06 23	06 59	07 32	13 06	13 52	14 45	15 42
N 40	06 15	06 48	07 18	13 17	14 05	14 58	15 54
35	06 08	06 39	07 06	13 26	14 16	15 09	16 05
30	06 01	06 30	06 56	13 35	14 25	15 19	16 15
20	05 47	06 14	06 38	13 49	14 42	15 36	16 32
N 10	05 34	06 00	06 22	14 02	14 56	15 51	16 46
0	05 20	05 45	06 07	14 14	15 10	16 05	16 59
S 10	05 03	05 30	05 52	14 26	15 23	16 19	17 13
20	04 44	05 12	05 36	14 39	15 37	16 34	17 27
30	04 19	04 51	05 17	14 54	15 54	16 51	17 44
35	04 03	04 38	05 06	15 03	16 04	17 01	17 54
40	03 44	04 23	04 54	15 13	16 15	17 12	18 05
45	03 19	04 04	04 39	15 24	16 28	17 26	18 17
S 50	02 44	03 40	04 20	15 39	16 44	17 42	18 33
52	02 25	03 28	04 11	15 45	16 51	17 50	18 40
54	02 02	03 14	04 02	15 53	16 59	17 58	18 49
56	01 28	02 58	03 50	16 01	17 09	18 08	18 58
58	////	02 38	03 38	16 10	17 19	18 19	19 08
S 60	////	02 12	03 22	16 21	17 32	18 32	19 20

Lat.	Sunset	Twilight Civil	Twilight Naut.	Moonset 19	Moonset 20	Moonset 21	Moonset 22
°	h m	h m	h m	h m	h m	h m	h m
N 72	■	14 50	16 34	05 38	07 43	□	10 29
N 70	13 13	15 19	16 47	05 03	06 42	08 04	08 54
68	14 10	15 40	16 57	04 38	06 08	07 22	08 14
66	14 44	15 57	17 06	04 19	05 43	06 54	07 47
64	15 08	16 11	17 14	04 03	05 23	06 32	07 26
62	15 27	16 23	17 21	03 50	05 08	06 15	07 09
60	15 42	16 33	17 27	03 39	04 54	06 00	06 54
N 58	15 55	16 42	17 32	03 30	04 43	05 48	06 42
56	16 07	16 50	17 37	03 22	04 33	05 37	06 32
54	16 17	16 57	17 42	03 15	04 25	05 28	06 22
52	16 25	17 04	17 46	03 08	04 17	05 19	06 14
50	16 33	17 10	17 50	03 02	04 10	05 12	06 07
45	16 50	17 23	17 59	02 49	03 55	04 56	05 51
N 40	17 04	17 34	18 07	02 39	03 43	04 43	05 38
35	17 16	17 43	18 14	02 30	03 32	04 31	05 26
30	17 26	17 52	18 21	02 22	03 23	04 22	05 17
20	17 44	18 08	18 34	02 08	03 07	04 05	05 00
N 10	18 00	18 22	18 48	01 57	02 53	03 50	04 45
0	18 14	18 37	19 02	01 46	02 41	03 36	04 31
S 10	18 29	18 52	19 18	01 35	02 28	03 22	04 17
20	18 45	19 09	19 38	01 23	02 14	03 07	04 03
30	19 04	19 30	20 02	01 09	01 58	02 51	03 46
35	19 15	19 43	20 18	01 02	01 49	02 41	03 36
40	19 27	19 59	20 37	00 53	01 39	02 29	03 24
45	19 42	20 17	21 02	00 42	01 27	02 16	03 11
S 50	20 01	20 41	21 36	00 30	01 12	02 00	02 55
52	20 09	20 53	21 54	00 24	01 05	01 52	02 47
54	20 19	21 06	22 18	00 18	00 57	01 44	02 38
56	20 30	21 22	22 50	00 11	00 49	01 35	02 29
58	20 43	21 42	////	00 03	00 39	01 24	02 18
S 60	20 58	22 06	////	24 28	00 28	01 11	02 05

Day	SUN Eqn. of Time 00^h	SUN Eqn. of Time 12^h	SUN Mer. Pass.	MOON Mer. Pass. Upper	MOON Mer. Pass. Lower	MOON Age	MOON Phase
d	m s	m s	h m	h m	h m	d	%
19	10 25	10 34	12 11	20 27	08 00	09	77
20	10 43	10 52	12 11	21 23	08 55	10	86
21	11 01	11 09	12 11	22 18	09 51	11	92

	UT	ARIES	VENUS −4·0		MARS +1·0		JUPITER −2·3		SATURN +0·5	
		GHA	GHA	Dec	GHA	Dec	GHA	Dec	GHA	Dec
d	h	° ′	° ′	° ′	° ′	° ′	° ′	° ′	° ′	° ′
22	00	120 47.4	213 15.1	S22 14.6	262 50.3	S13 21.6	306 45.1	N 4 02.0	228 43.1	S20 45.2
	01	135 49.8	228 14.2	14.8	277 51.5	22.0	321 47.6	02.0	243 45.3	45.2
	02	150 52.3	243 13.4	14.9	292 52.7	22.4	336 50.2	02.1	258 47.5	45.3
	03	165 54.8	258 12.5	. . 15.1	307 53.9	. . 22.8	351 52.8	. . 02.1	273 49.7	. . 45.3
	04	180 57.2	273 11.7	15.3	322 55.1	23.2	6 55.3	02.2	288 52.0	45.3
	05	195 59.7	288 10.8	15.4	337 56.3	23.6	21 57.9	02.3	303 54.2	45.3
	06	211 02.2	303 10.0	S22 15.6	352 57.4	S13 24.1	37 00.4	N 4 02.3	318 56.4	S20 45.4
	07	226 04.6	318 09.1	15.7	7 58.6	24.5	52 03.0	02.4	333 58.6	45.4
	08	241 07.1	333 08.3	15.9	22 59.8	24.9	67 05.6	02.4	349 00.8	45.4
F	09	256 09.5	348 07.4	. . 16.1	38 01.0	. . 25.3	82 08.1	. . 02.5	4 03.1	. . 45.4
R	10	271 12.0	3 06.6	16.2	53 02.2	25.7	97 10.7	02.5	19 05.3	45.5
I	11	286 14.5	18 05.7	16.4	68 03.4	26.1	112 13.3	02.6	34 07.5	45.5
D	12	301 16.9	33 04.9	S22 16.5	83 04.6	S13 26.5	127 15.8	N 4 02.6	49 09.7	S20 45.5
A	13	316 19.4	48 04.0	16.7	98 05.8	26.9	142 18.4	02.7	64 12.0	45.5
Y	14	331 21.9	63 03.2	16.8	113 07.0	27.3	157 20.9	02.8	79 14.2	45.6
	15	346 24.3	78 02.3	. . 17.0	128 08.2	. . 27.7	172 23.5	. . 02.8	94 16.4	. . 45.6
	16	1 26.8	93 01.5	17.2	143 09.4	28.1	187 26.1	02.9	109 18.6	45.6
	17	16 29.3	108 00.6	17.3	158 10.6	28.6	202 28.6	02.9	124 20.8	45.6
	18	31 31.7	122 59.8	S22 17.5	173 11.8	S13 29.0	217 31.2	N 4 03.0	139 23.1	S20 45.7
	19	46 34.2	137 58.9	17.6	188 13.0	29.4	232 33.8	03.0	154 25.3	45.7
	20	61 36.7	152 58.1	17.7	203 14.2	29.8	247 36.3	03.1	169 27.5	45.7
	21	76 39.1	167 57.2	. . 17.9	218 15.4	. . 30.2	262 38.9	. . 03.1	184 29.7	. . 45.7
	22	91 41.6	182 56.4	18.0	233 16.6	30.6	277 41.5	03.2	199 32.0	45.8
	23	106 44.0	197 55.5	18.2	248 17.8	31.0	292 44.0	03.3	214 34.2	45.8
23	00	121 46.5	212 54.6	S22 18.3	263 19.0	S13 31.4	307 46.6	N 4 03.3	229 36.4	S20 45.8
	01	136 49.0	227 53.8	18.5	278 20.2	31.8	322 49.2	03.4	244 38.6	45.8
	02	151 51.4	242 52.9	18.6	293 21.4	32.2	337 51.8	03.4	259 40.8	45.9
	03	166 53.9	257 52.1	. . 18.7	308 22.6	. . 32.6	352 54.3	. . 03.5	274 43.1	. . 45.9
	04	181 56.4	272 51.2	18.9	323 23.8	33.0	7 56.9	03.5	289 45.3	45.9
	05	196 58.8	287 50.4	19.0	338 25.0	33.4	22 59.5	03.6	304 47.5	45.9
	06	212 01.3	302 49.5	S22 19.2	353 26.2	S13 33.8	38 02.0	N 4 03.7	319 49.7	S20 46.0
	07	227 03.8	317 48.7	19.3	8 27.5	34.2	53 04.6	03.7	334 52.0	46.0
S	08	242 06.2	332 47.8	19.4	23 28.7	34.7	68 07.2	03.8	349 54.2	46.0
A	09	257 08.7	347 46.9	. . 19.6	38 29.9	. . 35.1	83 09.7	. . 03.8	4 56.4	. . 46.0
T	10	272 11.2	2 46.1	19.7	53 31.1	35.5	98 12.3	03.9	19 58.6	46.1
U	11	287 13.6	17 45.2	19.8	68 32.3	35.9	113 14.9	03.9	35 00.9	46.1
R	12	302 16.1	32 44.4	S22 19.9	83 33.5	S13 36.3	128 17.5	N 4 04.0	50 03.1	S20 46.1
D	13	317 18.5	47 43.5	20.1	98 34.7	36.7	143 20.0	04.1	65 05.3	46.1
A	14	332 21.0	62 42.7	20.2	113 35.9	37.1	158 22.6	04.1	80 07.5	46.2
Y	15	347 23.5	77 41.8	. . 20.3	128 37.1	. . 37.5	173 25.2	. . 04.2	95 09.8	. . 46.2
	16	2 25.9	92 41.0	20.5	143 38.3	37.9	188 27.7	04.2	110 12.0	46.2
	17	17 28.4	107 40.1	20.6	158 39.5	38.3	203 30.3	04.3	125 14.2	46.2
	18	32 30.9	122 39.2	S22 20.7	173 40.7	S13 38.7	218 32.9	N 4 04.4	140 16.4	S20 46.3
	19	47 33.3	137 38.4	20.8	188 41.9	39.1	233 35.5	04.4	155 18.7	46.3
	20	62 35.8	152 37.5	20.9	203 43.1	39.5	248 38.0	04.5	170 20.9	46.3
	21	77 38.3	167 36.7	. . 21.1	218 44.3	. . 39.9	263 40.6	. . 04.5	185 23.1	. . 46.3
	22	92 40.7	182 35.8	21.2	233 45.5	40.3	278 43.2	04.6	200 25.3	46.4
	23	107 43.2	197 34.9	21.3	248 46.7	40.7	293 45.8	04.6	215 27.6	46.4
24	00	122 45.7	212 34.1	S22 21.4	263 47.9	S13 41.1	308 48.3	N 4 04.7	230 29.8	S20 46.4
	01	137 48.1	227 33.2	21.5	278 49.1	41.5	323 50.9	04.8	245 32.0	46.4
	02	152 50.6	242 32.4	21.6	293 50.3	41.9	338 53.5	04.8	260 34.2	46.5
	03	167 53.0	257 31.5	. . 21.7	308 51.5	. . 42.3	353 56.1	. . 04.9	275 36.5	. . 46.5
	04	182 55.5	272 30.7	21.9	323 52.7	42.7	8 58.6	04.9	290 38.7	46.5
	05	197 58.0	287 29.8	22.0	338 53.9	43.1	24 01.2	05.0	305 40.9	46.5
	06	213 00.4	302 28.9	S22 22.1	353 55.1	S13 43.5	39 03.8	N 4 05.1	320 43.1	S20 46.5
	07	228 02.9	317 28.1	22.2	8 56.3	43.9	54 06.4	05.1	335 45.4	46.6
	08	243 05.4	332 27.2	22.3	23 57.5	44.3	69 08.9	05.2	350 47.6	46.6
S	09	258 07.8	347 26.4	. . 22.4	38 58.7	. . 44.7	84 11.5	. . 05.3	5 49.8	. . 46.6
U	10	273 10.3	2 25.5	22.5	54 00.0	45.1	99 14.1	05.3	20 52.1	46.6
N	11	288 12.8	17 24.6	22.6	69 01.2	45.5	114 16.7	05.4	35 54.3	46.7
D	12	303 15.2	32 23.8	S22 22.7	84 02.4	S13 45.9	129 19.3	N 4 05.4	50 56.5	S20 46.7
A	13	318 17.7	47 22.9	22.8	99 03.6	46.3	144 21.8	05.5	65 58.7	46.7
Y	14	333 20.1	62 22.1	22.9	114 04.8	46.7	159 24.4	05.6	81 01.0	46.7
	15	348 22.6	77 21.2	. . 23.0	129 06.0	. . 47.1	174 27.0	. . 05.6	96 03.2	. . 46.8
	16	3 25.1	92 20.3	23.1	144 07.2	47.5	189 29.6	05.7	111 05.4	46.8
	17	18 27.5	107 19.5	23.2	159 08.4	47.9	204 32.2	05.7	126 07.6	46.8
	18	33 30.0	122 18.6	S22 23.3	174 09.6	S13 48.3	219 34.7	N 4 05.8	141 09.9	S20 46.8
	19	48 32.5	137 17.8	23.4	189 10.8	48.7	234 37.3	05.9	156 12.1	46.9
	20	63 34.9	152 16.9	23.5	204 12.0	49.1	249 39.9	05.9	171 14.3	46.9
	21	78 37.4	167 16.0	. . 23.6	219 13.2	. . 49.5	264 42.5	. . 06.0	186 16.6	. . 46.9
	22	93 39.9	182 15.2	23.7	234 14.4	49.9	279 45.1	06.1	201 18.8	46.9
	23	108 42.3	197 14.3	23.8	249 15.6	50.3	294 47.6	06.1	216 21.0	47.0
		h m								
Mer. Pass.		15 50.3	*v* −0.9	*d* 0.1	*v* 1.2	*d* 0.4	*v* 2.6	*d* 0.1	*v* 2.2	*d* 0.0

STARS

Name	SHA	Dec
	° ′	° ′
Acamar	315 16.9	S40 14.8
Achernar	335 25.6	S57 09.7
Acrux	173 06.8	S63 11.0
Adhara	255 10.7	S29 00.0
Aldebaran	290 47.1	N16 32.3
Alioth	166 19.1	N55 52.1
Alkaid	152 57.6	N49 13.8
Al Na'ir	27 42.0	S46 53.1
Alnilam	275 44.3	S 1 11.8
Alphard	217 54.0	S 8 43.9
Alphecca	126 09.7	N26 39.6
Alpheratz	357 41.8	N29 10.8
Altair	62 06.8	N 8 54.8
Ankaa	353 14.2	S42 13.4
Antares	112 24.3	S26 27.8
Arcturus	145 54.2	N19 05.9
Atria	107 24.8	S69 02.9
Avior	234 16.5	S59 33.8
Bellatrix	278 29.8	N 6 21.6
Betelgeuse	270 59.1	N 7 24.3
Canopus	263 54.8	S52 42.6
Capella	280 31.4	N46 00.7
Deneb	49 30.7	N45 20.4
Denebola	182 31.7	N14 28.8
Diphda	348 54.2	S17 54.1
Dubhe	193 49.2	N61 39.6
Elnath	278 10.1	N28 37.1
Eltanin	90 45.8	N51 29.2
Enif	33 45.7	N 9 57.0
Fomalhaut	15 22.3	S29 32.3
Gacrux	171 58.5	S57 11.9
Gienah	175 50.3	S17 37.8
Hadar	148 45.2	S60 26.6
Hamal	327 58.7	N23 32.2
Kaus Aust.	83 41.8	S34 22.4
Kochab	137 20.6	N74 05.2
Markab	13 36.8	N15 17.5
Menkar	314 13.1	N 4 08.9
Menkent	148 05.4	S36 26.7
Miaplacidus	221 38.2	S69 47.0
Mirfak	308 37.5	N49 55.1
Nunki	75 56.5	S26 16.4
Peacock	53 17.1	S56 40.9
Pollux	243 25.2	N27 59.0
Procyon	244 57.5	N 5 10.7
Rasalhague	96 05.1	N12 33.0
Regulus	207 41.4	N11 53.1
Rigel	281 10.1	S 8 11.3
Rigil Kent.	139 49.3	S60 53.6
Sabik	102 10.7	S15 44.5
Schedar	349 38.6	N56 37.7
Shaula	96 19.8	S37 06.6
Sirius	258 31.8	S16 44.6
Spica	158 29.3	S11 14.6
Suhail	222 50.6	S43 30.0
Vega	80 38.1	N38 48.0
Zuben'ubi	137 03.5	S16 06.3

	SHA	Mer. Pass.
	° ′	h m
Venus	91 08.1	9 49
Mars	141 32.5	6 26
Jupiter	186 00.1	3 28
Saturn	107 49.9	8 40

UT	SUN GHA	SUN Dec	MOON GHA	v	MOON Dec	d	HP
d h	° ′	° ′	° ′	′	° ′	′	′
22 00 (FRIDAY)	177 10.4	S19 50.9	24 32.4	8.0	N18 19.7	0.9	57.6
01	192 10.3	50.4	38 59.4	8.0	18 18.8	0.9	57.6
02	207 10.1	49.8	53 26.4	8.0	18 17.9	1.1	57.6
03	222 09.9	. . 49.2	67 53.4	8.1	18 16.8	1.2	57.6
04	237 09.7	48.7	82 20.5	8.2	18 15.6	1.2	57.5
05	252 09.6	48.1	96 47.7	8.1	18 14.4	1.4	57.5
06	267 09.4	S19 47.5	111 14.8	8.2	N18 13.0	1.5	57.5
07	282 09.2	47.0	125 42.0	8.2	18 11.5	1.6	57.5
08	297 09.1	46.4	140 09.2	8.3	18 09.9	1.7	57.5
09	312 08.9	. . 45.8	154 36.5	8.2	18 08.2	1.8	57.4
10	327 08.7	45.3	169 03.7	8.4	18 06.4	2.0	57.4
11	342 08.6	44.7	183 31.1	8.3	18 04.4	2.0	57.4
12	357 08.4	S19 44.1	197 58.4	8.4	N18 02.4	2.1	57.4
13	12 08.2	43.6	212 25.8	8.4	18 00.3	2.2	57.4
14	27 08.0	43.0	226 53.2	8.5	17 58.1	2.4	57.3
15	42 07.9	. . 42.4	241 20.7	8.5	17 55.7	2.4	57.3
16	57 07.7	41.9	255 48.2	8.6	17 53.3	2.5	57.3
17	72 07.5	41.3	270 15.8	8.6	17 50.8	2.7	57.3
18	87 07.4	S19 40.7	284 43.4	8.6	N17 48.1	2.7	57.3
19	102 07.2	40.2	299 11.0	8.7	17 45.4	2.8	57.2
20	117 07.0	39.6	313 38.7	8.7	17 42.6	3.0	57.2
21	132 06.9	. . 39.0	328 06.4	8.7	17 39.6	3.0	57.2
22	147 06.7	38.4	342 34.1	8.8	17 36.6	3.1	57.2
23	162 06.5	37.9	357 01.9	8.9	17 33.5	3.3	57.1
23 00 (SATURDAY)	177 06.4	S19 37.3	11 29.8	8.9	N17 30.2	3.3	57.1
01	192 06.2	36.7	25 57.7	8.9	17 26.9	3.4	57.1
02	207 06.0	36.1	40 25.6	9.0	17 23.5	3.5	57.1
03	222 05.9	. . 35.6	54 53.6	9.0	17 20.0	3.7	57.1
04	237 05.7	35.0	69 21.6	9.1	17 16.3	3.7	57.0
05	252 05.6	34.4	83 49.7	9.1	17 12.6	3.8	57.0
06	267 05.4	S19 33.8	98 17.8	9.2	N17 08.8	3.9	57.0
07	282 05.2	33.2	112 46.0	9.2	17 04.9	4.0	57.0
08	297 05.1	32.7	127 14.2	9.3	17 00.9	4.0	57.0
09	312 04.9	. . 32.1	141 42.5	9.3	16 56.9	4.2	56.9
10	327 04.7	31.5	156 10.8	9.4	16 52.7	4.3	56.9
11	342 04.6	30.9	170 39.2	9.4	16 48.4	4.3	56.9
12	357 04.4	S19 30.3	185 07.6	9.5	N16 44.1	4.5	56.9
13	12 04.3	29.8	199 36.1	9.6	16 39.6	4.5	56.8
14	27 04.1	29.2	214 04.7	9.5	16 35.1	4.6	56.8
15	42 03.9	. . 28.6	228 33.2	9.7	16 30.5	4.7	56.8
16	57 03.8	28.0	243 01.9	9.7	16 25.8	4.8	56.8
17	72 03.6	27.4	257 30.6	9.7	16 21.0	4.9	56.8
18	87 03.5	S19 26.8	271 59.3	9.8	N16 16.1	5.0	56.7
19	102 03.3	26.2	286 28.1	9.9	16 11.1	5.0	56.7
20	117 03.1	25.7	300 57.0	9.9	16 06.1	5.1	56.7
21	132 03.0	. . 25.1	315 25.9	9.9	16 01.0	5.2	56.7
22	147 02.8	24.5	329 54.8	10.1	15 55.8	5.3	56.6
23	162 02.7	23.9	344 23.9	10.0	15 50.5	5.4	56.6
24 00 (SUNDAY)	177 02.5	S19 23.3	358 52.9	10.2	N15 45.1	5.5	56.6
01	192 02.4	22.7	13 22.1	10.1	15 39.6	5.5	56.6
02	207 02.2	22.1	27 51.2	10.3	15 34.1	5.6	56.6
03	222 02.0	. . 21.5	42 20.5	10.3	15 28.5	5.7	56.5
04	237 01.9	20.9	56 49.8	10.4	15 22.8	5.8	56.5
05	252 01.7	20.3	71 19.2	10.4	15 17.0	5.8	56.5
06	267 01.6	S19 19.7	85 48.6	10.4	N15 11.2	5.9	56.5
07	282 01.4	19.2	100 18.0	10.6	15 05.3	6.0	56.4
08	297 01.3	18.6	114 47.6	10.6	14 59.3	6.1	56.4
09	312 01.1	. . 18.0	129 17.2	10.6	14 53.2	6.1	56.4
10	327 01.0	17.4	143 46.8	10.7	14 47.1	6.2	56.4
11	342 00.8	16.8	158 16.5	10.8	14 40.9	6.3	56.3
12	357 00.7	S19 16.2	172 46.3	10.8	N14 34.6	6.3	56.3
13	12 00.5	15.6	187 16.1	10.9	14 28.3	6.4	56.3
14	27 00.3	15.0	201 46.0	10.9	14 21.9	6.5	56.3
15	42 00.2	. . 14.4	216 15.9	11.0	14 15.4	6.6	56.3
16	57 00.0	13.8	230 45.9	11.0	14 08.8	6.6	56.2
17	71 59.9	13.2	245 15.9	11.2	14 02.2	6.7	56.2
18	86 59.7	S19 12.6	259 46.1	11.1	N13 55.5	6.7	56.2
19	101 59.6	12.0	274 16.2	11.3	13 48.8	6.9	56.2
20	116 59.4	11.4	288 46.5	11.2	13 41.9	6.8	56.1
21	131 59.3	. . 10.8	303 16.7	11.4	13 35.1	7.0	56.1
22	146 59.1	10.2	317 47.1	11.4	13 28.1	7.0	56.1
23	161 59.0	09.6	332 17.5	11.4	N13 21.1	7.0	56.1
	SD 16.3	d 0.6	SD 15.6		15.5		15.3

Lat.	Twilight Naut.	Twilight Civil	Sunrise	Moonrise 22	Moonrise 23	Moonrise 24	Moonrise 25
°	h m	h m	h m	h m	h m	h m	h m
N 72	07 41	09 20	▬	11 05	13 19	15 12	16 59
N 70	07 29	08 54	10 45	12 40	14 07	15 42	17 18
68	07 19	08 34	09 59	13 19	14 38	16 04	17 33
66	07 11	08 18	09 29	13 47	15 01	16 22	17 45
64	07 04	08 05	09 07	14 08	15 18	16 36	17 55
62	06 57	07 54	08 49	14 25	15 33	16 47	18 03
60	06 52	07 44	08 35	14 39	15 46	16 57	18 11
N 58	06 47	07 36	08 22	14 51	15 56	17 06	18 17
56	06 42	07 28	08 11	15 01	16 05	17 13	18 23
54	06 38	07 21	08 02	15 10	16 14	17 20	18 28
52	06 34	07 15	07 53	15 18	16 21	17 26	18 32
50	06 30	07 10	07 46	15 26	16 28	17 32	18 37
45	06 22	06 57	07 30	15 42	16 42	17 44	18 45
N 40	06 14	06 47	07 16	15 54	16 53	17 53	18 53
35	06 07	06 38	07 05	16 05	17 03	18 02	18 59
30	06 00	06 29	06 55	16 15	17 12	18 09	19 05
20	05 47	06 14	06 38	16 32	17 27	18 21	19 15
N 10	05 34	06 00	06 22	16 46	17 40	18 33	19 23
0	05 21	05 46	06 08	16 59	17 52	18 43	19 31
S 10	05 05	05 31	05 54	17 13	18 05	18 53	19 39
20	04 46	05 14	05 38	17 27	18 18	19 04	19 47
30	04 22	04 54	05 20	17 44	18 32	19 17	19 57
35	04 07	04 41	05 09	17 54	18 41	19 24	20 02
40	03 48	04 26	04 57	18 05	18 51	19 32	20 09
45	03 24	04 08	04 43	18 17	19 02	19 42	20 16
S 50	02 51	03 45	04 25	18 33	19 16	19 53	20 25
52	02 34	03 34	04 17	18 40	19 23	19 58	20 29
54	02 12	03 21	04 07	18 49	19 30	20 04	20 33
56	01 42	03 05	03 57	18 58	19 38	20 11	20 38
58	00 49	02 47	03 45	19 08	19 47	20 18	20 43
S 60	////	02 24	03 30	19 20	19 57	20 26	20 49

Lat.	Sunset	Twilight Civil	Twilight Naut.	Moonset 22	Moonset 23	Moonset 24	Moonset 25
°	h m	h m	h m	h m	h m	h m	h m
N 72	▬	15 04	16 44	10 29	10 07	09 59	09 54
N 70	13 40	15 30	16 56	08 54	09 18	09 29	09 34
68	14 26	15 50	17 05	08 14	08 47	09 06	09 18
66	14 55	16 06	17 14	07 47	08 23	08 48	09 05
64	15 17	16 19	17 21	07 26	08 05	08 33	08 54
62	15 35	16 30	17 27	07 09	07 50	08 21	08 44
60	15 50	16 40	17 32	06 54	07 37	08 10	08 36
N 58	16 02	16 48	17 37	06 42	07 26	08 01	08 29
56	16 13	16 56	17 42	06 32	07 17	07 53	08 23
54	16 22	17 02	17 46	06 22	07 08	07 46	08 18
52	16 31	17 09	17 50	06 14	07 01	07 40	08 12
50	16 38	17 14	17 54	06 07	06 54	07 34	08 08
45	16 54	17 26	18 02	05 51	06 39	07 21	07 58
N 40	17 08	17 37	18 10	05 38	06 27	07 11	07 50
35	17 19	17 46	18 17	05 26	06 17	07 02	07 42
30	17 29	17 54	18 23	05 17	06 07	06 54	07 36
20	17 46	18 09	18 36	05 00	05 52	06 40	07 25
N 10	18 01	18 23	18 49	04 45	05 38	06 28	07 15
0	18 15	18 37	19 03	04 31	05 25	06 17	07 06
S 10	18 30	18 52	19 18	04 17	05 12	06 05	06 57
20	18 45	19 09	19 37	04 03	04 58	05 53	06 47
30	19 03	19 29	20 01	03 46	04 42	05 39	06 36
35	19 13	19 42	20 16	03 36	04 33	05 31	06 29
40	19 26	19 56	20 35	03 24	04 22	05 22	06 22
45	19 40	20 14	20 58	03 11	04 10	05 11	06 13
S 50	19 57	20 37	21 31	02 55	03 54	04 58	06 03
52	20 06	20 48	21 48	02 47	03 47	04 52	05 58
54	20 15	21 01	22 09	02 38	03 39	04 45	05 52
56	20 25	21 16	22 37	02 29	03 30	04 37	05 46
58	20 37	21 34	23 25	02 18	03 20	04 29	05 39
S 60	20 51	21 57	////	02 05	03 09	04 19	05 32

Day	SUN Eqn. of Time 00h	SUN Eqn. of Time 12h	SUN Mer. Pass.	MOON Mer. Pass. Upper	MOON Mer. Pass. Lower	MOON Age	MOON Phase
d	m s	m s	h m	h m	h m	d %	
22	11 18	11 26	12 11	23 12	10 45	12 97	○
23	11 34	11 42	12 12	24 05	11 39	13 99	
24	11 50	11 57	12 12	00 05	12 30	14 100	

Day	UT (d h)	ARIES GHA	VENUS −3·9 GHA	VENUS Dec	MARS +0·9 GHA	MARS Dec	JUPITER −2·3 GHA	JUPITER Dec	SATURN +0·5 GHA	SATURN Dec	STARS Name	SHA	Dec
MONDAY	25 00	123 44.8	212 13.4	S22 23.8	264 16.8	S13 50.7	309 50.2	N 4 06.2	231 23.2	S20 47.0	Acamar	315 17.0	S40 14.8
	01	138 47.3	227 12.6	23.9	279 18.1	51.1	324 52.8	06.2	246 25.5	47.0	Achernar	335 25.7	S57 09.7
	02	153 49.7	242 11.7	24.0	294 19.3	51.5	339 55.4	06.3	261 27.7	47.0	Acrux	173 06.8	S63 11.0
	03	168 52.2	257 10.9	24.1	309 20.5	51.9	354 58.0	06.4	276 29.9	47.1	Adhara	255 10.7	S29 00.0
	04	183 54.6	272 10.0	24.2	324 21.7	52.3	10 00.6	06.4	291 32.2	47.1	Aldebaran	290 47.1	N16 32.3
	05	198 57.1	287 09.1	24.3	339 22.9	52.7	25 03.1	06.5	306 34.4	47.1			
	06	213 59.6	302 08.3	S22 24.3	354 24.1	S13 53.1	40 05.7	N 4 06.6	321 36.6	S20 47.1	Alioth	166 19.0	N55 52.1
	07	229 02.0	317 07.4	24.4	9 25.3	53.5	55 08.3	06.6	336 38.8	47.1	Alkaid	152 57.5	N49 13.8
	08	244 04.5	332 06.6	24.5	24 26.5	53.9	70 10.9	06.7	351 41.1	47.2	Al Na'ir	27 42.0	S46 53.1
	09	259 07.0	347 05.7	24.6	39 27.7	54.3	85 13.5	06.7	6 43.3	47.2	Alnilam	275 44.3	S 1 11.8
	10	274 09.4	2 04.8	24.7	54 28.9	54.7	100 16.1	06.8	21 45.5	47.2	Alphard	217 54.0	S 8 43.9
	11	289 11.9	17 04.0	24.7	69 30.1	55.1	115 18.7	06.9	36 47.8	47.2			
	12	304 14.4	32 03.1	S22 24.8	84 31.3	S13 55.5	130 21.2	N 4 06.9	51 50.0	S20 47.3	Alphecca	126 09.7	N26 39.6
	13	319 16.8	47 02.2	24.9	99 32.6	55.9	145 23.8	07.0	66 52.2	47.3	Alpheratz	357 41.8	N29 10.8
	14	334 19.3	62 01.4	25.0	114 33.8	56.3	160 26.4	07.1	81 54.5	47.3	Altair	62 06.8	N 8 54.8
	15	349 21.8	77 00.5	25.0	129 35.0	56.7	175 29.0	07.1	96 56.7	47.3	Ankaa	353 14.2	S42 13.4
	16	4 24.2	91 59.6	25.1	144 36.2	57.1	190 31.6	07.2	111 58.9	47.4	Antares	112 24.3	S26 27.8
	17	19 26.7	106 58.8	25.2	159 37.4	57.5	205 34.2	07.3	127 01.1	47.4			
	18	34 29.1	121 57.9	S22 25.2	174 38.6	S13 57.9	220 36.8	N 4 07.3	142 03.4	S20 47.4	Arcturus	145 54.1	N19 05.9
	19	49 31.6	136 57.1	25.3	189 39.8	58.3	235 39.3	07.4	157 05.6	47.4	Atria	107 24.8	S69 02.9
	20	64 34.1	151 56.2	25.4	204 41.0	58.7	250 41.9	07.5	172 07.8	47.5	Avior	234 16.5	S59 33.8
	21	79 36.5	166 55.3	25.4	219 42.2	59.1	265 44.5	07.5	187 10.1	47.5	Bellatrix	278 29.8	N 6 21.6
	22	94 39.0	181 54.5	25.5	234 43.4	59.5	280 47.1	07.6	202 12.3	47.5	Betelgeuse	270 59.1	N 7 24.3
	23	109 41.5	196 53.6	25.5	249 44.7	13 59.8	295 49.7	07.6	217 14.5	47.5			
TUESDAY	26 00	124 43.9	211 52.7	S22 25.6	264 45.9	S14 00.2	310 52.3	N 4 07.7	232 16.8	S20 47.5	Canopus	263 54.9	S52 42.6
	01	139 46.4	226 51.9	25.7	279 47.1	00.6	325 54.9	07.8	247 19.0	47.6	Capella	280 31.4	N46 00.7
	02	154 48.9	241 51.0	25.7	294 48.3	01.0	340 57.5	07.8	262 21.2	47.6	Deneb	49 30.7	N45 20.4
	03	169 51.3	256 50.1	25.8	309 49.5	01.4	356 00.1	07.9	277 23.5	47.6	Denebola	182 31.7	N14 28.8
	04	184 53.8	271 49.3	25.8	324 50.7	01.8	11 02.6	08.0	292 25.7	47.6	Diphda	348 54.3	S17 54.1
	05	199 56.2	286 48.4	25.9	339 51.9	02.2	26 05.2	08.0	307 27.9	47.7			
	06	214 58.7	301 47.5	S22 25.9	354 53.1	S14 02.6	41 07.8	N 4 08.1	322 30.2	S20 47.7	Dubhe	193 49.2	N61 39.6
	07	230 01.2	316 46.7	26.0	9 54.4	03.0	56 10.4	08.2	337 32.4	47.7	Elnath	278 10.1	N28 37.1
	08	245 03.6	331 45.8	26.0	24 55.6	03.4	71 13.0	08.2	352 34.6	47.7	Eltanin	90 45.8	N51 29.2
	09	260 06.1	346 45.0	26.1	39 56.8	03.8	86 15.6	08.3	7 36.9	47.8	Enif	33 45.7	N 9 57.0
	10	275 08.6	1 44.1	26.1	54 58.0	04.2	101 18.2	08.4	22 39.1	47.8	Fomalhaut	15 22.4	S29 32.3
	11	290 11.0	16 43.2	26.2	69 59.2	04.6	116 20.8	08.4	37 41.3	47.8			
	12	305 13.5	31 42.4	S22 26.2	85 00.4	S14 05.0	131 23.4	N 4 08.5	52 43.6	S20 47.8	Gacrux	171 58.5	S57 11.9
	13	320 16.0	46 41.5	26.3	100 01.6	05.4	146 26.0	08.6	67 45.8	47.8	Gienah	175 50.3	S17 37.8
	14	335 18.4	61 40.6	26.3	115 02.8	05.7	161 28.6	08.6	82 48.0	47.9	Hadar	148 45.2	S60 26.6
	15	350 20.9	76 39.8	26.4	130 04.1	06.1	176 31.2	08.7	97 50.3	47.9	Hamal	327 58.7	N23 32.2
	16	5 23.4	91 38.9	26.4	145 05.3	06.5	191 33.8	08.8	112 52.5	47.9	Kaus Aust.	83 41.8	S34 22.4
	17	20 25.8	106 38.0	26.5	160 06.5	06.9	206 36.3	08.8	127 54.7	47.9			
	18	35 28.3	121 37.2	S22 26.5	175 07.7	S14 07.3	221 38.9	N 4 08.9	142 57.0	S20 48.0	Kochab	137 20.5	N74 05.2
	19	50 30.7	136 36.3	26.5	190 08.9	07.7	236 41.5	09.0	157 59.2	48.0	Markab	13 36.8	N15 17.5
	20	65 33.2	151 35.4	26.6	205 10.1	08.1	251 44.1	09.0	173 01.4	48.0	Menkar	314 13.1	N 4 08.9
	21	80 35.7	166 34.6	26.6	220 11.3	08.5	266 46.7	09.1	188 03.7	48.0	Menkent	148 05.4	S36 26.7
	22	95 38.1	181 33.7	26.6	235 12.6	08.9	281 49.3	09.2	203 05.9	48.1	Miaplacidus	221 38.2	S69 47.1
	23	110 40.6	196 32.8	26.7	250 13.8	09.3	296 51.9	09.2	218 08.1	48.1			
WEDNESDAY	27 00	125 43.1	211 32.0	S22 26.7	265 15.0	S14 09.7	311 54.5	N 4 09.3	233 10.4	S20 48.1	Mirfak	308 37.6	N49 55.1
	01	140 45.5	226 31.1	26.7	280 16.2	10.0	326 57.1	09.4	248 12.6	48.1	Nunki	75 56.5	S26 16.4
	02	155 48.0	241 30.2	26.8	295 17.4	10.4	341 59.7	09.5	263 14.8	48.1	Peacock	53 17.1	S56 40.9
	03	170 50.5	256 29.4	26.8	310 18.6	10.8	357 02.3	09.5	278 17.1	48.2	Pollux	243 25.2	N27 59.0
	04	185 52.9	271 28.5	26.8	325 19.8	11.2	12 04.9	09.6	293 19.3	48.2	Procyon	244 57.5	N 5 10.7
	05	200 55.4	286 27.6	26.9	340 21.1	11.6	27 07.5	09.7	308 21.5	48.2			
	06	215 57.9	301 26.8	S22 26.9	355 22.3	S14 12.0	42 10.1	N 4 09.7	323 23.8	S20 48.2	Rasalhague	96 05.1	N12 33.0
	07	231 00.3	316 25.9	26.9	10 23.5	12.4	57 12.7	09.8	338 26.0	48.3	Regulus	207 41.3	N11 53.1
	08	246 02.8	331 25.0	26.9	25 24.7	12.8	72 15.3	09.9	353 28.2	48.3	Rigel	281 10.1	S 8 11.3
	09	261 05.2	346 24.2	27.0	40 25.9	13.2	87 17.9	09.9	8 30.5	48.3	Rigil Kent.	139 49.2	S60 53.7
	10	276 07.7	1 23.3	27.0	55 27.1	13.5	102 20.5	10.0	23 32.7	48.3	Sabik	102 10.7	S15 44.5
	11	291 10.2	16 22.4	27.0	70 28.4	13.9	117 23.1	10.1	38 34.9	48.4			
	12	306 12.6	31 21.6	S22 27.0	85 29.6	S14 14.3	132 25.7	N 4 10.1	53 37.2	S20 48.4	Schedar	349 38.6	N56 37.7
	13	321 15.1	46 20.7	27.0	100 30.8	14.7	147 28.3	10.2	68 39.4	48.4	Shaula	96 19.8	S37 06.6
	14	336 17.6	61 19.8	27.1	115 32.0	15.1	162 30.9	10.3	83 41.6	48.4	Sirius	258 31.8	S16 44.6
	15	351 20.0	76 19.0	27.1	130 33.2	15.5	177 33.5	10.4	98 43.9	48.4	Spica	158 29.3	S11 14.6
	16	6 22.5	91 18.1	27.1	145 34.4	15.9	192 36.1	10.4	113 46.1	48.5	Suhail	222 50.6	S43 30.0
	17	21 25.0	106 17.2	27.1	160 35.7	16.3	207 38.7	10.5	128 48.4	48.5			
	18	36 27.4	121 16.4	S22 27.1	175 36.9	S14 16.6	222 41.3	N 4 10.6	143 50.6	S20 48.5	Vega	80 38.1	N38 48.0
	19	51 29.9	136 15.5	27.1	190 38.1	17.0	237 43.9	10.6	158 52.8	48.5	Zuben'ubi	137 03.5	S16 06.3
	20	66 32.3	151 14.6	27.1	205 39.3	17.4	252 46.5	10.7	173 55.1	48.6			
	21	81 34.8	166 13.8	27.1	220 40.5	17.8	267 49.1	10.8	188 57.3	48.6			
	22	96 37.3	181 12.9	27.1	235 41.7	18.2	282 51.7	10.8	203 59.5	48.6			
	23	111 39.7	196 12.0	27.1	250 43.0	18.6	297 54.3	10.9	219 01.8	48.6			
	Mer. Pass. (h m)	15 38.5	v −0.9	d 0.0	v 1.2	d 0.4	v 2.6	d 0.1	v 2.2	d 0.0			

	SHA (° ′)	Mer. Pass. (h m)
Venus	87 08.8	9 53
Mars	140 01.9	6 20
Jupiter	186 08.4	3 16
Saturn	107 32.8	8 30

UT	SUN GHA	SUN Dec	MOON GHA	v	MOON Dec	d	HP
d h	° ′	° ′	° ′	′	° ′	′	′
25 00	176 58.8	S19 09.0	346 47.9	11.6	N13 14.1	7.2	56.1
01	191 58.7	08.4	1 18.5	11.5	13 06.9	7.2	56.0
02	206 58.5	07.7	15 49.0	11.7	12 59.7	7.2	56.0
03	221 58.4	. . 07.1	30 19.7	11.6	12 52.5	7.3	56.0
04	236 58.3	06.5	44 50.3	11.8	12 45.2	7.3	56.0
05	251 58.1	05.9	59 21.1	11.8	12 37.9	7.5	55.9
06	266 58.0	S19 05.3	73 51.9	11.9	N12 30.4	7.4	55.9
07	281 57.8	04.7	88 22.8	11.9	12 23.0	7.5	55.9
08	296 57.7	04.1	102 53.7	12.0	12 15.5	7.6	55.9
09	311 57.5	. . 03.5	117 24.7	12.0	12 07.9	7.6	55.8
10	326 57.4	02.9	131 55.7	12.1	12 00.3	7.7	55.8
11	341 57.2	02.3	146 26.8	12.1	11 52.6	7.7	55.8
12	356 57.1	S19 01.7	160 57.9	12.2	N11 44.9	7.8	55.8
13	11 56.9	01.0	175 29.1	12.3	11 37.1	7.9	55.8
14	26 56.8	19 00.4	190 00.4	12.3	11 29.2	7.8	55.7
15	41 56.7	18 59.8	204 31.7	12.3	11 21.4	8.0	55.7
16	56 56.5	59.2	219 03.0	12.5	11 13.4	7.9	55.7
17	71 56.4	58.6	233 34.5	12.4	11 05.5	8.0	55.7
18	86 56.2	S18 58.0	248 05.9	12.5	N10 57.5	8.1	55.7
19	101 56.1	57.4	262 37.4	12.6	10 49.4	8.1	55.6
20	116 55.9	56.7	277 09.0	12.7	10 41.3	8.1	55.6
21	131 55.8	. . 56.1	291 40.7	12.6	10 33.2	8.2	55.6
22	146 55.7	55.5	306 12.3	12.8	10 25.0	8.3	55.6
23	161 55.5	54.9	320 44.1	12.8	10 16.7	8.2	55.5
26 00	176 55.4	S18 54.3	335 15.9	12.8	N10 08.5	8.4	55.5
01	191 55.2	53.6	349 47.7	12.9	10 00.1	8.3	55.5
02	206 55.1	53.0	4 19.6	13.0	9 51.8	8.4	55.5
03	221 55.0	. . 52.4	18 51.6	13.0	9 43.4	8.4	55.5
04	236 54.8	51.8	33 23.6	13.0	9 35.0	8.5	55.4
05	251 54.7	51.2	47 55.6	13.1	9 26.5	8.5	55.4
06	266 54.5	S18 50.5	62 27.7	13.1	N 9 18.0	8.5	55.4
07	281 54.4	49.9	76 59.8	13.2	9 09.5	8.6	55.4
08	296 54.3	49.3	91 32.0	13.3	9 00.9	8.6	55.4
09	311 54.1	. . 48.7	106 04.3	13.3	8 52.3	8.6	55.3
10	326 54.0	48.0	120 36.6	13.3	8 43.7	8.7	55.3
11	341 53.8	47.4	135 08.9	13.4	8 35.0	8.7	55.3
12	356 53.7	S18 46.8	149 41.3	13.4	N 8 26.3	8.7	55.3
13	11 53.6	46.2	164 13.7	13.5	8 17.6	8.8	55.3
14	26 53.4	45.5	178 46.2	13.5	8 08.8	8.8	55.2
15	41 53.3	. . 44.9	193 18.7	13.6	8 00.0	8.8	55.2
16	56 53.2	44.3	207 51.3	13.6	7 51.2	8.9	55.2
17	71 53.0	43.6	222 23.9	13.7	7 42.3	8.9	55.2
18	86 52.9	S18 43.0	236 56.6	13.7	N 7 33.4	8.9	55.2
19	101 52.8	42.4	251 29.3	13.7	7 24.5	8.9	55.1
20	116 52.6	41.8	266 02.0	13.8	7 15.6	8.9	55.1
21	131 52.5	. . 41.1	280 34.8	13.8	7 06.7	9.0	55.1
22	146 52.4	40.5	295 07.6	13.9	6 57.7	9.0	55.1
23	161 52.2	39.9	309 40.5	13.9	6 48.7	9.0	55.1
27 00	176 52.1	S18 39.2	324 13.4	14.0	N 6 39.7	9.1	55.0
01	191 52.0	38.6	338 46.4	14.0	6 30.6	9.1	55.0
02	206 51.8	38.0	353 19.4	14.0	6 21.5	9.0	55.0
03	221 51.7	. . 37.3	7 52.4	14.1	6 12.5	9.1	55.0
04	236 51.6	36.7	22 25.5	14.1	6 03.4	9.2	55.0
05	251 51.4	36.0	36 58.6	14.1	5 54.2	9.1	54.9
06	266 51.3	S18 35.4	51 31.7	14.2	N 5 45.1	9.2	54.9
07	281 51.2	34.8	66 04.9	14.2	5 35.9	9.2	54.9
08	296 51.0	34.1	80 38.1	14.3	5 26.7	9.2	54.9
09	311 50.9	. . 33.5	95 11.4	14.3	5 17.5	9.2	54.9
10	326 50.8	32.9	109 44.7	14.3	5 08.3	9.2	54.9
11	341 50.7	32.2	124 18.0	14.4	4 59.1	9.2	54.8
12	356 50.5	S18 31.6	138 51.4	14.4	N 4 49.9	9.3	54.8
13	11 50.4	30.9	153 24.8	14.4	4 40.6	9.3	54.8
14	26 50.3	30.3	167 58.2	14.5	4 31.3	9.3	54.8
15	41 50.1	. . 29.6	182 31.7	14.4	4 22.0	9.3	54.8
16	56 50.0	29.0	197 05.1	14.6	4 12.7	9.3	54.8
17	71 49.9	28.4	211 38.7	14.5	4 03.4	9.3	54.7
18	86 49.8	S18 27.7	226 12.2	14.6	N 3 54.1	9.3	54.7
19	101 49.6	27.1	240 45.8	14.6	3 44.8	9.3	54.7
20	116 49.5	26.4	255 19.4	14.6	3 35.5	9.4	54.7
21	131 49.4	. . 25.8	269 53.0	14.7	3 26.1	9.3	54.7
22	146 49.3	25.1	284 26.7	14.7	3 16.8	9.4	54.7
23	161 49.1	24.5	299 00.4	14.7	N 3 07.4	9.4	54.7
	SD 16.3	*d* 0.6	SD	15.2	15.1		14.9

Lat.	Twilight Naut.	Twilight Civil	Sunrise	Moonrise 25	Moonrise 26	Moonrise 27	Moonrise 28
°	h m	h m	h m	h m	h m	h m	h m
N 72	07 32	09 07	11 54	16 59	18 40	20 16	21 50
N 70	07 21	08 44	10 24	17 18	18 51	20 21	21 50
68	07 12	08 25	09 46	17 33	19 00	20 25	21 49
66	07 05	08 11	09 19	17 45	19 08	20 29	21 49
64	06 58	07 59	08 59	17 55	19 14	20 32	21 48
62	06 52	07 48	08 42	18 03	19 19	20 34	21 48
60	06 47	07 39	08 28	18 11	19 24	20 36	21 47
N 58	06 43	07 31	08 17	18 17	19 28	20 38	21 47
56	06 38	07 24	08 07	18 23	19 32	20 40	21 47
54	06 34	07 18	07 58	18 28	19 35	20 41	21 47
52	06 31	07 12	07 50	18 32	19 38	20 43	21 46
50	06 27	07 07	07 42	18 37	19 41	20 44	21 46
45	06 19	06 55	07 27	18 45	19 47	20 47	21 46
N 40	06 12	06 45	07 14	18 53	19 52	20 49	21 45
35	06 06	06 36	07 03	18 59	19 56	20 51	21 45
30	05 59	06 28	06 54	19 05	19 59	20 53	21 45
20	05 47	06 14	06 37	19 15	20 06	20 56	21 44
N 10	05 35	06 00	06 23	19 23	20 12	20 58	21 44
0	05 22	05 47	06 09	19 31	20 17	21 01	21 44
S 10	05 07	05 33	05 55	19 39	20 22	21 03	21 44
20	04 48	05 16	05 40	19 47	20 28	21 06	21 43
30	04 25	04 57	05 23	19 57	20 34	21 09	21 43
35	04 10	04 45	05 13	20 02	20 38	21 11	21 43
40	03 52	04 30	05 01	20 09	20 42	21 13	21 42
45	03 29	04 13	04 47	20 16	20 47	21 15	21 42
S 50	02 58	03 51	04 30	20 25	20 52	21 18	21 42
52	02 42	03 40	04 22	20 29	20 55	21 19	21 42
54	02 22	03 28	04 13	20 33	20 58	21 20	21 42
56	01 56	03 13	04 03	20 38	21 01	21 22	21 42
58	01 15	02 56	03 52	20 43	21 05	21 24	21 41
S 60	////	02 35	03 38	20 49	21 09	21 25	21 41

Lat.	Sunset	Twilight Civil	Twilight Naut.	Moonset 25	Moonset 26	Moonset 27	Moonset 28
°	h m	h m	h m	h m	h m	h m	h m
N 72	12 32	15 19	16 55	09 54	09 49	09 44	09 39
N 70	14 02	15 42	17 05	09 34	09 36	09 37	09 37
68	14 40	16 00	17 14	09 18	09 26	09 31	09 36
66	15 07	16 15	17 21	09 05	09 17	09 26	09 35
64	15 27	16 27	17 28	08 54	09 09	09 22	09 34
62	15 43	16 37	17 33	08 44	09 03	09 19	09 33
60	15 57	16 46	17 38	08 36	08 58	09 16	09 32
N 58	16 09	16 54	17 43	08 29	08 53	09 13	09 31
56	16 19	17 01	17 47	08 23	08 48	09 10	09 30
54	16 28	17 08	17 51	08 18	08 44	09 08	09 30
52	16 36	17 13	17 55	08 12	08 41	09 06	09 29
50	16 43	17 19	17 58	08 08	08 37	09 04	09 29
45	16 58	17 30	18 06	07 58	08 30	09 00	09 28
N 40	17 11	17 40	18 13	07 50	08 24	08 56	09 27
35	17 22	17 49	18 20	07 42	08 19	08 53	09 26
30	17 31	17 57	18 26	07 36	08 15	08 51	09 25
20	17 48	18 11	18 38	07 25	08 07	08 46	09 24
N 10	18 02	18 24	18 50	07 15	08 00	08 42	09 23
0	18 16	18 38	19 03	07 06	07 53	08 38	09 22
S 10	18 30	18 52	19 18	06 57	07 47	08 34	09 21
20	18 45	19 08	19 36	06 47	07 39	08 30	09 19
30	19 02	19 28	19 59	06 36	07 31	08 25	09 18
35	19 12	19 40	20 14	06 29	07 27	08 22	09 17
40	19 23	19 54	20 32	06 22	07 21	08 19	09 16
45	19 37	20 11	20 54	06 13	07 15	08 16	09 15
S 50	19 54	20 33	21 25	06 03	07 07	08 11	09 14
52	20 02	20 43	21 41	05 58	07 04	08 09	09 13
54	20 10	20 56	22 00	05 52	07 00	08 07	09 13
56	20 20	21 10	22 26	05 46	06 56	08 04	09 12
58	20 32	21 27	23 03	05 39	06 51	08 02	09 11
S 60	20 45	21 47	////	05 32	06 46	07 59	09 10

Day	SUN Eqn. of Time 00^h	SUN Eqn. of Time 12^h	SUN Mer. Pass.	MOON Mer. Pass. Upper	MOON Mer. Pass. Lower	MOON Age	MOON Phase
d	m s	m s	h m	h m	h m	d %	
25	12 04	12 11	12 12	00 55	13 19	15 98	
26	12 18	12 25	12 12	01 42	14 05	16 94	
27	12 31	12 38	12 13	02 28	14 50	17 89	

UT		ARIES	VENUS −3·9		MARS +0·9		JUPITER −2·3		SATURN +0·5	
		GHA	GHA	Dec	GHA	Dec	GHA	Dec	GHA	Dec
d	h	° ′	° ′	° ′	° ′	° ′	° ′	° ′	° ′	° ′
28	00	126 42.2	211 11.1	S22 27.2	265 44.2	S14 19.0	312 56.9	N 4 11.0	234 04.0	S20 48.6
	01	141 44.7	226 10.3	27.2	280 45.4	19.3	327 59.5	11.1	249 06.2	48.7
	02	156 47.1	241 09.4	27.2	295 46.6	19.7	343 02.1	11.1	264 08.5	48.7
	03	171 49.6	256 08.5	. . 27.2	310 47.8	. . 20.1	358 04.7	. . 11.2	279 10.7	. . 48.7
	04	186 52.1	271 07.7	27.2	325 49.1	20.5	13 07.3	11.3	294 13.0	48.7
	05	201 54.5	286 06.8	27.2	340 50.3	20.9	28 09.9	11.3	309 15.2	48.8
	06	216 57.0	301 05.9	S22 27.2	355 51.5	S14 21.3	43 12.5	N 4 11.4	324 17.4	S20 48.8
	07	231 59.5	316 05.1	27.2	10 52.7	21.7	58 15.1	11.5	339 19.7	48.8
T	08	247 01.9	331 04.2	27.2	25 53.9	22.0	73 17.7	11.6	354 21.9	48.8
H	09	262 04.4	346 03.3	. . 27.1	40 55.2	. . 22.4	88 20.3	. . 11.6	9 24.1	. . 48.8
U	10	277 06.8	1 02.5	27.1	55 56.4	22.8	103 22.9	11.7	24 26.4	48.9
R	11	292 09.3	16 01.6	27.1	70 57.6	23.2	118 25.5	11.8	39 28.6	48.9
S	12	307 11.8	31 00.7	S22 27.1	85 58.8	S14 23.6	133 28.2	N 4 11.9	54 30.9	S20 48.9
D	13	322 14.2	45 59.9	27.1	101 00.0	24.0	148 30.8	11.9	69 33.1	48.9
A	14	337 16.7	60 59.0	27.1	116 01.3	24.3	163 33.4	12.0	84 35.3	49.0
Y	15	352 19.2	75 58.1	. . 27.1	131 02.5	. . 24.7	178 36.0	. . 12.1	99 37.6	. . 49.0
	16	7 21.6	90 57.3	27.1	146 03.7	25.1	193 38.6	12.1	114 39.8	49.0
	17	22 24.1	105 56.4	27.1	161 04.9	25.5	208 41.2	12.2	129 42.1	49.0
	18	37 26.6	120 55.5	S22 27.0	176 06.2	S14 25.9	223 43.8	N 4 12.3	144 44.3	S20 49.0
	19	52 29.0	135 54.6	27.0	191 07.4	26.2	238 46.4	12.4	159 46.5	49.1
	20	67 31.5	150 53.8	27.0	206 08.6	26.6	253 49.0	12.4	174 48.8	49.1
	21	82 33.9	165 52.9	. . 27.0	221 09.8	. . 27.0	268 51.6	. . 12.5	189 51.0	. . 49.1
	22	97 36.4	180 52.0	27.0	236 11.0	27.4	283 54.2	12.6	204 53.3	49.1
	23	112 38.9	195 51.2	27.0	251 12.3	27.8	298 56.8	12.7	219 55.5	49.1
29	00	127 41.3	210 50.3	S22 26.9	266 13.5	S14 28.2	313 59.5	N 4 12.7	234 57.7	S20 49.2
	01	142 43.8	225 49.4	26.9	281 14.7	28.5	329 02.1	12.8	250 00.0	49.2
	02	157 46.3	240 48.6	26.9	296 15.9	28.9	344 04.7	12.9	265 02.2	49.2
	03	172 48.7	255 47.7	. . 26.9	311 17.2	. . 29.3	359 07.3	. . 13.0	280 04.5	. . 49.2
	04	187 51.2	270 46.8	26.8	326 18.4	29.7	14 09.9	13.0	295 06.7	49.3
	05	202 53.7	285 46.0	26.8	341 19.6	30.1	29 12.5	13.1	310 08.9	49.3
	06	217 56.1	300 45.1	S22 26.8	356 20.8	S14 30.4	44 15.1	N 4 13.2	325 11.2	S20 49.3
	07	232 58.6	315 44.2	26.7	11 22.0	30.8	59 17.7	13.3	340 13.4	49.3
	08	248 01.1	330 43.3	26.7	26 23.3	31.2	74 20.3	13.3	355 15.7	49.3
F	09	263 03.5	345 42.5	. . 26.7	41 24.5	. . 31.6	89 23.0	. . 13.4	10 17.9	. . 49.4
R	10	278 06.0	0 41.6	26.6	56 25.7	32.0	104 25.6	13.5	25 20.1	49.4
I	11	293 08.4	15 40.7	26.6	71 26.9	32.3	119 28.2	13.6	40 22.4	49.4
D	12	308 10.9	30 39.9	S22 26.6	86 28.2	S14 32.7	134 30.8	N 4 13.6	55 24.6	S20 49.4
A	13	323 13.4	45 39.0	26.5	101 29.4	33.1	149 33.4	13.7	70 26.9	49.5
Y	14	338 15.8	60 38.1	26.5	116 30.6	33.5	164 36.0	13.8	85 29.1	49.5
	15	353 18.3	75 37.3	. . 26.4	131 31.8	. . 33.9	179 38.6	. . 13.9	100 31.4	. . 49.5
	16	8 20.8	90 36.4	26.4	146 33.1	34.2	194 41.2	13.9	115 33.6	49.5
	17	23 23.2	105 35.5	26.4	161 34.3	34.6	209 43.9	14.0	130 35.8	49.5
	18	38 25.7	120 34.7	S22 26.3	176 35.5	S14 35.0	224 46.5	N 4 14.1	145 38.1	S20 49.6
	19	53 28.2	135 33.8	26.3	191 36.7	35.4	239 49.1	14.2	160 40.3	49.6
	20	68 30.6	150 32.9	26.2	206 38.0	35.7	254 51.7	14.2	175 42.6	49.6
	21	83 33.1	165 32.0	. . 26.2	221 39.2	. . 36.1	269 54.3	. . 14.3	190 44.8	. . 49.6
	22	98 35.6	180 31.2	26.1	236 40.4	36.5	284 56.9	14.4	205 47.0	49.6
	23	113 38.0	195 30.3	26.1	251 41.7	36.9	299 59.5	14.5	220 49.3	49.7
30	00	128 40.5	210 29.4	S22 26.0	266 42.9	S14 37.3	315 02.2	N 4 14.5	235 51.5	S20 49.7
	01	143 42.9	225 28.6	26.0	281 44.1	37.6	330 04.8	14.6	250 53.8	49.7
	02	158 45.4	240 27.7	25.9	296 45.3	38.0	345 07.4	14.7	265 56.0	49.7
	03	173 47.9	255 26.8	. . 25.9	311 46.6	. . 38.4	0 10.0	. . 14.8	280 58.3	. . 49.7
	04	188 50.3	270 26.0	25.8	326 47.8	38.8	15 12.6	14.8	296 00.5	49.8
	05	203 52.8	285 25.1	25.8	341 49.0	39.1	30 15.3	14.9	311 02.8	49.8
	06	218 55.3	300 24.2	S22 25.7	356 50.2	S14 39.5	45 17.9	N 4 15.0	326 05.0	S20 49.8
	07	233 57.7	315 23.3	25.6	11 51.5	39.9	60 20.5	15.1	341 07.2	49.8
S	08	249 00.2	330 22.5	25.6	26 52.7	40.3	75 23.1	15.2	356 09.5	49.9
A	09	264 02.7	345 21.6	. . 25.5	41 53.9	. . 40.6	90 25.7	. . 15.2	11 11.7	. . 49.9
T	10	279 05.1	0 20.7	25.5	56 55.2	41.0	105 28.3	15.3	26 14.0	49.9
U	11	294 07.6	15 19.9	25.4	71 56.4	41.4	120 31.0	15.4	41 16.2	49.9
R	12	309 10.0	30 19.0	S22 25.3	86 57.6	S14 41.8	135 33.6	N 4 15.5	56 18.5	S20 49.9
D	13	324 12.5	45 18.1	25.3	101 58.8	42.1	150 36.2	15.5	71 20.7	50.0
A	14	339 15.0	60 17.3	25.2	117 00.1	42.5	165 38.8	15.6	86 22.9	50.0
Y	15	354 17.4	75 16.4	. . 25.1	132 01.3	. . 42.9	180 41.4	. . 15.7	101 25.2	. . 50.0
	16	9 19.9	90 15.5	25.1	147 02.5	43.3	195 44.1	15.8	116 27.4	50.0
	17	24 22.4	105 14.7	25.0	162 03.8	43.6	210 46.7	15.9	131 29.7	50.0
	18	39 24.8	120 13.8	S22 24.9	177 05.0	S14 44.0	225 49.3	N 4 15.9	146 31.9	S20 50.1
	19	54 27.3	135 12.9	24.9	192 06.2	44.4	240 51.9	16.0	161 34.2	50.1
	20	69 29.8	150 12.0	24.8	207 07.5	44.8	255 54.5	16.1	176 36.4	50.1
	21	84 32.2	165 11.2	. . 24.7	222 08.7	. . 45.1	270 57.2	. . 16.2	191 38.7	. . 50.1
	22	99 34.7	180 10.3	24.6	237 09.9	45.5	285 59.8	16.3	206 40.9	50.1
	23	114 37.2	195 09.4	24.6	252 11.1	45.9	301 02.4	16.3	221 43.2	50.2
Mer. Pass.		h m 15 26.7	*v* −0.9	*d* 0.0	*v* 1.2	*d* 0.4	*v* 2.6	*d* 0.1	*v* 2.2	*d* 0.0

STARS

Name	SHA	Dec
	° ′	° ′
Acamar	315 17.0	S40 14.8
Achernar	335 25.7	S57 09.7
Acrux	173 06.7	S63 11.0
Adhara	255 10.8	S29 00.0
Aldebaran	290 47.1	N16 32.3
Alioth	166 19.0	N55 52.1
Alkaid	152 57.5	N49 13.8
Al Na'ir	27 42.0	S46 53.0
Alnilam	275 44.3	S 1 11.8
Alphard	217 54.0	S 8 43.9
Alphecca	126 09.6	N26 39.6
Alpheratz	357 41.8	N29 10.8
Altair	62 06.8	N 8 54.7
Ankaa	353 14.2	S42 13.4
Antares	112 24.2	S26 27.8
Arcturus	145 54.1	N19 05.9
Atria	107 24.7	S69 02.9
Avior	234 16.5	S59 33.9
Bellatrix	278 29.9	N 6 21.6
Betelgeuse	270 59.1	N 7 24.3
Canopus	263 54.9	S52 42.6
Capella	280 31.5	N46 00.7
Deneb	49 30.7	N45 20.4
Denebola	182 31.7	N14 28.8
Diphda	348 54.3	S17 54.1
Dubhe	193 49.1	N61 39.6
Elnath	278 10.1	N28 37.1
Eltanin	90 45.7	N51 29.2
Enif	33 45.7	N 9 57.0
Fomalhaut	15 22.4	S29 32.3
Gacrux	171 58.5	S57 12.0
Gienah	175 50.2	S17 37.8
Hadar	148 45.1	S60 26.7
Hamal	327 58.7	N23 32.2
Kaus Aust.	83 41.8	S34 22.4
Kochab	137 20.4	N74 05.1
Markab	13 36.8	N15 17.5
Menkar	314 13.1	N 4 08.9
Menkent	148 05.4	S36 26.7
Miaplacidus	221 38.2	S69 47.1
Mirfak	308 37.6	N49 55.1
Nunki	75 56.5	S26 16.4
Peacock	53 17.1	S56 40.9
Pollux	243 25.2	N27 59.0
Procyon	244 57.5	N 5 10.7
Rasalhague	96 05.0	N12 33.0
Regulus	207 41.3	N11 53.1
Rigel	281 10.1	S 8 11.3
Rigil Kent.	139 49.2	S60 53.7
Sabik	102 10.7	S15 44.5
Schedar	349 38.6	N56 37.7
Shaula	96 19.8	S37 06.6
Sirius	258 31.8	S16 44.6
Spica	158 29.3	S11 14.6
Suhail	222 50.6	S43 30.0
Vega	80 38.1	N38 48.0
Zuben'ubi	137 03.5	S16 06.3

	SHA	Mer. Pass.
	° ′	h m
Venus	83 09.0	9 57
Mars	138 32.1	6 15
Jupiter	186 18.1	3 04
Saturn	107 16.4	8 19

UT		SUN GHA	SUN Dec	MOON GHA	v	MOON Dec	d	HP
d	h	° ′	° ′	° ′	′	° ′	′	′
28	00	176 49.0	S18 23.8	313 34.1	14.8	N 2 58.0	9.3	54.6
	01	191 48.9	23.2	328 07.9	14.7	2 48.7	9.4	54.6
	02	206 48.8	22.5	342 41.6	14.8	2 39.3	9.4	54.6
	03	221 48.6	. . 21.9	357 15.4	14.9	2 29.9	9.4	54.6
	04	236 48.5	21.2	11 49.3	14.8	2 20.5	9.4	54.6
	05	251 48.4	20.6	26 23.1	14.9	2 11.1	9.4	54.6
	06	266 48.3	S18 19.9	40 57.0	14.9	N 2 01.7	9.4	54.6
T	07	281 48.2	19.3	55 30.9	14.9	1 52.3	9.4	54.5
H	08	296 48.0	18.6	70 04.8	14.9	1 42.9	9.4	54.5
U	09	311 47.9	. . 18.0	84 38.7	14.9	1 33.5	9.4	54.5
R	10	326 47.8	17.3	99 12.6	15.0	1 24.1	9.4	54.5
S	11	341 47.7	16.7	113 46.6	15.0	1 14.7	9.4	54.5
D	12	356 47.6	S18 16.0	128 20.6	15.0	N 1 05.3	9.4	54.5
A	13	11 47.4	15.4	142 54.6	15.0	0 55.9	9.4	54.5
Y	14	26 47.3	14.7	157 28.6	15.1	0 46.5	9.4	54.5
	15	41 47.2	. . 14.1	172 02.7	15.0	0 37.1	9.4	54.4
	16	56 47.1	13.4	186 36.7	15.1	0 27.7	9.4	54.4
	17	71 47.0	12.7	201 10.8	15.1	0 18.3	9.4	54.4
	18	86 46.8	S18 12.1	215 44.9	15.1	N 0 08.9	9.4	54.4
	19	101 46.7	11.4	230 19.0	15.1	S 0 00.5	9.4	54.4
	20	116 46.6	10.8	244 53.1	15.1	0 09.9	9.4	54.4
	21	131 46.5	. . 10.1	259 27.2	15.1	0 19.3	9.3	54.4
	22	146 46.4	09.4	274 01.3	15.2	0 28.6	9.4	54.4
	23	161 46.3	08.8	288 35.5	15.1	0 38.0	9.4	54.4
29	00	176 46.1	S18 08.1	303 09.6	15.2	S 0 47.4	9.3	54.4
	01	191 46.0	07.5	317 43.8	15.2	0 56.7	9.4	54.3
	02	206 45.9	06.8	332 18.0	15.2	1 06.1	9.3	54.3
	03	221 45.8	. . 06.1	346 52.2	15.1	1 15.4	9.3	54.3
	04	236 45.7	05.5	1 26.3	15.2	1 24.7	9.4	54.3
	05	251 45.6	04.8	16 00.5	15.2	1 34.1	9.3	54.3
	06	266 45.4	S18 04.1	30 34.7	15.3	S 1 43.4	9.3	54.3
	07	281 45.3	03.5	45 09.0	15.2	1 52.7	9.2	54.3
	08	296 45.2	02.8	59 43.2	15.2	2 01.9	9.3	54.3
F	09	311 45.1	. . 02.1	74 17.4	15.2	2 11.2	9.3	54.3
R	10	326 45.0	01.5	88 51.6	15.2	2 20.5	9.2	54.3
I	11	341 44.9	00.8	103 25.8	15.3	2 29.7	9.3	54.3
D	12	356 44.8	S18 00.1	118 00.1	15.2	S 2 39.0	9.2	54.3
A	13	11 44.7	17 59.5	132 34.3	15.2	2 48.2	9.2	54.3
Y	14	26 44.6	58.8	147 08.5	15.2	2 57.4	9.2	54.3
	15	41 44.4	. . 58.1	161 42.7	15.3	3 06.6	9.2	54.2
	16	56 44.3	57.5	176 17.0	15.2	3 15.8	9.2	54.2
	17	71 44.2	56.8	190 51.2	15.2	3 25.0	9.1	54.2
	18	86 44.1	S17 56.1	205 25.4	15.2	S 3 34.1	9.1	54.2
	19	101 44.0	55.5	219 59.6	15.3	3 43.2	9.1	54.2
	20	116 43.9	54.8	234 33.9	15.2	3 52.3	9.1	54.2
	21	131 43.8	. . 54.1	249 08.1	15.2	4 01.4	9.1	54.2
	22	146 43.7	53.4	263 42.3	15.2	4 10.5	9.1	54.2
	23	161 43.6	52.8	278 16.5	15.2	4 19.6	9.0	54.2
30	00	176 43.5	S17 52.1	292 50.7	15.2	S 4 28.6	9.0	54.2
	01	191 43.4	51.4	307 24.9	15.1	4 37.6	9.0	54.2
	02	206 43.2	50.7	321 59.0	15.2	4 46.6	9.0	54.2
	03	221 43.1	. . 50.1	336 33.2	15.2	4 55.6	9.0	54.2
	04	236 43.0	49.4	351 07.4	15.1	5 04.6	8.9	54.2
	05	251 42.9	48.7	5 41.5	15.2	5 13.5	8.9	54.2
	06	266 42.8	S17 48.0	20 15.7	15.1	S 5 22.4	8.9	54.2
S	07	281 42.7	47.3	34 49.8	15.1	5 31.3	8.9	54.2
A	08	296 42.6	46.7	49 23.9	15.1	5 40.2	8.8	54.2
T	09	311 42.5	. . 46.0	63 58.0	15.1	5 49.0	8.9	54.2
U	10	326 42.4	45.3	78 32.1	15.1	5 57.9	8.8	54.2
R	11	341 42.3	44.6	93 06.2	15.1	6 06.7	8.7	54.2
D	12	356 42.2	S17 43.9	107 40.3	15.0	S 6 15.4	8.8	54.2
A	13	11 42.1	43.3	122 14.3	15.1	6 24.2	8.7	54.2
Y	14	26 42.0	42.6	136 48.4	15.0	6 32.9	8.7	54.2
	15	41 41.9	. . 41.9	151 22.4	15.0	6 41.6	8.7	54.2
	16	56 41.8	41.2	165 56.4	15.0	6 50.3	8.6	54.2
	17	71 41.7	40.5	180 30.4	14.9	6 58.9	8.6	54.2
	18	86 41.6	S17 39.8	195 04.3	15.0	S 7 07.5	8.6	54.2
	19	101 41.5	39.2	209 38.3	14.9	7 16.1	8.5	54.2
	20	116 41.4	38.5	224 12.2	14.9	7 24.6	8.6	54.2
	21	131 41.3	. . 37.8	238 46.1	14.9	7 33.2	8.5	54.2
	22	146 41.2	37.1	253 20.0	14.8	7 41.7	8.4	54.2
	23	161 41.1	36.4	267 53.8	14.9	S 7 50.1	8.4	54.2
		SD 16.3	*d* 0.7	SD 14.8		14.8		14.8

Lat.	Twilight Naut.	Twilight Civil	Sunrise	Moonrise 28	Moonrise 29	Moonrise 30	Moonrise 31
°	h m	h m	h m	h m	h m	h m	h m
N 72	07 22	08 54	11 01	21 50	23 23	24 57	00 57
N 70	07 12	08 33	10 06	21 50	23 17	24 44	00 44
68	07 05	08 16	09 33	21 49	23 12	24 34	00 34
66	06 58	08 03	09 09	21 49	23 07	24 26	00 26
64	06 52	07 52	08 50	21 48	23 04	24 19	00 19
62	06 47	07 42	08 35	21 48	23 00	24 13	00 13
60	06 42	07 34	08 22	21 47	22 58	24 07	00 07
N 58	06 38	07 26	08 11	21 47	22 55	24 03	00 03
56	06 34	07 20	08 01	21 47	22 53	23 59	25 04
54	06 31	07 14	07 53	21 47	22 51	23 55	24 59
52	06 27	07 08	07 45	21 46	22 49	23 52	24 54
50	06 24	07 03	07 39	21 46	22 48	23 49	24 50
45	06 17	06 52	07 24	21 46	22 44	23 42	24 40
N 40	06 10	06 43	07 12	21 45	22 41	23 37	24 32
35	06 04	06 35	07 01	21 45	22 39	23 32	24 26
30	05 58	06 27	06 52	21 45	22 37	23 28	24 20
20	05 47	06 13	06 36	21 44	22 33	23 21	24 10
N 10	05 35	06 01	06 23	21 44	22 29	23 15	24 01
0	05 22	05 48	06 09	21 44	22 26	23 09	23 53
S 10	05 08	05 34	05 56	21 44	22 23	23 03	23 45
20	04 51	05 18	05 42	21 43	22 20	22 57	23 36
30	04 28	04 59	05 25	21 43	22 16	22 50	23 26
35	04 14	04 48	05 16	21 43	22 14	22 46	23 20
40	03 57	04 34	05 05	21 42	22 12	22 42	23 14
45	03 35	04 18	04 51	21 42	22 09	22 37	23 06
S 50	03 05	03 57	04 35	21 42	22 06	22 31	22 58
52	02 50	03 46	04 28	21 42	22 04	22 28	22 53
54	02 32	03 35	04 19	21 42	22 03	22 25	22 49
56	02 08	03 21	04 10	21 42	22 01	22 21	22 44
58	01 35	03 05	03 59	21 41	21 59	22 18	22 38
S 60	////	02 46	03 46	21 41	21 57	22 13	22 32

Lat.	Sunset	Twilight Civil	Twilight Naut.	Moonset 28	Moonset 29	Moonset 30	Moonset 31
°	h m	h m	h m	h m	h m	h m	h m
N 72	13 26	15 33	17 06	09 39	09 35	09 30	09 25
N 70	14 22	15 54	17 15	09 37	09 38	09 38	09 39
68	14 54	16 11	17 23	09 36	09 40	09 45	09 50
66	15 18	16 24	17 29	09 35	09 42	09 51	10 00
64	15 37	16 35	17 35	09 34	09 44	09 55	10 08
62	15 52	16 45	17 40	09 33	09 46	10 00	10 15
60	16 05	16 53	17 45	09 32	09 47	10 03	10 21
N 58	16 16	17 01	17 49	09 31	09 49	10 07	10 26
56	16 25	17 07	17 53	09 30	09 50	10 10	10 31
54	16 34	17 13	17 56	09 30	09 51	10 12	10 35
52	16 41	17 18	17 59	09 29	09 52	10 15	10 39
50	16 48	17 23	18 03	09 29	09 53	10 17	10 43
45	17 03	17 34	18 10	09 28	09 55	10 22	10 50
N 40	17 15	17 44	18 16	09 27	09 56	10 26	10 57
35	17 25	17 52	18 22	09 26	09 57	10 29	11 02
30	17 34	17 59	18 28	09 25	09 59	10 32	11 07
20	17 50	18 13	18 39	09 24	10 01	10 38	11 16
N 10	18 04	18 26	18 51	09 23	10 03	10 42	11 23
0	18 17	18 38	19 04	09 22	10 04	10 47	11 30
S 10	18 30	18 52	19 18	09 21	10 06	10 51	11 37
20	18 44	19 07	19 35	09 19	10 08	10 56	11 44
30	19 00	19 26	19 57	09 18	10 10	11 01	11 53
35	19 10	19 38	20 11	09 17	10 11	11 04	11 58
40	19 21	19 51	20 28	09 16	10 12	11 08	12 04
45	19 34	20 07	20 50	09 15	10 14	11 12	12 10
S 50	19 50	20 28	21 19	09 14	10 16	11 17	12 18
52	19 57	20 38	21 34	09 13	10 17	11 19	12 22
54	20 05	20 50	21 52	09 13	10 18	11 22	12 26
56	20 15	21 03	22 15	09 12	10 19	11 25	12 30
58	20 25	21 19	22 46	09 11	10 20	11 28	12 35
S 60	20 38	21 38	23 51	09 10	10 21	11 31	12 41

Day	SUN Eqn. of Time 00^h	SUN Eqn. of Time 12^h	SUN Mer. Pass.	MOON Mer. Pass. Upper	MOON Mer. Pass. Lower	MOON Age	MOON Phase
d	m s	m s	h m	h m	h m	d	%
28	12 44	12 50	12 13	03 11	15 33	18	82
29	12 55	13 01	12 13	03 54	16 15	19	74
30	13 06	13 11	12 13	04 37	16 58	20	65

UT		ARIES	VENUS −3·9		MARS +0·8		JUPITER −2·4		SATURN +0·5	
		GHA	GHA	Dec	GHA	Dec	GHA	Dec	GHA	Dec
d	h	° ′	° ′	° ′	° ′	° ′	° ′	° ′	° ′	° ′
31	00	129 39.6	210 08.6	S22 24.5	267 12.4	S14 46.3	316 05.0	N 4 16.4	236 45.4	S20 50.2
	01	144 42.1	225 07.7	24.4	282 13.6	46.6	331 07.7	16.5	251 47.6	50.2
	02	159 44.5	240 06.8	24.3	297 14.8	47.0	346 10.3	16.6	266 49.9	50.2
	03	174 47.0	255 06.0	. . 24.2	312 16.1	. . 47.4	1 12.9	. . 16.6	281 52.1	. . 50.3
	04	189 49.5	270 05.1	24.1	327 17.3	47.7	16 15.5	16.7	296 54.4	50.3
	05	204 51.9	285 04.2	24.1	342 18.5	48.1	31 18.2	16.8	311 56.6	50.3
	06	219 54.4	300 03.4	S22 24.0	357 19.8	S14 48.5	46 20.8	N 4 16.9	326 58.9	S20 50.3
	07	234 56.9	315 02.5	23.9	12 21.0	48.9	61 23.4	17.0	342 01.1	50.3
	08	249 59.3	330 01.6	23.8	27 22.2	49.2	76 26.0	17.0	357 03.4	50.4
SUNDAY	09	265 01.8	345 00.7	. . 23.7	42 23.5	. . 49.6	91 28.7	. . 17.1	12 05.6	. . 50.4
	10	280 04.3	359 59.9	23.6	57 24.7	50.0	106 31.3	17.2	27 07.9	50.4
	11	295 06.7	14 59.0	23.5	72 25.9	50.3	121 33.9	17.3	42 10.1	50.4
	12	310 09.2	29 58.1	S22 23.4	87 27.2	S14 50.7	136 36.5	N 4 17.4	57 12.4	S20 50.4
	13	325 11.6	44 57.3	23.3	102 28.4	51.1	151 39.2	17.5	72 14.6	50.5
	14	340 14.1	59 56.4	23.3	117 29.6	51.4	166 41.8	17.5	87 16.9	50.5
	15	355 16.6	74 55.5	. . 23.2	132 30.9	. . 51.8	181 44.4	. . 17.6	102 19.1	. . 50.5
	16	10 19.0	89 54.7	23.1	147 32.1	52.2	196 47.0	17.7	117 21.4	50.5
	17	25 21.5	104 53.8	23.0	162 33.3	52.6	211 49.7	17.8	132 23.6	50.5
	18	40 24.0	119 52.9	S22 22.9	177 34.6	S14 52.9	226 52.3	N 4 17.9	147 25.9	S20 50.6
	19	55 26.4	134 52.1	22.8	192 35.8	53.3	241 54.9	17.9	162 28.1	50.6
	20	70 28.9	149 51.2	22.7	207 37.0	53.7	256 57.6	18.0	177 30.3	50.6
	21	85 31.4	164 50.3	. . 22.6	222 38.3	. . 54.0	272 00.2	. . 18.1	192 32.6	. . 50.6
	22	100 33.8	179 49.4	22.5	237 39.5	54.4	287 02.8	18.2	207 34.8	50.6
	23	115 36.3	194 48.6	22.3	252 40.8	54.8	302 05.4	18.3	222 37.1	50.7
1	00	130 38.8	209 47.7	S22 22.2	267 42.0	S14 55.1	317 08.1	N 4 18.3	237 39.3	S20 50.7
	01	145 41.2	224 46.8	22.1	282 43.2	55.5	332 10.7	18.4	252 41.6	50.7
	02	160 43.7	239 46.0	22.0	297 44.5	55.9	347 13.3	18.5	267 43.8	50.7
	03	175 46.1	254 45.1	. . 21.9	312 45.7	. . 56.2	2 16.0	. . 18.6	282 46.1	. . 50.7
	04	190 48.6	269 44.2	21.8	327 46.9	56.6	17 18.6	18.7	297 48.3	50.8
	05	205 51.1	284 43.4	21.7	342 48.2	57.0	32 21.2	18.8	312 50.6	50.8
	06	220 53.5	299 42.5	S22 21.6	357 49.4	S14 57.3	47 23.9	N 4 18.8	327 52.8	S20 50.8
	07	235 56.0	314 41.6	21.5	12 50.6	57.7	62 26.5	18.9	342 55.1	50.8
	08	250 58.5	329 40.8	21.3	27 51.9	58.1	77 29.1	19.0	357 57.3	50.8
MONDAY	09	266 00.9	344 39.9	. . 21.2	42 53.1	. . 58.4	92 31.7	. . 19.1	12 59.6	. . 50.9
	10	281 03.4	359 39.0	21.1	57 54.4	58.8	107 34.4	19.2	28 01.8	50.9
	11	296 05.9	14 38.2	21.0	72 55.6	59.2	122 37.0	19.3	43 04.1	50.9
	12	311 08.3	29 37.3	S22 20.9	87 56.8	S14 59.5	137 39.6	N 4 19.3	58 06.3	S20 50.9
	13	326 10.8	44 36.4	20.8	102 58.1	14 59.9	152 42.3	19.4	73 08.6	50.9
	14	341 13.3	59 35.6	20.6	117 59.3	15 00.3	167 44.9	19.5	88 10.8	51.0
	15	356 15.7	74 34.7	. . 20.5	133 00.5	. . 00.6	182 47.5	. . 19.6	103 13.1	. . 51.0
	16	11 18.2	89 33.8	20.4	148 01.8	01.0	197 50.2	19.7	118 15.3	51.0
	17	26 20.6	104 32.9	20.3	163 03.0	01.4	212 52.8	19.8	133 17.6	51.0
	18	41 23.1	119 32.1	S22 20.1	178 04.3	S15 01.7	227 55.4	N 4 19.8	148 19.9	S20 51.0
	19	56 25.6	134 31.2	20.0	193 05.5	02.1	242 58.1	19.9	163 22.1	51.1
	20	71 28.0	149 30.3	19.9	208 06.7	02.5	258 00.7	20.0	178 24.4	51.1
	21	86 30.5	164 29.5	. . 19.7	223 08.0	. . 02.8	273 03.4	. . 20.1	193 26.6	. . 51.1
	22	101 33.0	179 28.6	19.6	238 09.2	03.2	288 06.0	20.2	208 28.9	51.1
	23	116 35.4	194 27.7	19.5	253 10.5	03.6	303 08.6	20.3	223 31.1	51.1
2	00	131 37.9	209 26.9	S22 19.3	268 11.7	S15 03.9	318 11.3	N 4 20.3	238 33.4	S20 51.2
	01	146 40.4	224 26.0	19.2	283 12.9	04.3	333 13.9	20.4	253 35.6	51.2
	02	161 42.8	239 25.1	19.1	298 14.2	04.7	348 16.5	20.5	268 37.9	51.2
	03	176 45.3	254 24.3	. . 18.9	313 15.4	. . 05.0	3 19.2	. . 20.6	283 40.1	. . 51.2
	04	191 47.7	269 23.4	18.8	328 16.7	05.4	18 21.8	20.7	298 42.4	51.2
	05	206 50.2	284 22.5	18.7	343 17.9	05.7	33 24.4	20.8	313 44.6	51.3
	06	221 52.7	299 21.7	S22 18.5	358 19.1	S15 06.1	48 27.1	N 4 20.9	328 46.9	S20 51.3
	07	236 55.1	314 20.8	18.4	13 20.4	06.5	63 29.7	20.9	343 49.1	51.3
	08	251 57.6	329 19.9	18.2	28 21.6	06.8	78 32.4	21.0	358 51.4	51.3
TUESDAY	09	267 00.1	344 19.1	. . 18.1	43 22.9	. . 07.2	93 35.0	. . 21.1	13 53.6	. . 51.3
	10	282 02.5	359 18.2	17.9	58 24.1	07.6	108 37.6	21.2	28 55.9	51.4
	11	297 05.0	14 17.3	17.8	73 25.4	07.9	123 40.3	21.3	43 58.1	51.4
	12	312 07.5	29 16.5	S22 17.6	88 26.6	S15 08.3	138 42.9	N 4 21.4	59 00.4	S20 51.4
	13	327 09.9	44 15.6	17.5	103 27.8	08.6	153 45.5	21.5	74 02.7	51.4
	14	342 12.4	59 14.7	17.3	118 29.1	09.0	168 48.2	21.5	89 04.9	51.4
	15	357 14.9	74 13.9	. . 17.2	133 30.3	. . 09.4	183 50.8	. . 21.6	104 07.2	. . 51.4
	16	12 17.3	89 13.0	17.0	148 31.6	09.7	198 53.5	21.7	119 09.4	51.5
	17	27 19.8	104 12.1	16.9	163 32.8	10.1	213 56.1	21.8	134 11.7	51.5
	18	42 22.2	119 11.3	S22 16.7	178 34.1	S15 10.4	228 58.8	N 4 21.9	149 13.9	S20 51.5
	19	57 24.7	134 10.4	16.6	193 35.3	10.8	244 01.4	22.0	164 16.2	51.5
	20	72 27.2	149 09.5	16.4	208 36.6	11.2	259 04.0	22.1	179 18.4	51.5
	21	87 29.6	164 08.7	. . 16.3	223 37.8	. . 11.5	274 06.7	. . 22.1	194 20.7	. . 51.6
	22	102 32.1	179 07.8	16.1	238 39.0	11.9	289 09.3	22.2	209 22.9	51.6
	23	117 34.6	194 06.9	15.9	253 40.3	12.2	304 12.0	22.3	224 25.2	51.6
Mer. Pass.	h m	15 14.9	v −0.9	d 0.1	v 1.2	d 0.4	v 2.6	d 0.1	v 2.3	d 0.0

STARS

Name	SHA	Dec
	° ′	° ′
Acamar	315 17.0	S40 14.8
Achernar	335 25.7	S57 09.7
Acrux	173 06.7	S63 11.1
Adhara	255 10.8	S29 00.0
Aldebaran	290 47.1	N16 32.3
Alioth	166 19.0	N55 52.1
Alkaid	152 57.5	N49 13.8
Al Na'ir	27 42.0	S46 53.0
Alnilam	275 44.3	S 1 11.8
Alphard	217 54.0	S 8 43.9
Alphecca	126 09.6	N26 39.6
Alpheratz	357 41.8	N29 10.8
Altair	62 06.8	N 8 54.7
Ankaa	353 14.2	S42 13.4
Antares	112 24.2	S26 27.8
Arcturus	145 54.1	N19 05.9
Atria	107 24.7	S69 02.9
Avior	234 16.6	S59 33.9
Bellatrix	278 29.9	N 6 21.6
Betelgeuse	270 59.1	N 7 24.3
Canopus	263 54.9	S52 42.7
Capella	280 31.5	N46 00.7
Deneb	49 30.7	N45 20.4
Denebola	182 31.6	N14 28.8
Diphda	348 54.3	S17 54.1
Dubhe	193 49.1	N61 39.6
Elnath	278 10.1	N28 37.1
Eltanin	90 45.7	N51 29.2
Enif	33 45.7	N 9 57.0
Fomalhaut	15 22.4	S29 32.3
Gacrux	171 58.4	S57 12.0
Gienah	175 50.2	S17 37.9
Hadar	148 45.1	S60 26.7
Hamal	327 58.7	N23 32.2
Kaus Aust.	83 41.8	S34 22.4
Kochab	137 20.4	N74 05.1
Markab	13 36.8	N15 17.5
Menkar	314 13.1	N 4 08.9
Menkent	148 05.3	S36 26.7
Miaplacidus	221 38.2	S69 47.1
Mirfak	308 37.6	N49 55.1
Nunki	75 56.4	S26 16.4
Peacock	53 17.1	S56 40.8
Pollux	243 25.2	N27 59.0
Procyon	244 57.5	N 5 10.7
Rasalhague	96 05.0	N12 33.0
Regulus	207 41.3	N11 53.1
Rigel	281 10.1	S 8 11.3
Rigil Kent.	139 49.2	S60 53.7
Sabik	102 10.7	S15 44.5
Schedar	349 38.6	N56 37.7
Shaula	96 19.8	S37 06.6
Sirius	258 31.8	S16 44.6
Spica	158 29.2	S11 14.7
Suhail	222 50.6	S43 30.0
Vega	80 38.1	N38 47.9
Zuben'ubi	137 03.4	S16 06.4

	SHA	Mer. Pass.
	° ′	h m
Venus	79 09.0	10 01
Mars	137 03.2	6 09
Jupiter	186 29.3	2 51
Saturn	107 00.6	8 08

UT d	UT h	SUN GHA	SUN Dec	MOON GHA	*v*	MOON Dec	*d*	HP
d	h	° ′	° ′	° ′	′	° ′	′	′
31	00	176 41.0	S17 35.7	282 27.7	14.8	S 7 58.5	8.4	54.2
	01	191 40.9	35.0	297 01.5	14.8	8 06.9	8.4	54.2
	02	206 40.8	34.3	311 35.3	14.8	8 15.3	8.3	54.2
	03	221 40.7	. . 33.7	326 09.1	14.7	8 23.6	8.3	54.2
	04	236 40.6	33.0	340 42.8	14.7	8 31.9	8.3	54.3
	05	251 40.5	32.3	355 16.5	14.7	8 40.2	8.2	54.3
	06	266 40.4	S17 31.6	9 50.2	14.7	S 8 48.4	8.2	54.3
	07	281 40.3	30.9	24 23.9	14.6	8 56.6	8.2	54.3
	08	296 40.2	30.2	38 57.5	14.6	9 04.8	8.1	54.3
S	09	311 40.1	. . 29.5	53 31.1	14.6	9 12.9	8.1	54.3
U	10	326 40.0	28.8	68 04.7	14.6	9 21.0	8.1	54.3
N	11	341 39.9	28.1	82 38.3	14.5	9 29.1	8.0	54.3
D	12	356 39.8	S17 27.4	97 11.8	14.5	S 9 37.1	7.9	54.3
A	13	11 39.7	26.7	111 45.3	14.4	9 45.0	8.0	54.3
Y	14	26 39.6	26.0	126 18.7	14.4	9 53.0	7.9	54.3
	15	41 39.5	. . 25.3	140 52.1	14.4	10 00.9	7.8	54.3
	16	56 39.4	24.6	155 25.5	14.4	10 08.7	7.9	54.3
	17	71 39.3	23.9	169 58.9	14.3	10 16.6	7.7	54.4
	18	86 39.2	S17 23.2	184 32.2	14.3	S10 24.3	7.8	54.4
	19	101 39.2	22.5	199 05.5	14.3	10 32.1	7.7	54.4
	20	116 39.1	21.8	213 38.8	14.2	10 39.8	7.6	54.4
	21	131 39.0	. . 21.1	228 12.0	14.2	10 47.4	7.6	54.4
	22	146 38.9	20.5	242 45.2	14.1	10 55.0	7.6	54.4
	23	161 38.8	19.7	257 18.3	14.1	11 02.6	7.5	54.4
1	00	176 38.7	S17 19.0	271 51.4	14.1	S11 10.1	7.5	54.4
	01	191 38.6	18.3	286 24.5	14.0	11 17.6	7.4	54.4
	02	206 38.5	17.6	300 57.5	14.0	11 25.0	7.4	54.5
	03	221 38.4	. . 16.9	315 30.5	14.0	11 32.4	7.3	54.5
	04	236 38.3	16.2	330 03.5	13.9	11 39.7	7.3	54.5
	05	251 38.2	15.5	344 36.4	13.9	11 47.0	7.3	54.5
	06	266 38.2	S17 14.8	359 09.3	13.8	S11 54.3	7.2	54.5
	07	281 38.1	14.1	13 42.1	13.8	12 01.5	7.1	54.5
	08	296 38.0	13.4	28 14.9	13.8	12 08.6	7.1	54.5
M	09	311 37.9	. . 12.7	42 47.7	13.7	12 15.7	7.1	54.5
O	10	326 37.8	12.0	57 20.4	13.6	12 22.8	7.0	54.6
N	11	341 37.7	11.3	71 53.0	13.7	12 29.8	6.9	54.6
D	12	356 37.6	S17 10.6	86 25.7	13.5	S12 36.7	6.9	54.6
A	13	11 37.5	09.9	100 58.2	13.6	12 43.6	6.9	54.6
Y	14	26 37.5	09.2	115 30.8	13.5	12 50.5	6.8	54.6
	15	41 37.4	. . 08.5	130 03.3	13.4	12 57.3	6.7	54.6
	16	56 37.3	07.8	144 35.7	13.4	13 04.0	6.7	54.7
	17	71 37.2	07.1	159 08.1	13.3	13 10.7	6.6	54.7
	18	86 37.1	S17 06.3	173 40.4	13.4	S13 17.3	6.6	54.7
	19	101 37.0	05.6	188 12.8	13.2	13 23.9	6.5	54.7
	20	116 36.9	04.9	202 45.0	13.2	13 30.4	6.5	54.7
	21	131 36.9	. . 04.2	217 17.2	13.2	13 36.9	6.4	54.7
	22	146 36.8	03.5	231 49.4	13.1	13 43.3	6.4	54.8
	23	161 36.7	02.8	246 21.5	13.1	13 49.7	6.3	54.8
2	00	176 36.6	S17 02.1	260 53.6	13.0	S13 56.0	6.2	54.8
	01	191 36.5	01.4	275 25.6	12.9	14 02.2	6.2	54.8
	02	206 36.4	17 00.6	289 57.5	12.9	14 08.4	6.1	54.8
	03	221 36.4	16 59.9	304 29.4	12.9	14 14.5	6.1	54.9
	04	236 36.3	59.2	319 01.3	12.8	14 20.6	6.0	54.9
	05	251 36.2	58.5	333 33.1	12.8	14 26.6	5.9	54.9
	06	266 36.1	S16 57.8	348 04.9	12.7	S14 32.5	5.9	54.9
	07	281 36.0	57.1	2 36.6	12.7	14 38.4	5.8	54.9
T	08	296 36.0	56.3	17 08.3	12.6	14 44.2	5.7	55.0
U	09	311 35.9	. . 55.6	31 39.9	12.5	14 49.9	5.7	55.0
E	10	326 35.8	54.9	46 11.4	12.5	14 55.6	5.6	55.0
S	11	341 35.7	54.2	60 42.9	12.5	15 01.2	5.6	55.0
D	12	356 35.6	S16 53.5	75 14.4	12.4	S15 06.8	5.5	55.0
A	13	11 35.6	52.7	89 45.8	12.3	15 12.3	5.4	55.1
Y	14	26 35.5	52.0	104 17.1	12.3	15 17.7	5.4	55.1
	15	41 35.4	. . 51.3	118 48.4	12.2	15 23.1	5.3	55.1
	16	56 35.3	50.6	133 19.6	12.2	15 28.4	5.2	55.1
	17	71 35.3	49.9	147 50.8	12.1	15 33.6	5.1	55.2
	18	86 35.2	S16 49.1	162 21.9	12.1	S15 38.7	5.1	55.2
	19	101 35.1	48.4	176 53.0	12.0	15 43.8	5.0	55.2
	20	116 35.0	47.7	191 24.0	12.0	15 48.8	5.0	55.2
	21	131 35.0	. . 47.0	205 55.0	11.9	15 53.8	4.8	55.3
	22	146 34.9	46.2	220 25.9	11.8	15 58.6	4.8	55.3
	23	161 34.8	45.5	234 56.7	11.8	S16 03.4	4.8	55.3
		SD 16.3	*d* 0.7	SD 14.8		14.9		15.0

Lat.	Twilight Naut.	Twilight Civil	Sunrise	Moonrise 31	Moonrise 1	Moonrise 2	Moonrise 3
°	h m	h m	h m	h m	h m	h m	h m
N 72	07 11	08 41	10 32	00 57	02 34	04 15	06 04
N 70	07 03	08 22	09 48	00 44	02 13	03 43	05 13
68	06 57	08 07	09 20	00 34	01 57	03 20	04 42
66	06 51	07 55	08 58	00 26	01 44	03 02	04 18
64	06 46	07 44	08 41	00 19	01 34	02 48	04 00
62	06 41	07 35	08 27	00 13	01 25	02 36	03 45
60	06 37	07 28	08 15	00 07	01 17	02 26	03 33
N 58	06 33	07 21	08 05	00 03	01 10	02 17	03 22
56	06 30	07 15	07 56	25 04	01 04	02 09	03 13
54	06 26	07 09	07 48	24 59	00 59	02 02	03 04
52	06 23	07 04	07 41	24 54	00 54	01 56	02 57
50	06 21	06 59	07 34	24 50	00 50	01 50	02 50
45	06 14	06 49	07 21	24 40	00 40	01 38	02 36
N 40	06 08	06 40	07 09	24 32	00 32	01 28	02 24
35	06 02	06 33	06 59	24 26	00 26	01 20	02 14
30	05 57	06 26	06 51	24 20	00 20	01 12	02 06
20	05 46	06 13	06 36	24 10	00 10	01 00	01 51
N 10	05 35	06 01	06 22	24 01	00 01	00 48	01 38
0	05 23	05 48	06 10	23 53	24 38	00 38	01 25
S 10	05 09	05 35	05 57	23 45	24 28	00 28	01 13
20	04 53	05 20	05 44	23 36	24 17	00 17	01 00
30	04 31	05 02	05 28	23 26	24 04	00 04	00 46
35	04 18	04 51	05 19	23 20	23 57	24 37	00 37
40	04 01	04 38	05 08	23 14	23 49	24 27	00 27
45	03 40	04 22	04 56	23 06	23 39	24 16	00 16
S 50	03 13	04 02	04 41	22 58	23 28	24 02	00 02
52	02 58	03 53	04 33	22 53	23 22	23 56	24 36
54	02 41	03 42	04 26	22 49	23 16	23 49	24 28
56	02 20	03 29	04 17	22 44	23 10	23 41	24 19
58	01 52	03 14	04 06	22 38	23 03	23 32	24 09
S 60	01 05	02 56	03 55	22 32	22 54	23 22	23 57

Lat.	Sunset	Twilight Civil	Twilight Naut.	Moonset 31	Moonset 1	Moonset 2	Moonset 3
°	h m	h m	h m	h m	h m	h m	h m
N 72	13 56	15 48	17 17	09 25	09 19	09 13	09 03
N 70	14 40	16 06	17 25	09 39	09 41	09 45	09 54
68	15 08	16 21	17 32	09 50	09 58	10 09	10 26
66	15 30	16 33	17 37	10 00	10 11	10 27	10 50
64	15 47	16 44	17 43	10 08	10 23	10 42	11 08
62	16 01	16 52	17 47	10 15	10 33	10 55	11 24
60	16 13	17 00	17 51	10 21	10 41	11 06	11 36
N 58	16 23	17 07	17 55	10 26	10 48	11 15	11 48
56	16 32	17 13	17 58	10 31	10 55	11 23	11 57
54	16 40	17 19	18 01	10 35	11 01	11 30	12 06
52	16 47	17 24	18 04	10 39	11 06	11 37	12 13
50	16 53	17 28	18 07	10 43	11 11	11 43	12 20
45	17 07	17 38	18 14	10 50	11 21	11 56	12 35
N 40	17 18	17 47	18 19	10 57	11 30	12 06	12 47
35	17 28	17 55	18 25	11 02	11 37	12 15	12 58
30	17 37	18 02	18 30	11 07	11 44	12 23	13 07
20	17 52	18 15	18 41	11 16	11 55	12 37	13 22
N 10	18 05	18 27	18 52	11 23	12 05	12 49	13 36
0	18 17	18 39	19 04	11 30	12 14	13 01	13 49
S 10	18 30	18 52	19 17	11 37	12 24	13 12	14 02
20	18 43	19 06	19 34	11 44	12 34	13 24	14 16
30	18 59	19 24	19 55	11 53	12 45	13 38	14 31
35	19 08	19 35	20 08	11 58	12 52	13 46	14 40
40	19 18	19 48	20 25	12 04	12 59	13 55	14 51
45	19 30	20 04	20 45	12 10	13 08	14 06	15 03
S 50	19 45	20 23	21 13	12 18	13 19	14 19	15 18
52	19 52	20 33	21 27	12 22	13 24	14 25	15 25
54	20 00	20 44	21 43	12 26	13 29	14 32	15 33
56	20 09	20 56	22 04	12 30	13 35	14 39	15 42
58	20 19	21 11	22 31	12 35	13 42	14 48	15 51
S 60	20 30	21 28	23 14	12 41	13 50	14 58	16 03

Day	SUN Eqn. of Time 00^h	SUN Eqn. of Time 12^h	SUN Mer. Pass.	MOON Mer. Pass. Upper	MOON Mer. Pass. Lower	MOON Age	MOON Phase
d	m s	m s	h m	h m	h m	d	%
31	13 16	13 21	12 13	05 19	17 41	21	56
1	13 25	13 29	12 13	06 03	18 26	22	47
2	13 33	13 37	12 14	06 49	19 13	23	37

UT (d h)	ARIES GHA	VENUS −3·9 GHA	VENUS Dec	MARS +0·8 GHA	MARS Dec	JUPITER −2·4 GHA	JUPITER Dec	SATURN +0·5 GHA	SATURN Dec
	° ′	° ′	° ′	° ′	° ′	° ′	° ′	° ′	° ′
3 00	132 37.0	209 06.1	S22 15.8	268 41.5	S15 12.6	319 14.6	N 4 22.4	239 27.5	S20 51.6
01	147 39.5	224 05.2	15.6	283 42.8	13.0	334 17.2	22.5	254 29.7	51.6
02	162 42.0	239 04.4	15.4	298 44.0	13.3	349 19.9	22.6	269 32.0	51.7
03	177 44.4	254 03.5	. . 15.3	313 45.3	. . 13.7	4 22.5	. . 22.7	284 34.2	. . 51.7
04	192 46.9	269 02.6	15.1	328 46.5	14.0	19 25.2	22.8	299 36.5	51.7
05	207 49.4	284 01.8	14.9	343 47.8	14.4	34 27.8	22.8	314 38.7	51.7
06	222 51.8	299 00.9	S22 14.8	358 49.0	S15 14.8	49 30.5	N 4 22.9	329 41.0	S20 51.7
W 07	237 54.3	314 00.0	14.6	13 50.3	15.1	64 33.1	23.0	344 43.2	51.8
E 08	252 56.7	328 59.2	14.4	28 51.5	15.5	79 35.7	23.1	359 45.5	51.8
D 09	267 59.2	343 58.3	. . 14.3	43 52.7	. . 15.8	94 38.4	. . 23.2	14 47.8	. . 51.8
N 10	283 01.7	358 57.4	14.1	58 54.0	16.2	109 41.0	23.3	29 50.0	51.8
E 11	298 04.1	13 56.6	13.9	73 55.2	16.5	124 43.7	23.4	44 52.3	51.8
S 12	313 06.6	28 55.7	S22 13.7	88 56.5	S15 16.9	139 46.3	N 4 23.5	59 54.5	S20 51.8
D 13	328 09.1	43 54.8	13.6	103 57.7	17.3	154 49.0	23.5	74 56.8	51.9
A 14	343 11.5	58 54.0	13.4	118 59.0	17.6	169 51.6	23.6	89 59.0	51.9
Y 15	358 14.0	73 53.1	. . 13.2	134 00.2	. . 18.0	184 54.3	. . 23.7	105 01.3	. . 51.9
16	13 16.5	88 52.2	13.0	149 01.5	18.3	199 56.9	23.8	120 03.6	51.9
17	28 18.9	103 51.4	12.8	164 02.7	18.7	214 59.6	23.9	135 05.8	51.9
18	43 21.4	118 50.5	S22 12.7	179 04.0	S15 19.0	230 02.2	N 4 24.0	150 08.1	S20 52.0
19	58 23.9	133 49.7	12.5	194 05.2	19.4	245 04.9	24.1	165 10.3	52.0
20	73 26.3	148 48.8	12.3	209 06.5	19.8	260 07.5	24.2	180 12.6	52.0
21	88 28.8	163 47.9	. . 12.1	224 07.7	. . 20.1	275 10.1	. . 24.3	195 14.8	. . 52.0
22	103 31.2	178 47.1	11.9	239 09.0	20.5	290 12.8	24.3	210 17.1	52.0
23	118 33.7	193 46.2	11.7	254 10.2	20.8	305 15.4	24.4	225 19.4	52.1
4 00	133 36.2	208 45.3	S22 11.5	269 11.5	S15 21.2	320 18.1	N 4 24.5	240 21.6	S20 52.1
01	148 38.6	223 44.5	11.3	284 12.7	21.5	335 20.7	24.6	255 23.9	52.1
02	163 41.1	238 43.6	11.2	299 14.0	21.9	350 23.4	24.7	270 26.1	52.1
03	178 43.6	253 42.8	. . 11.0	314 15.2	. . 22.2	5 26.0	. . 24.8	285 28.4	. . 52.1
04	193 46.0	268 41.9	10.8	329 16.5	22.6	20 28.7	24.9	300 30.7	52.1
05	208 48.5	283 41.0	10.6	344 17.7	22.9	35 31.3	25.0	315 32.9	52.2
06	223 51.0	298 40.2	S22 10.4	359 19.0	S15 23.3	50 34.0	N 4 25.1	330 35.2	S20 52.2
T 07	238 53.4	313 39.3	10.2	14 20.2	23.7	65 36.6	25.2	345 37.4	52.2
H 08	253 55.9	328 38.4	10.0	29 21.5	24.0	80 39.3	25.2	0 39.7	52.2
U 09	268 58.3	343 37.6	. . 09.8	44 22.7	. . 24.4	95 41.9	. . 25.3	15 42.0	. . 52.2
R 10	284 00.8	358 36.7	09.6	59 24.0	24.7	110 44.6	25.4	30 44.2	52.3
S 11	299 03.3	13 35.9	09.4	74 25.2	25.1	125 47.2	25.5	45 46.5	52.3
D 12	314 05.7	28 35.0	S22 09.2	89 26.5	S15 25.4	140 49.9	N 4 25.6	60 48.7	S20 52.3
A 13	329 08.2	43 34.1	09.0	104 27.8	25.8	155 52.5	25.7	75 51.0	52.3
Y 14	344 10.7	58 33.3	08.8	119 29.0	26.1	170 55.2	25.8	90 53.3	52.3
15	359 13.1	73 32.4	. . 08.6	134 30.3	. . 26.5	185 57.9	. . 25.9	105 55.5	. . 52.4
16	14 15.6	88 31.5	08.3	149 31.5	26.8	201 00.5	26.0	120 57.8	52.4
17	29 18.1	103 30.7	08.1	164 32.8	27.2	216 03.2	26.1	136 00.0	52.4
18	44 20.5	118 29.8	S22 07.9	179 34.0	S15 27.5	231 05.8	N 4 26.2	151 02.3	S20 52.4
19	59 23.0	133 29.0	07.7	194 35.3	27.9	246 08.5	26.2	166 04.6	52.4
20	74 25.5	148 28.1	07.5	209 36.5	28.2	261 11.1	26.3	181 06.8	52.4
21	89 27.9	163 27.2	. . 07.3	224 37.8	. . 28.6	276 13.8	. . 26.4	196 09.1	. . 52.5
22	104 30.4	178 26.4	07.1	239 39.0	28.9	291 16.4	26.5	211 11.3	52.5
23	119 32.8	193 25.5	06.9	254 40.3	29.3	306 19.1	26.6	226 13.6	52.5
5 00	134 35.3	208 24.7	S22 06.6	269 41.6	S15 29.6	321 21.7	N 4 26.7	241 15.9	S20 52.5
01	149 37.8	223 23.8	06.4	284 42.8	30.0	336 24.4	26.8	256 18.1	52.5
02	164 40.2	238 22.9	06.2	299 44.1	30.3	351 27.0	26.9	271 20.4	52.6
03	179 42.7	253 22.1	. . 06.0	314 45.3	. . 30.7	6 29.7	. . 27.0	286 22.7	. . 52.6
04	194 45.2	268 21.2	05.8	329 46.6	31.0	21 32.4	27.1	301 24.9	52.6
05	209 47.6	283 20.4	05.5	344 47.8	31.4	36 35.0	27.2	316 27.2	52.6
06	224 50.1	298 19.5	S22 05.3	359 49.1	S15 31.7	51 37.7	N 4 27.3	331 29.4	S20 52.6
07	239 52.6	313 18.7	05.1	14 50.3	32.1	66 40.3	27.4	346 31.7	52.6
08	254 55.0	328 17.8	04.9	29 51.6	32.4	81 43.0	27.4	1 34.0	52.7
F 09	269 57.5	343 16.9	. . 04.6	44 52.9	. . 32.8	96 45.6	. . 27.5	16 36.2	. . 52.7
R 10	285 00.0	358 16.1	04.4	59 54.1	33.1	111 48.3	27.6	31 38.5	52.7
I 11	300 02.4	13 15.2	04.2	74 55.4	33.5	126 51.0	27.7	46 40.8	52.7
D 12	315 04.9	28 14.4	S22 03.9	89 56.6	S15 33.8	141 53.6	N 4 27.8	61 43.0	S20 52.7
A 13	330 07.3	43 13.5	03.7	104 57.9	34.2	156 56.3	27.9	76 45.3	52.7
Y 14	345 09.8	58 12.6	03.5	119 59.2	34.5	171 58.9	28.0	91 47.5	52.8
15	0 12.3	73 11.8	. . 03.2	135 00.4	. . 34.9	187 01.6	. . 28.1	106 49.8	. . 52.8
16	15 14.7	88 10.9	03.0	150 01.7	35.2	202 04.2	28.2	121 52.1	52.8
17	30 17.2	103 10.1	02.8	165 02.9	35.6	217 06.9	28.3	136 54.3	52.8
18	45 19.7	118 09.2	S22 02.5	180 04.2	S15 35.9	232 09.6	N 4 28.4	151 56.6	S20 52.8
19	60 22.1	133 08.4	02.3	195 05.5	36.3	247 12.2	28.5	166 58.9	52.9
20	75 24.6	148 07.5	02.1	210 06.7	36.6	262 14.9	28.6	182 01.1	52.9
21	90 27.1	163 06.6	. . 01.8	225 08.0	. . 37.0	277 17.5	. . 28.7	197 03.4	. . 52.9
22	105 29.5	178 05.8	01.6	240 09.2	37.3	292 20.2	28.8	212 05.7	52.9
23	120 32.0	193 04.9	01.3	255 10.5	37.6	307 22.9	28.9	227 07.9	52.9
Mer. Pass. (h m)	15 03.1	v −0.9	d 0.2	v 1.3	d 0.4	v 2.7	d 0.1	v 2.3	d 0.0

STARS

Name	SHA ° ′	Dec ° ′
Acamar	315 17.0	S40 14.8
Achernar	335 25.7	S57 09.7
Acrux	173 06.7	S63 11.1
Adhara	255 10.8	S29 00.0
Aldebaran	290 47.1	N16 32.3
Alioth	166 19.0	N55 52.1
Alkaid	152 57.4	N49 13.8
Al Na'ir	27 42.0	S46 53.0
Alnilam	275 44.3	S 1 11.8
Alphard	217 54.0	S 8 43.9
Alphecca	126 09.6	N26 39.6
Alpheratz	357 41.8	N29 10.8
Altair	62 06.8	N 8 54.7
Ankaa	353 14.3	S42 13.4
Antares	112 24.2	S26 27.8
Arcturus	145 54.1	N19 05.8
Atria	107 24.6	S69 02.9
Avior	234 16.6	S59 33.9
Bellatrix	278 29.9	N 6 21.6
Betelgeuse	270 59.1	N 7 24.3
Canopus	263 54.9	S52 42.7
Capella	280 31.5	N46 00.7
Deneb	49 30.7	N45 20.3
Denebola	182 31.6	N14 28.8
Diphda	348 54.3	S17 54.1
Dubhe	193 49.1	N61 39.6
Elnath	278 10.1	N28 37.1
Eltanin	90 45.7	N51 29.2
Enif	33 45.7	N 9 57.0
Fomalhaut	15 22.4	S29 32.3
Gacrux	171 58.4	S57 12.0
Gienah	175 50.2	S17 37.9
Hadar	148 45.1	S60 26.7
Hamal	327 58.8	N23 32.2
Kaus Aust.	83 41.8	S34 22.3
Kochab	137 20.3	N74 05.1
Markab	13 36.8	N15 17.5
Menkar	314 13.1	N 4 08.9
Menkent	148 05.3	S36 26.7
Miaplacidus	221 38.2	S69 47.1
Mirfak	308 37.6	N49 55.1
Nunki	75 56.4	S26 16.4
Peacock	53 17.1	S56 40.8
Pollux	243 25.2	N27 59.0
Procyon	244 57.5	N 5 10.7
Rasalhague	96 05.0	N12 33.0
Regulus	207 41.3	N11 53.1
Rigel	281 10.1	S 8 11.3
Rigil Kent.	139 49.1	S60 53.7
Sabik	102 10.7	S15 44.5
Schedar	349 38.6	N56 37.7
Shaula	96 19.7	S37 06.6
Sirius	258 31.8	S16 44.7
Spica	158 29.2	S11 14.7
Suhail	222 50.6	S43 30.0
Vega	80 38.1	N38 47.9
Zuben'ubi	137 03.4	S16 06.4

	SHA ° ′	Mer. Pass. h m
Venus	75 09.2	10 06
Mars	135 35.3	6 03
Jupiter	186 41.9	2 38
Saturn	106 45.4	7 57

UT d h	SUN GHA ° ′	SUN Dec ° ′	MOON GHA ° ′	v ′	MOON Dec ° ′	d ′	HP ′
3 00	176 34.7	S16 44.8	249 27.5	11.8	S16 08.2	4.6	55.3
01	191 34.7	44.1	263 58.3	11.6	16 12.8	4.6	55.4
02	206 34.6	43.3	278 28.9	11.7	16 17.4	4.5	55.4
03	221 34.5	. . 42.6	292 59.6	11.5	16 21.9	4.4	55.4
04	236 34.4	41.9	307 30.1	11.5	16 26.3	4.4	55.4
05	251 34.4	41.1	322 00.6	11.5	16 30.7	4.2	55.5
06	266 34.3	S16 40.4	336 31.1	11.4	S16 34.9	4.2	55.5
W 07	281 34.2	39.7	351 01.5	11.4	16 39.1	4.2	55.5
E 08	296 34.1	39.0	5 31.9	11.2	16 43.3	4.0	55.5
D 09	311 34.1	. . 38.2	20 02.1	11.3	16 47.3	4.0	55.6
N 10	326 34.0	37.5	34 32.4	11.1	16 51.3	3.8	55.6
E 11	341 33.9	36.8	49 02.5	11.2	16 55.1	3.8	55.6
S 12	356 33.9	S16 36.0	63 32.7	11.0	S16 58.9	3.8	55.6
D 13	11 33.8	35.3	78 02.7	11.0	17 02.7	3.6	55.7
A 14	26 33.7	34.6	92 32.7	11.0	17 06.3	3.6	55.7
Y 15	41 33.7	. . 33.8	107 02.7	10.9	17 09.9	3.4	55.7
16	56 33.6	33.1	121 32.6	10.8	17 13.3	3.4	55.8
17	71 33.5	32.4	136 02.4	10.8	17 16.7	3.3	55.8
18	86 33.5	S16 31.6	150 32.2	10.7	S17 20.0	3.3	55.8
19	101 33.4	30.9	165 01.9	10.7	17 23.3	3.1	55.8
20	116 33.3	30.2	179 31.6	10.6	17 26.4	3.0	55.9
21	131 33.2	. . 29.4	194 01.2	10.5	17 29.4	3.0	55.9
22	146 33.2	28.7	208 30.7	10.5	17 32.4	2.9	55.9
23	161 33.1	27.9	223 00.2	10.5	17 35.3	2.8	56.0
4 00	176 33.0	S16 27.2	237 29.7	10.4	S17 38.1	2.7	56.0
01	191 33.0	26.5	251 59.1	10.3	17 40.8	2.6	56.0
02	206 32.9	25.7	266 28.4	10.3	17 43.4	2.5	56.1
03	221 32.9	. . 25.0	280 57.7	10.2	17 45.9	2.4	56.1
04	236 32.8	24.2	295 26.9	10.2	17 48.3	2.4	56.1
05	251 32.7	23.5	309 56.1	10.1	17 50.7	2.2	56.2
06	266 32.7	S16 22.8	324 25.2	10.1	S17 52.9	2.2	56.2
07	281 32.6	22.0	338 54.3	10.0	17 55.1	2.1	56.2
T 08	296 32.5	21.3	353 23.3	9.9	17 57.2	1.9	56.2
H 09	311 32.5	. . 20.5	7 52.2	9.9	17 59.1	1.9	56.3
U 10	326 32.4	19.8	22 21.1	9.9	18 01.0	1.8	56.3
R 11	341 32.3	19.1	36 50.0	9.8	18 02.8	1.7	56.3
S 12	356 32.3	S16 18.3	51 18.8	9.7	S18 04.5	1.6	56.4
D 13	11 32.2	17.6	65 47.5	9.7	18 06.1	1.5	56.4
A 14	26 32.2	16.8	80 16.2	9.7	18 07.6	1.4	56.4
Y 15	41 32.1	. . 16.1	94 44.9	9.6	18 09.0	1.3	56.5
16	56 32.0	15.3	109 13.5	9.5	18 10.3	1.2	56.5
17	71 32.0	14.6	123 42.0	9.5	18 11.5	1.1	56.5
18	86 31.9	S16 13.8	138 10.5	9.4	S18 12.6	1.0	56.6
19	101 31.9	13.1	152 38.9	9.4	18 13.6	0.9	56.6
20	116 31.8	12.3	167 07.3	9.4	18 14.5	0.9	56.6
21	131 31.7	. . 11.6	181 35.7	9.3	18 15.4	0.7	56.7
22	146 31.7	10.8	196 04.0	9.2	18 16.1	0.6	56.7
23	161 31.6	10.1	210 32.2	9.2	18 16.7	0.5	56.7
5 00	176 31.6	S16 09.3	225 00.4	9.2	S18 17.2	0.4	56.8
01	191 31.5	08.6	239 28.6	9.1	18 17.6	0.3	56.8
02	206 31.4	07.8	253 56.7	9.1	18 17.9	0.2	56.8
03	221 31.4	. . 07.1	268 24.8	9.0	18 18.1	0.1	56.9
04	236 31.3	06.3	282 52.8	8.9	18 18.2	0.1	56.9
05	251 31.3	05.6	297 20.7	9.0	18 18.3	0.1	56.9
06	266 31.2	S16 04.8	311 48.7	8.9	S18 18.2	0.2	57.0
07	281 31.2	04.1	326 16.6	8.8	18 18.0	0.4	57.0
08	296 31.1	03.3	340 44.4	8.8	18 17.6	0.4	57.0
F 09	311 31.1	. . 02.6	355 12.2	8.8	18 17.2	0.5	57.1
R 10	326 31.0	01.8	9 40.0	8.7	18 16.7	0.6	57.1
I 11	341 31.0	01.1	24 07.7	8.7	18 16.1	0.7	57.1
D 12	356 30.9	S16 00.3	38 35.4	8.6	S18 15.4	0.8	57.2
A 13	11 30.8	15 59.5	53 03.0	8.6	18 14.6	1.0	57.2
Y 14	26 30.8	58.8	67 30.6	8.6	18 13.6	1.0	57.2
15	41 30.7	. . 58.0	81 58.2	8.5	18 12.6	1.2	57.3
16	56 30.7	57.3	96 25.7	8.5	18 11.4	1.2	57.3
17	71 30.6	56.5	110 53.2	8.4	18 10.2	1.4	57.4
18	86 30.6	S15 55.8	125 20.6	8.5	S18 08.8	1.5	57.4
19	101 30.5	55.0	139 48.1	8.3	18 07.3	1.5	57.4
20	116 30.5	54.2	154 15.4	8.4	18 05.8	1.7	57.5
21	131 30.4	. . 53.5	168 42.8	8.3	18 04.1	1.8	57.5
22	146 30.4	52.7	183 10.1	8.3	18 02.3	1.9	57.5
23	161 30.3	52.0	197 37.4	8.2	S18 00.4	2.0	57.6
	SD 16.3	*d* 0.7	SD 15.2		15.4		15.6

Lat.	Twilight Naut.	Twilight Civil	Sunrise	Moonrise 3	4	5	6
°	h m	h m	h m	h m	h m	h m	h m
N 72	07 01	08 27	10 08	06 04	■	■	09 29
N 70	06 54	08 11	09 32	05 13	06 37	07 41	08 16
68	06 48	07 57	09 07	04 42	05 56	06 57	07 39
66	06 43	07 46	08 48	04 18	05 28	06 28	07 12
64	06 39	07 37	08 32	04 00	05 07	06 05	06 52
62	06 35	07 29	08 19	03 45	04 50	05 48	06 35
60	06 31	07 21	08 08	03 33	04 36	05 33	06 21
N 58	06 28	07 15	07 59	03 22	04 24	05 20	06 09
56	06 25	07 09	07 50	03 13	04 13	05 10	05 59
54	06 22	07 04	07 43	03 04	04 04	05 00	05 50
52	06 19	07 00	07 36	02 57	03 56	04 51	05 42
50	06 17	06 55	07 30	02 50	03 49	04 44	05 35
45	06 11	06 46	07 17	02 36	03 33	04 28	05 19
N 40	06 06	06 38	07 06	02 24	03 20	04 14	05 06
35	06 00	06 31	06 57	02 14	03 09	04 03	04 55
30	05 55	06 24	06 49	02 06	02 59	03 53	04 45
20	05 45	06 12	06 35	01 51	02 43	03 36	04 29
N 10	05 35	06 00	06 22	01 38	02 29	03 21	04 15
0	05 24	05 49	06 10	01 25	02 15	03 07	04 01
S 10	05 11	05 36	05 58	01 13	02 02	02 53	03 48
20	04 55	05 22	05 46	01 00	01 47	02 38	03 33
30	04 34	05 05	05 31	00 46	01 31	02 22	03 17
35	04 22	04 55	05 22	00 37	01 22	02 12	03 07
40	04 06	04 42	05 12	00 27	01 11	02 01	02 56
45	03 46	04 27	05 00	00 16	00 58	01 47	02 43
S 50	03 20	04 08	04 46	00 02	00 43	01 31	02 28
52	03 07	03 59	04 39	24 36	00 36	01 24	02 20
54	02 51	03 49	04 32	24 28	00 28	01 15	02 12
56	02 32	03 37	04 23	24 19	00 19	01 06	02 03
58	02 07	03 23	04 14	24 09	00 09	00 55	01 52
S 60	01 31	03 07	04 03	23 57	24 43	00 43	01 41

Lat.	Sunset	Twilight Civil	Twilight Naut.	Moonset 3	4	5	6
°	h m	h m	h m	h m	h m	h m	h m
N 72	14 21	16 02	17 29	09 03	■	■	11 05
N 70	14 57	16 18	17 35	09 54	10 14	10 59	12 17
68	15 22	16 32	17 41	10 26	10 55	11 44	12 55
66	15 41	16 43	17 46	10 50	11 23	12 13	13 21
64	15 57	16 52	17 50	11 08	11 45	12 35	13 41
62	16 10	17 00	17 54	11 24	12 02	12 53	13 57
60	16 21	17 07	17 58	11 36	12 16	13 08	14 11
N 58	16 30	17 13	18 01	11 48	12 29	13 20	14 22
56	16 38	17 19	18 04	11 57	12 39	13 31	14 33
54	16 46	17 24	18 06	12 06	12 49	13 40	14 42
52	16 52	17 29	18 09	12 13	12 57	13 49	14 49
50	16 58	17 33	18 12	12 20	13 04	13 56	14 57
45	17 11	17 42	18 17	12 35	13 20	14 13	15 12
N 40	17 22	17 50	18 23	12 47	13 34	14 26	15 24
35	17 31	17 58	18 28	12 58	13 45	14 37	15 35
30	17 39	18 04	18 33	13 07	13 55	14 47	15 44
20	17 53	18 16	18 42	13 22	14 11	15 04	16 00
N 10	18 06	18 27	18 53	13 36	14 26	15 19	16 14
0	18 17	18 39	19 04	13 49	14 40	15 33	16 27
S 10	18 29	18 51	19 17	14 02	14 54	15 47	16 40
20	18 42	19 05	19 32	14 16	15 08	16 01	16 54
30	18 57	19 22	19 53	14 31	15 25	16 18	17 10
35	19 05	19 33	20 05	14 40	15 35	16 28	17 19
40	19 15	19 45	20 21	14 51	15 46	16 39	17 29
45	19 27	19 59	20 40	15 03	15 59	16 52	17 41
S 50	19 41	20 18	21 06	15 18	16 15	17 08	17 56
52	19 47	20 27	21 19	15 25	16 22	17 15	18 03
54	19 55	20 37	21 35	15 33	16 31	17 24	18 10
56	20 03	20 49	21 53	15 42	16 40	17 33	18 19
58	20 12	21 02	22 17	15 51	16 51	17 43	18 28
S 60	20 23	21 18	22 51	16 03	17 03	17 56	18 39

Day	SUN Eqn. of Time 00^h	SUN Eqn. of Time 12^h	SUN Mer. Pass.	MOON Mer. Pass. Upper	MOON Mer. Pass. Lower	Age	Phase
d	m s	m s	h m	h m	h m	d %	
3	13 41	13 44	12 14	07 37	20 02	24 28	
4	13 48	13 51	12 14	08 27	20 53	25 19	◑
5	13 54	13 56	12 14	09 20	21 47	26 12	

Day	UT (d h)	ARIES GHA	VENUS −3·9 GHA	VENUS Dec	MARS +0·7 GHA	MARS Dec	JUPITER −2·4 GHA	JUPITER Dec	SATURN +0·5 GHA	SATURN Dec
		° ′	° ′	° ′	° ′	° ′	° ′	° ′	° ′	° ′
SATURDAY	6 00	135 34.5	208 04.1	S22 01.1	270 11.8	S15 38.0	322 25.5	N 4 28.9	242 10.2	S20 52.9
	01	150 36.9	223 03.2	00.8	285 13.0	38.3	337 28.2	29.0	257 12.5	53.0
	02	165 39.4	238 02.4	00.6	300 14.3	38.7	352 30.8	29.1	272 14.7	53.0
	03	180 41.8	253 01.5	. . 00.3	315 15.5	. . 39.0	7 33.5	. . 29.2	287 17.0	. . 53.0
	04	195 44.3	268 00.7	22 00.1	330 16.8	39.4	22 36.2	29.3	302 19.3	53.0
	05	210 46.8	282 59.8	21 59.8	345 18.1	39.7	37 38.8	29.4	317 21.5	53.0
	06	225 49.2	297 58.9	S21 59.6	0 19.3	S15 40.1	52 41.5	N 4 29.5	332 23.8	S20 53.0
	07	240 51.7	312 58.1	59.3	15 20.6	40.4	67 44.2	29.6	347 26.1	53.1
	08	255 54.2	327 57.2	59.1	30 21.9	40.8	82 46.8	29.7	2 28.3	53.1
	09	270 56.6	342 56.4	. . 58.8	45 23.1	. . 41.1	97 49.5	. . 29.8	17 30.6	. . 53.1
	10	285 59.1	357 55.5	58.6	60 24.4	41.4	112 52.1	29.9	32 32.9	53.1
	11	301 01.6	12 54.7	58.3	75 25.6	41.8	127 54.8	30.0	47 35.1	53.1
	12	316 04.0	27 53.8	S21 58.1	90 26.9	S15 42.1	142 57.5	N 4 30.1	62 37.4	S20 53.2
	13	331 06.5	42 53.0	57.8	105 28.2	42.5	158 00.1	30.2	77 39.7	53.2
	14	346 08.9	57 52.1	57.5	120 29.4	42.8	173 02.8	30.3	92 41.9	53.2
	15	1 11.4	72 51.3	. . 57.3	135 30.7	. . 43.2	188 05.5	. . 30.4	107 44.2	. . 53.2
	16	16 13.9	87 50.4	57.0	150 32.0	43.5	203 08.1	30.5	122 46.5	53.2
	17	31 16.3	102 49.5	56.7	165 33.2	43.8	218 10.8	30.6	137 48.7	53.2
	18	46 18.8	117 48.7	S21 56.5	180 34.5	S15 44.2	233 13.5	N 4 30.7	152 51.0	S20 53.3
	19	61 21.3	132 47.8	56.2	195 35.8	44.5	248 16.1	30.8	167 53.3	53.3
	20	76 23.7	147 47.0	55.9	210 37.0	44.9	263 18.8	30.9	182 55.5	53.3
	21	91 26.2	162 46.1	. . 55.7	225 38.3	. . 45.2	278 21.5	. . 31.0	197 57.8	. . 53.3
	22	106 28.7	177 45.3	55.4	240 39.6	45.6	293 24.1	31.0	213 00.1	53.3
	23	121 31.1	192 44.4	55.1	255 40.8	45.9	308 26.8	31.1	228 02.3	53.3
SUNDAY	7 00	136 33.6	207 43.6	S21 54.9	270 42.1	S15 46.2	323 29.5	N 4 31.2	243 04.6	S20 53.4
	01	151 36.1	222 42.7	54.6	285 43.4	46.6	338 32.1	31.3	258 06.9	53.4
	02	166 38.5	237 41.9	54.3	300 44.6	46.9	353 34.8	31.4	273 09.1	53.4
	03	181 41.0	252 41.0	. . 54.0	315 45.9	. . 47.3	8 37.5	. . 31.5	288 11.4	. . 53.4
	04	196 43.4	267 40.2	53.8	330 47.2	47.6	23 40.1	31.6	303 13.7	53.4
	05	211 45.9	282 39.3	53.5	345 48.4	47.9	38 42.8	31.7	318 15.9	53.4
	06	226 48.4	297 38.5	S21 53.2	0 49.7	S15 48.3	53 45.5	N 4 31.8	333 18.2	S20 53.5
	07	241 50.8	312 37.6	52.9	15 51.0	48.6	68 48.1	31.9	348 20.5	53.5
	08	256 53.3	327 36.8	52.6	30 52.2	49.0	83 50.8	32.0	3 22.8	53.5
	09	271 55.8	342 35.9	. . 52.4	45 53.5	. . 49.3	98 53.5	. . 32.1	18 25.0	. . 53.5
	10	286 58.2	357 35.1	52.1	60 54.8	49.6	113 56.1	32.2	33 27.3	53.5
	11	302 00.7	12 34.2	51.8	75 56.0	50.0	128 58.8	32.3	48 29.6	53.5
	12	317 03.2	27 33.4	S21 51.5	90 57.3	S15 50.3	144 01.5	N 4 32.4	63 31.8	S20 53.6
	13	332 05.6	42 32.5	51.2	105 58.6	50.7	159 04.1	32.5	78 34.1	53.6
	14	347 08.1	57 31.7	50.9	120 59.8	51.0	174 06.8	32.6	93 36.4	53.6
	15	2 10.6	72 30.8	. . 50.6	136 01.1	. . 51.3	189 09.5	. . 32.7	108 38.6	. . 53.6
	16	17 13.0	87 30.0	50.4	151 02.4	51.7	204 12.2	32.8	123 40.9	53.6
	17	32 15.5	102 29.1	50.1	166 03.7	52.0	219 14.8	32.9	138 43.2	53.6
	18	47 17.9	117 28.3	S21 49.8	181 04.9	S15 52.4	234 17.5	N 4 33.0	153 45.5	S20 53.7
	19	62 20.4	132 27.4	49.5	196 06.2	52.7	249 20.2	33.1	168 47.7	53.7
	20	77 22.9	147 26.6	49.2	211 07.5	53.0	264 22.8	33.2	183 50.0	53.7
	21	92 25.3	162 25.7	. . 48.9	226 08.7	. . 53.4	279 25.5	. . 33.3	198 52.3	. . 53.7
	22	107 27.8	177 24.9	48.6	241 10.0	53.7	294 28.2	33.4	213 54.5	53.7
	23	122 30.3	192 24.0	48.3	256 11.3	54.0	309 30.9	33.5	228 56.8	53.7
MONDAY	8 00	137 32.7	207 23.2	S21 48.0	271 12.6	S15 54.4	324 33.5	N 4 33.6	243 59.1	S20 53.8
	01	152 35.2	222 22.3	47.7	286 13.8	54.7	339 36.2	33.7	259 01.4	53.8
	02	167 37.7	237 21.5	47.4	301 15.1	55.1	354 38.9	33.8	274 03.6	53.8
	03	182 40.1	252 20.6	. . 47.1	316 16.4	. . 55.4	9 41.5	. . 33.9	289 05.9	. . 53.8
	04	197 42.6	267 19.8	46.8	331 17.7	55.7	24 44.2	34.0	304 08.2	53.8
	05	212 45.1	282 19.0	46.5	346 18.9	56.1	39 46.9	34.1	319 10.4	53.8
	06	227 47.5	297 18.1	S21 46.2	1 20.2	S15 56.4	54 49.6	N 4 34.2	334 12.7	S20 53.9
	07	242 50.0	312 17.3	45.9	16 21.5	56.7	69 52.2	34.3	349 15.0	53.9
	08	257 52.4	327 16.4	45.6	31 22.8	57.1	84 54.9	34.4	4 17.3	53.9
	09	272 54.9	342 15.6	. . 45.2	46 24.0	. . 57.4	99 57.6	. . 34.5	19 19.5	. . 53.9
	10	287 57.4	357 14.7	44.9	61 25.3	57.7	115 00.3	34.6	34 21.8	53.9
	11	302 59.8	12 13.9	44.6	76 26.6	58.1	130 02.9	34.7	49 24.1	53.9
	12	318 02.3	27 13.0	S21 44.3	91 27.9	S15 58.4	145 05.6	N 4 34.8	64 26.4	S20 54.0
	13	333 04.8	42 12.2	44.0	106 29.1	58.7	160 08.3	34.9	79 28.6	54.0
	14	348 07.2	57 11.4	43.7	121 30.4	59.1	175 11.0	35.0	94 30.9	54.0
	15	3 09.7	72 10.5	. . 43.4	136 31.7	. . 59.4	190 13.6	. . 35.1	109 33.2	. . 54.0
	16	18 12.2	87 09.7	43.1	151 33.0	15 59.8	205 16.3	35.2	124 35.5	54.0
	17	33 14.6	102 08.8	42.7	166 34.2	16 00.1	220 19.0	35.3	139 37.7	54.0
	18	48 17.1	117 08.0	S21 42.4	181 35.5	S16 00.4	235 21.7	N 4 35.4	154 40.0	S20 54.1
	19	63 19.5	132 07.1	42.1	196 36.8	00.8	250 24.3	35.5	169 42.3	54.1
	20	78 22.0	147 06.3	41.8	211 38.1	01.1	265 27.0	35.6	184 44.6	54.1
	21	93 24.5	162 05.4	. . 41.4	226 39.3	. . 01.4	280 29.7	. . 35.7	199 46.8	. . 54.1
	22	108 26.9	177 04.6	41.1	241 40.6	01.8	295 32.4	35.8	214 49.1	54.1
	23	123 29.4	192 03.8	40.8	256 41.9	02.1	310 35.1	35.9	229 51.4	54.1
	Mer. Pass. (h m)	14 51.3	v −0.8	d 0.3	v 1.3	d 0.3	v 2.7	d 0.1	v 2.3	d 0.0

STARS Name	SHA	Dec
	° ′	° ′
Acamar	315 17.0	S40 14.8
Achernar	335 25.8	S57 09.7
Acrux	173 06.6	S63 11.1
Adhara	255 10.8	S29 00.0
Aldebaran	290 47.2	N16 32.3
Alioth	166 18.9	N55 52.1
Alkaid	152 57.4	N49 13.8
Al Na'ir	27 42.0	S46 53.0
Alnilam	275 44.3	S 1 11.8
Alphard	217 54.0	S 8 43.9
Alphecca	126 09.6	N26 39.6
Alpheratz	357 41.8	N29 10.8
Altair	62 06.8	N 8 54.7
Ankaa	353 14.3	S42 13.4
Antares	112 24.2	S26 27.8
Arcturus	145 54.0	N19 05.8
Atria	107 24.6	S69 02.9
Avior	234 16.6	S59 33.9
Bellatrix	278 29.9	N 6 21.6
Betelgeuse	270 59.1	N 7 24.3
Canopus	263 54.9	S52 42.7
Capella	280 31.5	N46 00.7
Deneb	49 30.7	N45 20.3
Denebola	182 31.6	N14 28.8
Diphda	348 54.3	S17 54.1
Dubhe	193 49.1	N61 39.6
Elnath	278 10.1	N28 37.1
Eltanin	90 45.7	N51 29.2
Enif	33 45.7	N 9 57.0
Fomalhaut	15 22.4	S29 32.3
Gacrux	171 58.4	S57 12.0
Gienah	175 50.2	S17 37.9
Hadar	148 45.0	S60 26.7
Hamal	327 58.8	N23 32.2
Kaus Aust.	83 41.7	S34 22.3
Kochab	137 20.2	N74 05.1
Markab	13 36.8	N15 17.5
Menkar	314 13.1	N 4 08.9
Menkent	148 05.3	S36 26.7
Miaplacidus	221 38.2	S69 47.1
Mirfak	308 37.6	N49 55.1
Nunki	75 56.4	S26 16.4
Peacock	53 17.1	S56 40.8
Pollux	243 25.2	N27 59.0
Procyon	244 57.5	N 5 10.7
Rasalhague	96 05.0	N12 33.0
Regulus	207 41.3	N11 53.1
Rigel	281 10.1	S 8 11.3
Rigil Kent.	139 49.1	S60 53.7
Sabik	102 10.6	S15 44.5
Schedar	349 38.7	N56 37.7
Shaula	96 19.7	S37 06.6
Sirius	258 31.8	S16 44.7
Spica	158 29.2	S11 14.7
Suhail	222 50.6	S43 30.1
Vega	80 38.1	N38 47.9
Zuben'ubi	137 03.4	S16 06.4

	SHA	Mer. Pass.
	° ′	h m
Venus	71 10.0	10 10
Mars	134 08.5	5 57
Jupiter	186 55.9	2 26
Saturn	106 31.0	7 47

UT	SUN GHA	SUN Dec	MOON GHA	v	MOON Dec	d	HP
d h	° ′	° ′	° ′	′	° ′	′	′
6 00	176 30.3	S15 51.2	212 04.6	8.3	S17 58.4	2.1	57.6
01	191 30.2	50.4	226 31.9	8.2	17 56.3	2.3	57.6
02	206 30.2	49.7	240 59.1	8.1	17 54.0	2.3	57.7
03	221 30.1	. . 48.9	255 26.2	8.1	17 51.7	2.4	57.7
04	236 30.1	48.1	269 53.3	8.1	17 49.3	2.6	57.7
05	251 30.0	47.4	284 20.4	8.1	17 46.7	2.7	57.8
06	266 30.0	S15 46.6	298 47.5	8.1	S17 44.0	2.7	57.8
S 07	281 29.9	45.9	313 14.6	8.0	17 41.3	2.9	57.8
A 08	296 29.9	45.1	327 41.6	8.0	17 38.4	3.0	57.9
T 09	311 29.8	. . 44.3	342 08.6	8.0	17 35.4	3.1	57.9
U 10	326 29.8	43.6	356 35.6	7.9	17 32.3	3.2	57.9
R 11	341 29.8	42.8	11 02.5	8.0	17 29.1	3.3	58.0
D 12	356 29.7	S15 42.0	25 29.5	7.9	S17 25.8	3.4	58.0
A 13	11 29.7	41.3	39 56.4	7.8	17 22.4	3.6	58.0
Y 14	26 29.6	40.5	54 23.2	7.9	17 18.8	3.6	58.1
15	41 29.6	. . 39.7	68 50.1	7.9	17 15.2	3.8	58.1
16	56 29.5	39.0	83 17.0	7.8	17 11.4	3.8	58.1
17	71 29.5	38.2	97 43.8	7.8	17 07.6	4.0	58.2
18	86 29.4	S15 37.4	112 10.6	7.8	S17 03.6	4.0	58.2
19	101 29.4	36.6	126 37.4	7.8	16 59.6	4.2	58.2
20	116 29.4	35.9	141 04.2	7.7	16 55.4	4.3	58.3
21	131 29.3	. . 35.1	155 30.9	7.8	16 51.1	4.4	58.3
22	146 29.3	34.3	169 57.7	7.7	16 46.7	4.5	58.3
23	161 29.2	33.6	184 24.4	7.7	16 42.2	4.6	58.4
7 00	176 29.2	S15 32.8	198 51.1	7.7	S16 37.6	4.8	58.4
01	191 29.2	32.0	213 17.8	7.7	16 32.8	4.8	58.4
02	206 29.1	31.2	227 44.5	7.7	16 28.0	4.9	58.5
03	221 29.1	. . 30.5	242 11.2	7.7	16 23.1	5.1	58.5
04	236 29.0	29.7	256 37.9	7.6	16 18.0	5.1	58.5
05	251 29.0	28.9	271 04.5	7.7	16 12.9	5.3	58.6
06	266 29.0	S15 28.1	285 31.2	7.6	S16 07.6	5.3	58.6
07	281 28.9	27.4	299 57.8	7.7	16 02.3	5.5	58.6
08	296 28.9	26.6	314 24.5	7.6	15 56.8	5.5	58.7
S 09	311 28.8	. . 25.8	328 51.1	7.6	15 51.3	5.7	58.7
U 10	326 28.8	25.0	343 17.7	7.7	15 45.6	5.8	58.7
N 11	341 28.8	24.3	357 44.4	7.6	15 39.8	5.9	58.7
D 12	356 28.7	S15 23.5	12 11.0	7.6	S15 33.9	5.9	58.8
A 13	11 28.7	22.7	26 37.6	7.6	15 28.0	6.1	58.8
Y 14	26 28.7	21.9	41 04.2	7.6	15 21.9	6.2	58.8
15	41 28.6	. . 21.1	55 30.8	7.6	15 15.7	6.3	58.9
16	56 28.6	20.4	69 57.4	7.6	15 09.4	6.4	58.9
17	71 28.5	19.6	84 24.0	7.6	15 03.0	6.5	58.9
18	86 28.5	S15 18.8	98 50.6	7.6	S14 56.5	6.6	58.9
19	101 28.5	18.0	113 17.2	7.6	14 49.9	6.6	59.0
20	116 28.4	17.2	127 43.8	7.7	14 43.3	6.8	59.0
21	131 28.4	. . 16.5	142 10.5	7.6	14 36.5	6.9	59.0
22	146 28.4	15.7	156 37.1	7.6	14 29.6	7.0	59.1
23	161 28.3	14.9	171 03.7	7.6	14 22.6	7.0	59.1
8 00	176 28.3	S15 14.1	185 30.3	7.6	S14 15.6	7.2	59.1
01	191 28.3	13.3	199 56.9	7.6	14 08.4	7.3	59.1
02	206 28.2	12.5	214 23.5	7.7	14 01.1	7.3	59.2
03	221 28.2	. . 11.7	228 50.2	7.6	13 53.8	7.5	59.2
04	236 28.2	11.0	243 16.8	7.7	13 46.3	7.5	59.2
05	251 28.1	10.2	257 43.5	7.6	13 38.8	7.7	59.2
06	266 28.1	S15 09.4	272 10.1	7.7	S13 31.1	7.7	59.3
07	281 28.1	08.6	286 36.8	7.6	13 23.4	7.8	59.3
08	296 28.1	07.8	301 03.4	7.7	13 15.6	7.9	59.3
M 09	311 28.0	. . 07.0	315 30.1	7.7	13 07.7	8.0	59.3
O 10	326 28.0	06.2	329 56.8	7.7	12 59.7	8.1	59.4
N 11	341 28.0	05.5	344 23.5	7.7	12 51.6	8.2	59.4
D 12	356 27.9	S15 04.7	358 50.2	7.7	S12 43.4	8.2	59.4
A 13	11 27.9	03.9	13 16.9	7.7	12 35.2	8.4	59.4
Y 14	26 27.9	03.1	27 43.6	7.7	12 26.8	8.4	59.5
15	41 27.8	. . 02.3	42 10.3	7.8	12 18.4	8.5	59.5
16	56 27.8	01.5	56 37.1	7.7	12 09.9	8.6	59.5
17	71 27.8	15 00.7	71 03.8	7.8	12 01.3	8.7	59.5
18	86 27.8	S14 59.9	85 30.6	7.8	S11 52.6	8.7	59.6
19	101 27.7	59.1	99 57.4	7.8	11 43.9	8.9	59.6
20	116 27.7	58.3	114 24.2	7.8	11 35.0	8.9	59.6
21	131 27.7	. . 57.5	128 51.0	7.8	11 26.1	9.0	59.6
22	146 27.7	56.7	143 17.8	7.8	11 17.1	9.0	59.6
23	161 27.6	56.0	157 44.6	7.8	S11 08.1	9.2	59.7
	SD 16.2	*d* 0.8	SD 15.8		16.0		16.2

Lat.	Twilight Naut.	Twilight Civil	Sunrise	Moonrise 6	Moonrise 7	Moonrise 8	Moonrise 9
°	h m	h m	h m	h m	h m	h m	h m
N 72	06 49	08 14	09 47	09 29	09 12	09 04	08 58
N 70	06 44	07 59	09 16	08 16	08 32	08 40	08 43
68	06 39	07 47	08 54	07 39	08 05	08 21	08 31
66	06 35	07 37	08 37	07 12	07 44	08 05	08 21
64	06 31	07 29	08 23	06 52	07 27	07 53	08 13
62	06 28	07 21	08 11	06 35	07 13	07 42	08 06
60	06 25	07 15	08 01	06 21	07 01	07 33	07 59
N 58	06 22	07 09	07 52	06 09	06 51	07 25	07 54
56	06 20	07 04	07 44	05 59	06 42	07 18	07 49
54	06 17	06 59	07 37	05 50	06 34	07 11	07 44
52	06 15	06 55	07 31	05 42	06 27	07 06	07 40
50	06 13	06 51	07 25	05 35	06 20	07 00	07 36
45	06 08	06 42	07 13	05 19	06 06	06 49	07 28
N 40	06 03	06 35	07 03	05 06	05 55	06 40	07 22
35	05 58	06 28	06 54	04 55	05 45	06 32	07 16
30	05 54	06 22	06 47	04 45	05 36	06 25	07 11
20	05 44	06 11	06 33	04 29	05 21	06 12	07 02
N 10	05 35	06 00	06 22	04 15	05 08	06 02	06 54
0	05 24	05 49	06 11	04 01	04 56	05 52	06 47
S 10	05 12	05 37	05 59	03 48	04 44	05 42	06 40
20	04 57	05 24	05 47	03 33	04 31	05 31	06 32
30	04 37	05 08	05 33	03 17	04 16	05 18	06 23
35	04 25	04 58	05 25	03 07	04 07	05 11	06 18
40	04 10	04 46	05 16	02 56	03 57	05 03	06 12
45	03 52	04 32	05 05	02 43	03 46	04 54	06 05
S 50	03 27	04 14	04 51	02 28	03 32	04 42	05 57
52	03 15	04 06	04 45	02 20	03 25	04 37	05 53
54	03 00	03 56	04 38	02 12	03 18	04 31	05 49
56	02 43	03 45	04 30	02 03	03 10	04 24	05 44
58	02 21	03 32	04 21	01 52	03 00	04 17	05 39
S 60	01 51	03 17	04 11	01 41	02 50	04 08	05 33

Lat.	Sunset	Twilight Civil	Twilight Naut.	Moonset 6	Moonset 7	Moonset 8	Moonset 9
°	h m	h m	h m	h m	h m	h m	h m
N 72	14 43	16 16	17 41	11 05	13 18	15 21	17 22
N 70	15 13	16 31	17 46	12 17	13 57	15 45	17 36
68	15 35	16 42	17 51	12 55	14 24	16 03	17 46
66	15 53	16 52	17 55	13 21	14 44	16 17	17 55
64	16 07	17 01	17 58	13 41	15 00	16 29	18 02
62	16 18	17 08	18 01	13 57	15 14	16 39	18 08
60	16 28	17 14	18 04	14 11	15 25	16 47	18 14
N 58	16 37	17 20	18 07	14 22	15 35	16 54	18 18
56	16 45	17 25	18 09	14 33	15 43	17 01	18 23
54	16 52	17 30	18 12	14 42	15 51	17 07	18 26
52	16 58	17 34	18 14	14 49	15 58	17 12	18 30
50	17 04	17 38	18 16	14 57	16 04	17 17	18 33
45	17 16	17 46	18 21	15 12	16 17	17 27	18 39
N 40	17 26	17 54	18 26	15 24	16 28	17 35	18 45
35	17 34	18 00	18 31	15 35	16 37	17 43	18 50
30	17 42	18 07	18 35	15 44	16 45	17 49	18 54
20	17 55	18 18	18 44	16 00	16 59	18 00	19 01
N 10	18 07	18 28	18 53	16 14	17 11	18 09	19 07
0	18 18	18 39	19 04	16 27	17 23	18 18	19 13
S 10	18 29	18 51	19 16	16 40	17 34	18 27	19 19
20	18 41	19 04	19 31	16 54	17 46	18 36	19 25
30	18 55	19 20	19 50	17 10	17 59	18 47	19 32
35	19 03	19 30	20 02	17 19	18 07	18 53	19 35
40	19 12	19 41	20 17	17 29	18 16	18 59	19 40
45	19 23	19 55	20 35	17 41	18 26	19 07	19 45
S 50	19 36	20 13	21 00	17 56	18 39	19 17	19 51
52	19 42	20 21	21 12	18 03	18 45	19 21	19 54
54	19 49	20 30	21 26	18 10	18 51	19 26	19 57
56	19 57	20 41	21 43	18 19	18 58	19 31	20 00
58	20 05	20 54	22 04	18 28	19 06	19 37	20 04
S 60	20 15	21 09	22 33	18 39	19 15	19 44	20 08

Day	SUN Eqn. of Time 00h	SUN Eqn. of Time 12h	SUN Mer. Pass.	MOON Mer. Pass. Upper	MOON Mer. Pass. Lower	MOON Age	MOON Phase
d	m s	m s	h m	h m	h m	d	%
6	13 59	14 01	12 14	10 14	22 42	27	6
7	14 03	14 05	12 14	11 09	23 37	28	2
8	14 07	14 08	12 14	12 05	24 32	29	0

UT d h	ARIES GHA	VENUS −3·9 GHA	VENUS Dec	MARS +0·7 GHA	MARS Dec	JUPITER −2·4 GHA	JUPITER Dec	SATURN +0·5 GHA	SATURN Dec
	° ′	° ′	° ′	° ′	° ′	° ′	° ′	° ′	° ′
9 00	138 31.9	207 02.9	S21 40.5	271 43.2	S16 02.4	325 37.7	N 4 36.0	244 53.7	S20 54.2
01	153 34.3	222 02.1	40.1	286 44.5	02.7	340 40.4	36.1	259 55.9	54.2
02	168 36.8	237 01.2	39.8	301 45.7	03.1	355 43.1	36.2	274 58.2	54.2
03	183 39.3	252 00.4	. . 39.5	316 47.0	. . 03.4	10 45.8	. . 36.3	290 00.5	. . 54.2
04	198 41.7	266 59.6	39.2	331 48.3	03.7	25 48.4	36.4	305 02.8	54.2
05	213 44.2	281 58.7	38.8	346 49.6	04.1	40 51.1	36.5	320 05.0	54.2
06	228 46.7	296 57.9	S21 38.5	1 50.9	S16 04.4	55 53.8	N 4 36.6	335 07.3	S20 54.3
T 07	243 49.1	311 57.0	38.2	16 52.1	04.7	70 56.5	36.7	350 09.6	54.3
U 08	258 51.6	326 56.2	37.8	31 53.4	05.1	85 59.2	36.8	5 11.9	54.3
E 09	273 54.0	341 55.4	. . 37.5	46 54.7	. . 05.4	101 01.8	. . 36.9	20 14.1	. . 54.3
S 10	288 56.5	356 54.5	37.1	61 56.0	05.7	116 04.5	37.0	35 16.4	54.3
D 11	303 59.0	11 53.7	36.8	76 57.3	06.1	131 07.2	37.1	50 18.7	54.3
A 12	319 01.4	26 52.8	S21 36.5	91 58.5	S16 06.4	146 09.9	N 4 37.2	65 21.0	S20 54.3
Y 13	334 03.9	41 52.0	36.1	106 59.8	06.7	161 12.6	37.3	80 23.2	54.4
14	349 06.4	56 51.2	35.8	122 01.1	07.1	176 15.3	37.4	95 25.5	54.4
15	4 08.8	71 50.3	. . 35.4	137 02.4	. . 07.4	191 17.9	. . 37.5	110 27.8	. . 54.4
16	19 11.3	86 49.5	35.1	152 03.7	07.7	206 20.6	37.6	125 30.1	54.4
17	34 13.8	101 48.6	34.7	167 05.0	08.0	221 23.3	37.7	140 32.4	54.4
18	49 16.2	116 47.8	S21 34.4	182 06.2	S16 08.4	236 26.0	N 4 37.8	155 34.6	S20 54.4
19	64 18.7	131 47.0	34.1	197 07.5	08.7	251 28.7	37.9	170 36.9	54.5
20	79 21.2	146 46.1	33.7	212 08.8	09.0	266 31.3	38.0	185 39.2	54.5
21	94 23.6	161 45.3	. . 33.4	227 10.1	. . 09.4	281 34.0	. . 38.1	200 41.5	. . 54.5
22	109 26.1	176 44.5	33.0	242 11.4	09.7	296 36.7	38.2	215 43.8	54.5
23	124 28.5	191 43.6	32.7	257 12.7	10.0	311 39.4	38.4	230 46.0	54.5
10 00	139 31.0	206 42.8	S21 32.3	272 13.9	S16 10.3	326 42.1	N 4 38.5	245 48.3	S20 54.5
01	154 33.5	221 42.0	31.9	287 15.2	10.7	341 44.8	38.6	260 50.6	54.5
02	169 35.9	236 41.1	31.6	302 16.5	11.0	356 47.4	38.7	275 52.9	54.6
03	184 38.4	251 40.3	. . 31.2	317 17.8	. . 11.3	11 50.1	. . 38.8	290 55.1	. . 54.6
04	199 40.9	266 39.4	30.9	332 19.1	11.7	26 52.8	38.9	305 57.4	54.6
05	214 43.3	281 38.6	30.5	347 20.4	12.0	41 55.5	39.0	320 59.7	54.6
06	229 45.8	296 37.8	S21 30.2	2 21.7	S16 12.3	56 58.2	N 4 39.1	336 02.0	S20 54.6
W 07	244 48.3	311 36.9	29.8	17 22.9	12.6	72 00.9	39.2	351 04.3	54.6
E 08	259 50.7	326 36.1	29.4	32 24.2	13.0	87 03.6	39.3	6 06.5	54.7
D 09	274 53.2	341 35.3	. . 29.1	47 25.5	. . 13.3	102 06.2	. . 39.4	21 08.8	. . 54.7
N 10	289 55.6	356 34.4	28.7	62 26.8	13.6	117 08.9	39.5	36 11.1	54.7
E 11	304 58.1	11 33.6	28.3	77 28.1	13.9	132 11.6	39.6	51 13.4	54.7
S 12	320 00.6	26 32.8	S21 28.0	92 29.4	S16 14.3	147 14.3	N 4 39.7	66 15.7	S20 54.7
D 13	335 03.0	41 31.9	27.6	107 30.7	14.6	162 17.0	39.8	81 17.9	54.7
A 14	350 05.5	56 31.1	27.2	122 32.0	14.9	177 19.7	39.9	96 20.2	54.7
Y 15	5 08.0	71 30.3	. . 26.9	137 33.3	. . 15.2	192 22.4	. . 40.0	111 22.5	. . 54.8
16	20 10.4	86 29.4	26.5	152 34.5	15.6	207 25.0	40.1	126 24.8	54.8
17	35 12.9	101 28.6	26.1	167 35.8	15.9	222 27.7	40.2	141 27.1	54.8
18	50 15.4	116 27.8	S21 25.7	182 37.1	S16 16.2	237 30.4	N 4 40.3	156 29.4	S20 54.8
19	65 17.8	131 27.0	25.4	197 38.4	16.5	252 33.1	40.4	171 31.6	54.8
20	80 20.3	146 26.1	25.0	212 39.7	16.9	267 35.8	40.5	186 33.9	54.8
21	95 22.8	161 25.3	. . 24.6	227 41.0	. . 17.2	282 38.5	. . 40.6	201 36.2	. . 54.9
22	110 25.2	176 24.5	24.2	242 42.3	17.5	297 41.2	40.8	216 38.5	54.9
23	125 27.7	191 23.6	23.9	257 43.6	17.8	312 43.9	40.9	231 40.8	54.9
11 00	140 30.1	206 22.8	S21 23.5	272 44.9	S16 18.2	327 46.5	N 4 41.0	246 43.0	S20 54.9
01	155 32.6	221 22.0	23.1	287 46.2	18.5	342 49.2	41.1	261 45.3	54.9
02	170 35.1	236 21.1	22.7	302 47.4	18.8	357 51.9	41.2	276 47.6	54.9
03	185 37.5	251 20.3	. . 22.3	317 48.7	. . 19.1	12 54.6	. . 41.3	291 49.9	. . 54.9
04	200 40.0	266 19.5	22.0	332 50.0	19.4	27 57.3	41.4	306 52.2	55.0
05	215 42.5	281 18.7	21.6	347 51.3	19.8	43 00.0	41.5	321 54.5	55.0
06	230 44.9	296 17.8	S21 21.2	2 52.6	S16 20.1	58 02.7	N 4 41.6	336 56.7	S20 55.0
07	245 47.4	311 17.0	20.8	17 53.9	20.4	73 05.4	41.7	351 59.0	55.0
T 08	260 49.9	326 16.2	20.4	32 55.2	20.7	88 08.1	41.8	7 01.3	55.0
H 09	275 52.3	341 15.3	. . 20.0	47 56.5	. . 21.1	103 10.8	. . 41.9	22 03.6	. . 55.0
U 10	290 54.8	356 14.5	19.6	62 57.8	21.4	118 13.4	42.0	37 05.9	55.0
R 11	305 57.2	11 13.7	19.2	77 59.1	21.7	133 16.1	42.1	52 08.2	55.1
S 12	320 59.7	26 12.9	S21 18.8	93 00.4	S16 22.0	148 18.8	N 4 42.2	67 10.4	S20 55.1
D 13	336 02.2	41 12.0	18.4	108 01.7	22.3	163 21.5	42.3	82 12.7	55.1
A 14	351 04.6	56 11.2	18.1	123 03.0	22.7	178 24.2	42.4	97 15.0	55.1
Y 15	6 07.1	71 10.4	. . 17.7	138 04.3	. . 23.0	193 26.9	. . 42.6	112 17.3	. . 55.1
16	21 09.6	86 09.6	17.3	153 05.6	23.3	208 29.6	42.7	127 19.6	55.1
17	36 12.0	101 08.7	16.9	168 06.9	23.6	223 32.3	42.8	142 21.9	55.2
18	51 14.5	116 07.9	S21 16.5	183 08.2	S16 23.9	238 35.0	N 4 42.9	157 24.2	S20 55.2
19	66 17.0	131 07.1	16.1	198 09.5	24.3	253 37.7	43.0	172 26.4	55.2
20	81 19.4	146 06.3	15.7	213 10.8	24.6	268 40.4	43.1	187 28.7	55.2
21	96 21.9	161 05.4	. . 15.3	228 12.0	. . 24.9	283 43.1	. . 43.2	202 31.0	. . 55.2
22	111 24.4	176 04.6	14.8	243 13.3	25.2	298 45.8	43.3	217 33.3	55.2
23	126 26.8	191 03.8	14.4	258 14.6	25.5	313 48.5	43.4	232 35.6	55.2
Mer. Pass. (h m)	14 39.5	v −0.8	d 0.4	v 1.3	d 0.3	v 2.7	d 0.1	v 2.3	d 0.0

STARS

Name	SHA ° ′	Dec ° ′
Acamar	315 17.0	S40 14.8
Achernar	335 25.8	S57 09.7
Acrux	173 06.6	S63 11.1
Adhara	255 10.8	S29 00.0
Aldebaran	290 47.2	N16 32.3
Alioth	166 18.9	N55 52.1
Alkaid	152 57.4	N49 13.8
Al Na'ir	27 42.0	S46 53.0
Alnilam	275 44.3	S 1 11.8
Alphard	217 54.0	S 8 43.9
Alphecca	126 09.5	N26 39.6
Alpheratz	357 41.8	N29 10.8
Altair	62 06.8	N 8 54.7
Ankaa	353 14.3	S42 13.4
Antares	112 24.1	S26 27.8
Arcturus	145 54.0	N19 05.8
Atria	107 24.5	S69 02.9
Avior	234 16.6	S59 33.9
Bellatrix	278 29.9	N 6 21.6
Betelgeuse	270 59.1	N 7 24.3
Canopus	263 54.9	S52 42.7
Capella	280 31.5	N46 00.7
Deneb	49 30.6	N45 20.3
Denebola	182 31.6	N14 28.8
Diphda	348 54.3	S17 54.1
Dubhe	193 49.0	N61 39.6
Elnath	278 10.1	N28 37.1
Eltanin	90 45.6	N51 29.1
Enif	33 45.7	N 9 57.0
Fomalhaut	15 22.4	S29 32.3
Gacrux	171 58.4	S57 12.0
Gienah	175 50.2	S17 37.9
Hadar	148 45.0	S60 26.7
Hamal	327 58.8	N23 32.2
Kaus Aust.	83 41.7	S34 22.3
Kochab	137 20.2	N74 05.1
Markab	13 36.8	N15 17.5
Menkar	314 13.2	N 4 08.9
Menkent	148 05.3	S36 26.7
Miaplacidus	221 38.2	S69 47.2
Mirfak	308 37.7	N49 55.1
Nunki	75 56.4	S26 16.4
Peacock	53 17.1	S56 40.8
Pollux	243 25.2	N27 59.0
Procyon	244 57.5	N 5 10.7
Rasalhague	96 05.0	N12 33.0
Regulus	207 41.3	N11 53.1
Rigel	281 10.1	S 8 11.3
Rigil Kent.	139 49.0	S60 53.7
Sabik	102 10.6	S15 44.5
Schedar	349 38.7	N56 37.7
Shaula	96 19.7	S37 06.6
Sirius	258 31.9	S16 44.7
Spica	158 29.2	S11 14.7
Suhail	222 50.6	S43 30.1
Vega	80 38.0	N38 47.9
Zuben'ubi	137 03.4	S16 06.4

	SHA ° ′	Mer. Pass. h m
Venus	67 11.8	10 14
Mars	132 42.9	5 51
Jupiter	187 11.1	2 13
Saturn	106 17.3	7 36

	UT	SUN GHA	SUN Dec	MOON GHA	v	MOON Dec	d	HP
	d h	° ′	° ′	° ′	′	° ′	′	′
	9 00	176 27.6	S14 55.2	172 11.4	7.9	S10 58.9	9.2	59.7
	01	191 27.6	54.4	186 38.3	7.9	10 49.7	9.3	59.7
	02	206 27.6	53.6	201 05.2	7.9	10 40.4	9.4	59.7
	03	221 27.5	. . 52.8	215 32.1	7.9	10 31.0	9.4	59.7
	04	236 27.5	52.0	229 59.0	7.9	10 21.6	9.5	59.8
	05	251 27.5	51.2	244 25.9	7.9	10 12.1	9.6	59.8
	06	266 27.5	S14 50.4	258 52.8	8.0	S10 02.5	9.6	59.8
	07	281 27.4	49.6	273 19.8	7.9	9 52.9	9.7	59.8
T	08	296 27.4	48.8	287 46.7	8.0	9 43.2	9.8	59.8
U	09	311 27.4	. . 48.0	302 13.7	8.0	9 33.4	9.8	59.8
E	10	326 27.4	47.2	316 40.7	8.0	9 23.6	9.9	59.9
S	11	341 27.4	46.4	331 07.7	8.0	9 13.7	10.0	59.9
	12	356 27.3	S14 45.6	345 34.7	8.1	S 9 03.7	10.0	59.9
D	13	11 27.3	44.8	0 01.8	8.0	8 53.7	10.1	59.9
A	14	26 27.3	44.0	14 28.8	8.1	8 43.6	10.2	59.9
Y	15	41 27.3	. . 43.2	28 55.9	8.1	8 33.4	10.2	59.9
	16	56 27.3	42.4	43 23.0	8.1	8 23.2	10.2	59.9
	17	71 27.2	41.6	57 50.1	8.1	8 13.0	10.4	60.0
	18	86 27.2	S14 40.8	72 17.2	8.1	S 8 02.6	10.3	60.0
	19	101 27.2	40.0	86 44.3	8.2	7 52.3	10.5	60.0
	20	116 27.2	39.2	101 11.5	8.2	7 41.8	10.4	60.0
	21	131 27.2	. . 38.4	115 38.7	8.1	7 31.4	10.6	60.0
	22	146 27.2	37.6	130 05.8	8.2	7 20.8	10.5	60.0
	23	161 27.1	36.8	144 33.0	8.3	7 10.3	10.7	60.0
	10 00	176 27.1	S14 36.0	159 00.3	8.2	S 6 59.6	10.6	60.0
	01	191 27.1	35.2	173 27.5	8.2	6 49.0	10.8	60.1
	02	206 27.1	34.4	187 54.7	8.3	6 38.2	10.7	60.1
	03	221 27.1	. . 33.6	202 22.0	8.3	6 27.5	10.8	60.1
	04	236 27.1	32.7	216 49.3	8.3	6 16.7	10.9	60.1
	05	251 27.0	31.9	231 16.6	8.3	6 05.8	10.8	60.1
	06	266 27.0	S14 31.1	245 43.9	8.3	S 5 55.0	11.0	60.1
W	07	281 27.0	30.3	260 11.2	8.4	5 44.0	10.9	60.1
E	08	296 27.0	29.5	274 38.6	8.3	5 33.1	11.0	60.1
D	09	311 27.0	. . 28.7	289 05.9	8.4	5 22.1	11.1	60.1
N	10	326 27.0	27.9	303 33.3	8.4	5 11.0	11.0	60.1
E	11	341 27.0	27.1	318 00.7	8.4	5 00.0	11.1	60.1
S	12	356 26.9	S14 26.3	332 28.1	8.4	S 4 48.9	11.1	60.1
D	13	11 26.9	25.5	346 55.5	8.4	4 37.8	11.2	60.1
A	14	26 26.9	24.7	1 22.9	8.5	4 26.6	11.2	60.2
Y	15	41 26.9	. . 23.9	15 50.4	8.5	4 15.4	11.2	60.2
	16	56 26.9	23.0	30 17.9	8.4	4 04.2	11.2	60.2
	17	71 26.9	22.2	44 45.3	8.5	3 53.0	11.3	60.2
	18	86 26.9	S14 21.4	59 12.8	8.5	S 3 41.7	11.3	60.2
	19	101 26.9	20.6	73 40.3	8.5	3 30.4	11.3	60.2
	20	116 26.9	19.8	88 07.8	8.6	3 19.1	11.3	60.2
	21	131 26.9	. . 19.0	102 35.4	8.5	3 07.8	11.4	60.2
	22	146 26.8	18.2	117 02.9	8.5	2 56.4	11.4	60.2
	23	161 26.8	17.4	131 30.4	8.6	2 45.0	11.3	60.2
	11 00	176 26.8	S14 16.5	145 58.0	8.6	S 2 33.7	11.4	60.2
	01	191 26.8	15.7	160 25.6	8.6	2 22.3	11.5	60.2
	02	206 26.8	14.9	174 53.2	8.6	2 10.8	11.4	60.2
	03	221 26.8	. . 14.1	189 20.8	8.6	1 59.4	11.4	60.2
	04	236 26.8	13.3	203 48.4	8.6	1 48.0	11.5	60.2
	05	251 26.8	12.5	218 16.0	8.6	1 36.5	11.4	60.2
	06	266 26.8	S14 11.6	232 43.6	8.6	S 1 25.1	11.5	60.2
	07	281 26.8	10.8	247 11.2	8.7	1 13.6	11.5	60.2
T	08	296 26.8	10.0	261 38.9	8.6	1 02.1	11.4	60.2
H	09	311 26.8	. . 09.2	276 06.5	8.7	0 50.7	11.5	60.2
U	10	326 26.8	08.4	290 34.2	8.7	0 39.2	11.5	60.2
R	11	341 26.8	07.5	305 01.9	8.6	0 27.7	11.5	60.2
S	12	356 26.8	S14 06.7	319 29.5	8.7	S 0 16.2	11.4	60.2
D	13	11 26.7	05.9	333 57.2	8.7	S 0 04.8	11.5	60.2
	14	26 26.7	05.1	348 24.9	8.7	N 0 06.7	11.5	60.2
A	15	41 26.7	. . 04.3	2 52.6	8.7	0 18.2	11.5	60.2
Y	16	56 26.7	03.4	17 20.3	8.7	0 29.7	11.4	60.1
	17	71 26.7	02.6	31 48.0	8.8	0 41.1	11.5	60.1
	18	86 26.7	S14 01.8	46 15.8	8.7	N 0 52.6	11.4	60.1
	19	101 26.7	01.0	60 43.5	8.7	1 04.0	11.5	60.1
	20	116 26.7	14 00.2	75 11.2	8.7	1 15.5	11.4	60.1
	21	131 26.7	13 59.3	89 38.9	8.8	1 26.9	11.4	60.1
	22	146 26.7	58.5	104 06.7	8.7	1 38.3	11.4	60.1
	23	161 26.7	57.7	118 34.4	8.8	N 1 49.7	11.4	60.1
		SD 16.2	*d* 0.8	SD 16.3		16.4		16.4

Lat.	Twilight Naut.	Twilight Civil	Sunrise	Moonrise 9	Moonrise 10	Moonrise 11	Moonrise 12
°	h m	h m	h m	h m	h m	h m	h m
N 72	06 38	08 00	09 27	08 58	08 53	08 48	08 43
N 70	06 33	07 47	09 01	08 43	08 45	08 47	08 48
68	06 30	07 37	08 41	08 31	08 39	08 46	08 52
66	06 26	07 28	08 26	08 21	08 34	08 45	08 55
64	06 24	07 20	08 13	08 13	08 29	08 44	08 58
62	06 21	07 14	08 02	08 06	08 25	08 43	09 01
60	06 19	07 08	07 53	07 59	08 22	08 42	09 03
N 58	06 16	07 03	07 45	07 54	08 19	08 42	09 05
56	06 14	06 58	07 38	07 49	08 16	08 41	09 06
54	06 12	06 54	07 31	07 44	08 14	08 41	09 08
52	06 10	06 50	07 26	07 40	08 11	08 41	09 09
50	06 08	06 46	07 20	07 36	08 09	08 40	09 11
45	06 04	06 39	07 09	07 28	08 05	08 39	09 14
N 40	06 00	06 32	07 00	07 22	08 01	08 39	09 16
35	05 56	06 26	06 52	07 16	07 58	08 38	09 18
30	05 52	06 20	06 45	07 11	07 55	08 38	09 20
20	05 43	06 09	06 32	07 02	07 50	08 37	09 23
N 10	05 34	06 00	06 21	06 54	07 46	08 36	09 26
0	05 25	05 49	06 11	06 47	07 41	08 35	09 29
S 10	05 13	05 38	06 00	06 40	07 37	08 35	09 32
20	04 59	05 26	05 49	06 32	07 33	08 34	09 35
30	04 40	05 11	05 36	06 23	07 28	08 33	09 38
35	04 29	05 01	05 28	06 18	07 25	08 33	09 40
40	04 15	04 50	05 19	06 12	07 22	08 32	09 42
45	03 57	04 37	05 09	06 05	07 18	08 32	09 45
S 50	03 34	04 20	04 57	05 57	07 13	08 31	09 48
52	03 22	04 12	04 51	05 53	07 11	08 31	09 50
54	03 09	04 03	04 44	05 49	07 09	08 30	09 52
56	02 53	03 53	04 37	05 44	07 07	08 30	09 53
58	02 33	03 41	04 29	05 39	07 04	08 30	09 55
S 60	02 08	03 27	04 20	05 33	07 01	08 29	09 58

Lat.	Sunset	Twilight Civil	Twilight Naut.	Moonset 9	Moonset 10	Moonset 11	Moonset 12
°	h m	h m	h m	h m	h m	h m	h m
N 72	15 03	16 30	17 53	17 22	19 21	21 19	23 15
N 70	15 29	16 43	17 57	17 36	19 26	21 17	23 06
68	15 48	16 53	18 00	17 46	19 31	21 15	22 59
66	16 04	17 02	18 03	17 55	19 34	21 14	22 52
64	16 16	17 09	18 06	18 02	19 37	21 13	22 47
62	16 27	17 16	18 09	18 08	19 40	21 12	22 43
60	16 36	17 22	18 11	18 14	19 42	21 11	22 39
N 58	16 44	17 27	18 13	18 18	19 44	21 10	22 35
56	16 52	17 31	18 15	18 23	19 46	21 09	22 32
54	16 58	17 35	18 17	18 26	19 47	21 09	22 29
52	17 04	17 39	18 19	18 30	19 49	21 08	22 27
50	17 09	17 43	18 21	18 33	19 50	21 08	22 25
45	17 20	17 50	18 25	18 39	19 53	21 07	22 20
N 40	17 29	17 57	18 29	18 45	19 55	21 06	22 16
35	17 37	18 03	18 33	18 50	19 57	21 05	22 12
30	17 44	18 09	18 37	18 54	19 59	21 04	22 09
20	17 56	18 19	18 45	19 01	20 02	21 03	22 04
N 10	18 07	18 29	18 54	19 07	20 05	21 02	21 59
0	18 18	18 39	19 04	19 13	20 07	21 01	21 54
S 10	18 28	18 50	19 15	19 19	20 09	21 00	21 50
20	18 39	19 02	19 29	19 25	20 12	20 59	21 45
30	18 52	19 17	19 47	19 32	20 15	20 57	21 40
35	19 00	19 27	19 59	19 35	20 16	20 56	21 37
40	19 08	19 37	20 13	19 40	20 18	20 56	21 33
45	19 18	19 51	20 30	19 45	20 20	20 55	21 29
S 50	19 31	20 07	20 53	19 51	20 23	20 53	21 24
52	19 37	20 15	21 04	19 54	20 24	20 53	21 22
54	19 43	20 24	21 17	19 57	20 25	20 52	21 20
56	19 50	20 34	21 33	20 00	20 27	20 52	21 17
58	19 58	20 45	21 52	20 04	20 28	20 51	21 14
S 60	20 07	20 59	22 16	20 08	20 30	20 50	21 11

Day	SUN Eqn. of Time 00^h	SUN Eqn. of Time 12^h	SUN Mer. Pass.	MOON Mer. Pass. Upper	MOON Mer. Pass. Lower	MOON Age	MOON Phase
d	m s	m s	h m	h m	h m	d	%
9	14 09	14 11	12 14	13 00	00 32	01	1
10	14 11	14 12	12 14	13 54	01 27	02	5
11	14 13	14 13	12 14	14 48	02 21	03	11

d	h	ARIES GHA	VENUS −3·9 GHA	VENUS Dec	MARS +0·6 GHA	MARS Dec	JUPITER −2·4 GHA	JUPITER Dec	SATURN +0·5 GHA	SATURN Dec
		° ′	° ′	° ′	° ′	° ′	° ′	° ′	° ′	° ′
12	00	141 29.3	206 03.0	S21 14.0	273 15.9	S16 25.9	328 51.1	N 4 43.5	247 37.9	S20 55.3
	01	156 31.7	221 02.2	13.6	288 17.2	26.2	343 53.8	43.6	262 40.2	55.3
	02	171 34.2	236 01.3	13.2	303 18.5	26.5	358 56.5	43.7	277 42.4	55.3
	03	186 36.7	251 00.5	. . 12.8	318 19.8	. . 26.8	13 59.2	. . 43.8	292 44.7	. . 55.3
	04	201 39.1	265 59.7	12.4	333 21.1	27.1	29 01.9	43.9	307 47.0	55.3
	05	216 41.6	280 58.9	12.0	348 22.4	27.5	44 04.6	44.1	322 49.3	55.3
	06	231 44.1	295 58.0	S21 11.6	3 23.7	S16 27.8	59 07.3	N 4 44.2	337 51.6	S20 55.3
	07	246 46.5	310 57.2	11.2	18 25.0	28.1	74 10.0	44.3	352 53.9	55.4
	08	261 49.0	325 56.4	10.7	33 26.3	28.4	89 12.7	44.4	7 56.2	55.4
F	09	276 51.5	340 55.6	. . 10.3	48 27.6	. . 28.7	104 15.4	. . 44.5	22 58.5	. . 55.4
R	10	291 53.9	355 54.8	09.9	63 28.9	29.0	119 18.1	44.6	38 00.7	55.4
I	11	306 56.4	10 53.9	09.5	78 30.2	29.4	134 20.8	44.7	53 03.0	55.4
D	12	321 58.8	25 53.1	S21 09.1	93 31.5	S16 29.7	149 23.5	N 4 44.8	68 05.3	S20 55.4
A	13	337 01.3	40 52.3	08.7	108 32.8	30.0	164 26.2	44.9	83 07.6	55.4
Y	14	352 03.8	55 51.5	08.2	123 34.1	30.3	179 28.9	45.0	98 09.9	55.5
	15	7 06.2	70 50.7	. . 07.8	138 35.4	. . 30.6	194 31.6	. . 45.1	113 12.2	. . 55.5
	16	22 08.7	85 49.9	07.4	153 36.7	30.9	209 34.3	45.2	128 14.5	55.5
	17	37 11.2	100 49.0	07.0	168 38.1	31.3	224 37.0	45.4	143 16.8	55.5
	18	52 13.6	115 48.2	S21 06.5	183 39.4	S16 31.6	239 39.7	N 4 45.5	158 19.0	S20 55.5
	19	67 16.1	130 47.4	06.1	198 40.7	31.9	254 42.4	45.6	173 21.3	55.5
	20	82 18.6	145 46.6	05.7	213 42.0	32.2	269 45.1	45.7	188 23.6	55.5
	21	97 21.0	160 45.8	. . 05.3	228 43.3	. . 32.5	284 47.8	. . 45.8	203 25.9	. . 55.6
	22	112 23.5	175 44.9	04.8	243 44.6	32.8	299 50.5	45.9	218 28.2	55.6
	23	127 26.0	190 44.1	04.4	258 45.9	33.1	314 53.2	46.0	233 30.5	55.6
13	00	142 28.4	205 43.3	S21 04.0	273 47.2	S16 33.5	329 55.9	N 4 46.1	248 32.8	S20 55.6
	01	157 30.9	220 42.5	03.5	288 48.5	33.8	344 58.6	46.2	263 35.1	55.6
	02	172 33.3	235 41.7	03.1	303 49.8	34.1	0 01.3	46.3	278 37.4	55.6
	03	187 35.8	250 40.9	. . 02.7	318 51.1	. . 34.4	15 04.0	. . 46.4	293 39.7	. . 55.6
	04	202 38.3	265 40.1	02.2	333 52.4	34.7	30 06.7	46.6	308 41.9	55.7
	05	217 40.7	280 39.2	01.8	348 53.7	35.0	45 09.4	46.7	323 44.2	55.7
	06	232 43.2	295 38.4	S21 01.3	3 55.0	S16 35.3	60 12.1	N 4 46.8	338 46.5	S20 55.7
	07	247 45.7	310 37.6	00.9	18 56.3	35.6	75 14.8	46.9	353 48.8	55.7
S	08	262 48.1	325 36.8	00.5	33 57.6	36.0	90 17.5	47.0	8 51.1	55.7
A	09	277 50.6	340 36.0	21 00.0	48 58.9	. . 36.3	105 20.2	. . 47.1	23 53.4	. . 55.7
T	10	292 53.1	355 35.2	20 59.6	64 00.2	36.6	120 22.9	47.2	38 55.7	55.7
U	11	307 55.5	10 34.4	59.1	79 01.5	36.9	135 25.6	47.3	53 58.0	55.7
R	12	322 58.0	25 33.6	S20 58.7	94 02.9	S16 37.2	150 28.3	N 4 47.4	69 00.3	S20 55.8
D	13	338 00.5	40 32.7	58.2	109 04.2	37.5	165 31.0	47.5	84 02.6	55.8
A	14	353 02.9	55 31.9	57.8	124 05.5	37.8	180 33.7	47.7	99 04.9	55.8
Y	15	8 05.4	70 31.1	. . 57.3	139 06.8	. . 38.1	195 36.4	. . 47.8	114 07.1	. . 55.8
	16	23 07.8	85 30.3	56.9	154 08.1	38.5	210 39.1	47.9	129 09.4	55.8
	17	38 10.3	100 29.5	56.4	169 09.4	38.8	225 41.8	48.0	144 11.7	55.8
	18	53 12.8	115 28.7	S20 56.0	184 10.7	S16 39.1	240 44.5	N 4 48.1	159 14.0	S20 55.8
	19	68 15.2	130 27.9	55.5	199 12.0	39.4	255 47.2	48.2	174 16.3	55.9
	20	83 17.7	145 27.1	55.1	214 13.3	39.7	270 49.9	48.3	189 18.6	55.9
	21	98 20.2	160 26.3	. . 54.6	229 14.6	. . 40.0	285 52.6	. . 48.4	204 20.9	. . 55.9
	22	113 22.6	175 25.5	54.2	244 16.0	40.3	300 55.3	48.5	219 23.2	55.9
	23	128 25.1	190 24.6	53.7	259 17.3	40.6	315 58.0	48.7	234 25.5	55.9
14	00	143 27.6	205 23.8	S20 53.3	274 18.6	S16 40.9	331 00.7	N 4 48.8	249 27.8	S20 55.9
	01	158 30.0	220 23.0	52.8	289 19.9	41.3	346 03.4	48.9	264 30.1	55.9
	02	173 32.5	235 22.2	52.3	304 21.2	41.6	1 06.1	49.0	279 32.4	56.0
	03	188 34.9	250 21.4	. . 51.9	319 22.5	. . 41.9	16 08.8	. . 49.1	294 34.7	. . 56.0
	04	203 37.4	265 20.6	51.4	334 23.8	42.2	31 11.5	49.2	309 37.0	56.0
	05	218 39.9	280 19.8	50.9	349 25.1	42.5	46 14.2	49.3	324 39.2	56.0
	06	233 42.3	295 19.0	S20 50.5	4 26.5	S16 42.8	61 16.9	N 4 49.4	339 41.5	S20 56.0
	07	248 44.8	310 18.2	50.0	19 27.8	43.1	76 19.6	49.5	354 43.8	56.0
	08	263 47.3	325 17.4	49.5	34 29.1	43.4	91 22.3	49.7	9 46.1	56.0
S	09	278 49.7	340 16.6	. . 49.1	49 30.4	. . 43.7	106 25.1	. . 49.8	24 48.4	. . 56.0
U	10	293 52.2	355 15.8	48.6	64 31.7	44.0	121 27.8	49.9	39 50.7	56.1
N	11	308 54.7	10 15.0	48.1	79 33.0	44.3	136 30.5	50.0	54 53.0	56.1
D	12	323 57.1	25 14.2	S20 47.7	94 34.3	S16 44.6	151 33.2	N 4 50.1	69 55.3	S20 56.1
A	13	338 59.6	40 13.4	47.2	109 35.7	45.0	166 35.9	50.2	84 57.6	56.1
Y	14	354 02.1	55 12.6	46.7	124 37.0	45.3	181 38.6	50.3	99 59.9	56.1
	15	9 04.5	70 11.8	. . 46.2	139 38.3	. . 45.6	196 41.3	. . 50.4	115 02.2	. . 56.1
	16	24 07.0	85 11.0	45.8	154 39.6	45.9	211 44.0	50.6	130 04.5	56.1
	17	39 09.4	100 10.2	45.3	169 40.9	46.2	226 46.7	50.7	145 06.8	56.1
	18	54 11.9	115 09.4	S20 44.8	184 42.2	S16 46.5	241 49.4	N 4 50.8	160 09.1	S20 56.2
	19	69 14.4	130 08.6	44.3	199 43.6	46.8	256 52.1	50.9	175 11.4	56.2
	20	84 16.8	145 07.8	43.9	214 44.9	47.1	271 54.8	51.0	190 13.7	56.2
	21	99 19.3	160 07.0	. . 43.4	229 46.2	. . 47.4	286 57.5	. . 51.1	205 16.0	. . 56.2
	22	114 21.8	175 06.2	42.9	244 47.5	47.7	302 00.2	51.2	220 18.3	56.2
	23	129 24.2	190 05.3	42.4	259 48.8	48.0	317 03.0	51.3	235 20.6	56.2
Mer. Pass.		h m 14 27.7	v −0.8	d 0.4	v 1.3	d 0.3	v 2.7	d 0.1	v 2.3	d 0.0

STARS Name	SHA	Dec
	° ′	° ′
Acamar	315 17.1	S40 14.8
Achernar	335 25.8	S57 09.7
Acrux	173 06.6	S63 11.1
Adhara	255 10.8	S29 00.0
Aldebaran	290 47.2	N16 32.3
Alioth	166 18.9	N55 52.1
Alkaid	152 57.3	N49 13.8
Al Na'ir	27 42.0	S46 53.0
Alnilam	275 44.4	S 1 11.8
Alphard	217 54.0	S 8 43.9
Alphecca	126 09.5	N26 39.6
Alpheratz	357 41.9	N29 10.8
Altair	62 06.8	N 8 54.7
Ankaa	353 14.3	S42 13.4
Antares	112 24.1	S26 27.8
Arcturus	145 54.0	N19 05.8
Atria	107 24.5	S69 02.9
Avior	234 16.6	S59 34.0
Bellatrix	278 29.9	N 6 21.6
Betelgeuse	270 59.1	N 7 24.3
Canopus	263 55.0	S52 42.7
Capella	280 31.5	N46 00.7
Deneb	49 30.6	N45 20.3
Denebola	182 31.6	N14 28.8
Diphda	348 54.3	S17 54.1
Dubhe	193 49.0	N61 39.6
Elnath	278 10.1	N28 37.1
Eltanin	90 45.6	N51 29.1
Enif	33 45.7	N 9 56.9
Fomalhaut	15 22.4	S29 32.3
Gacrux	171 58.3	S57 12.0
Gienah	175 50.2	S17 37.9
Hadar	148 44.9	S60 26.7
Hamal	327 58.8	N23 32.2
Kaus Aust.	83 41.7	S34 22.3
Kochab	137 20.1	N74 05.1
Markab	13 36.8	N15 17.5
Menkar	314 13.2	N 4 08.9
Menkent	148 05.2	S36 26.7
Miaplacidus	221 38.2	S69 47.2
Mirfak	308 37.7	N49 55.1
Nunki	75 56.4	S26 16.4
Peacock	53 17.0	S56 40.8
Pollux	243 25.2	N27 59.0
Procyon	244 57.6	N 5 10.7
Rasalhague	96 04.9	N12 32.9
Regulus	207 41.3	N11 53.1
Rigel	281 10.2	S 8 11.3
Rigil Kent.	139 49.0	S60 53.7
Sabik	102 10.6	S15 44.5
Schedar	349 38.7	N56 37.6
Shaula	96 19.7	S37 06.6
Sirius	258 31.9	S16 44.7
Spica	158 29.2	S11 14.7
Suhail	222 50.6	S43 30.1
Vega	80 38.0	N38 47.9
Zuben'ubi	137 03.3	S16 06.4

	SHA	Mer. Pass.
	° ′	h m
Venus	63 14.9	10 18
Mars	131 18.8	5 44
Jupiter	187 27.4	2 00
Saturn	106 04.4	7 25

UT d	h	SUN GHA ° ′	SUN Dec ° ′	MOON GHA ° ′	v ′	MOON Dec ° ′	d ′	HP ′
12	00	176 26.7	S13 56.9	133 02.2	8.7	N 2 01.1	11.4	60.1
	01	191 26.7	56.0	147 29.9	8.8	2 12.5	11.3	60.1
	02	206 26.7	55.2	161 57.7	8.7	2 23.8	11.4	60.1
	03	221 26.7	. . 54.4	176 25.4	8.8	2 35.2	11.3	60.1
	04	236 26.7	53.6	190 53.2	8.7	2 46.5	11.3	60.1
	05	251 26.7	52.7	205 20.9	8.8	2 57.8	11.2	60.1
	06	266 26.7	S13 51.9	219 48.7	8.7	N 3 09.0	11.3	60.0
	07	281 26.7	51.1	234 16.4	8.8	3 20.3	11.2	60.0
	08	296 26.7	50.3	248 44.2	8.8	3 31.5	11.2	60.0
F	09	311 26.7	. . 49.4	263 12.0	8.7	3 42.7	11.2	60.0
R	10	326 26.7	48.6	277 39.7	8.8	3 53.9	11.1	60.0
I	11	341 26.7	47.8	292 07.5	8.7	4 05.0	11.1	60.0
D	12	356 26.7	S13 46.9	306 35.2	8.8	N 4 16.1	11.1	60.0
A	13	11 26.8	46.1	321 03.0	8.7	4 27.2	11.0	60.0
Y	14	26 26.8	45.3	335 30.7	8.8	4 38.2	11.0	60.0
	15	41 26.8	. . 44.5	349 58.5	8.7	4 49.2	11.0	60.0
	16	56 26.8	43.6	4 26.2	8.8	5 00.2	11.0	59.9
	17	71 26.8	42.8	18 54.0	8.7	5 11.2	10.9	59.9
	18	86 26.8	S13 42.0	33 21.7	8.8	N 5 22.1	10.8	59.9
	19	101 26.8	41.1	47 49.5	8.7	5 32.9	10.9	59.9
	20	116 26.8	40.3	62 17.2	8.8	5 43.8	10.7	59.9
	21	131 26.8	. . 39.5	76 45.0	8.7	5 54.5	10.8	59.9
	22	146 26.8	38.6	91 12.7	8.7	6 05.3	10.7	59.9
	23	161 26.8	37.8	105 40.4	8.7	6 16.0	10.6	59.8
13	00	176 26.8	S13 37.0	120 08.1	8.7	N 6 26.6	10.7	59.8
	01	191 26.8	36.1	134 35.8	8.7	6 37.3	10.5	59.8
	02	206 26.8	35.3	149 03.5	8.7	6 47.8	10.5	59.8
	03	221 26.8	. . 34.5	163 31.2	8.7	6 58.3	10.5	59.8
	04	236 26.9	33.6	177 58.9	8.7	7 08.8	10.4	59.8
	05	251 26.9	32.8	192 26.6	8.7	7 19.2	10.4	59.8
	06	266 26.9	S13 32.0	206 54.3	8.7	N 7 29.6	10.3	59.7
	07	281 26.9	31.1	221 22.0	8.6	7 39.9	10.3	59.7
S	08	296 26.9	30.3	235 49.6	8.7	7 50.2	10.2	59.7
A	09	311 26.9	. . 29.4	250 17.3	8.7	8 00.4	10.2	59.7
T	10	326 26.9	28.6	264 45.0	8.6	8 10.6	10.1	59.7
U	11	341 26.9	27.8	279 12.6	8.6	8 20.7	10.0	59.7
R	12	356 26.9	S13 26.9	293 40.2	8.6	N 8 30.7	10.0	59.6
D	13	11 27.0	26.1	308 07.8	8.7	8 40.7	9.9	59.6
A	14	26 27.0	25.3	322 35.5	8.6	8 50.6	9.9	59.6
Y	15	41 27.0	. . 24.4	337 03.1	8.6	9 00.5	9.8	59.6
	16	56 27.0	23.6	351 30.7	8.6	9 10.3	9.7	59.6
	17	71 27.0	22.7	5 58.3	8.5	9 20.0	9.7	59.6
	18	86 27.0	S13 21.9	20 25.8	8.6	N 9 29.7	9.6	59.5
	19	101 27.0	21.1	34 53.4	8.6	9 39.3	9.6	59.5
	20	116 27.0	20.2	49 21.0	8.5	9 48.9	9.5	59.5
	21	131 27.1	. . 19.4	63 48.5	8.5	9 58.4	9.4	59.5
	22	146 27.1	18.5	78 16.0	8.6	10 07.8	9.4	59.5
	23	161 27.1	17.7	92 43.6	8.5	10 17.2	9.2	59.5
14	00	176 27.1	S13 16.8	107 11.1	8.5	N10 26.4	9.3	59.4
	01	191 27.1	16.0	121 38.6	8.5	10 35.7	9.1	59.4
	02	206 27.1	15.2	136 06.1	8.5	10 44.8	9.1	59.4
	03	221 27.2	. . 14.3	150 33.6	8.4	10 53.9	9.0	59.4
	04	236 27.2	13.5	165 01.0	8.5	11 02.9	8.9	59.4
	05	251 27.2	12.6	179 28.5	8.4	11 11.8	8.8	59.3
	06	266 27.2	S13 11.8	193 55.9	8.5	N11 20.6	8.8	59.3
	07	281 27.2	10.9	208 23.4	8.4	11 29.4	8.7	59.3
	08	296 27.2	10.1	222 50.8	8.4	11 38.1	8.6	59.3
S	09	311 27.3	. . 09.2	237 18.2	8.4	11 46.7	8.6	59.3
U	10	326 27.3	08.4	251 45.6	8.4	11 55.3	8.5	59.2
N	11	341 27.3	07.5	266 13.0	8.4	12 03.8	8.3	59.2
D	12	356 27.3	S13 06.7	280 40.4	8.3	N12 12.1	8.4	59.2
A	13	11 27.3	05.8	295 07.7	8.4	12 20.5	8.2	59.2
Y	14	26 27.4	05.0	309 35.1	8.3	12 28.7	8.1	59.2
	15	41 27.4	. . 04.2	324 02.4	8.4	12 36.8	8.1	59.1
	16	56 27.4	03.3	338 29.8	8.3	12 44.9	8.0	59.1
	17	71 27.4	02.5	352 57.1	8.3	12 52.9	7.9	59.1
	18	86 27.5	S13 01.6	7 24.4	8.3	N13 00.8	7.8	59.1
	19	101 27.5	13 00.8	21 51.7	8.3	13 08.6	7.7	59.1
	20	116 27.5	12 59.9	36 19.0	8.3	13 16.3	7.7	59.0
	21	131 27.5	. . 59.1	50 46.3	8.2	13 24.0	7.5	59.0
	22	146 27.5	58.2	65 13.5	8.3	13 31.5	7.5	59.0
	23	161 27.6	57.4	79 40.8	8.2	N13 39.0	7.4	59.0
		SD 16.2	*d* 0.8	SD	16.3	16.3		16.1

Lat.	Twilight Naut.	Twilight Civil	Sunrise	Moonrise 12	13	14	15
°	h m	h m	h m	h m	h m	h m	h m
N 72	06 25	07 46	09 09	08 43	08 39	08 34	08 29
N 70	06 22	07 35	08 46	08 48	08 50	08 53	08 59
68	06 20	07 26	08 29	08 52	08 59	09 08	09 22
66	06 18	07 18	08 15	08 55	09 07	09 21	09 40
64	06 15	07 12	08 03	08 58	09 13	09 32	09 54
62	06 14	07 06	07 54	09 01	09 19	09 40	10 07
60	06 12	07 01	07 45	09 03	09 24	09 48	10 17
N 58	06 10	06 56	07 38	09 05	09 29	09 55	10 26
56	06 08	06 52	07 31	09 06	09 32	10 01	10 34
54	06 07	06 48	07 25	09 08	09 36	10 07	10 41
52	06 05	06 45	07 20	09 09	09 39	10 12	10 48
50	06 04	06 42	07 15	09 11	09 42	10 16	10 54
45	06 00	06 35	07 05	09 14	09 49	10 26	11 06
N 40	05 56	06 28	06 56	09 16	09 54	10 34	11 17
35	05 53	06 23	06 49	09 18	09 59	10 41	11 26
30	05 49	06 18	06 42	09 20	10 03	10 47	11 34
20	05 42	06 08	06 31	09 23	10 10	10 58	11 47
N 10	05 34	05 59	06 20	09 26	10 16	11 07	11 59
0	05 25	05 50	06 11	09 29	10 22	11 16	12 11
S 10	05 14	05 39	06 01	09 32	10 29	11 25	12 22
20	05 01	05 28	05 50	09 35	10 35	11 35	12 34
30	04 43	05 13	05 38	09 38	10 43	11 46	12 48
35	04 32	05 04	05 31	09 40	10 47	11 53	12 56
40	04 19	04 54	05 23	09 42	10 52	12 00	13 06
45	04 02	04 42	05 13	09 45	10 58	12 09	13 17
S 50	03 41	04 26	05 02	09 48	11 05	12 19	13 30
52	03 30	04 19	04 56	09 50	11 08	12 24	13 36
54	03 18	04 10	04 51	09 52	11 11	12 29	13 43
56	03 03	04 01	04 44	09 53	11 15	12 35	13 51
58	02 45	03 50	04 36	09 55	11 20	12 42	13 59
S 60	02 23	03 37	04 28	09 58	11 25	12 49	14 09

Lat.	Sunset	Twilight Civil	Twilight Naut.	Moonset 12	13	14	15
°	h m	h m	h m	h m	h m	h m	h m
N 72	15 21	16 44	18 05	23 15	25 12	01 12	03 11
N 70	15 44	16 55	18 08	23 06	24 55	00 55	02 41
68	16 01	17 04	18 10	22 59	24 41	00 41	02 20
66	16 15	17 12	18 12	22 52	24 29	00 29	02 03
64	16 26	17 18	18 14	22 47	24 20	00 20	01 49
62	16 36	17 24	18 16	22 43	24 12	00 12	01 37
60	16 44	17 29	18 18	22 39	24 05	00 05	01 27
N 58	16 52	17 33	18 20	22 35	23 59	25 19	01 19
56	16 58	17 37	18 21	22 32	23 53	25 11	01 11
54	17 04	17 41	18 23	22 29	23 48	25 04	01 04
52	17 09	17 44	18 24	22 27	23 44	24 58	00 58
50	17 14	17 48	18 26	22 25	23 40	24 53	00 53
45	17 24	17 55	18 29	22 20	23 31	24 41	00 41
N 40	17 33	18 01	18 32	22 16	23 24	24 32	00 32
35	17 40	18 06	18 36	22 12	23 18	24 23	00 23
30	17 47	18 11	18 39	22 09	23 13	24 16	00 16
20	17 58	18 21	18 47	22 04	23 04	24 03	00 03
N 10	18 08	18 30	18 55	21 59	22 56	23 52	24 49
0	18 18	18 39	19 04	21 54	22 48	23 42	24 37
S 10	18 27	18 49	19 14	21 50	22 40	23 32	24 25
20	18 38	19 01	19 27	21 45	22 32	23 21	24 11
30	18 50	19 15	19 44	21 40	22 23	23 09	23 56
35	18 57	19 23	19 55	21 37	22 18	23 01	23 48
40	19 05	19 34	20 08	21 33	22 12	22 53	23 38
45	19 14	19 46	20 25	21 29	22 05	22 44	23 26
S 50	19 25	20 01	20 46	21 24	21 57	22 32	23 12
52	19 31	20 08	20 56	21 22	21 53	22 27	23 06
54	19 37	20 17	21 09	21 20	21 49	22 21	22 59
56	19 43	20 26	21 23	21 17	21 44	22 15	22 51
58	19 50	20 37	21 40	21 14	21 39	22 07	22 42
S 60	19 59	20 49	22 01	21 11	21 33	21 59	22 31

Day	SUN Eqn. of Time 00^h	SUN Eqn. of Time 12^h	SUN Mer. Pass.	MOON Mer. Pass. Upper	MOON Mer. Pass. Lower	MOON Age	MOON Phase
d	m s	m s	h m	h m	h m	d %	
12	14 13	14 13	12 14	15 42	03 15	04 20	
13	14 13	14 12	12 14	16 35	04 08	05 30	
14	14 12	14 11	12 14	17 29	05 02	06 41	

UT	ARIES	VENUS −3·9		MARS +0·6		JUPITER −2·4		SATURN +0·5	
	GHA	GHA	Dec	GHA	Dec	GHA	Dec	GHA	Dec
d h	° ′	° ′	° ′	° ′	° ′	° ′	° ′	° ′	° ′
15 00	144 26.7	205 04.6	S20 41.9	274 50.2	S16 48.3	332 05.7	N 4 51.5	250 22.9	S20 56.2
01	159 29.2	220 03.8	41.4	289 51.5	48.6	347 08.4	51.6	265 25.2	56.3
02	174 31.6	235 03.0	41.0	304 52.8	48.9	2 11.1	51.7	280 27.5	56.3
03	189 34.1	250 02.2	. . 40.5	319 54.1	. . 49.2	17 13.8	. . 51.8	295 29.8	. . 56.3
04	204 36.6	265 01.4	40.0	334 55.4	49.5	32 16.5	51.9	310 32.1	56.3
05	219 39.0	280 00.6	39.5	349 56.8	49.8	47 19.2	52.0	325 34.4	56.3
06	234 41.5	294 59.8	S20 39.0	4 58.1	S16 50.1	62 21.9	N 4 52.1	340 36.7	S20 56.3
07	249 43.9	309 59.0	38.5	19 59.4	50.5	77 24.6	52.2	355 38.9	56.3
08	264 46.4	324 58.2	38.0	35 00.7	50.8	92 27.3	52.4	10 41.2	56.3
M 09	279 48.9	339 57.4	. . 37.5	50 02.0	. . 51.1	107 30.0	. . 52.5	25 43.5	. . 56.4
O 10	294 51.3	354 56.6	37.0	65 03.4	51.4	122 32.8	52.6	40 45.8	56.4
N 11	309 53.8	9 55.8	36.5	80 04.7	51.7	137 35.5	52.7	55 48.1	56.4
D 12	324 56.3	24 55.0	S20 36.0	95 06.0	S16 52.0	152 38.2	N 4 52.8	70 50.4	S20 56.4
A 13	339 58.7	39 54.2	35.5	110 07.3	52.3	167 40.9	52.9	85 52.7	56.4
Y 14	355 01.2	54 53.4	35.0	125 08.6	52.6	182 43.6	53.0	100 55.0	56.4
15	10 03.7	69 52.6	. . 34.5	140 10.0	. . 52.9	197 46.3	. . 53.2	115 57.3	. . 56.4
16	25 06.1	84 51.8	34.0	155 11.3	53.2	212 49.0	53.3	130 59.6	56.4
17	40 08.6	99 51.0	33.5	170 12.6	53.5	227 51.7	53.4	146 01.9	56.5
18	55 11.0	114 50.2	S20 33.0	185 13.9	S16 53.8	242 54.4	N 4 53.5	161 04.2	S20 56.5
19	70 13.5	129 49.4	32.5	200 15.3	54.1	257 57.2	53.6	176 06.5	56.5
20	85 16.0	144 48.6	32.0	215 16.6	54.4	272 59.9	53.7	191 08.8	56.5
21	100 18.4	159 47.8	. . 31.5	230 17.9	. . 54.7	288 02.6	. . 53.8	206 11.1	. . 56.5
22	115 20.9	174 47.0	31.0	245 19.2	55.0	303 05.3	54.0	221 13.4	56.5
23	130 23.4	189 46.3	30.5	260 20.6	55.3	318 08.0	54.1	236 15.7	56.5
16 00	145 25.8	204 45.5	S20 30.0	275 21.9	S16 55.6	333 10.7	N 4 54.2	251 18.0	S20 56.5
01	160 28.3	219 44.7	29.5	290 23.2	55.9	348 13.4	54.3	266 20.3	56.6
02	175 30.8	234 43.9	29.0	305 24.5	56.2	3 16.2	54.4	281 22.6	56.6
03	190 33.2	249 43.1	. . 28.5	320 25.9	. . 56.5	18 18.9	. . 54.5	296 24.9	. . 56.6
04	205 35.7	264 42.3	27.9	335 27.2	56.8	33 21.6	54.6	311 27.2	56.6
05	220 38.2	279 41.5	27.4	350 28.5	57.1	48 24.3	54.8	326 29.5	56.6
06	235 40.6	294 40.7	S20 26.9	5 29.9	S16 57.4	63 27.0	N 4 54.9	341 31.8	S20 56.6
07	250 43.1	309 39.9	26.4	20 31.2	57.7	78 29.7	55.0	356 34.2	56.6
T 08	265 45.5	324 39.1	25.9	35 32.5	58.0	93 32.4	55.1	11 36.5	56.6
U 09	280 48.0	339 38.4	. . 25.4	50 33.8	. . 58.3	108 35.2	. . 55.2	26 38.8	. . 56.7
E 10	295 50.5	354 37.6	24.8	65 35.2	58.6	123 37.9	55.3	41 41.1	56.7
S 11	310 52.9	9 36.8	24.3	80 36.5	58.9	138 40.6	55.5	56 43.4	56.7
D 12	325 55.4	24 36.0	S20 23.8	95 37.8	S16 59.2	153 43.3	N 4 55.6	71 45.7	S20 56.7
A 13	340 57.9	39 35.2	23.3	110 39.2	59.5	168 46.0	55.7	86 48.0	56.7
Y 14	356 00.3	54 34.4	22.7	125 40.5	16 59.8	183 48.7	55.8	101 50.3	56.7
15	11 02.8	69 33.6	. . 22.2	140 41.8	17 00.1	198 51.4	. . 55.9	116 52.6	. . 56.7
16	26 05.3	84 32.8	21.7	155 43.2	00.4	213 54.2	56.0	131 54.9	56.7
17	41 07.7	99 32.1	21.2	170 44.5	00.7	228 56.9	56.1	146 57.2	56.8
18	56 10.2	114 31.3	S20 20.6	185 45.8	S17 01.0	243 59.6	N 4 56.3	161 59.5	S20 56.8
19	71 12.7	129 30.5	20.1	200 47.2	01.3	259 02.3	56.4	177 01.8	56.8
20	86 15.1	144 29.7	19.6	215 48.5	01.6	274 05.0	56.5	192 04.1	56.8
21	101 17.6	159 28.9	. . 19.0	230 49.8	. . 01.9	289 07.7	. . 56.6	207 06.4	. . 56.8
22	116 20.0	174 28.1	18.5	245 51.2	02.2	304 10.5	56.7	222 08.7	56.8
23	131 22.5	189 27.4	18.0	260 52.5	02.5	319 13.2	56.8	237 11.0	56.8
17 00	146 25.0	204 26.6	S20 17.4	275 53.8	S17 02.8	334 15.9	N 4 57.0	252 13.3	S20 56.8
01	161 27.4	219 25.8	16.9	290 55.2	03.0	349 18.6	57.1	267 15.6	56.9
02	176 29.9	234 25.0	16.4	305 56.5	03.3	4 21.3	57.2	282 17.9	56.9
03	191 32.4	249 24.2	. . 15.8	320 57.8	. . 03.6	19 24.0	. . 57.3	297 20.2	. . 56.9
04	206 34.8	264 23.4	15.3	335 59.2	03.9	34 26.8	57.4	312 22.5	56.9
05	221 37.3	279 22.7	14.8	351 00.5	04.2	49 29.5	57.5	327 24.8	56.9
06	236 39.8	294 21.9	S20 14.2	6 01.8	S17 04.5	64 32.2	N 4 57.7	342 27.1	S20 56.9
W 07	251 42.2	309 21.1	13.7	21 03.2	04.8	79 34.9	57.8	357 29.4	56.9
E 08	266 44.7	324 20.3	13.1	36 04.5	05.1	94 37.6	57.9	12 31.7	56.9
D 09	281 47.2	339 19.5	. . 12.6	51 05.8	. . 05.4	109 40.4	. . 58.0	27 34.1	. . 56.9
N 10	296 49.6	354 18.8	12.0	66 07.2	05.7	124 43.1	58.1	42 36.4	57.0
E 11	311 52.1	9 18.0	11.5	81 08.5	06.0	139 45.8	58.2	57 38.7	57.0
S 12	326 54.5	24 17.2	S20 11.0	96 09.8	S17 06.3	154 48.5	N 4 58.4	72 41.0	S20 57.0
S 13	341 57.0	39 16.4	10.4	111 11.2	06.6	169 51.2	58.5	87 43.3	57.0
D 14	356 59.5	54 15.7	09.9	126 12.5	06.9	184 54.0	58.6	102 45.6	57.0
A 15	12 01.9	69 14.9	. . 09.3	141 13.9	. . 07.2	199 56.7	. . 58.7	117 47.9	. . 57.0
Y 16	27 04.4	84 14.1	08.8	156 15.2	07.5	214 59.4	58.8	132 50.2	57.0
17	42 06.9	99 13.3	08.2	171 16.5	07.8	230 02.1	58.9	147 52.5	57.0
18	57 09.3	114 12.6	S20 07.7	186 17.9	S17 08.1	245 04.8	N 4 59.1	162 54.8	S20 57.1
19	72 11.8	129 11.8	07.1	201 19.2	08.3	260 07.6	59.2	177 57.1	57.1
20	87 14.3	144 11.0	06.5	216 20.6	08.6	275 10.3	59.3	192 59.4	57.1
21	102 16.7	159 10.2	. . 06.0	231 21.9	. . 08.9	290 13.0	. . 59.4	208 01.7	. . 57.1
22	117 19.2	174 09.5	05.4	246 23.2	09.2	305 15.7	59.5	223 04.0	57.1
23	132 21.6	189 08.7	04.9	261 24.6	09.5	320 18.4	59.6	238 06.4	57.1
Mer. Pass.	h m 14 15.9	*v* −0.8	*d* 0.5	*v* 1.3	*d* 0.3	*v* 2.7	*d* 0.1	*v* 2.3	*d* 0.0

STARS

Name	SHA	Dec
	° ′	° ′
Acamar	315 17.1	S40 14.8
Achernar	335 25.8	S57 09.7
Acrux	173 06.5	S63 11.1
Adhara	255 10.8	S29 00.0
Aldebaran	290 47.2	N16 32.3
Alioth	166 18.8	N55 52.1
Alkaid	152 57.3	N49 13.8
Al Na'ir	27 42.0	S46 53.0
Alnilam	275 44.4	S 1 11.8
Alphard	217 54.0	S 8 44.0
Alphecca	126 09.5	N26 39.5
Alpheratz	357 41.9	N29 10.8
Altair	62 06.7	N 8 54.7
Ankaa	353 14.3	S42 13.4
Antares	112 24.1	S26 27.8
Arcturus	145 54.0	N19 05.8
Atria	107 24.4	S69 02.9
Avior	234 16.6	S59 34.0
Bellatrix	278 29.9	N 6 21.6
Betelgeuse	270 59.1	N 7 24.3
Canopus	263 55.0	S52 42.7
Capella	280 31.5	N46 00.7
Deneb	49 30.6	N45 20.3
Denebola	182 31.6	N14 28.8
Diphda	348 54.3	S17 54.1
Dubhe	193 49.0	N61 39.6
Elnath	278 10.1	N28 37.1
Eltanin	90 45.6	N51 29.1
Enif	33 45.7	N 9 56.9
Fomalhaut	15 22.4	S29 32.3
Gacrux	171 58.3	S57 12.0
Gienah	175 50.1	S17 37.9
Hadar	148 44.9	S60 26.7
Hamal	327 58.8	N23 32.2
Kaus Aust.	83 41.7	S34 22.3
Kochab	137 20.0	N74 05.1
Markab	13 36.8	N15 17.5
Menkar	314 13.2	N 4 08.9
Menkent	148 05.2	S36 26.7
Miaplacidus	221 38.2	S69 47.2
Mirfak	308 37.7	N49 55.1
Nunki	75 56.3	S26 16.4
Peacock	53 17.0	S56 40.8
Pollux	243 25.2	N27 59.0
Procyon	244 57.6	N 5 10.7
Rasalhague	96 04.9	N12 32.9
Regulus	207 41.3	N11 53.1
Rigel	281 10.2	S 8 11.4
Rigil Kent.	139 48.9	S60 53.7
Sabik	102 10.6	S15 44.5
Schedar	349 38.7	N56 37.6
Shaula	96 19.6	S37 06.6
Sirius	258 31.9	S16 44.7
Spica	158 29.1	S11 14.7
Suhail	222 50.6	S43 30.1
Vega	80 38.0	N38 47.9
Zuben'ubi	137 03.3	S16 06.4

	SHA	Mer. Pass.
	° ′	h m
Venus	59 19.6	10 22
Mars	129 56.1	5 38
Jupiter	187 44.9	1 47
Saturn	105 52.2	7 14

UT d	UT h	SUN GHA	SUN Dec	MOON GHA	v	MOON Dec	d	HP
d	h	° ′	° ′	° ′	′	° ′	′	′
15	00	176 27.6	S12 56.5	94 08.0	8.2	N13 46.4	7.2	58.9
	01	191 27.6	55.6	108 35.2	8.3	13 53.6	7.2	58.9
	02	206 27.6	54.8	123 02.5	8.2	14 00.8	7.1	58.9
	03	221 27.7	. . 53.9	137 29.7	8.2	14 07.9	7.1	58.9
	04	236 27.7	53.1	151 56.9	8.2	14 15.0	6.9	58.9
	05	251 27.7	52.2	166 24.1	8.1	14 21.9	6.8	58.8
	06	266 27.7	S12 51.4	180 51.2	8.2	N14 28.7	6.8	58.8
	07	281 27.8	50.5	195 18.4	8.2	14 35.5	6.6	58.8
	08	296 27.8	49.7	209 45.6	8.1	14 42.1	6.6	58.8
MONDAY	09	311 27.8	. . 48.8	224 12.7	8.2	14 48.7	6.4	58.7
	10	326 27.8	48.0	238 39.9	8.1	14 55.1	6.4	58.7
	11	341 27.9	47.1	253 07.0	8.1	15 01.5	6.3	58.7
	12	356 27.9	S12 46.3	267 34.1	8.1	N15 07.8	6.1	58.7
	13	11 27.9	45.4	282 01.2	8.2	15 13.9	6.1	58.7
	14	26 28.0	44.5	296 28.4	8.1	15 20.0	6.0	58.6
	15	41 28.0	. . 43.7	310 55.5	8.0	15 26.0	5.9	58.6
	16	56 28.0	42.8	325 22.5	8.1	15 31.9	5.8	58.6
	17	71 28.0	42.0	339 49.6	8.1	15 37.7	5.6	58.6
	18	86 28.1	S12 41.1	354 16.7	8.1	N15 43.3	5.6	58.5
	19	101 28.1	40.3	8 43.8	8.1	15 48.9	5.5	58.5
	20	116 28.1	39.4	23 10.9	8.0	15 54.4	5.4	58.5
	21	131 28.2	. . 38.5	37 37.9	8.1	15 59.8	5.3	58.5
	22	146 28.2	37.7	52 05.0	8.0	16 05.1	5.2	58.5
	23	161 28.2	36.8	66 32.0	8.1	16 10.3	5.1	58.4
16	00	176 28.3	S12 36.0	80 59.1	8.0	N16 15.4	4.9	58.4
	01	191 28.3	35.1	95 26.1	8.1	16 20.3	4.9	58.4
	02	206 28.3	34.2	109 53.2	8.0	16 25.2	4.8	58.4
	03	221 28.4	. . 33.4	124 20.2	8.1	16 30.0	4.7	58.3
	04	236 28.4	32.5	138 47.3	8.0	16 34.7	4.5	58.3
	05	251 28.4	31.6	153 14.3	8.0	16 39.2	4.5	58.3
	06	266 28.5	S12 30.8	167 41.3	8.1	N16 43.7	4.4	58.3
	07	281 28.5	29.9	182 08.4	8.0	16 48.1	4.2	58.3
	08	296 28.5	29.1	196 35.4	8.0	16 52.3	4.2	58.2
TUESDAY	09	311 28.6	. . 28.2	211 02.4	8.1	16 56.5	4.0	58.2
	10	326 28.6	27.3	225 29.5	8.0	17 00.5	4.0	58.2
	11	341 28.6	26.5	239 56.5	8.0	17 04.5	3.8	58.2
	12	356 28.7	S12 25.6	254 23.5	8.1	N17 08.3	3.7	58.1
	13	11 28.7	24.7	268 50.6	8.0	17 12.0	3.7	58.1
	14	26 28.7	23.9	283 17.6	8.1	17 15.7	3.5	58.1
	15	41 28.8	. . 23.0	297 44.7	8.0	17 19.2	3.4	58.1
	16	56 28.8	22.1	312 11.7	8.1	17 22.6	3.3	58.1
	17	71 28.8	21.3	326 38.8	8.0	17 25.9	3.2	58.0
	18	86 28.9	S12 20.4	341 05.8	8.1	N17 29.1	3.1	58.0
	19	101 28.9	19.5	355 32.9	8.1	17 32.2	3.0	58.0
	20	116 29.0	18.7	10 00.0	8.0	17 35.2	2.9	58.0
	21	131 29.0	. . 17.8	24 27.0	8.1	17 38.1	2.8	57.9
	22	146 29.0	16.9	38 54.1	8.1	17 40.9	2.6	57.9
	23	161 29.1	16.1	53 21.2	8.1	17 43.5	2.6	57.9
17	00	176 29.1	S12 15.2	67 48.3	8.1	N17 46.1	2.4	57.9
	01	191 29.2	14.3	82 15.4	8.1	17 48.5	2.4	57.8
	02	206 29.2	13.5	96 42.5	8.2	17 50.9	2.2	57.8
	03	221 29.2	. . 12.6	111 09.7	8.1	17 53.1	2.1	57.8
	04	236 29.3	11.7	125 36.8	8.1	17 55.2	2.1	57.8
	05	251 29.3	10.9	140 03.9	8.2	17 57.3	1.9	57.8
	06	266 29.4	S12 10.0	154 31.1	8.2	N17 59.2	1.8	57.7
	07	281 29.4	09.1	168 58.3	8.2	18 01.0	1.7	57.7
	08	296 29.4	08.2	183 25.5	8.2	18 02.7	1.6	57.7
WEDNESDAY	09	311 29.5	. . 07.4	197 52.7	8.2	18 04.3	1.5	57.7
	10	326 29.5	06.5	212 19.9	8.2	18 05.8	1.3	57.6
	11	341 29.6	05.6	226 47.1	8.3	18 07.1	1.3	57.6
	12	356 29.6	S12 04.8	241 14.4	8.2	N18 08.4	1.2	57.6
	13	11 29.6	03.9	255 41.6	8.3	18 09.6	1.0	57.6
	14	26 29.7	03.0	270 08.9	8.3	18 10.6	1.0	57.6
	15	41 29.7	. . 02.1	284 36.2	8.3	18 11.6	0.8	57.5
	16	56 29.8	01.3	299 03.5	8.4	18 12.4	0.7	57.5
	17	71 29.8	12 00.4	313 30.9	8.3	18 13.1	0.7	57.5
	18	86 29.9	S11 59.5	327 58.2	8.4	N18 13.8	0.5	57.5
	19	101 29.9	58.6	342 25.6	8.4	18 14.3	0.4	57.4
	20	116 30.0	57.8	356 53.0	8.5	18 14.7	0.3	57.4
	21	131 30.0	. . 56.9	11 20.5	8.4	18 15.0	0.2	57.4
	22	146 30.1	56.0	25 47.9	8.5	18 15.2	0.1	57.4
	23	161 30.1	55.1	40 15.4	8.5	N18 15.3	0.0	57.4
		SD 16.2	*d* 0.9	SD 16.0		15.8		15.7

Lat.	Twilight Naut.	Twilight Civil	Sunrise	Moonrise 15	Moonrise 16	Moonrise 17	Moonrise 18
°	h m	h m	h m	h m	h m	h m	h m
N 72	06 13	07 32	08 51	08 29	08 23	08 10	▭
N 70	06 11	07 23	08 32	08 59	09 12	09 38	10 30
68	06 10	07 15	08 16	09 22	09 43	10 18	11 11
66	06 08	07 08	08 04	09 40	10 07	10 45	11 39
64	06 07	07 03	07 53	09 54	10 25	11 06	12 00
62	06 06	06 58	07 45	10 07	10 40	11 23	12 17
60	06 05	06 53	07 37	10 17	10 53	11 37	12 31
N 58	06 03	06 49	07 30	10 26	11 04	11 49	12 44
56	06 02	06 46	07 24	10 34	11 13	12 00	12 54
54	06 01	06 42	07 19	10 41	11 22	12 09	13 03
52	06 00	06 39	07 14	10 48	11 30	12 17	13 12
50	05 59	06 37	07 10	10 54	11 36	12 25	13 19
45	05 56	06 30	07 00	11 06	11 51	12 41	13 35
N 40	05 53	06 25	06 52	11 17	12 03	12 54	13 48
35	05 50	06 20	06 46	11 26	12 14	13 05	13 59
30	05 47	06 15	06 40	11 34	12 23	13 15	14 09
20	05 41	06 06	06 29	11 47	12 39	13 32	14 25
N 10	05 33	05 58	06 20	11 59	12 52	13 46	14 40
0	05 25	05 50	06 11	12 11	13 05	14 00	14 54
S 10	05 15	05 40	06 02	12 22	13 18	14 14	15 07
20	05 02	05 29	05 52	12 34	13 32	14 28	15 22
30	04 46	05 16	05 41	12 48	13 48	14 45	15 39
35	04 36	05 08	05 34	12 56	13 58	14 55	15 48
40	04 23	04 58	05 27	13 06	14 08	15 07	16 00
45	04 08	04 46	05 18	13 17	14 21	15 20	16 13
S 50	03 48	04 32	05 07	13 30	14 36	15 36	16 29
52	03 38	04 25	05 02	13 36	14 43	15 44	16 36
54	03 26	04 17	04 57	13 43	14 51	15 52	16 44
56	03 13	04 08	04 51	13 51	15 00	16 02	16 54
58	02 57	03 58	04 44	13 59	15 10	16 13	17 04
S 60	02 37	03 47	04 36	14 09	15 22	16 25	17 16

Lat.	Sunset	Twilight Civil	Twilight Naut.	Moonset 15	Moonset 16	Moonset 17	Moonset 18
°	h m	h m	h m	h m	h m	h m	h m
N 72	15 39	16 58	18 18	03 11	05 11	07 19	▭
N 70	15 58	17 07	18 19	02 41	04 23	05 50	06 51
68	16 13	17 15	18 20	02 20	03 52	05 11	06 10
66	16 26	17 21	18 21	02 03	03 29	04 44	05 42
64	16 36	17 27	18 23	01 49	03 11	04 23	05 21
62	16 45	17 32	18 24	01 37	02 56	04 06	05 04
60	16 52	17 36	18 25	01 27	02 44	03 52	04 49
N 58	16 59	17 40	18 26	01 19	02 33	03 40	04 37
56	17 05	17 43	18 27	01 11	02 24	03 30	04 27
54	17 10	17 47	18 28	01 04	02 16	03 21	04 17
52	17 15	17 50	18 29	00 58	02 08	03 12	04 09
50	17 19	17 52	18 30	00 53	02 02	03 05	04 01
45	17 28	17 59	18 33	00 41	01 48	02 49	03 45
N 40	17 36	18 04	18 36	00 32	01 36	02 37	03 32
35	17 43	18 09	18 39	00 23	01 26	02 26	03 21
30	17 49	18 13	18 42	00 16	01 17	02 16	03 11
20	17 59	18 22	18 48	00 03	01 02	01 59	02 54
N 10	18 09	18 30	18 55	24 49	00 49	01 45	02 40
0	18 17	18 39	19 03	24 37	00 37	01 32	02 26
S 10	18 26	18 48	19 13	24 25	00 25	01 18	02 12
20	18 36	18 59	19 25	24 11	00 11	01 04	01 57
30	18 47	19 12	19 41	23 56	24 47	00 47	01 40
35	18 54	19 20	19 52	23 48	24 37	00 37	01 30
40	19 01	19 29	20 04	23 38	24 27	00 27	01 19
45	19 10	19 41	20 19	23 26	24 14	00 14	01 06
S 50	19 20	19 55	20 39	23 12	23 58	24 49	00 49
52	19 25	20 02	20 49	23 06	23 51	24 42	00 42
54	19 30	20 09	21 00	22 59	23 42	24 33	00 33
56	19 36	20 18	21 13	22 51	23 33	24 24	00 24
58	19 43	20 28	21 28	22 42	23 23	24 13	00 13
S 60	19 50	20 39	21 48	22 31	23 11	24 00	00 00

Day	SUN Eqn. of Time 00^h	SUN Eqn. of Time 12^h	SUN Mer. Pass.	MOON Mer. Pass. Upper	MOON Mer. Pass. Lower	MOON Age	MOON Phase
d	m s	m s	h m	h m	h m	d %	
15	14 10	14 08	12 14	18 24	05 56	07 52	
16	14 07	14 05	12 14	19 18	06 51	08 63	◐
17	14 04	14 02	12 14	20 13	07 46	09 73	

UT	ARIES	VENUS −3·9		MARS +0·5		JUPITER −2·5		SATURN +0·5		STARS		
d h	GHA ° ′	GHA ° ′	Dec ° ′	GHA ° ′	Dec ° ′	GHA ° ′	Dec ° ′	GHA ° ′	Dec ° ′	Name	SHA ° ′	Dec ° ′
18 00	147 24.1	204 07.9	S20 04.3	276 25.9	S17 09.8	335 21.2	N 4 59.8	253 08.7	S20 57.1	Acamar	315 17.1	S40 14.8
01	162 26.6	219 07.1	03.8	291 27.3	10.1	350 23.9	4 59.9	268 11.0	57.1	Achernar	335 25.9	S57 09.7
02	177 29.0	234 06.4	03.2	306 28.6	10.4	5 26.6	5 00.0	283 13.3	57.1	Acrux	173 06.5	S63 11.2
03	192 31.5	249 05.6	. . 02.6	321 29.9	. . 10.7	20 29.3	. . 00.1	298 15.6	. . 57.2	Adhara	255 10.8	S29 00.0
04	207 34.0	264 04.8	02.1	336 31.3	11.0	35 32.1	00.2	313 17.9	57.2	Aldebaran	290 47.2	N16 32.3
05	222 36.4	279 04.0	01.5	351 32.6	11.3	50 34.8	00.4	328 20.2	57.2			
06	237 38.9	294 03.3	S20 00.9	6 34.0	S17 11.6	65 37.5	N 5 00.5	343 22.5	S20 57.2	Alioth	166 18.8	N55 52.1
07	252 41.4	309 02.5	20 00.4	21 35.3	11.8	80 40.2	00.6	358 24.8	57.2	Alkaid	152 57.3	N49 13.8
T 08	267 43.8	324 01.7	19 59.8	36 36.7	12.1	95 42.9	00.7	13 27.1	57.2	Al Na'ir	27 42.0	S46 53.0
H 09	282 46.3	339 01.0	. . 59.2	51 38.0	. . 12.4	110 45.7	. . 00.8	28 29.4	. . 57.2	Alnilam	275 44.4	S 1 11.8
U 10	297 48.8	354 00.2	58.7	66 39.4	12.7	125 48.4	00.9	43 31.8	57.2	Alphard	217 54.0	S 8 44.0
R 11	312 51.2	8 59.4	58.1	81 40.7	13.0	140 51.1	01.1	58 34.1	57.2			
S 12	327 53.7	23 58.6	S19 57.5	96 42.0	S17 13.3	155 53.8	N 5 01.2	73 36.4	S20 57.3	Alphecca	126 09.5	N26 39.5
D 13	342 56.1	38 57.9	56.9	111 43.4	13.6	170 56.6	01.3	88 38.7	57.3	Alpheratz	357 41.9	N29 10.7
A 14	357 58.6	53 57.1	56.4	126 44.7	13.9	185 59.3	01.4	103 41.0	57.3	Altair	62 06.7	N 8 54.7
Y 15	13 01.1	68 56.3	. . 55.8	141 46.1	. . 14.2	201 02.0	. . 01.5	118 43.3	. . 57.3	Ankaa	353 14.3	S42 13.3
16	28 03.5	83 55.6	55.2	156 47.4	14.5	216 04.7	01.7	133 45.6	57.3	Antares	112 24.1	S26 27.8
17	43 06.0	98 54.8	54.7	171 48.8	14.7	231 07.5	01.8	148 47.9	57.3			
18	58 08.5	113 54.0	S19 54.1	186 50.1	S17 15.0	246 10.2	N 5 01.9	163 50.2	S20 57.3	Arcturus	145 54.0	N19 05.8
19	73 10.9	128 53.3	53.5	201 51.5	15.3	261 12.9	02.0	178 52.5	57.3	Atria	107 24.3	S69 02.9
20	88 13.4	143 52.5	52.9	216 52.8	15.6	276 15.6	02.1	193 54.9	57.3	Avior	234 16.6	S59 34.0
21	103 15.9	158 51.7	. . 52.3	231 54.2	. . 15.9	291 18.4	. . 02.2	208 57.2	. . 57.4	Bellatrix	278 29.9	N 6 21.6
22	118 18.3	173 51.0	51.8	246 55.5	16.2	306 21.1	02.4	223 59.5	57.4	Betelgeuse	270 59.2	N 7 24.3
23	133 20.8	188 50.2	51.2	261 56.9	16.5	321 23.8	02.5	239 01.8	57.4			
19 00	148 23.3	203 49.5	S19 50.6	276 58.2	S17 16.8	336 26.5	N 5 02.6	254 04.1	S20 57.4	Canopus	263 55.0	S52 42.7
01	163 25.7	218 48.7	50.0	291 59.6	17.0	351 29.3	02.7	269 06.4	57.4	Capella	280 31.6	N46 00.7
02	178 28.2	233 47.9	49.4	307 00.9	17.3	6 32.0	02.8	284 08.7	57.4	Deneb	49 30.6	N45 20.3
03	193 30.6	248 47.2	. . 48.8	322 02.3	. . 17.6	21 34.7	. . 03.0	299 11.0	. . 57.4	Denebola	182 31.5	N14 28.8
04	208 33.1	263 46.4	48.2	337 03.6	17.9	36 37.4	03.1	314 13.4	57.4	Diphda	348 54.3	S17 54.1
05	223 35.6	278 45.6	47.7	352 05.0	18.2	51 40.2	03.2	329 15.7	57.4			
06	238 38.0	293 44.9	S19 47.1	7 06.3	S17 18.5	66 42.9	N 5 03.3	344 18.0	S20 57.5	Dubhe	193 49.0	N61 39.6
07	253 40.5	308 44.1	46.5	22 07.7	18.8	81 45.6	03.4	359 20.3	57.5	Elnath	278 10.2	N28 37.1
08	268 43.0	323 43.4	45.9	37 09.0	19.1	96 48.3	03.6	14 22.6	57.5	Eltanin	90 45.6	N51 29.1
F 09	283 45.4	338 42.6	. . 45.3	52 10.4	. . 19.3	111 51.1	. . 03.7	29 24.9	. . 57.5	Enif	33 45.6	N 9 56.9
R 10	298 47.9	353 41.8	44.7	67 11.7	19.6	126 53.8	03.8	44 27.2	57.5	Fomalhaut	15 22.4	S29 32.3
I 11	313 50.4	8 41.1	44.1	82 13.1	19.9	141 56.5	03.9	59 29.6	57.5			
D 12	328 52.8	23 40.3	S19 43.5	97 14.4	S17 20.2	156 59.3	N 5 04.0	74 31.9	S20 57.5	Gacrux	171 58.3	S57 12.1
A 13	343 55.3	38 39.6	42.9	112 15.8	20.5	172 02.0	04.2	89 34.2	57.5	Gienah	175 50.1	S17 37.9
Y 14	358 57.8	53 38.8	42.3	127 17.1	20.8	187 04.7	04.3	104 36.5	57.5	Hadar	148 44.9	S60 26.7
15	14 00.2	68 38.0	. . 41.7	142 18.5	. . 21.0	202 07.4	. . 04.4	119 38.8	. . 57.6	Hamal	327 58.8	N23 32.2
16	29 02.7	83 37.3	41.1	157 19.9	21.3	217 10.2	04.5	134 41.1	57.6	Kaus Aust.	83 41.6	S34 22.3
17	44 05.1	98 36.5	40.5	172 21.2	21.6	232 12.9	04.6	149 43.4	57.6			
18	59 07.6	113 35.8	S19 39.9	187 22.6	S17 21.9	247 15.6	N 5 04.8	164 45.8	S20 57.6	Kochab	137 20.0	N74 05.1
19	74 10.1	128 35.0	39.3	202 23.9	22.2	262 18.4	04.9	179 48.1	57.6	Markab	13 36.8	N15 17.5
20	89 12.5	143 34.3	38.7	217 25.3	22.5	277 21.1	05.0	194 50.4	57.6	Menkar	314 13.2	N 4 08.9
21	104 15.0	158 33.5	. . 38.1	232 26.6	. . 22.8	292 23.8	. . 05.1	209 52.7	. . 57.6	Menkent	148 05.2	S36 26.8
22	119 17.5	173 32.7	37.5	247 28.0	23.0	307 26.5	05.2	224 55.0	57.6	Miaplacidus	221 38.2	S69 47.2
23	134 19.9	188 32.0	36.9	262 29.3	23.3	322 29.3	05.4	239 57.3	57.6			
20 00	149 22.4	203 31.2	S19 36.3	277 30.7	S17 23.6	337 32.0	N 5 05.5	254 59.6	S20 57.6	Mirfak	308 37.7	N49 55.1
01	164 24.9	218 30.5	35.7	292 32.1	23.9	352 34.7	05.6	270 02.0	57.7	Nunki	75 56.3	S26 16.4
02	179 27.3	233 29.7	35.1	307 33.4	24.2	7 37.5	05.7	285 04.3	57.7	Peacock	53 17.0	S56 40.8
03	194 29.8	248 29.0	. . 34.5	322 34.8	. . 24.4	22 40.2	. . 05.8	300 06.6	. . 57.7	Pollux	243 25.2	N27 59.0
04	209 32.2	263 28.2	33.8	337 36.1	24.7	37 42.9	06.0	315 08.9	57.7	Procyon	244 57.6	N 5 10.7
05	224 34.7	278 27.5	33.2	352 37.5	25.0	52 45.7	06.1	330 11.2	57.7			
06	239 37.2	293 26.7	S19 32.6	7 38.9	S17 25.3	67 48.4	N 5 06.2	345 13.5	S20 57.7	Rasalhague	96 04.9	N12 32.9
07	254 39.6	308 26.0	32.0	22 40.2	25.6	82 51.1	06.3	0 15.9	57.7	Regulus	207 41.3	N11 53.1
S 08	269 42.1	323 25.2	31.4	37 41.6	25.9	97 53.8	06.4	15 18.2	57.7	Rigel	281 10.2	S 8 11.4
A 09	284 44.6	338 24.5	. . 30.8	52 42.9	. . 26.1	112 56.6	. . 06.6	30 20.5	. . 57.7	Rigil Kent.	139 48.9	S60 53.7
T 10	299 47.0	353 23.7	30.2	67 44.3	26.4	127 59.3	06.7	45 22.8	57.8	Sabik	102 10.6	S15 44.5
U 11	314 49.5	8 23.0	29.5	82 45.7	26.7	143 02.0	06.8	60 25.1	57.8			
R 12	329 52.0	23 22.2	S19 28.9	97 47.0	S17 27.0	158 04.8	N 5 06.9	75 27.5	S20 57.8	Schedar	349 38.7	N56 37.6
D 13	344 54.4	38 21.5	28.3	112 48.4	27.3	173 07.5	07.1	90 29.8	57.8	Shaula	96 19.6	S37 06.6
A 14	359 56.9	53 20.7	27.7	127 49.7	27.5	188 10.2	07.2	105 32.1	57.8	Sirius	258 31.9	S16 44.7
Y 15	14 59.4	68 20.0	. . 27.0	142 51.1	. . 27.8	203 13.0	. . 07.3	120 34.4	. . 57.8	Spica	158 29.1	S11 14.7
16	30 01.8	83 19.2	26.4	157 52.5	28.1	218 15.7	07.4	135 36.7	57.8	Suhail	222 50.6	S43 30.1
17	45 04.3	98 18.5	25.8	172 53.8	28.4	233 18.4	07.5	150 39.0	57.8			
18	60 06.7	113 17.7	S19 25.2	187 55.2	S17 28.7	248 21.2	N 5 07.7	165 41.4	S20 57.8	Vega	80 38.0	N38 47.9
19	75 09.2	128 17.0	24.5	202 56.6	28.9	263 23.9	07.8	180 43.7	57.8	Zuben'ubi	137 03.3	S16 06.4
20	90 11.7	143 16.2	23.9	217 57.9	29.2	278 26.6	07.9	195 46.0	57.9			
21	105 14.1	158 15.5	. . 23.3	232 59.3	. . 29.5	293 29.4	. . 08.0	210 48.3	. . 57.9			
22	120 16.6	173 14.7	22.7	248 00.7	29.8	308 32.1	08.1	225 50.6	57.9			
23	135 19.1	188 14.0	22.0	263 02.0	30.1	323 34.8	08.3	240 53.0	57.9			
Mer. Pass.	h m 14 04.1	v −0.8	d 0.6	v 1.4	d 0.3	v 2.7	d 0.1	v 2.3	d 0.0			

	SHA ° ′	Mer. Pass. h m
Venus	55 26.2	10 25
Mars	128 35.0	5 32
Jupiter	188 03.3	1 34
Saturn	105 40.9	7 03

UT	SUN GHA	SUN Dec	MOON GHA	v	MOON Dec	d	HP
d h	° ′	° ′	° ′	′	° ′	′	′
18 00 (THURSDAY)	176 30.1	S11 54.3	54 42.9	8.5	N18 15.3	0.1	57.3
01	191 30.2	53.4	69 10.4	8.5	18 15.2	0.3	57.3
02	206 30.2	52.5	83 37.9	8.6	18 14.9	0.3	57.3
03	221 30.3	. . 51.6	98 05.5	8.6	18 14.6	0.4	57.3
04	236 30.3	50.7	112 33.1	8.6	18 14.2	0.6	57.2
05	251 30.4	49.9	127 00.7	8.7	18 13.6	0.6	57.2
06	266 30.4	S11 49.0	141 28.4	8.6	N18 13.0	0.7	57.2
07	281 30.5	48.1	155 56.0	8.7	18 12.3	0.9	57.2
08	296 30.5	47.2	170 23.7	8.8	18 11.4	1.0	57.2
09	311 30.6	. . 46.4	184 51.5	8.7	18 10.4	1.0	57.1
10	326 30.6	45.5	199 19.2	8.8	18 09.4	1.2	57.1
11	341 30.7	44.6	213 47.0	8.9	18 08.2	1.2	57.1
12	356 30.7	S11 43.7	228 14.9	8.8	N18 07.0	1.4	57.1
13	11 30.8	42.8	242 42.7	8.9	18 05.6	1.5	57.1
14	26 30.8	42.0	257 10.6	9.0	18 04.1	1.5	57.0
15	41 30.9	. . 41.1	271 38.6	8.9	18 02.6	1.7	57.0
16	56 30.9	40.2	286 06.5	9.0	18 00.9	1.8	57.0
17	71 31.0	39.3	300 34.5	9.0	17 59.1	1.8	57.0
18	86 31.0	S11 38.4	315 02.5	9.1	N17 57.3	2.0	56.9
19	101 31.1	37.5	329 30.6	9.1	17 55.3	2.1	56.9
20	116 31.1	36.7	343 58.7	9.1	17 53.2	2.1	56.9
21	131 31.2	. . 35.8	358 26.8	9.2	17 51.1	2.3	56.9
22	146 31.3	34.9	12 55.0	9.2	17 48.8	2.4	56.9
23	161 31.3	34.0	27 23.2	9.3	17 46.4	2.4	56.8
19 00 (FRIDAY)	176 31.4	S11 33.1	41 51.5	9.3	N17 44.0	2.6	56.8
01	191 31.4	32.2	56 19.8	9.3	17 41.4	2.6	56.8
02	206 31.5	31.4	70 48.1	9.3	17 38.8	2.8	56.8
03	221 31.5	. . 30.5	85 16.4	9.5	17 36.0	2.8	56.8
04	236 31.6	29.6	99 44.9	9.4	17 33.2	2.9	56.7
05	251 31.6	28.7	114 13.3	9.5	17 30.3	3.1	56.7
06	266 31.7	S11 27.8	128 41.8	9.5	N17 27.2	3.1	56.7
07	281 31.7	26.9	143 10.3	9.6	17 24.1	3.2	56.7
08	296 31.8	26.0	157 38.9	9.6	17 20.9	3.3	56.7
09	311 31.9	. . 25.2	172 07.5	9.6	17 17.6	3.4	56.6
10	326 31.9	24.3	186 36.1	9.7	17 14.2	3.5	56.6
11	341 32.0	23.4	201 04.8	9.8	17 10.7	3.6	56.6
12	356 32.0	S11 22.5	215 33.6	9.8	N17 07.1	3.7	56.6
13	11 32.1	21.6	230 02.4	9.8	17 03.4	3.8	56.5
14	26 32.1	20.7	244 31.2	9.9	16 59.6	3.8	56.5
15	41 32.2	. . 19.8	259 00.1	9.9	16 55.8	4.0	56.5
16	56 32.3	18.9	273 29.0	10.0	16 51.8	4.0	56.5
17	71 32.3	18.0	287 58.0	10.0	16 47.8	4.1	56.5
18	86 32.4	S11 17.2	302 27.0	10.0	N16 43.7	4.2	56.4
19	101 32.4	16.3	316 56.0	10.1	16 39.5	4.3	56.4
20	116 32.5	15.4	331 25.1	10.2	16 35.2	4.4	56.4
21	131 32.6	. . 14.5	345 54.3	10.2	16 30.8	4.5	56.4
22	146 32.6	13.6	0 23.5	10.2	16 26.3	4.5	56.4
23	161 32.7	12.7	14 52.7	10.3	16 21.8	4.7	56.3
20 00 (SATURDAY)	176 32.7	S11 11.8	29 22.0	10.3	N16 17.1	4.7	56.3
01	191 32.8	10.9	43 51.3	10.4	16 12.4	4.8	56.3
02	206 32.9	10.0	58 20.7	10.4	16 07.6	4.9	56.3
03	221 32.9	. . 09.1	72 50.1	10.5	16 02.7	4.9	56.3
04	236 33.0	08.2	87 19.6	10.5	15 57.8	5.1	56.2
05	251 33.1	07.4	101 49.1	10.6	15 52.7	5.1	56.2
06	266 33.1	S11 06.5	116 18.7	10.6	N15 47.6	5.2	56.2
07	281 33.2	05.6	130 48.3	10.7	15 42.4	5.3	56.2
08	296 33.2	04.7	145 18.0	10.7	15 37.1	5.3	56.2
09	311 33.3	. . 03.8	159 47.7	10.8	15 31.8	5.4	56.1
10	326 33.4	02.9	174 17.5	10.8	15 26.4	5.5	56.1
11	341 33.4	02.0	188 47.3	10.9	15 20.9	5.6	56.1
12	356 33.5	S11 01.1	203 17.2	10.9	N15 15.3	5.7	56.1
13	11 33.6	11 00.2	217 47.1	11.0	15 09.6	5.7	56.1
14	26 33.6	10 59.3	232 17.1	11.0	15 03.9	5.8	56.0
15	41 33.7	. . 58.4	246 47.1	11.1	14 58.1	5.9	56.0
16	56 33.8	57.5	261 17.2	11.1	14 52.2	5.9	56.0
17	71 33.8	56.6	275 47.3	11.1	14 46.3	6.1	56.0
18	86 33.9	S10 55.7	290 17.4	11.3	N14 40.2	6.1	56.0
19	101 34.0	54.8	304 47.7	11.2	14 34.1	6.1	56.0
20	116 34.0	53.9	319 17.9	11.3	14 28.0	6.2	55.9
21	131 34.1	. . 53.0	333 48.2	11.4	14 21.8	6.3	55.9
22	146 34.2	52.1	348 18.6	11.4	14 15.5	6.4	55.9
23	161 34.2	51.2	2 49.0	11.5	N14 09.1	6.4	55.9
	SD 16.2	*d* 0.9	SD 15.6		15.4		15.3

Lat.	Twilight Naut.	Twilight Civil	Sunrise	Moonrise 18	Moonrise 19	Moonrise 20	Moonrise 21
°	h m	h m	h m	h m	h m	h m	h m
N 72	06 00	07 18	08 34	▭	10 52	12 44	14 31
N 70	05 59	07 10	08 17	10 30	11 49	13 20	14 54
68	05 59	07 04	08 04	11 11	12 22	13 45	15 11
66	05 59	06 58	07 53	11 39	12 47	14 04	15 25
64	05 58	06 54	07 43	12 00	13 06	14 19	15 36
62	05 58	06 49	07 36	12 17	13 21	14 32	15 46
60	05 57	06 46	07 29	12 31	13 34	14 43	15 55
N 58	05 57	06 42	07 23	12 44	13 45	14 52	16 02
56	05 56	06 39	07 17	12 54	13 55	15 00	16 08
54	05 55	06 36	07 13	13 03	14 03	15 08	16 14
52	05 54	06 34	07 08	13 12	14 11	15 14	16 19
50	05 54	06 31	07 04	13 19	14 18	15 20	16 24
45	05 52	06 26	06 56	13 35	14 33	15 33	16 34
N 40	05 49	06 21	06 49	13 48	14 45	15 43	16 42
35	05 47	06 17	06 42	13 59	14 55	15 52	16 49
30	05 45	06 12	06 37	14 09	15 04	16 00	16 56
20	05 39	06 05	06 27	14 25	15 20	16 14	17 07
N 10	05 32	05 57	06 19	14 40	15 33	16 25	17 16
0	05 25	05 49	06 10	14 54	15 46	16 37	17 25
S 10	05 16	05 41	06 02	15 07	15 59	16 48	17 34
20	05 04	05 31	05 53	15 22	16 12	16 59	17 43
30	04 49	05 18	05 43	15 39	16 28	17 13	17 54
35	04 39	05 11	05 37	15 48	16 37	17 21	18 00
40	04 28	05 02	05 30	16 00	16 47	17 29	18 07
45	04 13	04 51	05 22	16 13	16 59	17 40	18 15
S 50	03 54	04 38	05 12	16 29	17 14	17 52	18 25
52	03 45	04 31	05 08	16 36	17 20	17 58	18 30
54	03 34	04 24	05 03	16 44	17 28	18 04	18 35
56	03 22	04 16	04 57	16 54	17 36	18 11	18 40
58	03 08	04 07	04 51	17 04	17 46	18 19	18 46
S 60	02 50	03 56	04 44	17 16	17 57	18 28	18 53

Lat.	Sunset	Twilight Civil	Twilight Naut.	Moonset 18	Moonset 19	Moonset 20	Moonset 21
°	h m	h m	h m	h m	h m	h m	h m
N 72	15 55	17 11	18 30	▭	08 20	08 13	08 08
N 70	16 12	17 19	18 30	06 51	07 22	07 37	07 44
68	16 25	17 25	18 30	06 10	06 48	07 12	07 26
66	16 36	17 31	18 31	05 42	06 24	06 52	07 11
64	16 45	17 36	18 31	05 21	06 04	06 36	06 59
62	16 53	17 40	18 31	05 04	05 49	06 23	06 48
60	17 00	17 43	18 32	04 49	05 35	06 11	06 39
N 58	17 06	17 47	18 32	04 37	05 24	06 01	06 32
56	17 11	17 50	18 33	04 27	05 14	05 53	06 25
54	17 16	17 52	18 34	04 17	05 05	05 45	06 18
52	17 20	17 55	18 34	04 09	04 57	05 38	06 13
50	17 24	17 57	18 35	04 01	04 50	05 32	06 08
45	17 33	18 03	18 37	03 45	04 35	05 19	05 57
N 40	17 40	18 07	18 39	03 32	04 23	05 08	05 48
35	17 46	18 12	18 41	03 21	04 12	04 58	05 40
30	17 51	18 16	18 44	03 11	04 03	04 50	05 33
20	18 01	18 23	18 49	02 54	03 46	04 35	05 21
N 10	18 09	18 31	18 55	02 40	03 32	04 23	05 10
0	18 17	18 38	19 03	02 26	03 19	04 11	05 00
S 10	18 25	18 47	19 12	02 12	03 06	03 59	04 50
20	18 34	18 57	19 23	01 57	02 52	03 46	04 39
30	18 44	19 09	19 38	01 40	02 35	03 31	04 27
35	18 50	19 16	19 48	01 30	02 26	03 22	04 20
40	18 57	19 25	19 59	01 19	02 15	03 13	04 12
45	19 05	19 36	20 14	01 06	02 02	03 01	04 02
S 50	19 14	19 49	20 32	00 49	01 46	02 47	03 50
52	19 19	19 55	20 41	00 42	01 39	02 41	03 45
54	19 24	20 02	20 51	00 33	01 31	02 33	03 39
56	19 29	20 10	21 03	00 24	01 22	02 25	03 32
58	19 35	20 19	21 17	00 13	01 11	02 16	03 25
S 60	19 42	20 29	21 35	00 00	00 59	02 06	03 16

Day	SUN Eqn. of Time 00^h	SUN Eqn. of Time 12^h	SUN Mer. Pass.	MOON Mer. Pass. Upper	MOON Mer. Pass. Lower	MOON Age	MOON Phase
d	m s	m s	h m	h m	h m	d	%
18	14 00	13 57	12 14	21 06	08 40	10	82
19	13 55	13 52	12 14	21 58	09 33	11	89
20	13 49	13 46	12 14	22 48	10 24	12	95

	UT	ARIES	VENUS −3·9		MARS +0·4		JUPITER −2·5		SATURN +0·5	
		GHA	GHA	Dec	GHA	Dec	GHA	Dec	GHA	Dec
	d h	° ′	° ′	° ′	° ′	° ′	° ′	° ′	° ′	° ′
	21 00	150 21.5	203 13.2	S19 21.4	278 03.4	S17 30.3	338 37.6	N 5 08.4	255 55.3	S20 57.9
	01	165 24.0	218 12.5	20.8	293 04.8	30.6	353 40.3	08.5	270 57.6	57.9
	02	180 26.5	233 11.8	20.1	308 06.1	30.9	8 43.0	08.6	285 59.9	57.9
	03	195 28.9	248 11.0	. . 19.5	323 07.5	. . 31.2	23 45.8	. . 08.8	301 02.2	. . 57.9
	04	210 31.4	263 10.3	18.9	338 08.9	31.4	38 48.5	08.9	316 04.6	57.9
	05	225 33.9	278 09.5	18.2	353 10.2	31.7	53 51.2	09.0	331 06.9	57.9
	06	240 36.3	293 08.8	S19 17.6	8 11.6	S17 32.0	68 54.0	N 5 09.1	346 09.2	S20 58.0
	07	255 38.8	308 08.0	17.0	23 13.0	32.3	83 56.7	09.2	1 11.5	58.0
	08	270 41.2	323 07.3	16.3	38 14.3	32.6	98 59.4	09.4	16 13.8	58.0
S	09	285 43.7	338 06.6	. . 15.7	53 15.7	. . 32.8	114 02.2	. . 09.5	31 16.2	. . 58.0
U	10	300 46.2	353 05.8	15.0	68 17.1	33.1	129 04.9	09.6	46 18.5	58.0
N	11	315 48.6	8 05.1	14.4	83 18.4	33.4	144 07.6	09.7	61 20.8	58.0
D	12	330 51.1	23 04.3	S19 13.8	98 19.8	S17 33.7	159 10.4	N 5 09.9	76 23.1	S20 58.0
A	13	345 53.6	38 03.6	13.1	113 21.2	33.9	174 13.1	10.0	91 25.5	58.0
Y	14	0 56.0	53 02.9	12.5	128 22.5	34.2	189 15.8	10.1	106 27.8	58.0
	15	15 58.5	68 02.1	. . 11.8	143 23.9	. . 34.5	204 18.6	. . 10.2	121 30.1	. . 58.0
	16	31 01.0	83 01.4	11.2	158 25.3	34.8	219 21.3	10.3	136 32.4	58.1
	17	46 03.4	98 00.6	10.5	173 26.7	35.0	234 24.0	10.5	151 34.7	58.1
	18	61 05.9	112 59.9	S19 09.9	188 28.0	S17 35.3	249 26.8	N 5 10.6	166 37.1	S20 58.1
	19	76 08.3	127 59.2	09.2	203 29.4	35.6	264 29.5	10.7	181 39.4	58.1
	20	91 10.8	142 58.4	08.6	218 30.8	35.9	279 32.2	10.8	196 41.7	58.1
	21	106 13.3	157 57.7	. . 07.9	233 32.1	. . 36.1	294 35.0	. . 11.0	211 44.0	. . 58.1
	22	121 15.7	172 57.0	07.3	248 33.5	36.4	309 37.7	11.1	226 46.4	58.1
	23	136 18.2	187 56.2	06.6	263 34.9	36.7	324 40.5	11.2	241 48.7	58.1
	22 00	151 20.7	202 55.5	S19 06.0	278 36.3	S17 37.0	339 43.2	N 5 11.3	256 51.0	S20 58.1
	01	166 23.1	217 54.8	05.3	293 37.6	37.2	354 45.9	11.4	271 53.3	58.1
	02	181 25.6	232 54.0	04.7	308 39.0	37.5	9 48.7	11.6	286 55.7	58.1
	03	196 28.1	247 53.3	. . 04.0	323 40.4	. . 37.8	24 51.4	. . 11.7	301 58.0	. . 58.2
	04	211 30.5	262 52.6	03.3	338 41.8	38.1	39 54.1	11.8	317 00.3	58.2
	05	226 33.0	277 51.8	02.7	353 43.1	38.3	54 56.9	11.9	332 02.6	58.2
	06	241 35.5	292 51.1	S19 02.0	8 44.5	S17 38.6	69 59.6	N 5 12.1	347 05.0	S20 58.2
	07	256 37.9	307 50.4	01.4	23 45.9	38.9	85 02.4	12.2	2 07.3	58.2
	08	271 40.4	322 49.6	00.7	38 47.3	39.2	100 05.1	12.3	17 09.6	58.2
M	09	286 42.8	337 48.9	19 00.0	53 48.7	. . 39.4	115 07.8	. . 12.4	32 11.9	. . 58.2
O	10	301 45.3	352 48.2	18 59.4	68 50.0	39.7	130 10.6	12.6	47 14.3	58.2
N	11	316 47.8	7 47.4	58.7	83 51.4	40.0	145 13.3	12.7	62 16.6	58.2
D	12	331 50.2	22 46.7	S18 58.0	98 52.8	S17 40.2	160 16.0	N 5 12.8	77 18.9	S20 58.2
A	13	346 52.7	37 46.0	57.4	113 54.2	40.5	175 18.8	12.9	92 21.2	58.3
Y	14	1 55.2	52 45.2	56.7	128 55.6	40.8	190 21.5	13.0	107 23.6	58.3
	15	16 57.6	67 44.5	. . 56.0	143 56.9	. . 41.1	205 24.3	. . 13.2	122 25.9	. . 58.3
	16	32 00.1	82 43.8	55.4	158 58.3	41.3	220 27.0	13.3	137 28.2	58.3
	17	47 02.6	97 43.1	54.7	173 59.7	41.6	235 29.7	13.4	152 30.5	58.3
	18	62 05.0	112 42.3	S18 54.0	189 01.1	S17 41.9	250 32.5	N 5 13.5	167 32.9	S20 58.3
	19	77 07.5	127 41.6	53.3	204 02.5	42.1	265 35.2	13.7	182 35.2	58.3
	20	92 09.9	142 40.9	52.7	219 03.8	42.4	280 38.0	13.8	197 37.5	58.3
	21	107 12.4	157 40.2	. . 52.0	234 05.2	. . 42.7	295 40.7	. . 13.9	212 39.8	. . 58.3
	22	122 14.9	172 39.4	51.3	249 06.6	43.0	310 43.4	14.0	227 42.2	58.3
	23	137 17.3	187 38.7	50.6	264 08.0	43.2	325 46.2	14.2	242 44.5	58.3
	23 00	152 19.8	202 38.0	S18 50.0	279 09.4	S17 43.5	340 48.9	N 5 14.3	257 46.8	S20 58.4
	01	167 22.3	217 37.3	49.3	294 10.8	43.8	355 51.7	14.4	272 49.2	58.4
	02	182 24.7	232 36.5	48.6	309 12.1	44.0	10 54.4	14.5	287 51.5	58.4
	03	197 27.2	247 35.8	. . 47.9	324 13.5	. . 44.3	25 57.1	. . 14.7	302 53.8	. . 58.4
	04	212 29.7	262 35.1	47.2	339 14.9	44.6	40 59.9	14.8	317 56.1	58.4
	05	227 32.1	277 34.4	46.6	354 16.3	44.8	56 02.6	14.9	332 58.5	58.4
	06	242 34.6	292 33.6	S18 45.9	9 17.7	S17 45.1	71 05.4	N 5 15.0	348 00.8	S20 58.4
	07	257 37.1	307 32.9	45.2	24 19.1	45.4	86 08.1	15.2	3 03.1	58.4
T	08	272 39.5	322 32.2	44.5	39 20.4	45.6	101 10.8	15.3	18 05.5	58.4
U	09	287 42.0	337 31.5	. . 43.8	54 21.8	. . 45.9	116 13.6	. . 15.4	33 07.8	. . 58.4
E	10	302 44.4	352 30.8	43.1	69 23.2	46.2	131 16.3	15.5	48 10.1	58.4
S	11	317 46.9	7 30.0	42.5	84 24.6	46.4	146 19.1	15.7	63 12.4	58.5
D	12	332 49.4	22 29.3	S18 41.8	99 26.0	S17 46.7	161 21.8	N 5 15.8	78 14.8	S20 58.5
A	13	347 51.8	37 28.6	41.1	114 27.4	47.0	176 24.5	15.9	93 17.1	58.5
Y	14	2 54.3	52 27.9	40.4	129 28.8	47.2	191 27.3	16.0	108 19.4	58.5
	15	17 56.8	67 27.2	. . 39.7	144 30.2	. . 47.5	206 30.0	. . 16.2	123 21.8	. . 58.5
	16	32 59.2	82 26.4	39.0	159 31.6	47.8	221 32.8	16.3	138 24.1	58.5
	17	48 01.7	97 25.7	38.3	174 32.9	48.0	236 35.5	16.4	153 26.4	58.5
	18	63 04.2	112 25.0	S18 37.6	189 34.3	S17 48.3	251 38.3	N 5 16.5	168 28.8	S20 58.5
	19	78 06.6	127 24.3	36.9	204 35.7	48.6	266 41.0	16.7	183 31.1	58.5
	20	93 09.1	142 23.6	36.2	219 37.1	48.8	281 43.7	16.8	198 33.4	58.5
	21	108 11.6	157 22.9	. . 35.5	234 38.5	. . 49.1	296 46.5	. . 16.9	213 35.7	. . 58.5
	22	123 14.0	172 22.1	34.8	249 39.9	49.4	311 49.2	17.0	228 38.1	58.5
	23	138 16.5	187 21.4	34.1	264 41.3	49.6	326 52.0	17.2	243 40.4	58.6
	Mer. Pass.	h m 13 52.3	v −0.7	d 0.7	v 1.4	d 0.3	v 2.7	d 0.1	v 2.3	d 0.0

STARS

Name	SHA	Dec
	° ′	° ′
Acamar	315 17.1	S40 14.8
Achernar	335 25.9	S57 09.7
Acrux	173 06.5	S63 11.2
Adhara	255 10.8	S29 00.1
Aldebaran	290 47.2	N16 32.3
Alioth	166 18.8	N55 52.1
Alkaid	152 57.3	N49 13.8
Al Na'ir	27 42.0	S46 53.0
Alnilam	275 44.4	S 1 11.8
Alphard	217 54.0	S 8 44.0
Alphecca	126 09.4	N26 39.5
Alpheratz	357 41.9	N29 10.7
Altair	62 06.7	N 8 54.7
Ankaa	353 14.3	S42 13.3
Antares	112 24.0	S26 27.8
Arcturus	145 53.9	N19 05.8
Atria	107 24.3	S69 02.9
Avior	234 16.6	S59 34.0
Bellatrix	278 29.9	N 6 21.6
Betelgeuse	270 59.2	N 7 24.3
Canopus	263 55.0	S52 42.7
Capella	280 31.6	N46 00.8
Deneb	49 30.6	N45 20.3
Denebola	182 31.5	N14 28.8
Diphda	348 54.3	S17 54.1
Dubhe	193 49.0	N61 39.7
Elnath	278 10.2	N28 37.1
Eltanin	90 45.5	N51 29.1
Enif	33 45.6	N 9 56.9
Fomalhaut	15 22.4	S29 32.3
Gacrux	171 58.3	S57 12.1
Gienah	175 50.1	S17 37.9
Hadar	148 44.8	S60 26.7
Hamal	327 58.8	N23 32.2
Kaus Aust.	83 41.6	S34 22.3
Kochab	137 19.9	N74 05.1
Markab	13 36.8	N15 17.5
Menkar	314 13.2	N 4 08.9
Menkent	148 05.2	S36 26.8
Miaplacidus	221 38.2	S69 47.2
Mirfak	308 37.7	N49 55.1
Nunki	75 56.3	S26 16.4
Peacock	53 17.0	S56 40.8
Pollux	243 25.2	N27 59.0
Procyon	244 57.6	N 5 10.7
Rasalhague	96 04.9	N12 32.9
Regulus	207 41.3	N11 53.1
Rigel	281 10.2	S 8 11.4
Rigil Kent.	139 48.9	S60 53.7
Sabik	102 10.5	S15 44.5
Schedar	349 38.7	N56 37.6
Shaula	96 19.6	S37 06.6
Sirius	258 31.9	S16 44.7
Spica	158 29.1	S11 14.7
Suhail	222 50.6	S43 30.1
Vega	80 38.0	N38 47.9
Zuben'ubi	137 03.3	S16 06.4

	SHA	Mer. Pass.
	° ′	h m
Venus	51 34.8	10 29
Mars	127 15.6	5 25
Jupiter	188 22.5	1 21
Saturn	105 30.3	6 52

INDEX TO SELECTED STARS, 2016

Name	No	Mag	SHA	Dec
			°	°
Acamar	**7**	3·2	315	S 40
Achernar	**5**	0·5	335	S 57
Acrux	**30**	1·3	173	S 63
Adhara	**19**	1·5	255	S 29
Aldebaran	**10**	0·9	291	N 17
Alioth	**32**	1·8	166	N 56
Alkaid	**34**	1·9	153	N 49
Al Na'ir	**55**	1·7	28	S 47
Alnilam	**15**	1·7	276	S 1
Alphard	**25**	2·0	218	S 9
Alphecca	**41**	2·2	126	N 27
Alpheratz	**1**	2·1	358	N 29
Altair	**51**	0·8	62	N 9
Ankaa	**2**	2·4	353	S 42
Antares	**42**	1·0	112	S 26
Arcturus	**37**	0·0	146	N 19
Atria	**43**	1·9	107	S 69
Avior	**22**	1·9	234	S 60
Bellatrix	**13**	1·6	278	N 6
Betelgeuse	**16**	Var.*	271	N 7
Canopus	**17**	−0·7	264	S 53
Capella	**12**	0·1	281	N 46
Deneb	**53**	1·3	50	N 45
Denebola	**28**	2·1	183	N 14
Diphda	**4**	2·0	349	S 18
Dubhe	**27**	1·8	194	N 62
Elnath	**14**	1·7	278	N 29
Eltanin	**47**	2·2	91	N 51
Enif	**54**	2·4	34	N 10
Fomalhaut	**56**	1·2	15	S 30
Gacrux	**31**	1·6	172	S 57
Gienah	**29**	2·6	176	S 18
Hadar	**35**	0·6	149	S 60
Hamal	**6**	2·0	328	N 24
Kaus Australis	**48**	1·9	84	S 34
Kochab	**40**	2·1	137	N 74
Markab	**57**	2·5	14	N 15
Menkar	**8**	2·5	314	N 4
Menkent	**36**	2·1	148	S 36
Miaplacidus	**24**	1·7	222	S 70
Mirfak	**9**	1·8	309	N 50
Nunki	**50**	2·0	76	S 26
Peacock	**52**	1·9	53	S 57
Pollux	**21**	1·1	243	N 28
Procyon	**20**	0·4	245	N 5
Rasalhague	**46**	2·1	96	N 13
Regulus	**26**	1·4	208	N 12
Rigel	**11**	0·1	281	S 8
Rigil Kentaurus	**38**	−0·3	140	S 61
Sabik	**44**	2·4	102	S 16
Schedar	**3**	2·2	350	N 57
Shaula	**45**	1·6	96	S 37
Sirius	**18**	−1·5	259	S 17
Spica	**33**	1·0	158	S 11
Suhail	**23**	2·2	223	S 44
Vega	**49**	0·0	81	N 39
Zubenelgenubi	**39**	2·8	137	S 16

No	Name	Mag	SHA	Dec
			°	°
1	*Alpheratz*	2·1	358	N 29
2	*Ankaa*	2·4	353	S 42
3	*Schedar*	2·2	350	N 57
4	*Diphda*	2·0	349	S 18
5	*Achernar*	0·5	335	S 57
6	*Hamal*	2·0	328	N 24
7	*Acamar*	3·2	315	S 40
8	*Menkar*	2·5	314	N 4
9	*Mirfak*	1·8	309	N 50
10	*Aldebaran*	0·9	291	N 17
11	*Rigel*	0·1	281	S 8
12	*Capella*	0·1	281	N 46
13	*Bellatrix*	1·6	278	N 6
14	*Elnath*	1·7	278	N 29
15	*Alnilam*	1·7	276	S 1
16	*Betelgeuse*	Var.*	271	N 7
17	*Canopus*	−0·7	264	S 53
18	*Sirius*	−1·5	259	S 17
19	*Adhara*	1·5	255	S 29
20	*Procyon*	0·4	245	N 5
21	*Pollux*	1·1	243	N 28
22	*Avior*	1·9	234	S 60
23	*Suhail*	2·2	223	S 44
24	*Miaplacidus*	1·7	222	S 70
25	*Alphard*	2·0	218	S 9
26	*Regulus*	1·4	208	N 12
27	*Dubhe*	1·8	194	N 62
28	*Denebola*	2·1	183	N 14
29	*Gienah*	2·6	176	S 18
30	*Acrux*	1·3	173	S 63
31	*Gacrux*	1·6	172	S 57
32	*Alioth*	1·8	166	N 56
33	*Spica*	1·0	158	S 11
34	*Alkaid*	1·9	153	N 49
35	*Hadar*	0·6	149	S 60
36	*Menkent*	2·1	148	S 36
37	*Arcturus*	0·0	146	N 19
38	*Rigil Kentaurus*	−0·3	140	S 61
39	*Zubenelgenubi*	2·8	137	S 16
40	*Kochab*	2·1	137	N 74
41	*Alphecca*	2·2	126	N 27
42	*Antares*	1·0	112	S 26
43	*Atria*	1·9	107	S 69
44	*Sabik*	2·4	102	S 16
45	*Shaula*	1·6	96	S 37
46	*Rasalhague*	2·1	96	N 13
47	*Eltanin*	2·2	91	N 51
48	*Kaus Australis*	1·9	84	S 34
49	*Vega*	0·0	81	N 39
50	*Nunki*	2·0	76	S 26
51	*Altair*	0·8	62	N 9
52	*Peacock*	1·9	53	S 57
53	*Deneb*	1·3	50	N 45
54	*Enif*	2·4	34	N 10
55	*Al Na'ir*	1·7	28	S 47
56	*Fomalhaut*	1·2	15	S 30
57	*Markab*	2·5	14	N 15

*0·1 — 1·2

ALTITUDE CORRECTION TABLES 10°-90°—SUN, STARS, PLANETS

SUN

OCT.—MAR. App. Alt.	Lower Limb	Upper Limb	APR.—SEPT. App. Alt.	Lower Limb	Upper Limb
° ′	′	′	° ′	′	′
9 33			9 39		
	+10·8	−21·5		+10·6	−21·2
9 45			9 50		
	+10·9	−21·4		+10·7	−21·1
9 56			10 02		
	+11·0	−21·3		+10·8	−21·0
10 08			10 14		
	+11·1	−21·2		+10·9	−20·9
10 20			10 27		
	+11·2	−21·1		+11·0	−20·8
10 33			10 40		
	+11·3	−21·0		+11·1	−20·7
10 46			10 53		
	+11·4	−20·9		+11·2	−20·6
11 00			11 07		
	+11·5	−20·8		+11·3	−20·5
11 15			11 22		
	+11·6	−20·7		+11·4	−20·4
11 30			11 37		
	+11·7	−20·6		+11·5	−20·3
11 45			11 53		
	+11·8	−20·5		+11·6	−20·2
12 01			12 10		
	+11·9	−20·4		+11·7	−20·1
12 18			12 27		
	+12·0	−20·3		+11·8	−20·0
12 36			12 45		
	+12·1	−20·2		+11·9	−19·9
12 54			13 04		
	+12·2	−20·1		+12·0	−19·8
13 14			13 24		
	+12·3	−20·0		+12·1	−19·7
13 34			13 44		
	+12·4	−19·9		+12·2	−19·6
13 55			14 06		
	+12·5	−19·8		+12·3	−19·5
14 17			14 29		
	+12·6	−19·7		+12·4	−19·4
14 41			14 53		
	+12·7	−19·6		+12·5	−19·3
15 05			15 18		
	+12·8	−19·5		+12·6	−19·2
15 31			15 45		
	+12·9	−19·4		+12·7	−19·1
15 59			16 13		
	+13·0	−19·3		+12·8	−19·0
16 27			16 43		
	+13·1	−19·2		+12·9	−18·9
16 58			17 14		
	+13·2	−19·1		+13·0	−18·8
17 30			17 47		
	+13·3	−19·0		+13·1	−18·7
18 05			18 23		
	+13·4	−18·9		+13·2	−18·6
18 41			19 00		
	+13·5	−18·8		+13·3	−18·5
19 20			19 41		
	+13·6	−18·7		+13·4	−18·4
20 02			20 24		
	+13·7	−18·6		+13·5	−18·3
20 46			21 10		
	+13·8	−18·5		+13·6	−18·2
21 34			21 59		
	+13·9	−18·4		+13·7	−18·1
22 25			22 52		
	+14·0	−18·3		+13·8	−18·0
23 20			23 49		
	+14·1	−18·2		+13·9	−17·9
24 20			24 51		
	+14·2	−18·1		+14·0	−17·8
25 24			25 58		
	+14·3	−18·0		+14·1	−17·7
26 34			27 11		
	+14·4	−17·9		+14·2	−17·6
27 50			28 31		
	+14·5	−17·8		+14·3	−17·5
29 13			29 58		
	+14·6	−17·7		+14·4	−17·4
30 44			31 33		
	+14·7	−17·6		+14·5	−17·3
32 24			33 18		
	+14·8	−17·5		+14·6	−17·2
34 15			35 15		
	+14·9	−17·4		+14·7	−17·1
36 17			37 24		
	+15·0	−17·3		+14·8	−17·0
38 34			39 48		
	+15·1	−17·2		+14·9	−16·9
41 06			42 28		
	+15·2	−17·1		+15·0	−16·8
43 56			45 29		
	+15·3	−17·0		+15·1	−16·7
47 07			48 52		
	+15·4	−16·9		+15·2	−16·6
50 43			52 41		
	+15·5	−16·8		+15·3	−16·5
54 46			56 59		
	+15·6	−16·7		+15·4	−16·4
59 21			61 50		
	+15·7	−16·6		+15·5	−16·3
64 28			67 15		
	+15·8	−16·5		+15·6	−16·2
70 10			73 14		
	+15·9	−16·4		+15·7	−16·1
76 24			79 42		
	+16·0	−16·3		+15·8	−16·0
83 05			86 31		
	+16·1	−16·2		+15·9	−15·9
90 00			90 00		

STARS AND PLANETS

App Alt.	Corrⁿ
° ′	′
9 55	
	−5·3
10 07	
	−5·2
10 20	
	−5·1
10 32	
	−5·0
10 46	
	−4·9
10 59	
	−4·8
11 14	
	−4·7
11 29	
	−4·6
11 44	
	−4·5
12 00	
	−4·4
12 17	
	−4·3
12 35	
	−4·2
12 53	
	−4·1
13 12	
	−4·0
13 32	
	−3·9
13 53	
	−3·8
14 16	
	−3·7
14 39	
	−3·6
15 03	
	−3·5
15 29	
	−3·4
15 56	
	−3·3
16 25	
	−3·2
16 55	
	−3·1
17 27	
	−3·0
18 01	
	−2·9
18 37	
	−2·8
19 16	
	−2·7
19 56	
	−2·6
20 40	
	−2·5
21 27	
	−2·4
22 17	
	−2·3
23 11	
	−2·2
24 09	
	−2·1
25 12	
	−2·0
26 20	
	−1·9
27 34	
	−1·8
28 54	
	−1·7
30 22	
	−1·6
31 58	
	−1·5
33 43	
	−1·4
35 38	
	−1·3
37 45	
	−1·2
40 06	
	−1·1
42 42	
	−1·0
45 34	
	−0·9
48 45	
	−0·8
52 16	
	−0·7
56 09	
	−0·6
60 26	
	−0·5
65 06	
	−0·4
70 09	
	−0·3
75 32	
	−0·2
81 12	
	−0·1
87 03	
	0·0
90 00	

App. Alt. — Additional Corrⁿ

2016

VENUS

Jan. 1–Dec. 3	
°	′
0	
	+0·1
60	

Dec. 4–Dec. 31	
°	′
0	
	+0·2
41	
	+0·1
76	

MARS

Jan. 1–Mar. 11 Sept. 16–Dec. 31	
°	′
0	
	+0·1
60	

Mar. 12–Apr. 30 July 5–Sept. 15	
°	′
0	
	+0·2
41	
	+0·1
76	

May 1–July 4	
°	′
0	
	+0·3
34	
	+0·2
60	
	+0·1
80	

DIP

Ht. of Eye	Corrⁿ	Ht. of Eye
m	′	ft.
2·4		8·0
	−2·8	
2·6		8·6
	−2·9	
2·8		9·2
	−3·0	
3·0		9·8
	−3·1	
3·2		10·5
	−3·2	
3·4		11·2
	−3·3	
3·6		11·9
	−3·4	
3·8		12·6
	−3·5	
4·0		13·3
	−3·6	
4·3		14·1
	−3·7	
4·5		14·9
	−3·8	
4·7		15·7
	−3·9	
5·0		16·5
	−4·0	
5·2		17·4
	−4·1	
5·5		18·3
	−4·2	
5·8		19·1
	−4·3	
6·1		20·1
	−4·4	
6·3		21·0
	−4·5	
6·6		22·0
	−4·6	
6·9		22·9
	−4·7	
7·2		23·9
	−4·8	
7·5		24·9
	−4·9	
7·9		26·0
	−5·0	
8·2		27·1
	−5·1	
8·5		28·1
	−5·2	
8·8		29·2
	−5·3	
9·2		30·4
	−5·4	
9·5		31·5
	−5·5	
9·9		32·7
	−5·6	
10·3		33·9
	−5·7	
10·6		35·1
	−5·8	
11·0		36·3
	−5·9	
11·4		37·6
	−6·0	
11·8		38·9
	−6·1	
12·2		40·1
	−6·2	
12·6		41·5
	−6·3	
13·0		42·8
	−6·4	
13·4		44·2
	−6·5	
13·8		45·5
	−6·6	
14·2		46·9
	−6·7	
14·7		48·4
	−6·8	
15·1		49·8
	−6·9	
15·5		51·3
	−7·0	
16·0		52·8
	−7·1	
16·5		54·3
	−7·2	
16·9		55·8
	−7·3	
17·4		57·4
	−7·4	
17·9		58·9
	−7·5	
18·4		60·5
	−7·6	
18·8		62·1
	−7·7	
19·3		63·8
	−7·8	
19·8		65·4
	−7·9	
20·4		67·1
	−8·0	
20·9		68·8
	−8·1	
21·4		70·5

Ht. of Eye	Corrⁿ
m	′
1·0	− 1·8
1·5	− 2·2
2·0	− 2·5
2·5	− 2·8
3·0	− 3·0
See table ←	
m	′
20	− 7·9
22	− 8·3
24	− 8·6
26	− 9·0
28	− 9·3
30	− 9·6
32	−10·0
34	−10·3
36	−10·6
38	−10·8
40	−11·1
42	−11·4
44	−11·7
46	−11·9
48	−12·2
ft.	′
2	− 1·4
4	− 1·9
6	− 2·4
8	− 2·7
10	− 3·1
See table ←	
ft.	′
70	− 8·1
75	− 8·4
80	− 8·7
85	− 8·9
90	− 9·2
95	− 9·5
100	− 9·7
105	− 9·9
110	−10·2
115	−10·4
120	−10·6
125	−10·8
130	−11·1
135	−11·3
140	−11·5
145	−11·7
150	−11·9
155	−12·1

App. Alt. = Apparent altitude = Sextant altitude corrected for index error and dip.

UT		SUN		MOON				
		GHA	Dec	GHA	*v*	Dec	*d*	HP
d	h	° ′	° ′	° ′	′	° ′	′	′
21	00	176 34.3	S10 50.3	17 19.5	11.5	N14 02.7	6.5	55.9
	01	191 34.4	49.4	31 50.0	11.6	13 56.2	6.6	55.8
	02	206 34.4	48.5	46 20.6	11.6	13 49.6	6.6	55.8
	03	221 34.5	. . 47.6	60 51.2	11.7	13 43.0	6.7	55.8
	04	236 34.6	46.7	75 21.9	11.7	13 36.3	6.8	55.8
	05	251 34.6	45.8	89 52.6	11.8	13 29.5	6.8	55.8
	06	266 34.7	S10 44.9	104 23.4	11.8	N13 22.7	6.8	55.7
	07	281 34.8	44.0	118 54.2	11.8	13 15.9	7.0	55.7
	08	296 34.9	43.1	133 25.0	12.0	13 08.9	7.0	55.7
S	09	311 34.9	. . 42.2	147 56.0	11.9	13 01.9	7.0	55.7
U	10	326 35.0	41.3	162 26.9	12.0	12 54.9	7.1	55.7
N	11	341 35.1	40.4	176 57.9	12.1	12 47.8	7.2	55.6
D	12	356 35.1	S10 39.5	191 29.0	12.1	N12 40.6	7.2	55.6
A	13	11 35.2	38.6	206 00.1	12.2	12 33.4	7.3	55.6
Y	14	26 35.3	37.7	220 31.3	12.2	12 26.1	7.4	55.6
	15	41 35.4	. . 36.8	235 02.5	12.3	12 18.7	7.3	55.6
	16	56 35.4	35.9	249 33.8	12.3	12 11.4	7.5	55.6
	17	71 35.5	35.0	264 05.1	12.3	12 03.9	7.5	55.5
	18	86 35.6	S10 34.1	278 36.4	12.4	N11 56.4	7.5	55.5
	19	101 35.6	33.2	293 07.8	12.5	11 48.9	7.6	55.5
	20	116 35.7	32.3	307 39.3	12.5	11 41.3	7.7	55.5
	21	131 35.8	. . 31.4	322 10.8	12.5	11 33.6	7.7	55.5
	22	146 35.9	30.5	336 42.3	12.6	11 25.9	7.7	55.4
	23	161 35.9	29.6	351 13.9	12.6	11 18.2	7.8	55.4
22	00	176 36.0	S10 28.7	5 45.5	12.7	N11 10.4	7.9	55.4
	01	191 36.1	27.8	20 17.2	12.8	11 02.5	7.9	55.4
	02	206 36.2	26.9	34 49.0	12.7	10 54.6	7.9	55.4
	03	221 36.2	. . 26.0	49 20.7	12.9	10 46.7	8.0	55.4
	04	236 36.3	25.0	63 52.6	12.8	10 38.7	8.0	55.3
	05	251 36.4	24.1	78 24.4	13.0	10 30.7	8.1	55.3
	06	266 36.5	S10 23.2	92 56.4	12.9	N10 22.6	8.1	55.3
	07	281 36.6	22.3	107 28.3	13.0	10 14.5	8.2	55.3
	08	296 36.6	21.4	122 00.3	13.1	10 06.3	8.2	55.3
M	09	311 36.7	. . 20.5	136 32.4	13.1	9 58.1	8.2	55.3
O	10	326 36.8	19.6	151 04.5	13.1	9 49.9	8.3	55.2
N	11	341 36.9	18.7	165 36.6	13.2	9 41.6	8.3	55.2
D	12	356 36.9	S10 17.8	180 08.8	13.2	N 9 33.3	8.4	55.2
A	13	11 37.0	16.9	194 41.0	13.3	9 24.9	8.4	55.2
Y	14	26 37.1	16.0	209 13.3	13.3	9 16.5	8.4	55.2
	15	41 37.2	. . 15.1	223 45.6	13.3	9 08.1	8.5	55.2
	16	56 37.3	14.1	238 17.9	13.4	8 59.6	8.5	55.1
	17	71 37.3	13.2	252 50.3	13.4	8 51.1	8.5	55.1
	18	86 37.4	S10 12.3	267 22.7	13.5	N 8 42.6	8.6	55.1
	19	101 37.5	11.4	281 55.2	13.5	8 34.0	8.6	55.1
	20	116 37.6	10.5	296 27.7	13.6	8 25.4	8.6	55.1
	21	131 37.7	. . 09.6	311 00.3	13.6	8 16.8	8.7	55.1
	22	146 37.7	08.7	325 32.9	13.6	8 08.1	8.7	55.0
	23	161 37.8	07.8	340 05.5	13.7	7 59.4	8.7	55.0
23	00	176 37.9	S10 06.9	354 38.2	13.7	N 7 50.7	8.8	55.0
	01	191 38.0	05.9	9 10.9	13.7	7 41.9	8.8	55.0
	02	206 38.1	05.0	23 43.6	13.8	7 33.1	8.8	55.0
	03	221 38.1	. . 04.1	38 16.4	13.8	7 24.3	8.9	55.0
	04	236 38.2	03.2	52 49.2	13.9	7 15.4	8.8	54.9
	05	251 38.3	02.3	67 22.1	13.9	7 06.6	8.9	54.9
	06	266 38.4	S10 01.4	81 55.0	13.9	N 6 57.7	9.0	54.9
	07	281 38.5	10 00.5	96 27.9	14.0	6 48.7	8.9	54.9
T	08	296 38.6	9 59.5	111 00.9	14.0	6 39.8	9.0	54.9
U	09	311 38.6	. . 58.6	125 33.9	14.0	6 30.8	9.0	54.9
E	10	326 38.7	57.7	140 06.9	14.1	6 21.8	9.0	54.9
S	11	341 38.8	56.8	154 40.0	14.1	6 12.8	9.0	54.8
D	12	356 38.9	S 9 55.9	169 13.1	14.1	N 6 03.8	9.1	54.8
A	13	11 39.0	55.0	183 46.2	14.1	5 54.7	9.1	54.8
Y	14	26 39.1	54.1	198 19.3	14.2	5 45.6	9.1	54.8
	15	41 39.2	. . 53.1	212 52.5	14.3	5 36.5	9.1	54.8
	16	56 39.2	52.2	227 25.8	14.2	5 27.4	9.1	54.8
	17	71 39.3	51.3	241 59.0	14.3	5 18.3	9.2	54.8
	18	86 39.4	S 9 50.4	256 32.3	14.3	N 5 09.1	9.2	54.7
	19	101 39.5	49.5	271 05.6	14.4	4 59.9	9.1	54.7
	20	116 39.6	48.6	285 39.0	14.4	4 50.8	9.3	54.7
	21	131 39.7	. . 47.6	300 12.4	14.4	4 41.5	9.2	54.7
	22	146 39.8	46.7	314 45.8	14.4	4 32.3	9.2	54.7
	23	161 39.8	45.8	329 19.2	14.5	N 4 23.1	9.3	54.7
		SD 16.2	*d* 0.9	SD 15.2		15.0		14.9

Lat.	Twilight Naut.	Twilight Civil	Sunrise	Moonrise 21	Moonrise 22	Moonrise 23	Moonrise 24
°	h m	h m	h m	h m	h m	h m	h m
N 72	05 46	07 04	08 17	14 31	16 13	17 50	19 25
N 70	05 47	06 58	08 03	14 54	16 27	17 57	19 26
68	05 48	06 53	07 51	15 11	16 38	18 04	19 28
66	05 49	06 48	07 41	15 25	16 47	18 09	19 29
64	05 49	06 44	07 33	15 36	16 55	18 13	19 30
62	05 49	06 41	07 26	15 46	17 02	18 16	19 30
60	05 49	06 38	07 20	15 55	17 07	18 20	19 31
N 58	05 49	06 35	07 15	16 02	17 12	18 22	19 32
56	05 49	06 32	07 10	16 08	17 17	18 25	19 32
54	05 49	06 30	07 06	16 14	17 21	18 27	19 33
52	05 49	06 28	07 02	16 19	17 24	18 29	19 33
50	05 48	06 26	06 59	16 24	17 28	18 31	19 34
45	05 47	06 21	06 51	16 34	17 35	18 35	19 35
N 40	05 46	06 17	06 44	16 42	17 41	18 38	19 35
35	05 44	06 13	06 39	16 49	17 46	18 41	19 36
30	05 42	06 10	06 34	16 56	17 50	18 44	19 37
20	05 37	06 03	06 25	17 07	17 58	18 48	19 38
N 10	05 32	05 56	06 18	17 16	18 05	18 52	19 38
0	05 25	05 49	06 10	17 25	18 11	18 56	19 39
S 10	05 16	05 41	06 03	17 34	18 18	19 00	19 40
20	05 06	05 32	05 55	17 43	18 24	19 03	19 41
30	04 52	05 21	05 45	17 54	18 32	19 08	19 42
35	04 43	05 14	05 40	18 00	18 36	19 10	19 43
40	04 32	05 05	05 34	18 07	18 42	19 13	19 43
45	04 18	04 56	05 26	18 15	18 47	19 17	19 44
S 50	04 01	04 43	05 18	18 25	18 54	19 21	19 45
52	03 52	04 37	05 14	18 30	18 57	19 22	19 46
54	03 42	04 31	05 09	18 35	19 01	19 24	19 46
56	03 31	04 23	05 04	18 40	19 05	19 27	19 47
58	03 18	04 15	04 59	18 46	19 09	19 29	19 47
S 60	03 02	04 05	04 52	18 53	19 14	19 32	19 48

Lat.	Sunset	Twilight Civil	Twilight Naut.	Moonset 21	Moonset 22	Moonset 23	Moonset 24
°	h m	h m	h m	h m	h m	h m	h m
N 72	16 11	17 25	18 43	08 08	08 03	07 59	07 54
N 70	16 26	17 31	18 42	07 44	07 48	07 50	07 50
68	16 37	17 36	18 41	07 26	07 35	07 42	07 47
66	16 47	17 41	18 40	07 11	07 25	07 36	07 44
64	16 55	17 44	18 39	06 59	07 16	07 30	07 42
62	17 02	17 48	18 39	06 48	07 09	07 25	07 40
60	17 08	17 51	18 39	06 39	07 02	07 21	07 38
N 58	17 13	17 53	18 39	06 32	06 56	07 18	07 37
56	17 18	17 56	18 39	06 25	06 51	07 14	07 35
54	17 22	17 58	18 39	06 18	06 47	07 11	07 34
52	17 26	18 00	18 39	06 13	06 43	07 09	07 33
50	17 29	18 02	18 40	06 08	06 39	07 06	07 32
45	17 37	18 07	18 41	05 57	06 30	07 01	07 29
N 40	17 43	18 11	18 42	05 48	06 24	06 57	07 27
35	17 49	18 14	18 44	05 40	06 18	06 53	07 26
30	17 54	18 18	18 46	05 33	06 12	06 49	07 24
20	18 02	18 24	18 50	05 21	06 03	06 43	07 22
N 10	18 10	18 31	18 56	05 10	05 55	06 38	07 19
0	18 17	18 38	19 02	05 00	05 47	06 33	07 17
S 10	18 24	18 46	19 11	04 50	05 40	06 28	07 15
20	18 32	18 55	19 21	04 39	05 32	06 22	07 12
30	18 41	19 06	19 35	04 27	05 22	06 16	07 09
35	18 47	19 13	19 44	04 20	05 17	06 13	07 08
40	18 53	19 21	19 54	04 12	05 10	06 09	07 06
45	19 00	19 31	20 08	04 02	05 03	06 04	07 04
S 50	19 08	19 43	20 25	03 50	04 54	05 58	07 01
52	19 12	19 48	20 33	03 45	04 50	05 56	07 00
54	19 17	19 55	20 43	03 39	04 46	05 53	06 59
56	19 22	20 02	20 54	03 32	04 41	05 49	06 57
58	19 27	20 10	21 07	03 25	04 35	05 46	06 56
S 60	19 33	20 20	21 22	03 16	04 29	05 42	06 54

Day	SUN Eqn. of Time 00^h	SUN Eqn. of Time 12^h	SUN Mer. Pass.	MOON Mer. Pass. Upper	MOON Mer. Pass. Lower	MOON Age	MOON Phase
d	m s	m s	h m	h m	h m	d %	
21	13 43	13 40	12 14	23 36	11 13	13 98	
22	13 36	13 32	12 14	24 22	11 59	14 100	○
23	13 29	13 25	12 13	00 22	12 44	15 99	

	UT	ARIES	VENUS −3·9		MARS +0·4		JUPITER −2·5		SATURN +0·5		STARS		
		GHA	GHA	Dec	GHA	Dec	GHA	Dec	GHA	Dec	Name	SHA	Dec
	d h	° ′	° ′	° ′	° ′	° ′	° ′	° ′	° ′	° ′		° ′	° ′
	24 00	153 18.9	202 20.7	S18 33.4	279 42.7	S17 49.9	341 54.7	N 5 17.3	258 42.7	S20 58.6	Acamar	315 17.1	S40 14.8
	01	168 21.4	217 20.0	32.7	294 44.1	50.2	356 57.5	17.4	273 45.1	58.6	Achernar	335 25.9	S57 09.7
	02	183 23.9	232 19.3	32.0	309 45.5	50.4	12 00.2	17.5	288 47.4	58.6	Acrux	173 06.5	S63 11.2
	03	198 26.3	247 18.6	. . 31.3	324 46.9	. . 50.7	27 02.9	. . 17.7	303 49.7	. . 58.6	Adhara	255 10.8	S29 00.1
	04	213 28.8	262 17.9	30.6	339 48.3	51.0	42 05.7	17.8	318 52.1	58.6	Aldebaran	290 47.2	N16 32.3
	05	228 31.3	277 17.2	29.9	354 49.6	51.2	57 08.4	17.9	333 54.4	58.6			
	06	243 33.7	292 16.4	S18 29.2	9 51.0	S17 51.5	72 11.2	N 5 18.0	348 56.7	S20 58.6	Alioth	166 18.8	N55 52.1
W	07	258 36.2	307 15.7	28.5	24 52.4	51.8	87 13.9	18.2	3 59.1	58.6	Alkaid	152 57.2	N49 13.8
E	08	273 38.7	322 15.0	27.8	39 53.8	52.0	102 16.7	18.3	19 01.4	58.6	Al Na'ir	27 42.0	S46 52.9
D	09	288 41.1	337 14.3	. . 27.1	54 55.2	. . 52.3	117 19.4	. . 18.4	34 03.7	. . 58.6	Alnilam	275 44.4	S 1 11.8
N	10	303 43.6	352 13.6	26.4	69 56.6	52.6	132 22.1	18.5	49 06.1	58.6	Alphard	217 54.0	S 8 44.0
E	11	318 46.0	7 12.9	25.7	84 58.0	52.8	147 24.9	18.7	64 08.4	58.7			
S	12	333 48.5	22 12.2	S18 25.0	99 59.4	S17 53.1	162 27.6	N 5 18.8	79 10.7	S20 58.7	Alphecca	126 09.4	N26 39.5
D	13	348 51.0	37 11.5	24.2	115 00.8	53.3	177 30.4	18.9	94 13.1	58.7	Alpheratz	357 41.9	N29 10.7
A	14	3 53.4	52 10.8	23.5	130 02.2	53.6	192 33.1	19.0	109 15.4	58.7	Altair	62 06.7	N 8 54.7
Y	15	18 55.9	67 10.1	. . 22.8	145 03.6	. . 53.9	207 35.9	. . 19.2	124 17.7	. . 58.7	Ankaa	353 14.3	S42 13.3
	16	33 58.4	82 09.4	22.1	160 05.0	54.1	222 38.6	19.3	139 20.1	58.7	Antares	112 24.0	S26 27.8
	17	49 00.8	97 08.6	21.4	175 06.4	54.4	237 41.4	19.4	154 22.4	58.7			
	18	64 03.3	112 07.9	S18 20.7	190 07.8	S17 54.7	252 44.1	N 5 19.5	169 24.7	S20 58.7	Arcturus	145 53.9	N19 05.8
	19	79 05.8	127 07.2	20.0	205 09.2	54.9	267 46.9	19.7	184 27.1	58.7	Atria	107 24.2	S69 02.9
	20	94 08.2	142 06.5	19.2	220 10.6	55.2	282 49.6	19.8	199 29.4	58.7	Avior	234 16.6	S59 34.0
	21	109 10.7	157 05.8	. . 18.5	235 12.0	. . 55.4	297 52.3	. . 19.9	214 31.7	. . 58.7	Bellatrix	278 29.9	N 6 21.6
	22	124 13.2	172 05.1	17.8	250 13.4	55.7	312 55.1	20.0	229 34.1	58.7	Betelgeuse	270 59.2	N 7 24.3
	23	139 15.6	187 04.4	17.1	265 14.8	56.0	327 57.8	20.2	244 36.4	58.8			
	25 00	154 18.1	202 03.7	S18 16.4	280 16.2	S17 56.2	343 00.6	N 5 20.3	259 38.8	S20 58.8	Canopus	263 55.0	S52 42.7
	01	169 20.5	217 03.0	15.6	295 17.6	56.5	358 03.3	20.4	274 41.1	58.8	Capella	280 31.6	N46 00.8
	02	184 23.0	232 02.3	14.9	310 19.0	56.7	13 06.1	20.5	289 43.4	58.8	Deneb	49 30.6	N45 20.2
	03	199 25.5	247 01.6	. . 14.2	325 20.4	. . 57.0	28 08.8	. . 20.7	304 45.8	. . 58.8	Denebola	182 31.5	N14 28.8
	04	214 27.9	262 00.9	13.5	340 21.8	57.3	43 11.6	20.8	319 48.1	58.8	Diphda	348 54.3	S17 54.1
	05	229 30.4	277 00.2	12.7	355 23.2	57.5	58 14.3	20.9	334 50.4	58.8			
	06	244 32.9	291 59.5	S18 12.0	10 24.6	S17 57.8	73 17.1	N 5 21.0	349 52.8	S20 58.8	Dubhe	193 49.0	N61 39.7
T	07	259 35.3	306 58.8	11.3	25 26.0	58.0	88 19.8	21.2	4 55.1	58.8	Elnath	278 10.2	N28 37.1
H	08	274 37.8	321 58.1	10.5	40 27.4	58.3	103 22.6	21.3	19 57.4	58.8	Eltanin	90 45.5	N51 29.1
U	09	289 40.3	336 57.4	. . 09.8	55 28.9	. . 58.6	118 25.3	. . 21.4	34 59.8	. . 58.8	Enif	33 45.6	N 9 56.9
R	10	304 42.7	351 56.7	09.1	70 30.3	58.8	133 28.0	21.6	50 02.1	58.8	Fomalhaut	15 22.4	S29 32.3
S	11	319 45.2	6 56.0	08.3	85 31.7	59.1	148 30.8	21.7	65 04.5	58.9			
D	12	334 47.6	21 55.3	S18 07.6	100 33.1	S17 59.3	163 33.5	N 5 21.8	80 06.8	S20 58.9	Gacrux	171 58.2	S57 12.1
A	13	349 50.1	36 54.6	06.9	115 34.5	59.6	178 36.3	21.9	95 09.1	58.9	Gienah	175 50.1	S17 37.9
Y	14	4 52.6	51 53.9	06.1	130 35.9	17 59.9	193 39.0	22.1	110 11.5	58.9	Hadar	148 44.8	S60 26.8
	15	19 55.0	66 53.2	. . 05.4	145 37.3	18 00.1	208 41.8	. . 22.2	125 13.8	. . 58.9	Hamal	327 58.8	N23 32.2
	16	34 57.5	81 52.5	04.7	160 38.7	00.4	223 44.5	22.3	140 16.1	58.9	Kaus Aust.	83 41.6	S34 22.3
	17	50 00.0	96 51.8	03.9	175 40.1	00.6	238 47.3	22.4	155 18.5	58.9			
	18	65 02.4	111 51.1	S18 03.2	190 41.5	S18 00.9	253 50.0	N 5 22.6	170 20.8	S20 58.9	Kochab	137 19.8	N74 05.1
	19	80 04.9	126 50.4	02.5	205 42.9	01.1	268 52.8	22.7	185 23.2	58.9	Markab	13 36.8	N15 17.5
	20	95 07.4	141 49.7	01.7	220 44.3	01.4	283 55.5	22.8	200 25.5	58.9	Menkar	314 13.2	N 4 08.9
	21	110 09.8	156 49.0	. . 01.0	235 45.8	. . 01.7	298 58.3	. . 22.9	215 27.8	. . 58.9	Menkent	148 05.1	S36 26.8
	22	125 12.3	171 48.3	18 00.2	250 47.2	01.9	314 01.0	23.1	230 30.2	58.9	Miaplacidus	221 38.2	S69 47.2
	23	140 14.8	186 47.6	17 59.5	265 48.6	02.2	329 03.8	23.2	245 32.5	58.9			
	26 00	155 17.2	201 47.0	S17 58.8	280 50.0	S18 02.4	344 06.5	N 5 23.3	260 34.9	S20 59.0	Mirfak	308 37.8	N49 55.1
	01	170 19.7	216 46.3	58.0	295 51.4	02.7	359 09.3	23.5	275 37.2	59.0	Nunki	75 56.3	S26 16.4
	02	185 22.1	231 45.6	57.3	310 52.8	02.9	14 12.0	23.6	290 39.5	59.0	Peacock	53 17.0	S56 40.7
	03	200 24.6	246 44.9	. . 56.5	325 54.2	. . 03.2	29 14.8	. . 23.7	305 41.9	. . 59.0	Pollux	243 25.2	N27 59.0
	04	215 27.1	261 44.2	55.8	340 55.6	03.5	44 17.5	23.8	320 44.2	59.0	Procyon	244 57.6	N 5 10.7
	05	230 29.5	276 43.5	55.0	355 57.0	03.7	59 20.3	24.0	335 46.6	59.0			
	06	245 32.0	291 42.8	S17 54.3	10 58.5	S18 04.0	74 23.0	N 5 24.1	350 48.9	S20 59.0	Rasalhague	96 04.9	N12 32.9
	07	260 34.5	306 42.1	53.5	25 59.9	04.2	89 25.8	24.2	5 51.2	59.0	Regulus	207 41.3	N11 53.1
	08	275 36.9	321 41.4	52.8	41 01.3	04.5	104 28.5	24.3	20 53.6	59.0	Rigel	281 10.2	S 8 11.4
F	09	290 39.4	336 40.7	. . 52.0	56 02.7	. . 04.7	119 31.3	. . 24.5	35 55.9	. . 59.0	Rigil Kent.	139 48.8	S60 53.7
R	10	305 41.9	351 40.0	51.3	71 04.1	05.0	134 34.0	24.6	50 58.3	59.0	Sabik	102 10.5	S15 44.5
I	11	320 44.3	6 39.4	50.5	86 05.5	05.2	149 36.8	24.7	66 00.6	59.0			
D	12	335 46.8	21 38.7	S17 49.8	101 07.0	S18 05.5	164 39.5	N 5 24.9	81 03.0	S20 59.0	Schedar	349 38.8	N56 37.6
A	13	350 49.2	36 38.0	49.0	116 08.4	05.8	179 42.3	25.0	96 05.3	59.0	Shaula	96 19.6	S37 06.6
Y	14	5 51.7	51 37.3	48.2	131 09.8	06.0	194 45.0	25.1	111 07.6	59.1	Sirius	258 31.9	S16 44.7
	15	20 54.2	66 36.6	. . 47.5	146 11.2	. . 06.3	209 47.8	. . 25.2	126 10.0	. . 59.1	Spica	158 29.1	S11 14.7
	16	35 56.6	81 35.9	46.7	161 12.6	06.5	224 50.5	25.4	141 12.3	59.1	Suhail	222 50.6	S43 30.1
	17	50 59.1	96 35.2	46.0	176 14.0	06.8	239 53.3	25.5	156 14.7	59.1			
	18	66 01.6	111 34.6	S17 45.2	191 15.5	S18 07.0	254 56.0	N 5 25.6	171 17.0	S20 59.1	Vega	80 37.9	N38 47.9
	19	81 04.0	126 33.9	44.5	206 16.9	07.3	269 58.8	25.7	186 19.4	59.1	Zuben'ubi	137 03.2	S16 06.4
	20	96 06.5	141 33.2	43.7	221 18.3	07.5	285 01.5	25.9	201 21.7	59.1			
	21	111 09.0	156 32.5	. . 42.9	236 19.7	. . 07.8	300 04.3	. . 26.0	216 24.0	. . 59.1			
	22	126 11.4	171 31.8	42.2	251 21.1	08.0	315 07.0	26.1	231 26.4	59.1			
	23	141 13.9	186 31.1	41.4	266 22.6	08.3	330 09.8	26.3	246 28.7	59.1			
	Mer. Pass.	h m 13 40.5	v −0.7	d 0.7	v 1.4	d 0.3	v 2.7	d 0.1	v 2.3	d 0.0			

	SHA	Mer. Pass.
	° ′	h m
Venus	47 45.6	10 32
Mars	125 58.1	5 18
Jupiter	188 42.5	1 08
Saturn	105 20.7	6 40

UT (d h)	SUN GHA	SUN Dec	MOON GHA	v	MOON Dec	d	HP
	° ′	° ′	° ′	′	° ′	′	′
24 00 (WEDNESDAY)	176 39.9	S 9 44.9	343 52.7	14.5	N 4 13.8	9.2	54.7
01	191 40.0	44.0	358 26.2	14.5	4 04.6	9.3	54.6
02	206 40.1	43.0	12 59.7	14.5	3 55.3	9.3	54.6
03	221 40.2	. . 42.1	27 33.2	14.6	3 46.0	9.3	54.6
04	236 40.3	41.2	42 06.8	14.6	3 36.7	9.3	54.6
05	251 40.4	40.3	56 40.4	14.6	3 27.4	9.3	54.6
06	266 40.5	S 9 39.4	71 14.0	14.6	N 3 18.1	9.3	54.6
07	281 40.6	38.4	85 47.6	14.7	3 08.8	9.3	54.6
08	296 40.6	37.5	100 21.3	14.7	2 59.5	9.4	54.6
09	311 40.7	. . 36.6	114 55.0	14.7	2 50.1	9.3	54.5
10	326 40.8	35.7	129 28.7	14.7	2 40.8	9.4	54.5
11	341 40.9	34.8	144 02.4	14.8	2 31.4	9.3	54.5
12	356 41.0	S 9 33.8	158 36.2	14.8	N 2 22.1	9.4	54.5
13	11 41.1	32.9	173 10.0	14.7	2 12.7	9.4	54.5
14	26 41.2	32.0	187 43.7	14.9	2 03.3	9.3	54.5
15	41 41.3	. . 31.1	202 17.6	14.8	1 54.0	9.4	54.5
16	56 41.4	30.2	216 51.4	14.8	1 44.6	9.4	54.5
17	71 41.5	29.2	231 25.2	14.9	1 35.2	9.4	54.4
18	86 41.6	S 9 28.3	245 59.1	14.9	N 1 25.8	9.4	54.4
19	101 41.7	27.4	260 33.0	14.9	1 16.4	9.3	54.4
20	116 41.7	26.5	275 06.9	14.9	1 07.1	9.4	54.4
21	131 41.8	. . 25.5	289 40.8	14.9	0 57.7	9.4	54.4
22	146 41.9	24.6	304 14.7	15.0	0 48.3	9.4	54.4
23	161 42.0	23.7	318 48.7	14.9	0 38.9	9.4	54.4
25 00 (THURSDAY)	176 42.1	S 9 22.8	333 22.6	15.0	N 0 29.5	9.3	54.4
01	191 42.2	21.8	347 56.6	15.0	0 20.2	9.4	54.4
02	206 42.3	20.9	2 30.6	15.0	0 10.8	9.4	54.3
03	221 42.4	. . 20.0	17 04.6	15.0	N 0 01.4	9.4	54.3
04	236 42.5	19.1	31 38.6	15.1	S 0 08.0	9.3	54.3
05	251 42.6	18.1	46 12.7	15.0	0 17.3	9.4	54.3
06	266 42.7	S 9 17.2	60 46.7	15.0	S 0 26.7	9.3	54.3
07	281 42.8	16.3	75 20.7	15.1	0 36.0	9.4	54.3
08	296 42.9	15.4	89 54.8	15.1	0 45.4	9.3	54.3
09	311 43.0	. . 14.4	104 28.9	15.0	0 54.7	9.3	54.3
10	326 43.1	13.5	119 02.9	15.1	1 04.0	9.4	54.3
11	341 43.2	12.6	133 37.0	15.1	1 13.4	9.3	54.3
12	356 43.3	S 9 11.6	148 11.1	15.1	S 1 22.7	9.3	54.3
13	11 43.4	10.7	162 45.2	15.1	1 32.0	9.3	54.3
14	26 43.5	09.8	177 19.3	15.1	1 41.3	9.3	54.2
15	41 43.6	. . 08.9	191 53.4	15.1	1 50.6	9.2	54.2
16	56 43.7	07.9	206 27.5	15.2	1 59.8	9.3	54.2
17	71 43.8	07.0	221 01.7	15.1	2 09.1	9.3	54.2
18	86 43.9	S 9 06.1	235 35.8	15.1	S 2 18.4	9.2	54.2
19	101 44.0	05.2	250 09.9	15.2	2 27.6	9.2	54.2
20	116 44.1	04.2	264 44.1	15.1	2 36.8	9.2	54.2
21	131 44.2	. . 03.3	279 18.2	15.1	2 46.0	9.2	54.2
22	146 44.3	02.4	293 52.3	15.2	2 55.2	9.2	54.2
23	161 44.4	01.4	308 26.5	15.1	3 04.4	9.2	54.2
26 00 (FRIDAY)	176 44.5	S 9 00.5	323 00.6	15.1	S 3 13.6	9.1	54.2
01	191 44.6	8 59.6	337 34.7	15.2	3 22.7	9.1	54.2
02	206 44.7	58.6	352 08.9	15.1	3 31.8	9.2	54.2
03	221 44.8	. . 57.7	6 43.0	15.2	3 41.0	9.1	54.2
04	236 44.9	56.8	21 17.2	15.1	3 50.1	9.0	54.2
05	251 45.0	55.8	35 51.3	15.1	3 59.1	9.1	54.1
06	266 45.1	S 8 54.9	50 25.4	15.1	S 4 08.2	9.0	54.1
07	281 45.2	54.0	64 59.5	15.2	4 17.2	9.1	54.1
08	296 45.3	53.1	79 33.7	15.1	4 26.3	9.0	54.1
09	311 45.4	. . 52.1	94 07.8	15.1	4 35.3	8.9	54.1
10	326 45.5	51.2	108 41.9	15.1	4 44.2	9.0	54.1
11	341 45.6	50.3	123 16.0	15.1	4 53.2	8.9	54.1
12	356 45.7	S 8 49.3	137 50.1	15.1	S 5 02.1	9.0	54.1
13	11 45.8	48.4	152 24.2	15.1	5 11.1	8.8	54.1
14	26 45.9	47.5	166 58.3	15.1	5 19.9	8.9	54.1
15	41 46.0	. . 46.5	181 32.4	15.0	5 28.8	8.9	54.1
16	56 46.1	45.6	196 06.4	15.1	5 37.7	8.8	54.1
17	71 46.2	44.7	210 40.5	15.1	5 46.5	8.8	54.1
18	86 46.3	S 8 43.7	225 14.6	15.0	S 5 55.3	8.7	54.1
19	101 46.4	42.8	239 48.6	15.0	6 04.0	8.8	54.1
20	116 46.5	41.8	254 22.6	15.1	6 12.8	8.7	54.1
21	131 46.6	. . 40.9	268 56.7	15.0	6 21.5	8.7	54.1
22	146 46.7	40.0	283 30.7	15.0	6 30.2	8.6	54.1
23	161 46.8	39.0	298 04.7	14.9	S 6 38.8	8.7	54.1
	SD 16.2	*d* 0.9	SD 14.9		14.8		14.7

Lat.	Twilight Naut.	Twilight Civil	Sunrise	Moonrise 24	25	26	27
°	h m	h m	h m	h m	h m	h m	h m
N 72	05 32	06 50	08 01	19 25	20 58	22 31	24 06
N 70	05 35	06 45	07 49	19 26	20 54	22 21	23 49
68	05 37	06 41	07 39	19 28	20 51	22 13	23 36
66	05 39	06 38	07 30	19 29	20 48	22 07	23 25
64	05 40	06 35	07 23	19 30	20 46	22 01	23 16
62	05 41	06 32	07 17	19 30	20 44	21 56	23 08
60	05 41	06 29	07 12	19 31	20 42	21 52	23 01
N 58	05 42	06 27	07 07	19 32	20 40	21 48	22 55
56	05 42	06 25	07 03	19 32	20 39	21 45	22 50
54	05 43	06 23	06 59	19 33	20 38	21 42	22 46
52	05 43	06 22	06 56	19 33	20 37	21 39	22 41
50	05 43	06 20	06 53	19 34	20 36	21 37	22 38
45	05 42	06 16	06 46	19 35	20 33	21 32	22 29
N 40	05 41	06 13	06 40	19 35	20 31	21 27	22 23
35	05 40	06 10	06 35	19 36	20 30	21 23	22 17
30	05 39	06 07	06 31	19 37	20 29	21 20	22 12
20	05 35	06 01	06 23	19 38	20 26	21 14	22 03
N 10	05 30	05 55	06 16	19 38	20 24	21 09	21 55
0	05 25	05 49	06 10	19 39	20 22	21 05	21 48
S 10	05 17	05 42	06 03	19 40	20 20	21 00	21 41
20	05 07	05 33	05 56	19 41	20 18	20 55	21 33
30	04 54	05 23	05 48	19 42	20 16	20 50	21 25
35	04 46	05 17	05 43	19 43	20 14	20 46	21 20
40	04 36	05 09	05 37	19 43	20 13	20 43	21 14
45	04 23	05 00	05 31	19 44	20 11	20 39	21 07
S 50	04 07	04 49	05 23	19 45	20 09	20 34	21 00
52	03 59	04 43	05 19	19 46	20 08	20 32	20 56
54	03 50	04 37	05 15	19 46	20 07	20 29	20 52
56	03 40	04 31	05 11	19 47	20 06	20 26	20 48
58	03 28	04 23	05 06	19 47	20 05	20 23	20 43
S 60	03 14	04 14	05 00	19 48	20 04	20 20	20 38

Lat.	Sunset	Twilight Civil	Twilight Naut.	Moonset 24	25	26	27
°	h m	h m	h m	h m	h m	h m	h m
N 72	16 27	17 38	18 57	07 54	07 50	07 45	07 41
N 70	16 39	17 43	18 54	07 50	07 51	07 51	07 52
68	16 49	17 47	18 51	07 47	07 52	07 56	08 02
66	16 57	17 50	18 50	07 44	07 53	08 01	08 10
64	17 04	17 53	18 48	07 42	07 53	08 04	08 16
62	17 10	17 56	18 47	07 40	07 54	08 07	08 22
60	17 16	17 58	18 46	07 38	07 54	08 10	08 27
N 58	17 20	18 00	18 46	07 37	07 55	08 13	08 32
56	17 24	18 02	18 45	07 35	07 55	08 15	08 36
54	17 28	18 04	18 45	07 34	07 55	08 17	08 39
52	17 31	18 05	18 45	07 33	07 56	08 19	08 42
50	17 34	18 07	18 45	07 32	07 56	08 20	08 45
45	17 41	18 11	18 45	07 29	07 57	08 24	08 52
N 40	17 47	18 14	18 45	07 27	07 57	08 27	08 57
35	17 51	18 17	18 46	07 26	07 58	08 29	09 02
30	17 56	18 20	18 48	07 24	07 58	08 32	09 06
20	18 03	18 26	18 51	07 22	07 59	08 36	09 13
N 10	18 10	18 31	18 56	07 19	07 59	08 39	09 20
0	18 16	18 37	19 02	07 17	08 00	08 43	09 25
S 10	18 23	18 44	19 09	07 15	08 01	08 46	09 31
20	18 30	18 52	19 19	07 12	08 01	08 49	09 38
30	18 38	19 03	19 31	07 09	08 02	08 53	09 45
35	18 43	19 09	19 40	07 08	08 02	08 56	09 49
40	18 48	19 16	19 50	07 06	08 02	08 58	09 54
45	18 55	19 25	20 02	07 04	08 03	09 01	09 59
S 50	19 02	19 36	20 18	07 01	08 04	09 05	10 06
52	19 06	19 42	20 25	07 00	08 04	09 07	10 09
54	19 10	19 47	20 34	06 59	08 04	09 09	10 12
56	19 14	19 54	20 44	06 57	08 04	09 11	10 16
58	19 19	20 01	20 56	06 56	08 05	09 13	10 20
S 60	19 24	20 10	21 10	06 54	08 05	09 15	10 25

Day	SUN Eqn. of Time 00h	SUN Eqn. of Time 12h	SUN Mer. Pass.	MOON Mer. Pass. Upper	MOON Mer. Pass. Lower	Age	Phase
d	m s	m s	h m	h m	h m	d	%
24	13 20	13 16	12 13	01 06	13 28	16	97
25	13 12	13 07	12 13	01 50	14 11	17	93
26	13 02	12 58	12 13	02 32	14 54	18	88

UT d	h	ARIES GHA	VENUS −3·9 GHA	VENUS Dec	MARS +0·3 GHA	MARS Dec	JUPITER −2·5 GHA	JUPITER Dec	SATURN +0·5 GHA	SATURN Dec
		° ′	° ′	° ′	° ′	° ′	° ′	° ′	° ′	° ′
27 SATURDAY	00	156 16.4	201 30.5	S17 40.6	281 24.0	S18 08.5	345 12.5	N 5 26.4	261 31.1	S20 59.1
	01	171 18.8	216 29.8	39.9	296 25.4	08.8	0 15.3	26.5	276 33.4	59.1
	02	186 21.3	231 29.1	39.1	311 26.8	09.0	15 18.0	26.6	291 35.8	59.1
	03	201 23.7	246 28.4	. . 38.3	326 28.3	. . 09.3	30 20.8	. . 26.8	306 38.1	. . 59.1
	04	216 26.2	261 27.7	37.6	341 29.7	09.5	45 23.5	26.9	321 40.4	59.2
	05	231 28.7	276 27.1	36.8	356 31.1	09.8	60 26.3	27.0	336 42.8	59.2
	06	246 31.1	291 26.4	S17 36.0	11 32.5	S18 10.0	75 29.0	N 5 27.1	351 45.1	S20 59.2
	07	261 33.6	306 25.7	35.3	26 34.0	10.3	90 31.8	27.3	6 47.5	59.2
	08	276 36.1	321 25.0	34.5	41 35.4	10.6	105 34.5	27.4	21 49.8	59.2
	09	291 38.5	336 24.3	. . 33.7	56 36.8	. . 10.8	120 37.3	. . 27.5	36 52.2	. . 59.2
	10	306 41.0	351 23.7	32.9	71 38.2	11.1	135 40.0	27.7	51 54.5	59.2
	11	321 43.5	6 23.0	32.2	86 39.7	11.3	150 42.8	27.8	66 56.9	59.2
	12	336 45.9	21 22.3	S17 31.4	101 41.1	S18 11.6	165 45.5	N 5 27.9	81 59.2	S20 59.2
	13	351 48.4	36 21.6	30.6	116 42.5	11.8	180 48.3	28.0	97 01.6	59.2
	14	6 50.9	51 21.0	29.8	131 43.9	12.1	195 51.0	28.2	112 03.9	59.2
	15	21 53.3	66 20.3	. . 29.1	146 45.4	. . 12.3	210 53.8	. . 28.3	127 06.2	. . 59.2
	16	36 55.8	81 19.6	28.3	161 46.8	12.6	225 56.5	28.4	142 08.6	59.2
	17	51 58.2	96 18.9	27.5	176 48.2	12.8	240 59.3	28.6	157 10.9	59.2
	18	67 00.7	111 18.3	S17 26.7	191 49.7	S18 13.0	256 02.1	N 5 28.7	172 13.3	S20 59.3
	19	82 03.2	126 17.6	25.9	206 51.1	13.3	271 04.8	28.8	187 15.6	59.3
	20	97 05.6	141 16.9	25.2	221 52.5	13.5	286 07.6	28.9	202 18.0	59.3
	21	112 08.1	156 16.2	. . 24.4	236 53.9	. . 13.8	301 10.3	. . 29.1	217 20.3	. . 59.3
	22	127 10.6	171 15.6	23.6	251 55.4	14.0	316 13.1	29.2	232 22.7	59.3
	23	142 13.0	186 14.9	22.8	266 56.8	14.3	331 15.8	29.3	247 25.0	59.3
28 SUNDAY	00	157 15.5	201 14.2	S17 22.0	281 58.2	S18 14.5	346 18.6	N 5 29.4	262 27.4	S20 59.3
	01	172 18.0	216 13.5	21.2	296 59.7	14.8	1 21.3	29.6	277 29.7	59.3
	02	187 20.4	231 12.9	20.4	312 01.1	15.0	16 24.1	29.7	292 32.1	59.3
	03	202 22.9	246 12.2	. . 19.7	327 02.5	. . 15.3	31 26.8	. . 29.8	307 34.4	. . 59.3
	04	217 25.3	261 11.5	18.9	342 04.0	15.5	46 29.6	30.0	322 36.8	59.3
	05	232 27.8	276 10.9	18.1	357 05.4	15.8	61 32.3	30.1	337 39.1	59.3
	06	247 30.3	291 10.2	S17 17.3	12 06.8	S18 16.0	76 35.1	N 5 30.2	352 41.5	S20 59.3
	07	262 32.7	306 09.5	16.5	27 08.3	16.3	91 37.9	30.3	7 43.8	59.3
	08	277 35.2	321 08.9	15.7	42 09.7	16.5	106 40.6	30.5	22 46.2	59.3
	09	292 37.7	336 08.2	. . 14.9	57 11.1	. . 16.8	121 43.4	. . 30.6	37 48.5	. . 59.4
	10	307 40.1	351 07.5	14.1	72 12.6	17.0	136 46.1	30.7	52 50.9	59.4
	11	322 42.6	6 06.9	13.3	87 14.0	17.3	151 48.9	30.9	67 53.2	59.4
	12	337 45.1	21 06.2	S17 12.5	102 15.5	S18 17.5	166 51.6	N 5 31.0	82 55.6	S20 59.4
	13	352 47.5	36 05.5	11.7	117 16.9	17.7	181 54.4	31.1	97 57.9	59.4
	14	7 50.0	51 04.9	10.9	132 18.3	18.0	196 57.1	31.2	113 00.3	59.4
	15	22 52.5	66 04.2	. . 10.1	147 19.8	. . 18.2	211 59.9	. . 31.4	128 02.6	. . 59.4
	16	37 54.9	81 03.5	09.3	162 21.2	18.5	227 02.6	31.5	143 05.0	59.4
	17	52 57.4	96 02.9	08.5	177 22.7	18.7	242 05.4	31.6	158 07.3	59.4
	18	67 59.8	111 02.2	S17 07.7	192 24.1	S18 19.0	257 08.2	N 5 31.8	173 09.7	S20 59.4
	19	83 02.3	126 01.5	06.9	207 25.5	19.2	272 10.9	31.9	188 12.0	59.4
	20	98 04.8	141 00.9	06.1	222 27.0	19.5	287 13.7	32.0	203 14.4	59.4
	21	113 07.2	156 00.2	. . 05.3	237 28.4	. . 19.7	302 16.4	. . 32.1	218 16.7	. . 59.4
	22	128 09.7	170 59.6	04.5	252 29.9	20.0	317 19.2	32.3	233 19.1	59.4
	23	143 12.2	185 58.9	03.7	267 31.3	20.2	332 21.9	32.4	248 21.4	59.4
29 MONDAY	00	158 14.6	200 58.2	S17 02.9	282 32.7	S18 20.4	347 24.7	N 5 32.5	263 23.8	S20 59.4
	01	173 17.1	215 57.6	02.1	297 34.2	20.7	2 27.4	32.7	278 26.1	59.5
	02	188 19.6	230 56.9	01.3	312 35.6	20.9	17 30.2	32.8	293 28.5	59.5
	03	203 22.0	245 56.3	17 00.5	327 37.1	. . 21.2	32 33.0	. . 32.9	308 30.8	. . 59.5
	04	218 24.5	260 55.6	16 59.7	342 38.5	21.4	47 35.7	33.0	323 33.2	59.5
	05	233 26.9	275 54.9	58.9	357 40.0	21.7	62 38.5	33.2	338 35.5	59.5
	06	248 29.4	290 54.3	S16 58.0	12 41.4	S18 21.9	77 41.2	N 5 33.3	353 37.9	S20 59.5
	07	263 31.9	305 53.6	57.2	27 42.9	22.1	92 44.0	33.4	8 40.2	59.5
	08	278 34.3	320 53.0	56.4	42 44.3	22.4	107 46.7	33.6	23 42.6	59.5
	09	293 36.8	335 52.3	. . 55.6	57 45.7	. . 22.6	122 49.5	. . 33.7	38 45.0	. . 59.5
	10	308 39.3	350 51.7	54.8	72 47.2	22.9	137 52.2	33.8	53 47.3	59.5
	11	323 41.7	5 51.0	54.0	87 48.6	23.1	152 55.0	34.0	68 49.7	59.5
	12	338 44.2	20 50.3	S16 53.2	102 50.1	S18 23.4	167 57.8	N 5 34.1	83 52.0	S20 59.5
	13	353 46.7	35 49.7	52.3	117 51.5	23.6	183 00.5	34.2	98 54.4	59.5
	14	8 49.1	50 49.0	51.5	132 53.0	23.8	198 03.3	34.3	113 56.7	59.5
	15	23 51.6	65 48.4	. . 50.7	147 54.4	. . 24.1	213 06.0	. . 34.5	128 59.1	. . 59.5
	16	38 54.1	80 47.7	49.9	162 55.9	24.3	228 08.8	34.6	144 01.4	59.5
	17	53 56.5	95 47.1	49.1	177 57.3	24.6	243 11.5	34.7	159 03.8	59.5
	18	68 59.0	110 46.4	S16 48.2	192 58.8	S18 24.8	258 14.3	N 5 34.9	174 06.1	S20 59.6
	19	84 01.4	125 45.8	47.4	208 00.2	25.0	273 17.1	35.0	189 08.5	59.6
	20	99 03.9	140 45.1	46.6	223 01.7	25.3	288 19.8	35.1	204 10.9	59.6
	21	114 06.4	155 44.5	. . 45.8	238 03.1	. . 25.5	303 22.6	. . 35.2	219 13.2	. . 59.6
	22	129 08.8	170 43.8	45.0	253 04.6	25.8	318 25.3	35.4	234 15.6	59.6
	23	144 11.3	185 43.2	44.1	268 06.1	26.0	333 28.1	35.5	249 17.9	59.6
Mer. Pass.		h m 13 28.8	v −0.7	d 0.8	v 1.4	d 0.2	v 2.8	d 0.1	v 2.4	d 0.0

STARS

Name	SHA	Dec
	° ′	° ′
Acamar	315 17.2	S40 14.8
Achernar	335 25.9	S57 09.6
Acrux	173 06.4	S63 11.2
Adhara	255 10.9	S29 00.1
Aldebaran	290 47.3	N16 32.3
Alioth	166 18.7	N55 52.2
Alkaid	152 57.2	N49 13.8
Al Na'ir	27 42.0	S46 52.9
Alnilam	275 44.4	S 1 11.8
Alphard	217 54.0	S 8 44.0
Alphecca	126 09.4	N26 39.5
Alpheratz	357 41.9	N29 10.7
Altair	62 06.7	N 8 54.7
Ankaa	353 14.3	S42 13.3
Antares	112 24.0	S26 27.8
Arcturus	145 53.9	N19 05.8
Atria	107 24.2	S69 02.9
Avior	234 16.7	S59 34.0
Bellatrix	278 30.0	N 6 21.5
Betelgeuse	270 59.2	N 7 24.3
Canopus	263 55.1	S52 42.7
Capella	280 31.6	N46 00.8
Deneb	49 30.6	N45 20.2
Denebola	182 31.5	N14 28.8
Diphda	348 54.3	S17 54.1
Dubhe	193 48.9	N61 39.7
Elnath	278 10.2	N28 37.1
Eltanin	90 45.5	N51 29.1
Enif	33 45.6	N 9 56.9
Fomalhaut	15 22.4	S29 32.3
Gacrux	171 58.2	S57 12.1
Gienah	175 50.1	S17 37.9
Hadar	148 44.8	S60 26.8
Hamal	327 58.9	N23 32.2
Kaus Aust.	83 41.6	S34 22.3
Kochab	137 19.8	N74 05.2
Markab	13 36.8	N15 17.5
Menkar	314 13.2	N 4 08.9
Menkent	148 05.1	S36 26.8
Miaplacidus	221 38.3	S69 47.3
Mirfak	308 37.8	N49 55.1
Nunki	75 56.3	S26 16.4
Peacock	53 16.9	S56 40.7
Pollux	243 25.2	N27 59.0
Procyon	244 57.6	N 5 10.7
Rasalhague	96 04.8	N12 32.9
Regulus	207 41.3	N11 53.1
Rigel	281 10.2	S 8 11.4
Rigil Kent.	139 48.8	S60 53.7
Sabik	102 10.5	S15 44.5
Schedar	349 38.8	N56 37.6
Shaula	96 19.5	S37 06.6
Sirius	258 31.9	S16 44.7
Spica	158 29.1	S11 14.7
Suhail	222 50.6	S43 30.2
Vega	80 37.9	N38 47.8
Zuben'ubi	137 03.2	S16 06.4

	SHA	Mer. Pass.
	° ′	h m
Venus	43 58.7	10 36
Mars	124 42.7	5 12
Jupiter	189 03.1	0 55
Saturn	105 11.9	6 29

	UT	SUN GHA	SUN Dec	MOON GHA	v	MOON Dec	d	HP
	d h	° ′	° ′	° ′	′	° ′	′	′
	27 00	176 46.9	S 8 38.1	312 38.6	15.0	S 6 47.5	8.6	54.1
	01	191 47.0	37.2	327 12.6	15.0	6 56.1	8.6	54.1
	02	206 47.1	36.2	341 46.6	14.9	7 04.7	8.5	54.1
	03	221 47.2	. . 35.3	356 20.5	14.9	7 13.2	8.5	54.1
	04	236 47.4	34.4	10 54.4	14.9	7 21.7	8.5	54.1
	05	251 47.5	33.4	25 28.3	14.9	7 30.2	8.4	54.1
	06	266 47.6	S 8 32.5	40 02.2	14.9	S 7 38.6	8.5	54.1
	07	281 47.7	31.5	54 36.1	14.9	7 47.1	8.3	54.1
S	08	296 47.8	30.6	69 10.0	14.8	7 55.4	8.4	54.1
A	09	311 47.9	. . 29.7	83 43.8	14.8	8 03.8	8.3	54.1
T	10	326 48.0	28.7	98 17.6	14.8	8 12.1	8.3	54.1
U	11	341 48.1	27.8	112 51.4	14.8	8 20.4	8.3	54.1
R	12	356 48.2	S 8 26.9	127 25.2	14.8	S 8 28.7	8.2	54.1
D	13	11 48.3	25.9	141 59.0	14.7	8 36.9	8.2	54.1
A	14	26 48.4	25.0	156 32.7	14.8	8 45.1	8.1	54.1
Y	15	41 48.5	. . 24.0	171 06.5	14.7	8 53.2	8.1	54.1
	16	56 48.7	23.1	185 40.2	14.6	9 01.3	8.1	54.1
	17	71 48.8	22.2	200 13.8	14.7	9 09.4	8.0	54.1
	18	86 48.9	S 8 21.2	214 47.5	14.6	S 9 17.4	8.0	54.1
	19	101 49.0	20.3	229 21.1	14.6	9 25.4	8.0	54.1
	20	116 49.1	19.3	243 54.7	14.6	9 33.4	7.9	54.1
	21	131 49.2	. . 18.4	258 28.3	14.6	9 41.3	7.9	54.1
	22	146 49.3	17.5	273 01.9	14.5	9 49.2	7.8	54.1
	23	161 49.4	16.5	287 35.4	14.5	9 57.0	7.8	54.1
	28 00	176 49.5	S 8 15.6	302 08.9	14.5	S10 04.8	7.7	54.1
	01	191 49.6	14.6	316 42.4	14.4	10 12.5	7.8	54.1
	02	206 49.8	13.7	331 15.8	14.5	10 20.3	7.6	54.2
	03	221 49.9	. . 12.8	345 49.3	14.4	10 27.9	7.7	54.2
	04	236 50.0	11.8	0 22.7	14.3	10 35.6	7.5	54.2
	05	251 50.1	10.9	14 56.0	14.4	10 43.1	7.6	54.2
	06	266 50.2	S 8 09.9	29 29.4	14.3	S10 50.7	7.5	54.2
	07	281 50.3	09.0	44 02.7	14.3	10 58.2	7.4	54.2
	08	296 50.4	08.0	58 36.0	14.2	11 05.6	7.4	54.2
S	09	311 50.5	. . 07.1	73 09.2	14.3	11 13.0	7.4	54.2
U	10	326 50.7	06.2	87 42.5	14.1	11 20.4	7.3	54.2
N	11	341 50.8	05.2	102 15.6	14.2	11 27.7	7.3	54.2
D	12	356 50.9	S 8 04.3	116 48.8	14.1	S11 35.0	7.2	54.2
A	13	11 51.0	03.3	131 21.9	14.1	11 42.2	7.2	54.2
Y	14	26 51.1	02.4	145 55.0	14.1	11 49.4	7.1	54.2
	15	41 51.2	. . 01.4	160 28.1	14.0	11 56.5	7.1	54.2
	16	56 51.3	8 00.5	175 01.1	14.0	12 03.6	7.0	54.3
	17	71 51.5	7 59.5	189 34.1	14.0	12 10.6	7.0	54.3
	18	86 51.6	S 7 58.6	204 07.1	13.9	S12 17.6	6.9	54.3
	19	101 51.7	57.7	218 40.0	13.9	12 24.5	6.8	54.3
	20	116 51.8	56.7	233 12.9	13.8	12 31.3	6.9	54.3
	21	131 51.9	. . 55.8	247 45.7	13.8	12 38.2	6.7	54.3
	22	146 52.0	54.8	262 18.5	13.8	12 44.9	6.7	54.3
	23	161 52.2	53.9	276 51.3	13.8	12 51.6	6.7	54.3
	29 00	176 52.3	S 7 52.9	291 24.1	13.7	S12 58.3	6.6	54.3
	01	191 52.4	52.0	305 56.8	13.6	13 04.9	6.6	54.4
	02	206 52.5	51.0	320 29.4	13.7	13 11.5	6.5	54.4
	03	221 52.6	. . 50.1	335 02.1	13.6	13 18.0	6.4	54.4
	04	236 52.7	49.1	349 34.7	13.5	13 24.4	6.4	54.4
	05	251 52.9	48.2	4 07.2	13.5	13 30.8	6.3	54.4
	06	266 53.0	S 7 47.3	18 39.7	13.5	S13 37.1	6.3	54.4
	07	281 53.1	46.3	33 12.2	13.4	13 43.4	6.2	54.4
	08	296 53.2	45.4	47 44.6	13.4	13 49.6	6.2	54.4
M	09	311 53.3	. . 44.4	62 17.0	13.4	13 55.8	6.1	54.5
O	10	326 53.5	43.5	76 49.4	13.3	14 01.9	6.0	54.5
N	11	341 53.6	42.5	91 21.7	13.2	14 07.9	6.0	54.5
D	12	356 53.7	S 7 41.6	105 53.9	13.3	S14 13.9	5.9	54.5
A	13	11 53.8	40.6	120 26.2	13.2	14 19.8	5.9	54.5
Y	14	26 53.9	39.7	134 58.4	13.1	14 25.7	5.8	54.5
	15	41 54.1	. . 38.7	149 30.5	13.1	14 31.5	5.7	54.6
	16	56 54.2	37.8	164 02.6	13.1	14 37.2	5.7	54.6
	17	71 54.3	36.8	178 34.7	13.0	14 42.9	5.6	54.6
	18	86 54.4	S 7 35.9	193 06.7	12.9	S14 48.5	5.5	54.6
	19	101 54.5	34.9	207 38.6	13.0	14 54.0	5.5	54.6
	20	116 54.7	34.0	222 10.6	12.8	14 59.5	5.4	54.6
	21	131 54.8	. . 33.0	236 42.4	12.9	15 04.9	5.4	54.7
	22	146 54.9	32.1	251 14.3	12.8	15 10.3	5.3	54.7
	23	161 55.0	31.1	265 46.1	12.7	S15 15.6	5.2	54.7
		SD 16.2	d 0.9	SD 14.7		14.8		14.9

Lat.	Twilight Naut.	Twilight Civil	Sunrise	Moonrise 27	Moonrise 28	Moonrise 29	Moonrise 1
°	h m	h m	h m	h m	h m	h m	h m
N 72	05 18	06 35	07 45	24 06	00 06	01 43	03 26
N 70	05 22	06 32	07 35	23 49	25 17	01 17	02 46
68	05 25	06 29	07 26	23 36	24 58	00 58	02 19
66	05 28	06 27	07 19	23 25	24 42	00 42	01 58
64	05 30	06 25	07 13	23 16	24 30	00 30	01 42
62	05 32	06 23	07 08	23 08	24 19	00 19	01 28
60	05 33	06 21	07 03	23 01	24 10	00 10	01 17
N 58	05 34	06 20	06 59	22 55	24 02	00 02	01 07
56	05 35	06 18	06 56	22 50	23 55	24 58	00 58
54	05 36	06 17	06 52	22 46	23 49	24 50	00 50
52	05 36	06 15	06 49	22 41	23 43	24 44	00 44
50	05 37	06 14	06 47	22 38	23 38	24 37	00 37
45	05 37	06 11	06 41	22 29	23 27	24 24	00 24
N 40	05 37	06 09	06 36	22 23	23 18	24 13	00 13
35	05 37	06 06	06 32	22 17	23 10	24 04	00 04
30	05 36	06 04	06 28	22 12	23 03	23 56	24 48
20	05 33	05 59	06 21	22 03	22 52	23 42	24 32
N 10	05 29	05 54	06 15	21 55	22 42	23 29	24 18
0	05 24	05 48	06 09	21 48	22 32	23 18	24 06
S 10	05 17	05 42	06 03	21 41	22 23	23 07	23 53
20	05 09	05 35	05 57	21 33	22 13	22 54	23 39
30	04 57	05 25	05 50	21 25	22 01	22 41	23 23
35	04 49	05 20	05 45	21 20	21 55	22 33	23 14
40	04 40	05 13	05 41	21 14	21 47	22 24	23 04
45	04 28	05 04	05 35	21 07	21 39	22 13	22 52
S 50	04 13	04 54	05 28	21 00	21 28	22 00	22 38
52	04 06	04 49	05 25	20 56	21 23	21 54	22 31
54	03 58	04 44	05 21	20 52	21 18	21 48	22 23
56	03 48	04 38	05 17	20 48	21 12	21 41	22 15
58	03 37	04 31	05 13	20 43	21 06	21 32	22 05
S 60	03 24	04 23	05 08	20 38	20 58	21 23	21 54

Lat.	Sunset	Twilight Civil	Twilight Naut.	Moonset 27	Moonset 28	Moonset 29	Moonset 1
°	h m	h m	h m	h m	h m	h m	h m
N 72	16 42	17 52	19 10	07 41	07 36	07 30	07 23
N 70	16 52	17 55	19 06	07 52	07 54	07 57	08 04
68	17 01	17 58	19 02	08 02	08 08	08 18	08 32
66	17 08	18 00	18 59	08 10	08 20	08 34	08 53
64	17 14	18 02	18 57	08 16	08 30	08 47	09 10
62	17 19	18 04	18 55	08 22	08 39	08 59	09 24
60	17 23	18 05	18 53	08 27	08 46	09 08	09 36
N 58	17 27	18 07	18 52	08 32	08 53	09 17	09 46
56	17 31	18 08	18 51	08 36	08 58	09 24	09 55
54	17 34	18 10	18 50	08 39	09 03	09 31	10 03
52	17 37	18 11	18 50	08 42	09 08	09 37	10 10
50	17 39	18 12	18 49	08 45	09 12	09 42	10 17
45	17 45	18 15	18 49	08 52	09 22	09 54	10 31
N 40	17 50	18 17	18 49	08 57	09 29	10 04	10 42
35	17 54	18 20	18 49	09 02	09 36	10 12	10 52
30	17 58	18 22	18 50	09 06	09 42	10 20	11 01
20	18 04	18 27	18 52	09 13	09 52	10 32	11 15
N 10	18 10	18 31	18 56	09 20	10 01	10 43	11 28
0	18 16	18 37	19 01	09 25	10 09	10 54	11 41
S 10	18 22	18 43	19 08	09 31	10 17	11 04	11 53
20	18 28	18 50	19 16	09 38	10 26	11 16	12 06
30	18 35	18 59	19 28	09 45	10 37	11 29	12 21
35	18 39	19 05	19 36	09 49	10 43	11 36	12 29
40	18 44	19 12	19 45	09 54	10 49	11 44	12 39
45	18 50	19 20	19 56	09 59	10 57	11 54	12 51
S 50	18 56	19 30	20 11	10 06	11 07	12 06	13 05
52	18 59	19 35	20 18	10 09	11 11	12 12	13 12
54	19 03	19 40	20 26	10 12	11 16	12 18	13 19
56	19 07	19 46	20 35	10 16	11 21	12 25	13 27
58	19 11	19 53	20 46	10 20	11 27	12 33	13 36
S 60	19 16	20 00	20 58	10 25	11 34	12 42	13 47

Day	SUN Eqn. of Time 00^h	SUN Eqn. of Time 12^h	SUN Mer. Pass.	MOON Mer. Pass. Upper	MOON Mer. Pass. Lower	MOON Age	MOON Phase
d	m s	m s	h m	h m	h m	d	%
27	12 53	12 47	12 13	03 15	15 37	19	81
28	12 42	12 37	12 13	03 58	16 21	20	73
29	12 31	12 25	12 12	04 43	17 06	21	64

UT d	UT h	ARIES GHA	VENUS −3·8 GHA	VENUS Dec	MARS +0·2 GHA	MARS Dec	JUPITER −2·5 GHA	JUPITER Dec	SATURN +0·5 GHA	SATURN Dec
		° ′	° ′	° ′	° ′	° ′	° ′	° ′	° ′	° ′
1	00	159 13.8	200 42.5	S16 43.3	283 07.5	S18 26.2	348 30.8	N 5 35.6	264 20.3	S20 59.6
	01	174 16.2	215 41.9	42.5	298 09.0	26.5	3 33.6	35.8	279 22.6	59.6
	02	189 18.7	230 41.2	41.6	313 10.4	26.7	18 36.4	35.9	294 25.0	59.6
	03	204 21.2	245 40.6	40.8	328 11.9	27.0	33 39.1	36.0	309 27.3	59.6
	04	219 23.6	260 39.9	40.0	343 13.3	27.2	48 41.9	36.1	324 29.7	59.6
	05	234 26.1	275 39.3	39.2	358 14.8	27.4	63 44.6	36.3	339 32.1	59.6
	06	249 28.6	290 38.6	S16 38.3	13 16.2	S18 27.7	78 47.4	N 5 36.4	354 34.4	S20 59.6
	07	264 31.0	305 38.0	37.5	28 17.7	27.9	93 50.2	36.5	9 36.8	59.6
T	08	279 33.5	320 37.3	36.7	43 19.2	28.1	108 52.9	36.7	24 39.1	59.6
U	09	294 35.9	335 36.7	35.8	58 20.6	28.4	123 55.7	36.8	39 41.5	59.6
E	10	309 38.4	350 36.1	35.0	73 22.1	28.6	138 58.4	36.9	54 43.9	59.6
S	11	324 40.9	5 35.4	34.2	88 23.5	28.9	154 01.2	37.1	69 46.2	59.7
D	12	339 43.3	20 34.8	S16 33.3	103 25.0	S18 29.1	169 03.9	N 5 37.2	84 48.6	S20 59.7
A	13	354 45.8	35 34.1	32.5	118 26.4	29.3	184 06.7	37.3	99 50.9	59.7
Y	14	9 48.3	50 33.5	31.6	133 27.9	29.6	199 09.5	37.4	114 53.3	59.7
	15	24 50.7	65 32.8	30.8	148 29.4	29.8	214 12.2	37.6	129 55.6	59.7
	16	39 53.2	80 32.2	30.0	163 30.8	30.0	229 15.0	37.7	144 58.0	59.7
	17	54 55.7	95 31.6	29.1	178 32.3	30.3	244 17.7	37.8	160 00.4	59.7
	18	69 58.1	110 30.9	S16 28.3	193 33.8	S18 30.5	259 20.5	N 5 38.0	175 02.7	S20 59.7
	19	85 00.6	125 30.3	27.4	208 35.2	30.8	274 23.3	38.1	190 05.1	59.7
	20	100 03.0	140 29.6	26.6	223 36.7	31.0	289 26.0	38.2	205 07.4	59.7
	21	115 05.5	155 29.0	25.8	238 38.1	31.2	304 28.8	38.3	220 09.8	59.7
	22	130 08.0	170 28.3	24.9	253 39.6	31.5	319 31.5	38.5	235 12.2	59.7
	23	145 10.4	185 27.7	24.1	268 41.1	31.7	334 34.3	38.6	250 14.5	59.7
2	00	160 12.9	200 27.1	S16 23.2	283 42.5	S18 31.9	349 37.1	N 5 38.7	265 16.9	S20 59.7
	01	175 15.4	215 26.4	22.4	298 44.0	32.2	4 39.8	38.9	280 19.2	59.7
	02	190 17.8	230 25.8	21.5	313 45.5	32.4	19 42.6	39.0	295 21.6	59.7
	03	205 20.3	245 25.2	20.7	328 46.9	32.6	34 45.3	39.1	310 24.0	59.7
	04	220 22.8	260 24.5	19.8	343 48.4	32.9	49 48.1	39.3	325 26.3	59.7
	05	235 25.2	275 23.9	19.0	358 49.9	33.1	64 50.8	39.4	340 28.7	59.7
	06	250 27.7	290 23.3	S16 18.1	13 51.3	S18 33.3	79 53.6	N 5 39.5	355 31.0	S20 59.8
W	07	265 30.2	305 22.6	17.3	28 52.8	33.6	94 56.4	39.6	10 33.4	59.8
E	08	280 32.6	320 22.0	16.4	43 54.3	33.8	109 59.1	39.8	25 35.8	59.8
D	09	295 35.1	335 21.3	15.6	58 55.8	34.0	125 01.9	39.9	40 38.1	59.8
N	10	310 37.5	350 20.7	14.7	73 57.2	34.3	140 04.6	40.0	55 40.5	59.8
E	11	325 40.0	5 20.1	13.9	88 58.7	34.5	155 07.4	40.2	70 42.9	59.8
S	12	340 42.5	20 19.4	S16 13.0	104 00.2	S18 34.7	170 10.2	N 5 40.3	85 45.2	S20 59.8
D	13	355 44.9	35 18.8	12.2	119 01.6	35.0	185 12.9	40.4	100 47.6	59.8
A	14	10 47.4	50 18.2	11.3	134 03.1	35.2	200 15.7	40.6	115 49.9	59.8
Y	15	25 49.9	65 17.5	10.4	149 04.6	35.4	215 18.4	40.7	130 52.3	59.8
	16	40 52.3	80 16.9	09.6	164 06.1	35.7	230 21.2	40.8	145 54.7	59.8
	17	55 54.8	95 16.3	08.7	179 07.5	35.9	245 24.0	40.9	160 57.0	59.8
	18	70 57.3	110 15.7	S16 07.9	194 09.0	S18 36.1	260 26.7	N 5 41.1	175 59.4	S20 59.8
	19	85 59.7	125 15.0	07.0	209 10.5	36.4	275 29.5	41.2	191 01.8	59.8
	20	101 02.2	140 14.4	06.1	224 11.9	36.6	290 32.3	41.3	206 04.1	59.8
	21	116 04.7	155 13.8	05.3	239 13.4	36.8	305 35.0	41.5	221 06.5	59.8
	22	131 07.1	170 13.1	04.4	254 14.9	37.1	320 37.8	41.6	236 08.9	59.8
	23	146 09.6	185 12.5	03.6	269 16.4	37.3	335 40.5	41.7	251 11.2	59.8
3	00	161 12.0	200 11.9	S16 02.7	284 17.9	S18 37.5	350 43.3	N 5 41.9	266 13.6	S20 59.8
	01	176 14.5	215 11.3	01.8	299 19.3	37.8	5 46.1	42.0	281 15.9	59.8
	02	191 17.0	230 10.6	01.0	314 20.8	38.0	20 48.8	42.1	296 18.3	59.9
	03	206 19.4	245 10.0	16 00.1	329 22.3	38.2	35 51.6	42.2	311 20.7	59.9
	04	221 21.9	260 09.4	15 59.2	344 23.8	38.5	50 54.3	42.4	326 23.0	59.9
	05	236 24.4	275 08.8	58.4	359 25.2	38.7	65 57.1	42.5	341 25.4	59.9
	06	251 26.8	290 08.1	S15 57.5	14 26.7	S18 38.9	80 59.9	N 5 42.6	356 27.8	S20 59.9
	07	266 29.3	305 07.5	56.6	29 28.2	39.1	96 02.6	42.8	11 30.1	59.9
T	08	281 31.8	320 06.9	55.7	44 29.7	39.4	111 05.4	42.9	26 32.5	59.9
H	09	296 34.2	335 06.3	54.9	59 31.2	39.6	126 08.1	43.0	41 34.9	59.9
U	10	311 36.7	350 05.6	54.0	74 32.7	39.8	141 10.9	43.2	56 37.2	59.9
R	11	326 39.2	5 05.0	53.1	89 34.1	40.1	156 13.7	43.3	71 39.6	59.9
S	12	341 41.6	20 04.4	S15 52.3	104 35.6	S18 40.3	171 16.4	N 5 43.4	86 42.0	S20 59.9
D	13	356 44.1	35 03.8	51.4	119 37.1	40.5	186 19.2	43.5	101 44.3	59.9
A	14	11 46.5	50 03.1	50.5	134 38.6	40.7	201 22.0	43.7	116 46.7	59.9
Y	15	26 49.0	65 02.5	49.6	149 40.1	41.0	216 24.7	43.8	131 49.1	59.9
	16	41 51.5	80 01.9	48.8	164 41.6	41.2	231 27.5	43.9	146 51.4	59.9
	17	56 53.9	95 01.3	47.9	179 43.0	41.4	246 30.2	44.1	161 53.8	59.9
	18	71 56.4	110 00.7	S15 47.0	194 44.5	S18 41.7	261 33.0	N 5 44.2	176 56.2	S20 59.9
	19	86 58.9	125 00.0	46.1	209 46.0	41.9	276 35.8	44.3	191 58.5	59.9
	20	102 01.3	139 59.4	45.2	224 47.5	42.1	291 38.5	44.5	207 00.9	59.9
	21	117 03.8	154 58.8	44.4	239 49.0	42.3	306 41.3	44.6	222 03.3	59.9
	22	132 06.3	169 58.2	43.5	254 50.5	42.6	321 44.0	44.7	237 05.7	59.9
	23	147 08.7	184 57.6	42.6	269 52.0	42.8	336 46.8	44.8	252 08.0	59.9
Mer. Pass.		h m 13 17.0	*v* −0.6	*d* 0.9	*v* 1.5	*d* 0.2	*v* 2.8	*d* 0.1	*v* 2.4	*d* 0.0

STARS

Name	SHA	Dec
	° ′	° ′
Acamar	315 17.2	S40 14.8
Achernar	335 25.9	S57 09.6
Acrux	173 06.4	S63 11.2
Adhara	255 10.9	S29 00.1
Aldebaran	290 47.3	N16 32.3
Alioth	166 18.7	N55 52.2
Alkaid	152 57.2	N49 13.8
Al Na'ir	27 42.0	S46 52.9
Alnilam	275 44.4	S 1 11.8
Alphard	217 54.0	S 8 44.0
Alphecca	126 09.4	N26 39.5
Alpheratz	357 41.9	N29 10.7
Altair	62 06.7	N 8 54.7
Ankaa	353 14.3	S42 13.3
Antares	112 24.0	S26 27.8
Arcturus	145 53.9	N19 05.8
Atria	107 24.1	S69 02.9
Avior	234 16.7	S59 34.0
Bellatrix	278 30.0	N 6 21.5
Betelgeuse	270 59.2	N 7 24.3
Canopus	263 55.1	S52 42.8
Capella	280 31.6	N46 00.8
Deneb	49 30.6	N45 20.2
Denebola	182 31.5	N14 28.8
Diphda	348 54.4	S17 54.1
Dubhe	193 48.9	N61 39.7
Elnath	278 10.2	N28 37.1
Eltanin	90 45.4	N51 29.1
Enif	33 45.6	N 9 56.9
Fomalhaut	15 22.4	S29 32.3
Gacrux	171 58.2	S57 12.1
Gienah	175 50.1	S17 38.0
Hadar	148 44.7	S60 26.8
Hamal	327 58.9	N23 32.2
Kaus Aust.	83 41.5	S34 22.3
Kochab	137 19.7	N74 05.2
Markab	13 36.8	N15 17.5
Menkar	314 13.3	N 4 08.9
Menkent	148 05.1	S36 26.8
Miaplacidus	221 38.3	S69 47.3
Mirfak	308 37.8	N49 55.1
Nunki	75 56.2	S26 16.4
Peacock	53 16.9	S56 40.7
Pollux	243 25.3	N27 59.0
Procyon	244 57.6	N 5 10.7
Rasalhague	96 04.8	N12 32.9
Regulus	207 41.3	N11 53.1
Rigel	281 10.2	S 8 11.4
Rigil Kent.	139 48.8	S60 53.8
Sabik	102 10.5	S15 44.5
Schedar	349 38.8	N56 37.6
Shaula	96 19.5	S37 06.6
Sirius	258 31.9	S16 44.7
Spica	158 29.1	S11 14.7
Suhail	222 50.6	S43 30.2
Vega	80 37.9	N38 47.8
Zuben'ubi	137 03.2	S16 06.4

	SHA	Mer. Pass.
	° ′	h m
Venus	40 14.2	10 39
Mars	123 29.6	5 05
Jupiter	189 24.1	0 41
Saturn	105 04.0	6 18

	UT	SUN GHA	SUN Dec	MOON GHA	*v*	MOON Dec	*d*	HP
	d h	° ′	° ′	° ′	′	° ′	′	′
	1 00	176 55.1	S 7 30.2	280 17.8	12.7	S15 20.8	5.1	54.7
	01	191 55.3	29.2	294 49.5	12.7	15 25.9	5.1	54.7
	02	206 55.4	28.3	309 21.2	12.6	15 31.0	5.0	54.7
	03	221 55.5	. . 27.3	323 52.8	12.5	15 36.0	5.0	54.8
	04	236 55.6	26.4	338 24.3	12.6	15 41.0	4.9	54.8
	05	251 55.8	25.4	352 55.9	12.4	15 45.9	4.8	54.8
	06	266 55.9	S 7 24.5	7 27.3	12.5	S15 50.7	4.7	54.8
	07	281 56.0	23.5	21 58.8	12.3	15 55.4	4.7	54.8
T	08	296 56.1	22.6	36 30.1	12.4	16 00.1	4.6	54.9
U	09	311 56.2	. . 21.6	51 01.5	12.2	16 04.7	4.5	54.9
E	10	326 56.4	20.7	65 32.7	12.3	16 09.2	4.5	54.9
S	11	341 56.5	19.7	80 04.0	12.2	16 13.7	4.3	54.9
D	12	356 56.6	S 7 18.7	94 35.2	12.1	S16 18.0	4.4	55.0
A	13	11 56.7	17.8	109 06.3	12.1	16 22.4	4.2	55.0
Y	14	26 56.9	16.8	123 37.4	12.0	16 26.6	4.1	55.0
	15	41 57.0	. . 15.9	138 08.4	12.0	16 30.7	4.1	55.0
	16	56 57.1	14.9	152 39.4	12.0	16 34.8	4.0	55.0
	17	71 57.2	14.0	167 10.4	11.9	16 38.8	4.0	55.1
	18	86 57.4	S 7 13.0	181 41.3	11.8	S16 42.8	3.8	55.1
	19	101 57.5	12.1	196 12.1	11.8	16 46.6	3.8	55.1
	20	116 57.6	11.1	210 42.9	11.8	16 50.4	3.7	55.1
	21	131 57.8	. . 10.2	225 13.7	11.7	16 54.1	3.6	55.2
	22	146 57.9	09.2	239 44.4	11.6	16 57.7	3.6	55.2
	23	161 58.0	08.3	254 15.0	11.7	17 01.3	3.5	55.2
	2 00	176 58.1	S 7 07.3	268 45.7	11.5	S17 04.8	3.3	55.2
	01	191 58.3	06.3	283 16.2	11.5	17 08.1	3.3	55.3
	02	206 58.4	05.4	297 46.7	11.5	17 11.4	3.3	55.3
	03	221 58.5	. . 04.4	312 17.2	11.4	17 14.7	3.1	55.3
	04	236 58.6	03.5	326 47.6	11.3	17 17.8	3.1	55.3
	05	251 58.8	02.5	341 17.9	11.4	17 20.9	3.0	55.4
	06	266 58.9	S 7 01.6	355 48.3	11.2	S17 23.9	2.8	55.4
W	07	281 59.0	7 00.6	10 18.5	11.2	17 26.7	2.9	55.4
E	08	296 59.2	6 59.6	24 48.7	11.2	17 29.6	2.7	55.4
D	09	311 59.3	. . 58.7	39 18.9	11.1	17 32.3	2.6	55.5
N	10	326 59.4	57.7	53 49.0	11.1	17 34.9	2.6	55.5
E	11	341 59.5	56.8	68 19.1	11.0	17 37.5	2.5	55.5
S	12	356 59.7	S 6 55.8	82 49.1	11.0	S17 40.0	2.4	55.6
D	13	11 59.8	54.9	97 19.1	10.9	17 42.4	2.3	55.6
A	14	26 59.9	53.9	111 49.0	10.9	17 44.7	2.2	55.6
Y	15	42 00.1	. . 52.9	126 18.9	10.8	17 46.9	2.1	55.6
	16	57 00.2	52.0	140 48.7	10.8	17 49.0	2.0	55.7
	17	72 00.3	51.0	155 18.5	10.7	17 51.0	2.0	55.7
	18	87 00.4	S 6 50.1	169 48.2	10.7	S17 53.0	1.8	55.7
	19	102 00.6	49.1	184 17.9	10.6	17 54.8	1.8	55.8
	20	117 00.7	48.2	198 47.5	10.6	17 56.6	1.7	55.8
	21	132 00.8	. . 47.2	213 17.1	10.5	17 58.3	1.6	55.8
	22	147 01.0	46.2	227 46.6	10.5	17 59.9	1.5	55.9
	23	162 01.1	45.3	242 16.1	10.5	18 01.4	1.4	55.9
	3 00	177 01.2	S 6 44.3	256 45.6	10.4	S18 02.8	1.3	55.9
	01	192 01.4	43.4	271 15.0	10.3	18 04.1	1.2	56.0
	02	207 01.5	42.4	285 44.3	10.3	18 05.3	1.1	56.0
	03	222 01.6	. . 41.4	300 13.6	10.3	18 06.4	1.1	56.0
	04	237 01.8	40.5	314 42.9	10.2	18 07.5	0.9	56.1
	05	252 01.9	39.5	329 12.1	10.2	18 08.4	0.9	56.1
	06	267 02.0	S 6 38.6	343 41.3	10.1	S18 09.3	0.7	56.1
	07	282 02.2	37.6	358 10.4	10.1	18 10.0	0.7	56.1
T	08	297 02.3	36.6	12 39.5	10.0	18 10.7	0.5	56.2
H	09	312 02.4	. . 35.7	27 08.5	10.0	18 11.2	0.5	56.2
U	10	327 02.6	34.7	41 37.5	9.9	18 11.7	0.4	56.3
R	11	342 02.7	33.8	56 06.4	9.9	18 12.1	0.3	56.3
S	12	357 02.8	S 6 32.8	70 35.3	9.8	S18 12.4	0.1	56.3
D	13	12 03.0	31.8	85 04.1	9.9	18 12.5	0.1	56.4
A	14	27 03.1	30.9	99 33.0	9.7	18 12.6	0.0	56.4
Y	15	42 03.2	. . 29.9	114 01.7	9.7	18 12.6	0.1	56.4
	16	57 03.4	28.9	128 30.4	9.7	18 12.5	0.2	56.5
	17	72 03.5	28.0	142 59.1	9.7	18 12.3	0.3	56.5
	18	87 03.6	S 6 27.0	157 27.8	9.6	S18 12.0	0.5	56.5
	19	102 03.8	26.1	171 56.4	9.5	18 11.5	0.5	56.6
	20	117 03.9	25.1	186 24.9	9.5	18 11.0	0.6	56.6
	21	132 04.0	. . 24.1	200 53.4	9.5	18 10.4	0.7	56.6
	22	147 04.2	23.2	215 21.9	9.4	18 09.7	0.8	56.7
	23	162 04.3	22.2	229 50.3	9.4	S18 08.9	0.9	56.7
		SD 16.2	*d* 1.0	SD 15.0		15.1		15.3

Lat.	Twilight Naut.	Twilight Civil	Sunrise	Moonrise 1	Moonrise 2	Moonrise 3	Moonrise 4
°	h m	h m	h m	h m	h m	h m	h m
N 72	05 03	06 21	07 29	03 26	05 18	■	■
N 70	05 09	06 19	07 21	02 46	04 11	05 24	06 12
68	05 13	06 18	07 14	02 19	03 35	04 41	05 31
66	05 17	06 16	07 08	01 58	03 10	04 13	05 03
64	05 20	06 15	07 03	01 42	02 50	03 51	04 42
62	05 23	06 14	06 58	01 28	02 34	03 33	04 25
60	05 25	06 13	06 54	01 17	02 20	03 19	04 10
N 58	05 26	06 12	06 51	01 07	02 09	03 07	03 58
56	05 28	06 11	06 48	00 58	01 59	02 56	03 47
54	05 29	06 10	06 45	00 50	01 50	02 47	03 38
52	05 30	06 09	06 43	00 44	01 42	02 38	03 30
50	05 31	06 08	06 41	00 37	01 35	02 31	03 22
45	05 32	06 06	06 36	00 24	01 20	02 15	03 06
N 40	05 33	06 04	06 31	00 13	01 08	02 01	02 53
35	05 33	06 02	06 28	00 04	00 57	01 50	02 42
30	05 33	06 01	06 24	24 48	00 48	01 40	02 32
20	05 31	05 57	06 19	24 32	00 32	01 24	02 15
N 10	05 28	05 53	06 14	24 18	00 18	01 09	02 01
0	05 24	05 48	06 09	24 06	00 06	00 55	01 47
S 10	05 18	05 43	06 04	23 53	24 42	00 42	01 33
20	05 10	05 36	05 58	23 39	24 27	00 27	01 19
30	04 59	05 28	05 52	23 23	24 10	00 10	01 02
35	04 52	05 22	05 48	23 14	24 01	00 01	00 52
40	04 43	05 16	05 44	23 04	23 50	24 41	00 41
45	04 33	05 09	05 39	22 52	23 37	24 28	00 28
S 50	04 19	05 00	05 33	22 38	23 21	24 12	00 12
52	04 12	04 55	05 30	22 31	23 14	24 05	00 05
54	04 05	04 50	05 27	22 23	23 06	23 56	24 56
56	03 56	04 45	05 24	22 15	22 56	23 47	24 48
58	03 46	04 39	05 20	22 05	22 46	23 37	24 38
S 60	03 35	04 32	05 16	21 54	22 34	23 24	24 26

Lat.	Sunset	Twilight Civil	Twilight Naut.	Moonset 1	Moonset 2	Moonset 3	Moonset 4
°	h m	h m	h m	h m	h m	h m	h m
N 72	16 57	18 06	19 24	07 23	07 11	■	■
N 70	17 05	18 07	19 18	08 04	08 18	08 50	09 50
68	17 12	18 08	19 13	08 32	08 55	09 33	10 31
66	17 18	18 10	19 09	08 53	09 21	10 01	10 59
64	17 23	18 11	19 06	09 10	09 41	10 23	11 20
62	17 27	18 12	19 03	09 24	09 57	10 41	11 37
60	17 31	18 13	19 01	09 36	10 11	10 55	11 51
N 58	17 34	18 14	18 59	09 46	10 22	11 08	12 03
56	17 37	18 14	18 57	09 55	10 33	11 18	12 14
54	17 40	18 15	18 56	10 03	10 42	11 28	12 23
52	17 42	18 16	18 55	10 10	10 50	11 36	12 31
50	17 44	18 17	18 54	10 17	10 57	11 44	12 39
45	17 49	18 19	18 53	10 31	11 12	12 00	12 55
N 40	17 53	18 20	18 52	10 42	11 25	12 13	13 07
35	17 57	18 22	18 52	10 52	11 36	12 25	13 18
30	18 00	18 24	18 52	11 01	11 45	12 34	13 28
20	18 06	18 28	18 53	11 15	12 02	12 51	13 45
N 10	18 11	18 32	18 56	11 28	12 16	13 06	13 59
0	18 15	18 36	19 00	11 41	12 29	13 20	14 12
S 10	18 20	18 41	19 06	11 53	12 43	13 34	14 26
20	18 26	18 48	19 14	12 06	12 57	13 48	14 40
30	18 32	18 56	19 24	12 21	13 13	14 05	14 56
35	18 35	19 01	19 31	12 29	13 23	14 15	15 06
40	18 39	19 07	19 40	12 39	13 33	14 26	15 17
45	18 44	19 14	19 50	12 51	13 46	14 39	15 29
S 50	18 50	19 23	20 04	13 05	14 02	14 55	15 45
52	18 53	19 28	20 10	13 12	14 09	15 03	15 52
54	18 56	19 32	20 17	13 19	14 17	15 11	16 00
56	18 59	19 38	20 26	13 27	14 26	15 20	16 09
58	19 03	19 44	20 35	13 36	14 36	15 31	16 19
S 60	19 07	19 51	20 47	13 47	14 48	15 43	16 30

Day	SUN Eqn. of Time 00^h	SUN Eqn. of Time 12^h	SUN Mer. Pass.	MOON Mer. Pass. Upper	MOON Mer. Pass. Lower	MOON Age	MOON Phase
d	m s	m s	h m	h m	h m	d	%
1	12 20	12 14	12 12	05 29	17 53	22	55
2	12 08	12 02	12 12	06 17	18 42	23	45
3	11 55	11 49	12 12	07 08	19 33	24	35

	UT d h	ARIES GHA ° ′	VENUS −3·8 GHA ° ′	Dec ° ′	MARS +0·2 GHA ° ′	Dec ° ′	JUPITER −2·5 GHA ° ′	Dec ° ′	SATURN +0·5 GHA ° ′	Dec ° ′
	4 00	162 11.2	199 57.0	S15 41.7	284 53.5	S18 43.0	351 49.6	N 5 45.0	267 10.4	S21 00.0
	01	177 13.6	214 56.3	40.8	299 54.9	43.2	6 52.3	45.1	282 12.8	00.0
	02	192 16.1	229 55.7	39.9	314 56.4	43.5	21 55.1	45.2	297 15.1	00.0
	03	207 18.6	244 55.1	. . 39.1	329 57.9	. . 43.7	36 57.9	. . 45.4	312 17.5	. . 00.0
	04	222 21.0	259 54.5	38.2	344 59.4	43.9	52 00.6	45.5	327 19.9	00.0
	05	237 23.5	274 53.9	37.3	0 00.9	44.2	67 03.4	45.6	342 22.2	00.0
	06	252 26.0	289 53.3	S15 36.4	15 02.4	S18 44.4	82 06.1	N 5 45.8	357 24.6	S21 00.0
	07	267 28.4	304 52.7	35.5	30 03.9	44.6	97 08.9	45.9	12 27.0	00.0
	08	282 30.9	319 52.0	34.6	45 05.4	44.8	112 11.7	46.0	27 29.3	00.0
F	09	297 33.4	334 51.4	. . 33.7	60 06.9	. . 45.1	127 14.4	. . 46.1	42 31.7	. . 00.0
R	10	312 35.8	349 50.8	32.8	75 08.4	45.3	142 17.2	46.3	57 34.1	00.0
I	11	327 38.3	4 50.2	31.9	90 09.9	45.5	157 20.0	46.4	72 36.5	00.0
D	12	342 40.8	19 49.6	S15 31.1	105 11.4	S18 45.7	172 22.7	N 5 46.5	87 38.8	S21 00.0
A	13	357 43.2	34 49.0	30.2	120 12.9	46.0	187 25.5	46.7	102 41.2	00.0
Y	14	12 45.7	49 48.4	29.3	135 14.4	46.2	202 28.2	46.8	117 43.6	00.0
	15	27 48.1	64 47.8	. . 28.4	150 15.9	. . 46.4	217 31.0	. . 46.9	132 45.9	. . 00.0
	16	42 50.6	79 47.2	27.5	165 17.4	46.6	232 33.8	47.1	147 48.3	00.0
	17	57 53.1	94 46.5	26.6	180 18.9	46.9	247 36.5	47.2	162 50.7	00.0
	18	72 55.5	109 45.9	S15 25.7	195 20.4	S18 47.1	262 39.3	N 5 47.3	177 53.1	S21 00.0
	19	87 58.0	124 45.3	24.8	210 21.9	47.3	277 42.1	47.4	192 55.4	00.0
	20	103 00.5	139 44.7	23.9	225 23.4	47.5	292 44.8	47.6	207 57.8	00.0
	21	118 02.9	154 44.1	. . 23.0	240 24.9	. . 47.7	307 47.6	. . 47.7	223 00.2	. . 00.0
	22	133 05.4	169 43.5	22.1	255 26.4	48.0	322 50.3	47.8	238 02.6	00.0
	23	148 07.9	184 42.9	21.2	270 27.9	48.2	337 53.1	48.0	253 04.9	00.0
	5 00	163 10.3	199 42.3	S15 20.3	285 29.4	S18 48.4	352 55.9	N 5 48.1	268 07.3	S21 00.1
	01	178 12.8	214 41.7	19.4	300 30.9	48.6	7 58.6	48.2	283 09.7	00.1
	02	193 15.3	229 41.1	18.5	315 32.4	48.9	23 01.4	48.4	298 12.0	00.1
	03	208 17.7	244 40.5	. . 17.6	330 33.9	. . 49.1	38 04.2	. . 48.5	313 14.4	. . 00.1
	04	223 20.2	259 39.9	16.7	345 35.4	49.3	53 06.9	48.6	328 16.8	00.1
	05	238 22.6	274 39.3	15.8	0 36.9	49.5	68 09.7	48.7	343 19.2	00.1
	06	253 25.1	289 38.7	S15 14.9	15 38.4	S18 49.8	83 12.5	N 5 48.9	358 21.5	S21 00.1
S	07	268 27.6	304 38.1	14.0	30 39.9	50.0	98 15.2	49.0	13 23.9	00.1
	08	283 30.0	319 37.5	13.0	45 41.4	50.2	113 18.0	49.1	28 26.3	00.1
A	09	298 32.5	334 36.9	. . 12.1	60 42.9	. . 50.4	128 20.7	. . 49.3	43 28.7	. . 00.1
T	10	313 35.0	349 36.3	11.2	75 44.4	50.6	143 23.5	49.4	58 31.0	00.1
U	11	328 37.4	4 35.7	10.3	90 45.9	50.9	158 26.3	49.5	73 33.4	00.1
R	12	343 39.9	19 35.1	S15 09.4	105 47.4	S18 51.1	173 29.0	N 5 49.7	88 35.8	S21 00.1
D	13	358 42.4	34 34.5	08.5	120 48.9	51.3	188 31.8	49.8	103 38.2	00.1
A	14	13 44.8	49 33.9	07.6	135 50.4	51.5	203 34.6	49.9	118 40.5	00.1
Y	15	28 47.3	64 33.3	. . 06.7	150 51.9	. . 51.7	218 37.3	. . 50.1	133 42.9	. . 00.1
	16	43 49.7	79 32.7	05.8	165 53.5	52.0	233 40.1	50.2	148 45.3	00.1
	17	58 52.2	94 32.1	04.9	180 55.0	52.2	248 42.9	50.3	163 47.7	00.1
	18	73 54.7	109 31.5	S15 03.9	195 56.5	S18 52.4	263 45.6	N 5 50.4	178 50.0	S21 00.1
	19	88 57.1	124 30.9	03.0	210 58.0	52.6	278 48.4	50.6	193 52.4	00.1
	20	103 59.6	139 30.3	02.1	225 59.5	52.8	293 51.1	50.7	208 54.8	00.1
	21	119 02.1	154 29.7	. . 01.2	241 01.0	. . 53.1	308 53.9	. . 50.8	223 57.2	. . 00.1
	22	134 04.5	169 29.1	15 00.3	256 02.5	53.3	323 56.7	51.0	238 59.6	00.1
	23	149 07.0	184 28.5	14 59.4	271 04.0	53.5	338 59.4	51.1	254 01.9	00.1
	6 00	164 09.5	199 27.9	S14 58.4	286 05.6	S18 53.7	354 02.2	N 5 51.2	269 04.3	S21 00.1
	01	179 11.9	214 27.3	57.5	301 07.1	53.9	9 05.0	51.4	284 06.7	00.1
	02	194 14.4	229 26.7	56.6	316 08.6	54.1	24 07.7	51.5	299 09.1	00.1
	03	209 16.9	244 26.1	. . 55.7	331 10.1	. . 54.4	39 10.5	. . 51.6	314 11.4	. . 00.2
	04	224 19.3	259 25.5	54.8	346 11.6	54.6	54 13.3	51.7	329 13.8	00.2
	05	239 21.8	274 24.9	53.8	1 13.1	54.8	69 16.0	51.9	344 16.2	00.2
	06	254 24.2	289 24.3	S14 52.9	16 14.7	S18 55.0	84 18.8	N 5 52.0	359 18.6	S21 00.2
	07	269 26.7	304 23.7	52.0	31 16.2	55.2	99 21.6	52.1	14 21.0	00.2
	08	284 29.2	319 23.2	51.1	46 17.7	55.5	114 24.3	52.3	29 23.3	00.2
S	09	299 31.6	334 22.6	. . 50.1	61 19.2	. . 55.7	129 27.1	. . 52.4	44 25.7	. . 00.2
U	10	314 34.1	349 22.0	49.2	76 20.7	55.9	144 29.8	52.5	59 28.1	00.2
N	11	329 36.6	4 21.4	48.3	91 22.3	56.1	159 32.6	52.7	74 30.5	00.2
D	12	344 39.0	19 20.8	S14 47.4	106 23.8	S18 56.3	174 35.4	N 5 52.8	89 32.9	S21 00.2
A	13	359 41.5	34 20.2	46.4	121 25.3	56.5	189 38.1	52.9	104 35.2	00.2
Y	14	14 44.0	49 19.6	45.5	136 26.8	56.8	204 40.9	53.0	119 37.6	00.2
	15	29 46.4	64 19.0	. . 44.6	151 28.4	. . 57.0	219 43.7	. . 53.2	134 40.0	. . 00.2
	16	44 48.9	79 18.4	43.6	166 29.9	57.2	234 46.4	53.3	149 42.4	00.2
	17	59 51.4	94 17.9	42.7	181 31.4	57.4	249 49.2	53.4	164 44.8	00.2
	18	74 53.8	109 17.3	S14 41.8	196 32.9	S18 57.6	264 52.0	N 5 53.6	179 47.1	S21 00.2
	19	89 56.3	124 16.7	40.8	211 34.4	57.8	279 54.7	53.7	194 49.5	00.2
	20	104 58.7	139 16.1	39.9	226 36.0	58.0	294 57.5	53.8	209 51.9	00.2
	21	120 01.2	154 15.5	. . 39.0	241 37.5	. . 58.3	310 00.3	. . 54.0	224 54.3	. . 00.2
	22	135 03.7	169 14.9	38.0	256 39.0	58.5	325 03.0	54.1	239 56.7	00.2
	23	150 06.1	184 14.3	37.1	271 40.6	58.7	340 05.8	54.2	254 59.0	00.2
	Mer. Pass.	h m 13 05.2	*v* −0.6	*d* 0.9	*v* 1.5	*d* 0.2	*v* 2.8	*d* 0.1	*v* 2.4	*d* 0.0

STARS

Name	SHA ° ′	Dec ° ′
Acamar	315 17.2	S40 14.8
Achernar	335 25.9	S57 09.6
Acrux	173 06.4	S63 11.2
Adhara	255 10.9	S29 00.1
Aldebaran	290 47.3	N16 32.3
Alioth	166 18.7	N55 52.2
Alkaid	152 57.2	N49 13.8
Al Na'ir	27 41.9	S46 52.9
Alnilam	275 44.4	S 1 11.8
Alphard	217 54.0	S 8 44.0
Alphecca	126 09.3	N26 39.5
Alpheratz	357 41.9	N29 10.7
Altair	62 06.7	N 8 54.7
Ankaa	353 14.3	S42 13.3
Antares	112 23.9	S26 27.8
Arcturus	145 53.9	N19 05.8
Atria	107 24.1	S69 02.9
Avior	234 16.7	S59 34.1
Bellatrix	278 30.0	N 6 21.5
Betelgeuse	270 59.2	N 7 24.3
Canopus	263 55.1	S52 42.8
Capella	280 31.7	N46 00.8
Deneb	49 30.5	N45 20.2
Denebola	182 31.5	N14 28.8
Diphda	348 54.4	S17 54.1
Dubhe	193 48.9	N61 39.7
Elnath	278 10.2	N28 37.1
Eltanin	90 45.4	N51 29.1
Enif	33 45.6	N 9 56.9
Fomalhaut	15 22.4	S29 32.3
Gacrux	171 58.2	S57 12.1
Gienah	175 50.1	S17 38.0
Hadar	148 44.7	S60 26.8
Hamal	327 58.9	N23 32.2
Kaus Aust.	83 41.5	S34 22.3
Kochab	137 19.7	N74 05.2
Markab	13 36.8	N15 17.5
Menkar	314 13.3	N 4 08.9
Menkent	148 05.1	S36 26.8
Miaplacidus	221 38.3	S69 47.3
Mirfak	308 37.8	N49 55.1
Nunki	75 56.2	S26 16.4
Peacock	53 16.9	S56 40.7
Pollux	243 25.3	N27 59.0
Procyon	244 57.6	N 5 10.7
Rasalhague	96 04.8	N12 32.9
Regulus	207 41.3	N11 53.1
Rigel	281 10.3	S 8 11.4
Rigil Kent.	139 48.7	S60 53.8
Sabik	102 10.4	S15 44.5
Schedar	349 38.8	N56 37.6
Shaula	96 19.5	S37 06.6
Sirius	258 31.9	S16 44.7
Spica	158 29.0	S11 14.7
Suhail	222 50.6	S43 30.2
Vega	80 37.9	N38 47.8
Zuben'ubi	137 03.2	S16 06.4

	SHA ° ′	Mer. Pass. h m
Venus	36 32.0	10 42
Mars	122 19.0	4 58
Jupiter	189 45.6	0 28
Saturn	104 57.0	6 07

Day	UT (d h)	SUN GHA	SUN Dec	MOON GHA	v	MOON Dec	d	HP
		° ′	° ′	° ′	′	° ′	′	′
FRIDAY	4 00	177 04.5	S 6 21.2	244 18.7	9.4	S18 08.0	1.0	56.7
	01	192 04.6	20.3	258 47.1	9.3	18 07.0	1.2	56.8
	02	207 04.7	19.3	273 15.4	9.3	18 05.8	1.2	56.8
	03	222 04.9	. . 18.4	287 43.7	9.2	18 04.6	1.3	56.9
	04	237 05.0	17.4	302 11.9	9.2	18 03.3	1.4	56.9
	05	252 05.1	16.4	316 40.1	9.1	18 01.9	1.6	56.9
	06	267 05.3	S 6 15.5	331 08.2	9.2	S18 00.3	1.6	57.0
	07	282 05.4	14.5	345 36.4	9.1	17 58.7	1.7	57.0
	08	297 05.5	13.5	0 04.5	9.0	17 57.0	1.9	57.0
	09	312 05.7	. . 12.6	14 32.5	9.0	17 55.1	1.9	57.1
	10	327 05.8	11.6	29 00.5	9.0	17 53.2	2.0	57.1
	11	342 06.0	10.6	43 28.5	9.0	17 51.2	2.2	57.2
	12	357 06.1	S 6 09.7	57 56.5	8.9	S17 49.0	2.2	57.2
	13	12 06.2	08.7	72 24.4	8.8	17 46.8	2.4	57.2
	14	27 06.4	07.7	86 52.2	8.9	17 44.4	2.5	57.3
	15	42 06.5	. . 06.8	101 20.1	8.8	17 41.9	2.5	57.3
	16	57 06.7	05.8	115 47.9	8.8	17 39.4	2.7	57.3
	17	72 06.8	04.9	130 15.7	8.7	17 36.7	2.8	57.4
	18	87 06.9	S 6 03.9	144 43.4	8.7	S17 33.9	2.8	57.4
	19	102 07.1	02.9	159 11.1	8.7	17 31.1	3.0	57.5
	20	117 07.2	02.0	173 38.8	8.7	17 28.1	3.1	57.5
	21	132 07.4	. . 01.0	188 06.5	8.6	17 25.0	3.2	57.5
	22	147 07.5	6 00.0	202 34.1	8.6	17 21.8	3.3	57.6
	23	162 07.6	5 59.1	217 01.7	8.6	17 18.5	3.4	57.6
SATURDAY	5 00	177 07.8	S 5 58.1	231 29.3	8.5	S17 15.1	3.5	57.7
	01	192 07.9	57.1	245 56.8	8.5	17 11.6	3.6	57.7
	02	207 08.1	56.2	260 24.3	8.5	17 08.0	3.8	57.7
	03	222 08.2	. . 55.2	274 51.8	8.5	17 04.2	3.8	57.8
	04	237 08.3	54.2	289 19.3	8.4	17 00.4	3.9	57.8
	05	252 08.5	53.3	303 46.7	8.4	16 56.5	4.1	57.8
	06	267 08.6	S 5 52.3	318 14.1	8.4	S16 52.4	4.1	57.9
	07	282 08.8	51.3	332 41.5	8.4	16 48.3	4.2	57.9
	08	297 08.9	50.3	347 08.9	8.3	16 44.1	4.4	58.0
	09	312 09.0	. . 49.4	1 36.2	8.3	16 39.7	4.5	58.0
	10	327 09.2	48.4	16 03.5	8.3	16 35.2	4.5	58.0
	11	342 09.3	47.4	30 30.8	8.3	16 30.7	4.7	58.1
	12	357 09.5	S 5 46.5	44 58.1	8.2	S16 26.0	4.8	58.1
	13	12 09.6	45.5	59 25.3	8.3	16 21.2	4.8	58.2
	14	27 09.8	44.5	73 52.6	8.2	16 16.4	5.0	58.2
	15	42 09.9	. . 43.6	88 19.8	8.1	16 11.4	5.1	58.2
	16	57 10.0	42.6	102 46.9	8.2	16 06.3	5.2	58.3
	17	72 10.2	41.6	117 14.1	8.2	16 01.1	5.3	58.3
	18	87 10.3	S 5 40.7	131 41.3	8.1	S15 55.8	5.4	58.4
	19	102 10.5	39.7	146 08.4	8.1	15 50.4	5.5	58.4
	20	117 10.6	38.7	160 35.5	8.1	15 44.9	5.6	58.4
	21	132 10.8	. . 37.8	175 02.6	8.1	15 39.3	5.7	58.5
	22	147 10.9	36.8	189 29.7	8.0	15 33.6	5.8	58.5
	23	162 11.1	35.8	203 56.7	8.0	15 27.8	5.9	58.5
SUNDAY	6 00	177 11.2	S 5 34.8	218 23.7	8.1	S15 21.9	6.0	58.6
	01	192 11.3	33.9	232 50.8	8.0	15 15.9	6.1	58.6
	02	207 11.5	32.9	247 17.8	8.0	15 09.8	6.2	58.7
	03	222 11.6	. . 31.9	261 44.8	8.0	15 03.6	6.3	58.7
	04	237 11.8	31.0	276 11.8	7.9	14 57.3	6.4	58.7
	05	252 11.9	30.0	290 38.7	8.0	14 50.9	6.5	58.8
	06	267 12.1	S 5 29.0	305 05.7	7.9	S14 44.4	6.7	58.8
	07	282 12.2	28.0	319 32.6	7.9	14 37.7	6.7	58.9
	08	297 12.4	27.1	333 59.5	8.0	14 31.0	6.8	58.9
	09	312 12.5	. . 26.1	348 26.5	7.9	14 24.2	6.9	58.9
	10	327 12.7	25.1	2 53.4	7.9	14 17.3	7.0	59.0
	11	342 12.8	24.2	17 20.3	7.8	14 10.3	7.1	59.0
	12	357 13.0	S 5 23.2	31 47.1	7.9	S14 03.2	7.2	59.0
	13	12 13.1	22.2	46 14.0	7.9	13 56.0	7.3	59.1
	14	27 13.2	21.2	60 40.9	7.8	13 48.7	7.3	59.1
	15	42 13.4	. . 20.3	75 07.7	7.9	13 41.4	7.5	59.2
	16	57 13.5	19.3	89 34.6	7.8	13 33.9	7.6	59.2
	17	72 13.7	18.3	104 01.4	7.8	13 26.3	7.7	59.2
	18	87 13.8	S 5 17.4	118 28.2	7.9	S13 18.6	7.7	59.3
	19	102 14.0	16.4	132 55.1	7.8	13 10.9	7.9	59.3
	20	117 14.1	15.4	147 21.9	7.8	13 03.0	7.9	59.3
	21	132 14.3	. . 14.4	161 48.7	7.8	12 55.1	8.1	59.4
	22	147 14.4	13.5	176 15.5	7.8	12 47.0	8.1	59.4
	23	162 14.6	12.5	190 42.3	7.8	S12 38.9	8.2	59.4
		SD 16.1	*d* 1.0	SD 15.6		15.8		16.1

Lat.	Twilight Naut.	Twilight Civil	Sunrise	Moonrise 4	Moonrise 5	Moonrise 6	Moonrise 7
°	h m	h m	h m	h m	h m	h m	h m
N 72	04 47	06 06	07 14	■	07 28	07 19	07 13
N 70	04 55	06 06	07 07	06 12	06 36	06 48	06 53
68	05 01	06 05	07 01	05 31	06 04	06 25	06 38
66	05 06	06 05	06 56	05 03	05 40	06 06	06 25
64	05 10	06 05	06 52	04 42	05 22	05 52	06 15
62	05 13	06 04	06 49	04 25	05 06	05 39	06 06
60	05 16	06 04	06 46	04 10	04 53	05 29	05 58
N 58	05 18	06 04	06 43	03 58	04 42	05 20	05 51
56	05 20	06 03	06 40	03 47	04 33	05 11	05 45
54	05 22	06 03	06 38	03 38	04 24	05 04	05 39
52	05 23	06 02	06 36	03 30	04 16	04 58	05 34
50	05 25	06 02	06 34	03 22	04 09	04 52	05 30
45	05 27	06 01	06 30	03 06	03 55	04 39	05 20
N 40	05 28	06 00	06 27	02 53	03 42	04 29	05 12
35	05 29	05 59	06 24	02 42	03 32	04 20	05 05
30	05 30	05 57	06 21	02 32	03 23	04 12	04 59
20	05 29	05 54	06 16	02 15	03 07	03 58	04 48
N 10	05 27	05 51	06 12	02 01	02 53	03 46	04 39
0	05 23	05 47	06 08	01 47	02 40	03 35	04 30
S 10	05 18	05 43	06 04	01 33	02 28	03 24	04 21
20	05 11	05 37	05 59	01 19	02 14	03 12	04 12
30	05 01	05 30	05 54	01 02	01 58	02 58	04 01
35	04 55	05 25	05 51	00 52	01 49	02 50	03 55
40	04 47	05 20	05 47	00 41	01 38	02 41	03 48
45	04 37	05 13	05 43	00 28	01 26	02 30	03 39
S 50	04 25	05 05	05 38	00 12	01 11	02 17	03 29
52	04 19	05 01	05 36	00 05	01 04	02 11	03 25
54	04 12	04 57	05 33	24 56	00 56	02 05	03 20
56	04 04	04 52	05 30	24 48	00 48	01 57	03 14
58	03 55	04 46	05 27	24 38	00 38	01 49	03 08
S 60	03 45	04 40	05 23	24 26	00 26	01 39	03 00

Lat.	Sunset	Twilight Civil	Twilight Naut.	Moonset 4	Moonset 5	Moonset 6	Moonset 7
°	h m	h m	h m	h m	h m	h m	h m
N 72	17 11	18 19	19 39	■	10 27	12 31	14 32
N 70	17 18	18 19	19 31	09 50	11 18	13 01	14 50
68	17 23	18 19	19 24	10 31	11 50	13 23	15 04
66	17 28	18 19	19 19	10 59	12 13	13 40	15 16
64	17 32	18 20	19 15	11 20	12 31	13 54	15 25
62	17 35	18 20	19 11	11 37	12 46	14 06	15 33
60	17 38	18 20	19 08	11 51	12 59	14 16	15 40
N 58	17 41	18 20	19 06	12 03	13 09	14 25	15 46
56	17 43	18 21	19 04	12 14	13 19	14 32	15 52
54	17 46	18 21	19 02	12 23	13 27	14 39	15 57
52	17 48	18 21	19 00	12 31	13 35	14 45	16 01
50	17 49	18 22	18 59	12 39	13 41	14 51	16 05
45	17 53	18 23	18 57	12 55	13 56	15 02	16 13
N 40	17 57	18 24	18 55	13 07	14 07	15 12	16 20
35	17 59	18 25	18 54	13 18	14 17	15 20	16 26
30	18 02	18 26	18 54	13 28	14 26	15 28	16 32
20	18 07	18 29	18 54	13 45	14 41	15 40	16 41
N 10	18 11	18 32	18 56	13 59	14 54	15 51	16 49
0	18 15	18 35	19 00	14 12	15 06	16 01	16 56
S 10	18 19	18 40	19 04	14 26	15 18	16 11	17 04
20	18 23	18 45	19 11	14 40	15 31	16 22	17 11
30	18 28	18 52	19 21	14 56	15 46	16 34	17 20
35	18 31	18 57	19 27	15 06	15 55	16 41	17 25
40	18 35	19 02	19 35	15 17	16 04	16 49	17 31
45	18 39	19 09	19 44	15 29	16 16	16 58	17 38
S 50	18 44	19 17	19 56	15 45	16 29	17 09	17 45
52	18 46	19 21	20 02	15 52	16 36	17 14	17 49
54	18 48	19 25	20 09	16 00	16 43	17 20	17 53
56	18 51	19 29	20 17	16 09	16 50	17 26	17 57
58	18 54	19 35	20 25	16 19	16 59	17 33	18 02
S 60	18 58	19 41	20 36	16 30	17 09	17 41	18 08

Day	SUN Eqn. of Time 00^h	SUN Eqn. of Time 12^h	SUN Mer. Pass.	MOON Mer. Pass. Upper	MOON Mer. Pass. Lower	MOON Age	MOON Phase
d	m s	m s	h m	h m	h m	d %	
4	11 42	11 36	12 12	08 00	20 26	25 25	
5	11 29	11 22	12 11	08 53	21 21	26 17	
6	11 15	11 08	12 11	09 48	22 16	27 9	

	UT	ARIES	VENUS −3·8		MARS +0·1		JUPITER −2·5		SATURN +0·5	
	d h	GHA ° ′	GHA ° ′	Dec ° ′	GHA ° ′	Dec ° ′	GHA ° ′	Dec ° ′	GHA ° ′	Dec ° ′
MONDAY	7 00	165 08.6	199 13.8	S14 36.2	286 42.1	S18 58.9	355 08.6	N 5 54.3	270 01.4	S21 00.2
	01	180 11.1	214 13.2	35.2	301 43.6	59.1	10 11.3	54.5	285 03.8	00.2
	02	195 13.5	229 12.6	34.3	316 45.1	59.3	25 14.1	54.6	300 06.2	00.2
	03	210 16.0	244 12.0	. . 33.4	331 46.7	. . 59.6	40 16.8	. . 54.7	315 08.6	. . 00.2
	04	225 18.5	259 11.4	32.4	346 48.2	18 59.8	55 19.6	54.9	330 11.0	00.2
	05	240 20.9	274 10.8	31.5	1 49.7	19 00.0	70 22.4	55.0	345 13.3	00.2
	06	255 23.4	289 10.3	S14 30.5	16 51.3	S19 00.2	85 25.1	N 5 55.1	0 15.7	S21 00.2
	07	270 25.8	304 09.7	29.6	31 52.8	00.4	100 27.9	55.3	15 18.1	00.2
	08	285 28.3	319 09.1	28.7	46 54.3	00.6	115 30.7	55.4	30 20.5	00.2
	09	300 30.8	334 08.5	. . 27.7	61 55.9	. . 00.8	130 33.4	. . 55.5	45 22.9	. . 00.2
	10	315 33.2	349 07.9	26.8	76 57.4	01.0	145 36.2	55.7	60 25.3	00.3
	11	330 35.7	4 07.4	25.8	91 58.9	01.3	160 39.0	55.8	75 27.6	00.3
	12	345 38.2	19 06.8	S14 24.9	107 00.5	S19 01.5	175 41.7	N 5 55.9	90 30.0	S21 00.3
	13	0 40.6	34 06.2	23.9	122 02.0	01.7	190 44.5	56.0	105 32.4	00.3
	14	15 43.1	49 05.6	23.0	137 03.5	01.9	205 47.3	56.2	120 34.8	00.3
	15	30 45.6	64 05.1	. . 22.0	152 05.1	. . 02.1	220 50.0	. . 56.3	135 37.2	. . 00.3
	16	45 48.0	79 04.5	21.1	167 06.6	02.3	235 52.8	56.4	150 39.6	00.3
	17	60 50.5	94 03.9	20.2	182 08.2	02.5	250 55.6	56.6	165 41.9	00.3
	18	75 53.0	109 03.3	S14 19.2	197 09.7	S19 02.7	265 58.3	N 5 56.7	180 44.3	S21 00.3
	19	90 55.4	124 02.7	18.3	212 11.2	03.0	281 01.1	56.8	195 46.7	00.3
	20	105 57.9	139 02.2	17.3	227 12.8	03.2	296 03.8	57.0	210 49.1	00.3
	21	121 00.3	154 01.6	. . 16.4	242 14.3	. . 03.4	311 06.6	. . 57.1	225 51.5	. . 00.3
	22	136 02.8	169 01.0	15.4	257 15.8	03.6	326 09.4	57.2	240 53.9	00.3
	23	151 05.3	184 00.5	14.4	272 17.4	03.8	341 12.1	57.3	255 56.3	00.3
TUESDAY	8 00	166 07.7	198 59.9	S14 13.5	287 18.9	S19 04.0	356 14.9	N 5 57.5	270 58.6	S21 00.3
	01	181 10.2	213 59.3	12.5	302 20.5	04.2	11 17.7	57.6	286 01.0	00.3
	02	196 12.7	228 58.7	11.6	317 22.0	04.4	26 20.4	57.7	301 03.4	00.3
	03	211 15.1	243 58.2	. . 10.6	332 23.6	. . 04.6	41 23.2	. . 57.9	316 05.8	. . 00.3
	04	226 17.6	258 57.6	09.7	347 25.1	04.8	56 26.0	58.0	331 08.2	00.3
	05	241 20.1	273 57.0	08.7	2 26.7	05.1	71 28.7	58.1	346 10.6	00.3
	06	256 22.5	288 56.5	S14 07.8	17 28.2	S19 05.3	86 31.5	N 5 58.3	1 13.0	S21 00.3
	07	271 25.0	303 55.9	06.8	32 29.7	05.5	101 34.3	58.4	16 15.4	00.3
	08	286 27.5	318 55.3	05.9	47 31.3	05.7	116 37.0	58.5	31 17.7	00.3
	09	301 29.9	333 54.7	. . 04.9	62 32.8	. . 05.9	131 39.8	. . 58.6	46 20.1	. . 00.3
	10	316 32.4	348 54.2	03.9	77 34.4	06.1	146 42.6	58.8	61 22.5	00.3
	11	331 34.8	3 53.6	03.0	92 35.9	06.3	161 45.3	58.9	76 24.9	00.3
	12	346 37.3	18 53.0	S14 02.0	107 37.5	S19 06.5	176 48.1	N 5 59.0	91 27.3	S21 00.3
	13	1 39.8	33 52.5	01.1	122 39.0	06.7	191 50.9	59.2	106 29.7	00.3
	14	16 42.2	48 51.9	14 00.1	137 40.6	06.9	206 53.6	59.3	121 32.1	00.3
	15	31 44.7	63 51.3	13 59.1	152 42.1	. . 07.1	221 56.4	. . 59.4	136 34.5	. . 00.3
	16	46 47.2	78 50.8	58.2	167 43.7	07.4	236 59.2	59.5	151 36.9	00.3
	17	61 49.6	93 50.2	57.2	182 45.2	07.6	252 01.9	59.7	166 39.2	00.3
	18	76 52.1	108 49.6	S13 56.2	197 46.8	S19 07.8	267 04.7	N 5 59.8	181 41.6	S21 00.3
	19	91 54.6	123 49.1	55.3	212 48.3	08.0	282 07.4	5 59.9	196 44.0	00.3
	20	106 57.0	138 48.5	54.3	227 49.9	08.2	297 10.2	6 00.1	211 46.4	00.3
	21	121 59.5	153 47.9	. . 53.3	242 51.4	. . 08.4	312 13.0	. . 00.2	226 48.8	. . 00.3
	22	137 01.9	168 47.4	52.4	257 53.0	08.6	327 15.7	00.3	241 51.2	00.3
	23	152 04.4	183 46.8	51.4	272 54.6	08.8	342 18.5	00.5	256 53.6	00.3
WEDNESDAY	9 00	167 06.9	198 46.3	S13 50.4	287 56.1	S19 09.0	357 21.3	N 6 00.6	271 56.0	S21 00.3
	01	182 09.3	213 45.7	49.5	302 57.7	09.2	12 24.0	00.7	286 58.4	00.3
	02	197 11.8	228 45.1	48.5	317 59.2	09.4	27 26.8	00.8	302 00.8	00.4
	03	212 14.3	243 44.6	. . 47.5	333 00.8	. . 09.6	42 29.6	. . 01.0	317 03.1	. . 00.4
	04	227 16.7	258 44.0	46.6	348 02.3	09.8	57 32.3	01.1	332 05.5	00.4
	05	242 19.2	273 43.5	45.6	3 03.9	10.0	72 35.1	01.2	347 07.9	00.4
	06	257 21.7	288 42.9	S13 44.6	18 05.5	S19 10.2	87 37.9	N 6 01.4	2 10.3	S21 00.4
	07	272 24.1	303 42.3	43.6	33 07.0	10.4	102 40.6	01.5	17 12.7	00.4
	08	287 26.6	318 41.8	42.7	48 08.6	10.7	117 43.4	01.6	32 15.1	00.4
	09	302 29.1	333 41.2	. . 41.7	63 10.1	. . 10.9	132 46.2	. . 01.8	47 17.5	. . 00.4
	10	317 31.5	348 40.7	40.7	78 11.7	11.1	147 48.9	01.9	62 19.9	00.4
	11	332 34.0	3 40.1	39.7	93 13.3	11.3	162 51.7	02.0	77 22.3	00.4
	12	347 36.4	18 39.5	S13 38.8	108 14.8	S19 11.5	177 54.5	N 6 02.1	92 24.7	S21 00.4
	13	2 38.9	33 39.0	37.8	123 16.4	11.7	192 57.2	02.3	107 27.1	00.4
	14	17 41.4	48 38.4	36.8	138 18.0	11.9	208 00.0	02.4	122 29.5	00.4
	15	32 43.8	63 37.9	. . 35.8	153 19.5	. . 12.1	223 02.8	. . 02.5	137 31.9	. . 00.4
	16	47 46.3	78 37.3	34.8	168 21.1	12.3	238 05.5	02.7	152 34.2	00.4
	17	62 48.8	93 36.8	33.9	183 22.7	12.5	253 08.3	02.8	167 36.6	00.4
	18	77 51.2	108 36.2	S13 32.9	198 24.2	S19 12.7	268 11.1	N 6 02.9	182 39.0	S21 00.4
	19	92 53.7	123 35.7	31.9	213 25.8	12.9	283 13.8	03.0	197 41.4	00.4
	20	107 56.2	138 35.1	30.9	228 27.4	13.1	298 16.6	03.2	212 43.8	00.4
	21	122 58.6	153 34.5	. . 29.9	243 28.9	. . 13.3	313 19.3	. . 03.3	227 46.2	. . 00.4
	22	138 01.1	168 34.0	29.0	258 30.5	13.5	328 22.1	03.4	242 48.6	00.4
	23	153 03.5	183 33.4	28.0	273 32.1	13.7	343 24.9	03.6	257 51.0	00.4
	Mer. Pass.	h m 12 53.4	v −0.6	d 1.0	v 1.5	d 0.2	v 2.8	d 0.1	v 2.4	d 0.0

STARS Name	SHA ° ′	Dec ° ′
Acamar	315 17.2	S40 14.8
Achernar	335 26.0	S57 09.6
Acrux	173 06.4	S63 11.3
Adhara	255 10.9	S29 00.1
Aldebaran	290 47.3	N16 32.3
Alioth	166 18.7	N55 52.2
Alkaid	152 57.1	N49 13.8
Al Na'ir	27 41.9	S46 52.9
Alnilam	275 44.5	S 1 11.8
Alphard	217 54.0	S 8 44.0
Alphecca	126 09.3	N26 39.5
Alpheratz	357 41.9	N29 10.7
Altair	62 06.6	N 8 54.7
Ankaa	353 14.3	S42 13.3
Antares	112 23.9	S26 27.8
Arcturus	145 53.8	N19 05.8
Atria	107 24.0	S69 02.9
Avior	234 16.7	S59 34.1
Bellatrix	278 30.0	N 6 21.5
Betelgeuse	270 59.2	N 7 24.3
Canopus	263 55.1	S52 42.8
Capella	280 31.7	N46 00.8
Deneb	49 30.5	N45 20.2
Denebola	182 31.5	N14 28.8
Diphda	348 54.4	S17 54.1
Dubhe	193 48.9	N61 39.7
Elnath	278 10.2	N28 37.1
Eltanin	90 45.4	N51 29.1
Enif	33 45.6	N 9 56.9
Fomalhaut	15 22.3	S29 32.3
Gacrux	171 58.2	S57 12.2
Gienah	175 50.1	S17 38.0
Hadar	148 44.7	S60 26.8
Hamal	327 58.9	N23 32.2
Kaus Aust.	83 41.5	S34 22.3
Kochab	137 19.6	N74 05.2
Markab	13 36.8	N15 17.5
Menkar	314 13.3	N 4 08.9
Menkent	148 05.1	S36 26.8
Miaplacidus	221 38.3	S69 47.3
Mirfak	308 37.8	N49 55.1
Nunki	75 56.2	S26 16.4
Peacock	53 16.8	S56 40.7
Pollux	243 25.3	N27 59.0
Procyon	244 57.6	N 5 10.7
Rasalhague	96 04.8	N12 32.9
Regulus	207 41.3	N11 53.1
Rigel	281 10.3	S 8 11.4
Rigil Kent.	139 48.7	S60 53.8
Sabik	102 10.4	S15 44.5
Schedar	349 38.8	N56 37.5
Shaula	96 19.4	S37 06.6
Sirius	258 32.0	S16 44.7
Spica	158 29.0	S11 14.8
Suhail	222 50.7	S43 30.2
Vega	80 37.8	N38 47.8
Zuben'ubi	137 03.2	S16 06.4

	SHA ° ′	Mer. Pass. h m
Venus	32 52.1	10 44
Mars	121 11.2	4 50
Jupiter	190 07.2	0 15
Saturn	104 50.9	5 55

UT	SUN GHA	SUN Dec	MOON GHA	v	MOON Dec	d	HP
d h	° ′	° ′	° ′	′	° ′	′	′
7 00	177 14.7	S 5 11.5	205 09.1	7.7	S12 30.7	8.3	59.5
01	192 14.9	10.6	219 35.8	7.8	12 22.4	8.4	59.5
02	207 15.0	09.6	234 02.6	7.8	12 14.0	8.5	59.5
03	222 15.2	. . 08.6	248 29.4	7.8	12 05.5	8.5	59.6
04	237 15.3	07.6	262 56.2	7.7	11 57.0	8.7	59.6
05	252 15.5	06.7	277 22.9	7.8	11 48.3	8.7	59.6
06	267 15.6	S 5 05.7	291 49.7	7.7	S11 39.6	8.8	59.7
07	282 15.8	04.7	306 16.4	7.8	11 30.8	8.9	59.7
M 08	297 15.9	03.7	320 43.2	7.7	11 21.9	9.0	59.7
O 09	312 16.1	. . 02.8	335 09.9	7.8	11 12.9	9.1	59.8
N 10	327 16.2	01.8	349 36.7	7.7	11 03.8	9.1	59.8
D 11	342 16.4	5 00.8	4 03.4	7.7	10 54.7	9.2	59.8
A 12	357 16.5	S 4 59.8	18 30.1	7.8	S10 45.5	9.3	59.9
Y 13	12 16.7	58.9	32 56.9	7.7	10 36.2	9.4	59.9
14	27 16.8	57.9	47 23.6	7.7	10 26.8	9.4	59.9
15	42 17.0	. . 56.9	61 50.3	7.8	10 17.4	9.6	60.0
16	57 17.1	55.9	76 17.1	7.7	10 07.8	9.6	60.0
17	72 17.3	55.0	90 43.8	7.7	9 58.2	9.6	60.0
18	87 17.4	S 4 54.0	105 10.5	7.7	S 9 48.6	9.8	60.0
19	102 17.6	53.0	119 37.2	7.8	9 38.8	9.8	60.1
20	117 17.7	52.0	134 04.0	7.7	9 29.0	9.9	60.1
21	132 17.9	. . 51.1	148 30.7	7.7	9 19.1	10.0	60.1
22	147 18.0	50.1	162 57.4	7.7	9 09.1	10.0	60.2
23	162 18.2	49.1	177 24.1	7.7	8 59.1	10.1	60.2
8 00	177 18.3	S 4 48.1	191 50.8	7.8	S 8 49.0	10.1	60.2
01	192 18.5	47.2	206 17.6	7.7	8 38.9	10.2	60.2
02	207 18.7	46.2	220 44.3	7.7	8 28.7	10.3	60.3
03	222 18.8	. . 45.2	235 11.0	7.7	8 18.4	10.4	60.3
04	237 19.0	44.2	249 37.7	7.7	8 08.0	10.4	60.3
05	252 19.1	43.3	264 04.4	7.8	7 57.6	10.5	60.3
06	267 19.3	S 4 42.3	278 31.2	7.7	S 7 47.1	10.5	60.4
07	282 19.4	41.3	292 57.9	7.7	7 36.6	10.6	60.4
T 08	297 19.6	40.3	307 24.6	7.7	7 26.0	10.6	60.4
U 09	312 19.7	. . 39.3	321 51.3	7.7	7 15.4	10.7	60.4
E 10	327 19.9	38.4	336 18.0	7.7	7 04.7	10.8	60.5
S 11	342 20.0	37.4	350 44.7	7.8	6 53.9	10.8	60.5
D 12	357 20.2	S 4 36.4	5 11.5	7.7	S 6 43.1	10.8	60.5
A 13	12 20.3	35.4	19 38.2	7.7	6 32.3	10.9	60.5
Y 14	27 20.5	34.5	34 04.9	7.7	6 21.4	11.0	60.6
15	42 20.7	. . 33.5	48 31.6	7.7	6 10.4	11.0	60.6
16	57 20.8	32.5	62 58.3	7.7	5 59.4	11.0	60.6
17	72 21.0	31.5	77 25.0	7.7	5 48.4	11.1	60.6
18	87 21.1	S 4 30.6	91 51.7	7.8	S 5 37.3	11.1	60.6
19	102 21.3	29.6	106 18.5	7.7	5 26.2	11.2	60.7
20	117 21.4	28.6	120 45.2	7.7	5 15.0	11.2	60.7
21	132 21.6	. . 27.6	135 11.9	7.7	5 03.8	11.3	60.7
22	147 21.7	26.6	149 38.6	7.7	4 52.5	11.3	60.7
23	162 21.9	25.7	164 05.3	7.7	S 4 41.2	11.3	60.7
9 00	177 22.1	S 4 24.7	A total eclipse of the Sun occurs on this date. See page 5.				
01	192 22.2	23.7					
02	207 22.4	22.7					
03	222 22.5	. . 21.7					
04	237 22.7	20.8					
05	252 22.8	19.8					
W 06	267 23.0	S 4 18.8	265 12.3	7.7	S 3 21.2	11.5	60.8
E 07	282 23.2	17.8	279 39.0	7.7	3 09.7	11.6	60.8
D 08	297 23.3	16.9	294 05.7	7.7	2 58.1	11.6	60.9
N 09	312 23.5	. . 15.9	308 32.4	7.7	2 46.5	11.6	60.9
E 10	327 23.6	14.9	322 59.1	7.7	2 34.9	11.6	60.9
S 11	342 23.8	13.9	337 25.8	7.7	2 23.3	11.7	60.9
D 12	357 23.9	S 4 12.9	351 52.5	7.7	S 2 11.6	11.7	60.9
A 13	12 24.1	12.0	6 19.2	7.7	1 59.9	11.6	60.9
Y 14	27 24.3	11.0	20 45.9	7.7	1 48.3	11.7	60.9
15	42 24.4	. . 10.0	35 12.6	7.7	1 36.6	11.8	60.9
16	57 24.6	09.0	49 39.3	7.7	1 24.8	11.7	60.9
17	72 24.7	08.0	64 06.0	7.7	1 13.1	11.7	60.9
18	87 24.9	S 4 07.1	78 32.7	7.7	S 1 01.4	11.8	60.9
19	102 25.1	06.1	92 59.4	7.6	0 49.6	11.8	61.0
20	117 25.2	05.1	107 26.0	7.7	0 37.8	11.7	61.0
21	132 25.4	. . 04.1	121 52.7	7.7	0 26.1	11.8	61.0
22	147 25.5	03.1	136 19.4	7.7	0 14.3	11.8	61.0
23	162 25.7	02.2	150 46.1	7.6	S 0 02.5	11.7	61.0
	SD 16.1	d 1.0	SD 16.3		16.5		16.6

Lat.	Twilight Naut.	Twilight Civil	Sunrise	Moonrise 7	Moonrise 8	Moonrise 9	Moonrise 10
°	h m	h m	h m	h m	h m	h m	h m
N 72	04 31	05 51	06 58	07 13	07 08	07 03	06 58
N 70	04 41	05 52	06 53	06 53	06 56	06 58	07 00
68	04 48	05 53	06 49	06 38	06 47	06 55	07 01
66	04 54	05 54	06 45	06 25	06 40	06 52	07 03
64	04 59	05 55	06 42	06 15	06 33	06 49	07 04
62	05 04	05 55	06 39	06 06	06 27	06 47	07 05
60	05 07	05 55	06 37	05 58	06 22	06 44	07 06
N 58	05 10	05 56	06 35	05 51	06 18	06 43	07 06
56	05 13	05 56	06 33	05 45	06 14	06 41	07 07
54	05 15	05 56	06 31	05 39	06 11	06 40	07 08
52	05 17	05 56	06 29	05 34	06 07	06 38	07 08
50	05 18	05 56	06 28	05 30	06 05	06 37	07 09
45	05 22	05 56	06 25	05 20	05 58	06 34	07 10
N 40	05 24	05 55	06 22	05 12	05 53	06 32	07 11
35	05 25	05 55	06 20	05 05	05 48	06 30	07 12
30	05 26	05 54	06 18	04 59	05 44	06 29	07 12
20	05 26	05 52	06 14	04 48	05 37	06 26	07 14
N 10	05 25	05 50	06 11	04 39	05 31	06 23	07 15
0	05 23	05 47	06 07	04 30	05 25	06 21	07 16
S 10	05 18	05 43	06 04	04 21	05 19	06 18	07 17
20	05 12	05 38	06 00	04 12	05 13	06 16	07 18
30	05 04	05 32	05 56	04 01	05 06	06 13	07 20
35	04 58	05 28	05 53	03 55	05 02	06 11	07 21
40	04 51	05 23	05 50	03 48	04 58	06 09	07 22
45	04 42	05 17	05 47	03 39	04 52	06 07	07 23
S 50	04 31	05 10	05 43	03 29	04 46	06 04	07 24
52	04 25	05 07	05 41	03 25	04 43	06 03	07 25
54	04 19	05 03	05 39	03 20	04 39	06 02	07 26
56	04 12	04 58	05 37	03 14	04 36	06 01	07 27
58	04 04	04 54	05 34	03 08	04 32	05 59	07 27
S 60	03 54	04 48	05 31	03 00	04 27	05 57	07 28

Lat.	Sunset	Twilight Civil	Twilight Naut.	Moonset 7	Moonset 8	Moonset 9	Moonset 10
°	h m	h m	h m	h m	h m	h m	h m
N 72	17 25	18 33	19 53	14 32	16 33	18 34	20 34
N 70	17 30	18 31	19 44	14 50	16 42	18 35	20 28
68	17 35	18 30	19 36	15 04	16 49	18 36	20 24
66	17 38	18 29	19 29	15 16	16 55	18 37	20 20
64	17 41	18 28	19 24	15 25	17 01	18 38	20 16
62	17 44	18 28	19 20	15 33	17 05	18 39	20 14
60	17 46	18 27	19 16	15 40	17 09	18 40	20 11
N 58	17 48	18 27	19 13	15 46	17 12	18 40	20 09
56	17 50	18 27	19 10	15 52	17 15	18 41	20 07
54	17 51	18 27	19 08	15 57	17 18	18 41	20 05
52	17 53	18 27	19 06	16 01	17 20	18 42	20 03
50	17 54	18 26	19 04	16 05	17 23	18 42	20 02
45	17 57	18 27	19 01	16 13	17 27	18 43	19 59
N 40	18 00	18 27	18 58	16 20	17 31	18 44	19 56
35	18 02	18 27	18 57	16 26	17 35	18 44	19 54
30	18 04	18 28	18 56	16 32	17 38	18 45	19 52
20	18 08	18 30	18 55	16 41	17 43	18 45	19 48
N 10	18 11	18 32	18 56	16 49	17 47	18 46	19 45
0	18 14	18 35	18 59	16 56	17 52	18 47	19 42
S 10	18 17	18 38	19 03	17 04	17 56	18 47	19 39
20	18 21	18 43	19 09	17 11	18 00	18 48	19 36
30	18 25	18 49	19 17	17 20	18 05	18 49	19 33
35	18 27	18 53	19 23	17 25	18 08	18 49	19 31
40	18 30	18 57	19 30	17 31	18 11	18 50	19 28
45	18 33	19 03	19 38	17 38	18 15	18 50	19 26
S 50	18 37	19 10	19 49	17 45	18 19	18 51	19 22
52	18 39	19 13	19 55	17 49	18 21	18 51	19 21
54	18 41	19 17	20 01	17 53	18 23	18 51	19 19
56	18 43	19 21	20 08	17 57	18 25	18 52	19 18
58	18 46	19 26	20 16	18 02	18 28	18 52	19 16
S 60	18 49	19 31	20 25	18 08	18 31	18 52	19 13

Day	SUN Eqn. of Time 00h	SUN Eqn. of Time 12h	SUN Mer. Pass.	MOON Mer. Pass. Upper	MOON Mer. Pass. Lower	MOON Age	MOON Phase
d	m s	m s	h m	h m	h m	d	%
7	11 01	10 54	12 11	10 43	23 11	28	4
8	10 47	10 40	12 11	11 38	24 06	29	1
9	10 32	10 25	12 10	12 34	00 06	00	0

UT	ARIES	VENUS −3·8		MARS +0·0		JUPITER −2·5		SATURN +0·4		STARS		
d h	GHA	GHA	Dec	GHA	Dec	GHA	Dec	GHA	Dec	Name	SHA	Dec
	° ′	° ′	° ′	° ′	° ′	° ′	° ′	° ′	° ′		° ′	° ′
10 00	168 06.0	198 32.9	S13 27.0	288 33.6	S19 13.9	358 27.6	N 6 03.7	272 53.4	S21 00.4	Acamar	315 17.2	S40 14.8
01	183 08.5	213 32.3	26.0	303 35.2	14.1	13 30.4	03.8	287 55.8	00.4	Achernar	335 26.0	S57 09.6
02	198 10.9	228 31.8	25.0	318 36.8	14.3	28 33.2	04.0	302 58.2	00.4	Acrux	173 06.4	S63 11.3
03	213 13.4	243 31.2	. . 24.0	333 38.4	. . 14.5	43 35.9	. . 04.1	318 00.6	. . 00.4	Adhara	255 10.9	S29 00.1
04	228 15.9	258 30.7	23.0	348 39.9	14.7	58 38.7	04.2	333 03.0	00.4	Aldebaran	290 47.3	N16 32.3
05	243 18.3	273 30.1	22.1	3 41.5	14.9	73 41.5	04.3	348 05.4	00.4			
06	258 20.8	288 29.6	S13 21.1	18 43.1	S19 15.1	88 44.2	N 6 04.5	3 07.8	S21 00.4	Alioth	166 18.7	N55 52.2
07	273 23.3	303 29.0	20.1	33 44.7	15.3	103 47.0	04.6	18 10.2	00.4	Alkaid	152 57.1	N49 13.8
T 08	288 25.7	318 28.5	19.1	48 46.2	15.5	118 49.8	04.7	33 12.6	00.4	Al Na'ir	27 41.9	S46 52.9
H 09	303 28.2	333 27.9	. . 18.1	63 47.8	. . 15.7	133 52.5	. . 04.9	48 15.0	. . 00.4	Alnilam	275 44.5	S 1 11.9
U 10	318 30.7	348 27.4	17.1	78 49.4	15.9	148 55.3	05.0	63 17.4	00.4	Alphard	217 54.0	S 8 44.0
R 11	333 33.1	3 26.8	16.1	93 51.0	16.1	163 58.1	05.1	78 19.8	00.4			
S 12	348 35.6	18 26.3	S13 15.1	108 52.5	S19 16.3	179 00.8	N 6 05.2	93 22.2	S21 00.4	Alphecca	126 09.3	N26 39.5
D 13	3 38.0	33 25.8	14.1	123 54.1	16.5	194 03.6	05.4	108 24.6	00.4	Alpheratz	357 41.9	N29 10.7
A 14	18 40.5	48 25.2	13.1	138 55.7	16.7	209 06.4	05.5	123 27.0	00.4	Altair	62 06.6	N 8 54.7
Y 15	33 43.0	63 24.7	. . 12.1	153 57.3	. . 16.9	224 09.1	. . 05.6	138 29.3	. . 00.4	Ankaa	353 14.3	S42 13.3
16	48 45.4	78 24.1	11.2	168 58.9	17.1	239 11.9	05.8	153 31.7	00.4	Antares	112 23.9	S26 27.8
17	63 47.9	93 23.6	10.2	184 00.4	17.3	254 14.7	05.9	168 34.1	00.4			
18	78 50.4	108 23.0	S13 09.2	199 02.0	S19 17.5	269 17.4	N 6 06.0	183 36.5	S21 00.4	Arcturus	145 53.8	N19 05.8
19	93 52.8	123 22.5	08.2	214 03.6	17.7	284 20.2	06.1	198 38.9	00.4	Atria	107 24.0	S69 02.9
20	108 55.3	138 21.9	07.2	229 05.2	17.9	299 22.9	06.3	213 41.3	00.4	Avior	234 16.7	S59 34.1
21	123 57.8	153 21.4	. . 06.2	244 06.8	. . 18.1	314 25.7	. . 06.4	228 43.7	. . 00.4	Bellatrix	278 30.0	N 6 21.5
22	139 00.2	168 20.9	05.2	259 08.4	18.3	329 28.5	06.5	243 46.1	00.4	Betelgeuse	270 59.2	N 7 24.3
23	154 02.7	183 20.3	04.2	274 09.9	18.5	344 31.2	06.7	258 48.5	00.4			
11 00	169 05.1	198 19.8	S13 03.2	289 11.5	S19 18.7	359 34.0	N 6 06.8	273 50.9	S21 00.4	Canopus	263 55.2	S52 42.8
01	184 07.6	213 19.2	02.2	304 13.1	18.9	14 36.8	06.9	288 53.3	00.4	Capella	280 31.7	N46 00.8
02	199 10.1	228 18.7	01.2	319 14.7	19.1	29 39.5	07.1	303 55.7	00.4	Deneb	49 30.5	N45 20.2
03	214 12.5	243 18.2	13 00.2	334 16.3	. . 19.3	44 42.3	. . 07.2	318 58.1	. . 00.4	Denebola	182 31.5	N14 28.8
04	229 15.0	258 17.6	12 59.2	349 17.9	19.5	59 45.1	07.3	334 00.5	00.4	Diphda	348 54.4	S17 54.1
05	244 17.5	273 17.1	58.2	4 19.5	19.7	74 47.8	07.4	349 02.9	00.4			
06	259 19.9	288 16.5	S12 57.2	19 21.0	S19 19.9	89 50.6	N 6 07.6	4 05.3	S21 00.4	Dubhe	193 48.9	N61 39.7
07	274 22.4	303 16.0	56.2	34 22.6	20.1	104 53.4	07.7	19 07.7	00.4	Elnath	278 10.3	N28 37.1
08	289 24.9	318 15.5	55.2	49 24.2	20.3	119 56.1	07.8	34 10.1	00.4	Eltanin	90 45.4	N51 29.1
F 09	304 27.3	333 14.9	. . 54.2	64 25.8	. . 20.5	134 58.9	. . 08.0	49 12.5	. . 00.4	Enif	33 45.6	N 9 56.9
R 10	319 29.8	348 14.4	53.1	79 27.4	20.7	150 01.7	08.1	64 14.9	00.4	Fomalhaut	15 22.3	S29 32.2
I 11	334 32.3	3 13.8	52.1	94 29.0	20.9	165 04.4	08.2	79 17.3	00.4			
D 12	349 34.7	18 13.3	S12 51.1	109 30.6	S19 21.1	180 07.2	N 6 08.3	94 19.7	S21 00.4	Gacrux	171 58.2	S57 12.2
A 13	4 37.2	33 12.8	50.1	124 32.2	21.3	195 09.9	08.5	109 22.1	00.4	Gienah	175 50.0	S17 38.0
Y 14	19 39.6	48 12.2	49.1	139 33.8	21.5	210 12.7	08.6	124 24.5	00.4	Hadar	148 44.6	S60 26.8
15	34 42.1	63 11.7	. . 48.1	154 35.4	. . 21.7	225 15.5	. . 08.7	139 27.0	. . 00.4	Hamal	327 58.9	N23 32.2
16	49 44.6	78 11.2	47.1	169 37.0	21.9	240 18.2	08.9	154 29.4	00.4	Kaus Aust.	83 41.5	S34 22.3
17	64 47.0	93 10.6	46.1	184 38.6	22.1	255 21.0	09.0	169 31.8	00.4			
18	79 49.5	108 10.1	S12 45.1	199 40.2	S19 22.3	270 23.8	N 6 09.1	184 34.2	S21 00.4	Kochab	137 19.6	N74 05.2
19	94 52.0	123 09.6	44.1	214 41.8	22.5	285 26.5	09.2	199 36.6	00.4	Markab	13 36.8	N15 17.4
20	109 54.4	138 09.0	43.1	229 43.4	22.7	300 29.3	09.4	214 39.0	00.4	Menkar	314 13.3	N 4 08.9
21	124 56.9	153 08.5	. . 42.0	244 45.0	. . 22.8	315 32.1	. . 09.5	229 41.4	. . 00.4	Menkent	148 05.0	S36 26.8
22	139 59.4	168 08.0	41.0	259 46.6	23.0	330 34.8	09.6	244 43.8	00.4	Miaplacidus	221 38.4	S69 47.3
23	155 01.8	183 07.4	40.0	274 48.2	23.2	345 37.6	09.8	259 46.2	00.5			
12 00	170 04.3	198 06.9	S12 39.0	289 49.8	S19 23.4	0 40.4	N 6 09.9	274 48.6	S21 00.5	Mirfak	308 37.9	N49 55.1
01	185 06.7	213 06.4	38.0	304 51.4	23.6	15 43.1	10.0	289 51.0	00.5	Nunki	75 56.2	S26 16.4
02	200 09.2	228 05.9	37.0	319 53.0	23.8	30 45.9	10.1	304 53.4	00.5	Peacock	53 16.8	S56 40.7
03	215 11.7	243 05.3	. . 36.0	334 54.6	. . 24.0	45 48.7	. . 10.3	319 55.8	. . 00.5	Pollux	243 25.3	N27 59.0
04	230 14.1	258 04.8	34.9	349 56.2	24.2	60 51.4	10.4	334 58.2	00.5	Procyon	244 57.6	N 5 10.7
05	245 16.6	273 04.3	33.9	4 57.8	24.4	75 54.2	10.5	350 00.6	00.5			
06	260 19.1	288 03.7	S12 32.9	19 59.4	S19 24.6	90 56.9	N 6 10.6	5 03.0	S21 00.5	Rasalhague	96 04.8	N12 32.9
07	275 21.5	303 03.2	31.9	35 01.0	24.8	105 59.7	10.8	20 05.4	00.5	Regulus	207 41.3	N11 53.1
S 08	290 24.0	318 02.7	30.9	50 02.6	25.0	121 02.5	10.9	35 07.8	00.5	Rigel	281 10.3	S 8 11.4
A 09	305 26.5	333 02.2	. . 29.9	65 04.2	. . 25.2	136 05.2	. . 11.0	50 10.2	. . 00.5	Rigil Kent.	139 48.7	S60 53.8
T 10	320 28.9	348 01.6	28.8	80 05.8	25.4	151 08.0	11.2	65 12.6	00.5	Sabik	102 10.4	S15 44.5
U 11	335 31.4	3 01.1	27.8	95 07.4	25.6	166 10.8	11.3	80 15.0	00.5			
R 12	350 33.9	18 00.6	S12 26.8	110 09.0	S19 25.8	181 13.5	N 6 11.4	95 17.4	S21 00.5	Schedar	349 38.8	N56 37.5
D 13	5 36.3	33 00.0	25.8	125 10.6	25.9	196 16.3	11.5	110 19.8	00.5	Shaula	96 19.4	S37 06.6
A 14	20 38.8	47 59.5	24.7	140 12.2	26.1	211 19.1	11.7	125 22.3	00.5	Sirius	258 32.0	S16 44.7
Y 15	35 41.2	62 59.0	. . 23.7	155 13.9	. . 26.3	226 21.8	. . 11.8	140 24.7	. . 00.5	Spica	158 29.0	S11 14.8
16	50 43.7	77 58.5	22.7	170 15.5	26.5	241 24.6	11.9	155 27.1	00.5	Suhail	222 50.7	S43 30.2
17	65 46.2	92 57.9	21.7	185 17.1	26.7	256 27.3	12.1	170 29.5	00.5			
18	80 48.6	107 57.4	S12 20.7	200 18.7	S19 26.9	271 30.1	N 6 12.2	185 31.9	S21 00.5	Vega	80 37.8	N38 47.8
19	95 51.1	122 56.9	19.6	215 20.3	27.1	286 32.9	12.3	200 34.3	00.5	Zuben'ubi	137 03.2	S16 06.4
20	110 53.6	137 56.4	18.6	230 21.9	27.3	301 35.6	12.4	215 36.7	00.5		SHA	Mer. Pass.
21	125 56.0	152 55.9	. . 17.6	245 23.5	. . 27.5	316 38.4	. . 12.6	230 39.1	. . 00.5		° ′	h m
22	140 58.5	167 55.3	16.5	260 25.1	27.7	331 41.2	12.7	245 41.5	00.5	Venus	29 14.6	10 47
23	156 01.0	182 54.8	15.5	275 26.8	27.9	346 43.9	12.8	260 43.9	00.5	Mars	120 06.4	4 43
	h m									Jupiter	190 28.9	0 02
Mer. Pass.	12 41.6	v −0.5	d 1.0	v 1.6	d 0.2	v 2.8	d 0.1	v 2.4	d 0.0	Saturn	104 45.8	5 44

UT	d h	SUN GHA	SUN Dec	MOON GHA	v	MOON Dec	d	HP
		° ′	° ′	° ′	′	° ′	′	′
	10 00	177 25.9	S 4 01.2	165 12.7	7.7	N 0 09.2	11.8	61.0
	01	192 26.0	4 00.2	179 39.4	7.7	0 21.0	11.8	61.0
	02	207 26.2	3 59.2	194 06.1	7.6	0 32.8	11.7	61.0
	03	222 26.3	. . 58.2	208 32.7	7.7	0 44.5	11.8	61.0
	04	237 26.5	57.3	222 59.4	7.6	0 56.3	11.8	61.0
	05	252 26.7	56.3	237 26.0	7.6	1 08.1	11.7	61.0
	06	267 26.8	S 3 55.3	251 52.6	7.7	N 1 19.8	11.8	61.0
	07	282 27.0	54.3	266 19.3	7.6	1 31.6	11.7	61.0
T	08	297 27.1	53.3	280 45.9	7.6	1 43.3	11.7	61.0
H	09	312 27.3	. . 52.3	295 12.5	7.7	1 55.0	11.7	61.0
U	10	327 27.5	51.4	309 39.2	7.6	2 06.7	11.7	61.0
R	11	342 27.6	50.4	324 05.8	7.6	2 18.4	11.7	61.0
S	12	357 27.8	S 3 49.4	338 32.4	7.6	N 2 30.1	11.6	61.0
D	13	12 28.0	48.4	352 59.0	7.6	2 41.7	11.7	61.0
A	14	27 28.1	47.4	7 25.6	7.6	2 53.4	11.6	61.0
Y	15	42 28.3	. . 46.5	21 52.2	7.5	3 05.0	11.6	61.0
	16	57 28.4	45.5	36 18.7	7.6	3 16.6	11.6	61.0
	17	72 28.6	44.5	50 45.3	7.6	3 28.2	11.5	61.0
	18	87 28.8	S 3 43.5	65 11.9	7.6	N 3 39.7	11.5	61.0
	19	102 28.9	42.5	79 38.5	7.5	3 51.2	11.5	61.0
	20	117 29.1	41.6	94 05.0	7.6	4 02.7	11.5	60.9
	21	132 29.3	. . 40.6	108 31.6	7.5	4 14.2	11.4	60.9
	22	147 29.4	39.6	122 58.1	7.5	4 25.6	11.4	60.9
	23	162 29.6	38.6	137 24.6	7.6	4 37.0	11.4	60.9
	11 00	177 29.7	S 3 37.6	151 51.2	7.5	N 4 48.4	11.3	60.9
	01	192 29.9	36.6	166 17.7	7.5	4 59.7	11.3	60.9
	02	207 30.1	35.7	180 44.2	7.5	5 11.0	11.3	60.9
	03	222 30.2	. . 34.7	195 10.7	7.5	5 22.3	11.2	60.9
	04	237 30.4	33.7	209 37.2	7.5	5 33.5	11.2	60.9
	05	252 30.6	32.7	224 03.7	7.5	5 44.7	11.1	60.9
	06	267 30.7	S 3 31.7	238 30.2	7.4	N 5 55.8	11.1	60.9
	07	282 30.9	30.7	252 56.6	7.5	6 06.9	11.0	60.8
	08	297 31.1	29.8	267 23.1	7.4	6 17.9	11.0	60.8
F	09	312 31.2	. . 28.8	281 49.5	7.5	6 28.9	11.0	60.8
R	10	327 31.4	27.8	296 16.0	7.4	6 39.9	10.9	60.8
I	11	342 31.5	26.8	310 42.4	7.4	6 50.8	10.8	60.8
D	12	357 31.7	S 3 25.8	325 08.8	7.5	N 7 01.6	10.8	60.8
A	13	12 31.9	24.8	339 35.3	7.4	7 12.4	10.8	60.8
Y	14	27 32.0	23.9	354 01.7	7.4	7 23.2	10.7	60.8
	15	42 32.2	. . 22.9	8 28.1	7.4	7 33.9	10.6	60.7
	16	57 32.4	21.9	22 54.5	7.4	7 44.5	10.6	60.7
	17	72 32.5	20.9	37 20.9	7.3	7 55.1	10.5	60.7
	18	87 32.7	S 3 19.9	51 47.2	7.4	N 8 05.6	10.4	60.7
	19	102 32.9	18.9	66 13.6	7.3	8 16.0	10.5	60.7
	20	117 33.0	18.0	80 39.9	7.4	8 26.5	10.3	60.7
	21	132 33.2	. . 17.0	95 06.3	7.3	8 36.8	10.3	60.6
	22	147 33.4	16.0	109 32.6	7.4	8 47.1	10.2	60.6
	23	162 33.5	15.0	123 59.0	7.3	8 57.3	10.1	60.6
	12 00	177 33.7	S 3 14.0	138 25.3	7.3	N 9 07.4	10.1	60.6
	01	192 33.9	13.0	152 51.6	7.3	9 17.5	10.0	60.6
	02	207 34.0	12.1	167 17.9	7.3	9 27.5	10.0	60.5
	03	222 34.2	. . 11.1	181 44.2	7.3	9 37.5	9.8	60.5
	04	237 34.4	10.1	196 10.5	7.3	9 47.3	9.8	60.5
	05	252 34.5	09.1	210 36.8	7.2	9 57.1	9.8	60.5
	06	267 34.7	S 3 08.1	225 03.0	7.3	N10 06.9	9.6	60.5
	07	282 34.9	07.1	239 29.3	7.2	10 16.5	9.6	60.4
S	08	297 35.0	06.1	253 55.5	7.3	10 26.1	9.5	60.4
A	09	312 35.2	. . 05.2	268 21.8	7.2	10 35.6	9.4	60.4
T	10	327 35.4	04.2	282 48.0	7.3	10 45.0	9.4	60.4
U	11	342 35.5	03.2	297 14.3	7.2	10 54.4	9.3	60.3
R	12	357 35.7	S 3 02.2	311 40.5	7.2	N11 03.7	9.2	60.3
D	13	12 35.9	01.2	326 06.7	7.2	11 12.9	9.1	60.3
A	14	27 36.1	3 00.2	340 32.9	7.2	11 22.0	9.0	60.3
Y	15	42 36.2	2 59.3	354 59.1	7.2	11 31.0	8.9	60.3
	16	57 36.4	58.3	9 25.3	7.2	11 39.9	8.9	60.2
	17	72 36.6	57.3	23 51.5	7.2	11 48.8	8.8	60.2
	18	87 36.7	S 2 56.3	38 17.7	7.2	N11 57.6	8.7	60.2
	19	102 36.9	55.3	52 43.9	7.1	12 06.3	8.6	60.2
	20	117 37.1	54.3	67 10.0	7.2	12 14.9	8.5	60.1
	21	132 37.2	. . 53.3	81 36.2	7.1	12 23.4	8.4	60.1
	22	147 37.4	52.4	96 02.3	7.2	12 31.8	8.4	60.1
	23	162 37.6	51.4	110 28.5	7.2	N12 40.2	8.2	60.1
		SD 16.1	*d* 1.0	SD 16.6		16.6		16.4

Lat.	Twilight Naut.	Twilight Civil	Sunrise	Moonrise 10	Moonrise 11	Moonrise 12	Moonrise 13
°	h m	h m	h m	h m	h m	h m	h m
N 72	04 15	05 36	06 43	06 58	06 54	06 49	06 44
N 70	04 26	05 39	06 39	07 00	07 02	07 05	07 10
68	04 35	05 41	06 36	07 01	07 09	07 18	07 30
66	04 42	05 43	06 33	07 03	07 14	07 28	07 46
64	04 48	05 44	06 31	07 04	07 19	07 37	07 59
62	04 54	05 45	06 29	07 05	07 24	07 45	08 10
60	04 58	05 46	06 28	07 06	07 27	07 51	08 19
N 58	05 02	05 47	06 26	07 06	07 31	07 57	08 27
56	05 05	05 48	06 25	07 07	07 34	08 02	08 35
54	05 08	05 49	06 24	07 08	07 36	08 07	08 41
52	05 10	05 49	06 23	07 08	07 39	08 11	08 47
50	05 12	05 49	06 22	07 09	07 41	08 15	08 53
45	05 16	05 50	06 19	07 10	07 46	08 23	09 04
N 40	05 19	05 50	06 17	07 11	07 50	08 30	09 14
35	05 21	05 51	06 16	07 12	07 53	08 37	09 22
30	05 23	05 50	06 14	07 12	07 57	08 42	09 29
20	05 24	05 50	06 12	07 14	08 02	08 51	09 42
N 10	05 24	05 48	06 09	07 15	08 07	09 00	09 53
0	05 22	05 46	06 07	07 16	08 12	09 08	10 04
S 10	05 19	05 43	06 04	07 17	08 16	09 15	10 14
20	05 13	05 39	06 01	07 18	08 21	09 24	10 26
30	05 06	05 34	05 58	07 20	08 27	09 34	10 39
35	05 01	05 31	05 56	07 21	08 30	09 39	10 46
40	04 54	05 26	05 54	07 22	08 34	09 46	10 55
45	04 46	05 21	05 51	07 23	08 39	09 53	11 05
S 50	04 36	05 15	05 48	07 24	08 44	10 02	11 17
52	04 31	05 12	05 46	07 25	08 47	10 07	11 23
54	04 26	05 09	05 45	07 26	08 49	10 11	11 29
56	04 19	05 05	05 43	07 27	08 52	10 16	11 37
58	04 12	05 01	05 41	07 27	08 56	10 22	11 45
S 60	04 03	04 56	05 39	07 28	08 59	10 29	11 54

Lat.	Sunset	Twilight Civil	Twilight Naut.	Moonset 10	Moonset 11	Moonset 12	Moonset 13
°	h m	h m	h m	h m	h m	h m	h m
N 72	17 39	18 47	20 09	20 34	22 36	24 38	00 38
N 70	17 43	18 44	19 57	20 28	22 22	24 13	00 13
68	17 46	18 41	19 47	20 24	22 11	23 55	25 33
66	17 48	18 39	19 40	20 20	22 01	23 40	25 12
64	17 50	18 37	19 33	20 16	21 54	23 28	24 56
62	17 52	18 36	19 28	20 14	21 47	23 18	24 42
60	17 53	18 35	19 24	20 11	21 41	23 09	24 31
N 58	17 55	18 34	19 20	20 09	21 36	23 01	24 21
56	17 56	18 33	19 16	20 07	21 32	22 54	24 12
54	17 57	18 32	19 14	20 05	21 28	22 48	24 04
52	17 58	18 32	19 11	20 03	21 24	22 43	23 57
50	17 59	18 31	19 09	20 02	21 21	22 38	23 51
45	18 01	18 30	19 05	19 59	21 14	22 28	23 38
N 40	18 03	18 30	19 01	19 56	21 08	22 19	23 27
35	18 05	18 30	18 59	19 54	21 03	22 11	23 17
30	18 06	18 30	18 58	19 52	20 59	22 05	23 09
20	18 09	18 31	18 56	19 48	20 51	21 53	22 55
N 10	18 11	18 32	18 56	19 45	20 44	21 44	22 42
0	18 13	18 34	18 58	19 42	20 38	21 34	22 31
S 10	18 16	18 37	19 01	19 39	20 32	21 25	22 19
20	18 18	18 40	19 06	19 36	20 25	21 15	22 07
30	18 21	18 45	19 13	19 33	20 17	21 04	21 52
35	18 23	18 49	19 18	19 31	20 13	20 57	21 44
40	18 25	18 53	19 25	19 28	20 08	20 50	21 35
45	18 28	18 57	19 32	19 26	20 02	20 41	21 24
S 50	18 31	19 03	19 42	19 22	19 55	20 31	21 11
52	18 32	19 06	19 47	19 21	19 52	20 26	21 05
54	18 34	19 10	19 53	19 19	19 49	20 21	20 58
56	18 36	19 13	19 59	19 18	19 45	20 15	20 50
58	18 37	19 17	20 06	19 16	19 41	20 09	20 42
S 60	18 40	19 22	20 14	19 13	19 36	20 02	20 32

Day	SUN Eqn. of Time 00^h	SUN Eqn. of Time 12^h	SUN Mer. Pass.	MOON Mer. Pass. Upper	MOON Mer. Pass. Lower	MOON Age	MOON Phase
d	m s	m s	h m	h m	h m	d	%
10	10 17	10 09	12 10	13 29	01 01	01	3
11	10 01	09 53	12 10	14 25	01 57	02	9
12	09 46	09 37	12 10	15 21	02 53	03	16

UT d h	ARIES GHA	VENUS −3·8 GHA	Dec	MARS +0·0 GHA	Dec	JUPITER −2·5 GHA	Dec	SATURN +0·4 GHA	Dec
	° ′	° ′	° ′	° ′	° ′	° ′	° ′	° ′	° ′
13 00	171 03.4	197 54.3	S12 14.5	290 28.4	S19 28.1	1 46.7	N 6 12.9	275 46.3	S21 00.5
01	186 05.9	212 53.8	13.5	305 30.0	28.2	16 49.5	13.1	290 48.7	00.5
02	201 08.4	227 53.2	12.4	320 31.6	28.4	31 52.2	13.2	305 51.1	00.5
03	216 10.8	242 52.7	· · 11.4	335 33.2	· · 28.6	46 55.0	· · 13.3	320 53.6	· · 00.5
04	231 13.3	257 52.2	10.4	350 34.8	28.8	61 57.8	13.5	335 56.0	00.5
05	246 15.7	272 51.7	09.3	5 36.5	29.0	77 00.5	13.6	350 58.4	00.5
06	261 18.2	287 51.2	S12 08.3	20 38.1	S19 29.2	92 03.3	N 6 13.7	6 00.8	S21 00.5
07	276 20.7	302 50.7	07.3	35 39.7	29.4	107 06.0	13.8	21 03.2	00.5
08	291 23.1	317 50.1	06.2	50 41.3	29.6	122 08.8	14.0	36 05.6	00.5
S 09	306 25.6	332 49.6	· · 05.2	65 43.0	· · 29.8	137 11.6	· · 14.1	51 08.0	· · 00.5
U 10	321 28.1	347 49.1	04.2	80 44.6	30.0	152 14.3	14.2	66 10.4	00.5
N 11	336 30.5	2 48.6	03.1	95 46.2	30.1	167 17.1	14.3	81 12.8	00.5
D 12	351 33.0	17 48.1	S12 02.1	110 47.8	S19 30.3	182 19.9	N 6 14.5	96 15.2	S21 00.5
A 13	6 35.5	32 47.6	01.1	125 49.4	30.5	197 22.6	14.6	111 17.7	00.5
Y 14	21 37.9	47 47.0	12 00.0	140 51.1	30.7	212 25.4	14.7	126 20.1	00.5
15	36 40.4	62 46.5	11 59.0	155 52.7	· · 30.9	227 28.1	· · 14.9	141 22.5	· · 00.5
16	51 42.8	77 46.0	58.0	170 54.3	31.1	242 30.9	15.0	156 24.9	00.5
17	66 45.3	92 45.5	56.9	185 56.0	31.3	257 33.7	15.1	171 27.3	00.5
18	81 47.8	107 45.0	S11 55.9	200 57.6	S19 31.5	272 36.4	N 6 15.2	186 29.7	S21 00.5
19	96 50.2	122 44.5	54.8	215 59.2	31.6	287 39.2	15.4	201 32.1	00.5
20	111 52.7	137 44.0	53.8	231 00.8	31.8	302 42.0	15.5	216 34.5	00.5
21	126 55.2	152 43.4	· · 52.8	246 02.5	· · 32.0	317 44.7	· · 15.6	231 36.9	· · 00.5
22	141 57.6	167 42.9	51.7	261 04.1	32.2	332 47.5	15.7	246 39.4	00.5
23	157 00.1	182 42.4	50.7	276 05.7	32.4	347 50.3	15.9	261 41.8	00.5
14 00	172 02.6	197 41.9	S11 49.6	291 07.4	S19 32.6	2 53.0	N 6 16.0	276 44.2	S21 00.5
01	187 05.0	212 41.4	48.6	306 09.0	32.8	17 55.8	16.1	291 46.6	00.5
02	202 07.5	227 40.9	47.6	321 10.6	33.0	32 58.5	16.3	306 49.0	00.5
03	217 10.0	242 40.4	· · 46.5	336 12.3	· · 33.1	48 01.3	· · 16.4	321 51.4	· · 00.5
04	232 12.4	257 39.9	45.5	351 13.9	33.3	63 04.1	16.5	336 53.8	00.5
05	247 14.9	272 39.4	44.4	6 15.5	33.5	78 06.8	16.6	351 56.2	00.5
06	262 17.3	287 38.9	S11 43.4	21 17.2	S19 33.7	93 09.6	N 6 16.8	6 58.7	S21 00.5
07	277 19.8	302 38.3	42.3	36 18.8	33.9	108 12.4	16.9	22 01.1	00.5
08	292 22.3	317 37.8	41.3	51 20.4	34.1	123 15.1	17.0	37 03.5	00.5
M 09	307 24.7	332 37.3	· · 40.2	66 22.1	· · 34.3	138 17.9	· · 17.1	52 05.9	· · 00.5
O 10	322 27.2	347 36.8	39.2	81 23.7	34.4	153 20.6	17.3	67 08.3	00.5
N 11	337 29.7	2 36.3	38.1	96 25.4	34.6	168 23.4	17.4	82 10.7	00.5
D 12	352 32.1	17 35.8	S11 37.1	111 27.0	S19 34.8	183 26.2	N 6 17.5	97 13.1	S21 00.5
A 13	7 34.6	32 35.3	36.1	126 28.6	35.0	198 28.9	17.6	112 15.6	00.5
Y 14	22 37.1	47 34.8	35.0	141 30.3	35.2	213 31.7	17.8	127 18.0	00.5
15	37 39.5	62 34.3	· · 34.0	156 31.9	· · 35.4	228 34.4	· · 17.9	142 20.4	· · 00.5
16	52 42.0	77 33.8	32.9	171 33.6	35.6	243 37.2	18.0	157 22.8	00.5
17	67 44.5	92 33.3	31.9	186 35.2	35.7	258 40.0	18.1	172 25.2	00.5
18	82 46.9	107 32.8	S11 30.8	201 36.9	S19 35.9	273 42.7	N 6 18.3	187 27.6	S21 00.5
19	97 49.4	122 32.3	29.7	216 38.5	36.1	288 45.5	18.4	202 30.1	00.5
20	112 51.8	137 31.8	28.7	231 40.1	36.3	303 48.3	18.5	217 32.5	00.5
21	127 54.3	152 31.3	· · 27.6	246 41.8	· · 36.5	318 51.0	· · 18.7	232 34.9	· · 00.5
22	142 56.8	167 30.8	26.6	261 43.4	36.7	333 53.8	18.8	247 37.3	00.5
23	157 59.2	182 30.3	25.5	276 45.1	36.8	348 56.5	18.9	262 39.7	00.5
15 00	173 01.7	197 29.8	S11 24.5	291 46.7	S19 37.0	3 59.3	N 6 19.0	277 42.1	S21 00.5
01	188 04.2	212 29.3	23.4	306 48.4	37.2	19 02.1	19.2	292 44.6	00.5
02	203 06.6	227 28.8	22.4	321 50.0	37.4	34 04.8	19.3	307 47.0	00.5
03	218 09.1	242 28.3	· · 21.3	336 51.7	· · 37.6	49 07.6	· · 19.4	322 49.4	· · 00.5
04	233 11.6	257 27.8	20.3	351 53.3	37.8	64 10.3	19.5	337 51.8	00.5
05	248 14.0	272 27.3	19.2	6 55.0	37.9	79 13.1	19.7	352 54.2	00.5
06	263 16.5	287 26.8	S11 18.1	21 56.6	S19 38.1	94 15.9	N 6 19.8	7 56.6	S21 00.5
07	278 18.9	302 26.3	17.1	36 58.3	38.3	109 18.6	19.9	22 59.1	00.5
T 08	293 21.4	317 25.8	16.0	52 00.0	38.5	124 21.4	20.0	38 01.5	00.5
U 09	308 23.9	332 25.3	· · 15.0	67 01.6	· · 38.7	139 24.2	· · 20.2	53 03.9	· · 00.5
E 10	323 26.3	347 24.8	13.9	82 03.3	38.8	154 26.9	20.3	68 06.3	00.5
S 11	338 28.8	2 24.3	12.8	97 04.9	39.0	169 29.7	20.4	83 08.7	00.5
D 12	353 31.3	17 23.8	S11 11.8	112 06.6	S19 39.2	184 32.4	N 6 20.5	98 11.2	S21 00.5
A 13	8 33.7	32 23.3	10.7	127 08.2	39.4	199 35.2	20.7	113 13.6	00.5
Y 14	23 36.2	47 22.8	09.7	142 09.9	39.6	214 38.0	20.8	128 16.0	00.5
15	38 38.7	62 22.3	· · 08.6	157 11.6	· · 39.8	229 40.7	· · 20.9	143 18.4	· · 00.5
16	53 41.1	77 21.8	07.5	172 13.2	39.9	244 43.5	21.0	158 20.8	00.5
17	68 43.6	92 21.3	06.5	187 14.9	40.1	259 46.2	21.2	173 23.3	00.5
18	83 46.1	107 20.8	S11 05.4	202 16.5	S19 40.3	274 49.0	N 6 21.3	188 25.7	S21 00.5
19	98 48.5	122 20.3	04.3	217 18.2	40.5	289 51.8	21.4	203 28.1	00.4
20	113 51.0	137 19.8	03.3	232 19.9	40.7	304 54.5	21.5	218 30.5	00.4
21	128 53.4	152 19.3	· · 02.2	247 21.5	· · 40.8	319 57.3	· · 21.7	233 32.9	· · 00.4
22	143 55.9	167 18.8	01.1	262 23.2	41.0	335 00.0	21.8	248 35.4	00.4
23	158 58.4	182 18.3	00.1	277 24.8	41.2	350 02.8	21.9	263 37.8	00.4
Mer. Pass.	h m 12 29.8	*v* −0.5	*d* 1.0	*v* 1.6	*d* 0.2	*v* 2.8	*d* 0.1	*v* 2.4	*d* 0.0

STARS Name	SHA	Dec
	° ′	° ′
Acamar	315 17.2	S40 14.8
Achernar	335 26.0	S57 09.6
Acrux	173 06.4	S63 11.3
Adhara	255 10.9	S29 00.1
Aldebaran	290 47.3	N16 32.3
Alioth	166 18.6	N55 52.2
Alkaid	152 57.1	N49 13.8
Al Na'ir	27 41.9	S46 52.9
Alnilam	275 44.5	S 1 11.9
Alphard	217 54.0	S 8 44.0
Alphecca	126 09.3	N26 39.5
Alpheratz	357 41.9	N29 10.7
Altair	62 06.6	N 8 54.7
Ankaa	353 14.3	S42 13.3
Antares	112 23.9	S26 27.8
Arcturus	145 53.8	N19 05.8
Atria	107 23.9	S69 02.9
Avior	234 16.8	S59 34.1
Bellatrix	278 30.0	N 6 21.5
Betelgeuse	270 59.3	N 7 24.3
Canopus	263 55.2	S52 42.8
Capella	280 31.7	N46 00.8
Deneb	49 30.5	N45 20.2
Denebola	182 31.5	N14 28.8
Diphda	348 54.4	S17 54.1
Dubhe	193 48.9	N61 39.7
Elnath	278 10.3	N28 37.1
Eltanin	90 45.3	N51 29.1
Enif	33 45.6	N 9 56.9
Fomalhaut	15 22.3	S29 32.2
Gacrux	171 58.1	S57 12.2
Gienah	175 50.0	S17 38.0
Hadar	148 44.6	S60 26.8
Hamal	327 58.9	N23 32.2
Kaus Aust.	83 41.4	S34 22.3
Kochab	137 19.5	N74 05.2
Markab	13 36.8	N15 17.4
Menkar	314 13.3	N 4 08.9
Menkent	148 05.0	S36 26.8
Miaplacidus	221 38.4	S69 47.3
Mirfak	308 37.9	N49 55.0
Nunki	75 56.2	S26 16.4
Peacock	53 16.8	S56 40.7
Pollux	243 25.3	N27 59.0
Procyon	244 57.6	N 5 10.7
Rasalhague	96 04.7	N12 32.9
Regulus	207 41.3	N11 53.1
Rigel	281 10.3	S 8 11.4
Rigil Kent.	139 48.6	S60 53.8
Sabik	102 10.4	S15 44.5
Schedar	349 38.8	N56 37.5
Shaula	96 19.4	S37 06.6
Sirius	258 32.0	S16 44.7
Spica	158 29.0	S11 14.8
Suhail	222 50.7	S43 30.2
Vega	80 37.8	N38 47.8
Zuben'ubi	137 03.1	S16 06.4

	SHA	Mer. Pass.
	° ′	h m
Venus	25 39.3	10 50
Mars	119 04.8	4 35
Jupiter	190 50.5	23 44
Saturn	104 41.6	5 32

UT	SUN GHA	SUN Dec	MOON GHA	v	MOON Dec	d	HP
d h	° ′	° ′	° ′	′	° ′	′	′
13 00	177 37.7	S 2 50.4	124 54.7	7.1	N12 48.4	8.2	60.0
01	192 37.9	49.4	139 20.8	7.1	12 56.6	8.1	60.0
02	207 38.1	48.4	153 46.9	7.2	13 04.7	7.9	60.0
03	222 38.3	. . 47.4	168 13.1	7.1	13 12.6	7.9	59.9
04	237 38.4	46.4	182 39.2	7.1	13 20.5	7.8	59.9
05	252 38.6	45.5	197 05.3	7.2	13 28.3	7.7	59.9
06	267 38.8	S 2 44.5	211 31.5	7.1	N13 36.0	7.6	59.9
07	282 38.9	43.5	225 57.6	7.1	13 43.6	7.5	59.8
S 08	297 39.1	42.5	240 23.7	7.1	13 51.1	7.4	59.8
U 09	312 39.3	. . 41.5	254 49.8	7.1	13 58.5	7.3	59.8
N 10	327 39.4	40.5	269 15.9	7.2	14 05.8	7.2	59.7
D 11	342 39.6	39.5	283 42.1	7.1	14 13.0	7.2	59.7
A 12	357 39.8	S 2 38.6	298 08.2	7.1	N14 20.2	7.0	59.7
Y 13	12 40.0	37.6	312 34.3	7.1	14 27.2	6.9	59.7
14	27 40.1	36.6	327 00.4	7.1	14 34.1	6.8	59.6
15	42 40.3	. . 35.6	341 26.5	7.2	14 40.9	6.7	59.6
16	57 40.5	34.6	355 52.7	7.1	14 47.6	6.6	59.6
17	72 40.6	33.6	10 18.8	7.1	14 54.2	6.5	59.5
18	87 40.8	S 2 32.6	24 44.9	7.1	N15 00.7	6.4	59.5
19	102 41.0	31.7	39 11.0	7.2	15 07.1	6.3	59.5
20	117 41.2	30.7	53 37.2	7.1	15 13.4	6.2	59.4
21	132 41.3	. . 29.7	68 03.3	7.1	15 19.6	6.1	59.4
22	147 41.5	28.7	82 29.4	7.2	15 25.7	6.0	59.4
23	162 41.7	27.7	96 55.6	7.1	15 31.7	5.9	59.4
14 00	177 41.9	S 2 26.7	111 21.7	7.2	N15 37.6	5.8	59.3
01	192 42.0	25.7	125 47.9	7.1	15 43.4	5.6	59.3
02	207 42.2	24.7	140 14.0	7.2	15 49.0	5.6	59.3
03	222 42.4	. . 23.8	154 40.2	7.2	15 54.6	5.4	59.2
04	237 42.5	22.8	169 06.4	7.1	16 00.0	5.4	59.2
05	252 42.7	21.8	183 32.5	7.2	16 05.4	5.2	59.2
06	267 42.9	S 2 20.8	197 58.7	7.2	N16 10.6	5.1	59.1
07	282 43.1	19.8	212 24.9	7.2	16 15.7	5.1	59.1
08	297 43.2	18.8	226 51.1	7.3	16 20.8	4.9	59.1
M 09	312 43.4	. . 17.8	241 17.4	7.2	16 25.7	4.8	59.0
O 10	327 43.6	16.9	255 43.6	7.2	16 30.5	4.7	59.0
N 11	342 43.8	15.9	270 09.8	7.3	16 35.2	4.6	59.0
D 12	357 43.9	S 2 14.9	284 36.1	7.2	N16 39.8	4.4	58.9
A 13	12 44.1	13.9	299 02.3	7.3	16 44.2	4.4	58.9
Y 14	27 44.3	12.9	313 28.6	7.3	16 48.6	4.3	58.9
15	42 44.5	. . 11.9	327 54.9	7.3	16 52.9	4.1	58.8
16	57 44.6	10.9	342 21.2	7.3	16 57.0	4.0	58.8
17	72 44.8	09.9	356 47.5	7.4	17 01.0	4.0	58.8
18	87 45.0	S 2 09.0	11 13.9	7.3	N17 05.0	3.8	58.7
19	102 45.2	08.0	25 40.2	7.4	17 08.8	3.7	58.7
20	117 45.3	07.0	40 06.6	7.3	17 12.5	3.6	58.7
21	132 45.5	. . 06.0	54 32.9	7.5	17 16.1	3.4	58.7
22	147 45.7	05.0	68 59.4	7.4	17 19.5	3.4	58.6
23	162 45.9	04.0	83 25.8	7.4	17 22.9	3.3	58.6
15 00	177 46.0	S 2 03.0	97 52.2	7.5	N17 26.2	3.1	58.6
01	192 46.2	02.0	112 18.7	7.4	17 29.3	3.0	58.5
02	207 46.4	01.1	126 45.1	7.5	17 32.3	3.0	58.5
03	222 46.6	2 00.1	141 11.6	7.6	17 35.3	2.8	58.5
04	237 46.7	1 59.1	155 38.2	7.5	17 38.1	2.7	58.4
05	252 46.9	58.1	170 04.7	7.6	17 40.8	2.6	58.4
06	267 47.1	S 1 57.1	184 31.3	7.6	N17 43.4	2.4	58.4
07	282 47.3	56.1	198 57.9	7.6	17 45.8	2.4	58.3
T 08	297 47.4	55.1	213 24.5	7.6	17 48.2	2.2	58.3
U 09	312 47.6	. . 54.1	227 51.1	7.7	17 50.4	2.2	58.3
E 10	327 47.8	53.2	242 17.8	7.7	17 52.6	2.0	58.2
S 11	342 48.0	52.2	256 44.5	7.7	17 54.6	1.9	58.2
D 12	357 48.1	S 1 51.2	271 11.2	7.8	N17 56.5	1.8	58.2
A 13	12 48.3	50.2	285 38.0	7.7	17 58.3	1.7	58.1
Y 14	27 48.5	49.2	300 04.7	7.8	18 00.0	1.6	58.1
15	42 48.7	. . 48.2	314 31.5	7.9	18 01.6	1.5	58.1
16	57 48.9	47.2	328 58.4	7.8	18 03.1	1.4	58.0
17	72 49.0	46.2	343 25.2	7.9	18 04.5	1.2	58.0
18	87 49.2	S 1 45.3	357 52.1	7.9	N18 05.7	1.2	58.0
19	102 49.4	44.3	12 19.0	8.0	18 06.9	1.0	57.9
20	117 49.6	43.3	26 46.0	8.0	18 07.9	0.9	57.9
21	132 49.7	. . 42.3	41 13.0	8.0	18 08.8	0.8	57.9
22	147 49.9	41.3	55 40.0	8.1	18 09.6	0.7	57.8
23	162 50.1	40.3	70 07.1	8.0	N18 10.3	0.6	57.8
	SD 16.1	d 1.0	SD 16.3		16.1		15.8

Lat.	Twilight Naut.	Twilight Civil	Sunrise	Moonrise 13	Moonrise 14	Moonrise 15	Moonrise 16
°	h m	h m	h m	h m	h m	h m	h m
N 72	03 57	05 20	06 27	06 44	06 39	06 33	□
N 70	04 11	05 25	06 25	07 10	07 20	07 42	08 26
68	04 21	05 28	06 23	07 30	07 49	08 19	09 06
66	04 30	05 31	06 22	07 46	08 10	08 45	09 34
64	04 37	05 34	06 21	07 59	08 27	09 05	09 56
62	04 43	05 36	06 20	08 10	08 41	09 22	10 13
60	04 49	05 37	06 19	08 19	08 53	09 36	10 27
N 58	04 53	05 39	06 18	08 27	09 04	09 47	10 39
56	04 57	05 40	06 17	08 35	09 13	09 58	10 50
54	05 00	05 41	06 16	08 41	09 21	10 07	10 59
52	05 03	05 42	06 16	08 47	09 28	10 15	11 08
50	05 05	05 43	06 15	08 53	09 35	10 22	11 15
45	05 11	05 45	06 14	09 04	09 49	10 38	11 31
N 40	05 14	05 46	06 13	09 14	10 00	10 51	11 44
35	05 17	05 46	06 12	09 22	10 10	11 02	11 55
30	05 19	05 47	06 11	09 29	10 19	11 11	12 05
20	05 21	05 47	06 09	09 42	10 34	11 28	12 22
N 10	05 22	05 46	06 07	09 53	10 47	11 42	12 36
0	05 21	05 45	06 06	10 04	11 00	11 56	12 50
S 10	05 19	05 43	06 04	10 14	11 12	12 09	13 04
20	05 14	05 40	06 02	10 26	11 26	12 24	13 19
30	05 08	05 36	06 00	10 39	11 41	12 41	13 36
35	05 03	05 33	05 58	10 46	11 50	12 50	13 45
40	04 58	05 30	05 57	10 55	12 01	13 01	13 57
45	04 51	05 26	05 55	11 05	12 13	13 15	14 10
S 50	04 42	05 20	05 53	11 17	12 27	13 31	14 26
52	04 37	05 18	05 52	11 23	12 34	13 38	14 33
54	04 32	05 15	05 51	11 29	12 42	13 47	14 42
56	04 26	05 12	05 49	11 37	12 51	13 56	14 51
58	04 20	05 08	05 48	11 45	13 00	14 07	15 02
S 60	04 12	05 04	05 46	11 54	13 11	14 19	15 14

Lat.	Sunset	Twilight Civil	Twilight Naut.	Moonset 13	Moonset 14	Moonset 15	Moonset 16
°	h m	h m	h m	h m	h m	h m	h m
N 72	17 53	19 01	20 25	00 38	02 41	04 45	□
N 70	17 55	18 56	20 11	00 13	02 01	03 36	04 47
68	17 57	18 52	20 00	25 33	01 33	02 59	04 06
66	17 58	18 49	19 50	25 12	01 12	02 33	03 38
64	17 59	18 46	19 43	24 56	00 56	02 13	03 17
62	18 00	18 44	19 37	24 42	00 42	01 57	03 00
60	18 01	18 42	19 31	24 31	00 31	01 44	02 45
N 58	18 02	18 41	19 27	24 21	00 21	01 32	02 33
56	18 02	18 39	19 23	24 12	00 12	01 22	02 22
54	18 03	18 38	19 20	24 04	00 04	01 13	02 13
52	18 03	18 37	19 17	23 57	25 05	01 05	02 05
50	18 04	18 36	19 14	23 51	24 58	00 58	01 57
45	18 05	18 34	19 09	23 38	24 43	00 43	01 41
N 40	18 06	18 33	19 05	23 27	24 30	00 30	01 28
35	18 07	18 32	19 02	23 17	24 19	00 19	01 17
30	18 08	18 32	19 00	23 09	24 10	00 10	01 07
20	18 09	18 31	18 57	22 55	23 54	24 50	00 50
N 10	18 11	18 32	18 56	22 42	23 40	24 36	00 36
0	18 12	18 33	18 57	22 31	23 27	24 22	00 22
S 10	18 14	18 35	18 59	22 19	23 14	24 08	00 08
20	18 16	18 38	19 03	22 07	22 59	23 53	24 48
30	18 18	18 42	19 10	21 52	22 43	23 36	24 31
35	18 19	18 44	19 14	21 44	22 34	23 27	24 21
40	18 21	18 48	19 19	21 35	22 23	23 15	24 10
45	18 22	18 52	19 26	21 24	22 11	23 02	23 57
S 50	18 24	18 57	19 35	21 11	21 56	22 46	23 41
52	18 25	18 59	19 40	21 05	21 48	22 38	23 34
54	18 26	19 02	19 45	20 58	21 41	22 30	23 26
56	18 28	19 05	19 50	20 50	21 32	22 20	23 16
58	18 29	19 09	19 56	20 42	21 22	22 10	23 06
S 60	18 31	19 13	20 04	20 32	21 10	21 57	22 54

Day	SUN Eqn. of Time 00^h	SUN Eqn. of Time 12^h	SUN Mer. Pass.	MOON Mer. Pass. Upper	MOON Mer. Pass. Lower	MOON Age	MOON Phase
d	m s	m s	h m	h m	h m	d %	
13	09 29	09 21	12 09	16 17	03 49	04 26	
14	09 13	09 05	12 09	17 13	04 45	05 37	
15	08 56	08 48	12 09	18 09	05 41	06 48	

	UT	ARIES	VENUS −3·8		MARS −0·1		JUPITER −2·5		SATURN +0·4	
	d h	GHA ° ′	GHA ° ′	Dec ° ′	GHA ° ′	Dec ° ′	GHA ° ′	Dec ° ′	GHA ° ′	Dec ° ′
	16 00	174 00.8	197 17.8	S10 59.0	292 26.5	S19 41.4	5 05.6	N 6 22.0	278 40.2	S21 00.4
	01	189 03.3	212 17.4	57.9	307 28.2	41.6	20 08.3	22.2	293 42.6	00.4
	02	204 05.8	227 16.9	56.9	322 29.8	41.7	35 11.1	22.3	308 45.1	00.4
	03	219 08.2	242 16.4	. . 55.8	337 31.5	. . 41.9	50 13.8	. . 22.4	323 47.5	. . 00.4
	04	234 10.7	257 15.9	54.7	352 33.2	42.1	65 16.6	22.5	338 49.9	00.4
	05	249 13.2	272 15.4	53.7	7 34.8	42.3	80 19.4	22.7	353 52.3	00.4
	06	264 15.6	287 14.9	S10 52.6	22 36.5	S19 42.4	95 22.1	N 6 22.8	8 54.7	S21 00.4
W	07	279 18.1	302 14.4	51.5	37 38.2	42.6	110 24.9	22.9	23 57.2	00.4
E	08	294 20.6	317 13.9	50.4	52 39.9	42.8	125 27.6	23.0	38 59.6	00.4
D	09	309 23.0	332 13.4	. . 49.4	67 41.5	. . 43.0	140 30.4	. . 23.2	54 02.0	. . 00.4
N	10	324 25.5	347 12.9	48.3	82 43.2	43.2	155 33.2	23.3	69 04.4	00.4
E	11	339 27.9	2 12.5	47.2	97 44.9	43.3	170 35.9	23.4	84 06.9	00.4
S	12	354 30.4	17 12.0	S10 46.1	112 46.5	S19 43.5	185 38.7	N 6 23.5	99 09.3	S21 00.4
D	13	9 32.9	32 11.5	45.1	127 48.2	43.7	200 41.4	23.7	114 11.7	00.4
A	14	24 35.3	47 11.0	44.0	142 49.9	43.9	215 44.2	23.8	129 14.1	00.4
Y	15	39 37.8	62 10.5	. . 42.9	157 51.6	. . 44.0	230 47.0	. . 23.9	144 16.6	. . 00.4
	16	54 40.3	77 10.0	41.8	172 53.3	44.2	245 49.7	24.0	159 19.0	00.4
	17	69 42.7	92 09.5	40.8	187 54.9	44.4	260 52.5	24.2	174 21.4	00.4
	18	84 45.2	107 09.1	S10 39.7	202 56.6	S19 44.6	275 55.2	N 6 24.3	189 23.8	S21 00.4
	19	99 47.7	122 08.6	38.6	217 58.3	44.8	290 58.0	24.4	204 26.3	00.4
	20	114 50.1	137 08.1	37.5	233 00.0	44.9	306 00.8	24.5	219 28.7	00.4
	21	129 52.6	152 07.6	. . 36.5	248 01.6	. . 45.1	321 03.5	. . 24.7	234 31.1	. . 00.4
	22	144 55.1	167 07.1	35.4	263 03.3	45.3	336 06.3	24.8	249 33.5	00.4
	23	159 57.5	182 06.6	34.3	278 05.0	45.5	351 09.0	24.9	264 36.0	00.4
	17 00	175 00.0	197 06.1	S10 33.2	293 06.7	S19 45.6	6 11.8	N 6 25.0	279 38.4	S21 00.4
	01	190 02.4	212 05.7	32.1	308 08.4	45.8	21 14.5	25.2	294 40.8	00.4
	02	205 04.9	227 05.2	31.1	323 10.1	46.0	36 17.3	25.3	309 43.2	00.4
	03	220 07.4	242 04.7	. . 30.0	338 11.7	. . 46.2	51 20.1	. . 25.4	324 45.7	. . 00.4
	04	235 09.8	257 04.2	28.9	353 13.4	46.3	66 22.8	25.5	339 48.1	00.4
	05	250 12.3	272 03.7	27.8	8 15.1	46.5	81 25.6	25.6	354 50.5	00.4
	06	265 14.8	287 03.3	S10 26.7	23 16.8	S19 46.7	96 28.3	N 6 25.8	9 52.9	S21 00.4
	07	280 17.2	302 02.8	25.7	38 18.5	46.9	111 31.1	25.9	24 55.4	00.4
T	08	295 19.7	317 02.3	24.6	53 20.2	47.0	126 33.9	26.0	39 57.8	00.4
H	09	310 22.2	332 01.8	. . 23.5	68 21.9	. . 47.2	141 36.6	. . 26.1	55 00.2	. . 00.4
U	10	325 24.6	347 01.3	22.4	83 23.6	47.4	156 39.4	26.3	70 02.7	00.4
R	11	340 27.1	2 00.9	21.3	98 25.2	47.6	171 42.1	26.4	85 05.1	00.4
S	12	355 29.5	17 00.4	S10 20.2	113 26.9	S19 47.7	186 44.9	N 6 26.5	100 07.5	S21 00.4
D	13	10 32.0	31 59.9	19.1	128 28.6	47.9	201 47.6	26.6	115 09.9	00.4
A	14	25 34.5	46 59.4	18.1	143 30.3	48.1	216 50.4	26.8	130 12.4	00.4
Y	15	40 36.9	61 58.9	. . 17.0	158 32.0	. . 48.3	231 53.2	. . 26.9	145 14.8	. . 00.4
	16	55 39.4	76 58.5	15.9	173 33.7	48.4	246 55.9	27.0	160 17.2	00.4
	17	70 41.9	91 58.0	14.8	188 35.4	48.6	261 58.7	27.1	175 19.7	00.4
	18	85 44.3	106 57.5	S10 13.7	203 37.1	S19 48.8	277 01.4	N 6 27.3	190 22.1	S21 00.4
	19	100 46.8	121 57.0	12.6	218 38.8	48.9	292 04.2	27.4	205 24.5	00.4
	20	115 49.3	136 56.6	11.5	233 40.5	49.1	307 06.9	27.5	220 26.9	00.4
	21	130 51.7	151 56.1	. . 10.4	248 42.2	. . 49.3	322 09.7	. . 27.6	235 29.4	. . 00.4
	22	145 54.2	166 55.6	09.3	263 43.9	49.5	337 12.5	27.7	250 31.8	00.4
	23	160 56.7	181 55.1	08.3	278 45.6	49.6	352 15.2	27.9	265 34.2	00.4
	18 00	175 59.1	196 54.7	S10 07.2	293 47.3	S19 49.8	7 18.0	N 6 28.0	280 36.7	S21 00.4
	01	191 01.6	211 54.2	06.1	308 49.0	50.0	22 20.7	28.1	295 39.1	00.4
	02	206 04.0	226 53.7	05.0	323 50.7	50.2	37 23.5	28.2	310 41.5	00.4
	03	221 06.5	241 53.2	. . 03.9	338 52.4	. . 50.3	52 26.2	. . 28.4	325 44.0	. . 00.4
	04	236 09.0	256 52.8	02.8	353 54.1	50.5	67 29.0	28.5	340 46.4	00.4
	05	251 11.4	271 52.3	01.7	8 55.8	50.7	82 31.8	28.6	355 48.8	00.4
	06	266 13.9	286 51.8	S10 00.6	23 57.5	S19 50.8	97 34.5	N 6 28.7	10 51.2	S21 00.4
	07	281 16.4	301 51.4	9 59.5	38 59.2	51.0	112 37.3	28.8	25 53.7	00.4
	08	296 18.8	316 50.9	58.4	54 00.9	51.2	127 40.0	29.0	40 56.1	00.4
F	09	311 21.3	331 50.4	. . 57.3	69 02.6	. . 51.4	142 42.8	. . 29.1	55 58.5	. . 00.4
R	10	326 23.8	346 49.9	56.2	84 04.3	51.5	157 45.5	29.2	71 01.0	00.4
I	11	341 26.2	1 49.5	55.1	99 06.0	51.7	172 48.3	29.3	86 03.4	00.4
D	12	356 28.7	16 49.0	S 9 54.0	114 07.7	S19 51.9	187 51.0	N 6 29.5	101 05.8	S21 00.4
A	13	11 31.2	31 48.5	52.9	129 09.4	52.0	202 53.8	29.6	116 08.3	00.4
Y	14	26 33.6	46 48.1	51.8	144 11.2	52.2	217 56.6	29.7	131 10.7	00.4
	15	41 36.1	61 47.6	. . 50.7	159 12.9	. . 52.4	232 59.3	. . 29.8	146 13.1	. . 00.4
	16	56 38.5	76 47.1	49.6	174 14.6	52.5	248 02.1	29.9	161 15.6	00.4
	17	71 41.0	91 46.7	48.5	189 16.3	52.7	263 04.8	30.1	176 18.0	00.4
	18	86 43.5	106 46.2	S 9 47.4	204 18.0	S19 52.9	278 07.6	N 6 30.2	191 20.4	S21 00.3
	19	101 45.9	121 45.7	46.3	219 19.7	53.1	293 10.3	30.3	206 22.9	00.3
	20	116 48.4	136 45.3	45.2	234 21.4	53.2	308 13.1	30.4	221 25.3	00.3
	21	131 50.9	151 44.8	. . 44.1	249 23.1	. . 53.4	323 15.8	. . 30.6	236 27.7	. . 00.3
	22	146 53.3	166 44.3	43.0	264 24.9	53.6	338 18.6	30.7	251 30.2	00.3
	23	161 55.8	181 43.9	41.9	279 26.6	53.7	353 21.4	30.8	266 32.6	00.3
	Mer. Pass.	h m 12 18.0	v −0.5	d 1.1	v 1.7	d 0.2	v 2.8	d 0.1	v 2.4	d 0.0

STARS

Name	SHA ° ′	Dec ° ′
Acamar	315 17.2	S40 14.8
Achernar	335 26.0	S57 09.6
Acrux	173 06.3	S63 11.3
Adhara	255 10.9	S29 00.1
Aldebaran	290 47.3	N16 32.3
Alioth	166 18.6	N55 52.2
Alkaid	152 57.1	N49 13.8
Al Na'ir	27 41.9	S46 52.9
Alnilam	275 44.5	S 1 11.9
Alphard	217 54.0	S 8 44.0
Alphecca	126 09.3	N26 39.5
Alpheratz	357 41.9	N29 10.7
Altair	62 06.6	N 8 54.7
Ankaa	353 14.3	S42 13.2
Antares	112 23.8	S26 27.8
Arcturus	145 53.8	N19 05.8
Atria	107 23.8	S69 02.9
Avior	234 16.8	S59 34.1
Bellatrix	278 30.0	N 6 21.5
Betelgeuse	270 59.3	N 7 24.3
Canopus	263 55.2	S52 42.8
Capella	280 31.7	N46 00.8
Deneb	49 30.5	N45 20.2
Denebola	182 31.5	N14 28.8
Diphda	348 54.4	S17 54.1
Dubhe	193 48.9	N61 39.8
Elnath	278 10.3	N28 37.1
Eltanin	90 45.3	N51 29.1
Enif	33 45.6	N 9 56.9
Fomalhaut	15 22.3	S29 32.2
Gacrux	171 58.1	S57 12.2
Gienah	175 50.0	S17 38.0
Hadar	148 44.6	S60 26.8
Hamal	327 58.9	N23 32.2
Kaus Aust.	83 41.4	S34 22.3
Kochab	137 19.5	N74 05.2
Markab	13 36.8	N15 17.4
Menkar	314 13.3	N 4 08.9
Menkent	148 05.0	S36 26.9
Miaplacidus	221 38.4	S69 47.4
Mirfak	308 37.9	N49 55.0
Nunki	75 56.1	S26 16.4
Peacock	53 16.8	S56 40.7
Pollux	243 25.3	N27 59.0
Procyon	244 57.6	N 5 10.7
Rasalhague	96 04.7	N12 32.9
Regulus	207 41.3	N11 53.1
Rigel	281 10.3	S 8 11.4
Rigil Kent.	139 48.6	S60 53.8
Sabik	102 10.3	S15 44.5
Schedar	349 38.8	N56 37.5
Shaula	96 19.4	S37 06.6
Sirius	258 32.0	S16 44.7
Spica	158 29.0	S11 14.8
Suhail	222 50.7	S43 30.2
Vega	80 37.8	N38 47.8
Zuben'ubi	137 03.1	S16 06.5

	SHA ° ′	Mer. Pass. h m
Venus	22 06.2	10 52
Mars	118 06.7	4 27
Jupiter	191 11.8	23 31
Saturn	104 38.4	5 21

	UT d h	SUN GHA ° ′	SUN Dec ° ′	MOON GHA ° ′	MOON *v* ′	MOON Dec ° ′	MOON *d* ′	MOON HP ′
	16 00	177 50.3	S 1 39.3	84 34.1	8.2	N18 10.9	0.5	57.8
	01	192 50.4	38.3	99 01.3	8.1	18 11.4	0.4	57.7
	02	207 50.6	37.3	113 28.4	8.2	18 11.8	0.3	57.7
	03	222 50.8	. . 36.4	127 55.6	8.3	18 12.1	0.2	57.7
	04	237 51.0	35.4	142 22.9	8.2	18 12.3	0.0	57.7
	05	252 51.2	34.4	156 50.1	8.3	18 12.3	0.0	57.6
	06	267 51.3	S 1 33.4	171 17.4	8.4	N18 12.3	0.2	57.6
W	07	282 51.5	32.4	185 44.8	8.4	18 12.1	0.2	57.6
E	08	297 51.7	31.4	200 12.2	8.4	18 11.9	0.4	57.5
D	09	312 51.9	. . 30.4	214 39.6	8.4	18 11.5	0.5	57.5
N	10	327 52.1	29.4	229 07.0	8.5	18 11.0	0.5	57.5
E	11	342 52.2	28.5	243 34.5	8.6	18 10.5	0.7	57.4
S	12	357 52.4	S 1 27.5	258 02.1	8.6	N18 09.8	0.8	57.4
D	13	12 52.6	26.5	272 29.7	8.6	18 09.0	0.9	57.4
	14	27 52.8	25.5	286 57.3	8.6	18 08.1	1.0	57.3
A	15	42 53.0	. . 24.5	301 24.9	8.8	18 07.1	1.1	57.3
Y	16	57 53.1	23.5	315 52.7	8.7	18 06.0	1.2	57.3
	17	72 53.3	22.5	330 20.4	8.8	18 04.8	1.3	57.3
	18	87 53.5	S 1 21.5	344 48.2	8.8	N18 03.5	1.4	57.2
	19	102 53.7	20.6	359 16.0	8.9	18 02.1	1.5	57.2
	20	117 53.8	19.6	13 43.9	8.9	18 00.6	1.6	57.2
	21	132 54.0	. . 18.6	28 11.8	9.0	17 59.0	1.7	57.1
	22	147 54.2	17.6	42 39.8	9.0	17 57.3	1.8	57.1
	23	162 54.4	16.6	57 07.8	9.1	17 55.5	1.9	57.1
	17 00	177 54.6	S 1 15.6	71 35.9	9.1	N17 53.6	2.0	57.0
	01	192 54.7	14.6	86 04.0	9.2	17 51.6	2.1	57.0
	02	207 54.9	13.6	100 32.2	9.2	17 49.5	2.2	57.0
	03	222 55.1	. . 12.6	115 00.4	9.2	17 47.3	2.3	57.0
	04	237 55.3	11.7	129 28.6	9.3	17 45.0	2.4	56.9
	05	252 55.5	10.7	143 56.9	9.4	17 42.6	2.4	56.9
	06	267 55.7	S 1 09.7	158 25.3	9.4	N17 40.2	2.6	56.9
	07	282 55.8	08.7	172 53.7	9.4	17 37.6	2.7	56.8
T	08	297 56.0	07.7	187 22.1	9.5	17 34.9	2.8	56.8
H	09	312 56.2	. . 06.7	201 50.6	9.6	17 32.1	2.8	56.8
U	10	327 56.4	05.7	216 19.2	9.5	17 29.3	3.0	56.8
R	11	342 56.6	04.7	230 47.7	9.7	17 26.3	3.0	56.7
S	12	357 56.7	S 1 03.7	245 16.4	9.7	N17 23.3	3.2	56.7
D	13	12 56.9	02.8	259 45.1	9.7	17 20.1	3.2	56.7
A	14	27 57.1	01.8	274 13.8	9.8	17 16.9	3.3	56.7
Y	15	42 57.3	1 00.8	288 42.6	9.9	17 13.6	3.4	56.6
	16	57 57.5	0 59.8	303 11.5	9.9	17 10.2	3.5	56.6
	17	72 57.6	58.8	317 40.4	9.9	17 06.7	3.6	56.6
	18	87 57.8	S 0 57.8	332 09.3	10.0	N17 03.1	3.7	56.5
	19	102 58.0	56.8	346 38.3	10.0	16 59.4	3.8	56.5
	20	117 58.2	55.8	1 07.3	10.1	16 55.6	3.8	56.5
	21	132 58.4	. . 54.9	15 36.4	10.2	16 51.8	4.0	56.5
	22	147 58.6	53.9	30 05.6	10.2	16 47.8	4.0	56.4
	23	162 58.7	52.9	44 34.8	10.3	16 43.8	4.1	56.4
	18 00	177 58.9	S 0 51.9	59 04.1	10.3	N16 39.7	4.2	56.4
	01	192 59.1	50.9	73 33.4	10.3	16 35.5	4.3	56.4
	02	207 59.3	49.9	88 02.7	10.5	16 31.2	4.3	56.3
	03	222 59.5	. . 48.9	102 32.2	10.4	16 26.9	4.5	56.3
	04	237 59.6	47.9	117 01.6	10.5	16 22.4	4.5	56.3
	05	252 59.8	46.9	131 31.1	10.6	16 17.9	4.6	56.3
	06	268 00.0	S 0 46.0	146 00.7	10.6	N16 13.3	4.7	56.2
	07	283 00.2	45.0	160 30.3	10.7	16 08.6	4.8	56.2
	08	298 00.4	44.0	175 00.0	10.7	16 03.8	4.8	56.2
F	09	313 00.6	. . 43.0	189 29.7	10.8	15 59.0	5.0	56.2
R	10	328 00.7	42.0	203 59.5	10.9	15 54.0	5.0	56.1
I	11	343 00.9	41.0	218 29.4	10.9	15 49.0	5.0	56.1
D	12	358 01.1	S 0 40.0	232 59.3	10.9	N15 44.0	5.2	56.1
A	13	13 01.3	39.0	247 29.2	11.0	15 38.8	5.2	56.1
Y	14	28 01.5	38.1	261 59.2	11.0	15 33.6	5.3	56.0
	15	43 01.7	. . 37.1	276 29.2	11.1	15 28.3	5.4	56.0
	16	58 01.8	36.1	290 59.3	11.2	15 22.9	5.5	56.0
	17	73 02.0	35.1	305 29.5	11.2	15 17.4	5.5	56.0
	18	88 02.2	S 0 34.1	319 59.7	11.3	N15 11.9	5.6	55.9
	19	103 02.4	33.1	334 30.0	11.3	15 06.3	5.7	55.9
	20	118 02.6	32.1	349 00.3	11.3	15 00.6	5.7	55.9
	21	133 02.8	. . 31.1	3 30.6	11.5	14 54.9	5.8	55.9
	22	148 02.9	30.1	18 01.1	11.4	14 49.1	5.9	55.8
	23	163 03.1	29.2	32 31.5	11.5	N14 43.2	6.0	55.8
		SD 16.1	*d* 1.0	SD 15.6		15.5		15.3

Lat. °	Twilight Naut. h m	Twilight Civil h m	Sunrise h m	Moonrise 16 h m	Moonrise 17 h m	Moonrise 18 h m	Moonrise 19 h m
N 72	03 38	05 04	06 12	▭	08 31	10 24	12 10
N 70	03 55	05 11	06 11	08 26	09 37	11 04	12 36
68	04 07	05 15	06 11	09 06	10 13	11 31	12 56
66	04 18	05 20	06 11	09 34	10 38	11 52	13 11
64	04 26	05 23	06 10	09 56	10 58	12 09	13 24
62	04 33	05 26	06 10	10 13	11 14	12 22	13 35
60	04 39	05 28	06 10	10 27	11 27	12 34	13 44
N 58	04 44	05 30	06 09	10 39	11 39	12 44	13 52
56	04 48	05 32	06 09	10 50	11 49	12 53	13 59
54	04 52	05 34	06 09	10 59	11 58	13 00	14 05
52	04 56	05 35	06 09	11 08	12 06	13 07	14 11
50	04 59	05 36	06 09	11 15	12 13	13 13	14 16
45	05 05	05 39	06 08	11 31	12 28	13 27	14 27
N 40	05 09	05 41	06 08	11 44	12 40	13 38	14 36
35	05 13	05 42	06 07	11 55	12 51	13 47	14 44
30	05 16	05 43	06 07	12 05	13 00	13 55	14 50
20	05 19	05 44	06 06	12 22	13 16	14 10	15 02
N 10	05 20	05 45	06 06	12 36	13 30	14 22	15 12
0	05 20	05 44	06 05	12 50	13 43	14 34	15 22
S 10	05 19	05 43	06 04	13 04	13 56	14 45	15 32
20	05 15	05 41	06 03	13 19	14 10	14 58	15 42
30	05 10	05 38	06 02	13 36	14 26	15 12	15 54
35	05 06	05 36	06 01	13 45	14 35	15 20	16 00
40	05 01	05 33	06 00	13 57	14 46	15 29	16 08
45	04 55	05 30	05 59	14 10	14 58	15 40	16 17
S 50	04 47	05 25	05 58	14 26	15 13	15 53	16 27
52	04 43	05 23	05 57	14 33	15 20	15 59	16 32
54	04 38	05 21	05 56	14 42	15 28	16 06	16 38
56	04 33	05 18	05 55	14 51	15 37	16 14	16 44
58	04 28	05 15	05 55	15 02	15 47	16 22	16 51
S 60	04 21	05 12	05 54	15 14	15 58	16 32	16 58

Lat. °	Sunset h m	Twilight Civil h m	Twilight Naut. h m	Moonset 16 h m	Moonset 17 h m	Moonset 18 h m	Moonset 19 h m
N 72	18 07	19 15	20 42	▭	06 33	06 27	06 22
N 70	18 07	19 09	20 25	04 47	05 27	05 46	05 55
68	18 08	19 03	20 12	04 06	04 51	05 18	05 34
66	18 08	18 59	20 02	03 38	04 25	04 56	05 18
64	18 08	18 55	19 53	03 17	04 05	04 39	05 05
62	18 08	18 52	19 46	03 00	03 48	04 25	04 53
60	18 08	18 50	19 39	02 45	03 35	04 13	04 44
N 58	18 08	18 47	19 34	02 33	03 23	04 03	04 35
56	18 08	18 46	19 29	02 22	03 13	03 54	04 28
54	18 09	18 44	19 25	02 13	03 04	03 46	04 21
52	18 09	18 42	19 22	02 05	02 56	03 39	04 15
50	18 09	18 41	19 19	01 57	02 49	03 32	04 09
45	18 09	18 38	19 13	01 41	02 33	03 18	03 58
N 40	18 09	18 36	19 08	01 28	02 20	03 07	03 48
35	18 10	18 35	19 04	01 17	02 10	02 57	03 39
30	18 10	18 34	19 01	01 07	02 00	02 48	03 32
20	18 10	18 32	18 58	00 50	01 44	02 33	03 19
N 10	18 11	18 32	18 56	00 36	01 29	02 20	03 08
0	18 11	18 32	18 56	00 22	01 16	02 08	02 57
S 10	18 12	18 33	18 58	00 08	01 02	01 55	02 47
20	18 13	18 35	19 01	24 48	00 48	01 42	02 35
30	18 14	18 38	19 06	24 31	00 31	01 27	02 22
35	18 15	18 40	19 10	24 21	00 21	01 18	02 14
40	18 16	18 43	19 14	24 10	00 10	01 07	02 06
45	18 17	18 46	19 20	23 57	24 56	00 56	01 55
S 50	18 18	18 50	19 28	23 41	24 41	00 41	01 43
52	18 18	18 52	19 32	23 34	24 34	00 34	01 37
54	18 19	18 54	19 37	23 26	24 27	00 27	01 31
56	18 20	18 57	19 41	23 16	24 18	00 18	01 24
58	18 21	19 00	19 47	23 06	24 09	00 09	01 16
S 60	18 21	19 03	19 54	22 54	23 58	25 07	01 07

Day	SUN Eqn. of Time 00^h	SUN Eqn. of Time 12^h	SUN Mer. Pass.	MOON Mer. Pass. Upper	MOON Mer. Pass. Lower	MOON Age	MOON Phase
d	m s	m s	h m	h m	h m	d	%
16	08 39	08 31	12 09	19 03	06 36	07	59
17	08 22	08 13	12 08	19 55	07 29	08	69
18	08 05	07 56	12 08	20 45	08 21	09	78

2016 MARCH 19, 20, 21 (SAT., SUN., MON.)

Day	UT d h	ARIES GHA ° ′	VENUS −3·8 GHA ° ′	VENUS Dec ° ′	MARS −0·2 GHA ° ′	MARS Dec ° ′	JUPITER −2·5 GHA ° ′	JUPITER Dec ° ′	SATURN +0·4 GHA ° ′	SATURN Dec ° ′
SATURDAY	19 00	176 58.3	196 43.4	S 9 40.8	294 28.3	S19 53.9	8 24.1	N 6 30.9	281 35.0	S21 00.3
	01	192 00.7	211 42.9	39.7	309 30.0	54.1	23 26.9	31.0	296 37.5	00.3
	02	207 03.2	226 42.5	38.6	324 31.7	54.2	38 29.6	31.2	311 39.9	00.3
	03	222 05.6	241 42.0	. . 37.5	339 33.5	. . 54.4	53 32.4	. . 31.3	326 42.4	. . 00.3
	04	237 08.1	256 41.5	36.4	354 35.2	54.6	68 35.1	31.4	341 44.8	00.3
	05	252 10.6	271 41.1	35.3	9 36.9	54.7	83 37.9	31.5	356 47.2	00.3
	06	267 13.0	286 40.6	S 9 34.2	24 38.6	S19 54.9	98 40.6	N 6 31.7	11 49.7	S21 00.3
	07	282 15.5	301 40.1	33.1	39 40.3	55.1	113 43.4	31.8	26 52.1	00.3
	08	297 18.0	316 39.7	32.0	54 42.1	55.2	128 46.1	31.9	41 54.5	00.3
	09	312 20.4	331 39.2	. . 30.9	69 43.8	. . 55.4	143 48.9	. . 32.0	56 57.0	. . 00.3
	10	327 22.9	346 38.8	29.8	84 45.5	55.6	158 51.6	32.1	71 59.4	00.3
	11	342 25.4	1 38.3	28.7	99 47.2	55.7	173 54.4	32.3	87 01.8	00.3
	12	357 27.8	16 37.8	S 9 27.6	114 49.0	S19 55.9	188 57.2	N 6 32.4	102 04.3	S21 00.3
	13	12 30.3	31 37.4	26.5	129 50.7	56.1	203 59.9	32.5	117 06.7	00.3
	14	27 32.8	46 36.9	25.3	144 52.4	56.2	219 02.7	32.6	132 09.2	00.3
	15	42 35.2	61 36.5	. . 24.2	159 54.1	. . 56.4	234 05.4	. . 32.7	147 11.6	. . 00.3
	16	57 37.7	76 36.0	23.1	174 55.9	56.6	249 08.2	32.9	162 14.0	00.3
	17	72 40.1	91 35.5	22.0	189 57.6	56.7	264 10.9	33.0	177 16.5	00.3
	18	87 42.6	106 35.1	S 9 20.9	204 59.3	S19 56.9	279 13.7	N 6 33.1	192 18.9	S21 00.3
	19	102 45.1	121 34.6	19.8	220 01.1	57.1	294 16.4	33.2	207 21.3	00.3
	20	117 47.5	136 34.2	18.7	235 02.8	57.2	309 19.2	33.3	222 23.8	00.3
	21	132 50.0	151 33.7	. . 17.6	250 04.5	. . 57.4	324 21.9	. . 33.5	237 26.2	. . 00.3
	22	147 52.5	166 33.2	16.5	265 06.3	57.6	339 24.7	33.6	252 28.7	00.3
	23	162 54.9	181 32.8	15.3	280 08.0	57.7	354 27.4	33.7	267 31.1	00.3
SUNDAY	20 00	177 57.4	196 32.3	S 9 14.2	295 09.7	S19 57.9	9 30.2	N 6 33.8	282 33.5	S21 00.3
	01	192 59.9	211 31.9	13.1	310 11.5	58.1	24 32.9	33.9	297 36.0	00.3
	02	208 02.3	226 31.4	12.0	325 13.2	58.2	39 35.7	34.1	312 38.4	00.3
	03	223 04.8	241 31.0	. . 10.9	340 15.0	. . 58.4	54 38.4	. . 34.2	327 40.9	. . 00.3
	04	238 07.3	256 30.5	09.8	355 16.7	58.6	69 41.2	34.3	342 43.3	00.3
	05	253 09.7	271 30.0	08.7	10 18.4	58.7	84 44.0	34.4	357 45.7	00.3
	06	268 12.2	286 29.6	S 9 07.5	25 20.2	S19 58.9	99 46.7	N 6 34.6	12 48.2	S21 00.3
	07	283 14.6	301 29.1	06.4	40 21.9	59.1	114 49.5	34.7	27 50.6	00.3
	08	298 17.1	316 28.7	05.3	55 23.7	59.2	129 52.2	34.8	42 53.1	00.3
	09	313 19.6	331 28.2	. . 04.2	70 25.4	. . 59.4	144 55.0	. . 34.9	57 55.5	. . 00.3
	10	328 22.0	346 27.8	03.1	85 27.1	59.6	159 57.7	35.0	72 57.9	00.3
	11	343 24.5	1 27.3	02.0	100 28.9	59.7	175 00.5	35.1	88 00.4	00.3
	12	358 27.0	16 26.9	S 9 00.8	115 30.6	S19 59.9	190 03.2	N 6 35.3	103 02.8	S21 00.2
	13	13 29.4	31 26.4	8 59.7	130 32.4	20 00.0	205 06.0	35.4	118 05.3	00.2
	14	28 31.9	46 26.0	58.6	145 34.1	00.2	220 08.7	35.5	133 07.7	00.2
	15	43 34.4	61 25.5	. . 57.5	160 35.9	. . 00.4	235 11.5	. . 35.6	148 10.2	. . 00.2
	16	58 36.8	76 25.1	56.4	175 37.6	00.5	250 14.2	35.7	163 12.6	00.2
	17	73 39.3	91 24.6	55.2	190 39.4	00.7	265 17.0	35.9	178 15.0	00.2
	18	88 41.7	106 24.2	S 8 54.1	205 41.1	S20 00.9	280 19.7	N 6 36.0	193 17.5	S21 00.2
	19	103 44.2	121 23.7	53.0	220 42.9	01.0	295 22.5	36.1	208 19.9	00.2
	20	118 46.7	136 23.3	51.9	235 44.6	01.2	310 25.2	36.2	223 22.4	00.2
	21	133 49.1	151 22.8	. . 50.8	250 46.4	. . 01.3	325 28.0	. . 36.3	238 24.8	. . 00.2
	22	148 51.6	166 22.4	49.6	265 48.1	01.5	340 30.7	36.5	253 27.3	00.2
	23	163 54.1	181 21.9	48.5	280 49.9	01.7	355 33.5	36.6	268 29.7	00.2
MONDAY	21 00	178 56.5	196 21.5	S 8 47.4	295 51.6	S20 01.8	10 36.2	N 6 36.7	283 32.1	S21 00.2
	01	193 59.0	211 21.0	46.3	310 53.4	02.0	25 39.0	36.8	298 34.6	00.2
	02	209 01.5	226 20.6	45.1	325 55.2	02.2	40 41.7	36.9	313 37.0	00.2
	03	224 03.9	241 20.1	. . 44.0	340 56.9	. . 02.3	55 44.5	. . 37.1	328 39.5	. . 00.2
	04	239 06.4	256 19.7	42.9	355 58.7	02.5	70 47.2	37.2	343 41.9	00.2
	05	254 08.9	271 19.2	41.8	11 00.4	02.6	85 50.0	37.3	358 44.4	00.2
	06	269 11.3	286 18.8	S 8 40.6	26 02.2	S20 02.8	100 52.7	N 6 37.4	13 46.8	S21 00.2
	07	284 13.8	301 18.3	39.5	41 03.9	03.0	115 55.5	37.5	28 49.3	00.2
	08	299 16.2	316 17.9	38.4	56 05.7	03.1	130 58.2	37.7	43 51.7	00.2
	09	314 18.7	331 17.4	. . 37.3	71 07.5	. . 03.3	146 01.0	. . 37.8	58 54.1	. . 00.2
	10	329 21.2	346 17.0	36.1	86 09.2	03.4	161 03.7	37.9	73 56.6	00.2
	11	344 23.6	1 16.5	35.0	101 11.0	03.6	176 06.5	38.0	88 59.0	00.2
	12	359 26.1	16 16.1	S 8 33.9	116 12.8	S20 03.8	191 09.2	N 6 38.1	104 01.5	S21 00.2
	13	14 28.6	31 15.6	32.7	131 14.5	03.9	206 12.0	38.2	119 03.9	00.2
	14	29 31.0	46 15.2	31.6	146 16.3	04.1	221 14.7	38.4	134 06.4	00.2
	15	44 33.5	61 14.7	. . 30.5	161 18.1	. . 04.2	236 17.5	. . 38.5	149 08.8	. . 00.2
	16	59 36.0	76 14.3	29.4	176 19.8	04.4	251 20.2	38.6	164 11.3	00.2
	17	74 38.4	91 13.9	28.2	191 21.6	04.6	266 23.0	38.7	179 13.7	00.2
	18	89 40.9	106 13.4	S 8 27.1	206 23.4	S20 04.7	281 25.7	N 6 38.8	194 16.2	S21 00.2
	19	104 43.3	121 13.0	26.0	221 25.1	04.9	296 28.5	39.0	209 18.6	00.2
	20	119 45.8	136 12.5	24.8	236 26.9	05.0	311 31.2	39.1	224 21.1	00.2
	21	134 48.3	151 12.1	. . 23.7	251 28.7	. . 05.2	326 33.9	. . 39.2	239 23.5	. . 00.2
	22	149 50.7	166 11.6	22.6	266 30.4	05.4	341 36.7	39.3	254 26.0	00.1
	23	164 53.2	181 11.2	21.4	281 32.2	05.5	356 39.4	39.4	269 28.4	00.1
	Mer. Pass. (h m)	12 06.2	*v* −0.5	*d* 1.1	*v* 1.7	*d* 0.2	*v* 2.8	*d* 0.1	*v* 2.4	*d* 0.0

STARS

Name	SHA ° ′	Dec ° ′
Acamar	315 17.3	S40 14.8
Achernar	335 26.0	S57 09.5
Acrux	173 06.3	S63 11.3
Adhara	255 11.0	S29 00.1
Aldebaran	290 47.3	N16 32.3
Alioth	166 18.6	N55 52.2
Alkaid	152 57.1	N49 13.8
Al Na'ir	27 41.9	S46 52.8
Alnilam	275 44.5	S 1 11.9
Alphard	217 54.0	S 8 44.0
Alphecca	126 09.2	N26 39.5
Alpheratz	357 41.9	N29 10.7
Altair	62 06.6	N 8 54.7
Ankaa	353 14.3	S42 13.2
Antares	112 23.8	S26 27.9
Arcturus	145 53.8	N19 05.8
Atria	107 23.8	S69 02.9
Avior	234 16.8	S59 34.1
Bellatrix	278 30.1	N 6 21.5
Betelgeuse	270 59.3	N 7 24.3
Canopus	263 55.3	S52 42.8
Capella	280 31.8	N46 00.8
Deneb	49 30.4	N45 20.2
Denebola	182 31.5	N14 28.8
Diphda	348 54.4	S17 54.1
Dubhe	193 48.9	N61 39.8
Elnath	278 10.3	N28 37.1
Eltanin	90 45.3	N51 29.1
Enif	33 45.5	N 9 56.9
Fomalhaut	15 22.3	S29 32.2
Gacrux	171 58.1	S57 12.2
Gienah	175 50.0	S17 38.0
Hadar	148 44.6	S60 26.9
Hamal	327 58.9	N23 32.2
Kaus Aust.	83 41.4	S34 22.3
Kochab	137 19.4	N74 05.2
Markab	13 36.8	N15 17.4
Menkar	314 13.3	N 4 08.9
Menkent	148 05.0	S36 26.9
Miaplacidus	221 38.5	S69 47.4
Mirfak	308 37.9	N49 55.0
Nunki	75 56.1	S26 16.4
Peacock	53 16.7	S56 40.7
Pollux	243 25.3	N27 59.0
Procyon	244 57.7	N 5 10.7
Rasalhague	96 04.7	N12 32.9
Regulus	207 41.3	N11 53.1
Rigel	281 10.3	S 8 11.4
Rigil Kent.	139 48.6	S60 53.8
Sabik	102 10.3	S15 44.5
Schedar	349 38.8	N56 37.5
Shaula	96 19.3	S37 06.6
Sirius	258 32.0	S16 44.7
Spica	158 29.0	S11 14.8
Suhail	222 50.7	S43 30.2
Vega	80 37.7	N38 47.8
Zuben'ubi	137 03.1	S16 06.5

	SHA ° ′	Mer. Pass. h m
Venus	18 34.9	10 54
Mars	117 12.3	4 19
Jupiter	191 32.8	23 18
Saturn	104 36.1	5 09

	UT	SUN GHA	SUN Dec	MOON GHA	v	MOON Dec	d	HP
	d h	° ′	° ′	° ′	′	° ′	′	′
	19 00	178 03.3	S 0 28.2	47 02.0	11.6	N14 37.2	6.0	55.8
	01	193 03.5	27.2	61 32.6	11.6	14 31.2	6.1	55.8
	02	208 03.7	26.2	76 03.2	11.7	14 25.1	6.1	55.8
	03	223 03.9	. . 25.2	90 33.9	11.7	14 19.0	6.3	55.7
	04	238 04.0	24.2	105 04.6	11.8	14 12.7	6.2	55.7
	05	253 04.2	23.2	119 35.4	11.9	14 06.5	6.4	55.7
	06	268 04.4	S 0 22.2	134 06.3	11.8	N14 00.1	6.4	55.7
	07	283 04.6	21.3	148 37.1	12.0	13 53.7	6.5	55.6
S	08	298 04.8	20.3	163 08.1	12.0	13 47.2	6.5	55.6
A	09	313 05.0	. . 19.3	177 39.1	12.0	13 40.7	6.6	55.6
T	10	328 05.2	18.3	192 10.1	12.1	13 34.1	6.7	55.6
U	11	343 05.3	17.3	206 41.2	12.1	13 27.4	6.7	55.6
R	12	358 05.5	S 0 16.3	221 12.3	12.2	N13 20.7	6.8	55.5
D	13	13 05.7	15.3	235 43.5	12.2	13 13.9	6.8	55.5
A	14	28 05.9	14.3	250 14.7	12.3	13 07.1	6.9	55.5
Y	15	43 06.1	. . 13.3	264 46.0	12.3	13 00.2	7.0	55.5
	16	58 06.3	12.4	279 17.3	12.4	12 53.2	7.0	55.5
	17	73 06.4	11.4	293 48.7	12.5	12 46.2	7.1	55.4
	18	88 06.6	S 0 10.4	308 20.2	12.4	N12 39.1	7.1	55.4
	19	103 06.8	09.4	322 51.6	12.6	12 32.0	7.2	55.4
	20	118 07.0	08.4	337 23.2	12.5	12 24.8	7.2	55.4
	21	133 07.2	. . 07.4	351 54.7	12.7	12 17.6	7.3	55.4
	22	148 07.4	06.4	6 26.4	12.6	12 10.3	7.3	55.3
	23	163 07.6	05.4	20 58.0	12.7	12 03.0	7.4	55.3
	20 00	178 07.7	S 0 04.5	35 29.7	12.8	N11 55.6	7.5	55.3
	01	193 07.9	03.5	50 01.5	12.8	11 48.1	7.5	55.3
	02	208 08.1	02.5	64 33.3	12.9	11 40.6	7.5	55.3
	03	223 08.3	. . 01.5	79 05.2	12.9	11 33.1	7.6	55.2
	04	238 08.5	S 00.5	93 37.1	12.9	11 25.5	7.6	55.2
	05	253 08.7	N 00.5	108 09.0	13.0	11 17.9	7.7	55.2
	06	268 08.9	N 0 01.5	122 41.0	13.0	N11 10.2	7.8	55.2
	07	283 09.0	02.5	137 13.0	13.1	11 02.4	7.7	55.2
	08	298 09.2	03.4	151 45.1	13.1	10 54.7	7.9	55.2
S	09	313 09.4	. . 04.4	166 17.2	13.2	10 46.8	7.8	55.1
U	10	328 09.6	05.4	180 49.4	13.2	10 39.0	8.0	55.1
N	11	343 09.8	06.4	195 21.6	13.3	10 31.0	7.9	55.1
D	12	358 10.0	N 0 07.4	209 53.9	13.2	N10 23.1	8.0	55.1
A	13	13 10.2	08.4	224 26.1	13.4	10 15.1	8.1	55.1
Y	14	28 10.3	09.4	238 58.5	13.4	10 07.0	8.0	55.1
	15	43 10.5	. . 10.4	253 30.9	13.4	9 59.0	8.2	55.0
	16	58 10.7	11.3	268 03.3	13.4	9 50.8	8.1	55.0
	17	73 10.9	12.3	282 35.7	13.5	9 42.7	8.2	55.0
	18	88 11.1	N 0 13.3	297 08.2	13.6	N 9 34.5	8.3	55.0
	19	103 11.3	14.3	311 40.8	13.5	9 26.2	8.3	55.0
	20	118 11.5	15.3	326 13.3	13.7	9 17.9	8.3	55.0
	21	133 11.7	. . 16.3	340 46.0	13.6	9 09.6	8.3	54.9
	22	148 11.8	17.3	355 18.6	13.7	9 01.3	8.4	54.9
	23	163 12.0	18.3	9 51.3	13.7	8 52.9	8.5	54.9
	21 00	178 12.2	N 0 19.2	24 24.0	13.8	N 8 44.4	8.4	54.9
	01	193 12.4	20.2	38 56.8	13.8	8 36.0	8.5	54.9
	02	208 12.6	21.2	53 29.6	13.8	8 27.5	8.5	54.9
	03	223 12.8	. . 22.2	68 02.4	13.9	8 19.0	8.6	54.8
	04	238 13.0	23.2	82 35.3	13.9	8 10.4	8.6	54.8
	05	253 13.1	24.2	97 08.2	14.0	8 01.8	8.6	54.8
	06	268 13.3	N 0 25.2	111 41.2	14.0	N 7 53.2	8.7	54.8
	07	283 13.5	26.2	126 14.2	14.0	7 44.5	8.6	54.8
	08	298 13.7	27.1	140 47.2	14.0	7 35.9	8.7	54.8
M	09	313 13.9	. . 28.1	155 20.2	14.1	7 27.2	8.8	54.8
O	10	328 14.1	29.1	169 53.3	14.1	7 18.4	8.8	54.7
N	11	343 14.3	30.1	184 26.4	14.2	7 09.6	8.7	54.7
D	12	358 14.5	N 0 31.1	198 59.6	14.1	N 7 00.9	8.9	54.7
A	13	13 14.6	32.1	213 32.7	14.3	6 52.0	8.8	54.7
Y	14	28 14.8	33.1	228 06.0	14.2	6 43.2	8.9	54.7
	15	43 15.0	. . 34.0	242 39.2	14.3	6 34.3	8.9	54.7
	16	58 15.2	35.0	257 12.5	14.3	6 25.4	8.9	54.7
	17	73 15.4	36.0	271 45.8	14.3	6 16.5	8.9	54.6
	18	88 15.6	N 0 37.0	286 19.1	14.4	N 6 07.6	9.0	54.6
	19	103 15.8	38.0	300 52.5	14.3	5 58.6	9.0	54.6
	20	118 16.0	39.0	315 25.8	14.5	5 49.6	9.0	54.6
	21	133 16.1	. . 40.0	329 59.3	14.4	5 40.6	9.0	54.6
	22	148 16.3	40.9	344 32.7	14.5	5 31.6	9.1	54.6
	23	163 16.5	41.9	359 06.2	14.5	N 5 22.5	9.0	54.6
		SD 16.1	*d* 1.0	SD 15.1		15.0		14.9

Lat.	Twilight Naut.	Twilight Civil	Sunrise	Moonrise 19	20	21	22
°	h m	h m	h m	h m	h m	h m	h m
N 72	03 19	04 48	05 56	12 10	13 52	15 29	17 04
N 70	03 38	04 56	05 57	12 36	14 09	15 39	17 08
68	03 53	05 03	05 58	12 56	14 22	15 47	17 11
66	04 05	05 08	05 59	13 11	14 32	15 53	17 13
64	04 14	05 12	06 00	13 24	14 41	15 59	17 15
62	04 22	05 16	06 00	13 35	14 49	16 03	17 17
60	04 29	05 19	06 01	13 44	14 56	16 07	17 19
N 58	04 35	05 22	06 01	13 52	15 01	16 11	17 20
56	04 40	05 24	06 01	13 59	15 06	16 14	17 21
54	04 45	05 26	06 02	14 05	15 11	16 17	17 22
52	04 48	05 28	06 02	14 11	15 15	16 19	17 23
50	04 52	05 30	06 02	14 16	15 19	16 22	17 24
45	04 59	05 33	06 03	14 27	15 27	16 27	17 26
N 40	05 04	05 36	06 03	14 36	15 34	16 31	17 28
35	05 09	05 38	06 03	14 44	15 40	16 35	17 29
30	05 12	05 40	06 04	14 50	15 45	16 38	17 31
20	05 16	05 42	06 04	15 02	15 54	16 44	17 33
N 10	05 19	05 43	06 04	15 12	16 01	16 49	17 35
0	05 19	05 43	06 04	15 22	16 08	16 53	17 37
S 10	05 19	05 43	06 04	15 32	16 16	16 58	17 38
20	05 16	05 42	06 04	15 42	16 23	17 03	17 40
30	05 12	05 40	06 04	15 54	16 32	17 08	17 43
35	05 09	05 38	06 03	16 00	16 37	17 11	17 44
40	05 04	05 36	06 03	16 08	16 43	17 15	17 45
45	04 59	05 33	06 03	16 17	16 49	17 19	17 47
S 50	04 52	05 30	06 02	16 27	16 57	17 24	17 49
52	04 49	05 28	06 02	16 32	17 01	17 26	17 50
54	04 45	05 27	06 02	16 38	17 05	17 29	17 51
56	04 40	05 24	06 02	16 44	17 09	17 32	17 52
58	04 35	05 22	06 01	16 51	17 14	17 35	17 53
S 60	04 29	05 19	06 01	16 58	17 20	17 38	17 55

Lat.	Sunset	Twilight Civil	Twilight Naut.	Moonset 19	20	21	22
°	h m	h m	h m	h m	h m	h m	h m
N 72	18 21	19 30	21 01	06 22	06 17	06 13	06 08
N 70	18 20	19 21	20 41	05 55	05 59	06 01	06 03
68	18 18	19 15	20 25	05 34	05 45	05 52	05 58
66	18 17	19 09	20 13	05 18	05 33	05 45	05 54
64	18 17	19 04	20 03	05 05	05 23	05 38	05 51
62	18 16	19 01	19 55	04 53	05 15	05 32	05 48
60	18 15	18 57	19 47	04 44	05 08	05 28	05 45
N 58	18 15	18 54	19 41	04 35	05 01	05 23	05 43
56	18 15	18 52	19 36	04 28	04 55	05 19	05 41
54	18 14	18 50	19 32	04 21	04 50	05 16	05 39
52	18 14	18 48	19 28	04 15	04 46	05 13	05 37
50	18 14	18 46	19 24	04 09	04 41	05 10	05 36
45	18 13	18 42	19 17	03 58	04 32	05 03	05 32
N 40	18 12	18 39	19 11	03 48	04 25	04 58	05 29
35	18 12	18 37	19 07	03 39	04 18	04 53	05 27
30	18 12	18 36	19 03	03 32	04 12	04 49	05 25
20	18 11	18 33	18 59	03 19	04 02	04 42	05 21
N 10	18 11	18 32	18 56	03 08	03 53	04 36	05 17
0	18 11	18 31	18 55	02 57	03 45	04 30	05 14
S 10	18 10	18 31	18 56	02 47	03 36	04 24	05 11
20	18 10	18 32	18 58	02 35	03 27	04 18	05 07
30	18 11	18 34	19 02	02 22	03 17	04 11	05 04
35	18 11	18 36	19 05	02 14	03 11	04 06	05 01
40	18 11	18 38	19 09	02 06	03 04	04 01	04 59
45	18 11	18 40	19 15	01 55	02 56	03 56	04 56
S 50	18 11	18 44	19 22	01 43	02 46	03 49	04 52
52	18 12	18 45	19 25	01 37	02 41	03 46	04 50
54	18 12	18 47	19 29	01 31	02 37	03 43	04 48
56	18 12	18 49	19 33	01 24	02 31	03 39	04 46
58	18 12	18 51	19 38	01 16	02 25	03 35	04 44
S 60	18 12	18 54	19 44	01 07	02 18	03 30	04 41

Day	SUN Eqn. of Time 00^h	SUN Eqn. of Time 12^h	SUN Mer. Pass.	MOON Mer. Pass. Upper	MOON Mer. Pass. Lower	Age	Phase
d	m s	m s	h m	h m	h m	d %	
19	07 47	07 38	12 08	21 33	09 10	10 86	
20	07 29	07 20	12 07	22 19	09 57	11 92	
21	07 12	07 03	12 07	23 04	10 42	12 96	

UT	ARIES	VENUS −3·8		MARS −0·3		JUPITER −2·5		SATURN +0·4	
d h	GHA ° ′	GHA ° ′	Dec ° ′	GHA ° ′	Dec ° ′	GHA ° ′	Dec ° ′	GHA ° ′	Dec ° ′
22 00 (TUESDAY)	179 55.7	196 10.8	S 8 20.3	296 34.0	S20 05.7	11 42.2	N 6 39.5	284 30.9	S21 00.1
01	194 58.1	211 10.3	19.2	311 35.8	05.8	26 44.9	39.7	299 33.3	00.1
02	210 00.6	226 09.9	18.0	326 37.5	06.0	41 47.7	39.8	314 35.7	00.1
03	225 03.1	241 09.4	. . 16.9	341 39.3	. . 06.1	56 50.4	. . 39.9	329 38.2	. . 00.1
04	240 05.5	256 09.0	15.8	356 41.1	06.3	71 53.2	40.0	344 40.6	00.1
05	255 08.0	271 08.6	14.6	11 42.9	06.5	86 55.9	40.1	359 43.1	00.1
06	270 10.5	286 08.1	S 8 13.5	26 44.7	S20 06.6	101 58.7	N 6 40.2	14 45.5	S21 00.1
07	285 12.9	301 07.7	12.4	41 46.4	06.8	117 01.4	40.4	29 48.0	00.1
08	300 15.4	316 07.2	11.2	56 48.2	06.9	132 04.2	40.5	44 50.4	00.1
09	315 17.8	331 06.8	. . 10.1	71 50.0	. . 07.1	147 06.9	. . 40.6	59 52.9	. . 00.1
10	330 20.3	346 06.4	09.0	86 51.8	07.3	162 09.7	40.7	74 55.3	00.1
11	345 22.8	1 05.9	07.8	101 53.6	07.4	177 12.4	40.8	89 57.8	00.1
12	0 25.2	16 05.5	S 8 06.7	116 55.3	S20 07.6	192 15.2	N 6 40.9	105 00.2	S21 00.1
13	15 27.7	31 05.0	05.5	131 57.1	07.7	207 17.9	41.1	120 02.7	00.1
14	30 30.2	46 04.6	04.4	146 58.9	07.9	222 20.6	41.2	135 05.1	00.1
15	45 32.6	61 04.2	. . 03.3	162 00.7	. . 08.0	237 23.4	. . 41.3	150 07.6	. . 00.1
16	60 35.1	76 03.7	02.1	177 02.5	08.2	252 26.1	41.4	165 10.0	00.1
17	75 37.6	91 03.3	8 01.0	192 04.3	08.3	267 28.9	41.5	180 12.5	00.1
18	90 40.0	106 02.9	S 7 59.8	207 06.1	S20 08.5	282 31.6	N 6 41.6	195 15.0	S21 00.1
19	105 42.5	121 02.4	58.7	222 07.8	08.7	297 34.4	41.8	210 17.4	00.1
20	120 44.9	136 02.0	57.6	237 09.6	08.8	312 37.1	41.9	225 19.9	00.1
21	135 47.4	151 01.6	. . 56.4	252 11.4	. . 09.0	327 39.9	. . 42.0	240 22.3	. . 00.1
22	150 49.9	166 01.1	55.3	267 13.2	09.1	342 42.6	42.1	255 24.8	00.1
23	165 52.3	181 00.7	54.1	282 15.0	09.3	357 45.4	42.2	270 27.2	00.1
23 00 (WEDNESDAY)	180 54.8	196 00.2	S 7 53.0	297 16.8	S20 09.4	12 48.1	N 6 42.3	285 29.7	S21 00.1
01	195 57.3	210 59.8	51.9	312 18.6	09.6	27 50.8	42.5	300 32.1	00.1
02	210 59.7	225 59.4	50.7	327 20.4	09.7	42 53.6	42.6	315 34.6	00.0
03	226 02.2	240 58.9	. . 49.6	342 22.2	. . 09.9	57 56.3	. . 42.7	330 37.0	. . 00.0
04	241 04.7	255 58.5	48.4	357 24.0	10.1	72 59.1	42.8	345 39.5	00.0
05	256 07.1	270 58.1	47.3	12 25.8	10.2	88 01.8	42.9	0 41.9	00.0
06	271 09.6	285 57.6	S 7 46.1	27 27.6	S20 10.4	103 04.6	N 6 43.0	15 44.4	S21 00.0
07	286 12.1	300 57.2	45.0	42 29.4	10.5	118 07.3	43.2	30 46.8	00.0
08	301 14.5	315 56.8	43.8	57 31.2	10.7	133 10.1	43.3	45 49.3	00.0
09	316 17.0	330 56.4	. . 42.7	72 33.0	. . 10.8	148 12.8	. . 43.4	60 51.7	. . 00.0
10	331 19.4	345 55.9	41.6	87 34.8	11.0	163 15.5	43.5	75 54.2	00.0
11	346 21.9	0 55.5	40.4	102 36.6	11.1	178 18.3	43.6	90 56.7	00.0
12	1 24.4	15 55.1	S 7 39.3	117 38.4	S20 11.3	193 21.0	N 6 43.7	105 59.1	S21 00.0
13	16 26.8	30 54.6	38.1	132 40.2	11.4	208 23.8	43.9	121 01.6	00.0
14	31 29.3	45 54.2	37.0	147 42.0	11.6	223 26.5	44.0	136 04.0	00.0
15	46 31.8	60 53.8	. . 35.8	162 43.8	. . 11.7	238 29.3	. . 44.1	151 06.5	. . 00.0
16	61 34.2	75 53.3	34.7	177 45.6	11.9	253 32.0	44.2	166 08.9	00.0
17	76 36.7	90 52.9	33.5	192 47.4	12.1	268 34.7	44.3	181 11.4	00.0
18	91 39.2	105 52.5	S 7 32.4	207 49.2	S20 12.2	283 37.5	N 6 44.4	196 13.8	S21 00.0
19	106 41.6	120 52.0	31.2	222 51.0	12.4	298 40.2	44.5	211 16.3	00.0
20	121 44.1	135 51.6	30.1	237 52.9	12.5	313 43.0	44.7	226 18.8	00.0
21	136 46.5	150 51.2	. . 28.9	252 54.7	. . 12.7	328 45.7	. . 44.8	241 21.2	. . 00.0
22	151 49.0	165 50.8	27.8	267 56.5	12.8	343 48.5	44.9	256 23.7	00.0
23	166 51.5	180 50.3	26.6	282 58.3	13.0	358 51.2	45.0	271 26.1	00.0
24 00 (THURSDAY)	181 53.9	195 49.9	S 7 25.5	298 00.1	S20 13.1	13 53.9	N 6 45.1	286 28.6	S21 00.0
01	196 56.4	210 49.5	24.3	313 01.9	13.3	28 56.7	45.2	301 31.0	00.0
02	211 58.9	225 49.1	23.2	328 03.7	13.4	43 59.4	45.3	316 33.5	21 00.0
03	227 01.3	240 48.6	. . 22.0	343 05.6	. . 13.6	59 02.2	. . 45.5	331 36.0	20 59.9
04	242 03.8	255 48.2	20.9	358 07.4	13.7	74 04.9	45.6	346 38.4	59.9
05	257 06.3	270 47.8	19.7	13 09.2	13.9	89 07.6	45.7	1 40.9	59.9
06	272 08.7	285 47.3	S 7 18.6	28 11.0	S20 14.0	104 10.4	N 6 45.8	16 43.3	S20 59.9
07	287 11.2	300 46.9	17.4	43 12.8	14.2	119 13.1	45.9	31 45.8	59.9
08	302 13.7	315 46.5	16.3	58 14.6	14.3	134 15.9	46.0	46 48.3	59.9
09	317 16.1	330 46.1	. . 15.1	73 16.5	. . 14.5	149 18.6	. . 46.1	61 50.7	. . 59.9
10	332 18.6	345 45.6	13.9	88 18.3	14.6	164 21.3	46.3	76 53.2	59.9
11	347 21.0	0 45.2	12.8	103 20.1	14.8	179 24.1	46.4	91 55.6	59.9
12	2 23.5	15 44.8	S 7 11.6	118 21.9	S20 14.9	194 26.8	N 6 46.5	106 58.1	S20 59.9
13	17 26.0	30 44.4	10.5	133 23.8	15.1	209 29.6	46.6	122 00.5	59.9
14	32 28.4	45 43.9	09.3	148 25.6	15.2	224 32.3	46.7	137 03.0	59.9
15	47 30.9	60 43.5	. . 08.2	163 27.4	. . 15.4	239 35.0	. . 46.8	152 05.5	. . 59.9
16	62 33.4	75 43.1	07.0	178 29.2	15.5	254 37.8	46.9	167 07.9	59.9
17	77 35.8	90 42.7	05.9	193 31.1	15.7	269 40.5	47.1	182 10.4	59.9
18	92 38.3	105 42.3	S 7 04.7	208 32.9	S20 15.8	284 43.3	N 6 47.2	197 12.8	S20 59.9
19	107 40.8	120 41.8	03.5	223 34.7	16.0	299 46.0	47.3	212 15.3	59.9
20	122 43.2	135 41.4	02.4	238 36.6	16.1	314 48.7	47.4	227 17.8	59.9
21	137 45.7	150 41.0	. . 01.2	253 38.4	. . 16.3	329 51.5	. . 47.5	242 20.2	. . 59.9
22	152 48.2	165 40.6	7 00.1	268 40.2	16.4	344 54.2	47.6	257 22.7	59.9
23	167 50.6	180 40.1	S 6 58.9	283 42.1	16.6	359 57.0	47.7	272 25.2	59.9
Mer. Pass.	h m 11 54.4	v −0.4	d 1.1	v 1.8	d 0.2	v 2.7	d 0.1	v 2.5	d 0.0

STARS Name	SHA ° ′	Dec ° ′
Acamar	315 17.3	S40 14.8
Achernar	335 26.0	S57 09.5
Acrux	173 06.3	S63 11.3
Adhara	255 11.0	S29 00.1
Aldebaran	290 47.4	N16 32.3
Alioth	166 18.6	N55 52.2
Alkaid	152 57.1	N49 13.9
Al Na'ir	27 41.9	S46 52.8
Alnilam	275 44.5	S 1 11.8
Alphard	217 54.0	S 8 44.0
Alphecca	126 09.2	N26 39.5
Alpheratz	357 41.9	N29 10.7
Altair	62 06.5	N 8 54.7
Ankaa	353 14.3	S42 13.2
Antares	112 23.8	S26 27.9
Arcturus	145 53.8	N19 05.8
Atria	107 23.7	S69 02.9
Avior	234 16.9	S59 34.1
Bellatrix	278 30.1	N 6 21.5
Betelgeuse	270 59.3	N 7 24.3
Canopus	263 55.3	S52 42.8
Capella	280 31.8	N46 00.8
Deneb	49 30.4	N45 20.2
Denebola	182 31.5	N14 28.8
Diphda	348 54.4	S17 54.1
Dubhe	193 48.9	N61 39.8
Elnath	278 10.3	N28 37.1
Eltanin	90 45.2	N51 29.1
Enif	33 45.5	N 9 56.9
Fomalhaut	15 22.3	S29 32.2
Gacrux	171 58.1	S57 12.2
Gienah	175 50.0	S17 38.0
Hadar	148 44.5	S60 26.9
Hamal	327 58.9	N23 32.2
Kaus Aust.	83 41.4	S34 22.3
Kochab	137 19.4	N74 05.2
Markab	13 36.8	N15 17.4
Menkar	314 13.3	N 4 08.9
Menkent	148 05.0	S36 26.9
Miaplacidus	221 38.5	S69 47.4
Mirfak	308 37.9	N49 55.0
Nunki	75 56.1	S26 16.4
Peacock	53 16.7	S56 40.7
Pollux	243 25.3	N27 59.0
Procyon	244 57.7	N 5 10.7
Rasalhague	96 04.7	N12 32.9
Regulus	207 41.3	N11 53.1
Rigel	281 10.3	S 8 11.4
Rigil Kent.	139 48.6	S60 53.8
Sabik	102 10.3	S15 44.5
Schedar	349 38.8	N56 37.5
Shaula	96 19.3	S37 06.6
Sirius	258 32.0	S16 44.7
Spica	158 29.0	S11 14.8
Suhail	222 50.7	S43 30.3
Vega	80 37.7	N38 47.8
Zuben'ubi	137 03.1	S16 06.5

	SHA ° ′	Mer. Pass. h m
Venus	15 05.4	10 56
Mars	116 22.0	4 10
Jupiter	191 53.3	23 05
Saturn	104 34.9	4 57

Day	UT (d h)	SUN GHA (° ′)	SUN Dec (° ′)	MOON GHA (° ′)	v (′)	MOON Dec (° ′)	d (′)	HP (′)
22	00	178 16.7	N 0 42.9	13 39.7	14.5	N 5 13.5	9.1	54.6
	01	193 16.9	43.9	28 13.2	14.5	5 04.4	9.1	54.5
	02	208 17.1	44.9	42 46.7	14.6	4 55.3	9.2	54.5
	03	223 17.3	. . 45.9	57 20.3	14.6	4 46.1	9.1	54.5
	04	238 17.5	46.9	71 53.9	14.6	4 37.0	9.1	54.5
	05	253 17.6	47.9	86 27.5	14.7	4 27.9	9.2	54.5
	06	268 17.8	N 0 48.8	101 01.2	14.6	N 4 18.7	9.2	54.5
	07	283 18.0	49.8	115 34.8	14.7	4 09.5	9.2	54.5
T	08	298 18.2	50.8	130 08.5	14.7	4 00.3	9.2	54.5
U	09	313 18.4	. . 51.8	144 42.2	14.8	3 51.1	9.2	54.4
E	10	328 18.6	52.8	159 16.0	14.7	3 41.9	9.3	54.4
S	11	343 18.8	53.8	173 49.7	14.8	3 32.6	9.2	54.4
D	12	358 19.0	N 0 54.8	188 23.5	14.8	N 3 23.4	9.3	54.4
A	13	13 19.2	55.7	202 57.3	14.8	3 14.1	9.2	54.4
Y	14	28 19.3	56.7	217 31.1	14.8	3 04.9	9.3	54.4
	15	43 19.5	. . 57.7	232 04.9	14.9	2 55.6	9.3	54.4
	16	58 19.7	58.7	246 38.8	14.8	2 46.3	9.3	54.4
	17	73 19.9	0 59.7	261 12.6	14.9	2 37.0	9.3	54.4
	18	88 20.1	N 1 00.7	275 46.5	14.9	N 2 27.7	9.3	54.4
	19	103 20.3	01.6	290 20.4	14.9	2 18.4	9.3	54.3
	20	118 20.5	02.6	304 54.3	14.9	2 09.1	9.3	54.3
	21	133 20.7	. . 03.6	319 28.2	15.0	1 59.8	9.4	54.3
	22	148 20.9	04.6	334 02.2	14.9	1 50.4	9.3	54.3
	23	163 21.0	05.6	348 36.1	15.0	1 41.1	9.3	54.3
23	00	178 21.2	N 1 06.6	3 10.1	15.0	N 1 31.8	9.4	54.3
	01	193 21.4	07.6	17 44.1	15.0	1 22.4	9.3	54.3
	02	208 21.6	08.5	32 18.1	15.0	1 13.1	9.4	54.3
	03	223 21.8	. . 09.5	46 52.1	15.0	1 03.7	9.3	54.3
	04	238 22.0	10.5	61 26.1	15.1	0 54.4	9.3	54.3
	05	253 22.2	11.5	76 00.2	15.0	0 45.1	9.4	54.2
	06	268 22.4	N 1 12.5	90 34.2	15.1	N 0 35.7	9.3	54.2
W	07	283 22.5	13.5	105 08.3	15.0	0 26.4	9.4	54.2
E	08	298 22.7	14.5	119 42.3	15.1	0 17.0	9.3	54.2
D	09	313 22.9	. . 15.4	134 16.4	15.1	N 0 07.7	9.4	54.2
N	10	328 23.1	16.4	148 50.5	15.1	S 0 01.7	9.3	54.2
E	11	343 23.3	17.4	163 24.6	15.1	0 11.0	9.3	54.2
S	12	358 23.5	N 1 18.4	177 58.7	15.1	S 0 20.3	9.4	54.2
D	13	13 23.7	19.4	192 32.8	15.1	0 29.7	9.3	54.2
A	14	28 23.9	20.4	207 06.9	15.1	0 39.0	9.3	54.2
Y	15	43 24.1	. . 21.3	221 41.0	15.2	0 48.3	9.3	54.2
	16	58 24.3	22.3	236 15.2	15.1	0 57.6	9.3	54.2
	17	73 24.4	23.3	250 49.3	15.1	1 06.9	9.3	54.2
	18	88 24.6	N 1 24.3	265 23.4	15.2	S 1 16.2	9.3	54.1
	19	103 24.8	25.3	279 57.6	15.1	1 25.5	9.3	54.1
	20	118 25.0	26.3	294 31.7	15.2	1 34.8	9.3	54.1
	21	133 25.2	. . 27.2	309 05.9	15.1	1 44.1	9.3	54.1
	22	148 25.4	28.2	323 40.0	15.1	1 53.4	9.2	54.1
	23	163 25.6	29.2	338 14.1	15.2	2 02.6	9.3	54.1
24	00	178 25.8	N 1 30.2	352 48.3	15.2	S 2 11.9	9.2	54.1
	01	193 26.0	31.2	7 22.5	15.1	2 21.1	9.3	54.1
	02	208 26.1	32.2	21 56.6	15.2	2 30.4	9.2	54.1
	03	223 26.3	. . 33.2	36 30.8	15.1	2 39.6	9.2	54.1
	04	238 26.5	34.1	51 04.9	15.2	2 48.8	9.2	54.1
	05	253 26.7	35.1	65 39.1	15.1	2 58.0	9.1	54.1
	06	268 26.9	N 1 36.1	80 13.2	15.2	S 3 07.1	9.2	54.1
T	07	283 27.1	37.1	94 47.4	15.1	3 16.3	9.1	54.1
H	08	298 27.3	38.1	109 21.5	15.1	3 25.4	9.2	54.1
U	09	313 27.5	. . 39.0	123 55.6	15.2	3 34.6	9.1	54.1
R	10	328 27.7	40.0	138 29.8	15.1	3 43.7	9.1	54.1
S	11	343 27.8	41.0	153 03.9	15.1	3 52.8	9.0	54.1
D	12	358 28.0	N 1 42.0	167 38.0	15.2	S 4 01.8	9.1	54.0
A	13	13 28.2	43.0	182 12.2	15.1	4 10.9	9.0	54.0
Y	14	28 28.4	44.0	196 46.3	15.1	4 19.9	9.1	54.0
	15	43 28.6	. . 44.9	211 20.4	15.1	4 29.0	9.0	54.0
	16	58 28.8	45.9	225 54.5	15.1	4 38.0	8.9	54.0
	17	73 29.0	46.9	240 28.6	15.1	4 46.9	9.0	54.0
	18	88 29.2	N 1 47.9	255 02.7	15.1	S 4 55.9	8.9	54.0
	19	103 29.4	48.9	269 36.8	15.0	5 04.8	9.0	54.0
	20	118 29.6	49.9	284 10.8	15.1	5 13.8	8.9	54.0
	21	133 29.7	. . 50.8	298 44.9	15.1	5 22.7	8.8	54.0
	22	148 29.9	51.8	313 19.0	15.0	5 31.5	8.9	54.0
	23	163 30.1	52.8	327 53.0	15.1	S 5 40.4	8.8	54.0
		SD 16.1	*d* 1.0	SD 14.8		14.8		14.7

Lat. (°)	Twilight Naut. (h m)	Twilight Civil (h m)	Sunrise (h m)	Moonrise 22 (h m)	Moonrise 23 (h m)	Moonrise 24 (h m)	Moonrise 25 (h m)
N 72	02 57	04 32	05 41	17 04	18 38	20 11	21 45
N 70	03 20	04 41	05 44	17 08	18 35	20 03	21 30
68	03 37	04 49	05 46	17 11	18 34	19 56	21 19
66	03 51	04 56	05 47	17 13	18 32	19 51	21 10
64	04 02	05 01	05 49	17 15	18 31	19 47	21 02
62	04 11	05 06	05 50	17 17	18 30	19 43	20 55
60	04 19	05 10	05 51	17 19	18 29	19 40	20 49
N 58	04 26	05 13	05 52	17 20	18 29	19 37	20 44
56	04 32	05 16	05 53	17 21	18 28	19 34	20 40
54	04 37	05 19	05 54	17 22	18 27	19 32	20 36
52	04 41	05 21	05 55	17 23	18 27	19 29	20 32
50	04 45	05 23	05 56	17 24	18 26	19 28	20 29
45	04 53	05 28	05 57	17 26	18 25	19 23	20 21
N 40	04 59	05 31	05 58	17 28	18 24	19 20	20 15
35	05 04	05 34	05 59	17 29	18 23	19 17	20 10
30	05 08	05 36	06 00	17 31	18 23	19 14	20 06
20	05 14	05 39	06 01	17 33	18 21	19 10	19 58
N 10	05 17	05 41	06 02	17 35	18 20	19 06	19 51
0	05 19	05 43	06 03	17 37	18 19	19 02	19 45
S 10	05 19	05 43	06 04	17 38	18 18	18 58	19 39
20	05 17	05 43	06 05	17 40	18 17	18 54	19 32
30	05 14	05 42	06 05	17 43	18 16	18 50	19 24
35	05 11	05 41	06 06	17 44	18 16	18 47	19 20
40	05 08	05 39	06 06	17 45	18 15	18 45	19 15
45	05 03	05 37	06 07	17 47	18 14	18 41	19 09
S 50	04 57	05 35	06 07	17 49	18 13	18 37	19 03
52	04 54	05 34	06 07	17 50	18 13	18 36	19 00
54	04 51	05 32	06 08	17 51	18 12	18 34	18 56
56	04 47	05 31	06 08	17 52	18 12	18 32	18 52
58	04 42	05 29	06 08	17 53	18 11	18 29	18 48
S 60	04 37	05 27	06 08	17 55	18 10	18 26	18 44

Lat. (°)	Sunset (h m)	Twilight Civil (h m)	Twilight Naut. (h m)	Moonset 22 (h m)	Moonset 23 (h m)	Moonset 24 (h m)	Moonset 25 (h m)
N 72	18 35	19 45	21 21	06 08	06 04	05 59	05 55
N 70	18 32	19 34	20 57	06 03	06 03	06 04	06 04
68	18 29	19 26	20 39	05 58	06 03	06 07	06 12
66	18 27	19 19	20 25	05 54	06 02	06 10	06 19
64	18 26	19 14	20 13	05 51	06 02	06 13	06 24
62	18 24	19 09	20 04	05 48	06 01	06 15	06 29
60	18 23	19 05	19 56	05 45	06 01	06 17	06 33
N 58	18 22	19 01	19 49	05 43	06 01	06 19	06 37
56	18 21	18 58	19 43	05 41	06 01	06 20	06 40
54	18 20	18 55	19 38	05 39	06 00	06 22	06 43
52	18 19	18 53	19 33	05 37	06 00	06 23	06 46
50	18 18	18 51	19 29	05 36	06 00	06 24	06 49
45	18 17	18 46	19 21	05 32	06 00	06 27	06 54
N 40	18 15	18 43	19 14	05 29	05 59	06 29	06 59
35	18 14	18 40	19 09	05 27	05 59	06 31	07 03
30	18 13	18 37	19 05	05 25	05 59	06 32	07 06
20	18 12	18 34	19 00	05 21	05 58	06 35	07 12
N 10	18 11	18 32	18 56	05 17	05 58	06 38	07 18
0	18 10	18 30	18 54	05 14	05 57	06 40	07 23
S 10	18 09	18 30	18 54	05 11	05 57	06 42	07 28
20	18 08	18 30	18 55	05 07	05 56	06 45	07 33
30	18 07	18 31	18 59	05 04	05 56	06 48	07 39
35	18 06	18 32	19 01	05 01	05 55	06 49	07 43
40	18 06	18 33	19 04	04 59	05 55	06 51	07 47
45	18 05	18 35	19 09	04 56	05 55	06 53	07 51
S 50	18 05	18 37	19 15	04 52	05 54	06 56	07 57
52	18 05	18 38	19 18	04 50	05 54	06 57	08 00
54	18 04	18 39	19 21	04 48	05 54	06 58	08 02
56	18 04	18 41	19 25	04 46	05 53	07 00	08 06
58	18 04	18 43	19 29	04 44	05 53	07 01	08 09
S 60	18 03	18 45	19 34	04 41	05 53	07 03	08 13

Day (d)	SUN Eqn. of Time 00^h (m s)	SUN Eqn. of Time 12^h (m s)	SUN Mer. Pass. (h m)	MOON Mer. Pass. Upper (h m)	MOON Mer. Pass. Lower (h m)	MOON Age (d)	MOON Phase (%)
22	06 54	06 45	12 07	23 47	11 25	13	99
23	06 35	06 26	12 06	24 30	12 08	14	100
24	06 17	06 08	12 06	00 30	12 51	15	99

UT	ARIES	VENUS −3·8		MARS −0·4		JUPITER −2·4		SATURN +0·4	
	GHA	GHA	Dec	GHA	Dec	GHA	Dec	GHA	Dec
d h	° ′	° ′	° ′	° ′	° ′	° ′	° ′	° ′	° ′
25 00	182 53.1	195 39.7	S 6 57.7	298 43.9	S20 16.7	14 59.7	N 6 47.8	287 27.6	S20 59.9
01	197 55.5	210 39.3	56.6	313 45.7	16.9	30 02.4	48.0	302 30.1	59.9
02	212 58.0	225 38.9	55.4	328 47.6	17.0	45 05.2	48.1	317 32.5	59.8
03	228 00.5	240 38.5	. . 54.3	343 49.4	. . 17.2	60 07.9	. . 48.2	332 35.0	. . 59.8
04	243 02.9	255 38.0	53.1	358 51.2	17.3	75 10.7	48.3	347 37.5	59.8
05	258 05.4	270 37.6	51.9	13 53.1	17.5	90 13.4	48.4	2 39.9	59.8
06	273 07.9	285 37.2	S 6 50.8	28 54.9	S20 17.6	105 16.1	N 6 48.5	17 42.4	S20 59.8
07	288 10.3	300 36.8	49.6	43 56.8	17.8	120 18.9	48.6	32 44.9	59.8
08	303 12.8	315 36.4	48.5	58 58.6	17.9	135 21.6	48.7	47 47.3	59.8
F 09	318 15.3	330 35.9	. . 47.3	74 00.4	. . 18.1	150 24.3	. . 48.9	62 49.8	. . 59.8
R 10	333 17.7	345 35.5	46.1	89 02.3	18.2	165 27.1	49.0	77 52.2	59.8
I 11	348 20.2	0 35.1	45.0	104 04.1	18.4	180 29.8	49.1	92 54.7	59.8
D 12	3 22.6	15 34.7	S 6 43.8	119 06.0	S20 18.5	195 32.6	N 6 49.2	107 57.2	S20 59.8
A 13	18 25.1	30 34.3	42.6	134 07.8	18.6	210 35.3	49.3	122 59.6	59.8
Y 14	33 27.6	45 33.9	41.5	149 09.7	18.8	225 38.0	49.4	138 02.1	59.8
15	48 30.0	60 33.4	. . 40.3	164 11.5	. . 18.9	240 40.8	. . 49.5	153 04.6	. . 59.8
16	63 32.5	75 33.0	39.2	179 13.4	19.1	255 43.5	49.6	168 07.0	59.8
17	78 35.0	90 32.6	38.0	194 15.2	19.2	270 46.2	49.8	183 09.5	59.8
18	93 37.4	105 32.2	S 6 36.8	209 17.1	S20 19.4	285 49.0	N 6 49.9	198 12.0	S20 59.8
19	108 39.9	120 31.8	35.7	224 18.9	19.5	300 51.7	50.0	213 14.4	59.8
20	123 42.4	135 31.4	34.5	239 20.8	19.7	315 54.4	50.1	228 16.9	59.8
21	138 44.8	150 30.9	. . 33.3	254 22.6	. . 19.8	330 57.2	. . 50.2	243 19.4	. . 59.8
22	153 47.3	165 30.5	32.2	269 24.5	20.0	345 59.9	50.3	258 21.8	59.8
23	168 49.8	180 30.1	31.0	284 26.3	20.1	1 02.7	50.4	273 24.3	59.7
26 00	183 52.2	195 29.7	S 6 29.8	299 28.2	S20 20.3	16 05.4	N 6 50.5	288 26.7	S20 59.7
01	198 54.7	210 29.3	28.7	314 30.0	20.4	31 08.1	50.6	303 29.2	59.7
02	213 57.1	225 28.9	27.5	329 31.9	20.5	46 10.9	50.8	318 31.7	59.7
03	228 59.6	240 28.4	. . 26.3	344 33.8	. . 20.7	61 13.6	. . 50.9	333 34.1	. . 59.7
04	244 02.1	255 28.0	25.2	359 35.6	20.8	76 16.3	51.0	348 36.6	59.7
05	259 04.5	270 27.6	24.0	14 37.5	21.0	91 19.1	51.1	3 39.1	59.7
06	274 07.0	285 27.2	S 6 22.8	29 39.3	S20 21.1	106 21.8	N 6 51.2	18 41.5	S20 59.7
07	289 09.5	300 26.8	21.7	44 41.2	21.3	121 24.5	51.3	33 44.0	59.7
S 08	304 11.9	315 26.4	20.5	59 43.1	21.4	136 27.3	51.4	48 46.5	59.7
A 09	319 14.4	330 26.0	. . 19.3	74 44.9	. . 21.6	151 30.0	. . 51.5	63 49.0	. . 59.7
T 10	334 16.9	345 25.6	18.1	89 46.8	21.7	166 32.7	51.6	78 51.4	59.7
U 11	349 19.3	0 25.1	17.0	104 48.7	21.9	181 35.5	51.7	93 53.9	59.7
R 12	4 21.8	15 24.7	S 6 15.8	119 50.5	S20 22.0	196 38.2	N 6 51.9	108 56.4	S20 59.7
D 13	19 24.2	30 24.3	14.6	134 52.4	22.1	211 40.9	52.0	123 58.8	59.7
A 14	34 26.7	45 23.9	13.5	149 54.3	22.3	226 43.7	52.1	139 01.3	59.7
Y 15	49 29.2	60 23.5	. . 12.3	164 56.1	. . 22.4	241 46.4	. . 52.2	154 03.8	. . 59.7
16	64 31.6	75 23.1	11.1	179 58.0	22.6	256 49.1	52.3	169 06.2	59.7
17	79 34.1	90 22.7	09.9	194 59.9	22.7	271 51.9	52.4	184 08.7	59.7
18	94 36.6	105 22.3	S 6 08.8	210 01.8	S20 22.9	286 54.6	N 6 52.5	199 11.2	S20 59.6
19	109 39.0	120 21.9	07.6	225 03.6	23.0	301 57.3	52.6	214 13.6	59.6
20	124 41.5	135 21.4	06.4	240 05.5	23.1	317 00.1	52.7	229 16.1	59.6
21	139 44.0	150 21.0	. . 05.3	255 07.4	. . 23.3	332 02.8	. . 52.8	244 18.6	. . 59.6
22	154 46.4	165 20.6	04.1	270 09.3	23.4	347 05.5	53.0	259 21.0	59.6
23	169 48.9	180 20.2	02.9	285 11.1	23.6	2 08.3	53.1	274 23.5	59.6
27 00	184 51.4	195 19.8	S 6 01.7	300 13.0	S20 23.7	17 11.0	N 6 53.2	289 26.0	S20 59.6
01	199 53.8	210 19.4	6 00.6	315 14.9	23.9	32 13.7	53.3	304 28.5	59.6
02	214 56.3	225 19.0	5 59.4	330 16.8	24.0	47 16.5	53.4	319 30.9	59.6
03	229 58.7	240 18.6	. . 58.2	345 18.6	. . 24.1	62 19.2	. . 53.5	334 33.4	. . 59.6
04	245 01.2	255 18.2	57.0	0 20.5	24.3	77 21.9	53.6	349 35.9	59.6
05	260 03.7	270 17.8	55.9	15 22.4	24.4	92 24.6	53.7	4 38.3	59.6
06	275 06.1	285 17.4	S 5 54.7	30 24.3	S20 24.6	107 27.4	N 6 53.8	19 40.8	S20 59.6
07	290 08.6	300 16.9	53.5	45 26.2	24.7	122 30.1	53.9	34 43.3	59.6
08	305 11.1	315 16.5	52.3	60 28.1	24.8	137 32.8	54.0	49 45.8	59.6
S 09	320 13.5	330 16.1	. . 51.1	75 29.9	. . 25.0	152 35.6	. . 54.2	64 48.2	. . 59.6
U 10	335 16.0	345 15.7	50.0	90 31.8	25.1	167 38.3	54.3	79 50.7	59.6
N 11	350 18.5	0 15.3	48.8	105 33.7	25.3	182 41.0	54.4	94 53.2	59.6
D 12	5 20.9	15 14.9	S 5 47.6	120 35.6	S20 25.4	197 43.8	N 6 54.5	109 55.6	S20 59.6
A 13	20 23.4	30 14.5	46.4	135 37.5	25.6	212 46.5	54.6	124 58.1	59.5
Y 14	35 25.9	45 14.1	45.3	150 39.4	25.7	227 49.2	54.7	140 00.6	59.5
15	50 28.3	60 13.7	. . 44.1	165 41.3	. . 25.8	242 52.0	. . 54.8	155 03.1	. . 59.5
16	65 30.8	75 13.3	42.9	180 43.2	26.0	257 54.7	54.9	170 05.5	59.5
17	80 33.2	90 12.9	41.7	195 45.1	26.1	272 57.4	55.0	185 08.0	59.5
18	95 35.7	105 12.5	S 5 40.5	210 47.0	S20 26.3	288 00.1	N 6 55.1	200 10.5	S20 59.5
19	110 38.2	120 12.1	39.4	225 48.9	26.4	303 02.9	55.2	215 13.0	59.5
20	125 40.6	135 11.7	38.2	240 50.8	26.5	318 05.6	55.3	230 15.4	59.5
21	140 43.1	150 11.3	. . 37.0	255 52.7	. . 26.7	333 08.3	. . 55.5	245 17.9	. . 59.5
22	155 45.6	165 10.9	35.8	270 54.6	26.8	348 11.1	55.6	260 20.4	59.5
23	170 48.0	180 10.5	34.6	285 56.5	27.0	3 13.8	55.7	275 22.9	59.5
Mer. Pass.	h m 11 42.6	*v* −0.4	*d* 1.2	*v* 1.9	*d* 0.1	*v* 2.7	*d* 0.1	*v* 2.5	*d* 0.0

STARS		
Name	SHA	Dec
	° ′	° ′
Acamar	315 17.3	S40 14.8
Achernar	335 26.0	S57 09.5
Acrux	173 06.3	S63 11.4
Adhara	255 11.0	S29 00.1
Aldebaran	290 47.4	N16 32.3
Alioth	166 18.6	N55 52.3
Alkaid	152 57.1	N49 13.9
Al Na'ir	27 41.8	S46 52.8
Alnilam	275 44.5	S 1 11.8
Alphard	217 54.0	S 8 44.0
Alphecca	126 09.2	N26 39.6
Alpheratz	357 41.9	N29 10.6
Altair	62 06.5	N 8 54.7
Ankaa	353 14.3	S42 13.2
Antares	112 23.8	S26 27.9
Arcturus	145 53.8	N19 05.8
Atria	107 23.7	S69 02.9
Avior	234 16.9	S59 34.1
Bellatrix	278 30.1	N 6 21.5
Betelgeuse	270 59.3	N 7 24.3
Canopus	263 55.3	S52 42.8
Capella	280 31.8	N46 00.7
Deneb	49 30.4	N45 20.2
Denebola	182 31.5	N14 28.8
Diphda	348 54.4	S17 54.1
Dubhe	193 48.9	N61 39.8
Elnath	278 10.3	N28 37.1
Eltanin	90 45.2	N51 29.1
Enif	33 45.5	N 9 56.9
Fomalhaut	15 22.3	S29 32.2
Gacrux	171 58.1	S57 12.3
Gienah	175 50.0	S17 38.0
Hadar	148 44.5	S60 26.9
Hamal	327 58.9	N23 32.1
Kaus Aust.	83 41.3	S34 22.3
Kochab	137 19.3	N74 05.2
Markab	13 36.8	N15 17.4
Menkar	314 13.3	N 4 08.9
Menkent	148 05.0	S36 26.9
Miaplacidus	221 38.5	S69 47.4
Mirfak	308 38.0	N49 55.0
Nunki	75 56.1	S26 16.4
Peacock	53 16.7	S56 40.6
Pollux	243 25.4	N27 59.0
Procyon	244 57.7	N 5 10.7
Rasalhague	96 04.7	N12 32.9
Regulus	207 41.3	N11 53.1
Rigel	281 10.4	S 8 11.4
Rigil Kent.	139 48.5	S60 53.9
Sabik	102 10.3	S15 44.5
Schedar	349 38.8	N56 37.5
Shaula	96 19.3	S37 06.6
Sirius	258 32.1	S16 44.7
Spica	158 29.0	S11 14.8
Suhail	222 50.7	S43 30.3
Vega	80 37.7	N38 47.8
Zuben'ubi	137 03.1	S16 06.5

	SHA	Mer. Pass.
	° ′	h m
Venus	11 37.5	10 58
Mars	115 36.0	4 02
Jupiter	192 13.2	22 51
Saturn	104 34.5	4 45

	UT	SUN GHA	SUN Dec	MOON GHA	v	MOON Dec	d	HP
	d h	° ′	° ′	° ′	′	° ′	′	′
	25 00	178 30.3	N 1 53.8	342 27.1	15.0	S 5 49.2	8.8	54.0
	01	193 30.5	54.8	357 01.1	15.0	5 58.0	8.8	54.0
	02	208 30.7	55.8	11 35.1	15.0	6 06.8	8.7	54.0
	03	223 30.9	. . 56.7	26 09.1	15.0	6 15.5	8.7	54.0
	04	238 31.1	57.7	40 43.1	15.0	6 24.2	8.7	54.0
	05	253 31.3	58.7	55 17.1	14.9	6 32.9	8.7	54.0
	06	268 31.4	N 1 59.7	69 51.0	15.0	S 6 41.6	8.6	54.0
	07	283 31.6	2 00.7	84 25.0	14.9	6 50.2	8.7	54.0
	08	298 31.8	01.6	98 58.9	14.9	6 58.9	8.5	54.0
F	09	313 32.0	. . 02.6	113 32.8	14.9	7 07.4	8.6	54.0
R	10	328 32.2	03.6	128 06.7	14.9	7 16.0	8.5	54.0
I	11	343 32.4	04.6	142 40.6	14.9	7 24.5	8.5	54.0
D	12	358 32.6	N 2 05.6	157 14.5	14.8	S 7 33.0	8.5	54.0
A	13	13 32.8	06.5	171 48.3	14.9	7 41.5	8.4	54.0
Y	14	28 33.0	07.5	186 22.2	14.8	7 49.9	8.4	54.0
	15	43 33.2	. . 08.5	200 56.0	14.8	7 58.3	8.3	54.0
	16	58 33.3	09.5	215 29.8	14.8	8 06.6	8.4	54.0
	17	73 33.5	10.5	230 03.6	14.8	8 15.0	8.2	54.0
	18	88 33.7	N 2 11.5	244 37.4	14.7	S 8 23.2	8.3	54.0
	19	103 33.9	12.4	259 11.1	14.7	8 31.5	8.2	54.0
	20	118 34.1	13.4	273 44.8	14.8	8 39.7	8.2	54.0
	21	133 34.3	. . 14.4	288 18.6	14.6	8 47.9	8.2	54.0
	22	148 34.5	15.4	302 52.2	14.7	8 56.1	8.1	54.0
	23	163 34.7	16.4	317 25.9	14.7	9 04.2	8.0	54.0
	26 00	178 34.9	N 2 17.3	331 59.6	14.6	S 9 12.2	8.1	54.0
	01	193 35.1	18.3	346 33.2	14.6	9 20.3	8.0	54.0
	02	208 35.2	19.3	1 06.8	14.6	9 28.3	7.9	54.0
	03	223 35.4	. . 20.3	15 40.4	14.5	9 36.2	8.0	54.0
	04	238 35.6	21.3	30 13.9	14.6	9 44.2	7.8	54.0
	05	253 35.8	22.2	44 47.5	14.5	9 52.0	7.9	54.0
	06	268 36.0	N 2 23.2	59 21.0	14.5	S 9 59.9	7.8	54.0
	07	283 36.2	24.2	73 54.5	14.4	10 07.7	7.7	54.0
S	08	298 36.4	25.2	88 27.9	14.5	10 15.4	7.7	54.0
A	09	313 36.6	. . 26.2	103 01.4	14.4	10 23.1	7.7	54.0
T	10	328 36.8	27.1	117 34.8	14.4	10 30.8	7.6	54.0
U	11	343 36.9	28.1	132 08.2	14.3	10 38.4	7.6	54.0
R	12	358 37.1	N 2 29.1	146 41.5	14.4	S10 46.0	7.5	54.0
D	13	13 37.3	30.1	161 14.9	14.3	10 53.5	7.5	54.0
A	14	28 37.5	31.0	175 48.2	14.2	11 01.0	7.5	54.0
Y	15	43 37.7	. . 32.0	190 21.4	14.3	11 08.5	7.4	54.0
	16	58 37.9	33.0	204 54.7	14.2	11 15.9	7.3	54.1
	17	73 38.1	34.0	219 27.9	14.2	11 23.2	7.3	54.1
	18	88 38.3	N 2 35.0	234 01.1	14.2	S11 30.5	7.3	54.1
	19	103 38.5	35.9	248 34.3	14.1	11 37.8	7.2	54.1
	20	118 38.7	36.9	263 07.4	14.2	11 45.0	7.2	54.1
	21	133 38.8	. . 37.9	277 40.6	14.0	11 52.2	7.1	54.1
	22	148 39.0	38.9	292 13.6	14.1	11 59.3	7.0	54.1
	23	163 39.2	39.9	306 46.7	14.0	12 06.3	7.0	54.1
	27 00	178 39.4	N 2 40.8	321 19.7	14.0	S12 13.3	7.0	54.1
	01	193 39.6	41.8	335 52.7	14.0	12 20.3	6.9	54.1
	02	208 39.8	42.8	350 25.7	13.9	12 27.2	6.9	54.1
	03	223 40.0	. . 43.8	4 58.6	13.9	12 34.1	6.8	54.1
	04	238 40.2	44.7	19 31.5	13.9	12 40.9	6.7	54.1
	05	253 40.4	45.7	34 04.4	13.8	12 47.6	6.7	54.1
	06	268 40.6	N 2 46.7	48 37.2	13.8	S12 54.3	6.6	54.1
	07	283 40.7	47.7	63 10.0	13.8	13 00.9	6.6	54.1
	08	298 40.9	48.7	77 42.8	13.7	13 07.5	6.6	54.2
S	09	313 41.1	. . 49.6	92 15.5	13.7	13 14.1	6.4	54.2
U	10	328 41.3	50.6	106 48.2	13.7	13 20.5	6.5	54.2
N	11	343 41.5	51.6	121 20.9	13.6	13 27.0	6.3	54.2
D	12	358 41.7	N 2 52.6	135 53.5	13.7	S13 33.3	6.3	54.2
A	13	13 41.9	53.5	150 26.2	13.5	13 39.6	6.3	54.2
Y	14	28 42.1	54.5	164 58.7	13.6	13 45.9	6.2	54.2
	15	43 42.3	. . 55.5	179 31.3	13.5	13 52.1	6.1	54.2
	16	58 42.4	56.5	194 03.8	13.4	13 58.2	6.0	54.2
	17	73 42.6	57.4	208 36.2	13.5	14 04.2	6.1	54.2
	18	88 42.8	N 2 58.4	223 08.7	13.4	S14 10.3	5.9	54.2
	19	103 43.0	2 59.4	237 41.1	13.3	14 16.2	5.9	54.3
	20	118 43.2	3 00.4	252 13.4	13.4	14 22.1	5.8	54.3
	21	133 43.4	. . 01.4	266 45.8	13.3	14 27.9	5.8	54.3
	22	148 43.6	02.3	281 18.1	13.2	14 33.7	5.7	54.3
	23	163 43.8	03.3	295 50.3	13.2	S14 39.4	5.6	54.3
		SD 16.1	d 1.0	SD 14.7		14.7		14.8

Lat.	Twilight Naut.	Twilight Civil	Sunrise	Moonrise 25	Moonrise 26	Moonrise 27	Moonrise 28
°	h m	h m	h m	h m	h m	h m	h m
N 72	02 34	04 15	05 25	21 45	23 21	25 01	01 01
N 70	03 01	04 26	05 30	21 30	22 59	24 27	00 27
68	03 21	04 36	05 33	21 19	22 41	24 03	00 03
66	03 37	04 44	05 36	21 10	22 27	23 44	24 57
64	03 50	04 50	05 38	21 02	22 16	23 29	24 38
62	04 00	04 56	05 41	20 55	22 06	23 16	24 23
60	04 09	05 00	05 42	20 49	21 58	23 05	24 10
N 58	04 16	05 04	05 44	20 44	21 51	22 56	23 59
56	04 23	05 08	05 45	20 40	21 45	22 48	23 49
54	04 29	05 11	05 47	20 36	21 39	22 41	23 41
52	04 34	05 14	05 48	20 32	21 34	22 35	23 34
50	04 38	05 17	05 49	20 29	21 29	22 29	23 27
45	04 47	05 22	05 51	20 21	21 19	22 16	23 12
N 40	04 54	05 26	05 53	20 15	21 11	22 06	23 00
35	05 00	05 30	05 55	20 10	21 04	21 57	22 50
30	05 04	05 32	05 56	20 06	20 58	21 49	22 41
20	05 11	05 37	05 59	19 58	20 47	21 36	22 26
N 10	05 15	05 40	06 01	19 51	20 37	21 25	22 13
0	05 18	05 42	06 02	19 45	20 29	21 14	22 00
S 10	05 19	05 43	06 04	19 39	20 20	21 03	21 48
20	05 18	05 44	06 06	19 32	20 11	20 52	21 35
30	05 16	05 43	06 07	19 24	20 00	20 39	21 20
35	05 14	05 43	06 08	19 20	19 54	20 31	21 11
40	05 11	05 42	06 09	19 15	19 48	20 23	21 01
45	05 07	05 41	06 10	19 09	19 40	20 13	20 50
S 50	05 02	05 40	06 12	19 03	19 30	20 01	20 36
52	04 59	05 39	06 12	19 00	19 26	19 55	20 29
54	04 56	05 38	06 13	18 56	19 21	19 49	20 22
56	04 53	05 37	06 14	18 52	19 16	19 42	20 14
58	04 49	05 36	06 15	18 48	19 10	19 35	20 05
S 60	04 45	05 34	06 16	18 44	19 03	19 26	19 54

Lat.	Sunset	Twilight Civil	Twilight Naut.	Moonset 25	Moonset 26	Moonset 27	Moonset 28
°	h m	h m	h m	h m	h m	h m	h m
N 72	18 48	20 00	21 44	05 55	05 50	05 44	05 38
N 70	18 44	19 48	21 15	06 04	06 06	06 08	06 13
68	18 40	19 38	20 53	06 12	06 18	06 26	06 38
66	18 37	19 30	20 37	06 19	06 29	06 41	06 58
64	18 34	19 23	20 24	06 24	06 37	06 53	07 13
62	18 32	19 17	20 13	06 29	06 45	07 03	07 26
60	18 30	19 12	20 04	06 33	06 51	07 12	07 38
N 58	18 28	19 08	19 56	06 37	06 57	07 20	07 47
56	18 27	19 04	19 50	06 40	07 02	07 27	07 56
54	18 25	19 01	19 44	06 43	07 07	07 33	08 03
52	18 24	18 58	19 39	06 46	07 11	07 39	08 10
50	18 23	18 56	19 34	06 49	07 15	07 44	08 16
45	18 21	18 50	19 25	06 54	07 23	07 55	08 29
N 40	18 19	18 46	19 18	06 59	07 30	08 04	08 40
35	18 17	18 42	19 12	07 03	07 36	08 11	08 50
30	18 15	18 39	19 07	07 06	07 41	08 18	08 58
20	18 13	18 35	19 01	07 12	07 50	08 30	09 12
N 10	18 11	18 32	18 56	07 18	07 58	08 41	09 24
0	18 09	18 29	18 53	07 23	08 06	08 50	09 36
S 10	18 07	18 28	18 52	07 28	08 14	09 00	09 48
20	18 05	18 27	18 53	07 33	08 22	09 11	10 00
30	18 03	18 27	18 55	07 39	08 31	09 23	10 14
35	18 02	18 27	18 57	07 43	08 36	09 29	10 23
40	18 01	18 28	18 59	07 47	08 42	09 37	10 32
45	18 00	18 29	19 03	07 51	08 49	09 47	10 43
S 50	17 58	18 30	19 08	07 57	08 58	09 58	10 57
52	17 58	18 31	19 10	08 00	09 02	10 03	11 03
54	17 57	18 32	19 13	08 02	09 06	10 09	11 10
56	17 56	18 33	19 16	08 06	09 11	10 15	11 18
58	17 55	18 34	19 20	08 09	09 16	10 22	11 26
S 60	17 54	18 36	19 24	08 13	09 22	10 30	11 36

Day	SUN Eqn. of Time 00^h	SUN Eqn. of Time 12^h	SUN Mer. Pass.	MOON Mer. Pass. Upper	MOON Mer. Pass. Lower	MOON Age	MOON Phase
d	m s	m s	h m	h m	h m	d	%
25	05 59	05 50	12 06	01 12	13 34	16	96
26	05 41	05 32	12 06	01 55	14 17	17	92
27	05 23	05 14	12 05	02 39	15 02	18	86

2016 MARCH 28, 29, 30 (MON., TUES., WED.)

UT		ARIES	VENUS −3·8		MARS −0·5		JUPITER −2·4		SATURN +0·4	
d	h	GHA ° ′	GHA ° ′	Dec ° ′	GHA ° ′	Dec ° ′	GHA ° ′	Dec ° ′	GHA ° ′	Dec ° ′
28 MONDAY	00	185 50.5	195 10.1	S 5 33.5	300 58.4	S20 27.1	18 16.5	N 6 55.8	290 25.3	S20 59.5
	01	200 53.0	210 09.6	32.3	316 00.3	27.2	33 19.2	55.9	305 27.8	59.5
	02	215 55.4	225 09.2	31.1	331 02.2	27.4	48 22.0	56.0	320 30.3	59.5
	03	230 57.9	240 08.8	. . 29.9	346 04.1	. . 27.5	63 24.7	. . 56.1	335 32.8	. . 59.5
	04	246 00.3	255 08.4	28.7	1 06.0	27.6	78 27.4	56.2	350 35.2	59.5
	05	261 02.8	270 08.0	27.6	16 07.9	27.8	93 30.1	56.3	5 37.7	59.5
	06	276 05.3	285 07.6	S 5 26.4	31 09.8	S20 27.9	108 32.9	N 6 56.4	20 40.2	S20 59.5
	07	291 07.7	300 07.2	25.2	46 11.7	28.1	123 35.6	56.5	35 42.7	59.4
	08	306 10.2	315 06.8	24.0	61 13.6	28.2	138 38.3	56.6	50 45.1	59.4
	09	321 12.7	330 06.4	. . 22.8	76 15.5	. . 28.3	153 41.1	. . 56.7	65 47.6	. . 59.4
	10	336 15.1	345 06.0	21.6	91 17.4	28.5	168 43.8	56.9	80 50.1	59.4
	11	351 17.6	0 05.6	20.5	106 19.3	28.6	183 46.5	57.0	95 52.6	59.4
	12	6 20.1	15 05.2	S 5 19.3	121 21.2	S20 28.8	198 49.2	N 6 57.1	110 55.0	S20 59.4
	13	21 22.5	30 04.8	18.1	136 23.1	28.9	213 52.0	57.2	125 57.5	59.4
	14	36 25.0	45 04.4	16.9	151 25.1	29.0	228 54.7	57.3	141 00.0	59.4
	15	51 27.5	60 04.0	. . 15.7	166 27.0	. . 29.2	243 57.4	. . 57.4	156 02.5	. . 59.4
	16	66 29.9	75 03.6	14.5	181 28.9	29.3	259 00.1	57.5	171 05.0	59.4
	17	81 32.4	90 03.2	13.3	196 30.8	29.4	274 02.9	57.6	186 07.4	59.4
	18	96 34.8	105 02.8	S 5 12.2	211 32.7	S20 29.6	289 05.6	N 6 57.7	201 09.9	S20 59.4
	19	111 37.3	120 02.4	11.0	226 34.6	29.7	304 08.3	57.8	216 12.4	59.4
	20	126 39.8	135 02.0	09.8	241 36.6	29.9	319 11.0	57.9	231 14.9	59.4
	21	141 42.2	150 01.6	. . 08.6	256 38.5	. . 30.0	334 13.8	. . 58.0	246 17.3	. . 59.4
	22	156 44.7	165 01.2	07.4	271 40.4	30.1	349 16.5	58.1	261 19.8	59.4
	23	171 47.2	180 00.8	06.2	286 42.3	30.3	4 19.2	58.2	276 22.3	59.4
29 TUESDAY	00	186 49.6	195 00.4	S 5 05.0	301 44.2	S20 30.4	19 21.9	N 6 58.3	291 24.8	S20 59.3
	01	201 52.1	210 00.0	03.9	316 46.2	30.5	34 24.7	58.4	306 27.3	59.3
	02	216 54.6	224 59.6	02.7	331 48.1	30.7	49 27.4	58.5	321 29.7	59.3
	03	231 57.0	239 59.2	. . 01.5	346 50.0	. . 30.8	64 30.1	. . 58.7	336 32.2	. . 59.3
	04	246 59.5	254 58.8	5 00.3	1 51.9	30.9	79 32.8	58.8	351 34.7	59.3
	05	262 02.0	269 58.4	4 59.1	16 53.9	31.1	94 35.6	58.9	6 37.2	59.3
	06	277 04.4	284 58.0	S 4 57.9	31 55.8	S20 31.2	109 38.3	N 6 59.0	21 39.7	S20 59.3
	07	292 06.9	299 57.6	56.7	46 57.7	31.4	124 41.0	59.1	36 42.1	59.3
	08	307 09.3	314 57.2	55.5	61 59.7	31.5	139 43.7	59.2	51 44.6	59.3
	09	322 11.8	329 56.8	. . 54.3	77 01.6	. . 31.6	154 46.4	. . 59.3	66 47.1	. . 59.3
	10	337 14.3	344 56.4	53.2	92 03.5	31.8	169 49.2	59.4	81 49.6	59.3
	11	352 16.7	359 56.1	52.0	107 05.5	31.9	184 51.9	59.5	96 52.1	59.3
	12	7 19.2	14 55.7	S 4 50.8	122 07.4	S20 32.0	199 54.6	N 6 59.6	111 54.6	S20 59.3
	13	22 21.7	29 55.3	49.6	137 09.3	32.2	214 57.3	59.7	126 57.0	59.3
	14	37 24.1	44 54.9	48.4	152 11.3	32.3	230 00.1	59.8	141 59.5	59.3
	15	52 26.6	59 54.5	. . 47.2	167 13.2	. . 32.4	245 02.8	6 59.9	157 02.0	. . 59.3
	16	67 29.1	74 54.1	46.0	182 15.1	32.6	260 05.5	7 00.0	172 04.5	59.2
	17	82 31.5	89 53.7	44.8	197 17.1	32.7	275 08.2	00.1	187 07.0	59.2
	18	97 34.0	104 53.3	S 4 43.6	212 19.0	S20 32.8	290 10.9	N 7 00.2	202 09.4	S20 59.2
	19	112 36.4	119 52.9	42.4	227 21.0	33.0	305 13.7	00.3	217 11.9	59.2
	20	127 38.9	134 52.5	41.2	242 22.9	33.1	320 16.4	00.4	232 14.4	59.2
	21	142 41.4	149 52.1	. . 40.1	257 24.8	. . 33.2	335 19.1	. . 00.5	247 16.9	. . 59.2
	22	157 43.8	164 51.7	38.9	272 26.8	33.4	350 21.8	00.6	262 19.4	59.2
	23	172 46.3	179 51.3	37.7	287 28.7	33.5	5 24.6	00.7	277 21.9	59.2
30 WEDNESDAY	00	187 48.8	194 50.9	S 4 36.5	302 30.7	S20 33.6	20 27.3	N 7 00.8	292 24.3	S20 59.2
	01	202 51.2	209 50.5	35.3	317 32.6	33.8	35 30.0	00.9	307 26.8	59.2
	02	217 53.7	224 50.1	34.1	332 34.6	33.9	50 32.7	01.1	322 29.3	59.2
	03	232 56.2	239 49.7	. . 32.9	347 36.5	. . 34.0	65 35.4	. . 01.2	337 31.8	. . 59.2
	04	247 58.6	254 49.3	31.7	2 38.5	34.2	80 38.2	01.3	352 34.3	59.2
	05	263 01.1	269 48.9	30.5	17 40.4	34.3	95 40.9	01.4	7 36.8	59.2
	06	278 03.6	284 48.6	S 4 29.3	32 42.4	S20 34.4	110 43.6	N 7 01.5	22 39.2	S20 59.2
	07	293 06.0	299 48.2	28.1	47 44.3	34.6	125 46.3	01.6	37 41.7	59.1
	08	308 08.5	314 47.8	26.9	62 46.3	34.7	140 49.0	01.7	52 44.2	59.1
	09	323 10.9	329 47.4	. . 25.7	77 48.3	. . 34.8	155 51.7	. . 01.8	67 46.7	. . 59.1
	10	338 13.4	344 47.0	24.5	92 50.2	35.0	170 54.5	01.9	82 49.2	59.1
	11	353 15.9	359 46.6	23.3	107 52.2	35.1	185 57.2	02.0	97 51.7	59.1
	12	8 18.3	14 46.2	S 4 22.1	122 54.1	S20 35.2	200 59.9	N 7 02.1	112 54.2	S20 59.1
	13	23 20.8	29 45.8	20.9	137 56.1	35.4	216 02.6	02.2	127 56.6	59.1
	14	38 23.3	44 45.4	19.7	152 58.0	35.5	231 05.3	02.3	142 59.1	59.1
	15	53 25.7	59 45.0	. . 18.6	168 00.0	. . 35.6	246 08.1	. . 02.4	158 01.6	. . 59.1
	16	68 28.2	74 44.6	17.4	183 02.0	35.8	261 10.8	02.5	173 04.1	59.1
	17	83 30.7	89 44.2	16.2	198 03.9	35.9	276 13.5	02.6	188 06.6	59.1
	18	98 33.1	104 43.8	S 4 15.0	213 05.9	S20 36.0	291 16.2	N 7 02.7	203 09.1	S20 59.1
	19	113 35.6	119 43.5	13.8	228 07.9	36.1	306 18.9	02.8	218 11.6	59.1
	20	128 38.1	134 43.1	12.6	243 09.8	36.3	321 21.6	02.9	233 14.1	59.1
	21	143 40.5	149 42.7	. . 11.4	258 11.8	. . 36.4	336 24.4	. . 03.0	248 16.5	. . 59.1
	22	158 43.0	164 42.3	10.2	273 13.8	36.5	351 27.1	03.1	263 19.0	59.0
	23	173 45.4	179 41.9	09.0	288 15.7	36.7	6 29.8	03.2	278 21.5	59.0
Mer. Pass.		h m 11 30.8	v −0.4	d 1.2	v 1.9	d 0.1	v 2.7	d 0.1	v 2.5	d 0.0

STARS

Name	SHA ° ′	Dec ° ′
Acamar	315 17.3	S40 14.8
Achernar	335 26.0	S57 09.5
Acrux	173 06.3	S63 11.4
Adhara	255 11.0	S29 00.1
Aldebaran	290 47.4	N16 32.2
Alioth	166 18.6	N55 52.3
Alkaid	152 57.0	N49 13.9
Al Na'ir	27 41.8	S46 52.8
Alnilam	275 44.6	S 1 11.9
Alphard	217 54.0	S 8 44.0
Alphecca	126 09.2	N26 39.6
Alpheratz	357 41.9	N29 10.6
Altair	62 06.5	N 8 54.7
Ankaa	353 14.3	S42 13.2
Antares	112 23.8	S26 27.9
Arcturus	145 53.7	N19 05.8
Atria	107 23.6	S69 03.0
Avior	234 16.9	S59 34.1
Bellatrix	278 30.1	N 6 21.5
Betelgeuse	270 59.3	N 7 24.3
Canopus	263 55.3	S52 42.8
Capella	280 31.8	N46 00.7
Deneb	49 30.4	N45 20.1
Denebola	182 31.5	N14 28.8
Diphda	348 54.4	S17 54.0
Dubhe	193 49.0	N61 39.8
Elnath	278 10.4	N28 37.1
Eltanin	90 45.2	N51 29.1
Enif	33 45.5	N 9 56.9
Fomalhaut	15 22.3	S29 32.2
Gacrux	171 58.1	S57 12.3
Gienah	175 50.0	S17 38.0
Hadar	148 44.5	S60 26.9
Hamal	327 58.9	N23 32.1
Kaus Aust.	83 41.3	S34 22.3
Kochab	137 19.3	N74 05.3
Markab	13 36.7	N15 17.4
Menkar	314 13.3	N 4 08.9
Menkent	148 05.0	S36 26.9
Miaplacidus	221 38.6	S69 47.4
Mirfak	308 38.0	N49 55.0
Nunki	75 56.0	S26 16.4
Peacock	53 16.6	S56 40.6
Pollux	243 25.4	N27 59.0
Procyon	244 57.7	N 5 10.7
Rasalhague	96 04.6	N12 32.9
Regulus	207 41.3	N11 53.1
Rigel	281 10.4	S 8 11.4
Rigil Kent.	139 48.5	S60 53.9
Sabik	102 10.3	S15 44.5
Schedar	349 38.8	N56 37.5
Shaula	96 19.3	S37 06.6
Sirius	258 32.1	S16 44.7
Spica	158 29.0	S11 14.8
Suhail	222 50.8	S43 30.3
Vega	80 37.7	N38 47.8
Zuben'ubi	137 03.1	S16 06.5

	SHA ° ′	Mer. Pass. h m
Venus	8 10.8	11 00
Mars	114 54.6	3 53
Jupiter	192 32.3	22 38
Saturn	104 35.2	4 34

	UT	SUN GHA	SUN Dec	MOON GHA	v	MOON Dec	d	HP
	d h	° ′	° ′	° ′	′	° ′	′	′
	28 00	178 44.0	N 3 04.3	310 22.5	13.2	S14 45.0	5.6	54.3
	01	193 44.1	05.3	324 54.7	13.2	14 50.6	5.5	54.3
	02	208 44.3	06.2	339 26.9	13.1	14 56.1	5.5	54.3
	03	223 44.5	. . 07.2	353 59.0	13.0	15 01.6	5.3	54.3
	04	238 44.7	08.2	8 31.0	13.1	15 06.9	5.4	54.4
	05	253 44.9	09.2	23 03.1	13.0	15 12.3	5.2	54.4
	06	268 45.1	N 3 10.1	37 35.1	12.9	S15 17.5	5.2	54.4
	07	283 45.3	11.1	52 07.0	13.0	15 22.7	5.1	54.4
	08	298 45.5	12.1	66 39.0	12.8	15 27.8	5.1	54.4
M	09	313 45.7	. . 13.1	81 10.8	12.9	15 32.9	4.9	54.4
O	10	328 45.8	14.0	95 42.7	12.8	15 37.8	4.9	54.4
N	11	343 46.0	15.0	110 14.5	12.8	15 42.7	4.9	54.5
D	12	358 46.2	N 3 16.0	124 46.3	12.7	S15 47.6	4.8	54.5
A	13	13 46.4	17.0	139 18.0	12.7	15 52.4	4.7	54.5
Y	14	28 46.6	17.9	153 49.7	12.7	15 57.1	4.6	54.5
	15	43 46.8	. . 18.9	168 21.4	12.6	16 01.7	4.6	54.5
	16	58 47.0	19.9	182 53.0	12.6	16 06.3	4.4	54.5
	17	73 47.2	20.9	197 24.6	12.5	16 10.7	4.5	54.5
	18	88 47.4	N 3 21.8	211 56.1	12.5	S16 15.2	4.3	54.6
	19	103 47.5	22.8	226 27.6	12.5	16 19.5	4.3	54.6
	20	118 47.7	23.8	240 59.1	12.4	16 23.8	4.2	54.6
	21	133 47.9	. . 24.7	255 30.5	12.4	16 28.0	4.1	54.6
	22	148 48.1	25.7	270 01.9	12.3	16 32.1	4.1	54.6
	23	163 48.3	26.7	284 33.2	12.3	16 36.2	3.9	54.6
	29 00	178 48.5	N 3 27.7	299 04.5	12.3	S16 40.1	3.9	54.7
	01	193 48.7	28.6	313 35.8	12.2	16 44.0	3.9	54.7
	02	208 48.9	29.6	328 07.0	12.2	16 47.9	3.7	54.7
	03	223 49.1	. . 30.6	342 38.2	12.2	16 51.6	3.7	54.7
	04	238 49.2	31.6	357 09.4	12.1	16 55.3	3.6	54.7
	05	253 49.4	32.5	11 40.5	12.1	16 58.9	3.5	54.8
	06	268 49.6	N 3 33.5	26 11.6	12.0	S17 02.4	3.4	54.8
	07	283 49.8	34.5	40 42.6	12.0	17 05.8	3.4	54.8
T	08	298 50.0	35.4	55 13.6	12.0	17 09.2	3.3	54.8
U	09	313 50.2	. . 36.4	69 44.6	11.9	17 12.5	3.2	54.8
E	10	328 50.4	37.4	84 15.5	11.9	17 15.7	3.1	54.9
S	11	343 50.6	38.4	98 46.4	11.8	17 18.8	3.0	54.9
D	12	358 50.8	N 3 39.3	113 17.2	11.8	S17 21.8	3.0	54.9
A	13	13 50.9	40.3	127 48.0	11.8	17 24.8	2.9	54.9
Y	14	28 51.1	41.3	142 18.8	11.7	17 27.7	2.8	54.9
	15	43 51.3	. . 42.3	156 49.5	11.7	17 30.5	2.7	55.0
	16	58 51.5	43.2	171 20.2	11.6	17 33.2	2.6	55.0
	17	73 51.7	44.2	185 50.8	11.6	17 35.8	2.5	55.0
	18	88 51.9	N 3 45.2	200 21.4	11.6	S17 38.3	2.5	55.0
	19	103 52.1	46.1	214 52.0	11.5	17 40.8	2.4	55.0
	20	118 52.3	47.1	229 22.5	11.5	17 43.2	2.3	55.1
	21	133 52.4	. . 48.1	243 53.0	11.5	17 45.5	2.2	55.1
	22	148 52.6	49.0	258 23.5	11.4	17 47.7	2.1	55.1
	23	163 52.8	50.0	272 53.9	11.4	17 49.8	2.1	55.1
	30 00	178 53.0	N 3 51.0	287 24.3	11.3	S17 51.9	1.9	55.2
	01	193 53.2	52.0	301 54.6	11.3	17 53.8	1.9	55.2
	02	208 53.4	52.9	316 24.9	11.3	17 55.7	1.8	55.2
	03	223 53.6	. . 53.9	330 55.2	11.2	17 57.5	1.7	55.2
	04	238 53.8	54.9	345 25.4	11.2	17 59.2	1.6	55.3
	05	253 53.9	55.8	359 55.6	11.2	18 00.8	1.5	55.3
	06	268 54.1	N 3 56.8	14 25.8	11.1	S18 02.3	1.4	55.3
W	07	283 54.3	57.8	28 55.9	11.1	18 03.7	1.4	55.3
E	08	298 54.5	58.7	43 26.0	11.0	18 05.1	1.2	55.4
D	09	313 54.7	3 59.7	57 56.0	11.0	18 06.3	1.2	55.4
N	10	328 54.9	4 00.7	72 26.0	11.0	18 07.5	1.1	55.4
E	11	343 55.1	01.7	86 56.0	10.9	18 08.6	1.0	55.4
S	12	358 55.3	N 4 02.6	101 25.9	10.9	S18 09.6	0.9	55.5
D	13	13 55.4	03.6	115 55.8	10.9	18 10.5	0.8	55.5
A	14	28 55.6	04.6	130 25.7	10.8	18 11.3	0.7	55.5
Y	15	43 55.8	. . 05.5	144 55.5	10.8	18 12.0	0.6	55.5
	16	58 56.0	06.5	159 25.3	10.7	18 12.6	0.5	55.6
	17	73 56.2	07.5	173 55.0	10.8	18 13.1	0.5	55.6
	18	88 56.4	N 4 08.4	188 24.8	10.7	S18 13.6	0.3	55.6
	19	103 56.6	09.4	202 54.5	10.6	18 13.9	0.3	55.7
	20	118 56.8	10.4	217 24.1	10.6	18 14.2	0.1	55.7
	21	133 56.9	. . 11.3	231 53.7	10.6	18 14.3	0.1	55.7
	22	148 57.1	12.3	246 23.3	10.6	18 14.4	0.0	55.7
	23	163 57.3	13.3	260 52.9	10.5	S18 14.4	0.1	55.8
		SD 16.0	*d* 1.0	SD 14.8		15.0		15.1

Lat.	Twilight Naut.	Twilight Civil	Sunrise	Moonrise 28	Moonrise 29	Moonrise 30	Moonrise 31
°	h m	h m	h m	h m	h m	h m	h m
N 72	02 07	03 57	05 10	01 01	02 48	■	■
N 70	02 41	04 11	05 16	00 27	01 53	03 11	04 09
68	03 04	04 22	05 20	00 03	01 21	02 30	03 26
66	03 23	04 31	05 24	24 57	00 57	02 02	02 57
64	03 37	04 39	05 28	24 38	00 38	01 41	02 35
62	03 49	04 45	05 31	24 23	00 23	01 24	02 18
60	03 59	04 51	05 33	24 10	00 10	01 10	02 03
N 58	04 07	04 56	05 36	23 59	24 58	00 58	01 51
56	04 14	05 00	05 38	23 49	24 47	00 47	01 40
54	04 20	05 04	05 39	23 41	24 38	00 38	01 30
52	04 26	05 07	05 41	23 34	24 30	00 30	01 22
50	04 31	05 10	05 43	23 27	24 22	00 22	01 14
45	04 41	05 16	05 46	23 12	24 06	00 06	00 58
N 40	04 49	05 21	05 48	23 00	23 53	24 45	00 45
35	04 55	05 25	05 51	22 50	23 42	24 34	00 34
30	05 01	05 29	05 53	22 41	23 33	24 24	00 24
20	05 08	05 34	05 56	22 26	23 16	24 07	00 07
N 10	05 13	05 38	05 59	22 13	23 02	23 52	24 43
0	05 17	05 41	06 01	22 00	22 48	23 38	24 29
S 10	05 18	05 43	06 04	21 48	22 35	23 24	24 16
20	05 19	05 44	06 06	21 35	22 21	23 10	24 02
30	05 17	05 45	06 09	21 20	22 04	22 53	23 45
35	05 16	05 45	06 11	21 11	21 55	22 43	23 36
40	05 14	05 45	06 12	21 01	21 44	22 32	23 25
45	05 11	05 45	06 14	20 50	21 31	22 19	23 12
S 50	05 07	05 44	06 17	20 36	21 16	22 03	22 57
52	05 05	05 44	06 18	20 29	21 09	21 55	22 50
54	05 02	05 43	06 19	20 22	21 01	21 47	22 41
56	04 59	05 43	06 20	20 14	20 52	21 38	22 32
58	04 56	05 42	06 21	20 05	20 42	21 27	22 22
S 60	04 53	05 41	06 23	19 54	20 30	21 15	22 10

Lat.	Sunset	Twilight Civil	Twilight Naut.	Moonset 28	Moonset 29	Moonset 30	Moonset 31
°	h m	h m	h m	h m	h m	h m	h m
N 72	19 02	20 16	22 11	05 38	05 29	■	■
N 70	18 56	20 01	21 34	06 13	06 24	06 46	07 33
68	18 51	19 50	21 09	06 38	06 57	07 28	08 16
66	18 47	19 40	20 50	06 58	07 21	07 56	08 45
64	18 43	19 32	20 35	07 13	07 40	08 17	09 07
62	18 40	19 26	20 23	07 26	07 56	08 35	09 24
60	18 37	19 20	20 13	07 38	08 09	08 49	09 39
N 58	18 35	19 15	20 04	07 47	08 20	09 01	09 51
56	18 33	19 11	19 57	07 56	08 30	09 12	10 02
54	18 31	19 07	19 50	08 03	08 39	09 21	10 11
52	18 29	19 04	19 45	08 10	08 47	09 29	10 20
50	18 28	19 00	19 40	08 16	08 54	09 37	10 27
45	18 24	18 54	19 29	08 29	09 08	09 53	10 43
N 40	18 22	18 49	19 21	08 40	09 21	10 06	10 57
35	18 19	18 45	19 14	08 50	09 31	10 17	11 08
30	18 17	18 41	19 09	08 58	09 41	10 27	11 18
20	18 14	18 36	19 01	09 12	09 56	10 44	11 34
N 10	18 11	18 32	18 56	09 24	10 10	10 59	11 49
0	18 08	18 29	18 53	09 36	10 23	11 12	12 03
S 10	18 05	18 26	18 51	09 48	10 36	11 26	12 16
20	18 03	18 25	18 50	10 00	10 50	11 41	12 31
30	18 00	18 24	18 51	10 14	11 06	11 57	12 48
35	17 58	18 23	18 53	10 23	11 15	12 07	12 57
40	17 56	18 23	18 55	10 32	11 26	12 18	13 08
45	17 54	18 23	18 57	10 43	11 38	12 31	13 21
S 50	17 52	18 24	19 01	10 57	11 53	12 47	13 37
52	17 51	18 24	19 03	11 03	12 01	12 55	13 44
54	17 50	18 25	19 06	11 10	12 08	13 03	13 53
56	17 48	18 25	19 08	11 18	12 17	13 12	14 02
58	17 47	18 26	19 11	11 26	12 27	13 23	14 12
S 60	17 45	18 27	19 15	11 36	12 39	13 35	14 24

Day	SUN Eqn. of Time 00^h	SUN Eqn. of Time 12^h	SUN Mer. Pass.	MOON Mer. Pass. Upper	MOON Mer. Pass. Lower	MOON Age	MOON Phase
d	m s	m s	h m	h m	h m	d %	
28	05 05	04 55	12 05	03 25	15 48	19 79	
29	04 46	04 37	12 05	04 12	16 36	20 71	
30	04 28	04 19	12 04	05 00	17 25	21 61	

UT d	UT h	ARIES GHA	VENUS −3·8 GHA	VENUS Dec	MARS −0·5 GHA	MARS Dec	JUPITER −2·4 GHA	JUPITER Dec	SATURN +0·3 GHA	SATURN Dec
		° ′	° ′	° ′	° ′	° ′	° ′	° ′	° ′	° ′
31 THURSDAY	00	188 47.9	194 41.5	S 4 07.8	303 17.7	S20 36.8	21 32.5	N 7 03.3	293 24.0	S20 59.0
	01	203 50.4	209 41.1	06.6	318 19.7	36.9	36 35.2	03.4	308 26.5	59.0
	02	218 52.8	224 40.7	05.4	333 21.7	37.1	51 37.9	03.5	323 29.0	59.0
	03	233 55.3	239 40.3	. . 04.2	348 23.6	. . 37.2	66 40.7	. . 03.6	338 31.5	. . 59.0
	04	248 57.8	254 39.9	03.0	3 25.6	37.3	81 43.4	03.7	353 34.0	59.0
	05	264 00.2	269 39.6	01.8	18 27.6	37.5	96 46.1	03.8	8 36.5	59.0
	06	279 02.7	284 39.2	S 4 00.6	33 29.6	S20 37.6	111 48.8	N 7 03.9	23 38.9	S20 59.0
	07	294 05.2	299 38.8	3 59.4	48 31.5	37.7	126 51.5	04.0	38 41.4	59.0
	08	309 07.6	314 38.4	58.2	63 33.5	37.8	141 54.2	04.1	53 43.9	59.0
	09	324 10.1	329 38.0	. . 57.0	78 35.5	. . 38.0	156 56.9	. . 04.2	68 46.4	. . 59.0
	10	339 12.5	344 37.6	55.8	93 37.5	38.1	171 59.7	04.3	83 48.9	59.0
	11	354 15.0	359 37.2	54.6	108 39.5	38.2	187 02.4	04.4	98 51.4	59.0
	12	9 17.5	14 36.8	S 3 53.4	123 41.4	S20 38.4	202 05.1	N 7 04.5	113 53.9	S20 59.0
	13	24 19.9	29 36.5	52.2	138 43.4	38.5	217 07.8	04.6	128 56.4	58.9
	14	39 22.4	44 36.1	51.0	153 45.4	38.6	232 10.5	04.7	143 58.9	58.9
	15	54 24.9	59 35.7	. . 49.8	168 47.4	. . 38.7	247 13.2	. . 04.8	159 01.4	. . 58.9
	16	69 27.3	74 35.3	48.6	183 49.4	38.9	262 15.9	04.9	174 03.8	58.9
	17	84 29.8	89 34.9	47.4	198 51.4	39.0	277 18.7	05.0	189 06.3	58.9
	18	99 32.3	104 34.5	S 3 46.2	213 53.4	S20 39.1	292 21.4	N 7 05.1	204 08.8	S20 58.9
	19	114 34.7	119 34.1	45.0	228 55.3	39.3	307 24.1	05.2	219 11.3	58.9
	20	129 37.2	134 33.7	43.8	243 57.3	39.4	322 26.8	05.3	234 13.8	58.9
	21	144 39.7	149 33.4	. . 42.6	258 59.3	. . 39.5	337 29.5	. . 05.4	249 16.3	. . 58.9
	22	159 42.1	164 33.0	41.4	274 01.3	39.6	352 32.2	05.5	264 18.8	58.9
	23	174 44.6	179 32.6	40.2	289 03.3	39.8	7 34.9	05.6	279 21.3	58.9
1 FRIDAY	00	189 47.0	194 32.2	S 3 39.0	304 05.3	S20 39.9	22 37.6	N 7 05.7	294 23.8	S20 58.9
	01	204 49.5	209 31.8	37.8	319 07.3	40.0	37 40.4	05.8	309 26.3	58.9
	02	219 52.0	224 31.4	36.5	334 09.3	40.2	52 43.1	05.9	324 28.8	58.9
	03	234 54.4	239 31.0	. . 35.3	349 11.3	. . 40.3	67 45.8	. . 06.0	339 31.3	. . 58.8
	04	249 56.9	254 30.7	34.1	4 13.3	40.4	82 48.5	06.1	354 33.7	58.8
	05	264 59.4	269 30.3	32.9	19 15.3	40.5	97 51.2	06.2	9 36.2	58.8
	06	280 01.8	284 29.9	S 3 31.7	34 17.3	S20 40.7	112 53.9	N 7 06.3	24 38.7	S20 58.8
	07	295 04.3	299 29.5	30.5	49 19.3	40.8	127 56.6	06.4	39 41.2	58.8
	08	310 06.8	314 29.1	29.3	64 21.3	40.9	142 59.3	06.5	54 43.7	58.8
	09	325 09.2	329 28.7	. . 28.1	79 23.3	. . 41.0	158 02.0	. . 06.6	69 46.2	. . 58.8
	10	340 11.7	344 28.3	26.9	94 25.3	41.2	173 04.8	06.7	84 48.7	58.8
	11	355 14.2	359 28.0	25.7	109 27.3	41.3	188 07.5	06.8	99 51.2	58.8
	12	10 16.6	14 27.6	S 3 24.5	124 29.3	S20 41.4	203 10.2	N 7 06.9	114 53.7	S20 58.8
	13	25 19.1	29 27.2	23.3	139 31.3	41.5	218 12.9	07.0	129 56.2	58.8
	14	40 21.5	44 26.8	22.1	154 33.4	41.7	233 15.6	07.1	144 58.7	58.8
	15	55 24.0	59 26.4	. . 20.9	169 35.4	. . 41.8	248 18.3	. . 07.2	160 01.2	. . 58.8
	16	70 26.5	74 26.0	19.7	184 37.4	41.9	263 21.0	07.3	175 03.7	58.7
	17	85 28.9	89 25.7	18.5	199 39.4	42.0	278 23.7	07.4	190 06.2	58.7
	18	100 31.4	104 25.3	S 3 17.3	214 41.4	S20 42.2	293 26.4	N 7 07.5	205 08.7	S20 58.7
	19	115 33.9	119 24.9	16.1	229 43.4	42.3	308 29.1	07.6	220 11.2	58.7
	20	130 36.3	134 24.5	14.9	244 45.4	42.4	323 31.8	07.7	235 13.7	58.7
	21	145 38.8	149 24.1	. . 13.6	259 47.5	. . 42.5	338 34.5	. . 07.8	250 16.2	. . 58.7
	22	160 41.3	164 23.7	12.4	274 49.5	42.7	353 37.3	07.9	265 18.7	58.7
	23	175 43.7	179 23.4	11.2	289 51.5	42.8	8 40.0	08.0	280 21.2	58.7
2 SATURDAY	00	190 46.2	194 23.0	S 3 10.0	304 53.5	S20 42.9	23 42.7	N 7 08.1	295 23.7	S20 58.7
	01	205 48.6	209 22.6	08.8	319 55.5	43.0	38 45.4	08.2	310 26.1	58.7
	02	220 51.1	224 22.2	07.6	334 57.6	43.2	53 48.1	08.3	325 28.6	58.7
	03	235 53.6	239 21.8	. . 06.4	349 59.6	. . 43.3	68 50.8	. . 08.4	340 31.1	. . 58.7
	04	250 56.0	254 21.4	05.2	5 01.6	43.4	83 53.5	08.5	355 33.6	58.7
	05	265 58.5	269 21.1	04.0	20 03.6	43.5	98 56.2	08.6	10 36.1	58.7
	06	281 01.0	284 20.7	S 3 02.8	35 05.7	S20 43.7	113 58.9	N 7 08.7	25 38.6	S20 58.6
	07	296 03.4	299 20.3	01.6	50 07.7	43.8	129 01.6	08.8	40 41.1	58.6
	08	311 05.9	314 19.9	3 00.4	65 09.7	43.9	144 04.3	08.9	55 43.6	58.6
	09	326 08.4	329 19.5	2 59.2	80 11.8	. . 44.0	159 07.0	. . 08.9	70 46.1	. . 58.6
	10	341 10.8	344 19.2	57.9	95 13.8	44.2	174 09.7	09.0	85 48.6	58.6
	11	356 13.3	359 18.8	56.7	110 15.8	44.3	189 12.4	09.1	100 51.1	58.6
	12	11 15.8	14 18.4	S 2 55.5	125 17.9	S20 44.4	204 15.1	N 7 09.2	115 53.6	S20 58.6
	13	26 18.2	29 18.0	54.3	140 19.9	44.5	219 17.8	09.3	130 56.1	58.6
	14	41 20.7	44 17.6	53.1	155 21.9	44.7	234 20.6	09.4	145 58.6	58.6
	15	56 23.1	59 17.3	. . 51.9	170 24.0	. . 44.8	249 23.3	. . 09.5	161 01.1	. . 58.6
	16	71 25.6	74 16.9	50.7	185 26.0	44.9	264 26.0	09.6	176 03.6	58.6
	17	86 28.1	89 16.5	49.5	200 28.0	45.0	279 28.7	09.7	191 06.1	58.6
	18	101 30.5	104 16.1	S 2 48.3	215 30.1	S20 45.1	294 31.4	N 7 09.8	206 08.6	S20 58.6
	19	116 33.0	119 15.7	47.1	230 32.1	45.3	309 34.1	09.9	221 11.1	58.5
	20	131 35.5	134 15.4	45.8	245 34.2	45.4	324 36.8	10.0	236 13.6	58.5
	21	146 37.9	149 15.0	. . 44.6	260 36.2	. . 45.5	339 39.5	. . 10.1	251 16.1	. . 58.5
	22	161 40.4	164 14.6	43.4	275 38.3	45.6	354 42.2	10.2	266 18.6	58.5
	23	176 42.9	179 14.2	42.2	290 40.3	45.8	9 44.9	10.3	281 21.1	58.5
Mer. Pass.		h m 11 19.0	*v* −0.4	*d* 1.2	*v* 2.0	*d* 0.1	*v* 2.7	*d* 0.1	*v* 2.5	*d* 0.0

STARS

Name	SHA	Dec
	° ′	° ′
Acamar	315 17.3	S40 14.7
Achernar	335 26.1	S57 09.5
Acrux	173 06.3	S63 11.4
Adhara	255 11.0	S29 00.1
Aldebaran	290 47.4	N16 32.2
Alioth	166 18.6	N55 52.3
Alkaid	152 57.0	N49 13.9
Al Na'ir	27 41.8	S46 52.8
Alnilam	275 44.6	S 1 11.8
Alphard	217 54.0	S 8 44.0
Alphecca	126 09.2	N26 39.6
Alpheratz	357 41.9	N29 10.6
Altair	62 06.5	N 8 54.7
Ankaa	353 14.3	S42 13.2
Antares	112 23.7	S26 27.9
Arcturus	145 53.7	N19 05.8
Atria	107 23.6	S69 03.0
Avior	234 16.9	S59 34.1
Bellatrix	278 30.1	N 6 21.5
Betelgeuse	270 59.3	N 7 24.3
Canopus	263 55.4	S52 42.8
Capella	280 31.8	N46 00.7
Deneb	49 30.4	N45 20.1
Denebola	182 31.5	N14 28.8
Diphda	348 54.4	S17 54.0
Dubhe	193 49.0	N61 39.8
Elnath	278 10.4	N28 37.1
Eltanin	90 45.2	N51 29.1
Enif	33 45.5	N 9 56.9
Fomalhaut	15 22.3	S29 32.2
Gacrux	171 58.1	S57 12.3
Gienah	175 50.0	S17 38.0
Hadar	148 44.5	S60 26.9
Hamal	327 58.9	N23 32.1
Kaus Aust.	83 41.3	S34 22.3
Kochab	137 19.3	N74 05.3
Markab	13 36.7	N15 17.4
Menkar	314 13.3	N 4 08.9
Menkent	148 04.9	S36 26.9
Miaplacidus	221 38.6	S69 47.4
Mirfak	308 38.0	N49 55.0
Nunki	75 56.0	S26 16.4
Peacock	53 16.6	S56 40.6
Pollux	243 25.4	N27 59.0
Procyon	244 57.7	N 5 10.7
Rasalhague	96 04.6	N12 32.9
Regulus	207 41.3	N11 53.1
Rigel	281 10.4	S 8 11.4
Rigil Kent.	139 48.5	S60 53.9
Sabik	102 10.2	S15 44.5
Schedar	349 38.8	N56 37.4
Shaula	96 19.2	S37 06.6
Sirius	258 32.1	S16 44.7
Spica	158 28.9	S11 14.8
Suhail	222 50.8	S43 30.3
Vega	80 37.6	N38 47.8
Zuben'ubi	137 03.0	S16 06.5

	SHA	Mer. Pass.
	° ′	h m
Venus	4 45.2	11 02
Mars	114 18.3	3 43
Jupiter	192 50.6	22 25
Saturn	104 36.7	4 22

UT (d h)	SUN GHA ° ′	SUN Dec ° ′	MOON GHA ° ′	v ′	MOON Dec ° ′	d ′	HP ′
31 00 THURSDAY	178 57.5	N 4 14.2	275 22.4	10.5	S18 14.3	0.3	55.8
01	193 57.7	15.2	289 51.9	10.4	18 14.0	0.3	55.8
02	208 57.9	16.2	304 21.3	10.4	18 13.7	0.4	55.9
03	223 58.1	. . 17.1	318 50.7	10.4	18 13.3	0.5	55.9
04	238 58.2	18.1	333 20.1	10.4	18 12.8	0.6	55.9
05	253 58.4	19.1	347 49.5	10.3	18 12.2	0.6	55.9
06	268 58.6	N 4 20.0	2 18.8	10.3	S18 11.6	0.8	56.0
07	283 58.8	21.0	16 48.1	10.2	18 10.8	0.9	56.0
08	298 59.0	22.0	31 17.3	10.3	18 09.9	1.0	56.0
09	313 59.2	. . 22.9	45 46.6	10.2	18 08.9	1.1	56.1
10	328 59.4	23.9	60 15.8	10.1	18 07.8	1.1	56.1
11	343 59.6	24.9	74 44.9	10.2	18 06.7	1.3	56.1
12	358 59.7	N 4 25.8	89 14.1	10.1	S18 05.4	1.4	56.2
13	13 59.9	26.8	103 43.2	10.1	18 04.0	1.4	56.2
14	29 00.1	27.8	118 12.3	10.0	18 02.6	1.6	56.2
15	44 00.3	. . 28.7	132 41.3	10.0	18 01.0	1.6	56.3
16	59 00.5	29.7	147 10.3	10.0	17 59.4	1.8	56.3
17	74 00.7	30.7	161 39.3	10.0	17 57.6	1.8	56.3
18	89 00.9	N 4 31.6	176 08.3	9.9	S17 55.8	2.0	56.4
19	104 01.0	32.6	190 37.2	9.9	17 53.8	2.0	56.4
20	119 01.2	33.6	205 06.1	9.9	17 51.8	2.2	56.4
21	134 01.4	. . 34.5	219 35.0	9.8	17 49.6	2.2	56.5
22	149 01.6	35.5	234 03.8	9.9	17 47.4	2.3	56.5
23	164 01.8	36.5	248 32.7	9.8	17 45.1	2.5	56.5
1 00 FRIDAY	179 02.0	N 4 37.4	263 01.5	9.7	S17 42.6	2.5	56.6
01	194 02.2	38.4	277 30.2	9.8	17 40.1	2.7	56.6
02	209 02.3	39.3	291 59.0	9.7	17 37.4	2.7	56.6
03	224 02.5	. . 40.3	306 27.7	9.7	17 34.7	2.8	56.7
04	239 02.7	41.3	320 56.4	9.7	17 31.9	3.0	56.7
05	254 02.9	42.2	335 25.1	9.6	17 28.9	3.0	56.8
06	269 03.1	N 4 43.2	349 53.7	9.6	S17 25.9	3.1	56.8
07	284 03.3	44.2	4 22.3	9.6	17 22.8	3.3	56.8
08	299 03.4	45.1	18 50.9	9.6	17 19.5	3.3	56.9
09	314 03.6	. . 46.1	33 19.5	9.5	17 16.2	3.4	56.9
10	329 03.8	47.1	47 48.0	9.6	17 12.8	3.6	56.9
11	344 04.0	48.0	62 16.6	9.5	17 09.2	3.6	57.0
12	359 04.2	N 4 49.0	76 45.1	9.4	S17 05.6	3.7	57.0
13	14 04.4	49.9	91 13.5	9.5	17 01.9	3.8	57.0
14	29 04.6	50.9	105 42.0	9.4	16 58.1	4.0	57.1
15	44 04.7	. . 51.9	120 10.4	9.4	16 54.1	4.0	57.1
16	59 04.9	52.8	134 38.8	9.4	16 50.1	4.1	57.2
17	74 05.1	53.8	149 07.2	9.4	16 46.0	4.2	57.2
18	89 05.3	N 4 54.7	163 35.6	9.3	S16 41.8	4.4	57.2
19	104 05.5	55.7	178 03.9	9.4	16 37.4	4.4	57.3
20	119 05.7	56.7	192 32.3	9.3	16 33.0	4.5	57.3
21	134 05.8	. . 57.6	207 00.6	9.3	16 28.5	4.6	57.3
22	149 06.0	58.6	221 28.9	9.2	16 23.9	4.7	57.4
23	164 06.2	4 59.6	235 57.1	9.3	16 19.2	4.9	57.4
2 00 SATURDAY	179 06.4	N 5 00.5	250 25.4	9.2	S16 14.3	4.9	57.5
01	194 06.6	01.5	264 53.6	9.2	16 09.4	5.0	57.5
02	209 06.8	02.4	279 21.8	9.2	16 04.4	5.1	57.5
03	224 06.9	. . 03.4	293 50.0	9.2	15 59.3	5.2	57.6
04	239 07.1	04.4	308 18.2	9.1	15 54.1	5.3	57.6
05	254 07.3	05.3	322 46.3	9.1	15 48.8	5.4	57.7
06	269 07.5	N 5 06.3	337 14.4	9.2	S15 43.4	5.5	57.7
07	284 07.7	07.2	351 42.6	9.1	15 37.9	5.6	57.7
08	299 07.9	08.2	6 10.7	9.0	15 32.3	5.7	57.8
09	314 08.1	. . 09.2	20 38.7	9.1	15 26.6	5.8	57.8
10	329 08.2	10.1	35 06.8	9.1	15 20.8	5.9	57.9
11	344 08.4	11.1	49 34.9	9.0	15 14.9	6.0	57.9
12	359 08.6	N 5 12.0	64 02.9	9.0	S15 08.9	6.1	57.9
13	14 08.8	13.0	78 30.9	9.0	15 02.8	6.1	58.0
14	29 09.0	13.9	92 58.9	9.0	14 56.7	6.3	58.0
15	44 09.1	. . 14.9	107 26.9	8.9	14 50.4	6.4	58.1
16	59 09.3	15.9	121 54.8	9.0	14 44.0	6.4	58.1
17	74 09.5	16.8	136 22.8	8.9	14 37.6	6.6	58.1
18	89 09.7	N 5 17.8	150 50.7	9.0	S14 31.0	6.6	58.2
19	104 09.9	18.7	165 18.7	8.9	14 24.4	6.8	58.2
20	119 10.1	19.7	179 46.6	8.8	14 17.6	6.8	58.3
21	134 10.2	. . 20.6	194 14.4	8.9	14 10.8	6.9	58.3
22	149 10.4	21.6	208 42.3	8.9	14 03.9	7.0	58.3
23	164 10.6	22.6	223 10.2	8.8	S13 56.9	7.1	58.4
	SD 16.0	*d* 1.0	SD 15.3		15.5		15.8

Lat. °	Twilight Naut. h m	Twilight Civil h m	Sunrise h m	Moonrise 31 h m	Moonrise 1 h m	Moonrise 2 h m	Moonrise 3 h m
N 72	01 33	03 39	04 54	■	05 48	05 35	05 28
N 70	02 18	03 55	05 01	04 09	04 41	04 56	05 03
68	02 46	04 08	05 08	03 26	04 04	04 29	04 44
66	03 07	04 19	05 13	02 57	03 38	04 08	04 29
64	03 24	04 28	05 17	02 35	03 18	03 51	04 16
62	03 37	04 35	05 21	02 18	03 02	03 37	04 05
60	03 48	04 41	05 24	02 03	02 48	03 26	03 56
N 58	03 57	04 47	05 27	01 51	02 36	03 15	03 48
56	04 05	04 52	05 30	01 40	02 26	03 06	03 41
54	04 12	04 56	05 32	01 30	02 17	02 59	03 35
52	04 18	05 00	05 34	01 22	02 09	02 51	03 29
50	04 24	05 03	05 36	01 14	02 02	02 45	03 24
45	04 35	05 10	05 40	00 58	01 46	02 31	03 13
N 40	04 44	05 16	05 44	00 45	01 34	02 20	03 03
35	04 51	05 21	05 46	00 34	01 23	02 10	02 55
30	04 57	05 25	05 49	00 24	01 13	02 02	02 48
20	05 05	05 31	05 53	00 07	00 57	01 47	02 36
N 10	05 11	05 36	05 57	24 43	00 43	01 34	02 25
0	05 16	05 40	06 00	24 29	00 29	01 22	02 15
S 10	05 18	05 43	06 04	24 16	00 16	01 10	02 05
20	05 20	05 45	06 07	24 02	00 02	00 57	01 54
30	05 19	05 47	06 11	23 45	24 42	00 42	01 42
35	05 18	05 48	06 13	23 36	24 33	00 33	01 34
40	05 17	05 48	06 15	23 25	24 23	00 23	01 26
45	05 15	05 49	06 18	23 12	24 12	00 12	01 17
S 50	05 11	05 49	06 21	22 57	23 58	25 05	01 05
52	05 10	05 49	06 23	22 50	23 51	25 00	01 00
54	05 08	05 49	06 24	22 41	23 44	24 54	00 54
56	05 06	05 49	06 26	22 32	23 36	24 47	00 47
58	05 03	05 49	06 28	22 22	23 27	24 40	00 40
S 60	05 00	05 48	06 30	22 10	23 16	24 31	00 31

Lat. °	Sunset h m	Twilight Civil h m	Twilight Naut. h m	Moonset 31 h m	Moonset 1 h m	Moonset 2 h m	Moonset 3 h m
N 72	19 17	20 33	22 47	■	07 42	09 44	11 43
N 70	19 09	20 16	21 56	07 33	08 48	10 23	12 06
68	19 02	20 02	21 26	08 16	09 25	10 49	12 24
66	18 57	19 51	21 04	08 45	09 50	11 09	12 39
64	18 52	19 42	20 47	09 07	10 10	11 26	12 51
62	18 48	19 34	20 33	09 24	10 26	11 39	13 00
60	18 45	19 28	20 22	09 39	10 39	11 50	13 09
N 58	18 42	19 22	20 12	09 51	10 51	12 00	13 16
56	18 39	19 17	20 04	10 02	11 01	12 08	13 23
54	18 37	19 13	19 57	10 11	11 10	12 16	13 29
52	18 34	19 09	19 51	10 20	11 18	12 23	13 34
50	18 32	19 05	19 45	10 27	11 25	12 29	13 39
45	18 28	18 58	19 33	10 43	11 40	12 42	13 49
N 40	18 25	18 52	19 24	10 57	11 52	12 53	13 58
35	18 22	18 47	19 17	11 08	12 03	13 02	14 05
30	18 19	18 43	19 11	11 18	12 12	13 10	14 11
20	18 14	18 37	19 02	11 34	12 28	13 24	14 22
N 10	18 11	18 32	18 56	11 49	12 42	13 36	14 32
0	18 07	18 28	18 52	12 03	12 54	13 47	14 40
S 10	18 04	18 25	18 49	12 16	13 07	13 58	14 49
20	18 00	18 22	18 48	12 31	13 21	14 10	14 59
30	17 56	18 20	18 48	12 48	13 36	14 24	15 09
35	17 54	18 19	18 48	12 57	13 45	14 31	15 15
40	17 51	18 19	18 50	13 08	13 56	14 40	15 22
45	17 49	18 18	18 52	13 21	14 08	14 51	15 30
S 50	17 45	18 18	18 55	13 37	14 22	15 03	15 40
52	17 44	18 17	18 57	13 44	14 29	15 09	15 44
54	17 42	18 17	18 58	13 53	14 37	15 15	15 49
56	17 40	18 17	19 00	14 02	14 45	15 22	15 54
58	17 38	18 17	19 03	14 12	14 54	15 30	16 00
S 60	17 36	18 18	19 06	14 24	15 05	15 39	16 07

Day d	SUN Eqn. of Time 00h m s	SUN Eqn. of Time 12h m s	SUN Mer. Pass. h m	MOON Mer. Pass. Upper h m	MOON Mer. Pass. Lower h m	MOON Age d	MOON Phase %
31	04 10	04 01	12 04	05 50	18 16	22	52
1	03 53	03 44	12 04	06 42	19 08	23	41
2	03 35	03 26	12 03	07 34	20 01	24	31

UT d	h	ARIES GHA	VENUS −3·8 GHA	VENUS Dec	MARS −0·6 GHA	MARS Dec	JUPITER −2·4 GHA	JUPITER Dec	SATURN +0·3 GHA	SATURN Dec	STARS Name	SHA	Dec
		° ′	° ′	° ′	° ′	° ′	° ′	° ′	° ′	° ′		° ′	° ′
3	00	191 45.3	194 13.8	S 2 41.0	305 42.3	S20 45.9	24 47.6	N 7 10.4	296 23.6	S20 58.5	Acamar	315 17.3	S40 14.7
	01	206 47.8	209 13.5	39.8	320 44.4	46.0	39 50.3	10.5	311 26.1	58.5	Achernar	335 26.1	S57 09.5
	02	221 50.3	224 13.1	38.6	335 46.4	46.1	54 53.0	10.6	326 28.6	58.5	Acrux	173 06.3	S63 11.4
	03	236 52.7	239 12.7	37.4	350 48.5	46.2	69 55.7	10.7	341 31.1	58.5	Adhara	255 11.0	S29 00.1
	04	251 55.2	254 12.3	36.2	5 50.5	46.4	84 58.4	10.8	356 33.6	58.5	Aldebaran	290 47.4	N16 32.2
	05	266 57.6	269 11.9	34.9	20 52.6	46.5	100 01.1	10.9	11 36.1	58.5			
	06	282 00.1	284 11.6	S 2 33.7	35 54.6	S20 46.6	115 03.8	N 7 11.0	26 38.6	S20 58.5	Alioth	166 18.6	N55 52.3
	07	297 02.6	299 11.2	32.5	50 56.7	46.7	130 06.5	11.0	41 41.1	58.4	Alkaid	152 57.0	N49 13.9
	08	312 05.0	314 10.8	31.3	65 58.8	46.8	145 09.2	11.1	56 43.6	58.4	Al Na'ir	27 41.8	S46 52.8
S	09	327 07.5	329 10.4	30.1	81 00.8	47.0	160 11.9	11.2	71 46.2	58.4	Alnilam	275 44.6	S 1 11.8
U	10	342 10.0	344 10.0	28.9	96 02.9	47.1	175 14.6	11.3	86 48.7	58.4	Alphard	217 54.0	S 8 44.0
N	11	357 12.4	359 09.7	27.7	111 04.9	47.2	190 17.3	11.4	101 51.2	58.4			
D	12	12 14.9	14 09.3	S 2 26.5	126 07.0	S20 47.3	205 20.0	N 7 11.5	116 53.7	S20 58.4	Alphecca	126 09.2	N26 39.6
A	13	27 17.4	29 08.9	25.2	141 09.1	47.4	220 22.7	11.6	131 56.2	58.4	Alpheratz	357 41.9	N29 10.6
Y	14	42 19.8	44 08.5	24.0	156 11.1	47.6	235 25.4	11.7	146 58.7	58.4	Altair	62 06.5	N 8 54.7
	15	57 22.3	59 08.2	22.8	171 13.2	47.7	250 28.1	11.8	162 01.2	58.4	Ankaa	353 14.3	S42 13.2
	16	72 24.7	74 07.8	21.6	186 15.2	47.8	265 30.8	11.9	177 03.7	58.4	Antares	112 23.7	S26 27.9
	17	87 27.2	89 07.4	20.4	201 17.3	47.9	280 33.5	12.0	192 06.2	58.4			
	18	102 29.7	104 07.0	S 2 19.2	216 19.4	S20 48.0	295 36.2	N 7 12.1	207 08.7	S20 58.4	Arcturus	145 53.7	N19 05.8
	19	117 32.1	119 06.6	18.0	231 21.4	48.2	310 38.9	12.2	222 11.2	58.4	Atria	107 23.5	S69 03.0
	20	132 34.6	134 06.3	16.8	246 23.5	48.3	325 41.6	12.3	237 13.7	58.3	Avior	234 17.0	S59 34.2
	21	147 37.1	149 05.9	15.5	261 25.6	48.4	340 44.3	12.4	252 16.2	58.3	Bellatrix	278 30.1	N 6 21.5
	22	162 39.5	164 05.5	14.3	276 27.7	48.5	355 47.0	12.5	267 18.7	58.3	Betelgeuse	270 59.4	N 7 24.3
	23	177 42.0	179 05.1	13.1	291 29.7	48.6	10 49.7	12.5	282 21.2	58.3			
4	00	192 44.5	194 04.8	S 2 11.9	306 31.8	S20 48.8	25 52.4	N 7 12.6	297 23.7	S20 58.3	Canopus	263 55.4	S52 42.8
	01	207 46.9	209 04.4	10.7	321 33.9	48.9	40 55.1	12.7	312 26.2	58.3	Capella	280 31.9	N46 00.7
	02	222 49.4	224 04.0	09.5	336 35.9	49.0	55 57.8	12.8	327 28.7	58.3	Deneb	49 30.3	N45 20.1
	03	237 51.9	239 03.6	08.2	351 38.0	49.1	71 00.5	12.9	342 31.2	58.3	Denebola	182 31.5	N14 28.8
	04	252 54.3	254 03.3	07.0	6 40.1	49.2	86 03.2	13.0	357 33.7	58.3	Diphda	348 54.4	S17 54.0
	05	267 56.8	269 02.9	05.8	21 42.2	49.4	101 05.9	13.1	12 36.2	58.3			
	06	282 59.2	284 02.5	S 2 04.6	36 44.3	S20 49.5	116 08.6	N 7 13.2	27 38.8	S20 58.3	Dubhe	193 49.0	N61 39.8
	07	298 01.7	299 02.1	03.4	51 46.3	49.6	131 11.3	13.3	42 41.3	58.3	Elnath	278 10.4	N28 37.1
	08	313 04.2	314 01.8	02.2	66 48.4	49.7	146 14.0	13.4	57 43.8	58.2	Eltanin	90 45.1	N51 29.1
M	09	328 06.6	329 01.4	2 01.0	81 50.5	49.8	161 16.7	13.5	72 46.3	58.2	Enif	33 45.5	N 9 56.9
O	10	343 09.1	344 01.0	1 59.7	96 52.6	49.9	176 19.4	13.6	87 48.8	58.2	Fomalhaut	15 22.3	S29 32.2
N	11	358 11.6	359 00.6	58.5	111 54.7	50.1	191 22.1	13.7	102 51.3	58.2			
D	12	13 14.0	14 00.3	S 1 57.3	126 56.8	S20 50.2	206 24.7	N 7 13.7	117 53.8	S20 58.2	Gacrux	171 58.1	S57 12.3
A	13	28 16.5	28 59.9	56.1	141 58.9	50.3	221 27.4	13.8	132 56.3	58.2	Gienah	175 50.0	S17 38.0
Y	14	43 19.0	43 59.5	54.9	157 00.9	50.4	236 30.1	13.9	147 58.8	58.2	Hadar	148 44.5	S60 26.9
	15	58 21.4	58 59.1	53.7	172 03.0	50.5	251 32.8	14.0	163 01.3	58.2	Hamal	327 58.9	N23 32.1
	16	73 23.9	73 58.7	52.4	187 05.1	50.7	266 35.5	14.1	178 03.8	58.2	Kaus Aust.	83 41.3	S34 22.3
	17	88 26.4	88 58.4	51.2	202 07.2	50.8	281 38.2	14.2	193 06.3	58.2			
	18	103 28.8	103 58.0	S 1 50.0	217 09.3	S20 50.9	296 40.9	N 7 14.3	208 08.8	S20 58.2	Kochab	137 19.2	N74 05.3
	19	118 31.3	118 57.6	48.8	232 11.4	51.0	311 43.6	14.4	223 11.4	58.2	Markab	13 36.7	N15 17.4
	20	133 33.7	133 57.2	47.6	247 13.5	51.1	326 46.3	14.5	238 13.9	58.1	Menkar	314 13.3	N 4 08.9
	21	148 36.2	148 56.9	46.4	262 15.6	51.2	341 49.0	14.6	253 16.4	58.1	Menkent	148 04.9	S36 26.9
	22	163 38.7	163 56.5	45.1	277 17.7	51.4	356 51.7	14.7	268 18.9	58.1	Miaplacidus	221 38.6	S69 47.4
	23	178 41.1	178 56.1	43.9	292 19.8	51.5	11 54.4	14.7	283 21.4	58.1			
5	00	193 43.6	193 55.8	S 1 42.7	307 21.9	S20 51.6	26 57.1	N 7 14.8	298 23.9	S20 58.1	Mirfak	308 38.0	N49 55.0
	01	208 46.1	208 55.4	41.5	322 24.0	51.7	41 59.8	14.9	313 26.4	58.1	Nunki	75 56.0	S26 16.4
	02	223 48.5	223 55.0	40.3	337 26.1	51.8	57 02.5	15.0	328 28.9	58.1	Peacock	53 16.6	S56 40.6
	03	238 51.0	238 54.6	39.1	352 28.2	51.9	72 05.2	15.1	343 31.4	58.1	Pollux	243 25.4	N27 59.1
	04	253 53.5	253 54.3	37.8	7 30.3	52.0	87 07.8	15.2	358 33.9	58.1	Procyon	244 57.7	N 5 10.7
	05	268 55.9	268 53.9	36.6	22 32.4	52.2	102 10.5	15.3	13 36.5	58.1			
	06	283 58.4	283 53.5	S 1 35.4	37 34.5	S20 52.3	117 13.2	N 7 15.4	28 39.0	S20 58.1	Rasalhague	96 04.6	N12 32.9
	07	299 00.8	298 53.1	34.2	52 36.6	52.4	132 15.9	15.5	43 41.5	58.0	Regulus	207 41.3	N11 53.1
T	08	314 03.3	313 52.8	33.0	67 38.7	52.5	147 18.6	15.6	58 44.0	58.0	Rigel	281 10.4	S 8 11.4
U	09	329 05.8	328 52.4	31.8	82 40.8	52.6	162 21.3	15.6	73 46.5	58.0	Rigil Kent.	139 48.5	S60 53.9
E	10	344 08.2	343 52.0	30.5	97 43.0	52.7	177 24.0	15.7	88 49.0	58.0	Sabik	102 10.2	S15 44.5
S	11	359 10.7	358 51.6	29.3	112 45.1	52.9	192 26.7	15.8	103 51.5	58.0			
D	12	14 13.2	13 51.3	S 1 28.1	127 47.2	S20 53.0	207 29.4	N 7 15.9	118 54.0	S20 58.0	Schedar	349 38.8	N56 37.4
A	13	29 15.6	28 50.9	26.9	142 49.3	53.1	222 32.1	16.0	133 56.5	58.0	Shaula	96 19.2	S37 06.6
Y	14	44 18.1	43 50.5	25.7	157 51.4	53.2	237 34.8	16.1	148 59.1	58.0	Sirius	258 32.1	S16 44.7
	15	59 20.6	58 50.1	24.4	172 53.5	53.3	252 37.4	16.2	164 01.6	58.0	Spica	158 28.9	S11 14.8
	16	74 23.0	73 49.8	23.2	187 55.7	53.4	267 40.1	16.3	179 04.1	58.0	Suhail	222 50.8	S43 30.3
	17	89 25.5	88 49.4	22.0	202 57.8	53.5	282 42.8	16.4	194 06.6	58.0			
	18	104 28.0	103 49.0	S 1 20.8	217 59.9	S20 53.7	297 45.5	N 7 16.4	209 09.1	S20 58.0	Vega	80 37.6	N38 47.8
	19	119 30.4	118 48.7	19.6	233 02.0	53.8	312 48.2	16.5	224 11.6	57.9	Zuben'ubi	137 03.0	S16 06.5
	20	134 32.9	133 48.3	18.3	248 04.1	53.9	327 50.9	16.6	239 14.1	57.9			
	21	149 35.3	148 47.9	17.1	263 06.3	54.0	342 53.6	16.7	254 16.7	57.9			
	22	164 37.8	163 47.5	15.9	278 08.4	54.1	357 56.3	16.8	269 19.2	57.9			
	23	179 40.3	178 47.2	14.7	293 10.5	54.2	12 59.0	16.9	284 21.7	57.9			
Mer. Pass.		h m 11 07.2	v −0.4	d 1.2	v 2.1	d 0.1	v 2.7	d 0.1	v 2.5	d 0.0			

	SHA	Mer. Pass.
	° ′	h m
Venus	1 20.3	11 04
Mars	113 47.3	3 33
Jupiter	193 07.9	22 13
Saturn	104 39.3	4 10

UT		SUN GHA	SUN Dec	MOON GHA	v	MOON Dec	d	HP
d	h	° ′	° ′	° ′	′	° ′	′	′
3 SUNDAY	00	179 10.8	N 5 23.5	237 38.0	8.9	S13 49.8	7.2	58.4
	01	194 11.0	24.5	252 05.9	8.8	13 42.6	7.3	58.5
	02	209 11.2	25.4	266 33.7	8.8	13 35.3	7.4	58.5
	03	224 11.3	. . 26.4	281 01.5	8.8	13 27.9	7.5	58.5
	04	239 11.5	27.3	295 29.3	8.7	13 20.4	7.6	58.6
	05	254 11.7	28.3	309 57.0	8.8	13 12.8	7.6	58.6
	06	269 11.9	N 5 29.3	324 24.8	8.7	S13 05.2	7.7	58.7
	07	284 12.1	30.2	338 52.5	8.8	12 57.5	7.9	58.7
	08	299 12.2	31.2	353 20.3	8.7	12 49.6	7.9	58.7
	09	314 12.4	. . 32.1	7 48.0	8.7	12 41.7	8.0	58.8
	10	329 12.6	33.1	22 15.7	8.7	12 33.7	8.1	58.8
	11	344 12.8	34.0	36 43.4	8.7	12 25.6	8.2	58.9
	12	359 13.0	N 5 35.0	51 11.1	8.6	S12 17.4	8.2	58.9
	13	14 13.2	35.9	65 38.7	8.7	12 09.2	8.4	58.9
	14	29 13.3	36.9	80 06.4	8.6	12 00.8	8.4	59.0
	15	44 13.5	. . 37.9	94 34.0	8.7	11 52.4	8.5	59.0
	16	59 13.7	38.8	109 01.7	8.6	11 43.9	8.6	59.1
	17	74 13.9	39.8	123 29.3	8.6	11 35.3	8.7	59.1
	18	89 14.1	N 5 40.7	137 56.9	8.6	S11 26.6	8.7	59.1
	19	104 14.2	41.7	152 24.5	8.6	11 17.9	8.8	59.2
	20	119 14.4	42.6	166 52.1	8.5	11 09.1	9.0	59.2
	21	134 14.6	. . 43.6	181 19.6	8.6	11 00.1	8.9	59.2
	22	149 14.8	44.5	195 47.2	8.5	10 51.2	9.1	59.3
	23	164 15.0	45.5	210 14.7	8.5	10 42.1	9.2	59.3
4 MONDAY	00	179 15.1	N 5 46.4	224 42.2	8.5	S10 32.9	9.2	59.4
	01	194 15.3	47.4	239 09.7	8.5	10 23.7	9.3	59.4
	02	209 15.5	48.3	253 37.2	8.5	10 14.4	9.4	59.4
	03	224 15.7	. . 49.3	268 04.7	8.5	10 05.0	9.4	59.5
	04	239 15.9	50.2	282 32.2	8.5	9 55.6	9.5	59.5
	05	254 16.0	51.2	296 59.7	8.4	9 46.1	9.6	59.6
	06	269 16.2	N 5 52.1	311 27.1	8.4	S 9 36.5	9.7	59.6
	07	284 16.4	53.1	325 54.5	8.5	9 26.8	9.8	59.6
	08	299 16.6	54.0	340 22.0	8.4	9 17.0	9.8	59.7
	09	314 16.8	. . 55.0	354 49.4	8.4	9 07.2	9.8	59.7
	10	329 16.9	56.0	9 16.8	8.3	8 57.4	10.0	59.7
	11	344 17.1	56.9	23 44.1	8.4	8 47.4	10.0	59.8
	12	359 17.3	N 5 57.9	38 11.5	8.4	S 8 37.4	10.1	59.8
	13	14 17.5	58.8	52 38.9	8.3	8 27.3	10.1	59.8
	14	29 17.7	5 59.8	67 06.2	8.3	8 17.2	10.2	59.9
	15	44 17.8	6 00.7	81 33.5	8.3	8 07.0	10.3	59.9
	16	59 18.0	01.7	96 00.8	8.3	7 56.7	10.3	60.0
	17	74 18.2	02.6	110 28.1	8.3	7 46.4	10.4	60.0
	18	89 18.4	N 6 03.6	124 55.4	8.3	S 7 36.0	10.5	60.0
	19	104 18.6	04.5	139 22.7	8.2	7 25.5	10.5	60.1
	20	119 18.7	05.5	153 49.9	8.3	7 15.0	10.6	60.1
	21	134 18.9	. . 06.4	168 17.2	8.2	7 04.4	10.6	60.1
	22	149 19.1	07.4	182 44.4	8.2	6 53.8	10.7	60.2
	23	164 19.3	08.3	197 11.6	8.2	6 43.1	10.7	60.2
5 TUESDAY	00	179 19.5	N 6 09.2	211 38.8	8.2	S 6 32.4	10.8	60.2
	01	194 19.6	10.2	226 06.0	8.2	6 21.6	10.9	60.3
	02	209 19.8	11.1	240 33.2	8.1	6 10.7	10.8	60.3
	03	224 20.0	. . 12.1	255 00.3	8.1	5 59.9	11.0	60.3
	04	239 20.2	13.0	269 27.4	8.2	5 48.9	11.0	60.4
	05	254 20.3	14.0	283 54.6	8.1	5 37.9	11.0	60.4
	06	269 20.5	N 6 14.9	298 21.7	8.0	S 5 26.9	11.1	60.4
	07	284 20.7	15.9	312 48.7	8.1	5 15.8	11.2	60.4
	08	299 20.9	16.8	327 15.8	8.1	5 04.6	11.1	60.5
	09	314 21.1	. . 17.8	341 42.9	8.0	4 53.5	11.3	60.5
	10	329 21.2	18.7	356 09.9	8.0	4 42.2	11.2	60.5
	11	344 21.4	19.7	10 36.9	8.0	4 31.0	11.3	60.6
	12	359 21.6	N 6 20.6	25 03.9	8.0	S 4 19.7	11.4	60.6
	13	14 21.8	21.6	39 30.9	8.0	4 08.3	11.3	60.6
	14	29 21.9	22.5	53 57.9	7.9	3 57.0	11.5	60.6
	15	44 22.1	. . 23.5	68 24.8	7.9	3 45.5	11.4	60.7
	16	59 22.3	24.4	82 51.7	7.9	3 34.1	11.5	60.7
	17	74 22.5	25.3	97 18.6	7.9	3 22.6	11.5	60.7
	18	89 22.7	N 6 26.3	111 45.5	7.9	S 3 11.1	11.6	60.8
	19	104 22.8	27.2	126 12.4	7.9	2 59.5	11.5	60.8
	20	119 23.0	28.2	140 39.3	7.8	2 48.0	11.6	60.8
	21	134 23.2	. . 29.1	155 06.1	7.8	2 36.4	11.7	60.8
	22	149 23.4	30.1	169 32.9	7.8	2 24.7	11.6	60.9
	23	164 23.5	31.0	183 59.7	7.8	S 2 13.1	11.7	60.9
		SD 16.0	d 1.0	SD 16.0		16.3		16.5

Lat.	Twilight Naut.	Twilight Civil	Sunrise	Moonrise 3	Moonrise 4	Moonrise 5	Moonrise 6
°	h m	h m	h m	h m	h m	h m	h m
N 72	00 39	03 20	04 38	05 28	05 22	05 17	05 12
N 70	01 51	03 39	04 47	05 03	05 07	05 09	05 11
68	02 27	03 54	04 55	04 44	04 55	05 03	05 10
66	02 51	04 06	05 01	04 29	04 45	04 57	05 08
64	03 10	04 16	05 07	04 16	04 36	04 52	05 08
62	03 25	04 25	05 11	04 05	04 29	04 48	05 07
60	03 37	04 32	05 15	03 56	04 22	04 45	05 06
N 58	03 47	04 38	05 19	03 48	04 16	04 42	05 05
56	03 56	04 43	05 22	03 41	04 11	04 39	05 05
54	04 04	04 48	05 25	03 35	04 07	04 36	05 04
52	04 11	04 53	05 27	03 29	04 03	04 34	05 04
50	04 17	04 57	05 30	03 24	03 59	04 32	05 03
45	04 29	05 05	05 35	03 13	03 51	04 27	05 03
N 40	04 39	05 11	05 39	03 03	03 44	04 23	05 02
35	04 47	05 17	05 42	02 55	03 38	04 20	05 01
30	04 53	05 21	05 45	02 48	03 33	04 17	05 01
20	05 03	05 29	05 51	02 36	03 24	04 12	05 00
N 10	05 10	05 34	05 55	02 25	03 16	04 07	04 59
0	05 15	05 39	06 00	02 15	03 09	04 03	04 58
S 10	05 18	05 43	06 04	02 05	03 01	03 59	04 57
20	05 20	05 46	06 08	01 54	02 53	03 54	04 56
30	05 21	05 49	06 13	01 42	02 44	03 49	04 56
35	05 21	05 50	06 15	01 34	02 39	03 46	04 55
40	05 20	05 51	06 18	01 26	02 33	03 43	04 54
45	05 18	05 52	06 22	01 17	02 26	03 39	04 54
S 50	05 16	05 54	06 26	01 05	02 18	03 34	04 53
52	05 15	05 54	06 28	01 00	02 14	03 32	04 53
54	05 13	05 54	06 30	00 54	02 10	03 29	04 52
56	05 12	05 55	06 32	00 47	02 05	03 27	04 52
58	05 10	05 55	06 34	00 40	02 00	03 24	04 51
S 60	05 07	05 56	06 37	00 31	01 54	03 21	04 51

Lat.	Sunset	Twilight Civil	Twilight Naut.	Moonset 3	Moonset 4	Moonset 5	Moonset 6
°	h m	h m	h m	h m	h m	h m	h m
N 72	19 31	20 51	////	11 43	13 41	15 41	17 41
N 70	19 21	20 30	22 23	12 06	13 55	15 46	17 39
68	19 13	20 15	21 44	12 24	14 06	15 51	17 38
66	19 07	20 02	21 19	12 39	14 14	15 54	17 37
64	19 01	19 52	20 59	12 51	14 22	15 57	17 36
62	18 56	19 43	20 44	13 00	14 28	16 00	17 35
60	18 52	19 36	20 31	13 09	14 34	16 03	17 34
N 58	18 48	19 29	20 21	13 16	14 39	16 05	17 33
56	18 45	19 24	20 11	13 23	14 43	16 06	17 33
54	18 42	19 19	20 03	13 29	14 47	16 08	17 32
52	18 40	19 14	19 57	13 34	14 50	16 10	17 31
50	18 37	19 10	19 50	13 39	14 53	16 11	17 31
45	18 32	19 02	19 38	13 49	15 00	16 14	17 30
N 40	18 28	18 55	19 28	13 58	15 06	16 16	17 29
35	18 24	18 50	19 20	14 05	15 11	16 19	17 28
30	18 21	18 45	19 13	14 11	15 15	16 20	17 28
20	18 15	18 37	19 03	14 22	15 22	16 24	17 26
N 10	18 10	18 32	18 56	14 32	15 28	16 26	17 25
0	18 06	18 27	18 51	14 40	15 34	16 29	17 24
S 10	18 02	18 23	18 47	14 49	15 40	16 31	17 23
20	17 57	18 20	18 45	14 59	15 46	16 34	17 22
30	17 53	18 17	18 44	15 09	15 53	16 37	17 21
35	17 50	18 15	18 44	15 15	15 58	16 39	17 20
40	17 47	18 14	18 45	15 22	16 02	16 41	17 19
45	17 43	18 13	18 46	15 30	16 07	16 43	17 18
S 50	17 39	18 11	18 49	15 40	16 14	16 46	17 17
52	17 37	18 11	18 50	15 44	16 16	16 47	17 17
54	17 35	18 10	18 51	15 49	16 20	16 48	17 16
56	17 33	18 10	18 53	15 54	16 23	16 49	17 15
58	17 30	18 09	18 55	16 00	16 27	16 51	17 15
S 60	17 27	18 09	18 57	16 07	16 31	16 53	17 14

Day	SUN Eqn. of Time 00^h	SUN Eqn. of Time 12^h	SUN Mer. Pass.	MOON Mer. Pass. Upper	MOON Mer. Pass. Lower	Age	Phase
d	m s	m s	h m	h m	h m	d %	
3	03 17	03 08	12 03	08 28	20 54	25 21	
4	03 00	02 51	12 03	09 21	21 49	26 13	
5	02 43	02 34	12 03	10 16	22 43	27 6	

UT	ARIES	VENUS −3·8		MARS −0·7		JUPITER −2·4		SATURN +0·3	
	GHA	GHA	Dec	GHA	Dec	GHA	Dec	GHA	Dec
d h	° ′	° ′	° ′	° ′	° ′	° ′	° ′	° ′	° ′
6 00	194 42.7	193 46.8	S 1 13.5	308 12.6	S20 54.3	28 01.6	N 7 17.0	299 24.2	S20 57.9
01	209 45.2	208 46.4	12.2	323 14.8	54.5	43 04.3	17.1	314 26.7	57.9
02	224 47.7	223 46.0	11.0	338 16.9	54.6	58 07.0	17.2	329 29.2	57.9
03	239 50.1	238 45.7	. . 09.8	353 19.0	. . 54.7	73 09.7	. . 17.2	344 31.7	. . 57.9
04	254 52.6	253 45.3	08.6	8 21.2	54.8	88 12.4	17.3	359 34.3	57.9
05	269 55.1	268 44.9	07.4	23 23.3	54.9	103 15.1	17.4	14 36.8	57.9
W 06	284 57.5	283 44.6	S 1 06.1	38 25.4	S20 55.0	118 17.8	N 7 17.5	29 39.3	S20 57.8
E 07	300 00.0	298 44.2	04.9	53 27.6	55.1	133 20.5	17.6	44 41.8	57.8
D 08	315 02.4	313 43.8	03.7	68 29.7	55.2	148 23.1	17.7	59 44.3	57.8
N 09	330 04.9	328 43.4	. . 02.5	83 31.9	. . 55.4	163 25.8	. . 17.8	74 46.8	. . 57.8
E 10	345 07.4	343 43.1	01.3	98 34.0	55.5	178 28.5	17.8	89 49.3	57.8
S 11	0 09.8	358 42.7	1 00.0	113 36.1	55.6	193 31.2	17.9	104 51.9	57.8
D 12	15 12.3	13 42.3	S 0 58.8	128 38.3	S20 55.7	208 33.9	N 7 18.0	119 54.4	S20 57.8
A 13	30 14.8	28 42.0	57.6	143 40.4	55.8	223 36.6	18.1	134 56.9	57.8
Y 14	45 17.2	43 41.6	56.4	158 42.6	55.9	238 39.2	18.2	149 59.4	57.8
15	60 19.7	58 41.2	. . 55.2	173 44.7	. . 56.0	253 41.9	. . 18.3	165 01.9	. . 57.8
16	75 22.2	73 40.8	53.9	188 46.9	56.1	268 44.6	18.4	180 04.4	57.8
17	90 24.6	88 40.5	52.7	203 49.0	56.2	283 47.3	18.5	195 07.0	57.7
18	105 27.1	103 40.1	S 0 51.5	218 51.1	S20 56.4	298 50.0	N 7 18.5	210 09.5	S20 57.7
19	120 29.6	118 39.7	50.3	233 53.3	56.5	313 52.7	18.6	225 12.0	57.7
20	135 32.0	133 39.4	49.1	248 55.5	56.6	328 55.4	18.7	240 14.5	57.7
21	150 34.5	148 39.0	. . 47.8	263 57.6	. . 56.7	343 58.0	. . 18.8	255 17.0	. . 57.7
22	165 36.9	163 38.6	46.6	278 59.8	56.8	359 00.7	18.9	270 19.6	57.7
23	180 39.4	178 38.2	45.4	294 01.9	56.9	14 03.4	19.0	285 22.1	57.7
7 00	195 41.9	193 37.9	S 0 44.2	309 04.1	S20 57.0	29 06.1	N 7 19.1	300 24.6	S20 57.7
01	210 44.3	208 37.5	43.0	324 06.2	57.1	44 08.8	19.1	315 27.1	57.7
02	225 46.8	223 37.1	41.7	339 08.4	57.2	59 11.4	19.2	330 29.6	57.7
03	240 49.3	238 36.8	. . 40.5	354 10.5	. . 57.4	74 14.1	. . 19.3	345 32.1	. . 57.6
04	255 51.7	253 36.4	39.3	9 12.7	57.5	89 16.8	19.4	0 34.7	57.6
05	270 54.2	268 36.0	38.1	24 14.9	57.6	104 19.5	19.5	15 37.2	57.6
06	285 56.7	283 35.6	S 0 36.8	39 17.0	S20 57.7	119 22.2	N 7 19.6	30 39.7	S20 57.6
T 07	300 59.1	298 35.3	35.6	54 19.2	57.8	134 24.9	19.7	45 42.2	57.6
H 08	316 01.6	313 34.9	34.4	69 21.4	57.9	149 27.5	19.7	60 44.7	57.6
U 09	331 04.0	328 34.5	. . 33.2	84 23.5	. . 58.0	164 30.2	. . 19.8	75 47.3	. . 57.6
R 10	346 06.5	343 34.2	32.0	99 25.7	58.1	179 32.9	19.9	90 49.8	57.6
S 11	1 09.0	358 33.8	30.7	114 27.9	58.2	194 35.6	20.0	105 52.3	57.6
D 12	16 11.4	13 33.4	S 0 29.5	129 30.0	S20 58.3	209 38.3	N 7 20.1	120 54.8	S20 57.6
A 13	31 13.9	28 33.1	28.3	144 32.2	58.4	224 40.9	20.2	135 57.3	57.6
Y 14	46 16.4	43 32.7	27.1	159 34.4	58.6	239 43.6	20.2	150 59.9	57.5
15	61 18.8	58 32.3	. . 25.8	174 36.6	. . 58.7	254 46.3	. . 20.3	166 02.4	. . 57.5
16	76 21.3	73 31.9	24.6	189 38.7	58.8	269 49.0	20.4	181 04.9	57.5
17	91 23.8	88 31.6	23.4	204 40.9	58.9	284 51.6	20.5	196 07.4	57.5
18	106 26.2	103 31.2	S 0 22.2	219 43.1	S20 59.0	299 54.3	N 7 20.6	211 10.0	S20 57.5
19	121 28.7	118 30.8	21.0	234 45.3	59.1	314 57.0	20.7	226 12.5	57.5
20	136 31.2	133 30.5	19.7	249 47.4	59.2	329 59.7	20.7	241 15.0	57.5
21	151 33.6	148 30.1	. . 18.5	264 49.6	. . 59.3	345 02.4	. . 20.8	256 17.5	. . 57.5
22	166 36.1	163 29.7	17.3	279 51.8	59.4	0 05.0	20.9	271 20.0	57.5
23	181 38.5	178 29.4	16.1	294 54.0	59.5	15 07.7	21.0	286 22.6	57.5
8 00	196 41.0	193 29.0	S 0 14.8	309 56.2	S20 59.6	30 10.4	N 7 21.1	301 25.1	S20 57.4
01	211 43.5	208 28.6	13.6	324 58.4	59.7	45 13.1	21.2	316 27.6	57.4
02	226 45.9	223 28.2	12.4	340 00.5	20 59.9	60 15.7	21.2	331 30.1	57.4
03	241 48.4	238 27.9	. . 11.2	355 02.7	21 00.0	75 18.4	. . 21.3	346 32.7	. . 57.4
04	256 50.9	253 27.5	10.0	10 04.9	00.1	90 21.1	21.4	1 35.2	57.4
05	271 53.3	268 27.1	08.7	25 07.1	00.2	105 23.8	21.5	16 37.7	57.4
06	286 55.8	283 26.8	S 0 07.5	40 09.3	S21 00.3	120 26.5	N 7 21.6	31 40.2	S20 57.4
07	301 58.3	298 26.4	06.3	55 11.5	00.4	135 29.1	21.7	46 42.8	57.4
08	317 00.7	313 26.0	05.1	70 13.7	00.5	150 31.8	21.7	61 45.3	57.4
F 09	332 03.2	328 25.7	. . 03.8	85 15.9	. . 00.6	165 34.5	. . 21.8	76 47.8	. . 57.4
R 10	347 05.7	343 25.3	02.6	100 18.1	00.7	180 37.2	21.9	91 50.3	57.3
I 11	2 08.1	358 24.9	01.4	115 20.3	00.8	195 39.8	22.0	106 52.9	57.3
D 12	17 10.6	13 24.5	S 0 00.2	130 22.5	S21 00.9	210 42.5	N 7 22.1	121 55.4	S20 57.3
A 13	32 13.0	28 24.2	N 01.1	145 24.7	01.0	225 45.2	22.2	136 57.9	57.3
Y 14	47 15.5	43 23.8	02.3	160 26.9	01.1	240 47.8	22.2	152 00.4	57.3
15	62 18.0	58 23.4	. . 03.5	175 29.1	. . 01.2	255 50.5	. . 22.3	167 03.0	. . 57.3
16	77 20.4	73 23.1	04.7	190 31.3	01.4	270 53.2	22.4	182 05.5	57.3
17	92 22.9	88 22.7	06.0	205 33.5	01.5	285 55.9	22.5	197 08.0	57.3
18	107 25.4	103 22.3	N 0 07.2	220 35.7	S21 01.6	300 58.5	N 7 22.6	212 10.5	S20 57.3
19	122 27.8	118 22.0	08.4	235 37.9	01.7	316 01.2	22.6	227 13.1	57.3
20	137 30.3	133 21.6	09.6	250 40.1	01.8	331 03.9	22.7	242 15.6	57.2
21	152 32.8	148 21.2	. . 10.8	265 42.3	. . 01.9	346 06.6	. . 22.8	257 18.1	. . 57.2
22	167 35.2	163 20.9	12.1	280 44.5	02.0	1 09.2	22.9	272 20.6	57.2
23	182 37.7	178 20.5	13.3	295 46.8	02.1	16 11.9	23.0	287 23.2	57.2
Mer. Pass.	h m 10 55.4	v −0.4	d 1.2	v 2.2	d 0.1	v 2.7	d 0.1	v 2.5	d 0.0

STARS Name	SHA	Dec
	° ′	° ′
Acamar	315 17.3	S40 14.7
Achernar	335 26.1	S57 09.5
Acrux	173 06.3	S63 11.4
Adhara	255 11.1	S29 00.1
Aldebaran	290 47.4	N16 32.2
Alioth	166 18.6	N55 52.3
Alkaid	152 57.0	N49 13.9
Al Na'ir	27 41.8	S46 52.8
Alnilam	275 44.6	S 1 11.8
Alphard	217 54.1	S 8 44.0
Alphecca	126 09.1	N26 39.6
Alpheratz	357 41.8	N29 10.6
Altair	62 06.4	N 8 54.7
Ankaa	353 14.3	S42 13.2
Antares	112 23.7	S26 27.9
Arcturus	145 53.7	N19 05.9
Atria	107 23.5	S69 03.0
Avior	234 17.0	S59 34.2
Bellatrix	278 30.1	N 6 21.5
Betelgeuse	270 59.4	N 7 24.3
Canopus	263 55.4	S52 42.8
Capella	280 31.9	N46 00.7
Deneb	49 30.3	N45 20.1
Denebola	182 31.5	N14 28.8
Diphda	348 54.4	S17 54.0
Dubhe	193 49.0	N61 39.9
Elnath	278 10.4	N28 37.1
Eltanin	90 45.1	N51 29.1
Enif	33 45.5	N 9 56.9
Fomalhaut	15 22.2	S29 32.2
Gacrux	171 58.1	S57 12.3
Gienah	175 50.0	S17 38.0
Hadar	148 44.5	S60 26.9
Hamal	327 58.9	N23 32.1
Kaus Aust.	83 41.2	S34 22.3
Kochab	137 19.2	N74 05.3
Markab	13 36.7	N15 17.4
Menkar	314 13.4	N 4 08.9
Menkent	148 04.9	S36 26.9
Miaplacidus	221 38.7	S69 47.4
Mirfak	308 38.0	N49 55.0
Nunki	75 56.0	S26 16.4
Peacock	53 16.5	S56 40.6
Pollux	243 25.4	N27 59.1
Procyon	244 57.7	N 5 10.7
Rasalhague	96 04.6	N12 32.9
Regulus	207 41.3	N11 53.1
Rigel	281 10.4	S 8 11.4
Rigil Kent.	139 48.4	S60 53.9
Sabik	102 10.2	S15 44.5
Schedar	349 38.8	N56 37.4
Shaula	96 19.2	S37 06.6
Sirius	258 32.1	S16 44.7
Spica	158 28.9	S11 14.8
Suhail	222 50.8	S43 30.3
Vega	80 37.6	N38 47.8
Zuben'ubi	137 03.0	S16 06.5

	SHA	Mer. Pass.
	° ′	h m
Venus	357 56.0	11 06
Mars	113 22.2	3 23
Jupiter	193 24.2	22 00
Saturn	104 42.7	3 58

UT d h	SUN GHA ° ′	SUN Dec ° ′	MOON GHA ° ′	v ′	MOON Dec ° ′	d ′	HP ′
6 00 (WEDNESDAY)	179 23.7	N 6 32.0	198 26.5	7.7	S 2 01.4	11.7	60.9
01	194 23.9	32.9	212 53.2	7.8	1 49.7	11.7	60.9
02	209 24.1	33.8	227 20.0	7.7	1 38.0	11.8	60.9
03	224 24.2	. . 34.8	241 46.7	7.7	1 26.2	11.7	61.0
04	239 24.4	35.7	256 13.4	7.7	1 14.5	11.8	61.0
05	254 24.6	36.7	270 40.1	7.6	1 02.7	11.8	61.0
06	269 24.8	N 6 37.6	285 06.7	7.7	S 0 50.9	11.8	61.0
07	284 24.9	38.6	299 33.4	7.6	0 39.1	11.9	61.0
08	299 25.1	39.5	314 00.0	7.6	0 27.2	11.8	61.1
09	314 25.3	. . 40.4	328 26.6	7.5	0 15.4	11.8	61.1
10	329 25.5	41.4	342 53.1	7.6	S 0 03.6	11.9	61.1
11	344 25.6	42.3	357 19.7	7.5	N 0 08.3	11.8	61.1
12	359 25.8	N 6 43.3	11 46.2	7.5	N 0 20.1	11.9	61.1
13	14 26.0	44.2	26 12.7	7.5	0 32.0	11.9	61.2
14	29 26.2	45.2	40 39.2	7.4	0 43.9	11.8	61.2
15	44 26.3	. . 46.1	55 05.6	7.5	0 55.7	11.9	61.2
16	59 26.5	47.0	69 32.1	7.4	1 07.6	11.9	61.2
17	74 26.7	48.0	83 58.5	7.3	1 19.5	11.8	61.2
18	89 26.9	N 6 48.9	98 24.8	7.4	N 1 31.3	11.9	61.2
19	104 27.0	49.9	112 51.2	7.3	1 43.2	11.8	61.2
20	119 27.2	50.8	127 17.5	7.4	1 55.0	11.9	61.3
21	134 27.4	. . 51.7	141 43.9	7.2	2 06.9	11.8	61.3
22	149 27.6	52.7	156 10.1	7.3	2 18.7	11.9	61.3
23	164 27.7	53.6	170 36.4	7.3	2 30.6	11.8	61.3
7 00 (THURSDAY)	179 27.9	N 6 54.6	185 02.7	7.2	N 2 42.4	11.8	61.3
01	194 28.1	55.5	199 28.9	7.2	2 54.2	11.8	61.3
02	209 28.3	56.4	213 55.1	7.1	3 06.0	11.7	61.3
03	224 28.4	. . 57.4	228 21.2	7.2	3 17.7	11.8	61.3
04	239 28.6	58.3	242 47.4	7.1	3 29.5	11.7	61.3
05	254 28.8	6 59.2	257 13.5	7.1	3 41.2	11.7	61.3
06	269 29.0	N 7 00.2	271 39.6	7.0	N 3 52.9	11.7	61.4
07	284 29.1	01.1	286 05.6	7.1	4 04.6	11.7	61.4
08	299 29.3	02.1	300 31.7	7.0	4 16.3	11.6	61.4
09	314 29.5	. . 03.0	314 57.7	7.0	4 27.9	11.6	61.4
10	329 29.7	03.9	329 23.7	7.0	4 39.5	11.6	61.4
11	344 29.8	04.9	343 49.7	6.9	4 51.1	11.5	61.4
12	359 30.0	N 7 05.8	358 15.6	6.9	N 5 02.6	11.6	61.4
13	14 30.2	06.7	12 41.5	6.9	5 14.2	11.4	61.4
14	29 30.3	07.7	27 07.4	6.9	5 25.6	11.5	61.4
15	44 30.5	. . 08.6	41 33.3	6.8	5 37.1	11.4	61.4
16	59 30.7	09.6	55 59.1	6.8	5 48.5	11.4	61.4
17	74 30.9	10.5	70 24.9	6.8	5 59.9	11.3	61.4
18	89 31.0	N 7 11.4	84 50.7	6.8	N 6 11.2	11.3	61.4
19	104 31.2	12.4	99 16.5	6.7	6 22.5	11.2	61.4
20	119 31.4	13.3	113 42.2	6.7	6 33.7	11.2	61.4
21	134 31.5	. . 14.2	128 07.9	6.7	6 44.9	11.2	61.4
22	149 31.7	15.2	142 33.6	6.7	6 56.1	11.1	61.4
23	164 31.9	16.1	156 59.3	6.6	7 07.2	11.0	61.4
8 00 (FRIDAY)	179 32.1	N 7 17.0	171 24.9	6.6	N 7 18.2	11.0	61.4
01	194 32.2	18.0	185 50.5	6.6	7 29.2	11.0	61.4
02	209 32.4	18.9	200 16.1	6.6	7 40.2	10.9	61.4
03	224 32.6	. . 19.8	214 41.7	6.5	7 51.1	10.8	61.4
04	239 32.7	20.8	229 07.2	6.5	8 01.9	10.8	61.4
05	254 32.9	21.7	243 32.7	6.5	8 12.7	10.7	61.4
06	269 33.1	N 7 22.6	257 58.2	6.5	N 8 23.4	10.7	61.3
07	284 33.3	23.6	272 23.7	6.4	8 34.1	10.6	61.3
08	299 33.4	24.5	286 49.1	6.4	8 44.7	10.5	61.3
09	314 33.6	. . 25.4	301 14.5	6.4	8 55.2	10.5	61.3
10	329 33.8	26.4	315 39.9	6.4	9 05.7	10.4	61.3
11	344 33.9	27.3	330 05.3	6.3	9 16.1	10.3	61.3
12	359 34.1	N 7 28.2	344 30.6	6.4	N 9 26.4	10.3	61.3
13	14 34.3	29.2	358 56.0	6.3	9 36.7	10.2	61.3
14	29 34.5	30.1	13 21.3	6.2	9 46.9	10.2	61.3
15	44 34.6	. . 31.0	27 46.5	6.3	9 57.1	10.0	61.3
16	59 34.8	32.0	42 11.8	6.2	10 07.1	10.0	61.2
17	74 35.0	32.9	56 37.0	6.2	10 17.1	9.9	61.2
18	89 35.1	N 7 33.8	71 02.2	6.2	N10 27.0	9.8	61.2
19	104 35.3	34.7	85 27.4	6.2	10 36.8	9.8	61.2
20	119 35.5	35.7	99 52.6	6.2	10 46.6	9.7	61.2
21	134 35.6	. . 36.6	114 17.8	6.1	10 56.3	9.6	61.2
22	149 35.8	37.5	128 42.9	6.1	11 05.9	9.5	61.2
23	164 36.0	38.5	143 08.0	6.1	N11 15.4	9.4	61.1
	SD 16.0	d 0.9	SD 16.7		16.7		16.7

Lat. °	Twilight Naut. h m	Twilight Civil h m	Sunrise h m	Moonrise 6 h m	Moonrise 7 h m	Moonrise 8 h m	Moonrise 9 h m
N 72	////	02 59	04 22	05 12	05 08	05 03	04 58
N 70	01 18	03 22	04 33	05 11	05 12	05 15	05 19
68	02 05	03 39	04 42	05 10	05 16	05 24	05 35
66	02 34	03 53	04 50	05 08	05 20	05 32	05 48
64	02 55	04 04	04 56	05 08	05 23	05 39	05 59
62	03 12	04 14	05 01	05 07	05 25	05 45	06 09
60	03 26	04 22	05 06	05 06	05 27	05 50	06 17
N 58	03 37	04 29	05 10	05 05	05 29	05 55	06 24
56	03 47	04 35	05 14	05 05	05 31	05 59	06 30
54	03 56	04 41	05 17	05 04	05 33	06 03	06 36
52	04 03	04 46	05 20	05 04	05 34	06 06	06 41
50	04 10	04 50	05 23	05 03	05 35	06 09	06 46
45	04 23	04 59	05 29	05 03	05 38	06 16	06 56
N 40	04 34	05 06	05 34	05 02	05 41	06 21	07 04
35	04 42	05 13	05 38	05 01	05 43	06 26	07 12
30	04 49	05 18	05 42	05 01	05 45	06 30	07 18
20	05 00	05 26	05 48	05 00	05 48	06 38	07 29
N 10	05 08	05 33	05 54	04 59	05 51	06 44	07 39
0	05 14	05 38	05 59	04 58	05 54	06 51	07 49
S 10	05 18	05 43	06 04	04 57	05 57	06 57	07 58
20	05 21	05 47	06 09	04 56	06 00	07 04	08 08
30	05 23	05 50	06 14	04 56	06 03	07 12	08 20
35	05 23	05 52	06 18	04 55	06 05	07 16	08 27
40	05 23	05 54	06 21	04 54	06 08	07 21	08 34
45	05 22	05 56	06 26	04 54	06 10	07 28	08 43
S 50	05 21	05 58	06 31	04 53	06 14	07 35	08 54
52	05 20	05 59	06 33	04 53	06 15	07 38	08 59
54	05 19	06 00	06 35	04 52	06 17	07 42	09 05
56	05 18	06 01	06 38	04 52	06 19	07 46	09 11
58	05 16	06 02	06 41	04 51	06 21	07 51	09 18
S 60	05 14	06 03	06 44	04 51	06 23	07 56	09 26

Lat. °	Sunset h m	Twilight Civil h m	Twilight Naut. h m	Moonset 6 h m	Moonset 7 h m	Moonset 8 h m	Moonset 9 h m
N 72	19 46	21 10	////	17 41	19 44	21 50	23 58
N 70	19 34	20 46	23 00	17 39	19 35	21 31	23 25
68	19 24	20 28	22 06	17 38	19 27	21 16	23 02
66	19 17	20 14	21 35	17 37	19 21	21 04	22 44
64	19 10	20 02	21 12	17 36	19 15	20 54	22 29
62	19 04	19 52	20 55	17 35	19 10	20 46	22 17
60	18 59	19 44	20 41	17 34	19 06	20 38	22 06
N 58	18 55	19 37	20 29	17 33	19 03	20 32	21 57
56	18 51	19 30	20 19	17 33	19 00	20 26	21 49
54	18 48	19 25	20 10	17 32	18 57	20 21	21 42
52	18 45	19 20	20 03	17 31	18 54	20 17	21 36
50	18 42	19 15	19 56	17 31	18 52	20 12	21 30
45	18 36	19 06	19 42	17 30	18 47	20 04	21 18
N 40	18 31	18 58	19 31	17 29	18 43	19 56	21 08
35	18 26	18 52	19 23	17 28	18 39	19 50	20 59
30	18 23	18 47	19 15	17 28	18 36	19 44	20 52
20	18 16	18 38	19 04	17 26	18 30	19 35	20 39
N 10	18 10	18 32	18 56	17 25	18 25	19 26	20 27
0	18 05	18 26	18 50	17 24	18 21	19 18	20 16
S 10	18 00	18 21	18 46	17 23	18 16	19 10	20 06
20	17 55	18 17	18 43	17 22	18 11	19 02	19 54
30	17 49	18 13	18 41	17 21	18 06	18 52	19 41
35	17 46	18 11	18 40	17 20	18 02	18 47	19 34
40	17 42	18 09	18 41	17 19	17 59	18 40	19 25
45	17 38	18 07	18 41	17 18	17 55	18 33	19 15
S 50	17 33	18 05	18 42	17 17	17 50	18 25	19 03
52	17 30	18 04	18 43	17 17	17 47	18 21	18 58
54	17 28	18 03	18 44	17 16	17 45	18 16	18 52
56	17 25	18 02	18 45	17 15	17 42	18 11	18 45
58	17 22	18 01	18 46	17 15	17 39	18 06	18 37
S 60	17 18	18 00	18 48	17 14	17 36	18 00	18 29

Day	SUN Eqn. of Time 00^h	SUN Eqn. of Time 12^h	SUN Mer. Pass.	MOON Mer. Pass. Upper	MOON Mer. Pass. Lower	MOON Age	MOON Phase
d	m s	m s	h m	h m	h m	d	%
6	02 26	02 17	12 02	11 11	23 39	28	1
7	02 09	02 00	12 02	12 07	24 36	00	0
8	01 52	01 44	12 02	13 04	00 36	01	2

UT (d h)	ARIES GHA	VENUS −3·8 GHA	VENUS Dec	MARS −0·8 GHA	MARS Dec	JUPITER −2·4 GHA	JUPITER Dec	SATURN +0·3 GHA	SATURN Dec
	° ′	° ′	° ′	° ′	° ′	° ′	° ′	° ′	° ′
9 00 (SATURDAY)	197 40.1	193 20.1	N 0 14.5	310 49.0	S21 02.2	31 14.6	N 7 23.0	302 25.7	S20 57.2
01	212 42.6	208 19.7	15.7	325 51.2	02.3	46 17.2	23.1	317 28.2	57.2
02	227 45.1	223 19.4	17.0	340 53.4	02.4	61 19.9	23.2	332 30.7	57.2
03	242 47.5	238 19.0	. . 18.2	355 55.6	. . 02.5	76 22.6	. . 23.3	347 33.3	. . 57.2
04	257 50.0	253 18.6	19.4	10 57.8	02.6	91 25.3	23.4	2 35.8	57.2
05	272 52.5	268 18.3	20.6	26 00.1	02.7	106 27.9	23.4	17 38.3	57.2
06	287 54.9	283 17.9	N 0 21.9	41 02.3	S21 02.8	121 30.6	N 7 23.5	32 40.9	S20 57.1
07	302 57.4	298 17.5	23.1	56 04.5	02.9	136 33.3	23.6	47 43.4	57.1
08	317 59.9	313 17.2	24.3	71 06.7	03.0	151 35.9	23.7	62 45.9	57.1
09	333 02.3	328 16.8	. . 25.5	86 09.0	. . 03.1	166 38.6	. . 23.8	77 48.4	. . 57.1
10	348 04.8	343 16.4	26.8	101 11.2	03.2	181 41.3	23.8	92 51.0	57.1
11	3 07.3	358 16.1	28.0	116 13.4	03.3	196 43.9	23.9	107 53.5	57.1
12	18 09.7	13 15.7	N 0 29.2	131 15.6	S21 03.4	211 46.6	N 7 24.0	122 56.0	S20 57.1
13	33 12.2	28 15.3	30.4	146 17.9	03.5	226 49.3	24.1	137 58.6	57.1
14	48 14.6	43 15.0	31.6	161 20.1	03.7	241 51.9	24.2	153 01.1	57.1
15	63 17.1	58 14.6	. . 32.9	176 22.3	. . 03.8	256 54.6	. . 24.2	168 03.6	. . 57.1
16	78 19.6	73 14.2	34.1	191 24.6	03.9	271 57.3	24.3	183 06.1	57.0
17	93 22.0	88 13.8	35.3	206 26.8	04.0	287 00.0	24.4	198 08.7	57.0
18	108 24.5	103 13.5	N 0 36.5	221 29.0	S21 04.1	302 02.6	N 7 24.5	213 11.2	S20 57.0
19	123 27.0	118 13.1	37.8	236 31.3	04.2	317 05.3	24.6	228 13.7	57.0
20	138 29.4	133 12.7	39.0	251 33.5	04.3	332 08.0	24.6	243 16.3	57.0
21	153 31.9	148 12.4	. . 40.2	266 35.7	. . 04.4	347 10.6	. . 24.7	258 18.8	. . 57.0
22	168 34.4	163 12.0	41.4	281 38.0	04.5	2 13.3	24.8	273 21.3	57.0
23	183 36.8	178 11.6	42.7	296 40.2	04.6	17 16.0	24.9	288 23.9	57.0
10 00 (SUNDAY)	198 39.3	193 11.3	N 0 43.9	311 42.5	S21 04.7	32 18.6	N 7 24.9	303 26.4	S20 57.0
01	213 41.7	208 10.9	45.1	326 44.7	04.8	47 21.3	25.0	318 28.9	57.0
02	228 44.2	223 10.5	46.3	341 47.0	04.9	62 23.9	25.1	333 31.4	56.9
03	243 46.7	238 10.2	. . 47.6	356 49.2	. . 05.0	77 26.6	. . 25.2	348 34.0	. . 56.9
04	258 49.1	253 09.8	48.8	11 51.5	05.1	92 29.3	25.3	3 36.5	56.9
05	273 51.6	268 09.4	50.0	26 53.7	05.2	107 31.9	25.3	18 39.0	56.9
06	288 54.1	283 09.1	N 0 51.2	41 56.0	S21 05.3	122 34.6	N 7 25.4	33 41.6	S20 56.9
07	303 56.5	298 08.7	52.5	56 58.2	05.4	137 37.3	25.5	48 44.1	56.9
08	318 59.0	313 08.3	53.7	72 00.5	05.5	152 39.9	25.6	63 46.6	56.9
09	334 01.5	328 08.0	. . 54.9	87 02.7	. . 05.6	167 42.6	. . 25.6	78 49.2	. . 56.9
10	349 03.9	343 07.6	56.1	102 05.0	05.7	182 45.3	25.7	93 51.7	56.9
11	4 06.4	358 07.2	57.3	117 07.2	05.8	197 47.9	25.8	108 54.2	56.8
12	19 08.9	13 06.8	N 0 58.6	132 09.5	S21 05.9	212 50.6	N 7 25.9	123 56.8	S20 56.8
13	34 11.3	28 06.5	0 59.8	147 11.7	06.0	227 53.2	25.9	138 59.3	56.8
14	49 13.8	43 06.1	1 01.0	162 14.0	06.1	242 55.9	26.0	154 01.8	56.8
15	64 16.2	58 05.7	. . 02.2	177 16.3	. . 06.2	257 58.6	. . 26.1	169 04.4	. . 56.8
16	79 18.7	73 05.4	03.5	192 18.5	06.3	273 01.2	26.2	184 06.9	56.8
17	94 21.2	88 05.0	04.7	207 20.8	06.4	288 03.9	26.2	199 09.4	56.8
18	109 23.6	103 04.6	N 1 05.9	222 23.1	S21 06.5	303 06.6	N 7 26.3	214 12.0	S20 56.8
19	124 26.1	118 04.3	07.1	237 25.3	06.6	318 09.2	26.4	229 14.5	56.8
20	139 28.6	133 03.9	08.4	252 27.6	06.7	333 11.9	26.5	244 17.0	56.8
21	154 31.0	148 03.5	. . 09.6	267 29.9	. . 06.8	348 14.5	. . 26.6	259 19.6	. . 56.7
22	169 33.5	163 03.2	10.8	282 32.1	06.9	3 17.2	26.6	274 22.1	56.7
23	184 36.0	178 02.8	12.0	297 34.4	07.0	18 19.9	26.7	289 24.6	56.7
11 00 (MONDAY)	199 38.4	193 02.4	N 1 13.3	312 36.7	S21 07.1	33 22.5	N 7 26.8	304 27.2	S20 56.7
01	214 40.9	208 02.1	14.5	327 39.0	07.2	48 25.2	26.9	319 29.7	56.7
02	229 43.4	223 01.7	15.7	342 41.2	07.3	63 27.8	26.9	334 32.3	56.7
03	244 45.8	238 01.3	. . 16.9	357 43.5	. . 07.4	78 30.5	. . 27.0	349 34.8	. . 56.7
04	259 48.3	253 00.9	18.2	12 45.8	07.5	93 33.2	27.1	4 37.3	56.7
05	274 50.7	268 00.6	19.4	27 48.1	07.6	108 35.8	27.2	19 39.9	56.7
06	289 53.2	283 00.2	N 1 20.6	42 50.4	S21 07.7	123 38.5	N 7 27.2	34 42.4	S20 56.6
07	304 55.7	297 59.8	21.8	57 52.6	07.8	138 41.1	27.3	49 44.9	56.6
08	319 58.1	312 59.5	23.0	72 54.9	07.9	153 43.8	27.4	64 47.5	56.6
09	335 00.6	327 59.1	. . 24.3	87 57.2	. . 08.0	168 46.5	. . 27.4	79 50.0	. . 56.6
10	350 03.1	342 58.7	25.5	102 59.5	08.1	183 49.1	27.5	94 52.5	56.6
11	5 05.5	357 58.4	26.7	118 01.8	08.2	198 51.8	27.6	109 55.1	56.6
12	20 08.0	12 58.0	N 1 27.9	133 04.1	S21 08.3	213 54.4	N 7 27.7	124 57.6	S20 56.6
13	35 10.5	27 57.6	29.2	148 06.4	08.4	228 57.1	27.7	140 00.2	56.6
14	50 12.9	42 57.3	30.4	163 08.6	08.5	243 59.7	27.8	155 02.7	56.6
15	65 15.4	57 56.9	. . 31.6	178 10.9	. . 08.6	259 02.4	. . 27.9	170 05.2	. . 56.5
16	80 17.9	72 56.5	32.8	193 13.2	08.7	274 05.0	28.0	185 07.8	56.5
17	95 20.3	87 56.2	34.1	208 15.5	08.8	289 07.7	28.0	200 10.3	56.5
18	110 22.8	102 55.8	N 1 35.3	223 17.8	S21 08.9	304 10.4	N 7 28.1	215 12.8	S20 56.5
19	125 25.2	117 55.4	36.5	238 20.1	09.0	319 13.0	28.2	230 15.4	56.5
20	140 27.7	132 55.0	37.7	253 22.4	09.1	334 15.7	28.3	245 17.9	56.5
21	155 30.2	147 54.7	. . 39.0	268 24.7	. . 09.2	349 18.3	. . 28.3	260 20.5	. . 56.5
22	170 32.6	162 54.3	40.2	283 27.0	09.3	4 21.0	28.4	275 23.0	56.5
23	185 35.1	177 53.9	41.4	298 29.3	09.4	19 23.6	28.5	290 25.5	56.5
Mer. Pass.	h m 10 43.6	v −0.4	d 1.2	v 2.3	d 0.1	v 2.7	d 0.1	v 2.5	d 0.0

STARS

Name	SHA	Dec
	° ′	° ′
Acamar	315 17.3	S40 14.7
Achernar	335 26.1	S57 09.4
Acrux	173 06.3	S63 11.4
Adhara	255 11.1	S29 00.1
Aldebaran	290 47.4	N16 32.2
Alioth	166 18.6	N55 52.3
Alkaid	152 57.0	N49 13.9
Al Na'ir	27 41.7	S46 52.8
Alnilam	275 44.6	S 1 11.8
Alphard	217 54.1	S 8 44.0
Alphecca	126 09.1	N26 39.6
Alpheratz	357 41.8	N29 10.6
Altair	62 06.4	N 8 54.7
Ankaa	353 14.3	S42 13.1
Antares	112 23.7	S26 27.9
Arcturus	145 53.7	N19 05.9
Atria	107 23.4	S69 03.0
Avior	234 17.0	S59 34.2
Bellatrix	278 30.1	N 6 21.5
Betelgeuse	270 59.4	N 7 24.3
Canopus	263 55.4	S52 42.8
Capella	280 31.9	N46 00.7
Deneb	49 30.3	N45 20.1
Denebola	182 31.5	N14 28.8
Diphda	348 54.3	S17 54.0
Dubhe	193 49.0	N61 39.9
Elnath	278 10.4	N28 37.1
Eltanin	90 45.1	N51 29.1
Enif	33 45.4	N 9 56.9
Fomalhaut	15 22.2	S29 32.1
Gacrux	171 58.1	S57 12.3
Gienah	175 50.0	S17 38.0
Hadar	148 44.4	S60 27.0
Hamal	327 58.9	N23 32.1
Kaus Aust.	83 41.2	S34 22.3
Kochab	137 19.2	N74 05.3
Markab	13 36.7	N15 17.4
Menkar	314 13.4	N 4 08.9
Menkent	148 04.9	S36 26.9
Miaplacidus	221 38.7	S69 47.5
Mirfak	308 38.0	N49 55.0
Nunki	75 55.9	S26 16.3
Peacock	53 16.5	S56 40.6
Pollux	243 25.4	N27 59.1
Procyon	244 57.8	N 5 10.7
Rasalhague	96 04.5	N12 32.9
Regulus	207 41.3	N11 53.1
Rigel	281 10.4	S 8 11.3
Rigil Kent.	139 48.4	S60 53.9
Sabik	102 10.2	S15 44.5
Schedar	349 38.8	N56 37.4
Shaula	96 19.2	S37 06.6
Sirius	258 32.1	S16 44.7
Spica	158 28.9	S11 14.8
Suhail	222 50.8	S43 30.3
Vega	80 37.6	N38 47.8
Zuben'ubi	137 03.0	S16 06.5

	SHA	Mer. Pass.
	° ′	h m
Venus	354 32.0	11 08
Mars	113 03.2	3 13
Jupiter	193 39.3	21 47
Saturn	104 47.1	3 46

UT d h		SUN GHA ° ′	SUN Dec ° ′	MOON GHA ° ′	v ′	MOON Dec ° ′	d ′	HP ′
9 00		179 36.2	N 7 39.4	157 33.1	6.1	N11 24.8	9.4	61.1
01		194 36.3	40.3	171 58.2	6.0	11 34.2	9.2	61.1
02		209 36.5	41.2	186 23.2	6.1	11 43.4	9.2	61.1
03		224 36.7	. . 42.2	200 48.3	6.0	11 52.6	9.1	61.1
04		239 36.8	43.1	215 13.3	6.0	12 01.7	9.0	61.1
05		254 37.0	44.0	229 38.3	6.0	12 10.7	8.9	61.0
06		269 37.2	N 7 45.0	244 03.3	6.0	N12 19.6	8.8	61.0
07		284 37.3	45.9	258 28.3	6.0	12 28.4	8.7	61.0
08	S	299 37.5	46.8	272 53.3	5.9	12 37.1	8.7	61.0
09	A	314 37.7	. . 47.7	287 18.2	5.9	12 45.8	8.5	61.0
10	T	329 37.8	48.7	301 43.1	6.0	12 54.3	8.4	60.9
11	U	344 38.0	49.6	316 08.1	5.9	13 02.7	8.4	60.9
12	R	359 38.2	N 7 50.5	330 33.0	5.9	N13 11.1	8.2	60.9
13	D	14 38.3	51.4	344 57.9	5.8	13 19.3	8.2	60.9
14	A	29 38.5	52.4	359 22.7	5.9	13 27.5	8.0	60.8
15	Y	44 38.7	. . 53.3	13 47.6	5.9	13 35.5	7.9	60.8
16		59 38.8	54.2	28 12.5	5.8	13 43.4	7.9	60.8
17		74 39.0	55.1	42 37.3	5.9	13 51.3	7.7	60.8
18		89 39.2	N 7 56.1	57 02.2	5.8	N13 59.0	7.7	60.7
19		104 39.3	57.0	71 27.0	5.9	14 06.7	7.5	60.7
20		119 39.5	57.9	85 51.9	5.8	14 14.2	7.4	60.7
21		134 39.7	. . 58.8	100 16.7	5.8	14 21.6	7.4	60.7
22		149 39.8	7 59.8	114 41.5	5.8	14 29.0	7.2	60.6
23		164 40.0	8 00.7	129 06.3	5.8	14 36.2	7.1	60.6
10 00		179 40.2	N 8 01.6	143 31.1	5.8	N14 43.3	7.0	60.6
01		194 40.3	02.5	157 55.9	5.9	14 50.3	6.9	60.6
02		209 40.5	03.5	172 20.8	5.8	14 57.2	6.8	60.5
03		224 40.7	. . 04.4	186 45.6	5.8	15 04.0	6.6	60.5
04		239 40.8	05.3	201 10.4	5.8	15 10.6	6.6	60.5
05		254 41.0	06.2	215 35.2	5.8	15 17.2	6.4	60.4
06		269 41.2	N 8 07.2	230 00.0	5.8	N15 23.6	6.4	60.4
07		284 41.3	08.1	244 24.8	5.8	15 30.0	6.2	60.4
08		299 41.5	09.0	258 49.6	5.8	15 36.2	6.1	60.3
09	S	314 41.7	. . 09.9	273 14.4	5.8	15 42.3	6.0	60.3
10	U	329 41.8	10.8	287 39.2	5.8	15 48.3	5.9	60.3
11	N	344 42.0	11.8	302 04.0	5.9	15 54.2	5.8	60.3
12	D	359 42.2	N 8 12.7	316 28.9	5.8	N16 00.0	5.6	60.2
13	A	14 42.3	13.6	330 53.7	5.8	16 05.6	5.5	60.2
14	Y	29 42.5	14.5	345 18.5	5.9	16 11.1	5.5	60.2
15		44 42.7	. . 15.4	359 43.4	5.8	16 16.6	5.3	60.1
16		59 42.8	16.4	14 08.2	5.9	16 21.9	5.2	60.1
17		74 43.0	17.3	28 33.1	5.9	16 27.1	5.0	60.1
18		89 43.2	N 8 18.2	42 58.0	5.9	N16 32.1	5.0	60.0
19		104 43.3	19.1	57 22.9	5.9	16 37.1	4.8	60.0
20		119 43.5	20.0	71 47.8	5.9	16 41.9	4.7	60.0
21		134 43.6	. . 21.0	86 12.7	6.0	16 46.6	4.6	59.9
22		149 43.8	21.9	100 37.7	5.9	16 51.2	4.5	59.9
23		164 44.0	22.8	115 02.6	6.0	16 55.7	4.4	59.9
11 00		179 44.1	N 8 23.7	129 27.6	6.0	N17 00.1	4.2	59.8
01		194 44.3	24.6	143 52.6	6.0	17 04.3	4.1	59.8
02		209 44.5	25.5	158 17.6	6.0	17 08.4	4.0	59.7
03		224 44.6	. . 26.5	172 42.6	6.0	17 12.4	3.9	59.7
04		239 44.8	27.4	187 07.6	6.1	17 16.3	3.7	59.7
05		254 45.0	28.3	201 32.7	6.1	17 20.0	3.7	59.6
06		269 45.1	N 8 29.2	215 57.8	6.1	N17 23.7	3.5	59.6
07		284 45.3	30.1	230 22.9	6.2	17 27.2	3.4	59.6
08		299 45.4	31.0	244 48.1	6.1	17 30.6	3.3	59.5
09	M	314 45.6	. . 32.0	259 13.2	6.2	17 33.9	3.1	59.5
10	O	329 45.8	32.9	273 38.4	6.2	17 37.0	3.1	59.5
11	N	344 45.9	33.8	288 03.6	6.3	17 40.1	2.9	59.4
12	D	359 46.1	N 8 34.7	302 28.9	6.3	N17 43.0	2.8	59.4
13	A	14 46.3	35.6	316 54.2	6.3	17 45.8	2.6	59.3
14	Y	29 46.4	36.5	331 19.5	6.3	17 48.4	2.6	59.3
15		44 46.6	. . 37.4	345 44.8	6.4	17 51.0	2.4	59.3
16		59 46.7	38.4	0 10.2	6.4	17 53.4	2.4	59.2
17		74 46.9	39.3	14 35.6	6.4	17 55.8	2.1	59.2
18		89 47.1	N 8 40.2	29 01.0	6.5	N17 57.9	2.1	59.2
19		104 47.2	41.1	43 26.5	6.5	18 00.0	2.0	59.1
20		119 47.4	42.0	57 52.0	6.6	18 02.0	1.8	59.1
21		134 47.5	. . 42.9	72 17.6	6.5	18 03.8	1.7	59.0
22		149 47.7	43.8	86 43.1	6.7	18 05.5	1.6	59.0
23		164 47.9	44.7	101 08.8	6.6	N18 07.1	1.5	59.0
		SD 16.0	*d* 0.9	SD 16.6		16.4		16.2

Lat. °	Twilight Naut. h m	Twilight Civil h m	Sunrise h m	Moonrise 9 h m	Moonrise 10 h m	Moonrise 11 h m	Moonrise 12 h m
N 72	////	02 37	04 05	04 58	04 53	04 46	▭
N 70	////	03 04	04 18	05 19	05 26	05 42	06 16
68	01 39	03 24	04 29	05 35	05 51	06 16	06 57
66	02 15	03 40	04 38	05 48	06 10	06 41	07 25
64	02 40	03 53	04 45	05 59	06 25	07 00	07 47
62	02 59	04 03	04 52	06 09	06 38	07 16	08 04
60	03 14	04 12	04 57	06 17	06 49	07 29	08 19
N 58	03 27	04 20	05 02	06 24	06 58	07 40	08 31
56	03 38	04 27	05 06	06 30	07 07	07 50	08 41
54	03 47	04 33	05 10	06 36	07 14	07 59	08 51
52	03 55	04 38	05 14	06 41	07 21	08 07	08 59
50	04 02	04 43	05 17	06 46	07 27	08 14	09 07
45	04 17	04 53	05 24	06 56	07 40	08 29	09 23
N 40	04 29	05 02	05 29	07 04	07 51	08 42	09 36
35	04 38	05 08	05 34	07 12	08 00	08 52	09 47
30	04 45	05 14	05 38	07 18	08 09	09 02	09 57
20	04 57	05 23	05 46	07 29	08 23	09 18	10 14
N 10	05 06	05 31	05 52	07 39	08 35	09 32	10 29
0	05 13	05 37	05 58	07 49	08 47	09 46	10 43
S 10	05 18	05 42	06 04	07 58	08 59	09 59	10 57
20	05 22	05 47	06 10	08 08	09 12	10 13	11 11
30	05 24	05 52	06 16	08 20	09 26	10 30	11 28
35	05 25	05 55	06 20	08 27	09 35	10 39	11 38
40	05 26	05 57	06 24	08 34	09 45	10 50	11 50
45	05 26	06 00	06 29	08 43	09 56	11 03	12 03
S 50	05 25	06 03	06 35	08 54	10 10	11 19	12 19
52	05 25	06 04	06 38	08 59	10 16	11 26	12 27
54	05 24	06 05	06 41	09 05	10 24	11 35	12 36
56	05 23	06 06	06 44	09 11	10 32	11 44	12 45
58	05 23	06 08	06 48	09 18	10 41	11 54	12 56
S 60	05 21	06 10	06 52	09 26	10 51	12 06	13 09

Lat. °	Sunset h m	Twilight Civil h m	Twilight Naut. h m	Moonset 9 h m	Moonset 10 h m	Moonset 11 h m	Moonset 12 h m
N 72	20 01	21 31	////	23 58	26 08	02 08	▭
N 70	19 47	21 03	////	23 25	25 12	01 12	02 38
68	19 36	20 42	22 32	23 02	24 38	00 38	01 57
66	19 27	20 25	21 53	22 44	24 14	00 14	01 29
64	19 19	20 12	21 26	22 29	23 55	25 08	01 08
62	19 12	20 01	21 07	22 17	23 40	24 50	00 50
60	19 07	19 52	20 51	22 06	23 27	24 36	00 36
N 58	19 02	19 44	20 38	21 57	23 16	24 24	00 24
56	18 57	19 37	20 27	21 49	23 06	24 13	00 13
54	18 53	19 31	20 17	21 42	22 58	24 04	00 04
52	18 50	19 25	20 09	21 36	22 50	23 56	24 52
50	18 47	19 20	20 02	21 30	22 43	23 48	24 44
45	18 40	19 10	19 46	21 18	22 28	23 32	24 28
N 40	18 34	19 02	19 35	21 08	22 16	23 19	24 15
35	18 29	18 55	19 25	20 59	22 06	23 08	24 04
30	18 24	18 49	19 17	20 52	21 57	22 58	23 55
20	18 17	18 39	19 05	20 39	21 41	22 41	23 38
N 10	18 10	18 32	18 56	20 27	21 28	22 27	23 23
0	18 04	18 25	18 50	20 16	21 15	22 13	23 09
S 10	17 59	18 20	18 44	20 06	21 02	21 59	22 55
20	17 53	18 15	18 40	19 54	20 49	21 45	22 41
30	17 46	18 10	18 38	19 41	20 33	21 28	22 24
35	17 42	18 07	18 37	19 34	20 24	21 18	22 14
40	17 37	18 05	18 36	19 25	20 14	21 07	22 03
45	17 32	18 02	18 36	19 15	20 02	20 54	21 49
S 50	17 26	17 59	18 36	19 03	19 48	20 37	21 33
52	17 24	17 58	18 37	18 58	19 41	20 30	21 25
54	17 21	17 56	18 37	18 52	19 33	20 22	21 17
56	17 17	17 55	18 38	18 45	19 25	20 12	21 07
58	17 14	17 53	18 39	18 37	19 15	20 02	20 57
S 60	17 10	17 52	18 40	18 29	19 05	19 49	20 44

Day d	SUN Eqn. of Time 00^h m s	SUN Eqn. of Time 12^h m s	SUN Mer. Pass. h m	MOON Mer. Pass. Upper h m	MOON Mer. Pass. Lower h m	MOON Age d	MOON Phase %
9	01 36	01 28	12 01	14 03	01 33	02	6
10	01 20	01 12	12 01	15 01	02 32	03	13
11	01 04	00 56	12 01	15 59	03 30	04	22

2016 APRIL 12, 13, 14 (TUES., WED., THURS.)

UT d	h	ARIES GHA	VENUS −3·8 GHA	VENUS Dec	MARS −0·9 GHA	MARS Dec	JUPITER −2·4 GHA	JUPITER Dec	SATURN +0·3 GHA	SATURN Dec	STARS Name	SHA	Dec
		° ′	° ′	° ′	° ′	° ′	° ′	° ′	° ′	° ′		° ′	° ′
12	00	200 37.6	192 53.6	N 1 42.6	313 31.6	S21 09.5	34 26.3	N 7 28.6	305 28.1	S20 56.4	Acamar	315 17.3	S40 14.7
	01	215 40.0	207 53.2	43.8	328 33.9	09.6	49 28.9	28.6	320 30.6	56.4	Achernar	335 26.1	S57 09.4
	02	230 42.5	222 52.8	45.1	343 36.2	09.7	64 31.6	28.7	335 33.2	56.4	Acrux	173 06.3	S63 11.5
	03	245 45.0	237 52.5	. . 46.3	358 38.5	. . 09.8	79 34.2	. . 28.8	350 35.7	. . 56.4	Adhara	255 11.1	S29 00.1
	04	260 47.4	252 52.1	47.5	13 40.8	09.9	94 36.9	28.8	5 38.2	56.4	Aldebaran	290 47.4	N16 32.2
	05	275 49.9	267 51.7	48.7	28 43.2	09.9	109 39.6	28.9	20 40.8	56.4			
	06	290 52.3	282 51.4	N 1 50.0	43 45.5	S21 10.0	124 42.2	N 7 29.0	35 43.3	S20 56.4	Alioth	166 18.6	N55 52.3
	07	305 54.8	297 51.0	51.2	58 47.8	10.1	139 44.9	29.1	50 45.9	56.4	Alkaid	152 57.0	N49 13.9
T	08	320 57.3	312 50.6	52.4	73 50.1	10.2	154 47.5	29.1	65 48.4	56.4	Al Na'ir	27 41.7	S46 52.7
U	09	335 59.7	327 50.3	. . 53.6	88 52.4	. . 10.3	169 50.2	. . 29.2	80 50.9	. . 56.3	Alnilam	275 44.6	S 1 11.8
E	10	351 02.2	342 49.9	54.9	103 54.7	10.4	184 52.8	29.3	95 53.5	56.3	Alphard	217 54.1	S 8 44.0
S	11	6 04.7	357 49.5	56.1	118 57.0	10.5	199 55.5	29.3	110 56.0	56.3			
D	12	21 07.1	12 49.1	N 1 57.3	133 59.4	S21 10.6	214 58.1	N 7 29.4	125 58.6	S20 56.3	Alphecca	126 09.1	N26 39.6
A	13	36 09.6	27 48.8	58.5	149 01.7	10.7	230 00.8	29.5	141 01.1	56.3	Alpheratz	357 41.8	N29 10.6
Y	14	51 12.1	42 48.4	1 59.7	164 04.0	10.8	245 03.4	29.6	156 03.7	56.3	Altair	62 06.4	N 8 54.7
	15	66 14.5	57 48.0	2 01.0	179 06.3	. . 10.9	260 06.1	. . 29.6	171 06.2	. . 56.3	Ankaa	353 14.3	S42 13.1
	16	81 17.0	72 47.7	02.2	194 08.7	11.0	275 08.7	29.7	186 08.7	56.3	Antares	112 23.7	S26 27.9
	17	96 19.5	87 47.3	03.4	209 11.0	11.1	290 11.4	29.8	201 11.3	56.3			
	18	111 21.9	102 46.9	N 2 04.6	224 13.3	S21 11.2	305 14.0	N 7 29.8	216 13.8	S20 56.2	Arcturus	145 53.7	N19 05.9
	19	126 24.4	117 46.6	05.9	239 15.6	11.3	320 16.7	29.9	231 16.4	56.2	Atria	107 23.4	S69 03.0
	20	141 26.8	132 46.2	07.1	254 18.0	11.4	335 19.3	30.0	246 18.9	56.2	Avior	234 17.1	S59 34.2
	21	156 29.3	147 45.8	. . 08.3	269 20.3	. . 11.5	350 22.0	. . 30.0	261 21.4	. . 56.2	Bellatrix	278 30.2	N 6 21.5
	22	171 31.8	162 45.4	09.5	284 22.6	11.6	5 24.6	30.1	276 24.0	56.2	Betelgeuse	270 59.4	N 7 24.3
	23	186 34.2	177 45.1	10.7	299 25.0	11.7	20 27.3	30.2	291 26.5	56.2			
13	00	201 36.7	192 44.7	N 2 12.0	314 27.3	S21 11.8	35 29.9	N 7 30.3	306 29.1	S20 56.2	Canopus	263 55.5	S52 42.8
	01	216 39.2	207 44.3	13.2	329 29.6	11.9	50 32.6	30.3	321 31.6	56.2	Capella	280 31.9	N46 00.7
	02	231 41.6	222 44.0	14.4	344 32.0	11.9	65 35.2	30.4	336 34.2	56.2	Deneb	49 30.3	N45 20.1
	03	246 44.1	237 43.6	. . 15.6	359 34.3	. . 12.0	80 37.9	. . 30.5	351 36.7	. . 56.1	Denebola	182 31.5	N14 28.8
	04	261 46.6	252 43.2	16.9	14 36.6	12.1	95 40.5	30.5	6 39.3	56.1	Diphda	348 54.3	S17 54.0
	05	276 49.0	267 42.9	18.1	29 39.0	12.2	110 43.1	30.6	21 41.8	56.1			
	06	291 51.5	282 42.5	N 2 19.3	44 41.3	S21 12.3	125 45.8	N 7 30.7	36 44.3	S20 56.1	Dubhe	193 49.0	N61 39.9
W	07	306 54.0	297 42.1	20.5	59 43.7	12.4	140 48.4	30.7	51 46.9	56.1	Elnath	278 10.4	N28 37.1
E	08	321 56.4	312 41.7	21.7	74 46.0	12.5	155 51.1	30.8	66 49.4	56.1	Eltanin	90 45.0	N51 29.1
D	09	336 58.9	327 41.4	. . 23.0	89 48.4	. . 12.6	170 53.7	. . 30.9	81 52.0	. . 56.1	Enif	33 45.4	N 9 56.9
N	10	352 01.3	342 41.0	24.2	104 50.7	12.7	185 56.4	31.0	96 54.5	56.1	Fomalhaut	15 22.2	S29 32.1
E	11	7 03.8	357 40.6	25.4	119 53.0	12.8	200 59.0	31.0	111 57.1	56.1			
S	12	22 06.3	12 40.3	N 2 26.6	134 55.4	S21 12.9	216 01.7	N 7 31.1	126 59.6	S20 56.0	Gacrux	171 58.1	S57 12.4
D	13	37 08.7	27 39.9	27.8	149 57.8	13.0	231 04.3	31.2	142 02.2	56.0	Gienah	175 50.0	S17 38.1
A	14	52 11.2	42 39.5	29.1	165 00.1	13.1	246 07.0	31.2	157 04.7	56.0	Hadar	148 44.4	S60 27.0
Y	15	67 13.7	57 39.2	. . 30.3	180 02.5	. . 13.2	261 09.6	. . 31.3	172 07.2	. . 56.0	Hamal	327 58.9	N23 32.1
	16	82 16.1	72 38.8	31.5	195 04.8	13.3	276 12.2	31.4	187 09.8	56.0	Kaus Aust.	83 41.2	S34 22.3
	17	97 18.6	87 38.4	32.7	210 07.2	13.3	291 14.9	31.4	202 12.3	56.0			
	18	112 21.1	102 38.0	N 2 34.0	225 09.5	S21 13.4	306 17.5	N 7 31.5	217 14.9	S20 56.0	Kochab	137 19.2	N74 05.3
	19	127 23.5	117 37.7	35.2	240 11.9	13.5	321 20.2	31.6	232 17.4	56.0	Markab	13 36.7	N15 17.4
	20	142 26.0	132 37.3	36.4	255 14.2	13.6	336 22.8	31.6	247 20.0	55.9	Menkar	314 13.4	N 4 08.9
	21	157 28.5	147 36.9	. . 37.6	270 16.6	. . 13.7	351 25.5	. . 31.7	262 22.5	. . 55.9	Menkent	148 04.9	S36 26.9
	22	172 30.9	162 36.6	38.8	285 19.0	13.8	6 28.1	31.8	277 25.1	55.9	Miaplacidus	221 38.8	S69 47.5
	23	187 33.4	177 36.2	40.1	300 21.3	13.9	21 30.7	31.8	292 27.6	55.9			
14	00	202 35.8	192 35.8	N 2 41.3	315 23.7	S21 14.0	36 33.4	N 7 31.9	307 30.2	S20 55.9	Mirfak	308 38.0	N49 55.0
	01	217 38.3	207 35.4	42.5	330 26.1	14.1	51 36.0	32.0	322 32.7	55.9	Nunki	75 55.9	S26 16.3
	02	232 40.8	222 35.1	43.7	345 28.4	14.2	66 38.7	32.0	337 35.3	55.9	Peacock	53 16.5	S56 40.6
	03	247 43.2	237 34.7	. . 44.9	0 30.8	. . 14.3	81 41.3	. . 32.1	352 37.8	. . 55.9	Pollux	243 25.4	N27 59.1
	04	262 45.7	252 34.3	46.2	15 33.2	14.4	96 44.0	32.2	7 40.4	55.9	Procyon	244 57.8	N 5 10.7
	05	277 48.2	267 34.0	47.4	30 35.5	14.4	111 46.6	32.2	22 42.9	55.8			
	06	292 50.6	282 33.6	N 2 48.6	45 37.9	S21 14.5	126 49.2	N 7 32.3	37 45.5	S20 55.8	Rasalhague	96 04.5	N12 32.9
	07	307 53.1	297 33.2	49.8	60 40.3	14.6	141 51.9	32.4	52 48.0	55.8	Regulus	207 41.3	N11 53.1
T	08	322 55.6	312 32.8	51.0	75 42.7	14.7	156 54.5	32.4	67 50.6	55.8	Rigel	281 10.4	S 8 11.3
H	09	337 58.0	327 32.5	. . 52.3	90 45.0	. . 14.8	171 57.2	. . 32.5	82 53.1	. . 55.8	Rigil Kent.	139 48.4	S60 53.9
U	10	353 00.5	342 32.1	53.5	105 47.4	14.9	186 59.8	32.6	97 55.7	55.8	Sabik	102 10.2	S15 44.5
R	11	8 02.9	357 31.7	54.7	120 49.8	15.0	202 02.4	32.6	112 58.2	55.8			
S	12	23 05.4	12 31.4	N 2 55.9	135 52.2	S21 15.1	217 05.1	N 7 32.7	128 00.7	S20 55.8	Schedar	349 38.8	N56 37.4
D	13	38 07.9	27 31.0	57.1	150 54.6	15.2	232 07.7	32.8	143 03.3	55.7	Shaula	96 19.1	S37 06.6
A	14	53 10.3	42 30.6	58.4	165 56.9	15.3	247 10.3	32.8	158 05.8	55.7	Sirius	258 32.1	S16 44.7
Y	15	68 12.8	57 30.2	2 59.6	180 59.3	. . 15.4	262 13.0	. . 32.9	173 08.4	. . 55.7	Spica	158 28.9	S11 14.8
	16	83 15.3	72 29.9	3 00.8	196 01.7	15.4	277 15.6	33.0	188 10.9	55.7	Suhail	222 50.8	S43 30.3
	17	98 17.7	87 29.5	02.0	211 04.1	15.5	292 18.3	33.0	203 13.5	55.7			
	18	113 20.2	102 29.1	N 3 03.2	226 06.5	S21 15.6	307 20.9	N 7 33.1	218 16.0	S20 55.7	Vega	80 37.5	N38 47.8
	19	128 22.7	117 28.8	04.4	241 08.9	15.7	322 23.5	33.2	233 18.6	55.7	Zuben'ubi	137 03.0	S16 06.5
	20	143 25.1	132 28.4	05.7	256 11.3	15.8	337 26.2	33.2	248 21.2	55.7			
	21	158 27.6	147 28.0	. . 06.9	271 13.7	. . 15.9	352 28.8	. . 33.3	263 23.7	. . 55.7			
	22	173 30.1	162 27.6	08.1	286 16.1	16.0	7 31.4	33.4	278 26.3	55.6			
	23	188 32.5	177 27.3	09.3	301 18.5	16.1	22 34.1	33.4	293 28.8	55.6			
Mer. Pass.		h m 10 31.8	*v* −0.4	*d* 1.2	*v* 2.4	*d* 0.1	*v* 2.6	*d* 0.1	*v* 2.5	*d* 0.0			

	SHA	Mer. Pass.
	° ′	h m
Venus	351 08.0	11 09
Mars	112 50.6	3 02
Jupiter	193 53.2	21 34
Saturn	104 52.4	3 33

UT d h	SUN GHA ° ′	SUN Dec ° ′	MOON GHA ° ′	v ′	MOON Dec ° ′	d ′	HP ′
12 00	179 48.0	N 8 45.7	115 34.4	6.7	N18 08.6	1.4	58.9
01	194 48.2	46.6	130 00.1	6.8	18 10.0	1.2	58.9
02	209 48.3	47.5	144 25.9	6.8	18 11.2	1.1	58.9
03	224 48.5	. . 48.4	158 51.7	6.8	18 12.3	1.0	58.8
04	239 48.7	49.3	173 17.5	6.8	18 13.3	0.9	58.8
05	254 48.8	50.2	187 43.3	7.0	18 14.2	0.8	58.7
06	269 49.0	N 8 51.1	202 09.3	6.9	N18 15.0	0.7	58.7
T 07	284 49.1	52.0	216 35.2	7.0	18 15.7	0.5	58.7
U 08	299 49.3	52.9	231 01.2	7.1	18 16.2	0.4	58.6
E 09	314 49.5	. . 53.9	245 27.3	7.1	18 16.6	0.4	58.6
S 10	329 49.6	54.8	259 53.4	7.1	18 17.0	0.2	58.5
D 11	344 49.8	55.7	274 19.5	7.2	18 17.2	0.0	58.5
A 12	359 49.9	N 8 56.6	288 45.7	7.3	N18 17.2	0.0	58.5
Y 13	14 50.1	57.5	303 12.0	7.3	18 17.2	0.1	58.4
14	29 50.3	58.4	317 38.3	7.3	18 17.1	0.3	58.4
15	44 50.4	8 59.3	332 04.6	7.4	18 16.8	0.4	58.3
16	59 50.6	9 00.2	346 31.0	7.5	18 16.4	0.4	58.3
17	74 50.7	01.1	0 57.5	7.5	18 16.0	0.6	58.3
18	89 50.9	N 9 02.0	15 24.0	7.5	N18 15.4	0.7	58.2
19	104 51.1	02.9	29 50.5	7.6	18 14.7	0.9	58.2
20	119 51.2	03.8	44 17.1	7.7	18 13.8	0.9	58.2
21	134 51.4	. . 04.7	58 43.8	7.7	18 12.9	1.0	58.1
22	149 51.5	05.6	73 10.5	7.8	18 11.9	1.1	58.1
23	164 51.7	06.6	87 37.3	7.8	18 10.8	1.3	58.0
13 00	179 51.8	N 9 07.5	102 04.1	7.9	N18 09.5	1.4	58.0
01	194 52.0	08.4	116 31.0	8.0	18 08.1	1.4	58.0
02	209 52.2	09.3	130 58.0	8.0	18 06.7	1.6	57.9
03	224 52.3	. . 10.2	145 25.0	8.0	18 05.1	1.7	57.9
04	239 52.5	11.1	159 52.0	8.2	18 03.4	1.7	57.9
05	254 52.6	12.0	174 19.2	8.1	18 01.7	1.9	57.8
06	269 52.8	N 9 12.9	188 46.3	8.3	N17 59.8	2.0	57.8
W 07	284 52.9	13.8	203 13.6	8.3	17 57.8	2.1	57.7
E 08	299 53.1	14.7	217 40.9	8.4	17 55.7	2.2	57.7
D 09	314 53.3	. . 15.6	232 08.3	8.4	17 53.5	2.3	57.7
N 10	329 53.4	16.5	246 35.7	8.5	17 51.2	2.4	57.6
E 11	344 53.6	17.4	261 03.2	8.5	17 48.8	2.5	57.6
S 12	359 53.7	N 9 18.3	275 30.7	8.6	N17 46.3	2.6	57.6
D 13	14 53.9	19.2	289 58.3	8.7	17 43.7	2.7	57.5
A 14	29 54.0	20.1	304 26.0	8.7	17 41.0	2.8	57.5
Y 15	44 54.2	. . 21.0	318 53.7	8.8	17 38.2	2.8	57.4
16	59 54.3	21.9	333 21.5	8.9	17 35.4	3.0	57.4
17	74 54.5	22.8	347 49.4	8.9	17 32.4	3.1	57.4
18	89 54.7	N 9 23.7	2 17.3	9.0	N17 29.3	3.2	57.3
19	104 54.8	24.6	16 45.3	9.1	17 26.1	3.3	57.3
20	119 55.0	25.5	31 13.4	9.1	17 22.8	3.3	57.3
21	134 55.1	. . 26.4	45 41.5	9.2	17 19.5	3.5	57.2
22	149 55.3	27.3	60 09.7	9.2	17 16.0	3.5	57.2
23	164 55.4	28.2	74 37.9	9.4	17 12.5	3.7	57.1
14 00	179 55.6	N 9 29.1	89 06.3	9.3	N17 08.8	3.7	57.1
01	194 55.7	30.0	103 34.6	9.5	17 05.1	3.8	57.1
02	209 55.9	30.9	118 03.1	9.5	17 01.3	3.9	57.0
03	224 56.0	. . 31.8	132 31.6	9.6	16 57.4	4.0	57.0
04	239 56.2	32.7	147 00.2	9.6	16 53.4	4.1	57.0
05	254 56.4	33.6	161 28.8	9.7	16 49.3	4.2	56.9
06	269 56.5	N 9 34.5	175 57.5	9.8	N16 45.1	4.3	56.9
T 07	284 56.7	35.4	190 26.3	9.9	16 40.8	4.3	56.9
H 08	299 56.8	36.3	204 55.2	9.9	16 36.5	4.4	56.8
U 09	314 57.0	. . 37.2	219 24.1	9.9	16 32.1	4.5	56.8
R 10	329 57.1	38.1	233 53.0	10.1	16 27.6	4.6	56.8
S 11	344 57.3	39.0	248 22.1	10.1	16 23.0	4.7	56.7
D 12	359 57.4	N 9 39.9	262 51.2	10.1	N16 18.3	4.8	56.7
A 13	14 57.6	40.8	277 20.3	10.3	16 13.5	4.8	56.7
Y 14	29 57.7	41.7	291 49.6	10.3	16 08.7	5.0	56.6
15	44 57.9	. . 42.6	306 18.9	10.4	16 03.7	5.0	56.6
16	59 58.0	43.5	320 48.3	10.4	15 58.7	5.0	56.6
17	74 58.2	44.3	335 17.7	10.5	15 53.7	5.2	56.5
18	89 58.3	N 9 45.2	349 47.2	10.5	N15 48.5	5.2	56.5
19	104 58.5	46.1	4 16.7	10.7	15 43.3	5.3	56.5
20	119 58.6	47.0	18 46.4	10.7	15 38.0	5.4	56.4
21	134 58.8	. . 47.9	33 16.1	10.7	15 32.6	5.5	56.4
22	149 58.9	48.8	47 45.8	10.9	15 27.1	5.5	56.4
23	164 59.1	49.7	62 15.7	10.8	N15 21.6	5.6	56.3
	SD 16.0	*d* 0.9	SD 15.9		15.7		15.4

Lat.	Twilight Naut. h m	Twilight Civil h m	Sunrise h m	Moonrise 12 h m	Moonrise 13 h m	Moonrise 14 h m	Moonrise 15 h m
N 72	////	02 12	03 48	▭	05 54	07 58	09 48
N 70	////	02 45	04 04	06 16	07 20	08 46	10 19
68	01 05	03 08	04 16	06 57	07 59	09 16	10 41
66	01 54	03 26	04 26	07 25	08 26	09 39	10 58
64	02 24	03 41	04 35	07 47	08 47	09 57	11 12
62	02 45	03 53	04 42	08 04	09 04	10 11	11 24
60	03 03	04 03	04 48	08 19	09 18	10 24	11 34
N 58	03 17	04 11	04 54	08 31	09 29	10 34	11 42
56	03 28	04 19	04 59	08 41	09 40	10 43	11 50
54	03 39	04 25	05 03	08 51	09 49	10 52	11 57
52	03 47	04 31	05 07	08 59	09 57	10 59	12 03
50	03 55	04 37	05 11	09 07	10 04	11 06	12 08
45	04 11	04 48	05 18	09 23	10 20	11 20	12 20
N 40	04 24	04 57	05 25	09 36	10 33	11 31	12 30
35	04 34	05 04	05 30	09 47	10 44	11 41	12 38
30	04 42	05 11	05 35	09 57	10 53	11 50	12 46
20	04 55	05 21	05 43	10 14	11 10	12 05	12 58
N 10	05 04	05 29	05 51	10 29	11 24	12 18	13 09
0	05 12	05 36	05 57	10 43	11 38	12 30	13 20
S 10	05 18	05 42	06 04	10 57	11 51	12 42	13 30
20	05 22	05 48	06 10	11 11	12 06	12 55	13 41
30	05 26	05 54	06 18	11 28	12 22	13 10	13 54
35	05 27	05 57	06 22	11 38	12 32	13 19	14 01
40	05 29	06 00	06 27	11 50	12 43	13 29	14 09
45	05 29	06 03	06 33	12 03	12 55	13 40	14 19
S 50	05 30	06 07	06 40	12 19	13 11	13 54	14 30
52	05 30	06 09	06 43	12 27	13 18	14 01	14 36
54	05 29	06 10	06 46	12 36	13 26	14 08	14 42
56	05 29	06 12	06 50	12 45	13 35	14 16	14 48
58	05 29	06 14	06 54	12 56	13 46	14 25	14 55
S 60	05 28	06 16	06 59	13 09	13 58	14 35	15 04

Lat.	Sunset h m	Twilight Civil h m	Twilight Naut. h m	Moonset 12 h m	Moonset 13 h m	Moonset 14 h m	Moonset 15 h m
N 72	20 16	21 56	////	▭	04 57	04 44	04 38
N 70	20 00	21 21	////	02 38	03 31	03 55	04 06
68	19 47	20 56	23 10	01 57	02 51	03 24	03 44
66	19 37	20 38	22 13	01 29	02 24	03 01	03 26
64	19 28	20 23	21 42	01 08	02 03	02 43	03 11
62	19 21	20 11	21 19	00 50	01 46	02 28	02 59
60	19 14	20 00	21 01	00 36	01 32	02 15	02 48
N 58	19 09	19 51	20 47	00 24	01 20	02 04	02 39
56	19 04	19 44	20 35	00 13	01 09	01 55	02 31
54	18 59	19 37	20 24	00 04	01 00	01 46	02 24
52	18 55	19 31	20 15	24 52	00 52	01 39	02 17
50	18 51	19 25	20 07	24 44	00 44	01 32	02 11
45	18 43	19 14	19 51	24 28	00 28	01 17	01 59
N 40	18 37	19 05	19 38	24 15	00 15	01 05	01 48
35	18 31	18 57	19 28	24 04	00 04	00 55	01 39
30	18 26	18 51	19 20	23 55	24 45	00 45	01 31
20	18 18	18 40	19 06	23 38	24 30	00 30	01 18
N 10	18 10	18 32	18 57	23 23	24 16	00 16	01 06
0	18 04	18 25	18 49	23 09	24 03	00 03	00 54
S 10	17 57	18 18	18 43	22 55	23 50	24 43	00 43
20	17 50	18 12	18 38	22 41	23 36	24 31	00 31
30	17 42	18 07	18 34	22 24	23 20	24 17	00 17
35	17 38	18 03	18 33	22 14	23 11	24 09	00 09
40	17 33	18 00	18 32	22 03	23 01	23 59	24 58
45	17 27	17 57	18 31	21 49	22 48	23 48	24 49
S 50	17 20	17 53	18 30	21 33	22 33	23 35	24 39
52	17 17	17 51	18 30	21 25	22 26	23 29	24 34
54	17 14	17 49	18 30	21 17	22 18	23 22	24 28
56	17 10	17 48	18 31	21 07	22 09	23 15	24 22
58	17 06	17 46	18 31	20 57	21 59	23 06	24 15
S 60	17 01	17 43	18 31	20 44	21 47	22 56	24 07

Day	SUN Eqn. of Time 00^h m s	SUN Eqn. of Time 12^h m s	SUN Mer. Pass. h m	MOON Mer. Pass. Upper h m	MOON Mer. Pass. Lower h m	MOON Age d	MOON Phase %
12	00 48	00 41	12 01	16 56	04 28	05	32
13	00 33	00 25	12 00	17 51	05 24	06	43
14	00 18	00 11	12 00	18 42	06 17	07	54

UT		ARIES	VENUS −3·8		MARS −1·0		JUPITER −2·3		SATURN +0·3		STARS		
		GHA	GHA	Dec	GHA	Dec	GHA	Dec	GHA	Dec	Name	SHA	Dec
d	h	° ′	° ′	° ′	° ′	° ′	° ′	° ′	° ′	° ′		° ′	° ′
15	00	203 35.0	192 26.9	N 3 10.5	316 20.9	S21 16.2	37 36.7	N 7 33.5	308 31.4	S20 55.6	Acamar	315 17.3	S40 14.7
	01	218 37.4	207 26.5	11.8	331 23.3	16.2	52 39.3	33.5	323 33.9	55.6	Achernar	335 26.1	S57 09.4
	02	233 39.9	222 26.1	13.0	346 25.7	16.3	67 42.0	33.6	338 36.5	55.6	Acrux	173 06.3	S63 11.5
	03	248 42.4	237 25.8	. . 14.2	1 28.1	. . 16.4	82 44.6	. . 33.7	353 39.0	. . 55.6	Adhara	255 11.1	S29 00.1
	04	263 44.8	252 25.4	15.4	16 30.5	16.5	97 47.3	33.7	8 41.6	55.6	Aldebaran	290 47.4	N16 32.2
	05	278 47.3	267 25.0	16.6	31 32.9	16.6	112 49.9	33.8	23 44.1	55.6			
	06	293 49.8	282 24.7	N 3 17.8	46 35.3	S21 16.7	127 52.5	N 7 33.9	38 46.7	S20 55.5	Alioth	166 18.6	N55 52.4
	07	308 52.2	297 24.3	19.1	61 37.7	16.8	142 55.2	33.9	53 49.2	55.5	Alkaid	152 57.0	N49 14.0
	08	323 54.7	312 23.9	20.3	76 40.1	16.9	157 57.8	34.0	68 51.8	55.5	Al Na'ir	27 41.7	S46 52.7
F	09	338 57.2	327 23.5	. . 21.5	91 42.5	. . 17.0	173 00.4	. . 34.1	83 54.3	. . 55.5	Alnilam	275 44.6	S 1 11.8
R	10	353 59.6	342 23.2	22.7	106 44.9	17.0	188 03.1	34.1	98 56.9	55.5	Alphard	217 54.1	S 8 44.0
I	11	9 02.1	357 22.8	23.9	121 47.3	17.1	203 05.7	34.2	113 59.4	55.5			
D	12	24 04.6	12 22.4	N 3 25.1	136 49.7	S21 17.2	218 08.3	N 7 34.2	129 02.0	S20 55.5	Alphecca	126 09.1	N26 39.6
A	13	39 07.0	27 22.0	26.4	151 52.1	17.3	233 11.0	34.3	144 04.5	55.5	Alpheratz	357 41.8	N29 10.6
Y	14	54 09.5	42 21.7	27.6	166 54.5	17.4	248 13.6	34.4	159 07.1	55.4	Altair	62 06.4	N 8 54.7
	15	69 11.9	57 21.3	. . 28.8	181 57.0	. . 17.5	263 16.2	. . 34.4	174 09.6	. . 55.4	Ankaa	353 14.3	S42 13.1
	16	84 14.4	72 20.9	30.0	196 59.4	17.6	278 18.8	34.5	189 12.2	55.4	Antares	112 23.6	S26 27.9
	17	99 16.9	87 20.5	31.2	212 01.8	17.7	293 21.5	34.6	204 14.8	55.4			
	18	114 19.3	102 20.2	N 3 32.4	227 04.2	S21 17.7	308 24.1	N 7 34.6	219 17.3	S20 55.4	Arcturus	145 53.7	N19 05.9
	19	129 21.8	117 19.8	33.7	242 06.6	17.8	323 26.7	34.7	234 19.9	55.4	Atria	107 23.3	S69 03.0
	20	144 24.3	132 19.4	34.9	257 09.1	17.9	338 29.4	34.7	249 22.4	55.4	Avior	234 17.1	S59 34.2
	21	159 26.7	147 19.0	. . 36.1	272 11.5	. . 18.0	353 32.0	. . 34.8	264 25.0	. . 55.4	Bellatrix	278 30.2	N 6 21.6
	22	174 29.2	162 18.7	37.3	287 13.9	18.1	8 34.6	34.9	279 27.5	55.3	Betelgeuse	270 59.4	N 7 24.3
	23	189 31.7	177 18.3	38.5	302 16.3	18.2	23 37.3	34.9	294 30.1	55.3			
16	00	204 34.1	192 17.9	N 3 39.7	317 18.8	S21 18.3	38 39.9	N 7 35.0	309 32.6	S20 55.3	Canopus	263 55.5	S52 42.8
	01	219 36.6	207 17.5	41.0	332 21.2	18.4	53 42.5	35.1	324 35.2	55.3	Capella	280 31.9	N46 00.7
	02	234 39.0	222 17.2	42.2	347 23.6	18.4	68 45.1	35.1	339 37.7	55.3	Deneb	49 30.2	N45 20.1
	03	249 41.5	237 16.8	. . 43.4	2 26.1	. . 18.5	83 47.8	. . 35.2	354 40.3	. . 55.3	Denebola	182 31.5	N14 28.8
	04	264 44.0	252 16.4	44.6	17 28.5	18.6	98 50.4	35.2	9 42.9	55.3	Diphda	348 54.3	S17 54.0
	05	279 46.4	267 16.0	45.8	32 30.9	18.7	113 53.0	35.3	24 45.4	55.3			
	06	294 48.9	282 15.7	N 3 47.0	47 33.4	S21 18.8	128 55.7	N 7 35.4	39 48.0	S20 55.2	Dubhe	193 49.0	N61 39.9
S	07	309 51.4	297 15.3	48.3	62 35.8	18.9	143 58.3	35.4	54 50.5	55.2	Elnath	278 10.4	N28 37.1
A	08	324 53.8	312 14.9	49.5	77 38.2	19.0	159 00.9	35.5	69 53.1	55.2	Eltanin	90 45.0	N51 29.1
T	09	339 56.3	327 14.5	. . 50.7	92 40.7	. . 19.0	174 03.5	. . 35.5	84 55.6	. . 55.2	Enif	33 45.4	N 9 56.9
U	10	354 58.8	342 14.2	51.9	107 43.1	19.1	189 06.2	35.6	99 58.2	55.2	Fomalhaut	15 22.2	S29 32.1
R	11	10 01.2	357 13.8	53.1	122 45.6	19.2	204 08.8	35.7	115 00.8	55.2			
D	12	25 03.7	12 13.4	N 3 54.3	137 48.0	S21 19.3	219 11.4	N 7 35.7	130 03.3	S20 55.2	Gacrux	171 58.1	S57 12.4
A	13	40 06.2	27 13.0	55.5	152 50.5	19.4	234 14.0	35.8	145 05.9	55.2	Gienah	175 50.0	S17 38.1
Y	14	55 08.6	42 12.7	56.8	167 52.9	19.5	249 16.7	35.8	160 08.4	55.1	Hadar	148 44.4	S60 27.0
	15	70 11.1	57 12.3	. . 58.0	182 55.4	. . 19.5	264 19.3	. . 35.9	175 11.0	. . 55.1	Hamal	327 58.9	N23 32.1
	16	85 13.5	72 11.9	3 59.2	197 57.8	19.6	279 21.9	36.0	190 13.5	55.1	Kaus Aust.	83 41.2	S34 22.3
	17	100 16.0	87 11.5	4 00.4	213 00.3	19.7	294 24.6	36.0	205 16.1	55.1			
	18	115 18.5	102 11.2	N 4 01.6	228 02.7	S21 19.8	309 27.2	N 7 36.1	220 18.7	S20 55.1	Kochab	137 19.1	N74 05.3
	19	130 20.9	117 10.8	02.8	243 05.2	19.9	324 29.8	36.1	235 21.2	55.1	Markab	13 36.7	N15 17.4
	20	145 23.4	132 10.4	04.0	258 07.6	20.0	339 32.4	36.2	250 23.8	55.1	Menkar	314 13.4	N 4 08.9
	21	160 25.9	147 10.0	. . 05.2	273 10.1	. . 20.1	354 35.0	. . 36.3	265 26.3	. . 55.1	Menkent	148 04.9	S36 26.9
	22	175 28.3	162 09.6	06.5	288 12.5	20.1	9 37.7	36.3	280 28.9	55.0	Miaplacidus	221 38.8	S69 47.5
	23	190 30.8	177 09.3	07.7	303 15.0	20.2	24 40.3	36.4	295 31.5	55.0			
17	00	205 33.3	192 08.9	N 4 08.9	318 17.5	S21 20.3	39 42.9	N 7 36.4	310 34.0	S20 55.0	Mirfak	308 38.0	N49 55.0
	01	220 35.7	207 08.5	10.1	333 19.9	20.4	54 45.5	36.5	325 36.6	55.0	Nunki	75 55.9	S26 16.3
	02	235 38.2	222 08.1	11.3	348 22.4	20.5	69 48.2	36.6	340 39.1	55.0	Peacock	53 16.4	S56 40.6
	03	250 40.7	237 07.8	. . 12.5	3 24.8	. . 20.6	84 50.8	. . 36.6	355 41.7	. . 55.0	Pollux	243 25.5	N27 59.1
	04	265 43.1	252 07.4	13.7	18 27.3	20.6	99 53.4	36.7	10 44.2	55.0	Procyon	244 57.8	N 5 10.7
	05	280 45.6	267 07.0	14.9	33 29.8	20.7	114 56.0	36.7	25 46.8	55.0			
	06	295 48.0	282 06.6	N 4 16.2	48 32.2	S21 20.8	129 58.7	N 7 36.8	40 49.4	S20 54.9	Rasalhague	96 04.5	N12 32.9
	07	310 50.5	297 06.2	17.4	63 34.7	20.9	145 01.3	36.8	55 51.9	54.9	Regulus	207 41.3	N11 53.1
	08	325 53.0	312 05.9	18.6	78 37.2	21.0	160 03.9	36.9	70 54.5	54.9	Rigel	281 10.4	S 8 11.3
S	09	340 55.4	327 05.5	. . 19.8	93 39.7	. . 21.1	175 06.5	. . 37.0	85 57.0	. . 54.9	Rigil Kent.	139 48.4	S60 54.0
U	10	355 57.9	342 05.1	21.0	108 42.1	21.1	190 09.1	37.0	100 59.6	54.9	Sabik	102 10.1	S15 44.5
N	11	11 00.4	357 04.7	22.2	123 44.6	21.2	205 11.8	37.1	116 02.2	54.9			
D	12	26 02.8	12 04.4	N 4 23.4	138 47.1	S21 21.3	220 14.4	N 7 37.1	131 04.7	S20 54.9	Schedar	349 38.8	N56 37.4
A	13	41 05.3	27 04.0	24.6	153 49.6	21.4	235 17.0	37.2	146 07.3	54.9	Shaula	96 19.1	S37 06.6
Y	14	56 07.8	42 03.6	25.8	168 52.0	21.5	250 19.6	37.2	161 09.9	54.8	Sirius	258 32.1	S16 44.7
	15	71 10.2	57 03.2	. . 27.1	183 54.5	. . 21.5	265 22.2	. . 37.3	176 12.4	. . 54.8	Spica	158 28.9	S11 14.8
	16	86 12.7	72 02.8	28.3	198 57.0	21.6	280 24.8	37.4	191 15.0	54.8	Suhail	222 50.9	S43 30.3
	17	101 15.1	87 02.5	29.5	213 59.5	21.7	295 27.5	37.4	206 17.5	54.8			
	18	116 17.6	102 02.1	N 4 30.7	229 02.0	S21 21.8	310 30.1	N 7 37.5	221 20.1	S20 54.8	Vega	80 37.5	N38 47.8
	19	131 20.1	117 01.7	31.9	244 04.5	21.9	325 32.7	37.5	236 22.7	54.8	Zuben'ubi	137 03.0	S16 06.5
	20	146 22.5	132 01.3	33.1	259 07.0	22.0	340 35.3	37.6	251 25.2	54.8		SHA	Mer. Pass.
	21	161 25.0	147 00.9	. . 34.3	274 09.4	. . 22.0	355 37.9	. . 37.6	266 27.8	. . 54.8		° ′	h m
	22	176 27.5	162 00.6	35.5	289 11.9	22.1	10 40.6	37.7	281 30.4	54.7	Venus	347 43.8	11 11
	23	191 29.9	177 00.2	36.7	304 14.4	22.2	25 43.2	37.8	296 32.9	54.7	Mars	112 44.7	2 50
Mer. Pass.		h m 10 20.0	v −0.4	d 1.2	v 2.4	d 0.1	v 2.6	d 0.1	v 2.6	d 0.0	Jupiter	194 05.8	21 22
											Saturn	104 58.5	3 21

Day	UT (d h)	SUN GHA (° ′)	SUN Dec (° ′)	MOON GHA (° ′)	v (′)	MOON Dec (° ′)	d (′)	HP (′)
FRIDAY	15 00	179 59.2	N 9 50.6	76 45.5	11.0	N15 16.0	5.7	56.3
	01	194 59.4	51.5	91 15.5	11.0	15 10.3	5.8	56.3
	02	209 59.5	52.4	105 45.5	11.1	15 04.5	5.8	56.2
	03	224 59.7	. . 53.3	120 15.6	11.1	14 58.7	5.9	56.2
	04	239 59.9	54.2	134 45.7	11.3	14 52.8	5.9	56.2
	05	255 00.0	55.1	149 16.0	11.2	14 46.9	6.1	56.2
	06	270 00.2	N 9 55.9	163 46.2	11.4	N14 40.8	6.0	56.1
	07	285 00.3	56.8	178 16.6	11.4	14 34.8	6.2	56.1
	08	300 00.5	57.7	192 47.0	11.4	14 28.6	6.2	56.1
	09	315 00.6	. . 58.6	207 17.4	11.5	14 22.4	6.3	56.0
	10	330 00.7	9 59.5	221 47.9	11.6	14 16.1	6.4	56.0
	11	345 00.9	10 00.4	236 18.5	11.7	14 09.7	6.4	56.0
	12	0 01.0	N10 01.3	250 49.2	11.7	N14 03.3	6.5	55.9
	13	15 01.2	02.2	265 19.9	11.8	13 56.8	6.5	55.9
	14	30 01.3	03.1	279 50.7	11.8	13 50.3	6.7	55.9
	15	45 01.5	. . 03.9	294 21.5	11.9	13 43.6	6.6	55.9
	16	60 01.6	04.8	308 52.4	11.9	13 37.0	6.8	55.8
	17	75 01.8	05.7	323 23.3	12.0	13 30.2	6.7	55.8
	18	90 01.9	N10 06.6	337 54.3	12.1	N13 23.5	6.9	55.8
	19	105 02.1	07.5	352 25.4	12.1	13 16.6	6.9	55.8
	20	120 02.2	08.4	6 56.5	12.2	13 09.7	7.0	55.7
	21	135 02.4	. . 09.3	21 27.7	12.3	13 02.7	7.0	55.7
	22	150 02.5	10.2	35 59.0	12.3	12 55.7	7.0	55.7
	23	165 02.7	11.0	50 30.3	12.3	12 48.7	7.2	55.6
SATURDAY	16 00	180 02.8	N10 11.9	65 01.6	12.4	N12 41.5	7.2	55.6
	01	195 03.0	12.8	79 33.0	12.5	12 34.3	7.2	55.6
	02	210 03.1	13.7	94 04.5	12.5	12 27.1	7.3	55.6
	03	225 03.3	. . 14.6	108 36.0	12.6	12 19.8	7.3	55.5
	04	240 03.4	15.5	123 07.6	12.6	12 12.5	7.4	55.5
	05	255 03.6	16.3	137 39.2	12.7	12 05.1	7.5	55.5
	06	270 03.7	N10 17.2	152 10.9	12.8	N11 57.6	7.4	55.5
	07	285 03.9	18.1	166 42.7	12.8	11 50.2	7.6	55.4
	08	300 04.0	19.0	181 14.5	12.8	11 42.6	7.6	55.4
	09	315 04.1	. . 19.9	195 46.3	12.9	11 35.0	7.6	55.4
	10	330 04.3	20.8	210 18.2	13.0	11 27.4	7.7	55.4
	11	345 04.4	21.6	224 50.2	13.0	11 19.7	7.7	55.3
	12	0 04.6	N10 22.5	239 22.2	13.0	N11 12.0	7.8	55.3
	13	15 04.7	23.4	253 54.2	13.2	11 04.2	7.8	55.3
	14	30 04.9	24.3	268 26.4	13.1	10 56.4	7.9	55.3
	15	45 05.0	. . 25.2	282 58.5	13.2	10 48.5	7.9	55.2
	16	60 05.2	26.0	297 30.7	13.3	10 40.6	7.9	55.2
	17	75 05.3	26.9	312 03.0	13.3	10 32.7	8.0	55.2
	18	90 05.5	N10 27.8	326 35.3	13.3	N10 24.7	8.0	55.2
	19	105 05.6	28.7	341 07.6	13.4	10 16.7	8.1	55.2
	20	120 05.7	29.6	355 40.0	13.5	10 08.6	8.1	55.1
	21	135 05.9	. . 30.4	10 12.5	13.5	10 00.5	8.2	55.1
	22	150 06.0	31.3	24 45.0	13.5	9 52.3	8.2	55.1
	23	165 06.2	32.2	39 17.5	13.6	9 44.1	8.2	55.1
SUNDAY	17 00	180 06.3	N10 33.1	53 50.1	13.6	N 9 35.9	8.3	55.1
	01	195 06.5	34.0	68 22.7	13.7	9 27.6	8.3	55.0
	02	210 06.6	34.8	82 55.4	13.7	9 19.3	8.3	55.0
	03	225 06.7	. . 35.7	97 28.1	13.8	9 11.0	8.4	55.0
	04	240 06.9	36.6	112 00.9	13.8	9 02.6	8.4	55.0
	05	255 07.0	37.5	126 33.7	13.8	8 54.2	8.4	55.0
	06	270 07.2	N10 38.3	141 06.5	13.9	N 8 45.8	8.5	54.9
	07	285 07.3	39.2	155 39.4	13.9	8 37.3	8.5	54.9
	08	300 07.5	40.1	170 12.3	14.0	8 28.8	8.5	54.9
	09	315 07.6	. . 41.0	184 45.3	14.0	8 20.3	8.6	54.9
	10	330 07.7	41.8	199 18.3	14.1	8 11.7	8.6	54.9
	11	345 07.9	42.7	213 51.4	14.0	8 03.1	8.6	54.8
	12	0 08.0	N10 43.6	228 24.4	14.2	N 7 54.5	8.7	54.8
	13	15 08.2	44.5	242 57.6	14.1	7 45.8	8.7	54.8
	14	30 08.3	45.3	257 30.7	14.2	7 37.1	8.7	54.8
	15	45 08.4	. . 46.2	272 03.9	14.2	7 28.4	8.7	54.8
	16	60 08.6	47.1	286 37.1	14.3	7 19.7	8.8	54.7
	17	75 08.7	48.0	301 10.4	14.3	7 10.9	8.8	54.7
	18	90 08.9	N10 48.8	315 43.7	14.3	N 7 02.1	8.8	54.7
	19	105 09.0	49.7	330 17.0	14.4	6 53.3	8.9	54.7
	20	120 09.2	50.6	344 50.4	14.4	6 44.4	8.8	54.7
	21	135 09.3	. . 51.4	359 23.8	14.4	6 35.6	8.9	54.7
	22	150 09.4	52.3	13 57.2	14.5	6 26.7	9.0	54.6
	23	165 09.6	53.2	28 30.7	14.5	N 6 17.7	8.9	54.6
		SD 16.0	*d* 0.9	SD 15.2		15.1		14.9

Lat. (°)	Twilight Naut. (h m)	Twilight Civil (h m)	Sunrise (h m)	Moonrise 15 (h m)	Moonrise 16 (h m)	Moonrise 17 (h m)	Moonrise 18 (h m)
N 72	////	01 44	03 31	09 48	11 32	13 11	14 46
N 70	////	02 25	03 49	10 19	11 52	13 23	14 52
68	////	02 52	04 03	10 41	12 07	13 32	14 56
66	01 30	03 12	04 15	10 58	12 19	13 40	15 00
64	02 06	03 29	04 24	11 12	12 29	13 47	15 03
62	02 31	03 42	04 32	11 24	12 38	13 52	15 06
60	02 50	03 53	04 39	11 34	12 45	13 57	15 08
N 58	03 06	04 02	04 46	11 42	12 52	14 01	15 10
56	03 19	04 11	04 51	11 50	12 58	14 05	15 12
54	03 30	04 18	04 56	11 57	13 03	14 09	15 14
52	03 39	04 24	05 00	12 03	13 07	14 12	15 15
50	03 48	04 30	05 04	12 08	13 12	14 14	15 17
45	04 05	04 42	05 13	12 20	13 21	14 21	15 20
N 40	04 18	04 52	05 20	12 30	13 28	14 26	15 22
35	04 29	05 00	05 26	12 38	13 35	14 30	15 24
30	04 38	05 07	05 32	12 46	13 40	14 34	15 26
20	04 52	05 19	05 41	12 58	13 50	14 41	15 30
N 10	05 03	05 28	05 49	13 09	13 59	14 46	15 33
0	05 11	05 35	05 56	13 20	14 07	14 52	15 35
S 10	05 18	05 42	06 04	13 30	14 15	14 57	15 38
20	05 23	05 49	06 11	13 41	14 23	15 03	15 41
30	05 28	05 56	06 20	13 54	14 33	15 10	15 44
35	05 30	05 59	06 25	14 01	14 39	15 14	15 46
40	05 31	06 03	06 30	14 09	14 45	15 18	15 49
45	05 33	06 07	06 37	14 19	14 53	15 23	15 51
S 50	05 34	06 11	06 44	14 30	15 01	15 29	15 54
52	05 34	06 13	06 48	14 36	15 05	15 32	15 55
54	05 35	06 16	06 52	14 42	15 10	15 35	15 57
56	05 35	06 18	06 56	14 48	15 15	15 38	15 59
58	05 35	06 20	07 01	14 55	15 20	15 42	16 00
S 60	05 35	06 23	07 06	15 04	15 27	15 46	16 02

Lat. (°)	Sunset (h m)	Twilight Civil (h m)	Twilight Naut. (h m)	Moonset 15 (h m)	Moonset 16 (h m)	Moonset 17 (h m)	Moonset 18 (h m)
N 72	20 32	22 25	////	04 38	04 32	04 28	04 23
N 70	20 14	21 40	////	04 06	04 12	04 14	04 16
68	19 59	21 12	////	03 44	03 56	04 04	04 09
66	19 47	20 50	22 38	03 26	03 42	03 55	04 04
64	19 37	20 34	21 58	03 11	03 31	03 47	04 00
62	19 29	20 20	21 32	02 59	03 22	03 40	03 56
60	19 22	20 09	21 12	02 48	03 14	03 35	03 53
N 58	19 15	19 59	20 56	02 39	03 07	03 30	03 50
56	19 10	19 50	20 43	02 31	03 00	03 25	03 47
54	19 05	19 43	20 31	02 24	02 55	03 21	03 45
52	19 00	19 36	20 22	02 17	02 50	03 18	03 42
50	18 56	19 30	20 13	02 11	02 45	03 14	03 40
45	18 47	19 18	19 55	01 59	02 35	03 07	03 36
N 40	18 40	19 08	19 42	01 48	02 26	03 01	03 32
35	18 34	19 00	19 31	01 39	02 19	02 56	03 29
30	18 28	18 53	19 22	01 31	02 13	02 51	03 26
20	18 19	18 41	19 08	01 18	02 02	02 43	03 21
N 10	18 11	18 32	18 57	01 06	01 52	02 36	03 17
0	18 03	18 24	18 48	00 54	01 43	02 29	03 13
S 10	17 56	18 17	18 42	00 43	01 33	02 22	03 09
20	17 48	18 10	18 36	00 31	01 24	02 15	03 04
30	17 39	18 03	18 31	00 17	01 12	02 06	02 59
35	17 34	18 00	18 29	00 09	01 06	02 01	02 56
40	17 28	17 56	18 27	24 58	00 58	01 56	02 53
45	17 22	17 52	18 26	24 49	00 49	01 50	02 49
S 50	17 14	17 47	18 25	24 39	00 39	01 42	02 44
52	17 11	17 45	18 24	24 34	00 34	01 38	02 42
54	17 07	17 43	18 24	24 28	00 28	01 34	02 40
56	17 02	17 40	18 24	24 22	00 22	01 30	02 37
58	16 58	17 38	18 23	24 15	00 15	01 25	02 34
S 60	16 52	17 35	18 23	24 07	00 07	01 19	02 31

Day	SUN Eqn. of Time 00^h	SUN Eqn. of Time 12^h	SUN Mer. Pass.	MOON Mer. Pass. Upper	MOON Mer. Pass. Lower	MOON Age	MOON Phase
d	m s	m s	h m	h m	h m	d	%
15	00 03	00 04	12 00	19 31	07 07	08	64
16	00 11	00 18	12 00	20 18	07 55	09	73
17	00 25	00 32	11 59	21 02	08 40	10	81

	UT	ARIES	VENUS −3·8		MARS −1·1		JUPITER −2·3		SATURN +0·2	
		GHA	GHA	Dec	GHA	Dec	GHA	Dec	GHA	Dec
	d h	° ′	° ′	° ′	° ′	° ′	° ′	° ′	° ′	° ′
	18 00	206 32.4	191 59.8	N 4 37.9	319 16.9	S21 22.3	40 45.8	N 7 37.8	311 35.5	S20 54.7
	01	221 34.9	206 59.4	39.2	334 19.4	22.4	55 48.4	37.9	326 38.0	54.7
	02	236 37.3	221 59.0	40.4	349 21.9	22.4	70 51.0	37.9	341 40.6	54.7
	03	251 39.8	236 58.7	. . 41.6	4 24.4	. . 22.5	85 53.6	. . 38.0	356 43.2	. . 54.7
	04	266 42.3	251 58.3	42.8	19 26.9	22.6	100 56.3	38.0	11 45.7	54.7
	05	281 44.7	266 57.9	44.0	34 29.4	22.7	115 58.9	38.1	26 48.3	54.6
	06	296 47.2	281 57.5	N 4 45.2	49 31.9	S21 22.8	131 01.5	N 7 38.1	41 50.9	S20 54.6
	07	311 49.6	296 57.1	46.4	64 34.4	22.8	146 04.1	38.2	56 53.4	54.6
	08	326 52.1	311 56.7	47.6	79 36.9	22.9	161 06.7	38.3	71 56.0	54.6
MONDAY	09	341 54.6	326 56.4	. . 48.8	94 39.4	. . 23.0	176 09.3	. . 38.3	86 58.6	. . 54.6
	10	356 57.0	341 56.0	50.0	109 41.9	23.1	191 11.9	38.4	102 01.1	54.6
	11	11 59.5	356 55.6	51.2	124 44.4	23.2	206 14.6	38.4	117 03.7	54.6
	12	27 02.0	11 55.2	N 4 52.4	139 46.9	S21 23.2	221 17.2	N 7 38.5	132 06.2	S20 54.6
	13	42 04.4	26 54.8	53.6	154 49.5	23.3	236 19.8	38.5	147 08.8	54.5
	14	57 06.9	41 54.5	54.9	169 52.0	23.4	251 22.4	38.6	162 11.4	54.5
	15	72 09.4	56 54.1	. . 56.1	184 54.5	. . 23.5	266 25.0	. . 38.6	177 13.9	. . 54.5
	16	87 11.8	71 53.7	57.3	199 57.0	23.6	281 27.6	38.7	192 16.5	54.5
	17	102 14.3	86 53.3	58.5	214 59.5	23.6	296 30.2	38.7	207 19.1	54.5
	18	117 16.7	101 52.9	N 4 59.7	230 02.0	S21 23.7	311 32.8	N 7 38.8	222 21.6	S20 54.5
	19	132 19.2	116 52.5	5 00.9	245 04.5	23.8	326 35.5	38.9	237 24.2	54.5
	20	147 21.7	131 52.2	02.1	260 07.1	23.9	341 38.1	38.9	252 26.8	54.5
	21	162 24.1	146 51.8	. . 03.3	275 09.6	. . 24.0	356 40.7	. . 39.0	267 29.3	. . 54.4
	22	177 26.6	161 51.4	04.5	290 12.1	24.0	11 43.3	39.0	282 31.9	54.4
	23	192 29.1	176 51.0	05.7	305 14.6	24.1	26 45.9	39.1	297 34.5	54.4
	19 00	207 31.5	191 50.6	N 5 06.9	320 17.2	S21 24.2	41 48.5	N 7 39.1	312 37.0	S20 54.4
	01	222 34.0	206 50.2	08.1	335 19.7	24.3	56 51.1	39.2	327 39.6	54.4
	02	237 36.5	221 49.9	09.3	350 22.2	24.3	71 53.7	39.2	342 42.2	54.4
	03	252 38.9	236 49.5	. . 10.5	5 24.7	. . 24.4	86 56.3	. . 39.3	357 44.7	. . 54.4
	04	267 41.4	251 49.1	11.7	20 27.3	24.5	101 58.9	39.3	12 47.3	54.3
	05	282 43.9	266 48.7	12.9	35 29.8	24.6	117 01.6	39.4	27 49.9	54.3
	06	297 46.3	281 48.3	N 5 14.1	50 32.3	S21 24.7	132 04.2	N 7 39.4	42 52.4	S20 54.3
	07	312 48.8	296 47.9	15.3	65 34.9	24.7	147 06.8	39.5	57 55.0	54.3
	08	327 51.2	311 47.6	16.5	80 37.4	24.8	162 09.4	39.5	72 57.6	54.3
TUESDAY	09	342 53.7	326 47.2	. . 17.7	95 40.0	. . 24.9	177 12.0	. . 39.6	88 00.1	. . 54.3
	10	357 56.2	341 46.8	18.9	110 42.5	25.0	192 14.6	39.6	103 02.7	54.3
	11	12 58.6	356 46.4	20.2	125 45.0	25.0	207 17.2	39.7	118 05.3	54.3
	12	28 01.1	11 46.0	N 5 21.4	140 47.6	S21 25.1	222 19.8	N 7 39.7	133 07.8	S20 54.2
	13	43 03.6	26 45.6	22.6	155 50.1	25.2	237 22.4	39.8	148 10.4	54.2
	14	58 06.0	41 45.2	23.8	170 52.7	25.3	252 25.0	39.9	163 13.0	54.2
	15	73 08.5	56 44.9	. . 25.0	185 55.2	. . 25.3	267 27.6	. . 39.9	178 15.6	. . 54.2
	16	88 11.0	71 44.5	26.2	200 57.8	25.4	282 30.2	40.0	193 18.1	54.2
	17	103 13.4	86 44.1	27.4	216 00.3	25.5	297 32.8	40.0	208 20.7	54.2
	18	118 15.9	101 43.7	N 5 28.6	231 02.9	S21 25.6	312 35.4	N 7 40.1	223 23.3	S20 54.2
	19	133 18.3	116 43.3	29.8	246 05.4	25.7	327 38.0	40.1	238 25.8	54.1
	20	148 20.8	131 42.9	31.0	261 08.0	25.7	342 40.7	40.2	253 28.4	54.1
	21	163 23.3	146 42.5	. . 32.2	276 10.5	. . 25.8	357 43.3	. . 40.2	268 31.0	. . 54.1
	22	178 25.7	161 42.1	33.4	291 13.1	25.9	12 45.9	40.3	283 33.5	54.1
	23	193 28.2	176 41.8	34.6	306 15.6	26.0	27 48.5	40.3	298 36.1	54.1
	20 00	208 30.7	191 41.4	N 5 35.8	321 18.2	S21 26.0	42 51.1	N 7 40.4	313 38.7	S20 54.1
	01	223 33.1	206 41.0	37.0	336 20.8	26.1	57 53.7	40.4	328 41.3	54.1
	02	238 35.6	221 40.6	38.2	351 23.3	26.2	72 56.3	40.5	343 43.8	54.0
	03	253 38.1	236 40.2	. . 39.4	6 25.9	. . 26.3	87 58.9	. . 40.5	358 46.4	. . 54.0
	04	268 40.5	251 39.8	40.6	21 28.4	26.3	103 01.5	40.6	13 49.0	54.0
	05	283 43.0	266 39.4	41.8	36 31.0	26.4	118 04.1	40.6	28 51.5	54.0
	06	298 45.5	281 39.0	N 5 43.0	51 33.6	S21 26.5	133 06.7	N 7 40.7	43 54.1	S20 54.0
	07	313 47.9	296 38.7	44.2	66 36.1	26.6	148 09.3	40.7	58 56.7	54.0
	08	328 50.4	311 38.3	45.4	81 38.7	26.6	163 11.9	40.8	73 59.2	54.0
WEDNESDAY	09	343 52.8	326 37.9	. . 46.6	96 41.3	. . 26.7	178 14.5	. . 40.8	89 01.8	. . 54.0
	10	358 55.3	341 37.5	47.8	111 43.9	26.8	193 17.1	40.9	104 04.4	53.9
	11	13 57.8	356 37.1	49.0	126 46.4	26.9	208 19.7	40.9	119 07.0	53.9
	12	29 00.2	11 36.7	N 5 50.2	141 49.0	S21 26.9	223 22.3	N 7 41.0	134 09.5	S20 53.9
	13	44 02.7	26 36.3	51.4	156 51.6	27.0	238 24.9	41.0	149 12.1	53.9
	14	59 05.2	41 35.9	52.6	171 54.2	27.1	253 27.5	41.1	164 14.7	53.9
	15	74 07.6	56 35.5	. . 53.8	186 56.7	. . 27.2	268 30.1	. . 41.1	179 17.3	. . 53.9
	16	89 10.1	71 35.1	55.0	201 59.3	27.2	283 32.7	41.1	194 19.8	53.9
	17	104 12.6	86 34.8	56.1	217 01.9	27.3	298 35.3	41.2	209 22.4	53.8
	18	119 15.0	101 34.4	N 5 57.3	232 04.5	S21 27.4	313 37.9	N 7 41.2	224 25.0	S20 53.8
	19	134 17.5	116 34.0	58.5	247 07.1	27.4	328 40.5	41.3	239 27.5	53.8
	20	149 20.0	131 33.6	5 59.7	262 09.7	27.5	343 43.1	41.3	254 30.1	53.8
	21	164 22.4	146 33.2	6 00.9	277 12.3	. . 27.6	358 45.7	. . 41.4	269 32.7	. . 53.8
	22	179 24.9	161 32.8	02.1	292 14.8	27.7	13 48.3	41.4	284 35.3	53.8
	23	194 27.3	176 32.4	03.3	307 17.4	27.7	28 50.9	41.5	299 37.8	53.8
	Mer. Pass.	h m 10 08.2	v −0.4	d 1.2	v 2.5	d 0.1	v 2.6	d 0.1	v 2.6	d 0.0

STARS

Name	SHA	Dec
	° ′	° ′
Acamar	315 17.4	S40 14.7
Achernar	335 26.1	S57 09.4
Acrux	173 06.3	S63 11.5
Adhara	255 11.1	S29 00.1
Aldebaran	290 47.5	N16 32.2
Alioth	166 18.6	N55 52.4
Alkaid	152 57.0	N49 14.0
Al Na'ir	27 41.7	S46 52.7
Alnilam	275 44.6	S 1 11.8
Alphard	217 54.1	S 8 44.0
Alphecca	126 09.1	N26 39.6
Alpheratz	357 41.8	N29 10.6
Altair	62 06.4	N 8 54.7
Ankaa	353 14.3	S42 13.1
Antares	112 23.6	S26 27.9
Arcturus	145 53.7	N19 05.9
Atria	107 23.3	S69 03.0
Avior	234 17.1	S59 34.2
Bellatrix	278 30.2	N 6 21.6
Betelgeuse	270 59.4	N 7 24.3
Canopus	263 55.5	S52 42.7
Capella	280 31.9	N46 00.7
Deneb	49 30.2	N45 20.1
Denebola	182 31.5	N14 28.8
Diphda	348 54.3	S17 54.0
Dubhe	193 49.1	N61 39.9
Elnath	278 10.4	N28 37.1
Eltanin	90 45.0	N51 29.1
Enif	33 45.4	N 9 56.9
Fomalhaut	15 22.2	S29 32.1
Gacrux	171 58.1	S57 12.4
Gienah	175 50.0	S17 38.1
Hadar	148 44.4	S60 27.0
Hamal	327 58.9	N23 32.1
Kaus Aust.	83 41.1	S34 22.3
Kochab	137 19.1	N74 05.4
Markab	13 36.6	N15 17.4
Menkar	314 13.4	N 4 08.9
Menkent	148 04.9	S36 27.0
Miaplacidus	221 38.9	S69 47.5
Mirfak	308 38.0	N49 54.9
Nunki	75 55.9	S26 16.3
Peacock	53 16.4	S56 40.6
Pollux	243 25.5	N27 59.1
Procyon	244 57.8	N 5 10.7
Rasalhague	96 04.5	N12 32.9
Regulus	207 41.4	N11 53.1
Rigel	281 10.4	S 8 11.3
Rigil Kent.	139 48.4	S60 54.0
Sabik	102 10.1	S15 44.5
Schedar	349 38.8	N56 37.4
Shaula	96 19.1	S37 06.6
Sirius	258 32.2	S16 44.7
Spica	158 28.9	S11 14.8
Suhail	222 50.9	S43 30.3
Vega	80 37.5	N38 47.8
Zuben'ubi	137 03.0	S16 06.5

	SHA	Mer. Pass.
	° ′	h m
Venus	344 19.1	11 13
Mars	112 45.6	2 38
Jupiter	194 17.0	21 09
Saturn	105 05.5	3 09

	UT	SUN GHA	SUN Dec	MOON GHA	v	MOON Dec	d	HP
	d h	° ′	° ′	° ′	′	° ′	′	′
	18 00	180 09.7	N10 54.1	43 04.2	14.5	N 6 08.8	9.0	54.6
	01	195 09.8	54.9	57 37.7	14.6	5 59.8	8.9	54.6
	02	210 10.0	55.8	72 11.3	14.5	5 50.9	9.0	54.6
	03	225 10.1	. . 56.7	86 44.8	14.7	5 41.9	9.1	54.6
	04	240 10.3	57.5	101 18.5	14.6	5 32.8	9.0	54.6
	05	255 10.4	58.4	115 52.1	14.7	5 23.8	9.1	54.5
	06	270 10.5	N10 59.3	130 25.8	14.7	N 5 14.7	9.0	54.5
	07	285 10.7	11 00.1	144 59.5	14.7	5 05.7	9.1	54.5
	08	300 10.8	01.0	159 33.2	14.7	4 56.6	9.2	54.5
M	09	315 11.0	. . 01.9	174 06.9	14.8	4 47.4	9.1	54.5
O	10	330 11.1	02.8	188 40.7	14.8	4 38.3	9.1	54.5
N	11	345 11.2	03.6	203 14.5	14.8	4 29.2	9.2	54.5
D	12	0 11.4	N11 04.5	217 48.3	14.9	N 4 20.0	9.2	54.4
A	13	15 11.5	05.4	232 22.2	14.8	4 10.8	9.2	54.4
Y	14	30 11.6	06.2	246 56.0	14.9	4 01.6	9.2	54.4
	15	45 11.8	. . 07.1	261 29.9	14.9	3 52.4	9.2	54.4
	16	60 11.9	07.9	276 03.8	14.9	3 43.2	9.2	54.4
	17	75 12.1	08.8	290 37.7	15.0	3 34.0	9.2	54.4
	18	90 12.2	N11 09.7	305 11.7	15.0	N 3 24.8	9.3	54.4
	19	105 12.3	10.5	319 45.7	14.9	3 15.5	9.2	54.4
	20	120 12.5	11.4	334 19.6	15.1	3 06.3	9.3	54.3
	21	135 12.6	. . 12.3	348 53.7	15.0	2 57.0	9.3	54.3
	22	150 12.7	13.1	3 27.7	15.0	2 47.7	9.3	54.3
	23	165 12.9	14.0	18 01.7	15.1	2 38.4	9.3	54.3
	19 00	180 13.0	N11 14.9	32 35.8	15.0	N 2 29.1	9.3	54.3
	01	195 13.1	15.7	47 09.8	15.1	2 19.8	9.3	54.3
	02	210 13.3	16.6	61 43.9	15.1	2 10.5	9.3	54.3
	03	225 13.4	. . 17.4	76 18.0	15.1	2 01.2	9.3	54.3
	04	240 13.5	18.3	90 52.1	15.2	1 51.9	9.4	54.3
	05	255 13.7	19.2	105 26.3	15.1	1 42.5	9.3	54.2
	06	270 13.8	N11 20.0	120 00.4	15.2	N 1 33.2	9.3	54.2
	07	285 14.0	20.9	134 34.6	15.1	1 23.9	9.4	54.2
T	08	300 14.1	21.8	149 08.7	15.2	1 14.5	9.3	54.2
U	09	315 14.2	. . 22.6	163 42.9	15.2	1 05.2	9.4	54.2
E	10	330 14.4	23.5	178 17.1	15.2	0 55.8	9.3	54.2
S	11	345 14.5	24.3	192 51.3	15.2	0 46.5	9.3	54.2
D	12	0 14.6	N11 25.2	207 25.5	15.2	N 0 37.2	9.4	54.2
A	13	15 14.8	26.1	221 59.7	15.2	0 27.8	9.3	54.2
Y	14	30 14.9	26.9	236 33.9	15.3	0 18.5	9.4	54.2
	15	45 15.0	. . 27.8	251 08.2	15.2	N 0 09.1	9.3	54.2
	16	60 15.2	28.6	265 42.4	15.3	S 0 00.2	9.4	54.1
	17	75 15.3	29.5	280 16.7	15.2	0 09.6	9.3	54.1
	18	90 15.4	N11 30.3	294 50.9	15.3	S 0 18.9	9.4	54.1
	19	105 15.6	31.2	309 25.2	15.2	0 28.3	9.3	54.1
	20	120 15.7	32.1	323 59.4	15.3	0 37.6	9.3	54.1
	21	135 15.8	. . 32.9	338 33.7	15.2	0 46.9	9.3	54.1
	22	150 15.9	33.8	353 07.9	15.3	0 56.2	9.4	54.1
	23	165 16.1	34.6	7 42.2	15.3	1 05.6	9.3	54.1
	20 00	180 16.2	N11 35.5	22 16.5	15.3	S 1 14.9	9.3	54.1
	01	195 16.3	36.3	36 50.8	15.2	1 24.2	9.3	54.1
	02	210 16.5	37.2	51 25.0	15.3	1 33.5	9.3	54.1
	03	225 16.6	. . 38.0	65 59.3	15.3	1 42.8	9.3	54.1
	04	240 16.7	38.9	80 33.6	15.3	1 52.1	9.2	54.1
	05	255 16.9	39.7	95 07.9	15.2	2 01.3	9.3	54.1
	06	270 17.0	N11 40.6	109 42.1	15.3	S 2 10.6	9.3	54.1
W	07	285 17.1	41.5	124 16.4	15.3	2 19.9	9.2	54.0
E	08	300 17.3	42.3	138 50.7	15.2	2 29.1	9.2	54.0
D	09	315 17.4	. . 43.2	153 24.9	15.3	2 38.3	9.3	54.0
N	10	330 17.5	44.0	167 59.2	15.3	2 47.6	9.2	54.0
E	11	345 17.6	44.9	182 33.5	15.2	2 56.8	9.2	54.0
S	12	0 17.8	N11 45.7	197 07.7	15.3	S 3 06.0	9.2	54.0
D	13	15 17.9	46.6	211 42.0	15.2	3 15.2	9.1	54.0
A	14	30 18.0	47.4	226 16.2	15.2	3 24.3	9.2	54.0
Y	15	45 18.2	. . 48.3	240 50.4	15.3	3 33.5	9.1	54.0
	16	60 18.3	49.1	255 24.7	15.2	3 42.6	9.2	54.0
	17	75 18.4	50.0	269 58.9	15.2	3 51.8	9.1	54.0
	18	90 18.5	N11 50.8	284 33.1	15.2	S 4 00.9	9.1	54.0
	19	105 18.7	51.7	299 07.3	15.2	4 10.0	9.1	54.0
	20	120 18.8	52.5	313 41.5	15.2	4 19.1	9.0	54.0
	21	135 18.9	. . 53.4	328 15.7	15.2	4 28.1	9.1	54.0
	22	150 19.0	54.2	342 49.9	15.2	4 37.2	9.0	54.0
	23	165 19.2	55.0	357 24.1	15.1	S 4 46.2	9.0	54.0
		SD 15.9	d 0.9	SD	14.8	14.8		14.7

Lat.	Twilight Naut.	Twilight Civil	Sunrise	Moonrise 18	19	20	21
°	h m	h m	h m	h m	h m	h m	h m
N 72	////	01 06	03 13	14 46	16 20	17 52	19 26
N 70	////	02 02	03 34	14 52	16 19	17 47	19 14
68	////	02 35	03 50	14 56	16 19	17 42	19 04
66	00 57	02 58	04 03	15 00	16 19	17 38	18 56
64	01 46	03 16	04 14	15 03	16 19	17 34	18 50
62	02 16	03 31	04 23	15 06	16 19	17 32	18 44
60	02 38	03 43	04 31	15 08	16 19	17 29	18 39
N 58	02 55	03 53	04 38	15 10	16 19	17 27	18 35
56	03 09	04 03	04 44	15 12	16 19	17 25	18 31
54	03 21	04 10	04 49	15 14	16 19	17 23	18 27
52	03 32	04 17	04 54	15 15	16 19	17 21	18 24
50	03 41	04 24	04 58	15 17	16 19	17 20	18 21
45	03 59	04 37	05 08	15 20	16 18	17 17	18 15
N 40	04 14	04 48	05 16	15 22	16 18	17 14	18 10
35	04 25	04 56	05 23	15 24	16 18	17 12	18 05
30	04 35	05 04	05 29	15 26	16 18	17 10	18 01
20	04 50	05 16	05 39	15 30	16 18	17 06	17 55
N 10	05 01	05 26	05 48	15 33	16 18	17 03	17 49
0	05 10	05 35	05 56	15 35	16 18	17 00	17 43
S 10	05 18	05 42	06 04	15 38	16 18	16 58	17 38
20	05 24	05 50	06 12	15 41	16 18	16 55	17 32
30	05 29	05 57	06 22	15 44	16 18	16 51	17 25
35	05 32	06 01	06 27	15 46	16 18	16 49	17 22
40	05 34	06 06	06 33	15 49	16 18	16 47	17 17
45	05 36	06 10	06 40	15 51	16 18	16 45	17 12
S 50	05 38	06 16	06 49	15 54	16 18	16 42	17 07
52	05 39	06 18	06 53	15 55	16 18	16 41	17 04
54	05 40	06 21	06 57	15 57	16 18	16 39	17 01
56	05 40	06 24	07 02	15 59	16 18	16 37	16 58
58	05 41	06 27	07 07	16 00	16 18	16 36	16 54
S 60	05 41	06 30	07 13	16 02	16 18	16 34	16 50

Lat.	Sunset	Twilight Civil	Twilight Naut.	Moonset 18	19	20	21
°	h m	h m	h m	h m	h m	h m	h m
N 72	20 49	23 08	////	04 23	04 18	04 14	04 09
N 70	20 28	22 03	////	04 16	04 16	04 16	04 16
68	20 11	21 28	////	04 09	04 14	04 18	04 23
66	19 58	21 04	23 15	04 04	04 12	04 20	04 28
64	19 46	20 45	22 18	04 00	04 11	04 22	04 33
62	19 37	20 30	21 46	03 56	04 10	04 23	04 37
60	19 29	20 17	21 23	03 53	04 09	04 24	04 40
N 58	19 22	20 06	21 06	03 50	04 08	04 25	04 43
56	19 16	19 57	20 51	03 47	04 07	04 26	04 46
54	19 10	19 49	20 39	03 45	04 06	04 27	04 49
52	19 05	19 42	20 28	03 42	04 06	04 28	04 51
50	19 01	19 36	20 19	03 40	04 05	04 29	04 53
45	18 51	19 22	20 00	03 36	04 04	04 30	04 57
N 40	18 43	19 11	19 45	03 32	04 02	04 32	05 01
35	18 36	19 02	19 34	03 29	04 01	04 33	05 04
30	18 30	18 55	19 24	03 26	04 00	04 34	05 07
20	18 20	18 42	19 09	03 21	03 59	04 36	05 12
N 10	18 11	18 32	18 57	03 17	03 57	04 37	05 17
0	18 02	18 23	18 48	03 13	03 56	04 39	05 21
S 10	17 54	18 16	18 40	03 09	03 55	04 40	05 25
20	17 46	18 08	18 34	03 04	03 53	04 41	05 30
30	17 36	18 00	18 28	02 59	03 51	04 43	05 35
35	17 30	17 56	18 26	02 56	03 51	04 44	05 38
40	17 24	17 52	18 23	02 53	03 49	04 45	05 41
45	17 17	17 47	18 21	02 49	03 48	04 47	05 45
S 50	17 08	17 41	18 19	02 44	03 47	04 48	05 49
52	17 04	17 39	18 18	02 42	03 46	04 49	05 51
54	17 00	17 36	18 17	02 40	03 45	04 50	05 54
56	16 55	17 34	18 17	02 37	03 44	04 50	05 56
58	16 50	17 30	18 16	02 34	03 43	04 51	05 59
S 60	16 44	17 27	18 15	02 31	03 42	04 52	06 02

Day	SUN Eqn. of Time 00^h	SUN Eqn. of Time 12^h	SUN Mer. Pass.	MOON Mer. Pass. Upper	MOON Mer. Pass. Lower	Age	Phase
d	m s	m s	h m	h m	h m	d	%
18	00 39	00 45	11 59	21 46	09 24	11	88
19	00 52	00 58	11 59	22 28	10 07	12	94
20	01 05	01 11	11 59	23 11	10 49	13	97

UT	ARIES	VENUS −3·8		MARS −1·2		JUPITER −2·3		SATURN +0·2	
	GHA	GHA	Dec	GHA	Dec	GHA	Dec	GHA	Dec
d h	° ′	° ′	° ′	° ′	° ′	° ′	° ′	° ′	° ′
21 00	209 29.8	191 32.0	N 6 04.5	322 20.0	S21 27.8	43 53.5	N 7 41.5	314 40.4	S20 53.7
01	224 32.3	206 31.6	05.7	337 22.6	27.9	58 56.1	41.6	329 43.0	53.7
02	239 34.7	221 31.2	06.9	352 25.2	28.0	73 58.7	41.6	344 45.6	53.7
03	254 37.2	236 30.8	. . 08.1	7 27.8	. . 28.0	89 01.3	. . 41.7	359 48.1	. . 53.7
04	269 39.7	251 30.4	09.3	22 30.4	28.1	104 03.9	41.7	14 50.7	53.7
05	284 42.1	266 30.1	10.5	37 33.0	28.2	119 06.5	41.8	29 53.3	53.7
06	299 44.6	281 29.7	N 6 11.7	52 35.6	S21 28.2	134 09.0	N 7 41.8	44 55.9	S20 53.7
07	314 47.1	296 29.3	12.9	67 38.2	28.3	149 11.6	41.9	59 58.4	53.6
T 08	329 49.5	311 28.9	14.1	82 40.8	28.4	164 14.2	41.9	75 01.0	53.6
H 09	344 52.0	326 28.5	. . 15.3	97 43.4	. . 28.5	179 16.8	. . 42.0	90 03.6	. . 53.6
U 10	359 54.4	341 28.1	16.5	112 46.0	28.5	194 19.4	42.0	105 06.2	53.6
R 11	14 56.9	356 27.7	17.7	127 48.6	28.6	209 22.0	42.0	120 08.7	53.6
S 12	29 59.4	11 27.3	N 6 18.8	142 51.2	S21 28.7	224 24.6	N 7 42.1	135 11.3	S20 53.6
D 13	45 01.8	26 26.9	20.0	157 53.9	28.7	239 27.2	42.1	150 13.9	53.6
A 14	60 04.3	41 26.5	21.2	172 56.5	28.8	254 29.8	42.2	165 16.5	53.6
Y 15	75 06.8	56 26.1	. . 22.4	187 59.1	. . 28.9	269 32.4	. . 42.2	180 19.0	. . 53.5
16	90 09.2	71 25.7	23.6	203 01.7	29.0	284 35.0	42.3	195 21.6	53.5
17	105 11.7	86 25.3	24.8	218 04.3	29.0	299 37.6	42.3	210 24.2	53.5
18	120 14.2	101 24.9	N 6 26.0	233 06.9	S21 29.1	314 40.2	N 7 42.4	225 26.8	S20 53.5
19	135 16.6	116 24.5	27.2	248 09.5	29.2	329 42.8	42.4	240 29.4	53.5
20	150 19.1	131 24.1	28.4	263 12.2	29.2	344 45.4	42.5	255 31.9	53.5
21	165 21.6	146 23.7	. . 29.6	278 14.8	. . 29.3	359 47.9	. . 42.5	270 34.5	. . 53.5
22	180 24.0	161 23.3	30.8	293 17.4	29.4	14 50.5	42.5	285 37.1	53.4
23	195 26.5	176 23.0	32.0	308 20.0	29.4	29 53.1	42.6	300 39.7	53.4
22 00	210 28.9	191 22.6	N 6 33.1	323 22.7	S21 29.5	44 55.7	N 7 42.6	315 42.2	S20 53.4
01	225 31.4	206 22.2	34.3	338 25.3	29.6	59 58.3	42.7	330 44.8	53.4
02	240 33.9	221 21.8	35.5	353 27.9	29.7	75 00.9	42.7	345 47.4	53.4
03	255 36.3	236 21.4	. . 36.7	8 30.6	. . 29.7	90 03.5	. . 42.8	0 50.0	. . 53.4
04	270 38.8	251 21.0	37.9	23 33.2	29.8	105 06.1	42.8	15 52.6	53.4
05	285 41.3	266 20.6	39.1	38 35.8	29.9	120 08.7	42.9	30 55.1	53.3
06	300 43.7	281 20.2	N 6 40.3	53 38.5	S21 29.9	135 11.3	N 7 42.9	45 57.7	S20 53.3
07	315 46.2	296 19.8	41.5	68 41.1	30.0	150 13.8	42.9	61 00.3	53.3
08	330 48.7	311 19.4	42.7	83 43.7	30.1	165 16.4	43.0	76 02.9	53.3
F 09	345 51.1	326 19.0	. . 43.8	98 46.4	. . 30.1	180 19.0	. . 43.0	91 05.4	. . 53.3
R 10	0 53.6	341 18.6	45.0	113 49.0	30.2	195 21.6	43.1	106 08.0	53.3
I 11	15 56.0	356 18.2	46.2	128 51.6	30.3	210 24.2	43.1	121 10.6	53.3
D 12	30 58.5	11 17.8	N 6 47.4	143 54.3	S21 30.3	225 26.8	N 7 43.2	136 13.2	S20 53.2
A 13	46 01.0	26 17.4	48.6	158 56.9	30.4	240 29.4	43.2	151 15.8	53.2
Y 14	61 03.4	41 17.0	49.8	173 59.6	30.5	255 31.9	43.2	166 18.3	53.2
15	76 05.9	56 16.6	. . 51.0	189 02.2	. . 30.5	270 34.5	. . 43.3	181 20.9	. . 53.2
16	91 08.4	71 16.2	52.1	204 04.9	30.6	285 37.1	43.3	196 23.5	53.2
17	106 10.8	86 15.8	53.3	219 07.5	30.7	300 39.7	43.4	211 26.1	53.2
18	121 13.3	101 15.4	N 6 54.5	234 10.2	S21 30.8	315 42.3	N 7 43.4	226 28.7	S20 53.2
19	136 15.8	116 15.0	55.7	249 12.8	30.8	330 44.9	43.5	241 31.2	53.1
20	151 18.2	131 14.6	56.9	264 15.5	30.9	345 47.5	43.5	256 33.8	53.1
21	166 20.7	146 14.2	. . 58.1	279 18.1	. . 31.0	0 50.0	. . 43.5	271 36.4	. . 53.1
22	181 23.2	161 13.8	6 59.3	294 20.8	31.0	15 52.6	43.6	286 39.0	53.1
23	196 25.6	176 13.4	7 00.4	309 23.5	31.1	30 55.2	43.6	301 41.6	53.1
23 00	211 28.1	191 13.0	N 7 01.6	324 26.1	S21 31.2	45 57.8	N 7 43.7	316 44.1	S20 53.1
01	226 30.5	206 12.6	02.8	339 28.8	31.2	61 00.4	43.7	331 46.7	53.1
02	241 33.0	221 12.2	04.0	354 31.4	31.3	76 03.0	43.7	346 49.3	53.0
03	256 35.5	236 11.8	. . 05.2	9 34.1	. . 31.4	91 05.5	. . 43.8	1 51.9	. . 53.0
04	271 37.9	251 11.4	06.4	24 36.8	31.4	106 08.1	43.8	16 54.5	53.0
05	286 40.4	266 11.0	07.5	39 39.4	31.5	121 10.7	43.9	31 57.1	53.0
06	301 42.9	281 10.6	N 7 08.7	54 42.1	S21 31.6	136 13.3	N 7 43.9	46 59.6	S20 53.0
07	316 45.3	296 10.2	09.9	69 44.8	31.6	151 15.9	43.9	62 02.2	53.0
S 08	331 47.8	311 09.8	11.1	84 47.4	31.7	166 18.5	44.0	77 04.8	52.9
A 09	346 50.3	326 09.4	. . 12.3	99 50.1	. . 31.8	181 21.0	. . 44.0	92 07.4	. . 52.9
T 10	1 52.7	341 09.0	13.5	114 52.8	31.8	196 23.6	44.1	107 10.0	52.9
U 11	16 55.2	356 08.5	14.6	129 55.5	31.9	211 26.2	44.1	122 12.5	52.9
R 12	31 57.7	11 08.1	N 7 15.8	144 58.1	S21 31.9	226 28.8	N 7 44.2	137 15.1	S20 52.9
D 13	47 00.1	26 07.7	17.0	160 00.8	32.0	241 31.4	44.2	152 17.7	52.9
A 14	62 02.6	41 07.3	18.2	175 03.5	32.1	256 33.9	44.2	167 20.3	52.9
Y 15	77 05.0	56 06.9	. . 19.4	190 06.2	. . 32.1	271 36.5	. . 44.3	182 22.9	. . 52.8
16	92 07.5	71 06.5	20.5	205 08.9	32.2	286 39.1	44.3	197 25.5	52.8
17	107 10.0	86 06.1	21.7	220 11.5	32.3	301 41.7	44.3	212 28.0	52.8
18	122 12.4	101 05.7	N 7 22.9	235 14.2	S21 32.3	316 44.3	N 7 44.4	227 30.6	S20 52.8
19	137 14.9	116 05.3	24.1	250 16.9	32.4	331 46.8	44.4	242 33.2	52.8
20	152 17.4	131 04.9	25.2	265 19.6	32.5	346 49.4	44.5	257 35.8	52.8
21	167 19.8	146 04.5	. . 26.4	280 22.3	. . 32.5	1 52.0	. . 44.5	272 38.4	. . 52.8
22	182 22.3	161 04.1	27.6	295 25.0	32.6	16 54.6	44.5	287 41.0	52.7
23	197 24.8	176 03.7	28.8	310 27.7	32.7	31 57.1	44.6	302 43.6	52.7
Mer. Pass.	h m 9 56.4	v −0.4	d 1.2	v 2.6	d 0.1	v 2.6	d 0.0	v 2.6	d 0.0

STARS Name	SHA	Dec
	° ′	° ′
Acamar	315 17.4	S40 14.6
Achernar	335 26.1	S57 09.4
Acrux	173 06.3	S63 11.5
Adhara	255 11.1	S29 00.1
Aldebaran	290 47.5	N16 32.2
Alioth	166 18.6	N55 52.4
Alkaid	152 57.0	N49 14.0
Al Na'ir	27 41.6	S46 52.7
Alnilam	275 44.6	S 1 11.8
Alphard	217 54.1	S 8 44.0
Alphecca	126 09.1	N26 39.6
Alpheratz	357 41.8	N29 10.6
Altair	62 06.3	N 8 54.7
Ankaa	353 14.3	S42 13.1
Antares	112 23.6	S26 27.9
Arcturus	145 53.7	N19 05.9
Atria	107 23.2	S69 03.0
Avior	234 17.2	S59 34.2
Bellatrix	278 30.2	N 6 21.6
Betelgeuse	270 59.4	N 7 24.3
Canopus	263 55.5	S52 42.7
Capella	280 31.9	N46 00.7
Deneb	49 30.2	N45 20.1
Denebola	182 31.5	N14 28.8
Diphda	348 54.3	S17 54.0
Dubhe	193 49.1	N61 39.9
Elnath	278 10.5	N28 37.0
Eltanin	90 45.0	N51 29.1
Enif	33 45.4	N 9 56.9
Fomalhaut	15 22.2	S29 32.1
Gacrux	171 58.1	S57 12.4
Gienah	175 50.0	S17 38.1
Hadar	148 44.4	S60 27.0
Hamal	327 58.9	N23 32.1
Kaus Aust.	83 41.1	S34 22.3
Kochab	137 19.1	N74 05.4
Markab	13 36.6	N15 17.4
Menkar	314 13.4	N 4 08.9
Menkent	148 04.9	S36 27.0
Miaplacidus	221 38.9	S69 47.5
Mirfak	308 38.0	N49 54.9
Nunki	75 55.8	S26 16.3
Peacock	53 16.3	S56 40.6
Pollux	243 25.5	N27 59.1
Procyon	244 57.8	N 5 10.7
Rasalhague	96 04.5	N12 32.9
Regulus	207 41.4	N11 53.1
Rigel	281 10.5	S 8 11.3
Rigil Kent.	139 48.4	S60 54.0
Sabik	102 10.1	S15 44.5
Schedar	349 38.7	N56 37.4
Shaula	96 19.1	S37 06.6
Sirius	258 32.2	S16 44.7
Spica	158 28.9	S11 14.8
Suhail	222 50.9	S43 30.3
Vega	80 37.5	N38 47.9
Zuben'ubi	137 03.0	S16 06.5
	SHA	Mer. Pass.
	° ′	h m
Venus	340 53.6	11 15
Mars	112 53.7	2 26
Jupiter	194 26.8	20 57
Saturn	105 13.3	2 57

UT	SUN GHA	SUN Dec	MOON GHA	v	MOON Dec	d	HP
d h	° ′	° ′	° ′	′	° ′	′	′
21 00	180 19.3	N11 55.9	11 58.2	15.2	S 4 55.2	9.0	54.0
01	195 19.4	56.7	26 32.4	15.1	5 04.2	8.9	54.0
02	210 19.6	57.6	41 06.5	15.2	5 13.1	9.0	54.0
03	225 19.7	. . 58.4	55 40.7	15.1	5 22.1	8.9	54.0
04	240 19.8	11 59.3	70 14.8	15.1	5 31.0	8.9	54.0
05	255 19.9	12 00.1	84 48.9	15.1	5 39.9	8.9	54.0
06	270 20.1	N12 01.0	99 23.0	15.0	S 5 48.8	8.8	54.0
07	285 20.2	01.8	113 57.0	15.1	5 57.6	8.8	54.0
08	300 20.3	02.7	128 31.1	15.0	6 06.4	8.8	54.0
09	315 20.4	. . 03.5	143 05.1	15.1	6 15.2	8.8	54.0
10	330 20.6	04.3	157 39.2	15.0	6 24.0	8.8	54.0
11	345 20.7	05.2	172 13.2	15.0	6 32.8	8.7	54.0
12	0 20.8	N12 06.0	186 47.2	14.9	S 6 41.5	8.7	54.0
13	15 20.9	06.9	201 21.1	15.0	6 50.2	8.6	54.0
14	30 21.1	07.7	215 55.1	15.0	6 58.8	8.7	54.0
15	45 21.2	. . 08.6	230 29.1	14.9	7 07.5	8.6	54.0
16	60 21.3	09.4	245 03.0	14.9	7 16.1	8.6	54.0
17	75 21.4	10.2	259 36.9	14.9	7 24.7	8.5	54.0
18	90 21.6	N12 11.1	274 10.8	14.8	S 7 33.2	8.6	54.0
19	105 21.7	11.9	288 44.6	14.9	7 41.8	8.4	54.0
20	120 21.8	12.8	303 18.5	14.8	7 50.2	8.5	54.0
21	135 21.9	. . 13.6	317 52.3	14.8	7 58.7	8.4	54.0
22	150 22.0	14.4	332 26.1	14.8	8 07.1	8.4	54.0
23	165 22.2	15.3	346 59.9	14.8	8 15.5	8.4	54.0
22 00	180 22.3	N12 16.1	1 33.7	14.7	S 8 23.9	8.3	54.0
01	195 22.4	17.0	16 07.4	14.7	8 32.2	8.3	54.0
02	210 22.5	17.8	30 41.1	14.7	8 40.5	8.3	54.0
03	225 22.7	. . 18.6	45 14.8	14.7	8 48.8	8.2	54.0
04	240 22.8	19.5	59 48.5	14.7	8 57.0	8.2	54.0
05	255 22.9	20.3	74 22.2	14.6	9 05.2	8.1	54.0
06	270 23.0	N12 21.1	88 55.8	14.6	S 9 13.3	8.1	54.0
07	285 23.1	22.0	103 29.4	14.6	9 21.4	8.1	54.0
08	300 23.3	22.8	118 03.0	14.5	9 29.5	8.0	54.0
09	315 23.4	. . 23.7	132 36.5	14.6	9 37.5	8.0	54.0
10	330 23.5	24.5	147 10.1	14.5	9 45.5	8.0	54.0
11	345 23.6	25.3	161 43.6	14.4	9 53.5	7.9	54.0
12	0 23.7	N12 26.2	176 17.0	14.5	S10 01.4	7.9	54.0
13	15 23.9	27.0	190 50.5	14.4	10 09.3	7.8	54.0
14	30 24.0	27.8	205 23.9	14.4	10 17.1	7.8	54.0
15	45 24.1	. . 28.7	219 57.3	14.4	10 24.9	7.8	54.0
16	60 24.2	29.5	234 30.7	14.3	10 32.7	7.7	54.0
17	75 24.3	30.3	249 04.0	14.3	10 40.4	7.6	54.0
18	90 24.5	N12 31.2	263 37.3	14.3	S10 48.0	7.7	54.0
19	105 24.6	32.0	278 10.6	14.3	10 55.7	7.5	54.0
20	120 24.7	32.8	292 43.9	14.2	11 03.2	7.6	54.0
21	135 24.8	. . 33.7	307 17.1	14.2	11 10.8	7.4	54.0
22	150 24.9	34.5	321 50.3	14.2	11 18.2	7.5	54.0
23	165 25.0	35.3	336 23.5	14.1	11 25.7	7.4	54.0
23 00	180 25.2	N12 36.1	350 56.6	14.1	S11 33.1	7.3	54.0
01	195 25.3	37.0	5 29.7	14.1	11 40.4	7.3	54.0
02	210 25.4	37.8	20 02.8	14.0	11 47.7	7.2	54.0
03	225 25.5	. . 38.6	34 35.8	14.0	11 54.9	7.2	54.1
04	240 25.6	39.5	49 08.8	14.0	12 02.1	7.2	54.1
05	255 25.7	40.3	63 41.8	14.0	12 09.3	7.1	54.1
06	270 25.9	N12 41.1	78 14.8	13.9	S12 16.4	7.0	54.1
07	285 26.0	41.9	92 47.7	13.9	12 23.4	7.0	54.1
08	300 26.1	42.8	107 20.6	13.9	12 30.4	6.9	54.1
09	315 26.2	. . 43.6	121 53.5	13.8	12 37.3	6.9	54.1
10	330 26.3	44.4	136 26.3	13.8	12 44.2	6.9	54.1
11	345 26.4	45.3	150 59.1	13.7	12 51.1	6.7	54.1
12	0 26.6	N12 46.1	165 31.8	13.8	S12 57.8	6.8	54.1
13	15 26.7	46.9	180 04.6	13.7	13 04.6	6.6	54.1
14	30 26.8	47.7	194 37.3	13.6	13 11.2	6.6	54.1
15	45 26.9	. . 48.6	209 09.9	13.6	13 17.8	6.6	54.1
16	60 27.0	49.4	223 42.5	13.6	13 24.4	6.5	54.1
17	75 27.1	50.2	238 15.1	13.6	13 30.9	6.4	54.1
18	90 27.2	N12 51.0	252 47.7	13.5	S13 37.3	6.4	54.2
19	105 27.3	51.8	267 20.2	13.5	13 43.7	6.4	54.2
20	120 27.5	52.7	281 52.7	13.5	13 50.1	6.2	54.2
21	135 27.6	. . 53.5	296 25.2	13.4	13 56.3	6.2	54.2
22	150 27.7	54.3	310 57.6	13.4	14 02.5	6.2	54.2
23	165 27.8	55.1	325 30.0	13.3	S14 08.7	6.1	54.2
	SD 15.9	*d* 0.8	SD	14.7	14.7		14.7

Lat.	Twilight Naut.	Twilight Civil	Sunrise	Moonrise 21	Moonrise 22	Moonrise 23	Moonrise 24
°	h m	h m	h m	h m	h m	h m	h m
N 72	////	////	02 54	19 26	21 02	22 42	24 28
N 70	////	01 36	03 18	19 14	20 43	22 12	23 41
68	////	02 16	03 37	19 04	20 27	21 50	23 10
66	////	02 43	03 51	18 56	20 15	21 33	22 48
64	01 24	03 03	04 03	18 50	20 05	21 19	22 30
62	02 00	03 20	04 13	18 44	19 56	21 07	22 15
60	02 25	03 33	04 22	18 39	19 48	20 57	22 03
N 58	02 44	03 45	04 30	18 35	19 42	20 48	21 52
56	02 59	03 54	04 36	18 31	19 36	20 41	21 43
54	03 13	04 03	04 42	18 27	19 31	20 34	21 35
52	03 24	04 11	04 48	18 24	19 26	20 28	21 28
50	03 33	04 17	04 53	18 21	19 22	20 22	21 21
45	03 53	04 32	05 03	18 15	19 13	20 10	21 07
N 40	04 09	04 43	05 12	18 10	19 05	20 01	20 56
35	04 21	04 53	05 19	18 05	18 59	19 52	20 46
30	04 31	05 01	05 25	18 01	18 53	19 45	20 37
20	04 47	05 14	05 37	17 55	18 43	19 33	20 22
N 10	04 59	05 25	05 46	17 49	18 35	19 22	20 10
0	05 09	05 34	05 55	17 43	18 27	19 11	19 58
S 10	05 18	05 42	06 04	17 38	18 19	19 01	19 46
20	05 25	05 51	06 13	17 32	18 10	18 50	19 33
30	05 31	05 59	06 24	17 25	18 01	18 38	19 18
35	05 34	06 04	06 30	17 22	17 55	18 31	19 10
40	05 37	06 09	06 36	17 17	17 49	18 23	19 00
45	05 40	06 14	06 44	17 12	17 42	18 14	18 49
S 50	05 42	06 20	06 54	17 07	17 33	18 02	18 36
52	05 43	06 23	06 58	17 04	17 29	17 57	18 29
54	05 45	06 26	07 03	17 01	17 25	17 51	18 22
56	05 46	06 29	07 08	16 58	17 20	17 45	18 15
58	05 47	06 33	07 14	16 54	17 14	17 38	18 06
S 60	05 48	06 37	07 20	16 50	17 08	17 30	17 56

Lat.	Sunset	Twilight Civil	Twilight Naut.	Moonset 21	Moonset 22	Moonset 23	Moonset 24
°	h m	h m	h m	h m	h m	h m	h m
N 72	21 07	////	////	04 09	04 03	03 58	03 51
N 70	20 42	22 30	////	04 16	04 17	04 19	04 22
68	20 23	21 46	////	04 23	04 28	04 35	04 45
66	20 08	21 18	////	04 28	04 37	04 48	05 03
64	19 56	20 56	22 41	04 33	04 45	04 59	05 18
62	19 45	20 40	22 02	04 37	04 52	05 09	05 30
60	19 36	20 26	21 36	04 40	04 57	05 17	05 41
N 58	19 29	20 14	21 16	04 43	05 03	05 24	05 50
56	19 22	20 04	21 00	04 46	05 07	05 31	05 58
54	19 16	19 55	20 46	04 49	05 11	05 36	06 05
52	19 10	19 48	20 35	04 51	05 15	05 41	06 11
50	19 05	19 41	20 25	04 53	05 18	05 46	06 17
45	18 55	19 26	20 05	04 57	05 26	05 56	06 30
N 40	18 46	19 15	19 49	05 01	05 32	06 05	06 40
35	18 38	19 05	19 37	05 04	05 37	06 12	06 49
30	18 32	18 57	19 26	05 07	05 42	06 18	06 57
20	18 21	18 43	19 10	05 12	05 50	06 29	07 10
N 10	18 11	18 32	18 58	05 17	05 57	06 39	07 22
0	18 02	18 23	18 48	05 21	06 04	06 48	07 33
S 10	17 53	18 14	18 39	05 25	06 11	06 57	07 45
20	17 43	18 06	18 32	05 30	06 18	07 07	07 57
30	17 33	17 57	18 25	05 35	06 26	07 18	08 10
35	17 27	17 53	18 22	05 38	06 31	07 25	08 18
40	17 20	17 48	18 19	05 41	06 36	07 32	08 27
45	17 12	17 42	18 17	05 45	06 43	07 41	08 38
S 50	17 03	17 36	18 14	05 49	06 50	07 51	08 51
52	16 58	17 33	18 13	05 51	06 54	07 56	08 57
54	16 53	17 30	18 11	05 54	06 58	08 01	09 03
56	16 48	17 27	18 10	05 56	07 02	08 07	09 11
58	16 42	17 23	18 09	05 59	07 07	08 14	09 19
S 60	16 35	17 19	18 08	06 02	07 12	08 21	09 28

Day	SUN Eqn. of Time 00^h	SUN Eqn. of Time 12^h	SUN Mer. Pass.	MOON Mer. Pass. Upper	MOON Mer. Pass. Lower	MOON Age	MOON Phase
d	m s	m s	h m	h m	h m	d	%
21	01 17	01 23	11 59	23 54	11 32	14	99
22	01 29	01 35	11 58	24 37	12 15	15	100
23	01 40	01 46	11 58	00 37	13 00	16	98

d	UT h	ARIES GHA	VENUS −3·9 GHA	VENUS Dec	MARS −1·3 GHA	MARS Dec	JUPITER −2·3 GHA	JUPITER Dec	SATURN +0·2 GHA	SATURN Dec
		° ′	° ′	° ′	° ′	° ′	° ′	° ′	° ′	° ′
24	00	212 27.2	191 03.3	N 7 30.0	325 30.4	S21 32.7	46 59.7	N 7 44.6	317 46.1	S20 52.7
	01	227 29.7	206 02.9	31.1	340 33.1	32.8	62 02.3	44.7	332 48.7	52.7
	02	242 32.1	221 02.5	32.3	355 35.8	32.9	77 04.9	44.7	347 51.3	52.7
	03	257 34.6	236 02.1	. . 33.5	10 38.5	. . 32.9	92 07.4	. . 44.7	2 53.9	. . 52.7
	04	272 37.1	251 01.6	34.7	25 41.2	33.0	107 10.0	44.8	17 56.5	52.7
	05	287 39.5	266 01.2	35.8	40 43.9	33.0	122 12.6	44.8	32 59.1	52.6
	06	302 42.0	281 00.8	N 7 37.0	55 46.6	S21 33.1	137 15.2	N 7 44.9	48 01.7	S20 52.6
	07	317 44.5	296 00.4	38.2	70 49.3	33.2	152 17.7	44.9	63 04.2	52.6
	08	332 46.9	311 00.0	39.4	85 52.0	33.2	167 20.3	44.9	78 06.8	52.6
SUNDAY	09	347 49.4	325 59.6	. . 40.5	100 54.7	. . 33.3	182 22.9	. . 45.0	93 09.4	. . 52.6
	10	2 51.9	340 59.2	41.7	115 57.4	33.4	197 25.5	45.0	108 12.0	52.6
	11	17 54.3	355 58.8	42.9	131 00.1	33.4	212 28.0	45.0	123 14.6	52.6
	12	32 56.8	10 58.4	N 7 44.1	146 02.8	S21 33.5	227 30.6	N 7 45.1	138 17.2	S20 52.5
	13	47 59.3	25 58.0	45.2	161 05.5	33.5	242 33.2	45.1	153 19.8	52.5
	14	63 01.7	40 57.6	46.4	176 08.2	33.6	257 35.8	45.1	168 22.3	52.5
	15	78 04.2	55 57.1	. . 47.6	191 11.0	. . 33.7	272 38.3	. . 45.2	183 24.9	. . 52.5
	16	93 06.6	70 56.7	48.8	206 13.7	33.7	287 40.9	45.2	198 27.5	52.5
	17	108 09.1	85 56.3	49.9	221 16.4	33.8	302 43.5	45.3	213 30.1	52.5
	18	123 11.6	100 55.9	N 7 51.1	236 19.1	S21 33.9	317 46.1	N 7 45.3	228 32.7	S20 52.4
	19	138 14.0	115 55.5	52.3	251 21.8	33.9	332 48.6	45.3	243 35.3	52.4
	20	153 16.5	130 55.1	53.5	266 24.6	34.0	347 51.2	45.4	258 37.9	52.4
	21	168 19.0	145 54.7	. . 54.6	281 27.3	. . 34.0	2 53.8	. . 45.4	273 40.5	. . 52.4
	22	183 21.4	160 54.3	55.8	296 30.0	34.1	17 56.3	45.4	288 43.0	52.4
	23	198 23.9	175 53.9	57.0	311 32.7	34.2	32 58.9	45.5	303 45.6	52.4
25	00	213 26.4	190 53.4	N 7 58.1	326 35.5	S21 34.2	48 01.5	N 7 45.5	318 48.2	S20 52.4
	01	228 28.8	205 53.0	7 59.3	341 38.2	34.3	63 04.0	45.5	333 50.8	52.3
	02	243 31.3	220 52.6	8 00.5	356 40.9	34.3	78 06.6	45.6	348 53.4	52.3
	03	258 33.8	235 52.2	. . 01.6	11 43.7	. . 34.4	93 09.2	. . 45.6	3 56.0	. . 52.3
	04	273 36.2	250 51.8	02.8	26 46.4	34.5	108 11.8	45.7	18 58.6	52.3
	05	288 38.7	265 51.4	04.0	41 49.1	34.5	123 14.3	45.7	34 01.2	52.3
	06	303 41.1	280 51.0	N 8 05.2	56 51.9	S21 34.6	138 16.9	N 7 45.7	49 03.7	S20 52.3
	07	318 43.6	295 50.5	06.3	71 54.6	34.6	153 19.5	45.8	64 06.3	52.3
	08	333 46.1	310 50.1	07.5	86 57.3	34.7	168 22.0	45.8	79 08.9	52.2
MONDAY	09	348 48.5	325 49.7	. . 08.7	102 00.1	. . 34.8	183 24.6	. . 45.8	94 11.5	. . 52.2
	10	3 51.0	340 49.3	09.8	117 02.8	34.8	198 27.2	45.9	109 14.1	52.2
	11	18 53.5	355 48.9	11.0	132 05.6	34.9	213 29.7	45.9	124 16.7	52.2
	12	33 55.9	10 48.5	N 8 12.2	147 08.3	S21 34.9	228 32.3	N 7 45.9	139 19.3	S20 52.2
	13	48 58.4	25 48.0	13.3	162 11.1	35.0	243 34.9	46.0	154 21.9	52.2
	14	64 00.9	40 47.6	14.5	177 13.8	35.1	258 37.4	46.0	169 24.5	52.1
	15	79 03.3	55 47.2	. . 15.7	192 16.6	. . 35.1	273 40.0	. . 46.0	184 27.1	. . 52.1
	16	94 05.8	70 46.8	16.8	207 19.3	35.2	288 42.6	46.1	199 29.6	52.1
	17	109 08.2	85 46.4	18.0	222 22.1	35.2	303 45.1	46.1	214 32.2	52.1
	18	124 10.7	100 46.0	N 8 19.2	237 24.8	S21 35.3	318 47.7	N 7 46.1	229 34.8	S20 52.1
	19	139 13.2	115 45.5	20.3	252 27.6	35.3	333 50.2	46.2	244 37.4	52.1
	20	154 15.6	130 45.1	21.5	267 30.3	35.4	348 52.8	46.2	259 40.0	52.1
	21	169 18.1	145 44.7	. . 22.6	282 33.1	. . 35.5	3 55.4	. . 46.2	274 42.6	. . 52.0
	22	184 20.6	160 44.3	23.8	297 35.8	35.5	18 57.9	46.3	289 45.2	52.0
	23	199 23.0	175 43.9	25.0	312 38.6	35.6	34 00.5	46.3	304 47.8	52.0
26	00	214 25.5	190 43.5	N 8 26.1	327 41.4	S21 35.6	49 03.1	N 7 46.3	319 50.4	S20 52.0
	01	229 28.0	205 43.0	27.3	342 44.1	35.7	64 05.6	46.4	334 53.0	52.0
	02	244 30.4	220 42.6	28.5	357 46.9	35.8	79 08.2	46.4	349 55.6	52.0
	03	259 32.9	235 42.2	. . 29.6	12 49.7	. . 35.8	94 10.8	. . 46.4	4 58.1	. . 51.9
	04	274 35.4	250 41.8	30.8	27 52.4	35.9	109 13.3	46.5	20 00.7	51.9
	05	289 37.8	265 41.4	31.9	42 55.2	35.9	124 15.9	46.5	35 03.3	51.9
	06	304 40.3	280 40.9	N 8 33.1	57 58.0	S21 36.0	139 18.4	N 7 46.5	50 05.9	S20 51.9
	07	319 42.7	295 40.5	34.3	73 00.7	36.0	154 21.0	46.6	65 08.5	51.9
	08	334 45.2	310 40.1	35.4	88 03.5	36.1	169 23.6	46.6	80 11.1	51.9
TUESDAY	09	349 47.7	325 39.7	. . 36.6	103 06.3	. . 36.1	184 26.1	. . 46.6	95 13.7	. . 51.9
	10	4 50.1	340 39.3	37.7	118 09.1	36.2	199 28.7	46.6	110 16.3	51.8
	11	19 52.6	355 38.8	38.9	133 11.8	36.3	214 31.2	46.7	125 18.9	51.8
	12	34 55.1	10 38.4	N 8 40.1	148 14.6	S21 36.3	229 33.8	N 7 46.7	140 21.5	S20 51.8
	13	49 57.5	25 38.0	41.2	163 17.4	36.4	244 36.4	46.7	155 24.1	51.8
	14	65 00.0	40 37.6	42.4	178 20.2	36.4	259 38.9	46.8	170 26.7	51.8
	15	80 02.5	55 37.1	. . 43.5	193 23.0	. . 36.5	274 41.5	. . 46.8	185 29.3	. . 51.8
	16	95 04.9	70 36.7	44.7	208 25.8	36.5	289 44.0	46.8	200 31.9	51.7
	17	110 07.4	85 36.3	45.9	223 28.5	36.6	304 46.6	46.9	215 34.5	51.7
	18	125 09.9	100 35.9	N 8 47.0	238 31.3	S21 36.7	319 49.2	N 7 46.9	230 37.0	S20 51.7
	19	140 12.3	115 35.4	48.2	253 34.1	36.7	334 51.7	46.9	245 39.6	51.7
	20	155 14.8	130 35.0	49.3	268 36.9	36.8	349 54.3	47.0	260 42.2	51.7
	21	170 17.2	145 34.6	. . 50.5	283 39.7	. . 36.8	4 56.8	. . 47.0	275 44.8	. . 51.7
	22	185 19.7	160 34.2	51.6	298 42.5	36.9	19 59.4	47.0	290 47.4	51.7
	23	200 22.2	175 33.7	52.8	313 45.3	36.9	35 01.9	47.0	305 50.0	51.6
Mer. Pass.	h m	9 44.6	v −0.4	d 1.2	v 2.7	d 0.1	v 2.6	d 0.0	v 2.6	d 0.0

STARS

Name	SHA ° ′	Dec ° ′
Acamar	315 17.4	S40 14.6
Achernar	335 26.0	S57 09.3
Acrux	173 06.4	S63 11.5
Adhara	255 11.2	S29 00.1
Aldebaran	290 47.5	N16 32.2
Alioth	166 18.6	N55 52.4
Alkaid	152 57.0	N49 14.0
Al Na'ir	27 41.6	S46 52.7
Alnilam	275 44.7	S 1 11.8
Alphard	217 54.1	S 8 44.0
Alphecca	126 09.1	N26 39.6
Alpheratz	357 41.8	N29 10.6
Altair	62 06.3	N 8 54.7
Ankaa	353 14.3	S42 13.1
Antares	112 23.6	S26 27.9
Arcturus	145 53.7	N19 05.9
Atria	107 23.2	S69 03.0
Avior	234 17.2	S59 34.2
Bellatrix	278 30.2	N 6 21.6
Betelgeuse	270 59.4	N 7 24.3
Canopus	263 55.6	S52 42.7
Capella	280 32.0	N46 00.7
Deneb	49 30.1	N45 20.1
Denebola	182 31.5	N14 28.8
Diphda	348 54.3	S17 54.0
Dubhe	193 49.1	N61 39.9
Elnath	278 10.5	N28 37.0
Eltanin	90 44.9	N51 29.1
Enif	33 45.3	N 9 56.9
Fomalhaut	15 22.1	S29 32.1
Gacrux	171 58.1	S57 12.4
Gienah	175 50.0	S17 38.1
Hadar	148 44.4	S60 27.0
Hamal	327 58.9	N23 32.1
Kaus Aust.	83 41.1	S34 22.3
Kochab	137 19.1	N74 05.4
Markab	13 36.6	N15 17.4
Menkar	314 13.4	N 4 08.9
Menkent	148 04.9	S36 27.0
Miaplacidus	221 38.9	S69 47.5
Mirfak	308 38.0	N49 54.9
Nunki	75 55.8	S26 16.3
Peacock	53 16.3	S56 40.6
Pollux	243 25.5	N27 59.1
Procyon	244 57.8	N 5 10.7
Rasalhague	96 04.5	N12 32.9
Regulus	207 41.4	N11 53.1
Rigel	281 10.5	S 8 11.3
Rigil Kent.	139 48.4	S60 54.0
Sabik	102 10.1	S15 44.5
Schedar	349 38.7	N56 37.4
Shaula	96 19.0	S37 06.6
Sirius	258 32.2	S16 44.7
Spica	158 28.9	S11 14.8
Suhail	222 50.9	S43 30.3
Vega	80 37.5	N38 47.9
Zuben'ubi	137 03.0	S16 06.5

	SHA ° ′	Mer. Pass. h m
Venus	337 27.1	11 17
Mars	113 09.1	2 13
Jupiter	194 35.1	20 44
Saturn	105 21.9	2 44

UT	SUN GHA	SUN Dec	MOON GHA	v	MOON Dec	d	HP
d h	° ′	° ′	° ′	′	° ′	′	′
24 00	180 27.9	N12 56.0	340 02.3	13.4	S14 14.8	6.0	54.2
01	195 28.0	56.8	354 34.7	13.3	14 20.8	6.0	54.2
02	210 28.1	57.6	9 07.0	13.2	14 26.8	5.9	54.2
03	225 28.3	. . 58.4	23 39.2	13.2	14 32.7	5.8	54.2
04	240 28.4	12 59.2	38 11.4	13.2	14 38.5	5.8	54.2
05	255 28.5	13 00.1	52 43.6	13.1	14 44.3	5.7	54.2
06	270 28.6	N13 00.9	67 15.7	13.2	S14 50.0	5.6	54.3
07	285 28.7	01.7	81 47.9	13.0	14 55.6	5.6	54.3
08	300 28.8	02.5	96 19.9	13.1	15 01.2	5.5	54.3
S 09	315 28.9	. . 03.3	110 52.0	13.0	15 06.7	5.5	54.3
U 10	330 29.0	04.2	125 24.0	12.9	15 12.2	5.4	54.3
N 11	345 29.1	05.0	139 55.9	13.0	15 17.6	5.3	54.3
D 12	0 29.2	N13 05.8	154 27.9	12.9	S15 22.9	5.3	54.3
A 13	15 29.4	06.6	168 59.8	12.8	15 28.2	5.1	54.3
Y 14	30 29.5	07.4	183 31.6	12.9	15 33.3	5.2	54.3
15	45 29.6	. . 08.2	198 03.5	12.7	15 38.5	5.0	54.3
16	60 29.7	09.1	212 35.2	12.8	15 43.5	5.0	54.4
17	75 29.8	09.9	227 07.0	12.7	15 48.5	4.9	54.4
18	90 29.9	N13 10.7	241 38.7	12.7	S15 53.4	4.8	54.4
19	105 30.0	11.5	256 10.4	12.6	15 58.2	4.8	54.4
20	120 30.1	12.3	270 42.0	12.7	16 03.0	4.7	54.4
21	135 30.2	. . 13.1	285 13.7	12.5	16 07.7	4.6	54.4
22	150 30.3	13.9	299 45.2	12.6	16 12.3	4.6	54.4
23	165 30.4	14.8	314 16.8	12.5	16 16.9	4.4	54.4
25 00	180 30.5	N13 15.6	328 48.3	12.4	S16 21.3	4.4	54.5
01	195 30.7	16.4	343 19.7	12.5	16 25.7	4.4	54.5
02	210 30.8	17.2	357 51.2	12.4	16 30.1	4.2	54.5
03	225 30.9	. . 18.0	12 22.6	12.3	16 34.3	4.2	54.5
04	240 31.0	18.8	26 53.9	12.4	16 38.5	4.1	54.5
05	255 31.1	19.6	41 25.3	12.3	16 42.6	4.0	54.5
06	270 31.2	N13 20.4	55 56.6	12.2	S16 46.6	4.0	54.5
07	285 31.3	21.2	70 27.8	12.3	16 50.6	3.9	54.5
08	300 31.4	22.1	84 59.1	12.1	16 54.5	3.8	54.6
M 09	315 31.5	. . 22.9	99 30.2	12.2	16 58.3	3.7	54.6
O 10	330 31.6	23.7	114 01.4	12.1	17 02.0	3.6	54.6
N 11	345 31.7	24.5	128 32.5	12.1	17 05.6	3.6	54.6
D 12	0 31.8	N13 25.3	143 03.6	12.1	S17 09.2	3.5	54.6
A 13	15 31.9	26.1	157 34.7	12.0	17 12.7	3.4	54.6
Y 14	30 32.0	26.9	172 05.7	12.0	17 16.1	3.3	54.6
15	45 32.1	. . 27.7	186 36.7	11.9	17 19.4	3.3	54.7
16	60 32.2	28.5	201 07.6	11.9	17 22.7	3.1	54.7
17	75 32.3	29.3	215 38.5	11.9	17 25.8	3.1	54.7
18	90 32.4	N13 30.1	230 09.4	11.9	S17 28.9	3.0	54.7
19	105 32.5	30.9	244 40.3	11.8	17 31.9	2.9	54.7
20	120 32.7	31.7	259 11.1	11.8	17 34.8	2.9	54.7
21	135 32.8	. . 32.5	273 41.9	11.7	17 37.7	2.7	54.8
22	150 32.9	33.3	288 12.6	11.8	17 40.4	2.7	54.8
23	165 33.0	34.1	302 43.4	11.6	17 43.1	2.6	54.8
26 00	180 33.1	N13 35.0	317 14.0	11.7	S17 45.7	2.5	54.8
01	195 33.2	35.8	331 44.7	11.6	17 48.2	2.4	54.8
02	210 33.3	36.6	346 15.3	11.6	17 50.6	2.4	54.8
03	225 33.4	. . 37.4	0 45.9	11.6	17 53.0	2.2	54.9
04	240 33.5	38.2	15 16.5	11.5	17 55.2	2.2	54.9
05	255 33.6	39.0	29 47.0	11.5	17 57.4	2.1	54.9
06	270 33.7	N13 39.8	44 17.5	11.5	S17 59.5	2.0	54.9
07	285 33.8	40.6	58 48.0	11.4	18 01.5	1.9	54.9
T 08	300 33.9	41.4	73 18.4	11.4	18 03.4	1.8	54.9
U 09	315 34.0	. . 42.2	87 48.8	11.4	18 05.2	1.7	55.0
E 10	330 34.1	43.0	102 19.2	11.4	18 06.9	1.7	55.0
S 11	345 34.2	43.8	116 49.6	11.3	18 08.6	1.5	55.0
12	0 34.3	N13 44.6	131 19.9	11.3	S18 10.1	1.5	55.0
D 13	15 34.4	45.4	145 50.2	11.3	18 11.6	1.4	55.0
A 14	30 34.5	46.2	160 20.5	11.2	18 13.0	1.3	55.1
Y 15	45 34.6	. . 47.0	174 50.7	11.2	18 14.3	1.2	55.1
16	60 34.7	47.8	189 20.9	11.2	18 15.5	1.1	55.1
17	75 34.8	48.5	203 51.1	11.1	18 16.6	1.0	55.1
18	90 34.9	N13 49.3	218 21.2	11.2	S18 17.6	1.0	55.1
19	105 35.0	50.1	232 51.4	11.1	18 18.6	0.8	55.2
20	120 35.1	50.9	247 21.5	11.0	18 19.4	0.8	55.2
21	135 35.2	. . 51.7	261 51.5	11.1	18 20.2	0.7	55.2
22	150 35.3	52.5	276 21.6	11.0	18 20.9	0.5	55.2
23	165 35.3	53.3	290 51.6	11.0	S18 21.4	0.5	55.2
	SD 15.9	*d* 0.8	SD 14.8		14.9		15.0

Lat.	Twilight Naut.	Twilight Civil	Sunrise	Moonrise 24	25	26	27
°	h m	h m	h m	h m	h m	h m	h m
N 72	////	////	02 35	24 28	00 28	02 43	▬
N 70	////	01 01	03 02	23 41	25 03	01 03	02 10
68	////	01 56	03 23	23 10	24 24	00 24	01 25
66	////	02 27	03 39	22 48	23 56	24 55	00 55
64	00 53	02 51	03 53	22 30	23 36	24 33	00 33
62	01 42	03 09	04 04	22 15	23 19	24 15	00 15
60	02 11	03 23	04 14	22 03	23 05	24 00	00 00
N 58	02 32	03 36	04 22	21 52	22 53	23 47	24 35
56	02 50	03 46	04 29	21 43	22 42	23 37	24 25
54	03 04	03 56	04 36	21 35	22 33	23 27	24 15
52	03 16	04 04	04 41	21 28	22 25	23 19	24 07
50	03 26	04 11	04 47	21 21	22 18	23 11	23 59
45	03 48	04 26	04 58	21 07	22 02	22 55	23 43
N 40	04 04	04 39	05 07	20 56	21 49	22 41	23 30
35	04 17	04 49	05 15	20 46	21 38	22 30	23 19
30	04 28	04 57	05 22	20 37	21 29	22 20	23 09
20	04 45	05 12	05 34	20 22	21 13	22 03	22 53
N 10	04 58	05 23	05 45	20 10	20 58	21 48	22 38
0	05 09	05 33	05 54	19 58	20 45	21 34	22 24
S 10	05 18	05 42	06 04	19 46	20 32	21 20	22 11
20	05 25	05 52	06 14	19 33	20 18	21 05	21 56
30	05 33	06 01	06 25	19 18	20 02	20 49	21 39
35	05 36	06 06	06 32	19 10	19 52	20 39	21 29
40	05 40	06 11	06 39	19 00	19 42	20 28	21 18
45	05 43	06 17	06 48	18 49	19 29	20 14	21 05
S 50	05 46	06 24	06 58	18 36	19 14	19 58	20 49
52	05 48	06 28	07 03	18 29	19 07	19 51	20 42
54	05 49	06 31	07 08	18 22	18 59	19 42	20 33
56	05 51	06 35	07 14	18 15	18 50	19 33	20 24
58	05 52	06 39	07 20	18 06	18 40	19 22	20 13
S 60	05 54	06 43	07 28	17 56	18 29	19 10	20 01

Lat.	Sunset	Twilight Civil	Twilight Naut.	Moonset 24	25	26	27
°	h m	h m	h m	h m	h m	h m	h m
N 72	21 27	////	////	03 51	03 42	03 06	▬
N 70	20 57	23 09	////	04 22	04 30	04 46	05 22
68	20 36	22 06	////	04 45	05 01	05 26	06 07
66	20 19	21 33	////	05 03	05 24	05 54	06 37
64	20 05	21 08	23 15	05 18	05 42	06 15	06 59
62	19 54	20 50	22 19	05 30	05 57	06 32	07 17
60	19 44	20 35	21 49	05 41	06 10	06 46	07 32
N 58	19 35	20 22	21 26	05 50	06 20	06 58	07 45
56	19 28	20 11	21 09	05 58	06 30	07 09	07 56
54	19 21	20 02	20 54	06 05	06 38	07 18	08 05
52	19 15	19 53	20 42	06 11	06 46	07 26	08 14
50	19 10	19 46	20 31	06 17	06 53	07 34	08 21
45	18 58	19 30	20 09	06 30	07 07	07 50	08 38
N 40	18 49	19 18	19 53	06 40	07 19	08 03	08 51
35	18 41	19 08	19 40	06 49	07 30	08 14	09 02
30	18 34	18 59	19 29	06 57	07 39	08 24	09 12
20	18 22	18 44	19 11	07 10	07 54	08 40	09 29
N 10	18 11	18 33	18 58	07 22	08 08	08 55	09 44
0	18 01	18 23	18 47	07 33	08 20	09 09	09 58
S 10	17 52	18 13	18 38	07 45	08 33	09 22	10 12
20	17 41	18 04	18 30	07 57	08 47	09 37	10 27
30	17 30	17 55	18 23	08 10	09 02	09 54	10 44
35	17 23	17 49	18 19	08 18	09 11	10 03	10 54
40	17 16	17 44	18 16	08 27	09 22	10 14	11 05
45	17 07	17 38	18 12	08 38	09 34	10 27	11 18
S 50	16 57	17 31	18 08	08 51	09 48	10 43	11 34
52	16 52	17 27	18 07	08 57	09 55	10 51	11 42
54	16 47	17 24	18 05	09 03	10 03	10 59	11 50
56	16 41	17 20	18 04	09 11	10 12	11 08	12 00
58	16 35	17 16	18 02	09 19	10 21	11 19	12 10
S 60	16 27	17 12	18 01	09 28	10 32	11 31	12 22

Day	SUN Eqn. of Time 00^h	SUN Eqn. of Time 12^h	SUN Mer. Pass.	MOON Mer. Pass. Upper	MOON Mer. Pass. Lower	Age	Phase
d	m s	m s	h m	h m	h m	d %	
24	01 51	01 57	11 58	01 22	13 45	17 95	
25	02 02	02 07	11 58	02 09	14 33	18 90	
26	02 12	02 17	11 58	02 57	15 21	19 84	

UT	ARIES	VENUS −3·9		MARS −1·4		JUPITER −2·3		SATURN +0·2	
d h	GHA ° ′	GHA ° ′	Dec ° ′	GHA ° ′	Dec ° ′	GHA ° ′	Dec ° ′	GHA ° ′	Dec ° ′
27 00 WEDNESDAY	215 24.6	190 33.3	N 8 53.9	328 48.1	S21 37.0	50 04.5	N 7 47.1	320 52.6	S20 51.6
01	230 27.1	205 32.9	55.1	343 50.9	37.0	65 07.1	47.1	335 55.2	51.6
02	245 29.6	220 32.5	56.3	358 53.7	37.1	80 09.6	47.1	350 57.8	51.6
03	260 32.0	235 32.0	. . 57.4	13 56.5	. . 37.1	95 12.2	. . 47.2	6 00.4	. . 51.6
04	275 34.5	250 31.6	58.6	28 59.3	37.2	110 14.7	47.2	21 03.0	51.6
05	290 37.0	265 31.2	8 59.7	44 02.1	37.3	125 17.3	47.2	36 05.6	51.5
06	305 39.4	280 30.8	N 9 00.9	59 04.9	S21 37.3	140 19.8	N 7 47.3	51 08.2	S20 51.5
07	320 41.9	295 30.3	02.0	74 07.7	37.4	155 22.4	47.3	66 10.8	51.5
08	335 44.4	310 29.9	03.2	89 10.5	37.4	170 24.9	47.3	81 13.4	51.5
09	350 46.8	325 29.5	. . 04.3	104 13.3	. . 37.5	185 27.5	. . 47.3	96 16.0	. . 51.5
10	5 49.3	340 29.0	05.5	119 16.1	37.5	200 30.0	47.4	111 18.6	51.5
11	20 51.7	355 28.6	06.6	134 18.9	37.6	215 32.6	47.4	126 21.2	51.5
12	35 54.2	10 28.2	N 9 07.8	149 21.8	S21 37.6	230 35.1	N 7 47.4	141 23.8	S20 51.4
13	50 56.7	25 27.8	08.9	164 24.6	37.7	245 37.7	47.5	156 26.4	51.4
14	65 59.1	40 27.3	10.1	179 27.4	37.7	260 40.3	47.5	171 29.0	51.4
15	81 01.6	55 26.9	. . 11.2	194 30.2	. . 37.8	275 42.8	. . 47.5	186 31.6	. . 51.4
16	96 04.1	70 26.5	12.4	209 33.0	37.8	290 45.4	47.5	201 34.2	51.4
17	111 06.5	85 26.0	13.5	224 35.9	37.9	305 47.9	47.6	216 36.7	51.4
18	126 09.0	100 25.6	N 9 14.7	239 38.7	S21 37.9	320 50.5	N 7 47.6	231 39.3	S20 51.3
19	141 11.5	115 25.2	15.8	254 41.5	38.0	335 53.0	47.6	246 41.9	51.3
20	156 13.9	130 24.7	17.0	269 44.3	38.0	350 55.6	47.6	261 44.5	51.3
21	171 16.4	145 24.3	. . 18.1	284 47.2	. . 38.1	5 58.1	. . 47.7	276 47.1	. . 51.3
22	186 18.8	160 23.9	19.3	299 50.0	38.1	21 00.7	47.7	291 49.7	51.3
23	201 21.3	175 23.4	20.4	314 52.8	38.2	36 03.2	47.7	306 52.3	51.3
28 00 THURSDAY	216 23.8	190 23.0	N 9 21.6	329 55.6	S21 38.2	51 05.8	N 7 47.8	321 54.9	S20 51.2
01	231 26.2	205 22.6	22.7	344 58.5	38.3	66 08.3	47.8	336 57.5	51.2
02	246 28.7	220 22.1	23.9	0 01.3	38.3	81 10.9	47.8	352 00.1	51.2
03	261 31.2	235 21.7	. . 25.0	15 04.1	. . 38.4	96 13.4	. . 47.8	7 02.7	. . 51.2
04	276 33.6	250 21.3	26.1	30 07.0	38.4	111 16.0	47.9	22 05.3	51.2
05	291 36.1	265 20.8	27.3	45 09.8	38.5	126 18.5	47.9	37 07.9	51.2
06	306 38.6	280 20.4	N 9 28.4	60 12.7	S21 38.5	141 21.0	N 7 47.9	52 10.5	S20 51.2
07	321 41.0	295 20.0	29.6	75 15.5	38.6	156 23.6	47.9	67 13.1	51.1
08	336 43.5	310 19.5	30.7	90 18.3	38.6	171 26.1	48.0	82 15.7	51.1
09	351 46.0	325 19.1	. . 31.9	105 21.2	. . 38.7	186 28.7	. . 48.0	97 18.3	. . 51.1
10	6 48.4	340 18.7	33.0	120 24.0	38.7	201 31.2	48.0	112 20.9	51.1
11	21 50.9	355 18.2	34.2	135 26.9	38.8	216 33.8	48.0	127 23.5	51.1
12	36 53.3	10 17.8	N 9 35.3	150 29.7	S21 38.8	231 36.3	N 7 48.1	142 26.1	S20 51.1
13	51 55.8	25 17.4	36.4	165 32.6	38.9	246 38.9	48.1	157 28.7	51.0
14	66 58.3	40 16.9	37.6	180 35.4	38.9	261 41.4	48.1	172 31.3	51.0
15	82 00.7	55 16.5	. . 38.7	195 38.3	. . 39.0	276 44.0	. . 48.1	187 33.9	. . 51.0
16	97 03.2	70 16.1	39.9	210 41.1	39.0	291 46.5	48.2	202 36.5	51.0
17	112 05.7	85 15.6	41.0	225 44.0	39.1	306 49.1	48.2	217 39.1	51.0
18	127 08.1	100 15.2	N 9 42.1	240 46.8	S21 39.1	321 51.6	N 7 48.2	232 41.7	S20 51.0
19	142 10.6	115 14.7	43.3	255 49.7	39.2	336 54.1	48.2	247 44.3	50.9
20	157 13.1	130 14.3	44.4	270 52.6	39.2	351 56.7	48.3	262 46.9	50.9
21	172 15.5	145 13.9	. . 45.6	285 55.4	. . 39.3	6 59.2	. . 48.3	277 49.5	. . 50.9
22	187 18.0	160 13.4	46.7	300 58.3	39.3	22 01.8	48.3	292 52.1	50.9
23	202 20.5	175 13.0	47.8	316 01.1	39.4	37 04.3	48.3	307 54.7	50.9
29 00 FRIDAY	217 22.9	190 12.5	N 9 49.0	331 04.0	S21 39.4	52 06.9	N 7 48.4	322 57.3	S20 50.9
01	232 25.4	205 12.1	50.1	346 06.9	39.5	67 09.4	48.4	337 59.9	50.9
02	247 27.8	220 11.7	51.2	1 09.7	39.5	82 11.9	48.4	353 02.5	50.8
03	262 30.3	235 11.2	. . 52.4	16 12.6	. . 39.6	97 14.5	. . 48.4	8 05.1	. . 50.8
04	277 32.8	250 10.8	53.5	31 15.5	39.6	112 17.0	48.5	23 07.7	50.8
05	292 35.2	265 10.3	54.7	46 18.4	39.7	127 19.6	48.5	38 10.3	50.8
06	307 37.7	280 09.9	N 9 55.8	61 21.2	S21 39.7	142 22.1	N 7 48.5	53 12.9	S20 50.8
07	322 40.2	295 09.5	56.9	76 24.1	39.8	157 24.6	48.5	68 15.5	50.8
08	337 42.6	310 09.0	58.1	91 27.0	39.8	172 27.2	48.5	83 18.1	50.7
09	352 45.1	325 08.6	9 59.2	106 29.9	. . 39.8	187 29.7	. . 48.6	98 20.7	. . 50.7
10	7 47.6	340 08.1	10 00.3	121 32.7	39.9	202 32.3	48.6	113 23.3	50.7
11	22 50.0	355 07.7	01.5	136 35.6	39.9	217 34.8	48.6	128 26.0	50.7
12	37 52.5	10 07.2	N10 02.6	151 38.5	S21 40.0	232 37.3	N 7 48.6	143 28.6	S20 50.7
13	52 54.9	25 06.8	03.7	166 41.4	40.0	247 39.9	48.7	158 31.2	50.7
14	67 57.4	40 06.3	04.9	181 44.3	40.1	262 42.4	48.7	173 33.8	50.6
15	82 59.9	55 05.9	. . 06.0	196 47.2	. . 40.1	277 45.0	. . 48.7	188 36.4	. . 50.6
16	98 02.3	70 05.5	07.1	211 50.1	40.2	292 47.5	48.7	203 39.0	50.6
17	113 04.8	85 05.0	08.3	226 52.9	40.2	307 50.0	48.7	218 41.6	50.6
18	128 07.3	100 04.6	N10 09.4	241 55.8	S21 40.3	322 52.6	N 7 48.8	233 44.2	S20 50.6
19	143 09.7	115 04.1	10.5	256 58.7	40.3	337 55.1	48.8	248 46.8	50.6
20	158 12.2	130 03.7	11.6	272 01.6	40.3	352 57.6	48.8	263 49.4	50.5
21	173 14.7	145 03.2	. . 12.8	287 04.5	. . 40.4	8 00.2	. . 48.8	278 52.0	. . 50.5
22	188 17.1	160 02.8	13.9	302 07.4	40.4	23 02.7	48.9	293 54.6	50.5
23	203 19.6	175 02.3	15.0	317 10.3	40.5	38 05.2	48.9	308 57.2	50.5
Mer. Pass.	h m 9 32.8	v −0.4	d 1.1	v 2.8	d 0.0	v 2.5	d 0.0	v 2.6	d 0.0

STARS Name	SHA ° ′	Dec ° ′
Acamar	315 17.4	S40 14.6
Achernar	335 26.0	S57 09.3
Acrux	173 06.4	S63 11.5
Adhara	255 11.2	S29 00.1
Aldebaran	290 47.5	N16 32.2
Alioth	166 18.6	N55 52.4
Alkaid	152 57.0	N49 14.0
Al Na'ir	27 41.6	S46 52.7
Alnilam	275 44.7	S 1 11.8
Alphard	217 54.1	S 8 44.0
Alphecca	126 09.1	N26 39.6
Alpheratz	357 41.8	N29 10.6
Altair	62 06.3	N 8 54.7
Ankaa	353 14.2	S42 13.0
Antares	112 23.6	S26 27.9
Arcturus	145 53.7	N19 05.9
Atria	107 23.2	S69 03.0
Avior	234 17.2	S59 34.2
Bellatrix	278 30.2	N 6 21.6
Betelgeuse	270 59.4	N 7 24.3
Canopus	263 55.6	S52 42.7
Capella	280 32.0	N46 00.7
Deneb	49 30.1	N45 20.1
Denebola	182 31.5	N14 28.8
Diphda	348 54.3	S17 53.9
Dubhe	193 49.1	N61 39.9
Elnath	278 10.5	N28 37.0
Eltanin	90 44.9	N51 29.1
Enif	33 45.3	N 9 56.9
Fomalhaut	15 22.1	S29 32.1
Gacrux	171 58.1	S57 12.4
Gienah	175 50.0	S17 38.1
Hadar	148 44.4	S60 27.1
Hamal	327 58.9	N23 32.1
Kaus Aust.	83 41.1	S34 22.3
Kochab	137 19.1	N74 05.4
Markab	13 36.6	N15 17.4
Menkar	314 13.4	N 4 08.9
Menkent	148 04.9	S36 27.0
Miaplacidus	221 39.0	S69 47.5
Mirfak	308 38.0	N49 54.9
Nunki	75 55.8	S26 16.3
Peacock	53 16.3	S56 40.6
Pollux	243 25.5	N27 59.1
Procyon	244 57.8	N 5 10.7
Rasalhague	96 04.4	N12 33.0
Regulus	207 41.4	N11 53.1
Rigel	281 10.5	S 8 11.3
Rigil Kent.	139 48.3	S60 54.0
Sabik	102 10.1	S15 44.5
Schedar	349 38.7	N56 37.3
Shaula	96 19.0	S37 06.6
Sirius	258 32.2	S16 44.7
Spica	158 28.9	S11 14.8
Suhail	222 50.9	S43 30.3
Vega	80 37.4	N38 47.9
Zuben'ubi	137 02.9	S16 06.5

	SHA ° ′	Mer. Pass. h m
Venus	333 59.2	11 19
Mars	113 31.9	2 00
Jupiter	194 42.0	20 32
Saturn	105 31.2	2 32

	UT	SUN GHA	SUN Dec	MOON GHA	*v*	MOON Dec	*d*	HP
	d h	° ′	° ′	° ′	′	° ′	′	′
	27 00	180 35.4	N13 54.1	305 21.6	11.0	S18 21.9	0.4	55.3
	01	195 35.5	54.9	319 51.6	10.9	18 22.3	0.3	55.3
	02	210 35.6	55.7	334 21.5	10.9	18 22.6	0.2	55.3
	03	225 35.7	. . 56.5	348 51.4	10.9	18 22.8	0.2	55.3
	04	240 35.8	57.3	3 21.3	10.9	18 23.0	0.0	55.3
	05	255 35.9	58.1	17 51.2	10.8	18 23.0	0.1	55.4
	06	270 36.0	N13 58.9	32 21.0	10.9	S18 22.9	0.1	55.4
W	07	285 36.1	13 59.7	46 50.9	10.8	18 22.8	0.3	55.4
E	08	300 36.2	14 00.5	61 20.7	10.8	18 22.5	0.3	55.4
D	09	315 36.3	. . 01.2	75 50.5	10.7	18 22.2	0.5	55.5
N	10	330 36.4	02.0	90 20.2	10.7	18 21.7	0.5	55.5
E	11	345 36.5	02.8	104 49.9	10.8	18 21.2	0.6	55.5
S	12	0 36.6	N14 03.6	119 19.7	10.7	S18 20.6	0.7	55.5
D	13	15 36.7	04.4	133 49.4	10.6	18 19.9	0.9	55.6
A	14	30 36.8	05.2	148 19.0	10.7	18 19.0	0.9	55.6
Y	15	45 36.9	. . 06.0	162 48.7	10.6	18 18.1	1.0	55.6
	16	60 37.0	06.8	177 18.3	10.6	18 17.1	1.0	55.6
	17	75 37.1	07.5	191 47.9	10.6	18 16.1	1.2	55.7
	18	90 37.2	N14 08.3	206 17.5	10.6	S18 14.9	1.3	55.7
	19	105 37.2	09.1	220 47.1	10.5	18 13.6	1.4	55.7
	20	120 37.3	09.9	235 16.6	10.6	18 12.2	1.5	55.7
	21	135 37.4	. . 10.7	249 46.2	10.5	18 10.7	1.5	55.8
	22	150 37.5	11.5	264 15.7	10.5	18 09.2	1.7	55.8
	23	165 37.6	12.3	278 45.2	10.5	18 07.5	1.7	55.8
	28 00	180 37.7	N14 13.0	293 14.7	10.4	S18 05.8	1.9	55.8
	01	195 37.8	13.8	307 44.1	10.5	18 03.9	1.9	55.9
	02	210 37.9	14.6	322 13.6	10.4	18 02.0	2.1	55.9
	03	225 38.0	. . 15.4	336 43.0	10.4	17 59.9	2.1	55.9
	04	240 38.1	16.2	351 12.4	10.4	17 57.8	2.2	55.9
	05	255 38.2	17.0	5 41.8	10.4	17 55.6	2.4	56.0
	06	270 38.2	N14 17.7	20 11.2	10.3	S17 53.2	2.4	56.0
	07	285 38.3	18.5	34 40.5	10.4	17 50.8	2.5	56.0
T	08	300 38.4	19.3	49 09.9	10.3	17 48.3	2.6	56.0
H	09	315 38.5	. . 20.1	63 39.2	10.3	17 45.7	2.7	56.1
U	10	330 38.6	20.9	78 08.5	10.3	17 43.0	2.8	56.1
R	11	345 38.7	21.6	92 37.8	10.3	17 40.2	2.9	56.1
S	12	0 38.8	N14 22.4	107 07.1	10.3	S17 37.3	3.0	56.2
D	13	15 38.9	23.2	121 36.4	10.3	17 34.3	3.1	56.2
A	14	30 39.0	24.0	136 05.7	10.2	17 31.2	3.2	56.2
Y	15	45 39.0	. . 24.8	150 34.9	10.3	17 28.0	3.2	56.2
	16	60 39.1	25.5	165 04.2	10.2	17 24.8	3.4	56.3
	17	75 39.2	26.3	179 33.4	10.2	17 21.4	3.5	56.3
	18	90 39.3	N14 27.1	194 02.6	10.2	S17 17.9	3.5	56.3
	19	105 39.4	27.9	208 31.8	10.2	17 14.4	3.7	56.4
	20	120 39.5	28.6	223 01.0	10.2	17 10.7	3.7	56.4
	21	135 39.6	. . 29.4	237 30.2	10.1	17 07.0	3.9	56.4
	22	150 39.7	30.2	251 59.3	10.2	17 03.1	3.9	56.4
	23	165 39.7	31.0	266 28.5	10.1	16 59.2	4.1	56.5
	29 00	180 39.8	N14 31.8	280 57.6	10.2	S16 55.1	4.1	56.5
	01	195 39.9	32.5	295 26.8	10.1	16 51.0	4.2	56.5
	02	210 40.0	33.3	309 55.9	10.1	16 46.8	4.3	56.6
	03	225 40.1	. . 34.1	324 25.0	10.1	16 42.5	4.4	56.6
	04	240 40.2	34.8	338 54.1	10.1	16 38.1	4.5	56.6
	05	255 40.3	35.6	353 23.2	10.1	16 33.6	4.6	56.7
	06	270 40.3	N14 36.4	7 52.3	10.0	S16 29.0	4.7	56.7
	07	285 40.4	37.2	22 21.3	10.1	16 24.3	4.8	56.7
	08	300 40.5	37.9	36 50.4	10.1	16 19.5	4.9	56.8
F	09	315 40.6	. . 38.7	51 19.5	10.0	16 14.6	4.9	56.8
R	10	330 40.7	39.5	65 48.5	10.0	16 09.7	5.1	56.8
I	11	345 40.8	40.2	80 17.5	10.1	16 04.6	5.1	56.9
D	12	0 40.8	N14 41.0	94 46.6	10.0	S15 59.5	5.3	56.9
A	13	15 40.9	41.8	109 15.6	10.0	15 54.2	5.3	56.9
Y	14	30 41.0	42.5	123 44.6	10.0	15 48.9	5.4	57.0
	15	45 41.1	. . 43.3	138 13.6	10.0	15 43.5	5.6	57.0
	16	60 41.2	44.1	152 42.6	10.0	15 37.9	5.6	57.0
	17	75 41.2	44.9	167 11.6	10.0	15 32.3	5.7	57.1
	18	90 41.3	N14 45.6	181 40.6	9.9	S15 26.6	5.8	57.1
	19	105 41.4	46.4	196 09.5	10.0	15 20.8	5.8	57.1
	20	120 41.5	47.2	210 38.5	10.0	15 15.0	6.0	57.2
	21	135 41.6	. . 47.9	225 07.5	9.9	15 09.0	6.1	57.2
	22	150 41.7	48.7	239 36.4	9.9	15 02.9	6.1	57.2
	23	165 41.7	49.4	254 05.3	10.0	S14 56.8	6.3	57.3
		SD 15.9	*d* 0.8	SD		15.1	15.3	15.5

Lat.	Twilight Naut.	Twilight Civil	Sunrise	Moonrise 27	28	29	30
°	h m	h m	h m	h m	h m	h m	h m
N 72	////	////	02 13	■	■	03 56	03 46
N 70	////	////	02 46	02 10	02 49	03 07	03 16
68	////	01 32	03 09	01 25	02 08	02 36	02 53
66	////	02 11	03 28	00 55	01 40	02 13	02 36
64	////	02 37	03 42	00 33	01 19	01 54	02 21
62	01 21	02 57	03 55	00 15	01 02	01 39	02 09
60	01 56	03 14	04 05	00 00	00 47	01 27	01 59
N 58	02 21	03 27	04 14	24 35	00 35	01 16	01 50
56	02 40	03 39	04 22	24 25	00 25	01 06	01 42
54	02 55	03 49	04 29	24 15	00 15	00 58	01 34
52	03 08	03 57	04 35	24 07	00 07	00 50	01 28
50	03 19	04 05	04 41	23 59	24 43	00 43	01 22
45	03 42	04 21	04 53	23 43	24 29	00 29	01 10
N 40	03 59	04 34	05 04	23 30	24 16	00 16	00 59
35	04 13	04 45	05 12	23 19	24 06	00 06	00 51
30	04 24	04 54	05 20	23 09	23 57	24 43	00 43
20	04 43	05 10	05 32	22 53	23 42	24 29	00 29
N 10	04 57	05 22	05 44	22 38	23 28	24 18	00 18
0	05 08	05 33	05 54	22 24	23 15	24 06	00 06
S 10	05 18	05 43	06 04	22 11	23 02	23 55	24 49
20	05 26	05 52	06 15	21 56	22 49	23 44	24 40
30	05 34	06 03	06 27	21 39	22 33	23 30	24 29
35	05 38	06 08	06 34	21 29	22 24	23 22	24 23
40	05 42	06 14	06 42	21 18	22 14	23 13	24 16
45	05 46	06 21	06 52	21 05	22 01	23 03	24 08
S 50	05 51	06 29	07 03	20 49	21 47	22 50	23 58
52	05 52	06 32	07 08	20 42	21 40	22 44	23 54
54	05 54	06 36	07 13	20 33	21 32	22 37	23 48
56	05 56	06 40	07 20	20 24	21 23	22 30	23 43
58	05 58	06 45	07 27	20 13	21 14	22 22	23 37
S 60	06 00	06 50	07 35	20 01	21 02	22 12	23 29

Lat.	Sunset	Twilight Civil	Twilight Naut.	Moonset 27	28	29	30
°	h m	h m	h m	h m	h m	h m	h m
N 72	21 48	////	////	■	■	07 07	09 05
N 70	21 13	////	////	05 22	06 28	07 56	09 34
68	20 49	22 30	////	06 07	07 08	08 26	09 56
66	20 30	21 49	////	06 37	07 36	08 49	10 13
64	20 15	21 21	////	06 59	07 57	09 07	10 26
62	20 02	21 00	22 40	07 17	08 14	09 22	10 38
60	19 51	20 44	22 03	07 32	08 28	09 34	10 48
N 58	19 42	20 30	21 37	07 45	08 40	09 44	10 56
56	19 34	20 18	21 18	07 56	08 51	09 54	11 04
54	19 27	20 08	21 02	08 05	09 00	10 02	11 10
52	19 20	19 59	20 49	08 14	09 08	10 09	11 16
50	19 15	19 51	20 37	08 21	09 15	10 16	11 22
45	19 02	19 34	20 14	08 38	09 31	10 30	11 33
N 40	18 52	19 21	19 57	08 51	09 44	10 41	11 43
35	18 43	19 10	19 43	09 02	09 55	10 51	11 51
30	18 36	19 01	19 31	09 12	10 05	11 00	11 58
20	18 23	18 46	19 13	09 29	10 21	11 15	12 10
N 10	18 11	18 33	18 58	09 44	10 35	11 28	12 21
0	18 01	18 22	18 47	09 58	10 49	11 40	12 31
S 10	17 50	18 12	18 37	10 12	11 02	11 52	12 41
20	17 40	18 02	18 28	10 27	11 16	12 04	12 52
30	17 27	17 52	18 20	10 44	11 32	12 19	13 04
35	17 20	17 46	18 16	10 54	11 42	12 27	13 11
40	17 12	17 40	18 12	11 05	11 52	12 37	13 18
45	17 03	17 33	18 08	11 18	12 05	12 48	13 28
S 50	16 52	17 25	18 04	11 34	12 20	13 02	13 38
52	16 46	17 22	18 02	11 42	12 27	13 08	13 44
54	16 41	17 18	18 00	11 50	12 35	13 15	13 49
56	16 34	17 14	17 58	12 00	12 44	13 22	13 55
58	16 27	17 09	17 56	12 10	12 54	13 31	14 02
S 60	16 19	17 04	17 54	12 22	13 06	13 41	14 10

Day	SUN Eqn. of Time 00^h	12^h	Mer. Pass.	MOON Mer. Pass. Upper	Lower	Age	Phase
d	m s	m s	h m	h m	h m	d	%
27	02 22	02 26	11 58	03 46	16 11	20	76
28	02 31	02 35	11 57	04 36	17 02	21	67
29	02 39	02 43	11 57	05 27	17 53	22	57

	UT	ARIES	VENUS −3·9		MARS −1·5		JUPITER −2·3		SATURN +0·2	
		GHA	GHA	Dec	GHA	Dec	GHA	Dec	GHA	Dec
	d h	° ′	° ′	° ′	° ′	° ′	° ′	° ′	° ′	° ′
	30 00	218 22.1	190 01.9	N10 16.2	332 13.2	S21 40.5	53 07.8	N 7 48.9	323 59.8	S20 50.5
	01	233 24.5	205 01.4	17.3	347 16.1	40.6	68 10.3	48.9	339 02.4	50.5
	02	248 27.0	220 01.0	18.4	2 19.0	40.6	83 12.9	48.9	354 05.0	50.4
	03	263 29.4	235 00.5	. . 19.5	17 21.9	. . 40.7	98 15.4	. . 49.0	9 07.6	. . 50.4
	04	278 31.9	250 00.1	20.7	32 24.8	40.7	113 17.9	49.0	24 10.2	50.4
	05	293 34.4	264 59.6	21.8	47 27.7	40.7	128 20.5	49.0	39 12.8	50.4
	06	308 36.8	279 59.2	N10 22.9	62 30.6	S21 40.8	143 23.0	N 7 49.0	54 15.4	S20 50.4
	07	323 39.3	294 58.7	24.0	77 33.5	40.8	158 25.5	49.0	69 18.0	50.4
S	08	338 41.8	309 58.3	25.2	92 36.5	40.9	173 28.1	49.1	84 20.6	50.3
A	09	353 44.2	324 57.8	. . 26.3	107 39.4	. . 40.9	188 30.6	. . 49.1	99 23.2	. . 50.3
T	10	8 46.7	339 57.4	27.4	122 42.3	41.0	203 33.1	49.1	114 25.9	50.3
U	11	23 49.2	354 56.9	28.5	137 45.2	41.0	218 35.6	49.1	129 28.5	50.3
R	12	38 51.6	9 56.5	N10 29.7	152 48.1	S21 41.0	233 38.2	N 7 49.1	144 31.1	S20 50.3
D	13	53 54.1	24 56.0	30.8	167 51.0	41.1	248 40.7	49.2	159 33.7	50.3
A	14	68 56.6	39 55.6	31.9	182 53.9	41.1	263 43.2	49.2	174 36.3	50.3
Y	15	83 59.0	54 55.1	. . 33.0	197 56.9	. . 41.2	278 45.8	. . 49.2	189 38.9	. . 50.2
	16	99 01.5	69 54.7	34.2	212 59.8	41.2	293 48.3	49.2	204 41.5	50.2
	17	114 03.9	84 54.2	35.3	228 02.7	41.3	308 50.8	49.2	219 44.1	50.2
	18	129 06.4	99 53.8	N10 36.4	243 05.6	S21 41.3	323 53.4	N 7 49.2	234 46.7	S20 50.2
	19	144 08.9	114 53.3	37.5	258 08.6	41.3	338 55.9	49.3	249 49.3	50.2
	20	159 11.3	129 52.9	38.6	273 11.5	41.4	353 58.4	49.3	264 51.9	50.2
	21	174 13.8	144 52.4	. . 39.8	288 14.4	. . 41.4	9 01.0	. . 49.3	279 54.5	. . 50.1
	22	189 16.3	159 51.9	40.9	303 17.3	41.5	24 03.5	49.3	294 57.1	50.1
	23	204 18.7	174 51.5	42.0	318 20.3	41.5	39 06.0	49.3	309 59.7	50.1
	1 00	219 21.2	189 51.0	N10 43.1	333 23.2	S21 41.5	54 08.5	N 7 49.4	325 02.3	S20 50.1
	01	234 23.7	204 50.6	44.2	348 26.1	41.6	69 11.1	49.4	340 05.0	50.1
	02	249 26.1	219 50.1	45.3	3 29.1	41.6	84 13.6	49.4	355 07.6	50.1
	03	264 28.6	234 49.7	. . 46.5	18 32.0	. . 41.7	99 16.1	. . 49.4	10 10.2	. . 50.0
	04	279 31.0	249 49.2	47.6	33 35.0	41.7	114 18.7	49.4	25 12.8	50.0
	05	294 33.5	264 48.8	48.7	48 37.9	41.7	129 21.2	49.4	40 15.4	50.0
	06	309 36.0	279 48.3	N10 49.8	63 40.8	S21 41.8	144 23.7	N 7 49.5	55 18.0	S20 50.0
	07	324 38.4	294 47.8	50.9	78 43.8	41.8	159 26.2	49.5	70 20.6	50.0
	08	339 40.9	309 47.4	52.0	93 46.7	41.9	174 28.8	49.5	85 23.2	50.0
S	09	354 43.4	324 46.9	. . 53.2	108 49.7	. . 41.9	189 31.3	. . 49.5	100 25.8	. . 49.9
U	10	9 45.8	339 46.5	54.3	123 52.6	41.9	204 33.8	49.5	115 28.4	49.9
N	11	24 48.3	354 46.0	55.4	138 55.6	42.0	219 36.3	49.5	130 31.0	49.9
D	12	39 50.8	9 45.5	N10 56.5	153 58.5	S21 42.0	234 38.9	N 7 49.6	145 33.6	S20 49.9
A	13	54 53.2	24 45.1	57.6	169 01.5	42.0	249 41.4	49.6	160 36.3	49.9
Y	14	69 55.7	39 44.6	58.7	184 04.4	42.1	264 43.9	49.6	175 38.9	49.9
	15	84 58.2	54 44.2	10 59.8	199 07.4	. . 42.1	279 46.4	. . 49.6	190 41.5	. . 49.8
	16	100 00.6	69 43.7	11 00.9	214 10.3	42.2	294 49.0	49.6	205 44.1	49.8
	17	115 03.1	84 43.2	02.1	229 13.3	42.2	309 51.5	49.6	220 46.7	49.8
	18	130 05.5	99 42.8	N11 03.2	244 16.3	S21 42.2	324 54.0	N 7 49.7	235 49.3	S20 49.8
	19	145 08.0	114 42.3	04.3	259 19.2	42.3	339 56.5	49.7	250 51.9	49.8
	20	160 10.5	129 41.9	05.4	274 22.2	42.3	354 59.0	49.7	265 54.5	49.8
	21	175 12.9	144 41.4	. . 06.5	289 25.1	. . 42.3	10 01.6	. . 49.7	280 57.1	. . 49.7
	22	190 15.4	159 40.9	07.6	304 28.1	42.4	25 04.1	49.7	295 59.7	49.7
	23	205 17.9	174 40.5	08.7	319 31.1	42.4	40 06.6	49.7	311 02.4	49.7
	2 00	220 20.3	189 40.0	N11 09.8	334 34.0	S21 42.5	55 09.1	N 7 49.7	326 05.0	S20 49.7
	01	235 22.8	204 39.5	10.9	349 37.0	42.5	70 11.7	49.8	341 07.6	49.7
	02	250 25.3	219 39.1	12.0	4 40.0	42.5	85 14.2	49.8	356 10.2	49.7
	03	265 27.7	234 38.6	. . 13.1	19 42.9	. . 42.6	100 16.7	. . 49.8	11 12.8	. . 49.6
	04	280 30.2	249 38.1	14.2	34 45.9	42.6	115 19.2	49.8	26 15.4	49.6
	05	295 32.7	264 37.7	15.3	49 48.9	42.6	130 21.7	49.8	41 18.0	49.6
	06	310 35.1	279 37.2	N11 16.5	64 51.9	S21 42.7	145 24.3	N 7 49.8	56 20.6	S20 49.6
	07	325 37.6	294 36.7	17.6	79 54.8	42.7	160 26.8	49.8	71 23.2	49.6
	08	340 40.0	309 36.3	18.7	94 57.8	42.7	175 29.3	49.9	86 25.9	49.6
M	09	355 42.5	324 35.8	. . 19.8	110 00.8	. . 42.8	190 31.8	. . 49.9	101 28.5	. . 49.5
O	10	10 45.0	339 35.3	20.9	125 03.8	42.8	205 34.3	49.9	116 31.1	49.5
N	11	25 47.4	354 34.9	22.0	140 06.8	42.9	220 36.8	49.9	131 33.7	49.5
D	12	40 49.9	9 34.4	N11 23.1	155 09.7	S21 42.9	235 39.4	N 7 49.9	146 36.3	S20 49.5
A	13	55 52.4	24 33.9	24.2	170 12.7	42.9	250 41.9	49.9	161 38.9	49.5
Y	14	70 54.8	39 33.5	25.3	185 15.7	43.0	265 44.4	49.9	176 41.5	49.5
	15	85 57.3	54 33.0	. . 26.4	200 18.7	. . 43.0	280 46.9	. . 50.0	191 44.1	. . 49.4
	16	100 59.8	69 32.5	27.5	215 21.7	43.0	295 49.4	50.0	206 46.8	49.4
	17	116 02.2	84 32.1	28.6	230 24.7	43.1	310 51.9	50.0	221 49.4	49.4
	18	131 04.7	99 31.6	N11 29.7	245 27.7	S21 43.1	325 54.5	N 7 50.0	236 52.0	S20 49.4
	19	146 07.1	114 31.1	30.8	260 30.7	43.1	340 57.0	50.0	251 54.6	49.4
	20	161 09.6	129 30.6	31.9	275 33.7	43.2	355 59.5	50.0	266 57.2	49.3
	21	176 12.1	144 30.2	. . 33.0	290 36.6	. . 43.2	11 02.0	. . 50.0	281 59.8	. . 49.3
	22	191 14.5	159 29.7	34.1	305 39.6	43.2	26 04.5	50.0	297 02.4	49.3
	23	206 17.0	174 29.2	35.2	320 42.6	43.3	41 07.0	50.1	312 05.0	49.3
	Mer. Pass.	h m 9 21.1	v −0.5	d 1.1	v 3.0	d 0.0	v 2.5	d 0.0	v 2.6	d 0.0

STARS

Name	SHA	Dec
	° ′	° ′
Acamar	315 17.4	S40 14.6
Achernar	335 26.0	S57 09.3
Acrux	173 06.4	S63 11.5
Adhara	255 11.2	S29 00.1
Aldebaran	290 47.5	N16 32.2
Alioth	166 18.6	N55 52.4
Alkaid	152 57.0	N49 14.0
Al Na'ir	27 41.6	S46 52.7
Alnilam	275 44.7	S 1 11.8
Alphard	217 54.1	S 8 44.0
Alphecca	126 09.0	N26 39.7
Alpheratz	357 41.7	N29 10.6
Altair	62 06.3	N 8 54.7
Ankaa	353 14.2	S42 13.0
Antares	112 23.5	S26 27.9
Arcturus	145 53.7	N19 05.9
Atria	107 23.1	S69 03.1
Avior	234 17.2	S59 34.2
Bellatrix	278 30.2	N 6 21.6
Betelgeuse	270 59.4	N 7 24.3
Canopus	263 55.6	S52 42.7
Capella	280 32.0	N46 00.7
Deneb	49 30.1	N45 20.2
Denebola	182 31.5	N14 28.8
Diphda	348 54.3	S17 53.9
Dubhe	193 49.1	N61 39.9
Elnath	278 10.5	N28 37.0
Eltanin	90 44.9	N51 29.2
Enif	33 45.3	N 9 56.9
Fomalhaut	15 22.1	S29 32.1
Gacrux	171 58.1	S57 12.4
Gienah	175 50.0	S17 38.1
Hadar	148 44.4	S60 27.1
Hamal	327 58.9	N23 32.1
Kaus Aust.	83 41.0	S34 22.3
Kochab	137 19.1	N74 05.4
Markab	13 36.6	N15 17.4
Menkar	314 13.4	N 4 08.9
Menkent	148 04.9	S36 27.0
Miaplacidus	221 39.0	S69 47.5
Mirfak	308 38.0	N49 54.9
Nunki	75 55.8	S26 16.3
Peacock	53 16.2	S56 40.6
Pollux	243 25.5	N27 59.1
Procyon	244 57.8	N 5 10.7
Rasalhague	96 04.4	N12 33.0
Regulus	207 41.4	N11 53.1
Rigel	281 10.5	S 8 11.3
Rigil Kent.	139 48.3	S60 54.0
Sabik	102 10.1	S15 44.5
Schedar	349 38.7	N56 37.3
Shaula	96 19.0	S37 06.7
Sirius	258 32.2	S16 44.7
Spica	158 28.9	S11 14.8
Suhail	222 50.9	S43 30.3
Vega	80 37.4	N38 47.9
Zuben'ubi	137 02.9	S16 06.5

	SHA	Mer. Pass.
	° ′	h m
Venus	330 29.8	11 21
Mars	114 02.0	1 46
Jupiter	194 47.3	20 20
Saturn	105 41.2	2 19

Day	UT	SUN GHA	SUN Dec	MOON GHA	v	MOON Dec	d	HP
	d h	° ′	° ′	° ′	′	° ′	′	′
SATURDAY	30 00	180 41.8	N14 50.2	268 34.3	9.9	S14 50.5	6.3	57.3
	01	195 41.9	51.0	283 03.2	9.9	14 44.2	6.4	57.3
	02	210 42.0	51.7	297 32.1	9.9	14 37.8	6.5	57.4
	03	225 42.1	. . 52.5	312 01.0	9.9	14 31.3	6.6	57.4
	04	240 42.1	53.3	326 29.9	9.9	14 24.7	6.7	57.4
	05	255 42.2	54.0	340 58.8	9.9	14 18.0	6.7	57.5
	06	270 42.3	N14 54.8	355 27.7	9.9	S14 11.3	6.9	57.5
	07	285 42.4	55.6	9 56.6	9.9	14 04.4	6.9	57.5
	08	300 42.4	56.3	24 25.5	9.8	13 57.5	7.0	57.6
	09	315 42.5	. . 57.1	38 54.3	9.9	13 50.5	7.1	57.6
	10	330 42.6	57.8	53 23.2	9.8	13 43.4	7.2	57.6
	11	345 42.7	58.6	67 52.0	9.9	13 36.2	7.3	57.7
	12	0 42.8	N14 59.4	82 20.9	9.8	S13 28.9	7.3	57.7
	13	15 42.8	15 00.1	96 49.7	9.9	13 21.6	7.5	57.7
	14	30 42.9	00.9	111 18.6	9.8	13 14.1	7.5	57.8
	15	45 43.0	. . 01.6	125 47.4	9.8	13 06.6	7.6	57.8
	16	60 43.1	02.4	140 16.2	9.8	12 59.0	7.7	57.9
	17	75 43.1	03.1	154 45.0	9.8	12 51.3	7.8	57.9
	18	90 43.2	N15 03.9	169 13.8	9.8	S12 43.5	7.8	57.9
	19	105 43.3	04.7	183 42.6	9.8	12 35.7	7.9	58.0
	20	120 43.4	05.4	198 11.4	9.7	12 27.8	8.1	58.0
	21	135 43.4	. . 06.2	212 40.1	9.8	12 19.7	8.0	58.0
	22	150 43.5	06.9	227 08.9	9.8	12 11.7	8.2	58.1
	23	165 43.6	07.7	241 37.7	9.7	12 03.5	8.3	58.1
SUNDAY	1 00	180 43.7	N15 08.4	256 06.4	9.8	S11 55.2	8.3	58.1
	01	195 43.7	09.2	270 35.2	9.7	11 46.9	8.4	58.2
	02	210 43.8	09.9	285 03.9	9.7	11 38.5	8.4	58.2
	03	225 43.9	. . 10.7	299 32.6	9.7	11 30.1	8.6	58.2
	04	240 44.0	11.4	314 01.3	9.7	11 21.5	8.6	58.3
	05	255 44.0	12.2	328 30.0	9.7	11 12.9	8.7	58.3
	06	270 44.1	N15 12.9	342 58.7	9.7	S11 04.2	8.8	58.4
	07	285 44.2	13.7	357 27.4	9.7	10 55.4	8.8	58.4
	08	300 44.2	14.5	11 56.1	9.6	10 46.6	9.0	58.4
	09	315 44.3	. . 15.2	26 24.7	9.7	10 37.6	9.0	58.5
	10	330 44.4	16.0	40 53.4	9.6	10 28.6	9.0	58.5
	11	345 44.5	16.7	55 22.0	9.7	10 19.6	9.2	58.5
	12	0 44.5	N15 17.4	69 50.7	9.6	S10 10.4	9.2	58.6
	13	15 44.6	18.2	84 19.3	9.6	10 01.2	9.2	58.6
	14	30 44.7	18.9	98 47.9	9.6	9 52.0	9.4	58.7
	15	45 44.7	. . 19.7	113 16.5	9.6	9 42.6	9.4	58.7
	16	60 44.8	20.4	127 45.1	9.5	9 33.2	9.5	58.7
	17	75 44.9	21.2	142 13.6	9.6	9 23.7	9.5	58.8
	18	90 45.0	N15 21.9	156 42.2	9.5	S 9 14.2	9.6	58.8
	19	105 45.0	22.7	171 10.7	9.6	9 04.6	9.7	58.8
	20	120 45.1	23.4	185 39.3	9.5	8 54.9	9.7	58.9
	21	135 45.2	. . 24.2	200 07.8	9.5	8 45.2	9.8	58.9
	22	150 45.2	24.9	214 36.3	9.5	8 35.4	9.9	58.9
	23	165 45.3	25.7	229 04.8	9.5	8 25.5	9.9	59.0
MONDAY	2 00	180 45.4	N15 26.4	243 33.3	9.4	S 8 15.6	10.0	59.0
	01	195 45.4	27.1	258 01.7	9.5	8 05.6	10.0	59.1
	02	210 45.5	27.9	272 30.2	9.4	7 55.6	10.1	59.1
	03	225 45.6	. . 28.6	286 58.6	9.4	7 45.5	10.2	59.1
	04	240 45.6	29.4	301 27.0	9.4	7 35.3	10.2	59.2
	05	255 45.7	30.1	315 55.4	9.4	7 25.1	10.3	59.2
	06	270 45.8	N15 30.9	330 23.8	9.4	S 7 14.8	10.3	59.2
	07	285 45.8	31.6	344 52.2	9.3	7 04.5	10.4	59.3
	08	300 45.9	32.3	359 20.5	9.3	6 54.1	10.4	59.3
	09	315 46.0	. . 33.1	13 48.8	9.4	6 43.7	10.5	59.3
	10	330 46.0	33.8	28 17.2	9.2	6 33.2	10.6	59.4
	11	345 46.1	34.6	42 45.4	9.3	6 22.6	10.6	59.4
	12	0 46.2	N15 35.3	57 13.7	9.3	S 6 12.0	10.6	59.4
	13	15 46.2	36.0	71 42.0	9.2	6 01.4	10.7	59.5
	14	30 46.3	36.8	86 10.2	9.2	5 50.7	10.7	59.5
	15	45 46.4	. . 37.5	100 38.4	9.2	5 40.0	10.8	59.5
	16	60 46.4	38.2	115 06.6	9.2	5 29.2	10.9	59.6
	17	75 46.5	39.0	129 34.8	9.1	5 18.3	10.8	59.6
	18	90 46.6	N15 39.7	144 02.9	9.2	S 5 07.5	11.0	59.6
	19	105 46.6	40.4	158 31.1	9.1	4 56.5	10.9	59.7
	20	120 46.7	41.2	172 59.2	9.1	4 45.6	11.0	59.7
	21	135 46.8	. . 41.9	187 27.3	9.0	4 34.6	11.1	59.8
	22	150 46.8	42.7	201 55.3	9.1	4 23.5	11.1	59.8
	23	165 46.9	43.4	216 23.4	9.0	S 4 12.4	11.1	59.8
		SD 15.9	*d* 0.7	SD	15.7	16.0		16.2

Lat.	Twilight Naut.	Twilight Civil	Sunrise	Moonrise 30	Moonrise 1	Moonrise 2	Moonrise 3
°	h m	h m	h m	h m	h m	h m	h m
N 72	////	////	01 49	03 46	03 39	03 33	03 28
N 70	////	////	02 29	03 16	03 20	03 22	03 23
68	////	01 03	02 56	02 53	03 05	03 13	03 19
66	////	01 53	03 16	02 36	02 52	03 05	03 16
64	////	02 23	03 32	02 21	02 42	02 58	03 13
62	00 55	02 46	03 46	02 09	02 33	02 53	03 11
60	01 40	03 04	03 57	01 59	02 25	02 48	03 08
N 58	02 08	03 18	04 07	01 50	02 18	02 43	03 07
56	02 29	03 31	04 15	01 42	02 12	02 39	03 05
54	02 46	03 41	04 23	01 34	02 07	02 36	03 03
52	03 00	03 51	04 30	01 28	02 02	02 33	03 02
50	03 12	03 59	04 36	01 22	01 57	02 30	03 01
45	03 36	04 17	04 49	01 10	01 48	02 23	02 58
N 40	03 55	04 30	05 00	00 59	01 40	02 18	02 55
35	04 09	04 42	05 09	00 51	01 33	02 13	02 53
30	04 21	04 52	05 17	00 43	01 27	02 09	02 51
20	04 40	05 08	05 31	00 29	01 16	02 02	02 48
N 10	04 55	05 21	05 43	00 18	01 07	01 56	02 46
0	05 07	05 32	05 54	00 06	00 58	01 50	02 43
S 10	05 18	05 43	06 05	24 49	00 49	01 44	02 40
20	05 27	05 53	06 16	24 40	00 40	01 38	02 38
30	05 36	06 04	06 29	24 29	00 29	01 31	02 35
35	05 40	06 10	06 37	24 23	00 23	01 27	02 33
40	05 45	06 17	06 45	24 16	00 16	01 22	02 31
45	05 50	06 24	06 55	24 08	00 08	01 17	02 29
S 50	05 55	06 33	07 07	23 58	25 10	01 10	02 26
52	05 57	06 37	07 13	23 54	25 07	01 07	02 24
54	05 59	06 41	07 19	23 48	25 04	01 04	02 23
56	06 01	06 45	07 26	23 43	25 00	01 00	02 21
58	06 04	06 51	07 33	23 37	24 56	00 56	02 20
S 60	06 06	06 56	07 42	23 29	24 52	00 52	02 18

Lat.	Sunset	Twilight Civil	Twilight Naut.	Moonset 30	Moonset 1	Moonset 2	Moonset 3
°	h m	h m	h m	h m	h m	h m	h m
N 72	22 12	////	////	09 05	11 00	12 55	14 51
N 70	21 30	////	////	09 34	11 18	13 04	14 53
68	21 02	23 03	////	09 56	11 32	13 12	14 55
66	20 41	22 06	////	10 13	11 43	13 18	14 56
64	20 24	21 34	////	10 26	11 52	13 23	14 57
62	20 10	21 11	23 09	10 38	12 00	13 28	14 58
60	19 59	20 53	22 18	10 48	12 07	13 32	14 59
N 58	19 49	20 38	21 49	10 56	12 13	13 35	15 00
56	19 40	20 25	21 27	11 04	12 19	13 38	15 01
54	19 32	20 14	21 10	11 10	12 24	13 41	15 01
52	19 26	20 05	20 56	11 16	12 28	13 43	15 02
50	19 19	19 56	20 43	11 22	12 32	13 46	15 02
45	19 06	19 38	20 19	11 33	12 40	13 50	15 03
N 40	18 55	19 24	20 00	11 43	12 47	13 55	15 04
35	18 46	19 13	19 46	11 51	12 53	13 58	15 05
30	18 38	19 03	19 33	11 58	12 59	14 01	15 06
20	18 24	18 47	19 14	12 10	13 08	14 06	15 07
N 10	18 12	18 33	18 59	12 21	13 16	14 11	15 08
0	18 00	18 22	18 47	12 31	13 23	14 15	15 08
S 10	17 49	18 11	18 36	12 41	13 30	14 19	15 09
20	17 38	18 01	18 27	12 52	13 38	14 24	15 10
30	17 25	17 49	18 18	13 04	13 47	14 29	15 11
35	17 17	17 43	18 13	13 11	13 52	14 32	15 12
40	17 08	17 37	18 09	13 18	13 58	14 35	15 12
45	16 58	17 29	18 04	13 28	14 04	14 39	15 13
S 50	16 46	17 20	17 59	13 38	14 12	14 43	15 14
52	16 41	17 17	17 57	13 44	14 16	14 45	15 14
54	16 35	17 12	17 54	13 49	14 20	14 48	15 14
56	16 28	17 08	17 52	13 55	14 24	14 50	15 15
58	16 20	17 03	17 49	14 02	14 29	14 53	15 15
S 60	16 11	16 57	17 47	14 10	14 34	14 56	15 16

Day	SUN Eqn. of Time 00h	SUN Eqn. of Time 12h	SUN Mer. Pass.	MOON Mer. Pass. Upper	MOON Mer. Pass. Lower	Age	Phase
d	m s	m s	h m	h m	h m	d	%
30	02 47	02 51	11 57	06 19	18 45	23	46
1	02 55	02 58	11 57	07 11	19 37	24	36
2	03 01	03 05	11 57	08 03	20 29	25	25

UT	ARIES	VENUS −3·9		MARS −1·6		JUPITER −2·2		SATURN +0·2		STARS		
d h	GHA ° ′	GHA ° ′	Dec ° ′	GHA ° ′	Dec ° ′	GHA ° ′	Dec ° ′	GHA ° ′	Dec ° ′	Name	SHA ° ′	Dec ° ′
3 00 (TUESDAY)	221 19.5	189 28.7	N11 36.3	335 45.6	S21 43.3	56 09.6	N 7 50.1	327 07.7	S20 49.3	Acamar	315 17.4	S40 14.6
01	236 21.9	204 28.3	37.4	350 48.6	43.3	71 12.1	50.1	342 10.3	49.3	Achernar	335 26.0	S57 09.3
02	251 24.4	219 27.8	38.5	5 51.6	43.4	86 14.6	50.1	357 12.9	49.2	Acrux	173 06.4	S63 11.6
03	266 26.9	234 27.3	. . 39.6	20 54.6	. . 43.4	101 17.1	. . 50.1	12 15.5	. . 49.2	Adhara	255 11.2	S29 00.1
04	281 29.3	249 26.9	40.6	35 57.7	43.4	116 19.6	50.1	27 18.1	49.2	Aldebaran	290 47.5	N16 32.2
05	296 31.8	264 26.4	41.7	51 00.7	43.4	131 22.1	50.1	42 20.7	49.2			
06	311 34.3	279 25.9	N11 42.8	66 03.7	S21 43.5	146 24.6	N 7 50.1	57 23.3	S20 49.2	Alioth	166 18.6	N55 52.4
07	326 36.7	294 25.4	43.9	81 06.7	43.5	161 27.1	50.1	72 26.0	49.2	Alkaid	152 57.0	N49 14.0
08	341 39.2	309 25.0	45.0	96 09.7	43.5	176 29.7	50.2	87 28.6	49.1	Al Na'ir	27 41.5	S46 52.7
09	356 41.6	324 24.5	. . 46.1	111 12.7	. . 43.6	191 32.2	. . 50.2	102 31.2	. . 49.1	Alnilam	275 44.7	S 1 11.8
10	11 44.1	339 24.0	47.2	126 15.7	43.6	206 34.7	50.2	117 33.8	49.1	Alphard	217 54.2	S 8 44.0
11	26 46.6	354 23.5	48.3	141 18.7	43.6	221 37.2	50.2	132 36.4	49.1			
12	41 49.0	9 23.0	N11 49.4	156 21.7	S21 43.7	236 39.7	N 7 50.2	147 39.0	S20 49.1	Alphecca	126 09.0	N26 39.7
13	56 51.5	24 22.6	50.5	171 24.8	43.7	251 42.2	50.2	162 41.6	49.1	Alpheratz	357 41.7	N29 10.6
14	71 54.0	39 22.1	51.6	186 27.8	43.7	266 44.7	50.2	177 44.3	49.0	Altair	62 06.2	N 8 54.7
15	86 56.4	54 21.6	. . 52.7	201 30.8	. . 43.8	281 47.2	. . 50.2	192 46.9	. . 49.0	Ankaa	353 14.2	S42 13.0
16	101 58.9	69 21.1	53.7	216 33.8	43.8	296 49.7	50.2	207 49.5	49.0	Antares	112 23.5	S26 27.9
17	117 01.4	84 20.7	54.8	231 36.8	43.8	311 52.2	50.2	222 52.1	49.0			
18	132 03.8	99 20.2	N11 55.9	246 39.9	S21 43.8	326 54.8	N 7 50.3	237 54.7	S20 49.0	Arcturus	145 53.7	N19 05.9
19	147 06.3	114 19.7	57.0	261 42.9	43.9	341 57.3	50.3	252 57.3	49.0	Atria	107 23.1	S69 03.1
20	162 08.8	129 19.2	58.1	276 45.9	43.9	356 59.8	50.3	268 00.0	48.9	Avior	234 17.3	S59 34.2
21	177 11.2	144 18.7	11 59.2	291 48.9	. . 43.9	12 02.3	. . 50.3	283 02.6	. . 48.9	Bellatrix	278 30.2	N 6 21.6
22	192 13.7	159 18.3	12 00.3	306 52.0	44.0	27 04.8	50.3	298 05.2	48.9	Betelgeuse	270 59.5	N 7 24.3
23	207 16.1	174 17.8	01.4	321 55.0	44.0	42 07.3	50.3	313 07.8	48.9			
4 00 (WEDNESDAY)	222 18.6	189 17.3	N12 02.4	336 58.0	S21 44.0	57 09.8	N 7 50.3	328 10.4	S20 48.9	Canopus	263 55.6	S52 42.7
01	237 21.1	204 16.8	03.5	352 01.1	44.1	72 12.3	50.3	343 13.0	48.9	Capella	280 32.0	N46 00.7
02	252 23.5	219 16.3	04.6	7 04.1	44.1	87 14.8	50.3	358 15.7	48.8	Deneb	49 30.1	N45 20.2
03	267 26.0	234 15.8	. . 05.7	22 07.1	. . 44.1	102 17.3	. . 50.3	13 18.3	. . 48.8	Denebola	182 31.5	N14 28.8
04	282 28.5	249 15.4	06.8	37 10.2	44.1	117 19.8	50.3	28 20.9	48.8	Diphda	348 54.3	S17 53.9
05	297 30.9	264 14.9	07.9	52 13.2	44.2	132 22.3	50.4	43 23.5	48.8			
06	312 33.4	279 14.4	N12 08.9	67 16.3	S21 44.2	147 24.8	N 7 50.4	58 26.1	S20 48.8	Dubhe	193 49.2	N61 40.0
07	327 35.9	294 13.9	10.0	82 19.3	44.2	162 27.3	50.4	73 28.7	48.7	Elnath	278 10.5	N28 37.0
08	342 38.3	309 13.4	11.1	97 22.3	44.2	177 29.8	50.4	88 31.4	48.7	Eltanin	90 44.9	N51 29.2
09	357 40.8	324 12.9	. . 12.2	112 25.4	. . 44.3	192 32.3	. . 50.4	103 34.0	. . 48.7	Enif	33 45.3	N 9 56.9
10	12 43.2	339 12.5	13.3	127 28.4	44.3	207 34.9	50.4	118 36.6	48.7	Fomalhaut	15 22.1	S29 32.1
11	27 45.7	354 12.0	14.3	142 31.5	44.3	222 37.4	50.4	133 39.2	48.7			
12	42 48.2	9 11.5	N12 15.4	157 34.5	S21 44.4	237 39.9	N 7 50.4	148 41.8	S20 48.7	Gacrux	171 58.1	S57 12.4
13	57 50.6	24 11.0	16.5	172 37.6	44.4	252 42.4	50.4	163 44.4	48.6	Gienah	175 50.0	S17 38.1
14	72 53.1	39 10.5	17.6	187 40.6	44.4	267 44.9	50.4	178 47.1	48.6	Hadar	148 44.4	S60 27.1
15	87 55.6	54 10.0	. . 18.7	202 43.7	. . 44.4	282 47.4	. . 50.4	193 49.7	. . 48.6	Hamal	327 58.9	N23 32.1
16	102 58.0	69 09.5	19.7	217 46.7	44.5	297 49.9	50.4	208 52.3	48.6	Kaus Aust.	83 41.0	S34 22.3
17	118 00.5	84 09.0	20.8	232 49.8	44.5	312 52.4	50.4	223 54.9	48.6			
18	133 03.0	99 08.6	N12 21.9	247 52.8	S21 44.5	327 54.9	N 7 50.5	238 57.5	S20 48.6	Kochab	137 19.1	N74 05.4
19	148 05.4	114 08.1	23.0	262 55.9	44.5	342 57.4	50.5	254 00.2	48.5	Markab	13 36.6	N15 17.4
20	163 07.9	129 07.6	24.0	277 59.0	44.6	357 59.9	50.5	269 02.8	48.5	Menkar	314 13.4	N 4 08.9
21	178 10.4	144 07.1	. . 25.1	293 02.0	. . 44.6	13 02.4	. . 50.5	284 05.4	. . 48.5	Menkent	148 04.9	S36 27.0
22	193 12.8	159 06.6	26.2	308 05.1	44.6	28 04.9	50.5	299 08.0	48.5	Miaplacidus	221 39.1	S69 47.5
23	208 15.3	174 06.1	27.3	323 08.1	44.6	43 07.4	50.5	314 10.6	48.5			
5 00 (THURSDAY)	223 17.7	189 05.6	N12 28.3	338 11.2	S21 44.7	58 09.9	N 7 50.5	329 13.3	S20 48.5	Mirfak	308 38.0	N49 54.9
01	238 20.2	204 05.1	29.4	353 14.3	44.7	73 12.4	50.5	344 15.9	48.4	Nunki	75 55.7	S26 16.3
02	253 22.7	219 04.6	30.5	8 17.3	44.7	88 14.9	50.5	359 18.5	48.4	Peacock	53 16.2	S56 40.6
03	268 25.1	234 04.1	. . 31.6	23 20.4	. . 44.7	103 17.4	. . 50.5	14 21.1	. . 48.4	Pollux	243 25.5	N27 59.1
04	283 27.6	249 03.6	32.6	38 23.5	44.8	118 19.9	50.5	29 23.7	48.4	Procyon	244 57.9	N 5 10.7
05	298 30.1	264 03.2	33.7	53 26.5	44.8	133 22.4	50.5	44 26.4	48.4			
06	313 32.5	279 02.7	N12 34.8	68 29.6	S21 44.8	148 24.9	N 7 50.5	59 29.0	S20 48.3	Rasalhague	96 04.4	N12 33.0
07	328 35.0	294 02.2	35.8	83 32.7	44.8	163 27.4	50.5	74 31.6	48.3	Regulus	207 41.4	N11 53.1
08	343 37.5	309 01.7	36.9	98 35.8	44.8	178 29.9	50.5	89 34.2	48.3	Rigel	281 10.5	S 8 11.3
09	358 39.9	324 01.2	. . 38.0	113 38.8	. . 44.9	193 32.4	. . 50.5	104 36.8	. . 48.3	Rigil Kent.	139 48.3	S60 54.0
10	13 42.4	339 00.7	39.0	128 41.9	44.9	208 34.9	50.5	119 39.5	48.3	Sabik	102 10.0	S15 44.5
11	28 44.8	354 00.2	40.1	143 45.0	44.9	223 37.4	50.5	134 42.1	48.3			
12	43 47.3	8 59.7	N12 41.2	158 48.1	S21 44.9	238 39.9	N 7 50.5	149 44.7	S20 48.2	Schedar	349 38.7	N56 37.3
13	58 49.8	23 59.2	42.2	173 51.2	45.0	253 42.4	50.6	164 47.3	48.2	Shaula	96 19.0	S37 06.7
14	73 52.2	38 58.7	43.3	188 54.2	45.0	268 44.8	50.6	179 49.9	48.2	Sirius	258 32.2	S16 44.7
15	88 54.7	53 58.2	. . 44.4	203 57.3	. . 45.0	283 47.3	. . 50.6	194 52.6	. . 48.2	Spica	158 28.9	S11 14.8
16	103 57.2	68 57.7	45.4	219 00.4	45.0	298 49.8	50.6	209 55.2	48.2	Suhail	222 51.0	S43 30.3
17	118 59.6	83 57.2	46.5	234 03.5	45.0	313 52.3	50.6	224 57.8	48.2			
18	134 02.1	98 56.7	N12 47.6	249 06.6	S21 45.1	328 54.8	N 7 50.6	240 00.4	S20 48.1	Vega	80 37.4	N38 47.9
19	149 04.6	113 56.2	48.6	264 09.7	45.1	343 57.3	50.6	255 03.0	48.1	Zuben'ubi	137 02.9	S16 06.5
20	164 07.0	128 55.7	49.7	279 12.8	45.1	358 59.8	50.6	270 05.7	48.1			
21	179 09.5	143 55.2	. . 50.8	294 15.8	. . 45.1	14 02.3	. . 50.6	285 08.3	. . 48.1			
22	194 12.0	158 54.7	51.8	309 18.9	45.2	29 04.8	50.6	300 10.9	48.1			
23	209 14.4	173 54.2	52.9	324 22.0	45.2	44 07.3	50.6	315 13.5	48.0			
Mer. Pass.	h m 9 09.3	v −0.5	d 1.1	v 3.0	d 0.0	v 2.5	d 0.0	v 2.6	d 0.0			

	SHA ° ′	Mer. Pass. h m
Venus	326 58.7	11 23
Mars	114 39.4	1 32
Jupiter	194 51.2	20 08
Saturn	105 51.8	2 07

UT	SUN GHA	SUN Dec	MOON GHA	v	MOON Dec	d	HP
d h	° ′	° ′	° ′	′	° ′	′	′
3 00	180 46.9	N15 44.1	230 51.4	9.0	S 4 01.3	11.2	59.9
01	195 47.0	44.8	245 19.4	8.9	3 50.1	11.2	59.9
02	210 47.1	45.6	259 47.3	9.0	3 38.9	11.2	59.9
03	225 47.1	. . 46.3	274 15.3	8.9	3 27.7	11.3	59.9
04	240 47.2	47.0	288 43.2	8.9	3 16.4	11.3	60.0
05	255 47.3	47.8	303 11.1	8.9	3 05.1	11.3	60.0
06	270 47.3	N15 48.5	317 39.0	8.8	S 2 53.8	11.3	60.0
07	285 47.4	49.2	332 06.8	8.8	2 42.5	11.4	60.1
T 08	300 47.4	50.0	346 34.6	8.8	2 31.1	11.5	60.1
U 09	315 47.5	. . 50.7	1 02.4	8.7	2 19.6	11.4	60.1
E 10	330 47.6	51.4	15 30.1	8.8	2 08.2	11.5	60.2
S 11	345 47.6	52.2	29 57.9	8.7	1 56.7	11.5	60.2
D 12	0 47.7	N15 52.9	44 25.6	8.6	S 1 45.2	11.5	60.2
A 13	15 47.7	53.6	58 53.2	8.7	1 33.7	11.5	60.3
Y 14	30 47.8	54.3	73 20.9	8.6	1 22.2	11.6	60.3
15	45 47.9	. . 55.1	87 48.5	8.5	1 10.6	11.6	60.3
16	60 47.9	55.8	102 16.0	8.6	0 59.0	11.6	60.3
17	75 48.0	56.5	116 43.6	8.5	0 47.4	11.6	60.4
18	90 48.0	N15 57.2	131 11.1	8.5	S 0 35.8	11.6	60.4
19	105 48.1	58.0	145 38.6	8.4	0 24.2	11.7	60.4
20	120 48.1	58.7	160 06.0	8.4	0 12.5	11.6	60.5
21	135 48.2	15 59.4	174 33.4	8.4	S 0 00.9	11.7	60.5
22	150 48.3	16 00.1	189 00.8	8.4	N 0 10.8	11.7	60.5
23	165 48.3	00.9	203 28.2	8.3	0 22.5	11.7	60.5
4 00	180 48.4	N16 01.6	217 55.5	8.2	N 0 34.2	11.7	60.6
01	195 48.4	02.3	232 22.7	8.3	0 45.9	11.7	60.6
02	210 48.5	03.0	246 50.0	8.2	0 57.6	11.7	60.6
03	225 48.5	. . 03.7	261 17.2	8.2	1 09.3	11.7	60.6
04	240 48.6	04.5	275 44.4	8.1	1 21.0	11.7	60.7
05	255 48.7	05.2	290 11.5	8.1	1 32.7	11.7	60.7
06	270 48.7	N16 05.9	304 38.6	8.1	N 1 44.4	11.7	60.7
W 07	285 48.8	06.6	319 05.7	8.0	1 56.1	11.7	60.7
E 08	300 48.8	07.3	333 32.7	8.0	2 07.8	11.7	60.8
D 09	315 48.9	. . 08.1	347 59.7	7.9	2 19.5	11.7	60.8
N 10	330 48.9	08.8	2 26.6	7.9	2 31.2	11.7	60.8
E 11	345 49.0	09.5	16 53.5	7.9	2 42.9	11.7	60.8
S 12	0 49.0	N16 10.2	31 20.4	7.8	N 2 54.6	11.7	60.8
D 13	15 49.1	10.9	45 47.2	7.8	3 06.3	11.7	60.9
A 14	30 49.1	11.6	60 14.0	7.8	3 18.0	11.6	60.9
Y 15	45 49.2	. . 12.3	74 40.8	7.7	3 29.6	11.7	60.9
16	60 49.2	13.1	89 07.5	7.7	3 41.3	11.6	60.9
17	75 49.3	13.8	103 34.2	7.6	3 52.9	11.6	60.9
18	90 49.3	N16 14.5	118 00.8	7.6	N 4 04.5	11.6	61.0
19	105 49.4	15.2	132 27.4	7.5	4 16.1	11.5	61.0
20	120 49.5	15.9	146 53.9	7.6	4 27.6	11.6	61.0
21	135 49.5	. . 16.6	161 20.5	7.4	4 39.2	11.5	61.0
22	150 49.6	17.3	175 46.9	7.5	4 50.7	11.5	61.0
23	165 49.6	18.1	190 13.4	7.3	5 02.2	11.5	61.0
5 00	180 49.7	N16 18.8	204 39.7	7.4	N 5 13.7	11.4	61.1
01	195 49.7	19.5	219 06.1	7.3	5 25.1	11.4	61.1
02	210 49.8	20.2	233 32.4	7.2	5 36.5	11.4	61.1
03	225 49.8	. . 20.9	247 58.6	7.3	5 47.9	11.4	61.1
04	240 49.9	21.6	262 24.9	7.1	5 59.3	11.3	61.1
05	255 49.9	22.3	276 51.0	7.2	6 10.6	11.3	61.1
06	270 50.0	N16 23.0	291 17.2	7.1	N 6 21.9	11.2	61.1
07	285 50.0	23.7	305 43.3	7.0	6 33.1	11.2	61.2
T 08	300 50.1	24.4	320 09.3	7.0	6 44.3	11.2	61.2
H 09	315 50.1	. . 25.1	334 35.3	7.0	6 55.5	11.1	61.2
U 10	330 50.1	25.8	349 01.3	6.9	7 06.6	11.1	61.2
R 11	345 50.2	26.6	3 27.2	6.9	7 17.7	11.0	61.2
S 12	0 50.2	N16 27.3	17 53.1	6.8	N 7 28.7	11.0	61.2
D 13	15 50.3	28.0	32 18.9	6.8	7 39.7	11.0	61.2
A 14	30 50.3	28.7	46 44.7	6.7	7 50.7	10.9	61.2
Y 15	45 50.4	. . 29.4	61 10.4	6.7	8 01.6	10.8	61.2
16	60 50.4	30.1	75 36.1	6.7	8 12.4	10.8	61.2
17	75 50.5	30.8	90 01.8	6.6	8 23.2	10.7	61.2
18	90 50.5	N16 31.5	104 27.4	6.6	N 8 33.9	10.7	61.3
19	105 50.6	32.2	118 53.0	6.5	8 44.6	10.6	61.3
20	120 50.6	32.9	133 18.5	6.5	8 55.2	10.6	61.3
21	135 50.7	. . 33.6	147 44.0	6.5	9 05.8	10.5	61.3
22	150 50.7	34.3	162 09.5	6.4	9 16.3	10.4	61.3
23	165 50.8	35.0	176 34.9	6.3	N 9 26.7	10.4	61.3
	SD 15.9	d 0.7	SD 16.4		16.6		16.7

Lat.	Twilight Naut.	Twilight Civil	Sunrise	Moonrise 3	Moonrise 4	Moonrise 5	Moonrise 6
°	h m	h m	h m	h m	h m	h m	h m
N 72	////	////	01 21	03 28	03 23	03 18	03 12
N 70	////	////	02 10	03 23	03 24	03 25	03 28
68	////	////	02 41	03 19	03 25	03 32	03 40
66	////	01 33	03 04	03 16	03 26	03 37	03 51
64	////	02 09	03 22	03 13	03 27	03 42	03 59
62	////	02 34	03 37	03 11	03 28	03 46	04 07
60	01 23	02 54	03 49	03 08	03 29	03 50	04 14
N 58	01 56	03 10	03 59	03 07	03 29	03 53	04 19
56	02 19	03 23	04 09	03 05	03 30	03 56	04 25
54	02 37	03 35	04 17	03 03	03 30	03 58	04 29
52	02 53	03 45	04 24	03 02	03 31	04 01	04 33
50	03 05	03 53	04 31	03 01	03 31	04 03	04 37
45	03 31	04 12	04 45	02 58	03 32	04 07	04 46
N 40	03 50	04 26	04 56	02 55	03 33	04 11	04 53
35	04 06	04 39	05 06	02 53	03 33	04 15	04 59
30	04 18	04 49	05 14	02 51	03 34	04 18	05 04
20	04 38	05 06	05 29	02 48	03 35	04 23	05 13
N 10	04 54	05 20	05 42	02 46	03 36	04 28	05 22
0	05 07	05 32	05 53	02 43	03 37	04 32	05 29
S 10	05 18	05 43	06 05	02 40	03 38	04 37	05 37
20	05 28	05 54	06 17	02 38	03 39	04 42	05 46
30	05 38	06 06	06 31	02 35	03 40	04 47	05 55
35	05 43	06 13	06 39	02 33	03 41	04 50	06 01
40	05 48	06 20	06 48	02 31	03 42	04 54	06 07
45	05 53	06 28	06 59	02 29	03 43	04 58	06 15
S 50	05 58	06 37	07 12	02 26	03 44	05 04	06 24
52	06 01	06 41	07 18	02 24	03 44	05 06	06 28
54	06 03	06 46	07 24	02 23	03 45	05 09	06 33
56	06 06	06 51	07 31	02 21	03 45	05 11	06 38
58	06 09	06 56	07 40	02 20	03 46	05 15	06 44
S 60	06 12	07 02	07 49	02 18	03 47	05 18	06 50

Lat.	Sunset	Twilight Civil	Twilight Naut.	Moonset 3	Moonset 4	Moonset 5	Moonset 6
°	h m	h m	h m	h m	h m	h m	h m
N 72	22 43	////	////	14 51	16 51	18 54	21 02
N 70	21 48	////	////	14 53	16 46	18 41	20 38
68	21 16	////	////	14 55	16 41	18 30	20 19
66	20 52	22 27	////	14 56	16 38	18 21	20 04
64	20 34	21 48	////	14 57	16 34	18 13	19 52
62	20 19	21 22	////	14 58	16 32	18 07	19 41
60	20 06	21 02	22 37	14 59	16 29	18 01	19 32
N 58	19 56	20 46	22 02	15 00	16 27	17 56	19 25
56	19 46	20 32	21 37	15 01	16 26	17 52	19 18
54	19 38	20 20	21 18	15 01	16 24	17 48	19 12
52	19 30	20 10	21 03	15 02	16 23	17 45	19 06
50	19 24	20 01	20 50	15 02	16 21	17 41	19 01
45	19 10	19 43	20 24	15 03	16 18	17 35	18 51
N 40	18 58	19 28	20 04	15 04	16 16	17 29	18 42
35	18 48	19 16	19 48	15 05	16 14	17 24	18 35
30	18 40	19 05	19 36	15 06	16 12	17 19	18 28
20	18 25	18 48	19 15	15 07	16 08	17 12	18 16
N 10	18 12	18 34	19 00	15 08	16 06	17 05	18 07
0	18 00	18 22	18 47	15 08	16 03	16 59	17 57
S 10	17 48	18 10	18 36	15 09	16 00	16 53	17 48
20	17 36	17 59	18 25	15 10	15 57	16 46	17 38
30	17 22	17 47	18 15	15 11	15 54	16 39	17 27
35	17 14	17 40	18 11	15 12	15 52	16 35	17 20
40	17 05	17 33	18 05	15 12	15 50	16 30	17 13
45	16 54	17 25	18 00	15 13	15 47	16 24	17 04
S 50	16 41	17 16	17 54	15 14	15 44	16 17	16 54
52	16 35	17 12	17 52	15 14	15 43	16 14	16 49
54	16 29	17 07	17 49	15 14	15 42	16 11	16 44
56	16 21	17 02	17 46	15 15	15 40	16 07	16 38
58	16 13	16 56	17 44	15 15	15 38	16 03	16 31
S 60	16 04	16 50	17 40	15 16	15 36	15 58	16 24

Day	SUN Eqn. of Time 00^h	SUN Eqn. of Time 12^h	SUN Mer. Pass.	MOON Mer. Pass. Upper	MOON Mer. Pass. Lower	MOON Age	MOON Phase
d	m s	m s	h m	h m	h m	d %	
3	03 08	03 11	11 57	08 56	21 23	26 16	
4	03 13	03 16	11 57	09 50	22 18	27 8	
5	03 19	03 21	11 57	10 46	23 14	28 3	

	UT	ARIES	VENUS −3·9		MARS −1·7		JUPITER −2·2		SATURN +0·1	
		GHA	GHA	Dec	GHA	Dec	GHA	Dec	GHA	Dec
	d h	° ′	° ′	° ′	° ′	° ′	° ′	° ′	° ′	° ′
	6 00	224 16.9	188 53.7	N12 53.9	339 25.1	S21 45.2	59 09.8	N 7 50.6	330 16.1	S20 48.0
	01	239 19.3	203 53.2	55.0	354 28.2	45.2	74 12.3	50.6	345 18.8	48.0
	02	254 21.8	218 52.7	56.1	9 31.3	45.2	89 14.8	50.6	0 21.4	48.0
	03	269 24.3	233 52.2	. . 57.1	24 34.4	. . 45.3	104 17.3	. . 50.6	15 24.0	. . 48.0
	04	284 26.7	248 51.7	58.2	39 37.5	45.3	119 19.8	50.6	30 26.6	48.0
	05	299 29.2	263 51.2	12 59.2	54 40.6	45.3	134 22.2	50.6	45 29.3	47.9
	06	314 31.7	278 50.7	N13 00.3	69 43.7	S21 45.3	149 24.7	N 7 50.6	60 31.9	S20 47.9
	07	329 34.1	293 50.2	01.4	84 46.8	45.3	164 27.2	50.6	75 34.5	47.9
	08	344 36.6	308 49.7	02.4	99 49.9	45.4	179 29.7	50.6	90 37.1	47.9
F	09	359 39.1	323 49.2	. . 03.5	114 53.0	. . 45.4	194 32.2	. . 50.6	105 39.8	. . 47.9
R	10	14 41.5	338 48.7	04.5	129 56.1	45.4	209 34.7	50.6	120 42.4	47.9
I	11	29 44.0	353 48.2	05.6	144 59.3	45.4	224 37.2	50.6	135 45.0	47.8
D	12	44 46.5	8 47.7	N13 06.6	160 02.4	S21 45.4	239 39.7	N 7 50.6	150 47.6	S20 47.8
A	13	59 48.9	23 47.2	07.7	175 05.5	45.4	254 42.2	50.6	165 50.2	47.8
Y	14	74 51.4	38 46.7	08.7	190 08.6	45.5	269 44.7	50.6	180 52.9	47.8
	15	89 53.8	53 46.2	. . 09.8	205 11.7	. . 45.5	284 47.1	. . 50.6	195 55.5	. . 47.8
	16	104 56.3	68 45.6	10.8	220 14.8	45.5	299 49.6	50.6	210 58.1	47.7
	17	119 58.8	83 45.1	11.9	235 17.9	45.5	314 52.1	50.6	226 00.7	47.7
	18	135 01.2	98 44.6	N13 12.9	250 21.1	S21 45.5	329 54.6	N 7 50.6	241 03.4	S20 47.7
	19	150 03.7	113 44.1	14.0	265 24.2	45.5	344 57.1	50.6	256 06.0	47.7
	20	165 06.2	128 43.6	15.0	280 27.3	45.6	359 59.6	50.6	271 08.6	47.7
	21	180 08.6	143 43.1	. . 16.1	295 30.4	. . 45.6	15 02.1	. . 50.6	286 11.2	. . 47.7
	22	195 11.1	158 42.6	17.1	310 33.5	45.6	30 04.6	50.6	301 13.9	47.6
	23	210 13.6	173 42.1	18.2	325 36.7	45.6	45 07.0	50.6	316 16.5	47.6
	7 00	225 16.0	188 41.6	N13 19.2	340 39.8	S21 45.6	60 09.5	N 7 50.6	331 19.1	S20 47.6
	01	240 18.5	203 41.1	20.3	355 42.9	45.6	75 12.0	50.6	346 21.7	47.6
	02	255 20.9	218 40.6	21.3	10 46.0	45.7	90 14.5	50.6	1 24.4	47.6
	03	270 23.4	233 40.0	. . 22.4	25 49.2	. . 45.7	105 17.0	. . 50.6	16 27.0	. . 47.5
	04	285 25.9	248 39.5	23.4	40 52.3	45.7	120 19.5	50.6	31 29.6	47.5
	05	300 28.3	263 39.0	24.5	55 55.4	45.7	135 21.9	50.6	46 32.2	47.5
	06	315 30.8	278 38.5	N13 25.5	70 58.6	S21 45.7	150 24.4	N 7 50.6	61 34.9	S20 47.5
S	07	330 33.3	293 38.0	26.6	86 01.7	45.7	165 26.9	50.6	76 37.5	47.5
	08	345 35.7	308 37.5	27.6	101 04.8	45.8	180 29.4	50.6	91 40.1	47.5
A	09	0 38.2	323 37.0	. . 28.6	116 08.0	. . 45.8	195 31.9	. . 50.6	106 42.7	. . 47.4
T	10	15 40.7	338 36.5	29.7	131 11.1	45.8	210 34.4	50.6	121 45.4	47.4
U	11	30 43.1	353 35.9	30.7	146 14.2	45.8	225 36.8	50.6	136 48.0	47.4
R	12	45 45.6	8 35.4	N13 31.8	161 17.4	S21 45.8	240 39.3	N 7 50.6	151 50.6	S20 47.4
D	13	60 48.1	23 34.9	32.8	176 20.5	45.8	255 41.8	50.6	166 53.2	47.4
A	14	75 50.5	38 34.4	33.8	191 23.7	45.8	270 44.3	50.6	181 55.9	47.4
Y	15	90 53.0	53 33.9	. . 34.9	206 26.8	. . 45.9	285 46.8	. . 50.6	196 58.5	. . 47.3
	16	105 55.4	68 33.4	35.9	221 29.9	45.9	300 49.3	50.6	212 01.1	47.3
	17	120 57.9	83 32.8	37.0	236 33.1	45.9	315 51.7	50.6	227 03.7	47.3
	18	136 00.4	98 32.3	N13 38.0	251 36.2	S21 45.9	330 54.2	N 7 50.6	242 06.4	S20 47.3
	19	151 02.8	113 31.8	39.0	266 39.4	45.9	345 56.7	50.6	257 09.0	47.3
	20	166 05.3	128 31.3	40.1	281 42.5	45.9	0 59.2	50.6	272 11.6	47.2
	21	181 07.8	143 30.8	. . 41.1	296 45.7	. . 45.9	16 01.6	. . 50.6	287 14.2	. . 47.2
	22	196 10.2	158 30.3	42.1	311 48.8	45.9	31 04.1	50.6	302 16.9	47.2
	23	211 12.7	173 29.7	43.2	326 52.0	46.0	46 06.6	50.6	317 19.5	47.2
	8 00	226 15.2	188 29.2	N13 44.2	341 55.1	S21 46.0	61 09.1	N 7 50.6	332 22.1	S20 47.2
	01	241 17.6	203 28.7	45.2	356 58.3	46.0	76 11.6	50.6	347 24.8	47.2
	02	256 20.1	218 28.2	46.3	12 01.4	46.0	91 14.0	50.6	2 27.4	47.1
	03	271 22.6	233 27.6	. . 47.3	27 04.6	. . 46.0	106 16.5	. . 50.6	17 30.0	. . 47.1
	04	286 25.0	248 27.1	48.3	42 07.8	46.0	121 19.0	50.6	32 32.6	47.1
	05	301 27.5	263 26.6	49.4	57 10.9	46.0	136 21.5	50.6	47 35.3	47.1
	06	316 29.9	278 26.1	N13 50.4	72 14.1	S21 46.0	151 24.0	N 7 50.6	62 37.9	S20 47.1
	07	331 32.4	293 25.6	51.4	87 17.2	46.0	166 26.4	50.6	77 40.5	47.0
	08	346 34.9	308 25.0	52.5	102 20.4	46.1	181 28.9	50.5	92 43.1	47.0
S	09	1 37.3	323 24.5	. . 53.5	117 23.6	. . 46.1	196 31.4	. . 50.5	107 45.8	. . 47.0
U	10	16 39.8	338 24.0	54.5	132 26.7	46.1	211 33.9	50.5	122 48.4	47.0
N	11	31 42.3	353 23.5	55.5	147 29.9	46.1	226 36.3	50.5	137 51.0	47.0
D	12	46 44.7	8 22.9	N13 56.6	162 33.1	S21 46.1	241 38.8	N 7 50.5	152 53.7	S20 47.0
A	13	61 47.2	23 22.4	57.6	177 36.2	46.1	256 41.3	50.5	167 56.3	46.9
Y	14	76 49.7	38 21.9	58.6	192 39.4	46.1	271 43.8	50.5	182 58.9	46.9
	15	91 52.1	53 21.4	13 59.7	207 42.6	. . 46.1	286 46.2	. . 50.5	198 01.5	. . 46.9
	16	106 54.6	68 20.8	14 00.7	222 45.8	46.1	301 48.7	50.5	213 04.2	46.9
	17	121 57.1	83 20.3	01.7	237 48.9	46.1	316 51.2	50.5	228 06.8	46.9
	18	136 59.5	98 19.8	N14 02.7	252 52.1	S21 46.1	331 53.6	N 7 50.5	243 09.4	S20 46.8
	19	152 02.0	113 19.2	03.7	267 55.3	46.2	346 56.1	50.5	258 12.1	46.8
	20	167 04.4	128 18.7	04.8	282 58.5	46.2	1 58.6	50.5	273 14.7	46.8
	21	182 06.9	143 18.2	. . 05.8	298 01.6	. . 46.2	17 01.1	. . 50.5	288 17.3	. . 46.8
	22	197 09.4	158 17.7	06.8	313 04.8	46.2	32 03.5	50.5	303 20.0	46.8
	23	212 11.8	173 17.1	07.8	328 08.0	46.2	47 06.0	50.5	318 22.6	46.8
	Mer. Pass.	h m 8 57.5	*v* −0.5	*d* 1.0	*v* 3.1	*d* 0.0	*v* 2.5	*d* 0.0	*v* 2.6	*d* 0.0

STARS

Name	SHA	Dec
	° ′	° ′
Acamar	315 17.4	S40 14.6
Achernar	335 26.0	S57 09.3
Acrux	173 06.4	S63 11.6
Adhara	255 11.2	S29 00.1
Aldebaran	290 47.5	N16 32.2
Alioth	166 18.6	N55 52.5
Alkaid	152 57.0	N49 14.1
Al Na'ir	27 41.5	S46 52.7
Alnilam	275 44.7	S 1 11.8
Alphard	217 54.2	S 8 44.0
Alphecca	126 09.0	N26 39.7
Alpheratz	357 41.7	N29 10.6
Altair	62 06.2	N 8 54.7
Ankaa	353 14.2	S42 13.0
Antares	112 23.5	S26 27.9
Arcturus	145 53.7	N19 05.9
Atria	107 23.1	S69 03.1
Avior	234 17.3	S59 34.2
Bellatrix	278 30.2	N 6 21.6
Betelgeuse	270 59.5	N 7 24.3
Canopus	263 55.7	S52 42.7
Capella	280 32.0	N46 00.7
Deneb	49 30.0	N45 20.2
Denebola	182 31.5	N14 28.8
Diphda	348 54.2	S17 53.9
Dubhe	193 49.2	N61 40.0
Elnath	278 10.5	N28 37.0
Eltanin	90 44.8	N51 29.2
Enif	33 45.3	N 9 56.9
Fomalhaut	15 22.1	S29 32.0
Gacrux	171 58.2	S57 12.5
Gienah	175 50.0	S17 38.1
Hadar	148 44.4	S60 27.1
Hamal	327 58.9	N23 32.1
Kaus Aust.	83 41.0	S34 22.3
Kochab	137 19.1	N74 05.5
Markab	13 36.5	N15 17.4
Menkar	314 13.4	N 4 09.0
Menkent	148 04.9	S36 27.0
Miaplacidus	221 39.1	S69 47.5
Mirfak	308 38.0	N49 54.9
Nunki	75 55.7	S26 16.3
Peacock	53 16.2	S56 40.6
Pollux	243 25.6	N27 59.1
Procyon	244 57.9	N 5 10.7
Rasalhague	96 04.4	N12 33.0
Regulus	207 41.4	N11 53.1
Rigel	281 10.5	S 8 11.3
Rigil Kent.	139 48.3	S60 54.1
Sabik	102 10.0	S15 44.5
Schedar	349 38.6	N56 37.3
Shaula	96 18.9	S37 06.7
Sirius	258 32.2	S16 44.7
Spica	158 28.9	S11 14.8
Suhail	222 51.0	S43 30.3
Vega	80 37.4	N38 47.9
Zuben'ubi	137 02.9	S16 06.5

	SHA	Mer. Pass.
	° ′	h m
Venus	323 25.6	11 26
Mars	115 23.8	1 17
Jupiter	194 53.5	19 56
Saturn	106 03.1	1 54

UT d h		SUN GHA	SUN Dec	MOON GHA	*v*	MOON Dec	*d*	HP
		° ′	° ′	° ′	′	° ′	′	′
6 00		180 50.8	N16 35.7	191 00.2	6.4	N 9 37.1	10.3	61.3
01		195 50.8	36.4	205 25.6	6.2	9 47.4	10.3	61.3
02		210 50.9	37.1	219 50.8	6.3	9 57.7	10.2	61.3
03		225 50.9	. . 37.8	234 16.1	6.2	10 07.9	10.1	61.3
04		240 51.0	38.5	248 41.3	6.1	10 18.0	10.0	61.3
05		255 51.0	39.2	263 06.4	6.1	10 28.0	10.0	61.3
06		270 51.1	N16 39.9	277 31.5	6.1	N10 38.0	9.9	61.3
07		285 51.1	40.6	291 56.6	6.1	10 47.9	9.8	61.3
08		300 51.1	41.3	306 21.7	6.0	10 57.7	9.8	61.3
09	F	315 51.2	. . 42.0	320 46.7	5.9	11 07.5	9.6	61.3
10	R	330 51.2	42.7	335 11.6	5.9	11 17.1	9.6	61.3
11	I	345 51.3	43.3	349 36.5	5.9	11 26.7	9.5	61.3
12	D	0 51.3	N16 44.0	4 01.4	5.9	N11 36.2	9.5	61.3
13	A	15 51.4	44.7	18 26.3	5.8	11 45.7	9.3	61.3
14	Y	30 51.4	45.4	32 51.1	5.8	11 55.0	9.3	61.3
15		45 51.4	. . 46.1	47 15.9	5.7	12 04.3	9.1	61.2
16		60 51.5	46.8	61 40.6	5.7	12 13.4	9.1	61.2
17		75 51.5	47.5	76 05.3	5.7	12 22.5	9.0	61.2
18		90 51.6	N16 48.2	90 30.0	5.6	N12 31.5	8.9	61.2
19		105 51.6	48.9	104 54.6	5.6	12 40.4	8.8	61.2
20		120 51.6	49.6	119 19.2	5.6	12 49.2	8.8	61.2
21		135 51.7	. . 50.3	133 43.8	5.5	12 58.0	8.6	61.2
22		150 51.7	51.0	148 08.3	5.5	13 06.6	8.5	61.2
23		165 51.8	51.6	162 32.8	5.5	13 15.1	8.5	61.2
7 00		180 51.8	N16 52.3	176 57.3	5.4	N13 23.6	8.3	61.2
01		195 51.8	53.0	191 21.7	5.5	13 31.9	8.2	61.2
02		210 51.9	53.7	205 46.2	5.3	13 40.1	8.2	61.1
03		225 51.9	. . 54.4	220 10.5	5.4	13 48.3	8.0	61.1
04		240 52.0	55.1	234 34.9	5.3	13 56.3	8.0	61.1
05		255 52.0	55.8	248 59.2	5.3	14 04.3	7.8	61.1
06		270 52.0	N16 56.4	263 23.5	5.3	N14 12.1	7.7	61.1
07		285 52.1	57.1	277 47.8	5.3	14 19.8	7.7	61.1
08	S	300 52.1	57.8	292 12.1	5.2	14 27.5	7.5	61.1
09	A	315 52.1	. . 58.5	306 36.3	5.2	14 35.0	7.4	61.0
10	T	330 52.2	59.2	321 00.5	5.2	14 42.4	7.3	61.0
11	U	345 52.2	16 59.9	335 24.7	5.2	14 49.7	7.2	61.0
12	R	0 52.2	N17 00.5	349 48.9	5.1	N14 56.9	7.1	61.0
13	D	15 52.3	01.2	4 13.0	5.2	15 04.0	6.9	61.0
14	A	30 52.3	01.9	18 37.2	5.1	15 10.9	6.9	61.0
15	Y	45 52.4	. . 02.6	33 01.3	5.1	15 17.8	6.8	60.9
16		60 52.4	03.3	47 25.4	5.1	15 24.6	6.6	60.9
17		75 52.4	03.9	61 49.5	5.0	15 31.2	6.5	60.9
18		90 52.5	N17 04.6	76 13.5	5.1	N15 37.7	6.4	60.9
19		105 52.5	05.3	90 37.6	5.0	15 44.1	6.3	60.9
20		120 52.5	06.0	105 01.6	5.1	15 50.4	6.2	60.8
21		135 52.6	. . 06.7	119 25.7	5.0	15 56.6	6.0	60.8
22		150 52.6	07.3	133 49.7	5.0	16 02.6	6.0	60.8
23		165 52.6	08.0	148 13.7	5.0	16 08.6	5.8	60.8
8 00		180 52.7	N17 08.7	162 37.7	5.0	N16 14.4	5.7	60.7
01		195 52.7	09.4	177 01.7	5.0	16 20.1	5.6	60.7
02		210 52.7	10.0	191 25.7	5.0	16 25.7	5.4	60.7
03		225 52.8	. . 10.7	205 49.7	5.0	16 31.1	5.3	60.7
04		240 52.8	11.4	220 13.7	5.0	16 36.4	5.3	60.7
05		255 52.8	12.1	234 37.7	5.0	16 41.7	5.0	60.6
06		270 52.9	N17 12.7	249 01.7	4.9	N16 46.7	5.0	60.6
07		285 52.9	13.4	263 25.6	5.0	16 51.7	4.8	60.6
08		300 52.9	14.1	277 49.6	5.0	16 56.5	4.8	60.5
09	S	315 52.9	. . 14.8	292 13.6	5.0	17 01.3	4.6	60.5
10	U	330 53.0	15.4	306 37.6	5.0	17 05.9	4.4	60.5
11	N	345 53.0	16.1	321 01.6	5.0	17 10.3	4.4	60.5
12	D	0 53.0	N17 16.8	335 25.6	5.1	N17 14.7	4.2	60.4
13	A	15 53.1	17.4	349 49.7	5.0	17 18.9	4.1	60.4
14	Y	30 53.1	18.1	4 13.7	5.0	17 23.0	3.9	60.4
15		45 53.1	. . 18.8	18 37.7	5.1	17 26.9	3.9	60.3
16		60 53.2	19.4	33 01.8	5.1	17 30.8	3.7	60.3
17		75 53.2	20.1	47 25.9	5.0	17 34.5	3.6	60.3
18		90 53.2	N17 20.8	61 49.9	5.1	N17 38.1	3.4	60.3
19		105 53.2	21.4	76 14.0	5.2	17 41.5	3.4	60.2
20		120 53.3	22.1	90 38.2	5.1	17 44.9	3.2	60.2
21		135 53.3	. . 22.8	105 02.3	5.2	17 48.1	3.0	60.2
22		150 53.3	23.4	119 26.5	5.1	17 51.1	3.0	60.1
23		165 53.3	24.1	133 50.6	5.2	N17 54.1	2.8	60.1
		SD 15.9	*d* 0.7	SD 16.7		16.6		16.5

Lat.	Twilight Naut.	Twilight Civil	Sunrise	Moonrise 6	7	8	9
°	h m	h m	h m	h m	h m	h m	h m
N 72	////	////	00 39	03 12	03 06	02 59	02 38
N 70	////	////	01 51	03 28	03 32	03 42	04 05
68	////	////	02 27	03 40	03 52	04 12	04 45
66	////	01 09	02 52	03 51	04 08	04 34	05 12
64	////	01 54	03 12	03 59	04 22	04 52	05 33
62	////	02 22	03 28	04 07	04 33	05 06	05 50
60	01 01	02 44	03 41	04 14	04 42	05 18	06 04
N 58	01 42	03 01	03 52	04 19	04 51	05 29	06 16
56	02 08	03 16	04 02	04 25	04 58	05 38	06 27
54	02 29	03 28	04 11	04 29	05 05	05 47	06 36
52	02 45	03 38	04 19	04 33	05 11	05 54	06 45
50	02 59	03 48	04 26	04 37	05 16	06 01	06 52
45	03 26	04 07	04 40	04 46	05 28	06 15	07 08
N 40	03 46	04 23	04 53	04 53	05 38	06 27	07 21
35	04 02	04 35	05 03	04 59	05 46	06 37	07 32
30	04 16	04 46	05 12	05 04	05 53	06 46	07 42
20	04 37	05 04	05 27	05 13	06 06	07 02	07 59
N 10	04 53	05 19	05 41	05 22	06 18	07 15	08 14
0	05 06	05 31	05 53	05 29	06 28	07 28	08 28
S 10	05 18	05 43	06 05	05 37	06 39	07 41	08 42
20	05 29	05 55	06 18	05 46	06 51	07 55	08 57
30	05 39	06 08	06 33	05 55	07 04	08 10	09 14
35	05 45	06 15	06 41	06 01	07 11	08 20	09 24
40	05 50	06 22	06 51	06 07	07 20	08 30	09 35
45	05 56	06 31	07 02	06 15	07 31	08 43	09 49
S 50	06 02	06 41	07 16	06 24	07 43	08 58	10 05
52	06 05	06 46	07 22	06 28	07 49	09 05	10 13
54	06 08	06 51	07 29	06 33	07 55	09 13	10 21
56	06 11	06 56	07 37	06 38	08 03	09 22	10 31
58	06 14	07 02	07 46	06 44	08 11	09 32	10 42
S 60	06 18	07 09	07 56	06 50	08 20	09 43	10 55

Lat.	Sunset	Twilight Civil	Twilight Naut.	Moonset 6	7	8	9
°	h m	h m	h m	h m	h m	h m	h m
N 72	23 44	////	////	21 02	23 15	25 42	01 42
N 70	22 08	////	////	20 38	22 32	24 15	00 15
68	21 30	////	////	20 19	22 04	23 36	24 45
66	21 04	22 53	////	20 04	21 42	23 09	24 16
64	20 43	22 04	////	19 52	21 25	22 48	23 54
62	20 27	21 34	////	19 41	21 11	22 31	23 36
60	20 14	21 12	22 59	19 32	20 59	22 17	23 22
N 58	20 02	20 54	22 15	19 25	20 49	22 05	23 09
56	19 52	20 39	21 47	19 18	20 40	21 55	22 58
54	19 43	20 27	21 27	19 12	20 32	21 46	22 49
52	19 35	20 16	21 10	19 06	20 25	21 37	22 40
50	19 28	20 06	20 56	19 01	20 19	21 30	22 33
45	19 13	19 47	20 28	18 51	20 05	21 14	22 17
N 40	19 01	19 31	20 08	18 42	19 54	21 01	22 03
35	18 51	19 18	19 51	18 35	19 44	20 51	21 52
30	18 41	19 07	19 38	18 28	19 36	20 41	21 42
20	18 26	18 49	19 17	18 16	19 21	20 24	21 25
N 10	18 12	18 35	19 00	18 07	19 09	20 10	21 10
0	18 00	18 22	18 47	17 57	18 57	19 57	20 56
S 10	17 48	18 10	18 35	17 48	18 45	19 43	20 42
20	17 35	17 58	18 24	17 38	18 32	19 29	20 27
30	17 20	17 45	18 13	17 27	18 18	19 12	20 09
35	17 11	17 38	18 08	17 20	18 09	19 03	19 59
40	17 01	17 30	18 02	17 13	18 00	18 52	19 48
45	16 50	17 21	17 57	17 04	17 49	18 39	19 34
S 50	16 36	17 11	17 50	16 54	17 35	18 23	19 18
52	16 30	17 07	17 47	16 49	17 29	18 16	19 10
54	16 23	17 02	17 44	16 44	17 22	18 08	19 01
56	16 15	16 56	17 41	16 38	17 14	17 59	18 52
58	16 06	16 50	17 38	16 31	17 06	17 48	18 41
S 60	15 56	16 44	17 34	16 24	16 56	17 37	18 28

Day	SUN Eqn. of Time 00^h	SUN Eqn. of Time 12^h	SUN Mer. Pass.	MOON Mer. Pass. Upper	MOON Mer. Pass. Lower	MOON Age	MOON Phase
d	m s	m s	h m	h m	h m	d	%
6	03 23	03 25	11 57	11 43	24 13	29	0
7	03 27	03 29	11 57	12 42	00 13	01	1
8	03 31	03 32	11 56	13 42	01 12	02	4

UT	ARIES	VENUS −3·9		MARS −1·8		JUPITER −2·2		SATURN +0·1		STARS		
d h	GHA ° ′	GHA ° ′	Dec ° ′	GHA ° ′	Dec ° ′	GHA ° ′	Dec ° ′	GHA ° ′	Dec ° ′	Name	SHA ° ′	Dec ° ′
9 00	227 14.3	188 16.6	N14 08.9	343 11.2	S21 46.2	62 08.5	N 7 50.5	333 25.2	S20 46.7	Acamar	315 17.3	S40 14.6
01	242 16.8	203 16.1	09.9	358 14.4	46.2	77 10.9	50.5	348 27.8	46.7	Achernar	335 26.0	S57 09.3
02	257 19.2	218 15.5	10.9	13 17.5	46.2	92 13.4	50.5	3 30.5	46.7	Acrux	173 06.4	S63 11.6
03	272 21.7	233 15.0	. . 11.9	28 20.7	. . 46.2	107 15.9	. . 50.4	18 33.1	. . 46.7	Adhara	255 11.2	S29 00.1
04	287 24.2	248 14.5	12.9	43 23.9	46.2	122 18.4	50.4	33 35.7	46.7	Aldebaran	290 47.5	N16 32.2
05	302 26.6	263 13.9	13.9	58 27.1	46.2	137 20.8	50.4	48 38.4	46.6			
06	317 29.1	278 13.4	N14 15.0	73 30.3	S21 46.2	152 23.3	N 7 50.4	63 41.0	S20 46.6	Alioth	166 18.7	N55 52.5
07	332 31.5	293 12.9	16.0	88 33.5	46.2	167 25.8	50.4	78 43.6	46.6	Alkaid	152 57.0	N49 14.1
08	347 34.0	308 12.3	17.0	103 36.7	46.2	182 28.2	50.4	93 46.3	46.6	Al Na'ir	27 41.5	S46 52.6
M 09	2 36.5	323 11.8	. . 18.0	118 39.9	. . 46.3	197 30.7	. . 50.4	108 48.9	. . 46.6	Alnilam	275 44.7	S 1 11.8
O 10	17 38.9	338 11.3	19.0	133 43.1	46.3	212 33.2	50.4	123 51.5	46.5	Alphard	217 54.2	S 8 44.0
N 11	32 41.4	353 10.7	20.0	148 46.2	46.3	227 35.6	50.4	138 54.1	46.5			
D 12	47 43.9	8 10.2	N14 21.1	163 49.4	S21 46.3	242 38.1	N 7 50.4	153 56.8	S20 46.5	Alphecca	126 09.0	N26 39.7
A 13	62 46.3	23 09.7	22.1	178 52.6	46.3	257 40.6	50.4	168 59.4	46.5	Alpheratz	357 41.7	N29 10.6
Y 14	77 48.8	38 09.1	23.1	193 55.8	46.3	272 43.0	50.4	184 02.0	46.5	Altair	62 06.2	N 8 54.7
15	92 51.3	53 08.6	. . 24.1	208 59.0	. . 46.3	287 45.5	. . 50.4	199 04.7	. . 46.5	Ankaa	353 14.2	S42 13.0
16	107 53.7	68 08.1	25.1	224 02.2	46.3	302 48.0	50.4	214 07.3	46.4	Antares	112 23.5	S26 27.9
17	122 56.2	83 07.5	26.1	239 05.4	46.3	317 50.4	50.3	229 09.9	46.4			
18	137 58.7	98 07.0	N14 27.1	254 08.6	S21 46.3	332 52.9	N 7 50.3	244 12.6	S20 46.4	Arcturus	145 53.7	N19 05.9
19	153 01.1	113 06.4	28.1	269 11.8	46.3	347 55.4	50.3	259 15.2	46.4	Atria	107 23.0	S69 03.1
20	168 03.6	128 05.9	29.1	284 15.0	46.3	2 57.8	50.3	274 17.8	46.4	Avior	234 17.3	S59 34.2
21	183 06.0	143 05.4	. . 30.1	299 18.2	. . 46.3	18 00.3	. . 50.3	289 20.5	. . 46.3	Bellatrix	278 30.2	N 6 21.6
22	198 08.5	158 04.8	31.1	314 21.4	46.3	33 02.8	50.3	304 23.1	46.3	Betelgeuse	270 59.5	N 7 24.3
23	213 11.0	173 04.3	32.2	329 24.7	46.3	48 05.2	50.3	319 25.7	46.3			
10 00	228 13.4	188 03.7	N14 33.2	344 27.9	S21 46.3	63 07.7	N 7 50.3	334 28.3	S20 46.3	Canopus	263 55.7	S52 42.7
01	243 15.9	203 03.2	34.2	359 31.1	46.3	78 10.2	50.3	349 31.0	46.3	Capella	280 32.0	N46 00.7
02	258 18.4	218 02.7	35.2	14 34.3	46.3	93 12.6	50.3	4 33.6	46.3	Deneb	49 30.0	N45 20.2
03	273 20.8	233 02.1	. . 36.2	29 37.5	. . 46.3	108 15.1	. . 50.3	19 36.2	. . 46.2	Denebola	182 31.5	N14 28.8
04	288 23.3	248 01.6	37.2	44 40.7	46.3	123 17.6	50.2	34 38.9	46.2	Diphda	348 54.2	S17 53.9
05	303 25.8	263 01.0	38.2	59 43.9	46.3	138 20.0	50.2	49 41.5	46.2			
06	318 28.2	278 00.5	N14 39.2	74 47.1	S21 46.3	153 22.5	N 7 50.2	64 44.1	S20 46.2	Dubhe	193 49.2	N61 40.0
07	333 30.7	293 00.0	40.2	89 50.4	46.3	168 24.9	50.2	79 46.8	46.2	Elnath	278 10.5	N28 37.0
T 08	348 33.2	307 59.4	41.2	104 53.6	46.3	183 27.4	50.2	94 49.4	46.1	Eltanin	90 44.8	N51 29.2
U 09	3 35.6	322 58.9	. . 42.2	119 56.8	. . 46.3	198 29.9	. . 50.2	109 52.0	. . 46.1	Enif	33 45.2	N 9 57.0
E 10	18 38.1	337 58.3	43.2	135 00.0	46.3	213 32.3	50.2	124 54.7	46.1	Fomalhaut	15 22.0	S29 32.0
S 11	33 40.5	352 57.8	44.2	150 03.2	46.3	228 34.8	50.2	139 57.3	46.1			
D 12	48 43.0	7 57.2	N14 45.2	165 06.4	S21 46.3	243 37.2	N 7 50.2	154 59.9	S20 46.1	Gacrux	171 58.2	S57 12.5
A 13	63 45.5	22 56.7	46.2	180 09.7	46.3	258 39.7	50.2	170 02.6	46.1	Gienah	175 50.0	S17 38.1
Y 14	78 47.9	37 56.1	47.2	195 12.9	46.3	273 42.2	50.1	185 05.2	46.0	Hadar	148 44.4	S60 27.1
15	93 50.4	52 55.6	. . 48.2	210 16.1	. . 46.3	288 44.6	. . 50.1	200 07.8	. . 46.0	Hamal	327 58.9	N23 32.1
16	108 52.9	67 55.0	49.2	225 19.3	46.3	303 47.1	50.1	215 10.5	46.0	Kaus Aust.	83 41.0	S34 22.3
17	123 55.3	82 54.5	50.2	240 22.6	46.3	318 49.5	50.1	230 13.1	46.0			
18	138 57.8	97 53.9	N14 51.1	255 25.8	S21 46.3	333 52.0	N 7 50.1	245 15.7	S20 46.0	Kochab	137 19.1	N74 05.5
19	154 00.3	112 53.4	52.1	270 29.0	46.3	348 54.5	50.1	260 18.4	45.9	Markab	13 36.5	N15 17.5
20	169 02.7	127 52.8	53.1	285 32.2	46.3	3 56.9	50.1	275 21.0	45.9	Menkar	314 13.3	N 4 09.0
21	184 05.2	142 52.3	. . 54.1	300 35.5	. . 46.3	18 59.4	. . 50.1	290 23.6	. . 45.9	Menkent	148 04.8	S36 27.0
22	199 07.7	157 51.7	55.1	315 38.7	46.3	34 01.8	50.0	305 26.3	45.9	Miaplacidus	221 39.2	S69 47.5
23	214 10.1	172 51.2	56.1	330 41.9	46.3	49 04.3	50.0	320 28.9	45.9			
11 00	229 12.6	187 50.6	N14 57.1	345 45.2	S21 46.3	64 06.7	N 7 50.0	335 31.5	S20 45.8	Mirfak	308 38.0	N49 54.9
01	244 15.0	202 50.1	58.1	0 48.4	46.3	79 09.2	50.0	350 34.2	45.8	Nunki	75 55.7	S26 16.3
02	259 17.5	217 49.5	14 59.1	15 51.6	46.3	94 11.7	50.0	5 36.8	45.8	Peacock	53 16.1	S56 40.6
03	274 20.0	232 49.0	15 00.1	30 54.9	. . 46.3	109 14.1	. . 50.0	20 39.4	. . 45.8	Pollux	243 25.6	N27 59.1
04	289 22.4	247 48.4	01.1	45 58.1	46.3	124 16.6	50.0	35 42.1	45.8	Procyon	244 57.9	N 5 10.7
05	304 24.9	262 47.9	02.0	61 01.4	46.3	139 19.0	50.0	50 44.7	45.8			
06	319 27.4	277 47.3	N15 03.0	76 04.6	S21 46.3	154 21.5	N 7 49.9	65 47.4	S20 45.7	Rasalhague	96 04.4	N12 33.0
W 07	334 29.8	292 46.8	04.0	91 07.8	46.3	169 23.9	49.9	80 50.0	45.7	Regulus	207 41.4	N11 53.1
E 08	349 32.3	307 46.2	05.0	106 11.1	46.3	184 26.4	49.9	95 52.6	45.7	Rigel	281 10.5	S 8 11.3
D 09	4 34.8	322 45.7	. . 06.0	121 14.3	. . 46.3	199 28.8	. . 49.9	110 55.3	. . 45.7	Rigil Kent.	139 48.3	S60 54.1
N 10	19 37.2	337 45.1	07.0	136 17.6	46.3	214 31.3	49.9	125 57.9	45.7	Sabik	102 10.0	S15 44.5
E 11	34 39.7	352 44.6	08.0	151 20.8	46.3	229 33.8	49.9	141 00.5	45.6			
S 12	49 42.2	7 44.0	N15 08.9	166 24.1	S21 46.3	244 36.2	N 7 49.9	156 03.2	S20 45.6	Schedar	349 38.6	N56 37.3
D 13	64 44.6	22 43.4	09.9	181 27.3	46.3	259 38.7	49.9	171 05.8	45.6	Shaula	96 18.9	S37 06.7
A 14	79 47.1	37 42.9	10.9	196 30.5	46.3	274 41.1	49.8	186 08.4	45.6	Sirius	258 32.2	S16 44.7
Y 15	94 49.5	52 42.3	. . 11.9	211 33.8	. . 46.3	289 43.6	. . 49.8	201 11.1	. . 45.6	Spica	158 28.9	S11 14.8
16	109 52.0	67 41.8	12.9	226 37.0	46.3	304 46.0	49.8	216 13.7	45.5	Suhail	222 51.0	S43 30.3
17	124 54.5	82 41.2	13.8	241 40.3	46.3	319 48.5	49.8	231 16.3	45.5			
18	139 56.9	97 40.6	N15 14.8	256 43.5	S21 46.3	334 50.9	N 7 49.8	246 19.0	S20 45.5	Vega	80 37.3	N38 47.9
19	154 59.4	112 40.1	15.8	271 46.8	46.3	349 53.4	49.8	261 21.6	45.5	Zuben'ubi	137 02.9	S16 06.5
20	170 01.9	127 39.5	16.8	286 50.0	46.3	4 55.8	49.8	276 24.2	45.5			
21	185 04.3	142 39.0	. . 17.7	301 53.3	. . 46.3	19 58.3	. . 49.7	291 26.9	. . 45.5			
22	200 06.8	157 38.4	18.7	316 56.6	46.3	35 00.7	49.7	306 29.5	45.4			
23	215 09.3	172 37.8	19.7	331 59.8	46.2	50 03.2	49.7	321 32.2	45.4			
Mer. Pass.	h m 8 45.7	v −0.5	d 1.0	v 3.2	d 0.0	v 2.5	d 0.0	v 2.6	d 0.0			

	SHA ° ′	Mer. Pass. h m
Venus	319 50.3	11 28
Mars	116 14.4	1 02
Jupiter	194 54.3	19 44
Saturn	106 14.9	1 42

	UT	SUN GHA	SUN Dec	MOON GHA	v	MOON Dec	d	HP
	d h	° ′	° ′	° ′	′	° ′	′	′
	9 00	180 53.4	N17 24.8	148 14.8	5.3	N17 56.9	2.7	60.1
	01	195 53.4	25.4	162 39.1	5.2	17 59.6	2.6	60.0
	02	210 53.4	26.1	177 03.3	5.3	18 02.2	2.4	60.0
	03	225 53.5	. . 26.8	191 27.6	5.3	18 04.6	2.3	60.0
	04	240 53.5	27.4	205 51.9	5.3	18 06.9	2.2	59.9
	05	255 53.5	28.1	220 16.2	5.4	18 09.1	2.0	59.9
	06	270 53.5	N17 28.7	234 40.6	5.4	N18 11.1	2.0	59.9
	07	285 53.6	29.4	249 05.0	5.4	18 13.1	1.8	59.8
	08	300 53.6	30.1	263 29.4	5.5	18 14.9	1.6	59.8
M	09	315 53.6	. . 30.7	277 53.9	5.5	18 16.5	1.6	59.8
O	10	330 53.6	31.4	292 18.4	5.5	18 18.1	1.4	59.7
N	11	345 53.7	32.0	306 42.9	5.6	18 19.5	1.3	59.7
D	12	0 53.7	N17 32.7	321 07.5	5.6	N18 20.8	1.2	59.7
A	13	15 53.7	33.4	335 32.1	5.7	18 22.0	1.0	59.6
Y	14	30 53.7	34.0	349 56.8	5.7	18 23.0	0.9	59.6
	15	45 53.8	. . 34.7	4 21.5	5.7	18 23.9	0.8	59.5
	16	60 53.8	35.3	18 46.2	5.8	18 24.7	0.7	59.5
	17	75 53.8	36.0	33 11.0	5.9	18 25.4	0.5	59.5
	18	90 53.8	N17 36.6	47 35.9	5.8	N18 25.9	0.5	59.4
	19	105 53.8	37.3	62 00.7	6.0	18 26.4	0.2	59.4
	20	120 53.9	37.9	76 25.7	5.9	18 26.6	0.2	59.4
	21	135 53.9	. . 38.6	90 50.6	6.1	18 26.8	0.1	59.3
	22	150 53.9	39.2	105 15.7	6.0	18 26.9	0.1	59.3
	23	165 53.9	39.9	119 40.7	6.2	18 26.8	0.2	59.2
	10 00	180 54.0	N17 40.6	134 05.9	6.1	N18 26.6	0.3	59.2
	01	195 54.0	41.2	148 31.0	6.3	18 26.3	0.4	59.2
	02	210 54.0	41.9	162 56.3	6.3	18 25.9	0.6	59.1
	03	225 54.0	. . 42.5	177 21.6	6.3	18 25.3	0.7	59.1
	04	240 54.0	43.2	191 46.9	6.4	18 24.6	0.7	59.1
	05	255 54.1	43.8	206 12.3	6.5	18 23.9	1.0	59.0
	06	270 54.1	N17 44.5	220 37.8	6.5	N18 22.9	1.0	59.0
	07	285 54.1	45.1	235 03.3	6.5	18 21.9	1.1	58.9
T	08	300 54.1	45.7	249 28.8	6.7	18 20.8	1.3	58.9
U	09	315 54.1	. . 46.4	263 54.5	6.7	18 19.5	1.4	58.9
E	10	330 54.2	47.0	278 20.2	6.7	18 18.1	1.4	58.8
S	11	345 54.2	47.7	292 45.9	6.9	18 16.7	1.7	58.8
D	12	0 54.2	N17 48.3	307 11.8	6.8	N18 15.0	1.7	58.7
A	13	15 54.2	49.0	321 37.6	7.0	18 13.3	1.8	58.7
Y	14	30 54.2	49.6	336 03.6	7.0	18 11.5	1.9	58.7
	15	45 54.2	. . 50.3	350 29.6	7.1	18 09.6	2.1	58.6
	16	60 54.3	50.9	4 55.7	7.1	18 07.5	2.2	58.6
	17	75 54.3	51.6	19 21.8	7.3	18 05.3	2.2	58.5
	18	90 54.3	N17 52.2	33 48.1	7.2	N18 03.1	2.4	58.5
	19	105 54.3	52.8	48 14.3	7.4	18 00.7	2.5	58.5
	20	120 54.3	53.5	62 40.7	7.4	17 58.2	2.6	58.4
	21	135 54.3	. . 54.1	77 07.1	7.5	17 55.6	2.7	58.4
	22	150 54.4	54.8	91 33.6	7.6	17 52.9	2.8	58.3
	23	165 54.4	55.4	106 00.2	7.6	17 50.1	2.9	58.3
	11 00	180 54.4	N17 56.0	120 26.8	7.7	N17 47.2	3.0	58.3
	01	195 54.4	56.7	134 53.5	7.8	17 44.2	3.2	58.2
	02	210 54.4	57.3	149 20.3	7.8	17 41.0	3.2	58.2
	03	225 54.4	. . 58.0	163 47.1	7.9	17 37.8	3.3	58.1
	04	240 54.5	58.6	178 14.0	8.0	17 34.5	3.4	58.1
	05	255 54.5	59.2	192 41.0	8.1	17 31.1	3.6	58.1
	06	270 54.5	N17 59.9	207 08.1	8.1	N17 27.5	3.6	58.0
W	07	285 54.5	18 00.5	221 35.2	8.3	17 23.9	3.7	58.0
E	08	300 54.5	01.1	236 02.5	8.2	17 20.2	3.8	57.9
D	09	315 54.5	. . 01.8	250 29.7	8.4	17 16.4	3.9	57.9
N	10	330 54.5	02.4	264 57.1	8.5	17 12.5	4.0	57.9
E	11	345 54.5	03.0	279 24.6	8.5	17 08.5	4.1	57.8
S	12	0 54.6	N18 03.7	293 52.1	8.6	N17 04.4	4.2	57.8
	13	15 54.6	04.3	308 19.7	8.6	17 00.2	4.3	57.7
D	14	30 54.6	04.9	322 47.3	8.8	16 55.9	4.4	57.7
A	15	45 54.6	. . 05.6	337 15.1	8.8	16 51.5	4.5	57.7
Y	16	60 54.6	06.2	351 42.9	8.9	16 47.0	4.5	57.6
	17	75 54.6	06.8	6 10.8	9.0	16 42.5	4.7	57.6
	18	90 54.6	N18 07.5	20 38.8	9.0	N16 37.8	4.7	57.5
	19	105 54.6	08.1	35 06.8	9.1	16 33.1	4.8	57.5
	20	120 54.7	08.7	49 34.9	9.2	16 28.3	5.0	57.5
	21	135 54.7	. . 09.3	64 03.1	9.3	16 23.3	5.0	57.4
	22	150 54.7	10.0	78 31.4	9.4	16 18.3	5.0	57.4
	23	165 54.7	10.6	92 59.8	9.4	N16 13.3	5.2	57.3
		SD 15.9	*d* 0.6	SD	16.3	16.0		15.7

Lat.	Twilight Naut.	Twilight Civil	Sunrise	Moonrise 9	Moonrise 10	Moonrise 11	Moonrise 12
°	h m	h m	h m	h m	h m	h m	h m
N 72	▭	▭	▭	02 38	▭	05 13	07 15
N 70	////	////	01 28	04 05	04 55	06 17	07 52
68	////	////	02 12	04 45	05 38	06 52	08 18
66	////	00 35	02 40	05 12	06 07	07 18	08 38
64	////	01 37	03 02	05 33	06 29	07 37	08 53
62	////	02 10	03 19	05 50	06 46	07 53	09 07
60	00 31	02 34	03 34	06 04	07 01	08 07	09 18
N 58	01 27	02 53	03 46	06 16	07 13	08 18	09 27
56	01 58	03 08	03 56	06 27	07 24	08 28	09 36
54	02 20	03 21	04 05	06 36	07 34	08 37	09 43
52	02 37	03 33	04 14	06 45	07 42	08 45	09 50
50	02 52	03 43	04 21	06 52	07 50	08 52	09 56
45	03 21	04 03	04 37	07 08	08 06	09 07	10 09
N 40	03 42	04 19	04 49	07 21	08 19	09 19	10 20
35	03 59	04 33	05 00	07 32	08 30	09 30	10 29
30	04 13	04 44	05 10	07 42	08 40	09 39	10 37
20	04 35	05 02	05 26	07 59	08 57	09 55	10 51
N 10	04 52	05 18	05 40	08 14	09 12	10 09	11 03
0	05 06	05 31	05 53	08 28	09 26	10 22	11 14
S 10	05 18	05 44	06 06	08 42	09 40	10 35	11 25
20	05 30	05 56	06 19	08 57	09 55	10 48	11 37
30	05 41	06 10	06 35	09 14	10 12	11 04	11 51
35	05 47	06 17	06 44	09 24	10 22	11 13	11 59
40	05 53	06 25	06 54	09 35	10 33	11 24	12 08
45	05 59	06 34	07 06	09 49	10 47	11 36	12 18
S 50	06 06	06 45	07 20	10 05	11 03	11 51	12 31
52	06 09	06 50	07 27	10 13	11 10	11 58	12 37
54	06 12	06 55	07 34	10 21	11 19	12 06	12 43
56	06 16	07 01	07 43	10 31	11 28	12 14	12 51
58	06 19	07 07	07 52	10 42	11 39	12 24	12 59
S 60	06 23	07 15	08 03	10 55	11 52	12 35	13 08

Lat.	Sunset	Twilight Civil	Twilight Naut.	Moonset 9	Moonset 10	Moonset 11	Moonset 12
°	h m	h m	h m	h m	h m	h m	h m
N 72	▭	▭	▭	01 42	▭	03 08	02 57
N 70	22 32	////	////	00 15	01 28	02 04	02 19
68	21 45	////	////	24 45	00 45	01 28	01 52
66	21 15	23 38	////	24 16	00 16	01 02	01 32
64	20 53	22 20	////	23 54	24 42	00 42	01 16
62	20 36	21 46	////	23 36	24 26	00 26	01 02
60	20 21	21 21	23 40	23 22	24 12	00 12	00 50
N 58	20 09	21 02	22 30	23 09	24 00	00 00	00 40
56	19 58	20 46	21 58	22 58	23 50	24 31	00 31
54	19 49	20 33	21 35	22 49	23 41	24 24	00 24
52	19 40	20 21	21 17	22 40	23 33	24 17	00 17
50	19 33	20 11	21 02	22 33	23 26	24 10	00 10
45	19 17	19 51	20 33	22 17	23 11	23 56	24 36
N 40	19 04	19 34	20 12	22 03	22 58	23 45	24 26
35	18 53	19 21	19 54	21 52	22 47	23 35	24 18
30	18 43	19 09	19 40	21 42	22 37	23 27	24 11
20	18 27	18 51	19 18	21 25	22 21	23 12	23 59
N 10	18 13	18 35	19 01	21 10	22 06	22 59	23 48
0	18 00	18 22	18 47	20 56	21 53	22 47	23 38
S 10	17 47	18 09	18 34	20 42	21 39	22 35	23 28
20	17 33	17 56	18 23	20 27	21 25	22 22	23 17
30	17 18	17 43	18 12	20 09	21 08	22 07	23 04
35	17 09	17 35	18 06	19 59	20 58	21 58	22 57
40	16 58	17 27	18 00	19 48	20 47	21 48	22 48
45	16 46	17 18	17 53	19 34	20 34	21 36	22 39
S 50	16 32	17 07	17 46	19 18	20 18	21 22	22 27
52	16 25	17 02	17 43	19 10	20 11	21 15	22 21
54	16 18	16 57	17 40	19 01	20 02	21 08	22 15
56	16 09	16 51	17 36	18 52	19 53	20 59	22 08
58	16 00	16 45	17 33	18 41	19 42	20 50	22 01
S 60	15 49	16 37	17 28	18 28	19 30	20 39	21 52

Day	SUN Eqn. of Time 00^h	SUN Eqn. of Time 12^h	SUN Mer. Pass.	MOON Mer. Pass. Upper	MOON Mer. Pass. Lower	MOON Age	MOON Phase
d	m s	m s	h m	h m	h m	d %	
9	03 33	03 35	11 56	14 42	02 12	03 11	
10	03 36	03 37	11 56	15 40	03 11	04 19	
11	03 38	03 38	11 56	16 34	04 07	05 28	

	UT	ARIES	VENUS −3·9		MARS −1·8		JUPITER −2·2		SATURN +0·1	
		GHA	GHA	Dec	GHA	Dec	GHA	Dec	GHA	Dec
	d h	° ′	° ′	° ′	° ′	° ′	° ′	° ′	° ′	° ′
	12 00	230 11.7	187 37.3	N15 20.7	347 03.1	S21 46.2	65 05.6	N 7 49.7	336 34.8	S20 45.4
	01	245 14.2	202 36.7	21.7	2 06.3	46.2	80 08.1	49.7	351 37.4	45.4
	02	260 16.6	217 36.2	22.6	17 09.6	46.2	95 10.5	49.7	6 40.1	45.4
	03	275 19.1	232 35.6	. . 23.6	32 12.8	. . 46.2	110 13.0	. . 49.7	21 42.7	. . 45.3
	04	290 21.6	247 35.0	24.6	47 16.1	46.2	125 15.4	49.6	36 45.3	45.3
	05	305 24.0	262 34.5	25.5	62 19.4	46.2	140 17.9	49.6	51 48.0	45.3
	06	320 26.5	277 33.9	N15 26.5	77 22.6	S21 46.2	155 20.3	N 7 49.6	66 50.6	S20 45.3
	07	335 29.0	292 33.3	27.5	92 25.9	46.2	170 22.8	49.6	81 53.2	45.3
T	08	350 31.4	307 32.8	28.5	107 29.2	46.2	185 25.2	49.6	96 55.9	45.2
H	09	5 33.9	322 32.2	. . 29.4	122 32.4	. . 46.2	200 27.7	. . 49.6	111 58.5	. . 45.2
U	10	20 36.4	337 31.6	30.4	137 35.7	46.2	215 30.1	49.5	127 01.2	45.2
R	11	35 38.8	352 31.1	31.4	152 39.0	46.2	230 32.6	49.5	142 03.8	45.2
S	12	50 41.3	7 30.5	N15 32.3	167 42.2	S21 46.2	245 35.0	N 7 49.5	157 06.4	S20 45.2
D	13	65 43.8	22 29.9	33.3	182 45.5	46.1	260 37.4	49.5	172 09.1	45.2
A	14	80 46.2	37 29.4	34.3	197 48.8	46.1	275 39.9	49.5	187 11.7	45.1
Y	15	95 48.7	52 28.8	. . 35.2	212 52.0	. . 46.1	290 42.3	. . 49.5	202 14.3	. . 45.1
	16	110 51.1	67 28.2	36.2	227 55.3	46.1	305 44.8	49.4	217 17.0	45.1
	17	125 53.6	82 27.7	37.1	242 58.6	46.1	320 47.2	49.4	232 19.6	45.1
	18	140 56.1	97 27.1	N15 38.1	258 01.9	S21 46.1	335 49.7	N 7 49.4	247 22.3	S20 45.1
	19	155 58.5	112 26.5	39.1	273 05.1	46.1	350 52.1	49.4	262 24.9	45.0
	20	171 01.0	127 25.9	40.0	288 08.4	46.1	5 54.6	49.4	277 27.5	45.0
	21	186 03.5	142 25.4	. . 41.0	303 11.7	. . 46.1	20 57.0	. . 49.4	292 30.2	. . 45.0
	22	201 05.9	157 24.8	42.0	318 15.0	46.1	35 59.4	49.3	307 32.8	45.0
	23	216 08.4	172 24.2	42.9	333 18.2	46.1	51 01.9	49.3	322 35.5	45.0
	13 00	231 10.9	187 23.7	N15 43.9	348 21.5	S21 46.0	66 04.3	N 7 49.3	337 38.1	S20 44.9
	01	246 13.3	202 23.1	44.8	3 24.8	46.0	81 06.8	49.3	352 40.7	44.9
	02	261 15.8	217 22.5	45.8	18 28.1	46.0	96 09.2	49.3	7 43.4	44.9
	03	276 18.3	232 21.9	. . 46.7	33 31.4	. . 46.0	111 11.7	. . 49.2	22 46.0	. . 44.9
	04	291 20.7	247 21.4	47.7	48 34.6	46.0	126 14.1	49.2	37 48.6	44.9
	05	306 23.2	262 20.8	48.7	63 37.9	46.0	141 16.5	49.2	52 51.3	44.9
	06	321 25.6	277 20.2	N15 49.6	78 41.2	S21 46.0	156 19.0	N 7 49.2	67 53.9	S20 44.8
	07	336 28.1	292 19.6	50.6	93 44.5	46.0	171 21.4	49.2	82 56.6	44.8
	08	351 30.6	307 19.1	51.5	108 47.8	46.0	186 23.9	49.2	97 59.2	44.8
F	09	6 33.0	322 18.5	. . 52.5	123 51.1	. . 45.9	201 26.3	. . 49.1	113 01.8	. . 44.8
R	10	21 35.5	337 17.9	53.4	138 54.4	45.9	216 28.7	49.1	128 04.5	44.8
I	11	36 38.0	352 17.3	54.4	153 57.7	45.9	231 31.2	49.1	143 07.1	44.7
D	12	51 40.4	7 16.8	N15 55.3	169 00.9	S21 45.9	246 33.6	N 7 49.1	158 09.8	S20 44.7
A	13	66 42.9	22 16.2	56.3	184 04.2	45.9	261 36.1	49.1	173 12.4	44.7
Y	14	81 45.4	37 15.6	57.2	199 07.5	45.9	276 38.5	49.0	188 15.0	44.7
	15	96 47.8	52 15.0	. . 58.2	214 10.8	. . 45.9	291 40.9	. . 49.0	203 17.7	. . 44.7
	16	111 50.3	67 14.4	15 59.1	229 14.1	45.9	306 43.4	49.0	218 20.3	44.6
	17	126 52.7	82 13.9	16 00.1	244 17.4	45.8	321 45.8	49.0	233 23.0	44.6
	18	141 55.2	97 13.3	N16 01.0	259 20.7	S21 45.8	336 48.3	N 7 49.0	248 25.6	S20 44.6
	19	156 57.7	112 12.7	02.0	274 24.0	45.8	351 50.7	48.9	263 28.2	44.6
	20	172 00.1	127 12.1	02.9	289 27.3	45.8	6 53.1	48.9	278 30.9	44.6
	21	187 02.6	142 11.5	. . 03.8	304 30.6	. . 45.8	21 55.6	. . 48.9	293 33.5	. . 44.5
	22	202 05.1	157 10.9	04.8	319 33.9	45.8	36 58.0	48.9	308 36.2	44.5
	23	217 07.5	172 10.4	05.7	334 37.2	45.8	52 00.4	48.9	323 38.8	44.5
	14 00	232 10.0	187 09.8	N16 06.7	349 40.5	S21 45.7	67 02.9	N 7 48.8	338 41.4	S20 44.5
	01	247 12.5	202 09.2	07.6	4 43.8	45.7	82 05.3	48.8	353 44.1	44.5
	02	262 14.9	217 08.6	08.6	19 47.1	45.7	97 07.7	48.8	8 46.7	44.5
	03	277 17.4	232 08.0	. . 09.5	34 50.4	. . 45.7	112 10.2	. . 48.8	23 49.4	. . 44.4
	04	292 19.9	247 07.4	10.4	49 53.7	45.7	127 12.6	48.7	38 52.0	44.4
	05	307 22.3	262 06.9	11.4	64 57.0	45.7	142 15.0	48.7	53 54.6	44.4
	06	322 24.8	277 06.3	N16 12.3	80 00.3	S21 45.6	157 17.5	N 7 48.7	68 57.3	S20 44.4
	07	337 27.2	292 05.7	13.2	95 03.6	45.6	172 19.9	48.7	83 59.9	44.4
S	08	352 29.7	307 05.1	14.2	110 06.9	45.6	187 22.3	48.7	99 02.6	44.3
A	09	7 32.2	322 04.5	. . 15.1	125 10.2	. . 45.6	202 24.8	. . 48.6	114 05.2	. . 44.3
T	10	22 34.6	337 03.9	16.1	140 13.5	45.6	217 27.2	48.6	129 07.8	44.3
U	11	37 37.1	352 03.3	17.0	155 16.9	45.6	232 29.6	48.6	144 10.5	44.3
R	12	52 39.6	7 02.7	N16 17.9	170 20.2	S21 45.5	247 32.1	N 7 48.6	159 13.1	S20 44.3
D	13	67 42.0	22 02.1	18.9	185 23.5	45.5	262 34.5	48.5	174 15.8	44.2
A	14	82 44.5	37 01.6	19.8	200 26.8	45.5	277 36.9	48.5	189 18.4	44.2
Y	15	97 47.0	52 01.0	. . 20.7	215 30.1	. . 45.5	292 39.4	. . 48.5	204 21.1	. . 44.2
	16	112 49.4	67 00.4	21.6	230 33.4	45.5	307 41.8	48.5	219 23.7	44.2
	17	127 51.9	81 59.8	22.6	245 36.7	45.5	322 44.2	48.5	234 26.3	44.2
	18	142 54.4	96 59.2	N16 23.5	260 40.0	S21 45.4	337 46.7	N 7 48.4	249 29.0	S20 44.1
	19	157 56.8	111 58.6	24.4	275 43.4	45.4	352 49.1	48.4	264 31.6	44.1
	20	172 59.3	126 58.0	25.4	290 46.7	45.4	7 51.5	48.4	279 34.3	44.1
	21	188 01.7	141 57.4	. . 26.3	305 50.0	. . 45.4	22 54.0	. . 48.4	294 36.9	. . 44.1
	22	203 04.2	156 56.8	27.2	320 53.3	45.4	37 56.4	48.3	309 39.5	44.1
	23	218 06.7	171 56.2	28.1	335 56.6	45.3	52 58.8	48.3	324 42.2	44.0
	Mer. Pass.	h m 8 33.9	v −0.6	d 1.0	v 3.3	d 0.0	v 2.4	d 0.0	v 2.6	d 0.0

STARS

Name	SHA	Dec
	° ′	° ′
Acamar	315 17.3	S40 14.5
Achernar	335 26.0	S57 09.2
Acrux	173 06.4	S63 11.6
Adhara	255 11.2	S29 00.0
Aldebaran	290 47.5	N16 32.2
Alioth	166 18.7	N55 52.5
Alkaid	152 57.0	N49 14.1
Al Na'ir	27 41.4	S46 52.6
Alnilam	275 44.7	S 1 11.8
Alphard	217 54.2	S 8 44.0
Alphecca	126 09.0	N26 39.7
Alpheratz	357 41.7	N29 10.6
Altair	62 06.2	N 8 54.8
Ankaa	353 14.1	S42 13.0
Antares	112 23.5	S26 27.9
Arcturus	145 53.7	N19 05.9
Atria	107 23.0	S69 03.1
Avior	234 17.4	S59 34.2
Bellatrix	278 30.2	N 6 21.6
Betelgeuse	270 59.5	N 7 24.3
Canopus	263 55.7	S52 42.7
Capella	280 32.0	N46 00.7
Deneb	49 30.0	N45 20.2
Denebola	182 31.5	N14 28.8
Diphda	348 54.2	S17 53.9
Dubhe	193 49.2	N61 40.0
Elnath	278 10.5	N28 37.0
Eltanin	90 44.8	N51 29.2
Enif	33 45.2	N 9 57.0
Fomalhaut	15 22.0	S29 32.0
Gacrux	171 58.2	S57 12.5
Gienah	175 50.1	S17 38.1
Hadar	148 44.4	S60 27.1
Hamal	327 58.9	N23 32.1
Kaus Aust.	83 40.9	S34 22.3
Kochab	137 19.1	N74 05.5
Markab	13 36.5	N15 17.5
Menkar	314 13.3	N 4 09.0
Menkent	148 04.8	S36 27.0
Miaplacidus	221 39.2	S69 47.5
Mirfak	308 38.0	N49 54.9
Nunki	75 55.7	S26 16.3
Peacock	53 16.1	S56 40.6
Pollux	243 25.6	N27 59.1
Procyon	244 57.9	N 5 10.7
Rasalhague	96 04.4	N12 33.0
Regulus	207 41.4	N11 53.1
Rigel	281 10.5	S 8 11.3
Rigil Kent.	139 48.3	S60 54.1
Sabik	102 10.0	S15 44.5
Schedar	349 38.6	N56 37.3
Shaula	96 18.9	S37 06.7
Sirius	258 32.2	S16 44.7
Spica	158 28.9	S11 14.8
Suhail	222 51.0	S43 30.3
Vega	80 37.3	N38 47.9
Zuben'ubi	137 02.9	S16 06.5

	SHA	Mer. Pass.
	° ′	h m
Venus	316 12.8	11 31
Mars	117 10.7	0 46
Jupiter	194 53.5	19 33
Saturn	106 27.2	1 29

UT d	h	SUN GHA	SUN Dec	MOON GHA	v	MOON Dec	d	HP
		° ′	° ′	° ′	′	° ′	′	′
12	00	180 54.7	N18 11.2	107 28.2	9.5	N16 08.1	5.2	57.3
	01	195 54.7	11.9	121 56.7	9.6	16 02.9	5.4	57.3
	02	210 54.7	12.5	136 25.3	9.7	15 57.5	5.4	57.2
	03	225 54.7	. . 13.1	150 54.0	9.7	15 52.1	5.5	57.2
	04	240 54.7	13.7	165 22.7	9.9	15 46.6	5.5	57.2
	05	255 54.7	14.4	179 51.6	9.9	15 41.1	5.7	57.1
	06	270 54.7	N18 15.0	194 20.5	9.9	N15 35.4	5.7	57.1
T	07	285 54.8	15.6	208 49.4	10.1	15 29.7	5.8	57.0
H	08	300 54.8	16.2	223 18.5	10.1	15 23.9	5.9	57.0
U	09	315 54.8	. . 16.8	237 47.6	10.2	15 18.0	5.9	57.0
R	10	330 54.8	17.5	252 16.8	10.3	15 12.1	6.0	56.9
S	11	345 54.8	18.1	266 46.1	10.3	15 06.1	6.1	56.9
D	12	0 54.8	N18 18.7	281 15.4	10.5	N15 00.0	6.2	56.9
A	13	15 54.8	19.3	295 44.9	10.5	14 53.8	6.2	56.8
Y	14	30 54.8	19.9	310 14.4	10.6	14 47.6	6.3	56.8
	15	45 54.8	. . 20.6	324 44.0	10.6	14 41.3	6.4	56.7
	16	60 54.8	21.2	339 13.6	10.8	14 34.9	6.4	56.7
	17	75 54.8	21.8	353 43.4	10.8	14 28.5	6.5	56.7
	18	90 54.8	N18 22.4	8 13.2	10.8	N14 22.0	6.6	56.6
	19	105 54.8	23.0	22 43.0	11.0	14 15.4	6.6	56.6
	20	120 54.8	23.6	37 13.0	11.0	14 08.8	6.7	56.6
	21	135 54.8	. . 24.3	51 43.0	11.1	14 02.1	6.8	56.5
	22	150 54.8	24.9	66 13.1	11.2	13 55.3	6.8	56.5
	23	165 54.9	25.5	80 43.3	11.2	13 48.5	6.9	56.5
13	00	180 54.9	N18 26.1	95 13.5	11.3	N13 41.6	6.9	56.4
	01	195 54.9	26.7	109 43.8	11.4	13 34.7	7.1	56.4
	02	210 54.9	27.3	124 14.2	11.5	13 27.6	7.0	56.4
	03	225 54.9	. . 27.9	138 44.7	11.5	13 20.6	7.1	56.3
	04	240 54.9	28.6	153 15.2	11.6	13 13.5	7.2	56.3
	05	255 54.9	29.2	167 45.8	11.7	13 06.3	7.3	56.3
	06	270 54.9	N18 29.8	182 16.5	11.7	N12 59.0	7.3	56.2
	07	285 54.9	30.4	196 47.2	11.8	12 51.7	7.3	56.2
	08	300 54.9	31.0	211 18.0	11.9	12 44.4	7.4	56.2
F	09	315 54.9	. . 31.6	225 48.9	11.9	12 37.0	7.5	56.1
R	10	330 54.9	32.2	240 19.8	12.0	12 29.5	7.5	56.1
I	11	345 54.9	32.8	254 50.8	12.1	12 22.0	7.5	56.1
D	12	0 54.9	N18 33.4	269 21.9	12.1	N12 14.5	7.6	56.0
A	13	15 54.9	34.0	283 53.0	12.2	12 06.9	7.7	56.0
Y	14	30 54.9	34.6	298 24.2	12.3	11 59.2	7.7	56.0
	15	45 54.9	. . 35.3	312 55.5	12.3	11 51.5	7.7	55.9
	16	60 54.9	35.9	327 26.8	12.4	11 43.8	7.8	55.9
	17	75 54.9	36.5	341 58.2	12.5	11 36.0	7.9	55.9
	18	90 54.9	N18 37.1	356 29.7	12.5	N11 28.1	7.9	55.8
	19	105 54.9	37.7	11 01.2	12.6	11 20.2	7.9	55.8
	20	120 54.9	38.3	25 32.8	12.7	11 12.3	8.0	55.8
	21	135 54.9	. . 38.9	40 04.5	12.7	11 04.3	8.0	55.8
	22	150 54.9	39.5	54 36.2	12.7	10 56.3	8.1	55.7
	23	165 54.9	40.1	69 07.9	12.9	10 48.2	8.1	55.7
14	00	180 54.9	N18 40.7	83 39.8	12.8	N10 40.1	8.2	55.7
	01	195 54.9	41.3	98 11.6	13.0	10 31.9	8.2	55.6
	02	210 54.9	41.9	112 43.6	13.0	10 23.7	8.2	55.6
	03	225 54.9	. . 42.5	127 15.6	13.1	10 15.5	8.3	55.6
	04	240 54.9	43.1	141 47.7	13.1	10 07.2	8.3	55.6
	05	255 54.9	43.7	156 19.8	13.1	9 58.9	8.3	55.5
	06	270 54.9	N18 44.3	170 51.9	13.3	N 9 50.6	8.4	55.5
S	07	285 54.9	44.9	185 24.2	13.2	9 42.2	8.4	55.5
A	08	300 54.9	45.5	199 56.4	13.4	9 33.8	8.5	55.4
T	09	315 54.9	. . 46.1	214 28.8	13.4	9 25.3	8.5	55.4
U	10	330 54.9	46.7	229 01.2	13.4	9 16.8	8.5	55.4
R	11	345 54.8	47.2	243 33.6	13.5	9 08.3	8.6	55.4
D	12	0 54.8	N18 47.8	258 06.1	13.5	N 8 59.7	8.6	55.3
A	13	15 54.8	48.4	272 38.6	13.6	8 51.1	8.6	55.3
Y	14	30 54.8	49.0	287 11.2	13.7	8 42.5	8.6	55.3
	15	45 54.8	. . 49.6	301 43.9	13.7	8 33.9	8.7	55.3
	16	60 54.8	50.2	316 16.6	13.7	8 25.2	8.7	55.2
	17	75 54.8	50.8	330 49.3	13.8	8 16.5	8.8	55.2
	18	90 54.8	N18 51.4	345 22.1	13.8	N 8 07.7	8.8	55.2
	19	105 54.8	52.0	359 54.9	13.9	7 58.9	8.7	55.2
	20	120 54.8	52.6	14 27.8	14.0	7 50.2	8.9	55.1
	21	135 54.8	. . 53.2	29 00.8	13.9	7 41.3	8.8	55.1
	22	150 54.8	53.8	43 33.7	14.0	7 32.5	8.9	55.1
	23	165 54.8	54.3	58 06.7	14.1	N 7 23.6	8.9	55.1
		SD 15.9	*d* 0.6	SD 15.5		15.3		15.1

Lat.	Twilight Naut.	Twilight Civil	Sunrise	Moonrise 12	Moonrise 13	Moonrise 14	Moonrise 15
°	h m	h m	h m	h m	h m	h m	h m
N 72	▭	▭	▭	07 15	09 05	10 48	12 25
N 70	////	////	01 00	07 52	09 28	11 02	12 33
68	////	////	01 56	08 18	09 46	11 14	12 39
66	////	////	02 29	08 38	10 01	11 23	12 45
64	////	01 19	02 52	08 53	10 12	11 31	12 49
62	////	01 58	03 11	09 07	10 22	11 38	12 53
60	////	02 24	03 26	09 18	10 31	11 44	12 56
N 58	01 11	02 45	03 39	09 27	10 38	11 49	12 59
56	01 47	03 01	03 50	09 36	10 45	11 54	13 02
54	02 11	03 15	04 00	09 43	10 51	11 58	13 04
52	02 30	03 27	04 09	09 50	10 56	12 02	13 06
50	02 46	03 37	04 16	09 56	11 01	12 05	13 08
45	03 16	03 59	04 33	10 09	11 11	12 12	13 12
N 40	03 38	04 16	04 46	10 20	11 20	12 18	13 16
35	03 56	04 30	04 58	10 29	11 27	12 24	13 19
30	04 10	04 42	05 08	10 37	11 33	12 28	13 21
20	04 33	05 01	05 25	10 51	11 44	12 36	13 26
N 10	04 51	05 17	05 39	11 03	11 54	12 43	13 30
0	05 06	05 31	05 53	11 14	12 03	12 50	13 34
S 10	05 19	05 44	06 06	11 25	12 12	12 56	13 38
20	05 31	05 57	06 21	11 37	12 22	13 03	13 42
30	05 43	06 11	06 37	11 51	12 33	13 11	13 46
35	05 49	06 19	06 46	11 59	12 39	13 15	13 49
40	05 55	06 28	06 57	12 08	12 46	13 20	13 52
45	06 02	06 38	07 09	12 18	12 55	13 26	13 55
S 50	06 10	06 49	07 24	12 31	13 05	13 34	13 59
52	06 13	06 54	07 32	12 37	13 09	13 37	14 01
54	06 16	07 00	07 39	12 43	13 14	13 40	14 03
56	06 20	07 06	07 48	12 51	13 20	13 44	14 06
58	06 24	07 13	07 58	12 59	13 26	13 49	14 08
S 60	06 29	07 21	08 10	13 08	13 33	13 54	14 11

Lat.	Sunset	Twilight Civil	Twilight Naut.	Moonset 12	Moonset 13	Moonset 14	Moonset 15
°	h m	h m	h m	h m	h m	h m	h m
N 72	▭	▭	▭	02 57	02 50	02 45	02 39
N 70	23 03	////	////	02 19	02 26	02 29	02 30
68	22 01	////	////	01 52	02 07	02 16	02 22
66	21 27	////	////	01 32	01 52	02 05	02 16
64	21 03	22 39	////	01 16	01 39	01 56	02 10
62	20 44	21 58	////	01 02	01 28	01 49	02 05
60	20 28	21 31	////	00 50	01 19	01 42	02 01
N 58	20 15	21 10	22 47	00 40	01 11	01 36	01 57
56	20 04	20 53	22 09	00 31	01 04	01 31	01 54
54	19 54	20 39	21 44	00 24	00 58	01 26	01 51
52	19 45	20 27	21 25	00 17	00 52	01 22	01 48
50	19 37	20 16	21 08	00 10	00 47	01 18	01 45
45	19 20	19 55	20 38	24 36	00 36	01 10	01 40
N 40	19 07	19 37	20 15	24 26	00 26	01 03	01 35
35	18 55	19 23	19 57	24 18	00 18	00 57	01 31
30	18 45	19 11	19 43	24 11	00 11	00 51	01 28
20	18 28	18 52	19 20	23 59	24 42	00 42	01 22
N 10	18 14	18 36	19 02	23 48	24 34	00 34	01 16
0	18 00	18 22	18 47	23 38	24 26	00 26	01 11
S 10	17 46	18 08	18 34	23 28	24 18	00 18	01 06
20	17 32	17 55	18 22	23 17	24 09	00 09	01 00
30	17 16	17 41	18 10	23 04	24 00	00 00	00 54
35	17 06	17 33	18 04	22 57	23 54	24 50	00 50
40	16 55	17 24	17 57	22 48	23 48	24 46	00 46
45	16 43	17 15	17 50	22 39	23 40	24 41	00 41
S 50	16 28	17 03	17 43	22 27	23 32	24 35	00 35
52	16 21	16 58	17 39	22 21	23 27	24 33	00 33
54	16 13	16 52	17 36	22 15	23 23	24 30	00 30
56	16 04	16 46	17 32	22 08	23 18	24 26	00 26
58	15 54	16 39	17 28	22 01	23 12	24 23	00 23
S 60	15 42	16 31	17 23	21 52	23 06	24 19	00 19

Day	SUN Eqn. of Time 00^h	SUN Eqn. of Time 12^h	SUN Mer. Pass.	MOON Mer. Pass. Upper	MOON Mer. Pass. Lower	MOON Age	MOON Phase
d	m s	m s	h m	h m	h m	d %	
12	03 39	03 39	11 56	17 26	05 01	06 38	
13	03 39	03 40	11 56	18 14	05 51	07 48	◐
14	03 40	03 39	11 56	19 00	06 38	08 58	

UT	ARIES	VENUS −3·9		MARS −1·9		JUPITER −2·2		SATURN +0·1		STARS		
	GHA	GHA	Dec	GHA	Dec	GHA	Dec	GHA	Dec	Name	SHA	Dec
d h	° ′	° ′	° ′	° ′	° ′	° ′	° ′	° ′	° ′		° ′	° ′
15 00	233 09.1	186 55.6	N16 29.1	350 59.9	S21 45.3	68 01.2	N 7 48.3	339 44.8	S20 44.0	Acamar	315 17.3	S40 14.5
01	248 11.6	201 55.0	30.0	6 03.3	45.3	83 03.7	48.3	354 47.5	44.0	Achernar	335 26.0	S57 09.2
02	263 14.1	216 54.4	30.9	21 06.6	45.3	98 06.1	48.2	9 50.1	44.0	Acrux	173 06.5	S63 11.6
03	278 16.5	231 53.8	. . 31.8	36 09.9	. . 45.3	113 08.5	. . 48.2	24 52.8	. . 44.0	Adhara	255 11.2	S29 00.0
04	293 19.0	246 53.2	32.8	51 13.2	45.3	128 11.0	48.2	39 55.4	44.0	Aldebaran	290 47.5	N16 32.2
05	308 21.5	261 52.6	33.7	66 16.6	45.2	143 13.4	48.2	54 58.0	43.9			
06	323 23.9	276 52.0	N16 34.6	81 19.9	S21 45.2	158 15.8	N 7 48.1	70 00.7	S20 43.9	Alioth	166 18.7	N55 52.5
07	338 26.4	291 51.5	35.5	96 23.2	45.2	173 18.2	48.1	85 03.3	43.9	Alkaid	152 57.0	N49 14.1
08	353 28.8	306 50.9	36.4	111 26.5	45.2	188 20.7	48.1	100 06.0	43.9	Al Na'ir	27 41.4	S46 52.6
S 09	8 31.3	321 50.3	. . 37.4	126 29.9	. . 45.1	203 23.1	. . 48.1	115 08.6	. . 43.9	Alnilam	275 44.7	S 1 11.8
U 10	23 33.8	336 49.7	38.3	141 33.2	45.1	218 25.5	48.0	130 11.3	43.8	Alphard	217 54.2	S 8 44.0
N 11	38 36.2	351 49.1	39.2	156 36.5	45.1	233 27.9	48.0	145 13.9	43.8			
D 12	53 38.7	6 48.5	N16 40.1	171 39.8	S21 45.1	248 30.4	N 7 48.0	160 16.5	S20 43.8	Alphecca	126 09.0	N26 39.7
A 13	68 41.2	21 47.9	41.0	186 43.2	45.1	263 32.8	48.0	175 19.2	43.8	Alpheratz	357 41.6	N29 10.6
Y 14	83 43.6	36 47.2	41.9	201 46.5	45.0	278 35.2	47.9	190 21.8	43.8	Altair	62 06.2	N 8 54.8
15	98 46.1	51 46.6	. . 42.9	216 49.8	. . 45.0	293 37.6	. . 47.9	205 24.5	. . 43.7	Ankaa	353 14.1	S42 13.0
16	113 48.6	66 46.0	43.8	231 53.2	45.0	308 40.1	47.9	220 27.1	43.7	Antares	112 23.5	S26 27.9
17	128 51.0	81 45.4	44.7	246 56.5	45.0	323 42.5	47.9	235 29.8	43.7			
18	143 53.5	96 44.8	N16 45.6	261 59.8	S21 45.0	338 44.9	N 7 47.8	250 32.4	S20 43.7	Arcturus	145 53.7	N19 05.9
19	158 56.0	111 44.2	46.5	277 03.2	44.9	353 47.3	47.8	265 35.0	43.7	Atria	107 23.0	S69 03.1
20	173 58.4	126 43.6	47.4	292 06.5	44.9	8 49.8	47.8	280 37.7	43.6	Avior	234 17.4	S59 34.2
21	189 00.9	141 43.0	. . 48.3	307 09.8	. . 44.9	23 52.2	. . 47.8	295 40.3	. . 43.6	Bellatrix	278 30.2	N 6 21.6
22	204 03.3	156 42.4	49.2	322 13.2	44.9	38 54.6	47.7	310 43.0	43.6	Betelgeuse	270 59.5	N 7 24.3
23	219 05.8	171 41.8	50.1	337 16.5	44.8	53 57.0	47.7	325 45.6	43.6			
16 00	234 08.3	186 41.2	N16 51.0	352 19.8	S21 44.8	68 59.4	N 7 47.7	340 48.3	S20 43.6	Canopus	263 55.7	S52 42.7
01	249 10.7	201 40.6	52.0	7 23.2	44.8	84 01.9	47.7	355 50.9	43.5	Capella	280 32.0	N46 00.7
02	264 13.2	216 40.0	52.9	22 26.5	44.8	99 04.3	47.6	10 53.6	43.5	Deneb	49 30.0	N45 20.2
03	279 15.7	231 39.4	. . 53.8	37 29.9	. . 44.7	114 06.7	. . 47.6	25 56.2	. . 43.5	Denebola	182 31.5	N14 28.9
04	294 18.1	246 38.8	54.7	52 33.2	44.7	129 09.1	47.6	40 58.8	43.5	Diphda	348 54.2	S17 53.9
05	309 20.6	261 38.2	55.6	67 36.5	44.7	144 11.5	47.6	56 01.5	43.5			
06	324 23.1	276 37.6	N16 56.5	82 39.9	S21 44.7	159 14.0	N 7 47.5	71 04.1	S20 43.4	Dubhe	193 49.3	N61 40.0
07	339 25.5	291 37.0	57.4	97 43.2	44.6	174 16.4	47.5	86 06.8	43.4	Elnath	278 10.5	N28 37.0
08	354 28.0	306 36.3	58.3	112 46.6	44.6	189 18.8	47.5	101 09.4	43.4	Eltanin	90 44.8	N51 29.2
M 09	9 30.4	321 35.7	16 59.2	127 49.9	. . 44.6	204 21.2	. . 47.4	116 12.1	. . 43.4	Enif	33 45.2	N 9 57.0
O 10	24 32.9	336 35.1	17 00.1	142 53.3	44.6	219 23.6	47.4	131 14.7	43.4	Fomalhaut	15 22.0	S29 32.0
N 11	39 35.4	351 34.5	01.0	157 56.6	44.5	234 26.1	47.4	146 17.4	43.4			
D 12	54 37.8	6 33.9	N17 01.9	172 59.9	S21 44.5	249 28.5	N 7 47.4	161 20.0	S20 43.3	Gacrux	171 58.2	S57 12.5
A 13	69 40.3	21 33.3	02.8	188 03.3	44.5	264 30.9	47.3	176 22.6	43.3	Gienah	175 50.1	S17 38.1
Y 14	84 42.8	36 32.7	03.7	203 06.6	44.5	279 33.3	47.3	191 25.3	43.3	Hadar	148 44.4	S60 27.1
15	99 45.2	51 32.1	. . 04.6	218 10.0	. . 44.4	294 35.7	. . 47.3	206 27.9	. . 43.3	Hamal	327 58.8	N23 32.1
16	114 47.7	66 31.4	05.5	233 13.3	44.4	309 38.2	47.2	221 30.6	43.3	Kaus Aust.	83 40.9	S34 22.3
17	129 50.2	81 30.8	06.4	248 16.7	44.4	324 40.6	47.2	236 33.2	43.2			
18	144 52.6	96 30.2	N17 07.3	263 20.0	S21 44.4	339 43.0	N 7 47.2	251 35.9	S20 43.2	Kochab	137 19.1	N74 05.5
19	159 55.1	111 29.6	08.1	278 23.4	44.3	354 45.4	47.2	266 38.5	43.2	Markab	13 36.5	N15 17.5
20	174 57.6	126 29.0	09.0	293 26.7	44.3	9 47.8	47.1	281 41.2	43.2	Menkar	314 13.3	N 4 09.0
21	190 00.0	141 28.4	. . 09.9	308 30.1	. . 44.3	24 50.2	. . 47.1	296 43.8	. . 43.2	Menkent	148 04.8	S36 27.0
22	205 02.5	156 27.8	10.8	323 33.4	44.3	39 52.6	47.1	311 46.5	43.1	Miaplacidus	221 39.3	S69 47.5
23	220 04.9	171 27.1	11.7	338 36.8	44.2	54 55.1	47.0	326 49.1	43.1			
17 00	235 07.4	186 26.5	N17 12.6	353 40.1	S21 44.2	69 57.5	N 7 47.0	341 51.8	S20 43.1	Mirfak	308 38.0	N49 54.9
01	250 09.9	201 25.9	13.5	8 43.5	44.2	84 59.9	47.0	356 54.4	43.1	Nunki	75 55.7	S26 16.3
02	265 12.3	216 25.3	14.4	23 46.9	44.1	100 02.3	47.0	11 57.0	43.1	Peacock	53 16.0	S56 40.6
03	280 14.8	231 24.7	. . 15.3	38 50.2	. . 44.1	115 04.7	. . 46.9	26 59.7	. . 43.0	Pollux	243 25.6	N27 59.1
04	295 17.3	246 24.0	16.1	53 53.6	44.1	130 07.1	46.9	42 02.3	43.0	Procyon	244 57.9	N 5 10.7
05	310 19.7	261 23.4	17.0	68 56.9	44.1	145 09.5	46.9	57 05.0	43.0			
06	325 22.2	276 22.8	N17 17.9	84 00.3	S21 44.0	160 12.0	N 7 46.8	72 07.6	S20 43.0	Rasalhague	96 04.3	N12 33.0
07	340 24.7	291 22.2	18.8	99 03.6	44.0	175 14.4	46.8	87 10.3	43.0	Regulus	207 41.4	N11 53.1
T 08	355 27.1	306 21.6	19.7	114 07.0	44.0	190 16.8	46.8	102 12.9	42.9	Rigel	281 10.5	S 8 11.3
U 09	10 29.6	321 20.9	. . 20.6	129 10.4	. . 43.9	205 19.2	. . 46.7	117 15.6	. . 42.9	Rigil Kent.	139 48.3	S60 54.1
E 10	25 32.1	336 20.3	21.4	144 13.7	43.9	220 21.6	46.7	132 18.2	42.9	Sabik	102 10.0	S15 44.5
S 11	40 34.5	351 19.7	22.3	159 17.1	43.9	235 24.0	46.7	147 20.9	42.9			
D 12	55 37.0	6 19.1	N17 23.2	174 20.4	S21 43.8	250 26.4	N 7 46.6	162 23.5	S20 42.9	Schedar	349 38.6	N56 37.3
A 13	70 39.4	21 18.4	24.1	189 23.8	43.8	265 28.8	46.6	177 26.2	42.8	Shaula	96 18.9	S37 06.7
Y 14	85 41.9	36 17.8	25.0	204 27.2	43.8	280 31.3	46.6	192 28.8	42.8	Sirius	258 32.3	S16 44.7
15	100 44.4	51 17.2	. . 25.8	219 30.5	. . 43.8	295 33.7	. . 46.6	207 31.4	. . 42.8	Spica	158 28.9	S11 14.8
16	115 46.8	66 16.6	26.7	234 33.9	43.7	310 36.1	46.5	222 34.1	42.8	Suhail	222 51.0	S43 30.3
17	130 49.3	81 15.9	27.6	249 37.2	43.7	325 38.5	46.5	237 36.7	42.8			
18	145 51.8	96 15.3	N17 28.5	264 40.6	S21 43.7	340 40.9	N 7 46.5	252 39.4	S20 42.7	Vega	80 37.3	N38 47.9
19	160 54.2	111 14.7	29.3	279 44.0	43.6	355 43.3	46.4	267 42.0	42.7	Zuben'ubi	137 02.9	S16 06.5
20	175 56.7	126 14.1	30.2	294 47.3	43.6	10 45.7	46.4	282 44.7	42.7		SHA	Mer. Pass.
21	190 59.2	141 13.4	. . 31.1	309 50.7	. . 43.6	25 48.1	. . 46.4	297 47.3	. . 42.7		° ′	h m
22	206 01.6	156 12.8	32.0	324 54.1	43.5	40 50.5	46.3	312 50.0	42.7	Venus	312 32.9	11 34
23	221 04.1	171 12.2	32.8	339 57.4	43.5	55 52.9	46.3	327 52.6	42.6	Mars	118 11.6	0 31
Mer. Pass.	h m 8 22.1	*v* −0.6	*d* 0.9	*v* 3.3	*d* 0.0	*v* 2.4	*d* 0.0	*v* 2.6	*d* 0.0	Jupiter	194 51.2	19 21
										Saturn	106 40.0	1 17

Day	UT d h	SUN GHA ° ′	SUN Dec ° ′	MOON GHA ° ′	v ′	MOON Dec ° ′	d ′	HP ′
	15 00	180 54.8	N18 54.9	72 39.8	14.1	N 7 14.7	8.9	55.0
	01	195 54.8	55.5	87 12.9	14.1	7 05.8	9.0	55.0
	02	210 54.8	56.1	101 46.0	14.2	6 56.8	9.0	55.0
	03	225 54.7	. . 56.7	116 19.2	14.3	6 47.8	9.0	55.0
	04	240 54.7	57.3	130 52.5	14.2	6 38.8	9.0	55.0
	05	255 54.7	57.9	145 25.7	14.3	6 29.8	9.0	54.9
	06	270 54.7	N18 58.4	159 59.0	14.4	N 6 20.8	9.1	54.9
	07	285 54.7	59.0	174 32.4	14.4	6 11.7	9.1	54.9
	08	300 54.7	18 59.6	189 05.8	14.4	6 02.6	9.1	54.9
SUNDAY	09	315 54.7	19 00.2	203 39.2	14.4	5 53.5	9.1	54.8
	10	330 54.7	00.8	218 12.6	14.5	5 44.4	9.1	54.8
	11	345 54.7	01.4	232 46.1	14.5	5 35.3	9.2	54.8
	12	0 54.7	N19 01.9	247 19.6	14.6	N 5 26.1	9.1	54.8
	13	15 54.7	02.5	261 53.2	14.6	5 17.0	9.2	54.8
	14	30 54.6	03.1	276 26.8	14.6	5 07.8	9.2	54.7
	15	45 54.6	. . 03.7	291 00.4	14.7	4 58.6	9.3	54.7
	16	60 54.6	04.3	305 34.1	14.6	4 49.3	9.2	54.7
	17	75 54.6	04.8	320 07.7	14.8	4 40.1	9.2	54.7
	18	90 54.6	N19 05.4	334 41.5	14.7	N 4 30.9	9.3	54.7
	19	105 54.6	06.0	349 15.2	14.8	4 21.6	9.3	54.7
	20	120 54.6	06.6	3 49.0	14.8	4 12.3	9.3	54.6
	21	135 54.6	. . 07.1	18 22.8	14.8	4 03.0	9.3	54.6
	22	150 54.5	07.7	32 56.6	14.9	3 53.7	9.3	54.6
	23	165 54.5	08.3	47 30.5	14.9	3 44.4	9.3	54.6
	16 00	180 54.5	N19 08.9	62 04.4	14.9	N 3 35.1	9.3	54.6
	01	195 54.5	09.4	76 38.3	14.9	3 25.8	9.4	54.6
	02	210 54.5	10.0	91 12.2	14.9	3 16.4	9.3	54.5
	03	225 54.5	. . 10.6	105 46.1	15.0	3 07.1	9.4	54.5
	04	240 54.5	11.1	120 20.1	15.0	2 57.7	9.3	54.5
	05	255 54.5	11.7	134 54.1	15.0	2 48.4	9.4	54.5
	06	270 54.4	N19 12.3	149 28.1	15.1	N 2 39.0	9.4	54.5
	07	285 54.4	12.9	164 02.2	15.1	2 29.6	9.4	54.5
	08	300 54.4	13.4	178 36.3	15.0	2 20.2	9.3	54.4
MONDAY	09	315 54.4	. . 14.0	193 10.3	15.1	2 10.9	9.4	54.4
	10	330 54.4	14.6	207 44.4	15.2	2 01.5	9.4	54.4
	11	345 54.4	15.1	222 18.6	15.1	1 52.1	9.4	54.4
	12	0 54.3	N19 15.7	236 52.7	15.1	N 1 42.7	9.5	54.4
	13	15 54.3	16.3	251 26.8	15.2	1 33.2	9.4	54.4
	14	30 54.3	16.8	266 01.0	15.2	1 23.8	9.4	54.4
	15	45 54.3	. . 17.4	280 35.2	15.2	1 14.4	9.4	54.3
	16	60 54.3	18.0	295 09.4	15.2	1 05.0	9.4	54.3
	17	75 54.3	18.5	309 43.6	15.2	0 55.6	9.4	54.3
	18	90 54.2	N19 19.1	324 17.8	15.3	N 0 46.2	9.4	54.3
	19	105 54.2	19.7	338 52.1	15.2	0 36.8	9.4	54.3
	20	120 54.2	20.2	353 26.3	15.3	0 27.4	9.4	54.3
	21	135 54.2	. . 20.8	8 00.6	15.2	0 18.0	9.5	54.3
	22	150 54.2	21.3	22 34.8	15.3	N 0 08.5	9.4	54.3
	23	165 54.2	21.9	37 09.1	15.3	S 0 00.9	9.4	54.3
	17 00	180 54.1	N19 22.5	51 43.4	15.3	S 0 10.3	9.4	54.2
	01	195 54.1	23.0	66 17.7	15.3	0 19.7	9.4	54.2
	02	210 54.1	23.6	80 52.0	15.3	0 29.1	9.4	54.2
	03	225 54.1	. . 24.1	95 26.3	15.3	0 38.5	9.4	54.2
	04	240 54.1	24.7	110 00.6	15.3	0 47.9	9.3	54.2
	05	255 54.0	25.3	124 34.9	15.4	0 57.2	9.4	54.2
	06	270 54.0	N19 25.8	139 09.3	15.3	S 1 06.6	9.4	54.2
	07	285 54.0	26.4	153 43.6	15.3	1 16.0	9.4	54.2
	08	300 54.0	26.9	168 17.9	15.4	1 25.4	9.3	54.2
TUESDAY	09	315 54.0	. . 27.5	182 52.3	15.3	1 34.7	9.4	54.2
	10	330 53.9	28.0	197 26.6	15.3	1 44.1	9.3	54.2
	11	345 53.9	28.6	212 00.9	15.4	1 53.4	9.3	54.1
	12	0 53.9	N19 29.1	226 35.3	15.3	S 2 02.7	9.4	54.1
	13	15 53.9	29.7	241 09.6	15.4	2 12.1	9.3	54.1
	14	30 53.8	30.2	255 44.0	15.3	2 21.4	9.3	54.1
	15	45 53.8	. . 30.8	270 18.3	15.3	2 30.7	9.3	54.1
	16	60 53.8	31.4	284 52.6	15.4	2 40.0	9.2	54.1
	17	75 53.8	31.9	299 27.0	15.3	2 49.2	9.3	54.1
	18	90 53.8	N19 32.5	314 01.3	15.3	S 2 58.5	9.2	54.1
	19	105 53.7	33.0	328 35.6	15.3	3 07.7	9.3	54.1
	20	120 53.7	33.6	343 09.9	15.3	3 17.0	9.2	54.1
	21	135 53.7	. . 34.1	357 44.2	15.4	3 26.2	9.2	54.1
	22	150 53.7	34.6	12 18.6	15.3	3 35.4	9.2	54.1
	23	165 53.6	35.2	26 52.9	15.3	S 3 44.6	9.2	54.1
		SD 15.8	*d* 0.6	SD 14.9		14.8		14.8

Lat. °	Twilight Naut. h m	Twilight Civil h m	Sunrise h m	Moonrise 15 h m	Moonrise 16 h m	Moonrise 17 h m	Moonrise 18 h m
N 72	▭	▭	▭	12 25	14 00	15 33	17 06
N 70	////	////	00 06	12 33	14 02	15 29	16 57
68	////	////	01 39	12 39	14 03	15 26	16 49
66	////	////	02 17	12 45	14 05	15 23	16 42
64	////	00 57	02 43	12 49	14 06	15 21	16 37
62	////	01 45	03 03	12 53	14 07	15 19	16 32
60	////	02 15	03 19	12 56	14 07	15 18	16 28
N 58	00 51	02 37	03 33	12 59	14 08	15 16	16 24
56	01 35	02 54	03 45	13 02	14 09	15 15	16 21
54	02 02	03 09	03 55	13 04	14 09	15 14	16 18
52	02 23	03 22	04 04	13 06	14 10	15 13	16 15
50	02 40	03 33	04 12	13 08	14 10	15 12	16 13
45	03 11	03 55	04 30	13 12	14 11	15 10	16 08
N 40	03 35	04 13	04 44	13 16	14 12	15 08	16 04
35	03 53	04 27	04 55	13 19	14 13	15 06	16 00
30	04 08	04 40	05 06	13 21	14 14	15 05	15 57
20	04 32	05 00	05 23	13 26	14 15	15 03	15 51
N 10	04 50	05 16	05 39	13 30	14 16	15 01	15 46
0	05 05	05 31	05 53	13 34	14 17	14 59	15 42
S 10	05 19	05 45	06 07	13 38	14 18	14 57	15 37
20	05 32	05 58	06 22	13 42	14 19	14 55	15 32
30	05 44	06 13	06 39	13 46	14 20	14 53	15 27
35	05 51	06 21	06 48	13 49	14 21	14 52	15 24
40	05 57	06 30	07 00	13 52	14 22	14 51	15 20
45	06 05	06 41	07 13	13 55	14 22	14 49	15 16
S 50	06 13	06 53	07 29	13 59	14 24	14 47	15 11
52	06 17	06 58	07 36	14 01	14 24	14 46	15 09
54	06 20	07 04	07 44	14 03	14 25	14 45	15 07
56	06 25	07 11	07 54	14 06	14 25	14 44	15 04
58	06 29	07 18	08 04	14 08	14 26	14 43	15 01
S 60	06 34	07 26	08 16	14 11	14 27	14 42	14 58

Lat. °	Sunset h m	Twilight Civil h m	Twilight Naut. h m	Moonset 15 h m	Moonset 16 h m	Moonset 17 h m	Moonset 18 h m
N 72	▭	▭	▭	02 39	02 34	02 29	02 24
N 70	▭	▭	▭	02 30	02 30	02 30	02 30
68	22 19	////	////	02 22	02 27	02 31	02 35
66	21 39	////	////	02 16	02 24	02 31	02 39
64	21 13	23 03	////	02 10	02 21	02 32	02 42
62	20 52	22 11	////	02 05	02 19	02 32	02 45
60	20 35	21 41	////	02 01	02 17	02 33	02 48
N 58	20 21	21 18	23 09	01 57	02 16	02 33	02 51
56	20 09	21 00	22 21	01 54	02 14	02 33	02 53
54	19 59	20 45	21 53	01 51	02 13	02 34	02 55
52	19 50	20 32	21 32	01 48	02 12	02 34	02 56
50	19 41	20 21	21 15	01 45	02 10	02 34	02 58
45	19 24	19 58	20 42	01 40	02 08	02 35	03 01
N 40	19 10	19 41	20 19	01 35	02 06	02 35	03 04
35	18 58	19 26	20 00	01 31	02 04	02 35	03 07
30	18 47	19 14	19 45	01 28	02 02	02 36	03 09
20	18 30	18 53	19 21	01 22	02 00	02 36	03 13
N 10	18 14	18 37	19 03	01 16	01 57	02 37	03 16
0	18 00	18 22	18 47	01 11	01 55	02 37	03 20
S 10	17 46	18 08	18 34	01 06	01 52	02 38	03 23
20	17 31	17 54	18 21	01 00	01 50	02 38	03 26
30	17 14	17 39	18 08	00 54	01 47	02 39	03 30
35	17 04	17 31	18 02	00 50	01 45	02 39	03 32
40	16 53	17 22	17 55	00 46	01 43	02 39	03 35
45	16 40	17 12	17 47	00 41	01 41	02 39	03 38
S 50	16 24	17 00	17 39	00 35	01 38	02 40	03 41
52	16 16	16 54	17 36	00 33	01 37	02 40	03 43
54	16 08	16 48	17 32	00 30	01 35	02 40	03 45
56	15 59	16 41	17 28	00 26	01 34	02 41	03 47
58	15 48	16 34	17 23	00 23	01 32	02 41	03 49
S 60	15 36	16 26	17 18	00 19	01 30	02 41	03 51

Day d	SUN Eqn. of Time 00^h m s	SUN Eqn. of Time 12^h m s	SUN Mer. Pass. h m	MOON Mer. Pass. Upper h m	MOON Mer. Pass. Lower h m	MOON Age d	MOON Phase %
15	03 39	03 39	11 56	19 44	07 23	09	67
16	03 38	03 37	11 56	20 27	08 06	10	76
17	03 37	03 36	11 56	21 09	08 48	11	84

UT (d h)	ARIES GHA	VENUS −3·9 GHA	VENUS Dec	MARS −2·0 GHA	MARS Dec	JUPITER −2·1 GHA	JUPITER Dec	SATURN +0·1 GHA	SATURN Dec
	° ′	° ′	° ′	° ′	° ′	° ′	° ′	° ′	° ′
18 00 (WEDNESDAY)	236 06.5	186 11.5	N17 33.7	355 00.8	S21 43.5	70 55.3	N 7 46.3	342 55.3	S20 42.6
01	251 09.0	201 10.9	34.6	10 04.2	43.4	85 57.8	46.2	357 57.9	42.6
02	266 11.5	216 10.3	35.4	25 07.5	43.4	101 00.2	46.2	13 00.6	42.6
03	281 13.9	231 09.7	. . 36.3	40 10.9	. . 43.4	116 02.6	. . 46.2	28 03.2	. . 42.6
04	296 16.4	246 09.0	37.2	55 14.3	43.3	131 05.0	46.1	43 05.9	42.5
05	311 18.9	261 08.4	38.0	70 17.7	43.3	146 07.4	46.1	58 08.5	42.5
06	326 21.3	276 07.8	N17 38.9	85 21.0	S21 43.3	161 09.8	N 7 46.1	73 11.2	S20 42.5
07	341 23.8	291 07.1	39.8	100 24.4	43.2	176 12.2	46.0	88 13.8	42.5
08	356 26.3	306 06.5	40.6	115 27.8	43.2	191 14.6	46.0	103 16.5	42.5
09	11 28.7	321 05.9	. . 41.5	130 31.1	. . 43.2	206 17.0	. . 46.0	118 19.1	. . 42.5
10	26 31.2	336 05.2	42.4	145 34.5	43.1	221 19.4	45.9	133 21.7	42.4
11	41 33.7	351 04.6	43.2	160 37.9	43.1	236 21.8	45.9	148 24.4	42.4
12	56 36.1	6 04.0	N17 44.1	175 41.3	S21 43.1	251 24.2	N 7 45.9	163 27.0	S20 42.4
13	71 38.6	21 03.3	45.0	190 44.6	43.0	266 26.6	45.8	178 29.7	42.4
14	86 41.0	36 02.7	45.8	205 48.0	43.0	281 29.0	45.8	193 32.3	42.4
15	101 43.5	51 02.1	. . 46.7	220 51.4	. . 43.0	296 31.4	. . 45.8	208 35.0	. . 42.3
16	116 46.0	66 01.4	47.5	235 54.8	42.9	311 33.8	45.7	223 37.6	42.3
17	131 48.4	81 00.8	48.4	250 58.1	42.9	326 36.2	45.7	238 40.3	42.3
18	146 50.9	96 00.1	N17 49.2	266 01.5	S21 42.9	341 38.6	N 7 45.7	253 42.9	S20 42.3
19	161 53.4	110 59.5	50.1	281 04.9	42.8	356 41.0	45.6	268 45.6	42.3
20	176 55.8	125 58.9	51.0	296 08.3	42.8	11 43.4	45.6	283 48.2	42.2
21	191 58.3	140 58.2	. . 51.8	311 11.7	. . 42.8	26 45.8	. . 45.6	298 50.9	. . 42.2
22	207 00.8	155 57.6	52.7	326 15.0	42.7	41 48.2	45.5	313 53.5	42.2
23	222 03.2	170 56.9	53.5	341 18.4	42.7	56 50.6	45.5	328 56.2	42.2
19 00 (THURSDAY)	237 05.7	185 56.3	N17 54.4	356 21.8	S21 42.7	71 53.0	N 7 45.5	343 58.8	S20 42.2
01	252 08.2	200 55.7	55.2	11 25.2	42.6	86 55.5	45.4	359 01.5	42.1
02	267 10.6	215 55.0	56.1	26 28.6	42.6	101 57.9	45.4	14 04.1	42.1
03	282 13.1	230 54.4	. . 56.9	41 31.9	. . 42.5	117 00.3	. . 45.3	29 06.8	. . 42.1
04	297 15.5	245 53.7	57.8	56 35.3	42.5	132 02.7	45.3	44 09.4	42.1
05	312 18.0	260 53.1	58.6	71 38.7	42.5	147 05.1	45.3	59 12.1	42.1
06	327 20.5	275 52.4	N17 59.5	86 42.1	S21 42.4	162 07.5	N 7 45.2	74 14.7	S20 42.0
07	342 22.9	290 51.8	18 00.3	101 45.5	42.4	177 09.8	45.2	89 17.4	42.0
08	357 25.4	305 51.2	01.1	116 48.9	42.4	192 12.2	45.2	104 20.0	42.0
09	12 27.9	320 50.5	. . 02.0	131 52.2	. . 42.3	207 14.6	. . 45.1	119 22.7	. . 42.0
10	27 30.3	335 49.9	02.8	146 55.6	42.3	222 17.0	45.1	134 25.3	42.0
11	42 32.8	350 49.2	03.7	161 59.0	42.2	237 19.4	45.1	149 28.0	41.9
12	57 35.3	5 48.6	N18 04.5	177 02.4	S21 42.2	252 21.8	N 7 45.0	164 30.6	S20 41.9
13	72 37.7	20 47.9	05.4	192 05.8	42.2	267 24.2	45.0	179 33.3	41.9
14	87 40.2	35 47.3	06.2	207 09.2	42.1	282 26.6	44.9	194 35.9	41.9
15	102 42.6	50 46.6	. . 07.0	222 12.6	. . 42.1	297 29.0	. . 44.9	209 38.6	. . 41.9
16	117 45.1	65 46.0	07.9	237 15.9	42.0	312 31.4	44.9	224 41.2	41.8
17	132 47.6	80 45.3	08.7	252 19.3	42.0	327 33.8	44.8	239 43.9	41.8
18	147 50.0	95 44.7	N18 09.6	267 22.7	S21 42.0	342 36.2	N 7 44.8	254 46.5	S20 41.8
19	162 52.5	110 44.0	10.4	282 26.1	41.9	357 38.6	44.8	269 49.2	41.8
20	177 55.0	125 43.4	11.2	297 29.5	41.9	12 41.0	44.7	284 51.8	41.8
21	192 57.4	140 42.7	. . 12.1	312 32.9	. . 41.9	27 43.4	. . 44.7	299 54.5	. . 41.7
22	207 59.9	155 42.1	12.9	327 36.3	41.8	42 45.8	44.6	314 57.1	41.7
23	223 02.4	170 41.4	13.7	342 39.7	41.8	57 48.2	44.6	329 59.8	41.7
20 00 (FRIDAY)	238 04.8	185 40.8	N18 14.6	357 43.1	S21 41.7	72 50.6	N 7 44.6	345 02.4	S20 41.7
01	253 07.3	200 40.1	15.4	12 46.5	41.7	87 53.0	44.5	0 05.1	41.7
02	268 09.8	215 39.5	16.2	27 49.8	41.7	102 55.4	44.5	15 07.7	41.6
03	283 12.2	230 38.8	. . 17.0	42 53.2	. . 41.6	117 57.8	. . 44.5	30 10.4	. . 41.6
04	298 14.7	245 38.2	17.9	57 56.6	41.6	133 00.2	44.4	45 13.0	41.6
05	313 17.1	260 37.5	18.7	73 00.0	41.5	148 02.6	44.4	60 15.7	41.6
06	328 19.6	275 36.9	N18 19.5	88 03.4	S21 41.5	163 04.9	N 7 44.3	75 18.3	S20 41.6
07	343 22.1	290 36.2	20.4	103 06.8	41.4	178 07.3	44.3	90 21.0	41.5
08	358 24.5	305 35.5	21.2	118 10.2	41.4	193 09.7	44.3	105 23.6	41.5
09	13 27.0	320 34.9	. . 22.0	133 13.6	. . 41.4	208 12.1	. . 44.2	120 26.3	. . 41.5
10	28 29.5	335 34.2	22.8	148 17.0	41.3	223 14.5	44.2	135 28.9	41.5
11	43 31.9	350 33.6	23.7	163 20.4	41.3	238 16.9	44.1	150 31.6	41.5
12	58 34.4	5 32.9	N18 24.5	178 23.8	S21 41.2	253 19.3	N 7 44.1	165 34.2	S20 41.4
13	73 36.9	20 32.3	25.3	193 27.2	41.2	268 21.7	44.1	180 36.9	41.4
14	88 39.3	35 31.6	26.1	208 30.6	41.2	283 24.1	44.0	195 39.5	41.4
15	103 41.8	50 30.9	. . 26.9	223 34.0	. . 41.1	298 26.5	. . 44.0	210 42.2	. . 41.4
16	118 44.3	65 30.3	27.8	238 37.4	41.1	313 28.9	43.9	225 44.8	41.4
17	133 46.7	80 29.6	28.6	253 40.8	41.0	328 31.2	43.9	240 47.5	41.3
18	148 49.2	95 29.0	N18 29.4	268 44.2	S21 41.0	343 33.6	N 7 43.9	255 50.1	S20 41.3
19	163 51.6	110 28.3	30.2	283 47.6	40.9	358 36.0	43.8	270 52.8	41.3
20	178 54.1	125 27.6	31.0	298 51.0	40.9	13 38.4	43.8	285 55.4	41.3
21	193 56.6	140 27.0	. . 31.8	313 54.4	. . 40.8	28 40.8	. . 43.7	300 58.1	. . 41.3
22	208 59.0	155 26.3	32.6	328 57.8	40.8	43 43.2	43.7	316 00.7	41.2
23	224 01.5	170 25.6	33.5	344 01.2	40.8	58 45.6	43.7	331 03.4	41.2
Mer. Pass.	h m 8 10.3	v −0.6	d 0.8	v 3.4	d 0.0	v 2.4	d 0.0	v 2.6	d 0.0

STARS

Name	SHA	Dec
	° ′	° ′
Acamar	315 17.3	S40 14.5
Achernar	335 25.9	S57 09.2
Acrux	173 06.5	S63 11.6
Adhara	255 11.3	S29 00.0
Aldebaran	290 47.5	N16 32.2
Alioth	166 18.7	N55 52.5
Alkaid	152 57.0	N49 14.1
Al Na'ir	27 41.4	S46 52.6
Alnilam	275 44.7	S 1 11.8
Alphard	217 54.2	S 8 44.0
Alphecca	126 09.0	N26 39.7
Alpheratz	357 41.6	N29 10.6
Altair	62 06.1	N 8 54.8
Ankaa	353 14.1	S42 12.9
Antares	112 23.5	S26 27.9
Arcturus	145 53.7	N19 06.0
Atria	107 22.9	S69 03.1
Avior	234 17.4	S59 34.2
Bellatrix	278 30.2	N 6 21.6
Betelgeuse	270 59.5	N 7 24.3
Canopus	263 55.7	S52 42.7
Capella	280 32.0	N46 00.6
Deneb	49 29.9	N45 20.2
Denebola	182 31.5	N14 28.9
Diphda	348 54.2	S17 53.9
Dubhe	193 49.3	N61 40.0
Elnath	278 10.5	N28 37.0
Eltanin	90 44.8	N51 29.2
Enif	33 45.2	N 9 57.0
Fomalhaut	15 22.0	S29 32.0
Gacrux	171 58.2	S57 12.5
Gienah	175 50.1	S17 38.1
Hadar	148 44.4	S60 27.1
Hamal	327 58.8	N23 32.1
Kaus Aust.	83 40.9	S34 22.3
Kochab	137 19.1	N74 05.5
Markab	13 36.5	N15 17.5
Menkar	314 13.3	N 4 09.0
Menkent	148 04.8	S36 27.0
Miaplacidus	221 39.3	S69 47.5
Mirfak	308 38.0	N49 54.9
Nunki	75 55.6	S26 16.3
Peacock	53 16.0	S56 40.5
Pollux	243 25.6	N27 59.1
Procyon	244 57.9	N 5 10.7
Rasalhague	96 04.3	N12 33.0
Regulus	207 41.5	N11 53.1
Rigel	281 10.5	S 8 11.3
Rigil Kent.	139 48.3	S60 54.1
Sabik	102 10.0	S15 44.5
Schedar	349 38.5	N56 37.3
Shaula	96 18.9	S37 06.7
Sirius	258 32.3	S16 44.7
Spica	158 28.9	S11 14.8
Suhail	222 51.1	S43 30.3
Vega	80 37.3	N38 47.9
Zuben'ubi	137 02.9	S16 06.5

	SHA	Mer. Pass.
	° ′	h m
Venus	308 50.6	11 37
Mars	119 16.1	0 14
Jupiter	194 47.4	19 09
Saturn	106 53.1	1 04

UT d h	SUN GHA ° ′	SUN Dec ° ′	MOON GHA ° ′	v ′	MOON Dec ° ′	d ′	HP ′
18 00 (WEDNESDAY)	180 53.6	N19 35.7	41 27.2	15.2	S 3 53.8	9.2	54.1
01	195 53.6	36.3	56 01.4	15.3	4 03.0	9.1	54.1
02	210 53.6	36.8	70 35.7	15.3	4 12.1	9.1	54.1
03	225 53.5	. . 37.4	85 10.0	15.3	4 21.2	9.1	54.1
04	240 53.5	37.9	99 44.3	15.2	4 30.3	9.1	54.1
05	255 53.5	38.5	114 18.5	15.2	4 39.4	9.1	54.0
06	270 53.5	N19 39.0	128 52.7	15.3	S 4 48.5	9.1	54.0
07	285 53.4	39.5	143 27.0	15.2	4 57.6	9.0	54.0
08	300 53.4	40.1	158 01.2	15.2	5 06.6	9.0	54.0
09	315 53.4	. . 40.6	172 35.4	15.2	5 15.6	9.0	54.0
10	330 53.4	41.2	187 09.6	15.2	5 24.6	9.0	54.0
11	345 53.3	41.7	201 43.8	15.1	5 33.6	8.9	54.0
12	0 53.3	N19 42.3	216 17.9	15.2	S 5 42.5	9.0	54.0
13	15 53.3	42.8	230 52.1	15.1	5 51.5	8.9	54.0
14	30 53.2	43.3	245 26.2	15.1	6 00.4	8.8	54.0
15	45 53.2	. . 43.9	260 00.3	15.1	6 09.2	8.9	54.0
16	60 53.2	44.4	274 34.4	15.1	6 18.1	8.8	54.0
17	75 53.2	44.9	289 08.5	15.1	6 26.9	8.8	54.0
18	90 53.1	N19 45.5	303 42.6	15.0	S 6 35.7	8.8	54.0
19	105 53.1	46.0	318 16.6	15.1	6 44.5	8.8	54.0
20	120 53.1	46.5	332 50.7	15.0	6 53.3	8.7	54.0
21	135 53.0	. . 47.1	347 24.7	15.0	7 02.0	8.7	54.0
22	150 53.0	47.6	1 58.7	14.9	7 10.7	8.6	54.0
23	165 53.0	48.1	16 32.6	15.0	7 19.3	8.7	54.0
19 00 (THURSDAY)	180 53.0	N19 48.7	31 06.6	14.9	S 7 28.0	8.6	54.0
01	195 52.9	49.2	45 40.5	14.9	7 36.6	8.6	54.0
02	210 52.9	49.7	60 14.4	14.9	7 45.2	8.5	54.0
03	225 52.9	. . 50.3	74 48.3	14.9	7 53.7	8.6	54.0
04	240 52.8	50.8	89 22.2	14.8	8 02.3	8.4	54.0
05	255 52.8	51.3	103 56.0	14.8	8 10.7	8.5	54.0
06	270 52.8	N19 51.9	118 29.8	14.8	S 8 19.2	8.4	54.0
07	285 52.7	52.4	133 03.6	14.8	8 27.6	8.4	54.0
08	300 52.7	52.9	147 37.4	14.7	8 36.0	8.4	54.0
09	315 52.7	. . 53.4	162 11.1	14.7	8 44.4	8.3	54.0
10	330 52.6	54.0	176 44.8	14.7	8 52.7	8.3	54.0
11	345 52.6	54.5	191 18.5	14.7	9 01.0	8.2	54.0
12	0 52.6	N19 55.0	205 52.2	14.6	S 9 09.2	8.2	54.0
13	15 52.5	55.5	220 25.8	14.6	9 17.4	8.2	54.0
14	30 52.5	56.1	234 59.4	14.6	9 25.6	8.2	54.0
15	45 52.5	. . 56.6	249 33.0	14.6	9 33.8	8.1	54.0
16	60 52.4	57.1	264 06.6	14.5	9 41.9	8.0	54.0
17	75 52.4	57.6	278 40.1	14.5	9 49.9	8.0	54.1
18	90 52.4	N19 58.2	293 13.6	14.5	S 9 57.9	8.0	54.1
19	105 52.3	58.7	307 47.1	14.4	10 05.9	8.0	54.1
20	120 52.3	59.2	322 20.5	14.4	10 13.9	7.9	54.1
21	135 52.3	19 59.7	336 53.9	14.4	10 21.8	7.8	54.1
22	150 52.2	20 00.2	351 27.3	14.3	10 29.6	7.9	54.1
23	165 52.2	00.8	6 00.6	14.3	10 37.5	7.7	54.1
20 00 (FRIDAY)	180 52.2	N20 01.3	20 33.9	14.3	S10 45.2	7.8	54.1
01	195 52.1	01.8	35 07.2	14.3	10 53.0	7.7	54.1
02	210 52.1	02.3	49 40.5	14.2	11 00.7	7.6	54.1
03	225 52.1	. . 02.8	64 13.7	14.2	11 08.3	7.6	54.1
04	240 52.0	03.4	78 46.9	14.1	11 15.9	7.6	54.1
05	255 52.0	03.9	93 20.0	14.1	11 23.5	7.5	54.1
06	270 52.0	N20 04.4	107 53.1	14.1	S11 31.0	7.4	54.1
07	285 51.9	04.9	122 26.2	14.1	11 38.4	7.4	54.1
08	300 51.9	05.4	136 59.3	14.0	11 45.8	7.4	54.1
09	315 51.8	. . 05.9	151 32.3	14.0	11 53.2	7.3	54.1
10	330 51.8	06.4	166 05.3	13.9	12 00.5	7.3	54.1
11	345 51.8	06.9	180 38.2	13.9	12 07.8	7.2	54.1
12	0 51.7	N20 07.5	195 11.1	13.9	S12 15.0	7.2	54.1
13	15 51.7	08.0	209 44.0	13.9	12 22.2	7.1	54.2
14	30 51.6	08.5	224 16.9	13.8	12 29.3	7.1	54.2
15	45 51.6	. . 09.0	238 49.7	13.7	12 36.4	7.0	54.2
16	60 51.6	09.5	253 22.4	13.8	12 43.4	7.0	54.2
17	75 51.5	10.0	267 55.2	13.7	12 50.4	6.9	54.2
18	90 51.5	N20 10.5	282 27.9	13.6	S12 57.3	6.8	54.2
19	105 51.4	11.0	297 00.5	13.6	13 04.1	6.8	54.2
20	120 51.4	11.5	311 33.1	13.6	13 10.9	6.8	54.2
21	135 51.4	. . 12.0	326 05.7	13.6	13 17.7	6.7	54.2
22	150 51.3	12.5	340 38.3	13.5	13 24.4	6.6	54.2
23	165 51.3	13.0	355 10.8	13.5	S13 31.0	6.6	54.2
	SD 15.8	*d* 0.5	SD 14.7		14.7		14.8

Lat. °	Twilight Naut. h m	Twilight Civil h m	Sunrise h m	Moonrise 18 h m	Moonrise 19 h m	Moonrise 20 h m	Moonrise 21 h m
N 72	▭	▭	▭	17 06	18 42	20 21	22 07
N 70	▭	▭	▭	16 57	18 25	19 55	21 26
68	////	////	01 21	16 49	18 12	19 35	20 58
66	////	////	02 05	16 42	18 01	19 20	20 37
64	////	00 25	02 33	16 37	17 52	19 07	20 20
62	////	01 32	02 55	16 32	17 44	18 56	20 06
60	////	02 05	03 13	16 28	17 38	18 47	19 55
N 58	00 22	02 29	03 27	16 24	17 32	18 39	19 45
56	01 23	02 48	03 40	16 21	17 27	18 32	19 36
54	01 54	03 03	03 50	16 18	17 22	18 26	19 28
52	02 16	03 17	04 00	16 15	17 18	18 20	19 21
50	02 34	03 28	04 08	16 13	17 14	18 15	19 15
45	03 07	03 52	04 26	16 08	17 06	18 04	19 02
N 40	03 31	04 10	04 41	16 04	16 59	17 55	18 51
35	03 50	04 25	04 53	16 00	16 53	17 47	18 41
30	04 06	04 38	05 04	15 57	16 48	17 40	18 33
20	04 30	04 59	05 22	15 51	16 40	17 29	18 19
N 10	04 49	05 16	05 38	15 46	16 32	17 19	18 06
0	05 05	05 31	05 53	15 42	16 25	17 09	17 55
S 10	05 19	05 45	06 07	15 37	16 18	16 59	17 43
20	05 33	06 00	06 23	15 32	16 10	16 49	17 31
30	05 46	06 15	06 40	15 27	16 01	16 38	17 17
35	05 53	06 23	06 51	15 24	15 56	16 31	17 09
40	06 00	06 33	07 02	15 20	15 51	16 24	17 00
45	06 08	06 44	07 16	15 16	15 44	16 15	16 49
S 50	06 16	06 56	07 33	15 11	15 37	16 05	16 36
52	06 20	07 02	07 40	15 09	15 33	16 00	16 31
54	06 24	07 08	07 49	15 07	15 29	15 55	16 24
56	06 29	07 15	07 59	15 04	15 25	15 49	16 17
58	06 34	07 23	08 10	15 01	15 20	15 42	16 08
S 60	06 39	07 32	08 23	14 58	15 15	15 35	15 59

Lat. °	Sunset h m	Twilight Civil h m	Twilight Naut. h m	Moonset 18 h m	Moonset 19 h m	Moonset 20 h m	Moonset 21 h m
N 72	▭	▭	▭	02 24	02 19	02 13	02 06
N 70	▭	▭	▭	02 30	02 30	02 31	02 33
68	22 39	////	////	02 35	02 39	02 45	02 54
66	21 52	////	////	02 39	02 47	02 57	03 10
64	21 22	////	////	02 42	02 54	03 07	03 23
62	21 00	22 25	////	02 45	03 00	03 15	03 35
60	20 42	21 51	////	02 48	03 04	03 23	03 45
N 58	20 27	21 26	////	02 51	03 09	03 29	03 53
56	20 15	21 07	22 34	02 53	03 13	03 35	04 01
54	20 04	20 51	22 02	02 55	03 16	03 40	04 07
52	19 54	20 38	21 39	02 56	03 20	03 45	04 13
50	19 45	20 26	21 21	02 58	03 23	03 49	04 19
45	19 27	20 02	20 47	03 01	03 29	03 58	04 31
N 40	19 12	19 44	20 22	03 04	03 34	04 06	04 40
35	19 00	19 28	20 03	03 07	03 39	04 13	04 49
30	18 49	19 16	19 47	03 09	03 43	04 18	04 56
20	18 31	18 55	19 23	03 13	03 50	04 29	05 09
N 10	18 15	18 37	19 04	03 16	03 56	04 38	05 20
0	18 00	18 22	18 48	03 20	04 02	04 46	05 31
S 10	17 45	18 08	18 33	03 23	04 08	04 54	05 41
20	17 30	17 53	18 20	03 26	04 14	05 03	05 53
30	17 12	17 38	18 07	03 30	04 22	05 13	06 06
35	17 02	17 29	18 00	03 32	04 26	05 19	06 13
40	16 50	17 20	17 53	03 35	04 30	05 26	06 22
45	16 37	17 09	17 45	03 38	04 36	05 34	06 32
S 50	16 20	16 56	17 36	03 41	04 42	05 43	06 44
52	16 12	16 50	17 32	03 43	04 45	05 48	06 50
54	16 03	16 44	17 28	03 45	04 49	05 53	06 56
56	15 54	16 37	17 24	03 47	04 53	05 58	07 03
58	15 43	16 29	17 19	03 49	04 57	06 04	07 11
S 60	15 30	16 21	17 13	03 51	05 01	06 11	07 19

Day d	SUN Eqn. of Time 00^h m s	SUN Eqn. of Time 12^h m s	SUN Mer. Pass. h m	MOON Mer. Pass. Upper h m	MOON Mer. Pass. Lower h m	MOON Age d	MOON Phase %
18	03 35	03 33	11 56	21 52	09 31	12	90
19	03 32	03 30	11 56	22 35	10 13	13	95
20	03 29	03 27	11 57	23 20	10 57	14	98

	UT d h	ARIES GHA ° ′	VENUS −3·9 GHA ° ′	VENUS Dec ° ′	MARS −2·1 GHA ° ′	MARS Dec ° ′	JUPITER −2·1 GHA ° ′	JUPITER Dec ° ′	SATURN +0·1 GHA ° ′	SATURN Dec ° ′
	21 00	239 04.0	185 25.0	N18 34.3	359 04.6	S21 40.7	73 48.0	N 7 43.6	346 06.1	S20 41.2
	01	254 06.4	200 24.3	35.1	14 08.0	40.7	88 50.4	43.6	1 08.7	41.2
	02	269 08.9	215 23.6	35.9	29 11.4	40.6	103 52.7	43.5	16 11.4	41.2
	03	284 11.4	230 23.0	. . 36.7	44 14.8	. . 40.6	118 55.1	. . 43.5	31 14.0	. . 41.1
	04	299 13.8	245 22.3	37.5	59 18.2	40.5	133 57.5	43.5	46 16.7	41.1
	05	314 16.3	260 21.6	38.3	74 21.6	40.5	148 59.9	43.4	61 19.3	41.1
	06	329 18.7	275 21.0	N18 39.1	89 25.0	S21 40.4	164 02.3	N 7 43.4	76 22.0	S20 41.1
	07	344 21.2	290 20.3	39.9	104 28.4	40.4	179 04.7	43.3	91 24.6	41.1
S	08	359 23.7	305 19.6	40.7	119 31.8	40.4	194 07.1	43.3	106 27.3	41.0
A	09	14 26.1	320 19.0	. . 41.5	134 35.2	. . 40.3	209 09.4	. . 43.2	121 29.9	. . 41.0
T	10	29 28.6	335 18.3	42.3	149 38.6	40.3	224 11.8	43.2	136 32.6	41.0
U	11	44 31.1	350 17.6	43.1	164 42.0	40.2	239 14.2	43.2	151 35.2	41.0
R	12	59 33.5	5 17.0	N18 43.9	179 45.4	S21 40.2	254 16.6	N 7 43.1	166 37.9	S20 41.0
D	13	74 36.0	20 16.3	44.7	194 48.8	40.1	269 19.0	43.1	181 40.5	40.9
A	14	89 38.5	35 15.6	45.5	209 52.2	40.1	284 21.4	43.0	196 43.2	40.9
Y	15	104 40.9	50 15.0	. . 46.3	224 55.6	. . 40.0	299 23.7	. . 43.0	211 45.8	. . 40.9
	16	119 43.4	65 14.3	47.1	239 59.0	40.0	314 26.1	42.9	226 48.5	40.9
	17	134 45.9	80 13.6	47.9	255 02.4	39.9	329 28.5	42.9	241 51.1	40.9
	18	149 48.3	95 12.9	N18 48.7	270 05.8	S21 39.9	344 30.9	N 7 42.9	256 53.8	S20 40.8
	19	164 50.8	110 12.3	49.5	285 09.2	39.9	359 33.3	42.8	271 56.4	40.8
	20	179 53.2	125 11.6	50.3	300 12.6	39.8	14 35.7	42.8	286 59.1	40.8
	21	194 55.7	140 10.9	. . 51.1	315 16.0	. . 39.8	29 38.0	. . 42.7	302 01.8	. . 40.8
	22	209 58.2	155 10.2	51.9	330 19.4	39.7	44 40.4	42.7	317 04.4	40.8
	23	225 00.6	170 09.6	52.7	345 22.8	39.7	59 42.8	42.6	332 07.1	40.7
	22 00	240 03.1	185 08.9	N18 53.5	0 26.2	S21 39.6	74 45.2	N 7 42.6	347 09.7	S20 40.7
	01	255 05.6	200 08.2	54.3	15 29.7	39.6	89 47.6	42.6	2 12.4	40.7
	02	270 08.0	215 07.5	55.1	30 33.1	39.5	104 49.9	42.5	17 15.0	40.7
	03	285 10.5	230 06.9	. . 55.9	45 36.5	. . 39.5	119 52.3	. . 42.5	32 17.7	. . 40.7
	04	300 13.0	245 06.2	56.7	60 39.9	39.4	134 54.7	42.4	47 20.3	40.6
	05	315 15.4	260 05.5	57.4	75 43.3	39.4	149 57.1	42.4	62 23.0	40.6
	06	330 17.9	275 04.8	N18 58.2	90 46.7	S21 39.3	164 59.5	N 7 42.3	77 25.6	S20 40.6
	07	345 20.4	290 04.1	59.0	105 50.1	39.3	180 01.8	42.3	92 28.3	40.6
	08	0 22.8	305 03.5	18 59.8	120 53.5	39.2	195 04.2	42.2	107 30.9	40.6
S	09	15 25.3	320 02.8	19 00.6	135 56.9	. . 39.2	210 06.6	. . 42.2	122 33.6	. . 40.5
U	10	30 27.7	335 02.1	01.4	151 00.3	39.1	225 09.0	42.2	137 36.2	40.5
N	11	45 30.2	350 01.4	02.1	166 03.7	39.1	240 11.3	42.1	152 38.9	40.5
D	12	60 32.7	5 00.7	N19 02.9	181 07.1	S21 39.0	255 13.7	N 7 42.1	167 41.6	S20 40.5
A	13	75 35.1	20 00.1	03.7	196 10.6	39.0	270 16.1	42.0	182 44.2	40.5
Y	14	90 37.6	34 59.4	04.5	211 14.0	38.9	285 18.5	42.0	197 46.9	40.4
	15	105 40.1	49 58.7	. . 05.3	226 17.4	. . 38.9	300 20.9	. . 41.9	212 49.5	. . 40.4
	16	120 42.5	64 58.0	06.0	241 20.8	38.8	315 23.2	41.9	227 52.2	40.4
	17	135 45.0	79 57.3	06.8	256 24.2	38.8	330 25.6	41.8	242 54.8	40.4
	18	150 47.5	94 56.6	N19 07.6	271 27.6	S21 38.7	345 28.0	N 7 41.8	257 57.5	S20 40.4
	19	165 49.9	109 56.0	08.4	286 31.0	38.7	0 30.4	41.7	273 00.1	40.3
	20	180 52.4	124 55.3	09.1	301 34.4	38.6	15 32.7	41.7	288 02.8	40.3
	21	195 54.8	139 54.6	. . 09.9	316 37.8	. . 38.6	30 35.1	. . 41.7	303 05.4	. . 40.3
	22	210 57.3	154 53.9	10.7	331 41.3	38.5	45 37.5	41.6	318 08.1	40.3
	23	225 59.8	169 53.2	11.5	346 44.7	38.5	60 39.9	41.6	333 10.7	40.3
	23 00	241 02.2	184 52.5	N19 12.2	1 48.1	S21 38.4	75 42.2	N 7 41.5	348 13.4	S20 40.2
	01	256 04.7	199 51.8	13.0	16 51.5	38.4	90 44.6	41.5	3 16.1	40.2
	02	271 07.2	214 51.2	13.8	31 54.9	38.3	105 47.0	41.4	18 18.7	40.2
	03	286 09.6	229 50.5	. . 14.5	46 58.3	. . 38.3	120 49.3	. . 41.4	33 21.4	. . 40.2
	04	301 12.1	244 49.8	15.3	62 01.7	38.2	135 51.7	41.3	48 24.0	40.2
	05	316 14.6	259 49.1	16.1	77 05.1	38.2	150 54.1	41.3	63 26.7	40.1
	06	331 17.0	274 48.4	N19 16.8	92 08.5	S21 38.1	165 56.5	N 7 41.2	78 29.3	S20 40.1
	07	346 19.5	289 47.7	17.6	107 12.0	38.1	180 58.8	41.2	93 32.0	40.1
	08	1 22.0	304 47.0	18.4	122 15.4	38.0	196 01.2	41.1	108 34.6	40.1
M	09	16 24.4	319 46.3	. . 19.1	137 18.8	. . 38.0	211 03.6	. . 41.1	123 37.3	. . 40.1
O	10	31 26.9	334 45.6	19.9	152 22.2	37.9	226 06.0	41.0	138 39.9	40.0
N	11	46 29.3	349 44.9	20.6	167 25.6	37.8	241 08.3	41.0	153 42.6	40.0
D	12	61 31.8	4 44.2	N19 21.4	182 29.0	S21 37.8	256 10.7	N 7 41.0	168 45.3	S20 40.0
A	13	76 34.3	19 43.6	22.2	197 32.4	37.7	271 13.1	40.9	183 47.9	40.0
Y	14	91 36.7	34 42.9	22.9	212 35.9	37.7	286 15.4	40.9	198 50.6	40.0
	15	106 39.2	49 42.2	. . 23.7	227 39.3	. . 37.6	301 17.8	. . 40.8	213 53.2	. . 39.9
	16	121 41.7	64 41.5	24.4	242 42.7	37.6	316 20.2	40.8	228 55.9	39.9
	17	136 44.1	79 40.8	25.2	257 46.1	37.5	331 22.5	40.7	243 58.5	39.9
	18	151 46.6	94 40.1	N19 25.9	272 49.5	S21 37.5	346 24.9	N 7 40.7	259 01.2	S20 39.9
	19	166 49.1	109 39.4	26.7	287 52.9	37.4	1 27.3	40.6	274 03.8	39.9
	20	181 51.5	124 38.7	27.4	302 56.3	37.4	16 29.6	40.6	289 06.5	39.8
	21	196 54.0	139 38.0	. . 28.2	317 59.8	. . 37.3	31 32.0	. . 40.5	304 09.1	. . 39.8
	22	211 56.5	154 37.3	29.0	333 03.2	37.3	46 34.4	40.5	319 11.8	39.8
	23	226 58.9	169 36.6	29.7	348 06.6	37.2	61 36.8	40.4	334 14.5	39.8
	Mer. Pass.	h m 7 58.5	*v* −0.7	*d* 0.8	*v* 3.4	*d* 0.0	*v* 2.4	*d* 0.0	*v* 2.7	*d* 0.0

STARS

Name	SHA ° ′	Dec ° ′
Acamar	315 17.3	S40 14.5
Achernar	335 25.9	S57 09.2
Acrux	173 06.5	S63 11.6
Adhara	255 11.3	S29 00.0
Aldebaran	290 47.5	N16 32.2
Alioth	166 18.7	N55 52.5
Alkaid	152 57.0	N49 14.1
Al Na'ir	27 41.4	S46 52.6
Alnilam	275 44.7	S 1 11.8
Alphard	217 54.2	S 8 44.0
Alphecca	126 09.0	N26 39.7
Alpheratz	357 41.6	N29 10.6
Altair	62 06.1	N 8 54.8
Ankaa	353 14.1	S42 12.9
Antares	112 23.5	S26 27.9
Arcturus	145 53.7	N19 06.0
Atria	107 22.9	S69 03.1
Avior	234 17.4	S59 34.1
Bellatrix	278 30.2	N 6 21.6
Betelgeuse	270 59.5	N 7 24.3
Canopus	263 55.7	S52 42.6
Capella	280 32.0	N46 00.6
Deneb	49 29.9	N45 20.2
Denebola	182 31.6	N14 28.9
Diphda	348 54.2	S17 53.9
Dubhe	193 49.3	N61 40.0
Elnath	278 10.5	N28 37.0
Eltanin	90 44.7	N51 29.3
Enif	33 45.1	N 9 57.0
Fomalhaut	15 21.9	S29 32.0
Gacrux	171 58.2	S57 12.5
Gienah	175 50.1	S17 38.1
Hadar	148 44.4	S60 27.2
Hamal	327 58.8	N23 32.1
Kaus Aust.	83 40.9	S34 22.3
Kochab	137 19.2	N74 05.5
Markab	13 36.4	N15 17.5
Menkar	314 13.3	N 4 09.0
Menkent	148 04.8	S36 27.0
Miaplacidus	221 39.3	S69 47.5
Mirfak	308 38.0	N49 54.9
Nunki	75 55.6	S26 16.3
Peacock	53 16.0	S56 40.5
Pollux	243 25.6	N27 59.1
Procyon	244 57.9	N 5 10.7
Rasalhague	96 04.3	N12 33.0
Regulus	207 41.5	N11 53.2
Rigel	281 10.5	S 8 11.3
Rigil Kent.	139 48.3	S60 54.1
Sabik	102 10.0	S15 44.5
Schedar	349 38.5	N56 37.3
Shaula	96 18.9	S37 06.7
Sirius	258 32.3	S16 44.6
Spica	158 28.9	S11 14.8
Suhail	222 51.1	S43 30.3
Vega	80 37.3	N38 48.0
Zuben'ubi	137 02.9	S16 06.5

	SHA ° ′	Mer. Pass. h m
Venus	305 05.8	11 40
Mars	120 23.1	23 53
Jupiter	194 42.1	18 58
Saturn	107 06.6	0 51

UT d h		SUN GHA	SUN Dec	MOON GHA	v	Dec	d	HP
		° ′	° ′	° ′	′	° ′	′	′
21 00		180 51.2	N20 13.5	9 43.3	13.4	S13 37.6	6.5	54.2
01		195 51.2	14.0	24 15.7	13.4	13 44.1	6.5	54.2
02		210 51.2	14.6	38 48.1	13.4	13 50.6	6.4	54.3
03		225 51.1	. . 15.1	53 20.5	13.3	13 57.0	6.3	54.3
04		240 51.1	15.6	67 52.8	13.3	14 03.3	6.3	54.3
05		255 51.0	16.1	82 25.1	13.2	14 09.6	6.2	54.3
06		270 51.0	N20 16.6	96 57.3	13.2	S14 15.8	6.2	54.3
07		285 51.0	17.1	111 29.5	13.2	14 22.0	6.1	54.3
08	S	300 50.9	17.6	126 01.7	13.1	14 28.1	6.0	54.3
09	A	315 50.9	. . 18.1	140 33.8	13.1	14 34.1	6.0	54.3
10	T	330 50.8	18.6	155 05.9	13.0	14 40.1	5.9	54.3
11	U	345 50.8	19.0	169 37.9	13.1	14 46.0	5.9	54.3
12	R	0 50.7	N20 19.5	184 10.0	12.9	S14 51.9	5.8	54.4
13	D	15 50.7	20.0	198 41.9	13.0	14 57.7	5.7	54.4
14	A	30 50.6	20.5	213 13.9	12.9	15 03.4	5.6	54.4
15	Y	45 50.6	. . 21.0	227 45.8	12.8	15 09.0	5.6	54.4
16		60 50.6	21.5	242 17.6	12.8	15 14.6	5.6	54.4
17		75 50.5	22.0	256 49.4	12.8	15 20.2	5.4	54.4
18		90 50.5	N20 22.5	271 21.2	12.7	S15 25.6	5.4	54.4
19		105 50.4	23.0	285 52.9	12.7	15 31.0	5.3	54.4
20		120 50.4	23.5	300 24.6	12.7	15 36.3	5.3	54.4
21		135 50.3	. . 24.0	314 56.3	12.6	15 41.6	5.2	54.4
22		150 50.3	24.5	329 27.9	12.6	15 46.8	5.1	54.5
23		165 50.2	25.0	343 59.5	12.5	15 51.9	5.0	54.5
22 00		180 50.2	N20 25.5	358 31.0	12.6	S15 56.9	5.0	54.5
01		195 50.1	25.9	13 02.6	12.4	16 01.9	4.9	54.5
02		210 50.1	26.4	27 34.0	12.4	16 06.8	4.8	54.5
03		225 50.0	. . 26.9	42 05.4	12.4	16 11.6	4.8	54.5
04		240 50.0	27.4	56 36.8	12.4	16 16.4	4.7	54.5
05		255 50.0	27.9	71 08.2	12.3	16 21.1	4.6	54.5
06		270 49.9	N20 28.4	85 39.5	12.3	S16 25.7	4.5	54.6
07		285 49.9	28.9	100 10.8	12.2	16 30.2	4.5	54.6
08		300 49.8	29.4	114 42.0	12.2	16 34.7	4.3	54.6
09	S	315 49.8	. . 29.8	129 13.2	12.2	16 39.0	4.4	54.6
10	U	330 49.7	30.3	143 44.4	12.1	16 43.4	4.2	54.6
11	N	345 49.7	30.8	158 15.5	12.1	16 47.6	4.1	54.6
12	D	0 49.6	N20 31.3	172 46.6	12.0	S16 51.7	4.1	54.6
13	A	15 49.6	31.8	187 17.6	12.0	16 55.8	4.0	54.6
14	Y	30 49.5	32.2	201 48.6	12.0	16 59.8	3.9	54.7
15		45 49.5	. . 32.7	216 19.6	11.9	17 03.7	3.9	54.7
16		60 49.4	33.2	230 50.5	11.9	17 07.6	3.7	54.7
17		75 49.4	33.7	245 21.4	11.9	17 11.3	3.7	54.7
18		90 49.3	N20 34.2	259 52.3	11.8	S17 15.0	3.6	54.7
19		105 49.3	34.6	274 23.1	11.8	17 18.6	3.6	54.7
20		120 49.2	35.1	288 53.9	11.8	17 22.2	3.4	54.7
21		135 49.2	. . 35.6	303 24.7	11.7	17 25.6	3.4	54.8
22		150 49.1	36.1	317 55.4	11.7	17 29.0	3.2	54.8
23		165 49.1	36.5	332 26.1	11.6	17 32.2	3.2	54.8
23 00		180 49.0	N20 37.0	346 56.7	11.6	S17 35.4	3.1	54.8
01		195 49.0	37.5	1 27.3	11.6	17 38.5	3.1	54.8
02		210 48.9	38.0	15 57.9	11.6	17 41.6	2.9	54.8
03		225 48.8	. . 38.4	30 28.5	11.5	17 44.5	2.9	54.8
04		240 48.8	38.9	44 59.0	11.5	17 47.4	2.8	54.9
05		255 48.7	39.4	59 29.5	11.4	17 50.2	2.7	54.9
06		270 48.7	N20 39.9	73 59.9	11.4	S17 52.9	2.6	54.9
07		285 48.6	40.3	88 30.3	11.4	17 55.5	2.5	54.9
08		300 48.6	40.8	103 00.7	11.4	17 58.0	2.4	54.9
09	M	315 48.5	. . 41.3	117 31.1	11.3	18 00.4	2.4	54.9
10	O	330 48.5	41.7	132 01.4	11.3	18 02.8	2.2	55.0
11	N	345 48.4	42.2	146 31.7	11.3	18 05.0	2.2	55.0
12	D	0 48.4	N20 42.7	161 02.0	11.2	S18 07.2	2.1	55.0
13	A	15 48.3	43.1	175 32.2	11.2	18 09.3	2.0	55.0
14	Y	30 48.3	43.6	190 02.4	11.2	18 11.3	1.9	55.0
15		45 48.2	. . 44.1	204 32.6	11.1	18 13.2	1.8	55.0
16		60 48.1	44.5	219 02.7	11.1	18 15.0	1.7	55.0
17		75 48.1	45.0	233 32.8	11.1	18 16.7	1.7	55.1
18		90 48.0	N20 45.5	248 02.9	11.1	S18 18.4	1.5	55.1
19		105 48.0	45.9	262 33.0	11.0	18 19.9	1.5	55.1
20		120 47.9	46.4	277 03.0	11.0	18 21.4	1.4	55.1
21		135 47.9	. . 46.9	291 33.0	11.0	18 22.8	1.3	55.1
22		150 47.8	47.3	306 03.0	10.9	18 24.1	1.2	55.1
23		165 47.7	47.8	320 32.9	11.0	S18 25.3	1.1	55.2
		SD 15.8	*d* 0.5	SD 14.8		14.9		15.0

Lat.	Twilight Naut.	Twilight Civil	Sunrise	Moonrise 21	22	23	24
°	h m	h m	h m	h m	h m	h m	h m
N 72	□	□	□	22 07	24 09	00 09	■
N 70	□	□	□	21 26	22 53	24 09	00 09
68	////	////	00 59	20 58	22 16	23 23	24 13
66	////	////	01 52	20 37	21 49	22 53	23 43
64	////	////	02 24	20 20	21 29	22 30	23 21
62	////	01 18	02 48	20 06	21 13	22 12	23 03
60	////	01 55	03 06	19 55	20 59	21 57	22 48
N 58	////	02 21	03 22	19 45	20 47	21 45	22 35
56	01 10	02 42	03 35	19 36	20 37	21 34	22 25
54	01 45	02 58	03 46	19 28	20 28	21 24	22 15
52	02 09	03 12	03 56	19 21	20 20	21 16	22 06
50	02 28	03 24	04 05	19 15	20 13	21 08	21 59
45	03 03	03 48	04 24	19 02	19 58	20 52	21 42
N 40	03 28	04 07	04 39	18 51	19 45	20 38	21 29
35	03 48	04 23	04 52	18 41	19 35	20 27	21 17
30	04 04	04 36	05 03	18 33	19 25	20 17	21 07
20	04 29	04 58	05 22	18 19	19 09	20 00	20 50
N 10	04 49	05 15	05 38	18 06	18 55	19 45	20 35
0	05 05	05 31	05 53	17 55	18 42	19 31	20 21
S 10	05 20	05 46	06 08	17 43	18 29	19 17	20 07
20	05 34	06 01	06 24	17 31	18 15	19 03	19 52
30	05 47	06 17	06 42	17 17	18 00	18 46	19 35
35	05 54	06 25	06 53	17 09	17 51	18 36	19 25
40	06 02	06 35	07 05	17 00	17 40	18 25	19 14
45	06 10	06 46	07 19	16 49	17 28	18 12	19 01
S 50	06 20	07 00	07 36	16 36	17 13	17 56	18 44
52	06 24	07 06	07 44	16 31	17 06	17 48	18 37
54	06 28	07 12	07 53	16 24	16 58	17 40	18 28
56	06 33	07 20	08 04	16 17	16 50	17 30	18 19
58	06 38	07 28	08 15	16 08	16 40	17 20	18 08
S 60	06 44	07 37	08 29	15 59	16 29	17 07	17 55

Lat.	Sunset	Twilight Civil	Twilight Naut.	Moonset 21	22	23	24
°	h m	h m	h m	h m	h m	h m	h m
N 72	□	□	□	02 06	01 56	01 33	■
N 70	□	□	□	02 33	02 38	02 49	03 16
68	23 03	////	////	02 54	03 06	03 27	04 02
66	22 05	////	////	03 10	03 28	03 54	04 32
64	21 32	////	////	03 23	03 45	04 15	04 55
62	21 08	22 40	////	03 35	03 59	04 31	05 13
60	20 49	22 01	////	03 45	04 11	04 45	05 28
N 58	20 33	21 34	////	03 53	04 22	04 57	05 41
56	20 20	21 13	22 47	04 01	04 31	05 07	05 52
54	20 08	20 57	22 11	04 07	04 39	05 17	06 01
52	19 58	20 43	21 46	04 13	04 46	05 25	06 10
50	19 49	20 30	21 27	04 19	04 53	05 32	06 18
45	19 30	20 06	20 51	04 31	05 07	05 48	06 34
N 40	19 15	19 46	20 26	04 40	05 18	06 01	06 48
35	19 02	19 31	20 06	04 49	05 28	06 12	06 59
30	18 51	19 18	19 50	04 56	05 37	06 21	07 09
20	18 32	18 56	19 24	05 09	05 52	06 38	07 26
N 10	18 16	18 38	19 05	05 20	06 05	06 52	07 41
0	18 00	18 22	18 48	05 31	06 18	07 06	07 55
S 10	17 45	18 08	18 33	05 41	06 30	07 19	08 09
20	17 29	17 53	18 20	05 53	06 43	07 34	08 24
30	17 11	17 37	18 06	06 06	06 58	07 50	08 41
35	17 00	17 28	17 59	06 13	07 07	08 00	08 51
40	16 48	17 18	17 51	06 22	07 17	08 11	09 03
45	16 34	17 07	17 43	06 32	07 29	08 24	09 16
S 50	16 17	16 53	17 33	06 44	07 43	08 40	09 32
52	16 09	16 47	17 29	06 50	07 50	08 47	09 40
54	15 59	16 41	17 25	06 56	07 57	08 55	09 49
56	15 49	16 33	17 20	07 03	08 05	09 04	09 58
58	15 38	16 25	17 15	07 11	08 15	09 15	10 09
S 60	15 24	16 16	17 09	07 19	08 26	09 27	10 22

Day	SUN Eqn. of Time 00^h	12^h	Mer. Pass.	MOON Mer. Pass. Upper	Lower	Age	Phase
d	m s	m s	h m	h m	h m	d %	
21	03 25	03 23	11 57	24 06	11 43	15 100	○
22	03 21	03 19	11 57	00 06	12 30	16 99	
23	03 16	03 14	11 57	00 54	13 18	17 97	

UT d	h	ARIES GHA	VENUS −3·9 GHA	Dec	MARS −2·0 GHA	Dec	JUPITER −2·1 GHA	Dec	SATURN +0·0 GHA	Dec
		° ′	° ′	° ′	° ′	° ′	° ′	° ′	° ′	° ′
24	00	242 01.4	184 35.9	N19 30.4	3 10.0	S21 37.1	76 39.1	N 7 40.4	349 17.1	S20 39.8
	01	257 03.8	199 35.2	31.2	18 13.4	37.1	91 41.5	40.3	4 19.8	39.7
	02	272 06.3	214 34.5	31.9	33 16.8	37.0	106 43.9	40.3	19 22.4	39.7
	03	287 08.8	229 33.8	. . 32.7	48 20.2	. . 37.0	121 46.2	. . 40.2	34 25.1	. . 39.7
	04	302 11.2	244 33.1	33.4	63 23.7	36.9	136 48.6	40.2	49 27.7	39.7
	05	317 13.7	259 32.4	34.2	78 27.1	36.9	151 51.0	40.1	64 30.4	39.7
	06	332 16.2	274 31.7	N19 34.9	93 30.5	S21 36.8	166 53.3	N 7 40.1	79 33.0	S20 39.6
	07	347 18.6	289 31.0	35.7	108 33.9	36.8	181 55.7	40.0	94 35.7	39.6
T	08	2 21.1	304 30.3	36.4	123 37.3	36.7	196 58.0	40.0	109 38.4	39.6
U	09	17 23.6	319 29.6	. . 37.1	138 40.7	. . 36.7	212 00.4	. . 39.9	124 41.0	. . 39.6
E	10	32 26.0	334 28.9	37.9	153 44.2	36.6	227 02.8	39.9	139 43.7	39.6
S	11	47 28.5	349 28.2	38.6	168 47.6	36.5	242 05.1	39.8	154 46.3	39.5
D	12	62 31.0	4 27.5	N19 39.4	183 51.0	S21 36.5	257 07.5	N 7 39.8	169 49.0	S20 39.5
A	13	77 33.4	19 26.8	40.1	198 54.4	36.4	272 09.9	39.7	184 51.6	39.5
Y	14	92 35.9	34 26.1	40.8	213 57.8	36.4	287 12.2	39.7	199 54.3	39.5
	15	107 38.3	49 25.3	. . 41.6	229 01.2	. . 36.3	302 14.6	. . 39.6	214 57.0	. . 39.5
	16	122 40.8	64 24.6	42.3	244 04.7	36.3	317 17.0	39.6	229 59.6	39.4
	17	137 43.3	79 23.9	43.0	259 08.1	36.2	332 19.3	39.5	245 02.3	39.4
	18	152 45.7	94 23.2	N19 43.8	274 11.5	S21 36.1	347 21.7	N 7 39.5	260 04.9	S20 39.4
	19	167 48.2	109 22.5	44.5	289 14.9	36.1	2 24.0	39.4	275 07.6	39.4
	20	182 50.7	124 21.8	45.2	304 18.3	36.0	17 26.4	39.4	290 10.2	39.4
	21	197 53.1	139 21.1	. . 46.0	319 21.7	. . 36.0	32 28.8	. . 39.3	305 12.9	. . 39.3
	22	212 55.6	154 20.4	46.7	334 25.1	35.9	47 31.1	39.3	320 15.5	39.3
	23	227 58.1	169 19.7	47.4	349 28.6	35.9	62 33.5	39.2	335 18.2	39.3
25	00	243 00.5	184 19.0	N19 48.1	4 32.0	S21 35.8	77 35.9	N 7 39.2	350 20.9	S20 39.3
	01	258 03.0	199 18.3	48.9	19 35.4	35.7	92 38.2	39.1	5 23.5	39.3
	02	273 05.5	214 17.6	49.6	34 38.8	35.7	107 40.6	39.0	20 26.2	39.2
	03	288 07.9	229 16.8	. . 50.3	49 42.2	. . 35.6	122 42.9	. . 39.0	35 28.8	. . 39.2
	04	303 10.4	244 16.1	51.0	64 45.6	35.6	137 45.3	38.9	50 31.5	39.2
	05	318 12.8	259 15.4	51.8	79 49.1	35.5	152 47.7	38.9	65 34.1	39.2
	06	333 15.3	274 14.7	N19 52.5	94 52.5	S21 35.4	167 50.0	N 7 38.8	80 36.8	S20 39.2
W	07	348 17.8	289 14.0	53.2	109 55.9	35.4	182 52.4	38.8	95 39.5	39.1
E	08	3 20.2	304 13.3	53.9	124 59.3	35.3	197 54.7	38.7	110 42.1	39.1
D	09	18 22.7	319 12.6	. . 54.7	140 02.7	. . 35.3	212 57.1	. . 38.7	125 44.8	. . 39.1
N	10	33 25.2	334 11.8	55.4	155 06.1	35.2	227 59.4	38.6	140 47.4	39.1
E	11	48 27.6	349 11.1	56.1	170 09.6	35.2	243 01.8	38.6	155 50.1	39.1
S	12	63 30.1	4 10.4	N19 56.8	185 13.0	S21 35.1	258 04.2	N 7 38.5	170 52.7	S20 39.0
D	13	78 32.6	19 09.7	57.5	200 16.4	35.0	273 06.5	38.5	185 55.4	39.0
A	14	93 35.0	34 09.0	58.2	215 19.8	35.0	288 08.9	38.4	200 58.0	39.0
Y	15	108 37.5	49 08.3	. . 58.9	230 23.2	. . 34.9	303 11.2	. . 38.4	216 00.7	. . 39.0
	16	123 39.9	64 07.5	19 59.7	245 26.6	34.9	318 13.6	38.3	231 03.4	39.0
	17	138 42.4	79 06.8	20 00.4	260 30.1	34.8	333 15.9	38.3	246 06.0	38.9
	18	153 44.9	94 06.1	N20 01.1	275 33.5	S21 34.7	348 18.3	N 7 38.2	261 08.7	S20 38.9
	19	168 47.3	109 05.4	01.8	290 36.9	34.7	3 20.7	38.1	276 11.3	38.9
	20	183 49.8	124 04.7	02.5	305 40.3	34.6	18 23.0	38.1	291 14.0	38.9
	21	198 52.3	139 03.9	. . 03.2	320 43.7	. . 34.6	33 25.4	. . 38.0	306 16.6	. . 38.9
	22	213 54.7	154 03.2	03.9	335 47.1	34.5	48 27.7	38.0	321 19.3	38.8
	23	228 57.2	169 02.5	04.6	350 50.5	34.4	63 30.1	37.9	336 22.0	38.8
26	00	243 59.7	184 01.8	N20 05.3	5 54.0	S21 34.4	78 32.4	N 7 37.9	351 24.6	S20 38.8
	01	259 02.1	199 01.1	06.0	20 57.4	34.3	93 34.8	37.8	6 27.3	38.8
	02	274 04.6	214 00.3	06.7	36 00.8	34.3	108 37.1	37.8	21 29.9	38.8
	03	289 07.1	228 59.6	. . 07.4	51 04.2	. . 34.2	123 39.5	. . 37.7	36 32.6	. . 38.7
	04	304 09.5	243 58.9	08.1	66 07.6	34.1	138 41.8	37.7	51 35.2	38.7
	05	319 12.0	258 58.2	08.8	81 11.0	34.1	153 44.2	37.6	66 37.9	38.7
	06	334 14.4	273 57.4	N20 09.5	96 14.4	S21 34.0	168 46.5	N 7 37.5	81 40.6	S20 38.7
	07	349 16.9	288 56.7	10.2	111 17.9	34.0	183 48.9	37.5	96 43.2	38.6
T	08	4 19.4	303 56.0	10.9	126 21.3	33.9	198 51.2	37.4	111 45.9	38.6
H	09	19 21.8	318 55.3	. . 11.6	141 24.7	. . 33.8	213 53.6	. . 37.4	126 48.5	. . 38.6
U	10	34 24.3	333 54.5	12.3	156 28.1	33.8	228 56.0	37.3	141 51.2	38.6
R	11	49 26.8	348 53.8	13.0	171 31.5	33.7	243 58.3	37.3	156 53.8	38.6
S	12	64 29.2	3 53.1	N20 13.7	186 34.9	S21 33.6	259 00.7	N 7 37.2	171 56.5	S20 38.5
D	13	79 31.7	18 52.4	14.4	201 38.3	33.6	274 03.0	37.2	186 59.2	38.5
A	14	94 34.2	33 51.6	15.1	216 41.8	33.5	289 05.4	37.1	202 01.8	38.5
Y	15	109 36.6	48 50.9	. . 15.8	231 45.2	. . 33.5	304 07.7	. . 37.0	217 04.5	. . 38.5
	16	124 39.1	63 50.2	16.5	246 48.6	33.4	319 10.1	37.0	232 07.1	38.5
	17	139 41.6	78 49.4	17.1	261 52.0	33.3	334 12.4	36.9	247 09.8	38.4
	18	154 44.0	93 48.7	N20 17.8	276 55.4	S21 33.3	349 14.8	N 7 36.9	262 12.5	S20 38.4
	19	169 46.5	108 48.0	18.5	291 58.8	33.2	4 17.1	36.8	277 15.1	38.4
	20	184 48.9	123 47.2	19.2	307 02.2	33.1	19 19.5	36.8	292 17.8	38.4
	21	199 51.4	138 46.5	. . 19.9	322 05.7	. . 33.1	34 21.8	. . 36.7	307 20.4	. . 38.4
	22	214 53.9	153 45.8	20.6	337 09.1	33.0	49 24.1	36.6	322 23.1	38.3
	23	229 56.3	168 45.0	21.3	352 12.5	33.0	64 26.5	36.6	337 25.7	38.3
Mer. Pass.		h m 7 46.7	v −0.7	d 0.7	v 3.4	d 0.1	v 2.4	d 0.1	v 2.7	d 0.0

STARS

Name	SHA	Dec
	° ′	° ′
Acamar	315 17.3	S40 14.5
Achernar	335 25.9	S57 09.2
Acrux	173 06.5	S63 11.6
Adhara	255 11.3	S29 00.0
Aldebaran	290 47.5	N16 32.2
Alioth	166 18.7	N55 52.5
Alkaid	152 57.0	N49 14.1
Al Na'ir	27 41.3	S46 52.6
Alnilam	275 44.7	S 1 11.8
Alphard	217 54.2	S 8 44.0
Alphecca	126 09.0	N26 39.7
Alpheratz	357 41.6	N29 10.6
Altair	62 06.1	N 8 54.8
Ankaa	353 14.1	S42 12.9
Antares	112 23.4	S26 27.9
Arcturus	145 53.7	N19 06.0
Atria	107 22.9	S69 03.2
Avior	234 17.5	S59 34.1
Bellatrix	278 30.2	N 6 21.6
Betelgeuse	270 59.5	N 7 24.3
Canopus	263 55.7	S52 42.6
Capella	280 32.0	N46 00.6
Deneb	49 29.9	N45 20.2
Denebola	182 31.6	N14 28.9
Diphda	348 54.1	S17 53.8
Dubhe	193 49.4	N61 40.0
Elnath	278 10.5	N28 37.0
Eltanin	90 44.7	N51 29.3
Enif	33 45.1	N 9 57.0
Fomalhaut	15 21.9	S29 32.0
Gacrux	171 58.2	S57 12.5
Gienah	175 50.1	S17 38.1
Hadar	148 44.4	S60 27.2
Hamal	327 58.8	N23 32.1
Kaus Aust.	83 40.9	S34 22.3
Kochab	137 19.2	N74 05.5
Markab	13 36.4	N15 17.5
Menkar	314 13.3	N 4 09.0
Menkent	148 04.8	S36 27.0
Miaplacidus	221 39.4	S69 47.5
Mirfak	308 38.0	N49 54.8
Nunki	75 55.6	S26 16.3
Peacock	53 15.9	S56 40.5
Pollux	243 25.6	N27 59.1
Procyon	244 57.9	N 5 10.7
Rasalhague	96 04.3	N12 33.0
Regulus	207 41.5	N11 53.2
Rigel	281 10.5	S 8 11.3
Rigil Kent.	139 48.3	S60 54.1
Sabik	102 09.9	S15 44.5
Schedar	349 38.5	N56 37.3
Shaula	96 18.8	S37 06.7
Sirius	258 32.3	S16 44.6
Spica	158 28.9	S11 14.8
Suhail	222 51.1	S43 30.3
Vega	80 37.3	N38 48.0
Zuben'ubi	137 02.9	S16 06.5

	SHA	Mer. Pass.
	° ′	h m
Venus	301 18.5	11 43
Mars	121 31.5	23 36
Jupiter	194 35.3	18 47
Saturn	107 20.3	0 38

UT	SUN GHA	SUN Dec	MOON GHA	v	MOON Dec	d	HP
d h	° ′	° ′	° ′	′	° ′	′	′
24 00	180 47.7	N20 48.2	335 02.9	10.9	S18 26.4	1.0	55.2
01	195 47.6	48.7	349 32.8	10.8	18 27.4	0.9	55.2
02	210 47.6	49.2	4 02.6	10.9	18 28.3	0.8	55.2
03	225 47.5	. . 49.6	18 32.5	10.8	18 29.1	0.7	55.2
04	240 47.5	50.1	33 02.3	10.8	18 29.8	0.7	55.3
05	255 47.4	50.5	47 32.1	10.8	18 30.5	0.5	55.3
06	270 47.3	N20 51.0	62 01.9	10.8	S18 31.0	0.5	55.3
07	285 47.3	51.4	76 31.7	10.7	18 31.5	0.3	55.3
T 08	300 47.2	51.9	91 01.4	10.7	18 31.8	0.3	55.3
U 09	315 47.2	. . 52.3	105 31.1	10.7	18 32.1	0.2	55.3
E 10	330 47.1	52.8	120 00.8	10.7	18 32.3	0.1	55.4
S 11	345 47.0	53.3	134 30.5	10.6	18 32.4	0.1	55.4
D 12	0 47.0	N20 53.7	149 00.1	10.7	S18 32.3	0.1	55.4
13	15 46.9	54.2	163 29.8	10.6	18 32.2	0.2	55.4
A 14	30 46.9	54.6	177 59.4	10.6	18 32.0	0.3	55.4
Y 15	45 46.8	. . 55.1	192 29.0	10.6	18 31.7	0.4	55.5
16	60 46.7	55.5	206 58.6	10.5	18 31.3	0.4	55.5
17	75 46.7	56.0	221 28.1	10.6	18 30.9	0.6	55.5
18	90 46.6	N20 56.4	235 57.7	10.5	S18 30.3	0.7	55.5
19	105 46.6	56.9	250 27.2	10.5	18 29.6	0.8	55.5
20	120 46.5	57.3	264 56.7	10.5	18 28.8	0.8	55.6
21	135 46.4	. . 57.8	279 26.2	10.5	18 28.0	1.0	55.6
22	150 46.4	58.2	293 55.7	10.5	18 27.0	1.1	55.6
23	165 46.3	58.6	308 25.2	10.4	18 25.9	1.1	55.6
25 00	180 46.2	N20 59.1	322 54.6	10.5	S18 24.8	1.3	55.6
01	195 46.2	20 59.5	337 24.1	10.4	18 23.5	1.3	55.7
02	210 46.1	21 00.0	351 53.5	10.4	18 22.2	1.4	55.7
03	225 46.1	. . 00.4	6 22.9	10.4	18 20.8	1.6	55.7
04	240 46.0	00.9	20 52.3	10.4	18 19.2	1.6	55.7
05	255 45.9	01.3	35 21.7	10.4	18 17.6	1.7	55.7
06	270 45.9	N21 01.7	49 51.1	10.3	S18 15.9	1.9	55.8
W 07	285 45.8	02.2	64 20.4	10.4	18 14.0	1.9	55.8
E 08	300 45.7	02.6	78 49.8	10.4	18 12.1	2.0	55.8
D 09	315 45.7	. . 03.1	93 19.2	10.3	18 10.1	2.1	55.8
N 10	330 45.6	03.5	107 48.5	10.3	18 08.0	2.2	55.8
E 11	345 45.5	03.9	122 17.8	10.3	18 05.8	2.3	55.9
S 12	0 45.5	N21 04.4	136 47.1	10.4	S18 03.5	2.4	55.9
D 13	15 45.4	04.8	151 16.5	10.3	18 01.1	2.5	55.9
A 14	30 45.3	05.3	165 45.8	10.3	17 58.6	2.6	55.9
Y 15	45 45.3	. . 05.7	180 15.1	10.3	17 56.0	2.6	55.9
16	60 45.2	06.1	194 44.4	10.2	17 53.4	2.8	56.0
17	75 45.2	06.6	209 13.6	10.3	17 50.6	2.9	56.0
18	90 45.1	N21 07.0	223 42.9	10.3	S17 47.7	3.0	56.0
19	105 45.0	07.4	238 12.2	10.3	17 44.7	3.0	56.0
20	120 45.0	07.9	252 41.5	10.2	17 41.7	3.2	56.1
21	135 44.9	. . 08.3	267 10.7	10.3	17 38.5	3.2	56.1
22	150 44.8	08.7	281 40.0	10.3	17 35.3	3.4	56.1
23	165 44.7	09.1	296 09.3	10.2	17 31.9	3.4	56.1
26 00	180 44.7	N21 09.6	310 38.5	10.3	S17 28.5	3.5	56.1
01	195 44.6	10.0	325 07.8	10.2	17 25.0	3.7	56.2
02	210 44.5	10.4	339 37.0	10.3	17 21.3	3.7	56.2
03	225 44.5	. . 10.9	354 06.3	10.2	17 17.6	3.8	56.2
04	240 44.4	11.3	8 35.5	10.2	17 13.8	3.9	56.2
05	255 44.3	11.7	23 04.7	10.3	17 09.9	4.0	56.3
06	270 44.3	N21 12.1	37 34.0	10.2	S17 05.9	4.1	56.3
T 07	285 44.2	12.6	52 03.2	10.3	17 01.8	4.2	56.3
08	300 44.1	13.0	66 32.5	10.2	16 57.6	4.3	56.3
H 09	315 44.1	. . 13.4	81 01.7	10.2	16 53.3	4.3	56.4
U 10	330 44.0	13.8	95 30.9	10.3	16 49.0	4.5	56.4
R 11	345 43.9	14.3	110 00.2	10.2	16 44.5	4.6	56.4
S 12	0 43.9	N21 14.7	124 29.4	10.3	S16 39.9	4.6	56.4
D 13	15 43.8	15.1	138 58.7	10.2	16 35.3	4.7	56.4
A 14	30 43.7	15.5	153 27.9	10.3	16 30.6	4.9	56.5
Y 15	45 43.6	. . 16.0	167 57.2	10.2	16 25.7	4.9	56.5
16	60 43.6	16.4	182 26.4	10.2	16 20.8	5.0	56.5
17	75 43.5	16.8	196 55.6	10.3	16 15.8	5.1	56.5
18	90 43.4	N21 17.2	211 24.9	10.2	S16 10.7	5.2	56.6
19	105 43.4	17.6	225 54.1	10.3	16 05.5	5.3	56.6
20	120 43.3	18.0	240 23.4	10.3	16 00.2	5.3	56.6
21	135 43.2	. . 18.5	254 52.7	10.2	15 54.9	5.5	56.6
22	150 43.1	18.9	269 21.9	10.3	15 49.4	5.5	56.7
23	165 43.1	19.3	283 51.2	10.2	S15 43.9	5.7	56.7
	SD 15.8	*d* 0.4	SD		15.1	15.2	15.4

Lat.	Twilight Naut.	Twilight Civil	Sunrise	Moonrise 24	25	26	27
°	h m	h m	h m	h m	h m	h m	h m
N 72	▭	▭	▭	■	■	02 23	02 07
N 70	▭	▭	▭	00 09	00 58	01 21	01 30
68	////	////	00 28	24 13	00 13	00 45	01 05
66	////	////	01 40	23 43	24 19	00 19	00 45
64	////	////	02 16	23 21	24 00	00 00	00 29
62	////	01 02	02 41	23 03	23 44	24 15	00 15
60	////	01 46	03 00	22 48	23 30	24 04	00 04
N 58	////	02 14	03 17	22 35	23 18	23 54	24 24
56	00 56	02 36	03 30	22 25	23 08	23 45	24 17
54	01 36	02 53	03 42	22 15	22 59	23 38	24 11
52	02 03	03 08	03 52	22 06	22 51	23 31	24 05
50	02 23	03 20	04 02	21 59	22 44	23 25	24 00
45	03 00	03 46	04 21	21 42	22 29	23 11	23 49
N 40	03 26	04 05	04 37	21 29	22 16	23 00	23 40
35	03 46	04 21	04 50	21 17	22 05	22 50	23 33
30	04 02	04 35	05 01	21 07	21 56	22 42	23 26
20	04 28	04 57	05 21	20 50	21 40	22 28	23 14
N 10	04 49	05 15	05 38	20 35	21 25	22 15	23 04
0	05 05	05 31	05 53	20 21	21 12	22 03	22 54
S 10	05 20	05 46	06 09	20 07	20 59	21 51	22 44
20	05 35	06 02	06 25	19 52	20 45	21 39	22 34
30	05 49	06 18	06 44	19 35	20 28	21 24	22 22
35	05 56	06 27	06 55	19 25	20 19	21 16	22 15
40	06 04	06 38	07 07	19 14	20 08	21 06	22 07
45	06 13	06 49	07 22	19 01	19 55	20 55	21 58
S 50	06 23	07 03	07 40	18 44	19 40	20 41	21 47
52	06 27	07 09	07 48	18 37	19 33	20 35	21 42
54	06 32	07 16	07 58	18 28	19 25	20 28	21 36
56	06 37	07 24	08 08	18 19	19 15	20 20	21 30
58	06 42	07 32	08 21	18 08	19 05	20 11	21 23
S 60	06 48	07 42	08 35	17 55	18 53	20 00	21 14

Lat.	Sunset	Twilight Civil	Twilight Naut.	Moonset 24	25	26	27
°	h m	h m	h m	h m	h m	h m	h m
N 72	▭	▭	▭	■	■	04 32	06 35
N 70	▭	▭	▭	03 16	04 12	05 35	07 11
68	23 50	////	////	04 02	04 57	06 10	07 36
66	22 17	////	////	04 32	05 26	06 35	07 55
64	21 41	////	////	04 55	05 48	06 54	08 11
62	21 15	22 57	////	05 13	06 06	07 10	08 23
60	20 55	22 11	////	05 28	06 21	07 24	08 34
N 58	20 39	21 42	////	05 41	06 33	07 35	08 44
56	20 25	21 20	23 03	05 52	06 44	07 45	08 52
54	20 13	21 02	22 20	06 01	06 54	07 53	08 59
52	20 02	20 47	21 53	06 10	07 02	08 01	09 06
50	19 53	20 35	21 32	06 18	07 10	08 08	09 12
45	19 33	20 09	20 55	06 34	07 26	08 23	09 24
N 40	19 18	19 49	20 29	06 48	07 39	08 35	09 35
35	19 04	19 33	20 08	06 59	07 51	08 46	09 44
30	18 53	19 20	19 52	07 09	08 00	08 55	09 52
20	18 33	18 57	19 26	07 26	08 17	09 10	10 05
N 10	18 16	18 39	19 05	07 41	08 32	09 24	10 17
0	18 01	18 23	18 49	07 55	08 46	09 37	10 28
S 10	17 45	18 07	18 33	08 09	09 00	09 49	10 38
20	17 29	17 52	18 19	08 24	09 14	10 03	10 50
30	17 10	17 36	18 05	08 41	09 31	10 18	11 03
35	16 59	17 26	17 57	08 51	09 41	10 27	11 11
40	16 46	17 16	17 49	09 03	09 52	10 37	11 19
45	16 32	17 04	17 41	09 16	10 05	10 49	11 29
S 50	16 14	16 51	17 31	09 32	10 21	11 03	11 41
52	16 05	16 44	17 27	09 40	10 28	11 10	11 47
54	15 56	16 37	17 22	09 49	10 36	11 17	11 53
56	15 45	16 30	17 17	09 58	10 45	11 26	12 00
58	15 33	16 21	17 11	10 09	10 56	11 35	12 07
S 60	15 19	16 11	17 05	10 22	11 08	11 45	12 16

Day	SUN Eqn. of Time 00^h	12^h	Mer. Pass.	MOON Mer. Pass. Upper	Lower	Age	Phase
d	m s	m s	h m	h m	h m	d %	
24	03 11	03 08	11 57	01 43	14 08	18 93	
25	03 05	03 02	11 57	02 34	14 59	19 88	
26	02 59	02 56	11 57	03 24	15 50	20 80	

Day	UT d h	ARIES GHA ° ′	VENUS −3·9 GHA ° ′	VENUS Dec ° ′	MARS −2·0 GHA ° ′	MARS Dec ° ′	JUPITER −2·1 GHA ° ′	JUPITER Dec ° ′	SATURN +0·0 GHA ° ′	SATURN Dec ° ′	STARS Name	SHA ° ′	Dec ° ′
FRIDAY	27 00	244 58.8	183 44.3	N20 21.9	7 15.9	S21 32.9	79 28.8	N 7 36.5	352 28.4	S20 38.3	Acamar	315 17.3	S40 14.5
	01	260 01.3	198 43.6	22.6	22 19.3	32.8	94 31.2	36.5	7 31.1	38.3	Achernar	335 25.9	S57 09.2
	02	275 03.7	213 42.8	23.3	37 22.7	32.8	109 33.5	36.4	22 33.7	38.3	Acrux	173 06.5	S63 11.6
	03	290 06.2	228 42.1	. . 24.0	52 26.1	. . 32.7	124 35.9	. . 36.4	37 36.4	. . 38.2	Adhara	255 11.3	S29 00.0
	04	305 08.7	243 41.4	24.7	67 29.5	32.6	139 38.2	36.3	52 39.0	38.2	Aldebaran	290 47.4	N16 32.3
	05	320 11.1	258 40.6	25.3	82 33.0	32.6	154 40.6	36.2	67 41.7	38.2			
	06	335 13.6	273 39.9	N20 26.0	97 36.4	S21 32.5	169 42.9	N 7 36.2	82 44.4	S20 38.2	Alioth	166 18.7	N55 52.5
	07	350 16.1	288 39.2	26.7	112 39.8	32.4	184 45.3	36.1	97 47.0	38.2	Alkaid	152 57.1	N49 14.1
	08	5 18.5	303 38.4	27.4	127 43.2	32.4	199 47.6	36.1	112 49.7	38.1	Al Na'ir	27 41.3	S46 52.6
	09	20 21.0	318 37.7	. . 28.0	142 46.6	. . 32.3	214 50.0	. . 36.0	127 52.3	. . 38.1	Alnilam	275 44.7	S 1 11.8
	10	35 23.4	333 37.0	28.7	157 50.0	32.3	229 52.3	35.9	142 55.0	38.1	Alphard	217 54.2	S 8 44.0
	11	50 25.9	348 36.2	29.4	172 53.4	32.2	244 54.6	35.9	157 57.6	38.1			
	12	65 28.4	3 35.5	N20 30.0	187 56.8	S21 32.1	259 57.0	N 7 35.8	173 00.3	S20 38.1	Alphecca	126 09.0	N26 39.8
	13	80 30.8	18 34.7	30.7	203 00.2	32.1	274 59.3	35.8	188 03.0	38.0	Alpheratz	357 41.5	N29 10.6
	14	95 33.3	33 34.0	31.4	218 03.6	32.0	290 01.7	35.7	203 05.6	38.0	Altair	62 06.1	N 8 54.8
	15	110 35.8	48 33.3	. . 32.1	233 07.1	. . 31.9	305 04.0	. . 35.7	218 08.3	. . 38.0	Ankaa	353 14.0	S42 12.9
	16	125 38.2	63 32.5	32.7	248 10.5	31.9	320 06.4	35.6	233 10.9	38.0	Antares	112 23.4	S26 27.9
	17	140 40.7	78 31.8	33.4	263 13.9	31.8	335 08.7	35.5	248 13.6	38.0			
	18	155 43.2	93 31.0	N20 34.0	278 17.3	S21 31.7	350 11.1	N 7 35.5	263 16.3	S20 37.9	Arcturus	145 53.7	N19 06.0
	19	170 45.6	108 30.3	34.7	293 20.7	31.7	5 13.4	35.4	278 18.9	37.9	Atria	107 22.9	S69 03.2
	20	185 48.1	123 29.6	35.4	308 24.1	31.6	20 15.7	35.4	293 21.6	37.9	Avior	234 17.5	S59 34.1
	21	200 50.5	138 28.8	. . 36.0	323 27.5	. . 31.5	35 18.1	. . 35.3	308 24.2	. . 37.9	Bellatrix	278 30.2	N 6 21.6
	22	215 53.0	153 28.1	36.7	338 30.9	31.5	50 20.4	35.2	323 26.9	37.9	Betelgeuse	270 59.5	N 7 24.3
	23	230 55.5	168 27.3	37.4	353 34.3	31.4	65 22.8	35.2	338 29.5	37.8			
SATURDAY	28 00	245 57.9	183 26.6	N20 38.0	8 37.7	S21 31.3	80 25.1	N 7 35.1	353 32.2	S20 37.8	Canopus	263 55.8	S52 42.6
	01	261 00.4	198 25.8	38.7	23 41.1	31.3	95 27.4	35.1	8 34.9	37.8	Capella	280 32.0	N46 00.6
	02	276 02.9	213 25.1	39.3	38 44.6	31.2	110 29.8	35.0	23 37.5	37.8	Deneb	49 29.8	N45 20.2
	03	291 05.3	228 24.3	. . 40.0	53 48.0	. . 31.1	125 32.1	. . 34.9	38 40.2	. . 37.8	Denebola	182 31.6	N14 28.9
	04	306 07.8	243 23.6	40.6	68 51.4	31.1	140 34.5	34.9	53 42.8	37.7	Diphda	348 54.1	S17 53.8
	05	321 10.3	258 22.9	41.3	83 54.8	31.0	155 36.8	34.8	68 45.5	37.7			
	06	336 12.7	273 22.1	N20 41.9	98 58.2	S21 30.9	170 39.1	N 7 34.8	83 48.2	S20 37.7	Dubhe	193 49.4	N61 40.0
	07	351 15.2	288 21.4	42.6	114 01.6	30.9	185 41.5	34.7	98 50.8	37.7	Elnath	278 10.5	N28 37.0
	08	6 17.7	303 20.6	43.2	129 05.0	30.8	200 43.8	34.6	113 53.5	37.7	Eltanin	90 44.7	N51 29.3
	09	21 20.1	318 19.9	. . 43.9	144 08.4	. . 30.8	215 46.2	. . 34.6	128 56.1	. . 37.6	Enif	33 45.1	N 9 57.0
	10	36 22.6	333 19.1	44.5	159 11.8	30.7	230 48.5	34.5	143 58.8	37.6	Fomalhaut	15 21.9	S29 32.0
	11	51 25.0	348 18.4	45.2	174 15.2	30.6	245 50.8	34.4	159 01.5	37.6			
	12	66 27.5	3 17.6	N20 45.8	189 18.6	S21 30.6	260 53.2	N 7 34.4	174 04.1	S20 37.6	Gacrux	171 58.2	S57 12.5
	13	81 30.0	18 16.9	46.5	204 22.0	30.5	275 55.5	34.3	189 06.8	37.6	Gienah	175 50.1	S17 38.1
	14	96 32.4	33 16.1	47.1	219 25.4	30.4	290 57.8	34.3	204 09.4	37.5	Hadar	148 44.4	S60 27.2
	15	111 34.9	48 15.4	. . 47.8	234 28.8	. . 30.4	306 00.2	. . 34.2	219 12.1	. . 37.5	Hamal	327 58.8	N23 32.1
	16	126 37.4	63 14.6	48.4	249 32.2	30.3	321 02.5	34.1	234 14.7	37.5	Kaus Aust.	83 40.8	S34 22.3
	17	141 39.8	78 13.9	49.1	264 35.6	30.2	336 04.9	34.1	249 17.4	37.5			
	18	156 42.3	93 13.1	N20 49.7	279 39.0	S21 30.2	351 07.2	N 7 34.0	264 20.1	S20 37.5	Kochab	137 19.2	N74 05.6
	19	171 44.8	108 12.4	50.3	294 42.4	30.1	6 09.5	34.0	279 22.7	37.4	Markab	13 36.4	N15 17.5
	20	186 47.2	123 11.6	51.0	309 45.8	30.0	21 11.9	33.9	294 25.4	37.4	Menkar	314 13.3	N 4 09.0
	21	201 49.7	138 10.8	. . 51.6	324 49.2	. . 29.9	36 14.2	. . 33.8	309 28.0	. . 37.4	Menkent	148 04.8	S36 27.0
	22	216 52.2	153 10.1	52.3	339 52.6	29.9	51 16.5	33.8	324 30.7	37.4	Miaplacidus	221 39.4	S69 47.5
	23	231 54.6	168 09.3	52.9	354 56.0	29.8	66 18.9	33.7	339 33.4	37.4			
SUNDAY	29 00	246 57.1	183 08.6	N20 53.5	9 59.4	S21 29.7	81 21.2	N 7 33.6	354 36.0	S20 37.3	Mirfak	308 37.9	N49 54.8
	01	261 59.5	198 07.8	54.2	25 02.8	29.7	96 23.5	33.6	9 38.7	37.3	Nunki	75 55.6	S26 16.3
	02	277 02.0	213 07.1	54.8	40 06.2	29.6	111 25.9	33.5	24 41.3	37.3	Peacock	53 15.9	S56 40.5
	03	292 04.5	228 06.3	. . 55.4	55 09.6	. . 29.5	126 28.2	. . 33.5	39 44.0	. . 37.3	Pollux	243 25.6	N27 59.1
	04	307 06.9	243 05.6	56.1	70 13.0	29.5	141 30.5	33.4	54 46.7	37.3	Procyon	244 57.9	N 5 10.7
	05	322 09.4	258 04.8	56.7	85 16.4	29.4	156 32.9	33.3	69 49.3	37.2			
	06	337 11.9	273 04.0	N20 57.3	100 19.8	S21 29.3	171 35.2	N 7 33.3	84 52.0	S20 37.2	Rasalhague	96 04.3	N12 33.0
	07	352 14.3	288 03.3	57.9	115 23.2	29.3	186 37.5	33.2	99 54.6	37.2	Regulus	207 41.5	N11 53.2
	08	7 16.8	303 02.5	58.6	130 26.6	29.2	201 39.9	33.1	114 57.3	37.2	Rigel	281 10.5	S 8 11.2
	09	22 19.3	318 01.8	. . 59.2	145 30.0	. . 29.1	216 42.2	. . 33.1	130 00.0	. . 37.2	Rigil Kent.	139 48.3	S60 54.1
	10	37 21.7	333 01.0	20 59.8	160 33.4	29.1	231 44.5	33.0	145 02.6	37.1	Sabik	102 09.9	S15 44.5
	11	52 24.2	348 00.2	21 00.4	175 36.8	29.0	246 46.9	32.9	160 05.3	37.1			
	12	67 26.6	2 59.5	N21 01.1	190 40.2	S21 28.9	261 49.2	N 7 32.9	175 07.9	S20 37.1	Schedar	349 38.4	N56 37.3
	13	82 29.1	17 58.7	01.7	205 43.6	28.9	276 51.5	32.8	190 10.6	37.1	Shaula	96 18.8	S37 06.7
	14	97 31.6	32 58.0	02.3	220 47.0	28.8	291 53.9	32.8	205 13.3	37.0	Sirius	258 32.3	S16 44.6
	15	112 34.0	47 57.2	. . 02.9	235 50.4	. . 28.7	306 56.2	. . 32.7	220 15.9	. . 37.0	Spica	158 28.9	S11 14.8
	16	127 36.5	62 56.4	03.5	250 53.8	28.7	321 58.5	32.6	235 18.6	37.0	Suhail	222 51.1	S43 30.3
	17	142 39.0	77 55.7	04.2	265 57.2	28.6	337 00.9	32.6	250 21.2	37.0			
	18	157 41.4	92 54.9	N21 04.8	281 00.6	S21 28.5	352 03.2	N 7 32.5	265 23.9	S20 37.0	Vega	80 37.2	N38 48.0
	19	172 43.9	107 54.1	05.4	296 04.0	28.4	7 05.5	32.4	280 26.6	36.9	Zuben'ubi	137 02.9	S16 06.5
	20	187 46.4	122 53.4	06.0	311 07.4	28.4	22 07.8	32.4	295 29.2	36.9			
	21	202 48.8	137 52.6	. . 06.6	326 10.8	. . 28.3	37 10.2	. . 32.3	310 31.9	. . 36.9			
	22	217 51.3	152 51.9	07.2	341 14.2	28.2	52 12.5	32.2	325 34.5	36.9			
	23	232 53.8	167 51.1	07.8	356 17.6	28.2	67 14.8	32.2	340 37.2	36.9			
	Mer. Pass. h m	7 34.9	*v* −0.7	*d* 0.6	*v* 3.4	*d* 0.1	*v* 2.3	*d* 0.1	*v* 2.7	*d* 0.0			

	SHA ° ′	Mer. Pass. h m
Venus	297 28.6	11 47
Mars	122 39.8	23 20
Jupiter	194 27.2	18 35
Saturn	107 34.3	0 26

d	UT h	SUN GHA ° ′	SUN Dec ° ′	MOON GHA ° ′	v ′	MOON Dec ° ′	d ′	HP ′
27	00	180 43.0	N21 19.7	298 20.4	10.3	S15 38.2	5.7	56.7
	01	195 42.9	20.1	312 49.7	10.3	15 32.5	5.8	56.7
	02	210 42.8	20.5	327 19.0	10.3	15 26.7	5.9	56.8
	03	225 42.8	. . 20.9	341 48.3	10.2	15 20.8	6.0	56.8
	04	240 42.7	21.4	356 17.5	10.3	15 14.8	6.1	56.8
	05	255 42.6	21.8	10 46.8	10.3	15 08.7	6.1	56.8
	06	270 42.5	N21 22.2	25 16.1	10.3	S15 02.6	6.2	56.9
	07	285 42.5	22.6	39 45.4	10.3	14 56.4	6.4	56.9
	08	300 42.4	23.0	54 14.7	10.3	14 50.0	6.4	56.9
F	09	315 42.3	. . 23.4	68 44.0	10.3	14 43.6	6.5	57.0
R	10	330 42.2	23.8	83 13.3	10.3	14 37.1	6.5	57.0
I	11	345 42.2	24.2	97 42.6	10.3	14 30.6	6.7	57.0
D	12	0 42.1	N21 24.6	112 11.9	10.3	S14 23.9	6.7	57.0
A	13	15 42.0	25.0	126 41.2	10.3	14 17.2	6.9	57.1
Y	14	30 41.9	25.4	141 10.5	10.4	14 10.3	6.9	57.1
	15	45 41.9	. . 25.8	155 39.9	10.3	14 03.4	7.0	57.1
	16	60 41.8	26.3	170 09.2	10.3	13 56.4	7.0	57.1
	17	75 41.7	26.7	184 38.5	10.4	13 49.4	7.2	57.2
	18	90 41.6	N21 27.1	199 07.9	10.3	S13 42.2	7.2	57.2
	19	105 41.6	27.5	213 37.2	10.4	13 35.0	7.3	57.2
	20	120 41.5	27.9	228 06.6	10.3	13 27.7	7.4	57.2
	21	135 41.4	. . 28.3	242 35.9	10.4	13 20.3	7.5	57.3
	22	150 41.3	28.7	257 05.3	10.3	13 12.8	7.5	57.3
	23	165 41.3	29.1	271 34.6	10.4	13 05.3	7.6	57.3
28	00	180 41.2	N21 29.5	286 04.0	10.4	S12 57.7	7.7	57.4
	01	195 41.1	29.9	300 33.4	10.3	12 50.0	7.8	57.4
	02	210 41.0	30.3	315 02.7	10.4	12 42.2	7.8	57.4
	03	225 40.9	. . 30.7	329 32.1	10.4	12 34.4	7.9	57.4
	04	240 40.9	31.1	344 01.5	10.4	12 26.5	8.0	57.5
	05	255 40.8	31.5	358 30.9	10.3	12 18.5	8.1	57.5
	06	270 40.7	N21 31.8	13 00.2	10.4	S12 10.4	8.2	57.5
	07	285 40.6	32.2	27 29.6	10.4	12 02.2	8.2	57.5
S	08	300 40.5	32.6	41 59.0	10.4	11 54.0	8.3	57.6
A	09	315 40.5	. . 33.0	56 28.4	10.4	11 45.7	8.3	57.6
T	10	330 40.4	33.4	70 57.8	10.4	11 37.4	8.4	57.6
U	11	345 40.3	33.8	85 27.2	10.4	11 29.0	8.5	57.7
R	12	0 40.2	N21 34.2	99 56.6	10.4	S11 20.5	8.6	57.7
D	13	15 40.1	34.6	114 26.0	10.4	11 11.9	8.6	57.7
A	14	30 40.1	35.0	128 55.4	10.4	11 03.3	8.7	57.7
Y	15	45 40.0	. . 35.4	143 24.8	10.4	10 54.6	8.8	57.8
	16	60 39.9	35.8	157 54.2	10.4	10 45.8	8.9	57.8
	17	75 39.8	36.2	172 23.6	10.4	10 36.9	8.9	57.8
	18	90 39.7	N21 36.5	186 53.0	10.4	S10 28.0	8.9	57.9
	19	105 39.7	36.9	201 22.4	10.4	10 19.1	9.1	57.9
	20	120 39.6	37.3	215 51.8	10.4	10 10.0	9.1	57.9
	21	135 39.5	. . 37.7	230 21.2	10.4	10 00.9	9.1	57.9
	22	150 39.4	38.1	244 50.6	10.4	9 51.8	9.2	58.0
	23	165 39.3	38.5	259 20.0	10.4	9 42.6	9.3	58.0
29	00	180 39.2	N21 38.9	273 49.4	10.4	S 9 33.3	9.4	58.0
	01	195 39.2	39.2	288 18.8	10.4	9 23.9	9.4	58.1
	02	210 39.1	39.6	302 48.2	10.3	9 14.5	9.4	58.1
	03	225 39.0	. . 40.0	317 17.5	10.4	9 05.1	9.6	58.1
	04	240 38.9	40.4	331 46.9	10.4	8 55.5	9.6	58.1
	05	255 38.8	40.8	346 16.3	10.4	8 45.9	9.6	58.2
	06	270 38.7	N21 41.1	0 45.7	10.4	S 8 36.3	9.7	58.2
	07	285 38.7	41.5	15 15.1	10.3	8 26.6	9.7	58.2
	08	300 38.6	41.9	29 44.4	10.4	8 16.9	9.9	58.3
S	09	315 38.5	. . 42.3	44 13.8	10.3	8 07.0	9.8	58.3
U	10	330 38.4	42.7	58 43.1	10.4	7 57.2	9.9	58.3
N	11	345 38.3	43.0	73 12.5	10.3	7 47.3	10.0	58.4
D	12	0 38.2	N21 43.4	87 41.8	10.4	S 7 37.3	10.0	58.4
A	13	15 38.2	43.8	102 11.2	10.3	7 27.3	10.1	58.4
Y	14	30 38.1	44.2	116 40.5	10.3	7 17.2	10.1	58.4
	15	45 38.0	. . 44.5	131 09.8	10.3	7 07.1	10.2	58.5
	16	60 37.9	44.9	145 39.1	10.3	6 56.9	10.2	58.5
	17	75 37.8	45.3	160 08.4	10.3	6 46.7	10.3	58.5
	18	90 37.7	N21 45.6	174 37.7	10.3	S 6 36.4	10.3	58.6
	19	105 37.6	46.0	189 07.0	10.3	6 26.1	10.4	58.6
	20	120 37.6	46.4	203 36.3	10.2	6 15.7	10.4	58.6
	21	135 37.5	. . 46.8	218 05.5	10.3	6 05.3	10.4	58.6
	22	150 37.4	47.1	232 34.8	10.2	5 54.9	10.5	58.7
	23	165 37.3	47.5	247 04.0	10.2	S 5 44.4	10.6	58.7
		SD 15.8	*d* 0.4	SD		15.5	15.7	15.9

Lat.	Twilight Naut.	Twilight Civil	Sunrise	Moonrise 27	Moonrise 28	Moonrise 29	Moonrise 30
°	h m	h m	h m	h m	h m	h m	h m
N 72	▭	▭	▭	02 07	01 58	01 51	01 45
N 70	▭	▭	▭	01 30	01 35	01 37	01 38
68	▭	▭	▭	01 05	01 17	01 25	01 32
66	////	////	01 28	00 45	01 02	01 16	01 26
64	////	////	02 07	00 29	00 50	01 08	01 22
62	////	00 43	02 34	00 15	00 40	01 01	01 18
60	////	01 37	02 55	00 04	00 31	00 54	01 15
N 58	////	02 08	03 12	24 24	00 24	00 49	01 12
56	00 39	02 30	03 26	24 17	00 17	00 44	01 09
54	01 28	02 49	03 38	24 11	00 11	00 40	01 07
52	01 57	03 04	03 49	24 05	00 05	00 36	01 05
50	02 18	03 17	03 59	24 00	00 00	00 33	01 03
45	02 56	03 43	04 19	23 49	24 25	00 25	00 58
N 40	03 23	04 03	04 35	23 40	24 18	00 18	00 55
35	03 44	04 20	04 49	23 33	24 13	00 13	00 51
30	04 01	04 34	05 00	23 26	24 08	00 08	00 49
20	04 28	04 56	05 20	23 14	23 59	24 44	00 44
N 10	04 48	05 15	05 38	23 04	23 52	24 40	00 40
0	05 06	05 31	05 54	22 54	23 45	24 36	00 36
S 10	05 21	05 47	06 10	22 44	23 38	24 32	00 32
20	05 36	06 03	06 26	22 34	23 30	24 27	00 27
30	05 50	06 20	06 46	22 22	23 21	24 22	00 22
35	05 58	06 29	06 57	22 15	23 17	24 20	00 20
40	06 06	06 40	07 10	22 07	23 11	24 17	00 17
45	06 15	06 52	07 25	21 58	23 04	24 13	00 13
S 50	06 25	07 06	07 43	21 47	22 56	24 08	00 08
52	06 30	07 13	07 52	21 42	22 53	24 06	00 06
54	06 35	07 20	08 02	21 36	22 49	24 04	00 04
56	06 40	07 28	08 13	21 30	22 44	24 02	00 02
58	06 46	07 37	08 25	21 23	22 39	23 59	25 21
S 60	06 52	07 47	08 40	21 14	22 33	23 56	25 21

Lat.	Sunset	Twilight Civil	Twilight Naut.	Moonset 27	Moonset 28	Moonset 29	Moonset 30
°	h m	h m	h m	h m	h m	h m	h m
N 72	▭	▭	▭	06 35	08 30	10 23	12 15
N 70	▭	▭	▭	07 11	08 52	10 35	12 20
68	▭	▭	▭	07 36	09 09	10 45	12 25
66	22 31	////	////	07 55	09 22	10 54	12 28
64	21 50	////	////	08 11	09 34	11 01	12 31
62	21 22	23 19	////	08 23	09 43	11 07	12 33
60	21 01	22 20	////	08 34	09 51	11 12	12 36
N 58	20 44	21 49	////	08 44	09 58	11 16	12 38
56	20 29	21 26	23 22	08 52	10 04	11 20	12 39
54	20 17	21 07	22 29	08 59	10 10	11 24	12 41
52	20 06	20 52	22 00	09 06	10 15	11 27	12 42
50	19 56	20 39	21 38	09 12	10 19	11 30	12 43
45	19 36	20 12	20 59	09 24	10 29	11 37	12 46
N 40	19 20	19 52	20 32	09 35	10 37	11 42	12 48
35	19 06	19 35	20 11	09 44	10 44	11 46	12 50
30	18 55	19 21	19 54	09 52	10 50	11 50	12 52
20	18 34	18 59	19 27	10 05	11 01	11 57	12 55
N 10	18 17	18 40	19 06	10 17	11 10	12 03	12 58
0	18 01	18 23	18 49	10 28	11 18	12 09	13 00
S 10	17 45	18 08	18 34	10 38	11 27	12 15	13 02
20	17 28	17 52	18 19	10 50	11 36	12 20	13 05
30	17 09	17 35	18 04	11 03	11 46	12 27	13 08
35	16 57	17 25	17 56	11 11	11 52	12 31	13 09
40	16 45	17 15	17 48	11 19	11 58	12 35	13 11
45	16 30	17 03	17 39	11 29	12 06	12 40	13 13
S 50	16 11	16 48	17 29	11 41	12 15	12 46	13 15
52	16 02	16 42	17 24	11 47	12 19	12 49	13 16
54	15 52	16 34	17 19	11 53	12 24	12 52	13 18
56	15 41	16 27	17 14	12 00	12 29	12 55	13 19
58	15 29	16 18	17 08	12 07	12 35	12 58	13 20
S 60	15 14	16 08	17 02	12 16	12 41	13 03	13 22

Day	SUN Eqn. of Time 00^h	SUN Eqn. of Time 12^h	SUN Mer. Pass.	MOON Mer. Pass. Upper	MOON Mer. Pass. Lower	MOON Age	MOON Phase
d	m s	m s	h m	h m	h m	d	%
27	02 52	02 49	11 57	04 15	16 41	21	71
28	02 45	02 41	11 57	05 06	17 32	22	61
29	02 37	02 33	11 57	05 57	18 22	23	50

UT	ARIES	VENUS −4·0		MARS −2·0		JUPITER −2·1		SATURN +0·0		STARS		
	GHA	GHA	Dec	GHA	Dec	GHA	Dec	GHA	Dec	Name	SHA	Dec
d h	° ′	° ′	° ′	° ′	° ′	° ′	° ′	° ′	° ′		° ′	° ′
30 00 MONDAY	247 56.2	182 50.3	N21 08.5	11 20.9	S21 28.1	82 17.2	N 7 32.1	355 39.9	S20 36.8	Acamar	315 17.3	S40 14.4
01	262 58.7	197 49.6	09.1	26 24.3	28.0	97 19.5	32.0	10 42.5	36.8	Achernar	335 25.8	S57 09.1
02	278 01.1	212 48.8	09.7	41 27.7	28.0	112 21.8	32.0	25 45.2	36.8	Acrux	173 06.6	S63 11.6
03	293 03.6	227 48.0	10.3	56 31.1	27.9	127 24.1	31.9	40 47.8	36.8	Adhara	255 11.3	S29 00.0
04	308 06.1	242 47.3	10.9	71 34.5	27.8	142 26.5	31.8	55 50.5	36.8	Aldebaran	290 47.4	N16 32.3
05	323 08.5	257 46.5	11.5	86 37.9	27.8	157 28.8	31.8	70 53.1	36.7			
06	338 11.0	272 45.7	N21 12.1	101 41.3	S21 27.7	172 31.1	N 7 31.7	85 55.8	S20 36.7	Alioth	166 18.8	N55 52.5
07	353 13.5	287 44.9	12.7	116 44.7	27.6	187 33.4	31.6	100 58.5	36.7	Alkaid	152 57.1	N49 14.2
08	8 15.9	302 44.2	13.3	131 48.1	27.5	202 35.8	31.6	116 01.1	36.7	Al Na'ir	27 41.3	S46 52.6
09	23 18.4	317 43.4	13.9	146 51.5	27.5	217 38.1	31.5	131 03.8	36.7	Alnilam	275 44.7	S 1 11.8
10	38 20.9	332 42.6	14.5	161 54.8	27.4	232 40.4	31.4	146 06.4	36.6	Alphard	217 54.3	S 8 44.0
11	53 23.3	347 41.9	15.1	176 58.2	27.3	247 42.7	31.4	161 09.1	36.6			
12	68 25.8	2 41.1	N21 15.7	192 01.6	S21 27.3	262 45.1	N 7 31.3	176 11.8	S20 36.6	Alphecca	126 09.0	N26 39.8
13	83 28.3	17 40.3	16.3	207 05.0	27.2	277 47.4	31.2	191 14.4	36.6	Alpheratz	357 41.5	N29 10.6
14	98 30.7	32 39.6	16.9	222 08.4	27.1	292 49.7	31.2	206 17.1	36.6	Altair	62 06.1	N 8 54.8
15	113 33.2	47 38.8	17.5	237 11.8	27.1	307 52.0	31.1	221 19.8	36.5	Ankaa	353 14.0	S42 12.9
16	128 35.6	62 38.0	18.1	252 15.2	27.0	322 54.4	31.0	236 22.4	36.5	Antares	112 23.4	S26 27.9
17	143 38.1	77 37.2	18.7	267 18.5	26.9	337 56.7	31.0	251 25.1	36.5			
18	158 40.6	92 36.5	N21 19.3	282 21.9	S21 26.8	352 59.0	N 7 30.9	266 27.7	S20 36.5	Arcturus	145 53.7	N19 06.0
19	173 43.0	107 35.7	19.9	297 25.3	26.8	8 01.3	30.8	281 30.4	36.5	Atria	107 22.8	S69 03.2
20	188 45.5	122 34.9	20.5	312 28.7	26.7	23 03.7	30.8	296 33.1	36.4	Avior	234 17.5	S59 34.1
21	203 48.0	137 34.1	21.0	327 32.1	26.6	38 06.0	30.7	311 35.7	36.4	Bellatrix	278 30.2	N 6 21.6
22	218 50.4	152 33.4	21.6	342 35.5	26.6	53 08.3	30.6	326 38.4	36.4	Betelgeuse	270 59.5	N 7 24.3
23	233 52.9	167 32.6	22.2	357 38.8	26.5	68 10.6	30.6	341 41.0	36.4			
31 00 TUESDAY	248 55.4	182 31.8	N21 22.8	12 42.2	S21 26.4	83 13.0	N 7 30.5	356 43.7	S20 36.4	Canopus	263 55.8	S52 42.6
01	263 57.8	197 31.0	23.4	27 45.6	26.4	98 15.3	30.4	11 46.4	36.3	Capella	280 32.0	N46 00.6
02	279 00.3	212 30.3	24.0	42 49.0	26.3	113 17.6	30.4	26 49.0	36.3	Deneb	49 29.8	N45 20.2
03	294 02.7	227 29.5	24.6	57 52.4	26.2	128 19.9	30.3	41 51.7	36.3	Denebola	182 31.6	N14 28.9
04	309 05.2	242 28.7	25.1	72 55.7	26.1	143 22.2	30.2	56 54.3	36.3	Diphda	348 54.1	S17 53.8
05	324 07.7	257 27.9	25.7	87 59.1	26.1	158 24.6	30.2	71 57.0	36.3			
06	339 10.1	272 27.1	N21 26.3	103 02.5	S21 26.0	173 26.9	N 7 30.1	86 59.7	S20 36.2	Dubhe	193 49.4	N61 40.0
07	354 12.6	287 26.4	26.9	118 05.9	25.9	188 29.2	30.0	102 02.3	36.2	Elnath	278 10.5	N28 37.0
08	9 15.1	302 25.6	27.5	133 09.3	25.9	203 31.5	30.0	117 05.0	36.2	Eltanin	90 44.7	N51 29.3
09	24 17.5	317 24.8	28.0	148 12.6	25.8	218 33.8	29.9	132 07.6	36.2	Enif	33 45.1	N 9 57.0
10	39 20.0	332 24.0	28.6	163 16.0	25.7	233 36.2	29.8	147 10.3	36.2	Fomalhaut	15 21.9	S29 32.0
11	54 22.5	347 23.2	29.2	178 19.4	25.6	248 38.5	29.7	162 13.0	36.1			
12	69 24.9	2 22.5	N21 29.8	193 22.8	S21 25.6	263 40.8	N 7 29.7	177 15.6	S20 36.1	Gacrux	171 58.3	S57 12.5
13	84 27.4	17 21.7	30.3	208 26.1	25.5	278 43.1	29.6	192 18.3	36.1	Gienah	175 50.1	S17 38.1
14	99 29.9	32 20.9	30.9	223 29.5	25.4	293 45.4	29.5	207 20.9	36.1	Hadar	148 44.4	S60 27.2
15	114 32.3	47 20.1	31.5	238 32.9	25.4	308 47.7	29.5	222 23.6	36.1	Hamal	327 58.8	N23 32.1
16	129 34.8	62 19.3	32.0	253 36.2	25.3	323 50.1	29.4	237 26.3	36.0	Kaus Aust.	83 40.8	S34 22.3
17	144 37.2	77 18.5	32.6	268 39.6	25.2	338 52.4	29.3	252 28.9	36.0			
18	159 39.7	92 17.8	N21 33.2	283 43.0	S21 25.1	353 54.7	N 7 29.3	267 31.6	S20 36.0	Kochab	137 19.2	N74 05.6
19	174 42.2	107 17.0	33.7	298 46.4	25.1	8 57.0	29.2	282 34.2	36.0	Markab	13 36.4	N15 17.5
20	189 44.6	122 16.2	34.3	313 49.7	25.0	23 59.3	29.1	297 36.9	36.0	Menkar	314 13.3	N 4 09.0
21	204 47.1	137 15.4	34.9	328 53.1	24.9	39 01.6	29.1	312 39.6	35.9	Menkent	148 04.9	S36 27.1
22	219 49.6	152 14.6	35.4	343 56.5	24.9	54 04.0	29.0	327 42.2	35.9	Miaplacidus	221 39.5	S69 47.5
23	234 52.0	167 13.8	36.0	358 59.8	24.8	69 06.3	28.9	342 44.9	35.9			
1 00 WEDNESDAY	249 54.5	182 13.0	N21 36.6	14 03.2	S21 24.7	84 08.6	N 7 28.8	357 47.5	S20 35.9	Mirfak	308 37.9	N49 54.8
01	264 57.0	197 12.3	37.1	29 06.6	24.6	99 10.9	28.8	12 50.2	35.9	Nunki	75 55.6	S26 16.3
02	279 59.4	212 11.5	37.7	44 09.9	24.6	114 13.2	28.7	27 52.9	35.8	Peacock	53 15.9	S56 40.6
03	295 01.9	227 10.7	38.2	59 13.3	24.5	129 15.5	28.6	42 55.5	35.8	Pollux	243 25.6	N27 59.1
04	310 04.3	242 09.9	38.8	74 16.7	24.4	144 17.9	28.6	57 58.2	35.8	Procyon	244 57.9	N 5 10.8
05	325 06.8	257 09.1	39.4	89 20.0	24.4	159 20.2	28.5	73 00.8	35.8			
06	340 09.3	272 08.3	N21 39.9	104 23.4	S21 24.3	174 22.5	N 7 28.4	88 03.5	S20 35.8	Rasalhague	96 04.3	N12 33.1
07	355 11.7	287 07.5	40.5	119 26.8	24.2	189 24.8	28.3	103 06.2	35.7	Regulus	207 41.5	N11 53.2
08	10 14.2	302 06.7	41.0	134 30.1	24.1	204 27.1	28.3	118 08.8	35.7	Rigel	281 10.5	S 8 11.2
09	25 16.7	317 05.9	41.6	149 33.5	24.1	219 29.4	28.2	133 11.5	35.7	Rigil Kent.	139 48.3	S60 54.1
10	40 19.1	332 05.2	42.1	164 36.9	24.0	234 31.7	28.1	148 14.1	35.7	Sabik	102 09.9	S15 44.5
11	55 21.6	347 04.4	42.7	179 40.2	23.9	249 34.1	28.1	163 16.8	35.6			
12	70 24.1	2 03.6	N21 43.2	194 43.6	S21 23.9	264 36.4	N 7 28.0	178 19.5	S20 35.6	Schedar	349 38.4	N56 37.3
13	85 26.5	17 02.8	43.8	209 46.9	23.8	279 38.7	27.9	193 22.1	35.6	Shaula	96 18.8	S37 06.7
14	100 29.0	32 02.0	44.3	224 50.3	23.7	294 41.0	27.8	208 24.8	35.6	Sirius	258 32.3	S16 44.6
15	115 31.5	47 01.2	44.9	239 53.7	23.6	309 43.3	27.8	223 27.5	35.6	Spica	158 28.9	S11 14.8
16	130 33.9	62 00.4	45.4	254 57.0	23.6	324 45.6	27.7	238 30.1	35.5	Suhail	222 51.1	S43 30.3
17	145 36.4	76 59.6	45.9	270 00.4	23.5	339 47.9	27.6	253 32.8	35.5			
18	160 38.8	91 58.8	N21 46.5	285 03.7	S21 23.4	354 50.2	N 7 27.6	268 35.4	S20 35.5	Vega	80 37.2	N38 48.0
19	175 41.3	106 58.0	47.0	300 07.1	23.3	9 52.5	27.5	283 38.1	35.5	Zuben'ubi	137 02.9	S16 06.5
20	190 43.8	121 57.2	47.6	315 10.4	23.3	24 54.9	27.4	298 40.8	35.5			
21	205 46.2	136 56.4	48.1	330 13.8	23.2	39 57.2	27.3	313 43.4	35.4			
22	220 48.7	151 55.6	48.6	345 17.2	23.1	54 59.5	27.3	328 46.1	35.4			
23	235 51.2	166 54.8	49.2	0 20.5	23.1	70 01.8	27.2	343 48.7	35.4			
Mer. Pass.	h m 7 23.1	v −0.8	d 0.6	v 3.4	d 0.1	v 2.3	d 0.1	v 2.7	d 0.0			

	SHA	Mer. Pass.
	° ′	h m
Venus	293 36.4	11 50
Mars	123 46.9	23 04
Jupiter	194 17.6	18 24
Saturn	107 48.3	0 13

UT		SUN GHA	SUN Dec	MOON GHA	v	MOON Dec	d	HP
d	h	° ′	° ′	° ′	′	° ′	′	′
30	00	180 37.2	N21 47.9	261 33.2	10.2	S 5 33.8	10.5	58.7
	01	195 37.1	48.2	276 02.4	10.2	5 23.3	10.7	58.8
	02	210 37.0	48.6	290 31.6	10.2	5 12.6	10.6	58.8
	03	225 36.9	. . 49.0	305 00.8	10.2	5 02.0	10.7	58.8
	04	240 36.9	49.3	319 30.0	10.1	4 51.3	10.7	58.8
	05	255 36.8	49.7	333 59.1	10.2	4 40.6	10.8	58.9
	06	270 36.7	N21 50.1	348 28.3	10.1	S 4 29.8	10.8	58.9
	07	285 36.6	50.4	2 57.4	10.1	4 19.0	10.9	58.9
	08	300 36.5	50.8	17 26.5	10.1	4 08.1	10.9	59.0
M	09	315 36.4	. . 51.1	31 55.6	10.0	3 57.2	10.9	59.0
O	10	330 36.3	51.5	46 24.6	10.1	3 46.3	10.9	59.0
N	11	345 36.2	51.9	60 53.7	10.0	3 35.4	11.0	59.0
D	12	0 36.1	N21 52.2	75 22.7	10.0	S 3 24.4	11.0	59.1
A	13	15 36.0	52.6	89 51.7	10.0	3 13.4	11.0	59.1
Y	14	30 36.0	52.9	104 20.7	9.9	3 02.4	11.1	59.1
	15	45 35.9	. . 53.3	118 49.6	10.0	2 51.3	11.1	59.2
	16	60 35.8	53.7	133 18.6	9.9	2 40.2	11.1	59.2
	17	75 35.7	54.0	147 47.5	9.9	2 29.1	11.1	59.2
	18	90 35.6	N21 54.4	162 16.4	9.9	S 2 18.0	11.2	59.2
	19	105 35.5	54.7	176 45.3	9.8	2 06.8	11.2	59.3
	20	120 35.4	55.1	191 14.1	9.8	1 55.6	11.2	59.3
	21	135 35.3	. . 55.4	205 42.9	9.8	1 44.4	11.2	59.3
	22	150 35.2	55.8	220 11.7	9.8	1 33.2	11.3	59.4
	23	165 35.1	56.1	234 40.5	9.8	1 21.9	11.2	59.4
31	00	180 35.0	N21 56.5	249 09.3	9.7	S 1 10.7	11.3	59.4
	01	195 35.0	56.8	263 38.0	9.7	0 59.4	11.3	59.4
	02	210 34.9	57.2	278 06.7	9.6	0 48.1	11.4	59.5
	03	225 34.8	. . 57.5	292 35.3	9.7	0 36.7	11.3	59.5
	04	240 34.7	57.9	307 04.0	9.6	0 25.4	11.3	59.5
	05	255 34.6	58.2	321 32.6	9.5	0 14.1	11.4	59.5
	06	270 34.5	N21 58.6	336 01.1	9.6	S 0 02.7	11.4	59.6
	07	285 34.4	58.9	350 29.7	9.5	N 0 08.7	11.3	59.6
T	08	300 34.3	59.3	4 58.2	9.4	0 20.0	11.4	59.6
U	09	315 34.2	21 59.6	19 26.6	9.5	0 31.4	11.4	59.6
E	10	330 34.1	22 00.0	33 55.1	9.4	0 42.8	11.4	59.7
S	11	345 34.0	00.3	48 23.5	9.4	0 54.2	11.4	59.7
D	12	0 33.9	N22 00.7	62 51.9	9.3	N 1 05.6	11.5	59.7
A	13	15 33.8	01.0	77 20.2	9.3	1 17.1	11.4	59.7
Y	14	30 33.7	01.4	91 48.5	9.3	1 28.5	11.4	59.8
	15	45 33.6	. . 01.7	106 16.8	9.2	1 39.9	11.4	59.8
	16	60 33.5	02.0	120 45.0	9.2	1 51.3	11.4	59.8
	17	75 33.5	02.4	135 13.2	9.2	2 02.7	11.4	59.8
	18	90 33.4	N22 02.7	149 41.4	9.1	N 2 14.1	11.4	59.9
	19	105 33.3	03.1	164 09.5	9.1	2 25.5	11.4	59.9
	20	120 33.2	03.4	178 37.6	9.0	2 36.9	11.4	59.9
	21	135 33.1	. . 03.7	193 05.6	9.0	2 48.3	11.4	59.9
	22	150 33.0	04.1	207 33.6	9.0	2 59.7	11.4	60.0
	23	165 32.9	04.4	222 01.6	8.9	3 11.1	11.4	60.0
1	00	180 32.8	N22 04.7	236 29.5	8.9	N 3 22.5	11.3	60.0
	01	195 32.7	05.1	250 57.4	8.8	3 33.8	11.4	60.0
	02	210 32.6	05.4	265 25.2	8.8	3 45.2	11.3	60.0
	03	225 32.5	. . 05.8	279 53.0	8.8	3 56.5	11.3	60.1
	04	240 32.4	06.1	294 20.8	8.7	4 07.8	11.3	60.1
	05	255 32.3	06.4	308 48.5	8.7	4 19.1	11.3	60.1
	06	270 32.2	N22 06.8	323 16.2	8.6	N 4 30.4	11.3	60.1
W	07	285 32.1	07.1	337 43.8	8.6	4 41.7	11.2	60.1
E	08	300 32.0	07.4	352 11.4	8.5	4 52.9	11.3	60.2
D	09	315 31.9	. . 07.7	6 38.9	8.5	5 04.2	11.2	60.2
N	10	330 31.8	08.1	21 06.4	8.4	5 15.4	11.2	60.2
E	11	345 31.7	08.4	35 33.8	8.4	5 26.6	11.1	60.2
S	12	0 31.6	N22 08.7	50 01.2	8.4	N 5 37.7	11.1	60.2
D	13	15 31.5	09.1	64 28.6	8.3	5 48.8	11.1	60.3
A	14	30 31.4	09.4	78 55.9	8.3	5 59.9	11.1	60.3
Y	15	45 31.3	. . 09.7	93 23.2	8.2	6 11.0	11.0	60.3
	16	60 31.2	10.0	107 50.4	8.1	6 22.0	11.0	60.3
	17	75 31.1	10.4	122 17.5	8.1	6 33.0	11.0	60.3
	18	90 31.0	N22 10.7	136 44.6	8.1	N 6 44.0	10.9	60.4
	19	105 30.9	11.0	151 11.7	8.0	6 54.9	10.9	60.4
	20	120 30.8	11.3	165 38.7	8.0	7 05.8	10.9	60.4
	21	135 30.7	. . 11.7	180 05.7	7.9	7 16.7	10.8	60.4
	22	150 30.6	12.0	194 32.6	7.9	7 27.5	10.8	60.4
	23	165 30.5	12.3	208 59.5	7.8	N 7 38.3	10.7	60.4
		SD 15.8	*d* 0.3	SD 16.1		16.3		16.4

Lat.	Twilight Naut.	Twilight Civil	Sunrise	Moonrise 30	Moonrise 31	Moonrise 1	Moonrise 2
°	h m	h m	h m	h m	h m	h m	h m
N 72	□	□	□	01 45	01 39	01 34	01 28
N 70	□	□	□	01 38	01 38	01 39	01 40
68	□	□	□	01 32	01 37	01 43	01 49
66	////	////	01 15	01 26	01 36	01 46	01 57
64	////	////	01 59	01 22	01 35	01 49	02 04
62	////	00 13	02 28	01 18	01 35	01 51	02 10
60	////	01 28	02 50	01 15	01 34	01 53	02 15
N 58	////	02 01	03 08	01 12	01 33	01 55	02 19
56	00 12	02 25	03 23	01 09	01 33	01 57	02 23
54	01 20	02 44	03 35	01 07	01 33	01 59	02 27
52	01 51	03 00	03 46	01 05	01 32	02 00	02 30
50	02 14	03 14	03 56	01 03	01 32	02 01	02 33
45	02 53	03 41	04 17	00 58	01 31	02 04	02 40
N 40	03 21	04 01	04 34	00 55	01 30	02 07	02 45
35	03 43	04 18	04 47	00 51	01 30	02 09	02 50
30	04 00	04 33	05 00	00 49	01 29	02 11	02 54
20	04 27	04 56	05 20	00 44	01 28	02 14	03 01
N 10	04 48	05 15	05 38	00 40	01 28	02 17	03 08
0	05 06	05 32	05 54	00 36	01 27	02 20	03 14
S 10	05 22	05 48	06 10	00 32	01 26	02 22	03 20
20	05 37	06 04	06 28	00 27	01 26	02 26	03 27
30	05 52	06 21	06 47	00 22	01 25	02 29	03 35
35	06 00	06 31	06 59	00 20	01 25	02 31	03 39
40	06 08	06 42	07 12	00 17	01 24	02 33	03 44
45	06 18	06 54	07 27	00 13	01 23	02 36	03 50
S 50	06 28	07 09	07 46	00 08	01 23	02 39	03 57
52	06 33	07 16	07 55	00 06	01 23	02 41	04 01
54	06 38	07 23	08 05	00 04	01 22	02 42	04 04
56	06 43	07 31	08 17	00 02	01 22	02 44	04 08
58	06 49	07 40	08 30	25 21	01 21	02 46	04 13
S 60	06 56	07 51	08 45	25 21	01 21	02 49	04 18

Lat.	Sunset	Twilight Civil	Twilight Naut.	Moonset 30	Moonset 31	Moonset 1	Moonset 2
°	h m	h m	h m	h m	h m	h m	h m
N 72	□	□	□	12 15	14 10	16 07	18 10
N 70	□	□	□	12 20	14 08	15 58	17 51
68	□	□	□	12 25	14 06	15 50	17 37
66	22 45	////	////	12 28	14 05	15 44	17 25
64	21 58	////	////	12 31	14 04	15 39	17 15
62	21 29	////	////	12 33	14 03	15 34	17 07
60	21 06	22 30	////	12 36	14 02	15 30	17 00
N 58	20 49	21 56	////	12 38	14 01	15 27	16 53
56	20 34	21 31	////	12 39	14 00	15 24	16 48
54	20 21	21 12	22 38	12 41	14 00	15 21	16 43
52	20 10	20 56	22 06	12 42	13 59	15 18	16 38
50	20 00	20 43	21 43	12 43	13 59	15 16	16 34
45	19 39	20 15	21 03	12 46	13 58	15 11	16 25
N 40	19 22	19 54	20 35	12 48	13 57	15 07	16 18
35	19 08	19 37	20 13	12 50	13 56	15 03	16 12
30	18 56	19 23	19 56	12 52	13 55	15 00	16 06
20	18 36	19 00	19 29	12 55	13 54	14 55	15 57
N 10	18 18	18 41	19 07	12 58	13 53	14 50	15 48
0	18 01	18 24	18 50	13 00	13 52	14 45	15 41
S 10	17 45	18 08	18 34	13 02	13 51	14 41	15 33
20	17 28	17 51	18 19	13 05	13 50	14 36	15 25
30	17 08	17 34	18 04	13 08	13 48	14 30	15 15
35	16 56	17 24	17 56	13 09	13 48	14 27	15 10
40	16 43	17 13	17 47	13 11	13 47	14 24	15 04
45	16 28	17 01	17 38	13 13	13 46	14 20	14 56
S 50	16 09	16 46	17 27	13 15	13 44	14 15	14 48
52	16 00	16 39	17 22	13 16	13 44	14 13	14 44
54	15 50	16 32	17 17	13 18	13 43	14 10	14 40
56	15 38	16 24	17 12	13 19	13 43	14 07	14 35
58	15 25	16 15	17 06	13 20	13 42	14 04	14 30
S 60	15 10	16 04	16 59	13 22	13 41	14 01	14 24

Day	SUN Eqn. of Time 00^h	SUN Eqn. of Time 12^h	SUN Mer. Pass.	MOON Mer. Pass. Upper	MOON Mer. Pass. Lower	MOON Age	MOON Phase
d	m s	m s	h m	h m	h m	d	%
30	02 29	02 25	11 58	06 48	19 13	24	39
31	02 20	02 16	11 58	07 39	20 06	25	28
1	02 11	02 07	11 58	08 32	21 00	26	18

	UT	ARIES	VENUS −4·0		MARS −1·9		JUPITER −2·0		SATURN +0·0	
		GHA	GHA	Dec	GHA	Dec	GHA	Dec	GHA	Dec
	d h	° ′	° ′	° ′	° ′	° ′	° ′	° ′	° ′	° ′
	2 00	250 53.6	181 54.0	N21 49.7	15 23.9	S21 23.0	85 04.1	N 7 27.1	358 51.4	S20 35.4
	01	265 56.1	196 53.2	50.2	30 27.2	22.9	100 06.4	27.0	13 54.1	35.4
	02	280 58.6	211 52.4	50.8	45 30.6	22.8	115 08.7	27.0	28 56.7	35.3
	03	296 01.0	226 51.6	. . 51.3	60 33.9	. . 22.8	130 11.0	. . 26.9	43 59.4	. . 35.3
	04	311 03.5	241 50.8	51.8	75 37.3	22.7	145 13.3	26.8	59 02.0	35.3
	05	326 06.0	256 50.0	52.4	90 40.6	22.6	160 15.6	26.7	74 04.7	35.3
	06	341 08.4	271 49.2	N21 52.9	105 44.0	S21 22.6	175 17.9	N 7 26.7	89 07.4	S20 35.3
	07	356 10.9	286 48.4	53.4	120 47.3	22.5	190 20.2	26.6	104 10.0	35.2
T	08	11 13.3	301 47.6	54.0	135 50.7	22.4	205 22.6	26.5	119 12.7	35.2
H	09	26 15.8	316 46.8	. . 54.5	150 54.0	. . 22.3	220 24.9	. . 26.5	134 15.3	. . 35.2
U	10	41 18.3	331 46.0	55.0	165 57.4	22.3	235 27.2	26.4	149 18.0	35.2
R	11	56 20.7	346 45.2	55.5	181 00.7	22.2	250 29.5	26.3	164 20.7	35.2
S	12	71 23.2	1 44.4	N21 56.1	196 04.0	S21 22.1	265 31.8	N 7 26.2	179 23.3	S20 35.1
D	13	86 25.7	16 43.6	56.6	211 07.4	22.0	280 34.1	26.2	194 26.0	35.1
A	14	101 28.1	31 42.8	57.1	226 10.7	22.0	295 36.4	26.1	209 28.7	35.1
Y	15	116 30.6	46 42.0	. . 57.6	241 14.1	. . 21.9	310 38.7	. . 26.0	224 31.3	. . 35.1
	16	131 33.1	61 41.2	58.1	256 17.4	21.8	325 41.0	25.9	239 34.0	35.1
	17	146 35.5	76 40.4	58.7	271 20.8	21.8	340 43.3	25.9	254 36.6	35.0
	18	161 38.0	91 39.6	N21 59.2	286 24.1	S21 21.7	355 45.6	N 7 25.8	269 39.3	S20 35.0
	19	176 40.4	106 38.8	21 59.7	301 27.4	21.6	10 47.9	25.7	284 42.0	35.0
	20	191 42.9	121 38.0	22 00.2	316 30.8	21.5	25 50.2	25.6	299 44.6	35.0
	21	206 45.4	136 37.2	. . 00.7	331 34.1	. . 21.5	40 52.5	. . 25.6	314 47.3	. . 35.0
	22	221 47.8	151 36.4	01.2	346 37.5	21.4	55 54.8	25.5	329 49.9	34.9
	23	236 50.3	166 35.6	01.7	1 40.8	21.3	70 57.1	25.4	344 52.6	34.9
	3 00	251 52.8	181 34.8	N22 02.3	16 44.1	S21 21.2	85 59.4	N 7 25.3	359 55.3	S20 34.9
	01	266 55.2	196 34.0	02.8	31 47.5	21.2	101 01.7	25.2	14 57.9	34.9
	02	281 57.7	211 33.2	03.3	46 50.8	21.1	116 04.0	25.2	30 00.6	34.9
	03	297 00.2	226 32.4	. . 03.8	61 54.1	. . 21.0	131 06.3	. . 25.1	45 03.2	. . 34.8
	04	312 02.6	241 31.6	04.3	76 57.5	21.0	146 08.6	25.0	60 05.9	34.8
	05	327 05.1	256 30.8	04.8	92 00.8	20.9	161 10.9	24.9	75 08.6	34.8
	06	342 07.6	271 29.9	N22 05.3	107 04.1	S21 20.8	176 13.2	N 7 24.9	90 11.2	S20 34.8
	07	357 10.0	286 29.1	05.8	122 07.5	20.7	191 15.5	24.8	105 13.9	34.8
	08	12 12.5	301 28.3	06.3	137 10.8	20.7	206 17.8	24.7	120 16.5	34.7
F	09	27 14.9	316 27.5	. . 06.8	152 14.1	. . 20.6	221 20.1	. . 24.6	135 19.2	. . 34.7
R	10	42 17.4	331 26.7	07.3	167 17.5	20.5	236 22.4	24.6	150 21.9	34.7
I	11	57 19.9	346 25.9	07.8	182 20.8	20.5	251 24.7	24.5	165 24.5	34.7
D	12	72 22.3	1 25.1	N22 08.3	197 24.1	S21 20.4	266 27.0	N 7 24.4	180 27.2	S20 34.7
A	13	87 24.8	16 24.3	08.8	212 27.4	20.3	281 29.3	24.3	195 29.9	34.6
Y	14	102 27.3	31 23.5	09.3	227 30.8	20.2	296 31.6	24.3	210 32.5	34.6
	15	117 29.7	46 22.7	. . 09.8	242 34.1	. . 20.2	311 33.9	. . 24.2	225 35.2	. . 34.6
	16	132 32.2	61 21.8	10.3	257 37.4	20.1	326 36.2	24.1	240 37.8	34.6
	17	147 34.7	76 21.0	10.8	272 40.7	20.0	341 38.5	24.0	255 40.5	34.6
	18	162 37.1	91 20.2	N22 11.3	287 44.1	S21 19.9	356 40.8	N 7 23.9	270 43.2	S20 34.5
	19	177 39.6	106 19.4	11.7	302 47.4	19.9	11 43.1	23.9	285 45.8	34.5
	20	192 42.1	121 18.6	12.2	317 50.7	19.8	26 45.4	23.8	300 48.5	34.5
	21	207 44.5	136 17.8	. . 12.7	332 54.0	. . 19.7	41 47.7	. . 23.7	315 51.1	. . 34.5
	22	222 47.0	151 17.0	13.2	347 57.3	19.7	56 50.0	23.6	330 53.8	34.5
	23	237 49.4	166 16.1	13.7	3 00.7	19.6	71 52.3	23.6	345 56.5	34.4
	4 00	252 51.9	181 15.3	N22 14.2	18 04.0	S21 19.5	86 54.6	N 7 23.5	0 59.1	S20 34.4
	01	267 54.4	196 14.5	14.7	33 07.3	19.4	101 56.9	23.4	16 01.8	34.4
	02	282 56.8	211 13.7	15.1	48 10.6	19.4	116 59.2	23.3	31 04.4	34.4
	03	297 59.3	226 12.9	. . 15.6	63 13.9	. . 19.3	132 01.5	. . 23.2	46 07.1	. . 34.4
	04	313 01.8	241 12.1	16.1	78 17.2	19.2	147 03.8	23.2	61 09.8	34.3
	05	328 04.2	256 11.2	16.6	93 20.6	19.2	162 06.1	23.1	76 12.4	34.3
	06	343 06.7	271 10.4	N22 17.1	108 23.9	S21 19.1	177 08.4	N 7 23.0	91 15.1	S20 34.3
	07	358 09.2	286 09.6	17.5	123 27.2	19.0	192 10.7	22.9	106 17.7	34.3
S	08	13 11.6	301 08.8	18.0	138 30.5	18.9	207 13.0	22.8	121 20.4	34.3
A	09	28 14.1	316 08.0	. . 18.5	153 33.8	. . 18.9	222 15.3	. . 22.8	136 23.1	. . 34.2
T	10	43 16.6	331 07.2	19.0	168 37.1	18.8	237 17.6	22.7	151 25.7	34.2
U	11	58 19.0	346 06.3	19.4	183 40.4	18.7	252 19.9	22.6	166 28.4	34.2
R	12	73 21.5	1 05.5	N22 19.9	198 43.7	S21 18.6	267 22.2	N 7 22.5	181 31.0	S20 34.2
D	13	88 23.9	16 04.7	20.4	213 47.0	18.6	282 24.5	22.4	196 33.7	34.2
A	14	103 26.4	31 03.9	20.8	228 50.3	18.5	297 26.8	22.4	211 36.4	34.1
Y	15	118 28.9	46 03.1	. . 21.3	243 53.6	. . 18.4	312 29.0	. . 22.3	226 39.0	. . 34.1
	16	133 31.3	61 02.2	21.8	258 56.9	18.4	327 31.3	22.2	241 41.7	34.1
	17	148 33.8	76 01.4	22.2	274 00.3	18.3	342 33.6	22.1	256 44.4	34.1
	18	163 36.3	91 00.6	N22 22.7	289 03.6	S21 18.2	357 35.9	N 7 22.0	271 47.0	S20 34.1
	19	178 38.7	105 59.8	23.2	304 06.9	18.1	12 38.2	22.0	286 49.7	34.0
	20	193 41.2	120 58.9	23.6	319 10.2	18.1	27 40.5	21.9	301 52.3	34.0
	21	208 43.7	135 58.1	. . 24.1	334 13.5	. . 18.0	42 42.8	. . 21.8	316 55.0	. . 34.0
	22	223 46.1	150 57.3	24.5	349 16.8	17.9	57 45.1	21.7	331 57.7	34.0
	23	238 48.6	165 56.5	25.0	4 20.1	17.9	72 47.4	21.6	347 00.3	34.0
	Mer. Pass.	h m 7 11.3	v −0.8	d 0.5	v 3.3	d 0.1	v 2.3	d 0.1	v 2.7	d 0.0

STARS		
Name	SHA	Dec
	° ′	° ′
Acamar	315 17.3	S40 14.4
Achernar	335 25.8	S57 09.1
Acrux	173 06.6	S63 11.6
Adhara	255 11.3	S29 00.0
Aldebaran	290 47.4	N16 32.3
Alioth	166 18.8	N55 52.5
Alkaid	152 57.1	N49 14.2
Al Na'ir	27 41.2	S46 52.6
Alnilam	275 44.7	S 1 11.8
Alphard	217 54.3	S 8 44.0
Alphecca	126 09.0	N26 39.8
Alpheratz	357 41.5	N29 10.6
Altair	62 06.0	N 8 54.8
Ankaa	353 14.0	S42 12.9
Antares	112 23.4	S26 27.9
Arcturus	145 53.7	N19 06.0
Atria	107 22.8	S69 03.2
Avior	234 17.5	S59 34.1
Bellatrix	278 30.2	N 6 21.6
Betelgeuse	270 59.5	N 7 24.3
Canopus	263 55.8	S52 42.6
Capella	280 32.0	N46 00.6
Deneb	49 29.8	N45 20.3
Denebola	182 31.6	N14 28.9
Diphda	348 54.1	S17 53.8
Dubhe	193 49.4	N61 40.0
Elnath	278 10.5	N28 37.0
Eltanin	90 44.7	N51 29.3
Enif	33 45.1	N 9 57.0
Fomalhaut	15 21.8	S29 31.9
Gacrux	171 58.3	S57 12.5
Gienah	175 50.1	S17 38.1
Hadar	148 44.4	S60 27.2
Hamal	327 58.7	N23 32.1
Kaus Aust.	83 40.8	S34 22.3
Kochab	137 19.3	N74 05.6
Markab	13 36.3	N15 17.5
Menkar	314 13.3	N 4 09.0
Menkent	148 04.9	S36 27.1
Miaplacidus	221 39.5	S69 47.5
Mirfak	308 37.9	N49 54.8
Nunki	75 55.5	S26 16.3
Peacock	53 15.8	S56 40.6
Pollux	243 25.6	N27 59.1
Procyon	244 57.9	N 5 10.8
Rasalhague	96 04.3	N12 33.1
Regulus	207 41.5	N11 53.2
Rigel	281 10.5	S 8 11.2
Rigil Kent.	139 48.3	S60 54.2
Sabik	102 09.9	S15 44.5
Schedar	349 38.4	N56 37.3
Shaula	96 18.8	S37 06.7
Sirius	258 32.3	S16 44.6
Spica	158 28.9	S11 14.8
Suhail	222 51.1	S43 30.3
Vega	80 37.2	N38 48.0
Zuben'ubi	137 02.9	S16 06.5

	SHA	Mer. Pass.
	° ′	h m
Venus	289 42.0	11 54
Mars	124 51.4	22 48
Jupiter	194 06.7	18 13
Saturn	108 02.5	0 00

Day	UT (d h)	SUN GHA (° ′)	SUN Dec (° ′)	MOON GHA (° ′)	v (′)	MOON Dec (° ′)	d (′)	HP (′)
THURSDAY	2 00	180 30.4	N22 12.6	223 26.3	7.7	N 7 49.0	10.7	60.4
	01	195 30.3	12.9	237 53.0	7.8	7 59.7	10.7	60.5
	02	210 30.2	13.3	252 19.8	7.6	8 10.4	10.6	60.5
	03	225 30.1	. . 13.6	266 46.4	7.6	8 21.0	10.5	60.5
	04	240 30.0	13.9	281 13.0	7.6	8 31.5	10.6	60.5
	05	255 29.9	14.2	295 39.6	7.5	8 42.1	10.4	60.5
	06	270 29.8	N22 14.5	310 06.1	7.5	N 8 52.5	10.4	60.5
	07	285 29.7	14.8	324 32.6	7.4	9 02.9	10.4	60.5
	08	300 29.6	15.2	338 59.0	7.3	9 13.3	10.3	60.6
	09	315 29.5	. . 15.5	353 25.3	7.3	9 23.6	10.2	60.6
	10	330 29.4	15.8	7 51.6	7.3	9 33.8	10.2	60.6
	11	345 29.3	16.1	22 17.9	7.2	9 44.0	10.1	60.6
	12	0 29.2	N22 16.4	36 44.1	7.1	N 9 54.1	10.1	60.6
	13	15 29.1	16.7	51 10.2	7.1	10 04.2	10.0	60.6
	14	30 29.0	17.0	65 36.3	7.1	10 14.2	9.9	60.6
	15	45 28.9	. . 17.3	80 02.4	7.0	10 24.1	9.9	60.6
	16	60 28.8	17.6	94 28.4	6.9	10 34.0	9.8	60.6
	17	75 28.7	18.0	108 54.3	6.9	10 43.8	9.7	60.6
	18	90 28.6	N22 18.3	123 20.2	6.8	N10 53.5	9.7	60.7
	19	105 28.5	18.6	137 46.0	6.8	11 03.2	9.6	60.7
	20	120 28.4	18.9	152 11.8	6.8	11 12.8	9.5	60.7
	21	135 28.3	. . 19.2	166 37.6	6.7	11 22.3	9.5	60.7
	22	150 28.2	19.5	181 03.3	6.6	11 31.8	9.3	60.7
	23	165 28.1	19.8	195 28.9	6.6	11 41.1	9.4	60.7
FRIDAY	3 00	180 27.9	N22 20.1	209 54.5	6.5	N11 50.5	9.2	60.7
	01	195 27.8	20.4	224 20.0	6.5	11 59.7	9.1	60.7
	02	210 27.7	20.7	238 45.5	6.5	12 08.8	9.1	60.7
	03	225 27.6	. . 21.0	253 11.0	6.3	12 17.9	9.0	60.7
	04	240 27.5	21.3	267 36.3	6.4	12 26.9	8.9	60.7
	05	255 27.4	21.6	282 01.7	6.3	12 35.8	8.8	60.7
	06	270 27.3	N22 21.9	296 27.0	6.2	N12 44.6	8.7	60.7
	07	285 27.2	22.2	310 52.2	6.2	12 53.3	8.7	60.7
	08	300 27.1	22.5	325 17.4	6.2	13 02.0	8.6	60.7
	09	315 27.0	. . 22.8	339 42.6	6.1	13 10.6	8.4	60.7
	10	330 26.9	23.1	354 07.7	6.0	13 19.0	8.4	60.7
	11	345 26.8	23.4	8 32.7	6.1	13 27.4	8.3	60.7
	12	0 26.7	N22 23.7	22 57.8	5.9	N13 35.7	8.2	60.7
	13	15 26.6	24.0	37 22.7	6.0	13 43.9	8.1	60.7
	14	30 26.5	24.3	51 47.7	5.8	13 52.0	8.0	60.7
	15	45 26.4	. . 24.6	66 12.5	5.9	14 00.0	7.9	60.7
	16	60 26.3	24.9	80 37.4	5.8	14 07.9	7.9	60.7
	17	75 26.1	25.2	95 02.2	5.7	14 15.8	7.7	60.7
	18	90 26.0	N22 25.4	109 26.9	5.8	N14 23.5	7.6	60.7
	19	105 25.9	25.7	123 51.7	5.6	14 31.1	7.5	60.7
	20	120 25.8	26.0	138 16.3	5.7	14 38.6	7.4	60.7
	21	135 25.7	. . 26.3	152 41.0	5.6	14 46.0	7.3	60.7
	22	150 25.6	26.6	167 05.6	5.5	14 53.3	7.2	60.7
	23	165 25.5	26.9	181 30.1	5.6	15 00.5	7.1	60.7
SATURDAY	4 00	180 25.4	N22 27.2	195 54.7	5.5	N15 07.6	7.0	60.7
	01	195 25.3	27.5	210 19.2	5.4	15 14.6	6.9	60.7
	02	210 25.2	27.8	224 43.6	5.4	15 21.5	6.8	60.7
	03	225 25.1	. . 28.0	239 08.0	5.4	15 28.3	6.7	60.7
	04	240 25.0	28.3	253 32.4	5.4	15 35.0	6.5	60.6
	05	255 24.8	28.6	267 56.8	5.3	15 41.5	6.5	60.6
	06	270 24.7	N22 28.9	282 21.1	5.3	N15 48.0	6.3	60.6
	07	285 24.6	29.2	296 45.4	5.3	15 54.3	6.3	60.6
	08	300 24.5	29.5	311 09.7	5.2	16 00.6	6.1	60.6
	09	315 24.4	. . 29.7	325 33.9	5.2	16 06.7	6.0	60.6
	10	330 24.3	30.0	339 58.1	5.2	16 12.7	5.8	60.6
	11	345 24.2	30.3	354 22.3	5.2	16 18.5	5.8	60.6
	12	0 24.1	N22 30.6	8 46.5	5.1	N16 24.3	5.6	60.6
	13	15 24.0	30.9	23 10.6	5.2	16 29.9	5.6	60.6
	14	30 23.9	31.1	37 34.8	5.1	16 35.5	5.4	60.5
	15	45 23.7	. . 31.4	51 58.9	5.0	16 40.9	5.3	60.5
	16	60 23.6	31.7	66 22.9	5.1	16 46.2	5.1	60.5
	17	75 23.5	32.0	80 47.0	5.0	16 51.3	5.1	60.5
	18	90 23.4	N22 32.2	95 11.0	5.1	N16 56.4	4.9	60.5
	19	105 23.3	32.5	109 35.1	5.0	17 01.3	4.8	60.5
	20	120 23.2	32.8	123 59.1	5.0	17 06.1	4.7	60.5
	21	135 23.1	. . 33.1	138 23.1	5.0	17 10.8	4.6	60.4
	22	150 23.0	33.3	152 47.1	5.0	17 15.4	4.4	60.4
	23	165 22.9	33.6	167 11.1	4.9	N17 19.8	4.3	60.4
		SD 15.8	d 0.3	SD	16.5		16.5	16.5

Lat.	Twilight Naut.	Twilight Civil	Sunrise	Moonrise 2	Moonrise 3	Moonrise 4	Moonrise 5
°	h m	h m	h m	h m	h m	h m	h m
N 72	▭	▭	▭	01 28	01 22	01 15	01 02
N 70	▭	▭	▭	01 40	01 42	01 48	02 01
68	▭	▭	▭	01 49	01 58	02 12	02 36
66	////	////	01 02	01 57	02 11	02 31	03 02
64	////	////	01 52	02 04	02 22	02 47	03 21
62	////	////	02 23	02 10	02 32	03 00	03 37
60	////	01 19	02 46	02 15	02 40	03 11	03 51
N 58	////	01 56	03 04	02 19	02 47	03 20	04 02
56	////	02 21	03 20	02 23	02 53	03 29	04 12
54	01 12	02 41	03 33	02 27	02 59	03 36	04 21
52	01 46	02 57	03 44	02 30	03 04	03 43	04 29
50	02 10	03 11	03 54	02 33	03 08	03 49	04 36
45	02 51	03 39	04 15	02 40	03 18	04 02	04 52
N 40	03 19	04 00	04 32	02 45	03 27	04 13	05 05
35	03 41	04 17	04 47	02 50	03 34	04 22	05 15
30	03 59	04 32	04 59	02 54	03 40	04 31	05 25
20	04 27	04 56	05 20	03 01	03 52	04 45	05 41
N 10	04 48	05 15	05 38	03 08	04 01	04 57	05 56
0	05 06	05 32	05 55	03 14	04 11	05 09	06 09
S 10	05 22	05 48	06 11	03 20	04 20	05 21	06 23
20	05 38	06 05	06 29	03 27	04 30	05 34	06 37
30	05 53	06 23	06 49	03 35	04 42	05 49	06 54
35	06 01	06 33	07 01	03 39	04 48	05 57	07 04
40	06 10	06 44	07 14	03 44	04 56	06 07	07 15
45	06 20	06 56	07 30	03 50	05 05	06 18	07 28
S 50	06 31	07 12	07 49	03 57	05 16	06 32	07 44
52	06 35	07 18	07 59	04 01	05 21	06 39	07 51
54	06 41	07 26	08 09	04 04	05 26	06 46	08 00
56	06 46	07 35	08 21	04 08	05 32	06 54	08 09
58	06 52	07 44	08 34	04 13	05 39	07 03	08 20
S 60	06 59	07 55	08 50	04 18	05 47	07 14	08 32

Lat.	Sunset	Twilight Civil	Twilight Naut.	Moonset 2	Moonset 3	Moonset 4	Moonset 5
°	h m	h m	h m	h m	h m	h m	h m
N 72	▭	▭	▭	18 10	20 19	22 37	▭
N 70	▭	▭	▭	17 51	19 46	21 38	23 11
68	▭	▭	▭	17 37	19 23	21 03	22 27
66	22 59	////	////	17 25	19 05	20 39	21 58
64	22 06	////	////	17 15	18 50	20 20	21 36
62	21 35	////	////	17 07	18 38	20 04	21 18
60	21 12	22 40	////	17 00	18 28	19 51	21 03
N 58	20 53	22 02	////	16 53	18 19	19 39	20 51
56	20 38	21 36	////	16 48	18 11	19 30	20 40
54	20 24	21 16	22 47	16 43	18 04	19 21	20 31
52	20 13	21 00	22 12	16 38	17 58	19 13	20 22
50	20 03	20 46	21 48	16 34	17 52	19 06	20 15
45	19 41	20 18	21 06	16 25	17 40	18 52	19 58
N 40	19 24	19 57	20 37	16 18	17 30	18 39	19 45
35	19 10	19 39	20 16	16 12	17 21	18 29	19 34
30	18 58	19 25	19 58	16 06	17 13	18 20	19 24
20	18 37	19 01	19 30	15 57	17 00	18 04	19 07
N 10	18 19	18 42	19 08	15 48	16 49	17 50	18 52
0	18 02	18 24	18 50	15 41	16 38	17 38	18 38
S 10	17 45	18 08	18 34	15 33	16 28	17 25	18 24
20	17 28	17 51	18 19	15 25	16 16	17 11	18 09
30	17 07	17 34	18 03	15 15	16 03	16 56	17 52
35	16 56	17 24	17 55	15 10	15 56	16 47	17 42
40	16 42	17 12	17 46	15 04	15 47	16 36	17 30
45	16 26	17 00	17 37	14 56	15 37	16 24	17 17
S 50	16 07	16 45	17 26	14 48	15 26	16 09	17 01
52	15 58	16 38	17 21	14 44	15 20	16 03	16 53
54	15 47	16 30	17 16	14 40	15 14	15 55	16 44
56	15 36	16 22	17 10	14 35	15 07	15 47	16 35
58	15 22	16 12	17 04	14 30	15 00	15 37	16 24
S 60	15 06	16 01	16 57	14 24	14 51	15 26	16 11

Day	SUN Eqn. of Time 00^h	SUN Eqn. of Time 12^h	SUN Mer. Pass.	MOON Mer. Pass. Upper	MOON Mer. Pass. Lower	MOON Age	MOON Phase
d	m s	m s	h m	h m	h m	d	%
2	02 02	01 57	11 58	09 27	21 56	27	10
3	01 52	01 47	11 58	10 24	22 54	28	4 ●
4	01 42	01 37	11 58	11 23	23 53	29	1

	UT	ARIES	VENUS −4·0		MARS −1·9		JUPITER −2·0		SATURN +0·0	
		GHA	GHA	Dec	GHA	Dec	GHA	Dec	GHA	Dec
	d h	° ′	° ′	° ′	° ′	° ′	° ′	° ′	° ′	° ′
	5 00	253 51.0	180 55.7	N22 25.5	19 23.3	S21 17.8	87 49.7	N 7 21.6	2 03.0	S20 33.9
	01	268 53.5	195 54.8	25.9	34 26.6	17.7	102 52.0	21.5	17 05.6	33.9
	02	283 56.0	210 54.0	26.4	49 29.9	17.6	117 54.3	21.4	32 08.3	33.9
	03	298 58.4	225 53.2	. . 26.8	64 33.2	. . 17.6	132 56.5	. . 21.3	47 11.0	. . 33.9
	04	314 00.9	240 52.4	27.3	79 36.5	17.5	147 58.8	21.2	62 13.6	33.9
	05	329 03.4	255 51.5	27.7	94 39.8	17.4	163 01.1	21.2	77 16.3	33.8
	06	344 05.8	270 50.7	N22 28.2	109 43.1	S21 17.4	178 03.4	N 7 21.1	92 18.9	S20 33.8
	07	359 08.3	285 49.9	28.6	124 46.4	17.3	193 05.7	21.0	107 21.6	33.8
	08	14 10.8	300 49.0	29.1	139 49.7	17.2	208 08.0	20.9	122 24.3	33.8
S	09	29 13.2	315 48.2	. . 29.5	154 53.0	. . 17.1	223 10.3	. . 20.8	137 26.9	. . 33.8
U	10	44 15.7	330 47.4	30.0	169 56.3	17.1	238 12.6	20.7	152 29.6	33.7
N	11	59 18.2	345 46.6	30.4	184 59.6	17.0	253 14.9	20.7	167 32.2	33.7
D	12	74 20.6	0 45.7	N22 30.9	200 02.8	S21 16.9	268 17.1	N 7 20.6	182 34.9	S20 33.7
A	13	89 23.1	15 44.9	31.3	215 06.1	16.9	283 19.4	20.5	197 37.6	33.7
Y	14	104 25.5	30 44.1	31.8	230 09.4	16.8	298 21.7	20.4	212 40.2	33.7
	15	119 28.0	45 43.2	. . 32.2	245 12.7	. . 16.7	313 24.0	. . 20.3	227 42.9	. . 33.6
	16	134 30.5	60 42.4	32.6	260 16.0	16.6	328 26.3	20.3	242 45.5	33.6
	17	149 32.9	75 41.6	33.1	275 19.3	16.6	343 28.6	20.2	257 48.2	33.6
	18	164 35.4	90 40.8	N22 33.5	290 22.5	S21 16.5	358 30.9	N 7 20.1	272 50.9	S20 33.6
	19	179 37.9	105 39.9	33.9	305 25.8	16.4	13 33.1	20.0	287 53.5	33.6
	20	194 40.3	120 39.1	34.4	320 29.1	16.4	28 35.4	19.9	302 56.2	33.5
	21	209 42.8	135 38.3	. . 34.8	335 32.4	. . 16.3	43 37.7	. . 19.8	317 58.9	. . 33.5
	22	224 45.3	150 37.4	35.3	350 35.7	16.2	58 40.0	19.8	333 01.5	33.5
	23	239 47.7	165 36.6	35.7	5 38.9	16.2	73 42.3	19.7	348 04.2	33.5
	6 00	254 50.2	180 35.8	N22 36.1	20 42.2	S21 16.1	88 44.6	N 7 19.6	3 06.8	S20 33.5
	01	269 52.7	195 34.9	36.5	35 45.5	16.0	103 46.9	19.5	18 09.5	33.4
	02	284 55.1	210 34.1	37.0	50 48.7	15.9	118 49.1	19.4	33 12.2	33.4
	03	299 57.6	225 33.3	. . 37.4	65 52.0	. . 15.9	133 51.4	. . 19.3	48 14.8	. . 33.4
	04	315 00.0	240 32.4	37.8	80 55.3	15.8	148 53.7	19.3	63 17.5	33.4
	05	330 02.5	255 31.6	38.3	95 58.6	15.7	163 56.0	19.2	78 20.1	33.4
	06	345 05.0	270 30.8	N22 38.7	111 01.8	S21 15.7	178 58.3	N 7 19.1	93 22.8	S20 33.3
	07	0 07.4	285 29.9	39.1	126 05.1	15.6	194 00.6	19.0	108 25.5	33.3
	08	15 09.9	300 29.1	39.5	141 08.4	15.5	209 02.8	18.9	123 28.1	33.3
M	09	30 12.4	315 28.3	. . 39.9	156 11.6	. . 15.4	224 05.1	. . 18.8	138 30.8	. . 33.3
O	10	45 14.8	330 27.4	40.4	171 14.9	15.4	239 07.4	18.8	153 33.4	33.3
N	11	60 17.3	345 26.6	40.8	186 18.2	15.3	254 09.7	18.7	168 36.1	33.2
D	12	75 19.8	0 25.8	N22 41.2	201 21.4	S21 15.2	269 12.0	N 7 18.6	183 38.8	S20 33.2
A	13	90 22.2	15 24.9	41.6	216 24.7	15.2	284 14.2	18.5	198 41.4	33.2
Y	14	105 24.7	30 24.1	42.0	231 27.9	15.1	299 16.5	18.4	213 44.1	33.2
	15	120 27.2	45 23.3	. . 42.4	246 31.2	. . 15.0	314 18.8	. . 18.3	228 46.7	. . 33.2
	16	135 29.6	60 22.4	42.8	261 34.5	15.0	329 21.1	18.2	243 49.4	33.1
	17	150 32.1	75 21.6	43.3	276 37.7	14.9	344 23.4	18.2	258 52.1	33.1
	18	165 34.5	90 20.8	N22 43.7	291 41.0	S21 14.8	359 25.6	N 7 18.1	273 54.7	S20 33.1
	19	180 37.0	105 20.0	44.1	306 44.2	14.8	14 27.9	18.0	288 57.4	33.1
	20	195 39.5	120 19.2	44.4	321 47.5	14.7	29 30.2	17.9	304 00.0	33.1
	21	210 41.9	135 18.4	. . 44.7	336 50.7	. . 14.6	44 32.5	. . 17.8	319 02.7	. . 33.0
	22	225 44.4	150 17.1	44.8	351 54.0	14.5	59 34.8	17.7	334 05.4	33.0
	23	240 46.9	165 16.3	45.7	6 57.2	14.5	74 37.0	17.6	349 08.0	33.0
	7 00	255 49.3	180 15.5	N22 46.1	22 00.5	S21 14.4	89 39.3	N 7 17.6	4 10.7	S20 33.0
	01	270 51.8	195 14.7	46.5	37 03.7	14.3	104 41.6	17.5	19 13.3	33.0
	02	285 54.3	210 13.9	46.9	52 07.0	14.3	119 43.9	17.4	34 16.0	32.9
	03	300 56.7	225 13.1	. . 47.3	67 10.2	. . 14.2	134 46.2	. . 17.3	49 18.7	. . 32.9
	04	315 59.2	240 12.3	47.7	82 13.5	14.1	149 48.4	17.2	64 21.3	32.9
	05	331 01.7	255 11.4	48.1	97 16.7	14.1	164 50.7	17.1	79 24.0	32.9
	06	346 04.1	270 10.6	N22 48.5	112 20.0	S21 14.0	179 53.0	N 7 17.0	94 26.6	S20 32.9
	07	1 06.6	285 09.7	48.9	127 23.2	13.9	194 55.3	17.0	109 29.3	32.8
T	08	16 09.0	300 08.9	49.3	142 26.5	13.9	209 57.5	16.9	124 32.0	32.8
U	09	31 11.5	315 08.1	. . 49.7	157 29.7	. . 13.8	224 59.8	. . 16.8	139 34.6	. . 32.8
E	10	46 14.0	330 07.2	50.1	172 32.9	13.7	240 02.1	16.7	154 37.3	32.8
S	11	61 16.4	345 06.4	50.5	187 36.2	13.7	255 04.4	16.6	169 39.9	32.8
D	12	76 18.9	0 05.5	N22 50.9	202 39.4	S21 13.6	270 06.6	N 7 16.5	184 42.6	S20 32.7
A	13	91 21.4	15 04.7	51.3	217 42.7	13.5	285 08.9	16.4	199 45.3	32.7
Y	14	106 23.8	30 03.9	51.7	232 45.9	13.4	300 11.2	16.3	214 47.9	32.7
	15	121 26.3	45 03.0	. . 52.1	247 49.1	. . 13.4	315 13.5	. . 16.3	229 50.6	. . 32.7
	16	136 28.8	60 02.2	52.4	262 52.4	13.3	330 15.7	16.2	244 53.2	32.7
	17	151 31.2	75 01.3	52.8	277 55.6	13.2	345 18.0	16.1	259 55.9	32.6
	18	166 33.7	90 00.5	N22 53.2	292 58.8	S21 13.2	0 20.3	N 7 16.0	274 58.6	S20 32.6
	19	181 36.2	104 59.6	53.6	308 02.1	13.1	15 22.6	15.9	290 01.2	32.6
	20	196 38.6	119 58.8	54.0	323 05.3	13.0	30 24.8	15.8	305 03.9	32.6
	21	211 41.1	134 57.9	. . 54.4	338 08.5	. . 13.0	45 27.1	. . 15.7	320 06.5	. . 32.6
	22	226 43.5	149 57.1	54.7	353 11.7	12.9	60 29.4	15.6	335 09.2	32.5
	23	241 46.0	164 56.2	55.1	8 15.0	12.8	75 31.7	15.6	350 11.9	32.5
	Mer. Pass.	h m 6 59.5	*v* −0.8	*d* 0.4	*v* 3.3	*d* 0.1	*v* 2.3	*d* 0.1	*v* 2.7	*d* 0.0

STARS

Name	SHA	Dec
	° ′	° ′
Acamar	315 17.3	S40 14.4
Achernar	335 25.8	S57 09.1
Acrux	173 06.6	S63 11.7
Adhara	255 11.3	S29 00.0
Aldebaran	290 47.4	N16 32.3
Alioth	166 18.8	N55 52.5
Alkaid	152 57.1	N49 14.2
Al Na'ir	27 41.2	S46 52.6
Alnilam	275 44.7	S 1 11.8
Alphard	217 54.3	S 8 44.0
Alphecca	126 09.0	N26 39.8
Alpheratz	357 41.5	N29 10.6
Altair	62 06.0	N 8 54.8
Ankaa	353 14.0	S42 12.9
Antares	112 23.4	S26 27.9
Arcturus	145 53.7	N19 06.0
Atria	107 22.8	S69 03.2
Avior	234 17.6	S59 34.1
Bellatrix	278 30.2	N 6 21.6
Betelgeuse	270 59.5	N 7 24.3
Canopus	263 55.8	S52 42.6
Capella	280 32.0	N46 00.6
Deneb	49 29.8	N45 20.3
Denebola	182 31.6	N14 28.9
Diphda	348 54.1	S17 53.8
Dubhe	193 49.5	N61 40.0
Elnath	278 10.5	N28 37.0
Eltanin	90 44.7	N51 29.3
Enif	33 45.0	N 9 57.0
Fomalhaut	15 21.8	S29 31.9
Gacrux	171 58.3	S57 12.5
Gienah	175 50.1	S17 38.1
Hadar	148 44.4	S60 27.2
Hamal	327 58.7	N23 32.1
Kaus Aust.	83 40.8	S34 22.3
Kochab	137 19.3	N74 05.6
Markab	13 36.3	N15 17.5
Menkar	314 13.2	N 4 09.0
Menkent	148 04.9	S36 27.1
Miaplacidus	221 39.5	S69 47.5
Mirfak	308 37.9	N49 54.8
Nunki	75 55.5	S26 16.3
Peacock	53 15.8	S56 40.6
Pollux	243 25.6	N27 59.1
Procyon	244 57.9	N 5 10.8
Rasalhague	96 04.3	N12 33.1
Regulus	207 41.5	N11 53.2
Rigel	281 10.5	S 8 11.2
Rigil Kent.	139 48.3	S60 54.2
Sabik	102 09.9	S15 44.5
Schedar	349 38.3	N56 37.3
Shaula	96 18.8	S37 06.7
Sirius	258 32.3	S16 44.6
Spica	158 28.9	S11 14.8
Suhail	222 51.1	S43 30.3
Vega	80 37.2	N38 48.0
Zuben'ubi	137 02.9	S16 06.5

	SHA	Mer. Pass.
	° ′	h m
Venus	285 45.6	11 58
Mars	125 52.0	22 32
Jupiter	193 54.4	18 02
Saturn	108 16.6	23 43

	UT d h	SUN GHA ° ′	SUN Dec ° ′	MOON GHA ° ′	v ′	MOON Dec ° ′	d ′	HP ′
	5 00	180 22.7	N22 33.9	181 35.0	5.0	N17 24.1	4.2	60.4
	01	195 22.6	34.2	195 59.0	4.9	17 28.3	4.0	60.4
	02	210 22.5	34.4	210 22.9	5.0	17 32.3	4.0	60.4
	03	225 22.4	. . 34.7	224 46.9	4.9	17 36.3	3.8	60.3
	04	240 22.3	35.0	239 10.8	5.0	17 40.1	3.7	60.3
	05	255 22.2	35.2	253 34.8	4.9	17 43.8	3.5	60.3
	06	270 22.1	N22 35.5	267 58.7	5.0	N17 47.3	3.4	60.3
	07	285 22.0	35.8	282 22.7	4.9	17 50.7	3.3	60.3
	08	300 21.8	36.0	296 46.6	5.0	17 54.0	3.2	60.2
S	09	315 21.7	. . 36.3	311 10.6	4.9	17 57.2	3.0	60.2
U	10	330 21.6	36.6	325 34.5	5.0	18 00.2	3.0	60.2
N	11	345 21.5	36.8	339 58.5	4.9	18 03.2	2.7	60.2
D	12	0 21.4	N22 37.1	354 22.4	5.0	N18 05.9	2.7	60.2
A	13	15 21.3	37.3	8 46.4	5.0	18 08.6	2.5	60.1
Y	14	30 21.2	37.6	23 10.4	5.0	18 11.1	2.4	60.1
	15	45 21.1	. . 37.9	37 34.4	5.0	18 13.5	2.3	60.1
	16	60 20.9	38.1	51 58.4	5.1	18 15.8	2.1	60.1
	17	75 20.8	38.4	66 22.5	5.0	18 17.9	2.0	60.0
	18	90 20.7	N22 38.6	80 46.5	5.1	N18 19.9	1.9	60.0
	19	105 20.6	38.9	95 10.6	5.0	18 21.8	1.8	60.0
	20	120 20.5	39.2	109 34.6	5.1	18 23.6	1.6	60.0
	21	135 20.4	. . 39.4	123 58.7	5.2	18 25.2	1.5	59.9
	22	150 20.3	39.7	138 22.9	5.1	18 26.7	1.3	59.9
	23	165 20.1	39.9	152 47.0	5.2	18 28.0	1.3	59.9
	6 00	180 20.0	N22 40.2	167 11.2	5.2	N18 29.3	1.1	59.9
	01	195 19.9	40.4	181 35.4	5.2	18 30.4	0.9	59.8
	02	210 19.8	40.7	195 59.6	5.3	18 31.3	0.9	59.8
	03	225 19.7	. . 40.9	210 23.9	5.3	18 32.2	0.7	59.8
	04	240 19.6	41.2	224 48.2	5.3	18 32.9	0.6	59.7
	05	255 19.4	41.4	239 12.5	5.4	18 33.5	0.5	59.7
	06	270 19.3	N22 41.7	253 36.9	5.4	N18 34.0	0.3	59.7
	07	285 19.2	42.0	268 01.3	5.4	18 34.3	0.2	59.7
	08	300 19.1	42.2	282 25.7	5.4	18 34.5	0.1	59.6
M	09	315 19.0	. . 42.4	296 50.1	5.5	18 34.6	0.0	59.6
O	10	330 18.9	42.7	311 14.6	5.6	18 34.6	0.2	59.6
N	11	345 18.7	42.9	325 39.2	5.6	18 34.4	0.3	59.5
D	12	0 18.6	N22 43.2	340 03.8	5.6	N18 34.1	0.4	59.5
A	13	15 18.5	43.4	354 28.4	5.7	18 33.7	0.6	59.5
Y	14	30 18.4	43.7	8 53.1	5.7	18 33.1	0.6	59.5
	15	45 18.3	. . 43.9	23 17.8	5.8	18 32.5	0.8	59.4
	16	60 18.2	44.2	37 42.6	5.8	18 31.7	1.0	59.4
	17	75 18.0	44.4	52 07.4	5.9	18 30.7	1.0	59.4
	18	90 17.9	N22 44.7	66 32.3	5.9	N18 29.7	1.2	59.3
	19	105 17.8	44.9	80 57.2	5.9	18 28.5	1.2	59.3
	20	120 17.7	45.1	95 22.1	6.1	18 27.3	1.4	59.3
	21	135 17.6	. . 45.4	109 47.2	6.0	18 25.9	1.6	59.2
	22	150 17.5	45.6	124 12.2	6.2	18 24.3	1.6	59.2
	23	165 17.3	45.9	138 37.4	6.2	18 22.7	1.8	59.2
	7 00	180 17.2	N22 46.1	153 02.6	6.2	N18 20.9	1.8	59.1
	01	195 17.1	46.3	167 27.8	6.3	18 19.1	2.0	59.1
	02	210 17.0	46.6	181 53.1	6.4	18 17.1	2.1	59.1
	03	225 16.9	. . 46.8	196 18.5	6.4	18 15.0	2.3	59.0
	04	240 16.7	47.0	210 43.9	6.5	18 12.7	2.3	59.0
	05	255 16.6	47.3	225 09.4	6.5	18 10.4	2.5	59.0
	06	270 16.5	N22 47.5	239 34.9	6.6	N18 07.9	2.5	58.9
	07	285 16.4	47.7	254 00.5	6.7	18 05.4	2.7	58.9
T	08	300 16.3	48.0	268 26.2	6.7	18 02.7	2.8	58.9
U	09	315 16.2	. . 48.2	282 51.9	6.8	17 59.9	2.9	58.8
E	10	330 16.0	48.4	297 17.7	6.9	17 57.0	3.0	58.8
S	11	345 15.9	48.7	311 43.6	6.9	17 54.0	3.2	58.7
D	12	0 15.8	N22 48.9	326 09.5	7.0	N17 50.8	3.2	58.7
A	13	15 15.7	49.1	340 35.5	7.1	17 47.6	3.3	58.7
Y	14	30 15.6	49.4	355 01.6	7.2	17 44.3	3.5	58.6
	15	45 15.4	. . 49.6	9 27.8	7.2	17 40.8	3.5	58.6
	16	60 15.3	49.8	23 54.0	7.3	17 37.3	3.7	58.6
	17	75 15.2	50.0	38 20.3	7.3	17 33.6	3.8	58.5
	18	90 15.1	N22 50.3	52 46.6	7.5	N17 29.8	3.8	58.5
	19	105 15.0	50.5	67 13.1	7.5	17 26.0	4.0	58.5
	20	120 14.8	50.7	81 39.6	7.5	17 22.0	4.1	58.4
	21	135 14.7	. . 50.9	96 06.1	7.7	17 17.9	4.1	58.4
	22	150 14.6	51.2	110 32.8	7.7	17 13.8	4.3	58.4
	23	165 14.5	51.4	124 59.5	7.8	N17 09.5	4.4	58.3
		SD 15.8	*d* 0.2	SD 16.4		16.2		16.0

Lat. °	Twilight Naut. h m	Twilight Civil h m	Sunrise h m	Moonrise 5 h m	Moonrise 6 h m	Moonrise 7 h m	Moonrise 8 h m
N 72	▭	▭	▭	01 02	▭	▭	04 26
N 70	▭	▭	▭	02 01	02 34	03 42	05 15
68	▭	▭	▭	02 36	03 18	04 23	05 46
66	////	////	00 48	03 02	03 47	04 51	06 10
64	////	////	01 46	03 21	04 09	05 13	06 28
62	////	////	02 19	03 37	04 27	05 30	06 42
60	////	01 11	02 42	03 51	04 42	05 44	06 55
N 58	////	01 51	03 01	04 02	04 54	05 56	07 06
56	////	02 17	03 17	04 12	05 05	06 07	07 15
54	01 05	02 38	03 31	04 21	05 15	06 16	07 23
52	01 42	02 55	03 42	04 29	05 23	06 25	07 31
50	02 06	03 09	03 53	04 36	05 31	06 32	07 37
45	02 49	03 37	04 14	04 52	05 48	06 48	07 52
N 40	03 18	03 59	04 31	05 05	06 01	07 01	08 03
35	03 40	04 17	04 46	05 15	06 12	07 12	08 13
30	03 58	04 31	04 59	05 25	06 22	07 22	08 22
20	04 26	04 55	05 20	05 41	06 40	07 39	08 37
N 10	04 48	05 15	05 38	05 56	06 55	07 53	08 50
0	05 07	05 33	05 55	06 09	07 09	08 07	09 03
S 10	05 23	05 49	06 12	06 23	07 23	08 21	09 15
20	05 39	06 06	06 30	06 37	07 38	08 35	09 28
30	05 54	06 24	06 50	06 54	07 56	08 52	09 43
35	06 03	06 34	07 02	07 04	08 06	09 02	09 52
40	06 12	06 46	07 16	07 15	08 17	09 13	10 02
45	06 22	06 59	07 32	07 28	08 31	09 26	10 13
S 50	06 33	07 14	07 52	07 44	08 48	09 42	10 27
52	06 38	07 21	08 01	07 51	08 56	09 50	10 34
54	06 43	07 29	08 12	08 00	09 04	09 58	10 41
56	06 49	07 37	08 24	08 09	09 14	10 07	10 49
58	06 55	07 47	08 38	08 20	09 25	10 18	10 58
S 60	07 02	07 58	08 54	08 32	09 38	10 30	11 08

Lat. °	Sunset h m	Twilight Civil h m	Twilight Naut. h m	Moonset 5 h m	Moonset 6 h m	Moonset 7 h m	Moonset 8 h m
N 72	▭	▭	▭	▭	▭	▭	01 20
N 70	▭	▭	▭	23 11	24 06	00 06	00 30
68	▭	▭	▭	22 27	23 25	23 58	24 17
66	23 14	////	////	21 58	22 56	23 34	23 59
64	22 13	////	////	21 36	22 34	23 16	23 44
62	21 40	////	////	21 18	22 17	23 01	23 32
60	21 16	22 49	////	21 03	22 02	22 48	23 22
N 58	20 57	22 08	////	20 51	21 50	22 37	23 12
56	20 41	21 41	////	20 40	21 39	22 27	23 04
54	20 27	21 20	22 55	20 31	21 30	22 18	22 57
52	20 16	21 03	22 17	20 22	21 21	22 11	22 51
50	20 05	20 49	21 52	20 15	21 14	22 04	22 45
45	19 44	20 21	21 09	19 58	20 58	21 49	22 32
N 40	19 26	19 59	20 40	19 45	20 44	21 37	22 22
35	19 12	19 41	20 18	19 34	20 33	21 26	22 13
30	18 59	19 26	19 59	19 24	20 23	21 17	22 05
20	18 38	19 02	19 31	19 07	20 06	21 01	21 51
N 10	18 19	18 42	19 09	18 52	19 51	20 47	21 39
0	18 02	18 25	18 51	18 38	19 37	20 34	21 28
S 10	17 46	18 08	18 34	18 24	19 23	20 21	21 17
20	17 28	17 51	18 19	18 09	19 08	20 07	21 04
30	17 07	17 33	18 03	17 52	18 51	19 51	20 50
35	16 55	17 23	17 55	17 42	18 40	19 41	20 42
40	16 41	17 12	17 46	17 30	18 29	19 30	20 33
45	16 25	16 59	17 36	17 17	18 15	19 18	20 22
S 50	16 05	16 43	17 25	17 01	17 59	19 02	20 09
52	15 56	16 36	17 20	16 53	17 51	18 55	20 03
54	15 45	16 28	17 14	16 44	17 42	18 47	19 56
56	15 33	16 20	17 08	16 35	17 32	18 38	19 48
58	15 19	16 10	17 02	16 24	17 21	18 28	19 39
S 60	15 03	15 59	16 55	16 11	17 08	18 16	19 29

Day	SUN Eqn. of Time 00^h	SUN Eqn. of Time 12^h	SUN Mer. Pass.	MOON Mer. Pass. Upper	MOON Mer. Pass. Lower	MOON Age	MOON Phase
d	m s	m s	h m	h m	h m	d %	
5	01 31	01 26	11 59	12 23	24 53	00 0	
6	01 20	01 15	11 59	13 23	00 53	01 3	
7	01 09	01 03	11 59	14 21	01 52	02 8	

	UT	ARIES	VENUS −4·0		MARS −1·9		JUPITER −2·0		SATURN +0·0	
	d h	GHA ° ′	GHA ° ′	Dec ° ′	GHA ° ′	Dec ° ′	GHA ° ′	Dec ° ′	GHA ° ′	Dec ° ′
	8 00	256 48.5	179 55.4	N22 55.5	23 18.2	S21 12.8	90 33.9	N 7 15.5	5 14.5	S20 32.5
	01	271 50.9	194 54.5	55.9	38 21.4	12.7	105 36.2	15.4	20 17.2	32.5
	02	286 53.4	209 53.7	56.2	53 24.6	12.6	120 38.5	15.3	35 19.8	32.5
	03	301 55.9	224 52.8	. . 56.6	68 27.9	. . 12.6	135 40.7	. . 15.2	50 22.5	. . 32.4
	04	316 58.3	239 52.0	57.0	83 31.1	12.5	150 43.0	15.1	65 25.2	32.4
	05	332 00.8	254 51.2	57.3	98 34.3	12.4	165 45.3	15.0	80 27.8	32.4
	06	347 03.3	269 50.3	N22 57.7	113 37.5	S21 12.4	180 47.6	N 7 14.9	95 30.5	S20 32.4
W	07	2 05.7	284 49.5	58.1	128 40.7	12.3	195 49.8	14.9	110 33.1	32.4
E	08	17 08.2	299 48.6	58.5	143 44.0	12.2	210 52.1	14.8	125 35.8	32.3
D	09	32 10.6	314 47.8	. . 58.8	158 47.2	. . 12.2	225 54.4	. . 14.7	140 38.5	. . 32.3
N	10	47 13.1	329 46.9	59.2	173 50.4	12.1	240 56.6	14.6	155 41.1	32.3
E	11	62 15.6	344 46.0	59.6	188 53.6	12.0	255 58.9	14.5	170 43.8	32.3
S	12	77 18.0	359 45.2	N22 59.9	203 56.8	S21 12.0	271 01.2	N 7 14.4	185 46.4	S20 32.3
D	13	92 20.5	14 44.3	23 00.3	219 00.0	11.9	286 03.5	14.3	200 49.1	32.2
A	14	107 23.0	29 43.5	00.6	234 03.2	11.8	301 05.7	14.2	215 51.8	32.2
Y	15	122 25.4	44 42.6	. . 01.0	249 06.4	. . 11.8	316 08.0	. . 14.1	230 54.4	. . 32.2
	16	137 27.9	59 41.8	01.4	264 09.6	11.7	331 10.3	14.0	245 57.1	32.2
	17	152 30.4	74 40.9	01.7	279 12.9	11.6	346 12.5	14.0	260 59.7	32.2
	18	167 32.8	89 40.1	N23 02.1	294 16.1	S21 11.6	1 14.8	N 7 13.9	276 02.4	S20 32.1
	19	182 35.3	104 39.2	02.4	309 19.3	11.5	16 17.1	13.8	291 05.1	32.1
	20	197 37.8	119 38.4	02.8	324 22.5	11.5	31 19.3	13.7	306 07.7	32.1
	21	212 40.2	134 37.5	. . 03.1	339 25.7	. . 11.4	46 21.6	. . 13.6	321 10.4	. . 32.1
	22	227 42.7	149 36.7	03.5	354 28.9	11.3	61 23.9	13.5	336 13.0	32.1
	23	242 45.1	164 35.8	03.8	9 32.1	11.3	76 26.1	13.4	351 15.7	32.0
	9 00	257 47.6	179 35.0	N23 04.2	24 35.3	S21 11.2	91 28.4	N 7 13.3	6 18.4	S20 32.0
	01	272 50.1	194 34.1	04.5	39 38.5	11.1	106 30.7	13.2	21 21.0	32.0
	02	287 52.5	209 33.2	04.9	54 41.7	11.1	121 32.9	13.1	36 23.7	32.0
	03	302 55.0	224 32.4	. . 05.2	69 44.9	. . 11.0	136 35.2	. . 13.0	51 26.3	. . 32.0
	04	317 57.5	239 31.5	05.6	84 48.0	10.9	151 37.5	13.0	66 29.0	31.9
	05	332 59.9	254 30.7	05.9	99 51.2	10.9	166 39.7	12.9	81 31.6	31.9
	06	348 02.4	269 29.8	N23 06.2	114 54.4	S21 10.8	181 42.0	N 7 12.8	96 34.3	S20 31.9
	07	3 04.9	284 29.0	06.6	129 57.6	10.7	196 44.3	12.7	111 37.0	31.9
T	08	18 07.3	299 28.1	06.9	145 00.8	10.7	211 46.5	12.6	126 39.6	31.9
H	09	33 09.8	314 27.3	. . 07.3	160 04.0	. . 10.6	226 48.8	. . 12.5	141 42.3	. . 31.8
U	10	48 12.3	329 26.4	07.6	175 07.2	10.6	241 51.1	12.4	156 44.9	31.8
R	11	63 14.7	344 25.5	07.9	190 10.4	10.5	256 53.3	12.3	171 47.6	31.8
S	12	78 17.2	359 24.7	N23 08.3	205 13.6	S21 10.4	271 55.6	N 7 12.2	186 50.3	S20 31.8
D	13	93 19.6	14 23.8	08.6	220 16.7	10.4	286 57.8	12.1	201 52.9	31.8
A	14	108 22.1	29 23.0	08.9	235 19.9	10.3	302 00.1	12.0	216 55.6	31.7
Y	15	123 24.6	44 22.1	. . 09.3	250 23.1	. . 10.2	317 02.4	. . 12.0	231 58.2	. . 31.7
	16	138 27.0	59 21.2	09.6	265 26.3	10.2	332 04.6	11.9	247 00.9	31.7
	17	153 29.5	74 20.4	09.9	280 29.5	10.1	347 06.9	11.8	262 03.6	31.7
	18	168 32.0	89 19.5	N23 10.3	295 32.6	S21 10.0	2 09.2	N 7 11.7	277 06.2	S20 31.7
	19	183 34.4	104 18.7	10.6	310 35.8	10.0	17 11.4	11.6	292 08.9	31.6
	20	198 36.9	119 17.8	10.9	325 39.0	09.9	32 13.7	11.5	307 11.5	31.6
	21	213 39.4	134 16.9	. . 11.2	340 42.2	. . 09.9	47 15.9	. . 11.4	322 14.2	. . 31.6
	22	228 41.8	149 16.1	11.6	355 45.3	09.8	62 18.2	11.3	337 16.8	31.6
	23	243 44.3	164 15.2	11.9	10 48.5	09.7	77 20.5	11.2	352 19.5	31.6
	10 00	258 46.8	179 14.4	N23 12.2	25 51.7	S21 09.7	92 22.7	N 7 11.1	7 22.2	S20 31.6
	01	273 49.2	194 13.5	12.5	40 54.8	09.6	107 25.0	11.0	22 24.8	31.5
	02	288 51.7	209 12.6	12.8	55 58.0	09.6	122 27.3	10.9	37 27.5	31.5
	03	303 54.1	224 11.8	. . 13.2	71 01.2	. . 09.5	137 29.5	. . 10.8	52 30.1	. . 31.5
	04	318 56.6	239 10.9	13.5	86 04.3	09.4	152 31.8	10.7	67 32.8	31.5
	05	333 59.1	254 10.0	13.8	101 07.5	09.4	167 34.0	10.6	82 35.5	31.5
	06	349 01.5	269 09.2	N23 14.1	116 10.7	S21 09.3	182 36.3	N 7 10.6	97 38.1	S20 31.4
	07	4 04.0	284 08.3	14.4	131 13.8	09.2	197 38.5	10.5	112 40.8	31.4
	08	19 06.5	299 07.5	14.7	146 17.0	09.2	212 40.8	10.4	127 43.4	31.4
F	09	34 08.9	314 06.6	. . 15.0	161 20.1	. . 09.1	227 43.1	. . 10.3	142 46.1	. . 31.4
R	10	49 11.4	329 05.7	15.4	176 23.3	09.1	242 45.3	10.2	157 48.7	31.4
I	11	64 13.9	344 04.9	15.7	191 26.5	09.0	257 47.6	10.1	172 51.4	31.3
D	12	79 16.3	359 04.0	N23 16.0	206 29.6	S21 08.9	272 49.8	N 7 10.0	187 54.1	S20 31.3
A	13	94 18.8	14 03.1	16.3	221 32.8	08.9	287 52.1	09.9	202 56.7	31.3
Y	14	109 21.2	29 02.3	16.6	236 35.9	08.8	302 54.4	09.8	217 59.4	31.3
	15	124 23.7	44 01.4	. . 16.9	251 39.1	. . 08.8	317 56.6	. . 09.7	233 02.0	. . 31.3
	16	139 26.2	59 00.5	17.2	266 42.2	08.7	332 58.9	09.6	248 04.7	31.2
	17	154 28.6	73 59.7	17.5	281 45.4	08.6	348 01.1	09.5	263 07.4	31.2
	18	169 31.1	88 58.8	N23 17.8	296 48.5	S21 08.6	3 03.4	N 7 09.4	278 10.0	S20 31.2
	19	184 33.6	103 57.9	18.1	311 51.7	08.5	18 05.6	09.3	293 12.7	31.2
	20	199 36.0	118 57.1	18.4	326 54.8	08.5	33 07.9	09.2	308 15.3	31.2
	21	214 38.5	133 56.2	. . 18.7	341 58.0	. . 08.4	48 10.2	. . 09.1	323 18.0	. . 31.1
	22	229 41.0	148 55.3	19.0	357 01.1	08.3	63 12.4	09.0	338 20.6	31.1
	23	244 43.4	163 54.5	19.3	12 04.2	08.3	78 14.7	08.9	353 23.3	31.1
	Mer. Pass.	h m 6 47.7	v −0.9	d 0.3	v 3.2	d 0.1	v 2.3	d 0.1	v 2.7	d 0.0

STARS

Name	SHA ° ′	Dec ° ′
Acamar	315 17.2	S40 14.4
Achernar	335 25.8	S57 09.1
Acrux	173 06.6	S63 11.7
Adhara	255 11.3	S29 00.0
Aldebaran	290 47.4	N16 32.3
Alioth	166 18.8	N55 52.6
Alkaid	152 57.1	N49 14.2
Al Na'ir	27 41.2	S46 52.6
Alnilam	275 44.7	S 1 11.7
Alphard	217 54.3	S 8 44.0
Alphecca	126 09.0	N26 39.8
Alpheratz	357 41.4	N29 10.7
Altair	62 06.0	N 8 54.8
Ankaa	353 13.9	S42 12.9
Antares	112 23.4	S26 27.9
Arcturus	145 53.7	N19 06.0
Atria	107 22.8	S69 03.2
Avior	234 17.6	S59 34.1
Bellatrix	278 30.2	N 6 21.6
Betelgeuse	270 59.5	N 7 24.4
Canopus	263 55.8	S52 42.6
Capella	280 31.9	N46 00.6
Deneb	49 29.7	N45 20.3
Denebola	182 31.6	N14 28.9
Diphda	348 54.0	S17 53.8
Dubhe	193 49.5	N61 40.0
Elnath	278 10.5	N28 37.0
Eltanin	90 44.7	N51 29.4
Enif	33 45.0	N 9 57.0
Fomalhaut	15 21.8	S29 31.9
Gacrux	171 58.3	S57 12.5
Gienah	175 50.1	S17 38.1
Hadar	148 44.4	S60 27.2
Hamal	327 58.7	N23 32.1
Kaus Aust.	83 40.8	S34 22.3
Kochab	137 19.3	N74 05.6
Markab	13 36.3	N15 17.5
Menkar	314 13.2	N 4 09.0
Menkent	148 04.9	S36 27.1
Miaplacidus	221 39.6	S69 47.5
Mirfak	308 37.9	N49 54.8
Nunki	75 55.5	S26 16.3
Peacock	53 15.8	S56 40.6
Pollux	243 25.6	N27 59.1
Procyon	244 57.9	N 5 10.8
Rasalhague	96 04.2	N12 33.1
Regulus	207 41.5	N11 53.2
Rigel	281 10.5	S 8 11.2
Rigil Kent.	139 48.4	S60 54.2
Sabik	102 09.9	S15 44.5
Schedar	349 38.3	N56 37.3
Shaula	96 18.8	S37 06.7
Sirius	258 32.3	S16 44.6
Spica	158 28.9	S11 14.8
Suhail	222 51.2	S43 30.3
Vega	80 37.2	N38 48.1
Zuben'ubi	137 02.9	S16 06.5

	SHA ° ′	Mer. Pass. h m
Venus	281 47.3	12 02
Mars	126 47.7	22 17
Jupiter	193 40.8	17 51
Saturn	108 30.7	23 31

UT	SUN GHA	SUN Dec	MOON GHA	*v*	MOON Dec	*d*	HP
d h	° ′	° ′	° ′	′	° ′	′	′
8 00	180 14.4	N22 51.6	139 26.3	7.9	N17 05.1	4.5	58.3
01	195 14.2	51.8	153 53.2	8.0	17 00.6	4.5	58.2
02	210 14.1	52.0	168 20.2	8.0	16 56.1	4.7	58.2
03	225 14.0	. . 52.3	182 47.2	8.1	16 51.4	4.7	58.2
04	240 13.9	52.5	197 14.3	8.2	16 46.7	4.9	58.1
05	255 13.7	52.7	211 41.5	8.2	16 41.8	4.9	58.1
06	270 13.6	N22 52.9	226 08.7	8.4	N16 36.9	5.0	58.1
W 07	285 13.5	53.1	240 36.1	8.4	16 31.9	5.2	58.0
E 08	300 13.4	53.3	255 03.5	8.5	16 26.7	5.2	58.0
D 09	315 13.3	. . 53.6	269 31.0	8.6	16 21.5	5.3	57.9
N 10	330 13.1	53.8	283 58.6	8.6	16 16.2	5.4	57.9
E 11	345 13.0	54.0	298 26.2	8.8	16 10.8	5.4	57.9
S 12	0 12.9	N22 54.2	312 54.0	8.8	N16 05.4	5.6	57.8
D 13	15 12.8	54.4	327 21.8	8.9	15 59.8	5.6	57.8
A 14	30 12.7	54.6	341 49.7	9.0	15 54.2	5.7	57.8
Y 15	45 12.5	. . 54.8	356 17.7	9.0	15 48.5	5.9	57.7
16	60 12.4	55.0	10 45.7	9.1	15 42.6	5.8	57.7
17	75 12.3	55.3	25 13.8	9.3	15 36.8	6.0	57.6
18	90 12.2	N22 55.5	39 42.1	9.3	N15 30.8	6.1	57.6
19	105 12.0	55.7	54 10.4	9.3	15 24.7	6.1	57.6
20	120 11.9	55.9	68 38.7	9.5	15 18.6	6.2	57.5
21	135 11.8	. . 56.1	83 07.2	9.5	15 12.4	6.3	57.5
22	150 11.7	56.3	97 35.7	9.6	15 06.1	6.3	57.5
23	165 11.5	56.5	112 04.3	9.7	14 59.8	6.5	57.4
9 00	180 11.4	N22 56.7	126 33.0	9.8	N14 53.3	6.5	57.4
01	195 11.3	56.9	141 01.8	9.8	14 46.8	6.5	57.3
02	210 11.2	57.1	155 30.6	10.0	14 40.3	6.7	57.3
03	225 11.1	. . 57.3	169 59.6	10.0	14 33.6	6.7	57.3
04	240 10.9	57.5	184 28.6	10.1	14 26.9	6.8	57.2
05	255 10.8	57.7	198 57.7	10.1	14 20.1	6.8	57.2
06	270 10.7	N22 57.9	213 26.8	10.3	N14 13.3	6.9	57.2
07	285 10.6	58.1	227 56.1	10.3	14 06.4	7.0	57.1
T 08	300 10.4	58.3	242 25.4	10.4	13 59.4	7.1	57.1
H 09	315 10.3	. . 58.5	256 54.8	10.5	13 52.3	7.1	57.1
U 10	330 10.2	58.7	271 24.3	10.6	13 45.2	7.2	57.0
R 11	345 10.1	58.9	285 53.9	10.6	13 38.0	7.2	57.0
S 12	0 09.9	N22 59.1	300 23.5	10.7	N13 30.8	7.3	56.9
D 13	15 09.8	59.3	314 53.2	10.8	13 23.5	7.4	56.9
A 14	30 09.7	59.5	329 23.0	10.9	13 16.1	7.4	56.9
Y 15	45 09.6	. . 59.7	343 52.9	10.9	13 08.7	7.5	56.8
16	60 09.4	22 59.9	358 22.8	11.0	13 01.2	7.5	56.8
17	75 09.3	23 00.1	12 52.8	11.1	12 53.7	7.6	56.8
18	90 09.2	N23 00.3	27 22.9	11.2	N12 46.1	7.7	56.7
19	105 09.1	00.5	41 53.1	11.2	12 38.4	7.7	56.7
20	120 08.9	00.6	56 23.3	11.4	12 30.7	7.7	56.7
21	135 08.8	. . 00.8	70 53.7	11.3	12 23.0	7.8	56.6
22	150 08.7	01.0	85 24.0	11.5	12 15.2	7.9	56.6
23	165 08.6	01.2	99 54.5	11.5	12 07.3	7.9	56.6
10 00	180 08.4	N23 01.4	114 25.0	11.6	N11 59.4	7.9	56.5
01	195 08.3	01.6	128 55.6	11.7	11 51.5	8.1	56.5
02	210 08.2	01.8	143 26.3	11.8	11 43.4	8.0	56.5
03	225 08.1	. . 02.0	157 57.1	11.8	11 35.4	8.1	56.4
04	240 07.9	02.1	172 27.9	11.9	11 27.3	8.2	56.4
05	255 07.8	02.3	186 58.8	11.9	11 19.1	8.2	56.4
06	270 07.7	N23 02.5	201 29.7	12.1	N11 10.9	8.2	56.3
07	285 07.6	02.7	216 00.8	12.1	11 02.7	8.3	56.3
08	300 07.4	02.9	230 31.9	12.1	10 54.4	8.3	56.3
F 09	315 07.3	. . 03.1	245 03.0	12.3	10 46.1	8.4	56.2
R 10	330 07.2	03.2	259 34.3	12.3	10 37.7	8.4	56.2
I 11	345 07.1	03.4	274 05.6	12.3	10 29.3	8.4	56.2
D 12	0 06.9	N23 03.6	288 36.9	12.4	N10 20.9	8.5	56.1
A 13	15 06.8	03.8	303 08.3	12.5	10 12.4	8.6	56.1
Y 14	30 06.7	04.0	317 39.8	12.6	10 03.8	8.5	56.1
15	45 06.5	. . 04.1	332 11.4	12.6	9 55.3	8.6	56.0
16	60 06.4	04.3	346 43.0	12.7	9 46.7	8.7	56.0
17	75 06.3	04.5	1 14.7	12.7	9 38.0	8.6	56.0
18	90 06.2	N23 04.7	15 46.4	12.8	N 9 29.4	8.7	55.9
19	105 06.0	04.8	30 18.2	12.9	9 20.7	8.8	55.9
20	120 05.9	05.0	44 50.1	12.9	9 11.9	8.7	55.9
21	135 05.8	. . 05.2	59 22.0	13.0	9 03.2	8.9	55.8
22	150 05.7	05.4	73 54.0	13.1	8 54.3	8.8	55.8
23	165 05.5	05.5	88 26.1	13.1	N 8 45.5	8.9	55.8
	SD 15.8	*d* 0.2	SD 15.8		15.5		15.3

Lat.	Twilight Naut.	Twilight Civil	Sunrise	Moonrise 8	Moonrise 9	Moonrise 10	Moonrise 11
°	h m	h m	h m	h m	h m	h m	h m
N 72	▭	▭	▭	04 26	06 26	08 15	09 58
N 70	▭	▭	▭	05 15	06 55	08 34	10 08
68	▭	▭	▭	05 46	07 17	08 48	10 17
66	////	////	00 32	06 10	07 34	09 00	10 24
64	////	////	01 40	06 28	07 48	09 10	10 30
62	////	////	02 15	06 42	08 00	09 18	10 35
60	////	01 04	02 40	06 55	08 10	09 25	10 39
N 58	////	01 47	02 59	07 06	08 18	09 31	10 43
56	////	02 15	03 15	07 15	08 26	09 37	10 47
54	00 58	02 36	03 29	07 23	08 33	09 42	10 50
52	01 38	02 53	03 41	07 31	08 39	09 46	10 53
50	02 04	03 07	03 51	07 37	08 44	09 50	10 55
45	02 47	03 36	04 13	07 52	08 56	09 59	11 01
N 40	03 17	03 58	04 31	08 03	09 05	10 06	11 06
35	03 40	04 16	04 46	08 13	09 14	10 13	11 10
30	03 58	04 31	04 58	08 22	09 21	10 18	11 13
20	04 26	04 55	05 20	08 37	09 34	10 28	11 19
N 10	04 48	05 15	05 38	08 50	09 44	10 36	11 25
0	05 07	05 33	05 56	09 03	09 55	10 44	11 30
S 10	05 24	05 50	06 13	09 15	10 05	10 51	11 35
20	05 40	06 07	06 31	09 28	10 16	11 00	11 40
30	05 56	06 25	06 52	09 43	10 28	11 09	11 46
35	06 04	06 36	07 04	09 52	10 35	11 14	11 50
40	06 13	06 47	07 18	10 02	10 44	11 20	11 54
45	06 23	07 00	07 34	10 13	10 53	11 28	11 58
S 50	06 35	07 16	07 54	10 27	11 05	11 36	12 04
52	06 40	07 23	08 04	10 34	11 10	11 40	12 06
54	06 45	07 31	08 15	10 41	11 16	11 44	12 09
56	06 51	07 40	08 27	10 49	11 22	11 49	12 12
58	06 58	07 50	08 41	10 58	11 29	11 54	12 15
S 60	07 05	08 01	08 58	11 08	11 38	12 00	12 19

Lat.	Sunset	Twilight Civil	Twilight Naut.	Moonset 8	Moonset 9	Moonset 10	Moonset 11
°	h m	h m	h m	h m	h m	h m	h m
N 72	▭	▭	▭	01 20	01 10	01 03	00 57
N 70	▭	▭	▭	00 30	00 39	00 43	00 45
68	▭	▭	▭	24 17	00 17	00 28	00 35
66	23 33	////	////	23 59	24 15	00 15	00 27
64	22 20	////	////	23 44	24 04	00 04	00 20
62	21 45	////	////	23 32	23 55	24 13	00 13
60	21 20	22 57	////	23 22	23 47	24 08	00 08
N 58	21 00	22 13	////	23 12	23 41	24 03	00 03
56	20 44	21 45	////	23 04	23 34	23 59	24 21
54	20 30	21 24	23 02	22 57	23 29	23 55	24 19
52	20 18	21 06	22 22	22 51	23 24	23 52	24 17
50	20 08	20 52	21 56	22 45	23 19	23 49	24 15
45	19 46	20 23	21 12	22 32	23 09	23 42	24 11
N 40	19 28	20 01	20 42	22 22	23 01	23 36	24 08
35	19 13	19 43	20 19	22 13	22 54	23 31	24 05
30	19 00	19 28	20 01	22 05	22 48	23 27	24 03
20	18 39	19 03	19 32	21 51	22 37	23 19	23 58
N 10	18 20	18 43	19 10	21 39	22 28	23 12	23 55
0	18 03	18 25	18 52	21 28	22 19	23 06	23 51
S 10	17 46	18 09	18 35	21 17	22 09	23 00	23 47
20	17 28	17 52	18 19	21 04	22 00	22 53	23 44
30	17 07	17 33	18 03	20 50	21 49	22 45	23 39
35	16 55	17 23	17 54	20 42	21 42	22 40	23 36
40	16 41	17 11	17 45	20 33	21 35	22 35	23 34
45	16 25	16 58	17 35	20 22	21 26	22 29	23 30
S 50	16 04	16 42	17 24	20 09	21 16	22 22	23 26
52	15 55	16 35	17 19	20 03	21 11	22 18	23 24
54	15 44	16 27	17 13	19 56	21 05	22 14	23 22
56	15 32	16 18	17 07	19 48	20 59	22 10	23 20
58	15 17	16 09	17 01	19 39	20 53	22 06	23 17
S 60	15 01	15 57	16 53	19 29	20 45	22 00	23 14

Day	SUN Eqn. of Time 00^h	SUN Eqn. of Time 12^h	SUN Mer. Pass.	MOON Mer. Pass. Upper	MOON Mer. Pass. Lower	MOON Age	MOON Phase
d	m s	m s	h m	h m	h m	d %	
8	00 58	00 52	11 59	15 15	02 48	03 15	
9	00 46	00 40	11 59	16 07	03 41	04 23	
10	00 34	00 28	12 00	16 55	04 31	05 32	

UT d	UT h	ARIES GHA ° ′	VENUS −4·0 GHA ° ′	VENUS Dec ° ′	MARS −1·8 GHA ° ′	MARS Dec ° ′	JUPITER −2·0 GHA ° ′	JUPITER Dec ° ′	SATURN +0·0 GHA ° ′	SATURN Dec ° ′
11	00	259 45.9	178 53.6	N23 19.6	27 07.4	S21 08.2	93 16.9	N 7 08.9	8 26.0	S20 31.1
	01	274 48.4	193 52.7	19.9	42 10.5	08.2	108 19.2	08.8	23 28.6	31.1
	02	289 50.8	208 51.9	20.1	57 13.7	08.1	123 21.4	08.7	38 31.3	31.0
	03	304 53.3	223 51.0	. . 20.4	72 16.8	. . 08.0	138 23.7	. . 08.6	53 33.9	. . 31.0
	04	319 55.7	238 50.1	20.7	87 19.9	08.0	153 25.9	08.5	68 36.6	31.0
	05	334 58.2	253 49.3	21.0	102 23.1	07.9	168 28.2	08.4	83 39.3	31.0
	06	350 00.7	268 48.4	N23 21.3	117 26.2	S21 07.9	183 30.4	N 7 08.3	98 41.9	S20 31.0
	07	5 03.1	283 47.5	21.6	132 29.3	07.8	198 32.7	08.2	113 44.6	30.9
SATURDAY	08	20 05.6	298 46.7	21.9	147 32.5	07.8	213 35.0	08.1	128 47.2	30.9
	09	35 08.1	313 45.8	. . 22.1	162 35.6	. . 07.7	228 37.2	. . 08.0	143 49.9	. . 30.9
	10	50 10.5	328 44.9	22.4	177 38.7	07.6	243 39.5	07.9	158 52.5	30.9
	11	65 13.0	343 44.0	22.7	192 41.8	07.6	258 41.7	07.8	173 55.2	30.9
	12	80 15.5	358 43.2	N23 23.0	207 45.0	S21 07.5	273 44.0	N 7 07.7	188 57.9	S20 30.9
	13	95 17.9	13 42.3	23.3	222 48.1	07.5	288 46.2	07.6	204 00.5	30.8
	14	110 20.4	28 41.4	23.5	237 51.2	07.4	303 48.5	07.5	219 03.2	30.8
	15	125 22.9	43 40.6	. . 23.8	252 54.3	. . 07.4	318 50.7	. . 07.4	234 05.8	. . 30.8
	16	140 25.3	58 39.7	24.1	267 57.5	07.3	333 53.0	07.3	249 08.5	30.8
	17	155 27.8	73 38.8	24.4	283 00.6	07.2	348 55.2	07.2	264 11.1	30.8
	18	170 30.2	88 38.0	N23 24.6	298 03.7	S21 07.2	3 57.5	N 7 07.1	279 13.8	S20 30.7
	19	185 32.7	103 37.1	24.9	313 06.8	07.1	18 59.7	07.0	294 16.5	30.7
	20	200 35.2	118 36.2	25.2	328 09.9	07.1	34 02.0	06.9	309 19.1	30.7
	21	215 37.6	133 35.3	. . 25.4	343 13.0	. . 07.0	49 04.2	. . 06.8	324 21.8	. . 30.7
	22	230 40.1	148 34.5	25.7	358 16.1	07.0	64 06.5	06.7	339 24.4	30.7
	23	245 42.6	163 33.6	26.0	13 19.3	06.9	79 08.7	06.6	354 27.1	30.6
12	00	260 45.0	178 32.7	N23 26.2	28 22.4	S21 06.9	94 11.0	N 7 06.5	9 29.7	S20 30.6
	01	275 47.5	193 31.8	26.5	43 25.5	06.8	109 13.2	06.4	24 32.4	30.6
	02	290 50.0	208 31.0	26.8	58 28.6	06.7	124 15.5	06.3	39 35.1	30.6
	03	305 52.4	223 30.1	. . 27.0	73 31.7	. . 06.7	139 17.7	. . 06.2	54 37.7	. . 30.6
	04	320 54.9	238 29.2	27.3	88 34.8	06.6	154 20.0	06.1	69 40.4	30.5
	05	335 57.3	253 28.4	27.5	103 37.9	06.6	169 22.2	06.0	84 43.0	30.5
	06	350 59.8	268 27.5	N23 27.8	118 41.0	S21 06.5	184 24.5	N 7 05.9	99 45.7	S20 30.5
	07	6 02.3	283 26.6	28.1	133 44.1	06.5	199 26.7	05.8	114 48.3	30.5
	08	21 04.7	298 25.7	28.3	148 47.2	06.4	214 29.0	05.7	129 51.0	30.5
SUNDAY	09	36 07.2	313 24.9	. . 28.6	163 50.3	. . 06.4	229 31.2	. . 05.6	144 53.7	. . 30.4
	10	51 09.7	328 24.0	28.8	178 53.4	06.3	244 33.5	05.5	159 56.3	30.4
	11	66 12.1	343 23.1	29.1	193 56.5	06.3	259 35.7	05.5	174 59.0	30.4
	12	81 14.6	358 22.2	N23 29.3	208 59.6	S21 06.2	274 37.9	N 7 05.4	190 01.6	S20 30.4
	13	96 17.1	13 21.4	29.6	224 02.7	06.1	289 40.2	05.3	205 04.3	30.4
	14	111 19.5	28 20.5	29.8	239 05.8	06.1	304 42.4	05.2	220 06.9	30.4
	15	126 22.0	43 19.6	. . 30.1	254 08.9	. . 06.0	319 44.7	. . 05.1	235 09.6	. . 30.3
	16	141 24.5	58 18.7	30.3	269 12.0	06.0	334 46.9	05.0	250 12.2	30.3
	17	156 26.9	73 17.8	30.6	284 15.0	05.9	349 49.2	04.9	265 14.9	30.3
	18	171 29.4	88 17.0	N23 30.8	299 18.1	S21 05.9	4 51.4	N 7 04.8	280 17.6	S20 30.3
	19	186 31.8	103 16.1	31.0	314 21.2	05.8	19 53.7	04.7	295 20.2	30.3
	20	201 34.3	118 15.2	31.3	329 24.3	05.8	34 55.9	04.6	310 22.9	30.2
	21	216 36.8	133 14.3	. . 31.5	344 27.4	. . 05.7	49 58.2	. . 04.5	325 25.5	. . 30.2
	22	231 39.2	148 13.5	31.8	359 30.5	05.7	65 00.4	04.4	340 28.2	30.2
	23	246 41.7	163 12.6	32.0	14 33.5	05.6	80 02.6	04.3	355 30.8	30.2
13	00	261 44.2	178 11.7	N23 32.2	29 36.6	S21 05.6	95 04.9	N 7 04.2	10 33.5	S20 30.2
	01	276 46.6	193 10.8	32.5	44 39.7	05.5	110 07.1	04.1	25 36.2	30.1
	02	291 49.1	208 09.9	32.7	59 42.8	05.5	125 09.4	04.0	40 38.8	30.1
	03	306 51.6	223 09.1	. . 32.9	74 45.8	. . 05.4	140 11.6	. . 03.9	55 41.5	. . 30.1
	04	321 54.0	238 08.2	33.2	89 48.9	05.4	155 13.9	03.8	70 44.1	30.1
	05	336 56.5	253 07.3	33.4	104 52.0	05.3	170 16.1	03.7	85 46.8	30.1
	06	351 59.0	268 06.4	N23 33.6	119 55.1	S21 05.3	185 18.3	N 7 03.6	100 49.4	S20 30.0
	07	7 01.4	283 05.6	33.8	134 58.1	05.2	200 20.6	03.5	115 52.1	30.0
	08	22 03.9	298 04.7	34.1	150 01.2	05.2	215 22.8	03.4	130 54.7	30.0
MONDAY	09	37 06.3	313 03.8	. . 34.3	165 04.3	. . 05.1	230 25.1	. . 03.3	145 57.4	. . 30.0
	10	52 08.8	328 02.9	34.5	180 07.3	05.1	245 27.3	03.2	161 00.1	30.0
	11	67 11.3	343 02.0	34.7	195 10.4	05.0	260 29.6	03.0	176 02.7	30.0
	12	82 13.7	358 01.2	N23 35.0	210 13.5	S21 05.0	275 31.8	N 7 02.9	191 05.4	S20 29.9
	13	97 16.2	13 00.3	35.2	225 16.5	04.9	290 34.0	02.8	206 08.0	29.9
	14	112 18.7	27 59.4	35.4	240 19.6	04.9	305 36.3	02.7	221 10.7	29.9
	15	127 21.1	42 58.5	. . 35.6	255 22.6	. . 04.8	320 38.5	. . 02.6	236 13.3	. . 29.9
	16	142 23.6	57 57.6	35.8	270 25.7	04.8	335 40.8	02.5	251 16.0	29.9
	17	157 26.1	72 56.8	36.1	285 28.7	04.7	350 43.0	02.4	266 18.6	29.8
	18	172 28.5	87 55.9	N23 36.3	300 31.8	S21 04.7	5 45.2	N 7 02.3	281 21.3	S20 29.8
	19	187 31.0	102 55.0	36.5	315 34.9	04.6	20 47.5	02.2	296 24.0	29.8
	20	202 33.4	117 54.1	36.7	330 37.9	04.6	35 49.7	02.1	311 26.6	29.8
	21	217 35.9	132 53.2	. . 36.9	345 41.0	. . 04.5	50 52.0	. . 02.0	326 29.3	. . 29.8
	22	232 38.4	147 52.3	37.1	0 44.0	04.5	65 54.2	01.9	341 31.9	29.7
	23	247 40.8	162 51.5	37.3	15 47.1	04.4	80 56.4	01.8	356 34.6	29.7
Mer. Pass.		h m 6 35.9	v −0.9	d 0.2	v 3.1	d 0.1	v 2.2	d 0.1	v 2.7	d 0.0

STARS

Name	SHA ° ′	Dec ° ′
Acamar	315 17.2	S40 14.4
Achernar	335 25.7	S57 09.1
Acrux	173 06.6	S63 11.7
Adhara	255 11.3	S28 59.9
Aldebaran	290 47.4	N16 32.3
Alioth	166 18.8	N55 52.6
Alkaid	152 57.1	N49 14.2
Al Na'ir	27 41.1	S46 52.6
Alnilam	275 44.7	S 1 11.7
Alphard	217 54.3	S 8 44.0
Alphecca	126 09.0	N26 39.8
Alpheratz	357 41.4	N29 10.7
Altair	62 06.0	N 8 54.8
Ankaa	353 13.9	S42 12.8
Antares	112 23.4	S26 27.9
Arcturus	145 53.7	N19 06.0
Atria	107 22.8	S69 03.2
Avior	234 17.6	S59 34.1
Bellatrix	278 30.2	N 6 21.6
Betelgeuse	270 59.5	N 7 24.4
Canopus	263 55.8	S52 42.5
Capella	280 31.9	N46 00.6
Deneb	49 29.7	N45 20.3
Denebola	182 31.6	N14 28.9
Diphda	348 54.0	S17 53.8
Dubhe	193 49.5	N61 40.0
Elnath	278 10.5	N28 37.0
Eltanin	90 44.7	N51 29.4
Enif	33 45.0	N 9 57.1
Fomalhaut	15 21.8	S29 31.9
Gacrux	171 58.3	S57 12.5
Gienah	175 50.1	S17 38.1
Hadar	148 44.4	S60 27.2
Hamal	327 58.7	N23 32.1
Kaus Aust.	83 40.8	S34 22.3
Kochab	137 19.4	N74 05.6
Markab	13 36.3	N15 17.5
Menkar	314 13.2	N 4 09.0
Menkent	148 04.9	S36 27.1
Miaplacidus	221 39.6	S69 47.5
Mirfak	308 37.8	N49 54.8
Nunki	75 55.5	S26 16.3
Peacock	53 15.7	S56 40.6
Pollux	243 25.6	N27 59.1
Procyon	244 57.9	N 5 10.8
Rasalhague	96 04.2	N12 33.1
Regulus	207 41.5	N11 53.2
Rigel	281 10.5	S 8 11.2
Rigil Kent.	139 48.4	S60 54.2
Sabik	102 09.9	S15 44.5
Schedar	349 38.3	N56 37.3
Shaula	96 18.8	S37 06.7
Sirius	258 32.3	S16 44.6
Spica	158 28.9	S11 14.8
Suhail	222 51.2	S43 30.3
Vega	80 37.2	N38 48.1
Zuben'ubi	137 02.9	S16 06.5

	SHA ° ′	Mer. Pass. h m
Venus	277 47.7	12 07
Mars	127 37.3	22 02
Jupiter	193 25.9	17 41
Saturn	108 44.7	23 18

	UT (d h)	SUN GHA	SUN Dec	MOON GHA	v	Dec	d	HP
		° ′	° ′	° ′	′	° ′	′	′
	11 00	180 05.4	N23 05.7	102 58.2	13.1	N 8 36.6	8.9	55.8
	01	195 05.3	05.9	117 30.3	13.2	8 27.7	8.9	55.7
	02	210 05.1	06.0	132 02.5	13.3	8 18.8	8.9	55.7
	03	225 05.0	. . 06.2	146 34.8	13.3	8 09.9	9.0	55.7
	04	240 04.9	06.4	161 07.1	13.4	8 00.9	9.0	55.6
	05	255 04.8	06.5	175 39.5	13.4	7 51.9	9.1	55.6
	06	270 04.6	N23 06.7	190 11.9	13.5	N 7 42.8	9.0	55.6
	07	285 04.5	06.9	204 44.4	13.6	7 33.8	9.1	55.6
S	08	300 04.4	07.0	219 17.0	13.6	7 24.7	9.1	55.5
A	09	315 04.3	. . 07.2	233 49.6	13.6	7 15.6	9.1	55.5
T	10	330 04.1	07.4	248 22.2	13.7	7 06.5	9.2	55.5
U	11	345 04.0	07.5	262 54.9	13.7	6 57.3	9.2	55.4
R	12	0 03.9	N23 07.7	277 27.6	13.8	N 6 48.1	9.2	55.4
D	13	15 03.7	07.9	292 00.4	13.8	6 38.9	9.2	55.4
A	14	30 03.6	08.0	306 33.2	13.9	6 29.7	9.2	55.4
Y	15	45 03.5	. . 08.2	321 06.1	14.0	6 20.5	9.3	55.3
	16	60 03.4	08.3	335 39.1	13.9	6 11.2	9.2	55.3
	17	75 03.2	08.5	350 12.0	14.0	6 02.0	9.3	55.3
	18	90 03.1	N23 08.7	4 45.0	14.1	N 5 52.7	9.3	55.3
	19	105 03.0	08.8	19 18.1	14.1	5 43.4	9.4	55.2
	20	120 02.8	09.0	33 51.2	14.2	5 34.0	9.3	55.2
	21	135 02.7	. . 09.1	48 24.4	14.1	5 24.7	9.4	55.2
	22	150 02.6	09.3	62 57.5	14.3	5 15.3	9.3	55.2
	23	165 02.5	09.4	77 30.8	14.2	5 06.0	9.4	55.1
	12 00	180 02.3	N23 09.6	92 04.0	14.3	N 4 56.6	9.4	55.1
	01	195 02.2	09.7	106 37.3	14.4	4 47.2	9.4	55.1
	02	210 02.1	09.9	121 10.7	14.4	4 37.8	9.4	55.1
	03	225 01.9	. . 10.0	135 44.1	14.4	4 28.4	9.5	55.0
	04	240 01.8	10.2	150 17.5	14.4	4 18.9	9.4	55.0
	05	255 01.7	10.3	164 50.9	14.5	4 09.5	9.5	55.0
	06	270 01.5	N23 10.5	179 24.4	14.6	N 4 00.0	9.4	55.0
	07	285 01.4	10.6	193 58.0	14.5	3 50.6	9.5	55.0
	08	300 01.3	10.8	208 31.5	14.6	3 41.1	9.5	54.9
S	09	315 01.2	. . 10.9	223 05.1	14.6	3 31.6	9.5	54.9
U	10	330 01.0	11.1	237 38.7	14.7	3 22.1	9.5	54.9
N	11	345 00.9	11.2	252 12.4	14.7	3 12.6	9.5	54.9
D	12	0 00.8	N23 11.4	266 46.1	14.7	N 3 03.1	9.5	54.9
A	13	15 00.6	11.5	281 19.8	14.7	2 53.6	9.5	54.8
Y	14	30 00.5	11.7	295 53.5	14.8	2 44.1	9.5	54.8
	15	45 00.4	. . 11.8	310 27.3	14.8	2 34.6	9.5	54.8
	16	60 00.2	12.0	325 01.1	14.8	2 25.1	9.5	54.8
	17	75 00.1	12.1	339 34.9	14.8	2 15.6	9.6	54.8
	18	90 00.0	N23 12.2	354 08.7	14.9	N 2 06.0	9.5	54.7
	19	104 59.9	12.4	8 42.6	14.9	1 56.5	9.5	54.7
	20	119 59.7	12.5	23 16.5	14.9	1 47.0	9.6	54.7
	21	134 59.6	. . 12.7	37 50.4	15.0	1 37.4	9.5	54.7
	22	149 59.5	12.8	52 24.4	14.9	1 27.9	9.5	54.7
	23	164 59.3	12.9	66 58.3	15.0	1 18.4	9.6	54.6
	13 00	179 59.2	N23 13.1	81 32.3	15.0	N 1 08.8	9.5	54.6
	01	194 59.1	13.2	96 06.3	15.1	0 59.3	9.5	54.6
	02	209 58.9	13.3	110 40.4	15.0	0 49.8	9.6	54.6
	03	224 58.8	. . 13.5	125 14.4	15.1	0 40.2	9.5	54.6
	04	239 58.7	13.6	139 48.5	15.0	0 30.7	9.5	54.6
	05	254 58.6	13.7	154 22.5	15.1	0 21.2	9.5	54.6
	06	269 58.4	N23 13.9	168 56.6	15.1	N 0 11.7	9.5	54.5
	07	284 58.3	14.0	183 30.7	15.2	N 0 02.2	9.6	54.5
	08	299 58.2	14.1	198 04.9	15.1	S 0 07.4	9.5	54.5
M	09	314 58.0	. . 14.3	212 39.0	15.1	0 16.9	9.5	54.5
O	10	329 57.9	14.4	227 13.1	15.2	0 26.4	9.5	54.5
N	11	344 57.8	14.5	241 47.3	15.2	0 35.9	9.4	54.5
D	12	359 57.6	N23 14.7	256 21.5	15.2	S 0 45.3	9.5	54.5
A	13	14 57.5	14.8	270 55.7	15.2	0 54.8	9.5	54.4
Y	14	29 57.4	14.9	285 29.9	15.2	1 04.3	9.5	54.4
	15	44 57.2	. . 15.0	300 04.1	15.2	1 13.8	9.4	54.4
	16	59 57.1	15.2	314 38.3	15.2	1 23.2	9.5	54.4
	17	74 57.0	15.3	329 12.5	15.2	1 32.7	9.4	54.4
	18	89 56.8	N23 15.4	343 46.7	15.2	S 1 42.1	9.4	54.4
	19	104 56.7	15.5	358 20.9	15.3	1 51.5	9.4	54.4
	20	119 56.6	15.7	12 55.2	15.2	2 00.9	9.4	54.4
	21	134 56.4	. . 15.8	27 29.4	15.3	2 10.3	9.4	54.3
	22	149 56.3	15.9	42 03.7	15.2	2 19.7	9.4	54.3
	23	164 56.2	16.0	56 37.9	15.3	S 2 29.1	9.4	54.3
		SD 15.8	*d* 0.1	SD 15.1		14.9		14.8

Lat.	Twilight Naut.	Twilight Civil	Sunrise	Moonrise 11	Moonrise 12	Moonrise 13	Moonrise 14
°	h m	h m	h m	h m	h m	h m	h m
N 72	▭	▭	▭	09 58	11 35	13 09	14 43
N 70	▭	▭	▭	10 08	11 39	13 08	14 36
68	▭	▭	▭	10 17	11 43	13 07	14 30
66	////	////	00 06	10 24	11 46	13 06	14 25
64	////	////	01 36	10 30	11 48	13 05	14 21
62	////	////	02 12	10 35	11 50	13 04	14 17
60	////	00 58	02 37	10 39	11 52	13 04	14 14
N 58	////	01 44	02 57	10 43	11 54	13 03	14 11
56	////	02 12	03 14	10 47	11 55	13 02	14 09
54	00 53	02 34	03 28	10 50	11 57	13 02	14 07
52	01 35	02 52	03 40	10 53	11 58	13 02	14 05
50	02 02	03 06	03 51	10 55	11 59	13 01	14 03
45	02 46	03 36	04 13	11 01	12 01	13 00	13 59
N 40	03 16	03 58	04 31	11 06	12 03	13 00	13 56
35	03 39	04 16	04 45	11 10	12 05	12 59	13 53
30	03 58	04 31	04 58	11 13	12 07	12 59	13 50
20	04 26	04 56	05 20	11 19	12 09	12 58	13 46
N 10	04 49	05 16	05 39	11 25	12 12	12 57	13 42
0	05 08	05 34	05 56	11 30	12 14	12 57	13 39
S 10	05 24	05 51	06 14	11 35	12 16	12 56	13 36
20	05 40	06 08	06 32	11 40	12 18	12 55	13 32
30	05 57	06 27	06 53	11 46	12 21	12 54	13 28
35	06 05	06 37	07 05	11 50	12 22	12 54	13 25
40	06 15	06 49	07 19	11 54	12 24	12 54	13 23
45	06 25	07 02	07 36	11 58	12 26	12 53	13 20
S 50	06 36	07 18	07 56	12 04	12 29	12 52	13 16
52	06 42	07 25	08 06	12 06	12 30	12 52	13 14
54	06 47	07 33	08 17	12 09	12 31	12 52	13 13
56	06 53	07 42	08 29	12 12	12 32	12 51	13 11
58	07 00	07 52	08 44	12 15	12 34	12 51	13 08
S 60	07 07	08 04	09 01	12 19	12 35	12 51	13 06

Lat.	Sunset	Twilight Civil	Twilight Naut.	Moonset 11	Moonset 12	Moonset 13	Moonset 14
°	h m	h m	h m	h m	h m	h m	h m
N 72	▭	▭	▭	00 57	00 52	00 47	00 41
N 70	▭	▭	▭	00 45	00 45	00 45	00 45
68	▭	▭	▭	00 35	00 40	00 44	00 48
66	▭	▭	▭	00 27	00 36	00 43	00 51
64	22 25	////	////	00 20	00 32	00 43	00 53
62	21 49	////	////	00 13	00 29	00 42	00 55
60	21 23	23 04	////	00 08	00 26	00 41	00 57
N 58	21 03	22 17	////	00 03	00 23	00 41	00 58
56	20 46	21 48	////	24 21	00 21	00 40	01 00
54	20 32	21 26	23 09	24 19	00 19	00 40	01 01
52	20 20	21 09	22 26	24 17	00 17	00 40	01 02
50	20 10	20 54	21 59	24 15	00 15	00 39	01 03
45	19 47	20 25	21 14	24 11	00 11	00 39	01 05
N 40	19 29	20 02	20 44	24 08	00 08	00 38	01 07
35	19 15	19 44	20 21	24 05	00 05	00 37	01 09
30	19 02	19 29	20 02	24 03	00 03	00 37	01 10
20	18 40	19 04	19 34	23 58	24 36	00 36	01 13
N 10	18 21	18 44	19 11	23 55	24 35	00 35	01 15
0	18 04	18 26	18 52	23 51	24 34	00 34	01 17
S 10	17 46	18 09	18 35	23 47	24 34	00 34	01 19
20	17 28	17 52	18 19	23 44	24 33	00 33	01 21
30	17 07	17 33	18 03	23 39	24 32	00 32	01 24
35	16 55	17 23	17 54	23 36	24 31	00 31	01 25
40	16 41	17 11	17 45	23 34	24 31	00 31	01 27
45	16 24	16 58	17 35	23 30	24 30	00 30	01 29
S 50	16 04	16 42	17 23	23 26	24 29	00 29	01 31
52	15 54	16 35	17 18	23 24	24 29	00 29	01 32
54	15 43	16 27	17 13	23 22	24 28	00 28	01 33
56	15 30	16 18	17 07	23 20	24 28	00 28	01 34
58	15 16	16 08	17 00	23 17	24 27	00 27	01 36
S 60	14 59	15 56	16 53	23 14	24 26	00 26	01 37

Day	SUN Eqn. of Time 00^h	SUN Eqn. of Time 12^h	SUN Mer. Pass.	MOON Mer. Pass. Upper	MOON Mer. Pass. Lower	Age	Phase
d	m s	m s	h m	h m	h m	d %	
11	00 22	00 16	12 00	17 40	05 18	06 42	
12	00 10	00 03	12 00	18 24	06 02	07 52	◑
13	00 03	00 09	12 00	19 07	06 46	08 61	

UT		ARIES	VENUS −4·0		MARS −1·7		JUPITER −2·0		SATURN +0·1	
		GHA	GHA	Dec	GHA	Dec	GHA	Dec	GHA	Dec
d	h	° ′	° ′	° ′	° ′	° ′	° ′	° ′	° ′	° ′
14	00	262 43.3	177 50.6	N23 37.5	30 50.1	S21 04.4	95 58.7	N 7 01.7	11 37.2	S20 29.7
	01	277 45.8	192 49.7	37.7	45 53.1	04.3	111 00.9	01.6	26 39.9	29.7
	02	292 48.2	207 48.8	37.9	60 56.2	04.3	126 03.1	01.5	41 42.5	29.7
	03	307 50.7	222 47.9	. . 38.1	75 59.2	. . 04.2	141 05.4	. . 01.4	56 45.2	. . 29.6
	04	322 53.2	237 47.1	38.4	91 02.3	04.2	156 07.6	01.3	71 47.9	29.6
	05	337 55.6	252 46.2	38.6	106 05.3	04.1	171 09.9	01.2	86 50.5	29.6
	06	352 58.1	267 45.3	N23 38.8	121 08.3	S21 04.1	186 12.1	N 7 01.1	101 53.2	S20 29.6
	07	8 00.6	282 44.4	39.0	136 11.4	04.1	201 14.3	01.0	116 55.8	29.6
	08	23 03.0	297 43.5	39.1	151 14.4	04.0	216 16.6	00.9	131 58.5	29.6
	09	38 05.5	312 42.6	. . 39.3	166 17.4	. . 04.0	231 18.8	. . 00.8	147 01.1	. . 29.5
	10	53 07.9	327 41.7	39.5	181 20.5	03.9	246 21.0	00.7	162 03.8	29.5
TUESDAY	11	68 10.4	342 40.9	39.7	196 23.5	03.9	261 23.3	00.6	177 06.4	29.5
	12	83 12.9	357 40.0	N23 39.9	211 26.5	S21 03.8	276 25.5	N 7 00.5	192 09.1	S20 29.5
	13	98 15.3	12 39.1	40.1	226 29.6	03.8	291 27.7	00.4	207 11.7	29.5
	14	113 17.8	27 38.2	40.3	241 32.6	03.7	306 30.0	00.3	222 14.4	29.4
	15	128 20.3	42 37.3	. . 40.5	256 35.6	. . 03.7	321 32.2	. . 00.2	237 17.1	. . 29.4
	16	143 22.7	57 36.4	40.7	271 38.6	03.7	336 34.5	00.1	252 19.7	29.4
	17	158 25.2	72 35.6	40.9	286 41.7	03.6	351 36.7	7 00.0	267 22.4	29.4
	18	173 27.7	87 34.7	N23 41.1	301 44.7	S21 03.6	6 38.9	N 6 59.9	282 25.0	S20 29.4
	19	188 30.1	102 33.8	41.2	316 47.7	03.5	21 41.2	59.8	297 27.7	29.3
	20	203 32.6	117 32.9	41.4	331 50.7	03.5	36 43.4	59.7	312 30.3	29.3
	21	218 35.0	132 32.0	. . 41.6	346 53.7	. . 03.4	51 45.6	. . 59.6	327 33.0	. . 29.3
	22	233 37.5	147 31.1	41.8	1 56.8	03.4	66 47.9	59.4	342 35.6	29.3
	23	248 40.0	162 30.2	42.0	16 59.8	03.3	81 50.1	59.3	357 38.3	29.3
15	00	263 42.4	177 29.4	N23 42.1	32 02.8	S21 03.3	96 52.3	N 6 59.2	12 40.9	S20 29.3
	01	278 44.9	192 28.5	42.3	47 05.8	03.3	111 54.6	59.1	27 43.6	29.2
	02	293 47.4	207 27.6	42.5	62 08.8	03.2	126 56.8	59.0	42 46.2	29.2
	03	308 49.8	222 26.7	. . 42.7	77 11.8	. . 03.2	141 59.0	. . 58.9	57 48.9	. . 29.2
	04	323 52.3	237 25.8	42.8	92 14.8	03.1	157 01.2	58.8	72 51.6	29.2
	05	338 54.8	252 24.9	43.0	107 17.8	03.1	172 03.5	58.7	87 54.2	29.2
	06	353 57.2	267 24.0	N23 43.2	122 20.8	S21 03.0	187 05.7	N 6 58.6	102 56.9	S20 29.1
	07	8 59.7	282 23.2	43.4	137 23.8	03.0	202 07.9	58.5	117 59.5	29.1
	08	24 02.2	297 22.3	43.5	152 26.8	03.0	217 10.2	58.4	133 02.2	29.1
	09	39 04.6	312 21.4	. . 43.7	167 29.8	. . 02.9	232 12.4	. . 58.3	148 04.8	. . 29.1
	10	54 07.1	327 20.5	43.9	182 32.8	02.9	247 14.6	58.2	163 07.5	29.1
WEDNESDAY	11	69 09.5	342 19.6	44.0	197 35.8	02.8	262 16.9	58.1	178 10.1	29.0
	12	84 12.0	357 18.7	N23 44.2	212 38.8	S21 02.8	277 19.1	N 6 58.0	193 12.8	S20 29.0
	13	99 14.5	12 17.8	44.4	227 41.8	02.8	292 21.3	57.9	208 15.4	29.0
	14	114 16.9	27 16.9	44.5	242 44.8	02.7	307 23.6	57.8	223 18.1	29.0
	15	129 19.4	42 16.1	. . 44.7	257 47.8	. . 02.7	322 25.8	. . 57.7	238 20.7	. . 29.0
	16	144 21.9	57 15.2	44.8	272 50.8	02.6	337 28.0	57.6	253 23.4	29.0
	17	159 24.3	72 14.3	45.0	287 53.8	02.6	352 30.2	57.4	268 26.1	28.9
	18	174 26.8	87 13.4	N23 45.1	302 56.8	S21 02.6	7 32.5	N 6 57.3	283 28.7	S20 28.9
	19	189 29.3	102 12.5	45.3	317 59.8	02.5	22 34.7	57.2	298 31.4	28.9
	20	204 31.7	117 11.6	45.5	333 02.8	02.5	37 36.9	57.1	313 34.0	28.9
	21	219 34.2	132 10.7	. . 45.6	348 05.7	. . 02.4	52 39.2	. . 57.0	328 36.7	. . 28.9
	22	234 36.7	147 09.8	45.8	3 08.7	02.4	67 41.4	56.9	343 39.3	28.8
	23	249 39.1	162 08.9	45.9	18 11.7	02.4	82 43.6	56.8	358 42.0	28.8
16	00	264 41.6	177 08.1	N23 46.1	33 14.7	S21 02.3	97 45.8	N 6 56.7	13 44.6	S20 28.8
	01	279 44.0	192 07.2	46.2	48 17.7	02.3	112 48.1	56.6	28 47.3	28.8
	02	294 46.5	207 06.3	46.4	63 20.6	02.3	127 50.3	56.5	43 49.9	28.8
	03	309 49.0	222 05.4	. . 46.5	78 23.6	. . 02.2	142 52.5	. . 56.4	58 52.6	. . 28.7
	04	324 51.4	237 04.5	46.6	93 26.6	02.2	157 54.7	56.3	73 55.2	28.7
	05	339 53.9	252 03.6	46.8	108 29.6	02.1	172 57.0	56.2	88 57.9	28.7
	06	354 56.4	267 02.7	N23 46.9	123 32.5	S21 02.1	187 59.2	N 6 56.1	104 00.5	S20 28.7
	07	9 58.8	282 01.8	47.1	138 35.5	02.1	203 01.4	55.9	119 03.2	28.7
	08	25 01.3	297 00.9	47.2	153 38.5	02.0	218 03.7	55.8	134 05.8	28.7
	09	40 03.8	312 00.0	. . 47.3	168 41.4	. . 02.0	233 05.9	. . 55.7	149 08.5	. . 28.6
	10	55 06.2	326 59.2	47.5	183 44.4	02.0	248 08.1	55.6	164 11.1	28.6
THURSDAY	11	70 08.7	341 58.3	47.6	198 47.4	01.9	263 10.3	55.5	179 13.8	28.6
	12	85 11.1	356 57.4	N23 47.8	213 50.3	S21 01.9	278 12.6	N 6 55.4	194 16.4	S20 28.6
	13	100 13.6	11 56.5	47.9	228 53.3	01.8	293 14.8	55.3	209 19.1	28.6
	14	115 16.1	26 55.6	48.0	243 56.2	01.8	308 17.0	55.2	224 21.8	28.5
	15	130 18.5	41 54.7	. . 48.2	258 59.2	. . 01.8	323 19.2	. . 55.1	239 24.4	. . 28.5
	16	145 21.0	56 53.8	48.3	274 02.2	01.7	338 21.4	55.0	254 27.1	28.5
	17	160 23.5	71 52.9	48.4	289 05.1	01.7	353 23.7	54.9	269 29.7	28.5
	18	175 25.9	86 52.0	N23 48.5	304 08.1	S21 01.7	8 25.9	N 6 54.8	284 32.4	S20 28.5
	19	190 28.4	101 51.1	48.7	319 11.0	01.6	23 28.1	54.7	299 35.0	28.5
	20	205 30.9	116 50.2	48.8	334 14.0	01.6	38 30.3	54.5	314 37.7	28.4
	21	220 33.3	131 49.3	. . 48.9	349 16.9	. . 01.6	53 32.6	. . 54.4	329 40.3	. . 28.4
	22	235 35.8	146 48.5	49.0	4 19.9	01.5	68 34.8	54.3	344 43.0	28.4
	23	250 38.3	161 47.6	49.2	19 22.8	01.5	83 37.0	54.2	359 45.6	28.4
Mer. Pass.		h m 6 24.1	v −0.9	d 0.2	v 3.0	d 0.0	v 2.2	d 0.1	v 2.7	d 0.0

STARS

Name	SHA	Dec
	° ′	° ′
Acamar	315 17.2	S40 14.4
Achernar	335 25.7	S57 09.1
Acrux	173 06.7	S63 11.7
Adhara	255 11.3	S28 59.9
Aldebaran	290 47.4	N16 32.3
Alioth	166 18.9	N55 52.6
Alkaid	152 57.1	N49 14.2
Al Na'ir	27 41.1	S46 52.6
Alnilam	275 44.7	S 1 11.7
Alphard	217 54.3	S 8 44.0
Alphecca	126 09.0	N26 39.8
Alpheratz	357 41.4	N29 10.7
Altair	62 06.0	N 8 54.9
Ankaa	353 13.9	S42 12.8
Antares	112 23.4	S26 27.9
Arcturus	145 53.7	N19 06.0
Atria	107 22.8	S69 03.2
Avior	234 17.6	S59 34.1
Bellatrix	278 30.2	N 6 21.6
Betelgeuse	270 59.5	N 7 24.4
Canopus	263 55.8	S52 42.5
Capella	280 31.9	N46 00.6
Deneb	49 29.7	N45 20.3
Denebola	182 31.6	N14 28.9
Diphda	348 54.0	S17 53.8
Dubhe	193 49.5	N61 40.0
Elnath	278 10.5	N28 37.0
Eltanin	90 44.7	N51 29.4
Enif	33 45.0	N 9 57.1
Fomalhaut	15 21.7	S29 31.9
Gacrux	171 58.4	S57 12.5
Gienah	175 50.1	S17 38.1
Hadar	148 44.5	S60 27.2
Hamal	327 58.7	N23 32.1
Kaus Aust.	83 40.7	S34 22.3
Kochab	137 19.4	N74 05.6
Markab	13 36.2	N15 17.6
Menkar	314 13.2	N 4 09.0
Menkent	148 04.9	S36 27.1
Miaplacidus	221 39.7	S69 47.4
Mirfak	308 37.8	N49 54.8
Nunki	75 55.5	S26 16.3
Peacock	53 15.7	S56 40.6
Pollux	243 25.6	N27 59.1
Procyon	244 57.9	N 5 10.8
Rasalhague	96 04.2	N12 33.1
Regulus	207 41.5	N11 53.2
Rigel	281 10.5	S 8 11.2
Rigil Kent.	139 48.4	S60 54.2
Sabik	102 09.9	S15 44.5
Schedar	349 38.2	N56 37.3
Shaula	96 18.7	S37 06.7
Sirius	258 32.3	S16 44.6
Spica	158 29.0	S11 14.8
Suhail	222 51.2	S43 30.3
Vega	80 37.2	N38 48.1
Zuben'ubi	137 02.9	S16 06.5

	SHA	Mer. Pass.
	° ′	h m
Venus	273 46.9	12 11
Mars	128 20.3	21 47
Jupiter	193 09.9	17 30
Saturn	108 58.5	23 05

UT d	h	SUN GHA	SUN Dec	MOON GHA	v	MOON Dec	d	HP
d	h	° ′	° ′	° ′	′	° ′	′	′
14	00	179 56.1	N23 16.1	71 12.2	15.2	S 2 38.5	9.3	54.3
	01	194 55.9	16.3	85 46.4	15.3	2 47.8	9.4	54.3
	02	209 55.8	16.4	100 20.7	15.2	2 57.2	9.3	54.3
	03	224 55.7	. . 16.5	114 54.9	15.3	3 06.5	9.3	54.3
	04	239 55.5	16.6	129 29.2	15.3	3 15.8	9.3	54.3
	05	254 55.4	16.7	144 03.5	15.2	3 25.1	9.3	54.3
	06	269 55.3	N23 16.8	158 37.7	15.3	S 3 34.4	9.2	54.3
	07	284 55.1	17.0	173 12.0	15.2	3 43.6	9.3	54.2
TUESDAY	08	299 55.0	17.1	187 46.2	15.2	3 52.9	9.2	54.2
	09	314 54.9	. . 17.2	202 20.4	15.3	4 02.1	9.2	54.2
	10	329 54.7	17.3	216 54.7	15.2	4 11.3	9.2	54.2
	11	344 54.6	17.4	231 28.9	15.2	4 20.5	9.2	54.2
	12	359 54.5	N23 17.5	246 03.1	15.3	S 4 29.7	9.1	54.2
	13	14 54.3	17.6	260 37.4	15.2	4 38.8	9.2	54.2
	14	29 54.2	17.7	275 11.6	15.2	4 48.0	9.1	54.2
	15	44 54.1	. . 17.8	289 45.8	15.2	4 57.1	9.1	54.2
	16	59 53.9	18.0	304 20.0	15.1	5 06.2	9.0	54.2
	17	74 53.8	18.1	318 54.1	15.2	5 15.2	9.1	54.2
	18	89 53.7	N23 18.2	333 28.3	15.2	S 5 24.3	9.0	54.2
	19	104 53.5	18.3	348 02.5	15.1	5 33.3	9.0	54.2
	20	119 53.4	18.4	2 36.6	15.2	5 42.3	9.0	54.2
	21	134 53.3	. . 18.5	17 10.8	15.1	5 51.3	8.9	54.2
	22	149 53.1	18.6	31 44.9	15.1	6 00.2	9.0	54.2
	23	164 53.0	18.7	46 19.0	15.1	6 09.2	8.9	54.2
15	00	179 52.9	N23 18.8	60 53.1	15.1	S 6 18.1	8.9	54.2
	01	194 52.7	18.9	75 27.2	15.1	6 27.0	8.8	54.2
	02	209 52.6	19.0	90 01.3	15.0	6 35.8	8.8	54.2
	03	224 52.5	. . 19.1	104 35.3	15.0	6 44.6	8.8	54.1
	04	239 52.3	19.2	119 09.3	15.1	6 53.4	8.8	54.1
	05	254 52.2	19.3	133 43.4	15.0	7 02.2	8.7	54.1
	06	269 52.1	N23 19.4	148 17.4	14.9	S 7 10.9	8.7	54.1
WEDNESDAY	07	284 51.9	19.5	162 51.3	15.0	7 19.6	8.7	54.1
	08	299 51.8	19.6	177 25.3	14.9	7 28.3	8.7	54.1
	09	314 51.7	. . 19.7	191 59.2	15.0	7 37.0	8.6	54.1
	10	329 51.5	19.8	206 33.2	14.9	7 45.6	8.6	54.1
	11	344 51.4	19.9	221 07.1	14.8	7 54.2	8.6	54.1
	12	359 51.3	N23 20.0	235 40.9	14.9	S 8 02.8	8.5	54.1
	13	14 51.1	20.1	250 14.8	14.8	8 11.3	8.5	54.1
	14	29 51.0	20.2	264 48.6	14.8	8 19.8	8.4	54.1
	15	44 50.9	. . 20.2	279 22.4	14.8	8 28.2	8.5	54.1
	16	59 50.7	20.3	293 56.2	14.8	8 36.7	8.4	54.1
	17	74 50.6	20.4	308 30.0	14.7	8 45.1	8.3	54.1
	18	89 50.5	N23 20.5	323 03.7	14.7	S 8 53.4	8.3	54.1
	19	104 50.3	20.6	337 37.4	14.7	9 01.7	8.3	54.1
	20	119 50.2	20.7	352 11.1	14.7	9 10.0	8.3	54.1
	21	134 50.1	. . 20.8	6 44.8	14.6	9 18.3	8.2	54.1
	22	149 49.9	20.9	21 18.4	14.6	9 26.5	8.2	54.2
	23	164 49.8	21.0	35 52.0	14.6	9 34.7	8.1	54.2
16	00	179 49.7	N23 21.0	50 25.6	14.5	S 9 42.8	8.1	54.2
	01	194 49.5	21.1	64 59.1	14.5	9 50.9	8.1	54.2
	02	209 49.4	21.2	79 32.6	14.5	9 59.0	8.0	54.2
	03	224 49.3	. . 21.3	94 06.1	14.5	10 07.0	8.0	54.2
	04	239 49.1	21.4	108 39.6	14.4	10 15.0	7.9	54.2
	05	254 49.0	21.5	123 13.0	14.4	10 22.9	7.9	54.2
	06	269 48.9	N23 21.5	137 46.4	14.4	S10 30.8	7.9	54.2
THURSDAY	07	284 48.7	21.6	152 19.8	14.3	10 38.7	7.8	54.2
	08	299 48.6	21.7	166 53.1	14.3	10 46.5	7.8	54.2
	09	314 48.5	. . 21.8	181 26.4	14.3	10 54.3	7.7	54.2
	10	329 48.3	21.9	195 59.7	14.2	11 02.0	7.7	54.2
	11	344 48.2	21.9	210 32.9	14.2	11 09.7	7.6	54.2
	12	359 48.1	N23 22.0	225 06.1	14.1	S11 17.3	7.6	54.2
	13	14 47.9	22.1	239 39.2	14.2	11 24.9	7.6	54.2
	14	29 47.8	22.2	254 12.4	14.1	11 32.5	7.5	54.2
	15	44 47.7	. . 22.2	268 45.5	14.0	11 40.0	7.4	54.2
	16	59 47.5	22.3	283 18.5	14.0	11 47.4	7.4	54.2
	17	74 47.4	22.4	297 51.5	14.0	11 54.8	7.4	54.2
	18	89 47.3	N23 22.5	312 24.5	14.0	S12 02.2	7.3	54.2
	19	104 47.1	22.5	326 57.5	13.9	12 09.5	7.2	54.3
	20	119 47.0	22.6	341 30.4	13.8	12 16.7	7.3	54.3
	21	134 46.9	. . 22.7	356 03.2	13.9	12 24.0	7.1	54.3
	22	149 46.7	22.7	10 36.1	13.8	12 31.1	7.1	54.3
	23	164 46.6	22.8	25 08.9	13.7	S12 38.2	7.1	54.3
		SD 15.8	d 0.1	SD 14.8		14.8		14.8

Lat.	Twilight Naut.	Twilight Civil	Sunrise	Moonrise 14	Moonrise 15	Moonrise 16	Moonrise 17
°	h m	h m	h m	h m	h m	h m	h m
N 72	▭	▭	▭	14 43	16 18	17 56	19 39
N 70	▭	▭	▭	14 36	16 04	17 34	19 05
68	▭	▭	▭	14 30	15 53	17 17	18 40
66	▭	▭	▭	14 25	15 44	17 03	18 21
64	////	////	01 33	14 21	15 36	16 52	18 06
62	////	////	02 10	14 17	15 30	16 42	17 53
60	////	00 53	02 36	14 14	15 24	16 34	17 43
N 58	////	01 41	02 56	14 11	15 19	16 27	17 33
56	////	02 11	03 13	14 09	15 15	16 20	17 25
54	00 48	02 33	03 27	14 07	15 11	16 15	17 18
52	01 33	02 51	03 39	14 05	15 07	16 10	17 12
50	02 01	03 06	03 50	14 03	15 04	16 05	17 06
45	02 46	03 35	04 13	13 59	14 57	15 55	16 53
N 40	03 16	03 58	04 31	13 56	14 51	15 47	16 43
35	03 39	04 16	04 46	13 53	14 46	15 40	16 34
30	03 58	04 31	04 59	13 50	14 42	15 34	16 26
20	04 27	04 56	05 20	13 46	14 34	15 23	16 13
N 10	04 49	05 16	05 39	13 42	14 28	15 14	16 02
0	05 08	05 34	05 57	13 39	14 22	15 06	15 51
S 10	05 25	05 51	06 14	13 36	14 16	14 57	15 40
20	05 41	06 09	06 33	13 32	14 09	14 48	15 29
30	05 58	06 28	06 54	13 28	14 02	14 37	15 16
35	06 06	06 38	07 06	13 25	13 58	14 32	15 08
40	06 16	06 50	07 20	13 23	13 53	14 25	14 59
45	06 26	07 03	07 37	13 20	13 47	14 17	14 50
S 50	06 38	07 19	07 58	13 16	13 41	14 08	14 38
52	06 43	07 27	08 08	13 14	13 38	14 03	14 32
54	06 49	07 35	08 19	13 13	13 34	13 59	14 26
56	06 55	07 44	08 31	13 11	13 31	13 53	14 19
58	07 01	07 54	08 46	13 08	13 27	13 47	14 12
S 60	07 09	08 06	09 03	13 06	13 22	13 41	14 03

Lat.	Sunset	Twilight Civil	Twilight Naut.	Moonset 14	Moonset 15	Moonset 16	Moonset 17
°	h m	h m	h m	h m	h m	h m	h m
N 72	▭	▭	▭	00 41	00 36	00 30	00 23
N 70	▭	▭	▭	00 45	00 45	00 45	00 46
68	▭	▭	▭	00 48	00 52	00 57	01 04
66	▭	▭	▭	00 51	00 58	01 07	01 19
64	22 29	////	////	00 53	01 04	01 16	01 31
62	21 52	////	////	00 55	01 08	01 23	01 41
60	21 25	23 10	////	00 57	01 12	01 30	01 50
N 58	21 05	22 20	////	00 58	01 16	01 35	01 57
56	20 48	21 51	////	01 00	01 19	01 40	02 04
54	20 34	21 29	23 14	01 01	01 22	01 45	02 10
52	20 22	21 11	22 29	01 02	01 25	01 49	02 16
50	20 11	20 56	22 01	01 03	01 27	01 53	02 21
45	19 49	20 26	21 16	01 05	01 32	02 01	02 32
N 40	19 31	20 04	20 45	01 07	01 37	02 08	02 41
35	19 16	19 45	20 22	01 09	01 40	02 13	02 48
30	19 03	19 30	20 03	01 10	01 44	02 19	02 55
20	18 41	19 05	19 34	01 13	01 50	02 27	03 07
N 10	18 22	18 45	19 12	01 15	01 55	02 35	03 17
0	18 04	18 27	18 53	01 17	02 00	02 43	03 27
S 10	17 47	18 10	18 36	01 19	02 04	02 50	03 37
20	17 28	17 52	18 20	01 21	02 09	02 58	03 47
30	17 07	17 34	18 03	01 24	02 15	03 07	03 59
35	16 55	17 23	17 55	01 25	02 19	03 12	04 06
40	16 41	17 11	17 45	01 27	02 23	03 18	04 14
45	16 24	16 58	17 35	01 29	02 27	03 25	04 23
S 50	16 03	16 42	17 23	01 31	02 32	03 33	04 34
52	15 54	16 34	17 18	01 32	02 35	03 37	04 39
54	15 42	16 26	17 12	01 33	02 38	03 42	04 45
56	15 30	16 17	17 06	01 34	02 41	03 46	04 52
58	15 15	16 07	17 00	01 36	02 44	03 52	04 59
S 60	14 58	15 55	16 52	01 37	02 48	03 57	05 07

Day	SUN Eqn. of Time 00^h	SUN Eqn. of Time 12^h	SUN Mer. Pass.	MOON Mer. Pass. Upper	MOON Mer. Pass. Lower	MOON Age	MOON Phase
d	m s	m s	h m	h m	h m	d	%
14	00 16	00 22	12 00	19 49	07 28	09	70
15	00 28	00 35	12 01	20 32	08 11	10	78
16	00 41	00 47	12 01	21 16	08 54	11	86

	UT	ARIES	VENUS −3·9		MARS −1·7		JUPITER −1·9		SATURN +0·1	
	d h	GHA	GHA	Dec	GHA	Dec	GHA	Dec	GHA	Dec
		° ′	° ′	° ′	° ′	° ′	° ′	° ′	° ′	° ′
	17 00	265 40.7	176 46.7	N23 49.3	34 25.8	S21 01.5	98 39.2	N 6 54.1	14 48.3	S20 28.4
	01	280 43.2	191 45.8	49.4	49 28.7	01.4	113 41.5	54.0	29 50.9	28.3
	02	295 45.6	206 44.9	49.5	64 31.6	01.4	128 43.7	53.9	44 53.6	28.3
	03	310 48.1	221 44.0	. . 49.6	79 34.6	. . 01.4	143 45.9	. . 53.8	59 56.2	. . 28.3
	04	325 50.6	236 43.1	49.7	94 37.5	01.3	158 48.1	53.7	74 58.9	28.3
	05	340 53.0	251 42.2	49.9	109 40.5	01.3	173 50.3	53.6	90 01.5	28.3
	06	355 55.5	266 41.3	N23 50.0	124 43.4	S21 01.3	188 52.6	N 6 53.4	105 04.2	S20 28.3
	07	10 58.0	281 40.4	50.1	139 46.3	01.2	203 54.8	53.3	120 06.8	28.2
	08	26 00.4	296 39.5	50.2	154 49.3	01.2	218 57.0	53.2	135 09.5	28.2
F	09	41 02.9	311 38.6	. . 50.3	169 52.2	. . 01.2	233 59.2	. . 53.1	150 12.1	. . 28.2
R	10	56 05.4	326 37.7	50.4	184 55.1	01.2	249 01.4	53.0	165 14.8	28.2
I	11	71 07.8	341 36.9	50.5	199 58.1	01.1	264 03.7	52.9	180 17.4	28.2
D	12	86 10.3	356 36.0	N23 50.6	215 01.0	S21 01.1	279 05.9	N 6 52.8	195 20.1	S20 28.1
A	13	101 12.8	11 35.1	50.7	230 03.9	01.1	294 08.1	52.7	210 22.7	28.1
Y	14	116 15.2	26 34.2	50.8	245 06.8	01.0	309 10.3	52.6	225 25.4	28.1
	15	131 17.7	41 33.3	. . 50.9	260 09.8	. . 01.0	324 12.5	. . 52.5	240 28.0	. . 28.1
	16	146 20.1	56 32.4	51.0	275 12.7	01.0	339 14.8	52.3	255 30.7	28.1
	17	161 22.6	71 31.5	51.1	290 15.6	00.9	354 17.0	52.2	270 33.3	28.0
	18	176 25.1	86 30.6	N23 51.2	305 18.5	S21 00.9	9 19.2	N 6 52.1	285 36.0	S20 28.0
	19	191 27.5	101 29.7	51.3	320 21.4	00.9	24 21.4	52.0	300 38.6	28.0
	20	206 30.0	116 28.8	51.4	335 24.4	00.9	39 23.6	51.9	315 41.3	28.0
	21	221 32.5	131 27.9	. . 51.5	350 27.3	. . 00.8	54 25.8	. . 51.8	330 43.9	. . 28.0
	22	236 34.9	146 27.0	51.6	5 30.2	00.8	69 28.1	51.7	345 46.6	28.0
	23	251 37.4	161 26.1	51.7	20 33.1	00.8	84 30.3	51.6	0 49.2	27.9
	18 00	266 39.9	176 25.2	N23 51.8	35 36.0	S21 00.7	99 32.5	N 6 51.5	15 51.9	S20 27.9
	01	281 42.3	191 24.3	51.9	50 38.9	00.7	114 34.7	51.3	30 54.5	27.9
	02	296 44.8	206 23.4	52.0	65 41.8	00.7	129 36.9	51.2	45 57.2	27.9
	03	311 47.3	221 22.6	. . 52.0	80 44.7	. . 00.7	144 39.1	. . 51.1	60 59.8	. . 27.9
	04	326 49.7	236 21.7	52.1	95 47.6	00.6	159 41.4	51.0	76 02.5	27.8
	05	341 52.2	251 20.8	52.2	110 50.5	00.6	174 43.6	50.9	91 05.1	27.8
	06	356 54.6	266 19.9	N23 52.3	125 53.4	S21 00.6	189 45.8	N 6 50.8	106 07.8	S20 27.8
S	07	11 57.1	281 19.0	52.4	140 56.3	00.6	204 48.0	50.7	121 10.4	27.8
	08	26 59.6	296 18.1	52.5	155 59.2	00.5	219 50.2	50.6	136 13.1	27.8
A	09	42 02.0	311 17.2	. . 52.5	171 02.1	. . 00.5	234 52.4	. . 50.5	151 15.7	. . 27.8
T	10	57 04.5	326 16.3	52.6	186 05.0	00.5	249 54.7	50.3	166 18.4	27.7
U	11	72 07.0	341 15.4	52.7	201 07.9	00.4	264 56.9	50.2	181 21.0	27.7
R	12	87 09.4	356 14.5	N23 52.8	216 10.8	S21 00.4	279 59.1	N 6 50.1	196 23.7	S20 27.7
D	13	102 11.9	11 13.6	52.9	231 13.7	00.4	295 01.3	50.0	211 26.3	27.7
A	14	117 14.4	26 12.7	52.9	246 16.6	00.4	310 03.5	49.9	226 29.0	27.7
	15	132 16.8	41 11.8	. . 53.0	261 19.5	. . 00.3	325 05.7	. . 49.8	241 31.6	. . 27.7
Y	16	147 19.3	56 10.9	53.1	276 22.4	00.3	340 07.9	49.7	256 34.3	27.6
	17	162 21.7	71 10.0	53.1	291 25.3	00.3	355 10.1	49.6	271 36.9	27.6
	18	177 24.2	86 09.1	N23 53.2	306 28.1	S21 00.3	10 12.4	N 6 49.4	286 39.6	S20 27.6
	19	192 26.7	101 08.2	53.3	321 31.0	00.3	25 14.6	49.3	301 42.2	27.6
	20	207 29.1	116 07.3	53.3	336 33.9	00.2	40 16.8	49.2	316 44.9	27.6
	21	222 31.6	131 06.4	. . 53.4	351 36.8	. . 00.2	55 19.0	. . 49.1	331 47.5	. . 27.5
	22	237 34.1	146 05.5	53.5	6 39.7	00.2	70 21.2	49.0	346 50.2	27.5
	23	252 36.5	161 04.7	53.5	21 42.5	00.2	85 23.4	48.9	1 52.8	27.5
	19 00	267 39.0	176 03.8	N23 53.6	36 45.4	S21 00.1	100 25.6	N 6 48.8	16 55.5	S20 27.5
	01	282 41.5	191 02.9	53.7	51 48.3	00.1	115 27.8	48.6	31 58.1	27.5
	02	297 43.9	206 02.0	53.7	66 51.2	00.1	130 30.1	48.5	47 00.8	27.5
	03	312 46.4	221 01.1	. . 53.8	81 54.0	. . 00.1	145 32.3	. . 48.4	62 03.4	. . 27.4
	04	327 48.9	236 00.2	53.8	96 56.9	00.0	160 34.5	48.3	77 06.1	27.4
	05	342 51.3	250 59.3	53.9	111 59.8	00.0	175 36.7	48.2	92 08.7	27.4
	06	357 53.8	265 58.4	N23 53.9	127 02.6	S21 00.0	190 38.9	N 6 48.1	107 11.4	S20 27.4
	07	12 56.2	280 57.5	54.0	142 05.5	00.0	205 41.1	48.0	122 14.0	27.4
	08	27 58.7	295 56.6	54.0	157 08.4	21 00.0	220 43.3	47.8	137 16.7	27.3
S	09	43 01.2	310 55.7	. . 54.1	172 11.2	20 59.9	235 45.5	. . 47.7	152 19.3	. . 27.3
U	10	58 03.6	325 54.8	54.1	187 14.1	59.9	250 47.7	47.6	167 22.0	27.3
N	11	73 06.1	340 53.9	54.2	202 16.9	59.9	265 49.9	47.5	182 24.6	27.3
D	12	88 08.6	355 53.0	N23 54.2	217 19.8	S20 59.9	280 52.2	N 6 47.4	197 27.2	S20 27.3
A	13	103 11.0	10 52.1	54.3	232 22.7	59.9	295 54.4	47.3	212 29.9	27.3
Y	14	118 13.5	25 51.2	54.3	247 25.5	59.8	310 56.6	47.2	227 32.5	27.2
	15	133 16.0	40 50.3	. . 54.4	262 28.4	. . 59.8	325 58.8	. . 47.0	242 35.2	. . 27.2
	16	148 18.4	55 49.4	54.4	277 31.2	59.8	341 01.0	46.9	257 37.8	27.2
	17	163 20.9	70 48.5	54.4	292 34.1	59.8	356 03.2	46.8	272 40.5	27.2
	18	178 23.4	85 47.6	N23 54.5	307 36.9	S20 59.8	11 05.4	N 6 46.7	287 43.1	S20 27.2
	19	193 25.8	100 46.7	54.5	322 39.8	59.8	26 07.6	46.6	302 45.8	27.2
	20	208 28.3	115 45.8	54.6	337 42.6	59.7	41 09.8	46.5	317 48.4	27.1
	21	223 30.7	130 44.9	. . 54.6	352 45.4	. . 59.7	56 12.0	. . 46.4	332 51.1	. . 27.1
	22	238 33.2	145 44.0	54.6	7 48.3	59.7	71 14.2	46.2	347 53.7	27.1
	23	253 35.7	160 43.1	54.7	22 51.1	59.7	86 16.4	46.1	2 56.4	27.1
	Mer. Pass.	h m 6 12.3	v −0.9	d 0.1	v 2.9	d 0.0	v 2.2	d 0.1	v 2.6	d 0.0

STARS

Name	SHA	Dec
	° ′	° ′
Acamar	315 17.2	S40 14.4
Achernar	335 25.7	S57 09.1
Acrux	173 06.7	S63 11.7
Adhara	255 11.3	S28 59.9
Aldebaran	290 47.4	N16 32.3
Alioth	166 18.9	N55 52.6
Alkaid	152 57.1	N49 14.2
Al Na'ir	27 41.1	S46 52.6
Alnilam	275 44.7	S 1 11.7
Alphard	217 54.3	S 8 44.0
Alphecca	126 09.0	N26 39.8
Alpheratz	357 41.4	N29 10.7
Altair	62 06.0	N 8 54.9
Ankaa	353 13.9	S42 12.8
Antares	112 23.4	S26 27.9
Arcturus	145 53.7	N19 06.0
Atria	107 22.8	S69 03.3
Avior	234 17.6	S59 34.1
Bellatrix	278 30.2	N 6 21.6
Betelgeuse	270 59.5	N 7 24.4
Canopus	263 55.8	S52 42.5
Capella	280 31.9	N46 00.6
Deneb	49 29.7	N45 20.3
Denebola	182 31.6	N14 28.9
Diphda	348 54.0	S17 53.8
Dubhe	193 49.6	N61 40.0
Elnath	278 10.4	N28 37.0
Eltanin	90 44.7	N51 29.4
Enif	33 44.9	N 9 57.1
Fomalhaut	15 21.7	S29 31.9
Gacrux	171 58.4	S57 12.5
Gienah	175 50.2	S17 38.1
Hadar	148 44.5	S60 27.2
Hamal	327 58.6	N23 32.1
Kaus Aust.	83 40.7	S34 22.3
Kochab	137 19.4	N74 05.6
Markab	13 36.2	N15 17.6
Menkar	314 13.2	N 4 09.0
Menkent	148 04.9	S36 27.1
Miaplacidus	221 39.7	S69 47.4
Mirfak	308 37.8	N49 54.8
Nunki	75 55.5	S26 16.3
Peacock	53 15.7	S56 40.6
Pollux	243 25.6	N27 59.0
Procyon	244 57.9	N 5 10.8
Rasalhague	96 04.2	N12 33.1
Regulus	207 41.5	N11 53.2
Rigel	281 10.5	S 8 11.2
Rigil Kent.	139 48.4	S60 54.2
Sabik	102 09.9	S15 44.5
Schedar	349 38.2	N56 37.3
Shaula	96 18.7	S37 06.7
Sirius	258 32.3	S16 44.6
Spica	158 29.0	S11 14.8
Suhail	222 51.2	S43 30.2
Vega	80 37.2	N38 48.1
Zuben'ubi	137 02.9	S16 06.5

	SHA	Mer. Pass.
	° ′	h m
Venus	269 45.4	12 15
Mars	128 56.1	21 33
Jupiter	192 52.6	17 19
Saturn	109 12.0	22 53

UT	SUN GHA	SUN Dec	MOON GHA	v	MOON Dec	d	HP
d h	° ′	° ′	° ′	′	° ′	′	′
17 00	179 46.4	N23 22.9	39 41.6	13.7	S12 45.3	7.0	54.3
01	194 46.3	22.9	54 14.3	13.7	12 52.3	6.9	54.3
02	209 46.2	23.0	68 47.0	13.7	12 59.2	6.9	54.3
03	224 46.0	. . 23.1	83 19.7	13.6	13 06.1	6.9	54.3
04	239 45.9	23.1	97 52.3	13.5	13 13.0	6.8	54.3
05	254 45.8	23.2	112 24.8	13.5	13 19.8	6.7	54.3
06	269 45.6	N23 23.3	126 57.3	13.5	S13 26.5	6.7	54.3
07	284 45.5	23.3	141 29.8	13.4	13 33.2	6.6	54.4
08	299 45.4	23.4	156 02.2	13.4	13 39.8	6.6	54.4
F 09	314 45.2	. . 23.5	170 34.6	13.4	13 46.4	6.5	54.4
R 10	329 45.1	23.5	185 07.0	13.3	13 52.9	6.4	54.4
I 11	344 45.0	23.6	199 39.3	13.3	13 59.3	6.4	54.4
D 12	359 44.8	N23 23.6	214 11.6	13.2	S14 05.7	6.4	54.4
A 13	14 44.7	23.7	228 43.8	13.2	14 12.1	6.2	54.4
Y 14	29 44.6	23.8	243 16.0	13.1	14 18.3	6.2	54.4
15	44 44.4	. . 23.8	257 48.1	13.1	14 24.5	6.2	54.4
16	59 44.3	23.9	272 20.2	13.1	14 30.7	6.1	54.4
17	74 44.2	23.9	286 52.3	13.0	14 36.8	6.0	54.5
18	89 44.0	N23 24.0	301 24.3	13.0	S14 42.8	6.0	54.5
19	104 43.9	24.0	315 56.3	12.9	14 48.8	5.9	54.5
20	119 43.8	24.1	330 28.2	12.9	14 54.7	5.8	54.5
21	134 43.6	. . 24.1	345 00.1	12.8	15 00.5	5.8	54.5
22	149 43.5	24.2	359 31.9	12.8	15 06.3	5.7	54.5
23	164 43.4	24.2	14 03.7	12.8	15 12.0	5.6	54.5
18 00	179 43.2	N23 24.3	28 35.5	12.7	S15 17.6	5.6	54.5
01	194 43.1	24.3	43 07.2	12.7	15 23.2	5.5	54.6
02	209 42.9	24.4	57 38.9	12.6	15 28.7	5.4	54.6
03	224 42.8	. . 24.4	72 10.5	12.6	15 34.1	5.4	54.6
04	239 42.7	24.5	86 42.1	12.5	15 39.5	5.3	54.6
05	254 42.5	24.5	101 13.6	12.5	15 44.8	5.2	54.6
06	269 42.4	N23 24.6	115 45.1	12.5	S15 50.0	5.2	54.6
S 07	284 42.3	24.6	130 16.6	12.4	15 55.2	5.1	54.6
A 08	299 42.1	24.7	144 48.0	12.3	16 00.3	5.0	54.7
T 09	314 42.0	. . 24.7	159 19.3	12.3	16 05.3	4.9	54.7
U 10	329 41.9	24.8	173 50.6	12.3	16 10.2	4.9	54.7
R 11	344 41.7	24.8	188 21.9	12.2	16 15.1	4.8	54.7
D 12	359 41.6	N23 24.8	202 53.1	12.2	S16 19.9	4.7	54.7
A 13	14 41.5	24.9	217 24.3	12.2	16 24.6	4.7	54.7
Y 14	29 41.3	24.9	231 55.5	12.1	16 29.3	4.6	54.7
15	44 41.2	. . 25.0	246 26.6	12.0	16 33.9	4.5	54.8
16	59 41.1	25.0	260 57.6	12.0	16 38.4	4.4	54.8
17	74 40.9	25.0	275 28.6	12.0	16 42.8	4.3	54.8
18	89 40.8	N23 25.1	289 59.6	11.9	S16 47.1	4.3	54.8
19	104 40.7	25.1	304 30.5	11.9	16 51.4	4.2	54.8
20	119 40.5	25.2	319 01.4	11.9	16 55.6	4.1	54.8
21	134 40.4	. . 25.2	333 32.3	11.8	16 59.7	4.1	54.8
22	149 40.2	25.2	348 03.1	11.7	17 03.8	3.9	54.9
23	164 40.1	25.3	2 33.8	11.7	17 07.7	3.9	54.9
19 00	179 40.0	N23 25.3	17 04.5	11.7	S17 11.6	3.8	54.9
01	194 39.8	25.3	31 35.2	11.6	17 15.4	3.7	54.9
02	209 39.7	25.4	46 05.8	11.6	17 19.1	3.7	54.9
03	224 39.6	. . 25.4	60 36.4	11.6	17 22.8	3.5	54.9
04	239 39.4	25.4	75 07.0	11.5	17 26.3	3.5	55.0
05	254 39.3	25.5	89 37.5	11.4	17 29.8	3.4	55.0
06	269 39.2	N23 25.5	104 07.9	11.5	S17 33.2	3.3	55.0
07	284 39.0	25.5	118 38.4	11.4	17 36.5	3.3	55.0
08	299 38.9	25.5	133 08.8	11.3	17 39.8	3.1	55.0
S 09	314 38.8	. . 25.6	147 39.1	11.3	17 42.9	3.1	55.0
U 10	329 38.6	25.6	162 09.4	11.3	17 46.0	2.9	55.1
N 11	344 38.5	25.6	176 39.7	11.2	17 48.9	2.9	55.1
D 12	359 38.4	N23 25.6	191 09.9	11.2	S17 51.8	2.8	55.1
A 13	14 38.2	25.7	205 40.1	11.1	17 54.6	2.7	55.1
Y 14	29 38.1	25.7	220 10.2	11.2	17 57.3	2.7	55.1
15	44 37.9	. . 25.7	234 40.4	11.0	18 00.0	2.5	55.1
16	59 37.8	25.7	249 10.4	11.1	18 02.5	2.4	55.2
17	74 37.7	25.8	263 40.5	11.0	18 04.9	2.4	55.2
18	89 37.5	N23 25.8	278 10.5	11.0	S18 07.3	2.3	55.2
19	104 37.4	25.8	292 40.5	10.9	18 09.6	2.2	55.2
20	119 37.3	25.8	307 10.4	10.9	18 11.8	2.1	55.2
21	134 37.1	. . 25.8	321 40.3	10.9	18 13.9	2.0	55.3
22	149 37.0	25.9	336 10.2	10.8	18 15.9	1.9	55.3
23	164 36.9	25.9	350 40.0	10.8	S18 17.8	1.8	55.3
	SD 15.8	*d* 0.0	SD 14.8		14.9		15.0

Lat.	Twilight Naut.	Twilight Civil	Sunrise	Moonrise 17	Moonrise 18	Moonrise 19	Moonrise 20
°	h m	h m	h m	h m	h m	h m	h m
N 72	□	□	□	19 39	21 33	■	■
N 70	□	□	□	19 05	20 35	21 59	23 00
68	□	□	□	18 40	20 01	21 14	22 12
66	□	□	□	18 21	19 37	20 45	21 42
64	////	////	01 31	18 06	19 18	20 23	21 19
62	////	////	02 09	17 53	19 02	20 05	21 01
60	////	00 50	02 36	17 43	18 49	19 51	20 45
N 58	////	01 40	02 56	17 33	18 38	19 38	20 33
56	////	02 10	03 13	17 25	18 28	19 28	20 22
54	00 46	02 33	03 27	17 18	18 20	19 18	20 12
52	01 32	02 51	03 39	17 12	18 12	19 10	20 03
50	02 00	03 06	03 50	17 06	18 05	19 02	19 55
45	02 46	03 35	04 13	16 53	17 50	18 46	19 39
N 40	03 16	03 58	04 31	16 43	17 38	18 33	19 25
35	03 39	04 16	04 46	16 34	17 28	18 22	19 14
30	03 58	04 31	04 59	16 26	17 19	18 12	19 03
20	04 27	04 56	05 21	16 13	17 04	17 55	18 46
N 10	04 50	05 17	05 40	16 02	16 50	17 40	18 31
0	05 09	05 35	05 58	15 51	16 38	17 27	18 17
S 10	05 26	05 52	06 15	15 40	16 25	17 13	18 03
20	05 42	06 10	06 34	15 29	16 12	16 58	17 48
30	05 58	06 28	06 55	15 16	15 57	16 42	17 31
35	06 07	06 39	07 07	15 08	15 48	16 32	17 21
40	06 17	06 51	07 21	14 59	15 38	16 21	17 09
45	06 27	07 04	07 38	14 50	15 26	16 08	16 56
S 50	06 39	07 20	07 59	14 38	15 12	15 52	16 39
52	06 44	07 28	08 09	14 32	15 06	15 45	16 32
54	06 50	07 36	08 20	14 26	14 58	15 37	16 23
56	06 56	07 45	08 33	14 19	14 50	15 28	16 13
58	07 03	07 55	08 47	14 12	14 41	15 17	16 03
S 60	07 10	08 07	09 05	14 03	14 31	15 06	15 50

Lat.	Sunset	Twilight Civil	Twilight Naut.	Moonset 17	Moonset 18	Moonset 19	Moonset 20
°	h m	h m	h m	h m	h m	h m	h m
N 72	□	□	□	00 23	{00 14 / 23 58}	■	■
N 70	□	□	□	00 46	00 49	00 57	01 16
68	□	□	□	01 04	01 14	01 31	02 00
66	□	□	□	01 19	01 34	01 56	02 29
64	22 32	////	////	01 31	01 50	02 16	02 52
62	21 53	////	////	01 41	02 03	02 32	03 09
60	21 27	23 13	////	01 50	02 14	02 45	03 24
N 58	21 07	22 22	////	01 57	02 24	02 56	03 37
56	20 50	21 52	////	02 04	02 32	03 06	03 48
54	20 35	21 30	23 17	02 10	02 40	03 15	03 57
52	20 23	21 12	22 30	02 16	02 47	03 23	04 06
50	20 12	20 57	22 03	02 21	02 53	03 30	04 13
45	19 50	20 27	21 17	02 32	03 06	03 45	04 30
N 40	19 32	20 05	20 46	02 41	03 17	03 58	04 43
35	19 17	19 46	20 23	02 48	03 27	04 08	04 55
30	19 04	19 31	20 04	02 55	03 35	04 18	05 05
20	18 41	19 06	19 35	03 07	03 49	04 34	05 22
N 10	18 23	18 46	19 13	03 17	04 02	04 48	05 37
0	18 05	18 27	18 54	03 27	04 13	05 01	05 51
S 10	17 47	18 10	18 37	03 37	04 25	05 14	06 05
20	17 29	17 53	18 20	03 47	04 37	05 28	06 20
30	17 08	17 34	18 04	03 59	04 52	05 45	06 37
35	16 55	17 23	17 55	04 06	05 00	05 54	06 47
40	16 41	17 12	17 46	04 14	05 10	06 05	06 58
45	16 24	16 58	17 35	04 23	05 21	06 17	07 11
S 50	16 04	16 42	17 24	04 34	05 34	06 33	07 28
52	15 54	16 35	17 18	04 39	05 41	06 40	07 35
54	15 42	16 26	17 13	04 45	05 48	06 48	07 44
56	15 30	16 17	17 06	04 52	05 55	06 57	07 53
58	15 15	16 07	17 00	04 59	06 04	07 07	08 04
S 60	14 58	15 55	16 52	05 07	06 14	07 19	08 17

Day	SUN Eqn. of Time 00^h	SUN Eqn. of Time 12^h	SUN Mer. Pass.	MOON Mer. Pass. Upper	MOON Mer. Pass. Lower	Age	Phase
d	m s	m s	h m	h m	h m	d %	
17	00 54	01 00	12 01	22 02	09 39	12 92	○
18	01 07	01 13	12 01	22 49	10 25	13 96	
19	01 20	01 26	12 01	23 39	11 14	14 99	

UT	ARIES	VENUS −3·9		MARS −1·6		JUPITER −1·9		SATURN +0·1	
	GHA	GHA	Dec	GHA	Dec	GHA	Dec	GHA	Dec
d h	° ′	° ′	° ′	° ′	° ′	° ′	° ′	° ′	° ′
20 00 (MONDAY)	268 38.1	175 42.3	N23 54.7	37 54.0	S20 59.7	101 18.6	N 6 46.0	17 59.0	S20 27.1
01	283 40.6	190 41.4	54.7	52 56.8	59.7	116 20.9	45.9	33 01.7	27.0
02	298 43.1	205 40.5	54.7	67 59.6	59.6	131 23.1	45.8	48 04.3	27.0
03	313 45.5	220 39.6	. . 54.8	83 02.5	. . 59.6	146 25.3	. . 45.7	63 07.0	. . 27.0
04	328 48.0	235 38.7	54.8	98 05.3	59.6	161 27.5	45.5	78 09.6	27.0
05	343 50.5	250 37.8	54.8	113 08.1	59.6	176 29.7	45.4	93 12.3	27.0
06	358 52.9	265 36.9	N23 54.9	128 11.0	S20 59.6	191 31.9	N 6 45.3	108 14.9	S20 27.0
07	13 55.4	280 36.0	54.9	143 13.8	59.6	206 34.1	45.2	123 17.5	26.9
08	28 57.9	295 35.1	54.9	158 16.6	59.5	221 36.3	45.1	138 20.2	26.9
09	44 00.3	310 34.2	. . 54.9	173 19.5	. . 59.5	236 38.5	. . 45.0	153 22.8	. . 26.9
10	59 02.8	325 33.3	54.9	188 22.3	59.5	251 40.7	44.8	168 25.5	26.9
11	74 05.2	340 32.4	55.0	203 25.1	59.5	266 42.9	44.7	183 28.1	26.9
12	89 07.7	355 31.5	N23 55.0	218 27.9	S20 59.5	281 45.1	N 6 44.6	198 30.8	S20 26.9
13	104 10.2	10 30.6	55.0	233 30.7	59.5	296 47.3	44.5	213 33.4	26.8
14	119 12.6	25 29.7	55.0	248 33.6	59.5	311 49.5	44.4	228 36.1	26.8
15	134 15.1	40 28.8	. . 55.0	263 36.4	. . 59.4	326 51.7	. . 44.3	243 38.7	. . 26.8
16	149 17.6	55 27.9	55.0	278 39.2	59.4	341 53.9	44.1	258 41.4	26.8
17	164 20.0	70 27.0	55.0	293 42.0	59.4	356 56.1	44.0	273 44.0	26.8
18	179 22.5	85 26.1	N23 55.0	308 44.8	S20 59.4	11 58.3	N 6 43.9	288 46.7	S20 26.7
19	194 25.0	100 25.2	55.1	323 47.6	59.4	27 00.5	43.8	303 49.3	26.7
20	209 27.4	115 24.3	55.1	338 50.4	59.4	42 02.7	43.7	318 51.9	26.7
21	224 29.9	130 23.4	. . 55.1	353 53.3	. . 59.4	57 04.9	. . 43.6	333 54.6	. . 26.7
22	239 32.4	145 22.5	55.1	8 56.1	59.4	72 07.1	43.4	348 57.2	26.7
23	254 34.8	160 21.6	55.1	23 58.9	59.3	87 09.3	43.3	3 59.9	26.7
21 00 (TUESDAY)	269 37.3	175 20.7	N23 55.1	39 01.7	S20 59.3	102 11.5	N 6 43.2	19 02.5	S20 26.6
01	284 39.7	190 19.8	55.1	54 04.5	59.3	117 13.7	43.1	34 05.2	26.6
02	299 42.2	205 18.9	55.1	69 07.3	59.3	132 15.9	43.0	49 07.8	26.6
03	314 44.7	220 18.0	. . 55.1	84 10.1	. . 59.3	147 18.1	. . 42.9	64 10.5	. . 26.6
04	329 47.1	235 17.1	55.1	99 12.9	59.3	162 20.3	42.7	79 13.1	26.6
05	344 49.6	250 16.2	55.1	114 15.7	59.3	177 22.5	42.6	94 15.8	26.6
06	359 52.1	265 15.3	N23 55.1	129 18.5	S20 59.3	192 24.7	N 6 42.5	109 18.4	S20 26.5
07	14 54.5	280 14.5	55.1	144 21.3	59.3	207 26.9	42.4	124 21.0	26.5
08	29 57.0	295 13.6	55.1	159 24.0	59.3	222 29.1	42.3	139 23.7	26.5
09	44 59.5	310 12.7	. . 55.0	174 26.8	. . 59.2	237 31.3	. . 42.1	154 26.3	. . 26.5
10	60 01.9	325 11.8	55.0	189 29.6	59.2	252 33.5	42.0	169 29.0	26.5
11	75 04.4	340 10.9	55.0	204 32.4	59.2	267 35.7	41.9	184 31.6	26.5
12	90 06.8	355 10.0	N23 55.0	219 35.2	S20 59.2	282 37.9	N 6 41.8	199 34.3	S20 26.4
13	105 09.3	10 09.1	55.0	234 38.0	59.2	297 40.1	41.7	214 36.9	26.4
14	120 11.8	25 08.2	55.0	249 40.8	59.2	312 42.3	41.5	229 39.6	26.4
15	135 14.2	40 07.3	. . 55.0	264 43.5	. . 59.2	327 44.5	. . 41.4	244 42.2	. . 26.4
16	150 16.7	55 06.4	54.9	279 46.3	59.2	342 46.7	41.3	259 44.8	26.4
17	165 19.2	70 05.5	54.9	294 49.1	59.2	357 48.9	41.2	274 47.5	26.4
18	180 21.6	85 04.6	N23 54.9	309 51.9	S20 59.2	12 51.1	N 6 41.1	289 50.1	S20 26.3
19	195 24.1	100 03.7	54.9	324 54.7	59.2	27 53.3	40.9	304 52.8	26.3
20	210 26.6	115 02.8	54.9	339 57.4	59.2	42 55.5	40.8	319 55.4	26.3
21	225 29.0	130 01.9	. . 54.8	355 00.2	. . 59.2	57 57.7	. . 40.7	334 58.1	. . 26.3
22	240 31.5	145 01.0	54.8	10 03.0	59.2	72 59.9	40.6	350 00.7	26.3
23	255 34.0	160 00.1	54.8	25 05.7	59.2	88 02.1	40.5	5 03.4	26.2
22 00 (WEDNESDAY)	270 36.4	174 59.2	N23 54.8	40 08.5	S20 59.1	103 04.3	N 6 40.4	20 06.0	S20 26.2
01	285 38.9	189 58.3	54.7	55 11.3	59.1	118 06.5	40.2	35 08.6	26.2
02	300 41.3	204 57.4	54.7	70 14.0	59.1	133 08.7	40.1	50 11.3	26.2
03	315 43.8	219 56.5	. . 54.7	85 16.8	. . 59.1	148 10.9	. . 40.0	65 13.9	. . 26.2
04	330 46.3	234 55.6	54.6	100 19.6	59.1	163 13.1	39.9	80 16.6	26.2
05	345 48.7	249 54.7	54.6	115 22.3	59.1	178 15.3	39.8	95 19.2	26.1
06	0 51.2	264 53.8	N23 54.6	130 25.1	S20 59.1	193 17.5	N 6 39.6	110 21.9	S20 26.1
07	15 53.7	279 52.9	54.5	145 27.8	59.1	208 19.7	39.5	125 24.5	26.1
08	30 56.1	294 52.0	54.5	160 30.6	59.1	223 21.9	39.4	140 27.1	26.1
09	45 58.6	309 51.1	. . 54.5	175 33.4	. . 59.1	238 24.1	. . 39.3	155 29.8	. . 26.1
10	61 01.1	324 50.2	54.4	190 36.1	59.1	253 26.3	39.1	170 32.4	26.1
11	76 03.5	339 49.3	54.4	205 38.9	59.1	268 28.5	39.0	185 35.1	26.0
12	91 06.0	354 48.4	N23 54.3	220 41.6	S20 59.1	283 30.7	N 6 38.9	200 37.7	S20 26.0
13	106 08.5	9 47.6	54.3	235 44.4	59.1	298 32.8	38.8	215 40.4	26.0
14	121 10.9	24 46.7	54.2	250 47.1	59.1	313 35.0	38.7	230 43.0	26.0
15	136 13.4	39 45.8	. . 54.2	265 49.8	. . 59.1	328 37.2	. . 38.5	245 45.6	. . 26.0
16	151 15.8	54 44.9	54.2	280 52.6	59.1	343 39.4	38.4	260 48.3	26.0
17	166 18.3	69 44.0	54.1	295 55.3	59.1	358 41.6	38.3	275 50.9	25.9
18	181 20.8	84 43.1	N23 54.1	310 58.1	S20 59.1	13 43.8	N 6 38.2	290 53.6	S20 25.9
19	196 23.2	99 42.2	54.0	326 00.8	59.1	28 46.0	38.1	305 56.2	25.9
20	211 25.7	114 41.3	54.0	341 03.5	59.1	43 48.2	37.9	320 58.9	25.9
21	226 28.2	129 40.4	. . 53.9	356 06.3	. . 59.1	58 50.4	. . 37.8	336 01.5	. . 25.9
22	241 30.6	144 39.5	53.8	11 09.0	59.1	73 52.6	37.7	351 04.1	25.9
23	256 33.1	159 38.6	53.8	26 11.8	59.1	88 54.8	37.6	6 06.8	25.8
Mer. Pass.	h m 6 00.5	v −0.9	d 0.0	v 2.8	d 0.0	v 2.2	d 0.1	v 2.6	d 0.0

STARS

Name	SHA	Dec
	° ′	° ′
Acamar	315 17.2	S40 14.3
Achernar	335 25.6	S57 09.0
Acrux	173 06.7	S63 11.7
Adhara	255 11.3	S28 59.9
Aldebaran	290 47.4	N16 32.3
Alioth	166 18.9	N55 52.6
Alkaid	152 57.2	N49 14.2
Al Na'ir	27 41.0	S46 52.6
Alnilam	275 44.6	S 1 11.7
Alphard	217 54.3	S 8 44.0
Alphecca	126 09.0	N26 39.8
Alpheratz	357 41.3	N29 10.7
Altair	62 05.9	N 8 54.9
Ankaa	353 13.8	S42 12.8
Antares	112 23.4	S26 27.9
Arcturus	145 53.7	N19 06.0
Atria	107 22.8	S69 03.3
Avior	234 17.6	S59 34.1
Bellatrix	278 30.2	N 6 21.6
Betelgeuse	270 59.4	N 7 24.4
Canopus	263 55.8	S52 42.5
Capella	280 31.9	N46 00.6
Deneb	49 29.7	N45 20.3
Denebola	182 31.6	N14 28.9
Diphda	348 53.9	S17 53.7
Dubhe	193 49.6	N61 40.0
Elnath	278 10.4	N28 37.0
Eltanin	90 44.7	N51 29.4
Enif	33 44.9	N 9 57.1
Fomalhaut	15 21.7	S29 31.9
Gacrux	171 58.4	S57 12.5
Gienah	175 50.2	S17 38.1
Hadar	148 44.5	S60 27.2
Hamal	327 58.6	N23 32.2
Kaus Aust.	83 40.7	S34 22.3
Kochab	137 19.5	N74 05.7
Markab	13 36.2	N15 17.6
Menkar	314 13.2	N 4 09.1
Menkent	148 04.9	S36 27.1
Miaplacidus	221 39.7	S69 47.4
Mirfak	308 37.8	N49 54.8
Nunki	75 55.4	S26 16.3
Peacock	53 15.6	S56 40.6
Pollux	243 25.6	N27 59.0
Procyon	244 57.9	N 5 10.8
Rasalhague	96 04.2	N12 33.1
Regulus	207 41.5	N11 53.2
Rigel	281 10.4	S 8 11.2
Rigil Kent.	139 48.4	S60 54.2
Sabik	102 09.9	S15 44.5
Schedar	349 38.2	N56 37.3
Shaula	96 18.7	S37 06.7
Sirius	258 32.3	S16 44.6
Spica	158 29.0	S11 14.8
Suhail	222 51.2	S43 30.2
Vega	80 37.1	N38 48.1
Zuben'ubi	137 02.9	S16 06.5

	SHA	Mer. Pass.
	° ′	h m
Venus	265 43.5	12 19
Mars	129 24.4	21 20
Jupiter	192 34.3	17 09
Saturn	109 25.2	22 40

	UT	SUN GHA	SUN Dec	MOON GHA	*v*	MOON Dec	*d*	HP
	d h	° ′	° ′	° ′	′	° ′	′	′
	20 00	179 36.7	N23 25.9	5 09.8	10.7	S18 19.6	1.8	55.3
	01	194 36.6	25.9	19 39.5	10.8	18 21.4	1.6	55.3
	02	209 36.5	25.9	34 09.3	10.7	18 23.0	1.6	55.3
	03	224 36.3	. . 25.9	48 39.0	10.6	18 24.6	1.4	55.4
	04	239 36.2	26.0	63 08.6	10.7	18 26.0	1.4	55.4
	05	254 36.1	26.0	77 38.3	10.6	18 27.4	1.3	55.4
	06	269 35.9	N23 26.0	92 07.9	10.5	S18 28.7	1.1	55.4
	07	284 35.8	26.0	106 37.4	10.6	18 29.8	1.1	55.4
	08	299 35.7	26.0	121 07.0	10.5	18 30.9	1.0	55.5
M	09	314 35.5	. . 26.0	135 36.5	10.5	18 31.9	0.9	55.5
O	10	329 35.4	26.0	150 06.0	10.4	18 32.8	0.8	55.5
N	11	344 35.2	26.0	164 35.4	10.5	18 33.6	0.7	55.5
D	12	359 35.1	N23 26.0	179 04.9	10.4	S18 34.3	0.6	55.5
A	13	14 35.0	26.0	193 34.3	10.3	18 34.9	0.6	55.5
Y	14	29 34.8	26.1	208 03.6	10.4	18 35.5	0.4	55.6
	15	44 34.7	. . 26.1	222 33.0	10.3	18 35.9	0.3	55.6
	16	59 34.6	26.1	237 02.3	10.3	18 36.2	0.2	55.6
	17	74 34.4	26.1	251 31.6	10.3	18 36.4	0.2	55.6
	18	89 34.3	N23 26.1	266 00.9	10.2	S18 36.6	0.0	55.6
	19	104 34.2	26.1	280 30.1	10.2	18 36.6	0.0	55.7
	20	119 34.0	26.1	294 59.3	10.3	18 36.6	0.2	55.7
	21	134 33.9	. . 26.1	309 28.6	10.1	18 36.4	0.3	55.7
	22	149 33.8	26.1	323 57.7	10.2	18 36.1	0.3	55.7
	23	164 33.6	26.1	338 26.9	10.1	18 35.8	0.4	55.7
	21 00	179 33.5	N23 26.1	352 56.0	10.2	S18 35.4	0.6	55.8
	01	194 33.4	26.1	7 25.2	10.1	18 34.8	0.6	55.8
	02	209 33.2	26.1	21 54.3	10.0	18 34.2	0.8	55.8
	03	224 33.1	. . 26.1	36 23.3	10.1	18 33.4	0.8	55.8
	04	239 33.0	26.1	50 52.4	10.1	18 32.6	0.9	55.8
	05	254 32.8	26.1	65 21.5	10.0	18 31.7	1.1	55.9
	06	269 32.7	N23 26.1	79 50.5	10.0	S18 30.6	1.1	55.9
	07	284 32.6	26.1	94 19.5	10.0	18 29.5	1.2	55.9
T	08	299 32.4	26.0	108 48.5	10.0	18 28.3	1.4	55.9
U	09	314 32.3	. . 26.0	123 17.5	10.0	18 26.9	1.4	55.9
E	10	329 32.1	26.0	137 46.5	9.9	18 25.5	1.5	56.0
S	11	344 32.0	26.0	152 15.4	10.0	18 24.0	1.6	56.0
D	12	359 31.9	N23 26.0	166 44.4	9.9	S18 22.4	1.8	56.0
A	13	14 31.7	26.0	181 13.3	9.9	18 20.6	1.8	56.0
Y	14	29 31.6	26.0	195 42.2	9.9	18 18.8	1.9	56.0
	15	44 31.5	. . 26.0	210 11.1	9.9	18 16.9	2.0	56.1
	16	59 31.3	26.0	224 40.0	9.9	18 14.9	2.1	56.1
	17	74 31.2	26.0	239 08.9	9.9	18 12.8	2.3	56.1
	18	89 31.1	N23 25.9	253 37.8	9.8	S18 10.5	2.3	56.1
	19	104 30.9	25.9	268 06.6	9.9	18 08.2	2.4	56.1
	20	119 30.8	25.9	282 35.5	9.9	18 05.8	2.5	56.2
	21	134 30.7	. . 25.9	297 04.4	9.8	18 03.3	2.6	56.2
	22	149 30.5	25.9	311 33.2	9.8	18 00.7	2.7	56.2
	23	164 30.4	25.9	326 02.0	9.9	17 58.0	2.8	56.2
	22 00	179 30.3	N23 25.8	340 30.9	9.8	S17 55.2	2.9	56.3
	01	194 30.1	25.8	354 59.7	9.8	17 52.3	3.0	56.3
	02	209 30.0	25.8	9 28.5	9.8	17 49.3	3.1	56.3
	03	224 29.9	. . 25.8	23 57.3	9.9	17 46.2	3.2	56.3
	04	239 29.7	25.8	38 26.2	9.8	17 43.0	3.3	56.3
	05	254 29.6	25.7	52 55.0	9.8	17 39.7	3.4	56.4
	06	269 29.5	N23 25.7	67 23.8	9.8	S17 36.3	3.5	56.4
W	07	284 29.3	25.7	81 52.6	9.8	17 32.8	3.6	56.4
E	08	299 29.2	25.7	96 21.4	9.8	17 29.2	3.7	56.4
D	09	314 29.1	. . 25.7	110 50.2	9.8	17 25.5	3.7	56.4
N	10	329 28.9	25.6	125 19.0	9.8	17 21.8	3.9	56.5
E	11	344 28.8	25.6	139 47.8	9.8	17 17.9	4.0	56.5
S	12	359 28.7	N23 25.6	154 16.6	9.8	S17 13.9	4.0	56.5
D	13	14 28.5	25.5	168 45.4	9.9	17 09.9	4.2	56.5
A	14	29 28.4	25.5	183 14.3	9.8	17 05.7	4.3	56.5
Y	15	44 28.2	. . 25.5	197 43.1	9.8	17 01.4	4.3	56.6
	16	59 28.1	25.5	212 11.9	9.8	16 57.1	4.4	56.6
	17	74 28.0	25.4	226 40.7	9.8	16 52.7	4.6	56.6
	18	89 27.8	N23 25.4	241 09.5	9.9	S16 48.1	4.6	56.6
	19	104 27.7	25.4	255 38.4	9.8	16 43.5	4.7	56.6
	20	119 27.6	25.3	270 07.2	9.8	16 38.8	4.9	56.7
	21	134 27.4	. . 25.3	284 36.0	9.9	16 33.9	4.9	56.7
	22	149 27.3	25.3	299 04.9	9.8	16 29.0	5.0	56.7
	23	164 27.2	25.2	313 33.7	9.9	S16 24.0	5.1	56.7
		SD 15.8	*d* 0.0	SD 15.1		15.3		15.4

Lat.	Twilight Naut.	Twilight Civil	Sunrise	Moonrise 20	Moonrise 21	Moonrise 22	Moonrise 23
°	h m	h m	h m	h m	h m	h m	h m
N 72	□	□	□	■	■	01 09	00 28
N 70	□	□	□	23 00	23 31	23 44	23 50
68	□	□	□	22 12	22 51	23 15	23 29
66	□	□	□	21 42	22 24	22 53	23 13
64	////	////	01 31	21 19	22 03	22 35	22 59
62	////	////	02 09	21 01	21 45	22 21	22 48
60	////	00 49	02 36	20 45	21 31	22 08	22 38
N 58	////	01 40	02 56	20 33	21 19	21 58	22 30
56	////	02 11	03 13	20 22	21 09	21 48	22 22
54	00 45	02 33	03 27	20 12	20 59	21 40	22 15
52	01 32	02 51	03 40	20 03	20 51	21 33	22 09
50	02 00	03 06	03 51	19 55	20 43	21 26	22 04
45	02 46	03 36	04 13	19 39	20 28	21 12	21 52
N 40	03 17	03 58	04 31	19 25	20 14	21 00	21 42
35	03 40	04 17	04 46	19 14	20 03	20 50	21 34
30	03 59	04 32	04 59	19 03	19 53	20 41	21 26
20	04 28	04 57	05 22	18 46	19 37	20 26	21 13
N 10	04 50	05 18	05 41	18 31	19 22	20 13	21 02
0	05 09	05 36	05 58	18 17	19 08	20 00	20 52
S 10	05 26	05 53	06 16	18 03	18 55	19 47	20 41
20	05 43	06 10	06 34	17 48	18 40	19 34	20 30
30	05 59	06 29	06 55	17 31	18 23	19 19	20 17
35	06 08	06 40	07 08	17 21	18 13	19 10	20 09
40	06 17	06 51	07 22	17 09	18 02	19 00	20 01
45	06 28	07 05	07 39	16 56	17 49	18 48	19 50
S 50	06 40	07 21	08 00	16 39	17 33	18 33	19 38
52	06 45	07 29	08 10	16 32	17 26	18 26	19 33
54	06 51	07 37	08 21	16 23	17 17	18 19	19 26
56	06 57	07 46	08 33	16 13	17 08	18 10	19 19
58	07 04	07 56	08 48	16 03	16 57	18 01	19 12
S 60	07 11	08 08	09 06	15 50	16 45	17 50	19 03

Lat.	Sunset	Twilight Civil	Twilight Naut.	Moonset 20	Moonset 21	Moonset 22	Moonset 23
°	h m	h m	h m	h m	h m	h m	h m
N 72	□	□	□	■	■	01 38	04 06
N 70	□	□	□	01 16	01 59	03 15	04 50
68	□	□	□	02 00	02 47	03 55	05 19
66	□	□	□	02 29	03 18	04 22	05 40
64	22 32	////	////	02 52	03 41	04 43	05 57
62	21 54	////	////	03 09	03 59	05 00	06 11
60	21 28	23 14	////	03 24	04 14	05 14	06 23
N 58	21 07	22 23	////	03 37	04 27	05 26	06 33
56	20 50	21 53	////	03 48	04 38	05 36	06 42
54	20 36	21 31	23 18	03 57	04 47	05 45	06 50
52	20 24	21 13	22 31	04 06	04 56	05 53	06 57
50	20 13	20 58	22 03	04 13	05 04	06 01	07 03
45	19 50	20 28	21 18	04 30	05 20	06 16	07 17
N 40	19 32	20 05	20 47	04 43	05 34	06 29	07 28
35	19 17	19 47	20 24	04 55	05 45	06 40	07 38
30	19 04	19 32	20 05	05 05	05 55	06 49	07 46
20	18 42	19 07	19 36	05 22	06 13	07 06	08 01
N 10	18 23	18 46	19 13	05 37	06 28	07 20	08 13
0	18 06	18 28	18 54	05 51	06 42	07 33	08 25
S 10	17 48	18 11	18 37	06 05	06 56	07 46	08 36
20	17 30	17 54	18 21	06 20	07 11	08 00	08 49
30	17 08	17 35	18 05	06 37	07 28	08 16	09 03
35	16 56	17 24	17 56	06 47	07 38	08 26	09 11
40	16 42	17 12	17 46	06 58	07 49	08 36	09 20
45	16 25	16 59	17 36	07 11	08 02	08 49	09 31
S 50	16 04	16 43	17 24	07 28	08 18	09 04	09 44
52	15 54	16 35	17 19	07 35	08 26	09 11	09 50
54	15 43	16 27	17 13	07 44	08 34	09 19	09 57
56	15 30	16 18	17 07	07 53	08 44	09 27	10 04
58	15 16	16 08	17 00	08 04	08 55	09 37	10 12
S 60	14 58	15 56	16 53	08 17	09 07	09 48	10 22

Day	SUN Eqn. of Time 00^h	SUN Eqn. of Time 12^h	SUN Mer. Pass.	MOON Mer. Pass. Upper	MOON Mer. Pass. Lower	MOON Age	MOON Phase
d	m s	m s	h m	h m	h m	d %	
20	01 33	01 39	12 02	24 29	12 04	15 100	
21	01 46	01 52	12 02	00 29	12 55	16 99	
22	01 59	02 05	12 02	01 21	13 47	17 96	

UT	ARIES	VENUS −3·9		MARS −1·6		JUPITER −1·9		SATURN +0·1		STARS		
	GHA	GHA	Dec	GHA	Dec	GHA	Dec	GHA	Dec	Name	SHA	Dec
d h	° ′	° ′	° ′	° ′	° ′	° ′	° ′	° ′	° ′		° ′	° ′
23 00	271 35.6	174 37.7	N23 53.7	41 14.5	S20 59.1	103 57.0	N 6 37.4	21 09.4	S20 25.8	Acamar	315 17.1	S40 14.3
01	286 38.0	189 36.8	53.7	56 17.2	59.1	118 59.2	37.3	36 12.1	25.8	Achernar	335 25.6	S57 09.0
02	301 40.5	204 35.9	53.6	71 19.9	59.1	134 01.3	37.2	51 14.7	25.8	Acrux	173 06.7	S63 11.7
03	316 43.0	219 35.0	. . 53.6	86 22.7	. . 59.1	149 03.5	. . 37.1	66 17.3	. . 25.8	Adhara	255 11.3	S28 59.9
04	331 45.4	234 34.1	53.5	101 25.4	59.1	164 05.7	37.0	81 20.0	25.8	Aldebaran	290 47.3	N16 32.3
05	346 47.9	249 33.2	53.4	116 28.1	59.1	179 07.9	36.8	96 22.6	25.7			
06	1 50.3	264 32.3	N23 53.4	131 30.8	S20 59.1	194 10.1	N 6 36.7	111 25.3	S20 25.7	Alioth	166 18.9	N55 52.6
07	16 52.8	279 31.4	53.3	146 33.6	59.1	209 12.3	36.6	126 27.9	25.7	Alkaid	152 57.2	N49 14.2
T 08	31 55.3	294 30.5	53.2	161 36.3	59.1	224 14.5	36.5	141 30.6	25.7	Al Na'ir	27 41.0	S46 52.6
H 09	46 57.7	309 29.6	. . 53.2	176 39.0	. . 59.1	239 16.7	. . 36.3	156 33.2	. . 25.7	Alnilam	275 44.6	S 1 11.7
U 10	62 00.2	324 28.7	53.1	191 41.7	59.1	254 18.9	36.2	171 35.8	25.7	Alphard	217 54.3	S 8 44.0
R 11	77 02.7	339 27.8	53.0	206 44.4	59.1	269 21.1	36.1	186 38.5	25.6			
S 12	92 05.1	354 27.0	N23 53.0	221 47.1	S20 59.1	284 23.2	N 6 36.0	201 41.1	S20 25.6	Alphecca	126 09.0	N26 39.8
D 13	107 07.6	9 26.1	52.9	236 49.9	59.1	299 25.4	35.9	216 43.8	25.6	Alpheratz	357 41.3	N29 10.7
A 14	122 10.1	24 25.2	52.8	251 52.6	59.1	314 27.6	35.7	231 46.4	25.6	Altair	62 05.9	N 8 54.9
Y 15	137 12.5	39 24.3	. . 52.7	266 55.3	. . 59.2	329 29.8	. . 35.6	246 49.0	. . 25.6	Ankaa	353 13.8	S42 12.8
16	152 15.0	54 23.4	52.7	281 58.0	59.2	344 32.0	35.5	261 51.7	25.6	Antares	112 23.4	S26 27.9
17	167 17.4	69 22.5	52.6	297 00.7	59.2	359 34.2	35.4	276 54.3	25.5			
18	182 19.9	84 21.6	N23 52.5	312 03.4	S20 59.2	14 36.4	N 6 35.2	291 57.0	S20 25.5	Arcturus	145 53.7	N19 06.0
19	197 22.4	99 20.7	52.4	327 06.1	59.2	29 38.6	35.1	306 59.6	25.5	Atria	107 22.8	S69 03.3
20	212 24.8	114 19.8	52.3	342 08.8	59.2	44 40.7	35.0	322 02.2	25.5	Avior	234 17.7	S59 34.0
21	227 27.3	129 18.9	. . 52.3	357 11.5	. . 59.2	59 42.9	. . 34.9	337 04.9	. . 25.5	Bellatrix	278 30.2	N 6 21.6
22	242 29.8	144 18.0	52.2	12 14.2	59.2	74 45.1	34.7	352 07.5	25.5	Betelgeuse	270 59.4	N 7 24.4
23	257 32.2	159 17.1	52.1	27 16.9	59.2	89 47.3	34.6	7 10.2	25.4			
24 00	272 34.7	174 16.2	N23 52.0	42 19.6	S20 59.2	104 49.5	N 6 34.5	22 12.8	S20 25.4	Canopus	263 55.8	S52 42.5
01	287 37.2	189 15.3	51.9	57 22.3	59.2	119 51.7	34.4	37 15.4	25.4	Capella	280 31.9	N46 00.6
02	302 39.6	204 14.4	51.8	72 25.0	59.2	134 53.9	34.2	52 18.1	25.4	Deneb	49 29.6	N45 20.4
03	317 42.1	219 13.5	. . 51.7	87 27.7	. . 59.2	149 56.1	. . 34.1	67 20.7	. . 25.4	Denebola	182 31.6	N14 28.9
04	332 44.6	234 12.6	51.6	102 30.4	59.2	164 58.2	34.0	82 23.4	25.4	Diphda	348 53.9	S17 53.7
05	347 47.0	249 11.7	51.5	117 33.0	59.3	180 00.4	33.9	97 26.0	25.3			
06	2 49.5	264 10.9	N23 51.4	132 35.7	S20 59.3	195 02.6	N 6 33.7	112 28.6	S20 25.3	Dubhe	193 49.6	N61 40.0
07	17 51.9	279 10.0	51.4	147 38.4	59.3	210 04.8	33.6	127 31.3	25.3	Elnath	278 10.4	N28 37.0
08	32 54.4	294 09.1	51.3	162 41.1	59.3	225 07.0	33.5	142 33.9	25.3	Eltanin	90 44.7	N51 29.4
F 09	47 56.9	309 08.2	. . 51.2	177 43.8	. . 59.3	240 09.2	. . 33.4	157 36.6	. . 25.3	Enif	33 44.9	N 9 57.1
R 10	62 59.3	324 07.3	51.1	192 46.5	59.3	255 11.3	33.3	172 39.2	25.3	Fomalhaut	15 21.7	S29 31.9
I 11	78 01.8	339 06.4	51.0	207 49.1	59.3	270 13.5	33.1	187 41.8	25.2			
D 12	93 04.3	354 05.5	N23 50.9	222 51.8	S20 59.3	285 15.7	N 6 33.0	202 44.5	S20 25.2	Gacrux	171 58.4	S57 12.5
A 13	108 06.7	9 04.6	50.8	237 54.5	59.3	300 17.9	32.9	217 47.1	25.2	Gienah	175 50.2	S17 38.1
Y 14	123 09.2	24 03.7	50.7	252 57.2	59.3	315 20.1	32.8	232 49.8	25.2	Hadar	148 44.5	S60 27.3
15	138 11.7	39 02.8	. . 50.5	267 59.8	. . 59.4	330 22.3	. . 32.6	247 52.4	. . 25.2	Hamal	327 58.6	N23 32.2
16	153 14.1	54 01.9	50.4	283 02.5	59.4	345 24.4	32.5	262 55.0	25.2	Kaus Aust.	83 40.7	S34 22.3
17	168 16.6	69 01.0	50.3	298 05.2	59.4	0 26.6	32.4	277 57.7	25.1			
18	183 19.1	84 00.1	N23 50.2	313 07.9	S20 59.4	15 28.8	N 6 32.2	293 00.3	S20 25.1	Kochab	137 19.5	N74 05.7
19	198 21.5	98 59.2	50.1	328 10.5	59.4	30 31.0	32.1	308 02.9	25.1	Markab	13 36.2	N15 17.6
20	213 24.0	113 58.4	50.0	343 13.2	59.4	45 33.2	32.0	323 05.6	25.1	Menkar	314 13.1	N 4 09.1
21	228 26.4	128 57.5	. . 49.9	358 15.8	. . 59.4	60 35.4	. . 31.9	338 08.2	. . 25.1	Menkent	148 04.9	S36 27.1
22	243 28.9	143 56.6	49.8	13 18.5	59.4	75 37.5	31.7	353 10.9	25.1	Miaplacidus	221 39.8	S69 47.4
23	258 31.4	158 55.7	49.7	28 21.2	59.5	90 39.7	31.6	8 13.5	25.0			
25 00	273 33.8	173 54.8	N23 49.5	43 23.8	S20 59.5	105 41.9	N 6 31.5	23 16.1	S20 25.0	Mirfak	308 37.7	N49 54.8
01	288 36.3	188 53.9	49.4	58 26.5	59.5	120 44.1	31.4	38 18.8	25.0	Nunki	75 55.4	S26 16.3
02	303 38.8	203 53.0	49.3	73 29.1	59.5	135 46.3	31.2	53 21.4	25.0	Peacock	53 15.6	S56 40.6
03	318 41.2	218 52.1	. . 49.2	88 31.8	. . 59.5	150 48.5	. . 31.1	68 24.0	. . 25.0	Pollux	243 25.6	N27 59.0
04	333 43.7	233 51.2	49.1	103 34.5	59.5	165 50.6	31.0	83 26.7	25.0	Procyon	244 57.9	N 5 10.8
05	348 46.2	248 50.3	48.9	118 37.1	59.5	180 52.8	30.9	98 29.3	25.0			
06	3 48.6	263 49.4	N23 48.8	133 39.8	S20 59.6	195 55.0	N 6 30.7	113 32.0	S20 24.9	Rasalhague	96 04.2	N12 33.1
07	18 51.1	278 48.5	48.7	148 42.4	59.6	210 57.2	30.6	128 34.6	24.9	Regulus	207 41.5	N11 53.2
S 08	33 53.6	293 47.6	48.6	163 45.0	59.6	225 59.4	30.5	143 37.2	24.9	Rigel	281 10.4	S 8 11.2
A 09	48 56.0	308 46.8	. . 48.4	178 47.7	. . 59.6	241 01.5	. . 30.4	158 39.9	. . 24.9	Rigil Kent.	139 48.4	S60 54.2
T 10	63 58.5	323 45.9	48.3	193 50.3	59.6	256 03.7	30.2	173 42.5	24.9	Sabik	102 09.9	S15 44.5
U 11	79 00.9	338 45.0	48.2	208 53.0	59.6	271 05.9	30.1	188 45.1	24.9			
R 12	94 03.4	353 44.1	N23 48.1	223 55.6	S20 59.7	286 08.1	N 6 30.0	203 47.8	S20 24.8	Schedar	349 38.1	N56 37.3
D 13	109 05.9	8 43.2	47.9	238 58.3	59.7	301 10.3	29.8	218 50.4	24.8	Shaula	96 18.7	S37 06.7
A 14	124 08.3	23 42.3	47.8	254 00.9	59.7	316 12.4	29.7	233 53.1	24.8	Sirius	258 32.3	S16 44.5
Y 15	139 10.8	38 41.4	. . 47.7	269 03.5	. . 59.7	331 14.6	. . 29.6	248 55.7	. . 24.8	Spica	158 29.0	S11 14.8
16	154 13.3	53 40.5	47.5	284 06.2	59.7	346 16.8	29.5	263 58.3	24.8	Suhail	222 51.2	S43 30.2
17	169 15.7	68 39.6	47.4	299 08.8	59.7	1 19.0	29.3	279 01.0	24.8			
18	184 18.2	83 38.7	N23 47.2	314 11.4	S20 59.8	16 21.1	N 6 29.2	294 03.6	S20 24.7	Vega	80 37.1	N38 48.1
19	199 20.7	98 37.8	47.1	329 14.1	59.8	31 23.3	29.1	309 06.2	24.7	Zuben'ubi	137 02.9	S16 06.5
20	214 23.1	113 37.0	47.0	344 16.7	59.8	46 25.5	29.0	324 08.9	24.7		SHA	Mer. Pass.
21	229 25.6	128 36.1	. . 46.8	359 19.3	. . 59.8	61 27.7	. . 28.8	339 11.5	. . 24.7		° ′	h m
22	244 28.0	143 35.2	46.7	14 21.9	59.8	76 29.9	28.7	354 14.2	24.7	Venus	261 41.5	12 24
23	259 30.5	158 34.3	46.5	29 24.6	59.9	91 32.0	28.6	9 16.8	24.7	Mars	129 44.9	21 07
	h m									Jupiter	192 14.8	16 58
Mer. Pass.	5 48.7	*v* −0.9	*d* 0.1	*v* 2.7	*d* 0.0	*v* 2.2	*d* 0.1	*v* 2.6	*d* 0.0	Saturn	109 38.1	22 27

UT d h		SUN GHA ° ′	SUN Dec ° ′	MOON GHA ° ′	v ′	MOON Dec ° ′	d ′	HP ′
23 00	THURSDAY	179 27.0	N23 25.2	328 02.6	9.9	S16 18.9	5.2	56.8
01		194 26.9	25.2	342 31.5	9.8	16 13.7	5.2	56.8
02		209 26.8	25.1	357 00.3	9.9	16 08.5	5.4	56.8
03		224 26.6	. . 25.1	11 29.2	9.9	16 03.1	5.5	56.8
04		239 26.5	25.1	25 58.1	9.9	15 57.6	5.5	56.8
05		254 26.4	25.0	40 27.0	9.9	15 52.1	5.7	56.9
06		269 26.2	N23 25.0	54 55.9	9.9	S15 46.4	5.7	56.9
07		284 26.1	24.9	69 24.8	9.9	15 40.7	5.8	56.9
08		299 26.0	24.9	83 53.7	9.9	15 34.9	5.9	56.9
09		314 25.8	. . 24.9	98 22.6	10.0	15 29.0	6.0	56.9
10		329 25.7	24.8	112 51.6	9.9	15 23.0	6.1	57.0
11		344 25.6	24.8	127 20.5	10.0	15 16.9	6.1	57.0
12		359 25.4	N23 24.7	141 49.5	10.0	S15 10.8	6.3	57.0
13		14 25.3	24.7	156 18.5	9.9	15 04.5	6.3	57.0
14		29 25.2	24.6	170 47.4	10.0	14 58.2	6.5	57.0
15		44 25.0	. . 24.6	185 16.4	10.0	14 51.7	6.5	57.1
16		59 24.9	24.5	199 45.4	10.0	14 45.2	6.6	57.1
17		74 24.8	24.5	214 14.4	10.1	14 38.6	6.6	57.1
18		89 24.6	N23 24.4	228 43.5	10.0	S14 32.0	6.8	57.1
19		104 24.5	24.4	243 12.5	10.1	14 25.2	6.9	57.2
20		119 24.4	24.3	257 41.6	10.0	14 18.3	6.9	57.2
21		134 24.2	. . 24.3	272 10.6	10.1	14 11.4	7.0	57.2
22		149 24.1	24.2	286 39.7	10.1	14 04.4	7.1	57.2
23		164 24.0	24.2	301 08.8	10.1	13 57.3	7.1	57.2
24 00	FRIDAY	179 23.8	N23 24.1	315 37.9	10.1	S13 50.2	7.3	57.3
01		194 23.7	24.1	330 07.0	10.1	13 42.9	7.3	57.3
02		209 23.6	24.0	344 36.1	10.1	13 35.6	7.4	57.3
03		224 23.4	. . 24.0	359 05.2	10.2	13 28.2	7.5	57.3
04		239 23.3	23.9	13 34.4	10.2	13 20.7	7.6	57.3
05		254 23.2	23.9	28 03.6	10.1	13 13.1	7.6	57.4
06		269 23.0	N23 23.8	42 32.7	10.2	S13 05.5	7.7	57.4
07		284 22.9	23.8	57 01.9	10.2	12 57.8	7.8	57.4
08		299 22.8	23.7	71 31.1	10.2	12 50.0	7.9	57.4
09		314 22.6	. . 23.6	86 00.3	10.2	12 42.1	7.9	57.4
10		329 22.5	23.6	100 29.5	10.3	12 34.2	8.0	57.5
11		344 22.4	23.5	114 58.8	10.2	12 26.2	8.1	57.5
12		359 22.3	N23 23.5	129 28.0	10.3	S12 18.1	8.1	57.5
13		14 22.1	23.4	143 57.3	10.3	12 10.0	8.3	57.5
14		29 22.0	23.3	158 26.6	10.3	12 01.7	8.2	57.6
15		44 21.9	. . 23.3	172 55.9	10.3	11 53.5	8.4	57.6
16		59 21.7	23.2	187 25.2	10.3	11 45.1	8.4	57.6
17		74 21.6	23.1	201 54.5	10.3	11 36.7	8.5	57.6
18		89 21.5	N23 23.1	216 23.8	10.3	S11 28.2	8.6	57.6
19		104 21.3	23.0	230 53.1	10.4	11 19.6	8.6	57.7
20		119 21.2	22.9	245 22.5	10.3	11 11.0	8.7	57.7
21		134 21.1	. . 22.9	259 51.8	10.4	11 02.3	8.8	57.7
22		149 20.9	22.8	274 21.2	10.4	10 53.5	8.8	57.7
23		164 20.8	22.7	288 50.6	10.4	10 44.7	8.9	57.7
25 00	SATURDAY	179 20.7	N23 22.7	303 20.0	10.4	S10 35.8	9.0	57.8
01		194 20.5	22.6	317 49.4	10.4	10 26.8	9.0	57.8
02		209 20.4	22.5	332 18.8	10.4	10 17.8	9.1	57.8
03		224 20.3	. . 22.5	346 48.2	10.4	10 08.7	9.1	57.8
04		239 20.1	22.4	1 17.6	10.5	9 59.6	9.2	57.8
05		254 20.0	22.3	15 47.1	10.4	9 50.4	9.3	57.9
06		269 19.9	N23 22.2	30 16.5	10.5	S 9 41.1	9.3	57.9
07		284 19.7	22.2	44 46.0	10.5	9 31.8	9.4	57.9
08		299 19.6	22.1	59 15.5	10.4	9 22.4	9.4	57.9
09		314 19.5	. . 22.0	73 44.9	10.5	9 13.0	9.5	57.9
10		329 19.3	21.9	88 14.4	10.5	9 03.5	9.6	58.0
11		344 19.2	21.9	102 43.9	10.5	8 53.9	9.6	58.0
12		359 19.1	N23 21.8	117 13.4	10.5	S 8 44.3	9.6	58.0
13		14 19.0	21.7	131 42.9	10.5	8 34.7	9.7	58.0
14		29 18.8	21.6	146 12.4	10.6	8 25.0	9.8	58.0
15		44 18.7	. . 21.5	160 42.0	10.5	8 15.2	9.8	58.1
16		59 18.6	21.5	175 11.5	10.5	8 05.4	9.9	58.1
17		74 18.4	21.4	189 41.0	10.6	7 55.5	9.9	58.1
18		89 18.3	N23 21.3	204 10.6	10.5	S 7 45.6	9.9	58.1
19		104 18.2	21.2	218 40.1	10.6	7 35.7	10.0	58.1
20		119 18.0	21.1	233 09.7	10.5	7 25.7	10.1	58.2
21		134 17.9	. . 21.1	247 39.2	10.6	7 15.6	10.1	58.2
22		149 17.8	21.0	262 08.8	10.5	7 05.5	10.1	58.2
23		164 17.6	20.9	276 38.3	10.6	S 6 55.4	10.2	58.2
		SD 15.8	*d* 0.1	SD 15.5		15.7		15.8

Lat. °	Twilight Naut. h m	Twilight Civil h m	Sunrise h m	Moonrise 23 h m	Moonrise 24 h m	Moonrise 25 h m	Moonrise 26 h m
N 72	▭	▭	▭	00 28	00 17	00 09	{00 03 / 23 57}
N 70	▭	▭	▭	23 50	23 52	23 53	23 53
68	▭	▭	▭	23 29	23 39	23 45	23 51
66	▭	▭	▭	23 13	23 27	23 38	23 48
64	////	////	01 33	22 59	23 18	23 33	23 46
62	////	////	02 11	22 48	23 10	23 28	23 44
60	////	00 51	02 37	22 38	23 03	23 23	23 43
N 58	////	01 42	02 57	22 30	22 56	23 20	23 41
56	////	02 12	03 14	22 22	22 51	23 16	23 40
54	00 47	02 34	03 28	22 15	22 46	23 13	23 39
52	01 34	02 52	03 41	22 09	22 41	23 10	23 38
50	02 01	03 07	03 52	22 04	22 37	23 08	23 37
45	02 47	03 37	04 14	21 52	22 28	23 02	23 34
N 40	03 18	03 59	04 32	21 42	22 21	22 58	23 33
35	03 41	04 18	04 47	21 34	22 15	22 53	23 31
30	03 59	04 33	05 00	21 26	22 09	22 50	23 30
20	04 28	04 58	05 22	21 13	21 59	22 44	23 28
N 10	04 51	05 18	05 41	21 02	21 51	22 38	23 25
0	05 10	05 36	05 59	20 52	21 43	22 33	23 24
S 10	05 27	05 53	06 16	20 41	21 34	22 28	23 22
20	05 43	06 11	06 35	20 30	21 26	22 22	23 20
30	06 00	06 30	06 56	20 17	21 16	22 16	23 17
35	06 09	06 40	07 08	20 09	21 10	22 13	23 16
40	06 18	06 52	07 23	20 01	21 04	22 09	23 15
45	06 28	07 06	07 39	19 50	20 56	22 04	23 13
S 50	06 40	07 22	08 00	19 38	20 47	21 58	23 11
52	06 45	07 29	08 10	19 33	20 43	21 55	23 10
54	06 51	07 37	08 21	19 26	20 38	21 53	23 09
56	06 57	07 46	08 34	19 19	20 33	21 49	23 08
58	07 04	07 57	08 48	19 12	20 27	21 46	23 06
S 60	07 11	08 08	09 06	19 03	20 21	21 42	23 05

Lat. °	Sunset h m	Twilight Civil h m	Twilight Naut. h m	Moonset 23 h m	Moonset 24 h m	Moonset 25 h m	Moonset 26 h m
N 72	▭	▭	▭	04 06	06 05	07 59	09 50
N 70	▭	▭	▭	04 50	06 31	08 14	09 58
68	▭	▭	▭	05 19	06 51	08 27	10 04
66	▭	▭	▭	05 40	07 06	08 37	10 09
64	22 32	////	////	05 57	07 19	08 45	10 14
62	21 54	////	////	06 11	07 30	08 52	10 17
60	21 28	23 13	////	06 23	07 39	08 58	10 21
N 58	21 07	22 23	////	06 33	07 47	09 04	10 24
56	20 51	21 53	////	06 42	07 54	09 09	10 26
54	20 36	21 31	23 17	06 50	08 00	09 13	10 28
52	20 24	21 13	22 31	06 57	08 05	09 17	10 31
50	20 13	20 58	22 03	07 03	08 11	09 20	10 32
45	19 51	20 28	21 18	07 17	08 21	09 28	10 36
N 40	19 33	20 06	20 47	07 28	08 30	09 34	10 40
35	19 18	19 47	20 24	07 38	08 38	09 40	10 43
30	19 05	19 32	20 06	07 46	08 45	09 45	10 45
20	18 43	19 07	19 36	08 01	08 56	09 53	10 50
N 10	18 24	18 47	19 14	08 13	09 07	10 00	10 54
0	18 06	18 29	18 55	08 25	09 16	10 07	10 57
S 10	17 49	18 12	18 38	08 36	09 25	10 13	11 01
20	17 30	17 54	18 22	08 49	09 35	10 20	11 04
30	17 09	17 35	18 05	09 03	09 47	10 28	11 09
35	16 57	17 25	17 57	09 11	09 53	10 33	11 11
40	16 43	17 13	17 47	09 20	10 00	10 38	11 14
45	16 26	17 00	17 37	09 31	10 09	10 44	11 17
S 50	16 05	16 43	17 25	09 44	10 19	10 51	11 20
52	15 55	16 36	17 20	09 50	10 24	10 54	11 22
54	15 44	16 28	17 14	09 57	10 29	10 58	11 24
56	15 31	16 19	17 08	10 04	10 35	11 02	11 26
58	15 17	16 09	17 01	10 12	10 41	11 06	11 28
S 60	14 59	15 57	16 54	10 22	10 49	11 11	11 31

Day	SUN Eqn. of Time 00^h	SUN Eqn. of Time 12^h	SUN Mer. Pass.	MOON Mer. Pass. Upper	MOON Mer. Pass. Lower	MOON Age	MOON Phase
d	m s	m s	h m	h m	h m	d	%
23	02 12	02 18	12 02	02 12	14 38	18	90
24	02 24	02 31	12 03	03 04	15 29	19	83
25	02 37	02 43	12 03	03 55	16 20	20	74

	UT	ARIES GHA	VENUS −3·9 GHA	VENUS Dec	MARS −1·5 GHA	MARS Dec	JUPITER −1·9 GHA	JUPITER Dec	SATURN +0·1 GHA	SATURN Dec
	d h	° ′	° ′	° ′	° ′	° ′	° ′	° ′	° ′	° ′
	26 00	274 33.0	173 33.4	N23 46.4	44 27.2	S20 59.9	106 34.2	N 6 28.4	24 19.4	S20 24.6
	01	289 35.4	188 32.5	46.2	59 29.8	59.9	121 36.4	28.3	39 22.1	24.6
	02	304 37.9	203 31.6	46.1	74 32.4	59.9	136 38.6	28.2	54 24.7	24.6
	03	319 40.4	218 30.7	. . 46.0	89 35.1	20 59.9	151 40.7	. . 28.1	69 27.3	. . 24.6
	04	334 42.8	233 29.8	45.8	104 37.7	21 00.0	166 42.9	27.9	84 30.0	24.6
	05	349 45.3	248 29.0	45.6	119 40.3	00.0	181 45.1	27.8	99 32.6	24.6
	06	4 47.8	263 28.1	N23 45.5	134 42.9	S21 00.0	196 47.3	N 6 27.7	114 35.2	S20 24.6
	07	19 50.2	278 27.2	45.3	149 45.5	00.0	211 49.4	27.5	129 37.9	24.5
	08	34 52.7	293 26.3	45.2	164 48.1	00.0	226 51.6	27.4	144 40.5	24.5
S	09	49 55.2	308 25.4	. . 45.0	179 50.7	. . 00.1	241 53.8	. . 27.3	159 43.1	. . 24.5
U	10	64 57.6	323 24.5	44.9	194 53.3	00.1	256 56.0	27.2	174 45.8	24.5
N	11	80 00.1	338 23.6	44.7	209 55.9	00.1	271 58.1	27.0	189 48.4	24.5
D	12	95 02.5	353 22.7	N23 44.6	224 58.5	S21 00.1	287 00.3	N 6 26.9	204 51.0	S20 24.5
A	13	110 05.0	8 21.8	44.4	240 01.2	00.2	302 02.5	26.8	219 53.7	24.4
Y	14	125 07.5	23 21.0	44.2	255 03.8	00.2	317 04.7	26.6	234 56.3	24.4
	15	140 09.9	38 20.1	. . 44.1	270 06.4	. . 00.2	332 06.8	. . 26.5	249 59.0	. . 24.4
	16	155 12.4	53 19.2	43.9	285 09.0	00.2	347 09.0	26.4	265 01.6	24.4
	17	170 14.9	68 18.3	43.7	300 11.5	00.3	2 11.2	26.3	280 04.2	24.4
	18	185 17.3	83 17.4	N23 43.6	315 14.1	S21 00.3	17 13.4	N 6 26.1	295 06.9	S20 24.4
	19	200 19.8	98 16.5	43.4	330 16.7	00.3	32 15.5	26.0	310 09.5	24.3
	20	215 22.3	113 15.6	43.2	345 19.3	00.3	47 17.7	25.9	325 12.1	24.3
	21	230 24.7	128 14.7	. . 43.1	0 21.9	. . 00.4	62 19.9	. . 25.7	340 14.8	. . 24.3
	22	245 27.2	143 13.9	42.9	15 24.5	00.4	77 22.1	25.6	355 17.4	24.3
	23	260 29.6	158 13.0	42.7	30 27.1	00.4	92 24.2	25.5	10 20.0	24.3
	27 00	275 32.1	173 12.1	N23 42.5	45 29.7	S21 00.4	107 26.4	N 6 25.3	25 22.7	S20 24.3
	01	290 34.6	188 11.2	42.4	60 32.3	00.5	122 28.6	25.2	40 25.3	24.3
	02	305 37.0	203 10.3	42.2	75 34.9	00.5	137 30.7	25.1	55 27.9	24.2
	03	320 39.5	218 09.4	. . 42.0	90 37.4	. . 00.5	152 32.9	. . 25.0	70 30.6	. . 24.2
	04	335 42.0	233 08.5	41.8	105 40.0	00.5	167 35.1	24.8	85 33.2	24.2
	05	350 44.4	248 07.7	41.6	120 42.6	00.6	182 37.3	24.7	100 35.8	24.2
	06	5 46.9	263 06.8	N23 41.5	135 45.2	S21 00.6	197 39.4	N 6 24.6	115 38.5	S20 24.2
	07	20 49.4	278 05.9	41.3	150 47.7	00.6	212 41.6	24.4	130 41.1	24.2
	08	35 51.8	293 05.0	41.1	165 50.3	00.7	227 43.8	24.3	145 43.7	24.1
M	09	50 54.3	308 04.1	. . 40.9	180 52.9	. . 00.7	242 45.9	. . 24.2	160 46.4	. . 24.1
O	10	65 56.8	323 03.2	40.7	195 55.5	00.7	257 48.1	24.0	175 49.0	24.1
N	11	80 59.2	338 02.3	40.5	210 58.0	00.8	272 50.3	23.9	190 51.6	24.1
D	12	96 01.7	353 01.5	N23 40.3	226 00.6	S21 00.8	287 52.4	N 6 23.8	205 54.3	S20 24.1
A	13	111 04.1	8 00.6	40.1	241 03.2	00.8	302 54.6	23.6	220 56.9	24.1
Y	14	126 06.6	22 59.7	40.0	256 05.7	00.8	317 56.8	23.5	235 59.5	24.1
	15	141 09.1	37 58.8	. . 39.8	271 08.3	. . 00.9	332 59.0	. . 23.4	251 02.2	. . 24.0
	16	156 11.5	52 57.9	39.6	286 10.9	00.9	348 01.1	23.3	266 04.8	24.0
	17	171 14.0	67 57.0	39.4	301 13.4	00.9	3 03.3	23.1	281 07.4	24.0
	18	186 16.5	82 56.2	N23 39.2	316 16.0	S21 01.0	18 05.5	N 6 23.0	296 10.1	S20 24.0
	19	201 18.9	97 55.3	39.0	331 18.5	01.0	33 07.6	22.9	311 12.7	24.0
	20	216 21.4	112 54.4	38.8	346 21.1	01.0	48 09.8	22.7	326 15.3	24.0
	21	231 23.9	127 53.5	. . 38.6	1 23.7	. . 01.1	63 12.0	. . 22.6	341 17.9	. . 23.9
	22	246 26.3	142 52.6	38.4	16 26.2	01.1	78 14.1	22.5	356 20.6	23.9
	23	261 28.8	157 51.7	38.2	31 28.8	01.1	93 16.3	22.3	11 23.2	23.9
	28 00	276 31.3	172 50.9	N23 38.0	46 31.3	S21 01.2	108 18.5	N 6 22.2	26 25.8	S20 23.9
	01	291 33.7	187 50.0	37.8	61 33.9	01.2	123 20.6	22.1	41 28.5	23.9
	02	306 36.2	202 49.1	37.6	76 36.4	01.2	138 22.8	21.9	56 31.1	23.9
	03	321 38.6	217 48.2	. . 37.4	91 38.9	. . 01.3	153 25.0	. . 21.8	71 33.7	. . 23.9
	04	336 41.1	232 47.3	37.1	106 41.5	01.3	168 27.1	21.7	86 36.4	23.8
	05	351 43.6	247 46.5	36.9	121 44.0	01.3	183 29.3	21.5	101 39.0	23.8
	06	6 46.0	262 45.6	N23 36.7	136 46.6	S21 01.4	198 31.5	N 6 21.4	116 41.6	S20 23.8
	07	21 48.5	277 44.7	36.5	151 49.1	01.4	213 33.6	21.3	131 44.3	23.8
T	08	36 51.0	292 43.8	36.3	166 51.7	01.4	228 35.8	21.1	146 46.9	23.8
U	09	51 53.4	307 42.9	. . 36.1	181 54.2	. . 01.5	243 38.0	. . 21.0	161 49.5	. . 23.8
E	10	66 55.9	322 42.0	35.9	196 56.7	01.5	258 40.1	20.9	176 52.2	23.7
S	11	81 58.4	337 41.2	35.6	211 59.3	01.5	273 42.3	20.7	191 54.8	23.7
D	12	97 00.8	352 40.3	N23 35.4	227 01.8	S21 01.6	288 44.5	N 6 20.6	206 57.4	S20 23.7
A	13	112 03.3	7 39.4	35.2	242 04.3	01.6	303 46.6	20.5	222 00.0	23.7
Y	14	127 05.7	22 38.5	35.0	257 06.8	01.7	318 48.8	20.3	237 02.7	23.7
	15	142 08.2	37 37.6	. . 34.8	272 09.4	. . 01.7	333 51.0	. . 20.2	252 05.3	. . 23.7
	16	157 10.7	52 36.8	34.5	287 11.9	01.7	348 53.1	20.1	267 07.9	23.7
	17	172 13.1	67 35.9	34.3	302 14.4	01.8	3 55.3	19.9	282 10.6	23.6
	18	187 15.6	82 35.0	N23 34.1	317 16.9	S21 01.8	18 57.4	N 6 19.8	297 13.2	S20 23.6
	19	202 18.1	97 34.1	33.9	332 19.5	01.8	33 59.6	19.7	312 15.8	23.6
	20	217 20.5	112 33.2	33.6	347 22.0	01.9	49 01.8	19.5	327 18.5	23.6
	21	232 23.0	127 32.4	. . 33.4	2 24.5	. . 01.9	64 03.9	. . 19.4	342 21.1	. . 23.6
	22	247 25.5	142 31.5	33.2	17 27.0	02.0	79 06.1	19.3	357 23.7	23.6
	23	262 27.9	157 30.6	32.9	32 29.5	02.0	94 08.3	19.1	12 26.3	23.6
	Mer. Pass.	h m 5 36.9	*v* −0.9	*d* 0.2	*v* 2.6	*d* 0.0	*v* 2.2	*d* 0.1	*v* 2.6	*d* 0.0

STARS

Name	SHA	Dec
	° ′	° ′
Acamar	315 17.1	S40 14.3
Achernar	335 25.6	S57 09.0
Acrux	173 06.8	S63 11.7
Adhara	255 11.3	S28 59.9
Aldebaran	290 47.3	N16 32.3
Alioth	166 18.9	N55 52.6
Alkaid	152 57.2	N49 14.2
Al Na'ir	27 41.0	S46 52.6
Alnilam	275 44.6	S 1 11.7
Alphard	217 54.3	S 8 43.9
Alphecca	126 09.0	N26 39.9
Alpheratz	357 41.3	N29 10.7
Altair	62 05.9	N 8 54.9
Ankaa	353 13.8	S42 12.8
Antares	112 23.4	S26 27.9
Arcturus	145 53.7	N19 06.1
Atria	107 22.8	S69 03.3
Avior	234 17.7	S59 34.0
Bellatrix	278 30.1	N 6 21.6
Betelgeuse	270 59.4	N 7 24.4
Canopus	263 55.8	S52 42.5
Capella	280 31.9	N46 00.6
Deneb	49 29.6	N45 20.4
Denebola	182 31.7	N14 28.9
Diphda	348 53.9	S17 53.7
Dubhe	193 49.6	N61 40.0
Elnath	278 10.4	N28 37.0
Eltanin	90 44.7	N51 29.4
Enif	33 44.9	N 9 57.1
Fomalhaut	15 21.6	S29 31.9
Gacrux	171 58.4	S57 12.5
Gienah	175 50.2	S17 38.1
Hadar	148 44.5	S60 27.3
Hamal	327 58.6	N23 32.2
Kaus Aust.	83 40.7	S34 22.3
Kochab	137 19.6	N74 05.7
Markab	13 36.2	N15 17.6
Menkar	314 13.1	N 4 09.1
Menkent	148 04.9	S36 27.1
Miaplacidus	221 39.8	S69 47.4
Mirfak	308 37.7	N49 54.8
Nunki	75 55.4	S26 16.3
Peacock	53 15.6	S56 40.6
Pollux	243 25.6	N27 59.0
Procyon	244 57.9	N 5 10.8
Rasalhague	96 04.2	N12 33.1
Regulus	207 41.6	N11 53.2
Rigel	281 10.4	S 8 11.2
Rigil Kent.	139 48.4	S60 54.2
Sabik	102 09.9	S15 44.5
Schedar	349 38.1	N56 37.3
Shaula	96 18.7	S37 06.7
Sirius	258 32.3	S16 44.5
Spica	158 29.0	S11 14.8
Suhail	222 51.2	S43 30.2
Vega	80 37.1	N38 48.1
Zuben'ubi	137 02.9	S16 06.5

	SHA	Mer. Pass.
	° ′	h m
Venus	257 40.0	12 28
Mars	129 57.6	20 54
Jupiter	191 54.3	16 48
Saturn	109 50.5	22 15

UT		SUN GHA	SUN Dec	MOON GHA	*v*	MOON Dec	*d*	HP
	d h	° ′	° ′	° ′	′	° ′	′	′
	26 00	179 17.5	N23 20.8	291 07.9	10.6	S 6 45.2	10.2	58.2
	01	194 17.4	20.7	305 37.5	10.5	6 35.0	10.3	58.3
	02	209 17.3	20.6	320 07.0	10.6	6 24.7	10.3	58.3
	03	224 17.1	. . 20.5	334 36.6	10.6	6 14.4	10.4	58.3
	04	239 17.0	20.4	349 06.2	10.5	6 04.0	10.3	58.3
	05	254 16.9	20.3	3 35.7	10.6	5 53.7	10.5	58.3
	06	269 16.7	N23 20.3	18 05.3	10.6	S 5 43.2	10.4	58.4
	07	284 16.6	20.2	32 34.9	10.5	5 32.8	10.5	58.4
	08	299 16.5	20.1	47 04.4	10.6	5 22.3	10.6	58.4
S	09	314 16.3	. . 20.0	61 34.0	10.5	5 11.7	10.6	58.4
U	10	329 16.2	19.9	76 03.5	10.6	5 01.1	10.6	58.4
N	11	344 16.1	19.8	90 33.1	10.6	4 50.5	10.6	58.5
D	12	359 16.0	N23 19.7	105 02.7	10.5	S 4 39.9	10.7	58.5
A	13	14 15.8	19.6	119 32.2	10.6	4 29.2	10.7	58.5
Y	14	29 15.7	19.5	134 01.8	10.5	4 18.5	10.7	58.5
	15	44 15.6	. . 19.4	148 31.3	10.5	4 07.8	10.8	58.5
	16	59 15.4	19.3	163 00.8	10.6	3 57.0	10.8	58.6
	17	74 15.3	19.2	177 30.4	10.5	3 46.2	10.8	58.6
	18	89 15.2	N23 19.1	191 59.9	10.5	S 3 35.4	10.8	58.6
	19	104 15.0	19.0	206 29.4	10.5	3 24.6	10.9	58.6
	20	119 14.9	18.9	220 58.9	10.5	3 13.7	10.9	58.6
	21	134 14.8	. . 18.8	235 28.4	10.5	3 02.8	10.9	58.7
	22	149 14.7	18.7	249 57.9	10.5	2 51.9	11.0	58.7
	23	164 14.5	18.6	264 27.4	10.4	2 40.9	10.9	58.7
	27 00	179 14.4	N23 18.5	278 56.8	10.5	S 2 30.0	11.0	58.7
	01	194 14.3	18.4	293 26.3	10.4	2 19.0	11.0	58.7
	02	209 14.1	18.3	307 55.7	10.4	2 08.0	11.1	58.8
	03	224 14.0	. . 18.2	322 25.1	10.5	1 56.9	11.0	58.8
	04	239 13.9	18.1	336 54.6	10.4	1 45.9	11.1	58.8
	05	254 13.8	18.0	351 24.0	10.4	1 34.8	11.0	58.8
	06	269 13.6	N23 17.9	5 53.4	10.3	S 1 23.8	11.1	58.8
	07	284 13.5	17.8	20 22.7	10.4	1 12.7	11.1	58.8
	08	299 13.4	17.6	34 52.1	10.3	1 01.6	11.1	58.9
M	09	314 13.2	. . 17.5	49 21.4	10.4	0 50.5	11.2	58.9
O	10	329 13.1	17.4	63 50.8	10.3	0 39.3	11.1	58.9
N	11	344 13.0	17.3	78 20.1	10.3	0 28.2	11.1	58.9
D	12	359 12.9	N23 17.2	92 49.4	10.2	S 0 17.1	11.2	58.9
A	13	14 12.7	17.1	107 18.6	10.3	S 0 05.9	11.1	59.0
Y	14	29 12.6	17.0	121 47.9	10.2	N 0 05.2	11.2	59.0
	15	44 12.5	. . 16.9	136 17.1	10.2	0 16.4	11.2	59.0
	16	59 12.3	16.7	150 46.3	10.2	0 27.6	11.2	59.0
	17	74 12.2	16.6	165 15.5	10.2	0 38.8	11.1	59.0
	18	89 12.1	N23 16.5	179 44.7	10.1	N 0 49.9	11.2	59.0
	19	104 12.0	16.4	194 13.8	10.1	1 01.1	11.2	59.1
	20	119 11.8	16.3	208 42.9	10.1	1 12.3	11.2	59.1
	21	134 11.7	. . 16.2	223 12.0	10.1	1 23.5	11.1	59.1
	22	149 11.6	16.0	237 41.1	10.1	1 34.6	11.2	59.1
	23	164 11.4	15.9	252 10.2	10.0	1 45.8	11.2	59.1
	28 00	179 11.3	N23 15.8	266 39.2	10.0	N 1 57.0	11.2	59.1
	01	194 11.2	15.7	281 08.2	9.9	2 08.2	11.1	59.2
	02	209 11.1	15.6	295 37.1	10.0	2 19.3	11.2	59.2
	03	224 10.9	. . 15.4	310 06.1	9.9	2 30.5	11.1	59.2
	04	239 10.8	15.3	324 35.0	9.9	2 41.6	11.2	59.2
	05	254 10.7	15.2	339 03.9	9.8	2 52.8	11.1	59.2
	06	269 10.6	N23 15.1	353 32.7	9.8	N 3 03.9	11.1	59.2
	07	284 10.4	14.9	8 01.5	9.8	3 15.0	11.1	59.3
T	08	299 10.3	14.8	22 30.3	9.8	3 26.1	11.1	59.3
U	09	314 10.2	. . 14.7	36 59.1	9.7	3 37.2	11.1	59.3
E	10	329 10.0	14.6	51 27.8	9.7	3 48.3	11.0	59.3
S	11	344 09.9	14.4	65 56.5	9.7	3 59.3	11.1	59.3
D	12	359 09.8	N23 14.3	80 25.2	9.6	N 4 10.4	11.0	59.3
A	13	14 09.7	14.2	94 53.8	9.6	4 21.4	11.0	59.4
Y	14	29 09.5	14.0	109 22.4	9.5	4 32.4	11.0	59.4
	15	44 09.4	. . 13.9	123 50.9	9.6	4 43.4	11.0	59.4
	16	59 09.3	13.8	138 19.5	9.4	4 54.4	10.9	59.4
	17	74 09.2	13.6	152 47.9	9.5	5 05.3	10.9	59.4
	18	89 09.0	N23 13.5	167 16.4	9.4	N 5 16.2	10.9	59.4
	19	104 08.9	13.4	181 44.8	9.4	5 27.1	10.9	59.4
	20	119 08.8	13.2	196 13.2	9.3	5 38.0	10.8	59.5
	21	134 08.7	. . 13.1	210 41.5	9.3	5 48.8	10.8	59.5
	22	149 08.5	13.0	225 09.8	9.2	5 59.6	10.8	59.5
	23	164 08.4	12.8	239 38.0	9.3	N 6 10.4	10.8	59.5
		SD 15.8	*d* 0.1	SD	15.9		16.1	16.2

Lat.	Twilight Naut.	Twilight Civil	Sunrise	Moonrise 26	Moonrise 27	Moonrise 28	Moonrise 29
°	h m	h m	h m	h m	h m	h m	h m
N 72	▭	▭	▭	{00 03 / 23 57}	23 51	23 46	23 40
N 70	▭	▭	▭	23 53	23 54	23 54	23 56
68	▭	▭	▭	23 51	23 56	24 01	00 01
66	▭	▭	▭	23 48	23 57	24 07	00 07
64	////	////	01 36	23 46	23 59	24 12	00 12
62	////	////	02 13	23 44	24 00	00 00	00 17
60	////	00 56	02 39	23 43	24 01	00 01	00 21
N 58	////	01 44	02 59	23 41	24 02	00 02	00 24
56	////	02 14	03 16	23 40	24 03	00 03	00 27
54	00 51	02 36	03 30	23 39	24 04	00 04	00 30
52	01 36	02 53	03 42	23 38	24 04	00 04	00 32
50	02 03	03 08	03 53	23 37	24 05	00 05	00 35
45	02 48	03 38	04 15	23 34	24 07	00 07	00 40
N 40	03 19	04 00	04 33	23 33	24 08	00 08	00 44
35	03 42	04 19	04 48	23 31	24 09	00 09	00 48
30	04 00	04 34	05 01	23 30	24 10	00 10	00 51
20	04 29	04 59	05 23	23 28	24 12	00 12	00 57
N 10	04 52	05 19	05 42	23 25	24 13	00 13	01 02
0	05 11	05 37	05 59	23 24	24 14	00 14	01 07
S 10	05 28	05 54	06 17	23 22	24 16	00 16	01 11
20	05 44	06 11	06 35	23 20	24 18	00 18	01 17
30	06 00	06 30	06 56	23 17	24 19	00 19	01 23
35	06 09	06 41	07 09	23 16	24 20	00 20	01 26
40	06 18	06 52	07 23	23 15	24 22	00 22	01 30
45	06 28	07 06	07 39	23 13	24 23	00 23	01 35
S 50	06 40	07 22	08 00	23 11	24 25	00 25	01 40
52	06 45	07 29	08 10	23 10	24 26	00 26	01 43
54	06 51	07 37	08 21	23 09	24 27	00 27	01 45
56	06 57	07 46	08 33	23 08	24 27	00 27	01 49
58	07 04	07 56	08 48	23 06	24 29	00 29	01 52
S 60	07 11	08 08	09 05	23 05	24 30	00 30	01 56

Lat.	Sunset	Twilight Civil	Twilight Naut.	Moonset 26	Moonset 27	Moonset 28	Moonset 29
°	h m	h m	h m	h m	h m	h m	h m
N 72	▭	▭	▭	09 50	11 42	13 35	15 32
N 70	▭	▭	▭	09 58	11 43	13 29	15 18
68	▭	▭	▭	10 04	11 43	13 24	15 06
66	▭	▭	▭	10 09	11 44	13 20	14 57
64	22 30	////	////	10 14	11 44	13 16	14 49
62	21 53	////	////	10 17	11 44	13 13	14 42
60	21 27	23 09	////	10 21	11 45	13 10	14 36
N 58	21 07	22 21	////	10 24	11 45	13 08	14 31
56	20 50	21 52	////	10 26	11 45	13 06	14 27
54	20 36	21 30	23 14	10 28	11 45	13 04	14 23
52	20 24	21 13	22 30	10 31	11 46	13 02	14 19
50	20 13	20 58	22 03	10 32	11 46	13 00	14 16
45	19 51	20 28	21 18	10 36	11 46	12 57	14 09
N 40	19 33	20 06	20 47	10 40	11 46	12 54	14 03
35	19 18	19 48	20 24	10 43	11 47	12 52	13 58
30	19 05	19 32	20 06	10 45	11 47	12 49	13 53
20	18 43	19 08	19 37	10 50	11 47	12 46	13 45
N 10	18 24	18 47	19 14	10 54	11 47	12 42	13 38
0	18 07	18 29	18 56	10 57	11 48	12 39	13 32
S 10	17 49	18 12	18 39	11 01	11 48	12 36	13 25
20	17 31	17 55	18 23	11 04	11 48	12 33	13 19
30	17 10	17 36	18 06	11 09	11 48	12 29	13 11
35	16 58	17 26	17 57	11 11	11 48	12 27	13 06
40	16 44	17 14	17 48	11 14	11 49	12 24	13 01
45	16 27	17 01	17 38	11 17	11 49	12 21	12 55
S 50	16 06	16 45	17 26	11 20	11 49	12 18	12 48
52	15 57	16 37	17 21	11 22	11 49	12 16	12 45
54	15 45	16 29	17 15	11 24	11 49	12 14	12 42
56	15 33	16 20	17 09	11 26	11 49	12 13	12 38
58	15 18	16 10	17 03	11 28	11 49	12 10	12 34
S 60	15 01	15 58	16 55	11 31	11 49	12 08	12 29

Day	SUN Eqn. of Time 00^h	SUN Eqn. of Time 12^h	SUN Mer. Pass.	MOON Mer. Pass. Upper	MOON Mer. Pass. Lower	MOON Age	MOON Phase
d	m s	m s	h m	h m	h m	d %	
26	02 50	02 56	12 03	04 45	17 10	21 64	
27	03 02	03 08	12 03	05 36	18 01	22 53	
28	03 14	03 21	12 03	06 27	18 53	23 42	

Day	UT d h	ARIES GHA ° ′	VENUS −3·9 GHA ° ′	VENUS Dec ° ′	MARS −1·4 GHA ° ′	MARS Dec ° ′	JUPITER −1·9 GHA ° ′	JUPITER Dec ° ′	SATURN +0·1 GHA ° ′	SATURN Dec ° ′
WEDNESDAY	29 00	277 30.4	172 29.7	N23 32.7	47 32.1	S21 02.0	109 10.4	N 6 19.0	27 29.0	S20 23.5
	01	292 32.9	187 28.9	32.5	62 34.6	02.1	124 12.6	18.9	42 31.6	23.5
	02	307 35.3	202 28.0	32.2	77 37.1	02.1	139 14.8	18.7	57 34.2	23.5
	03	322 37.8	217 27.1	. . 32.0	92 39.6	. . 02.2	154 16.9	. . 18.6	72 36.9	. . 23.5
	04	337 40.2	232 26.2	31.8	107 42.1	02.2	169 19.1	18.5	87 39.5	23.5
	05	352 42.7	247 25.3	31.5	122 44.6	02.2	184 21.2	18.3	102 42.1	23.5
	06	7 45.2	262 24.5	N23 31.3	137 47.1	S21 02.3	199 23.4	N 6 18.2	117 44.7	S20 23.4
	07	22 47.6	277 23.6	31.0	152 49.6	02.3	214 25.6	18.1	132 47.4	23.4
	08	37 50.1	292 22.7	30.8	167 52.1	02.4	229 27.7	17.9	147 50.0	23.4
	09	52 52.6	307 21.8	. . 30.6	182 54.6	. . 02.4	244 29.9	. . 17.8	162 52.6	. . 23.4
	10	67 55.0	322 21.0	30.3	197 57.1	02.4	259 32.0	17.7	177 55.3	23.4
	11	82 57.5	337 20.1	30.1	212 59.6	02.5	274 34.2	17.5	192 57.9	23.4
	12	98 00.0	352 19.2	N23 29.8	228 02.1	S21 02.5	289 36.4	N 6 17.4	208 00.5	S20 23.4
	13	113 02.4	7 18.3	29.6	243 04.6	02.6	304 38.5	17.3	223 03.1	23.3
	14	128 04.9	22 17.5	29.3	258 07.1	02.6	319 40.7	17.1	238 05.8	23.3
	15	143 07.4	37 16.6	. . 29.1	273 09.6	. . 02.7	334 42.8	. . 17.0	253 08.4	. . 23.3
	16	158 09.8	52 15.7	28.8	288 12.1	02.7	349 45.0	16.9	268 11.0	23.3
	17	173 12.3	67 14.8	28.6	303 14.6	02.8	4 47.2	16.7	283 13.7	23.3
	18	188 14.7	82 14.0	N23 28.3	318 17.0	S21 02.8	19 49.3	N 6 16.6	298 16.3	S20 23.3
	19	203 17.2	97 13.1	28.0	333 19.5	02.8	34 51.5	16.5	313 18.9	23.3
	20	218 19.7	112 12.2	27.8	348 22.0	02.9	49 53.6	16.3	328 21.5	23.2
	21	233 22.1	127 11.3	. . 27.5	3 24.5	. . 02.9	64 55.8	. . 16.2	343 24.2	. . 23.2
	22	248 24.6	142 10.5	27.3	18 27.0	03.0	79 58.0	16.0	358 26.8	23.2
	23	263 27.1	157 09.6	27.0	33 29.5	03.0	95 00.1	15.9	13 29.4	23.2
THURSDAY	30 00	278 29.5	172 08.7	N23 26.7	48 31.9	S21 03.1	110 02.3	N 6 15.8	28 32.0	S20 23.2
	01	293 32.0	187 07.8	26.5	63 34.4	03.1	125 04.4	15.6	43 34.7	23.2
	02	308 34.5	202 07.0	26.2	78 36.9	03.2	140 06.6	15.5	58 37.3	23.2
	03	323 36.9	217 06.1	. . 25.9	93 39.4	. . 03.2	155 08.8	. . 15.4	73 39.9	. . 23.1
	04	338 39.4	232 05.2	25.7	108 41.8	03.3	170 10.9	15.2	88 42.6	23.1
	05	353 41.8	247 04.4	25.4	123 44.3	03.3	185 13.1	15.1	103 45.2	23.1
	06	8 44.3	262 03.5	N23 25.1	138 46.8	S21 03.4	200 15.2	N 6 15.0	118 47.8	S20 23.1
	07	23 46.8	277 02.6	24.9	153 49.2	03.4	215 17.4	14.8	133 50.4	23.1
	08	38 49.2	292 01.7	24.6	168 51.7	03.5	230 19.5	14.7	148 53.1	23.1
	09	53 51.7	307 00.9	. . 24.3	183 54.2	. . 03.5	245 21.7	. . 14.5	163 55.7	. . 23.1
	10	68 54.2	322 00.0	24.1	198 56.6	03.6	260 23.9	14.4	178 58.3	23.0
	11	83 56.6	336 59.1	23.8	213 59.1	03.6	275 26.0	14.3	194 00.9	23.0
	12	98 59.1	351 58.3	N23 23.5	229 01.5	S21 03.7	290 28.2	N 6 14.1	209 03.6	S20 23.0
	13	114 01.6	6 57.4	23.2	244 04.0	03.7	305 30.3	14.0	224 06.2	23.0
	14	129 04.0	21 56.5	22.9	259 06.5	03.8	320 32.5	13.9	239 08.8	23.0
	15	144 06.5	36 55.6	. . 22.7	274 08.9	. . 03.8	335 34.6	. . 13.7	254 11.4	. . 23.0
	16	159 09.0	51 54.8	22.4	289 11.4	03.9	350 36.8	13.6	269 14.1	23.0
	17	174 11.4	66 53.9	22.1	304 13.8	03.9	5 38.9	13.4	284 16.7	22.9
	18	189 13.9	81 53.0	N23 21.8	319 16.3	S21 04.0	20 41.1	N 6 13.3	299 19.3	S20 22.9
	19	204 16.3	96 52.2	21.5	334 18.7	04.0	35 43.2	13.2	314 21.9	22.9
	20	219 18.8	111 51.3	21.2	349 21.2	04.1	50 45.4	13.0	329 24.6	22.9
	21	234 21.3	126 50.4	. . 21.0	4 23.6	. . 04.1	65 47.6	. . 12.9	344 27.2	. . 22.9
	22	249 23.7	141 49.6	20.7	19 26.1	04.2	80 49.7	12.8	359 29.8	22.9
	23	264 26.2	156 48.7	20.4	34 28.5	04.2	95 51.9	12.6	14 32.4	22.9
FRIDAY	1 00	279 28.7	171 47.8	N23 20.1	49 30.9	S21 04.3	110 54.0	N 6 12.5	29 35.1	S20 22.8
	01	294 31.1	186 47.0	19.8	64 33.4	04.3	125 56.2	12.3	44 37.7	22.8
	02	309 33.6	201 46.1	19.5	79 35.8	04.4	140 58.3	12.2	59 40.3	22.8
	03	324 36.1	216 45.2	. . 19.2	94 38.3	. . 04.4	156 00.5	. . 12.1	74 42.9	. . 22.8
	04	339 38.5	231 44.4	18.9	109 40.7	04.5	171 02.6	11.9	89 45.6	22.8
	05	354 41.0	246 43.5	18.6	124 43.1	04.5	186 04.8	11.8	104 48.2	22.8
	06	9 43.5	261 42.6	N23 18.3	139 45.6	S21 04.6	201 06.9	N 6 11.7	119 50.8	S20 22.8
	07	24 45.9	276 41.8	18.0	154 48.0	04.6	216 09.1	11.5	134 53.4	22.7
	08	39 48.4	291 40.9	17.7	169 50.4	04.7	231 11.2	11.4	149 56.1	22.7
	09	54 50.8	306 40.0	. . 17.4	184 52.8	. . 04.8	246 13.4	. . 11.2	164 58.7	. . 22.7
	10	69 53.3	321 39.2	17.1	199 55.3	04.8	261 15.5	11.1	180 01.3	22.7
	11	84 55.8	336 38.3	16.8	214 57.7	04.9	276 17.7	11.0	195 03.9	22.7
	12	99 58.2	351 37.4	N23 16.5	230 00.1	S21 04.9	291 19.9	N 6 10.8	210 06.5	S20 22.7
	13	115 00.7	6 36.6	16.2	245 02.5	05.0	306 22.0	10.7	225 09.2	22.7
	14	130 03.2	21 35.7	15.9	260 05.0	05.0	321 24.2	10.5	240 11.8	22.6
	15	145 05.6	36 34.8	. . 15.6	275 07.4	. . 05.1	336 26.3	. . 10.4	255 14.4	. . 22.6
	16	160 08.1	51 34.0	15.3	290 09.8	05.2	351 28.5	10.3	270 17.0	22.6
	17	175 10.6	66 33.1	15.0	305 12.2	05.2	6 30.6	10.1	285 19.7	22.6
	18	190 13.0	81 32.3	N23 14.6	320 14.6	S21 05.3	21 32.8	N 6 10.0	300 22.3	S20 22.6
	19	205 15.5	96 31.4	14.3	335 17.0	05.3	36 34.9	09.9	315 24.9	22.6
	20	220 18.0	111 30.5	14.0	350 19.4	05.4	51 37.1	09.7	330 27.5	22.6
	21	235 20.4	126 29.7	. . 13.7	5 21.9	. . 05.4	66 39.2	. . 09.6	345 30.1	. . 22.5
	22	250 22.9	141 28.8	13.4	20 24.3	05.5	81 41.4	09.4	0 32.8	22.5
	23	265 25.3	156 27.9	13.1	35 26.7	05.6	96 43.5	09.3	15 35.4	22.5
	Mer. Pass.	h m 5 25.1	v −0.9	d 0.3	v 2.5	d 0.0	v 2.2	d 0.1	v 2.6	d 0.0

STARS Name	SHA ° ′	Dec ° ′
Acamar	315 17.1	S40 14.3
Achernar	335 25.5	S57 09.0
Acrux	173 06.8	S63 11.7
Adhara	255 11.3	S28 59.9
Aldebaran	290 47.3	N16 32.3
Alioth	166 19.0	N55 52.6
Alkaid	152 57.2	N49 14.2
Al Na'ir	27 41.0	S46 52.6
Alnilam	275 44.6	S 1 11.7
Alphard	217 54.3	S 8 43.9
Alphecca	126 09.0	N26 39.9
Alpheratz	357 41.3	N29 10.7
Altair	62 05.9	N 8 54.9
Ankaa	353 13.7	S42 12.8
Antares	112 23.4	S26 27.9
Arcturus	145 53.7	N19 06.1
Atria	107 22.8	S69 03.3
Avior	234 17.7	S59 34.0
Bellatrix	278 30.1	N 6 21.7
Betelgeuse	270 59.4	N 7 24.4
Canopus	263 55.8	S52 42.4
Capella	280 31.9	N46 00.6
Deneb	49 29.6	N45 20.4
Denebola	182 31.7	N14 28.9
Diphda	348 53.9	S17 53.7
Dubhe	193 49.6	N61 40.0
Elnath	278 10.4	N28 37.0
Eltanin	90 44.7	N51 29.5
Enif	33 44.9	N 9 57.1
Fomalhaut	15 21.6	S29 31.9
Gacrux	171 58.5	S57 12.5
Gienah	175 50.2	S17 38.0
Hadar	148 44.6	S60 27.3
Hamal	327 58.5	N23 32.2
Kaus Aust.	83 40.7	S34 22.4
Kochab	137 19.6	N74 05.7
Markab	13 36.1	N15 17.6
Menkar	314 13.1	N 4 09.1
Menkent	148 04.9	S36 27.1
Miaplacidus	221 39.8	S69 47.4
Mirfak	308 37.7	N49 54.8
Nunki	75 55.4	S26 16.3
Peacock	53 15.6	S56 40.6
Pollux	243 25.6	N27 59.0
Procyon	244 57.9	N 5 10.8
Rasalhague	96 04.2	N12 33.1
Regulus	207 41.6	N11 53.2
Rigel	281 10.4	S 8 11.1
Rigil Kent.	139 48.5	S60 54.2
Sabik	102 09.9	S15 44.5
Schedar	349 38.1	N56 37.3
Shaula	96 18.7	S37 06.7
Sirius	258 32.3	S16 44.5
Spica	158 29.0	S11 14.8
Suhail	222 51.2	S43 30.2
Vega	80 37.1	N38 48.2
Zuben'ubi	137 02.9	S16 06.5

	SHA ° ′	Mer. Pass. h m
Venus	253 39.2	12 32
Mars	130 02.4	20 42
Jupiter	191 32.8	16 37
Saturn	110 02.5	22 02

UT d	UT h	SUN GHA	SUN Dec	MOON GHA	MOON v	MOON Dec	MOON d	MOON HP
		° ′	° ′	° ′	′	° ′	′	′
29	00	179 08.3	N23 12.7	254 06.3	9.1	N 6 21.2	10.7	59.5
	01	194 08.2	12.6	268 34.4	9.2	6 31.9	10.7	59.5
	02	209 08.0	12.4	283 02.6	9.1	6 42.6	10.6	59.5
	03	224 07.9	. . 12.3	297 30.7	9.0	6 53.2	10.6	59.6
	04	239 07.8	12.1	311 58.7	9.0	7 03.8	10.6	59.6
	05	254 07.7	12.0	326 26.7	9.0	7 14.4	10.5	59.6
	06	269 07.5	N23 11.8	340 54.7	8.9	N 7 24.9	10.5	59.6
W	07	284 07.4	11.7	355 22.6	8.9	7 35.4	10.5	59.6
E	08	299 07.3	11.6	9 50.5	8.8	7 45.9	10.4	59.6
D	09	314 07.2	. . 11.4	24 18.3	8.8	7 56.3	10.4	59.6
N	10	329 07.0	11.3	38 46.1	8.7	8 06.7	10.3	59.6
E	11	344 06.9	11.1	53 13.8	8.7	8 17.0	10.3	59.6
S	12	359 06.8	N23 11.0	67 41.5	8.7	N 8 27.3	10.2	59.7
D	13	14 06.7	10.8	82 09.2	8.6	8 37.5	10.2	59.7
A	14	29 06.5	10.7	96 36.8	8.6	8 47.7	10.2	59.7
Y	15	44 06.4	. . 10.5	111 04.4	8.5	8 57.9	10.0	59.7
	16	59 06.3	10.4	125 31.9	8.5	9 07.9	10.1	59.7
	17	74 06.2	10.2	139 59.4	8.4	9 18.0	10.0	59.7
	18	89 06.0	N23 10.1	154 26.8	8.3	N 9 28.0	9.9	59.7
	19	104 05.9	09.9	168 54.1	8.4	9 37.9	9.9	59.7
	20	119 05.8	09.8	183 21.5	8.2	9 47.8	9.8	59.7
	21	134 05.7	. . 09.6	197 48.7	8.3	9 57.6	9.8	59.8
	22	149 05.5	09.5	212 16.0	8.2	10 07.4	9.7	59.8
	23	164 05.4	09.3	226 43.2	8.1	10 17.1	9.6	59.8
30	00	179 05.3	N23 09.2	241 10.3	8.1	N10 26.7	9.6	59.8
	01	194 05.2	09.0	255 37.4	8.0	10 36.3	9.5	59.8
	02	209 05.1	08.9	270 04.4	8.0	10 45.8	9.4	59.8
	03	224 04.9	. . 08.7	284 31.4	7.9	10 55.2	9.4	59.8
	04	239 04.8	08.5	298 58.3	7.9	11 04.6	9.4	59.8
	05	254 04.7	08.4	313 25.2	7.9	11 14.0	9.2	59.8
	06	269 04.6	N23 08.2	327 52.1	7.8	N11 23.2	9.2	59.8
T	07	284 04.4	08.1	342 18.9	7.7	11 32.4	9.1	59.8
H	08	299 04.3	07.9	356 45.6	7.7	11 41.5	9.1	59.8
U	09	314 04.2	. . 07.8	11 12.3	7.6	11 50.6	8.9	59.8
R	10	329 04.1	07.6	25 38.9	7.6	11 59.5	8.9	59.9
S	11	344 03.9	07.4	40 05.5	7.6	12 08.4	8.9	59.9
D	12	359 03.8	N23 07.3	54 32.1	7.5	N12 17.3	8.7	59.9
A	13	14 03.7	07.1	68 58.6	7.4	12 26.0	8.7	59.9
Y	14	29 03.6	06.9	83 25.0	7.4	12 34.7	8.6	59.9
	15	44 03.5	. . 06.8	97 51.4	7.4	12 43.3	8.5	59.9
	16	59 03.3	06.6	112 17.8	7.3	12 51.8	8.4	59.9
	17	74 03.2	06.4	126 44.1	7.2	13 00.2	8.4	59.9
	18	89 03.1	N23 06.3	141 10.3	7.2	N13 08.6	8.3	59.9
	19	104 03.0	06.1	155 36.5	7.2	13 16.9	8.2	59.9
	20	119 02.9	05.9	170 02.7	7.1	13 25.1	8.1	59.9
	21	134 02.7	. . 05.8	184 28.8	7.1	13 33.2	8.0	59.9
	22	149 02.6	05.6	198 54.9	7.0	13 41.2	7.9	59.9
	23	164 02.5	05.4	213 20.9	7.0	13 49.1	7.8	59.9
1	00	179 02.4	N23 05.3	227 46.9	6.9	N13 56.9	7.8	59.9
	01	194 02.2	05.1	242 12.8	6.9	14 04.7	7.7	59.9
	02	209 02.1	04.9	256 38.7	6.8	14 12.4	7.5	59.9
	03	224 02.0	. . 04.7	271 04.5	6.8	14 19.9	7.5	59.9
	04	239 01.9	04.6	285 30.3	6.7	14 27.4	7.4	59.9
	05	254 01.8	04.4	299 56.0	6.7	14 34.8	7.3	59.9
	06	269 01.6	N23 04.2	314 21.7	6.7	N14 42.1	7.2	59.9
	07	284 01.5	04.0	328 47.4	6.6	14 49.3	7.1	59.9
	08	299 01.4	03.9	343 13.0	6.6	14 56.4	7.0	59.9
F	09	314 01.3	. . 03.7	357 38.6	6.5	15 03.4	6.9	59.9
R	10	329 01.2	03.5	12 04.1	6.5	15 10.3	6.8	59.9
I	11	344 01.0	03.3	26 29.6	6.5	15 17.1	6.7	59.9
D	12	359 00.9	N23 03.1	40 55.1	6.4	N15 23.8	6.6	59.9
A	13	14 00.8	03.0	55 20.5	6.3	15 30.4	6.5	59.9
Y	14	29 00.7	02.8	69 45.8	6.4	15 36.9	6.3	59.9
	15	44 00.6	. . 02.6	84 11.2	6.3	15 43.2	6.3	59.9
	16	59 00.4	02.4	98 36.5	6.2	15 49.5	6.2	59.9
	17	74 00.3	02.2	113 01.7	6.2	15 55.7	6.1	59.9
	18	89 00.2	N23 02.0	127 26.9	6.2	N16 01.8	6.0	59.9
	19	104 00.1	01.9	141 52.1	6.2	16 07.8	5.8	59.9
	20	119 00.0	01.7	156 17.3	6.1	16 13.6	5.8	59.9
	21	133 59.9	. . 01.5	170 42.4	6.1	16 19.4	5.6	59.9
	22	148 59.7	01.3	185 07.5	6.0	16 25.0	5.5	59.9
	23	163 59.6	01.1	199 32.5	6.1	N16 30.5	5.5	59.9
		SD 15.8	*d* 0.2	SD 16.3		16.3		16.3

Lat.	Twilight Naut.	Twilight Civil	Sunrise	Moonrise 29	Moonrise 30	Moonrise 1	Moonrise 2
°	h m	h m	h m	h m	h m	h m	h m
N 72	▭	▭	▭	23 40	23 33	23 24	22 50
N 70	▭	▭	▭	23 56	23 59	24 08	00 08
68	▭	▭	▭	00 01	00 09	00 20	00 37
66	////	////	00 12	00 07	00 19	00 36	00 59
64	////	////	01 40	00 12	00 28	00 49	01 17
62	////	////	02 16	00 17	00 36	01 00	01 32
60	////	01 02	02 42	00 21	00 43	01 10	01 44
N 58	////	01 48	03 01	00 24	00 49	01 18	01 55
56	////	02 16	03 18	00 27	00 54	01 26	02 04
54	00 57	02 38	03 32	00 30	00 59	01 32	02 12
52	01 39	02 56	03 44	00 32	01 03	01 38	02 20
50	02 06	03 10	03 55	00 35	01 07	01 44	02 27
45	02 50	03 40	04 17	00 40	01 16	01 56	02 41
N 40	03 20	04 02	04 35	00 44	01 23	02 05	02 53
35	03 43	04 20	04 49	00 48	01 29	02 14	03 03
30	04 02	04 35	05 02	00 51	01 34	02 21	03 12
20	04 30	04 59	05 24	00 57	01 44	02 34	03 28
N 10	04 53	05 20	05 43	01 02	01 52	02 46	03 41
0	05 11	05 38	06 00	01 07	02 00	02 56	03 54
S 10	05 28	05 55	06 17	01 11	02 08	03 07	04 07
20	05 44	06 12	06 36	01 17	02 17	03 19	04 21
30	06 00	06 30	06 57	01 23	02 27	03 32	04 36
35	06 09	06 41	07 09	01 26	02 33	03 40	04 46
40	06 18	06 52	07 23	01 30	02 39	03 48	04 56
45	06 28	07 06	07 39	01 35	02 47	03 59	05 09
S 50	06 40	07 21	08 00	01 40	02 56	04 11	05 24
52	06 45	07 29	08 09	01 43	03 00	04 17	05 31
54	06 51	07 37	08 20	01 45	03 05	04 24	05 39
56	06 57	07 46	08 33	01 49	03 10	04 31	05 47
58	07 03	07 56	08 47	01 52	03 16	04 39	05 58
S 60	07 11	08 07	09 04	01 56	03 23	04 48	06 09

Lat.	Sunset	Twilight Civil	Twilight Naut.	Moonset 29	Moonset 30	Moonset 1	Moonset 2
°	h m	h m	h m	h m	h m	h m	h m
N 72	▭	▭	▭	15 32	17 34	19 43	22 19
N 70	▭	▭	▭	15 18	17 09	19 00	20 42
68	▭	▭	▭	15 06	16 50	18 31	20 02
66	23 44	////	////	14 57	16 35	18 09	19 35
64	22 26	////	////	14 49	16 22	17 52	19 14
62	21 51	////	////	14 42	16 12	17 38	18 57
60	21 25	23 04	////	14 36	16 03	17 26	18 43
N 58	21 06	22 19	////	14 31	15 55	17 16	18 31
56	20 49	21 50	////	14 27	15 48	17 07	18 20
54	20 35	21 29	23 09	14 23	15 42	16 59	18 11
52	20 23	21 11	22 27	14 19	15 36	16 52	18 03
50	20 13	20 57	22 01	14 16	15 32	16 46	17 56
45	19 50	20 28	21 17	14 09	15 21	16 32	17 40
N 40	19 33	20 05	20 47	14 03	15 12	16 21	17 27
35	19 18	19 48	20 24	13 58	15 04	16 11	17 16
30	19 05	19 33	20 06	13 53	14 58	16 03	17 06
20	18 43	19 08	19 37	13 45	14 46	15 48	16 50
N 10	18 25	18 48	19 15	13 38	14 36	15 35	16 35
0	18 07	18 30	18 56	13 32	14 27	15 23	16 22
S 10	17 50	18 13	18 39	13 25	14 17	15 12	16 08
20	17 32	17 56	18 23	13 19	14 07	14 59	15 54
30	17 11	17 37	18 07	13 11	13 56	14 45	15 37
35	16 59	17 27	17 59	13 06	13 49	14 36	15 28
40	16 45	17 15	17 49	13 01	13 42	14 27	15 17
45	16 28	17 02	17 39	12 55	13 33	14 16	15 04
S 50	16 08	16 46	17 28	12 48	13 23	14 02	14 48
52	15 58	16 39	17 23	12 45	13 18	13 56	14 41
54	15 47	16 31	17 17	12 42	13 13	13 49	14 33
56	15 35	16 22	17 11	12 38	13 07	13 41	14 24
58	15 21	16 12	17 04	12 34	13 00	13 33	14 13
S 60	15 04	16 01	16 57	12 29	12 53	13 23	14 02

Day	SUN Eqn. of Time 00^h	SUN Eqn. of Time 12^h	SUN Mer. Pass.	MOON Mer. Pass. Upper	MOON Mer. Pass. Lower	MOON Age	MOON Phase
d	m s	m s	h m	h m	h m	d %	
29	03 27	03 33	12 04	07 19	19 46	24 31	
30	03 39	03 44	12 04	08 13	20 41	25 20	
1	03 50	03 56	12 04	09 10	21 39	26 12	

UT	ARIES	VENUS −3·9		MARS −1·4		JUPITER −1·9		SATURN +0·2	
	GHA	GHA	Dec	GHA	Dec	GHA	Dec	GHA	Dec
d h	° ′	° ′	° ′	° ′	° ′	° ′	° ′	° ′	° ′
2 00	280 27.8	171 27.1	N23 12.7	50 29.1	S21 05.6	111 45.7	N 6 09.2	30 38.0	S20 22.5
01	295 30.3	186 26.2	12.4	65 31.5	05.7	126 47.8	09.0	45 40.6	22.5
02	310 32.7	201 25.4	12.1	80 33.9	05.7	141 50.0	08.9	60 43.3	22.5
03	325 35.2	216 24.5	. . 11.8	95 36.3	. . 05.8	156 52.1	. . 08.7	75 45.9	. . 22.5
04	340 37.7	231 23.6	11.5	110 38.7	05.9	171 54.2	08.6	90 48.5	22.4
05	355 40.1	246 22.8	11.1	125 41.1	05.9	186 56.4	08.5	105 51.1	22.4
06	10 42.6	261 21.9	N23 10.8	140 43.5	S21 06.0	201 58.5	N 6 08.3	120 53.7	S20 22.4
07	25 45.1	276 21.1	10.5	155 45.9	06.0	217 00.7	08.2	135 56.4	22.4
S 08	40 47.5	291 20.2	10.1	170 48.3	06.1	232 02.8	08.0	150 59.0	22.4
A 09	55 50.0	306 19.3	. . 09.8	185 50.7	. . 06.2	247 05.0	. . 07.9	166 01.6	. . 22.4
T 10	70 52.4	321 18.5	09.5	200 53.0	06.2	262 07.1	07.8	181 04.2	22.4
U 11	85 54.9	336 17.6	09.1	215 55.4	06.3	277 09.3	07.6	196 06.8	22.4
R 12	100 57.4	351 16.8	N23 08.8	230 57.8	S21 06.4	292 11.4	N 6 07.5	211 09.5	S20 22.3
D 13	115 59.8	6 15.9	08.5	246 00.2	06.4	307 13.6	07.3	226 12.1	22.3
A 14	131 02.3	21 15.0	08.1	261 02.6	06.5	322 15.7	07.2	241 14.7	22.3
Y 15	146 04.8	36 14.2	. . 07.8	276 05.0	. . 06.6	337 17.9	. . 07.1	256 17.3	. . 22.3
16	161 07.2	51 13.3	07.5	291 07.4	06.6	352 20.0	06.9	271 19.9	22.3
17	176 09.7	66 12.5	07.1	306 09.7	06.7	7 22.2	06.8	286 22.6	22.3
18	191 12.2	81 11.6	N23 06.8	321 12.1	S21 06.7	22 24.3	N 6 06.6	301 25.2	S20 22.3
19	206 14.6	96 10.8	06.4	336 14.5	06.8	37 26.5	06.5	316 27.8	22.2
20	221 17.1	111 09.9	06.1	351 16.9	06.9	52 28.6	06.3	331 30.4	22.2
21	236 19.6	126 09.1	. . 05.8	6 19.2	. . 06.9	67 30.7	. . 06.2	346 33.0	. . 22.2
22	251 22.0	141 08.2	05.4	21 21.6	07.0	82 32.9	06.1	1 35.7	22.2
23	266 24.5	156 07.3	05.1	36 24.0	07.1	97 35.0	05.9	16 38.3	22.2
3 00	281 26.9	171 06.5	N23 04.7	51 26.4	S21 07.1	112 37.2	N 6 05.8	31 40.9	S20 22.2
01	296 29.4	186 05.6	04.4	66 28.7	07.2	127 39.3	05.6	46 43.5	22.2
02	311 31.9	201 04.8	04.0	81 31.1	07.3	142 41.5	05.5	61 46.1	22.2
03	326 34.3	216 03.9	. . 03.7	96 33.5	. . 07.3	157 43.6	. . 05.4	76 48.8	. . 22.1
04	341 36.8	231 03.1	03.3	111 35.8	07.4	172 45.8	05.2	91 51.4	22.1
05	356 39.3	246 02.2	03.0	126 38.2	07.5	187 47.9	05.1	106 54.0	22.1
06	11 41.7	261 01.4	N23 02.6	141 40.5	S21 07.5	202 50.0	N 6 04.9	121 56.6	S20 22.1
07	26 44.2	276 00.5	02.2	156 42.9	07.6	217 52.2	04.8	136 59.2	22.1
08	41 46.7	290 59.7	01.9	171 45.3	07.7	232 54.3	04.6	152 01.9	22.1
S 09	56 49.1	305 58.8	. . 01.5	186 47.6	. . 07.7	247 56.5	. . 04.5	167 04.5	. . 22.1
U 10	71 51.6	320 58.0	01.2	201 50.0	07.8	262 58.6	04.4	182 07.1	22.0
N 11	86 54.1	335 57.1	00.8	216 52.3	07.9	278 00.8	04.2	197 09.7	22.0
D 12	101 56.5	350 56.2	N23 00.4	231 54.7	S21 08.0	293 02.9	N 6 04.1	212 12.3	S20 22.0
A 13	116 59.0	5 55.4	23 00.1	246 57.0	08.0	308 05.0	03.9	227 14.9	22.0
Y 14	132 01.4	20 54.5	22 59.7	261 59.4	08.1	323 07.2	03.8	242 17.6	22.0
15	147 03.9	35 53.7	. . 59.3	277 01.7	. . 08.2	338 09.3	. . 03.6	257 20.2	. . 22.0
16	162 06.4	50 52.8	59.0	292 04.1	08.2	353 11.5	03.5	272 22.8	22.0
17	177 08.8	65 52.0	58.6	307 06.4	08.3	8 13.6	03.4	287 25.4	22.0
18	192 11.3	80 51.1	N22 58.2	322 08.7	S21 08.4	23 15.8	N 6 03.2	302 28.0	S20 21.9
19	207 13.8	95 50.3	57.9	337 11.1	08.5	38 17.9	03.1	317 30.6	21.9
20	222 16.2	110 49.4	57.5	352 13.4	08.5	53 20.0	02.9	332 33.3	21.9
21	237 18.7	125 48.6	. . 57.1	7 15.8	. . 08.6	68 22.2	. . 02.8	347 35.9	. . 21.9
22	252 21.2	140 47.7	56.8	22 18.1	08.7	83 24.3	02.6	2 38.5	21.9
23	267 23.6	155 46.9	56.4	37 20.4	08.7	98 26.5	02.5	17 41.1	21.9
4 00	282 26.1	170 46.1	N22 56.0	52 22.8	S21 08.8	113 28.6	N 6 02.4	32 43.7	S20 21.9
01	297 28.6	185 45.2	55.6	67 25.1	08.9	128 30.7	02.2	47 46.3	21.8
02	312 31.0	200 44.4	55.2	82 27.4	09.0	143 32.9	02.1	62 49.0	21.8
03	327 33.5	215 43.5	. . 54.9	97 29.8	. . 09.0	158 35.0	. . 01.9	77 51.6	. . 21.8
04	342 35.9	230 42.7	54.5	112 32.1	09.1	173 37.2	01.8	92 54.2	21.8
05	357 38.4	245 41.8	54.1	127 34.4	09.2	188 39.3	01.6	107 56.8	21.8
06	12 40.9	260 41.0	N22 53.7	142 36.7	S21 09.3	203 41.4	N 6 01.5	122 59.4	S20 21.8
07	27 43.3	275 40.1	53.3	157 39.1	09.3	218 43.6	01.4	138 02.0	21.8
08	42 45.8	290 39.3	53.0	172 41.4	09.4	233 45.7	01.2	153 04.7	21.8
M 09	57 48.3	305 38.4	. . 52.6	187 43.7	. . 09.5	248 47.9	. . 01.1	168 07.3	. . 21.7
O 10	72 50.7	320 37.6	52.2	202 46.0	09.6	263 50.0	00.9	183 09.9	21.7
N 11	87 53.2	335 36.7	51.8	217 48.3	09.6	278 52.1	00.8	198 12.5	21.7
D 12	102 55.7	350 35.9	N22 51.4	232 50.7	S21 09.7	293 54.3	N 6 00.6	213 15.1	S20 21.7
A 13	117 58.1	5 35.1	51.0	247 53.0	09.8	308 56.4	00.5	228 17.7	21.7
Y 14	133 00.6	20 34.2	50.6	262 55.3	09.9	323 58.6	00.3	243 20.4	21.7
15	148 03.1	35 33.4	. . 50.2	277 57.6	. . 09.9	339 00.7	. . 00.2	258 23.0	. . 21.7
16	163 05.5	50 32.5	49.8	292 59.9	10.0	354 02.8	6 00.1	273 25.6	21.7
17	178 08.0	65 31.7	49.4	308 02.2	10.1	9 05.0	5 59.9	288 28.2	21.6
18	193 10.4	80 30.8	N22 49.0	323 04.5	S21 10.2	24 07.1	N 5 59.8	303 30.8	S20 21.6
19	208 12.9	95 30.0	48.6	338 06.8	10.3	39 09.2	59.6	318 33.4	21.6
20	223 15.4	110 29.2	48.2	353 09.1	10.3	54 11.4	59.5	333 36.0	21.6
21	238 17.8	125 28.3	. . 47.8	8 11.4	. . 10.4	69 13.5	. . 59.3	348 38.7	. . 21.6
22	253 20.3	140 27.5	47.4	23 13.7	10.5	84 15.6	59.2	3 41.3	21.6
23	268 22.8	155 26.6	47.0	38 16.0	10.6	99 17.8	59.0	18 43.9	21.6
Mer. Pass.	h m 5 13.3	v −0.9	d 0.4	v 2.4	d 0.1	v 2.1	d 0.1	v 2.6	d 0.0

STARS Name	SHA	Dec
	° ′	° ′
Acamar	315 17.1	S40 14.3
Achernar	335 25.5	S57 09.0
Acrux	173 06.8	S63 11.7
Adhara	255 11.3	S28 59.9
Aldebaran	290 47.3	N16 32.3
Alioth	166 19.0	N55 52.6
Alkaid	152 57.2	N49 14.2
Al Na'ir	27 40.9	S46 52.6
Alnilam	275 44.6	S 1 11.7
Alphard	217 54.3	S 8 43.9
Alphecca	126 09.0	N26 39.9
Alpheratz	357 41.2	N29 10.7
Altair	62 05.9	N 8 54.9
Ankaa	353 13.7	S42 12.8
Antares	112 23.4	S26 27.9
Arcturus	145 53.7	N19 06.1
Atria	107 22.8	S69 03.3
Avior	234 17.7	S59 34.0
Bellatrix	278 30.1	N 6 21.7
Betelgeuse	270 59.4	N 7 24.4
Canopus	263 55.8	S52 42.4
Capella	280 31.8	N46 00.6
Deneb	49 29.6	N45 20.4
Denebola	182 31.7	N14 28.9
Diphda	348 53.9	S17 53.7
Dubhe	193 49.7	N61 40.0
Elnath	278 10.4	N28 37.0
Eltanin	90 44.7	N51 29.5
Enif	33 44.8	N 9 57.1
Fomalhaut	15 21.6	S29 31.9
Gacrux	171 58.5	S57 12.5
Gienah	175 50.2	S17 38.0
Hadar	148 44.6	S60 27.3
Hamal	327 58.5	N23 32.2
Kaus Aust.	83 40.7	S34 22.4
Kochab	137 19.7	N74 05.7
Markab	13 36.1	N15 17.6
Menkar	314 13.1	N 4 09.1
Menkent	148 04.9	S36 27.1
Miaplacidus	221 39.8	S69 47.4
Mirfak	308 37.7	N49 54.8
Nunki	75 55.4	S26 16.3
Peacock	53 15.5	S56 40.6
Pollux	243 25.6	N27 59.0
Procyon	244 57.9	N 5 10.8
Rasalhague	96 04.2	N12 33.2
Regulus	207 41.6	N11 53.2
Rigel	281 10.4	S 8 11.1
Rigil Kent.	139 48.5	S60 54.2
Sabik	102 09.8	S15 44.5
Schedar	349 38.0	N56 37.3
Shaula	96 18.7	S37 06.7
Sirius	258 32.3	S16 44.5
Spica	158 29.0	S11 14.8
Suhail	222 51.2	S43 30.2
Vega	80 37.1	N38 48.2
Zuben'ubi	137 02.9	S16 06.5

	SHA	Mer. Pass.
	° ′	h m
Venus	249 39.5	12 36
Mars	129 59.4	20 31
Jupiter	191 10.2	16 27
Saturn	110 14.0	21 49

UT		SUN GHA	SUN Dec	MOON GHA	v	MOON Dec	d	HP
	d h	° ′	° ′	° ′	′	° ′	′	′
SATURDAY	2 00	178 59.5	N23 00.9	213 57.6	6.0	N16 36.0	5.3	59.9
	01	193 59.4	00.7	228 22.6	5.9	16 41.3	5.2	59.9
	02	208 59.3	00.5	242 47.5	5.9	16 46.5	5.0	59.9
	03	223 59.1	. . 00.4	257 12.4	6.0	16 51.5	5.0	59.8
	04	238 59.0	00.2	271 37.4	5.8	16 56.5	4.9	59.8
	05	253 58.9	23 00.0	286 02.2	5.9	17 01.4	4.7	59.8
	06	268 58.8	N22 59.8	300 27.1	5.8	N17 06.1	4.6	59.8
	07	283 58.7	59.6	314 51.9	5.8	17 10.7	4.5	59.8
	08	298 58.6	59.4	329 16.7	5.8	17 15.2	4.4	59.8
	09	313 58.4	. . 59.2	343 41.5	5.8	17 19.6	4.3	59.8
	10	328 58.3	59.0	358 06.3	5.7	17 23.9	4.1	59.8
	11	343 58.2	58.8	12 31.0	5.8	17 28.0	4.0	59.8
	12	358 58.1	N22 58.6	26 55.8	5.7	N17 32.0	4.0	59.8
	13	13 58.0	58.4	41 20.5	5.7	17 36.0	3.7	59.8
	14	28 57.9	58.2	55 45.2	5.6	17 39.7	3.7	59.8
	15	43 57.7	. . 58.0	70 09.8	5.7	17 43.4	3.6	59.7
	16	58 57.6	57.8	84 34.5	5.7	17 47.0	3.4	59.7
	17	73 57.5	57.6	98 59.2	5.6	17 50.4	3.3	59.7
	18	88 57.4	N22 57.4	113 23.8	5.6	N17 53.7	3.2	59.7
	19	103 57.3	57.2	127 48.4	5.6	17 56.9	3.0	59.7
	20	118 57.2	57.0	142 13.0	5.7	17 59.9	3.0	59.7
	21	133 57.0	. . 56.8	156 37.7	5.6	18 02.9	2.8	59.7
	22	148 56.9	56.6	171 02.3	5.6	18 05.7	2.7	59.7
	23	163 56.8	56.4	185 26.9	5.6	18 08.4	2.5	59.6
SUNDAY	3 00	178 56.7	N22 56.2	199 51.5	5.6	N18 10.9	2.5	59.6
	01	193 56.6	56.0	214 16.1	5.6	18 13.4	2.3	59.6
	02	208 56.5	55.8	228 40.7	5.6	18 15.7	2.2	59.6
	03	223 56.3	. . 55.6	243 05.3	5.6	18 17.9	2.0	59.6
	04	238 56.2	55.4	257 29.9	5.6	18 19.9	2.0	59.6
	05	253 56.1	55.2	271 54.5	5.6	18 21.9	1.8	59.6
	06	268 56.0	N22 55.0	286 19.1	5.6	N18 23.7	1.7	59.5
	07	283 55.9	54.7	300 43.7	5.6	18 25.4	1.5	59.5
	08	298 55.8	54.5	315 08.3	5.6	18 26.9	1.5	59.5
	09	313 55.7	. . 54.3	329 32.9	5.6	18 28.4	1.3	59.5
	10	328 55.5	54.1	343 57.5	5.7	18 29.7	1.2	59.5
	11	343 55.4	53.9	358 22.2	5.6	18 30.9	1.0	59.5
	12	358 55.3	N22 53.7	12 46.8	5.7	N18 31.9	1.0	59.4
	13	13 55.2	53.5	27 11.5	5.7	18 32.9	0.8	59.4
	14	28 55.1	53.3	41 36.2	5.7	18 33.7	0.7	59.4
	15	43 55.0	. . 53.0	56 00.9	5.7	18 34.4	0.5	59.4
	16	58 54.9	52.8	70 25.6	5.8	18 34.9	0.5	59.4
	17	73 54.8	52.6	84 50.4	5.7	18 35.4	0.3	59.4
	18	88 54.6	N22 52.4	99 15.1	5.8	N18 35.7	0.2	59.3
	19	103 54.5	52.2	113 39.9	5.8	18 35.9	0.0	59.3
	20	118 54.4	52.0	128 04.7	5.9	18 35.9	0.0	59.3
	21	133 54.3	. . 51.7	142 29.6	5.8	18 35.9	0.2	59.3
	22	148 54.2	51.5	156 54.4	5.9	18 35.7	0.3	59.3
	23	163 54.1	51.3	171 19.3	5.9	18 35.4	0.5	59.2
MONDAY	4 00	178 54.0	N22 51.1	185 44.2	6.0	N18 34.9	0.5	59.2
	01	193 53.9	50.9	200 09.2	5.9	18 34.4	0.7	59.2
	02	208 53.7	50.6	214 34.1	6.0	18 33.7	0.8	59.2
	03	223 53.6	. . 50.4	228 59.1	6.1	18 32.9	0.9	59.2
	04	238 53.5	50.2	243 24.2	6.0	18 32.0	1.1	59.1
	05	253 53.4	50.0	257 49.2	6.2	18 30.9	1.1	59.1
	06	268 53.3	N22 49.7	272 14.4	6.1	N18 29.8	1.3	59.1
	07	283 53.2	49.5	286 39.5	6.2	18 28.5	1.4	59.1
	08	298 53.1	49.3	301 04.7	6.2	18 27.1	1.5	59.0
	09	313 53.0	. . 49.0	315 29.9	6.3	18 25.6	1.7	59.0
	10	328 52.9	48.8	329 55.2	6.3	18 23.9	1.8	59.0
	11	343 52.7	48.6	344 20.5	6.4	18 22.1	1.8	59.0
	12	358 52.6	N22 48.4	358 45.9	6.4	N18 20.3	2.0	58.9
	13	13 52.5	48.1	13 11.3	6.4	18 18.3	2.2	58.9
	14	28 52.4	47.9	27 36.7	6.5	18 16.1	2.2	58.9
	15	43 52.3	. . 47.7	42 02.2	6.5	18 13.9	2.3	58.9
	16	58 52.2	47.4	56 27.7	6.6	18 11.6	2.5	58.8
	17	73 52.1	47.2	70 53.3	6.7	18 09.1	2.6	58.8
	18	88 52.0	N22 47.0	85 19.0	6.7	N18 06.5	2.7	58.8
	19	103 51.9	46.7	99 44.7	6.7	18 03.8	2.8	58.8
	20	118 51.8	46.5	114 10.4	6.8	18 01.0	2.9	58.7
	21	133 51.6	. . 46.3	128 36.2	6.8	17 58.1	3.0	58.7
	22	148 51.5	46.0	143 02.0	6.9	17 55.1	3.2	58.7
	23	163 51.4	45.8	157 27.9	7.0	N17 51.9	3.2	58.7
		SD 15.8	*d* 0.2	SD 16.3		16.2		16.1

Lat.	Twilight Naut.	Twilight Civil	Sunrise	Moonrise 2	Moonrise 3	Moonrise 4	Moonrise 5
°	h m	h m	h m	h m	h m	h m	h m
N 72	▭	▭	▭	22 50	▭	▭	01 27
N 70	▭	▭	▭	00 08	00 28	01 15	02 38
68	▭	▭	▭	00 37	01 08	02 00	03 15
66	////	////	00 38	00 59	01 36	02 30	03 41
64	////	////	01 46	01 17	01 57	02 52	04 01
62	////	////	02 20	01 32	02 14	03 10	04 18
60	////	01 09	02 45	01 44	02 28	03 25	04 31
N 58	////	01 52	03 04	01 55	02 41	03 37	04 43
56	////	02 20	03 20	02 04	02 51	03 48	04 53
54	01 04	02 41	03 34	02 12	03 01	03 58	05 02
52	01 43	02 58	03 46	02 20	03 09	04 06	05 10
50	02 09	03 13	03 57	02 27	03 17	04 14	05 17
45	02 53	03 41	04 19	02 41	03 33	04 30	05 32
N 40	03 22	04 03	04 36	02 53	03 46	04 44	05 45
35	03 45	04 21	04 51	03 03	03 57	04 55	05 56
30	04 03	04 36	05 03	03 12	04 07	05 05	06 05
20	04 31	05 00	05 25	03 28	04 24	05 22	06 21
N 10	04 54	05 20	05 43	03 41	04 39	05 37	06 35
0	05 12	05 38	06 01	03 54	04 53	05 51	06 48
S 10	05 29	05 55	06 18	04 07	05 07	06 05	07 02
20	05 44	06 12	06 36	04 21	05 22	06 20	07 16
30	06 00	06 30	06 56	04 36	05 39	06 38	07 32
35	06 09	06 41	07 09	04 46	05 49	06 48	07 41
40	06 18	06 52	07 22	04 56	06 00	06 59	07 52
45	06 28	07 05	07 39	05 09	06 14	07 13	08 04
S 50	06 39	07 21	07 59	05 24	06 31	07 29	08 19
52	06 44	07 28	08 08	05 31	06 38	07 37	08 26
54	06 50	07 36	08 19	05 39	06 47	07 46	08 34
56	06 56	07 45	08 31	05 47	06 57	07 55	08 43
58	07 02	07 54	08 45	05 58	07 08	08 06	08 53
S 60	07 09	08 06	09 02	06 09	07 21	08 19	09 04

Lat.	Sunset	Twilight Civil	Twilight Naut.	Moonset 2	Moonset 3	Moonset 4	Moonset 5
°	h m	h m	h m	h m	h m	h m	h m
N 72	▭	▭	▭	22 19	▭	23 47	23 30
N 70	▭	▭	▭	20 42	21 58	22 35	22 50
68	▭	▭	▭	20 02	21 13	21 58	22 23
66	23 25	////	////	19 35	20 43	21 31	22 02
64	22 21	////	////	19 14	20 21	21 11	21 45
62	21 47	////	////	18 57	20 03	20 54	21 32
60	21 23	22 57	////	18 43	19 48	20 40	21 20
N 58	21 04	22 15	////	18 31	19 36	20 28	21 10
56	20 48	21 48	////	18 20	19 25	20 18	21 01
54	20 34	21 27	23 03	18 11	19 15	20 09	20 53
52	20 22	21 10	22 24	18 03	19 06	20 01	20 45
50	20 12	20 55	21 59	17 56	18 59	19 53	20 39
45	19 50	20 27	21 16	17 40	18 42	19 38	20 25
N 40	19 32	20 05	20 46	17 27	18 29	19 25	20 14
35	19 18	19 47	20 24	17 16	18 17	19 14	20 04
30	19 05	19 32	20 05	17 06	18 07	19 04	19 55
20	18 44	19 08	19 37	16 50	17 50	18 47	19 40
N 10	18 25	18 48	19 15	16 35	17 35	18 33	19 27
0	18 08	18 30	18 57	16 22	17 21	18 19	19 15
S 10	17 51	18 14	18 40	16 08	17 07	18 05	19 02
20	17 33	17 57	18 24	15 54	16 51	17 50	18 49
30	17 12	17 38	18 08	15 37	16 34	17 33	18 34
35	17 00	17 28	18 00	15 28	16 24	17 24	18 25
40	16 46	17 17	17 51	15 17	16 12	17 12	18 15
45	16 30	17 04	17 41	15 04	15 59	16 59	18 03
S 50	16 10	16 48	17 29	14 48	15 42	16 43	17 48
52	16 00	16 41	17 24	14 41	15 34	16 35	17 41
54	15 50	16 33	17 19	14 33	15 25	16 27	17 34
56	15 38	16 24	17 13	14 24	15 16	16 17	17 25
58	15 23	16 14	17 07	14 13	15 05	16 06	17 16
S 60	15 07	16 03	16 59	14 02	14 52	15 54	17 05

Day	SUN Eqn. of Time 00^h	SUN Eqn. of Time 12^h	SUN Mer. Pass.	MOON Mer. Pass. Upper	MOON Mer. Pass. Lower	Age	Phase
d	m s	m s	h m	h m	h m	d %	
2	04 02	04 07	12 04	10 08	22 37	27 5	●
3	04 13	04 18	12 04	11 07	23 36	28 1	
4	04 24	04 29	12 04	12 05	24 34	00 0	

UT	ARIES GHA	VENUS −3·9 GHA	VENUS Dec	MARS −1·3 GHA	MARS Dec	JUPITER −1·8 GHA	JUPITER Dec	SATURN +0·2 GHA	SATURN Dec	STARS Name	SHA	Dec
d h	° ′	° ′	° ′	° ′	° ′	° ′	° ′	° ′	° ′		° ′	° ′
5 00 (Tuesday)	283 25.2	170 25.8	N22 46.6	53 18.3	S21 10.6	114 19.9	N 5 58.9	33 46.5	S20 21.6	Acamar	315 17.1	S40 14.3
01	298 27.7	185 25.0	46.2	68 20.6	10.7	129 22.1	58.8	48 49.1	21.5	Achernar	335 25.5	S57 09.0
02	313 30.2	200 24.1	45.8	83 22.9	10.8	144 24.2	58.6	63 51.7	21.5	Acrux	173 06.9	S63 11.7
03	328 32.6	215 23.3	. . 45.4	98 25.2	. . 10.9	159 26.3	. . 58.5	78 54.3	. . 21.5	Adhara	255 11.3	S28 59.8
04	343 35.1	230 22.4	45.0	113 27.5	11.0	174 28.5	58.3	93 56.9	21.5	Aldebaran	290 47.3	N16 32.3
05	358 37.6	245 21.6	44.6	128 29.8	11.0	189 30.6	58.2	108 59.6	21.5			
06	13 40.0	260 20.8	N22 44.2	143 32.1	S21 11.1	204 32.7	N 5 58.0	124 02.2	S20 21.5	Alioth	166 19.0	N55 52.6
07	28 42.5	275 19.9	43.8	158 34.4	11.2	219 34.9	57.9	139 04.8	21.5	Alkaid	152 57.2	N49 14.2
08	43 44.9	290 19.1	43.3	173 36.7	11.3	234 37.0	57.7	154 07.4	21.5	Al Na'ir	27 40.9	S46 52.6
09	58 47.4	305 18.3	. . 42.9	188 39.0	. . 11.4	249 39.1	. . 57.6	169 10.0	. . 21.4	Alnilam	275 44.6	S 1 11.7
10	73 49.9	320 17.4	42.5	203 41.2	11.5	264 41.3	57.4	184 12.6	21.4	Alphard	217 54.3	S 8 43.9
11	88 52.3	335 16.6	42.1	218 43.5	11.5	279 43.4	57.3	199 15.2	21.4			
12	103 54.8	350 15.7	N22 41.7	233 45.8	S21 11.6	294 45.5	N 5 57.2	214 17.8	S20 21.4	Alphecca	126 09.0	N26 39.9
13	118 57.3	5 14.9	41.3	248 48.1	11.7	309 47.7	57.0	229 20.5	21.4	Alpheratz	357 41.2	N29 10.7
14	133 59.7	20 14.1	40.8	263 50.4	11.8	324 49.8	56.9	244 23.1	21.4	Altair	62 05.9	N 8 54.9
15	149 02.2	35 13.2	. . 40.4	278 52.6	. . 11.9	339 51.9	. . 56.7	259 25.7	. . 21.4	Ankaa	353 13.7	S42 12.8
16	164 04.7	50 12.4	40.0	293 54.9	12.0	354 54.1	56.6	274 28.3	21.4	Antares	112 23.4	S26 27.9
17	179 07.1	65 11.6	39.6	308 57.2	12.0	9 56.2	56.4	289 30.9	21.3			
18	194 09.6	80 10.7	N22 39.1	323 59.5	S21 12.1	24 58.3	N 5 56.3	304 33.5	S20 21.3	Arcturus	145 53.7	N19 06.1
19	209 12.0	95 09.9	38.7	339 01.7	12.2	40 00.5	56.1	319 36.1	21.3	Atria	107 22.8	S69 03.3
20	224 14.5	110 09.1	38.3	354 04.0	12.3	55 02.6	56.0	334 38.7	21.3	Avior	234 17.7	S59 34.0
21	239 17.0	125 08.2	. . 37.9	9 06.3	. . 12.4	70 04.7	. . 55.8	349 41.4	. . 21.3	Bellatrix	278 30.1	N 6 21.7
22	254 19.4	140 07.4	37.4	24 08.5	12.5	85 06.9	55.7	4 44.0	21.3	Betelgeuse	270 59.4	N 7 24.4
23	269 21.9	155 06.6	37.0	39 10.8	12.6	100 09.0	55.5	19 46.6	21.3			
6 00 (Wednesday)	284 24.4	170 05.7	N22 36.6	54 13.1	S21 12.6	115 11.1	N 5 55.4	34 49.2	S20 21.3	Canopus	263 55.8	S52 42.4
01	299 26.8	185 04.9	36.1	69 15.3	12.7	130 13.3	55.2	49 51.8	21.2	Capella	280 31.8	N46 00.5
02	314 29.3	200 04.1	35.7	84 17.6	12.8	145 15.4	55.1	64 54.4	21.2	Deneb	49 29.6	N45 20.4
03	329 31.8	215 03.2	. . 35.3	99 19.8	. . 12.9	160 17.5	. . 55.0	79 57.0	. . 21.2	Denebola	182 31.7	N14 28.9
04	344 34.2	230 02.4	34.8	114 22.1	13.0	175 19.7	54.8	94 59.6	21.2	Diphda	348 53.8	S17 53.7
05	359 36.7	245 01.6	34.4	129 24.3	13.1	190 21.8	54.7	110 02.2	21.2			
06	14 39.2	260 00.8	N22 34.0	144 26.6	S21 13.2	205 23.9	N 5 54.5	125 04.9	S20 21.2	Dubhe	193 49.7	N61 40.0
07	29 41.6	274 59.9	33.5	159 28.9	13.2	220 26.1	54.4	140 07.5	21.2	Elnath	278 10.4	N28 37.0
08	44 44.1	289 59.1	33.1	174 31.1	13.3	235 28.2	54.2	155 10.1	21.2	Eltanin	90 44.7	N51 29.5
09	59 46.5	304 58.3	. . 32.6	189 33.4	. . 13.4	250 30.3	. . 54.1	170 12.7	. . 21.1	Enif	33 44.8	N 9 57.1
10	74 49.0	319 57.4	32.2	204 35.6	13.5	265 32.4	53.9	185 15.3	21.1	Fomalhaut	15 21.6	S29 31.9
11	89 51.5	334 56.6	31.7	219 37.8	13.6	280 34.6	53.8	200 17.9	21.1			
12	104 53.9	349 55.8	N22 31.3	234 40.1	S21 13.7	295 36.7	N 5 53.6	215 20.5	S20 21.1	Gacrux	171 58.5	S57 12.5
13	119 56.4	4 55.0	30.9	249 42.3	13.8	310 38.8	53.5	230 23.1	21.1	Gienah	175 50.2	S17 38.0
14	134 58.9	19 54.1	30.4	264 44.6	13.9	325 41.0	53.3	245 25.7	21.1	Hadar	148 44.6	S60 27.3
15	150 01.3	34 53.3	. . 30.0	279 46.8	. . 14.0	340 43.1	. . 53.2	260 28.3	. . 21.1	Hamal	327 58.5	N23 32.2
16	165 03.8	49 52.5	29.5	294 49.1	14.1	355 45.2	53.0	275 30.9	21.1	Kaus Aust.	83 40.7	S34 22.4
17	180 06.3	64 51.6	29.1	309 51.3	14.1	10 47.4	52.9	290 33.6	21.1			
18	195 08.7	79 50.8	N22 28.6	324 53.5	S21 14.2	25 49.5	N 5 52.7	305 36.2	S20 21.0	Kochab	137 19.7	N74 05.7
19	210 11.2	94 50.0	28.1	339 55.8	14.3	40 51.6	52.6	320 38.8	21.0	Markab	13 36.1	N15 17.6
20	225 13.7	109 49.2	27.7	354 58.0	14.4	55 53.7	52.4	335 41.4	21.0	Menkar	314 13.1	N 4 09.1
21	240 16.1	124 48.3	. . 27.2	10 00.2	. . 14.5	70 55.9	. . 52.3	350 44.0	. . 21.0	Menkent	148 04.9	S36 27.1
22	255 18.6	139 47.5	26.8	25 02.5	14.6	85 58.0	52.1	5 46.6	21.0	Miaplacidus	221 39.9	S69 47.4
23	270 21.0	154 46.7	26.3	40 04.7	14.7	101 00.1	52.0	20 49.2	21.0			
7 00 (Thursday)	285 23.5	169 45.9	N22 25.9	55 06.9	S21 14.8	116 02.3	N 5 51.8	35 51.8	S20 21.0	Mirfak	308 37.6	N49 54.8
01	300 26.0	184 45.1	25.4	70 09.2	14.9	131 04.4	51.7	50 54.4	21.0	Nunki	75 55.4	S26 16.3
02	315 28.4	199 44.2	24.9	85 11.4	15.0	146 06.5	51.5	65 57.0	20.9	Peacock	53 15.5	S56 40.6
03	330 30.9	214 43.4	. . 24.5	100 13.6	. . 15.1	161 08.6	. . 51.4	80 59.6	. . 20.9	Pollux	243 25.6	N27 59.0
04	345 33.4	229 42.6	24.0	115 15.8	15.2	176 10.8	51.2	96 02.2	20.9	Procyon	244 57.9	N 5 10.8
05	0 35.8	244 41.8	23.5	130 18.0	15.3	191 12.9	51.1	111 04.8	20.9			
06	15 38.3	259 40.9	N22 23.1	145 20.3	S21 15.3	206 15.0	N 5 51.0	126 07.5	S20 20.9	Rasalhague	96 04.2	N12 33.2
07	30 40.8	274 40.1	22.6	160 22.5	15.4	221 17.1	50.8	141 10.1	20.9	Regulus	207 41.6	N11 53.2
08	45 43.2	289 39.3	22.1	175 24.7	15.5	236 19.3	50.7	156 12.7	20.9	Rigel	281 10.4	S 8 11.1
09	60 45.7	304 38.5	. . 21.7	190 26.9	. . 15.6	251 21.4	. . 50.5	171 15.3	. . 20.9	Rigil Kent.	139 48.5	S60 54.2
10	75 48.2	319 37.7	21.2	205 29.1	15.7	266 23.5	50.4	186 17.9	20.9	Sabik	102 09.8	S15 44.5
11	90 50.6	334 36.8	20.7	220 31.3	15.8	281 25.7	50.2	201 20.5	20.8			
12	105 53.1	349 36.0	N22 20.3	235 33.6	S21 15.9	296 27.8	N 5 50.1	216 23.1	S20 20.8	Schedar	349 38.0	N56 37.3
13	120 55.5	4 35.2	19.8	250 35.8	16.0	311 29.9	49.9	231 25.7	20.8	Shaula	96 18.7	S37 06.7
14	135 58.0	19 34.4	19.3	265 38.0	16.1	326 32.0	49.8	246 28.3	20.8	Sirius	258 32.2	S16 44.5
15	151 00.5	34 33.6	. . 18.8	280 40.2	. . 16.2	341 34.2	. . 49.6	261 30.9	. . 20.8	Spica	158 29.0	S11 14.8
16	166 02.9	49 32.8	18.4	295 42.4	16.3	356 36.3	49.5	276 33.5	20.8	Suhail	222 51.2	S43 30.2
17	181 05.4	64 31.9	17.9	310 44.6	16.4	11 38.4	49.3	291 36.1	20.8			
18	196 07.9	79 31.1	N22 17.4	325 46.8	S21 16.5	26 40.5	N 5 49.2	306 38.7	S20 20.8	Vega	80 37.1	N38 48.2
19	211 10.3	94 30.3	16.9	340 49.0	16.6	41 42.7	49.0	321 41.3	20.8	Zuben'ubi	137 02.9	S16 06.5
20	226 12.8	109 29.5	16.4	355 51.2	16.7	56 44.8	48.9	336 43.9	20.7			
21	241 15.3	124 28.7	. . 16.0	10 53.4	. . 16.8	71 46.9	. . 48.7	351 46.5	. . 20.7			
22	256 17.7	139 27.9	15.5	25 55.6	16.9	86 49.0	48.6	6 49.2	20.7			
23	271 20.2	154 27.0	15.0	40 57.8	17.0	101 51.1	48.4	21 51.8	20.7			
Mer. Pass.	h m 5 01.5	v −0.8	d 0.4	v 2.2	d 0.1	v 2.1	d 0.1	v 2.6	d 0.0			

	SHA	Mer. Pass.
	° ′	h m
Venus	245 41.4	12 40
Mars	129 48.7	20 20
Jupiter	190 46.8	16 17
Saturn	110 24.8	21 37

d	h	SUN GHA	SUN Dec	MOON GHA	v	MOON Dec	d	HP
		° ′	° ′	° ′	′	° ′	′	′
5	00	178 51.3	N22 45.6	171 53.9	7.0	N17 48.7	3.4	58.6
	01	193 51.2	45.3	186 19.9	7.1	17 45.3	3.4	58.6
	02	208 51.1	45.1	200 46.0	7.1	17 41.9	3.6	58.6
	03	223 51.0	. . 44.8	215 12.1	7.2	17 38.3	3.7	58.5
	04	238 50.9	44.6	229 38.3	7.3	17 34.6	3.8	58.5
	05	253 50.8	44.3	244 04.6	7.3	17 30.8	3.9	58.5
	06	268 50.7	N22 44.1	258 30.9	7.4	N17 26.9	4.0	58.5
	07	283 50.6	43.9	272 57.3	7.4	17 22.9	4.1	58.4
TUESDAY	08	298 50.5	43.6	287 23.7	7.5	17 18.8	4.2	58.4
	09	313 50.3	. . 43.4	301 50.2	7.6	17 14.6	4.3	58.4
	10	328 50.2	43.1	316 16.8	7.6	17 10.3	4.4	58.4
	11	343 50.1	42.9	330 43.4	7.7	17 05.9	4.5	58.3
	12	358 50.0	N22 42.6	345 10.1	7.8	N17 01.4	4.6	58.3
	13	13 49.9	42.4	359 36.9	7.8	16 56.8	4.7	58.3
	14	28 49.8	42.1	14 03.7	7.9	16 52.1	4.8	58.2
	15	43 49.7	. . 41.9	28 30.6	7.9	16 47.3	4.9	58.2
	16	58 49.6	41.6	42 57.5	8.1	16 42.4	5.0	58.2
	17	73 49.5	41.4	57 24.6	8.1	16 37.4	5.0	58.1
	18	88 49.4	N22 41.1	71 51.7	8.1	N16 32.4	5.2	58.1
	19	103 49.3	40.9	86 18.8	8.3	16 27.2	5.3	58.1
	20	118 49.2	40.6	100 46.1	8.3	16 21.9	5.4	58.1
	21	133 49.1	. . 40.4	115 13.4	8.4	16 16.5	5.4	58.0
	22	148 49.0	40.1	129 40.8	8.4	16 11.1	5.5	58.0
	23	163 48.9	39.9	144 08.2	8.6	16 05.6	5.7	58.0
6	00	178 48.8	N22 39.6	158 35.8	8.6	N15 59.9	5.7	57.9
	01	193 48.7	39.4	173 03.4	8.6	15 54.2	5.8	57.9
	02	208 48.5	39.1	187 31.0	8.8	15 48.4	5.9	57.9
	03	223 48.4	. . 38.9	201 58.8	8.8	15 42.5	5.9	57.8
	04	238 48.3	38.6	216 26.6	8.9	15 36.6	6.1	57.8
	05	253 48.2	38.3	230 54.5	8.9	15 30.5	6.1	57.8
	06	268 48.1	N22 38.1	245 22.4	9.1	N15 24.4	6.3	57.7
WEDNESDAY	07	283 48.0	37.8	259 50.5	9.1	15 18.1	6.2	57.7
	08	298 47.9	37.6	274 18.6	9.1	15 11.9	6.4	57.7
	09	313 47.8	. . 37.3	288 46.7	9.3	15 05.5	6.5	57.6
	10	328 47.7	37.0	303 15.0	9.3	14 59.0	6.5	57.6
	11	343 47.6	36.8	317 43.3	9.4	14 52.5	6.6	57.6
	12	358 47.5	N22 36.5	332 11.7	9.5	N14 45.9	6.7	57.6
	13	13 47.4	36.3	346 40.2	9.5	14 39.2	6.8	57.5
	14	28 47.3	36.0	1 08.7	9.7	14 32.4	6.8	57.5
	15	43 47.2	. . 35.7	15 37.4	9.7	14 25.6	6.9	57.5
	16	58 47.1	35.5	30 06.1	9.7	14 18.7	7.0	57.4
	17	73 47.0	35.2	44 34.8	9.9	14 11.7	7.0	57.4
	18	88 46.9	N22 34.9	59 03.7	9.9	N14 04.7	7.1	57.4
	19	103 46.8	34.7	73 32.6	10.0	13 57.6	7.2	57.3
	20	118 46.7	34.4	88 01.6	10.1	13 50.4	7.2	57.3
	21	133 46.6	. . 34.1	102 30.7	10.1	13 43.2	7.3	57.3
	22	148 46.5	33.9	116 59.8	10.2	13 35.9	7.4	57.2
	23	163 46.4	33.6	131 29.0	10.3	13 28.5	7.5	57.2
7	00	178 46.3	N22 33.3	145 58.3	10.4	N13 21.0	7.5	57.2
	01	193 46.2	33.0	160 27.7	10.4	13 13.5	7.5	57.1
	02	208 46.1	32.8	174 57.1	10.5	13 06.0	7.6	57.1
	03	223 46.0	. . 32.5	189 26.6	10.6	12 58.4	7.7	57.1
	04	238 45.9	32.2	203 56.2	10.7	12 50.7	7.8	57.0
	05	253 45.8	32.0	218 25.9	10.7	12 42.9	7.8	57.0
	06	268 45.7	N22 31.7	232 55.6	10.8	N12 35.1	7.8	57.0
	07	283 45.6	31.4	247 25.4	10.9	12 27.3	7.9	56.9
THURSDAY	08	298 45.5	31.1	261 55.3	10.9	12 19.4	8.0	56.9
	09	313 45.4	. . 30.9	276 25.2	11.1	12 11.4	8.0	56.9
	10	328 45.3	30.6	290 55.3	11.0	12 03.4	8.1	56.8
	11	343 45.2	30.3	305 25.3	11.2	11 55.3	8.1	56.8
	12	358 45.1	N22 30.0	319 55.5	11.2	N11 47.2	8.2	56.8
	13	13 45.0	29.7	334 25.7	11.3	11 39.0	8.2	56.8
	14	28 44.9	29.5	348 56.0	11.4	11 30.8	8.3	56.7
	15	43 44.8	. . 29.2	3 26.4	11.4	11 22.5	8.3	56.7
	16	58 44.7	28.9	17 56.8	11.5	11 14.2	8.3	56.7
	17	73 44.6	28.6	32 27.3	11.6	11 05.9	8.5	56.6
	18	88 44.5	N22 28.3	46 57.9	11.7	N10 57.4	8.4	56.6
	19	103 44.4	28.0	61 28.6	11.7	10 49.0	8.5	56.6
	20	118 44.3	27.8	75 59.3	11.7	10 40.5	8.6	56.5
	21	133 44.2	. . 27.5	90 30.0	11.9	10 31.9	8.5	56.5
	22	148 44.1	27.2	105 00.9	11.9	10 23.4	8.7	56.5
	23	163 44.0	26.9	119 31.8	12.0	N10 14.7	8.6	56.4
		SD 15.8	*d* 0.3	SD	15.9		15.7	15.5

Lat.	Twilight Naut.	Twilight Civil	Sunrise	Moonrise 5	Moonrise 6	Moonrise 7	Moonrise 8
°	h m	h m	h m	h m	h m	h m	h m
N 72	▭	▭	▭	01 27	03 39	05 35	07 23
N 70	▭	▭	▭	02 38	04 17	05 59	07 37
68	▭	▭	▭	03 15	04 44	06 17	07 48
66	////	////	00 55	03 41	05 04	06 31	07 58
64	////	////	01 52	04 01	05 20	06 43	08 05
62	////	////	02 25	04 18	05 34	06 53	08 12
60	////	01 18	02 49	04 31	05 45	07 02	08 18
N 58	////	01 57	03 08	04 43	05 55	07 09	08 23
56	////	02 24	03 24	04 53	06 03	07 16	08 27
54	01 12	02 44	03 37	05 02	06 11	07 21	08 31
52	01 48	03 01	03 49	05 10	06 18	07 27	08 35
50	02 13	03 15	03 59	05 17	06 24	07 31	08 38
45	02 55	03 44	04 21	05 32	06 37	07 42	08 46
N 40	03 24	04 05	04 38	05 45	06 48	07 50	08 52
35	03 47	04 23	04 52	05 56	06 57	07 58	08 57
30	04 05	04 38	05 05	06 05	07 05	08 04	09 01
20	04 33	05 02	05 26	06 21	07 19	08 15	09 09
N 10	04 54	05 21	05 44	06 35	07 31	08 25	09 16
0	05 13	05 39	06 01	06 48	07 43	08 34	09 22
S 10	05 29	05 55	06 18	07 02	07 54	08 43	09 29
20	05 45	06 12	06 36	07 16	08 06	08 53	09 35
30	06 00	06 30	06 56	07 32	08 20	09 04	09 43
35	06 09	06 40	07 08	07 41	08 28	09 10	09 48
40	06 18	06 51	07 22	07 52	08 37	09 17	09 53
45	06 27	07 04	07 38	08 04	08 48	09 26	09 58
S 50	06 38	07 20	07 58	08 19	09 01	09 36	10 05
52	06 43	07 27	08 07	08 26	09 07	09 40	10 09
54	06 49	07 34	08 17	08 34	09 13	09 45	10 12
56	06 55	07 43	08 29	08 43	09 21	09 51	10 16
58	07 01	07 53	08 43	08 53	09 29	09 57	10 20
S 60	07 08	08 04	08 59	09 04	09 38	10 04	10 25

Lat.	Sunset	Twilight Civil	Twilight Naut.	Moonset 5	Moonset 6	Moonset 7	Moonset 8
°	h m	h m	h m	h m	h m	h m	h m
N 72	▭	▭	▭	23 30	23 22	23 15	23 09
N 70	▭	▭	▭	22 50	22 57	22 59	23 00
68	▭	▭	▭	22 23	22 38	22 47	22 53
66	23 10	////	////	22 02	22 22	22 36	22 47
64	22 15	////	////	21 45	22 10	22 27	22 41
62	21 43	////	////	21 32	21 59	22 20	22 36
60	21 20	22 49	////	21 20	21 50	22 13	22 32
N 58	21 01	22 11	////	21 10	21 42	22 07	22 29
56	20 45	21 45	////	21 01	21 35	22 02	22 26
54	20 32	21 24	22 56	20 53	21 28	21 58	22 23
52	20 20	21 08	22 20	20 45	21 22	21 53	22 20
50	20 10	20 54	21 56	20 39	21 17	21 49	22 18
45	19 49	20 25	21 14	20 25	21 06	21 41	22 12
N 40	19 32	20 04	20 45	20 14	20 56	21 34	22 08
35	19 17	19 47	20 23	20 04	20 48	21 28	22 04
30	19 05	19 32	20 05	19 55	20 41	21 23	22 01
20	18 44	19 08	19 37	19 40	20 29	21 13	21 55
N 10	18 25	18 48	19 15	19 27	20 18	21 05	21 49
0	18 08	18 31	18 57	19 15	20 08	20 57	21 44
S 10	17 52	18 14	18 41	19 02	19 57	20 50	21 39
20	17 34	17 58	18 25	18 49	19 46	20 41	21 34
30	17 14	17 40	18 09	18 34	19 34	20 32	21 28
35	17 02	17 30	18 01	18 25	19 26	20 26	21 24
40	16 48	17 18	17 52	18 15	19 18	20 20	21 20
45	16 32	17 06	17 42	18 03	19 08	20 12	21 16
S 50	16 12	16 50	17 31	17 48	18 56	20 03	21 10
52	16 03	16 43	17 26	17 41	18 50	19 59	21 07
54	15 53	16 36	17 21	17 34	18 44	19 55	21 04
56	15 41	16 27	17 15	17 25	18 37	19 50	21 01
58	15 27	16 17	17 09	17 16	18 29	19 44	20 58
S 60	15 11	16 06	17 02	17 05	18 21	19 38	20 54

Day	SUN Eqn. of Time 00^h	SUN Eqn. of Time 12^h	SUN Mer. Pass.	MOON Mer. Pass. Upper	MOON Mer. Pass. Lower	MOON Age	MOON Phase
d	m s	m s	h m	h m	h m	d %	
5	04 35	04 40	12 05	13 02	00 34	01 2	●
6	04 45	04 50	12 05	13 55	01 29	02 5	
7	04 55	04 59	12 05	14 46	02 21	03 11	

UT d h	ARIES GHA ° ′	VENUS −3·9 GHA ° ′	VENUS Dec ° ′	MARS −1·2 GHA ° ′	MARS Dec ° ′	JUPITER −1·8 GHA ° ′	JUPITER Dec ° ′	SATURN +0·2 GHA ° ′	SATURN Dec ° ′
8 00	286 22.6	169 26.2	N22 14.5	56 00.0	S21 17.1	116 53.3	N 5 48.3	36 54.4	S20 20.7
01	301 25.1	184 25.4	14.0	71 02.2	17.2	131 55.4	48.1	51 57.0	20.7
02	316 27.6	199 24.6	13.5	86 04.4	17.3	146 57.5	48.0	66 59.6	20.7
03	331 30.0	214 23.8	. . 13.0	101 06.5	. . 17.4	161 59.6	. . 47.8	82 02.2	. . 20.7
04	346 32.5	229 23.0	12.5	116 08.7	17.5	177 01.8	47.7	97 04.8	20.7
05	1 35.0	244 22.2	12.1	131 10.9	17.6	192 03.9	47.5	112 07.4	20.6
06	16 37.4	259 21.4	N22 11.6	146 13.1	S21 17.7	207 06.0	N 5 47.4	127 10.0	S20 20.6
07	31 39.9	274 20.5	11.1	161 15.3	17.8	222 08.1	47.2	142 12.6	20.6
08	46 42.4	289 19.7	10.6	176 17.5	17.9	237 10.3	47.0	157 15.2	20.6
F 09	61 44.8	304 18.9	. . 10.1	191 19.7	. . 18.0	252 12.4	. . 46.9	172 17.8	. . 20.6
R 10	76 47.3	319 18.1	09.6	206 21.8	18.1	267 14.5	46.7	187 20.4	20.6
I 11	91 49.8	334 17.3	09.1	221 24.0	18.2	282 16.6	46.6	202 23.0	20.6
D 12	106 52.2	349 16.5	N22 08.6	236 26.2	S21 18.3	297 18.7	N 5 46.4	217 25.6	S20 20.6
A 13	121 54.7	4 15.7	08.1	251 28.4	18.4	312 20.9	46.3	232 28.2	20.6
Y 14	136 57.1	19 14.9	07.6	266 30.5	18.5	327 23.0	46.1	247 30.8	20.5
15	151 59.6	34 14.1	. . 07.1	281 32.7	. . 18.6	342 25.1	. . 46.0	262 33.4	. . 20.5
16	167 02.1	49 13.3	06.6	296 34.9	18.7	357 27.2	45.8	277 36.0	20.5
17	182 04.5	64 12.5	06.1	311 37.1	18.8	12 29.4	45.7	292 38.6	20.5
18	197 07.0	79 11.6	N22 05.6	326 39.2	S21 18.9	27 31.5	N 5 45.5	307 41.2	S20 20.5
19	212 09.5	94 10.8	05.0	341 41.4	19.0	42 33.6	45.4	322 43.8	20.5
20	227 11.9	109 10.0	04.5	356 43.6	19.1	57 35.7	45.2	337 46.4	20.5
21	242 14.4	124 09.2	. . 04.0	11 45.7	. . 19.2	72 37.8	. . 45.1	352 49.0	. . 20.5
22	257 16.9	139 08.4	03.5	26 47.9	19.3	87 40.0	44.9	7 51.6	20.5
23	272 19.3	154 07.6	03.0	41 50.0	19.4	102 42.1	44.8	22 54.2	20.4
9 00	287 21.8	169 06.8	N22 02.5	56 52.2	S21 19.5	117 44.2	N 5 44.6	37 56.8	S20 20.4
01	302 24.3	184 06.0	02.0	71 54.4	19.6	132 46.3	44.5	52 59.4	20.4
02	317 26.7	199 05.2	01.5	86 56.5	19.8	147 48.4	44.3	68 02.0	20.4
03	332 29.2	214 04.4	. . 00.9	101 58.7	. . 19.9	162 50.6	. . 44.2	83 04.6	. . 20.4
04	347 31.6	229 03.6	22 00.4	117 00.8	20.0	177 52.7	44.0	98 07.3	20.4
05	2 34.1	244 02.8	21 59.9	132 03.0	20.1	192 54.8	43.9	113 09.9	20.4
06	17 36.6	259 02.0	N21 59.4	147 05.1	S21 20.2	207 56.9	N 5 43.7	128 12.5	S20 20.4
07	32 39.0	274 01.2	58.9	162 07.3	20.3	222 59.0	43.6	143 15.1	20.4
S 08	47 41.5	289 00.4	58.3	177 09.4	20.4	238 01.1	43.4	158 17.7	20.3
A 09	62 44.0	303 59.6	. . 57.8	192 11.6	. . 20.5	253 03.3	. . 43.3	173 20.3	. . 20.3
T 10	77 46.4	318 58.8	57.3	207 13.7	20.6	268 05.4	43.1	188 22.9	20.3
U 11	92 48.9	333 58.0	56.8	222 15.9	20.7	283 07.5	42.9	203 25.5	20.3
R 12	107 51.4	348 57.2	N21 56.2	237 18.0	S21 20.8	298 09.6	N 5 42.8	218 28.1	S20 20.3
D 13	122 53.8	3 56.4	55.7	252 20.1	20.9	313 11.7	42.6	233 30.7	20.3
A 14	137 56.3	18 55.6	55.2	267 22.3	21.0	328 13.9	42.5	248 33.3	20.3
Y 15	152 58.7	33 54.8	. . 54.7	282 24.4	. . 21.1	343 16.0	. . 42.3	263 35.9	. . 20.3
16	168 01.2	48 54.0	54.1	297 26.6	21.3	358 18.1	42.2	278 38.5	20.3
17	183 03.7	63 53.2	53.6	312 28.7	21.4	13 20.2	42.0	293 41.1	20.3
18	198 06.1	78 52.4	N21 53.1	327 30.8	S21 21.5	28 22.3	N 5 41.9	308 43.7	S20 20.2
19	213 08.6	93 51.6	52.5	342 33.0	21.6	43 24.4	41.7	323 46.3	20.2
20	228 11.1	108 50.8	52.0	357 35.1	21.7	58 26.6	41.6	338 48.9	20.2
21	243 13.5	123 50.0	. . 51.5	12 37.2	. . 21.8	73 28.7	. . 41.4	353 51.5	. . 20.2
22	258 16.0	138 49.2	50.9	27 39.4	21.9	88 30.8	41.3	8 54.1	20.2
23	273 18.5	153 48.4	50.4	42 41.5	22.0	103 32.9	41.1	23 56.7	20.2
10 00	288 20.9	168 47.6	N21 49.8	57 43.6	S21 22.1	118 35.0	N 5 41.0	38 59.2	S20 20.2
01	303 23.4	183 46.8	49.3	72 45.7	22.3	133 37.1	40.8	54 01.8	20.2
02	318 25.9	198 46.0	48.8	87 47.9	22.4	148 39.3	40.6	69 04.4	20.2
03	333 28.3	213 45.2	. . 48.2	102 50.0	. . 22.5	163 41.4	. . 40.5	84 07.0	. . 20.1
04	348 30.8	228 44.4	47.7	117 52.1	22.6	178 43.5	40.3	99 09.6	20.1
05	3 33.2	243 43.7	47.1	132 54.2	22.7	193 45.6	40.2	114 12.2	20.1
06	18 35.7	258 42.9	N21 46.6	147 56.3	S21 22.8	208 47.7	N 5 40.0	129 14.8	S20 20.1
07	33 38.2	273 42.1	46.0	162 58.5	22.9	223 49.8	39.9	144 17.4	20.1
08	48 40.6	288 41.3	45.5	178 00.6	23.0	238 51.9	39.7	159 20.0	20.1
S 09	63 43.1	303 40.5	. . 44.9	193 02.7	. . 23.2	253 54.1	. . 39.6	174 22.6	. . 20.1
U 10	78 45.6	318 39.7	44.4	208 04.8	23.3	268 56.2	39.4	189 25.2	20.1
N 11	93 48.0	333 38.9	43.8	223 06.9	23.4	283 58.3	39.3	204 27.8	20.1
D 12	108 50.5	348 38.1	N21 43.3	238 09.0	S21 23.5	299 00.4	N 5 39.1	219 30.4	S20 20.1
A 13	123 53.0	3 37.3	42.7	253 11.1	23.6	314 02.5	38.9	234 33.0	20.0
Y 14	138 55.4	18 36.5	42.2	268 13.2	23.7	329 04.6	38.8	249 35.6	20.0
15	153 57.9	33 35.8	. . 41.6	283 15.3	. . 23.8	344 06.7	. . 38.6	264 38.2	. . 20.0
16	169 00.3	48 35.0	41.1	298 17.4	24.0	359 08.9	38.5	279 40.8	20.0
17	184 02.8	63 34.2	40.5	313 19.5	24.1	14 11.0	38.3	294 43.4	20.0
18	199 05.3	78 33.4	N21 39.9	328 21.6	S21 24.2	29 13.1	N 5 38.2	309 46.0	S20 20.0
19	214 07.7	93 32.6	39.4	343 23.7	24.3	44 15.2	38.0	324 48.6	20.0
20	229 10.2	108 31.8	38.8	358 25.8	24.4	59 17.3	37.9	339 51.2	20.0
21	244 12.7	123 31.0	. . 38.3	13 27.9	. . 24.5	74 19.4	. . 37.7	354 53.8	. . 20.0
22	259 15.1	138 30.2	37.7	28 30.0	24.7	89 21.5	37.6	9 56.4	20.0
23	274 17.6	153 29.5	37.1	43 32.1	24.8	104 23.6	37.4	24 59.0	19.9
Mer. Pass. (h m)	4 49.8	v −0.8	d 0.5	v 2.1	d 0.1	v 2.1	d 0.2	v 2.6	d 0.0

STARS

Name	SHA ° ′	Dec ° ′
Acamar	315 17.0	S40 14.3
Achernar	335 25.4	S57 09.0
Acrux	173 06.9	S63 11.7
Adhara	255 11.3	S28 59.8
Aldebaran	290 47.3	N16 32.3
Alioth	166 19.0	N55 52.6
Alkaid	152 57.3	N49 14.2
Al Na'ir	27 40.9	S46 52.6
Alnilam	275 44.6	S 1 11.7
Alphard	217 54.3	S 8 43.9
Alphecca	126 09.0	N26 39.9
Alpheratz	357 41.2	N29 10.7
Altair	62 05.9	N 8 54.9
Ankaa	353 13.6	S42 12.8
Antares	112 23.4	S26 27.9
Arcturus	145 53.8	N19 06.1
Atria	107 22.8	S69 03.3
Avior	234 17.7	S59 34.0
Bellatrix	278 30.1	N 6 21.7
Betelgeuse	270 59.4	N 7 24.4
Canopus	263 55.8	S52 42.4
Capella	280 31.8	N46 00.5
Deneb	49 29.6	N45 20.4
Denebola	182 31.7	N14 28.9
Diphda	348 53.8	S17 53.7
Dubhe	193 49.7	N61 40.0
Elnath	278 10.3	N28 37.0
Eltanin	90 44.7	N51 29.5
Enif	33 44.8	N 9 57.2
Fomalhaut	15 21.5	S29 31.9
Gacrux	171 58.5	S57 12.5
Gienah	175 50.2	S17 38.0
Hadar	148 44.6	S60 27.3
Hamal	327 58.5	N23 32.2
Kaus Aust.	83 40.7	S34 22.4
Kochab	137 19.8	N74 05.7
Markab	13 36.1	N15 17.6
Menkar	314 13.0	N 4 09.1
Menkent	148 05.0	S36 27.1
Miaplacidus	221 39.9	S69 47.4
Mirfak	308 37.6	N49 54.8
Nunki	75 55.4	S26 16.3
Peacock	53 15.5	S56 40.6
Pollux	243 25.6	N27 59.0
Procyon	244 57.9	N 5 10.8
Rasalhague	96 04.2	N12 33.2
Regulus	207 41.6	N11 53.2
Rigel	281 10.4	S 8 11.1
Rigil Kent.	139 48.5	S60 54.3
Sabik	102 09.8	S15 44.5
Schedar	349 37.9	N56 37.4
Shaula	96 18.7	S37 06.7
Sirius	258 32.2	S16 44.5
Spica	158 29.0	S11 14.8
Suhail	222 51.3	S43 30.2
Vega	80 37.1	N38 48.2
Zuben'ubi	137 02.9	S16 06.5

	SHA ° ′	Mer. Pass. h m
Venus	241 45.0	12 44
Mars	129 30.4	20 10
Jupiter	190 22.4	16 07
Saturn	110 35.1	21 24

	UT	SUN GHA	SUN Dec	MOON GHA	v	MOON Dec	d	HP
	d h	° ′	° ′	° ′	′	° ′	′	′
	8 00	178 43.9	N22 26.6	134 02.8	12.0	N10 06.1	8.7	56.4
	01	193 43.8	26.3	148 33.8	12.1	9 57.4	8.8	56.4
	02	208 43.7	26.0	163 04.9	12.2	9 48.6	8.8	56.3
	03	223 43.6	. . 25.8	177 36.1	12.2	9 39.8	8.8	56.3
	04	238 43.5	25.5	192 07.3	12.3	9 31.0	8.8	56.3
	05	253 43.4	25.2	206 38.6	12.4	9 22.2	8.9	56.3
	06	268 43.3	N22 24.9	221 10.0	12.4	N 9 13.3	8.9	56.2
	07	283 43.2	24.6	235 41.4	12.5	9 04.4	9.0	56.2
	08	298 43.2	24.3	250 12.9	12.5	8 55.4	9.0	56.2
F	09	313 43.1	. . 24.0	264 44.4	12.6	8 46.4	9.0	56.1
R	10	328 43.0	23.7	279 16.0	12.7	8 37.4	9.1	56.1
I	11	343 42.9	23.4	293 47.7	12.7	8 28.3	9.0	56.1
D	12	358 42.8	N22 23.1	308 19.4	12.8	N 8 19.3	9.1	56.1
A	13	13 42.7	22.8	322 51.2	12.8	8 10.2	9.2	56.0
Y	14	28 42.6	22.5	337 23.0	12.9	8 01.0	9.1	56.0
	15	43 42.5	. . 22.2	351 54.9	12.9	7 51.9	9.2	56.0
	16	58 42.4	21.9	6 26.8	13.0	7 42.7	9.3	55.9
	17	73 42.3	21.6	20 58.8	13.1	7 33.4	9.2	55.9
	18	88 42.2	N22 21.3	35 30.9	13.1	N 7 24.2	9.3	55.9
	19	103 42.1	21.0	50 03.0	13.2	7 14.9	9.2	55.8
	20	118 42.0	20.7	64 35.2	13.2	7 05.7	9.4	55.8
	21	133 41.9	. . 20.4	79 07.4	13.3	6 56.3	9.3	55.8
	22	148 41.8	20.1	93 39.7	13.3	6 47.0	9.3	55.8
	23	163 41.7	19.8	108 12.0	13.3	6 37.7	9.4	55.7
	9 00	178 41.7	N22 19.5	122 44.3	13.5	N 6 28.3	9.4	55.7
	01	193 41.6	19.2	137 16.8	13.4	6 18.9	9.4	55.7
	02	208 41.5	18.9	151 49.2	13.6	6 09.5	9.4	55.7
	03	223 41.4	. . 18.6	166 21.8	13.5	6 00.1	9.5	55.6
	04	238 41.3	18.3	180 54.3	13.7	5 50.6	9.5	55.6
	05	253 41.2	18.0	195 27.0	13.6	5 41.1	9.4	55.6
	06	268 41.1	N22 17.7	209 59.6	13.7	N 5 31.7	9.5	55.6
S	07	283 41.0	17.4	224 32.3	13.8	5 22.2	9.5	55.5
	08	298 40.9	17.1	239 05.1	13.8	5 12.7	9.5	55.5
A	09	313 40.8	. . 16.8	253 37.9	13.8	5 03.2	9.6	55.5
T	10	328 40.7	16.5	268 10.7	13.9	4 53.6	9.5	55.4
U	11	343 40.7	16.2	282 43.6	13.9	4 44.1	9.6	55.4
R	12	358 40.6	N22 15.8	297 16.5	14.0	N 4 34.5	9.6	55.4
D	13	13 40.5	15.5	311 49.5	14.0	4 24.9	9.5	55.4
A	14	28 40.4	15.2	326 22.5	14.1	4 15.4	9.6	55.3
Y	15	43 40.3	. . 14.9	340 55.6	14.1	4 05.8	9.6	55.3
	16	58 40.2	14.6	355 28.7	14.1	3 56.2	9.6	55.3
	17	73 40.1	14.3	10 01.8	14.1	3 46.6	9.6	55.3
	18	88 40.0	N22 14.0	24 34.9	14.2	N 3 37.0	9.6	55.3
	19	103 39.9	13.6	39 08.1	14.3	3 27.4	9.7	55.2
	20	118 39.8	13.3	53 41.4	14.3	3 17.7	9.6	55.2
	21	133 39.8	. . 13.0	68 14.7	14.3	3 08.1	9.6	55.2
	22	148 39.7	12.7	82 48.0	14.3	2 58.5	9.7	55.2
	23	163 39.6	12.4	97 21.3	14.4	2 48.8	9.6	55.1
	10 00	178 39.5	N22 12.1	111 54.7	14.4	N 2 39.2	9.7	55.1
	01	193 39.4	11.7	126 28.1	14.4	2 29.5	9.6	55.1
	02	208 39.3	11.4	141 01.5	14.5	2 19.9	9.7	55.1
	03	223 39.2	. . 11.1	155 35.0	14.5	2 10.2	9.6	55.1
	04	238 39.1	10.8	170 08.5	14.5	2 00.6	9.7	55.0
	05	253 39.1	10.5	184 42.0	14.6	1 50.9	9.6	55.0
	06	268 39.0	N22 10.1	199 15.6	14.6	N 1 41.3	9.7	55.0
	07	283 38.9	09.8	213 49.2	14.6	1 31.6	9.6	55.0
	08	298 38.8	09.5	228 22.8	14.7	1 22.0	9.7	54.9
S	09	313 38.7	. . 09.2	242 56.5	14.6	1 12.3	9.6	54.9
U	10	328 38.6	08.8	257 30.1	14.7	1 02.7	9.7	54.9
N	11	343 38.5	08.5	272 03.8	14.7	0 53.0	9.6	54.9
D	12	358 38.5	N22 08.2	286 37.5	14.8	N 0 43.4	9.6	54.9
A	13	13 38.4	07.9	301 11.3	14.7	0 33.8	9.7	54.9
Y	14	28 38.3	07.5	315 45.0	14.8	0 24.1	9.6	54.8
	15	43 38.2	. . 07.2	330 18.8	14.8	0 14.5	9.6	54.8
	16	58 38.1	06.9	344 52.6	14.8	N 0 04.9	9.6	54.8
	17	73 38.0	06.5	359 26.4	14.9	S 0 04.7	9.6	54.8
	18	88 38.0	N22 06.2	14 00.3	14.8	S 0 14.3	9.6	54.8
	19	103 37.9	05.9	28 34.1	14.9	0 23.9	9.6	54.7
	20	118 37.8	05.5	43 08.0	14.9	0 33.5	9.6	54.7
	21	133 37.7	. . 05.2	57 41.9	14.9	0 43.1	9.5	54.7
	22	148 37.6	04.9	72 15.8	15.0	0 52.6	9.6	54.7
	23	163 37.5	04.5	86 49.8	14.9	S 1 02.2	9.6	54.7
		SD 15.8	*d* 0.3	SD 15.3		15.1		15.0

Lat.	Twilight Naut.	Twilight Civil	Sunrise	Moonrise 8	Moonrise 9	Moonrise 10	Moonrise 11
°	h m	h m	h m	h m	h m	h m	h m
N 72	▭	▭	▭	07 23	09 04	10 41	12 16
N 70	▭	▭	▭	07 37	09 11	10 42	12 11
68	▭	▭	▭	07 48	09 17	10 43	12 07
66	////	////	01 10	07 58	09 22	10 44	12 04
64	////	////	02 00	08 05	09 26	10 45	12 02
62	////	////	02 31	08 12	09 30	10 45	11 59
60	////	01 27	02 54	08 18	09 33	10 46	11 57
N 58	////	02 03	03 12	08 23	09 35	10 46	11 56
56	////	02 29	03 27	08 27	09 38	10 47	11 54
54	01 20	02 48	03 40	08 31	09 40	10 47	11 53
52	01 54	03 05	03 52	08 35	09 42	10 47	11 51
50	02 17	03 19	04 02	08 38	09 44	10 48	11 50
45	02 58	03 46	04 23	08 46	09 48	10 48	11 48
N 40	03 27	04 07	04 40	08 52	09 51	10 49	11 46
35	03 49	04 25	04 54	08 57	09 54	10 49	11 44
30	04 06	04 39	05 06	09 01	09 56	10 50	11 42
20	04 34	05 03	05 27	09 09	10 01	10 51	11 39
N 10	04 55	05 22	05 45	09 16	10 04	10 51	11 37
0	05 13	05 39	06 02	09 22	10 08	10 52	11 35
S 10	05 29	05 56	06 18	09 29	10 11	10 53	11 33
20	05 45	06 12	06 36	09 35	10 15	10 53	11 30
30	06 00	06 30	06 56	09 43	10 20	10 54	11 28
35	06 08	06 40	07 07	09 48	10 22	10 55	11 26
40	06 17	06 51	07 21	09 53	10 25	10 55	11 25
45	06 26	07 03	07 36	09 58	10 28	10 56	11 23
S 50	06 37	07 18	07 56	10 05	10 32	10 57	11 20
52	06 42	07 25	08 05	10 09	10 34	10 57	11 19
54	06 47	07 33	08 15	10 12	10 36	10 57	11 18
56	06 53	07 41	08 27	10 16	10 38	10 58	11 17
58	06 59	07 50	08 40	10 20	10 40	10 58	11 16
S 60	07 06	08 01	08 56	10 25	10 43	10 59	11 14

Lat.	Sunset	Twilight Civil	Twilight Naut.	Moonset 8	Moonset 9	Moonset 10	Moonset 11
°	h m	h m	h m	h m	h m	h m	h m
N 72	▭	▭	▭	23 09	23 04	22 59	22 53
N 70	▭	▭	▭	23 00	23 00	23 00	23 00
68	▭	▭	▭	22 53	22 57	23 01	23 05
66	22 57	////	////	22 47	22 55	23 02	23 10
64	22 09	////	////	22 41	22 53	23 03	23 14
62	21 38	////	////	22 36	22 51	23 04	23 17
60	21 16	22 41	////	22 32	22 49	23 05	23 20
N 58	20 58	22 06	////	22 29	22 48	23 05	23 23
56	20 43	21 41	////	22 26	22 46	23 06	23 25
54	20 30	21 21	22 48	22 23	22 45	23 06	23 27
52	20 18	21 05	22 16	22 20	22 44	23 07	23 29
50	20 08	20 51	21 52	22 18	22 43	23 07	23 31
45	19 47	20 24	21 12	22 12	22 41	23 08	23 35
N 40	19 31	20 03	20 43	22 08	22 39	23 09	23 38
35	19 16	19 46	20 22	22 04	22 37	23 10	23 41
30	19 04	19 31	20 04	22 01	22 36	23 10	23 44
20	18 43	19 08	19 37	21 55	22 34	23 11	23 48
N 10	18 26	18 48	19 15	21 49	22 31	23 12	23 52
0	18 09	18 31	18 57	21 44	22 29	23 13	23 55
S 10	17 52	18 15	18 41	21 39	22 27	23 13	23 59
20	17 35	17 59	18 26	21 34	22 25	23 14	24 03
30	17 15	17 41	18 11	21 28	22 22	23 15	24 07
35	17 03	17 31	18 03	21 24	22 21	23 16	24 10
40	16 50	17 20	17 54	21 20	22 19	23 16	24 13
45	16 34	17 08	17 44	21 16	22 17	23 17	24 16
S 50	16 15	16 53	17 34	21 10	22 15	23 18	24 20
52	16 06	16 46	17 29	21 07	22 13	23 18	24 22
54	15 56	16 38	17 24	21 04	22 12	23 19	24 24
56	15 44	16 30	17 18	21 01	22 11	23 19	24 26
58	15 31	16 21	17 12	20 58	22 09	23 19	24 28
S 60	15 15	16 10	17 05	20 54	22 08	23 20	24 31

Day	SUN Eqn. of Time 00^h	SUN Eqn. of Time 12^h	SUN Mer. Pass.	MOON Mer. Pass. Upper	MOON Mer. Pass. Lower	MOON Age	MOON Phase
d	m s	m s	h m	h m	h m	d	%
8	05 04	05 09	12 05	15 33	03 10	04	18
9	05 13	05 18	12 05	16 19	03 56	05	27
10	05 22	05 26	12 05	17 02	04 41	06	36

UT d h	ARIES GHA ° ′	VENUS −3·9 GHA ° ′	VENUS Dec ° ′	MARS −1·2 GHA ° ′	MARS Dec ° ′	JUPITER −1·8 GHA ° ′	JUPITER Dec ° ′	SATURN +0·2 GHA ° ′	SATURN Dec ° ′
11 00 (MONDAY)	289 20.1	168 28.7	N21 36.6	58 34.2	S21 24.9	119 25.8	N 5 37.2	40 01.6	S20 19.9
01	304 22.5	183 27.9	36.0	73 36.3	25.0	134 27.9	37.1	55 04.2	19.9
02	319 25.0	198 27.1	35.4	88 38.4	25.1	149 30.0	36.9	70 06.8	19.9
03	334 27.5	213 26.3	. . 34.9	103 40.5	. . 25.2	164 32.1	. . 36.8	85 09.4	. . 19.9
04	349 29.9	228 25.5	34.3	118 42.6	25.4	179 34.2	36.6	100 12.0	19.9
05	4 32.4	243 24.8	33.7	133 44.7	25.5	194 36.3	36.5	115 14.6	19.9
06	19 34.8	258 24.0	N21 33.1	148 46.8	S21 25.6	209 38.4	N 5 36.3	130 17.1	S20 19.9
07	34 37.3	273 23.2	32.6	163 48.8	25.7	224 40.5	36.2	145 19.7	19.9
08	49 39.8	288 22.4	32.0	178 50.9	25.8	239 42.6	36.0	160 22.3	19.9
09	64 42.2	303 21.6	. . 31.4	193 53.0	. . 26.0	254 44.8	. . 35.8	175 24.9	. . 19.8
10	79 44.7	318 20.9	30.8	208 55.1	26.1	269 46.9	35.7	190 27.5	19.8
11	94 47.2	333 20.1	30.3	223 57.2	26.2	284 49.0	35.5	205 30.1	19.8
12	109 49.6	348 19.3	N21 29.7	238 59.2	S21 26.3	299 51.1	N 5 35.4	220 32.7	S20 19.8
13	124 52.1	3 18.5	29.1	254 01.3	26.4	314 53.2	35.2	235 35.3	19.8
14	139 54.6	18 17.7	28.5	269 03.4	26.6	329 55.3	35.1	250 37.9	19.8
15	154 57.0	33 17.0	. . 27.9	284 05.5	. . 26.7	344 57.4	. . 34.9	265 40.5	. . 19.8
16	169 59.5	48 16.2	27.4	299 07.5	26.8	359 59.5	34.7	280 43.1	19.8
17	185 02.0	63 15.4	26.8	314 09.6	26.9	15 01.6	34.6	295 45.7	19.8
18	200 04.4	78 14.6	N21 26.2	329 11.7	S21 27.0	30 03.7	N 5 34.4	310 48.3	S20 19.8
19	215 06.9	93 13.9	25.6	344 13.7	27.2	45 05.9	34.3	325 50.9	19.7
20	230 09.3	108 13.1	25.0	359 15.8	27.3	60 08.0	34.1	340 53.5	19.7
21	245 11.8	123 12.3	. . 24.4	14 17.9	. . 27.4	75 10.1	. . 34.0	355 56.1	. . 19.7
22	260 14.3	138 11.5	23.8	29 19.9	27.5	90 12.2	33.8	10 58.6	19.7
23	275 16.7	153 10.8	23.2	44 22.0	27.7	105 14.3	33.7	26 01.2	19.7
12 00 (TUESDAY)	290 19.2	168 10.0	N21 22.7	59 24.1	S21 27.8	120 16.4	N 5 33.5	41 03.8	S20 19.7
01	305 21.7	183 09.2	22.1	74 26.1	27.9	135 18.5	33.3	56 06.4	19.7
02	320 24.1	198 08.4	21.5	89 28.2	28.0	150 20.6	33.2	71 09.0	19.7
03	335 26.6	213 07.7	. . 20.9	104 30.2	. . 28.1	165 22.7	. . 33.0	86 11.6	. . 19.7
04	350 29.1	228 06.9	20.3	119 32.3	28.3	180 24.8	32.9	101 14.2	19.7
05	5 31.5	243 06.1	19.7	134 34.3	28.4	195 26.9	32.7	116 16.8	19.7
06	20 34.0	258 05.3	N21 19.1	149 36.4	S21 28.5	210 29.0	N 5 32.6	131 19.4	S20 19.6
07	35 36.4	273 04.6	18.5	164 38.4	28.6	225 31.1	32.4	146 22.0	19.6
08	50 38.9	288 03.8	17.9	179 40.5	28.8	240 33.3	32.2	161 24.6	19.6
09	65 41.4	303 03.0	. . 17.3	194 42.5	. . 28.9	255 35.4	. . 32.1	176 27.2	. . 19.6
10	80 43.8	318 02.3	16.7	209 44.6	29.0	270 37.5	31.9	191 29.7	19.6
11	95 46.3	333 01.5	16.1	224 46.6	29.1	285 39.6	31.8	206 32.3	19.6
12	110 48.8	348 00.7	N21 15.5	239 48.7	S21 29.3	300 41.7	N 5 31.6	221 34.9	S20 19.6
13	125 51.2	3 00.0	14.9	254 50.7	29.4	315 43.8	31.4	236 37.5	19.6
14	140 53.7	17 59.2	14.3	269 52.8	29.5	330 45.9	31.3	251 40.1	19.6
15	155 56.2	32 58.4	. . 13.7	284 54.8	. . 29.7	345 48.0	. . 31.1	266 42.7	. . 19.6
16	170 58.6	47 57.7	13.0	299 56.8	29.8	0 50.1	31.0	281 45.3	19.6
17	186 01.1	62 56.9	12.4	314 58.9	29.9	15 52.2	30.8	296 47.9	19.5
18	201 03.6	77 56.1	N21 11.8	330 00.9	S21 30.0	30 54.3	N 5 30.7	311 50.5	S20 19.5
19	216 06.0	92 55.4	11.2	345 03.0	30.2	45 56.4	30.5	326 53.1	19.5
20	231 08.5	107 54.6	10.6	0 05.0	30.3	60 58.5	30.3	341 55.6	19.5
21	246 10.9	122 53.8	. . 10.0	15 07.0	. . 30.4	76 00.6	. . 30.2	356 58.2	. . 19.5
22	261 13.4	137 53.1	09.4	30 09.1	30.5	91 02.7	30.0	12 00.8	19.5
23	276 15.9	152 52.3	08.8	45 11.1	30.7	106 04.8	29.9	27 03.4	19.5
13 00 (WEDNESDAY)	291 18.3	167 51.5	N21 08.1	60 13.1	S21 30.8	121 06.9	N 5 29.7	42 06.0	S20 19.5
01	306 20.8	182 50.8	07.5	75 15.1	30.9	136 09.0	29.5	57 08.6	19.5
02	321 23.3	197 50.0	06.9	90 17.2	31.1	151 11.2	29.4	72 11.2	19.5
03	336 25.7	212 49.3	. . 06.3	105 19.2	. . 31.2	166 13.3	. . 29.2	87 13.8	. . 19.5
04	351 28.2	227 48.5	05.7	120 21.2	31.3	181 15.4	29.1	102 16.4	19.4
05	6 30.7	242 47.7	05.0	135 23.2	31.5	196 17.5	28.9	117 18.9	19.4
06	21 33.1	257 47.0	N21 04.4	150 25.3	S21 31.6	211 19.6	N 5 28.8	132 21.5	S20 19.4
07	36 35.6	272 46.2	03.8	165 27.3	31.7	226 21.7	28.6	147 24.1	19.4
08	51 38.1	287 45.5	03.2	180 29.3	31.8	241 23.8	28.4	162 26.7	19.4
09	66 40.5	302 44.7	. . 02.5	195 31.3	. . 32.0	256 25.9	. . 28.3	177 29.3	. . 19.4
10	81 43.0	317 43.9	01.9	210 33.3	32.1	271 28.0	28.1	192 31.9	19.4
11	96 45.4	332 43.2	01.3	225 35.3	32.2	286 30.1	28.0	207 34.5	19.4
12	111 47.9	347 42.4	N21 00.7	240 37.3	S21 32.4	301 32.2	N 5 27.8	222 37.1	S20 19.4
13	126 50.4	2 41.7	21 00.0	255 39.4	32.5	316 34.3	27.6	237 39.6	19.4
14	141 52.8	17 40.9	20 59.4	270 41.4	32.6	331 36.4	27.5	252 42.2	19.4
15	156 55.3	32 40.2	. . 58.8	285 43.4	. . 32.8	346 38.5	. . 27.3	267 44.8	. . 19.4
16	171 57.8	47 39.4	58.1	300 45.4	32.9	1 40.6	27.2	282 47.4	19.3
17	187 00.2	62 38.6	57.5	315 47.4	33.0	16 42.7	27.0	297 50.0	19.3
18	202 02.7	77 37.9	N20 56.9	330 49.4	S21 33.2	31 44.8	N 5 26.8	312 52.6	S20 19.3
19	217 05.2	92 37.1	56.2	345 51.4	33.3	46 46.9	26.7	327 55.2	19.3
20	232 07.6	107 36.4	55.6	0 53.4	33.4	61 49.0	26.5	342 57.8	19.3
21	247 10.1	122 35.6	. . 54.9	15 55.4	. . 33.6	76 51.1	. . 26.4	358 00.3	. . 19.3
22	262 12.5	137 34.9	54.3	30 57.4	33.7	91 53.2	26.2	13 02.9	19.3
23	277 15.0	152 34.1	53.7	45 59.4	33.8	106 55.3	26.0	28 05.5	19.3
Mer. Pass.	h m 4 38.0	v −0.8	d 0.6	v 2.0	d 0.1	v 2.1	d 0.2	v 2.6	d 0.0

STARS

Name	SHA ° ′	Dec ° ′
Acamar	315 17.0	S40 14.2
Achernar	335 25.4	S57 09.0
Acrux	173 06.9	S63 11.7
Adhara	255 11.3	S28 59.8
Aldebaran	290 47.2	N16 32.3
Alioth	166 19.0	N55 52.6
Alkaid	152 57.3	N49 14.2
Al Na'ir	27 40.9	S46 52.6
Alnilam	275 44.6	S 1 11.7
Alphard	217 54.3	S 8 43.9
Alphecca	126 09.1	N26 39.9
Alpheratz	357 41.2	N29 10.8
Altair	62 05.9	N 8 54.9
Ankaa	353 13.6	S42 12.8
Antares	112 23.4	S26 27.9
Arcturus	145 53.8	N19 06.1
Atria	107 22.8	S69 03.4
Avior	234 17.7	S59 34.0
Bellatrix	278 30.1	N 6 21.7
Betelgeuse	270 59.4	N 7 24.4
Canopus	263 55.8	S52 42.4
Capella	280 31.8	N46 00.5
Deneb	49 29.6	N45 20.5
Denebola	182 31.7	N14 28.9
Diphda	348 53.8	S17 53.7
Dubhe	193 49.7	N61 39.9
Elnath	278 10.3	N28 37.0
Eltanin	90 44.7	N51 29.5
Enif	33 44.8	N 9 57.2
Fomalhaut	15 21.5	S29 31.9
Gacrux	171 58.6	S57 12.5
Gienah	175 50.2	S17 38.0
Hadar	148 44.6	S60 27.3
Hamal	327 58.5	N23 32.2
Kaus Aust.	83 40.7	S34 22.4
Kochab	137 19.8	N74 05.7
Markab	13 36.0	N15 17.7
Menkar	314 13.0	N 4 09.1
Menkent	148 05.0	S36 27.1
Miaplacidus	221 39.9	S69 47.3
Mirfak	308 37.6	N49 54.8
Nunki	75 55.4	S26 16.3
Peacock	53 15.5	S56 40.6
Pollux	243 25.6	N27 59.0
Procyon	244 57.9	N 5 10.8
Rasalhague	96 04.2	N12 33.2
Regulus	207 41.6	N11 53.2
Rigel	281 10.4	S 8 11.1
Rigil Kent.	139 48.6	S60 54.3
Sabik	102 09.9	S15 44.5
Schedar	349 37.9	N56 37.4
Shaula	96 18.7	S37 06.7
Sirius	258 32.2	S16 44.5
Spica	158 29.0	S11 14.8
Suhail	222 51.3	S43 30.2
Vega	80 37.1	N38 48.2
Zuben'ubi	137 03.0	S16 06.5

	SHA ° ′	Mer. Pass. h m
Venus	237 50.8	12 48
Mars	129 04.9	20 00
Jupiter	189 57.2	15 57
Saturn	110 44.6	21 12

Day	UT	SUN GHA	SUN Dec	MOON GHA	MOON v	MOON Dec	MOON d	MOON HP
	d h	° ′	° ′	° ′	′	° ′	′	′
MONDAY	11 00	178 37.5	N22 04.2	101 23.7	15.0	S 1 11.8	9.5	54.7
	01	193 37.4	03.9	115 57.7	14.9	1 21.3	9.5	54.6
	02	208 37.3	03.5	130 31.6	15.0	1 30.8	9.5	54.6
	03	223 37.2	. . 03.2	145 05.6	15.0	1 40.3	9.6	54.6
	04	238 37.1	02.9	159 39.6	15.0	1 49.9	9.4	54.6
	05	253 37.0	02.5	174 13.6	15.0	1 59.3	9.5	54.6
	06	268 37.0	N22 02.2	188 47.6	15.1	S 2 08.8	9.5	54.6
	07	283 36.9	01.8	203 21.7	15.0	2 18.3	9.4	54.6
	08	298 36.8	01.5	217 55.7	15.0	2 27.7	9.5	54.5
	09	313 36.7	. . 01.2	232 29.7	15.1	2 37.2	9.4	54.5
	10	328 36.6	00.8	247 03.8	15.0	2 46.6	9.4	54.5
	11	343 36.6	00.5	261 37.8	15.1	2 56.0	9.4	54.5
	12	358 36.5	N22 00.1	276 11.9	15.1	S 3 05.4	9.4	54.5
	13	13 36.4	21 59.8	290 46.0	15.0	3 14.8	9.3	54.5
	14	28 36.3	59.4	305 20.0	15.1	3 24.1	9.3	54.5
	15	43 36.2	. . 59.1	319 54.1	15.1	3 33.4	9.4	54.5
	16	58 36.2	58.8	334 28.2	15.1	3 42.8	9.3	54.4
	17	73 36.1	58.4	349 02.3	15.0	3 52.1	9.2	54.4
	18	88 36.0	N21 58.1	3 36.3	15.1	S 4 01.3	9.3	54.4
	19	103 35.9	57.7	18 10.4	15.1	4 10.6	9.2	54.4
	20	118 35.8	57.4	32 44.5	15.1	4 19.8	9.2	54.4
	21	133 35.8	. . 57.0	47 18.6	15.1	4 29.0	9.2	54.4
	22	148 35.7	56.7	61 52.7	15.0	4 38.2	9.2	54.4
	23	163 35.6	56.3	76 26.7	15.1	4 47.4	9.2	54.4
TUESDAY	12 00	178 35.5	N21 56.0	91 00.8	15.1	S 4 56.6	9.1	54.4
	01	193 35.4	55.6	105 34.9	15.0	5 05.7	9.1	54.4
	02	208 35.4	55.3	120 08.9	15.1	5 14.8	9.1	54.4
	03	223 35.3	. . 54.9	134 43.0	15.0	5 23.9	9.0	54.3
	04	238 35.2	54.6	149 17.0	15.1	5 32.9	9.0	54.3
	05	253 35.1	54.2	163 51.1	15.0	5 41.9	9.0	54.3
	06	268 35.1	N21 53.9	178 25.1	15.0	S 5 50.9	9.0	54.3
	07	283 35.0	53.5	192 59.1	15.1	5 59.9	9.0	54.3
	08	298 34.9	53.1	207 33.2	15.0	6 08.9	8.9	54.3
	09	313 34.8	. . 52.8	222 07.2	15.0	6 17.8	8.9	54.3
	10	328 34.8	52.4	236 41.2	15.0	6 26.7	8.9	54.3
	11	343 34.7	52.1	251 15.2	14.9	6 35.6	8.8	54.3
	12	358 34.6	N21 51.7	265 49.1	15.0	S 6 44.4	8.8	54.3
	13	13 34.5	51.4	280 23.1	15.0	6 53.2	8.8	54.3
	14	28 34.5	51.0	294 57.1	14.9	7 02.0	8.7	54.3
	15	43 34.4	. . 50.6	309 31.0	14.9	7 10.7	8.8	54.3
	16	58 34.3	50.3	324 04.9	14.9	7 19.5	8.6	54.3
	17	73 34.2	49.9	338 38.8	14.9	7 28.1	8.7	54.3
	18	88 34.2	N21 49.5	353 12.7	14.9	S 7 36.8	8.6	54.3
	19	103 34.1	49.2	7 46.6	14.9	7 45.4	8.6	54.3
	20	118 34.0	48.8	22 20.5	14.8	7 54.0	8.6	54.3
	21	133 33.9	. . 48.5	36 54.3	14.8	8 02.6	8.5	54.2
	22	148 33.9	48.1	51 28.1	14.8	8 11.1	8.5	54.2
	23	163 33.8	47.7	66 01.9	14.8	8 19.6	8.5	54.2
WEDNESDAY	13 00	178 33.7	N21 47.4	80 35.7	14.8	S 8 28.1	8.4	54.2
	01	193 33.6	47.0	95 09.5	14.7	8 36.5	8.4	54.2
	02	208 33.6	46.6	109 43.2	14.8	8 44.9	8.3	54.2
	03	223 33.5	. . 46.3	124 17.0	14.7	8 53.2	8.3	54.2
	04	238 33.4	45.9	138 50.7	14.6	9 01.5	8.3	54.2
	05	253 33.4	45.5	153 24.3	14.7	9 09.8	8.3	54.2
	06	268 33.3	N21 45.2	167 58.0	14.6	S 9 18.1	8.2	54.2
	07	283 33.2	44.8	182 31.6	14.6	9 26.3	8.1	54.2
	08	298 33.1	44.4	197 05.2	14.6	9 34.4	8.1	54.2
	09	313 33.1	. . 44.0	211 38.8	14.6	9 42.5	8.1	54.2
	10	328 33.0	43.7	226 12.4	14.5	9 50.6	8.1	54.2
	11	343 32.9	43.3	240 45.9	14.5	9 58.7	8.0	54.2
	12	358 32.9	N21 42.9	255 19.4	14.5	S10 06.7	7.9	54.2
	13	13 32.8	42.5	269 52.9	14.4	10 14.6	8.0	54.2
	14	28 32.7	42.2	284 26.3	14.5	10 22.6	7.8	54.3
	15	43 32.7	. . 41.8	298 59.8	14.4	10 30.4	7.9	54.3
	16	58 32.6	41.4	313 33.2	14.3	10 38.3	7.8	54.3
	17	73 32.5	41.0	328 06.5	14.4	10 46.1	7.7	54.3
	18	88 32.4	N21 40.7	342 39.9	14.3	S10 53.8	7.7	54.3
	19	103 32.4	40.3	357 13.2	14.2	11 01.5	7.7	54.3
	20	118 32.3	39.9	11 46.4	14.3	11 09.2	7.6	54.3
	21	133 32.2	. . 39.5	26 19.7	14.2	11 16.8	7.6	54.3
	22	148 32.2	39.1	40 52.9	14.1	11 24.4	7.5	54.3
	23	163 32.1	38.8	55 26.0	14.2	S11 31.9	7.5	54.3
		SD 15.8	*d* 0.4	SD	14.8	14.8		14.8

Lat.	Twilight Naut.	Twilight Civil	Sunrise	Moonrise 11	Moonrise 12	Moonrise 13	Moonrise 14
°	h m	h m	h m	h m	h m	h m	h m
N 72	▭	▭	▭	12 16	13 50	15 26	17 07
N 70	▭	▭	▭	12 11	13 39	15 08	16 38
68	▭	▭	▭	12 07	13 31	14 54	16 18
66	////	////	01 24	12 04	13 24	14 43	16 01
64	////	////	02 08	12 02	13 18	14 33	15 48
62	////	00 23	02 37	11 59	13 12	14 25	15 37
60	////	01 36	02 59	11 57	13 08	14 18	15 27
N 58	////	02 10	03 16	11 56	13 04	14 12	15 19
56	00 21	02 34	03 31	11 54	13 00	14 06	15 11
54	01 29	02 53	03 44	11 53	12 57	14 01	15 05
52	01 59	03 09	03 55	11 51	12 54	13 57	14 59
50	02 22	03 22	04 05	11 50	12 52	13 53	14 54
45	03 02	03 49	04 25	11 48	12 46	13 44	14 42
N 40	03 29	04 10	04 42	11 46	12 42	13 37	14 33
35	03 51	04 27	04 56	11 44	12 38	13 31	14 25
30	04 08	04 41	05 08	11 42	12 34	13 26	14 18
20	04 35	05 04	05 28	11 39	12 28	13 16	14 06
N 10	04 56	05 23	05 46	11 37	12 23	13 08	13 55
0	05 14	05 40	06 02	11 35	12 18	13 01	13 45
S 10	05 30	05 56	06 18	11 33	12 13	12 53	13 35
20	05 45	06 12	06 35	11 30	12 07	12 45	13 25
30	06 00	06 29	06 55	11 28	12 02	12 36	13 13
35	06 07	06 39	07 06	11 26	11 58	12 31	13 06
40	06 16	06 50	07 20	11 25	11 54	12 25	12 59
45	06 25	07 02	07 35	11 23	11 50	12 19	12 50
S 50	06 36	07 16	07 54	11 20	11 45	12 10	12 39
52	06 40	07 23	08 03	11 19	11 42	12 07	12 34
54	06 45	07 30	08 13	11 18	11 40	12 03	12 28
56	06 51	07 39	08 24	11 17	11 37	11 58	12 22
58	06 57	07 48	08 37	11 16	11 33	11 53	12 15
S 60	07 03	07 58	08 52	11 14	11 30	11 47	12 08

Lat.	Sunset	Twilight Civil	Twilight Naut.	Moonset 11	Moonset 12	Moonset 13	Moonset 14
°	h m	h m	h m	h m	h m	h m	h m
N 72	▭	▭	▭	22 53	22 48	22 41	22 34
N 70	▭	▭	▭	23 00	23 00	23 01	23 03
68	▭	▭	▭	23 05	23 10	23 16	23 25
66	22 44	////	////	23 10	23 18	23 28	23 42
64	22 01	////	////	23 14	23 25	23 39	23 56
62	21 33	23 36	////	23 17	23 31	23 48	24 08
60	21 11	22 32	////	23 20	23 37	23 55	24 18
N 58	20 54	22 00	////	23 23	23 42	24 02	00 02
56	20 39	21 36	23 39	23 25	23 46	24 08	00 08
54	20 27	21 17	22 40	23 27	23 50	24 14	00 14
52	20 16	21 02	22 10	23 29	23 53	24 19	00 19
50	20 06	20 49	21 48	23 31	23 56	24 23	00 23
45	19 46	20 22	21 09	23 35	24 03	00 03	00 33
N 40	19 29	20 01	20 41	23 38	24 09	00 09	00 41
35	19 15	19 44	20 20	23 41	24 14	00 14	00 47
30	19 03	19 30	20 03	23 44	24 18	00 18	00 54
20	18 43	19 07	19 36	23 48	24 25	00 25	01 04
N 10	18 26	18 48	19 15	23 52	24 32	00 32	01 13
0	18 09	18 32	18 57	23 55	24 38	00 38	01 22
S 10	17 53	18 16	18 42	23 59	24 45	00 45	01 31
20	17 36	18 00	18 27	24 03	00 03	00 51	01 40
30	17 16	17 42	18 12	24 07	00 07	00 59	01 51
35	17 05	17 33	18 04	24 10	00 10	01 03	01 57
40	16 52	17 22	17 56	24 13	00 13	01 08	02 04
45	16 37	17 10	17 46	24 16	00 16	01 14	02 12
S 50	16 18	16 55	17 36	24 20	00 20	01 21	02 22
52	16 09	16 49	17 31	24 22	00 22	01 24	02 27
54	15 59	16 41	17 26	24 24	00 24	01 28	02 32
56	15 48	16 33	17 21	24 26	00 26	01 32	02 37
58	15 35	16 24	17 15	24 28	00 28	01 36	02 44
S 60	15 20	16 14	17 09	24 31	00 31	01 41	02 51

Day	SUN Eqn. of Time 00^h	SUN Eqn. of Time 12^h	SUN Mer. Pass.	MOON Mer. Pass. Upper	MOON Mer. Pass. Lower	MOON Age	MOON Phase
d	m s	m s	h m	h m	h m	d %	
11	05 30	05 34	12 06	17 45	05 24	07 45	
12	05 38	05 41	12 06	18 28	06 07	08 55	
13	05 45	05 48	12 06	19 11	06 50	09 64	

	UT	ARIES	VENUS −3·9		MARS −1·1		JUPITER −1·8		SATURN +0·2	
	d h	GHA ° ′	GHA ° ′	Dec ° ′	GHA ° ′	Dec ° ′	GHA ° ′	Dec ° ′	GHA ° ′	Dec ° ′
	14 00	292 17.5	167 33.4	N20 53.0	61 01.4	S21 34.0	121 57.4	N 5 25.9	43 08.1	S20 19.3
	01	307 19.9	182 32.6	52.4	76 03.4	34.1	136 59.5	25.7	58 10.7	19.3
	02	322 22.4	197 31.9	51.7	91 05.4	34.2	152 01.6	25.6	73 13.3	19.3
	03	337 24.9	212 31.1	. . 51.1	106 07.4	. . 34.4	167 03.7	. . 25.4	88 15.9	. . 19.2
	04	352 27.3	227 30.4	50.4	121 09.4	34.5	182 05.8	25.2	103 18.4	19.2
	05	7 29.8	242 29.6	49.8	136 11.4	34.6	197 07.9	25.1	118 21.0	19.2
	06	22 32.3	257 28.9	N20 49.1	151 13.4	S21 34.8	212 10.0	N 5 24.9	133 23.6	S20 19.2
	07	37 34.7	272 28.1	48.5	166 15.3	34.9	227 12.1	24.8	148 26.2	19.2
THURSDAY	08	52 37.2	287 27.4	47.8	181 17.3	35.0	242 14.2	24.6	163 28.8	19.2
	09	67 39.7	302 26.6	. . 47.2	196 19.3	. . 35.2	257 16.3	. . 24.4	178 31.4	. . 19.2
	10	82 42.1	317 25.9	46.5	211 21.3	35.3	272 18.4	24.3	193 33.9	19.2
	11	97 44.6	332 25.1	45.9	226 23.3	35.5	287 20.5	24.1	208 36.5	19.2
	12	112 47.0	347 24.4	N20 45.2	241 25.3	S21 35.6	302 22.6	N 5 24.0	223 39.1	S20 19.2
	13	127 49.5	2 23.6	44.6	256 27.2	35.7	317 24.7	23.8	238 41.7	19.2
	14	142 52.0	17 22.9	43.9	271 29.2	35.9	332 26.8	23.6	253 44.3	19.2
	15	157 54.4	32 22.2	. . 43.3	286 31.2	. . 36.0	347 28.9	. . 23.5	268 46.9	. . 19.2
	16	172 56.9	47 21.4	42.6	301 33.2	36.1	2 31.0	23.3	283 49.4	19.1
	17	187 59.4	62 20.7	41.9	316 35.1	36.3	17 33.1	23.1	298 52.0	19.1
	18	203 01.8	77 19.9	N20 41.3	331 37.1	S21 36.4	32 35.2	N 5 23.0	313 54.6	S20 19.1
	19	218 04.3	92 19.2	40.6	346 39.1	36.6	47 37.3	22.8	328 57.2	19.1
	20	233 06.8	107 18.4	40.0	1 41.1	36.7	62 39.4	22.7	343 59.8	19.1
	21	248 09.2	122 17.7	. . 39.3	16 43.0	. . 36.8	77 41.5	. . 22.5	359 02.4	. . 19.1
	22	263 11.7	137 17.0	38.6	31 45.0	37.0	92 43.6	22.3	14 04.9	19.1
	23	278 14.2	152 16.2	38.0	46 47.0	37.1	107 45.7	22.2	29 07.5	19.1
	15 00	293 16.6	167 15.5	N20 37.3	61 48.9	S21 37.3	122 47.8	N 5 22.0	44 10.1	S20 19.1
	01	308 19.1	182 14.7	36.6	76 50.9	37.4	137 49.9	21.9	59 12.7	19.1
	02	323 21.5	197 14.0	36.0	91 52.9	37.5	152 52.0	21.7	74 15.3	19.1
	03	338 24.0	212 13.3	. . 35.3	106 54.8	. . 37.7	167 54.1	. . 21.5	89 17.9	. . 19.1
	04	353 26.5	227 12.5	34.6	121 56.8	37.8	182 56.2	21.4	104 20.4	19.0
	05	8 28.9	242 11.8	34.0	136 58.7	38.0	197 58.3	21.2	119 23.0	19.0
	06	23 31.4	257 11.0	N20 33.3	152 00.7	S21 38.1	213 00.4	N 5 21.0	134 25.6	S20 19.0
	07	38 33.9	272 10.3	32.6	167 02.7	38.2	228 02.5	20.9	149 28.2	19.0
	08	53 36.3	287 09.6	31.9	182 04.6	38.4	243 04.6	20.7	164 30.8	19.0
FRIDAY	09	68 38.8	302 08.8	. . 31.3	197 06.6	. . 38.5	258 06.6	. . 20.6	179 33.3	. . 19.0
	10	83 41.3	317 08.1	30.6	212 08.5	38.7	273 08.7	20.4	194 35.9	19.0
	11	98 43.7	332 07.4	29.9	227 10.5	38.8	288 10.8	20.2	209 38.5	19.0
	12	113 46.2	347 06.6	N20 29.2	242 12.4	S21 39.0	303 12.9	N 5 20.1	224 41.1	S20 19.0
	13	128 48.6	2 05.9	28.5	257 14.4	39.1	318 15.0	19.9	239 43.7	19.0
	14	143 51.1	17 05.2	27.9	272 16.3	39.2	333 17.1	19.7	254 46.2	19.0
	15	158 53.6	32 04.4	. . 27.2	287 18.3	. . 39.4	348 19.2	. . 19.6	269 48.8	. . 19.0
	16	173 56.0	47 03.7	26.5	302 20.2	39.5	3 21.3	19.4	284 51.4	19.0
	17	188 58.5	62 03.0	25.8	317 22.2	39.7	18 23.4	19.3	299 54.0	18.9
	18	204 01.0	77 02.2	N20 25.1	332 24.1	S21 39.8	33 25.5	N 5 19.1	314 56.6	S20 18.9
	19	219 03.4	92 01.5	24.4	347 26.0	40.0	48 27.6	18.9	329 59.1	18.9
	20	234 05.9	107 00.8	23.8	2 28.0	40.1	63 29.7	18.8	345 01.7	18.9
	21	249 08.4	122 00.0	. . 23.1	17 29.9	. . 40.2	78 31.8	. . 18.6	0 04.3	. . 18.9
	22	264 10.8	136 59.3	22.4	32 31.9	40.4	93 33.9	18.4	15 06.9	18.9
	23	279 13.3	151 58.6	21.7	47 33.8	40.5	108 36.0	18.3	30 09.5	18.9
	16 00	294 15.8	166 57.9	N20 21.0	62 35.7	S21 40.7	123 38.1	N 5 18.1	45 12.0	S20 18.9
	01	309 18.2	181 57.1	20.3	77 37.7	40.8	138 40.2	18.0	60 14.6	18.9
	02	324 20.7	196 56.4	19.6	92 39.6	41.0	153 42.3	17.8	75 17.2	18.9
	03	339 23.1	211 55.7	. . 18.9	107 41.5	. . 41.1	168 44.3	. . 17.6	90 19.8	. . 18.9
	04	354 25.6	226 54.9	18.2	122 43.5	41.3	183 46.4	17.5	105 22.4	18.9
	05	9 28.1	241 54.2	17.5	137 45.4	41.4	198 48.5	17.3	120 24.9	18.9
	06	24 30.5	256 53.5	N20 16.8	152 47.3	S21 41.6	213 50.6	N 5 17.1	135 27.5	S20 18.9
	07	39 33.0	271 52.8	16.1	167 49.2	41.7	228 52.7	17.0	150 30.1	18.8
SATURDAY	08	54 35.5	286 52.0	15.4	182 51.2	41.8	243 54.8	16.8	165 32.7	18.8
	09	69 37.9	301 51.3	. . 14.7	197 53.1	. . 42.0	258 56.9	. . 16.6	180 35.2	. . 18.8
	10	84 40.4	316 50.6	14.0	212 55.0	42.1	273 59.0	16.5	195 37.8	18.8
	11	99 42.9	331 49.9	13.3	227 56.9	42.3	289 01.1	16.3	210 40.4	18.8
	12	114 45.3	346 49.2	N20 12.6	242 58.9	S21 42.4	304 03.2	N 5 16.1	225 43.0	S20 18.8
	13	129 47.8	1 48.4	11.9	258 00.8	42.6	319 05.3	16.0	240 45.5	18.8
	14	144 50.3	16 47.7	11.2	273 02.7	42.7	334 07.4	15.8	255 48.1	18.8
	15	159 52.7	31 47.0	. . 10.5	288 04.6	. . 42.9	349 09.5	. . 15.7	270 50.7	. . 18.8
	16	174 55.2	46 46.3	09.8	303 06.5	43.0	4 11.5	15.5	285 53.3	18.8
	17	189 57.6	61 45.5	09.1	318 08.4	43.2	19 13.6	15.3	300 55.9	18.8
	18	205 00.1	76 44.8	N20 08.4	333 10.4	S21 43.3	34 15.7	N 5 15.2	315 58.4	S20 18.8
	19	220 02.6	91 44.1	07.7	348 12.3	43.5	49 17.8	15.0	331 01.0	18.8
	20	235 05.0	106 43.4	07.0	3 14.2	43.6	64 19.9	14.8	346 03.6	18.8
	21	250 07.5	121 42.7	. . 06.3	18 16.1	. . 43.8	79 22.0	. . 14.7	1 06.2	. . 18.7
	22	265 10.0	136 42.0	05.5	33 18.0	43.9	94 24.1	14.5	16 08.7	18.7
	23	280 12.4	151 41.2	04.8	48 19.9	44.1	109 26.2	14.3	31 11.3	18.7
	Mer. Pass.	h m 4 26.2	v −0.7	d 0.7	v 1.9	d 0.1	v 2.1	d 0.2	v 2.6	d 0.0

STARS Name	SHA ° ′	Dec ° ′
Acamar	315 17.0	S40 14.2
Achernar	335 25.4	S57 09.0
Acrux	173 06.9	S63 11.7
Adhara	255 11.3	S28 59.8
Aldebaran	290 47.2	N16 32.3
Alioth	166 19.1	N55 52.6
Alkaid	152 57.3	N49 14.2
Al Na'ir	27 40.8	S46 52.6
Alnilam	275 44.5	S 1 11.7
Alphard	217 54.3	S 8 43.9
Alphecca	126 09.1	N26 39.9
Alpheratz	357 41.2	N29 10.8
Altair	62 05.9	N 8 55.0
Ankaa	353 13.6	S42 12.8
Antares	112 23.4	S26 27.9
Arcturus	145 53.8	N19 06.1
Atria	107 22.8	S69 03.4
Avior	234 17.7	S59 33.9
Bellatrix	278 30.1	N 6 21.7
Betelgeuse	270 59.4	N 7 24.4
Canopus	263 55.7	S52 42.4
Capella	280 31.8	N46 00.5
Deneb	49 29.5	N45 20.5
Denebola	182 31.7	N14 28.9
Diphda	348 53.8	S17 53.7
Dubhe	193 49.7	N61 39.9
Elnath	278 10.3	N28 37.0
Eltanin	90 44.7	N51 29.5
Enif	33 44.8	N 9 57.2
Fomalhaut	15 21.5	S29 31.9
Gacrux	171 58.6	S57 12.5
Gienah	175 50.2	S17 38.0
Hadar	148 44.7	S60 27.3
Hamal	327 58.4	N23 32.2
Kaus Aust.	83 40.7	S34 22.4
Kochab	137 19.9	N74 05.7
Markab	13 36.0	N15 17.7
Menkar	314 13.0	N 4 09.1
Menkent	148 05.0	S36 27.1
Miaplacidus	221 39.9	S69 47.3
Mirfak	308 37.5	N49 54.8
Nunki	75 55.4	S26 16.3
Peacock	53 15.5	S56 40.6
Pollux	243 25.6	N27 59.0
Procyon	244 57.9	N 5 10.8
Rasalhague	96 04.2	N12 33.2
Regulus	207 41.6	N11 53.2
Rigel	281 10.3	S 8 11.1
Rigil Kent.	139 48.6	S60 54.3
Sabik	102 09.9	S15 44.5
Schedar	349 37.9	N56 37.4
Shaula	96 18.7	S37 06.8
Sirius	258 32.2	S16 44.5
Spica	158 29.0	S11 14.8
Suhail	222 51.3	S43 30.1
Vega	80 37.1	N38 48.2
Zuben'ubi	137 03.0	S16 06.5

	SHA ° ′	Mer. Pass. h m
Venus	233 58.9	12 52
Mars	128 32.3	19 50
Jupiter	189 31.2	15 47
Saturn	110 53.5	21 00

UT d h	SUN GHA ° ′	SUN Dec ° ′	MOON GHA ° ′	v ′	MOON Dec ° ′	d ′	HP ′
14 00	178 32.0	N21 38.4	69 59.2	14.1	S11 39.4	7.4	54.3
01	193 32.0	38.0	84 32.3	14.1	11 46.8	7.4	54.3
02	208 31.9	37.6	99 05.4	14.0	11 54.2	7.3	54.3
03	223 31.8	. . 37.2	113 38.4	14.0	12 01.5	7.3	54.3
04	238 31.8	36.8	128 11.4	14.0	12 08.8	7.2	54.3
05	253 31.7	36.5	142 44.4	13.9	12 16.0	7.2	54.3
06	268 31.6	N21 36.1	157 17.3	13.9	S12 23.2	7.1	54.3
T 07	283 31.6	35.7	171 50.2	13.9	12 30.3	7.1	54.3
H 08	298 31.5	35.3	186 23.1	13.8	12 37.4	7.0	54.3
U 09	313 31.4	. . 34.9	200 55.9	13.8	12 44.4	7.0	54.3
R 10	328 31.4	34.5	215 28.7	13.7	12 51.4	6.9	54.4
S 11	343 31.3	34.1	230 01.4	13.7	12 58.3	6.9	54.4
D 12	358 31.2	N21 33.8	244 34.1	13.7	S13 05.2	6.8	54.4
A 13	13 31.2	33.4	259 06.8	13.6	13 12.0	6.8	54.4
Y 14	28 31.1	33.0	273 39.4	13.6	13 18.8	6.7	54.4
15	43 31.1	. . 32.6	288 12.0	13.6	13 25.5	6.6	54.4
16	58 31.0	32.2	302 44.6	13.5	13 32.1	6.6	54.4
17	73 30.9	31.8	317 17.1	13.4	13 38.7	6.6	54.4
18	88 30.9	N21 31.4	331 49.5	13.5	S13 45.3	6.4	54.4
19	103 30.8	31.0	346 22.0	13.3	13 51.7	6.5	54.4
20	118 30.7	30.6	0 54.3	13.4	13 58.2	6.3	54.4
21	133 30.7	. . 30.2	15 26.7	13.3	14 04.5	6.3	54.5
22	148 30.6	29.8	29 59.0	13.2	14 10.8	6.3	54.5
23	163 30.5	29.4	44 31.2	13.3	14 17.1	6.1	54.5
15 00	178 30.5	N21 29.0	59 03.5	13.1	S14 23.2	6.2	54.5
01	193 30.4	28.6	73 35.6	13.2	14 29.4	6.0	54.5
02	208 30.4	28.2	88 07.8	13.1	14 35.4	6.0	54.5
03	223 30.3	. . 27.8	102 39.9	13.0	14 41.4	6.0	54.5
04	238 30.2	27.4	117 11.9	13.0	14 47.4	5.8	54.5
05	253 30.2	27.0	131 43.9	12.9	14 53.2	5.8	54.6
06	268 30.1	N21 26.6	146 15.8	13.0	S14 59.0	5.8	54.6
07	283 30.1	26.2	160 47.8	12.8	15 04.8	5.7	54.6
08	298 30.0	25.8	175 19.6	12.8	15 10.5	5.6	54.6
F 09	313 29.9	. . 25.4	189 51.4	12.8	15 16.1	5.5	54.6
R 10	328 29.9	25.0	204 23.2	12.8	15 21.6	5.5	54.6
I 11	343 29.8	24.6	218 55.0	12.6	15 27.1	5.4	54.6
D 12	358 29.8	N21 24.2	233 26.6	12.7	S15 32.5	5.4	54.7
A 13	13 29.7	23.8	247 58.3	12.6	15 37.9	5.2	54.7
Y 14	28 29.6	23.4	262 29.9	12.5	15 43.1	5.2	54.7
15	43 29.6	. . 23.0	277 01.4	12.5	15 48.3	5.2	54.7
16	58 29.5	22.6	291 32.9	12.5	15 53.5	5.1	54.7
17	73 29.5	22.2	306 04.4	12.4	15 58.6	5.0	54.7
18	88 29.4	N21 21.8	320 35.8	12.4	S16 03.6	4.9	54.7
19	103 29.3	21.4	335 07.2	12.3	16 08.5	4.8	54.8
20	118 29.3	21.0	349 38.5	12.2	16 13.3	4.8	54.8
21	133 29.2	. . 20.5	4 09.7	12.3	16 18.1	4.7	54.8
22	148 29.2	20.1	18 41.0	12.2	16 22.8	4.7	54.8
23	163 29.1	19.7	33 12.2	12.1	16 27.5	4.5	54.8
16 00	178 29.1	N21 19.3	47 43.3	12.1	S16 32.0	4.5	54.8
01	193 29.0	18.9	62 14.4	12.0	16 36.5	4.4	54.9
02	208 28.9	18.5	76 45.4	12.0	16 40.9	4.4	54.9
03	223 28.9	. . 18.1	91 16.4	11.9	16 45.3	4.2	54.9
04	238 28.8	17.7	105 47.3	11.9	16 49.5	4.2	54.9
05	253 28.8	17.2	120 18.2	11.9	16 53.7	4.1	54.9
06	268 28.7	N21 16.8	134 49.1	11.8	S16 57.8	4.1	54.9
S 07	283 28.7	16.4	149 19.9	11.8	17 01.9	3.9	55.0
08	298 28.6	16.0	163 50.7	11.7	17 05.8	3.9	55.0
A 09	313 28.6	. . 15.6	178 21.4	11.7	17 09.7	3.8	55.0
T 10	328 28.5	15.2	192 52.1	11.6	17 13.5	3.7	55.0
U 11	343 28.5	14.7	207 22.7	11.6	17 17.2	3.6	55.0
R 12	358 28.4	N21 14.3	221 53.3	11.5	S17 20.8	3.6	55.1
D 13	13 28.3	13.9	236 23.8	11.5	17 24.4	3.4	55.1
A 14	28 28.3	13.5	250 54.3	11.4	17 27.8	3.4	55.1
Y 15	43 28.2	. . 13.1	265 24.7	11.4	17 31.2	3.3	55.1
16	58 28.2	12.6	279 55.1	11.4	17 34.5	3.2	55.1
17	73 28.1	12.2	294 25.5	11.3	17 37.7	3.2	55.2
18	88 28.1	N21 11.8	308 55.8	11.2	S17 40.9	3.0	55.2
19	103 28.0	11.4	323 26.0	11.3	17 43.9	3.0	55.2
20	118 28.0	10.9	337 56.3	11.1	17 46.9	2.9	55.2
21	133 27.9	. . 10.5	352 26.4	11.2	17 49.8	2.8	55.2
22	148 27.9	10.1	6 56.6	11.1	17 52.6	2.7	55.3
23	163 27.8	09.7	21 26.7	11.0	S17 55.3	2.6	55.3
	SD 15.8	*d* 0.4	SD 14.8		14.9		15.0

Lat. °	Twilight Naut. h m	Twilight Civil h m	Sunrise h m	Moonrise 14 h m	Moonrise 15 h m	Moonrise 16 h m	Moonrise 17 h m
N 72	▭	▭	▭	17 07	18 54	21 11	■
N 70	▭	▭	▭	16 38	18 09	19 37	20 50
68	▭	▭	▭	16 18	17 40	18 57	20 03
66	////	////	01 37	16 01	17 18	18 30	19 33
64	////	////	02 17	15 48	17 01	18 09	19 10
62	////	00 53	02 44	15 37	16 46	17 52	18 52
60	////	01 46	03 04	15 27	16 34	17 38	18 37
N 58	////	02 17	03 21	15 19	16 24	17 27	18 24
56	00 48	02 40	03 35	15 11	16 15	17 16	18 13
54	01 37	02 58	03 48	15 05	16 07	17 07	18 03
52	02 06	03 13	03 58	14 59	16 00	16 59	17 55
50	02 27	03 26	04 08	14 54	15 54	16 52	17 47
45	03 05	03 52	04 28	14 42	15 40	16 36	17 30
N 40	03 32	04 12	04 44	14 33	15 28	16 23	17 17
35	03 53	04 29	04 58	14 25	15 19	16 13	17 05
30	04 10	04 42	05 09	14 18	15 10	16 03	16 55
20	04 36	05 05	05 29	14 06	14 56	15 47	16 38
N 10	04 57	05 24	05 46	13 55	14 43	15 33	16 23
0	05 14	05 40	06 02	13 45	14 31	15 19	16 09
S 10	05 30	05 56	06 18	13 35	14 20	15 06	15 55
20	05 44	06 11	06 35	13 25	14 07	14 52	15 40
30	05 59	06 28	06 54	13 13	13 53	14 36	15 23
35	06 07	06 38	07 05	13 06	13 45	14 27	15 14
40	06 15	06 48	07 18	12 59	13 35	14 16	15 02
45	06 24	07 00	07 33	12 50	13 24	14 04	14 49
S 50	06 34	07 14	07 51	12 39	13 11	13 49	14 33
52	06 38	07 21	08 00	12 34	13 05	13 42	14 25
54	06 43	07 28	08 10	12 28	12 58	13 34	14 17
56	06 48	07 36	08 21	12 22	12 51	13 25	14 07
58	06 54	07 44	08 33	12 15	12 42	13 15	13 57
S 60	07 00	07 54	08 48	12 08	12 33	13 04	13 44

Lat. °	Sunset h m	Twilight Civil h m	Twilight Naut. h m	Moonset 14 h m	Moonset 15 h m	Moonset 16 h m	Moonset 17 h m
N 72	▭	▭	▭	22 34	22 23	21 46	■
N 70	▭	▭	▭	23 03	23 08	23 21	23 52
68	▭	▭	▭	23 25	23 38	24 01	00 01
66	22 31	////	////	23 42	24 00	00 00	00 28
64	21 53	////	////	23 56	24 18	00 18	00 49
62	21 27	23 13	////	24 08	00 08	00 33	01 06
60	21 06	22 23	////	24 18	00 18	00 45	01 21
N 58	20 50	21 53	////	00 02	00 26	00 56	01 33
56	20 36	21 31	23 18	00 08	00 34	01 05	01 43
54	20 24	21 13	22 32	00 14	00 41	01 14	01 53
52	20 13	20 58	22 04	00 19	00 47	01 21	02 01
50	20 03	20 45	21 44	00 23	00 53	01 28	02 08
45	19 44	20 19	21 06	00 33	01 05	01 42	02 24
N 40	19 28	19 59	20 39	00 41	01 15	01 54	02 37
35	19 14	19 43	20 18	00 47	01 24	02 04	02 48
30	19 02	19 29	20 02	00 54	01 32	02 13	02 58
20	18 43	19 07	19 35	01 04	01 45	02 28	03 15
N 10	18 26	18 48	19 15	01 13	01 56	02 42	03 30
0	18 10	18 32	18 58	01 22	02 07	02 54	03 43
S 10	17 54	18 16	18 42	01 31	02 18	03 07	03 57
20	17 37	18 01	18 28	01 40	02 30	03 20	04 12
30	17 18	17 44	18 13	01 51	02 43	03 36	04 28
35	17 07	17 35	18 06	01 57	02 51	03 45	04 38
40	16 54	17 24	17 58	02 04	03 00	03 55	04 49
45	16 39	17 12	17 49	02 12	03 10	04 07	05 02
S 50	16 21	16 58	17 39	02 22	03 22	04 21	05 18
52	16 12	16 52	17 34	02 27	03 28	04 28	05 26
54	16 03	16 45	17 30	02 32	03 35	04 36	05 34
56	15 52	16 37	17 24	02 37	03 42	04 44	05 43
58	15 39	16 28	17 19	02 44	03 50	04 54	05 54
S 60	15 25	16 18	17 13	02 51	03 59	05 05	06 06

Day d	SUN Eqn. of Time 00^h m s	SUN Eqn. of Time 12^h m s	SUN Mer. Pass. h m	MOON Mer. Pass. Upper h m	MOON Mer. Pass. Lower h m	MOON Age d	MOON %	Phase
14	05 52	05 55	12 06	19 56	07 34	10	73	
15	05 58	06 01	12 06	20 43	08 19	11	81	◐
16	06 04	06 06	12 06	21 31	09 07	12	88	

	UT	ARIES	VENUS −3·9		MARS −1·0		JUPITER −1·8		SATURN +0·3	
	d h	GHA ° ′	GHA ° ′	Dec ° ′	GHA ° ′	Dec ° ′	GHA ° ′	Dec ° ′	GHA ° ′	Dec ° ′
	17 00	295 14.9	166 40.5	N20 04.1	63 21.8	S21 44.2	124 28.3	N 5 14.2	46 13.9	S20 18.7
	01	310 17.4	181 39.8	03.4	78 23.7	44.4	139 30.4	14.0	61 16.5	18.7
	02	325 19.8	196 39.1	02.7	93 25.6	44.5	154 32.5	13.8	76 19.0	18.7
	03	340 22.3	211 38.4	. . 02.0	108 27.5	. . 44.7	169 34.5	. . 13.7	91 21.6	. . 18.7
	04	355 24.8	226 37.7	01.3	123 29.4	44.8	184 36.6	13.5	106 24.2	18.7
	05	10 27.2	241 36.9	20 00.5	138 31.3	45.0	199 38.7	13.4	121 26.8	18.7
	06	25 29.7	256 36.2	N19 59.8	153 33.2	S21 45.1	214 40.8	N 5 13.2	136 29.3	S20 18.7
	07	40 32.1	271 35.5	59.1	168 35.1	45.3	229 42.9	13.0	151 31.9	18.7
	08	55 34.6	286 34.8	58.4	183 37.0	45.4	244 45.0	12.9	166 34.5	18.7
S	09	70 37.1	301 34.1	. . 57.6	198 38.9	. . 45.6	259 47.1	. . 12.7	181 37.1	. . 18.7
U	10	85 39.5	316 33.4	56.9	213 40.8	45.7	274 49.2	12.5	196 39.6	18.7
N	11	100 42.0	331 32.7	56.2	228 42.7	45.9	289 51.3	12.4	211 42.2	18.6
D	12	115 44.5	346 32.0	N19 55.5	243 44.6	S21 46.0	304 53.3	N 5 12.2	226 44.8	S20 18.6
A	13	130 46.9	1 31.2	54.7	258 46.5	46.2	319 55.4	12.0	241 47.3	18.6
Y	14	145 49.4	16 30.5	54.0	273 48.3	46.3	334 57.5	11.9	256 49.9	18.6
	15	160 51.9	31 29.8	. . 53.3	288 50.2	. . 46.5	349 59.6	. . 11.7	271 52.5	. . 18.6
	16	175 54.3	46 29.1	52.6	303 52.1	46.6	5 01.7	11.5	286 55.1	18.6
	17	190 56.8	61 28.4	51.8	318 54.0	46.8	20 03.8	11.4	301 57.6	18.6
	18	205 59.3	76 27.7	N19 51.1	333 55.9	S21 46.9	35 05.9	N 5 11.2	317 00.2	S20 18.6
	19	221 01.7	91 27.0	50.4	348 57.8	47.1	50 08.0	11.0	332 02.8	18.6
	20	236 04.2	106 26.3	49.6	3 59.7	47.3	65 10.0	10.9	347 05.4	18.6
	21	251 06.6	121 25.6	. . 48.9	19 01.5	. . 47.4	80 12.1	. . 10.7	2 07.9	. . 18.6
	22	266 09.1	136 24.9	48.1	34 03.4	47.6	95 14.2	10.5	17 10.5	18.6
	23	281 11.6	151 24.2	47.4	49 05.3	47.7	110 16.3	10.4	32 13.1	18.6
	18 00	296 14.0	166 23.5	N19 46.7	64 07.2	S21 47.9	125 18.4	N 5 10.2	47 15.6	S20 18.6
	01	311 16.5	181 22.8	45.9	79 09.0	48.0	140 20.5	10.0	62 18.2	18.6
	02	326 19.0	196 22.1	45.2	94 10.9	48.2	155 22.6	09.9	77 20.8	18.6
	03	341 21.4	211 21.4	. . 44.5	109 12.8	. . 48.3	170 24.7	. . 09.7	92 23.4	. . 18.5
	04	356 23.9	226 20.7	43.7	124 14.7	48.5	185 26.7	09.5	107 25.9	18.5
	05	11 26.4	241 19.9	43.0	139 16.5	48.6	200 28.8	09.4	122 28.5	18.5
	06	26 28.8	256 19.2	N19 42.2	154 18.4	S21 48.8	215 30.9	N 5 09.2	137 31.1	S20 18.5
	07	41 31.3	271 18.5	41.5	169 20.3	49.0	230 33.0	09.0	152 33.6	18.5
	08	56 33.7	286 17.8	40.7	184 22.1	49.1	245 35.1	08.9	167 36.2	18.5
M	09	71 36.2	301 17.1	. . 40.0	199 24.0	. . 49.3	260 37.2	. . 08.7	182 38.8	. . 18.5
O	10	86 38.7	316 16.4	39.2	214 25.9	49.4	275 39.3	08.5	197 41.4	18.5
N	11	101 41.1	331 15.7	38.5	229 27.7	49.6	290 41.3	08.4	212 43.9	18.5
D	12	116 43.6	346 15.0	N19 37.7	244 29.6	S21 49.7	305 43.4	N 5 08.2	227 46.5	S20 18.5
A	13	131 46.1	1 14.4	37.0	259 31.4	49.9	320 45.5	08.0	242 49.1	18.5
Y	14	146 48.5	16 13.7	36.2	274 33.3	50.1	335 47.6	07.9	257 51.6	18.5
	15	161 51.0	31 13.0	. . 35.5	289 35.2	. . 50.2	350 49.7	. . 07.7	272 54.2	. . 18.5
	16	176 53.5	46 12.3	34.7	304 37.0	50.4	5 51.8	07.5	287 56.8	18.5
	17	191 55.9	61 11.6	34.0	319 38.9	50.5	20 53.8	07.4	302 59.3	18.5
	18	206 58.4	76 10.9	N19 33.2	334 40.7	S21 50.7	35 55.9	N 5 07.2	318 01.9	S20 18.5
	19	222 00.9	91 10.2	32.5	349 42.6	50.8	50 58.0	07.0	333 04.5	18.4
	20	237 03.3	106 09.5	31.7	4 44.4	51.0	66 00.1	06.9	348 07.0	18.4
	21	252 05.8	121 08.8	. . 31.0	19 46.3	. . 51.2	81 02.2	. . 06.7	3 09.6	. . 18.4
	22	267 08.2	136 08.1	30.2	34 48.1	51.3	96 04.3	06.5	18 12.2	18.4
	23	282 10.7	151 07.4	29.4	49 50.0	51.5	111 06.3	06.4	33 14.8	18.4
	19 00	297 13.2	166 06.7	N19 28.7	64 51.8	S21 51.6	126 08.4	N 5 06.2	48 17.3	S20 18.4
	01	312 15.6	181 06.0	27.9	79 53.7	51.8	141 10.5	06.0	63 19.9	18.4
	02	327 18.1	196 05.3	27.1	94 55.5	52.0	156 12.6	05.9	78 22.5	18.4
	03	342 20.6	211 04.6	. . 26.4	109 57.3	. . 52.1	171 14.7	. . 05.7	93 25.0	. . 18.4
	04	357 23.0	226 03.9	25.6	124 59.2	52.3	186 16.8	05.5	108 27.6	18.4
	05	12 25.5	241 03.2	24.9	140 01.0	52.4	201 18.8	05.4	123 30.2	18.4
	06	27 28.0	256 02.6	N19 24.1	155 02.9	S21 52.6	216 20.9	N 5 05.2	138 32.7	S20 18.4
	07	42 30.4	271 01.9	23.3	170 04.7	52.8	231 23.0	05.0	153 35.3	18.4
T	08	57 32.9	286 01.2	22.6	185 06.5	52.9	246 25.1	04.9	168 37.9	18.4
U	09	72 35.4	301 00.5	. . 21.8	200 08.4	. . 53.1	261 27.2	. . 04.7	183 40.4	. . 18.4
E	10	87 37.8	315 59.8	21.0	215 10.2	53.2	276 29.3	04.5	198 43.0	18.4
S	11	102 40.3	330 59.1	20.2	230 12.1	53.4	291 31.3	04.3	213 45.6	18.4
D	12	117 42.7	345 58.4	N19 19.5	245 13.9	S21 53.6	306 33.4	N 5 04.2	228 48.1	S20 18.4
A	13	132 45.2	0 57.7	18.7	260 15.7	53.7	321 35.5	04.0	243 50.7	18.3
Y	14	147 47.7	15 57.1	17.9	275 17.5	53.9	336 37.6	03.8	258 53.3	18.3
	15	162 50.1	30 56.4	. . 17.1	290 19.4	. . 54.1	351 39.7	. . 03.7	273 55.8	. . 18.3
	16	177 52.6	45 55.7	16.4	305 21.2	54.2	6 41.7	03.5	288 58.4	18.3
	17	192 55.1	60 55.0	15.6	320 23.0	54.4	21 43.8	03.3	304 01.0	18.3
	18	207 57.5	75 54.3	N19 14.8	335 24.9	S21 54.5	36 45.9	N 5 03.2	319 03.5	S20 18.3
	19	223 00.0	90 53.6	14.0	350 26.7	54.7	51 48.0	03.0	334 06.1	18.3
	20	238 02.5	105 53.0	13.3	5 28.5	54.9	66 50.1	02.8	349 08.6	18.3
	21	253 04.9	120 52.3	. . 12.5	20 30.3	. . 55.0	81 52.1	. . 02.7	4 11.2	. . 18.3
	22	268 07.4	135 51.6	11.7	35 32.1	55.2	96 54.2	02.5	19 13.8	18.3
	23	283 09.9	150 50.9	10.9	50 34.0	55.4	111 56.3	02.3	34 16.3	18.3
	Mer. Pass.	h m 4 14.4	v −0.7	d 0.8	v 1.9	d 0.2	v 2.1	d 0.2	v 2.6	d 0.0

STARS

Name	SHA ° ′	Dec ° ′
Acamar	315 17.0	S40 14.2
Achernar	335 25.3	S57 09.0
Acrux	173 07.0	S63 11.7
Adhara	255 11.2	S28 59.8
Aldebaran	290 47.2	N16 32.3
Alioth	166 19.1	N55 52.6
Alkaid	152 57.3	N49 14.2
Al Na'ir	27 40.8	S46 52.6
Alnilam	275 44.5	S 1 11.6
Alphard	217 54.3	S 8 43.9
Alphecca	126 09.1	N26 39.9
Alpheratz	357 41.1	N29 10.8
Altair	62 05.9	N 8 55.0
Ankaa	353 13.6	S42 12.8
Antares	112 23.4	S26 27.9
Arcturus	145 53.8	N19 06.1
Atria	107 22.8	S69 03.4
Avior	234 17.7	S59 33.9
Bellatrix	278 30.0	N 6 21.7
Betelgeuse	270 59.3	N 7 24.4
Canopus	263 55.7	S52 42.3
Capella	280 31.7	N46 00.5
Deneb	49 29.5	N45 20.5
Denebola	182 31.7	N14 28.9
Diphda	348 53.7	S17 53.7
Dubhe	193 49.8	N61 39.9
Elnath	278 10.3	N28 37.0
Eltanin	90 44.7	N51 29.6
Enif	33 44.8	N 9 57.2
Fomalhaut	15 21.5	S29 31.9
Gacrux	171 58.6	S57 12.5
Gienah	175 50.2	S17 38.0
Hadar	148 44.7	S60 27.3
Hamal	327 58.4	N23 32.2
Kaus Aust.	83 40.7	S34 22.4
Kochab	137 19.9	N74 05.7
Markab	13 36.0	N15 17.7
Menkar	314 13.0	N 4 09.1
Menkent	148 05.0	S36 27.1
Miaplacidus	221 39.9	S69 47.3
Mirfak	308 37.5	N49 54.8
Nunki	75 55.4	S26 16.3
Peacock	53 15.4	S56 40.6
Pollux	243 25.6	N27 59.0
Procyon	244 57.9	N 5 10.8
Rasalhague	96 04.2	N12 33.2
Regulus	207 41.6	N11 53.2
Rigel	281 10.3	S 8 11.1
Rigil Kent.	139 48.6	S60 54.3
Sabik	102 09.9	S15 44.5
Schedar	349 37.8	N56 37.4
Shaula	96 18.7	S37 06.8
Sirius	258 32.2	S16 44.5
Spica	158 29.0	S11 14.8
Suhail	222 51.3	S43 30.1
Vega	80 37.1	N38 48.2
Zuben'ubi	137 03.0	S16 06.5

	SHA ° ′	Mer. Pass. h m
Venus	230 09.4	12 55
Mars	127 53.1	19 41
Jupiter	189 04.4	15 37
Saturn	111 01.6	20 47

UT d h	SUN GHA ° ′	SUN Dec ° ′	MOON GHA ° ′	v ′	MOON Dec ° ′	d ′	HP ′
17 00	178 27.8	N21 09.2	35 56.7	11.0	S17 57.9	2.5	55.3
01	193 27.7	08.8	50 26.7	11.0	18 00.4	2.5	55.3
02	208 27.7	08.4	64 56.7	10.9	18 02.9	2.3	55.3
03	223 27.6	. . 08.0	79 26.6	10.9	18 05.2	2.3	55.4
04	238 27.6	07.5	93 56.5	10.8	18 07.5	2.2	55.4
05	253 27.5	07.1	108 26.3	10.8	18 09.7	2.1	55.4
06	268 27.5	N21 06.7	122 56.1	10.7	S18 11.8	2.0	55.4
07	283 27.4	06.2	137 25.8	10.7	18 13.8	1.9	55.4
08	298 27.4	05.8	151 55.5	10.7	18 15.7	1.8	55.5
S 09	313 27.3	. . 05.4	166 25.2	10.6	18 17.5	1.7	55.5
U 10	328 27.3	04.9	180 54.8	10.6	18 19.2	1.7	55.5
N 11	343 27.2	04.5	195 24.4	10.6	18 20.9	1.5	55.5
D 12	358 27.2	N21 04.1	209 54.0	10.5	S18 22.4	1.4	55.6
A 13	13 27.1	03.6	224 23.5	10.5	18 23.8	1.4	55.6
Y 14	28 27.1	03.2	238 53.0	10.4	18 25.2	1.3	55.6
15	43 27.0	. . 02.8	253 22.4	10.4	18 26.5	1.1	55.6
16	58 27.0	02.3	267 51.8	10.4	18 27.6	1.1	55.7
17	73 26.9	01.9	282 21.2	10.3	18 28.7	1.0	55.7
18	88 26.9	N21 01.4	296 50.5	10.3	S18 29.7	0.9	55.7
19	103 26.8	01.0	311 19.8	10.3	18 30.6	0.8	55.7
20	118 26.8	00.6	325 49.1	10.2	18 31.4	0.7	55.7
21	133 26.8	21 00.1	340 18.3	10.2	18 32.1	0.6	55.8
22	148 26.7	20 59.7	354 47.5	10.1	18 32.7	0.5	55.8
23	163 26.7	59.2	9 16.6	10.1	18 33.2	0.4	55.8
18 00	178 26.6	N20 58.8	23 45.7	10.1	S18 33.6	0.3	55.8
01	193 26.6	58.4	38 14.8	10.1	18 33.9	0.2	55.9
02	208 26.5	57.9	52 43.9	10.0	18 34.1	0.1	55.9
03	223 26.5	. . 57.5	67 12.9	10.0	18 34.2	0.0	55.9
04	238 26.4	57.0	81 41.9	10.0	18 34.2	0.1	55.9
05	253 26.4	56.6	96 10.9	9.9	18 34.1	0.2	56.0
06	268 26.3	N20 56.1	110 39.8	9.9	S18 33.9	0.2	56.0
07	283 26.3	55.7	125 08.7	9.9	18 33.7	0.4	56.0
08	298 26.3	55.2	139 37.6	9.9	18 33.3	0.5	56.0
M 09	313 26.2	. . 54.8	154 06.5	9.8	18 32.8	0.6	56.1
O 10	328 26.2	54.4	168 35.3	9.8	18 32.2	0.7	56.1
N 11	343 26.1	53.9	183 04.1	9.8	18 31.5	0.7	56.1
D 12	358 26.1	N20 53.5	197 32.9	9.7	S18 30.8	0.9	56.1
A 13	13 26.0	53.0	212 01.6	9.7	18 29.9	1.0	56.1
Y 14	28 26.0	52.6	226 30.3	9.7	18 28.9	1.1	56.2
15	43 26.0	. . 52.1	240 59.0	9.7	18 27.8	1.1	56.2
16	58 25.9	51.7	255 27.7	9.6	18 26.7	1.3	56.2
17	73 25.9	51.2	269 56.3	9.7	18 25.4	1.4	56.2
18	88 25.8	N20 50.7	284 25.0	9.6	S18 24.0	1.5	56.3
19	103 25.8	50.3	298 53.6	9.6	18 22.5	1.6	56.3
20	118 25.8	49.8	313 22.2	9.5	18 20.9	1.6	56.3
21	133 25.7	. . 49.4	327 50.7	9.6	18 19.3	1.8	56.3
22	148 25.7	48.9	342 19.3	9.5	18 17.5	1.9	56.4
23	163 25.6	48.5	356 47.8	9.5	18 15.6	2.0	56.4
19 00	178 25.6	N20 48.0	11 16.3	9.5	S18 13.6	2.1	56.4
01	193 25.6	47.6	25 44.8	9.5	18 11.5	2.2	56.4
02	208 25.5	47.1	40 13.3	9.5	18 09.3	2.3	56.5
03	223 25.5	. . 46.6	54 41.8	9.4	18 07.0	2.3	56.5
04	238 25.4	46.2	69 10.2	9.4	18 04.7	2.5	56.5
05	253 25.4	45.7	83 38.6	9.4	18 02.2	2.6	56.5
06	268 25.4	N20 45.3	98 07.0	9.4	S17 59.6	2.7	56.6
07	283 25.3	44.8	112 35.4	9.4	17 56.9	2.8	56.6
T 08	298 25.3	44.3	127 03.8	9.4	17 54.1	2.9	56.6
U 09	313 25.3	. . 43.9	141 32.2	9.4	17 51.2	3.0	56.6
E 10	328 25.2	43.4	156 00.6	9.3	17 48.2	3.1	56.7
S 11	343 25.2	43.0	170 28.9	9.4	17 45.1	3.2	56.7
D 12	358 25.1	N20 42.5	184 57.3	9.3	S17 41.9	3.3	56.7
A 13	13 25.1	42.0	199 25.6	9.3	17 38.6	3.4	56.7
Y 14	28 25.1	41.6	213 53.9	9.4	17 35.2	3.5	56.8
15	43 25.0	. . 41.1	228 22.3	9.3	17 31.7	3.6	56.8
16	58 25.0	40.6	242 50.6	9.3	17 28.1	3.7	56.8
17	73 25.0	40.2	257 18.9	9.3	17 24.4	3.8	56.8
18	88 24.9	N20 39.7	271 47.2	9.3	S17 20.6	3.9	56.9
19	103 24.9	39.2	286 15.5	9.3	17 16.7	4.0	56.9
20	118 24.9	38.8	300 43.8	9.2	17 12.7	4.1	56.9
21	133 24.8	. . 38.3	315 12.0	9.3	17 08.6	4.2	56.9
22	148 24.8	37.8	329 40.3	9.3	17 04.4	4.3	57.0
23	163 24.8	37.3	344 08.6	9.3	S17 00.1	4.4	57.0
	SD 15.8	d 0.4	SD 15.1		15.3		15.5

Lat. °	Twilight Naut. h m	Twilight Civil h m	Sunrise h m	Moonrise 17 h m	Moonrise 18 h m	Moonrise 19 h m	Moonrise 20 h m
N 72	☐	☐	☐	■	■	22 50	22 35
N 70	☐	☐	☐	20 50	21 35	21 54	22 03
68	////	////	00 38	20 03	20 51	21 21	21 39
66	////	////	01 50	19 33	20 22	20 56	21 20
64	////	////	02 25	19 10	19 59	20 37	21 05
62	////	01 12	02 51	18 52	19 42	20 21	20 52
60	////	01 56	03 10	18 37	19 27	20 08	20 42
N 58	////	02 24	03 26	18 24	19 14	19 57	20 32
56	01 06	02 46	03 40	18 13	19 04	19 47	20 24
54	01 46	03 03	03 52	18 03	18 54	19 38	20 17
52	02 12	03 17	04 02	17 55	18 45	19 31	20 10
50	02 33	03 30	04 11	17 47	18 38	19 24	20 04
45	03 09	03 55	04 31	17 30	18 21	19 08	19 51
N 40	03 35	04 15	04 46	17 17	18 08	18 56	19 40
35	03 56	04 31	05 00	17 05	17 57	18 45	19 31
30	04 12	04 44	05 11	16 55	17 47	18 36	19 23
20	04 38	05 06	05 30	16 38	17 30	18 20	19 09
N 10	04 58	05 24	05 47	16 23	17 15	18 06	18 57
0	05 15	05 41	06 03	16 09	17 01	17 53	18 46
S 10	05 30	05 56	06 18	15 55	16 47	17 40	18 34
20	05 44	06 11	06 34	15 40	16 32	17 26	18 22
30	05 58	06 27	06 53	15 23	16 15	17 10	18 08
35	06 05	06 36	07 04	15 14	16 05	17 01	18 00
40	06 13	06 47	07 16	15 02	15 54	16 50	17 51
45	06 22	06 58	07 31	14 49	15 40	16 38	17 40
S 50	06 31	07 12	07 48	14 33	15 24	16 22	17 27
52	06 36	07 18	07 57	14 25	15 16	16 15	17 21
54	06 40	07 25	08 06	14 17	15 08	16 07	17 14
56	06 45	07 32	08 17	14 07	14 58	15 58	17 06
58	06 51	07 41	08 29	13 57	14 47	15 48	16 58
S 60	06 56	07 50	08 43	13 44	14 35	15 37	16 48

Lat. °	Sunset h m	Twilight Civil h m	Twilight Naut. h m	Moonset 17 h m	Moonset 18 h m	Moonset 19 h m	Moonset 20 h m
N 72	☐	☐	☐	■	■	■	01 30
N 70	☐	☐	☐	23 52	24 55	00 55	02 25
68	23 23	////	////	00 01	00 39	01 39	02 58
66	22 19	////	////	00 28	01 10	02 08	03 22
64	21 45	////	////	00 49	01 33	02 30	03 41
62	21 20	22 56	////	01 06	01 51	02 47	03 56
60	21 01	22 14	////	01 21	02 06	03 02	04 09
N 58	20 45	21 46	////	01 33	02 19	03 14	04 20
56	20 31	21 25	23 02	01 43	02 30	03 25	04 29
54	20 20	21 08	22 24	01 53	02 39	03 35	04 38
52	20 10	20 54	21 58	02 01	02 48	03 43	04 45
50	20 00	20 42	21 38	02 08	02 56	03 51	04 52
45	19 41	20 17	21 02	02 24	03 12	04 07	05 07
N 40	19 26	19 57	20 37	02 37	03 26	04 20	05 18
35	19 13	19 41	20 16	02 48	03 37	04 31	05 29
30	19 01	19 28	20 00	02 58	03 47	04 41	05 37
20	18 42	19 06	19 34	03 15	04 05	04 58	05 53
N 10	18 25	18 48	19 14	03 30	04 20	05 12	06 06
0	18 10	18 32	18 58	03 43	04 34	05 26	06 18
S 10	17 55	18 17	18 43	03 57	04 48	05 39	06 31
20	17 38	18 02	18 29	04 12	05 03	05 54	06 44
30	17 20	17 45	18 15	04 28	05 20	06 11	06 59
35	17 09	17 36	18 07	04 38	05 30	06 20	07 07
40	16 57	17 26	18 00	04 49	05 42	06 31	07 17
45	16 42	17 15	17 51	05 02	05 55	06 44	07 29
S 50	16 24	17 01	17 42	05 18	06 11	07 00	07 43
52	16 16	16 55	17 37	05 26	06 19	07 07	07 49
54	16 07	16 48	17 33	05 34	06 28	07 15	07 56
56	15 56	16 41	17 28	05 43	06 37	07 24	08 04
58	15 44	16 32	17 23	05 54	06 48	07 34	08 13
S 60	15 30	16 23	17 17	06 06	07 01	07 46	08 23

Day	SUN Eqn. of Time 00^h	SUN Eqn. of Time 12^h	SUN Mer. Pass.	MOON Mer. Pass. Upper	MOON Mer. Pass. Lower	Age	Phase
d	m s	m s	h m	h m	h m	d %	
17	06 09	06 11	12 06	22 22	09 56	13 93	
18	06 13	06 16	12 06	23 13	10 47	14 98	(full moon symbol)
19	06 18	06 19	12 06	24 06	11 39	15 100	

UT	ARIES	VENUS −3·9		MARS −1·0		JUPITER −1·8		SATURN +0·3		STARS		
	GHA	GHA	Dec	GHA	Dec	GHA	Dec	GHA	Dec	Name	SHA	Dec
d h	° ′	° ′	° ′	° ′	° ′	° ′	° ′	° ′	° ′		° ′	° ′
20 00	298 12.3	165 50.2	N19 10.1	65 35.8	S21 55.5	126 58.4	N 5 02.2	49 18.9	S20 18.3	Acamar	315 16.9	S40 14.2
01	313 14.8	180 49.6	09.3	80 37.6	55.7	142 00.5	02.0	64 21.5	18.3	Achernar	335 25.3	S57 09.0
02	328 17.2	195 48.9	08.6	95 39.4	55.8	157 02.5	01.8	79 24.0	18.3	Acrux	173 07.0	S63 11.7
03	343 19.7	210 48.2	. . 07.8	110 41.2	. . 56.0	172 04.6	. . 01.6	94 26.6	. . 18.3	Adhara	255 11.2	S28 59.8
04	358 22.2	225 47.5	07.0	125 43.0	56.2	187 06.7	01.5	109 29.2	18.3	Aldebaran	290 47.2	N16 32.3
05	13 24.6	240 46.8	06.2	140 44.9	56.3	202 08.8	01.3	124 31.7	18.3			
WEDNESDAY 06	28 27.1	255 46.2	N19 05.4	155 46.7	S21 56.5	217 10.9	N 5 01.1	139 34.3	S20 18.3	Alioth	166 19.1	N55 52.6
07	43 29.6	270 45.5	04.6	170 48.5	56.7	232 12.9	01.0	154 36.9	18.3	Alkaid	152 57.3	N49 14.2
08	58 32.0	285 44.8	03.8	185 50.3	56.8	247 15.0	00.8	169 39.4	18.2	Al Na'ir	27 40.8	S46 52.6
09	73 34.5	300 44.1	. . 03.0	200 52.1	. . 57.0	262 17.1	. . 00.6	184 42.0	. . 18.2	Alnilam	275 44.5	S 1 11.6
10	88 37.0	315 43.5	02.2	215 53.9	57.2	277 19.2	00.5	199 44.5	18.2	Alphard	217 54.3	S 8 43.9
11	103 39.4	330 42.8	01.4	230 55.7	57.3	292 21.3	00.3	214 47.1	18.2			
12	118 41.9	345 42.1	N19 00.7	245 57.5	S21 57.5	307 23.3	N 5 00.1	229 49.7	S20 18.2	Alphecca	126 09.1	N26 39.9
13	133 44.3	0 41.4	18 59.9	260 59.3	57.7	322 25.4	4 59.9	244 52.2	18.2	Alpheratz	357 41.1	N29 10.8
14	148 46.8	15 40.8	59.1	276 01.1	57.8	337 27.5	59.8	259 54.8	18.2	Altair	62 05.8	N 8 55.0
15	163 49.3	30 40.1	. . 58.3	291 02.9	. . 58.0	352 29.6	. . 59.6	274 57.4	. . 18.2	Ankaa	353 13.5	S42 12.7
16	178 51.7	45 39.4	57.5	306 04.7	58.2	7 31.7	59.4	289 59.9	18.2	Antares	112 23.4	S26 27.9
17	193 54.2	60 38.7	56.7	321 06.5	58.3	22 33.7	59.3	305 02.5	18.2			
18	208 56.7	75 38.1	N18 55.9	336 08.3	S21 58.5	37 35.8	N 4 59.1	320 05.0	S20 18.2	Arcturus	145 53.8	N19 06.1
19	223 59.1	90 37.4	55.1	351 10.1	58.7	52 37.9	58.9	335 07.6	18.2	Atria	107 22.9	S69 03.4
20	239 01.6	105 36.7	54.3	6 11.9	58.8	67 40.0	58.8	350 10.2	18.2	Avior	234 17.7	S59 33.9
21	254 04.1	120 36.1	. . 53.5	21 13.7	. . 59.0	82 42.0	. . 58.6	5 12.7	. . 18.2	Bellatrix	278 30.0	N 6 21.7
22	269 06.5	135 35.4	52.7	36 15.5	59.2	97 44.1	58.4	20 15.3	18.2	Betelgeuse	270 59.3	N 7 24.4
23	284 09.0	150 34.7	51.9	51 17.3	59.3	112 46.2	58.2	35 17.8	18.2			
21 00	299 11.5	165 34.1	N18 51.0	66 19.1	S21 59.5	127 48.3	N 4 58.1	50 20.4	S20 18.2	Canopus	263 55.7	S52 42.3
01	314 13.9	180 33.4	50.2	81 20.9	59.7	142 50.3	57.9	65 23.0	18.2	Capella	280 31.7	N46 00.5
02	329 16.4	195 32.7	49.4	96 22.6	21 59.8	157 52.4	57.7	80 25.5	18.2	Deneb	49 29.5	N45 20.5
03	344 18.8	210 32.1	. . 48.6	111 24.4	22 00.0	172 54.5	. . 57.6	95 28.1	. . 18.2	Denebola	182 31.7	N14 28.9
04	359 21.3	225 31.4	47.8	126 26.2	00.2	187 56.6	57.4	110 30.6	18.1	Diphda	348 53.7	S17 53.7
05	14 23.8	240 30.7	47.0	141 28.0	00.3	202 58.7	57.2	125 33.2	18.1			
THURSDAY 06	29 26.2	255 30.1	N18 46.2	156 29.8	S22 00.5	218 00.7	N 4 57.1	140 35.8	S20 18.1	Dubhe	193 49.8	N61 39.9
07	44 28.7	270 29.4	45.4	171 31.6	00.7	233 02.8	56.9	155 38.3	18.1	Elnath	278 10.3	N28 37.0
08	59 31.2	285 28.7	44.6	186 33.3	00.8	248 04.9	56.7	170 40.9	18.1	Eltanin	90 44.7	N51 29.6
09	74 33.6	300 28.1	. . 43.8	201 35.1	. . 01.0	263 07.0	. . 56.5	185 43.4	. . 18.1	Enif	33 44.7	N 9 57.2
10	89 36.1	315 27.4	42.9	216 36.9	01.2	278 09.0	56.4	200 46.0	18.1	Fomalhaut	15 21.5	S29 31.9
11	104 38.6	330 26.7	42.1	231 38.7	01.3	293 11.1	56.2	215 48.6	18.1			
12	119 41.0	345 26.1	N18 41.3	246 40.5	S22 01.5	308 13.2	N 4 56.0	230 51.1	S20 18.1	Gacrux	171 58.6	S57 12.5
13	134 43.5	0 25.4	40.5	261 42.2	01.7	323 15.3	55.9	245 53.7	18.1	Gienah	175 50.2	S17 38.0
14	149 46.0	15 24.8	39.7	276 44.0	01.9	338 17.3	55.7	260 56.2	18.1	Hadar	148 44.7	S60 27.3
15	164 48.4	30 24.1	. . 38.9	291 45.8	. . 02.0	353 19.4	. . 55.5	275 58.8	. . 18.1	Hamal	327 58.4	N23 32.2
16	179 50.9	45 23.4	38.0	306 47.6	02.2	8 21.5	55.3	291 01.4	18.1	Kaus Aust.	83 40.7	S34 22.4
17	194 53.3	60 22.8	37.2	321 49.3	02.4	23 23.6	55.2	306 03.9	18.1			
18	209 55.8	75 22.1	N18 36.4	336 51.1	S22 02.5	38 25.6	N 4 55.0	321 06.5	S20 18.1	Kochab	137 20.0	N74 05.7
19	224 58.3	90 21.5	35.6	351 52.9	02.7	53 27.7	54.8	336 09.0	18.1	Markab	13 36.0	N15 17.7
20	240 00.7	105 20.8	34.7	6 54.6	02.9	68 29.8	54.7	351 11.6	18.1	Menkar	314 12.9	N 4 09.1
21	255 03.2	120 20.2	. . 33.9	21 56.4	. . 03.1	83 31.8	. . 54.5	6 14.1	. . 18.1	Menkent	148 05.0	S36 27.1
22	270 05.7	135 19.5	33.1	36 58.2	03.2	98 33.9	54.3	21 16.7	18.1	Miaplacidus	221 40.0	S69 47.3
23	285 08.1	150 18.8	32.3	51 59.9	03.4	113 36.0	54.1	36 19.3	18.1			
22 00	300 10.6	165 18.2	N18 31.4	67 01.7	S22 03.6	128 38.1	N 4 54.0	51 21.8	S20 18.1	Mirfak	308 37.5	N49 54.8
01	315 13.1	180 17.5	30.6	82 03.4	03.7	143 40.1	53.8	66 24.4	18.1	Nunki	75 55.4	S26 16.3
02	330 15.5	195 16.9	29.8	97 05.2	03.9	158 42.2	53.6	81 26.9	18.1	Peacock	53 15.4	S56 40.6
03	345 18.0	210 16.2	. . 29.0	112 07.0	. . 04.1	173 44.3	. . 53.4	96 29.5	. . 18.0	Pollux	243 25.6	N27 59.0
04	0 20.4	225 15.6	28.1	127 08.7	04.3	188 46.4	53.3	111 32.0	18.0	Procyon	244 57.9	N 5 10.8
05	15 22.9	240 14.9	27.3	142 10.5	04.4	203 48.4	53.1	126 34.6	18.0			
FRIDAY 06	30 25.4	255 14.3	N18 26.5	157 12.2	S22 04.6	218 50.5	N 4 52.9	141 37.2	S20 18.0	Rasalhague	96 04.2	N12 33.2
07	45 27.8	270 13.6	25.6	172 14.0	04.8	233 52.6	52.8	156 39.7	18.0	Regulus	207 41.6	N11 53.2
08	60 30.3	285 13.0	24.8	187 15.7	04.9	248 54.7	52.6	171 42.3	18.0	Rigel	281 10.3	S 8 11.1
09	75 32.8	300 12.3	. . 24.0	202 17.5	. . 05.1	263 56.7	. . 52.4	186 44.8	. . 18.0	Rigil Kent.	139 48.6	S60 54.3
10	90 35.2	315 11.7	23.1	217 19.2	05.3	278 58.8	52.2	201 47.4	18.0	Sabik	102 09.9	S15 44.5
11	105 37.7	330 11.0	22.3	232 21.0	05.5	294 00.9	52.1	216 49.9	18.0			
12	120 40.2	345 10.4	N18 21.4	247 22.7	S22 05.6	309 02.9	N 4 51.9	231 52.5	S20 18.0	Schedar	349 37.8	N56 37.4
13	135 42.6	0 09.7	20.6	262 24.5	05.8	324 05.0	51.7	246 55.0	18.0	Shaula	96 18.7	S37 06.8
14	150 45.1	15 09.1	19.8	277 26.2	06.0	339 07.1	51.6	261 57.6	18.0	Sirius	258 32.2	S16 44.4
15	165 47.6	30 08.4	. . 18.9	292 28.0	. . 06.2	354 09.2	. . 51.4	277 00.2	. . 18.0	Spica	158 29.1	S11 14.8
16	180 50.0	45 07.8	18.1	307 29.7	06.3	9 11.2	51.2	292 02.7	18.0	Suhail	222 51.3	S43 30.1
17	195 52.5	60 07.1	17.2	322 31.5	06.5	24 13.3	51.0	307 05.3	18.0			
18	210 54.9	75 06.5	N18 16.4	337 33.2	S22 06.7	39 15.4	N 4 50.9	322 07.8	S20 18.0	Vega	80 37.1	N38 48.3
19	225 57.4	90 05.8	15.6	352 35.0	06.9	54 17.4	50.7	337 10.4	18.0	Zuben'ubi	137 03.0	S16 06.5
20	240 59.9	105 05.2	14.7	7 36.7	07.0	69 19.5	50.5	352 12.9	18.0		SHA	Mer. Pass.
21	256 02.3	120 04.5	. . 13.9	22 38.4	. . 07.2	84 21.6	. . 50.3	7 15.5	. . 18.0		° ′	h m
22	271 04.8	135 03.9	13.0	37 40.2	07.4	99 23.7	50.2	22 18.0	18.0	Venus	226 22.6	12 58
23	286 07.3	150 03.3	12.2	52 41.9	07.6	114 25.7	50.0	37 20.6	18.0	Mars	127 07.6	19 32
Mer. Pass.	h m 4 02.6	v −0.7	d 0.8	v 1.8	d 0.2	v 2.1	d 0.2	v 2.6	d 0.0	Jupiter	188 36.8	15 27
										Saturn	111 09.0	20 35

Day	UT (h)	SUN GHA (° ′)	SUN Dec (° ′)	MOON GHA (° ′)	v (′)	MOON Dec (° ′)	d (′)	HP (′)
20	00	178 24.7	N20 36.9	358 36.9	9.2	S16 55.7	4.5	57.0
	01	193 24.7	36.4	13 05.1	9.3	16 51.2	4.6	57.0
	02	208 24.6	35.9	27 33.4	9.3	16 46.6	4.7	57.1
	03	223 24.6	. . 35.5	42 01.7	9.3	16 41.9	4.8	57.1
	04	238 24.6	35.0	56 30.0	9.2	16 37.1	4.8	57.1
	05	253 24.6	34.5	70 58.2	9.3	16 32.3	5.0	57.1
	06	268 24.5	N20 34.0	85 26.5	9.3	S16 27.3	5.1	57.1
W	07	283 24.5	33.6	99 54.8	9.2	16 22.2	5.2	57.2
E	08	298 24.5	33.1	114 23.0	9.3	16 17.0	5.2	57.2
D	09	313 24.4	. . 32.6	128 51.3	9.3	16 11.8	5.4	57.2
N	10	328 24.4	32.1	143 19.6	9.3	16 06.4	5.4	57.2
E	11	343 24.4	31.7	157 47.9	9.3	16 01.0	5.6	57.3
S	12	358 24.3	N20 31.2	172 16.2	9.3	S15 55.4	5.6	57.3
	13	13 24.3	30.7	186 44.5	9.3	15 49.8	5.8	57.3
D	14	28 24.3	30.2	201 12.8	9.3	15 44.0	5.8	57.3
A	15	43 24.2	. . 29.7	215 41.1	9.3	15 38.2	5.9	57.4
Y	16	58 24.2	29.3	230 09.4	9.3	15 32.3	6.0	57.4
	17	73 24.2	28.8	244 37.7	9.3	15 26.3	6.1	57.4
	18	88 24.1	N20 28.3	259 06.0	9.3	S15 20.2	6.2	57.4
	19	103 24.1	27.8	273 34.3	9.4	15 14.0	6.3	57.4
	20	118 24.1	27.3	288 02.7	9.3	15 07.7	6.4	57.5
	21	133 24.1	. . 26.8	302 31.0	9.4	15 01.3	6.5	57.5
	22	148 24.0	26.4	316 59.4	9.3	14 54.8	6.5	57.5
	23	163 24.0	25.9	331 27.7	9.4	14 48.3	6.7	57.5
21	00	178 24.0	N20 25.4	345 56.1	9.4	S14 41.6	6.7	57.6
	01	193 23.9	24.9	0 24.5	9.4	14 34.9	6.8	57.6
	02	208 23.9	24.4	14 52.9	9.4	14 28.1	6.9	57.6
	03	223 23.9	. . 23.9	29 21.3	9.4	14 21.2	7.0	57.6
	04	238 23.9	23.4	43 49.7	9.4	14 14.2	7.1	57.6
	05	253 23.8	23.0	58 18.1	9.4	14 07.1	7.1	57.7
	06	268 23.8	N20 22.5	72 46.5	9.5	S14 00.0	7.3	57.7
T	07	283 23.8	22.0	87 15.0	9.4	13 52.7	7.3	57.7
	08	298 23.8	21.5	101 43.4	9.5	13 45.4	7.4	57.7
H	09	313 23.7	. . 21.0	116 11.9	9.5	13 38.0	7.5	57.8
U	10	328 23.7	20.5	130 40.4	9.5	13 30.5	7.6	57.8
R	11	343 23.7	20.0	145 08.9	9.5	13 22.9	7.6	57.8
S	12	358 23.7	N20 19.5	159 37.4	9.5	S13 15.3	7.8	57.8
D	13	13 23.6	19.0	174 05.9	9.5	13 07.5	7.8	57.8
A	14	28 23.6	18.5	188 34.4	9.6	12 59.7	7.9	57.9
Y	15	43 23.6	. . 18.0	203 03.0	9.5	12 51.8	7.9	57.9
	16	58 23.6	17.5	217 31.5	9.6	12 43.9	8.1	57.9
	17	73 23.5	17.1	232 00.1	9.6	12 35.8	8.1	57.9
	18	88 23.5	N20 16.6	246 28.7	9.6	S12 27.7	8.2	57.9
	19	103 23.5	16.1	260 57.3	9.6	12 19.5	8.3	58.0
	20	118 23.5	15.6	275 25.9	9.6	12 11.2	8.3	58.0
	21	133 23.4	. . 15.1	289 54.5	9.7	12 02.9	8.4	58.0
	22	148 23.4	14.6	304 23.2	9.6	11 54.5	8.5	58.0
	23	163 23.4	14.1	318 51.8	9.7	11 46.0	8.6	58.0
22	00	178 23.4	N20 13.6	333 20.5	9.7	S11 37.4	8.6	58.1
	01	193 23.4	13.1	347 49.2	9.7	11 28.8	8.7	58.1
	02	208 23.3	12.6	2 17.9	9.7	11 20.1	8.8	58.1
	03	223 23.3	. . 12.1	16 46.6	9.7	11 11.3	8.8	58.1
	04	238 23.3	11.6	31 15.3	9.8	11 02.5	8.9	58.1
	05	253 23.3	11.1	45 44.1	9.7	10 53.6	9.0	58.2
	06	268 23.3	N20 10.6	60 12.8	9.8	S10 44.6	9.0	58.2
	07	283 23.2	10.1	74 41.6	9.8	10 35.6	9.1	58.2
	08	298 23.2	09.5	89 10.4	9.8	10 26.5	9.2	58.2
F	09	313 23.2	. . 09.0	103 39.2	9.8	10 17.3	9.2	58.2
R	10	328 23.2	08.5	118 08.0	9.8	10 08.1	9.3	58.2
I	11	343 23.2	08.0	132 36.8	9.8	9 58.8	9.3	58.3
D	12	358 23.1	N20 07.5	147 05.6	9.9	S 9 49.5	9.4	58.3
A	13	13 23.1	07.0	161 34.5	9.8	9 40.1	9.5	58.3
Y	14	28 23.1	06.5	176 03.3	9.9	9 30.6	9.5	58.3
	15	43 23.1	. . 06.0	190 32.2	9.9	9 21.1	9.6	58.3
	16	58 23.1	05.5	205 01.1	9.9	9 11.5	9.6	58.4
	17	73 23.0	05.0	219 30.0	9.9	9 01.9	9.7	58.4
	18	88 23.0	N20 04.5	233 58.9	10.0	S 8 52.2	9.8	58.4
	19	103 23.0	04.0	248 27.9	9.9	8 42.4	9.8	58.4
	20	118 23.0	03.5	262 56.8	10.0	8 32.6	9.9	58.4
	21	133 23.0	. . 02.9	277 25.8	9.9	8 22.7	9.9	58.4
	22	148 23.0	02.4	291 54.7	10.0	8 12.8	9.9	58.4
	23	163 22.9	01.9	306 23.7	10.0	S 8 02.9	10.0	58.5
		SD 15.8	*d* 0.5	SD 15.6		15.8		15.9

Lat. (°)	Twilight Naut. (h m)	Twilight Civil (h m)	Sunrise (h m)	Moonrise 20 (h m)	Moonrise 21 (h m)	Moonrise 22 (h m)	Moonrise 23 (h m)
N 72	▭	▭	▭	22 35	22 27	22 20	22 14
N 70	▭	▭	▭	22 03	22 06	22 08	22 08
68	////	////	01 09	21 39	21 50	21 58	22 04
66	////	////	02 03	21 20	21 37	21 49	22 00
64	////	////	02 35	21 05	21 26	21 42	21 56
62	////	01 28	02 58	20 52	21 17	21 36	21 54
60	////	02 06	03 17	20 42	21 09	21 31	21 51
N 58	////	02 32	03 32	20 32	21 01	21 26	21 49
56	01 20	02 52	03 45	20 24	20 55	21 22	21 47
54	01 55	03 08	03 56	20 17	20 49	21 18	21 45
52	02 19	03 22	04 06	20 10	20 44	21 15	21 43
50	02 38	03 34	04 15	20 04	20 40	21 12	21 42
45	03 13	03 59	04 34	19 51	20 30	21 05	21 38
N 40	03 38	04 18	04 49	19 40	20 21	20 59	21 36
35	03 58	04 33	05 02	19 31	20 14	20 55	21 33
30	04 14	04 46	05 13	19 23	20 08	20 50	21 31
20	04 39	05 08	05 32	19 09	19 57	20 43	21 27
N 10	04 59	05 25	05 48	18 57	19 47	20 36	21 24
0	05 15	05 41	06 03	18 46	19 38	20 30	21 21
S 10	05 30	05 55	06 18	18 34	19 29	20 24	21 18
20	05 43	06 10	06 34	18 22	19 19	20 17	21 15
30	05 57	06 26	06 52	18 08	19 08	20 09	21 11
35	06 04	06 35	07 02	18 00	19 02	20 05	21 09
40	06 11	06 45	07 14	17 51	18 54	20 00	21 07
45	06 20	06 56	07 28	17 40	18 46	19 54	21 04
S 50	06 29	07 09	07 45	17 27	18 36	19 47	21 01
52	06 33	07 15	07 53	17 21	18 31	19 44	20 59
54	06 37	07 21	08 02	17 14	18 25	19 40	20 57
56	06 42	07 29	08 12	17 06	18 20	19 37	20 55
58	06 47	07 37	08 24	16 58	18 13	19 32	20 53
S 60	06 52	07 46	08 37	16 48	18 06	19 27	20 51

Lat. (°)	Sunset (h m)	Twilight Civil (h m)	Twilight Naut. (h m)	Moonset 20 (h m)	Moonset 21 (h m)	Moonset 22 (h m)	Moonset 23 (h m)
N 72	▭	▭	▭	01 30	03 35	05 32	07 26
N 70	▭	▭	▭	02 25	04 06	05 51	07 36
68	22 56	////	////	02 58	04 29	06 06	07 45
66	22 07	////	////	03 22	04 47	06 18	07 52
64	21 36	////	////	03 41	05 01	06 28	07 57
62	21 13	22 41	////	03 56	05 13	06 36	08 02
60	20 55	22 04	////	04 09	05 23	06 44	08 07
N 58	20 40	21 39	////	04 20	05 32	06 50	08 10
56	20 27	21 19	22 49	04 29	05 40	06 56	08 14
54	20 16	21 03	22 15	04 38	05 47	07 01	08 17
52	20 06	20 50	21 52	04 45	05 53	07 05	08 19
50	19 57	20 38	21 33	04 52	05 59	07 09	08 22
45	19 39	20 14	20 59	05 07	06 11	07 18	08 27
N 40	19 24	19 55	20 34	05 18	06 21	07 25	08 32
35	19 11	19 39	20 14	05 29	06 29	07 32	08 35
30	19 00	19 26	19 58	05 37	06 37	07 37	08 39
20	18 41	19 05	19 33	05 53	06 49	07 47	08 45
N 10	18 25	18 48	19 14	06 06	07 00	07 55	08 50
0	18 10	18 32	18 58	06 18	07 11	08 03	08 54
S 10	17 55	18 17	18 43	06 31	07 21	08 11	08 59
20	17 39	18 03	18 30	06 44	07 32	08 19	09 04
30	17 21	17 47	18 16	06 59	07 45	08 28	09 09
35	17 11	17 38	18 09	07 07	07 52	08 33	09 13
40	16 59	17 29	18 02	07 17	08 00	08 39	09 16
45	16 45	17 17	17 54	07 29	08 09	08 46	09 20
S 50	16 28	17 04	17 45	07 43	08 21	08 54	09 25
52	16 20	16 59	17 41	07 49	08 26	08 58	09 27
54	16 11	16 52	17 36	07 56	08 32	09 02	09 30
56	16 01	16 45	17 32	08 04	08 38	09 07	09 33
58	15 50	16 37	17 27	08 13	08 45	09 12	09 35
S 60	15 36	16 28	17 21	08 23	08 53	09 18	09 39

Day	SUN Eqn. of Time 00^h (m s)	SUN Eqn. of Time 12^h (m s)	SUN Mer. Pass. (h m)	MOON Mer. Pass. Upper (h m)	MOON Mer. Pass. Lower (h m)	MOON Age (d)	MOON Phase (%)
20	06 21	06 23	12 06	00 06	12 32	16	100
21	06 24	06 25	12 06	00 58	13 24	17	97
22	06 26	06 27	12 06	01 50	14 16	18	92

	UT d h	ARIES GHA	VENUS −3·9 GHA	VENUS Dec	MARS −0·9 GHA	MARS Dec	JUPITER −1·8 GHA	JUPITER Dec	SATURN +0·3 GHA	SATURN Dec
		° ′	° ′	° ′	° ′	° ′	° ′	° ′	° ′	° ′
	23 00	301 09.7	165 02.6	N18 11.3	67 43.6	S22 07.7	129 27.8	N 4 49.8	52 23.1	S20 18.0
	01	316 12.2	180 02.0	10.5	82 45.4	07.9	144 29.9	49.6	67 25.7	18.0
	02	331 14.7	195 01.3	09.6	97 47.1	08.1	159 31.9	49.5	82 28.2	18.0
	03	346 17.1	210 00.7	. . 08.8	112 48.8	. . 08.3	174 34.0	. . 49.3	97 30.8	. . 18.0
	04	1 19.6	225 00.0	07.9	127 50.6	08.4	189 36.1	49.1	112 33.4	18.0
	05	16 22.1	239 59.4	07.1	142 52.3	08.6	204 38.1	49.0	127 35.9	18.0
	06	31 24.5	254 58.8	N18 06.2	157 54.0	S22 08.8	219 40.2	N 4 48.8	142 38.5	S20 17.9
	07	46 27.0	269 58.1	05.4	172 55.8	09.0	234 42.3	48.6	157 41.0	17.9
S	08	61 29.4	284 57.5	04.5	187 57.5	09.1	249 44.4	48.4	172 43.6	17.9
A	09	76 31.9	299 56.8	. . 03.7	202 59.2	. . 09.3	264 46.4	. . 48.3	187 46.1	. . 17.9
T	10	91 34.4	314 56.2	02.8	218 00.9	09.5	279 48.5	48.1	202 48.7	17.9
U	11	106 36.8	329 55.6	01.9	233 02.7	09.7	294 50.6	47.9	217 51.2	17.9
R	12	121 39.3	344 54.9	N18 01.1	248 04.4	S22 09.8	309 52.6	N 4 47.7	232 53.8	S20 17.9
D	13	136 41.8	359 54.3	18 00.2	263 06.1	10.0	324 54.7	47.6	247 56.3	17.9
A	14	151 44.2	14 53.7	17 59.4	278 07.8	10.2	339 56.8	47.4	262 58.9	17.9
Y	15	166 46.7	29 53.0	. . 58.5	293 09.5	. . 10.4	354 58.8	. . 47.2	278 01.4	. . 17.9
	16	181 49.2	44 52.4	57.6	308 11.3	10.6	10 00.9	47.0	293 04.0	17.9
	17	196 51.6	59 51.8	56.8	323 13.0	10.7	25 03.0	46.9	308 06.5	17.9
	18	211 54.1	74 51.1	N17 55.9	338 14.7	S22 10.9	40 05.0	N 4 46.7	323 09.1	S20 17.9
	19	226 56.5	89 50.5	55.0	353 16.4	11.1	55 07.1	46.5	338 11.6	17.9
	20	241 59.0	104 49.9	54.2	8 18.1	11.3	70 09.2	46.3	353 14.2	17.9
	21	257 01.5	119 49.2	. . 53.3	23 19.8	. . 11.4	85 11.2	. . 46.2	8 16.7	. . 17.9
	22	272 03.9	134 48.6	52.4	38 21.5	11.6	100 13.3	46.0	23 19.3	17.9
	23	287 06.4	149 48.0	51.6	53 23.3	11.8	115 15.4	45.8	38 21.8	17.9
	24 00	302 08.9	164 47.3	N17 50.7	68 25.0	S22 12.0	130 17.4	N 4 45.6	53 24.4	S20 17.9
	01	317 11.3	179 46.7	49.8	83 26.7	12.2	145 19.5	45.5	68 26.9	17.9
	02	332 13.8	194 46.1	49.0	98 28.4	12.3	160 21.6	45.3	83 29.5	17.9
	03	347 16.3	209 45.4	. . 48.1	113 30.1	. . 12.5	175 23.6	. . 45.1	98 32.0	. . 17.9
	04	2 18.7	224 44.8	47.2	128 31.8	12.7	190 25.7	44.9	113 34.6	17.9
	05	17 21.2	239 44.2	46.4	143 33.5	12.9	205 27.8	44.8	128 37.1	17.9
	06	32 23.7	254 43.6	N17 45.5	158 35.2	S22 13.1	220 29.8	N 4 44.6	143 39.7	S20 17.9
	07	47 26.1	269 42.9	44.6	173 36.9	13.2	235 31.9	44.4	158 42.2	17.9
	08	62 28.6	284 42.3	43.7	188 38.6	13.4	250 34.0	44.2	173 44.8	17.9
S	09	77 31.0	299 41.7	. . 42.9	203 40.3	. . 13.6	265 36.0	. . 44.1	188 47.3	. . 17.9
U	10	92 33.5	314 41.0	42.0	218 42.0	13.8	280 38.1	43.9	203 49.9	17.9
N	11	107 36.0	329 40.4	41.1	233 43.7	14.0	295 40.2	43.7	218 52.4	17.9
D	12	122 38.4	344 39.8	N17 40.2	248 45.4	S22 14.1	310 42.2	N 4 43.5	233 55.0	S20 17.9
A	13	137 40.9	359 39.2	39.3	263 47.1	14.3	325 44.3	43.4	248 57.5	17.9
Y	14	152 43.4	14 38.5	38.5	278 48.8	14.5	340 46.4	43.2	264 00.1	17.8
	15	167 45.8	29 37.9	. . 37.6	293 50.5	. . 14.7	355 48.4	. . 43.0	279 02.6	. . 17.8
	16	182 48.3	44 37.3	36.7	308 52.2	14.9	10 50.5	42.8	294 05.1	17.8
	17	197 50.8	59 36.7	35.8	323 53.8	15.0	25 52.6	42.7	309 07.7	17.8
	18	212 53.2	74 36.1	N17 34.9	338 55.5	S22 15.2	40 54.6	N 4 42.5	324 10.2	S20 17.8
	19	227 55.7	89 35.4	34.0	353 57.2	15.4	55 56.7	42.3	339 12.8	17.8
	20	242 58.2	104 34.8	33.2	8 58.9	15.6	70 58.8	42.1	354 15.3	17.8
	21	258 00.6	119 34.2	. . 32.3	24 00.6	. . 15.8	86 00.8	. . 42.0	9 17.9	. . 17.8
	22	273 03.1	134 33.6	31.4	39 02.3	15.9	101 02.9	41.8	24 20.4	17.8
	23	288 05.5	149 33.0	30.5	54 04.0	16.1	116 05.0	41.6	39 23.0	17.8
	25 00	303 08.0	164 32.3	N17 29.6	69 05.6	S22 16.3	131 07.0	N 4 41.4	54 25.5	S20 17.8
	01	318 10.5	179 31.7	28.7	84 07.3	16.5	146 09.1	41.3	69 28.1	17.8
	02	333 12.9	194 31.1	27.8	99 09.0	16.7	161 11.1	41.1	84 30.6	17.8
	03	348 15.4	209 30.5	. . 26.9	114 10.7	. . 16.9	176 13.2	. . 40.9	99 33.2	. . 17.8
	04	3 17.9	224 29.9	26.0	129 12.4	17.0	191 15.3	40.7	114 35.7	17.8
	05	18 20.3	239 29.3	25.1	144 14.0	17.2	206 17.3	40.6	129 38.2	17.8
	06	33 22.8	254 28.6	N17 24.2	159 15.7	S22 17.4	221 19.4	N 4 40.4	144 40.8	S20 17.8
	07	48 25.3	269 28.0	23.4	174 17.4	17.6	236 21.5	40.2	159 43.3	17.8
	08	63 27.7	284 27.4	22.5	189 19.1	17.8	251 23.5	40.0	174 45.9	17.8
M	09	78 30.2	299 26.8	. . 21.6	204 20.7	. . 18.0	266 25.6	. . 39.9	189 48.4	. . 17.8
O	10	93 32.6	314 26.2	20.7	219 22.4	18.1	281 27.7	39.7	204 51.0	17.8
N	11	108 35.1	329 25.6	19.8	234 24.1	18.3	296 29.7	39.5	219 53.5	17.8
D	12	123 37.6	344 25.0	N17 18.9	249 25.7	S22 18.5	311 31.8	N 4 39.3	234 56.1	S20 17.8
A	13	138 40.0	359 24.4	18.0	264 27.4	18.7	326 33.8	39.1	249 58.6	17.8
Y	14	153 42.5	14 23.7	17.1	279 29.1	18.9	341 35.9	39.0	265 01.1	17.8
	15	168 45.0	29 23.1	. . 16.2	294 30.7	. . 19.1	356 38.0	. . 38.8	280 03.7	. . 17.8
	16	183 47.4	44 22.5	15.3	309 32.4	19.2	11 40.0	38.6	295 06.2	17.8
	17	198 49.9	59 21.9	14.4	324 34.1	19.4	26 42.1	38.4	310 08.8	17.8
	18	213 52.4	74 21.3	N17 13.5	339 35.7	S22 19.6	41 44.2	N 4 38.3	325 11.3	S20 17.8
	19	228 54.8	89 20.7	12.5	354 37.4	19.8	56 46.2	38.1	340 13.9	17.8
	20	243 57.3	104 20.1	11.6	9 39.1	20.0	71 48.3	37.9	355 16.4	17.8
	21	258 59.8	119 19.5	. . 10.7	24 40.7	. . 20.2	86 50.3	. . 37.7	10 18.9	. . 17.8
	22	274 02.2	134 18.9	09.8	39 42.4	20.4	101 52.4	37.6	25 21.5	17.8
	23	289 04.7	149 18.3	08.9	54 44.0	20.5	116 54.5	37.4	40 24.0	17.8
	Mer. Pass.	h m 3 50.8	v −0.6	d 0.9	v 1.7	d 0.2	v 2.1	d 0.2	v 2.5	d 0.0

STARS

Name	SHA	Dec
	° ′	° ′
Acamar	315 16.9	S40 14.2
Achernar	335 25.3	S57 09.0
Acrux	173 07.0	S63 11.6
Adhara	255 11.2	S28 59.8
Aldebaran	290 47.2	N16 32.3
Alioth	166 19.1	N55 52.6
Alkaid	152 57.4	N49 14.2
Al Na'ir	27 40.8	S46 52.6
Alnilam	275 44.5	S 1 11.6
Alphard	217 54.3	S 8 43.9
Alphecca	126 09.1	N26 39.9
Alpheratz	357 41.1	N29 10.8
Altair	62 05.8	N 8 55.0
Ankaa	353 13.5	S42 12.7
Antares	112 23.4	S26 27.9
Arcturus	145 53.8	N19 06.1
Atria	107 22.9	S69 03.4
Avior	234 17.7	S59 33.9
Bellatrix	278 30.0	N 6 21.7
Betelgeuse	270 59.3	N 7 24.4
Canopus	263 55.7	S52 42.3
Capella	280 31.7	N46 00.5
Deneb	49 29.5	N45 20.5
Denebola	182 31.7	N14 28.9
Diphda	348 53.7	S17 53.6
Dubhe	193 49.8	N61 39.9
Elnath	278 10.2	N28 37.0
Eltanin	90 44.7	N51 29.6
Enif	33 44.7	N 9 57.2
Fomalhaut	15 21.4	S29 31.9
Gacrux	171 58.6	S57 12.5
Gienah	175 50.3	S17 38.0
Hadar	148 44.7	S60 27.3
Hamal	327 58.4	N23 32.2
Kaus Aust.	83 40.7	S34 22.4
Kochab	137 20.0	N74 05.7
Markab	13 36.0	N15 17.7
Menkar	314 12.9	N 4 09.2
Menkent	148 05.0	S36 27.1
Miaplacidus	221 40.0	S69 47.3
Mirfak	308 37.4	N49 54.8
Nunki	75 55.4	S26 16.3
Peacock	53 15.4	S56 40.7
Pollux	243 25.6	N27 59.0
Procyon	244 57.9	N 5 10.8
Rasalhague	96 04.2	N12 33.2
Regulus	207 41.6	N11 53.2
Rigel	281 10.3	S 8 11.1
Rigil Kent.	139 48.6	S60 54.3
Sabik	102 09.9	S15 44.5
Schedar	349 37.8	N56 37.4
Shaula	96 18.7	S37 06.8
Sirius	258 32.2	S16 44.4
Spica	158 29.1	S11 14.8
Suhail	222 51.3	S43 30.1
Vega	80 37.1	N38 48.3
Zuben'ubi	137 03.0	S16 06.5

	SHA	Mer. Pass.
	° ′	h m
Venus	222 38.5	13 01
Mars	126 16.1	19 24
Jupiter	188 08.6	15 17
Saturn	111 15.5	20 23

	UT	SUN GHA	SUN Dec	MOON GHA	v	MOON Dec	d	HP
	d h	° ′	° ′	° ′	′	° ′	′	′
	23 00	178 22.9	N20 01.4	320 52.7	10.0	S 7 52.9	10.1	58.5
	01	193 22.9	00.9	335 21.7	10.0	7 42.8	10.1	58.5
	02	208 22.9	20 00.4	349 50.7	10.0	7 32.7	10.1	58.5
	03	223 22.9	19 59.9	4 19.7	10.1	7 22.6	10.2	58.5
	04	238 22.9	59.3	18 48.8	10.0	7 12.4	10.3	58.5
	05	253 22.8	58.8	33 17.8	10.1	7 02.1	10.3	58.6
	06	268 22.8	N19 58.3	47 46.9	10.0	S 6 51.8	10.3	58.6
S	07	283 22.8	57.8	62 15.9	10.1	6 41.5	10.4	58.6
A	08	298 22.8	57.3	76 45.0	10.1	6 31.1	10.4	58.6
T	09	313 22.8	. . 56.8	91 14.1	10.1	6 20.7	10.4	58.6
U	10	328 22.8	56.2	105 43.2	10.1	6 10.3	10.5	58.6
R	11	343 22.8	55.7	120 12.3	10.1	5 59.8	10.5	58.6
D	12	358 22.7	N19 55.2	134 41.4	10.1	S 5 49.3	10.6	58.7
A	13	13 22.7	54.7	149 10.5	10.1	5 38.7	10.6	58.7
Y	14	28 22.7	54.1	163 39.6	10.1	5 28.1	10.6	58.7
	15	43 22.7	. . 53.6	178 08.7	10.2	5 17.5	10.7	58.7
	16	58 22.7	53.1	192 37.9	10.1	5 06.8	10.7	58.7
	17	73 22.7	52.6	207 07.0	10.1	4 56.1	10.7	58.7
	18	88 22.7	N19 52.1	221 36.1	10.2	S 4 45.4	10.8	58.7
	19	103 22.7	51.5	236 05.3	10.1	4 34.6	10.8	58.8
	20	118 22.6	51.0	250 34.4	10.2	4 23.8	10.8	58.8
	21	133 22.6	. . 50.5	265 03.6	10.2	4 13.0	10.9	58.8
	22	148 22.6	50.0	279 32.8	10.1	4 02.1	10.8	58.8
	23	163 22.6	49.4	294 01.9	10.2	3 51.3	10.9	58.8
	24 00	178 22.6	N19 48.9	308 31.1	10.2	S 3 40.4	10.9	58.8
	01	193 22.6	48.4	323 00.3	10.1	3 29.5	11.0	58.8
	02	208 22.6	47.8	337 29.4	10.2	3 18.5	11.0	58.8
	03	223 22.6	. . 47.3	351 58.6	10.2	3 07.5	11.0	58.9
	04	238 22.6	46.8	6 27.8	10.1	2 56.5	11.0	58.9
	05	253 22.6	46.3	20 56.9	10.2	2 45.5	11.0	58.9
	06	268 22.5	N19 45.7	35 26.1	10.2	S 2 34.5	11.0	58.9
	07	283 22.5	45.2	49 55.3	10.2	2 23.5	11.1	58.9
	08	298 22.5	44.7	64 24.5	10.1	2 12.4	11.1	58.9
S	09	313 22.5	. . 44.1	78 53.6	10.2	2 01.3	11.1	58.9
U	10	328 22.5	43.6	93 22.8	10.1	1 50.2	11.1	58.9
N	11	343 22.5	43.1	107 51.9	10.2	1 39.1	11.1	58.9
D	12	358 22.5	N19 42.5	122 21.1	10.2	S 1 28.0	11.1	59.0
A	13	13 22.5	42.0	136 50.3	10.1	1 16.9	11.2	59.0
Y	14	28 22.5	41.5	151 19.4	10.2	1 05.7	11.1	59.0
	15	43 22.5	. . 40.9	165 48.6	10.1	0 54.6	11.2	59.0
	16	58 22.5	40.4	180 17.7	10.1	0 43.4	11.1	59.0
	17	73 22.5	39.8	194 46.8	10.2	0 32.3	11.2	59.0
	18	88 22.5	N19 39.3	209 16.0	10.1	S 0 21.1	11.2	59.0
	19	103 22.5	38.8	223 45.1	10.1	S 0 09.9	11.2	59.0
	20	118 22.5	38.2	238 14.2	10.1	N 0 01.3	11.1	59.0
	21	133 22.4	. . 37.7	252 43.3	10.1	0 12.4	11.2	59.0
	22	148 22.4	37.2	267 12.4	10.1	0 23.6	11.2	59.0
	23	163 22.4	36.6	281 41.5	10.0	0 34.8	11.2	59.1
	25 00	178 22.4	N19 36.1	296 10.5	10.1	N 0 46.0	11.2	59.1
	01	193 22.4	35.5	310 39.6	10.0	0 57.2	11.1	59.1
	02	208 22.4	35.0	325 08.6	10.1	1 08.3	11.2	59.1
	03	223 22.4	. . 34.4	339 37.7	10.0	1 19.5	11.2	59.1
	04	238 22.4	33.9	354 06.7	10.0	1 30.7	11.1	59.1
	05	253 22.4	33.4	8 35.7	10.0	1 41.8	11.2	59.1
	06	268 22.4	N19 32.8	23 04.7	10.0	N 1 53.0	11.1	59.1
	07	283 22.4	32.3	37 33.7	10.0	2 04.1	11.2	59.1
	08	298 22.4	31.7	52 02.7	9.9	2 15.3	11.1	59.1
M	09	313 22.4	. . 31.2	66 31.6	10.0	2 26.4	11.1	59.1
O	10	328 22.4	30.6	81 00.6	9.9	2 37.5	11.1	59.1
N	11	343 22.4	30.1	95 29.5	9.9	2 48.6	11.1	59.1
D	12	358 22.4	N19 29.5	109 58.4	9.9	N 2 59.7	11.1	59.2
A	13	13 22.4	29.0	124 27.3	9.9	3 10.8	11.0	59.2
Y	14	28 22.4	28.4	138 56.2	9.8	3 21.8	11.1	59.2
	15	43 22.4	. . 27.9	153 25.0	9.9	3 32.9	11.0	59.2
	16	58 22.4	27.3	167 53.9	9.8	3 43.9	11.0	59.2
	17	73 22.4	26.8	182 22.7	9.8	3 54.9	11.0	59.2
	18	88 22.4	N19 26.2	196 51.5	9.7	N 4 05.9	10.9	59.2
	19	103 22.4	25.7	211 20.2	9.8	4 16.8	10.9	59.2
	20	118 22.4	25.1	225 49.0	9.7	4 27.7	11.0	59.2
	21	133 22.4	. . 24.6	240 17.7	9.7	4 38.7	10.8	59.2
	22	148 22.4	24.0	254 46.4	9.7	4 49.5	10.9	59.2
	23	163 22.4	23.5	269 15.1	9.7	N 5 00.4	10.8	59.2
		SD 15.8	*d* 0.5	SD	16.0	16.1		16.1

Lat.	Twilight Naut.	Twilight Civil	Sunrise	Moonrise 23	Moonrise 24	Moonrise 25	Moonrise 26
°	h m	h m	h m	h m	h m	h m	h m
N 72	▭	▭	▭	22 14	22 08	22 03	21 57
N 70	▭	▭	▭	22 08	22 09	22 09	22 10
68	////	////	01 31	22 04	22 09	22 14	22 21
66	////	////	02 15	22 00	22 09	22 19	22 30
64	////	00 36	02 44	21 56	22 09	22 23	22 38
62	////	01 42	03 06	21 54	22 10	22 26	22 44
60	////	02 16	03 23	21 51	22 10	22 29	22 50
N 58	00 33	02 39	03 38	21 49	22 10	22 31	22 55
56	01 33	02 58	03 50	21 47	22 10	22 34	22 59
54	02 04	03 14	04 01	21 45	22 10	22 36	23 03
52	02 26	03 27	04 10	21 43	22 10	22 38	23 07
50	02 44	03 39	04 19	21 42	22 10	22 40	23 10
45	03 18	04 02	04 37	21 38	22 11	22 43	23 18
N 40	03 42	04 20	04 51	21 36	22 11	22 47	23 24
35	04 01	04 35	05 04	21 33	22 11	22 49	23 29
30	04 16	04 48	05 14	21 31	22 11	22 52	23 34
20	04 41	05 09	05 33	21 27	22 12	22 56	23 42
N 10	05 00	05 26	05 48	21 24	22 12	23 00	23 49
0	05 15	05 41	06 03	21 21	22 12	23 04	23 56
S 10	05 29	05 55	06 17	21 18	22 13	23 07	24 03
20	05 43	06 09	06 33	21 15	22 13	23 11	24 11
30	05 56	06 25	06 50	21 11	22 13	23 16	24 19
35	06 02	06 33	07 00	21 09	22 14	23 19	24 24
40	06 09	06 42	07 12	21 07	22 14	23 22	24 30
45	06 17	06 53	07 25	21 04	22 14	23 25	24 36
S 50	06 26	07 06	07 42	21 01	22 15	23 29	24 44
52	06 30	07 11	07 49	20 59	22 15	23 31	24 48
54	06 34	07 18	07 58	20 57	22 15	23 33	24 52
56	06 38	07 24	08 08	20 55	22 15	23 36	24 56
58	06 43	07 32	08 19	20 53	22 16	23 38	25 01
S 60	06 48	07 41	08 31	20 51	22 16	23 41	25 07

Lat.	Sunset	Twilight Civil	Twilight Naut.	Moonset 23	Moonset 24	Moonset 25	Moonset 26
°	h m	h m	h m	h m	h m	h m	h m
N 72	▭	▭	▭	07 26	09 19	11 12	13 06
N 70	▭	▭	▭	07 36	09 22	11 08	12 55
68	22 36	////	////	07 45	09 24	11 05	12 46
66	21 54	////	////	07 52	09 26	11 02	12 38
64	21 27	23 25	////	07 57	09 28	11 00	12 32
62	21 05	22 27	////	08 02	09 30	10 58	12 26
60	20 48	21 55	////	08 07	09 31	10 56	12 22
N 58	20 34	21 32	23 29	08 10	09 32	10 55	12 17
56	20 22	21 13	22 36	08 14	09 33	10 53	12 14
54	20 11	20 58	22 07	08 17	09 34	10 52	12 10
52	20 02	20 45	21 45	08 19	09 35	10 51	12 07
50	19 53	20 33	21 27	08 22	09 36	10 50	12 05
45	19 36	20 10	20 54	08 27	09 37	10 48	11 59
N 40	19 21	19 52	20 30	08 32	09 39	10 46	11 54
35	19 09	19 37	20 12	08 35	09 40	10 45	11 50
30	18 58	19 25	19 56	08 39	09 41	10 43	11 46
20	18 40	19 04	19 32	08 45	09 42	10 41	11 40
N 10	18 25	18 47	19 13	08 50	09 44	10 39	11 34
0	18 10	18 32	18 58	08 54	09 45	10 37	11 29
S 10	17 56	18 18	18 44	08 59	09 47	10 35	11 23
20	17 40	18 04	18 31	09 04	09 48	10 32	11 18
30	17 23	17 49	18 18	09 09	09 50	10 30	11 11
35	17 13	17 40	18 11	09 13	09 51	10 29	11 08
40	17 02	17 31	18 04	09 16	09 52	10 27	11 03
45	16 48	17 20	17 56	09 20	09 53	10 25	10 58
S 50	16 32	17 08	17 48	09 25	09 54	10 23	10 53
52	16 24	17 02	17 44	09 27	09 55	10 22	10 50
54	16 15	16 56	17 40	09 30	09 56	10 21	10 47
56	16 06	16 49	17 36	09 33	09 56	10 20	10 44
58	15 55	16 41	17 31	09 35	09 57	10 18	10 40
S 60	15 42	16 33	17 26	09 39	09 58	10 17	10 36

Day	SUN Eqn. of Time 00h	SUN Eqn. of Time 12h	SUN Mer. Pass.	MOON Mer. Pass. Upper	MOON Mer. Pass. Lower	MOON Age	MOON Phase
d	m s	m s	h m	h m	h m	d	%
23	06 28	06 29	12 06	02 42	15 08	19	86
24	06 30	06 30	12 06	03 33	15 59	20	77
25	06 30	06 30	12 07	04 24	16 50	21	67

UT	ARIES	VENUS −3·9		MARS −0·9		JUPITER −1·8		SATURN +0·3	
	GHA	GHA	Dec	GHA	Dec	GHA	Dec	GHA	Dec
d h	° ′	° ′	° ′	° ′	° ′	° ′	° ′	° ′	° ′
26 00	304 07.1	164 17.7	N17 08.0	69 45.7	S22 20.7	131 56.5	N 4 37.2	55 26.6	S20 17.8
01	319 09.6	179 17.0	07.1	84 47.3	20.9	146 58.6	37.0	70 29.1	17.8
02	334 12.1	194 16.4	06.2	99 49.0	21.1	162 00.6	36.8	85 31.6	17.8
03	349 14.5	209 15.8	. . 05.3	114 50.7	. . 21.3	177 02.7	. . 36.7	100 34.2	. . 17.8
04	4 17.0	224 15.2	04.4	129 52.3	21.5	192 04.8	36.5	115 36.7	17.8
05	19 19.5	239 14.6	03.5	144 54.0	21.6	207 06.8	36.3	130 39.3	17.8
06	34 21.9	254 14.0	N17 02.5	159 55.6	S22 21.8	222 08.9	N 4 36.1	145 41.8	S20 17.8
T 07	49 24.4	269 13.4	01.6	174 57.3	22.0	237 10.9	36.0	160 44.4	17.8
U 08	64 26.9	284 12.8	17 00.7	189 58.9	22.2	252 13.0	35.8	175 46.9	17.8
E 09	79 29.3	299 12.2	16 59.8	205 00.6	. . 22.4	267 15.1	. . 35.6	190 49.4	. . 17.8
S 10	94 31.8	314 11.6	58.9	220 02.2	22.6	282 17.1	35.4	205 52.0	17.7
D 11	109 34.2	329 11.0	58.0	235 03.8	22.8	297 19.2	35.2	220 54.5	17.7
A 12	124 36.7	344 10.4	N16 57.0	250 05.5	S22 23.0	312 21.2	N 4 35.1	235 57.1	S20 17.7
Y 13	139 39.2	359 09.8	56.1	265 07.1	23.1	327 23.3	34.9	250 59.6	17.7
14	154 41.6	14 09.2	55.2	280 08.8	23.3	342 25.4	34.7	266 02.1	17.7
15	169 44.1	29 08.6	. . 54.3	295 10.4	. . 23.5	357 27.4	. . 34.5	281 04.7	. . 17.7
16	184 46.6	44 08.0	53.4	310 12.1	23.7	12 29.5	34.4	296 07.2	17.7
17	199 49.0	59 07.4	52.4	325 13.7	23.9	27 31.5	34.2	311 09.8	17.7
18	214 51.5	74 06.8	N16 51.5	340 15.3	S22 24.1	42 33.6	N 4 34.0	326 12.3	S20 17.7
19	229 54.0	89 06.2	50.6	355 17.0	24.3	57 35.7	33.8	341 14.8	17.7
20	244 56.4	104 05.6	49.7	10 18.6	24.4	72 37.7	33.6	356 17.4	17.7
21	259 58.9	119 05.0	. . 48.7	25 20.2	. . 24.6	87 39.8	. . 33.5	11 19.9	. . 17.7
22	275 01.4	134 04.5	47.8	40 21.9	24.8	102 41.8	33.3	26 22.4	17.7
23	290 03.8	149 03.9	46.9	55 23.5	25.0	117 43.9	33.1	41 25.0	17.7
27 00	305 06.3	164 03.3	N16 46.0	70 25.1	S22 25.2	132 45.9	N 4 32.9	56 27.5	S20 17.7
01	320 08.7	179 02.7	45.0	85 26.8	25.4	147 48.0	32.8	71 30.1	17.7
02	335 11.2	194 02.1	44.1	100 28.4	25.6	162 50.1	32.6	86 32.6	17.7
03	350 13.7	209 01.5	. . 43.2	115 30.0	. . 25.8	177 52.1	. . 32.4	101 35.1	. . 17.7
04	5 16.1	224 00.9	42.2	130 31.6	26.0	192 54.2	32.2	116 37.7	17.7
05	20 18.6	239 00.3	41.3	145 33.3	26.1	207 56.2	32.0	131 40.2	17.7
06	35 21.1	253 59.7	N16 40.4	160 34.9	S22 26.3	222 58.3	N 4 31.9	146 42.7	S20 17.7
W 07	50 23.5	268 59.1	39.4	175 36.5	26.5	238 00.4	31.7	161 45.3	17.7
E 08	65 26.0	283 58.5	38.5	190 38.1	26.7	253 02.4	31.5	176 47.8	17.7
D 09	80 28.5	298 57.9	. . 37.6	205 39.8	. . 26.9	268 04.5	. . 31.3	191 50.4	. . 17.7
N 10	95 30.9	313 57.4	36.6	220 41.4	27.1	283 06.5	31.1	206 52.9	17.7
E 11	110 33.4	328 56.8	35.7	235 43.0	27.3	298 08.6	31.0	221 55.4	17.7
S 12	125 35.9	343 56.2	N16 34.8	250 44.6	S22 27.5	313 10.6	N 4 30.8	236 58.0	S20 17.7
D 13	140 38.3	358 55.6	33.8	265 46.2	27.7	328 12.7	30.6	252 00.5	17.7
A 14	155 40.8	13 55.0	32.9	280 47.8	27.8	343 14.7	30.4	267 03.0	17.7
Y 15	170 43.2	28 54.4	. . 31.9	295 49.5	. . 28.0	358 16.8	. . 30.2	282 05.6	. . 17.7
16	185 45.7	43 53.8	31.0	310 51.1	28.2	13 18.9	30.1	297 08.1	17.7
17	200 48.2	58 53.2	30.1	325 52.7	28.4	28 20.9	29.9	312 10.6	17.7
18	215 50.6	73 52.7	N16 29.1	340 54.3	S22 28.6	43 23.0	N 4 29.7	327 13.2	S20 17.7
19	230 53.1	88 52.1	28.2	355 55.9	28.8	58 25.0	29.5	342 15.7	17.7
20	245 55.6	103 51.5	27.2	10 57.5	29.0	73 27.1	29.4	357 18.2	17.7
21	260 58.0	118 50.9	. . 26.3	25 59.1	. . 29.2	88 29.1	. . 29.2	12 20.8	. . 17.7
22	276 00.5	133 50.3	25.3	41 00.7	29.4	103 31.2	29.0	27 23.3	17.7
23	291 03.0	148 49.7	24.4	56 02.3	29.6	118 33.2	28.8	42 25.8	17.7
28 00	306 05.4	163 49.2	N16 23.4	71 03.9	S22 29.7	133 35.3	N 4 28.6	57 28.4	S20 17.7
01	321 07.9	178 48.6	22.5	86 05.6	29.9	148 37.4	28.5	72 30.9	17.7
02	336 10.3	193 48.0	21.5	101 07.2	30.1	163 39.4	28.3	87 33.5	17.7
03	351 12.8	208 47.4	. . 20.6	116 08.8	. . 30.3	178 41.5	. . 28.1	102 36.0	. . 17.7
04	6 15.3	223 46.8	19.6	131 10.4	30.5	193 43.5	27.9	117 38.5	17.7
05	21 17.7	238 46.3	18.7	146 12.0	30.7	208 45.6	27.7	132 41.1	17.7
06	36 20.2	253 45.7	N16 17.7	161 13.6	S22 30.9	223 47.6	N 4 27.6	147 43.6	S20 17.7
07	51 22.7	268 45.1	16.8	176 15.2	31.1	238 49.7	27.4	162 46.1	17.7
T 08	66 25.1	283 44.5	15.8	191 16.8	31.3	253 51.7	27.2	177 48.6	17.7
H 09	81 27.6	298 44.0	. . 14.9	206 18.3	. . 31.5	268 53.8	. . 27.0	192 51.2	. . 17.7
U 10	96 30.1	313 43.4	13.9	221 19.9	31.7	283 55.8	26.8	207 53.7	17.7
R 11	111 32.5	328 42.8	13.0	236 21.5	31.8	298 57.9	26.7	222 56.2	17.7
S 12	126 35.0	343 42.2	N16 12.0	251 23.1	S22 32.0	314 00.0	N 4 26.5	237 58.8	S20 17.7
D 13	141 37.5	358 41.6	11.1	266 24.7	32.2	329 02.0	26.3	253 01.3	17.7
A 14	156 39.9	13 41.1	10.1	281 26.3	32.4	344 04.1	26.1	268 03.8	17.7
Y 15	171 42.4	28 40.5	. . 09.1	296 27.9	. . 32.6	359 06.1	. . 25.9	283 06.4	. . 17.7
16	186 44.8	43 39.9	08.2	311 29.5	32.8	14 08.2	25.7	298 08.9	17.7
17	201 47.3	58 39.4	07.2	326 31.1	33.0	29 10.2	25.6	313 11.4	17.7
18	216 49.8	73 38.8	N16 06.3	341 32.7	S22 33.2	44 12.3	N 4 25.4	328 14.0	S20 17.7
19	231 52.2	88 38.2	05.3	356 34.3	33.4	59 14.3	25.2	343 16.5	17.7
20	246 54.7	103 37.6	04.3	11 35.8	33.6	74 16.4	25.0	358 19.0	17.7
21	261 57.2	118 37.1	. . 03.4	26 37.4	. . 33.8	89 18.4	. . 24.8	13 21.6	. . 17.7
22	276 59.6	133 36.5	02.4	41 39.0	34.0	104 20.5	24.7	28 24.1	17.7
23	292 02.1	148 35.9	01.5	56 40.6	34.2	119 22.5	24.5	43 26.6	17.7
Mer. Pass.	h m 3 39.0	*v* −0.6	*d* 0.9	*v* 1.6	*d* 0.2	*v* 2.1	*d* 0.2	*v* 2.5	*d* 0.0

STARS

Name	SHA	Dec
	° ′	° ′
Acamar	315 16.9	S40 14.2
Achernar	335 25.2	S57 09.0
Acrux	173 07.1	S63 11.6
Adhara	255 11.2	S28 59.8
Aldebaran	290 47.1	N16 32.3
Alioth	166 19.2	N55 52.6
Alkaid	152 57.4	N49 14.2
Al Na'ir	27 40.7	S46 52.6
Alnilam	275 44.5	S 1 11.6
Alphard	217 54.3	S 8 43.9
Alphecca	126 09.1	N26 39.9
Alpheratz	357 41.1	N29 10.8
Altair	62 05.8	N 8 55.0
Ankaa	353 13.5	S42 12.7
Antares	112 23.4	S26 27.9
Arcturus	145 53.8	N19 06.1
Atria	107 22.9	S69 03.4
Avior	234 17.7	S59 33.9
Bellatrix	278 30.0	N 6 21.7
Betelgeuse	270 59.3	N 7 24.4
Canopus	263 55.7	S52 42.3
Capella	280 31.7	N46 00.5
Deneb	49 29.5	N45 20.5
Denebola	182 31.7	N14 28.9
Diphda	348 53.7	S17 53.6
Dubhe	193 49.8	N61 39.9
Elnath	278 10.2	N28 37.0
Eltanin	90 44.7	N51 29.6
Enif	33 44.7	N 9 57.2
Fomalhaut	15 21.4	S29 31.9
Gacrux	171 58.7	S57 12.5
Gienah	175 50.3	S17 38.0
Hadar	148 44.8	S60 27.3
Hamal	327 58.3	N23 32.2
Kaus Aust.	83 40.7	S34 22.4
Kochab	137 20.1	N74 05.7
Markab	13 36.0	N15 17.7
Menkar	314 12.9	N 4 09.2
Menkent	148 05.0	S36 27.1
Miaplacidus	221 40.0	S69 47.3
Mirfak	308 37.4	N49 54.8
Nunki	75 55.4	S26 16.3
Peacock	53 15.4	S56 40.7
Pollux	243 25.6	N27 59.0
Procyon	244 57.9	N 5 10.8
Rasalhague	96 04.2	N12 33.2
Regulus	207 41.6	N11 53.2
Rigel	281 10.3	S 8 11.1
Rigil Kent.	139 48.7	S60 54.3
Sabik	102 09.9	S15 44.5
Schedar	349 37.7	N56 37.4
Shaula	96 18.7	S37 06.8
Sirius	258 32.2	S16 44.4
Spica	158 29.1	S11 14.7
Suhail	222 51.3	S43 30.1
Vega	80 37.1	N38 48.3
Zuben'ubi	137 03.0	S16 06.5

	SHA	Mer. Pass.
	° ′	h m
Venus	218 57.0	13 04
Mars	125 18.8	19 16
Jupiter	187 39.7	15 07
Saturn	111 21.2	20 11

UT		SUN GHA	SUN Dec	MOON GHA	v	MOON Dec	d	HP
d	h	° ′	° ′	° ′	′	° ′	′	′
26	00	178 22.4	N19 22.9	283 43.8	9.6	N 5 11.2	10.8	59.2
	01	193 22.4	22.4	298 12.4	9.6	5 22.0	10.8	59.2
	02	208 22.4	21.8	312 41.0	9.6	5 32.8	10.8	59.2
	03	223 22.4	. . 21.2	327 09.6	9.6	5 43.6	10.7	59.2
	04	238 22.4	20.7	341 38.2	9.5	5 54.3	10.6	59.2
	05	253 22.4	20.1	356 06.7	9.5	6 04.9	10.7	59.3
	06	268 22.4	N19 19.6	10 35.2	9.5	N 6 15.6	10.6	59.3
	07	283 22.4	19.0	25 03.7	9.4	6 26.2	10.6	59.3
T	08	298 22.4	18.5	39 32.1	9.5	6 36.8	10.5	59.3
U	09	313 22.4	. . 17.9	54 00.6	9.4	6 47.3	10.5	59.3
E	10	328 22.4	17.3	68 29.0	9.3	6 57.8	10.4	59.3
S	11	343 22.4	16.8	82 57.3	9.4	7 08.2	10.5	59.3
D	12	358 22.4	N19 16.2	97 25.7	9.3	N 7 18.7	10.3	59.3
A	13	13 22.5	15.7	111 54.0	9.3	7 29.0	10.4	59.3
Y	14	28 22.5	15.1	126 22.3	9.2	7 39.4	10.3	59.3
	15	43 22.5	. . 14.5	140 50.5	9.2	7 49.7	10.2	59.3
	16	58 22.5	14.0	155 18.7	9.2	7 59.9	10.2	59.3
	17	73 22.5	13.4	169 46.9	9.2	8 10.1	10.1	59.3
	18	88 22.5	N19 12.8	184 15.1	9.1	N 8 20.2	10.1	59.3
	19	103 22.5	12.3	198 43.2	9.1	8 30.3	10.1	59.3
	20	118 22.5	11.7	213 11.3	9.0	8 40.4	10.0	59.3
	21	133 22.5	. . 11.1	227 39.3	9.0	8 50.4	9.9	59.3
	22	148 22.5	10.6	242 07.3	9.0	9 00.3	9.9	59.3
	23	163 22.5	10.0	256 35.3	9.0	9 10.2	9.9	59.3
27	00	178 22.5	N19 09.4	271 03.3	8.9	N 9 20.1	9.8	59.3
	01	193 22.5	08.9	285 31.2	8.9	9 29.9	9.7	59.3
	02	208 22.5	08.3	299 59.1	8.8	9 39.6	9.7	59.3
	03	223 22.5	. . 07.7	314 26.9	8.8	9 49.3	9.6	59.3
	04	238 22.6	07.2	328 54.7	8.8	9 58.9	9.5	59.3
	05	253 22.6	06.6	343 22.5	8.8	10 08.4	9.5	59.3
	06	268 22.6	N19 06.0	357 50.3	8.7	N10 17.9	9.5	59.3
W	07	283 22.6	05.4	12 18.0	8.6	10 27.4	9.4	59.3
E	08	298 22.6	04.9	26 45.6	8.7	10 36.8	9.3	59.3
D	09	313 22.6	. . 04.3	41 13.3	8.6	10 46.1	9.2	59.3
N	10	328 22.6	03.7	55 40.9	8.5	10 55.3	9.2	59.3
E	11	343 22.6	03.2	70 08.4	8.6	11 04.5	9.1	59.3
S	12	358 22.6	N19 02.6	84 36.0	8.4	N11 13.6	9.0	59.3
D	13	13 22.6	02.0	99 03.4	8.5	11 22.6	9.0	59.3
A	14	28 22.7	01.4	113 30.9	8.4	11 31.6	8.9	59.3
Y	15	43 22.7	. . 00.8	127 58.3	8.4	11 40.5	8.9	59.3
	16	58 22.7	19 00.3	142 25.7	8.3	11 49.4	8.7	59.3
	17	73 22.7	18 59.7	156 53.0	8.3	11 58.1	8.7	59.3
	18	88 22.7	N18 59.1	171 20.3	8.3	N12 06.8	8.6	59.3
	19	103 22.7	58.5	185 47.6	8.2	12 15.4	8.6	59.3
	20	118 22.7	58.0	200 14.8	8.2	12 24.0	8.4	59.3
	21	133 22.7	. . 57.4	214 42.0	8.1	12 32.4	8.4	59.3
	22	148 22.8	56.8	229 09.1	8.1	12 40.8	8.3	59.3
	23	163 22.8	56.2	243 36.2	8.1	12 49.1	8.3	59.3
28	00	178 22.8	N18 55.6	258 03.3	8.0	N12 57.4	8.1	59.3
	01	193 22.8	55.1	272 30.3	8.0	13 05.5	8.1	59.3
	02	208 22.8	54.5	286 57.3	8.0	13 13.6	8.0	59.3
	03	223 22.8	. . 53.9	301 24.3	7.9	13 21.6	7.9	59.3
	04	238 22.8	53.3	315 51.2	7.9	13 29.5	7.8	59.3
	05	253 22.9	52.7	330 18.1	7.8	13 37.3	7.7	59.3
	06	268 22.9	N18 52.1	344 44.9	7.8	N13 45.0	7.7	59.3
	07	283 22.9	51.6	359 11.7	7.8	13 52.7	7.6	59.3
T	08	298 22.9	51.0	13 38.5	7.8	14 00.3	7.4	59.3
H	09	313 22.9	. . 50.4	28 05.3	7.6	14 07.7	7.4	59.3
U	10	328 22.9	49.8	42 31.9	7.7	14 15.1	7.3	59.3
R	11	343 23.0	49.2	56 58.6	7.6	14 22.4	7.2	59.3
S	12	358 23.0	N18 48.6	71 25.2	7.6	N14 29.6	7.2	59.3
D	13	13 23.0	48.0	85 51.8	7.6	14 36.8	7.0	59.3
A	14	28 23.0	47.4	100 18.4	7.5	14 43.8	6.9	59.3
Y	15	43 23.0	. . 46.9	114 44.9	7.5	14 50.7	6.9	59.3
	16	58 23.0	46.3	129 11.4	7.4	14 57.6	6.7	59.3
	17	73 23.1	45.7	143 37.8	7.5	15 04.3	6.7	59.3
	18	88 23.1	N18 45.1	158 04.3	7.3	N15 11.0	6.5	59.2
	19	103 23.1	44.5	172 30.6	7.4	15 17.5	6.5	59.2
	20	118 23.1	43.9	186 57.0	7.3	15 24.0	6.3	59.2
	21	133 23.1	. . 43.3	201 23.3	7.3	15 30.3	6.3	59.2
	22	148 23.1	42.7	215 49.6	7.2	15 36.6	6.1	59.2
	23	163 23.2	42.1	230 15.8	7.3	N15 42.7	6.1	59.2
		SD 15.8	*d* 0.6	SD 16.2		16.2		16.1

Lat.	Twilight Naut.	Twilight Civil	Sunrise	Moonrise 26	Moonrise 27	Moonrise 28	Moonrise 29
°	h m	h m	h m	h m	h m	h m	h m
N 72	▭	▭	▭	21 57	21 51	21 44	21 31
N 70	////	////	00 15	22 10	22 13	22 19	22 33
68	////	////	01 50	22 21	22 30	22 45	23 09
66	////	////	02 27	22 30	22 44	23 04	23 34
64	////	01 08	02 53	22 38	22 56	23 20	23 54
62	////	01 56	03 14	22 44	23 06	23 33	24 10
60	////	02 25	03 30	22 50	23 14	23 45	24 24
N 58	01 02	02 47	03 44	22 55	23 22	23 55	24 35
56	01 46	03 05	03 55	22 59	23 29	24 03	00 03
54	02 13	03 20	04 06	23 03	23 34	24 11	00 11
52	02 33	03 32	04 15	23 07	23 40	24 18	00 18
50	02 50	03 43	04 23	23 10	23 45	24 24	00 24
45	03 22	04 06	04 40	23 18	23 55	24 37	00 37
N 40	03 45	04 23	04 54	23 24	24 04	00 04	00 49
35	04 03	04 38	05 06	23 29	24 12	00 12	00 58
30	04 18	04 50	05 16	23 34	24 19	00 19	01 07
20	04 42	05 10	05 34	23 42	24 30	00 30	01 21
N 10	05 00	05 27	05 49	23 49	24 41	00 41	01 34
0	05 16	05 41	06 03	23 56	24 50	00 50	01 46
S 10	05 29	05 55	06 17	24 03	00 03	01 00	01 58
20	05 42	06 08	06 32	24 11	00 11	01 10	02 11
30	05 54	06 23	06 48	24 19	00 19	01 23	02 26
35	06 01	06 31	06 58	24 24	00 24	01 30	02 34
40	06 07	06 40	07 09	24 30	00 30	01 38	02 44
45	06 15	06 50	07 22	24 36	00 36	01 47	02 56
S 50	06 23	07 02	07 38	24 44	00 44	01 58	03 10
52	06 26	07 08	07 45	24 48	00 48	02 03	03 17
54	06 30	07 13	07 53	24 52	00 52	02 09	03 24
56	06 34	07 20	08 03	24 56	00 56	02 16	03 32
58	06 38	07 27	08 13	25 01	01 01	02 23	03 41
S 60	06 43	07 35	08 25	25 07	01 07	02 31	03 52

Lat.	Sunset	Twilight Civil	Twilight Naut.	Moonset 26	Moonset 27	Moonset 28	Moonset 29
°	h m	h m	h m	h m	h m	h m	h m
N 72	▭	▭	▭	13 06	15 04	17 06	19 17
N 70	23 30	////	////	12 55	14 43	16 32	18 16
68	22 18	////	////	12 46	14 27	16 07	17 41
66	21 42	////	////	12 38	14 14	15 48	17 16
64	21 17	22 58	////	12 32	14 03	15 33	16 56
62	20 57	22 14	////	12 26	13 54	15 20	16 40
60	20 41	21 45	////	12 22	13 47	15 09	16 27
N 58	20 28	21 24	23 05	12 17	13 40	15 00	16 16
56	20 16	21 06	22 24	12 14	13 34	14 52	16 06
54	20 06	20 52	21 58	12 10	13 28	14 45	15 57
52	19 57	20 40	21 38	12 07	13 24	14 38	15 49
50	19 49	20 29	21 21	12 05	13 19	14 32	15 42
45	19 32	20 06	20 50	11 59	13 10	14 20	15 27
N 40	19 18	19 49	20 27	11 54	13 02	14 09	15 15
35	19 07	19 35	20 09	11 50	12 55	14 00	15 04
30	18 56	19 23	19 54	11 46	12 49	13 53	14 55
20	18 39	19 03	19 31	11 40	12 39	13 39	14 39
N 10	18 24	18 46	19 12	11 34	12 30	13 28	14 26
0	18 10	18 32	18 57	11 29	12 22	13 17	14 13
S 10	17 56	18 18	18 44	11 23	12 13	13 06	14 00
20	17 41	18 05	18 31	11 18	12 05	12 54	13 46
30	17 25	17 50	18 19	11 11	11 54	12 41	13 30
35	17 15	17 42	18 13	11 08	11 49	12 33	13 21
40	17 04	17 33	18 06	11 03	11 42	12 24	13 11
45	16 51	17 23	17 59	10 58	11 34	12 14	12 59
S 50	16 36	17 11	17 51	10 53	11 25	12 02	12 44
52	16 28	17 06	17 47	10 50	11 21	11 56	12 37
54	16 20	17 00	17 44	10 47	11 16	11 50	12 29
56	16 11	16 54	17 40	10 44	11 11	11 43	12 21
58	16 01	16 46	17 35	10 40	11 05	11 35	12 11
S 60	15 49	16 38	17 31	10 36	10 59	11 26	12 00

Day	SUN Eqn. of Time 00^h	SUN Eqn. of Time 12^h	SUN Mer. Pass.	MOON Mer. Pass. Upper	MOON Mer. Pass. Lower	MOON Age	MOON Phase
d	m s	m s	h m	h m	h m	d %	
26	06 30	06 30	12 07	05 16	17 42	22 55	
27	06 30	06 29	12 06	06 09	18 36	23 44	
28	06 29	06 28	12 06	07 03	19 31	24 33	

	UT d h	ARIES GHA	VENUS −3·9 GHA	VENUS Dec	MARS −0·8 GHA	MARS Dec	JUPITER −1·7 GHA	JUPITER Dec	SATURN +0·3 GHA	SATURN Dec
		° ′	° ′	° ′	° ′	° ′	° ′	° ′	° ′	° ′
	29 00	307 04.6	163 35.4	N16 00.5	71 42.2	S22 34.3	134 24.6	N 4 24.3	58 29.1	S20 17.7
	01	322 07.0	178 34.8	15 59.5	86 43.7	34.5	149 26.6	24.1	73 31.7	17.7
	02	337 09.5	193 34.2	58.6	101 45.3	34.7	164 28.7	23.9	88 34.2	17.7
	03	352 12.0	208 33.7	. . 57.6	116 46.9	. . 34.9	179 30.7	. . 23.8	103 36.7	. . 17.7
	04	7 14.4	223 33.1	56.6	131 48.5	35.1	194 32.8	23.6	118 39.3	17.7
	05	22 16.9	238 32.5	55.6	146 50.0	35.3	209 34.9	23.4	133 41.8	17.7
	06	37 19.3	253 32.0	N15 54.7	161 51.6	S22 35.5	224 36.9	N 4 23.2	148 44.3	S20 17.7
	07	52 21.8	268 31.4	53.7	176 53.2	35.7	239 39.0	23.0	163 46.9	17.7
	08	67 24.3	283 30.8	52.7	191 54.8	35.9	254 41.0	22.9	178 49.4	17.7
F	09	82 26.7	298 30.3	. . 51.8	206 56.3	. . 36.1	269 43.1	. . 22.7	193 51.9	. . 17.7
R	10	97 29.2	313 29.7	50.8	221 57.9	36.3	284 45.1	22.5	208 54.4	17.7
I	11	112 31.7	328 29.1	49.8	236 59.5	36.5	299 47.2	22.3	223 57.0	17.7
D	12	127 34.1	343 28.6	N15 48.8	252 01.0	S22 36.7	314 49.2	N 4 22.1	238 59.5	S20 17.7
A	13	142 36.6	358 28.0	47.9	267 02.6	36.9	329 51.3	21.9	254 02.0	17.7
Y	14	157 39.1	13 27.4	46.9	282 04.2	37.1	344 53.3	21.8	269 04.6	17.7
	15	172 41.5	28 26.9	. . 45.9	297 05.7	. . 37.3	359 55.4	. . 21.6	284 07.1	. . 17.7
	16	187 44.0	43 26.3	44.9	312 07.3	37.4	14 57.4	21.4	299 09.6	17.7
	17	202 46.5	58 25.8	44.0	327 08.9	37.6	29 59.5	21.2	314 12.1	17.7
	18	217 48.9	73 25.2	N15 43.0	342 10.4	S22 37.8	45 01.5	N 4 21.0	329 14.7	S20 17.7
	19	232 51.4	88 24.6	42.0	357 12.0	38.0	60 03.6	20.9	344 17.2	17.7
	20	247 53.8	103 24.1	41.0	12 13.6	38.2	75 05.6	20.7	359 19.7	17.7
	21	262 56.3	118 23.5	. . 40.0	27 15.1	. . 38.4	90 07.7	. . 20.5	14 22.2	. . 17.7
	22	277 58.8	133 23.0	39.1	42 16.7	38.6	105 09.7	20.3	29 24.8	17.7
	23	293 01.2	148 22.4	38.1	57 18.2	38.8	120 11.8	20.1	44 27.3	17.7
	30 00	308 03.7	163 21.8	N15 37.1	72 19.8	S22 39.0	135 13.8	N 4 19.9	59 29.8	S20 17.7
	01	323 06.2	178 21.3	36.1	87 21.3	39.2	150 15.9	19.8	74 32.3	17.7
	02	338 08.6	193 20.7	35.1	102 22.9	39.4	165 17.9	19.6	89 34.9	17.7
	03	353 11.1	208 20.2	. . 34.1	117 24.4	. . 39.6	180 20.0	. . 19.4	104 37.4	. . 17.7
	04	8 13.6	223 19.6	33.2	132 26.0	39.8	195 22.0	19.2	119 39.9	17.7
	05	23 16.0	238 19.1	32.2	147 27.5	40.0	210 24.1	19.0	134 42.4	17.7
	06	38 18.5	253 18.5	N15 31.2	162 29.1	S22 40.2	225 26.1	N 4 18.8	149 45.0	S20 17.7
	07	53 21.0	268 18.0	30.2	177 30.6	40.4	240 28.2	18.7	164 47.5	17.7
S	08	68 23.4	283 17.4	29.2	192 32.2	40.6	255 30.2	18.5	179 50.0	17.7
A	09	83 25.9	298 16.8	. . 28.2	207 33.7	. . 40.8	270 32.2	. . 18.3	194 52.5	. . 17.7
T	10	98 28.3	313 16.3	27.2	222 35.3	41.0	285 34.3	18.1	209 55.1	17.7
U	11	113 30.8	328 15.7	26.2	237 36.8	41.2	300 36.3	17.9	224 57.6	17.7
R	12	128 33.3	343 15.2	N15 25.2	252 38.4	S22 41.4	315 38.4	N 4 17.7	240 00.1	S20 17.7
D	13	143 35.7	358 14.6	24.2	267 39.9	41.6	330 40.4	17.6	255 02.6	17.7
A	14	158 38.2	13 14.1	23.3	282 41.5	41.8	345 42.5	17.4	270 05.2	17.7
Y	15	173 40.7	28 13.5	. . 22.3	297 43.0	. . 42.0	0 44.5	. . 17.2	285 07.7	. . 17.7
	16	188 43.1	43 13.0	21.3	312 44.5	42.1	15 46.6	17.0	300 10.2	17.7
	17	203 45.6	58 12.4	20.3	327 46.1	42.3	30 48.6	16.8	315 12.7	17.7
	18	218 48.1	73 11.9	N15 19.3	342 47.6	S22 42.5	45 50.7	N 4 16.6	330 15.3	S20 17.7
	19	233 50.5	88 11.3	18.3	357 49.1	42.7	60 52.7	16.5	345 17.8	17.7
	20	248 53.0	103 10.8	17.3	12 50.7	42.9	75 54.8	16.3	0 20.3	17.7
	21	263 55.4	118 10.2	. . 16.3	27 52.2	. . 43.1	90 56.8	. . 16.1	15 22.8	. . 17.7
	22	278 57.9	133 09.7	15.3	42 53.8	43.3	105 58.9	15.9	30 25.3	17.7
	23	294 00.4	148 09.2	14.3	57 55.3	43.5	121 00.9	15.7	45 27.9	17.7
	31 00	309 02.8	163 08.6	N15 13.3	72 56.8	S22 43.7	136 03.0	N 4 15.5	60 30.4	S20 17.7
	01	324 05.3	178 08.1	12.3	87 58.3	43.9	151 05.0	15.4	75 32.9	17.7
	02	339 07.8	193 07.5	11.3	102 59.9	44.1	166 07.1	15.2	90 35.4	17.7
	03	354 10.2	208 07.0	. . 10.3	118 01.4	. . 44.3	181 09.1	. . 15.0	105 38.0	. . 17.7
	04	9 12.7	223 06.4	09.3	133 02.9	44.5	196 11.1	14.8	120 40.5	17.7
	05	24 15.2	238 05.9	08.3	148 04.5	44.7	211 13.2	14.6	135 43.0	17.7
	06	39 17.6	253 05.3	N15 07.3	163 06.0	S22 44.9	226 15.2	N 4 14.4	150 45.5	S20 17.7
	07	54 20.1	268 04.8	06.3	178 07.5	45.1	241 17.3	14.3	165 48.0	17.7
	08	69 22.6	283 04.3	05.3	193 09.0	45.3	256 19.3	14.1	180 50.6	17.7
S	09	84 25.0	298 03.7	. . 04.3	208 10.6	. . 45.5	271 21.4	. . 13.9	195 53.1	. . 17.7
U	10	99 27.5	313 03.2	03.2	223 12.1	45.7	286 23.4	13.7	210 55.6	17.7
N	11	114 29.9	328 02.6	02.2	238 13.6	45.9	301 25.5	13.5	225 58.1	17.7
D	12	129 32.4	343 02.1	N15 01.2	253 15.1	S22 46.1	316 27.5	N 4 13.3	241 00.6	S20 17.7
A	13	144 34.9	358 01.6	15 00.2	268 16.6	46.3	331 29.6	13.2	256 03.2	17.7
Y	14	159 37.3	13 01.0	14 59.2	283 18.1	46.5	346 31.6	13.0	271 05.7	17.7
	15	174 39.8	28 00.5	. . 58.2	298 19.7	. . 46.7	1 33.6	. . 12.8	286 08.2	. . 17.7
	16	189 42.3	42 59.9	57.2	313 21.2	46.9	16 35.7	12.6	301 10.7	17.7
	17	204 44.7	57 59.4	56.2	328 22.7	47.1	31 37.7	12.4	316 13.2	17.7
	18	219 47.2	72 58.9	N14 55.2	343 24.2	S22 47.3	46 39.8	N 4 12.2	331 15.8	S20 17.7
	19	234 49.7	87 58.3	54.1	358 25.7	47.5	61 41.8	12.1	346 18.3	17.7
	20	249 52.1	102 57.8	53.1	13 27.2	47.7	76 43.9	11.9	1 20.8	17.7
	21	264 54.6	117 57.3	. . 52.1	28 28.7	. . 47.9	91 45.9	. . 11.7	16 23.3	. . 17.7
	22	279 57.1	132 56.7	51.1	43 30.2	48.1	106 48.0	11.5	31 25.8	17.7
	23	294 59.5	147 56.2	50.1	58 31.8	48.3	121 50.0	11.3	46 28.4	17.7
	Mer. Pass.	h m 3 27.2	*v* −0.6	*d* 1.0	*v* 1.5	*d* 0.2	*v* 2.0	*d* 0.2	*v* 2.5	*d* 0.0

STARS

Name	SHA	Dec
	° ′	° ′
Acamar	315 16.9	S40 14.2
Achernar	335 25.2	S57 08.9
Acrux	173 07.1	S63 11.6
Adhara	255 11.2	S28 59.7
Aldebaran	290 47.1	N16 32.3
Alioth	166 19.2	N55 52.6
Alkaid	152 57.4	N49 14.2
Al Na'ir	27 40.7	S46 52.6
Alnilam	275 44.5	S 1 11.6
Alphard	217 54.3	S 8 43.9
Alphecca	126 09.1	N26 39.9
Alpheratz	357 41.0	N29 10.8
Altair	62 05.8	N 8 55.0
Ankaa	353 13.5	S42 12.7
Antares	112 23.4	S26 27.9
Arcturus	145 53.8	N19 06.1
Atria	107 22.9	S69 03.4
Avior	234 17.7	S59 33.9
Bellatrix	278 30.0	N 6 21.7
Betelgeuse	270 59.3	N 7 24.4
Canopus	263 55.7	S52 42.3
Capella	280 31.6	N46 00.5
Deneb	49 29.5	N45 20.6
Denebola	182 31.7	N14 28.9
Diphda	348 53.6	S17 53.6
Dubhe	193 49.8	N61 39.9
Elnath	278 10.2	N28 37.0
Eltanin	90 44.7	N51 29.6
Enif	33 44.7	N 9 57.2
Fomalhaut	15 21.4	S29 31.9
Gacrux	171 58.7	S57 12.5
Gienah	175 50.3	S17 38.0
Hadar	148 44.8	S60 27.3
Hamal	327 58.3	N23 32.3
Kaus Aust.	83 40.7	S34 22.4
Kochab	137 20.2	N74 05.7
Markab	13 35.9	N15 17.7
Menkar	314 12.9	N 4 09.2
Menkent	148 05.0	S36 27.1
Miaplacidus	221 40.0	S69 47.3
Mirfak	308 37.4	N49 54.8
Nunki	75 55.4	S26 16.3
Peacock	53 15.4	S56 40.7
Pollux	243 25.5	N27 59.0
Procyon	244 57.9	N 5 10.8
Rasalhague	96 04.2	N12 33.2
Regulus	207 41.6	N11 53.2
Rigel	281 10.2	S 8 11.1
Rigil Kent.	139 48.7	S60 54.3
Sabik	102 09.9	S15 44.5
Schedar	349 37.7	N56 37.4
Shaula	96 18.7	S37 06.8
Sirius	258 32.2	S16 44.4
Spica	158 29.1	S11 14.7
Suhail	222 51.3	S43 30.1
Vega	80 37.1	N38 48.3
Zuben'ubi	137 03.0	S16 06.5

	SHA	Mer. Pass.
	° ′	h m
Venus	215 18.1	13 07
Mars	124 16.1	19 09
Jupiter	187 10.1	14 57
Saturn	111 26.1	19 59

	UT	SUN GHA	SUN Dec	MOON GHA	*v*	MOON Dec	*d*	HP
	d h	° ′	° ′	° ′	′	° ′	′	′
	29 00	178 23.2	N18 41.5	244 42.1	7.2	N15 48.8	6.0	59.2
	01	193 23.2	40.9	259 08.3	7.1	15 54.8	5.8	59.2
	02	208 23.2	40.3	273 34.4	7.1	16 00.6	5.8	59.2
	03	223 23.2	. . 39.7	288 00.5	7.1	16 06.4	5.6	59.2
	04	238 23.3	39.1	302 26.6	7.1	16 12.0	5.6	59.2
	05	253 23.3	38.6	316 52.7	7.1	16 17.6	5.4	59.2
	06	268 23.3	N18 38.0	331 18.8	7.0	N16 23.0	5.4	59.2
	07	283 23.3	37.4	345 44.8	7.0	16 28.4	5.2	59.2
	08	298 23.4	36.8	0 10.8	6.9	16 33.6	5.1	59.2
F	09	313 23.4	. . 36.2	14 36.7	7.0	16 38.7	5.1	59.2
R	10	328 23.4	35.6	29 02.7	6.9	16 43.8	4.9	59.2
I	11	343 23.4	35.0	43 28.6	6.9	16 48.7	4.8	59.1
D	12	358 23.4	N18 34.4	57 54.5	6.8	N16 53.5	4.7	59.1
A	13	13 23.5	33.8	72 20.3	6.9	16 58.2	4.5	59.1
Y	14	28 23.5	33.2	86 46.2	6.8	17 02.7	4.5	59.1
	15	43 23.5	. . 32.6	101 12.0	6.8	17 07.2	4.4	59.1
	16	58 23.5	32.0	115 37.8	6.8	17 11.6	4.2	59.1
	17	73 23.6	31.3	130 03.6	6.7	17 15.8	4.2	59.1
	18	88 23.6	N18 30.7	144 29.3	6.8	N17 20.0	4.0	59.1
	19	103 23.6	30.1	158 55.1	6.7	17 24.0	3.9	59.1
	20	118 23.6	29.5	173 20.8	6.7	17 27.9	3.8	59.1
	21	133 23.7	. . 28.9	187 46.5	6.7	17 31.7	3.7	59.1
	22	148 23.7	28.3	202 12.2	6.6	17 35.4	3.6	59.0
	23	163 23.7	27.7	216 37.8	6.7	17 39.0	3.4	59.0
	30 00	178 23.7	N18 27.1	231 03.5	6.6	N17 42.4	3.4	59.0
	01	193 23.8	26.5	245 29.1	6.7	17 45.8	3.2	59.0
	02	208 23.8	25.9	259 54.8	6.6	17 49.0	3.1	59.0
	03	223 23.8	. . 25.3	274 20.4	6.6	17 52.1	3.0	59.0
	04	238 23.8	24.7	288 46.0	6.6	17 55.1	2.9	59.0
	05	253 23.9	24.1	303 11.6	6.6	17 58.0	2.8	59.0
	06	268 23.9	N18 23.5	317 37.2	6.6	N18 00.8	2.6	59.0
	07	283 23.9	22.9	332 02.8	6.6	18 03.4	2.6	59.0
S	08	298 24.0	22.2	346 28.4	6.5	18 06.0	2.4	58.9
A	09	313 24.0	. . 21.6	0 53.9	6.6	18 08.4	2.3	58.9
T	10	328 24.0	21.0	15 19.5	6.6	18 10.7	2.1	58.9
U	11	343 24.0	20.4	29 45.1	6.5	18 12.8	2.1	58.9
R	12	358 24.1	N18 19.8	44 10.6	6.6	N18 14.9	1.9	58.9
D	13	13 24.1	19.2	58 36.2	6.5	18 16.8	1.9	58.9
A	14	28 24.1	18.6	73 01.7	6.6	18 18.7	1.7	58.9
Y	15	43 24.2	. . 17.9	87 27.3	6.6	18 20.4	1.6	58.9
	16	58 24.2	17.3	101 52.9	6.5	18 22.0	1.4	58.8
	17	73 24.2	16.7	116 18.4	6.6	18 23.4	1.4	58.8
	18	88 24.3	N18 16.1	130 44.0	6.6	N18 24.8	1.2	58.8
	19	103 24.3	15.5	145 09.6	6.5	18 26.0	1.1	58.8
	20	118 24.3	14.9	159 35.1	6.6	18 27.1	1.0	58.8
	21	133 24.3	. . 14.3	174 00.7	6.6	18 28.1	0.9	58.8
	22	148 24.4	13.6	188 26.3	6.6	18 29.0	0.7	58.8
	23	163 24.4	13.0	202 51.9	6.6	18 29.7	0.7	58.8
	31 00	178 24.4	N18 12.4	217 17.5	6.6	N18 30.4	0.5	58.7
	01	193 24.5	11.8	231 43.1	6.7	18 30.9	0.4	58.7
	02	208 24.5	11.2	246 08.8	6.6	18 31.3	0.2	58.7
	03	223 24.5	. . 10.5	260 34.4	6.7	18 31.5	0.2	58.7
	04	238 24.6	09.9	275 00.1	6.7	18 31.7	0.0	58.7
	05	253 24.6	09.3	289 25.8	6.7	18 31.7	0.0	58.7
	06	268 24.6	N18 08.7	303 51.5	6.7	N18 31.7	0.2	58.6
	07	283 24.7	08.0	318 17.2	6.7	18 31.5	0.3	58.6
	08	298 24.7	07.4	332 42.9	6.8	18 31.2	0.5	58.6
S	09	313 24.7	. . 06.8	347 08.7	6.7	18 30.7	0.5	58.6
U	10	328 24.8	06.2	1 34.4	6.8	18 30.2	0.7	58.6
N	11	343 24.8	05.5	16 00.2	6.9	18 29.5	0.8	58.6
D	12	358 24.8	N18 04.9	30 26.1	6.8	N18 28.7	0.9	58.6
A	13	13 24.9	04.3	44 51.9	6.9	18 27.8	1.0	58.5
Y	14	28 24.9	03.7	59 17.8	6.9	18 26.8	1.1	58.5
	15	43 25.0	. . 03.0	73 43.7	6.9	18 25.7	1.3	58.5
	16	58 25.0	02.4	88 09.6	6.9	18 24.4	1.3	58.5
	17	73 25.0	01.8	102 35.5	7.0	18 23.1	1.5	58.5
	18	88 25.1	N18 01.2	117 01.5	7.0	N18 21.6	1.6	58.5
	19	103 25.1	18 00.5	131 27.5	7.1	18 20.0	1.7	58.4
	20	118 25.1	17 59.9	145 53.6	7.1	18 18.3	1.8	58.4
	21	133 25.2	. . 59.3	160 19.7	7.1	18 16.5	2.0	58.4
	22	148 25.2	58.6	174 45.8	7.1	18 14.5	2.0	58.4
	23	163 25.3	58.0	189 11.9	7.2	N18 12.5	2.2	58.4
		SD 15.8	*d* 0.6	SD 16.1		16.0		16.0

Lat.	Twilight Naut.	Twilight Civil	Sunrise	Moonrise 29	Moonrise 30	Moonrise 31	Moonrise 1
°	h m	h m	h m	h m	h m	h m	h m
N 72	▭	▭	▭	21 31	▭	▭	▭
N 70	////	////	01 11	22 33	23 06	24 12	00 12
68	////	////	02 07	23 09	23 50	24 53	00 53
66	////	////	02 39	23 34	24 19	00 19	01 21
64	////	01 30	03 03	23 54	24 41	00 41	01 43
62	////	02 09	03 22	24 10	00 10	00 59	02 00
60	////	02 35	03 37	24 24	00 24	01 13	02 14
N 58	01 21	02 55	03 50	24 35	00 35	01 26	02 26
56	01 57	03 12	04 01	00 03	00 45	01 37	02 37
54	02 21	03 26	04 11	00 11	00 54	01 46	02 46
52	02 41	03 37	04 19	00 18	01 02	01 55	02 54
50	02 56	03 48	04 27	00 24	01 10	02 02	03 02
45	03 26	04 09	04 43	00 37	01 25	02 19	03 18
N 40	03 49	04 26	04 57	00 49	01 38	02 32	03 31
35	04 06	04 40	05 08	00 58	01 49	02 44	03 42
30	04 21	04 52	05 18	01 07	01 58	02 54	03 52
20	04 43	05 11	05 35	01 21	02 15	03 11	04 08
N 10	05 01	05 27	05 49	01 34	02 29	03 26	04 23
0	05 16	05 41	06 03	01 46	02 43	03 40	04 36
S 10	05 29	05 54	06 16	01 58	02 56	03 54	04 50
20	05 41	06 07	06 30	02 11	03 11	04 09	05 05
30	05 52	06 21	06 47	02 26	03 27	04 26	05 21
35	05 58	06 29	06 56	02 34	03 37	04 36	05 31
40	06 05	06 37	07 06	02 44	03 48	04 48	05 42
45	06 12	06 47	07 19	02 56	04 01	05 02	05 55
S 50	06 19	06 58	07 34	03 10	04 17	05 18	06 11
52	06 22	07 03	07 41	03 17	04 25	05 26	06 18
54	06 26	07 09	07 49	03 24	04 33	05 35	06 27
56	06 30	07 15	07 57	03 32	04 43	05 44	06 36
58	06 34	07 22	08 07	03 41	04 53	05 56	06 46
S 60	06 38	07 30	08 18	03 52	05 06	06 08	06 58

Lat.	Sunset	Twilight Civil	Twilight Naut.	Moonset 29	Moonset 30	Moonset 31	Moonset 1
°	h m	h m	h m	h m	h m	h m	h m
N 72	▭	▭	▭	19 17	▭	▭	21 47
N 70	22 53	////	////	18 16	19 42	20 35	20 58
68	22 02	////	////	17 41	18 59	19 53	20 26
66	21 31	////	////	17 16	18 30	19 25	20 03
64	21 07	22 38	////	16 56	18 08	19 04	19 44
62	20 49	22 01	////	16 40	17 50	18 46	19 29
60	20 34	21 35	////	16 27	17 35	18 32	19 16
N 58	20 22	21 16	22 46	16 16	17 23	18 20	19 05
56	20 11	20 59	22 13	16 06	17 12	18 09	18 55
54	20 01	20 46	21 49	15 57	17 03	17 59	18 47
52	19 53	20 34	21 30	15 49	16 54	17 51	18 39
50	19 45	20 24	21 15	15 42	16 47	17 43	18 32
45	19 29	20 03	20 45	15 27	16 30	17 27	18 17
N 40	19 15	19 46	20 23	15 15	16 17	17 14	18 05
35	19 04	19 32	20 06	15 04	16 06	17 03	17 55
30	18 54	19 20	19 52	14 55	15 56	16 53	17 46
20	18 38	19 01	19 29	14 39	15 39	16 36	17 30
N 10	18 23	18 46	19 12	14 26	15 24	16 21	17 16
0	18 10	18 32	18 57	14 13	15 10	16 07	17 03
S 10	17 57	18 19	18 44	14 00	14 56	15 53	16 50
20	17 43	18 06	18 32	13 46	14 41	15 38	16 36
30	17 27	17 52	18 21	13 30	14 24	15 21	16 20
35	17 17	17 44	18 15	13 21	14 14	15 11	16 10
40	17 07	17 36	18 08	13 11	14 03	14 59	16 00
45	16 54	17 26	18 02	12 59	13 49	14 46	15 47
S 50	16 40	17 15	17 54	12 44	13 33	14 29	15 32
52	16 33	17 10	17 51	12 37	13 25	14 21	15 24
54	16 25	17 04	17 48	12 29	13 17	14 13	15 16
56	16 16	16 58	17 44	12 21	13 07	14 03	15 07
58	16 06	16 52	17 40	12 11	12 56	13 52	14 57
S 60	15 55	16 44	17 36	12 00	12 44	13 39	14 45

Day	SUN Eqn. of Time 00^h	SUN Eqn. of Time 12^h	SUN Mer. Pass.	MOON Mer. Pass. Upper	MOON Mer. Pass. Lower	MOON Age	MOON Phase
d	m s	m s	h m	h m	h m	d %	
29	06 27	06 26	12 06	07 59	20 28	25 22	
30	06 25	06 24	12 06	08 56	21 25	26 14	
31	06 22	06 21	12 06	09 53	22 22	27 7	

UT d h	ARIES GHA	VENUS −3·8 GHA	VENUS Dec	MARS −0·8 GHA	MARS Dec	JUPITER −1·7 GHA	JUPITER Dec	SATURN +0·3 GHA	SATURN Dec	STARS Name	SHA	Dec
	° ′	° ′	° ′	° ′	° ′	° ′	° ′	° ′	° ′		° ′	° ′
1 00 (MONDAY)	310 02.0	162 55.7	N14 49.1	73 33.3	S22 48.5	136 52.0	N 4 11.1	61 30.9	S20 17.7	Acamar	315 16.8	S40 14.2
01	325 04.4	177 55.1	48.0	88 34.8	48.7	151 54.1	10.9	76 33.4	17.7	Achernar	335 25.2	S57 08.9
02	340 06.9	192 54.6	47.0	103 36.3	48.9	166 56.1	10.8	91 35.9	17.7	Acrux	173 07.1	S63 11.6
03	355 09.4	207 54.1	. . 46.0	118 37.8	. . 49.1	181 58.2	. . 10.6	106 38.4	. . 17.7	Adhara	255 11.2	S28 59.7
04	10 11.8	222 53.5	45.0	133 39.3	49.3	197 00.2	10.4	121 40.9	17.7	Aldebaran	290 47.1	N16 32.3
05	25 14.3	237 53.0	44.0	148 40.8	49.5	212 02.3	10.2	136 43.5	17.7			
06	40 16.8	252 52.5	N14 42.9	163 42.3	S22 49.7	227 04.3	N 4 10.0	151 46.0	S20 17.7	Alioth	166 19.2	N55 52.6
07	55 19.2	267 51.9	41.9	178 43.8	49.9	242 06.3	09.8	166 48.5	17.8	Alkaid	152 57.4	N49 14.2
08	70 21.7	282 51.4	40.9	193 45.3	50.1	257 08.4	09.7	181 51.0	17.8	Al Na'ir	27 40.7	S46 52.6
09	85 24.2	297 50.9	. . 39.9	208 46.8	. . 50.3	272 10.4	. . 09.5	196 53.5	. . 17.8	Alnilam	275 44.4	S 1 11.6
10	100 26.6	312 50.3	38.9	223 48.3	50.5	287 12.5	09.3	211 56.0	17.8	Alphard	217 54.3	S 8 43.9
11	115 29.1	327 49.8	37.8	238 49.8	50.7	302 14.5	09.1	226 58.6	17.8			
12	130 31.6	342 49.3	N14 36.8	253 51.3	S22 50.9	317 16.6	N 4 08.9	242 01.1	S20 17.8	Alphecca	126 09.1	N26 39.9
13	145 34.0	357 48.8	35.8	268 52.8	51.1	332 18.6	08.7	257 03.6	17.8	Alpheratz	357 41.0	N29 10.8
14	160 36.5	12 48.2	34.8	283 54.3	51.3	347 20.6	08.5	272 06.1	17.8	Altair	62 05.8	N 8 55.0
15	175 38.9	27 47.7	. . 33.7	298 55.8	. . 51.5	2 22.7	. . 08.4	287 08.6	. . 17.8	Ankaa	353 13.4	S42 12.7
16	190 41.4	42 47.2	32.7	313 57.2	51.7	17 24.7	08.2	302 11.1	17.8	Antares	112 23.4	S26 27.9
17	205 43.9	57 46.7	31.7	328 58.7	51.9	32 26.8	08.0	317 13.6	17.8			
18	220 46.3	72 46.1	N14 30.6	344 00.2	S22 52.1	47 28.8	N 4 07.8	332 16.2	S20 17.8	Arcturus	145 53.8	N19 06.1
19	235 48.8	87 45.6	29.6	359 01.7	52.3	62 30.9	07.6	347 18.7	17.8	Atria	107 23.0	S69 03.4
20	250 51.3	102 45.1	28.6	14 03.2	52.5	77 32.9	07.4	2 21.2	17.8	Avior	234 17.7	S59 33.8
21	265 53.7	117 44.6	. . 27.5	29 04.7	. . 52.7	92 34.9	. . 07.2	17 23.7	. . 17.8	Bellatrix	278 29.9	N 6 21.7
22	280 56.2	132 44.0	26.5	44 06.2	52.9	107 37.0	07.1	32 26.2	17.8	Betelgeuse	270 59.3	N 7 24.4
23	295 58.7	147 43.5	25.5	59 07.7	53.1	122 39.0	06.9	47 28.7	17.8			
2 00 (TUESDAY)	311 01.1	162 43.0	N14 24.5	74 09.1	S22 53.3	137 41.1	N 4 06.7	62 31.2	S20 17.8	Canopus	263 55.6	S52 42.3
01	326 03.6	177 42.5	23.4	89 10.6	53.5	152 43.1	06.5	77 33.8	17.8	Capella	280 31.6	N46 00.5
02	341 06.0	192 42.0	22.4	104 12.1	53.7	167 45.1	06.3	92 36.3	17.8	Deneb	49 29.5	N45 20.6
03	356 08.5	207 41.4	. . 21.3	119 13.6	. . 53.9	182 47.2	. . 06.1	107 38.8	. . 17.8	Denebola	182 31.7	N14 28.9
04	11 11.0	222 40.9	20.3	134 15.1	54.1	197 49.2	05.9	122 41.3	17.8	Diphda	348 53.6	S17 53.6
05	26 13.4	237 40.4	19.3	149 16.5	54.3	212 51.3	05.8	137 43.8	17.8			
06	41 15.9	252 39.9	N14 18.2	164 18.0	S22 54.5	227 53.3	N 4 05.6	152 46.3	S20 17.8	Dubhe	193 49.8	N61 39.9
07	56 18.4	267 39.4	17.2	179 19.5	54.7	242 55.3	05.4	167 48.8	17.8	Elnath	278 10.2	N28 37.0
08	71 20.8	282 38.8	16.2	194 21.0	54.9	257 57.4	05.2	182 51.4	17.8	Eltanin	90 44.7	N51 29.6
09	86 23.3	297 38.3	. . 15.1	209 22.5	. . 55.1	272 59.4	. . 05.0	197 53.9	. . 17.8	Enif	33 44.7	N 9 57.2
10	101 25.8	312 37.8	14.1	224 23.9	55.3	288 01.5	04.8	212 56.4	17.8	Fomalhaut	15 21.4	S29 31.9
11	116 28.2	327 37.3	13.0	239 25.4	55.5	303 03.5	04.6	227 58.9	17.8			
12	131 30.7	342 36.8	N14 12.0	254 26.9	S22 55.7	318 05.5	N 4 04.5	243 01.4	S20 17.8	Gacrux	171 58.7	S57 12.5
13	146 33.2	357 36.2	11.0	269 28.3	55.9	333 07.6	04.3	258 03.9	17.8	Gienah	175 50.3	S17 38.0
14	161 35.6	12 35.7	09.9	284 29.8	56.1	348 09.6	04.1	273 06.4	17.8	Hadar	148 44.8	S60 27.3
15	176 38.1	27 35.2	. . 08.9	299 31.3	. . 56.3	3 11.7	. . 03.9	288 08.9	. . 17.8	Hamal	327 58.3	N23 32.3
16	191 40.5	42 34.7	07.8	314 32.7	56.5	18 13.7	03.7	303 11.4	17.8	Kaus Aust.	83 40.7	S34 22.4
17	206 43.0	57 34.2	06.8	329 34.2	56.7	33 15.7	03.5	318 14.0	17.8			
18	221 45.5	72 33.7	N14 05.7	344 35.7	S22 56.9	48 17.8	N 4 03.3	333 16.5	S20 17.8	Kochab	137 20.2	N74 05.7
19	236 47.9	87 33.2	04.7	359 37.1	57.1	63 19.8	03.1	348 19.0	17.8	Markab	13 35.9	N15 17.7
20	251 50.4	102 32.6	03.6	14 38.6	57.3	78 21.9	03.0	3 21.5	17.8	Menkar	314 12.9	N 4 09.2
21	266 52.9	117 32.1	. . 02.6	29 40.1	. . 57.5	93 23.9	. . 02.8	18 24.0	. . 17.8	Menkent	148 05.1	S36 27.1
22	281 55.3	132 31.6	01.6	44 41.5	57.7	108 25.9	02.6	33 26.5	17.8	Miaplacidus	221 40.0	S69 47.2
23	296 57.8	147 31.1	14 00.5	59 43.0	57.9	123 28.0	02.4	48 29.0	17.8			
3 00 (WEDNESDAY)	312 00.3	162 30.6	N13 59.5	74 44.5	S22 58.1	138 30.0	N 4 02.2	63 31.5	S20 17.8	Mirfak	308 37.3	N49 54.8
01	327 02.7	177 30.1	58.4	89 45.9	58.3	153 32.1	02.0	78 34.0	17.8	Nunki	75 55.4	S26 16.3
02	342 05.2	192 29.6	57.4	104 47.4	58.5	168 34.1	01.8	93 36.5	17.8	Peacock	53 15.4	S56 40.7
03	357 07.7	207 29.1	. . 56.3	119 48.8	. . 58.7	183 36.1	. . 01.7	108 39.1	. . 17.9	Pollux	243 25.5	N27 59.0
04	12 10.1	222 28.6	55.2	134 50.3	58.9	198 38.2	01.5	123 41.6	17.9	Procyon	244 57.8	N 5 10.8
05	27 12.6	237 28.1	54.2	149 51.7	59.1	213 40.2	01.3	138 44.1	17.9			
06	42 15.0	252 27.5	N13 53.1	164 53.2	S22 59.3	228 42.2	N 4 01.1	153 46.6	S20 17.9	Rasalhague	96 04.2	N12 33.2
07	57 17.5	267 27.0	52.1	179 54.7	59.5	243 44.3	00.9	168 49.1	17.9	Regulus	207 41.6	N11 53.2
08	72 20.0	282 26.5	51.0	194 56.1	22 59.7	258 46.3	00.7	183 51.6	17.9	Rigel	281 10.2	S 8 11.0
09	87 22.4	297 26.0	. . 50.0	209 57.6	23 00.0	273 48.4	. . 00.5	198 54.1	. . 17.9	Rigil Kent.	139 48.7	S60 54.3
10	102 24.9	312 25.5	48.9	224 59.0	00.2	288 50.4	00.3	213 56.6	17.9	Sabik	102 09.9	S15 44.5
11	117 27.4	327 25.0	47.9	240 00.5	00.4	303 52.4	00.2	228 59.1	17.9			
12	132 29.8	342 24.5	N13 46.8	255 01.9	S23 00.6	318 54.5	N 4 00.0	244 01.6	S20 17.9	Schedar	349 37.7	N56 37.4
13	147 32.3	357 24.0	45.8	270 03.4	00.8	333 56.5	3 59.8	259 04.1	17.9	Shaula	96 18.7	S37 06.8
14	162 34.8	12 23.5	44.7	285 04.8	01.0	348 58.5	59.6	274 06.6	17.9	Sirius	258 32.1	S16 44.4
15	177 37.2	27 23.0	. . 43.6	300 06.2	. . 01.2	4 00.6	. . 59.4	289 09.1	. . 17.9	Spica	158 29.1	S11 14.7
16	192 39.7	42 22.5	42.6	315 07.7	01.4	19 02.6	59.2	304 11.7	17.9	Suhail	222 51.3	S43 30.1
17	207 42.2	57 22.0	41.5	330 09.1	01.6	34 04.7	59.0	319 14.2	17.9			
18	222 44.6	72 21.5	N13 40.5	345 10.6	S23 01.8	49 06.7	N 3 58.8	334 16.7	S20 17.9	Vega	80 37.1	N38 48.3
19	237 47.1	87 21.0	39.4	0 12.0	02.0	64 08.7	58.7	349 19.2	17.9	Zuben'ubi	137 03.0	S16 06.5
20	252 49.5	102 20.5	38.3	15 13.5	02.2	79 10.8	58.5	4 21.7	17.9			
21	267 52.0	117 20.0	. . 37.3	30 14.9	. . 02.4	94 12.8	. . 58.3	19 24.2	. . 17.9			
22	282 54.5	132 19.5	36.2	45 16.3	02.6	109 14.8	58.1	34 26.7	17.9			
23	297 56.9	147 19.0	35.1	60 17.8	02.8	124 16.9	57.9	49 29.2	17.9			
Mer. Pass. (h m)	3 15.4	v −0.5	d 1.0	v 1.5	d 0.2	v 2.0	d 0.2	v 2.5	d 0.0			

	SHA (° ′)	Mer. Pass. (h m)
Venus	211 41.9	13 10
Mars	123 08.0	19 02
Jupiter	186 39.9	14 47
Saturn	111 30.1	19 47

	UT	SUN GHA	SUN Dec	MOON GHA	v	MOON Dec	d	HP
	d h	° ′	° ′	° ′	′	° ′	′	′
	1 00	178 25.3	N17 57.4	203 38.1	7.2	N18 10.3	2.2	58.3
	01	193 25.3	56.7	218 04.3	7.3	18 08.1	2.4	58.3
	02	208 25.4	56.1	232 30.6	7.3	18 05.7	2.5	58.3
	03	223 25.4	. . 55.5	246 56.9	7.3	18 03.2	2.6	58.3
	04	238 25.4	54.8	261 23.2	7.4	18 00.6	2.7	58.3
	05	253 25.5	54.2	275 49.6	7.4	17 57.9	2.9	58.2
	06	268 25.5	N17 53.6	290 16.0	7.4	N17 55.0	2.9	58.2
	07	283 25.6	52.9	304 42.4	7.5	17 52.1	3.0	58.2
	08	298 25.6	52.3	319 08.9	7.6	17 49.1	3.2	58.2
M	09	313 25.6	. . 51.7	333 35.5	7.6	17 45.9	3.2	58.2
O	10	328 25.7	51.0	348 02.1	7.6	17 42.7	3.4	58.1
N	11	343 25.7	50.4	2 28.7	7.7	17 39.3	3.5	58.1
D	12	358 25.8	N17 49.8	16 55.4	7.7	N17 35.8	3.5	58.1
A	13	13 25.8	49.1	31 22.1	7.8	17 32.3	3.7	58.1
Y	14	28 25.9	48.5	45 48.9	7.8	17 28.6	3.8	58.1
	15	43 25.9	. . 47.8	60 15.7	7.9	17 24.8	3.9	58.0
	16	58 25.9	47.2	74 42.6	7.9	17 20.9	3.9	58.0
	17	73 26.0	46.6	89 09.5	8.0	17 17.0	4.1	58.0
	18	88 26.0	N17 45.9	103 36.5	8.0	N17 12.9	4.2	58.0
	19	103 26.1	45.3	118 03.5	8.1	17 08.7	4.3	58.0
	20	118 26.1	44.6	132 30.6	8.1	17 04.4	4.4	57.9
	21	133 26.2	. . 44.0	146 57.7	8.2	17 00.0	4.4	57.9
	22	148 26.2	43.4	161 24.9	8.2	16 55.6	4.6	57.9
	23	163 26.2	42.7	175 52.1	8.3	16 51.0	4.7	57.9
	2 00	178 26.3	N17 42.1	190 19.4	8.3	N16 46.3	4.8	57.8
	01	193 26.3	41.4	204 46.7	8.4	16 41.5	4.8	57.8
	02	208 26.4	40.8	219 14.1	8.5	16 36.7	5.0	57.8
	03	223 26.4	. . 40.1	233 41.6	8.5	16 31.7	5.0	57.8
	04	238 26.5	39.5	248 09.1	8.6	16 26.7	5.2	57.8
	05	253 26.5	38.8	262 36.7	8.6	16 21.5	5.2	57.7
	06	268 26.6	N17 38.2	277 04.3	8.7	N16 16.3	5.3	57.7
	07	283 26.6	37.5	291 32.0	8.7	16 11.0	5.4	57.7
T	08	298 26.7	36.9	305 59.7	8.9	16 05.6	5.5	57.7
U	09	313 26.7	. . 36.3	320 27.6	8.8	16 00.1	5.6	57.6
E	10	328 26.8	35.6	334 55.4	8.9	15 54.5	5.7	57.6
S	11	343 26.8	35.0	349 23.3	9.0	15 48.8	5.7	57.6
D	12	358 26.8	N17 34.3	3 51.3	9.1	N15 43.1	5.9	57.6
A	13	13 26.9	33.7	18 19.4	9.1	15 37.2	5.9	57.5
Y	14	28 26.9	33.0	32 47.5	9.2	15 31.3	6.0	57.5
	15	43 27.0	. . 32.4	47 15.7	9.2	15 25.3	6.1	57.5
	16	58 27.0	31.7	61 43.9	9.3	15 19.2	6.2	57.5
	17	73 27.1	31.1	76 12.2	9.3	15 13.0	6.3	57.5
	18	88 27.1	N17 30.4	90 40.5	9.5	N15 06.7	6.3	57.4
	19	103 27.2	29.7	105 09.0	9.4	15 00.4	6.4	57.4
	20	118 27.2	29.1	119 37.4	9.6	14 54.0	6.5	57.4
	21	133 27.3	. . 28.4	134 06.0	9.6	14 47.5	6.6	57.4
	22	148 27.3	27.8	148 34.6	9.7	14 40.9	6.6	57.3
	23	163 27.4	27.1	163 03.3	9.7	14 34.3	6.7	57.3
	3 00	178 27.4	N17 26.5	177 32.0	9.8	N14 27.6	6.8	57.3
	01	193 27.5	25.8	192 00.8	9.8	14 20.8	6.9	57.3
	02	208 27.5	25.2	206 29.6	10.0	14 13.9	6.9	57.2
	03	223 27.6	. . 24.5	220 58.6	10.0	14 07.0	7.1	57.2
	04	238 27.6	23.8	235 27.6	10.0	13 59.9	7.0	57.2
	05	253 27.7	23.2	249 56.6	10.1	13 52.9	7.2	57.2
	06	268 27.8	N17 22.5	264 25.7	10.2	N13 45.7	7.2	57.1
W	07	283 27.8	21.9	278 54.9	10.2	13 38.5	7.3	57.1
E	08	298 27.9	21.2	293 24.1	10.4	13 31.2	7.3	57.1
D	09	313 27.9	. . 20.5	307 53.5	10.3	13 23.9	7.4	57.1
N	10	328 28.0	19.9	322 22.8	10.5	13 16.5	7.5	57.0
E	11	343 28.0	19.2	336 52.3	10.5	13 09.0	7.6	57.0
S	12	358 28.1	N17 18.6	351 21.8	10.5	N13 01.4	7.6	57.0
D	13	13 28.1	17.9	5 51.3	10.7	12 53.8	7.6	56.9
A	14	28 28.2	17.2	20 21.0	10.6	12 46.2	7.7	56.9
Y	15	43 28.2	. . 16.6	34 50.6	10.8	12 38.5	7.8	56.9
	16	58 28.3	15.9	49 20.4	10.8	12 30.7	7.9	56.9
	17	73 28.3	15.3	63 50.2	10.9	12 22.8	7.9	56.8
	18	88 28.4	N17 14.6	78 20.1	10.9	N12 14.9	7.9	56.8
	19	103 28.5	13.9	92 50.0	11.1	12 07.0	8.0	56.8
	20	118 28.5	13.3	107 20.1	11.0	11 59.0	8.1	56.8
	21	133 28.6	. . 12.6	121 50.1	11.2	11 50.9	8.1	56.7
	22	148 28.6	11.9	136 20.3	11.1	11 42.8	8.2	56.7
	23	163 28.7	11.3	150 50.4	11.3	N11 34.6	8.2	56.7
		SD 15.8	*d* 0.6	SD		15.8	15.7	15.5

Lat.	Twilight Naut.	Twilight Civil	Sunrise	Moonrise 1	Moonrise 2	Moonrise 3	Moonrise 4
°	h m	h m	h m	h m	h m	h m	h m
N 72	▭	▭	▭	▭	00 56	02 56	04 47
N 70	////	////	01 38	00 12	01 45	03 25	05 05
68	////	////	02 22	00 53	02 16	03 47	05 19
66	////	00 44	02 51	01 21	02 39	04 04	05 31
64	////	01 48	03 12	01 43	02 57	04 18	05 40
62	////	02 21	03 30	02 00	03 12	04 29	05 49
60	00 40	02 44	03 44	02 14	03 24	04 39	05 56
N 58	01 37	03 03	03 56	02 26	03 35	04 48	06 02
56	02 08	03 18	04 06	02 37	03 44	04 55	06 07
54	02 30	03 32	04 16	02 46	03 52	05 02	06 12
52	02 48	03 43	04 24	02 54	04 00	05 08	06 17
50	03 02	03 53	04 31	03 02	04 06	05 13	06 21
45	03 31	04 13	04 47	03 18	04 20	05 25	06 29
N 40	03 52	04 29	05 00	03 31	04 32	05 34	06 36
35	04 09	04 43	05 10	03 42	04 42	05 43	06 43
30	04 23	04 54	05 20	03 52	04 51	05 50	06 48
20	04 45	05 12	05 36	04 08	05 06	06 02	06 57
N 10	05 02	05 28	05 50	04 23	05 19	06 13	07 06
0	05 16	05 41	06 03	04 36	05 31	06 24	07 13
S 10	05 28	05 54	06 16	04 50	05 44	06 34	07 21
20	05 39	06 06	06 29	05 05	05 57	06 45	07 29
30	05 51	06 19	06 44	05 21	06 12	06 57	07 38
35	05 56	06 27	06 53	05 31	06 20	07 04	07 44
40	06 02	06 35	07 03	05 42	06 30	07 12	07 50
45	06 08	06 44	07 15	05 55	06 42	07 22	07 57
S 50	06 15	06 54	07 29	06 11	06 56	07 33	08 05
52	06 18	06 59	07 36	06 18	07 02	07 38	08 09
54	06 21	07 04	07 43	06 27	07 09	07 44	08 13
56	06 25	07 10	07 52	06 36	07 17	07 51	08 18
58	06 28	07 16	08 01	06 46	07 26	07 58	08 23
S 60	06 32	07 23	08 11	06 58	07 37	08 06	08 29

Lat.	Sunset	Twilight Civil	Twilight Naut.	Moonset 1	Moonset 2	Moonset 3	Moonset 4
°	h m	h m	h m	h m	h m	h m	h m
N 72	▭	▭	▭	21 47	21 38	21 31	21 26
N 70	22 27	////	////	20 58	21 07	21 12	21 14
68	21 46	////	////	20 26	20 45	20 56	21 04
66	21 19	23 15	////	20 03	20 27	20 44	20 56
64	20 58	22 20	////	19 44	20 13	20 33	20 49
62	20 41	21 49	////	19 29	20 00	20 24	20 43
60	20 27	21 26	23 21	19 16	19 50	20 16	20 37
N 58	20 15	21 07	22 31	19 05	19 41	20 09	20 33
56	20 05	20 52	22 02	18 55	19 33	20 03	20 29
54	19 56	20 39	21 40	18 47	19 26	19 58	20 25
52	19 48	20 28	21 23	18 39	19 19	19 53	20 21
50	19 40	20 19	21 09	18 32	19 13	19 48	20 18
45	19 25	19 58	20 40	18 17	19 01	19 38	20 12
N 40	19 12	19 42	20 19	18 05	18 50	19 30	20 06
35	19 02	19 29	20 03	17 55	18 41	19 23	20 01
30	18 52	19 18	19 49	17 46	18 34	19 17	19 57
20	18 36	19 00	19 27	17 30	18 20	19 06	19 49
N 10	18 22	18 45	19 10	17 16	18 08	18 57	19 43
0	18 10	18 31	18 57	17 03	17 57	18 48	19 36
S 10	17 57	18 19	18 44	16 50	17 45	18 39	19 30
20	17 44	18 07	18 33	16 36	17 33	18 29	19 23
30	17 28	17 53	18 22	16 20	17 19	18 18	19 15
35	17 19	17 46	18 17	16 10	17 11	18 12	19 11
40	17 09	17 38	18 11	16 00	17 02	18 04	19 06
45	16 58	17 29	18 05	15 47	16 51	17 56	19 00
S 50	16 44	17 19	17 58	15 32	16 38	17 45	18 52
52	16 37	17 14	17 55	15 24	16 31	17 40	18 49
54	16 30	17 09	17 52	15 16	16 25	17 35	18 45
56	16 22	17 03	17 48	15 07	16 17	17 29	18 41
58	16 12	16 57	17 45	14 57	16 08	17 22	18 37
S 60	16 02	16 50	17 41	14 45	15 58	17 15	18 32

Day	SUN Eqn. of Time 00h	SUN Eqn. of Time 12h	SUN Mer. Pass.	MOON Mer. Pass. Upper	MOON Mer. Pass. Lower	MOON Age	MOON Phase
d	m s	m s	h m	h m	h m	d	%
1	06 19	06 17	12 06	10 50	23 17	28	2
2	06 15	06 13	12 06	11 44	24 10	29	0
3	06 10	06 08	12 06	12 36	00 10	01	0

UT d h	ARIES GHA	VENUS −3·8 GHA	VENUS Dec	MARS −0·7 GHA	MARS Dec	JUPITER −1·7 GHA	JUPITER Dec	SATURN +0·4 GHA	SATURN Dec
	° ′	° ′	° ′	° ′	° ′	° ′	° ′	° ′	° ′
4 00	312 59.4	162 18.5	N13 34.1	75 19.2	S23 03.0	139 18.9	N 3 57.7	64 31.7	S20 17.9
01	328 01.9	177 18.0	33.0	90 20.7	03.2	154 20.9	57.5	79 34.2	17.9
02	343 04.3	192 17.5	32.0	105 22.1	03.4	169 23.0	57.3	94 36.7	17.9
03	358 06.8	207 17.0	. . 30.9	120 23.5	. . 03.6	184 25.0	. . 57.1	109 39.2	. . 17.9
04	13 09.3	222 16.5	29.8	135 25.0	03.8	199 27.1	57.0	124 41.7	17.9
05	28 11.7	237 16.0	28.8	150 26.4	04.0	214 29.1	56.8	139 44.2	17.9
06	43 14.2	252 15.5	N13 27.7	165 27.8	S23 04.2	229 31.1	N 3 56.6	154 46.7	S20 17.9
07	58 16.6	267 15.0	26.6	180 29.3	04.4	244 33.2	56.4	169 49.2	17.9
08	73 19.1	282 14.5	25.5	195 30.7	04.6	259 35.2	56.2	184 51.7	17.9
09	88 21.6	297 14.0	. . 24.5	210 32.1	. . 04.8	274 37.2	. . 56.0	199 54.2	. . 17.9
10	103 24.0	312 13.5	23.4	225 33.5	05.0	289 39.3	55.8	214 56.8	18.0
11	118 26.5	327 13.0	22.3	240 35.0	05.2	304 41.3	55.6	229 59.3	18.0
12	133 29.0	342 12.5	N13 21.3	255 36.4	S23 05.4	319 43.3	N 3 55.5	245 01.8	S20 18.0
13	148 31.4	357 12.0	20.2	270 37.8	05.6	334 45.4	55.3	260 04.3	18.0
14	163 33.9	12 11.5	19.1	285 39.2	05.9	349 47.4	55.1	275 06.8	18.0
15	178 36.4	27 11.0	. . 18.0	300 40.7	. . 06.1	4 49.4	. . 54.9	290 09.3	. . 18.0
16	193 38.8	42 10.6	17.0	315 42.1	06.3	19 51.5	54.7	305 11.8	18.0
17	208 41.3	57 10.1	15.9	330 43.5	06.5	34 53.5	54.5	320 14.3	18.0
18	223 43.8	72 09.6	N13 14.8	345 44.9	S23 06.7	49 55.5	N 3 54.3	335 16.8	S20 18.0
19	238 46.2	87 09.1	13.7	0 46.3	06.9	64 57.6	54.1	350 19.3	18.0
20	253 48.7	102 08.6	12.7	15 47.8	07.1	79 59.6	53.9	5 21.8	18.0
21	268 51.1	117 08.1	. . 11.6	30 49.2	. . 07.3	95 01.6	. . 53.8	20 24.3	. . 18.0
22	283 53.6	132 07.6	10.5	45 50.6	07.5	110 03.7	53.6	35 26.8	18.0
23	298 56.1	147 07.1	09.4	60 52.0	07.7	125 05.7	53.4	50 29.3	18.0
5 00	313 58.5	162 06.6	N13 08.4	75 53.4	S23 07.9	140 07.7	N 3 53.2	65 31.8	S20 18.0
01	329 01.0	177 06.1	07.3	90 54.8	08.1	155 09.8	53.0	80 34.3	18.0
02	344 03.5	192 05.7	06.2	105 56.3	08.3	170 11.8	52.8	95 36.8	18.0
03	359 05.9	207 05.2	. . 05.1	120 57.7	. . 08.5	185 13.8	. . 52.6	110 39.3	. . 18.0
04	14 08.4	222 04.7	04.0	135 59.1	08.7	200 15.9	52.4	125 41.8	18.0
05	29 10.9	237 04.2	02.9	151 00.5	08.9	215 17.9	52.2	140 44.3	18.0
06	44 13.3	252 03.7	N13 01.9	166 01.9	S23 09.1	230 19.9	N 3 52.1	155 46.8	S20 18.0
07	59 15.8	267 03.2	13 00.8	181 03.3	09.3	245 22.0	51.9	170 49.3	18.0
08	74 18.2	282 02.7	12 59.7	196 04.7	09.5	260 24.0	51.7	185 51.8	18.0
09	89 20.7	297 02.3	. . 58.6	211 06.1	. . 09.7	275 26.0	. . 51.5	200 54.3	. . 18.0
10	104 23.2	312 01.8	57.5	226 07.5	09.9	290 28.1	51.3	215 56.8	18.0
11	119 25.6	327 01.3	56.4	241 08.9	10.2	305 30.1	51.1	230 59.3	18.1
12	134 28.1	342 00.8	N12 55.4	256 10.3	S23 10.4	320 32.1	N 3 50.9	246 01.8	S20 18.1
13	149 30.6	357 00.3	54.3	271 11.7	10.6	335 34.2	50.7	261 04.3	18.1
14	164 33.0	11 59.8	53.2	286 13.1	10.8	350 36.2	50.5	276 06.8	18.1
15	179 35.5	26 59.4	. . 52.1	301 14.5	. . 11.0	5 38.2	. . 50.3	291 09.3	. . 18.1
16	194 38.0	41 58.9	51.0	316 15.9	11.2	20 40.3	50.2	306 11.8	18.1
17	209 40.4	56 58.4	49.9	331 17.3	11.4	35 42.3	50.0	321 14.3	18.1
18	224 42.9	71 57.9	N12 48.8	346 18.7	S23 11.6	50 44.3	N 3 49.8	336 16.8	S20 18.1
19	239 45.4	86 57.4	47.7	1 20.1	11.8	65 46.4	49.6	351 19.3	18.1
20	254 47.8	101 57.0	46.6	16 21.5	12.0	80 48.4	49.4	6 21.8	18.1
21	269 50.3	116 56.5	. . 45.6	31 22.9	. . 12.2	95 50.4	. . 49.2	21 24.3	. . 18.1
22	284 52.7	131 56.0	44.5	46 24.3	12.4	110 52.5	49.0	36 26.8	18.1
23	299 55.2	146 55.5	43.4	61 25.7	12.6	125 54.5	48.8	51 29.3	18.1
6 00	314 57.7	161 55.0	N12 42.3	76 27.1	S23 12.8	140 56.5	N 3 48.6	66 31.8	S20 18.1
01	330 00.1	176 54.6	41.2	91 28.5	13.0	155 58.5	48.4	81 34.3	18.1
02	345 02.6	191 54.1	40.1	106 29.9	13.2	171 00.6	48.3	96 36.8	18.1
03	0 05.1	206 53.6	. . 39.0	121 31.3	. . 13.4	186 02.6	. . 48.1	111 39.3	. . 18.1
04	15 07.5	221 53.1	37.9	136 32.7	13.6	201 04.6	47.9	126 41.7	18.1
05	30 10.0	236 52.7	36.8	151 34.1	13.8	216 06.7	47.7	141 44.2	18.1
06	45 12.5	251 52.2	N12 35.7	166 35.4	S23 14.0	231 08.7	N 3 47.5	156 46.7	S20 18.1
07	60 14.9	266 51.7	34.6	181 36.8	14.3	246 10.7	47.3	171 49.2	18.1
08	75 17.4	281 51.2	33.5	196 38.2	14.5	261 12.8	47.1	186 51.7	18.1
09	90 19.9	296 50.8	. . 32.4	211 39.6	. . 14.7	276 14.8	. . 46.9	201 54.2	. . 18.2
10	105 22.3	311 50.3	31.3	226 41.0	14.9	291 16.8	46.7	216 56.7	18.2
11	120 24.8	326 49.8	30.2	241 42.4	15.1	306 18.9	46.5	231 59.2	18.2
12	135 27.2	341 49.3	N12 29.1	256 43.7	S23 15.3	321 20.9	N 3 46.4	247 01.7	S20 18.2
13	150 29.7	356 48.9	28.0	271 45.1	15.5	336 22.9	46.2	262 04.2	18.2
14	165 32.2	11 48.4	26.9	286 46.5	15.7	351 24.9	46.0	277 06.7	18.2
15	180 34.6	26 47.9	. . 25.8	301 47.9	. . 15.9	6 27.0	. . 45.8	292 09.2	. . 18.2
16	195 37.1	41 47.5	24.7	316 49.3	16.1	21 29.0	45.6	307 11.7	18.2
17	210 39.6	56 47.0	23.6	331 50.6	16.3	36 31.0	45.4	322 14.2	18.2
18	225 42.0	71 46.5	N12 22.5	346 52.0	S23 16.5	51 33.1	N 3 45.2	337 16.7	S20 18.2
19	240 44.5	86 46.1	21.4	1 53.4	16.7	66 35.1	45.0	352 19.2	18.2
20	255 47.0	101 45.6	20.3	16 54.8	16.9	81 37.1	44.8	7 21.7	18.2
21	270 49.4	116 45.1	. . 19.2	31 56.1	. . 17.1	96 39.1	. . 44.6	22 24.2	. . 18.2
22	285 51.9	131 44.7	18.1	46 57.5	17.3	111 41.2	44.4	37 26.7	18.2
23	300 54.3	146 44.2	17.0	61 58.9	17.5	126 43.2	44.3	52 29.1	18.2
Mer. Pass. (h m)	3 03.6	v −0.5	d 1.1	v 1.4	d 0.2	v 2.0	d 0.2	v 2.5	d 0.0

STARS Name	SHA	Dec
	° ′	° ′
Acamar	315 16.8	S40 14.2
Achernar	335 25.1	S57 08.9
Acrux	173 07.1	S63 11.6
Adhara	255 11.2	S28 59.7
Aldebaran	290 47.1	N16 32.3
Alioth	166 19.2	N55 52.5
Alkaid	152 57.4	N49 14.2
Al Na'ir	27 40.7	S46 52.6
Alnilam	275 44.4	S 1 11.6
Alphard	217 54.3	S 8 43.9
Alphecca	126 09.1	N26 39.9
Alpheratz	357 41.0	N29 10.8
Altair	62 05.8	N 8 55.0
Ankaa	353 13.4	S42 12.7
Antares	112 23.5	S26 27.9
Arcturus	145 53.9	N19 06.1
Atria	107 23.0	S69 03.4
Avior	234 17.7	S59 33.8
Bellatrix	278 29.9	N 6 21.7
Betelgeuse	270 59.2	N 7 24.4
Canopus	263 55.6	S52 42.3
Capella	280 31.6	N46 00.5
Deneb	49 29.5	N45 20.6
Denebola	182 31.8	N14 28.9
Diphda	348 53.6	S17 53.6
Dubhe	193 49.8	N61 39.9
Elnath	278 10.2	N28 37.0
Eltanin	90 44.8	N51 29.6
Enif	33 44.7	N 9 57.2
Fomalhaut	15 21.4	S29 31.9
Gacrux	171 58.7	S57 12.5
Gienah	175 50.3	S17 38.0
Hadar	148 44.8	S60 27.3
Hamal	327 58.3	N23 32.3
Kaus Aust.	83 40.7	S34 22.4
Kochab	137 20.3	N74 05.7
Markab	13 35.9	N15 17.7
Menkar	314 12.8	N 4 09.2
Menkent	148 05.1	S36 27.1
Miaplacidus	221 40.0	S69 47.2
Mirfak	308 37.3	N49 54.8
Nunki	75 55.4	S26 16.3
Peacock	53 15.4	S56 40.7
Pollux	243 25.5	N27 59.0
Procyon	244 57.8	N 5 10.8
Rasalhague	96 04.3	N12 33.2
Regulus	207 41.6	N11 53.2
Rigel	281 10.2	S 8 11.0
Rigil Kent.	139 48.8	S60 54.3
Sabik	102 09.9	S15 44.5
Schedar	349 37.6	N56 37.5
Shaula	96 18.7	S37 06.8
Sirius	258 32.1	S16 44.4
Spica	158 29.1	S11 14.7
Suhail	222 51.3	S43 30.0
Vega	80 37.1	N38 48.3
Zuben'ubi	137 03.0	S16 06.5
	SHA	**Mer. Pass.**
	° ′	h m
Venus	208 08.1	13 12
Mars	121 54.9	18 55
Jupiter	186 09.2	14 38
Saturn	111 33.2	19 35

UT d	h	SUN GHA ° ′	SUN Dec ° ′	MOON GHA ° ′	v ′	MOON Dec ° ′	d ′	HP ′
4	00	178 28.7	N17 10.6	165 20.7	11.3	N11 26.4	8.3	56.7
	01	193 28.8	09.9	179 51.0	11.4	11 18.1	8.3	56.6
	02	208 28.9	09.3	194 21.4	11.4	11 09.8	8.4	56.6
	03	223 28.9	. . 08.6	208 51.8	11.6	11 01.4	8.4	56.6
	04	238 29.0	07.9	223 22.4	11.5	10 53.0	8.5	56.6
	05	253 29.0	07.2	237 52.9	11.6	10 44.5	8.5	56.5
	06	268 29.1	N17 06.6	252 23.5	11.7	N10 36.0	8.5	56.5
T	07	283 29.1	05.9	266 54.2	11.8	10 27.5	8.6	56.5
H	08	298 29.2	05.2	281 25.0	11.8	10 18.9	8.7	56.5
U	09	313 29.3	. . 04.6	295 55.8	11.8	10 10.2	8.6	56.4
R	10	328 29.3	03.9	310 26.6	12.0	10 01.6	8.8	56.4
S	11	343 29.4	03.2	324 57.6	11.9	9 52.8	8.7	56.4
D	12	358 29.4	N17 02.5	339 28.5	12.1	N 9 44.1	8.8	56.4
A	13	13 29.5	01.9	353 59.6	12.1	9 35.3	8.9	56.3
Y	14	28 29.6	01.2	8 30.7	12.1	9 26.4	8.9	56.3
	15	43 29.6	17 00.5	23 01.8	12.2	9 17.5	8.9	56.3
	16	58 29.7	16 59.9	37 33.0	12.3	9 08.6	8.9	56.2
	17	73 29.8	59.2	52 04.3	12.3	8 59.7	9.0	56.2
	18	88 29.8	N16 58.5	66 35.6	12.4	N 8 50.7	9.0	56.2
	19	103 29.9	57.8	81 07.0	12.4	8 41.7	9.1	56.2
	20	118 29.9	57.1	95 38.4	12.5	8 32.6	9.1	56.1
	21	133 30.0	. . 56.5	110 09.9	12.5	8 23.5	9.1	56.1
	22	148 30.1	55.8	124 41.4	12.6	8 14.4	9.1	56.1
	23	163 30.1	55.1	139 13.0	12.7	8 05.3	9.2	56.1
5	00	178 30.2	N16 54.4	153 44.7	12.7	N 7 56.1	9.2	56.0
	01	193 30.3	53.8	168 16.4	12.7	7 46.9	9.2	56.0
	02	208 30.3	53.1	182 48.1	12.8	7 37.7	9.3	56.0
	03	223 30.4	. . 52.4	197 19.9	12.9	7 28.4	9.3	56.0
	04	238 30.5	51.7	211 51.8	12.9	7 19.1	9.3	55.9
	05	253 30.5	51.0	226 23.7	13.0	7 09.8	9.3	55.9
	06	268 30.6	N16 50.4	240 55.7	13.0	N 7 00.5	9.4	55.9
	07	283 30.6	49.7	255 27.7	13.0	6 51.1	9.4	55.9
	08	298 30.7	49.0	269 59.7	13.1	6 41.7	9.4	55.8
F	09	313 30.8	. . 48.3	284 31.8	13.2	6 32.3	9.4	55.8
R	10	328 30.8	47.6	299 04.0	13.2	6 22.9	9.5	55.8
I	11	343 30.9	46.9	313 36.2	13.2	6 13.4	9.4	55.8
D	12	358 31.0	N16 46.3	328 08.4	13.3	N 6 04.0	9.5	55.7
A	13	13 31.0	45.6	342 40.7	13.3	5 54.5	9.5	55.7
Y	14	28 31.1	44.9	357 13.0	13.4	5 45.0	9.5	55.7
	15	43 31.2	. . 44.2	11 45.4	13.4	5 35.5	9.6	55.7
	16	58 31.2	43.5	26 17.8	13.5	5 25.9	9.5	55.7
	17	73 31.3	42.8	40 50.3	13.5	5 16.4	9.6	55.6
	18	88 31.4	N16 42.1	55 22.8	13.6	N 5 06.8	9.6	55.6
	19	103 31.5	41.4	69 55.4	13.6	4 57.2	9.6	55.6
	20	118 31.5	40.8	84 28.0	13.6	4 47.6	9.6	55.6
	21	133 31.6	. . 40.1	99 00.6	13.7	4 38.0	9.6	55.5
	22	148 31.7	39.4	113 33.3	13.7	4 28.4	9.6	55.5
	23	163 31.7	38.7	128 06.0	13.7	4 18.8	9.6	55.5
6	00	178 31.8	N16 38.0	142 38.7	13.8	N 4 09.2	9.7	55.5
	01	193 31.9	37.3	157 11.5	13.9	3 59.5	9.7	55.4
	02	208 31.9	36.6	171 44.4	13.8	3 49.8	9.6	55.4
	03	223 32.0	. . 35.9	186 17.2	14.0	3 40.2	9.7	55.4
	04	238 32.1	35.2	200 50.2	13.9	3 30.5	9.7	55.4
	05	253 32.2	34.5	215 23.1	14.0	3 20.8	9.7	55.4
	06	268 32.2	N16 33.9	229 56.1	14.0	N 3 11.1	9.6	55.3
S	07	283 32.3	33.2	244 29.1	14.0	3 01.5	9.7	55.3
A	08	298 32.4	32.5	259 02.1	14.1	2 51.8	9.7	55.3
T	09	313 32.4	. . 31.8	273 35.2	14.1	2 42.1	9.8	55.3
U	10	328 32.5	31.1	288 08.3	14.2	2 32.3	9.7	55.2
R	11	343 32.6	30.4	302 41.5	14.2	2 22.6	9.7	55.2
D	12	358 32.7	N16 29.7	317 14.7	14.2	N 2 12.9	9.7	55.2
A	13	13 32.7	29.0	331 47.9	14.2	2 03.2	9.7	55.2
Y	14	28 32.8	28.3	346 21.1	14.3	1 53.5	9.7	55.2
	15	43 32.9	. . 27.6	0 54.4	14.3	1 43.8	9.7	55.1
	16	58 33.0	26.9	15 27.7	14.3	1 34.1	9.7	55.1
	17	73 33.0	26.2	30 01.0	14.4	1 24.4	9.7	55.1
	18	88 33.1	N16 25.5	44 34.4	14.4	N 1 14.7	9.7	55.1
	19	103 33.2	24.8	59 07.8	14.4	1 05.0	9.7	55.1
	20	118 33.3	24.1	73 41.2	14.4	0 55.3	9.7	55.0
	21	133 33.3	. . 23.4	88 14.6	14.5	0 45.6	9.7	55.0
	22	148 33.4	22.7	102 48.1	14.5	0 35.9	9.7	55.0
	23	163 33.5	22.0	117 21.6	14.5	N 0 26.2	9.7	55.0
		SD 15.8	*d* 0.7	SD 15.4		15.2		15.0

Lat. °	Twilight Naut. h m	Twilight Civil h m	Sunrise h m	Moonrise 4 h m	Moonrise 5 h m	Moonrise 6 h m	Moonrise 7 h m
N 72	////	////	00 47	04 47	06 31	08 10	09 47
N 70	////	////	02 00	05 05	06 41	08 14	09 45
68	////	////	02 37	05 19	06 50	08 18	09 43
66	////	01 18	03 02	05 31	06 56	08 20	09 42
64	////	02 03	03 22	05 40	07 02	08 22	09 41
62	////	02 32	03 38	05 49	07 07	08 24	09 40
60	01 11	02 54	03 51	05 56	07 12	08 26	09 39
N 58	01 52	03 11	04 02	06 02	07 15	08 28	09 38
56	02 18	03 25	04 12	06 07	07 19	08 29	09 37
54	02 38	03 38	04 21	06 12	07 22	08 30	09 37
52	02 55	03 48	04 29	06 17	07 25	08 31	09 36
50	03 08	03 58	04 35	06 21	07 27	08 32	09 36
45	03 35	04 17	04 50	06 29	07 33	08 34	09 35
N 40	03 56	04 32	05 02	06 36	07 37	08 36	09 34
35	04 12	04 45	05 13	06 43	07 41	08 38	09 33
30	04 25	04 56	05 22	06 48	07 44	08 39	09 32
20	04 46	05 14	05 37	06 57	07 50	08 42	09 31
N 10	05 02	05 28	05 50	07 06	07 56	08 44	09 30
0	05 16	05 41	06 02	07 13	08 00	08 46	09 29
S 10	05 27	05 53	06 15	07 21	08 05	08 48	09 29
20	05 38	06 05	06 28	07 29	08 11	08 50	09 28
30	05 49	06 17	06 42	07 38	08 16	08 52	09 27
35	05 54	06 24	06 51	07 44	08 20	08 54	09 26
40	05 59	06 32	07 00	07 50	08 24	08 55	09 25
45	06 05	06 40	07 11	07 57	08 28	08 57	09 24
S 50	06 11	06 50	07 25	08 05	08 33	08 59	09 24
52	06 14	06 54	07 31	08 09	08 36	09 00	09 23
54	06 17	06 59	07 38	08 13	08 39	09 01	09 23
56	06 20	07 05	07 46	08 18	08 42	09 02	09 22
58	06 23	07 10	07 54	08 23	08 45	09 04	09 22
S 60	06 27	07 17	08 04	08 29	08 48	09 05	09 21

Lat. °	Sunset h m	Twilight Civil h m	Twilight Naut. h m	Moonset 4 h m	Moonset 5 h m	Moonset 6 h m	Moonset 7 h m
N 72	23 09	////	////	21 26	21 20	21 15	21 10
N 70	22 06	////	////	21 14	21 14	21 14	21 14
68	21 31	////	////	21 04	21 09	21 14	21 18
66	21 07	22 46	////	20 56	21 05	21 13	21 21
64	20 48	22 04	////	20 49	21 01	21 12	21 23
62	20 32	21 37	////	20 43	20 58	21 12	21 25
60	20 19	21 16	22 54	20 37	20 55	21 12	21 27
N 58	20 08	20 59	22 16	20 33	20 53	21 11	21 29
56	19 58	20 45	21 51	20 29	20 51	21 11	21 31
54	19 50	20 33	21 31	20 25	20 49	21 11	21 32
52	19 42	20 22	21 15	20 21	20 47	21 10	21 33
50	19 35	20 13	21 02	20 18	20 45	21 10	21 34
45	19 21	19 54	20 35	20 12	20 42	21 10	21 37
N 40	19 09	19 39	20 15	20 06	20 39	21 09	21 39
35	18 59	19 26	19 59	20 01	20 36	21 09	21 41
30	18 50	19 16	19 46	19 57	20 34	21 09	21 43
20	18 35	18 58	19 25	19 49	20 29	21 08	21 45
N 10	18 22	18 44	19 09	19 43	20 26	21 07	21 48
0	18 09	18 31	18 56	19 36	20 22	21 07	21 50
S 10	17 57	18 19	18 44	19 30	20 19	21 06	21 53
20	17 45	18 07	18 34	19 23	20 15	21 06	21 55
30	17 30	17 55	18 24	19 15	20 11	21 05	21 58
35	17 22	17 48	18 19	19 11	20 08	21 05	21 59
40	17 12	17 41	18 13	19 06	20 06	21 04	22 01
45	17 01	17 32	18 08	19 00	20 02	21 04	22 03
S 50	16 48	17 23	18 01	18 52	19 58	21 03	22 06
52	16 42	17 18	17 59	18 49	19 57	21 03	22 07
54	16 35	17 13	17 56	18 45	19 55	21 02	22 08
56	16 27	17 08	17 53	18 41	19 52	21 02	22 10
58	16 18	17 02	17 50	18 37	19 50	21 01	22 11
S 60	16 09	16 56	17 46	18 32	19 47	21 01	22 13

Day	SUN Eqn. of Time 00^h	SUN Eqn. of Time 12^h	SUN Mer. Pass.	MOON Mer. Pass. Upper	MOON Mer. Pass. Lower	MOON Age	MOON Phase
d	m s	m s	h m	h m	h m	d	%
4	06 05	06 02	12 06	13 25	01 01	02	3
5	05 59	05 56	12 06	14 11	01 48	03	7
6	05 53	05 50	12 06	14 56	02 34	04	14

UT	ARIES	VENUS −3·8		MARS −0·6		JUPITER −1·7		SATURN +0·4	
d h	GHA ° ′	GHA ° ′	Dec ° ′	GHA ° ′	Dec ° ′	GHA ° ′	Dec ° ′	GHA ° ′	Dec ° ′
7 00	315 56.8	161 43.7	N12 15.9	77 00.2	S23 17.8	141 45.2	N 3 44.1	67 31.6	S20 18.2
01	330 59.3	176 43.2	14.8	92 01.6	18.0	156 47.3	43.9	82 34.1	18.2
02	346 01.7	191 42.8	13.6	107 03.0	18.2	171 49.3	43.7	97 36.6	18.2
03	1 04.2	206 42.3	. . 12.5	122 04.4	. . 18.4	186 51.3	. . 43.5	112 39.1	. . 18.2
04	16 06.7	221 41.9	11.4	137 05.7	18.6	201 53.3	43.3	127 41.6	18.2
05	31 09.1	236 41.4	10.3	152 07.1	18.8	216 55.4	43.1	142 44.1	18.3
06	46 11.6	251 40.9	N12 09.2	167 08.5	S23 19.0	231 57.4	N 3 42.9	157 46.6	S20 18.3
07	61 14.1	266 40.5	08.1	182 09.8	19.2	246 59.4	42.7	172 49.1	18.3
S 08	76 16.5	281 40.0	07.0	197 11.2	19.4	262 01.5	42.5	187 51.6	18.3
U 09	91 19.0	296 39.5	. . 05.9	212 12.5	. . 19.6	277 03.5	. . 42.3	202 54.1	. . 18.3
N 10	106 21.5	311 39.1	04.8	227 13.9	19.8	292 05.5	42.1	217 56.6	18.3
D 11	121 23.9	326 38.6	03.6	242 15.3	20.0	307 07.5	42.0	232 59.1	18.3
A 12	136 26.4	341 38.1	N12 02.5	257 16.6	S23 20.2	322 09.6	N 3 41.8	248 01.5	S20 18.3
Y 13	151 28.8	356 37.7	01.4	272 18.0	20.4	337 11.6	41.6	263 04.0	18.3
14	166 31.3	11 37.2	12 00.3	287 19.3	20.6	352 13.6	41.4	278 06.5	18.3
15	181 33.8	26 36.8	11 59.2	302 20.7	. . 20.8	7 15.6	. . 41.2	293 09.0	. . 18.3
16	196 36.2	41 36.3	58.1	317 22.1	21.0	22 17.7	41.0	308 11.5	18.3
17	211 38.7	56 35.8	57.0	332 23.4	21.3	37 19.7	40.8	323 14.0	18.3
18	226 41.2	71 35.4	N11 55.8	347 24.8	S23 21.5	52 21.7	N 3 40.6	338 16.5	S20 18.3
19	241 43.6	86 34.9	54.7	2 26.1	21.7	67 23.8	40.4	353 19.0	18.3
20	256 46.1	101 34.5	53.6	17 27.5	21.9	82 25.8	40.2	8 21.5	18.3
21	271 48.6	116 34.0	. . 52.5	32 28.8	. . 22.1	97 27.8	. . 40.0	23 24.0	. . 18.3
22	286 51.0	131 33.6	51.4	47 30.2	22.3	112 29.8	39.8	38 26.4	18.3
23	301 53.5	146 33.1	50.2	62 31.5	22.5	127 31.9	39.7	53 28.9	18.4
8 00	316 55.9	161 32.6	N11 49.1	77 32.9	S23 22.7	142 33.9	N 3 39.5	68 31.4	S20 18.4
01	331 58.4	176 32.2	48.0	92 34.2	22.9	157 35.9	39.3	83 33.9	18.4
02	347 00.9	191 31.7	46.9	107 35.6	23.1	172 37.9	39.1	98 36.4	18.4
03	2 03.3	206 31.3	. . 45.8	122 36.9	. . 23.3	187 40.0	. . 38.9	113 38.9	. . 18.4
04	17 05.8	221 30.8	44.6	137 38.3	23.5	202 42.0	38.7	128 41.4	18.4
05	32 08.3	236 30.4	43.5	152 39.6	23.7	217 44.0	38.5	143 43.9	18.4
06	47 10.7	251 29.9	N11 42.4	167 40.9	S23 23.9	232 46.0	N 3 38.3	158 46.3	S20 18.4
07	62 13.2	266 29.5	41.3	182 42.3	24.1	247 48.1	38.1	173 48.8	18.4
08	77 15.7	281 29.0	40.1	197 43.6	24.3	262 50.1	37.9	188 51.3	18.4
M 09	92 18.1	296 28.5	. . 39.0	212 45.0	. . 24.6	277 52.1	. . 37.7	203 53.8	. . 18.4
O 10	107 20.6	311 28.1	37.9	227 46.3	24.8	292 54.1	37.5	218 56.3	18.4
N 11	122 23.1	326 27.6	36.8	242 47.7	25.0	307 56.2	37.3	233 58.8	18.4
D 12	137 25.5	341 27.2	N11 35.6	257 49.0	S23 25.2	322 58.2	N 3 37.2	249 01.3	S20 18.4
A 13	152 28.0	356 26.7	34.5	272 50.3	25.4	338 00.2	37.0	264 03.8	18.4
Y 14	167 30.4	11 26.3	33.4	287 51.7	25.6	353 02.2	36.8	279 06.2	18.4
15	182 32.9	26 25.8	. . 32.3	302 53.0	. . 25.8	8 04.3	. . 36.6	294 08.7	. . 18.4
16	197 35.4	41 25.4	31.1	317 54.3	26.0	23 06.3	36.4	309 11.2	18.5
17	212 37.8	56 24.9	30.0	332 55.7	26.2	38 08.3	36.2	324 13.7	18.5
18	227 40.3	71 24.5	N11 28.9	347 57.0	S23 26.4	53 10.3	N 3 36.0	339 16.2	S20 18.5
19	242 42.8	86 24.0	27.7	2 58.3	26.6	68 12.4	35.8	354 18.7	18.5
20	257 45.2	101 23.6	26.6	17 59.7	26.8	83 14.4	35.6	9 21.2	18.5
21	272 47.7	116 23.1	. . 25.5	33 01.0	. . 27.0	98 16.4	. . 35.4	24 23.6	. . 18.5
22	287 50.2	131 22.7	24.3	48 02.3	27.2	113 18.4	35.2	39 26.1	18.5
23	302 52.6	146 22.3	23.2	63 03.7	27.4	128 20.5	35.0	54 28.6	18.5
9 00	317 55.1	161 21.8	N11 22.1	78 05.0	S23 27.6	143 22.5	N 3 34.8	69 31.1	S20 18.5
01	332 57.6	176 21.4	20.9	93 06.3	27.9	158 24.5	34.6	84 33.6	18.5
02	348 00.0	191 20.9	19.8	108 07.6	28.1	173 26.5	34.4	99 36.1	18.5
03	3 02.5	206 20.5	. . 18.7	123 09.0	. . 28.3	188 28.6	. . 34.3	114 38.5	. . 18.5
04	18 04.9	221 20.0	17.5	138 10.3	28.5	203 30.6	34.1	129 41.0	18.5
05	33 07.4	236 19.6	16.4	153 11.6	28.7	218 32.6	33.9	144 43.5	18.5
06	48 09.9	251 19.1	N11 15.3	168 12.9	S23 28.9	233 34.6	N 3 33.7	159 46.0	S20 18.5
07	63 12.3	266 18.7	14.1	183 14.3	29.1	248 36.7	33.5	174 48.5	18.5
T 08	78 14.8	281 18.2	13.0	198 15.6	29.3	263 38.7	33.3	189 51.0	18.6
U 09	93 17.3	296 17.8	. . 11.9	213 16.9	. . 29.5	278 40.7	. . 33.1	204 53.4	. . 18.6
E 10	108 19.7	311 17.4	10.7	228 18.2	29.7	293 42.7	32.9	219 55.9	18.6
S 11	123 22.2	326 16.9	09.6	243 19.5	29.9	308 44.7	32.7	234 58.4	18.6
D 12	138 24.7	341 16.5	N11 08.4	258 20.9	S23 30.1	323 46.8	N 3 32.5	250 00.9	S20 18.6
A 13	153 27.1	356 16.0	07.3	273 22.2	30.3	338 48.8	32.3	265 03.4	18.6
Y 14	168 29.6	11 15.6	06.2	288 23.5	30.5	353 50.8	32.1	280 05.9	18.6
15	183 32.0	26 15.2	. . 05.0	303 24.8	. . 30.7	8 52.8	. . 31.9	295 08.3	. . 18.6
16	198 34.5	41 14.7	03.9	318 26.1	31.0	23 54.9	31.7	310 10.8	18.6
17	213 37.0	56 14.3	02.7	333 27.4	31.2	38 56.9	31.5	325 13.3	18.6
18	228 39.4	71 13.8	N11 01.6	348 28.7	S23 31.4	53 58.9	N 3 31.4	340 15.8	S20 18.6
19	243 41.9	86 13.4	11 00.5	3 30.1	31.6	69 00.9	31.2	355 18.3	18.6
20	258 44.4	101 13.0	10 59.3	18 31.4	31.8	84 03.0	31.0	10 20.7	18.6
21	273 46.8	116 12.5	. . 58.2	33 32.7	. . 32.0	99 05.0	. . 30.8	25 23.2	. . 18.6
22	288 49.3	131 12.1	57.0	48 34.0	32.2	114 07.0	30.6	40 25.7	18.7
23	303 51.8	146 11.6	55.9	63 35.3	32.4	129 09.0	30.4	55 28.2	18.7
Mer. Pass.	h m 2 51.8	*v* −0.5	*d* 1.1	*v* 1.3	*d* 0.2	*v* 2.0	*d* 0.2	*v* 2.5	*d* 0.0

STARS

Name	SHA ° ′	Dec ° ′
Acamar	315 16.8	S40 14.2
Achernar	335 25.1	S57 08.9
Acrux	173 07.2	S63 11.6
Adhara	255 11.2	S28 59.7
Aldebaran	290 47.1	N16 32.3
Alioth	166 19.2	N55 52.5
Alkaid	152 57.4	N49 14.2
Al Na'ir	27 40.7	S46 52.6
Alnilam	275 44.4	S 1 11.6
Alphard	217 54.3	S 8 43.9
Alphecca	126 09.2	N26 39.9
Alpheratz	357 41.0	N29 10.9
Altair	62 05.8	N 8 55.0
Ankaa	353 13.4	S42 12.7
Antares	112 23.5	S26 27.9
Arcturus	145 53.9	N19 06.1
Atria	107 23.0	S69 03.4
Avior	234 17.7	S59 33.8
Bellatrix	278 29.9	N 6 21.7
Betelgeuse	270 59.2	N 7 24.5
Canopus	263 55.6	S52 42.2
Capella	280 31.5	N46 00.5
Deneb	49 29.5	N45 20.6
Denebola	182 31.8	N14 28.9
Diphda	348 53.6	S17 53.6
Dubhe	193 49.8	N61 39.9
Elnath	278 10.1	N28 37.0
Eltanin	90 44.8	N51 29.6
Enif	33 44.7	N 9 57.3
Fomalhaut	15 21.4	S29 31.9
Gacrux	171 58.7	S57 12.5
Gienah	175 50.3	S17 38.0
Hadar	148 44.9	S60 27.3
Hamal	327 58.2	N23 32.3
Kaus Aust.	83 40.7	S34 22.4
Kochab	137 20.3	N74 05.7
Markab	13 35.9	N15 17.8
Menkar	314 12.8	N 4 09.2
Menkent	148 05.1	S36 27.1
Miaplacidus	221 40.0	S69 47.2
Mirfak	308 37.3	N49 54.8
Nunki	75 55.4	S26 16.3
Peacock	53 15.4	S56 40.7
Pollux	243 25.5	N27 59.0
Procyon	244 57.8	N 5 10.8
Rasalhague	96 04.3	N12 33.2
Regulus	207 41.6	N11 53.2
Rigel	281 10.2	S 8 11.0
Rigil Kent.	139 48.8	S60 54.3
Sabik	102 09.9	S15 44.5
Schedar	349 37.6	N56 37.5
Shaula	96 18.7	S37 06.8
Sirius	258 32.1	S16 44.4
Spica	158 29.1	S11 14.7
Suhail	222 51.3	S43 30.0
Vega	80 37.2	N38 48.3
Zuben'ubi	137 03.0	S16 06.5

	SHA ° ′	Mer. Pass. h m
Venus	204 36.7	13 14
Mars	120 36.9	18 48
Jupiter	185 37.9	14 28
Saturn	111 35.5	19 23

Day	UT	SUN GHA	SUN Dec	MOON GHA	v	MOON Dec	d	HP
	d h	° ′	° ′	° ′	′	° ′	′	′
7	00	178 33.6	N16 21.3	131 55.1	14.5	N 0 16.5	9.7	55.0
	01	193 33.6	20.6	146 28.6	14.6	N 0 06.8	9.6	54.9
	02	208 33.7	19.9	161 02.2	14.5	S 0 02.8	9.7	54.9
	03	223 33.8	. . 19.2	175 35.7	14.6	0 12.5	9.6	54.9
	04	238 33.9	18.5	190 09.3	14.6	0 22.1	9.7	54.9
	05	253 33.9	17.8	204 42.9	14.7	0 31.8	9.6	54.9
	06	268 34.0	N16 17.1	219 16.6	14.6	S 0 41.4	9.6	54.9
	07	283 34.1	16.4	233 50.2	14.7	0 51.0	9.6	54.8
S	08	298 34.2	15.7	248 23.9	14.7	1 00.6	9.6	54.8
U	09	313 34.3	. . 15.0	262 57.6	14.7	1 10.2	9.6	54.8
N	10	328 34.3	14.3	277 31.3	14.7	1 19.8	9.6	54.8
D	11	343 34.4	13.6	292 05.0	14.8	1 29.4	9.6	54.8
A	12	358 34.5	N16 12.9	306 38.8	14.7	S 1 39.0	9.5	54.8
Y	13	13 34.6	12.2	321 12.5	14.8	1 48.5	9.6	54.7
	14	28 34.6	11.4	335 46.3	14.8	1 58.1	9.5	54.7
	15	43 34.7	. . 10.7	350 20.1	14.8	2 07.6	9.5	54.7
	16	58 34.8	10.0	4 53.9	14.8	2 17.1	9.5	54.7
	17	73 34.9	09.3	19 27.7	14.8	2 26.6	9.5	54.7
	18	88 35.0	N16 08.6	34 01.5	14.8	S 2 36.1	9.4	54.7
	19	103 35.1	07.9	48 35.3	14.8	2 45.5	9.5	54.6
	20	118 35.1	07.2	63 09.1	14.9	2 55.0	9.4	54.6
	21	133 35.2	. . 06.5	77 43.0	14.8	3 04.4	9.4	54.6
	22	148 35.3	05.8	92 16.8	14.9	3 13.8	9.4	54.6
	23	163 35.4	05.1	106 50.7	14.9	3 23.2	9.4	54.6
8	00	178 35.5	N16 04.3	121 24.6	14.8	S 3 32.6	9.3	54.6
	01	193 35.5	03.6	135 58.4	14.9	3 41.9	9.3	54.6
	02	208 35.6	02.9	150 32.3	14.9	3 51.2	9.3	54.5
	03	223 35.7	. . 02.2	165 06.2	14.9	4 00.5	9.3	54.5
	04	238 35.8	01.5	179 40.1	14.9	4 09.8	9.3	54.5
	05	253 35.9	00.8	194 14.0	14.9	4 19.1	9.2	54.5
	06	268 36.0	N16 00.1	208 47.9	14.9	S 4 28.3	9.2	54.5
	07	283 36.0	15 59.4	223 21.8	14.9	4 37.5	9.2	54.5
M	08	298 36.1	58.6	237 55.7	14.9	4 46.7	9.2	54.5
O	09	313 36.2	. . 57.9	252 29.6	14.9	4 55.9	9.1	54.5
N	10	328 36.3	57.2	267 03.5	14.9	5 05.0	9.1	54.5
D	11	343 36.4	56.5	281 37.4	14.9	5 14.1	9.1	54.4
A	12	358 36.5	N15 55.8	296 11.3	14.9	S 5 23.2	9.1	54.4
Y	13	13 36.6	55.1	310 45.2	14.9	5 32.3	9.0	54.4
	14	28 36.6	54.3	325 19.1	14.9	5 41.3	9.1	54.4
	15	43 36.7	. . 53.6	339 53.0	14.9	5 50.4	8.9	54.4
	16	58 36.8	52.9	354 26.9	14.9	5 59.3	9.0	54.4
	17	73 36.9	52.2	9 00.8	14.9	6 08.3	8.9	54.4
	18	88 37.0	N15 51.5	23 34.7	14.8	S 6 17.2	8.9	54.4
	19	103 37.1	50.7	38 08.5	14.9	6 26.1	8.9	54.4
	20	118 37.2	50.0	52 42.4	14.9	6 35.0	8.8	54.4
	21	133 37.3	. . 49.3	67 16.3	14.8	6 43.8	8.8	54.3
	22	148 37.3	48.6	81 50.1	14.9	6 52.6	8.8	54.3
	23	163 37.4	47.9	96 24.0	14.8	7 01.4	8.7	54.3
9	00	178 37.5	N15 47.1	110 57.8	14.9	S 7 10.1	8.8	54.3
	01	193 37.6	46.4	125 31.7	14.8	7 18.9	8.6	54.3
	02	208 37.7	45.7	140 05.5	14.8	7 27.5	8.7	54.3
	03	223 37.8	. . 45.0	154 39.3	14.8	7 36.2	8.6	54.3
	04	238 37.9	44.2	169 13.1	14.8	7 44.8	8.6	54.3
	05	253 38.0	43.5	183 46.9	14.7	7 53.4	8.5	54.3
	06	268 38.1	N15 42.8	198 20.6	14.8	S 8 01.9	8.5	54.3
T	07	283 38.1	42.1	212 54.4	14.8	8 10.4	8.5	54.3
U	08	298 38.2	41.3	227 28.2	14.7	8 18.9	8.4	54.3
E	09	313 38.3	. . 40.6	242 01.9	14.7	8 27.3	8.4	54.3
S	10	328 38.4	39.9	256 35.6	14.7	8 35.7	8.4	54.3
D	11	343 38.5	39.2	271 09.3	14.7	8 44.1	8.3	54.3
A	12	358 38.6	N15 38.4	285 43.0	14.7	S 8 52.4	8.3	54.3
Y	13	13 38.7	37.7	300 16.7	14.6	9 00.7	8.2	54.3
	14	28 38.8	37.0	314 50.3	14.6	9 08.9	8.2	54.3
	15	43 38.9	. . 36.2	329 23.9	14.7	9 17.1	8.2	54.3
	16	58 39.0	35.5	343 57.6	14.6	9 25.3	8.1	54.3
	17	73 39.1	34.8	358 31.2	14.5	9 33.4	8.1	54.2
	18	88 39.2	N15 34.1	13 04.7	14.6	S 9 41.5	8.1	54.2
	19	103 39.3	33.3	27 38.3	14.5	9 49.6	8.0	54.2
	20	118 39.3	32.6	42 11.8	14.5	9 57.6	7.9	54.2
	21	133 39.4	. . 31.9	56 45.3	14.5	10 05.5	7.9	54.2
	22	148 39.5	31.1	71 18.8	14.5	10 13.4	7.9	54.2
	23	163 39.6	30.4	85 52.3	14.4	S10 21.3	7.9	54.2
		SD 15.8	*d* 0.7	SD	14.9		14.8	14.8

Lat.	Twilight Naut.	Twilight Civil	Sunrise	Moonrise 7	Moonrise 8	Moonrise 9	Moonrise 10
°	h m	h m	h m	h m	h m	h m	h m
N 72	////	////	01 29	09 47	11 22	12 57	14 35
N 70	////	////	02 19	09 45	11 14	12 42	14 12
68	////	////	02 51	09 43	11 07	12 31	13 54
66	////	01 42	03 13	09 42	11 02	12 21	13 40
64	////	02 18	03 31	09 41	10 58	12 13	13 28
62	////	02 43	03 46	09 40	10 54	12 07	13 18
60	01 31	03 03	03 58	09 39	10 50	12 01	13 10
N 58	02 04	03 19	04 09	09 38	10 47	11 56	13 03
56	02 28	03 32	04 18	09 37	10 45	11 51	12 56
54	02 46	03 44	04 26	09 37	10 42	11 47	12 50
52	03 02	03 54	04 33	09 36	10 40	11 43	12 45
50	03 15	04 03	04 40	09 36	10 38	11 40	12 41
45	03 40	04 21	04 54	09 35	10 34	11 33	12 30
N 40	03 59	04 36	05 05	09 34	10 31	11 26	12 22
35	04 15	04 48	05 15	09 33	10 28	11 21	12 15
30	04 27	04 58	05 23	09 32	10 25	11 17	12 09
20	04 47	05 15	05 38	09 31	10 20	11 09	11 58
N 10	05 03	05 29	05 50	09 30	10 16	11 02	11 48
0	05 16	05 41	06 02	09 29	10 13	10 56	11 39
S 10	05 27	05 52	06 14	09 29	10 09	10 49	11 31
20	05 37	06 03	06 26	09 28	10 05	10 42	11 21
30	05 46	06 15	06 40	09 27	10 00	10 35	11 11
35	05 51	06 21	06 48	09 26	09 58	10 30	11 05
40	05 56	06 28	06 57	09 25	09 55	10 26	10 58
45	06 01	06 36	07 07	09 24	09 52	10 20	10 50
S 50	06 07	06 45	07 20	09 24	09 48	10 13	10 40
52	06 09	06 49	07 26	09 23	09 46	10 10	10 36
54	06 12	06 54	07 32	09 23	09 44	10 06	10 31
56	06 14	06 59	07 39	09 22	09 42	10 03	10 25
58	06 17	07 04	07 47	09 22	09 39	09 58	10 19
S 60	06 20	07 10	07 57	09 21	09 37	09 54	10 13

Lat.	Sunset	Twilight Civil	Twilight Naut.	Moonset 7	Moonset 8	Moonset 9	Moonset 10
°	h m	h m	h m	h m	h m	h m	h m
N 72	22 33	////	////	21 10	21 04	20 59	20 52
N 70	21 47	////	////	21 14	21 14	21 15	21 16
68	21 17	23 33	////	21 18	21 22	21 27	21 35
66	20 55	22 24	////	21 21	21 29	21 38	21 50
64	20 38	21 49	////	21 23	21 34	21 47	22 02
62	20 23	21 25	23 37	21 25	21 39	21 55	22 13
60	20 11	21 06	22 35	21 27	21 43	22 01	22 22
N 58	20 01	20 50	22 03	21 29	21 47	22 07	22 30
56	19 52	20 37	21 40	21 31	21 51	22 12	22 37
54	19 44	20 26	21 23	21 32	21 54	22 17	22 43
52	19 37	20 16	21 08	21 33	21 56	22 21	22 48
50	19 30	20 07	20 55	21 34	21 59	22 25	22 53
45	19 17	19 49	20 30	21 37	22 05	22 33	23 04
N 40	19 05	19 35	20 11	21 39	22 09	22 40	23 14
35	18 56	19 23	19 56	21 41	22 13	22 46	23 22
30	18 47	19 13	19 43	21 43	22 17	22 52	23 28
20	18 33	18 56	19 23	21 45	22 23	23 01	23 41
N 10	18 21	18 42	19 08	21 48	22 28	23 09	23 51
0	18 09	18 30	18 55	21 50	22 33	23 17	24 01
S 10	17 58	18 19	18 45	21 53	22 38	23 24	24 11
20	17 46	18 08	18 35	21 55	22 44	23 32	24 21
30	17 32	17 57	18 25	21 58	22 50	23 42	24 34
35	17 24	17 50	18 20	21 59	22 54	23 47	24 41
40	17 15	17 43	18 16	22 01	22 58	23 53	24 49
45	17 05	17 36	18 10	22 03	23 02	24 00	00 00
S 50	16 52	17 26	18 05	22 06	23 08	24 09	00 09
52	16 46	17 22	18 03	22 07	23 11	24 13	00 13
54	16 40	17 18	18 00	22 08	23 13	24 17	00 17
56	16 33	17 13	17 58	22 10	23 17	24 22	00 22
58	16 25	17 08	17 55	22 11	23 20	24 28	00 28
S 60	16 15	17 02	17 52	22 13	23 24	24 34	00 34

Day	SUN Eqn. of Time 00^h	SUN Eqn. of Time 12^h	SUN Mer. Pass.	MOON Mer. Pass. Upper	MOON Mer. Pass. Lower	MOON Age	MOON Phase
d	m s	m s	h m	h m	h m	d %	
7	05 46	05 42	12 06	15 40	03 18	05 21	
8	05 38	05 34	12 06	16 23	04 01	06 29	
9	05 30	05 26	12 05	17 06	04 44	07 38	

2016 AUGUST 10, 11, 12 (WED., THURS., FRI.)

UT		ARIES	VENUS −3·8		MARS −0·6		JUPITER −1·7		SATURN +0·4	
	d h	GHA ° ′	GHA ° ′	Dec ° ′	GHA ° ′	Dec ° ′	GHA ° ′	Dec ° ′	GHA ° ′	Dec ° ′
	10 00	318 54.2	161 11.2	N10 54.7	78 36.6	S23 32.6	144 11.0	N 3 30.2	70 30.7	S20 18.7
	01	333 56.7	176 10.8	53.6	93 37.9	32.8	159 13.1	30.0	85 33.1	18.7
	02	348 59.2	191 10.3	52.4	108 39.2	33.0	174 15.1	29.8	100 35.6	18.7
	03	4 01.6	206 09.9	. . 51.3	123 40.5	. . 33.2	189 17.1	. . 29.6	115 38.1	. . 18.7
	04	19 04.1	221 09.5	50.2	138 41.8	33.4	204 19.1	29.4	130 40.6	18.7
	05	34 06.5	236 09.0	49.0	153 43.1	33.6	219 21.1	29.2	145 43.1	18.7
	06	49 09.0	251 08.6	N10 47.9	168 44.4	S23 33.8	234 23.2	N 3 29.0	160 45.5	S20 18.7
W	07	64 11.5	266 08.2	46.7	183 45.7	34.0	249 25.2	28.8	175 48.0	18.7
E	08	79 13.9	281 07.7	45.6	198 47.0	34.3	264 27.2	28.6	190 50.5	18.7
D	09	94 16.4	296 07.3	. . 44.4	213 48.3	. . 34.5	279 29.2	. . 28.4	205 53.0	. . 18.7
N	10	109 18.9	311 06.9	43.3	228 49.6	34.7	294 31.3	28.2	220 55.5	18.7
E	11	124 21.3	326 06.4	42.1	243 50.9	34.9	309 33.3	28.1	235 57.9	18.7
S	12	139 23.8	341 06.0	N10 41.0	258 52.2	S23 35.1	324 35.3	N 3 27.9	251 00.4	S20 18.7
D	13	154 26.3	356 05.6	39.8	273 53.5	35.3	339 37.3	27.7	266 02.9	18.8
A	14	169 28.7	11 05.1	38.7	288 54.8	35.5	354 39.3	27.5	281 05.4	18.8
Y	15	184 31.2	26 04.7	. . 37.5	303 56.1	. . 35.7	9 41.4	. . 27.3	296 07.8	. . 18.8
	16	199 33.6	41 04.3	36.3	318 57.4	35.9	24 43.4	27.1	311 10.3	18.8
	17	214 36.1	56 03.8	35.2	333 58.7	36.1	39 45.4	26.9	326 12.8	18.8
	18	229 38.6	71 03.4	N10 34.0	349 00.0	S23 36.3	54 47.4	N 3 26.7	341 15.3	S20 18.8
	19	244 41.0	86 03.0	32.9	4 01.3	36.5	69 49.4	26.5	356 17.8	18.8
	20	259 43.5	101 02.6	31.7	19 02.6	36.7	84 51.5	26.3	11 20.2	18.8
	21	274 46.0	116 02.1	. . 30.6	34 03.9	. . 36.9	99 53.5	. . 26.1	26 22.7	. . 18.8
	22	289 48.4	131 01.7	29.4	49 05.2	37.1	114 55.5	25.9	41 25.2	18.8
	23	304 50.9	146 01.3	28.3	64 06.4	37.3	129 57.5	25.7	56 27.7	18.8
	11 00	319 53.4	161 00.8	N10 27.1	79 07.7	S23 37.5	144 59.5	N 3 25.5	71 30.1	S20 18.8
	01	334 55.8	176 00.4	25.9	94 09.0	37.8	160 01.6	25.3	86 32.6	18.8
	02	349 58.3	191 00.0	24.8	109 10.3	38.0	175 03.6	25.1	101 35.1	18.9
	03	5 00.8	205 59.6	. . 23.6	124 11.6	. . 38.2	190 05.6	. . 24.9	116 37.6	. . 18.9
	04	20 03.2	220 59.1	22.5	139 12.9	38.4	205 07.6	24.7	131 40.0	18.9
	05	35 05.7	235 58.7	21.3	154 14.2	38.6	220 09.6	24.5	146 42.5	18.9
	06	50 08.1	250 58.3	N10 20.2	169 15.4	S23 38.8	235 11.6	N 3 24.3	161 45.0	S20 18.9
	07	65 10.6	265 57.9	19.0	184 16.7	39.0	250 13.7	24.2	176 47.5	18.9
T	08	80 13.1	280 57.4	17.8	199 18.0	39.2	265 15.7	24.0	191 49.9	18.9
H	09	95 15.5	295 57.0	. . 16.7	214 19.3	. . 39.4	280 17.7	. . 23.8	206 52.4	. . 18.9
U	10	110 18.0	310 56.6	15.5	229 20.6	39.6	295 19.7	23.6	221 54.9	18.9
R	11	125 20.5	325 56.2	14.3	244 21.8	39.8	310 21.7	23.4	236 57.4	18.9
S	12	140 22.9	340 55.8	N10 13.2	259 23.1	S23 40.0	325 23.8	N 3 23.2	251 59.8	S20 18.9
D	13	155 25.4	355 55.3	12.0	274 24.4	40.2	340 25.8	23.0	267 02.3	18.9
A	14	170 27.9	10 54.9	10.9	289 25.7	40.4	355 27.8	22.8	282 04.8	18.9
Y	15	185 30.3	25 54.5	. . 09.7	304 26.9	. . 40.6	10 29.8	. . 22.6	297 07.3	. . 19.0
	16	200 32.8	40 54.1	08.5	319 28.2	40.8	25 31.8	22.4	312 09.7	19.0
	17	215 35.3	55 53.6	07.4	334 29.5	41.0	40 33.9	22.2	327 12.2	19.0
	18	230 37.7	70 53.2	N10 06.2	349 30.8	S23 41.2	55 35.9	N 3 22.0	342 14.7	S20 19.0
	19	245 40.2	85 52.8	05.0	4 32.0	41.5	70 37.9	21.8	357 17.1	19.0
	20	260 42.6	100 52.4	03.9	19 33.3	41.7	85 39.9	21.6	12 19.6	19.0
	21	275 45.1	115 52.0	. . 02.7	34 34.6	. . 41.9	100 41.9	. . 21.4	27 22.1	. . 19.0
	22	290 47.6	130 51.5	01.5	49 35.8	42.1	115 43.9	21.2	42 24.6	19.0
	23	305 50.0	145 51.1	10 00.4	64 37.1	42.3	130 46.0	21.0	57 27.0	19.0
	12 00	320 52.5	160 50.7	N 9 59.2	79 38.4	S23 42.5	145 48.0	N 3 20.8	72 29.5	S20 19.0
	01	335 55.0	175 50.3	58.0	94 39.6	42.7	160 50.0	20.6	87 32.0	19.0
	02	350 57.4	190 49.9	56.9	109 40.9	42.9	175 52.0	20.4	102 34.4	19.0
	03	5 59.9	205 49.5	. . 55.7	124 42.2	. . 43.1	190 54.0	. . 20.2	117 36.9	. . 19.1
	04	21 02.4	220 49.0	54.5	139 43.4	43.3	205 56.0	20.0	132 39.4	19.1
	05	36 04.8	235 48.6	53.4	154 44.7	43.5	220 58.1	19.8	147 41.9	19.1
	06	51 07.3	250 48.2	N 9 52.2	169 46.0	S23 43.7	236 00.1	N 3 19.6	162 44.3	S20 19.1
	07	66 09.7	265 47.8	51.0	184 47.2	43.9	251 02.1	19.5	177 46.8	19.1
	08	81 12.2	280 47.4	49.8	199 48.5	44.1	266 04.1	19.3	192 49.3	19.1
F	09	96 14.7	295 47.0	. . 48.7	214 49.7	. . 44.3	281 06.1	. . 19.1	207 51.7	. . 19.1
R	10	111 17.1	310 46.6	47.5	229 51.0	44.5	296 08.1	18.9	222 54.2	19.1
I	11	126 19.6	325 46.1	46.3	244 52.3	44.7	311 10.2	18.7	237 56.7	19.1
D	12	141 22.1	340 45.7	N 9 45.1	259 53.5	S23 44.9	326 12.2	N 3 18.5	252 59.2	S20 19.1
A	13	156 24.5	355 45.3	44.0	274 54.8	45.1	341 14.2	18.3	268 01.6	19.1
Y	14	171 27.0	10 44.9	42.8	289 56.0	45.4	356 16.2	18.1	283 04.1	19.1
	15	186 29.5	25 44.5	. . 41.6	304 57.3	. . 45.6	11 18.2	. . 17.9	298 06.6	. . 19.2
	16	201 31.9	40 44.1	40.4	319 58.5	45.8	26 20.2	17.7	313 09.0	19.2
	17	216 34.4	55 43.7	39.3	334 59.8	46.0	41 22.3	17.5	328 11.5	19.2
	18	231 36.9	70 43.3	N 9 38.1	350 01.0	S23 46.2	56 24.3	N 3 17.3	343 14.0	S20 19.2
	19	246 39.3	85 42.8	36.9	5 02.3	46.4	71 26.3	17.1	358 16.4	19.2
	20	261 41.8	100 42.4	35.7	20 03.5	46.6	86 28.3	16.9	13 18.9	19.2
	21	276 44.2	115 42.0	. . 34.6	35 04.8	. . 46.8	101 30.3	. . 16.7	28 21.4	. . 19.2
	22	291 46.7	130 41.6	33.4	50 06.0	47.0	116 32.3	16.5	43 23.8	19.2
	23	306 49.2	145 41.2	32.2	65 07.3	47.2	131 34.4	16.3	58 26.3	19.2
	Mer. Pass.	h m 2 40.0	*v* −0.4	*d* 1.2	*v* 1.3	*d* 0.2	*v* 2.0	*d* 0.2	*v* 2.5	*d* 0.0

STARS

Name	SHA ° ′	Dec ° ′
Acamar	315 16.7	S40 14.2
Achernar	335 25.1	S57 08.9
Acrux	173 07.2	S63 11.6
Adhara	255 11.1	S28 59.7
Aldebaran	290 47.0	N16 32.4
Alioth	166 19.2	N55 52.5
Alkaid	152 57.5	N49 14.2
Al Na'ir	27 40.7	S46 52.6
Alnilam	275 44.4	S 1 11.6
Alphard	217 54.3	S 8 43.9
Alphecca	126 09.2	N26 39.9
Alpheratz	357 41.0	N29 10.9
Altair	62 05.8	N 8 55.0
Ankaa	353 13.4	S42 12.8
Antares	112 23.5	S26 27.9
Arcturus	145 53.9	N19 06.1
Atria	107 23.1	S69 03.4
Avior	234 17.7	S59 33.8
Bellatrix	278 29.9	N 6 21.7
Betelgeuse	270 59.2	N 7 24.5
Canopus	263 55.6	S52 42.2
Capella	280 31.5	N46 00.5
Deneb	49 29.5	N45 20.6
Denebola	182 31.8	N14 28.9
Diphda	348 53.6	S17 53.6
Dubhe	193 49.8	N61 39.8
Elnath	278 10.1	N28 37.0
Eltanin	90 44.8	N51 29.6
Enif	33 44.7	N 9 57.3
Fomalhaut	15 21.3	S29 31.9
Gacrux	171 58.8	S57 12.5
Gienah	175 50.3	S17 38.0
Hadar	148 44.9	S60 27.3
Hamal	327 58.2	N23 32.3
Kaus Aust.	83 40.7	S34 22.4
Kochab	137 20.4	N74 05.7
Markab	13 35.9	N15 17.8
Menkar	314 12.8	N 4 09.2
Menkent	148 05.1	S36 27.1
Miaplacidus	221 40.0	S69 47.2
Mirfak	308 37.3	N49 54.8
Nunki	75 55.4	S26 16.3
Peacock	53 15.4	S56 40.7
Pollux	243 25.5	N27 59.0
Procyon	244 57.8	N 5 10.8
Rasalhague	96 04.3	N12 33.3
Regulus	207 41.6	N11 53.2
Rigel	281 10.2	S 8 11.0
Rigil Kent.	139 48.8	S60 54.3
Sabik	102 09.9	S15 44.5
Schedar	349 37.6	N56 37.5
Shaula	96 18.8	S37 06.8
Sirius	258 32.1	S16 44.4
Spica	158 29.1	S11 14.7
Suhail	222 51.3	S43 30.0
Vega	80 37.2	N38 48.3
Zuben'ubi	137 03.1	S16 06.5

	SHA ° ′	Mer. Pass. h m
Venus	201 07.5	13 16
Mars	119 14.4	18 42
Jupiter	185 06.2	14 18
Saturn	111 36.8	19 11

Day	UT (d h)	SUN GHA (° ′)	SUN Dec (° ′)	MOON GHA (° ′)	v (′)	MOON Dec (° ′)	d (′)	HP (′)
WEDNESDAY	10 00	178 39.7	N15 29.7	100 25.7	14.5	S10 29.2	7.7	54.2
	01	193 39.8	28.9	114 59.2	14.4	10 36.9	7.8	54.2
	02	208 39.9	28.2	129 32.6	14.3	10 44.7	7.7	54.2
	03	223 40.0	. . 27.5	144 05.9	14.4	10 52.4	7.6	54.2
	04	238 40.1	26.7	158 39.3	14.3	11 00.0	7.6	54.2
	05	253 40.2	26.0	173 12.6	14.3	11 07.6	7.6	54.2
	06	268 40.3	N15 25.3	187 45.9	14.3	S11 15.2	7.5	54.2
	07	283 40.4	24.5	202 19.2	14.2	11 22.7	7.5	54.2
	08	298 40.5	23.8	216 52.4	14.2	11 30.2	7.4	54.2
	09	313 40.6	. . 23.0	231 25.6	14.2	11 37.6	7.4	54.3
	10	328 40.7	22.3	245 58.8	14.2	11 45.0	7.3	54.3
	11	343 40.8	21.6	260 32.0	14.1	11 52.3	7.3	54.3
	12	358 40.9	N15 20.8	275 05.1	14.1	S11 59.6	7.2	54.3
	13	13 41.0	20.1	289 38.2	14.1	12 06.8	7.1	54.3
	14	28 41.1	19.4	304 11.3	14.0	12 13.9	7.2	54.3
	15	43 41.2	. . 18.6	318 44.3	14.0	12 21.1	7.0	54.3
	16	58 41.3	17.9	333 17.3	14.0	12 28.1	7.0	54.3
	17	73 41.4	17.1	347 50.3	13.9	12 35.1	7.0	54.3
	18	88 41.5	N15 16.4	2 23.2	13.9	S12 42.1	6.9	54.3
	19	103 41.6	15.7	16 56.1	13.9	12 49.0	6.9	54.3
	20	118 41.7	14.9	31 29.0	13.8	12 55.9	6.8	54.3
	21	133 41.8	. . 14.2	46 01.8	13.8	13 02.7	6.7	54.3
	22	148 41.9	13.4	60 34.6	13.8	13 09.4	6.7	54.3
	23	163 42.0	12.7	75 07.4	13.8	13 16.1	6.7	54.3
THURSDAY	11 00	178 42.1	N15 11.9	89 40.2	13.7	S13 22.8	6.5	54.3
	01	193 42.2	11.2	104 12.9	13.6	13 29.3	6.6	54.3
	02	208 42.3	10.5	118 45.5	13.7	13 35.9	6.4	54.3
	03	223 42.4	. . 09.7	133 18.2	13.5	13 42.3	6.4	54.3
	04	238 42.5	09.0	147 50.7	13.6	13 48.7	6.4	54.4
	05	253 42.6	08.2	162 23.3	13.5	13 55.1	6.3	54.4
	06	268 42.7	N15 07.5	176 55.8	13.5	S14 01.4	6.2	54.4
	07	283 42.8	06.7	191 28.3	13.5	14 07.6	6.2	54.4
	08	298 42.9	06.0	206 00.8	13.4	14 13.8	6.1	54.4
	09	313 43.0	. . 05.2	220 33.2	13.3	14 19.9	6.0	54.4
	10	328 43.1	04.5	235 05.5	13.4	14 25.9	6.0	54.4
	11	343 43.2	03.7	249 37.9	13.2	14 31.9	6.0	54.4
	12	358 43.3	N15 03.0	264 10.1	13.3	S14 37.9	5.8	54.4
	13	13 43.4	02.2	278 42.4	13.2	14 43.7	5.8	54.4
	14	28 43.5	01.5	293 14.6	13.2	14 49.5	5.8	54.5
	15	43 43.6	. . 00.7	307 46.8	13.1	14 55.3	5.7	54.5
	16	58 43.7	15 00.0	322 18.9	13.1	15 01.0	5.6	54.5
	17	73 43.8	14 59.2	336 51.0	13.0	15 06.6	5.5	54.5
	18	88 43.9	N14 58.5	351 23.0	13.0	S15 12.1	5.5	54.5
	19	103 44.0	57.7	5 55.0	13.0	15 17.6	5.4	54.5
	20	118 44.2	57.0	20 27.0	12.9	15 23.0	5.4	54.5
	21	133 44.3	. . 56.2	34 58.9	12.9	15 28.4	5.2	54.5
	22	148 44.4	55.5	49 30.8	12.8	15 33.6	5.3	54.6
	23	163 44.5	54.7	64 02.6	12.8	15 38.9	5.1	54.6
FRIDAY	12 00	178 44.6	N14 54.0	78 34.4	12.8	S15 44.0	5.1	54.6
	01	193 44.7	53.2	93 06.2	12.7	15 49.1	5.0	54.6
	02	208 44.8	52.5	107 37.9	12.6	15 54.1	4.9	54.6
	03	223 44.9	. . 51.7	122 09.5	12.7	15 59.0	4.9	54.6
	04	238 45.0	51.0	136 41.2	12.5	16 03.9	4.8	54.6
	05	253 45.1	50.2	151 12.7	12.6	16 08.7	4.7	54.7
	06	268 45.2	N14 49.5	165 44.3	12.5	S16 13.4	4.7	54.7
	07	283 45.3	48.7	180 15.8	12.4	16 18.1	4.6	54.7
	08	298 45.4	47.9	194 47.2	12.4	16 22.7	4.5	54.7
	09	313 45.6	. . 47.2	209 18.6	12.4	16 27.2	4.4	54.7
	10	328 45.7	46.4	223 50.0	12.3	16 31.6	4.4	54.7
	11	343 45.8	45.7	238 21.3	12.3	16 36.0	4.3	54.8
	12	358 45.9	N14 44.9	252 52.6	12.2	S16 40.3	4.2	54.8
	13	13 46.0	44.2	267 23.8	12.2	16 44.5	4.1	54.8
	14	28 46.1	43.4	281 55.0	12.1	16 48.6	4.1	54.8
	15	43 46.2	. . 42.6	296 26.1	12.1	16 52.7	4.0	54.8
	16	58 46.3	41.9	310 57.2	12.0	16 56.7	3.9	54.8
	17	73 46.4	41.1	325 28.2	12.0	17 00.6	3.8	54.9
	18	88 46.5	N14 40.4	339 59.2	12.0	S17 04.4	3.7	54.9
	19	103 46.7	39.6	354 30.2	11.9	17 08.1	3.7	54.9
	20	118 46.8	38.8	9 01.1	11.9	17 11.8	3.6	54.9
	21	133 46.9	. . 38.1	23 32.0	11.8	17 15.4	3.5	54.9
	22	148 47.0	37.3	38 02.8	11.7	17 18.9	3.5	55.0
	23	163 47.1	36.6	52 33.5	11.8	S17 22.4	3.3	55.0
		SD 15.8	*d* 0.7	SD 14.8		14.8		14.9

Lat.	Twilight Naut. (h m)	Twilight Civil (h m)	Sunrise (h m)	Moonrise 10 (h m)	Moonrise 11 (h m)	Moonrise 12 (h m)	Moonrise 13 (h m)
N 72	////	////	01 57	14 35	16 17	18 09	■
N 70	////	////	02 37	14 12	15 41	17 10	18 30
68	////	01 10	03 04	13 54	15 16	16 35	17 47
66	////	02 01	03 24	13 40	14 57	16 11	17 18
64	////	02 32	03 41	13 28	14 42	15 52	16 56
62	01 02	02 54	03 54	13 18	14 29	15 36	16 38
60	01 48	03 12	04 05	13 10	14 18	15 23	16 24
N 58	02 16	03 27	04 15	13 03	14 08	15 12	16 11
56	02 38	03 39	04 24	12 56	14 00	15 02	16 00
54	02 54	03 50	04 31	12 50	13 53	14 54	15 51
52	03 09	03 59	04 38	12 45	13 46	14 46	15 43
50	03 21	04 08	04 44	12 41	13 40	14 39	15 35
45	03 45	04 25	04 57	12 30	13 28	14 24	15 19
N 40	04 03	04 39	05 08	12 22	13 17	14 12	15 06
35	04 18	04 50	05 17	12 15	13 08	14 02	14 55
30	04 30	05 00	05 25	12 09	13 01	13 53	14 45
20	04 49	05 16	05 39	11 58	12 47	13 37	14 28
N 10	05 03	05 29	05 51	11 48	12 35	13 24	14 13
0	05 15	05 40	06 02	11 39	12 24	13 11	14 00
S 10	05 26	05 51	06 13	11 31	12 14	12 59	13 46
20	05 35	06 01	06 24	11 21	12 02	12 45	13 32
30	05 44	06 12	06 37	11 11	11 49	12 30	13 15
35	05 48	06 18	06 44	11 05	11 41	12 21	13 05
40	05 53	06 25	06 53	10 58	11 33	12 11	12 54
45	05 57	06 32	07 03	10 50	11 22	11 59	12 41
S 50	06 02	06 40	07 15	10 40	11 10	11 45	12 26
52	06 04	06 44	07 20	10 36	11 05	11 39	12 18
54	06 06	06 48	07 26	10 31	10 59	11 31	12 10
56	06 09	06 53	07 33	10 25	10 52	11 23	12 01
58	06 11	06 58	07 40	10 19	10 44	11 14	11 51
S 60	06 14	07 03	07 49	10 13	10 35	11 03	11 39

Lat.	Sunset (h m)	Twilight Civil (h m)	Twilight Naut. (h m)	Moonset 10 (h m)	Moonset 11 (h m)	Moonset 12 (h m)	Moonset 13 (h m)
N 72	22 06	////	////	20 52	20 44	20 30	■
N 70	21 29	////	////	21 16	21 20	21 29	21 51
68	21 03	22 51	////	21 35	21 46	22 04	22 34
66	20 43	22 04	////	21 50	22 06	22 29	23 04
64	20 27	21 35	////	22 02	22 22	22 49	23 26
62	20 14	21 13	22 59	22 13	22 35	23 05	23 43
60	20 03	20 56	22 17	22 22	22 47	23 18	23 58
N 58	19 54	20 42	21 51	22 30	22 56	23 29	24 11
56	19 45	20 29	21 30	22 37	23 05	23 39	24 21
54	19 38	20 19	21 14	22 43	23 13	23 48	24 31
52	19 31	20 10	21 00	22 48	23 20	23 56	24 39
50	19 25	20 02	20 48	22 53	23 26	24 03	00 03
45	19 12	19 44	20 24	23 04	23 39	24 18	00 18
N 40	19 02	19 31	20 06	23 14	23 50	24 31	00 31
35	18 53	19 20	19 52	23 22	24 00	00 00	00 42
30	18 45	19 10	19 40	23 28	24 08	00 08	00 51
20	18 31	18 54	19 21	23 41	24 22	00 22	01 07
N 10	18 19	18 41	19 07	23 51	24 35	00 35	01 21
0	18 09	18 30	18 55	24 01	00 01	00 47	01 34
S 10	17 58	18 19	18 45	24 11	00 11	00 59	01 48
20	17 46	18 09	18 35	24 21	00 21	01 11	02 02
30	17 34	17 58	18 27	24 34	00 34	01 26	02 18
35	17 26	17 52	18 22	24 41	00 41	01 34	02 27
40	17 18	17 46	18 18	24 49	00 49	01 44	02 38
45	17 08	17 39	18 14	00 00	00 58	01 55	02 51
S 50	16 56	17 30	18 09	00 09	01 09	02 09	03 06
52	16 51	17 27	18 07	00 13	01 15	02 15	03 13
54	16 45	17 23	18 05	00 17	01 20	02 22	03 21
56	16 38	17 18	18 02	00 22	01 27	02 30	03 30
58	16 31	17 13	18 00	00 28	01 34	02 39	03 40
S 60	16 22	17 08	17 58	00 34	01 42	02 49	03 52

Day	SUN Eqn. of Time 00^h	SUN Eqn. of Time 12^h	SUN Mer. Pass.	MOON Mer. Pass. Upper	MOON Mer. Pass. Lower	MOON Age	MOON Phase
d	m s	m s	h m	h m	h m	d	%
10	05 21	05 17	12 05	17 50	05 28	08	48
11	05 12	05 07	12 05	18 36	06 13	09	57
12	05 02	04 57	12 05	19 23	06 59	10	66

UT d	UT h	ARIES GHA	VENUS −3·8 GHA	VENUS Dec	MARS −0·5 GHA	MARS Dec	JUPITER −1·7 GHA	JUPITER Dec	SATURN +0·4 GHA	SATURN Dec
		° ′	° ′	° ′	° ′	° ′	° ′	° ′	° ′	° ′
13	00	321 51.6	160 40.8	N 9 31.0	80 08.5	S23 47.4	146 36.4	N 3 16.1	73 28.8	S20 19.2
	01	336 54.1	175 40.4	29.9	95 09.8	47.6	161 38.4	15.9	88 31.2	19.2
	02	351 56.6	190 40.0	28.7	110 11.0	47.8	176 40.4	15.7	103 33.7	19.3
	03	6 59.0	205 39.6	. . 27.5	125 12.3	. . 48.0	191 42.4	. . 15.5	118 36.2	. . 19.3
	04	22 01.5	220 39.2	26.3	140 13.5	48.2	206 44.4	15.3	133 38.6	19.3
	05	37 04.0	235 38.8	25.1	155 14.8	48.4	221 46.4	15.1	148 41.1	19.3
	06	52 06.4	250 38.3	N 9 24.0	170 16.0	S23 48.6	236 48.5	N 3 14.9	163 43.6	S20 19.3
	07	67 08.9	265 37.9	22.8	185 17.3	48.8	251 50.5	14.7	178 46.0	19.3
S	08	82 11.4	280 37.5	21.6	200 18.5	49.0	266 52.5	14.5	193 48.5	19.3
A	09	97 13.8	295 37.1	. . 20.4	215 19.7	. . 49.2	281 54.5	. . 14.3	208 51.0	. . 19.3
T	10	112 16.3	310 36.7	19.2	230 21.0	49.4	296 56.5	14.1	223 53.4	19.3
U	11	127 18.7	325 36.3	18.0	245 22.2	49.6	311 58.5	13.9	238 55.9	19.3
R	12	142 21.2	340 35.9	N 9 16.9	260 23.4	S23 49.9	327 00.5	N 3 13.7	253 58.4	S20 19.3
D	13	157 23.7	355 35.5	15.7	275 24.7	50.1	342 02.6	13.5	269 00.8	19.4
A	14	172 26.1	10 35.1	14.5	290 25.9	50.3	357 04.6	13.4	284 03.3	19.4
Y	15	187 28.6	25 34.7	. . 13.3	305 27.2	. . 50.5	12 06.6	. . 13.2	299 05.8	. . 19.4
	16	202 31.1	40 34.3	12.1	320 28.4	50.7	27 08.6	13.0	314 08.2	19.4
	17	217 33.5	55 33.9	10.9	335 29.6	50.9	42 10.6	12.8	329 10.7	19.4
	18	232 36.0	70 33.5	N 9 09.7	350 30.9	S23 51.1	57 12.6	N 3 12.6	344 13.2	S20 19.4
	19	247 38.5	85 33.1	08.6	5 32.1	51.3	72 14.6	12.4	359 15.6	19.4
	20	262 40.9	100 32.7	07.4	20 33.3	51.5	87 16.7	12.2	14 18.1	19.4
	21	277 43.4	115 32.3	. . 06.2	35 34.6	. . 51.7	102 18.7	. . 12.0	29 20.5	. . 19.4
	22	292 45.9	130 31.9	05.0	50 35.8	51.9	117 20.7	11.8	44 23.0	19.4
	23	307 48.3	145 31.5	03.8	65 37.0	52.1	132 22.7	11.6	59 25.5	19.4
14	00	322 50.8	160 31.1	N 9 02.6	80 38.2	S23 52.3	147 24.7	N 3 11.4	74 27.9	S20 19.5
	01	337 53.2	175 30.7	01.4	95 39.5	52.5	162 26.7	11.2	89 30.4	19.5
	02	352 55.7	190 30.3	9 00.2	110 40.7	52.7	177 28.7	11.0	104 32.9	19.5
	03	7 58.2	205 29.9	8 59.0	125 41.9	. . 52.9	192 30.8	. . 10.8	119 35.3	. . 19.5
	04	23 00.6	220 29.5	57.9	140 43.1	53.1	207 32.8	10.6	134 37.8	19.5
	05	38 03.1	235 29.1	56.7	155 44.4	53.3	222 34.8	10.4	149 40.2	19.5
	06	53 05.6	250 28.7	N 8 55.5	170 45.6	S23 53.5	237 36.8	N 3 10.2	164 42.7	S20 19.5
	07	68 08.0	265 28.3	54.3	185 46.8	53.7	252 38.8	10.0	179 45.2	19.5
	08	83 10.5	280 27.9	53.1	200 48.0	53.9	267 40.8	09.8	194 47.6	19.5
S	09	98 13.0	295 27.5	. . 51.9	215 49.3	. . 54.1	282 42.8	. . 09.6	209 50.1	. . 19.5
U	10	113 15.4	310 27.1	50.7	230 50.5	54.3	297 44.8	09.4	224 52.6	19.5
N	11	128 17.9	325 26.7	49.5	245 51.7	54.5	312 46.9	09.2	239 55.0	19.6
D	12	143 20.3	340 26.3	N 8 48.3	260 52.9	S23 54.7	327 48.9	N 3 09.0	254 57.5	S20 19.6
A	13	158 22.8	355 25.9	47.1	275 54.1	54.9	342 50.9	08.8	269 59.9	19.6
Y	14	173 25.3	10 25.5	45.9	290 55.4	55.1	357 52.9	08.6	285 02.4	19.6
	15	188 27.7	25 25.1	. . 44.7	305 56.6	. . 55.3	12 54.9	. . 08.4	300 04.9	. . 19.6
	16	203 30.2	40 24.7	43.5	320 57.8	55.5	27 56.9	08.2	315 07.3	19.6
	17	218 32.7	55 24.3	42.3	335 59.0	55.8	42 58.9	08.0	330 09.8	19.6
	18	233 35.1	70 23.9	N 8 41.1	351 00.2	S23 56.0	58 00.9	N 3 07.8	345 12.2	S20 19.6
	19	248 37.6	85 23.5	39.9	6 01.4	56.2	73 03.0	07.6	0 14.7	19.6
	20	263 40.1	100 23.1	38.8	21 02.6	56.4	88 05.0	07.4	15 17.2	19.6
	21	278 42.5	115 22.7	. . 37.6	36 03.9	. . 56.6	103 07.0	. . 07.2	30 19.6	. . 19.7
	22	293 45.0	130 22.4	36.4	51 05.1	56.8	118 09.0	07.0	45 22.1	19.7
	23	308 47.5	145 22.0	35.2	66 06.3	57.0	133 11.0	06.8	60 24.5	19.7
15	00	323 49.9	160 21.6	N 8 34.0	81 07.5	S23 57.2	148 13.0	N 3 06.6	75 27.0	S20 19.7
	01	338 52.4	175 21.2	32.8	96 08.7	57.4	163 15.0	06.4	90 29.5	19.7
	02	353 54.8	190 20.8	31.6	111 09.9	57.6	178 17.0	06.2	105 31.9	19.7
	03	8 57.3	205 20.4	. . 30.4	126 11.1	. . 57.8	193 19.0	. . 06.0	120 34.4	. . 19.7
	04	23 59.8	220 20.0	29.2	141 12.3	58.0	208 21.1	05.8	135 36.8	19.7
	05	39 02.2	235 19.6	28.0	156 13.5	58.2	223 23.1	05.6	150 39.3	19.7
	06	54 04.7	250 19.2	N 8 26.8	171 14.7	S23 58.4	238 25.1	N 3 05.4	165 41.7	S20 19.7
	07	69 07.2	265 18.8	25.6	186 15.9	58.6	253 27.1	05.2	180 44.2	19.8
	08	84 09.6	280 18.4	24.4	201 17.1	58.8	268 29.1	05.0	195 46.7	19.8
M	09	99 12.1	295 18.1	. . 23.2	216 18.3	. . 59.0	283 31.1	. . 04.8	210 49.1	. . 19.8
O	10	114 14.6	310 17.7	22.0	231 19.5	59.2	298 33.1	04.6	225 51.6	19.8
N	11	129 17.0	325 17.3	20.7	246 20.7	59.4	313 35.1	04.4	240 54.0	19.8
D	12	144 19.5	340 16.9	N 8 19.5	261 21.9	S23 59.6	328 37.1	N 3 04.2	255 56.5	S20 19.8
A	13	159 22.0	355 16.5	18.3	276 23.1	23 59.8	343 39.2	04.0	270 58.9	19.8
Y	14	174 24.4	10 16.1	17.1	291 24.3	24 00.0	358 41.2	03.8	286 01.4	19.8
	15	189 26.9	25 15.7	. . 15.9	306 25.5	. . 00.2	13 43.2	. . 03.6	301 03.9	. . 19.8
	16	204 29.3	40 15.3	14.7	321 26.7	00.4	28 45.2	03.4	316 06.3	19.8
	17	219 31.8	55 14.9	13.5	336 27.9	00.6	43 47.2	03.2	331 08.8	19.9
	18	234 34.3	70 14.6	N 8 12.3	351 29.1	S24 00.8	58 49.2	N 3 03.0	346 11.2	S20 19.9
	19	249 36.7	85 14.2	11.1	6 30.3	01.0	73 51.2	02.8	1 13.7	19.9
	20	264 39.2	100 13.8	09.9	21 31.5	01.2	88 53.2	02.6	16 16.1	19.9
	21	279 41.7	115 13.4	. . 08.7	36 32.7	. . 01.4	103 55.2	. . 02.4	31 18.6	. . 19.9
	22	294 44.1	130 13.0	07.5	51 33.9	01.6	118 57.2	02.2	46 21.0	19.9
	23	309 46.6	145 12.6	06.3	66 35.1	01.8	133 59.2	02.0	61 23.5	19.9
Mer. Pass.		h m 2 28.2	v −0.4	d 1.2	v 1.2	d 0.2	v 2.0	d 0.2	v 2.5	d 0.0

STARS

Name	SHA	Dec
	° ′	° ′
Acamar	315 16.7	S40 14.2
Achernar	335 25.0	S57 09.0
Acrux	173 07.2	S63 11.6
Adhara	255 11.1	S28 59.7
Aldebaran	290 47.0	N16 32.4
Alioth	166 19.3	N55 52.5
Alkaid	152 57.5	N49 14.2
Al Na'ir	27 40.7	S46 52.6
Alnilam	275 44.4	S 1 11.6
Alphard	217 54.3	S 8 43.8
Alphecca	126 09.2	N26 39.9
Alpheratz	357 41.0	N29 10.9
Altair	62 05.8	N 8 55.0
Ankaa	353 13.4	S42 12.8
Antares	112 23.5	S26 27.9
Arcturus	145 53.9	N19 06.1
Atria	107 23.1	S69 03.4
Avior	234 17.7	S59 33.8
Bellatrix	278 29.9	N 6 21.7
Betelgeuse	270 59.2	N 7 24.5
Canopus	263 55.6	S52 42.2
Capella	280 31.5	N46 00.5
Deneb	49 29.5	N45 20.6
Denebola	182 31.8	N14 28.9
Diphda	348 53.5	S17 53.6
Dubhe	193 49.8	N61 39.8
Elnath	278 10.1	N28 37.0
Eltanin	90 44.8	N51 29.7
Enif	33 44.7	N 9 57.3
Fomalhaut	15 21.3	S29 31.9
Gacrux	171 58.8	S57 12.5
Gienah	175 50.3	S17 38.0
Hadar	148 44.9	S60 27.3
Hamal	327 58.2	N23 32.3
Kaus Aust.	83 40.7	S34 22.4
Kochab	137 20.4	N74 05.7
Markab	13 35.9	N15 17.8
Menkar	314 12.8	N 4 09.2
Menkent	148 05.1	S36 27.1
Miaplacidus	221 40.0	S69 47.2
Mirfak	308 37.2	N49 54.8
Nunki	75 55.4	S26 16.3
Peacock	53 15.4	S56 40.7
Pollux	243 25.5	N27 59.0
Procyon	244 57.8	N 5 10.8
Rasalhague	96 04.3	N12 33.3
Regulus	207 41.6	N11 53.2
Rigel	281 10.2	S 8 11.0
Rigil Kent.	139 48.8	S60 54.2
Sabik	102 09.9	S15 44.5
Schedar	349 37.6	N56 37.5
Shaula	96 18.8	S37 06.8
Sirius	258 32.1	S16 44.4
Spica	158 29.1	S11 14.7
Suhail	222 51.3	S43 30.0
Vega	80 37.2	N38 48.4
Zuben'ubi	137 03.1	S16 06.5

	SHA	Mer. Pass.
	° ′	h m
Venus	197 40.3	13 18
Mars	117 47.5	18 36
Jupiter	184 33.9	14 08
Saturn	111 37.2	18 59

	UT	SUN GHA	SUN Dec	MOON GHA	*v*	MOON Dec	*d*	HP
	d h	° ′	° ′	° ′	′	° ′	′	′
	13 00	178 47.2	N14 35.8	67 04.3	11.7	S17 25.7	3.3	55.0
	01	193 47.3	35.0	81 35.0	11.6	17 29.0	3.2	55.0
	02	208 47.4	34.3	96 05.6	11.6	17 32.2	3.1	55.0
	03	223 47.6	. . 33.5	110 36.2	11.5	17 35.3	3.0	55.1
	04	238 47.7	32.7	125 06.7	11.5	17 38.3	3.0	55.1
	05	253 47.8	32.0	139 37.2	11.5	17 41.3	2.8	55.1
	06	268 47.9	N14 31.2	154 07.7	11.4	S17 44.1	2.8	55.1
	07	283 48.0	30.4	168 38.1	11.4	17 46.9	2.7	55.2
S	08	298 48.1	29.7	183 08.5	11.3	17 49.6	2.6	55.2
A	09	313 48.2	. . 28.9	197 38.8	11.3	17 52.2	2.5	55.2
T	10	328 48.4	28.1	212 09.1	11.2	17 54.7	2.5	55.2
U	11	343 48.5	27.4	226 39.3	11.2	17 57.2	2.3	55.2
R	12	358 48.6	N14 26.6	241 09.5	11.2	S17 59.5	2.3	55.3
D	13	13 48.7	25.8	255 39.7	11.1	18 01.8	2.2	55.3
A	14	28 48.8	25.1	270 09.8	11.1	18 04.0	2.0	55.3
Y	15	43 48.9	. . 24.3	284 39.9	11.0	18 06.0	2.0	55.3
	16	58 49.1	23.5	299 09.9	11.0	18 08.0	2.0	55.4
	17	73 49.2	22.8	313 39.9	10.9	18 10.0	1.8	55.4
	18	88 49.3	N14 22.0	328 09.8	10.9	S18 11.8	1.7	55.4
	19	103 49.4	21.2	342 39.7	10.8	18 13.5	1.6	55.4
	20	118 49.5	20.4	357 09.5	10.9	18 15.1	1.6	55.5
	21	133 49.6	. . 19.7	11 39.4	10.7	18 16.7	1.5	55.5
	22	148 49.8	18.9	26 09.1	10.8	18 18.2	1.3	55.5
	23	163 49.9	18.1	40 38.9	10.6	18 19.5	1.3	55.5
	14 00	178 50.0	N14 17.4	55 08.5	10.7	S18 20.8	1.2	55.6
	01	193 50.1	16.6	69 38.2	10.6	18 22.0	1.1	55.6
	02	208 50.2	15.8	84 07.8	10.6	18 23.1	1.0	55.6
	03	223 50.4	. . 15.0	98 37.4	10.5	18 24.1	0.9	55.6
	04	238 50.5	14.3	113 06.9	10.5	18 25.0	0.8	55.7
	05	253 50.6	13.5	127 36.4	10.4	18 25.8	0.7	55.7
	06	268 50.7	N14 12.7	142 05.8	10.4	S18 26.5	0.6	55.7
	07	283 50.8	11.9	156 35.2	10.4	18 27.1	0.6	55.7
	08	298 51.0	11.2	171 04.6	10.3	18 27.7	0.4	55.8
S	09	313 51.1	. . 10.4	185 33.9	10.3	18 28.1	0.3	55.8
U	10	328 51.2	09.6	200 03.2	10.3	18 28.4	0.3	55.8
N	11	343 51.3	08.8	214 32.5	10.2	18 28.7	0.1	55.9
D	12	358 51.4	N14 08.1	229 01.7	10.2	S18 28.8	0.1	55.9
A	13	13 51.6	07.3	243 30.9	10.1	18 28.9	0.1	55.9
Y	14	28 51.7	06.5	258 00.0	10.1	18 28.8	0.1	55.9
	15	43 51.8	. . 05.7	272 29.1	10.1	18 28.7	0.2	56.0
	16	58 51.9	05.0	286 58.2	10.1	18 28.5	0.4	56.0
	17	73 52.1	04.2	301 27.3	10.0	18 28.1	0.4	56.0
	18	88 52.2	N14 03.4	315 56.3	9.9	S18 27.7	0.6	56.1
	19	103 52.3	02.6	330 25.2	10.0	18 27.1	0.6	56.1
	20	118 52.4	01.8	344 54.2	9.9	18 26.5	0.7	56.1
	21	133 52.6	. . 01.1	359 23.1	9.9	18 25.8	0.9	56.1
	22	148 52.7	14 00.3	13 52.0	9.8	18 24.9	0.9	56.2
	23	163 52.8	13 59.5	28 20.8	9.8	18 24.0	1.0	56.2
	15 00	178 52.9	N13 58.7	42 49.6	9.8	S18 23.0	1.2	56.2
	01	193 53.0	57.9	57 18.4	9.8	18 21.8	1.2	56.3
	02	208 53.2	57.1	71 47.2	9.7	18 20.6	1.3	56.3
	03	223 53.3	. . 56.4	86 15.9	9.7	18 19.3	1.4	56.3
	04	238 53.4	55.6	100 44.6	9.7	18 17.9	1.6	56.3
	05	253 53.5	54.8	115 13.3	9.6	18 16.3	1.6	56.4
	06	268 53.7	N13 54.0	129 41.9	9.6	S18 14.7	1.7	56.4
	07	283 53.8	53.2	144 10.5	9.6	18 13.0	1.9	56.4
	08	298 53.9	52.4	158 39.1	9.5	18 11.1	1.9	56.5
M	09	313 54.1	. . 51.7	173 07.6	9.6	18 09.2	2.1	56.5
O	10	328 54.2	50.9	187 36.2	9.5	18 07.1	2.1	56.5
N	11	343 54.3	50.1	202 04.7	9.5	18 05.0	2.2	56.6
D	12	358 54.4	N13 49.3	216 33.2	9.4	S18 02.8	2.4	56.6
A	13	13 54.6	48.5	231 01.6	9.5	18 00.4	2.4	56.6
Y	14	28 54.7	47.7	245 30.1	9.4	17 58.0	2.6	56.6
	15	43 54.8	. . 46.9	259 58.5	9.3	17 55.4	2.6	56.7
	16	58 54.9	46.2	274 26.8	9.4	17 52.8	2.8	56.7
	17	73 55.1	45.4	288 55.2	9.4	17 50.0	2.8	56.7
	18	88 55.2	N13 44.6	303 23.6	9.3	S17 47.2	3.0	56.8
	19	103 55.3	43.8	317 51.9	9.3	17 44.2	3.0	56.8
	20	118 55.5	43.0	332 20.2	9.3	17 41.2	3.2	56.8
	21	133 55.6	. . 42.2	346 48.5	9.2	17 38.0	3.2	56.9
	22	148 55.7	41.4	1 16.7	9.3	17 34.8	3.4	56.9
	23	163 55.8	40.6	15 45.0	9.2	S17 31.4	3.4	56.9
		SD 15.8	*d* 0.8	SD		15.1	15.2	15.4

Lat.	Twilight Naut.	Twilight Civil	Sunrise	Moonrise 13	Moonrise 14	Moonrise 15	Moonrise 16
°	h m	h m	h m	h m	h m	h m	h m
N 72	////	////	02 20	■	■	21 13	20 52
N 70	////	////	02 53	18 30	19 29	19 58	20 12
68	////	01 38	03 17	17 47	18 43	19 21	19 44
66	////	02 18	03 35	17 18	18 13	18 54	19 23
64	////	02 44	03 50	16 56	17 50	18 33	19 06
62	01 28	03 05	04 02	16 38	17 32	18 17	18 52
60	02 03	03 21	04 13	16 24	17 17	18 03	18 40
N 58	02 28	03 34	04 22	16 11	17 05	17 51	18 30
56	02 47	03 46	04 30	16 00	16 54	17 40	18 21
54	03 02	03 56	04 37	15 51	16 44	17 31	18 13
52	03 15	04 05	04 43	15 43	16 35	17 23	18 05
50	03 27	04 12	04 49	15 35	16 28	17 16	17 59
45	03 49	04 29	05 01	15 19	16 11	17 00	17 45
N 40	04 07	04 42	05 11	15 06	15 58	16 47	17 34
35	04 20	04 53	05 19	14 55	15 46	16 36	17 24
30	04 32	05 02	05 27	14 45	15 36	16 27	17 15
20	04 50	05 17	05 40	14 28	15 19	16 10	17 00
N 10	05 04	05 29	05 51	14 13	15 04	15 56	16 47
0	05 15	05 40	06 01	14 00	14 50	15 42	16 35
S 10	05 25	05 50	06 11	13 46	14 36	15 29	16 23
20	05 33	05 59	06 22	13 32	14 21	15 14	16 10
30	05 41	06 10	06 34	13 15	14 04	14 58	15 55
35	05 45	06 15	06 41	13 05	13 54	14 48	15 46
40	05 49	06 21	06 49	12 54	13 43	14 37	15 36
45	05 53	06 28	06 58	12 41	13 30	14 24	15 24
S 50	05 57	06 35	07 09	12 26	13 13	14 08	15 10
52	05 59	06 39	07 14	12 18	13 06	14 01	15 04
54	06 01	06 43	07 20	12 10	12 57	13 53	14 56
56	06 03	06 47	07 26	12 01	12 48	13 43	14 48
58	06 05	06 51	07 33	11 51	12 37	13 33	14 39
S 60	06 07	06 56	07 41	11 39	12 24	13 21	14 28

Lat.	Sunset	Twilight Civil	Twilight Naut.	Moonset 13	Moonset 14	Moonset 15	Moonset 16
°	h m	h m	h m	h m	h m	h m	h m
N 72	21 43	////	////	■	■	22 42	24 55
N 70	21 12	23 54	////	21 51	22 38	23 57	25 34
68	20 49	22 24	////	22 34	23 24	24 34	00 34
66	20 31	21 47	////	23 04	23 54	25 00	01 00
64	20 17	21 21	23 55	23 26	24 16	00 16	01 21
62	20 05	21 02	22 35	23 43	24 34	00 34	01 37
60	19 55	20 46	22 02	23 58	24 49	00 49	01 51
N 58	19 46	20 33	21 38	24 11	00 11	01 01	02 02
56	19 38	20 22	21 20	24 21	00 21	01 12	02 13
54	19 31	20 12	21 05	24 31	00 31	01 22	02 21
52	19 25	20 03	20 52	24 39	00 39	01 30	02 29
50	19 19	19 55	20 41	00 03	00 47	01 38	02 37
45	19 07	19 39	20 19	00 18	01 03	01 54	02 52
N 40	18 58	19 27	20 02	00 31	01 17	02 08	03 04
35	18 49	19 16	19 48	00 42	01 28	02 19	03 15
30	18 42	19 07	19 37	00 51	01 38	02 29	03 24
20	18 29	18 52	19 19	01 07	01 55	02 46	03 40
N 10	18 18	18 40	19 05	01 21	02 10	03 01	03 54
0	18 08	18 29	18 54	01 34	02 24	03 15	04 07
S 10	17 58	18 19	18 44	01 48	02 38	03 29	04 20
20	17 47	18 10	18 36	02 02	02 53	03 44	04 34
30	17 35	18 00	18 28	02 18	03 10	04 00	04 50
35	17 28	17 54	18 24	02 27	03 19	04 10	04 59
40	17 21	17 49	18 21	02 38	03 31	04 22	05 09
45	17 11	17 42	18 17	02 51	03 44	04 35	05 22
S 50	17 01	17 34	18 13	03 06	04 00	04 51	05 36
52	16 56	17 31	18 11	03 13	04 08	04 58	05 43
54	16 50	17 27	18 09	03 21	04 16	05 07	05 51
56	16 44	17 23	18 07	03 30	04 26	05 16	05 59
58	16 37	17 19	18 05	03 40	04 37	05 26	06 09
S 60	16 29	17 14	18 03	03 52	04 49	05 39	06 20

Day	SUN Eqn. of Time 00^h	SUN Eqn. of Time 12^h	SUN Mer. Pass.	MOON Mer. Pass. Upper	MOON Mer. Pass. Lower	MOON Age	MOON Phase
d	m s	m s	h m	h m	h m	d %	
13	04 51	04 46	12 05	20 12	07 47	11 75	
14	04 40	04 34	12 05	21 03	08 37	12 83	
15	04 29	04 23	12 04	21 55	09 28	13 90	

UT		ARIES	VENUS −3·8		MARS −0·5		JUPITER −1·7		SATURN +0·4	
d	h	GHA	GHA	Dec	GHA	Dec	GHA	Dec	GHA	Dec
		° ′	° ′	° ′	° ′	° ′	° ′	° ′	° ′	° ′
16 TUESDAY	00	324 49.1	160 12.2	N 8 05.1	81 36.3	S24 02.0	149 01.3	N 3 01.8	76 26.0	S20 19.9
	01	339 51.5	175 11.9	03.9	96 37.5	02.2	164 03.3	01.6	91 28.4	19.9
	02	354 54.0	190 11.5	02.7	111 38.7	02.4	179 05.3	01.4	106 30.9	20.0
	03	9 56.5	205 11.1	. . 01.5	126 39.9	. . 02.6	194 07.3	. . 01.2	121 33.3	. . 20.0
	04	24 58.9	220 10.7	8 00.2	141 41.1	02.8	209 09.3	01.0	136 35.8	20.0
	05	40 01.4	235 10.3	7 59.0	156 42.2	03.0	224 11.3	00.8	151 38.2	20.0
	06	55 03.8	250 09.9	N 7 57.8	171 43.4	S24 03.2	239 13.3	N 3 00.6	166 40.7	S20 20.0
	07	70 06.3	265 09.6	56.6	186 44.6	03.4	254 15.3	00.4	181 43.1	20.0
	08	85 08.8	280 09.2	55.4	201 45.8	03.6	269 17.3	00.2	196 45.6	20.0
	09	100 11.2	295 08.8	. . 54.2	216 47.0	. . 03.8	284 19.3	3 00.0	211 48.0	. . 20.0
	10	115 13.7	310 08.4	53.0	231 48.2	04.0	299 21.3	2 59.9	226 50.5	20.0
	11	130 16.2	325 08.0	51.8	246 49.3	04.2	314 23.4	59.7	241 52.9	20.1
	12	145 18.6	340 07.7	N 7 50.6	261 50.5	S24 04.4	329 25.4	N 2 59.5	256 55.4	S20 20.1
	13	160 21.1	355 07.3	49.3	276 51.7	04.6	344 27.4	59.3	271 57.9	20.1
	14	175 23.6	10 06.9	48.1	291 52.9	04.8	359 29.4	59.1	287 00.3	20.1
	15	190 26.0	25 06.5	. . 46.9	306 54.1	. . 05.0	14 31.4	. . 58.9	302 02.8	. . 20.1
	16	205 28.5	40 06.1	45.7	321 55.3	05.2	29 33.4	58.7	317 05.2	20.1
	17	220 30.9	55 05.8	44.5	336 56.4	05.4	44 35.4	58.5	332 07.7	20.1
	18	235 33.4	70 05.4	N 7 43.3	351 57.6	S24 05.6	59 37.4	N 2 58.3	347 10.1	S20 20.1
	19	250 35.9	85 05.0	42.1	6 58.8	05.8	74 39.4	58.1	2 12.6	20.1
	20	265 38.3	100 04.6	40.8	22 00.0	06.0	89 41.4	57.9	17 15.0	20.2
	21	280 40.8	115 04.2	. . 39.6	37 01.1	. . 06.2	104 43.4	. . 57.7	32 17.5	. . 20.2
	22	295 43.3	130 03.9	38.4	52 02.3	06.4	119 45.4	57.5	47 19.9	20.2
	23	310 45.7	145 03.5	37.2	67 03.5	06.6	134 47.5	57.3	62 22.4	20.2
17 WEDNESDAY	00	325 48.2	160 03.1	N 7 36.0	82 04.7	S24 06.8	149 49.5	N 2 57.1	77 24.8	S20 20.2
	01	340 50.7	175 02.7	34.8	97 05.8	07.0	164 51.5	56.9	92 27.3	20.2
	02	355 53.1	190 02.4	33.6	112 07.0	07.2	179 53.5	56.7	107 29.7	20.2
	03	10 55.6	205 02.0	. . 32.3	127 08.2	. . 07.4	194 55.5	. . 56.5	122 32.2	. . 20.2
	04	25 58.1	220 01.6	31.1	142 09.3	07.6	209 57.5	56.3	137 34.6	20.2
	05	41 00.5	235 01.2	29.9	157 10.5	07.8	224 59.5	56.0	152 37.1	20.3
	06	56 03.0	250 00.9	N 7 28.7	172 11.7	S24 08.0	240 01.5	N 2 55.8	167 39.5	S20 20.3
	07	71 05.4	265 00.5	27.5	187 12.8	08.2	255 03.5	55.6	182 42.0	20.3
	08	86 07.9	280 00.1	26.2	202 14.0	08.4	270 05.5	55.4	197 44.4	20.3
	09	101 10.4	294 59.7	. . 25.0	217 15.2	. . 08.6	285 07.5	. . 55.2	212 46.9	. . 20.3
	10	116 12.8	309 59.4	23.8	232 16.3	08.8	300 09.5	55.0	227 49.3	20.3
	11	131 15.3	324 59.0	22.6	247 17.5	09.0	315 11.5	54.8	242 51.8	20.3
	12	146 17.8	339 58.6	N 7 21.4	262 18.7	S24 09.2	330 13.5	N 2 54.6	257 54.2	S20 20.3
	13	161 20.2	354 58.2	20.1	277 19.8	09.4	345 15.6	54.4	272 56.7	20.3
	14	176 22.7	9 57.9	18.9	292 21.0	09.6	0 17.6	54.2	287 59.1	20.4
	15	191 25.2	24 57.5	. . 17.7	307 22.2	. . 09.8	15 19.6	. . 54.0	303 01.6	. . 20.4
	16	206 27.6	39 57.1	16.5	322 23.3	10.0	30 21.6	53.8	318 04.0	20.4
	17	221 30.1	54 56.7	15.3	337 24.5	10.2	45 23.6	53.6	333 06.4	20.4
	18	236 32.6	69 56.4	N 7 14.0	352 25.6	S24 10.4	60 25.6	N 2 53.4	348 08.9	S20 20.4
	19	251 35.0	84 56.0	12.8	7 26.8	10.6	75 27.6	53.2	3 11.3	20.4
	20	266 37.5	99 55.6	11.6	22 28.0	10.8	90 29.6	53.0	18 13.8	20.4
	21	281 39.9	114 55.3	. . 10.4	37 29.1	. . 11.0	105 31.6	. . 52.8	33 16.2	. . 20.4
	22	296 42.4	129 54.9	09.1	52 30.3	11.2	120 33.6	52.6	48 18.7	20.5
	23	311 44.9	144 54.5	07.9	67 31.4	11.4	135 35.6	52.4	63 21.1	20.5
18 THURSDAY	00	326 47.3	159 54.1	N 7 06.7	82 32.6	S24 11.6	150 37.6	N 2 52.2	78 23.6	S20 20.5
	01	341 49.8	174 53.8	05.5	97 33.7	11.8	165 39.6	52.0	93 26.0	20.5
	02	356 52.3	189 53.4	04.2	112 34.9	12.0	180 41.6	51.8	108 28.5	20.5
	03	11 54.7	204 53.0	. . 03.0	127 36.1	. . 12.2	195 43.6	. . 51.6	123 30.9	. . 20.5
	04	26 57.2	219 52.7	01.8	142 37.2	12.3	210 45.6	51.4	138 33.4	20.5
	05	41 59.7	234 52.3	7 00.6	157 38.4	12.5	225 47.6	51.2	153 35.8	20.5
	06	57 02.1	249 51.9	N 6 59.3	172 39.5	S24 12.7	240 49.7	N 2 51.0	168 38.2	S20 20.5
	07	72 04.6	264 51.6	58.1	187 40.7	12.9	255 51.7	50.8	183 40.7	20.6
	08	87 07.0	279 51.2	56.9	202 41.8	13.1	270 53.7	50.6	198 43.1	20.6
	09	102 09.5	294 50.8	. . 55.7	217 43.0	. . 13.3	285 55.7	. . 50.4	213 45.6	. . 20.6
	10	117 12.0	309 50.5	54.4	232 44.1	13.5	300 57.7	50.2	228 48.0	20.6
	11	132 14.4	324 50.1	53.2	247 45.3	13.7	315 59.7	50.0	243 50.5	20.6
	12	147 16.9	339 49.7	N 6 52.0	262 46.4	S24 13.9	331 01.7	N 2 49.8	258 52.9	S20 20.6
	13	162 19.4	354 49.4	50.7	277 47.5	14.1	346 03.7	49.6	273 55.4	20.6
	14	177 21.8	9 49.0	49.5	292 48.7	14.3	1 05.7	49.4	288 57.8	20.6
	15	192 24.3	24 48.6	. . 48.3	307 49.8	. . 14.5	16 07.7	. . 49.2	304 00.2	. . 20.7
	16	207 26.8	39 48.3	47.1	322 51.0	14.7	31 09.7	49.0	319 02.7	20.7
	17	222 29.2	54 47.9	45.8	337 52.1	14.9	46 11.7	48.8	334 05.1	20.7
	18	237 31.7	69 47.5	N 6 44.6	352 53.3	S24 15.1	61 13.7	N 2 48.6	349 07.6	S20 20.7
	19	252 34.2	84 47.2	43.4	7 54.4	15.3	76 15.7	48.4	4 10.0	20.7
	20	267 36.6	99 46.8	42.1	22 55.5	15.5	91 17.7	48.2	19 12.5	20.7
	21	282 39.1	114 46.4	. . 40.9	37 56.7	. . 15.7	106 19.7	. . 48.0	34 14.9	. . 20.7
	22	297 41.5	129 46.1	39.7	52 57.8	15.9	121 21.7	47.8	49 17.3	20.7
	23	312 44.0	144 45.7	38.4	67 59.0	16.1	136 23.7	47.6	64 19.8	20.8
Mer. Pass.		h m 2 16.4	*v* −0.4	*d* 1.2	*v* 1.2	*d* 0.2	*v* 2.0	*d* 0.2	*v* 2.4	*d* 0.0

STARS

Name	SHA	Dec
	° ′	° ′
Acamar	315 16.7	S40 14.2
Achernar	335 25.0	S57 09.0
Acrux	173 07.2	S63 11.6
Adhara	255 11.1	S28 59.7
Aldebaran	290 47.0	N16 32.4
Alioth	166 19.3	N55 52.5
Alkaid	152 57.5	N49 14.2
Al Na'ir	27 40.6	S46 52.6
Alnilam	275 44.4	S 1 11.6
Alphard	217 54.3	S 8 43.8
Alphecca	126 09.2	N26 39.9
Alpheratz	357 40.9	N29 10.9
Altair	62 05.8	N 8 55.0
Ankaa	353 13.3	S42 12.8
Antares	112 23.5	S26 27.9
Arcturus	145 53.9	N19 06.1
Atria	107 23.1	S69 03.4
Avior	234 17.7	S59 33.8
Bellatrix	278 29.9	N 6 21.7
Betelgeuse	270 59.2	N 7 24.5
Canopus	263 55.5	S52 42.2
Capella	280 31.5	N46 00.5
Deneb	49 29.5	N45 20.6
Denebola	182 31.8	N14 28.9
Diphda	348 53.5	S17 53.6
Dubhe	193 49.8	N61 39.8
Elnath	278 10.1	N28 37.0
Eltanin	90 44.8	N51 29.7
Enif	33 44.7	N 9 57.3
Fomalhaut	15 21.3	S29 31.9
Gacrux	171 58.8	S57 12.4
Gienah	175 50.3	S17 38.0
Hadar	148 44.9	S60 27.2
Hamal	327 58.2	N23 32.3
Kaus Aust.	83 40.7	S34 22.4
Kochab	137 20.5	N74 05.7
Markab	13 35.9	N15 17.8
Menkar	314 12.8	N 4 09.2
Menkent	148 05.1	S36 27.0
Miaplacidus	221 40.0	S69 47.2
Mirfak	308 37.2	N49 54.8
Nunki	75 55.4	S26 16.3
Peacock	53 15.4	S56 40.7
Pollux	243 25.5	N27 59.0
Procyon	244 57.8	N 5 10.8
Rasalhague	96 04.3	N12 33.3
Regulus	207 41.6	N11 53.2
Rigel	281 10.1	S 8 11.0
Rigil Kent.	139 48.9	S60 54.2
Sabik	102 09.9	S15 44.5
Schedar	349 37.5	N56 37.5
Shaula	96 18.8	S37 06.8
Sirius	258 32.1	S16 44.4
Spica	158 29.1	S11 14.7
Suhail	222 51.2	S43 30.0
Vega	80 37.2	N38 48.4
Zuben'ubi	137 03.1	S16 06.5

	SHA	Mer. Pass.
	° ′	h m
Venus	194 14.9	13 20
Mars	116 16.5	18 30
Jupiter	184 01.3	13 59
Saturn	111 36.6	18 47

UT d	UT h	SUN GHA ° ′	SUN Dec ° ′	MOON GHA ° ′	MOON *v* ′	MOON Dec ° ′	MOON *d* ′	MOON HP ′
16	00	178 56.0	N13 39.8	30 13.2	9.2	S17 28.0	3.6	57.0
	01	193 56.1	39.0	44 41.4	9.2	17 24.4	3.7	57.0
	02	208 56.2	38.3	59 09.6	9.2	17 20.7	3.7	57.0
	03	223 56.4	. . 37.5	73 37.8	9.1	17 17.0	3.9	57.0
	04	238 56.5	36.7	88 05.9	9.2	17 13.1	4.0	57.1
	05	253 56.6	35.9	102 34.1	9.1	17 09.1	4.0	57.1
	06	268 56.8	N13 35.1	117 02.2	9.1	S17 05.1	4.2	57.1
	07	283 56.9	34.3	131 30.3	9.1	17 00.9	4.3	57.2
TUESDAY	08	298 57.0	33.5	145 58.4	9.1	16 56.6	4.3	57.2
	09	313 57.2	. . 32.7	160 26.5	9.1	16 52.3	4.5	57.2
	10	328 57.3	31.9	174 54.6	9.1	16 47.8	4.6	57.3
	11	343 57.4	31.1	189 22.7	9.0	16 43.2	4.6	57.3
	12	358 57.6	N13 30.3	203 50.7	9.1	S16 38.6	4.8	57.3
	13	13 57.7	29.5	218 18.8	9.0	16 33.8	4.9	57.4
	14	28 57.8	28.7	232 46.8	9.0	16 28.9	5.0	57.4
	15	43 58.0	. . 27.9	247 14.8	9.1	16 23.9	5.0	57.4
	16	58 58.1	27.1	261 42.9	9.0	16 18.9	5.2	57.4
	17	73 58.2	26.3	276 10.9	9.0	16 13.7	5.3	57.5
	18	88 58.4	N13 25.5	290 38.9	9.0	S16 08.4	5.3	57.5
	19	103 58.5	24.7	305 06.9	8.9	16 03.1	5.5	57.5
	20	118 58.6	23.9	319 34.8	9.0	15 57.6	5.5	57.6
	21	133 58.8	. . 23.1	334 02.8	9.0	15 52.1	5.7	57.6
	22	148 58.9	22.3	348 30.8	9.0	15 46.4	5.7	57.6
	23	163 59.0	21.5	2 58.8	8.9	15 40.7	5.9	57.7
17	00	178 59.2	N13 20.7	17 26.7	9.0	S15 34.8	5.9	57.7
	01	193 59.3	19.9	31 54.7	9.0	15 28.9	6.1	57.7
	02	208 59.4	19.1	46 22.7	8.9	15 22.8	6.1	57.7
	03	223 59.6	. . 18.3	60 50.6	9.0	15 16.7	6.2	57.8
	04	238 59.7	17.5	75 18.6	8.9	15 10.5	6.4	57.8
	05	253 59.8	16.7	89 46.5	8.9	15 04.1	6.4	57.8
	06	269 00.0	N13 15.9	104 14.4	9.0	S14 57.7	6.5	57.9
WEDNESDAY	07	284 00.1	15.1	118 42.4	8.9	14 51.2	6.6	57.9
	08	299 00.3	14.3	133 10.3	9.0	14 44.6	6.7	57.9
	09	314 00.4	. . 13.5	147 38.3	8.9	14 37.9	6.8	58.0
	10	329 00.5	12.7	162 06.2	9.0	14 31.1	6.8	58.0
	11	344 00.7	11.9	176 34.2	8.9	14 24.3	7.0	58.0
	12	359 00.8	N13 11.1	191 02.1	8.9	S14 17.3	7.1	58.0
	13	14 01.0	10.3	205 30.0	9.0	14 10.2	7.1	58.1
	14	29 01.1	09.5	219 58.0	8.9	14 03.1	7.2	58.1
	15	44 01.2	. . 08.7	234 25.9	9.0	13 55.9	7.4	58.1
	16	59 01.4	07.9	248 53.9	8.9	13 48.5	7.4	58.2
	17	74 01.5	07.1	263 21.8	9.0	13 41.1	7.5	58.2
	18	89 01.6	N13 06.3	277 49.8	8.9	S13 33.6	7.6	58.2
	19	104 01.8	05.5	292 17.7	9.0	13 26.0	7.6	58.2
	20	119 01.9	04.7	306 45.7	9.0	13 18.4	7.8	58.3
	21	134 02.1	. . 03.9	321 13.7	8.9	13 10.6	7.8	58.3
	22	149 02.2	03.1	335 41.6	9.0	13 02.8	7.9	58.3
	23	164 02.3	02.3	350 09.6	9.0	12 54.9	8.0	58.3
18	00	179 02.5	N13 01.4	4 37.6	8.9	S12 46.9	8.1	58.4
	01	194 02.6	13 00.6	19 05.5	9.0	12 38.8	8.2	58.4
	02	209 02.8	12 59.8	33 33.5	9.0	12 30.6	8.2	58.4
	03	224 02.9	. . 59.0	48 01.5	9.0	12 22.4	8.4	58.4
	04	239 03.1	58.2	62 29.5	9.0	12 14.0	8.4	58.5
	05	254 03.2	57.4	76 57.5	9.0	12 05.6	8.5	58.5
	06	269 03.3	N12 56.6	91 25.5	9.0	S11 57.1	8.5	58.5
THURSDAY	07	284 03.5	55.8	105 53.5	9.0	11 48.6	8.7	58.6
	08	299 03.6	55.0	120 21.5	9.1	11 39.9	8.7	58.6
	09	314 03.8	. . 54.2	134 49.6	9.0	11 31.2	8.8	58.6
	10	329 03.9	53.3	149 17.6	9.0	11 22.4	8.8	58.6
	11	344 04.0	52.5	163 45.6	9.1	11 13.6	9.0	58.7
	12	359 04.2	N12 51.7	178 13.7	9.0	S11 04.6	9.0	58.7
	13	14 04.3	50.9	192 41.7	9.1	10 55.6	9.1	58.7
	14	29 04.5	50.1	207 09.8	9.0	10 46.5	9.1	58.7
	15	44 04.6	. . 49.3	221 37.8	9.1	10 37.4	9.2	58.7
	16	59 04.8	48.5	236 05.9	9.1	10 28.2	9.3	58.8
	17	74 04.9	47.6	250 34.0	9.1	10 18.9	9.4	58.8
	18	89 05.1	N12 46.8	265 02.1	9.0	S10 09.5	9.4	58.8
	19	104 05.2	46.0	279 30.1	9.1	10 00.1	9.5	58.8
	20	119 05.3	45.2	293 58.2	9.1	9 50.6	9.5	58.9
	21	134 05.5	. . 44.4	308 26.3	9.2	9 41.1	9.7	58.9
	22	149 05.6	43.6	322 54.5	9.1	9 31.4	9.6	58.9
	23	164 05.8	42.8	337 22.6	9.1	S 9 21.8	9.8	58.9
		SD 15.8	*d* 0.8	SD 15.6		15.8		16.0

Lat.	Twilight Naut. h m	Twilight Civil h m	Sunrise h m	Moonrise 16 h m	Moonrise 17 h m	Moonrise 18 h m	Moonrise 19 h m
N 72	////	////	02 40	20 52	20 42	20 35	20 29
N 70	////	01 05	03 08	20 12	20 17	20 20	20 21
68	////	02 01	03 29	19 44	19 58	20 08	20 15
66	////	02 33	03 46	19 23	19 43	19 57	20 09
64	00 57	02 57	03 59	19 06	19 30	19 49	20 04
62	01 47	03 15	04 10	18 52	19 19	19 41	20 00
60	02 17	03 30	04 20	18 40	19 10	19 35	19 57
N 58	02 38	03 42	04 28	18 30	19 02	19 29	19 53
56	02 56	03 53	04 35	18 21	18 55	19 24	19 50
54	03 10	04 02	04 42	18 13	18 48	19 20	19 48
52	03 22	04 10	04 48	18 05	18 43	19 16	19 45
50	03 32	04 17	04 53	17 59	18 37	19 12	19 43
45	03 54	04 33	05 04	17 45	18 26	19 04	19 39
N 40	04 10	04 45	05 14	17 34	18 17	18 57	19 35
35	04 23	04 55	05 22	17 24	18 09	18 51	19 31
30	04 34	05 04	05 29	17 15	18 01	18 46	19 28
20	04 51	05 18	05 41	17 00	17 49	18 37	19 23
N 10	05 04	05 29	05 51	16 47	17 38	18 29	19 18
0	05 15	05 39	06 01	16 35	17 28	18 21	19 14
S 10	05 24	05 49	06 10	16 23	17 18	18 14	19 10
20	05 31	05 57	06 20	16 10	17 07	18 06	19 05
30	05 39	06 07	06 31	15 55	16 55	17 57	19 00
35	05 42	06 12	06 38	15 46	16 47	17 51	18 57
40	05 45	06 17	06 45	15 36	16 39	17 45	18 53
45	05 49	06 23	06 54	15 24	16 30	17 38	18 49
S 50	05 52	06 30	07 04	15 10	16 18	17 30	18 45
52	05 54	06 33	07 08	15 04	16 13	17 26	18 42
54	05 55	06 37	07 14	14 56	16 07	17 22	18 40
56	05 57	06 40	07 19	14 48	16 00	17 17	18 37
58	05 58	06 44	07 26	14 39	15 53	17 12	18 34
S 60	06 00	06 49	07 33	14 28	15 44	17 06	18 31

Lat.	Sunset h m	Twilight Civil h m	Twilight Naut. h m	Moonset 16 h m	Moonset 17 h m	Moonset 18 h m	Moonset 19 h m
N 72	21 23	////	////	24 55	00 55	02 55	04 53
N 70	20 56	22 51	////	25 34	01 34	03 19	05 06
68	20 36	22 01	////	00 34	02 01	03 37	05 17
66	20 20	21 31	////	01 00	02 21	03 51	05 26
64	20 07	21 08	23 00	01 21	02 38	04 03	05 34
62	19 56	20 51	22 16	01 37	02 51	04 13	05 40
60	19 46	20 36	21 48	01 51	03 03	04 22	05 45
N 58	19 38	20 24	21 27	02 02	03 12	04 29	05 50
56	19 31	20 14	21 10	02 13	03 21	04 36	05 55
54	19 25	20 04	20 56	02 21	03 29	04 42	05 58
52	19 19	19 56	20 44	02 29	03 35	04 47	06 02
50	19 14	19 49	20 34	02 37	03 42	04 52	06 05
45	19 03	19 34	20 13	02 52	03 55	05 02	06 12
N 40	18 53	19 22	19 57	03 04	04 06	05 10	06 18
35	18 46	19 12	19 44	03 15	04 15	05 18	06 22
30	18 39	19 04	19 33	03 24	04 23	05 24	06 27
20	18 27	18 50	19 17	03 40	04 37	05 35	06 34
N 10	18 17	18 38	19 04	03 54	04 49	05 45	06 40
0	18 07	18 29	18 53	04 07	05 00	05 53	06 46
S 10	17 58	18 19	18 44	04 20	05 12	06 02	06 52
20	17 48	18 11	18 37	04 34	05 24	06 12	06 59
30	17 37	18 01	18 30	04 50	05 37	06 22	07 06
35	17 31	17 57	18 26	04 59	05 45	06 28	07 10
40	17 23	17 51	18 23	05 09	05 54	06 35	07 14
45	17 15	17 45	18 20	05 22	06 04	06 43	07 20
S 50	17 05	17 39	18 16	05 36	06 17	06 53	07 26
52	17 00	17 35	18 15	05 43	06 23	06 57	07 29
54	16 55	17 32	18 14	05 51	06 29	07 02	07 32
56	16 50	17 29	18 12	05 59	06 36	07 08	07 35
58	16 43	17 25	18 11	06 09	06 44	07 14	07 39
S 60	16 36	17 20	18 09	06 20	06 53	07 20	07 43

Day	SUN Eqn. of Time 00^h	SUN Eqn. of Time 12^h	SUN Mer. Pass.	MOON Mer. Pass. Upper	MOON Mer. Pass. Lower	MOON Age	MOON Phase
d	m s	m s	h m	h m	h m	d %	
16	04 16	04 10	12 04	22 48	10 21	14 96	○
17	04 04	03 57	12 04	23 41	11 14	15 99	
18	03 50	03 44	12 04	24 34	12 07	16 100	

2016 AUGUST 19, 20, 21 (FRI., SAT., SUN.)

Day	UT	ARIES	VENUS −3·8		MARS −0·5		JUPITER −1·7		SATURN +0·4	
		GHA	GHA	Dec	GHA	Dec	GHA	Dec	GHA	Dec
	d h	° ′	° ′	° ′	° ′	° ′	° ′	° ′	° ′	° ′
	19 00	327 46.5	159 45.3	N 6 37.2	83 00.1	S24 16.3	151 25.7	N 2 47.4	79 22.2	S20 20.8
	01	342 48.9	174 45.0	36.0	98 01.2	16.5	166 27.7	47.2	94 24.7	20.8
	02	357 51.4	189 44.6	34.7	113 02.4	16.7	181 29.7	47.0	109 27.1	20.8
	03	12 53.9	204 44.3	. . 33.5	128 03.5	. . 16.9	196 31.7	. . 46.8	124 29.6	. . 20.8
	04	27 56.3	219 43.9	32.3	143 04.6	17.0	211 33.8	46.6	139 32.0	20.8
	05	42 58.8	234 43.5	31.0	158 05.8	17.2	226 35.8	46.4	154 34.4	20.8
	06	58 01.3	249 43.2	N 6 29.8	173 06.9	S24 17.4	241 37.8	N 2 46.2	169 36.9	S20 20.8
	07	73 03.7	264 42.8	28.6	188 08.0	17.6	256 39.8	46.0	184 39.3	20.9
	08	88 06.2	279 42.5	27.3	203 09.2	17.8	271 41.8	45.8	199 41.8	20.9
F	09	103 08.7	294 42.1	. . 26.1	218 10.3	. . 18.0	286 43.8	. . 45.6	214 44.2	. . 20.9
R	10	118 11.1	309 41.7	24.9	233 11.4	18.2	301 45.8	45.4	229 46.6	20.9
I	11	133 13.6	324 41.4	23.6	248 12.6	18.4	316 47.8	45.2	244 49.1	20.9
D	12	148 16.0	339 41.0	N 6 22.4	263 13.7	S24 18.6	331 49.8	N 2 45.0	259 51.5	S20 20.9
A	13	163 18.5	354 40.6	21.2	278 14.8	18.8	346 51.8	44.8	274 54.0	20.9
Y	14	178 21.0	9 40.3	19.9	293 16.0	19.0	1 53.8	44.6	289 56.4	20.9
	15	193 23.4	24 39.9	. . 18.7	308 17.1	. . 19.2	16 55.8	. . 44.4	304 58.8	. . 21.0
	16	208 25.9	39 39.6	17.4	323 18.2	19.4	31 57.8	44.2	320 01.3	21.0
	17	223 28.4	54 39.2	16.2	338 19.3	19.6	46 59.8	44.0	335 03.7	21.0
	18	238 30.8	69 38.9	N 6 15.0	353 20.5	S24 19.8	62 01.8	N 2 43.8	350 06.2	S20 21.0
	19	253 33.3	84 38.5	13.7	8 21.6	20.0	77 03.8	43.6	5 08.6	21.0
	20	268 35.8	99 38.1	12.5	23 22.7	20.1	92 05.8	43.4	20 11.0	21.0
	21	283 38.2	114 37.8	. . 11.3	38 23.8	. . 20.3	107 07.8	. . 43.2	35 13.5	. . 21.0
	22	298 40.7	129 37.4	10.0	53 25.0	20.5	122 09.8	43.0	50 15.9	21.0
	23	313 43.1	144 37.1	08.8	68 26.1	20.7	137 11.8	42.8	65 18.3	21.1
	20 00	328 45.6	159 36.7	N 6 07.5	83 27.2	S24 20.9	152 13.8	N 2 42.6	80 20.8	S20 21.1
	01	343 48.1	174 36.3	06.3	98 28.3	21.1	167 15.8	42.4	95 23.2	21.1
	02	358 50.5	189 36.0	05.1	113 29.4	21.3	182 17.8	42.2	110 25.7	21.1
	03	13 53.0	204 35.6	. . 03.8	128 30.6	. . 21.5	197 19.8	. . 42.0	125 28.1	. . 21.1
	04	28 55.5	219 35.3	02.6	143 31.7	21.7	212 21.8	41.7	140 30.5	21.1
	05	43 57.9	234 34.9	01.3	158 32.8	21.9	227 23.8	41.5	155 33.0	21.1
	06	59 00.4	249 34.6	N 6 00.1	173 33.9	S24 22.1	242 25.8	N 2 41.3	170 35.4	S20 21.1
	07	74 02.9	264 34.2	5 58.9	188 35.0	22.3	257 27.8	41.1	185 37.8	21.2
S	08	89 05.3	279 33.9	57.6	203 36.1	22.5	272 29.8	40.9	200 40.3	21.2
A	09	104 07.8	294 33.5	. . 56.4	218 37.3	. . 22.7	287 31.8	. . 40.7	215 42.7	. . 21.2
T	10	119 10.3	309 33.1	55.1	233 38.4	22.8	302 33.8	40.5	230 45.1	21.2
U	11	134 12.7	324 32.8	53.9	248 39.5	23.0	317 35.8	40.3	245 47.6	21.2
R	12	149 15.2	339 32.4	N 5 52.6	263 40.6	S24 23.2	332 37.8	N 2 40.1	260 50.0	S20 21.2
D	13	164 17.6	354 32.1	51.4	278 41.7	23.4	347 39.8	39.9	275 52.5	21.2
A	14	179 20.1	9 31.7	50.2	293 42.8	23.6	2 41.8	39.7	290 54.9	21.3
Y	15	194 22.6	24 31.4	. . 48.9	308 43.9	. . 23.8	17 43.8	. . 39.5	305 57.3	. . 21.3
	16	209 25.0	39 31.0	47.7	323 45.0	24.0	32 45.8	39.3	320 59.8	21.3
	17	224 27.5	54 30.7	46.4	338 46.1	24.2	47 47.8	39.1	336 02.2	21.3
	18	239 30.0	69 30.3	N 5 45.2	353 47.3	S24 24.4	62 49.8	N 2 38.9	351 04.6	S20 21.3
	19	254 32.4	84 30.0	43.9	8 48.4	24.6	77 51.8	38.7	6 07.1	21.3
	20	269 34.9	99 29.6	42.7	23 49.5	24.8	92 53.8	38.5	21 09.5	21.3
	21	284 37.4	114 29.3	. . 41.4	38 50.6	. . 24.9	107 55.8	. . 38.3	36 11.9	. . 21.3
	22	299 39.8	129 28.9	40.2	53 51.7	25.1	122 57.8	38.1	51 14.4	21.4
	23	314 42.3	144 28.6	39.0	68 52.8	25.3	137 59.8	37.9	66 16.8	21.4
	21 00	329 44.7	159 28.2	N 5 37.7	83 53.9	S24 25.5	153 01.8	N 2 37.7	81 19.2	S20 21.4
	01	344 47.2	174 27.9	36.5	98 55.0	25.7	168 03.8	37.5	96 21.7	21.4
	02	359 49.7	189 27.5	35.2	113 56.1	25.9	183 05.8	37.3	111 24.1	21.4
	03	14 52.1	204 27.1	. . 34.0	128 57.2	. . 26.1	198 07.8	. . 37.1	126 26.5	. . 21.4
	04	29 54.6	219 26.8	32.7	143 58.3	26.3	213 09.8	36.9	141 29.0	21.4
	05	44 57.1	234 26.4	31.5	158 59.4	26.5	228 11.8	36.7	156 31.4	21.5
	06	59 59.5	249 26.1	N 5 30.2	174 00.5	S24 26.7	243 13.8	N 2 36.5	171 33.8	S20 21.5
	07	75 02.0	264 25.7	29.0	189 01.6	26.8	258 15.8	36.3	186 36.3	21.5
	08	90 04.5	279 25.4	27.7	204 02.7	27.0	273 17.8	36.1	201 38.7	21.5
S	09	105 06.9	294 25.1	. . 26.5	219 03.8	. . 27.2	288 19.8	. . 35.9	216 41.1	. . 21.5
U	10	120 09.4	309 24.7	25.2	234 04.9	27.4	303 21.8	35.7	231 43.6	21.5
N	11	135 11.9	324 24.4	24.0	249 06.0	27.6	318 23.8	35.5	246 46.0	21.5
D	12	150 14.3	339 24.0	N 5 22.7	264 07.1	S24 27.8	333 25.8	N 2 35.3	261 48.4	S20 21.6
A	13	165 16.8	354 23.7	21.5	279 08.2	28.0	348 27.8	35.0	276 50.8	21.6
Y	14	180 19.2	9 23.3	20.2	294 09.3	28.2	3 29.8	34.8	291 53.3	21.6
	15	195 21.7	24 23.0	. . 19.0	309 10.4	. . 28.4	18 31.8	. . 34.6	306 55.7	. . 21.6
	16	210 24.2	39 22.6	17.7	324 11.5	28.5	33 33.8	34.4	321 58.1	21.6
	17	225 26.6	54 22.3	16.5	339 12.5	28.7	48 35.8	34.2	337 00.6	21.6
	18	240 29.1	69 21.9	N 5 15.2	354 13.6	S24 28.9	63 37.8	N 2 34.0	352 03.0	S20 21.6
	19	255 31.6	84 21.6	14.0	9 14.7	29.1	78 39.8	33.8	7 05.4	21.6
	20	270 34.0	99 21.2	12.7	24 15.8	29.3	93 41.8	33.6	22 07.9	21.7
	21	285 36.5	114 20.9	. . 11.5	39 16.9	. . 29.5	108 43.8	. . 33.4	37 10.3	. . 21.7
	22	300 39.0	129 20.5	10.2	54 18.0	29.7	123 45.8	33.2	52 12.7	21.7
	23	315 41.4	144 20.2	09.0	69 19.1	29.9	138 47.8	33.0	67 15.2	21.7
	Mer. Pass.	h m 2 04.6	*v* −0.4	*d* 1.2	*v* 1.1	*d* 0.2	*v* 2.0	*d* 0.2	*v* 2.4	*d* 0.0

STARS

Name	SHA	Dec
	° ′	° ′
Acamar	315 16.7	S40 14.2
Achernar	335 25.0	S57 09.0
Acrux	173 07.2	S63 11.6
Adhara	255 11.1	S28 59.7
Aldebaran	290 47.0	N16 32.4
Alioth	166 19.3	N55 52.5
Alkaid	152 57.5	N49 14.2
Al Na'ir	27 40.6	S46 52.6
Alnilam	275 44.3	S 1 11.6
Alphard	217 54.3	S 8 43.8
Alphecca	126 09.2	N26 39.9
Alpheratz	357 40.9	N29 10.9
Altair	62 05.8	N 8 55.0
Ankaa	353 13.3	S42 12.8
Antares	112 23.5	S26 27.9
Arcturus	145 53.9	N19 06.1
Atria	107 23.2	S69 03.5
Avior	234 17.7	S59 33.7
Bellatrix	278 29.8	N 6 21.7
Betelgeuse	270 59.1	N 7 24.5
Canopus	263 55.5	S52 42.2
Capella	280 31.4	N46 00.5
Deneb	49 29.5	N45 20.7
Denebola	182 31.8	N14 28.9
Diphda	348 53.5	S17 53.6
Dubhe	193 49.8	N61 39.8
Elnath	278 10.0	N28 37.0
Eltanin	90 44.9	N51 29.7
Enif	33 44.7	N 9 57.3
Fomalhaut	15 21.3	S29 31.9
Gacrux	171 58.8	S57 12.4
Gienah	175 50.3	S17 38.0
Hadar	148 45.0	S60 27.2
Hamal	327 58.1	N23 32.3
Kaus Aust.	83 40.7	S34 22.4
Kochab	137 20.5	N74 05.7
Markab	13 35.9	N15 17.8
Menkar	314 12.7	N 4 09.2
Menkent	148 05.1	S36 27.0
Miaplacidus	221 40.0	S69 47.1
Mirfak	308 37.2	N49 54.8
Nunki	75 55.4	S26 16.3
Peacock	53 15.4	S56 40.7
Pollux	243 25.4	N27 59.0
Procyon	244 57.8	N 5 10.9
Rasalhague	96 04.3	N12 33.3
Regulus	207 41.6	N11 53.2
Rigel	281 10.1	S 8 11.0
Rigil Kent.	139 48.9	S60 54.2
Sabik	102 09.9	S15 44.5
Schedar	349 37.5	N56 37.5
Shaula	96 18.8	S37 06.8
Sirius	258 32.1	S16 44.4
Spica	158 29.1	S11 14.7
Suhail	222 51.2	S43 30.0
Vega	80 37.2	N38 48.4
Zuben'ubi	137 03.1	S16 06.5

	SHA	Mer. Pass.
	° ′	h m
Venus	190 51.1	13 22
Mars	114 41.6	18 25
Jupiter	183 28.2	13 49
Saturn	111 35.2	18 36

UT		SUN GHA	SUN Dec	MOON GHA	v	MOON Dec	d	HP
d	h	° ′	° ′	° ′	′	° ′	′	′
19	00	179 05.9	N12 41.9	351 50.7	9.1	S 9 12.0	9.8	59.0
	01	194 06.1	41.1	6 18.8	9.2	9 02.2	9.8	59.0
	02	209 06.2	40.3	20 47.0	9.1	8 52.4	10.0	59.0
	03	224 06.4	. . 39.5	35 15.1	9.2	8 42.4	9.9	59.0
	04	239 06.5	38.7	49 43.3	9.2	8 32.5	10.1	59.0
	05	254 06.7	37.8	64 11.5	9.1	8 22.4	10.1	59.1
	06	269 06.8	N12 37.0	78 39.6	9.2	S 8 12.3	10.1	59.1
	07	284 07.0	36.2	93 07.8	9.2	8 02.2	10.2	59.1
	08	299 07.1	35.4	107 36.0	9.2	7 52.0	10.3	59.1
F	09	314 07.3	. . 34.6	122 04.2	9.2	7 41.7	10.3	59.1
R	10	329 07.4	33.8	136 32.4	9.2	7 31.4	10.3	59.2
I	11	344 07.5	32.9	151 00.6	9.2	7 21.1	10.4	59.2
D	12	359 07.7	N12 32.1	165 28.8	9.2	S 7 10.7	10.5	59.2
A	13	14 07.8	31.3	179 57.0	9.2	7 00.2	10.5	59.2
Y	14	29 08.0	30.5	194 25.2	9.3	6 49.7	10.5	59.2
	15	44 08.1	. . 29.6	208 53.5	9.2	6 39.2	10.6	59.2
	16	59 08.3	28.8	223 21.7	9.2	6 28.6	10.7	59.3
	17	74 08.4	28.0	237 49.9	9.3	6 17.9	10.6	59.3
	18	89 08.6	N12 27.2	252 18.2	9.2	S 6 07.3	10.8	59.3
	19	104 08.7	26.4	266 46.4	9.3	5 56.5	10.7	59.3
	20	119 08.9	25.5	281 14.7	9.3	5 45.8	10.8	59.3
	21	134 09.0	. . 24.7	295 43.0	9.2	5 35.0	10.8	59.3
	22	149 09.2	23.9	310 11.2	9.3	5 24.2	10.9	59.4
	23	164 09.3	23.1	324 39.5	9.3	5 13.3	10.9	59.4
20	00	179 09.5	N12 22.2	339 07.8	9.3	S 5 02.4	11.0	59.4
	01	194 09.6	21.4	353 36.1	9.2	4 51.4	10.9	59.4
	02	209 09.8	20.6	8 04.3	9.3	4 40.5	11.1	59.4
	03	224 09.9	. . 19.8	22 32.6	9.3	4 29.4	11.0	59.4
	04	239 10.1	18.9	37 00.9	9.3	4 18.4	11.1	59.4
	05	254 10.2	18.1	51 29.2	9.3	4 07.3	11.1	59.5
	06	269 10.4	N12 17.3	65 57.5	9.3	S 3 56.2	11.1	59.5
S	07	284 10.6	16.4	80 25.8	9.3	3 45.1	11.1	59.5
A	08	299 10.7	15.6	94 54.1	9.3	3 34.0	11.2	59.5
T	09	314 10.9	. . 14.8	109 22.4	9.3	3 22.8	11.2	59.5
U	10	329 11.0	14.0	123 50.7	9.3	3 11.6	11.2	59.5
R	11	344 11.2	13.1	138 19.0	9.3	3 00.4	11.3	59.5
D	12	359 11.3	N12 12.3	152 47.3	9.3	S 2 49.1	11.2	59.5
A	13	14 11.5	11.5	167 15.6	9.3	2 37.9	11.3	59.5
Y	14	29 11.6	10.6	181 43.9	9.3	2 26.6	11.3	59.6
	15	44 11.8	. . 09.8	196 12.2	9.3	2 15.3	11.3	59.6
	16	59 11.9	09.0	210 40.5	9.3	2 04.0	11.4	59.6
	17	74 12.1	08.2	225 08.8	9.3	1 52.6	11.3	59.6
	18	89 12.2	N12 07.3	239 37.1	9.3	S 1 41.3	11.4	59.6
	19	104 12.4	06.5	254 05.4	9.3	1 29.9	11.3	59.6
	20	119 12.5	05.7	268 33.7	9.3	1 18.6	11.4	59.6
	21	134 12.7	. . 04.8	283 02.0	9.3	1 07.2	11.4	59.6
	22	149 12.9	04.0	297 30.3	9.3	0 55.8	11.4	59.6
	23	164 13.0	03.2	311 58.6	9.3	0 44.4	11.4	59.6
21	00	179 13.2	N12 02.3	326 26.9	9.3	S 0 33.0	11.4	59.6
	01	194 13.3	01.5	340 55.2	9.2	0 21.6	11.4	59.7
	02	209 13.5	12 00.7	355 23.4	9.3	S 0 10.2	11.4	59.7
	03	224 13.6	11 59.8	9 51.7	9.3	N 0 01.2	11.5	59.7
	04	239 13.8	59.0	24 20.0	9.2	0 12.7	11.4	59.7
	05	254 14.0	58.2	38 48.2	9.3	0 24.1	11.4	59.7
	06	269 14.1	N11 57.3	53 16.5	9.2	N 0 35.5	11.4	59.7
	07	284 14.3	56.5	67 44.7	9.3	0 46.9	11.4	59.7
	08	299 14.4	55.7	82 13.0	9.2	0 58.3	11.4	59.7
S	09	314 14.6	. . 54.8	96 41.2	9.2	1 09.7	11.4	59.7
U	10	329 14.7	54.0	111 09.4	9.3	1 21.1	11.4	59.7
N	11	344 14.9	53.1	125 37.7	9.2	1 32.5	11.4	59.7
D	12	359 15.1	N11 52.3	140 05.9	9.2	N 1 43.9	11.4	59.7
A	13	14 15.2	51.5	154 34.1	9.2	1 55.3	11.3	59.7
Y	14	29 15.4	50.6	169 02.3	9.1	2 06.6	11.4	59.7
	15	44 15.5	. . 49.8	183 30.4	9.2	2 18.0	11.3	59.7
	16	59 15.7	49.0	197 58.6	9.2	2 29.3	11.3	59.7
	17	74 15.8	48.1	212 26.8	9.1	2 40.6	11.4	59.7
	18	89 16.0	N11 47.3	226 54.9	9.2	N 2 52.0	11.2	59.7
	19	104 16.2	46.4	241 23.1	9.1	3 03.2	11.3	59.7
	20	119 16.3	45.6	255 51.2	9.1	3 14.5	11.3	59.7
	21	134 16.5	. . 44.8	270 19.3	9.1	3 25.8	11.2	59.7
	22	149 16.6	43.9	284 47.4	9.1	3 37.0	11.2	59.7
	23	164 16.8	43.1	299 15.5	9.1	N 3 48.2	11.2	59.7
		SD 15.8	*d* 0.8	SD 16.1		16.2		16.3

Lat.	Twilight Naut.	Twilight Civil	Sunrise	Moonrise 19	Moonrise 20	Moonrise 21	Moonrise 22
°	h m	h m	h m	h m	h m	h m	h m
N 72	////	////	02 59	20 29	20 24	20 18	20 13
N 70	////	01 39	03 23	20 21	20 22	20 23	20 24
68	////	02 20	03 41	20 15	20 20	20 26	20 33
66	////	02 48	03 56	20 09	20 19	20 29	20 40
64	01 27	03 08	04 08	20 04	20 18	20 32	20 46
62	02 04	03 25	04 18	20 00	20 17	20 34	20 52
60	02 29	03 38	04 27	19 57	20 16	20 36	20 57
N 58	02 48	03 49	04 35	19 53	20 16	20 38	21 01
56	03 04	03 59	04 41	19 50	20 15	20 39	21 05
54	03 17	04 08	04 47	19 48	20 14	20 41	21 08
52	03 29	04 16	04 53	19 45	20 14	20 42	21 11
50	03 38	04 22	04 58	19 43	20 13	20 43	21 14
45	03 58	04 37	05 08	19 39	20 12	20 46	21 20
N 40	04 14	04 48	05 17	19 35	20 11	20 48	21 25
35	04 26	04 57	05 24	19 31	20 10	20 50	21 30
30	04 36	05 06	05 30	19 28	20 10	20 51	21 34
20	04 52	05 19	05 41	19 23	20 09	20 54	21 41
N 10	05 04	05 29	05 51	19 18	20 08	20 57	21 47
0	05 14	05 39	06 00	19 14	20 07	20 59	21 53
S 10	05 22	05 47	06 09	19 10	20 06	21 02	21 58
20	05 29	05 55	06 18	19 05	20 05	21 05	22 05
30	05 36	06 04	06 28	19 00	20 04	21 08	22 12
35	05 39	06 08	06 34	18 57	20 03	21 10	22 16
40	05 42	06 13	06 41	18 53	20 02	21 12	22 21
45	05 44	06 19	06 49	18 49	20 01	21 14	22 26
S 50	05 47	06 25	06 58	18 45	20 00	21 17	22 33
52	05 48	06 27	07 02	18 42	20 00	21 18	22 36
54	05 49	06 30	07 07	18 40	20 00	21 20	22 40
56	05 50	06 34	07 12	18 37	19 59	21 21	22 43
58	05 51	06 37	07 18	18 34	19 58	21 23	22 48
S 60	05 52	06 41	07 24	18 31	19 58	21 25	22 52

Lat.	Sunset	Twilight Civil	Twilight Naut.	Moonset 19	Moonset 20	Moonset 21	Moonset 22
°	h m	h m	h m	h m	h m	h m	h m
N 72	21 03	////	////	04 53	06 49	08 44	10 41
N 70	20 40	22 20	////	05 06	06 55	08 43	10 32
68	20 22	21 41	////	05 17	06 59	08 42	10 25
66	20 08	21 15	////	05 26	07 03	08 41	10 19
64	19 56	20 55	22 33	05 34	07 06	08 40	10 14
62	19 46	20 39	21 58	05 40	07 09	08 39	10 10
60	19 38	20 26	21 34	05 45	07 12	08 39	10 06
N 58	19 30	20 15	21 15	05 50	07 14	08 38	10 03
56	19 24	20 06	21 00	05 55	07 16	08 38	10 00
54	19 18	19 57	20 47	05 58	07 17	08 37	09 58
52	19 13	19 50	20 36	06 02	07 19	08 37	09 55
50	19 08	19 43	20 27	06 05	07 20	08 37	09 53
45	18 58	19 29	20 07	06 12	07 23	08 36	09 48
N 40	18 49	19 18	19 52	06 18	07 26	08 35	09 45
35	18 42	19 08	19 40	06 22	07 28	08 35	09 41
30	18 36	19 00	19 30	06 27	07 30	08 34	09 38
20	18 25	18 47	19 14	06 34	07 33	08 33	09 33
N 10	18 15	18 37	19 02	06 40	07 36	08 32	09 29
0	18 07	18 28	18 52	06 46	07 39	08 32	09 25
S 10	17 58	18 19	18 44	06 52	07 42	08 31	09 20
20	17 49	18 11	18 37	06 59	07 44	08 30	09 16
30	17 39	18 03	18 31	07 06	07 48	08 29	09 11
35	17 33	17 59	18 28	07 10	07 49	08 28	09 08
40	17 26	17 54	18 26	07 14	07 51	08 28	09 05
45	17 18	17 49	18 23	07 20	07 54	08 27	09 01
S 50	17 09	17 43	18 20	07 26	07 56	08 26	08 56
52	17 05	17 40	18 19	07 29	07 58	08 26	08 54
54	17 00	17 37	18 18	07 32	07 59	08 25	08 52
56	16 55	17 34	18 17	07 35	08 00	08 25	08 49
58	16 49	17 31	18 16	07 39	08 02	08 24	08 46
S 60	16 43	17 27	18 15	07 43	08 04	08 23	08 43

Day	SUN Eqn. of Time 00ʰ	SUN Eqn. of Time 12ʰ	SUN Mer. Pass.	MOON Mer. Pass. Upper	MOON Mer. Pass. Lower	MOON Age	MOON Phase
d	m s	m s	h m	h m	h m	d %	
19	03 37	03 30	12 03	00 34	13 00	17 98	
20	03 22	03 15	12 03	01 27	13 53	18 94	○
21	03 08	03 00	12 03	02 19	14 45	19 88	

2016 AUGUST 22, 23, 24 (MON., TUES., WED.)

UT d	h	ARIES GHA	VENUS −3·8 GHA	VENUS Dec	MARS −0·4 GHA	MARS Dec	JUPITER −1·7 GHA	JUPITER Dec	SATURN +0·4 GHA	SATURN Dec
		° ′	° ′	° ′	° ′	° ′	° ′	° ′	° ′	° ′
22 MONDAY	00	330 43.9	159 19.8	N 5 07.7	84 20.2	S24 30.0	153 49.8	N 2 32.8	82 17.6	S20 21.7
	01	345 46.3	174 19.5	06.5	99 21.3	30.2	168 51.8	32.6	97 20.0	21.7
	02	0 48.8	189 19.1	05.2	114 22.3	30.4	183 53.8	32.4	112 22.4	21.7
	03	15 51.3	204 18.8	. . 04.0	129 23.4	. . 30.6	198 55.8	. . 32.2	127 24.9	. . 21.8
	04	30 53.7	219 18.5	02.7	144 24.5	30.8	213 57.8	32.0	142 27.3	21.8
	05	45 56.2	234 18.1	01.5	159 25.6	31.0	228 59.8	31.8	157 29.7	21.8
	06	60 58.7	249 17.8	N 5 00.2	174 26.7	S24 31.2	244 01.8	N 2 31.6	172 32.2	S20 21.8
	07	76 01.1	264 17.4	4 59.0	189 27.8	31.4	259 03.8	31.4	187 34.6	21.8
	08	91 03.6	279 17.1	57.7	204 28.8	31.5	274 05.8	31.2	202 37.0	21.8
	09	106 06.1	294 16.7	. . 56.4	219 29.9	. . 31.7	289 07.8	. . 31.0	217 39.4	. . 21.8
	10	121 08.5	309 16.4	55.2	234 31.0	31.9	304 09.8	30.8	232 41.9	21.9
	11	136 11.0	324 16.0	53.9	249 32.1	32.1	319 11.8	30.6	247 44.3	21.9
	12	151 13.5	339 15.7	N 4 52.7	264 33.2	S24 32.3	334 13.8	N 2 30.4	262 46.7	S20 21.9
	13	166 15.9	354 15.4	51.4	279 34.2	32.5	349 15.8	30.2	277 49.1	21.9
	14	181 18.4	9 15.0	50.2	294 35.3	32.7	4 17.8	30.0	292 51.6	21.9
	15	196 20.8	24 14.7	. . 48.9	309 36.4	. . 32.8	19 19.8	. . 29.7	307 54.0	. . 21.9
	16	211 23.3	39 14.3	47.7	324 37.5	33.0	34 21.8	29.5	322 56.4	21.9
	17	226 25.8	54 14.0	46.4	339 38.6	33.2	49 23.8	29.3	337 58.8	22.0
	18	241 28.2	69 13.6	N 4 45.1	354 39.6	S24 33.4	64 25.8	N 2 29.1	353 01.3	S20 22.0
	19	256 30.7	84 13.3	43.9	9 40.7	33.6	79 27.8	28.9	8 03.7	22.0
	20	271 33.2	99 13.0	42.6	24 41.8	33.8	94 29.8	28.7	23 06.1	22.0
	21	286 35.6	114 12.6	. . 41.4	39 42.8	. . 33.9	109 31.8	. . 28.5	38 08.6	. . 22.0
	22	301 38.1	129 12.3	40.1	54 43.9	34.1	124 33.8	28.3	53 11.0	22.0
	23	316 40.6	144 11.9	38.9	69 45.0	34.3	139 35.8	28.1	68 13.4	22.1
23 TUESDAY	00	331 43.0	159 11.6	N 4 37.6	84 46.1	S24 34.5	154 37.8	N 2 27.9	83 15.8	S20 22.1
	01	346 45.5	174 11.2	36.3	99 47.1	34.7	169 39.8	27.7	98 18.3	22.1
	02	1 48.0	189 10.9	35.1	114 48.2	34.9	184 41.8	27.5	113 20.7	22.1
	03	16 50.4	204 10.6	. . 33.8	129 49.3	. . 35.1	199 43.8	. . 27.3	128 23.1	. . 22.1
	04	31 52.9	219 10.2	32.6	144 50.3	35.2	214 45.8	27.1	143 25.5	22.1
	05	46 55.3	234 09.9	31.3	159 51.4	35.4	229 47.8	26.9	158 27.9	22.1
	06	61 57.8	249 09.5	N 4 30.0	174 52.5	S24 35.6	244 49.8	N 2 26.7	173 30.4	S20 22.2
	07	77 00.3	264 09.2	28.8	189 53.5	35.8	259 51.8	26.5	188 32.8	22.2
	08	92 02.7	279 08.9	27.5	204 54.6	36.0	274 53.8	26.3	203 35.2	22.2
	09	107 05.2	294 08.5	. . 26.3	219 55.7	. . 36.2	289 55.7	. . 26.1	218 37.6	. . 22.2
	10	122 07.7	309 08.2	25.0	234 56.7	36.3	304 57.7	25.9	233 40.1	22.2
	11	137 10.1	324 07.8	23.7	249 57.8	36.5	319 59.7	25.7	248 42.5	22.2
	12	152 12.6	339 07.5	N 4 22.5	264 58.9	S24 36.7	335 01.7	N 2 25.5	263 44.9	S20 22.2
	13	167 15.1	354 07.2	21.2	279 59.9	36.9	350 03.7	25.2	278 47.3	22.3
	14	182 17.5	9 06.8	20.0	295 01.0	37.1	5 05.7	25.0	293 49.8	22.3
	15	197 20.0	24 06.5	. . 18.7	310 02.0	. . 37.3	20 07.7	. . 24.8	308 52.2	. . 22.3
	16	212 22.4	39 06.2	17.4	325 03.1	37.4	35 09.7	24.6	323 54.6	22.3
	17	227 24.9	54 05.8	16.2	340 04.2	37.6	50 11.7	24.4	338 57.0	22.3
	18	242 27.4	69 05.5	N 4 14.9	355 05.2	S24 37.8	65 13.7	N 2 24.2	353 59.4	S20 22.3
	19	257 29.8	84 05.1	13.7	10 06.3	38.0	80 15.7	24.0	9 01.9	22.3
	20	272 32.3	99 04.8	12.4	25 07.3	38.2	95 17.7	23.8	24 04.3	22.4
	21	287 34.8	114 04.5	. . 11.1	40 08.4	. . 38.3	110 19.7	. . 23.6	39 06.7	. . 22.4
	22	302 37.2	129 04.1	09.9	55 09.4	38.5	125 21.7	23.4	54 09.1	22.4
	23	317 39.7	144 03.8	08.6	70 10.5	38.7	140 23.7	23.2	69 11.6	22.4
24 WEDNESDAY	00	332 42.2	159 03.5	N 4 07.3	85 11.6	S24 38.9	155 25.7	N 2 23.0	84 14.0	S20 22.4
	01	347 44.6	174 03.1	06.1	100 12.6	39.1	170 27.7	22.8	99 16.4	22.4
	02	2 47.1	189 02.8	04.8	115 13.7	39.2	185 29.7	22.6	114 18.8	22.5
	03	17 49.6	204 02.4	. . 03.5	130 14.7	. . 39.4	200 31.7	. . 22.4	129 21.2	. . 22.5
	04	32 52.0	219 02.1	02.3	145 15.8	39.6	215 33.7	22.2	144 23.7	22.5
	05	47 54.5	234 01.8	4 01.0	160 16.8	39.8	230 35.7	22.0	159 26.1	22.5
	06	62 56.9	249 01.4	N 3 59.8	175 17.9	S24 40.0	245 37.7	N 2 21.8	174 28.5	S20 22.5
	07	77 59.4	264 01.1	58.5	190 18.9	40.2	260 39.7	21.6	189 30.9	22.5
	08	93 01.9	279 00.8	57.2	205 20.0	40.3	275 41.6	21.4	204 33.3	22.5
	09	108 04.3	294 00.4	. . 56.0	220 21.0	. . 40.5	290 43.6	. . 21.1	219 35.8	. . 22.6
	10	123 06.8	309 00.1	54.7	235 22.1	40.7	305 45.6	20.9	234 38.2	22.6
	11	138 09.3	323 59.8	53.4	250 23.1	40.9	320 47.6	20.7	249 40.6	22.6
	12	153 11.7	338 59.4	N 3 52.2	265 24.2	S24 41.0	335 49.6	N 2 20.5	264 43.0	S20 22.6
	13	168 14.2	353 59.1	50.9	280 25.2	41.2	350 51.6	20.3	279 45.4	22.6
	14	183 16.7	8 58.8	49.6	295 26.3	41.4	5 53.6	20.1	294 47.8	22.6
	15	198 19.1	23 58.4	. . 48.4	310 27.3	. . 41.6	20 55.6	. . 19.9	309 50.3	. . 22.7
	16	213 21.6	38 58.1	47.1	325 28.3	41.8	35 57.6	19.7	324 52.7	22.7
	17	228 24.1	53 57.8	45.8	340 29.4	41.9	50 59.6	19.5	339 55.1	22.7
	18	243 26.5	68 57.4	N 3 44.6	355 30.4	S24 42.1	66 01.6	N 2 19.3	354 57.5	S20 22.7
	19	258 29.0	83 57.1	43.3	10 31.5	42.3	81 03.6	19.1	9 59.9	22.7
	20	273 31.4	98 56.8	42.0	25 32.5	42.5	96 05.6	18.9	25 02.3	22.7
	21	288 33.9	113 56.4	. . 40.8	40 33.6	. . 42.7	111 07.6	. . 18.7	40 04.8	. . 22.7
	22	303 36.4	128 56.1	39.5	55 34.6	42.8	126 09.6	18.5	55 07.2	22.8
	23	318 38.8	143 55.8	38.2	70 35.6	43.0	141 11.6	18.3	70 09.6	22.8
Mer. Pass.		h m 1 52.8	*v* −0.3	*d* 1.3	*v* 1.1	*d* 0.2	*v* 2.0	*d* 0.2	*v* 2.4	*d* 0.0

STARS

Name	SHA	Dec
	° ′	° ′
Acamar	315 16.6	S40 14.2
Achernar	335 24.9	S57 09.0
Acrux	173 07.3	S63 11.6
Adhara	255 11.1	S28 59.7
Aldebaran	290 47.0	N16 32.4
Alioth	166 19.3	N55 52.5
Alkaid	152 57.5	N49 14.2
Al Na'ir	27 40.6	S46 52.6
Alnilam	275 44.3	S 1 11.6
Alphard	217 54.3	S 8 43.8
Alphecca	126 09.2	N26 39.9
Alpheratz	357 40.9	N29 10.9
Altair	62 05.9	N 8 55.1
Ankaa	353 13.3	S42 12.8
Antares	112 23.5	S26 27.9
Arcturus	145 53.9	N19 06.1
Atria	107 23.2	S69 03.5
Avior	234 17.6	S59 33.7
Bellatrix	278 29.8	N 6 21.7
Betelgeuse	270 59.1	N 7 24.5
Canopus	263 55.5	S52 42.2
Capella	280 31.4	N46 00.5
Deneb	49 29.5	N45 20.7
Denebola	182 31.8	N14 28.9
Diphda	348 53.5	S17 53.6
Dubhe	193 49.9	N61 39.8
Elnath	278 10.0	N28 37.0
Eltanin	90 44.9	N51 29.7
Enif	33 44.7	N 9 57.3
Fomalhaut	15 21.3	S29 31.9
Gacrux	171 58.8	S57 12.4
Gienah	175 50.3	S17 38.0
Hadar	148 45.0	S60 27.2
Hamal	327 58.1	N23 32.3
Kaus Aust.	83 40.7	S34 22.4
Kochab	137 20.6	N74 05.7
Markab	13 35.8	N15 17.8
Menkar	314 12.7	N 4 09.2
Menkent	148 05.2	S36 27.0
Miaplacidus	221 40.0	S69 47.1
Mirfak	308 37.1	N49 54.9
Nunki	75 55.4	S26 16.3
Peacock	53 15.4	S56 40.8
Pollux	243 25.4	N27 59.0
Procyon	244 57.7	N 5 10.9
Rasalhague	96 04.3	N12 33.3
Regulus	207 41.6	N11 53.2
Rigel	281 10.1	S 8 11.0
Rigil Kent.	139 48.9	S60 54.2
Sabik	102 10.0	S15 44.5
Schedar	349 37.5	N56 37.5
Shaula	96 18.8	S37 06.8
Sirius	258 32.0	S16 44.4
Spica	158 29.2	S11 14.7
Suhail	222 51.2	S43 30.0
Vega	80 37.2	N38 48.4
Zuben'ubi	137 03.1	S16 06.5

	SHA	Mer. Pass.
	° ′	h m
Venus	187 28.6	13 24
Mars	113 03.0	18 20
Jupiter	182 54.8	13 40
Saturn	111 32.8	18 24

UT d	UT h	SUN GHA	SUN Dec	MOON GHA	MOON v	MOON Dec	MOON d	MOON HP
		° ′	° ′	° ′	′	° ′	′	′
22	00	179 17.0	N11 42.2	313 43.6	9.1	N 3 59.4	11.1	59.7
	01	194 17.1	41.4	328 11.7	9.0	4 10.5	11.2	59.7
	02	209 17.3	40.5	342 39.7	9.0	4 21.7	11.1	59.7
	03	224 17.4	. . 39.7	357 07.7	9.1	4 32.8	11.1	59.7
	04	239 17.6	38.9	11 35.8	9.0	4 43.9	11.0	59.7
	05	254 17.8	38.0	26 03.8	9.0	4 54.9	11.0	59.7
	06	269 17.9	N11 37.2	40 31.8	8.9	N 5 05.9	11.0	59.7
	07	284 18.1	36.3	54 59.7	9.0	5 16.9	11.0	59.7
	08	299 18.3	35.5	69 27.7	8.9	5 27.9	10.9	59.7
MONDAY	09	314 18.4	. . 34.6	83 55.6	9.0	5 38.8	10.9	59.7
	10	329 18.6	33.8	98 23.6	8.9	5 49.7	10.8	59.7
	11	344 18.7	33.0	112 51.5	8.9	6 00.5	10.8	59.7
	12	359 18.9	N11 32.1	127 19.4	8.8	N 6 11.3	10.8	59.7
	13	14 19.1	31.3	141 47.2	8.9	6 22.1	10.7	59.7
	14	29 19.2	30.4	156 15.1	8.8	6 32.8	10.7	59.7
	15	44 19.4	. . 29.6	170 42.9	8.8	6 43.5	10.7	59.7
	16	59 19.6	28.7	185 10.7	8.8	6 54.2	10.6	59.7
	17	74 19.7	27.9	199 38.5	8.8	7 04.8	10.5	59.7
	18	89 19.9	N11 27.0	214 06.3	8.8	N 7 15.3	10.5	59.7
	19	104 20.0	26.2	228 34.1	8.7	7 25.8	10.5	59.7
	20	119 20.2	25.3	243 01.8	8.7	7 36.3	10.4	59.7
	21	134 20.4	. . 24.5	257 29.5	8.7	7 46.7	10.4	59.7
	22	149 20.5	23.6	271 57.2	8.7	7 57.1	10.3	59.7
	23	164 20.7	22.8	286 24.9	8.6	8 07.4	10.3	59.7
23	00	179 20.9	N11 22.0	300 52.5	8.7	N 8 17.7	10.2	59.7
	01	194 21.0	21.1	315 20.2	8.6	8 27.9	10.1	59.7
	02	209 21.2	20.3	329 47.8	8.6	8 38.0	10.1	59.7
	03	224 21.4	. . 19.4	344 15.4	8.5	8 48.1	10.1	59.7
	04	239 21.5	18.6	358 42.9	8.6	8 58.2	10.0	59.6
	05	254 21.7	17.7	13 10.5	8.5	9 08.2	9.9	59.6
	06	269 21.9	N11 16.9	27 38.0	8.5	N 9 18.1	9.9	59.6
	07	284 22.0	16.0	42 05.5	8.5	9 28.0	9.8	59.6
TUESDAY	08	299 22.2	15.2	56 33.0	8.4	9 37.8	9.7	59.6
	09	314 22.4	. . 14.3	71 00.4	8.4	9 47.5	9.7	59.6
	10	329 22.5	13.4	85 27.8	8.5	9 57.2	9.6	59.6
	11	344 22.7	12.6	99 55.3	8.3	10 06.8	9.6	59.6
	12	359 22.9	N11 11.7	114 22.6	8.4	N10 16.4	9.5	59.6
	13	14 23.0	10.9	128 50.0	8.3	10 25.9	9.4	59.6
	14	29 23.2	10.0	143 17.3	8.3	10 35.3	9.3	59.6
	15	44 23.4	. . 09.2	157 44.6	8.3	10 44.6	9.3	59.6
	16	59 23.5	08.3	172 11.9	8.3	10 53.9	9.2	59.6
	17	74 23.7	07.5	186 39.2	8.2	11 03.1	9.2	59.5
	18	89 23.9	N11 06.6	201 06.4	8.2	N11 12.3	9.0	59.5
	19	104 24.0	05.8	215 33.6	8.2	11 21.3	9.0	59.5
	20	119 24.2	04.9	230 00.8	8.2	11 30.3	9.0	59.5
	21	134 24.4	. . 04.1	244 28.0	8.1	11 39.3	8.8	59.5
	22	149 24.5	03.2	258 55.1	8.1	11 48.1	8.8	59.5
	23	164 24.7	02.3	273 22.2	8.1	11 56.9	8.7	59.5
24	00	179 24.9	N11 01.5	287 49.3	8.1	N12 05.6	8.6	59.5
	01	194 25.0	11 00.6	302 16.4	8.0	12 14.2	8.5	59.5
	02	209 25.2	10 59.8	316 43.4	8.0	12 22.7	8.5	59.5
	03	224 25.4	. . 58.9	331 10.4	8.0	12 31.2	8.4	59.4
	04	239 25.5	58.1	345 37.4	8.0	12 39.6	8.3	59.4
	05	254 25.7	57.2	0 04.4	7.9	12 47.9	8.2	59.4
	06	269 25.9	N10 56.3	14 31.3	7.9	N12 56.1	8.1	59.4
WEDNESDAY	07	284 26.1	55.5	28 58.2	7.9	13 04.2	8.1	59.4
	08	299 26.2	54.6	43 25.1	7.9	13 12.3	7.9	59.4
	09	314 26.4	. . 53.8	57 52.0	7.8	13 20.2	7.9	59.4
	10	329 26.6	52.9	72 18.8	7.9	13 28.1	7.8	59.4
	11	344 26.7	52.1	86 45.7	7.8	13 35.9	7.7	59.4
	12	359 26.9	N10 51.2	101 12.5	7.7	N13 43.6	7.6	59.3
	13	14 27.1	50.3	115 39.2	7.8	13 51.2	7.5	59.3
	14	29 27.2	49.5	130 06.0	7.7	13 58.7	7.5	59.3
	15	44 27.4	. . 48.6	144 32.7	7.7	14 06.2	7.3	59.3
	16	59 27.6	47.8	158 59.4	7.7	14 13.5	7.2	59.3
	17	74 27.8	46.9	173 26.1	7.7	14 20.7	7.2	59.3
	18	89 27.9	N10 46.0	187 52.8	7.6	N14 27.9	7.1	59.3
	19	104 28.1	45.2	202 19.4	7.6	14 35.0	6.9	59.3
	20	119 28.3	44.3	216 46.0	7.6	14 41.9	6.9	59.2
	21	134 28.4	. . 43.4	231 12.6	7.6	14 48.8	6.8	59.2
	22	149 28.6	42.6	245 39.2	7.6	14 55.6	6.7	59.2
	23	164 28.8	41.7	260 05.8	7.5	N15 02.3	6.5	59.2
		SD 15.8	*d* 0.9	SD	16.3	16.2		16.2

Lat.	Twilight Naut.	Twilight Civil	Sunrise	Moonrise 22	23	24	25
°	h m	h m	h m	h m	h m	h m	h m
N 72	////	01 05	03 16	20 13	20 07	20 01	19 52
N 70	////	02 04	03 37	20 24	20 26	20 31	20 42
68	////	02 37	03 53	20 33	20 41	20 54	21 14
66	00 57	03 01	04 06	20 40	20 53	21 11	21 38
64	01 49	03 19	04 17	20 46	21 04	21 26	21 56
62	02 19	03 34	04 26	20 52	21 13	21 38	22 11
60	02 41	03 46	04 34	20 57	21 20	21 49	22 24
N 58	02 58	03 57	04 41	21 01	21 27	21 58	22 35
56	03 12	04 06	04 47	21 05	21 33	22 06	22 45
54	03 25	04 14	04 53	21 08	21 38	22 13	22 54
52	03 35	04 21	04 58	21 11	21 43	22 19	23 01
50	03 44	04 27	05 02	21 14	21 47	22 25	23 08
45	04 03	04 40	05 12	21 20	21 57	22 38	23 23
N 40	04 17	04 51	05 19	21 25	22 05	22 48	23 35
35	04 29	05 00	05 26	21 30	22 12	22 57	23 46
30	04 38	05 07	05 32	21 34	22 18	23 05	23 55
20	04 53	05 20	05 42	21 41	22 28	23 18	24 11
N 10	05 05	05 30	05 51	21 47	22 38	23 30	24 25
0	05 14	05 38	05 59	21 53	22 47	23 42	24 38
S 10	05 21	05 46	06 07	21 58	22 56	23 53	24 51
20	05 27	05 53	06 16	22 05	23 05	24 05	00 05
30	05 33	06 01	06 25	22 12	23 16	24 19	00 19
35	05 35	06 05	06 30	22 16	23 22	24 28	00 28
40	05 37	06 09	06 37	22 21	23 30	24 37	00 37
45	05 40	06 14	06 44	22 26	23 38	24 48	00 48
S 50	05 41	06 19	06 52	22 33	23 48	25 01	01 01
52	05 42	06 21	06 56	22 36	23 53	25 07	01 07
54	05 43	06 24	07 00	22 40	23 58	25 14	01 14
56	05 43	06 27	07 05	22 43	24 04	00 04	01 22
58	05 44	06 30	07 10	22 48	24 11	00 11	01 30
S 60	05 45	06 33	07 16	22 52	24 18	00 18	01 40

Lat.	Sunset	Twilight Civil	Twilight Naut.	Moonset 22	23	24	25
°	h m	h m	h m	h m	h m	h m	h m
N 72	20 45	22 46	////	10 41	12 39	14 40	16 45
N 70	20 25	21 54	////	10 32	12 21	14 10	15 56
68	20 09	21 23	////	10 25	12 08	13 49	15 25
66	19 56	21 00	22 57	10 19	11 57	13 32	15 02
64	19 46	20 43	22 11	10 14	11 47	13 18	14 43
62	19 37	20 28	21 42	10 10	11 40	13 07	14 29
60	19 29	20 16	21 21	10 06	11 33	12 57	14 16
N 58	19 22	20 06	21 04	10 03	11 27	12 48	14 05
56	19 16	19 57	20 50	10 00	11 22	12 41	13 56
54	19 11	19 50	20 39	09 58	11 17	12 34	13 48
52	19 06	19 43	20 28	09 55	11 13	12 28	13 40
50	19 02	19 37	20 19	09 53	11 09	12 23	13 34
45	18 53	19 24	20 01	09 48	11 01	12 11	13 19
N 40	18 45	19 13	19 47	09 45	10 54	12 02	13 08
35	18 38	19 04	19 36	09 41	10 48	11 53	12 58
30	18 32	18 57	19 26	09 38	10 42	11 46	12 49
20	18 22	18 45	19 11	09 33	10 33	11 34	12 34
N 10	18 14	18 35	19 00	09 29	10 26	11 23	12 21
0	18 06	18 27	18 51	09 25	10 18	11 13	12 08
S 10	17 58	18 19	18 44	09 20	10 11	11 03	11 56
20	17 50	18 12	18 38	09 16	10 03	10 52	11 43
30	17 40	18 05	18 33	09 11	09 54	10 39	11 28
35	17 35	18 01	18 30	09 08	09 49	10 32	11 19
40	17 29	17 57	18 28	09 05	09 43	10 24	11 09
45	17 22	17 52	18 26	09 01	09 36	10 15	10 58
S 50	17 14	17 47	18 24	08 56	09 28	10 03	10 44
52	17 10	17 44	18 24	08 54	09 24	09 58	10 37
54	17 06	17 42	18 23	08 52	09 20	09 52	10 30
56	17 01	17 39	18 23	08 49	09 16	09 46	10 22
58	16 56	17 36	18 22	08 46	09 11	09 39	10 13
S 60	16 50	17 33	18 22	08 43	09 05	09 31	10 02

Day	SUN Eqn. of Time 00^h	SUN Eqn. of Time 12^h	SUN Mer. Pass.	MOON Mer. Pass. Upper	MOON Mer. Pass. Lower	MOON Age	MOON Phase
d	m s	m s	h m	h m	h m	d %	
22	02 52	02 45	12 03	03 12	15 39	20 79	
23	02 37	02 29	12 02	04 05	16 32	21 69	
24	02 21	02 13	12 02	05 00	17 27	22 58	

UT	Day	ARIES GHA	VENUS −3·8 GHA	VENUS Dec	MARS −0·4 GHA	MARS Dec	JUPITER −1·7 GHA	JUPITER Dec	SATURN +0·5 GHA	SATURN Dec
d h		° ′	° ′	° ′	° ′	° ′	° ′	° ′	° ′	° ′
25 00	THURSDAY	333 41.3	158 55.4	N 3 37.0	85 36.7	S24 43.2	156 13.6	N 2 18.1	85 12.0	S20 22.8
01		348 43.8	173 55.1	35.7	100 37.7	43.4	171 15.6	17.9	100 14.4	22.8
02		3 46.2	188 54.8	34.4	115 38.7	43.5	186 17.5	17.7	115 16.8	22.8
03		18 48.7	203 54.4	. . 33.2	130 39.8	. . 43.7	201 19.5	. . 17.4	130 19.3	. . 22.8
04		33 51.2	218 54.1	31.9	145 40.8	43.9	216 21.5	17.2	145 21.7	22.9
05		48 53.6	233 53.8	30.6	160 41.9	44.1	231 23.5	17.0	160 24.1	22.9
06		63 56.1	248 53.4	N 3 29.3	175 42.9	S24 44.3	246 25.5	N 2 16.8	175 26.5	S20 22.9
07		78 58.5	263 53.1	28.1	190 43.9	44.4	261 27.5	16.6	190 28.9	22.9
08		94 01.0	278 52.8	26.8	205 45.0	44.6	276 29.5	16.4	205 31.3	22.9
09		109 03.5	293 52.4	. . 25.5	220 46.0	. . 44.8	291 31.5	. . 16.2	220 33.8	. . 22.9
10		124 05.9	308 52.1	24.3	235 47.0	45.0	306 33.5	16.0	235 36.2	23.0
11		139 08.4	323 51.8	23.0	250 48.1	45.1	321 35.5	15.8	250 38.6	23.0
12		154 10.9	338 51.4	N 3 21.7	265 49.1	S24 45.3	336 37.5	N 2 15.6	265 41.0	S20 23.0
13		169 13.3	353 51.1	20.5	280 50.1	45.5	351 39.5	15.4	280 43.4	23.0
14		184 15.8	8 50.8	19.2	295 51.1	45.7	6 41.5	15.2	295 45.8	23.0
15		199 18.3	23 50.5	. . 17.9	310 52.2	. . 45.8	21 43.5	. . 15.0	310 48.2	. . 23.0
16		214 20.7	38 50.1	16.6	325 53.2	46.0	36 45.5	14.8	325 50.7	23.1
17		229 23.2	53 49.8	15.4	340 54.2	46.2	51 47.4	14.6	340 53.1	23.1
18		244 25.7	68 49.5	N 3 14.1	355 55.3	S24 46.4	66 49.4	N 2 14.4	355 55.5	S20 23.1
19		259 28.1	83 49.1	12.8	10 56.3	46.5	81 51.4	14.1	10 57.9	23.1
20		274 30.6	98 48.8	11.6	25 57.3	46.7	96 53.4	13.9	26 00.3	23.1
21		289 33.0	113 48.5	. . 10.3	40 58.3	. . 46.9	111 55.4	. . 13.7	41 02.7	. . 23.1
22		304 35.5	128 48.1	09.0	55 59.4	47.1	126 57.4	13.5	56 05.1	23.2
23		319 38.0	143 47.8	07.7	71 00.4	47.2	141 59.4	13.3	71 07.5	23.2
26 00	FRIDAY	334 40.4	158 47.5	N 3 06.5	86 01.4	S24 47.4	157 01.4	N 2 13.1	86 10.0	S20 23.2
01		349 42.9	173 47.2	05.2	101 02.4	47.6	172 03.4	12.9	101 12.4	23.2
02		4 45.4	188 46.8	03.9	116 03.4	47.8	187 05.4	12.7	116 14.8	23.2
03		19 47.8	203 46.5	. . 02.7	131 04.5	. . 47.9	202 07.4	. . 12.5	131 17.2	. . 23.2
04		34 50.3	218 46.2	01.4	146 05.5	48.1	217 09.4	12.3	146 19.6	23.2
05		49 52.8	233 45.8	3 00.1	161 06.5	48.3	232 11.4	12.1	161 22.0	23.3
06		64 55.2	248 45.5	N 2 58.8	176 07.5	S24 48.5	247 13.3	N 2 11.9	176 24.4	S20 23.3
07		79 57.7	263 45.2	57.6	191 08.5	48.6	262 15.3	11.7	191 26.8	23.3
08		95 00.2	278 44.9	56.3	206 09.6	48.8	277 17.3	11.5	206 29.2	23.3
09		110 02.6	293 44.5	. . 55.0	221 10.6	. . 49.0	292 19.3	. . 11.3	221 31.7	. . 23.3
10		125 05.1	308 44.2	53.7	236 11.6	49.2	307 21.3	11.0	236 34.1	23.3
11		140 07.5	323 43.9	52.5	251 12.6	49.3	322 23.3	10.8	251 36.5	23.4
12		155 10.0	338 43.6	N 2 51.2	266 13.6	S24 49.5	337 25.3	N 2 10.6	266 38.9	S20 23.4
13		170 12.5	353 43.2	49.9	281 14.6	49.7	352 27.3	10.4	281 41.3	23.4
14		185 14.9	8 42.9	48.6	296 15.7	49.8	7 29.3	10.2	296 43.7	23.4
15		200 17.4	23 42.6	. . 47.4	311 16.7	. . 50.0	22 31.3	. . 10.0	311 46.1	. . 23.4
16		215 19.9	38 42.2	46.1	326 17.7	50.2	37 33.3	09.8	326 48.5	23.4
17		230 22.3	53 41.9	44.8	341 18.7	50.4	52 35.3	09.6	341 50.9	23.5
18		245 24.8	68 41.6	N 2 43.5	356 19.7	S24 50.5	67 37.2	N 2 09.4	356 53.3	S20 23.5
19		260 27.3	83 41.3	42.3	11 20.7	50.7	82 39.2	09.2	11 55.8	23.5
20		275 29.7	98 40.9	41.0	26 21.7	50.9	97 41.2	09.0	26 58.2	23.5
21		290 32.2	113 40.6	. . 39.7	41 22.7	. . 51.0	112 43.2	. . 08.8	42 00.6	. . 23.5
22		305 34.7	128 40.3	38.4	56 23.7	51.2	127 45.2	08.6	57 03.0	23.5
23		320 37.1	143 40.0	37.2	71 24.7	51.4	142 47.2	08.4	72 05.4	23.6
27 00	SATURDAY	335 39.6	158 39.6	N 2 35.9	86 25.8	S24 51.6	157 49.2	N 2 08.2	87 07.8	S20 23.6
01		350 42.0	173 39.3	34.6	101 26.8	51.7	172 51.2	07.9	102 10.2	23.6
02		5 44.5	188 39.0	33.3	116 27.8	51.9	187 53.2	07.7	117 12.6	23.6
03		20 47.0	203 38.7	. . 32.1	131 28.8	. . 52.1	202 55.2	. . 07.5	132 15.0	. . 23.6
04		35 49.4	218 38.3	30.8	146 29.8	52.2	217 57.2	07.3	147 17.4	23.7
05		50 51.9	233 38.0	29.5	161 30.8	52.4	232 59.1	07.1	162 19.8	23.7
06		65 54.4	248 37.7	N 2 28.2	176 31.8	S24 52.6	248 01.1	N 2 06.9	177 22.2	S20 23.7
07		80 56.8	263 37.4	27.0	191 32.8	52.7	263 03.1	06.7	192 24.6	23.7
08		95 59.3	278 37.0	25.7	206 33.8	52.9	278 05.1	06.5	207 27.1	23.7
09		111 01.8	293 36.7	. . 24.4	221 34.8	. . 53.1	293 07.1	. . 06.3	222 29.5	. . 23.7
10		126 04.2	308 36.4	23.1	236 35.8	53.2	308 09.1	06.1	237 31.9	23.8
11		141 06.7	323 36.1	21.8	251 36.8	53.4	323 11.1	05.9	252 34.3	23.8
12		156 09.1	338 35.7	N 2 20.6	266 37.8	S24 53.6	338 13.1	N 2 05.7	267 36.7	S20 23.8
13		171 11.6	353 35.4	19.3	281 38.8	53.8	353 15.1	05.5	282 39.1	23.8
14		186 14.1	8 35.1	18.0	296 39.8	53.9	8 17.1	05.3	297 41.5	23.8
15		201 16.5	23 34.8	. . 16.7	311 40.8	. . 54.1	23 19.0	. . 05.0	312 43.9	. . 23.8
16		216 19.0	38 34.4	15.5	326 41.8	54.3	38 21.0	04.8	327 46.3	23.9
17		231 21.5	53 34.1	14.2	341 42.8	54.4	53 23.0	04.6	342 48.7	23.9
18		246 23.9	68 33.8	N 2 12.9	356 43.8	S24 54.6	68 25.0	N 2 04.4	357 51.1	S20 23.9
19		261 26.4	83 33.5	11.6	11 44.8	54.8	83 27.0	04.2	12 53.5	23.9
20		276 28.9	98 33.1	10.3	26 45.8	54.9	98 29.0	04.0	27 55.9	23.9
21		291 31.3	113 32.8	. . 09.1	41 46.8	. . 55.1	113 31.0	. . 03.8	42 58.3	. . 23.9
22		306 33.8	128 32.5	07.8	56 47.8	55.3	128 33.0	03.6	58 00.7	24.0
23		321 36.3	143 32.2	06.5	71 48.7	55.4	143 35.0	03.4	73 03.1	24.0
Mer. Pass.		h m 1 41.0	v −0.3	d 1.3	v 1.0	d 0.2	v 2.0	d 0.2	v 2.4	d 0.0

STARS

Name	SHA	Dec
	° ′	° ′
Acamar	315 16.6	S40 14.2
Achernar	335 24.9	S57 09.0
Acrux	173 07.3	S63 11.5
Adhara	255 11.1	S28 59.7
Aldebaran	290 46.9	N16 32.4
Alioth	166 19.3	N55 52.5
Alkaid	152 57.5	N49 14.2
Al Na'ir	27 40.6	S46 52.7
Alnilam	275 44.3	S 1 11.6
Alphard	217 54.3	S 8 43.8
Alphecca	126 09.2	N26 40.0
Alpheratz	357 40.9	N29 10.9
Altair	62 05.9	N 8 55.1
Ankaa	353 13.3	S42 12.8
Antares	112 23.6	S26 27.9
Arcturus	145 53.9	N19 06.1
Atria	107 23.2	S69 03.5
Avior	234 17.6	S59 33.7
Bellatrix	278 29.8	N 6 21.8
Betelgeuse	270 59.1	N 7 24.5
Canopus	263 55.5	S52 42.2
Capella	280 31.4	N46 00.5
Deneb	49 29.5	N45 20.7
Denebola	182 31.8	N14 28.9
Diphda	348 53.5	S17 53.6
Dubhe	193 49.9	N61 39.8
Elnath	278 10.0	N28 37.0
Eltanin	90 44.9	N51 29.7
Enif	33 44.7	N 9 57.3
Fomalhaut	15 21.3	S29 31.9
Gacrux	171 58.8	S57 12.4
Gienah	175 50.3	S17 38.0
Hadar	148 45.0	S60 27.2
Hamal	327 58.1	N23 32.3
Kaus Aust.	83 40.7	S34 22.4
Kochab	137 20.7	N74 05.7
Markab	13 35.8	N15 17.8
Menkar	314 12.7	N 4 09.2
Menkent	148 05.2	S36 27.0
Miaplacidus	221 40.0	S69 47.1
Mirfak	308 37.1	N49 54.9
Nunki	75 55.4	S26 16.3
Peacock	53 15.4	S56 40.8
Pollux	243 25.4	N27 59.0
Procyon	244 57.7	N 5 10.9
Rasalhague	96 04.3	N12 33.3
Regulus	207 41.6	N11 53.2
Rigel	281 10.1	S 8 11.0
Rigil Kent.	139 48.9	S60 54.2
Sabik	102 10.0	S15 44.5
Schedar	349 37.5	N56 37.6
Shaula	96 18.8	S37 06.8
Sirius	258 32.0	S16 44.3
Spica	158 29.2	S11 14.7
Suhail	222 51.2	S43 30.0
Vega	80 37.2	N38 48.4
Zuben'ubi	137 03.1	S16 06.5

	SHA	Mer. Pass.
	° ′	h m
Venus	184 07.1	13 25
Mars	111 21.0	18 15
Jupiter	182 21.0	13 30
Saturn	111 29.5	18 12

UT d h		SUN GHA ° ′	SUN Dec ° ′	MOON GHA ° ′	v ′	MOON Dec ° ′	d ′	HP ′
25 00		179 29.0	N10 40.9	274 32.3	7.5	N15 08.8	6.5	59.2
01		194 29.1	40.0	288 58.8	7.5	15 15.3	6.4	59.2
02		209 29.3	39.1	303 25.3	7.5	15 21.7	6.3	59.2
03		224 29.5	. . 38.3	317 51.8	7.4	15 28.0	6.2	59.1
04		239 29.7	37.4	332 18.2	7.5	15 34.2	6.1	59.1
05		254 29.8	36.5	346 44.7	7.4	15 40.3	6.0	59.1
06		269 30.0	N10 35.7	1 11.1	7.4	N15 46.3	5.9	59.1
07		284 30.2	34.8	15 37.5	7.4	15 52.2	5.7	59.1
08	T	299 30.4	33.9	30 03.9	7.3	15 57.9	5.7	59.1
09	H	314 30.5	. . 33.1	44 30.2	7.4	16 03.6	5.6	59.1
10	U	329 30.7	32.2	58 56.6	7.3	16 09.2	5.5	59.0
11	R	344 30.9	31.3	73 22.9	7.4	16 14.7	5.3	59.0
12	S	359 31.1	N10 30.5	87 49.3	7.3	N16 20.0	5.3	59.0
13	D	14 31.2	29.6	102 15.6	7.3	16 25.3	5.2	59.0
14	A	29 31.4	28.7	116 41.9	7.2	16 30.5	5.0	59.0
15	Y	44 31.6	. . 27.9	131 08.1	7.3	16 35.5	4.9	59.0
16		59 31.8	27.0	145 34.4	7.3	16 40.4	4.9	59.0
17		74 31.9	26.1	160 00.7	7.2	16 45.3	4.7	58.9
18		89 32.1	N10 25.3	174 26.9	7.2	N16 50.0	4.6	58.9
19		104 32.3	24.4	188 53.1	7.2	16 54.6	4.5	58.9
20		119 32.5	23.5	203 19.3	7.3	16 59.1	4.4	58.9
21		134 32.6	. . 22.7	217 45.6	7.2	17 03.5	4.3	58.9
22		149 32.8	21.8	232 11.8	7.2	17 07.8	4.2	58.9
23		164 33.0	20.9	246 38.0	7.1	17 12.0	4.1	58.8
26 00		179 33.2	N10 20.0	261 04.1	7.2	N17 16.1	3.9	58.8
01		194 33.3	19.2	275 30.3	7.2	17 20.0	3.9	58.8
02		209 33.5	18.3	289 56.5	7.1	17 23.9	3.7	58.8
03		224 33.7	. . 17.4	304 22.6	7.2	17 27.6	3.7	58.8
04		239 33.9	16.6	318 48.8	7.2	17 31.3	3.5	58.8
05		254 34.1	15.7	333 15.0	7.1	17 34.8	3.4	58.7
06		269 34.2	N10 14.8	347 41.1	7.2	N17 38.2	3.3	58.7
07		284 34.4	13.9	2 07.3	7.1	17 41.5	3.2	58.7
08		299 34.6	13.1	16 33.4	7.1	17 44.7	3.0	58.7
09	F	314 34.8	. . 12.2	30 59.5	7.2	17 47.7	3.0	58.7
10	R	329 34.9	11.3	45 25.7	7.1	17 50.7	2.8	58.7
11	I	344 35.1	10.4	59 51.8	7.2	17 53.5	2.7	58.6
12	D	359 35.3	N10 09.6	74 18.0	7.1	N17 56.2	2.6	58.6
13	A	14 35.5	08.7	88 44.1	7.2	17 58.8	2.5	58.6
14	Y	29 35.7	07.8	103 10.3	7.1	18 01.3	2.4	58.6
15		44 35.8	. . 07.0	117 36.4	7.2	18 03.7	2.3	58.6
16		59 36.0	06.1	132 02.6	7.1	18 06.0	2.1	58.6
17		74 36.2	05.2	146 28.7	7.2	18 08.1	2.1	58.5
18		89 36.4	N10 04.3	160 54.9	7.1	N18 10.2	1.9	58.5
19		104 36.6	03.5	175 21.0	7.2	18 12.1	1.8	58.5
20		119 36.7	02.6	189 47.2	7.2	18 13.9	1.7	58.5
21		134 36.9	. . 01.7	204 13.4	7.2	18 15.6	1.6	58.5
22		149 37.1	10 00.8	218 39.6	7.2	18 17.2	1.5	58.5
23		164 37.3	9 59.9	233 05.8	7.2	18 18.7	1.3	58.4
27 00		179 37.5	N 9 59.1	247 32.0	7.2	N18 20.0	1.2	58.4
01		194 37.6	58.2	261 58.2	7.3	18 21.2	1.2	58.4
02		209 37.8	57.3	276 24.5	7.2	18 22.4	1.0	58.4
03		224 38.0	. . 56.4	290 50.7	7.3	18 23.4	0.9	58.4
04		239 38.2	55.6	305 17.0	7.2	18 24.3	0.7	58.3
05		254 38.4	54.7	319 43.2	7.3	18 25.0	0.7	58.3
06		269 38.5	N 9 53.8	334 09.5	7.3	N18 25.7	0.6	58.3
07		284 38.7	52.9	348 35.8	7.4	18 26.3	0.4	58.3
08	S	299 38.9	52.0	3 02.2	7.3	18 26.7	0.3	58.3
09	A	314 39.1	. . 51.2	17 28.5	7.4	18 27.0	0.2	58.3
10	T	329 39.3	50.3	31 54.9	7.3	18 27.2	0.1	58.2
11	U	344 39.5	49.4	46 21.2	7.4	18 27.3	0.0	58.2
12	R	359 39.6	N 9 48.5	60 47.6	7.5	N18 27.3	0.2	58.2
13	D	14 39.8	47.6	75 14.1	7.4	18 27.1	0.2	58.2
14	A	29 40.0	46.8	89 40.5	7.5	18 26.9	0.4	58.2
15	Y	44 40.2	. . 45.9	104 07.0	7.5	18 26.5	0.4	58.1
16		59 40.4	45.0	118 33.5	7.5	18 26.1	0.6	58.1
17		74 40.6	44.1	133 00.0	7.5	18 25.5	0.7	58.1
18		89 40.7	N 9 43.2	147 26.5	7.6	N18 24.8	0.8	58.1
19		104 40.9	42.4	161 53.1	7.6	18 24.0	1.0	58.1
20		119 41.1	41.5	176 19.7	7.6	18 23.0	1.0	58.0
21		134 41.3	. . 40.6	190 46.3	7.6	18 22.0	1.1	58.0
22		149 41.5	39.7	205 12.9	7.7	18 20.9	1.3	58.0
23		164 41.7	38.8	219 39.6	7.7	N18 19.6	1.4	58.0
		SD 15.9	*d* 0.9	SD 16.1		16.0		15.9

Lat. °	Twilight Naut. h m	Twilight Civil h m	Sunrise h m	Moonrise 25 h m	Moonrise 26 h m	Moonrise 27 h m	Moonrise 28 h m
N 72	////	01 43	03 32	19 52	▭	▭	22 24
N 70	////	02 25	03 51	20 42	21 07	22 00	23 23
68	////	02 53	04 05	21 14	21 48	22 43	23 58
66	01 29	03 14	04 16	21 38	22 16	23 12	24 23
64	02 07	03 30	04 26	21 56	22 38	23 33	24 42
62	02 32	03 43	04 34	22 11	22 55	23 51	24 58
60	02 52	03 55	04 41	22 24	23 09	24 05	00 05
N 58	03 07	04 04	04 48	22 35	23 22	24 18	00 18
56	03 21	04 13	04 53	22 45	23 32	24 28	00 28
54	03 32	04 20	04 58	22 54	23 42	24 38	00 38
52	03 41	04 26	05 02	23 01	23 50	24 46	00 46
50	03 50	04 32	05 06	23 08	23 58	24 54	00 54
45	04 07	04 44	05 15	23 23	24 14	00 14	01 10
N 40	04 20	04 54	05 22	23 35	24 27	00 27	01 23
35	04 31	05 02	05 28	23 46	24 38	00 38	01 34
30	04 40	05 09	05 34	23 55	24 48	00 48	01 44
20	04 54	05 21	05 43	24 11	00 11	01 05	02 01
N 10	05 05	05 30	05 51	24 25	00 25	01 20	02 16
0	05 13	05 37	05 58	24 38	00 38	01 34	02 30
S 10	05 20	05 44	06 06	24 51	00 51	01 48	02 44
20	05 25	05 51	06 13	00 05	01 05	02 03	02 58
30	05 30	05 58	06 22	00 19	01 21	02 20	03 15
35	05 32	06 01	06 27	00 28	01 30	02 30	03 25
40	05 33	06 05	06 32	00 37	01 41	02 42	03 36
45	05 35	06 09	06 38	00 48	01 54	02 55	03 50
S 50	05 36	06 13	06 46	01 01	02 09	03 11	04 06
52	05 36	06 15	06 50	01 07	02 17	03 19	04 13
54	05 36	06 17	06 53	01 14	02 25	03 28	04 22
56	05 37	06 20	06 58	01 22	02 34	03 37	04 31
58	05 37	06 22	07 02	01 30	02 44	03 48	04 42
S 60	05 37	06 25	07 07	01 40	02 56	04 01	04 54

Lat. °	Sunset h m	Twilight Civil h m	Twilight Naut. h m	Moonset 25 h m	Moonset 26 h m	Moonset 27 h m	Moonset 28 h m
N 72	20 27	22 11	////	16 45	▭	▭	20 03
N 70	20 09	21 32	////	15 56	17 28	18 32	19 03
68	19 56	21 06	23 53	15 25	16 47	17 49	18 28
66	19 45	20 46	22 27	15 02	16 19	17 20	18 03
64	19 35	20 30	21 52	14 43	15 58	16 58	17 43
62	19 27	20 18	21 27	14 29	15 41	16 41	17 27
60	19 20	20 07	21 09	14 16	15 27	16 26	17 14
N 58	19 14	19 57	20 53	14 05	15 15	16 14	17 02
56	19 09	19 49	20 41	13 56	15 04	16 03	16 52
54	19 04	19 42	20 30	13 48	14 55	15 54	16 43
52	19 00	19 36	20 20	13 40	14 47	15 45	16 35
50	18 56	19 30	20 12	13 34	14 39	15 38	16 28
45	18 47	19 18	19 55	13 19	14 23	15 21	16 13
N 40	18 40	19 08	19 42	13 08	14 10	15 08	16 00
35	18 34	19 00	19 31	12 58	13 59	14 57	15 49
30	18 29	18 54	19 23	12 49	13 49	14 47	15 40
20	18 20	18 42	19 09	12 34	13 33	14 30	15 24
N 10	18 12	18 34	18 58	12 21	13 18	14 15	15 09
0	18 05	18 26	18 50	12 08	13 05	14 01	14 56
S 10	17 58	18 19	18 44	11 56	12 51	13 47	14 42
20	17 50	18 13	18 38	11 43	12 36	13 32	14 28
30	17 42	18 06	18 34	11 28	12 20	13 14	14 11
35	17 37	18 03	18 32	11 19	12 10	13 04	14 02
40	17 32	17 59	18 31	11 09	11 59	12 53	13 51
45	17 25	17 55	18 29	10 58	11 46	12 39	13 38
S 50	17 18	17 51	18 28	10 44	11 30	12 23	13 22
52	17 15	17 49	18 28	10 37	11 23	12 15	13 14
54	17 11	17 47	18 28	10 30	11 14	12 07	13 06
56	17 07	17 45	18 28	10 22	11 05	11 57	12 57
58	17 02	17 42	18 28	10 13	10 55	11 46	12 46
S 60	16 57	17 40	18 28	10 02	10 43	11 33	12 34

Day d	SUN Eqn. of Time 00^h m s	SUN Eqn. of Time 12^h m s	SUN Mer. Pass. h m	MOON Mer. Pass. Upper h m	MOON Mer. Pass. Lower h m	MOON Age d	MOON Phase %
25	02 04	01 56	12 02	05 55	18 23	23	46
26	01 48	01 39	12 02	06 51	19 19	24	35
27	01 31	01 22	12 01	07 47	20 15	25	25

UT		ARIES	VENUS −3·8		MARS −0·3		JUPITER −1·7		SATURN +0·5	
		GHA	GHA	Dec	GHA	Dec	GHA	Dec	GHA	Dec
d	h	° ′	° ′	° ′	° ′	° ′	° ′	° ′	° ′	° ′
28	00	336 38.7	158 31.8	N 2 05.2	86 49.7	S24 55.6	158 37.0	N 2 03.2	88 05.5	S20 24.0
	01	351 41.2	173 31.5	03.9	101 50.7	55.8	173 38.9	03.0	103 07.9	24.0
	02	6 43.6	188 31.2	02.7	116 51.7	55.9	188 40.9	02.8	118 10.3	24.0
	03	21 46.1	203 30.9	. . 01.4	131 52.7	. . 56.1	203 42.9	. . 02.6	133 12.7	. . 24.1
	04	36 48.6	218 30.6	2 00.1	146 53.7	56.3	218 44.9	02.3	148 15.1	24.1
	05	51 51.0	233 30.2	1 58.8	161 54.7	56.4	233 46.9	02.1	163 17.6	24.1
	06	66 53.5	248 29.9	N 1 57.5	176 55.7	S24 56.6	248 48.9	N 2 01.9	178 20.0	S20 24.1
	07	81 56.0	263 29.6	56.3	191 56.7	56.8	263 50.9	01.7	193 22.4	24.1
	08	96 58.4	278 29.3	55.0	206 57.6	56.9	278 52.9	01.5	208 24.8	24.1
S	09	112 00.9	293 28.9	. . 53.7	221 58.6	. . 57.1	293 54.9	. . 01.3	223 27.2	. . 24.2
U	10	127 03.4	308 28.6	52.4	236 59.6	57.3	308 56.8	01.1	238 29.6	24.2
N	11	142 05.8	323 28.3	51.1	252 00.6	57.4	323 58.8	00.9	253 32.0	24.2
D	12	157 08.3	338 28.0	N 1 49.9	267 01.6	S24 57.6	339 00.8	N 2 00.7	268 34.4	S20 24.2
A	13	172 10.8	353 27.7	48.6	282 02.6	57.7	354 02.8	00.5	283 36.8	24.2
Y	14	187 13.2	8 27.3	47.3	297 03.6	57.9	9 04.8	00.3	298 39.2	24.2
	15	202 15.7	23 27.0	. . 46.0	312 04.5	. . 58.1	24 06.8	2 00.1	313 41.6	. . 24.3
	16	217 18.1	38 26.7	44.7	327 05.5	58.2	39 08.8	1 59.9	328 44.0	24.3
	17	232 20.6	53 26.4	43.5	342 06.5	58.4	54 10.8	59.6	343 46.4	24.3
	18	247 23.1	68 26.0	N 1 42.2	357 07.5	S24 58.6	69 12.8	N 1 59.4	358 48.8	S20 24.3
	19	262 25.5	83 25.7	40.9	12 08.5	58.7	84 14.7	59.2	13 51.2	24.3
	20	277 28.0	98 25.4	39.6	27 09.4	58.9	99 16.7	59.0	28 53.6	24.4
	21	292 30.5	113 25.1	. . 38.3	42 10.4	. . 59.1	114 18.7	. . 58.8	43 56.0	. . 24.4
	22	307 32.9	128 24.8	37.0	57 11.4	59.2	129 20.7	58.6	58 58.4	24.4
	23	322 35.4	143 24.4	35.8	72 12.4	59.4	144 22.7	58.4	74 00.8	24.4
29	00	337 37.9	158 24.1	N 1 34.5	87 13.4	S24 59.5	159 24.7	N 1 58.2	89 03.2	S20 24.4
	01	352 40.3	173 23.8	33.2	102 14.3	59.7	174 26.7	58.0	104 05.6	24.4
	02	7 42.8	188 23.5	31.9	117 15.3	24 59.9	189 28.7	57.8	119 08.0	24.5
	03	22 45.2	203 23.2	. . 30.6	132 16.3	25 00.0	204 30.6	. . 57.6	134 10.4	. . 24.5
	04	37 47.7	218 22.8	29.3	147 17.3	00.2	219 32.6	57.4	149 12.8	24.5
	05	52 50.2	233 22.5	28.1	162 18.2	00.4	234 34.6	57.1	164 15.2	24.5
	06	67 52.6	248 22.2	N 1 26.8	177 19.2	S25 00.5	249 36.6	N 1 56.9	179 17.6	S20 24.5
	07	82 55.1	263 21.9	25.5	192 20.2	00.7	264 38.6	56.7	194 20.0	24.6
	08	97 57.6	278 21.6	24.2	207 21.1	00.8	279 40.6	56.5	209 22.4	24.6
M	09	113 00.0	293 21.2	. . 22.9	222 22.1	. . 01.0	294 42.6	. . 56.3	224 24.8	. . 24.6
O	10	128 02.5	308 20.9	21.7	237 23.1	01.2	309 44.6	56.1	239 27.2	24.6
N	11	143 05.0	323 20.6	20.4	252 24.1	01.3	324 46.5	55.9	254 29.6	24.6
D	12	158 07.4	338 20.3	N 1 19.1	267 25.0	S25 01.5	339 48.5	N 1 55.7	269 32.0	S20 24.6
A	13	173 09.9	353 20.0	17.8	282 26.0	01.6	354 50.5	55.5	284 34.4	24.7
Y	14	188 12.4	8 19.6	16.5	297 27.0	01.8	9 52.5	55.3	299 36.7	24.7
	15	203 14.8	23 19.3	. . 15.2	312 27.9	. . 02.0	24 54.5	. . 55.1	314 39.1	. . 24.7
	16	218 17.3	38 19.0	14.0	327 28.9	02.1	39 56.5	54.9	329 41.5	24.7
	17	233 19.7	53 18.7	12.7	342 29.9	02.3	54 58.5	54.6	344 43.9	24.7
	18	248 22.2	68 18.4	N 1 11.4	357 30.8	S25 02.4	70 00.5	N 1 54.4	359 46.3	S20 24.8
	19	263 24.7	83 18.0	10.1	12 31.8	02.6	85 02.4	54.2	14 48.7	24.8
	20	278 27.1	98 17.7	08.8	27 32.8	02.8	100 04.4	54.0	29 51.1	24.8
	21	293 29.6	113 17.4	. . 07.5	42 33.7	. . 02.9	115 06.4	. . 53.8	44 53.5	. . 24.8
	22	308 32.1	128 17.1	06.2	57 34.7	03.1	130 08.4	53.6	59 55.9	24.8
	23	323 34.5	143 16.8	05.0	72 35.6	03.2	145 10.4	53.4	74 58.3	24.8
30	00	338 37.0	158 16.4	N 1 03.7	87 36.6	S25 03.4	160 12.4	N 1 53.2	90 00.7	S20 24.9
	01	353 39.5	173 16.1	02.4	102 37.6	03.5	175 14.4	53.0	105 03.1	24.9
	02	8 41.9	188 15.8	1 01.1	117 38.5	03.7	190 16.4	52.8	120 05.5	24.9
	03	23 44.4	203 15.5	0 59.8	132 39.5	. . 03.9	205 18.3	. . 52.6	135 07.9	. . 24.9
	04	38 46.9	218 15.2	58.5	147 40.4	04.0	220 20.3	52.4	150 10.3	24.9
	05	53 49.3	233 14.8	57.3	162 41.4	04.2	235 22.3	52.1	165 12.7	25.0
	06	68 51.8	248 14.5	N 0 56.0	177 42.4	S25 04.3	250 24.3	N 1 51.9	180 15.1	S20 25.0
	07	83 54.2	263 14.2	54.7	192 43.3	04.5	265 26.3	51.7	195 17.5	25.0
T	08	98 56.7	278 13.9	53.4	207 44.3	04.7	280 28.3	51.5	210 19.9	25.0
U	09	113 59.2	293 13.6	. . 52.1	222 45.2	. . 04.8	295 30.3	. . 51.3	225 22.3	. . 25.0
E	10	129 01.6	308 13.3	50.8	237 46.2	05.0	310 32.2	51.1	240 24.7	25.1
S	11	144 04.1	323 12.9	49.5	252 47.1	05.1	325 34.2	50.9	255 27.0	25.1
D	12	159 06.6	338 12.6	N 0 48.3	267 48.1	S25 05.3	340 36.2	N 1 50.7	270 29.4	S20 25.1
A	13	174 09.0	353 12.3	47.0	282 49.1	05.4	355 38.2	50.5	285 31.8	25.1
Y	14	189 11.5	8 12.0	45.7	297 50.0	05.6	10 40.2	50.3	300 34.2	25.1
	15	204 14.0	23 11.7	. . 44.4	312 51.0	. . 05.7	25 42.2	. . 50.1	315 36.6	. . 25.1
	16	219 16.4	38 11.3	43.1	327 51.9	05.9	40 44.2	49.8	330 39.0	25.2
	17	234 18.9	53 11.0	41.8	342 52.9	06.1	55 46.1	49.6	345 41.4	25.2
	18	249 21.3	68 10.7	N 0 40.5	357 53.8	S25 06.2	70 48.1	N 1 49.4	0 43.8	S20 25.2
	19	264 23.8	83 10.4	39.3	12 54.8	06.4	85 50.1	49.2	15 46.2	25.2
	20	279 26.3	98 10.1	38.0	27 55.7	06.5	100 52.1	49.0	30 48.6	25.2
	21	294 28.7	113 09.8	. . 36.7	42 56.7	. . 06.7	115 54.1	. . 48.8	45 51.0	. . 25.3
	22	309 31.2	128 09.4	35.4	57 57.6	06.8	130 56.1	48.6	60 53.4	25.3
	23	324 33.7	143 09.1	34.1	72 58.6	07.0	145 58.1	48.4	75 55.8	25.3
Mer. Pass.		h m 1 29.2	*v* −0.3	*d* 1.3	*v* 1.0	*d* 0.2	*v* 2.0	*d* 0.2	*v* 2.4	*d* 0.0

STARS

Name	SHA	Dec
	° ′	° ′
Acamar	315 16.6	S40 14.1
Achernar	335 24.9	S57 09.0
Acrux	173 07.3	S63 11.5
Adhara	255 11.0	S28 59.6
Aldebaran	290 46.9	N16 32.4
Alioth	166 19.3	N55 52.5
Alkaid	152 57.6	N49 14.2
Al Na'ir	27 40.6	S46 52.7
Alnilam	275 44.3	S 1 11.6
Alphard	217 54.3	S 8 43.8
Alphecca	126 09.3	N26 39.9
Alpheratz	357 40.9	N29 10.9
Altair	62 05.9	N 8 55.1
Ankaa	353 13.3	S42 12.8
Antares	112 23.6	S26 27.9
Arcturus	145 54.0	N19 06.1
Atria	107 23.3	S69 03.5
Avior	234 17.6	S59 33.7
Bellatrix	278 29.8	N 6 21.8
Betelgeuse	270 59.1	N 7 24.5
Canopus	263 55.4	S52 42.2
Capella	280 31.3	N46 00.5
Deneb	49 29.5	N45 20.7
Denebola	182 31.8	N14 28.9
Diphda	348 53.5	S17 53.6
Dubhe	193 49.8	N61 39.8
Elnath	278 10.0	N28 37.0
Eltanin	90 44.9	N51 29.7
Enif	33 44.7	N 9 57.3
Fomalhaut	15 21.3	S29 31.9
Gacrux	171 58.8	S57 12.4
Gienah	175 50.3	S17 37.9
Hadar	148 45.0	S60 27.2
Hamal	327 58.1	N23 32.3
Kaus Aust.	83 40.7	S34 22.4
Kochab	137 20.7	N74 05.7
Markab	13 35.8	N15 17.8
Menkar	314 12.7	N 4 09.2
Menkent	148 05.2	S36 27.0
Miaplacidus	221 40.0	S69 47.1
Mirfak	308 37.1	N49 54.9
Nunki	75 55.4	S26 16.3
Peacock	53 15.4	S56 40.8
Pollux	243 25.4	N27 59.0
Procyon	244 57.7	N 5 10.9
Rasalhague	96 04.3	N12 33.3
Regulus	207 41.6	N11 53.2
Rigel	281 10.0	S 8 11.0
Rigil Kent.	139 49.0	S60 54.2
Sabik	102 10.0	S15 44.5
Schedar	349 37.4	N56 37.6
Shaula	96 18.8	S37 06.8
Sirius	258 32.0	S16 44.3
Spica	158 29.2	S11 14.7
Suhail	222 51.2	S43 29.9
Vega	80 37.3	N38 48.4
Zuben'ubi	137 03.1	S16 06.5

	SHA	Mer. Pass.
	° ′	h m
Venus	180 46.3	13 27
Mars	109 35.5	18 10
Jupiter	181 46.8	13 21
Saturn	111 25.3	18 01

	UT (d h)	SUN GHA ° ′	SUN Dec ° ′	MOON GHA ° ′	v ′	MOON Dec ° ′	d ′	HP ′
	28 00	179 41.8	N 9 37.9	234 06.3	7.7	N18 18.2	1.4	58.0
	01	194 42.0	37.1	248 33.0	7.8	18 16.8	1.6	58.0
	02	209 42.2	36.2	262 59.8	7.8	18 15.2	1.7	57.9
	03	224 42.4	. . 35.3	277 26.6	7.8	18 13.5	1.8	57.9
	04	239 42.6	34.4	291 53.4	7.9	18 11.7	1.9	57.9
	05	254 42.8	33.5	306 20.3	7.9	18 09.8	2.0	57.9
	06	269 42.9	N 9 32.6	320 47.2	8.0	N18 07.8	2.2	57.9
	07	284 43.1	31.7	335 14.2	7.9	18 05.6	2.2	57.8
	08	299 43.3	30.9	349 41.1	8.0	18 03.4	2.3	57.8
S	09	314 43.5	. . 30.0	4 08.1	8.1	18 01.1	2.5	57.8
U	10	329 43.7	29.1	18 35.2	8.1	17 58.6	2.5	57.8
N	11	344 43.9	28.2	33 02.3	8.1	17 56.1	2.7	57.8
D	12	359 44.1	N 9 27.3	47 29.4	8.2	N17 53.4	2.8	57.7
A	13	14 44.2	26.4	61 56.6	8.2	17 50.6	2.8	57.7
Y	14	29 44.4	25.5	76 23.8	8.2	17 47.8	3.0	57.7
	15	44 44.6	. . 24.6	90 51.0	8.3	17 44.8	3.1	57.7
	16	59 44.8	23.8	105 18.3	8.3	17 41.7	3.1	57.7
	17	74 45.0	22.9	119 45.6	8.4	17 38.6	3.3	57.6
	18	89 45.2	N 9 22.0	134 13.0	8.4	N17 35.3	3.4	57.6
	19	104 45.4	21.1	148 40.4	8.4	17 31.9	3.5	57.6
	20	119 45.6	20.2	163 07.8	8.5	17 28.4	3.5	57.6
	21	134 45.7	. . 19.3	177 35.3	8.6	17 24.9	3.7	57.6
	22	149 45.9	18.4	192 02.9	8.6	17 21.2	3.8	57.5
	23	164 46.1	17.5	206 30.5	8.6	17 17.4	3.9	57.5
	29 00	179 46.3	N 9 16.6	220 58.1	8.7	N17 13.5	3.9	57.5
	01	194 46.5	15.8	235 25.8	8.7	17 09.6	4.1	57.5
	02	209 46.7	14.9	249 53.5	8.8	17 05.5	4.2	57.5
	03	224 46.9	. . 14.0	264 21.3	8.8	17 01.3	4.2	57.4
	04	239 47.1	13.1	278 49.1	8.9	16 57.1	4.4	57.4
	05	254 47.2	12.2	293 17.0	8.9	16 52.7	4.4	57.4
	06	269 47.4	N 9 11.3	307 44.9	9.0	N16 48.3	4.5	57.4
	07	284 47.6	10.4	322 12.9	9.0	16 43.8	4.7	57.4
	08	299 47.8	09.5	336 40.9	9.0	16 39.1	4.7	57.3
M	09	314 48.0	. . 08.6	351 08.9	9.2	16 34.4	4.8	57.3
O	10	329 48.2	07.7	5 37.1	9.1	16 29.6	4.9	57.3
N	11	344 48.4	06.8	20 05.2	9.3	16 24.7	5.0	57.3
D	12	359 48.6	N 9 05.9	34 33.5	9.2	N16 19.7	5.1	57.3
A	13	14 48.8	05.1	49 01.7	9.3	16 14.6	5.2	57.2
Y	14	29 48.9	04.2	63 30.0	9.4	16 09.4	5.2	57.2
	15	44 49.1	. . 03.3	77 58.4	9.4	16 04.2	5.4	57.2
	16	59 49.3	02.4	92 26.8	9.5	15 58.8	5.4	57.2
	17	74 49.5	01.5	106 55.3	9.6	15 53.4	5.5	57.2
	18	89 49.7	N 9 00.6	121 23.9	9.5	N15 47.9	5.6	57.1
	19	104 49.9	8 59.7	135 52.4	9.7	15 42.3	5.7	57.1
	20	119 50.1	58.8	150 21.1	9.7	15 36.6	5.7	57.1
	21	134 50.3	. . 57.9	164 49.8	9.7	15 30.9	5.9	57.1
	22	149 50.5	57.0	179 18.5	9.8	15 25.0	5.9	57.1
	23	164 50.7	56.1	193 47.3	9.9	15 19.1	6.0	57.0
	30 00	179 50.9	N 8 55.2	208 16.2	9.9	N15 13.1	6.1	57.0
	01	194 51.0	54.3	222 45.1	9.9	15 07.0	6.1	57.0
	02	209 51.2	53.4	237 14.0	10.1	15 00.9	6.3	57.0
	03	224 51.4	. . 52.5	251 43.1	10.0	14 54.6	6.3	56.9
	04	239 51.6	51.6	266 12.1	10.2	14 48.3	6.4	56.9
	05	254 51.8	50.7	280 41.3	10.1	14 41.9	6.5	56.9
	06	269 52.0	N 8 49.8	295 10.4	10.3	N14 35.4	6.5	56.9
	07	284 52.2	48.9	309 39.7	10.3	14 28.9	6.6	56.9
T	08	299 52.4	48.0	324 09.0	10.3	14 22.3	6.7	56.8
U	09	314 52.6	. . 47.1	338 38.3	10.4	14 15.6	6.7	56.8
E	10	329 52.8	46.2	353 07.7	10.5	14 08.9	6.9	56.8
S	11	344 53.0	45.3	7 37.2	10.5	14 02.0	6.9	56.8
D	12	359 53.2	N 8 44.4	22 06.7	10.6	N13 55.1	6.9	56.8
	13	14 53.4	43.5	36 36.3	10.6	13 48.2	7.1	56.7
A	14	29 53.5	42.6	51 05.9	10.7	13 41.1	7.1	56.7
Y	15	44 53.7	. . 41.7	65 35.6	10.7	13 34.0	7.1	56.7
	16	59 53.9	40.8	80 05.3	10.8	13 26.9	7.3	56.7
	17	74 54.1	39.9	94 35.1	10.9	13 19.6	7.3	56.7
	18	89 54.3	N 8 39.0	109 05.0	10.9	N13 12.3	7.3	56.6
	19	104 54.5	38.1	123 34.9	10.9	13 05.0	7.4	56.6
	20	119 54.7	37.2	138 04.8	11.0	12 57.6	7.5	56.6
	21	134 54.9	. . 36.3	152 34.8	11.1	12 50.1	7.6	56.6
	22	149 55.1	35.4	167 04.9	11.1	12 42.5	7.6	56.5
	23	164 55.3	34.5	181 35.0	11.2	N12 34.9	7.6	56.5
		SD 15.9	d 0.9	SD	15.7		15.6	15.5

Lat. °	Twilight Naut. h m	Twilight Civil h m	Sunrise h m	Moonrise 28 h m	Moonrise 29 h m	Moonrise 30 h m	Moonrise 31 h m
N 72	////	02 11	03 48	22 24	24 24	00 24	02 16
N 70	////	02 44	04 04	23 23	25 00	01 00	02 38
68	01 01	03 08	04 16	23 58	25 24	01 24	02 55
66	01 53	03 26	04 26	24 23	00 23	01 44	03 09
64	02 23	03 41	04 35	24 42	00 42	01 59	03 20
62	02 45	03 53	04 42	24 58	00 58	02 12	03 29
60	03 02	04 03	04 49	00 05	01 11	02 23	03 38
N 58	03 16	04 11	04 54	00 18	01 22	02 32	03 45
56	03 28	04 19	04 59	00 28	01 32	02 40	03 51
54	03 39	04 26	05 03	00 38	01 40	02 48	03 57
52	03 47	04 32	05 07	00 46	01 48	02 54	04 02
50	03 55	04 37	05 11	00 54	01 55	03 00	04 06
45	04 11	04 48	05 19	01 10	02 10	03 13	04 16
N 40	04 24	04 57	05 25	01 23	02 22	03 23	04 24
35	04 34	05 05	05 31	01 34	02 33	03 32	04 31
30	04 42	05 11	05 35	01 44	02 42	03 40	04 38
20	04 55	05 21	05 44	02 01	02 57	03 53	04 48
N 10	05 05	05 30	05 51	02 16	03 11	04 05	04 57
0	05 12	05 37	05 57	02 30	03 24	04 16	05 06
S 10	05 18	05 43	06 04	02 44	03 37	04 27	05 15
20	05 23	05 49	06 11	02 58	03 50	04 39	05 24
30	05 26	05 54	06 18	03 15	04 06	04 52	05 35
35	05 28	05 57	06 23	03 25	04 15	05 00	05 41
40	05 29	06 00	06 28	03 36	04 26	05 09	05 48
45	05 30	06 04	06 33	03 50	04 38	05 19	05 56
S 50	05 30	06 07	06 40	04 06	04 52	05 32	06 05
52	05 30	06 09	06 43	04 13	04 59	05 37	06 10
54	05 30	06 11	06 46	04 22	05 07	05 44	06 15
56	05 29	06 12	06 50	04 31	05 15	05 51	06 20
58	05 29	06 14	06 54	04 42	05 25	05 59	06 26
S 60	05 28	06 16	06 59	04 54	05 36	06 08	06 33

Lat. °	Sunset h m	Twilight Civil h m	Twilight Naut. h m	Moonset 28 h m	Moonset 29 h m	Moonset 30 h m	Moonset 31 h m
N 72	20 10	21 44	////	20 03	19 53	19 46	19 40
N 70	19 55	21 12	////	19 03	19 17	19 23	19 25
68	19 43	20 50	22 49	18 28	18 51	19 05	19 13
66	19 33	20 32	22 03	18 03	18 31	18 50	19 03
64	19 25	20 18	21 34	17 43	18 15	18 38	18 55
62	19 17	20 07	21 13	17 27	18 02	18 28	18 48
60	19 11	19 57	20 57	17 14	17 50	18 19	18 42
N 58	19 06	19 48	20 43	17 02	17 41	18 11	18 36
56	19 01	19 41	20 31	16 52	17 32	18 04	18 31
54	18 57	19 34	20 21	16 43	17 24	17 58	18 27
52	18 53	19 29	20 13	16 35	17 17	17 53	18 23
50	18 50	19 23	20 05	16 28	17 11	17 48	18 19
45	18 42	19 12	19 49	16 13	16 58	17 37	18 11
N 40	18 36	19 04	19 37	16 00	16 46	17 28	18 04
35	18 30	18 56	19 27	15 49	16 37	17 20	17 59
30	18 26	18 50	19 19	15 40	16 29	17 13	17 54
20	18 18	18 40	19 06	15 24	16 14	17 01	17 45
N 10	18 11	18 32	18 57	15 09	16 01	16 50	17 37
0	18 04	18 25	18 49	14 56	15 49	16 41	17 29
S 10	17 58	18 19	18 44	14 42	15 37	16 31	17 22
20	17 51	18 13	18 39	14 28	15 24	16 20	17 14
30	17 44	18 08	18 36	14 11	15 10	16 08	17 05
35	17 39	18 05	18 34	14 02	15 01	16 00	17 00
40	17 35	18 02	18 33	13 51	14 51	15 52	16 53
45	17 29	17 59	18 33	13 38	14 39	15 43	16 46
S 50	17 22	17 55	18 33	13 22	14 25	15 31	16 38
52	17 19	17 54	18 33	13 14	14 19	15 26	16 34
54	17 16	17 52	18 33	13 06	14 12	15 20	16 30
56	17 12	17 50	18 33	12 57	14 03	15 13	16 25
58	17 08	17 48	18 34	12 46	13 54	15 06	16 19
S 60	17 04	17 46	18 34	12 34	13 43	14 58	16 13

Day	SUN Eqn. of Time 00^h	SUN Eqn. of Time 12^h	SUN Mer. Pass.	MOON Mer. Pass. Upper	MOON Mer. Pass. Lower	MOON Age	MOON Phase
d	m s	m s	h m	h m	h m	d %	
28	01 13	01 04	12 01	08 43	21 10	26 16	
29	00 55	00 46	12 01	09 37	22 03	27 9	
30	00 37	00 28	12 00	10 28	22 53	28 4	

UT	ARIES	VENUS −3·8		MARS −0·3		JUPITER −1·7		SATURN +0·5	
	GHA	GHA	Dec	GHA	Dec	GHA	Dec	GHA	Dec
d h	° ′	° ′	° ′	° ′	° ′	° ′	° ′	° ′	° ′
31 00	339 36.1	158 08.8	N 0 32.8	87 59.5	S25 07.1	161 00.0	N 1 48.2	90 58.1	S20 25.3
01	354 38.6	173 08.5	31.5	103 00.5	07.3	176 02.0	48.0	106 00.5	25.3
02	9 41.1	188 08.2	30.3	118 01.4	07.4	191 04.0	47.8	121 02.9	25.4
03	24 43.5	203 07.9	. . 29.0	133 02.3	. . 07.6	206 06.0	. . 47.5	136 05.3	. . 25.4
04	39 46.0	218 07.5	27.7	148 03.3	07.7	221 08.0	47.3	151 07.7	25.4
05	54 48.5	233 07.2	26.4	163 04.2	07.9	236 10.0	47.1	166 10.1	25.4
06	69 50.9	248 06.9	N 0 25.1	178 05.2	S25 08.1	251 12.0	N 1 46.9	181 12.5	S20 25.4
W 07	84 53.4	263 06.6	23.8	193 06.1	08.2	266 13.9	46.7	196 14.9	25.5
E 08	99 55.8	278 06.3	22.5	208 07.1	08.4	281 15.9	46.5	211 17.3	25.5
D 09	114 58.3	293 06.0	. . 21.3	223 08.0	. . 08.5	296 17.9	. . 46.3	226 19.7	. . 25.5
N 10	130 00.8	308 05.6	20.0	238 08.9	08.7	311 19.9	46.1	241 22.0	25.5
E 11	145 03.2	323 05.3	18.7	253 09.9	08.8	326 21.9	45.9	256 24.4	25.5
S 12	160 05.7	338 05.0	N 0 17.4	268 10.8	S25 09.0	341 23.9	N 1 45.7	271 26.8	S20 25.5
D 13	175 08.2	353 04.7	16.1	283 11.8	09.1	356 25.8	45.5	286 29.2	25.6
A 14	190 10.6	8 04.4	14.8	298 12.7	09.3	11 27.8	45.2	301 31.6	25.6
Y 15	205 13.1	23 04.1	. . 13.5	313 13.6	. . 09.4	26 29.8	. . 45.0	316 34.0	. . 25.6
16	220 15.6	38 03.7	12.2	328 14.6	09.6	41 31.8	44.8	331 36.4	25.6
17	235 18.0	53 03.4	11.0	343 15.5	09.7	56 33.8	44.6	346 38.8	25.6
18	250 20.5	68 03.1	N 0 09.7	358 16.5	S25 09.9	71 35.8	N 1 44.4	1 41.2	S20 25.7
19	265 23.0	83 02.8	08.4	13 17.4	10.0	86 37.8	44.2	16 43.5	25.7
20	280 25.4	98 02.5	07.1	28 18.3	10.2	101 39.7	44.0	31 45.9	25.7
21	295 27.9	113 02.2	. . 05.8	43 19.3	. . 10.3	116 41.7	. . 43.8	46 48.3	. . 25.7
22	310 30.3	128 01.8	04.5	58 20.2	10.5	131 43.7	43.6	61 50.7	25.7
23	325 32.8	143 01.5	03.2	73 21.1	10.6	146 45.7	43.4	76 53.1	25.8
1 00	340 35.3	158 01.2	N 0 01.9	88 22.1	S25 10.8	161 47.7	N 1 43.1	91 55.5	S20 25.8
01	355 37.7	173 00.9	N 00.7	103 23.0	10.9	176 49.7	42.9	106 57.9	25.8
02	10 40.2	188 00.6	S 00.6	118 23.9	11.1	191 51.6	42.7	122 00.3	25.8
03	25 42.7	203 00.3	. . 01.9	133 24.8	. . 11.2	206 53.6	. . 42.5	137 02.6	. . 25.8
04	40 45.1	217 59.9	03.2	148 25.8	11.4	221 55.6	42.3	152 05.0	25.9
05	55 47.6	232 59.6	04.5	163 26.7	11.5	236 57.6	42.1	167 07.4	25.9
06	70 50.1	247 59.3	S 0 05.8	178 27.6	S25 11.7	251 59.6	N 1 41.9	182 09.8	S20 25.9
07	85 52.5	262 59.0	07.1	193 28.6	11.8	267 01.6	41.7	197 12.2	25.9
T 08	100 55.0	277 58.7	08.4	208 29.5	12.0	282 03.5	41.5	212 14.6	25.9
H 09	115 57.4	292 58.4	. . 09.6	223 30.4	. . 12.1	297 05.5	. . 41.3	227 17.0	. . 26.0
U 10	130 59.9	307 58.0	10.9	238 31.3	12.2	312 07.5	41.1	242 19.3	26.0
R 11	146 02.4	322 57.7	12.2	253 32.3	12.4	327 09.5	40.8	257 21.7	26.0
S 12	161 04.8	337 57.4	S 0 13.5	268 33.2	S25 12.5	342 11.5	N 1 40.6	272 24.1	S20 26.0
D 13	176 07.3	352 57.1	14.8	283 34.1	12.7	357 13.5	40.4	287 26.5	26.0
A 14	191 09.8	7 56.8	16.1	298 35.1	12.8	12 15.4	40.2	302 28.9	26.1
Y 15	206 12.2	22 56.5	. . 17.4	313 36.0	. . 13.0	27 17.4	. . 40.0	317 31.3	. . 26.1
16	221 14.7	37 56.1	18.7	328 36.9	13.1	42 19.4	39.8	332 33.6	26.1
17	236 17.2	52 55.8	19.9	343 37.8	13.3	57 21.4	39.6	347 36.0	26.1
18	251 19.6	67 55.5	S 0 21.2	358 38.7	S25 13.4	72 23.4	N 1 39.4	2 38.4	S20 26.1
19	266 22.1	82 55.2	22.5	13 39.7	13.6	87 25.4	39.2	17 40.8	26.2
20	281 24.6	97 54.9	23.8	28 40.6	13.7	102 27.3	39.0	32 43.2	26.2
21	296 27.0	112 54.6	. . 25.1	43 41.5	. . 13.8	117 29.3	. . 38.7	47 45.6	. . 26.2
22	311 29.5	127 54.2	26.4	58 42.4	14.0	132 31.3	38.5	62 47.9	26.2
23	326 31.9	142 53.9	27.7	73 43.3	14.1	147 33.3	38.3	77 50.3	26.2
2 00	341 34.4	157 53.6	S 0 29.0	88 44.3	S25 14.3	162 35.3	N 1 38.1	92 52.7	S20 26.3
01	356 36.9	172 53.3	30.3	103 45.2	14.4	177 37.3	37.9	107 55.1	26.3
02	11 39.3	187 53.0	31.5	118 46.1	14.6	192 39.2	37.7	122 57.5	26.3
03	26 41.8	202 52.7	. . 32.8	133 47.0	. . 14.7	207 41.2	. . 37.5	137 59.9	. . 26.3
04	41 44.3	217 52.4	34.1	148 47.9	14.9	222 43.2	37.3	153 02.2	26.3
05	56 46.7	232 52.0	35.4	163 48.8	15.0	237 45.2	37.1	168 04.6	26.4
06	71 49.2	247 51.7	S 0 36.7	178 49.8	S25 15.1	252 47.2	N 1 36.9	183 07.0	S20 26.4
07	86 51.7	262 51.4	38.0	193 50.7	15.3	267 49.2	36.6	198 09.4	26.4
08	101 54.1	277 51.1	39.3	208 51.6	15.4	282 51.1	36.4	213 11.8	26.4
F 09	116 56.6	292 50.8	. . 40.6	223 52.5	. . 15.6	297 53.1	. . 36.2	228 14.2	. . 26.4
R 10	131 59.0	307 50.5	41.9	238 53.4	15.7	312 55.1	36.0	243 16.5	26.5
I 11	147 01.5	322 50.1	43.1	253 54.3	15.9	327 57.1	35.8	258 18.9	26.5
D 12	162 04.0	337 49.8	S 0 44.4	268 55.2	S25 16.0	342 59.1	N 1 35.6	273 21.3	S20 26.5
A 13	177 06.4	352 49.5	45.7	283 56.1	16.1	358 01.1	35.4	288 23.7	26.5
Y 14	192 08.9	7 49.2	47.0	298 57.1	16.3	13 03.0	35.2	303 26.1	26.5
15	207 11.4	22 48.9	. . 48.3	313 58.0	. . 16.4	28 05.0	. . 35.0	318 28.4	. . 26.6
16	222 13.8	37 48.6	49.6	328 58.9	16.6	43 07.0	34.8	333 30.8	26.6
17	237 16.3	52 48.3	50.9	343 59.8	16.7	58 09.0	34.5	348 33.2	26.6
18	252 18.8	67 47.9	S 0 52.2	359 00.7	S25 16.8	73 11.0	N 1 34.3	3 35.6	S20 26.6
19	267 21.2	82 47.6	53.4	14 01.6	17.0	88 12.9	34.1	18 38.0	26.7
20	282 23.7	97 47.3	54.7	29 02.5	17.1	103 14.9	33.9	33 40.3	26.7
21	297 26.2	112 47.0	. . 56.0	44 03.4	. . 17.3	118 16.9	. . 33.7	48 42.7	. . 26.7
22	312 28.6	127 46.7	57.3	59 04.3	17.4	133 18.9	33.5	63 45.1	26.7
23	327 31.1	142 46.4	58.6	74 05.2	17.5	148 20.9	33.3	78 47.5	26.7
Mer. Pass.	h m 1 17.4	v −0.3	d 1.3	v 0.9	d 0.1	v 2.0	d 0.2	v 2.4	d 0.0

STARS Name	SHA	Dec
	° ′	° ′
Acamar	315 16.6	S40 14.1
Achernar	335 24.9	S57 09.0
Acrux	173 07.3	S63 11.5
Adhara	255 11.0	S28 59.6
Aldebaran	290 46.9	N16 32.4
Alioth	166 19.3	N55 52.5
Alkaid	152 57.6	N49 14.2
Al Na'ir	27 40.6	S46 52.7
Alnilam	275 44.2	S 1 11.6
Alphard	217 54.3	S 8 43.8
Alphecca	126 09.3	N26 39.9
Alpheratz	357 40.9	N29 11.0
Altair	62 05.9	N 8 55.1
Ankaa	353 13.2	S42 12.8
Antares	112 23.6	S26 27.9
Arcturus	145 54.0	N19 06.1
Atria	107 23.3	S69 03.5
Avior	234 17.6	S59 33.7
Bellatrix	278 29.7	N 6 21.8
Betelgeuse	270 59.1	N 7 24.5
Canopus	263 55.4	S52 42.2
Capella	280 31.3	N46 00.5
Deneb	49 29.5	N45 20.7
Denebola	182 31.8	N14 28.9
Diphda	348 53.5	S17 53.6
Dubhe	193 49.8	N61 39.7
Elnath	278 09.9	N28 37.0
Eltanin	90 44.9	N51 29.7
Enif	33 44.7	N 9 57.3
Fomalhaut	15 21.3	S29 31.9
Gacrux	171 58.9	S57 12.4
Gienah	175 50.3	S17 37.9
Hadar	148 45.1	S60 27.2
Hamal	327 58.1	N23 32.3
Kaus Aust.	83 40.8	S34 22.4
Kochab	137 20.8	N74 05.7
Markab	13 35.8	N15 17.8
Menkar	314 12.6	N 4 09.2
Menkent	148 05.2	S36 27.0
Miaplacidus	221 39.9	S69 47.1
Mirfak	308 37.0	N49 54.9
Nunki	75 55.4	S26 16.3
Peacock	53 15.4	S56 40.8
Pollux	243 25.4	N27 59.0
Procyon	244 57.7	N 5 10.9
Rasalhague	96 04.4	N12 33.3
Regulus	207 41.5	N11 53.2
Rigel	281 10.0	S 8 11.0
Rigil Kent.	139 49.0	S60 54.2
Sabik	102 10.0	S15 44.5
Schedar	349 37.4	N56 37.6
Shaula	96 18.8	S37 06.8
Sirius	258 32.0	S16 44.3
Spica	158 29.2	S11 14.7
Suhail	222 51.2	S43 29.9
Vega	80 37.3	N38 48.4
Zuben'ubi	137 03.1	S16 06.4

	SHA	Mer. Pass.
	° ′	h m
Venus	177 25.9	13 28
Mars	107 46.8	18 05
Jupiter	181 12.4	13 11
Saturn	111 20.2	17 49

	UT	SUN GHA	SUN Dec	MOON GHA	*v*	MOON Dec	*d*	HP
	d h	° ′	° ′	° ′	′	° ′	′	′
	31 00	179 55.5	N 8 33.6	196 05.2	11.2	N12 27.3	7.8	56.5
	01	194 55.7	32.7	210 35.4	11.3	12 19.5	7.7	56.5
	02	209 55.9	31.8	225 05.7	11.4	12 11.8	7.9	56.5
	03	224 56.1	. . 30.9	239 36.1	11.4	12 03.9	7.9	56.4
	04	239 56.3	30.0	254 06.5	11.4	11 56.0	7.9	56.4
	05	254 56.5	29.1	268 36.9	11.5	11 48.1	8.0	56.4
	06	269 56.7	N 8 28.2	283 07.4	11.6	N11 40.1	8.1	56.4
W	07	284 56.8	27.3	297 38.0	11.6	11 32.0	8.1	56.4
E	08	299 57.0	26.4	312 08.6	11.6	11 23.9	8.1	56.3
D	09	314 57.2	. . 25.5	326 39.2	11.8	11 15.8	8.2	56.3
	10	329 57.4	24.6	341 10.0	11.7	11 07.6	8.3	56.3
N	11	344 57.6	23.7	355 40.7	11.9	10 59.3	8.3	56.3
E	12	359 57.8	N 8 22.8	10 11.6	11.8	N10 51.0	8.4	56.3
S	13	14 58.0	21.9	24 42.4	12.0	10 42.6	8.4	56.2
D	14	29 58.2	21.0	39 13.4	11.9	10 34.2	8.4	56.2
A	15	44 58.4	. . 20.1	53 44.3	12.1	10 25.8	8.5	56.2
Y	16	59 58.6	19.2	68 15.4	12.0	10 17.3	8.5	56.2
	17	74 58.8	18.3	82 46.4	12.2	10 08.8	8.6	56.1
	18	89 59.0	N 8 17.4	97 17.6	12.2	N10 00.2	8.6	56.1
	19	104 59.2	16.5	111 48.8	12.2	9 51.6	8.7	56.1
	20	119 59.4	15.5	126 20.0	12.3	9 42.9	8.7	56.1
	21	134 59.6	. . 14.6	140 51.3	12.3	9 34.2	8.7	56.1
	22	149 59.8	13.7	155 22.6	12.4	9 25.5	8.8	56.0
	23	165 00.0	12.8	169 54.0	12.4	9 16.7	8.8	56.0
	1 00	180 00.2	N 8 11.9	184 25.4	12.5	N 9 07.9	8.9	56.0
	01	195 00.4	11.0	198 56.9	12.5	8 59.0	8.9	56.0
	02	210 00.6	10.1	213 28.4	12.6	8 50.1	8.9	56.0
	03	225 00.8	. . 09.2	228 00.0	12.6	8 41.2	9.0	55.9
	04	240 01.0	08.3	242 31.6	12.7	8 32.2	9.0	55.9
	05	255 01.2	07.4	257 03.3	12.7	N 8 23.2	9.0	55.9
	06	270 01.4	N 8 06.5	An annular eclipse of the Sun occurs on this date. See page 5.				
	07	285 01.6	05.6					
T	08	300 01.8	04.6					
H	09	315 02.0	. . 03.7					
U	10	330 02.2	02.8					
R	11	345 02.4	01.9					
S	12	0 02.6	N 8 01.0	358 46.2	13.1	N 7 19.3	9.2	55.7
D	13	15 02.8	8 00.1	13 18.3	13.0	7 10.1	9.3	55.7
A	14	30 03.0	7 59.2	27 50.3	13.1	7 00.8	9.2	55.7
Y	15	45 03.2	. . 58.3	42 22.4	13.2	6 51.6	9.4	55.7
	16	60 03.4	57.4	56 54.6	13.2	6 42.2	9.3	55.7
	17	75 03.6	56.5	71 26.8	13.2	6 32.9	9.4	55.6
	18	90 03.8	N 7 55.5	85 59.0	13.3	N 6 23.5	9.4	55.6
	19	105 04.0	54.6	100 31.3	13.3	6 14.1	9.4	55.6
	20	120 04.2	53.7	115 03.6	13.4	6 04.7	9.4	55.6
	21	135 04.4	. . 52.8	129 36.0	13.4	5 55.3	9.4	55.6
	22	150 04.6	51.9	144 08.4	13.4	5 45.9	9.5	55.5
	23	165 04.8	51.0	158 40.8	13.5	5 36.4	9.5	55.5
	2 00	180 05.0	N 7 50.1	173 13.3	13.5	N 5 26.9	9.5	55.5
	01	195 05.2	49.2	187 45.8	13.6	5 17.4	9.5	55.5
	02	210 05.4	48.2	202 18.4	13.6	5 07.9	9.6	55.5
	03	225 05.6	. . 47.3	216 51.0	13.6	4 58.3	9.5	55.4
	04	240 05.8	46.4	231 23.6	13.6	4 48.8	9.6	55.4
	05	255 06.0	45.5	245 56.2	13.7	4 39.2	9.6	55.4
	06	270 06.2	N 7 44.6	260 28.9	13.8	N 4 29.6	9.5	55.4
	07	285 06.4	43.7	275 01.7	13.7	4 20.1	9.7	55.4
	08	300 06.6	42.8	289 34.4	13.8	4 10.4	9.6	55.4
F	09	315 06.8	. . 41.8	304 07.2	13.9	4 00.8	9.6	55.3
R	10	330 07.0	40.9	318 40.1	13.8	3 51.2	9.6	55.3
I	11	345 07.2	40.0	333 12.9	13.9	3 41.6	9.7	55.3
D	12	0 07.4	N 7 39.1	347 45.8	14.0	N 3 31.9	9.6	55.3
A	13	15 07.6	38.2	2 18.8	13.9	3 22.3	9.7	55.3
Y	14	30 07.8	37.3	16 51.7	14.0	3 12.6	9.7	55.2
	15	45 08.0	. . 36.3	31 24.7	14.0	3 02.9	9.7	55.2
	16	60 08.2	35.4	45 57.7	14.1	2 53.2	9.6	55.2
	17	75 08.4	34.5	60 30.8	14.1	2 43.6	9.7	55.2
	18	90 08.6	N 7 33.6	75 03.9	14.1	N 2 33.9	9.7	55.2
	19	105 08.8	32.7	89 37.0	14.1	2 24.2	9.7	55.1
	20	120 09.0	31.8	104 10.1	14.2	2 14.5	9.7	55.1
	21	135 09.2	. . 30.8	118 43.3	14.1	2 04.8	9.7	55.1
	22	150 09.4	29.9	133 16.4	14.3	1 55.1	9.7	55.1
	23	165 09.6	29.0	147 49.7	14.2	N 1 45.4	9.7	55.1
		SD 15.9	*d* 0.9	SD	15.3		15.2	15.1

Lat.	Twilight Naut.	Twilight Civil	Sunrise	Moonrise 31	Moonrise 1	Moonrise 2	Moonrise 3
°	h m	h m	h m	h m	h m	h m	h m
N 72	////	02 34	04 03	02 16	04 02	05 42	07 20
N 70	////	03 01	04 17	02 38	04 15	05 49	07 20
68	01 34	03 22	04 27	02 55	04 25	05 54	07 21
66	02 12	03 38	04 36	03 09	04 34	05 58	07 21
64	02 37	03 51	04 44	03 20	04 41	06 02	07 21
62	02 57	04 02	04 50	03 29	04 48	06 05	07 21
60	03 12	04 11	04 56	03 38	04 53	06 08	07 22
N 58	03 25	04 19	05 01	03 45	04 58	06 10	07 22
56	03 36	04 25	05 05	03 51	05 02	06 13	07 22
54	03 45	04 32	05 09	03 57	05 06	06 15	07 22
52	03 53	04 37	05 12	04 02	05 09	06 16	07 22
50	04 01	04 42	05 15	04 06	05 13	06 18	07 22
45	04 16	04 52	05 22	04 16	05 19	06 22	07 23
N 40	04 27	05 00	05 28	04 24	05 25	06 24	07 23
35	04 36	05 07	05 33	04 31	05 30	06 27	07 23
30	04 44	05 13	05 37	04 38	05 34	06 29	07 23
20	04 56	05 22	05 44	04 48	05 41	06 33	07 23
N 10	05 05	05 29	05 51	04 57	05 48	06 36	07 24
0	05 11	05 36	05 57	05 06	05 54	06 40	07 24
S 10	05 17	05 41	06 02	05 15	06 00	06 43	07 24
20	05 20	05 46	06 08	05 24	06 06	06 46	07 25
30	05 23	05 51	06 15	05 35	06 14	06 50	07 25
35	05 24	05 53	06 19	05 41	06 18	06 52	07 25
40	05 24	05 56	06 23	05 48	06 23	06 55	07 26
45	05 24	05 58	06 28	05 56	06 28	06 58	07 26
S 50	05 24	06 01	06 34	06 05	06 35	07 01	07 26
52	05 23	06 02	06 36	06 10	06 38	07 03	07 26
54	05 23	06 04	06 39	06 15	06 41	07 05	07 27
56	05 22	06 05	06 42	06 20	06 45	07 07	07 27
58	05 21	06 06	06 46	06 26	06 49	07 09	07 27
S 60	05 20	06 08	06 50	06 33	06 53	07 11	07 27

Lat.	Sunset	Twilight Civil	Twilight Naut.	Moonset 31	Moonset 1	Moonset 2	Moonset 3
°	h m	h m	h m	h m	h m	h m	h m
N 72	19 53	21 20	////	19 40	19 35	19 30	19 25
N 70	19 40	20 54	23 31	19 25	19 26	19 27	19 27
68	19 30	20 34	22 17	19 13	19 20	19 24	19 29
66	19 21	20 19	21 43	19 03	19 14	19 22	19 30
64	19 14	20 06	21 18	18 55	19 09	19 21	19 31
62	19 08	19 56	21 00	18 48	19 04	19 19	19 33
60	19 02	19 47	20 45	18 42	19 01	19 18	19 34
N 58	18 58	19 39	20 32	18 36	18 57	19 16	19 34
56	18 53	19 33	20 22	18 31	18 54	19 15	19 35
54	18 50	19 27	20 13	18 27	18 52	19 14	19 36
52	18 46	19 21	20 05	18 23	18 49	19 13	19 37
50	18 43	19 17	19 58	18 19	18 47	19 13	19 37
45	18 37	19 07	19 43	18 11	18 42	19 11	19 38
N 40	18 31	18 59	19 32	18 04	18 38	19 09	19 39
35	18 26	18 52	19 23	17 59	18 34	19 08	19 40
30	18 22	18 46	19 15	17 54	18 31	19 07	19 41
20	18 15	18 37	19 03	17 45	18 26	19 05	19 43
N 10	18 09	18 30	18 55	17 37	18 21	19 03	19 44
0	18 03	18 24	18 48	17 29	18 16	19 01	19 45
S 10	17 58	18 19	18 43	17 22	18 11	18 59	19 46
20	17 52	18 14	18 40	17 14	18 06	18 58	19 47
30	17 45	18 09	18 37	17 05	18 01	18 55	19 49
35	17 41	18 07	18 36	17 00	17 57	18 54	19 50
40	17 37	18 05	18 36	16 53	17 54	18 53	19 50
45	17 33	18 02	18 36	16 46	17 49	18 51	19 51
S 50	17 27	17 59	18 37	16 38	17 44	18 49	19 53
52	17 24	17 58	18 37	16 34	17 42	18 48	19 53
54	17 21	17 57	18 38	16 30	17 39	18 47	19 54
56	17 18	17 56	18 39	16 25	17 36	18 46	19 55
58	17 15	17 54	18 40	16 19	17 33	18 45	19 55
S 60	17 11	17 53	18 41	16 13	17 29	18 43	19 56

Day	SUN Eqn. of Time 00^h	SUN Eqn. of Time 12^h	SUN Mer. Pass.	MOON Mer. Pass. Upper	MOON Mer. Pass. Lower	MOON Age	MOON Phase
d	m s	m s	h m	h m	h m	d	%
31	00 18	00 09	12 00	11 18	23 42	29	1
1	00 00	00 10	12 00	12 05	24 28	00	0
2	00 19	00 29	12 00	12 50	00 28	01	1

UT d h	ARIES GHA ° ′	VENUS −3·8 GHA ° ′	Dec ° ′	MARS −0·2 GHA ° ′	Dec ° ′	JUPITER −1·7 GHA ° ′	Dec ° ′	SATURN +0·5 GHA ° ′	Dec ° ′	STARS Name	SHA ° ′	Dec ° ′
3 00 (SATURDAY)	342 33.5	157 46.0	S 0 59.9	89 06.1	S25 17.7	163 22.9	N 1 33.1	93 49.8	S20 26.8	Acamar	315 16.5	S40 14.2
01	357 36.0	172 45.7	1 01.2	104 07.0	17.8	178 24.8	32.9	108 52.2	26.8	Achernar	335 24.8	S57 09.0
02	12 38.5	187 45.4	02.5	119 07.9	18.0	193 26.8	32.6	123 54.6	26.8	Acrux	173 07.3	S63 11.5
03	27 40.9	202 45.1	. . 03.8	134 08.8	. . 18.1	208 28.8	. . 32.4	138 57.0	. . 26.8	Adhara	255 11.0	S28 59.6
04	42 43.4	217 44.8	05.0	149 09.7	18.2	223 30.8	32.2	153 59.4	26.8	Aldebaran	290 46.9	N16 32.4
05	57 45.9	232 44.5	06.3	164 10.6	18.4	238 32.8	32.0	169 01.7	26.9			
06	72 48.3	247 44.1	S 1 07.6	179 11.5	S25 18.5	253 34.7	N 1 31.8	184 04.1	S20 26.9	Alioth	166 19.4	N55 52.4
07	87 50.8	262 43.8	08.9	194 12.4	18.7	268 36.7	31.6	199 06.5	26.9	Alkaid	152 57.6	N49 14.2
08	102 53.3	277 43.5	10.2	209 13.3	18.8	283 38.7	31.4	214 08.9	26.9	Al Na'ir	27 40.6	S46 52.7
09	117 55.7	292 43.2	. . 11.5	224 14.2	. . 18.9	298 40.7	. . 31.2	229 11.2	. . 26.9	Alnilam	275 44.2	S 1 11.6
10	132 58.2	307 42.9	12.8	239 15.1	19.1	313 42.7	31.0	244 13.6	27.0	Alphard	217 54.2	S 8 43.8
11	148 00.7	322 42.6	14.1	254 16.0	19.2	328 44.7	30.8	259 16.0	27.0			
12	163 03.1	337 42.3	S 1 15.4	269 16.9	S25 19.3	343 46.6	N 1 30.5	274 18.4	S20 27.0	Alphecca	126 09.3	N26 39.9
13	178 05.6	352 41.9	16.6	284 17.8	19.5	358 48.6	30.3	289 20.8	27.0	Alpheratz	357 40.9	N29 11.0
14	193 08.0	7 41.6	17.9	299 18.7	19.6	13 50.6	30.1	304 23.1	27.0	Altair	62 05.9	N 8 55.1
15	208 10.5	22 41.3	. . 19.2	314 19.6	. . 19.7	28 52.6	. . 29.9	319 25.5	. . 27.1	Ankaa	353 13.2	S42 12.8
16	223 13.0	37 41.0	20.5	329 20.5	19.9	43 54.6	29.7	334 27.9	27.1	Antares	112 23.6	S26 27.9
17	238 15.4	52 40.7	21.8	344 21.4	20.0	58 56.5	29.5	349 30.3	27.1			
18	253 17.9	67 40.4	S 1 23.1	359 22.3	S25 20.2	73 58.5	N 1 29.3	4 32.6	S20 27.1	Arcturus	145 54.0	N19 06.1
19	268 20.4	82 40.0	24.4	14 23.2	20.3	89 00.5	29.1	19 35.0	27.2	Atria	107 23.4	S69 03.5
20	283 22.8	97 39.7	25.7	29 24.1	20.4	104 02.5	28.9	34 37.4	27.2	Avior	234 17.6	S59 33.7
21	298 25.3	112 39.4	. . 26.9	44 25.0	. . 20.6	119 04.5	. . 28.6	49 39.8	. . 27.2	Bellatrix	278 29.7	N 6 21.8
22	313 27.8	127 39.1	28.2	59 25.9	20.7	134 06.4	28.4	64 42.1	27.2	Betelgeuse	270 59.0	N 7 24.5
23	328 30.2	142 38.8	29.5	74 26.8	20.8	149 08.4	28.2	79 44.5	27.2			
4 00 (SUNDAY)	343 32.7	157 38.5	S 1 30.8	89 27.7	S25 21.0	164 10.4	N 1 28.0	94 46.9	S20 27.3	Canopus	263 55.4	S52 42.1
01	358 35.1	172 38.2	32.1	104 28.6	21.1	179 12.4	27.8	109 49.3	27.3	Capella	280 31.3	N46 00.5
02	13 37.6	187 37.8	33.4	119 29.4	21.2	194 14.4	27.6	124 51.6	27.3	Deneb	49 29.6	N45 20.7
03	28 40.1	202 37.5	. . 34.7	134 30.3	. . 21.4	209 16.3	. . 27.4	139 54.0	. . 27.3	Denebola	182 31.8	N14 28.9
04	43 42.5	217 37.2	36.0	149 31.2	21.5	224 18.3	27.2	154 56.4	27.3	Diphda	348 53.4	S17 53.6
05	58 45.0	232 36.9	37.3	164 32.1	21.6	239 20.3	27.0	169 58.8	27.4			
06	73 47.5	247 36.6	S 1 38.5	179 33.0	S25 21.8	254 22.3	N 1 26.7	185 01.1	S20 27.4	Dubhe	193 49.8	N61 39.7
07	88 49.9	262 36.3	39.8	194 33.9	21.9	269 24.3	26.5	200 03.5	27.4	Elnath	278 09.9	N28 37.0
08	103 52.4	277 35.9	41.1	209 34.8	22.0	284 26.3	26.3	215 05.9	27.4	Eltanin	90 45.0	N51 29.7
09	118 54.9	292 35.6	. . 42.4	224 35.7	. . 22.2	299 28.2	. . 26.1	230 08.2	. . 27.4	Enif	33 44.7	N 9 57.3
10	133 57.3	307 35.3	43.7	239 36.5	22.3	314 30.2	25.9	245 10.6	27.5	Fomalhaut	15 21.3	S29 31.9
11	148 59.8	322 35.0	45.0	254 37.4	22.4	329 32.2	25.7	260 13.0	27.5			
12	164 02.3	337 34.7	S 1 46.3	269 38.3	S25 22.5	344 34.2	N 1 25.5	275 15.4	S20 27.5	Gacrux	171 58.9	S57 12.4
13	179 04.7	352 34.4	47.6	284 39.2	22.7	359 36.2	25.3	290 17.7	27.5	Gienah	175 50.3	S17 37.9
14	194 07.2	7 34.0	48.8	299 40.1	22.8	14 38.1	25.1	305 20.1	27.6	Hadar	148 45.1	S60 27.2
15	209 09.6	22 33.7	. . 50.1	314 41.0	. . 22.9	29 40.1	. . 24.8	320 22.5	. . 27.6	Hamal	327 58.0	N23 32.4
16	224 12.1	37 33.4	51.4	329 41.8	23.1	44 42.1	24.6	335 24.9	27.6	Kaus Aust.	83 40.8	S34 22.4
17	239 14.6	52 33.1	52.7	344 42.7	23.2	59 44.1	24.4	350 27.2	27.6			
18	254 17.0	67 32.8	S 1 54.0	359 43.6	S25 23.3	74 46.1	N 1 24.2	5 29.6	S20 27.6	Kochab	137 20.8	N74 05.7
19	269 19.5	82 32.5	55.3	14 44.5	23.5	89 48.0	24.0	20 32.0	27.7	Markab	13 35.8	N15 17.8
20	284 22.0	97 32.1	56.6	29 45.4	23.6	104 50.0	23.8	35 34.3	27.7	Menkar	314 12.6	N 4 09.2
21	299 24.4	112 31.8	. . 57.9	44 46.2	. . 23.7	119 52.0	. . 23.6	50 36.7	. . 27.7	Menkent	148 05.2	S36 27.0
22	314 26.9	127 31.5	1 59.1	59 47.1	23.9	134 54.0	23.4	65 39.1	27.7	Miaplacidus	221 39.9	S69 47.1
23	329 29.4	142 31.2	2 00.4	74 48.0	24.0	149 56.0	23.2	80 41.5	27.8			
5 00 (MONDAY)	344 31.8	157 30.9	S 2 01.7	89 48.9	S25 24.1	164 57.9	N 1 22.9	95 43.8	S20 27.8	Mirfak	308 37.0	N49 54.9
01	359 34.3	172 30.6	03.0	104 49.8	24.2	179 59.9	22.7	110 46.2	27.8	Nunki	75 55.4	S26 16.4
02	14 36.7	187 30.3	04.3	119 50.6	24.4	195 01.9	22.5	125 48.6	27.8	Peacock	53 15.4	S56 40.8
03	29 39.2	202 29.9	. . 05.6	134 51.5	. . 24.5	210 03.9	. . 22.3	140 50.9	. . 27.8	Pollux	243 25.4	N27 59.0
04	44 41.7	217 29.6	06.9	149 52.4	24.6	225 05.8	22.1	155 53.3	27.9	Procyon	244 57.7	N 5 10.9
05	59 44.1	232 29.3	08.2	164 53.3	24.7	240 07.8	21.9	170 55.7	27.9			
06	74 46.6	247 29.0	S 2 09.4	179 54.1	S25 24.9	255 09.8	N 1 21.7	185 58.0	S20 27.9	Rasalhague	96 04.4	N12 33.3
07	89 49.1	262 28.7	10.7	194 55.0	25.0	270 11.8	21.5	201 00.4	27.9	Regulus	207 41.5	N11 53.2
08	104 51.5	277 28.4	12.0	209 55.9	25.1	285 13.8	21.3	216 02.8	27.9	Rigel	281 10.0	S 8 11.0
09	119 54.0	292 28.0	. . 13.3	224 56.8	. . 25.3	300 15.7	. . 21.0	231 05.1	. . 28.0	Rigil Kent.	139 49.0	S60 54.2
10	134 56.5	307 27.7	14.6	239 57.6	25.4	315 17.7	20.8	246 07.5	28.0	Sabik	102 10.0	S15 44.5
11	149 58.9	322 27.4	15.9	254 58.5	25.5	330 19.7	20.6	261 09.9	28.0			
12	165 01.4	337 27.1	S 2 17.2	269 59.4	S25 25.6	345 21.7	N 1 20.4	276 12.3	S20 28.0	Schedar	349 37.4	N56 37.6
13	180 03.9	352 26.8	18.5	285 00.2	25.8	0 23.7	20.2	291 14.6	28.1	Shaula	96 18.9	S37 06.8
14	195 06.3	7 26.4	19.7	300 01.1	25.9	15 25.6	20.0	306 17.0	28.1	Sirius	258 32.0	S16 44.3
15	210 08.8	22 26.1	. . 21.0	315 02.0	. . 26.0	30 27.6	. . 19.8	321 19.4	. . 28.1	Spica	158 29.2	S11 14.7
16	225 11.2	37 25.8	22.3	330 02.9	26.1	45 29.6	19.6	336 21.7	28.1	Suhail	222 51.2	S43 29.9
17	240 13.7	52 25.5	23.6	345 03.7	26.3	60 31.6	19.4	351 24.1	28.1			
18	255 16.2	67 25.2	S 2 24.9	0 04.6	S25 26.4	75 33.6	N 1 19.1	6 26.5	S20 28.2	Vega	80 37.3	N38 48.4
19	270 18.6	82 24.9	26.2	15 05.5	26.5	90 35.5	18.9	21 28.8	28.2	Zuben'ubi	137 03.1	S16 06.4
20	285 21.1	97 24.5	27.5	30 06.3	26.6	105 37.5	18.7	36 31.2	28.2			
21	300 23.6	112 24.2	. . 28.8	45 07.2	. . 26.8	120 39.5	. . 18.5	51 33.6	. . 28.2			
22	315 26.0	127 23.9	30.0	60 08.1	26.9	135 41.5	18.3	66 35.9	28.3			
23	330 28.5	142 23.6	31.3	75 08.9	27.0	150 43.5	18.1	81 38.3	28.3			
Mer. Pass. (h m)	1 05.6	v −0.3	d 1.3	v 0.9	d 0.1	v 2.0	d 0.2	v 2.4	d 0.0			

	SHA ° ′	Mer. Pass. h m
Venus	174 05.8	13 30
Mars	105 55.0	18 01
Jupiter	180 37.7	13 02
Saturn	111 14.2	17 38

Day	UT (h)	SUN GHA	SUN Dec	MOON GHA	v	MOON Dec	d	HP
d	h	° ′	° ′	° ′	′	° ′	′	′
3 SATURDAY	00	180 09.8	N 7 28.1	162 22.9	14.3	N 1 35.7	9.7	55.1
	01	195 10.0	27.2	176 56.2	14.3	1 26.0	9.7	55.0
	02	210 10.2	26.3	191 29.5	14.3	1 16.3	9.7	55.0
	03	225 10.4	. . 25.3	206 02.8	14.3	1 06.6	9.7	55.0
	04	240 10.6	24.4	220 36.1	14.4	0 56.9	9.7	55.0
	05	255 10.8	23.5	235 09.5	14.3	0 47.2	9.7	55.0
	06	270 11.0	N 7 22.6	249 42.8	14.4	N 0 37.5	9.7	54.9
	07	285 11.2	21.7	264 16.2	14.5	0 27.8	9.7	54.9
	08	300 11.4	20.7	278 49.7	14.4	0 18.1	9.7	54.9
	09	315 11.7	. . 19.8	293 23.1	14.5	N 0 08.4	9.7	54.9
	10	330 11.9	18.9	307 56.6	14.5	S 0 01.3	9.6	54.9
	11	345 12.1	18.0	322 30.1	14.5	0 10.9	9.7	54.9
	12	0 12.3	N 7 17.1	337 03.6	14.5	S 0 20.6	9.6	54.8
	13	15 12.5	16.1	351 37.1	14.5	0 30.2	9.7	54.8
	14	30 12.7	15.2	6 10.6	14.6	0 39.9	9.6	54.8
	15	45 12.9	. . 14.3	20 44.2	14.5	0 49.5	9.6	54.8
	16	60 13.1	13.4	35 17.7	14.6	0 59.1	9.7	54.8
	17	75 13.3	12.5	49 51.3	14.6	1 08.8	9.6	54.8
	18	90 13.5	N 7 11.5	64 24.9	14.6	S 1 18.4	9.6	54.8
	19	105 13.7	10.6	78 58.5	14.7	1 28.0	9.5	54.7
	20	120 13.9	09.7	93 32.2	14.6	1 37.5	9.6	54.7
	21	135 14.1	. . 08.8	108 05.8	14.7	1 47.1	9.6	54.7
	22	150 14.3	07.8	122 39.5	14.6	1 56.7	9.5	54.7
	23	165 14.5	06.9	137 13.1	14.7	2 06.2	9.5	54.7
4 SUNDAY	00	180 14.7	N 7 06.0	151 46.8	14.7	S 2 15.7	9.5	54.7
	01	195 14.9	05.1	166 20.5	14.7	2 25.2	9.5	54.6
	02	210 15.1	04.2	180 54.2	14.7	2 34.7	9.5	54.6
	03	225 15.4	. . 03.2	195 27.9	14.8	2 44.2	9.5	54.6
	04	240 15.6	02.3	210 01.7	14.7	2 53.7	9.4	54.6
	05	255 15.8	01.4	224 35.4	14.7	3 03.1	9.4	54.6
	06	270 16.0	N 7 00.5	239 09.1	14.8	S 3 12.5	9.5	54.6
	07	285 16.2	6 59.5	253 42.9	14.7	3 22.0	9.3	54.6
	08	300 16.4	58.6	268 16.6	14.8	3 31.3	9.4	54.6
	09	315 16.6	. . 57.7	282 50.4	14.8	3 40.7	9.4	54.5
	10	330 16.8	56.8	297 24.2	14.7	3 50.1	9.3	54.5
	11	345 17.0	55.8	311 57.9	14.8	3 59.4	9.3	54.5
	12	0 17.2	N 6 54.9	326 31.7	14.8	S 4 08.7	9.3	54.5
	13	15 17.4	54.0	341 05.5	14.8	4 18.0	9.2	54.5
	14	30 17.6	53.1	355 39.3	14.8	4 27.2	9.3	54.5
	15	45 17.8	. . 52.1	10 13.1	14.7	4 36.5	9.2	54.5
	16	60 18.0	51.2	24 46.8	14.8	4 45.7	9.2	54.5
	17	75 18.3	50.3	39 20.6	14.8	4 54.9	9.1	54.4
	18	90 18.5	N 6 49.4	53 54.4	14.8	S 5 04.0	9.1	54.4
	19	105 18.7	48.4	68 28.2	14.8	5 13.1	9.2	54.4
	20	120 18.9	47.5	83 02.0	14.8	5 22.3	9.0	54.4
	21	135 19.1	. . 46.6	97 35.8	14.8	5 31.3	9.1	54.4
	22	150 19.3	45.6	112 09.6	14.8	5 40.4	9.0	54.4
	23	165 19.5	44.7	126 43.4	14.8	5 49.4	9.0	54.4
5 MONDAY	00	180 19.7	N 6 43.8	141 17.2	14.8	S 5 58.4	9.0	54.4
	01	195 19.9	42.9	155 51.0	14.8	6 07.4	8.9	54.4
	02	210 20.1	41.9	170 24.8	14.8	6 16.3	8.9	54.3
	03	225 20.3	. . 41.0	184 58.6	14.7	6 25.2	8.9	54.3
	04	240 20.5	40.1	199 32.3	14.8	6 34.1	8.9	54.3
	05	255 20.8	39.1	214 06.1	14.8	6 43.0	8.8	54.3
	06	270 21.0	N 6 38.2	228 39.9	14.7	S 6 51.8	8.8	54.3
	07	285 21.2	37.3	243 13.6	14.8	7 00.6	8.7	54.3
	08	300 21.4	36.4	257 47.4	14.7	7 09.3	8.8	54.3
	09	315 21.6	. . 35.4	272 21.1	14.8	7 18.1	8.6	54.3
	10	330 21.8	34.5	286 54.9	14.7	7 26.7	8.7	54.3
	11	345 22.0	33.6	301 28.6	14.7	7 35.4	8.6	54.3
	12	0 22.2	N 6 32.6	316 02.3	14.8	S 7 44.0	8.6	54.3
	13	15 22.4	31.7	330 36.1	14.7	7 52.6	8.5	54.2
	14	30 22.6	30.8	345 09.8	14.7	8 01.1	8.5	54.2
	15	45 22.9	. . 29.9	359 43.5	14.7	8 09.6	8.5	54.2
	16	60 23.1	28.9	14 17.2	14.6	8 18.1	8.5	54.2
	17	75 23.3	28.0	28 50.8	14.7	8 26.6	8.4	54.2
	18	90 23.5	N 6 27.1	43 24.5	14.6	S 8 35.0	8.3	54.2
	19	105 23.7	26.1	57 58.1	14.7	8 43.3	8.3	54.2
	20	120 23.9	25.2	72 31.8	14.6	8 51.6	8.3	54.2
	21	135 24.1	. . 24.3	87 05.4	14.6	8 59.9	8.3	54.2
	22	150 24.3	23.3	101 39.0	14.6	9 08.2	8.2	54.2
	23	165 24.5	22.4	116 12.6	14.6	S 9 16.4	8.1	54.2
		SD 15.9	*d* 0.9	SD 14.9		14.8		14.8

Lat.	Twilight Naut.	Twilight Civil	Sunrise	Moonrise 3	Moonrise 4	Moonrise 5	Moonrise 6
°	h m	h m	h m	h m	h m	h m	h m
N 72	////	02 54	04 18	07 20	08 55	10 30	12 07
N 70	01 09	03 18	04 29	07 20	08 50	10 19	11 48
68	01 59	03 35	04 38	07 21	08 45	10 09	11 33
66	02 29	03 49	04 46	07 21	08 42	10 02	11 20
64	02 51	04 01	04 52	07 21	08 39	09 55	11 10
62	03 08	04 10	04 58	07 21	08 36	09 50	11 02
60	03 22	04 19	05 03	07 22	08 34	09 45	10 55
N 58	03 33	04 26	05 07	07 22	08 32	09 40	10 48
56	03 43	04 32	05 11	07 22	08 30	09 37	10 42
54	03 52	04 37	05 14	07 22	08 28	09 33	10 37
52	03 59	04 42	05 17	07 22	08 27	09 30	10 33
50	04 06	04 47	05 20	07 22	08 25	09 27	10 29
45	04 20	04 56	05 26	07 23	08 22	09 21	10 20
N 40	04 30	05 03	05 31	07 23	08 20	09 16	10 12
35	04 39	05 09	05 35	07 23	08 18	09 12	10 06
30	04 46	05 15	05 39	07 23	08 16	09 08	10 00
20	04 57	05 23	05 45	07 23	08 13	09 02	09 50
N 10	05 05	05 29	05 51	07 24	08 10	08 56	09 42
0	05 11	05 35	05 56	07 24	08 07	08 51	09 34
S 10	05 15	05 39	06 00	07 24	08 05	08 45	09 26
20	05 18	05 44	06 06	07 25	08 02	08 40	09 18
30	05 20	05 47	06 11	07 25	07 59	08 33	09 09
35	05 20	05 49	06 15	07 25	07 57	08 30	09 03
40	05 20	05 51	06 18	07 26	07 55	08 26	08 57
45	05 19	05 53	06 22	07 26	07 53	08 21	08 50
S 50	05 18	05 55	06 27	07 26	07 50	08 15	08 41
52	05 17	05 56	06 30	07 26	07 49	08 13	08 38
54	05 16	05 57	06 32	07 27	07 48	08 10	08 33
56	05 15	05 58	06 35	07 27	07 46	08 07	08 29
58	05 13	05 58	06 38	07 27	07 45	08 03	08 23
S 60	05 11	05 59	06 41	07 27	07 43	07 59	08 17

Lat.	Sunset	Twilight Civil	Twilight Naut.	Moonset 3	Moonset 4	Moonset 5	Moonset 6
°	h m	h m	h m	h m	h m	h m	h m
N 72	19 37	20 58	////	19 25	19 19	19 14	19 08
N 70	19 26	20 36	22 37	19 27	19 27	19 27	19 28
68	19 17	20 19	21 53	19 29	19 33	19 38	19 45
66	19 10	20 06	21 24	19 30	19 38	19 47	19 58
64	19 03	19 55	21 03	19 31	19 42	19 54	20 08
62	18 58	19 45	20 47	19 33	19 46	20 01	20 18
60	18 53	19 37	20 33	19 34	19 50	20 07	20 26
N 58	18 49	19 30	20 22	19 34	19 52	20 12	20 33
56	18 46	19 24	20 12	19 35	19 55	20 16	20 39
54	18 42	19 19	20 04	19 36	19 57	20 20	20 45
52	18 39	19 14	19 57	19 37	20 00	20 24	20 50
50	18 37	19 10	19 50	19 37	20 02	20 27	20 54
45	18 31	19 01	19 37	19 38	20 06	20 34	21 04
N 40	18 26	18 54	19 26	19 39	20 09	20 40	21 13
35	18 22	18 48	19 18	19 40	20 13	20 45	21 20
30	18 18	18 43	19 11	19 41	20 15	20 50	21 26
20	18 12	18 35	19 01	19 43	20 20	20 58	21 37
N 10	18 07	18 28	18 53	19 44	20 24	21 05	21 46
0	18 02	18 23	18 47	19 45	20 28	21 12	21 55
S 10	17 57	18 18	18 43	19 46	20 32	21 18	22 04
20	17 52	18 14	18 40	19 47	20 37	21 25	22 14
30	17 47	18 11	18 39	19 49	20 41	21 33	22 25
35	17 44	18 09	18 38	19 50	20 44	21 38	22 32
40	17 40	18 07	18 39	19 50	20 47	21 43	22 39
45	17 36	18 05	18 39	19 51	20 51	21 49	22 47
S 50	17 31	18 04	18 41	19 53	20 55	21 57	22 57
52	17 29	18 03	18 42	19 53	20 57	22 00	23 02
54	17 27	18 02	18 43	19 54	21 00	22 04	23 07
56	17 24	18 01	18 44	19 55	21 02	22 08	23 13
58	17 21	18 00	18 46	19 55	21 05	22 13	23 20
S 60	17 18	18 00	18 48	19 56	21 08	22 18	23 27

Day	SUN Eqn. of Time 00^h	SUN Eqn. of Time 12^h	SUN Mer. Pass.	MOON Mer. Pass. Upper	MOON Mer. Pass. Lower	MOON Age	MOON Phase
d	m s	m s	h m	h m	h m	d %	
3	00 39	00 49	11 59	13 35	01 13	02 4	
4	00 59	01 08	11 59	14 18	01 56	03 9	
5	01 18	01 28	11 59	15 01	02 39	04 16	

UT	ARIES	VENUS −3·8		MARS −0·2		JUPITER −1·7		SATURN +0·5	
	GHA	GHA	Dec	GHA	Dec	GHA	Dec	GHA	Dec
d h	° ′	° ′	° ′	° ′	° ′	° ′	° ′	° ′	° ′
6 00	345 31.0	157 23.3	S 2 32.6	90 09.8	S25 27.1	165 45.4	N 1 17.9	96 40.7	S20 28.3
01	0 33.4	172 23.0	33.9	105 10.6	27.2	180 47.4	17.7	111 43.0	28.3
02	15 35.9	187 22.6	35.2	120 11.5	27.4	195 49.4	17.4	126 45.4	28.3
03	30 38.3	202 22.3	. . 36.5	135 12.4	. . 27.5	210 51.4	. . 17.2	141 47.8	. . 28.4
04	45 40.8	217 22.0	37.8	150 13.2	27.6	225 53.3	17.0	156 50.1	28.4
05	60 43.3	232 21.7	39.0	165 14.1	27.7	240 55.3	16.8	171 52.5	28.4
06	75 45.7	247 21.4	S 2 40.3	180 15.0	S25 27.9	255 57.3	N 1 16.6	186 54.9	S20 28.4
07	90 48.2	262 21.1	41.6	195 15.8	28.0	270 59.3	16.4	201 57.2	28.5
T 08	105 50.7	277 20.7	42.9	210 16.7	28.1	286 01.3	16.2	216 59.6	28.5
U 09	120 53.1	292 20.4	. . 44.2	225 17.5	. . 28.2	301 03.2	. . 16.0	232 01.9	. . 28.5
E 10	135 55.6	307 20.1	45.5	240 18.4	28.3	316 05.2	15.8	247 04.3	28.5
S 11	150 58.1	322 19.8	46.8	255 19.3	28.5	331 07.2	15.5	262 06.7	28.5
D 12	166 00.5	337 19.5	S 2 48.0	270 20.1	S25 28.6	346 09.2	N 1 15.3	277 09.0	S20 28.6
A 13	181 03.0	352 19.1	49.3	285 21.0	28.7	1 11.2	15.1	292 11.4	28.6
Y 14	196 05.5	7 18.8	50.6	300 21.8	28.8	16 13.1	14.9	307 13.8	28.6
15	211 07.9	22 18.5	. . 51.9	315 22.7	. . 28.9	31 15.1	. . 14.7	322 16.1	. . 28.6
16	226 10.4	37 18.2	53.2	330 23.5	29.1	46 17.1	14.5	337 18.5	28.7
17	241 12.8	52 17.9	54.5	345 24.4	29.2	61 19.1	14.3	352 20.9	28.7
18	256 15.3	67 17.6	S 2 55.8	0 25.3	S25 29.3	76 21.0	N 1 14.1	7 23.2	S20 28.7
19	271 17.8	82 17.2	57.0	15 26.1	29.4	91 23.0	13.8	22 25.6	28.7
20	286 20.2	97 16.9	58.3	30 27.0	29.5	106 25.0	13.6	37 28.0	28.7
21	301 22.7	112 16.6	2 59.6	45 27.8	. . 29.7	121 27.0	. . 13.4	52 30.3	. . 28.8
22	316 25.2	127 16.3	3 00.9	60 28.7	29.8	136 29.0	13.2	67 32.7	28.8
23	331 27.6	142 16.0	02.2	75 29.5	29.9	151 30.9	13.0	82 35.0	28.8
7 00	346 30.1	157 15.6	S 3 03.5	90 30.4	S25 30.0	166 32.9	N 1 12.8	97 37.4	S20 28.8
01	1 32.6	172 15.3	04.8	105 31.2	30.1	181 34.9	12.6	112 39.8	28.9
02	16 35.0	187 15.0	06.0	120 32.1	30.2	196 36.9	12.4	127 42.1	28.9
03	31 37.5	202 14.7	. . 07.3	135 32.9	. . 30.4	211 38.8	. . 12.2	142 44.5	. . 28.9
04	46 40.0	217 14.4	08.6	150 33.8	30.5	226 40.8	11.9	157 46.8	28.9
05	61 42.4	232 14.0	09.9	165 34.6	30.6	241 42.8	11.7	172 49.2	29.0
06	76 44.9	247 13.7	S 3 11.2	180 35.5	S25 30.7	256 44.8	N 1 11.5	187 51.6	S20 29.0
W 07	91 47.3	262 13.4	12.5	195 36.3	30.8	271 46.8	11.3	202 53.9	29.0
E 08	106 49.8	277 13.1	13.7	210 37.2	30.9	286 48.7	11.1	217 56.3	29.0
D 09	121 52.3	292 12.8	. . 15.0	225 38.0	. . 31.1	301 50.7	. . 10.9	232 58.7	. . 29.0
N 10	136 54.7	307 12.5	16.3	240 38.9	31.2	316 52.7	10.7	248 01.0	29.1
E 11	151 57.2	322 12.1	17.6	255 39.7	31.3	331 54.7	10.5	263 03.4	29.1
S 12	166 59.7	337 11.8	S 3 18.9	270 40.5	S25 31.4	346 56.6	N 1 10.2	278 05.7	S20 29.1
D 13	182 02.1	352 11.5	20.2	285 41.4	31.5	1 58.6	10.0	293 08.1	29.1
A 14	197 04.6	7 11.2	21.4	300 42.2	31.6	17 00.6	09.8	308 10.5	29.2
Y 15	212 07.1	22 10.9	. . 22.7	315 43.1	. . 31.7	32 02.6	. . 09.6	323 12.8	. . 29.2
16	227 09.5	37 10.5	24.0	330 43.9	31.9	47 04.5	09.4	338 15.2	29.2
17	242 12.0	52 10.2	25.3	345 44.8	32.0	62 06.5	09.2	353 17.5	29.2
18	257 14.4	67 09.9	S 3 26.6	0 45.6	S25 32.1	77 08.5	N 1 09.0	8 19.9	S20 29.2
19	272 16.9	82 09.6	27.9	15 46.5	32.2	92 10.5	08.8	23 22.3	29.3
20	287 19.4	97 09.2	29.1	30 47.3	32.3	107 12.5	08.5	38 24.6	29.3
21	302 21.8	112 08.9	. . 30.4	45 48.1	. . 32.4	122 14.4	. . 08.3	53 27.0	. . 29.3
22	317 24.3	127 08.6	31.7	60 49.0	32.5	137 16.4	08.1	68 29.3	29.3
23	332 26.8	142 08.3	33.0	75 49.8	32.6	152 18.4	07.9	83 31.7	29.4
8 00	347 29.2	157 08.0	S 3 34.3	90 50.7	S25 32.8	167 20.4	N 1 07.7	98 34.0	S20 29.4
01	2 31.7	172 07.6	35.6	105 51.5	32.9	182 22.3	07.5	113 36.4	29.4
02	17 34.2	187 07.3	36.8	120 52.3	33.0	197 24.3	07.3	128 38.8	29.4
03	32 36.6	202 07.0	. . 38.1	135 53.2	. . 33.1	212 26.3	. . 07.1	143 41.1	. . 29.5
04	47 39.1	217 06.7	39.4	150 54.0	33.2	227 28.3	06.8	158 43.5	29.5
05	62 41.6	232 06.4	40.7	165 54.8	33.3	242 30.2	06.6	173 45.8	29.5
06	77 44.0	247 06.0	S 3 42.0	180 55.7	S25 33.4	257 32.2	N 1 06.4	188 48.2	S20 29.5
07	92 46.5	262 05.7	43.2	195 56.5	33.5	272 34.2	06.2	203 50.5	29.6
T 08	107 48.9	277 05.4	44.5	210 57.3	33.6	287 36.2	06.0	218 52.9	29.6
H 09	122 51.4	292 05.1	. . 45.8	225 58.2	. . 33.7	302 38.2	. . 05.8	233 55.3	. . 29.6
U 10	137 53.9	307 04.8	47.1	240 59.0	33.9	317 40.1	05.6	248 57.6	29.6
R 11	152 56.3	322 04.4	48.4	255 59.9	34.0	332 42.1	05.4	264 00.0	29.6
S 12	167 58.8	337 04.1	S 3 49.7	271 00.7	S25 34.1	347 44.1	N 1 05.1	279 02.3	S20 29.7
D 13	183 01.3	352 03.8	50.9	286 01.5	34.2	2 46.1	04.9	294 04.7	29.7
A 14	198 03.7	7 03.5	52.2	301 02.3	34.3	17 48.0	04.7	309 07.0	29.7
Y 15	213 06.2	22 03.1	. . 53.5	316 03.2	. . 34.4	32 50.0	. . 04.5	324 09.4	. . 29.7
16	228 08.7	37 02.8	54.8	331 04.0	34.5	47 52.0	04.3	339 11.8	29.8
17	243 11.1	52 02.5	56.1	346 04.8	34.6	62 54.0	04.1	354 14.1	29.8
18	258 13.6	67 02.2	S 3 57.3	1 05.7	S25 34.7	77 55.9	N 1 03.9	9 16.5	S20 29.8
19	273 16.1	82 01.9	58.6	16 06.5	34.8	92 57.9	03.7	24 18.8	29.8
20	288 18.5	97 01.5	3 59.9	31 07.3	34.9	107 59.9	03.4	39 21.2	29.9
21	303 21.0	112 01.2	4 01.2	46 08.2	. . 35.0	123 01.9	. . 03.2	54 23.5	. . 29.9
22	318 23.4	127 00.9	02.5	61 09.0	35.1	138 03.8	03.0	69 25.9	29.9
23	333 25.9	142 00.6	03.7	76 09.8	35.2	153 05.8	02.8	84 28.2	29.9
Mer. Pass.	h m 0 53.8	v −0.3	d 1.3	v 0.8	d 0.1	v 2.0	d 0.2	v 2.4	d 0.0

STARS Name	SHA	Dec
	° ′	° ′
Acamar	315 16.5	S40 14.2
Achernar	335 24.8	S57 09.0
Acrux	173 07.3	S63 11.5
Adhara	255 11.0	S28 59.6
Aldebaran	290 46.8	N16 32.4
Alioth	166 19.4	N55 52.4
Alkaid	152 57.6	N49 14.2
Al Na'ir	27 40.6	S46 52.7
Alnilam	275 44.2	S 1 11.6
Alphard	217 54.2	S 8 43.8
Alphecca	126 09.3	N26 39.9
Alpheratz	357 40.9	N29 11.0
Altair	62 05.9	N 8 55.1
Ankaa	353 13.2	S42 12.8
Antares	112 23.6	S26 27.9
Arcturus	145 54.0	N19 06.1
Atria	107 23.4	S69 03.5
Avior	234 17.5	S59 33.7
Bellatrix	278 29.7	N 6 21.8
Betelgeuse	270 59.0	N 7 24.5
Canopus	263 55.4	S52 42.1
Capella	280 31.3	N46 00.5
Deneb	49 29.6	N45 20.7
Denebola	182 31.8	N14 28.9
Diphda	348 53.4	S17 53.6
Dubhe	193 49.8	N61 39.7
Elnath	278 09.9	N28 37.0
Eltanin	90 45.0	N51 29.7
Enif	33 44.7	N 9 57.3
Fomalhaut	15 21.3	S29 31.9
Gacrux	171 58.9	S57 12.4
Gienah	175 50.3	S17 37.9
Hadar	148 45.1	S60 27.2
Hamal	327 58.0	N23 32.4
Kaus Aust.	83 40.8	S34 22.4
Kochab	137 20.9	N74 05.6
Markab	13 35.8	N15 17.8
Menkar	314 12.6	N 4 09.2
Menkent	148 05.2	S36 27.0
Miaplacidus	221 39.9	S69 47.1
Mirfak	308 37.0	N49 54.9
Nunki	75 55.5	S26 16.4
Peacock	53 15.4	S56 40.8
Pollux	243 25.3	N27 59.0
Procyon	244 57.7	N 5 10.9
Rasalhague	96 04.4	N12 33.3
Regulus	207 41.5	N11 53.2
Rigel	281 10.0	S 8 11.0
Rigil Kent.	139 49.1	S60 54.2
Sabik	102 10.0	S15 44.5
Schedar	349 37.4	N56 37.6
Shaula	96 18.9	S37 06.8
Sirius	258 31.9	S16 44.3
Spica	158 29.2	S11 14.7
Suhail	222 51.2	S43 29.9
Vega	80 37.3	N38 48.4
Zuben'ubi	137 03.2	S16 06.4

	SHA	Mer. Pass.
	° ′	h m
Venus	170 45.5	13 31
Mars	104 00.3	17 57
Jupiter	180 02.8	12 52
Saturn	111 07.3	17 27

UT		SUN GHA	SUN Dec	MOON GHA	v	MOON Dec	d	HP
d	h	° ′	° ′	° ′	′	° ′	′	′
6	00	180 24.7	N 6 21.5	130 46.2	14.6	S 9 24.5	8.1	54.2
	01	195 25.0	20.5	145 19.8	14.5	9 32.6	8.1	54.2
	02	210 25.2	19.6	159 53.3	14.6	9 40.7	8.1	54.2
	03	225 25.4	. . 18.7	174 26.9	14.5	9 48.8	8.0	54.2
	04	240 25.6	17.7	189 00.4	14.5	9 56.8	7.9	54.2
	05	255 25.8	16.8	203 33.9	14.5	10 04.7	7.9	54.2
	06	270 26.0	N 6 15.9	218 07.4	14.5	S10 12.6	7.9	54.2
	07	285 26.2	14.9	232 40.9	14.4	10 20.5	7.8	54.2
T	08	300 26.4	14.0	247 14.3	14.4	10 28.3	7.8	54.1
U	09	315 26.7	. . 13.1	261 47.7	14.4	10 36.1	7.7	54.1
E	10	330 26.9	12.1	276 21.1	14.4	10 43.8	7.7	54.1
S	11	345 27.1	11.2	290 54.5	14.4	10 51.5	7.6	54.1
D	12	0 27.3	N 6 10.3	305 27.9	14.4	S10 59.1	7.6	54.1
A	13	15 27.5	09.3	320 01.3	14.3	11 06.7	7.5	54.1
Y	14	30 27.7	08.4	334 34.6	14.3	11 14.2	7.5	54.1
	15	45 27.9	. . 07.5	349 07.9	14.3	11 21.7	7.5	54.1
	16	60 28.1	06.5	3 41.2	14.2	11 29.2	7.3	54.1
	17	75 28.3	05.6	18 14.4	14.3	11 36.5	7.4	54.1
	18	90 28.6	N 6 04.7	32 47.7	14.2	S11 43.9	7.3	54.1
	19	105 28.8	03.7	47 20.9	14.2	11 51.2	7.2	54.1
	20	120 29.0	02.8	61 54.1	14.2	11 58.4	7.2	54.1
	21	135 29.2	. . 01.9	76 27.3	14.1	12 05.6	7.2	54.1
	22	150 29.4	00.9	91 00.4	14.1	12 12.8	7.0	54.1
	23	165 29.6	6 00.0	105 33.5	14.1	12 19.8	7.1	54.1
7	00	180 29.8	N 5 59.0	120 06.6	14.1	S12 26.9	7.0	54.1
	01	195 30.1	58.1	134 39.7	14.0	12 33.9	6.9	54.1
	02	210 30.3	57.2	149 12.7	14.0	12 40.8	6.9	54.1
	03	225 30.5	. . 56.2	163 45.7	14.0	12 47.7	6.8	54.1
	04	240 30.7	55.3	178 18.7	14.0	12 54.5	6.8	54.1
	05	255 30.9	54.4	192 51.7	13.9	13 01.3	6.7	54.1
	06	270 31.1	N 5 53.4	207 24.6	13.9	S13 08.0	6.6	54.2
W	07	285 31.3	52.5	221 57.5	13.9	13 14.6	6.6	54.2
E	08	300 31.5	51.6	236 30.4	13.9	13 21.2	6.6	54.2
D	09	315 31.8	. . 50.6	251 03.3	13.8	13 27.8	6.4	54.2
N	10	330 32.0	49.7	265 36.1	13.8	13 34.2	6.5	54.2
E	11	345 32.2	48.7	280 08.9	13.7	13 40.7	6.3	54.2
S	12	0 32.4	N 5 47.8	294 41.6	13.7	S13 47.0	6.3	54.2
D	13	15 32.6	46.9	309 14.3	13.7	13 53.3	6.3	54.2
A	14	30 32.8	45.9	323 47.0	13.7	13 59.6	6.2	54.2
Y	15	45 33.0	. . 45.0	338 19.7	13.6	14 05.8	6.1	54.2
	16	60 33.3	44.0	352 52.3	13.6	14 11.9	6.1	54.2
	17	75 33.5	43.1	7 24.9	13.6	14 18.0	6.0	54.2
	18	90 33.7	N 5 42.2	21 57.5	13.5	S14 24.0	5.9	54.2
	19	105 33.9	41.2	36 30.0	13.6	14 29.9	5.9	54.2
	20	120 34.1	40.3	51 02.6	13.4	14 35.8	5.8	54.2
	21	135 34.3	. . 39.3	65 35.0	13.5	14 41.6	5.8	54.2
	22	150 34.6	38.4	80 07.5	13.4	14 47.4	5.7	54.2
	23	165 34.8	37.5	94 39.9	13.3	14 53.1	5.6	54.2
8	00	180 35.0	N 5 36.5	109 12.2	13.4	S14 58.7	5.6	54.3
	01	195 35.2	35.6	123 44.6	13.3	15 04.3	5.5	54.3
	02	210 35.4	34.6	138 16.9	13.3	15 09.8	5.4	54.3
	03	225 35.6	. . 33.7	152 49.2	13.2	15 15.2	5.4	54.3
	04	240 35.8	32.8	167 21.4	13.2	15 20.6	5.3	54.3
	05	255 36.1	31.8	181 53.6	13.2	15 25.9	5.3	54.3
	06	270 36.3	N 5 30.9	196 25.8	13.1	S15 31.2	5.1	54.3
T	07	285 36.5	29.9	210 57.9	13.1	15 36.3	5.1	54.3
H	08	300 36.7	29.0	225 30.0	13.0	15 41.4	5.1	54.3
U	09	315 36.9	. . 28.1	240 02.0	13.1	15 46.5	4.9	54.3
R	10	330 37.1	27.1	254 34.1	12.9	15 51.4	4.9	54.4
S	11	345 37.4	26.2	269 06.0	13.0	15 56.3	4.9	54.4
D	12	0 37.6	N 5 25.2	283 38.0	12.9	S16 01.2	4.7	54.4
A	13	15 37.8	24.3	298 09.9	12.9	16 05.9	4.7	54.4
Y	14	30 38.0	23.3	312 41.8	12.8	16 10.6	4.6	54.4
	15	45 38.2	. . 22.4	327 13.6	12.8	16 15.2	4.6	54.4
	16	60 38.4	21.5	341 45.4	12.8	16 19.8	4.4	54.4
	17	75 38.7	20.5	356 17.2	12.7	16 24.2	4.4	54.4
	18	90 38.9	N 5 19.6	10 48.9	12.7	S16 28.6	4.4	54.5
	19	105 39.1	18.6	25 20.6	12.6	16 33.0	4.2	54.5
	20	120 39.3	17.7	39 52.2	12.7	16 37.2	4.2	54.5
	21	135 39.5	. . 16.7	54 23.9	12.5	16 41.4	4.1	54.5
	22	150 39.7	15.8	68 55.4	12.6	16 45.5	4.0	54.5
	23	165 40.0	14.9	83 27.0	12.5	S16 49.5	4.0	54.5
		SD 15.9	*d* 0.9	SD 14.8		14.8		14.8

Lat.	Twilight Naut.	Twilight Civil	Sunrise	Moonrise 6	Moonrise 7	Moonrise 8	Moonrise 9
°	h m	h m	h m	h m	h m	h m	h m
N 72	00 08	03 13	04 32	12 07	13 46	15 31	17 43
N 70	01 42	03 33	04 42	11 48	13 17	14 45	16 09
68	02 19	03 48	04 49	11 33	12 55	14 15	15 29
66	02 44	04 00	04 56	11 20	12 38	13 53	15 02
64	03 03	04 10	05 01	11 10	12 24	13 35	14 41
62	03 19	04 19	05 06	11 02	12 13	13 21	14 24
60	03 31	04 26	05 10	10 55	12 03	13 09	14 10
N 58	03 42	04 33	05 13	10 48	11 54	12 58	13 59
56	03 51	04 38	05 17	10 42	11 47	12 49	13 48
54	03 58	04 43	05 19	10 37	11 40	12 41	13 39
52	04 05	04 47	05 22	10 33	11 34	12 34	13 31
50	04 11	04 51	05 24	10 29	11 29	12 27	13 24
45	04 24	05 00	05 29	10 20	11 17	12 13	13 08
N 40	04 34	05 06	05 34	10 12	11 07	12 02	12 55
35	04 41	05 12	05 37	10 06	10 59	11 52	12 44
30	04 48	05 16	05 40	10 00	10 52	11 44	12 35
20	04 58	05 24	05 46	09 50	10 39	11 29	12 19
N 10	05 05	05 29	05 50	09 42	10 29	11 16	12 04
0	05 10	05 34	05 55	09 34	10 19	11 04	11 51
S 10	05 13	05 38	05 59	09 26	10 08	10 52	11 38
20	05 15	05 41	06 03	09 18	09 58	10 40	11 24
30	05 16	05 44	06 08	09 09	09 46	10 25	11 08
35	05 16	05 45	06 10	09 03	09 39	10 17	10 59
40	05 15	05 46	06 13	08 57	09 31	10 07	10 48
45	05 14	05 48	06 17	08 50	09 21	09 56	10 35
S 50	05 11	05 49	06 21	08 41	09 10	09 43	10 20
52	05 10	05 49	06 23	08 38	09 05	09 37	10 13
54	05 09	05 50	06 25	08 33	08 59	09 30	10 05
56	05 07	05 50	06 27	08 29	08 53	09 22	09 57
58	05 05	05 50	06 29	08 23	08 46	09 13	09 47
S 60	05 03	05 51	06 32	08 17	08 38	09 04	09 35

Lat.	Sunset	Twilight Civil	Twilight Naut.	Moonset 6	Moonset 7	Moonset 8	Moonset 9
°	h m	h m	h m	h m	h m	h m	h m
N 72	19 21	20 38	23 11	19 08	19 01	18 51	18 18
N 70	19 11	20 19	22 05	19 28	19 31	19 38	19 53
68	19 04	20 05	21 31	19 45	19 54	20 09	20 32
66	18 58	19 53	21 07	19 58	20 12	20 31	21 00
64	18 53	19 43	20 49	20 08	20 26	20 49	21 21
62	18 48	19 35	20 34	20 18	20 38	21 04	21 38
60	18 44	19 28	20 22	20 26	20 49	21 17	21 52
N 58	18 41	19 22	20 12	20 33	20 58	21 27	22 04
56	18 38	19 16	20 03	20 39	21 06	21 37	22 15
54	18 35	19 11	19 56	20 45	21 13	21 45	22 24
52	18 33	19 07	19 49	20 50	21 19	21 53	22 32
50	18 30	19 03	19 43	20 54	21 25	22 00	22 40
45	18 25	18 55	19 31	21 04	21 37	22 14	22 56
N 40	18 21	18 49	19 21	21 13	21 47	22 26	23 09
35	18 18	18 43	19 14	21 20	21 56	22 36	23 20
30	18 15	18 39	19 07	21 26	22 04	22 45	23 30
20	18 10	18 32	18 58	21 37	22 18	23 01	23 46
N 10	18 05	18 26	18 51	21 46	22 29	23 14	24 01
0	18 01	18 22	18 46	21 55	22 40	23 27	24 15
S 10	17 57	18 18	18 43	22 04	22 51	23 39	24 28
20	17 53	18 15	18 41	22 14	23 03	23 53	24 43
30	17 48	18 12	18 40	22 25	23 17	24 08	00 08
35	17 46	18 11	18 40	22 32	23 25	24 17	00 17
40	17 43	18 10	18 41	22 39	23 34	24 28	00 28
45	17 40	18 09	18 43	22 47	23 44	24 40	00 40
S 50	17 36	18 08	18 45	22 57	23 57	24 54	00 54
52	17 34	18 08	18 47	23 02	24 03	00 03	01 01
54	17 32	18 07	18 48	23 07	24 09	00 09	01 09
56	17 30	18 07	18 50	23 13	24 17	00 17	01 17
58	17 27	18 07	18 52	23 20	24 25	00 25	01 27
S 60	17 25	18 06	18 55	23 27	24 34	00 34	01 38

Day	SUN Eqn. of Time 00^h	SUN Eqn. of Time 12^h	SUN Mer. Pass.	MOON Mer. Pass. Upper	MOON Mer. Pass. Lower	MOON Age	MOON Phase
d	m s	m s	h m	h m	h m	d %	
6	01 39	01 49	11 58	15 45	03 23	05 23	
7	01 59	02 09	11 58	16 29	04 07	06 32	
8	02 19	02 30	11 58	17 15	04 52	07 41	

UT d	UT h	ARIES GHA	VENUS −3·8 GHA	VENUS Dec	MARS −0·2 GHA	MARS Dec	JUPITER −1·7 GHA	JUPITER Dec	SATURN +0·5 GHA	SATURN Dec	STARS Name	SHA	Dec
		° ′	° ′	° ′	° ′	° ′	° ′	° ′	° ′	° ′		° ′	° ′
9 FRIDAY	00	348 28.4	157 00.2	S 4 05.0	91 10.6	S25 35.4	168 07.8	N 1 02.6	99 30.6	S20 30.0	Acamar	315 16.5	S40 14.2
	01	3 30.8	171 59.9	06.3	106 11.5	35.5	183 09.8	02.4	114 32.9	30.0	Achernar	335 24.8	S57 09.0
	02	18 33.3	186 59.6	07.6	121 12.3	35.6	198 11.7	02.2	129 35.3	30.0	Acrux	173 07.3	S63 11.5
	03	33 35.8	201 59.3	. . 08.9	136 13.1	. . 35.7	213 13.7	. . 02.0	144 37.7	. . 30.0	Adhara	255 11.0	S28 59.6
	04	48 38.2	216 58.9	10.1	151 13.9	35.8	228 15.7	01.7	159 40.0	30.0	Aldebaran	290 46.8	N16 32.4
	05	63 40.7	231 58.6	11.4	166 14.8	35.9	243 17.7	01.5	174 42.4	30.1			
	06	78 43.2	246 58.3	S 4 12.7	181 15.6	S25 36.0	258 19.7	N 1 01.3	189 44.7	S20 30.1	Alioth	166 19.4	N55 52.4
	07	93 45.6	261 58.0	14.0	196 16.4	36.1	273 21.6	01.1	204 47.1	30.1	Alkaid	152 57.6	N49 14.2
	08	108 48.1	276 57.7	15.3	211 17.2	36.2	288 23.6	00.9	219 49.4	30.1	Al Na'ir	27 40.6	S46 52.7
	09	123 50.5	291 57.3	. . 16.5	226 18.1	. . 36.3	303 25.6	. . 00.7	234 51.8	. . 30.2	Alnilam	275 44.2	S 1 11.6
	10	138 53.0	306 57.0	17.8	241 18.9	36.4	318 27.6	00.5	249 54.1	30.2	Alphard	217 54.2	S 8 43.8
	11	153 55.5	321 56.7	19.1	256 19.7	36.5	333 29.5	00.3	264 56.5	30.2			
	12	168 57.9	336 56.4	S 4 20.4	271 20.5	S25 36.6	348 31.5	N 1 00.0	279 58.8	S20 30.2	Alphecca	126 09.3	N26 39.9
	13	184 00.4	351 56.0	21.6	286 21.3	36.7	3 33.5	0 59.8	295 01.2	30.3	Alpheratz	357 40.8	N29 11.0
	14	199 02.9	6 55.7	22.9	301 22.2	36.8	18 35.5	59.6	310 03.5	30.3	Altair	62 05.9	N 8 55.1
	15	214 05.3	21 55.4	. . 24.2	316 23.0	. . 36.9	33 37.4	. . 59.4	325 05.9	. . 30.3	Ankaa	353 13.2	S42 12.8
	16	229 07.8	36 55.1	25.5	331 23.8	37.0	48 39.4	59.2	340 08.2	30.3	Antares	112 23.6	S26 27.9
	17	244 10.3	51 54.7	26.8	346 24.6	37.1	63 41.4	59.0	355 10.6	30.4			
	18	259 12.7	66 54.4	S 4 28.0	1 25.4	S25 37.2	78 43.4	N 0 58.8	10 12.9	S20 30.4	Arcturus	145 54.0	N19 06.1
	19	274 15.2	81 54.1	29.3	16 26.3	37.3	93 45.3	58.6	25 15.3	30.4	Atria	107 23.4	S69 03.5
	20	289 17.7	96 53.8	30.6	31 27.1	37.4	108 47.3	58.3	40 17.6	30.4	Avior	234 17.5	S59 33.7
	21	304 20.1	111 53.4	. . 31.9	46 27.9	. . 37.5	123 49.3	. . 58.1	55 20.0	. . 30.5	Bellatrix	278 29.7	N 6 21.8
	22	319 22.6	126 53.1	33.1	61 28.7	37.6	138 51.3	57.9	70 22.3	30.5	Betelgeuse	270 59.0	N 7 24.5
	23	334 25.0	141 52.8	34.4	76 29.5	37.7	153 53.2	57.7	85 24.7	30.5			
10 SATURDAY	00	349 27.5	156 52.5	S 4 35.7	91 30.3	S25 37.8	168 55.2	N 0 57.5	100 27.0	S20 30.5	Canopus	263 55.3	S52 42.1
	01	4 30.0	171 52.1	37.0	106 31.2	37.9	183 57.2	57.3	115 29.4	30.5	Capella	280 31.2	N46 00.5
	02	19 32.4	186 51.8	38.3	121 32.0	38.0	198 59.2	57.1	130 31.7	30.6	Deneb	49 29.6	N45 20.7
	03	34 34.9	201 51.5	. . 39.5	136 32.8	. . 38.1	214 01.1	. . 56.9	145 34.1	. . 30.6	Denebola	182 31.8	N14 28.9
	04	49 37.4	216 51.2	40.8	151 33.6	38.2	229 03.1	56.6	160 36.4	30.6	Diphda	348 53.4	S17 53.6
	05	64 39.8	231 50.8	42.1	166 34.4	38.3	244 05.1	56.4	175 38.8	30.6			
	06	79 42.3	246 50.5	S 4 43.4	181 35.2	S25 38.4	259 07.1	N 0 56.2	190 41.1	S20 30.7	Dubhe	193 49.8	N61 39.7
	07	94 44.8	261 50.2	44.6	196 36.0	38.5	274 09.0	56.0	205 43.5	30.7	Elnath	278 09.9	N28 37.0
	08	109 47.2	276 49.8	45.9	211 36.8	38.6	289 11.0	55.8	220 45.8	30.7	Eltanin	90 45.0	N51 29.7
	09	124 49.7	291 49.5	. . 47.2	226 37.7	. . 38.7	304 13.0	. . 55.6	235 48.2	. . 30.7	Enif	33 44.7	N 9 57.3
	10	139 52.2	306 49.2	48.5	241 38.5	38.8	319 15.0	55.4	250 50.5	30.8	Fomalhaut	15 21.3	S29 31.9
	11	154 54.6	321 48.9	49.7	256 39.3	38.9	334 16.9	55.2	265 52.9	30.8			
	12	169 57.1	336 48.5	S 4 51.0	271 40.1	S25 39.0	349 18.9	N 0 54.9	280 55.2	S20 30.8	Gacrux	171 58.9	S57 12.4
	13	184 59.5	351 48.2	52.3	286 40.9	39.1	4 20.9	54.7	295 57.6	30.8	Gienah	175 50.3	S17 37.9
	14	200 02.0	6 47.9	53.6	301 41.7	39.2	19 22.9	54.5	310 59.9	30.9	Hadar	148 45.1	S60 27.2
	15	215 04.5	21 47.6	. . 54.8	316 42.5	. . 39.3	34 24.8	. . 54.3	326 02.3	. . 30.9	Hamal	327 58.0	N23 32.4
	16	230 06.9	36 47.2	56.1	331 43.3	39.4	49 26.8	54.1	341 04.6	30.9	Kaus Aust.	83 40.8	S34 22.4
	17	245 09.4	51 46.9	57.4	346 44.1	39.5	64 28.8	53.9	356 07.0	30.9			
	18	260 11.9	66 46.6	S 4 58.7	1 44.9	S25 39.5	79 30.8	N 0 53.7	11 09.3	S20 31.0	Kochab	137 20.9	N74 05.6
	19	275 14.3	81 46.2	4 59.9	16 45.7	39.6	94 32.7	53.4	26 11.7	31.0	Markab	13 35.8	N15 17.9
	20	290 16.8	96 45.9	5 01.2	31 46.5	39.7	109 34.7	53.2	41 14.0	31.0	Menkar	314 12.6	N 4 09.2
	21	305 19.3	111 45.6	. . 02.5	46 47.3	. . 39.8	124 36.7	. . 53.0	56 16.4	. . 31.0	Menkent	148 05.2	S36 27.0
	22	320 21.7	126 45.3	03.7	61 48.2	39.9	139 38.7	52.8	71 18.7	31.1	Miaplacidus	221 39.9	S69 47.0
	23	335 24.2	141 44.9	05.0	76 49.0	40.0	154 40.6	52.6	86 21.0	31.1			
11 SUNDAY	00	350 26.6	156 44.6	S 5 06.3	91 49.8	S25 40.1	169 42.6	N 0 52.4	101 23.4	S20 31.1	Mirfak	308 36.9	N49 54.9
	01	5 29.1	171 44.3	07.6	106 50.6	40.2	184 44.6	52.2	116 25.7	31.1	Nunki	75 55.5	S26 16.4
	02	20 31.6	186 43.9	08.8	121 51.4	40.3	199 46.6	52.0	131 28.1	31.2	Peacock	53 15.5	S56 40.8
	03	35 34.0	201 43.6	. . 10.1	136 52.2	. . 40.4	214 48.5	. . 51.7	146 30.4	. . 31.2	Pollux	243 25.3	N27 59.0
	04	50 36.5	216 43.3	11.4	151 53.0	40.5	229 50.5	51.5	161 32.8	31.2	Procyon	244 57.6	N 5 10.9
	05	65 39.0	231 43.0	12.7	166 53.8	40.6	244 52.5	51.3	176 35.1	31.2			
	06	80 41.4	246 42.6	S 5 13.9	181 54.6	S25 40.7	259 54.4	N 0 51.1	191 37.5	S20 31.3	Rasalhague	96 04.4	N12 33.3
	07	95 43.9	261 42.3	15.2	196 55.4	40.8	274 56.4	50.9	206 39.8	31.3	Regulus	207 41.5	N11 53.2
	08	110 46.4	276 42.0	16.5	211 56.2	40.8	289 58.4	50.7	221 42.2	31.3	Rigel	281 10.0	S 8 11.0
	09	125 48.8	291 41.6	. . 17.7	226 57.0	. . 40.9	305 00.4	. . 50.5	236 44.5	. . 31.3	Rigil Kent.	139 49.1	S60 54.2
	10	140 51.3	306 41.3	19.0	241 57.8	41.0	320 02.3	50.3	251 46.8	31.4	Sabik	102 10.0	S15 44.5
	11	155 53.8	321 41.0	20.3	256 58.6	41.1	335 04.3	50.0	266 49.2	31.4			
	12	170 56.2	336 40.6	S 5 21.6	271 59.4	S25 41.2	350 06.3	N 0 49.8	281 51.5	S20 31.4	Schedar	349 37.4	N56 37.6
	13	185 58.7	351 40.3	22.8	287 00.2	41.3	5 08.3	49.6	296 53.9	31.4	Shaula	96 18.9	S37 06.8
	14	201 01.1	6 40.0	24.1	302 01.0	41.4	20 10.2	49.4	311 56.2	31.5	Sirius	258 31.9	S16 44.3
	15	216 03.6	21 39.6	. . 25.4	317 01.8	. . 41.5	35 12.2	. . 49.2	326 58.6	. . 31.5	Spica	158 29.2	S11 14.7
	16	231 06.1	36 39.3	26.6	332 02.6	41.6	50 14.2	49.0	342 00.9	31.5	Suhail	222 51.2	S43 29.9
	17	246 08.5	51 39.0	27.9	347 03.3	41.6	65 16.2	48.8	357 03.3	31.5			
	18	261 11.0	66 38.7	S 5 29.2	2 04.1	S25 41.7	80 18.1	N 0 48.5	12 05.6	S20 31.6	Vega	80 37.3	N38 48.4
	19	276 13.5	81 38.3	30.4	17 04.9	41.8	95 20.1	48.3	27 07.9	31.6	Zuben'ubi	137 03.2	S16 06.4
	20	291 15.9	96 38.0	31.7	32 05.7	41.9	110 22.1	48.1	42 10.3	31.6			
	21	306 18.4	111 37.7	. . 33.0	47 06.5	. . 42.0	125 24.1	. . 47.9	57 12.6	. . 31.6			
	22	321 20.9	126 37.3	34.3	62 07.3	42.1	140 26.0	47.7	72 15.0	31.7			
	23	336 23.3	141 37.0	35.5	77 08.1	42.2	155 28.0	47.5	87 17.3	31.7			
Mer. Pass.		h m 0 42.1	v −0.3	d 1.3	v 0.8	d 0.1	v 2.0	d 0.2	v 2.3	d 0.0			

	SHA ° ′	Mer. Pass. h m
Venus	167 24.9	13 33
Mars	102 02.8	17 53
Jupiter	179 27.7	12 43
Saturn	110 59.5	17 15

	UT (d h)	SUN GHA (° ′)	SUN Dec (° ′)	MOON GHA (° ′)	MOON *v* (′)	MOON Dec (° ′)	MOON *d* (′)	MOON HP (′)
	9 00	180 40.2	N 5 13.9	97 58.5	12.4	S16 53.5	3.9	54.5
	01	195 40.4	13.0	112 29.9	12.4	16 57.4	3.8	54.6
	02	210 40.6	12.0	127 01.3	12.4	17 01.2	3.7	54.6
	03	225 40.8	. . 11.1	141 32.7	12.4	17 04.9	3.7	54.6
	04	240 41.0	10.1	156 04.1	12.3	17 08.6	3.6	54.6
	05	255 41.3	09.2	170 35.4	12.2	17 12.2	3.5	54.6
	06	270 41.5	N 5 08.2	185 06.6	12.3	S17 15.7	3.4	54.6
	07	285 41.7	07.3	199 37.9	12.1	17 19.1	3.3	54.7
	08	300 41.9	06.4	214 09.0	12.2	17 22.4	3.3	54.7
F	09	315 42.1	. . 05.4	228 40.2	12.1	17 25.7	3.2	54.7
R	10	330 42.3	04.5	243 11.3	12.1	17 28.9	3.1	54.7
I	11	345 42.6	03.5	257 42.4	12.0	17 32.0	3.0	54.7
D	12	0 42.8	N 5 02.6	272 13.4	12.0	S17 35.0	2.9	54.7
A	13	15 43.0	01.6	286 44.4	11.9	17 37.9	2.9	54.8
Y	14	30 43.2	5 00.7	301 15.3	12.0	17 40.8	2.8	54.8
	15	45 43.4	4 59.7	315 46.3	11.8	17 43.6	2.7	54.8
	16	60 43.7	58.8	330 17.1	11.9	17 46.3	2.6	54.8
	17	75 43.9	57.8	344 48.0	11.8	17 48.9	2.5	54.8
	18	90 44.1	N 4 56.9	359 18.8	11.7	S17 51.4	2.5	54.9
	19	105 44.3	55.9	13 49.5	11.8	17 53.9	2.3	54.9
	20	120 44.5	55.0	28 20.3	11.6	17 56.2	2.3	54.9
	21	135 44.7	. . 54.1	42 50.9	11.7	17 58.5	2.2	54.9
	22	150 45.0	53.1	57 21.6	11.6	18 00.7	2.1	54.9
	23	165 45.2	52.2	71 52.2	11.5	18 02.8	2.0	55.0
	10 00	180 45.4	N 4 51.2	86 22.7	11.6	S18 04.8	2.0	55.0
	01	195 45.6	50.3	100 53.3	11.5	18 06.8	1.8	55.0
	02	210 45.8	49.3	115 23.8	11.4	18 08.6	1.8	55.0
	03	225 46.1	. . 48.4	129 54.2	11.4	18 10.4	1.7	55.1
	04	240 46.3	47.4	144 24.6	11.4	18 12.1	1.6	55.1
	05	255 46.5	46.5	158 55.0	11.3	18 13.7	1.5	55.1
	06	270 46.7	N 4 45.5	173 25.3	11.3	S18 15.2	1.4	55.1
	07	285 46.9	44.6	187 55.6	11.3	18 16.6	1.3	55.2
S	08	300 47.1	43.6	202 25.9	11.2	18 17.9	1.2	55.2
A	09	315 47.4	. . 42.7	216 56.1	11.2	18 19.1	1.2	55.2
T	10	330 47.6	41.7	231 26.3	11.1	18 20.3	1.1	55.2
U	11	345 47.8	40.8	245 56.4	11.2	18 21.4	0.9	55.3
R	12	0 48.0	N 4 39.8	260 26.6	11.0	S18 22.3	0.9	55.3
D	13	15 48.2	38.9	274 56.6	11.1	18 23.2	0.8	55.3
A	14	30 48.5	37.9	289 26.7	11.0	18 24.0	0.7	55.3
Y	15	45 48.7	. . 37.0	303 56.7	10.9	18 24.7	0.6	55.4
	16	60 48.9	36.0	318 26.6	11.0	18 25.3	0.5	55.4
	17	75 49.1	35.1	332 56.6	10.9	18 25.8	0.4	55.4
	18	90 49.3	N 4 34.1	347 26.5	10.8	S18 26.2	0.4	55.4
	19	105 49.6	33.2	1 56.3	10.8	18 26.6	0.2	55.5
	20	120 49.8	32.2	16 26.1	10.8	18 26.8	0.2	55.5
	21	135 50.0	. . 31.3	30 55.9	10.8	18 27.0	0.0	55.5
	22	150 50.2	30.3	45 25.7	10.7	18 27.0	0.0	55.5
	23	165 50.4	29.4	59 55.4	10.7	18 27.0	0.2	55.6
	11 00	180 50.7	N 4 28.4	74 25.1	10.6	S18 26.8	0.2	55.6
	01	195 50.9	27.5	88 54.7	10.7	18 26.6	0.3	55.6
	02	210 51.1	26.5	103 24.4	10.5	18 26.3	0.4	55.7
	03	225 51.3	. . 25.6	117 53.9	10.6	18 25.9	0.6	55.7
	04	240 51.5	24.6	132 23.5	10.5	18 25.3	0.6	55.7
	05	255 51.8	23.7	146 53.0	10.5	18 24.7	0.7	55.7
	06	270 52.0	N 4 22.7	161 22.5	10.4	S18 24.0	0.8	55.8
	07	285 52.2	21.8	175 51.9	10.5	18 23.2	0.9	55.8
	08	300 52.4	20.8	190 21.4	10.4	18 22.3	1.0	55.8
S	09	315 52.6	. . 19.9	204 50.8	10.3	18 21.3	1.0	55.9
U	10	330 52.9	18.9	219 20.1	10.3	18 20.3	1.2	55.9
N	11	345 53.1	18.0	233 49.4	10.3	18 19.1	1.3	55.9
D	12	0 53.3	N 4 17.0	248 18.7	10.3	S18 17.8	1.4	56.0
A	13	15 53.5	16.1	262 48.0	10.2	18 16.4	1.5	56.0
Y	14	30 53.8	15.1	277 17.2	10.2	18 14.9	1.5	56.0
	15	45 54.0	. . 14.1	291 46.4	10.2	18 13.4	1.7	56.1
	16	60 54.2	13.2	306 15.6	10.2	18 11.7	1.8	56.1
	17	75 54.4	12.2	320 44.8	10.1	18 09.9	1.9	56.1
	18	90 54.6	N 4 11.3	335 13.9	10.1	S18 08.0	1.9	56.2
	19	105 54.9	10.3	349 43.0	10.0	18 06.1	2.1	56.2
	20	120 55.1	09.4	4 12.0	10.1	18 04.0	2.1	56.2
	21	135 55.3	. . 08.4	18 41.1	10.0	18 01.9	2.3	56.3
	22	150 55.5	07.5	33 10.1	9.9	17 59.6	2.4	56.3
	23	165 55.7	06.5	47 39.0	10.0	S17 57.2	2.4	56.3
		SD 15.9	*d* 0.9	SD 14.9		15.1		15.2

Lat. (°)	Twilight Naut. (h m)	Twilight Civil (h m)	Sunrise (h m)	Moonrise 9 (h m)	Moonrise 10 (h m)	Moonrise 11 (h m)	Moonrise 12 (h m)
N 72	01 20	03 30	04 46	17 43	■	■	19 10
N 70	02 08	03 47	04 54	16 09	17 17	17 59	18 18
68	02 37	04 00	05 00	15 29	16 32	17 17	17 46
66	02 59	04 11	05 05	15 02	16 02	16 48	17 22
64	03 15	04 20	05 10	14 41	15 39	16 27	17 03
62	03 29	04 27	05 14	14 24	15 21	16 09	16 48
60	03 40	04 34	05 17	14 10	15 06	15 55	16 35
N 58	03 49	04 39	05 20	13 59	14 54	15 42	16 24
56	03 58	04 44	05 22	13 48	14 43	15 32	16 14
54	04 05	04 49	05 25	13 39	14 33	15 22	16 06
52	04 11	04 53	05 27	13 31	14 25	15 14	15 58
50	04 16	04 56	05 29	13 24	14 17	15 06	15 51
45	04 28	05 03	05 33	13 08	14 01	14 50	15 36
N 40	04 37	05 09	05 36	12 55	13 47	14 37	15 24
35	04 44	05 14	05 39	12 44	13 36	14 26	15 14
30	04 50	05 18	05 42	12 35	13 26	14 16	15 04
20	04 58	05 24	05 46	12 19	13 09	13 59	14 49
N 10	05 05	05 29	05 50	12 04	12 54	13 44	14 35
0	05 09	05 33	05 54	11 51	12 40	13 30	14 22
S 10	05 11	05 36	05 57	11 38	12 26	13 16	14 09
20	05 13	05 38	06 00	11 24	12 11	13 02	13 55
30	05 12	05 40	06 04	11 08	11 54	12 45	13 39
35	05 12	05 41	06 06	10 59	11 44	12 35	13 30
40	05 10	05 42	06 09	10 48	11 33	12 24	13 20
45	05 08	05 42	06 11	10 35	11 20	12 11	13 07
S 50	05 05	05 42	06 14	10 20	11 04	11 55	12 52
52	05 03	05 42	06 16	10 13	10 56	11 47	12 45
54	05 01	05 42	06 17	10 05	10 48	11 39	12 37
56	04 59	05 42	06 19	09 57	10 39	11 29	12 29
58	04 57	05 42	06 21	09 47	10 28	11 18	12 19
S 60	04 54	05 42	06 23	09 35	10 16	11 06	12 07

Lat. (°)	Sunset (h m)	Twilight Civil (h m)	Twilight Naut. (h m)	Moonset 9 (h m)	Moonset 10 (h m)	Moonset 11 (h m)	Moonset 12 (h m)
N 72	19 05	20 19	22 23	18 18	■	■	22 08
N 70	18 57	20 03	21 40	19 53	20 26	21 30	22 59
68	18 51	19 51	21 12	20 32	21 12	22 12	23 30
66	18 46	19 40	20 51	21 00	21 42	22 40	23 54
64	18 42	19 32	20 35	21 21	22 04	23 01	24 12
62	18 38	19 24	20 22	21 38	22 22	23 19	24 27
60	18 35	19 18	20 11	21 52	22 37	23 33	24 39
N 58	18 32	19 13	20 02	22 04	22 50	23 45	24 50
56	18 30	19 08	19 54	22 15	23 01	23 56	25 00
54	18 28	19 04	19 47	22 24	23 10	24 05	00 05
52	18 26	19 00	19 41	22 32	23 19	24 13	00 13
50	18 24	18 57	19 36	22 40	23 27	24 21	00 21
45	18 20	18 49	19 25	22 56	23 43	24 37	00 37
N 40	18 16	18 44	19 16	23 09	23 57	24 50	00 50
35	18 14	18 39	19 09	23 20	24 08	00 08	01 01
30	18 11	18 35	19 03	23 30	24 18	00 18	01 10
20	18 07	18 29	18 55	23 46	24 35	00 35	01 27
N 10	18 03	18 24	18 49	24 01	00 01	00 50	01 41
0	18 00	18 21	18 45	24 15	00 15	01 04	01 55
S 10	17 57	18 18	18 42	24 28	00 28	01 18	02 08
20	17 54	18 16	18 41	24 43	00 43	01 33	02 23
30	17 50	18 14	18 42	00 08	00 59	01 50	02 39
35	17 48	18 13	18 43	00 17	01 09	02 00	02 49
40	17 46	18 13	18 44	00 28	01 20	02 11	02 59
45	17 43	18 12	18 46	00 40	01 33	02 24	03 12
S 50	17 40	18 12	18 50	00 54	01 49	02 41	03 28
52	17 39	18 12	18 51	01 01	01 57	02 48	03 35
54	17 37	18 12	18 53	01 09	02 05	02 57	03 43
56	17 35	18 13	18 56	01 17	02 14	03 06	03 52
58	17 34	18 13	18 58	01 27	02 25	03 17	04 02
S 60	17 32	18 13	19 02	01 38	02 37	03 29	04 13

Day	SUN Eqn. of Time 00^h	SUN Eqn. of Time 12^h	SUN Mer. Pass.	MOON Mer. Pass. Upper	MOON Mer. Pass. Lower	MOON Age	MOON Phase
d	m s	m s	h m	h m	h m	d	%
9	02 40	02 51	11 57	18 03	05 39	08	50
10	03 01	03 12	11 57	18 52	06 27	09	60
11	03 22	03 33	11 56	19 43	07 17	10	69

UT		ARIES	VENUS −3·9		MARS −0·1		JUPITER −1·7		SATURN +0·5	
d h		GHA	GHA	Dec	GHA	Dec	GHA	Dec	GHA	Dec
		° ′	° ′	° ′	° ′	° ′	° ′	° ′	° ′	° ′
12 00		351 25.8	156 36.7	S 5 36.8	92 08.9	S25 42.3	170 30.0	N 0 47.3	102 19.7	S20 31.7
01		6 28.3	171 36.3	38.1	107 09.7	42.3	185 32.0	47.1	117 22.0	31.7
02		21 30.7	186 36.0	39.3	122 10.5	42.4	200 33.9	46.8	132 24.3	31.8
03		36 33.2	201 35.7	. . 40.6	137 11.3	. . 42.5	215 35.9	. . 46.6	147 26.7	. . 31.8
04		51 35.6	216 35.3	41.9	152 12.1	42.6	230 37.9	46.4	162 29.0	31.8
05		66 38.1	231 35.0	43.1	167 12.9	42.7	245 39.8	46.2	177 31.4	31.8
06		81 40.6	246 34.7	S 5 44.4	182 13.6	S25 42.8	260 41.8	N 0 46.0	192 33.7	S20 31.9
07		96 43.0	261 34.3	45.7	197 14.4	42.9	275 43.8	45.8	207 36.0	31.9
08		111 45.5	276 34.0	46.9	212 15.2	42.9	290 45.8	45.6	222 38.4	31.9
09	M	126 48.0	291 33.7	. . 48.2	227 16.0	. . 43.0	305 47.7	. . 45.3	237 40.7	. . 31.9
10	O	141 50.4	306 33.3	49.5	242 16.8	43.1	320 49.7	45.1	252 43.1	32.0
11	N	156 52.9	321 33.0	50.7	257 17.6	43.2	335 51.7	44.9	267 45.4	32.0
12	D	171 55.4	336 32.7	S 5 52.0	272 18.4	S25 43.3	350 53.7	N 0 44.7	282 47.8	S20 32.0
13	A	186 57.8	351 32.3	53.3	287 19.2	43.4	5 55.6	44.5	297 50.1	32.0
14	Y	202 00.3	6 32.0	54.5	302 19.9	43.4	20 57.6	44.3	312 52.4	32.1
15		217 02.7	21 31.7	. . 55.8	317 20.7	. . 43.5	35 59.6	. . 44.1	327 54.8	. . 32.1
16		232 05.2	36 31.3	57.1	332 21.5	43.6	51 01.6	43.9	342 57.1	32.1
17		247 07.7	51 31.0	58.3	347 22.3	43.7	66 03.5	43.6	357 59.5	32.1
18		262 10.1	66 30.6	S 5 59.6	2 23.1	S25 43.8	81 05.5	N 0 43.4	13 01.8	S20 32.2
19		277 12.6	81 30.3	6 00.9	17 23.9	43.8	96 07.5	43.2	28 04.1	32.2
20		292 15.1	96 30.0	02.1	32 24.7	43.9	111 09.4	43.0	43 06.5	32.2
21		307 17.5	111 29.6	. . 03.4	47 25.4	. . 44.0	126 11.4	. . 42.8	58 08.8	. . 32.2
22		322 20.0	126 29.3	04.7	62 26.2	44.1	141 13.4	42.6	73 11.1	32.3
23		337 22.5	141 29.0	05.9	77 27.0	44.2	156 15.4	42.4	88 13.5	32.3
13 00		352 24.9	156 28.6	S 6 07.2	92 27.8	S25 44.2	171 17.3	N 0 42.1	103 15.8	S20 32.3
01		7 27.4	171 28.3	08.4	107 28.6	44.3	186 19.3	41.9	118 18.2	32.3
02		22 29.9	186 28.0	09.7	122 29.3	44.4	201 21.3	41.7	133 20.5	32.4
03		37 32.3	201 27.6	. . 11.0	137 30.1	. . 44.5	216 23.3	. . 41.5	148 22.8	. . 32.4
04		52 34.8	216 27.3	12.2	152 30.9	44.6	231 25.2	41.3	163 25.2	32.4
05		67 37.2	231 26.9	13.5	167 31.7	44.6	246 27.2	41.1	178 27.5	32.4
06		82 39.7	246 26.6	S 6 14.8	182 32.5	S25 44.7	261 29.2	N 0 40.9	193 29.9	S20 32.5
07		97 42.2	261 26.3	16.0	197 33.2	44.8	276 31.2	40.7	208 32.2	32.5
08	T	112 44.6	276 25.9	17.3	212 34.0	44.9	291 33.1	40.4	223 34.5	32.5
09	U	127 47.1	291 25.6	. . 18.5	227 34.8	. . 45.0	306 35.1	. . 40.2	238 36.9	. . 32.5
10	E	142 49.6	306 25.3	19.8	242 35.6	45.0	321 37.1	40.0	253 39.2	32.6
11	S	157 52.0	321 24.9	21.1	257 36.3	45.1	336 39.0	39.8	268 41.5	32.6
12	D	172 54.5	336 24.6	S 6 22.3	272 37.1	S25 45.2	351 41.0	N 0 39.6	283 43.9	S20 32.6
13	A	187 57.0	351 24.2	23.6	287 37.9	45.3	6 43.0	39.4	298 46.2	32.6
14	Y	202 59.4	6 23.9	24.9	302 38.7	45.3	21 45.0	39.2	313 48.5	32.7
15		218 01.9	21 23.6	. . 26.1	317 39.4	. . 45.4	36 46.9	. . 38.9	328 50.9	. . 32.7
16		233 04.4	36 23.2	27.4	332 40.2	45.5	51 48.9	38.7	343 53.2	32.7
17		248 06.8	51 22.9	28.6	347 41.0	45.6	66 50.9	38.5	358 55.6	32.7
18		263 09.3	66 22.5	S 6 29.9	2 41.8	S25 45.6	81 52.9	N 0 38.3	13 57.9	S20 32.8
19		278 11.7	81 22.2	31.2	17 42.5	45.7	96 54.8	38.1	29 00.2	32.8
20		293 14.2	96 21.9	32.4	32 43.3	45.8	111 56.8	37.9	44 02.6	32.8
21		308 16.7	111 21.5	. . 33.7	47 44.1	. . 45.9	126 58.8	. . 37.7	59 04.9	. . 32.9
22		323 19.1	126 21.2	34.9	62 44.9	45.9	142 00.7	37.4	74 07.2	32.9
23		338 21.6	141 20.8	36.2	77 45.6	46.0	157 02.7	37.2	89 09.6	32.9
14 00		353 24.1	156 20.5	S 6 37.4	92 46.4	S25 46.1	172 04.7	N 0 37.0	104 11.9	S20 32.9
01		8 26.5	171 20.2	38.7	107 47.2	46.1	187 06.7	36.8	119 14.2	33.0
02		23 29.0	186 19.8	40.0	122 47.9	46.2	202 08.6	36.6	134 16.6	33.0
03		38 31.5	201 19.5	. . 41.2	137 48.7	. . 46.3	217 10.6	. . 36.4	149 18.9	. . 33.0
04		53 33.9	216 19.1	42.5	152 49.5	46.4	232 12.6	36.2	164 21.2	33.0
05		68 36.4	231 18.8	43.7	167 50.2	46.4	247 14.5	36.0	179 23.6	33.1
06		83 38.8	246 18.4	S 6 45.0	182 51.0	S25 46.5	262 16.5	N 0 35.7	194 25.9	S20 33.1
07	W	98 41.3	261 18.1	46.3	197 51.8	46.6	277 18.5	35.5	209 28.2	33.1
08	E	113 43.8	276 17.8	47.5	212 52.5	46.6	292 20.5	35.3	224 30.6	33.1
09	D	128 46.2	291 17.4	. . 48.8	227 53.3	. . 46.7	307 22.4	. . 35.1	239 32.9	. . 33.2
10	N	143 48.7	306 17.1	50.0	242 54.1	46.8	322 24.4	34.9	254 35.2	33.2
11	E	158 51.2	321 16.7	51.3	257 54.8	46.9	337 26.4	34.7	269 37.6	33.2
12	S	173 53.6	336 16.4	S 6 52.5	272 55.6	S25 46.9	352 28.4	N 0 34.5	284 39.9	S20 33.2
13		188 56.1	351 16.0	53.8	287 56.4	47.0	7 30.3	34.2	299 42.2	33.3
14	D	203 58.6	6 15.7	55.0	302 57.1	47.1	22 32.3	34.0	314 44.6	33.3
15	A	219 01.0	21 15.4	. . 56.3	317 57.9	. . 47.1	37 34.3	. . 33.8	329 46.9	. . 33.3
16	Y	234 03.5	36 15.0	57.6	332 58.7	47.2	52 36.2	33.6	344 49.2	33.3
17		249 06.0	51 14.7	6 58.8	347 59.4	47.3	67 38.2	33.4	359 51.6	33.4
18		264 08.4	66 14.3	S 7 00.1	3 00.2	S25 47.3	82 40.2	N 0 33.2	14 53.9	S20 33.4
19		279 10.9	81 14.0	01.3	18 01.0	47.4	97 42.2	33.0	29 56.2	33.4
20		294 13.3	96 13.6	02.6	33 01.7	47.5	112 44.1	32.7	44 58.6	33.5
21		309 15.8	111 13.3	. . 03.8	48 02.5	. . 47.5	127 46.1	. . 32.5	60 00.9	. . 33.5
22		324 18.3	126 12.9	05.1	63 03.2	47.6	142 48.1	32.3	75 03.2	33.5
23		339 20.7	141 12.6	06.3	78 04.0	47.7	157 50.0	32.1	90 05.5	33.5
Mer. Pass.		h m 0 30.3	v −0.3	d 1.3	v 0.8	d 0.1	v 2.0	d 0.2	v 2.3	d 0.0

STARS

Name	SHA	Dec
	° ′	° ′
Acamar	315 16.5	S40 14.2
Achernar	335 24.8	S57 09.0
Acrux	173 07.3	S63 11.5
Adhara	255 10.9	S28 59.6
Aldebaran	290 46.8	N16 32.4
Alioth	166 19.4	N55 52.4
Alkaid	152 57.6	N49 14.1
Al Na'ir	27 40.6	S46 52.7
Alnilam	275 44.2	S 1 11.5
Alphard	217 54.2	S 8 43.8
Alphecca	126 09.3	N26 39.9
Alpheratz	357 40.8	N29 11.0
Altair	62 05.9	N 8 55.1
Ankaa	353 13.2	S42 12.8
Antares	112 23.6	S26 27.9
Arcturus	145 54.0	N19 06.1
Atria	107 23.5	S69 03.5
Avior	234 17.5	S59 33.6
Bellatrix	278 29.7	N 6 21.8
Betelgeuse	270 59.0	N 7 24.5
Canopus	263 55.3	S52 42.1
Capella	280 31.2	N46 00.5
Deneb	49 29.6	N45 20.8
Denebola	182 31.8	N14 28.9
Diphda	348 53.4	S17 53.6
Dubhe	193 49.8	N61 39.7
Elnath	278 09.9	N28 37.0
Eltanin	90 45.1	N51 29.7
Enif	33 44.7	N 9 57.3
Fomalhaut	15 21.3	S29 31.9
Gacrux	171 58.9	S57 12.3
Gienah	175 50.3	S17 37.9
Hadar	148 45.1	S60 27.2
Hamal	327 58.0	N23 32.4
Kaus Aust.	83 40.8	S34 22.4
Kochab	137 21.0	N74 05.6
Markab	13 35.8	N15 17.9
Menkar	314 12.6	N 4 09.3
Menkent	148 05.2	S36 27.0
Miaplacidus	221 39.8	S69 47.0
Mirfak	308 36.9	N49 54.9
Nunki	75 55.5	S26 16.4
Peacock	53 15.5	S56 40.8
Pollux	243 25.3	N27 59.0
Procyon	244 57.6	N 5 10.9
Rasalhague	96 04.4	N12 33.3
Regulus	207 41.5	N11 53.2
Rigel	281 09.9	S 8 11.0
Rigil Kent.	139 49.1	S60 54.2
Sabik	102 10.0	S15 44.5
Schedar	349 37.4	N56 37.7
Shaula	96 18.9	S37 06.8
Sirius	258 31.9	S16 44.3
Spica	158 29.2	S11 14.7
Suhail	222 51.1	S43 29.9
Vega	80 37.3	N38 48.4
Zuben'ubi	137 03.2	S16 06.4

	SHA	Mer. Pass.
	° ′	h m
Venus	164 03.7	13 34
Mars	100 02.9	17 49
Jupiter	178 52.4	12 33
Saturn	110 50.9	17 04

	UT	SUN GHA	SUN Dec	MOON GHA	*v*	MOON Dec	*d*	HP
	d h	° ′	° ′	° ′	′	° ′	′	′
	12 00	180 56.0	N 4 05.6	62 08.0	9.9	S17 54.8	2.6	56.4
	01	195 56.2	04.6	76 36.9	9.9	17 52.2	2.6	56.4
	02	210 56.4	03.7	91 05.8	9.9	17 49.6	2.8	56.4
	03	225 56.6	. . 02.7	105 34.7	9.8	17 46.8	2.8	56.5
	04	240 56.8	01.7	120 03.5	9.9	17 44.0	3.0	56.5
	05	255 57.1	4 00.8	134 32.4	9.8	17 41.0	3.0	56.5
	06	270 57.3	N 3 59.8	149 01.2	9.7	S17 38.0	3.2	56.6
	07	285 57.5	58.9	163 29.9	9.8	17 34.8	3.2	56.6
	08	300 57.7	57.9	177 58.7	9.7	17 31.6	3.4	56.6
M	09	315 58.0	. . 57.0	192 27.4	9.7	17 28.2	3.4	56.7
O	10	330 58.2	56.0	206 56.1	9.7	17 24.8	3.6	56.7
N	11	345 58.4	55.1	221 24.8	9.7	17 21.2	3.6	56.7
D	12	0 58.6	N 3 54.1	235 53.5	9.6	S17 17.6	3.8	56.8
A	13	15 58.8	53.2	250 22.1	9.6	17 13.8	3.8	56.8
Y	14	30 59.1	52.2	264 50.7	9.6	17 10.0	4.0	56.8
	15	45 59.3	. . 51.2	279 19.3	9.6	17 06.0	4.0	56.9
	16	60 59.5	50.3	293 47.9	9.5	17 02.0	4.2	56.9
	17	75 59.7	49.3	308 16.4	9.6	16 57.8	4.2	56.9
	18	91 00.0	N 3 48.4	322 45.0	9.5	S16 53.6	4.4	57.0
	19	106 00.2	47.4	337 13.5	9.5	16 49.2	4.4	57.0
	20	121 00.4	46.5	351 42.0	9.5	16 44.8	4.5	57.0
	21	136 00.6	. . 45.5	6 10.5	9.4	16 40.3	4.7	57.1
	22	151 00.8	44.5	20 38.9	9.5	16 35.6	4.7	57.1
	23	166 01.1	43.6	35 07.4	9.4	16 30.9	4.8	57.2
	13 00	181 01.3	N 3 42.6	49 35.8	9.4	S16 26.1	5.0	57.2
	01	196 01.5	41.7	64 04.2	9.4	16 21.1	5.0	57.2
	02	211 01.7	40.7	78 32.6	9.4	16 16.1	5.1	57.3
	03	226 02.0	. . 39.8	93 01.0	9.3	16 11.0	5.3	57.3
	04	241 02.2	38.8	107 29.3	9.4	16 05.7	5.3	57.3
	05	256 02.4	37.9	121 57.7	9.3	16 00.4	5.4	57.4
	06	271 02.6	N 3 36.9	136 26.0	9.3	S15 55.0	5.5	57.4
	07	286 02.8	35.9	150 54.3	9.3	15 49.5	5.6	57.4
T	08	301 03.1	35.0	165 22.6	9.3	15 43.9	5.8	57.5
U	09	316 03.3	. . 34.0	179 50.9	9.2	15 38.1	5.8	57.5
E	10	331 03.5	33.1	194 19.1	9.3	15 32.3	5.9	57.6
S	11	346 03.7	32.1	208 47.4	9.2	15 26.4	6.0	57.6
D	12	1 04.0	N 3 31.1	223 15.6	9.2	S15 20.4	6.1	57.6
A	13	16 04.2	30.2	237 43.8	9.2	15 14.3	6.1	57.7
Y	14	31 04.4	29.2	252 12.0	9.2	15 08.2	6.3	57.7
	15	46 04.6	. . 28.3	266 40.2	9.2	15 01.9	6.4	57.7
	16	61 04.9	27.3	281 08.4	9.2	14 55.5	6.5	57.8
	17	76 05.1	26.4	295 36.6	9.2	14 49.0	6.5	57.8
	18	91 05.3	N 3 25.4	310 04.8	9.1	S14 42.5	6.7	57.9
	19	106 05.5	24.4	324 32.9	9.2	14 35.8	6.8	57.9
	20	121 05.7	23.5	339 01.1	9.1	14 29.0	6.8	57.9
	21	136 06.0	. . 22.5	353 29.2	9.1	14 22.2	6.9	58.0
	22	151 06.2	21.6	7 57.3	9.1	14 15.3	7.1	58.0
	23	166 06.4	20.6	22 25.4	9.1	14 08.2	7.1	58.0
	14 00	181 06.6	N 3 19.6	36 53.5	9.1	S14 01.1	7.2	58.1
	01	196 06.9	18.7	51 21.6	9.1	13 53.9	7.3	58.1
	02	211 07.1	17.7	65 49.7	9.0	13 46.6	7.4	58.1
	03	226 07.3	. . 16.8	80 17.7	9.1	13 39.2	7.4	58.2
	04	241 07.5	15.8	94 45.8	9.0	13 31.8	7.6	58.2
	05	256 07.8	14.8	109 13.8	9.1	13 24.2	7.7	58.3
	06	271 08.0	N 3 13.9	123 41.9	9.0	S13 16.5	7.7	58.3
W	07	286 08.2	12.9	138 09.9	9.0	13 08.8	7.8	58.3
E	08	301 08.4	12.0	152 37.9	9.0	13 01.0	7.9	58.4
D	09	316 08.6	. . 11.0	167 05.9	9.0	12 53.1	8.0	58.4
N	10	331 08.9	10.0	181 33.9	9.0	12 45.1	8.1	58.4
E	11	346 09.1	09.1	196 01.9	9.0	12 37.0	8.2	58.5
S	12	1 09.3	N 3 08.1	210 29.9	9.0	S12 28.8	8.2	58.5
D	13	16 09.5	07.2	224 57.9	9.0	12 20.6	8.3	58.5
A	14	31 09.8	06.2	239 25.9	9.0	12 12.3	8.5	58.6
Y	15	46 10.0	. . 05.2	253 53.9	8.9	12 03.8	8.5	58.6
	16	61 10.2	04.3	268 21.8	9.0	11 55.3	8.5	58.6
	17	76 10.4	03.3	282 49.8	8.9	11 46.8	8.7	58.7
	18	91 10.7	N 3 02.4	297 17.7	9.0	S11 38.1	8.7	58.7
	19	106 10.9	01.4	311 45.7	8.9	11 29.4	8.8	58.8
	20	121 11.1	3 00.4	326 13.6	8.9	11 20.6	8.9	58.8
	21	136 11.3	2 59.5	340 41.5	8.9	11 11.7	9.0	58.8
	22	151 11.6	58.5	355 09.4	9.0	11 02.7	9.0	58.9
	23	166 11.8	57.5	9 37.4	8.9	S10 53.7	9.2	58.9
		SD 15.9	*d* 1.0	SD 15.5		15.7		15.9

Lat.	Twilight Naut.	Twilight Civil	Sunrise	Moonrise 12	13	14	15
°	h m	h m	h m	h m	h m	h m	h m
N 72	01 53	03 46	05 00	19 10	18 58	18 50	18 44
N 70	02 29	04 01	05 06	18 18	18 27	18 31	18 33
68	02 53	04 12	05 11	17 46	18 04	18 15	18 23
66	03 12	04 21	05 15	17 22	17 46	18 03	18 16
64	03 27	04 29	05 18	17 03	17 31	17 52	18 09
62	03 39	04 36	05 21	16 48	17 19	17 43	18 03
60	03 49	04 41	05 24	16 35	17 08	17 35	17 58
N 58	03 57	04 46	05 26	16 24	16 59	17 28	17 54
56	04 04	04 50	05 28	16 14	16 51	17 22	17 50
54	04 11	04 54	05 30	16 06	16 44	17 17	17 47
52	04 17	04 58	05 32	15 58	16 37	17 12	17 43
50	04 22	05 01	05 33	15 51	16 31	17 07	17 40
45	04 32	05 07	05 37	15 36	16 19	16 58	17 34
N 40	04 40	05 12	05 39	15 24	16 08	16 49	17 29
35	04 46	05 16	05 42	15 14	15 59	16 42	17 24
30	04 51	05 20	05 44	15 04	15 51	16 36	17 20
20	04 59	05 25	05 47	14 49	15 38	16 26	17 13
N 10	05 04	05 29	05 50	14 35	15 26	16 16	17 07
0	05 08	05 32	05 52	14 22	15 14	16 07	17 01
S 10	05 10	05 34	05 55	14 09	15 03	15 59	16 55
20	05 10	05 36	05 58	13 55	14 51	15 49	16 49
30	05 09	05 36	06 00	13 39	14 37	15 38	16 41
35	05 07	05 37	06 02	13 30	14 29	15 32	16 37
40	05 05	05 37	06 04	13 20	14 20	15 25	16 33
45	05 02	05 36	06 06	13 07	14 10	15 17	16 27
S 50	04 58	05 36	06 08	12 52	13 57	15 07	16 21
52	04 56	05 35	06 09	12 45	13 51	15 02	16 18
54	04 54	05 35	06 10	12 37	13 44	14 57	16 14
56	04 51	05 34	06 11	12 29	13 37	14 51	16 11
58	04 48	05 34	06 13	12 19	13 28	14 45	16 06
S 60	04 44	05 33	06 14	12 07	13 19	14 38	16 02

Lat.	Sunset	Twilight Civil	Twilight Naut.	Moonset 12	13	14	15
°	h m	h m	h m	h m	h m	h m	h m
N 72	18 49	20 01	21 51	22 08	24 09	00 09	02 08
N 70	18 43	19 48	21 17	22 59	24 40	00 40	02 26
68	18 39	19 37	20 54	23 30	25 02	01 02	02 40
66	18 35	19 28	20 36	23 54	25 19	01 19	02 52
64	18 31	19 20	20 22	24 12	00 12	01 33	03 01
62	18 29	19 14	20 10	24 27	00 27	01 45	03 09
60	18 26	19 08	20 01	24 39	00 39	01 55	03 16
N 58	18 24	19 04	19 52	24 50	00 50	02 03	03 23
56	18 22	19 00	19 45	25 00	01 00	02 11	03 28
54	18 20	18 56	19 39	00 05	01 08	02 18	03 33
52	18 19	18 53	19 34	00 13	01 15	02 24	03 37
50	18 17	18 50	19 29	00 21	01 22	02 29	03 41
45	18 14	18 44	19 19	00 37	01 36	02 41	03 50
N 40	18 12	18 39	19 11	00 50	01 48	02 51	03 57
35	18 09	18 35	19 04	01 01	01 58	02 59	04 03
30	18 07	18 31	18 59	01 10	02 07	03 06	04 08
20	18 04	18 26	18 52	01 27	02 22	03 19	04 17
N 10	18 01	18 22	18 47	01 41	02 35	03 30	04 25
0	17 59	18 20	18 44	01 55	02 47	03 40	04 33
S 10	17 57	18 18	18 42	02 08	02 59	03 50	04 40
20	17 54	18 16	18 42	02 23	03 12	04 00	04 48
30	17 52	18 15	18 43	02 39	03 27	04 13	04 57
35	17 50	18 15	18 45	02 49	03 35	04 20	05 02
40	17 49	18 16	18 47	02 59	03 45	04 28	05 08
45	17 47	18 16	18 50	03 12	03 56	04 37	05 14
S 50	17 44	18 17	18 54	03 28	04 10	04 48	05 22
52	17 44	18 17	18 56	03 35	04 16	04 53	05 26
54	17 42	18 18	18 59	03 43	04 23	04 59	05 30
56	17 41	18 18	19 02	03 52	04 31	05 05	05 34
58	17 40	18 19	19 05	04 02	04 40	05 12	05 39
S 60	17 39	18 20	19 09	04 13	04 50	05 20	05 45

Day	SUN Eqn. of Time 00^h	SUN Eqn. of Time 12^h	SUN Mer. Pass.	MOON Mer. Pass. Upper	MOON Mer. Pass. Lower	MOON Age	MOON Phase
d	m s	m s	h m	h m	h m	d	%
12	03 43	03 54	11 56	20 34	08 08	11	78
13	04 05	04 15	11 56	21 27	09 01	12	87
14	04 26	04 37	11 55	22 20	09 54	13	93

Day	UT d h	ARIES GHA	VENUS −3·9 GHA	VENUS Dec	MARS −0·1 GHA	MARS Dec	JUPITER −1·7 GHA	JUPITER Dec	SATURN +0·5 GHA	SATURN Dec
		° ′	° ′	° ′	° ′	° ′	° ′	° ′	° ′	° ′
THURSDAY	15 00	354 23.2	156 12.3	S 7 07.6	93 04.8	S25 47.7	172 52.0	N 0 31.9	105 07.9	S20 33.6
	01	9 25.7	171 11.9	08.8	108 05.5	47.8	187 54.0	31.7	120 10.2	33.6
	02	24 28.1	186 11.6	10.1	123 06.3	47.9	202 56.0	31.5	135 12.5	33.6
	03	39 30.6	201 11.2	. . 11.3	138 07.0	. . 47.9	217 57.9	. . 31.3	150 14.9	. . 33.6
	04	54 33.1	216 10.9	12.6	153 07.8	48.0	232 59.9	31.0	165 17.2	33.7
	05	69 35.5	231 10.5	13.8	168 08.6	48.1	248 01.9	30.8	180 19.5	33.7
	06	84 38.0	246 10.2	S 7 15.1	183 09.3	S25 48.1	263 03.8	N 0 30.6	195 21.9	S20 33.7
	07	99 40.5	261 09.8	16.4	198 10.1	48.2	278 05.8	30.4	210 24.2	33.7
	08	114 42.9	276 09.5	17.6	213 10.8	48.2	293 07.8	30.2	225 26.5	33.8
	09	129 45.4	291 09.1	. . 18.9	228 11.6	. . 48.3	308 09.8	. . 30.0	240 28.8	. . 33.8
	10	144 47.8	306 08.8	20.1	243 12.3	48.4	323 11.7	29.8	255 31.2	33.8
	11	159 50.3	321 08.4	21.4	258 13.1	48.4	338 13.7	29.5	270 33.5	33.8
	12	174 52.8	336 08.1	S 7 22.6	273 13.9	S25 48.5	353 15.7	N 0 29.3	285 35.8	S20 33.9
	13	189 55.2	351 07.7	23.9	288 14.6	48.6	8 17.6	29.1	300 38.2	33.9
	14	204 57.7	6 07.4	25.1	303 15.4	48.6	23 19.6	28.9	315 40.5	33.9
	15	220 00.2	21 07.0	. . 26.4	318 16.1	. . 48.7	38 21.6	. . 28.7	330 42.8	. . 34.0
	16	235 02.6	36 06.7	27.6	333 16.9	48.7	53 23.6	28.5	345 45.1	34.0
	17	250 05.1	51 06.3	28.8	348 17.6	48.8	68 25.5	28.3	0 47.5	34.0
	18	265 07.6	66 06.0	S 7 30.1	3 18.4	S25 48.9	83 27.5	N 0 28.0	15 49.8	S20 34.0
	19	280 10.0	81 05.6	31.3	18 19.1	48.9	98 29.5	27.8	30 52.1	34.1
	20	295 12.5	96 05.3	32.6	33 19.9	49.0	113 31.4	27.6	45 54.5	34.1
	21	310 14.9	111 04.9	. . 33.8	48 20.6	. . 49.0	128 33.4	. . 27.4	60 56.8	. . 34.1
	22	325 17.4	126 04.6	35.1	63 21.4	49.1	143 35.4	27.2	75 59.1	34.1
	23	340 19.9	141 04.2	36.3	78 22.1	49.2	158 37.4	27.0	91 01.4	34.2
FRIDAY	16 00	355 22.3	156 03.9	S 7 37.6	93 22.9	S25 49.2	173 39.3	N 0 26.8	106 03.8	S20 34.2
	01	10 24.8	171 03.5	38.8	108 23.6	49.3	188 41.3	26.5	121 06.1	34.2
	02	25 27.3	186 03.2	40.1	123 24.4	49.3	203 43.3	26.3	136 08.4	34.2
	03	40 29.7	201 02.8	. . 41.3	138 25.1	. . 49.4	218 45.2	. . 26.1	151 10.7	. . 34.3
	04	55 32.2	216 02.5	42.6	153 25.9	49.5	233 47.2	25.9	166 13.1	34.3
	05	70 34.7	231 02.1	43.8	168 26.6	49.5	248 49.2	25.7	181 15.4	34.3
	06	85 37.1	246 01.8	S 7 45.1	183 27.4	S25 49.6	263 51.2	N 0 25.5	196 17.7	S20 34.4
	07	100 39.6	261 01.4	46.3	198 28.1	49.6	278 53.1	25.3	211 20.1	34.4
	08	115 42.1	276 01.1	47.5	213 28.9	49.7	293 55.1	25.1	226 22.4	34.4
	09	130 44.5	291 00.7	. . 48.8	228 29.6	. . 49.7	308 57.1	. . 24.8	241 24.7	. . 34.4
	10	145 47.0	306 00.4	50.0	243 30.4	49.8	323 59.0	24.6	256 27.0	34.5
	11	160 49.4	321 00.0	51.3	258 31.1	49.8	339 01.0	24.4	271 29.4	34.5
	12	175 51.9	335 59.7	S 7 52.5	273 31.9	S25 49.9	354 03.0	N 0 24.2	286 31.7	S20 34.5
	13	190 54.4	350 59.3	53.8	288 32.6	50.0	9 05.0	24.0	301 34.0	34.5
	14	205 56.8	5 59.0	55.0	303 33.3	50.0	24 06.9	23.8	316 36.3	34.6
	15	220 59.3	20 58.6	. . 56.2	318 34.1	. . 50.1	39 08.9	. . 23.6	331 38.7	. . 34.6
	16	236 01.8	35 58.2	57.5	333 34.8	50.1	54 10.9	23.3	346 41.0	34.6
	17	251 04.2	50 57.9	7 58.7	348 35.6	50.2	69 12.8	23.1	1 43.3	34.7
	18	266 06.7	65 57.5	S 8 00.0	3 36.3	S25 50.2	84 14.8	N 0 22.9	16 45.6	S20 34.7
	19	281 09.2	80 57.2	01.2	18 37.1	50.3	99 16.8	22.7	31 48.0	34.7
	20	296 11.6	95 56.8	02.5	33 37.8	50.3	114 18.8	22.5	46 50.3	34.7
	21	311 14.1	110 56.5	. . 03.7	48 38.5	. . 50.4	129 20.7	. . 22.3	61 52.6	. . 34.8
	22	326 16.5	125 56.1	04.9	63 39.3	50.4	144 22.7	22.1	76 54.9	34.8
	23	341 19.0	140 55.8	06.2	78 40.0	50.5	159 24.7	21.8	91 57.2	34.8
SATURDAY	17 00	356 21.5	155 55.4	S 8 07.4	93 40.8	S25 50.5	174 26.6	N 0 21.6	106 59.6	S20 34.8
	01	11 23.9	170 55.0	08.7	108 41.5	50.6	189 28.6	21.4	122 01.9	34.9
	02	26 26.4	185 54.7	09.9	123 42.2	50.6	204 30.6	21.2	137 04.2	34.9
	03	41 28.9	200 54.3	. . 11.1	138 43.0	. . 50.7	219 32.5	. . 21.0	152 06.5	. . 34.9
	04	56 31.3	215 54.0	12.4	153 43.7	50.7	234 34.5	20.8	167 08.9	35.0
	05	71 33.8	230 53.6	13.6	168 44.5	50.8	249 36.5	20.6	182 11.2	35.0
	06	86 36.3	245 53.3	S 8 14.9	183 45.2	S25 50.8	264 38.5	N 0 20.3	197 13.5	S20 35.0
	07	101 38.7	260 52.9	16.1	198 45.9	50.9	279 40.4	20.1	212 15.8	35.0
	08	116 41.2	275 52.5	17.3	213 46.7	50.9	294 42.4	19.9	227 18.1	35.1
	09	131 43.7	290 52.2	. . 18.6	228 47.4	. . 51.0	309 44.4	. . 19.7	242 20.5	. . 35.1
	10	146 46.1	305 51.8	19.8	243 48.1	51.0	324 46.3	19.5	257 22.8	35.1
	11	161 48.6	320 51.5	21.0	258 48.9	51.1	339 48.3	19.3	272 25.1	35.1
	12	176 51.0	335 51.1	S 8 22.3	273 49.6	S25 51.1	354 50.3	N 0 19.1	287 27.4	S20 35.2
	13	191 53.5	350 50.7	23.5	288 50.3	51.2	9 52.3	18.8	302 29.8	35.2
	14	206 56.0	5 50.4	24.7	303 51.1	51.2	24 54.2	18.6	317 32.1	35.2
	15	221 58.4	20 50.0	. . 26.0	318 51.8	. . 51.3	39 56.2	. . 18.4	332 34.4	. . 35.3
	16	237 00.9	35 49.7	27.2	333 52.6	51.3	54 58.2	18.2	347 36.7	35.3
	17	252 03.4	50 49.3	28.5	348 53.3	51.4	70 00.1	18.0	2 39.0	35.3
	18	267 05.8	65 48.9	S 8 29.7	3 54.0	S25 51.4	85 02.1	N 0 17.8	17 41.4	S20 35.3
	19	282 08.3	80 48.6	30.9	18 54.7	51.5	100 04.1	17.6	32 43.7	35.4
	20	297 10.8	95 48.2	32.2	33 55.5	51.5	115 06.0	17.3	47 46.0	35.4
	21	312 13.2	110 47.9	. . 33.4	48 56.2	. . 51.5	130 08.0	. . 17.1	62 48.3	. . 35.4
	22	327 15.7	125 47.5	34.6	63 56.9	51.6	145 10.0	16.9	77 50.6	35.4
	23	342 18.1	140 47.1	35.9	78 57.7	51.6	160 12.0	16.7	92 53.0	35.5
	Mer. Pass.	h m 0 18.5	v −0.4	d 1.2	v 0.7	d 0.1	v 2.0	d 0.2	v 2.3	d 0.0

STARS

Name	SHA	Dec
	° ′	° ′
Acamar	315 16.5	S40 14.2
Achernar	335 24.7	S57 09.0
Acrux	173 07.4	S63 11.4
Adhara	255 10.9	S28 59.6
Aldebaran	290 46.8	N16 32.4
Alioth	166 19.4	N55 52.4
Alkaid	152 57.6	N49 14.1
Al Na'ir	27 40.6	S46 52.7
Alnilam	275 44.1	S 1 11.5
Alphard	217 54.2	S 8 43.8
Alphecca	126 09.3	N26 39.9
Alpheratz	357 40.8	N29 11.0
Altair	62 05.9	N 8 55.1
Ankaa	353 13.2	S42 12.8
Antares	112 23.7	S26 27.9
Arcturus	145 54.0	N19 06.1
Atria	107 23.5	S69 03.5
Avior	234 17.5	S59 33.6
Bellatrix	278 29.6	N 6 21.8
Betelgeuse	270 59.0	N 7 24.5
Canopus	263 55.3	S52 42.1
Capella	280 31.2	N46 00.5
Deneb	49 29.6	N45 20.8
Denebola	182 31.8	N14 28.9
Diphda	348 53.4	S17 53.6
Dubhe	193 49.8	N61 39.7
Elnath	278 09.8	N28 37.0
Eltanin	90 45.1	N51 29.7
Enif	33 44.7	N 9 57.3
Fomalhaut	15 21.3	S29 31.9
Gacrux	171 58.9	S57 12.3
Gienah	175 50.3	S17 37.9
Hadar	148 45.2	S60 27.2
Hamal	327 58.0	N23 32.4
Kaus Aust.	83 40.8	S34 22.4
Kochab	137 21.0	N74 05.6
Markab	13 35.8	N15 17.9
Menkar	314 12.6	N 4 09.3
Menkent	148 05.2	S36 27.0
Miaplacidus	221 39.8	S69 47.0
Mirfak	308 36.9	N49 54.9
Nunki	75 55.5	S26 16.4
Peacock	53 15.5	S56 40.8
Pollux	243 25.3	N27 59.0
Procyon	244 57.6	N 5 10.9
Rasalhague	96 04.4	N12 33.3
Regulus	207 41.5	N11 53.2
Rigel	281 09.9	S 8 11.0
Rigil Kent.	139 49.1	S60 54.2
Sabik	102 10.1	S15 44.5
Schedar	349 37.4	N56 37.7
Shaula	96 18.9	S37 06.8
Sirius	258 31.9	S16 44.3
Spica	158 29.2	S11 14.7
Suhail	222 51.1	S43 29.9
Vega	80 37.4	N38 48.4
Zuben'ubi	137 03.2	S16 06.4

	SHA	Mer. Pass.
	° ′	h m
Venus	160 41.6	13 36
Mars	98 00.5	17 46
Jupiter	178 17.0	12 24
Saturn	110 41.4	16 53

	UT	SUN GHA	SUN Dec	MOON GHA	*v*	MOON Dec	*d*	HP
	d h	° ′	° ′	° ′	′	° ′	′	′
	15 00	181 12.0	N 2 56.6	24 05.3	8.9	S10 44.5	9.2	58.9
	01	196 12.2	55.6	38 33.2	8.9	10 35.3	9.2	59.0
	02	211 12.4	54.7	53 01.1	8.9	10 26.1	9.4	59.0
	03	226 12.7	. . 53.7	67 29.0	8.8	10 16.7	9.4	59.0
	04	241 12.9	52.7	81 56.8	8.9	10 07.3	9.5	59.1
	05	256 13.1	51.8	96 24.7	8.9	9 57.8	9.5	59.1
	06	271 13.3	N 2 50.8	110 52.6	8.8	S 9 48.3	9.6	59.1
	07	286 13.6	49.8	125 20.4	8.9	9 38.7	9.7	59.2
T	08	301 13.8	48.9	139 48.3	8.9	9 29.0	9.8	59.2
H	09	316 14.0	. . 47.9	154 16.2	8.8	9 19.2	9.8	59.2
U	10	331 14.2	47.0	168 44.0	8.8	9 09.4	9.9	59.2
R	11	346 14.5	46.0	183 11.8	8.9	8 59.5	10.0	59.3
S	12	1 14.7	N 2 45.0	197 39.7	8.8	S 8 49.5	10.0	59.3
D	13	16 14.9	44.1	212 07.5	8.8	8 39.5	10.1	59.3
A	14	31 15.1	43.1	226 35.3	8.8	8 29.4	10.1	59.4
Y	15	46 15.4	. . 42.1	241 03.1	8.8	8 19.3	10.2	59.4
	16	61 15.6	41.2	255 30.9	8.9	8 09.1	10.3	59.4
	17	76 15.8	40.2	269 58.8	8.7	7 58.8	10.3	59.5
	18	91 16.0	N 2 39.3	284 26.5	8.8	S 7 48.5	10.4	59.5
	19	106 16.3	38.3	298 54.3	8.8	7 38.1	10.5	59.5
	20	121 16.5	37.3	313 22.1	8.8	7 27.6	10.5	59.5
	21	136 16.7	. . 36.4	327 49.9	8.8	7 17.1	10.5	59.6
	22	151 16.9	35.4	342 17.7	8.7	7 06.6	10.6	59.6
	23	166 17.1	34.4	356 45.4	8.8	6 56.0	10.7	59.6
	16 00	181 17.4	N 2 33.5	11 13.2	8.7	S 6 45.3	10.7	59.7
	01	196 17.6	32.5	25 40.9	8.8	6 34.6	10.7	59.7
	02	211 17.8	31.5	40 08.7	8.7	6 23.9	10.8	59.7
	03	226 18.0	. . 30.6	54 36.4	8.7	6 13.1	10.9	59.7
	04	241 18.3	29.6	69 04.1	8.8	6 02.2	10.9	59.8
	05	256 18.5	28.7	83 31.9	8.7	5 51.3	10.9	59.8
	06	271 18.7	N 2 27.7	97 59.6	8.7	S 5 40.4	11.0	59.8
	07	286 18.9	26.7	112 27.3	8.7	5 29.4	11.0	59.8
	08	301 19.2	25.8	126 55.0	8.6	5 18.4	11.1	59.9
F	09	316 19.4	. . 24.8	141 22.6	8.7	5 07.3	11.1	59.9
R	10	331 19.6	23.8	155 50.3	8.7	4 56.2	11.2	59.9
I	11	346 19.8	22.9	170 18.0	8.7	4 45.0	11.2	59.9
D	12	1 20.1	N 2 21.9	184 45.7	8.6	S 4 33.8	11.2	60.0
A	13	16 20.3	20.9	199 13.3	8.7	4 22.6	11.3	60.0
Y	14	31 20.5	20.0	213 41.0	8.6	4 11.3	11.3	60.0
	15	46 20.7	. . 19.0	228 08.6	8.6	4 00.0	11.3	60.0
	16	61 21.0	18.0	242 36.2	8.6	3 48.7	11.4	60.1
	17	76 21.2	17.1	257 03.8	8.6	3 37.3	11.4	60.1
	18	91 21.4	N 2 16.1	271 31.4	8.6	S 3 25.9	11.4	60.1
	19	106 21.6	15.1	285 59.0	8.6	3 14.5	11.4	60.1
	20	121 21.9	14.2	300 26.6	8.6	3 03.1	11.5	60.1
	21	136 22.1	. . 13.2	314 54.2	8.5	2 51.6	11.5	60.2
	22	151 22.3	12.2	329 21.7	8.6	2 40.1	11.5	60.2
	23	166 22.5	11.3	343 49.3	8.5	2 28.6	11.6	60.2
	17 00	181 22.8	N 2 10.3	358 16.8	8.6	S 2 17.0	11.5	60.2
	01	196 23.0	09.4	12 44.4	8.5	2 05.5	11.6	60.2
	02	211 23.2	08.4	27 11.9	8.5	1 53.9	11.6	60.2
	03	226 23.4	. . 07.4	41 39.4	8.5	1 42.3	11.7	60.3
	04	241 23.6	06.5	56 06.9	8.4	1 30.6	11.6	60.3
	05	256 23.9	05.5	70 34.3	8.5	1 19.0	11.7	60.3
	06	271 24.1	N 2 04.5	85 01.8	8.5	S 1 07.3	11.6	60.3
	07	286 24.3	03.6	99 29.3	8.4	0 55.7	11.7	60.3
S	08	301 24.5	02.6	113 56.7	8.4	0 44.0	11.7	60.3
A	09	316 24.8	. . 01.6	128 24.1	8.4	0 32.3	11.7	60.4
T	10	331 25.0	2 00.7	142 51.5	8.4	0 20.6	11.7	60.4
U	11	346 25.2	1 59.7	157 18.9	8.4	S 0 08.9	11.7	60.4
R	12	1 25.4	N 1 58.7	171 46.3	8.4	N 0 02.8	11.7	60.4
D	13	16 25.7	57.8	186 13.7	8.3	0 14.5	11.7	60.4
A	14	31 25.9	56.8	200 41.0	8.4	0 26.2	11.8	60.4
Y	15	46 26.1	. . 55.8	215 08.4	8.3	0 38.0	11.7	60.4
	16	61 26.3	54.9	229 35.7	8.3	0 49.7	11.7	60.4
	17	76 26.6	53.9	244 03.0	8.3	1 01.4	11.7	60.5
	18	91 26.8	N 1 52.9	258 30.3	8.3	N 1 13.1	11.7	60.5
	19	106 27.0	52.0	272 57.6	8.2	1 24.8	11.8	60.5
	20	121 27.2	51.0	287 24.8	8.3	1 36.6	11.7	60.5
	21	136 27.5	. . 50.0	301 52.1	8.2	1 48.3	11.6	60.5
	22	151 27.7	49.0	316 19.3	8.2	1 59.9	11.7	60.5
	23	166 27.9	48.1	330 46.5	8.2	N 2 11.6	11.7	60.5
		SD 15.9	*d* 1.0	SD 16.2		16.3		16.5

Lat.	Twilight Naut.	Twilight Civil	Sunrise	Moonrise 15	Moonrise 16	Moonrise 17	Moonrise 18
°	h m	h m	h m	h m	h m	h m	h m
N 72	02 19	04 02	05 13	18 44	18 38	18 33	18 28
N 70	02 48	04 14	05 18	18 33	18 34	18 35	18 36
68	03 08	04 24	05 21	18 23	18 30	18 36	18 42
66	03 24	04 32	05 24	18 16	18 27	18 37	18 48
64	03 37	04 38	05 27	18 09	18 24	18 38	18 52
62	03 48	04 44	05 29	18 03	18 21	18 39	18 57
60	03 57	04 49	05 31	17 58	18 19	18 39	19 00
N 58	04 05	04 53	05 33	17 54	18 17	18 40	19 03
56	04 11	04 57	05 34	17 50	18 16	18 41	19 06
54	04 17	05 00	05 35	17 47	18 14	18 41	19 09
52	04 22	05 03	05 37	17 43	18 13	18 42	19 11
50	04 27	05 05	05 38	17 40	18 12	18 42	19 13
45	04 36	05 11	05 40	17 34	18 09	18 43	19 18
N 40	04 43	05 15	05 42	17 29	18 06	18 44	19 22
35	04 49	05 18	05 44	17 24	18 04	18 45	19 25
30	04 53	05 21	05 45	17 20	18 03	18 45	19 29
20	05 00	05 26	05 48	17 13	18 00	18 46	19 34
N 10	05 04	05 29	05 50	17 07	17 57	18 47	19 39
0	05 07	05 31	05 51	17 01	17 54	18 48	19 43
S 10	05 08	05 32	05 53	16 55	17 52	18 49	19 48
20	05 07	05 33	05 55	16 49	17 49	18 51	19 53
30	05 05	05 33	05 57	16 41	17 46	18 52	19 58
35	05 03	05 32	05 58	16 37	17 44	18 53	20 01
40	05 00	05 32	05 59	16 33	17 42	18 53	20 05
45	04 57	05 31	06 00	16 27	17 40	18 54	20 09
S 50	04 52	05 29	06 01	16 21	17 37	18 56	20 15
52	04 49	05 28	06 02	16 18	17 36	18 56	20 17
54	04 46	05 28	06 03	16 14	17 35	18 57	20 20
56	04 43	05 26	06 03	16 11	17 33	18 58	20 23
58	04 39	05 25	06 04	16 06	17 31	18 58	20 26
S 60	04 35	05 24	06 05	16 02	17 30	18 59	20 30

Lat.	Sunset	Twilight Civil	Twilight Naut.	Moonset 15	Moonset 16	Moonset 17	Moonset 18
°	h m	h m	h m	h m	h m	h m	h m
N 72	18 33	19 44	21 24	02 08	04 06	06 04	08 04
N 70	18 29	19 32	20 57	02 26	04 15	06 06	07 58
68	18 26	19 23	20 37	02 40	04 23	06 08	07 54
66	18 23	19 15	20 22	02 52	04 29	06 09	07 50
64	18 21	19 09	20 09	03 01	04 34	06 10	07 47
62	18 19	19 04	19 59	03 09	04 39	06 11	07 44
60	18 17	18 59	19 50	03 16	04 43	06 11	07 42
N 58	18 15	18 55	19 43	03 23	04 46	06 12	07 39
56	18 14	18 51	19 36	03 28	04 49	06 13	07 38
54	18 13	18 48	19 31	03 33	04 52	06 13	07 36
52	18 12	18 45	19 26	03 37	04 54	06 14	07 34
50	18 11	18 43	19 22	03 41	04 57	06 14	07 33
45	18 08	18 38	19 12	03 50	05 02	06 15	07 30
N 40	18 07	18 34	19 06	03 57	05 06	06 16	07 27
35	18 05	18 30	19 00	04 03	05 09	06 17	07 25
30	18 04	18 28	18 56	04 08	05 12	06 17	07 23
20	18 01	18 23	18 49	04 17	05 17	06 18	07 20
N 10	18 00	18 21	18 45	04 25	05 22	06 19	07 17
0	17 58	18 19	18 43	04 33	05 26	06 20	07 14
S 10	17 56	18 17	18 42	04 40	05 30	06 21	07 11
20	17 55	18 17	18 42	04 48	05 35	06 21	07 09
30	17 53	18 17	18 45	04 57	05 40	06 22	07 05
35	17 52	18 18	18 47	05 02	05 43	06 23	07 03
40	17 51	18 18	18 50	05 08	05 46	06 23	07 01
45	17 50	18 19	18 54	05 14	05 50	06 24	06 58
S 50	17 49	18 21	18 59	05 22	05 54	06 25	06 55
52	17 48	18 22	19 01	05 26	05 56	06 25	06 54
54	17 48	18 23	19 04	05 30	05 58	06 25	06 52
56	17 47	18 24	19 08	05 34	06 01	06 26	06 51
58	17 46	18 25	19 12	05 39	06 03	06 26	06 49
S 60	17 46	18 27	19 16	05 45	06 06	06 27	06 47

Day	SUN Eqn. of Time 00^h	SUN Eqn. of Time 12^h	SUN Mer. Pass.	MOON Mer. Pass. Upper	MOON Mer. Pass. Lower	MOON Age	MOON Phase
d	m s	m s	h m	h m	h m	d %	
15	04 48	04 58	11 55	23 13	10 47	14 98	
16	05 09	05 20	11 55	24 07	11 40	15 100	
17	05 31	05 41	11 54	00 07	12 34	16 99	

UT	ARIES	VENUS −3·9		MARS −0·1		JUPITER −1·7		SATURN +0·5	
d h	GHA ° ′	GHA ° ′	Dec ° ′	GHA ° ′	Dec ° ′	GHA ° ′	Dec ° ′	GHA ° ′	Dec ° ′
18 00 SUNDAY	357 20.6	155 46.8	S 8 37.1	93 58.4	S25 51.7	175 13.9	N 0 16.5	107 55.3	S20 35.5
01	12 23.1	170 46.4	38.3	108 59.1	51.7	190 15.9	16.3	122 57.6	35.5
02	27 25.5	185 46.0	39.6	123 59.9	51.8	205 17.9	16.1	137 59.9	35.6
03	42 28.0	200 45.7	. . 40.8	139 00.6	. . 51.8	220 19.8	. . 15.8	153 02.2	. . 35.6
04	57 30.5	215 45.3	42.0	154 01.3	51.8	235 21.8	15.6	168 04.6	35.6
05	72 32.9	230 44.9	43.2	169 02.1	51.9	250 23.8	15.4	183 06.9	35.6
06	87 35.4	245 44.6	S 8 44.5	184 02.8	S25 51.9	265 25.7	N 0 15.2	198 09.2	S20 35.7
07	102 37.9	260 44.2	45.7	199 03.5	52.0	280 27.7	15.0	213 11.5	35.7
08	117 40.3	275 43.9	46.9	214 04.2	52.0	295 29.7	14.8	228 13.8	35.7
09	132 42.8	290 43.5	. . 48.2	229 05.0	. . 52.1	310 31.7	. . 14.6	243 16.1	. . 35.7
10	147 45.3	305 43.1	49.4	244 05.7	52.1	325 33.6	14.3	258 18.5	35.8
11	162 47.7	320 42.8	50.6	259 06.4	52.1	340 35.6	14.1	273 20.8	35.8
12	177 50.2	335 42.4	S 8 51.9	274 07.1	S25 52.2	355 37.6	N 0 13.9	288 23.1	S20 35.8
13	192 52.6	350 42.0	53.1	289 07.9	52.2	10 39.5	13.7	303 25.4	35.9
14	207 55.1	5 41.7	54.3	304 08.6	52.3	25 41.5	13.5	318 27.7	35.9
15	222 57.6	20 41.3	. . 55.5	319 09.3	. . 52.3	40 43.5	. . 13.3	333 30.1	. . 35.9
16	238 00.0	35 40.9	56.8	334 10.0	52.3	55 45.4	13.1	348 32.4	35.9
17	253 02.5	50 40.6	58.0	349 10.8	52.4	70 47.4	12.9	3 34.7	36.0
18	268 05.0	65 40.2	S 8 59.2	4 11.5	S25 52.4	85 49.4	N 0 12.6	18 37.0	S20 36.0
19	283 07.4	80 39.8	9 00.5	19 12.2	52.4	100 51.4	12.4	33 39.3	36.0
20	298 09.9	95 39.4	01.7	34 12.9	52.5	115 53.3	12.2	48 41.6	36.1
21	313 12.4	110 39.1	. . 02.9	49 13.7	. . 52.5	130 55.3	. . 12.0	63 43.9	. . 36.1
22	328 14.8	125 38.7	04.1	64 14.4	52.6	145 57.3	11.8	78 46.3	36.1
23	343 17.3	140 38.3	05.4	79 15.1	52.6	160 59.2	11.6	93 48.6	36.1
19 00 MONDAY	358 19.7	155 38.0	S 9 06.6	94 15.8	S25 52.6	176 01.2	N 0 11.4	108 50.9	S20 36.2
01	13 22.2	170 37.6	07.8	109 16.5	52.7	191 03.2	11.1	123 53.2	36.2
02	28 24.7	185 37.2	09.0	124 17.3	52.7	206 05.1	10.9	138 55.5	36.2
03	43 27.1	200 36.9	. . 10.3	139 18.0	. . 52.7	221 07.1	. . 10.7	153 57.8	. . 36.2
04	58 29.6	215 36.5	11.5	154 18.7	52.8	236 09.1	10.5	169 00.2	36.3
05	73 32.1	230 36.1	12.7	169 19.4	52.8	251 11.1	10.3	184 02.5	36.3
06	88 34.5	245 35.8	S 9 13.9	184 20.1	S25 52.8	266 13.0	N 0 10.1	199 04.8	S20 36.3
07	103 37.0	260 35.4	15.1	199 20.9	52.9	281 15.0	09.9	214 07.1	36.4
08	118 39.5	275 35.0	16.4	214 21.6	52.9	296 17.0	09.6	229 09.4	36.4
09	133 41.9	290 34.6	. . 17.6	229 22.3	. . 52.9	311 18.9	. . 09.4	244 11.7	. . 36.4
10	148 44.4	305 34.3	18.8	244 23.0	53.0	326 20.9	09.2	259 14.0	36.4
11	163 46.9	320 33.9	20.0	259 23.7	53.0	341 22.9	09.0	274 16.4	36.5
12	178 49.3	335 33.5	S 9 21.3	274 24.4	S25 53.0	356 24.8	N 0 08.8	289 18.7	S20 36.5
13	193 51.8	350 33.1	22.5	289 25.2	53.1	11 26.8	08.6	304 21.0	36.5
14	208 54.2	5 32.8	23.7	304 25.9	53.1	26 28.8	08.4	319 23.3	36.6
15	223 56.7	20 32.4	. . 24.9	319 26.6	. . 53.1	41 30.8	. . 08.1	334 25.6	. . 36.6
16	238 59.2	35 32.0	26.1	334 27.3	53.2	56 32.7	07.9	349 27.9	36.6
17	254 01.6	50 31.6	27.4	349 28.0	53.2	71 34.7	07.7	4 30.2	36.6
18	269 04.1	65 31.3	S 9 28.6	4 28.7	S25 53.2	86 36.7	N 0 07.5	19 32.6	S20 36.7
19	284 06.6	80 30.9	29.8	19 29.5	53.3	101 38.6	07.3	34 34.9	36.7
20	299 09.0	95 30.5	31.0	34 30.2	53.3	116 40.6	07.1	49 37.2	36.7
21	314 11.5	110 30.1	. . 32.2	49 30.9	. . 53.3	131 42.6	. . 06.9	64 39.5	. . 36.8
22	329 14.0	125 29.8	33.4	64 31.6	53.3	146 44.5	06.6	79 41.8	36.8
23	344 16.4	140 29.4	34.7	79 32.3	53.4	161 46.5	06.4	94 44.1	36.8
20 00 TUESDAY	359 18.9	155 29.0	S 9 35.9	94 33.0	S25 53.4	176 48.5	N 0 06.2	109 46.4	S20 36.8
01	14 21.4	170 28.6	37.1	109 33.7	53.4	191 50.4	06.0	124 48.7	36.9
02	29 23.8	185 28.3	38.3	124 34.4	53.5	206 52.4	05.8	139 51.1	36.9
03	44 26.3	200 27.9	. . 39.5	139 35.2	. . 53.5	221 54.4	. . 05.6	154 53.4	. . 36.9
04	59 28.7	215 27.5	40.7	154 35.9	53.5	236 56.4	05.4	169 55.7	37.0
05	74 31.2	230 27.1	42.0	169 36.6	53.5	251 58.3	05.1	184 58.0	37.0
06	89 33.7	245 26.8	S 9 43.2	184 37.3	S25 53.6	267 00.3	N 0 04.9	200 00.3	S20 37.0
07	104 36.1	260 26.4	44.4	199 38.0	53.6	282 02.3	04.7	215 02.6	37.0
08	119 38.6	275 26.0	45.6	214 38.7	53.6	297 04.2	04.5	230 04.9	37.1
09	134 41.1	290 25.6	. . 46.8	229 39.4	. . 53.6	312 06.2	. . 04.3	245 07.2	. . 37.1
10	149 43.5	305 25.2	48.0	244 40.1	53.7	327 08.2	04.1	260 09.5	37.1
11	164 46.0	320 24.9	49.2	259 40.8	53.7	342 10.1	03.9	275 11.8	37.2
12	179 48.5	335 24.5	S 9 50.5	274 41.5	S25 53.7	357 12.1	N 0 03.6	290 14.2	S20 37.2
13	194 50.9	350 24.1	51.7	289 42.2	53.7	12 14.1	03.4	305 16.5	37.2
14	209 53.4	5 23.7	52.9	304 42.9	53.8	27 16.0	03.2	320 18.8	37.2
15	224 55.8	20 23.3	. . 54.1	319 43.7	. . 53.8	42 18.0	. . 03.0	335 21.1	. . 37.3
16	239 58.3	35 23.0	55.3	334 44.4	53.8	57 20.0	02.8	350 23.4	37.3
17	255 00.8	50 22.6	56.5	349 45.1	53.8	72 22.0	02.6	5 25.7	37.3
18	270 03.2	65 22.2	S 9 57.7	4 45.8	S25 53.9	87 23.9	N 0 02.4	20 28.0	S20 37.4
19	285 05.7	80 21.8	9 58.9	19 46.5	53.9	102 25.9	02.1	35 30.3	37.4
20	300 08.2	95 21.4	10 00.1	34 47.2	53.9	117 27.9	01.9	50 32.6	37.4
21	315 10.6	110 21.0	. . 01.3	49 47.9	. . 53.9	132 29.8	. . 01.7	65 34.9	. . 37.4
22	330 13.1	125 20.7	02.6	64 48.6	53.9	147 31.8	01.5	80 37.3	37.5
23	345 15.6	140 20.3	03.8	79 49.3	54.0	162 33.8	01.3	95 39.6	37.5
Mer. Pass.	h m 0 06.7	*v* −0.4	*d* 1.2	*v* 0.7	*d* 0.0	*v* 2.0	*d* 0.2	*v* 2.3	*d* 0.0

STARS

Name	SHA ° ′	Dec ° ′
Acamar	315 16.4	S40 14.2
Achernar	335 24.7	S57 09.0
Acrux	173 07.4	S63 11.4
Adhara	255 10.9	S28 59.6
Aldebaran	290 46.8	N16 32.4
Alioth	166 19.4	N55 52.4
Alkaid	152 57.7	N49 14.1
Al Na'ir	27 40.6	S46 52.7
Alnilam	275 44.1	S 1 11.5
Alphard	217 54.2	S 8 43.8
Alphecca	126 09.4	N26 39.9
Alpheratz	357 40.8	N29 11.0
Altair	62 05.9	N 8 55.1
Ankaa	353 13.2	S42 12.8
Antares	112 23.7	S26 27.9
Arcturus	145 54.0	N19 06.1
Atria	107 23.6	S69 03.5
Avior	234 17.4	S59 33.6
Bellatrix	278 29.6	N 6 21.8
Betelgeuse	270 58.9	N 7 24.5
Canopus	263 55.2	S52 42.1
Capella	280 31.1	N46 00.5
Deneb	49 29.6	N45 20.8
Denebola	182 31.8	N14 28.9
Diphda	348 53.4	S17 53.6
Dubhe	193 49.8	N61 39.6
Elnath	278 09.8	N28 37.0
Eltanin	90 45.1	N51 29.7
Enif	33 44.7	N 9 57.3
Fomalhaut	15 21.3	S29 31.9
Gacrux	171 58.9	S57 12.3
Gienah	175 50.3	S17 37.9
Hadar	148 45.2	S60 27.1
Hamal	327 58.0	N23 32.4
Kaus Aust.	83 40.9	S34 22.4
Kochab	137 21.1	N74 05.6
Markab	13 35.8	N15 17.9
Menkar	314 12.5	N 4 09.3
Menkent	148 05.3	S36 27.0
Miaplacidus	221 39.8	S69 47.0
Mirfak	308 36.9	N49 54.9
Nunki	75 55.5	S26 16.4
Peacock	53 15.5	S56 40.8
Pollux	243 25.3	N27 59.0
Procyon	244 57.6	N 5 10.9
Rasalhague	96 04.4	N12 33.3
Regulus	207 41.5	N11 53.2
Rigel	281 09.9	S 8 11.0
Rigil Kent.	139 49.1	S60 54.2
Sabik	102 10.1	S15 44.5
Schedar	349 37.3	N56 37.7
Shaula	96 19.0	S37 06.8
Sirius	258 31.9	S16 44.3
Spica	158 29.2	S11 14.7
Suhail	222 51.1	S43 29.9
Vega	80 37.4	N38 48.4
Zuben'ubi	137 03.2	S16 06.4

	SHA ° ′	Mer. Pass. h m
Venus	157 18.2	13 38
Mars	95 56.1	17 42
Jupiter	177 41.5	12 14
Saturn	110 31.1	16 42

UT d h	SUN GHA ° ′	SUN Dec ° ′	MOON GHA ° ′	v ′	MOON Dec ° ′	d ′	HP ′
18 00	181 28.1	N 1 47.1	345 13.7	8.2	N 2 23.3	11.7	60.5
01	196 28.4	46.1	359 40.9	8.1	2 35.0	11.6	60.5
02	211 28.6	45.2	14 08.0	8.2	2 46.6	11.6	60.5
03	226 28.8	. . 44.2	28 35.2	8.1	2 58.2	11.7	60.5
04	241 29.0	43.2	43 02.3	8.1	3 09.9	11.6	60.6
05	256 29.2	42.3	57 29.4	8.1	3 21.5	11.5	60.6
06	271 29.5	N 1 41.3	71 56.5	8.0	N 3 33.0	11.6	60.6
07	286 29.7	40.3	86 23.5	8.1	3 44.6	11.5	60.6
S 08	301 29.9	39.4	100 50.6	8.0	3 56.1	11.5	60.6
U 09	316 30.1	. . 38.4	115 17.6	8.0	4 07.6	11.5	60.6
N 10	331 30.4	37.4	129 44.6	8.0	4 19.1	11.5	60.6
D 11	346 30.6	36.5	144 11.6	8.0	4 30.6	11.4	60.6
A 12	1 30.8	N 1 35.5	158 38.6	7.9	N 4 42.0	11.4	60.6
Y 13	16 31.0	34.5	173 05.5	7.9	4 53.4	11.4	60.6
14	31 31.3	33.6	187 32.4	7.9	5 04.8	11.3	60.6
15	46 31.5	. . 32.6	201 59.3	7.9	5 16.1	11.3	60.6
16	61 31.7	31.6	216 26.2	7.9	5 27.4	11.3	60.6
17	76 31.9	30.7	230 53.1	7.8	5 38.7	11.2	60.6
18	91 32.2	N 1 29.7	245 19.9	7.8	N 5 49.9	11.2	60.6
19	106 32.4	28.7	259 46.7	7.8	6 01.1	11.2	60.6
20	121 32.6	27.7	274 13.5	7.8	6 12.3	11.1	60.6
21	136 32.8	. . 26.8	288 40.3	7.8	6 23.4	11.0	60.6
22	151 33.0	25.8	303 07.1	7.7	6 34.4	11.1	60.6
23	166 33.3	24.8	317 33.8	7.7	6 45.5	11.0	60.6
19 00	181 33.5	N 1 23.9	332 00.5	7.7	N 6 56.5	10.9	60.6
01	196 33.7	22.9	346 27.2	7.7	7 07.4	10.9	60.6
02	211 33.9	21.9	0 53.9	7.6	7 18.3	10.8	60.6
03	226 34.2	. . 21.0	15 20.5	7.7	7 29.1	10.8	60.6
04	241 34.4	20.0	29 47.2	7.6	7 39.9	10.7	60.6
05	256 34.6	19.0	44 13.8	7.5	7 50.6	10.7	60.6
06	271 34.8	N 1 18.1	58 40.3	7.6	N 8 01.3	10.7	60.6
07	286 35.1	17.1	73 06.9	7.5	8 12.0	10.5	60.5
08	301 35.3	16.1	87 33.4	7.5	8 22.5	10.5	60.5
M 09	316 35.5	. . 15.1	101 59.9	7.5	8 33.0	10.5	60.5
O 10	331 35.7	14.2	116 26.4	7.5	8 43.5	10.4	60.5
N 11	346 35.9	13.2	130 52.9	7.5	8 53.9	10.3	60.5
D 12	1 36.2	N 1 12.2	145 19.4	7.4	N 9 04.2	10.3	60.5
A 13	16 36.4	11.3	159 45.8	7.4	9 14.5	10.2	60.5
Y 14	31 36.6	10.3	174 12.2	7.4	9 24.7	10.2	60.5
15	46 36.8	. . 09.3	188 38.6	7.3	9 34.9	10.1	60.5
16	61 37.1	08.4	203 04.9	7.3	9 45.0	10.0	60.5
17	76 37.3	07.4	217 31.2	7.4	9 55.0	9.9	60.5
18	91 37.5	N 1 06.4	231 57.6	7.2	N10 04.9	9.9	60.5
19	106 37.7	05.4	246 23.8	7.3	10 14.8	9.8	60.4
20	121 38.0	04.5	260 50.1	7.3	10 24.6	9.7	60.4
21	136 38.2	. . 03.5	275 16.4	7.2	10 34.3	9.7	60.4
22	151 38.4	02.5	289 42.6	7.2	10 44.0	9.6	60.4
23	166 38.6	01.6	304 08.8	7.2	10 53.6	9.5	60.4
20 00	181 38.8	N 1 00.6	318 35.0	7.1	N11 03.1	9.4	60.4
01	196 39.1	0 59.6	333 01.1	7.2	11 12.5	9.4	60.4
02	211 39.3	58.7	347 27.3	7.1	11 21.9	9.3	60.4
03	226 39.5	. . 57.7	1 53.4	7.1	11 31.2	9.2	60.3
04	241 39.7	56.7	16 19.5	7.1	11 40.4	9.1	60.3
05	256 40.0	55.7	30 45.6	7.0	11 49.5	9.0	60.3
06	271 40.2	N 0 54.8	45 11.6	7.1	N11 58.5	9.0	60.3
07	286 40.4	53.8	59 37.7	7.0	12 07.5	8.8	60.3
T 08	301 40.6	52.8	74 03.7	7.0	12 16.3	8.8	60.3
U 09	316 40.8	. . 51.9	88 29.7	6.9	12 25.1	8.7	60.3
E 10	331 41.1	50.9	102 55.6	7.0	12 33.8	8.6	60.2
S 11	346 41.3	49.9	117 21.6	6.9	12 42.4	8.5	60.2
D 12	1 41.5	N 0 48.9	131 47.5	7.0	N12 50.9	8.5	60.2
A 13	16 41.7	48.0	146 13.5	6.9	12 59.4	8.3	60.2
Y 14	31 42.0	47.0	160 39.4	6.9	13 07.7	8.2	60.2
15	46 42.2	. . 46.0	175 05.3	6.8	13 15.9	8.2	60.2
16	61 42.4	45.1	189 31.1	6.9	13 24.1	8.1	60.1
17	76 42.6	44.1	203 57.0	6.8	13 32.2	7.9	60.1
18	91 42.8	N 0 43.1	218 22.8	6.8	N13 40.1	7.9	60.1
19	106 43.1	42.1	232 48.6	6.8	13 48.0	7.8	60.1
20	121 43.3	41.2	247 14.4	6.8	13 55.8	7.7	60.1
21	136 43.5	. . 40.2	261 40.2	6.8	14 03.5	7.6	60.1
22	151 43.7	39.2	276 06.0	6.8	14 11.1	7.4	60.0
23	166 44.0	38.3	290 31.8	6.7	N14 18.5	7.4	60.0
	SD 15.9	*d* 1.0	SD 16.5		16.5		16.4

Lat. °	Twilight Naut. h m	Twilight Civil h m	Sunrise h m	Moonrise 18 h m	Moonrise 19 h m	Moonrise 20 h m	Moonrise 21 h m
N 72	02 41	04 17	05 27	18 28	18 22	18 16	18 08
N 70	03 05	04 27	05 30	18 36	18 38	18 42	18 50
68	03 22	04 35	05 32	18 42	18 50	19 01	19 19
66	03 36	04 42	05 34	18 48	19 00	19 17	19 41
64	03 48	04 47	05 35	18 52	19 09	19 30	19 58
62	03 57	04 52	05 37	18 57	19 17	19 41	20 12
60	04 05	04 56	05 38	19 00	19 23	19 51	20 24
N 58	04 12	05 00	05 39	19 03	19 29	19 59	20 35
56	04 18	05 03	05 40	19 06	19 34	20 06	20 44
54	04 23	05 05	05 41	19 09	19 39	20 13	20 52
52	04 27	05 08	05 42	19 11	19 43	20 19	21 00
50	04 31	05 10	05 42	19 13	19 47	20 24	21 06
45	04 40	05 14	05 44	19 18	19 55	20 36	21 20
N 40	04 46	05 18	05 45	19 22	20 02	20 45	21 32
35	04 51	05 21	05 46	19 25	20 08	20 54	21 42
30	04 55	05 23	05 47	19 29	20 14	21 01	21 51
20	05 01	05 26	05 48	19 34	20 23	21 14	22 06
N 10	05 04	05 28	05 49	19 39	20 31	21 25	22 20
0	05 06	05 30	05 50	19 43	20 39	21 35	22 32
S 10	05 06	05 30	05 51	19 48	20 47	21 46	22 45
20	05 05	05 30	05 52	19 53	20 55	21 57	22 59
30	05 01	05 29	05 53	19 58	21 05	22 10	23 14
35	04 59	05 28	05 53	20 01	21 10	22 18	23 23
40	04 55	05 27	05 54	20 05	21 17	22 27	23 34
45	04 51	05 25	05 54	20 09	21 24	22 37	23 46
S 50	04 45	05 23	05 55	20 15	21 33	22 49	24 01
52	04 42	05 21	05 55	20 17	21 37	22 55	24 08
54	04 39	05 20	05 55	20 20	21 42	23 01	24 16
56	04 35	05 18	05 55	20 23	21 47	23 08	24 24
58	04 30	05 17	05 56	20 26	21 53	23 17	24 34
S 60	04 25	05 15	05 56	20 30	21 59	23 26	24 46

Lat. °	Sunset h m	Twilight Civil h m	Twilight Naut. h m	Moonset 18 h m	Moonset 19 h m	Moonset 20 h m	Moonset 21 h m
N 72	18 18	19 27	21 01	08 04	10 05	12 09	14 16
N 70	18 15	19 17	20 38	07 58	09 51	11 44	13 35
68	18 13	19 10	20 21	07 54	09 40	11 26	13 07
66	18 12	19 03	20 08	07 50	09 31	11 11	12 46
64	18 10	18 58	19 57	07 47	09 24	10 59	12 29
62	18 09	18 53	19 48	07 44	09 17	10 49	12 15
60	18 08	18 50	19 40	07 42	09 12	10 40	12 04
N 58	18 07	18 46	19 33	07 39	09 07	10 32	11 53
56	18 06	18 43	19 28	07 38	09 02	10 26	11 45
54	18 05	18 41	19 23	07 36	08 59	10 20	11 37
52	18 05	18 38	19 18	07 34	08 55	10 14	11 30
50	18 04	18 36	19 14	07 33	08 52	10 09	11 24
45	18 03	18 32	19 06	07 30	08 45	09 59	11 10
N 40	18 02	18 29	19 00	07 27	08 39	09 50	10 59
35	18 01	18 26	18 55	07 25	08 34	09 43	10 49
30	18 00	18 24	18 52	07 23	08 30	09 36	10 41
20	17 59	18 21	18 46	07 20	08 22	09 25	10 27
N 10	17 58	18 19	18 43	07 17	08 16	09 15	10 14
0	17 57	18 18	18 42	07 14	08 09	09 06	10 02
S 10	17 56	18 17	18 41	07 11	08 03	08 56	09 51
20	17 55	18 17	18 43	07 09	07 57	08 46	09 38
30	17 55	18 19	18 46	07 05	07 49	08 35	09 24
35	17 54	18 20	18 49	07 03	07 45	08 29	09 16
40	17 54	18 21	18 53	07 01	07 40	08 21	09 06
45	17 54	18 23	18 57	06 58	07 34	08 13	08 55
S 50	17 53	18 26	19 04	06 55	07 28	08 03	08 42
52	17 53	18 27	19 07	06 54	07 24	07 58	08 36
54	17 53	18 28	19 10	06 52	07 21	07 53	08 29
56	17 53	18 30	19 14	06 51	07 17	07 47	08 22
58	17 53	18 32	19 18	06 49	07 13	07 41	08 13
S 60	17 52	18 34	19 24	06 47	07 08	07 33	08 03

Day d	SUN Eqn. of Time 00^h m s	SUN Eqn. of Time 12^h m s	SUN Mer. Pass. h m	MOON Mer. Pass. Upper h m	MOON Mer. Pass. Lower h m	MOON Age d	%	Phase
18	05 52	06 03	11 54	01 01	13 29	17	96	
19	06 14	06 24	11 54	01 56	14 24	18	90	
20	06 35	06 46	11 53	02 52	15 20	19	81	

Day	UT d h	ARIES GHA ° ′	VENUS −3·9 GHA ° ′	VENUS Dec ° ′	MARS +0·0 GHA ° ′	MARS Dec ° ′	JUPITER −1·7 GHA ° ′	JUPITER Dec ° ′	SATURN +0·5 GHA ° ′	SATURN Dec ° ′
WEDNESDAY	21 00	0 18.0	155 19.9	S10 05.0	94 50.0	S25 54.0	177 35.7	N 0 01.1	110 41.9	S20 37.5
	01	15 20.5	170 19.5	06.2	109 50.7	54.0	192 37.7	00.9	125 44.2	37.6
	02	30 23.0	185 19.1	07.4	124 51.4	54.0	207 39.7	00.6	140 46.5	37.6
	03	45 25.4	200 18.7	. . 08.6	139 52.1	. . 54.1	222 41.6	. . 00.4	155 48.8	. . 37.6
	04	60 27.9	215 18.4	09.8	154 52.8	54.1	237 43.6	N 00.2	170 51.1	37.6
	05	75 30.3	230 18.0	11.0	169 53.5	54.1	252 45.6	00.0	185 53.4	37.7
	06	90 32.8	245 17.6	S10 12.2	184 54.2	S25 54.1	267 47.6	S 0 00.2	200 55.7	S20 37.7
	07	105 35.3	260 17.2	13.4	199 54.9	54.1	282 49.5	00.4	215 58.0	37.7
	08	120 37.7	275 16.8	14.6	214 55.6	54.1	297 51.5	00.6	231 00.3	37.8
	09	135 40.2	290 16.4	. . 15.8	229 56.3	. . 54.2	312 53.5	. . 00.9	246 02.6	. . 37.8
	10	150 42.7	305 16.0	17.0	244 57.0	54.2	327 55.4	01.1	261 04.9	37.8
	11	165 45.1	320 15.7	18.2	259 57.7	54.2	342 57.4	01.3	276 07.3	37.8
	12	180 47.6	335 15.3	S10 19.4	274 58.4	S25 54.2	357 59.4	S 0 01.5	291 09.6	S20 37.9
	13	195 50.1	350 14.9	20.6	289 59.1	54.2	13 01.3	01.7	306 11.9	37.9
	14	210 52.5	5 14.5	21.8	304 59.8	54.2	28 03.3	01.9	321 14.2	37.9
	15	225 55.0	20 14.1	. . 23.0	320 00.5	. . 54.3	43 05.3	. . 02.1	336 16.5	. . 38.0
	16	240 57.5	35 13.7	24.2	335 01.2	54.3	58 07.2	02.4	351 18.8	38.0
	17	255 59.9	50 13.3	25.5	350 01.9	54.3	73 09.2	02.6	6 21.1	38.0
	18	271 02.4	65 12.9	S10 26.7	5 02.6	S25 54.3	88 11.2	S 0 02.8	21 23.4	S20 38.0
	19	286 04.8	80 12.5	27.9	20 03.3	54.3	103 13.1	03.0	36 25.7	38.1
	20	301 07.3	95 12.2	29.1	35 04.0	54.3	118 15.1	03.2	51 28.0	38.1
	21	316 09.8	110 11.8	. . 30.3	50 04.7	. . 54.3	133 17.1	. . 03.4	66 30.3	. . 38.1
	22	331 12.2	125 11.4	31.5	65 05.4	54.4	148 19.1	03.6	81 32.6	38.2
	23	346 14.7	140 11.0	32.7	80 06.1	54.4	163 21.0	03.9	96 34.9	38.2
THURSDAY	22 00	1 17.2	155 10.6	S10 33.9	95 06.8	S25 54.4	178 23.0	S 0 04.1	111 37.2	S20 38.2
	01	16 19.6	170 10.2	35.0	110 07.5	54.4	193 25.0	04.3	126 39.5	38.2
	02	31 22.1	185 09.8	36.2	125 08.1	54.4	208 26.9	04.5	141 41.8	38.3
	03	46 24.6	200 09.4	. . 37.4	140 08.8	. . 54.4	223 28.9	. . 04.7	156 44.1	. . 38.3
	04	61 27.0	215 09.0	38.6	155 09.5	54.4	238 30.9	04.9	171 46.4	38.3
	05	76 29.5	230 08.6	39.8	170 10.2	54.4	253 32.8	05.1	186 48.7	38.4
	06	91 31.9	245 08.2	S10 41.0	185 10.9	S25 54.5	268 34.8	S 0 05.4	201 51.0	S20 38.4
	07	106 34.4	260 07.8	42.2	200 11.6	54.5	283 36.8	05.6	216 53.4	38.4
	08	121 36.9	275 07.4	43.4	215 12.3	54.5	298 38.7	05.8	231 55.7	38.4
	09	136 39.3	290 07.0	. . 44.6	230 13.0	. . 54.5	313 40.7	. . 06.0	246 58.0	. . 38.5
	10	151 41.8	305 06.7	45.8	245 13.7	54.5	328 42.7	06.2	262 00.3	38.5
	11	166 44.3	320 06.3	47.0	260 14.4	54.5	343 44.6	06.4	277 02.6	38.5
	12	181 46.7	335 05.9	S10 48.2	275 15.1	S25 54.5	358 46.6	S 0 06.6	292 04.9	S20 38.6
	13	196 49.2	350 05.5	49.4	290 15.8	54.5	13 48.6	06.9	307 07.2	38.6
	14	211 51.7	5 05.1	50.6	305 16.4	54.5	28 50.5	07.1	322 09.5	38.6
	15	226 54.1	20 04.7	. . 51.8	320 17.1	. . 54.5	43 52.5	. . 07.3	337 11.8	. . 38.7
	16	241 56.6	35 04.3	53.0	335 17.8	54.5	58 54.5	07.5	352 14.1	38.7
	17	256 59.1	50 03.9	54.2	350 18.5	54.6	73 56.5	07.7	7 16.4	38.7
	18	272 01.5	65 03.5	S10 55.4	5 19.2	S25 54.6	88 58.4	S 0 07.9	22 18.7	S20 38.7
	19	287 04.0	80 03.1	56.6	20 19.9	54.6	104 00.4	08.1	37 21.0	38.8
	20	302 06.4	95 02.7	57.7	35 20.6	54.6	119 02.4	08.4	52 23.3	38.8
	21	317 08.9	110 02.3	10 58.9	50 21.3	. . 54.6	134 04.3	. . 08.6	67 25.6	. . 38.8
	22	332 11.4	125 01.9	11 00.1	65 21.9	54.6	149 06.3	08.8	82 27.9	38.9
	23	347 13.8	140 01.5	01.3	80 22.6	54.6	164 08.3	09.0	97 30.2	38.9
FRIDAY	23 00	2 16.3	155 01.1	S11 02.5	95 23.3	S25 54.6	179 10.2	S 0 09.2	112 32.5	S20 38.9
	01	17 18.8	170 00.7	03.7	110 24.0	54.6	194 12.2	09.4	127 34.8	38.9
	02	32 21.2	185 00.3	04.9	125 24.7	54.6	209 14.2	09.6	142 37.1	39.0
	03	47 23.7	199 59.9	. . 06.1	140 25.4	. . 54.6	224 16.1	. . 09.9	157 39.4	. . 39.0
	04	62 26.2	214 59.5	07.3	155 26.1	54.6	239 18.1	10.1	172 41.7	39.0
	05	77 28.6	229 59.1	08.4	170 26.7	54.6	254 20.1	10.3	187 44.0	39.1
	06	92 31.1	244 58.7	S11 09.6	185 27.4	S25 54.6	269 22.0	S 0 10.5	202 46.3	S20 39.1
	07	107 33.6	259 58.3	10.8	200 28.1	54.6	284 24.0	10.7	217 48.6	39.1
	08	122 36.0	274 57.9	12.0	215 28.8	54.6	299 26.0	10.9	232 50.9	39.2
	09	137 38.5	289 57.5	. . 13.2	230 29.5	. . 54.6	314 27.9	. . 11.1	247 53.2	. . 39.2
	10	152 40.9	304 57.1	14.4	245 30.2	54.6	329 29.9	11.4	262 55.5	39.2
	11	167 43.4	319 56.7	15.6	260 30.8	54.6	344 31.9	11.6	277 57.8	39.2
	12	182 45.9	334 56.3	S11 16.7	275 31.5	S25 54.6	359 33.9	S 0 11.8	293 00.1	S20 39.3
	13	197 48.3	349 55.9	17.9	290 32.2	54.6	14 35.8	12.0	308 02.4	39.3
	14	212 50.8	4 55.5	19.1	305 32.9	54.6	29 37.8	12.2	323 04.7	39.3
	15	227 53.3	19 55.1	. . 20.3	320 33.6	. . 54.6	44 39.8	. . 12.4	338 07.0	. . 39.4
	16	242 55.7	34 54.6	21.5	335 34.2	54.6	59 41.7	12.6	353 09.3	39.4
	17	257 58.2	49 54.2	22.6	350 34.9	54.6	74 43.7	12.9	8 11.6	39.4
	18	273 00.7	64 53.8	S11 23.8	5 35.6	S25 54.6	89 45.7	S 0 13.1	23 13.9	S20 39.4
	19	288 03.1	79 53.4	25.0	20 36.3	54.6	104 47.6	13.3	38 16.2	39.5
	20	303 05.6	94 53.0	26.2	35 37.0	54.6	119 49.6	13.5	53 18.5	39.5
	21	318 08.1	109 52.6	. . 27.4	50 37.6	. . 54.6	134 51.6	. . 13.7	68 20.8	. . 39.5
	22	333 10.5	124 52.2	28.6	65 38.3	54.6	149 53.5	13.9	83 23.1	39.6
	23	348 13.0	139 51.8	29.7	80 39.0	54.6	164 55.5	14.1	98 25.4	39.6
	Mer. Pass.	h m 23 50.9	v −0.4	d 1.2	v 0.7	d 0.0	v 2.0	d 0.2	v 2.3	d 0.0

STARS

Name	SHA ° ′	Dec ° ′
Acamar	315 16.4	S40 14.2
Achernar	335 24.7	S57 09.0
Acrux	173 07.4	S63 11.4
Adhara	255 10.9	S28 59.6
Aldebaran	290 46.7	N16 32.4
Alioth	166 19.4	N55 52.4
Alkaid	152 57.7	N49 14.1
Al Na'ir	27 40.6	S46 52.7
Alnilam	275 44.1	S 1 11.5
Alphard	217 54.2	S 8 43.8
Alphecca	126 09.4	N26 39.9
Alpheratz	357 40.8	N29 11.0
Altair	62 05.9	N 8 55.1
Ankaa	353 13.2	S42 12.8
Antares	112 23.7	S26 27.9
Arcturus	145 54.0	N19 06.0
Atria	107 23.6	S69 03.4
Avior	234 17.4	S59 33.6
Bellatrix	278 29.6	N 6 21.8
Betelgeuse	270 58.9	N 7 24.5
Canopus	263 55.2	S52 42.1
Capella	280 31.1	N46 00.5
Deneb	49 29.6	N45 20.8
Denebola	182 31.8	N14 28.9
Diphda	348 53.4	S17 53.6
Dubhe	193 49.8	N61 39.6
Elnath	278 09.8	N28 37.0
Eltanin	90 45.1	N51 29.7
Enif	33 44.7	N 9 57.3
Fomalhaut	15 21.3	S29 31.9
Gacrux	171 58.9	S57 12.3
Gienah	175 50.3	S17 37.9
Hadar	148 45.2	S60 27.1
Hamal	327 58.0	N23 32.4
Kaus Aust.	83 40.9	S34 22.4
Kochab	137 21.1	N74 05.6
Markab	13 35.8	N15 17.9
Menkar	314 12.5	N 4 09.3
Menkent	148 05.3	S36 27.0
Miaplacidus	221 39.7	S69 47.0
Mirfak	308 36.8	N49 54.9
Nunki	75 55.5	S26 16.4
Peacock	53 15.5	S56 40.8
Pollux	243 25.2	N27 59.0
Procyon	244 57.6	N 5 10.9
Rasalhague	96 04.5	N12 33.3
Regulus	207 41.5	N11 53.2
Rigel	281 09.9	S 8 11.0
Rigil Kent.	139 49.2	S60 54.2
Sabik	102 10.1	S15 44.5
Schedar	349 37.3	N56 37.7
Shaula	96 19.0	S37 06.8
Sirius	258 31.8	S16 44.3
Spica	158 29.2	S11 14.7
Suhail	222 51.1	S43 29.9
Vega	80 37.4	N38 48.4
Zuben'ubi	137 03.2	S16 06.4

	SHA ° ′	Mer. Pass. h m
Venus	153 53.4	13 40
Mars	93 49.6	17 39
Jupiter	177 05.8	12 05
Saturn	110 20.1	16 31

	UT	SUN GHA	SUN Dec	MOON GHA	*v*	MOON Dec	*d*	HP
	d h	° ′	° ′	° ′	′	° ′	′	′
	21 00	181 44.2	N 0 37.3	304 57.5	6.7	N14 25.9	7.3	60.0
	01	196 44.4	36.3	319 23.2	6.7	14 33.2	7.2	60.0
	02	211 44.6	35.3	333 48.9	6.8	14 40.4	7.1	60.0
	03	226 44.8	. . 34.4	348 14.7	6.6	14 47.5	7.0	59.9
	04	241 45.1	33.4	2 40.3	6.7	14 54.5	6.8	59.9
	05	256 45.3	32.4	17 06.0	6.7	15 01.3	6.8	59.9
	06	271 45.5	N 0 31.5	31 31.7	6.7	N15 08.1	6.7	59.9
W	07	286 45.7	30.5	45 57.4	6.6	15 14.8	6.6	59.8
E	08	301 46.0	29.5	60 23.0	6.7	15 21.4	6.4	59.8
D	09	316 46.2	. . 28.5	74 48.7	6.6	15 27.8	6.4	59.8
N	10	331 46.4	27.6	89 14.3	6.6	15 34.2	6.2	59.8
E	11	346 46.6	26.6	103 39.9	6.6	15 40.4	6.2	59.8
	12	1 46.8	N 0 25.6	118 05.5	6.6	N15 46.6	6.0	59.7
S	13	16 47.1	24.7	132 31.1	6.6	15 52.6	5.9	59.7
D	14	31 47.3	23.7	146 56.7	6.6	15 58.5	5.8	59.7
A	15	46 47.5	. . 22.7	161 22.3	6.6	16 04.3	5.7	59.7
Y	16	61 47.7	21.7	175 47.9	6.6	16 10.0	5.6	59.6
	17	76 47.9	20.8	190 13.5	6.6	16 15.6	5.5	59.6
	18	91 48.2	N 0 19.8	204 39.1	6.6	N16 21.1	5.4	59.6
	19	106 48.4	18.8	219 04.7	6.6	16 26.5	5.2	59.6
	20	121 48.6	17.8	233 30.3	6.6	16 31.7	5.2	59.5
	21	136 48.8	. . 16.9	247 55.9	6.5	16 36.9	5.0	59.5
	22	151 49.0	15.9	262 21.4	6.6	16 41.9	4.9	59.5
	23	166 49.3	14.9	276 47.0	6.6	16 46.8	4.8	59.5
	22 00	181 49.5	N 0 14.0	291 12.6	6.6	N16 51.6	4.7	59.5
	01	196 49.7	13.0	305 38.2	6.6	16 56.3	4.6	59.4
	02	211 49.9	12.0	320 03.8	6.5	17 00.9	4.4	59.4
	03	226 50.1	. . 11.0	334 29.3	6.6	17 05.3	4.4	59.4
	04	241 50.4	10.1	348 54.9	6.6	17 09.7	4.2	59.4
	05	256 50.6	09.1	3 20.5	6.6	17 13.9	4.1	59.3
	06	271 50.8	N 0 08.1	17 46.1	6.6	N17 18.0	4.0	59.3
	07	286 51.0	07.1	32 11.7	6.6	17 22.0	3.9	59.3
T	08	301 51.2	06.2	46 37.3	6.7	17 25.9	3.8	59.2
H	09	316 51.5	. . 05.2	61 03.0	6.6	17 29.7	3.7	59.2
U	10	331 51.7	04.2	75 28.6	6.6	17 33.4	3.5	59.2
R	11	346 51.9	03.3	89 54.2	6.7	17 36.9	3.4	59.2
S	12	1 52.1	N 0 02.3	104 19.9	6.6	N17 40.3	3.3	59.1
D	13	16 52.3	01.3	118 45.5	6.7	17 43.6	3.2	59.1
A	14	31 52.6	N 00.3	133 11.2	6.7	17 46.8	3.1	59.1
Y	15	46 52.8	S 00.6	147 36.9	6.7	17 49.9	2.9	59.1
	16	61 53.0	01.6	162 02.6	6.7	17 52.8	2.8	59.0
	17	76 53.2	02.6	176 28.3	6.7	17 55.6	2.8	59.0
	18	91 53.4	S 0 03.6	190 54.0	6.7	N17 58.4	2.6	59.0
	19	106 53.7	04.5	205 19.7	6.8	18 01.0	2.4	59.0
	20	121 53.9	05.5	219 45.5	6.8	18 03.4	2.4	58.9
	21	136 54.1	. . 06.5	234 11.3	6.8	18 05.8	2.2	58.9
	22	151 54.3	07.4	248 37.1	6.8	18 08.0	2.2	58.9
	23	166 54.5	08.4	263 02.9	6.8	18 10.2	2.0	58.9
	23 00	181 54.8	S 0 09.4	277 28.7	6.8	N18 12.2	1.9	58.8
	01	196 55.0	10.4	291 54.5	6.9	18 14.1	1.7	58.8
	02	211 55.2	11.3	306 20.4	6.9	18 15.8	1.7	58.8
	03	226 55.4	. . 12.3	320 46.3	6.9	18 17.5	1.5	58.7
	04	241 55.6	13.3	335 12.2	7.0	18 19.0	1.5	58.7
	05	256 55.9	14.3	349 38.2	6.9	18 20.5	1.3	58.7
	06	271 56.1	S 0 15.2	4 04.1	7.0	N18 21.8	1.1	58.7
	07	286 56.3	16.2	18 30.1	7.0	18 22.9	1.1	58.6
	08	301 56.5	17.2	32 56.1	7.1	18 24.0	1.0	58.6
F	09	316 56.7	. . 18.2	47 22.2	7.0	18 25.0	0.8	58.6
R	10	331 56.9	19.1	61 48.2	7.1	18 25.8	0.7	58.6
I	11	346 57.2	20.1	76 14.3	7.2	18 26.5	0.6	58.5
D	12	1 57.4	S 0 21.1	90 40.5	7.1	N18 27.1	0.5	58.5
A	13	16 57.6	22.0	105 06.6	7.2	18 27.6	0.4	58.5
Y	14	31 57.8	23.0	119 32.8	7.2	18 28.0	0.3	58.4
	15	46 58.0	. . 24.0	133 59.0	7.3	18 28.3	0.1	58.4
	16	61 58.3	25.0	148 25.3	7.3	18 28.4	0.0	58.4
	17	76 58.5	25.9	162 51.6	7.3	18 28.4	0.1	58.4
	18	91 58.7	S 0 26.9	177 17.9	7.3	N18 28.3	0.2	58.3
	19	106 58.9	27.9	191 44.2	7.4	18 28.1	0.3	58.3
	20	121 59.1	28.9	206 10.6	7.5	18 27.8	0.4	58.3
	21	136 59.3	. . 29.8	220 37.1	7.4	18 27.4	0.5	58.3
	22	151 59.6	30.8	235 03.5	7.5	18 26.9	0.7	58.2
	23	166 59.8	31.8	249 30.0	7.6	N18 26.2	0.7	58.2
		SD 16.0	*d* 1.0	SD 16.3		16.1		15.9

Lat.	Twilight Naut.	Twilight Civil	Sunrise	Moonrise 21	22	23	24
°	h m	h m	h m	h m	h m	h m	h m
N 72	03 00	04 31	05 40	18 08	17 50	▭	19 54
N 70	03 20	04 40	05 41	18 50	19 10	19 53	21 08
68	03 36	04 46	05 42	19 19	19 48	20 37	21 46
66	03 48	04 52	05 43	19 41	20 15	21 06	22 12
64	03 58	04 56	05 44	19 58	20 36	21 28	22 32
62	04 06	05 00	05 44	20 12	20 53	21 45	22 49
60	04 13	05 03	05 45	20 24	21 07	22 00	23 03
N 58	04 19	05 06	05 45	20 35	21 19	22 12	23 14
56	04 24	05 09	05 46	20 44	21 30	22 23	23 24
54	04 29	05 11	05 46	20 52	21 39	22 33	23 33
52	04 33	05 13	05 46	21 00	21 47	22 41	23 41
50	04 36	05 14	05 47	21 06	21 54	22 49	23 49
45	04 44	05 18	05 47	21 20	22 10	23 05	24 04
N 40	04 49	05 21	05 48	21 32	22 23	23 19	24 17
35	04 53	05 23	05 48	21 42	22 35	23 30	24 27
30	04 57	05 25	05 48	21 51	22 44	23 40	24 37
20	05 01	05 27	05 49	22 06	23 01	23 57	24 53
N 10	05 04	05 28	05 49	22 20	23 16	24 12	00 12
0	05 05	05 29	05 49	22 32	23 30	24 26	00 26
S 10	05 04	05 28	05 49	22 45	23 43	24 40	00 40
20	05 02	05 27	05 49	22 59	23 58	24 55	00 55
30	04 57	05 25	05 49	23 14	24 15	00 15	01 12
35	04 54	05 24	05 49	23 23	24 25	00 25	01 22
40	04 50	05 22	05 49	23 34	24 36	00 36	01 33
45	04 45	05 19	05 48	23 46	24 50	00 50	01 47
S 50	04 38	05 16	05 48	24 01	00 01	01 06	02 03
52	04 35	05 14	05 48	24 08	00 08	01 14	02 11
54	04 31	05 12	05 48	24 16	00 16	01 22	02 19
56	04 26	05 10	05 47	24 24	00 24	01 32	02 29
58	04 21	05 08	05 47	24 34	00 34	01 43	02 40
S 60	04 16	05 05	05 47	24 46	00 46	01 55	02 53

Lat.	Sunset	Twilight Civil	Twilight Naut.	Moonset 21	22	23	24
°	h m	h m	h m	h m	h m	h m	h m
N 72	18 02	19 10	20 40	14 16	16 34	▭	18 24
N 70	18 02	19 03	20 21	13 35	15 15	16 30	17 09
68	18 01	18 56	20 06	13 07	14 37	15 46	16 31
66	18 00	18 51	19 54	12 46	14 10	15 17	16 05
64	18 00	18 47	19 45	12 29	13 49	14 55	15 44
62	17 59	18 43	19 37	12 15	13 33	14 37	15 27
60	17 59	18 40	19 30	12 04	13 19	14 23	15 14
N 58	17 58	18 37	19 24	11 53	13 07	14 10	15 02
56	17 58	18 35	19 19	11 45	12 57	13 59	14 51
54	17 58	18 33	19 15	11 37	12 48	13 50	14 42
52	17 58	18 31	19 11	11 30	12 40	13 41	14 34
50	17 57	18 30	19 08	11 24	12 32	13 34	14 27
45	17 57	18 26	19 01	11 10	12 17	13 17	14 11
N 40	17 57	18 24	18 55	10 59	12 04	13 04	13 58
35	17 56	18 22	18 51	10 49	11 53	12 53	13 47
30	17 56	18 20	18 48	10 41	11 44	12 43	13 37
20	17 56	18 18	18 43	10 27	11 27	12 26	13 20
N 10	17 56	18 17	18 41	10 14	11 13	12 11	13 06
0	17 56	18 16	18 40	10 02	11 00	11 57	12 52
S 10	17 56	18 17	18 41	09 51	10 46	11 43	12 38
20	17 56	18 18	18 44	09 38	10 32	11 28	12 24
30	17 56	18 20	18 48	09 24	10 16	11 10	12 07
35	17 57	18 22	18 51	09 16	10 06	11 00	11 57
40	17 57	18 24	18 56	09 06	09 56	10 49	11 46
45	17 57	18 27	19 01	08 55	09 43	10 35	11 32
S 50	17 58	18 30	19 08	08 42	09 27	10 19	11 16
52	17 58	18 32	19 12	08 36	09 20	10 11	11 09
54	17 58	18 34	19 16	08 29	09 12	10 03	11 00
56	17 59	18 36	19 20	08 22	09 03	09 53	10 51
58	17 59	18 38	19 25	08 13	08 53	09 42	10 40
S 60	18 00	18 41	19 31	08 03	08 41	09 29	10 27

Day	SUN Eqn. of Time 00^h	SUN Eqn. of Time 12^h	SUN Mer. Pass.	MOON Mer. Pass. Upper	MOON Mer. Pass. Lower	MOON Age	MOON Phase
d	m s	m s	h m	h m	h m	d	%
21	06 56	07 07	11 53	03 49	16 17	20	71
22	07 17	07 28	11 53	04 46	17 15	21	60
23	07 39	07 49	11 52	05 43	18 11	22	49

UT d h		ARIES GHA	VENUS −3·9 GHA	VENUS Dec	MARS +0·0 GHA	MARS Dec	JUPITER −1·7 GHA	JUPITER Dec	SATURN +0·5 GHA	SATURN Dec
		° ′	° ′	° ′	° ′	° ′	° ′	° ′	° ′	° ′
24 00		3 15.4	154 51.4	S11 30.9	95 39.7	S25 54.6	179 57.5	S 0 14.4	113 27.7	S20 39.6
01		18 17.9	169 51.0	32.1	110 40.3	54.6	194 59.4	14.6	128 30.0	39.7
02		33 20.4	184 50.6	33.3	125 41.0	54.6	210 01.4	14.8	143 32.3	39.7
03		48 22.8	199 50.2	. . 34.4	140 41.7	. . 54.6	225 03.4	. . 15.0	158 34.6	. . 39.7
04		63 25.3	214 49.8	35.6	155 42.4	54.6	240 05.3	15.2	173 36.9	39.7
05		78 27.8	229 49.3	36.8	170 43.1	54.6	255 07.3	15.4	188 39.2	39.8
06		93 30.2	244 48.9	S11 38.0	185 43.7	S25 54.6	270 09.3	S 0 15.6	203 41.5	S20 39.8
07		108 32.7	259 48.5	39.1	200 44.4	54.6	285 11.2	15.9	218 43.7	39.8
08	S	123 35.2	274 48.1	40.3	215 45.1	54.6	300 13.2	16.1	233 46.0	39.9
09	A	138 37.6	289 47.7	. . 41.5	230 45.8	. . 54.6	315 15.2	. . 16.3	248 48.3	. . 39.9
10	T	153 40.1	304 47.3	42.7	245 46.4	54.5	330 17.1	16.5	263 50.6	39.9
11	U	168 42.5	319 46.9	43.8	260 47.1	54.5	345 19.1	16.7	278 52.9	40.0
12	R	183 45.0	334 46.5	S11 45.0	275 47.8	S25 54.5	0 21.1	S 0 16.9	293 55.2	S20 40.0
13	D	198 47.5	349 46.0	46.2	290 48.4	54.5	15 23.1	17.1	308 57.5	40.0
14	A	213 49.9	4 45.6	47.4	305 49.1	54.5	30 25.0	17.4	323 59.8	40.0
15	Y	228 52.4	19 45.2	. . 48.5	320 49.8	. . 54.5	45 27.0	. . 17.6	339 02.1	. . 40.1
16		243 54.9	34 44.8	49.7	335 50.5	54.5	60 29.0	17.8	354 04.4	40.1
17		258 57.3	49 44.4	50.9	350 51.1	54.5	75 30.9	18.0	9 06.7	40.1
18		273 59.8	64 44.0	S11 52.1	5 51.8	S25 54.5	90 32.9	S 0 18.2	24 09.0	S20 40.2
19		289 02.3	79 43.6	53.2	20 52.5	54.5	105 34.9	18.4	39 11.3	40.2
20		304 04.7	94 43.1	54.4	35 53.1	54.5	120 36.8	18.6	54 13.6	40.2
21		319 07.2	109 42.7	. . 55.6	50 53.8	. . 54.4	135 38.8	. . 18.9	69 15.9	. . 40.3
22		334 09.7	124 42.3	56.7	65 54.5	54.4	150 40.8	19.1	84 18.2	40.3
23		349 12.1	139 41.9	57.9	80 55.2	54.4	165 42.7	19.3	99 20.5	40.3
25 00		4 14.6	154 41.5	S11 59.1	95 55.8	S25 54.4	180 44.7	S 0 19.5	114 22.8	S20 40.3
01		19 17.0	169 41.1	12 00.2	110 56.5	54.4	195 46.7	19.7	129 25.1	40.4
02		34 19.5	184 40.6	01.4	125 57.2	54.4	210 48.6	19.9	144 27.3	40.4
03		49 22.0	199 40.2	. . 02.6	140 57.8	. . 54.4	225 50.6	. . 20.1	159 29.6	. . 40.4
04		64 24.4	214 39.8	03.7	155 58.5	54.4	240 52.6	20.4	174 31.9	40.5
05		79 26.9	229 39.4	04.9	170 59.2	54.3	255 54.5	20.6	189 34.2	40.5
06		94 29.4	244 39.0	S12 06.1	185 59.8	S25 54.3	270 56.5	S 0 20.8	204 36.5	S20 40.5
07		109 31.8	259 38.5	07.2	201 00.5	54.3	285 58.5	21.0	219 38.8	40.6
08		124 34.3	274 38.1	08.4	216 01.2	54.3	301 00.4	21.2	234 41.1	40.6
09	S	139 36.8	289 37.7	. . 09.6	231 01.8	. . 54.3	316 02.4	. . 21.4	249 43.4	. . 40.6
10	U	154 39.2	304 37.3	10.7	246 02.5	54.3	331 04.4	21.6	264 45.7	40.6
11	N	169 41.7	319 36.9	11.9	261 03.2	54.3	346 06.3	21.8	279 48.0	40.7
12	D	184 44.2	334 36.4	S12 13.0	276 03.8	S25 54.2	1 08.3	S 0 22.1	294 50.3	S20 40.7
13	A	199 46.6	349 36.0	14.2	291 04.5	54.2	16 10.3	22.3	309 52.6	40.7
14	Y	214 49.1	4 35.6	15.4	306 05.2	54.2	31 12.2	22.5	324 54.9	40.8
15		229 51.5	19 35.2	. . 16.5	321 05.8	. . 54.2	46 14.2	. . 22.7	339 57.2	. . 40.8
16		244 54.0	34 34.8	17.7	336 06.5	54.2	61 16.2	22.9	354 59.4	40.8
17		259 56.5	49 34.3	18.8	351 07.2	54.2	76 18.2	23.1	10 01.7	40.9
18		274 58.9	64 33.9	S12 20.0	6 07.8	S25 54.1	91 20.1	S 0 23.3	25 04.0	S20 40.9
19		290 01.4	79 33.5	21.2	21 08.5	54.1	106 22.1	23.6	40 06.3	40.9
20		305 03.9	94 33.1	22.3	36 09.1	54.1	121 24.1	23.8	55 08.6	40.9
21		320 06.3	109 32.6	. . 23.5	51 09.8	. . 54.1	136 26.0	. . 24.0	70 10.9	. . 41.0
22		335 08.8	124 32.2	24.6	66 10.5	54.1	151 28.0	24.2	85 13.2	41.0
23		350 11.3	139 31.8	25.8	81 11.1	54.0	166 30.0	24.4	100 15.5	41.0
26 00		5 13.7	154 31.4	S12 27.0	96 11.8	S25 54.0	181 31.9	S 0 24.6	115 17.8	S20 41.1
01		20 16.2	169 30.9	28.1	111 12.4	54.0	196 33.9	24.8	130 20.1	41.1
02		35 18.6	184 30.5	29.3	126 13.1	54.0	211 35.9	25.1	145 22.4	41.1
03		50 21.1	199 30.1	. . 30.4	141 13.8	. . 54.0	226 37.8	. . 25.3	160 24.6	. . 41.2
04		65 23.6	214 29.6	31.6	156 14.4	53.9	241 39.8	25.5	175 26.9	41.2
05		80 26.0	229 29.2	32.7	171 15.1	53.9	256 41.8	25.7	190 29.2	41.2
06		95 28.5	244 28.8	S12 33.9	186 15.7	S25 53.9	271 43.7	S 0 25.9	205 31.5	S20 41.3
07		110 31.0	259 28.4	35.0	201 16.4	53.9	286 45.7	26.1	220 33.8	41.3
08		125 33.4	274 27.9	36.2	216 17.1	53.8	301 47.7	26.3	235 36.1	41.3
09	M	140 35.9	289 27.5	. . 37.3	231 17.7	. . 53.8	316 49.6	. . 26.6	250 38.4	. . 41.3
10	O	155 38.4	304 27.1	38.5	246 18.4	53.8	331 51.6	26.8	265 40.7	41.4
11	N	170 40.8	319 26.6	39.6	261 19.0	53.8	346 53.6	27.0	280 43.0	41.4
12	D	185 43.3	334 26.2	S12 40.8	276 19.7	S25 53.7	1 55.5	S 0 27.2	295 45.2	S20 41.4
13	A	200 45.8	349 25.8	41.9	291 20.4	53.7	16 57.5	27.4	310 47.5	41.5
14	Y	215 48.2	4 25.3	43.1	306 21.0	53.7	31 59.5	27.6	325 49.8	41.5
15		230 50.7	19 24.9	. . 44.2	321 21.7	. . 53.7	47 01.4	. . 27.8	340 52.1	. . 41.5
16		245 53.1	34 24.5	45.4	336 22.3	53.6	62 03.4	28.1	355 54.4	41.6
17		260 55.6	49 24.0	46.5	351 23.0	53.6	77 05.4	28.3	10 56.7	41.6
18		275 58.1	64 23.6	S12 47.7	6 23.6	S25 53.6	92 07.3	S 0 28.5	25 59.0	S20 41.6
19		291 00.5	79 23.2	48.8	21 24.3	53.6	107 09.3	28.7	41 01.3	41.6
20		306 03.0	94 22.7	50.0	36 24.9	53.5	122 11.3	28.9	56 03.5	41.7
21		321 05.5	109 22.3	. . 51.1	51 25.6	. . 53.5	137 13.3	. . 29.1	71 05.8	. . 41.7
22		336 07.9	124 21.9	52.3	66 26.3	53.5	152 15.2	29.3	86 08.1	41.7
23		351 10.4	139 21.4	53.4	81 26.9	53.5	167 17.2	29.6	101 10.4	41.8
Mer. Pass.		h m 23 39.1	v −0.4	d 1.2	v 0.7	d 0.0	v 2.0	d 0.2	v 2.3	d 0.0

STARS Name	SHA	Dec
	° ′	° ′
Acamar	315 16.4	S40 14.2
Achernar	335 24.7	S57 09.1
Acrux	173 07.4	S63 11.4
Adhara	255 10.9	S28 59.6
Aldebaran	290 46.7	N16 32.4
Alioth	166 19.4	N55 52.3
Alkaid	152 57.7	N49 14.1
Al Na'ir	27 40.6	S46 52.8
Alnilam	275 44.1	S 1 11.5
Alphard	217 54.2	S 8 43.8
Alphecca	126 09.4	N26 39.9
Alpheratz	357 40.8	N29 11.0
Altair	62 06.0	N 8 55.1
Ankaa	353 13.2	S42 12.9
Antares	112 23.7	S26 27.9
Arcturus	145 54.0	N19 06.0
Atria	107 23.6	S69 03.4
Avior	234 17.4	S59 33.6
Bellatrix	278 29.6	N 6 21.8
Betelgeuse	270 58.9	N 7 24.5
Canopus	263 55.2	S52 42.1
Capella	280 31.1	N46 00.5
Deneb	49 29.7	N45 20.8
Denebola	182 31.8	N14 28.9
Diphda	348 53.4	S17 53.6
Dubhe	193 49.8	N61 39.6
Elnath	278 09.8	N28 37.0
Eltanin	90 45.2	N51 29.7
Enif	33 44.7	N 9 57.4
Fomalhaut	15 21.3	S29 31.9
Gacrux	171 58.9	S57 12.3
Gienah	175 50.3	S17 37.9
Hadar	148 45.2	S60 27.1
Hamal	327 57.9	N23 32.4
Kaus Aust.	83 40.9	S34 22.4
Kochab	137 21.2	N74 05.6
Markab	13 35.8	N15 17.9
Menkar	314 12.5	N 4 09.3
Menkent	148 05.3	S36 27.0
Miaplacidus	221 39.7	S69 47.0
Mirfak	308 36.8	N49 54.9
Nunki	75 55.5	S26 16.4
Peacock	53 15.5	S56 40.9
Pollux	243 25.2	N27 58.9
Procyon	244 57.5	N 5 10.9
Rasalhague	96 04.5	N12 33.3
Regulus	207 41.5	N11 53.2
Rigel	281 09.9	S 8 11.0
Rigil Kent.	139 49.2	S60 54.1
Sabik	102 10.1	S15 44.5
Schedar	349 37.3	N56 37.7
Shaula	96 19.0	S37 06.8
Sirius	258 31.8	S16 44.3
Spica	158 29.2	S11 14.7
Suhail	222 51.1	S43 29.9
Vega	80 37.4	N38 48.4
Zuben'ubi	137 03.2	S16 06.4

	SHA	Mer. Pass.
	° ′	h m
Venus	150 26.9	13 42
Mars	91 41.2	17 35
Jupiter	176 30.1	11 55
Saturn	110 08.2	16 20

Day	UT (d h)	SUN GHA (° ′)	SUN Dec (° ′)	MOON GHA (° ′)	v (′)	MOON Dec (° ′)	d (′)	HP (′)
SATURDAY	24 00	182 00.0	S 0 32.8	263 56.6	7.5	N18 25.5	0.9	58.2
	01	197 00.2	33.7	278 23.1	7.6	18 24.6	1.0	58.1
	02	212 00.4	34.7	292 49.7	7.7	18 23.6	1.1	58.1
	03	227 00.6	. . 35.7	307 16.4	7.7	18 22.5	1.2	58.1
	04	242 00.9	36.6	321 43.1	7.7	18 21.3	1.3	58.1
	05	257 01.1	37.6	336 09.8	7.8	18 20.0	1.5	58.0
	06	272 01.3	S 0 38.6	350 36.6	7.8	N18 18.5	1.5	58.0
	07	287 01.5	39.6	5 03.4	7.9	18 17.0	1.6	58.0
	08	302 01.7	40.5	19 30.3	7.9	18 15.4	1.8	58.0
	09	317 01.9	. . 41.5	33 57.2	8.0	18 13.6	1.9	57.9
	10	332 02.2	42.5	48 24.2	8.0	18 11.7	1.9	57.9
	11	347 02.4	43.5	62 51.2	8.0	18 09.8	2.1	57.9
	12	2 02.6	S 0 44.4	77 18.2	8.1	N18 07.7	2.2	57.8
	13	17 02.8	45.4	91 45.3	8.1	18 05.5	2.3	57.8
	14	32 03.0	46.4	106 12.4	8.2	18 03.2	2.4	57.8
	15	47 03.2	. . 47.4	120 39.6	8.2	18 00.8	2.4	57.8
	16	62 03.5	48.3	135 06.8	8.3	17 58.4	2.6	57.7
	17	77 03.7	49.3	149 34.1	8.4	17 55.8	2.7	57.7
	18	92 03.9	S 0 50.3	164 01.5	8.3	N17 53.1	2.8	57.7
	19	107 04.1	51.2	178 28.8	8.5	17 50.3	3.0	57.7
	20	122 04.3	52.2	192 56.3	8.4	17 47.3	3.0	57.6
	21	137 04.5	. . 53.2	207 23.7	8.6	17 44.3	3.1	57.6
	22	152 04.8	54.2	221 51.3	8.5	17 41.2	3.2	57.6
	23	167 05.0	55.1	236 18.8	8.7	17 38.0	3.3	57.6
SUNDAY	25 00	182 05.2	S 0 56.1	250 46.5	8.6	N17 34.7	3.4	57.5
	01	197 05.4	57.1	265 14.1	8.8	17 31.3	3.5	57.5
	02	212 05.6	58.1	279 41.9	8.8	17 27.8	3.6	57.5
	03	227 05.8	0 59.0	294 09.7	8.8	17 24.2	3.7	57.4
	04	242 06.0	1 00.0	308 37.5	8.9	17 20.5	3.8	57.4
	05	257 06.3	01.0	323 05.4	8.9	17 16.7	3.9	57.4
	06	272 06.5	S 1 02.0	337 33.3	9.0	N17 12.8	3.9	57.4
	07	287 06.7	02.9	352 01.3	9.1	17 08.9	4.1	57.3
	08	302 06.9	03.9	6 29.4	9.1	17 04.8	4.2	57.3
	09	317 07.1	. . 04.9	20 57.5	9.2	17 00.6	4.3	57.3
	10	332 07.3	05.9	35 25.7	9.2	16 56.3	4.3	57.3
	11	347 07.6	06.8	49 53.9	9.3	16 52.0	4.4	57.2
	12	2 07.8	S 1 07.8	64 22.2	9.3	N16 47.6	4.6	57.2
	13	17 08.0	08.8	78 50.5	9.4	16 43.0	4.6	57.2
	14	32 08.2	09.7	93 18.9	9.4	16 38.4	4.7	57.2
	15	47 08.4	. . 10.7	107 47.3	9.5	16 33.7	4.8	57.1
	16	62 08.6	11.7	122 15.8	9.5	16 28.9	4.9	57.1
	17	77 08.8	12.7	136 44.3	9.7	16 24.0	5.0	57.1
	18	92 09.1	S 1 13.6	151 13.0	9.6	N16 19.0	5.0	57.1
	19	107 09.3	14.6	165 41.6	9.7	16 14.0	5.2	57.0
	20	122 09.5	15.6	180 10.3	9.8	16 08.8	5.2	57.0
	21	137 09.7	. . 16.6	194 39.1	9.8	16 03.6	5.3	57.0
	22	152 09.9	17.5	209 07.9	9.9	15 58.3	5.4	57.0
	23	167 10.1	18.5	223 36.8	10.0	15 52.9	5.5	56.9
MONDAY	26 00	182 10.3	S 1 19.5	238 05.8	10.0	N15 47.4	5.6	56.9
	01	197 10.5	20.5	252 34.8	10.0	15 41.8	5.6	56.9
	02	212 10.8	21.4	267 03.8	10.2	15 36.2	5.7	56.9
	03	227 11.0	. . 22.4	281 33.0	10.1	15 30.5	5.8	56.8
	04	242 11.2	23.4	296 02.1	10.3	15 24.7	5.9	56.8
	05	257 11.4	24.4	310 31.4	10.3	15 18.8	5.9	56.8
	06	272 11.6	S 1 25.3	325 00.7	10.3	N15 12.9	6.1	56.8
	07	287 11.8	26.3	339 30.0	10.4	15 06.8	6.1	56.7
	08	302 12.0	27.3	353 59.4	10.5	15 00.7	6.2	56.7
	09	317 12.3	. . 28.2	8 28.9	10.5	14 54.5	6.2	56.7
	10	332 12.5	29.2	22 58.4	10.6	14 48.3	6.3	56.7
	11	347 12.7	30.2	37 28.0	10.6	14 42.0	6.4	56.6
	12	2 12.9	S 1 31.2	51 57.6	10.7	N14 35.6	6.5	56.6
	13	17 13.1	32.1	66 27.3	10.7	14 29.1	6.6	56.6
	14	32 13.3	33.1	80 57.0	10.8	14 22.5	6.6	56.6
	15	47 13.5	. . 34.1	95 26.8	10.9	14 15.9	6.6	56.6
	16	62 13.7	35.1	109 56.7	10.9	14 09.3	6.8	56.5
	17	77 14.0	36.0	124 26.6	11.0	14 02.5	6.8	56.5
	18	92 14.2	S 1 37.0	138 56.6	11.0	N13 55.7	6.9	56.5
	19	107 14.4	38.0	153 26.6	11.1	13 48.8	6.9	56.5
	20	122 14.6	39.0	167 56.7	11.1	13 41.9	7.1	56.4
	21	137 14.8	. . 39.9	182 26.8	11.2	13 34.8	7.0	56.4
	22	152 15.0	40.9	196 57.0	11.3	13 27.8	7.2	56.4
	23	167 15.2	41.9	211 27.3	11.3	N13 20.6	7.2	56.4
		SD 16.0	*d* 1.0	SD 15.8		15.6		15.4

Lat. (°)	Twilight Naut. (h m)	Twilight Civil (h m)	Sunrise (h m)	Moonrise 24 (h m)	Moonrise 25 (h m)	Moonrise 26 (h m)	Moonrise 27 (h m)
N 72	03 18	04 46	05 53	19 54	22 00	23 53	25 39
N 70	03 35	04 52	05 53	21 08	22 41	24 18	00 18
68	03 48	04 57	05 53	21 46	23 09	24 38	00 38
66	03 59	05 01	05 53	22 12	23 30	24 53	00 53
64	04 08	05 05	05 52	22 32	23 47	25 06	01 06
62	04 15	05 08	05 52	22 49	24 00	00 00	01 16
60	04 21	05 11	05 52	23 03	24 12	00 12	01 25
N 58	04 26	05 13	05 52	23 14	24 22	00 22	01 33
56	04 31	05 15	05 52	23 24	24 31	00 31	01 40
54	04 35	05 16	05 52	23 33	24 39	00 39	01 46
52	04 38	05 18	05 51	23 41	24 46	00 46	01 52
50	04 41	05 19	05 51	23 49	24 52	00 52	01 57
45	04 47	05 22	05 51	24 04	00 04	01 05	02 08
N 40	04 52	05 24	05 51	24 17	00 17	01 16	02 17
35	04 56	05 25	05 50	24 27	00 27	01 26	02 25
30	04 58	05 26	05 50	24 37	00 37	01 34	02 31
20	05 02	05 28	05 50	24 53	00 53	01 49	02 43
N 10	05 04	05 28	05 49	00 12	01 07	02 01	02 53
0	05 04	05 28	05 48	00 26	01 20	02 13	03 03
S 10	05 02	05 26	05 47	00 40	01 34	02 24	03 12
20	04 59	05 25	05 47	00 55	01 48	02 37	03 22
30	04 54	05 21	05 45	01 12	02 04	02 51	03 34
35	04 50	05 19	05 45	01 22	02 13	02 59	03 41
40	04 45	05 17	05 44	01 33	02 24	03 09	03 48
45	04 39	05 13	05 43	01 47	02 37	03 20	03 57
S 50	04 31	05 09	05 41	02 03	02 52	03 33	04 07
52	04 27	05 07	05 41	02 11	02 59	03 39	04 12
54	04 23	05 05	05 40	02 19	03 07	03 46	04 18
56	04 18	05 02	05 40	02 29	03 16	03 53	04 24
58	04 12	04 59	05 39	02 40	03 26	04 02	04 30
S 60	04 06	04 56	05 38	02 53	03 37	04 11	04 38

Lat. (°)	Sunset (h m)	Twilight Civil (h m)	Twilight Naut. (h m)	Moonset 24 (h m)	Moonset 25 (h m)	Moonset 26 (h m)	Moonset 27 (h m)
N 72	17 47	18 54	20 20	18 24	18 08	18 01	17 55
N 70	17 48	18 48	20 04	17 09	17 27	17 34	17 37
68	17 48	18 44	19 52	16 31	16 58	17 14	17 23
66	17 49	18 40	19 41	16 05	16 36	16 57	17 12
64	17 49	18 36	19 33	15 44	16 19	16 44	17 02
62	17 49	18 33	19 26	15 27	16 05	16 33	16 54
60	17 50	18 31	19 20	15 14	15 53	16 23	16 47
N 58	17 50	18 29	19 15	15 02	15 42	16 15	16 41
56	17 50	18 27	19 11	14 51	15 33	16 07	16 35
54	17 50	18 25	19 07	14 42	15 25	16 01	16 30
52	17 51	18 24	19 04	14 34	15 18	15 55	16 26
50	17 51	18 23	19 01	14 27	15 11	15 49	16 22
45	17 51	18 20	18 55	14 11	14 57	15 37	16 13
N 40	17 52	18 19	18 50	13 58	14 46	15 28	16 05
35	17 52	18 17	18 47	13 47	14 36	15 19	15 59
30	17 52	18 16	18 44	13 37	14 27	15 12	15 53
20	17 53	18 15	18 41	13 20	14 12	14 59	15 43
N 10	17 54	18 15	18 39	13 06	13 58	14 48	15 34
0	17 55	18 15	18 39	12 52	13 46	14 37	15 26
S 10	17 56	18 17	18 41	12 38	13 33	14 26	15 17
20	17 57	18 19	18 44	12 24	13 20	14 15	15 09
30	17 58	18 22	18 50	12 07	13 04	14 02	14 58
35	17 59	18 24	18 54	11 57	12 55	13 54	14 52
40	18 00	18 27	18 59	11 46	12 45	13 45	14 46
45	18 01	18 30	19 05	11 32	12 33	13 35	14 38
S 50	18 02	18 35	19 13	11 16	12 18	13 23	14 28
52	18 03	18 37	19 17	11 09	12 11	13 17	14 24
54	18 04	18 39	19 22	11 00	12 04	13 10	14 19
56	18 05	18 42	19 27	10 51	11 55	13 03	14 13
58	18 06	18 45	19 33	10 40	11 45	12 55	14 07
S 60	18 07	18 49	19 39	10 27	11 34	12 46	14 00

Day (d)	SUN Eqn. of Time 00^h (m s)	SUN Eqn. of Time 12^h (m s)	SUN Mer. Pass. (h m)	MOON Mer. Pass. Upper (h m)	MOON Mer. Pass. Lower (h m)	MOON Age (d)	MOON Phase (%)
24	08 00	08 10	11 52	06 39	19 06	23	38
25	08 20	08 31	11 51	07 33	19 59	24	28
26	08 41	08 51	11 51	08 25	20 50	25	19

UT		ARIES	VENUS −3·9		MARS +0·0		JUPITER −1·7		SATURN +0·5		STARS		
		GHA	GHA	Dec	GHA	Dec	GHA	Dec	GHA	Dec	Name	SHA	Dec
d	h	° ′	° ′	° ′	° ′	° ′	° ′	° ′	° ′	° ′		° ′	° ′
27	00	6 12.9	154 21.0	S12 54.6	96 27.6	S25 53.4	182 19.2	S 0 29.8	116 12.7	S20 41.8	Acamar	315 16.4	S40 14.2
	01	21 15.3	169 20.6	55.7	111 28.2	53.4	197 21.1	30.0	131 15.0	41.8	Achernar	335 24.7	S57 09.1
	02	36 17.8	184 20.1	56.9	126 28.9	53.4	212 23.1	30.2	146 17.3	41.9	Acrux	173 07.4	S63 11.4
	03	51 20.3	199 19.7	. . 58.0	141 29.5	. . 53.3	227 25.1	. . 30.4	161 19.6	. . 41.9	Adhara	255 10.8	S28 59.6
	04	66 22.7	214 19.3	12 59.1	156 30.2	53.3	242 27.0	30.6	176 21.8	41.9	Aldebaran	290 46.7	N16 32.4
	05	81 25.2	229 18.8	13 00.3	171 30.8	53.3	257 29.0	30.8	191 24.1	42.0			
	06	96 27.6	244 18.4	S13 01.4	186 31.5	S25 53.2	272 31.0	S 0 31.1	206 26.4	S20 42.0	Alioth	166 19.4	N55 52.3
	07	111 30.1	259 17.9	02.6	201 32.1	53.2	287 32.9	31.3	221 28.7	42.0	Alkaid	152 57.7	N49 14.1
T	08	126 32.6	274 17.5	03.7	216 32.8	53.2	302 34.9	31.5	236 31.0	42.0	Al Na'ir	27 40.7	S46 52.8
U	09	141 35.0	289 17.1	. . 04.8	231 33.4	. . 53.2	317 36.9	. . 31.7	251 33.3	. . 42.1	Alnilam	275 44.1	S 1 11.5
E	10	156 37.5	304 16.6	06.0	246 34.1	53.1	332 38.8	31.9	266 35.6	42.1	Alphard	217 54.1	S 8 43.8
S	11	171 40.0	319 16.2	07.1	261 34.7	53.1	347 40.8	32.1	281 37.8	42.1			
D	12	186 42.4	334 15.7	S13 08.3	276 35.4	S25 53.1	2 42.8	S 0 32.3	296 40.1	S20 42.2	Alphecca	126 09.4	N26 39.9
A	13	201 44.9	349 15.3	09.4	291 36.0	53.0	17 44.7	32.5	311 42.4	42.2	Alpheratz	357 40.8	N29 11.1
Y	14	216 47.4	4 14.9	10.5	306 36.7	53.0	32 46.7	32.8	326 44.7	42.2	Altair	62 06.0	N 8 55.1
	15	231 49.8	19 14.4	. . 11.7	321 37.3	. . 53.0	47 48.7	. . 33.0	341 47.0	. . 42.3	Ankaa	353 13.2	S42 12.9
	16	246 52.3	34 14.0	12.8	336 38.0	52.9	62 50.6	33.2	356 49.3	42.3	Antares	112 23.7	S26 27.9
	17	261 54.7	49 13.5	14.0	351 38.6	52.9	77 52.6	33.4	11 51.5	42.3			
	18	276 57.2	64 13.1	S13 15.1	6 39.3	S25 52.8	92 54.6	S 0 33.6	26 53.8	S20 42.4	Arcturus	145 54.0	N19 06.0
	19	291 59.7	79 12.6	16.2	21 39.9	52.8	107 56.5	33.8	41 56.1	42.4	Atria	107 23.7	S69 03.4
	20	307 02.1	94 12.2	17.4	36 40.6	52.8	122 58.5	34.0	56 58.4	42.4	Avior	234 17.4	S59 33.6
	21	322 04.6	109 11.8	. . 18.5	51 41.2	. . 52.7	138 00.5	. . 34.3	72 00.7	. . 42.4	Bellatrix	278 29.6	N 6 21.8
	22	337 07.1	124 11.3	19.6	66 41.9	52.7	153 02.4	34.5	87 03.0	42.5	Betelgeuse	270 58.9	N 7 24.5
	23	352 09.5	139 10.9	20.8	81 42.5	52.7	168 04.4	34.7	102 05.3	42.5			
28	00	7 12.0	154 10.4	S13 21.9	96 43.1	S25 52.6	183 06.4	S 0 34.9	117 07.5	S20 42.5	Canopus	263 55.2	S52 42.1
	01	22 14.5	169 10.0	23.0	111 43.8	52.6	198 08.3	35.1	132 09.8	42.6	Capella	280 31.0	N46 00.5
	02	37 16.9	184 09.5	24.2	126 44.4	52.6	213 10.3	35.3	147 12.1	42.6	Deneb	49 29.7	N45 20.8
	03	52 19.4	199 09.1	. . 25.3	141 45.1	. . 52.5	228 12.3	. . 35.5	162 14.4	. . 42.6	Denebola	182 31.8	N14 28.9
	04	67 21.9	214 08.6	26.4	156 45.7	52.5	243 14.2	35.8	177 16.7	42.7	Diphda	348 53.4	S17 53.6
	05	82 24.3	229 08.2	27.5	171 46.4	52.4	258 16.2	36.0	192 18.9	42.7			
	06	97 26.8	244 07.7	S13 28.7	186 47.0	S25 52.4	273 18.2	S 0 36.2	207 21.2	S20 42.7	Dubhe	193 49.8	N61 39.6
W	07	112 29.2	259 07.3	29.8	201 47.7	52.4	288 20.2	36.4	222 23.5	42.8	Elnath	278 09.7	N28 37.0
E	08	127 31.7	274 06.8	30.9	216 48.3	52.3	303 22.1	36.6	237 25.8	42.8	Eltanin	90 45.2	N51 29.7
D	09	142 34.2	289 06.4	. . 32.1	231 48.9	. . 52.3	318 24.1	. . 36.8	252 28.1	. . 42.8	Enif	33 44.7	N 9 57.4
N	10	157 36.6	304 05.9	33.2	246 49.6	52.2	333 26.1	37.0	267 30.4	42.9	Fomalhaut	15 21.3	S29 31.9
E	11	172 39.1	319 05.5	34.3	261 50.2	52.2	348 28.0	37.3	282 32.6	42.9			
S	12	187 41.6	334 05.0	S13 35.4	276 50.9	S25 52.2	3 30.0	S 0 37.5	297 34.9	S20 42.9	Gacrux	171 58.9	S57 12.3
D	13	202 44.0	349 04.6	36.6	291 51.5	52.1	18 32.0	37.7	312 37.2	42.9	Gienah	175 50.3	S17 37.9
A	14	217 46.5	4 04.1	37.7	306 52.2	52.1	33 33.9	37.9	327 39.5	43.0	Hadar	148 45.2	S60 27.1
Y	15	232 49.0	19 03.7	. . 38.8	321 52.8	. . 52.0	48 35.9	. . 38.1	342 41.8	. . 43.0	Hamal	327 57.9	N23 32.4
	16	247 51.4	34 03.2	39.9	336 53.4	52.0	63 37.9	38.3	357 44.0	43.0	Kaus Aust.	83 40.9	S34 22.4
	17	262 53.9	49 02.8	41.1	351 54.1	51.9	78 39.8	38.5	12 46.3	43.1			
	18	277 56.3	64 02.3	S13 42.2	6 54.7	S25 51.9	93 41.8	S 0 38.8	27 48.6	S20 43.1	Kochab	137 21.2	N74 05.6
	19	292 58.8	79 01.9	43.3	21 55.4	51.9	108 43.8	39.0	42 50.9	43.1	Markab	13 35.8	N15 17.9
	20	308 01.3	94 01.4	44.4	36 56.0	51.8	123 45.7	39.2	57 53.2	43.2	Menkar	314 12.5	N 4 09.3
	21	323 03.7	109 01.0	. . 45.5	51 56.6	. . 51.8	138 47.7	. . 39.4	72 55.5	. . 43.2	Menkent	148 05.3	S36 27.0
	22	338 06.2	124 00.5	46.7	66 57.3	51.7	153 49.7	39.6	87 57.7	43.2	Miaplacidus	221 39.7	S69 47.0
	23	353 08.7	139 00.0	47.8	81 57.9	51.7	168 51.6	39.8	103 00.0	43.3			
29	00	8 11.1	153 59.6	S13 48.9	96 58.6	S25 51.6	183 53.6	S 0 40.0	118 02.3	S20 43.3	Mirfak	308 36.8	N49 55.0
	01	23 13.6	168 59.1	50.0	111 59.2	51.6	198 55.6	40.2	133 04.6	43.3	Nunki	75 55.5	S26 16.4
	02	38 16.1	183 58.7	51.1	126 59.8	51.5	213 57.5	40.5	148 06.9	43.4	Peacock	53 15.6	S56 40.9
	03	53 18.5	198 58.2	. . 52.3	142 00.5	. . 51.5	228 59.5	. . 40.7	163 09.1	. . 43.4	Pollux	243 25.2	N27 58.9
	04	68 21.0	213 57.8	53.4	157 01.1	51.4	244 01.5	40.9	178 11.4	43.4	Procyon	244 57.5	N 5 10.9
	05	83 23.5	228 57.3	54.5	172 01.7	51.4	259 03.4	41.1	193 13.7	43.4			
	06	98 25.9	243 56.8	S13 55.6	187 02.4	S25 51.3	274 05.4	S 0 41.3	208 16.0	S20 43.5	Rasalhague	96 04.5	N12 33.3
	07	113 28.4	258 56.4	56.7	202 03.0	51.3	289 07.4	41.5	223 18.2	43.5	Regulus	207 41.5	N11 53.2
T	08	128 30.8	273 55.9	57.8	217 03.7	51.2	304 09.3	41.7	238 20.5	43.5	Rigel	281 09.8	S 8 11.0
H	09	143 33.3	288 55.5	13 59.0	232 04.3	. . 51.2	319 11.3	. . 42.0	253 22.8	. . 43.6	Rigil Kent.	139 49.2	S60 54.1
U	10	158 35.8	303 55.0	14 00.1	247 04.9	51.1	334 13.3	42.2	268 25.1	43.6	Sabik	102 10.1	S15 44.5
R	11	173 38.2	318 54.5	01.2	262 05.6	51.1	349 15.2	42.4	283 27.4	43.6			
S	12	188 40.7	333 54.1	S14 02.3	277 06.2	S25 51.0	4 17.2	S 0 42.6	298 29.6	S20 43.7	Schedar	349 37.3	N56 37.7
D	13	203 43.2	348 53.6	03.4	292 06.8	51.0	19 19.2	42.8	313 31.9	43.7	Shaula	96 19.0	S37 06.8
A	14	218 45.6	3 53.2	04.5	307 07.5	50.9	34 21.1	43.0	328 34.2	43.7	Sirius	258 31.8	S16 44.3
Y	15	233 48.1	18 52.7	. . 05.6	322 08.1	. . 50.9	49 23.1	. . 43.2	343 36.5	. . 43.8	Spica	158 29.2	S11 14.7
	16	248 50.6	33 52.2	06.7	337 08.7	50.8	64 25.1	43.5	358 38.8	43.8	Suhail	222 51.1	S43 29.8
	17	263 53.0	48 51.8	07.9	352 09.4	50.8	79 27.0	43.7	13 41.0	43.8			
	18	278 55.5	63 51.3	S14 09.0	7 10.0	S25 50.7	94 29.0	S 0 43.9	28 43.3	S20 43.9	Vega	80 37.4	N38 48.4
	19	293 58.0	78 50.8	10.1	22 10.6	50.7	109 31.0	44.1	43 45.6	43.9	Zuben'ubi	137 03.2	S16 06.4
	20	309 00.4	93 50.4	11.2	37 11.3	50.6	124 32.9	44.3	58 47.9	43.9			
	21	324 02.9	108 49.9	. . 12.3	52 11.9	. . 50.6	139 34.9	. . 44.5	73 50.1	. . 43.9			
	22	339 05.3	123 49.5	13.4	67 12.5	50.5	154 36.9	44.7	88 52.4	44.0			
	23	354 07.8	138 49.0	14.5	82 13.2	50.5	169 38.9	44.9	103 54.7	44.0			
Mer. Pass.		h m 23 27.3	*v* −0.5	*d* 1.1	*v* 0.6	*d* 0.0	*v* 2.0	*d* 0.2	*v* 2.3	*d* 0.0			

	SHA	Mer. Pass.
	° ′	h m
Venus	146 58.4	13 44
Mars	89 31.2	17 32
Jupiter	175 54.4	11 46
Saturn	109 55.5	16 09

UT	SUN GHA	SUN Dec	MOON GHA	v	MOON Dec	d	HP
d h	° ′	° ′	° ′	′	° ′	′	′
27 00 (TUESDAY)	182 15.4	S 1 42.8	225 57.6	11.3	N13 13.4	7.2	56.3
01	197 15.6	43.8	240 27.9	11.4	13 06.2	7.4	56.3
02	212 15.9	44.8	254 58.3	11.5	12 58.8	7.4	56.3
03	227 16.1	. . 45.8	269 28.8	11.5	12 51.4	7.4	56.3
04	242 16.3	46.7	283 59.3	11.6	12 44.0	7.5	56.3
05	257 16.5	47.7	298 29.9	11.6	12 36.5	7.6	56.2
06	272 16.7	S 1 48.7	313 00.5	11.7	N12 28.9	7.6	56.2
07	287 16.9	49.7	327 31.2	11.7	12 21.3	7.7	56.2
08	302 17.1	50.6	342 01.9	11.8	12 13.6	7.7	56.2
09	317 17.3	. . 51.6	356 32.7	11.9	12 05.9	7.8	56.1
10	332 17.5	52.6	11 03.6	11.9	11 58.1	7.8	56.1
11	347 17.7	53.6	25 34.5	11.9	11 50.3	7.9	56.1
12	2 18.0	S 1 54.5	40 05.4	12.0	N11 42.4	8.0	56.1
13	17 18.2	55.5	54 36.4	12.1	11 34.4	8.0	56.1
14	32 18.4	56.5	69 07.5	12.1	11 26.4	8.0	56.0
15	47 18.6	. . 57.4	83 38.6	12.1	11 18.4	8.1	56.0
16	62 18.8	58.4	98 09.7	12.2	11 10.3	8.1	56.0
17	77 19.0	1 59.4	112 40.9	12.3	11 02.2	8.2	56.0
18	92 19.2	S 2 00.4	127 12.2	12.3	N10 54.0	8.3	56.0
19	107 19.4	01.3	141 43.5	12.3	10 45.7	8.3	55.9
20	122 19.6	02.3	156 14.8	12.4	10 37.4	8.3	55.9
21	137 19.8	. . 03.3	170 46.2	12.5	10 29.1	8.4	55.9
22	152 20.1	04.3	185 17.7	12.5	10 20.7	8.4	55.9
23	167 20.3	05.2	199 49.2	12.5	10 12.3	8.4	55.8
28 00 (WEDNESDAY)	182 20.5	S 2 06.2	214 20.7	12.6	N10 03.9	8.6	55.8
01	197 20.7	07.2	228 52.3	12.6	9 55.3	8.5	55.8
02	212 20.9	08.1	243 23.9	12.7	9 46.8	8.6	55.8
03	227 21.1	. . 09.1	257 55.6	12.7	9 38.2	8.6	55.8
04	242 21.3	10.1	272 27.3	12.8	9 29.6	8.7	55.7
05	257 21.5	11.1	286 59.1	12.8	9 20.9	8.7	55.7
06	272 21.7	S 2 12.0	301 30.9	12.9	N 9 12.2	8.7	55.7
07	287 21.9	13.0	316 02.8	12.9	9 03.5	8.8	55.7
08	302 22.1	14.0	330 34.7	13.0	8 54.7	8.8	55.7
09	317 22.3	. . 15.0	345 06.7	13.0	8 45.9	8.9	55.6
10	332 22.6	15.9	359 38.7	13.0	8 37.0	8.9	55.6
11	347 22.8	16.9	14 10.7	13.1	8 28.1	8.9	55.6
12	2 23.0	S 2 17.9	28 42.8	13.1	N 8 19.2	8.9	55.6
13	17 23.2	18.8	43 14.9	13.2	8 10.3	9.0	55.6
14	32 23.4	19.8	57 47.1	13.2	8 01.3	9.0	55.6
15	47 23.6	. . 20.8	72 19.3	13.2	7 52.3	9.1	55.5
16	62 23.8	21.8	86 51.5	13.3	7 43.2	9.1	55.5
17	77 24.0	22.7	101 23.8	13.3	7 34.1	9.1	55.5
18	92 24.2	S 2 23.7	115 56.1	13.4	N 7 25.0	9.1	55.5
19	107 24.4	24.7	130 28.5	13.4	7 15.9	9.2	55.5
20	122 24.6	25.6	145 00.9	13.5	7 06.7	9.2	55.4
21	137 24.8	. . 26.6	159 33.4	13.4	6 57.5	9.2	55.4
22	152 25.0	27.6	174 05.8	13.6	6 48.3	9.2	55.4
23	167 25.2	28.6	188 38.4	13.5	6 39.1	9.3	55.4
29 00 (THURSDAY)	182 25.5	S 2 29.5	203 10.9	13.6	N 6 29.8	9.3	55.4
01	197 25.7	30.5	217 43.5	13.6	6 20.5	9.3	55.3
02	212 25.9	31.5	232 16.1	13.7	6 11.2	9.3	55.3
03	227 26.1	. . 32.4	246 48.8	13.7	6 01.9	9.4	55.3
04	242 26.3	33.4	261 21.5	13.7	5 52.5	9.3	55.3
05	257 26.5	34.4	275 54.2	13.8	5 43.2	9.4	55.3
06	272 26.7	S 2 35.4	290 27.0	13.8	N 5 33.8	9.5	55.3
07	287 26.9	36.3	304 59.8	13.8	5 24.3	9.4	55.2
08	302 27.1	37.3	319 32.6	13.9	5 14.9	9.4	55.2
09	317 27.3	. . 38.3	334 05.5	13.9	5 05.5	9.5	55.2
10	332 27.5	39.2	348 38.4	13.9	4 56.0	9.5	55.2
11	347 27.7	40.2	3 11.3	14.0	4 46.5	9.5	55.2
12	2 27.9	S 2 41.2	17 44.3	14.0	N 4 37.0	9.5	55.2
13	17 28.1	42.2	32 17.3	14.0	4 27.5	9.6	55.1
14	32 28.3	43.1	46 50.3	14.0	4 17.9	9.5	55.1
15	47 28.5	. . 44.1	61 23.3	14.1	4 08.4	9.6	55.1
16	62 28.7	45.1	75 56.4	14.1	3 58.8	9.5	55.1
17	77 28.9	46.0	90 29.5	14.1	3 49.3	9.6	55.1
18	92 29.1	S 2 47.0	105 02.6	14.2	N 3 39.7	9.6	55.1
19	107 29.3	48.0	119 35.8	14.2	3 30.1	9.6	55.0
20	122 29.6	49.0	134 09.0	14.2	3 20.5	9.6	55.0
21	137 29.8	. . 49.9	148 42.2	14.2	3 10.9	9.6	55.0
22	152 30.0	50.9	163 15.4	14.3	3 01.3	9.7	55.0
23	167 30.2	51.9	177 48.7	14.3	N 2 51.6	9.6	55.0
	SD 16.0	*d* 1.0	SD 15.3		15.1		15.0

Lat.	Twilight Naut.	Twilight Civil	Sunrise	Moonrise 27	Moonrise 28	Moonrise 29	Moonrise 30
°	h m	h m	h m	h m	h m	h m	h m
N 72	03 35	04 59	06 07	25 39	01 39	03 20	04 57
N 70	03 49	05 04	06 05	00 18	01 54	03 28	05 00
68	04 01	05 08	06 03	00 38	02 07	03 35	05 02
66	04 10	05 11	06 02	00 53	02 17	03 41	05 04
64	04 17	05 14	06 01	01 06	02 26	03 46	05 05
62	04 23	05 16	06 00	01 16	02 33	03 50	05 06
60	04 29	05 18	05 59	01 25	02 40	03 54	05 07
N 58	04 33	05 19	05 58	01 33	02 45	03 57	05 08
56	04 37	05 21	05 58	01 40	02 50	04 00	05 09
54	04 40	05 22	05 57	01 46	02 55	04 03	05 10
52	04 43	05 23	05 56	01 52	02 59	04 05	05 11
50	04 46	05 24	05 56	01 57	03 02	04 07	05 11
45	04 51	05 25	05 55	02 08	03 10	04 12	05 13
N 40	04 55	05 27	05 54	02 17	03 17	04 16	05 14
35	04 58	05 27	05 53	02 25	03 22	04 19	05 15
30	05 00	05 28	05 52	02 31	03 27	04 22	05 16
20	05 03	05 28	05 50	02 43	03 36	04 27	05 18
N 10	05 03	05 28	05 49	02 53	03 43	04 32	05 19
0	05 03	05 27	05 47	03 03	03 50	04 36	05 20
S 10	05 00	05 25	05 46	03 12	03 57	04 40	05 22
20	04 56	05 22	05 44	03 22	04 05	04 45	05 23
30	04 50	05 18	05 42	03 34	04 13	04 50	05 25
35	04 45	05 15	05 40	03 41	04 18	04 53	05 26
40	04 40	05 12	05 39	03 48	04 24	04 56	05 27
45	04 33	05 08	05 37	03 57	04 30	05 00	05 28
S 50	04 24	05 03	05 35	04 07	04 38	05 05	05 30
52	04 20	05 00	05 34	04 12	04 41	05 07	05 30
54	04 15	04 57	05 33	04 18	04 45	05 09	05 31
56	04 09	04 54	05 32	04 24	04 49	05 11	05 32
58	04 03	04 51	05 30	04 30	04 54	05 14	05 33
S 60	03 55	04 47	05 29	04 38	04 59	05 17	05 34

Lat.	Sunset	Twilight Civil	Twilight Naut.	Moonset 27	Moonset 28	Moonset 29	Moonset 30
°	h m	h m	h m	h m	h m	h m	h m
N 72	17 32	18 39	20 02	17 55	17 49	17 44	17 39
N 70	17 34	18 34	19 48	17 37	17 39	17 39	17 39
68	17 36	18 31	19 38	17 23	17 30	17 35	17 39
66	17 37	18 28	19 29	17 12	17 23	17 32	17 40
64	17 38	18 26	19 22	17 02	17 17	17 29	17 40
62	17 40	18 23	19 16	16 54	17 11	17 26	17 40
60	17 41	18 22	19 11	16 47	17 07	17 24	17 40
N 58	17 41	18 20	19 06	16 41	17 03	17 22	17 40
56	17 42	18 19	19 03	16 35	16 59	17 20	17 40
54	17 43	18 18	18 59	16 30	16 56	17 19	17 40
52	17 44	18 17	18 56	16 26	16 53	17 17	17 40
50	17 44	18 16	18 54	16 22	16 50	17 16	17 41
45	17 46	18 15	18 49	16 13	16 44	17 13	17 41
N 40	17 47	18 14	18 45	16 05	16 39	17 11	17 41
35	17 48	18 13	18 42	15 59	16 35	17 08	17 41
30	17 49	18 13	18 40	15 53	16 31	17 07	17 41
20	17 50	18 12	18 38	15 43	16 24	17 03	17 41
N 10	17 52	18 13	18 37	15 34	16 18	17 00	17 41
0	17 54	18 14	18 38	15 26	16 13	16 58	17 41
S 10	17 55	18 16	18 41	15 17	16 07	16 55	17 42
20	17 57	18 19	18 45	15 09	16 01	16 52	17 42
30	18 00	18 24	18 52	14 58	15 54	16 48	17 42
35	18 01	18 27	18 56	14 52	15 50	16 46	17 42
40	18 03	18 30	19 02	14 46	15 45	16 44	17 42
45	18 05	18 34	19 09	14 38	15 40	16 41	17 42
S 50	18 07	18 40	19 18	14 28	15 34	16 38	17 42
52	18 08	18 42	19 23	14 24	15 31	16 37	17 42
54	18 09	18 45	19 28	14 19	15 27	16 35	17 42
56	18 11	18 48	19 33	14 13	15 24	16 33	17 42
58	18 12	18 52	19 40	14 07	15 20	16 31	17 42
S 60	18 14	18 56	19 48	14 00	15 15	16 29	17 42

Day	SUN Eqn. of Time 00^h	SUN Eqn. of Time 12^h	SUN Mer. Pass.	MOON Mer. Pass. Upper	MOON Mer. Pass. Lower	MOON Age	MOON Phase
d	m s	m s	h m	h m	h m	d	%
27	09 01	09 11	11 51	09 14	21 38	26	12
28	09 21	09 31	11 50	10 01	22 24	27	6
29	09 41	09 51	11 50	10 47	23 09	28	2

UT d	UT h	ARIES GHA	VENUS −3·9 GHA	VENUS Dec	MARS +0·1 GHA	MARS Dec	JUPITER −1·7 GHA	JUPITER Dec	SATURN +0·5 GHA	SATURN Dec
		° ′	° ′	° ′	° ′	° ′	° ′	° ′	° ′	° ′
30 FRIDAY	00	9 10.3	153 48.5	S14 15.6	97 13.8	S25 50.4	184 40.8	S 0 45.2	118 57.0	S20 44.0
	01	24 12.7	168 48.1	16.7	112 14.4	50.4	199 42.8	45.4	133 59.2	44.1
	02	39 15.2	183 47.6	17.8	127 15.1	50.3	214 44.8	45.6	149 01.5	44.1
	03	54 17.7	198 47.1	. . 18.9	142 15.7	. . 50.2	229 46.7	. . 45.8	164 03.8	. . 44.1
	04	69 20.1	213 46.7	20.0	157 16.3	50.2	244 48.7	46.0	179 06.1	44.2
	05	84 22.6	228 46.2	21.1	172 17.0	50.1	259 50.7	46.2	194 08.3	44.2
	06	99 25.1	243 45.7	S14 22.2	187 17.6	S25 50.1	274 52.6	S 0 46.4	209 10.6	S20 44.2
	07	114 27.5	258 45.2	23.3	202 18.2	50.0	289 54.6	46.7	224 12.9	44.3
	08	129 30.0	273 44.8	24.4	217 18.8	50.0	304 56.6	46.9	239 15.2	44.3
	09	144 32.4	288 44.3	. . 25.5	232 19.5	. . 49.9	319 58.5	. . 47.1	254 17.5	. . 44.3
	10	159 34.9	303 43.8	26.6	247 20.1	49.8	335 00.5	47.3	269 19.7	44.4
	11	174 37.4	318 43.4	27.7	262 20.7	49.8	350 02.5	47.5	284 22.0	44.4
	12	189 39.8	333 42.9	S14 28.8	277 21.4	S25 49.7	5 04.4	S 0 47.7	299 24.3	S20 44.4
	13	204 42.3	348 42.4	29.9	292 22.0	49.7	20 06.4	47.9	314 26.6	44.5
	14	219 44.8	3 41.9	31.0	307 22.6	49.6	35 08.4	48.1	329 28.8	44.5
	15	234 47.2	18 41.5	. . 32.1	322 23.2	. . 49.5	50 10.3	. . 48.4	344 31.1	. . 44.5
	16	249 49.7	33 41.0	33.2	337 23.9	49.5	65 12.3	48.6	359 33.4	44.5
	17	264 52.2	48 40.5	34.3	352 24.5	49.4	80 14.3	48.8	14 35.6	44.6
	18	279 54.6	63 40.1	S14 35.4	7 25.1	S25 49.4	95 16.2	S 0 49.0	29 37.9	S20 44.6
	19	294 57.1	78 39.6	36.5	22 25.7	49.3	110 18.2	49.2	44 40.2	44.6
	20	309 59.6	93 39.1	37.6	37 26.4	49.2	125 20.2	49.4	59 42.5	44.7
	21	325 02.0	108 38.6	. . 38.7	52 27.0	. . 49.2	140 22.1	. . 49.6	74 44.7	. . 44.7
	22	340 04.5	123 38.2	39.8	67 27.6	49.1	155 24.1	49.9	89 47.0	44.7
	23	355 06.9	138 37.7	40.9	82 28.2	49.0	170 26.1	50.1	104 49.3	44.8
1 SATURDAY	00	10 09.4	153 37.2	S14 42.0	97 28.9	S25 49.0	185 28.0	S 0 50.3	119 51.6	S20 44.8
	01	25 11.9	168 36.7	43.1	112 29.5	48.9	200 30.0	50.5	134 53.8	44.8
	02	40 14.3	183 36.2	44.2	127 30.1	48.9	215 32.0	50.7	149 56.1	44.9
	03	55 16.8	198 35.8	. . 45.2	142 30.7	. . 48.8	230 33.9	. . 50.9	164 58.4	. . 44.9
	04	70 19.3	213 35.3	46.3	157 31.4	48.7	245 35.9	51.1	180 00.7	44.9
	05	85 21.7	228 34.8	47.4	172 32.0	48.7	260 37.9	51.3	195 02.9	45.0
	06	100 24.2	243 34.3	S14 48.5	187 32.6	S25 48.6	275 39.8	S 0 51.6	210 05.2	S20 45.0
	07	115 26.7	258 33.8	49.6	202 33.2	48.5	290 41.8	51.8	225 07.5	45.0
	08	130 29.1	273 33.4	50.7	217 33.9	48.5	305 43.8	52.0	240 09.7	45.1
	09	145 31.6	288 32.9	. . 51.8	232 34.5	. . 48.4	320 45.8	. . 52.2	255 12.0	. . 45.1
	10	160 34.0	303 32.4	52.9	247 35.1	48.3	335 47.7	52.4	270 14.3	45.1
	11	175 36.5	318 31.9	53.9	262 35.7	48.3	350 49.7	52.6	285 16.6	45.2
	12	190 39.0	333 31.4	S14 55.0	277 36.4	S25 48.2	5 51.7	S 0 52.8	300 18.8	S20 45.2
	13	205 41.4	348 31.0	56.1	292 37.0	48.1	20 53.6	53.1	315 21.1	45.2
	14	220 43.9	3 30.5	57.2	307 37.6	48.0	35 55.6	53.3	330 23.4	45.3
	15	235 46.4	18 30.0	. . 58.3	322 38.2	. . 48.0	50 57.6	. . 53.5	345 25.6	. . 45.3
	16	250 48.8	33 29.5	14 59.4	337 38.8	47.9	65 59.5	53.7	0 27.9	45.3
	17	265 51.3	48 29.0	15 00.4	352 39.5	47.8	81 01.5	53.9	15 30.2	45.3
	18	280 53.8	63 28.5	S15 01.5	7 40.1	S25 47.8	96 03.5	S 0 54.1	30 32.5	S20 45.4
	19	295 56.2	78 28.1	02.6	22 40.7	47.7	111 05.4	54.3	45 34.7	45.4
	20	310 58.7	93 27.6	03.7	37 41.3	47.6	126 07.4	54.5	60 37.0	45.4
	21	326 01.2	108 27.1	. . 04.8	52 41.9	. . 47.6	141 09.4	. . 54.8	75 39.3	. . 45.5
	22	341 03.6	123 26.6	05.8	67 42.6	47.5	156 11.3	55.0	90 41.5	45.5
	23	356 06.1	138 26.1	06.9	82 43.2	47.4	171 13.3	55.2	105 43.8	45.5
2 SUNDAY	00	11 08.5	153 25.6	S15 08.0	97 43.8	S25 47.3	186 15.3	S 0 55.4	120 46.1	S20 45.6
	01	26 11.0	168 25.1	09.1	112 44.4	47.3	201 17.2	55.6	135 48.3	45.6
	02	41 13.5	183 24.6	10.2	127 45.0	47.2	216 19.2	55.8	150 50.6	45.6
	03	56 15.9	198 24.2	. . 11.2	142 45.6	. . 47.1	231 21.2	. . 56.0	165 52.9	. . 45.7
	04	71 18.4	213 23.7	12.3	157 46.3	47.0	246 23.1	56.2	180 55.2	45.7
	05	86 20.9	228 23.2	13.4	172 46.9	47.0	261 25.1	56.5	195 57.4	45.7
	06	101 23.3	243 22.7	S15 14.5	187 47.5	S25 46.9	276 27.1	S 0 56.7	210 59.7	S20 45.8
	07	116 25.8	258 22.2	15.5	202 48.1	46.8	291 29.0	56.9	226 02.0	45.8
	08	131 28.3	273 21.7	16.6	217 48.7	46.7	306 31.0	57.1	241 04.2	45.8
	09	146 30.7	288 21.2	. . 17.7	232 49.3	. . 46.7	321 33.0	. . 57.3	256 06.5	. . 45.9
	10	161 33.2	303 20.7	18.7	247 50.0	46.6	336 34.9	57.5	271 08.8	45.9
	11	176 35.6	318 20.2	19.8	262 50.6	46.5	351 36.9	57.7	286 11.0	45.9
	12	191 38.1	333 19.7	S15 20.9	277 51.2	S25 46.4	6 38.9	S 0 58.0	301 13.3	S20 46.0
	13	206 40.6	348 19.2	22.0	292 51.8	46.4	21 40.9	58.2	316 15.6	46.0
	14	221 43.0	3 18.7	23.0	307 52.4	46.3	36 42.8	58.4	331 17.8	46.0
	15	236 45.5	18 18.2	. . 24.1	322 53.0	. . 46.2	51 44.8	. . 58.6	346 20.1	. . 46.1
	16	251 48.0	33 17.8	25.2	337 53.6	46.1	66 46.8	58.8	1 22.4	46.1
	17	266 50.4	48 17.3	26.2	352 54.3	46.0	81 48.7	59.0	16 24.6	46.1
	18	281 52.9	63 16.8	S15 27.3	7 54.9	S25 46.0	96 50.7	S 0 59.2	31 26.9	S20 46.1
	19	296 55.4	78 16.3	28.4	22 55.5	45.9	111 52.7	59.4	46 29.2	46.2
	20	311 57.8	93 15.8	29.4	37 56.1	45.8	126 54.6	59.7	61 31.4	46.2
	21	327 00.3	108 15.3	. . 30.5	52 56.7	. . 45.7	141 56.6	0 59.9	76 33.7	. . 46.2
	22	342 02.8	123 14.8	31.6	67 57.3	45.6	156 58.6	1 00.1	91 36.0	46.3
	23	357 05.2	138 14.3	32.6	82 57.9	45.6	172 00.5	S 1 00.3	106 38.2	46.3
Mer. Pass.		h m 23 15.6	*v* −0.5	*d* 1.1	*v* 0.6	*d* 0.1	*v* 2.0	*d* 0.2	*v* 2.3	*d* 0.0

STARS

Name	SHA	Dec
	° ′	° ′
Acamar	315 16.4	S40 14.2
Achernar	335 24.7	S57 09.1
Acrux	173 07.4	S63 11.4
Adhara	255 10.8	S28 59.6
Aldebaran	290 46.7	N16 32.4
Alioth	166 19.4	N55 52.3
Alkaid	152 57.7	N49 14.1
Al Na'ir	27 40.7	S46 52.8
Alnilam	275 44.0	S 1 11.5
Alphard	217 54.1	S 8 43.8
Alphecca	126 09.4	N26 39.9
Alpheratz	357 40.8	N29 11.1
Altair	62 06.0	N 8 55.1
Ankaa	353 13.2	S42 12.9
Antares	112 23.7	S26 27.9
Arcturus	145 54.0	N19 06.0
Atria	107 23.7	S69 03.4
Avior	234 17.3	S59 33.6
Bellatrix	278 29.5	N 6 21.8
Betelgeuse	270 58.9	N 7 24.5
Canopus	263 55.1	S52 42.1
Capella	280 31.0	N46 00.5
Deneb	49 29.7	N45 20.8
Denebola	182 31.8	N14 28.9
Diphda	348 53.4	S17 53.6
Dubhe	193 49.7	N61 39.6
Elnath	278 09.7	N28 37.0
Eltanin	90 45.2	N51 29.7
Enif	33 44.7	N 9 57.4
Fomalhaut	15 21.3	S29 31.9
Gacrux	171 58.9	S57 12.3
Gienah	175 50.3	S17 37.9
Hadar	148 45.2	S60 27.1
Hamal	327 57.9	N23 32.4
Kaus Aust.	83 40.9	S34 22.4
Kochab	137 21.2	N74 05.5
Markab	13 35.8	N15 17.9
Menkar	314 12.5	N 4 09.3
Menkent	148 05.3	S36 26.9
Miaplacidus	221 39.6	S69 47.0
Mirfak	308 36.8	N49 55.0
Nunki	75 55.6	S26 16.4
Peacock	53 15.6	S56 40.9
Pollux	243 25.2	N27 58.9
Procyon	244 57.5	N 5 10.9
Rasalhague	96 04.5	N12 33.3
Regulus	207 41.4	N11 53.1
Rigel	281 09.8	S 8 11.0
Rigil Kent.	139 49.2	S60 54.1
Sabik	102 10.1	S15 44.5
Schedar	349 37.3	N56 37.7
Shaula	96 19.0	S37 06.8
Sirius	258 31.8	S16 44.3
Spica	158 29.2	S11 14.7
Suhail	222 51.0	S43 29.8
Vega	80 37.5	N38 48.4
Zuben'ubi	137 03.2	S16 06.4

	SHA	Mer. Pass.
	° ′	h m
Venus	143 27.8	13 46
Mars	87 19.5	17 29
Jupiter	175 18.6	11 37
Saturn	109 42.2	15 58

UT d	h	SUN GHA ° ′	SUN Dec ° ′	MOON GHA ° ′	v ′	MOON Dec ° ′	d ′	HP ′
30	00	182 30.4	S 2 52.8	192 22.0	14.3	N 2 42.0	9.7	55.0
	01	197 30.6	53.8	206 55.3	14.3	2 32.3	9.6	54.9
	02	212 30.8	54.8	221 28.6	14.3	2 22.7	9.7	54.9
	03	227 31.0	. . 55.8	236 01.9	14.4	2 13.0	9.6	54.9
	04	242 31.2	56.7	250 35.3	14.4	2 03.4	9.7	54.9
	05	257 31.4	57.7	265 08.7	14.4	1 53.7	9.6	54.9
	06	272 31.6	S 2 58.7	279 42.1	14.5	N 1 44.1	9.7	54.9
	07	287 31.8	2 59.6	294 15.6	14.4	1 34.4	9.7	54.8
F	08	302 32.0	3 00.6	308 49.0	14.5	1 24.7	9.6	54.8
R	09	317 32.2	. . 01.6	323 22.5	14.5	1 15.1	9.7	54.8
I	10	332 32.4	02.5	337 56.0	14.5	1 05.4	9.7	54.8
D	11	347 32.6	03.5	352 29.5	14.5	0 55.7	9.7	54.8
A	12	2 32.8	S 3 04.5	7 03.0	14.6	N 0 46.0	9.6	54.8
Y	13	17 33.0	05.5	21 36.6	14.6	0 36.4	9.7	54.8
	14	32 33.2	06.4	36 10.2	14.5	0 26.7	9.7	54.7
	15	47 33.4	. . 07.4	50 43.7	14.6	0 17.0	9.6	54.7
	16	62 33.6	08.4	65 17.3	14.6	N 0 07.4	9.7	54.7
	17	77 33.8	09.3	79 50.9	14.7	S 0 02.3	9.6	54.7
	18	92 34.0	S 3 10.3	94 24.6	14.6	S 0 11.9	9.7	54.7
	19	107 34.2	11.3	108 58.2	14.7	0 21.6	9.6	54.7
	20	122 34.4	12.2	123 31.9	14.6	0 31.2	9.6	54.7
	21	137 34.6	. . 13.2	138 05.5	14.7	0 40.8	9.7	54.6
	22	152 34.8	14.2	152 39.2	14.7	0 50.5	9.6	54.6
	23	167 35.0	15.2	167 12.9	14.7	1 00.1	9.6	54.6
1	00	182 35.2	S 3 16.1	181 46.6	14.7	S 1 09.7	9.6	54.6
	01	197 35.4	17.1	196 20.3	14.7	1 19.3	9.6	54.6
	02	212 35.6	18.1	210 54.0	14.8	1 28.9	9.6	54.6
	03	227 35.8	. . 19.0	225 27.8	14.7	1 38.5	9.5	54.6
	04	242 36.0	20.0	240 01.5	14.8	1 48.0	9.6	54.6
	05	257 36.2	21.0	254 35.3	14.7	1 57.6	9.5	54.5
	06	272 36.4	S 3 21.9	269 09.0	14.8	S 2 07.1	9.6	54.5
S	07	287 36.6	22.9	283 42.8	14.8	2 16.7	9.5	54.5
A	08	302 36.8	23.9	298 16.6	14.8	2 26.2	9.5	54.5
T	09	317 37.0	. . 24.8	312 50.4	14.7	2 35.7	9.5	54.5
U	10	332 37.2	25.8	327 24.1	14.8	2 45.2	9.4	54.5
R	11	347 37.4	26.8	341 57.9	14.8	2 54.6	9.5	54.5
D	12	2 37.6	S 3 27.8	356 31.7	14.8	S 3 04.1	9.4	54.5
A	13	17 37.8	28.7	11 05.5	14.9	3 13.5	9.4	54.4
Y	14	32 38.0	29.7	25 39.4	14.8	3 22.9	9.4	54.4
	15	47 38.2	. . 30.7	40 13.2	14.8	3 32.3	9.4	54.4
	16	62 38.4	31.6	54 47.0	14.8	3 41.7	9.4	54.4
	17	77 38.6	32.6	69 20.8	14.8	3 51.1	9.3	54.4
	18	92 38.8	S 3 33.6	83 54.6	14.8	S 4 00.4	9.4	54.4
	19	107 39.0	34.5	98 28.4	14.9	4 09.8	9.3	54.4
	20	122 39.2	35.5	113 02.3	14.8	4 19.1	9.2	54.4
	21	137 39.4	. . 36.5	127 36.1	14.8	4 28.3	9.3	54.4
	22	152 39.6	37.4	142 09.9	14.8	4 37.6	9.2	54.3
	23	167 39.8	38.4	156 43.7	14.8	4 46.8	9.2	54.3
2	00	182 40.0	S 3 39.4	171 17.5	14.9	S 4 56.0	9.2	54.3
	01	197 40.2	40.3	185 51.4	14.8	5 05.2	9.2	54.3
	02	212 40.4	41.3	200 25.2	14.8	5 14.4	9.1	54.3
	03	227 40.6	. . 42.3	214 59.0	14.8	5 23.5	9.1	54.3
	04	242 40.8	43.2	229 32.8	14.8	5 32.6	9.1	54.3
	05	257 41.0	44.2	244 06.6	14.8	5 41.7	9.1	54.3
	06	272 41.2	S 3 45.2	258 40.4	14.8	S 5 50.8	9.0	54.3
	07	287 41.4	46.1	273 14.2	14.8	5 59.8	9.0	54.3
	08	302 41.6	47.1	287 48.0	14.8	6 08.8	9.0	54.2
S	09	317 41.8	. . 48.1	302 21.8	14.8	6 17.8	8.9	54.2
U	10	332 42.0	49.0	316 55.6	14.8	6 26.7	9.0	54.2
N	11	347 42.1	50.0	331 29.4	14.7	6 35.7	8.8	54.2
D	12	2 42.3	S 3 51.0	346 03.1	14.8	S 6 44.5	8.9	54.2
A	13	17 42.5	51.9	0 36.9	14.8	6 53.4	8.8	54.2
Y	14	32 42.7	52.9	15 10.7	14.7	7 02.2	8.8	54.2
	15	47 42.9	. . 53.9	29 44.4	14.8	7 11.0	8.8	54.2
	16	62 43.1	54.8	44 18.2	14.7	7 19.8	8.7	54.2
	17	77 43.3	55.8	58 51.9	14.7	7 28.5	8.7	54.2
	18	92 43.5	S 3 56.8	73 25.6	14.7	S 7 37.2	8.7	54.2
	19	107 43.7	57.7	87 59.3	14.7	7 45.9	8.6	54.2
	20	122 43.9	58.7	102 33.0	14.7	7 54.5	8.6	54.1
	21	137 44.1	3 59.7	117 06.7	14.7	8 03.1	8.5	54.1
	22	152 44.3	4 00.6	131 40.4	14.7	8 11.6	8.5	54.1
	23	167 44.5	S 4 01.6	146 14.1	14.6	S 8 20.1	8.5	54.1
		SD 16.0	*d* 1.0	SD 14.9		14.8		14.8

Lat.	Twilight Naut.	Twilight Civil	Sunrise	Moonrise 30	Moonrise 1	Moonrise 2	Moonrise 3
°	h m	h m	h m	h m	h m	h m	h m
N 72	03 51	05 13	06 20	04 57	06 33	08 08	09 44
N 70	04 03	05 16	06 17	05 00	06 30	07 59	09 28
68	04 12	05 19	06 14	05 02	06 27	07 51	09 15
66	04 20	05 21	06 12	05 04	06 25	07 45	09 04
64	04 26	05 22	06 10	05 05	06 23	07 40	08 56
62	04 32	05 24	06 08	05 06	06 21	07 35	08 48
60	04 36	05 25	06 06	05 07	06 20	07 31	08 42
N 58	04 40	05 26	06 05	05 08	06 19	07 28	08 36
56	04 43	05 27	06 04	05 09	06 17	07 25	08 31
54	04 46	05 27	06 02	05 10	06 16	07 22	08 26
52	04 48	05 28	06 01	05 11	06 16	07 19	08 22
50	04 51	05 28	06 00	05 11	06 15	07 17	08 19
45	04 55	05 29	05 58	05 13	06 13	07 12	08 11
N 40	04 58	05 30	05 57	05 14	06 11	07 08	08 04
35	05 00	05 30	05 55	05 15	06 10	07 05	07 58
30	05 02	05 30	05 54	05 16	06 09	07 01	07 53
20	05 03	05 29	05 51	05 18	06 07	06 56	07 45
N 10	05 03	05 28	05 49	05 19	06 05	06 51	07 37
0	05 02	05 26	05 46	05 20	06 04	06 47	07 30
S 10	04 58	05 23	05 44	05 22	06 02	06 43	07 23
20	04 53	05 19	05 41	05 23	06 01	06 38	07 16
30	04 46	05 14	05 38	05 25	05 59	06 33	07 08
35	04 41	05 11	05 36	05 26	05 58	06 30	07 03
40	04 35	05 07	05 34	05 27	05 57	06 27	06 57
45	04 27	05 02	05 31	05 28	05 55	06 23	06 51
S 50	04 17	04 56	05 28	05 30	05 54	06 18	06 44
52	04 12	04 53	05 27	05 30	05 53	06 16	06 40
54	04 07	04 50	05 25	05 31	05 52	06 14	06 36
56	04 00	04 46	05 24	05 32	05 51	06 11	06 32
58	03 53	04 42	05 22	05 33	05 50	06 08	06 28
S 60	03 45	04 37	05 20	05 34	05 49	06 05	06 22

Lat.	Sunset	Twilight Civil	Twilight Naut.	Moonset 30	Moonset 1	Moonset 2	Moonset 3
°	h m	h m	h m	h m	h m	h m	h m
N 72	17 16	18 23	19 44	17 39	17 33	17 28	17 22
N 70	17 20	18 20	19 33	17 39	17 39	17 39	17 40
68	17 23	18 18	19 24	17 39	17 43	17 48	17 54
66	17 26	18 16	19 17	17 40	17 47	17 55	18 05
64	17 28	18 15	19 11	17 40	17 50	18 02	18 15
62	17 30	18 14	19 06	17 40	17 53	18 07	18 23
60	17 31	18 13	19 01	17 40	17 56	18 12	18 30
N 58	17 33	18 12	18 58	17 40	17 58	18 16	18 37
56	17 34	18 11	18 54	17 40	18 00	18 20	18 42
54	17 36	18 11	18 52	17 40	18 02	18 24	18 47
52	17 37	18 10	18 49	17 40	18 03	18 27	18 52
50	17 38	18 10	18 47	17 41	18 05	18 30	18 56
45	17 40	18 09	18 43	17 41	18 08	18 36	19 05
N 40	17 42	18 09	18 40	17 41	18 11	18 41	19 13
35	17 44	18 09	18 38	17 41	18 13	18 45	19 19
30	17 45	18 09	18 37	17 41	18 15	18 49	19 25
20	17 48	18 10	18 35	17 41	18 19	18 56	19 35
N 10	17 50	18 11	18 36	17 41	18 22	19 02	19 43
0	17 53	18 13	18 38	17 41	18 25	19 08	19 52
S 10	17 55	18 16	18 41	17 42	18 28	19 14	20 00
20	17 58	18 20	18 46	17 42	18 31	19 20	20 09
30	18 02	18 26	18 54	17 42	18 34	19 27	20 19
35	18 03	18 29	18 59	17 42	18 36	19 31	20 24
40	18 06	18 33	19 05	17 42	18 39	19 35	20 31
45	18 08	18 38	19 13	17 42	18 42	19 40	20 39
S 50	18 12	18 44	19 23	17 42	18 45	19 47	20 48
52	18 13	18 47	19 28	17 42	18 46	19 50	20 52
54	18 15	18 51	19 34	17 42	18 48	19 53	20 57
56	18 17	18 54	19 40	17 42	18 50	19 57	21 02
58	18 19	18 59	19 48	17 42	18 52	20 00	21 08
S 60	18 21	19 04	19 56	17 42	18 54	20 05	21 15

Day	SUN Eqn. of Time 00^h	SUN Eqn. of Time 12^h	SUN Mer. Pass.	MOON Mer. Pass. Upper	MOON Mer. Pass. Lower	MOON Age	MOON Phase
d	m s	m s	h m	h m	h m	d %	
30	10 01	10 11	11 50	11 31	23 53	29 0	
1	10 20	10 30	11 50	12 14	24 36	00 0	●
2	10 40	10 49	11 49	12 57	00 36	01 2	

	UT	ARIES	VENUS −3·9		MARS +0·1		JUPITER −1·7		SATURN +0·5		STARS		
		GHA	GHA	Dec	GHA	Dec	GHA	Dec	GHA	Dec	Name	SHA	Dec
	d h	° ′	° ′	° ′	° ′	° ′	° ′	° ′	° ′	° ′		° ′	° ′
	3 00	12 07.7	153 13.8	S15 33.7	97 58.6	S25 45.5	187 02.5	S 1 00.5	121 40.5	S20 46.3	Acamar	315 16.4	S40 14.2
	01	27 10.1	168 13.3	34.7	112 59.2	45.4	202 04.5	00.7	136 42.8	46.4	Achernar	335 24.7	S57 09.1
	02	42 12.6	183 12.8	35.8	127 59.8	45.3	217 06.4	00.9	151 45.0	46.4	Acrux	173 07.3	S63 11.4
	03	57 15.1	198 12.3	. . 36.9	143 00.4	. . 45.2	232 08.4	. . 01.1	166 47.3	. . 46.4	Adhara	255 10.8	S28 59.6
	04	72 17.5	213 11.8	37.9	158 01.0	45.2	247 10.4	01.4	181 49.6	46.5	Aldebaran	290 46.7	N16 32.4
	05	87 20.0	228 11.3	39.0	173 01.6	45.1	262 12.3	01.6	196 51.8	46.5			
	06	102 22.5	243 10.8	S15 40.0	188 02.2	S25 45.0	277 14.3	S 1 01.8	211 54.1	S20 46.5	Alioth	166 19.4	N55 52.3
	07	117 24.9	258 10.3	41.1	203 02.8	44.9	292 16.3	02.0	226 56.4	46.6	Alkaid	152 57.7	N49 14.0
	08	132 27.4	273 09.8	42.2	218 03.4	44.8	307 18.2	02.2	241 58.6	46.6	Al Na'ir	27 40.7	S46 52.8
M	09	147 29.9	288 09.3	. . 43.2	233 04.0	. . 44.7	322 20.2	. . 02.4	257 00.9	. . 46.6	Alnilam	275 44.0	S 1 11.5
O	10	162 32.3	303 08.8	44.3	248 04.7	44.6	337 22.2	02.6	272 03.2	46.7	Alphard	217 54.1	S 8 43.8
N	11	177 34.8	318 08.3	45.3	263 05.3	44.6	352 24.1	02.8	287 05.4	46.7			
D	12	192 37.2	333 07.8	S15 46.4	278 05.9	S25 44.5	7 26.1	S 1 03.1	302 07.7	S20 46.7	Alphecca	126 09.4	N26 39.9
A	13	207 39.7	348 07.2	47.4	293 06.5	44.4	22 28.1	03.3	317 10.0	46.8	Alpheratz	357 40.8	N29 11.1
Y	14	222 42.2	3 06.7	48.5	308 07.1	44.3	37 30.1	03.5	332 12.2	46.8	Altair	62 06.0	N 8 55.1
	15	237 44.6	18 06.2	. . 49.5	323 07.7	. . 44.2	52 32.0	. . 03.7	347 14.5	. . 46.8	Ankaa	353 13.2	S42 12.9
	16	252 47.1	33 05.7	50.6	338 08.3	44.1	67 34.0	03.9	2 16.8	46.9	Antares	112 23.7	S26 27.9
	17	267 49.6	48 05.2	51.6	353 08.9	44.0	82 36.0	04.1	17 19.0	46.9			
	18	282 52.0	63 04.7	S15 52.7	8 09.5	S25 43.9	97 37.9	S 1 04.3	32 21.3	S20 46.9	Arcturus	145 54.1	N19 06.0
	19	297 54.5	78 04.2	53.7	23 10.1	43.9	112 39.9	04.5	47 23.5	47.0	Atria	107 23.8	S69 03.4
	20	312 57.0	93 03.7	54.8	38 10.7	43.8	127 41.9	04.8	62 25.8	47.0	Avior	234 17.3	S59 33.6
	21	327 59.4	108 03.2	. . 55.8	53 11.3	. . 43.7	142 43.8	. . 05.0	77 28.1	. . 47.0	Bellatrix	278 29.5	N 6 21.8
	22	343 01.9	123 02.7	56.9	68 12.0	43.6	157 45.8	05.2	92 30.3	47.1	Betelgeuse	270 58.8	N 7 24.5
	23	358 04.4	138 02.2	57.9	83 12.6	43.5	172 47.8	05.4	107 32.6	47.1			
	4 00	13 06.8	153 01.7	S15 59.0	98 13.2	S25 43.4	187 49.7	S 1 05.6	122 34.9	S20 47.1	Canopus	263 55.1	S52 42.1
	01	28 09.3	168 01.2	16 00.0	113 13.8	43.3	202 51.7	05.8	137 37.1	47.2	Capella	280 31.0	N46 00.5
	02	43 11.7	183 00.6	01.1	128 14.4	43.2	217 53.7	06.0	152 39.4	47.2	Deneb	49 29.7	N45 20.8
	03	58 14.2	198 00.1	. . 02.1	143 15.0	. . 43.1	232 55.6	. . 06.2	167 41.7	. . 47.2	Denebola	182 31.7	N14 28.8
	04	73 16.7	212 59.6	03.2	158 15.6	43.0	247 57.6	06.5	182 43.9	47.3	Diphda	348 53.4	S17 53.6
	05	88 19.1	227 59.1	04.2	173 16.2	42.9	262 59.6	06.7	197 46.2	47.3			
	06	103 21.6	242 58.6	S16 05.3	188 16.8	S25 42.9	278 01.5	S 1 06.9	212 48.4	S20 47.3	Dubhe	193 49.7	N61 39.6
	07	118 24.1	257 58.1	06.3	203 17.4	42.8	293 03.5	07.1	227 50.7	47.4	Elnath	278 09.7	N28 37.0
T	08	133 26.5	272 57.6	07.3	218 18.0	42.7	308 05.5	07.3	242 53.0	47.4	Eltanin	90 45.2	N51 29.7
U	09	148 29.0	287 57.1	. . 08.4	233 18.6	. . 42.6	323 07.4	. . 07.5	257 55.2	. . 47.4	Enif	33 44.7	N 9 57.4
E	10	163 31.5	302 56.5	09.4	248 19.2	42.5	338 09.4	07.7	272 57.5	47.4	Fomalhaut	15 21.3	S29 32.0
S	11	178 33.9	317 56.0	10.5	263 19.8	42.4	353 11.4	07.9	287 59.8	47.5			
D	12	193 36.4	332 55.5	S16 11.5	278 20.4	S25 42.3	8 13.4	S 1 08.2	303 02.0	S20 47.5	Gacrux	171 58.9	S57 12.2
	13	208 38.9	347 55.0	12.5	293 21.0	42.2	23 15.3	08.4	318 04.3	47.5	Gienah	175 50.3	S17 37.9
A	14	223 41.3	2 54.5	13.6	308 21.6	42.1	38 17.3	08.6	333 06.5	47.6	Hadar	148 45.2	S60 27.1
Y	15	238 43.8	17 54.0	. . 14.6	323 22.2	. . 42.0	53 19.3	. . 08.8	348 08.8	. . 47.6	Hamal	327 57.9	N23 32.4
	16	253 46.2	32 53.4	15.6	338 22.8	41.9	68 21.2	09.0	3 11.1	47.6	Kaus Aust.	83 40.9	S34 22.4
	17	268 48.7	47 52.9	16.7	353 23.4	41.8	83 23.2	09.2	18 13.3	47.7			
	18	283 51.2	62 52.4	S16 17.7	8 24.0	S25 41.7	98 25.2	S 1 09.4	33 15.6	S20 47.7	Kochab	137 21.3	N74 05.5
	19	298 53.6	77 51.9	18.7	23 24.6	41.6	113 27.1	09.6	48 17.8	47.7	Markab	13 35.8	N15 17.9
	20	313 56.1	92 51.4	19.8	38 25.2	41.5	128 29.1	09.9	63 20.1	47.8	Menkar	314 12.5	N 4 09.3
	21	328 58.6	107 50.8	. . 20.8	53 25.8	. . 41.4	143 31.1	. . 10.1	78 22.4	. . 47.8	Menkent	148 05.3	S36 26.9
	22	344 01.0	122 50.3	21.8	68 26.4	41.3	158 33.0	10.3	93 24.6	47.8	Miaplacidus	221 39.6	S69 47.0
	23	359 03.5	137 49.8	22.9	83 27.0	41.2	173 35.0	10.5	108 26.9	47.9			
	5 00	14 06.0	152 49.3	S16 23.9	98 27.6	S25 41.1	188 37.0	S 1 10.7	123 29.1	S20 47.9	Mirfak	308 36.7	N49 55.0
	01	29 08.4	167 48.8	24.9	113 28.2	41.0	203 38.9	10.9	138 31.4	47.9	Nunki	75 55.6	S26 16.4
	02	44 10.9	182 48.2	26.0	128 28.8	40.9	218 40.9	11.1	153 33.7	48.0	Peacock	53 15.6	S56 40.9
	03	59 13.3	197 47.7	. . 27.0	143 29.4	. . 40.8	233 42.9	. . 11.3	168 35.9	. . 48.0	Pollux	243 25.1	N27 58.9
	04	74 15.8	212 47.2	28.0	158 30.0	40.7	248 44.8	11.6	183 38.2	48.0	Procyon	244 57.5	N 5 10.8
	05	89 18.3	227 46.7	29.1	173 30.6	40.6	263 46.8	11.8	198 40.4	48.1			
	06	104 20.7	242 46.1	S16 30.1	188 31.2	S25 40.5	278 48.8	S 1 12.0	213 42.7	S20 48.1	Rasalhague	96 04.5	N12 33.3
W	07	119 23.2	257 45.6	31.1	203 31.8	40.4	293 50.8	12.2	228 45.0	48.1	Regulus	207 41.4	N11 53.1
E	08	134 25.7	272 45.1	32.1	218 32.4	40.3	308 52.7	12.4	243 47.2	48.2	Rigel	281 09.8	S 8 11.0
D	09	149 28.1	287 44.6	. . 33.2	233 33.0	. . 40.2	323 54.7	. . 12.6	258 49.5	. . 48.2	Rigil Kent.	139 49.2	S60 54.1
N	10	164 30.6	302 44.0	34.2	248 33.6	40.1	338 56.7	12.8	273 51.7	48.2	Sabik	102 10.1	S15 44.5
E	11	179 33.1	317 43.5	35.2	263 34.2	40.0	353 58.6	13.0	288 54.0	48.3			
S	12	194 35.5	332 43.0	S16 36.2	278 34.8	S25 39.9	9 00.6	S 1 13.3	303 56.3	S20 48.3	Schedar	349 37.3	N56 37.8
D	13	209 38.0	347 42.5	37.2	293 35.4	39.8	24 02.6	13.5	318 58.5	48.3	Shaula	96 19.0	S37 06.8
A	14	224 40.5	2 41.9	38.3	308 36.0	39.7	39 04.5	13.7	334 00.8	48.4	Sirius	258 31.8	S16 44.3
Y	15	239 42.9	17 41.4	. . 39.3	323 36.6	. . 39.6	54 06.5	. . 13.9	349 03.0	. . 48.4	Spica	158 29.2	S11 14.7
	16	254 45.4	32 40.9	40.3	338 37.2	39.5	69 08.5	14.1	4 05.3	48.4	Suhail	222 51.0	S43 29.8
	17	269 47.8	47 40.3	41.3	353 37.8	39.4	84 10.4	14.3	19 07.5	48.5			
	18	284 50.3	62 39.8	S16 42.3	8 38.4	S25 39.2	99 12.4	S 1 14.5	34 09.8	S20 48.5	Vega	80 37.5	N38 48.4
	19	299 52.8	77 39.3	43.4	23 39.0	39.1	114 14.4	14.7	49 12.1	48.5	Zuben'ubi	137 03.2	S16 06.4
	20	314 55.2	92 38.8	44.4	38 39.6	39.0	129 16.3	14.9	64 14.3	48.6		SHA	Mer. Pass.
	21	329 57.7	107 38.2	. . 45.4	53 40.2	. . 38.9	144 18.3	. . 15.2	79 16.6	. . 48.6		° ′	h m
	22	345 00.2	122 37.7	46.4	68 40.8	38.8	159 20.3	15.4	94 18.8	48.6	Venus	139 54.8	13 48
	23	0 02.6	137 37.2	47.4	83 41.4	38.7	174 22.3	15.6	109 21.1	48.7	Mars	85 06.3	17 26
		h m									Jupiter	174 42.9	11 27
	Mer. Pass.	23 03.8	*v* −0.5	*d* 1.0	*v* 0.6	*d* 0.1	*v* 2.0	*d* 0.2	*v* 2.3	*d* 0.0	Saturn	109 28.0	15 47

Day	UT	SUN GHA	SUN Dec	MOON GHA	v	MOON Dec	d	HP
	d h	° ′	° ′	° ′	′	° ′	′	′
	3 00	182 44.7	S 4 02.6	160 47.7	14.7	S 8 28.6	8.4	54.1
	01	197 44.9	03.5	175 21.4	14.6	8 37.0	8.4	54.1
	02	212 45.1	04.5	189 55.0	14.6	8 45.4	8.4	54.1
	03	227 45.3	. . 05.5	204 28.6	14.7	8 53.8	8.3	54.1
	04	242 45.5	06.4	219 02.3	14.5	9 02.1	8.3	54.1
	05	257 45.6	07.4	233 35.8	14.6	9 10.4	8.3	54.1
	06	272 45.8	S 4 08.4	248 09.4	14.6	S 9 18.7	8.2	54.1
	07	287 46.0	09.3	262 43.0	14.5	9 26.9	8.1	54.1
	08	302 46.2	10.3	277 16.5	14.6	9 35.0	8.1	54.1
MONDAY	09	317 46.4	. . 11.3	291 50.1	14.5	9 43.1	8.1	54.1
	10	332 46.6	12.2	306 23.6	14.5	9 51.2	8.1	54.1
	11	347 46.8	13.2	320 57.1	14.5	9 59.3	7.9	54.1
	12	2 47.0	S 4 14.2	335 30.6	14.5	S10 07.2	8.0	54.0
	13	17 47.2	15.1	350 04.1	14.4	10 15.2	7.9	54.0
	14	32 47.4	16.1	4 37.5	14.4	10 23.1	7.8	54.0
	15	47 47.6	. . 17.1	19 10.9	14.5	10 30.9	7.9	54.0
	16	62 47.8	18.0	33 44.4	14.4	10 38.8	7.7	54.0
	17	77 48.0	19.0	48 17.8	14.3	10 46.5	7.7	54.0
	18	92 48.1	S 4 19.9	62 51.1	14.4	S10 54.2	7.7	54.0
	19	107 48.3	20.9	77 24.5	14.3	11 01.9	7.6	54.0
	20	122 48.5	21.9	91 57.8	14.4	11 09.5	7.6	54.0
	21	137 48.7	. . 22.8	106 31.2	14.3	11 17.1	7.5	54.0
	22	152 48.9	23.8	121 04.5	14.3	11 24.6	7.5	54.0
	23	167 49.1	24.8	135 37.8	14.2	11 32.1	7.4	54.0
	4 00	182 49.3	S 4 25.7	150 11.0	14.3	S11 39.5	7.4	54.0
	01	197 49.5	26.7	164 44.3	14.2	11 46.9	7.4	54.0
	02	212 49.7	27.7	179 17.5	14.2	11 54.3	7.2	54.0
	03	227 49.9	. . 28.6	193 50.7	14.1	12 01.5	7.3	54.0
	04	242 50.1	29.6	208 23.8	14.2	12 08.8	7.1	54.0
	05	257 50.2	30.5	222 57.0	14.1	12 15.9	7.1	54.0
	06	272 50.4	S 4 31.5	237 30.1	14.1	S12 23.0	7.1	54.0
	07	287 50.6	32.5	252 03.2	14.1	12 30.1	7.0	54.0
TUESDAY	08	302 50.8	33.4	266 36.3	14.1	12 37.1	7.0	54.0
	09	317 51.0	. . 34.4	281 09.4	14.0	12 44.1	6.9	54.0
	10	332 51.2	35.4	295 42.4	14.0	12 51.0	6.8	54.0
	11	347 51.4	36.3	310 15.4	14.0	12 57.8	6.8	54.0
	12	2 51.6	S 4 37.3	324 48.4	14.0	S13 04.6	6.8	54.0
	13	17 51.8	38.3	339 21.4	13.9	13 11.4	6.6	54.0
	14	32 51.9	39.2	353 54.3	13.9	13 18.0	6.7	54.0
	15	47 52.1	. . 40.2	8 27.2	13.9	13 24.7	6.5	54.0
	16	62 52.3	41.1	23 00.1	13.9	13 31.2	6.5	54.0
	17	77 52.5	42.1	37 33.0	13.8	13 37.7	6.5	54.0
	18	92 52.7	S 4 43.1	52 05.8	13.8	S13 44.2	6.4	54.0
	19	107 52.9	44.0	66 38.6	13.8	13 50.6	6.3	54.0
	20	122 53.1	45.0	81 11.4	13.8	13 56.9	6.3	54.0
	21	137 53.3	. . 45.9	95 44.2	13.7	14 03.2	6.2	54.0
	22	152 53.4	46.9	110 16.9	13.7	14 09.4	6.1	54.0
	23	167 53.6	47.9	124 49.6	13.7	14 15.5	6.1	54.0
	5 00	182 53.8	S 4 48.8	139 22.3	13.6	S14 21.6	6.1	54.0
	01	197 54.0	49.8	153 54.9	13.6	14 27.7	5.9	54.0
	02	212 54.2	50.8	168 27.5	13.6	14 33.6	5.9	54.0
	03	227 54.4	. . 51.7	183 00.1	13.6	14 39.5	5.9	54.0
	04	242 54.6	52.7	197 32.7	13.5	14 45.4	5.7	54.0
	05	257 54.8	53.6	212 05.2	13.6	14 51.1	5.7	54.0
	06	272 54.9	S 4 54.6	226 37.8	13.4	S14 56.8	5.7	54.0
WEDNESDAY	07	287 55.1	55.6	241 10.2	13.5	15 02.5	5.6	54.0
	08	302 55.3	56.5	255 42.7	13.4	15 08.1	5.5	54.0
	09	317 55.5	. . 57.5	270 15.1	13.4	15 13.6	5.4	54.0
	10	332 55.7	58.4	284 47.5	13.4	15 19.0	5.4	54.1
	11	347 55.9	4 59.4	299 19.9	13.3	15 24.4	5.3	54.1
	12	2 56.1	S 5 00.4	313 52.2	13.3	S15 29.7	5.3	54.1
	13	17 56.2	01.3	328 24.5	13.3	15 35.0	5.2	54.1
	14	32 56.4	02.3	342 56.8	13.3	15 40.2	5.1	54.1
	15	47 56.6	. . 03.2	357 29.1	13.2	15 45.3	5.0	54.1
	16	62 56.8	04.2	12 01.3	13.2	15 50.3	5.0	54.1
	17	77 57.0	05.2	26 33.5	13.1	15 55.3	4.9	54.1
	18	92 57.2	S 5 06.1	41 05.6	13.1	S16 00.2	4.9	54.1
	19	107 57.3	07.1	55 37.7	13.1	16 05.1	4.7	54.1
	20	122 57.5	08.0	70 09.8	13.1	16 09.8	4.7	54.1
	21	137 57.7	. . 09.0	84 41.9	13.1	16 14.5	4.6	54.1
	22	152 57.9	10.0	99 14.0	13.0	16 19.1	4.6	54.1
	23	167 58.1	10.9	113 46.0	12.9	S16 23.7	4.5	54.1
		SD 16.0	d 1.0	SD 14.7		14.7		14.7

Lat.	Twilight Naut.	Twilight Civil	Sunrise	Moonrise 3	Moonrise 4	Moonrise 5	Moonrise 6
°	h m	h m	h m	h m	h m	h m	h m
N 72	04 06	05 27	06 34	09 44	11 23	13 06	15 01
N 70	04 16	05 28	06 29	09 28	10 57	12 26	13 52
68	04 24	05 29	06 25	09 15	10 38	11 59	13 16
66	04 30	05 30	06 21	09 04	10 23	11 39	12 50
64	04 35	05 31	06 18	08 56	10 10	11 22	12 30
62	04 40	05 32	06 16	08 48	10 00	11 09	12 14
60	04 43	05 32	06 13	08 42	09 51	10 57	12 01
N 58	04 47	05 32	06 11	08 36	09 43	10 48	11 49
56	04 49	05 33	06 10	08 31	09 36	10 39	11 39
54	04 52	05 33	06 08	08 26	09 30	10 31	11 30
52	04 54	05 33	06 06	08 22	09 24	10 25	11 22
50	04 55	05 33	06 05	08 19	09 19	10 18	11 15
45	04 59	05 33	06 02	08 11	09 08	10 05	11 00
N 40	05 01	05 32	06 00	08 04	09 00	09 54	10 48
35	05 03	05 32	05 57	07 58	08 52	09 45	10 37
30	05 04	05 31	05 55	07 53	08 45	09 37	10 28
20	05 04	05 30	05 52	07 45	08 34	09 23	10 12
N 10	05 03	05 27	05 48	07 37	08 24	09 11	09 58
0	05 01	05 25	05 45	07 30	08 14	08 59	09 46
S 10	04 56	05 21	05 42	07 23	08 05	08 48	09 33
20	04 51	05 16	05 38	07 16	07 55	08 36	09 19
30	04 42	05 10	05 34	07 08	07 44	08 22	09 03
35	04 36	05 06	05 32	07 03	07 37	08 14	08 54
40	04 30	05 02	05 29	06 57	07 30	08 05	08 44
45	04 21	04 56	05 26	06 51	07 22	07 55	08 32
S 50	04 10	04 49	05 22	06 44	07 11	07 42	08 17
52	04 04	04 46	05 20	06 40	07 07	07 36	08 10
54	03 58	04 42	05 18	06 36	07 01	07 30	08 03
56	03 51	04 38	05 16	06 32	06 56	07 23	07 54
58	03 44	04 33	05 13	06 28	06 49	07 14	07 45
S 60	03 34	04 28	05 10	06 22	06 42	07 05	07 34

Lat.	Sunset	Twilight Civil	Twilight Naut.	Moonset 3	Moonset 4	Moonset 5	Moonset 6
°	h m	h m	h m	h m	h m	h m	h m
N 72	17 01	18 08	19 28	17 22	17 15	17 06	16 47
N 70	17 06	18 07	19 18	17 40	17 41	17 46	17 56
68	17 11	18 06	19 11	17 54	18 01	18 13	18 33
66	17 14	18 05	19 05	18 05	18 18	18 34	18 59
64	17 17	18 05	19 00	18 15	18 31	18 51	19 19
62	17 20	18 04	18 56	18 23	18 42	19 05	19 35
60	17 22	18 04	18 52	18 30	18 51	19 17	19 49
N 58	17 25	18 04	18 49	18 37	19 00	19 27	20 01
56	17 26	18 03	18 46	18 42	19 07	19 36	20 11
54	17 28	18 03	18 44	18 47	19 14	19 44	20 20
52	17 30	18 03	18 42	18 52	19 20	19 51	20 28
50	17 31	18 03	18 41	18 56	19 25	19 58	20 35
45	17 34	18 04	18 38	19 05	19 37	20 12	20 51
N 40	17 37	18 04	18 35	19 13	19 46	20 23	21 04
35	17 39	18 05	18 34	19 19	19 55	20 33	21 15
30	17 41	18 05	18 33	19 25	20 02	20 42	21 24
20	17 45	18 07	18 33	19 35	20 15	20 56	21 41
N 10	17 49	18 10	18 34	19 43	20 26	21 09	21 55
0	17 52	18 13	18 37	19 52	20 36	21 21	22 08
S 10	17 55	18 16	18 41	20 00	20 46	21 34	22 22
20	17 59	18 21	18 47	20 09	20 57	21 47	22 36
30	18 03	18 27	18 56	20 19	21 10	22 02	22 52
35	18 06	18 31	19 01	20 24	21 18	22 10	23 02
40	18 09	18 36	19 08	20 31	21 26	22 20	23 13
45	18 12	18 42	19 17	20 39	21 36	22 32	23 26
S 50	18 16	18 49	19 29	20 48	21 48	22 46	23 41
52	18 18	18 53	19 34	20 52	21 53	22 52	23 49
54	18 20	18 56	19 40	20 57	21 59	23 00	23 57
56	18 23	19 01	19 47	21 02	22 06	23 08	24 06
58	18 25	19 06	19 56	21 08	22 14	23 17	24 16
S 60	18 28	19 11	20 05	21 15	22 23	23 28	24 28

Day	SUN Eqn. of Time 00^h	SUN Eqn. of Time 12^h	SUN Mer. Pass.	MOON Mer. Pass. Upper	MOON Mer. Pass. Lower	MOON Age	MOON Phase
d	m s	m s	h m	h m	h m	d	%
3	10 58	11 08	11 49	13 41	01 19	02	6
4	11 17	11 26	11 49	14 25	02 03	03	11
5	11 35	11 44	11 48	15 10	02 48	04	17

UT	ARIES	VENUS −3·9		MARS +0·1		JUPITER −1·7		SATURN +0·5	
	GHA	GHA	Dec	GHA	Dec	GHA	Dec	GHA	Dec
d h	° ′	° ′	° ′	° ′	° ′	° ′	° ′	° ′	° ′
6 00	15 05.1	152 36.6	S16 48.4	98 42.0	S25 38.6	189 24.2	S 1 15.8	124 23.3	S20 48.7
01	30 07.6	167 36.1	49.5	113 42.6	38.5	204 26.2	16.0	139 25.6	48.7
02	45 10.0	182 35.6	50.5	128 43.2	38.4	219 28.2	16.2	154 27.9	48.8
03	60 12.5	197 35.0	. . 51.5	143 43.8	. . 38.3	234 30.1	. . 16.4	169 30.1	. . 48.8
04	75 15.0	212 34.5	52.5	158 44.4	38.2	249 32.1	16.6	184 32.4	48.8
05	90 17.4	227 34.0	53.5	173 45.0	38.0	264 34.1	16.9	199 34.6	48.9
06	105 19.9	242 33.4	S16 54.5	188 45.5	S25 37.9	279 36.0	S 1 17.1	214 36.9	S20 48.9
07	120 22.3	257 32.9	55.5	203 46.1	37.8	294 38.0	17.3	229 39.1	48.9
T 08	135 24.8	272 32.3	56.5	218 46.7	37.7	309 40.0	17.5	244 41.4	49.0
H 09	150 27.3	287 31.8	. . 57.5	233 47.3	. . 37.6	324 41.9	. . 17.7	259 43.7	. . 49.0
U 10	165 29.7	302 31.3	58.5	248 47.9	37.5	339 43.9	17.9	274 45.9	49.0
R 11	180 32.2	317 30.7	16 59.5	263 48.5	37.4	354 45.9	18.1	289 48.2	49.1
S 12	195 34.7	332 30.2	S17 00.6	278 49.1	S25 37.3	9 47.9	S 1 18.3	304 50.4	S20 49.1
D 13	210 37.1	347 29.7	01.6	293 49.7	37.1	24 49.8	18.5	319 52.7	49.1
A 14	225 39.6	2 29.1	02.6	308 50.3	37.0	39 51.8	18.8	334 54.9	49.2
Y 15	240 42.1	17 28.6	. . 03.6	323 50.9	. . 36.9	54 53.8	. . 19.0	349 57.2	. . 49.2
16	255 44.5	32 28.0	04.6	338 51.5	36.8	69 55.7	19.2	4 59.4	49.2
17	270 47.0	47 27.5	05.6	353 52.1	36.7	84 57.7	19.4	20 01.7	49.3
18	285 49.4	62 26.9	S17 06.6	8 52.7	S25 36.6	99 59.7	S 1 19.6	35 03.9	S20 49.3
19	300 51.9	77 26.4	07.6	23 53.2	36.4	115 01.6	19.8	50 06.2	49.3
20	315 54.4	92 25.9	08.6	38 53.8	36.3	130 03.6	20.0	65 08.5	49.4
21	330 56.8	107 25.3	. . 09.6	53 54.4	. . 36.2	145 05.6	. . 20.2	80 10.7	. . 49.4
22	345 59.3	122 24.8	10.6	68 55.0	36.1	160 07.5	20.5	95 13.0	49.4
23	1 01.8	137 24.2	11.6	83 55.6	36.0	175 09.5	20.7	110 15.2	49.5
7 00	16 04.2	152 23.7	S17 12.6	98 56.2	S25 35.9	190 11.5	S 1 20.9	125 17.5	S20 49.5
01	31 06.7	167 23.1	13.6	113 56.8	35.7	205 13.5	21.1	140 19.7	49.5
02	46 09.2	182 22.6	14.6	128 57.4	35.6	220 15.4	21.3	155 22.0	49.6
03	61 11.6	197 22.1	. . 15.6	143 58.0	. . 35.5	235 17.4	. . 21.5	170 24.2	. . 49.6
04	76 14.1	212 21.5	16.5	158 58.6	35.4	250 19.4	21.7	185 26.5	49.6
05	91 16.6	227 21.0	17.5	173 59.1	35.3	265 21.3	21.9	200 28.7	49.7
06	106 19.0	242 20.4	S17 18.5	188 59.7	S25 35.1	280 23.3	S 1 22.1	215 31.0	S20 49.7
07	121 21.5	257 19.9	19.5	204 00.3	35.0	295 25.3	22.4	230 33.2	49.7
08	136 23.9	272 19.3	20.5	219 00.9	34.9	310 27.2	22.6	245 35.5	49.8
F 09	151 26.4	287 18.8	. . 21.5	234 01.5	. . 34.8	325 29.2	. . 22.8	260 37.8	. . 49.8
R 10	166 28.9	302 18.2	22.5	249 02.1	34.7	340 31.2	23.0	275 40.0	49.8
I 11	181 31.3	317 17.7	23.5	264 02.7	34.5	355 33.1	23.2	290 42.3	49.9
D 12	196 33.8	332 17.1	S17 24.5	279 03.3	S25 34.4	10 35.1	S 1 23.4	305 44.5	S20 49.9
A 13	211 36.3	347 16.6	25.5	294 03.8	34.3	25 37.1	23.6	320 46.8	49.9
Y 14	226 38.7	2 16.0	26.4	309 04.4	34.2	40 39.1	23.8	335 49.0	50.0
15	241 41.2	17 15.5	. . 27.4	324 05.0	. . 34.0	55 41.0	. . 24.0	350 51.3	. . 50.0
16	256 43.7	32 14.9	28.4	339 05.6	33.9	70 43.0	24.3	5 53.5	50.0
17	271 46.1	47 14.4	29.4	354 06.2	33.8	85 45.0	24.5	20 55.8	50.1
18	286 48.6	62 13.8	S17 30.4	9 06.8	S25 33.7	100 46.9	S 1 24.7	35 58.0	S20 50.1
19	301 51.1	77 13.2	31.4	24 07.4	33.5	115 48.9	24.9	51 00.3	50.1
20	316 53.5	92 12.7	32.4	39 07.9	33.4	130 50.9	25.1	66 02.5	50.2
21	331 56.0	107 12.1	. . 33.3	54 08.5	. . 33.3	145 52.8	. . 25.3	81 04.8	. . 50.2
22	346 58.4	122 11.6	34.3	69 09.1	33.2	160 54.8	25.5	96 07.0	50.2
23	2 00.9	137 11.0	35.3	84 09.7	33.0	175 56.8	25.7	111 09.3	50.3
8 00	17 03.4	152 10.5	S17 36.3	99 10.3	S25 32.9	190 58.7	S 1 25.9	126 11.5	S20 50.3
01	32 05.8	167 09.9	37.3	114 10.9	32.8	206 00.7	26.2	141 13.8	50.3
02	47 08.3	182 09.4	38.2	129 11.5	32.6	221 02.7	26.4	156 16.0	50.4
03	62 10.8	197 08.8	. . 39.2	144 12.0	. . 32.5	236 04.7	. . 26.6	171 18.3	. . 50.4
04	77 13.2	212 08.2	40.2	159 12.6	32.4	251 06.6	26.8	186 20.5	50.4
05	92 15.7	227 07.7	41.2	174 13.2	32.3	266 08.6	27.0	201 22.8	50.5
06	107 18.2	242 07.1	S17 42.1	189 13.8	S25 32.1	281 10.6	S 1 27.2	216 25.0	S20 50.5
07	122 20.6	257 06.6	43.1	204 14.4	32.0	296 12.5	27.4	231 27.3	50.5
S 08	137 23.1	272 06.0	44.1	219 15.0	31.9	311 14.5	27.6	246 29.5	50.6
A 09	152 25.5	287 05.4	. . 45.1	234 15.5	. . 31.7	326 16.5	. . 27.8	261 31.8	. . 50.6
T 10	167 28.0	302 04.9	46.0	249 16.1	31.6	341 18.4	28.1	276 34.0	50.6
U 11	182 30.5	317 04.3	47.0	264 16.7	31.5	356 20.4	28.3	291 36.3	50.7
R 12	197 32.9	332 03.8	S17 48.0	279 17.3	S25 31.3	11 22.4	S 1 28.5	306 38.5	S20 50.7
D 13	212 35.4	347 03.2	48.9	294 17.9	31.2	26 24.4	28.7	321 40.8	50.7
A 14	227 37.9	2 02.6	49.9	309 18.5	31.1	41 26.3	28.9	336 43.0	50.8
Y 15	242 40.3	17 02.1	. . 50.9	324 19.0	. . 30.9	56 28.3	. . 29.1	351 45.3	. . 50.8
16	257 42.8	32 01.5	51.8	339 19.6	30.8	71 30.3	29.3	6 47.5	50.8
17	272 45.3	47 00.9	52.8	354 20.2	30.7	86 32.2	29.5	21 49.8	50.9
18	287 47.7	62 00.4	S17 53.8	9 20.8	S25 30.5	101 34.2	S 1 29.7	36 52.0	S20 50.9
19	302 50.2	76 59.8	54.7	24 21.4	30.4	116 36.2	30.0	51 54.3	50.9
20	317 52.7	91 59.2	55.7	39 21.9	30.3	131 38.1	30.2	66 56.5	51.0
21	332 55.1	106 58.7	. . 56.7	54 22.5	. . 30.1	146 40.1	. . 30.4	81 58.8	. . 51.0
22	347 57.6	121 58.1	57.6	69 23.1	30.0	161 42.1	30.6	97 01.0	51.0
23	3 00.0	136 57.5	58.6	84 23.7	29.9	176 44.1	30.8	112 03.3	51.1
Mer. Pass.	h m 22 52.0	*v* −0.6	*d* 1.0	*v* 0.6	*d* 0.1	*v* 2.0	*d* 0.2	*v* 2.3	*d* 0.0

STARS Name	SHA	Dec
	° ′	° ′
Acamar	315 16.3	S40 14.2
Achernar	335 24.6	S57 09.1
Acrux	173 07.3	S63 11.4
Adhara	255 10.8	S28 59.6
Aldebaran	290 46.6	N16 32.4
Alioth	166 19.4	N55 52.3
Alkaid	152 57.7	N49 14.0
Al Na'ir	27 40.7	S46 52.8
Alnilam	275 44.0	S 1 11.6
Alphard	217 54.1	S 8 43.8
Alphecca	126 09.4	N26 39.9
Alpheratz	357 40.8	N29 11.1
Altair	62 06.0	N 8 55.1
Ankaa	353 13.2	S42 12.9
Antares	112 23.7	S26 27.9
Arcturus	145 54.1	N19 06.0
Atria	107 23.8	S69 03.4
Avior	234 17.3	S59 33.6
Bellatrix	278 29.5	N 6 21.8
Betelgeuse	270 58.8	N 7 24.5
Canopus	263 55.1	S52 42.1
Capella	280 31.0	N46 00.5
Deneb	49 29.7	N45 20.8
Denebola	182 31.7	N14 28.8
Diphda	348 53.4	S17 53.6
Dubhe	193 49.7	N61 39.5
Elnath	278 09.7	N28 37.0
Eltanin	90 45.3	N51 29.7
Enif	33 44.7	N 9 57.4
Fomalhaut	15 21.3	S29 32.0
Gacrux	171 58.9	S57 12.2
Gienah	175 50.3	S17 37.9
Hadar	148 45.2	S60 27.1
Hamal	327 57.9	N23 32.4
Kaus Aust.	83 40.9	S34 22.4
Kochab	137 21.3	N74 05.5
Markab	13 35.8	N15 17.9
Menkar	314 12.5	N 4 09.3
Menkent	148 05.3	S36 26.9
Miaplacidus	221 39.6	S69 46.9
Mirfak	308 36.7	N49 55.0
Nunki	75 55.6	S26 16.4
Peacock	53 15.6	S56 40.9
Pollux	243 25.1	N27 58.9
Procyon	244 57.5	N 5 10.8
Rasalhague	96 04.5	N12 33.3
Regulus	207 41.4	N11 53.1
Rigel	281 09.8	S 8 11.0
Rigil Kent.	139 49.2	S60 54.1
Sabik	102 10.2	S15 44.5
Schedar	349 37.3	N56 37.8
Shaula	96 19.1	S37 06.8
Sirius	258 31.7	S16 44.3
Spica	158 29.2	S11 14.7
Suhail	222 51.0	S43 29.8
Vega	80 37.5	N38 48.4
Zuben'ubi	137 03.2	S16 06.4

	SHA	Mer. Pass.
	° ′	h m
Venus	136 19.5	13 51
Mars	82 52.0	17 24
Jupiter	174 07.2	11 18
Saturn	109 13.2	15 36

UT	SUN GHA	SUN Dec	MOON GHA	v	MOON Dec	d	HP
d h	° ′	° ′	° ′	′	° ′	′	′
6 00	182 58.3	S 5 11.9	128 17.9	13.0	S16 28.2	4.4	54.2
01	197 58.4	12.8	142 49.9	12.9	16 32.6	4.3	54.2
02	212 58.6	13.8	157 21.8	12.9	16 36.9	4.3	54.2
03	227 58.8	. . 14.8	171 53.7	12.8	16 41.2	4.2	54.2
04	242 59.0	15.7	186 25.5	12.9	16 45.4	4.1	54.2
05	257 59.2	16.7	200 57.4	12.8	16 49.5	4.0	54.2
06	272 59.4	S 5 17.6	215 29.2	12.7	S16 53.5	4.0	54.2
T 07	287 59.5	18.6	230 00.9	12.8	16 57.5	3.9	54.2
H 08	302 59.7	19.5	244 32.7	12.7	17 01.4	3.8	54.2
U 09	317 59.9	. . 20.5	259 04.4	12.6	17 05.2	3.7	54.2
R 10	333 00.1	21.5	273 36.0	12.7	17 08.9	3.7	54.3
S 11	348 00.3	22.4	288 07.7	12.6	17 12.6	3.6	54.3
D 12	3 00.4	S 5 23.4	302 39.3	12.6	S17 16.2	3.5	54.3
A 13	18 00.6	24.3	317 10.9	12.5	17 19.7	3.4	54.3
Y 14	33 00.8	25.3	331 42.4	12.5	17 23.1	3.4	54.3
15	48 01.0	. . 26.2	346 13.9	12.5	17 26.5	3.3	54.3
16	63 01.2	27.2	0 45.4	12.5	17 29.8	3.1	54.3
17	78 01.3	28.2	15 16.9	12.4	17 32.9	3.2	54.3
18	93 01.5	S 5 29.1	29 48.3	12.4	S17 36.1	3.0	54.4
19	108 01.7	30.1	44 19.7	12.3	17 39.1	3.0	54.4
20	123 01.9	31.0	58 51.0	12.4	17 42.1	2.8	54.4
21	138 02.1	. . 32.0	73 22.4	12.3	17 44.9	2.8	54.4
22	153 02.2	32.9	87 53.7	12.2	17 47.7	2.8	54.4
23	168 02.4	33.9	102 24.9	12.3	17 50.5	2.6	54.4
7 00	183 02.6	S 5 34.9	116 56.2	12.2	S17 53.1	2.5	54.4
01	198 02.8	35.8	131 27.4	12.2	17 55.6	2.5	54.5
02	213 03.0	36.8	145 58.6	12.1	17 58.1	2.4	54.5
03	228 03.1	. . 37.7	160 29.7	12.1	18 00.5	2.3	54.5
04	243 03.3	38.7	175 00.8	12.1	18 02.8	2.2	54.5
05	258 03.5	39.6	189 31.9	12.1	18 05.0	2.2	54.5
06	273 03.7	S 5 40.6	204 03.0	12.0	S18 07.2	2.0	54.5
07	288 03.9	41.5	218 34.0	12.0	18 09.2	2.0	54.5
08	303 04.0	42.5	233 05.0	12.0	18 11.2	1.9	54.6
F 09	318 04.2	. . 43.4	247 36.0	11.9	18 13.1	1.8	54.6
R 10	333 04.4	44.4	262 06.9	11.9	18 14.9	1.7	54.6
I 11	348 04.6	45.4	276 37.8	11.9	18 16.6	1.6	54.6
D 12	3 04.7	S 5 46.3	291 08.7	11.8	S18 18.2	1.6	54.6
A 13	18 04.9	47.3	305 39.5	11.8	18 19.8	1.5	54.7
Y 14	33 05.1	48.2	320 10.3	11.8	18 21.3	1.3	54.7
15	48 05.3	. . 49.2	334 41.1	11.8	18 22.6	1.3	54.7
16	63 05.4	50.1	349 11.9	11.7	18 23.9	1.2	54.7
17	78 05.6	51.1	3 42.6	11.7	18 25.1	1.1	54.7
18	93 05.8	S 5 52.0	18 13.3	11.7	S18 26.2	1.1	54.8
19	108 06.0	53.0	32 44.0	11.7	18 27.3	0.9	54.8
20	123 06.1	53.9	47 14.7	11.6	18 28.2	0.9	54.8
21	138 06.3	. . 54.9	61 45.3	11.6	18 29.1	0.7	54.8
22	153 06.5	55.9	76 15.9	11.5	18 29.8	0.7	54.8
23	168 06.7	56.8	90 46.4	11.6	18 30.5	0.6	54.9
8 00	183 06.8	S 5 57.8	105 17.0	11.5	S18 31.1	0.5	54.9
01	198 07.0	58.7	119 47.5	11.5	18 31.6	0.4	54.9
02	213 07.2	5 59.7	134 18.0	11.4	18 32.0	0.3	54.9
03	228 07.4	6 00.6	148 48.4	11.4	18 32.3	0.2	54.9
04	243 07.5	01.6	163 18.8	11.4	18 32.5	0.2	55.0
05	258 07.7	02.5	177 49.2	11.4	18 32.7	0.0	55.0
06	273 07.9	S 6 03.5	192 19.6	11.4	S18 32.7	0.0	55.0
S 07	288 08.1	04.4	206 50.0	11.3	18 32.7	0.1	55.0
A 08	303 08.2	05.4	221 20.3	11.3	18 32.6	0.2	55.1
T 09	318 08.4	. . 06.3	235 50.6	11.2	18 32.4	0.4	55.1
U 10	333 08.6	07.3	250 20.8	11.3	18 32.0	0.4	55.1
R 11	348 08.8	08.2	264 51.1	11.2	18 31.6	0.5	55.1
D 12	3 08.9	S 6 09.2	279 21.3	11.2	S18 31.1	0.5	55.2
A 13	18 09.1	10.1	293 51.5	11.2	18 30.6	0.7	55.2
Y 14	33 09.3	11.1	308 21.7	11.1	18 29.9	0.8	55.2
15	48 09.4	. . 12.0	322 51.8	11.1	18 29.1	0.9	55.2
16	63 09.6	13.0	337 21.9	11.1	18 28.2	0.9	55.3
17	78 09.8	13.9	351 52.0	11.1	18 27.3	1.1	55.3
18	93 10.0	S 6 14.9	6 22.1	11.0	S18 26.2	1.1	55.3
19	108 10.1	15.8	20 52.1	11.0	18 25.1	1.2	55.3
20	123 10.3	16.8	35 22.1	11.0	18 23.9	1.4	55.4
21	138 10.5	. . 17.7	49 52.1	11.0	18 22.5	1.4	55.4
22	153 10.6	18.7	64 22.1	11.0	18 21.1	1.5	55.4
23	168 10.8	19.6	78 52.1	10.9	S18 19.6	1.6	55.5
	SD 16.0	d 1.0	SD 14.8		14.9		15.0

Lat.	Twilight Naut.	Twilight Civil	Sunrise	Moonrise 6	Moonrise 7	Moonrise 8	Moonrise 9
°	h m	h m	h m	h m	h m	h m	h m
N 72	04 21	05 40	06 48	15 01	▬	▬	17 38
N 70	04 29	05 40	06 41	13 52	15 08	16 00	16 26
68	04 35	05 40	06 36	13 16	14 23	15 14	15 49
66	04 40	05 40	06 31	12 50	13 53	14 44	15 22
64	04 44	05 40	06 27	12 30	13 31	14 22	15 02
62	04 48	05 39	06 24	12 14	13 13	14 04	14 45
60	04 51	05 39	06 21	12 01	12 58	13 49	14 31
N 58	04 53	05 39	06 18	11 49	12 46	13 36	14 20
56	04 55	05 38	06 16	11 39	12 35	13 25	14 09
54	04 57	05 38	06 13	11 30	12 25	13 16	14 00
52	04 59	05 38	06 12	11 22	12 17	13 07	13 52
50	05 00	05 37	06 10	11 15	12 09	12 59	13 45
45	05 02	05 36	06 06	11 00	11 53	12 43	13 29
N 40	05 04	05 35	06 03	10 48	11 40	12 29	13 16
35	05 05	05 34	06 00	10 37	11 28	12 18	13 05
30	05 05	05 33	05 57	10 28	11 19	12 08	12 56
20	05 05	05 30	05 52	10 12	11 02	11 51	12 39
N 10	05 03	05 27	05 48	09 58	10 47	11 36	12 25
0	05 00	05 24	05 44	09 46	10 33	11 22	12 12
S 10	04 55	05 19	05 40	09 33	10 19	11 08	11 58
20	04 48	05 14	05 36	09 19	10 05	10 53	11 44
30	04 38	05 07	05 31	09 03	09 48	10 36	11 27
35	04 32	05 02	05 28	08 54	09 38	10 26	11 18
40	04 24	04 57	05 24	08 44	09 27	10 14	11 07
45	04 15	04 50	05 20	08 32	09 14	10 01	10 54
S 50	04 03	04 42	05 15	08 17	08 58	09 45	10 38
52	03 57	04 39	05 13	08 10	08 50	09 37	10 31
54	03 50	04 34	05 11	08 03	08 42	09 28	10 23
56	03 42	04 30	05 08	07 54	08 33	09 19	10 13
58	03 34	04 24	05 05	07 45	08 22	09 08	10 03
S 60	03 24	04 18	05 01	07 34	08 10	08 55	09 51

Lat.	Sunset	Twilight Civil	Twilight Naut.	Moonset 6	Moonset 7	Moonset 8	Moonset 9
°	h m	h m	h m	h m	h m	h m	h m
N 72	16 45	17 53	19 12	16 47	▬	▬	19 16
N 70	16 52	17 53	19 04	17 56	18 19	19 09	20 27
68	16 58	17 54	18 58	18 33	19 04	19 55	21 04
66	17 03	17 54	18 53	18 59	19 34	20 24	21 30
64	17 07	17 54	18 49	19 19	19 57	20 47	21 50
62	17 10	17 55	18 46	19 35	20 15	21 05	22 06
60	17 13	17 55	18 43	19 49	20 30	21 20	22 20
N 58	17 16	17 55	18 41	20 01	20 42	21 32	22 32
56	17 19	17 56	18 39	20 11	20 53	21 43	22 42
54	17 21	17 56	18 37	20 20	21 03	21 53	22 51
52	17 23	17 57	18 36	20 28	21 11	22 01	22 58
50	17 25	17 57	18 34	20 35	21 19	22 09	23 06
45	17 29	17 58	18 32	20 51	21 35	22 25	23 21
N 40	17 32	17 59	18 31	21 04	21 49	22 39	23 33
35	17 35	18 01	18 30	21 15	22 00	22 50	23 44
30	17 38	18 02	18 30	21 24	22 10	23 00	23 53
20	17 43	18 05	18 30	21 41	22 27	23 17	24 09
N 10	17 47	18 08	18 32	21 55	22 42	23 32	24 23
0	17 51	18 12	18 36	22 08	22 56	23 46	24 36
S 10	17 55	18 16	18 41	22 22	23 10	23 59	24 49
20	18 00	18 22	18 48	22 36	23 25	24 14	00 14
30	18 05	18 29	18 58	22 52	23 42	24 31	00 31
35	18 08	18 34	19 04	23 02	23 52	24 41	00 41
40	18 12	18 39	19 12	23 13	24 04	00 04	00 52
45	18 16	18 46	19 22	23 26	24 17	00 17	01 05
S 50	18 21	18 54	19 34	23 41	24 33	00 33	01 21
52	18 23	18 58	19 40	23 49	24 41	00 41	01 29
54	18 26	19 02	19 47	23 57	24 50	00 50	01 37
56	18 29	19 07	19 55	24 06	00 06	00 59	01 46
58	18 32	19 13	20 04	24 16	00 16	01 10	01 57
S 60	18 36	19 19	20 14	24 28	00 28	01 22	02 09

Day	SUN Eqn. of Time 00^h	SUN Eqn. of Time 12^h	SUN Mer. Pass.	MOON Mer. Pass. Upper	MOON Mer. Pass. Lower	MOON Age	MOON Phase
d	m s	m s	h m	h m	h m	d	%
6	11 53	12 01	11 48	15 57	03 33	05	25
7	12 10	12 19	11 48	16 45	04 21	06	34
8	12 27	12 35	11 47	17 34	05 09	07	43

	UT	ARIES	VENUS −3·9		MARS +0·2		JUPITER −1·7		SATURN +0·5		STARS		
	d h	GHA ° ′	GHA ° ′	Dec ° ′	GHA ° ′	Dec ° ′	GHA ° ′	Dec ° ′	GHA ° ′	Dec ° ′	Name	SHA ° ′	Dec ° ′
	9 00	18 02.5	151 57.0	S17 59.5	99 24.3	S25 29.7	191 46.0	S 1 31.0	127 05.5	S20 51.1	Acamar	315 16.3	S40 14.2
	01	33 05.0	166 56.4	18 00.5	114 24.8	29.6	206 48.0	31.2	142 07.8	51.1	Achernar	335 24.6	S57 09.1
	02	48 07.4	181 55.8	01.5	129 25.4	29.4	221 50.0	31.4	157 10.0	51.2	Acrux	173 07.3	S63 11.3
	03	63 09.9	196 55.3	. . 02.4	144 26.0	. . 29.3	236 51.9	. . 31.6	172 12.2	. . 51.2	Adhara	255 10.7	S28 59.6
	04	78 12.4	211 54.7	03.4	159 26.6	29.2	251 53.9	31.9	187 14.5	51.2	Aldebaran	290 46.6	N16 32.4
	05	93 14.8	226 54.1	04.3	174 27.2	29.0	266 55.9	32.1	202 16.7	51.3			
	06	108 17.3	241 53.5	S18 05.3	189 27.7	S25 28.9	281 57.9	S 1 32.3	217 19.0	S20 51.3	Alioth	166 19.4	N55 52.3
	07	123 19.8	256 53.0	06.3	204 28.3	28.7	296 59.8	32.5	232 21.2	51.3	Alkaid	152 57.7	N49 14.0
	08	138 22.2	271 52.4	07.2	219 28.9	28.6	312 01.8	32.7	247 23.5	51.4	Al Na'ir	27 40.7	S46 52.8
S	09	153 24.7	286 51.8	. . 08.2	234 29.5	. . 28.5	327 03.8	. . 32.9	262 25.7	. . 51.4	Alnilam	275 44.0	S 1 11.6
U	10	168 27.2	301 51.3	09.1	249 30.1	28.3	342 05.7	33.1	277 28.0	51.4	Alphard	217 54.1	S 8 43.8
N	11	183 29.6	316 50.7	10.1	264 30.6	28.2	357 07.7	33.3	292 30.2	51.5			
D	12	198 32.1	331 50.1	S18 11.0	279 31.2	S25 28.0	12 09.7	S 1 33.5	307 32.5	S20 51.5	Alphecca	126 09.4	N26 39.9
A	13	213 34.5	346 49.5	12.0	294 31.8	27.9	27 11.6	33.7	322 34.7	51.5	Alpheratz	357 40.8	N29 11.1
Y	14	228 37.0	1 49.0	12.9	309 32.4	27.8	42 13.6	34.0	337 37.0	51.6	Altair	62 06.0	N 8 55.1
	15	243 39.5	16 48.4	. . 13.9	324 32.9	. . 27.6	57 15.6	. . 34.2	352 39.2	. . 51.6	Ankaa	353 13.2	S42 12.9
	16	258 41.9	31 47.8	14.8	339 33.5	27.5	72 17.6	34.4	7 41.4	51.6	Antares	112 23.8	S26 27.9
	17	273 44.4	46 47.2	15.8	354 34.1	27.3	87 19.5	34.6	22 43.7	51.7			
	18	288 46.9	61 46.7	S18 16.7	9 34.7	S25 27.2	102 21.5	S 1 34.8	37 45.9	S20 51.7	Arcturus	145 54.1	N19 06.0
	19	303 49.3	76 46.1	17.7	24 35.3	27.0	117 23.5	35.0	52 48.2	51.7	Atria	107 23.8	S69 03.4
	20	318 51.8	91 45.5	18.6	39 35.8	26.9	132 25.4	35.2	67 50.4	51.8	Avior	234 17.2	S59 33.6
	21	333 54.3	106 44.9	. . 19.5	54 36.4	. . 26.7	147 27.4	. . 35.4	82 52.7	. . 51.8	Bellatrix	278 29.5	N 6 21.8
	22	348 56.7	121 44.3	20.5	69 37.0	26.6	162 29.4	35.6	97 54.9	51.8	Betelgeuse	270 58.8	N 7 24.5
	23	3 59.2	136 43.8	21.4	84 37.6	26.5	177 31.4	35.9	112 57.2	51.9			
	10 00	19 01.7	151 43.2	S18 22.4	99 38.1	S25 26.3	192 33.3	S 1 36.1	127 59.4	S20 51.9	Canopus	263 55.0	S52 42.1
	01	34 04.1	166 42.6	23.3	114 38.7	26.2	207 35.3	36.3	143 01.7	51.9	Capella	280 30.9	N46 00.5
	02	49 06.6	181 42.0	24.3	129 39.3	26.0	222 37.3	36.5	158 03.9	52.0	Deneb	49 29.8	N45 20.8
	03	64 09.0	196 41.4	. . 25.2	144 39.9	. . 25.9	237 39.2	. . 36.7	173 06.1	. . 52.0	Denebola	182 31.7	N14 28.8
	04	79 11.5	211 40.9	26.1	159 40.4	25.7	252 41.2	36.9	188 08.4	52.0	Diphda	348 53.4	S17 53.7
	05	94 14.0	226 40.3	27.1	174 41.0	25.6	267 43.2	37.1	203 10.6	52.1			
	06	109 16.4	241 39.7	S18 28.0	189 41.6	S25 25.4	282 45.1	S 1 37.3	218 12.9	S20 52.1	Dubhe	193 49.7	N61 39.5
	07	124 18.9	256 39.1	28.9	204 42.2	25.3	297 47.1	37.5	233 15.1	52.1	Elnath	278 09.6	N28 37.0
	08	139 21.4	271 38.5	29.9	219 42.7	25.1	312 49.1	37.7	248 17.4	52.2	Eltanin	90 45.3	N51 29.7
M	09	154 23.8	286 37.9	. . 30.8	234 43.3	. . 25.0	327 51.1	. . 38.0	263 19.6	. . 52.2	Enif	33 44.7	N 9 57.4
O	10	169 26.3	301 37.3	31.8	249 43.9	24.8	342 53.0	38.2	278 21.9	52.2	Fomalhaut	15 21.3	S29 32.0
N	11	184 28.8	316 36.8	32.7	264 44.5	24.7	357 55.0	38.4	293 24.1	52.3			
D	12	199 31.2	331 36.2	S18 33.6	279 45.0	S25 24.5	12 57.0	S 1 38.6	308 26.3	S20 52.3	Gacrux	171 58.9	S57 12.2
A	13	214 33.7	346 35.6	34.6	294 45.6	24.4	27 58.9	38.8	323 28.6	52.3	Gienah	175 50.3	S17 37.9
Y	14	229 36.1	1 35.0	35.5	309 46.2	24.2	43 00.9	39.0	338 30.8	52.4	Hadar	148 45.2	S60 27.1
	15	244 38.6	16 34.4	. . 36.4	324 46.8	. . 24.1	58 02.9	. . 39.2	353 33.1	. . 52.4	Hamal	327 57.9	N23 32.4
	16	259 41.1	31 33.8	37.3	339 47.3	23.9	73 04.9	39.4	8 35.3	52.4	Kaus Aust.	83 41.0	S34 22.4
	17	274 43.5	46 33.2	38.3	354 47.9	23.8	88 06.8	39.6	23 37.6	52.5			
	18	289 46.0	61 32.6	S18 39.2	9 48.5	S25 23.6	103 08.8	S 1 39.8	38 39.8	S20 52.5	Kochab	137 21.3	N74 05.5
	19	304 48.5	76 32.1	40.1	24 49.1	23.4	118 10.8	40.1	53 42.0	52.6	Markab	13 35.8	N15 17.9
	20	319 50.9	91 31.5	41.1	39 49.6	23.3	133 12.7	40.3	68 44.3	52.6	Menkar	314 12.4	N 4 09.3
	21	334 53.4	106 30.9	. . 42.0	54 50.2	. . 23.1	148 14.7	. . 40.5	83 46.5	. . 52.6	Menkent	148 05.3	S36 26.9
	22	349 55.9	121 30.3	42.9	69 50.8	23.0	163 16.7	40.7	98 48.8	52.7	Miaplacidus	221 39.5	S69 46.9
	23	4 58.3	136 29.7	43.8	84 51.3	22.8	178 18.7	40.9	113 51.0	52.7			
	11 00	20 00.8	151 29.1	S18 44.7	99 51.9	S25 22.7	193 20.6	S 1 41.1	128 53.2	S20 52.7	Mirfak	308 36.7	N49 55.0
	01	35 03.3	166 28.5	45.7	114 52.5	22.5	208 22.6	41.3	143 55.5	52.8	Nunki	75 55.6	S26 16.4
	02	50 05.7	181 27.9	46.6	129 53.1	22.4	223 24.6	41.5	158 57.7	52.8	Peacock	53 15.7	S56 40.9
	03	65 08.2	196 27.3	. . 47.5	144 53.6	. . 22.2	238 26.5	. . 41.7	174 00.0	. . 52.8	Pollux	243 25.1	N27 58.9
	04	80 10.6	211 26.7	48.4	159 54.2	22.0	253 28.5	41.9	189 02.2	52.9	Procyon	244 57.4	N 5 10.8
	05	95 13.1	226 26.1	49.4	174 54.8	21.9	268 30.5	42.2	204 04.5	52.9			
	06	110 15.6	241 25.5	S18 50.3	189 55.3	S25 21.7	283 32.5	S 1 42.4	219 06.7	S20 52.9	Rasalhague	96 04.5	N12 33.3
	07	125 18.0	256 24.9	51.2	204 55.9	21.6	298 34.4	42.6	234 08.9	53.0	Regulus	207 41.4	N11 53.1
T	08	140 20.5	271 24.3	52.1	219 56.5	21.4	313 36.4	42.8	249 11.2	53.0	Rigel	281 09.8	S 8 11.0
U	09	155 23.0	286 23.7	. . 53.0	234 57.1	. . 21.2	328 38.4	. . 43.0	264 13.4	. . 53.0	Rigil Kent.	139 49.2	S60 54.1
E	10	170 25.4	301 23.2	53.9	249 57.6	21.1	343 40.3	43.2	279 15.7	53.1	Sabik	102 10.2	S15 44.5
S	11	185 27.9	316 22.6	54.8	264 58.2	20.9	358 42.3	43.4	294 17.9	53.1			
D	12	200 30.4	331 22.0	S18 55.8	279 58.8	S25 20.8	13 44.3	S 1 43.6	309 20.1	S20 53.1	Schedar	349 37.3	N56 37.8
A	13	215 32.8	346 21.4	56.7	294 59.3	20.6	28 46.3	43.8	324 22.4	53.2	Shaula	96 19.1	S37 06.8
Y	14	230 35.3	1 20.8	57.6	309 59.9	20.4	43 48.2	44.0	339 24.6	53.2	Sirius	258 31.7	S16 44.3
	15	245 37.8	16 20.2	. . 58.5	325 00.5	. . 20.3	58 50.2	. . 44.2	354 26.9	. . 53.2	Spica	158 29.2	S11 14.7
	16	260 40.2	31 19.6	18 59.4	340 01.0	20.1	73 52.2	44.5	9 29.1	53.3	Suhail	222 51.0	S43 29.8
	17	275 42.7	46 19.0	19 00.3	355 01.6	20.0	88 54.1	44.7	24 31.3	53.3			
	18	290 45.1	61 18.4	S19 01.2	10 02.2	S25 19.8	103 56.1	S 1 44.9	39 33.6	S20 53.3	Vega	80 37.5	N38 48.4
	19	305 47.6	76 17.8	02.1	25 02.7	19.6	118 58.1	45.1	54 35.8	53.4	Zuben'ubi	137 03.2	S16 06.4
	20	320 50.1	91 17.2	03.0	40 03.3	19.5	134 00.1	45.3	69 38.1	53.4			
	21	335 52.5	106 16.5	. . 03.9	55 03.9	. . 19.3	149 02.0	. . 45.5	84 40.3	. . 53.4			
	22	350 55.0	121 15.9	04.8	70 04.5	19.1	164 04.0	45.7	99 42.5	53.5			
	23	5 57.5	136 15.3	05.7	85 05.0	19.0	179 06.0	45.9	114 44.8	53.5			
	Mer. Pass.	h m 22 40.2	*v* −0.6	*d* 0.9	*v* 0.6	*d* 0.2	*v* 2.0	*d* 0.2	*v* 2.2	*d* 0.0			

	SHA ° ′	Mer. Pass. h m
Venus	132 41.5	13 54
Mars	80 36.5	17 21
Jupiter	173 31.7	11 08
Saturn	108 57.8	15 26

UT		SUN GHA	SUN Dec	MOON GHA	*v*	MOON Dec	*d*	HP
d	h	° ′	° ′	° ′	′	° ′	′	′
9	00	183 11.0	S 6 20.6	93 22.0	10.9	S18 18.0	1.7	55.5
	01	198 11.2	21.5	107 51.9	10.9	18 16.3	1.8	55.5
	02	213 11.3	22.5	122 21.8	10.8	18 14.5	1.9	55.5
	03	228 11.5	. . 23.4	136 51.6	10.9	18 12.6	1.9	55.6
	04	243 11.7	24.4	151 21.5	10.8	18 10.7	2.1	55.6
	05	258 11.8	25.3	165 51.3	10.8	18 08.6	2.2	55.6
	06	273 12.0	S 6 26.3	180 21.1	10.8	S18 06.4	2.3	55.7
	07	288 12.2	27.2	194 50.9	10.7	18 04.1	2.3	55.7
	08	303 12.3	28.2	209 20.6	10.7	18 01.8	2.5	55.7
S	09	318 12.5	. . 29.1	223 50.3	10.8	17 59.3	2.5	55.8
U	10	333 12.7	30.1	238 20.1	10.6	17 56.8	2.6	55.8
N	11	348 12.8	31.0	252 49.7	10.7	17 54.2	2.8	55.8
D	12	3 13.0	S 6 32.0	267 19.4	10.7	S17 51.4	2.8	55.8
A	13	18 13.2	32.9	281 49.1	10.6	17 48.6	2.9	55.9
Y	14	33 13.4	33.9	296 18.7	10.6	17 45.7	3.1	55.9
	15	48 13.5	. . 34.8	310 48.3	10.6	17 42.6	3.1	55.9
	16	63 13.7	35.8	325 17.9	10.6	17 39.5	3.2	56.0
	17	78 13.9	36.7	339 47.5	10.5	17 36.3	3.3	56.0
	18	93 14.0	S 6 37.6	354 17.0	10.5	S17 33.0	3.4	56.0
	19	108 14.2	38.6	8 46.5	10.6	17 29.6	3.5	56.1
	20	123 14.4	39.5	23 16.1	10.5	17 26.1	3.5	56.1
	21	138 14.5	. . 40.5	37 45.6	10.4	17 22.6	3.7	56.1
	22	153 14.7	41.4	52 15.0	10.5	17 18.9	3.8	56.2
	23	168 14.9	42.4	66 44.5	10.4	17 15.1	3.9	56.2
10	00	183 15.0	S 6 43.3	81 13.9	10.4	S17 11.2	3.9	56.2
	01	198 15.2	44.3	95 43.3	10.5	17 07.3	4.1	56.3
	02	213 15.3	45.2	110 12.8	10.3	17 03.2	4.2	56.3
	03	228 15.5	. . 46.2	124 42.1	10.4	16 59.0	4.2	56.3
	04	243 15.7	47.1	139 11.5	10.4	16 54.8	4.3	56.4
	05	258 15.8	48.0	153 40.9	10.3	16 50.5	4.5	56.4
	06	273 16.0	S 6 49.0	168 10.2	10.3	S16 46.0	4.5	56.4
	07	288 16.2	49.9	182 39.5	10.3	16 41.5	4.6	56.5
	08	303 16.3	50.9	197 08.8	10.3	16 36.9	4.7	56.5
M	09	318 16.5	. . 51.8	211 38.1	10.3	16 32.2	4.9	56.6
O	10	333 16.7	52.8	226 07.4	10.2	16 27.3	4.9	56.6
N	11	348 16.8	53.7	240 36.6	10.3	16 22.4	5.0	56.6
D	12	3 17.0	S 6 54.7	255 05.9	10.2	S16 17.4	5.1	56.7
A	13	18 17.2	55.6	269 35.1	10.2	16 12.3	5.1	56.7
Y	14	33 17.3	56.5	284 04.3	10.2	16 07.2	5.3	56.7
	15	48 17.5	. . 57.5	298 33.5	10.2	16 01.9	5.4	56.8
	16	63 17.6	58.4	313 02.7	10.1	15 56.5	5.5	56.8
	17	78 17.8	6 59.4	327 31.8	10.2	15 51.0	5.5	56.8
	18	93 18.0	S 7 00.3	342 01.0	10.1	S15 45.5	5.7	56.9
	19	108 18.1	01.3	356 30.1	10.1	15 39.8	5.7	56.9
	20	123 18.3	02.2	10 59.2	10.1	15 34.1	5.8	57.0
	21	138 18.5	. . 03.1	25 28.3	10.1	15 28.3	6.0	57.0
	22	153 18.6	04.1	39 57.4	10.1	15 22.3	6.0	57.0
	23	168 18.8	05.0	54 26.5	10.0	15 16.3	6.1	57.1
11	00	183 18.9	S 7 06.0	68 55.5	10.1	S15 10.2	6.2	57.1
	01	198 19.1	06.9	83 24.6	10.0	15 04.0	6.3	57.2
	02	213 19.3	07.9	97 53.6	10.0	14 57.7	6.3	57.2
	03	228 19.4	. . 08.8	112 22.6	10.0	14 51.4	6.5	57.2
	04	243 19.6	09.7	126 51.6	10.0	14 44.9	6.6	57.3
	05	258 19.7	10.7	141 20.6	10.0	14 38.3	6.6	57.3
	06	273 19.9	S 7 11.6	155 49.6	9.9	S14 31.7	6.7	57.3
	07	288 20.1	12.6	170 18.5	10.0	14 25.0	6.9	57.4
T	08	303 20.2	13.5	184 47.5	9.9	14 18.1	6.9	57.4
U	09	318 20.4	. . 14.4	199 16.4	9.9	14 11.2	7.0	57.5
E	10	333 20.5	15.4	213 45.3	9.9	14 04.2	7.1	57.5
S	11	348 20.7	16.3	228 14.2	9.9	13 57.1	7.1	57.5
D	12	3 20.9	S 7 17.3	242 43.1	9.9	S13 50.0	7.3	57.6
A	13	18 21.0	18.2	257 12.0	9.8	13 42.7	7.3	57.6
Y	14	33 21.2	19.1	271 40.8	9.9	13 35.4	7.5	57.7
	15	48 21.3	. . 20.1	286 09.7	9.8	13 27.9	7.5	57.7
	16	63 21.5	21.0	300 38.5	9.8	13 20.4	7.6	57.7
	17	78 21.6	22.0	315 07.3	9.8	13 12.8	7.7	57.8
	18	93 21.8	S 7 22.9	329 36.1	9.8	S13 05.1	7.8	57.8
	19	108 22.0	23.8	344 04.9	9.8	12 57.3	7.8	57.9
	20	123 22.1	24.8	358 33.7	9.8	12 49.5	8.0	57.9
	21	138 22.3	. . 25.7	13 02.5	9.7	12 41.5	8.0	57.9
	22	153 22.4	26.6	27 31.2	9.7	12 33.5	8.1	58.0
	23	168 22.6	27.6	41 59.9	9.7	S12 25.4	8.2	58.0
		SD 16.0	*d* 0.9	SD 15.2		15.4		15.7

Lat.	Twilight Naut.	Twilight Civil	Sunrise	Moonrise 9	Moonrise 10	Moonrise 11	Moonrise 12
°	h m	h m	h m	h m	h m	h m	h m
N 72	04 34	05 53	07 02	17 38	17 17	17 07	17 00
N 70	04 41	05 52	06 53	16 26	16 37	16 42	16 45
68	04 46	05 50	06 47	15 49	16 10	16 23	16 32
66	04 50	05 49	06 41	15 22	15 49	16 08	16 22
64	04 53	05 48	06 36	15 02	15 32	15 55	16 13
62	04 56	05 47	06 32	14 45	15 18	15 44	16 06
60	04 58	05 46	06 28	14 31	15 06	15 35	15 59
N 58	05 00	05 45	06 25	14 20	14 56	15 27	15 54
56	05 01	05 44	06 22	14 09	14 47	15 20	15 49
54	05 03	05 44	06 19	14 00	14 39	15 14	15 44
52	05 04	05 43	06 17	13 52	14 32	15 08	15 40
50	05 05	05 42	06 14	13 45	14 26	15 03	15 36
45	05 06	05 40	06 10	13 29	14 12	14 51	15 28
N 40	05 07	05 38	06 06	13 16	14 01	14 42	15 21
35	05 07	05 37	06 02	13 05	13 51	14 34	15 15
30	05 07	05 35	05 59	12 56	13 42	14 27	15 10
20	05 06	05 31	05 53	12 39	13 27	14 15	15 01
N 10	05 03	05 27	05 48	12 25	13 14	14 04	14 53
0	04 59	05 23	05 44	12 12	13 02	13 54	14 46
S 10	04 53	05 18	05 39	11 58	12 50	13 43	14 38
20	04 45	05 11	05 33	11 44	12 37	13 33	14 30
30	04 35	05 03	05 27	11 27	12 22	13 20	14 21
35	04 28	04 58	05 24	11 18	12 14	13 13	14 16
40	04 19	04 52	05 20	11 07	12 04	13 05	14 10
45	04 09	04 45	05 15	10 54	11 52	12 55	14 03
S 50	03 55	04 36	05 09	10 38	11 38	12 44	13 54
52	03 49	04 31	05 06	10 31	11 31	12 38	13 50
54	03 42	04 27	05 03	10 23	11 24	12 32	13 46
56	03 33	04 21	05 00	10 13	11 16	12 26	13 41
58	03 24	04 15	04 56	10 03	11 07	12 18	13 36
S 60	03 12	04 08	04 52	09 51	10 56	12 10	13 30

Lat.	Sunset	Twilight Civil	Twilight Naut.	Moonset 9	Moonset 10	Moonset 11	Moonset 12
°	h m	h m	h m	h m	h m	h m	h m
N 72	16 30	17 38	18 56	19 16	21 23	23 20	25 17
N 70	16 38	17 40	18 50	20 27	22 02	23 44	25 30
68	16 46	17 42	18 46	21 04	22 28	24 02	00 02
66	16 51	17 43	18 42	21 30	22 49	24 16	00 16
64	16 56	17 44	18 39	21 50	23 05	24 28	00 28
62	17 01	17 45	18 36	22 06	23 18	24 38	00 38
60	17 05	17 46	18 34	22 20	23 30	24 47	00 47
N 58	17 08	17 47	18 33	22 32	23 39	24 54	00 54
56	17 11	17 48	18 31	22 42	23 48	25 01	01 01
54	17 14	17 49	18 30	22 51	23 55	25 07	01 07
52	17 16	17 50	18 29	22 58	24 02	00 02	01 12
50	17 18	17 51	18 28	23 06	24 08	00 08	01 17
45	17 23	17 53	18 27	23 21	24 22	00 22	01 27
N 40	17 28	17 55	18 26	23 33	24 32	00 32	01 35
35	17 31	17 57	18 26	23 44	24 42	00 42	01 43
30	17 34	17 58	18 26	23 53	24 50	00 50	01 49
20	17 40	18 02	18 28	24 09	00 09	01 03	02 00
N 10	17 45	18 06	18 31	24 23	00 23	01 15	02 09
0	17 50	18 11	18 35	24 36	00 36	01 27	02 18
S 10	17 55	18 16	18 41	24 49	00 49	01 38	02 27
20	18 01	18 23	18 49	00 14	01 02	01 50	02 37
30	18 07	18 31	19 00	00 31	01 18	02 03	02 47
35	18 11	18 36	19 07	00 41	01 27	02 11	02 53
40	18 15	18 43	19 15	00 52	01 37	02 20	03 00
45	18 20	18 50	19 26	01 05	01 50	02 30	03 08
S 50	18 26	18 59	19 40	01 21	02 04	02 43	03 18
52	18 29	19 04	19 46	01 29	02 11	02 49	03 22
54	18 32	19 08	19 54	01 37	02 19	02 55	03 27
56	18 35	19 14	20 02	01 46	02 27	03 02	03 33
58	18 39	19 20	20 12	01 57	02 37	03 10	03 39
S 60	18 43	19 27	20 24	02 09	02 48	03 19	03 45

Day	SUN Eqn. of Time 00ʰ	SUN Eqn. of Time 12ʰ	SUN Mer. Pass.	MOON Mer. Pass. Upper	MOON Mer. Pass. Lower	MOON Age	MOON Phase
d	m s	m s	h m	h m	h m	d	%
9	12 44	12 52	11 47	18 24	05 59	08	53
10	13 00	13 08	11 47	19 14	06 49	09	63
11	13 15	13 23	11 47	20 06	07 40	10	73

UT		ARIES	VENUS −3·9		MARS +0·2		JUPITER −1·7		SATURN +0·5		STARS		
		GHA	GHA	Dec	GHA	Dec	GHA	Dec	GHA	Dec	Name	SHA	Dec
d h		° ′	° ′	° ′	° ′	° ′	° ′	° ′	° ′	° ′		° ′	° ′
12 00		20 59.9	151 14.7	S19 06.7	100 05.6	S25 18.8	194 07.9	S 1 46.1	129 47.0	S20 53.5	Acamar	315 16.3	S40 14.2
01		36 02.4	166 14.1	07.6	115 06.2	18.6	209 09.9	46.3	144 49.2	53.6	Achernar	335 24.6	S57 09.1
02		51 04.9	181 13.5	08.5	130 06.7	18.5	224 11.9	46.6	159 51.5	53.6	Acrux	173 07.3	S63 11.3
03		66 07.3	196 12.9	. . 09.4	145 07.3	. . 18.3	239 13.9	. . 46.8	174 53.7	. . 53.6	Adhara	255 10.7	S28 59.6
04		81 09.8	211 12.3	10.3	160 07.9	18.1	254 15.8	47.0	189 56.0	53.7	Aldebaran	290 46.6	N16 32.4
05		96 12.2	226 11.7	11.2	175 08.4	18.0	269 17.8	47.2	204 58.2	53.7			
06		111 14.7	241 11.1	S19 12.1	190 09.0	S25 17.8	284 19.8	S 1 47.4	220 00.4	S20 53.7	Alioth	166 19.4	N55 52.2
07	W	126 17.2	256 10.5	12.9	205 09.6	17.6	299 21.8	47.6	235 02.7	53.8	Alkaid	152 57.7	N49 14.0
08	E	141 19.6	271 09.9	13.8	220 10.1	17.5	314 23.7	47.8	250 04.9	53.8	Al Na'ir	27 40.7	S46 52.8
09	D	156 22.1	286 09.3	. . 14.7	235 10.7	. . 17.3	329 25.7	. . 48.0	265 07.2	. . 53.8	Alnilam	275 44.0	S 1 11.6
10	N	171 24.6	301 08.7	15.6	250 11.3	17.1	344 27.7	48.2	280 09.4	53.9	Alphard	217 54.1	S 8 43.8
11	E	186 27.0	316 08.1	16.5	265 11.8	17.0	359 29.6	48.4	295 11.6	53.9			
12	S	201 29.5	331 07.4	S19 17.4	280 12.4	S25 16.8	14 31.6	S 1 48.6	310 13.9	S20 53.9	Alphecca	126 09.5	N26 39.9
13	D	216 32.0	346 06.8	18.3	295 13.0	16.6	29 33.6	48.9	325 16.1	54.0	Alpheratz	357 40.8	N29 11.1
14	A	231 34.4	1 06.2	19.2	310 13.5	16.4	44 35.6	49.1	340 18.3	54.0	Altair	62 06.0	N 8 55.1
15	Y	246 36.9	16 05.6	. . 20.1	325 14.1	. . 16.3	59 37.5	. . 49.3	355 20.6	. . 54.1	Ankaa	353 13.2	S42 12.9
16		261 39.4	31 05.0	21.0	340 14.7	16.1	74 39.5	49.5	10 22.8	54.1	Antares	112 23.8	S26 27.9
17		276 41.8	46 04.4	21.9	355 15.2	15.9	89 41.5	49.7	25 25.1	54.1			
18		291 44.3	61 03.8	S19 22.8	10 15.8	S25 15.8	104 43.4	S 1 49.9	40 27.3	S20 54.2	Arcturus	145 54.1	N19 06.0
19		306 46.7	76 03.2	23.6	25 16.4	15.6	119 45.4	50.1	55 29.5	54.2	Atria	107 23.9	S69 03.4
20		321 49.2	91 02.5	24.5	40 16.9	15.4	134 47.4	50.3	70 31.8	54.2	Avior	234 17.2	S59 33.6
21		336 51.7	106 01.9	. . 25.4	55 17.5	. . 15.2	149 49.4	. . 50.5	85 34.0	. . 54.3	Bellatrix	278 29.5	N 6 21.8
22		351 54.1	121 01.3	26.3	70 18.1	15.1	164 51.3	50.7	100 36.2	54.3	Betelgeuse	270 58.8	N 7 24.5
23		6 56.6	136 00.7	27.2	85 18.6	14.9	179 53.3	50.9	115 38.5	54.3			
13 00		21 59.1	151 00.1	S19 28.1	100 19.2	S25 14.7	194 55.3	S 1 51.2	130 40.7	S20 54.4	Canopus	263 55.0	S52 42.1
01		37 01.5	165 59.5	29.0	115 19.7	14.5	209 57.3	51.4	145 42.9	54.4	Capella	280 30.9	N46 00.6
02		52 04.0	180 58.9	29.8	130 20.3	14.4	224 59.2	51.6	160 45.2	54.4	Deneb	49 29.8	N45 20.8
03		67 06.5	195 58.2	. . 30.7	145 20.9	. . 14.2	240 01.2	. . 51.8	175 47.4	. . 54.5	Denebola	182 31.7	N14 28.8
04		82 08.9	210 57.6	31.6	160 21.4	14.0	255 03.2	52.0	190 49.6	54.5	Diphda	348 53.4	S17 53.7
05		97 11.4	225 57.0	32.5	175 22.0	13.8	270 05.1	52.2	205 51.9	54.5			
06		112 13.8	240 56.4	S19 33.3	190 22.6	S25 13.6	285 07.1	S 1 52.4	220 54.1	S20 54.6	Dubhe	193 49.7	N61 39.5
07	T	127 16.3	255 55.8	34.2	205 23.1	13.5	300 09.1	52.6	235 56.4	54.6	Elnath	278 09.6	N28 37.0
08	H	142 18.8	270 55.1	35.1	220 23.7	13.3	315 11.1	52.8	250 58.6	54.6	Eltanin	90 45.3	N51 29.7
09	U	157 21.2	285 54.5	. . 36.0	235 24.3	. . 13.1	330 13.0	. . 53.0	266 00.8	. . 54.7	Enif	33 44.8	N 9 57.4
10	R	172 23.7	300 53.9	36.8	250 24.8	12.9	345 15.0	53.2	281 03.1	54.7	Fomalhaut	15 21.3	S29 32.0
11	S	187 26.2	315 53.3	37.7	265 25.4	12.8	0 17.0	53.4	296 05.3	54.7			
12	D	202 28.6	330 52.7	S19 38.6	280 26.0	S25 12.6	15 19.0	S 1 53.7	311 07.5	S20 54.8	Gacrux	171 58.9	S57 12.2
13	A	217 31.1	345 52.0	39.5	295 26.5	12.4	30 20.9	53.9	326 09.8	54.8	Gienah	175 50.3	S17 37.9
14	Y	232 33.6	0 51.4	40.3	310 27.1	12.2	45 22.9	54.1	341 12.0	54.8	Hadar	148 45.2	S60 27.1
15		247 36.0	15 50.8	. . 41.2	325 27.6	. . 12.0	60 24.9	. . 54.3	356 14.2	. . 54.9	Hamal	327 57.9	N23 32.4
16		262 38.5	30 50.2	42.1	340 28.2	11.8	75 26.8	54.5	11 16.5	54.9	Kaus Aust.	83 41.0	S34 22.4
17		277 41.0	45 49.5	42.9	355 28.8	11.7	90 28.8	54.7	26 18.7	54.9			
18		292 43.4	60 48.9	S19 43.8	10 29.3	S25 11.5	105 30.8	S 1 54.9	41 20.9	S20 55.0	Kochab	137 21.4	N74 05.5
19		307 45.9	75 48.3	44.7	25 29.9	11.3	120 32.8	55.1	56 23.2	55.0	Markab	13 35.8	N15 17.9
20		322 48.3	90 47.7	45.5	40 30.5	11.1	135 34.7	55.3	71 25.4	55.0	Menkar	314 12.4	N 4 09.3
21		337 50.8	105 47.0	. . 46.4	55 31.0	. . 10.9	150 36.7	. . 55.5	86 27.6	. . 55.1	Menkent	148 05.3	S36 26.9
22		352 53.3	120 46.4	47.3	70 31.6	10.7	165 38.7	55.7	101 29.9	55.1	Miaplacidus	221 39.5	S69 46.9
23		7 55.7	135 45.8	48.1	85 32.1	10.6	180 40.7	56.0	116 32.1	55.2			
14 00		22 58.2	150 45.1	S19 49.0	100 32.7	S25 10.4	195 42.6	S 1 56.2	131 34.3	S20 55.2	Mirfak	308 36.7	N49 55.0
01		38 00.7	165 44.5	49.9	115 33.3	10.2	210 44.6	56.4	146 36.6	55.2	Nunki	75 55.6	S26 16.4
02		53 03.1	180 43.9	50.7	130 33.8	10.0	225 46.6	56.6	161 38.8	55.3	Peacock	53 15.7	S56 40.9
03		68 05.6	195 43.3	. . 51.6	145 34.4	. . 09.8	240 48.6	. . 56.8	176 41.0	. . 55.3	Pollux	243 25.1	N27 58.9
04		83 08.1	210 42.6	52.4	160 34.9	09.6	255 50.5	57.0	191 43.3	55.3	Procyon	244 57.4	N 5 10.8
05		98 10.5	225 42.0	53.3	175 35.5	09.4	270 52.5	57.2	206 45.5	55.4			
06		113 13.0	240 41.4	S19 54.1	190 36.1	S25 09.3	285 54.5	S 1 57.4	221 47.7	S20 55.4	Rasalhague	96 04.5	N12 33.3
07		128 15.4	255 40.7	55.0	205 36.6	09.1	300 56.4	57.6	236 50.0	55.4	Regulus	207 41.4	N11 53.1
08		143 17.9	270 40.1	55.9	220 37.2	08.9	315 58.4	57.8	251 52.2	55.5	Rigel	281 09.7	S 8 11.0
09	F	158 20.4	285 39.5	. . 56.7	235 37.7	. . 08.7	331 00.4	. . 58.0	266 54.4	. . 55.5	Rigil Kent.	139 49.2	S60 54.1
10	R	173 22.8	300 38.8	57.6	250 38.3	08.5	346 02.4	58.2	281 56.7	55.5	Sabik	102 10.2	S15 44.5
11	I	188 25.3	315 38.2	58.4	265 38.9	08.3	1 04.3	58.4	296 58.9	55.6			
12	D	203 27.8	330 37.6	S19 59.3	280 39.4	S25 08.1	16 06.3	S 1 58.7	312 01.1	S20 55.6	Schedar	349 37.3	N56 37.8
13	A	218 30.2	345 36.9	20 00.1	295 40.0	07.9	31 08.3	58.9	327 03.4	55.6	Shaula	96 19.1	S37 06.8
14	Y	233 32.7	0 36.3	01.0	310 40.5	07.7	46 10.3	59.1	342 05.6	55.7	Sirius	258 31.7	S16 44.3
15		248 35.2	15 35.7	. . 01.8	325 41.1	. . 07.6	61 12.2	. . 59.3	357 07.8	. . 55.7	Spica	158 29.2	S11 14.7
16		263 37.6	30 35.0	02.7	340 41.7	07.4	76 14.2	59.5	12 10.1	55.7	Suhail	222 50.9	S43 29.8
17		278 40.1	45 34.4	03.5	355 42.2	07.2	91 16.2	59.7	27 12.3	55.8			
18		293 42.6	60 33.8	S20 04.4	10 42.8	S25 07.0	106 18.2	S 1 59.9	42 14.5	S20 55.8	Vega	80 37.5	N38 48.4
19		308 45.0	75 33.1	05.2	25 43.3	06.8	121 20.1	2 00.1	57 16.7	55.8	Zuben'ubi	137 03.2	S16 06.4
20		323 47.5	90 32.5	06.0	40 43.9	06.6	136 22.1	00.3	72 19.0	55.9		SHA	Mer.Pass.
21		338 49.9	105 31.8	. . 06.9	55 44.5	. . 06.4	151 24.1	. . 00.5	87 21.2	. . 55.9		° ′	h m
22		353 52.4	120 31.2	07.7	70 45.0	06.2	166 26.1	00.7	102 23.4	55.9	Venus	129 01.0	13 57
23		8 54.9	135 30.6	08.6	85 45.6	06.0	181 28.0	00.9	117 25.7	56.0	Mars	78 20.1	17 18
Mer. Pass.		h m 22 28.4	v −0.6	d 0.9	v 0.6	d 0.2	v 2.0	d 0.2	v 2.2	d 0.0	Jupiter	172 56.2	10 59
											Saturn	108 41.6	15 15

UT d	h	SUN GHA ° ′	SUN Dec ° ′	MOON GHA ° ′	v ′	MOON Dec ° ′	d ′	HP ′
12	00	183 22.7	S 7 28.5	56 28.6	9.7	S12 17.2	8.2	58.1
	01	198 22.9	29.5	70 57.3	9.7	12 09.0	8.4	58.1
	02	213 23.0	30.4	85 26.0	9.7	12 00.6	8.4	58.2
	03	228 23.2	. . 31.3	99 54.7	9.7	11 52.2	8.5	58.2
	04	243 23.4	32.3	114 23.4	9.6	11 43.7	8.6	58.2
	05	258 23.5	33.2	128 52.0	9.6	11 35.1	8.7	58.3
W	06	273 23.7	S 7 34.1	143 20.6	9.7	S11 26.4	8.7	58.3
E	07	288 23.8	35.1	157 49.3	9.6	11 17.7	8.8	58.4
D	08	303 24.0	36.0	172 17.9	9.6	11 08.9	8.9	58.4
N	09	318 24.1	. . 37.0	186 46.5	9.5	11 00.0	9.0	58.4
E	10	333 24.3	37.9	201 15.0	9.6	10 51.0	9.1	58.5
S	11	348 24.4	38.8	215 43.6	9.5	10 41.9	9.1	58.5
D	12	3 24.6	S 7 39.8	230 12.1	9.5	S10 32.8	9.2	58.6
A	13	18 24.7	40.7	244 40.6	9.5	10 23.6	9.2	58.6
Y	14	33 24.9	41.6	259 09.1	9.5	10 14.4	9.4	58.6
	15	48 25.1	. . 42.6	273 37.6	9.5	10 05.0	9.4	58.7
	16	63 25.2	43.5	288 06.1	9.5	9 55.6	9.5	58.7
	17	78 25.4	44.4	302 34.6	9.4	9 46.1	9.5	58.8
	18	93 25.5	S 7 45.4	317 03.0	9.4	S 9 36.6	9.7	58.8
	19	108 25.7	46.3	331 31.4	9.5	9 26.9	9.6	58.8
	20	123 25.8	47.2	345 59.9	9.3	9 17.3	9.8	58.9
	21	138 26.0	. . 48.2	0 28.2	9.4	9 07.5	9.8	58.9
	22	153 26.1	49.1	14 56.6	9.4	8 57.7	9.9	59.0
	23	168 26.3	50.0	29 25.0	9.3	8 47.8	10.0	59.0
13	00	183 26.4	S 7 51.0	43 53.3	9.3	S 8 37.8	10.0	59.0
	01	198 26.6	51.9	58 21.6	9.3	8 27.8	10.1	59.1
	02	213 26.7	52.8	72 49.9	9.3	8 17.7	10.1	59.1
	03	228 26.9	. . 53.8	87 18.2	9.3	8 07.6	10.3	59.2
	04	243 27.0	54.7	101 46.5	9.2	7 57.3	10.2	59.2
	05	258 27.2	55.6	116 14.7	9.3	7 47.1	10.4	59.2
	06	273 27.3	S 7 56.6	130 43.0	9.2	S 7 36.7	10.3	59.3
T	07	288 27.5	57.5	145 11.2	9.2	7 26.4	10.5	59.3
H	08	303 27.6	58.4	159 39.4	9.1	7 15.9	10.5	59.3
U	09	318 27.8	7 59.4	174 07.5	9.2	7 05.4	10.6	59.4
R	10	333 27.9	8 00.3	188 35.7	9.1	6 54.8	10.6	59.4
S	11	348 28.1	01.2	203 03.8	9.1	6 44.2	10.7	59.5
D	12	3 28.2	S 8 02.2	217 31.9	9.1	S 6 33.5	10.7	59.5
A	13	18 28.4	03.1	232 00.0	9.1	6 22.8	10.8	59.5
Y	14	33 28.5	04.0	246 28.1	9.0	6 12.0	10.8	59.6
	15	48 28.6	. . 04.9	260 56.1	9.1	6 01.2	10.9	59.6
	16	63 28.8	05.9	275 24.2	9.0	5 50.3	10.9	59.6
	17	78 28.9	06.8	289 52.2	9.0	5 39.4	11.0	59.7
	18	93 29.1	S 8 07.7	304 20.2	8.9	S 5 28.4	11.0	59.7
	19	108 29.2	08.7	318 48.1	8.9	5 17.4	11.1	59.8
	20	123 29.4	09.6	333 16.0	9.0	5 06.3	11.1	59.8
	21	138 29.5	. . 10.5	347 44.0	8.8	4 55.2	11.2	59.8
	22	153 29.7	11.4	2 11.8	8.9	4 44.0	11.2	59.9
	23	168 29.8	12.4	16 39.7	8.9	4 32.8	11.2	59.9
14	00	183 30.0	S 8 13.3	31 07.6	8.8	S 4 21.6	11.3	59.9
	01	198 30.1	14.2	45 35.4	8.8	4 10.3	11.3	60.0
	02	213 30.3	15.2	60 03.2	8.7	3 59.0	11.4	60.0
	03	228 30.4	. . 16.1	74 30.9	8.8	3 47.6	11.4	60.0
	04	243 30.5	17.0	88 58.7	8.7	3 36.2	11.4	60.1
	05	258 30.7	17.9	103 26.4	8.7	3 24.8	11.5	60.1
	06	273 30.8	S 8 18.9	117 54.1	8.6	S 3 13.3	11.5	60.1
	07	288 31.0	19.8	132 21.7	8.7	3 01.8	11.5	60.2
	08	303 31.1	20.7	146 49.4	8.6	2 50.3	11.6	60.2
F	09	318 31.3	. . 21.7	161 17.0	8.6	2 38.7	11.5	60.2
R	10	333 31.4	22.6	175 44.6	8.5	2 27.2	11.7	60.3
I	11	348 31.5	23.5	190 12.1	8.5	2 15.5	11.6	60.3
D	12	3 31.7	S 8 24.4	204 39.6	8.5	S 2 03.9	11.7	60.3
A	13	18 31.8	25.4	219 07.1	8.5	1 52.2	11.7	60.3
Y	14	33 32.0	26.3	233 34.6	8.5	1 40.5	11.7	60.4
	15	48 32.1	. . 27.2	248 02.1	8.4	1 28.8	11.7	60.4
	16	63 32.3	28.1	262 29.5	8.4	1 17.1	11.8	60.4
	17	78 32.4	29.1	276 56.9	8.3	1 05.3	11.8	60.5
	18	93 32.5	S 8 30.0	291 24.2	8.3	S 0 53.5	11.8	60.5
	19	108 32.7	30.9	305 51.5	8.3	0 41.7	11.8	60.5
	20	123 32.8	31.8	320 18.8	8.3	0 29.9	11.8	60.5
	21	138 33.0	. . 32.8	334 46.1	8.2	0 18.1	11.9	60.6
	22	153 33.1	33.7	349 13.3	8.2	S 0 06.2	11.8	60.6
	23	168 33.2	34.6	3 40.5	8.2	N 0 05.6	11.9	60.6
		SD 16.1	*d* 0.9	SD 16.0		16.2		16.4

Lat. °	Twilight Naut. h m	Twilight Civil h m	Sunrise h m	Moonrise 12 h m	Moonrise 13 h m	Moonrise 14 h m	Moonrise 15 h m
N 72	04 48	06 06	07 16	17 00	16 54	16 48	16 42
N 70	04 53	06 03	07 06	16 45	16 46	16 46	16 47
68	04 56	06 01	06 58	16 32	16 39	16 45	16 51
66	04 59	05 59	06 51	16 22	16 33	16 44	16 54
64	05 02	05 57	06 45	16 13	16 29	16 43	16 57
62	05 03	05 55	06 40	16 06	16 24	16 42	16 59
60	05 05	05 53	06 35	15 59	16 21	16 41	17 01
N 58	05 06	05 52	06 31	15 54	16 18	16 40	17 03
56	05 07	05 50	06 28	15 49	16 15	16 40	17 05
54	05 08	05 49	06 25	15 44	16 12	16 39	17 06
52	05 09	05 48	06 22	15 40	16 10	16 38	17 08
50	05 09	05 47	06 19	15 36	16 08	16 38	17 09
45	05 10	05 44	06 13	15 28	16 03	16 37	17 12
N 40	05 10	05 41	06 09	15 21	15 59	16 36	17 14
35	05 10	05 39	06 04	15 15	15 55	16 35	17 16
30	05 09	05 37	06 01	15 10	15 52	16 35	17 18
20	05 06	05 32	05 54	15 01	15 47	16 34	17 21
N 10	05 03	05 27	05 48	14 53	15 43	16 33	17 24
0	04 58	05 22	05 43	14 46	15 38	16 32	17 27
S 10	04 51	05 16	05 37	14 38	15 34	16 31	17 29
20	04 43	05 09	05 31	14 30	15 29	16 30	17 32
30	04 31	05 00	05 24	14 21	15 24	16 29	17 36
35	04 23	04 54	05 20	14 16	15 21	16 29	17 38
40	04 14	04 47	05 15	14 10	15 18	16 28	17 40
45	04 03	04 39	05 09	14 03	15 14	16 27	17 43
S 50	03 48	04 29	05 03	13 54	15 09	16 26	17 46
52	03 41	04 24	05 00	13 50	15 07	16 26	17 47
54	03 33	04 19	04 56	13 46	15 04	16 25	17 49
56	03 24	04 13	04 52	13 41	15 01	16 25	17 51
58	03 13	04 06	04 48	13 36	14 59	16 24	17 53
S 60	03 01	03 59	04 43	13 30	14 55	16 24	17 55

Lat. °	Sunset h m	Twilight Civil h m	Twilight Naut. h m	Moonset 12 h m	Moonset 13 h m	Moonset 14 h m	Moonset 15 h m
N 72	16 14	17 24	18 41	25 17	01 17	03 14	05 13
N 70	16 25	17 27	18 37	25 30	01 30	03 19	05 11
68	16 33	17 30	18 34	00 02	01 41	03 24	05 10
66	16 40	17 32	18 31	00 16	01 50	03 28	05 09
64	16 46	17 34	18 29	00 28	01 58	03 31	05 08
62	16 51	17 36	18 27	00 38	02 04	03 34	05 07
60	16 56	17 38	18 26	00 47	02 09	03 36	05 06
N 58	17 00	17 39	18 25	00 54	02 14	03 39	05 06
56	17 03	17 41	18 24	01 01	02 19	03 40	05 05
54	17 07	17 42	18 23	01 07	02 22	03 42	05 05
52	17 10	17 43	18 22	01 12	02 26	03 44	05 04
50	17 12	17 45	18 22	01 17	02 29	03 45	05 04
45	17 18	17 48	18 22	01 27	02 36	03 48	05 03
N 40	17 23	17 50	18 22	01 35	02 42	03 51	05 02
35	17 27	17 53	18 22	01 43	02 47	03 53	05 01
30	17 31	17 55	18 23	01 49	02 51	03 55	05 01
20	17 38	18 00	18 26	02 00	02 58	03 58	05 00
N 10	17 44	18 05	18 29	02 09	03 05	04 01	04 59
0	17 49	18 10	18 35	02 18	03 11	04 04	04 58
S 10	17 55	18 17	18 41	02 27	03 16	04 06	04 57
20	18 02	18 24	18 50	02 37	03 23	04 09	04 56
30	18 09	18 33	19 02	02 47	03 30	04 12	04 55
35	18 13	18 39	19 10	02 53	03 34	04 14	04 54
40	18 18	18 46	19 19	03 00	03 38	04 16	04 53
45	18 24	18 54	19 31	03 08	03 44	04 18	04 52
S 50	18 31	19 04	19 45	03 18	03 50	04 21	04 51
52	18 34	19 09	19 53	03 22	03 53	04 22	04 51
54	18 37	19 15	20 01	03 27	03 56	04 23	04 50
56	18 41	19 21	20 10	03 33	04 00	04 25	04 49
58	18 46	19 28	20 21	03 39	04 03	04 26	04 49
S 60	18 50	19 35	20 34	03 45	04 08	04 28	04 48

Day	SUN Eqn. of Time 00^h	SUN Eqn. of Time 12^h	SUN Mer. Pass.	MOON Mer. Pass. Upper	MOON Mer. Pass. Lower	MOON Age	MOON Phase
d	m s	m s	h m	h m	h m	d %	
12	13 31	13 38	11 46	20 58	08 32	11 82	
13	13 45	13 53	11 46	21 51	09 24	12 90	
14	14 00	14 06	11 46	22 45	10 18	13 96	

UT d	UT h	ARIES GHA	VENUS −3·9 GHA	VENUS Dec	MARS +0·2 GHA	MARS Dec	JUPITER −1·7 GHA	JUPITER Dec	SATURN +0·5 GHA	SATURN Dec
		° ′	° ′	° ′	° ′	° ′	° ′	° ′	° ′	° ′
15	00	23 57.3	150 29.9	S20 09.4	100 46.1	S25 05.8	196 30.0	S 2 01.2	132 27.9	S20 56.0
	01	38 59.8	165 29.3	10.3	115 46.7	05.6	211 32.0	01.4	147 30.1	56.0
	02	54 02.3	180 28.6	11.1	130 47.3	05.4	226 34.0	01.6	162 32.4	56.1
	03	69 04.7	195 28.0	. . 11.9	145 47.8	. . 05.2	241 35.9	. . 01.8	177 34.6	. . 56.1
	04	84 07.2	210 27.4	12.8	160 48.4	05.0	256 37.9	02.0	192 36.8	56.2
	05	99 09.7	225 26.7	13.6	175 48.9	04.8	271 39.9	02.2	207 39.0	56.2
	06	114 12.1	240 26.1	S20 14.4	190 49.5	S25 04.6	286 41.9	S 2 02.4	222 41.3	S20 56.2
	07	129 14.6	255 25.4	15.3	205 50.0	04.5	301 43.8	02.6	237 43.5	56.3
S	08	144 17.1	270 24.8	16.1	220 50.6	04.3	316 45.8	02.8	252 45.7	56.3
A	09	159 19.5	285 24.1	. . 16.9	235 51.2	. . 04.1	331 47.8	. . 03.0	267 48.0	. . 56.3
T	10	174 22.0	300 23.5	17.8	250 51.7	03.9	346 49.7	03.2	282 50.2	56.4
U	11	189 24.4	315 22.8	18.6	265 52.3	03.7	1 51.7	03.4	297 52.4	56.4
R	12	204 26.9	330 22.2	S20 19.4	280 52.8	S25 03.5	16 53.7	S 2 03.6	312 54.7	S20 56.4
D	13	219 29.4	345 21.6	20.3	295 53.4	03.3	31 55.7	03.9	327 56.9	56.5
A	14	234 31.8	0 20.9	21.1	310 53.9	03.1	46 57.6	04.1	342 59.1	56.5
Y	15	249 34.3	15 20.3	. . 21.9	325 54.5	. . 02.9	61 59.6	. . 04.3	358 01.3	. . 56.5
	16	264 36.8	30 19.6	22.7	340 55.1	02.7	77 01.6	04.5	13 03.6	56.6
	17	279 39.2	45 19.0	23.6	355 55.6	02.5	92 03.6	04.7	28 05.8	56.6
	18	294 41.7	60 18.3	S20 24.4	10 56.2	S25 02.3	107 05.5	S 2 04.9	43 08.0	S20 56.6
	19	309 44.2	75 17.7	25.2	25 56.7	02.1	122 07.5	05.1	58 10.3	56.7
	20	324 46.6	90 17.0	26.0	40 57.3	01.8	137 09.5	05.3	73 12.5	56.7
	21	339 49.1	105 16.4	. . 26.9	55 57.8	. . 01.6	152 11.5	. . 05.5	88 14.7	. . 56.7
	22	354 51.5	120 15.7	27.7	70 58.4	01.4	167 13.4	05.7	103 16.9	56.8
	23	9 54.0	135 15.1	28.5	85 59.0	01.2	182 15.4	05.9	118 19.2	56.8
16	00	24 56.5	150 14.4	S20 29.3	100 59.5	S25 01.0	197 17.4	S 2 06.1	133 21.4	S20 56.8
	01	39 58.9	165 13.8	30.1	116 00.1	00.8	212 19.4	06.3	148 23.6	56.9
	02	55 01.4	180 13.1	30.9	131 00.6	00.6	227 21.3	06.5	163 25.8	56.9
	03	70 03.9	195 12.4	. . 31.8	146 01.2	. . 00.4	242 23.3	. . 06.8	178 28.1	. . 56.9
	04	85 06.3	210 11.8	32.6	161 01.7	00.2	257 25.3	07.0	193 30.3	57.0
	05	100 08.8	225 11.1	33.4	176 02.3	25 00.0	272 27.3	07.2	208 32.5	57.0
	06	115 11.3	240 10.5	S20 34.2	191 02.8	S24 59.8	287 29.2	S 2 07.4	223 34.8	S20 57.0
	07	130 13.7	255 09.8	35.0	206 03.4	59.6	302 31.2	07.6	238 37.0	57.1
	08	145 16.2	270 09.2	35.8	221 04.0	59.4	317 33.2	07.8	253 39.2	57.1
S	09	160 18.7	285 08.5	. . 36.6	236 04.5	. . 59.2	332 35.2	. . 08.0	268 41.4	. . 57.2
U	10	175 21.1	300 07.9	37.4	251 05.1	59.0	347 37.1	08.2	283 43.7	57.2
N	11	190 23.6	315 07.2	38.3	266 05.6	58.8	2 39.1	08.4	298 45.9	57.2
D	12	205 26.0	330 06.5	S20 39.1	281 06.2	S24 58.6	17 41.1	S 2 08.6	313 48.1	S20 57.3
A	13	220 28.5	345 05.9	39.9	296 06.7	58.3	32 43.1	08.8	328 50.3	57.3
Y	14	235 31.0	0 05.2	40.7	311 07.3	58.1	47 45.0	09.0	343 52.6	57.3
	15	250 33.4	15 04.6	. . 41.5	326 07.8	. . 57.9	62 47.0	. . 09.2	358 54.8	. . 57.4
	16	265 35.9	30 03.9	42.3	341 08.4	57.7	77 49.0	09.4	13 57.0	57.4
	17	280 38.4	45 03.2	43.1	356 08.9	57.5	92 51.0	09.7	28 59.2	57.4
	18	295 40.8	60 02.6	S20 43.9	11 09.5	S24 57.3	107 52.9	S 2 09.9	44 01.5	S20 57.5
	19	310 43.3	75 01.9	44.7	26 10.0	57.1	122 54.9	10.1	59 03.7	57.5
	20	325 45.8	90 01.3	45.5	41 10.6	56.9	137 56.9	10.3	74 05.9	57.5
	21	340 48.2	105 00.6	. . 46.3	56 11.2	. . 56.7	152 58.9	. . 10.5	89 08.1	. . 57.6
	22	355 50.7	119 59.9	47.1	71 11.7	56.4	168 00.9	10.7	104 10.4	57.6
	23	10 53.1	134 59.3	47.9	86 12.3	56.2	183 02.8	10.9	119 12.6	57.6
17	00	25 55.6	149 58.6	S20 48.7	101 12.8	S24 56.0	198 04.8	S 2 11.1	134 14.8	S20 57.7
	01	40 58.1	164 57.9	49.5	116 13.4	55.8	213 06.8	11.3	149 17.0	57.7
	02	56 00.5	179 57.3	50.3	131 13.9	55.6	228 08.8	11.5	164 19.3	57.7
	03	71 03.0	194 56.6	. . 51.1	146 14.5	. . 55.4	243 10.7	. . 11.7	179 21.5	. . 57.8
	04	86 05.5	209 55.9	51.9	161 15.0	55.2	258 12.7	11.9	194 23.7	57.8
	05	101 07.9	224 55.3	52.6	176 15.6	54.9	273 14.7	12.1	209 25.9	57.8
	06	116 10.4	239 54.6	S20 53.4	191 16.1	S24 54.7	288 16.7	S 2 12.3	224 28.2	S20 57.9
	07	131 12.9	254 53.9	54.2	206 16.7	54.5	303 18.6	12.5	239 30.4	57.9
	08	146 15.3	269 53.3	55.0	221 17.2	54.3	318 20.6	12.8	254 32.6	58.0
M	09	161 17.8	284 52.6	. . 55.8	236 17.8	. . 54.1	333 22.6	. . 13.0	269 34.8	. . 58.0
O	10	176 20.3	299 51.9	56.6	251 18.3	53.9	348 24.6	13.2	284 37.1	58.0
N	11	191 22.7	314 51.3	57.4	266 18.9	53.6	3 26.5	13.4	299 39.3	58.1
D	12	206 25.2	329 50.6	S20 58.2	281 19.4	S24 53.4	18 28.5	S 2 13.6	314 41.5	S20 58.1
A	13	221 27.6	344 49.9	58.9	296 20.0	53.2	33 30.5	13.8	329 43.7	58.1
Y	14	236 30.1	359 49.3	20 59.7	311 20.6	53.0	48 32.5	14.0	344 46.0	58.2
	15	251 32.6	14 48.6	. . 21 00.5	326 21.1	. . 52.8	63 34.4	. . 14.2	359 48.2	. . 58.2
	16	266 35.0	29 47.9	01.3	341 21.7	52.5	78 36.4	14.4	14 50.4	58.2
	17	281 37.5	44 47.2	02.1	356 22.2	52.3	93 38.4	14.6	29 52.6	58.3
	18	296 40.0	59 46.6	S21 02.8	11 22.8	S24 52.1	108 40.4	S 2 14.8	44 54.9	S20 58.3
	19	311 42.4	74 45.9	03.6	26 23.3	51.9	123 42.3	15.0	59 57.1	58.3
	20	326 44.9	89 45.2	04.4	41 23.9	51.7	138 44.3	15.2	74 59.3	58.4
	21	341 47.4	104 44.6	. . 05.2	56 24.4	. . 51.4	153 46.3	. . 15.4	90 01.5	. . 58.4
	22	356 49.8	119 43.9	06.0	71 25.0	51.2	168 48.3	15.6	105 03.7	58.4
	23	11 52.3	134 43.2	06.7	86 25.5	51.0	183 50.3	15.8	120 06.0	58.5
Mer. Pass.		h m 22 16.6	v −0.7	d 0.8	v 0.6	d 0.2	v 2.0	d 0.2	v 2.2	d 0.0

STARS

Name	SHA	Dec
	° ′	° ′
Acamar	315 16.3	S40 14.3
Achernar	335 24.6	S57 09.2
Acrux	173 07.3	S63 11.3
Adhara	255 10.7	S28 59.6
Aldebaran	290 46.6	N16 32.4
Alioth	166 19.4	N55 52.2
Alkaid	152 57.7	N49 14.0
Al Na'ir	27 40.7	S46 52.8
Alnilam	275 43.9	S 1 11.6
Alphard	217 54.0	S 8 43.8
Alphecca	126 09.5	N26 39.9
Alpheratz	357 40.8	N29 11.1
Altair	62 06.1	N 8 55.1
Ankaa	353 13.2	S42 12.9
Antares	112 23.8	S26 27.9
Arcturus	145 54.1	N19 06.0
Atria	107 23.9	S69 03.4
Avior	234 17.2	S59 33.6
Bellatrix	278 29.4	N 6 21.8
Betelgeuse	270 58.7	N 7 24.5
Canopus	263 55.0	S52 42.1
Capella	280 30.9	N46 00.6
Deneb	49 29.8	N45 20.8
Denebola	182 31.7	N14 28.8
Diphda	348 53.4	S17 53.7
Dubhe	193 49.6	N61 39.5
Elnath	278 09.6	N28 37.0
Eltanin	90 45.3	N51 29.7
Enif	33 44.8	N 9 57.4
Fomalhaut	15 21.3	S29 32.0
Gacrux	171 58.9	S57 12.2
Gienah	175 50.3	S17 37.9
Hadar	148 45.2	S60 27.0
Hamal	327 57.9	N23 32.5
Kaus Aust.	83 41.0	S34 22.4
Kochab	137 21.4	N74 05.5
Markab	13 35.8	N15 17.9
Menkar	314 12.4	N 4 09.3
Menkent	148 05.3	S36 26.9
Miaplacidus	221 39.4	S69 46.9
Mirfak	308 36.7	N49 55.0
Nunki	75 55.6	S26 16.4
Peacock	53 15.7	S56 40.9
Pollux	243 25.0	N27 58.9
Procyon	244 57.4	N 5 10.8
Rasalhague	96 04.6	N12 33.3
Regulus	207 41.4	N11 53.1
Rigel	281 09.7	S 8 11.0
Rigil Kent.	139 49.3	S60 54.1
Sabik	102 10.2	S15 44.5
Schedar	349 37.3	N56 37.8
Shaula	96 19.1	S37 06.8
Sirius	258 31.7	S16 44.3
Spica	158 29.2	S11 14.7
Suhail	222 50.9	S43 29.8
Vega	80 37.6	N38 48.4
Zuben'ubi	137 03.3	S16 06.4

	SHA	Mer. Pass.
	° ′	h m
Venus	125 17.9	14 00
Mars	76 03.0	17 15
Jupiter	172 20.9	10 49
Saturn	108 24.9	15 04

Day	UT d h	SUN GHA ° ′	SUN Dec ° ′	MOON GHA ° ′	v ′	MOON Dec ° ′	d ′	HP ′
SATURDAY	15 00	183 33.4	S 8 35.5	18 07.7	8.1	N 0 17.5	11.8	60.6
	01	198 33.5	36.5	32 34.8	8.1	0 29.3	11.9	60.7
	02	213 33.7	37.4	47 01.9	8.1	0 41.2	11.9	60.7
	03	228 33.8	. . 38.3	61 29.0	8.0	0 53.1	11.9	60.7
	04	243 33.9	39.2	75 56.0	8.0	1 05.0	11.9	60.7
	05	258 34.1	40.1	90 23.0	8.0	1 16.9	11.9	60.8
	06	273 34.2	S 8 41.1	104 50.0	7.9	N 1 28.8	11.9	60.8
	07	288 34.4	42.0	119 16.9	7.9	1 40.7	11.9	60.8
	08	303 34.5	42.9	133 43.8	7.9	1 52.6	11.8	60.8
	09	318 34.6	. . 43.8	148 10.7	7.8	2 04.4	11.9	60.9
	10	333 34.8	44.8	162 37.5	7.8	2 16.3	11.9	60.9
	11	348 34.9	45.7	177 04.3	7.8	2 28.2	11.9	60.9
	12	3 35.0	S 8 46.6	191 31.1	7.7	N 2 40.1	11.8	60.9
	13	18 35.2	47.5	205 57.8	7.7	2 51.9	11.9	60.9
	14	33 35.3	48.4	220 24.5	7.7	3 03.8	11.8	61.0
	15	48 35.4	. . 49.4	234 51.2	7.6	3 15.6	11.8	61.0
	16	63 35.6	50.3	249 17.8	7.6	3 27.4	11.9	61.0
	17	78 35.7	51.2	263 44.4	7.5	3 39.3	11.7	61.0
	18	93 35.9	S 8 52.1	278 10.9	7.6	N 3 51.0	11.8	61.0
	19	108 36.0	53.0	292 37.5	7.4	4 02.8	11.8	61.0
	20	123 36.1	54.0	307 03.9	7.5	4 14.6	11.7	61.1
	21	138 36.3	. . 54.9	321 30.4	7.4	4 26.3	11.7	61.1
	22	153 36.4	55.8	335 56.8	7.3	4 38.0	11.7	61.1
	23	168 36.5	56.7	350 23.1	7.4	4 49.7	11.7	61.1
SUNDAY	16 00	183 36.7	S 8 57.6	4 49.5	7.3	N 5 01.4	11.6	61.1
	01	198 36.8	58.5	19 15.8	7.2	5 13.0	11.6	61.1
	02	213 36.9	8 59.5	33 42.0	7.2	5 24.6	11.6	61.1
	03	228 37.1	9 00.4	48 08.2	7.2	5 36.2	11.5	61.2
	04	243 37.2	01.3	62 34.4	7.2	5 47.7	11.5	61.2
	05	258 37.3	02.2	77 00.6	7.1	5 59.2	11.5	61.2
	06	273 37.5	S 9 03.1	91 26.7	7.0	N 6 10.7	11.4	61.2
	07	288 37.6	04.0	105 52.7	7.0	6 22.1	11.4	61.2
	08	303 37.7	05.0	120 18.7	7.0	6 33.5	11.4	61.2
	09	318 37.8	. . 05.9	134 44.7	7.0	6 44.9	11.3	61.2
	10	333 38.0	06.8	149 10.7	6.9	6 56.2	11.2	61.2
	11	348 38.1	07.7	163 36.6	6.9	7 07.4	11.3	61.2
	12	3 38.2	S 9 08.6	178 02.5	6.8	N 7 18.7	11.1	61.2
	13	18 38.4	09.5	192 28.3	6.8	7 29.8	11.2	61.2
	14	33 38.5	10.5	206 54.1	6.8	7 41.0	11.0	61.2
	15	48 38.6	. . 11.4	221 19.9	6.7	7 52.0	11.1	61.3
	16	63 38.8	12.3	235 45.6	6.7	8 03.1	10.9	61.3
	17	78 38.9	13.2	250 11.3	6.6	8 14.0	11.0	61.3
	18	93 39.0	S 9 14.1	264 36.9	6.6	N 8 25.0	10.8	61.3
	19	108 39.1	15.0	279 02.5	6.6	8 35.8	10.8	61.3
	20	123 39.3	15.9	293 28.1	6.6	8 46.6	10.8	61.3
	21	138 39.4	. . 16.9	307 53.7	6.4	8 57.4	10.7	61.3
	22	153 39.5	17.8	322 19.1	6.5	9 08.1	10.6	61.3
	23	168 39.7	18.7	336 44.6	6.4	9 18.7	10.5	61.3
MONDAY	17 00	183 39.8	S 9 19.6	351 10.0	6.4	N 9 29.2	10.5	61.3
	01	198 39.9	20.5	5 35.4	6.4	9 39.7	10.5	61.3
	02	213 40.0	21.4	20 00.8	6.3	9 50.2	10.3	61.3
	03	228 40.2	. . 22.3	34 26.1	6.3	10 00.5	10.3	61.3
	04	243 40.3	23.2	48 51.4	6.2	10 10.8	10.2	61.3
	05	258 40.4	24.2	63 16.6	6.2	10 21.0	10.2	61.3
	06	273 40.5	S 9 25.1	77 41.8	6.2	N10 31.2	10.1	61.3
	07	288 40.7	26.0	92 07.0	6.1	10 41.3	10.0	61.3
	08	303 40.8	26.9	106 32.1	6.2	10 51.3	9.9	61.3
	09	318 40.9	. . 27.8	120 57.3	6.0	11 01.2	9.8	61.2
	10	333 41.0	28.7	135 22.3	6.1	11 11.0	9.8	61.2
	11	348 41.2	29.6	149 47.4	6.0	11 20.8	9.7	61.2
	12	3 41.3	S 9 30.5	164 12.4	5.9	N11 30.5	9.6	61.2
	13	18 41.4	31.4	178 37.3	6.0	11 40.1	9.5	61.2
	14	33 41.5	32.4	193 02.3	5.9	11 49.6	9.4	61.2
	15	48 41.7	. . 33.3	207 27.2	5.9	11 59.0	9.4	61.2
	16	63 41.8	34.2	221 52.1	5.8	12 08.4	9.2	61.2
	17	78 41.9	35.1	236 16.9	5.8	12 17.6	9.2	61.2
	18	93 42.0	S 9 36.0	250 41.7	5.8	N12 26.8	9.1	61.2
	19	108 42.2	36.9	265 06.5	5.8	12 35.9	9.0	61.2
	20	123 42.3	37.8	279 31.3	5.7	12 44.9	8.9	61.2
	21	138 42.4	. . 38.7	293 56.0	5.7	12 53.8	8.8	61.1
	22	153 42.5	39.6	308 20.7	5.7	13 02.6	8.7	61.1
	23	168 42.6	40.5	322 45.4	5.6	N13 11.3	8.6	61.1
		SD 16.1	*d* 0.9	SD 16.6		16.7		16.7

Lat. °	Twilight Naut. h m	Twilight Civil h m	Sunrise h m	Moonrise 15 h m	Moonrise 16 h m	Moonrise 17 h m	Moonrise 18 h m
N 72	05 01	06 20	07 31	16 42	16 36	16 30	16 22
N 70	05 04	06 15	07 19	16 47	16 48	16 50	16 56
68	05 07	06 11	07 09	16 51	16 57	17 07	17 21
66	05 09	06 08	07 01	16 54	17 05	17 20	17 40
64	05 10	06 05	06 54	16 57	17 12	17 31	17 56
62	05 11	06 03	06 48	16 59	17 18	17 40	18 09
60	05 12	06 00	06 43	17 01	17 23	17 49	18 20
N 58	05 13	05 58	06 38	17 03	17 28	17 56	18 30
56	05 13	05 56	06 34	17 05	17 32	18 02	18 38
54	05 14	05 54	06 30	17 06	17 35	18 08	18 46
52	05 14	05 53	06 27	17 08	17 39	18 13	18 53
50	05 14	05 51	06 24	17 09	17 42	18 18	18 59
45	05 14	05 48	06 17	17 12	17 48	18 28	19 12
N 40	05 13	05 44	06 12	17 14	17 54	18 37	19 23
35	05 12	05 41	06 07	17 16	17 59	18 44	19 33
30	05 11	05 39	06 03	17 18	18 03	18 50	19 41
20	05 07	05 33	05 55	17 21	18 10	19 02	19 56
N 10	05 03	05 27	05 49	17 24	18 17	19 12	20 08
0	04 57	05 21	05 42	17 27	18 23	19 21	20 20
S 10	04 50	05 14	05 36	17 29	18 29	19 31	20 32
20	04 40	05 06	05 29	17 32	18 36	19 41	20 45
30	04 27	04 56	05 21	17 36	18 44	19 52	21 00
35	04 19	04 50	05 16	17 38	18 48	19 59	21 09
40	04 09	04 42	05 10	17 40	18 54	20 07	21 18
45	03 57	04 34	05 04	17 43	19 00	20 16	21 30
S 50	03 41	04 23	04 56	17 46	19 07	20 27	21 44
52	03 33	04 17	04 53	17 47	19 10	20 32	21 51
54	03 25	04 12	04 49	17 49	19 14	20 38	21 58
56	03 15	04 05	04 45	17 51	19 18	20 44	22 06
58	03 03	03 58	04 40	17 53	19 23	20 51	22 15
S 60	02 49	03 49	04 35	17 55	19 28	20 59	22 26

Lat. °	Sunset h m	Twilight Civil h m	Twilight Naut. h m	Moonset 15 h m	Moonset 16 h m	Moonset 17 h m	Moonset 18 h m
N 72	15 58	17 09	18 27	05 13	07 16	09 22	11 34
N 70	16 11	17 14	18 24	05 11	07 06	09 03	11 01
68	16 21	17 18	18 22	05 10	06 59	08 48	10 37
66	16 29	17 21	18 20	05 09	06 52	08 36	10 18
64	16 36	17 24	18 19	05 08	06 47	08 26	10 03
62	16 42	17 27	18 18	05 07	06 42	08 18	09 51
60	16 47	17 29	18 17	05 06	06 38	08 11	09 40
N 58	16 52	17 32	18 17	05 06	06 35	08 04	09 31
56	16 56	17 34	18 17	05 05	06 32	07 59	09 23
54	17 00	17 35	18 16	05 05	06 29	07 53	09 16
52	17 03	17 37	18 16	05 04	06 26	07 49	09 09
50	17 06	17 39	18 16	05 04	06 24	07 45	09 04
45	17 13	17 42	18 16	05 03	06 19	07 36	08 51
N 40	17 19	17 46	18 17	05 02	06 15	07 28	08 41
35	17 23	17 49	18 18	05 01	06 11	07 22	08 32
30	17 28	17 52	18 20	05 01	06 08	07 16	08 25
20	17 35	17 58	18 23	05 00	06 03	07 07	08 11
N 10	17 42	18 03	18 28	04 59	05 58	06 58	08 00
0	17 49	18 10	18 34	04 58	05 53	06 50	07 49
S 10	17 55	18 17	18 42	04 57	05 49	06 43	07 38
20	18 03	18 25	18 51	04 56	05 44	06 34	07 27
30	18 11	18 35	19 04	04 55	05 38	06 25	07 14
35	18 16	18 42	19 13	04 54	05 35	06 19	07 06
40	18 21	18 49	19 23	04 53	05 32	06 13	06 57
45	18 28	18 58	19 35	04 52	05 28	06 06	06 47
S 50	18 36	19 10	19 51	04 51	05 23	05 57	06 35
52	18 39	19 15	19 59	04 51	05 20	05 53	06 30
54	18 43	19 21	20 08	04 50	05 18	05 48	06 24
56	18 48	19 28	20 18	04 49	05 15	05 44	06 17
58	18 52	19 35	20 30	04 49	05 12	05 38	06 09
S 60	18 58	19 44	20 44	04 48	05 09	05 32	06 00

Day d	SUN Eqn. of Time 00^h m s	SUN Eqn. of Time 12^h m s	SUN Mer. Pass. h m	MOON Mer. Pass. Upper h m	MOON Mer. Pass. Lower h m	MOON Age d	%	Phase
15	14 13	14 20	11 46	23 40	11 12	14	99	○
16	14 26	14 33	11 45	24 37	12 08	15	100	
17	14 39	14 45	11 45	00 37	13 06	16	97	

	UT	ARIES	VENUS −3·9		MARS +0·3		JUPITER −1·7		SATURN +0·5		STARS		
	d h	GHA	GHA	Dec	GHA	Dec	GHA	Dec	GHA	Dec	Name	SHA	Dec
	18 00	26 54.8	149 42.5	S21 07.5	101 26.1	S24 50.8	198 52.2	S 2 16.1	135 08.2	S20 58.5	Acamar	315 16.3	S40 14.3
	01	41 57.2	164 41.8	08.3	116 26.6	50.5	213 54.2	16.3	150 10.4	58.5	Achernar	335 24.6	S57 09.2
	02	56 59.7	179 41.2	09.0	131 27.2	50.3	228 56.2	16.5	165 12.6	58.6	Acrux	173 07.3	S63 11.3
	03	72 02.1	194 40.5	. . 09.8	146 27.7	. . 50.1	243 58.2	. . 16.7	180 14.9	. . 58.6	Adhara	255 10.7	S28 59.6
	04	87 04.6	209 39.8	10.6	161 28.3	49.9	259 00.1	16.9	195 17.1	58.6	Aldebaran	290 46.6	N16 32.4
	05	102 07.1	224 39.1	11.4	176 28.8	49.6	274 02.1	17.1	210 19.3	58.7			
	06	117 09.5	239 38.5	S21 12.1	191 29.4	S24 49.4	289 04.1	S 2 17.3	225 21.5	S20 58.7	Alioth	166 19.4	N55 52.2
	07	132 12.0	254 37.8	12.9	206 29.9	49.2	304 06.1	17.5	240 23.7	58.8	Alkaid	152 57.7	N49 14.0
TUESDAY	08	147 14.5	269 37.1	13.7	221 30.5	49.0	319 08.0	17.7	255 26.0	58.8	Al Na'ir	27 40.8	S46 52.8
	09	162 16.9	284 36.4	. . 14.4	236 31.0	. . 48.7	334 10.0	. . 17.9	270 28.2	. . 58.8	Alnilam	275 43.9	S 1 11.6
	10	177 19.4	299 35.7	15.2	251 31.6	48.5	349 12.0	18.1	285 30.4	58.9	Alphard	217 54.0	S 8 43.8
	11	192 21.9	314 35.1	15.9	266 32.1	48.3	4 14.0	18.3	300 32.6	58.9			
	12	207 24.3	329 34.4	S21 16.7	281 32.7	S24 48.0	19 16.0	S 2 18.5	315 34.8	S20 58.9	Alphecca	126 09.5	N26 39.8
	13	222 26.8	344 33.7	17.5	296 33.2	47.8	34 17.9	18.7	330 37.1	59.0	Alpheratz	357 40.8	N29 11.1
	14	237 29.2	359 33.0	18.2	311 33.8	47.6	49 19.9	18.9	345 39.3	59.0	Altair	62 06.1	N 8 55.1
	15	252 31.7	14 32.3	. . 19.0	326 34.3	. . 47.4	64 21.9	. . 19.1	0 41.5	. . 59.0	Ankaa	353 13.2	S42 12.9
	16	267 34.2	29 31.6	19.7	341 34.9	47.1	79 23.9	19.3	15 43.7	59.1	Antares	112 23.8	S26 27.9
	17	282 36.6	44 31.0	20.5	356 35.4	46.9	94 25.8	19.6	30 45.9	59.1			
	18	297 39.1	59 30.3	S21 21.3	11 36.0	S24 46.7	109 27.8	S 2 19.8	45 48.2	S20 59.1	Arcturus	145 54.1	N19 06.0
	19	312 41.6	74 29.6	22.0	26 36.5	46.4	124 29.8	20.0	60 50.4	59.2	Atria	107 23.9	S69 03.4
	20	327 44.0	89 28.9	22.8	41 37.1	46.2	139 31.8	20.2	75 52.6	59.2	Avior	234 17.1	S59 33.6
	21	342 46.5	104 28.2	. . 23.5	56 37.6	. . 46.0	154 33.7	. . 20.4	90 54.8	. . 59.2	Bellatrix	278 29.4	N 6 21.8
	22	357 49.0	119 27.5	24.3	71 38.2	45.7	169 35.7	20.6	105 57.1	59.3	Betelgeuse	270 58.7	N 7 24.5
	23	12 51.4	134 26.8	25.0	86 38.7	45.5	184 37.7	20.8	120 59.3	59.3			
	19 00	27 53.9	149 26.2	S21 25.8	101 39.3	S24 45.3	199 39.7	S 2 21.0	136 01.5	S20 59.3	Canopus	263 54.9	S52 42.2
	01	42 56.4	164 25.5	26.5	116 39.8	45.0	214 41.7	21.2	151 03.7	59.4	Capella	280 30.8	N46 00.6
	02	57 58.8	179 24.8	27.3	131 40.4	44.8	229 43.6	21.4	166 05.9	59.4	Deneb	49 29.8	N45 20.8
	03	73 01.3	194 24.1	. . 28.0	146 40.9	. . 44.6	244 45.6	. . 21.6	181 08.1	. . 59.4	Denebola	182 31.7	N14 28.8
	04	88 03.7	209 23.4	28.8	161 41.5	44.3	259 47.6	21.8	196 10.4	59.5	Diphda	348 53.4	S17 53.7
	05	103 06.2	224 22.7	29.5	176 42.0	44.1	274 49.6	22.0	211 12.6	59.5			
	06	118 08.7	239 22.0	S21 30.3	191 42.6	S24 43.9	289 51.5	S 2 22.2	226 14.8	S20 59.6	Dubhe	193 49.6	N61 39.5
	07	133 11.1	254 21.3	31.0	206 43.1	43.6	304 53.5	22.4	241 17.0	59.6	Elnath	278 09.6	N28 37.0
	08	148 13.6	269 20.6	31.7	221 43.7	43.4	319 55.5	22.6	256 19.2	59.6	Eltanin	90 45.4	N51 29.7
WEDNESDAY	09	163 16.1	284 20.0	. . 32.5	236 44.2	. . 43.2	334 57.5	. . 22.8	271 21.5	. . 59.7	Enif	33 44.8	N 9 57.4
	10	178 18.5	299 19.3	33.2	251 44.7	42.9	349 59.5	23.0	286 23.7	59.7	Fomalhaut	15 21.3	S29 32.0
	11	193 21.0	314 18.6	34.0	266 45.3	42.7	5 01.4	23.2	301 25.9	59.7			
	12	208 23.5	329 17.9	S21 34.7	281 45.8	S24 42.4	20 03.4	S 2 23.5	316 28.1	S20 59.8	Gacrux	171 58.8	S57 12.2
	13	223 25.9	344 17.2	35.4	296 46.4	42.2	35 05.4	23.7	331 30.3	59.8	Gienah	175 50.3	S17 37.9
	14	238 28.4	359 16.5	36.2	311 46.9	42.0	50 07.4	23.9	346 32.6	59.8	Hadar	148 45.2	S60 27.0
	15	253 30.9	14 15.8	. . 36.9	326 47.5	. . 41.7	65 09.3	. . 24.1	1 34.8	. . 59.9	Hamal	327 57.9	N23 32.5
	16	268 33.3	29 15.1	37.6	341 48.0	41.5	80 11.3	24.3	16 37.0	59.9	Kaus Aust.	83 41.0	S34 22.4
	17	283 35.8	44 14.4	38.4	356 48.6	41.3	95 13.3	24.5	31 39.2	20 59.9			
	18	298 38.2	59 13.7	S21 39.1	11 49.1	S24 41.0	110 15.3	S 2 24.7	46 41.4	S21 00.0	Kochab	137 21.4	N74 05.4
	19	313 40.7	74 13.0	39.8	26 49.7	40.8	125 17.3	24.9	61 43.6	00.0	Markab	13 35.8	N15 17.9
	20	328 43.2	89 12.3	40.6	41 50.2	40.5	140 19.2	25.1	76 45.9	00.0	Menkar	314 12.4	N 4 09.3
	21	343 45.6	104 11.6	. . 41.3	56 50.8	. . 40.3	155 21.2	. . 25.3	91 48.1	. . 00.1	Menkent	148 05.3	S36 26.9
	22	358 48.1	119 10.9	42.0	71 51.3	40.0	170 23.2	25.5	106 50.3	00.1	Miaplacidus	221 39.4	S69 46.9
	23	13 50.6	134 10.2	42.7	86 51.9	39.8	185 25.2	25.7	121 52.5	00.1			
	20 00	28 53.0	149 09.5	S21 43.5	101 52.4	S24 39.6	200 27.2	S 2 25.9	136 54.7	S21 00.2	Mirfak	308 36.6	N49 55.0
	01	43 55.5	164 08.8	44.2	116 53.0	39.3	215 29.1	26.1	151 56.9	00.2	Nunki	75 55.7	S26 16.4
	02	58 58.0	179 08.1	44.9	131 53.5	39.1	230 31.1	26.3	166 59.2	00.3	Peacock	53 15.7	S56 40.9
	03	74 00.4	194 07.4	. . 45.6	146 54.1	. . 38.8	245 33.1	. . 26.5	182 01.4	. . 00.3	Pollux	243 25.0	N27 58.9
	04	89 02.9	209 06.7	46.4	161 54.6	38.6	260 35.1	26.7	197 03.6	00.3	Procyon	244 57.4	N 5 10.8
	05	104 05.4	224 06.0	47.1	176 55.1	38.3	275 37.0	26.9	212 05.8	00.4			
	06	119 07.8	239 05.3	S21 47.8	191 55.7	S24 38.1	290 39.0	S 2 27.1	227 08.0	S21 00.4	Rasalhague	96 04.6	N12 33.3
	07	134 10.3	254 04.6	48.5	206 56.2	37.8	305 41.0	27.3	242 10.2	00.4	Regulus	207 41.3	N11 53.1
	08	149 12.7	269 03.9	49.3	221 56.8	37.6	320 43.0	27.6	257 12.5	00.5	Rigel	281 09.7	S 8 11.0
THURSDAY	09	164 15.2	284 03.2	. . 50.0	236 57.3	. . 37.4	335 45.0	. . 27.8	272 14.7	. . 00.5	Rigil Kent.	139 49.3	S60 54.0
	10	179 17.7	299 02.5	50.7	251 57.9	37.1	350 46.9	28.0	287 16.9	00.5	Sabik	102 10.2	S15 44.5
	11	194 20.1	314 01.8	51.4	266 58.4	36.9	5 48.9	28.2	302 19.1	00.6			
	12	209 22.6	329 01.1	S21 52.1	281 59.0	S24 36.6	20 50.9	S 2 28.4	317 21.3	S21 00.6	Schedar	349 37.3	N56 37.8
	13	224 25.1	344 00.4	52.8	296 59.5	36.4	35 52.9	28.6	332 23.5	00.6	Shaula	96 19.1	S37 06.8
	14	239 27.5	358 59.7	53.5	312 00.1	36.1	50 54.9	28.8	347 25.8	00.7	Sirius	258 31.6	S16 44.3
	15	254 30.0	13 59.0	. . 54.3	327 00.6	. . 35.9	65 56.8	. . 29.0	2 28.0	. . 00.7	Spica	158 29.2	S11 14.7
	16	269 32.5	28 58.3	55.0	342 01.2	35.6	80 58.8	29.2	17 30.2	00.7	Suhail	222 50.9	S43 29.8
	17	284 34.9	43 57.6	55.7	357 01.7	35.4	96 00.8	29.4	32 32.4	00.8			
	18	299 37.4	58 56.9	S21 56.4	12 02.2	S24 35.1	111 02.8	S 2 29.6	47 34.6	S21 00.8	Vega	80 37.6	N38 48.4
	19	314 39.8	73 56.2	57.1	27 02.8	34.9	126 04.8	29.8	62 36.8	00.8	Zuben'ubi	137 03.3	S16 06.4
	20	329 42.3	88 55.4	57.8	42 03.3	34.6	141 06.7	30.0	77 39.0	00.9			
	21	344 44.8	103 54.7	. . 58.5	57 03.9	. . 34.4	156 08.7	. . 30.2	92 41.3	. . 00.9			
	22	359 47.2	118 54.0	59.2	72 04.4	34.1	171 10.7	30.4	107 43.5	01.0			
	23	14 49.7	133 53.3	59.9	87 05.0	33.9	186 12.7	30.6	122 45.7	01.0			
	Mer. Pass.	h m 22 04.8	v −0.7	d 0.7	v 0.5	d 0.2	v 2.0	d 0.2	v 2.2	d 0.0			

	SHA	Mer. Pass.
	° ′	h m
Venus	121 32.3	14 03
Mars	73 45.4	17 13
Jupiter	171 45.8	10 40
Saturn	108 07.6	14 54

UT		SUN GHA	SUN Dec	MOON GHA	v	MOON Dec	d	HP
d	h	° ′	° ′	° ′	′	° ′	′	′
18	00	183 42.8	S 9 41.4	337 10.0	5.7	N13 19.9	8.5	61.1
	01	198 42.9	42.3	351 34.7	5.6	13 28.4	8.4	61.1
	02	213 43.0	43.2	5 59.3	5.5	13 36.8	8.4	61.1
	03	228 43.1	. . 44.2	20 23.8	5.6	13 45.2	8.2	61.1
	04	243 43.3	45.1	34 48.4	5.5	13 53.4	8.1	61.1
	05	258 43.4	46.0	49 12.9	5.5	14 01.5	8.0	61.0
	06	273 43.5	S 9 46.9	63 37.4	5.5	N14 09.5	7.9	61.0
	07	288 43.6	47.8	78 01.9	5.5	14 17.4	7.8	61.0
T	08	303 43.7	48.7	92 26.4	5.4	14 25.2	7.7	61.0
U	09	318 43.8	. . 49.6	106 50.8	5.4	14 32.9	7.6	61.0
E	10	333 44.0	50.5	121 15.2	5.4	14 40.5	7.5	61.0
	11	348 44.1	51.4	135 39.6	5.4	14 48.0	7.4	60.9
S	12	3 44.2	S 9 52.3	150 04.0	5.4	N14 55.4	7.2	60.9
D	13	18 44.3	53.2	164 28.4	5.3	15 02.6	7.2	60.9
A	14	33 44.4	54.1	178 52.7	5.4	15 09.8	7.0	60.9
Y	15	48 44.6	. . 55.0	193 17.1	5.3	15 16.8	7.0	60.9
	16	63 44.7	55.9	207 41.4	5.3	15 23.8	6.8	60.8
	17	78 44.8	56.8	222 05.7	5.3	15 30.6	6.7	60.8
	18	93 44.9	S 9 57.7	236 30.0	5.3	N15 37.3	6.6	60.8
	19	108 45.0	58.6	250 54.3	5.2	15 43.9	6.4	60.8
	20	123 45.1	9 59.5	265 18.5	5.3	15 50.3	6.4	60.7
	21	138 45.3	10 00.4	279 42.8	5.3	15 56.7	6.2	60.7
	22	153 45.4	01.3	294 07.1	5.2	16 02.9	6.1	60.7
	23	168 45.5	02.2	308 31.3	5.3	16 09.0	6.0	60.7
19	00	183 45.6	S10 03.1	322 55.6	5.2	N16 15.0	5.9	60.7
	01	198 45.7	04.0	337 19.8	5.2	16 20.9	5.8	60.6
	02	213 45.8	04.9	351 44.0	5.3	16 26.7	5.6	60.6
	03	228 45.9	. . 05.8	6 08.3	5.2	16 32.3	5.6	60.6
	04	243 46.1	06.7	20 32.5	5.2	16 37.9	5.4	60.6
	05	258 46.2	07.6	34 56.7	5.3	16 43.3	5.2	60.5
	06	273 46.3	S10 08.5	49 21.0	5.2	N16 48.5	5.2	60.5
W	07	288 46.4	09.4	63 45.2	5.2	16 53.7	5.0	60.5
E	08	303 46.5	10.3	78 09.4	5.2	16 58.7	4.9	60.4
D	09	318 46.6	. . 11.2	92 33.6	5.3	17 03.6	4.8	60.4
N	10	333 46.7	12.1	106 57.9	5.2	17 08.4	4.7	60.4
E	11	348 46.8	13.0	121 22.1	5.3	17 13.1	4.5	60.4
S	12	3 46.9	S10 13.9	135 46.4	5.2	N17 17.6	4.4	60.3
	13	18 47.1	14.8	150 10.6	5.3	17 22.0	4.3	60.3
D	14	33 47.2	15.7	164 34.9	5.3	17 26.3	4.2	60.3
A	15	48 47.3	. . 16.6	178 59.2	5.3	17 30.5	4.0	60.3
Y	16	63 47.4	17.5	193 23.5	5.3	17 34.5	3.9	60.2
	17	78 47.5	18.4	207 47.8	5.3	17 38.4	3.8	60.2
	18	93 47.6	S10 19.3	222 12.1	5.3	N17 42.2	3.7	60.2
	19	108 47.7	20.2	236 36.4	5.3	17 45.9	3.5	60.1
	20	123 47.8	21.1	251 00.7	5.4	17 49.4	3.4	60.1
	21	138 47.9	. . 22.0	265 25.1	5.4	17 52.8	3.3	60.1
	22	153 48.0	22.9	279 49.5	5.4	17 56.1	3.1	60.0
	23	168 48.2	23.8	294 13.9	5.4	17 59.2	3.1	60.0
20	00	183 48.3	S10 24.7	308 38.3	5.4	N18 02.3	2.8	60.0
	01	198 48.4	25.6	323 02.7	5.5	18 05.1	2.8	59.9
	02	213 48.5	26.5	337 27.2	5.5	18 07.9	2.7	59.9
	03	228 48.6	. . 27.4	351 51.7	5.5	18 10.6	2.5	59.9
	04	243 48.7	28.3	6 16.2	5.5	18 13.1	2.4	59.9
	05	258 48.8	29.2	20 40.7	5.6	18 15.5	2.2	59.8
	06	273 48.9	S10 30.0	35 05.3	5.6	N18 17.7	2.2	59.8
T	07	288 49.0	30.9	49 29.9	5.6	18 19.9	2.0	59.8
H	08	303 49.1	31.8	63 54.5	5.6	18 21.9	1.9	59.7
	09	318 49.2	. . 32.7	78 19.1	5.7	18 23.8	1.7	59.7
U	10	333 49.3	33.6	92 43.8	5.7	18 25.5	1.6	59.7
R	11	348 49.4	34.5	107 08.5	5.8	18 27.1	1.5	59.6
S	12	3 49.5	S10 35.4	121 33.3	5.7	N18 28.6	1.4	59.6
D	13	18 49.6	36.3	135 58.0	5.9	18 30.0	1.3	59.6
A	14	33 49.7	37.2	150 22.9	5.8	18 31.3	1.1	59.5
Y	15	48 49.8	. . 38.1	164 47.7	5.9	18 32.4	1.0	59.5
	16	63 49.9	39.0	179 12.6	5.9	18 33.4	0.9	59.4
	17	78 50.0	39.9	193 37.5	6.0	18 34.3	0.7	59.4
	18	93 50.1	S10 40.8	208 02.5	6.0	N18 35.0	0.7	59.4
	19	108 50.3	41.6	222 27.5	6.1	18 35.7	0.5	59.3
	20	123 50.4	42.5	236 52.6	6.1	18 36.2	0.3	59.3
	21	138 50.5	. . 43.4	251 17.7	6.1	18 36.5	0.3	59.3
	22	153 50.6	44.3	265 42.8	6.2	18 36.8	0.1	59.2
	23	168 50.7	45.2	280 08.0	6.2	N18 36.9	0.0	59.2
		SD 16.1	d 0.9	SD 16.6		16.4		16.2

Lat.	Twilight Naut.	Twilight Civil	Sunrise	Moonrise 18	Moonrise 19	Moonrise 20	Moonrise 21
°	h m	h m	h m	h m	h m	h m	h m
N 72	05 14	06 33	07 46	16 22	16 07	▭	▭
N 70	05 16	06 27	07 32	16 56	17 09	17 42	18 49
68	05 17	06 22	07 20	17 21	17 45	18 27	19 31
66	05 18	06 17	07 11	17 40	18 11	18 56	19 59
64	05 18	06 14	07 03	17 56	18 31	19 18	20 21
62	05 19	06 10	06 56	18 09	18 47	19 36	20 38
60	05 19	06 07	06 50	18 20	19 00	19 51	20 52
N 58	05 19	06 05	06 45	18 30	19 12	20 04	21 04
56	05 19	06 02	06 40	18 38	19 22	20 15	21 15
54	05 19	06 00	06 36	18 46	19 31	20 24	21 24
52	05 19	05 58	06 32	18 53	19 39	20 33	21 33
50	05 18	05 56	06 29	18 59	19 47	20 41	21 40
45	05 17	05 51	06 21	19 12	20 02	20 57	21 56
N 40	05 16	05 48	06 15	19 23	20 15	21 10	22 09
35	05 14	05 44	06 10	19 33	20 26	21 22	22 20
30	05 13	05 40	06 05	19 41	20 35	21 32	22 30
20	05 08	05 34	05 56	19 56	20 52	21 49	22 47
N 10	05 03	05 27	05 49	20 08	21 06	22 04	23 02
0	04 56	05 21	05 42	20 20	21 20	22 18	23 15
S 10	04 48	05 13	05 34	20 32	21 33	22 33	23 29
20	04 38	05 04	05 26	20 45	21 48	22 48	23 44
30	04 24	04 53	05 17	21 00	22 05	23 05	24 00
35	04 15	04 46	05 12	21 09	22 15	23 15	24 10
40	04 04	04 38	05 06	21 18	22 26	23 27	24 21
45	03 51	04 28	04 59	21 30	22 39	23 41	24 34
S 50	03 34	04 16	04 50	21 44	22 55	23 57	24 50
52	03 26	04 10	04 46	21 51	23 03	24 05	00 05
54	03 16	04 04	04 42	21 58	23 11	24 14	00 14
56	03 05	03 57	04 37	22 06	23 20	24 24	00 24
58	02 52	03 49	04 32	22 15	23 31	24 35	00 35
S 60	02 37	03 39	04 26	22 26	23 44	24 48	00 48

Lat.	Sunset	Twilight Civil	Twilight Naut.	Moonset 18	Moonset 19	Moonset 20	Moonset 21
°	h m	h m	h m	h m	h m	h m	h m
N 72	15 42	16 55	18 13	11 34	13 54	▭	▭
N 70	15 56	17 01	18 12	11 01	12 52	14 23	15 16
68	16 08	17 06	18 11	10 37	12 17	13 38	14 34
66	16 18	17 11	18 10	10 18	11 52	13 09	14 05
64	16 26	17 15	18 10	10 03	11 32	12 47	13 44
62	16 33	17 18	18 10	09 51	11 16	12 29	13 26
60	16 39	17 21	18 09	09 40	11 03	12 14	13 12
N 58	16 44	17 24	18 09	09 31	10 52	12 02	12 59
56	16 49	17 27	18 10	09 23	10 42	11 51	12 48
54	16 53	17 29	18 10	09 16	10 33	11 41	12 39
52	16 57	17 31	18 10	09 09	10 25	11 33	12 31
50	17 00	17 33	18 10	09 04	10 18	11 25	12 23
45	17 08	17 38	18 12	08 51	10 03	11 09	12 07
N 40	17 14	17 42	18 13	08 41	09 51	10 55	11 53
35	17 20	17 45	18 15	08 32	09 40	10 44	11 42
30	17 25	17 49	18 17	08 25	09 31	10 34	11 32
20	17 33	17 56	18 21	08 11	09 15	10 17	11 15
N 10	17 41	18 02	18 27	08 00	09 02	10 02	11 00
0	17 48	18 09	18 34	07 49	08 49	09 48	10 46
S 10	17 56	18 17	18 42	07 38	08 36	09 34	10 32
20	18 04	18 26	18 53	07 27	08 22	09 19	10 17
30	18 13	18 38	19 07	07 14	08 06	09 02	09 59
35	18 18	18 44	19 16	07 06	07 57	08 52	09 49
40	18 24	18 53	19 26	06 57	07 47	08 40	09 38
45	18 32	19 03	19 40	06 47	07 34	08 27	09 24
S 50	18 40	19 15	19 57	06 35	07 20	08 10	09 08
52	18 44	19 21	20 06	06 30	07 13	08 03	09 00
54	18 49	19 27	20 15	06 24	07 05	07 54	08 51
56	18 54	19 35	20 27	06 17	06 56	07 45	08 41
58	18 59	19 43	20 40	06 09	06 47	07 34	08 30
S 60	19 06	19 53	20 56	06 00	06 36	07 21	08 17

Day	SUN Eqn. of Time 00^h	SUN Eqn. of Time 12^h	SUN Mer. Pass.	MOON Mer. Pass. Upper	MOON Mer. Pass. Lower	MOON Age	MOON Phase
d	m s	m s	h m	h m	h m	d %	
18	14 51	14 57	11 45	01 35	14 05	17 92	
19	15 02	15 08	11 45	02 34	15 04	18 84	
20	15 13	15 18	11 45	03 34	16 03	19 75	

2016 OCTOBER 21, 22, 23 (FRI., SAT., SUN.)

UT d h	ARIES GHA ° ′	VENUS −4·0 GHA ° ′	VENUS Dec ° ′	MARS +0·3 GHA ° ′	MARS Dec ° ′	JUPITER −1·7 GHA ° ′	JUPITER Dec ° ′	SATURN +0·5 GHA ° ′	SATURN Dec ° ′
21 00 (FRIDAY)	29 52.2	148 52.6	S22 00.6	102 05.5	S24 33.6	201 14.7	S 2 30.8	137 47.9	S21 01.0
01	44 54.6	163 51.9	01.3	117 06.1	33.4	216 16.6	31.0	152 50.1	01.1
02	59 57.1	178 51.2	02.0	132 06.6	33.1	231 18.6	31.2	167 52.3	01.1
03	74 59.6	193 50.5	. . 02.7	147 07.2	. . 32.8	246 20.6	. . 31.4	182 54.5	. . 01.1
04	90 02.0	208 49.8	03.4	162 07.7	32.6	261 22.6	31.6	197 56.8	01.2
05	105 04.5	223 49.0	04.1	177 08.2	32.3	276 24.5	31.8	212 59.0	01.2
06	120 07.0	238 48.3	S22 04.8	192 08.8	S24 32.1	291 26.5	S 2 32.0	228 01.2	S21 01.2
07	135 09.4	253 47.6	05.5	207 09.3	31.8	306 28.5	32.2	243 03.4	01.3
08	150 11.9	268 46.9	06.2	222 09.9	31.6	321 30.5	32.5	258 05.6	01.3
09	165 14.3	283 46.2	. . 06.9	237 10.4	. . 31.3	336 32.5	. . 32.7	273 07.8	. . 01.3
10	180 16.8	298 45.5	07.6	252 11.0	31.1	351 34.4	32.9	288 10.0	01.4
11	195 19.3	313 44.8	08.3	267 11.5	30.8	6 36.4	33.1	303 12.3	01.4
12	210 21.7	328 44.0	S22 09.0	282 12.1	S24 30.5	21 38.4	S 2 33.3	318 14.5	S21 01.4
13	225 24.2	343 43.3	09.6	297 12.6	30.3	36 40.4	33.5	333 16.7	01.5
14	240 26.7	358 42.6	10.3	312 13.1	30.0	51 42.4	33.7	348 18.9	01.5
15	255 29.1	13 41.9	. . 11.0	327 13.7	. . 29.8	66 44.3	. . 33.9	3 21.1	. . 01.5
16	270 31.6	28 41.2	11.7	342 14.2	29.5	81 46.3	34.1	18 23.3	01.6
17	285 34.1	43 40.5	12.4	357 14.8	29.3	96 48.3	34.3	33 25.5	01.6
18	300 36.5	58 39.7	S22 13.1	12 15.3	S24 29.0	111 50.3	S 2 34.5	48 27.8	S21 01.7
19	315 39.0	73 39.0	13.8	27 15.9	28.7	126 52.3	34.7	63 30.0	01.7
20	330 41.5	88 38.3	14.4	42 16.4	28.5	141 54.2	34.9	78 32.2	01.7
21	345 43.9	103 37.6	. . 15.1	57 17.0	. . 28.2	156 56.2	. . 35.1	93 34.4	. . 01.8
22	0 46.4	118 36.9	15.8	72 17.5	27.9	171 58.2	35.3	108 36.6	01.8
23	15 48.8	133 36.1	16.5	87 18.0	27.7	187 00.2	35.5	123 38.8	01.8
22 00 (SATURDAY)	30 51.3	148 35.4	S22 17.1	102 18.6	S24 27.4	202 02.2	S 2 35.7	138 41.0	S21 01.9
01	45 53.8	163 34.7	17.8	117 19.1	27.2	217 04.2	35.9	153 43.2	01.9
02	60 56.2	178 34.0	18.5	132 19.7	26.9	232 06.1	36.1	168 45.4	01.9
03	75 58.7	193 33.3	. . 19.2	147 20.2	. . 26.6	247 08.1	. . 36.3	183 47.7	. . 02.0
04	91 01.2	208 32.5	19.8	162 20.8	26.4	262 10.1	36.5	198 49.9	02.0
05	106 03.6	223 31.8	20.5	177 21.3	26.1	277 12.1	36.7	213 52.1	02.0
06	121 06.1	238 31.1	S22 21.2	192 21.8	S24 25.8	292 14.1	S 2 36.9	228 54.3	S21 02.1
07	136 08.6	253 30.4	21.9	207 22.4	25.6	307 16.0	37.1	243 56.5	02.1
08	151 11.0	268 29.6	22.5	222 22.9	25.3	322 18.0	37.3	258 58.7	02.1
09	166 13.5	283 28.9	. . 23.2	237 23.5	. . 25.0	337 20.0	. . 37.5	274 00.9	. . 02.2
10	181 16.0	298 28.2	23.9	252 24.0	24.8	352 22.0	37.7	289 03.1	02.2
11	196 18.4	313 27.5	24.5	267 24.6	24.5	7 24.0	37.9	304 05.3	02.3
12	211 20.9	328 26.7	S22 25.2	282 25.1	S24 24.2	22 25.9	S 2 38.2	319 07.6	S21 02.3
13	226 23.3	343 26.0	25.9	297 25.6	24.0	37 27.9	38.4	334 09.8	02.3
14	241 25.8	358 25.3	26.5	312 26.2	23.7	52 29.9	38.6	349 12.0	02.4
15	256 28.3	13 24.5	. . 27.2	327 26.7	. . 23.4	67 31.9	. . 38.8	4 14.2	. . 02.4
16	271 30.7	28 23.8	27.8	342 27.3	23.2	82 33.9	39.0	19 16.4	02.4
17	286 33.2	43 23.1	28.5	357 27.8	22.9	97 35.8	39.2	34 18.6	02.5
18	301 35.7	58 22.4	S22 29.2	12 28.4	S24 22.6	112 37.8	S 2 39.4	49 20.8	S21 02.5
19	316 38.1	73 21.6	29.8	27 28.9	22.4	127 39.8	39.6	64 23.0	02.5
20	331 40.6	88 20.9	30.5	42 29.4	22.1	142 41.8	39.8	79 25.2	02.6
21	346 43.1	103 20.2	. . 31.1	57 30.0	. . 21.8	157 43.8	. . 40.0	94 27.5	. . 02.6
22	1 45.5	118 19.4	31.8	72 30.5	21.6	172 45.8	40.2	109 29.7	02.6
23	16 48.0	133 18.7	32.4	87 31.1	21.3	187 47.7	40.4	124 31.9	02.7
23 00 (SUNDAY)	31 50.4	148 18.0	S22 33.1	102 31.6	S24 21.0	202 49.7	S 2 40.6	139 34.1	S21 02.7
01	46 52.9	163 17.2	33.7	117 32.1	20.7	217 51.7	40.8	154 36.3	02.7
02	61 55.4	178 16.5	34.4	132 32.7	20.5	232 53.7	41.0	169 38.5	02.8
03	76 57.8	193 15.8	. . 35.0	147 33.2	. . 20.2	247 55.7	. . 41.2	184 40.7	. . 02.8
04	92 00.3	208 15.0	35.7	162 33.8	19.9	262 57.6	41.4	199 42.9	02.8
05	107 02.8	223 14.3	36.3	177 34.3	19.6	277 59.6	41.6	214 45.1	02.9
06	122 05.2	238 13.6	S22 37.0	192 34.9	S24 19.4	293 01.6	S 2 41.8	229 47.3	S21 02.9
07	137 07.7	253 12.8	37.6	207 35.4	19.1	308 03.6	42.0	244 49.5	03.0
08	152 10.2	268 12.1	38.3	222 35.9	18.8	323 05.6	42.2	259 51.8	03.0
09	167 12.6	283 11.4	. . 38.9	237 36.5	. . 18.5	338 07.6	. . 42.4	274 54.0	. . 03.0
10	182 15.1	298 10.6	39.6	252 37.0	18.3	353 09.5	42.6	289 56.2	03.1
11	197 17.6	313 09.9	40.2	267 37.6	18.0	8 11.5	42.8	304 58.4	03.1
12	212 20.0	328 09.1	S22 40.8	282 38.1	S24 17.7	23 13.5	S 2 43.0	320 00.6	S21 03.1
13	227 22.5	343 08.4	41.5	297 38.7	17.4	38 15.5	43.2	335 02.8	03.2
14	242 24.9	358 07.7	42.1	312 39.2	17.2	53 17.5	43.4	350 05.0	03.2
15	257 27.4	13 06.9	. . 42.8	327 39.7	. . 16.9	68 19.4	. . 43.6	5 07.2	. . 03.2
16	272 29.9	28 06.2	43.4	342 40.3	16.6	83 21.4	43.8	20 09.4	03.3
17	287 32.3	43 05.5	44.0	357 40.8	16.3	98 23.4	44.0	35 11.6	03.3
18	302 34.8	58 04.7	S22 44.7	12 41.4	S24 16.0	113 25.4	S 2 44.2	50 13.8	S21 03.3
19	317 37.3	73 04.0	45.3	27 41.9	15.8	128 27.4	44.4	65 16.0	03.4
20	332 39.7	88 03.2	45.9	42 42.4	15.5	143 29.4	44.6	80 18.3	03.4
21	347 42.2	103 02.5	. . 46.5	57 43.0	. . 15.2	158 31.3	. . 44.8	95 20.5	. . 03.4
22	2 44.7	118 01.7	47.2	72 43.5	14.9	173 33.3	45.0	110 22.7	03.5
23	17 47.1	133 01.0	47.8	87 44.1	14.6	188 35.3	45.2	125 24.9	03.5
Mer. Pass. (h m)	21 53.0	*v* −0.7	*d* 0.7	*v* 0.5	*d* 0.3	*v* 2.0	*d* 0.2	*v* 2.2	*d* 0.0

STARS

Name	SHA ° ′	Dec ° ′
Acamar	315 16.3	S40 14.3
Achernar	335 24.6	S57 09.2
Acrux	173 07.3	S63 11.3
Adhara	255 10.6	S28 59.6
Aldebaran	290 46.5	N16 32.4
Alioth	166 19.4	N55 52.2
Alkaid	152 57.7	N49 13.9
Al Na'ir	27 40.8	S46 52.8
Alnilam	275 43.9	S 1 11.6
Alphard	217 54.0	S 8 43.8
Alphecca	126 09.5	N26 39.8
Alpheratz	357 40.8	N29 11.1
Altair	62 06.1	N 8 55.1
Ankaa	353 13.2	S42 13.0
Antares	112 23.8	S26 27.9
Arcturus	145 54.1	N19 06.0
Atria	107 23.9	S69 03.4
Avior	234 17.1	S59 33.6
Bellatrix	278 29.4	N 6 21.8
Betelgeuse	270 58.7	N 7 24.5
Canopus	263 54.9	S52 42.2
Capella	280 30.8	N46 00.6
Deneb	49 29.8	N45 20.8
Denebola	182 31.7	N14 28.8
Diphda	348 53.4	S17 53.7
Dubhe	193 49.6	N61 39.5
Elnath	278 09.5	N28 37.0
Eltanin	90 45.4	N51 29.7
Enif	33 44.8	N 9 57.4
Fomalhaut	15 21.3	S29 32.0
Gacrux	171 58.8	S57 12.2
Gienah	175 50.3	S17 37.9
Hadar	148 45.2	S60 27.0
Hamal	327 57.8	N23 32.5
Kaus Aust.	83 41.0	S34 22.4
Kochab	137 21.4	N74 05.4
Markab	13 35.8	N15 17.9
Menkar	314 12.4	N 4 09.3
Menkent	148 05.3	S36 26.9
Miaplacidus	221 39.3	S69 46.9
Mirfak	308 36.6	N49 55.0
Nunki	75 55.7	S26 16.4
Peacock	53 15.7	S56 40.9
Pollux	243 25.0	N27 58.9
Procyon	244 57.4	N 5 10.8
Rasalhague	96 04.6	N12 33.3
Regulus	207 41.3	N11 53.1
Rigel	281 09.7	S 8 11.0
Rigil Kent.	139 49.2	S60 54.0
Sabik	102 10.2	S15 44.5
Schedar	349 37.3	N56 37.8
Shaula	96 19.1	S37 06.8
Sirius	258 31.6	S16 44.3
Spica	158 29.2	S11 14.7
Suhail	222 50.9	S43 29.8
Vega	80 37.6	N38 48.4
Zuben'ubi	137 03.3	S16 06.4

	SHA ° ′	Mer. Pass. h m
Venus	117 44.1	14 06
Mars	71 27.3	17 10
Jupiter	171 10.9	10 30
Saturn	107 49.7	14 43

	UT	SUN GHA	SUN Dec	MOON GHA	v	MOON Dec	d	HP
	d h	° ′	° ′	° ′	′	° ′	′	′
21	00	183 50.8	S10 46.1	294 33.2	6.3	N18 36.9	0.1	59.2
	01	198 50.9	47.0	308 58.5	6.3	18 36.8	0.2	59.1
	02	213 51.0	47.9	323 23.8	6.4	18 36.6	0.3	59.1
	03	228 51.1	. . 48.7	337 49.2	6.4	18 36.3	0.5	59.1
	04	243 51.2	49.6	352 14.6	6.5	18 35.8	0.6	59.0
	05	258 51.3	50.5	6 40.1	6.5	18 35.2	0.7	59.0
	06	273 51.4	S10 51.4	21 05.6	6.6	N18 34.5	0.8	59.0
	07	288 51.5	52.3	35 31.2	6.7	18 33.7	1.0	58.9
	08	303 51.6	53.2	49 56.9	6.6	18 32.7	1.1	58.9
F	09	318 51.7	. . 54.1	64 22.5	6.8	18 31.6	1.1	58.8
R	10	333 51.7	55.0	78 48.3	6.8	18 30.5	1.3	58.8
I	11	348 51.8	55.8	93 14.1	6.8	18 29.2	1.4	58.8
D	12	3 51.9	S10 56.7	107 39.9	6.9	N18 27.8	1.6	58.7
A	13	18 52.0	57.6	122 05.8	7.0	18 26.2	1.6	58.7
Y	14	33 52.1	58.5	136 31.8	7.0	18 24.6	1.8	58.7
	15	48 52.2	10 59.4	150 57.8	7.1	18 22.8	1.8	58.6
	16	63 52.3	11 00.3	165 23.9	7.1	18 21.0	2.0	58.6
	17	78 52.4	01.1	179 50.0	7.2	18 19.0	2.1	58.6
	18	93 52.5	S11 02.0	194 16.2	7.3	N18 16.9	2.2	58.5
	19	108 52.6	02.9	208 42.5	7.3	18 14.7	2.3	58.5
	20	123 52.7	03.8	223 08.8	7.4	18 12.4	2.4	58.5
	21	138 52.8	. . 04.7	237 35.2	7.5	18 10.0	2.6	58.4
	22	153 52.9	05.6	252 01.7	7.5	18 07.4	2.6	58.4
	23	168 53.0	06.4	266 28.2	7.6	18 04.8	2.8	58.3
22	00	183 53.1	S11 07.3	280 54.8	7.6	N18 02.0	2.8	58.3
	01	198 53.2	08.2	295 21.4	7.7	17 59.2	3.0	58.3
	02	213 53.3	09.1	309 48.1	7.8	17 56.2	3.0	58.2
	03	228 53.4	. . 10.0	324 14.9	7.8	17 53.2	3.2	58.2
	04	243 53.5	10.9	338 41.7	7.9	17 50.0	3.3	58.2
	05	258 53.5	11.7	353 08.6	8.0	17 46.7	3.4	58.1
	06	273 53.6	S11 12.6	7 35.6	8.0	N17 43.3	3.4	58.1
	07	288 53.7	13.5	22 02.6	8.1	17 39.9	3.6	58.1
S	08	303 53.8	14.4	36 29.7	8.2	17 36.3	3.7	58.0
A	09	318 53.9	. . 15.3	50 56.9	8.2	17 32.6	3.8	58.0
T	10	333 54.0	16.1	65 24.1	8.3	17 28.8	3.8	58.0
U	11	348 54.1	17.0	79 51.4	8.4	17 25.0	4.0	57.9
R	12	3 54.2	S11 17.9	94 18.8	8.4	N17 21.0	4.1	57.9
D	13	18 54.3	18.8	108 46.2	8.6	17 16.9	4.1	57.8
A	14	33 54.4	19.6	123 13.8	8.5	17 12.8	4.3	57.8
Y	15	48 54.5	. . 20.5	137 41.3	8.7	17 08.5	4.4	57.8
	16	63 54.5	21.4	152 09.0	8.7	17 04.1	4.4	57.7
	17	78 54.6	22.3	166 36.7	8.8	16 59.7	4.5	57.7
	18	93 54.7	S11 23.2	181 04.5	8.9	N16 55.2	4.7	57.7
	19	108 54.8	24.0	195 32.4	8.9	16 50.5	4.7	57.6
	20	123 54.9	24.9	210 00.3	9.0	16 45.8	4.8	57.6
	21	138 55.0	. . 25.8	224 28.3	9.1	16 41.0	4.9	57.6
	22	153 55.1	26.7	238 56.4	9.1	16 36.1	5.0	57.5
	23	168 55.2	27.5	253 24.5	9.2	16 31.1	5.1	57.5
23	00	183 55.2	S11 28.4	267 52.7	9.3	N16 26.0	5.1	57.5
	01	198 55.3	29.3	282 21.0	9.3	16 20.9	5.3	57.4
	02	213 55.4	30.2	296 49.3	9.5	16 15.6	5.3	57.4
	03	228 55.5	. . 31.0	311 17.8	9.5	16 10.3	5.4	57.4
	04	243 55.6	31.9	325 46.3	9.5	16 04.9	5.5	57.3
	05	258 55.7	32.8	340 14.8	9.6	15 59.4	5.6	57.3
	06	273 55.7	S11 33.6	354 43.4	9.8	N15 53.8	5.7	57.3
	07	288 55.8	34.5	9 12.2	9.7	15 48.1	5.7	57.2
	08	303 55.9	35.4	23 40.9	9.9	15 42.4	5.8	57.2
S	09	318 56.0	. . 36.3	38 09.8	9.9	15 36.6	5.9	57.2
U	10	333 56.1	37.1	52 38.7	10.0	15 30.7	6.0	57.1
N	11	348 56.2	38.0	67 07.7	10.0	15 24.7	6.1	57.1
D	12	3 56.2	S11 38.9	81 36.7	10.2	N15 18.6	6.1	57.1
A	13	18 56.3	39.7	96 05.9	10.1	15 12.5	6.2	57.0
Y	14	33 56.4	40.6	110 35.0	10.3	15 06.3	6.3	57.0
	15	48 56.5	. . 41.5	125 04.3	10.3	15 00.0	6.4	57.0
	16	63 56.6	42.4	139 33.6	10.4	14 53.6	6.4	56.9
	17	78 56.7	43.2	154 03.0	10.5	14 47.2	6.5	56.9
	18	93 56.7	S11 44.1	168 32.5	10.6	N14 40.7	6.5	56.9
	19	108 56.8	45.0	183 02.1	10.6	14 34.2	6.7	56.8
	20	123 56.9	45.8	197 31.7	10.6	14 27.5	6.7	56.8
	21	138 57.0	. . 46.7	212 01.3	10.8	14 20.8	6.8	56.8
	22	153 57.1	47.6	226 31.1	10.8	14 14.0	6.8	56.7
	23	168 57.1	48.4	241 00.9	10.9	N14 07.2	6.9	56.7
		SD 16.1	d 0.9	SD 16.0		15.8		15.5

Lat.	Twilight Naut.	Twilight Civil	Sunrise	Moonrise 21	Moonrise 22	Moonrise 23	Moonrise 24
°	h m	h m	h m	h m	h m	h m	h m
N 72	05 27	06 46	08 02	▭	19 30	21 29	23 18
N 70	05 27	06 38	07 45	18 49	20 21	21 59	23 37
68	05 27	06 32	07 32	19 31	20 52	22 21	23 51
66	05 27	06 27	07 21	19 59	21 16	22 39	24 03
64	05 27	06 22	07 12	20 21	21 34	22 53	24 13
62	05 26	06 18	07 04	20 38	21 49	23 04	24 22
60	05 26	06 14	06 58	20 52	22 01	23 14	24 29
N 58	05 25	06 11	06 52	21 04	22 12	23 23	24 35
56	05 25	06 08	06 47	21 15	22 21	23 31	24 41
54	05 24	06 05	06 42	21 24	22 30	23 38	24 46
52	05 24	06 03	06 38	21 33	22 37	23 44	24 51
50	05 23	06 01	06 34	21 40	22 44	23 49	24 55
45	05 21	05 55	06 25	21 56	22 58	24 01	00 01
N 40	05 19	05 51	06 18	22 09	23 10	24 11	00 11
35	05 17	05 46	06 12	22 20	23 20	24 19	00 19
30	05 14	05 42	06 07	22 30	23 29	24 26	00 26
20	05 09	05 35	05 57	22 47	23 44	24 39	00 39
N 10	05 03	05 28	05 49	23 02	23 57	24 50	00 50
0	04 55	05 20	05 41	23 15	24 09	00 09	01 00
S 10	04 47	05 12	05 33	23 29	24 22	00 22	01 11
20	04 35	05 02	05 24	23 44	24 35	00 35	01 22
30	04 20	04 50	05 14	24 00	00 00	00 50	01 34
35	04 11	04 42	05 08	24 10	00 10	00 59	01 42
40	03 59	04 33	05 02	24 21	00 21	01 09	01 50
45	03 45	04 23	04 54	24 34	00 34	01 20	01 59
S 50	03 27	04 10	04 44	24 50	00 50	01 34	02 11
52	03 18	04 04	04 40	00 05	00 58	01 41	02 16
54	03 08	03 57	04 35	00 14	01 06	01 48	02 22
56	02 56	03 49	04 30	00 24	01 15	01 56	02 29
58	02 42	03 40	04 24	00 35	01 26	02 05	02 36
S 60	02 25	03 30	04 17	00 48	01 38	02 16	02 44

Lat.	Sunset	Twilight Civil	Twilight Naut.	Moonset 21	Moonset 22	Moonset 23	Moonset 24
°	h m	h m	h m	h m	h m	h m	h m
N 72	15 25	16 41	18 00	▭	16 29	16 19	16 11
N 70	15 42	16 49	18 00	15 16	15 38	15 47	15 51
68	15 55	16 55	18 00	14 34	15 06	15 24	15 35
66	16 06	17 01	18 00	14 05	14 42	15 06	15 22
64	16 16	17 05	18 01	13 44	14 24	14 51	15 11
62	16 23	17 10	18 01	13 26	14 08	14 39	15 02
60	16 30	17 13	18 02	13 12	13 55	14 29	14 54
N 58	16 36	17 17	18 02	12 59	13 44	14 19	14 47
56	16 41	17 20	18 03	12 48	13 35	14 11	14 41
54	16 46	17 22	18 04	12 39	13 26	14 04	14 35
52	16 50	17 25	18 04	12 31	13 18	13 58	14 30
50	16 54	17 27	18 05	12 23	13 11	13 52	14 26
45	17 03	17 33	18 07	12 07	12 56	13 39	14 16
N 40	17 10	17 38	18 09	11 53	12 44	13 28	14 07
35	17 16	17 42	18 11	11 42	12 34	13 19	14 00
30	17 22	17 46	18 14	11 32	12 24	13 11	13 54
20	17 31	17 54	18 19	11 15	12 09	12 58	13 43
N 10	17 40	18 01	18 26	11 00	11 55	12 46	13 33
0	17 48	18 09	18 33	10 46	11 42	12 34	13 24
S 10	17 56	18 17	18 42	10 32	11 28	12 23	13 15
20	18 05	18 27	18 54	10 17	11 14	12 11	13 05
30	18 15	18 40	19 09	09 59	10 58	11 56	12 54
35	18 21	18 47	19 19	09 49	10 49	11 48	12 47
40	18 28	18 56	19 30	09 38	10 38	11 39	12 40
45	18 36	19 07	19 45	09 24	10 25	11 28	12 31
S 50	18 45	19 20	20 04	09 08	10 10	11 15	12 20
52	18 50	19 27	20 13	09 00	10 02	11 08	12 15
54	18 55	19 34	20 23	08 51	09 54	11 01	12 10
56	19 00	19 42	20 35	08 41	09 45	10 54	12 04
58	19 06	19 51	20 50	08 30	09 35	10 45	11 57
S 60	19 13	20 01	21 07	08 17	09 23	10 35	11 49

Day	SUN Eqn. of Time 00ʰ	SUN Eqn. of Time 12ʰ	SUN Mer. Pass.	MOON Mer. Pass. Upper	MOON Mer. Pass. Lower	MOON Age	MOON Phase
d	m s	m s	h m	h m	h m	d %	
21	15 23	15 28	11 45	04 32	17 01	20 64	
22	15 32	15 37	11 44	05 28	17 56	21 53	◐
23	15 41	15 45	11 44	06 22	18 47	22 43	

	UT	ARIES	VENUS −4·0		MARS +0·3		JUPITER −1·7		SATURN +0·5	
		GHA	GHA	Dec	GHA	Dec	GHA	Dec	GHA	Dec
	d h	° ′	° ′	° ′	° ′	° ′	° ′	° ′	° ′	° ′
MONDAY	24 00	32 49.6	148 00.3	S22 48.4	102 44.6	S24 14.4	203 37.3	S 2 45.4	140 27.1	S21 03.6
	01	47 52.1	162 59.5	49.1	117 45.1	14.1	218 39.3	45.6	155 29.3	03.6
	02	62 54.5	177 58.8	49.7	132 45.7	13.8	233 41.3	45.8	170 31.5	03.6
	03	77 57.0	192 58.0	. . 50.3	147 46.2	. . 13.5	248 43.2	. . 46.0	185 33.7	. . 03.7
	04	92 59.4	207 57.3	50.9	162 46.8	13.2	263 45.2	46.2	200 35.9	03.7
	05	108 01.9	222 56.5	51.5	177 47.3	12.9	278 47.2	46.5	215 38.1	03.7
	06	123 04.4	237 55.8	S22 52.2	192 47.8	S24 12.7	293 49.2	S 2 46.7	230 40.3	S21 03.8
	07	138 06.8	252 55.0	52.8	207 48.4	12.4	308 51.2	46.9	245 42.5	03.8
	08	153 09.3	267 54.3	53.4	222 48.9	12.1	323 53.2	47.1	260 44.7	03.8
	09	168 11.8	282 53.6	. . 54.0	237 49.5	. . 11.8	338 55.1	. . 47.3	275 46.9	. . 03.9
	10	183 14.2	297 52.8	54.6	252 50.0	11.5	353 57.1	47.5	290 49.1	03.9
	11	198 16.7	312 52.1	55.3	267 50.5	11.2	8 59.1	47.7	305 51.4	03.9
	12	213 19.2	327 51.3	S22 55.9	282 51.1	S24 10.9	24 01.1	S 2 47.9	320 53.6	S21 04.0
	13	228 21.6	342 50.6	56.5	297 51.6	10.7	39 03.1	48.1	335 55.8	04.0
	14	243 24.1	357 49.8	57.1	312 52.2	10.4	54 05.1	48.3	350 58.0	04.0
	15	258 26.5	12 49.1	. . 57.7	327 52.7	. . 10.1	69 07.0	. . 48.5	6 00.2	. . 04.1
	16	273 29.0	27 48.3	58.3	342 53.2	09.8	84 09.0	48.7	21 02.4	04.1
	17	288 31.5	42 47.6	58.9	357 53.8	09.5	99 11.0	48.9	36 04.6	04.2
	18	303 33.9	57 46.8	S22 59.5	12 54.3	S24 09.2	114 13.0	S 2 49.1	51 06.8	S21 04.2
	19	318 36.4	72 46.1	23 00.1	27 54.9	08.9	129 15.0	49.3	66 09.0	04.2
	20	333 38.9	87 45.3	00.7	42 55.4	08.6	144 17.0	49.5	81 11.2	04.3
	21	348 41.3	102 44.6	. . 01.3	57 55.9	. . 08.4	159 18.9	. . 49.7	96 13.4	. . 04.3
	22	3 43.8	117 43.8	01.9	72 56.5	08.1	174 20.9	49.9	111 15.6	04.3
	23	18 46.3	132 43.1	02.5	87 57.0	07.8	189 22.9	50.1	126 17.8	04.4
TUESDAY	25 00	33 48.7	147 42.3	S23 03.1	102 57.6	S24 07.5	204 24.9	S 2 50.3	141 20.0	S21 04.4
	01	48 51.2	162 41.6	03.7	117 58.1	07.2	219 26.9	50.5	156 22.2	04.4
	02	63 53.7	177 40.8	04.3	132 58.6	06.9	234 28.9	50.7	171 24.4	04.5
	03	78 56.1	192 40.0	. . 04.9	147 59.2	. . 06.6	249 30.8	. . 50.9	186 26.6	. . 04.5
	04	93 58.6	207 39.3	05.5	162 59.7	06.3	264 32.8	51.1	201 28.8	04.5
	05	109 01.0	222 38.5	06.1	178 00.3	06.0	279 34.8	51.3	216 31.0	04.6
	06	124 03.5	237 37.8	S23 06.7	193 00.8	S24 05.7	294 36.8	S 2 51.5	231 33.2	S21 04.6
	07	139 06.0	252 37.0	07.3	208 01.3	05.4	309 38.8	51.7	246 35.5	04.6
	08	154 08.4	267 36.3	07.9	223 01.9	05.1	324 40.8	51.9	261 37.7	04.7
	09	169 10.9	282 35.5	. . 08.5	238 02.4	. . 04.8	339 42.8	. . 52.1	276 39.9	. . 04.7
	10	184 13.4	297 34.7	09.1	253 03.0	04.5	354 44.7	52.3	291 42.1	04.7
	11	199 15.8	312 34.0	09.7	268 03.5	04.2	9 46.7	52.5	306 44.3	04.8
	12	214 18.3	327 33.2	S23 10.3	283 04.0	S24 04.0	24 48.7	S 2 52.7	321 46.5	S21 04.8
	13	229 20.8	342 32.5	10.9	298 04.6	03.7	39 50.7	52.9	336 48.7	04.9
	14	244 23.2	357 31.7	11.4	313 05.1	03.4	54 52.7	53.1	351 50.9	04.9
	15	259 25.7	12 31.0	. . 12.0	328 05.7	. . 03.1	69 54.7	. . 53.3	6 53.1	. . 04.9
	16	274 28.2	27 30.2	12.6	343 06.2	02.8	84 56.6	53.5	21 55.3	05.0
	17	289 30.6	42 29.4	13.2	358 06.7	02.5	99 58.6	53.7	36 57.5	05.0
	18	304 33.1	57 28.7	S23 13.8	13 07.3	S24 02.2	115 00.6	S 2 53.9	51 59.7	S21 05.0
	19	319 35.5	72 27.9	14.4	28 07.8	01.9	130 02.6	54.1	67 01.9	05.1
	20	334 38.0	87 27.2	14.9	43 08.4	01.6	145 04.6	54.3	82 04.1	05.1
	21	349 40.5	102 26.4	. . 15.5	58 08.9	. . 01.3	160 06.6	. . 54.5	97 06.3	. . 05.1
	22	4 42.9	117 25.6	16.1	73 09.4	01.0	175 08.6	54.7	112 08.5	05.2
	23	19 45.4	132 24.9	16.7	88 10.0	00.7	190 10.5	54.9	127 10.7	05.2
WEDNESDAY	26 00	34 47.9	147 24.1	S23 17.2	103 10.5	S24 00.4	205 12.5	S 2 55.1	142 12.9	S21 05.2
	01	49 50.3	162 23.3	17.8	118 11.0	24 00.1	220 14.5	55.3	157 15.1	05.3
	02	64 52.8	177 22.6	18.4	133 11.6	23 59.8	235 16.5	55.5	172 17.3	05.3
	03	79 55.3	192 21.8	. . 19.0	148 12.1	. . 59.5	250 18.5	. . 55.7	187 19.5	. . 05.3
	04	94 57.7	207 21.0	19.5	163 12.7	59.2	265 20.5	55.9	202 21.7	05.4
	05	110 00.2	222 20.3	20.1	178 13.2	58.9	280 22.5	56.1	217 23.9	05.4
	06	125 02.6	237 19.5	S23 20.7	193 13.7	S23 58.6	295 24.4	S 2 56.3	232 26.1	S21 05.5
	07	140 05.1	252 18.8	21.2	208 14.3	58.2	310 26.4	56.5	247 28.3	05.5
	08	155 07.6	267 18.0	21.8	223 14.8	57.9	325 28.4	56.7	262 30.5	05.5
	09	170 10.0	282 17.2	. . 22.4	238 15.4	. . 57.6	340 30.4	. . 56.9	277 32.7	. . 05.6
	10	185 12.5	297 16.5	22.9	253 15.9	57.3	355 32.4	57.1	292 34.9	05.6
	11	200 15.0	312 15.7	23.5	268 16.4	57.0	10 34.4	57.3	307 37.1	05.6
	12	215 17.4	327 14.9	S23 24.0	283 17.0	S23 56.7	25 36.4	S 2 57.5	322 39.3	S21 05.7
	13	230 19.9	342 14.1	24.6	298 17.5	56.4	40 38.3	57.7	337 41.5	05.7
	14	245 22.4	357 13.4	25.2	313 18.0	56.1	55 40.3	57.9	352 43.7	05.7
	15	260 24.8	12 12.6	. . 25.7	328 18.6	. . 55.8	70 42.3	. . 58.1	7 45.9	. . 05.8
	16	275 27.3	27 11.8	26.3	343 19.1	55.5	85 44.3	58.3	22 48.1	05.8
	17	290 29.8	42 11.1	26.8	358 19.7	55.2	100 46.3	58.5	37 50.3	05.8
	18	305 32.2	57 10.3	S23 27.4	13 20.2	S23 54.9	115 48.3	S 2 58.7	52 52.5	S21 05.9
	19	320 34.7	72 09.5	27.9	28 20.7	54.6	130 50.3	58.9	67 54.7	05.9
	20	335 37.1	87 08.8	28.5	43 21.3	54.3	145 52.2	59.1	82 56.9	05.9
	21	350 39.6	102 08.0	. . 29.0	58 21.8	. . 54.0	160 54.2	. . 59.3	97 59.1	. . 06.0
	22	5 42.1	117 07.2	29.6	73 22.4	53.6	175 56.2	59.5	113 01.3	06.0
	23	20 44.5	132 06.4	30.1	88 22.9	53.3	190 58.2	59.7	128 03.5	06.1
	Mer. Pass.	h m 21 41.2	v −0.8	d 0.6	v 0.5	d 0.3	v 2.0	d 0.2	v 2.2	d 0.0

STARS

Name	SHA	Dec
	° ′	° ′
Acamar	315 16.3	S40 14.3
Achernar	335 24.6	S57 09.2
Acrux	173 07.2	S63 11.3
Adhara	255 10.6	S28 59.6
Aldebaran	290 46.5	N16 32.4
Alioth	166 19.4	N55 52.2
Alkaid	152 57.7	N49 13.9
Al Na'ir	27 40.8	S46 52.8
Alnilam	275 43.9	S 1 11.6
Alphard	217 54.0	S 8 43.8
Alphecca	126 09.5	N26 39.8
Alpheratz	357 40.8	N29 11.1
Altair	62 06.1	N 8 55.1
Ankaa	353 13.2	S42 13.0
Antares	112 23.8	S26 27.9
Arcturus	145 54.1	N19 06.0
Atria	107 24.0	S69 03.4
Avior	234 17.0	S59 33.6
Bellatrix	278 29.4	N 6 21.8
Betelgeuse	270 58.7	N 7 24.5
Canopus	263 54.9	S52 42.2
Capella	280 30.8	N46 00.6
Deneb	49 29.9	N45 20.8
Denebola	182 31.7	N14 28.8
Diphda	348 53.4	S17 53.7
Dubhe	193 49.6	N61 39.5
Elnath	278 09.5	N28 37.1
Eltanin	90 45.4	N51 29.7
Enif	33 44.8	N 9 57.4
Fomalhaut	15 21.3	S29 32.0
Gacrux	171 58.8	S57 12.2
Gienah	175 50.3	S17 37.9
Hadar	148 45.2	S60 27.0
Hamal	327 57.8	N23 32.5
Kaus Aust.	83 41.0	S34 22.4
Kochab	137 21.4	N74 05.4
Markab	13 35.9	N15 17.9
Menkar	314 12.4	N 4 09.3
Menkent	148 05.3	S36 26.9
Miaplacidus	221 39.3	S69 46.9
Mirfak	308 36.6	N49 55.0
Nunki	75 55.7	S26 16.4
Peacock	53 15.8	S56 40.9
Pollux	243 25.0	N27 58.9
Procyon	244 57.3	N 5 10.8
Rasalhague	96 04.6	N12 33.2
Regulus	207 41.3	N11 53.1
Rigel	281 09.7	S 8 11.0
Rigil Kent.	139 49.2	S60 54.0
Sabik	102 10.2	S15 44.5
Schedar	349 37.3	N56 37.9
Shaula	96 19.1	S37 06.8
Sirius	258 31.6	S16 44.4
Spica	158 29.2	S11 14.7
Suhail	222 50.8	S43 29.8
Vega	80 37.6	N38 48.4
Zuben'ubi	137 03.2	S16 06.4

	SHA	Mer. Pass.
	° ′	h m
Venus	113 53.6	14 10
Mars	69 08.8	17 08
Jupiter	170 36.2	10 21
Saturn	107 31.3	14 33

Day	UT d h	SUN GHA ° ′	SUN Dec ° ′	MOON GHA ° ′	v ′	MOON Dec ° ′	d ′	HP ′
MONDAY	24 00	183 57.2	S11 49.3	255 30.8	10.9	N14 00.3	7.0	56.7
	01	198 57.3	50.2	270 00.7	11.0	13 53.3	7.0	56.7
	02	213 57.4	51.0	284 30.7	11.1	13 46.3	7.1	56.6
	03	228 57.4	. . 51.9	299 00.8	11.1	13 39.2	7.2	56.6
	04	243 57.5	52.8	313 30.9	11.3	13 32.0	7.2	56.6
	05	258 57.6	53.6	328 01.2	11.2	13 24.8	7.3	56.5
	06	273 57.7	S11 54.5	342 31.4	11.4	N13 17.5	7.3	56.5
	07	288 57.8	55.4	357 01.8	11.4	13 10.2	7.4	56.5
	08	303 57.8	56.2	11 32.2	11.4	13 02.8	7.5	56.4
	09	318 57.9	. . 57.1	26 02.6	11.6	12 55.3	7.5	56.4
	10	333 58.0	58.0	40 33.2	11.6	12 47.8	7.6	56.4
	11	348 58.1	58.8	55 03.8	11.6	12 40.2	7.6	56.4
	12	3 58.1	S11 59.7	69 34.4	11.7	N12 32.6	7.7	56.3
	13	18 58.2	12 00.6	84 05.1	11.8	12 24.9	7.7	56.3
	14	33 58.3	01.4	98 35.9	11.9	12 17.2	7.8	56.3
	15	48 58.4	. . 02.3	113 06.8	11.9	12 09.4	7.9	56.2
	16	63 58.4	03.1	127 37.7	11.9	12 01.5	7.9	56.2
	17	78 58.5	04.0	142 08.6	12.0	11 53.6	7.9	56.2
	18	93 58.6	S12 04.9	156 39.6	12.1	N11 45.7	8.0	56.2
	19	108 58.6	05.7	171 10.7	12.2	11 37.7	8.1	56.1
	20	123 58.7	06.6	185 41.9	12.2	11 29.6	8.1	56.1
	21	138 58.8	. . 07.5	200 13.1	12.2	11 21.5	8.1	56.1
	22	153 58.9	08.3	214 44.3	12.3	11 13.4	8.2	56.0
	23	168 58.9	09.2	229 15.6	12.4	11 05.2	8.3	56.0
TUESDAY	25 00	183 59.0	S12 10.0	243 47.0	12.4	N10 56.9	8.2	56.0
	01	198 59.1	10.9	258 18.4	12.5	10 48.7	8.4	56.0
	02	213 59.1	11.8	272 49.9	12.5	10 40.3	8.3	55.9
	03	228 59.2	. . 12.6	287 21.4	12.6	10 32.0	8.4	55.9
	04	243 59.3	13.5	301 53.0	12.7	10 23.6	8.5	55.9
	05	258 59.4	14.3	316 24.7	12.7	10 15.1	8.5	55.9
	06	273 59.4	S12 15.2	330 56.4	12.7	N10 06.6	8.5	55.8
	07	288 59.5	16.0	345 28.1	12.9	9 58.1	8.6	55.8
	08	303 59.6	16.9	0 00.0	12.8	9 49.5	8.6	55.8
	09	318 59.6	. . 17.8	14 31.8	12.9	9 40.9	8.7	55.8
	10	333 59.7	18.6	29 03.7	13.0	9 32.2	8.7	55.7
	11	348 59.8	19.5	43 35.7	13.0	9 23.5	8.7	55.7
	12	3 59.8	S12 20.3	58 07.7	13.1	N 9 14.8	8.8	55.7
	13	18 59.9	21.2	72 39.8	13.1	9 06.0	8.8	55.7
	14	34 00.0	22.0	87 11.9	13.1	8 57.2	8.8	55.6
	15	49 00.0	. . 22.9	101 44.0	13.2	8 48.4	8.9	55.6
	16	64 00.1	23.7	116 16.2	13.3	8 39.5	8.9	55.6
	17	79 00.2	24.6	130 48.5	13.3	8 30.6	8.9	55.6
	18	94 00.2	S12 25.5	145 20.8	13.3	N 8 21.7	9.0	55.5
	19	109 00.3	26.3	159 53.1	13.4	8 12.7	9.0	55.5
	20	124 00.4	27.2	174 25.5	13.4	8 03.7	9.0	55.5
	21	139 00.4	. . 28.0	188 57.9	13.5	7 54.7	9.0	55.5
	22	154 00.5	28.9	203 30.4	13.5	7 45.7	9.1	55.5
	23	169 00.6	29.7	218 02.9	13.6	7 36.6	9.1	55.4
WEDNESDAY	26 00	184 00.6	S12 30.6	232 35.5	13.6	N 7 27.5	9.2	55.4
	01	199 00.7	31.4	247 08.1	13.7	7 18.3	9.1	55.4
	02	214 00.7	32.3	261 40.8	13.7	7 09.2	9.2	55.4
	03	229 00.8	. . 33.1	276 13.5	13.7	7 00.0	9.2	55.3
	04	244 00.9	34.0	290 46.2	13.8	6 50.8	9.3	55.3
	05	259 00.9	34.8	305 19.0	13.8	6 41.5	9.2	55.3
	06	274 01.0	S12 35.7	319 51.8	13.8	N 6 32.3	9.3	55.3
	07	289 01.1	36.5	334 24.6	13.9	6 23.0	9.3	55.3
	08	304 01.1	37.4	348 57.5	13.9	6 13.7	9.4	55.2
	09	319 01.2	. . 38.2	3 30.4	14.0	6 04.3	9.3	55.2
	10	334 01.2	39.1	18 03.4	14.0	5 55.0	9.4	55.2
	11	349 01.3	39.9	32 36.4	14.0	5 45.6	9.4	55.2
	12	4 01.4	S12 40.8	47 09.4	14.1	N 5 36.2	9.4	55.2
	13	19 01.4	41.6	61 42.5	14.1	5 26.8	9.4	55.1
	14	34 01.5	42.5	76 15.6	14.1	5 17.4	9.5	55.1
	15	49 01.5	. . 43.3	90 48.7	14.2	5 07.9	9.4	55.1
	16	64 01.6	44.2	105 21.9	14.2	4 58.5	9.5	55.1
	17	79 01.6	45.0	119 55.1	14.2	4 49.0	9.5	55.1
	18	94 01.7	S12 45.9	134 28.3	14.3	N 4 39.5	9.5	55.0
	19	109 01.8	46.7	149 01.6	14.2	4 30.0	9.5	55.0
	20	124 01.8	47.5	163 34.8	14.4	4 20.5	9.5	55.0
	21	139 01.9	. . 48.4	178 08.2	14.3	4 11.0	9.6	55.0
	22	154 01.9	49.2	192 41.5	14.4	4 01.4	9.5	55.0
	23	169 02.0	50.1	207 14.9	14.4	N 3 51.9	9.6	54.9
		SD 16.1	*d* 0.9	SD 15.3		15.2		15.0

Lat.	Twilight Naut.	Twilight Civil	Sunrise	Moonrise 24	Moonrise 25	Moonrise 26	Moonrise 27
°	h m	h m	h m	h m	h m	h m	h m
N 72	05 39	06 59	08 18	23 18	25 00	01 00	02 38
N 70	05 38	06 50	07 59	23 37	25 11	01 11	02 43
68	05 37	06 43	07 44	23 51	25 20	01 20	02 46
66	05 36	06 36	07 32	24 03	00 03	01 27	02 49
64	05 35	06 31	07 21	24 13	00 13	01 33	02 52
62	05 34	06 26	07 13	24 22	00 22	01 39	02 54
60	05 33	06 21	07 05	24 29	00 29	01 43	02 56
N 58	05 32	06 18	06 59	24 35	00 35	01 47	02 58
56	05 31	06 14	06 53	24 41	00 41	01 51	03 00
54	05 30	06 11	06 48	24 46	00 46	01 54	03 01
52	05 28	06 08	06 43	24 51	00 51	01 57	03 02
50	05 27	06 05	06 39	24 55	00 55	02 00	03 03
45	05 25	05 59	06 29	00 01	01 04	02 05	03 06
N 40	05 22	05 54	06 22	00 11	01 11	02 10	03 08
35	05 19	05 49	06 15	00 19	01 17	02 14	03 10
30	05 16	05 44	06 09	00 26	01 23	02 18	03 11
20	05 10	05 36	05 59	00 39	01 32	02 24	03 14
N 10	05 03	05 28	05 49	00 50	01 41	02 30	03 17
0	04 55	05 19	05 41	01 00	01 49	02 35	03 19
S 10	04 45	05 10	05 32	01 11	01 57	02 40	03 21
20	04 33	05 00	05 22	01 22	02 05	02 45	03 24
30	04 17	04 46	05 11	01 34	02 15	02 52	03 27
35	04 07	04 38	05 05	01 42	02 20	02 55	03 28
40	03 55	04 29	04 58	01 50	02 26	02 59	03 30
45	03 39	04 18	04 49	01 59	02 34	03 04	03 32
S 50	03 20	04 04	04 39	02 11	02 42	03 10	03 35
52	03 10	03 57	04 34	02 16	02 46	03 12	03 36
54	02 59	03 49	04 29	02 22	02 50	03 15	03 37
56	02 46	03 41	04 23	02 29	02 55	03 18	03 38
58	02 31	03 31	04 16	02 36	03 01	03 22	03 40
S 60	02 12	03 20	04 08	02 44	03 07	03 25	03 42

Lat.	Sunset	Twilight Civil	Twilight Naut.	Moonset 24	Moonset 25	Moonset 26	Moonset 27
°	h m	h m	h m	h m	h m	h m	h m
N 72	15 09	16 27	17 47	16 11	16 05	15 59	15 54
N 70	15 28	16 36	17 48	15 51	15 52	15 53	15 52
68	15 43	16 44	17 49	15 35	15 42	15 47	15 51
66	15 55	16 51	17 51	15 22	15 34	15 43	15 50
64	16 05	16 56	17 52	15 11	15 26	15 39	15 49
62	16 14	17 01	17 53	15 02	15 20	15 35	15 49
60	16 22	17 06	17 54	14 54	15 15	15 32	15 48
N 58	16 28	17 09	17 55	14 47	15 10	15 29	15 47
56	16 34	17 13	17 56	14 41	15 05	15 27	15 47
54	16 40	17 16	17 58	14 35	15 02	15 25	15 46
52	16 44	17 19	17 59	14 30	14 58	15 23	15 46
50	16 49	17 22	18 00	14 26	14 55	15 21	15 46
45	16 58	17 28	18 03	14 16	14 48	15 17	15 45
N 40	17 06	17 34	18 05	14 07	14 42	15 14	15 44
35	17 13	17 39	18 08	14 00	14 37	15 11	15 43
30	17 19	17 43	18 11	13 54	14 32	15 08	15 43
20	17 29	17 52	18 18	13 43	14 25	15 04	15 42
N 10	17 39	18 00	18 25	13 33	14 18	15 00	15 41
0	17 47	18 09	18 33	13 24	14 11	14 56	15 40
S 10	17 56	18 18	18 43	13 15	14 05	14 52	15 39
20	18 06	18 29	18 55	13 05	13 58	14 48	15 38
30	18 17	18 42	19 12	12 54	13 49	14 44	15 37
35	18 24	18 50	19 22	12 47	13 45	14 41	15 36
40	18 31	19 00	19 34	12 40	13 39	14 38	15 36
45	18 40	19 11	19 50	12 31	13 33	14 35	15 35
S 50	18 50	19 26	20 10	12 20	13 26	14 30	15 34
52	18 55	19 33	20 20	12 15	13 22	14 28	15 33
54	19 01	19 40	20 31	12 10	13 18	14 26	15 33
56	19 07	19 49	20 44	12 04	13 14	14 24	15 32
58	19 14	19 59	21 00	11 57	13 10	14 21	15 32
S 60	19 21	20 11	21 20	11 49	13 04	14 18	15 31

Day	SUN Eqn. of Time 00h	SUN Eqn. of Time 12h	SUN Mer. Pass.	MOON Mer. Pass. Upper	MOON Mer. Pass. Lower	MOON Age	MOON Phase
d	m s	m s	h m	h m	h m	d %	
24	15 49	15 52	11 44	07 12	19 36	23 33	
25	15 56	15 59	11 44	08 00	20 23	24 24	
26	16 02	16 05	11 44	08 46	21 08	25 16	

UT d h	ARIES GHA	VENUS −4·0 GHA	VENUS Dec	MARS +0·3 GHA	MARS Dec	JUPITER −1·7 GHA	JUPITER Dec	SATURN +0·5 GHA	SATURN Dec
	° ′	° ′	° ′	° ′	° ′	° ′	° ′	° ′	° ′
27 00 THURSDAY	35 47.0	147 05.7	S23 30.7	103 23.4	S23 53.0	206 00.2	S 2 59.9	143 05.7	S21 06.1
01	50 49.5	162 04.9	31.2	118 24.0	52.7	221 02.2	3 00.1	158 07.9	06.1
02	65 51.9	177 04.1	31.8	133 24.5	52.4	236 04.2	00.3	173 10.1	06.2
03	80 54.4	192 03.4	. . 32.3	148 25.0	. . 52.1	251 06.2	. . 00.5	188 12.3	. . 06.2
04	95 56.9	207 02.6	32.9	163 25.6	51.8	266 08.1	00.7	203 14.5	06.2
05	110 59.3	222 01.8	33.4	178 26.1	51.5	281 10.1	00.9	218 16.7	06.3
06	126 01.8	237 01.0	S23 34.0	193 26.7	S23 51.1	296 12.1	S 3 01.1	233 18.9	S21 06.3
07	141 04.2	252 00.3	34.5	208 27.2	50.8	311 14.1	01.3	248 21.1	06.3
08	156 06.7	266 59.5	35.0	223 27.7	50.5	326 16.1	01.5	263 23.3	06.4
09	171 09.2	281 58.7	. . 35.6	238 28.3	. . 50.2	341 18.1	. . 01.7	278 25.5	. . 06.4
10	186 11.6	296 57.9	36.1	253 28.8	49.9	356 20.1	01.9	293 27.7	06.4
11	201 14.1	311 57.1	36.6	268 29.3	49.6	11 22.1	02.1	308 29.9	06.5
12	216 16.6	326 56.4	S23 37.2	283 29.9	S23 49.3	26 24.0	S 3 02.3	323 32.1	S21 06.5
13	231 19.0	341 55.6	37.7	298 30.4	48.9	41 26.0	02.5	338 34.3	06.5
14	246 21.5	356 54.8	38.2	313 31.0	48.6	56 28.0	02.7	353 36.5	06.6
15	261 24.0	11 54.0	. . 38.8	328 31.5	. . 48.3	71 30.0	. . 02.9	8 38.7	. . 06.6
16	276 26.4	26 53.3	39.3	343 32.0	48.0	86 32.0	03.1	23 40.9	06.7
17	291 28.9	41 52.5	39.8	358 32.6	47.7	101 34.0	03.3	38 43.1	06.7
18	306 31.4	56 51.7	S23 40.4	13 33.1	S23 47.4	116 36.0	S 3 03.5	53 45.3	S21 06.7
19	321 33.8	71 50.9	40.9	28 33.6	47.0	131 38.0	03.7	68 47.5	06.8
20	336 36.3	86 50.1	41.4	43 34.2	46.7	146 39.9	03.9	83 49.7	06.8
21	351 38.7	101 49.4	. . 41.9	58 34.7	. . 46.4	161 41.9	. . 04.1	98 51.9	. . 06.8
22	6 41.2	116 48.6	42.5	73 35.3	46.1	176 43.9	04.3	113 54.1	06.9
23	21 43.7	131 47.8	43.0	88 35.8	45.8	191 45.9	04.5	128 56.3	06.9
28 00 FRIDAY	36 46.1	146 47.0	S23 43.5	103 36.3	S23 45.4	206 47.9	S 3 04.7	143 58.5	S21 06.9
01	51 48.6	161 46.2	44.0	118 36.9	45.1	221 49.9	04.9	159 00.7	07.0
02	66 51.1	176 45.5	44.5	133 37.4	44.8	236 51.9	05.1	174 02.9	07.0
03	81 53.5	191 44.7	. . 45.1	148 37.9	. . 44.5	251 53.9	. . 05.3	189 05.1	. . 07.0
04	96 56.0	206 43.9	45.6	163 38.5	44.2	266 55.8	05.5	204 07.3	07.1
05	111 58.5	221 43.1	46.1	178 39.0	43.8	281 57.8	05.7	219 09.5	07.1
06	127 00.9	236 42.3	S23 46.6	193 39.6	S23 43.5	296 59.8	S 3 05.9	234 11.7	S21 07.1
07	142 03.4	251 41.5	47.1	208 40.1	43.2	312 01.8	06.1	249 13.9	07.2
08	157 05.8	266 40.8	47.6	223 40.6	42.9	327 03.8	06.3	264 16.1	07.2
09	172 08.3	281 40.0	. . 48.1	238 41.2	. . 42.5	342 05.8	. . 06.5	279 18.3	. . 07.2
10	187 10.8	296 39.2	48.6	253 41.7	42.2	357 07.8	06.7	294 20.5	07.3
11	202 13.2	311 38.4	49.1	268 42.2	41.9	12 09.8	06.9	309 22.7	07.3
12	217 15.7	326 37.6	S23 49.7	283 42.8	S23 41.6	27 11.8	S 3 07.1	324 24.9	S21 07.4
13	232 18.2	341 36.8	50.2	298 43.3	41.2	42 13.7	07.3	339 27.1	07.4
14	247 20.6	356 36.0	50.7	313 43.9	40.9	57 15.7	07.5	354 29.3	07.4
15	262 23.1	11 35.3	. . 51.2	328 44.4	. . 40.6	72 17.7	. . 07.7	9 31.5	. . 07.5
16	277 25.6	26 34.5	51.7	343 44.9	40.3	87 19.7	07.9	24 33.7	07.5
17	292 28.0	41 33.7	52.2	358 45.5	39.9	102 21.7	08.1	39 35.9	07.5
18	307 30.5	56 32.9	S23 52.7	13 46.0	S23 39.6	117 23.7	S 3 08.2	54 38.1	S21 07.6
19	322 33.0	71 32.1	53.2	28 46.5	39.3	132 25.7	08.4	69 40.2	07.6
20	337 35.4	86 31.3	53.7	43 47.1	39.0	147 27.7	08.6	84 42.4	07.6
21	352 37.9	101 30.5	. . 54.2	58 47.6	. . 38.6	162 29.7	. . 08.8	99 44.6	. . 07.7
22	7 40.3	116 29.7	54.7	73 48.2	38.3	177 31.6	09.0	114 46.8	07.7
23	22 42.8	131 28.9	55.2	88 48.7	38.0	192 33.6	09.2	129 49.0	07.7
29 00 SATURDAY	37 45.3	146 28.2	S23 55.6	103 49.2	S23 37.6	207 35.6	S 3 09.4	144 51.2	S21 07.8
01	52 47.7	161 27.4	56.1	118 49.8	37.3	222 37.6	09.6	159 53.4	07.8
02	67 50.2	176 26.6	56.6	133 50.3	37.0	237 39.6	09.8	174 55.6	07.8
03	82 52.7	191 25.8	. . 57.1	148 50.8	. . 36.6	252 41.6	. . 10.0	189 57.8	. . 07.9
04	97 55.1	206 25.0	57.6	163 51.4	36.3	267 43.6	10.2	205 00.0	07.9
05	112 57.6	221 24.2	58.1	178 51.9	36.0	282 45.6	10.4	220 02.2	08.0
06	128 00.1	236 23.4	S23 58.6	193 52.4	S23 35.7	297 47.6	S 3 10.6	235 04.4	S21 08.0
07	143 02.5	251 22.6	59.1	208 53.0	35.3	312 49.6	10.8	250 06.6	08.0
08	158 05.0	266 21.8	23 59.5	223 53.5	35.0	327 51.5	11.0	265 08.8	08.1
09	173 07.5	281 21.0	24 00.0	238 54.1	. . 34.7	342 53.5	. . 11.2	280 11.0	. . 08.1
10	188 09.9	296 20.2	00.5	253 54.6	34.3	357 55.5	11.4	295 13.2	08.1
11	203 12.4	311 19.4	01.0	268 55.1	34.0	12 57.5	11.6	310 15.4	08.2
12	218 14.8	326 18.6	S24 01.5	283 55.7	S23 33.7	27 59.5	S 3 11.8	325 17.6	S21 08.2
13	233 17.3	341 17.8	02.0	298 56.2	33.3	43 01.5	12.0	340 19.8	08.2
14	248 19.8	356 17.1	02.4	313 56.7	33.0	58 03.5	12.2	355 22.0	08.3
15	263 22.2	11 16.3	. . 02.9	328 57.3	. . 32.6	73 05.5	. . 12.4	10 24.2	. . 08.3
16	278 24.7	26 15.5	03.4	343 57.8	32.3	88 07.5	12.6	25 26.3	08.3
17	293 27.2	41 14.7	03.9	358 58.4	32.0	103 09.5	12.8	40 28.5	08.4
18	308 29.6	56 13.9	S24 04.3	13 58.9	S23 31.6	118 11.4	S 3 13.0	55 30.7	S21 08.4
19	323 32.1	71 13.1	04.8	28 59.4	31.3	133 13.4	13.2	70 32.9	08.4
20	338 34.6	86 12.3	05.3	44 00.0	31.0	148 15.4	13.4	85 35.1	08.5
21	353 37.0	101 11.5	. . 05.7	59 00.5	. . 30.6	163 17.4	. . 13.6	100 37.3	. . 08.5
22	8 39.5	116 10.7	06.2	74 01.0	30.3	178 19.4	13.8	115 39.5	08.5
23	23 41.9	131 09.9	06.7	89 01.6	29.9	193 21.4	14.0	130 41.7	08.6
Mer. Pass. (h m)	21 29.4	v −0.8	d 0.5	v 0.5	d 0.3	v 2.0	d 0.2	v 2.2	d 0.0

STARS

Name	SHA	Dec
	° ′	° ′
Acamar	315 16.3	S40 14.3
Achernar	335 24.6	S57 09.2
Acrux	173 07.2	S63 11.3
Adhara	255 10.6	S28 59.6
Aldebaran	290 46.5	N16 32.4
Alioth	166 19.4	N55 52.2
Alkaid	152 57.7	N49 13.9
Al Na'ir	27 40.8	S46 52.9
Alnilam	275 43.9	S 1 11.6
Alphard	217 54.0	S 8 43.8
Alphecca	126 09.5	N26 39.8
Alpheratz	357 40.8	N29 11.1
Altair	62 06.1	N 8 55.1
Ankaa	353 13.2	S42 13.0
Antares	112 23.8	S26 27.9
Arcturus	145 54.1	N19 05.9
Atria	107 24.0	S69 03.4
Avior	234 17.0	S59 33.6
Bellatrix	278 29.4	N 6 21.8
Betelgeuse	270 58.7	N 7 24.5
Canopus	263 54.9	S52 42.2
Capella	280 30.8	N46 00.6
Deneb	49 29.9	N45 20.8
Denebola	182 31.7	N14 28.8
Diphda	348 53.4	S17 53.7
Dubhe	193 49.5	N61 39.4
Elnath	278 09.5	N28 37.1
Eltanin	90 45.4	N51 29.7
Enif	33 44.8	N 9 57.4
Fomalhaut	15 21.3	S29 32.0
Gacrux	171 58.8	S57 12.2
Gienah	175 50.2	S17 37.9
Hadar	148 45.2	S60 27.0
Hamal	327 57.8	N23 32.5
Kaus Aust.	83 41.1	S34 22.4
Kochab	137 21.5	N74 05.4
Markab	13 35.9	N15 17.9
Menkar	314 12.4	N 4 09.3
Menkent	148 05.3	S36 26.9
Miaplacidus	221 39.2	S69 46.9
Mirfak	308 36.6	N49 55.1
Nunki	75 55.7	S26 16.4
Peacock	53 15.8	S56 40.9
Pollux	243 24.9	N27 58.9
Procyon	244 57.3	N 5 10.8
Rasalhague	96 04.6	N12 33.2
Regulus	207 41.3	N11 53.1
Rigel	281 09.7	S 8 11.0
Rigil Kent.	139 49.3	S60 54.0
Sabik	102 10.2	S15 44.5
Schedar	349 37.3	N56 37.9
Shaula	96 19.1	S37 06.8
Sirius	258 31.6	S16 44.4
Spica	158 29.2	S11 14.7
Suhail	222 50.8	S43 29.8
Vega	80 37.6	N38 48.4
Zuben'ubi	137 03.3	S16 06.4

	SHA	Mer. Pass.
	° ′	h m
Venus	110 00.9	14 14
Mars	66 50.2	17 05
Jupiter	170 01.8	10 11
Saturn	107 12.4	14 22

UT d h	SUN GHA ° ′	SUN Dec ° ′	MOON GHA ° ′	v ′	MOON Dec ° ′	d ′	HP ′
27 00	184 02.0	S12 50.9	221 48.3	14.4	N 3 42.3	9.6	54.9
01	199 02.1	51.8	236 21.7	14.5	3 32.7	9.6	54.9
02	214 02.2	52.6	250 55.2	14.5	3 23.1	9.6	54.9
03	229 02.2	. . 53.5	265 28.7	14.5	3 13.5	9.6	54.9
04	244 02.3	54.3	280 02.2	14.5	3 03.9	9.6	54.9
05	259 02.3	55.1	294 35.7	14.6	2 54.3	9.6	54.8
06	274 02.4	S12 56.0	309 09.3	14.5	N 2 44.7	9.7	54.8
T 07	289 02.4	56.8	323 42.8	14.6	2 35.0	9.6	54.8
H 08	304 02.5	57.7	338 16.4	14.7	2 25.4	9.7	54.8
U 09	319 02.5	. . 58.5	352 50.1	14.6	2 15.7	9.6	54.8
R 10	334 02.6	12 59.3	7 23.7	14.7	2 06.1	9.7	54.8
S 11	349 02.6	13 00.2	21 57.4	14.6	1 56.4	9.6	54.7
D 12	4 02.7	S13 01.0	36 31.0	14.8	N 1 46.8	9.7	54.7
A 13	19 02.7	01.9	51 04.8	14.7	1 37.1	9.6	54.7
Y 14	34 02.8	02.7	65 38.5	14.7	1 27.5	9.7	54.7
15	49 02.8	. . 03.5	80 12.2	14.8	1 17.8	9.7	54.7
16	64 02.9	04.4	94 46.0	14.7	1 08.1	9.6	54.7
17	79 02.9	05.2	109 19.7	14.8	0 58.5	9.7	54.6
18	94 03.0	S13 06.1	123 53.5	14.8	N 0 48.8	9.6	54.6
19	109 03.0	06.9	138 27.3	14.9	0 39.2	9.7	54.6
20	124 03.1	07.7	153 01.2	14.8	0 29.5	9.7	54.6
21	139 03.1	. . 08.6	167 35.0	14.9	0 19.8	9.6	54.6
22	154 03.2	09.4	182 08.9	14.8	0 10.2	9.7	54.6
23	169 03.2	10.2	196 42.7	14.9	N 0 00.5	9.6	54.6
28 00	184 03.3	S13 11.1	211 16.6	14.9	S 0 09.1	9.7	54.5
01	199 03.3	11.9	225 50.5	14.9	0 18.8	9.6	54.5
02	214 03.4	12.7	240 24.4	14.9	0 28.4	9.7	54.5
03	229 03.4	. . 13.6	254 58.3	14.9	0 38.1	9.6	54.5
04	244 03.5	14.4	269 32.2	14.9	0 47.7	9.6	54.5
05	259 03.5	15.2	284 06.1	15.0	0 57.3	9.6	54.5
06	274 03.6	S13 16.1	298 40.1	14.9	S 1 06.9	9.6	54.5
07	289 03.6	16.9	313 14.0	15.0	1 16.5	9.6	54.5
08	304 03.6	17.7	327 48.0	14.9	1 26.1	9.6	54.4
F 09	319 03.7	. . 18.6	342 21.9	15.0	1 35.7	9.6	54.4
R 10	334 03.7	19.4	356 55.9	15.0	1 45.3	9.6	54.4
I 11	349 03.8	20.2	11 29.9	15.0	1 54.9	9.5	54.4
D 12	4 03.8	S13 21.1	26 03.9	14.9	S 2 04.4	9.6	54.4
A 13	19 03.9	21.9	40 37.8	15.0	2 14.0	9.5	54.4
Y 14	34 03.9	22.7	55 11.8	15.0	2 23.5	9.5	54.4
15	49 03.9	. . 23.6	69 45.8	15.0	2 33.0	9.5	54.4
16	64 04.0	24.4	84 19.8	15.0	2 42.5	9.5	54.3
17	79 04.0	25.2	98 53.8	15.0	2 52.0	9.5	54.3
18	94 04.1	S13 26.1	113 27.8	15.0	S 3 01.5	9.5	54.3
19	109 04.1	26.9	128 01.8	15.0	3 11.0	9.4	54.3
20	124 04.2	27.7	142 35.8	15.0	3 20.4	9.4	54.3
21	139 04.2	. . 28.5	157 09.8	15.0	3 29.8	9.4	54.3
22	154 04.2	29.4	171 43.8	15.0	3 39.2	9.4	54.3
23	169 04.3	30.2	186 17.8	15.0	3 48.6	9.4	54.3
29 00	184 04.3	S13 31.0	200 51.8	15.0	S 3 58.0	9.4	54.3
01	199 04.4	31.8	215 25.8	15.0	4 07.4	9.3	54.3
02	214 04.4	32.7	229 59.8	15.0	4 16.7	9.3	54.2
03	229 04.4	. . 33.5	244 33.8	15.0	4 26.0	9.3	54.2
04	244 04.5	34.3	259 07.8	15.0	4 35.3	9.3	54.2
05	259 04.5	35.1	273 41.8	15.0	4 44.6	9.3	54.2
06	274 04.5	S13 36.0	288 15.8	15.0	S 4 53.9	9.2	54.2
S 07	289 04.6	36.8	302 49.8	14.9	5 03.1	9.2	54.2
A 08	304 04.6	37.6	317 23.7	15.0	5 12.3	9.2	54.2
T 09	319 04.7	. . 38.4	331 57.7	15.0	5 21.5	9.1	54.2
U 10	334 04.7	39.3	346 31.7	14.9	5 30.6	9.2	54.2
R 11	349 04.7	40.1	1 05.6	15.0	5 39.8	9.1	54.2
D 12	4 04.8	S13 40.9	15 39.6	14.9	S 5 48.9	9.1	54.2
A 13	19 04.8	41.7	30 13.5	15.0	5 58.0	9.0	54.1
Y 14	34 04.8	42.6	44 47.5	14.9	6 07.0	9.1	54.1
15	49 04.9	. . 43.4	59 21.4	14.9	6 16.1	9.0	54.1
16	64 04.9	44.2	73 55.3	14.9	6 25.1	9.0	54.1
17	79 04.9	45.0	88 29.2	14.9	6 34.1	8.9	54.1
18	94 05.0	S13 45.8	103 03.1	14.9	S 6 43.0	8.9	54.1
19	109 05.0	46.7	117 37.0	14.9	6 51.9	8.9	54.1
20	124 05.0	47.5	132 10.9	14.8	7 00.8	8.9	54.1
21	139 05.1	. . 48.3	146 44.7	14.9	7 09.7	8.8	54.1
22	154 05.1	49.1	161 18.6	14.8	7 18.5	8.8	54.1
23	169 05.1	49.9	175 52.4	14.8	S 7 27.3	8.7	54.1
	SD 16.1	d 0.8	SD	14.9	14.8		14.8

Lat.	Twilight Naut. h m	Twilight Civil h m	Sunrise h m	Moonrise 27 h m	Moonrise 28 h m	Moonrise 29 h m	Moonrise 30 h m
N 72	05 52	07 13	08 35	02 38	04 14	05 49	07 24
N 70	05 49	07 02	08 13	02 43	04 12	05 41	07 11
68	05 47	06 53	07 56	02 46	04 11	05 36	07 00
66	05 45	06 45	07 42	02 49	04 10	05 31	06 50
64	05 43	06 39	07 31	02 52	04 10	05 27	06 43
62	05 41	06 33	07 21	02 54	04 09	05 23	06 36
60	05 39	06 28	07 13	02 56	04 09	05 20	06 31
N 58	05 38	06 24	07 06	02 58	04 08	05 17	06 26
56	05 36	06 20	06 59	03 00	04 08	05 15	06 21
54	05 35	06 16	06 53	03 01	04 07	05 13	06 17
52	05 33	06 13	06 48	03 02	04 07	05 11	06 14
50	05 32	06 10	06 44	03 03	04 07	05 09	06 11
45	05 29	06 03	06 33	03 06	04 06	05 05	06 04
N 40	05 25	05 57	06 25	03 08	04 05	05 02	05 58
35	05 22	05 52	06 18	03 10	04 05	04 59	05 53
30	05 18	05 47	06 11	03 11	04 04	04 56	05 48
20	05 11	05 37	06 00	03 14	04 04	04 52	05 41
N 10	05 03	05 28	05 50	03 17	04 03	04 49	05 34
0	04 54	05 19	05 40	03 19	04 02	04 45	05 28
S 10	04 44	05 09	05 31	03 21	04 02	04 42	05 22
20	04 31	04 58	05 20	03 24	04 01	04 38	05 16
30	04 14	04 43	05 09	03 27	04 00	04 34	05 08
35	04 03	04 35	05 02	03 28	04 00	04 32	05 04
40	03 50	04 25	04 54	03 30	04 00	04 29	04 59
45	03 34	04 13	04 44	03 32	03 59	04 26	04 54
S 50	03 13	03 57	04 33	03 35	03 59	04 22	04 47
52	03 02	03 50	04 28	03 36	03 58	04 21	04 44
54	02 50	03 42	04 22	03 37	03 58	04 19	04 41
56	02 36	03 33	04 16	03 38	03 58	04 17	04 37
58	02 19	03 22	04 08	03 40	03 57	04 15	04 33
S 60	01 58	03 10	04 00	03 42	03 57	04 12	04 29

Lat.	Sunset h m	Twilight Civil h m	Twilight Naut. h m	Moonset 27 h m	Moonset 28 h m	Moonset 29 h m	Moonset 30 h m
N 72	14 51	16 13	17 34	15 54	15 48	15 42	15 36
N 70	15 13	16 24	17 37	15 52	15 52	15 51	15 51
68	15 30	16 33	17 39	15 51	15 55	15 59	16 03
66	15 44	16 41	17 41	15 50	15 57	16 05	16 14
64	15 56	16 47	17 43	15 49	16 00	16 10	16 22
62	16 05	16 53	17 45	15 49	16 01	16 15	16 30
60	16 14	16 58	17 47	15 48	16 03	16 19	16 36
N 58	16 21	17 02	17 49	15 47	16 05	16 22	16 42
56	16 27	17 07	17 50	15 47	16 06	16 26	16 47
54	16 33	17 10	17 52	15 46	16 07	16 28	16 51
52	16 38	17 14	17 53	15 46	16 08	16 31	16 55
50	16 43	17 17	17 55	15 46	16 09	16 34	16 59
45	16 53	17 24	17 58	15 45	16 12	16 39	17 07
N 40	17 02	17 30	18 02	15 44	16 13	16 43	17 14
35	17 09	17 35	18 05	15 43	16 15	16 47	17 20
30	17 16	17 41	18 09	15 43	16 16	16 50	17 25
20	17 27	17 50	18 16	15 42	16 19	16 56	17 34
N 10	17 38	17 59	18 24	15 41	16 21	17 01	17 42
0	17 47	18 08	18 33	15 40	16 23	17 06	17 49
S 10	17 57	18 19	18 44	15 39	16 25	17 11	17 57
20	18 07	18 30	18 57	15 38	16 27	17 16	18 05
30	18 19	18 45	19 14	15 37	16 30	17 22	18 14
35	18 27	18 53	19 25	15 36	16 31	17 25	18 19
40	18 35	19 03	19 38	15 36	16 33	17 29	18 25
45	18 44	19 16	19 55	15 35	16 34	17 33	18 32
S 50	18 56	19 31	20 16	15 34	16 37	17 39	18 40
52	19 01	19 39	20 27	15 33	16 38	17 41	18 44
54	19 07	19 47	20 39	15 33	16 39	17 44	18 48
56	19 13	19 56	20 54	15 32	16 40	17 47	18 53
58	19 21	20 07	21 11	15 32	16 41	17 50	18 58
S 60	19 29	20 20	21 34	15 31	16 43	17 54	19 04

Day	SUN Eqn. of Time 00^h	SUN Eqn. of Time 12^h	SUN Mer. Pass.	MOON Mer. Pass. Upper	MOON Mer. Pass. Lower	MOON Age	MOON Phase
d	m s	m s	h m	h m	h m	d %	
27	16 08	16 11	11 44	09 30	21 51	26 9	●
28	16 13	16 15	11 44	10 13	22 34	27 5	
29	16 17	16 19	11 44	10 55	23 17	28 1	

Day	UT	ARIES	VENUS −4·0		MARS +0·4		JUPITER −1·7		SATURN +0·5		STARS		
		GHA	GHA	Dec	GHA	Dec	GHA	Dec	GHA	Dec	Name	SHA	Dec
	d h	° ′	° ′	° ′	° ′	° ′	° ′	° ′	° ′	° ′		° ′	° ′
	30 00	38 44.4	146 09.1	S24 07.1	104 02.1	S23 29.6	208 23.4	S 3 14.2	145 43.9	S21 08.6	Acamar	315 16.3	S40 14.3
	01	53 46.9	161 08.3	07.6	119 02.6	29.3	223 25.4	14.4	160 46.1	08.7	Achernar	335 24.6	S57 09.2
	02	68 49.3	176 07.5	08.1	134 03.2	28.9	238 27.4	14.6	175 48.3	08.7	Acrux	173 07.2	S63 11.3
	03	83 51.8	191 06.7	. . 08.5	149 03.7	. . 28.6	253 29.4	. . 14.8	190 50.5	. . 08.7	Adhara	255 10.6	S28 59.6
	04	98 54.3	206 05.9	09.0	164 04.3	28.2	268 31.4	15.0	205 52.7	08.8	Aldebaran	290 46.5	N16 32.4
	05	113 56.7	221 05.1	09.4	179 04.8	27.9	283 33.3	15.2	220 54.9	08.8			
	06	128 59.2	236 04.3	S24 09.9	194 05.3	S23 27.6	298 35.3	S 3 15.4	235 57.1	S21 08.8	Alioth	166 19.3	N55 52.1
	07	144 01.7	251 03.5	10.4	209 05.9	27.2	313 37.3	15.6	250 59.2	08.9	Alkaid	152 57.7	N49 13.9
	08	159 04.1	266 02.7	10.8	224 06.4	26.9	328 39.3	15.7	266 01.4	08.9	Al Na'ir	27 40.8	S46 52.9
S	09	174 06.6	281 01.9	. . 11.3	239 06.9	. . 26.5	343 41.3	. . 15.9	281 03.6	. . 08.9	Alnilam	275 43.9	S 1 11.6
U	10	189 09.1	296 01.1	11.7	254 07.5	26.2	358 43.3	16.1	296 05.8	09.0	Alphard	217 53.9	S 8 43.8
N	11	204 11.5	311 00.3	12.2	269 08.0	25.8	13 45.3	16.3	311 08.0	09.0			
D	12	219 14.0	325 59.5	S24 12.6	284 08.6	S23 25.5	28 47.3	S 3 16.5	326 10.2	S21 09.0	Alphecca	126 09.5	N26 39.8
A	13	234 16.4	340 58.7	13.1	299 09.1	25.2	43 49.3	16.7	341 12.4	09.1	Alpheratz	357 40.8	N29 11.1
Y	14	249 18.9	355 57.9	13.5	314 09.6	24.8	58 51.3	16.9	356 14.6	09.1	Altair	62 06.1	N 8 55.1
	15	264 21.4	10 57.1	. . 14.0	329 10.2	. . 24.5	73 53.3	. . 17.1	11 16.8	. . 09.1	Ankaa	353 13.2	S42 13.0
	16	279 23.8	25 56.3	14.4	344 10.7	24.1	88 55.3	17.3	26 19.0	09.2	Antares	112 23.8	S26 27.9
	17	294 26.3	40 55.5	14.9	359 11.2	23.8	103 57.3	17.5	41 21.2	09.2			
	18	309 28.8	55 54.7	S24 15.3	14 11.8	S23 23.4	118 59.2	S 3 17.7	56 23.4	S21 09.3	Arcturus	145 54.1	N19 05.9
	19	324 31.2	70 53.9	15.7	29 12.3	23.1	134 01.2	17.9	71 25.6	09.3	Atria	107 24.0	S69 03.3
	20	339 33.7	85 53.0	16.2	44 12.8	22.7	149 03.2	18.1	86 27.7	09.3	Avior	234 17.0	S59 33.6
	21	354 36.2	100 52.2	. . 16.6	59 13.4	. . 22.4	164 05.2	. . 18.3	101 29.9	. . 09.4	Bellatrix	278 29.3	N 6 21.8
	22	9 38.6	115 51.4	17.1	74 13.9	22.0	179 07.2	18.5	116 32.1	09.4	Betelgeuse	270 58.6	N 7 24.5
	23	24 41.1	130 50.6	17.5	89 14.5	21.7	194 09.2	18.7	131 34.3	09.4			
	31 00	39 43.5	145 49.8	S24 17.9	104 15.0	S23 21.3	209 11.2	S 3 18.9	146 36.5	S21 09.5	Canopus	263 54.8	S52 42.2
	01	54 46.0	160 49.0	18.4	119 15.5	21.0	224 13.2	19.1	161 38.7	09.5	Capella	280 30.7	N46 00.6
	02	69 48.5	175 48.2	18.8	134 16.1	20.6	239 15.2	19.3	176 40.9	09.5	Deneb	49 29.9	N45 20.8
	03	84 50.9	190 47.4	. . 19.2	149 16.6	. . 20.3	254 17.2	. . 19.5	191 43.1	. . 09.6	Denebola	182 31.6	N14 28.8
	04	99 53.4	205 46.6	19.7	164 17.1	19.9	269 19.2	19.7	206 45.3	09.6	Diphda	348 53.4	S17 53.7
	05	114 55.9	220 45.8	20.1	179 17.7	19.6	284 21.2	19.9	221 47.5	09.6			
	06	129 58.3	235 45.0	S24 20.5	194 18.2	S23 19.2	299 23.2	S 3 20.1	236 49.7	S21 09.7	Dubhe	193 49.5	N61 39.4
	07	145 00.8	250 44.2	21.0	209 18.8	18.9	314 25.1	20.3	251 51.9	09.7	Elnath	278 09.5	N28 37.1
	08	160 03.3	265 43.4	21.4	224 19.3	18.5	329 27.1	20.5	266 54.0	09.7	Eltanin	90 45.4	N51 29.6
M	09	175 05.7	280 42.6	. . 21.8	239 19.8	. . 18.2	344 29.1	. . 20.7	281 56.2	. . 09.8	Enif	33 44.8	N 9 57.4
O	10	190 08.2	295 41.8	22.2	254 20.4	17.8	359 31.1	20.8	296 58.4	09.8	Fomalhaut	15 21.3	S29 32.0
N	11	205 10.7	310 40.9	22.7	269 20.9	17.5	14 33.1	21.0	312 00.6	09.8			
D	12	220 13.1	325 40.1	S24 23.1	284 21.4	S23 17.1	29 35.1	S 3 21.2	327 02.8	S21 09.9	Gacrux	171 58.8	S57 12.2
A	13	235 15.6	340 39.3	23.5	299 22.0	16.8	44 37.1	21.4	342 05.0	09.9	Gienah	175 50.2	S17 37.9
Y	14	250 18.0	355 38.5	23.9	314 22.5	16.4	59 39.1	21.6	357 07.2	10.0	Hadar	148 45.2	S60 27.0
	15	265 20.5	10 37.7	. . 24.4	329 23.0	. . 16.1	74 41.1	. . 21.8	12 09.4	. . 10.0	Hamal	327 57.8	N23 32.5
	16	280 23.0	25 36.9	24.8	344 23.6	15.7	89 43.1	22.0	27 11.6	10.0	Kaus Aust.	83 41.1	S34 22.4
	17	295 25.4	40 36.1	25.2	359 24.1	15.3	104 45.1	22.2	42 13.8	10.1			
	18	310 27.9	55 35.3	S24 25.6	14 24.7	S23 15.0	119 47.1	S 3 22.4	57 15.9	S21 10.1	Kochab	137 21.5	N74 05.4
	19	325 30.4	70 34.5	26.0	29 25.2	14.6	134 49.1	22.6	72 18.1	10.1	Markab	13 35.9	N15 17.9
	20	340 32.8	85 33.6	26.4	44 25.7	14.3	149 51.1	22.8	87 20.3	10.2	Menkar	314 12.4	N 4 09.3
	21	355 35.3	100 32.8	. . 26.8	59 26.3	. . 13.9	164 53.1	. . 23.0	102 22.5	. . 10.2	Menkent	148 05.3	S36 26.9
	22	10 37.8	115 32.0	27.3	74 26.8	13.6	179 55.1	23.2	117 24.7	10.2	Miaplacidus	221 39.2	S69 46.9
	23	25 40.2	130 31.2	27.7	89 27.3	13.2	194 57.0	23.4	132 26.9	10.3			
	1 00	40 42.7	145 30.4	S24 28.1	104 27.9	S23 12.9	209 59.0	S 3 23.6	147 29.1	S21 10.3	Mirfak	308 36.6	N49 55.1
	01	55 45.2	160 29.6	28.5	119 28.4	12.5	225 01.0	23.8	162 31.3	10.3	Nunki	75 55.7	S26 16.4
	02	70 47.6	175 28.8	28.9	134 29.0	12.1	240 03.0	24.0	177 33.5	10.4	Peacock	53 15.8	S56 40.9
	03	85 50.1	190 28.0	. . 29.3	149 29.5	. . 11.8	255 05.0	. . 24.2	192 35.6	. . 10.4	Pollux	243 24.9	N27 58.9
	04	100 52.5	205 27.1	29.7	164 30.0	11.4	270 07.0	24.4	207 37.8	10.4	Procyon	244 57.3	N 5 10.8
	05	115 55.0	220 26.3	30.1	179 30.6	11.1	285 09.0	24.6	222 40.0	10.5			
	06	130 57.5	235 25.5	S24 30.5	194 31.1	S23 10.7	300 11.0	S 3 24.8	237 42.2	S21 10.5	Rasalhague	96 04.6	N12 33.2
	07	145 59.9	250 24.7	30.9	209 31.6	10.3	315 13.0	24.9	252 44.4	10.6	Regulus	207 41.3	N11 53.1
T	08	161 02.4	265 23.9	31.3	224 32.2	10.0	330 15.0	25.1	267 46.6	10.6	Rigel	281 09.6	S 8 11.0
U	09	176 04.9	280 23.1	. . 31.7	239 32.7	. . 09.6	345 17.0	. . 25.3	282 48.8	. . 10.6	Rigil Kent.	139 49.2	S60 54.0
E	10	191 07.3	295 22.3	32.1	254 33.2	09.2	0 19.0	25.5	297 51.0	10.7	Sabik	102 10.2	S15 44.5
S	11	206 09.8	310 21.4	32.5	269 33.8	08.9	15 21.0	25.7	312 53.2	10.7			
D	12	221 12.3	325 20.6	S24 32.9	284 34.3	S23 08.5	30 23.0	S 3 25.9	327 55.3	S21 10.7	Schedar	349 37.3	N56 37.9
A	13	236 14.7	340 19.8	33.3	299 34.9	08.2	45 25.0	26.1	342 57.5	10.8	Shaula	96 19.2	S37 06.8
Y	14	251 17.2	355 19.0	33.7	314 35.4	07.8	60 27.0	26.3	357 59.7	10.8	Sirius	258 31.6	S16 44.4
	15	266 19.6	10 18.2	. . 34.1	329 35.9	. . 07.4	75 29.0	. . 26.5	13 01.9	. . 10.8	Spica	158 29.2	S11 14.7
	16	281 22.1	25 17.4	34.5	344 36.5	07.1	90 31.0	26.7	28 04.1	10.9	Suhail	222 50.8	S43 29.8
	17	296 24.6	40 16.5	34.8	359 37.0	06.7	105 33.0	26.9	43 06.3	10.9			
	18	311 27.0	55 15.7	S24 35.2	14 37.5	S23 06.3	120 35.0	S 3 27.1	58 08.5	S21 10.9	Vega	80 37.7	N38 48.4
	19	326 29.5	70 14.9	35.6	29 38.1	06.0	135 36.9	27.3	73 10.7	11.0	Zuben'ubi	137 03.3	S16 06.4
	20	341 32.0	85 14.1	36.0	44 38.6	05.6	150 38.9	27.5	88 12.8	11.0		SHA	Mer. Pass.
	21	356 34.4	100 13.3	. . 36.4	59 39.2	. . 05.2	165 40.9	. . 27.7	103 15.0	. . 11.0		° ′	h m
	22	11 36.9	115 12.4	36.8	74 39.7	04.9	180 42.9	27.9	118 17.2	11.1	Venus	106 06.3	14 17
	23	26 39.4	130 11.6	37.1	89 40.2	04.5	195 44.9	28.1	133 19.4	11.1	Mars	64 31.4	17 02
		h m									Jupiter	169 27.6	10 02
	Mer. Pass.	21 17.6	v −0.8	d 0.4	v 0.5	d 0.4	v 2.0	d 0.2	v 2.2	d 0.0	Saturn	106 53.0	14 11

	UT	SUN GHA	SUN Dec	MOON GHA	*v*	MOON Dec	*d*	HP
	d h	° ′	° ′	° ′	′	° ′	′	′
	30 00	184 05.2	S13 50.7	190 26.2	14.8	S 7 36.0	8.8	54.1
	01	199 05.2	51.6	205 00.0	14.8	7 44.8	8.7	54.1
	02	214 05.2	52.4	219 33.8	14.8	7 53.5	8.6	54.1
	03	229 05.3	. . 53.2	234 07.6	14.8	8 02.1	8.7	54.0
	04	244 05.3	54.0	248 41.4	14.8	8 10.8	8.6	54.0
	05	259 05.3	54.8	263 15.2	14.7	8 19.4	8.5	54.0
	06	274 05.3	S13 55.6	277 48.9	14.7	S 8 27.9	8.5	54.0
	07	289 05.4	56.5	292 22.6	14.7	8 36.4	8.5	54.0
	08	304 05.4	57.3	306 56.3	14.7	8 44.9	8.5	54.0
S	09	319 05.4	. . 58.1	321 30.0	14.7	8 53.4	8.4	54.0
U	10	334 05.5	58.9	336 03.7	14.7	9 01.8	8.3	54.0
N	11	349 05.5	13 59.7	350 37.4	14.6	9 10.1	8.4	54.0
D	12	4 05.5	S14 00.5	5 11.0	14.6	S 9 18.5	8.3	54.0
A	13	19 05.5	01.3	19 44.6	14.6	9 26.8	8.2	54.0
Y	14	34 05.6	02.2	34 18.2	14.6	9 35.0	8.2	54.0
	15	49 05.6	. . 03.0	48 51.8	14.6	9 43.2	8.2	54.0
	16	64 05.6	03.8	63 25.4	14.5	9 51.4	8.1	54.0
	17	79 05.6	04.6	77 58.9	14.5	9 59.5	8.1	54.0
	18	94 05.7	S14 05.4	92 32.4	14.6	S10 07.6	8.1	54.0
	19	109 05.7	06.2	107 06.0	14.4	10 15.7	8.0	54.0
	20	124 05.7	07.0	121 39.4	14.5	10 23.7	7.9	54.0
	21	139 05.7	. . 07.8	136 12.9	14.5	10 31.6	7.9	54.0
	22	154 05.8	08.6	150 46.4	14.4	10 39.5	7.9	54.0
	23	169 05.8	09.5	165 19.8	14.4	10 47.4	7.8	54.0
	31 00	184 05.8	S14 10.3	179 53.2	14.4	S10 55.2	7.8	53.9
	01	199 05.8	11.1	194 26.6	14.3	11 03.0	7.7	53.9
	02	214 05.9	11.9	208 59.9	14.4	11 10.7	7.7	53.9
	03	229 05.9	. . 12.7	223 33.3	14.3	11 18.4	7.6	53.9
	04	244 05.9	13.5	238 06.6	14.3	11 26.0	7.6	53.9
	05	259 05.9	14.3	252 39.9	14.2	11 33.6	7.5	53.9
	06	274 06.0	S14 15.1	267 13.1	14.3	S11 41.1	7.5	53.9
	07	289 06.0	15.9	281 46.4	14.2	11 48.6	7.4	53.9
	08	304 06.0	16.7	296 19.6	14.2	11 56.0	7.4	53.9
M	09	319 06.0	. . 17.5	310 52.8	14.2	12 03.4	7.4	53.9
O	10	334 06.0	18.3	325 26.0	14.1	12 10.8	7.2	53.9
N	11	349 06.1	19.1	339 59.1	14.1	12 18.0	7.3	53.9
D	12	4 06.1	S14 19.9	354 32.2	14.1	S12 25.3	7.1	53.9
A	13	19 06.1	20.7	9 05.3	14.1	12 32.4	7.2	53.9
Y	14	34 06.1	21.5	23 38.4	14.1	12 39.6	7.0	53.9
	15	49 06.1	. . 22.3	38 11.5	14.0	12 46.6	7.1	53.9
	16	64 06.1	23.1	52 44.5	14.0	12 53.7	6.9	53.9
	17	79 06.2	23.9	67 17.5	14.0	13 00.6	6.9	53.9
	18	94 06.2	S14 24.7	81 50.5	13.9	S13 07.5	6.9	53.9
	19	109 06.2	25.5	96 23.4	13.9	13 14.4	6.8	53.9
	20	124 06.2	26.3	110 56.3	13.9	13 21.2	6.7	53.9
	21	139 06.2	. . 27.1	125 29.2	13.9	13 27.9	6.7	53.9
	22	154 06.2	27.9	140 02.1	13.8	13 34.6	6.6	53.9
	23	169 06.3	28.7	154 34.9	13.8	13 41.2	6.5	53.9
	1 00	184 06.3	S14 29.5	169 07.7	13.8	S13 47.7	6.5	53.9
	01	199 06.3	30.3	183 40.5	13.8	13 54.2	6.5	53.9
	02	214 06.3	31.1	198 13.3	13.7	14 00.7	6.4	53.9
	03	229 06.3	. . 31.9	212 46.0	13.7	14 07.1	6.3	53.9
	04	244 06.3	32.7	227 18.7	13.7	14 13.4	6.2	53.9
	05	259 06.3	33.5	241 51.4	13.6	14 19.6	6.2	53.9
	06	274 06.4	S14 34.3	256 24.0	13.6	S14 25.8	6.2	53.9
	07	289 06.4	35.1	270 56.6	13.6	14 32.0	6.1	53.9
T	08	304 06.4	35.9	285 29.2	13.6	14 38.1	6.0	53.9
U	09	319 06.4	. . 36.7	300 01.8	13.5	14 44.1	5.9	53.9
E	10	334 06.4	37.5	314 34.3	13.5	14 50.0	5.9	53.9
S	11	349 06.4	38.3	329 06.8	13.5	14 55.9	5.8	53.9
D	12	4 06.4	S14 39.1	343 39.3	13.5	S15 01.7	5.8	53.9
A	13	19 06.4	39.9	358 11.8	13.4	15 07.5	5.7	53.9
Y	14	34 06.4	40.7	12 44.2	13.4	15 13.2	5.6	53.9
	15	49 06.5	. . 41.5	27 16.6	13.4	15 18.8	5.5	54.0
	16	64 06.5	42.3	41 49.0	13.3	15 24.3	5.5	54.0
	17	79 06.5	43.1	56 21.3	13.3	15 29.8	5.5	54.0
	18	94 06.5	S14 43.9	70 53.6	13.3	S15 35.3	5.3	54.0
	19	109 06.5	44.7	85 25.9	13.2	15 40.6	5.3	54.0
	20	124 06.5	45.4	99 58.1	13.2	15 45.9	5.2	54.0
	21	139 06.5	. . 46.2	114 30.3	13.2	15 51.1	5.2	54.0
	22	154 06.5	47.0	129 02.5	13.2	15 56.3	5.0	54.0
	23	169 06.5	47.8	143 34.7	13.1	S16 01.3	5.1	54.0
		SD 16.1	*d* 0.8	SD 14.7		14.7		14.7

Lat.	Twilight Naut.	Twilight Civil	Sunrise	Moonrise 30	Moonrise 31	Moonrise 1	Moonrise 2
°	h m	h m	h m	h m	h m	h m	h m
N 72	06 04	07 26	08 53	07 24	09 03	10 45	12 38
N 70	06 00	07 14	08 27	07 11	08 40	10 11	11 40
68	05 56	07 03	08 08	07 00	08 23	09 46	11 06
66	05 53	06 55	07 53	06 50	08 10	09 27	10 41
64	05 51	06 47	07 40	06 43	07 58	09 12	10 22
62	05 48	06 41	07 30	06 36	07 49	08 59	10 07
60	05 46	06 35	07 21	06 31	07 40	08 49	09 54
N 58	05 44	06 30	07 13	06 26	07 33	08 39	09 42
56	05 42	06 26	07 06	06 21	07 27	08 31	09 33
54	05 40	06 22	06 59	06 17	07 21	08 24	09 24
52	05 38	06 18	06 54	06 14	07 16	08 17	09 17
50	05 36	06 15	06 49	06 11	07 12	08 12	09 10
45	05 32	06 07	06 37	06 04	07 02	07 59	08 55
N 40	05 28	06 00	06 28	05 58	06 54	07 49	08 43
35	05 24	05 54	06 20	05 53	06 47	07 40	08 33
30	05 20	05 49	06 13	05 48	06 40	07 32	08 24
20	05 12	05 38	06 01	05 41	06 30	07 19	08 08
N 10	05 04	05 29	05 50	05 34	06 20	07 07	07 55
0	04 54	05 19	05 40	05 28	06 12	06 56	07 42
S 10	04 43	05 08	05 30	05 22	06 03	06 46	07 30
20	04 29	04 56	05 19	05 16	05 54	06 34	07 16
30	04 11	04 41	05 06	05 08	05 44	06 21	07 01
35	03 59	04 32	04 58	05 04	05 38	06 14	06 52
40	03 46	04 21	04 50	04 59	05 31	06 05	06 42
45	03 28	04 08	04 40	04 54	05 23	05 55	06 31
S 50	03 06	03 52	04 28	04 47	05 14	05 43	06 17
52	02 55	03 44	04 22	04 44	05 09	05 38	06 10
54	02 42	03 35	04 16	04 41	05 05	05 32	06 03
56	02 26	03 25	04 09	04 37	04 59	05 25	05 55
58	02 07	03 14	04 01	04 33	04 54	05 17	05 45
S 60	01 43	03 00	03 52	04 29	04 47	05 08	05 35

Lat.	Sunset	Twilight Civil	Twilight Naut.	Moonset 30	Moonset 31	Moonset 1	Moonset 2
°	h m	h m	h m	h m	h m	h m	h m
N 72	14 33	15 59	17 22	15 36	15 28	15 19	15 02
N 70	14 58	16 12	17 26	15 51	15 52	15 54	16 01
68	15 18	16 22	17 29	16 03	16 10	16 20	16 35
66	15 33	16 31	17 32	16 14	16 24	16 39	17 00
64	15 46	16 39	17 35	16 22	16 37	16 55	17 19
62	15 57	16 45	17 38	16 30	16 47	17 08	17 35
60	16 06	16 51	17 40	16 36	16 56	17 19	17 49
N 58	16 14	16 56	17 42	16 42	17 03	17 29	18 00
56	16 21	17 00	17 44	16 47	17 10	17 38	18 10
54	16 27	17 04	17 46	16 51	17 16	17 45	18 19
52	16 33	17 08	17 48	16 55	17 22	17 52	18 27
50	16 38	17 12	17 50	16 59	17 27	17 58	18 34
45	16 49	17 20	17 54	17 07	17 38	18 11	18 49
N 40	16 58	17 26	17 58	17 14	17 47	18 22	19 02
35	17 06	17 33	18 02	17 20	17 54	18 32	19 12
30	17 13	17 38	18 06	17 25	18 01	18 40	19 22
20	17 26	17 48	18 15	17 34	18 13	18 54	19 38
N 10	17 37	17 58	18 23	17 42	18 24	19 07	19 52
0	17 47	18 08	18 33	17 49	18 33	19 18	20 05
S 10	17 57	18 19	18 45	17 57	18 43	19 30	20 18
20	18 09	18 32	18 59	18 05	18 53	19 43	20 32
30	18 22	18 47	19 17	18 14	19 05	19 57	20 48
35	18 29	18 56	19 29	18 19	19 12	20 05	20 58
40	18 38	19 07	19 43	18 25	19 20	20 15	21 08
45	18 48	19 20	20 00	18 32	19 29	20 26	21 21
S 50	19 01	19 37	20 23	18 40	19 41	20 40	21 36
52	19 06	19 45	20 34	18 44	19 46	20 46	21 44
54	19 13	19 54	20 48	18 48	19 52	20 53	21 52
56	19 20	20 04	21 04	18 53	19 58	21 01	22 01
58	19 28	20 16	21 23	18 58	20 05	21 10	22 11
S 60	19 37	20 29	21 48	19 04	20 13	21 20	22 22

	SUN			MOON			
Day	Eqn. of Time 00^h	Eqn. of Time 12^h	Mer. Pass.	Mer. Pass. Upper	Mer. Pass. Lower	Age	Phase
d	m s	m s	h m	h m	h m	d	%
30	16 21	16 22	11 44	11 39	24 00	29	0
31	16 23	16 24	11 44	12 23	00 00	01	1
1	16 25	16 26	11 44	13 07	00 45	02	3

	UT d h	ARIES GHA ° ′	VENUS −4·0 GHA ° ′	VENUS Dec ° ′	MARS +0·4 GHA ° ′	MARS Dec ° ′	JUPITER −1·7 GHA ° ′	JUPITER Dec ° ′	SATURN +0·5 GHA ° ′	SATURN Dec ° ′
	2 00	41 41.8	145 10.8	S24 37.5	104 40.8	S23 04.1	210 46.9	S 3 28.3	148 21.6	S21 11.1
	01	56 44.3	160 10.0	37.9	119 41.3	03.8	225 48.9	28.4	163 23.8	11.2
	02	71 46.8	175 09.2	38.3	134 41.8	03.4	240 50.9	28.6	178 26.0	11.2
	03	86 49.2	190 08.3	. . 38.7	149 42.4	. . 03.0	255 52.9	. . 28.8	193 28.2	. . 11.3
	04	101 51.7	205 07.5	39.0	164 42.9	02.7	270 54.9	29.0	208 30.3	11.3
	05	116 54.1	220 06.7	39.4	179 43.5	02.3	285 56.9	29.2	223 32.5	11.3
	06	131 56.6	235 05.9	S24 39.8	194 44.0	S23 01.9	300 58.9	S 3 29.4	238 34.7	S21 11.4
W	07	146 59.1	250 05.1	40.1	209 44.5	01.5	316 00.9	29.6	253 36.9	11.4
E	08	162 01.5	265 04.2	40.5	224 45.1	01.2	331 02.9	29.8	268 39.1	11.4
D	09	177 04.0	280 03.4	. . 40.9	239 45.6	. . 00.8	346 04.9	. . 30.0	283 41.3	. . 11.5
N	10	192 06.5	295 02.6	41.3	254 46.1	00.4	1 06.9	30.2	298 43.5	11.5
E	11	207 08.9	310 01.8	41.6	269 46.7	23 00.1	16 08.9	30.4	313 45.7	11.5
S	12	222 11.4	325 01.0	S24 42.0	284 47.2	S22 59.7	31 10.9	S 3 30.6	328 47.8	S21 11.6
D	13	237 13.9	340 00.1	42.4	299 47.8	59.3	46 12.9	30.8	343 50.0	11.6
A	14	252 16.3	354 59.3	42.7	314 48.3	58.9	61 14.9	31.0	358 52.2	11.6
Y	15	267 18.8	9 58.5	. . 43.1	329 48.8	. . 58.6	76 16.9	. . 31.2	13 54.4	. . 11.7
	16	282 21.3	24 57.7	43.4	344 49.4	58.2	91 18.9	31.4	28 56.6	11.7
	17	297 23.7	39 56.8	43.8	359 49.9	57.8	106 20.9	31.5	43 58.8	11.7
	18	312 26.2	54 56.0	S24 44.2	14 50.4	S22 57.4	121 22.9	S 3 31.7	59 01.0	S21 11.8
	19	327 28.6	69 55.2	44.5	29 51.0	57.1	136 24.9	31.9	74 03.1	11.8
	20	342 31.1	84 54.4	44.9	44 51.5	56.7	151 26.9	32.1	89 05.3	11.8
	21	357 33.6	99 53.5	. . 45.2	59 52.1	. . 56.3	166 28.9	. . 32.3	104 07.5	. . 11.9
	22	12 36.0	114 52.7	45.6	74 52.6	55.9	181 30.9	32.5	119 09.7	11.9
	23	27 38.5	129 51.9	45.9	89 53.1	55.6	196 32.9	32.7	134 11.9	12.0
	3 00	42 41.0	144 51.1	S24 46.3	104 53.7	S22 55.2	211 34.9	S 3 32.9	149 14.1	S21 12.0
	01	57 43.4	159 50.2	46.6	119 54.2	54.8	226 36.9	33.1	164 16.3	12.0
	02	72 45.9	174 49.4	47.0	134 54.7	54.4	241 38.8	33.3	179 18.4	12.1
	03	87 48.4	189 48.6	. . 47.3	149 55.3	. . 54.1	256 40.8	. . 33.5	194 20.6	. . 12.1
	04	102 50.8	204 47.8	47.7	164 55.8	53.7	271 42.8	33.7	209 22.8	12.1
	05	117 53.3	219 46.9	48.0	179 56.4	53.3	286 44.8	33.9	224 25.0	12.2
	06	132 55.8	234 46.1	S24 48.4	194 56.9	S22 52.9	301 46.8	S 3 34.1	239 27.2	S21 12.2
	07	147 58.2	249 45.3	48.7	209 57.4	52.5	316 48.8	34.3	254 29.4	12.2
T	08	163 00.7	264 44.5	49.0	224 58.0	52.2	331 50.8	34.4	269 31.5	12.3
H	09	178 03.1	279 43.6	. . 49.4	239 58.5	. . 51.8	346 52.8	. . 34.6	284 33.7	. . 12.3
U	10	193 05.6	294 42.8	49.7	254 59.0	51.4	1 54.8	34.8	299 35.9	12.3
R	11	208 08.1	309 42.0	50.1	269 59.6	51.0	16 56.8	35.0	314 38.1	12.4
S	12	223 10.5	324 41.1	S24 50.4	285 00.1	S22 50.6	31 58.8	S 3 35.2	329 40.3	S21 12.4
D	13	238 13.0	339 40.3	50.7	300 00.7	50.3	47 00.8	35.4	344 42.5	12.4
A	14	253 15.5	354 39.5	51.1	315 01.2	49.9	62 02.8	35.6	359 44.7	12.5
Y	15	268 17.9	9 38.7	. . 51.4	330 01.7	. . 49.5	77 04.8	. . 35.8	14 46.8	. . 12.5
	16	283 20.4	24 37.8	51.7	345 02.3	49.1	92 06.8	36.0	29 49.0	12.5
	17	298 22.9	39 37.0	52.1	0 02.8	48.7	107 08.8	36.2	44 51.2	12.6
	18	313 25.3	54 36.2	S24 52.4	15 03.4	S22 48.3	122 10.8	S 3 36.4	59 53.4	S21 12.6
	19	328 27.8	69 35.3	52.7	30 03.9	48.0	137 12.8	36.6	74 55.6	12.6
	20	343 30.2	84 34.5	53.0	45 04.4	47.6	152 14.8	36.8	89 57.8	12.7
	21	358 32.7	99 33.7	. . 53.4	60 05.0	. . 47.2	167 16.8	. . 36.9	104 59.9	. . 12.7
	22	13 35.2	114 32.9	53.7	75 05.5	46.8	182 18.8	37.1	120 02.1	12.8
	23	28 37.6	129 32.0	54.0	90 06.0	46.4	197 20.8	37.3	135 04.3	12.8
	4 00	43 40.1	144 31.2	S24 54.3	105 06.6	S22 46.0	212 22.8	S 3 37.5	150 06.5	S21 12.8
	01	58 42.6	159 30.4	54.6	120 07.1	45.6	227 24.8	37.7	165 08.7	12.9
	02	73 45.0	174 29.5	55.0	135 07.7	45.3	242 26.8	37.9	180 10.9	12.9
	03	88 47.5	189 28.7	. . 55.3	150 08.2	. . 44.9	257 28.8	. . 38.1	195 13.0	. . 12.9
	04	103 50.0	204 27.9	55.6	165 08.7	44.5	272 30.8	38.3	210 15.2	13.0
	05	118 52.4	219 27.0	55.9	180 09.3	44.1	287 32.8	38.5	225 17.4	13.0
	06	133 54.9	234 26.2	S24 56.2	195 09.8	S22 43.7	302 34.8	S 3 38.7	240 19.6	S21 13.0
	07	148 57.4	249 25.4	56.5	210 10.4	43.3	317 36.8	38.9	255 21.8	13.1
	08	163 59.8	264 24.5	56.9	225 10.9	42.9	332 38.8	39.1	270 24.0	13.1
F	09	179 02.3	279 23.7	. . 57.2	240 11.4	. . 42.5	347 40.8	. . 39.2	285 26.1	. . 13.1
R	10	194 04.7	294 22.9	57.5	255 12.0	42.1	2 42.8	39.4	300 28.3	13.2
I	11	209 07.2	309 22.0	57.8	270 12.5	41.8	17 44.8	39.6	315 30.5	13.2
D	12	224 09.7	324 21.2	S24 58.1	285 13.1	S22 41.4	32 46.8	S 3 39.8	330 32.7	S21 13.2
A	13	239 12.1	339 20.4	58.4	300 13.6	41.0	47 48.8	40.0	345 34.9	13.3
Y	14	254 14.6	354 19.5	58.7	315 14.1	40.6	62 50.8	40.2	0 37.1	13.3
	15	269 17.1	9 18.7	. . 59.0	330 14.7	. . 40.2	77 52.8	. . 40.4	15 39.2	. . 13.3
	16	284 19.5	24 17.9	59.3	345 15.2	39.8	92 54.8	40.6	30 41.4	13.4
	17	299 22.0	39 17.0	59.6	0 15.7	39.4	107 56.8	40.8	45 43.6	13.4
	18	314 24.5	54 16.2	S24 59.9	15 16.3	S22 39.0	122 58.8	S 3 41.0	60 45.8	S21 13.5
	19	329 26.9	69 15.4	25 00.2	30 16.8	38.6	138 00.8	41.2	75 48.0	13.5
	20	344 29.4	84 14.5	00.5	45 17.4	38.2	153 02.8	41.4	90 50.1	13.5
	21	359 31.9	99 13.7	. . 00.8	60 17.9	. . 37.8	168 04.8	. . 41.5	105 52.3	. . 13.6
	22	14 34.3	114 12.9	01.1	75 18.4	37.4	183 06.8	41.7	120 54.5	13.6
	23	29 36.8	129 12.0	01.4	90 19.0	37.0	198 08.8	41.9	135 56.7	13.6
	Mer. Pass.	h m 21 05.8	v −0.8	d 0.3	v 0.5	d 0.4	v 2.0	d 0.2	v 2.2	d 0.0

STARS

Name	SHA ° ′	Dec ° ′
Acamar	315 16.2	S40 14.3
Achernar	335 24.6	S57 09.2
Acrux	173 07.2	S63 11.2
Adhara	255 10.6	S28 59.7
Aldebaran	290 46.5	N16 32.4
Alioth	166 19.3	N55 52.1
Alkaid	152 57.7	N49 13.9
Al Na'ir	27 40.8	S46 52.9
Alnilam	275 43.8	S 1 11.6
Alphard	217 53.9	S 8 43.8
Alphecca	126 09.5	N26 39.8
Alpheratz	357 40.8	N29 11.1
Altair	62 06.1	N 8 55.1
Ankaa	353 13.2	S42 13.0
Antares	112 23.8	S26 27.9
Arcturus	145 54.0	N19 05.9
Atria	107 24.0	S69 03.3
Avior	234 16.9	S59 33.6
Bellatrix	278 29.3	N 6 21.7
Betelgeuse	270 58.6	N 7 24.5
Canopus	263 54.8	S52 42.2
Capella	280 30.7	N46 00.6
Deneb	49 29.9	N45 20.8
Denebola	182 31.6	N14 28.8
Diphda	348 53.4	S17 53.7
Dubhe	193 49.5	N61 39.4
Elnath	278 09.5	N28 37.1
Eltanin	90 45.5	N51 29.6
Enif	33 44.8	N 9 57.4
Fomalhaut	15 21.4	S29 32.0
Gacrux	171 58.7	S57 12.1
Gienah	175 50.2	S17 37.9
Hadar	148 45.2	S60 27.0
Hamal	327 57.8	N23 32.5
Kaus Aust.	83 41.1	S34 22.4
Kochab	137 21.5	N74 05.3
Markab	13 35.9	N15 17.9
Menkar	314 12.4	N 4 09.3
Menkent	148 05.3	S36 26.9
Miaplacidus	221 39.1	S69 46.9
Mirfak	308 36.5	N49 55.1
Nunki	75 55.7	S26 16.4
Peacock	53 15.9	S56 40.9
Pollux	243 24.9	N27 58.9
Procyon	244 57.3	N 5 10.8
Rasalhague	96 04.6	N12 33.2
Regulus	207 41.2	N11 53.1
Rigel	281 09.6	S 8 11.0
Rigil Kent.	139 49.2	S60 54.0
Sabik	102 10.2	S15 44.5
Schedar	349 37.3	N56 37.9
Shaula	96 19.2	S37 06.8
Sirius	258 31.5	S16 44.4
Spica	158 29.2	S11 14.7
Suhail	222 50.8	S43 29.8
Vega	80 37.7	N38 48.4
Zuben'ubi	137 03.2	S16 06.4

	SHA ° ′	Mer. Pass. h m
Venus	102 10.1	14 21
Mars	62 12.7	17 00
Jupiter	168 53.9	9 52
Saturn	106 33.1	14 01

UT d h	SUN GHA	SUN Dec	MOON GHA	v	MOON Dec	d	HP
	° ′	° ′	° ′	′	° ′	′	′
2 00	184 06.5	S14 48.6	158 06.8	13.2	S16 06.4	4.9	54.0
01	199 06.5	49.4	172 39.0	13.0	16 11.3	4.9	54.0
02	214 06.5	50.2	187 11.0	13.1	16 16.2	4.8	54.0
03	229 06.5	. . 51.0	201 43.1	13.0	16 21.0	4.7	54.0
04	244 06.6	51.8	216 15.1	13.0	16 25.7	4.6	54.0
05	259 06.6	52.5	230 47.1	13.0	16 30.3	4.6	54.0
06	274 06.6	S14 53.3	245 19.1	12.9	S16 34.9	4.5	54.0
W 07	289 06.6	54.1	259 51.0	12.9	16 39.4	4.5	54.0
E 08	304 06.6	54.9	274 22.9	12.9	16 43.9	4.3	54.0
D 09	319 06.6	. . 55.7	288 54.8	12.8	16 48.2	4.3	54.0
N 10	334 06.6	56.5	303 26.6	12.9	16 52.5	4.2	54.0
E 11	349 06.6	57.3	317 58.5	12.8	16 56.7	4.1	54.1
S 12	4 06.6	S14 58.0	332 30.3	12.7	S17 00.8	4.1	54.1
D 13	19 06.6	58.8	347 02.0	12.8	17 04.9	4.0	54.1
A 14	34 06.6	14 59.6	1 33.8	12.7	17 08.9	3.9	54.1
Y 15	49 06.6	15 00.4	16 05.5	12.7	17 12.8	3.8	54.1
16	64 06.6	01.2	30 37.2	12.6	17 16.6	3.8	54.1
17	79 06.6	02.0	45 08.8	12.7	17 20.4	3.7	54.1
18	94 06.6	S15 02.7	59 40.5	12.6	S17 24.1	3.6	54.1
19	109 06.6	03.5	74 12.1	12.6	17 27.7	3.5	54.1
20	124 06.6	04.3	88 43.7	12.5	17 31.2	3.4	54.1
21	139 06.6	. . 05.1	103 15.2	12.5	17 34.6	3.4	54.1
22	154 06.6	05.9	117 46.7	12.5	17 38.0	3.3	54.1
23	169 06.6	06.6	132 18.2	12.5	17 41.3	3.2	54.1
3 00	184 06.6	S15 07.4	146 49.7	12.5	S17 44.5	3.1	54.2
01	199 06.6	08.2	161 21.2	12.4	17 47.6	3.0	54.2
02	214 06.6	09.0	175 52.6	12.4	17 50.6	3.0	54.2
03	229 06.6	. . 09.7	190 24.0	12.3	17 53.6	2.9	54.2
04	244 06.6	10.5	204 55.3	12.4	17 56.5	2.8	54.2
05	259 06.6	11.3	219 26.7	12.3	17 59.3	2.7	54.2
06	274 06.6	S15 12.1	233 58.0	12.3	S18 02.0	2.6	54.2
T 07	289 06.6	12.9	248 29.3	12.3	18 04.6	2.6	54.2
H 08	304 06.6	13.6	263 00.6	12.2	18 07.2	2.5	54.2
U 09	319 06.6	. . 14.4	277 31.8	12.2	18 09.7	2.3	54.2
R 10	334 06.5	15.2	292 03.0	12.2	18 12.0	2.3	54.3
S 11	349 06.5	16.0	306 34.2	12.2	18 14.3	2.3	54.3
D 12	4 06.5	S15 16.7	321 05.4	12.1	S18 16.6	2.1	54.3
A 13	19 06.5	17.5	335 36.5	12.2	18 18.7	2.1	54.3
Y 14	34 06.5	18.3	350 07.7	12.1	18 20.8	1.9	54.3
15	49 06.5	. . 19.0	4 38.8	12.0	18 22.7	1.9	54.3
16	64 06.5	19.8	19 09.8	12.1	18 24.6	1.8	54.3
17	79 06.5	20.6	33 40.9	12.0	18 26.4	1.7	54.3
18	94 06.5	S15 21.4	48 11.9	12.0	S18 28.1	1.7	54.4
19	109 06.5	22.1	62 42.9	12.0	18 29.8	1.5	54.4
20	124 06.5	22.9	77 13.9	12.0	18 31.3	1.5	54.4
21	139 06.5	. . 23.7	91 44.9	11.9	18 32.8	1.3	54.4
22	154 06.5	24.4	106 15.8	11.9	18 34.1	1.3	54.4
23	169 06.4	25.2	120 46.7	11.9	18 35.4	1.2	54.4
4 00	184 06.4	S15 26.0	135 17.6	11.9	S18 36.6	1.1	54.4
01	199 06.4	26.7	149 48.5	11.9	18 37.7	1.0	54.5
02	214 06.4	27.5	164 19.4	11.8	18 38.7	1.0	54.5
03	229 06.4	. . 28.3	178 50.2	11.8	18 39.7	0.8	54.5
04	244 06.4	29.0	193 21.0	11.8	18 40.5	0.8	54.5
05	259 06.4	29.8	207 51.8	11.8	18 41.3	0.7	54.5
06	274 06.4	S15 30.6	222 22.6	11.8	S18 42.0	0.6	54.5
07	289 06.4	31.3	236 53.4	11.7	18 42.6	0.5	54.5
08	304 06.3	32.1	251 24.1	11.7	18 43.1	0.4	54.6
F 09	319 06.3	. . 32.9	265 54.8	11.7	18 43.5	0.3	54.6
R 10	334 06.3	33.6	280 25.5	11.7	18 43.8	0.2	54.6
I 11	349 06.3	34.4	294 56.2	11.7	18 44.0	0.2	54.6
D 12	4 06.3	S15 35.2	309 26.9	11.6	S18 44.2	0.0	54.6
A 13	19 06.3	35.9	323 57.5	11.7	18 44.2	0.0	54.6
Y 14	34 06.3	36.7	338 28.2	11.6	18 44.2	0.2	54.7
15	49 06.2	. . 37.5	352 58.8	11.6	18 44.0	0.2	54.7
16	64 06.2	38.2	7 29.4	11.6	18 43.8	0.3	54.7
17	79 06.2	39.0	22 00.0	11.5	18 43.5	0.4	54.7
18	94 06.2	S15 39.7	36 30.5	11.6	S18 43.1	0.5	54.7
19	109 06.2	40.5	51 01.1	11.5	18 42.6	0.5	54.8
20	124 06.2	41.3	65 31.6	11.5	18 42.1	0.7	54.8
21	139 06.1	. . 42.0	80 02.1	11.5	18 41.4	0.8	54.8
22	154 06.1	42.8	94 32.6	11.5	18 40.6	0.8	54.8
23	169 06.1	43.5	109 03.1	11.5	S18 39.8	0.9	54.8
	SD 16.2	*d* 0.8	SD 14.7		14.8		14.9

Lat.	Twilight Naut.	Twilight Civil	Sunrise	Moonrise 2	Moonrise 3	Moonrise 4	Moonrise 5
°	h m	h m	h m	h m	h m	h m	h m
N 72	06 16	07 40	09 12	12 38	■	■	■
N 70	06 10	07 26	08 43	11 40	13 02	14 05	14 37
68	06 06	07 14	08 21	11 06	12 18	13 15	13 54
66	06 02	07 04	08 04	10 41	11 48	12 44	13 26
64	05 59	06 56	07 50	10 22	11 26	12 20	13 04
62	05 56	06 49	07 38	10 07	11 08	12 02	12 46
60	05 53	06 42	07 28	09 54	10 54	11 47	12 32
N 58	05 50	06 37	07 20	09 42	10 41	11 34	12 19
56	05 48	06 32	07 12	09 33	10 30	11 23	12 08
54	05 45	06 27	07 05	09 24	10 21	11 13	11 59
52	05 43	06 23	06 59	09 17	10 12	11 04	11 50
50	05 41	06 19	06 54	09 10	10 05	10 56	11 43
45	05 36	06 11	06 42	08 55	09 49	10 39	11 27
N 40	05 31	06 03	06 32	08 43	09 36	10 26	11 13
35	05 27	05 57	06 23	08 33	09 24	10 14	11 02
30	05 22	05 51	06 16	08 24	09 14	10 04	10 52
20	05 14	05 40	06 03	08 08	08 58	09 47	10 35
N 10	05 04	05 29	05 51	07 55	08 43	09 31	10 20
0	04 54	05 19	05 40	07 42	08 29	09 17	10 06
S 10	04 42	05 07	05 29	07 30	08 16	09 03	09 52
20	04 27	04 54	05 17	07 16	08 01	08 48	09 37
30	04 08	04 38	05 03	07 01	07 44	08 31	09 20
35	03 56	04 28	04 55	06 52	07 35	08 21	09 10
40	03 41	04 17	04 46	06 42	07 24	08 09	08 59
45	03 23	04 03	04 35	06 31	07 11	07 56	08 46
S 50	02 59	03 46	04 22	06 17	06 55	07 39	08 30
52	02 47	03 37	04 16	06 10	06 48	07 31	08 22
54	02 33	03 28	04 09	06 03	06 39	07 23	08 13
56	02 16	03 17	04 02	05 55	06 30	07 13	08 04
58	01 55	03 05	03 53	05 45	06 20	07 02	07 53
S 60	01 27	02 50	03 44	05 35	06 08	06 49	07 40

Lat.	Sunset	Twilight Civil	Twilight Naut.	Moonset 2	Moonset 3	Moonset 4	Moonset 5
°	h m	h m	h m	h m	h m	h m	h m
N 72	14 13	15 45	17 10	15 02	■	■	■
N 70	14 43	16 00	17 15	16 01	16 16	16 54	18 03
68	15 05	16 12	17 20	16 35	17 01	17 43	18 45
66	15 22	16 22	17 24	17 00	17 31	18 15	19 14
64	15 36	16 30	17 27	17 19	17 53	18 38	19 36
62	15 48	16 37	17 30	17 35	18 11	18 56	19 53
60	15 58	16 44	17 33	17 49	18 26	19 12	20 07
N 58	16 07	16 49	17 36	18 00	18 38	19 25	20 20
56	16 14	16 54	17 39	18 10	18 49	19 36	20 30
54	16 21	16 59	17 41	18 19	18 59	19 46	20 40
52	16 27	17 03	17 43	18 27	19 07	19 54	20 48
50	16 33	17 07	17 45	18 34	19 15	20 02	20 55
45	16 45	17 16	17 51	18 49	19 31	20 19	21 11
N 40	16 55	17 23	17 55	19 02	19 45	20 32	21 24
35	17 04	17 30	18 00	19 12	19 56	20 44	21 36
30	17 11	17 36	18 04	19 22	20 06	20 54	21 45
20	17 24	17 47	18 13	19 38	20 23	21 12	22 02
N 10	17 36	17 58	18 23	19 52	20 38	21 27	22 16
0	17 47	18 08	18 33	20 05	20 52	21 41	22 30
S 10	17 58	18 20	18 46	20 18	21 06	21 55	22 43
20	18 10	18 33	19 01	20 32	21 21	22 10	22 58
30	18 24	18 50	19 20	20 48	21 38	22 27	23 14
35	18 32	18 59	19 32	20 58	21 48	22 37	23 24
40	18 42	19 11	19 47	21 08	22 00	22 49	23 34
45	18 52	19 25	20 05	21 21	22 13	23 02	23 47
S 50	19 06	19 43	20 30	21 36	22 30	23 19	24 03
52	19 12	19 51	20 42	21 44	22 37	23 26	24 10
54	19 19	20 01	20 56	21 52	22 46	23 35	24 18
56	19 27	20 12	21 14	22 01	22 56	23 45	24 27
58	19 35	20 24	21 35	22 11	23 06	23 55	24 37
S 60	19 45	20 39	22 05	22 22	23 19	24 08	00 08

Day	SUN Eqn. of Time 00^h	SUN Eqn. of Time 12^h	SUN Mer. Pass.	MOON Mer. Pass. Upper	MOON Mer. Pass. Lower	MOON Age	MOON Phase
d	m s	m s	h m	h m	h m	d	%
2	16 26	16 26	11 44	13 54	01 30	03	7
3	16 26	16 26	11 44	14 41	02 17	04	12
4	16 26	16 25	11 44	15 29	03 05	05	19

	UT	ARIES	VENUS −4·0		MARS +0·4		JUPITER −1·7		SATURN +0·5	
		GHA	GHA	Dec	GHA	Dec	GHA	Dec	GHA	Dec
	d h	° ′	° ′	° ′	° ′	° ′	° ′	° ′	° ′	° ′
	5 00	44 39.2	144 11.2	S25 01.7	105 19.5	S22 36.6	213 10.8	S 3 42.1	150 58.9	S21 13.7
	01	59 41.7	159 10.4	02.0	120 20.1	36.2	228 12.8	42.3	166 01.1	13.7
	02	74 44.2	174 09.5	02.3	135 20.6	35.8	243 14.8	42.5	181 03.2	13.7
	03	89 46.6	189 08.7	. . 02.5	150 21.1	. . 35.5	258 16.8	. . 42.7	196 05.4	. . 13.8
	04	104 49.1	204 07.9	02.8	165 21.7	35.1	273 18.8	42.9	211 07.6	13.8
	05	119 51.6	219 07.0	03.1	180 22.2	34.7	288 20.8	43.1	226 09.8	13.8
	06	134 54.0	234 06.2	S25 03.4	195 22.8	S22 34.3	303 22.8	S 3 43.3	241 12.0	S21 13.9
	07	149 56.5	249 05.4	03.7	210 23.3	33.9	318 24.8	43.5	256 14.1	13.9
S	08	164 59.0	264 04.5	04.0	225 23.8	33.5	333 26.8	43.6	271 16.3	13.9
A	09	180 01.4	279 03.7	. . 04.2	240 24.4	. . 33.1	348 28.9	. . 43.8	286 18.5	. . 14.0
T	10	195 03.9	294 02.9	04.5	255 24.9	32.7	3 30.9	44.0	301 20.7	14.0
U	11	210 06.4	309 02.0	04.8	270 25.5	32.3	18 32.9	44.2	316 22.9	14.0
R	12	225 08.8	324 01.2	S25 05.1	285 26.0	S22 31.9	33 34.9	S 3 44.4	331 25.0	S21 14.1
D	13	240 11.3	339 00.3	05.4	300 26.5	31.5	48 36.9	44.6	346 27.2	14.1
A	14	255 13.7	353 59.5	05.6	315 27.1	31.1	63 38.9	44.8	1 29.4	14.1
Y	15	270 16.2	8 58.7	. . 05.9	330 27.6	. . 30.7	78 40.9	. . 45.0	16 31.6	. . 14.2
	16	285 18.7	23 57.8	06.2	345 28.2	30.3	93 42.9	45.2	31 33.8	14.2
	17	300 21.1	38 57.0	06.4	0 28.7	29.9	108 44.9	45.4	46 35.9	14.3
	18	315 23.6	53 56.2	S25 06.7	15 29.2	S22 29.5	123 46.9	S 3 45.6	61 38.1	S21 14.3
	19	330 26.1	68 55.3	07.0	30 29.8	29.1	138 48.9	45.7	76 40.3	14.3
	20	345 28.5	83 54.5	07.3	45 30.3	28.7	153 50.9	45.9	91 42.5	14.4
	21	0 31.0	98 53.6	. . 07.5	60 30.9	. . 28.2	168 52.9	. . 46.1	106 44.7	. . 14.4
	22	15 33.5	113 52.8	07.8	75 31.4	27.8	183 54.9	46.3	121 46.8	14.4
	23	30 35.9	128 52.0	08.0	90 31.9	27.4	198 56.9	46.5	136 49.0	14.5
	6 00	45 38.4	143 51.1	S25 08.3	105 32.5	S22 27.0	213 58.9	S 3 46.7	151 51.2	S21 14.5
	01	60 40.8	158 50.3	08.6	120 33.0	26.6	229 00.9	46.9	166 53.4	14.5
	02	75 43.3	173 49.4	08.8	135 33.6	26.2	244 02.9	47.1	181 55.6	14.6
	03	90 45.8	188 48.6	. . 09.1	150 34.1	. . 25.8	259 04.9	. . 47.3	196 57.7	. . 14.6
	04	105 48.2	203 47.8	09.3	165 34.6	25.4	274 06.9	47.5	211 59.9	14.6
	05	120 50.7	218 46.9	09.6	180 35.2	25.0	289 08.9	47.6	227 02.1	14.7
	06	135 53.2	233 46.1	S25 09.9	195 35.7	S22 24.6	304 10.9	S 3 47.8	242 04.3	S21 14.7
	07	150 55.6	248 45.2	10.1	210 36.3	24.2	319 12.9	48.0	257 06.5	14.7
	08	165 58.1	263 44.4	10.4	225 36.8	23.8	334 14.9	48.2	272 08.6	14.8
S	09	181 00.6	278 43.6	. . 10.6	240 37.3	. . 23.4	349 16.9	. . 48.4	287 10.8	. . 14.8
U	10	196 03.0	293 42.7	10.9	255 37.9	23.0	4 18.9	48.6	302 13.0	14.8
N	11	211 05.5	308 41.9	11.1	270 38.4	22.6	19 20.9	48.8	317 15.2	14.9
D	12	226 08.0	323 41.0	S25 11.4	285 39.0	S22 22.2	34 22.9	S 3 49.0	332 17.4	S21 14.9
A	13	241 10.4	338 40.2	11.6	300 39.5	21.7	49 24.9	49.2	347 19.5	14.9
Y	14	256 12.9	353 39.4	11.8	315 40.1	21.3	64 26.9	49.3	2 21.7	15.0
	15	271 15.3	8 38.5	. . 12.1	330 40.6	. . 20.9	79 29.0	. . 49.5	17 23.9	. . 15.0
	16	286 17.8	23 37.7	12.3	345 41.1	20.5	94 31.0	49.7	32 26.1	15.0
	17	301 20.3	38 36.8	12.6	0 41.7	20.1	109 33.0	49.9	47 28.3	15.1
	18	316 22.7	53 36.0	S25 12.8	15 42.2	S22 19.7	124 35.0	S 3 50.1	62 30.4	S21 15.1
	19	331 25.2	68 35.2	13.1	30 42.8	19.3	139 37.0	50.3	77 32.6	15.2
	20	346 27.7	83 34.3	13.3	45 43.3	18.9	154 39.0	50.5	92 34.8	15.2
	21	1 30.1	98 33.5	. . 13.5	60 43.8	. . 18.5	169 41.0	. . 50.7	107 37.0	. . 15.2
	22	16 32.6	113 32.6	13.8	75 44.4	18.0	184 43.0	50.9	122 39.1	15.3
	23	31 35.1	128 31.8	14.0	90 44.9	17.6	199 45.0	51.0	137 41.3	15.3
	7 00	46 37.5	143 31.0	S25 14.2	105 45.5	S22 17.2	214 47.0	S 3 51.2	152 43.5	S21 15.3
	01	61 40.0	158 30.1	14.5	120 46.0	16.8	229 49.0	51.4	167 45.7	15.4
	02	76 42.5	173 29.3	14.7	135 46.6	16.4	244 51.0	51.6	182 47.9	15.4
	03	91 44.9	188 28.4	. . 14.9	150 47.1	. . 16.0	259 53.0	. . 51.8	197 50.0	. . 15.4
	04	106 47.4	203 27.6	15.1	165 47.6	15.6	274 55.0	52.0	212 52.2	15.5
	05	121 49.8	218 26.7	15.4	180 48.2	15.1	289 57.0	52.2	227 54.4	15.5
	06	136 52.3	233 25.9	S25 15.6	195 48.7	S22 14.7	304 59.0	S 3 52.4	242 56.6	S21 15.5
	07	151 54.8	248 25.1	15.8	210 49.3	14.3	320 01.0	52.6	257 58.7	15.6
	08	166 57.2	263 24.2	16.0	225 49.8	13.9	335 03.0	52.7	273 00.9	15.6
M	09	181 59.7	278 23.4	. . 16.3	240 50.3	. . 13.5	350 05.1	. . 52.9	288 03.1	. . 15.6
O	10	197 02.2	293 22.5	16.5	255 50.9	13.1	5 07.1	53.1	303 05.3	15.7
N	11	212 04.6	308 21.7	16.7	270 51.4	12.6	20 09.1	53.3	318 07.5	15.7
D	12	227 07.1	323 20.8	S25 16.9	285 52.0	S22 12.2	35 11.1	S 3 53.5	333 09.6	S21 15.7
A	13	242 09.6	338 20.0	17.1	300 52.5	11.8	50 13.1	53.7	348 11.8	15.8
Y	14	257 12.0	353 19.2	17.3	315 53.1	11.4	65 15.1	53.9	3 14.0	15.8
	15	272 14.5	8 18.3	. . 17.6	330 53.6	. . 11.0	80 17.1	. . 54.1	18 16.2	. . 15.8
	16	287 16.9	23 17.5	17.8	345 54.1	10.5	95 19.1	54.3	33 18.3	15.9
	17	302 19.4	38 16.6	18.0	0 54.7	10.1	110 21.1	54.4	48 20.5	15.9
	18	317 21.9	53 15.8	S25 18.2	15 55.2	S22 09.7	125 23.1	S 3 54.6	63 22.7	S21 15.9
	19	332 24.3	68 14.9	18.4	30 55.8	09.3	140 25.1	54.8	78 24.9	16.0
	20	347 26.8	83 14.1	18.6	45 56.3	08.9	155 27.1	55.0	93 27.0	16.0
	21	2 29.3	98 13.3	. . 18.8	60 56.9	. . 08.4	170 29.1	. . 55.2	108 29.2	. . 16.1
	22	17 31.7	113 12.4	19.0	75 57.4	08.0	185 31.1	55.4	123 31.4	16.1
	23	32 34.2	128 11.6	19.2	90 57.9	07.6	200 33.1	55.6	138 33.6	16.1
	Mer. Pass.	h m 20 54.0	v −0.8	d 0.2	v 0.5	d 0.4	v 2.0	d 0.2	v 2.2	d 0.0

STARS

Name	SHA	Dec
	° ′	° ′
Acamar	315 16.2	S40 14.3
Achernar	335 24.6	S57 09.3
Acrux	173 07.1	S63 11.2
Adhara	255 10.5	S28 59.7
Aldebaran	290 46.5	N16 32.4
Alioth	166 19.3	N55 52.1
Alkaid	152 57.7	N49 13.9
Al Na'ir	27 40.9	S46 52.9
Alnilam	275 43.8	S 1 11.6
Alphard	217 53.9	S 8 43.8
Alphecca	126 09.5	N26 39.8
Alpheratz	357 40.8	N29 11.1
Altair	62 06.1	N 8 55.1
Ankaa	353 13.2	S42 13.0
Antares	112 23.8	S26 27.9
Arcturus	145 54.0	N19 05.9
Atria	107 24.0	S69 03.3
Avior	234 16.9	S59 33.6
Bellatrix	278 29.3	N 6 21.7
Betelgeuse	270 58.6	N 7 24.5
Canopus	263 54.8	S52 42.2
Capella	280 30.7	N46 00.6
Deneb	49 29.9	N45 20.8
Denebola	182 31.6	N14 28.7
Diphda	348 53.4	S17 53.7
Dubhe	193 49.4	N61 39.4
Elnath	278 09.4	N28 37.1
Eltanin	90 45.5	N51 29.6
Enif	33 44.8	N 9 57.4
Fomalhaut	15 21.4	S29 32.0
Gacrux	171 58.7	S57 12.1
Gienah	175 50.2	S17 37.9
Hadar	148 45.2	S60 27.0
Hamal	327 57.8	N23 32.5
Kaus Aust.	83 41.1	S34 22.4
Kochab	137 21.5	N74 05.3
Markab	13 35.9	N15 17.9
Menkar	314 12.3	N 4 09.3
Menkent	148 05.2	S36 26.9
Miaplacidus	221 39.1	S69 46.9
Mirfak	308 36.5	N49 55.1
Nunki	75 55.7	S26 16.4
Peacock	53 15.9	S56 40.9
Pollux	243 24.9	N27 58.9
Procyon	244 57.2	N 5 10.8
Rasalhague	96 04.6	N12 33.2
Regulus	207 41.2	N11 53.1
Rigel	281 09.6	S 8 11.0
Rigil Kent.	139 49.2	S60 54.0
Sabik	102 10.2	S15 44.5
Schedar	349 37.3	N56 37.9
Shaula	96 19.2	S37 06.8
Sirius	258 31.5	S16 44.4
Spica	158 29.2	S11 14.7
Suhail	222 50.7	S43 29.8
Vega	80 37.7	N38 48.4
Zuben'ubi	137 03.2	S16 06.4

	SHA	Mer. Pass.
	° ′	h m
Venus	98 12.7	14 25
Mars	59 54.1	16 57
Jupiter	168 20.5	9 43
Saturn	106 12.8	13 51

UT		SUN GHA	SUN Dec	MOON GHA	v	MOON Dec	d	HP
d	h	° ′	° ′	° ′	′	° ′	′	′
5 SATURDAY	00	184 06.1	S15 44.3	123 33.6	11.4	S18 38.9	1.1	54.8
	01	199 06.1	45.0	138 04.0	11.5	18 37.8	1.1	54.9
	02	214 06.1	45.8	152 34.5	11.4	18 36.7	1.2	54.9
	03	229 06.0	. . 46.6	167 04.9	11.4	18 35.5	1.3	54.9
	04	244 06.0	47.3	181 35.3	11.4	18 34.2	1.4	54.9
	05	259 06.0	48.1	196 05.7	11.4	18 32.8	1.5	54.9
	06	274 06.0	S15 48.8	210 36.1	11.4	S18 31.3	1.6	55.0
	07	289 06.0	49.6	225 06.5	11.4	18 29.7	1.6	55.0
	08	304 05.9	50.3	239 36.9	11.3	18 28.1	1.8	55.0
	09	319 05.9	. . 51.1	254 07.2	11.4	18 26.3	1.8	55.0
	10	334 05.9	51.8	268 37.6	11.3	18 24.5	2.0	55.1
	11	349 05.9	52.6	283 07.9	11.3	18 22.5	2.0	55.1
	12	4 05.8	S15 53.3	297 38.2	11.3	S18 20.5	2.1	55.1
	13	19 05.8	54.1	312 08.5	11.3	18 18.4	2.2	55.1
	14	34 05.8	54.8	326 38.8	11.3	18 16.2	2.3	55.1
	15	49 05.8	. . 55.6	341 09.1	11.3	18 13.9	2.4	55.2
	16	64 05.7	56.4	355 39.4	11.2	18 11.5	2.5	55.2
	17	79 05.7	57.1	10 09.6	11.3	18 09.0	2.6	55.2
	18	94 05.7	S15 57.9	24 39.9	11.2	S18 06.4	2.6	55.2
	19	109 05.7	58.6	39 10.1	11.2	18 03.8	2.8	55.3
	20	124 05.6	15 59.3	53 40.3	11.3	18 01.0	2.9	55.3
	21	139 05.6	16 00.1	68 10.6	11.2	17 58.1	2.9	55.3
	22	154 05.6	00.8	82 40.8	11.2	17 55.2	3.0	55.3
	23	169 05.6	01.6	97 11.0	11.2	17 52.2	3.1	55.4
6 SUNDAY	00	184 05.5	S16 02.3	111 41.2	11.2	S17 49.1	3.3	55.4
	01	199 05.5	03.1	126 11.4	11.1	17 45.8	3.3	55.4
	02	214 05.5	03.8	140 41.5	11.2	17 42.5	3.4	55.4
	03	229 05.5	. . 04.6	155 11.7	11.2	17 39.1	3.4	55.5
	04	244 05.4	05.3	169 41.9	11.1	17 35.7	3.6	55.5
	05	259 05.4	06.1	184 12.0	11.2	17 32.1	3.7	55.5
	06	274 05.4	S16 06.8	198 42.2	11.1	S17 28.4	3.7	55.5
	07	289 05.3	07.6	213 12.3	11.1	17 24.7	3.9	55.6
	08	304 05.3	08.3	227 42.4	11.2	17 20.8	3.9	55.6
	09	319 05.3	. . 09.0	242 12.6	11.1	17 16.9	4.1	55.6
	10	334 05.2	09.8	256 42.7	11.1	17 12.8	4.1	55.7
	11	349 05.2	10.5	271 12.8	11.1	17 08.7	4.2	55.7
	12	4 05.2	S16 11.3	285 42.9	11.1	S17 04.5	4.3	55.7
	13	19 05.2	12.0	300 13.0	11.1	17 00.2	4.4	55.7
	14	34 05.1	12.7	314 43.1	11.0	16 55.8	4.4	55.8
	15	49 05.1	. . 13.5	329 13.1	11.1	16 51.4	4.6	55.8
	16	64 05.1	14.2	343 43.2	11.1	16 46.8	4.6	55.8
	17	79 05.0	15.0	358 13.3	11.0	16 42.2	4.8	55.9
	18	94 05.0	S16 15.7	12 43.3	11.1	S16 37.4	4.8	55.9
	19	109 05.0	16.4	27 13.4	11.0	16 32.6	4.9	55.9
	20	124 04.9	17.2	41 43.4	11.1	16 27.7	5.0	56.0
	21	139 04.9	. . 17.9	56 13.5	11.0	16 22.7	5.1	56.0
	22	154 04.9	18.6	70 43.5	11.0	16 17.6	5.2	56.0
	23	169 04.8	19.4	85 13.5	11.1	16 12.4	5.3	56.0
7 MONDAY	00	184 04.8	S16 20.1	99 43.6	11.0	S16 07.1	5.4	56.1
	01	199 04.7	20.9	114 13.6	11.0	16 01.7	5.4	56.1
	02	214 04.7	21.6	128 43.6	11.0	15 56.3	5.5	56.1
	03	229 04.7	. . 22.3	143 13.6	11.0	15 50.8	5.6	56.2
	04	244 04.6	23.1	157 43.6	11.0	15 45.2	5.8	56.2
	05	259 04.6	23.8	172 13.6	11.0	15 39.4	5.7	56.2
	06	274 04.6	S16 24.5	186 43.6	10.9	S15 33.7	5.9	56.3
	07	289 04.5	25.3	201 13.5	11.0	15 27.8	6.0	56.3
	08	304 04.5	26.0	215 43.5	11.0	15 21.8	6.0	56.3
	09	319 04.4	. . 26.7	230 13.5	10.9	15 15.8	6.2	56.4
	10	334 04.4	27.4	244 43.4	11.0	15 09.6	6.2	56.4
	11	349 04.4	28.2	259 13.4	10.9	15 03.4	6.3	56.4
	12	4 04.3	S16 28.9	273 43.3	11.0	S14 57.1	6.4	56.5
	13	19 04.3	29.6	288 13.3	10.9	14 50.7	6.4	56.5
	14	34 04.2	30.4	302 43.2	10.9	14 44.3	6.6	56.5
	15	49 04.2	. . 31.1	317 13.1	11.0	14 37.7	6.6	56.6
	16	64 04.2	31.8	331 43.1	10.9	14 31.1	6.7	56.6
	17	79 04.1	32.5	346 13.0	10.9	14 24.4	6.8	56.6
	18	94 04.1	S16 33.3	0 42.9	10.9	S14 17.6	6.9	56.7
	19	109 04.0	34.0	15 12.8	10.9	14 10.7	7.0	56.7
	20	124 04.0	34.7	29 42.7	10.9	14 03.7	7.0	56.7
	21	139 04.0	. . 35.5	44 12.6	10.8	13 56.7	7.2	56.8
	22	154 03.9	36.2	58 42.4	10.9	13 49.5	7.2	56.8
	23	169 03.9	36.9	73 12.3	10.9	S13 42.3	7.3	56.8
		SD 16.2	d 0.7	SD 15.0		15.2		15.4

Lat.	Twilight Naut.	Twilight Civil	Sunrise	Moonrise 5	6	7	8
°	h m	h m	h m	h m	h m	h m	h m
N 72	06 27	07 54	09 33	■	15 42	15 27	15 18
N 70	06 21	07 38	08 58	14 37	14 51	14 56	14 59
68	06 15	07 24	08 34	13 54	14 19	14 34	14 43
66	06 10	07 13	08 15	13 26	13 55	14 16	14 30
64	06 06	07 04	08 00	13 04	13 36	14 01	14 20
62	06 03	06 56	07 47	12 46	13 21	13 49	14 11
60	05 59	06 49	07 36	12 32	13 08	13 38	14 03
N 58	05 56	06 43	07 27	12 19	12 57	13 29	13 56
56	05 53	06 38	07 18	12 08	12 48	13 21	13 50
54	05 50	06 33	07 11	11 59	12 39	13 14	13 45
52	05 48	06 28	07 04	11 50	12 31	13 07	13 40
50	05 45	06 24	06 59	11 43	12 24	13 02	13 35
45	05 40	06 15	06 46	11 27	12 10	12 49	13 25
N 40	05 34	06 07	06 35	11 13	11 57	12 39	13 17
35	05 29	06 00	06 26	11 02	11 47	12 30	13 10
30	05 25	05 53	06 18	10 52	11 38	12 22	13 04
20	05 15	05 41	06 04	10 35	11 22	12 08	12 53
N 10	05 05	05 30	05 52	10 20	11 08	11 56	12 44
0	04 54	05 19	05 40	10 06	10 55	11 45	12 35
S 10	04 41	05 06	05 28	09 52	10 43	11 34	12 26
20	04 25	04 53	05 16	09 37	10 29	11 22	12 17
30	04 05	04 36	05 01	09 20	10 13	11 08	12 06
35	03 53	04 25	04 53	09 10	10 04	11 00	12 00
40	03 37	04 13	04 43	08 59	09 53	10 51	11 53
45	03 18	03 59	04 31	08 46	09 41	10 41	11 44
S 50	02 52	03 40	04 17	08 30	09 26	10 28	11 34
52	02 39	03 31	04 11	08 22	09 19	10 22	11 30
54	02 24	03 21	04 04	08 13	09 11	10 15	11 24
56	02 06	03 10	03 55	08 04	09 02	10 08	11 19
58	01 42	02 56	03 46	07 53	08 52	09 59	11 12
S 60	01 09	02 41	03 36	07 40	08 41	09 50	11 05

Lat.	Sunset	Twilight Civil	Twilight Naut.	Moonset 5	6	7	8
°	h m	h m	h m	h m	h m	h m	h m
N 72	13 53	15 32	16 58	■	18 41	20 40	22 33
N 70	14 28	15 48	17 05	18 03	19 32	21 10	22 52
68	14 52	16 02	17 11	18 45	20 03	21 32	23 06
66	15 11	16 13	17 16	19 14	20 27	21 49	23 17
64	15 27	16 22	17 20	19 36	20 45	22 03	23 27
62	15 40	16 30	17 24	19 53	21 00	22 14	23 35
60	15 50	16 37	17 27	20 07	21 12	22 24	23 42
N 58	16 00	16 43	17 30	20 20	21 23	22 33	23 48
56	16 08	16 49	17 33	20 30	21 32	22 41	23 54
54	16 16	16 54	17 36	20 40	21 41	22 47	23 59
52	16 22	16 58	17 39	20 48	21 48	22 53	24 03
50	16 28	17 03	17 41	20 55	21 55	22 59	24 07
45	16 41	17 12	17 47	21 11	22 09	23 10	24 16
N 40	16 52	17 20	17 52	21 24	22 20	23 20	24 23
35	17 01	17 27	17 57	21 36	22 30	23 28	24 29
30	17 09	17 34	18 02	21 45	22 39	23 36	24 34
20	17 23	17 46	18 12	22 02	22 54	23 48	24 44
N 10	17 35	17 57	18 22	22 16	23 07	23 59	24 52
0	17 47	18 09	18 34	22 30	23 19	24 09	00 09
S 10	17 59	18 21	18 47	22 43	23 31	24 19	00 19
20	18 12	18 35	19 02	22 58	23 44	24 30	00 30
30	18 27	18 52	19 23	23 14	23 59	24 42	00 42
35	18 35	19 03	19 36	23 24	24 07	00 07	00 49
40	18 45	19 15	19 51	23 34	24 17	00 17	00 57
45	18 57	19 30	20 11	23 47	24 28	00 28	01 06
S 50	19 11	19 48	20 37	24 03	00 03	00 42	01 17
52	19 18	19 57	20 50	24 10	00 10	00 48	01 22
54	19 25	20 08	21 05	24 18	00 18	00 55	01 28
56	19 33	20 19	21 24	24 27	00 27	01 03	01 34
58	19 43	20 33	21 49	24 37	00 37	01 12	01 41
S 60	19 53	20 49	22 24	00 08	00 49	01 22	01 49

Day	SUN Eqn. of Time 00^h	SUN Eqn. of Time 12^h	SUN Mer. Pass.	MOON Mer. Pass. Upper	MOON Mer. Pass. Lower	MOON Age	MOON Phase
d	m s	m s	h m	h m	h m	d %	
5	16 24	16 23	11 44	16 18	03 53	06 28	
6	16 22	16 21	11 44	17 07	04 43	07 37	
7	16 19	16 17	11 44	17 57	05 32	08 47	

Day	UT	ARIES	VENUS −4·0		MARS +0·4		JUPITER −1·7		SATURN +0·5	
		GHA	GHA	Dec	GHA	Dec	GHA	Dec	GHA	Dec
	d h	° ′	° ′	° ′	° ′	° ′	° ′	° ′	° ′	° ′
TUESDAY	8 00	47 36.7	143 10.7	S25 19.4	105 58.5	S22 07.2	215 35.2	S 3 55.8	153 35.7	S21 16.2
	01	62 39.1	158 09.9	19.6	120 59.0	06.7	230 37.2	55.9	168 37.9	16.2
	02	77 41.6	173 09.0	19.8	135 59.6	06.3	245 39.2	56.1	183 40.1	16.2
	03	92 44.1	188 08.2	. . 20.0	151 00.1	. . 05.9	260 41.2	. . 56.3	198 42.3	. . 16.3
	04	107 46.5	203 07.3	20.2	166 00.7	05.5	275 43.2	56.5	213 44.5	16.3
	05	122 49.0	218 06.5	20.4	181 01.2	05.0	290 45.2	56.7	228 46.6	16.3
	06	137 51.4	233 05.7	S25 20.6	196 01.8	S22 04.6	305 47.2	S 3 56.9	243 48.8	S21 16.4
	07	152 53.9	248 04.8	20.8	211 02.3	04.2	320 49.2	57.1	258 51.0	16.4
	08	167 56.4	263 04.0	21.0	226 02.8	03.8	335 51.2	57.3	273 53.2	16.4
	09	182 58.8	278 03.1	. . 21.2	241 03.4	. . 03.3	350 53.2	. . 57.4	288 55.3	. . 16.5
	10	198 01.3	293 02.3	21.4	256 03.9	02.9	5 55.2	57.6	303 57.5	16.5
	11	213 03.8	308 01.4	21.6	271 04.5	02.5	20 57.2	57.8	318 59.7	16.5
	12	228 06.2	323 00.6	S25 21.8	286 05.0	S22 02.1	35 59.3	S 3 58.0	334 01.9	S21 16.6
	13	243 08.7	337 59.7	21.9	301 05.6	01.6	51 01.3	58.2	349 04.0	16.6
	14	258 11.2	352 58.9	22.1	316 06.1	01.2	66 03.3	58.4	4 06.2	16.6
	15	273 13.6	7 58.0	. . 22.3	331 06.6	. . 00.8	81 05.3	. . 58.6	19 08.4	. . 16.7
	16	288 16.1	22 57.2	22.5	346 07.2	22 00.4	96 07.3	58.8	34 10.6	16.7
	17	303 18.6	37 56.4	22.7	1 07.7	21 59.9	111 09.3	58.9	49 12.7	16.7
	18	318 21.0	52 55.5	S25 22.8	16 08.3	S21 59.5	126 11.3	S 3 59.1	64 14.9	S21 16.8
	19	333 23.5	67 54.7	23.0	31 08.8	59.1	141 13.3	59.3	79 17.1	16.8
	20	348 25.9	82 53.8	23.2	46 09.4	58.6	156 15.3	59.5	94 19.3	16.8
	21	3 28.4	97 53.0	. . 23.4	61 09.9	. . 58.2	171 17.3	. . 59.7	109 21.4	. . 16.9
	22	18 30.9	112 52.1	23.6	76 10.5	57.8	186 19.3	3 59.9	124 23.6	16.9
	23	33 33.3	127 51.3	23.7	91 11.0	57.3	201 21.3	4 00.1	139 25.8	16.9
WEDNESDAY	9 00	48 35.8	142 50.4	S25 23.9	106 11.6	S21 56.9	216 23.4	S 4 00.2	154 28.0	S21 17.0
	01	63 38.3	157 49.6	24.1	121 12.1	56.5	231 25.4	00.4	169 30.1	17.0
	02	78 40.7	172 48.7	24.2	136 12.6	56.0	246 27.4	00.6	184 32.3	17.1
	03	93 43.2	187 47.9	. . 24.4	151 13.2	. . 55.6	261 29.4	. . 00.8	199 34.5	. . 17.1
	04	108 45.7	202 47.1	24.6	166 13.7	55.2	276 31.4	01.0	214 36.7	17.1
	05	123 48.1	217 46.2	24.7	181 14.3	54.7	291 33.4	01.2	229 38.8	17.2
	06	138 50.6	232 45.4	S25 24.9	196 14.8	S21 54.3	306 35.4	S 4 01.4	244 41.0	S21 17.2
	07	153 53.0	247 44.5	25.1	211 15.4	53.9	321 37.4	01.6	259 43.2	17.2
	08	168 55.5	262 43.7	25.2	226 15.9	53.4	336 39.4	01.7	274 45.4	17.3
	09	183 58.0	277 42.8	. . 25.4	241 16.5	. . 53.0	351 41.4	. . 01.9	289 47.5	. . 17.3
	10	199 00.4	292 42.0	25.5	256 17.0	52.6	6 43.5	02.1	304 49.7	17.3
	11	214 02.9	307 41.1	25.7	271 17.6	52.1	21 45.5	02.3	319 51.9	17.4
	12	229 05.4	322 40.3	S25 25.9	286 18.1	S21 51.7	36 47.5	S 4 02.5	334 54.1	S21 17.4
	13	244 07.8	337 39.4	26.0	301 18.6	51.3	51 49.5	02.7	349 56.2	17.4
	14	259 10.3	352 38.6	26.2	316 19.2	50.8	66 51.5	02.9	4 58.4	17.5
	15	274 12.8	7 37.7	. . 26.3	331 19.7	. . 50.4	81 53.5	. . 03.0	20 00.6	. . 17.5
	16	289 15.2	22 36.9	26.5	346 20.3	50.0	96 55.5	03.2	35 02.7	17.5
	17	304 17.7	37 36.1	26.6	1 20.8	49.5	111 57.5	03.4	50 04.9	17.6
	18	319 20.2	52 35.2	S25 26.8	16 21.4	S21 49.1	126 59.5	S 4 03.6	65 07.1	S21 17.6
	19	334 22.6	67 34.4	26.9	31 21.9	48.6	142 01.6	03.8	80 09.3	17.6
	20	349 25.1	82 33.5	27.1	46 22.5	48.2	157 03.6	04.0	95 11.4	17.7
	21	4 27.5	97 32.7	. . 27.2	61 23.0	. . 47.8	172 05.6	. . 04.2	110 13.6	. . 17.7
	22	19 30.0	112 31.8	27.4	76 23.6	47.3	187 07.6	04.3	125 15.8	17.7
	23	34 32.5	127 31.0	27.5	91 24.1	46.9	202 09.6	04.5	140 18.0	17.8
THURSDAY	10 00	49 34.9	142 30.1	S25 27.6	106 24.7	S21 46.4	217 11.6	S 4 04.7	155 20.1	S21 17.8
	01	64 37.4	157 29.3	27.8	121 25.2	46.0	232 13.6	04.9	170 22.3	17.8
	02	79 39.9	172 28.4	27.9	136 25.7	45.6	247 15.6	05.1	185 24.5	17.9
	03	94 42.3	187 27.6	. . 28.1	151 26.3	. . 45.1	262 17.7	. . 05.3	200 26.7	. . 17.9
	04	109 44.8	202 26.7	28.2	166 26.8	44.7	277 19.7	05.4	215 28.8	17.9
	05	124 47.3	217 25.9	28.3	181 27.4	44.2	292 21.7	05.6	230 31.0	18.0
	06	139 49.7	232 25.0	S25 28.5	196 27.9	S21 43.8	307 23.7	S 4 05.8	245 33.2	S21 18.0
	07	154 52.2	247 24.2	28.6	211 28.5	43.3	322 25.7	06.0	260 35.3	18.0
	08	169 54.7	262 23.4	28.7	226 29.0	42.9	337 27.7	06.2	275 37.5	18.1
	09	184 57.1	277 22.5	. . 28.9	241 29.6	. . 42.5	352 29.7	. . 06.4	290 39.7	. . 18.1
	10	199 59.6	292 21.7	29.0	256 30.1	42.0	7 31.7	06.6	305 41.9	18.1
	11	215 02.0	307 20.8	29.1	271 30.7	41.6	22 33.7	06.7	320 44.0	18.2
	12	230 04.5	322 20.0	S25 29.2	286 31.2	S21 41.1	37 35.8	S 4 06.9	335 46.2	S21 18.2
	13	245 07.0	337 19.1	29.4	301 31.8	40.7	52 37.8	07.1	350 48.4	18.3
	14	260 09.4	352 18.3	29.5	316 32.3	40.2	67 39.8	07.3	5 50.5	18.3
	15	275 11.9	7 17.4	. . 29.6	331 32.9	. . 39.8	82 41.8	. . 07.5	20 52.7	. . 18.3
	16	290 14.4	22 16.6	29.7	346 33.4	39.3	97 43.8	07.7	35 54.9	18.4
	17	305 16.8	37 15.7	29.9	1 34.0	38.9	112 45.8	07.9	50 57.1	18.4
	18	320 19.3	52 14.9	S25 30.0	16 34.5	S21 38.5	127 47.8	S 4 08.0	65 59.2	S21 18.4
	19	335 21.8	67 14.0	30.1	31 35.1	38.0	142 49.9	08.2	81 01.4	18.5
	20	350 24.2	82 13.2	30.2	46 35.6	37.6	157 51.9	08.4	96 03.6	18.5
	21	5 26.7	97 12.3	. . 30.3	61 36.2	. . 37.1	172 53.9	. . 08.6	111 05.8	. . 18.5
	22	20 29.1	112 11.5	30.4	76 36.7	36.7	187 55.9	08.8	126 07.9	18.6
	23	35 31.6	127 10.6	30.5	91 37.2	36.2	202 57.9	09.0	141 10.1	18.6
	Mer. Pass.	h m 20 42.2	*v* −0.8	*d* 0.2	*v* 0.5	*d* 0.4	*v* 2.0	*d* 0.2	*v* 2.2	*d* 0.0

STARS

Name	SHA	Dec
	° ′	° ′
Acamar	315 16.2	S40 14.4
Achernar	335 24.6	S57 09.3
Acrux	173 07.1	S63 11.2
Adhara	255 10.5	S28 59.7
Aldebaran	290 46.4	N16 32.4
Alioth	166 19.3	N55 52.1
Alkaid	152 57.7	N49 13.8
Al Na'ir	27 40.9	S46 52.9
Alnilam	275 43.8	S 1 11.6
Alphard	217 53.9	S 8 43.9
Alphecca	126 09.5	N26 39.8
Alpheratz	357 40.8	N29 11.2
Altair	62 06.2	N 8 55.1
Ankaa	353 13.2	S42 13.0
Antares	112 23.8	S26 27.9
Arcturus	145 54.0	N19 05.9
Atria	107 24.0	S69 03.3
Avior	234 16.9	S59 33.6
Bellatrix	278 29.3	N 6 21.7
Betelgeuse	270 58.6	N 7 24.5
Canopus	263 54.7	S52 42.2
Capella	280 30.7	N46 00.6
Deneb	49 30.0	N45 20.8
Denebola	182 31.6	N14 28.7
Diphda	348 53.4	S17 53.7
Dubhe	193 49.4	N61 39.4
Elnath	278 09.4	N28 37.1
Eltanin	90 45.5	N51 29.6
Enif	33 44.9	N 9 57.4
Fomalhaut	15 21.4	S29 32.0
Gacrux	171 58.7	S57 12.1
Gienah	175 50.2	S17 37.9
Hadar	148 45.2	S60 26.9
Hamal	327 57.8	N23 32.5
Kaus Aust.	83 41.1	S34 22.4
Kochab	137 21.5	N74 05.3
Markab	13 35.9	N15 17.9
Menkar	314 12.3	N 4 09.2
Menkent	148 05.2	S36 26.9
Miaplacidus	221 39.0	S69 46.9
Mirfak	308 36.5	N49 55.1
Nunki	75 55.7	S26 16.4
Peacock	53 15.9	S56 40.9
Pollux	243 24.8	N27 58.9
Procyon	244 57.2	N 5 10.8
Rasalhague	96 04.6	N12 33.2
Regulus	207 41.2	N11 53.1
Rigel	281 09.6	S 8 11.0
Rigil Kent.	139 49.2	S60 54.0
Sabik	102 10.2	S15 44.5
Schedar	349 37.3	N56 37.9
Shaula	96 19.2	S37 06.8
Sirius	258 31.5	S16 44.4
Spica	158 29.1	S11 14.7
Suhail	222 50.7	S43 29.8
Vega	80 37.7	N38 48.4
Zuben'ubi	137 03.2	S16 06.4

	SHA	Mer. Pass.
	° ′	h m
Venus	94 14.6	14 29
Mars	57 35.8	16 55
Jupiter	167 47.6	9 33
Saturn	105 52.2	13 40

UT d h	SUN GHA ° ′	SUN Dec ° ′	MOON GHA ° ′	v ′	Dec ° ′	d ′	HP ′
8 00 (TUESDAY)	184 03.8	S16 37.6	87 42.2	10.8	S13 35.0	7.3	56.9
01	199 03.8	38.4	102 12.0	10.9	13 27.7	7.5	56.9
02	214 03.7	39.1	116 41.9	10.8	13 20.2	7.5	57.0
03	229 03.7	. . 39.8	131 11.7	10.9	13 12.7	7.6	57.0
04	244 03.6	40.5	145 41.6	10.8	13 05.1	7.7	57.0
05	259 03.6	41.2	160 11.4	10.8	12 57.4	7.8	57.1
06	274 03.5	S16 42.0	174 41.2	10.8	S12 49.6	7.8	57.1
07	289 03.5	42.7	189 11.0	10.8	12 41.8	7.9	57.1
08	304 03.5	43.4	203 40.8	10.8	12 33.9	8.0	57.2
09	319 03.4	. . 44.1	218 10.6	10.8	12 25.9	8.1	57.2
10	334 03.4	44.8	232 40.4	10.7	12 17.8	8.1	57.2
11	349 03.3	45.6	247 10.1	10.8	12 09.7	8.3	57.3
12	4 03.3	S16 46.3	261 39.9	10.7	S12 01.4	8.3	57.3
13	19 03.2	47.0	276 09.6	10.8	11 53.1	8.3	57.4
14	34 03.2	47.7	290 39.4	10.7	11 44.8	8.5	57.4
15	49 03.1	. . 48.4	305 09.1	10.7	11 36.3	8.5	57.4
16	64 03.1	49.1	319 38.8	10.7	11 27.8	8.6	57.5
17	79 03.0	49.9	334 08.5	10.7	11 19.2	8.6	57.5
18	94 03.0	S16 50.6	348 38.2	10.7	S11 10.6	8.8	57.6
19	109 02.9	51.3	3 07.9	10.6	11 01.8	8.8	57.6
20	124 02.9	52.0	17 37.5	10.7	10 53.0	8.8	57.6
21	139 02.8	. . 52.7	32 07.2	10.6	10 44.2	9.0	57.7
22	154 02.8	53.4	46 36.8	10.6	10 35.2	9.0	57.7
23	169 02.7	54.1	61 06.4	10.6	10 26.2	9.1	57.7
9 00 (WEDNESDAY)	184 02.7	S16 54.9	75 36.0	10.6	S10 17.1	9.1	57.8
01	199 02.6	55.6	90 05.6	10.6	10 08.0	9.2	57.8
02	214 02.5	56.3	104 35.2	10.6	9 58.8	9.3	57.9
03	229 02.5	. . 57.0	119 04.8	10.5	9 49.5	9.4	57.9
04	244 02.4	57.7	133 34.3	10.6	9 40.1	9.4	57.9
05	259 02.4	58.4	148 03.9	10.5	9 30.7	9.5	58.0
06	274 02.3	S16 59.1	162 33.4	10.5	S 9 21.2	9.5	58.0
07	289 02.3	16 59.8	177 02.9	10.5	9 11.7	9.6	58.1
08	304 02.2	17 00.5	191 32.4	10.4	9 02.1	9.7	58.1
09	319 02.2	. . 01.2	206 01.8	10.5	8 52.4	9.7	58.1
10	334 02.1	01.9	220 31.3	10.4	8 42.7	9.8	58.2
11	349 02.0	02.7	235 00.7	10.4	8 32.9	9.9	58.2
12	4 02.0	S17 03.4	249 30.1	10.4	S 8 23.0	9.9	58.3
13	19 01.9	04.1	263 59.5	10.4	8 13.1	10.0	58.3
14	34 01.9	04.8	278 28.9	10.4	8 03.1	10.0	58.3
15	49 01.8	. . 05.5	292 58.3	10.3	7 53.1	10.1	58.4
16	64 01.8	06.2	307 27.6	10.3	7 43.0	10.1	58.4
17	79 01.7	06.9	321 56.9	10.3	7 32.9	10.2	58.5
18	94 01.6	S17 07.6	336 26.2	10.3	S 7 22.7	10.3	58.5
19	109 01.6	08.3	350 55.5	10.2	7 12.4	10.3	58.5
20	124 01.5	09.0	5 24.7	10.3	7 02.1	10.4	58.6
21	139 01.5	. . 09.7	19 54.0	10.2	6 51.7	10.4	58.6
22	154 01.4	10.4	34 23.2	10.1	6 41.3	10.5	58.7
23	169 01.3	11.1	48 52.3	10.2	6 30.8	10.5	58.7
10 00 (THURSDAY)	184 01.3	S17 11.8	63 21.5	10.1	S 6 20.3	10.6	58.7
01	199 01.2	12.5	77 50.6	10.1	6 09.7	10.6	58.8
02	214 01.2	13.2	92 19.7	10.1	5 59.1	10.7	58.8
03	229 01.1	. . 13.9	106 48.8	10.0	5 48.4	10.7	58.9
04	244 01.0	14.6	121 17.8	10.1	5 37.7	10.8	58.9
05	259 01.0	15.3	135 46.9	10.0	5 26.9	10.8	58.9
06	274 00.9	S17 16.0	150 15.9	9.9	S 5 16.1	10.9	59.0
07	289 00.8	16.7	164 44.8	10.0	5 05.2	10.9	59.0
08	304 00.8	17.4	179 13.8	9.9	4 54.3	10.9	59.1
09	319 00.7	. . 18.1	193 42.7	9.9	4 43.4	11.0	59.1
10	334 00.6	18.8	208 11.6	9.8	4 32.4	11.0	59.1
11	349 00.6	19.5	222 40.4	9.9	4 21.4	11.1	59.2
12	4 00.5	S17 20.1	237 09.3	9.7	S 4 10.3	11.1	59.2
13	19 00.4	20.8	251 38.0	9.8	3 59.2	11.2	59.3
14	34 00.4	21.5	266 06.8	9.7	3 48.0	11.2	59.3
15	49 00.3	. . 22.2	280 35.5	9.7	3 36.8	11.2	59.3
16	64 00.2	22.9	295 04.2	9.7	3 25.6	11.3	59.4
17	79 00.2	23.6	309 32.9	9.6	3 14.3	11.3	59.4
18	94 00.1	S17 24.3	324 01.5	9.6	S 3 03.0	11.3	59.5
19	109 00.0	25.0	338 30.1	9.6	2 51.7	11.4	59.5
20	124 00.0	25.7	352 58.7	9.5	2 40.3	11.4	59.5
21	138 59.9	. . 26.4	7 27.2	9.5	2 28.9	11.4	59.6
22	153 59.8	27.1	21 55.7	9.4	2 17.5	11.4	59.6
23	168 59.8	27.7	36 24.1	9.4	S 2 06.1	11.5	59.6
	SD 16.2	*d* 0.7	SD 15.6		15.9		16.1

Lat. °	Twilight Naut. h m	Twilight Civil h m	Sunrise h m	Moonrise 8 h m	Moonrise 9 h m	Moonrise 10 h m	Moonrise 11 h m
N 72	06 39	08 08	09 57	15 18	15 11	15 04	14 58
N 70	06 31	07 49	09 15	14 59	14 59	14 59	14 59
68	06 24	07 35	08 47	14 43	14 50	14 55	15 00
66	06 19	07 23	08 26	14 30	14 42	14 52	15 01
64	06 14	07 13	08 09	14 20	14 35	14 49	15 02
62	06 09	07 04	07 55	14 11	14 29	14 46	15 02
60	06 05	06 56	07 44	14 03	14 24	14 44	15 03
N 58	06 02	06 50	07 34	13 56	14 20	14 42	15 03
56	05 59	06 44	07 25	13 50	14 16	14 40	15 04
54	05 55	06 38	07 17	13 45	14 12	14 38	15 04
52	05 53	06 33	07 10	13 40	14 09	14 37	15 04
50	05 50	06 29	07 04	13 35	14 06	14 35	15 05
45	05 43	06 19	06 50	13 25	13 59	14 32	15 05
N 40	05 38	06 10	06 39	13 17	13 54	14 30	15 06
35	05 32	06 02	06 29	13 10	13 49	14 28	15 07
30	05 27	05 55	06 20	13 04	13 45	14 26	15 07
20	05 16	05 43	06 06	12 53	13 38	14 22	15 08
N 10	05 05	05 31	05 53	12 44	13 31	14 19	15 09
0	04 54	05 19	05 40	12 35	13 25	14 17	15 09
S 10	04 40	05 06	05 28	12 26	13 19	14 14	15 10
20	04 24	04 51	05 15	12 17	13 13	14 11	15 11
30	04 03	04 33	04 59	12 06	13 06	14 08	15 12
35	03 49	04 23	04 50	12 00	13 02	14 06	15 13
40	03 33	04 10	04 40	11 53	12 57	14 04	15 13
45	03 13	03 54	04 28	11 44	12 51	14 01	15 14
S 50	02 46	03 35	04 13	11 34	12 45	13 58	15 15
52	02 32	03 25	04 06	11 30	12 41	13 57	15 15
54	02 15	03 15	03 58	11 24	12 38	13 55	15 16
56	01 55	03 02	03 49	11 19	12 34	13 54	15 16
58	01 29	02 48	03 39	11 12	12 30	13 52	15 17
S 60	00 47	02 31	03 28	11 05	12 25	13 50	15 18

Lat. °	Sunset h m	Twilight Civil h m	Twilight Naut. h m	Moonset 8 h m	Moonset 9 h m	Moonset 10 h m	Moonset 11 h m
N 72	13 29	15 19	16 47	22 33	24 27	00 27	02 21
N 70	14 11	15 37	16 55	22 52	24 36	00 36	02 24
68	14 40	15 52	17 02	23 06	24 44	00 44	02 26
66	15 01	16 04	17 08	23 17	24 50	00 50	02 27
64	15 18	16 14	17 13	23 27	24 56	00 56	02 29
62	15 31	16 23	17 17	23 35	25 01	01 01	02 30
60	15 43	16 31	17 21	23 42	25 05	01 05	02 31
N 58	15 53	16 37	17 25	23 48	25 08	01 08	02 32
56	16 02	16 43	17 28	23 54	25 11	01 11	02 32
54	16 10	16 49	17 32	23 59	25 14	01 14	02 33
52	16 17	16 54	17 35	24 03	00 03	01 17	02 34
50	16 24	16 58	17 37	24 07	00 07	01 19	02 34
45	16 37	17 09	17 44	24 16	00 16	01 24	02 35
N 40	16 49	17 17	17 50	24 23	00 23	01 28	02 36
35	16 58	17 25	17 55	24 29	00 29	01 32	02 37
30	17 07	17 32	18 01	24 34	00 34	01 35	02 38
20	17 22	17 45	18 11	24 44	00 44	01 41	02 39
N 10	17 35	17 57	18 22	24 52	00 52	01 45	02 41
0	17 47	18 09	18 34	00 09	00 59	01 50	02 42
S 10	18 00	18 22	18 48	00 19	01 06	01 54	02 43
20	18 13	18 37	19 04	00 30	01 14	01 59	02 44
30	18 29	18 55	19 26	00 42	01 23	02 04	02 45
35	18 38	19 06	19 39	00 49	01 28	02 07	02 45
40	18 49	19 19	19 55	00 57	01 34	02 10	02 46
45	19 01	19 34	20 16	01 06	01 41	02 14	02 47
S 50	19 16	19 54	20 44	01 17	01 49	02 19	02 48
52	19 23	20 04	20 58	01 22	01 53	02 21	02 48
54	19 31	20 15	21 15	01 28	01 57	02 23	02 49
56	19 40	20 27	21 36	01 34	02 01	02 26	02 49
58	19 50	20 42	22 03	01 41	02 06	02 29	02 50
S 60	20 01	21 00	22 48	01 49	02 12	02 32	02 51

Day	SUN Eqn. of Time 00^h	SUN Eqn. of Time 12^h	SUN Mer. Pass.	MOON Mer. Pass. Upper	MOON Mer. Pass. Lower	MOON Age	MOON Phase
d	m s	m s	h m	h m	h m	d %	
8	16 15	16 13	11 44	18 47	06 22	09 57	
9	16 11	16 08	11 44	19 38	07 12	10 68	
10	16 05	16 02	11 44	20 29	08 03	11 78	

	UT	ARIES	VENUS −4·1		MARS +0·5		JUPITER −1·7		SATURN +0·5	
		GHA	GHA	Dec	GHA	Dec	GHA	Dec	GHA	Dec
	d h	° ′	° ′	° ′	° ′	° ′	° ′	° ′	° ′	° ′
	11 00	50 34.1	142 09.8	S25 30.7	106 37.8	S21 35.8	217 59.9	S 4 09.1	156 12.3	S21 18.6
	01	65 36.5	157 09.0	30.8	121 38.3	35.3	233 01.9	09.3	171 14.4	18.7
	02	80 39.0	172 08.1	30.9	136 38.9	34.9	248 04.0	09.5	186 16.6	18.7
	03	95 41.5	187 07.3	. . 31.0	151 39.4	. . 34.4	263 06.0	. . 09.7	201 18.8	. . 18.7
	04	110 43.9	202 06.4	31.1	166 40.0	34.0	278 08.0	09.9	216 21.0	18.8
	05	125 46.4	217 05.6	31.2	181 40.5	33.5	293 10.0	10.1	231 23.1	18.8
	06	140 48.9	232 04.7	S25 31.3	196 41.1	S21 33.1	308 12.0	S 4 10.2	246 25.3	S21 18.8
	07	155 51.3	247 03.9	31.4	211 41.6	32.6	323 14.0	10.4	261 27.5	18.9
	08	170 53.8	262 03.0	31.5	226 42.2	32.2	338 16.0	10.6	276 29.6	18.9
F	09	185 56.3	277 02.2	. . 31.6	241 42.7	. . 31.7	353 18.1	. . 10.8	291 31.8	. . 18.9
R	10	200 58.7	292 01.3	31.7	256 43.3	31.2	8 20.1	11.0	306 34.0	19.0
I	11	216 01.2	307 00.5	31.8	271 43.8	30.8	23 22.1	11.2	321 36.1	19.0
D	12	231 03.6	321 59.6	S25 31.9	286 44.4	S21 30.3	38 24.1	S 4 11.3	336 38.3	S21 19.0
A	13	246 06.1	336 58.8	32.0	301 44.9	29.9	53 26.1	11.5	351 40.5	19.1
Y	14	261 08.6	351 57.9	32.1	316 45.5	29.4	68 28.1	11.7	6 42.7	19.1
	15	276 11.0	6 57.1	. . 32.2	331 46.0	. . 29.0	83 30.1	. . 11.9	21 44.8	. . 19.1
	16	291 13.5	21 56.3	32.3	346 46.6	28.5	98 32.2	12.1	36 47.0	19.2
	17	306 16.0	36 55.4	32.3	1 47.1	28.1	113 34.2	12.3	51 49.2	19.2
	18	321 18.4	51 54.6	S25 32.4	16 47.7	S21 27.6	128 36.2	S 4 12.4	66 51.3	S21 19.2
	19	336 20.9	66 53.7	32.5	31 48.2	27.2	143 38.2	12.6	81 53.5	19.3
	20	351 23.4	81 52.9	32.6	46 48.8	26.7	158 40.2	12.8	96 55.7	19.3
	21	6 25.8	96 52.0	. . 32.7	61 49.3	. . 26.2	173 42.2	. . 13.0	111 57.9	. . 19.3
	22	21 28.3	111 51.2	32.8	76 49.9	25.8	188 44.3	13.2	127 00.0	19.4
	23	36 30.7	126 50.3	32.9	91 50.4	25.3	203 46.3	13.4	142 02.2	19.4
	12 00	51 33.2	141 49.5	S25 32.9	106 51.0	S21 24.9	218 48.3	S 4 13.5	157 04.4	S21 19.4
	01	66 35.7	156 48.6	33.0	121 51.5	24.4	233 50.3	13.7	172 06.5	19.5
	02	81 38.1	171 47.8	33.1	136 52.1	24.0	248 52.3	13.9	187 08.7	19.5
	03	96 40.6	186 46.9	. . 33.2	151 52.6	. . 23.5	263 54.3	. . 14.1	202 10.9	. . 19.5
	04	111 43.1	201 46.1	33.2	166 53.2	23.0	278 56.3	14.3	217 13.0	19.6
	05	126 45.5	216 45.3	33.3	181 53.7	22.6	293 58.4	14.5	232 15.2	19.6
	06	141 48.0	231 44.4	S25 33.4	196 54.3	S21 22.1	309 00.4	S 4 14.6	247 17.4	S21 19.6
	07	156 50.5	246 43.6	33.5	211 54.9	21.7	324 02.4	14.8	262 19.6	19.7
S	08	171 52.9	261 42.7	33.5	226 55.4	21.2	339 04.4	15.0	277 21.7	19.7
A	09	186 55.4	276 41.9	. . 33.6	241 56.0	. . 20.7	354 06.4	. . 15.2	292 23.9	. . 19.7
T	10	201 57.9	291 41.0	33.7	256 56.5	20.3	9 08.5	15.4	307 26.1	19.8
U	11	217 00.3	306 40.2	33.7	271 57.1	19.8	24 10.5	15.6	322 28.2	19.8
R	12	232 02.8	321 39.3	S25 33.8	286 57.6	S21 19.3	39 12.5	S 4 15.7	337 30.4	S21 19.9
D	13	247 05.2	336 38.5	33.9	301 58.2	18.9	54 14.5	15.9	352 32.6	19.9
A	14	262 07.7	351 37.6	33.9	316 58.7	18.4	69 16.5	16.1	7 34.7	19.9
Y	15	277 10.2	6 36.8	. . 34.0	331 59.3	. . 18.0	84 18.5	. . 16.3	22 36.9	. . 20.0
	16	292 12.6	21 35.9	34.1	346 59.8	17.5	99 20.6	16.5	37 39.1	20.0
	17	307 15.1	36 35.1	34.1	2 00.4	17.0	114 22.6	16.6	52 41.2	20.0
	18	322 17.6	51 34.3	S25 34.2	17 00.9	S21 16.6	129 24.6	S 4 16.8	67 43.4	S21 20.1
	19	337 20.0	66 33.4	34.2	32 01.5	16.1	144 26.6	17.0	82 45.6	20.1
	20	352 22.5	81 32.6	34.3	47 02.0	15.6	159 28.6	17.2	97 47.8	20.1
	21	7 25.0	96 31.7	. . 34.3	62 02.6	. . 15.2	174 30.6	. . 17.4	112 49.9	. . 20.2
	22	22 27.4	111 30.9	34.4	77 03.1	14.7	189 32.7	17.6	127 52.1	20.2
	23	37 29.9	126 30.0	34.4	92 03.7	14.2	204 34.7	17.7	142 54.3	20.2
	13 00	52 32.4	141 29.2	S25 34.5	107 04.2	S21 13.8	219 36.7	S 4 17.9	157 56.4	S21 20.3
	01	67 34.8	156 28.3	34.5	122 04.8	13.3	234 38.7	18.1	172 58.6	20.3
	02	82 37.3	171 27.5	34.6	137 05.3	12.8	249 40.7	18.3	188 00.8	20.3
	03	97 39.7	186 26.7	. . 34.6	152 05.9	. . 12.4	264 42.8	. . 18.5	203 02.9	. . 20.4
	04	112 42.2	201 25.8	34.7	167 06.5	11.9	279 44.8	18.6	218 05.1	20.4
	05	127 44.7	216 25.0	34.7	182 07.0	11.4	294 46.8	18.8	233 07.3	20.4
	06	142 47.1	231 24.1	S25 34.8	197 07.6	S21 11.0	309 48.8	S 4 19.0	248 09.4	S21 20.5
	07	157 49.6	246 23.3	34.8	212 08.1	10.5	324 50.8	19.2	263 11.6	20.5
	08	172 52.1	261 22.4	34.8	227 08.7	10.0	339 52.9	19.4	278 13.8	20.5
S	09	187 54.5	276 21.6	. . 34.9	242 09.2	. . 09.6	354 54.9	. . 19.6	293 15.9	. . 20.6
U	10	202 57.0	291 20.7	34.9	257 09.8	09.1	9 56.9	19.7	308 18.1	20.6
N	11	217 59.5	306 19.9	35.0	272 10.3	08.6	24 58.9	19.9	323 20.3	20.6
D	12	233 01.9	321 19.1	S25 35.0	287 10.9	S21 08.1	40 00.9	S 4 20.1	338 22.4	S21 20.7
A	13	248 04.4	336 18.2	35.0	302 11.4	07.7	55 02.9	20.3	353 24.6	20.7
Y	14	263 06.8	351 17.4	35.1	317 12.0	07.2	70 05.0	20.5	8 26.8	20.7
	15	278 09.3	6 16.5	. . 35.1	332 12.5	. . 06.7	85 07.0	. . 20.6	23 28.9	. . 20.8
	16	293 11.8	21 15.7	35.1	347 13.1	06.3	100 09.0	20.8	38 31.1	20.8
	17	308 14.2	36 14.8	35.1	2 13.7	05.8	115 11.0	21.0	53 33.3	20.8
	18	323 16.7	51 14.0	S25 35.2	17 14.2	S21 05.3	130 13.1	S 4 21.2	68 35.4	S21 20.9
	19	338 19.2	66 13.2	35.2	32 14.8	04.8	145 15.1	21.4	83 37.6	20.9
	20	353 21.6	81 12.3	35.2	47 15.3	04.4	160 17.1	21.5	98 39.8	20.9
	21	8 24.1	96 11.5	. . 35.2	62 15.9	. . 03.9	175 19.1	. . 21.7	113 42.0	. . 21.0
	22	23 26.6	111 10.6	35.3	77 16.4	03.4	190 21.1	21.9	128 44.1	21.0
	23	38 29.0	126 09.8	35.3	92 17.0	02.9	205 23.2	22.1	143 46.3	21.0
	Mer. Pass.	h m 20 30.4	*v* −0.8	*d* 0.1	*v* 0.6	*d* 0.5	*v* 2.0	*d* 0.2	*v* 2.2	*d* 0.0

STARS

Name	SHA	Dec
	° ′	° ′
Acamar	315 16.2	S40 14.4
Achernar	335 24.7	S57 09.3
Acrux	173 07.1	S63 11.2
Adhara	255 10.5	S28 59.7
Aldebaran	290 46.4	N16 32.4
Alioth	166 19.3	N55 52.1
Alkaid	152 57.6	N49 13.8
Al Na'ir	27 40.9	S46 52.9
Alnilam	275 43.8	S 1 11.6
Alphard	217 53.8	S 8 43.9
Alphecca	126 09.5	N26 39.8
Alpheratz	357 40.9	N29 11.2
Altair	62 06.2	N 8 55.1
Ankaa	353 13.2	S42 13.0
Antares	112 23.8	S26 27.9
Arcturus	145 54.0	N19 05.9
Atria	107 24.1	S69 03.3
Avior	234 16.8	S59 33.6
Bellatrix	278 29.3	N 6 21.7
Betelgeuse	270 58.6	N 7 24.4
Canopus	263 54.7	S52 42.2
Capella	280 30.6	N46 00.6
Deneb	49 30.0	N45 20.8
Denebola	182 31.6	N14 28.7
Diphda	348 53.4	S17 53.7
Dubhe	193 49.4	N61 39.4
Elnath	278 09.4	N28 37.1
Eltanin	90 45.5	N51 29.6
Enif	33 44.9	N 9 57.4
Fomalhaut	15 21.4	S29 32.0
Gacrux	171 58.7	S57 12.1
Gienah	175 50.2	S17 37.9
Hadar	148 45.2	S60 26.9
Hamal	327 57.8	N23 32.5
Kaus Aust.	83 41.1	S34 22.4
Kochab	137 21.5	N74 05.3
Markab	13 35.9	N15 17.9
Menkar	314 12.3	N 4 09.2
Menkent	148 05.2	S36 26.9
Miaplacidus	221 39.0	S69 46.9
Mirfak	308 36.5	N49 55.1
Nunki	75 55.8	S26 16.4
Peacock	53 15.9	S56 40.9
Pollux	243 24.8	N27 58.9
Procyon	244 57.2	N 5 10.8
Rasalhague	96 04.6	N12 33.2
Regulus	207 41.2	N11 53.0
Rigel	281 09.6	S 8 11.0
Rigil Kent.	139 49.2	S60 54.0
Sabik	102 10.2	S15 44.5
Schedar	349 37.4	N56 37.9
Shaula	96 19.2	S37 06.8
Sirius	258 31.5	S16 44.4
Spica	158 29.1	S11 14.7
Suhail	222 50.7	S43 29.8
Vega	80 37.7	N38 48.4
Zuben'ubi	137 03.2	S16 06.4

	SHA	Mer. Pass.
	° ′	h m
Venus	90 16.3	14 34
Mars	55 17.8	16 52
Jupiter	167 15.1	9 24
Saturn	105 31.2	13 30

	UT	SUN GHA	SUN Dec	MOON GHA	v	MOON Dec	d	HP
	d h	° ′	° ′	° ′	′	° ′	′	′
	11 00	183 59.7	S17 28.4	50 52.5	9.4	S 1 54.6	11.5	59.7
	01	198 59.6	29.1	65 20.9	9.4	1 43.1	11.6	59.7
	02	213 59.6	29.8	79 49.3	9.3	1 31.5	11.5	59.8
	03	228 59.5	. . 30.5	94 17.6	9.2	1 20.0	11.6	59.8
	04	243 59.4	31.2	108 45.8	9.2	1 08.4	11.6	59.8
	05	258 59.3	31.9	123 14.0	9.2	0 56.8	11.6	59.9
	06	273 59.3	S17 32.5	137 42.2	9.2	S 0 45.2	11.7	59.9
	07	288 59.2	33.2	152 10.4	9.0	0 33.5	11.6	59.9
	08	303 59.1	33.9	166 38.4	9.1	0 21.9	11.7	60.0
F	09	318 59.0	. . 34.6	181 06.5	9.0	S 0 10.2	11.7	60.0
R	10	333 59.0	35.3	195 34.5	9.0	N 0 01.5	11.7	60.0
I	11	348 58.9	36.0	210 02.5	8.9	0 13.2	11.8	60.1
D	12	3 58.8	S17 36.6	224 30.4	8.9	N 0 25.0	11.7	60.1
A	13	18 58.8	37.3	238 58.3	8.8	0 36.7	11.7	60.2
Y	14	33 58.7	38.0	253 26.1	8.8	0 48.4	11.8	60.2
	15	48 58.6	. . 38.7	267 53.9	8.8	1 00.2	11.8	60.2
	16	63 58.5	39.4	282 21.7	8.7	1 12.0	11.7	60.3
	17	78 58.4	40.0	296 49.4	8.6	1 23.7	11.8	60.3
	18	93 58.4	S17 40.7	311 17.0	8.6	N 1 35.5	11.8	60.3
	19	108 58.3	41.4	325 44.6	8.6	1 47.3	11.8	60.4
	20	123 58.2	42.1	340 12.2	8.5	1 59.1	11.8	60.4
	21	138 58.1	. . 42.7	354 39.7	8.5	2 10.9	11.8	60.4
	22	153 58.1	43.4	9 07.2	8.4	2 22.7	11.7	60.5
	23	168 58.0	44.1	23 34.6	8.3	2 34.4	11.8	60.5
	12 00	183 57.9	S17 44.8	38 01.9	8.4	N 2 46.2	11.8	60.5
	01	198 57.8	45.4	52 29.3	8.2	2 58.0	11.8	60.5
	02	213 57.7	46.1	66 56.5	8.2	3 09.8	11.7	60.6
	03	228 57.7	. . 46.8	81 23.7	8.2	3 21.5	11.8	60.6
	04	243 57.6	47.5	95 50.9	8.1	3 33.3	11.8	60.6
	05	258 57.5	48.1	110 18.0	8.1	3 45.1	11.7	60.7
	06	273 57.4	S17 48.8	124 45.1	8.0	N 3 56.8	11.7	60.7
	07	288 57.3	49.5	139 12.1	7.9	4 08.5	11.7	60.7
S	08	303 57.3	50.1	153 39.0	7.9	4 20.2	11.7	60.7
A	09	318 57.2	. . 50.8	168 05.9	7.9	4 31.9	11.7	60.8
T	10	333 57.1	51.5	182 32.8	7.8	4 43.6	11.6	60.8
U	11	348 57.0	52.2	196 59.6	7.7	4 55.2	11.7	60.8
R	12	3 56.9	S17 52.8	211 26.3	7.7	N 5 06.9	11.6	60.9
D	13	18 56.8	53.5	225 53.0	7.6	5 18.5	11.6	60.9
A	14	33 56.8	54.2	240 19.6	7.6	5 30.1	11.6	60.9
Y	15	48 56.7	. . 54.8	254 46.2	7.5	5 41.7	11.5	60.9
	16	63 56.6	55.5	269 12.7	7.5	5 53.2	11.5	61.0
	17	78 56.5	56.2	283 39.2	7.4	6 04.7	11.5	61.0
	18	93 56.4	S17 56.8	298 05.6	7.4	N 6 16.2	11.4	61.0
	19	108 56.3	57.5	312 32.0	7.3	6 27.6	11.5	61.0
	20	123 56.3	58.1	326 58.3	7.2	6 39.1	11.3	61.1
	21	138 56.2	. . 58.8	341 24.5	7.2	6 50.4	11.4	61.1
	22	153 56.1	17 59.5	355 50.7	7.1	7 01.8	11.3	61.1
	23	168 56.0	18 00.1	10 16.8	7.1	7 13.1	11.3	61.1
	13 00	183 55.9	S18 00.8	24 42.9	7.0	N 7 24.4	11.2	61.1
	01	198 55.8	01.5	39 08.9	7.0	7 35.6	11.2	61.2
	02	213 55.7	02.1	53 34.9	6.9	7 46.8	11.1	61.2
	03	228 55.6	. . 02.8	68 00.8	6.8	7 57.9	11.1	61.2
	04	243 55.6	03.4	82 26.6	6.8	8 09.0	11.1	61.2
	05	258 55.5	04.1	96 52.4	6.7	8 20.1	11.0	61.2
	06	273 55.4	S18 04.8	111 18.1	6.7	N 8 31.1	10.9	61.2
	07	288 55.3	05.4	125 43.8	6.6	8 42.0	10.9	61.3
	08	303 55.2	06.1	140 09.4	6.6	8 52.9	10.9	61.3
S	09	318 55.1	. . 06.7	154 35.0	6.5	9 03.8	10.8	61.3
U	10	333 55.0	07.4	169 00.5	6.4	9 14.6	10.7	61.3
N	11	348 54.9	08.0	183 25.9	6.4	9 25.3	10.7	61.3
D	12	3 54.8	S18 08.7	197 51.3	6.3	N 9 36.0	10.6	61.3
A	13	18 54.7	09.3	212 16.6	6.3	9 46.6	10.5	61.4
Y	14	33 54.6	10.0	226 41.9	6.2	9 57.1	10.5	61.4
	15	48 54.6	. . 10.7	241 07.1	6.2	10 07.6	10.4	61.4
	16	63 54.5	11.3	255 32.3	6.1	10 18.0	10.4	61.4
	17	78 54.4	12.0	269 57.4	6.0	10 28.4	10.3	61.4
	18	93 54.3	S18 12.6	284 22.4	6.0	N10 38.7	10.2	61.4
	19	108 54.2	13.3	298 47.4	5.9	10 48.9	10.1	61.4
	20	123 54.1	13.9	313 12.3	5.9	10 59.0	10.1	61.4
	21	138 54.0	. . 14.6	327 37.2	5.8	11 09.1	10.0	61.4
	22	153 53.9	15.2	342 02.0	5.8	11 19.1	9.9	61.5
	23	168 53.8	15.9	356 26.8	5.7	N11 29.0	9.9	61.5
		SD 16.2	*d* 0.7	SD 16.4		16.6		16.7

Lat.	Twilight Naut.	Twilight Civil	Sunrise	Moonrise 11	Moonrise 12	Moonrise 13	Moonrise 14
°	h m	h m	h m	h m	h m	h m	h m
N 72	06 50	08 22	10 26	14 58	14 52	14 45	14 37
N 70	06 41	08 01	09 33	14 59	14 59	15 00	15 03
68	06 33	07 45	09 01	15 00	15 06	15 13	15 23
66	06 27	07 32	08 37	15 01	15 11	15 23	15 39
64	06 21	07 21	08 19	15 02	15 16	15 32	15 53
62	06 16	07 11	08 04	15 02	15 19	15 39	16 04
60	06 12	07 03	07 51	15 03	15 23	15 46	16 14
N 58	06 08	06 56	07 40	15 03	15 26	15 51	16 22
56	06 04	06 49	07 31	15 04	15 29	15 57	16 30
54	06 00	06 43	07 23	15 04	15 31	16 01	16 36
52	05 57	06 38	07 15	15 04	15 33	16 05	16 42
50	05 54	06 33	07 08	15 05	15 35	16 09	16 48
45	05 47	06 22	06 54	15 05	15 40	16 17	16 59
N 40	05 41	06 13	06 42	15 06	15 44	16 24	17 09
35	05 35	06 05	06 32	15 07	15 47	16 30	17 18
30	05 29	05 58	06 23	15 07	15 50	16 36	17 25
20	05 18	05 44	06 07	15 08	15 55	16 45	17 38
N 10	05 06	05 32	05 54	15 09	16 00	16 53	17 49
0	04 54	05 19	05 41	15 09	16 04	17 01	18 00
S 10	04 40	05 05	05 28	15 10	16 08	17 09	18 11
20	04 22	04 50	05 14	15 11	16 13	17 17	18 23
30	04 00	04 31	04 57	15 12	16 18	17 27	18 36
35	03 46	04 20	04 48	15 13	16 22	17 32	18 44
40	03 30	04 07	04 37	15 13	16 25	17 39	18 53
45	03 08	03 50	04 24	15 14	16 29	17 46	19 03
S 50	02 39	03 30	04 08	15 15	16 34	17 55	19 16
52	02 25	03 20	04 01	15 15	16 37	17 59	19 22
54	02 07	03 08	03 53	15 16	16 39	18 04	19 28
56	01 44	02 55	03 43	15 16	16 42	18 09	19 35
58	01 14	02 40	03 33	15 17	16 45	18 15	19 44
S 60	00 15	02 21	03 21	15 18	16 49	18 21	19 53

Lat.	Sunset	Twilight Civil	Twilight Naut.	Moonset 11	Moonset 12	Moonset 13	Moonset 14
°	h m	h m	h m	h m	h m	h m	h m
N 72	13 01	15 05	16 37	02 21	04 20	06 24	08 35
N 70	13 54	15 26	16 46	02 24	04 15	06 11	08 10
68	14 27	15 42	16 54	02 26	04 11	06 00	07 51
66	14 50	15 56	17 00	02 27	04 08	05 51	07 36
64	15 09	16 07	17 06	02 29	04 05	05 44	07 23
62	15 24	16 16	17 11	02 30	04 02	05 37	07 13
60	15 36	16 25	17 16	02 31	04 00	05 32	07 04
N 58	15 47	16 32	17 20	02 32	03 58	05 27	06 56
56	15 57	16 38	17 24	02 32	03 56	05 23	06 50
54	16 05	16 44	17 27	02 33	03 55	05 19	06 44
52	16 13	16 50	17 31	02 34	03 53	05 15	06 38
50	16 19	16 55	17 34	02 34	03 52	05 12	06 33
45	16 34	17 05	17 41	02 35	03 49	05 05	06 23
N 40	16 46	17 15	17 47	02 36	03 47	05 00	06 14
35	16 56	17 23	17 53	02 37	03 45	04 55	06 06
30	17 05	17 30	17 59	02 38	03 43	04 51	06 00
20	17 21	17 44	18 11	02 39	03 40	04 43	05 48
N 10	17 35	17 57	18 22	02 41	03 38	04 37	05 38
0	17 48	18 09	18 35	02 42	03 35	04 31	05 29
S 10	18 01	18 23	18 49	02 43	03 32	04 25	05 19
20	18 15	18 39	19 06	02 44	03 30	04 18	05 10
30	18 31	18 57	19 29	02 45	03 27	04 11	04 58
35	18 41	19 09	19 43	02 45	03 25	04 07	04 52
40	18 52	19 22	20 00	02 46	03 23	04 02	04 44
45	19 05	19 39	20 21	02 47	03 20	03 56	04 36
S 50	19 21	20 00	20 51	02 48	03 18	03 50	04 25
52	19 29	20 10	21 06	02 48	03 16	03 46	04 20
54	19 37	20 21	21 24	02 49	03 15	03 43	04 15
56	19 46	20 35	21 47	02 49	03 13	03 39	04 09
58	19 57	20 51	22 19	02 50	03 12	03 35	04 03
S 60	20 10	21 10	////	02 51	03 10	03 31	03 56

Day	SUN Eqn. of Time 00^h	SUN Eqn. of Time 12^h	SUN Mer. Pass.	MOON Mer. Pass. Upper	MOON Mer. Pass. Lower	MOON Age	MOON Phase
d	m s	m s	h m	h m	h m	d %	
11	15 59	15 55	11 44	21 22	08 55	12 86	
12	15 52	15 48	11 44	22 17	09 49	13 93	○
13	15 44	15 39	11 44	23 15	10 46	14 98	

UT d	h	ARIES GHA	VENUS −4·1 GHA	Dec	MARS +0·5 GHA	Dec	JUPITER −1·7 GHA	Dec	SATURN +0·5 GHA	Dec
		° ′	° ′	° ′	° ′	° ′	° ′	° ′	° ′	° ′
14 MONDAY	00	53 31.5	141 08.9	S25 35.3	107 17.5	S21 02.5	220 25.2	S 4 22.3	158 48.5	S21 21.1
	01	68 34.0	156 08.1	35.3	122 18.1	02.0	235 27.2	22.4	173 50.6	21.1
	02	83 36.4	171 07.3	35.3	137 18.7	01.5	250 29.2	22.6	188 52.8	21.1
	03	98 38.9	186 06.4	35.4	152 19.2	01.0	265 31.2	22.8	203 55.0	21.2
	04	113 41.3	201 05.6	35.4	167 19.8	00.6	280 33.3	23.0	218 57.1	21.2
	05	128 43.8	216 04.7	35.4	182 20.3	21 00.1	295 35.3	23.2	233 59.3	21.2
	06	143 46.3	231 03.9	S25 35.4	197 20.9	S20 59.6	310 37.3	S 4 23.3	249 01.5	S21 21.3
	07	158 48.7	246 03.0	35.4	212 21.4	59.1	325 39.3	23.5	264 03.6	21.3
	08	173 51.2	261 02.2	35.4	227 22.0	58.7	340 41.3	23.7	279 05.8	21.3
	09	188 53.7	276 01.4	35.4	242 22.5	58.2	355 43.4	23.9	294 08.0	21.4
	10	203 56.1	291 00.5	35.4	257 23.1	57.7	10 45.4	24.1	309 10.1	21.4
	11	218 58.6	305 59.7	35.4	272 23.7	57.2	25 47.4	24.2	324 12.3	21.4
	12	234 01.1	320 58.8	S25 35.4	287 24.2	S20 56.7	40 49.4	S 4 24.4	339 14.5	S21 21.5
	13	249 03.5	335 58.0	35.4	302 24.8	56.3	55 51.5	24.6	354 16.6	21.5
	14	264 06.0	350 57.1	35.4	317 25.3	55.8	70 53.5	24.8	9 18.8	21.5
	15	279 08.5	5 56.3	35.4	332 25.9	55.3	85 55.5	25.0	24 21.0	21.6
	16	294 10.9	20 55.5	35.4	347 26.4	54.8	100 57.5	25.1	39 23.1	21.6
	17	309 13.4	35 54.6	35.4	2 27.0	54.3	115 59.5	25.3	54 25.3	21.6
	18	324 15.8	50 53.8	S25 35.4	17 27.6	S20 53.9	131 01.6	S 4 25.5	69 27.5	S21 21.7
	19	339 18.3	65 52.9	35.4	32 28.1	53.4	146 03.6	25.7	84 29.6	21.7
	20	354 20.8	80 52.1	35.4	47 28.7	52.9	161 05.6	25.9	99 31.8	21.7
	21	9 23.2	95 51.3	35.4	62 29.2	52.4	176 07.6	26.0	114 33.9	21.8
	22	24 25.7	110 50.4	35.4	77 29.8	51.9	191 09.7	26.2	129 36.1	21.8
	23	39 28.2	125 49.6	35.4	92 30.3	51.4	206 11.7	26.4	144 38.3	21.8
15 TUESDAY	00	54 30.6	140 48.7	S25 35.4	107 30.9	S20 51.0	221 13.7	S 4 26.6	159 40.4	S21 21.9
	01	69 33.1	155 47.9	35.4	122 31.5	50.5	236 15.7	26.8	174 42.6	21.9
	02	84 35.6	170 47.1	35.4	137 32.0	50.0	251 17.8	26.9	189 44.8	21.9
	03	99 38.0	185 46.2	35.3	152 32.6	49.5	266 19.8	27.1	204 46.9	22.0
	04	114 40.5	200 45.4	35.3	167 33.1	49.0	281 21.8	27.3	219 49.1	22.0
	05	129 42.9	215 44.5	35.3	182 33.7	48.5	296 23.8	27.5	234 51.3	22.0
	06	144 45.4	230 43.7	S25 35.3	197 34.3	S20 48.0	311 25.8	S 4 27.7	249 53.4	S21 22.1
	07	159 47.9	245 42.9	35.3	212 34.8	47.6	326 27.9	27.8	264 55.6	22.1
	08	174 50.3	260 42.0	35.2	227 35.4	47.1	341 29.9	28.0	279 57.8	22.1
	09	189 52.8	275 41.2	35.2	242 35.9	46.6	356 31.9	28.2	294 59.9	22.2
	10	204 55.3	290 40.4	35.2	257 36.5	46.1	11 33.9	28.4	310 02.1	22.2
	11	219 57.7	305 39.5	35.2	272 37.1	45.6	26 36.0	28.5	325 04.3	22.2
	12	235 00.2	320 38.7	S25 35.1	287 37.6	S20 45.1	41 38.0	S 4 28.7	340 06.4	S21 22.3
	13	250 02.7	335 37.8	35.1	302 38.2	44.6	56 40.0	28.9	355 08.6	22.3
	14	265 05.1	350 37.0	35.1	317 38.7	44.1	71 42.0	29.1	10 10.8	22.3
	15	280 07.6	5 36.2	35.1	332 39.3	43.7	86 44.1	29.3	25 12.9	22.4
	16	295 10.1	20 35.3	35.0	347 39.8	43.2	101 46.1	29.4	40 15.1	22.4
	17	310 12.5	35 34.5	35.0	2 40.4	42.7	116 48.1	29.6	55 17.3	22.4
	18	325 15.0	50 33.6	S25 35.0	17 41.0	S20 42.2	131 50.1	S 4 29.8	70 19.4	S21 22.5
	19	340 17.4	65 32.8	34.9	32 41.5	41.7	146 52.2	30.0	85 21.6	22.5
	20	355 19.9	80 32.0	34.9	47 42.1	41.2	161 54.2	30.2	100 23.8	22.5
	21	10 22.4	95 31.1	34.8	62 42.6	40.7	176 56.2	30.3	115 25.9	22.6
	22	25 24.8	110 30.3	34.8	77 43.2	40.2	191 58.2	30.5	130 28.1	22.6
	23	40 27.3	125 29.5	34.8	92 43.8	39.7	207 00.3	30.7	145 30.2	22.6
16 WEDNESDAY	00	55 29.8	140 28.6	S25 34.7	107 44.3	S20 39.2	222 02.3	S 4 30.9	160 32.4	S21 22.7
	01	70 32.2	155 27.8	34.7	122 44.9	38.8	237 04.3	31.0	175 34.6	22.7
	02	85 34.7	170 27.0	34.6	137 45.5	38.3	252 06.3	31.2	190 36.7	22.7
	03	100 37.2	185 26.1	34.6	152 46.0	37.8	267 08.4	31.4	205 38.9	22.8
	04	115 39.6	200 25.3	34.5	167 46.6	37.3	282 10.4	31.6	220 41.1	22.8
	05	130 42.1	215 24.4	34.5	182 47.1	36.8	297 12.4	31.8	235 43.2	22.8
	06	145 44.6	230 23.6	S25 34.4	197 47.7	S20 36.3	312 14.4	S 4 31.9	250 45.4	S21 22.9
	07	160 47.0	245 22.8	34.4	212 48.3	35.8	327 16.5	32.1	265 47.6	22.9
	08	175 49.5	260 21.9	34.3	227 48.8	35.3	342 18.5	32.3	280 49.7	22.9
	09	190 51.9	275 21.1	34.3	242 49.4	34.8	357 20.5	32.5	295 51.9	23.0
	10	205 54.4	290 20.3	34.2	257 49.9	34.3	12 22.6	32.6	310 54.0	23.0
	11	220 56.9	305 19.4	34.2	272 50.5	33.8	27 24.6	32.8	325 56.2	23.0
	12	235 59.3	320 18.6	S25 34.1	287 51.1	S20 33.3	42 26.6	S 4 33.0	340 58.4	S21 23.1
	13	251 01.8	335 17.8	34.1	302 51.6	32.8	57 28.6	33.2	356 00.5	23.1
	14	266 04.3	350 16.9	34.0	317 52.2	32.3	72 30.7	33.3	11 02.7	23.1
	15	281 06.7	5 16.1	33.9	332 52.7	31.8	87 32.7	33.5	26 04.9	23.2
	16	296 09.2	20 15.3	33.9	347 53.3	31.3	102 34.7	33.7	41 07.0	23.2
	17	311 11.7	35 14.4	33.8	2 53.9	30.8	117 36.7	33.9	56 09.2	23.2
	18	326 14.1	50 13.6	S25 33.8	17 54.4	S20 30.3	132 38.8	S 4 34.1	71 11.4	S21 23.3
	19	341 16.6	65 12.8	33.7	32 55.0	29.8	147 40.8	34.2	86 13.5	23.3
	20	356 19.1	80 11.9	33.6	47 55.6	29.3	162 42.8	34.4	101 15.7	23.3
	21	11 21.5	95 11.1	33.5	62 56.1	28.8	177 44.9	34.6	116 17.8	23.4
	22	26 24.0	110 10.3	33.5	77 56.7	28.3	192 46.9	34.8	131 20.0	23.4
	23	41 26.4	125 09.4	33.4	92 57.2	27.8	207 48.9	34.9	146 22.2	23.4
Mer. Pass.		h m 20 18.6	v −0.8	d 0.0	v 0.6	d 0.5	v 2.0	d 0.2	v 2.2	d 0.0

STARS

Name	SHA	Dec
	° ′	° ′
Acamar	315 16.2	S40 14.4
Achernar	335 24.7	S57 09.3
Acrux	173 07.0	S63 11.2
Adhara	255 10.5	S28 59.7
Aldebaran	290 46.4	N16 32.4
Alioth	166 19.2	N55 52.1
Alkaid	152 57.6	N49 13.8
Al Na'ir	27 40.9	S46 52.9
Alnilam	275 43.8	S 1 11.6
Alphard	217 53.8	S 8 43.9
Alphecca	126 09.5	N26 39.7
Alpheratz	357 40.9	N29 11.2
Altair	62 06.2	N 8 55.1
Ankaa	353 13.2	S42 13.0
Antares	112 23.8	S26 27.9
Arcturus	145 54.0	N19 05.9
Atria	107 24.1	S69 03.3
Avior	234 16.8	S59 33.6
Bellatrix	278 29.3	N 6 21.7
Betelgeuse	270 58.6	N 7 24.4
Canopus	263 54.7	S52 42.2
Capella	280 30.6	N46 00.6
Deneb	49 30.0	N45 20.8
Denebola	182 31.5	N14 28.7
Diphda	348 53.4	S17 53.7
Dubhe	193 49.3	N61 39.4
Elnath	278 09.4	N28 37.1
Eltanin	90 45.5	N51 29.6
Enif	33 44.9	N 9 57.4
Fomalhaut	15 21.4	S29 32.0
Gacrux	171 58.6	S57 12.1
Gienah	175 50.1	S17 37.9
Hadar	148 45.1	S60 26.9
Hamal	327 57.8	N23 32.5
Kaus Aust.	83 41.1	S34 22.4
Kochab	137 21.5	N74 05.3
Markab	13 35.9	N15 17.9
Menkar	314 12.3	N 4 09.2
Menkent	148 05.2	S36 26.9
Miaplacidus	221 38.9	S69 46.9
Mirfak	308 36.5	N49 55.1
Nunki	75 55.8	S26 16.4
Peacock	53 15.9	S56 40.9
Pollux	243 24.8	N27 58.9
Procyon	244 57.2	N 5 10.8
Rasalhague	96 04.6	N12 33.2
Regulus	207 41.2	N11 53.0
Rigel	281 09.6	S 8 11.1
Rigil Kent.	139 49.2	S60 53.9
Sabik	102 10.2	S15 44.5
Schedar	349 37.4	N56 37.9
Shaula	96 19.2	S37 06.7
Sirius	258 31.5	S16 44.4
Spica	158 29.1	S11 14.7
Suhail	222 50.6	S43 29.9
Vega	80 37.7	N38 48.4
Zuben'ubi	137 03.2	S16 06.4

	SHA	Mer. Pass.
	° ′	h m
Venus	86 18.1	14 38
Mars	53 00.3	16 49
Jupiter	166 43.1	9 14
Saturn	105 09.8	13 19

Day	UT (h)	SUN GHA	SUN Dec	MOON GHA	v	MOON Dec	d	HP
d	h	° ′	° ′	° ′	′	° ′	′	′
14	00	183 53.7	S18 16.5	10 51.5	5.7	N11 38.9	9.8	61.5
	01	198 53.6	17.2	25 16.2	5.6	11 48.7	9.6	61.5
	02	213 53.5	17.8	39 40.8	5.6	11 58.3	9.6	61.5
	03	228 53.4	. . 18.5	54 05.4	5.5	12 07.9	9.6	61.5
	04	243 53.3	19.1	68 29.9	5.4	12 17.5	9.4	61.5
	05	258 53.2	19.7	82 54.3	5.4	12 26.9	9.3	61.5
	06	273 53.1	S18 20.4	97 18.7	5.4	N12 36.2	9.3	61.5
	07	288 53.0	21.0	111 43.1	5.3	12 45.5	9.2	61.5
	08	303 52.9	21.7	126 07.4	5.2	12 54.7	9.0	61.5
MONDAY	09	318 52.8	. . 22.3	140 31.6	5.3	13 03.7	9.0	61.5
	10	333 52.7	23.0	154 55.9	5.1	13 12.7	8.9	61.5
	11	348 52.6	23.6	169 20.0	5.1	13 21.6	8.8	61.5
	12	3 52.5	S18 24.3	183 44.1	5.1	N13 30.4	8.7	61.5
	13	18 52.4	24.9	198 08.2	5.0	13 39.1	8.6	61.5
	14	33 52.3	25.5	212 32.2	5.0	13 47.7	8.5	61.5
	15	48 52.2	. . 26.2	226 56.2	4.9	13 56.2	8.4	61.5
	16	63 52.1	26.8	241 20.1	4.9	14 04.6	8.3	61.5
	17	78 52.0	27.5	255 44.0	4.8	14 12.9	8.2	61.5
	18	93 51.9	S18 28.1	270 07.8	4.8	N14 21.1	8.1	61.5
	19	108 51.8	28.7	284 31.6	4.8	14 29.2	8.0	61.5
	20	123 51.7	29.4	298 55.4	4.7	14 37.2	7.8	61.5
	21	138 51.6	. . 30.0	313 19.1	4.7	14 45.0	7.8	61.5
	22	153 51.5	30.6	327 42.8	4.7	14 52.8	7.7	61.5
	23	168 51.4	31.3	342 06.5	4.6	15 00.5	7.5	61.5
15	00	183 51.3	S18 31.9	356 30.1	4.6	N15 08.0	7.4	61.5
	01	198 51.2	32.5	10 53.7	4.5	15 15.4	7.4	61.4
	02	213 51.1	33.2	25 17.2	4.5	15 22.8	7.2	61.4
	03	228 51.0	. . 33.8	39 40.7	4.5	15 30.0	7.1	61.4
	04	243 50.9	34.4	54 04.2	4.4	15 37.1	6.9	61.4
	05	258 50.7	35.1	68 27.6	4.4	15 44.0	6.9	61.4
	06	273 50.6	S18 35.7	82 51.0	4.4	N15 50.9	6.7	61.4
	07	288 50.5	36.3	97 14.4	4.4	15 57.6	6.6	61.4
TUESDAY	08	303 50.4	37.0	111 37.8	4.3	16 04.2	6.5	61.4
	09	318 50.3	. . 37.6	126 01.1	4.3	16 10.7	6.4	61.4
	10	333 50.2	38.2	140 24.4	4.3	16 17.1	6.2	61.4
	11	348 50.1	38.9	154 47.7	4.3	16 23.3	6.2	61.3
	12	3 50.0	S18 39.5	169 11.0	4.2	N16 29.5	6.0	61.3
	13	18 49.9	40.1	183 34.2	4.2	16 35.5	5.9	61.3
	14	33 49.8	40.7	197 57.4	4.2	16 41.4	5.7	61.3
	15	48 49.7	. . 41.4	212 20.6	4.2	16 47.1	5.6	61.3
	16	63 49.5	42.0	226 43.8	4.2	16 52.7	5.5	61.3
	17	78 49.4	42.6	241 07.0	4.2	16 58.2	5.4	61.2
	18	93 49.3	S18 43.2	255 30.2	4.1	N17 03.6	5.2	61.2
	19	108 49.2	43.9	269 53.3	4.1	17 08.8	5.1	61.2
	20	123 49.1	44.5	284 16.4	4.2	17 13.9	5.0	61.2
	21	138 49.0	. . 45.1	298 39.6	4.1	17 18.9	4.9	61.2
	22	153 48.9	45.7	313 02.7	4.1	17 23.8	4.7	61.1
	23	168 48.8	46.4	327 25.8	4.1	17 28.5	4.6	61.1
16	00	183 48.6	S18 47.0	341 48.9	4.1	N17 33.1	4.4	61.1
	01	198 48.5	47.6	356 12.0	4.1	17 37.5	4.3	61.1
	02	213 48.4	48.2	10 35.1	4.1	17 41.8	4.2	61.1
	03	228 48.3	. . 48.8	24 58.2	4.1	17 46.0	4.1	61.0
	04	243 48.2	49.5	39 21.3	4.1	17 50.1	3.9	61.0
	05	258 48.1	50.1	53 44.4	4.1	17 54.0	3.8	61.0
	06	273 48.0	S18 50.7	68 07.5	4.1	N17 57.8	3.6	61.0
	07	288 47.8	51.3	82 30.6	4.1	18 01.4	3.5	60.9
	08	303 47.7	51.9	96 53.7	4.2	18 04.9	3.4	60.9
	09	318 47.6	. . 52.5	111 16.9	4.1	18 08.3	3.3	60.9
	10	333 47.5	53.2	125 40.0	4.2	18 11.6	3.1	60.9
	11	348 47.4	53.8	140 03.2	4.1	18 14.7	2.9	60.8
WEDNESDAY	12	3 47.3	S18 54.4	154 26.3	4.2	N18 17.6	2.9	60.8
	13	18 47.1	55.0	168 49.5	4.2	18 20.5	2.7	60.8
	14	33 47.0	55.6	183 12.7	4.2	18 23.2	2.5	60.8
	15	48 46.9	. . 56.2	197 35.9	4.2	18 25.7	2.5	60.7
	16	63 46.8	56.8	211 59.1	4.3	18 28.2	2.3	60.7
	17	78 46.7	57.4	226 22.4	4.3	18 30.5	2.1	60.7
	18	93 46.5	S18 58.1	240 45.7	4.3	N18 32.6	2.0	60.7
	19	108 46.4	58.7	255 09.0	4.3	18 34.6	1.9	60.6
	20	123 46.3	59.3	269 32.3	4.4	18 36.5	1.7	60.6
	21	138 46.2	18 59.9	283 55.7	4.3	18 38.2	1.7	60.6
	22	153 46.0	19 00.5	298 19.0	4.5	18 39.9	1.4	60.5
	23	168 45.9	S19 01.1	312 42.5	4.4	N18 41.3	1.4	60.5
		SD 16.2	*d* 0.6	SD 16.8		16.7		16.6

Lat.	Twilight Naut.	Twilight Civil	Sunrise	Moonrise 14	15	16	17
°	h m	h m	h m	h m	h m	h m	h m
N 72	07 01	08 36	11 11	14 37	14 25	▭	▭
N 70	06 50	08 13	09 52	15 03	15 11	15 30	16 21
68	06 42	07 55	09 15	15 23	15 41	16 13	17 08
66	06 35	07 41	08 49	15 39	16 04	16 42	17 38
64	06 28	07 29	08 29	15 53	16 22	17 03	18 01
62	06 23	07 19	08 12	16 04	16 37	17 21	18 19
60	06 18	07 10	07 59	16 14	16 49	17 36	18 34
N 58	06 13	07 02	07 47	16 22	17 00	17 48	18 47
56	06 09	06 55	07 37	16 30	17 10	17 59	18 58
54	06 05	06 49	07 28	16 36	17 18	18 09	19 08
52	06 02	06 43	07 20	16 42	17 26	18 17	19 16
50	05 58	06 38	07 13	16 48	17 33	18 25	19 24
45	05 51	06 26	06 58	16 59	17 47	18 41	19 41
N 40	05 44	06 16	06 45	17 09	17 59	18 55	19 54
35	05 37	06 08	06 35	17 18	18 10	19 06	20 06
30	05 31	06 00	06 25	17 25	18 19	19 16	20 16
20	05 19	05 46	06 09	17 38	18 34	19 33	20 33
N 10	05 07	05 33	05 55	17 49	18 48	19 48	20 49
0	04 54	05 19	05 41	18 00	19 01	20 03	21 03
S 10	04 39	05 05	05 27	18 11	19 14	20 17	21 17
20	04 21	04 49	05 13	18 23	19 28	20 32	21 32
30	03 58	04 30	04 56	18 36	19 44	20 50	21 50
35	03 44	04 18	04 46	18 44	19 54	21 00	22 00
40	03 26	04 04	04 34	18 53	20 04	21 11	22 12
45	03 04	03 47	04 21	19 03	20 17	21 25	22 25
S 50	02 33	03 25	04 04	19 16	20 32	21 42	22 42
52	02 17	03 15	03 56	19 22	20 40	21 50	22 50
54	01 58	03 02	03 48	19 28	20 48	21 59	22 59
56	01 33	02 48	03 38	19 35	20 57	22 09	23 08
58	00 57	02 32	03 27	19 44	21 07	22 20	23 19
S 60	////	02 11	03 14	19 53	21 19	22 33	23 32

Lat.	Sunset	Twilight Civil	Twilight Naut.	Moonset 14	15	16	17
°	h m	h m	h m	h m	h m	h m	h m
N 72	12 18	14 52	16 27	08 35	10 54	▭	▭
N 70	13 36	15 15	16 38	08 10	10 09	11 58	13 15
68	14 14	15 33	16 46	07 51	09 39	11 16	12 28
66	14 40	15 48	16 54	07 36	09 17	10 48	11 58
64	15 00	16 00	17 00	07 23	09 00	10 26	11 35
62	15 16	16 10	17 06	07 13	08 46	10 09	11 16
60	15 30	16 19	17 11	07 04	08 33	09 54	11 01
N 58	15 41	16 27	17 15	06 56	08 23	09 42	10 48
56	15 51	16 34	17 20	06 50	08 14	09 31	10 37
54	16 00	16 40	17 23	06 44	08 06	09 22	10 27
52	16 08	16 46	17 27	06 38	07 59	09 13	10 19
50	16 15	16 51	17 30	06 33	07 52	09 06	10 11
45	16 31	17 03	17 38	06 23	07 38	08 50	09 54
N 40	16 43	17 12	17 45	06 14	07 27	08 37	09 41
35	16 54	17 21	17 52	06 06	07 17	08 26	09 29
30	17 04	17 29	17 58	06 00	07 09	08 16	09 19
20	17 20	17 43	18 10	05 48	06 54	07 59	09 01
N 10	17 35	17 57	18 22	05 38	06 41	07 44	08 46
0	17 48	18 10	18 35	05 29	06 29	07 30	08 32
S 10	18 02	18 24	18 50	05 19	06 17	07 17	08 17
20	18 17	18 40	19 08	05 10	06 04	07 02	08 02
30	18 34	19 00	19 32	04 58	05 50	06 45	07 44
35	18 44	19 12	19 46	04 52	05 41	06 35	07 34
40	18 56	19 26	20 04	04 44	05 32	06 24	07 22
45	19 09	19 43	20 27	04 36	05 20	06 11	07 08
S 50	19 26	20 05	20 58	04 25	05 07	05 55	06 51
52	19 34	20 16	21 14	04 20	05 00	05 48	06 43
54	19 43	20 28	21 34	04 15	04 53	05 39	06 34
56	19 53	20 43	21 59	04 09	04 46	05 30	06 24
58	20 04	21 00	22 38	04 03	04 37	05 20	06 13
S 60	20 18	21 21	////	03 56	04 27	05 07	06 00

Day	SUN Eqn. of Time 00^h	SUN Eqn. of Time 12^h	SUN Mer. Pass.	MOON Mer. Pass. Upper	MOON Mer. Pass. Lower	MOON Age	MOON Phase
d	m s	m s	h m	h m	h m	d %	
14	15 35	15 30	11 44	24 15	11 44	15 100	○
15	15 25	15 20	11 45	00 15	12 45	16 98	
16	15 15	15 09	11 45	01 16	13 47	17 94	

UT	ARIES	VENUS −4·1		MARS +0·5		JUPITER −1·7		SATURN +0·5		STARS		
	GHA	GHA	Dec	GHA	Dec	GHA	Dec	GHA	Dec	Name	SHA	Dec
d h	° ′	° ′	° ′	° ′	° ′	° ′	° ′	° ′	° ′		° ′	° ′
17 00	56 28.9	140 08.6	S25 33.3	107 57.8	S20 27.3	222 50.9	S 4 35.1	161 24.3	S21 23.5	Acamar	315 16.2	S40 14.4
01	71 31.4	155 07.8	33.3	122 58.4	26.8	237 53.0	35.3	176 26.5	23.5	Achernar	335 24.7	S57 09.3
02	86 33.8	170 06.9	33.2	137 58.9	26.3	252 55.0	35.5	191 28.7	23.5	Acrux	173 07.0	S63 11.2
03	101 36.3	185 06.1	. . 33.1	152 59.5	. . 25.8	267 57.0	. . 35.6	206 30.8	. . 23.6	Adhara	255 10.5	S28 59.7
04	116 38.8	200 05.3	33.0	168 00.1	25.3	282 59.1	35.8	221 33.0	23.6	Aldebaran	290 46.4	N16 32.4
05	131 41.2	215 04.4	33.0	183 00.6	24.8	298 01.1	36.0	236 35.2	23.6			
06	146 43.7	230 03.6	S25 32.9	198 01.2	S20 24.3	313 03.1	S 4 36.2	251 37.3	S21 23.7	Alioth	166 19.2	N55 52.0
07	161 46.2	245 02.8	32.8	213 01.8	23.8	328 05.1	36.4	266 39.5	23.7	Alkaid	152 57.6	N49 13.8
T 08	176 48.6	260 02.0	32.7	228 02.3	23.3	343 07.2	36.5	281 41.6	23.7	Al Na'ir	27 40.9	S46 52.9
H 09	191 51.1	275 01.1	. . 32.6	243 02.9	. . 22.8	358 09.2	. . 36.7	296 43.8	. . 23.8	Alnilam	275 43.7	S 1 11.6
U 10	206 53.6	290 00.3	32.5	258 03.5	22.3	13 11.2	36.9	311 46.0	23.8	Alphard	217 53.8	S 8 43.9
R 11	221 56.0	304 59.5	32.5	273 04.0	21.8	28 13.3	37.1	326 48.1	23.8			
S 12	236 58.5	319 58.6	S25 32.4	288 04.6	S20 21.3	43 15.3	S 4 37.2	341 50.3	S21 23.9	Alphecca	126 09.5	N26 39.7
D 13	252 00.9	334 57.8	32.3	303 05.1	20.8	58 17.3	37.4	356 52.5	23.9	Alpheratz	357 40.9	N29 11.2
A 14	267 03.4	349 57.0	32.2	318 05.7	20.3	73 19.3	37.6	11 54.6	23.9	Altair	62 06.2	N 8 55.1
Y 15	282 05.9	4 56.1	. . 32.1	333 06.3	. . 19.8	88 21.4	. . 37.8	26 56.8	. . 24.0	Ankaa	353 13.2	S42 13.1
16	297 08.3	19 55.3	32.0	348 06.8	19.3	103 23.4	37.9	41 58.9	24.0	Antares	112 23.8	S26 27.9
17	312 10.8	34 54.5	31.9	3 07.4	18.8	118 25.4	38.1	57 01.1	24.0			
18	327 13.3	49 53.7	S25 31.8	18 08.0	S20 18.3	133 27.5	S 4 38.3	72 03.3	S21 24.1	Arcturus	145 54.0	N19 05.9
19	342 15.7	64 52.8	31.7	33 08.5	17.8	148 29.5	38.5	87 05.4	24.1	Atria	107 24.0	S69 03.3
20	357 18.2	79 52.0	31.6	48 09.1	17.3	163 31.5	38.6	102 07.6	24.1	Avior	234 16.7	S59 33.6
21	12 20.7	94 51.2	. . 31.5	63 09.7	. . 16.8	178 33.6	. . 38.8	117 09.8	. . 24.2	Bellatrix	278 29.2	N 6 21.7
22	27 23.1	109 50.4	31.4	78 10.2	16.2	193 35.6	39.0	132 11.9	24.2	Betelgeuse	270 58.5	N 7 24.4
23	42 25.6	124 49.5	31.3	93 10.8	15.7	208 37.6	39.2	147 14.1	24.2			
18 00	57 28.1	139 48.7	S25 31.2	108 11.4	S20 15.2	223 39.6	S 4 39.3	162 16.2	S21 24.3	Canopus	263 54.7	S52 42.3
01	72 30.5	154 47.9	31.1	123 11.9	14.7	238 41.7	39.5	177 18.4	24.3	Capella	280 30.6	N46 00.6
02	87 33.0	169 47.0	31.0	138 12.5	14.2	253 43.7	39.7	192 20.6	24.3	Deneb	49 30.0	N45 20.8
03	102 35.4	184 46.2	. . 30.9	153 13.1	. . 13.7	268 45.7	. . 39.9	207 22.7	. . 24.4	Denebola	182 31.5	N14 28.7
04	117 37.9	199 45.4	30.8	168 13.6	13.2	283 47.8	40.0	222 24.9	24.4	Diphda	348 53.4	S17 53.7
05	132 40.4	214 44.6	30.7	183 14.2	12.7	298 49.8	40.2	237 27.0	24.4			
06	147 42.8	229 43.7	S25 30.6	198 14.8	S20 12.2	313 51.8	S 4 40.4	252 29.2	S21 24.5	Dubhe	193 49.3	N61 39.3
07	162 45.3	244 42.9	30.5	213 15.3	11.7	328 53.9	40.6	267 31.4	24.5	Elnath	278 09.4	N28 37.1
08	177 47.8	259 42.1	30.3	228 15.9	11.2	343 55.9	40.7	282 33.5	24.5	Eltanin	90 45.5	N51 29.6
F 09	192 50.2	274 41.3	. . 30.2	243 16.5	. . 10.6	358 57.9	. . 40.9	297 35.7	. . 24.6	Enif	33 44.9	N 9 57.4
R 10	207 52.7	289 40.4	30.1	258 17.0	10.1	14 00.0	41.1	312 37.9	24.6	Fomalhaut	15 21.4	S29 32.1
I 11	222 55.2	304 39.6	30.0	273 17.6	09.6	29 02.0	41.3	327 40.0	24.6			
D 12	237 57.6	319 38.8	S25 29.9	288 18.2	S20 09.1	44 04.0	S 4 41.4	342 42.2	S21 24.7	Gacrux	171 58.6	S57 12.1
A 13	253 00.1	334 38.0	29.8	303 18.7	08.6	59 06.1	41.6	357 44.3	24.7	Gienah	175 50.1	S17 37.9
Y 14	268 02.5	349 37.1	29.6	318 19.3	08.1	74 08.1	41.8	12 46.5	24.7	Hadar	148 45.1	S60 26.9
15	283 05.0	4 36.3	. . 29.5	333 19.9	. . 07.6	89 10.1	. . 42.0	27 48.7	. . 24.8	Hamal	327 57.8	N23 32.5
16	298 07.5	19 35.5	29.4	348 20.4	07.1	104 12.2	42.1	42 50.8	24.8	Kaus Aust.	83 41.1	S34 22.4
17	313 09.9	34 34.7	29.3	3 21.0	06.5	119 14.2	42.3	57 53.0	24.8			
18	328 12.4	49 33.8	S25 29.1	18 21.6	S20 06.0	134 16.2	S 4 42.5	72 55.1	S21 24.8	Kochab	137 21.5	N74 05.3
19	343 14.9	64 33.0	29.0	33 22.1	05.5	149 18.3	42.7	87 57.3	24.9	Markab	13 35.9	N15 17.9
20	358 17.3	79 32.2	28.9	48 22.7	05.0	164 20.3	42.8	102 59.5	24.9	Menkar	314 12.3	N 4 09.2
21	13 19.8	94 31.4	. . 28.8	63 23.3	. . 04.5	179 22.3	. . 43.0	118 01.6	. . 24.9	Menkent	148 05.2	S36 26.9
22	28 22.3	109 30.6	28.6	78 23.8	04.0	194 24.4	43.2	133 03.8	25.0	Miaplacidus	221 38.9	S69 46.9
23	43 24.7	124 29.7	28.5	93 24.4	03.4	209 26.4	43.3	148 05.9	25.0			
19 00	58 27.2	139 28.9	S25 28.4	108 25.0	S20 02.9	224 28.4	S 4 43.5	163 08.1	S21 25.0	Mirfak	308 36.5	N49 55.1
01	73 29.7	154 28.1	28.2	123 25.5	02.4	239 30.5	43.7	178 10.3	25.1	Nunki	75 55.8	S26 16.4
02	88 32.1	169 27.3	28.1	138 26.1	01.9	254 32.5	43.9	193 12.4	25.1	Peacock	53 16.0	S56 40.9
03	103 34.6	184 26.5	. . 28.0	153 26.7	. . 01.4	269 34.5	. . 44.0	208 14.6	. . 25.1	Pollux	243 24.8	N27 58.9
04	118 37.0	199 25.6	27.8	168 27.2	00.9	284 36.6	44.2	223 16.8	25.2	Procyon	244 57.2	N 5 10.8
05	133 39.5	214 24.8	27.7	183 27.8	20 00.3	299 38.6	44.4	238 18.9	25.2			
06	148 42.0	229 24.0	S25 27.5	198 28.4	S19 59.8	314 40.6	S 4 44.6	253 21.1	S21 25.2	Rasalhague	96 04.6	N12 33.2
07	163 44.4	244 23.2	27.4	213 29.0	59.3	329 42.7	44.7	268 23.2	25.3	Regulus	207 41.1	N11 53.0
S 08	178 46.9	259 22.4	27.3	228 29.5	58.8	344 44.7	44.9	283 25.4	25.3	Rigel	281 09.5	S 8 11.1
A 09	193 49.4	274 21.5	. . 27.1	243 30.1	. . 58.3	359 46.7	. . 45.1	298 27.6	. . 25.3	Rigil Kent.	139 49.2	S60 53.9
T 10	208 51.8	289 20.7	27.0	258 30.7	57.7	14 48.8	45.3	313 29.7	25.4	Sabik	102 10.2	S15 44.5
U 11	223 54.3	304 19.9	26.8	273 31.2	57.2	29 50.8	45.4	328 31.9	25.4			
R 12	238 56.8	319 19.1	S25 26.7	288 31.8	S19 56.7	44 52.8	S 4 45.6	343 34.0	S21 25.4	Schedar	349 37.4	N56 38.0
D 13	253 59.2	334 18.3	26.5	303 32.4	56.2	59 54.9	45.8	358 36.2	25.5	Shaula	96 19.2	S37 06.7
A 14	269 01.7	349 17.4	26.4	318 32.9	55.7	74 56.9	46.0	13 38.4	25.5	Sirius	258 31.4	S16 44.4
Y 15	284 04.2	4 16.6	. . 26.2	333 33.5	. . 55.1	89 58.9	. . 46.1	28 40.5	. . 25.5	Spica	158 29.1	S11 14.7
16	299 06.6	19 15.8	26.1	348 34.1	54.6	105 01.0	46.3	43 42.7	25.6	Suhail	222 50.6	S43 29.9
17	314 09.1	34 15.0	25.9	3 34.7	54.1	120 03.0	46.5	58 44.8	25.6			
18	329 11.5	49 14.2	S25 25.7	18 35.2	S19 53.6	135 05.0	S 4 46.6	73 47.0	S21 25.6	Vega	80 37.7	N38 48.3
19	344 14.0	64 13.4	25.6	33 35.8	53.1	150 07.1	46.8	88 49.2	25.7	Zuben'ubi	137 03.2	S16 06.4
20	359 16.5	79 12.5	25.4	48 36.4	52.5	165 09.1	47.0	103 51.3	25.7			
21	14 18.9	94 11.7	. . 25.3	63 36.9	. . 52.0	180 11.2	. . 47.2	118 53.5	. . 25.7			
22	29 21.4	109 10.9	25.1	78 37.5	51.5	195 13.2	47.3	133 55.6	25.8			
23	44 23.9	124 10.1	24.9	93 38.1	51.0	210 15.2	47.5	148 57.8	25.8			
Mer. Pass.	h m 20 06.8	*v* −0.8	*d* 0.1	*v* 0.6	*d* 0.5	*v* 2.0	*d* 0.2	*v* 2.2	*d* 0.0			

	SHA	Mer. Pass.
	° ′	h m
Venus	82 20.6	14 42
Mars	50 43.3	16 47
Jupiter	166 11.6	9 04
Saturn	104 48.2	13 09

UT	SUN GHA	SUN Dec	MOON GHA	v	MOON Dec	d	HP
d h	° ′	° ′	° ′	′	° ′	′	′
17 00	183 45.8	S19 01.7	327 05.9	4.5	N18 42.7	1.2	60.5
01	198 45.7	02.3	341 29.4	4.5	18 43.9	1.0	60.4
02	213 45.6	02.9	355 52.9	4.6	18 44.9	1.0	60.4
03	228 45.4	. . 03.5	10 16.5	4.6	18 45.9	0.8	60.4
04	243 45.3	04.1	24 40.1	4.6	18 46.7	0.6	60.3
05	258 45.2	04.7	39 03.7	4.7	18 47.3	0.5	60.3
06	273 45.1	S19 05.3	53 27.4	4.7	N18 47.8	0.4	60.3
T 07	288 44.9	05.9	67 51.1	4.7	18 48.2	0.3	60.2
H 08	303 44.8	06.5	82 14.8	4.8	18 48.5	0.1	60.2
U 09	318 44.7	. . 07.2	96 38.6	4.9	18 48.6	0.0	60.2
R 10	333 44.6	07.8	111 02.5	4.9	18 48.6	0.1	60.1
S 11	348 44.4	08.4	125 26.4	4.9	18 48.5	0.3	60.1
D 12	3 44.3	S19 09.0	139 50.3	5.0	N18 48.2	0.4	60.1
A 13	18 44.2	09.6	154 14.3	5.1	18 47.8	0.5	60.0
Y 14	33 44.0	10.2	168 38.4	5.1	18 47.3	0.7	60.0
15	48 43.9	. . 10.8	183 02.5	5.2	18 46.6	0.7	60.0
16	63 43.8	11.3	197 26.7	5.2	18 45.9	1.0	59.9
17	78 43.7	11.9	211 50.9	5.3	18 44.9	1.0	59.9
18	93 43.5	S19 12.5	226 15.2	5.3	N18 43.9	1.2	59.8
19	108 43.4	13.1	240 39.5	5.4	18 42.7	1.3	59.8
20	123 43.3	13.7	255 03.9	5.4	18 41.4	1.4	59.8
21	138 43.1	. . 14.3	269 28.3	5.5	18 40.0	1.5	59.7
22	153 43.0	14.9	283 52.8	5.6	18 38.5	1.7	59.7
23	168 42.9	15.5	298 17.4	5.7	18 36.8	1.8	59.7
18 00	183 42.7	S19 16.1	312 42.1	5.7	N18 35.0	1.9	59.6
01	198 42.6	16.7	327 06.8	5.7	18 33.1	2.1	59.6
02	213 42.5	17.3	341 31.5	5.9	18 31.0	2.1	59.5
03	228 42.4	. . 17.9	355 56.4	5.9	18 28.9	2.3	59.5
04	243 42.2	18.5	10 21.3	6.0	18 26.6	2.4	59.5
05	258 42.1	19.1	24 46.3	6.0	18 24.2	2.5	59.4
06	273 42.0	S19 19.7	39 11.3	6.1	N18 21.7	2.6	59.4
07	288 41.8	20.2	53 36.4	6.2	18 19.1	2.8	59.3
08	303 41.7	20.8	68 01.6	6.3	18 16.3	2.9	59.3
F 09	318 41.5	. . 21.4	82 26.9	6.3	18 13.4	3.0	59.3
R 10	333 41.4	22.0	96 52.2	6.4	18 10.4	3.0	59.2
I 11	348 41.3	22.6	111 17.6	6.5	18 07.4	3.3	59.2
D 12	3 41.1	S19 23.2	125 43.1	6.5	N18 04.1	3.3	59.2
A 13	18 41.0	23.8	140 08.6	6.7	18 00.8	3.4	59.1
Y 14	33 40.9	24.3	154 34.3	6.7	17 57.4	3.6	59.1
15	48 40.7	. . 24.9	169 00.0	6.8	17 53.8	3.6	59.0
16	63 40.6	25.5	183 25.8	6.8	17 50.2	3.8	59.0
17	78 40.5	26.1	197 51.6	7.0	17 46.4	3.8	59.0
18	93 40.3	S19 26.7	212 17.6	7.0	N17 42.6	4.0	58.9
19	108 40.2	27.3	226 43.6	7.1	17 38.6	4.1	58.9
20	123 40.0	27.8	241 09.7	7.2	17 34.5	4.2	58.8
21	138 39.9	. . 28.4	255 35.9	7.2	17 30.3	4.3	58.8
22	153 39.8	29.0	270 02.1	7.4	17 26.0	4.4	58.7
23	168 39.6	29.6	284 28.5	7.4	17 21.6	4.5	58.7
19 00	183 39.5	S19 30.2	298 54.9	7.5	N17 17.1	4.5	58.7
01	198 39.3	30.7	313 21.4	7.6	17 12.6	4.7	58.6
02	213 39.2	31.3	327 48.0	7.7	17 07.9	4.8	58.6
03	228 39.1	. . 31.9	342 14.7	7.7	17 03.1	4.9	58.5
04	243 38.9	32.5	356 41.4	7.9	16 58.2	5.0	58.5
05	258 38.8	33.0	11 08.3	7.9	16 53.2	5.1	58.5
06	273 38.6	S19 33.6	25 35.2	8.0	N16 48.1	5.1	58.4
S 07	288 38.5	34.2	40 02.2	8.1	16 43.0	5.3	58.4
A 08	303 38.3	34.8	54 29.3	8.2	16 37.7	5.4	58.3
T 09	318 38.2	. . 35.3	68 56.5	8.2	16 32.3	5.4	58.3
U 10	333 38.1	35.9	83 23.7	8.4	16 26.9	5.5	58.3
R 11	348 37.9	36.5	97 51.1	8.4	16 21.4	5.7	58.2
D 12	3 37.8	S19 37.1	112 18.5	8.5	N16 15.7	5.7	58.2
A 13	18 37.6	37.6	126 46.0	8.6	16 10.0	5.8	58.1
Y 14	33 37.5	38.2	141 13.6	8.7	16 04.2	5.8	58.1
15	48 37.3	. . 38.8	155 41.3	8.7	15 58.4	6.0	58.1
16	63 37.2	39.3	170 09.0	8.9	15 52.4	6.1	58.0
17	78 37.0	39.9	184 36.9	8.9	15 46.3	6.1	58.0
18	93 36.9	S19 40.5	199 04.8	9.0	N15 40.2	6.2	57.9
19	108 36.7	41.0	213 32.8	9.1	15 34.0	6.3	57.9
20	123 36.6	41.6	228 00.9	9.2	15 27.7	6.4	57.9
21	138 36.5	. . 42.2	242 29.1	9.3	15 21.3	6.4	57.8
22	153 36.3	42.7	256 57.4	9.3	15 14.9	6.5	57.8
23	168 36.2	43.3	271 25.7	9.5	N15 08.4	6.6	57.7
	SD 16.2	*d* 0.6	SD 16.4		16.1		15.9

Lat.	Twilight Naut.	Twilight Civil	Sunrise	Moonrise 17	Moonrise 18	Moonrise 19	Moonrise 20
°	h m	h m	h m	h m	h m	h m	h m
N 72	07 11	08 50	■	□	16 34	18 53	20 49
N 70	07 00	08 25	10 13	16 21	17 48	19 31	21 12
68	06 50	08 05	09 29	17 08	18 26	19 57	21 30
66	06 42	07 50	09 00	17 38	18 52	20 17	21 44
64	06 35	07 37	08 38	18 01	19 13	20 33	21 56
62	06 29	07 26	08 21	18 19	19 29	20 46	22 06
60	06 24	07 16	08 06	18 34	19 43	20 58	22 14
N 58	06 19	07 08	07 54	18 47	19 55	21 07	22 22
56	06 14	07 00	07 43	18 58	20 05	21 16	22 28
54	06 10	06 54	07 34	19 08	20 14	21 23	22 34
52	06 06	06 48	07 26	19 16	20 22	21 30	22 39
50	06 02	06 42	07 18	19 24	20 29	21 36	22 44
45	05 54	06 30	07 02	19 41	20 44	21 49	22 54
N 40	05 47	06 20	06 49	19 54	20 57	22 00	23 02
35	05 40	06 11	06 38	20 06	21 08	22 09	23 09
30	05 33	06 02	06 28	20 16	21 17	22 17	23 16
20	05 21	05 47	06 11	20 33	21 33	22 31	23 27
N 10	05 08	05 34	05 56	20 49	21 47	22 43	23 36
0	04 54	05 20	05 42	21 03	22 00	22 55	23 45
S 10	04 39	05 05	05 27	21 17	22 14	23 06	23 54
20	04 20	04 48	05 12	21 32	22 28	23 18	24 04
30	03 56	04 28	04 54	21 50	22 44	23 32	24 15
35	03 41	04 16	04 44	22 00	22 53	23 40	24 21
40	03 23	04 01	04 32	22 12	23 04	23 49	24 28
45	02 59	03 43	04 18	22 25	23 16	23 59	24 36
S 50	02 27	03 21	04 00	22 42	23 32	24 12	00 12
52	02 10	03 10	03 52	22 50	23 39	24 18	00 18
54	01 50	02 57	03 43	22 59	23 47	24 25	00 25
56	01 22	02 42	03 33	23 08	23 55	24 32	00 32
58	00 36	02 24	03 21	23 19	24 05	00 05	00 40
S 60	////	02 02	03 07	23 32	24 17	00 17	00 49

Lat.	Sunset	Twilight Civil	Twilight Naut.	Moonset 17	Moonset 18	Moonset 19	Moonset 20
°	h m	h m	h m	h m	h m	h m	h m
N 72	■	14 39	16 18	□	15 04	14 41	14 31
N 70	13 16	15 05	16 30	13 15	13 49	14 02	14 06
68	14 01	15 24	16 39	12 28	13 11	13 35	13 48
66	14 30	15 40	16 47	11 58	12 44	13 14	13 33
64	14 52	15 53	16 54	11 35	12 24	12 57	13 20
62	15 09	16 04	17 01	11 16	12 07	12 43	13 09
60	15 24	16 14	17 06	11 01	11 53	12 32	13 00
N 58	15 36	16 22	17 11	10 48	11 41	12 21	12 52
56	15 47	16 29	17 16	10 37	11 31	12 12	12 45
54	15 56	16 36	17 20	10 27	11 21	12 04	12 39
52	16 04	16 42	17 24	10 19	11 13	11 57	12 33
50	16 12	16 48	17 28	10 11	11 06	11 51	12 28
45	16 28	17 00	17 36	09 54	10 50	11 37	12 17
N 40	16 41	17 10	17 43	09 41	10 37	11 26	12 08
35	16 53	17 20	17 50	09 29	10 26	11 16	12 00
30	17 02	17 28	17 57	09 19	10 16	11 07	11 53
20	17 20	17 43	18 10	09 01	09 59	10 52	11 40
N 10	17 35	17 57	18 23	08 46	09 45	10 39	11 29
0	17 49	18 11	18 36	08 32	09 31	10 27	11 19
S 10	18 03	18 26	18 52	08 17	09 17	10 14	11 09
20	18 19	18 42	19 11	08 02	09 02	10 01	10 58
30	18 37	19 03	19 35	07 44	08 45	09 46	10 46
35	18 47	19 15	19 50	07 34	08 35	09 37	10 38
40	18 59	19 30	20 08	07 22	08 24	09 27	10 30
45	19 13	19 48	20 32	07 08	08 10	09 15	10 20
S 50	19 31	20 11	21 05	06 51	07 54	09 00	10 08
52	19 39	20 22	21 22	06 43	07 46	08 54	10 03
54	19 49	20 35	21 44	06 34	07 38	08 46	09 57
56	19 59	20 50	22 12	06 24	07 28	08 38	09 50
58	20 11	21 09	23 03	06 13	07 17	08 28	09 42
S 60	20 25	21 32	////	06 00	07 04	08 17	09 33

Day	SUN Eqn. of Time 00h	SUN Eqn. of Time 12h	SUN Mer. Pass.	MOON Mer. Pass. Upper	MOON Mer. Pass. Lower	Age	Phase
d	m s	m s	h m	h m	h m	d %	
17	15 03	14 57	11 45	02 17	14 47	18 88	◐
18	14 51	14 45	11 45	03 17	15 46	19 79	
19	14 38	14 31	11 45	04 14	16 41	20 69	

2016 NOVEMBER 20, 21, 22 (SUN., MON., TUES.)

UT	ARIES	VENUS −4·1		MARS +0·6		JUPITER −1·7		SATURN +0·5		STARS		
	GHA	GHA	Dec	GHA	Dec	GHA	Dec	GHA	Dec	Name	SHA	Dec
d h	° ′	° ′	° ′	° ′	° ′	° ′	° ′	° ′	° ′		° ′	° ′
20 00	59 26.3	139 09.3	S25 24.8	108 38.7	S19 50.4	225 17.3	S 4 47.7	164 00.0	S21 25.8	Acamar	315 16.2	S40 14.4
01	74 28.8	154 08.5	24.6	123 39.2	49.9	240 19.3	47.8	179 02.1	25.9	Achernar	335 24.7	S57 09.3
02	89 31.3	169 07.7	24.5	138 39.8	49.4	255 21.3	48.0	194 04.3	25.9	Acrux	173 07.0	S63 11.2
03	104 33.7	184 06.8	. . 24.3	153 40.4	. . 48.9	270 23.4	. . 48.2	209 06.4	. . 25.9	Adhara	255 10.4	S28 59.7
04	119 36.2	199 06.0	24.1	168 40.9	48.3	285 25.4	48.4	224 08.6	26.0	Aldebaran	290 46.4	N16 32.4
05	134 38.7	214 05.2	23.9	183 41.5	47.8	300 27.4	48.5	239 10.7	26.0			
06	149 41.1	229 04.4	S25 23.8	198 42.1	S19 47.3	315 29.5	S 4 48.7	254 12.9	S21 26.0	Alioth	166 19.2	N55 52.0
07	164 43.6	244 03.6	23.6	213 42.7	46.8	330 31.5	48.9	269 15.1	26.1	Alkaid	152 57.6	N49 13.8
08	179 46.0	259 02.8	23.4	228 43.2	46.2	345 33.6	49.1	284 17.2	26.1	Al Na'ir	27 40.9	S46 52.9
S 09	194 48.5	274 02.0	. . 23.3	243 43.8	. . 45.7	0 35.6	. . 49.2	299 19.4	. . 26.1	Alnilam	275 43.7	S 1 11.6
U 10	209 51.0	289 01.1	23.1	258 44.4	45.2	15 37.6	49.4	314 21.5	26.2	Alphard	217 53.8	S 8 43.9
N 11	224 53.4	304 00.3	22.9	273 44.9	44.6	30 39.7	49.6	329 23.7	26.2			
D 12	239 55.9	318 59.5	S25 22.7	288 45.5	S19 44.1	45 41.7	S 4 49.7	344 25.9	S21 26.2	Alphecca	126 09.5	N26 39.7
A 13	254 58.4	333 58.7	22.5	303 46.1	43.6	60 43.7	49.9	359 28.0	26.3	Alpheratz	357 40.9	N29 11.2
Y 14	270 00.8	348 57.9	22.4	318 46.7	43.1	75 45.8	50.1	14 30.2	26.3	Altair	62 06.2	N 8 55.1
15	285 03.3	3 57.1	. . 22.2	333 47.2	. . 42.5	90 47.8	. . 50.3	29 32.3	. . 26.3	Ankaa	353 13.2	S42 13.1
16	300 05.8	18 56.3	22.0	348 47.8	42.0	105 49.9	50.4	44 34.5	26.3	Antares	112 23.8	S26 27.9
17	315 08.2	33 55.5	21.8	3 48.4	41.5	120 51.9	50.6	59 36.7	26.4			
18	330 10.7	48 54.7	S25 21.6	18 49.0	S19 40.9	135 53.9	S 4 50.8	74 38.8	S21 26.4	Arcturus	145 54.0	N19 05.8
19	345 13.1	63 53.8	21.4	33 49.5	40.4	150 56.0	50.9	89 41.0	26.4	Atria	107 24.0	S69 03.3
20	0 15.6	78 53.0	21.3	48 50.1	39.9	165 58.0	51.1	104 43.1	26.5	Avior	234 16.7	S59 33.6
21	15 18.1	93 52.2	. . 21.1	63 50.7	. . 39.3	181 00.0	. . 51.3	119 45.3	. . 26.5	Bellatrix	278 29.2	N 6 21.7
22	30 20.5	108 51.4	20.9	78 51.3	38.8	196 02.1	51.5	134 47.4	26.5	Betelgeuse	270 58.5	N 7 24.4
23	45 23.0	123 50.6	20.7	93 51.8	38.3	211 04.1	51.6	149 49.6	26.6			
21 00	60 25.5	138 49.8	S25 20.5	108 52.4	S19 37.8	226 06.2	S 4 51.8	164 51.8	S21 26.6	Canopus	263 54.7	S52 42.3
01	75 27.9	153 49.0	20.3	123 53.0	37.2	241 08.2	52.0	179 53.9	26.6	Capella	280 30.6	N46 00.6
02	90 30.4	168 48.2	20.1	138 53.5	36.7	256 10.2	52.1	194 56.1	26.7	Deneb	49 30.0	N45 20.8
03	105 32.9	183 47.4	. . 19.9	153 54.1	. . 36.2	271 12.3	. . 52.3	209 58.2	. . 26.7	Denebola	182 31.5	N14 28.7
04	120 35.3	198 46.6	19.7	168 54.7	35.6	286 14.3	52.5	225 00.4	26.7	Diphda	348 53.4	S17 53.7
05	135 37.8	213 45.8	19.5	183 55.3	35.1	301 16.4	52.6	240 02.6	26.8			
06	150 40.3	228 45.0	S25 19.3	198 55.8	S19 34.6	316 18.4	S 4 52.8	255 04.7	S21 26.8	Dubhe	193 49.2	N61 39.3
07	165 42.7	243 44.2	19.1	213 56.4	34.0	331 20.4	53.0	270 06.9	26.8	Elnath	278 09.4	N28 37.1
08	180 45.2	258 43.4	18.9	228 57.0	33.5	346 22.5	53.2	285 09.0	26.9	Eltanin	90 45.6	N51 29.6
M 09	195 47.6	273 42.5	. . 18.7	243 57.6	. . 32.9	1 24.5	. . 53.3	300 11.2	. . 26.9	Enif	33 44.9	N 9 57.4
O 10	210 50.1	288 41.7	18.5	258 58.1	32.4	16 26.6	53.5	315 13.3	26.9	Fomalhaut	15 21.4	S29 32.1
N 11	225 52.6	303 40.9	18.3	273 58.7	31.9	31 28.6	53.7	330 15.5	27.0			
D 12	240 55.0	318 40.1	S25 18.1	288 59.3	S19 31.3	46 30.6	S 4 53.8	345 17.7	S21 27.0	Gacrux	171 58.6	S57 12.1
A 13	255 57.5	333 39.3	17.9	303 59.9	30.8	61 32.7	54.0	0 19.8	27.0	Gienah	175 50.1	S17 37.9
Y 14	271 00.0	348 38.5	17.6	319 00.4	30.3	76 34.7	54.2	15 22.0	27.1	Hadar	148 45.1	S60 26.9
15	286 02.4	3 37.7	. . 17.4	334 01.0	. . 29.7	91 36.8	. . 54.4	30 24.1	. . 27.1	Hamal	327 57.8	N23 32.5
16	301 04.9	18 36.9	17.2	349 01.6	29.2	106 38.8	54.5	45 26.3	27.1	Kaus Aust.	83 41.1	S34 22.4
17	316 07.4	33 36.1	17.0	4 02.2	28.7	121 40.8	54.7	60 28.5	27.2			
18	331 09.8	48 35.3	S25 16.8	19 02.8	S19 28.1	136 42.9	S 4 54.9	75 30.6	S21 27.2	Kochab	137 21.5	N74 05.2
19	346 12.3	63 34.5	16.6	34 03.3	27.6	151 44.9	55.0	90 32.8	27.2	Markab	13 35.9	N15 17.9
20	1 14.8	78 33.7	16.3	49 03.9	27.0	166 47.0	55.2	105 34.9	27.3	Menkar	314 12.3	N 4 09.2
21	16 17.2	93 32.9	. . 16.1	64 04.5	. . 26.5	181 49.0	. . 55.4	120 37.1	. . 27.3	Menkent	148 05.2	S36 26.9
22	31 19.7	108 32.1	15.9	79 05.1	26.0	196 51.0	55.5	135 39.2	27.3	Miaplacidus	221 38.8	S69 46.9
23	46 22.1	123 31.3	15.7	94 05.6	25.4	211 53.1	55.7	150 41.4	27.3			
22 00	61 24.6	138 30.5	S25 15.5	109 06.2	S19 24.9	226 55.1	S 4 55.9	165 43.6	S21 27.4	Mirfak	308 36.5	N49 55.1
01	76 27.1	153 29.7	15.2	124 06.8	24.3	241 57.2	56.0	180 45.7	27.4	Nunki	75 55.8	S26 16.4
02	91 29.5	168 28.9	15.0	139 07.4	23.8	256 59.2	56.2	195 47.9	27.4	Peacock	53 16.0	S56 40.9
03	106 32.0	183 28.1	. . 14.8	154 07.9	. . 23.3	272 01.3	. . 56.4	210 50.0	. . 27.5	Pollux	243 24.7	N27 58.9
04	121 34.5	198 27.3	14.6	169 08.5	22.7	287 03.3	56.6	225 52.2	27.5	Procyon	244 57.1	N 5 10.8
05	136 36.9	213 26.5	14.3	184 09.1	22.2	302 05.3	56.7	240 54.3	27.5			
06	151 39.4	228 25.7	S25 14.1	199 09.7	S19 21.6	317 07.4	S 4 56.9	255 56.5	S21 27.6	Rasalhague	96 04.6	N12 33.2
07	166 41.9	243 24.9	13.9	214 10.3	21.1	332 09.4	57.1	270 58.7	27.6	Regulus	207 41.1	N11 53.0
T 08	181 44.3	258 24.1	13.6	229 10.8	20.5	347 11.5	57.2	286 00.8	27.6	Rigel	281 09.5	S 8 11.1
U 09	196 46.8	273 23.3	. . 13.4	244 11.4	. . 20.0	2 13.5	. . 57.4	301 03.0	. . 27.7	Rigil Kent.	139 49.1	S60 53.9
E 10	211 49.2	288 22.5	13.2	259 12.0	19.5	17 15.6	57.6	316 05.1	27.7	Sabik	102 10.2	S15 44.5
S 11	226 51.7	303 21.7	12.9	274 12.6	18.9	32 17.6	57.7	331 07.3	27.7			
D 12	241 54.2	318 20.9	S25 12.7	289 13.1	S19 18.4	47 19.6	S 4 57.9	346 09.4	S21 27.8	Schedar	349 37.4	N56 38.0
A 13	256 56.6	333 20.1	12.4	304 13.7	17.8	62 21.7	58.1	1 11.6	27.8	Shaula	96 19.2	S37 06.7
Y 14	271 59.1	348 19.3	12.2	319 14.3	17.3	77 23.7	58.2	16 13.8	27.8	Sirius	258 31.4	S16 44.4
15	287 01.6	3 18.6	. . 12.0	334 14.9	. . 16.7	92 25.8	. . 58.4	31 15.9	. . 27.9	Spica	158 29.1	S11 14.7
16	302 04.0	18 17.8	11.7	349 15.5	16.2	107 27.8	58.6	46 18.1	27.9	Suhail	222 50.6	S43 29.9
17	317 06.5	33 17.0	11.5	4 16.0	15.6	122 29.9	58.7	61 20.2	27.9			
18	332 09.0	48 16.2	S25 11.2	19 16.6	S19 15.1	137 31.9	S 4 58.9	76 22.4	S21 28.0	Vega	80 37.7	N38 48.3
19	347 11.4	63 15.4	11.0	34 17.2	14.6	152 33.9	59.1	91 24.5	28.0	Zuben'ubi	137 03.2	S16 06.4
20	2 13.9	78 14.6	10.7	49 17.8	14.0	167 36.0	59.3	106 26.7	28.0			
21	17 16.4	93 13.8	. . 10.5	64 18.4	. . 13.5	182 38.0	. . 59.4	121 28.9	. . 28.0			
22	32 18.8	108 13.0	10.2	79 18.9	12.9	197 40.1	59.6	136 31.0	28.1			
23	47 21.3	123 12.2	10.0	94 19.5	12.4	212 42.1	59.8	151 33.2	28.1			
Mer. Pass.	h m 19 55.0	v −0.8	d 0.2	v 0.6	d 0.5	v 2.0	d 0.2	v 2.2	d 0.0			

	SHA	Mer. Pass.
	° ′	h m
Venus	78 24.3	14 45
Mars	48 26.9	16 44
Jupiter	165 40.7	8 54
Saturn	104 26.3	12 59

UT (d h)	SUN GHA	SUN Dec	MOON GHA	v	MOON Dec	d	HP
	° ′	° ′	° ′	′	° ′	′	′
20 00	183 36.0	S19 43.9	285 54.2	9.5	N15 01.8	6.7	57.7
01	198 35.9	44.4	300 22.7	9.6	14 55.1	6.8	57.7
02	213 35.7	45.0	314 51.3	9.7	14 48.3	6.8	57.6
03	228 35.6	. . 45.6	329 20.0	9.7	14 41.5	6.9	57.6
04	243 35.4	46.1	343 48.7	9.9	14 34.6	6.9	57.5
05	258 35.3	46.7	358 17.6	9.9	14 27.7	7.1	57.5
06	273 35.1	S19 47.2	12 46.5	10.0	N14 20.6	7.1	57.5
07	288 35.0	47.8	27 15.5	10.1	14 13.5	7.1	57.4
08	303 34.8	48.4	41 44.6	10.2	14 06.4	7.3	57.4
S 09	318 34.7	. . 48.9	56 13.8	10.3	13 59.1	7.3	57.3
U 10	333 34.5	49.5	70 43.1	10.3	13 51.8	7.3	57.3
N 11	348 34.3	50.0	85 12.4	10.4	13 44.5	7.5	57.3
D 12	3 34.2	S19 50.6	99 41.8	10.5	N13 37.0	7.5	57.2
A 13	18 34.0	51.1	114 11.3	10.6	13 29.5	7.5	57.2
Y 14	33 33.9	51.7	128 40.9	10.7	13 22.0	7.6	57.2
15	48 33.7	. . 52.2	143 10.6	10.7	13 14.4	7.7	57.1
16	63 33.6	52.8	157 40.3	10.8	13 06.7	7.7	57.1
17	78 33.4	53.4	172 10.1	10.9	12 59.0	7.8	57.0
18	93 33.3	S19 53.9	186 40.0	11.0	N12 51.2	7.8	57.0
19	108 33.1	54.5	201 10.0	11.0	12 43.4	7.9	57.0
20	123 33.0	55.0	215 40.0	11.1	12 35.5	8.0	56.9
21	138 32.8	. . 55.6	230 10.1	11.2	12 27.5	8.0	56.9
22	153 32.6	56.1	244 40.3	11.3	12 19.5	8.1	56.9
23	168 32.5	56.7	259 10.6	11.3	12 11.4	8.1	56.8
21 00	183 32.3	S19 57.2	273 40.9	11.5	N12 03.3	8.1	56.8
01	198 32.2	57.8	288 11.4	11.5	11 55.2	8.2	56.7
02	213 32.0	58.3	302 41.9	11.5	11 47.0	8.3	56.7
03	228 31.9	. . 58.8	317 12.4	11.7	11 38.7	8.3	56.7
04	243 31.7	59.4	331 43.1	11.7	11 30.4	8.4	56.6
05	258 31.5	19 59.9	346 13.8	11.7	11 22.0	8.4	56.6
06	273 31.4	S20 00.5	0 44.5	11.9	N11 13.6	8.4	56.6
07	288 31.2	01.0	15 15.4	11.9	11 05.2	8.5	56.5
08	303 31.1	01.6	29 46.3	12.0	10 56.7	8.5	56.5
M 09	318 30.9	. . 02.1	44 17.3	12.1	10 48.2	8.6	56.5
O 10	333 30.7	02.7	58 48.4	12.1	10 39.6	8.6	56.4
N 11	348 30.6	03.2	73 19.5	12.2	10 31.0	8.7	56.4
D 12	3 30.4	S20 03.7	87 50.7	12.2	N10 22.3	8.7	56.4
A 13	18 30.2	04.3	102 21.9	12.3	10 13.6	8.7	56.3
Y 14	33 30.1	04.8	116 53.2	12.4	10 04.9	8.8	56.3
15	48 29.9	. . 05.4	131 24.6	12.5	9 56.1	8.8	56.3
16	63 29.8	05.9	145 56.1	12.5	9 47.3	8.8	56.2
17	78 29.6	06.4	160 27.6	12.6	9 38.5	8.9	56.2
18	93 29.4	S20 07.0	174 59.2	12.6	N 9 29.6	9.0	56.2
19	108 29.3	07.5	189 30.8	12.7	9 20.6	8.9	56.1
20	123 29.1	08.1	204 02.5	12.8	9 11.7	9.0	56.1
21	138 28.9	. . 08.6	218 34.3	12.8	9 02.7	9.0	56.1
22	153 28.8	09.1	233 06.1	12.9	8 53.7	9.1	56.0
23	168 28.6	09.7	247 38.0	12.9	8 44.6	9.0	56.0
22 00	183 28.4	S20 10.2	262 09.9	13.0	N 8 35.6	9.2	56.0
01	198 28.3	10.7	276 41.9	13.1	8 26.4	9.1	55.9
02	213 28.1	11.3	291 14.0	13.1	8 17.3	9.2	55.9
03	228 27.9	. . 11.8	305 46.1	13.1	8 08.1	9.2	55.9
04	243 27.8	12.3	320 18.2	13.2	7 58.9	9.2	55.8
05	258 27.6	12.8	334 50.4	13.3	7 49.7	9.2	55.8
06	273 27.4	S20 13.4	349 22.7	13.3	N 7 40.5	9.3	55.8
07	288 27.3	13.9	3 55.0	13.4	7 31.2	9.3	55.8
T 08	303 27.1	14.4	18 27.4	13.4	7 21.9	9.3	55.7
U 09	318 26.9	. . 15.0	32 59.8	13.5	7 12.6	9.4	55.7
E 10	333 26.8	15.5	47 32.3	13.6	7 03.2	9.4	55.7
S 11	348 26.6	16.0	62 04.9	13.5	6 53.8	9.4	55.6
D 12	3 26.4	S20 16.5	76 37.4	13.7	N 6 44.4	9.4	55.6
A 13	18 26.2	17.1	91 10.1	13.6	6 35.0	9.4	55.6
Y 14	33 26.1	17.6	105 42.7	13.8	6 25.6	9.5	55.6
15	48 25.9	. . 18.1	120 15.5	13.7	6 16.1	9.4	55.5
16	63 25.7	18.6	134 48.2	13.8	6 06.7	9.5	55.5
17	78 25.6	19.2	149 21.0	13.9	5 57.2	9.5	55.5
18	93 25.4	S20 19.7	163 53.9	13.9	N 5 47.7	9.6	55.5
19	108 25.2	20.2	178 26.8	14.0	5 38.1	9.5	55.4
20	123 25.0	20.7	192 59.8	13.9	5 28.6	9.6	55.4
21	138 24.9	. . 21.2	207 32.7	14.1	5 19.0	9.5	55.4
22	153 24.7	21.8	222 05.8	14.0	5 09.5	9.6	55.3
23	168 24.5	22.3	236 38.8	14.2	N 4 59.9	9.6	55.3
	SD 16.2	*d* 0.5	SD 15.6		15.4		15.2

Lat.	Twilight Naut.	Twilight Civil	Sunrise	Moonrise 20	Moonrise 21	Moonrise 22	Moonrise 23
°	h m	h m	h m	h m	h m	h m	h m
N 72	07 22	09 05	▬	20 49	22 37	24 17	00 17
N 70	07 09	08 36	10 39	21 12	22 50	24 24	00 24
68	06 58	08 15	09 44	21 30	23 01	24 30	00 30
66	06 50	07 58	09 11	21 44	23 10	24 34	00 34
64	06 42	07 44	08 48	21 56	23 18	24 38	00 38
62	06 35	07 32	08 29	22 06	23 24	24 42	00 42
60	06 29	07 22	08 14	22 14	23 30	24 44	00 44
N 58	06 24	07 14	08 01	22 22	23 35	24 47	00 47
56	06 19	07 06	07 49	22 28	23 39	24 49	00 49
54	06 15	06 59	07 39	22 34	23 43	24 51	00 51
52	06 10	06 52	07 31	22 39	23 47	24 53	00 53
50	06 07	06 46	07 23	22 44	23 50	24 55	00 55
45	05 58	06 34	07 06	22 54	23 57	24 59	00 59
N 40	05 50	06 23	06 52	23 02	24 03	00 03	01 02
35	05 42	06 13	06 41	23 09	24 08	00 08	01 05
30	05 36	06 05	06 30	23 16	24 12	00 12	01 07
20	05 22	05 49	06 13	23 27	24 20	00 20	01 11
N 10	05 09	05 35	05 57	23 36	24 27	00 27	01 15
0	04 55	05 20	05 42	23 45	24 33	00 33	01 18
S 10	04 39	05 05	05 28	23 54	24 39	00 39	01 21
20	04 20	04 48	05 12	24 04	00 04	00 46	01 25
30	03 55	04 27	04 53	24 15	00 15	00 53	01 29
35	03 39	04 14	04 42	24 21	00 21	00 58	01 31
40	03 20	03 59	04 30	24 28	00 28	01 02	01 34
45	02 56	03 40	04 15	24 36	00 36	01 08	01 37
S 50	02 22	03 17	03 57	00 12	00 46	01 15	01 41
52	02 04	03 05	03 48	00 18	00 51	01 18	01 42
54	01 41	02 51	03 39	00 25	00 56	01 21	01 44
56	01 09	02 36	03 28	00 32	01 01	01 25	01 46
58	////	02 17	03 15	00 40	01 07	01 29	01 48
S 60	////	01 52	03 00	00 49	01 14	01 34	01 51

Lat.	Sunset	Twilight Civil	Twilight Naut.	Moonset 20	Moonset 21	Moonset 22	Moonset 23
°	h m	h m	h m	h m	h m	h m	h m
N 72	▬	14 26	16 09	14 31	14 23	14 17	14 11
N 70	12 52	14 55	16 22	14 06	14 08	14 08	14 07
68	13 47	15 16	16 33	13 48	13 55	14 01	14 05
66	14 20	15 33	16 42	13 33	13 45	13 55	14 02
64	14 44	15 47	16 49	13 20	13 37	13 49	14 00
62	15 02	15 59	16 56	13 09	13 29	13 45	13 59
60	15 18	16 09	17 02	13 00	13 23	13 41	13 57
N 58	15 31	16 18	17 07	12 52	13 17	13 38	13 56
56	15 42	16 26	17 12	12 45	13 12	13 34	13 55
54	15 52	16 33	17 17	12 39	13 07	13 32	13 54
52	16 01	16 39	17 21	12 33	13 03	13 29	13 53
50	16 09	16 45	17 25	12 28	12 59	13 27	13 52
45	16 26	16 58	17 34	12 17	12 51	13 22	13 50
N 40	16 39	17 09	17 42	12 08	12 44	13 17	13 48
35	16 51	17 18	17 49	12 00	12 38	13 14	13 47
30	17 01	17 27	17 56	11 53	12 33	13 10	13 45
20	17 19	17 43	18 10	11 40	12 24	13 05	13 43
N 10	17 35	17 57	18 23	11 29	12 16	13 00	13 41
0	17 50	18 12	18 37	11 19	12 08	12 55	13 39
S 10	18 04	18 27	18 53	11 09	12 01	12 50	13 37
20	18 21	18 44	19 13	10 58	11 53	12 45	13 35
30	18 39	19 06	19 37	10 46	11 43	12 39	13 33
35	18 50	19 18	19 53	10 38	11 38	12 35	13 31
40	19 03	19 34	20 13	10 30	11 32	12 31	13 30
45	19 17	19 52	20 37	10 20	11 24	12 27	13 28
S 50	19 36	20 16	21 12	10 08	11 16	12 21	13 26
52	19 45	20 28	21 30	10 03	11 11	12 19	13 25
54	19 54	20 42	21 54	09 57	11 07	12 16	13 24
56	20 05	20 58	22 26	09 50	11 02	12 13	13 22
58	20 18	21 18	////	09 42	10 56	12 10	13 21
S 60	20 33	21 43	////	09 33	10 50	12 06	13 19

Day	SUN Eqn. of Time 00^h	SUN Eqn. of Time 12^h	SUN Mer. Pass.	MOON Mer. Pass. Upper	MOON Mer. Pass. Lower	MOON Age	MOON Phase (%)
d	m s	m s	h m	h m	h m	d	%
20	14 24	14 17	11 46	05 07	17 32	21	59
21	14 10	14 02	11 46	05 57	18 21	22	49
22	13 54	13 46	11 46	06 44	19 06	23	39

UT d h	ARIES GHA	VENUS −4·1 GHA	VENUS Dec	MARS +0·6 GHA	MARS Dec	JUPITER −1·8 GHA	JUPITER Dec	SATURN +0·5 GHA	SATURN Dec
	° ′	° ′	° ′	° ′	° ′	° ′	° ′	° ′	° ′
23 00	62 23.7	138 11.4	S25 09.7	109 20.1	S19 11.8	227 44.2	S 4 59.9	166 35.3	S21 28.1
01	77 26.2	153 10.6	09.5	124 20.7	11.3	242 46.2	5 00.1	181 37.5	28.2
02	92 28.7	168 09.8	09.2	139 21.3	10.7	257 48.3	00.3	196 39.6	28.2
03	107 31.1	183 09.0	. . 09.0	154 21.8	. . 10.2	272 50.3	. . 00.4	211 41.8	. . 28.2
04	122 33.6	198 08.3	08.7	169 22.4	09.6	287 52.4	00.6	226 43.9	28.3
05	137 36.1	213 07.5	08.4	184 23.0	09.1	302 54.4	00.8	241 46.1	28.3
W 06	152 38.5	228 06.7	S25 08.2	199 23.6	S19 08.5	317 56.4	S 5 00.9	256 48.3	S21 28.3
E 07	167 41.0	243 05.9	07.9	214 24.2	08.0	332 58.5	01.1	271 50.4	28.4
D 08	182 43.5	258 05.1	07.7	229 24.7	07.4	348 00.5	01.3	286 52.6	28.4
N 09	197 45.9	273 04.3	. . 07.4	244 25.3	. . 06.9	3 02.6	. . 01.4	301 54.7	. . 28.4
E 10	212 48.4	288 03.5	07.1	259 25.9	06.3	18 04.6	01.6	316 56.9	28.5
S 11	227 50.9	303 02.7	06.9	274 26.5	05.8	33 06.7	01.8	331 59.0	28.5
D 12	242 53.3	318 01.9	S25 06.6	289 27.1	S19 05.2	48 08.7	S 5 01.9	347 01.2	S21 28.5
A 13	257 55.8	333 01.2	06.3	304 27.6	04.7	63 10.8	02.1	2 03.3	28.6
Y 14	272 58.2	348 00.4	06.0	319 28.2	04.1	78 12.8	02.3	17 05.5	28.6
15	288 00.7	2 59.6	. . 05.8	334 28.8	. . 03.6	93 14.9	. . 02.4	32 07.7	. . 28.6
16	303 03.2	17 58.8	05.5	349 29.4	03.0	108 16.9	02.6	47 09.8	28.7
17	318 05.6	32 58.0	05.2	4 30.0	02.5	123 19.0	02.8	62 12.0	28.7
18	333 08.1	47 57.2	S25 05.0	19 30.6	S19 01.9	138 21.0	S 5 02.9	77 14.1	S21 28.7
19	348 10.6	62 56.5	04.7	34 31.1	01.4	153 23.0	03.1	92 16.3	28.7
20	3 13.0	77 55.7	04.4	49 31.7	00.8	168 25.1	03.3	107 18.4	28.8
21	18 15.5	92 54.9	. . 04.1	64 32.3	19 00.2	183 27.1	. . 03.4	122 20.6	. . 28.8
22	33 18.0	107 54.1	03.8	79 32.9	18 59.7	198 29.2	03.6	137 22.8	28.8
23	48 20.4	122 53.3	03.6	94 33.5	59.1	213 31.2	03.8	152 24.9	28.9
24 00	63 22.9	137 52.5	S25 03.3	109 34.1	S18 58.6	228 33.3	S 5 03.9	167 27.1	S21 28.9
01	78 25.3	152 51.8	03.0	124 34.6	58.0	243 35.3	04.1	182 29.2	28.9
02	93 27.8	167 51.0	02.7	139 35.2	57.5	258 37.4	04.3	197 31.4	29.0
03	108 30.3	182 50.2	. . 02.4	154 35.8	. . 56.9	273 39.4	. . 04.4	212 33.5	. . 29.0
04	123 32.7	197 49.4	02.1	169 36.4	56.4	288 41.5	04.6	227 35.7	29.0
05	138 35.2	212 48.6	01.8	184 37.0	55.8	303 43.5	04.8	242 37.8	29.1
06	153 37.7	227 47.9	S25 01.5	199 37.6	S18 55.2	318 45.6	S 5 04.9	257 40.0	S21 29.1
T 07	168 40.1	242 47.1	01.3	214 38.1	54.7	333 47.6	05.1	272 42.1	29.1
H 08	183 42.6	257 46.3	01.0	229 38.7	54.1	348 49.7	05.3	287 44.3	29.2
U 09	198 45.1	272 45.5	. . 00.7	244 39.3	. . 53.6	3 51.7	. . 05.4	302 46.5	. . 29.2
R 10	213 47.5	287 44.7	00.4	259 39.9	53.0	18 53.8	05.6	317 48.6	29.2
S 11	228 50.0	302 44.0	25 00.1	274 40.5	52.5	33 55.8	05.8	332 50.8	29.3
D 12	243 52.5	317 43.2	S24 59.8	289 41.1	S18 51.9	48 57.9	S 5 05.9	347 52.9	S21 29.3
A 13	258 54.9	332 42.4	59.5	304 41.6	51.3	63 59.9	06.1	2 55.1	29.3
Y 14	273 57.4	347 41.6	59.2	319 42.2	50.8	79 02.0	06.3	17 57.2	29.3
15	288 59.8	2 40.9	. . 58.9	334 42.8	. . 50.2	94 04.0	. . 06.4	32 59.4	. . 29.4
16	304 02.3	17 40.1	58.6	349 43.4	49.7	109 06.1	06.6	48 01.5	29.4
17	319 04.8	32 39.3	58.3	4 44.0	49.1	124 08.1	06.8	63 03.7	29.4
18	334 07.2	47 38.5	S24 58.0	19 44.6	S18 48.5	139 10.2	S 5 06.9	78 05.9	S21 29.5
19	349 09.7	62 37.7	57.7	34 45.2	48.0	154 12.2	07.1	93 08.0	29.5
20	4 12.2	77 37.0	57.4	49 45.7	47.4	169 14.3	07.3	108 10.2	29.5
21	19 14.6	92 36.2	. . 57.0	64 46.3	. . 46.8	184 16.3	. . 07.4	123 12.3	. . 29.6
22	34 17.1	107 35.4	56.7	79 46.9	46.3	199 18.4	07.6	138 14.5	29.6
23	49 19.6	122 34.7	56.4	94 47.5	45.7	214 20.4	07.7	153 16.6	29.6
25 00	64 22.0	137 33.9	S24 56.1	109 48.1	S18 45.2	229 22.5	S 5 07.9	168 18.8	S21 29.7
01	79 24.5	152 33.1	55.8	124 48.7	44.6	244 24.5	08.1	183 20.9	29.7
02	94 26.9	167 32.3	55.5	139 49.3	44.0	259 26.6	08.2	198 23.1	29.7
03	109 29.4	182 31.6	. . 55.2	154 49.8	. . 43.5	274 28.6	. . 08.4	213 25.2	. . 29.8
04	124 31.9	197 30.8	54.9	169 50.4	42.9	289 30.7	08.6	228 27.4	29.8
05	139 34.3	212 30.0	54.5	184 51.0	42.3	304 32.7	08.7	243 29.6	29.8
06	154 36.8	227 29.3	S24 54.2	199 51.6	S18 41.8	319 34.8	S 5 08.9	258 31.7	S21 29.8
07	169 39.3	242 28.5	53.9	214 52.2	41.2	334 36.8	09.1	273 33.9	29.9
08	184 41.7	257 27.7	53.6	229 52.8	40.6	349 38.9	09.2	288 36.0	29.9
F 09	199 44.2	272 27.0	. . 53.3	244 53.4	. . 40.1	4 40.9	. . 09.4	303 38.2	. . 29.9
R 10	214 46.7	287 26.2	52.9	259 53.9	39.5	19 43.0	09.6	318 40.3	30.0
I 11	229 49.1	302 25.4	52.6	274 54.5	38.9	34 45.0	09.7	333 42.5	30.0
D 12	244 51.6	317 24.6	S24 52.3	289 55.1	S18 38.4	49 47.1	S 5 09.9	348 44.6	S21 30.0
A 13	259 54.1	332 23.9	51.9	304 55.7	37.8	64 49.1	10.1	3 46.8	30.1
Y 14	274 56.5	347 23.1	51.6	319 56.3	37.2	79 51.2	10.2	18 48.9	30.1
15	289 59.0	2 22.4	. . 51.3	334 56.9	. . 36.7	94 53.2	. . 10.4	33 51.1	. . 30.1
16	305 01.4	17 21.6	51.0	349 57.5	36.1	109 55.3	10.5	48 53.2	30.2
17	320 03.9	32 20.8	50.6	4 58.1	35.5	124 57.3	10.7	63 55.4	30.2
18	335 06.4	47 20.1	S24 50.3	19 58.6	S18 35.0	139 59.4	S 5 10.9	78 57.6	S21 30.2
19	350 08.8	62 19.3	50.0	34 59.2	34.4	155 01.5	11.0	93 59.7	30.3
20	5 11.3	77 18.5	49.6	49 59.8	33.8	170 03.5	11.2	109 01.9	30.3
21	20 13.8	92 17.8	. . 49.3	65 00.4	. . 33.3	185 05.6	. . 11.4	124 04.0	. . 30.3
22	35 16.2	107 17.0	48.9	80 01.0	32.7	200 07.6	11.5	139 06.2	30.3
23	50 18.7	122 16.2	48.6	95 01.6	32.1	215 09.7	11.7	154 08.3	30.4
Mer. Pass. (h m)	19 43.2	v −0.8	d 0.3	v 0.6	d 0.6	v 2.0	d 0.2	v 2.2	d 0.0

STARS

Name	SHA	Dec
	° ′	° ′
Acamar	315 16.2	S40 14.4
Achernar	335 24.7	S57 09.3
Acrux	173 06.9	S63 11.2
Adhara	255 10.4	S28 59.7
Aldebaran	290 46.4	N16 32.4
Alioth	166 19.2	N55 52.0
Alkaid	152 57.6	N49 13.8
Al Na'ir	27 41.0	S46 52.9
Alnilam	275 43.7	S 1 11.6
Alphard	217 53.8	S 8 43.9
Alphecca	126 09.5	N26 39.7
Alpheratz	357 40.9	N29 11.2
Altair	62 06.2	N 8 55.0
Ankaa	353 13.3	S42 13.1
Antares	112 23.8	S26 27.9
Arcturus	145 54.0	N19 05.8
Atria	107 24.1	S69 03.2
Avior	234 16.7	S59 33.7
Bellatrix	278 29.2	N 6 21.7
Betelgeuse	270 58.5	N 7 24.4
Canopus	263 54.6	S52 42.3
Capella	280 30.6	N46 00.6
Deneb	49 30.1	N45 20.8
Denebola	182 31.5	N14 28.7
Diphda	348 53.4	S17 53.8
Dubhe	193 49.2	N61 39.3
Elnath	278 09.3	N28 37.1
Eltanin	90 45.6	N51 29.5
Enif	33 44.9	N 9 57.3
Fomalhaut	15 21.4	S29 32.1
Gacrux	171 58.5	S57 12.1
Gienah	175 50.1	S17 37.9
Hadar	148 45.1	S60 26.9
Hamal	327 57.8	N23 32.5
Kaus Aust.	83 41.1	S34 22.4
Kochab	137 21.4	N74 05.2
Markab	13 35.9	N15 17.9
Menkar	314 12.3	N 4 09.2
Menkent	148 05.2	S36 26.9
Miaplacidus	221 38.8	S69 47.0
Mirfak	308 36.5	N49 55.2
Nunki	75 55.8	S26 16.4
Peacock	53 16.0	S56 40.9
Pollux	243 24.7	N27 58.9
Procyon	244 57.1	N 5 10.8
Rasalhague	96 04.7	N12 33.2
Regulus	207 41.1	N11 53.0
Rigel	281 09.5	S 8 11.1
Rigil Kent.	139 49.1	S60 53.9
Sabik	102 10.2	S15 44.5
Schedar	349 37.4	N56 38.0
Shaula	96 19.2	S37 06.7
Sirius	258 31.4	S16 44.4
Spica	158 29.1	S11 14.7
Suhail	222 50.6	S43 29.9
Vega	80 37.8	N38 48.3
Zuben'ubi	137 03.2	S16 06.4

	SHA	Mer. Pass.
	° ′	h m
Venus	74 29.7	14 49
Mars	46 11.2	16 41
Jupiter	165 10.4	8 45
Saturn	104 04.2	12 48

UT (d h)	SUN GHA ° ′	SUN Dec ° ′	MOON GHA ° ′	v ′	MOON Dec ° ′	d ′	HP ′
23 00	183 24.3	S20 22.8	251 12.0	14.1	N 4 50.3	9.6	55.3
01	198 24.2	23.3	265 45.1	14.2	4 40.7	9.7	55.3
02	213 24.0	23.8	280 18.3	14.2	4 31.0	9.6	55.2
03	228 23.8	. . 24.3	294 51.5	14.3	4 21.4	9.6	55.2
04	243 23.6	24.9	309 24.8	14.3	4 11.8	9.7	55.2
05	258 23.5	25.4	323 58.1	14.3	4 02.1	9.7	55.2
W 06	273 23.3	S20 25.9	338 31.4	14.4	N 3 52.4	9.7	55.1
E 07	288 23.1	26.4	353 04.8	14.4	3 42.7	9.6	55.1
D 08	303 22.9	26.9	7 38.2	14.4	3 33.1	9.7	55.1
N 09	318 22.8	. . 27.4	22 11.6	14.5	3 23.4	9.7	55.1
E 10	333 22.6	27.9	36 45.1	14.5	3 13.7	9.7	55.1
S 11	348 22.4	28.5	51 18.6	14.5	3 04.0	9.8	55.0
D 12	3 22.2	S20 29.0	65 52.1	14.6	N 2 54.2	9.7	55.0
A 13	18 22.0	29.5	80 25.7	14.6	2 44.5	9.7	55.0
Y 14	33 21.9	30.0	94 59.3	14.6	2 34.8	9.7	55.0
15	48 21.7	. . 30.5	109 32.9	14.6	2 25.1	9.8	54.9
16	63 21.5	31.0	124 06.5	14.7	2 15.3	9.7	54.9
17	78 21.3	31.5	138 40.2	14.7	2 05.6	9.7	54.9
18	93 21.1	S20 32.0	153 13.9	14.7	N 1 55.9	9.8	54.9
19	108 21.0	32.5	167 47.6	14.7	1 46.1	9.7	54.9
20	123 20.8	33.0	182 21.3	14.8	1 36.4	9.7	54.8
21	138 20.6	. . 33.5	196 55.1	14.8	1 26.7	9.8	54.8
22	153 20.4	34.0	211 28.9	14.8	1 16.9	9.7	54.8
23	168 20.2	34.5	226 02.7	14.9	1 07.2	9.8	54.8
24 00	183 20.1	S20 35.0	240 36.6	14.8	N 0 57.4	9.7	54.8
01	198 19.9	35.5	255 10.4	14.9	0 47.7	9.7	54.7
02	213 19.7	36.0	269 44.3	14.9	0 38.0	9.8	54.7
03	228 19.5	. . 36.5	284 18.2	14.9	0 28.2	9.7	54.7
04	243 19.3	37.0	298 52.1	14.9	0 18.5	9.7	54.7
05	258 19.1	37.5	313 26.0	15.0	N 0 08.8	9.7	54.7
06	273 19.0	S20 38.0	328 00.0	14.9	S 0 00.9	9.7	54.6
T 07	288 18.8	38.5	342 33.9	15.0	0 10.6	9.7	54.6
H 08	303 18.6	39.0	357 07.9	15.0	0 20.3	9.7	54.6
U 09	318 18.4	. . 39.5	11 41.9	15.0	0 30.0	9.7	54.6
R 10	333 18.2	40.0	26 15.9	15.1	0 39.7	9.7	54.6
S 11	348 18.0	40.5	40 50.0	15.0	0 49.4	9.7	54.6
D 12	3 17.8	S20 41.0	55 24.0	15.0	S 0 59.1	9.7	54.5
A 13	18 17.7	41.5	69 58.0	15.1	1 08.8	9.6	54.5
Y 14	33 17.5	42.0	84 32.1	15.1	1 18.4	9.7	54.5
15	48 17.3	. . 42.5	99 06.2	15.0	1 28.1	9.6	54.5
16	63 17.1	43.0	113 40.2	15.1	1 37.7	9.6	54.5
17	78 16.9	43.5	128 14.3	15.1	1 47.3	9.7	54.5
18	93 16.7	S20 44.0	142 48.4	15.1	S 1 57.0	9.6	54.5
19	108 16.5	44.5	157 22.5	15.1	2 06.6	9.5	54.4
20	123 16.3	44.9	171 56.6	15.2	2 16.1	9.6	54.4
21	138 16.1	. . 45.4	186 30.8	15.1	2 25.7	9.6	54.4
22	153 16.0	45.9	201 04.9	15.1	2 35.3	9.5	54.4
23	168 15.8	46.4	215 39.0	15.1	2 44.8	9.6	54.4
25 00	183 15.6	S20 46.9	230 13.1	15.2	S 2 54.4	9.5	54.4
01	198 15.4	47.4	244 47.3	15.1	3 03.9	9.5	54.4
02	213 15.2	47.9	259 21.4	15.1	3 13.4	9.5	54.3
03	228 15.0	. . 48.3	273 55.5	15.2	3 22.9	9.5	54.3
04	243 14.8	48.8	288 29.7	15.1	3 32.4	9.4	54.3
05	258 14.6	49.3	303 03.8	15.2	3 41.8	9.4	54.3
06	273 14.4	S20 49.8	317 38.0	15.1	S 3 51.2	9.5	54.3
07	288 14.2	50.3	332 12.1	15.2	4 00.7	9.4	54.3
08	303 14.0	50.8	346 46.3	15.1	4 10.1	9.3	54.3
F 09	318 13.8	. . 51.2	1 20.4	15.1	4 19.4	9.4	54.3
R 10	333 13.6	51.7	15 54.5	15.2	4 28.8	9.3	54.2
I 11	348 13.5	52.2	30 28.7	15.1	4 38.1	9.3	54.2
D 12	3 13.3	S20 52.7	45 02.8	15.1	S 4 47.4	9.3	54.2
A 13	18 13.1	53.2	59 36.9	15.2	4 56.7	9.3	54.2
Y 14	33 12.9	53.6	74 11.1	15.1	5 06.0	9.3	54.2
15	48 12.7	. . 54.1	88 45.2	15.1	5 15.3	9.2	54.2
16	63 12.5	54.6	103 19.3	15.1	5 24.5	9.2	54.2
17	78 12.3	55.1	117 53.4	15.1	5 33.7	9.2	54.2
18	93 12.1	S20 55.5	132 27.5	15.1	S 5 42.9	9.1	54.2
19	108 11.9	56.0	147 01.6	15.1	5 52.0	9.1	54.2
20	123 11.7	56.5	161 35.7	15.0	6 01.1	9.1	54.1
21	138 11.5	. . 56.9	176 09.7	15.1	6 10.2	9.1	54.1
22	153 11.3	57.4	190 43.8	15.1	6 19.3	9.0	54.1
23	168 11.1	57.9	205 17.9	15.0	S 6 28.3	9.1	54.1
	SD 16.2	*d* 0.5	SD 15.0		14.9		14.8

Lat.	Twilight Naut. h m	Twilight Civil h m	Sunrise h m	Moonrise 23 h m	Moonrise 24 h m	Moonrise 25 h m	Moonrise 26 h m
N 72	07 31	09 19	■	00 17	01 54	03 29	05 05
N 70	07 17	08 47	11 17	00 24	01 55	03 24	04 53
68	07 06	08 24	09 59	00 30	01 56	03 20	04 44
66	06 57	08 06	09 23	00 34	01 56	03 17	04 36
64	06 48	07 52	08 57	00 38	01 57	03 14	04 30
62	06 41	07 39	08 37	00 42	01 57	03 11	04 25
60	06 35	07 28	08 21	00 44	01 57	03 09	04 20
N 58	06 29	07 19	08 07	00 47	01 58	03 07	04 16
56	06 24	07 11	07 55	00 49	01 58	03 05	04 12
54	06 19	07 03	07 45	00 51	01 58	03 04	04 09
52	06 15	06 57	07 36	00 53	01 58	03 02	04 06
50	06 10	06 51	07 27	00 55	01 59	03 01	04 03
45	06 01	06 37	07 10	00 59	01 59	02 58	03 57
N 40	05 53	06 26	06 56	01 02	01 59	02 56	03 52
35	05 45	06 16	06 43	01 05	02 00	02 54	03 48
30	05 38	06 07	06 33	01 07	02 00	02 52	03 44
20	05 24	05 51	06 14	01 11	02 01	02 49	03 38
N 10	05 10	05 36	05 58	01 15	02 01	02 47	03 32
0	04 55	05 21	05 43	01 18	02 01	02 44	03 27
S 10	04 39	05 05	05 28	01 21	02 02	02 42	03 22
20	04 19	04 47	05 11	01 25	02 02	02 39	03 16
30	03 54	04 26	04 52	01 29	02 03	02 36	03 10
35	03 37	04 12	04 41	01 31	02 03	02 35	03 06
40	03 18	03 57	04 28	01 34	02 04	02 33	03 02
45	02 52	03 38	04 13	01 37	02 04	02 31	02 58
S 50	02 17	03 13	03 54	01 41	02 05	02 28	02 52
52	01 57	03 01	03 45	01 42	02 05	02 27	02 50
54	01 33	02 47	03 35	01 44	02 05	02 26	02 47
56	00 56	02 30	03 23	01 46	02 06	02 24	02 44
58	////	02 09	03 10	01 48	02 06	02 23	02 40
S 60	////	01 43	02 55	01 51	02 06	02 21	02 37

Lat.	Sunset h m	Twilight Civil h m	Twilight Naut. h m	Moonset 23 h m	Moonset 24 h m	Moonset 25 h m	Moonset 26 h m
N 72	■	14 14	16 01	14 11	14 05	13 58	13 52
N 70	12 16	14 45	16 15	14 07	14 06	14 05	14 05
68	13 34	15 08	16 27	14 05	14 08	14 11	14 15
66	14 10	15 27	16 36	14 02	14 09	14 16	14 24
64	14 36	15 41	16 45	14 00	14 10	14 20	14 31
62	14 56	15 54	16 52	13 59	14 11	14 24	14 38
60	15 12	16 05	16 58	13 57	14 12	14 27	14 43
N 58	15 26	16 14	17 04	13 56	14 13	14 30	14 48
56	15 38	16 22	17 09	13 55	14 14	14 33	14 53
54	15 48	16 30	17 14	13 54	14 14	14 35	14 57
52	15 58	16 36	17 19	13 53	14 15	14 37	15 00
50	16 06	16 43	17 23	13 52	14 15	14 39	15 04
45	16 23	16 56	17 32	13 50	14 16	14 43	15 11
N 40	16 38	17 07	17 41	13 48	14 17	14 47	15 17
35	16 50	17 17	17 48	13 47	14 18	14 50	15 22
30	17 01	17 26	17 56	13 45	14 19	14 52	15 26
20	17 19	17 43	18 10	13 43	14 20	14 57	15 34
N 10	17 35	17 58	18 23	13 41	14 21	15 01	15 41
0	17 50	18 13	18 38	13 39	14 22	15 05	15 48
S 10	18 06	18 28	18 55	13 37	14 23	15 09	15 54
20	18 22	18 46	19 15	13 35	14 24	15 13	16 01
30	18 42	19 08	19 40	13 33	14 25	15 17	16 09
35	18 53	19 22	19 57	13 31	14 26	15 20	16 14
40	19 06	19 37	20 17	13 30	14 27	15 23	16 19
45	19 21	19 57	20 43	13 28	14 28	15 27	16 25
S 50	19 41	20 22	21 19	13 26	14 29	15 31	16 32
52	19 50	20 34	21 38	13 25	14 29	15 33	16 36
54	20 00	20 48	22 04	13 24	14 30	15 35	16 40
56	20 11	21 05	22 42	13 22	14 30	15 37	16 44
58	20 25	21 26	////	13 21	14 31	15 40	16 48
S 60	20 41	21 54	////	13 19	14 32	15 43	16 53

Day	SUN Eqn. of Time 00^h m s	SUN Eqn. of Time 12^h m s	SUN Mer. Pass. h m	MOON Mer. Pass. Upper h m	MOON Mer. Pass. Lower h m	MOON Age d	MOON Phase %
23	13 38	13 29	11 47	07 29	19 50	24	29
24	13 21	13 12	11 47	08 12	20 33	25	21
25	13 03	12 53	11 47	08 54	21 16	26	14

UT		ARIES	VENUS −4·2		MARS +0·6		JUPITER −1·8		SATURN +0·5	
		GHA	GHA	Dec	GHA	Dec	GHA	Dec	GHA	Dec
d	h	° ′	° ′	° ′	° ′	° ′	° ′	° ′	° ′	° ′
26	00	65 21.2	137 15.5	S24 48.3	110 02.2	S18 31.6	230 11.7	S 5 11.9	169 10.5	S21 30.4
	01	80 23.6	152 14.7	47.9	125 02.8	31.0	245 13.8	12.0	184 12.6	30.4
	02	95 26.1	167 14.0	47.6	140 03.4	30.4	260 15.8	12.2	199 14.8	30.5
	03	110 28.6	182 13.2	. . 47.2	155 03.9	. . 29.8	275 17.9	. . 12.3	214 16.9	. . 30.5
	04	125 31.0	197 12.4	46.9	170 04.5	29.3	290 19.9	12.5	229 19.1	30.5
	05	140 33.5	212 11.7	46.5	185 05.1	28.7	305 22.0	12.7	244 21.2	30.6
	06	155 35.9	227 10.9	S24 46.2	200 05.7	S18 28.1	320 24.0	S 5 12.8	259 23.4	S21 30.6
	07	170 38.4	242 10.2	45.8	215 06.3	27.6	335 26.1	13.0	274 25.6	30.6
SATURDAY	08	185 40.9	257 09.4	45.5	230 06.9	27.0	350 28.2	13.2	289 27.7	30.7
	09	200 43.3	272 08.6	. . 45.1	245 07.5	. . 26.4	5 30.2	. . 13.3	304 29.9	. . 30.7
	10	215 45.8	287 07.9	44.8	260 08.1	25.8	20 32.3	13.5	319 32.0	30.7
	11	230 48.3	302 07.1	44.4	275 08.7	25.3	35 34.3	13.6	334 34.2	30.8
	12	245 50.7	317 06.4	S24 44.1	290 09.3	S18 24.7	50 36.4	S 5 13.8	349 36.3	S21 30.8
	13	260 53.2	332 05.6	43.7	305 09.8	24.1	65 38.4	14.0	4 38.5	30.8
	14	275 55.7	347 04.9	43.4	320 10.4	23.5	80 40.5	14.1	19 40.6	30.8
	15	290 58.1	2 04.1	. . 43.0	335 11.0	. . 23.0	95 42.5	. . 14.3	34 42.8	. . 30.9
	16	306 00.6	17 03.4	42.6	350 11.6	22.4	110 44.6	14.5	49 44.9	30.9
	17	321 03.0	32 02.6	42.3	5 12.2	21.8	125 46.7	14.6	64 47.1	30.9
	18	336 05.5	47 01.8	S24 41.9	20 12.8	S18 21.2	140 48.7	S 5 14.8	79 49.2	S21 31.0
	19	351 08.0	62 01.1	41.5	35 13.4	20.7	155 50.8	14.9	94 51.4	31.0
	20	6 10.4	77 00.3	41.2	50 14.0	20.1	170 52.8	15.1	109 53.5	31.0
	21	21 12.9	91 59.6	. . 40.8	65 14.6	. . 19.5	185 54.9	. . 15.3	124 55.7	. . 31.1
	22	36 15.4	106 58.8	40.4	80 15.2	18.9	200 56.9	15.4	139 57.9	31.1
	23	51 17.8	121 58.1	40.1	95 15.8	18.4	215 59.0	15.6	155 00.0	31.1
27	00	66 20.3	136 57.3	S24 39.7	110 16.4	S18 17.8	231 01.1	S 5 15.8	170 02.2	S21 31.2
	01	81 22.8	151 56.6	39.3	125 16.9	17.2	246 03.1	15.9	185 04.3	31.2
	02	96 25.2	166 55.8	39.0	140 17.5	16.6	261 05.2	16.1	200 06.5	31.2
	03	111 27.7	181 55.1	. . 38.6	155 18.1	. . 16.1	276 07.2	. . 16.2	215 08.6	. . 31.2
	04	126 30.2	196 54.3	38.2	170 18.7	15.5	291 09.3	16.4	230 10.8	31.3
	05	141 32.6	211 53.6	37.8	185 19.3	14.9	306 11.3	16.6	245 12.9	31.3
	06	156 35.1	226 52.8	S24 37.5	200 19.9	S18 14.3	321 13.4	S 5 16.7	260 15.1	S21 31.3
	07	171 37.5	241 52.1	37.1	215 20.5	13.7	336 15.5	16.9	275 17.2	31.4
	08	186 40.0	256 51.4	36.7	230 21.1	13.2	351 17.5	17.0	290 19.4	31.4
SUNDAY	09	201 42.5	271 50.6	. . 36.3	245 21.7	. . 12.6	6 19.6	. . 17.2	305 21.5	. . 31.4
	10	216 44.9	286 49.9	35.9	260 22.3	12.0	21 21.6	17.4	320 23.7	31.5
	11	231 47.4	301 49.1	35.6	275 22.9	11.4	36 23.7	17.5	335 25.8	31.5
	12	246 49.9	316 48.4	S24 35.2	290 23.5	S18 10.8	51 25.8	S 5 17.7	350 28.0	S21 31.5
	13	261 52.3	331 47.6	34.8	305 24.1	10.3	66 27.8	17.8	5 30.1	31.6
	14	276 54.8	346 46.9	34.4	320 24.7	09.7	81 29.9	18.0	20 32.3	31.6
	15	291 57.3	1 46.1	. . 34.0	335 25.3	. . 09.1	96 31.9	. . 18.2	35 34.4	. . 31.6
	16	306 59.7	16 45.4	33.6	350 25.8	08.5	111 34.0	18.3	50 36.6	31.6
	17	322 02.2	31 44.7	33.2	5 26.4	07.9	126 36.0	18.5	65 38.8	31.7
	18	337 04.7	46 43.9	S24 32.8	20 27.0	S18 07.3	141 38.1	S 5 18.7	80 40.9	S21 31.7
	19	352 07.1	61 43.2	32.5	35 27.6	06.8	156 40.2	18.8	95 43.1	31.7
	20	7 09.6	76 42.4	32.1	50 28.2	06.2	171 42.2	19.0	110 45.2	31.8
	21	22 12.0	91 41.7	. . 31.7	65 28.8	. . 05.6	186 44.3	. . 19.1	125 47.4	. . 31.8
	22	37 14.5	106 41.0	31.3	80 29.4	05.0	201 46.3	19.3	140 49.5	31.8
	23	52 17.0	121 40.2	30.9	95 30.0	04.4	216 48.4	19.5	155 51.7	31.9
28	00	67 19.4	136 39.5	S24 30.5	110 30.6	S18 03.8	231 50.5	S 5 19.6	170 53.8	S21 31.9
	01	82 21.9	151 38.7	30.1	125 31.2	03.3	246 52.5	19.8	185 56.0	31.9
	02	97 24.4	166 38.0	29.7	140 31.8	02.7	261 54.6	19.9	200 58.1	32.0
	03	112 26.8	181 37.3	. . 29.3	155 32.4	. . 02.1	276 56.7	. . 20.1	216 00.3	. . 32.0
	04	127 29.3	196 36.5	28.9	170 33.0	01.5	291 58.7	20.3	231 02.4	32.0
	05	142 31.8	211 35.8	28.5	185 33.6	00.9	307 00.8	20.4	246 04.6	32.0
	06	157 34.2	226 35.1	S24 28.1	200 34.2	S18 00.3	322 02.8	S 5 20.6	261 06.7	S21 32.1
	07	172 36.7	241 34.3	27.7	215 34.8	17 59.7	337 04.9	20.7	276 08.9	32.1
	08	187 39.1	256 33.6	27.2	230 35.4	59.1	352 07.0	20.9	291 11.0	32.1
MONDAY	09	202 41.6	271 32.8	. . 26.8	245 36.0	. . 58.6	7 09.0	. . 21.1	306 13.2	. . 32.2
	10	217 44.1	286 32.1	26.4	260 36.6	58.0	22 11.1	21.2	321 15.3	32.2
	11	232 46.5	301 31.4	26.0	275 37.2	57.4	37 13.1	21.4	336 17.5	32.2
	12	247 49.0	316 30.7	S24 25.6	290 37.8	S17 56.8	52 15.2	S 5 21.5	351 19.6	S21 32.3
	13	262 51.5	331 29.9	25.2	305 38.4	56.2	67 17.3	21.7	6 21.8	32.3
	14	277 53.9	346 29.2	24.8	320 39.0	55.6	82 19.3	21.8	21 23.9	32.3
	15	292 56.4	1 28.5	. . 24.4	335 39.5	. . 55.0	97 21.4	. . 22.0	36 26.1	. . 32.3
	16	307 58.9	16 27.7	23.9	350 40.1	54.4	112 23.5	22.2	51 28.2	32.4
	17	323 01.3	31 27.0	23.5	5 40.7	53.9	127 25.5	22.3	66 30.4	32.4
	18	338 03.8	46 26.3	S24 23.1	20 41.3	S17 53.3	142 27.6	S 5 22.5	81 32.5	S21 32.4
	19	353 06.3	61 25.5	22.7	35 41.9	52.7	157 29.6	22.6	96 34.7	32.5
	20	8 08.7	76 24.8	22.3	50 42.5	52.1	172 31.7	22.8	111 36.9	32.5
	21	23 11.2	91 24.1	. . 21.8	65 43.1	. . 51.5	187 33.8	. . 23.0	126 39.0	. . 32.5
	22	38 13.6	106 23.4	21.4	80 43.7	50.9	202 35.8	23.1	141 41.2	32.6
	23	53 16.1	121 22.6	21.0	95 44.3	50.3	217 37.9	23.3	156 43.3	32.6
Mer. Pass.		h m 19 31.4	v −0.7	d 0.4	v 0.6	d 0.6	v 2.1	d 0.2	v 2.2	d 0.0

STARS		
Name	SHA	Dec
	° ′	° ′
Acamar	315 16.2	S40 14.4
Achernar	335 24.7	S57 09.4
Acrux	173 06.9	S63 11.2
Adhara	255 10.4	S28 59.7
Aldebaran	290 46.4	N16 32.4
Alioth	166 19.1	N55 52.0
Alkaid	152 57.6	N49 13.7
Al Na'ir	27 41.0	S46 52.9
Alnilam	275 43.7	S 1 11.6
Alphard	217 53.7	S 8 43.9
Alphecca	126 09.5	N26 39.7
Alpheratz	357 40.9	N29 11.2
Altair	62 06.2	N 8 55.0
Ankaa	353 13.3	S42 13.1
Antares	112 23.8	S26 27.9
Arcturus	145 54.0	N19 05.8
Atria	107 24.0	S69 03.2
Avior	234 16.6	S59 33.7
Bellatrix	278 29.2	N 6 21.7
Betelgeuse	270 58.5	N 7 24.4
Canopus	263 54.6	S52 42.3
Capella	280 30.5	N46 00.6
Deneb	49 30.1	N45 20.8
Denebola	182 31.5	N14 28.7
Diphda	348 53.4	S17 53.8
Dubhe	193 49.2	N61 39.3
Elnath	278 09.3	N28 37.1
Eltanin	90 45.6	N51 29.5
Enif	33 44.9	N 9 57.3
Fomalhaut	15 21.4	S29 32.1
Gacrux	171 58.5	S57 12.1
Gienah	175 50.1	S17 37.9
Hadar	148 45.0	S60 26.9
Hamal	327 57.8	N23 32.5
Kaus Aust.	83 41.1	S34 22.4
Kochab	137 21.4	N74 05.2
Markab	13 36.0	N15 17.9
Menkar	314 12.3	N 4 09.2
Menkent	148 05.1	S36 26.9
Miaplacidus	221 38.7	S69 47.0
Mirfak	308 36.5	N49 55.2
Nunki	75 55.8	S26 16.4
Peacock	53 16.0	S56 40.9
Pollux	243 24.7	N27 58.9
Procyon	244 57.1	N 5 10.7
Rasalhague	96 04.7	N12 33.2
Regulus	207 41.1	N11 53.0
Rigel	281 09.5	S 8 11.1
Rigil Kent.	139 49.1	S60 53.9
Sabik	102 10.2	S15 44.5
Schedar	349 37.4	N56 38.0
Shaula	96 19.2	S37 06.7
Sirius	258 31.4	S16 44.5
Spica	158 29.0	S11 14.7
Suhail	222 50.5	S43 29.9
Vega	80 37.8	N38 48.3
Zuben'ubi	137 03.2	S16 06.4

	SHA	Mer. Pass.
	° ′	h m
Venus	70 37.0	14 53
Mars	43 56.1	16 38
Jupiter	164 40.8	8 35
Saturn	103 41.9	12 38

UT	SUN GHA	SUN Dec	MOON GHA	v	MOON Dec	d	HP
d h	° ′	° ′	° ′	′	° ′	′	′
26 00	183 10.9	S20 58.4	219 51.9	15.0	S 6 37.4	8.9	54.1
01	198 10.7	58.8	234 25.9	15.1	6 46.3	9.0	54.1
02	213 10.5	59.3	249 00.0	15.0	6 55.3	8.9	54.1
03	228 10.3	20 59.8	263 34.0	15.0	7 04.2	8.9	54.1
04	243 10.1	21 00.2	278 08.0	14.9	7 13.1	8.9	54.1
05	258 09.9	00.7	292 41.9	15.0	7 22.0	8.8	54.1
06	273 09.7	S21 01.2	307 15.9	15.0	S 7 30.8	8.8	54.1
S 07	288 09.5	01.6	321 49.9	14.9	7 39.6	8.8	54.1
A 08	303 09.3	02.1	336 23.8	14.9	7 48.4	8.7	54.0
T 09	318 09.1	. . 02.6	350 57.7	14.9	7 57.1	8.7	54.0
U 10	333 08.9	03.0	5 31.6	14.9	8 05.8	8.7	54.0
R 11	348 08.7	03.5	20 05.5	14.9	8 14.5	8.7	54.0
D 12	3 08.5	S21 03.9	34 39.4	14.9	S 8 23.2	8.6	54.0
A 13	18 08.3	04.4	49 13.3	14.8	8 31.8	8.5	54.0
Y 14	33 08.1	04.9	63 47.1	14.8	8 40.3	8.6	54.0
15	48 07.9	. . 05.3	78 20.9	14.8	8 48.9	8.5	54.0
16	63 07.7	05.8	92 54.7	14.8	8 57.4	8.4	54.0
17	78 07.5	06.2	107 28.5	14.8	9 05.8	8.4	54.0
18	93 07.3	S21 06.7	122 02.3	14.7	S 9 14.2	8.4	54.0
19	108 07.1	07.2	136 36.0	14.7	9 22.6	8.3	54.0
20	123 06.9	07.6	151 09.7	14.7	9 30.9	8.3	54.0
21	138 06.7	. . 08.1	165 43.4	14.7	9 39.2	8.3	54.0
22	153 06.4	08.5	180 17.1	14.7	9 47.5	8.2	54.0
23	168 06.2	09.0	194 50.8	14.6	9 55.7	8.2	54.0
27 00	183 06.0	S21 09.4	209 24.4	14.6	S10 03.9	8.2	54.0
01	198 05.8	09.9	223 58.0	14.6	10 12.1	8.0	54.0
02	213 05.6	10.3	238 31.6	14.6	10 20.1	8.1	54.0
03	228 05.4	. . 10.8	253 05.2	14.5	10 28.2	8.0	54.0
04	243 05.2	11.2	267 38.7	14.6	10 36.2	8.0	54.0
05	258 05.0	11.7	282 12.3	14.5	10 44.2	7.9	54.0
06	273 04.8	S21 12.1	296 45.8	14.4	S10 52.1	7.9	54.0
07	288 04.6	12.6	311 19.2	14.5	11 00.0	7.8	53.9
08	303 04.4	13.0	325 52.7	14.4	11 07.8	7.8	53.9
S 09	318 04.2	. . 13.5	340 26.1	14.4	11 15.6	7.7	53.9
U 10	333 04.0	13.9	354 59.5	14.4	11 23.3	7.7	53.9
N 11	348 03.7	14.4	9 32.9	14.3	11 31.0	7.7	53.9
D 12	3 03.5	S21 14.8	24 06.2	14.3	S11 38.7	7.6	53.9
A 13	18 03.3	15.3	38 39.5	14.3	11 46.3	7.5	53.9
Y 14	33 03.1	15.7	53 12.8	14.3	11 53.8	7.5	53.9
15	48 02.9	. . 16.2	67 46.1	14.2	12 01.3	7.5	53.9
16	63 02.7	16.6	82 19.3	14.2	12 08.8	7.4	53.9
17	78 02.5	17.0	96 52.5	14.2	12 16.2	7.3	53.9
18	93 02.3	S21 17.5	111 25.7	14.1	S12 23.5	7.3	53.9
19	108 02.1	17.9	125 58.8	14.1	12 30.8	7.2	53.9
20	123 01.8	18.4	140 31.9	14.1	12 38.0	7.2	53.9
21	138 01.6	. . 18.8	155 05.0	14.1	12 45.2	7.2	53.9
22	153 01.4	19.2	169 38.1	14.0	12 52.4	7.0	53.9
23	168 01.2	19.7	184 11.1	14.0	12 59.4	7.1	53.9
28 00	183 01.0	S21 20.1	198 44.1	14.0	S13 06.5	7.0	53.9
01	198 00.8	20.6	213 17.1	13.9	13 13.5	6.9	53.9
02	213 00.6	21.0	227 50.0	13.9	13 20.4	6.8	53.9
03	228 00.3	. . 21.4	242 22.9	13.9	13 27.2	6.8	53.9
04	243 00.1	21.9	256 55.8	13.9	13 34.0	6.8	53.9
05	257 59.9	22.3	271 28.7	13.8	13 40.8	6.7	53.9
06	272 59.7	S21 22.7	286 01.5	13.8	S13 47.5	6.6	53.9
07	287 59.5	23.2	300 34.3	13.7	13 54.1	6.6	53.9
08	302 59.3	23.6	315 07.0	13.7	14 00.7	6.5	53.9
M 09	317 59.1	. . 24.0	329 39.7	13.7	14 07.2	6.5	53.9
O 10	332 58.8	24.4	344 12.4	13.7	14 13.7	6.3	54.0
N 11	347 58.6	24.9	358 45.1	13.6	14 20.0	6.4	54.0
D 12	2 58.4	S21 25.3	13 17.7	13.6	S14 26.4	6.3	54.0
A 13	17 58.2	25.7	27 50.3	13.6	14 32.7	6.2	54.0
Y 14	32 58.0	26.2	42 22.9	13.5	14 38.9	6.1	54.0
15	47 57.7	. . 26.6	56 55.4	13.5	14 45.0	6.1	54.0
16	62 57.5	27.0	71 27.9	13.5	14 51.1	6.0	54.0
17	77 57.3	27.4	86 00.4	13.4	14 57.1	6.0	54.0
18	92 57.1	S21 27.9	100 32.8	13.4	S15 03.1	5.9	54.0
19	107 56.9	28.3	115 05.2	13.4	15 09.0	5.8	54.0
20	122 56.6	28.7	129 37.6	13.3	15 14.8	5.8	54.0
21	137 56.4	. . 29.1	144 09.9	13.3	15 20.6	5.7	54.0
22	152 56.2	29.5	158 42.2	13.3	15 26.3	5.6	54.0
23	167 56.0	30.0	173 14.5	13.2	S15 31.9	5.6	54.0
	SD 16.2	*d* 0.4	SD 14.7		14.7		14.7

Lat.	Twilight Naut.	Twilight Civil	Sunrise	Moonrise 26	Moonrise 27	Moonrise 28	Moonrise 29
°	h m	h m	h m	h m	h m	h m	h m
N 72	07 41	09 33	▬	05 05	06 42	08 24	10 14
N 70	07 26	08 58	▬	04 53	06 23	07 54	09 25
68	07 13	08 33	10 15	04 44	06 08	07 32	08 54
66	07 03	08 14	09 34	04 36	05 56	07 15	08 31
64	06 54	07 58	09 06	04 30	05 46	07 01	08 13
62	06 47	07 45	08 44	04 25	05 37	06 49	07 58
60	06 40	07 34	08 27	04 20	05 30	06 39	07 46
N 58	06 34	07 24	08 13	04 16	05 24	06 31	07 35
56	06 28	07 16	08 01	04 12	05 18	06 23	07 26
54	06 23	07 08	07 50	04 09	05 13	06 16	07 18
52	06 19	07 01	07 40	04 06	05 08	06 10	07 11
50	06 14	06 55	07 32	04 03	05 04	06 05	07 04
45	06 04	06 41	07 14	03 57	04 55	05 53	06 50
N 40	05 56	06 29	06 59	03 52	04 48	05 43	06 38
35	05 48	06 19	06 46	03 48	04 41	05 35	06 28
30	05 40	06 09	06 35	03 44	04 36	05 28	06 20
20	05 26	05 53	06 16	03 38	04 26	05 15	06 05
N 10	05 11	05 37	06 00	03 32	04 18	05 04	05 52
0	04 56	05 22	05 44	03 27	04 10	04 54	05 40
S 10	04 39	05 06	05 28	03 22	04 02	04 44	05 28
20	04 19	04 47	05 11	03 16	03 54	04 33	05 15
30	03 53	04 25	04 52	03 10	03 45	04 21	05 00
35	03 36	04 11	04 40	03 06	03 39	04 14	04 52
40	03 15	03 55	04 27	03 02	03 33	04 06	04 42
45	02 49	03 35	04 11	02 58	03 26	03 57	04 31
S 50	02 12	03 10	03 51	02 52	03 18	03 46	04 17
52	01 51	02 57	03 42	02 50	03 14	03 41	04 11
54	01 24	02 42	03 31	02 47	03 09	03 35	04 04
56	00 41	02 24	03 19	02 44	03 05	03 29	03 56
58	////	02 03	03 06	02 40	03 00	03 22	03 48
S 60	////	01 34	02 49	02 37	02 54	03 14	03 38

Lat.	Sunset	Twilight Civil	Twilight Naut.	Moonset 26	Moonset 27	Moonset 28	Moonset 29
°	h m	h m	h m	h m	h m	h m	h m
N 72	▬	14 01	15 54	13 52	13 44	13 34	13 19
N 70	▬	14 36	16 09	14 05	14 04	14 05	14 09
68	13 19	15 01	16 21	14 15	14 20	14 28	14 41
66	14 01	15 21	16 32	14 24	14 33	14 46	15 04
64	14 29	15 36	16 40	14 31	14 44	15 01	15 22
62	14 50	15 50	16 48	14 38	14 54	15 13	15 38
60	15 08	16 01	16 55	14 43	15 02	15 23	15 50
N 58	15 22	16 11	17 01	14 48	15 09	15 32	16 01
56	15 35	16 19	17 07	14 53	15 15	15 40	16 11
54	15 45	16 27	17 12	14 57	15 20	15 48	16 19
52	15 55	16 34	17 17	15 00	15 26	15 54	16 27
50	16 03	16 40	17 21	15 04	15 30	16 00	16 34
45	16 22	16 54	17 31	15 11	15 40	16 12	16 49
N 40	16 36	17 06	17 40	15 17	15 48	16 23	17 01
35	16 49	17 17	17 48	15 22	15 55	16 32	17 11
30	17 00	17 26	17 55	15 26	16 02	16 40	17 20
20	17 19	17 43	18 10	15 34	16 13	16 53	17 36
N 10	17 36	17 58	18 24	15 41	16 22	17 05	17 49
0	17 51	18 14	18 39	15 48	16 31	17 16	18 02
S 10	18 07	18 30	18 57	15 54	16 40	17 27	18 15
20	18 24	18 48	19 17	16 01	16 50	17 39	18 29
30	18 44	19 11	19 43	16 09	17 01	17 53	18 45
35	18 56	19 25	20 00	16 14	17 07	18 01	18 54
40	19 09	19 41	20 21	16 19	17 15	18 10	19 04
45	19 25	20 01	20 47	16 25	17 23	18 20	19 16
S 50	19 45	20 27	21 25	16 32	17 33	18 33	19 31
52	19 54	20 40	21 46	16 36	17 38	18 39	19 38
54	20 05	20 55	22 14	16 40	17 43	18 46	19 46
56	20 17	21 13	23 00	16 44	17 49	18 53	19 55
58	20 31	21 35	////	16 48	17 56	19 02	20 05
S 60	20 48	22 05	////	16 53	18 03	19 11	20 16

Day	SUN Eqn. of Time 00^h	SUN Eqn. of Time 12^h	SUN Mer. Pass.	MOON Mer. Pass. Upper	MOON Mer. Pass. Lower	MOON Age	MOON Phase
d	m s	m s	h m	h m	h m	d %	
26	12 44	12 34	11 47	09 37	21 59	27 8	●
27	12 25	12 15	11 48	10 21	22 43	28 4	
28	12 04	11 54	11 48	11 05	23 28	29 1	

UT		ARIES	VENUS −4·2		MARS +0·6		JUPITER −1·8		SATURN +0·5	
		GHA	GHA	Dec	GHA	Dec	GHA	Dec	GHA	Dec
d	h	° ′	° ′	° ′	° ′	° ′	° ′	° ′	° ′	° ′
29	00	68 18.6	136 21.9	S24 20.6	110 44.9	S17 49.7	232 40.0	S 5 23.4	171 45.5	S21 32.6
	01	83 21.0	151 21.2	20.1	125 45.5	49.1	247 42.0	23.6	186 47.6	32.7
	02	98 23.5	166 20.5	19.7	140 46.1	48.5	262 44.1	23.8	201 49.8	32.7
	03	113 26.0	181 19.7	. . 19.3	155 46.7	. . 47.9	277 46.2	. . 23.9	216 51.9	. . 32.7
	04	128 28.4	196 19.0	18.8	170 47.3	47.4	292 48.2	24.1	231 54.1	32.7
	05	143 30.9	211 18.3	18.4	185 47.9	46.8	307 50.3	24.2	246 56.2	32.8
	06	158 33.4	226 17.6	S24 18.0	200 48.5	S17 46.2	322 52.3	S 5 24.4	261 58.4	S21 32.8
	07	173 35.8	241 16.8	17.5	215 49.1	45.6	337 54.4	24.5	277 00.5	32.8
T	08	188 38.3	256 16.1	17.1	230 49.7	45.0	352 56.5	24.7	292 02.7	32.9
U	09	203 40.8	271 15.4	. . 16.7	245 50.3	. . 44.4	7 58.5	. . 24.9	307 04.8	. . 32.9
E	10	218 43.2	286 14.7	16.2	260 50.9	43.8	23 00.6	25.0	322 07.0	32.9
S	11	233 45.7	301 14.0	15.8	275 51.5	43.2	38 02.7	25.2	337 09.1	33.0
D	12	248 48.1	316 13.2	S24 15.3	290 52.1	S17 42.6	53 04.7	S 5 25.3	352 11.3	S21 33.0
A	13	263 50.6	331 12.5	14.9	305 52.7	42.0	68 06.8	25.5	7 13.4	33.0
Y	14	278 53.1	346 11.8	14.5	320 53.3	41.4	83 08.9	25.6	22 15.6	33.0
	15	293 55.5	1 11.1	. . 14.0	335 53.9	. . 40.8	98 10.9	. . 25.8	37 17.7	. . 33.1
	16	308 58.0	16 10.4	13.6	350 54.5	40.2	113 13.0	26.0	52 19.9	33.1
	17	324 00.5	31 09.6	13.1	5 55.1	39.6	128 15.1	26.1	67 22.0	33.1
	18	339 02.9	46 08.9	S24 12.7	20 55.7	S17 39.0	143 17.1	S 5 26.3	82 24.2	S21 33.2
	19	354 05.4	61 08.2	12.2	35 56.3	38.4	158 19.2	26.4	97 26.3	33.2
	20	9 07.9	76 07.5	11.8	50 56.9	37.8	173 21.3	26.6	112 28.5	33.2
	21	24 10.3	91 06.8	. . 11.3	65 57.5	. . 37.2	188 23.3	. . 26.7	127 30.6	. . 33.3
	22	39 12.8	106 06.1	10.9	80 58.1	36.6	203 25.4	26.9	142 32.8	33.3
	23	54 15.3	121 05.4	10.4	95 58.7	36.0	218 27.5	27.1	157 34.9	33.3
30	00	69 17.7	136 04.6	S24 10.0	110 59.3	S17 35.4	233 29.5	S 5 27.2	172 37.1	S21 33.3
	01	84 20.2	151 03.9	09.5	125 59.9	34.8	248 31.6	27.4	187 39.2	33.4
	02	99 22.6	166 03.2	09.1	141 00.5	34.2	263 33.7	27.5	202 41.4	33.4
	03	114 25.1	181 02.5	. . 08.6	156 01.1	. . 33.6	278 35.7	. . 27.7	217 43.5	. . 33.4
	04	129 27.6	196 01.8	08.1	171 01.7	33.0	293 37.8	27.8	232 45.7	33.5
	05	144 30.0	211 01.1	07.7	186 02.3	32.4	308 39.9	28.0	247 47.8	33.5
	06	159 32.5	226 00.4	S24 07.2	201 03.0	S17 31.8	323 41.9	S 5 28.2	262 50.0	S21 33.5
W	07	174 35.0	240 59.7	06.8	216 03.6	31.2	338 44.0	28.3	277 52.1	33.6
E	08	189 37.4	255 59.0	06.3	231 04.2	30.6	353 46.1	28.5	292 54.3	33.6
D	09	204 39.9	270 58.3	. . 05.8	246 04.8	. . 30.0	8 48.1	. . 28.6	307 56.4	. . 33.6
N	10	219 42.4	285 57.5	05.4	261 05.4	29.4	23 50.2	28.8	322 58.6	33.6
E	11	234 44.8	300 56.8	04.9	276 06.0	28.8	38 52.3	28.9	338 00.7	33.7
S	12	249 47.3	315 56.1	S24 04.4	291 06.6	S17 28.2	53 54.4	S 5 29.1	353 02.9	S21 33.7
D	13	264 49.7	330 55.4	04.0	306 07.2	27.6	68 56.4	29.2	8 05.0	33.7
A	14	279 52.2	345 54.7	03.5	321 07.8	27.0	83 58.5	29.4	23 07.2	33.8
Y	15	294 54.7	0 54.0	. . 03.0	336 08.4	. . 26.4	99 00.6	. . 29.6	38 09.3	. . 33.8
	16	309 57.1	15 53.3	02.5	351 09.0	25.8	114 02.6	29.7	53 11.5	33.8
	17	324 59.6	30 52.6	02.1	6 09.6	25.2	129 04.7	29.9	68 13.6	33.9
	18	340 02.1	45 51.9	S24 01.6	21 10.2	S17 24.6	144 06.8	S 5 30.0	83 15.8	S21 33.9
	19	355 04.5	60 51.2	01.1	36 10.8	24.0	159 08.8	30.2	98 17.9	33.9
	20	10 07.0	75 50.5	00.6	51 11.4	23.4	174 10.9	30.3	113 20.1	33.9
	21	25 09.5	90 49.8	24 00.2	66 12.0	. . 22.8	189 13.0	. . 30.5	128 22.2	. . 34.0
	22	40 11.9	105 49.1	23 59.7	81 12.6	22.2	204 15.0	30.6	143 24.4	34.0
	23	55 14.4	120 48.4	59.2	96 13.2	21.6	219 17.1	30.8	158 26.5	34.0
1	00	70 16.9	135 47.7	S23 58.7	111 13.8	S17 21.0	234 19.2	S 5 31.0	173 28.7	S21 34.1
	01	85 19.3	150 47.0	58.2	126 14.4	20.4	249 21.3	31.1	188 30.8	34.1
	02	100 21.8	165 46.3	57.8	141 15.0	19.8	264 23.3	31.3	203 33.0	34.1
	03	115 24.2	180 45.6	. . 57.3	156 15.6	. . 19.2	279 25.4	. . 31.4	218 35.1	. . 34.2
	04	130 26.7	195 44.9	56.8	171 16.2	18.6	294 27.5	31.6	233 37.3	34.2
	05	145 29.2	210 44.2	56.3	186 16.8	18.0	309 29.5	31.7	248 39.4	34.2
	06	160 31.6	225 43.5	S23 55.8	201 17.5	S17 17.3	324 31.6	S 5 31.9	263 41.6	S21 34.2
	07	175 34.1	240 42.8	55.3	216 18.1	16.7	339 33.7	32.0	278 43.7	34.3
T	08	190 36.6	255 42.1	54.8	231 18.7	16.1	354 35.8	32.2	293 45.9	34.3
H	09	205 39.0	270 41.4	. . 54.3	246 19.3	. . 15.5	9 37.8	. . 32.4	308 48.0	. . 34.3
U	10	220 41.5	285 40.8	53.8	261 19.9	14.9	24 39.9	32.5	323 50.2	34.4
R	11	235 44.0	300 40.1	53.3	276 20.5	14.3	39 42.0	32.7	338 52.3	34.4
S	12	250 46.4	315 39.4	S23 52.9	291 21.1	S17 13.7	54 44.1	S 5 32.8	353 54.5	S21 34.4
D	13	265 48.9	330 38.7	52.4	306 21.7	13.1	69 46.1	33.0	8 56.6	34.4
A	14	280 51.4	345 38.0	51.9	321 22.3	12.5	84 48.2	33.1	23 58.8	34.5
Y	15	295 53.8	0 37.3	. . 51.4	336 22.9	. . 11.9	99 50.3	. . 33.3	39 00.9	. . 34.5
	16	310 56.3	15 36.6	50.9	351 23.5	11.3	114 52.3	33.4	54 03.1	34.5
	17	325 58.7	30 35.9	50.4	6 24.1	10.7	129 54.4	33.6	69 05.2	34.6
	18	341 01.2	45 35.2	S23 49.9	21 24.7	S17 10.0	144 56.5	S 5 33.7	84 07.4	S21 34.6
	19	356 03.7	60 34.5	49.4	36 25.3	09.4	159 58.6	33.9	99 09.5	34.6
	20	11 06.1	75 33.9	48.8	51 26.0	08.8	175 00.6	34.0	114 11.7	34.7
	21	26 08.6	90 33.2	. . 48.3	66 26.6	. . 08.2	190 02.7	. . 34.2	129 13.8	. . 34.7
	22	41 11.1	105 32.5	47.8	81 27.2	07.6	205 04.8	34.4	144 16.0	34.7
	23	56 13.5	120 31.8	47.3	96 27.8	07.0	220 06.9	34.5	159 18.1	34.7
Mer. Pass.		h m 19 19.6	v −0.7	d 0.5	v 0.6	d 0.6	v 2.1	d 0.2	v 2.2	d 0.0

STARS		
Name	SHA	Dec
	° ′	° ′
Acamar	315 16.2	S40 14.5
Achernar	335 24.7	S57 09.4
Acrux	173 06.8	S63 11.2
Adhara	255 10.4	S28 59.8
Aldebaran	290 46.4	N16 32.4
Alioth	166 19.1	N55 52.0
Alkaid	152 57.5	N49 13.7
Al Na'ir	27 41.0	S46 52.9
Alnilam	275 43.7	S 1 11.6
Alphard	217 53.7	S 8 43.9
Alphecca	126 09.4	N26 39.7
Alpheratz	357 40.9	N29 11.2
Altair	62 06.2	N 8 55.0
Ankaa	353 13.3	S42 13.1
Antares	112 23.8	S26 27.9
Arcturus	145 53.9	N19 05.8
Atria	107 24.0	S69 03.2
Avior	234 16.6	S59 33.7
Bellatrix	278 29.2	N 6 21.7
Betelgeuse	270 58.5	N 7 24.4
Canopus	263 54.6	S52 42.3
Capella	280 30.5	N46 00.6
Deneb	49 30.1	N45 20.8
Denebola	182 31.4	N14 28.7
Diphda	348 53.4	S17 53.8
Dubhe	193 49.1	N61 39.3
Elnath	278 09.3	N28 37.1
Eltanin	90 45.6	N51 29.5
Enif	33 44.9	N 9 57.3
Fomalhaut	15 21.5	S29 32.1
Gacrux	171 58.5	S57 12.1
Gienah	175 50.0	S17 37.9
Hadar	148 45.0	S60 26.9
Hamal	327 57.8	N23 32.5
Kaus Aust.	83 41.1	S34 22.4
Kochab	137 21.4	N74 05.2
Markab	13 36.0	N15 17.9
Menkar	314 12.3	N 4 09.2
Menkent	148 05.1	S36 26.9
Miaplacidus	221 38.7	S69 47.0
Mirfak	308 36.5	N49 55.2
Nunki	75 55.8	S26 16.4
Peacock	53 16.0	S56 40.9
Pollux	243 24.7	N27 58.9
Procyon	244 57.1	N 5 10.7
Rasalhague	96 04.7	N12 33.2
Regulus	207 41.0	N11 53.0
Rigel	281 09.5	S 8 11.1
Rigil Kent.	139 49.1	S60 53.9
Sabik	102 10.2	S15 44.5
Schedar	349 37.4	N56 38.0
Shaula	96 19.2	S37 06.7
Sirius	258 31.4	S16 44.5
Spica	158 29.0	S11 14.7
Suhail	222 50.5	S43 29.9
Vega	80 37.8	N38 48.3
Zuben'ubi	137 03.2	S16 06.4

	SHA	Mer. Pass.
	° ′	h m
Venus	66 46.9	14 56
Mars	41 41.6	16 35
Jupiter	164 11.8	8 25
Saturn	103 19.4	12 28

UT		SUN GHA	SUN Dec	MOON GHA	v	MOON Dec	d	HP
d h		° ′	° ′	° ′	′	° ′	′	′
29 00	TUESDAY	182 55.8	S21 30.4	187 46.7	13.2	S15 37.5	5.5	54.0
01		197 55.5	30.8	202 18.9	13.2	15 43.0	5.4	54.0
02		212 55.3	31.2	216 51.1	13.2	15 48.4	5.3	54.0
03		227 55.1	. . 31.6	231 23.3	13.1	15 53.7	5.3	54.0
04		242 54.9	32.1	245 55.4	13.1	15 59.0	5.3	54.0
05		257 54.7	32.5	260 27.5	13.0	16 04.3	5.1	54.0
06		272 54.4	S21 32.9	274 59.5	13.0	S16 09.4	5.1	54.0
07		287 54.2	33.3	289 31.5	13.0	16 14.5	5.0	54.0
08		302 54.0	33.7	304 03.5	13.0	16 19.5	4.9	54.0
09		317 53.8	. . 34.1	318 35.5	12.9	16 24.4	4.9	54.0
10		332 53.5	34.6	333 07.4	12.9	16 29.3	4.8	54.0
11		347 53.3	35.0	347 39.3	12.8	16 34.1	4.7	54.1
12		2 53.1	S21 35.4	2 11.1	12.8	S16 38.8	4.7	54.1
13		17 52.9	35.8	16 42.9	12.8	16 43.5	4.5	54.1
14		32 52.6	36.2	31 14.7	12.8	16 48.0	4.5	54.1
15		47 52.4	. . 36.6	45 46.5	12.7	16 52.5	4.5	54.1
16		62 52.2	37.0	60 18.2	12.7	16 57.0	4.3	54.1
17		77 52.0	37.4	74 49.9	12.7	17 01.3	4.3	54.1
18		92 51.7	S21 37.8	89 21.6	12.6	S17 05.6	4.2	54.1
19		107 51.5	38.2	103 53.2	12.6	17 09.8	4.1	54.1
20		122 51.3	38.6	118 24.8	12.6	17 13.9	4.0	54.1
21		137 51.1	. . 39.0	132 56.4	12.5	17 17.9	4.0	54.1
22		152 50.8	39.5	147 27.9	12.5	17 21.9	3.9	54.1
23		167 50.6	39.9	161 59.4	12.5	17 25.8	3.8	54.1
30 00	WEDNESDAY	182 50.4	S21 40.3	176 30.9	12.5	S17 29.6	3.7	54.1
01		197 50.1	40.7	191 02.4	12.4	17 33.3	3.7	54.1
02		212 49.9	41.1	205 33.8	12.4	17 37.0	3.6	54.2
03		227 49.7	. . 41.5	220 05.2	12.4	17 40.6	3.5	54.2
04		242 49.5	41.9	234 36.6	12.3	17 44.1	3.4	54.2
05		257 49.2	42.3	249 07.9	12.3	17 47.5	3.3	54.2
06		272 49.0	S21 42.7	263 39.2	12.3	S17 50.8	3.3	54.2
07		287 48.8	43.1	278 10.5	12.2	17 54.1	3.1	54.2
08		302 48.5	43.5	292 41.7	12.3	17 57.2	3.1	54.2
09		317 48.3	. . 43.9	307 13.0	12.2	18 00.3	3.0	54.2
10		332 48.1	44.2	321 44.2	12.1	18 03.3	3.0	54.2
11		347 47.8	44.6	336 15.3	12.2	18 06.3	2.8	54.2
12		2 47.6	S21 45.0	350 46.5	12.1	S18 09.1	2.8	54.2
13		17 47.4	45.4	5 17.6	12.1	18 11.9	2.6	54.3
14		32 47.2	45.8	19 48.7	12.1	18 14.5	2.6	54.3
15		47 46.9	. . 46.2	34 19.8	12.0	18 17.1	2.5	54.3
16		62 46.7	46.6	48 50.8	12.0	18 19.6	2.4	54.3
17		77 46.5	47.0	63 21.8	12.0	18 22.0	2.4	54.3
18		92 46.2	S21 47.4	77 52.8	12.0	S18 24.4	2.2	54.3
19		107 46.0	47.8	92 23.8	11.9	18 26.6	2.2	54.3
20		122 45.8	48.2	106 54.7	11.9	18 28.8	2.1	54.3
21		137 45.5	. . 48.6	121 25.6	11.9	18 30.9	2.0	54.3
22		152 45.3	48.9	135 56.5	11.9	18 32.9	1.9	54.3
23		167 45.0	49.3	150 27.4	11.8	18 34.8	1.8	54.4
1 00	THURSDAY	182 44.8	S21 49.7	164 58.2	11.9	S18 36.6	1.7	54.4
01		197 44.6	50.1	179 29.1	11.8	18 38.3	1.7	54.4
02		212 44.3	50.5	193 59.9	11.8	18 40.0	1.5	54.4
03		227 44.1	. . 50.9	208 30.7	11.7	18 41.5	1.5	54.4
04		242 43.9	51.2	223 01.4	11.8	18 43.0	1.4	54.4
05		257 43.6	51.6	237 32.2	11.7	18 44.4	1.3	54.4
06		272 43.4	S21 52.0	252 02.9	11.7	S18 45.7	1.2	54.4
07		287 43.2	52.4	266 33.6	11.7	18 46.9	1.1	54.4
08		302 42.9	52.8	281 04.3	11.6	18 48.0	1.1	54.5
09		317 42.7	. . 53.2	295 34.9	11.7	18 49.1	0.9	54.5
10		332 42.5	53.5	310 05.6	11.6	18 50.0	0.9	54.5
11		347 42.2	53.9	324 36.2	11.6	18 50.9	0.7	54.5
12		2 42.0	S21 54.3	339 06.8	11.6	S18 51.6	0.7	54.5
13		17 41.7	54.7	353 37.4	11.6	18 52.3	0.6	54.5
14		32 41.5	55.0	8 08.0	11.5	18 52.9	0.5	54.5
15		47 41.3	. . 55.4	22 38.5	11.6	18 53.4	0.4	54.5
16		62 41.0	55.8	37 09.1	11.5	18 53.8	0.3	54.6
17		77 40.8	56.2	51 39.6	11.5	18 54.1	0.2	54.6
18		92 40.5	S21 56.5	66 10.1	11.5	S18 54.3	0.1	54.6
19		107 40.3	56.9	80 40.6	11.5	18 54.4	0.1	54.6
20		122 40.1	57.3	95 11.1	11.5	18 54.5	0.1	54.6
21		137 39.8	. . 57.6	109 41.6	11.4	18 54.4	0.1	54.6
22		152 39.6	58.0	124 12.0	11.5	18 54.3	0.2	54.6
23		167 39.3	58.4	138 42.5	11.4	S18 54.1	0.4	54.7
		SD 16.2	*d* 0.4	SD 14.7		14.8		14.9

Lat.	Twilight Naut.	Twilight Civil	Sunrise	Moonrise 29	Moonrise 30	Moonrise 1	Moonrise 2
°	h m	h m	h m	h m	h m	h m	h m
N 72	07 49	09 47	▬	10 14	▬	▬	▬
N 70	07 33	09 09	▬	09 25	10 53	12 06	12 49
68	07 20	08 42	10 33	08 54	10 10	11 15	12 01
66	07 09	08 22	09 45	08 31	09 42	10 43	11 30
64	07 00	08 05	09 14	08 13	09 20	10 19	11 07
62	06 52	07 51	08 52	07 58	09 03	10 00	10 48
60	06 45	07 40	08 34	07 46	08 49	09 45	10 33
N 58	06 38	07 29	08 19	07 35	08 36	09 32	10 20
56	06 33	07 20	08 06	07 26	08 26	09 21	10 09
54	06 27	07 12	07 55	07 18	08 17	09 11	09 59
52	06 22	07 05	07 45	07 11	08 08	09 02	09 50
50	06 18	06 58	07 36	07 04	08 01	08 54	09 43
45	06 07	06 44	07 17	06 50	07 45	08 37	09 26
N 40	05 58	06 32	07 02	06 38	07 32	08 23	09 12
35	05 50	06 21	06 49	06 28	07 21	08 12	09 01
30	05 42	06 12	06 38	06 20	07 11	08 02	08 50
20	05 27	05 54	06 18	06 05	06 55	07 44	08 33
N 10	05 13	05 39	06 01	05 52	06 40	07 29	08 18
0	04 57	05 23	05 45	05 40	06 27	07 15	08 03
S 10	04 39	05 06	05 29	05 28	06 13	07 00	07 49
20	04 19	04 47	05 12	05 15	05 59	06 45	07 34
30	03 52	04 24	04 51	05 00	05 42	06 28	07 17
35	03 35	04 10	04 39	04 52	05 33	06 18	07 06
40	03 14	03 54	04 26	04 42	05 22	06 06	06 55
45	02 46	03 33	04 09	04 31	05 09	05 53	06 41
S 50	02 08	03 07	03 49	04 17	04 54	05 36	06 25
52	01 46	02 54	03 39	04 11	04 47	05 28	06 17
54	01 16	02 38	03 29	04 04	04 39	05 20	06 08
56	00 22	02 20	03 16	03 56	04 30	05 10	05 58
58	////	01 56	03 02	03 48	04 20	04 59	05 47
S 60	////	01 25	02 44	03 38	04 08	04 46	05 34

Lat.	Sunset	Twilight Civil	Twilight Naut.	Moonset 29	Moonset 30	Moonset 1	Moonset 2
°	h m	h m	h m	h m	h m	h m	h m
N 72	▬	13 50	15 48	13 19	▬	▬	▬
N 70	▬	14 28	16 04	14 09	14 19	14 45	15 44
68	13 04	14 55	16 17	14 41	15 01	15 37	16 32
66	13 52	15 16	16 28	15 04	15 30	16 09	17 03
64	14 23	15 32	16 37	15 22	15 52	16 33	17 26
62	14 45	15 46	16 45	15 38	16 10	16 52	17 45
60	15 04	15 58	16 52	15 50	16 24	17 07	18 00
N 58	15 19	16 08	16 59	16 01	16 37	17 20	18 12
56	15 31	16 17	17 05	16 11	16 47	17 32	18 23
54	15 43	16 25	17 10	16 19	16 57	17 41	18 33
52	15 53	16 32	17 15	16 27	17 05	17 50	18 42
50	16 01	16 39	17 19	16 34	17 13	17 58	18 50
45	16 20	16 53	17 30	16 49	17 29	18 15	19 06
N 40	16 35	17 05	17 39	17 01	17 43	18 29	19 20
35	16 48	17 16	17 47	17 11	17 54	18 41	19 31
30	17 00	17 26	17 55	17 20	18 04	18 51	19 41
20	17 19	17 43	18 10	17 36	18 21	19 08	19 58
N 10	17 36	17 59	18 25	17 49	18 36	19 24	20 13
0	17 52	18 15	18 41	18 02	18 50	19 38	20 27
S 10	18 09	18 32	18 58	18 15	19 04	19 52	20 41
20	18 26	18 50	19 19	18 29	19 18	20 08	20 56
30	18 47	19 14	19 46	18 45	19 36	20 25	21 13
35	18 59	19 28	20 03	18 54	19 45	20 35	21 23
40	19 12	19 44	20 25	19 04	19 57	20 47	21 34
45	19 29	20 05	20 52	19 16	20 10	21 01	21 47
S 50	19 49	20 32	21 31	19 31	20 27	21 17	22 03
52	19 59	20 45	21 54	19 38	20 34	21 25	22 11
54	20 10	21 01	22 24	19 46	20 43	21 34	22 19
56	20 23	21 19	23 24	19 55	20 52	21 44	22 29
58	20 37	21 43	////	20 05	21 03	21 55	22 39
S 60	20 55	22 16	////	20 16	21 16	22 08	22 52

Day	SUN Eqn. of Time 00^h	SUN Eqn. of Time 12^h	SUN Mer. Pass.	MOON Mer. Pass. Upper	MOON Mer. Pass. Lower	MOON Age	MOON Phase
d	m s	m s	h m	h m	h m	d	%
29	11 44	11 33	11 48	11 51	24 14	30	0
30	11 22	11 11	11 49	12 38	00 14	01	1
1	11 00	10 48	11 49	13 26	01 02	02	4

Day	UT (d h)	ARIES GHA	VENUS −4·2 GHA	VENUS Dec	MARS +0·7 GHA	MARS Dec	JUPITER −1·8 GHA	JUPITER Dec	SATURN +0·5 GHA	SATURN Dec
		° ′	° ′	° ′	° ′	° ′	° ′	° ′	° ′	° ′
FRIDAY	2 00	71 16.0	135 31.1	S23 46.8	111 28.4	S17 06.4	235 08.9	S 5 34.7	174 20.3	S21 34.8
	01	86 18.5	150 30.4	46.3	126 29.0	05.8	250 11.0	34.8	189 22.4	34.8
	02	101 20.9	165 29.7	45.8	141 29.6	05.2	265 13.1	35.0	204 24.6	34.8
	03	116 23.4	180 29.1	. . 45.3	156 30.2	. . 04.5	280 15.2	. . 35.1	219 26.7	. . 34.9
	04	131 25.9	195 28.4	44.8	171 30.8	03.9	295 17.2	35.3	234 28.9	34.9
	05	146 28.3	210 27.7	44.3	186 31.4	03.3	310 19.3	35.4	249 31.0	34.9
	06	161 30.8	225 27.0	S23 43.7	201 32.0	S17 02.7	325 21.4	S 5 35.6	264 33.2	S21 35.0
	07	176 33.2	240 26.3	43.2	216 32.6	02.1	340 23.5	35.7	279 35.3	35.0
	08	191 35.7	255 25.7	42.7	231 33.3	01.5	355 25.5	35.9	294 37.5	35.0
	09	206 38.2	270 25.0	. . 42.2	246 33.9	. . 00.9	10 27.6	. . 36.0	309 39.6	. . 35.0
	10	221 40.6	285 24.3	41.7	261 34.5	17 00.2	25 29.7	36.2	324 41.8	35.1
	11	236 43.1	300 23.6	41.1	276 35.1	16 59.6	40 31.8	36.3	339 43.9	35.1
	12	251 45.6	315 22.9	S23 40.6	291 35.7	S16 59.0	55 33.8	S 5 36.5	354 46.1	S21 35.1
	13	266 48.0	330 22.3	40.1	306 36.3	58.4	70 35.9	36.6	9 48.2	35.2
	14	281 50.5	345 21.6	39.6	321 36.9	57.8	85 38.0	36.8	24 50.4	35.2
	15	296 53.0	0 20.9	. . 39.1	336 37.5	. . 57.2	100 40.1	. . 36.9	39 52.5	. . 35.2
	16	311 55.4	15 20.2	38.5	351 38.1	56.5	115 42.1	37.1	54 54.7	35.2
	17	326 57.9	30 19.6	38.0	6 38.8	55.9	130 44.2	37.3	69 56.8	35.3
	18	342 00.4	45 18.9	S23 37.5	21 39.4	S16 55.3	145 46.3	S 5 37.4	84 59.0	S21 35.3
	19	357 02.8	60 18.2	36.9	36 40.0	54.7	160 48.4	37.6	100 01.1	35.3
	20	12 05.3	75 17.6	36.4	51 40.6	54.1	175 50.4	37.7	115 03.3	35.4
	21	27 07.7	90 16.9	. . 35.9	66 41.2	. . 53.5	190 52.5	. . 37.9	130 05.4	. . 35.4
	22	42 10.2	105 16.2	35.3	81 41.8	52.8	205 54.6	38.0	145 07.6	35.4
	23	57 12.7	120 15.5	34.8	96 42.4	52.2	220 56.7	38.2	160 09.7	35.4
SATURDAY	3 00	72 15.1	135 14.9	S23 34.3	111 43.0	S16 51.6	235 58.8	S 5 38.3	175 11.9	S21 35.5
	01	87 17.6	150 14.2	33.7	126 43.6	51.0	251 00.8	38.5	190 14.0	35.5
	02	102 20.1	165 13.5	33.2	141 44.3	50.4	266 02.9	38.6	205 16.2	35.5
	03	117 22.5	180 12.9	. . 32.7	156 44.9	. . 49.8	281 05.0	. . 38.8	220 18.3	. . 35.6
	04	132 25.0	195 12.2	32.1	171 45.5	49.1	296 07.1	38.9	235 20.5	35.6
	05	147 27.5	210 11.5	31.6	186 46.1	48.5	311 09.2	39.1	250 22.6	35.6
	06	162 29.9	225 10.9	S23 31.0	201 46.7	S16 47.9	326 11.2	S 5 39.2	265 24.8	S21 35.7
	07	177 32.4	240 10.2	30.5	216 47.3	47.3	341 13.3	39.4	280 26.9	35.7
	08	192 34.8	255 09.5	30.0	231 47.9	46.7	356 15.4	39.5	295 29.1	35.7
	09	207 37.3	270 08.9	. . 29.4	246 48.5	. . 46.0	11 17.5	. . 39.7	310 31.2	. . 35.7
	10	222 39.8	285 08.2	28.9	261 49.2	45.4	26 19.5	39.8	325 33.4	35.8
	11	237 42.2	300 07.5	28.3	276 49.8	44.8	41 21.6	40.0	340 35.5	35.8
	12	252 44.7	315 06.9	S23 27.8	291 50.4	S16 44.2	56 23.7	S 5 40.1	355 37.7	S21 35.8
	13	267 47.2	330 06.2	27.2	306 51.0	43.5	71 25.8	40.3	10 39.8	35.9
	14	282 49.6	345 05.6	26.7	321 51.6	42.9	86 27.9	40.4	25 42.0	35.9
	15	297 52.1	0 04.9	. . 26.1	336 52.2	. . 42.3	101 29.9	. . 40.6	40 44.1	. . 35.9
	16	312 54.6	15 04.2	25.6	351 52.8	41.7	116 32.0	40.7	55 46.3	35.9
	17	327 57.0	30 03.6	25.0	6 53.5	41.1	131 34.1	40.9	70 48.4	36.0
	18	342 59.5	45 02.9	S23 24.4	21 54.1	S16 40.4	146 36.2	S 5 41.0	85 50.6	S21 36.0
	19	358 02.0	60 02.3	23.9	36 54.7	39.8	161 38.3	41.2	100 52.7	36.0
	20	13 04.4	75 01.6	23.3	51 55.3	39.2	176 40.4	41.3	115 54.9	36.1
	21	28 06.9	90 01.0	. . 22.8	66 55.9	. . 38.6	191 42.4	. . 41.5	130 57.0	. . 36.1
	22	43 09.3	105 00.3	22.2	81 56.5	37.9	206 44.5	41.6	145 59.2	36.1
	23	58 11.8	119 59.6	21.7	96 57.1	37.3	221 46.6	41.8	161 01.3	36.1
SUNDAY	4 00	73 14.3	134 59.0	S23 21.1	111 57.8	S16 36.7	236 48.7	S 5 41.9	176 03.5	S21 36.2
	01	88 16.7	149 58.3	20.5	126 58.4	36.1	251 50.8	42.1	191 05.6	36.2
	02	103 19.2	164 57.7	20.0	141 59.0	35.4	266 52.8	42.2	206 07.8	36.2
	03	118 21.7	179 57.0	. . 19.4	156 59.6	. . 34.8	281 54.9	. . 42.4	221 09.9	. . 36.3
	04	133 24.1	194 56.4	18.8	172 00.2	34.2	296 57.0	42.5	236 12.1	36.3
	05	148 26.6	209 55.7	18.3	187 00.8	33.6	311 59.1	42.7	251 14.2	36.3
	06	163 29.1	224 55.1	S23 17.7	202 01.5	S16 32.9	327 01.2	S 5 42.8	266 16.3	S21 36.3
	07	178 31.5	239 54.4	17.1	217 02.1	32.3	342 03.3	43.0	281 18.5	36.4
	08	193 34.0	254 53.8	16.6	232 02.7	31.7	357 05.3	43.1	296 20.6	36.4
	09	208 36.5	269 53.1	. . 16.0	247 03.3	. . 31.1	12 07.4	. . 43.3	311 22.8	. . 36.4
	10	223 38.9	284 52.5	15.4	262 03.9	30.4	27 09.5	43.4	326 24.9	36.5
	11	238 41.4	299 51.8	14.8	277 04.5	29.8	42 11.6	43.6	341 27.1	36.5
	12	253 43.8	314 51.2	S23 14.3	292 05.2	S16 29.2	57 13.7	S 5 43.7	356 29.2	S21 36.5
	13	268 46.3	329 50.6	13.7	307 05.8	28.5	72 15.8	43.9	11 31.4	36.6
	14	283 48.8	344 49.9	13.1	322 06.4	27.9	87 17.8	44.0	26 33.5	36.6
	15	298 51.2	359 49.3	. . 12.5	337 07.0	. . 27.3	102 19.9	. . 44.2	41 35.7	. . 36.6
	16	313 53.7	14 48.6	12.0	352 07.6	26.7	117 22.0	44.3	56 37.8	36.6
	17	328 56.2	29 48.0	11.4	7 08.2	26.0	132 24.1	44.5	71 40.0	36.7
	18	343 58.6	44 47.3	S23 10.8	22 08.9	S16 25.4	147 26.2	S 5 44.6	86 42.1	S21 36.7
	19	359 01.1	59 46.7	10.2	37 09.5	24.8	162 28.3	44.8	101 44.3	36.7
	20	14 03.6	74 46.1	09.6	52 10.1	24.1	177 30.3	44.9	116 46.4	36.8
	21	29 06.0	89 45.4	. . 09.0	67 10.7	. . 23.5	192 32.4	. . 45.1	131 48.6	. . 36.8
	22	44 08.5	104 44.8	08.5	82 11.3	22.9	207 34.5	45.2	146 50.7	36.8
	23	59 11.0	119 44.1	07.9	97 12.0	22.2	222 36.6	45.4	161 52.9	36.8
	Mer. Pass.	h m 19 07.8	*v* −0.7	*d* 0.5	*v* 0.6	*d* 0.6	*v* 2.1	*d* 0.2	*v* 2.1	*d* 0.0

STARS

Name	SHA	Dec
	° ′	° ′
Acamar	315 16.2	S40 14.5
Achernar	335 24.8	S57 09.4
Acrux	173 06.8	S63 11.2
Adhara	255 10.4	S28 59.8
Aldebaran	290 46.3	N16 32.4
Alioth	166 19.1	N55 52.0
Alkaid	152 57.5	N49 13.7
Al Na'ir	27 41.0	S46 52.9
Alnilam	275 43.7	S 1 11.7
Alphard	217 53.7	S 8 43.9
Alphecca	126 09.4	N26 39.7
Alpheratz	357 40.9	N29 11.2
Altair	62 06.2	N 8 55.0
Ankaa	353 13.3	S42 13.1
Antares	112 23.8	S26 27.9
Arcturus	145 53.9	N19 05.8
Atria	107 24.0	S69 03.2
Avior	234 16.6	S59 33.7
Bellatrix	278 29.2	N 6 21.7
Betelgeuse	270 58.5	N 7 24.4
Canopus	263 54.6	S52 42.3
Capella	280 30.5	N46 00.7
Deneb	49 30.1	N45 20.8
Denebola	182 31.4	N14 28.6
Diphda	348 53.4	S17 53.8
Dubhe	193 49.1	N61 39.3
Elnath	278 09.3	N28 37.1
Eltanin	90 45.6	N51 29.5
Enif	33 44.9	N 9 57.3
Fomalhaut	15 21.5	S29 32.1
Gacrux	171 58.4	S57 12.1
Gienah	175 50.0	S17 37.9
Hadar	148 45.0	S60 26.9
Hamal	327 57.8	N23 32.5
Kaus Aust.	83 41.1	S34 22.4
Kochab	137 21.4	N74 05.2
Markab	13 36.0	N15 17.9
Menkar	314 12.3	N 4 09.2
Menkent	148 05.1	S36 26.9
Miaplacidus	221 38.6	S69 47.0
Mirfak	308 36.5	N49 55.2
Nunki	75 55.8	S26 16.4
Peacock	53 16.0	S56 40.9
Pollux	243 24.6	N27 58.9
Procyon	244 57.1	N 5 10.7
Rasalhague	96 04.6	N12 33.1
Regulus	207 41.0	N11 53.0
Rigel	281 09.5	S 8 11.1
Rigil Kent.	139 49.0	S60 53.9
Sabik	102 10.2	S15 44.5
Schedar	349 37.5	N56 38.0
Shaula	96 19.2	S37 06.7
Sirius	258 31.4	S16 44.5
Spica	158 29.0	S11 14.8
Suhail	222 50.5	S43 29.9
Vega	80 37.8	N38 48.3
Zuben'ubi	137 03.1	S16 06.4

	SHA	Mer. Pass.
	° ′	h m
Venus	62 59.7	15 00
Mars	39 27.9	16 32
Jupiter	163 43.6	8 15
Saturn	102 56.7	12 17

	UT	SUN GHA	SUN Dec	MOON GHA	v	MOON Dec	d	HP
	d h	° ′	° ′	° ′	′	° ′	′	′
	2 00	182 39.1	S21 58.8	153 12.9	11.4	S18 53.7	0.4	54.7
	01	197 38.9	59.1	167 43.3	11.4	18 53.3	0.5	54.7
	02	212 38.6	59.5	182 13.7	11.4	18 52.8	0.6	54.7
	03	227 38.4	21 59.9	196 44.1	11.4	18 52.2	0.7	54.7
	04	242 38.1	22 00.2	211 14.5	11.4	18 51.5	0.7	54.7
	05	257 37.9	00.6	225 44.9	11.3	18 50.8	0.9	54.7
	06	272 37.6	S22 00.9	240 15.2	11.4	S18 49.9	1.0	54.8
	07	287 37.4	01.3	254 45.6	11.3	18 48.9	1.0	54.8
	08	302 37.2	01.7	269 15.9	11.4	18 47.9	1.2	54.8
F	09	317 36.9	. . 02.0	283 46.3	11.3	18 46.7	1.2	54.8
R	10	332 36.7	02.4	298 16.6	11.3	18 45.5	1.3	54.8
I	11	347 36.4	02.8	312 46.9	11.3	18 44.2	1.5	54.8
D	12	2 36.2	S22 03.1	327 17.2	11.3	S18 42.7	1.5	54.9
A	13	17 35.9	03.5	341 47.5	11.3	18 41.2	1.6	54.9
Y	14	32 35.7	03.8	356 17.8	11.3	18 39.6	1.7	54.9
	15	47 35.4	. . 04.2	10 48.1	11.3	18 37.9	1.8	54.9
	16	62 35.2	04.5	25 18.4	11.3	18 36.1	1.9	54.9
	17	77 35.0	04.9	39 48.7	11.2	18 34.2	1.9	54.9
	18	92 34.7	S22 05.3	54 18.9	11.3	S18 32.3	2.1	55.0
	19	107 34.5	05.6	68 49.2	11.3	18 30.2	2.1	55.0
	20	122 34.2	06.0	83 19.5	11.2	18 28.1	2.3	55.0
	21	137 34.0	. . 06.3	97 49.7	11.3	18 25.8	2.3	55.0
	22	152 33.7	06.7	112 20.0	11.2	18 23.5	2.5	55.0
	23	167 33.5	07.0	126 50.2	11.3	18 21.0	2.5	55.0
	3 00	182 33.2	S22 07.4	141 20.5	11.2	S18 18.5	2.6	55.1
	01	197 33.0	07.7	155 50.7	11.3	18 15.9	2.7	55.1
	02	212 32.7	08.1	170 21.0	11.2	18 13.2	2.8	55.1
	03	227 32.5	. . 08.4	184 51.2	11.3	18 10.4	2.9	55.1
	04	242 32.2	08.8	199 21.5	11.2	18 07.5	2.9	55.1
	05	257 32.0	09.1	213 51.7	11.3	18 04.6	3.1	55.2
	06	272 31.7	S22 09.5	228 22.0	11.2	S18 01.5	3.2	55.2
S	07	287 31.5	09.8	242 52.2	11.2	17 58.3	3.2	55.2
	08	302 31.2	10.1	257 22.4	11.3	17 55.1	3.3	55.2
A	09	317 31.0	. . 10.5	271 52.7	11.2	17 51.8	3.5	55.2
T	10	332 30.7	10.8	286 22.9	11.3	17 48.3	3.5	55.2
U	11	347 30.5	11.2	300 53.2	11.2	17 44.8	3.6	55.3
R	12	2 30.2	S22 11.5	315 23.4	11.3	S17 41.2	3.7	55.3
D	13	17 30.0	11.9	329 53.7	11.2	17 37.5	3.8	55.3
A	14	32 29.7	12.2	344 23.9	11.3	17 33.7	3.8	55.3
Y	15	47 29.5	. . 12.5	358 54.2	11.2	17 29.9	4.0	55.3
	16	62 29.2	12.9	13 24.4	11.3	17 25.9	4.0	55.4
	17	77 29.0	13.2	27 54.7	11.2	17 21.9	4.2	55.4
	18	92 28.7	S22 13.5	42 24.9	11.3	S17 17.7	4.2	55.4
	19	107 28.5	13.9	56 55.2	11.2	17 13.5	4.3	55.4
	20	122 28.2	14.2	71 25.4	11.3	17 09.2	4.4	55.5
	21	137 28.0	. . 14.6	85 55.7	11.3	17 04.8	4.5	55.5
	22	152 27.7	14.9	100 26.0	11.2	17 00.3	4.6	55.5
	23	167 27.5	15.2	114 56.2	11.3	16 55.7	4.7	55.5
	4 00	182 27.2	S22 15.6	129 26.5	11.3	S16 51.0	4.7	55.5
	01	197 27.0	15.9	143 56.8	11.3	16 46.3	4.8	55.6
	02	212 26.7	16.2	158 27.1	11.3	16 41.5	5.0	55.6
	03	227 26.5	. . 16.5	172 57.4	11.2	16 36.5	5.0	55.6
	04	242 26.2	16.9	187 27.6	11.3	16 31.5	5.1	55.6
	05	257 25.9	17.2	201 57.9	11.3	16 26.4	5.1	55.7
	06	272 25.7	S22 17.5	216 28.2	11.4	S16 21.3	5.3	55.7
	07	287 25.4	17.9	230 58.6	11.3	16 16.0	5.4	55.7
	08	302 25.2	18.2	245 28.9	11.3	16 10.6	5.4	55.7
S	09	317 24.9	. . 18.5	259 59.2	11.3	16 05.2	5.5	55.7
U	10	332 24.7	18.8	274 29.5	11.3	15 59.7	5.6	55.8
N	11	347 24.4	19.2	288 59.8	11.4	15 54.1	5.7	55.8
D	12	2 24.2	S22 19.5	303 30.2	11.3	S15 48.4	5.8	55.8
A	13	17 23.9	19.8	318 00.5	11.3	15 42.6	5.8	55.8
Y	14	32 23.6	20.1	332 30.8	11.4	15 36.8	5.9	55.9
	15	47 23.4	. . 20.5	347 01.2	11.3	15 30.9	6.0	55.9
	16	62 23.1	20.8	1 31.5	11.4	15 24.9	6.1	55.9
	17	77 22.9	21.1	16 01.9	11.4	15 18.8	6.2	55.9
	18	92 22.6	S22 21.4	30 32.3	11.3	S15 12.6	6.3	56.0
	19	107 22.4	21.7	45 02.6	11.4	15 06.3	6.3	56.0
	20	122 22.1	22.0	59 33.0	11.4	15 00.0	6.4	56.0
	21	137 21.8	. . 22.4	74 03.4	11.4	14 53.6	6.5	56.0
	22	152 21.6	22.7	88 33.8	11.4	14 47.1	6.6	56.1
	23	167 21.3	23.0	103 04.2	11.3	S14 40.5	6.6	56.1
		SD 16.3	*d* 0.3	SD 14.9		15.1		15.2

Lat.	Twilight Naut.	Twilight Civil	Sunrise	Moonrise 2	Moonrise 3	Moonrise 4	Moonrise 5
°	h m	h m	h m	h m	h m	h m	h m
N 72	07 57	10 01	▬	▬	14 16	13 50	13 39
N 70	07 40	09 19	▬	12 49	13 06	13 13	13 15
68	07 26	08 50	10 51	12 01	12 29	12 46	12 56
66	07 15	08 28	09 55	11 30	12 03	12 26	12 42
64	07 05	08 11	09 22	11 07	11 43	12 09	12 29
62	06 57	07 57	08 59	10 48	11 26	11 56	12 19
60	06 49	07 45	08 40	10 33	11 12	11 44	12 10
N 58	06 43	07 34	08 24	10 20	11 01	11 34	12 02
56	06 37	07 25	08 11	10 09	10 50	11 25	11 55
54	06 31	07 16	07 59	09 59	10 41	11 18	11 49
52	06 26	07 09	07 49	09 50	10 33	11 11	11 43
50	06 21	07 02	07 40	09 43	10 26	11 04	11 38
45	06 10	06 47	07 21	09 26	10 10	10 51	11 27
N 40	06 01	06 35	07 05	09 12	09 58	10 39	11 18
35	05 52	06 24	06 52	09 01	09 47	10 30	11 10
30	05 44	06 14	06 40	08 50	09 37	10 21	11 03
20	05 29	05 56	06 20	08 33	09 21	10 07	10 51
N 10	05 14	05 40	06 03	08 18	09 06	09 54	10 41
0	04 58	05 24	05 46	08 03	08 53	09 42	10 31
S 10	04 40	05 07	05 30	07 49	08 39	09 30	10 21
20	04 19	04 48	05 12	07 34	08 25	09 17	10 10
30	03 51	04 24	04 51	07 17	08 08	09 02	09 58
35	03 34	04 10	04 39	07 06	07 59	08 54	09 51
40	03 12	03 53	04 25	06 55	07 48	08 44	09 43
45	02 44	03 32	04 08	06 41	07 35	08 33	09 34
S 50	02 04	03 04	03 47	06 25	07 19	08 19	09 23
52	01 41	02 51	03 37	06 17	07 12	08 12	09 17
54	01 09	02 35	03 26	06 08	07 03	08 05	09 12
56	////	02 15	03 13	05 58	06 54	07 57	09 05
58	////	01 51	02 58	05 47	06 44	07 48	08 58
S 60	////	01 16	02 40	05 34	06 32	07 37	08 50

Lat.	Sunset	Twilight Civil	Twilight Naut.	Moonset 2	Moonset 3	Moonset 4	Moonset 5
°	h m	h m	h m	h m	h m	h m	h m
N 72	▬	13 38	15 42	▬	16 00	18 09	20 02
N 70	▬	14 21	15 59	15 44	17 10	18 45	20 25
68	12 48	14 49	16 13	16 32	17 46	19 11	20 42
66	13 44	15 11	16 24	17 03	18 12	19 31	20 56
64	14 17	15 28	16 34	17 26	18 32	19 47	21 07
62	14 41	15 43	16 43	17 45	18 48	20 00	21 17
60	15 00	15 55	16 50	18 00	19 01	20 11	21 25
N 58	15 16	16 05	16 57	18 12	19 13	20 20	21 33
56	15 29	16 15	17 03	18 23	19 23	20 29	21 39
54	15 41	16 23	17 09	18 33	19 32	20 36	21 45
52	15 51	16 31	17 14	18 42	19 40	20 43	21 50
50	16 00	16 38	17 18	18 50	19 47	20 49	21 54
45	16 19	16 52	17 29	19 06	20 02	21 01	22 04
N 40	16 35	17 05	17 39	19 20	20 14	21 12	22 12
35	16 48	17 16	17 47	19 31	20 25	21 21	22 20
30	17 00	17 26	17 55	19 41	20 34	21 29	22 26
20	17 20	17 44	18 11	19 58	20 50	21 43	22 36
N 10	17 37	18 00	18 26	20 13	21 04	21 54	22 46
0	17 54	18 16	18 42	20 27	21 16	22 05	22 54
S 10	18 10	18 33	19 00	20 41	21 29	22 16	23 03
20	18 28	18 52	19 21	20 56	21 43	22 28	23 12
30	18 49	19 16	19 49	21 13	21 58	22 41	23 22
35	19 01	19 30	20 06	21 23	22 07	22 49	23 28
40	19 15	19 48	20 28	21 34	22 18	22 58	23 35
45	19 32	20 09	20 57	21 47	22 30	23 08	23 43
S 50	19 53	20 36	21 37	22 03	22 44	23 20	23 52
52	20 03	20 50	22 01	22 11	22 51	23 26	23 57
54	20 15	21 06	22 34	22 19	22 58	23 32	24 01
56	20 28	21 26	////	22 29	23 07	23 39	24 07
58	20 43	21 51	////	22 39	23 16	23 47	24 12
S 60	21 01	22 27	////	22 52	23 27	23 56	24 19

Day	SUN Eqn. of Time 00^h	SUN Eqn. of Time 12^h	SUN Mer. Pass.	MOON Mer. Pass. Upper	MOON Mer. Pass. Lower	MOON Age	MOON Phase
d	m s	m s	h m	h m	h m	d %	
2	10 37	10 25	11 50	14 15	01 51	03 8	
3	10 13	10 01	11 50	15 05	02 40	04 14	
4	09 49	09 37	11 50	15 54	03 29	05 22	

UT d	UT h	ARIES GHA	VENUS −4·2 GHA	VENUS Dec	MARS +0·7 GHA	MARS Dec	JUPITER −1·8 GHA	JUPITER Dec	SATURN +0·4 GHA	SATURN Dec
		° ′	° ′	° ′	° ′	° ′	° ′	° ′	° ′	° ′
5	00	74 13.4	134 43.5	S23 07.3	112 12.6	S16 21.6	237 38.7	S 5 45.5	176 55.0	S21 36.9
	01	89 15.9	149 42.9	06.7	127 13.2	21.0	252 40.8	45.7	191 57.2	36.9
	02	104 18.3	164 42.2	06.1	142 13.8	20.4	267 42.9	45.8	206 59.3	36.9
	03	119 20.8	179 41.6	. . 05.5	157 14.4	. . 19.7	282 44.9	. . 45.9	222 01.5	. . 37.0
	04	134 23.3	194 41.0	04.9	172 15.1	19.1	297 47.0	46.1	237 03.6	37.0
	05	149 25.7	209 40.3	04.3	187 15.7	18.5	312 49.1	46.2	252 05.8	37.0
	06	164 28.2	224 39.7	S23 03.7	202 16.3	S16 17.8	327 51.2	S 5 46.4	267 07.9	S21 37.0
	07	179 30.7	239 39.1	03.1	217 16.9	17.2	342 53.3	46.5	282 10.1	37.1
	08	194 33.1	254 38.4	02.5	232 17.5	16.6	357 55.4	46.7	297 12.2	37.1
M	09	209 35.6	269 37.8	. . 02.0	247 18.2	. . 15.9	12 57.5	. . 46.8	312 14.4	. . 37.1
O	10	224 38.1	284 37.2	01.4	262 18.8	15.3	27 59.5	47.0	327 16.5	37.2
N	11	239 40.5	299 36.5	00.8	277 19.4	14.7	43 01.6	47.1	342 18.7	37.2
D	12	254 43.0	314 35.9	S23 00.2	292 20.0	S16 14.0	58 03.7	S 5 47.3	357 20.8	S21 37.2
A	13	269 45.4	329 35.3	22 59.6	307 20.6	13.4	73 05.8	47.4	12 23.0	37.2
Y	14	284 47.9	344 34.6	58.9	322 21.3	12.8	88 07.9	47.6	27 25.1	37.3
	15	299 50.4	359 34.0	. . 58.3	337 21.9	. . 12.1	103 10.0	. . 47.7	42 27.2	. . 37.3
	16	314 52.8	14 33.4	57.7	352 22.5	11.5	118 12.1	47.9	57 29.4	37.3
	17	329 55.3	29 32.8	57.1	7 23.1	10.8	133 14.2	48.0	72 31.5	37.4
	18	344 57.8	44 32.1	S22 56.5	22 23.7	S16 10.2	148 16.2	S 5 48.2	87 33.7	S21 37.4
	19	0 00.2	59 31.5	55.9	37 24.4	09.6	163 18.3	48.3	102 35.8	37.4
	20	15 02.7	74 30.9	55.3	52 25.0	08.9	178 20.4	48.4	117 38.0	37.4
	21	30 05.2	89 30.3	. . 54.7	67 25.6	. . 08.3	193 22.5	. . 48.6	132 40.1	. . 37.5
	22	45 07.6	104 29.6	54.1	82 26.2	07.7	208 24.6	48.7	147 42.3	37.5
	23	60 10.1	119 29.0	53.5	97 26.8	07.0	223 26.7	48.9	162 44.4	37.5
6	00	75 12.6	134 28.4	S22 52.9	112 27.5	S16 06.4	238 28.8	S 5 49.0	177 46.6	S21 37.5
	01	90 15.0	149 27.8	52.3	127 28.1	05.8	253 30.9	49.2	192 48.7	37.6
	02	105 17.5	164 27.2	51.6	142 28.7	05.1	268 33.0	49.3	207 50.9	37.6
	03	120 19.9	179 26.5	. . 51.0	157 29.3	. . 04.5	283 35.1	. . 49.5	222 53.0	. . 37.6
	04	135 22.4	194 25.9	50.4	172 30.0	03.8	298 37.1	49.6	237 55.2	37.7
	05	150 24.9	209 25.3	49.8	187 30.6	03.2	313 39.2	49.8	252 57.3	37.7
	06	165 27.3	224 24.7	S22 49.2	202 31.2	S16 02.6	328 41.3	S 5 49.9	267 59.5	S21 37.7
	07	180 29.8	239 24.1	48.5	217 31.8	01.9	343 43.4	50.1	283 01.6	37.7
T	08	195 32.3	254 23.4	47.9	232 32.5	01.3	358 45.5	50.2	298 03.8	37.8
U	09	210 34.7	269 22.8	. . 47.3	247 33.1	. . 00.6	13 47.6	. . 50.3	313 05.9	. . 37.8
E	10	225 37.2	284 22.2	46.7	262 33.7	16 00.0	28 49.7	50.5	328 08.1	37.8
S	11	240 39.7	299 21.6	46.1	277 34.3	15 59.4	43 51.8	50.6	343 10.2	37.9
D	12	255 42.1	314 21.0	S22 45.4	292 35.0	S15 58.7	58 53.9	S 5 50.8	358 12.4	S21 37.9
A	13	270 44.6	329 20.4	44.8	307 35.6	58.1	73 56.0	50.9	13 14.5	37.9
Y	14	285 47.1	344 19.8	44.2	322 36.2	57.4	88 58.0	51.1	28 16.7	37.9
	15	300 49.5	359 19.2	. . 43.5	337 36.8	. . 56.8	104 00.1	. . 51.2	43 18.8	. . 38.0
	16	315 52.0	14 18.5	42.9	352 37.5	56.2	119 02.2	51.4	58 21.0	38.0
	17	330 54.4	29 17.9	42.3	7 38.1	55.5	134 04.3	51.5	73 23.1	38.0
	18	345 56.9	44 17.3	S22 41.7	22 38.7	S15 54.9	149 06.4	S 5 51.7	88 25.2	S21 38.1
	19	0 59.4	59 16.7	41.0	37 39.3	54.2	164 08.5	51.8	103 27.4	38.1
	20	16 01.8	74 16.1	40.4	52 40.0	53.6	179 10.6	51.9	118 29.5	38.1
	21	31 04.3	89 15.5	. . 39.8	67 40.6	. . 53.0	194 12.7	. . 52.1	133 31.7	. . 38.1
	22	46 06.8	104 14.9	39.1	82 41.2	52.3	209 14.8	52.2	148 33.8	38.2
	23	61 09.2	119 14.3	38.5	97 41.8	51.7	224 16.9	52.4	163 36.0	38.2
7	00	76 11.7	134 13.7	S22 37.8	112 42.5	S15 51.0	239 19.0	S 5 52.5	178 38.1	S21 38.2
	01	91 14.2	149 13.1	37.2	127 43.1	50.4	254 21.1	52.7	193 40.3	38.3
	02	106 16.6	164 12.5	36.6	142 43.7	49.7	269 23.2	52.8	208 42.4	38.3
	03	121 19.1	179 11.9	. . 35.9	157 44.3	. . 49.1	284 25.3	. . 53.0	223 44.6	. . 38.3
	04	136 21.5	194 11.3	35.3	172 45.0	48.4	299 27.3	53.1	238 46.7	38.3
	05	151 24.0	209 10.7	34.6	187 45.6	47.8	314 29.4	53.2	253 48.9	38.4
	06	166 26.5	224 10.1	S22 34.0	202 46.2	S15 47.2	329 31.5	S 5 53.4	268 51.0	S21 38.4
W	07	181 28.9	239 09.5	33.4	217 46.8	46.5	344 33.6	53.5	283 53.2	38.4
E	08	196 31.4	254 08.9	32.7	232 47.5	45.9	359 35.7	53.7	298 55.3	38.4
D	09	211 33.9	269 08.3	. . 32.1	247 48.1	. . 45.2	14 37.8	. . 53.8	313 57.5	. . 38.5
N	10	226 36.3	284 07.7	31.4	262 48.7	44.6	29 39.9	54.0	328 59.6	38.5
E	11	241 38.8	299 07.1	30.8	277 49.4	43.9	44 42.0	54.1	344 01.8	38.5
S	12	256 41.3	314 06.5	S22 30.1	292 50.0	S15 43.3	59 44.1	S 5 54.2	359 03.9	S21 38.6
D	13	271 43.7	329 05.9	29.5	307 50.6	42.6	74 46.2	54.4	14 06.1	38.6
A	14	286 46.2	344 05.3	28.8	322 51.2	42.0	89 48.3	54.5	29 08.2	38.6
Y	15	301 48.7	359 04.7	. . 28.2	337 51.9	. . 41.3	104 50.4	. . 54.7	44 10.4	. . 38.6
	16	316 51.1	14 04.1	27.5	352 52.5	40.7	119 52.5	54.8	59 12.5	38.7
	17	331 53.6	29 03.5	26.8	7 53.1	40.1	134 54.6	55.0	74 14.6	38.7
	18	346 56.0	44 02.9	S22 26.2	22 53.8	S15 39.4	149 56.7	S 5 55.1	89 16.8	S21 38.7
	19	1 58.5	59 02.3	25.5	37 54.4	38.8	164 58.8	55.2	104 18.9	38.8
	20	17 01.0	74 01.8	24.9	52 55.0	38.1	180 00.9	55.4	119 21.1	38.8
	21	32 03.4	89 01.2	. . 24.2	67 55.6	. . 37.5	195 03.0	. . 55.5	134 23.2	. . 38.8
	22	47 05.9	104 00.6	23.6	82 56.3	36.8	210 05.1	55.7	149 25.4	38.8
	23	62 08.4	119 00.0	22.9	97 56.9	36.2	225 07.2	55.8	164 27.5	38.9
Mer. Pass.		h m 18 56.1	v −0.6	d 0.6	v 0.6	d 0.6	v 2.1	d 0.1	v 2.1	d 0.0

STARS Name	SHA	Dec
	° ′	° ′
Acamar	315 16.2	S40 14.5
Achernar	335 24.8	S57 09.4
Acrux	173 06.8	S63 11.2
Adhara	255 10.3	S28 59.8
Aldebaran	290 46.3	N16 32.4
Alioth	166 19.0	N55 51.9
Alkaid	152 57.5	N49 13.7
Al Na'ir	27 41.0	S46 52.9
Alnilam	275 43.7	S 1 11.7
Alphard	217 53.7	S 8 43.9
Alphecca	126 09.4	N26 39.6
Alpheratz	357 40.9	N29 11.2
Altair	62 06.2	N 8 55.0
Ankaa	353 13.3	S42 13.1
Antares	112 23.8	S26 27.9
Arcturus	145 53.9	N19 05.8
Atria	107 24.0	S69 03.2
Avior	234 16.6	S59 33.7
Bellatrix	278 29.2	N 6 21.7
Betelgeuse	270 58.4	N 7 24.4
Canopus	263 54.6	S52 42.4
Capella	280 30.5	N46 00.7
Deneb	49 30.1	N45 20.8
Denebola	182 31.4	N14 28.6
Diphda	348 53.4	S17 53.8
Dubhe	193 49.0	N61 39.3
Elnath	278 09.3	N28 37.1
Eltanin	90 45.6	N51 29.5
Enif	33 44.9	N 9 57.3
Fomalhaut	15 21.5	S29 32.1
Gacrux	171 58.4	S57 12.1
Gienah	175 50.0	S17 38.0
Hadar	148 44.9	S60 26.9
Hamal	327 57.8	N23 32.5
Kaus Aust.	83 41.1	S34 22.4
Kochab	137 21.3	N74 05.1
Markab	13 36.0	N15 17.9
Menkar	314 12.3	N 4 09.2
Menkent	148 05.1	S36 26.9
Miaplacidus	221 38.6	S69 47.0
Mirfak	308 36.5	N49 55.2
Nunki	75 55.8	S26 16.4
Peacock	53 16.1	S56 40.9
Pollux	243 24.6	N27 58.9
Procyon	244 57.0	N 5 10.7
Rasalhague	96 04.6	N12 33.1
Regulus	207 41.0	N11 53.0
Rigel	281 09.5	S 8 11.1
Rigil Kent.	139 49.0	S60 53.9
Sabik	102 10.2	S15 44.5
Schedar	349 37.5	N56 38.0
Shaula	96 19.2	S37 06.7
Sirius	258 31.3	S16 44.5
Spica	158 29.0	S11 14.8
Suhail	222 50.4	S43 29.9
Vega	80 37.8	N38 48.3
Zuben'ubi	137 03.1	S16 06.4

	SHA	Mer. Pass.
	° ′	h m
Venus	59 15.8	15 03
Mars	37 14.9	16 29
Jupiter	163 16.2	8 05
Saturn	102 34.0	12 07

UT		SUN GHA	SUN Dec	MOON GHA	v	MOON Dec	d	HP
d h		° ′	° ′	° ′	′	° ′	′	′
5 00		182 21.1	S22 23.3	117 34.5	11.4	S14 33.9	6.8	56.1
01		197 20.8	23.6	132 04.9	11.4	14 27.1	6.8	56.1
02		212 20.5	23.9	146 35.3	11.5	14 20.3	6.9	56.2
03		227 20.3	. . 24.2	161 05.8	11.4	14 13.4	6.9	56.2
04		242 20.0	24.6	175 36.2	11.4	14 06.5	7.1	56.2
05		257 19.8	24.9	190 06.6	11.4	13 59.4	7.1	56.2
06		272 19.5	S22 25.2	204 37.0	11.4	S13 52.3	7.2	56.3
07		287 19.2	25.5	219 07.4	11.5	13 45.1	7.3	56.3
08		302 19.0	25.8	233 37.9	11.4	13 37.8	7.3	56.3
09	M	317 18.7	. . 26.1	248 08.3	11.4	13 30.5	7.4	56.4
10	O	332 18.5	26.4	262 38.7	11.5	13 23.1	7.5	56.4
11	N	347 18.2	26.7	277 09.2	11.4	13 15.6	7.6	56.4
12	D	2 17.9	S22 27.0	291 39.6	11.5	S13 08.0	7.6	56.4
13	A	17 17.7	27.3	306 10.1	11.4	13 00.4	7.7	56.5
14	Y	32 17.4	27.6	320 40.5	11.5	12 52.7	7.8	56.5
15		47 17.1	. . 27.9	335 11.0	11.5	12 44.9	7.8	56.5
16		62 16.9	28.2	349 41.5	11.4	12 37.1	8.0	56.6
17		77 16.6	28.5	4 11.9	11.5	12 29.1	8.0	56.6
18		92 16.4	S22 28.8	18 42.4	11.4	S12 21.1	8.0	56.6
19		107 16.1	29.1	33 12.8	11.5	12 13.1	8.2	56.6
20		122 15.8	29.4	47 43.3	11.5	12 04.9	8.2	56.7
21		137 15.6	. . 29.7	62 13.8	11.4	11 56.7	8.2	56.7
22		152 15.3	30.0	76 44.2	11.5	11 48.5	8.4	56.7
23		167 15.0	30.3	91 14.7	11.5	11 40.1	8.4	56.8
6 00		182 14.8	S22 30.6	105 45.2	11.4	S11 31.7	8.4	56.8
01		197 14.5	30.9	120 15.6	11.5	11 23.3	8.6	56.8
02		212 14.2	31.2	134 46.1	11.5	11 14.7	8.6	56.8
03		227 14.0	. . 31.5	149 16.6	11.4	11 06.1	8.6	56.9
04		242 13.7	31.8	163 47.0	11.5	10 57.5	8.8	56.9
05		257 13.4	32.1	178 17.5	11.5	10 48.7	8.8	56.9
06		272 13.2	S22 32.4	192 48.0	11.4	S10 39.9	8.8	57.0
07		287 12.9	32.7	207 18.4	11.5	10 31.1	9.0	57.0
08	T	302 12.6	33.0	221 48.9	11.4	10 22.1	8.9	57.0
09	U	317 12.4	. . 33.3	236 19.3	11.5	10 13.2	9.1	57.1
10	E	332 12.1	33.6	250 49.8	11.4	10 04.1	9.1	57.1
11	S	347 11.8	33.8	265 20.2	11.5	9 55.0	9.2	57.1
12	D	2 11.6	S22 34.1	279 50.7	11.4	S 9 45.8	9.2	57.2
13	A	17 11.3	34.4	294 21.1	11.5	9 36.6	9.3	57.2
14	Y	32 11.0	34.7	308 51.6	11.4	9 27.3	9.3	57.2
15		47 10.8	. . 35.0	323 22.0	11.4	9 18.0	9.4	57.2
16		62 10.5	35.3	337 52.4	11.4	9 08.6	9.5	57.3
17		77 10.2	35.5	352 22.8	11.4	8 59.1	9.5	57.3
18		92 10.0	S22 35.8	6 53.2	11.4	S 8 49.6	9.6	57.3
19		107 09.7	36.1	21 23.6	11.4	8 40.0	9.6	57.4
20		122 09.4	36.4	35 54.0	11.4	8 30.4	9.7	57.4
21		137 09.2	. . 36.7	50 24.4	11.4	8 20.7	9.7	57.4
22		152 08.9	37.0	64 54.8	11.3	8 11.0	9.8	57.5
23		167 08.6	37.2	79 25.1	11.4	8 01.2	9.8	57.5
7 00		182 08.4	S22 37.5	93 55.5	11.3	S 7 51.4	9.9	57.5
01		197 08.1	37.8	108 25.8	11.4	7 41.5	10.0	57.6
02		212 07.8	38.1	122 56.2	11.3	7 31.5	9.9	57.6
03		227 07.5	. . 38.3	137 26.5	11.3	7 21.6	10.1	57.6
04		242 07.3	38.6	151 56.8	11.3	7 11.5	10.1	57.7
05		257 07.0	38.9	166 27.1	11.3	7 01.4	10.1	57.7
06		272 06.7	S22 39.2	180 57.4	11.2	S 6 51.3	10.2	57.7
07	W	287 06.5	39.4	195 27.6	11.3	6 41.1	10.2	57.8
08	E	302 06.2	39.7	209 57.9	11.2	6 30.9	10.3	57.8
09	D	317 05.9	. . 40.0	224 28.1	11.2	6 20.6	10.3	57.8
10	N	332 05.6	40.2	238 58.3	11.2	6 10.3	10.4	57.9
11	E	347 05.4	40.5	253 28.5	11.2	5 59.9	10.4	57.9
12	S	2 05.1	S22 40.8	267 58.7	11.2	S 5 49.5	10.5	57.9
13	D	17 04.8	41.1	282 28.9	11.1	5 39.0	10.5	58.0
14	A	32 04.6	41.3	296 59.0	11.2	5 28.5	10.5	58.0
15	Y	47 04.3	. . 41.6	311 29.2	11.1	5 18.0	10.6	58.0
16		62 04.0	41.9	325 59.3	11.1	5 07.4	10.6	58.1
17		77 03.7	42.1	340 29.4	11.0	4 56.8	10.7	58.1
18		92 03.5	S22 42.4	354 59.4	11.1	S 4 46.1	10.7	58.1
19		107 03.2	42.6	9 29.5	11.0	4 35.4	10.7	58.2
20		122 02.9	42.9	23 59.5	11.0	4 24.7	10.8	58.2
21		137 02.6	. . 43.2	38 29.5	11.0	4 13.9	10.8	58.2
22		152 02.4	43.4	52 59.5	10.9	4 03.1	10.8	58.3
23		167 02.1	43.7	67 29.4	11.0	S 3 52.3	10.9	58.3
		SD 16.3	*d* 0.3	SD		15.4	15.6	15.8

Lat.	Twilight Naut.	Twilight Civil	Sunrise	Moonrise 5	Moonrise 6	Moonrise 7	Moonrise 8
°	h m	h m	h m	h m	h m	h m	h m
N 72	08 04	10 15	■	13 39	13 30	13 23	13 16
N 70	07 47	09 28	■	13 15	13 15	13 15	13 14
68	07 32	08 57	11 13	12 56	13 03	13 08	13 13
66	07 20	08 35	10 05	12 42	12 53	13 03	13 11
64	07 10	08 17	09 30	12 29	12 45	12 58	13 10
62	07 01	08 02	09 05	12 19	12 38	12 54	13 09
60	06 53	07 49	08 45	12 10	12 31	12 51	13 08
N 58	06 47	07 38	08 29	12 02	12 26	12 47	13 08
56	06 40	07 29	08 15	11 55	12 21	12 45	13 07
54	06 35	07 20	08 03	11 49	12 17	12 42	13 06
52	06 29	07 12	07 53	11 43	12 13	12 40	13 06
50	06 24	07 05	07 43	11 38	12 09	12 38	13 05
45	06 13	06 50	07 24	11 27	12 01	12 33	13 04
N 40	06 04	06 37	07 08	11 18	11 54	12 29	13 03
35	05 55	06 26	06 54	11 10	11 49	12 26	13 03
30	05 46	06 16	06 42	11 03	11 44	12 23	13 02
20	05 31	05 58	06 22	10 51	11 35	12 18	13 01
N 10	05 15	05 42	06 04	10 41	11 27	12 13	13 00
0	04 59	05 25	05 47	10 31	11 20	12 09	12 59
S 10	04 41	05 08	05 31	10 21	11 13	12 05	12 58
20	04 19	04 48	05 12	10 10	11 05	12 00	12 57
30	03 51	04 24	04 51	09 58	10 56	11 55	12 56
35	03 33	04 10	04 39	09 51	10 51	11 52	12 55
40	03 11	03 52	04 25	09 43	10 45	11 49	12 54
45	02 42	03 31	04 07	09 34	10 38	11 45	12 54
S 50	02 01	03 03	03 46	09 23	10 30	11 40	12 53
52	01 36	02 49	03 36	09 17	10 26	11 38	12 52
54	01 01	02 32	03 24	09 12	10 22	11 36	12 52
56	////	02 12	03 11	09 05	10 17	11 33	12 51
58	////	01 46	02 55	08 58	10 12	11 30	12 51
S 60	////	01 08	02 37	08 50	10 06	11 27	12 50

Lat.	Sunset	Twilight Civil	Twilight Naut.	Moonset 5	Moonset 6	Moonset 7	Moonset 8
°	h m	h m	h m	h m	h m	h m	h m
N 72	■	13 27	15 37	20 02	21 53	23 43	25 36
N 70	■	14 14	15 55	20 25	22 06	23 49	25 34
68	12 29	14 45	16 10	20 42	22 16	23 53	25 33
66	13 37	15 07	16 22	20 56	22 25	23 57	25 32
64	14 12	15 25	16 32	21 07	22 32	24 00	00 00
62	14 37	15 40	16 41	21 17	22 39	24 03	00 03
60	14 57	15 53	16 49	21 25	22 44	24 06	00 06
N 58	15 13	16 04	16 56	21 33	22 49	24 08	00 08
56	15 27	16 13	17 02	21 39	22 53	24 10	00 10
54	15 39	16 22	17 08	21 45	22 57	24 11	00 11
52	15 49	16 30	17 13	21 50	23 00	24 13	00 13
50	15 59	16 37	17 18	21 54	23 03	24 14	00 14
45	16 19	16 52	17 29	22 04	23 10	24 17	00 17
N 40	16 35	17 05	17 39	22 12	23 15	24 20	00 20
35	16 48	17 16	17 48	22 20	23 20	24 22	00 22
30	17 00	17 26	17 56	22 26	23 24	24 24	00 24
20	17 20	17 44	18 12	22 36	23 31	24 27	00 27
N 10	17 38	18 01	18 27	22 46	23 37	24 30	00 30
0	17 55	18 17	18 43	22 54	23 43	24 33	00 33
S 10	18 12	18 35	19 02	23 03	23 49	24 35	00 35
20	18 30	18 54	19 23	23 12	23 55	24 38	00 38
30	18 51	19 18	19 51	23 22	24 02	00 02	00 41
35	19 04	19 33	20 09	23 28	24 06	00 06	00 43
40	19 18	19 51	20 32	23 35	24 10	00 10	00 45
45	19 35	20 12	21 01	23 43	24 16	00 16	00 47
S 50	19 57	20 40	21 43	23 52	24 22	00 22	00 50
52	20 07	20 55	22 08	23 57	24 25	00 25	00 51
54	20 19	21 11	22 44	24 01	00 01	00 28	00 52
56	20 32	21 32	////	24 07	00 07	00 31	00 54
58	20 48	21 58	////	24 12	00 12	00 35	00 55
S 60	21 07	22 37	////	24 19	00 19	00 39	00 57

Day	SUN Eqn. of Time 00^h	SUN Eqn. of Time 12^h	SUN Mer. Pass.	MOON Mer. Pass. Upper	MOON Mer. Pass. Lower	MOON Age	MOON Phase
d	m s	m s	h m	h m	h m	d	%
5	09 25	09 12	11 51	16 43	04 18	06	31
6	09 00	08 47	11 51	17 32	05 07	07	41
7	08 34	08 21	11 52	18 21	05 56	08	51

Day	UT (d h)	ARIES GHA	VENUS −4·2 GHA	VENUS Dec	MARS +0·7 GHA	MARS Dec	JUPITER −1·8 GHA	JUPITER Dec	SATURN +0·4 GHA	SATURN Dec
		° ′	° ′	° ′	° ′	° ′	° ′	° ′	° ′	° ′
THURSDAY	8 00	77 10.8	133 59.4	S22 22.2	112 57.5	S15 35.5	240 09.3	S 5 56.0	179 29.7	S21 38.9
	01	92 13.3	148 58.8	21.6	127 58.2	34.9	255 11.4	56.1	194 31.8	38.9
	02	107 15.8	163 58.2	20.9	142 58.8	34.2	270 13.5	56.2	209 34.0	38.9
	03	122 18.2	178 57.6	. . 20.2	157 59.4	. . 33.6	285 15.6	. . 56.4	224 36.1	. . 39.0
	04	137 20.7	193 57.1	19.6	173 00.0	32.9	300 17.6	56.5	239 38.3	39.0
	05	152 23.2	208 56.5	18.9	188 00.7	32.3	315 19.7	56.7	254 40.4	39.0
	06	167 25.6	223 55.9	S22 18.2	203 01.3	S15 31.6	330 21.8	S 5 56.8	269 42.6	S21 39.1
	07	182 28.1	238 55.3	17.6	218 01.9	31.0	345 23.9	57.0	284 44.7	39.1
	08	197 30.5	253 54.7	16.9	233 02.6	30.3	0 26.0	57.1	299 46.9	39.1
	09	212 33.0	268 54.2	. . 16.2	248 03.2	. . 29.7	15 28.1	. . 57.2	314 49.0	. . 39.1
	10	227 35.5	283 53.6	15.5	263 03.8	29.0	30 30.2	57.4	329 51.2	39.2
	11	242 37.9	298 53.0	14.9	278 04.5	28.4	45 32.3	57.5	344 53.3	39.2
	12	257 40.4	313 52.4	S22 14.2	293 05.1	S15 27.7	60 34.4	S 5 57.7	359 55.5	S21 39.2
	13	272 42.9	328 51.8	13.5	308 05.7	27.1	75 36.5	57.8	14 57.6	39.2
	14	287 45.3	343 51.3	12.8	323 06.4	26.4	90 38.6	57.9	29 59.7	39.3
	15	302 47.8	358 50.7	. . 12.2	338 07.0	. . 25.8	105 40.7	. . 58.1	45 01.9	. . 39.3
	16	317 50.3	13 50.1	11.5	353 07.6	25.1	120 42.8	58.2	60 04.0	39.3
	17	332 52.7	28 49.5	10.8	8 08.3	24.4	135 44.9	58.4	75 06.2	39.4
	18	347 55.2	43 49.0	S22 10.1	23 08.9	S15 23.8	150 47.0	S 5 58.5	90 08.3	S21 39.4
	19	2 57.6	58 48.4	09.5	38 09.5	23.1	165 49.1	58.6	105 10.5	39.4
	20	18 00.1	73 47.8	08.8	53 10.2	22.5	180 51.2	58.8	120 12.6	39.4
	21	33 02.6	88 47.3	. . 08.1	68 10.8	. . 21.8	195 53.3	. . 58.9	135 14.8	. . 39.5
	22	48 05.0	103 46.7	07.4	83 11.4	21.2	210 55.4	59.1	150 16.9	39.5
	23	63 07.5	118 46.1	06.7	98 12.1	20.5	225 57.5	59.2	165 19.1	39.5
FRIDAY	9 00	78 10.0	133 45.5	S22 06.0	113 12.7	S15 19.9	240 59.6	S 5 59.4	180 21.2	S21 39.5
	01	93 12.4	148 45.0	05.3	128 13.3	19.2	256 01.7	59.5	195 23.4	39.6
	02	108 14.9	163 44.4	04.7	143 14.0	18.6	271 03.8	59.6	210 25.5	39.6
	03	123 17.4	178 43.8	. . 04.0	158 14.6	. . 17.9	286 05.9	. . 59.8	225 27.7	. . 39.6
	04	138 19.8	193 43.3	03.3	173 15.2	17.2	301 08.0	5 59.9	240 29.8	39.7
	05	153 22.3	208 42.7	02.6	188 15.9	16.6	316 10.2	6 00.1	255 32.0	39.7
	06	168 24.8	223 42.1	S22 01.9	203 16.5	S15 15.9	331 12.3	S 6 00.2	270 34.1	S21 39.7
	07	183 27.2	238 41.6	01.2	218 17.1	15.3	346 14.4	00.3	285 36.3	39.7
	08	198 29.7	253 41.0	22 00.5	233 17.8	14.6	1 16.5	00.5	300 38.4	39.8
	09	213 32.1	268 40.5	21 59.8	248 18.4	. . 14.0	16 18.6	. . 00.6	315 40.6	. . 39.8
	10	228 34.6	283 39.9	59.1	263 19.0	13.3	31 20.7	00.8	330 42.7	39.8
	11	243 37.1	298 39.3	58.4	278 19.7	12.6	46 22.8	00.9	345 44.8	39.8
	12	258 39.5	313 38.8	S21 57.7	293 20.3	S15 12.0	61 24.9	S 6 01.0	0 47.0	S21 39.9
	13	273 42.0	328 38.2	57.0	308 20.9	11.3	76 27.0	01.2	15 49.1	39.9
	14	288 44.5	343 37.7	56.3	323 21.6	10.7	91 29.1	01.3	30 51.3	39.9
	15	303 46.9	358 37.1	. . 55.6	338 22.2	. . 10.0	106 31.2	. . 01.4	45 53.4	. . 40.0
	16	318 49.4	13 36.5	54.9	353 22.8	09.4	121 33.3	01.6	60 55.6	40.0
	17	333 51.9	28 36.0	54.2	8 23.5	08.7	136 35.4	01.7	75 57.7	40.0
	18	348 54.3	43 35.4	S21 53.5	23 24.1	S15 08.0	151 37.5	S 6 01.9	90 59.9	S21 40.0
	19	3 56.8	58 34.9	52.8	38 24.8	07.4	166 39.6	02.0	106 02.0	40.1
	20	18 59.3	73 34.3	52.1	53 25.4	06.7	181 41.7	02.1	121 04.2	40.1
	21	34 01.7	88 33.8	. . 51.4	68 26.0	. . 06.1	196 43.8	. . 02.3	136 06.3	. . 40.1
	22	49 04.2	103 33.2	50.7	83 26.7	05.4	211 45.9	02.4	151 08.5	40.1
	23	64 06.6	118 32.7	50.0	98 27.3	04.7	226 48.0	02.6	166 10.6	40.2
SATURDAY	10 00	79 09.1	133 32.1	S21 49.3	113 27.9	S15 04.1	241 50.1	S 6 02.7	181 12.8	S21 40.2
	01	94 11.6	148 31.6	48.6	128 28.6	03.4	256 52.2	02.8	196 14.9	40.2
	02	109 14.0	163 31.0	47.8	143 29.2	02.8	271 54.3	03.0	211 17.1	40.3
	03	124 16.5	178 30.5	. . 47.1	158 29.9	. . 02.1	286 56.4	. . 03.1	226 19.2	. . 40.3
	04	139 19.0	193 29.9	46.4	173 30.5	01.4	301 58.5	03.3	241 21.4	40.3
	05	154 21.4	208 29.4	45.7	188 31.1	00.8	317 00.7	03.4	256 23.5	40.3
	06	169 23.9	223 28.8	S21 45.0	203 31.8	S15 00.1	332 02.8	S 6 03.5	271 25.7	S21 40.4
	07	184 26.4	238 28.3	44.3	218 32.4	14 59.5	347 04.9	03.7	286 27.8	40.4
	08	199 28.8	253 27.7	43.6	233 33.0	58.8	2 07.0	03.8	301 29.9	40.4
	09	214 31.3	268 27.2	. . 42.8	248 33.7	. . 58.1	17 09.1	. . 03.9	316 32.1	. . 40.4
	10	229 33.7	283 26.7	42.1	263 34.3	57.5	32 11.2	04.1	331 34.2	40.5
	11	244 36.2	298 26.1	41.4	278 35.0	56.8	47 13.3	04.2	346 36.4	40.5
	12	259 38.7	313 25.6	S21 40.7	293 35.6	S14 56.1	62 15.4	S 6 04.4	1 38.5	S21 40.5
	13	274 41.1	328 25.0	39.9	308 36.2	55.5	77 17.5	04.5	16 40.7	40.5
	14	289 43.6	343 24.5	39.2	323 36.9	54.8	92 19.6	04.6	31 42.8	40.6
	15	304 46.1	358 24.0	. . 38.5	338 37.5	. . 54.1	107 21.7	. . 04.8	46 45.0	. . 40.6
	16	319 48.5	13 23.4	37.8	353 38.2	53.5	122 23.8	04.9	61 47.1	40.6
	17	334 51.0	28 22.9	37.0	8 38.8	52.8	137 25.9	05.0	76 49.3	40.7
	18	349 53.5	43 22.3	S21 36.3	23 39.4	S14 52.2	152 28.0	S 6 05.2	91 51.4	S21 40.7
	19	4 55.9	58 21.8	35.6	38 40.1	51.5	167 30.2	05.3	106 53.6	40.7
	20	19 58.4	73 21.3	34.9	53 40.7	50.8	182 32.3	05.5	121 55.7	40.7
	21	35 00.9	88 20.7	. . 34.1	68 41.4	. . 50.2	197 34.4	. . 05.6	136 57.9	. . 40.8
	22	50 03.3	103 20.2	33.4	83 42.0	49.5	212 36.5	05.7	152 00.0	40.8
	23	65 05.8	118 19.7	32.7	98 42.6	48.8	227 38.6	05.9	167 02.2	40.8
	Mer. Pass.	h m 18 44.3	v −0.6	d 0.7	v 0.6	d 0.7	v 2.1	d 0.1	v 2.1	d 0.0

STARS

Name	SHA	Dec
	° ′	° ′
Acamar	315 16.3	S40 14.5
Achernar	335 24.8	S57 09.4
Acrux	173 06.7	S63 11.2
Adhara	255 10.3	S28 59.8
Aldebaran	290 46.3	N16 32.4
Alioth	166 19.0	N55 51.9
Alkaid	152 57.5	N49 13.7
Al Na'ir	27 41.0	S46 52.9
Alnilam	275 43.7	S 1 11.7
Alphard	217 53.6	S 8 43.9
Alphecca	126 09.4	N26 39.6
Alpheratz	357 40.9	N29 11.2
Altair	62 06.2	N 8 55.0
Ankaa	353 13.3	S42 13.1
Antares	112 23.8	S26 27.9
Arcturus	145 53.9	N19 05.8
Atria	107 24.0	S69 03.2
Avior	234 16.5	S59 33.7
Bellatrix	278 29.2	N 6 21.7
Betelgeuse	270 58.4	N 7 24.4
Canopus	263 54.6	S52 42.4
Capella	280 30.5	N46 00.7
Deneb	49 30.1	N45 20.8
Denebola	182 31.4	N14 28.6
Diphda	348 53.4	S17 53.8
Dubhe	193 49.0	N61 39.3
Elnath	278 09.3	N28 37.1
Eltanin	90 45.6	N51 29.5
Enif	33 45.0	N 9 57.3
Fomalhaut	15 21.5	S29 32.1
Gacrux	171 58.4	S57 12.1
Gienah	175 50.0	S17 38.0
Hadar	148 44.9	S60 26.9
Hamal	327 57.8	N23 32.5
Kaus Aust.	83 41.1	S34 22.4
Kochab	137 21.3	N74 05.1
Markab	13 36.0	N15 17.9
Menkar	314 12.3	N 4 09.2
Menkent	148 05.1	S36 26.9
Miaplacidus	221 38.5	S69 47.0
Mirfak	308 36.5	N49 55.2
Nunki	75 55.8	S26 16.4
Peacock	53 16.1	S56 40.9
Pollux	243 24.6	N27 58.9
Procyon	244 57.0	N 5 10.7
Rasalhague	96 04.6	N12 33.1
Regulus	207 41.0	N11 53.0
Rigel	281 09.5	S 8 11.1
Rigil Kent.	139 49.0	S60 53.9
Sabik	102 10.2	S15 44.5
Schedar	349 37.5	N56 38.0
Shaula	96 19.2	S37 06.7
Sirius	258 31.3	S16 44.5
Spica	158 29.0	S11 14.8
Suhail	222 50.4	S43 29.9
Vega	80 37.8	N38 48.3
Zuben'ubi	137 03.1	S16 06.5

	SHA	Mer. Pass.
	° ′	h m
Venus	55 35.6	15 06
Mars	35 02.7	16 26
Jupiter	162 49.7	7 55
Saturn	102 11.3	11 57

UT d h	SUN GHA ° ′	SUN Dec ° ′	MOON GHA ° ′	v ′	Dec ° ′	d ′	HP ′
8 00 THURSDAY	182 01.8	S22 43.9	81 59.4	10.9	S 3 41.4	10.9	58.4
01	197 01.6	44.2	96 29.3	10.8	3 30.5	10.9	58.4
02	212 01.3	44.5	110 59.1	10.9	3 19.6	11.0	58.4
03	227 01.0	. . 44.7	125 29.0	10.8	3 08.6	11.0	58.5
04	242 00.7	45.0	139 58.8	10.8	2 57.6	11.0	58.5
05	257 00.5	45.2	154 28.6	10.7	2 46.6	11.1	58.5
06	272 00.2	S22 45.5	168 58.3	10.8	S 2 35.5	11.1	58.6
07	286 59.9	45.7	183 28.1	10.7	2 24.4	11.1	58.6
08	301 59.6	46.0	197 57.8	10.7	2 13.3	11.1	58.6
09	316 59.3	. . 46.2	212 27.5	10.6	2 02.2	11.2	58.7
10	331 59.1	46.5	226 57.1	10.6	1 51.0	11.2	58.7
11	346 58.8	46.7	241 26.7	10.6	1 39.8	11.2	58.7
12	1 58.5	S22 47.0	255 56.3	10.5	S 1 28.6	11.2	58.8
13	16 58.2	47.2	270 25.8	10.5	1 17.4	11.3	58.8
14	31 58.0	47.5	284 55.3	10.5	1 06.1	11.2	58.8
15	46 57.7	. . 47.7	299 24.8	10.4	0 54.9	11.3	58.9
16	61 57.4	48.0	313 54.2	10.4	0 43.6	11.3	58.9
17	76 57.1	48.2	328 23.6	10.3	0 32.3	11.4	58.9
18	91 56.9	S22 48.5	342 52.9	10.4	S 0 20.9	11.3	59.0
19	106 56.6	48.7	357 22.3	10.2	S 0 09.6	11.4	59.0
20	121 56.3	49.0	11 51.5	10.3	N 0 01.8	11.3	59.0
21	136 56.0	. . 49.2	26 20.8	10.2	0 13.1	11.4	59.1
22	151 55.7	49.5	40 50.0	10.1	0 24.5	11.4	59.1
23	166 55.5	49.7	55 19.1	10.1	0 35.9	11.4	59.1
9 00 FRIDAY	181 55.2	S22 49.9	69 48.2	10.1	N 0 47.3	11.4	59.2
01	196 54.9	50.2	84 17.3	10.0	0 58.7	11.4	59.2
02	211 54.6	50.4	98 46.3	10.0	1 10.1	11.5	59.2
03	226 54.3	. . 50.7	113 15.3	9.9	1 21.6	11.4	59.3
04	241 54.1	50.9	127 44.2	9.9	1 33.0	11.4	59.3
05	256 53.8	51.1	142 13.1	9.9	1 44.4	11.5	59.3
06	271 53.5	S22 51.4	156 42.0	9.8	N 1 55.9	11.4	59.4
07	286 53.2	51.6	171 10.8	9.7	2 07.3	11.5	59.4
08	301 52.9	51.8	185 39.5	9.7	2 18.8	11.4	59.4
09	316 52.7	. . 52.1	200 08.2	9.7	2 30.2	11.5	59.5
10	331 52.4	52.3	214 36.9	9.6	2 41.7	11.4	59.5
11	346 52.1	52.5	229 05.5	9.5	2 53.1	11.5	59.5
12	1 51.8	S22 52.8	243 34.0	9.5	N 3 04.6	11.4	59.6
13	16 51.5	53.0	258 02.5	9.5	3 16.0	11.4	59.6
14	31 51.3	53.2	272 31.0	9.4	3 27.4	11.4	59.6
15	46 51.0	. . 53.5	286 59.4	9.3	3 38.8	11.5	59.7
16	61 50.7	53.7	301 27.7	9.3	3 50.3	11.4	59.7
17	76 50.4	53.9	315 56.0	9.3	4 01.7	11.4	59.7
18	91 50.1	S22 54.1	330 24.3	9.1	N 4 13.1	11.3	59.8
19	106 49.9	54.4	344 52.4	9.2	4 24.4	11.4	59.8
20	121 49.6	54.6	359 20.6	9.0	4 35.8	11.4	59.8
21	136 49.3	. . 54.8	13 48.6	9.0	4 47.2	11.3	59.9
22	151 49.0	55.0	28 16.6	9.0	4 58.5	11.3	59.9
23	166 48.7	55.3	42 44.6	8.9	5 09.8	11.3	59.9
10 00 SATURDAY	181 48.4	S22 55.5	57 12.5	8.8	N 5 21.1	11.3	60.0
01	196 48.2	55.7	71 40.3	8.8	5 32.4	11.3	60.0
02	211 47.9	55.9	86 08.1	8.7	5 43.7	11.2	60.0
03	226 47.6	. . 56.1	100 35.8	8.7	5 54.9	11.2	60.0
04	241 47.3	56.4	115 03.5	8.6	6 06.1	11.2	60.1
05	256 47.0	56.6	129 31.1	8.5	6 17.3	11.2	60.1
06	271 46.7	S22 56.8	143 58.6	8.5	N 6 28.5	11.1	60.1
07	286 46.5	57.0	158 26.1	8.4	6 39.6	11.1	60.2
08	301 46.2	57.2	172 53.5	8.4	6 50.7	11.1	60.2
09	316 45.9	. . 57.4	187 20.9	8.3	7 01.8	11.0	60.2
10	331 45.6	57.7	201 48.2	8.2	7 12.8	11.0	60.2
11	346 45.3	57.9	216 15.4	8.2	7 23.8	11.0	60.3
12	1 45.0	S22 58.1	230 42.6	8.1	N 7 34.8	10.9	60.3
13	16 44.7	58.3	245 09.7	8.0	7 45.7	10.9	60.3
14	31 44.5	58.5	259 36.7	8.0	7 56.6	10.9	60.3
15	46 44.2	. . 58.7	274 03.7	7.9	8 07.5	10.8	60.4
16	61 43.9	58.9	288 30.6	7.8	8 18.3	10.8	60.4
17	76 43.6	59.1	302 57.4	7.8	8 29.1	10.7	60.4
18	91 43.3	S22 59.3	317 24.2	7.7	N 8 39.8	10.7	60.4
19	106 43.0	59.5	331 50.9	7.7	8 50.5	10.6	60.5
20	121 42.7	22 59.7	346 17.6	7.5	9 01.1	10.6	60.5
21	136 42.5	23 00.0	0 44.1	7.5	9 11.7	10.6	60.5
22	151 42.2	00.2	15 10.6	7.5	9 22.3	10.5	60.5
23	166 41.9	00.4	29 37.1	7.4	N 9 32.8	10.4	60.6
	SD 16.3	*d* 0.2	SD 16.0		16.2		16.4

Lat. °	Twilight Naut. h m	Twilight Civil h m	Sunrise h m	Moonrise 8 h m	Moonrise 9 h m	Moonrise 10 h m	Moonrise 11 h m
N 72	08 11	10 27	▬	13 16	13 09	13 02	12 55
N 70	07 52	09 36	▬	13 14	13 14	13 13	13 14
68	07 37	09 04	▬	13 13	13 17	13 22	13 30
66	07 25	08 40	10 14	13 11	13 20	13 30	13 43
64	07 14	08 22	09 36	13 10	13 23	13 36	13 54
62	07 05	08 06	09 10	13 09	13 25	13 42	14 03
60	06 57	07 53	08 50	13 08	13 27	13 47	14 11
N 58	06 50	07 42	08 33	13 08	13 28	13 51	14 17
56	06 44	07 32	08 19	13 07	13 30	13 55	14 24
54	06 38	07 24	08 07	13 06	13 31	13 58	14 29
52	06 32	07 16	07 56	13 06	13 33	14 02	14 34
50	06 27	07 09	07 47	13 05	13 34	14 04	14 39
45	06 16	06 53	07 27	13 04	13 36	14 11	14 49
N 40	06 06	06 40	07 10	13 03	13 39	14 16	14 57
35	05 57	06 28	06 57	13 03	13 40	14 21	15 04
30	05 48	06 18	06 44	13 02	13 42	14 25	15 10
20	05 33	06 00	06 24	13 01	13 45	14 32	15 21
N 10	05 17	05 43	06 06	13 00	13 48	14 38	15 31
0	05 00	05 26	05 49	12 59	13 50	14 44	15 40
S 10	04 42	05 09	05 32	12 58	13 53	14 50	15 49
20	04 20	04 49	05 13	12 57	13 55	14 56	15 59
30	03 51	04 24	04 52	12 56	13 59	15 04	16 11
35	03 33	04 10	04 39	12 55	14 00	15 08	16 17
40	03 11	03 52	04 24	12 54	14 02	15 13	16 25
45	02 41	03 30	04 07	12 54	14 05	15 18	16 34
S 50	01 58	03 01	03 45	12 53	14 08	15 25	16 44
52	01 33	02 47	03 35	12 52	14 09	15 28	16 49
54	00 55	02 30	03 23	12 52	14 11	15 32	16 55
56	////	02 09	03 09	12 51	14 12	15 36	17 01
58	////	01 42	02 53	12 51	14 14	15 40	17 08
S 60	////	01 00	02 34	12 50	14 16	15 45	17 15

Lat. °	Sunset h m	Twilight Civil h m	Twilight Naut. h m	Moonset 8 h m	Moonset 9 h m	Moonset 10 h m	Moonset 11 h m
N 72	▬	13 18	15 34	25 36	01 36	03 32	05 36
N 70	▬	14 09	15 53	25 34	01 34	03 24	05 18
68	▬	14 41	16 07	25 33	01 33	03 16	05 03
66	13 31	15 05	16 20	25 32	01 32	03 10	04 52
64	14 08	15 23	16 30	00 00	01 31	03 06	04 42
62	14 35	15 38	16 40	00 03	01 31	03 01	04 34
60	14 55	15 51	16 48	00 06	01 30	02 58	04 27
N 58	15 12	16 03	16 55	00 08	01 30	02 54	04 21
56	15 26	16 12	17 01	00 10	01 29	02 51	04 16
54	15 38	16 21	17 07	00 11	01 29	02 49	04 11
52	15 49	16 29	17 13	00 13	01 28	02 46	04 06
50	15 58	16 36	17 18	00 14	01 28	02 44	04 02
45	16 18	16 52	17 29	00 17	01 27	02 39	03 54
N 40	16 35	17 05	17 39	00 20	01 27	02 36	03 47
35	16 48	17 16	17 48	00 22	01 26	02 32	03 41
30	17 00	17 27	17 56	00 24	01 25	02 29	03 35
20	17 21	17 45	18 12	00 27	01 25	02 24	03 26
N 10	17 39	18 02	18 28	00 30	01 24	02 20	03 18
0	17 56	18 19	18 45	00 33	01 23	02 15	03 10
S 10	18 13	18 36	19 03	00 35	01 22	02 11	03 03
20	18 32	18 56	19 25	00 38	01 21	02 07	02 55
30	18 53	19 21	19 54	00 41	01 20	02 01	02 45
35	19 06	19 36	20 12	00 43	01 20	01 59	02 40
40	19 21	19 53	20 35	00 45	01 19	01 55	02 34
45	19 38	20 15	21 04	00 47	01 18	01 51	02 27
S 50	20 00	20 44	21 48	00 50	01 18	01 47	02 19
52	20 11	20 59	22 14	00 51	01 17	01 45	02 15
54	20 23	21 16	22 53	00 52	01 17	01 42	02 11
56	20 36	21 37	////	00 54	01 16	01 40	02 06
58	20 52	22 05	////	00 55	01 16	01 37	02 01
S 60	21 12	22 47	////	00 57	01 15	01 34	01 55

Day	SUN Eqn. of Time 00^h	SUN Eqn. of Time 12^h	SUN Mer. Pass.	MOON Mer. Pass. Upper	MOON Mer. Pass. Lower	MOON Age	MOON Phase
d	m s	m s	h m	h m	h m	d %	
8	08 08	07 55	11 52	19 11	06 46	09 62	
9	07 41	07 28	11 53	20 03	07 37	10 73	
10	07 14	07 01	11 53	20 57	08 29	11 83	

2016 DECEMBER 11, 12, 13 (SUN., MON., TUES.)

UT d	h	ARIES GHA	VENUS −4·3 GHA	VENUS Dec	MARS +0·7 GHA	MARS Dec	JUPITER −1·8 GHA	JUPITER Dec	SATURN +0·4 GHA	SATURN Dec
		° ′	° ′	° ′	° ′	° ′	° ′	° ′	° ′	° ′
11	00	80 08.2	133 19.1	S21 31.9	113 43.3	S14 48.2	242 40.7	S 6 06.0	182 04.3	S21 40.8
	01	95 10.7	148 18.6	31.2	128 43.9	47.5	257 42.8	06.1	197 06.5	40.9
	02	110 13.2	163 18.1	30.5	143 44.6	46.8	272 44.9	06.3	212 08.6	40.9
	03	125 15.6	178 17.6	. . 29.7	158 45.2	. . 46.2	287 47.0	. . 06.4	227 10.8	. . 40.9
	04	140 18.1	193 17.0	29.0	173 45.8	45.5	302 49.1	06.5	242 12.9	40.9
	05	155 20.6	208 16.5	28.3	188 46.5	44.8	317 51.3	06.7	257 15.0	41.0
	06	170 23.0	223 16.0	S21 27.5	203 47.1	S14 44.2	332 53.4	S 6 06.8	272 17.2	S21 41.0
	07	185 25.5	238 15.4	26.8	218 47.8	43.5	347 55.5	07.0	287 19.3	41.0
	08	200 28.0	253 14.9	26.0	233 48.4	42.8	2 57.6	07.1	302 21.5	41.1
S	09	215 30.4	268 14.4	. . 25.3	248 49.1	. . 42.2	17 59.7	. . 07.2	317 23.6	. . 41.1
U	10	230 32.9	283 13.9	24.6	263 49.7	41.5	33 01.8	07.4	332 25.8	41.1
N	11	245 35.4	298 13.3	23.8	278 50.3	40.8	48 03.9	07.5	347 27.9	41.1
D	12	260 37.8	313 12.8	S21 23.1	293 51.0	S14 40.2	63 06.0	S 6 07.6	2 30.1	S21 41.2
A	13	275 40.3	328 12.3	22.3	308 51.6	39.5	78 08.1	07.8	17 32.2	41.2
Y	14	290 42.7	343 11.8	21.6	323 52.3	38.8	93 10.3	07.9	32 34.4	41.2
	15	305 45.2	358 11.3	. . 20.8	338 52.9	. . 38.1	108 12.4	. . 08.0	47 36.5	. . 41.2
	16	320 47.7	13 10.7	20.1	353 53.6	37.5	123 14.5	08.2	62 38.7	41.3
	17	335 50.1	28 10.2	19.3	8 54.2	36.8	138 16.6	08.3	77 40.8	41.3
	18	350 52.6	43 09.7	S21 18.6	23 54.8	S14 36.1	153 18.7	S 6 08.4	92 43.0	S21 41.3
	19	5 55.1	58 09.2	17.8	38 55.5	35.5	168 20.8	08.6	107 45.1	41.3
	20	20 57.5	73 08.7	17.1	53 56.1	34.8	183 22.9	08.7	122 47.3	41.4
	21	36 00.0	88 08.2	. . 16.3	68 56.8	. . 34.1	198 25.0	. . 08.8	137 49.4	. . 41.4
	22	51 02.5	103 07.6	15.6	83 57.4	33.5	213 27.2	09.0	152 51.6	41.4
	23	66 04.9	118 07.1	14.8	98 58.1	32.8	228 29.3	09.1	167 53.7	41.5
12	00	81 07.4	133 06.6	S21 14.1	113 58.7	S14 32.1	243 31.4	S 6 09.3	182 55.8	S21 41.5
	01	96 09.8	148 06.1	13.3	128 59.4	31.4	258 33.5	09.4	197 58.0	41.5
	02	111 12.3	163 05.6	12.6	144 00.0	30.8	273 35.6	09.5	213 00.1	41.5
	03	126 14.8	178 05.1	. . 11.8	159 00.6	. . 30.1	288 37.7	. . 09.7	228 02.3	. . 41.6
	04	141 17.2	193 04.6	11.0	174 01.3	29.4	303 39.8	09.8	243 04.4	41.6
	05	156 19.7	208 04.1	10.3	189 01.9	28.8	318 42.0	09.9	258 06.6	41.6
	06	171 22.2	223 03.6	S21 09.5	204 02.6	S14 28.1	333 44.1	S 6 10.1	273 08.7	S21 41.6
	07	186 24.6	238 03.0	08.8	219 03.2	27.4	348 46.2	10.2	288 10.9	41.7
	08	201 27.1	253 02.5	08.0	234 03.9	26.7	3 48.3	10.3	303 13.0	41.7
M	09	216 29.6	268 02.0	. . 07.2	249 04.5	. . 26.1	18 50.4	. . 10.5	318 15.2	. . 41.7
O	10	231 32.0	283 01.5	06.5	264 05.2	25.4	33 52.5	10.6	333 17.3	41.7
N	11	246 34.5	298 01.0	05.7	279 05.8	24.7	48 54.6	10.7	348 19.5	41.8
D	12	261 37.0	313 00.5	S21 04.9	294 06.5	S14 24.0	63 56.8	S 6 10.9	3 21.6	S21 41.8
A	13	276 39.4	328 00.0	04.2	309 07.1	23.4	78 58.9	11.0	18 23.8	41.8
Y	14	291 41.9	342 59.5	03.4	324 07.7	22.7	94 01.0	11.1	33 25.9	41.8
	15	306 44.3	357 59.0	. . 02.6	339 08.4	. . 22.0	109 03.1	. . 11.3	48 28.1	. . 41.9
	16	321 46.8	12 58.5	01.9	354 09.0	21.3	124 05.2	11.4	63 30.2	41.9
	17	336 49.3	27 58.0	01.1	9 09.7	20.7	139 07.3	11.5	78 32.4	41.9
	18	351 51.7	42 57.5	S21 00.3	24 10.3	S14 20.0	154 09.5	S 6 11.7	93 34.5	S21 42.0
	19	6 54.2	57 57.0	20 59.5	39 11.0	19.3	169 11.6	11.8	108 36.7	42.0
	20	21 56.7	72 56.5	58.8	54 11.6	18.6	184 13.7	11.9	123 38.8	42.0
	21	36 59.1	87 56.0	. . 58.0	69 12.3	. . 18.0	199 15.8	. . 12.1	138 40.9	. . 42.0
	22	52 01.6	102 55.5	57.2	84 12.9	17.3	214 17.9	12.2	153 43.1	42.1
	23	67 04.1	117 55.0	56.4	99 13.6	16.6	229 20.0	12.3	168 45.2	42.1
13	00	82 06.5	132 54.6	S20 55.7	114 14.2	S14 15.9	244 22.2	S 6 12.5	183 47.4	S21 42.1
	01	97 09.0	147 54.1	54.9	129 14.9	15.3	259 24.3	12.6	198 49.5	42.1
	02	112 11.5	162 53.6	54.1	144 15.5	14.6	274 26.4	12.7	213 51.7	42.2
	03	127 13.9	177 53.1	. . 53.3	159 16.2	. . 13.9	289 28.5	. . 12.9	228 53.8	. . 42.2
	04	142 16.4	192 52.6	52.5	174 16.8	13.2	304 30.6	13.0	243 56.0	42.2
	05	157 18.8	207 52.1	51.8	189 17.5	12.6	319 32.8	13.1	258 58.1	42.2
	06	172 21.3	222 51.6	S20 51.0	204 18.1	S14 11.9	334 34.9	S 6 13.3	274 00.3	S21 42.3
	07	187 23.8	237 51.1	50.2	219 18.8	11.2	349 37.0	13.4	289 02.4	42.3
T	08	202 26.2	252 50.6	49.4	234 19.4	10.5	4 39.1	13.5	304 04.6	42.3
U	09	217 28.7	267 50.1	. . 48.6	249 20.1	. . 09.8	19 41.2	. . 13.7	319 06.7	. . 42.3
E	10	232 31.2	282 49.7	47.8	264 20.7	09.2	34 43.4	13.8	334 08.9	42.4
S	11	247 33.6	297 49.2	47.1	279 21.4	08.5	49 45.5	13.9	349 11.0	42.4
D	12	262 36.1	312 48.7	S20 46.3	294 22.0	S14 07.8	64 47.6	S 6 14.0	4 13.2	S21 42.4
A	13	277 38.6	327 48.2	45.5	309 22.7	07.1	79 49.7	14.2	19 15.3	42.4
Y	14	292 41.0	342 47.7	44.7	324 23.3	06.4	94 51.8	14.3	34 17.5	42.5
	15	307 43.5	357 47.2	. . 43.9	339 24.0	. . 05.8	109 54.0	. . 14.4	49 19.6	. . 42.5
	16	322 46.0	12 46.8	43.1	354 24.6	05.1	124 56.1	14.6	64 21.7	42.5
	17	337 48.4	27 46.3	42.3	9 25.3	04.4	139 58.2	14.7	79 23.9	42.5
	18	352 50.9	42 45.8	S20 41.5	24 25.9	S14 03.7	155 00.3	S 6 14.8	94 26.0	S21 42.6
	19	7 53.3	57 45.3	40.7	39 26.6	03.0	170 02.4	15.0	109 28.2	42.6
	20	22 55.8	72 44.9	39.9	54 27.2	02.4	185 04.6	15.1	124 30.3	42.6
	21	37 58.3	87 44.4	. . 39.1	69 27.9	. . 01.7	200 06.7	. . 15.2	139 32.5	. . 42.7
	22	53 00.7	102 43.9	38.3	84 28.5	01.0	215 08.8	15.4	154 34.6	42.7
	23	68 03.2	117 43.4	37.5	99 29.2	00.3	230 10.9	15.5	169 36.8	42.7
Mer. Pass.		h m 18 32.5	*v* −0.5	*d* 0.8	*v* 0.6	*d* 0.7	*v* 2.1	*d* 0.1	*v* 2.1	*d* 0.0

STARS

Name	SHA	Dec
	° ′	° ′
Acamar	315 16.3	S40 14.5
Achernar	335 24.8	S57 09.4
Acrux	173 06.7	S63 11.2
Adhara	255 10.3	S28 59.8
Aldebaran	290 46.3	N16 32.4
Alioth	166 19.0	N55 51.9
Alkaid	152 57.4	N49 13.7
Al Na'ir	27 41.1	S46 52.9
Alnilam	275 43.7	S 1 11.7
Alphard	217 53.6	S 8 44.0
Alphecca	126 09.4	N26 39.6
Alpheratz	357 41.0	N29 11.2
Altair	62 06.2	N 8 55.0
Ankaa	353 13.3	S42 13.1
Antares	112 23.7	S26 27.9
Arcturus	145 53.9	N19 05.7
Atria	107 24.0	S69 03.2
Avior	234 16.5	S59 33.7
Bellatrix	278 29.2	N 6 21.7
Betelgeuse	270 58.4	N 7 24.4
Canopus	263 54.5	S52 42.4
Capella	280 30.5	N46 00.7
Deneb	49 30.2	N45 20.8
Denebola	182 31.3	N14 28.6
Diphda	348 53.5	S17 53.8
Dubhe	193 48.9	N61 39.3
Elnath	278 09.3	N28 37.1
Eltanin	90 45.6	N51 29.4
Enif	33 45.0	N 9 57.3
Fomalhaut	15 21.5	S29 32.1
Gacrux	171 58.3	S57 12.1
Gienah	175 49.9	S17 38.0
Hadar	148 44.9	S60 26.9
Hamal	327 57.8	N23 32.5
Kaus Aust.	83 41.1	S34 22.4
Kochab	137 21.3	N74 05.1
Markab	13 36.0	N15 17.9
Menkar	314 12.3	N 4 09.2
Menkent	148 05.0	S36 26.9
Miaplacidus	221 38.5	S69 47.0
Mirfak	308 36.5	N49 55.2
Nunki	75 55.8	S26 16.4
Peacock	53 16.1	S56 40.9
Pollux	243 24.6	N27 58.8
Procyon	244 57.0	N 5 10.7
Rasalhague	96 04.6	N12 33.1
Regulus	207 40.9	N11 53.0
Rigel	281 09.5	S 8 11.1
Rigil Kent.	139 49.0	S60 53.9
Sabik	102 10.2	S15 44.5
Schedar	349 37.5	N56 38.0
Shaula	96 19.2	S37 06.7
Sirius	258 31.3	S16 44.5
Spica	158 28.9	S11 14.8
Suhail	222 50.4	S43 30.0
Vega	80 37.8	N38 48.2
Zuben'ubi	137 03.1	S16 06.5

	SHA	Mer. Pass.
	° ′	h m
Venus	51 59.2	15 08
Mars	32 51.3	16 23
Jupiter	162 24.0	7 45
Saturn	101 48.5	11 47

Day	UT (d h)	SUN GHA	SUN Dec	MOON GHA	v	MOON Dec	d	HP
		° ′	° ′	° ′	′	° ′	′	′
11	00	181 41.6	S23 00.6	44 03.5	7.3	N 9 43.2	10.4	60.6
	01	196 41.3	00.8	58 29.8	7.2	9 53.6	10.3	60.6
	02	211 41.0	01.0	72 56.0	7.2	10 03.9	10.3	60.6
	03	226 40.7	. . 01.2	87 22.2	7.1	10 14.2	10.2	60.7
	04	241 40.4	01.4	101 48.3	7.0	10 24.4	10.1	60.7
	05	256 40.2	01.6	116 14.3	7.0	10 34.5	10.1	60.7
	06	271 39.9	S23 01.8	130 40.3	6.9	N10 44.6	10.1	60.7
	07	286 39.6	02.0	145 06.2	6.8	10 54.7	9.9	60.7
	08	301 39.3	02.2	159 32.0	6.8	11 04.6	9.9	60.8
S	09	316 39.0	. . 02.4	173 57.8	6.7	11 14.5	9.8	60.8
U	10	331 38.7	02.5	188 23.5	6.6	11 24.3	9.8	60.8
N	11	346 38.4	02.7	202 49.1	6.6	11 34.1	9.7	60.8
D	12	1 38.1	S23 02.9	217 14.7	6.5	N11 43.8	9.6	60.8
A	13	16 37.8	03.1	231 40.2	6.4	11 53.4	9.5	60.9
Y	14	31 37.6	03.3	246 05.6	6.4	12 02.9	9.5	60.9
	15	46 37.3	. . 03.5	260 31.0	6.3	12 12.4	9.4	60.9
	16	61 37.0	03.7	274 56.3	6.2	12 21.8	9.3	60.9
	17	76 36.7	03.9	289 21.5	6.1	12 31.1	9.2	60.9
	18	91 36.4	S23 04.1	303 46.6	6.1	N12 40.3	9.2	60.9
	19	106 36.1	04.3	318 11.7	6.1	12 49.5	9.1	61.0
	20	121 35.8	04.5	332 36.8	5.9	12 58.6	9.0	61.0
	21	136 35.5	. . 04.6	347 01.7	5.9	13 07.6	8.9	61.0
	22	151 35.2	04.8	1 26.6	5.9	13 16.5	8.8	61.0
	23	166 35.0	05.0	15 51.5	5.7	13 25.3	8.7	61.0
12	00	181 34.7	S23 05.2	30 16.2	5.7	N13 34.0	8.6	61.0
	01	196 34.4	05.4	44 40.9	5.7	13 42.6	8.6	61.0
	02	211 34.1	05.6	59 05.6	5.6	13 51.2	8.4	61.0
	03	226 33.8	. . 05.7	73 30.2	5.5	13 59.6	8.4	61.1
	04	241 33.5	05.9	87 54.7	5.5	14 08.0	8.2	61.1
	05	256 33.2	06.1	102 19.2	5.4	14 16.2	8.2	61.1
	06	271 32.9	S23 06.3	116 43.6	5.3	N14 24.4	8.0	61.1
	07	286 32.6	06.5	131 07.9	5.3	14 32.4	8.0	61.1
	08	301 32.3	06.6	145 32.2	5.2	14 40.4	7.9	61.1
M	09	316 32.0	. . 06.8	159 56.4	5.2	14 48.3	7.7	61.1
O	10	331 31.7	07.0	174 20.6	5.1	14 56.0	7.7	61.1
N	11	346 31.5	07.2	188 44.7	5.0	15 03.7	7.5	61.1
D	12	1 31.2	S23 07.3	203 08.7	5.0	N15 11.2	7.5	61.1
A	13	16 30.9	07.5	217 32.7	4.9	15 18.7	7.3	61.1
Y	14	31 30.6	07.7	231 56.6	4.9	15 26.0	7.3	61.1
	15	46 30.3	. . 07.9	246 20.5	4.9	15 33.3	7.1	61.2
	16	61 30.0	08.0	260 44.4	4.7	15 40.4	7.0	61.2
	17	76 29.7	08.2	275 08.1	4.8	15 47.4	6.9	61.2
	18	91 29.4	S23 08.4	289 31.9	4.7	N15 54.3	6.8	61.2
	19	106 29.1	08.5	303 55.6	4.6	16 01.1	6.6	61.2
	20	121 28.8	08.7	318 19.2	4.6	16 07.7	6.6	61.2
	21	136 28.5	. . 08.9	332 42.8	4.5	16 14.3	6.4	61.2
	22	151 28.2	09.0	347 06.3	4.5	16 20.7	6.3	61.2
	23	166 27.9	09.2	1 29.8	4.5	16 27.0	6.2	61.2
13	00	181 27.6	S23 09.4	15 53.3	4.4	N16 33.2	6.1	61.2
	01	196 27.3	09.5	30 16.7	4.4	16 39.3	5.9	61.2
	02	211 27.1	09.7	44 40.1	4.3	16 45.2	5.9	61.2
	03	226 26.8	. . 09.9	59 03.4	4.3	16 51.1	5.7	61.2
	04	241 26.5	10.0	73 26.7	4.2	16 56.8	5.6	61.2
	05	256 26.2	10.2	87 49.9	4.3	17 02.4	5.4	61.2
	06	271 25.9	S23 10.3	102 13.2	4.1	N17 07.8	5.3	61.2
	07	286 25.6	10.5	116 36.3	4.2	17 13.1	5.3	61.2
T	08	301 25.3	10.7	130 59.5	4.1	17 18.4	5.0	61.2
U	09	316 25.0	. . 10.8	145 22.6	4.1	17 23.4	5.0	61.1
E	10	331 24.7	11.0	159 45.7	4.1	17 28.4	4.8	61.1
S	11	346 24.4	11.1	174 08.8	4.0	17 33.2	4.7	61.1
D	12	1 24.1	S23 11.3	188 31.8	4.0	N17 37.9	4.5	61.1
A	13	16 23.8	11.4	202 54.8	4.0	17 42.4	4.5	61.1
	14	31 23.5	11.6	217 17.8	4.0	17 46.9	4.3	61.1
Y	15	46 23.2	. . 11.7	231 40.8	3.9	17 51.2	4.1	61.1
	16	61 22.9	11.9	246 03.7	3.9	17 55.3	4.0	61.1
	17	76 22.6	12.0	260 26.6	3.9	17 59.3	3.9	61.1
	18	91 22.3	S23 12.2	274 49.5	3.9	N18 03.2	3.8	61.1
	19	106 22.0	12.3	289 12.4	3.9	18 07.0	3.6	61.1
	20	121 21.7	12.5	303 35.3	3.9	18 10.6	3.5	61.1
	21	136 21.4	. . 12.6	317 58.2	3.8	18 14.1	3.3	61.0
	22	151 21.1	12.8	332 21.0	3.9	18 17.4	3.2	61.0
	23	166 20.8	12.9	346 43.9	3.8	N18 20.6	3.1	61.0
		SD 16.3	*d* 0.2	SD		16.6	16.7	16.7

Lat.	Twilight Naut.	Twilight Civil	Sunrise	Moonrise 11	12	13	14
°	h m	h m	h m	h m	h m	h m	h m
N 72	08 16	10 38	▬	12 55	12 45	12 23	▭
N 70	07 57	09 43	▬	13 14	13 18	13 28	13 56
68	07 42	09 09	▬	13 30	13 42	14 04	14 44
66	07 29	08 45	10 22	13 43	14 01	14 30	15 15
64	07 18	08 26	09 42	13 54	14 17	14 50	15 38
62	07 09	08 10	09 15	14 03	14 30	15 06	15 57
60	07 01	07 57	08 54	14 11	14 41	15 20	16 12
N 58	06 53	07 46	08 37	14 17	14 50	15 32	16 25
56	06 47	07 36	08 23	14 24	14 59	15 42	16 36
54	06 41	07 27	08 10	14 29	15 06	15 51	16 46
52	06 35	07 19	07 59	14 34	15 13	15 59	16 55
50	06 30	07 11	07 50	14 39	15 19	16 07	17 03
45	06 18	06 56	07 29	14 49	15 32	16 22	17 19
N 40	06 08	06 42	07 13	14 57	15 43	16 35	17 33
35	05 59	06 31	06 59	15 04	15 52	16 46	17 45
30	05 50	06 20	06 47	15 10	16 01	16 56	17 55
20	05 34	06 02	06 26	15 21	16 15	17 12	18 13
N 10	05 18	05 45	06 07	15 31	16 27	17 27	18 28
0	05 02	05 28	05 50	15 40	16 39	17 41	18 43
S 10	04 43	05 10	05 33	15 49	16 51	17 54	18 57
20	04 21	04 50	05 14	15 59	17 04	18 09	19 13
30	03 52	04 25	04 52	16 11	17 19	18 26	19 30
35	03 33	04 10	04 40	16 17	17 27	18 36	19 41
40	03 11	03 52	04 25	16 25	17 37	18 47	19 53
45	02 41	03 30	04 07	16 34	17 49	19 01	20 07
S 50	01 57	03 01	03 45	16 44	18 03	19 17	20 24
52	01 30	02 46	03 34	16 49	18 09	19 25	20 32
54	00 49	02 29	03 22	16 55	18 16	19 33	20 41
56	////	02 07	03 08	17 01	18 25	19 43	20 51
58	////	01 39	02 52	17 08	18 34	19 54	21 02
S 60	////	00 54	02 32	17 15	18 44	20 06	21 16

Lat.	Sunset	Twilight Civil	Twilight Naut.	Moonset 11	12	13	14
°	h m	h m	h m	h m	h m	h m	h m
N 72	▬	13 09	15 31	05 36	07 48	10 16	▭
N 70	▬	14 05	15 51	05 18	07 16	09 13	10 54
68	▬	14 38	16 06	05 03	06 52	08 37	10 06
66	13 26	15 03	16 19	04 52	06 34	08 12	09 36
64	14 06	15 22	16 30	04 42	06 20	07 52	09 13
62	14 33	15 37	16 39	04 34	06 07	07 36	08 54
60	14 54	15 51	16 47	04 27	05 57	07 23	08 39
N 58	15 11	16 02	16 54	04 21	05 48	07 12	08 26
56	15 25	16 12	17 01	04 16	05 40	07 02	08 15
54	15 37	16 21	17 07	04 11	05 33	06 53	08 05
52	15 48	16 29	17 13	04 06	05 27	06 45	07 57
50	15 58	16 36	17 18	04 02	05 21	06 38	07 49
45	16 18	16 52	17 29	03 54	05 09	06 23	07 32
N 40	16 35	17 05	17 39	03 47	04 59	06 11	07 19
35	16 49	17 17	17 49	03 41	04 50	06 00	07 07
30	17 01	17 27	17 57	03 35	04 43	05 51	06 57
20	17 22	17 46	18 14	03 26	04 30	05 35	06 40
N 10	17 40	18 03	18 30	03 18	04 19	05 21	06 24
0	17 58	18 20	18 46	03 10	04 08	05 08	06 10
S 10	18 15	18 38	19 05	03 03	03 57	04 55	05 56
20	18 34	18 58	19 27	02 55	03 46	04 42	05 41
30	18 56	19 23	19 56	02 45	03 33	04 26	05 23
35	19 08	19 38	20 15	02 40	03 26	04 17	05 13
40	19 23	19 56	20 37	02 34	03 17	04 06	05 01
45	19 41	20 18	21 08	02 27	03 07	03 54	04 48
S 50	20 03	20 47	21 52	02 19	02 56	03 39	04 31
52	20 14	21 02	22 19	02 15	02 50	03 32	04 23
54	20 26	21 20	23 01	02 11	02 44	03 25	04 14
56	20 40	21 41	////	02 06	02 37	03 16	04 05
58	20 56	22 10	////	02 01	02 30	03 06	03 53
S 60	21 16	22 56	////	01 55	02 21	02 55	03 41

Day	SUN Eqn. of Time 00^h	SUN Eqn. of Time 12^h	SUN Mer. Pass.	MOON Mer. Pass. Upper	MOON Mer. Pass. Lower	Age	%	Phase
d	m s	m s	h m	h m	h m	d	%	
11	06 47	06 33	11 53	21 54	09 25	12	91	
12	06 19	06 05	11 54	22 54	10 24	13	96	○
13	05 51	05 37	11 54	23 55	11 24	14	99	

UT	ARIES	VENUS −4·3		MARS +0·8		JUPITER −1·9		SATURN +0·4		STARS		
	GHA	GHA	Dec	GHA	Dec	GHA	Dec	GHA	Dec	Name	SHA	Dec
d h	° ′	° ′	° ′	° ′	° ′	° ′	° ′	° ′	° ′		° ′	° ′
14 00	83 05.7	132 43.0	S20 36.7	114 29.8	S13 59.6	245 13.1	S 6 15.6	184 38.9	S21 42.7	Acamar	315 16.3	S40 14.5
01	98 08.1	147 42.5	35.9	129 30.5	59.0	260 15.2	15.8	199 41.1	42.8	Achernar	335 24.8	S57 09.4
02	113 10.6	162 42.0	35.1	144 31.1	58.3	275 17.3	15.9	214 43.2	42.8	Acrux	173 06.6	S63 11.2
03	128 13.1	177 41.5	. . 34.3	159 31.8	. . 57.6	290 19.4	. . 16.0	229 45.4	. . 42.8	Adhara	255 10.3	S28 59.8
04	143 15.5	192 41.1	33.5	174 32.4	56.9	305 21.5	16.1	244 47.5	42.8	Aldebaran	290 46.3	N16 32.4
05	158 18.0	207 40.6	32.7	189 33.1	56.2	320 23.7	16.3	259 49.7	42.9			
06	173 20.5	222 40.1	S20 31.9	204 33.8	S13 55.5	335 25.8	S 6 16.4	274 51.8	S21 42.9	Alioth	166 19.0	N55 51.9
W 07	188 22.9	237 39.7	31.1	219 34.4	54.9	350 27.9	16.5	289 54.0	42.9	Alkaid	152 57.4	N49 13.6
E 08	203 25.4	252 39.2	30.3	234 35.1	54.2	5 30.0	16.7	304 56.1	42.9	Al Na'ir	27 41.1	S46 52.9
D 09	218 27.8	267 38.7	. . 29.5	249 35.7	. . 53.5	20 32.2	. . 16.8	319 58.3	. . 43.0	Alnilam	275 43.6	S 1 11.7
N 10	233 30.3	282 38.3	28.7	264 36.4	52.8	35 34.3	16.9	335 00.4	43.0	Alphard	217 53.6	S 8 44.0
E 11	248 32.8	297 37.8	27.9	279 37.0	52.1	50 36.4	17.1	350 02.6	43.0			
S 12	263 35.2	312 37.3	S20 27.1	294 37.7	S13 51.4	65 38.5	S 6 17.2	5 04.7	S21 43.0	Alphecca	126 09.4	N26 39.6
D 13	278 37.7	327 36.9	26.3	309 38.3	50.8	80 40.7	17.3	20 06.8	43.1	Alpheratz	357 41.0	N29 11.2
A 14	293 40.2	342 36.4	25.5	324 39.0	50.1	95 42.8	17.4	35 09.0	43.1	Altair	62 06.2	N 8 55.0
Y 15	308 42.6	357 35.9	. . 24.7	339 39.6	. . 49.4	110 44.9	. . 17.6	50 11.1	. . 43.1	Ankaa	353 13.4	S42 13.1
16	323 45.1	12 35.5	23.8	354 40.3	48.7	125 47.0	17.7	65 13.3	43.1	Antares	112 23.7	S26 27.9
17	338 47.6	27 35.0	23.0	9 40.9	48.0	140 49.2	17.8	80 15.4	43.2			
18	353 50.0	42 34.6	S20 22.2	24 41.6	S13 47.3	155 51.3	S 6 18.0	95 17.6	S21 43.2	Arcturus	145 53.8	N19 05.7
19	8 52.5	57 34.1	21.4	39 42.3	46.7	170 53.4	18.1	110 19.7	43.2	Atria	107 23.9	S69 03.2
20	23 55.0	72 33.7	20.6	54 42.9	46.0	185 55.5	18.2	125 21.9	43.2	Avior	234 16.5	S59 33.8
21	38 57.4	87 33.2	. . 19.8	69 43.6	. . 45.3	200 57.7	. . 18.3	140 24.0	. . 43.3	Bellatrix	278 29.1	N 6 21.7
22	53 59.9	102 32.7	18.9	84 44.2	44.6	215 59.8	18.5	155 26.2	43.3	Betelgeuse	270 58.4	N 7 24.4
23	69 02.3	117 32.3	18.1	99 44.9	43.9	231 01.9	18.6	170 28.3	43.3			
15 00	84 04.8	132 31.8	S20 17.3	114 45.5	S13 43.2	246 04.0	S 6 18.7	185 30.5	S21 43.3	Canopus	263 54.5	S52 42.4
01	99 07.3	147 31.4	16.5	129 46.2	42.5	261 06.2	18.9	200 32.6	43.4	Capella	280 30.5	N46 00.7
02	114 09.7	162 30.9	15.7	144 46.8	41.8	276 08.3	19.0	215 34.8	43.4	Deneb	49 30.2	N45 20.8
03	129 12.2	177 30.5	. . 14.8	159 47.5	. . 41.2	291 10.4	. . 19.1	230 36.9	. . 43.4	Denebola	182 31.3	N14 28.6
04	144 14.7	192 30.0	14.0	174 48.2	40.5	306 12.6	19.2	245 39.1	43.4	Diphda	348 53.5	S17 53.8
05	159 17.1	207 29.6	13.2	189 48.8	39.8	321 14.7	19.4	260 41.2	43.5			
06	174 19.6	222 29.1	S20 12.4	204 49.5	S13 39.1	336 16.8	S 6 19.5	275 43.4	S21 43.5	Dubhe	193 48.9	N61 39.3
T 07	189 22.1	237 28.7	11.5	219 50.1	38.4	351 18.9	19.6	290 45.5	43.5	Elnath	278 09.2	N28 37.1
H 08	204 24.5	252 28.2	10.7	234 50.8	37.7	6 21.1	19.8	305 47.7	43.5	Eltanin	90 45.6	N51 29.4
U 09	219 27.0	267 27.8	. . 09.9	249 51.4	. . 37.0	21 23.2	. . 19.9	320 49.8	. . 43.6	Enif	33 45.0	N 9 57.3
R 10	234 29.4	282 27.3	09.1	264 52.1	36.3	36 25.3	20.0	335 51.9	43.6	Fomalhaut	15 21.5	S29 32.1
S 11	249 31.9	297 26.9	08.2	279 52.8	35.7	51 27.5	20.1	350 54.1	43.6			
D 12	264 34.4	312 26.4	S20 07.4	294 53.4	S13 35.0	66 29.6	S 6 20.3	5 56.2	S21 43.6	Gacrux	171 58.3	S57 12.1
A 13	279 36.8	327 26.0	06.6	309 54.1	34.3	81 31.7	20.4	20 58.4	43.7	Gienah	175 49.9	S17 38.0
Y 14	294 39.3	342 25.6	05.7	324 54.7	33.6	96 33.8	20.5	36 00.5	43.7	Hadar	148 44.8	S60 26.9
15	309 41.8	357 25.1	. . 04.9	339 55.4	. . 32.9	111 36.0	. . 20.7	51 02.7	. . 43.7	Hamal	327 57.8	N23 32.5
16	324 44.2	12 24.7	04.1	354 56.0	32.2	126 38.1	20.8	66 04.8	43.7	Kaus Aust.	83 41.1	S34 22.4
17	339 46.7	27 24.2	03.2	9 56.7	31.5	141 40.2	20.9	81 07.0	43.8			
18	354 49.2	42 23.8	S20 02.4	24 57.4	S13 30.8	156 42.4	S 6 21.0	96 09.1	S21 43.8	Kochab	137 21.2	N74 05.1
19	9 51.6	57 23.4	01.6	39 58.0	30.1	171 44.5	21.2	111 11.3	43.8	Markab	13 36.0	N15 17.9
20	24 54.1	72 22.9	20 00.7	54 58.7	29.4	186 46.6	21.3	126 13.4	43.8	Menkar	314 12.3	N 4 09.2
21	39 56.6	87 22.5	19 59.9	69 59.3	. . 28.8	201 48.7	. . 21.4	141 15.6	. . 43.9	Menkent	148 05.0	S36 26.9
22	54 59.0	102 22.1	59.1	85 00.0	28.1	216 50.9	21.5	156 17.7	43.9	Miaplacidus	221 38.4	S69 47.0
23	70 01.5	117 21.6	58.2	100 00.7	27.4	231 53.0	21.7	171 19.9	43.9			
16 00	85 03.9	132 21.2	S19 57.4	115 01.3	S13 26.7	246 55.1	S 6 21.8	186 22.0	S21 43.9	Mirfak	308 36.5	N49 55.2
01	100 06.4	147 20.8	56.5	130 02.0	26.0	261 57.3	21.9	201 24.2	44.0	Nunki	75 55.8	S26 16.4
02	115 08.9	162 20.3	55.7	145 02.6	25.3	276 59.4	22.0	216 26.3	44.0	Peacock	53 16.1	S56 40.8
03	130 11.3	177 19.9	. . 54.9	160 03.3	. . 24.6	292 01.5	. . 22.2	231 28.5	. . 44.0	Pollux	243 24.6	N27 58.8
04	145 13.8	192 19.5	54.0	175 04.0	23.9	307 03.7	22.3	246 30.6	44.0	Procyon	244 57.0	N 5 10.7
05	160 16.3	207 19.0	53.2	190 04.6	23.2	322 05.8	22.4	261 32.8	44.1			
06	175 18.7	222 18.6	S19 52.3	205 05.3	S13 22.5	337 07.9	S 6 22.6	276 34.9	S21 44.1	Rasalhague	96 04.6	N12 33.1
07	190 21.2	237 18.2	51.5	220 05.9	21.8	352 10.1	22.7	291 37.1	44.1	Regulus	207 40.9	N11 52.9
08	205 23.7	252 17.7	50.6	235 06.6	21.1	7 12.2	22.8	306 39.2	44.1	Rigel	281 09.5	S 8 11.1
F 09	220 26.1	267 17.3	. . 49.8	250 07.3	. . 20.5	22 14.3	. . 22.9	321 41.4	. . 44.2	Rigil Kent.	139 48.9	S60 53.9
R 10	235 28.6	282 16.9	48.9	265 07.9	19.8	37 16.5	23.1	336 43.5	44.2	Sabik	102 10.2	S15 44.5
I 11	250 31.1	297 16.5	48.1	280 08.6	19.1	52 18.6	23.2	351 45.6	44.2			
D 12	265 33.5	312 16.0	S19 47.2	295 09.2	S13 18.4	67 20.7	S 6 23.3	6 47.8	S21 44.2	Schedar	349 37.5	N56 38.0
A 13	280 36.0	327 15.6	46.4	310 09.9	17.7	82 22.9	23.4	21 49.9	44.3	Shaula	96 19.1	S37 06.7
Y 14	295 38.4	342 15.2	45.5	325 10.6	17.0	97 25.0	23.6	36 52.1	44.3	Sirius	258 31.3	S16 44.5
15	310 40.9	357 14.8	. . 44.7	340 11.2	. . 16.3	112 27.1	. . 23.7	51 54.2	. . 44.3	Spica	158 28.9	S11 14.8
16	325 43.4	12 14.4	43.8	355 11.9	15.6	127 29.3	23.8	66 56.4	44.3	Suhail	222 50.4	S43 30.0
17	340 45.8	27 13.9	43.0	10 12.6	14.9	142 31.4	23.9	81 58.5	44.4			
18	355 48.3	42 13.5	S19 42.1	25 13.2	S13 14.2	157 33.5	S 6 24.1	97 00.7	S21 44.4	Vega	80 37.8	N38 48.2
19	10 50.8	57 13.1	41.3	40 13.9	13.5	172 35.7	24.2	112 02.8	44.4	Zuben'ubi	137 03.1	S16 06.5
20	25 53.2	72 12.7	40.4	55 14.5	12.8	187 37.8	24.3	127 05.0	44.4		SHA	Mer.Pass.
21	40 55.7	87 12.3	. . 39.5	70 15.2	. . 12.1	202 39.9	. . 24.4	142 07.1	. . 44.5		° ′	h m
22	55 58.2	102 11.9	38.7	85 15.9	11.4	217 42.1	24.6	157 09.3	44.5	Venus	48 27.0	15 10
23	71 00.6	117 11.4	37.8	100 16.5	10.7	232 44.2	24.7	172 11.4	44.5	Mars	30 40.7	16 20
	h m									Jupiter	161 59.2	7 35
Mer. Pass.	18 20.7	v −0.4	d 0.8	v 0.7	d 0.7	v 2.1	d 0.1	v 2.1	d 0.0	Saturn	101 25.7	11 36

UT	SUN GHA	SUN Dec	MOON GHA	v	MOON Dec	d	HP
d h	° ′	° ′	° ′	′	° ′	′	′
14 00 (WEDNESDAY)	181 20.5	S23 13.1	1 06.7	3.9	N18 23.7	3.0	61.0
01	196 20.2	13.2	15 29.6	3.8	18 26.7	2.8	61.0
02	211 20.0	13.4	29 52.4	3.8	18 29.5	2.6	61.0
03	226 19.7	. . 13.5	44 15.2	3.8	18 32.1	2.5	61.0
04	241 19.4	13.7	58 38.0	3.9	18 34.6	2.4	60.9
05	256 19.1	13.8	73 00.9	3.8	18 37.0	2.3	60.9
06	271 18.8	S23 13.9	87 23.7	3.8	N18 39.3	2.1	60.9
07	286 18.5	14.1	101 46.5	3.9	18 41.4	1.9	60.9
08	301 18.2	14.2	116 09.4	3.8	18 43.3	1.8	60.9
09	316 17.9	. . 14.4	130 32.2	3.9	18 45.1	1.7	60.9
10	331 17.6	14.5	144 55.1	3.9	18 46.8	1.6	60.8
11	346 17.3	14.6	159 18.0	3.9	18 48.4	1.4	60.8
12	1 17.0	S23 14.8	173 40.9	3.9	N18 49.8	1.3	60.8
13	16 16.7	14.9	188 03.8	3.9	18 51.1	1.1	60.8
14	31 16.4	15.0	202 26.7	3.9	18 52.2	1.0	60.8
15	46 16.1	. . 15.2	216 49.6	4.0	18 53.2	0.8	60.7
16	61 15.8	15.3	231 12.6	4.0	18 54.0	0.7	60.7
17	76 15.5	15.4	245 35.6	4.0	18 54.7	0.6	60.7
18	91 15.2	S23 15.6	259 58.6	4.0	N18 55.3	0.4	60.7
19	106 14.9	15.7	274 21.6	4.1	18 55.7	0.3	60.7
20	121 14.6	15.8	288 44.7	4.1	18 56.0	0.2	60.6
21	136 14.3	. . 15.9	303 07.8	4.1	18 56.2	0.0	60.6
22	151 14.0	16.1	317 30.9	4.2	18 56.2	0.1	60.6
23	166 13.7	16.2	331 54.1	4.2	18 56.1	0.3	60.6
15 00 (THURSDAY)	181 13.4	S23 16.3	346 17.3	4.2	N18 55.8	0.4	60.5
01	196 13.1	16.5	0 40.5	4.3	18 55.4	0.5	60.5
02	211 12.8	16.6	15 03.8	4.3	18 54.9	0.7	60.5
03	226 12.5	. . 16.7	29 27.1	4.4	18 54.2	0.8	60.5
04	241 12.2	16.8	43 50.5	4.4	18 53.4	0.9	60.4
05	256 11.9	16.9	58 13.9	4.4	18 52.5	1.1	60.4
06	271 11.6	S23 17.1	72 37.3	4.5	N18 51.4	1.2	60.4
07	286 11.3	17.2	87 00.8	4.5	18 50.2	1.3	60.3
08	301 11.0	17.3	101 24.3	4.6	18 48.9	1.5	60.3
09	316 10.7	. . 17.4	115 47.9	4.6	18 47.4	1.6	60.3
10	331 10.4	17.5	130 11.5	4.7	18 45.8	1.7	60.3
11	346 10.1	17.7	144 35.2	4.8	18 44.1	1.9	60.2
12	1 09.8	S23 17.8	158 59.0	4.8	N18 42.2	2.0	60.2
13	16 09.5	17.9	173 22.8	4.8	18 40.2	2.1	60.2
14	31 09.2	18.0	187 46.6	4.9	18 38.1	2.3	60.1
15	46 08.9	. . 18.1	202 10.5	5.0	18 35.8	2.3	60.1
16	61 08.6	18.2	216 34.5	5.1	18 33.5	2.6	60.1
17	76 08.3	18.3	230 58.6	5.0	18 30.9	2.6	60.0
18	91 08.0	S23 18.5	245 22.6	5.2	N18 28.3	2.7	60.0
19	106 07.7	18.6	259 46.8	5.2	18 25.6	2.9	60.0
20	121 07.4	18.7	274 11.0	5.3	18 22.7	3.0	59.9
21	136 07.1	. . 18.8	288 35.3	5.4	18 19.7	3.2	59.9
22	151 06.8	18.9	302 59.7	5.4	18 16.5	3.2	59.9
23	166 06.4	19.0	317 24.1	5.5	18 13.3	3.4	59.8
16 00 (FRIDAY)	181 06.1	S23 19.1	331 48.6	5.6	N18 09.9	3.5	59.8
01	196 05.8	19.2	346 13.2	5.6	18 06.4	3.6	59.8
02	211 05.5	19.3	0 37.8	5.7	18 02.8	3.7	59.7
03	226 05.2	. . 19.4	15 02.5	5.8	17 59.1	3.8	59.7
04	241 04.9	19.5	29 27.3	5.9	17 55.3	4.0	59.7
05	256 04.6	19.6	43 52.2	5.9	17 51.3	4.0	59.6
06	271 04.3	S23 19.7	58 17.1	6.0	N17 47.3	4.2	59.6
07	286 04.0	19.8	72 42.1	6.1	17 43.1	4.3	59.6
08	301 03.7	19.9	87 07.2	6.1	17 38.8	4.4	59.5
09	316 03.4	. . 20.0	101 32.3	6.3	17 34.4	4.6	59.5
10	331 03.1	20.1	115 57.6	6.3	17 29.8	4.6	59.5
11	346 02.8	20.2	130 22.9	6.4	17 25.2	4.7	59.4
12	1 02.5	S23 20.3	144 48.3	6.5	N17 20.5	4.8	59.4
13	16 02.2	20.4	159 13.8	6.6	17 15.7	5.0	59.3
14	31 01.9	20.5	173 39.4	6.6	17 10.7	5.0	59.3
15	46 01.6	. . 20.6	188 05.0	6.7	17 05.7	5.2	59.3
16	61 01.3	20.7	202 30.7	6.9	17 00.5	5.3	59.2
17	76 01.0	20.8	216 56.6	6.9	16 55.2	5.3	59.2
18	91 00.7	S23 20.9	231 22.5	6.9	N16 49.9	5.5	59.2
19	106 00.4	21.0	245 48.4	7.1	16 44.4	5.5	59.1
20	121 00.1	21.1	260 14.5	7.2	16 38.9	5.7	59.1
21	135 59.8	. . 21.2	274 40.7	7.2	16 33.2	5.7	59.0
22	150 59.5	21.3	289 06.9	7.3	16 27.5	5.9	59.0
23	165 59.2	21.3	303 33.2	7.5	N16 21.6	5.9	59.0
	SD 16.3	d 0.1	SD 16.6		16.4		16.2

Lat.	Twilight Naut.	Twilight Civil	Sunrise	Moonrise 14	Moonrise 15	Moonrise 16	Moonrise 17
°	h m	h m	h m	h m	h m	h m	h m
N 72	08 21	10 48	■	□	□	15 54	18 05
N 70	08 01	09 48	■	13 56	15 06	16 48	18 35
68	07 45	09 14	■	14 44	15 52	17 21	18 57
66	07 32	08 49	10 28	15 15	16 22	17 44	19 14
64	07 21	08 29	09 47	15 38	16 44	18 03	19 28
62	07 12	08 13	09 19	15 57	17 02	18 18	19 40
60	07 03	08 00	08 57	16 12	17 17	18 31	19 50
N 58	06 56	07 48	08 40	16 25	17 29	18 42	19 59
56	06 49	07 38	08 26	16 36	17 40	18 52	20 06
54	06 43	07 29	08 13	16 46	17 50	19 00	20 13
52	06 37	07 21	08 02	16 55	17 58	19 08	20 19
50	06 32	07 14	07 52	17 03	18 06	19 14	20 25
45	06 21	06 58	07 32	17 19	18 22	19 29	20 36
N 40	06 10	06 44	07 15	17 33	18 36	19 41	20 46
35	06 01	06 33	07 01	17 45	18 47	19 51	20 54
30	05 52	06 22	06 48	17 55	18 57	20 00	21 02
20	05 36	06 03	06 27	18 13	19 14	20 15	21 14
N 10	05 20	05 46	06 09	18 28	19 29	20 29	21 25
0	05 03	05 29	05 52	18 43	19 43	20 41	21 35
S 10	04 44	05 11	05 34	18 57	19 57	20 54	21 46
20	04 22	04 51	05 15	19 13	20 12	21 07	21 57
30	03 53	04 26	04 53	19 30	20 29	21 22	22 09
35	03 34	04 11	04 40	19 41	20 39	21 31	22 16
40	03 11	03 53	04 25	19 53	20 51	21 41	22 25
45	02 41	03 30	04 08	20 07	21 04	21 53	22 34
S 50	01 56	03 01	03 45	20 24	21 21	22 07	22 46
52	01 28	02 46	03 34	20 32	21 28	22 14	22 51
54	00 44	02 28	03 22	20 41	21 37	22 21	22 57
56	////	02 06	03 08	20 51	21 46	22 29	23 03
58	////	01 37	02 51	21 02	21 57	22 39	23 10
S 60	////	00 49	02 31	21 16	22 10	22 49	23 19

Lat.	Sunset	Twilight Civil	Twilight Naut.	Moonset 14	Moonset 15	Moonset 16	Moonset 17
°	h m	h m	h m	h m	h m	h m	h m
N 72	■	13 03	15 30	□	□	13 08	12 52
N 70	■	14 02	15 50	10 54	11 52	12 14	12 21
68	■	14 37	16 05	10 06	11 07	11 40	11 58
66	13 23	15 02	16 18	09 36	10 37	11 16	11 40
64	14 04	15 21	16 29	09 13	10 14	10 57	11 25
62	14 32	15 37	16 39	08 54	09 56	10 41	11 13
60	14 53	15 51	16 47	08 39	09 41	10 28	11 02
N 58	15 10	16 02	16 55	08 26	09 28	10 16	10 53
56	15 25	16 12	17 01	08 15	09 17	10 06	10 45
54	15 38	16 21	17 07	08 05	09 07	09 58	10 38
52	15 49	16 29	17 13	07 57	08 59	09 50	10 31
50	15 58	16 37	17 18	07 49	08 51	09 43	10 25
45	16 19	16 53	17 30	07 32	08 34	09 28	10 13
N 40	16 36	17 06	17 40	07 19	08 21	09 15	10 02
35	16 50	17 18	17 50	07 07	08 09	09 04	09 53
30	17 02	17 29	17 58	06 57	07 59	08 55	09 45
20	17 23	17 47	18 15	06 40	07 41	08 39	09 31
N 10	17 42	18 05	18 31	06 24	07 26	08 25	09 19
0	17 59	18 22	18 48	06 10	07 12	08 11	09 08
S 10	18 17	18 40	19 07	05 56	06 57	07 58	08 56
20	18 35	19 00	19 29	05 41	06 42	07 44	08 44
30	18 57	19 25	19 58	05 23	06 24	07 27	08 30
35	19 10	19 40	20 17	05 13	06 14	07 17	08 21
40	19 25	19 58	20 40	05 01	06 02	07 06	08 12
45	19 43	20 21	21 10	04 48	05 48	06 53	08 01
S 50	20 06	20 50	21 55	04 31	05 31	06 38	07 47
52	20 17	21 05	22 23	04 23	05 23	06 30	07 41
54	20 29	21 23	23 08	04 14	05 14	06 22	07 34
56	20 43	21 45	////	04 05	05 04	06 13	07 26
58	21 00	22 15	////	03 53	04 53	06 02	07 18
S 60	21 20	23 03	////	03 41	04 39	05 50	07 08

Day	SUN Eqn. of Time 00^h	SUN Eqn. of Time 12^h	SUN Mer. Pass.	MOON Mer. Pass. Upper	MOON Mer. Pass. Lower	Age	Phase
d	m s	m s	h m	h m	h m	d	%
14	05 23	05 08	11 55	24 57	12 26	15	99
15	04 54	04 40	11 55	00 57	13 28	16	97
16	04 25	04 11	11 56	01 57	14 26	17	91

UT	ARIES	VENUS −4·3		MARS +0·8		JUPITER −1·9		SATURN +0·5	
d h	GHA ° ′	GHA ° ′	Dec ° ′	GHA ° ′	Dec ° ′	GHA ° ′	Dec ° ′	GHA ° ′	Dec ° ′
17 00	86 03.1	132 11.0	S19 37.0	115 17.2	S13 10.0	247 46.4	S 6 24.8	187 13.6	S21 44.5
01	101 05.6	147 10.6	36.1	130 17.9	09.3	262 48.5	24.9	202 15.7	44.6
02	116 08.0	162 10.2	35.2	145 18.5	08.6	277 50.6	25.1	217 17.9	44.6
03	131 10.5	177 09.8	. . 34.4	160 19.2	. . 07.9	292 52.8	. . 25.2	232 20.0	. . 44.6
04	146 12.9	192 09.4	33.5	175 19.8	07.2	307 54.9	25.3	247 22.2	44.6
05	161 15.4	207 09.0	32.7	190 20.5	06.6	322 57.0	25.4	262 24.3	44.7
06	176 17.9	222 08.6	S19 31.8	205 21.2	S13 05.9	337 59.2	S 6 25.6	277 26.5	S21 44.7
S 07	191 20.3	237 08.2	30.9	220 21.8	05.2	353 01.3	25.7	292 28.6	44.7
A 08	206 22.8	252 07.7	30.1	235 22.5	04.5	8 03.4	25.8	307 30.8	44.7
T 09	221 25.3	267 07.3	. . 29.2	250 23.2	. . 03.8	23 05.6	. . 25.9	322 32.9	. . 44.8
U 10	236 27.7	282 06.9	28.3	265 23.8	03.1	38 07.7	26.0	337 35.1	44.8
R 11	251 30.2	297 06.5	27.5	280 24.5	02.4	53 09.9	26.2	352 37.2	44.8
D 12	266 32.7	312 06.1	S19 26.6	295 25.2	S13 01.7	68 12.0	S 6 26.3	7 39.4	S21 44.8
A 13	281 35.1	327 05.7	25.7	310 25.8	01.0	83 14.1	26.4	22 41.5	44.9
Y 14	296 37.6	342 05.3	24.8	325 26.5	13 00.3	98 16.3	26.5	37 43.6	44.9
15	311 40.1	357 04.9	. . 24.0	340 27.2	12 59.6	113 18.4	. . 26.7	52 45.8	. . 44.9
16	326 42.5	12 04.5	23.1	355 27.8	58.9	128 20.6	26.8	67 47.9	44.9
17	341 45.0	27 04.1	22.2	10 28.5	58.2	143 22.7	26.9	82 50.1	45.0
18	356 47.4	42 03.7	S19 21.3	25 29.2	S12 57.5	158 24.8	S 6 27.0	97 52.2	S21 45.0
19	11 49.9	57 03.3	20.5	40 29.8	56.8	173 27.0	27.2	112 54.4	45.0
20	26 52.4	72 02.9	19.6	55 30.5	56.1	188 29.1	27.3	127 56.5	45.0
21	41 54.8	87 02.5	. . 18.7	70 31.1	. . 55.4	203 31.2	. . 27.4	142 58.7	. . 45.1
22	56 57.3	102 02.1	17.8	85 31.8	54.7	218 33.4	27.5	158 00.8	45.1
23	71 59.8	117 01.7	17.0	100 32.5	54.0	233 35.5	27.6	173 03.0	45.1
18 00	87 02.2	132 01.3	S19 16.1	115 33.1	S12 53.3	248 37.7	S 6 27.8	188 05.1	S21 45.1
01	102 04.7	147 01.0	15.2	130 33.8	52.6	263 39.8	27.9	203 07.3	45.2
02	117 07.2	162 00.6	14.3	145 34.5	51.9	278 42.0	28.0	218 09.4	45.2
03	132 09.6	177 00.2	. . 13.4	160 35.1	. . 51.2	293 44.1	. . 28.1	233 11.6	. . 45.2
04	147 12.1	191 59.8	12.6	175 35.8	50.5	308 46.2	28.3	248 13.7	45.2
05	162 14.5	206 59.4	11.7	190 36.5	49.8	323 48.4	28.4	263 15.9	45.2
06	177 17.0	221 59.0	S19 10.8	205 37.2	S12 49.1	338 50.5	S 6 28.5	278 18.0	S21 45.3
07	192 19.5	236 58.6	09.9	220 37.8	48.4	353 52.7	28.6	293 20.2	45.3
08	207 21.9	251 58.2	09.0	235 38.5	47.7	8 54.8	28.7	308 22.3	45.3
S 09	222 24.4	266 57.8	. . 08.1	250 39.2	. . 47.0	23 56.9	. . 28.9	323 24.5	. . 45.3
U 10	237 26.9	281 57.5	07.2	265 39.8	46.3	38 59.1	29.0	338 26.6	45.4
N 11	252 29.3	296 57.1	06.4	280 40.5	45.6	54 01.2	29.1	353 28.8	45.4
D 12	267 31.8	311 56.7	S19 05.5	295 41.2	S12 44.9	69 03.4	S 6 29.2	8 30.9	S21 45.4
A 13	282 34.3	326 56.3	04.6	310 41.8	44.1	84 05.5	29.3	23 33.1	45.4
Y 14	297 36.7	341 55.9	03.7	325 42.5	43.4	99 07.7	29.5	38 35.2	45.5
15	312 39.2	356 55.5	. . 02.8	340 43.2	. . 42.7	114 09.8	. . 29.6	53 37.4	. . 45.5
16	327 41.7	11 55.2	01.9	355 43.8	42.0	129 11.9	29.7	68 39.5	45.5
17	342 44.1	26 54.8	01.0	10 44.5	41.3	144 14.1	29.8	83 41.7	45.5
18	357 46.6	41 54.4	S19 00.1	25 45.2	S12 40.6	159 16.2	S 6 30.0	98 43.8	S21 45.6
19	12 49.0	56 54.0	18 59.2	40 45.8	39.9	174 18.4	30.1	113 46.0	45.6
20	27 51.5	71 53.7	58.3	55 46.5	39.2	189 20.5	30.2	128 48.1	45.6
21	42 54.0	86 53.3	. . 57.4	70 47.2	. . 38.5	204 22.7	. . 30.3	143 50.3	. . 45.6
22	57 56.4	101 52.9	56.5	85 47.8	37.8	219 24.8	30.4	158 52.4	45.7
23	72 58.9	116 52.5	55.6	100 48.5	37.1	234 27.0	30.6	173 54.5	45.7
19 00	88 01.4	131 52.2	S18 54.7	115 49.2	S12 36.4	249 29.1	S 6 30.7	188 56.7	S21 45.7
01	103 03.8	146 51.8	53.8	130 49.9	35.7	264 31.2	30.8	203 58.8	45.7
02	118 06.3	161 51.4	52.9	145 50.5	35.0	279 33.4	30.9	219 01.0	45.8
03	133 08.8	176 51.0	. . 52.0	160 51.2	. . 34.3	294 35.5	. . 31.0	234 03.1	. . 45.8
04	148 11.2	191 50.7	51.1	175 51.9	33.6	309 37.7	31.2	249 05.3	45.8
05	163 13.7	206 50.3	50.2	190 52.5	32.9	324 39.8	31.3	264 07.4	45.8
06	178 16.2	221 49.9	S18 49.3	205 53.2	S12 32.2	339 42.0	S 6 31.4	279 09.6	S21 45.9
07	193 18.6	236 49.6	48.4	220 53.9	31.5	354 44.1	31.5	294 11.7	45.9
08	208 21.1	251 49.2	47.5	235 54.6	30.8	9 46.3	31.6	309 13.9	45.9
M 09	223 23.5	266 48.8	. . 46.6	250 55.2	. . 30.0	24 48.4	. . 31.8	324 16.0	. . 45.9
O 10	238 26.0	281 48.5	45.7	265 55.9	29.3	39 50.6	31.9	339 18.2	45.9
N 11	253 28.5	296 48.1	44.8	280 56.6	28.6	54 52.7	32.0	354 20.3	46.0
D 12	268 30.9	311 47.8	S18 43.9	295 57.2	S12 27.9	69 54.9	S 6 32.1	9 22.5	S21 46.0
A 13	283 33.4	326 47.4	43.0	310 57.9	27.2	84 57.0	32.2	24 24.6	46.0
Y 14	298 35.9	341 47.0	42.1	325 58.6	26.5	99 59.2	32.4	39 26.8	46.0
15	313 38.3	356 46.7	. . 41.2	340 59.3	. . 25.8	115 01.3	. . 32.5	54 28.9	. . 46.1
16	328 40.8	11 46.3	40.3	355 59.9	25.1	130 03.5	32.6	69 31.1	46.1
17	343 43.3	26 46.0	39.4	11 00.6	24.4	145 05.6	32.7	84 33.2	46.1
18	358 45.7	41 45.6	S18 38.4	26 01.3	S12 23.7	160 07.7	S 6 32.8	99 35.4	S21 46.1
19	13 48.2	56 45.2	37.5	41 01.9	23.0	175 09.9	32.9	114 37.5	46.2
20	28 50.6	71 44.9	36.6	56 02.6	22.3	190 12.0	33.1	129 39.7	46.2
21	43 53.1	86 44.5	. . 35.7	71 03.3	. . 21.6	205 14.2	. . 33.2	144 41.8	. . 46.2
22	58 55.6	101 44.2	34.8	86 04.0	20.8	220 16.3	33.3	159 44.0	46.2
23	73 58.0	116 43.8	33.9	101 04.6	20.1	235 18.5	33.4	174 46.1	46.3
Mer. Pass.	h m 18 08.9	*v* −0.4	*d* 0.9	*v* 0.7	*d* 0.7	*v* 2.1	*d* 0.1	*v* 2.1	*d* 0.0

STARS Name	SHA ° ′	Dec ° ′
Acamar	315 16.3	S40 14.5
Achernar	335 24.8	S57 09.4
Acrux	173 06.6	S63 11.2
Adhara	255 10.3	S28 59.8
Aldebaran	290 46.3	N16 32.4
Alioth	166 18.9	N55 51.9
Alkaid	152 57.4	N49 13.6
Al Na'ir	27 41.1	S46 52.9
Alnilam	275 43.6	S 1 11.7
Alphard	217 53.6	S 8 44.0
Alphecca	126 09.4	N26 39.6
Alpheratz	357 41.0	N29 11.2
Altair	62 06.2	N 8 55.0
Ankaa	353 13.4	S42 13.1
Antares	112 23.7	S26 27.9
Arcturus	145 53.8	N19 05.7
Atria	107 23.9	S69 03.1
Avior	234 16.4	S59 33.8
Bellatrix	278 29.1	N 6 21.7
Betelgeuse	270 58.4	N 7 24.4
Canopus	263 54.5	S52 42.4
Capella	280 30.4	N46 00.7
Deneb	49 30.2	N45 20.8
Denebola	182 31.3	N14 28.6
Diphda	348 53.5	S17 53.8
Dubhe	193 48.8	N61 39.3
Elnath	278 09.2	N28 37.1
Eltanin	90 45.6	N51 29.4
Enif	33 45.0	N 9 57.3
Fomalhaut	15 21.5	S29 32.1
Gacrux	171 58.2	S57 12.1
Gienah	175 49.9	S17 38.0
Hadar	148 44.8	S60 26.9
Hamal	327 57.8	N23 32.5
Kaus Aust.	83 41.1	S34 22.4
Kochab	137 21.2	N74 05.1
Markab	13 36.0	N15 17.9
Menkar	314 12.3	N 4 09.2
Menkent	148 05.0	S36 26.9
Miaplacidus	221 38.4	S69 47.0
Mirfak	308 36.5	N49 55.2
Nunki	75 55.8	S26 16.4
Peacock	53 16.1	S56 40.8
Pollux	243 24.5	N27 58.8
Procyon	244 57.0	N 5 10.7
Rasalhague	96 04.6	N12 33.1
Regulus	207 40.9	N11 52.9
Rigel	281 09.4	S 8 11.2
Rigil Kent.	139 48.9	S60 53.9
Sabik	102 10.2	S15 44.5
Schedar	349 37.5	N56 38.0
Shaula	96 19.1	S37 06.7
Sirius	258 31.3	S16 44.5
Spica	158 28.9	S11 14.8
Suhail	222 50.3	S43 30.0
Vega	80 37.8	N38 48.2
Zuben'ubi	137 03.0	S16 06.5

	SHA ° ′	Mer. Pass. h m
Venus	44 59.1	15 12
Mars	28 30.9	16 17
Jupiter	161 35.4	7 24
Saturn	101 02.9	11 26

UT	Day	SUN GHA	SUN Dec	MOON GHA	v	MOON Dec	d	HP
d h		° ′	° ′	° ′	′	° ′	′	′
17 00	SATURDAY	180 58.9	S23 21.4	317 59.7	7.5	N16 15.7	6.0	58.9
01		195 58.6	21.5	332 26.2	7.5	16 09.7	6.2	58.9
02		210 58.2	21.6	346 52.7	7.7	16 03.5	6.2	58.8
03		225 57.9	. . 21.7	1 19.4	7.8	15 57.3	6.3	58.8
04		240 57.6	21.8	15 46.2	7.8	15 51.0	6.4	58.8
05		255 57.3	21.9	30 13.0	8.0	15 44.6	6.4	58.7
06		270 57.0	S23 21.9	44 40.0	8.0	N15 38.2	6.6	58.7
07		285 56.7	22.0	59 07.0	8.1	15 31.6	6.6	58.6
08		300 56.4	22.1	73 34.1	8.2	15 25.0	6.8	58.6
09		315 56.1	. . 22.2	88 01.3	8.3	15 18.2	6.8	58.6
10		330 55.8	22.3	102 28.6	8.4	15 11.4	6.9	58.5
11		345 55.5	22.3	116 56.0	8.5	15 04.5	6.9	58.5
12		0 55.2	S23 22.4	131 23.5	8.5	N14 57.6	7.1	58.4
13		15 54.9	22.5	145 51.0	8.7	14 50.5	7.1	58.4
14		30 54.6	22.6	160 18.7	8.7	14 43.4	7.2	58.4
15		45 54.3	. . 22.6	174 46.4	8.9	14 36.2	7.3	58.3
16		60 54.0	22.7	189 14.3	8.9	14 28.9	7.3	58.3
17		75 53.7	22.8	203 42.2	9.0	14 21.6	7.4	58.2
18		90 53.4	S23 22.9	218 10.2	9.1	N14 14.2	7.5	58.2
19		105 53.1	22.9	232 38.3	9.2	14 06.7	7.6	58.2
20		120 52.7	23.0	247 06.5	9.2	13 59.1	7.6	58.1
21		135 52.4	. . 23.1	261 34.7	9.4	13 51.5	7.7	58.1
22		150 52.1	23.1	276 03.1	9.4	13 43.8	7.8	58.0
23		165 51.8	23.2	290 31.5	9.6	13 36.0	7.8	58.0
18 00	SUNDAY	180 51.5	S23 23.3	305 00.1	9.6	N13 28.2	7.9	58.0
01		195 51.2	23.4	319 28.7	9.7	13 20.3	8.0	57.9
02		210 50.9	23.4	333 57.4	9.8	13 12.3	8.0	57.9
03		225 50.6	. . 23.5	348 26.2	9.9	13 04.3	8.0	57.8
04		240 50.3	23.5	2 55.1	9.9	12 56.3	8.2	57.8
05		255 50.0	23.6	17 24.0	10.1	12 48.1	8.2	57.8
06		270 49.7	S23 23.7	31 53.1	10.1	N12 39.9	8.2	57.7
07		285 49.4	23.7	46 22.2	10.2	12 31.7	8.3	57.7
08		300 49.1	23.8	60 51.4	10.3	12 23.4	8.4	57.6
09		315 48.8	. . 23.9	75 20.7	10.4	12 15.0	8.4	57.6
10		330 48.4	23.9	89 50.1	10.5	12 06.6	8.5	57.6
11		345 48.1	24.0	104 19.6	10.5	11 58.1	8.5	57.5
12		0 47.8	S23 24.0	118 49.1	10.7	N11 49.6	8.6	57.5
13		15 47.5	24.1	133 18.8	10.7	11 41.0	8.6	57.4
14		30 47.2	24.1	147 48.5	10.8	11 32.4	8.6	57.4
15		45 46.9	. . 24.2	162 18.3	10.8	11 23.8	8.8	57.4
16		60 46.6	24.3	176 48.1	11.0	11 15.0	8.7	57.3
17		75 46.3	24.3	191 18.1	11.0	11 06.3	8.8	57.3
18		90 46.0	S23 24.4	205 48.1	11.1	N10 57.5	8.9	57.2
19		105 45.7	24.4	220 18.2	11.2	10 48.6	8.9	57.2
20		120 45.4	24.5	234 48.4	11.3	10 39.7	8.9	57.2
21		135 45.1	. . 24.5	249 18.7	11.3	10 30.8	9.0	57.1
22		150 44.8	24.6	263 49.0	11.5	10 21.8	9.0	57.1
23		165 44.4	24.6	278 19.5	11.4	10 12.8	9.0	57.1
19 00	MONDAY	180 44.1	S23 24.7	292 49.9	11.6	N10 03.8	9.1	57.0
01		195 43.8	24.7	307 20.5	11.7	9 54.7	9.2	57.0
02		210 43.5	24.8	321 51.2	11.7	9 45.5	9.1	56.9
03		225 43.2	. . 24.8	336 21.9	11.8	9 36.4	9.2	56.9
04		240 42.9	24.9	350 52.7	11.8	9 27.2	9.3	56.9
05		255 42.6	24.9	5 23.5	12.0	9 17.9	9.2	56.8
06		270 42.3	S23 24.9	19 54.5	12.0	N 9 08.7	9.3	56.8
07		285 42.0	25.0	34 25.5	12.0	8 59.4	9.4	56.8
08		300 41.7	25.0	48 56.5	12.2	8 50.0	9.3	56.7
09		315 41.4	. . 25.1	63 27.7	12.2	8 40.7	9.4	56.7
10		330 41.1	25.1	77 58.9	12.3	8 31.3	9.4	56.6
11		345 40.7	25.1	92 30.2	12.3	8 21.9	9.5	56.6
12		0 40.4	S23 25.2	107 01.5	12.4	N 8 12.4	9.5	56.6
13		15 40.1	25.2	121 32.9	12.5	8 02.9	9.5	56.5
14		30 39.8	25.3	136 04.4	12.6	7 53.4	9.5	56.5
15		45 39.5	. . 25.3	150 36.0	12.6	7 43.9	9.6	56.5
16		60 39.2	25.3	165 07.6	12.6	7 34.3	9.5	56.4
17		75 38.9	25.4	179 39.2	12.8	7 24.8	9.6	56.4
18		90 38.6	S23 25.4	194 11.0	12.7	N 7 15.2	9.6	56.4
19		105 38.3	25.4	208 42.7	12.9	7 05.6	9.7	56.3
20		120 38.0	25.5	223 14.6	12.9	6 55.9	9.7	56.3
21		135 37.6	. . 25.5	237 46.5	13.0	6 46.2	9.6	56.2
22		150 37.3	25.5	252 18.5	13.0	6 36.6	9.7	56.2
23		165 37.0	25.6	266 50.5	13.1	N 6 26.9	9.7	56.2
		SD 16.3	*d* 0.1	SD 15.9		15.7		15.4

Lat.	Twilight Naut.	Twilight Civil	Sunrise	Moonrise 17	Moonrise 18	Moonrise 19	Moonrise 20
°	h m	h m	h m	h m	h m	h m	h m
N 72	08 24	10 54	■	18 05	20 01	21 48	23 29
N 70	08 04	09 52	■	18 35	20 19	21 58	23 32
68	07 48	09 17	■	18 57	20 33	22 06	23 35
66	07 35	08 52	10 32	19 14	20 45	22 12	23 37
64	07 24	08 32	09 50	19 28	20 54	22 18	23 39
62	07 14	08 16	09 22	19 40	21 02	22 23	23 40
60	07 06	08 02	09 00	19 50	21 09	22 27	23 42
N 58	06 58	07 51	08 43	19 59	21 15	22 30	23 43
56	06 51	07 41	08 28	20 06	21 21	22 34	23 44
54	06 45	07 31	08 15	20 13	21 26	22 37	23 45
52	06 40	07 23	08 04	20 19	21 30	22 39	23 46
50	06 34	07 16	07 54	20 25	21 34	22 42	23 47
45	06 22	07 00	07 34	20 36	21 43	22 47	23 49
N 40	06 12	06 46	07 17	20 46	21 50	22 51	23 50
35	06 03	06 34	07 03	20 54	21 56	22 55	23 52
30	05 54	06 24	06 50	21 02	22 01	22 58	23 53
20	05 37	06 05	06 29	21 14	22 10	23 04	23 55
N 10	05 21	05 48	06 10	21 25	22 19	23 09	23 57
0	05 04	05 31	05 53	21 35	22 26	23 14	23 59
S 10	04 45	05 12	05 35	21 46	22 34	23 18	24 00
20	04 23	04 52	05 17	21 57	22 42	23 23	24 02
30	03 54	04 27	04 54	22 09	22 51	23 29	24 04
35	03 35	04 12	04 41	22 16	22 56	23 32	24 05
40	03 12	03 54	04 26	22 25	23 02	23 36	24 07
45	02 41	03 31	04 08	22 34	23 09	23 40	24 08
S 50	01 56	03 01	03 46	22 46	23 17	23 45	24 10
52	01 28	02 46	03 35	22 51	23 21	23 47	24 11
54	00 42	02 28	03 23	22 57	23 25	23 50	24 12
56	////	02 06	03 08	23 03	23 30	23 53	24 13
58	////	01 36	02 52	23 10	23 35	23 56	24 14
S 60	////	00 46	02 31	23 19	23 41	23 59	24 15

Lat.	Sunset	Twilight Civil	Twilight Naut.	Moonset 17	Moonset 18	Moonset 19	Moonset 20
°	h m	h m	h m	h m	h m	h m	h m
N 72	■	12 59	15 30	12 52	12 43	12 35	12 29
N 70	■	14 01	15 50	12 21	12 23	12 24	12 23
68	■	14 36	16 06	11 58	12 08	12 14	12 19
66	13 21	15 02	16 19	11 40	11 55	12 06	12 15
64	14 03	15 21	16 30	11 25	11 45	12 00	12 11
62	14 32	15 37	16 39	11 13	11 36	11 54	12 08
60	14 53	15 51	16 48	11 02	11 28	11 49	12 06
N 58	15 11	16 03	16 55	10 53	11 21	11 44	12 04
56	15 26	16 13	17 02	10 45	11 15	11 40	12 02
54	15 38	16 22	17 08	10 38	11 10	11 36	12 00
52	15 49	16 30	17 14	10 31	11 05	11 33	11 58
50	15 59	16 38	17 19	10 25	11 00	11 30	11 56
45	16 20	16 54	17 31	10 13	10 51	11 24	11 53
N 40	16 37	17 07	17 41	10 02	10 43	11 18	11 50
35	16 51	17 19	17 51	09 53	10 36	11 13	11 48
30	17 03	17 30	18 00	09 45	10 29	11 09	11 46
20	17 25	17 49	18 16	09 31	10 19	11 02	11 42
N 10	17 43	18 06	18 32	09 19	10 09	10 55	11 39
0	18 01	18 23	18 49	09 08	10 00	10 49	11 35
S 10	18 18	18 41	19 08	08 56	09 51	10 43	11 32
20	18 37	19 02	19 31	08 44	09 41	10 36	11 29
30	18 59	19 27	20 00	08 30	09 30	10 29	11 25
35	19 12	19 42	20 19	08 21	09 24	10 24	11 22
40	19 27	20 00	20 42	08 12	09 17	10 19	11 20
45	19 45	20 23	21 13	08 01	09 08	10 13	11 17
S 50	20 08	20 52	21 58	07 47	08 58	10 06	11 13
52	20 19	21 08	22 26	07 41	08 53	10 03	11 11
54	20 31	21 26	23 13	07 34	08 48	10 00	11 10
56	20 45	21 48	////	07 26	08 42	09 56	11 08
58	21 02	22 18	////	07 18	08 35	09 51	11 05
S 60	21 23	23 09	////	07 08	08 27	09 46	11 03

Day	SUN Eqn. of Time 00^h	SUN Eqn. of Time 12^h	SUN Mer. Pass.	MOON Mer. Pass. Upper	MOON Mer. Pass. Lower	MOON Age	MOON Phase
d	m s	m s	h m	h m	h m	d %	
17	03 56	03 41	11 56	02 55	15 22	18 84	
18	03 27	03 12	11 57	03 48	16 13	19 75	
19	02 57	02 42	11 57	04 38	17 01	20 66	

2016 DECEMBER 20, 21, 22 (TUES., WED., THURS.)

	UT	ARIES	VENUS −4·3		MARS +0·8		JUPITER −1·9		SATURN +0·5	
		GHA	GHA	Dec	GHA	Dec	GHA	Dec	GHA	Dec
	d h	° ′	° ′	° ′	° ′	° ′	° ′	° ′	° ′	° ′
	20 00	89 00.5	131 43.5	S18 33.0	116 05.3	S12 19.4	250 20.6	S 6 33.5	189 48.3	S21 46.3
	01	104 03.0	146 43.1	32.0	131 06.0	18.7	265 22.8	33.7	204 50.4	46.3
	02	119 05.4	161 42.8	31.1	146 06.7	18.0	280 24.9	33.8	219 52.6	46.3
	03	134 07.9	176 42.4	. . 30.2	161 07.3	. . 17.3	295 27.1	. . 33.9	234 54.7	. . 46.3
	04	149 10.4	191 42.1	29.3	176 08.0	16.6	310 29.2	34.0	249 56.9	46.4
	05	164 12.8	206 41.7	28.4	191 08.7	15.9	325 31.4	34.1	264 59.0	46.4
	06	179 15.3	221 41.4	S18 27.4	206 09.4	S12 15.2	340 33.6	S 6 34.2	280 01.2	S21 46.4
	07	194 17.8	236 41.0	26.5	221 10.0	14.5	355 35.7	34.4	295 03.3	46.4
T	08	209 20.2	251 40.7	25.6	236 10.7	13.7	10 37.9	34.5	310 05.5	46.5
U	09	224 22.7	266 40.3	. . 24.7	251 11.4	. . 13.0	25 40.0	. . 34.6	325 07.6	. . 46.5
E	10	239 25.1	281 40.0	23.8	266 12.1	12.3	40 42.2	34.7	340 09.8	46.5
	11	254 27.6	296 39.6	22.8	281 12.7	11.6	55 44.3	34.8	355 11.9	46.5
S	12	269 30.1	311 39.3	S18 21.9	296 13.4	S12 10.9	70 46.5	S 6 34.9	10 14.1	S21 46.6
D	13	284 32.5	326 39.0	21.0	311 14.1	10.2	85 48.6	35.1	25 16.2	46.6
A	14	299 35.0	341 38.6	20.1	326 14.8	09.5	100 50.8	35.2	40 18.4	46.6
Y	15	314 37.5	356 38.3	. . 19.1	341 15.4	. . 08.8	115 52.9	. . 35.3	55 20.5	. . 46.6
	16	329 39.9	11 37.9	18.2	356 16.1	08.1	130 55.1	35.4	70 22.7	46.7
	17	344 42.4	26 37.6	17.3	11 16.8	07.3	145 57.2	35.5	85 24.8	46.7
	18	359 44.9	41 37.3	S18 16.3	26 17.5	S12 06.6	160 59.4	S 6 35.6	100 27.0	S21 46.7
	19	14 47.3	56 36.9	15.4	41 18.1	05.9	176 01.5	35.8	115 29.1	46.7
	20	29 49.8	71 36.6	14.5	56 18.8	05.2	191 03.7	35.9	130 31.3	46.7
	21	44 52.3	86 36.3	. . 13.5	71 19.5	. . 04.5	206 05.8	. . 36.0	145 33.4	. . 46.8
	22	59 54.7	101 35.9	12.6	86 20.2	03.8	221 08.0	36.1	160 35.6	46.8
	23	74 57.2	116 35.6	11.7	101 20.8	03.1	236 10.2	36.2	175 37.7	46.8
	21 00	89 59.6	131 35.3	S18 10.7	116 21.5	S12 02.3	251 12.3	S 6 36.3	190 39.9	S21 46.8
	01	105 02.1	146 34.9	09.8	131 22.2	01.6	266 14.5	36.5	205 42.0	46.9
	02	120 04.6	161 34.6	08.9	146 22.9	00.9	281 16.6	36.6	220 44.2	46.9
	03	135 07.0	176 34.3	. . 07.9	161 23.6	12 00.2	296 18.8	. . 36.7	235 46.3	. . 46.9
	04	150 09.5	191 34.0	07.0	176 24.2	11 59.5	311 20.9	36.8	250 48.5	46.9
	05	165 12.0	206 33.6	06.1	191 24.9	58.8	326 23.1	36.9	265 50.6	47.0
	06	180 14.4	221 33.3	S18 05.1	206 25.6	S11 58.1	341 25.2	S 6 37.0	280 52.8	S21 47.0
W	07	195 16.9	236 33.0	04.2	221 26.3	57.3	356 27.4	37.2	295 54.9	47.0
E	08	210 19.4	251 32.6	03.3	236 26.9	56.6	11 29.6	37.3	310 57.1	47.0
D	09	225 21.8	266 32.3	. . 02.3	251 27.6	. . 55.9	26 31.7	. . 37.4	325 59.2	. . 47.0
	10	240 24.3	281 32.0	01.4	266 28.3	55.2	41 33.9	37.5	341 01.4	47.1
N	11	255 26.7	296 31.7	18 00.4	281 29.0	54.5	56 36.0	37.6	356 03.5	47.1
E	12	270 29.2	311 31.4	S17 59.5	296 29.7	S11 53.8	71 38.2	S 6 37.7	11 05.7	S21 47.1
S	13	285 31.7	326 31.0	58.5	311 30.3	53.1	86 40.3	37.8	26 07.8	47.1
D	14	300 34.1	341 30.7	57.6	326 31.0	52.3	101 42.5	38.0	41 10.0	47.2
A	15	315 36.6	356 30.4	. . 56.7	341 31.7	. . 51.6	116 44.7	. . 38.1	56 12.1	. . 47.2
Y	16	330 39.1	11 30.1	55.7	356 32.4	50.9	131 46.8	38.2	71 14.3	47.2
	17	345 41.5	26 29.8	54.8	11 33.0	50.2	146 49.0	38.3	86 16.4	47.2
	18	0 44.0	41 29.4	S17 53.8	26 33.7	S11 49.5	161 51.1	S 6 38.4	101 18.6	S21 47.3
	19	15 46.5	56 29.1	52.9	41 34.4	48.8	176 53.3	38.5	116 20.7	47.3
	20	30 48.9	71 28.8	51.9	56 35.1	48.0	191 55.4	38.6	131 22.9	47.3
	21	45 51.4	86 28.5	. . 51.0	71 35.8	. . 47.3	206 57.6	. . 38.8	146 25.0	. . 47.3
	22	60 53.9	101 28.2	50.0	86 36.4	46.6	221 59.8	38.9	161 27.2	47.3
	23	75 56.3	116 27.9	49.1	101 37.1	45.9	237 01.9	39.0	176 29.3	47.4
	22 00	90 58.8	131 27.6	S17 48.1	116 37.8	S11 45.2	252 04.1	S 6 39.1	191 31.5	S21 47.4
	01	106 01.2	146 27.3	47.2	131 38.5	44.5	267 06.2	39.2	206 33.6	47.4
	02	121 03.7	161 27.0	46.2	146 39.2	43.7	282 08.4	39.3	221 35.8	47.4
	03	136 06.2	176 26.6	. . 45.3	161 39.8	. . 43.0	297 10.6	. . 39.4	236 37.9	. . 47.5
	04	151 08.6	191 26.3	44.3	176 40.5	42.3	312 12.7	39.5	251 40.1	47.5
	05	166 11.1	206 26.0	43.4	191 41.2	41.6	327 14.9	39.7	266 42.2	47.5
	06	181 13.6	221 25.7	S17 42.4	206 41.9	S11 40.9	342 17.1	S 6 39.8	281 44.4	S21 47.5
	07	196 16.0	236 25.4	41.4	221 42.6	40.1	357 19.2	39.9	296 46.5	47.5
T	08	211 18.5	251 25.1	40.5	236 43.3	39.4	12 21.4	40.0	311 48.7	47.6
H	09	226 21.0	266 24.8	. . 39.5	251 43.9	. . 38.7	27 23.5	. . 40.1	326 50.8	. . 47.6
U	10	241 23.4	281 24.5	38.6	266 44.6	38.0	42 25.7	40.2	341 53.0	47.6
R	11	256 25.9	296 24.2	37.6	281 45.3	37.3	57 27.9	40.3	356 55.1	47.6
S	12	271 28.4	311 23.9	S17 36.7	296 46.0	S11 36.5	72 30.0	S 6 40.5	11 57.3	S21 47.7
D	13	286 30.8	326 23.6	35.7	311 46.7	35.8	87 32.2	40.6	26 59.4	47.7
A	14	301 33.3	341 23.3	34.7	326 47.3	35.1	102 34.3	40.7	42 01.6	47.7
	15	316 35.7	356 23.0	. . 33.8	341 48.0	. . 34.4	117 36.5	. . 40.8	57 03.7	. . 47.7
Y	16	331 38.2	11 22.7	32.8	356 48.7	33.7	132 38.7	40.9	72 05.9	47.8
	17	346 40.7	26 22.4	31.8	11 49.4	32.9	147 40.8	41.0	87 08.0	47.8
	18	1 43.1	41 22.1	S17 30.9	26 50.1	S11 32.2	162 43.0	S 6 41.1	102 10.2	S21 47.8
	19	16 45.6	56 21.8	29.9	41 50.8	31.5	177 45.2	41.2	117 12.3	47.8
	20	31 48.1	71 21.5	29.0	56 51.4	30.8	192 47.3	41.3	132 14.5	47.8
	21	46 50.5	86 21.2	. . 28.0	71 52.1	. . 30.1	207 49.5	. . 41.5	147 16.6	. . 47.9
	22	61 53.0	101 21.0	27.0	86 52.8	29.3	222 51.7	41.6	162 18.8	47.9
	23	76 55.5	116 20.7	26.1	101 53.5	28.6	237 53.8	41.7	177 20.9	47.9
	Mer. Pass.	h m 17 57.1	v −0.3	d 0.9	v 0.7	d 0.7	v 2.2	d 0.1	v 2.1	d 0.0

STARS

Name	SHA	Dec
	° ′	° ′
Acamar	315 16.3	S40 14.5
Achernar	335 24.9	S57 09.4
Acrux	173 06.5	S63 11.2
Adhara	255 10.3	S28 59.9
Aldebaran	290 46.3	N16 32.4
Alioth	166 18.9	N55 51.9
Alkaid	152 57.4	N49 13.6
Al Na'ir	27 41.1	S46 52.9
Alnilam	275 43.6	S 1 11.7
Alphard	217 53.5	S 8 44.0
Alphecca	126 09.3	N26 39.6
Alpheratz	357 41.0	N29 11.2
Altair	62 06.2	N 8 55.0
Ankaa	353 13.4	S42 13.1
Antares	112 23.7	S26 27.9
Arcturus	145 53.8	N19 05.7
Atria	107 23.9	S69 03.1
Avior	234 16.4	S59 33.8
Bellatrix	278 29.1	N 6 21.7
Betelgeuse	270 58.4	N 7 24.4
Canopus	263 54.5	S52 42.4
Capella	280 30.4	N46 00.7
Deneb	49 30.2	N45 20.7
Denebola	182 31.3	N14 28.6
Diphda	348 53.5	S17 53.8
Dubhe	193 48.8	N61 39.3
Elnath	278 09.2	N28 37.1
Eltanin	90 45.6	N51 29.4
Enif	33 45.0	N 9 57.3
Fomalhaut	15 21.5	S29 32.1
Gacrux	171 58.2	S57 12.1
Gienah	175 49.9	S17 38.0
Hadar	148 44.7	S60 26.9
Hamal	327 57.9	N23 32.5
Kaus Aust.	83 41.1	S34 22.4
Kochab	137 21.2	N74 05.1
Markab	13 36.0	N15 17.9
Menkar	314 12.3	N 4 09.2
Menkent	148 05.0	S36 26.9
Miaplacidus	221 38.4	S69 47.1
Mirfak	308 36.5	N49 55.2
Nunki	75 55.8	S26 16.4
Peacock	53 16.1	S56 40.8
Pollux	243 24.5	N27 58.8
Procyon	244 57.0	N 5 10.7
Rasalhague	96 04.6	N12 33.1
Regulus	207 40.9	N11 52.9
Rigel	281 09.4	S 8 11.2
Rigil Kent.	139 48.8	S60 53.9
Sabik	102 10.2	S15 44.5
Schedar	349 37.6	N56 38.0
Shaula	96 19.1	S37 06.7
Sirius	258 31.3	S16 44.6
Spica	158 28.9	S11 14.8
Suhail	222 50.3	S43 30.0
Vega	80 37.8	N38 48.2
Zuben'ubi	137 03.0	S16 06.5

	SHA	Mer. Pass.
	° ′	h m
Venus	41 35.6	15 14
Mars	26 21.9	16 14
Jupiter	161 12.7	7 14
Saturn	100 40.2	11 16

UT		SUN GHA	SUN Dec	MOON GHA	v	MOON Dec	d	HP
d	h	° ′	° ′	° ′	′	° ′	′	′
20	00	180 36.7	S23 25.6	281 22.6	13.1	N 6 17.2	9.8	56.1
	01	195 36.4	25.6	295 54.7	13.2	6 07.4	9.7	56.1
	02	210 36.1	25.6	310 26.9	13.3	5 57.7	9.8	56.1
	03	225 35.8	. . 25.7	324 59.2	13.3	5 47.9	9.8	56.0
	04	240 35.5	25.7	339 31.5	13.4	5 38.1	9.8	56.0
	05	255 35.2	25.7	354 03.9	13.4	5 28.3	9.8	56.0
	06	270 34.9	S23 25.7	8 36.3	13.5	N 5 18.5	9.8	55.9
	07	285 34.6	25.8	23 08.8	13.5	5 08.7	9.8	55.9
T	08	300 34.2	25.8	37 41.3	13.5	4 58.9	9.9	55.9
U	09	315 33.9	. . 25.8	52 13.8	13.7	4 49.0	9.8	55.9
E	10	330 33.6	25.8	66 46.5	13.6	4 39.2	9.9	55.8
S	11	345 33.3	25.8	81 19.1	13.7	4 29.3	9.9	55.8
D	12	0 33.0	S23 25.9	95 51.8	13.8	N 4 19.4	9.8	55.8
A	13	15 32.7	25.9	110 24.6	13.8	4 09.6	9.9	55.7
Y	14	30 32.4	25.9	124 57.4	13.8	3 59.7	9.9	55.7
	15	45 32.1	. . 25.9	139 30.2	13.9	3 49.8	9.9	55.7
	16	60 31.8	25.9	154 03.1	14.0	3 39.9	9.9	55.6
	17	75 31.5	25.9	168 36.1	13.9	3 30.0	9.9	55.6
	18	90 31.1	S23 26.0	183 09.0	14.1	N 3 20.1	9.9	55.6
	19	105 30.8	26.0	197 42.1	14.0	3 10.2	10.0	55.5
	20	120 30.5	26.0	212 15.1	14.1	3 00.2	9.9	55.5
	21	135 30.2	. . 26.0	226 48.2	14.2	2 50.3	9.9	55.5
	22	150 29.9	26.0	241 21.4	14.1	2 40.4	9.9	55.5
	23	165 29.6	26.0	255 54.5	14.2	2 30.5	9.9	55.4
21	00	180 29.3	S23 26.0	270 27.7	14.3	N 2 20.6	10.0	55.4
	01	195 29.0	26.0	285 01.0	14.3	2 10.6	9.9	55.4
	02	210 28.7	26.0	299 34.3	14.3	2 00.7	9.9	55.3
	03	225 28.3	. . 26.0	314 07.6	14.4	1 50.8	9.9	55.3
	04	240 28.0	26.1	328 41.0	14.3	1 40.9	9.9	55.3
	05	255 27.7	26.1	343 14.3	14.5	1 31.0	10.0	55.3
	06	270 27.4	S23 26.1	357 47.8	14.4	N 1 21.0	9.9	55.2
W	07	285 27.1	26.1	12 21.2	14.5	1 11.1	9.9	55.2
E	08	300 26.8	26.1	26 54.7	14.5	1 01.2	9.9	55.2
D	09	315 26.5	. . 26.1	41 28.2	14.5	0 51.3	9.9	55.2
N	10	330 26.2	26.1	56 01.7	14.6	0 41.4	9.9	55.1
E	11	345 25.9	26.1	70 35.3	14.6	0 31.5	9.9	55.1
S	12	0 25.6	S23 26.1	85 08.9	14.6	N 0 21.6	9.8	55.1
D	13	15 25.2	26.1	99 42.5	14.7	0 11.8	9.9	55.1
A	14	30 24.9	26.1	114 16.2	14.6	N 0 01.9	9.9	55.0
Y	15	45 24.6	. . 26.1	128 49.8	14.7	S 0 08.0	9.8	55.0
	16	60 24.3	26.1	143 23.5	14.8	0 17.8	9.9	55.0
	17	75 24.0	26.1	157 57.3	14.7	0 27.7	9.8	55.0
	18	90 23.7	S23 26.1	172 31.0	14.8	S 0 37.5	9.8	54.9
	19	105 23.4	26.0	187 04.8	14.7	0 47.3	9.8	54.9
	20	120 23.1	26.0	201 38.5	14.8	0 57.1	9.8	54.9
	21	135 22.8	. . 26.0	216 12.3	14.9	1 06.9	9.8	54.9
	22	150 22.4	26.0	230 46.2	14.8	1 16.7	9.8	54.9
	23	165 22.1	26.0	245 20.0	14.9	1 26.5	9.8	54.8
22	00	180 21.8	S23 26.0	259 53.9	14.8	S 1 36.3	9.7	54.8
	01	195 21.5	26.0	274 27.7	14.9	1 46.0	9.7	54.8
	02	210 21.2	26.0	289 01.6	14.9	1 55.7	9.8	54.8
	03	225 20.9	. . 26.0	303 35.5	15.0	2 05.5	9.7	54.8
	04	240 20.6	25.9	318 09.5	14.9	2 15.2	9.7	54.7
	05	255 20.3	25.9	332 43.4	14.9	2 24.9	9.6	54.7
	06	270 20.0	S23 25.9	347 17.3	15.0	S 2 34.5	9.7	54.7
T	07	285 19.6	25.9	1 51.3	14.9	2 44.2	9.6	54.7
H	08	300 19.3	25.9	16 25.2	15.0	2 53.8	9.6	54.7
U	09	315 19.0	. . 25.9	30 59.2	15.0	3 03.4	9.6	54.6
R	10	330 18.7	25.8	45 33.2	15.0	3 13.0	9.6	54.6
S	11	345 18.4	25.8	60 07.2	15.0	3 22.6	9.6	54.6
D	12	0 18.1	S23 25.8	74 41.2	15.0	S 3 32.2	9.5	54.6
A	13	15 17.8	25.8	89 15.2	15.0	3 41.7	9.5	54.6
Y	14	30 17.5	25.8	103 49.2	15.1	3 51.2	9.5	54.5
	15	45 17.2	. . 25.7	118 23.3	15.0	4 00.7	9.5	54.5
	16	60 16.8	25.7	132 57.3	15.0	4 10.2	9.5	54.5
	17	75 16.5	25.7	147 31.3	15.1	4 19.7	9.4	54.5
	18	90 16.2	S23 25.7	162 05.4	15.0	S 4 29.1	9.4	54.5
	19	105 15.9	25.6	176 39.4	15.0	4 38.5	9.4	54.5
	20	120 15.6	25.6	191 13.4	15.1	4 47.9	9.4	54.5
	21	135 15.3	. . 25.6	205 47.5	15.0	4 57.3	9.3	54.4
	22	150 15.0	25.6	220 21.5	15.1	5 06.6	9.3	54.4
	23	165 14.7	25.5	234 55.6	15.0	S 5 15.9	9.3	54.4
		SD 16.3	d 0.0	SD 15.2		15.0		14.9

Lat.	Twilight Naut.	Twilight Civil	Sunrise	Moonrise 20	Moonrise 21	Moonrise 22	Moonrise 23
°	h m	h m	h m	h m	h m	h m	h m
N 72	08 26	10 58	▬	23 29	25 06	01 06	02 41
N 70	08 06	09 55	▬	23 32	25 03	01 03	02 33
68	07 50	09 19	▬	23 35	25 01	01 01	02 25
66	07 37	08 54	10 35	23 37	24 59	00 59	02 20
64	07 25	08 34	09 52	23 39	24 57	00 57	02 15
62	07 16	08 18	09 24	23 40	24 56	00 56	02 10
60	07 07	08 04	09 02	23 42	24 55	00 55	02 07
N 58	07 00	07 53	08 45	23 43	24 54	00 54	02 03
56	06 53	07 42	08 30	23 44	24 53	00 53	02 00
54	06 47	07 33	08 17	23 45	24 52	00 52	01 58
52	06 41	07 25	08 06	23 46	24 51	00 51	01 55
50	06 36	07 18	07 56	23 47	24 51	00 51	01 53
45	06 24	07 01	07 35	23 49	24 49	00 49	01 49
N 40	06 14	06 48	07 18	23 50	24 48	00 48	01 45
35	06 04	06 36	07 04	23 52	24 47	00 47	01 41
30	05 56	06 25	06 52	23 53	24 46	00 46	01 38
20	05 39	06 07	06 31	23 55	24 45	00 45	01 33
N 10	05 23	05 49	06 12	23 57	24 43	00 43	01 29
0	05 06	05 32	05 55	23 59	24 42	00 42	01 25
S 10	04 47	05 14	05 37	24 00	00 00	00 41	01 21
20	04 24	04 53	05 18	24 02	00 02	00 39	01 16
30	03 55	04 28	04 56	24 04	00 04	00 38	01 12
35	03 36	04 13	04 43	24 05	00 05	00 37	01 09
40	03 13	03 55	04 28	24 07	00 07	00 36	01 06
45	02 42	03 32	04 10	24 08	00 08	00 35	01 02
S 50	01 57	03 02	03 47	24 10	00 10	00 34	00 58
52	01 29	02 47	03 36	24 11	00 11	00 33	00 56
54	00 41	02 29	03 24	24 12	00 12	00 33	00 53
56	////	02 07	03 10	24 13	00 13	00 32	00 51
58	////	01 37	02 53	24 14	00 14	00 31	00 48
S 60	////	00 46	02 32	24 15	00 15	00 30	00 45

Lat.	Sunset	Twilight Civil	Twilight Naut.	Moonset 20	Moonset 21	Moonset 22	Moonset 23
°	h m	h m	h m	h m	h m	h m	h m
N 72	▬	12 59	15 31	12 29	12 22	12 16	12 09
N 70	▬	14 02	15 51	12 23	12 22	12 21	12 20
68	▬	14 37	16 07	12 19	12 22	12 25	12 29
66	13 22	15 03	16 20	12 15	12 22	12 29	12 36
64	14 04	15 23	16 31	12 11	12 22	12 31	12 42
62	14 33	15 39	16 41	12 08	12 21	12 34	12 47
60	14 54	15 52	16 49	12 06	12 21	12 36	12 52
N 58	15 12	16 04	16 57	12 04	12 21	12 38	12 56
56	15 27	16 14	17 03	12 02	12 21	12 40	13 00
54	15 39	16 23	17 10	12 00	12 21	12 42	13 03
52	15 51	16 32	17 15	11 58	12 21	12 43	13 06
50	16 01	16 39	17 21	11 56	12 21	12 44	13 09
45	16 21	16 55	17 32	11 53	12 21	12 47	13 14
N 40	16 38	17 09	17 43	11 50	12 20	12 50	13 19
35	16 52	17 21	17 52	11 48	12 20	12 52	13 24
30	17 05	17 31	18 01	11 46	12 20	12 54	13 28
20	17 26	17 50	18 18	11 42	12 20	12 57	13 34
N 10	17 45	18 07	18 34	11 39	12 20	13 00	13 40
0	18 02	18 25	18 51	11 35	12 20	13 03	13 45
S 10	18 20	18 43	19 10	11 32	12 19	13 05	13 51
20	18 39	19 03	19 32	11 29	12 19	13 08	13 57
30	19 01	19 28	20 02	11 25	12 19	13 11	14 04
35	19 14	19 44	20 20	11 22	12 19	13 13	14 07
40	19 29	20 02	20 44	11 20	12 18	13 15	14 12
45	19 47	20 24	21 14	11 17	12 18	13 18	14 17
S 50	20 10	20 54	22 00	11 13	12 18	13 21	14 23
52	20 20	21 09	22 28	11 11	12 18	13 22	14 26
54	20 33	21 27	23 15	11 10	12 18	13 24	14 29
56	20 47	21 50	////	11 08	12 17	13 25	14 32
58	21 04	22 20	////	11 05	12 17	13 27	14 36
S 60	21 24	23 11	////	11 03	12 17	13 29	14 40

Day	SUN Eqn. of Time 00^h	SUN Eqn. of Time 12^h	SUN Mer. Pass.	MOON Mer. Pass. Upper	MOON Mer. Pass. Lower	MOON Age	MOON Phase
d	m s	m s	h m	h m	h m	d %	
20	02 28	02 13	11 58	05 24	17 47	21 56	
21	01 58	01 43	11 58	06 09	18 31	22 46	◐
22	01 28	01 13	11 59	06 52	19 14	23 37	

UT d	h	ARIES GHA	VENUS −4·4 GHA	VENUS Dec	MARS +0·8 GHA	MARS Dec	JUPITER −1·9 GHA	JUPITER Dec	SATURN +0·5 GHA	SATURN Dec
		° ′	° ′	° ′	° ′	° ′	° ′	° ′	° ′	° ′
23	00	91 57.9	131 20.4	S17 25.1	116 54.2	S11 27.9	252 56.0	S 6 41.8	192 23.1	S21 47.9
	01	107 00.4	146 20.1	24.1	131 54.9	27.2	267 58.2	41.9	207 25.2	48.0
	02	122 02.8	161 19.8	23.1	146 55.5	26.5	283 00.3	42.0	222 27.4	48.0
	03	137 05.3	176 19.5	. . 22.2	161 56.2	. . 25.7	298 02.5	. . 42.1	237 29.5	. . 48.0
	04	152 07.8	191 19.2	21.2	176 56.9	25.0	313 04.7	42.2	252 31.7	48.0
	05	167 10.2	206 18.9	20.2	191 57.6	24.3	328 06.8	42.4	267 33.8	48.0
	06	182 12.7	221 18.6	S17 19.3	206 58.3	S11 23.6	343 09.0	S 6 42.5	282 36.0	S21 48.1
	07	197 15.2	236 18.4	18.3	221 59.0	22.8	358 11.1	42.6	297 38.1	48.1
	08	212 17.6	251 18.1	17.3	236 59.6	22.1	13 13.3	42.7	312 40.3	48.1
F	09	227 20.1	266 17.8	. . 16.3	252 00.3	. . 21.4	28 15.5	. . 42.8	327 42.4	. . 48.1
R	10	242 22.6	281 17.5	15.4	267 01.0	20.7	43 17.6	42.9	342 44.6	48.2
I	11	257 25.0	296 17.2	14.4	282 01.7	19.9	58 19.8	43.0	357 46.7	48.2
D	12	272 27.5	311 17.0	S17 13.4	297 02.4	S11 19.2	73 22.0	S 6 43.1	12 48.9	S21 48.2
A	13	287 30.0	326 16.7	12.4	312 03.1	18.5	88 24.2	43.2	27 51.0	48.2
Y	14	302 32.4	341 16.4	11.5	327 03.8	17.8	103 26.3	43.3	42 53.2	48.2
	15	317 34.9	356 16.1	. . 10.5	342 04.4	. . 17.1	118 28.5	. . 43.5	57 55.3	. . 48.3
	16	332 37.3	11 15.9	09.5	357 05.1	16.3	133 30.7	43.6	72 57.5	48.3
	17	347 39.8	26 15.6	08.5	12 05.8	15.6	148 32.8	43.7	87 59.6	48.3
	18	2 42.3	41 15.3	S17 07.6	27 06.5	S11 14.9	163 35.0	S 6 43.8	103 01.8	S21 48.3
	19	17 44.7	56 15.0	06.6	42 07.2	14.2	178 37.2	43.9	118 03.9	48.4
	20	32 47.2	71 14.8	05.6	57 07.9	13.4	193 39.3	44.0	133 06.1	48.4
	21	47 49.7	86 14.5	. . 04.6	72 08.6	. . 12.7	208 41.5	. . 44.1	148 08.2	. . 48.4
	22	62 52.1	101 14.2	03.6	87 09.2	12.0	223 43.7	44.2	163 10.4	48.4
	23	77 54.6	116 13.9	02.6	102 09.9	11.3	238 45.8	44.3	178 12.5	48.4
24	00	92 57.1	131 13.7	S17 01.7	117 10.6	S11 10.5	253 48.0	S 6 44.4	193 14.7	S21 48.5
	01	107 59.5	146 13.4	17 00.7	132 11.3	09.8	268 50.2	44.6	208 16.8	48.5
	02	123 02.0	161 13.1	16 59.7	147 12.0	09.1	283 52.4	44.7	223 19.0	48.5
	03	138 04.5	176 12.9	. . 58.7	162 12.7	. . 08.4	298 54.5	. . 44.8	238 21.1	. . 48.5
	04	153 06.9	191 12.6	57.7	177 13.4	07.6	313 56.7	44.9	253 23.3	48.6
	05	168 09.4	206 12.3	56.7	192 14.1	06.9	328 58.9	45.0	268 25.4	48.6
	06	183 11.8	221 12.1	S16 55.7	207 14.7	S11 06.2	344 01.0	S 6 45.1	283 27.6	S21 48.6
S	07	198 14.3	236 11.8	54.8	222 15.4	05.4	359 03.2	45.2	298 29.7	48.6
A	08	213 16.8	251 11.6	53.8	237 16.1	04.7	14 05.4	45.3	313 31.9	48.6
T	09	228 19.2	266 11.3	. . 52.8	252 16.8	. . 04.0	29 07.6	. . 45.4	328 34.1	. . 48.7
U	10	243 21.7	281 11.0	51.8	267 17.5	03.3	44 09.7	45.5	343 36.2	48.7
R	11	258 24.2	296 10.8	50.8	282 18.2	02.5	59 11.9	45.6	358 38.4	48.7
D	12	273 26.6	311 10.5	S16 49.8	297 18.9	S11 01.8	74 14.1	S 6 45.7	13 40.5	S21 48.7
A	13	288 29.1	326 10.3	48.8	312 19.6	01.1	89 16.2	45.9	28 42.7	48.8
Y	14	303 31.6	341 10.0	47.8	327 20.2	11 00.4	104 18.4	46.0	43 44.8	48.8
	15	318 34.0	356 09.7	. . 46.8	342 20.9	10 59.6	119 20.6	. . 46.1	58 47.0	. . 48.8
	16	333 36.5	11 09.5	45.8	357 21.6	58.9	134 22.8	46.2	73 49.1	48.8
	17	348 38.9	26 09.2	44.8	12 22.3	58.2	149 24.9	46.3	88 51.3	48.8
	18	3 41.4	41 09.0	S16 43.8	27 23.0	S10 57.4	164 27.1	S 6 46.4	103 53.4	S21 48.9
	19	18 43.9	56 08.7	42.8	42 23.7	56.7	179 29.3	46.5	118 55.6	48.9
	20	33 46.3	71 08.5	41.9	57 24.4	56.0	194 31.5	46.6	133 57.7	48.9
	21	48 48.8	86 08.2	. . 40.9	72 25.1	. . 55.3	209 33.6	. . 46.7	148 59.9	. . 48.9
	22	63 51.3	101 08.0	39.9	87 25.8	54.5	224 35.8	46.8	164 02.0	49.0
	23	78 53.7	116 07.7	38.9	102 26.4	53.8	239 38.0	46.9	179 04.2	49.0
25	00	93 56.2	131 07.5	S16 37.9	117 27.1	S10 53.1	254 40.2	S 6 47.0	194 06.3	S21 49.0
	01	108 58.7	146 07.2	36.9	132 27.8	52.3	269 42.3	47.1	209 08.5	49.0
	02	124 01.1	161 07.0	35.9	147 28.5	51.6	284 44.5	47.2	224 10.6	49.0
	03	139 03.6	176 06.8	. . 34.9	162 29.2	. . 50.9	299 46.7	. . 47.4	239 12.8	. . 49.1
	04	154 06.1	191 06.5	33.9	177 29.9	50.2	314 48.9	47.5	254 14.9	49.1
	05	169 08.5	206 06.3	32.9	192 30.6	49.4	329 51.0	47.6	269 17.1	49.1
	06	184 11.0	221 06.0	S16 31.9	207 31.3	S10 48.7	344 53.2	S 6 47.7	284 19.2	S21 49.1
	07	199 13.4	236 05.8	30.8	222 32.0	48.0	359 55.4	47.8	299 21.4	49.1
	08	214 15.9	251 05.5	29.8	237 32.7	47.2	14 57.6	47.9	314 23.5	49.2
S	09	229 18.4	266 05.3	. . 28.8	252 33.3	. . 46.5	29 59.7	. . 48.0	329 25.7	. . 49.2
U	10	244 20.8	281 05.1	27.8	267 34.0	45.8	45 01.9	48.1	344 27.8	49.2
N	11	259 23.3	296 04.8	26.8	282 34.7	45.0	60 04.1	48.2	359 30.0	49.2
D	12	274 25.8	311 04.6	S16 25.8	297 35.4	S10 44.3	75 06.3	S 6 48.3	14 32.2	S21 49.3
A	13	289 28.2	326 04.3	24.8	312 36.1	43.6	90 08.5	48.4	29 34.3	49.3
Y	14	304 30.7	341 04.1	23.8	327 36.8	42.8	105 10.6	48.5	44 36.5	49.3
	15	319 33.2	356 03.9	. . 22.8	342 37.5	. . 42.1	120 12.8	. . 48.6	59 38.6	. . 49.3
	16	334 35.6	11 03.6	21.8	357 38.2	41.4	135 15.0	48.7	74 40.8	49.3
	17	349 38.1	26 03.4	20.8	12 38.9	40.7	150 17.2	48.8	89 42.9	49.4
	18	4 40.6	41 03.2	S16 19.8	27 39.6	S10 39.9	165 19.3	S 6 48.9	104 45.1	S21 49.4
	19	19 43.0	56 03.0	18.8	42 40.3	39.2	180 21.5	49.0	119 47.2	49.4
	20	34 45.5	71 02.7	17.7	57 41.0	38.5	195 23.7	49.2	134 49.4	49.4
	21	49 47.9	86 02.5	. . 16.7	72 41.7	. . 37.7	210 25.9	. . 49.3	149 51.5	. . 49.4
	22	64 50.4	101 02.3	15.7	87 42.3	37.0	225 28.1	49.4	164 53.7	49.5
	23	79 52.9	116 02.0	14.7	102 43.0	36.3	240 30.2	49.5	179 55.8	49.5
Mer. Pass.		h m 17 45.3	*v* −0.3	*d* 1.0	*v* 0.7	*d* 0.7	*v* 2.2	*d* 0.1	*v* 2.2	*d* 0.0

STARS

Name	SHA	Dec
	° ′	° ′
Acamar	315 16.3	S40 14.6
Achernar	335 24.9	S57 09.4
Acrux	173 06.5	S63 11.2
Adhara	255 10.3	S28 59.9
Aldebaran	290 46.3	N16 32.4
Alioth	166 18.8	N55 51.9
Alkaid	152 57.3	N49 13.6
Al Na'ir	27 41.1	S46 52.9
Alnilam	275 43.6	S 1 11.7
Alphard	217 53.5	S 8 44.0
Alphecca	126 09.3	N26 39.5
Alpheratz	357 41.0	N29 11.2
Altair	62 06.2	N 8 55.0
Ankaa	353 13.4	S42 13.1
Antares	112 23.7	S26 27.9
Arcturus	145 53.8	N19 05.7
Atria	107 23.9	S69 03.1
Avior	234 16.4	S59 33.8
Bellatrix	278 29.1	N 6 21.7
Betelgeuse	270 58.4	N 7 24.4
Canopus	263 54.5	S52 42.5
Capella	280 30.4	N46 00.7
Deneb	49 30.2	N45 20.7
Denebola	182 31.2	N14 28.6
Diphda	348 53.5	S17 53.8
Dubhe	193 48.8	N61 39.3
Elnath	278 09.2	N28 37.1
Eltanin	90 45.6	N51 29.4
Enif	33 45.0	N 9 57.3
Fomalhaut	15 21.5	S29 32.1
Gacrux	171 58.2	S57 12.1
Gienah	175 49.8	S17 38.0
Hadar	148 44.7	S60 26.9
Hamal	327 57.9	N23 32.5
Kaus Aust.	83 41.1	S34 22.4
Kochab	137 21.1	N74 05.0
Markab	13 36.0	N15 17.9
Menkar	314 12.3	N 4 09.2
Menkent	148 04.9	S36 26.9
Miaplacidus	221 38.3	S69 47.1
Mirfak	308 36.5	N49 55.2
Nunki	75 55.8	S26 16.4
Peacock	53 16.1	S56 40.8
Pollux	243 24.5	N27 58.8
Procyon	244 56.9	N 5 10.7
Rasalhague	96 04.6	N12 33.1
Regulus	207 40.8	N11 52.9
Rigel	281 09.4	S 8 11.2
Rigil Kent.	139 48.8	S60 53.9
Sabik	102 10.2	S15 44.5
Schedar	349 37.6	N56 38.0
Shaula	96 19.1	S37 06.7
Sirius	258 31.3	S16 44.6
Spica	158 28.8	S11 14.8
Suhail	222 50.3	S43 30.0
Vega	80 37.8	N38 48.2
Zuben'ubi	137 03.0	S16 06.5

	SHA	Mer. Pass.
	° ′	h m
Venus	38 16.6	15 15
Mars	24 13.6	16 11
Jupiter	160 51.0	7 04
Saturn	100 17.6	11 05

	UT d h	SUN GHA ° ′	SUN Dec ° ′	MOON GHA ° ′	*v* ′	MOON Dec ° ′	*d* ′	HP ′
	23 00	180 14.4	S23 25.5	249 29.6	15.0	S 5 25.2	9.3	54.4
	01	195 14.0	25.5	264 03.6	15.1	5 34.5	9.2	54.4
	02	210 13.7	25.4	278 37.7	15.0	5 43.7	9.2	54.4
	03	225 13.4	. . 25.4	293 11.7	15.1	5 52.9	9.2	54.4
	04	240 13.1	25.4	307 45.8	15.0	6 02.1	9.1	54.3
	05	255 12.8	25.3	322 19.8	15.0	6 11.2	9.2	54.3
	06	270 12.5	S23 25.3	336 53.8	15.0	S 6 20.4	9.1	54.3
	07	285 12.2	25.3	351 27.8	15.0	6 29.5	9.0	54.3
	08	300 11.9	25.2	6 01.8	15.0	6 38.5	9.1	54.3
F	09	315 11.6	. . 25.2	20 35.8	15.0	6 47.6	9.0	54.3
R	10	330 11.2	25.2	35 09.8	15.0	6 56.6	8.9	54.3
I	11	345 10.9	25.1	49 43.8	15.0	7 05.5	9.0	54.3
D	12	0 10.6	S23 25.1	64 17.8	15.0	S 7 14.5	8.9	54.2
A	13	15 10.3	25.0	78 51.8	14.9	7 23.4	8.9	54.2
Y	14	30 10.0	25.0	93 25.7	15.0	7 32.3	8.8	54.2
	15	45 09.7	. . 25.0	107 59.7	14.9	7 41.1	8.8	54.2
	16	60 09.4	24.9	122 33.6	14.9	7 49.9	8.8	54.2
	17	75 09.1	24.9	137 07.5	14.9	7 58.7	8.7	54.2
	18	90 08.7	S23 24.8	151 41.4	14.9	S 8 07.4	8.7	54.2
	19	105 08.4	24.8	166 15.3	14.9	8 16.1	8.7	54.2
	20	120 08.1	24.7	180 49.2	14.9	8 24.8	8.6	54.2
	21	135 07.8	. . 24.7	195 23.1	14.8	8 33.4	8.6	54.2
	22	150 07.5	24.6	209 56.9	14.9	8 42.0	8.6	54.1
	23	165 07.2	24.6	224 30.8	14.8	8 50.6	8.5	54.1
	24 00	180 06.9	S23 24.5	239 04.6	14.8	S 8 59.1	8.5	54.1
	01	195 06.6	24.5	253 38.4	14.8	9 07.6	8.4	54.1
	02	210 06.3	24.4	268 12.2	14.8	9 16.0	8.4	54.1
	03	225 06.0	. . 24.4	282 46.0	14.7	9 24.4	8.4	54.1
	04	240 05.6	24.3	297 19.7	14.8	9 32.8	8.3	54.1
	05	255 05.3	24.3	311 53.5	14.7	9 41.1	8.3	54.1
	06	270 05.0	S23 24.2	326 27.2	14.7	S 9 49.4	8.2	54.1
	07	285 04.7	24.2	341 00.9	14.6	9 57.6	8.2	54.1
S	08	300 04.4	24.1	355 34.5	14.7	10 05.8	8.2	54.1
A	09	315 04.1	. . 24.0	10 08.2	14.6	10 14.0	8.1	54.1
T	10	330 03.8	24.0	24 41.8	14.6	10 22.1	8.1	54.1
U	11	345 03.5	23.9	39 15.4	14.6	10 30.2	8.0	54.1
R	12	0 03.2	S23 23.9	53 49.0	14.6	S10 38.2	8.0	54.1
D	13	15 02.8	23.8	68 22.6	14.5	10 46.2	7.9	54.1
A	14	30 02.5	23.8	82 56.1	14.5	10 54.1	7.9	54.1
Y	15	45 02.2	. . 23.7	97 29.6	14.5	11 02.0	7.9	54.1
	16	60 01.9	23.6	112 03.1	14.5	11 09.9	7.8	54.0
	17	75 01.6	23.6	126 36.6	14.4	11 17.7	7.7	54.0
	18	90 01.3	S23 23.5	141 10.0	14.4	S11 25.4	7.7	54.0
	19	105 01.0	23.4	155 43.4	14.4	11 33.1	7.7	54.0
	20	120 00.7	23.4	170 16.8	14.4	11 40.8	7.6	54.0
	21	135 00.4	. . 23.3	184 50.2	14.3	11 48.4	7.6	54.0
	22	150 00.0	23.2	199 23.5	14.3	11 56.0	7.5	54.0
	23	164 59.7	23.2	213 56.8	14.3	12 03.5	7.4	54.0
	25 00	179 59.4	S23 23.1	228 30.1	14.2	S12 10.9	7.5	54.0
	01	194 59.1	23.0	243 03.3	14.3	12 18.4	7.3	54.0
	02	209 58.8	23.0	257 36.6	14.1	12 25.7	7.3	54.0
	03	224 58.5	. . 22.9	272 09.7	14.2	12 33.0	7.3	54.0
	04	239 58.2	22.8	286 42.9	14.1	12 40.3	7.2	54.0
	05	254 57.9	22.7	301 16.0	14.1	12 47.5	7.1	54.0
	06	269 57.6	S23 22.7	315 49.1	14.1	S12 54.6	7.1	54.0
	07	284 57.3	22.6	330 22.2	14.0	13 01.7	7.1	54.0
	08	299 56.9	22.5	344 55.2	14.1	13 08.8	7.0	54.0
S	09	314 56.6	. . 22.4	359 28.3	13.9	13 15.8	6.9	54.0
U	10	329 56.3	22.4	14 01.2	14.0	13 22.7	6.9	54.0
N	11	344 56.0	22.3	28 34.2	13.9	13 29.6	6.8	54.0
D	12	359 55.7	S23 22.2	43 07.1	13.9	S13 36.4	6.8	54.0
A	13	14 55.4	22.1	57 40.0	13.8	13 43.2	6.7	54.0
Y	14	29 55.1	22.0	72 12.8	13.8	13 49.9	6.6	54.0
	15	44 54.8	. . 22.0	86 45.6	13.8	13 56.5	6.6	54.0
	16	59 54.5	21.9	101 18.4	13.8	14 03.1	6.5	54.0
	17	74 54.2	21.8	115 51.2	13.7	14 09.6	6.5	54.0
	18	89 53.8	S23 21.7	130 23.9	13.6	S14 16.1	6.4	54.0
	19	104 53.5	21.6	144 56.5	13.7	14 22.5	6.4	54.0
	20	119 53.2	21.5	159 29.2	13.6	14 28.9	6.3	54.0
	21	134 52.9	. . 21.5	174 01.8	13.6	14 35.2	6.2	54.1
	22	149 52.6	21.4	188 34.4	13.5	14 41.4	6.2	54.1
	23	164 52.3	21.3	203 06.9	13.5	S14 47.6	6.1	54.1
		SD 16.3	*d* 0.1	SD	14.8		14.7	14.7

Lat. °	Twilight Naut. h m	Twilight Civil h m	Sunrise h m	Moonrise 23 h m	Moonrise 24 h m	Moonrise 25 h m	Moonrise 26 h m
N 72	08 27	10 57	▬	02 41	04 18	05 58	07 44
N 70	08 07	09 55	▬	02 33	04 02	05 33	07 04
68	07 51	09 20	▬	02 25	03 50	05 14	06 37
66	07 38	08 55	10 35	02 20	03 39	04 59	06 16
64	07 27	08 35	09 53	02 15	03 31	04 46	06 00
62	07 17	08 19	09 25	02 10	03 24	04 36	05 46
60	07 09	08 06	09 03	02 07	03 17	04 27	05 35
N 58	07 01	07 54	08 46	02 03	03 12	04 19	05 25
56	06 54	07 44	08 31	02 00	03 07	04 12	05 16
54	06 48	07 34	08 18	01 58	03 02	04 06	05 09
52	06 43	07 26	08 07	01 55	02 58	04 01	05 02
50	06 37	07 19	07 57	01 53	02 55	03 56	04 56
45	06 25	07 03	07 37	01 49	02 47	03 45	04 42
N 40	06 15	06 49	07 20	01 45	02 41	03 36	04 31
35	06 06	06 37	07 06	01 41	02 35	03 29	04 22
30	05 57	06 27	06 53	01 38	02 30	03 22	04 14
20	05 40	06 08	06 32	01 33	02 22	03 11	04 00
N 10	05 24	05 51	06 13	01 29	02 15	03 01	03 48
0	05 07	05 33	05 56	01 25	02 08	02 51	03 36
S 10	04 48	05 15	05 38	01 21	02 01	02 42	03 25
20	04 26	04 55	05 19	01 16	01 54	02 32	03 13
30	03 57	04 30	04 57	01 12	01 46	02 21	02 59
35	03 38	04 15	04 44	01 09	01 41	02 15	02 51
40	03 15	03 56	04 29	01 06	01 36	02 08	02 42
45	02 44	03 34	04 11	01 02	01 30	01 59	02 32
S 50	01 58	03 04	03 49	00 58	01 22	01 49	02 19
52	01 31	02 49	03 38	00 56	01 19	01 44	02 13
54	00 44	02 31	03 26	00 53	01 15	01 39	02 07
56	////	02 09	03 11	00 51	01 11	01 34	01 59
58	////	01 39	02 54	00 48	01 07	01 27	01 51
S 60	////	00 48	02 34	00 45	01 02	01 20	01 42

Lat. °	Sunset h m	Twilight Civil h m	Twilight Naut. h m	Moonset 23 h m	Moonset 24 h m	Moonset 25 h m	Moonset 26 h m
N 72	▬	13 02	15 33	12 09	12 02	11 53	11 41
N 70	▬	14 04	15 53	12 20	12 19	12 19	12 21
68	▬	14 40	16 09	12 29	12 33	12 39	12 49
66	13 24	15 05	16 22	12 36	12 44	12 55	13 10
64	14 07	15 24	16 33	12 42	12 54	13 08	13 27
62	14 35	15 41	16 43	12 47	13 02	13 19	13 41
60	14 56	15 54	16 51	12 52	13 09	13 29	13 53
N 58	15 14	16 06	16 58	12 56	13 15	13 37	14 04
56	15 29	16 16	17 05	13 00	13 21	13 45	14 13
54	15 41	16 25	17 11	13 03	13 26	13 51	14 21
52	15 52	16 33	17 17	13 06	13 30	13 57	14 28
50	16 02	16 41	17 22	13 09	13 34	14 02	14 34
45	16 23	16 57	17 34	13 14	13 43	14 14	14 48
N 40	16 40	17 10	17 44	13 19	13 50	14 24	15 00
35	16 54	17 22	17 54	13 24	13 57	14 32	15 10
30	17 06	17 33	18 03	13 28	14 02	14 39	15 18
20	17 28	17 52	18 19	13 34	14 12	14 52	15 33
N 10	17 46	18 09	18 35	13 40	14 21	15 03	15 46
0	18 04	18 26	18 52	13 45	14 29	15 13	15 59
S 10	18 21	18 44	19 11	13 51	14 37	15 23	16 11
20	18 40	19 05	19 34	13 57	14 45	15 34	16 24
30	19 02	19 30	20 03	14 04	14 55	15 47	16 39
35	19 15	19 45	20 22	14 07	15 01	15 54	16 48
40	19 30	20 03	20 45	14 12	15 07	16 03	16 58
45	19 48	20 26	21 15	14 17	15 15	16 13	17 09
S 50	20 11	20 55	22 01	14 23	15 24	16 25	17 24
52	20 22	21 10	22 29	14 26	15 28	16 30	17 30
54	20 34	21 28	23 15	14 29	15 33	16 36	17 38
56	20 48	21 51	////	14 32	15 38	16 43	17 46
58	21 05	22 20	////	14 36	15 44	16 51	17 55
S 60	21 25	23 11	////	14 40	15 51	16 59	18 06

Day	SUN Eqn. of Time 00^h	SUN Eqn. of Time 12^h	SUN Mer. Pass.	MOON Mer. Pass. Upper	MOON Mer. Pass. Lower	MOON Age	MOON Phase
d	m s	m s	h m	h m	h m	d	%
23	00 58	00 43	11 59	07 35	19 57	24	28
24	00 28	00 13	12 00	08 18	20 40	25	20
25	00 02	00 17	12 00	09 02	21 25	26	13

	UT (d h)	ARIES GHA	VENUS −4·4 GHA	VENUS Dec	MARS +0·9 GHA	MARS Dec	JUPITER −1·9 GHA	JUPITER Dec	SATURN +0·5 GHA	SATURN Dec
		° ′	° ′	° ′	° ′	° ′	° ′	° ′	° ′	° ′
	26 00	94 55.3	131 01.8	S16 13.7	117 43.7	S10 35.5	255 32.4	S 6 49.6	194 58.0	S21 49.5
	01	109 57.8	146 01.6	12.7	132 44.4	34.8	270 34.6	49.7	210 00.1	49.5
	02	125 00.3	161 01.4	11.7	147 45.1	34.1	285 36.8	49.8	225 02.3	49.6
	03	140 02.7	176 01.1	. . 10.6	162 45.8	. . 33.3	300 39.0	. . 49.9	240 04.4	. . 49.6
	04	155 05.2	191 00.9	09.6	177 46.5	32.6	315 41.2	50.0	255 06.6	49.6
	05	170 07.7	206 00.7	08.6	192 47.2	31.9	330 43.3	50.1	270 08.7	49.6
	06	185 10.1	221 00.5	S16 07.6	207 47.9	S10 31.1	345 45.5	S 6 50.2	285 10.9	S21 49.6
	07	200 12.6	236 00.2	06.6	222 48.6	30.4	0 47.7	50.3	300 13.1	49.7
	08	215 15.1	251 00.0	05.6	237 49.3	29.7	15 49.9	50.4	315 15.2	49.7
M	09	230 17.5	265 59.8	. . 04.5	252 50.0	. . 28.9	30 52.1	. . 50.5	330 17.4	. . 49.7
O	10	245 20.0	280 59.6	03.5	267 50.7	28.2	45 54.2	50.6	345 19.5	49.7
N	11	260 22.4	295 59.4	02.5	282 51.4	27.5	60 56.4	50.7	0 21.7	49.7
D	12	275 24.9	310 59.2	S16 01.5	297 52.1	S10 26.7	75 58.6	S 6 50.8	15 23.8	S21 49.8
A	13	290 27.4	325 58.9	16 00.5	312 52.8	26.0	91 00.8	50.9	30 26.0	49.8
Y	14	305 29.8	340 58.7	15 59.4	327 53.4	25.3	106 03.0	51.0	45 28.1	49.8
	15	320 32.3	355 58.5	. . 58.4	342 54.1	. . 24.5	121 05.2	. . 51.1	60 30.3	. . 49.8
	16	335 34.8	10 58.3	57.4	357 54.8	23.8	136 07.3	51.2	75 32.4	49.9
	17	350 37.2	25 58.1	56.4	12 55.5	23.0	151 09.5	51.3	90 34.6	49.9
	18	5 39.7	40 57.9	S15 55.3	27 56.2	S10 22.3	166 11.7	S 6 51.4	105 36.7	S21 49.9
	19	20 42.2	55 57.7	54.3	42 56.9	21.6	181 13.9	51.5	120 38.9	49.9
	20	35 44.6	70 57.5	53.3	57 57.6	20.8	196 16.1	51.6	135 41.0	49.9
	21	50 47.1	85 57.3	. . 52.3	72 58.3	. . 20.1	211 18.3	. . 51.7	150 43.2	. . 50.0
	22	65 49.5	100 57.1	51.2	87 59.0	19.4	226 20.5	51.8	165 45.3	50.0
	23	80 52.0	115 56.8	50.2	102 59.7	18.6	241 22.6	51.9	180 47.5	50.0
	27 00	95 54.5	130 56.6	S15 49.2	118 00.4	S10 17.9	256 24.8	S 6 52.1	195 49.7	S21 50.0
	01	110 56.9	145 56.4	48.2	133 01.1	17.2	271 27.0	52.2	210 51.8	50.0
	02	125 59.4	160 56.2	47.1	148 01.8	16.4	286 29.2	52.3	225 54.0	50.1
	03	141 01.9	175 56.0	. . 46.1	163 02.5	. . 15.7	301 31.4	. . 52.4	240 56.1	. . 50.1
	04	156 04.3	190 55.8	45.1	178 03.2	14.9	316 33.6	52.5	255 58.3	50.1
	05	171 06.8	205 55.6	44.0	193 03.9	14.2	331 35.8	52.6	271 00.4	50.1
	06	186 09.3	220 55.4	S15 43.0	208 04.6	S10 13.5	346 37.9	S 6 52.7	286 02.6	S21 50.1
	07	201 11.7	235 55.2	42.0	223 05.3	12.7	1 40.1	52.8	301 04.7	50.2
T	08	216 14.2	250 55.0	40.9	238 06.0	12.0	16 42.3	52.9	316 06.9	50.2
U	09	231 16.7	265 54.8	. . 39.9	253 06.7	. . 11.3	31 44.5	. . 53.0	331 09.0	. . 50.2
E	10	246 19.1	280 54.6	38.9	268 07.4	10.5	46 46.7	53.1	346 11.2	50.2
S	11	261 21.6	295 54.4	37.8	283 08.1	09.8	61 48.9	53.2	1 13.3	50.2
D	12	276 24.0	310 54.2	S15 36.8	298 08.8	S10 09.1	76 51.1	S 6 53.3	16 15.5	S21 50.3
A	13	291 26.5	325 54.1	35.8	313 09.5	08.3	91 53.3	53.4	31 17.7	50.3
Y	14	306 29.0	340 53.9	34.7	328 10.2	07.6	106 55.5	53.5	46 19.8	50.3
	15	321 31.4	355 53.7	. . 33.7	343 10.9	. . 06.8	121 57.6	. . 53.6	61 22.0	. . 50.3
	16	336 33.9	10 53.5	32.7	358 11.6	06.1	136 59.8	53.7	76 24.1	50.4
	17	351 36.4	25 53.3	31.6	13 12.3	05.4	152 02.0	53.8	91 26.3	50.4
	18	6 38.8	40 53.1	S15 30.6	28 12.9	S10 04.6	167 04.2	S 6 53.9	106 28.4	S21 50.4
	19	21 41.3	55 52.9	29.5	43 13.6	03.9	182 06.4	54.0	121 30.6	50.4
	20	36 43.8	70 52.7	28.5	58 14.3	03.1	197 08.6	54.1	136 32.7	50.4
	21	51 46.2	85 52.5	. . 27.5	73 15.0	. . 02.4	212 10.8	. . 54.2	151 34.9	. . 50.5
	22	66 48.7	100 52.4	26.4	88 15.7	01.7	227 13.0	54.3	166 37.0	50.5
	23	81 51.2	115 52.2	25.4	103 16.4	00.9	242 15.2	54.4	181 39.2	50.5
	28 00	96 53.6	130 52.0	S15 24.3	118 17.1	S10 00.2	257 17.4	S 6 54.5	196 41.3	S21 50.5
	01	111 56.1	145 51.8	23.3	133 17.8	9 59.4	272 19.6	54.6	211 43.5	50.5
	02	126 58.5	160 51.6	22.2	148 18.5	58.7	287 21.7	54.7	226 45.7	50.6
	03	142 01.0	175 51.4	. . 21.2	163 19.2	. . 58.0	302 23.9	. . 54.8	241 47.8	. . 50.6
	04	157 03.5	190 51.3	20.2	178 19.9	57.2	317 26.1	54.9	256 50.0	50.6
	05	172 05.9	205 51.1	19.1	193 20.6	56.5	332 28.3	55.0	271 52.1	50.6
	06	187 08.4	220 50.9	S15 18.1	208 21.3	S 9 55.7	347 30.5	S 6 55.1	286 54.3	S21 50.6
W	07	202 10.9	235 50.7	17.0	223 22.0	55.0	2 32.7	55.2	301 56.4	50.7
E	08	217 13.3	250 50.5	16.0	238 22.7	54.3	17 34.9	55.3	316 58.6	50.7
D	09	232 15.8	265 50.4	. . 14.9	253 23.4	. . 53.5	32 37.1	. . 55.4	332 00.7	. . 50.7
N	10	247 18.3	280 50.2	13.9	268 24.1	52.8	47 39.3	55.5	347 02.9	50.7
E	11	262 20.7	295 50.0	12.8	283 24.8	52.0	62 41.5	55.6	2 05.0	50.7
S	12	277 23.2	310 49.9	S15 11.8	298 25.5	S 9 51.3	77 43.7	S 6 55.7	17 07.2	S21 50.8
S	13	292 25.7	325 49.7	10.7	313 26.2	50.6	92 45.9	55.8	32 09.4	50.8
D	14	307 28.1	340 49.5	09.7	328 26.9	49.8	107 48.1	55.9	47 11.5	50.8
A	15	322 30.6	355 49.3	. . 08.6	343 27.6	. . 49.1	122 50.3	. . 56.0	62 13.7	. . 50.8
Y	16	337 33.0	10 49.2	07.6	358 28.3	48.3	137 52.5	56.1	77 15.8	50.8
	17	352 35.5	25 49.0	06.5	13 29.0	47.6	152 54.6	56.2	92 18.0	50.9
	18	7 38.0	40 48.8	S15 05.5	28 29.7	S 9 46.8	167 56.8	S 6 56.3	107 20.1	S21 50.9
	19	22 40.4	55 48.7	04.4	43 30.4	46.1	182 59.0	56.4	122 22.3	50.9
	20	37 42.9	70 48.5	03.4	58 31.1	45.4	198 01.2	56.5	137 24.4	50.9
	21	52 45.4	85 48.3	. . 02.3	73 31.9	. . 44.6	213 03.4	. . 56.6	152 26.6	. . 50.9
	22	67 47.8	100 48.2	01.3	88 32.6	43.9	228 05.6	56.6	167 28.7	51.0
	23	82 50.3	115 48.0	00.2	103 33.3	43.1	243 07.8	56.7	182 30.9	51.0
	Mer. Pass.	h m 17 33.5	*v* −0.2	*d* 1.0	*v* 0.7	*d* 0.7	*v* 2.2	*d* 0.1	*v* 2.2	*d* 0.0

STARS

Name	SHA	Dec
	° ′	° ′
Acamar	315 16.3	S40 14.6
Achernar	335 24.9	S57 09.4
Acrux	173 06.4	S63 11.2
Adhara	255 10.3	S28 59.9
Aldebaran	290 46.3	N16 32.4
Alioth	166 18.8	N55 51.9
Alkaid	152 57.3	N49 13.6
Al Na'ir	27 41.1	S46 52.9
Alnilam	275 43.6	S 1 11.7
Alphard	217 53.5	S 8 44.0
Alphecca	126 09.3	N26 39.5
Alpheratz	357 41.0	N29 11.2
Altair	62 06.2	N 8 55.0
Ankaa	353 13.4	S42 13.1
Antares	112 23.7	S26 27.9
Arcturus	145 53.8	N19 05.7
Atria	107 23.8	S69 03.1
Avior	234 16.4	S59 33.8
Bellatrix	278 29.1	N 6 21.7
Betelgeuse	270 58.4	N 7 24.4
Canopus	263 54.5	S52 42.5
Capella	280 30.4	N46 00.7
Deneb	49 30.2	N45 20.7
Denebola	182 31.2	N14 28.6
Diphda	348 53.5	S17 53.8
Dubhe	193 48.7	N61 39.3
Elnath	278 09.2	N28 37.1
Eltanin	90 45.6	N51 29.4
Enif	33 45.0	N 9 57.3
Fomalhaut	15 21.6	S29 32.1
Gacrux	171 58.1	S57 12.1
Gienah	175 49.8	S17 38.0
Hadar	148 44.7	S60 26.9
Hamal	327 57.9	N23 32.5
Kaus Aust.	83 41.1	S34 22.4
Kochab	137 21.1	N74 05.0
Markab	13 36.1	N15 17.9
Menkar	314 12.3	N 4 09.2
Menkent	148 04.9	S36 26.9
Miaplacidus	221 38.3	S69 47.1
Mirfak	308 36.5	N49 55.2
Nunki	75 55.8	S26 16.3
Peacock	53 16.1	S56 40.8
Pollux	243 24.5	N27 58.8
Procyon	244 56.9	N 5 10.7
Rasalhague	96 04.6	N12 33.1
Regulus	207 40.8	N11 52.9
Rigel	281 09.4	S 8 11.2
Rigil Kent.	139 48.8	S60 53.9
Sabik	102 10.1	S15 44.5
Schedar	349 37.6	N56 38.0
Shaula	96 19.1	S37 06.7
Sirius	258 31.3	S16 44.6
Spica	158 28.8	S11 14.8
Suhail	222 50.3	S43 30.0
Vega	80 37.8	N38 48.2
Zuben'ubi	137 03.0	S16 06.5

	SHA	Mer. Pass.
	° ′	h m
Venus	35 02.2	15 16
Mars	22 05.9	16 07
Jupiter	160 30.4	6 53
Saturn	99 55.2	10 55

Day	UT	SUN GHA	SUN Dec	MOON GHA	v	MOON Dec	d	HP
	d h	° ′	° ′	° ′	′	° ′	′	′
MONDAY	26 00	179 52.0	S23 21.2	217 39.4	13.5	S14 53.7	6.0	54.1
	01	194 51.7	21.1	232 11.9	13.4	14 59.7	6.0	54.1
	02	209 51.4	21.0	246 44.3	13.4	15 05.7	5.9	54.1
	03	224 51.1	. . 20.9	261 16.7	13.4	15 11.6	5.8	54.1
	04	239 50.7	20.8	275 49.1	13.3	15 17.4	5.8	54.1
	05	254 50.4	20.7	290 21.4	13.3	15 23.2	5.7	54.1
	06	269 50.1	S23 20.6	304 53.7	13.3	S15 28.9	5.7	54.1
	07	284 49.8	20.5	319 26.0	13.2	15 34.6	5.6	54.1
	08	299 49.5	20.4	333 58.2	13.2	15 40.2	5.5	54.1
	09	314 49.2	. . 20.4	348 30.4	13.1	15 45.7	5.4	54.1
	10	329 48.9	20.3	3 02.5	13.1	15 51.1	5.4	54.1
	11	344 48.6	20.2	17 34.6	13.1	15 56.5	5.3	54.1
	12	359 48.3	S23 20.1	32 06.7	13.1	S16 01.8	5.3	54.1
	13	14 48.0	20.0	46 38.8	13.0	16 07.1	5.1	54.1
	14	29 47.7	19.9	61 10.8	12.9	16 12.2	5.1	54.1
	15	44 47.3	. . 19.8	75 42.7	13.0	16 17.3	5.1	54.1
	16	59 47.0	19.7	90 14.7	12.9	16 22.4	4.9	54.1
	17	74 46.7	19.6	104 46.6	12.8	16 27.3	4.9	54.2
	18	89 46.4	S23 19.4	119 18.4	12.8	S16 32.2	4.8	54.2
	19	104 46.1	19.3	133 50.2	12.8	16 37.0	4.8	54.2
	20	119 45.8	19.2	148 22.0	12.8	16 41.8	4.6	54.2
	21	134 45.5	. . 19.1	162 53.8	12.7	16 46.4	4.6	54.2
	22	149 45.2	19.0	177 25.5	12.7	16 51.0	4.6	54.2
	23	164 44.9	18.9	191 57.2	12.6	16 55.6	4.4	54.2
TUESDAY	27 00	179 44.6	S23 18.8	206 28.8	12.6	S17 00.0	4.4	54.2
	01	194 44.3	18.7	221 00.4	12.6	17 04.4	4.3	54.2
	02	209 44.0	18.6	235 32.0	12.5	17 08.7	4.2	54.2
	03	224 43.6	. . 18.5	250 03.5	12.5	17 12.9	4.1	54.2
	04	239 43.3	18.4	264 35.0	12.5	17 17.0	4.1	54.2
	05	254 43.0	18.3	279 06.5	12.4	17 21.1	4.0	54.3
	06	269 42.7	S23 18.1	293 37.9	12.4	S17 25.1	3.9	54.3
	07	284 42.4	18.0	308 09.3	12.4	17 29.0	3.8	54.3
	08	299 42.1	17.9	322 40.7	12.3	17 32.8	3.8	54.3
	09	314 41.8	. . 17.8	337 12.0	12.3	17 36.6	3.6	54.3
	10	329 41.5	17.7	351 43.3	12.2	17 40.2	3.6	54.3
	11	344 41.2	17.6	6 14.5	12.3	17 43.8	3.5	54.3
	12	359 40.9	S23 17.4	20 45.8	12.2	S17 47.3	3.5	54.3
	13	14 40.6	17.3	35 17.0	12.1	17 50.8	3.3	54.3
	14	29 40.3	17.2	49 48.1	12.1	17 54.1	3.3	54.3
	15	44 40.0	. . 17.1	64 19.2	12.1	17 57.4	3.2	54.4
	16	59 39.6	17.0	78 50.3	12.1	18 00.6	3.1	54.4
	17	74 39.3	16.8	93 21.4	12.0	18 03.7	3.0	54.4
	18	89 39.0	S23 16.7	107 52.4	12.0	S18 06.7	2.9	54.4
	19	104 38.7	16.6	122 23.4	11.9	18 09.6	2.9	54.4
	20	119 38.4	16.5	136 54.3	12.0	18 12.5	2.8	54.4
	21	134 38.1	. . 16.3	151 25.3	11.9	18 15.3	2.6	54.4
	22	149 37.8	16.2	165 56.2	11.8	18 17.9	2.6	54.4
	23	164 37.5	16.1	180 27.0	11.9	18 20.5	2.6	54.4
WEDNESDAY	28 00	179 37.2	S23 16.0	194 57.9	11.8	S18 23.1	2.4	54.5
	01	194 36.9	15.8	209 28.7	11.7	18 25.5	2.3	54.5
	02	209 36.6	15.7	223 59.4	11.8	18 27.8	2.3	54.5
	03	224 36.3	. . 15.6	238 30.2	11.7	18 30.1	2.2	54.5
	04	239 36.0	15.4	253 00.9	11.7	18 32.3	2.0	54.5
	05	254 35.7	15.3	267 31.6	11.6	18 34.3	2.0	54.5
	06	269 35.4	S23 15.2	282 02.2	11.7	S18 36.3	1.9	54.5
	07	284 35.0	15.0	296 32.9	11.6	18 38.2	1.9	54.5
	08	299 34.7	14.9	311 03.5	11.5	18 40.1	1.7	54.6
	09	314 34.4	. . 14.8	325 34.0	11.6	18 41.8	1.6	54.6
	10	329 34.1	14.6	340 04.6	11.5	18 43.4	1.6	54.6
	11	344 33.8	14.5	354 35.1	11.5	18 45.0	1.5	54.6
	12	359 33.5	S23 14.4	9 05.6	11.5	S18 46.5	1.3	54.6
	13	14 33.2	14.2	23 36.1	11.4	18 47.8	1.3	54.6
	14	29 32.9	14.1	38 06.5	11.4	18 49.1	1.2	54.6
	15	44 32.6	. . 14.0	52 36.9	11.4	18 50.3	1.1	54.6
	16	59 32.3	13.8	67 07.3	11.4	18 51.4	1.0	54.7
	17	74 32.0	13.7	81 37.7	11.4	18 52.4	1.0	54.7
	18	89 31.7	S23 13.5	96 08.1	11.3	S18 53.4	0.8	54.7
	19	104 31.4	13.4	110 38.4	11.3	18 54.2	0.7	54.7
	20	119 31.1	13.2	125 08.7	11.3	18 54.9	0.7	54.7
	21	134 30.8	. . 13.1	139 39.0	11.2	18 55.6	0.5	54.7
	22	149 30.5	12.9	154 09.2	11.3	18 56.1	0.5	54.7
	23	164 30.2	12.8	168 39.5	11.2	S18 56.6	0.4	54.8
		SD 16.3	d 0.1	SD 14.7		14.8		14.9

Lat.	Twilight Naut.	Twilight Civil	Sunrise	Moonrise 26	Moonrise 27	Moonrise 28	Moonrise 29
°	h m	h m	h m	h m	h m	h m	h m
N 72	08 27	10 54	■	07 44	09 54	■	■
N 70	08 07	09 54	■	07 04	08 35	09 57	10 54
68	07 51	09 20	■	06 37	07 57	09 08	10 02
66	07 38	08 55	10 34	06 16	07 30	08 36	09 29
64	07 27	08 35	09 53	06 00	07 10	08 13	09 06
62	07 18	08 19	09 25	05 46	06 53	07 54	08 47
60	07 09	08 06	09 03	05 35	06 40	07 39	08 31
N 58	07 02	07 54	08 46	05 25	06 28	07 26	08 18
56	06 55	07 44	08 32	05 16	06 18	07 15	08 07
54	06 49	07 35	08 19	05 09	06 09	07 05	07 57
52	06 43	07 27	08 08	05 02	06 01	06 57	07 48
50	06 38	07 20	07 58	04 56	05 54	06 49	07 40
45	06 27	07 04	07 38	04 42	05 38	06 32	07 23
N 40	06 16	06 50	07 21	04 31	05 26	06 19	07 09
35	06 07	06 39	07 07	04 22	05 15	06 07	06 57
30	05 58	06 28	06 54	04 14	05 06	05 57	06 47
20	05 42	06 09	06 33	04 00	04 50	05 40	06 29
N 10	05 26	05 52	06 15	03 48	04 36	05 25	06 14
0	05 09	05 35	05 58	03 36	04 23	05 11	06 00
S 10	04 50	05 17	05 40	03 25	04 10	04 57	05 45
20	04 27	04 57	05 21	03 13	03 56	04 42	05 30
30	03 58	04 32	04 59	02 59	03 40	04 25	05 12
35	03 40	04 17	04 46	02 51	03 31	04 15	05 02
40	03 17	03 58	04 31	02 42	03 21	04 03	04 51
45	02 46	03 36	04 13	02 32	03 08	03 50	04 37
S 50	02 01	03 06	03 51	02 19	02 54	03 34	04 20
52	01 34	02 51	03 40	02 13	02 47	03 26	04 12
54	00 49	02 34	03 28	02 07	02 39	03 18	04 03
56	////	02 12	03 14	01 59	02 30	03 08	03 53
58	////	01 42	02 57	01 51	02 21	02 57	03 42
S 60	////	00 53	02 37	01 42	02 10	02 45	03 29

Lat.	Sunset	Twilight Civil	Twilight Naut.	Moonset 26	Moonset 27	Moonset 28	Moonset 29
°	h m	h m	h m	h m	h m	h m	h m
N 72	■	13 09	15 36	11 41	11 08	■	■
N 70	■	14 09	15 56	12 21	12 27	12 45	13 31
68	■	14 43	16 12	12 49	13 06	13 35	14 23
66	13 29	15 08	16 25	13 10	13 33	14 06	14 55
64	14 10	15 27	16 36	13 27	13 54	14 30	15 19
62	14 38	15 43	16 45	13 41	14 10	14 48	15 38
60	14 59	15 57	16 53	13 53	14 24	15 04	15 53
N 58	15 16	16 08	17 01	14 04	14 36	15 17	16 06
56	15 31	16 18	17 07	14 13	14 47	15 28	16 17
54	15 44	16 27	17 14	14 21	14 56	15 38	16 27
52	15 55	16 36	17 19	14 28	15 04	15 47	16 36
50	16 04	16 43	17 24	14 34	15 11	15 55	16 44
45	16 25	16 59	17 36	14 48	15 27	16 11	17 01
N 40	16 42	17 12	17 46	15 00	15 40	16 25	17 15
35	16 56	17 24	17 56	15 10	15 51	16 37	17 26
30	17 08	17 35	18 04	15 18	16 01	16 47	17 37
20	17 29	17 53	18 21	15 33	16 18	17 05	17 54
N 10	17 48	18 10	18 37	15 46	16 32	17 20	18 09
0	18 05	18 28	18 54	15 59	16 46	17 34	18 24
S 10	18 22	18 46	19 13	16 11	16 59	17 48	18 38
20	18 41	19 06	19 35	16 24	17 14	18 04	18 53
30	19 03	19 31	20 04	16 39	17 31	18 21	19 10
35	19 16	19 46	20 23	16 48	17 40	18 31	19 20
40	19 31	20 04	20 46	16 58	17 51	18 43	19 32
45	19 49	20 26	21 16	17 09	18 04	18 57	19 46
S 50	20 11	20 56	22 01	17 24	18 20	19 14	20 02
52	20 22	21 11	22 28	17 30	18 28	19 21	20 10
54	20 34	21 29	23 12	17 38	18 36	19 30	20 18
56	20 48	21 50	////	17 46	18 45	19 40	20 28
58	21 05	22 20	////	17 55	18 56	19 51	20 39
S 60	21 25	23 07	////	18 06	19 08	20 04	20 52

Day	SUN Eqn. of Time 00h	SUN Eqn. of Time 12h	SUN Mer. Pass.	MOON Mer. Pass. Upper	MOON Mer. Pass. Lower	MOON Age	MOON Phase
d	m s	m s	h m	h m	h m	d %	
26	00 31	00 46	12 01	09 47	22 11	27 7	
27	01 01	01 16	12 01	10 34	22 58	28 3	
28	01 31	01 45	12 02	11 22	23 47	29 1	

	UT	ARIES	VENUS −4·4		MARS +0·9		JUPITER −1·9		SATURN +0·5	
		GHA	GHA	Dec	GHA	Dec	GHA	Dec	GHA	Dec
	d h	° ′	° ′	° ′	° ′	° ′	° ′	° ′	° ′	° ′
	29 00	97 52.8	130 47.8	S14 59.2	118 34.0	S 9 42.4	258 10.0	S 6 56.8	197 33.1	S21 51.0
	01	112 55.2	145 47.7	58.1	133 34.7	41.7	273 12.2	56.9	212 35.2	51.0
	02	127 57.7	160 47.5	57.1	148 35.4	40.9	288 14.4	57.0	227 37.4	51.0
	03	143 00.1	175 47.4	. . 56.0	163 36.1	. . 40.2	303 16.6	. . 57.1	242 39.5	. . 51.1
	04	158 02.6	190 47.2	54.9	178 36.8	39.4	318 18.8	57.2	257 41.7	51.1
	05	173 05.1	205 47.0	53.9	193 37.5	38.7	333 21.0	57.3	272 43.8	51.1
	06	188 07.5	220 46.9	S14 52.8	208 38.2	S 9 37.9	348 23.2	S 6 57.4	287 46.0	S21 51.1
	07	203 10.0	235 46.7	51.8	223 38.9	37.2	3 25.4	57.5	302 48.1	51.2
T	08	218 12.5	250 46.6	50.7	238 39.6	36.4	18 27.6	57.6	317 50.3	51.2
H	09	233 14.9	265 46.4	. . 49.6	253 40.3	. . 35.7	33 29.8	. . 57.7	332 52.5	. . 51.2
U	10	248 17.4	280 46.3	48.6	268 41.0	35.0	48 32.0	57.8	347 54.6	51.2
R	11	263 19.9	295 46.1	47.5	283 41.7	34.2	63 34.2	57.9	2 56.8	51.2
S	12	278 22.3	310 46.0	S14 46.5	298 42.4	S 9 33.5	78 36.4	S 6 58.0	17 58.9	S21 51.3
D	13	293 24.8	325 45.8	45.4	313 43.1	32.7	93 38.6	58.1	33 01.1	51.3
A	14	308 27.3	340 45.7	44.3	328 43.8	32.0	108 40.8	58.2	48 03.2	51.3
Y	15	323 29.7	355 45.5	. . 43.3	343 44.5	. . 31.2	123 43.0	. . 58.3	63 05.4	. . 51.3
	16	338 32.2	10 45.4	42.2	358 45.2	30.5	138 45.2	58.4	78 07.5	51.3
	17	353 34.6	25 45.2	41.2	13 45.9	29.7	153 47.4	58.5	93 09.7	51.4
	18	8 37.1	40 45.1	S14 40.1	28 46.6	S 9 29.0	168 49.6	S 6 58.6	108 11.9	S21 51.4
	19	23 39.6	55 44.9	39.0	43 47.3	28.3	183 51.8	58.7	123 14.0	51.4
	20	38 42.0	70 44.8	38.0	58 48.0	27.5	198 54.0	58.8	138 16.2	51.4
	21	53 44.5	85 44.6	. . 36.9	73 48.7	. . 26.8	213 56.2	. . 58.9	153 18.3	. . 51.4
	22	68 47.0	100 44.5	35.8	88 49.4	26.0	228 58.4	59.0	168 20.5	51.5
	23	83 49.4	115 44.4	34.8	103 50.1	25.3	244 00.6	59.1	183 22.6	51.5
	30 00	98 51.9	130 44.2	S14 33.7	118 50.8	S 9 24.5	259 02.8	S 6 59.2	198 24.8	S21 51.5
	01	113 54.4	145 44.1	32.6	133 51.5	23.8	274 05.0	59.2	213 27.0	51.5
	02	128 56.8	160 43.9	31.6	148 52.3	23.0	289 07.2	59.3	228 29.1	51.5
	03	143 59.3	175 43.8	. . 30.5	163 53.0	. . 22.3	304 09.4	. . 59.4	243 31.3	. . 51.6
	04	159 01.8	190 43.7	29.4	178 53.7	21.5	319 11.6	59.5	258 33.4	51.6
	05	174 04.2	205 43.5	28.3	193 54.4	20.8	334 13.8	59.6	273 35.6	51.6
	06	189 06.7	220 43.4	S14 27.3	208 55.1	S 9 20.1	349 16.0	S 6 59.7	288 37.7	S21 51.6
	07	204 09.1	235 43.3	26.2	223 55.8	19.3	4 18.2	59.8	303 39.9	51.6
	08	219 11.6	250 43.1	25.1	238 56.5	18.6	19 20.4	6 59.9	318 42.0	51.7
F	09	234 14.1	265 43.0	. . 24.1	253 57.2	. . 17.8	34 22.6	7 00.0	333 44.2	. . 51.7
R	10	249 16.5	280 42.9	23.0	268 57.9	17.1	49 24.9	00.1	348 46.4	51.7
I	11	264 19.0	295 42.7	21.9	283 58.6	16.3	64 27.1	00.2	3 48.5	51.7
D	12	279 21.5	310 42.6	S14 20.8	298 59.3	S 9 15.6	79 29.3	S 7 00.3	18 50.7	S21 51.7
A	13	294 23.9	325 42.5	19.8	314 00.0	14.8	94 31.5	00.4	33 52.8	51.7
Y	14	309 26.4	340 42.4	18.7	329 00.7	14.1	109 33.7	00.5	48 55.0	51.8
	15	324 28.9	355 42.2	. . 17.6	344 01.4	. . 13.3	124 35.9	. . 00.6	63 57.1	. . 51.8
	16	339 31.3	10 42.1	16.5	359 02.1	12.6	139 38.1	00.7	78 59.3	51.8
	17	354 33.8	25 42.0	15.5	14 02.8	11.8	154 40.3	00.8	94 01.5	51.8
	18	9 36.3	40 41.9	S14 14.4	29 03.6	S 9 11.1	169 42.5	S 7 00.8	109 03.6	S21 51.8
	19	24 38.7	55 41.7	13.3	44 04.3	10.3	184 44.7	00.9	124 05.8	51.9
	20	39 41.2	70 41.6	12.2	59 05.0	09.6	199 46.9	01.0	139 07.9	51.9
	21	54 43.6	85 41.5	. . 11.2	74 05.7	. . 08.8	214 49.1	. . 01.1	154 10.1	. . 51.9
	22	69 46.1	100 41.4	10.1	89 06.4	08.1	229 51.3	01.2	169 12.2	51.9
	23	84 48.6	115 41.2	09.0	104 07.1	07.3	244 53.5	01.3	184 14.4	51.9
	31 00	99 51.0	130 41.1	S14 07.9	119 07.8	S 9 06.6	259 55.7	S 7 01.4	199 16.6	S21 52.0
	01	114 53.5	145 41.0	06.8	134 08.5	05.8	274 58.0	01.5	214 18.7	52.0
	02	129 56.0	160 40.9	05.8	149 09.2	05.1	290 00.2	01.6	229 20.9	52.0
	03	144 58.4	175 40.8	. . 04.7	164 09.9	. . 04.3	305 02.4	. . 01.7	244 23.0	. . 52.0
	04	160 00.9	190 40.7	03.6	179 10.6	03.6	320 04.6	01.8	259 25.2	52.0
	05	175 03.4	205 40.5	02.5	194 11.3	02.9	335 06.8	01.9	274 27.3	52.1
	06	190 05.8	220 40.4	S14 01.4	209 12.0	S 9 02.1	350 09.0	S 7 02.0	289 29.5	S21 52.1
	07	205 08.3	235 40.3	14 00.4	224 12.8	01.4	5 11.2	02.1	304 31.7	52.1
S	08	220 10.8	250 40.2	13 59.3	239 13.5	9 00.6	20 13.4	02.1	319 33.8	52.1
A	09	235 13.2	265 40.1	. . 58.2	254 14.2	8 59.9	35 15.6	. . 02.2	334 36.0	. . 52.1
T	10	250 15.7	280 40.0	57.1	269 14.9	59.1	50 17.8	02.3	349 38.1	52.2
U	11	265 18.1	295 39.9	56.0	284 15.6	58.4	65 20.1	02.4	4 40.3	52.2
R	12	280 20.6	310 39.8	S13 54.9	299 16.3	S 8 57.6	80 22.3	S 7 02.5	19 42.4	S21 52.2
D	13	295 23.1	325 39.7	53.8	314 17.0	56.9	95 24.5	02.6	34 44.6	52.2
A	14	310 25.5	340 39.6	52.8	329 17.7	56.1	110 26.7	02.7	49 46.8	52.2
Y	15	325 28.0	355 39.5	. . 51.7	344 18.4	. . 55.4	125 28.9	. . 02.8	64 48.9	. . 52.3
	16	340 30.5	10 39.3	50.6	359 19.1	54.6	140 31.1	02.9	79 51.1	52.3
	17	355 32.9	25 39.2	49.5	14 19.9	53.9	155 33.3	03.0	94 53.2	52.3
	18	10 35.4	40 39.1	S13 48.4	29 20.6	S 8 53.1	170 35.5	S 7 03.1	109 55.4	S21 52.3
	19	25 37.9	55 39.0	47.3	44 21.3	52.3	185 37.7	03.1	124 57.5	52.3
	20	40 40.3	70 38.9	46.2	59 22.0	51.6	200 40.0	03.2	139 59.7	52.4
	21	55 42.8	85 38.8	. . 45.1	74 22.7	. . 50.8	215 42.2	. . 03.3	155 01.9	. . 52.4
	22	70 45.2	100 38.7	44.1	89 23.4	50.1	230 44.4	03.4	170 04.0	52.4
	23	85 47.7	115 38.6	43.0	104 24.1	49.3	245 46.6	03.5	185 06.2	52.4
	Mer. Pass.	h m 17 21.7	*v* −0.1	*d* 1.1	*v* 0.7	*d* 0.7	*v* 2.2	*d* 0.1	*v* 2.2	*d* 0.0

STARS

Name	SHA	Dec
	° ′	° ′
Acamar	315 16.3	S40 14.6
Achernar	335 24.9	S57 09.4
Acrux	173 06.4	S63 11.2
Adhara	255 10.2	S28 59.9
Aldebaran	290 46.3	N16 32.4
Alioth	166 18.8	N55 51.8
Alkaid	152 57.3	N49 13.6
Al Na'ir	27 41.1	S46 52.9
Alnilam	275 43.6	S 1 11.7
Alphard	217 53.5	S 8 44.0
Alphecca	126 09.3	N26 39.5
Alpheratz	357 41.0	N29 11.2
Altair	62 06.2	N 8 55.0
Ankaa	353 13.4	S42 13.1
Antares	112 23.6	S26 27.9
Arcturus	145 53.7	N19 05.7
Atria	107 23.8	S69 03.1
Avior	234 16.4	S59 33.8
Bellatrix	278 29.1	N 6 21.7
Betelgeuse	270 58.4	N 7 24.4
Canopus	263 54.5	S52 42.5
Capella	280 30.4	N46 00.7
Deneb	49 30.2	N45 20.7
Denebola	182 31.2	N14 28.6
Diphda	348 53.5	S17 53.8
Dubhe	193 48.7	N61 39.3
Elnath	278 09.2	N28 37.1
Eltanin	90 45.6	N51 29.3
Enif	33 45.0	N 9 57.3
Fomalhaut	15 21.6	S29 32.1
Gacrux	171 58.1	S57 12.1
Gienah	175 49.8	S17 38.0
Hadar	148 44.6	S60 26.9
Hamal	327 57.9	N23 32.5
Kaus Aust.	83 41.1	S34 22.4
Kochab	137 21.0	N74 05.0
Markab	13 36.1	N15 17.9
Menkar	314 12.3	N 4 09.2
Menkent	148 04.9	S36 26.9
Miaplacidus	221 38.2	S69 47.1
Mirfak	308 36.5	N49 55.3
Nunki	75 55.7	S26 16.3
Peacock	53 16.1	S56 40.8
Pollux	243 24.5	N27 58.8
Procyon	244 56.9	N 5 10.7
Rasalhague	96 04.6	N12 33.0
Regulus	207 40.8	N11 52.9
Rigel	281 09.4	S 8 11.2
Rigil Kent.	139 48.7	S60 53.9
Sabik	102 10.1	S15 44.5
Schedar	349 37.6	N56 38.0
Shaula	96 19.1	S37 06.7
Sirius	258 31.3	S16 44.6
Spica	158 28.8	S11 14.8
Suhail	222 50.3	S43 30.0
Vega	80 37.8	N38 48.1
Zuben'ubi	137 03.0	S16 06.5

	SHA	Mer. Pass.
	° ′	h m
Venus	31 52.3	15 17
Mars	19 58.9	16 04
Jupiter	160 10.9	6 43
Saturn	99 32.9	10 45

UT	SUN GHA	SUN Dec	MOON GHA	v	MOON Dec	d	HP
d h	° ′	° ′	° ′	′	° ′	′	′
29 00	179 29.9	S23 12.7	183 09.7	11.2	S18 57.0	0.3	54.8
01	194 29.6	12.5	197 39.9	11.2	18 57.3	0.2	54.8
02	209 29.3	12.4	212 10.1	11.1	18 57.5	0.1	54.8
03	224 28.9	. . 12.2	226 40.2	11.2	18 57.6	0.0	54.8
04	239 28.6	12.1	241 10.4	11.1	18 57.6	0.1	54.8
05	254 28.3	11.9	255 40.5	11.1	18 57.5	0.2	54.8
06	269 28.0	S23 11.8	270 10.6	11.1	S18 57.3	0.3	54.9
T 07	284 27.7	11.6	284 40.7	11.1	18 57.0	0.4	54.9
H 08	299 27.4	11.4	299 10.8	11.1	18 56.6	0.4	54.9
U 09	314 27.1	. . 11.3	313 40.9	11.0	18 56.2	0.6	54.9
R 10	329 26.8	11.1	328 10.9	11.0	18 55.6	0.6	54.9
S 11	344 26.5	11.0	342 40.9	11.1	18 55.0	0.8	54.9
D 12	359 26.2	S23 10.8	357 11.0	11.0	S18 54.2	0.8	55.0
A 13	14 25.9	10.7	11 41.0	11.0	18 53.4	0.9	55.0
Y 14	29 25.6	10.5	26 11.0	10.9	18 52.5	1.1	55.0
15	44 25.3	. . 10.3	40 40.9	11.0	18 51.4	1.1	55.0
16	59 25.0	10.2	55 10.9	11.0	18 50.3	1.2	55.0
17	74 24.7	10.0	69 40.9	10.9	18 49.1	1.3	55.0
18	89 24.4	S23 09.9	84 10.8	11.0	S18 47.8	1.4	55.1
19	104 24.1	09.7	98 40.8	10.9	18 46.4	1.5	55.1
20	119 23.8	09.5	113 10.7	10.9	18 44.9	1.6	55.1
21	134 23.5	. . 09.4	127 40.6	10.9	18 43.3	1.7	55.1
22	149 23.2	09.2	142 10.5	10.9	18 41.6	1.8	55.1
23	164 22.9	09.0	156 40.4	10.9	18 39.8	1.8	55.1
30 00	179 22.6	S23 08.9	171 10.3	10.9	S18 38.0	2.0	55.2
01	194 22.3	08.7	185 40.2	10.9	18 36.0	2.1	55.2
02	209 22.0	08.5	200 10.1	10.9	18 33.9	2.1	55.2
03	224 21.7	. . 08.4	214 40.0	10.8	18 31.8	2.3	55.2
04	239 21.4	08.2	229 09.8	10.9	18 29.5	2.3	55.2
05	254 21.1	08.0	243 39.7	10.9	18 27.2	2.5	55.2
06	269 20.8	S23 07.9	258 09.6	10.8	S18 24.7	2.5	55.3
07	284 20.5	07.7	272 39.4	10.9	18 22.2	2.6	55.3
08	299 20.2	07.5	287 09.3	10.8	18 19.6	2.7	55.3
F 09	314 19.9	. . 07.3	301 39.1	10.9	18 16.9	2.8	55.3
R 10	329 19.6	07.2	316 09.0	10.8	18 14.1	2.9	55.3
I 11	344 19.3	07.0	330 38.8	10.9	18 11.2	3.0	55.3
D 12	359 19.0	S23 06.8	345 08.7	10.8	S18 08.2	3.1	55.4
A 13	14 18.7	06.6	359 38.5	10.9	18 05.1	3.2	55.4
Y 14	29 18.4	06.5	14 08.4	10.8	18 01.9	3.3	55.4
15	44 18.1	. . 06.3	28 38.2	10.9	17 58.6	3.4	55.4
16	59 17.8	06.1	43 08.1	10.8	17 55.2	3.4	55.4
17	74 17.5	05.9	57 37.9	10.9	17 51.8	3.6	55.4
18	89 17.2	S23 05.7	72 07.8	10.8	S17 48.2	3.6	55.5
19	104 16.9	05.6	86 37.6	10.9	17 44.6	3.8	55.5
20	119 16.6	05.4	101 07.5	10.9	17 40.8	3.8	55.5
21	134 16.3	. . 05.2	115 37.4	10.8	17 37.0	3.9	55.5
22	149 16.0	05.0	130 07.2	10.9	17 33.1	4.0	55.5
23	164 15.7	04.8	144 37.1	10.9	17 29.1	4.1	55.6
31 00	179 15.4	S23 04.6	159 07.0	10.8	S17 25.0	4.2	55.6
01	194 15.1	04.5	173 36.8	10.9	17 20.8	4.3	55.6
02	209 14.8	04.3	188 06.7	10.9	17 16.5	4.4	55.6
03	224 14.5	. . 04.1	202 36.6	10.9	17 12.1	4.4	55.6
04	239 14.2	03.9	217 06.5	10.9	17 07.7	4.6	55.6
05	254 13.9	03.7	231 36.4	10.9	17 03.1	4.6	55.7
06	269 13.6	S23 03.5	246 06.3	10.9	S16 58.5	4.7	55.7
07	284 13.3	03.3	260 36.2	10.9	16 53.8	4.9	55.7
S 08	299 13.0	03.1	275 06.1	11.0	16 48.9	4.9	55.7
A 09	314 12.7	. . 02.9	289 36.1	10.9	16 44.0	5.0	55.7
T 10	329 12.4	02.7	304 06.0	11.0	16 39.0	5.0	55.8
U 11	344 12.1	02.5	318 36.0	10.9	16 34.0	5.2	55.8
R 12	359 11.8	S23 02.3	333 05.9	11.0	S16 28.8	5.2	55.8
D 13	14 11.5	02.2	347 35.9	10.9	16 23.6	5.4	55.8
A 14	29 11.2	02.0	2 05.8	11.0	16 18.2	5.4	55.8
Y 15	44 10.9	. . 01.8	16 35.8	11.0	16 12.8	5.5	55.9
16	59 10.6	01.6	31 05.8	11.0	16 07.3	5.6	55.9
17	74 10.3	01.4	45 35.8	11.0	16 01.7	5.7	55.9
18	89 10.0	S23 01.2	60 05.8	11.0	S15 56.0	5.8	55.9
19	104 09.7	01.0	74 35.8	11.1	15 50.2	5.8	55.9
20	119 09.4	00.8	89 05.9	11.0	15 44.4	5.9	56.0
21	134 09.1	. . 00.6	103 35.9	11.1	15 38.5	6.0	56.0
22	149 08.8	00.3	118 06.0	11.0	15 32.5	6.1	56.0
23	164 08.5	00.1	132 36.0	11.1	S15 26.4	6.2	56.0
	SD 16.3	*d* 0.2	SD 15.0		15.1		15.2

Lat.	Twilight Naut.	Twilight Civil	Sunrise	Moonrise 29	30	31	1
°	h m	h m	h m	h m	h m	h m	h m
N 72	08 25	10 47	▬	▬	▬	12 13	11 58
N 70	08 06	09 52	▬	10 54	11 19	11 27	11 30
68	07 51	09 18	▬	10 02	10 37	10 57	11 09
66	07 38	08 54	10 30	09 29	10 08	10 34	10 52
64	07 27	08 35	09 51	09 06	09 46	10 16	10 39
62	07 18	08 19	09 24	08 47	09 29	10 02	10 27
60	07 09	08 06	09 03	08 31	09 14	09 49	10 17
N 58	07 02	07 55	08 46	08 18	09 02	09 38	10 08
56	06 56	07 44	08 32	08 07	08 51	09 29	10 01
54	06 50	07 36	08 19	07 57	08 42	09 21	09 54
52	06 44	07 28	08 08	07 48	08 33	09 13	09 48
50	06 39	07 20	07 59	07 40	08 26	09 07	09 42
45	06 27	07 04	07 38	07 23	08 10	08 52	09 30
N 40	06 17	06 51	07 22	07 09	07 56	08 40	09 20
35	06 08	06 40	07 08	06 57	07 45	08 30	09 12
30	05 59	06 29	06 55	06 47	07 35	08 21	09 04
20	05 43	06 11	06 34	06 29	07 18	08 06	08 51
N 10	05 27	05 53	06 16	06 14	07 03	07 52	08 40
0	05 10	05 36	05 59	06 00	06 49	07 39	08 29
S 10	04 52	05 19	05 42	05 45	06 36	07 27	08 18
20	04 29	04 58	05 23	05 30	06 21	07 13	08 07
30	04 01	04 34	05 01	05 12	06 04	06 58	07 54
35	03 42	04 19	04 48	05 02	05 54	06 49	07 46
40	03 19	04 01	04 33	04 51	05 42	06 38	07 37
45	02 49	03 38	04 16	04 37	05 29	06 26	07 27
S 50	02 05	03 09	03 54	04 20	05 13	06 11	07 15
52	01 38	02 54	03 43	04 12	05 05	06 05	07 09
54	00 56	02 37	03 31	04 03	04 57	05 57	07 03
56	////	02 15	03 17	03 53	04 47	05 48	06 56
58	////	01 47	03 00	03 42	04 36	05 39	06 48
S 60	////	01 01	02 40	03 29	04 24	05 28	06 38

Lat.	Sunset	Twilight Civil	Twilight Naut.	Moonset 29	30	31	1
°	h m	h m	h m	h m	h m	h m	h m
N 72	▬	13 19	15 41	▬	▬	15 39	17 37
N 70	▬	14 14	16 00	13 31	14 50	16 25	18 04
68	▬	14 48	16 15	14 23	15 31	16 54	18 25
66	13 35	15 12	16 28	14 55	16 00	17 16	18 40
64	14 15	15 31	16 39	15 19	16 21	17 34	18 53
62	14 42	15 47	16 48	15 38	16 38	17 48	19 04
60	15 03	16 00	16 56	15 53	16 52	18 00	19 14
N 58	15 20	16 11	17 03	16 06	17 04	18 10	19 22
56	15 34	16 21	17 10	16 17	17 15	18 19	19 29
54	15 47	16 30	17 16	16 27	17 24	18 27	19 35
52	15 57	16 38	17 22	16 36	17 33	18 35	19 41
50	16 07	16 45	17 27	16 44	17 40	18 41	19 46
45	16 27	17 01	17 38	17 01	17 56	18 55	19 57
N 40	16 44	17 14	17 48	17 15	18 09	19 06	20 06
35	16 58	17 26	17 58	17 26	18 20	19 16	20 14
30	17 10	17 36	18 06	17 37	18 29	19 24	20 21
20	17 31	17 55	18 22	17 54	18 46	19 39	20 33
N 10	17 49	18 12	18 38	18 09	19 00	19 51	20 43
0	18 06	18 29	18 55	18 24	19 13	20 03	20 53
S 10	18 24	18 47	19 14	18 38	19 27	20 15	21 02
20	18 42	19 07	19 36	18 53	19 41	20 28	21 12
30	19 04	19 32	20 05	19 10	19 57	20 42	21 24
35	19 17	19 47	20 23	19 20	20 07	20 50	21 30
40	19 32	20 04	20 46	19 32	20 17	20 59	21 38
45	19 50	20 27	21 16	19 46	20 30	21 10	21 47
S 50	20 12	20 56	22 00	20 02	20 45	21 23	21 57
52	20 22	21 10	22 26	20 10	20 52	21 29	22 02
54	20 34	21 28	23 08	20 18	21 00	21 36	22 07
56	20 48	21 49	////	20 28	21 09	21 44	22 13
58	21 04	22 18	////	20 39	21 19	21 52	22 20
S 60	21 24	23 02	////	20 52	21 31	22 02	22 27

Day	SUN Eqn. of Time 00^h	SUN Eqn. of Time 12^h	SUN Mer. Pass.	MOON Mer. Pass. Upper	MOON Mer. Pass. Lower	Age	Phase
d	m s	m s	h m	h m	h m	d	%
29	02 00	02 15	12 02	12 12	24 37	00	0
30	02 29	02 44	12 03	13 01	00 37	01	2
31	02 58	03 12	12 03	13 51	01 26	02	5

EXPLANATION

PRINCIPLE AND ARRANGEMENT

1. *Object.* The object of this Almanac is to provide, in a convenient form, the data required for the practice of astronomical navigation at sea.

2. *Principle.* The main contents of the Almanac consist of data from which the *Greenwich Hour Angle* (GHA) and the *Declination* (Dec) of all the bodies used for navigation can be obtained for any instant of *Universal Time* (UT, specifically UT1, or previously Greenwich Mean Time (GMT)).

The *Local Hour Angle* (LHA) can then be obtained by means of the formula:

$$\text{LHA} = \text{GHA} \begin{smallmatrix} -\text{ west} \\ +\text{ east} \end{smallmatrix} \text{ longitude}$$

The remaining data consist of: times of rising and setting of the Sun and Moon, and times of twilight; miscellaneous calendarial and planning data and auxiliary tables, including a list of Standard Times; corrections to be applied to observed altitude.

For the Sun, Moon, and planets the GHA and Dec are tabulated directly for each hour of UT throughout the year. For the stars the *Sidereal Hour Angle* (SHA) is given, and the GHA is obtained from:

$$\text{GHA Star} = \text{GHA Aries} + \text{SHA Star}$$

The SHA and Dec of the stars change slowly and may be regarded as constant over periods of several days. GHA Aries, or the Greenwich Hour Angle of the first point of Aries (the Vernal Equinox), is tabulated for each hour. Permanent tables give the appropriate increments and corrections to the tabulated hourly values of GHA and Dec for the minutes and seconds of UT.

The six-volume series of *Sight Reduction Tables for Marine Navigation* (published in U.S.A. as Pub. No. 229) has been designed for the solution of the navigational triangle and is intended for use with *The Nautical Almanac*.

Two alternative procedures for sight reduction are described on pages 277–318. The first requires the use of programmable calculators or computers, while the second uses a set of concise tables that is given on pages 286–317.

The tabular accuracy is 0.′1 throughout. The time argument on the daily pages of this Almanac is UT1 denoted throughout by UT. This scale may differ from the broadcast time signals (UTC) by an amount which, if ignored, will introduce an error of up to 0.′2 in longitude determined from astronomical observations. The difference arises because the time argument depends on the variable rate of rotation of the Earth while the broadcast time signals are based on an atomic time-scale. Step adjustments of exactly one second are made to the time signals as required (normally at 24^h on December 31 and June 30) so that the difference between the time signals and UT, as used in this Almanac, may not exceed $0^s.9$. Those who require to reduce observations to a precision of better than 1^s must therefore obtain the correction (DUT1) to the time signals from coding in the signal, or from other sources; the required time is given by UT1=UTC+DUT1 to a precision of $0^s.1$. Alternatively, the longitude, when determined from astronomical observations, may be corrected by the corresponding amount shown in the following table:

Correction to time signals	Correction to longitude
$-0^s.9$ to $-0^s.7$	0.′2 to east
$-0^s.6$ to $-0^s.3$	0.′1 to east
$-0^s.2$ to $+0^s.2$	no correction
$+0^s.3$ to $+0^s.6$	0.′1 to west
$+0^s.7$ to $+0^s.9$	0.′2 to west

3. *Lay-out.* The ephemeral data for three days are presented on an opening of two pages: the left-hand page contains the data for the planets and stars; the right-hand page contains the data for the Sun and Moon, together with times of twilight, sunrise, sunset, moonrise and moonset.

The remaining contents are arranged as follows: for ease of reference the altitude-correction tables are given on pages A2, A3, A4, xxxiv and xxxv; calendar, Moon's phases, eclipses, and planet notes (i.e. data of general interest) precede the main tabulations. The Explanation is followed by information on standard times, star charts and list of star positions, sight reduction procedures and concise sight reduction tables, polar phenomena information and graphs, tables of increments and corrections and other auxiliary tables that are frequently used.

MAIN DATA

4. *Daily pages.* The daily pages give the GHA of Aries, the GHA and Dec of the Sun, Moon, and the four navigational planets, for each hour of UT. For the Moon, values of v and d are also tabulated for each hour to facilitate the correction of GHA and Dec to intermediate times; v and d for the Sun and planets change so slowly that they are given, at the foot of the appropriate columns, once only on the page; v is zero for Aries and negligible for the Sun, and is omitted. The SHA and Dec of the 57 selected stars, arranged in alphabetical order of proper name, are also given.

5. *Stars.* The SHA and Dec of 173 stars, including the 57 selected stars, are tabulated for each month on pages 268–273; no interpolation is required and the data can be used in precisely the same way as those for the selected stars on the daily pages. The stars are arranged in order of SHA.

The list of 173 includes all stars down to magnitude 3·0, together with a few fainter ones to fill the larger gaps. The 57 selected stars have been chosen from amongst these on account of brightness and distribution in the sky; they will suffice for the majority of observations.

The 57 selected stars are known by their proper names, but they are also numbered in descending order of SHA. In the list of 173 stars, the constellation names are always given on the left-hand page; on the facing page proper names are given where well-known names exist. Numbers for the selected stars are given in both columns.

An index to the selected stars, containing lists in both alphabetical and numerical order, is given on page xxxiii and is also reprinted on the bookmark.

6. *Increments and corrections.* The tables printed on tinted paper (pages ii–xxxi) at the back of the Almanac provide the increments and corrections for minutes and seconds to be applied to the hourly values of GHA and Dec. They consist of sixty tables, one for each minute, separated into two parts: increments to GHA for Sun and planets, Aries, and Moon for every minute and second; and, for each minute, corrections to be applied to GHA and Dec corresponding to the values of v and d given on the daily pages.

The increments are based on the following adopted hourly rates of increase of the GHA: Sun and planets, 15° precisely; Aries, 15° 02′.46; Moon, 14° 19′.0. The values of v on the daily pages are the excesses of the actual hourly motions over the adopted values; they are generally positive, except for Venus. The tabulated hourly values of the Sun's GHA have been adjusted to reduce to a minimum the error caused by treating v as negligible. The values of d on the daily pages are the hourly differences of the Dec. For the Moon, the true values of v and d are given for each hour; otherwise mean values are given for the three days on the page.

7. *Method of entry.* The UT of an observation is expressed as a day and hour, followed by a number of minutes and seconds. The tabular values of GHA and Dec, and, where necessary, the corresponding values of v and d, are taken directly from the daily pages for the day and hour of UT; this hour is always *before* the time of observation. SHA and Dec of the selected stars are also taken from the daily pages.

The table of Increments and Corrections for the minute of UT is then selected. For the GHA, the increment for minutes and seconds is taken from the appropriate column opposite the seconds of UT; the v-correction is taken from the second part of the same table opposite the value of v as given on the daily pages. Both increment and v-correction are to be added to the GHA, except for Venus when v is prefixed by a minus sign and the v-correction is to be subtracted. For the Dec there is no increment, but a d-correction is applied in the same way as the v-correction; d is given without sign on the daily pages and the sign of the correction is to be supplied by inspection of the Dec column. In many cases the correction may be applied mentally.

8. *Examples.* (a) Sun and Moon. Required the GHA and Dec of the Sun and Moon on 2016 November 9 at $15^h\ 47^m\ 13^s$ UT.

		SUN			MOON			
		GHA	Dec	d	GHA	v	Dec	d
		° ′	° ′	′	° ′	′	° ′	′
Daily page, November $9^d\ 15^h$		49 01·8	S 17 05·5	0·7	292 58·3	10·3	S 7 53·1	10·1
Increments for	$47^m\ 13^s$	11 48·3			11 16·0			
v or d corrections for	47^m		+0·6		+8·2		−8·0	
Sum for November $9^d\ 15^h\ 47^m\ 13^s$		60 50·1	S 17 06·1		304 22·5		S 7 45·1	

(b) Planets. Required the LHA and Dec of (i) Venus on 2016 November 9 at $13^h\ 28^m\ 38^s$ UT in longitude E 78° 33′; (ii) Jupiter on 2016 November 9 at $10^h\ 34^m\ 27^s$ UT in longitude W 83° 57′.

		VENUS					JUPITER			
		GHA	v	Dec	d		GHA	v	Dec	d
		° ′	′	° ′	′		° ′	′	° ′	′
Daily page, Nov. 9^d	(13^h)	337 39·4	−0·8	S 25 26·0	0·2	(10^h)	6 43·5	2·0	S 4 02·1	0·2
Increments (planets)	$(28^m\ 38^s)$	7 09·5				$(34^m\ 27^s)$	8 36·8			
v or d corrections	(28^m)	−0·4		+0·1		(34^m)	+1·2		+0·1	
Sum = GHA and Dec.		344 48·5		S 25 26·1			15 21·5		S 4 02·2	
Longitude	(east)	+ 78 33·0				(west)	− 83 57·0			
Multiples of 360°		−360					+360			
LHA planet		63 21·5					291 24·5			

(c) Stars. Required the GHA and Dec of (i) *Aldebaran* on 2016 November 9 at $7^h\ 21^m\ 13^s$ UT; (ii) *Vega* on 2016 November 9 at $20^h\ 06^m\ 19^s$ UT.

		Aldebaran			*Vega*	
		GHA	Dec		GHA	Dec
		° ′	° ′		° ′	° ′
Daily page (SHA and Dec)		290 46·4	N 16 32.4		80 37·7	N 38 48.4
Daily page (GHA Aries)	(7^h)	153 53·0		(20^h)	349 25·1	
Increments (Aries)	$(21^m\ 13^s)$	5 19·1		$(06^m\ 19^s)$	1 35·0	
Sum = GHA star		449 58·5			431 37·8	
Multiples of 360°		−360			−360	
GHA star		89 58·5			71 37·8	

9. *Polaris (Pole Star) tables.* The tables on pages 274–276 provide means by which the latitude can be deduced from an observed altitude of *Polaris*, and they also give its azimuth; their use is explained and illustrated on those pages. They are based on the following formula:

$$\text{Latitude} - H_O = -p\cos h + \tfrac{1}{2}p\ \sin p\ \sin^2 h\ \tan(\text{latitude})$$

where H_O = Apparent altitude (corrected for refraction)

p = polar distance of *Polaris* = 90° − Dec

h = local hour angle of *Polaris* = LHA Aries + SHA

a_0, which is a function of LHA Aries only, is the value of both terms of the above formula calculated for mean values of the SHA (316° 47′) and Dec (N 89° 20′.0) of *Polaris*, for a mean latitude of 50°, and adjusted by the addition of a constant (58′.8).

a_1, which is a function of LHA Aries and latitude, is the excess of the value of the second term over its mean value for latitude 50°, increased by a constant (0′.6) to make it always positive. a_2, which is a function of LHA Aries and date, is the correction to the first term for the variation of *Polaris* from its adopted mean position; it is increased by a constant (0′.6) to make it positive. The sum of the added constants is 1°, so that:

$$\text{Latitude} = \text{Apparent altitude (corrected for refraction)} - 1^\circ + a_0 + a_1 + a_2$$

RISING AND SETTING PHENOMENA

10. *General.* On the right-hand daily pages are given the times of sunrise and sunset, of the beginning and end of civil and nautical twilights, and of moonrise and moonset for a range of latitudes from N 72° to S 60°. These times, which are given to the nearest minute, are strictly the UT of the phenomena on the Greenwich meridian; they are given for every day for moonrise and moonset, but only for the middle day of the three on each page for the solar phenomena.

They are approximately the Local Mean Times (LMT) of the corresponding phenomena on other meridians; they can be formally interpolated if desired. The UT of a phenomenon is obtained from the LMT by:

$$\text{UT} = \text{LMT} \begin{array}{l} + \text{ west} \\ - \text{ east} \end{array} \text{longitude}$$

in which the longitude must first be converted to time by the table on page i or otherwise. Interpolation for latitude can be done mentally or with the aid of Table I on page xxxii.

The following symbols are used to indicate the conditions under which, in high latitudes, some of the phenomena do not occur:

□ Sun or Moon remains continuously above the horizon;

■ Sun or Moon remains continuously below the horizon;

//// twilight lasts all night.

Basis of the tabulations. At sunrise and sunset 16′ is allowed for semi-diameter and 34′ for horizontal refraction, so that at the times given the Sun's upper limb is on the visible horizon; all times refer to phenomena as seen from sea level with a clear horizon.

At the times given for the beginning and end of twilight, the Sun's zenith distance is 96° for civil, and 102° for nautical twilight. The degree of illumination at the times given for civil twilight (in good conditions and in the absence of other illumination) is such that the brightest stars are visible and the horizon is clearly defined. At the times given for nautical twilight the horizon is in general not visible, and it is too dark for observation with a marine sextant.

Times corresponding to other depressions of the Sun may be obtained by interpolation or, for depressions of more than 12°, less reliably, by extrapolation; times so obtained will be subject to considerable uncertainty near extreme conditions.

At moonrise and moonset, allowance is made for semi-diameter, parallax, and refraction (34′), so that at the times given the Moon's upper limb is on the visible horizon as seen from sea level.

Polar phenomena. Information and graphs concerning the rising and setting of the Sun and Moon and the duration of civil twilight for high latitudes are given on pages 320–325.

11. *Sunrise, sunset, twilight.* The tabulated times may be regarded, without serious error, as the LMT of the phenomena on any of the three days on the page and in any longitude. Precise times may normally be obtained by interpolating the tabular values for latitude and to the correct day and longitude, the latter being expressed as a fraction of a day by dividing it by 360°, positive for west and negative for east longitudes. In the extreme conditions near □, ■ or //// interpolation may not be possible in one direction, but accurate times are of little value in these circumstances.

Examples. Required the UT of (a) the beginning of morning twilights and sunrise on 2016 January 13 for latitude S 48° 55′, longitude E 75° 18′; (b) sunset and the end of evening twilights on 2016 January 15 for latitude N 67° 10′, longitude W 168° 05′.

	(a)	Twilight Nautical	Twilight Civil	Sunrise	(b)	Sunset	Twilight Civil	Twilight Nautical
		d h m	d h m	d h m		d h m	d h m	d h m
From p. 19								
LMT for Lat	S 45°	13 03 08	13 03 55	13 04 31	N 66°	15 14 21	15 15 41	15 16 52
Corr. to (p. xxxii, Table I)	S 48° 55′	−30	−20	−16	N 67° 10′	−24	−12	−6
Long (p. i)	E 75° 18′	−5 01	−5 01	−5 01	W 168° 05′	+11 12	+11 12	+11 12
UT		12 21 37	12 22 34	12 23 14		16 01 09	16 02 41	16 03 58

The LMT are strictly for January 14 (middle date on page) and 0° longitude; for more precise times it is necessary to interpolate, but rounding errors may accumulate to about 2^{m}.

(a) to January $13^{d} - 75°/360° = $ Jan. $12^{d}_{\cdot}8$, i.e. $\frac{1}{3}(1{\cdot}2) = 0{\cdot}4$ backwards towards the data for the same latitude interpolated similarly from page 17; the corrections are -2^{m} to nautical twilight, -2^{m} to civil twilight and -2^{m} to sunrise.

(b) to January $15^{d} + 168°/360° = $ Jan. $15^{d}_{\cdot}5$, i.e. $\frac{1}{3}(1{\cdot}5) = 0{\cdot}5$ forwards towards the data for the same latitude interpolated similarly from page 21; the corrections are $+8^{m}$ to sunset, $+4^{m}$ to civil twilight, and $+4^{m}$ to nautical twilight.

12. *Moonrise, moonset.* Precise times of moonrise and moonset are rarely needed; a glance at the tables will generally give sufficient indication of whether the Moon is available for observation and of the hours of rising and setting. If needed, precise times may be obtained as follows. Interpolate for latitude, using Table I on page xxxii, on the day wanted and also on the preceding day in east longitudes or the following day in west longitudes; take the difference between these times and interpolate for longitude by applying to the time for the day wanted the correction from Table II on page xxxii, so that the resulting time is between the two times used. In extreme conditions near ☐ or ■ interpolation for latitude or longitude may be possible only in one direction; accurate times are of little value in these circumstances.

To facilitate this interpolation, the times of moonrise and moonset are given for four days on each page; where no phenomenon occurs during a particular day (as happens once a month) the time of the phenomenon on the following day, increased by 24^{h}, is given; extra care must be taken when interpolating between two values, when one of those values exceeds 24^{h}. In practice it suffices to use the daily difference between the times for the nearest tabular latitude, and generally, to enter Table II with the nearest tabular arguments as in the examples below.

Examples. Required the UT of moonrise and moonset in latitude S 47° 10′, longitudes E 124° 00′ and W 78° 31′ on 2016 January 26.

	Longitude E 124° 00′ Moonrise	Longitude E 124° 00′ Moonset	Longitude W 78° 31′ Moonrise	Longitude W 78° 31′ Moonset
	d h m	d h m	d h m	d h m
LMT for Lat. S 45°	26 20 47	26 07 15	26 20 47	26 07 15
Lat correction (p. xxxii, Table I)	+02	−04	+02	−04
Long correction (p. xxxii, Table II)	−10	−20	+07	+13
Correct LMT	26 20 39	26 06 51	26 20 56	26 07 24
Longitude (p. i)	−8 16	−8 16	+5 14	+5 14
UT	26 12 23	25 22 35	27 02 10	26 12 38

ALTITUDE CORRECTION TABLES

13. *General.* In general, two corrections are given for application to altitudes observed with a marine sextant; additional corrections are required for Venus and Mars and also for very low altitudes.

Tables of the correction for dip of the horizon, due to height of eye above sea level, are given on pages A2 and xxxiv. Strictly this correction should be applied first and subtracted from the sextant altitude to give apparent altitude, which is the correct argument for the other tables.

Separate tables are given of the second correction for the Sun, for stars and planets (on pages A2 and A3), and for the Moon (on pages xxxiv and xxxv). For the Sun, values are given for both lower and upper limbs, for two periods of the year. The star tables are used for the planets, but additional corrections for parallax (page A2) are required for Venus and Mars. The Moon tables are in two parts: the main correction is a function of apparent altitude only and is tabulated for the lower limb (30′ must be subtracted to obtain the correction for the upper limb); the other, which is given for both lower and upper limbs, depends also on the horizontal parallax, which has to be taken from the daily pages.

An additional correction, given on page A4, is required for the change in the refraction, due to variations of pressure and temperature from the adopted standard conditions; it may generally be ignored for altitudes greater than 10°, except possibly in extreme conditions. The correction tables for the Sun, stars, and planets are in two parts; only those for altitudes greater than 10° are reprinted on the bookmark.

14. *Critical tables.* Some of the altitude correction tables are arranged as critical tables. In these, an interval of apparent altitude (or height of eye) corresponds to a single value of the correction; no interpolation is required. At a "critical" entry the upper of the two possible values of the correction is to be taken. For example, in the table of dip, a correction of −4′.1 corresponds to all values of the height of eye from 5·3 to 5·5 metres (17·5 to 18·3 feet) inclusive.

15. *Examples.* The following examples illustrate the use of the altitude correction tables; the sextant altitudes given are assumed to be taken on 2016 March 11 with a marine sextant at height 5·4 metres (18 feet), temperature −3°C and pressure 982 mb, the Moon sights being taken at about 10^{h} UT.

	SUN lower limb	SUN upper limb	MOON lower limb	MOON upper limb	VENUS	*Polaris*
	° ′	° ′	° ′	° ′	° ′	° ′
Sextant altitude	21 19·7	3 20·2	33 27·6	26 06·7	4 32·6	49 36·5
Dip, height 5·4 metres (18 feet)	−4·1	−4·1	−4·1	−4·1	−4·1	−4·1
Main correction	+13·8	−29·6	+57·4	+60·5	−10·8	−0·8
−30′ for upper limb (Moon)	—	—	—	−30·0	—	—
L, U correction for Moon	—	—	+8·5	+5·5	—	—
Additional correction for Venus	—	—	—	—	+0·1	—
Additional refraction correction	−0·1	−0·6	−0·1	−0·1	−0·5	0·0
Corrected sextant altitude	21 29·3	2 45·9	34 29·3	26 38·5	4 17·3	49 31·6

The main corrections have been taken out with apparent altitude (sextant altitude corrected for index error and dip) as argument, interpolating where possible. These refinements are rarely necessary.

16. *Composition of the Corrections.* The table for the dip of the sea horizon is based on the formula:

$$\text{Correction for dip} = -1'.76\sqrt{(\text{height of eye in metres})} = -0'.97\sqrt{(\text{height of eye in feet})}$$

The correction table for the Sun includes the effects of semi-diameter, parallax and mean refraction.

The correction tables for the stars and planets allow for the effect of mean refraction.

The phase correction for Venus has been incorporated in the tabulations for GHA and Dec, and no correction for phase is required. The additional corrections for Venus and Mars allow for parallax. Alternatively, the correction for parallax may be calculated from $p \cos H$, where p is the parallax and H is the altitude. In 2016 the values for p are:

	Jan. 1		Dec. 3		Dec. 31					
Venus		0′.1		0′.2						

	Jan. 1		Mar. 11		Apr. 30		July 4		Sept. 15		Dec. 31
Mars		0′.1		0′.2		0′.3		0′.2		0′.1	

The correction table for the Moon includes the effect of semi-diameter, parallax, augmentation and mean refraction.

Mean refraction is calculated for a temperature of 10°C (50°F), a pressure of 1010 mb (29·83 inches), humidity of 80% and wavelength 0·50169 μm.

17. *Bubble sextant observations.* When observing with a bubble sextant, no correction is necessary for dip, semi-diameter, or augmentation. The altitude corrections for the stars and planets on page A2 and on the bookmark should be used for the Sun as well as for the stars and planets; for the Moon, it is easiest to take the mean of the corrections for lower and upper limbs and subtract 15′ from the altitude; the correction for dip must not be applied.

AUXILIARY AND PLANNING DATA

18. *Sun and Moon.* On the daily pages are given: hourly values of the horizontal parallax of the Moon; the semi-diameters and the times of meridian passage of both Sun and Moon over the Greenwich meridian; the equation of time; the age of the Moon, the percent (%) illuminated and a symbol indicating the phase. The times of the phases of the Moon are given in UT on page 4. For the Moon, the semi-diameters for each of the three days are given at the foot of the column; for the Sun a single value is sufficient. Table II on page xxxii may be used for interpolating the time of the Moon's meridian passage for longitude. The equation of time is given daily at 00^h and 12^h UT. The sign is *positive* for unshaded values and *negative* for shaded values. To obtain apparent time add the equation of time to mean time when the sign is *positive*. Subtract the equation of time from mean time when the sign is *negative*. At 12^h UT, when the sign is *positive*, meridian passage of the Sun occurs *before* 12^h UT, otherwise it occurs *after* 12^h UT.

19. *Planets.* The magnitudes of the planets are given immediately following their names in the headings on the daily pages; also given, for the middle day of the three on the page, are their SHA at 00^h UT and their times of meridian passage.

The planet notes and diagram on pages 8 and 9 provide descriptive information as to the suitability of the planets for observation during the year, and of their positions and movements.

20. *Stars.* The time of meridian passage of the first point of Aries over the Greenwich meridian is given on the daily pages, for the middle day of the three on the page, to $0^m.1$. The interval between successive meridian passages is $23^h\ 56^m.1$ (24^h less $3^m.9$), so that times for intermediate days and other meridians can readily be derived. If a precise time is required, it may be obtained by finding the UT at which LHA Aries is zero.

The meridian passage of a star occurs when its LHA is zero, that is when LHA Aries + SHA = 360°. An approximate time can be obtained from the planet diagram on page 9.

The star charts on pages 266 and 267 are intended to assist identification. They show the relative positions of the stars in the sky as seen from the Earth and include all 173 stars used in the Almanac, together with a few others to complete the main constellation configurations. The local meridian at any time may be located on the chart by means of its SHA which is 360° − LHA Aries, or west longitude − GHA Aries.

21. *Star globe.* To set a star globe on which is printed a scale of LHA Aries, first set the globe for latitude and then rotate about the polar axis until the scale under the edge of the meridian circle reads LHA Aries.

To mark the positions of the Sun, Moon, and planets on the star globe, take the difference GHA Aries − GHA body and use this along the LHA Aries scale, in conjunction with the declination, to plot the position. GHA Aries − GHA body is most conveniently found by taking the difference when the GHA of the body is small (less than 15°), which happens once a day.

22. *Calendar.* On page 4 are given lists of ecclesiastical festivals, and of the principal anniversaries and holidays in the United Kingdom and the United States of America. The calendar on page 5 includes the day of the year as well as the day of the week.

Brief particulars are given, at the foot of page 5, of the solar and lunar eclipses occurring during the year; the times given are in UT. The principal features of the more important solar eclipses are shown on the maps on pages 6 and 7.

23. *Standard times.* The lists on pages 262–265 give the standard times used in most countries. In general no attempt is made to give details of the beginning and end of summer time, since they are liable to frequent changes at short notice. For the latest information consult Admiralty List of Radio Signals Volume 2 (NP 282) corrected by Section VI of the weekly edition of Admiralty Notices to Mariners.

The Date or Calendar Line is an arbitrary line, on either side of which the date differs by one day; when crossing this line on a westerly course, the date must be advanced one day; when crossing it on an easterly course, the date must be put back one day. The line is a modification of the line of the 180th meridian, and is drawn so as to include, as far as possible, islands of any one group, etc., on the same side of the line. It may be traced by starting at the South Pole and joining up to the following positions:

	°	°	°	°	°	°	°
Lat	S 51·0	S 45·0	S 15·0	S 5·0	N 48·0	N 53·0	N 65·5
Long	180·0	W 172·5	W 172·5	180·0	180·0	E 170·0	W 169·0

thence through the middle of the Diomede Islands to Lat N 68°·0, Long W 169°·0, passing east of Ostrov Vrangelya (Wrangel Island) to Lat N 75°·0, Long 180°·0, and thence to the North Pole.

ACCURACY

24. *Main data.* The quantities tabulated in this Almanac are generally correct to the nearest 0′·1; the exception is the Sun's GHA which is deliberately adjusted by up to 0′·15 to reduce the error due to ignoring the *v*-correction. The GHA and Dec at intermediate times cannot be obtained to this precision, since at least two quantities must be added; moreover, the *v*- and *d*-corrections are based on mean values of *v* and *d* and are taken from tables for the whole minute only. The largest error that can occur in the GHA or Dec of any body other than the Sun or Moon is less than 0′·2; it may reach 0′·25 for the GHA of the Sun and 0′·3 for that of the Moon.

In practice, it may be expected that only one third of the values of GHA and Dec taken out will have errors larger than 0′·05 and less than one tenth will have errors larger than 0′·1.

25. *Altitude corrections.* The errors in the altitude corrections are nominally of the same order as those in GHA and Dec, as they result from the addition of several quantities each correctly rounded off to 0′·1. But the actual values of the dip and of the refraction at low altitudes may, in extreme atmospheric conditions, differ considerably from the mean values used in the tables.

USE OF THIS ALMANAC IN 2017

This Almanac may be used for the Sun and stars in 2017 in the following manner.

For the Sun, take out the GHA and Dec for the same date but, for January and February, for a time $18^h\ 12^m\ 00^s$ *later* and, for March to December, for a time $5^h\ 48^m\ 00^s$ *earlier* than the UT of observation; in both cases add 87° 00′ to the GHA so obtained. The error, mainly due to planetary perturbations of the Earth, is unlikely to exceed 0′·4.

For the stars, calculate the GHA and Dec for the same date and the same time, but for January and February *add* 44′·0 and for March to December *subtract* 15′·1 from the GHA so found. The error due to incomplete correction for precession and nutation is unlikely to exceed 0′·4. If preferred, the same result can be obtained by using a time $18^h\ 12^m\ 00^s$ later for January and February, and $5^h\ 48^m\ 00^s$ earlier for March to December, than the UT of observation (as for the Sun) and adding 86° 59′·2 to the GHA (or adding 87° as for the Sun and subtracting 0′·8, for precession, from the SHA of the star).

The Almanac cannot be so used for the Moon or planets.

LIST I — PLACES FAST ON UTC (mainly those EAST OF GREENWICH)

The times given below should be *added* to UTC to give Standard Time / *subtracted* from Standard Time to give UTC.

	h	m
Admiralty Islands	10	
Afghanistan	04	30
Albania*	01	
Algeria	01	
Amirante Islands	04	
Andaman Islands	05	30
Angola	01	
Armenia	04	
Australia		
Australian Capital Territory*	10	
New South Wales*[1]	10	
Northern Territory	09	30
Queensland	10	
South Australia*	09	30
Tasmania*	10	
Victoria*	10	
Western Australia	08	
Whitsunday Islands	10	
Austria*†	01	
Azerbaijan*	04	
Bahrain	03	
Balearic Islands*†	01	
Bangladesh	06	
Belarus	03	
Belgium*†	01	
Benin	01	
Bosnia and Herzegovina*	01	
Botswana, Republic of	02	
Brunei	08	
Bulgaria*†	02	
Burma (Myanmar)	06	30
Burundi	02	
Cambodia	07	
Cameroon Republic	01	
Caroline Islands[2]	10	
Central African Republic	01	
Chad	01	
Chagos Archipelago & Diego Garcia	06	
Chatham Islands*	12	45
China, People's Republic of	08	
Christmas Island, Indian Ocean	07	
Cocos (Keeling) Islands	06	30
Comoro Islands (Comoros)	03	
Congo, Democratic Republic		
West: Kinshasa, Equateur	01	
East: Orientale, Kasai, Kivu, Shaba	02	
Congo Republic	01	
Corsica*†	01	
Crete*†	02	
Croatia*†	01	
Cyprus†: Ercan*, Larnaca*	02	
Czech Republic*†	01	
Denmark*†	01	
Djibouti	03	
Egypt*, Arab Republic of	02	
Equatorial Guinea, Republic of	01	
Bioko	01	
Eritrea	03	
Estonia*†	02	
Ethiopia	03	
Fiji*	12	
Finland*†	02	
France*†	01	
Gabon	01	
Georgia	04	
Germany*†	01	
Gibraltar*	01	
Greece*†	02	
Guam	10	
Hong Kong	08	
Hungary*†	01	
India	05	30
Indonesia, Republic of		
Bangka, Billiton, Java, West and Central Kalimantan, Madura, Sumatra	07	
Bali, Flores, South and East Kalimantan, Lombok, Sulawesi, Sumba, Sumbawa, West Timor	08	
Aru, Irian Jaya, Kai, Moluccas Tanimbar	09	
Iran*	03	30
Iraq	03	
Israel*	02	
Italy*†	01	
Jan Mayen Island*	01	
Japan	09	
Jordan	02	
Kazakhstan		
Western: Aktau, Uralsk, Atyrau	05	
Eastern & Central: Kzyl-Orda, Astana	06	
Kenya	03	
Kerguelen Islands	05	
Kiribati Republic		
Gilbert Islands	12	
Phoenix Islands[3]	13	
Line Islands[3]	14	
Korea, North	09	
Korea, South	09	
Kuwait	03	
Kyrgyzstan	06	
Laccadive Islands	05	30
Laos	07	

* Daylight-saving time may be kept in these places. † For Summer time dates see List II footnotes.

[1] Except Broken Hill Area* which keeps $09^h 30^m$.

[2] Except Pohnpei, Pingelap and Kosrae which keep 11^h and Palau which keeps 09^h.

[3] The Line and Phoenix Is. not part of the Kiribati Republic keep 10^h and 11^h, respectively, slow on UTC.

LIST I — (*continued*)

	h	m
Latvia*†	02	
Lebanon*	02	
Lesotho	02	
Libya	02	
Liechtenstein*	01	
Lithuania*†	02	
Lord Howe Island*	10	30
Luxembourg*†	01	
Macau	08	
Macedonia*, former Yugoslav Republic	01	
Madagascar, Democratic Republic of	03	
Malawi	02	
Malaysia, Malaya, Sabah, Sarawak	08	
Maldives, Republic of The	05	
Malta*†	01	
Mariana Islands	10	
Marshall Islands	12	
Mauritius	04	
Moldova*	02	
Monaco*	01	
Mongolia	08	
Montenegro*	01	
Mozambique	02	
Namibia*	01	
Nauru	12	
Nepal	05	45
Netherlands, The*†	01	
New Caledonia	11	
New Zealand*	12	
Nicobar Islands	05	30
Niger	01	
Nigeria, Republic of	01	
Norfolk Island	11	30
Norway*	01	
Novaya Zemlya	04	
Okinawa	09	
Oman	04	
Pagalu (Annobon Islands)	01	
Pakistan	05	
Palau Islands	09	
Papua New Guinea	10	
Pescadores Islands	08	
Philippine Republic	08	
Poland*†	01	
Qatar	03	
Reunion	04	
Romania*†	02	
Russia [1]		
Kaliningrad	02	
Moscow, St. Petersburg, Volgograd, Arkhangelsk, Astrakhan	03	
Samara	04	
Ekaterinburg, Ufa, Perm, Novyy Port	05	
Omsk, Novosibirsk, Tomsk	06	
Norilsk, Krasnoyarsk, Dikson	07	
Irkutsk, Bratsk, Ulan-Ude, Chita	08	
Tiksi, Yakutsk	09	
Vladivostok, Khabarovsk, Okhotsk, Magadan	10	
Sakhalin Island, Kuril Islands	11	
Petropavlovsk-K., Anadyr	12	
Rwanda	02	
Ryukyu Islands	09	
Samoa*	13	
Santa Cruz Islands	11	
Sardinia*†	01	
Saudi Arabia	03	
Schouten Islands	09	
Serbia*	01	
Seychelles	04	
Sicily*†	01	
Singapore	08	
Slovakia*†	01	
Slovenia*†	01	
Socotra	03	
Solomon Islands	11	
Somalia Republic	03	
South Africa, Republic of	02	
Spain*†	01	
Spanish Possessions in North Africa*	01	
Spitsbergen (Svalbard)*	01	
Sri Lanka	05	30
Sudan, Republic of	03	
Swaziland	02	
Sweden*†	01	
Switzerland*	01	
Syria (Syrian Arab Republic)*	02	
Taiwan	08	
Tajikistan	05	
Tanzania	03	
Thailand	07	
Timor-Leste	09	
Tonga	13	
Tunisia	01	
Turkey*	02	
Turkmenistan	05	
Tuvalu	12	
Uganda	03	
Ukraine*	02	
United Arab Emirates	04	
Uzbekistan	05	
Vanuatu, Republic of	11	
Vietnam, Socialist Republic of	07	
Yemen	03	
Zambia, Republic of	02	
Zimbabwe	02	

* Daylight-saving time may be kept in these places. † For Summer time dates see List II footnotes.

[1] The boundaries between the zones are irregular; listed are chief towns in each zone.

LIST II — PLACES NORMALLY KEEPING UTC

Ascension Island	Ghana	Irish Republic*†	Morocco*	Sierra Leone
Burkina-Faso	Great Britain†	Ivory Coast	Portugal*†	Togo Republic
Canary Islands*†	Guinea-Bissau	Liberia	Principe	Tristan da Cunha
Channel Islands†	Guinea Republic	Madeira*†	St. Helena	
Faeroes*, The	Iceland	Mali	São Tomé	
Gambia, The	Ireland, Northern†	Mauritania	Senegal	

* Daylight-saving time may be kept in these places.

† Summer time (daylight-saving time), one hour in advance of UTC, will be kept from 2016 March 27^{d} 01^{h} to October 30^{d} 01^{h} UTC (Ninth Summer Time Directive of the European Union). Ratification by member countries has not been verified.

LIST III — PLACES SLOW ON UTC (WEST OF GREENWICH)

The times given below should be *subtracted* from UTC to give Standard Time / *added* to Standard Time to give UTC.

	h	m
American Samoa	11	
Argentina	03	
Austral (Tubuai) Islands[1]	10	
Azores*†	01	
Bahamas*	05	
Barbados	04	
Belize	06	
Bermuda*	04	
Bolivia	04	
Brazil		
Fernando de Noronha I., Trindade I., Oceanic Is.	02	
N and NE coastal states, Tocantins, Minas Gerais*, Goiás*, Brasilia*, S and E coastal states*	03	
Mato Grosso do Sul*, E Amazonas, Rondônia, Mato Grosso*, Roraima	04	
Acre, W Amazonas	05	
British Antarctic Territory[2,3]	03	
Canada[3]‡		
Alberta*	07	
British Columbia*	08	
Labrador*	04	
Manitoba*	06	
New Brunswick*	04	
Newfoundland*	03	30
Nunavut*		
east of long. W. 85°	05	
long. W. 85° to W. 102°	06	
west of long. W. 102°	07	
Northwest Territories*	07	
Nova Scotia*	04	
Ontario, east of long. W. 90°*	05	
Ontario, west of long. W. 90°*	06	

	h	m
Canada (*continued*)		
Prince Edward Island*	04	
Quebec, east of long. W. 63°	04	
west of long. W. 63°*	05	
Saskatchewan	06	
Yukon*	08	
Cape Verde Islands	01	
Cayman Islands	05	
Chile*	04	
Colombia	05	
Cook Islands	10	
Costa Rica	06	
Cuba*	05	
Curaçao Island	04	
Dominican Republic	04	
Easter Island (I. de Pascua)*	06	
Ecuador	05	
El Salvador	06	
Falkland Islands	03	
Fernando de Noronha Island	02	
French Guiana	03	
Galápagos Islands	06	
Greenland		
Danmarkshavn, Mesters Vig	00	
General*	03	
Scoresby Sound*	01	
Thule*, Pituffik*	04	
Grenada	04	
Guadeloupe	04	
Guatemala	06	
Guyana, Republic of	04	

* Daylight-saving time may be kept in these places. ‡ Dates for DST are given at the end of List III.

1 This is the legal standard time, but local mean time is generally used.

2 Stations may use UTC.

3 Some areas may keep another time zone.

LIST III — (*continued*)

	h	m
Haiti*	05	
Honduras	06	
Jamaica	05	
Johnston Island	10	
Juan Fernandez Islands*	04	
Leeward Islands	04	
Marquesas Islands	09	30
Martinique	04	
Mexico		
General*	06	
Sonora, Sinaloa*, Nayarit*, Chihuahua*, Southern District of Lower California*	07	
Northern District of Lower California*	08	
Midway Islands	11	
Nicaragua	06	
Niue	11	
Panama, Republic of	05	
Paraguay*	04	
Peru	05	
Pitcairn Island	08	
Puerto Rico	04	
St. Pierre and Miquelon*	03	
Society Islands	10	
South Georgia	02	
Suriname	03	
Trindade Island, South Atlantic	02	
Trinidad and Tobago	04	
Tuamotu Archipelago	10	
Tubuai (Austral) Islands	10	
Turks and Caicos Islands*	05	
United States of America‡		
Alabama	06	
Alaska	09	
Aleutian Islands, east of W. 169° 30′	09	
Aleutian Islands, west of W. 169° 30′	10	
Arizona[1]	07	
Arkansas	06	
California	08	
Colorado	07	
Connecticut	05	
Delaware	05	
District of Columbia	05	
Florida[2]	05	
Georgia	05	
Hawaii[1]	10	

	h	m
United States of America‡(*continued*)		
Idaho, southern part	07	
northern part	08	
Illinois	06	
Indiana[2]	05	
Iowa	06	
Kansas[2]	06	
Kentucky, eastern part	05	
western part	06	
Louisiana	06	
Maine	05	
Maryland	05	
Massachusetts	05	
Michigan[2]	05	
Minnesota	06	
Mississippi	06	
Missouri	06	
Montana	07	
Nebraska, eastern part	06	
western part	07	
Nevada	08	
New Hampshire	05	
New Jersey	05	
New Mexico	07	
New York	05	
North Carolina	05	
North Dakota, eastern part	06	
western part	07	
Ohio	05	
Oklahoma	06	
Oregon[2]	08	
Pennsylvania	05	
Rhode Island	05	
South Carolina	05	
South Dakota, eastern part	06	
western part	07	
Tennessee, eastern part	05	
western part	06	
Texas[2]	06	
Utah	07	
Vermont	05	
Virginia	05	
Washington D.C.	05	
Washington	08	
West Virginia	05	
Wisconsin	06	
Wyoming	07	
Uruguay*	03	
Venezuela	04	30
Virgin Islands	04	
Windward Islands	04	

* Daylight-saving time may be kept in these places.

‡ Daylight-saving (Summer) time, one hour fast on the time given, is kept during 2016 from March 13 (second Sunday) to November 6 (first Sunday), changing at $02^h\ 00^m$ local clock time.

1 Exempt from keeping daylight-saving time, except for a portion of Arizona.

2 A small portion of the state is in another time zone.

NORTHERN STARS

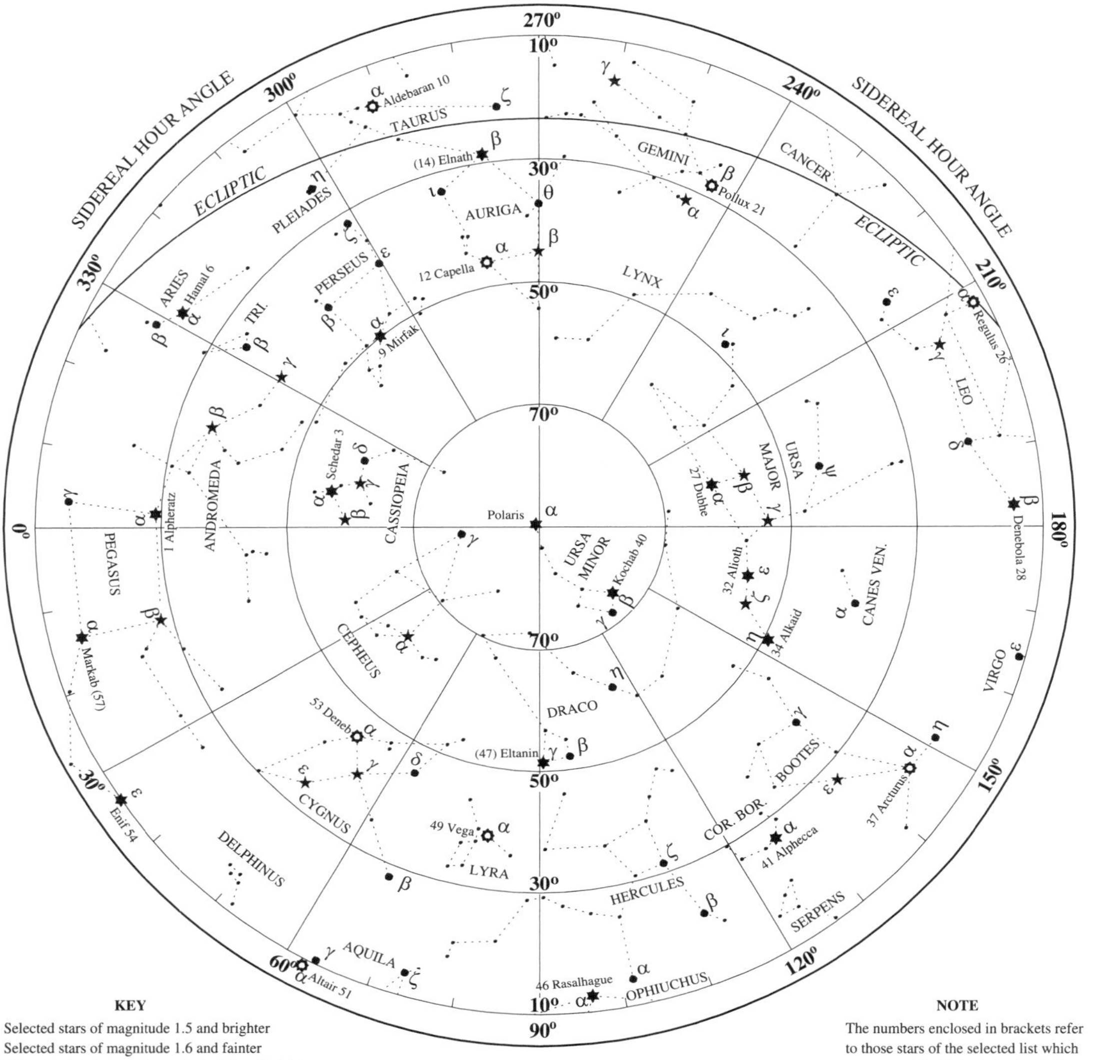

KEY

- Selected stars of magnitude 1.5 and brighter
- Selected stars of magnitude 1.6 and fainter
- Other tabulated stars of magnitude 2.5 and brighter
- Other tabulated stars of magnitude 2.6 and fainter
- Untabulated stars

NOTE

The numbers enclosed in brackets refer to those stars of the selected list which are not used in Sight Reduction Tables A.P. 3270, N.P. 303.

EQUATORIAL STARS (SHA 0° to 180°)

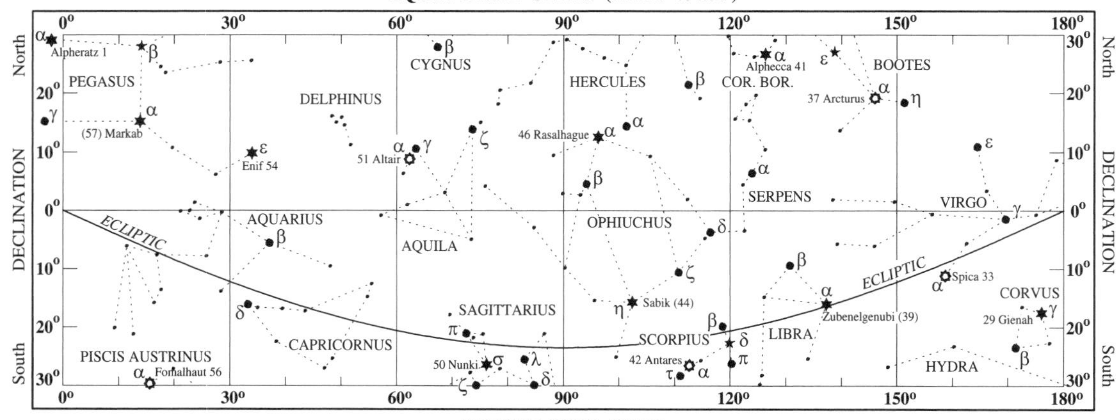

SIDEREAL HOUR ANGLE

SOUTHERN STARS

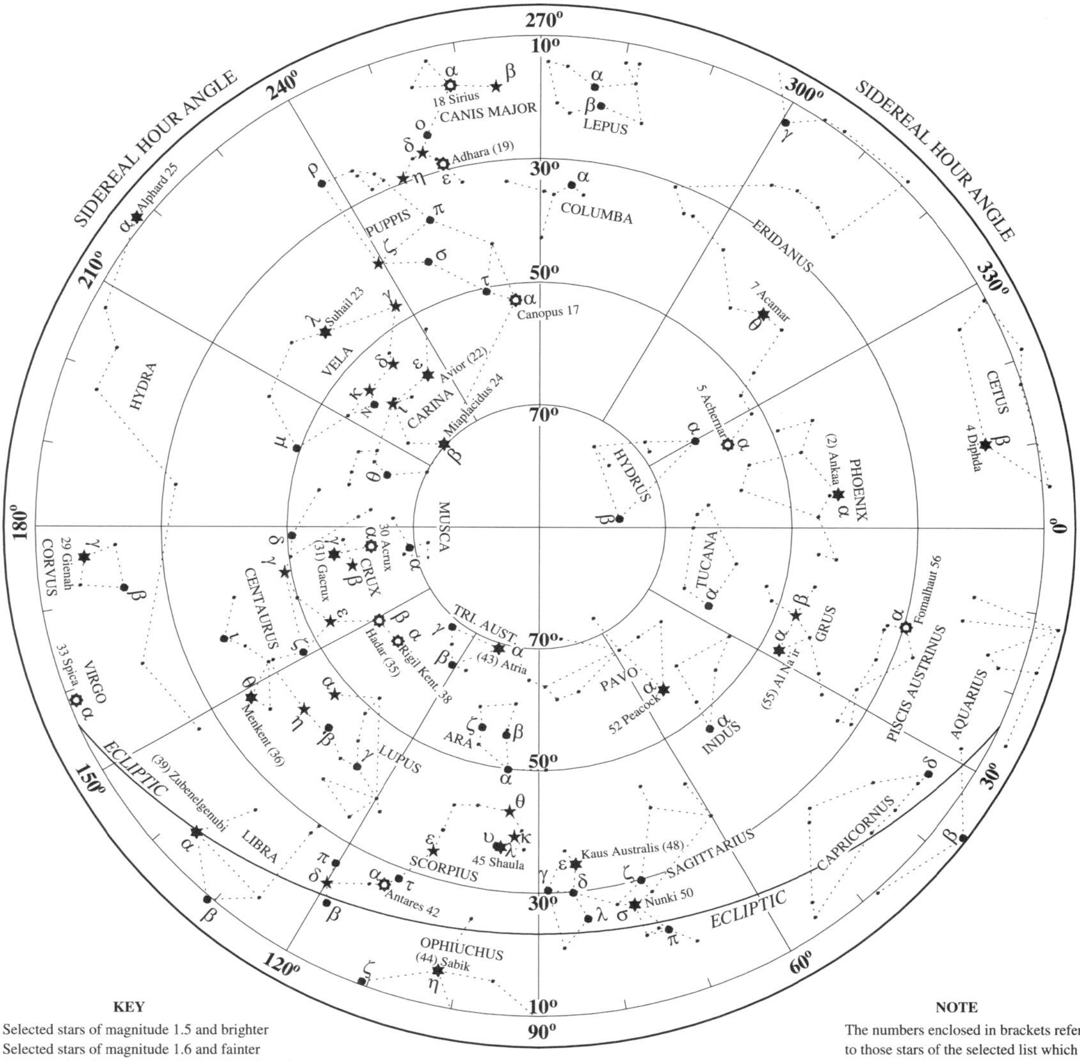

SIDEREAL HOUR ANGLE

270°
240°
210°
180°
150°
120°
90°
60°
30°
0°
300°
330°

CANIS MAJOR
18 Sirius
Adhara (19)
LEPUS
COLUMBA
PUPPIS
ERIDANUS
Canopus 17
Suhail 23
VELA
7 Acamar
HYDRA
CARINA
Avior (22)
Miaplacidus 24
5 Achernar
CETUS
4 Diphda
HYDRUS
(2) Ankaa
PHOENIX
MUSCA
30 Acrux
(31) Gacrux
CRUX
29 Gienah
CORVUS
CENTAURUS
TUCANA
Fomalhaut 56
GRUS
TRI. AUST.
(43) Atria
Hadar (35)
Rigil Kent. 38
PAVO
52 Peacock
(55) Al Na'ir
PISCIS AUSTRINUS
AQUARIUS
33 Spica
VIRGO
Menkent (36)
ARA
INDUS
LUPUS
ECLIPTIC
(39) Zubenelgenubi
LIBRA
45 Shaula
SCORPIUS
Kaus Australis (48)
SAGITTARIUS
CAPRICORNUS
Antares 42
Nunki 50
OPHIUCHUS
(44) Sabik
Alphard 25

KEY

- Selected stars of magnitude 1.5 and brighter
- Selected stars of magnitude 1.6 and fainter
- Other tabulated stars of magnitude 2.5 and brighter
- Other tabulated stars of magnitude 2.6 and fainter
- Untabulated stars

NOTE

The numbers enclosed in brackets refer to those stars of the selected list which are not used in Sight Reduction Tables A.P. 3270, N.P. 303.

EQUATORIAL STARS (SHA 180° to 360°)

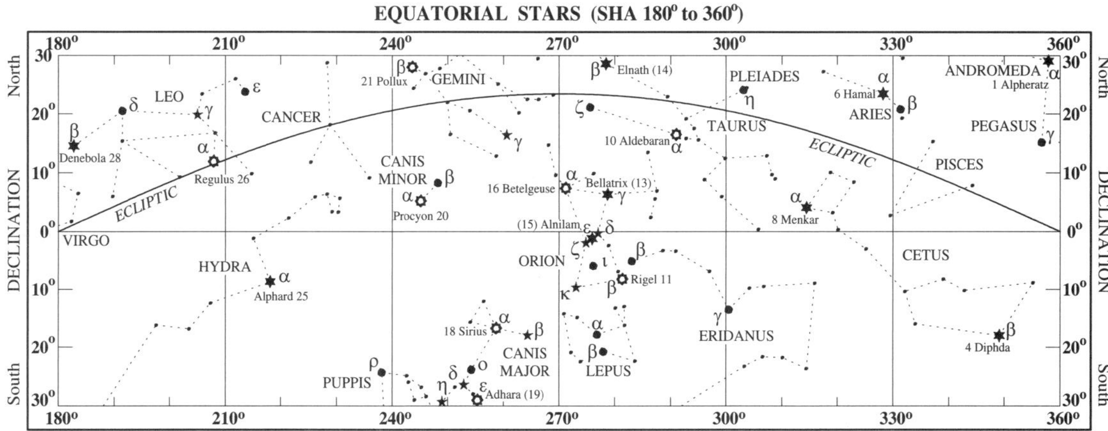

Mag.	Name and Number		SHA							Declination						
				JAN.	FEB.	MAR.	APR.	MAY	JUNE		JAN.	FEB.	MAR.	APR.	MAY	JUNE
			°	′	′	′	′	′	′	°	′	′	′	′	′	′
3·2	γ Cephei		**4**	59·7	60·3	60·4	60·2	59·6	58·8	N **77**	43·6	43·5	43·3	43·2	43·1	43·1
2·5	α Pegasi	57	**13**	36·8	36·8	36·8	36·7	36·5	36·2	N **15**	17·6	17·5	17·4	17·4	17·5	17·6
2·4	β Pegasi		**13**	51·8	51·9	51·9	51·8	51·6	51·3	N **28**	10·3	10·2	10·1	10·1	10·1	10·2
1·2	α Piscis Aust.	56	**15**	22·3	22·4	22·3	22·2	22·0	21·7	S **29**	32·4	32·3	32·2	32·1	32·0	31·9
2·1	β Gruis		**19**	06·2	06·3	06·2	06·0	05·8	05·5	S **46**	48·2	48·1	48·0	47·8	47·7	47·6
2·9	α Tucanæ		**25**	07·0	07·0	06·9	06·6	06·3	05·9	S **60**	10·9	10·8	10·6	10·5	10·4	10·3
1·7	α Gruis	55	**27**	42·0	42·0	41·9	41·7	41·4	41·1	S **46**	53·1	53·0	52·9	52·7	52·6	52·6
2·9	δ Capricorni		**33**	01·5	01·5	01·4	01·2	01·0	00·7	S **16**	03·3	03·2	03·2	03·1	03·1	03·0
2·4	ε Pegasi	54	**33**	45·7	45·7	45·6	45·4	45·2	45·0	N **9**	57·0	56·9	56·9	56·9	57·0	57·1
2·9	β Aquarii		**36**	54·3	54·3	54·2	54·0	53·8	53·5	S **5**	30·0	30·0	30·0	30·0	29·9	29·8
2·4	α Cephei		**40**	16·0	16·0	15·9	15·6	15·2	14·8	N **62**	39·4	39·3	39·1	39·1	39·1	39·2
2·5	ε Cygni		**48**	17·4	17·4	17·2	17·0	16·8	16·5	N **34**	02·0	01·9	01·8	01·7	01·8	01·9
1·3	α Cygni	53	**49**	30·7	30·6	30·5	30·2	30·0	29·7	N **45**	20·4	20·3	20·2	20·1	20·2	20·3
3·1	α Indi		**50**	20·3	20·2	20·0	19·7	19·4	19·1	S **47**	14·1	14·0	13·9	13·8	13·7	13·7
1·9	α Pavonis	52	**53**	17·2	17·0	16·8	16·4	16·1	15·7	S **56**	40·9	40·8	40·7	40·6	40·6	40·6
2·2	γ Cygni		**54**	18·3	18·2	18·1	17·8	17·6	17·3	N **40**	18·7	18·5	18·4	18·4	18·4	18·6
0·8	α Aquilæ	51	**62**	06·9	06·8	06·6	06·4	06·2	06·0	N **8**	54·8	54·7	54·7	54·7	54·8	54·9
2·7	γ Aquilæ		**63**	15·0	14·9	14·7	14·5	14·3	14·1	N **10**	39·3	39·2	39·2	39·2	39·2	39·3
2·9	δ Cygni		**63**	38·3	38·2	38·0	37·7	37·4	37·2	N **45**	10·4	10·2	10·1	10·1	10·2	10·3
3·1	β Cygni		**67**	09·8	09·7	09·6	09·3	09·1	08·9	N **27**	59·7	59·6	59·6	59·6	59·6	59·8
2·9	π Sagittarii		**72**	19·6	19·5	19·3	19·1	18·8	18·6	S **20**	59·7	59·7	59·7	59·7	59·6	59·6
3·0	ζ Aquilæ		**73**	28·1	28·0	27·8	27·6	27·4	27·2	N **13**	53·4	53·3	53·2	53·3	53·3	53·4
2·6	ζ Sagittarii		**74**	06·0	05·8	05·6	05·3	05·1	04·9	S **29**	51·2	51·2	51·2	51·1	51·1	51·1
2·0	σ Sagittarii	50	**75**	56·5	56·4	56·1	55·9	55·7	55·5	S **26**	16·4	16·4	16·4	16·3	16·3	16·3
0·0	α Lyræ	49	**80**	38·2	38·0	37·8	37·5	37·3	37·2	N **38**	48·0	47·9	47·8	47·8	47·9	48·1
2·8	λ Sagittarii		**82**	46·0	45·8	45·6	45·3	45·1	44·9	S **25**	24·5	24·5	24·5	24·5	24·5	24·5
1·9	ε Sagittarii	48	**83**	41·9	41·7	41·4	41·2	40·9	40·7	S **34**	22·4	22·3	22·3	22·3	22·3	22·3
2·7	δ Sagittarii		**84**	30·1	29·9	29·7	29·4	29·2	29·0	S **29**	49·0	49·0	49·0	49·0	49·0	49·0
3·0	γ Sagittarii		**88**	17·8	17·6	17·4	17·1	16·9	16·7	S **30**	25·2	25·2	25·2	25·2	25·2	25·2
2·2	γ Draconis	47	**90**	45·8	45·6	45·3	45·0	44·8	44·7	N **51**	29·3	29·1	29·1	29·1	29·2	29·4
2·8	β Ophiuchi		**93**	56·3	56·2	55·9	55·7	55·6	55·4	N **4**	33·8	33·7	33·7	33·7	33·8	33·8
2·4	κ Scorpii		**94**	06·4	06·2	05·9	05·6	05·4	05·2	S **39**	02·0	02·0	02·0	02·0	02·0	02·1
1·9	θ Scorpii		**95**	23·3	23·1	22·8	22·5	22·2	22·1	S **43**	00·2	00·1	00·1	00·2	00·2	00·2
2·1	α Ophiuchi	46	**96**	05·1	04·9	04·7	04·5	04·3	04·2	N **12**	33·0	32·9	32·9	32·9	33·0	33·1
1·6	λ Scorpii	45	**96**	19·9	19·7	19·4	19·1	18·9	18·7	S **37**	06·6	06·6	06·6	06·6	06·7	06·7
3·0	α Aræ		**96**	44·2	43·9	43·6	43·3	43·0	42·8	S **49**	53·0	52·9	52·9	53·0	53·0	53·1
2·7	υ Scorpii		**97**	02·5	02·3	02·0	01·8	01·5	01·4	S **37**	18·2	18·2	18·2	18·2	18·3	18·3
2·8	β Draconis		**97**	18·6	18·3	18·0	17·7	17·5	17·4	N **52**	17·4	17·3	17·2	17·3	17·4	17·5
2·8	β Aræ		**98**	21·0	20·6	20·3	19·9	19·6	19·4	S **55**	32·3	32·3	32·3	32·3	32·4	32·5
Var.‡	α Herculis		**101**	09·6	09·4	09·2	09·0	08·8	08·7	N **14**	22·4	22·3	22·3	22·3	22·4	22·5
2·4	η Ophiuchi	44	**102**	10·8	10·6	10·4	10·1	10·0	09·9	S **15**	44·5	44·5	44·5	44·5	44·5	44·5
3·1	ζ Aræ		**104**	61·2	60·8	60·4	60·1	59·8	59·6	S **56**	00·5	00·5	00·5	00·6	00·6	00·7
2·3	ε Scorpii		**107**	12·2	12·0	11·7	11·5	11·3	11·2	S **34**	19·0	19·0	19·1	19·1	19·1	19·2
1·9	α Triang. Aust.	43	**107**	25·0	24·5	23·9	23·3	23·0	22·8	S **69**	03·0	02·9	02·9	03·0	03·1	03·2
2·8	ζ Herculis		**109**	32·0	31·7	31·5	31·3	31·2	31·1	N **31**	34·4	34·3	34·3	34·4	34·5	34·6
2·6	ζ Ophiuchi		**110**	29·6	29·4	29·2	29·0	28·8	28·7	S **10**	35·8	35·8	35·9	35·9	35·9	35·8
2·8	τ Scorpii		**110**	47·0	46·8	46·5	46·3	46·1	46·0	S **28**	14·7	14·7	14·7	14·8	14·8	14·8
2·8	β Herculis		**112**	16·6	16·4	16·2	16·0	15·9	15·8	N **21**	27·3	27·2	27·2	27·3	27·3	27·5
1·0	α Scorpii	42	**112**	24·3	24·1	23·9	23·6	23·5	23·4	S **26**	27·8	27·8	27·8	27·9	27·9	27·9
2·7	η Draconis		**113**	57·4	57·1	56·7	56·4	56·2	56·2	N **61**	28·6	28·5	28·5	28·6	28·7	28·9
2·7	δ Ophiuchi		**116**	12·4	12·2	12·0	11·8	11·7	11·6	S **3**	44·0	44·0	44·1	44·1	44·0	44·0
2·6	β Scorpii		**118**	24·6	24·4	24·2	24·0	23·8	23·8	S **19**	50·7	50·8	50·8	50·8	50·9	50·9
2·3	δ Scorpii		**119**	40·9	40·7	40·5	40·3	40·1	40·1	S **22**	39·8	39·8	39·9	39·9	39·9	40·0
2·9	π Scorpii		**120**	02·8	02·6	02·3	02·1	02·0	01·9	S **26**	09·3	09·4	09·4	09·5	09·5	09·5
2·8	β Trianguli Aust.		**120**	51·8	51·3	50·9	50·5	50·2	50·2	S **63**	28·4	28·4	28·4	28·5	28·6	28·8
2·6	α Serpentis		**123**	44·3	44·1	43·9	43·7	43·6	43·6	N **6**	22·6	22·5	22·5	22·5	22·6	22·6
2·8	γ Lupi		**125**	57·0	56·7	56·4	56·2	56·0	56·0	S **41**	12·9	12·9	13·0	13·1	13·2	13·2
2·2	α Coronæ Bor.	41	**126**	09·7	09·5	09·3	09·1	09·0	09·0	N **26**	39·6	39·6	39·5	39·6	39·7	39·8

‡ 2·9 — 3·6

Mag.	Name and Number		SHA							Declination						
				JULY	AUG.	SEPT.	OCT.	NOV.	DEC.		JULY	AUG.	SEPT.	OCT.	NOV.	DEC.
			°	′	′	′	′	′	′	°	′	′	′	′	′	′
3·2	γ Cephei		**4**	58·0	57·5	57·2	57·4	57·8	58·5	N **77**	43·2	43·3	43·5	43·7	43·9	43·9
2·5	*Markab*	57	**13**	36·0	35·9	35·8	35·8	35·9	36·0	N **15**	17·7	17·8	17·9	17·9	17·9	17·9
2·4	*Scheat*		**13**	51·1	50·9	50·9	50·9	51·0	51·1	N **28**	10·3	10·4	10·6	10·6	10·7	10·7
1·2	*Fomalhaut*	56	**15**	21·5	21·3	21·3	21·3	21·4	21·5	S **29**	31·9	31·9	31·9	32·0	32·0	32·1
2·1	β Gruis		**19**	05·2	05·0	04·9	05·0	05·1	05·3	S **46**	47·6	47·7	47·8	47·9	47·9	48·0
2·9	α Tucanæ		**25**	05·5	05·3	05·2	05·4	05·6	05·9	S **60**	10·3	10·4	10·5	10·6	10·7	10·7
1·7	*Al Na'ir*	55	**27**	40·8	40·7	40·6	40·7	40·9	41·1	S **46**	52·6	52·6	52·7	52·8	52·9	52·9
2·9	δ Capricorni		**33**	00·5	00·4	00·4	00·5	00·6	00·7	S **16**	02·9	02·9	02·9	02·9	03·0	03·0
2·4	*Enif*	54	**33**	44·8	44·7	44·7	44·8	44·9	45·0	N **9**	57·2	57·3	57·3	57·4	57·4	57·3
2·9	β Aquarii		**36**	53·4	53·3	53·3	53·3	53·5	53·5	S **5**	29·7	29·7	29·6	29·7	29·7	29·7
2·4	*Alderamin*		**40**	14·6	14·5	14·6	14·9	15·2	15·5	N **62**	39·3	39·5	39·7	39·8	39·8	39·8
2·5	ε Cygni		**48**	16·4	16·3	16·4	16·5	16·7	16·8	N **34**	02·1	02·2	02·3	02·4	02·4	02·3
1·3	*Deneb*	53	**49**	29·5	29·5	29·6	29·8	30·0	30·2	N **45**	20·5	20·6	20·8	20·8	20·8	20·8
3·1	α Indi		**50**	18·9	18·8	18·8	19·0	19·2	19·3	S **47**	13·7	13·8	13·9	14·0	14·0	13·9
1·9	*Peacock*	52	**53**	15·5	15·4	15·5	15·7	15·9	16·1	S **56**	40·6	40·7	40·8	40·9	40·9	40·8
2·2	γ Cygni		**54**	17·2	17·2	17·3	17·5	17·7	17·8	N **40**	18·7	18·9	19·0	19·0	19·0	19·0
0·8	*Altair*	51	**62**	05·9	05·8	05·9	06·0	06·2	06·2	N **8**	55·0	55·0	55·1	55·1	55·1	55·0
2·7	γ Aquilæ		**63**	14·0	14·0	14·1	14·2	14·3	14·4	N **10**	39·4	39·5	39·6	39·6	39·6	39·5
2·9	δ Cygni		**63**	37·1	37·1	37·3	37·5	37·7	37·8	N **45**	10·5	10·6	10·7	10·8	10·7	10·6
3·1	*Albireo*		**67**	08·8	08·8	08·9	09·1	09·2	09·3	N **27**	59·9	60·0	60·1	60·1	60·1	60·0
2·9	π Sagittarii		**72**	18·5	18·5	18·6	18·8	18·9	18·9	S **20**	59·6	59·6	59·6	59·6	59·6	59·6
3·0	ζ Aquilæ		**73**	27·1	27·2	27·3	27·4	27·5	27·6	N **13**	53·5	53·6	53·7	53·7	53·6	53·6
2·6	ζ Sagittarii		**74**	04·8	04·8	04·9	05·0	05·2	05·2	S **29**	51·1	51·2	51·2	51·2	51·2	51·2
2·0	*Nunki*	50	**75**	55·4	55·4	55·5	55·6	55·8	55·8	S **26**	16·3	16·3	16·4	16·4	16·4	16·4
0·0	*Vega*	49	**80**	37·1	37·2	37·4	37·6	37·7	37·8	N **38**	48·2	48·4	48·4	48·4	48·4	48·2
2·8	λ Sagittarii		**82**	44·9	44·9	45·0	45·2	45·3	45·3	S **25**	24·5	24·5	24·5	24·5	24·5	24·5
1·9	*Kaus Australis*	48	**83**	40·7	40·7	40·8	41·0	41·1	41·1	S **34**	22·4	22·4	22·4	22·4	22·4	22·4
2·7	δ Sagittarii		**84**	28·9	29·0	29·1	29·2	29·4	29·3	S **29**	49·0	49·0	49·1	49·1	49·1	49·0
3·0	γ Sagittarii		**88**	16·7	16·7	16·8	17·0	17·1	17·1	S **30**	25·2	25·2	25·2	25·2	25·2	25·2
2·2	*Eltanin*	47	**90**	44·7	44·8	45·1	45·3	45·5	45·6	N **51**	29·5	29·7	29·7	29·7	29·6	29·4
2·8	β Ophiuchi		**93**	55·4	55·5	55·6	55·7	55·8	55·8	N **4**	33·9	34·0	34·0	34·0	33·9	33·9
2·4	κ Scorpii		**94**	05·2	05·3	05·4	05·6	05·7	05·7	S **39**	02·1	02·1	02·2	02·2	02·1	02·1
1·9	θ Scorpii		**95**	22·0	22·1	22·3	22·5	22·6	22·5	S **43**	00·3	00·4	00·4	00·4	00·3	00·2
2·1	*Rasalhague*	46	**96**	04·2	04·3	04·4	04·6	04·6	04·6	N **12**	33·2	33·3	33·3	33·3	33·2	33·1
1·6	*Shaula*	45	**96**	18·7	18·8	18·9	19·1	19·2	19·1	S **37**	06·8	06·8	06·8	06·8	06·7	06·7
3·0	α Aræ		**96**	42·8	42·9	43·1	43·3	43·4	43·4	S **49**	53·2	53·2	53·3	53·2	53·2	53·1
2·7	υ Scorpii		**97**	01·4	01·4	01·6	01·7	01·8	01·8	S **37**	18·3	18·4	18·4	18·4	18·3	18·3
2·8	β Draconis		**97**	17·5	17·6	17·9	18·2	18·3	18·4	N **52**	17·7	17·8	17·8	17·8	17·7	17·5
2·8	β Aræ		**98**	19·4	19·5	19·7	20·0	20·1	20·1	S **55**	32·6	32·6	32·7	32·6	32·6	32·5
Var.‡	α Herculis		**101**	08·7	08·8	08·9	09·1	09·2	09·1	N **14**	22·6	22·7	22·7	22·7	22·6	22·5
2·4	*Sabik*	44	**102**	09·9	09·9	10·0	10·2	10·2	10·2	S **15**	44·5	44·5	44·5	44·5	44·5	44·5
3·1	ζ Aræ		**104**	59·6	59·8	60·0	60·3	60·4	60·3	S **56**	00·8	00·9	00·9	00·9	00·8	00·7
2·3	ε Scorpii		**107**	11·2	11·3	11·4	11·6	11·6	11·6	S **34**	19·2	19·2	19·2	19·2	19·2	19·1
1·9	*Atria*	43	**107**	22·8	23·1	23·5	23·9	24·1	23·9	S **69**	03·4	03·4	03·5	03·4	03·3	03·2
2·8	ζ Herculis		**109**	31·1	31·2	31·4	31·6	31·7	31·6	N **31**	34·7	34·8	34·8	34·7	34·6	34·5
2·6	ζ Ophiuchi		**110**	28·7	28·8	28·9	29·1	29·1	29·0	S **10**	35·8	35·8	35·8	35·8	35·8	35·8
2·8	τ Scorpii		**110**	46·0	46·1	46·3	46·4	46·5	46·4	S **28**	14·8	14·8	14·8	14·8	14·8	14·8
2·8	β Herculis		**112**	15·8	15·9	16·1	16·2	16·3	16·2	N **21**	27·6	27·6	27·6	27·6	27·5	27·4
1·0	*Antares*	42	**112**	23·4	23·5	23·6	23·8	23·8	23·7	S **26**	27·9	27·9	27·9	27·9	27·9	27·9
2·7	η Draconis		**113**	56·4	56·7	57·0	57·3	57·5	57·5	N **61**	29·0	29·1	29·1	29·0	28·8	28·6
2·7	δ Ophiuchi		**116**	11·6	11·7	11·8	12·0	12·0	11·9	S **3**	44·0	43·9	43·9	43·9	44·0	44·0
2·6	β Scorpii		**118**	23·8	23·9	24·0	24·1	24·2	24·1	S **19**	50·9	50·8	50·8	50·8	50·8	50·8
2·3	*Dschubba*		**119**	40·1	40·2	40·3	40·4	40·5	40·4	S **22**	40·0	40·0	39·9	39·9	39·9	39·9
2·9	π Scorpii		**120**	02·0	02·1	02·2	02·3	02·3	02·2	S **26**	09·5	09·5	09·5	09·5	09·5	09·5
2·8	β Trianguli Aust.		**120**	50·3	50·5	50·8	51·1	51·2	51·0	S **63**	28·9	28·9	28·9	28·8	28·7	28·6
2·6	α Serpentis		**123**	43·6	43·7	43·8	43·9	44·0	43·9	N **6**	22·7	22·7	22·7	22·7	22·6	22·5
2·8	γ Lupi		**125**	56·0	56·2	56·4	56·5	56·5	56·3	S **41**	13·3	13·3	13·2	13·2	13·1	13·1
2·2	*Alphecca*	41	**126**	09·1	09·2	09·3	09·5	09·5	09·4	N **26**	39·9	39·9	39·9	39·9	39·7	39·6

‡ 2·9 — 3·6

Mag.	Name and Number		SHA							Declination						
				JAN.	FEB.	MAR.	APR.	MAY	JUNE		JAN.	FEB.	MAR.	APR.	MAY	JUNE
			°	′	′	′	′	′	′	°	′	′	′	′	′	′
3·1	γ Ursæ Minoris		**129**	50·1	49·5	49·0	48·6	48·5	48·7	**N 71**	46·4	46·4	46·4	46·5	46·7	46·8
2·9	γ Trianguli Aust.		**129**	53·8	53·2	52·7	52·3	52·1	52·1	**S 68**	43·8	43·9	43·9	44·1	44·2	44·4
2·6	β Libræ		**130**	32·1	31·8	31·6	31·5	31·4	31·4	**S 9**	26·4	26·4	26·5	26·5	26·5	26·5
2·7	β Lupi		**135**	06·2	05·9	05·7	05·5	05·4	05·4	**S 43**	11·6	11·6	11·7	11·8	11·9	12·0
2·8	α Libræ	39	**137**	03·6	03·3	03·1	03·0	02·9	02·9	**S 16**	06·3	06·4	06·4	06·5	06·5	06·5
2·1	β Ursæ Minoris	40	**137**	20·7	20·1	19·5	19·2	19·1	19·4	**N 74**	05·2	05·1	05·2	05·3	05·5	05·6
2·4	ε Bootis		**138**	34·9	34·7	34·4	34·3	34·2	34·3	**N 27**	00·4	00·3	00·3	00·4	00·5	00·6
2·3	α Lupi		**139**	15·0	14·7	14·4	14·2	14·1	14·1	**S 47**	27·1	27·1	27·2	27·3	27·4	27·5
−0·3	α Centauri	38	**139**	49·4	49·0	48·6	48·4	48·3	48·4	**S 60**	53·6	53·7	53·8	54·0	54·1	54·2
2·3	η Centauri		**140**	52·1	51·8	51·5	51·3	51·3	51·3	**S 42**	13·4	13·4	13·5	13·6	13·7	13·8
3·0	γ Bootis		**141**	49·4	49·1	48·9	48·7	48·7	48·8	**N 38**	14·2	14·1	14·1	14·2	14·4	14·5
0·0	α Bootis	37	**145**	54·2	54·0	53·8	53·7	53·7	53·7	**N 19**	05·9	05·8	05·8	05·9	05·9	06·0
2·1	θ Centauri	36	**148**	05·5	05·2	05·0	04·9	04·8	04·9	**S 36**	26·6	26·7	26·8	26·9	27·0	27·1
0·6	β Centauri	35	**148**	45·3	44·9	44·6	44·4	44·4	44·5	**S 60**	26·6	26·7	26·8	27·0	27·1	27·2
2·6	ζ Centauri		**150**	51·7	51·4	51·2	51·0	51·0	51·0	**S 47**	21·7	21·8	21·9	22·1	22·2	22·2
2·7	η Bootis		**151**	08·4	08·1	08·0	07·9	07·8	07·9	**N 18**	19·0	18·9	18·9	19·0	19·0	19·1
1·9	η Ursæ Majoris	34	**152**	57·6	57·3	57·1	57·0	57·0	57·1	**N 49**	13·8	13·8	13·8	13·9	14·1	14·2
2·3	ε Centauri		**154**	46·1	45·8	45·5	45·4	45·4	45·5	**S 53**	32·5	32·6	32·8	32·9	33·0	33·1
1·0	α Virginis	33	**158**	29·4	29·2	29·0	28·9	28·9	29·0	**S 11**	14·6	14·7	14·8	14·8	14·8	14·8
2·3	ζ Ursæ Majoris		**158**	51·7	51·3	51·1	51·0	51·1	51·2	**N 54**	50·3	50·3	50·3	50·5	50·6	50·7
2·8	ι Centauri		**159**	37·3	37·1	36·9	36·8	36·8	36·9	**S 36**	47·6	47·7	47·8	47·9	48·0	48·0
2·8	ε Virginis		**164**	15·4	15·2	15·0	15·0	15·0	15·0	**N 10**	52·3	52·3	52·2	52·3	52·3	52·4
2·9	α Canum Venat.		**165**	48·4	48·2	48·0	48·0	48·0	48·1	**N 38**	13·7	13·7	13·7	13·8	14·0	14·0
1·8	ε Ursæ Majoris	32	**166**	19·2	18·9	18·6	18·6	18·7	18·9	**N 55**	52·1	52·1	52·2	52·3	52·5	52·6
1·3	β Crucis		**167**	49·6	49·2	49·0	49·0	49·0	49·2	**S 59**	46·3	46·4	46·6	46·7	46·9	46·9
2·9	γ Virginis		**169**	22·8	22·6	22·5	22·5	22·5	22·6	**S 1**	32·3	32·3	32·4	32·4	32·4	32·3
2·2	γ Centauri		**169**	23·6	23·3	23·1	23·1	23·1	23·3	**S 49**	02·6	02·7	02·9	03·0	03·1	03·2
2·7	α Muscæ		**170**	27·0	26·6	26·3	26·2	26·4	26·7	**S 69**	13·1	13·2	13·4	13·6	13·7	13·8
2·7	β Corvi		**171**	11·4	11·2	11·0	11·0	11·0	11·1	**S 23**	29·0	29·1	29·2	29·3	29·3	29·3
1·6	γ Crucis	31	**171**	58·6	58·3	58·1	58·1	58·2	58·4	**S 57**	11·9	12·0	12·2	12·4	12·5	12·5
1·3	α Crucis	30	**173**	06·9	06·6	06·4	06·3	06·4	06·7	**S 63**	11·0	11·1	11·3	11·5	11·6	11·7
2·6	γ Corvi	29	**175**	50·3	50·2	50·0	50·0	50·1	50·1	**S 17**	37·8	37·9	38·0	38·1	38·1	38·1
2·6	δ Centauri		**177**	41·7	41·4	41·3	41·3	41·4	41·5	**S 50**	48·5	48·6	48·8	48·9	49·0	49·1
2·4	γ Ursæ Majoris		**181**	20·0	19·7	19·6	19·6	19·7	19·9	**N 53**	36·0	36·1	36·2	36·3	36·4	36·5
2·1	β Leonis	28	**182**	31·8	31·6	31·5	31·5	31·5	31·6	**N 14**	28·8	28·8	28·8	28·8	28·8	28·9
2·6	δ Leonis		**191**	15·5	15·3	15·2	15·3	15·3	15·4	**N 20**	26·0	25·9	26·0	26·0	26·1	26·1
3·0	ψ Ursæ Majoris		**192**	21·5	21·3	21·2	21·3	21·4	21·5	**N 44**	24·4	24·4	24·5	24·6	24·7	24·8
1·8	α Ursæ Majoris	27	**193**	49·3	49·0	48·9	49·0	49·3	49·5	**N 61**	39·5	39·6	39·8	39·9	40·0	40·0
2·4	β Ursæ Majoris		**194**	17·9	17·6	17·5	17·6	17·8	18·0	**N 56**	17·5	17·5	17·7	17·8	17·9	17·9
2·7	μ Velorum		**198**	07·5	07·4	07·3	07·4	07·6	07·8	**S 49**	30·2	30·4	30·5	30·7	30·7	30·7
2·8	θ Carinæ		**199**	06·2	06·0	05·9	06·1	06·4	06·7	**S 64**	28·6	28·7	28·9	29·1	29·2	29·2
2·3	γ Leonis		**204**	47·0	46·8	46·8	46·9	47·0	47·1	**N 19**	45·4	45·4	45·4	45·4	45·5	45·5
1·4	α Leonis	26	**207**	41·4	41·3	41·3	41·3	41·4	41·5	**N 11**	53·1	53·1	53·1	53·1	53·1	53·2
3·0	ε Leonis		**213**	18·4	18·3	18·3	18·4	18·5	18·6	**N 23**	41·8	41·8	41·8	41·8	41·9	41·9
3·1	N Velorum		**217**	03·6	03·5	03·6	03·8	04·1	04·3	**S 57**	06·3	06·5	06·7	06·8	06·8	06·8
2·0	α Hydræ	25	**217**	54·1	54·0	54·0	54·1	54·2	54·3	**S 8**	43·9	43·9	44·0	44·0	44·0	44·0
2·5	κ Velorum		**219**	20·1	20·1	20·2	20·4	20·6	20·8	**S 55**	04·8	05·0	05·1	05·2	05·2	05·2
2·2	ι Carinæ		**220**	36·4	36·4	36·5	36·7	37·0	37·3	**S 59**	20·6	20·8	20·9	21·0	21·1	21·0
1·7	β Carinæ	24	**221**	38·2	38·2	38·4	38·8	39·2	39·7	**S 69**	47·0	47·2	47·3	47·5	47·5	47·5
2·2	λ Velorum	23	**222**	50·7	50·6	50·7	50·8	51·0	51·2	**S 43**	29·9	30·1	30·2	30·3	30·3	30·3
3·1	ι Ursæ Majoris		**224**	55·2	55·1	55·1	55·3	55·5	55·6	**N 47**	58·4	58·5	58·6	58·7	58·7	58·7
2·0	δ Velorum		**228**	42·1	42·1	42·2	42·4	42·7	42·9	**S 54**	46·1	46·3	46·5	46·6	46·6	46·5
1·9	ε Carinæ	22	**234**	16·6	16·6	16·8	17·1	17·4	17·6	**S 59**	33·8	34·0	34·1	34·2	34·2	34·1
1·8	γ Velorum		**237**	29·0	29·0	29·2	29·4	29·6	29·7	**S 47**	23·2	23·4	23·5	23·5	23·5	23·4
2·8	ρ Puppis		**237**	56·2	56·2	56·3	56·4	56·5	56·6	**S 24**	21·2	21·4	21·5	21·5	21·5	21·4
2·3	ζ Puppis		**238**	57·3	57·3	57·4	57·6	57·8	57·9	**S 40**	03·1	03·2	03·3	03·4	03·4	03·3
1·1	β Geminorum	21	**243**	25·2	25·2	25·3	25·4	25·6	25·6	**N 27**	59·0	59·0	59·0	59·1	59·1	59·1
0·4	α Canis Minoris	20	**244**	57·6	57·6	57·6	57·8	57·9	57·9	**N 5**	10·8	10·7	10·7	10·7	10·7	10·8

Mag.	Name and Number		SHA °	JULY ′	AUG. ′	SEPT. ′	OCT. ′	NOV. ′	DEC. ′	Declination °	JULY ′	AUG. ′	SEPT. ′	OCT. ′	NOV. ′	DEC. ′
3·1	γ Ursæ Minoris		**129**	49·1	49·6	50·1	50·5	50·6	50·5	N **71**	46·9	47·0	46·9	46·8	46·6	46·4
2·9	γ Trianguli Aust.		**129**	52·3	52·6	53·0	53·3	53·3	53·0	S **68**	44·5	44·5	44·4	44·3	44·2	44·1
2·6	β Libræ		**130**	31·4	31·5	31·6	31·7	31·7	31·6	S **9**	26·4	26·4	26·4	26·4	26·4	26·5
2·7	β Lupi		**135**	05·5	05·6	05·8	05·9	05·8	05·7	S **43**	12·0	12·0	12·0	11·9	11·8	11·8
2·8	*Zubenelgenubi*	39	**137**	03·0	03·1	03·2	03·3	03·2	03·1	S **16**	06·5	06·5	06·4	06·4	06·4	06·5
2·1	*Kochab*	40	**137**	19·9	20·4	21·0	21·4	21·5	21·2	N **74**	05·7	05·7	05·6	05·5	05·3	05·1
2·4	ε Bootis		**138**	34·4	34·5	34·6	34·7	34·7	34·5	N **27**	00·7	00·7	00·7	00·6	00·4	00·3
2·3	α Lupi		**139**	14·2	14·4	14·6	14·7	14·6	14·4	S **47**	27·6	27·6	27·5	27·4	27·3	27·3
−0·3	*Rigil Kent.*	38	**139**	48·6	48·8	49·1	49·3	49·2	48·9	S **60**	54·3	54·2	54·2	54·1	53·9	53·9
2·3	η Centauri		**140**	51·4	51·5	51·7	51·8	51·7	51·5	S **42**	13·8	13·8	13·8	13·7	13·6	13·6
3·0	γ Bootis		**141**	48·9	49·0	49·2	49·3	49·2	49·1	N **38**	14·5	14·6	14·5	14·4	14·2	14·1
0·0	*Arcturus*	37	**145**	53·8	53·9	54·0	54·1	54·0	53·9	N **19**	06·1	06·1	06·1	06·0	05·9	05·7
2·1	*Menkent*	36	**148**	05·0	05·1	05·2	05·3	05·2	05·0	S **36**	27·1	27·1	27·0	26·9	26·9	26·9
0·6	*Hadar*	35	**148**	44·7	44·9	45·1	45·2	45·1	44·8	S **60**	27·3	27·3	27·2	27·0	26·9	26·9
2·6	ζ Centauri		**150**	51·2	51·3	51·5	51·5	51·4	51·2	S **47**	22·3	22·2	22·1	22·0	22·0	21·9
2·7	η Bootis		**151**	08·0	08·1	08·2	08·2	08·1	08·0	N **18**	19·2	19·2	19·2	19·1	19·0	18·8
1·9	*Alkaid*	34	**152**	57·3	57·5	57·6	57·7	57·6	57·4	N **49**	14·2	14·2	14·1	14·0	13·8	13·6
2·3	ε Centauri		**154**	45·7	45·9	46·0	46·1	45·9	45·7	S **53**	33·1	33·1	33·0	32·9	32·8	32·8
1·0	*Spica*	33	**158**	29·0	29·1	29·2	29·2	29·1	28·9	S **11**	14·8	14·7	14·7	14·7	14·7	14·8
2·3	*Mizar*		**158**	51·4	51·6	51·8	51·8	51·7	51·5	N **54**	50·7	50·7	50·6	50·4	50·2	50·1
2·8	ι Centauri		**159**	37·0	37·1	37·2	37·2	37·1	36·9	S **36**	48·0	48·0	47·9	47·8	47·8	47·8
2·8	ε Virginis		**164**	15·1	15·2	15·3	15·3	15·2	15·0	N **10**	52·4	52·4	52·4	52·4	52·3	52·1
2·9	*Cor Caroli*		**165**	48·2	48·4	48·4	48·4	48·3	48·1	N **38**	14·1	14·0	13·9	13·8	13·7	13·5
1·8	*Alioth*	32	**166**	19·1	19·3	19·4	19·4	19·3	19·0	N **55**	52·6	52·5	52·4	52·2	52·1	51·9
1·3	*Mimosa*		**167**	49·4	49·7	49·8	49·8	49·6	49·2	S **59**	46·9	46·9	46·7	46·6	46·5	46·5
2·9	γ Virginis		**169**	22·6	22·7	22·8	22·7	22·6	22·4	S **1**	32·3	32·3	32·3	32·3	32·4	32·4
2·2	*Muhlifain*		**169**	23·4	23·6	23·7	23·7	23·5	23·2	S **49**	03·2	03·1	03·0	02·9	02·8	02·8
2·7	α Muscæ		**170**	27·0	27·4	27·6	27·6	27·3	26·8	S **69**	13·8	13·8	13·6	13·5	13·4	13·3
2·7	β Corvi		**171**	11·2	11·3	11·3	11·3	11·2	10·9	S **23**	29·3	29·3	29·2	29·1	29·1	29·2
1·6	*Gacrux*	31	**171**	58·6	58·8	58·9	58·9	58·6	58·3	S **57**	12·5	12·5	12·3	12·2	12·1	12·1
1·3	*Acrux*	30	**173**	06·9	07·2	07·3	07·3	07·0	06·6	S **63**	11·7	11·6	11·5	11·3	11·2	11·2
2·6	*Gienah*	29	**175**	50·2	50·3	50·3	50·3	50·2	49·9	S **17**	38·0	38·0	37·9	37·9	37·9	38·0
2·6	δ Centauri		**177**	41·7	41·9	41·9	41·9	41·7	41·3	S **50**	49·0	49·0	48·8	48·7	48·7	48·7
2·4	*Phecda*		**181**	20·1	20·2	20·2	20·2	20·0	19·6	N **53**	36·5	36·4	36·2	36·1	35·9	35·8
2·1	*Denebola*	28	**182**	31·7	31·8	31·8	31·7	31·6	31·3	N **14**	28·9	28·9	28·9	28·8	28·7	28·6
2·6	δ Leonis		**191**	15·5	15·6	15·5	15·5	15·3	15·0	N **20**	26·1	26·1	26·0	26·0	25·9	25·7
3·0	ψ Ursæ Majoris		**192**	21·7	21·7	21·7	21·6	21·4	21·0	N **44**	24·7	24·7	24·5	24·4	24·3	24·2
1·8	*Dubhe*	27	**193**	49·7	49·8	49·8	49·6	49·3	48·9	N **61**	39·9	39·8	39·7	39·5	39·4	39·3
2·4	*Merak*		**194**	18·2	18·3	18·3	18·1	17·8	17·4	N **56**	17·8	17·7	17·6	17·4	17·3	17·2
2·7	μ Velorum		**198**	07·9	08·0	08·0	07·9	07·6	07·3	S **49**	30·7	30·5	30·4	30·3	30·3	30·3
2·8	θ Carinæ		**199**	07·0	07·1	07·1	06·9	06·6	06·1	S **64**	29·1	29·0	28·8	28·7	28·7	28·7
2·3	*Algeiba*		**204**	47·1	47·1	47·1	46·9	46·7	46·5	N **19**	45·5	45·5	45·5	45·4	45·3	45·2
1·4	*Regulus*	26	**207**	41·6	41·6	41·5	41·4	41·2	40·9	N **11**	53·2	53·2	53·2	53·1	53·0	52·9
3·0	ε Leonis		**213**	18·6	18·6	18·5	18·3	18·1	17·8	N **23**	41·9	41·9	41·8	41·7	41·7	41·6
3·1	N Velorum		**217**	04·5	04·5	04·4	04·2	03·8	03·5	S **57**	06·7	06·5	06·4	06·3	06·3	06·4
2·0	*Alphard*	25	**217**	54·3	54·3	54·2	54·1	53·8	53·6	S **8**	43·9	43·8	43·8	43·8	43·9	44·0
2·5	κ Velorum		**219**	21·0	21·0	20·9	20·6	20·3	20·0	S **55**	05·1	04·9	04·8	04·7	04·7	04·8
2·2	ι Carinæ		**220**	37·4	37·4	37·3	37·1	36·7	36·3	S **59**	20·9	20·7	20·6	20·5	20·5	20·6
1·7	*Miaplacidus*	24	**221**	39·9	40·0	39·8	39·4	38·9	38·4	S **69**	47·3	47·2	47·0	46·9	46·9	47·0
2·2	*Suhail*	23	**222**	51·3	51·3	51·1	50·9	50·7	50·4	S **43**	30·1	30·0	29·9	29·8	29·9	30·0
3·1	ι Ursæ Majoris		**224**	55·7	55·6	55·4	55·2	54·9	54·5	N **47**	58·6	58·5	58·4	58·3	58·2	58·2
2·0	δ Velorum		**228**	43·0	43·0	42·8	42·6	42·2	41·9	S **54**	46·4	46·2	46·1	46·0	46·0	46·2
1·9	*Avior*	22	**234**	17·7	17·7	17·5	17·2	16·8	16·5	S **59**	33·9	33·8	33·6	33·6	33·6	33·8
1·8	γ Velorum		**237**	29·8	29·7	29·5	29·3	29·0	28·7	S **47**	23·3	23·1	23·0	23·0	23·0	23·2
2·8	ρ Puppis		**237**	56·6	56·6	56·4	56·2	56·0	55·8	S **24**	21·3	21·2	21·1	21·1	21·1	21·2
2·3	ζ Puppis		**238**	57·9	57·8	57·7	57·4	57·2	56·9	S **40**	03·1	03·0	02·9	02·9	02·9	03·1
1·1	*Pollux*	21	**243**	25·6	25·5	25·3	25·1	24·8	24·6	N **27**	59·0	59·0	59·0	58·9	58·9	58·8
0·4	*Procyon*	20	**244**	57·9	57·8	57·6	57·4	57·2	57·0	N **5**	10·8	10·8	10·9	10·8	10·8	10·7

Mag.	Name and Number		SHA							Declination						
				JAN.	FEB.	MAR.	APR.	MAY	JUNE		JAN.	FEB.	MAR.	APR.	MAY	JUNE
			°	′	′	′	′	′	′	°	′	′	′	′	′	′
1·6	α Geminorum		**246**	05·4	05·4	05·5	05·6	05·7	05·8	N **31**	50·9	50·9	51·0	51·0	51·0	51·0
3·3	σ Puppis		**247**	33·4	33·4	33·6	33·8	34·0	34·1	S **43**	20·3	20·4	20·5	20·5	20·5	20·4
2·9	β Canis Minoris		**247**	59·4	59·4	59·5	59·6	59·7	59·7	N **8**	15·1	15·1	15·1	15·1	15·1	15·2
2·4	η Canis Majoris		**248**	48·6	48·7	48·8	49·0	49·1	49·2	S **29**	20·3	20·4	20·5	20·5	20·5	20·4
2·7	π Puppis		**250**	33·9	33·9	34·1	34·3	34·4	34·5	S **37**	07·8	08·0	08·1	08·1	08·0	07·9
1·8	δ Canis Majoris		**252**	43·9	44·0	44·1	44·3	44·4	44·5	S **26**	25·4	25·5	25·6	25·6	25·5	25·4
3·0	ο Canis Majoris		**254**	04·2	04·2	04·4	04·5	04·6	04·7	S **23**	51·7	51·8	51·9	51·9	51·8	51·7
1·5	ε Canis Majoris	19	**255**	10·7	10·8	10·9	11·1	11·2	11·3	S **28**	59·9	60·0	60·1	60·1	60·0	59·9
2·9	τ Puppis		**257**	24·4	24·5	24·7	25·0	25·2	25·3	S **50**	38·3	38·4	38·5	38·5	38·5	38·3
−1·5	α Canis Majoris	18	**258**	31·8	31·9	32·0	32·1	32·3	32·3	S **16**	44·6	44·7	44·7	44·7	44·7	44·6
1·9	γ Geminorum		**260**	20·1	20·1	20·3	20·4	20·5	20·5	N **16**	22·9	22·9	22·9	22·9	22·9	22·9
−0·7	α Carinæ	17	**263**	54·8	55·0	55·2	55·5	55·7	55·8	S **52**	42·6	42·7	42·8	42·8	42·7	42·5
2·0	β Canis Majoris		**264**	08·6	08·6	08·7	08·9	09·0	09·0	S **17**	58·1	58·2	58·3	58·3	58·2	58·1
2·6	θ Aurigæ		**269**	47·4	47·5	47·6	47·8	47·9	47·9	N **37**	12·6	12·6	12·7	12·7	12·6	12·6
1·9	β Aurigæ		**269**	49·0	49·1	49·2	49·4	49·5	49·5	N **44**	56·7	56·8	56·8	56·8	56·8	56·7
Var.‡	α Orionis	16	**270**	59·1	59·1	59·3	59·4	59·5	59·5	N **7**	24·3	24·3	24·3	24·3	24·3	24·4
2·1	κ Orionis		**272**	51·9	52·0	52·1	52·3	52·3	52·3	S **9**	40·1	40·2	40·2	40·2	40·2	40·1
1·9	ζ Orionis		**274**	36·2	36·2	36·4	36·5	36·6	36·6	S **1**	56·3	56·4	56·4	56·4	56·3	56·3
2·6	α Columbæ		**274**	56·2	56·3	56·5	56·7	56·8	56·8	S **34**	04·3	04·4	04·4	04·4	04·3	04·1
3·0	ζ Tauri		**275**	20·6	20·7	20·8	21·0	21·0	21·0	N **21**	08·9	08·9	08·9	08·9	08·9	08·9
1·7	ε Orionis	15	**275**	44·3	44·4	44·5	44·6	44·7	44·7	S **1**	11·8	11·8	11·9	11·8	11·8	11·7
2·8	ι Orionis		**275**	56·4	56·5	56·6	56·8	56·8	56·8	S **5**	54·3	54·3	54·3	54·3	54·3	54·2
2·6	α Leporis		**276**	38·1	38·2	38·4	38·5	38·6	38·6	S **17**	49·0	49·0	49·1	49·0	49·0	48·9
2·2	δ Orionis		**276**	47·3	47·4	47·5	47·6	47·7	47·7	S **0**	17·5	17·6	17·6	17·6	17·5	17·5
2·8	β Leporis		**277**	45·7	45·8	45·9	46·1	46·2	46·2	S **20**	45·1	45·2	45·2	45·2	45·1	45·0
1·7	β Tauri	14	**278**	10·1	10·1	10·3	10·4	10·5	10·5	N **28**	37·0	37·1	37·1	37·1	37·0	37·0
1·6	γ Orionis	13	**278**	29·8	29·9	30·0	30·2	30·2	30·2	N **6**	21·6	21·6	21·5	21·6	21·6	21·6
0·1	α Aurigæ	12	**280**	31·4	31·5	31·7	31·9	32·0	31·9	N **46**	00·7	00·7	00·8	00·7	00·7	00·6
0·1	β Orionis	11	**281**	10·1	10·2	10·3	10·4	10·5	10·5	S **8**	11·3	11·3	11·4	11·3	11·3	11·2
2·8	β Eridani		**282**	50·1	50·2	50·4	50·5	50·5	50·5	S **5**	04·2	04·3	04·3	04·3	04·2	04·1
2·7	ι Aurigæ		**285**	29·1	29·2	29·3	29·4	29·5	29·4	N **33**	11·3	11·3	11·3	11·3	11·3	11·2
0·9	α Tauri	10	**290**	47·1	47·2	47·3	47·4	47·5	47·4	N **16**	32·3	32·3	32·3	32·2	32·2	32·3
2·9	ε Persei		**300**	15·6	15·8	16·0	16·1	16·1	16·0	N **40**	03·3	03·3	03·3	03·2	03·2	03·1
3·0	γ Eridani		**300**	18·1	18·2	18·4	18·5	18·5	18·4	S **13**	28·1	28·1	28·1	28·1	28·0	27·9
2·9	ζ Persei		**301**	12·6	12·7	12·8	12·9	12·9	12·8	N **31**	55·8	55·8	55·7	55·7	55·7	55·6
2·9	η Tauri		**302**	53·1	53·3	53·4	53·5	53·5	53·4	N **24**	09·1	09·1	09·1	09·1	09·1	09·1
1·8	α Persei	9	**308**	37·5	37·7	37·9	38·0	38·0	37·8	N **49**	55·1	55·1	55·0	55·0	54·9	54·8
Var.§	β Persei		**312**	41·4	41·6	41·8	41·9	41·8	41·7	N **41**	01·0	01·0	01·0	00·9	00·8	00·8
2·5	α Ceti	8	**314**	13·1	13·2	13·3	13·4	13·3	13·2	N **4**	09·0	08·9	08·9	08·9	09·0	09·0
3·2	θ Eridani	7	**315**	16·9	17·1	17·2	17·3	17·3	17·2	S **40**	14·8	14·8	14·8	14·7	14·5	14·4
2·0	α Ursæ Minoris		**316**	46·7	59·8	71·6	78·4	77·5	69·7	N **89**	20·1	20·1	20·1	19·9	19·8	19·7
3·0	β Trianguli		**327**	22·3	22·4	22·6	22·6	22·5	22·3	N **35**	03·8	03·8	03·7	03·6	03·6	03·6
2·0	α Arietis	6	**327**	58·7	58·8	58·9	58·9	58·8	58·7	N **23**	32·2	32·2	32·2	32·1	32·1	32·1
2·3	γ Andromedæ		**328**	46·5	46·6	46·8	46·8	46·7	46·5	N **42**	24·5	24·4	24·3	24·3	24·2	24·2
2·9	α Hydri		**330**	11·0	11·3	11·6	11·7	11·6	11·4	S **61**	29·9	29·9	29·8	29·6	29·4	29·3
2·6	β Arietis		**331**	07·0	07·1	07·2	07·2	07·1	06·9	N **20**	53·1	53·1	53·1	53·0	53·0	53·1
0·5	α Eridani	5	**335**	25·6	25·8	26·0	26·1	26·0	25·7	S **57**	09·7	09·7	09·6	09·4	09·2	09·1
2·7	δ Cassiopeiæ		**338**	16·6	16·8	17·0	17·0	16·9	16·5	N **60**	19·3	19·2	19·1	19·0	18·9	18·9
2·1	β Andromedæ		**342**	20·4	20·5	20·6	20·6	20·5	20·2	N **35**	42·4	42·4	42·3	42·2	42·2	42·2
Var.‖	γ Cassiopeiæ		**345**	34·5	34·7	34·9	34·9	34·7	34·3	N **60**	48·4	48·4	48·2	48·1	48·0	48·0
2·0	β Ceti	4	**348**	54·2	54·3	54·4	54·3	54·2	54·0	S **17**	54·1	54·1	54·1	54·0	53·9	53·8
2·2	α Cassiopeiæ	3	**349**	38·5	38·7	38·8	38·8	38·6	38·2	N **56**	37·7	37·6	37·5	37·4	37·3	37·3
2·4	α Phœnicis	2	**353**	14·2	14·3	14·3	14·3	14·1	13·9	S **42**	13·4	13·4	13·3	13·1	13·0	12·8
2·8	β Hydri		**353**	22·5	23·1	23·3	23·2	22·8	22·1	S **77**	10·2	10·1	09·9	09·7	09·6	09·4
2·8	γ Pegasi		**356**	29·1	29·2	29·2	29·2	29·0	28·8	N **15**	16·4	16·3	16·3	16·3	16·3	16·4
2·3	β Cassiopeiæ		**357**	29·3	29·5	29·6	29·5	29·3	28·9	N **59**	14·5	14·4	14·3	14·2	14·1	14·1
2·1	α Andromedæ	1	**357**	41·8	41·9	41·9	41·8	41·6	41·4	N **29**	10·8	10·8	10·7	10·6	10·6	10·7

‡ 0·1 — 1·2 § 2·1 — 3·4 ‖ Irregular variable; 2014 mag. 2·1

Mag.	Name and Number		SHA	JULY	AUG.	SEPT.	OCT.	NOV.	DEC.	Declination	JULY	AUG.	SEPT.	OCT.	NOV.	DEC.
			°	′	′	′	′	′	′	°	′	′	′	′	′	′
1·6	*Castor*		**246**	05·7	05·6	05·4	05·2	04·9	04·7	**N 31**	50·9	50·9	50·9	50·8	50·8	50·8
3·3	σ Puppis		**247**	34·1	34·0	33·8	33·5	33·3	33·1	**S 43**	20·2	20·1	20·0	20·0	20·0	20·2
2·9	β Canis Minoris		**247**	59·7	59·6	59·4	59·2	59·0	58·8	**N 8**	15·2	15·2	15·2	15·2	15·2	15·1
2·4	η Canis Majoris		**248**	49·2	49·0	48·9	48·6	48·4	48·2	**S 29**	20·3	20·1	20·1	20·0	20·1	20·3
2·7	π Puppis		**250**	34·5	34·4	34·2	34·0	33·7	33·5	**S 37**	07·8	07·6	07·5	07·5	07·6	07·8
1·8	*Wezen*		**252**	44·4	44·3	44·1	43·9	43·7	43·5	**S 26**	25·3	25·2	25·1	25·1	25·2	25·3
3·0	ο Canis Majoris		**254**	04·7	04·5	04·3	04·1	03·9	03·7	**S 23**	51·6	51·5	51·4	51·4	51·5	51·6
1·5	*Adhara*	19	**255**	11·3	11·1	10·9	10·7	10·5	10·3	**S 28**	59·8	59·7	59·6	59·6	59·7	59·8
2·9	τ Puppis		**257**	25·3	25·2	24·9	24·6	24·3	24·1	**S 50**	38·2	38·0	37·9	37·9	38·0	38·2
−1·5	*Sirius*	18	**258**	32·2	32·1	31·9	31·7	31·5	31·3	**S 16**	44·5	44·4	44·3	44·3	44·4	44·5
1·9	*Alhena*		**260**	20·4	20·3	20·1	19·8	19·6	19·4	**N 16**	22·9	22·9	22·9	22·9	22·9	22·8
−0·7	*Canopus*	17	**263**	55·7	55·6	55·3	55·0	54·7	54·5	**S 52**	42·4	42·2	42·1	42·1	42·2	42·4
2·0	*Mirzam*		**264**	09·0	08·8	08·6	08·4	08·2	08·0	**S 17**	58·0	57·9	57·8	57·8	57·9	58·0
2·6	θ Aurigæ		**269**	47·7	47·5	47·2	47·0	46·7	46·5	**N 37**	12·5	12·5	12·5	12·5	12·5	12·6
1·9	*Menkalinan*		**269**	49·4	49·1	48·8	48·6	48·3	48·1	**N 44**	56·6	56·6	56·6	56·6	56·6	56·7
Var.‡	*Betelgeuse*	16	**270**	59·4	59·2	59·0	58·8	58·6	58·4	**N 7**	24·4	24·5	24·5	24·5	24·4	24·4
2·1	κ Orionis		**272**	52·2	52·1	51·9	51·7	51·5	51·3	**S 9**	40·0	39·9	39·8	39·9	39·9	40·0
1·9	*Alnitak*		**274**	36·4	36·3	36·1	35·9	35·7	35·5	**S 1**	56·2	56·1	56·1	56·1	56·2	56·2
2·6	*Phact*		**274**	56·7	56·5	56·3	56·0	55·8	55·7	**S 34**	04·0	03·9	03·8	03·8	04·0	04·1
3·0	ζ Tauri		**275**	20·9	20·7	20·4	20·2	20·0	19·9	**N 21**	08·9	08·9	09·0	09·0	09·0	08·9
1·7	*Alnilam*	15	**275**	44·6	44·4	44·2	44·0	43·8	43·6	**S 1**	11·7	11·6	11·5	11·6	11·6	11·7
2·8	ι Orionis		**275**	56·7	56·5	56·3	56·1	55·9	55·8	**S 5**	54·1	54·0	54·0	54·0	54·1	54·1
2·6	α Leporis		**276**	38·5	38·3	38·1	37·9	37·7	37·6	**S 17**	48·8	48·7	48·6	48·6	48·7	48·8
2·2	δ Orionis		**276**	47·6	47·4	47·2	47·0	46·8	46·7	**S 0**	17·4	17·3	17·3	17·3	17·3	17·4
2·8	β Leporis		**277**	46·0	45·9	45·6	45·4	45·3	45·1	**S 20**	44·9	44·8	44·7	44·8	44·8	45·0
1·7	*Elnath*	14	**278**	10·3	10·1	09·8	09·6	09·4	09·3	**N 28**	37·0	37·0	37·0	37·0	37·1	37·1
1·6	*Bellatrix*	13	**278**	30·1	29·9	29·7	29·4	29·3	29·1	**N 6**	21·7	21·7	21·8	21·8	21·7	21·7
0·1	*Capella*	12	**280**	31·8	31·5	31·2	30·9	30·6	30·5	**N 46**	00·5	00·5	00·5	00·6	00·6	00·7
0·1	*Rigel*	11	**281**	10·3	10·1	09·9	09·7	09·6	09·5	**S 8**	11·1	11·0	11·0	11·0	11·1	11·1
2·8	β Eridani		**282**	50·4	50·2	50·0	49·8	49·6	49·5	**S 5**	04·1	04·0	03·9	04·0	04·0	04·1
2·7	ι Aurigæ		**285**	29·3	29·0	28·8	28·5	28·3	28·2	**N 33**	11·2	11·2	11·3	11·3	11·3	11·4
0·9	*Aldebaran*	10	**290**	47·2	47·0	46·8	46·6	46·4	46·3	**N 16**	32·3	32·4	32·4	32·4	32·4	32·4
2·9	ε Persei		**300**	15·8	15·5	15·2	15·0	14·8	14·7	**N 40**	03·1	03·2	03·2	03·3	03·4	03·4
3·0	γ Eridani		**300**	18·3	18·0	17·8	17·6	17·5	17·5	**S 13**	27·8	27·7	27·7	27·7	27·8	27·9
2·9	ζ Persei		**301**	12·6	12·4	12·1	11·9	11·8	11·7	**N 31**	55·6	55·7	55·7	55·8	55·9	55·9
2·9	*Alcyone*		**302**	53·2	52·9	52·7	52·5	52·4	52·3	**N 24**	09·1	09·2	09·2	09·3	09·3	09·3
1·8	*Mirfak*	9	**308**	37·5	37·2	36·9	36·7	36·5	36·5	**N 49**	54·8	54·8	54·9	55·0	55·1	55·2
Var.§	*Algol*		**312**	41·4	41·1	40·8	40·7	40·5	40·5	**N 41**	00·8	00·9	00·9	01·0	01·1	01·2
2·5	*Menkar*	8	**314**	13·0	12·8	12·6	12·4	12·3	12·3	**N 4**	09·1	09·2	09·3	09·3	09·2	09·2
3·2	*Acamar*	7	**315**	17·0	16·7	16·5	16·3	16·2	16·3	**S 40**	14·2	14·2	14·2	14·2	14·4	14·5
2·0	*Polaris*		**316**	56·8	42·1	28·8	19·2	15·0	19·0	**N 89**	19·6	19·6	19·7	19·9	20·1	20·2
3·0	β Trianguli		**327**	22·1	21·8	21·6	21·4	21·4	21·4	**N 35**	03·6	03·7	03·8	03·9	04·0	04·0
2·0	*Hamal*	6	**327**	58·4	58·2	58·0	57·9	57·8	57·8	**N 23**	32·2	32·3	32·4	32·5	32·5	32·5
2·3	*Almak*		**328**	46·2	45·9	45·7	45·5	45·5	45·5	**N 42**	24·2	24·3	24·4	24·5	24·6	24·7
2·9	α Hydri		**330**	11·0	10·6	10·3	10·1	10·2	10·3	**S 61**	29·2	29·1	29·2	29·3	29·5	29·6
2·6	*Sheratan*		**331**	06·7	06·5	06·3	06·2	06·1	06·2	**N 20**	53·1	53·2	53·3	53·4	53·4	53·4
0·5	*Achernar*	5	**335**	25·4	25·0	24·8	24·6	24·7	24·8	**S 57**	09·0	09·0	09·0	09·1	09·3	09·4
2·7	*Ruchbah*		**338**	16·1	15·8	15·5	15·3	15·3	15·5	**N 60**	18·9	19·0	19·1	19·3	19·4	19·5
2·1	*Mirach*		**342**	20·0	19·7	19·6	19·5	19·5	19·5	**N 35**	42·2	42·4	42·5	42·6	42·7	42·7
Var.‖	γ Cassiopeiæ		**345**	33·9	33·6	33·3	33·2	33·3	33·4	**N 60**	48·0	48·1	48·3	48·5	48·6	48·7
2·0	*Diphda*	4	**348**	53·8	53·5	53·4	53·4	53·4	53·5	**S 17**	53·7	53·6	53·6	53·7	53·7	53·8
2·2	*Schedar*	3	**349**	37·9	37·6	37·4	37·3	37·4	37·5	**N 56**	37·4	37·5	37·7	37·8	37·9	38·0
2·4	*Ankaa*	2	**353**	13·6	13·3	13·2	13·2	13·2	13·4	**S 42**	12·8	12·8	12·8	12·9	13·0	13·1
2·8	β Hydri		**353**	21·4	20·6	20·2	20·2	20·5	21·1	**S 77**	09·4	09·4	09·6	09·7	09·9	09·9
2·8	*Algenib*		**356**	28·6	28·4	28·3	28·2	28·3	28·3	**N 15**	16·5	16·6	16·7	16·7	16·7	16·7
2·3	*Caph*		**357**	28·5	28·2	28·1	28·0	28·2	28·4	**N 59**	14·2	14·3	14·5	14·7	14·8	14·8
2·1	*Alpheratz*	1	**357**	41·2	40·9	40·8	40·8	40·9	41·0	**N 29**	10·8	10·9	11·0	11·1	11·2	11·2

‡ 0·1 — 1·2 § 2·1 — 3·4 ‖ Irregular variable; 2014 mag. 2·1

POLARIS (POLE STAR) TABLES, 2016

FOR DETERMINING LATITUDE FROM SEXTANT ALTITUDE AND FOR AZIMUTH

LHA ARIES	0° – 9°	10° – 19°	20° – 29°	30° – 39°	40° – 49°	50° – 59°	60° – 69°	70° – 79°	80° – 89°	90° – 99°	100° – 109°	110° – 119°
	a_0	a_0	a_0	a_0	a_0	a_0	a_0	a_0	a_0	a_0	a_0	a_0
°	° ′	° ′	° ′	° ′	° ′	° ′	° ′	° ′	° ′	° ′	° ′	° ′
0	0 29·8	0 25·4	0 22·1	0 19·9	0 18·9	0 19·1	0 20·5	0 23·1	0 26·9	0 31·6	0 37·1	0 43·3
1	29·3	25·0	21·8	19·7	18·8	19·2	20·7	23·5	27·3	32·1	37·7	43·9
2	28·8	24·7	21·5	19·6	18·8	19·3	21·0	23·8	27·7	32·6	38·3	44·6
3	28·4	24·3	21·3	19·4	18·8	19·4	21·2	24·2	28·2	33·1	38·9	45·2
4	27·9	24·0	21·1	19·3	18·8	19·5	21·4	24·5	28·6	33·7	39·5	45·9
5	0 27·5	0 23·6	0 20·8	0 19·2	0 18·8	0 19·7	0 21·7	0 24·9	0 29·1	0 34·2	0 40·1	0 46·5
6	27·0	23·3	20·6	19·1	18·8	19·8	22·0	25·3	29·6	34·8	40·7	47·2
7	26·6	23·0	20·4	19·0	18·9	20·0	22·2	25·6	30·1	35·3	41·4	47·9
8	26·2	22·7	20·2	19·0	18·9	20·1	22·5	26·0	30·5	35·9	42·0	48·6
9	25·8	22·4	20·0	18·9	19·0	20·3	22·8	26·4	31·0	36·5	42·6	49·2
10	0 25·4	0 22·1	0 19·9	0 18·9	0 19·1	0 20·5	0 23·1	0 26·9	0 31·6	0 37·1	0 43·3	0 49·9
Lat.	a_1	a_1	a_1	a_1	a_1	a_1	a_1	a_1	a_1	a_1	a_1	a_1
°	′	′	′	′	′	′	′	′	′	′	′	′
0	0·5	0·5	0·6	0·6	0·6	0·6	0·6	0·5	0·5	0·4	0·4	0·3
10	·5	·5	·6	·6	·6	·6	·6	·5	·5	·5	·4	·4
20	·5	·6	·6	·6	·6	·6	·6	·5	·5	·5	·5	·4
30	·5	·6	·6	·6	·6	·6	·6	·6	·5	·5	·5	·5
40	0·6	0·6	0·6	0·6	0·6	0·6	0·6	0·6	0·6	0·5	0·5	0·5
45	·6	·6	·6	·6	·6	·6	·6	·6	·6	·6	·6	·6
50	·6	·6	·6	·6	·6	·6	·6	·6	·6	·6	·6	·6
55	·6	·6	·6	·6	·6	·6	·6	·6	·6	·6	·6	·6
60	·6	·6	·6	·6	·6	·6	·6	·6	·7	·7	·7	·7
62	0·7	0·6	0·6	0·6	0·6	0·6	0·6	0·6	0·7	0·7	0·7	0·7
64	·7	·6	·6	·6	·6	·6	·6	·7	·7	·7	·8	·8
66	·7	·7	·6	·6	·6	·6	·6	·7	·7	·8	·8	·8
68	0·7	0·7	0·6	0·6	0·6	0·6	0·6	0·7	0·7	0·8	0·8	0·9
Month	a_2	a_2	a_2	a_2	a_2	a_2	a_2	a_2	a_2	a_2	a_2	a_2
	′	′	′	′	′	′	′	′	′	′	′	′
Jan.	0·7	0·7	0·7	0·7	0·7	0·7	0·7	0·7	0·7	0·7	0·7	0·6
Feb.	·6	·7	·7	·7	·8	·8	·8	·8	·8	·8	·8	·8
Mar.	·5	·5	·6	·6	·7	·7	·8	·8	·8	·9	·9	·9
Apr.	0·3	0·4	0·4	0·5	0·6	0·6	0·7	0·7	0·8	0·9	0·9	0·9
May	·2	·3	·3	·3	·4	·5	·5	·6	·7	·8	·8	·9
June	·2	·2	·2	·2	·3	·3	·4	·5	·5	·6	·7	·7
July	0·2	0·2	0·2	0·2	0·2	0·3	0·3	0·3	0·4	0·5	0·5	0·6
Aug.	·4	·3	·3	·3	·2	·2	·2	·3	·3	·3	·4	·4
Sept.	·5	·5	·4	·4	·3	·3	·3	·3	·3	·3	·3	·3
Oct.	0·7	0·7	0·6	0·5	0·5	0·4	0·4	0·3	0·3	0·3	0·3	0·3
Nov.	0·9	0·8	·8	·7	·7	·6	·5	·5	·4	·4	·3	·3
Dec.	1·0	1·0	0·9	0·9	0·8	0·8	0·7	0·6	0·6	0·5	0·4	0·4
Lat.	AZIMUTH											
°	°	°	°	°	°	°	°	°	°	°	°	°
0	0·4	0·3	0·2	0·1	0·0	359·9	359·8	359·6	359·6	359·5	359·4	359·4
20	0·4	0·3	0·2	0·1	0·0	359·9	359·7	359·6	359·5	359·4	359·4	359·3
40	0·5	0·4	0·3	0·1	0·0	359·8	359·7	359·5	359·4	359·3	359·2	359·2
50	0·6	0·5	0·3	0·2	0·0	359·8	359·6	359·4	359·3	359·2	359·1	359·0
55	0·7	0·6	0·4	0·2	0·0	359·8	359·6	359·4	359·2	359·1	359·0	358·9
60	0·8	0·6	0·4	0·2	0·0	359·7	359·5	359·3	359·1	358·9	358·8	358·7
65	1·0	0·8	0·5	0·2	359·9	359·7	359·4	359·2	358·9	358·7	358·6	358·5

Latitude = Apparent altitude (corrected for refraction) $-1° + a_0 + a_1 + a_2$

The table is entered with LHA Aries to determine the column to be used; each column refers to a range of 10°. a_0 is taken, with mental interpolation, from the upper table with the units of LHA Aries in degrees as argument; a_1, a_2 are taken, without interpolation, from the second and third tables with arguments latitude and month respectively. a_0, a_1, a_2, are always positive. The final table gives the azimuth of *Polaris*.

POLARIS (POLE STAR) TABLES, 2016

FOR DETERMINING LATITUDE FROM SEXTANT ALTITUDE AND FOR AZIMUTH

LHA ARIES	120° – 129°	130° – 139°	140° – 149°	150° – 159°	160° – 169°	170° – 179°	180° – 189°	190° – 199°	200° – 209°	210° – 219°	220° – 229°	230° – 239°
	a_0	a_0	a_0	a_0	a_0	a_0	a_0	a_0	a_0	a_0	a_0	a_0
°	° ′	° ′	° ′	° ′	° ′	° ′	° ′	° ′	° ′	° ′	° ′	° ′
0	0 49·9	0 56·8	1 03·8	1 10·6	1 17·0	1 22·9	1 28·1	1 32·3	1 35·6	1 37·8	1 38·7	1 38·5
1	50·6	57·5	04·5	11·3	17·7	23·5	28·5	32·7	35·9	37·9	38·8	38·4
2	51·3	58·2	05·2	11·9	18·3	24·0	29·0	33·1	36·1	38·0	38·8	38·3
3	52·0	58·9	05·9	12·6	18·9	24·6	29·5	33·4	36·4	38·2	38·8	38·2
4	52·7	0 59·6	06·6	13·2	19·5	25·1	29·9	33·8	36·6	38·3	38·8	38·1
5	0 53·4	1 00·3	1 07·2	1 13·9	1 20·1	1 25·6	1 30·3	1 34·1	1 36·8	1 38·4	1 38·8	1 38·0
6	54·0	01·0	07·9	14·5	20·7	26·1	30·8	34·4	37·0	38·5	38·8	37·8
7	54·7	01·7	08·6	15·2	21·2	26·6	31·2	34·7	37·2	38·6	38·7	37·7
8	55·4	02·4	09·3	15·8	21·8	27·1	31·6	35·0	37·4	38·6	38·7	37·5
9	56·1	03·1	09·9	16·4	22·4	27·6	32·0	35·3	37·6	38·7	38·6	37·3
10	0 56·8	1 03·8	1 10·6	1 17·0	1 22·9	1 28·1	1 32·3	1 35·6	1 37·8	1 38·7	1 38·5	1 37·1
Lat.	a_1	a_1	a_1	a_1	a_1	a_1	a_1	a_1	a_1	a_1	a_1	a_1
°	′	′	′	′	′	′	′	′	′	′	′	′
0	0·3	0·3	0·3	0·4	0·4	0·4	0·5	0·5	0·6	0·6	0·6	0·6
10	·4	·4	·4	·4	·4	·5	·5	·5	·6	·6	·6	·6
20	·4	·4	·4	·4	·5	·5	·5	·6	·6	·6	·6	·6
30	·5	·5	·5	·5	·5	·5	·5	·6	·6	·6	·6	·6
40	0·5	0·5	0·5	0·5	0·5	0·6	0·6	0·6	0·6	0·6	0·6	0·6
45	·6	·6	·6	·6	·6	·6	·6	·6	·6	·6	·6	·6
50	·6	·6	·6	·6	·6	·6	·6	·6	·6	·6	·6	·6
55	·7	·7	·7	·6	·6	·6	·6	·6	·6	·6	·6	·6
60	·7	·7	·7	·7	·7	·7	·6	·6	·6	·6	·6	·6
62	0·8	0·8	0·8	0·7	0·7	0·7	0·7	0·6	0·6	0·6	0·6	0·6
64	·8	·8	·8	·8	·7	·7	·7	·6	·6	·6	·6	·6
66	·8	·8	·8	·8	·8	·7	·7	·7	·6	·6	·6	·6
68	0·9	0·9	0·9	0·9	0·8	0·8	0·7	0·7	0·6	0·6	0·6	0·6
Month	a_2	a_2	a_2	a_2	a_2	a_2	a_2	a_2	a_2	a_2	a_2	a_2
	′	′	′	′	′	′	′	′	′	′	′	′
Jan.	0·6	0·6	0·6	0·6	0·5	0·5	0·5	0·5	0·5	0·5	0·5	0·5
Feb.	·8	·7	·7	·7	·6	·6	·6	·5	·5	·5	·4	·4
Mar.	0·9	0·9	0·9	0·8	·8	·8	·7	·7	·6	·6	·5	·5
Apr.	1·0	1·0	1·0	1·0	0·9	0·9	0·9	0·8	0·8	0·7	0·6	0·6
May	0·9	1·0	1·0	1·0	1·0	1·0	1·0	0·9	0·9	0·9	·8	·7
June	·8	0·9	0·9	1·0	1·0	1·0	1·0	1·0	1·0	1·0	0·9	·9
July	0·7	0·7	0·8	0·8	0·9	0·9	1·0	1·0	1·0	1·0	1·0	0·9
Aug.	·5	·6	·6	·7	·7	·8	0·8	0·9	0·9	0·9	1·0	1·0
Sept.	·4	·4	·4	·5	·6	·6	·7	·7	·8	·8	0·9	0·9
Oct.	0·3	0·3	0·3	0·3	0·4	0·4	0·5	0·5	0·6	0·7	0·7	0·8
Nov.	·2	·2	·2	·2	·3	·3	·3	·4	·4	·5	·5	·6
Dec.	0·3	0·3	0·2	0·2	0·2	0·2	0·2	0·2	0·3	0·3	0·4	0·4
Lat.	AZIMUTH											
°	°	°	°	°	°	°	°	°	°	°	°	°
0	359·3	359·3	359·3	359·4	359·4	359·5	359·6	359·7	359·8	359·9	0·0	0·1
20	359·3	359·3	359·3	359·3	359·4	359·5	359·6	359·7	359·8	359·9	0·0	0·1
40	359·1	359·1	359·1	359·2	359·3	359·4	359·5	359·6	359·7	359·9	0·0	0·2
50	359·0	359·0	359·0	359·0	359·1	359·2	359·4	359·5	359·7	359·9	0·0	0·2
55	358·8	358·8	358·9	358·9	359·0	359·1	359·3	359·5	359·6	359·8	0·0	0·2
60	358·7	358·7	358·7	358·8	358·9	359·0	359·2	359·4	359·6	359·8	0·0	0·3
65	358·4	358·4	358·5	358·5	358·7	358·8	359·0	359·3	359·5	359·8	0·0	0·3

ILLUSTRATION

On 2016 April 21 at $23^h\ 18^m\ 56^s$ UT in longitude W 37° 14′ the apparent altitude (corrected for refraction), H_O, of *Polaris* was 49° 31′.6

From the daily pages:	°	′
GHA Aries (23^h)	195	26·5
Increment ($18^m\ 56^s$)	4	44·8
Longitude (west)	−37	14
LHA Aries	162	57

	°	′
H_O	49	31·6
a_0 (argument 162° 57′)	1	18·9
a_1 (Lat 50° approx.)		0·6
a_2 (April)		0·9
Sum − 1° = Lat =	49	52·0

POLARIS (POLE STAR) TABLES, 2016

FOR DETERMINING LATITUDE FROM SEXTANT ALTITUDE AND FOR AZIMUTH

LHA ARIES	240° – 249°	250° – 259°	260° – 269°	270° – 279°	280° – 289°	290° – 299°	300° – 309°	310° – 319°	320° – 329°	330° – 339°	340° – 349°	350° – 359°
°	a_0 ° ′	a_0 ° ′	a_0 ° ′	a_0 ° ′	a_0 ° ′	a_0 ° ′	a_0 ° ′	a_0 ° ′	a_0 ° ′	a_0 ° ′	a_0 ° ′	a_0 ° ′
0	1 37·1	1 34·6	1 30·9	1 26·3	1 20·9	1 14·8	1 08·2	1 01·3	0 54·3	0 47·5	0 41·0	0 35·0
1	36·9	34·2	30·5	25·8	20·3	14·2	07·5	1 00·6	53·7	46·8	40·4	34·5
2	36·7	33·9	30·1	25·3	19·7	13·5	06·8	0 59·9	53·0	46·2	39·8	33·9
3	36·5	33·6	29·7	24·8	19·1	12·9	06·2	59·2	52·3	45·5	39·1	33·4
4	36·2	33·2	29·2	24·3	18·5	12·2	05·5	58·5	51·6	44·8	38·5	32·8
5	1 36·0	1 32·9	1 28·7	1 23·7	1 17·9	1 11·6	1 04·8	0 57·8	0 50·9	0 44·2	0 37·9	0 32·3
6	35·7	32·5	28·3	23·2	17·3	10·9	04·1	57·1	50·2	43·5	37·3	31·8
7	35·4	32·1	27·8	22·6	16·7	10·2	03·4	56·4	49·5	42·9	36·7	31·3
8	35·2	31·7	27·3	22·1	16·1	09·6	02·7	55·7	48·9	42·3	36·2	30·8
9	34·9	31·3	26·8	21·5	15·4	08·9	02·0	55·0	48·2	41·6	35·6	30·3
10	1 34·6	1 30·9	1 26·3	1 20·9	1 14·8	1 08·2	1 01·3	0 54·3	0 47·5	0 41·0	0 35·0	0 29·8
Lat. °	a_1 ′	a_1 ′	a_1 ′	a_1 ′	a_1 ′	a_1 ′	a_1 ′	a_1 ′	a_1 ′	a_1 ′	a_1 ′	a_1 ′
0	0·6	0·5	0·5	0·4	0·4	0·3	0·3	0·3	0·3	0·4	0·4	0·4
10	·6	·5	·5	·5	·4	·4	·4	·4	·4	·4	·4	·5
20	·6	·5	·5	·5	·5	·4	·4	·4	·4	·4	·5	·5
30	·6	·6	·5	·5	·5	·5	·5	·5	·5	·5	·5	·5
40	0·6	0·6	0·6	0·5	0·5	0·5	0·5	0·5	0·5	0·5	0·5	0·6
45	·6	·6	·6	·6	·6	·6	·6	·6	·6	·6	·6	·6
50	·6	·6	·6	·6	·6	·6	·6	·6	·6	·6	·6	·6
55	·6	·6	·6	·6	·6	·6	·7	·7	·7	·6	·6	·6
60	·6	·6	·7	·7	·7	·7	·7	·7	·7	·7	·7	·7
62	0·6	0·6	0·7	0·7	0·7	0·7	0·8	0·8	0·8	0·7	0·7	0·7
64	·6	·7	·7	·7	·8	·8	·8	·8	·8	·8	·7	·7
66	·6	·7	·7	·8	·8	·8	·8	·8	·8	·8	·8	·7
68	0·6	0·7	0·7	0·8	0·8	0·9	0·9	0·9	0·9	0·9	0·8	0·8
Month	a_2 ′	a_2 ′	a_2 ′	a_2 ′	a_2 ′	a_2 ′	a_2 ′	a_2 ′	a_2 ′	a_2 ′	a_2 ′	a_2 ′
Jan.	0·5	0·5	0·5	0·5	0·5	0·6	0·6	0·6	0·6	0·6	0·7	0·7
Feb.	·4	·4	·4	·4	·4	·4	·4	·5	·5	·5	·6	·6
Mar.	·4	·4	·4	·3	·3	·3	·3	·3	·3	·4	·4	·4
Apr.	0·5	0·5	0·4	0·3	0·3	0·3	0·2	0·2	0·2	0·2	0·3	0·3
May	·7	·6	·5	·4	·4	·3	·3	·2	·2	·2	·2	·2
June	·8	·7	·7	·6	·5	·5	·4	·3	·3	·2	·2	·2
July	0·9	0·9	0·8	0·7	0·7	0·6	0·5	0·5	0·4	0·4	0·3	0·3
Aug.	1·0	·9	·9	·9	·8	·8	·7	·6	·6	·5	·5	·4
Sept.	0·9	·9	·9	·9	·9	·9	·8	·8	·8	·7	·6	·6
Oct.	0·8	0·9	0·9	0·9	0·9	0·9	0·9	0·9	0·9	0·9	0·8	0·8
Nov.	·7	·7	·8	·8	·9	·9	1·0	1·0	1·0	1·0	0·9	0·9
Dec.	0·5	0·6	0·6	0·7	0·8	0·8	0·9	0·9	1·0	1·0	1·0	1·0
Lat.	AZIMUTH											
°	°	°	°	°	°	°	°	°	°	°	°	°
0	0·2	0·4	0·4	0·5	0·6	0·6	0·7	0·7	0·7	0·6	0·6	0·5
20	0·3	0·4	0·5	0·6	0·6	0·7	0·7	0·7	0·7	0·7	0·6	0·5
40	0·3	0·5	0·6	0·7	0·8	0·8	0·9	0·9	0·9	0·8	0·7	0·7
50	0·4	0·5	0·7	0·8	0·9	1·0	1·0	1·0	1·0	1·0	0·9	0·8
55	0·4	0·6	0·8	0·9	1·0	1·1	1·1	1·2	1·1	1·1	1·0	0·9
60	0·5	0·7	0·9	1·0	1·2	1·3	1·3	1·3	1·3	1·2	1·1	1·0
65	0·6	0·8	1·0	1·2	1·4	1·5	1·6	1·6	1·6	1·5	1·4	1·2

$$\text{Latitude} = \text{Apparent altitude (corrected for refraction)} - 1^\circ + a_0 + a_1 + a_2$$

The table is entered with LHA Aries to determine the column to be used; each column refers to a range of 10°. a_0 is taken, with mental interpolation, from the upper table with the units of LHA Aries in degrees as argument; a_1, a_2 are taken, without interpolation, from the second and third tables with arguments latitude and month respectively. a_0, a_1, a_2, are always positive. The final table gives the azimuth of *Polaris*.

SIGHT REDUCTION PROCEDURES

METHODS AND FORMULAE FOR DIRECT COMPUTATION

1. *Introduction.* In this section formulae and methods are provided for *calculating* position at sea from observed altitudes taken with a marine sextant using a computer or programmable calculator.

The method uses analogous concepts and similar terminology as that used in *manual* methods of astro-navigation, where position is found by plotting position lines from their intercept and azimuth on a marine chart.

The algorithms are presented in standard algebra suitable for translating into the programming language of the user's computer. The basic ephemeris data may be taken directly from the main tabular pages of a current version of *The Nautical Almanac.* Formulae are given for calculating altitude and azimuth from the *GHA* and *Dec* of a body, and the estimated position of the observer. Formulae are also given for reducing sextant observations to observed altitudes by applying the corrections for dip, refraction, parallax and semi-diameter.

The intercept and azimuth obtained from each observation determine a position line, and the observer should lie on or close to each position line. The method of least squares is used to calculate the fix by finding the position where the sum of the squares of the distances from the position lines is a minimum. The use of least squares has other advantages. For example, it is possible to improve the estimated position at the time of fix by repeating the calculation. It is also possible to include more observations in the solution and to reject doubtful ones.

2. *Notation.*

GHA = Greenwich hour angle. The range of *GHA* is from 0° to 360° starting at 0° on the Greenwich meridian increasing to the west, back to 360° on the Greenwich meridian.

SHA = sidereal hour angle. The range is 0° to 360°.

Dec = declination. The sign convention for declination is north is positive, south is negative. The range is from −90° at the south celestial pole to +90° at the north celestial pole.

Long = longitude. The sign convention is east is positive, west is negative. The range is −180° to +180°.

Lat = latitude. The sign convention is north is positive, south is negative. The range is from −90° to +90°.

LHA = *GHA* + *Long* = local hour angle. The *LHA* increases to the west from 0° on the local meridian to 360°.

H_C = calculated altitude. Above the horizon is positive, below the horizon is negative. The range is from −90° in the nadir to +90° in the zenith.

H_S = sextant altitude.

H = apparent altitude = sextant altitude corrected for instrumental error and dip.

H_O = observed altitude = apparent altitude corrected for refraction and, in appropriate cases, corrected for parallax and semi-diameter.

Z = Z_n= true azimuth. Z is measured from true north through east, south, west and back to north. The range is from 0° to 360°.

I = sextant index error.

D = dip of horizon.

R = atmospheric refraction.

HP = horizontal parallax of the Sun, Moon, Venus or Mars.
PA = parallax in altitude of the Sun, Moon, Venus or Mars.
SD = semi-diameter of the Sun or Moon.
p = intercept $= H_O - H_C$. Towards is positive, away is negative.
T = course or track, measured as for azimuth from the north.
V = speed in knots.

3. *Entering Basic Data.* When quantities such as *GHA* are entered, which in *The Nautical Almanac* are given in degrees and minutes, convert them to degrees and decimals of a degree by dividing the minutes by 60 and adding to the degrees; for example, if $GHA = 123° \; 45'.6$, enter the two numbers 123 and 45·6 into the memory and set $GHA = 123 + 45{\cdot}6/60 = 123°.7600$. Although four decimal places of a degree are shown in the examples, it is assumed that full precision is maintained in the calculations.

When using a computer or programmable calculator, write a subroutine to convert degrees and minutes to degrees and decimals. Scientific calculators usually have a special key for this purpose. For quantities like *Dec* which require a minus sign for southern declination, change the sign from plus to minus after the value has been converted to degrees and decimals, *e.g.* $Dec = S\,0° \; 12'.3 = S\,0°.2050 = -0°.2050$. Other quantities which require conversion are semi-diameter, horizontal parallax, longitude and latitude.

4. *Interpolation of GHA and Dec* The *GHA* and *Dec* of the Sun, Moon and planets are interpolated to the time of observation by direct calculation as follows: If the universal time is $a^h \; b^m \; c^s$, form the interpolation factor $x = b/60 + c/3600$. Enter the tabular value GHA_0 for the preceding hour (a) and the tabular value GHA_1 for the following hour ($a + 1$) then the interpolated value *GHA* is given by

$$GHA = GHA_0 + x(GHA_1 - GHA_0)$$

If the *GHA* passes through 360° between tabular values add 360° to GHA_1 before interpolation. If the interpolated value exceeds 360°, subtract 360° from *GHA*.

Similarly for declination, enter the tabular value Dec_0 for the preceding hour (a) and the tabular value Dec_1 for the following hour ($a + 1$), then the interpolated value *Dec* is given by

$$Dec = Dec_0 + x(Dec_1 - Dec_0)$$

5. *Example.* (a) Find the *GHA* and *Dec* of the Sun on 2016 February 13 at $14^h \; 47^m \; 13^s$ UT.

The interpolation factor $x = 47/60 + 13/3600 = 0^h.7869$

page 39 $14^h \; GHA_0 = 26° \; 27'.0 = 26°.4500$

$15^h \; GHA_1 = 41° \; 27'.0 = 41°.4500$

$14^h.7869 \; GHA = 26{\cdot}4500 + 0{\cdot}7869(41{\cdot}4500 - 26{\cdot}4500) = 38°.2542$

$14^h \; Dec_0 = S\,13° \; 25'.3 = -13°.4217$

$15^h \; Dec_1 = S\,13° \; 24'.4 = -13°.4067$

$14^h.7869 \; Dec = -13{\cdot}4217 + 0{\cdot}7869(-13{\cdot}4067 + 13{\cdot}4217) = -13°.4099$

GHA Aries is interpolated in the same way as *GHA* of a body. For a star the *SHA* and *Dec* are taken from the tabular page and do not require interpolation, then

$$GHA = GHA \text{ Aries} + SHA$$

where *GHA* Aries is interpolated to the time of observation.

(b) Find the *GHA* and *Dec* of *Vega* on 2016 February 13 at $14^h\ 47^m\ 13^s$ UT.

The interpolation factor $x = 0^h\!.7869$ as in the previous example

$$\text{page 38} \quad 14^h\ GHA\ \text{Aries}_0 = 353°\ 02'\!.9 = 353°\!.0483$$
$$15^h\ GHA\ \text{Aries}_1 = 8°\ 05'\!.4 = 368°\!.0900 \quad (360°\ \text{added})$$
$$14^h\!.7869\ GHA\ \text{Aries} = 353{\cdot}0483 + 0{\cdot}7869(368{\cdot}0900 - 353{\cdot}0483) = 364°\!.8853$$
$$SHA = 80°\ 38'\!.0 = 80°\!.6333$$
$$GHA = GHA\ \text{Aries} + SHA = 85°\!.5186 \quad (\text{multiple of } 360°\ \text{removed})$$
$$Dec = \text{N}\,38°\ 47'\!.9 = +38°\!.7983$$

6. *The calculated altitude and azimuth.* The calculated altitude H_C and true azimuth Z are determined from the *GHA* and *Dec* interpolated to the time of observation and from the *Long* and *Lat* estimated at the time of observation as follows:

Step 1. Calculate the local hour angle

$$LHA = GHA + Long$$

Add or subtract multiples of 360° to set *LHA* in the range 0° to 360°.

Step 2. Calculate S, C and the altitude H_C from

$$S = \sin Dec$$
$$C = \cos Dec \cos LHA$$
$$H_C = \sin^{-1}(S \sin Lat + C \cos Lat)$$

where $\sin^{-1}$ is the inverse function of sine.

Step 3. Calculate X and A from

$$X = (S \cos Lat - C \sin Lat)/\cos H_C$$
$$\text{If } X > +1 \quad \text{set} \quad X = +1$$
$$\text{If } X < -1 \quad \text{set} \quad X = -1$$
$$A = \cos^{-1} X$$

where $\cos^{-1}$ is the inverse function of cosine.

Step 4. Determine the azimuth Z

$$\text{If } LHA > 180° \quad \text{then} \quad Z = A$$
$$\text{Otherwise} \quad Z = 360° - A$$

7. *Example.* Find the calculated altitude H_C and azimuth Z when

$$GHA = 53° \quad Dec = \text{S}\,15° \quad Lat = \text{N}\,32° \quad Long = \text{W}\,16°$$

For the calculation

$$GHA = 53°\!.0000 \quad Dec = -15°\!.0000 \quad Lat = +32°\!.0000 \quad Long = -16°\!.0000$$

Step 1. $LHA = 53{\cdot}0000 - 16{\cdot}0000 = 37{\cdot}0000$

Step 2.

$$S = -0{\cdot}2588$$
$$C = +0{\cdot}9659 \times 0{\cdot}7986 = 0{\cdot}7714$$
$$\sin H_C = -0{\cdot}2588 \times 0{\cdot}5299 + 0{\cdot}7714 \times 0{\cdot}8480 = 0{\cdot}5171$$
$$H_C = 31°\!.1346$$

Step 3. $X = (-0{\cdot}2588 \times 0{\cdot}8480 - 0{\cdot}7714 \times 0{\cdot}5299)/0{\cdot}8560 = -0{\cdot}7340$

$A = 137^\circ\!.2239$

Step 4. Since $LHA \leq 180^\circ$ then $Z = 360^\circ - A = 222^\circ\!.7761$

8. *Reduction from sextant altitude to observed altitude.* The sextant altitude H_S is corrected for both dip and index error to produce the apparent altitude. The observed altitude H_O is calculated by applying a correction for refraction. For the Sun, Moon, Venus and Mars a correction for parallax is also applied to H, and for the Sun and Moon a further correction for semi-diameter is required. The corrections are calculated as follows:

Step 1. Calculate dip

$$D = 0^\circ\!.0293\sqrt{h}$$

where h is the height of eye above the horizon in metres.

Step 2. Calculate apparent altitude

$$H = H_S + I - D$$

where I is the sextant index error.

Step 3. Calculate refraction (R) at a standard temperature of 10° Celsius (C) and pressure of 1010 millibars (mb)

$$R_0 = 0^\circ\!.0167/\tan(H + 7{\cdot}32/(H + 4{\cdot}32))$$

If the temperature T° C and pressure P mb are known calculate the refraction from

$$R = fR_0 \qquad \text{where} \qquad f = 0{\cdot}28P/(T + 273)$$

$$\text{otherwise set} \qquad R = R_0$$

Step 4. Calculate the parallax in altitude (PA) from the horizontal parallax (HP) and the apparent altitude (H) for the Sun, Moon, Venus and Mars as follows:

$$PA = HP\cos H$$

For the Sun $HP = 0^\circ\!.0024$. This correction is very small and could be ignored.

For the Moon HP is taken for the nearest hour from the main tabular page and converted to degrees.

For Venus and Mars the HP is taken from the critical table at the bottom of page 259 and converted to degrees.

For the navigational stars and the remaining planets, Jupiter and Saturn set $PA = 0$.

If an error of $0'\!.2$ is significant the expression for the parallax in altitude for the Moon should include a small correction OB for the oblateness of the Earth as follows:

$$PA = HP\cos H + OB$$

$$\text{where} \quad OB = -0^\circ\!.0032\sin^2 Lat\,\cos H + 0^\circ\!.0032\sin(2Lat)\cos Z\,\sin H$$

At mid-latitudes and for altitudes of the Moon below 60° a simple approximation to OB is

$$OB = -0^\circ\!.0017\cos H$$

Step 5. Calculate the semi-diameter for the Sun and Moon as follows:

Sun: SD is taken from the main tabular page and converted to degrees.

Moon: $SD = 0\overset{\circ}{.}2724HP$ where HP is taken for the nearest hour from the main tabular page and converted to degrees.

Step 6. Calculate the observed altitude

$$H_O = H - R + PA \pm SD$$

where the plus sign is used if the lower limb of the Sun or Moon was observed and the minus sign if the upper limb was observed.

9. *Example.* The following example illustrates how to use a calculator to reduce the sextant altitude (H_S) to observed altitude (H_O); the sextant altitudes given are assumed to be taken on 2016 March 11 with a marine sextant, zero index error, at height 5·4 m, temperature −3° C and pressure 982 mb, the Moon sights are assumed to be taken at 10^h UT.

Body limb	Sun lower	Sun upper	Moon lower	Moon upper	Venus —	*Polaris* —
Sextant altitude:						
H_S	21·3283	3·3367	33·4600	26·1117	4·5433	49·6083
Step 1. Dip:						
$D = 0{\cdot}0293\sqrt{h}$	0·0681	0·0681	0·0681	0·0681	0·0681	0·0681
Step 2. Apparent altitude:						
$H = H_S + I - D$	21·2602	3·2686	33·3919	26·0436	4·4752	49·5402
Step 3. Refraction:						
R_0	0·0423	0·2256	0·0251	0·0338	0·1798	0·0142
f	1·0184	1·0184	1·0184	1·0184	1·0184	1·0184
$R = fR_0$	0·0431	0·2298	0·0256	0·0344	0·1831	0·0144
Step 4. Parallax:			(60′.8)	(60′.8)	(0′.1)	
HP	0·0024	0·0024	1·0133	1·0133	0·0017	—
Parallax in altitude:						
$PA = HP \cos H$	0·0022	0·0024	0·8461	0·9104	0·0017	—
Step 5. Semi-diameter:						
Sun : $SD = 16{\cdot}1/60$	0·2683	0·2683	—	—	—	—
Moon : $SD = 0{\cdot}2724HP$	—	—	0·2760	0·2760	—	—
Step 6. Observed altitude:						
$H_O = H - R + PA \pm SD$	21·4877	2·7729	34·4884	26·6436	4·2938	49·5258

Note that for the Moon the correction for the oblateness of the Earth of about $-0\overset{\circ}{.}0017 \cos H$, which equals $-0\overset{\circ}{.}0014$ for the lower limb and $-0\overset{\circ}{.}0015$ for the upper limb, has been ignored in the above calculation.

10. *Position from intercept and azimuth using a chart.* An estimate is made of the position at the adopted time of fix. The position at the time of observation is then calculated by dead reckoning from the time of fix. For example if the course (track) T and the speed V (in knots) of the observer are constant then *Long* and *Lat* at the time of observation are calculated from

$$Long = L_F + t\,(V/60)\sin T/\cos B_F$$
$$Lat = B_F + t\,(V/60)\cos T$$

where L_F and B_F are the estimated longitude and latitude at the time of fix and t is the time interval in hours from the time of fix to the time of observation, t is positive if the time of observation is after the time of fix and negative if it was before.

The position line of an observation is plotted on a chart using the intercept

$$p = H_O - H_C$$

and azimuth Z with origin at the calculated position (*Long*, *Lat*) at the time of observation, where H_C and Z are calculated using the method in section 6, page 279. Starting from this calculated position a line is drawn on the chart along the direction of the azimuth to the body. Convert p to nautical miles by multiplying by 60. The position line is drawn at right angles to the azimuth line, distance p from $(Long, Lat)$ towards the body if p is positive and distance p away from the body if p is negative. Provided there are no gross errors the navigator should be somewhere on or near the position line at the time of observation. Two or more position lines are required to determine a fix.

11. *Position from intercept and azimuth by calculation.* The position of the fix may be calculated from two or more sextant observations as follows.

If p_1, Z_1, are the intercept and azimuth of the first observation, p_2, Z_2, of the second observation and so on, form the summations

$$\begin{aligned}
A &= \cos^2 Z_1 + \cos^2 Z_2 + \cdots\\
B &= \cos Z_1 \sin Z_1 + \cos Z_2 \sin Z_2 + \cdots\\
C &= \sin^2 Z_1 + \sin^2 Z_2 + \cdots\\
D &= p_1 \cos Z_1 + p_2 \cos Z_2 + \cdots\\
E &= p_1 \sin Z_1 + p_2 \sin Z_2 + \cdots
\end{aligned}$$

where the number of terms in each summation is equal to the number of observations.

With $G = A\,C - B^2$, an improved estimate of the position at the time of fix (L_I, B_I) is given by

$$L_I = L_F + (A\,E - B\,D)/(G \cos B_F), \qquad B_I = B_F + (C\,D - B\,E)/G$$

Calculate the distance d between the initial estimated position (L_F, B_F) at the time of fix and the improved estimated position (L_I, B_I) in nautical miles from

$$d = 60\sqrt{((L_I - L_F)^2 \cos^2 B_F + (B_I - B_F)^2)}$$

If d exceeds about 20 nautical miles set $L_F = L_I$, $B_F = B_I$ and repeat the calculation until d, the distance between the position at the previous estimate and the improved estimate, is less than about 20 nautical miles.

12. *Example of direct computation.* Using the method described above, calculate the position of a ship on 2016 July 3 at $21^h\,00^m\,00^s$ UT from the marine sextant observations of the three stars *Regulus* (No. 26) at $20^h\,39^m\,23^s$ UT, *Antares* (No. 42) at $20^h\,45^m\,47^s$ UT and *Kochab* (No. 40) at $21^h\,10^m\,34^s$ UT, where the observed altitudes of the three stars corrected for the effects of refraction, dip and instrumental error, are $27^\circ\!.4792$, $25^\circ\!.7704$ and $47^\circ\!.5377$ respectively. The ship was travelling at a constant speed of 20 knots on a course of 325° during the period of observation, and the position of the ship at the time of fix $21^h\,00^m\,00^s$ UT is only known to the nearest whole degree W 15°, N 32°.

Intermediate values for the first iteration are shown in the table. *GHA* Aries was interpolated from the nearest tabular values on page 132. For the first iteration set $L_F = -15^\circ 0000$, $B_F = +32^\circ 0000$ at the time of fix at $21^h\ 00^m\ 00^s$ UT.

	First Iteration		
Body	*Regulus*	*Antares*	*Kochab*
No.	26	42	40
time of observation	$20^h\ 39^m\ 23^s$	$20^h\ 45^m\ 47^s$	$21^h\ 10^m\ 34^s$
H_O	27·4792	25·7704	47·5377
interpolation factor	0·6564	0·7631	0·1761
GHA Aries	232·1432	233·7476	239·9607
SHA (page 132)	207·6933	112·3900	137·3283
GHA	79·8365	346·1376	17·2890
Dec (page 132)	+11·8867	−26·4650	+74·0950
t	−0·3436	−0·2369	+0·1761
Long	−14·9225	−14·9466	−15·0397
Lat	+31·9062	+31·9353	+32·0481
Z	267·1304	151·4575	359·0801
H_C	27·4561	25·4646	47·9378
p	+0·0231	+0·3058	−0·4001

$$A = 1{\cdot}7739 \quad B = -0{\cdot}3858 \quad C = 1{\cdot}2261 \quad D = -0{\cdot}6698 \quad E = 0{\cdot}1295 \quad G = 2{\cdot}0261$$
$$(A\,E - B\,D)/(G \cos B_F) = -0{\cdot}0167, \qquad (C\,D - B\,E)/G = -0{\cdot}3807$$

An improved estimate of the position at the time of fix is

$$L_I = L_F - 0{\cdot}0167 = -15{\cdot}0167 \quad \text{and} \quad B_I = B_F - 0{\cdot}3807 = +31{\cdot}6193$$

Since the distance between the previous estimated position and the improved estimate $d = 22{\cdot}9$ nautical miles set $L_F = -15{\cdot}0167$, and $B_F = +31{\cdot}6193$ and repeat the calculation. The table shows the intermediate values of the calculation for the second iteration. In each iteration the quantities H_O, *GHA*, *Dec* and *t* do not change.

	Second Iteration		
Body	*Regulus*	*Antares*	*Kochab*
No.	26	42	40
Long	−14·9396	−14·9635	−15·0563
Lat	+31·5255	+31·5546	+31·6674
Z	267·3188	151·3551	359·0935
H_C	27·4890	25·7919	47·5574
p	−0·0098	−0·0216	−0·0197

$$A = 1{\cdot}7721 \quad B = -0{\cdot}3898 \quad C = 1{\cdot}2279 \quad D = -0{\cdot}0003 \quad E = -0{\cdot}0002 \quad G = 2{\cdot}0240$$
$$(A\,E - B\,D)/(G \cos B_F) = -0{\cdot}0003, \qquad (C\,D - B\,E)/G = -0{\cdot}0002$$

An improved estimate of the position at the time of fix is

$$L_I = L_F - 0{\cdot}0003 = -15{\cdot}0170 \quad \text{and} \quad B_I = B_F - 0{\cdot}0002 = +31{\cdot}6191$$

The distance between the previous estimated position and the improved estimated position $d = 0{\cdot}02$ nautical miles is so small that a third iteration would produce a negligible improvement to the estimate of the position.

USE OF CONCISE SIGHT REDUCTION TABLES

1. *Introduction.* The concise sight reduction tables given on pages 286 to 317 are intended for use when neither more extensive tables nor electronic computing aids are available. These "NAO sight reduction tables" provide for the reduction of the local hour angle and declination of a celestial object to azimuth and altitude, referred to an assumed position on the Earth, for use in the intercept method of celestial navigation which is now standard practice.

2. *Form of tables.* Entries in the reduction table are at a fixed interval of one degree for all latitudes and hour angles. A compact arrangement results from division of the navigational triangle into two right spherical triangles, so that the table has to be entered twice. Assumed latitude and local hour angle are the arguments for the first entry. The reduction table responds with the intermediate arguments A, B, and Z_1, where A is used as one of the arguments for the second entry to the table, B has to be incremented by the declination to produce the quantity F, and Z_1 is a component of the azimuth angle. The reduction table is then reentered with A and F and yields H, P, and Z_2 where H is the altitude, P is the complement of the parallactic angle, and Z_2 is the second component of the azimuth angle. It is usually necessary to adjust the tabular altitude for the fractional parts of the intermediate entering arguments to derive computed altitude, and an auxiliary table is provided for the purpose. Rules governing signs of the quantities which must be added or subtracted are given in the instructions and summarized on each tabular page. Azimuth angle is the sum of two components and is converted to true azimuth by familiar rules, repeated at the bottom of the tabular pages.

Tabular altitude and intermediate quantities are given to the nearest minute of arc, although errors of 2′ in computed altitude may accrue during adjustment for the minutes parts of entering arguments. Components of azimuth angle are stated to 0°1; for derived true azimuth, only whole degrees are warranted. Since objects near the zenith are difficult to observe with a marine sextant, they should be avoided; altitudes greater than about 80° are not suited to reduction by this method.

In many circumstances, the accuracy provided by these tables is sufficient. However, to maintain the full accuracy (0′1) of the ephemeral data in the almanac throughout their reduction to altitude and azimuth, more extensive tables or a calculator should be used.

3. *Use of Tables.*

Step 1. Determine the Greenwich hour angle (GHA) and Declination (Dec) of the body from the almanac. Select an assumed latitude (Lat) of integral degrees nearest to the estimated latitude. Choose an assumed longitude nearest to the estimated longitude such that the local hour angle

$$LHA = GHA \begin{matrix} -\text{ west} \\ +\text{ east} \end{matrix} \text{ longitude}$$

has integral degrees.

Step 2. Enter the reduction table with Lat and LHA as arguments. Record the quantities A, B and Z_1. Apply the rules for the sign of B and Z_1: B is minus if $90° < LHA < 270°$: Z_1 has the same sign as B. Set $A°$ = nearest whole degree of A and A' = minutes part of A. This step may be repeated for all reductions before leaving the latitude opening of the table.

Step 3. Record the declination Dec. Apply the rules for the sign of Dec: Dec is minus if the name of Dec (*i.e.* N or S) is contrary to latitude. Add B and Dec algebraically to produce F. If F is negative, the object is below the horizon (in sight reduction, this can occur when the objects are close to the horizon). Regard F as positive until step 7. Set $F°$ = nearest whole degree of F and F' = minutes part of F.

Step 4. Enter the reduction table a second time with $A°$ and $F°$ as arguments and record H, P, and Z_2. Set $P° =$ nearest whole degree of P and $Z_2° =$ nearest whole degree of Z_2.

Step 5. Enter the auxiliary table with F' and $P°$ as arguments to obtain $corr_1$ to H for F'. Apply the rule for the sign of $corr_1$: $corr_1$ is minus if $F < 90°$ and $F' > 29'$ or if $F > 90°$ and $F' < 30'$, otherwise $corr_1$ is plus.

Step 6. Enter the auxiliary table with A' and $Z_2°$ as arguments to obtain $corr_2$ to H for A'. Apply the rule for the sign of $corr_2$: $corr_2$ is minus if $A' < 30'$, otherwise $corr_2$ is plus.

Step 7. Calculate the computed altitude H_C as the sum of H, $corr_1$ and $corr_2$. Apply the rule for the sign of H_C: H_C is minus if F is negative.

Step 8. Apply the rule for the sign of Z_2: Z_2 is minus if $F > 90°$. If F is negative, replace Z_2 by $180° - Z_2$. Set the azimuth angle Z equal to the algebraic sum of Z_1 and Z_2 and ignore the resulting sign. Obtain the true azimuth Z_n from the rules

For N latitude, if	$LHA > 180°$	$Z_n = Z$
if	$LHA < 180°$	$Z_n = 360° - Z$
For S latitude, if	$LHA > 180°$	$Z_n = 180° - Z$
if	$LHA < 180°$	$Z_n = 180° + Z$

Observed altitude H_O is compared with H_C to obtain the altitude difference, which, with Z_n, is used to plot the position line.

4. *Example.* (a) Required the altitude and azimuth of *Schedar* on 2016 February 4 at UT 06[h] 33[m] from the estimated position 5° east, 53° north.

1. Assumed latitude	$Lat =$	53° N		
From the almanac	$GHA =$	221° 46′		
Assumed longitude		5° 14′ E		
Local hour angle	$LHA =$	227		
2. Reduction table, 1st entry				
$(Lat, LHA) = (53, 227)$	$A =$	26 07	$A° = 26$, $A' = 7$	
	$B =$	−27 12	$Z_1 = -49{\cdot}4$,	$90° < LHA < 270°$
3. From the almanac	$Dec =$	+56 38		*Lat* and *Dec* same
Sum $= B + Dec$	$F =$	+29 26	$F° = 29$, $F' = 26$	
4. Reduction table, 2nd entry				
$(A°, F°) = (26, 29)$	$H =$	25 50	$P° = 61$	
			$Z_2 = 76{\cdot}3, Z_2° = 76$	
5. Auxiliary table, 1st entry				
$(F', P°) = (26, 61)$	$corr_1 =$	+23		$F < 90°,\ F' < 29'$
Sum		26 13		
6. Auxiliary table, 2nd entry				
$(A', Z_2°) = (7, 76)$	$corr_2 =$	−2		$A' < 30'$
7. Sum = computed altitude	$H_C =$	+26° 11′		$F > 0°$
8. Azimuth, first component	$Z_1 =$	−49·4		same sign as B
second component	$Z_2 =$	+76·3		$F < 90°,\ F > 0°$
Sum = azimuth angle	$Z =$	26·9		
True azimuth	$Z_n =$	027°		N *Lat*, $LHA > 180°$

continued on page 318

SIGHT REDUCTION TABLE

B: (−) for 90° < LHA < 270°
Dec:(−) for Lat. contrary name

Z₁: same sign as B
Z₂: (−) for F > 90°

Lat. / A		0°			1°			2°			3°			4°			5°			Lat. / A	
LHA/F		A/H	B/P	Z_1/Z_2	A/H	B/P	Z_1/Z_2	A/H	B/P	Z_1/Z_2	A/H	B/P	Z_1/Z_2	A/H	B/P	Z_1/Z_2	A/H	B/P	Z_1/Z_2	LHA	
°	°	° ′	° ′	°	° ′	° ′	°	° ′	° ′	°	° ′	° ′	°	° ′	° ′	°	° ′	° ′	°	°	°
0	180	0 00	90 00	90·0	0 00	89 00	90·0	0 00	88 00	90·0	0 00	87 00	90·0	0 00	86 00	90·0	0 00	85 00	90·0	180	360
1	179	1 00	90 00	90·0	1 00	89 00	90·0	1 00	88 00	90·0	1 00	87 00	89·9	1 00	86 00	89·9	1 00	85 00	89·9	181	359
2	178	2 00	90 00	90·0	2 00	89 00	90·0	2 00	88 00	89·9	2 00	87 00	89·9	2 00	86 00	89·9	2 00	85 00	89·8	182	358
3	177	3 00	90 00	90·0	3 00	89 00	89·9	3 00	88 00	89·9	3 00	87 00	89·8	3 00	86 00	89·8	2 59	85 00	89·7	183	357
4	176	4 00	90 00	90·0	4 00	89 00	89·9	4 00	88 00	89·9	4 00	87 00	89·8	3 59	85 59	89·7	3 59	84 59	89·7	184	356
5	175	5 00	90 00	90·0	5 00	89 00	89·9	5 00	88 00	89·8	5 00	86 59	89·7	4 59	85 59	89·7	4 59	84 59	89·6	185	355
6	174	6 00	90 00	90·0	6 00	89 00	89·9	6 00	87 59	89·8	6 00	86 59	89·7	5 59	85 59	89·6	5 59	84 58	89·5	186	354
7	173	7 00	90 00	90·0	7 00	89 00	89·9	7 00	87 59	89·8	6 59	86 59	89·6	6 59	85 58	89·5	6 58	84 58	89·4	187	353
8	172	8 00	90 00	90·0	8 00	88 59	89·9	8 00	87 59	89·7	7 59	86 58	89·6	7 59	85 58	89·4	7 58	84 57	89·3	188	352
9	171	9 00	90 00	90·0	9 00	88 59	89·8	9 00	87 59	89·7	8 59	86 58	89·5	8 59	85 57	89·4	8 58	84 56	89·2	189	351
10	170	10 00	90 00	90·0	10 00	88 59	89·8	10 00	87 58	89·6	9 59	86 57	89·5	9 59	85 56	89·3	9 58	84 55	89·1	190	350
11	169	11 00	90 00	90·0	11 00	88 59	89·8	11 00	87 58	89·6	10 59	86 57	89·4	10 58	85 56	89·2	10 57	84 54	89·0	191	349
12	168	12 00	90 00	90·0	12 00	88 59	89·8	12 00	87 57	89·6	11 59	86 56	89·4	11 58	85 55	89·2	11 57	84 53	88·9	192	348
13	167	13 00	90 00	90·0	13 00	88 58	89·8	13 00	87 57	89·5	12 59	86 55	89·3	12 58	85 54	89·1	12 57	84 52	88·8	193	347
14	166	14 00	90 00	90·0	14 00	88 58	89·8	13 59	87 56	89·5	13 59	86 55	89·3	13 58	85 53	89·0	13 57	84 51	88·8	194	346
15	165	15 00	90 00	90·0	15 00	88 58	89·7	14 59	87 56	89·5	14 59	86 54	89·2	14 58	85 52	88·9	14 56	84 49	88·7	195	345
16	164	16 00	90 00	90·0	16 00	88 58	89·7	15 59	87 55	89·4	15 59	86 53	89·1	15 58	85 50	88·9	15 56	84 48	88·6	196	344
17	163	17 00	90 00	90·0	17 00	88 57	89·7	16 59	87 55	89·4	16 59	86 52	89·1	16 57	85 49	88·8	16 56	84 46	88·5	197	343
18	162	18 00	90 00	90·0	18 00	88 57	89·7	17 59	87 54	89·4	17 58	86 51	89·0	17 57	85 48	88·7	17 56	84 45	88·4	198	342
19	161	19 00	90 00	90·0	19 00	88 57	89·7	18 59	87 53	89·3	18 58	86 50	89·0	18 57	85 46	88·6	18 55	84 43	88·3	199	341
20	160	20 00	90 00	90·0	20 00	88 56	89·6	19 59	87 52	89·3	19 58	86 48	88·9	19 57	85 45	88·5	19 55	84 41	88·2	200	340
21	159	21 00	90 00	90·0	21 00	88 56	89·6	20 59	87 51	89·2	20 58	86 47	88·8	20 57	85 43	88·5	20 55	84 39	88·1	201	339
22	158	22 00	90 00	90·0	22 00	88 55	89·6	21 59	87 51	89·2	21 58	86 46	88·8	21 57	85 41	88·4	21 55	84 37	88·0	202	338
23	157	23 00	90 00	90·0	23 00	88 55	89·6	22 59	87 50	89·2	22 58	86 44	88·7	22 56	85 39	88·3	22 54	84 34	87·9	203	337
24	156	24 00	90 00	90·0	24 00	88 54	89·6	23 59	87 49	89·1	23 58	86 43	88·7	23 56	85 37	88·2	23 54	84 32	87·8	204	336
25	155	25 00	90 00	90·0	25 00	88 54	89·5	24 59	87 48	89·1	24 58	86 41	88·6	24 56	85 35	88·1	24 54	84 29	87·7	205	335
26	154	26 00	90 00	90·0	26 00	88 53	89·5	25 59	87 47	89·0	25 58	86 40	88·5	25 56	85 33	88·1	25 54	84 26	87·6	206	334
27	153	27 00	90 00	90·0	27 00	88 53	89·5	26 59	87 45	89·0	26 58	86 38	88·5	26 56	85 31	88·0	26 53	84 24	87·5	207	333
28	152	28 00	90 00	90·0	28 00	88 52	89·5	27 59	87 44	88·9	27 57	86 36	88·4	27 56	85 28	87·9	27 53	84 20	87·3	208	332
29	151	29 00	90 00	90·0	29 00	88 51	89·4	28 59	87 43	88·9	28 57	86 34	88·3	28 55	85 26	87·8	28 53	84 17	87·2	209	331
30	150	30 00	90 00	90·0	30 00	88 51	89·4	29 59	87 41	88·8	29 57	86 32	88·3	29 55	85 23	87·7	29 52	84 14	87·1	210	330
31	149	31 00	90 00	90·0	31 00	88 50	89·4	30 59	87 40	88·8	30 57	86 30	88·2	30 55	85 20	87·6	30 52	84 10	87·0	211	329
32	148	32 00	90 00	90·0	32 00	88 49	89·4	31 59	87 39	88·8	31 57	86 28	88·1	31 55	85 17	87·5	31 52	84 07	86·9	212	328
33	147	33 00	90 00	90·0	33 00	88 48	89·4	32 59	87 37	88·7	32 57	86 25	88·1	32 55	85 14	87·4	32 52	84 03	86·8	213	327
34	146	34 00	90 00	90·0	34 00	88 48	89·3	33 59	87 35	88·7	33 57	86 23	88·0	33 54	85 11	87·3	33 51	83 59	86·6	214	326
35	145	35 00	90 00	90·0	35 00	88 47	89·3	34 59	87 34	88·6	34 57	86 20	87·9	34 54	85 07	87·2	34 51	83 54	86·5	215	325
36	144	36 00	90 00	90·0	36 00	88 46	89·3	35 58	87 32	88·5	35 57	86 18	87·8	35 54	85 04	87·1	35 51	83 50	86·4	216	324
37	143	37 00	90 00	90·0	37 00	88 45	89·2	36 58	87 30	88·5	36 56	86 15	87·7	36 54	85 00	87·0	36 50	83 45	86·2	217	323
38	142	38 00	90 00	90·0	38 00	88 44	89·2	37 58	87 28	88·4	37 56	86 12	87·7	37 53	84 56	86·9	37 50	83 40	86·1	218	322
39	141	39 00	90 00	90·0	39 00	88 43	89·2	38 58	87 26	88·4	38 56	86 09	87·6	38 53	84 52	86·8	38 49	83 35	86·0	219	321
40	140	40 00	90 00	90·0	40 00	88 42	89·2	39 58	87 23	88·3	39 56	86 05	87·5	39 53	84 47	86·7	39 49	83 29	85·8	220	320
41	139	41 00	90 00	90·0	41 00	88 41	89·1	40 58	87 21	88·3	40 56	86 02	87·4	40 53	84 42	86·5	40 49	83 23	85·7	221	319
42	138	42 00	90 00	90·0	42 00	88 39	89·1	41 58	87 19	88·2	41 56	85 58	87·3	41 52	84 37	86·4	41 48	83 17	85·5	222	318
43	137	43 00	90 00	90·0	43 00	88 38	89·1	42 58	87 16	88·1	42 56	85 54	87·2	42 52	84 32	86·3	42 48	83 11	85·4	223	317
44	136	44 00	90 00	90·0	43 59	88 37	89·0	43 58	87 13	88·1	43 55	85 50	87·1	43 52	84 27	86·1	43 47	83 04	85·2	224	316
45	135	45 00	90 00	90·0	44 59	88 35	89·0	44 58	87 10	88·0	44 55	85 46	87·0	44 52	84 21	86·0	44 47	82 57	85·0	225	315

Lat. / A		0°			1°			2°			3°			4°			5°			Lat. / A	
LHA/F		A/H	B/P	Z_1/Z_2	A/H	B/P	Z_1/Z_2	A/H	B/P	Z_1/Z_2	A/H	B/P	Z_1/Z_2	A/H	B/P	Z_1/Z_2	A/H	B/P	Z_1/Z_2	LHA	
°	°	° ′	° ′	°	° ′	° ′	°	° ′	° ′	°	° ′	° ′	°	° ′	° ′	°	° ′	° ′	°	°	°
45	135	45 00	90 00	90·0	44 59	88 35	89·0	44 58	87 10	88·0	44 55	85 46	87·0	44 52	84 21	86·0	44 47	82 57	85·0	225	315
46	134	46 00	90 00	90·0	45 59	88 34	89·0	45 58	87 07	87·9	45 55	85 41	86·9	45 51	84 15	85·9	45 46	82 49	84·8	226	314
47	133	47 00	90 00	90·0	46 59	88 32	88·9	46 58	87 04	87·9	46 55	85 36	86·8	46 51	84 09	85·7	46 46	82 41	84·7	227	313
48	132	48 00	90 00	90·0	47 59	88 30	88·9	47 58	87 01	87·8	47 55	85 31	86·7	47 51	84 02	85·6	47 46	82 33	84·5	228	312
49	131	49 00	90 00	90·0	48 59	88 29	88·8	48 58	86 57	87·7	48 55	85 26	86·6	48 50	83 55	85·4	48 45	82 24	84·3	229	311
50	130	50 00	90 00	90·0	49 59	88 27	88·8	49 58	86 53	87·6	49 54	85 20	86·4	49 50	83 47	85·2	49 44	82 15	84·1	230	310
51	129	51 00	90 00	90·0	50 59	88 25	88·8	50 57	86 49	87·5	50 54	85 14	86·3	50 50	83 40	85·1	50 44	82 05	83·9	231	309
52	128	52 00	90 00	90·0	51 59	88 23	88·7	51 57	86 45	87·4	51 54	85 08	86·2	51 49	83 31	84·9	51 43	81 55	83·6	232	308
53	127	53 00	90 00	90·0	52 59	88 20	88·7	52 57	86 41	87·3	52 54	85 01	86·0	52 49	83 22	84·7	52 43	81 44	83·4	233	307
54	126	54 00	90 00	90·0	53 59	88 18	88·6	53 57	86 36	87·2	53 54	84 54	85·9	53 49	83 13	84·5	53 42	81 32	83·2	234	306
55	125	55 00	90 00	90·0	54 59	88 15	88·6	54 57	86 31	87·1	54 53	84 47	85·7	54 48	83 03	84·3	54 41	81 20	82·9	235	305
56	124	56 00	90 00	90·0	55 59	88 13	88·5	55 57	86 26	87·0	55 53	84 39	85·6	55 48	82 52	84·1	55 41	81 06	82·6	236	304
57	123	57 00	90 00	90·0	56 59	88 10	88·5	56 57	86 20	86·9	56 53	84 30	85·4	56 47	82 41	83·9	56 40	80 52	82·4	237	303
58	122	58 00	90 00	90·0	57 59	88 07	88·4	57 57	86 14	86·8	57 52	84 21	85·2	57 47	82 29	83·6	57 39	80 38	82·1	238	302
59	121	59 00	90 00	90·0	58 59	88 04	88·3	58 57	86 07	86·7	58 52	84 11	85·0	58 46	82 16	83·4	58 38	80 22	81·7	239	301
60	120	60 00	90 00	90·0	59 59	88 00	88·3	59 56	86 00	86·5	59 52	84 01	84·8	59 46	82 02	83·1	59 37	80 05	81·4	240	300
61	119	61 00	90 00	90·0	60 59	87 56	88·2	60 56	85 53	86·4	60 52	83 50	84·6	60 45	81 48	82·8	60 37	79 46	81·1	241	299
62	118	62 00	90 00	90·0	61 59	87 52	88·1	61 56	85 45	86·2	61 51	83 38	84·4	61 44	81 32	82·5	61 36	79 27	80·7	242	298
63	117	63 00	90 00	90·0	62 59	87 48	88·0	62 56	85 36	86·1	62 51	83 25	84·1	62 44	81 15	82·2	62 35	79 06	80·3	243	297
64	116	64 00	90 00	90·0	63 59	87 43	88·0	63 56	85 27	85·9	63 50	83 11	83·9	63 43	80 56	81·9	63 33	78 43	79·9	244	296
65	115	65 00	90 00	90·0	64 59	87 38	87·9	64 56	85 17	85·7	64 50	82 56	83·6	64 42	80 36	81·5	64 32	78 18	79·4	245	295
66	114	66 00	90 00	90·0	65 59	87 33	87·8	65 55	85 06	85·5	65 49	82 39	83·3	65 41	80 15	81·1	65 31	77 52	78·9	246	294
67	113	67 00	90 00	90·0	66 59	87 27	87·6	66 55	84 54	85·3	66 49	82 22	83·0	66 40	79 51	80·7	66 29	77 23	78·4	247	293
68	112	68 00	90 00	90·0	67 59	87 20	87·5	67 55	84 40	85·1	67 48	82 02	82·6	67 39	79 26	80·2	67 28	76 51	77·8	248	292
69	111	69 00	90 00	90·0	68 59	87 13	87·4	68 55	84 26	84·8	68 48	81 41	82·2	68 38	78 58	79·7	68 26	76 17	77·2	249	291
70	110	70 00	90 00	90·0	69 59	87 05	87·3	69 54	84 10	84·5	69 47	81 17	81·8	69 37	78 27	79·2	69 25	75 39	76·5	250	290
71	109	71 00	90 00	90·0	70 58	86 56	87·1	70 54	83 53	84·2	70 46	80 51	81·4	70 36	77 53	78·5	70 23	74 58	75·8	251	289
72	108	72 00	90 00	90·0	71 58	86 46	86·9	71 54	83 33	83·9	71 46	80 22	80·8	71 35	77 15	77·9	71 20	74 12	75·0	252	288
73	107	73 00	90 00	90·0	72 58	86 35	86·7	72 53	83 11	83·5	72 45	79 50	80·3	72 33	76 33	77·1	72 18	73 20	74·1	253	287
74	106	74 00	90 00	90·0	73 58	86 23	86·5	73 53	82 47	83·1	73 44	79 14	79·7	73 31	75 46	76·3	73 15	72 23	73·1	254	286
75	105	75 00	90 00	90·0	74 58	86 09	86·3	74 52	82 19	82·6	74 43	78 33	78·9	74 29	74 53	75·4	74 12	71 19	72·0	255	285
76	104	76 00	90 00	90·0	75 58	85 52	86·0	75 52	81 47	82·0	75 41	77 47	78·1	75 27	73 53	74·4	75 09	70 07	70·7	256	284
77	103	77 00	90 00	90·0	76 58	85 34	85·7	76 51	81 11	81·4	76 40	76 53	77·2	76 25	72 44	73·2	76 05	68 45	69·3	257	283
78	102	78 00	90 00	90·0	77 58	85 12	85·3	77 50	80 28	80·7	77 38	75 51	76·2	77 22	71 25	71·8	77 01	67 11	67·7	258	282
79	101	79 00	90 00	90·0	78 57	84 46	84·9	78 49	79 38	79·8	78 36	74 39	74·9	78 18	69 52	70·3	77 56	65 22	65·8	259	281
80	100	80 00	90 00	90·0	79 57	84 16	84·3	79 48	78 38	78·8	79 34	73 12	73·5	79 14	68 04	68·4	78 50	63 16	63·7	260	280
81	99	81 00	90 00	90·0	80 57	83 38	83·7	80 47	77 25	77·6	80 31	71 29	71·7	80 09	65 55	66·2	79 43	60 47	61·2	261	279
82	98	82 00	90 00	90·0	81 56	82 51	82·9	81 45	75 55	76·1	81 28	69 22	69·6	81 04	63 19	63·6	80 34	57 51	58·2	262	278
83	97	83 00	90 00	90·0	82 56	81 51	81·9	82 43	74 01	74·1	82 23	66 44	66·9	81 57	60 09	60·4	81 24	54 20	54·6	263	277
84	96	84 00	90 00	90·0	83 55	80 31	80·6	83 41	71 32	71·6	83 18	63 22	63·5	82 48	56 13	56·4	82 12	50 04	50·3	264	276
85	95	85 00	90 00	90·0	84 54	78 40	78·7	84 37	68 10	68·3	84 10	58 59	59·1	83 36	51 16	51·4	82 56	44 53	45·1	265	275
86	94	86 00	90 00	90·0	85 53	75 57	76·0	85 32	63 24	63·5	85 00	53 05	53·2	84 21	44 56	45·1	83 36	38 34	38·7	266	274
87	93	87 00	90 00	90·0	86 50	71 33	71·6	86 24	56 17	56·3	85 45	44 58	45·0	85 00	36 49	36·9	84 10	30 53	31·0	267	273
88	92	88 00	90 00	90·0	87 46	63 26	63·4	87 10	44 59	45·0	86 24	33 40	33·7	85 32	26 31	26·6	84 37	21 45	21·8	268	272
89	91	89 00	90 00	90·0	88 35	45 00	45·0	87 46	26 33	26·6	86 50	18 25	18·4	85 53	14 01	14·0	84 54	11 17	11·3	269	271
90	90	90 00	0 00	0·0	89 00	0 00	0·0	88 00	0 00	0·0	87 00	0 00	0·0	86 00	0 00	0·0	85 00	0 00	0·0	270	270

N. Lat: for LHA > 180° … $Z_n = Z$
for LHA < 180° … $Z_n = 360° - Z$

S. Lat.: for LHA > 180° … $Z_n = 180° - Z$
for LHA < 180° … $Z_n = 180° + Z$

SIGHT REDUCTION TABLE

B: (−) for 90° < LHA < 270°
Dec: (−) for Lat. contrary name

Z_1: same sign as B
Z_2: (−) for F > 90°

Lat. / A		6°			7°			8°			9°			10°			11°			Lat. / A	
LHA/F		A/H	B/P	Z_1/Z_2	A/H	B/P	Z_1/Z_2	A/H	B/P	Z_1/Z_2	A/H	B/P	Z_1/Z_2	A/H	B/P	Z_1/Z_2	A/H	B/P	Z_1/Z_2	LHA	
°	°	° ′	° ′	°	° ′	° ′	°	° ′	° ′	°	° ′	° ′	°	° ′	° ′	°	° ′	° ′	°	°	°
0	180	0 00	84 00	90·0	0 00	83 00	90·0	0 00	82 00	90·0	0 00	81 00	90·0	0 00	80 00	90·0	0 00	79 00	90·0	180	360
1	179	1 00	84 00	89·9	1 00	83 00	89·9	0 59	82 00	89·9	0 59	81 00	89·8	0 59	80 00	89·8	0 59	79 00	89·8	181	359
2	178	1 59	84 00	89·8	1 59	83 00	89·8	1 59	82 00	89·7	1 59	81 00	89·7	1 58	80 00	89·7	1 58	79 00	89·6	182	358
3	177	2 59	84 00	89·7	2 59	82 59	89·6	2 58	81 59	89·6	2 58	80 59	89·5	2 57	79 59	89·5	2 57	78 59	89·4	183	357
4	176	3 59	83 59	89·6	3 58	82 59	89·5	3 58	81 59	89·4	3 57	80 59	89·4	3 56	79 59	89·3	3 56	78 58	89·2	184	356
5	175	4 58	83 59	89·5	4 58	82 58	89·4	4 57	81 58	89·3	4 56	80 58	89·2	4 55	79 58	89·1	4 54	78 58	89·0	185	355
6	174	5 58	83 58	89·4	5 57	82 58	89·3	5 56	81 57	89·2	5 56	80 57	89·1	5 55	79 57	89·0	5 53	78 56	88·9	186	354
7	173	6 58	83 57	89·3	6 57	82 57	89·1	6 56	81 56	89·0	6 55	80 56	88·9	6 54	79 56	88·8	6 52	78 55	88·7	187	353
8	172	7 57	83 56	89·2	7 56	82 56	89·0	7 55	81 55	88·9	7 54	80 55	88·7	7 53	79 54	88·6	7 51	78 54	88·5	188	352
9	171	8 57	83 56	89·1	8 56	82 55	88·9	8 55	81 54	88·7	8 53	80 53	88·6	8 52	79 53	88·4	8 50	78 52	88·3	189	351
10	170	9 57	83 54	88·9	9 55	82 54	88·8	9 54	81 53	88·6	9 53	80 52	88·4	9 51	79 51	88·2	9 49	78 50	88·1	190	350
11	169	10 56	83 53	88·8	10 55	82 52	88·6	10 53	81 51	88·5	10 52	80 50	88·3	10 50	79 49	88·1	10 48	78 48	87·9	191	349
12	168	11 56	83 52	88·7	11 55	82 51	88·5	11 53	81 49	88·3	11 51	80 48	88·1	11 49	79 47	87·9	11 47	78 46	87·7	192	348
13	167	12 56	83 51	88·6	12 54	82 49	88·4	12 52	81 48	88·2	12 50	80 46	87·9	12 48	79 45	87·7	12 45	78 43	87·5	193	347
14	166	13 55	83 49	88·5	13 54	82 47	88·3	13 52	81 46	88·0	13 49	80 44	87·8	13 47	79 42	87·5	13 44	78 40	87·3	194	346
15	165	14 55	83 47	88·4	14 53	82 45	88·1	14 51	81 43	87·9	14 49	80 41	87·6	14 46	79 39	87·3	14 43	78 37	87·1	195	345
16	164	15 55	83 46	88·3	15 53	82 43	88·0	15 50	81 41	87·7	15 48	80 39	87·4	15 45	79 36	87·1	15 42	78 34	86·9	196	344
17	163	16 54	83 44	88·2	16 52	82 41	87·9	16 50	81 38	87·6	16 47	80 36	87·3	16 44	79 33	87·0	16 41	78 31	86·7	197	343
18	162	17 54	83 42	88·1	17 52	82 39	87·7	17 49	81 36	87·4	17 46	80 33	87·1	17 43	79 30	86·8	17 39	78 27	86·5	198	342
19	161	18 54	83 39	87·9	18 51	82 36	87·6	18 48	81 33	87·3	18 45	80 29	86·9	18 42	79 26	86·6	18 38	78 23	86·2	199	341
20	160	19 53	83 37	87·8	19 51	82 33	87·5	19 48	81 30	87·1	19 45	80 26	86·7	19 41	79 22	86·4	19 37	78 19	86·0	200	340
21	159	20 53	83 35	87·7	20 50	82 30	87·3	20 47	81 26	86·9	20 44	80 22	86·6	20 40	79 18	86·2	20 36	78 14	85·8	201	339
22	158	21 52	83 32	87·6	21 50	82 27	87·2	21 46	81 23	86·8	21 43	80 18	86·4	21 39	79 14	86·0	21 35	78 10	85·6	202	338
23	157	22 52	83 29	87·5	22 49	82 24	87·0	22 46	81 19	86·6	22 42	80 14	86·2	22 38	79 09	85·8	22 33	78 05	85·4	203	337
24	156	23 52	83 26	87·3	23 49	82 21	86·9	23 45	81 15	86·5	23 41	80 10	86·0	23 37	79 05	85·6	23 32	77 59	85·1	204	336
25	155	24 51	83 23	87·2	24 48	82 17	86·7	24 44	81 11	86·3	24 40	80 05	85·8	24 36	78 59	85·4	24 31	77 54	84·9	205	335
26	154	25 51	83 20	87·1	25 48	82 13	86·6	25 44	81 07	86·1	25 39	80 00	85·6	25 35	78 54	85·2	25 29	77 48	84·7	206	334
27	153	26 50	83 16	87·0	26 47	82 09	86·4	26 43	81 02	85·9	26 38	79 55	85·4	26 33	78 48	84·9	26 28	77 42	84·4	207	333
28	152	27 50	83 13	86·8	27 46	82 05	86·3	27 42	80 57	85·8	27 38	79 50	85·2	27 32	78 42	84·7	27 27	77 35	84·2	208	332
29	151	28 50	83 09	86·7	28 46	82 01	86·1	28 41	80 52	85·6	28 37	79 44	85·0	28 31	78 36	84·5	28 25	77 28	84·0	209	331
30	150	29 49	83 05	86·5	29 45	81 56	86·0	29 41	80 47	85·4	29 36	79 38	84·8	29 30	78 29	84·3	29 24	77 21	83·7	210	330
31	149	30 49	83 01	86·4	30 45	81 51	85·8	30 40	80 41	85·2	30 35	79 32	84·6	30 29	78 23	84·0	30 22	77 13	83·5	211	329
32	148	31 48	82 56	86·3	31 44	81 46	85·6	31 39	80 35	85·0	31 34	79 25	84·4	31 27	78 15	83·8	31 21	77 05	83·2	212	328
33	147	32 48	82 51	86·1	32 43	81 40	85·5	32 38	80 29	84·8	32 33	79 18	84·2	32 26	78 08	83·6	32 19	76 57	82·9	213	327
34	146	33 47	82 46	86·0	33 43	81 35	85·3	33 37	80 23	84·6	33 32	79 11	84·0	33 25	78 00	83·3	33 18	76 48	82·7	214	326
35	145	34 47	82 41	85·8	34 42	81 29	85·1	34 37	80 16	84·4	34 30	79 03	83·7	34 24	77 51	83·1	34 16	76 39	82·4	215	325
36	144	35 46	82 36	85·7	35 41	81 22	84·9	35 36	80 09	84·2	35 29	78 55	83·5	35 22	77 42	82·8	35 14	76 29	82·1	216	324
37	143	36 46	82 30	85·5	36 41	81 16	84·8	36 35	80 01	84·0	36 28	78 47	83·3	36 21	77 33	82·5	36 13	76 19	81·8	217	323
38	142	37 45	82 24	85·3	37 40	81 09	84·6	37 34	79 53	83·8	37 27	78 38	83·0	37 19	77 23	82·3	37 11	76 09	81·5	218	322
39	141	38 45	82 18	85·2	38 39	81 01	84·4	38 33	79 45	83·6	38 26	78 29	82·8	38 18	77 13	82·0	38 09	75 57	81·2	219	321
40	140	39 44	82 11	85·0	39 39	80 54	84·2	39 32	79 36	83·3	39 25	78 19	82·5	39 16	77 02	81·7	39 07	75 46	80·9	220	320
41	139	40 44	82 04	84·8	40 38	80 46	84·0	40 31	79 27	83·1	40 23	78 09	82·3	40 15	76 51	81·4	40 05	75 33	80·6	221	319
42	138	41 43	81 57	84·6	41 37	80 37	83·7	41 30	79 17	82·9	41 22	77 58	82·0	41 13	76 39	81·1	41 04	75 21	80·3	222	318
43	137	42 42	81 49	84·4	42 36	80 28	83·5	42 29	79 07	82·6	42 21	77 47	81·7	42 12	76 27	80·8	42 02	75 07	79·9	223	317
44	136	43 42	81 41	84·2	43 35	80 19	83·3	43 28	78 57	82·3	43 19	77 35	81·4	43 10	76 14	80·5	43 00	74 53	79·6	224	316
45	135	44 41	81 33	84·0	44 34	80 09	83·1	44 27	78 46	82·1	44 18	77 22	81·1	44 08	76 00	80·1	43 57	74 38	79·2	225	315

Lat. / A		6°			7°			8°			9°			10°			11°			Lat. / A	
LHA/F		A/H	B/P	Z_1/Z_2	A/H	B/P	Z_1/Z_2	A/H	B/P	Z_1/Z_2	A/H	B/P	Z_1/Z_2	A/H	B/P	Z_1/Z_2	A/H	B/P	Z_1/Z_2	LHA	
°	°	° ′	° ′	°	° ′	° ′	°	° ′	° ′	°	° ′	° ′	°	° ′	° ′	°	° ′	° ′	°	°	°
45	135	44 41	81 33	84·0	44 34	80 09	83·1	44 27	78 46	82·1	44 18	77 22	81·1	44 08	76 00	80·1	43 57	74 38	79·2	225	315
46	134	45 41	81 24	83·8	45 34	79 59	82·8	45 26	78 34	81·8	45 16	77 09	80·8	45 06	75 45	79·8	44 55	74 22	78·8	226	314
47	133	46 40	81 14	83·6	46 33	79 48	82·6	46 24	78 21	81·5	46 15	76 56	80·5	46 04	75 30	79·5	45 53	74 05	78·4	227	313
48	132	47 39	81 04	83·4	47 32	79 36	82·3	47 23	78 08	81·2	47 13	76 41	80·1	47 03	75 14	79·1	46 51	73 48	78·0	228	312
49	131	48 38	80 54	83·1	48 31	79 24	82·0	48 22	77 55	80·9	48 12	76 26	79·8	48 01	74 57	78·7	47 48	73 30	77·6	229	311
50	130	49 38	80 43	82·9	49 30	79 11	81·7	49 20	77 40	80·6	49 10	76 09	79·4	48 58	74 40	78·3	48 46	73 10	77·2	230	310
51	129	50 37	80 31	82·6	50 29	78 58	81·4	50 19	77 25	80·2	50 08	75 52	79·1	49 56	74 21	77·9	49 43	72 50	76·7	231	309
52	128	51 36	80 19	82·4	51 27	78 43	81·1	51 18	77 08	79·9	51 06	75 34	78·7	50 54	74 01	77·5	50 40	72 29	76·3	232	308
53	127	52 35	80 06	82·1	52 26	78 28	80·8	52 16	76 51	79·5	52 04	75 15	78·3	51 52	73 40	77·0	51 37	72 06	75·8	233	307
54	126	53 34	79 52	81·8	53 25	78 12	80·5	53 14	76 33	79·2	53 02	74 55	77·8	52 49	73 18	76·6	52 35	71 42	75·3	234	306
55	125	54 33	79 37	81·5	54 24	77 55	80·1	54 13	76 14	78·8	54 00	74 34	77·4	53 47	72 55	76·1	53 31	71 17	74·8	235	305
56	124	55 32	79 21	81·2	55 22	77 37	79·8	55 11	75 54	78·3	54 58	74 11	76·9	54 44	72 30	75·6	54 28	70 50	74·2	236	304
57	123	56 31	79 05	80·9	56 21	77 18	79·4	56 09	75 32	77·9	55 56	73 47	76·5	55 41	72 04	75·0	55 25	70 22	73·6	237	303
58	122	57 30	78 47	80·5	57 19	76 57	79·0	57 07	75 09	77·4	56 53	73 22	75·9	56 38	71 36	74·5	56 21	69 51	73·0	238	302
59	121	58 29	78 28	80·1	58 18	76 35	78·5	58 05	74 44	77·0	57 51	72 54	75·4	57 35	71 06	73·9	57 17	69 19	72·4	239	301
60	120	59 28	78 08	79·7	59 16	76 12	78·1	59 03	74 18	76·4	58 48	72 25	74·8	58 32	70 34	73·3	58 13	68 45	71·7	240	300
61	119	60 26	77 46	79·3	60 14	75 47	77·6	60 01	73 50	75·9	59 45	71 54	74·2	59 28	70 01	72·6	59 09	68 09	71·0	241	299
62	118	61 25	77 23	78·9	61 12	75 21	77·1	60 58	73 20	75·3	60 42	71 21	73·6	60 24	69 25	71·9	60 05	67 31	70·3	242	298
63	117	62 23	76 58	78·4	62 10	74 52	76·5	61 56	72 48	74·7	61 39	70 46	72·9	61 20	68 46	71·2	61 00	66 49	69·5	243	297
64	116	63 22	76 31	77·9	63 08	74 21	76·0	62 53	72 13	74·1	62 35	70 08	72·2	62 16	68 05	70·4	61 55	66 05	68·6	244	296
65	115	64 20	76 02	77·4	64 06	73 48	75·4	63 50	71 36	73·4	63 32	69 27	71·5	63 12	67 21	69·6	62 50	65 18	67·7	245	295
66	114	65 18	75 31	76·8	65 03	73 12	74·7	64 47	70 56	72·6	64 28	68 43	70·6	64 07	66 34	68·7	63 44	64 27	66·8	246	294
67	113	66 16	74 57	76·2	66 01	72 33	74·0	65 43	70 13	71·8	65 23	67 56	69·8	65 02	65 43	67·8	64 38	63 33	65·8	247	293
68	112	67 14	74 20	75·5	66 58	71 51	73·2	66 40	69 26	71·0	66 19	67 05	68·8	65 56	64 48	66·7	65 32	62 35	64·7	248	292
69	111	68 12	73 39	74·8	67 55	71 05	72·4	67 36	68 35	70·1	67 14	66 09	67·8	66 50	63 48	65·7	66 25	61 31	63·6	249	291
70	110	69 09	72 55	74·0	68 51	70 15	71·5	68 31	67 40	69·1	68 09	65 09	66·7	67 44	62 44	64·5	67 17	60 23	62·3	250	290
71	109	70 07	72 06	73·1	69 48	69 20	70·5	69 27	66 39	68·0	69 03	64 03	65·6	68 37	61 34	63·2	68 09	59 10	61·0	251	289
72	108	71 03	71 13	72·2	70 44	68 20	69·4	70 21	65 33	66·8	69 57	62 52	64·3	69 29	60 17	61·9	69 00	57 50	59·6	252	288
73	107	72 00	70 14	71·1	71 39	67 13	68·3	71 16	64 20	65·5	70 50	61 33	62·9	70 21	58 54	60·4	69 50	56 23	58·0	253	287
74	106	72 56	69 08	70·0	72 34	65 59	67·0	72 09	62 59	64·1	71 42	60 07	61·4	71 12	57 24	58·8	70 40	54 49	56·4	254	286
75	105	73 52	67 54	68·7	73 29	64 37	65·5	73 03	61 30	62·6	72 34	58 32	59·7	72 02	55 44	57·1	71 28	53 06	54·5	255	285
76	104	74 48	66 31	67·3	74 23	63 05	64·0	73 55	59 51	60·8	73 24	56 47	57·9	72 51	53 55	55·1	72 16	51 13	52·6	256	284
77	103	75 42	64 57	65·6	75 16	61 22	62·2	74 46	58 00	58·9	74 14	54 51	55·9	73 39	51 55	53·1	73 02	49 10	50·4	257	283
78	102	76 36	63 11	63·8	76 08	59 26	60·2	75 37	55 57	56·8	75 02	52 42	53·6	74 26	49 42	50·8	73 47	46 56	48·1	258	282
79	101	77 29	61 09	61·7	76 59	57 14	57·9	76 26	53 38	54·4	75 49	50 18	51·2	75 11	47 16	48·2	74 30	44 28	45·5	259	281
80	100	78 21	58 49	59·3	77 49	54 44	55·3	77 13	51 01	51·7	76 35	47 38	48·4	75 54	44 34	45·4	75 11	41 47	42·7	260	280
81	99	79 12	56 06	56·6	78 37	51 52	52·4	77 59	48 04	48·7	77 18	44 39	45·4	76 35	41 35	42·4	75 49	38 50	39·7	261	279
82	98	80 01	52 56	53·4	79 23	48 35	49·1	78 42	44 43	45·3	77 59	41 18	41·9	77 13	38 17	39·0	76 26	35 36	36·4	262	278
83	97	80 47	49 13	49·6	80 07	44 47	45·2	79 23	40 56	41·4	78 37	37 35	38·1	77 49	34 39	35·3	76 59	32 05	32·8	263	277
84	96	81 31	44 51	45·2	80 47	40 24	40·8	80 01	36 38	37·1	79 12	33 25	33·9	78 21	30 40	31·2	77 29	28 16	28·8	264	276
85	95	82 12	39 40	39·9	81 24	35 22	35·7	80 34	31 48	32·2	79 43	28 49	29·2	78 50	26 18	26·7	77 56	24 09	24·6	265	275
86	94	82 48	33 34	33·8	81 57	29 36	29·8	81 04	26 24	26·7	80 09	23 46	24·1	79 14	21 35	21·9	78 18	19 44	20·1	266	274
87	93	83 18	26 28	26·6	82 23	23 05	23·3	81 28	20 25	20·6	80 31	18 17	18·5	79 34	16 32	16·8	78 36	15 04	15·4	267	273
88	92	83 41	18 22	18·5	82 43	15 52	16·0	81 45	13 57	14·1	80 47	12 26	12·6	79 48	11 12	11·4	78 49	10 11	10·4	268	272
89	91	83 55	9 26	9·5	82 56	8 05	8·2	81 56	7 05	7·1	80 57	6 17	6·4	79 57	5 39	5·7	78 57	5 08	5·2	269	271
90	90	84 00	0 00	0·0	83 00	0 00	0·0	82 00	0 00	0·0	81 00	0 00	0·0	80 00	0 00	0·0	79 00	0 00	0·0	270	270

N. Lat: for LHA > 180° … $Z_n = Z$
for LHA < 180° … $Z_n = 360° - Z$

S. Lat.: for LHA > 180° … $Z_n = 180° - Z$
for LHA < 180° … $Z_n = 180° + Z$

SIGHT REDUCTION TABLE

B: (−) for 90° < LHA < 270°
Dec:(−) for Lat. contrary name

Z_1: same sign as B
Z_2: (−) for F > 90°

Lat. / A		12°			13°			14°			15°			16°			17°			Lat. / A	
LHA/F		A/H	B/P	Z_1/Z_2	A/H	B/P	Z_1/Z_2	A/H	B/P	Z_1/Z_2	A/H	B/P	Z_1/Z_2	A/H	B/P	Z_1/Z_2	A/H	B/P	Z_1/Z_2	LHA	
°	°	° ′	° ′	°	° ′	° ′	°	° ′	° ′	°	° ′	° ′	°	° ′	° ′	°	° ′	° ′	°	°	°
0	180	0 00	78 00	90·0	0 00	77 00	90·0	0 00	76 00	90·0	0 00	75 00	90·0	0 00	74 00	90·0	0 00	73 00	90·0	180	360
1	179	0 59	78 00	89·8	0 58	77 00	89·8	0 58	76 00	89·8	0 58	75 00	89·7	0 58	74 00	89·7	0 57	73 00	89·7	181	359
2	178	1 57	78 00	89·6	1 57	77 00	89·5	1 56	76 00	89·5	1 56	74 59	89·5	1 55	73 59	89·4	1 55	72 59	89·4	182	358
3	177	2 56	77 59	89·4	2 55	76 59	89·3	2 55	75 59	89·3	2 54	74 59	89·2	2 53	73 59	89·2	2 52	72 59	89·1	183	357
4	176	3 55	77 58	89·2	3 54	76 58	89·1	3 53	75 58	89·0	3 52	74 58	89·0	3 51	73 58	88·9	3 49	72 58	88·8	184	356
5	175	4 53	77 57	89·0	4 52	76 57	88·9	4 51	75 57	88·8	4 50	74 57	88·7	4 48	73 57	88·6	4 47	72 56	88·5	185	355
6	174	5 52	77 56	88·7	5 51	76 56	88·6	5 49	75 56	88·5	5 48	74 55	88·4	5 46	73 55	88·3	5 44	72 55	88·2	186	354
7	173	6 51	77 55	88·5	6 49	76 54	88·4	6 47	75 54	88·3	6 46	74 54	88·2	6 44	73 53	88·1	6 42	72 53	87·9	187	353
8	172	7 49	77 53	88·3	7 48	76 53	88·2	7 46	75 52	88·1	7 44	74 52	87·9	7 41	73 51	87·8	7 39	72 51	87·6	188	352
9	171	8 48	77 51	88·1	8 46	76 51	88·0	8 44	75 50	87·8	8 41	74 49	87·7	8 39	73 49	87·5	8 36	72 48	87·3	189	351
10	170	9 47	77 49	87·9	9 44	76 48	87·7	9 42	75 48	87·6	9 39	74 47	87·4	9 37	73 46	87·2	9 34	72 45	87·0	190	350
11	169	10 45	77 47	87·7	10 43	76 46	87·5	10 40	75 45	87·3	10 37	74 44	87·1	10 34	73 43	86·9	10 31	72 42	86·7	191	349
12	168	11 44	77 44	87·5	11 41	76 43	87·3	11 38	75 42	87·1	11 35	74 41	86·9	11 32	73 40	86·6	11 28	72 39	86·4	192	348
13	167	12 43	77 42	87·3	12 40	76 40	87·0	12 36	75 39	86·8	12 33	74 37	86·6	12 29	73 36	86·4	12 25	72 35	86·1	193	347
14	166	13 41	77 39	87·0	13 38	76 37	86·8	13 35	75 35	86·5	13 31	74 34	86·3	13 27	73 32	86·1	13 23	72 31	85·8	194	346
15	165	14 40	77 35	86·8	14 36	76 33	86·6	14 33	75 32	86·3	14 29	74 30	86·0	14 24	73 28	85·8	14 20	72 26	85·5	195	345
16	164	15 38	77 32	86·6	15 35	76 30	86·3	15 31	75 28	86·0	15 26	74 25	85·8	15 22	73 23	85·5	15 17	72 21	85·2	196	344
17	163	16 37	77 28	86·4	16 33	76 26	86·1	16 29	75 23	85·8	16 24	74 21	85·5	16 19	73 19	85·2	16 14	72 16	84·9	197	343
18	162	17 36	77 24	86·1	17 31	76 21	85·8	17 27	75 19	85·5	17 22	74 16	85·2	17 17	73 13	84·9	17 11	72 11	84·6	198	342
19	161	18 34	77 20	85·9	18 30	76 17	85·6	18 25	75 14	85·2	18 20	74 11	84·9	18 14	73 08	84·6	18 08	72 05	84·3	199	341
20	160	19 33	77 15	85·7	19 28	76 12	85·3	19 23	75 08	85·0	19 17	74 05	84·6	19 12	73 02	84·3	19 05	71 59	83·9	200	340
21	159	20 31	77 10	85·4	20 26	76 07	85·1	20 21	75 03	84·7	20 15	73 59	84·3	20 09	72 56	84·0	20 03	71 52	83·6	201	339
22	158	21 30	77 05	85·2	21 24	76 01	84·8	21 19	74 57	84·4	21 13	73 53	84·0	21 06	72 49	83·6	21 00	71 45	83·3	202	338
23	157	22 28	77 00	85·0	22 23	75 55	84·5	22 17	74 51	84·1	22 10	73 46	83·7	22 04	72 42	83·3	21 56	71 38	82·9	203	337
24	156	23 27	76 54	84·7	23 21	75 49	84·3	23 15	74 44	83·9	23 08	73 39	83·4	23 01	72 34	83·0	22 53	71 30	82·6	204	336
25	155	24 25	76 48	84·5	24 19	75 43	84·0	24 13	74 37	83·6	24 06	73 32	83·1	23 58	72 27	82·7	23 50	71 22	82·2	205	335
26	154	25 23	76 42	84·2	25 17	75 36	83·7	25 10	74 30	83·3	25 03	73 24	82·8	24 55	72 18	82·3	24 47	71 13	81·9	206	334
27	153	26 22	76 35	84·0	26 15	75 28	83·5	26 08	74 22	83·0	26 01	73 16	82·5	25 52	72 10	82·0	25 44	71 04	81·5	207	333
28	152	27 20	76 28	83·7	27 13	75 21	83·2	27 06	74 14	82·7	26 58	73 07	82·2	26 50	72 00	81·7	26 41	70 54	81·2	208	332
29	151	28 18	76 20	83·4	28 11	75 13	82·9	28 04	74 05	82·4	27 55	72 58	81·8	27 47	71 51	81·3	27 37	70 44	80·8	209	331
30	150	29 17	76 13	83·2	29 09	75 04	82·6	29 01	73 56	82·0	28 53	72 48	81·5	28 44	71 41	81·0	28 34	70 33	80·4	210	330
31	149	30 15	76 04	82·9	30 07	74 56	82·3	29 59	73 47	81·7	29 50	72 38	81·2	29 41	71 30	80·6	29 30	70 22	80·0	211	329
32	148	31 13	75 56	82·6	31 05	74 46	82·0	30 57	73 37	81·4	30 47	72 28	80·8	30 37	71 19	80·2	30 27	70 11	79·6	212	328
33	147	32 11	75 47	82·3	32 03	74 37	81·7	31 54	73 27	81·1	31 44	72 17	80·5	31 34	71 07	79·9	31 23	69 58	79·2	213	327
34	146	33 10	75 37	82·0	33 01	74 26	81·4	32 52	73 16	80·7	32 42	72 05	80·1	32 31	70 55	79·5	32 20	69 45	78·8	214	326
35	145	34 08	75 27	81·7	33 59	74 16	81·0	33 49	73 04	80·4	33 39	71 53	79·7	33 28	70 42	79·1	33 16	69 32	78·4	215	325
36	144	35 06	75 17	81·4	34 56	74 04	80·7	34 46	72 52	80·0	34 36	71 40	79·4	34 24	70 29	78·7	34 12	69 18	78·0	216	324
37	143	36 04	75 06	81·1	35 54	73 53	80·4	35 44	72 40	79·7	35 33	71 27	79·0	35 21	70 15	78·3	35 08	69 03	77·6	217	323
38	142	37 02	74 54	80·8	36 52	73 40	80·0	36 41	72 27	79·3	36 29	71 13	78·6	36 17	70 00	77·8	36 04	68 48	77·1	218	322
39	141	38 00	74 42	80·4	37 49	73 27	79·7	37 38	72 13	78·9	37 26	70 59	78·2	37 13	69 45	77·4	37 00	68 32	76·7	219	321
40	140	38 57	74 30	80·1	38 47	73 14	79·3	38 35	71 58	78·5	38 23	70 43	77·7	38 10	69 29	77·0	37 56	68 15	76·2	220	320
41	139	39 55	74 16	79·8	39 44	72 59	78·9	39 32	71 43	78·1	39 19	70 27	77·3	39 06	69 12	76·5	38 51	67 57	75·7	221	319
42	138	40 53	74 02	79·4	40 41	72 45	78·5	40 29	71 27	77·7	40 16	70 10	76·9	40 02	68 54	76·1	39 47	67 38	75·3	222	318
43	137	41 51	73 48	79·0	41 39	72 29	78·2	41 26	71 11	77·3	41 12	69 53	76·4	40 58	68 35	75·6	40 42	67 19	74·7	223	317
44	136	42 48	73 32	78·6	42 36	72 12	77·7	42 23	70 53	76·9	42 09	69 34	76·0	41 54	68 16	75·1	41 38	66 58	74·2	224	316
45	135	43 46	73 16	78·3	43 33	71 55	77·3	43 19	70 35	76·4	43 05	69 15	75·5	42 49	67 56	74·6	42 33	66 37	73·7	225	315

Lat. / A		12°			13°			14°			15°			16°			17°			Lat. / A	
LHA/F		A/H	B/P	Z_1/Z_2	A/H	B/P	Z_1/Z_2	A/H	B/P	Z_1/Z_2	A/H	B/P	Z_1/Z_2	A/H	B/P	Z_1/Z_2	A/H	B/P	Z_1/Z_2	LHA	
°	°	° ′	° ′	°	° ′	° ′	°	° ′	° ′	°	° ′	° ′	°	° ′	° ′	°	° ′	° ′	°	°	°
45	135	43 46	73 16	78·3	43 33	71 55	77·3	43 19	70 35	76·4	43 05	69 15	75·5	42 49	67 56	74·6	42 33	66 37	73·7	225	315
46	134	44 43	72 59	77·8	44 30	71 37	76·9	44 16	70 15	75·9	44 01	68 54	75·0	43 45	67 34	74·1	43 28	66 15	73·2	226	314
47	133	45 40	72 41	77·4	45 27	71 18	76·4	45 12	69 55	75·5	44 57	68 33	74·5	44 40	67 12	73·5	44 23	65 51	72·6	227	313
48	132	46 38	72 23	77·0	46 24	70 58	76·0	46 09	69 34	75·0	45 53	68 11	74·0	45 35	66 48	73·0	45 17	65 27	72·0	228	312
49	131	47 35	72 03	76·5	47 20	70 37	75·5	47 05	69 11	74·4	46 48	67 47	73·4	46 30	66 23	72·4	46 12	65 01	71·4	229	311
50	130	48 32	71 42	76·1	48 17	70 15	75·0	48 01	68 48	73·9	47 44	67 22	72·9	47 25	65 58	71·8	47 06	64 34	70·8	230	310
51	129	49 29	71 20	75·6	49 13	69 51	74·5	48 57	68 23	73·4	48 39	66 56	72·3	48 20	65 30	71·2	48 00	64 05	70·1	231	309
52	128	50 25	70 57	75·1	50 09	69 27	73·9	49 52	67 57	72·8	49 34	66 29	71·7	49 15	65 02	70·6	48 54	63 35	69·5	232	308
53	127	51 22	70 33	74·6	51 06	69 01	73·4	50 48	67 30	72·2	50 29	66 00	71·0	50 09	64 31	69·9	49 48	63 04	68·8	233	307
54	126	52 19	70 07	74·0	52 02	68 33	72·8	51 43	67 01	71·6	51 24	65 30	70·4	51 03	64 00	69·2	50 41	62 31	68·1	234	306
55	125	53 15	69 40	73·5	52 57	68 04	72·2	52 38	66 30	70·9	52 18	64 58	69·7	51 57	63 26	68·5	51 34	61 56	67·3	235	305
56	124	54 11	69 11	72·9	53 53	67 34	71·6	53 33	65 58	70·3	53 12	64 24	69·0	52 50	62 51	67·8	52 27	61 20	66·6	236	304
57	123	55 07	68 41	72·2	54 48	67 02	70·9	54 28	65 24	69·6	54 06	63 48	68·3	53 43	62 14	67·0	53 19	60 42	65·8	237	303
58	122	56 03	68 09	71·6	55 43	66 28	70·2	55 22	64 48	68·8	55 00	63 11	67·5	54 36	61 35	66·2	54 12	60 01	64·9	238	302
59	121	56 59	67 34	70·9	56 38	65 51	69·5	56 16	64 10	68·1	55 53	62 31	66·7	55 29	60 54	65·4	55 03	59 18	64·1	239	301
60	120	57 54	66 58	70·2	57 33	65 13	68·7	57 10	63 30	67·3	56 46	61 49	65·9	56 21	60 10	64·5	55 55	58 33	63·1	240	300
61	119	58 49	66 20	69·4	58 27	64 32	67·9	58 04	62 47	66·4	57 39	61 04	65·0	57 13	59 24	63·6	56 46	57 46	62·2	241	299
62	118	59 44	65 38	68·6	59 21	63 49	67·1	58 57	62 02	65·5	58 31	60 17	64·0	58 05	58 35	62·6	57 36	56 56	61·2	242	298
63	117	60 38	64 55	67·8	60 15	63 03	66·2	59 50	61 13	64·6	59 23	59 27	63·1	58 55	57 43	61·6	58 26	56 03	60·2	243	297
64	116	61 32	64 08	66·9	61 08	62 14	65·2	60 42	60 22	63·6	60 15	58 34	62·0	59 46	56 49	60·5	59 16	55 06	59·1	244	296
65	115	62 26	63 18	66·0	62 01	61 21	64·2	61 34	59 28	62·6	61 06	57 37	61·0	60 36	55 51	59·4	60 05	54 07	57·9	245	295
66	114	63 20	62 25	65·0	62 53	60 25	63·2	62 26	58 30	61·5	61 56	56 37	59·8	61 25	54 49	58·2	60 53	53 04	56·7	246	294
67	113	64 13	61 27	63·9	63 45	59 25	62·1	63 16	57 27	60·3	62 46	55 34	58·6	62 14	53 44	57·0	61 41	51 57	55·4	247	293
68	112	65 05	60 26	62·8	64 37	58 21	60·9	64 07	56 21	59·1	63 35	54 25	57·4	63 02	52 34	55·7	62 27	50 47	54·1	248	292
69	111	65 57	59 20	61·6	65 27	57 13	59·6	64 56	55 10	57·8	64 23	53 13	56·0	63 49	51 20	54·3	63 14	49 32	52·7	249	291
70	110	66 48	58 08	60·3	66 18	55 59	58·3	65 45	53 55	56·4	65 11	51 55	54·6	64 36	50 01	52·9	63 59	48 12	51·2	250	290
71	109	67 39	56 52	58·9	67 07	54 40	56·8	66 33	52 33	54·9	65 58	50 33	53·1	65 21	48 38	51·3	64 43	46 48	49·7	251	289
72	108	68 29	55 29	57·4	67 55	53 14	55·3	67 20	51 06	53·3	66 44	49 04	51·5	66 06	47 08	49·7	65 26	45 18	48·0	252	288
73	107	69 18	53 59	55·8	68 43	51 42	53·7	68 07	49 33	51·6	67 29	47 30	49·8	66 49	45 33	48·0	66 08	43 43	46·3	253	287
74	106	70 06	52 22	54·1	69 30	50 03	51·9	68 52	47 52	49·8	68 12	45 49	47·9	67 31	43 52	46·1	66 49	42 02	44·4	254	286
75	105	70 53	50 36	52·2	70 15	48 16	50·0	69 36	46 04	47·9	68 55	44 00	46·0	68 12	42 04	44·2	67 29	40 15	42·5	255	285
76	104	71 38	48 42	50·2	70 59	46 20	47·9	70 18	44 08	45·9	69 36	42 05	43·9	68 52	40 09	42·1	68 07	38 21	40·5	256	284
77	103	72 23	46 37	48·0	71 42	44 15	45·7	70 59	42 03	43·7	70 15	40 01	41·7	69 30	38 07	39·9	68 43	36 21	38·3	257	283
78	102	73 06	44 22	45·6	72 23	42 00	43·4	71 38	39 49	41·3	70 53	37 49	39·4	70 06	35 57	37·6	69 18	34 13	36·0	258	282
79	101	73 47	41 55	43·1	73 02	39 34	40·8	72 16	37 26	38·8	71 28	35 27	36·9	70 40	33 38	35·2	69 50	31 58	33·6	259	281
80	100	74 26	39 15	40·3	73 39	36 57	38·1	72 51	34 51	36·1	72 02	32 57	34·3	71 12	31 12	32·6	70 21	29 36	31·1	260	280
81	99	75 02	36 21	37·3	74 14	34 07	35·1	73 24	32 06	33·2	72 34	30 17	31·5	71 42	28 37	29·9	70 50	27 06	28·4	261	279
82	98	75 37	33 13	34·1	74 46	31 05	32·0	73 55	29 10	30·2	73 03	27 27	28·5	72 09	25 53	27·0	71 16	24 29	25·7	262	278
83	97	76 08	29 50	30·6	75 16	27 50	28·6	74 23	26 03	26·9	73 29	24 27	25·4	72 34	23 02	24·0	71 39	21 44	22·8	263	277
84	96	76 36	26 11	26·8	75 42	24 22	25·0	74 48	22 45	23·5	73 52	21 19	22·1	72 56	20 02	20·9	72 00	18 53	19·8	264	276
85	95	77 01	22 18	22·8	76 05	20 41	21·3	75 09	19 16	19·9	74 12	18 01	18·7	73 15	16 54	17·6	72 18	15 55	16·7	265	275
86	94	77 22	18 10	18·6	76 25	16 49	17·3	75 27	15 38	16·1	74 29	14 36	15·1	73 31	13 40	14·2	72 33	12 51	13·5	266	274
87	93	77 38	13 50	14·1	76 40	12 46	13·1	75 41	11 51	12·2	74 43	11 03	11·4	73 44	10 21	10·8	72 45	9 43	10·2	267	273
88	92	77 50	9 19	9·5	76 51	8 36	8·8	75 52	7 58	8·2	74 52	7 25	7·7	73 53	6 56	7·2	72 53	6 31	6·8	268	272
89	91	77 58	4 42	4·8	76 58	4 19	4·4	75 58	4 00	4·1	74 58	3 44	3·9	73 58	3 29	3·6	72 58	3 16	3·4	269	271
90	90	78 00	0 00	0·0	77 00	0 00	0·0	76 00	0 00	0·0	75 00	0 00	0·0	74 00	0 00	0·0	73 00	0 00	0·0	270	270

N. Lat: for LHA > 180° … $Z_n = Z$
for LHA < 180° … $Z_n = 360° - Z$

S. Lat.: for LHA > 180° … $Z_n = 180° - Z$
for LHA < 180° … $Z_n = 180° + Z$

SIGHT REDUCTION TABLE

B: (−) for 90° < LHA < 270°
Dec:(−) for Lat. contrary name

Z_1: same sign as B
Z_2: (−) for F > 90°

Lat. / A		18°			19°			20°			21°			22°			23°			Lat. / A	
LHA/F		A/H	B/P	Z_1/Z_2	A/H	B/P	Z_1/Z_2	A/H	B/P	Z_1/Z_2	A/H	B/P	Z_1/Z_2	A/H	B/P	Z_1/Z_2	A/H	B/P	Z_1/Z_2	LHA	
°	°	° ′	° ′	°	° ′	° ′	°	° ′	° ′	°	° ′	° ′	°	° ′	° ′	°	° ′	° ′	°	°	°
0	180	0 00	72 00	90·0	0 00	71 00	90·0	0 00	70 00	90·0	0 00	69 00	90·0	0 00	68 00	90·0	0 00	67 00	90·0	180	360
1	179	0 57	72 00	89·7	0 57	71 00	89·7	0 56	70 00	89·7	0 56	69 00	89·6	0 56	68 00	89·6	0 55	67 00	89·6	181	359
2	178	1 54	71 59	89·4	1 53	70 59	89·3	1 53	69 59	89·3	1 52	68 59	89·3	1 51	67 59	89·3	1 50	66 59	89·2	182	358
3	177	2 51	71 59	89·1	2 50	70 59	89·0	2 49	69 58	89·0	2 48	68 58	88·9	2 47	67 58	88·9	2 46	66 58	88·8	183	357
4	176	3 48	71 58	88·8	3 47	70 57	88·7	3 46	69 57	88·6	3 44	68 57	88·6	3 42	67 57	88·5	3 41	66 57	88·4	184	356
5	175	4 45	71 56	88·5	4 44	70 56	88·4	4 42	69 56	88·3	4 40	68 56	88·2	4 38	67 55	88·1	4 36	66 55	88·0	185	355
6	174	5 42	71 54	88·1	5 40	70 54	88·0	5 38	69 54	87·9	5 36	68 54	87·8	5 34	67 53	87·7	5 31	66 53	87·6	186	354
7	173	6 39	71 52	87·8	6 37	70 52	87·7	6 35	69 52	87·6	6 32	68 51	87·5	6 29	67 51	87·4	6 26	66 51	87·3	187	353
8	172	7 36	71 50	87·5	7 34	70 50	87·4	7 31	69 49	87·2	7 28	68 49	87·1	7 25	67 48	87·0	7 22	66 48	86·9	188	352
9	171	8 33	71 47	87·2	8 30	70 47	87·0	8 27	69 46	86·9	8 24	68 46	86·8	8 20	67 45	86·6	8 17	66 45	86·5	189	351
10	170	9 30	71 44	86·9	9 27	70 44	86·7	9 23	69 43	86·5	9 20	68 42	86·4	9 16	67 42	86·2	9 12	66 41	86·1	190	350
11	169	10 27	71 41	86·6	10 24	70 40	86·4	10 20	69 39	86·2	10 16	68 39	86·0	10 11	67 38	85·8	10 07	66 37	85·7	191	349
12	168	11 24	71 37	86·2	11 20	70 36	86·0	11 16	69 35	85·8	11 12	68 34	85·6	11 07	67 33	85·4	11 02	66 32	85·3	192	348
13	167	12 21	71 33	85·9	12 17	70 32	85·7	12 12	69 31	85·5	12 07	68 30	85·3	12 02	67 29	85·1	11 57	66 28	84·8	193	347
14	166	13 18	71 29	85·6	13 13	70 28	85·4	13 08	69 26	85·1	13 03	68 25	84·9	12 58	67 24	84·7	12 52	66 22	84·4	194	346
15	165	14 15	71 24	85·3	14 10	70 23	85·0	14 05	69 21	84·8	13 59	68 20	84·5	13 53	67 18	84·3	13 47	66 17	84·0	195	345
16	164	15 12	71 19	84·9	15 06	70 18	84·7	15 01	69 16	84·4	14 55	68 14	84·1	14 48	67 12	83·9	14 42	66 10	83·6	196	344
17	163	16 09	71 14	84·6	16 03	70 12	84·3	15 57	69 10	84·0	15 50	68 08	83·7	15 44	67 06	83·5	15 37	66 04	83·2	197	343
18	162	17 05	71 08	84·3	16 59	70 06	84·0	16 53	69 03	83·7	16 46	68 01	83·4	16 39	66 59	83·1	16 32	65 57	82·8	198	342
19	161	18 02	71 02	83·9	17 56	69 59	83·6	17 49	68 57	83·3	17 42	67 54	83·0	17 34	66 52	82·7	17 26	65 49	82·3	199	341
20	160	18 59	70 56	83·6	18 52	69 53	83·2	18 45	68 50	82·9	18 37	67 47	82·6	18 29	66 44	82·2	18 21	65 41	81·9	200	340
21	159	19 56	70 49	83·2	19 48	69 45	82·9	19 41	68 42	82·5	19 33	67 39	82·2	19 24	66 36	81·8	19 16	65 33	81·5	201	339
22	158	20 52	70 41	82·9	20 45	69 38	82·5	20 37	68 34	82·1	20 28	67 31	81·8	20 19	66 27	81·4	20 10	65 24	81·0	202	338
23	157	21 49	70 33	82·5	21 41	69 29	82·1	21 32	68 26	81·7	21 24	67 22	81·4	21 14	66 18	81·0	21 05	65 15	80·6	203	337
24	156	22 45	70 25	82·2	22 37	69 21	81·8	22 28	68 17	81·3	22 19	67 12	80·9	22 09	66 09	80·5	21 59	65 05	80·1	204	336
25	155	23 42	70 17	81·8	23 33	69 12	81·4	23 24	68 07	80·9	23 14	67 03	80·5	23 04	65 58	80·1	22 54	64 54	79·7	205	335
26	154	24 38	70 07	81·4	24 29	69 02	81·0	24 20	67 57	80·5	24 09	66 52	80·1	23 59	65 48	79·6	23 48	64 43	79·2	206	334
27	153	25 35	69 58	81·1	25 25	68 52	80·6	25 15	67 47	80·1	25 05	66 42	79·7	24 54	65 36	79·2	24 42	64 32	78·7	207	333
28	152	26 31	69 48	80·7	26 21	68 42	80·2	26 11	67 36	79·7	26 00	66 30	79·2	25 48	65 25	78·7	25 36	64 19	78·3	208	332
29	151	27 27	69 37	80·3	27 17	68 31	79·8	27 06	67 24	79·3	26 55	66 18	78·8	26 43	65 12	78·3	26 30	64 07	77·8	209	331
30	150	28 24	69 26	79·9	28 13	68 19	79·4	28 01	67 12	78·8	27 50	66 06	78·3	27 37	64 59	77·8	27 24	63 53	77·3	210	330
31	149	29 20	69 14	79·5	29 09	68 07	78·9	28 57	67 00	78·4	28 44	65 53	77·8	28 31	64 46	77·3	28 18	63 39	76·8	211	329
32	148	30 16	69 02	79·1	30 04	67 54	78·5	29 52	66 46	77·9	29 39	65 39	77·4	29 26	64 32	76·8	29 12	63 25	76·3	212	328
33	147	31 12	68 49	78·7	31 00	67 41	78·1	30 47	66 32	77·5	30 34	65 24	76·9	30 20	64 17	76·3	30 05	63 09	75·8	213	327
34	146	32 08	68 36	78·2	31 55	67 27	77·6	31 42	66 18	77·0	31 28	65 09	76·4	31 14	64 01	75·8	30 59	62 53	75·2	214	326
35	145	33 04	68 22	77·8	32 51	67 12	77·2	32 37	66 03	76·5	32 23	64 54	75·9	32 08	63 45	75·3	31 52	62 36	74·7	215	325
36	144	33 59	68 07	77·3	33 46	66 57	76·7	33 32	65 47	76·0	33 17	64 37	75·4	33 01	63 28	74·8	32 45	62 19	74·2	216	324
37	143	34 55	67 52	76·9	34 41	66 41	76·2	34 26	65 30	75·5	34 11	64 20	74·9	33 55	63 10	74·2	33 38	62 01	73·6	217	323
38	142	35 50	67 36	76·4	35 36	66 24	75·7	35 21	65 13	75·0	35 05	64 02	74·4	34 48	62 51	73·7	34 31	61 41	73·0	218	322
39	141	36 46	67 19	76·0	36 31	66 06	75·2	36 15	64 54	74·5	35 59	63 43	73·8	35 42	62 32	73·1	35 24	61 21	72·4	219	321
40	140	37 41	67 01	75·5	37 26	65 48	74·7	37 10	64 35	74·0	36 53	63 23	73·3	36 35	62 12	72·6	36 17	61 01	71·8	220	320
41	139	38 36	66 42	75·0	38 20	65 29	74·2	38 04	64 15	73·4	37 46	63 02	72·7	37 28	61 50	72·0	37 09	60 39	71·2	221	319
42	138	39 31	66 23	74·5	39 15	65 08	73·7	38 58	63 54	72·9	38 40	62 41	72·1	38 21	61 28	71·4	38 01	60 16	70·6	222	318
43	137	40 26	66 03	73·9	40 09	64 47	73·1	39 51	63 33	72·3	39 33	62 18	71·5	39 13	61 05	70·7	38 53	59 52	70·0	223	317
44	136	41 21	65 42	73·4	41 03	64 25	72·5	40 45	63 10	71·7	40 26	61 55	70·9	40 06	60 41	70·1	39 45	59 27	69·3	224	316
45	135	42 16	65 19	72·8	41 57	64 02	72·0	41 38	62 46	71·1	41 19	61 30	70·3	40 58	60 15	69·5	40 37	59 01	68·7	225	315

Lat. / A		18°			19°			20°			21°			22°			23°			Lat. / A	
LHA/F		A/H	B/P	Z_1/Z_2	A/H	B/P	Z_1/Z_2	A/H	B/P	Z_1/Z_2	A/H	B/P	Z_1/Z_2	A/H	B/P	Z_1/Z_2	A/H	B/P	Z_1/Z_2	LHA	
°	°	° ′	° ′	°	° ′	° ′	°	° ′	° ′	°	° ′	° ′	°	° ′	° ′	°	° ′	° ′	°	°	°
45	135	42 16	65 19	72·8	41 57	64 02	72·0	41 38	62 46	71·1	41 19	61 30	70·3	40 58	60 15	69·5	40 37	59 01	68·7	225	315
46	134	43 10	64 56	72·3	42 51	63 38	71·4	42 32	62 21	70·5	42 11	61 05	69·6	41 50	59 49	68·8	41 28	58 34	68·0	226	314
47	133	44 04	64 32	71·7	43 45	63 13	70·8	43 25	61 55	69·9	43 04	60 38	69·0	42 42	59 21	68·1	42 19	58 06	67·3	227	313
48	132	44 58	64 06	71·1	44 38	62 46	70·1	44 18	61 27	69·2	43 56	60 09	68·3	43 33	58 53	67·4	43 10	57 37	66·5	228	312
49	131	45 52	63 39	70·4	45 32	62 18	69·5	45 10	60 59	68·5	44 48	59 40	67·6	44 24	58 22	66·7	44 00	57 06	65·8	229	311
50	130	46 46	63 11	69·8	46 25	61 49	68·8	46 03	60 29	67·8	45 39	59 09	66·9	45 15	57 51	65·9	44 50	56 34	65·0	230	310
51	129	47 39	62 42	69·1	47 17	61 19	68·1	46 55	59 57	67·1	46 31	58 37	66·1	46 06	57 18	65·2	45 40	56 00	64·2	231	309
52	128	48 33	62 11	68·4	48 10	60 47	67·4	47 46	59 25	66·4	47 22	58 03	65·4	46 56	56 44	64·4	46 30	55 25	63·4	232	308
53	127	49 25	61 38	67·7	49 02	60 13	66·6	48 38	58 50	65·6	48 13	57 28	64·6	47 46	56 07	63·6	47 19	54 48	62·6	233	307
54	126	50 18	61 04	67·0	49 54	59 38	65·9	49 29	58 14	64·8	49 03	56 51	63·7	48 36	55 30	62·7	48 08	54 10	61·7	234	306
55	125	51 10	60 28	66·2	50 46	59 01	65·1	50 20	57 36	64·0	49 53	56 12	62·9	49 25	54 50	61·9	48 56	53 30	60·8	235	305
56	124	52 03	59 50	65·4	51 37	58 23	64·2	51 10	56 56	63·1	50 43	55 32	62·0	50 14	54 09	61·0	49 44	52 48	59·9	236	304
57	123	52 54	59 11	64·6	52 28	57 42	63·4	52 00	56 15	62·2	51 32	54 49	61·1	51 02	53 26	60·0	50 32	52 04	59·0	237	303
58	122	53 46	58 29	63·7	53 18	56 59	62·5	52 50	55 31	61·3	52 21	54 05	60·2	51 50	52 41	59·1	51 19	51 18	58·0	238	302
59	121	54 37	57 45	62·8	54 08	56 14	61·5	53 39	54 45	60·4	53 09	53 18	59·2	52 38	51 53	58·1	52 06	50 30	57·0	239	301
60	120	55 27	56 59	61·8	54 58	55 27	60·6	54 28	53 57	59·4	53 57	52 29	58·2	53 25	51 04	57·0	52 52	49 40	55·9	240	300
61	119	56 17	56 10	60·9	55 47	54 37	59·6	55 16	53 06	58·3	54 44	51 38	57·1	54 11	50 12	55·9	53 37	48 48	54·8	241	299
62	118	57 07	55 19	59·8	56 36	53 45	58·5	56 04	52 13	57·2	55 31	50 44	56·0	54 57	49 17	54·8	54 22	47 53	53·7	242	298
63	117	57 56	54 25	58·8	57 24	52 49	57·4	56 51	51 17	56·1	56 17	49 47	54·9	55 42	48 20	53·7	55 06	46 55	52·5	243	297
64	116	58 44	53 27	57·6	58 12	51 51	56·3	57 38	50 18	55·0	57 03	48 48	53·7	56 27	47 20	52·5	55 50	45 55	51·3	244	296
65	115	59 32	52 27	56·5	58 58	50 50	55·1	58 24	49 16	53·7	57 47	47 45	52·5	57 10	46 17	51·2	56 32	44 52	50·0	245	295
66	114	60 19	51 23	55·2	59 45	49 45	53·8	59 09	48 11	52·5	58 32	46 39	51·2	57 53	45 11	49·9	57 14	43 47	48·7	246	294
67	113	61 06	50 15	53·9	60 30	48 37	52·5	59 53	47 02	51·1	59 15	45 30	49·8	58 36	44 02	48·6	57 55	42 38	47·4	247	293
68	112	61 52	49 04	52·6	61 15	47 25	51·1	60 36	45 50	49·8	59 57	44 18	48·4	59 17	42 50	47·2	58 36	41 26	46·0	248	292
69	111	62 37	47 48	51·2	61 58	46 09	49·7	61 19	44 33	48·3	60 39	43 02	47·0	59 57	41 34	45·7	59 15	40 10	44·5	249	291
70	110	63 21	46 28	49·7	62 41	44 48	48·2	62 01	43 13	46·8	61 19	41 42	45·4	60 36	40 15	44·2	59 53	38 52	43·0	250	290
71	109	64 04	45 03	48·1	63 23	43 24	46·6	62 41	41 49	45·2	61 58	40 18	43·9	61 15	38 52	42·6	60 30	37 29	41·4	251	289
72	108	64 45	43 34	46·4	64 04	41 54	44·9	63 21	40 20	43·5	62 37	38 50	42·2	61 52	37 25	40·9	61 06	36 03	39·7	252	288
73	107	65 26	41 59	44·7	64 43	40 20	43·2	63 59	38 46	41·8	63 14	37 18	40·5	62 27	35 53	39·2	61 41	34 34	38·0	253	287
74	106	66 06	40 19	42·9	65 21	38 41	41·4	64 36	37 08	40·0	63 49	35 41	38·7	63 02	34 18	37·4	62 14	33 00	36·3	254	286
75	105	66 44	38 32	40·9	65 58	36 56	39·5	65 11	35 25	38·1	64 23	33 59	36·8	63 35	32 39	35·6	62 46	31 22	34·4	255	285
76	104	67 20	36 40	38·9	66 33	35 05	37·4	65 45	33 37	36·1	64 56	32 13	34·8	64 07	30 55	33·6	63 16	29 41	32·5	256	284
77	103	67 55	34 42	36·8	67 07	33 09	35·3	66 18	31 43	34·0	65 27	30 22	32·8	64 37	29 06	31·6	63 45	27 55	30·6	257	283
78	102	68 29	32 37	34·5	67 39	31 07	33·1	66 48	29 44	31·9	65 57	28 26	30·7	65 05	27 14	29·6	64 13	26 06	28·5	258	282
79	101	69 00	30 25	32·2	68 09	29 00	30·8	67 17	27 40	29·6	66 25	26 26	28·5	65 32	25 17	27·4	64 38	24 12	26·4	259	281
80	100	69 29	28 07	29·7	68 37	26 46	28·4	67 44	25 30	27·3	66 50	24 20	26·2	65 56	23 15	25·2	65 02	22 15	24·3	260	280
81	99	69 57	25 43	27·1	69 03	24 26	25·9	68 09	23 15	24·8	67 14	22 10	23·8	66 19	21 10	22·9	65 23	20 14	22·1	261	279
82	98	70 21	23 11	24·5	69 27	22 00	23·3	68 31	20 56	22·3	67 36	19 56	21·4	66 40	19 00	20·6	65 43	18 09	19·8	262	278
83	97	70 44	20 34	21·7	69 48	19 29	20·7	68 51	18 31	19·7	67 55	17 37	18·9	66 58	16 47	18·1	66 01	16 01	17·4	263	277
84	96	71 03	17 50	18·8	70 07	16 53	17·9	69 09	16 01	17·1	68 12	15 14	16·3	67 14	14 30	15·7	66 16	13 50	15·1	264	276
85	95	71 20	15 01	15·8	70 23	14 12	15·0	69 25	13 28	14·3	68 26	12 48	13·7	67 28	12 10	13·1	66 29	11 36	12·6	265	275
86	94	71 35	12 07	12·8	70 36	11 27	12·1	69 37	10 51	11·6	68 38	10 18	11·0	67 39	9 48	10·6	66 40	9 20	10·1	266	274
87	93	71 46	9 09	9·6	70 46	8 39	9·1	69 47	8 11	8·7	68 48	7 46	8·3	67 48	7 23	8·0	66 49	7 02	7·6	267	273
88	92	71 54	6 08	6·4	70 54	5 47	6·1	69 54	5 29	5·8	68 55	5 12	5·6	67 55	4 56	5·3	66 55	4 42	5·1	268	272
89	91	71 58	3 04	3·2	70 58	2 54	3·1	69 59	2 45	2·9	68 59	2 36	2·8	67 59	2 28	2·7	66 59	2 21	2·6	269	271
90	90	72 00	0 00	0·0	71 00	0 00	0·0	70 00	0 00	0·0	69 00	0 00	0·0	68 00	0 00	0·0	67 00	0 00	0·0	270	270

N. Lat: for LHA > 180° … $Z_n = Z$
for LHA < 180° … $Z_n = 360° - Z$

S. Lat.: for LHA > 180° … $Z_n = 180° - Z$
for LHA < 180° … $Z_n = 180° + Z$

SIGHT REDUCTION TABLE

B: (–) for 90° < LHA < 270°
Dec:(–) for Lat. contrary name

Z_1: same sign as B
Z_2: (–) for F > 90°

Lat. / A		24°			25°			26°			27°			28°			29°			Lat. / A	
LHA/F		A/H	B/P	Z_1/Z_2	A/H	B/P	Z_1/Z_2	A/H	B/P	Z_1/Z_2	A/H	B/P	Z_1/Z_2	A/H	B/P	Z_1/Z_2	A/H	B/P	Z_1/Z_2	LHA	
°	°	° ′	° ′	°	° ′	° ′	°	° ′	° ′	°	° ′	° ′	°	° ′	° ′	°	° ′	° ′	°	°	°
0	180	0 00	66 00	90·0	0 00	65 00	90·0	0 00	64 00	90·0	0 00	63 00	90·0	0 00	62 00	90·0	0 00	61 00	90·0	180	360
1	179	0 55	66 00	89·6	0 54	65 00	89·6	0 54	64 00	89·6	0 53	63 00	89·5	0 53	62 00	89·5	0 52	61 00	89·5	181	359
2	178	1 50	65 59	89·2	1 49	64 59	89·2	1 48	63 59	89·1	1 47	62 59	89·1	1 46	61 59	89·1	1 45	60 59	89·0	182	358
3	177	2 44	65 58	88·8	2 43	64 58	88·7	2 42	63 58	88·7	2 40	62 58	88·6	2 39	61 58	88·6	2 37	60 58	88·5	183	357
4	176	3 39	65 57	88·4	3 37	64 57	88·3	3 36	63 57	88·2	3 34	62 57	88·2	3 32	61 57	88·1	3 30	60 56	88·1	184	356
5	175	4 34	65 55	88·0	4 32	64 55	87·9	4 30	63 55	87·8	4 27	62 55	87·7	4 25	61 55	87·6	4 22	60 54	87·6	185	355
6	174	5 29	65 53	87·6	5 26	64 53	87·5	5 23	63 53	87·4	5 21	62 52	87·3	5 18	61 52	87·2	5 15	60 52	87·1	186	354
7	173	6 24	65 50	87·1	6 20	64 50	87·0	6 17	63 50	86·9	6 14	62 50	86·8	6 11	61 49	86·7	6 07	60 49	86·6	187	353
8	172	7 18	65 47	86·7	7 15	64 47	86·6	7 11	63 47	86·5	7 07	62 46	86·3	7 04	61 46	86·2	6 59	60 46	86·1	188	352
9	171	8 13	65 44	86·3	8 09	64 44	86·2	8 05	63 43	86·0	8 01	62 43	85·9	7 56	61 42	85·7	7 52	60 42	85·6	189	351
10	170	9 08	65 40	85·9	9 03	64 40	85·7	8 59	63 39	85·6	8 54	62 39	85·4	8 49	61 38	85·3	8 44	60 38	85·1	190	350
11	169	10 02	65 36	85·5	9 57	64 35	85·3	9 52	63 35	85·1	9 47	62 34	85·0	9 42	61 33	84·8	9 36	60 33	84·6	191	349
12	168	10 57	65 32	85·1	10 52	64 31	84·9	10 46	63 30	84·7	10 41	62 29	84·5	10 35	61 28	84·3	10 29	60 28	84·1	192	348
13	167	11 52	65 27	84·6	11 46	64 26	84·4	11 40	63 25	84·2	11 34	62 24	84·0	11 27	61 23	83·8	11 21	60 22	83·6	193	347
14	166	12 46	65 21	84·2	12 40	64 20	84·0	12 34	63 19	83·8	12 27	62 18	83·5	12 20	61 17	83·3	12 13	60 16	83·1	194	346
15	165	13 41	65 15	83·8	13 34	64 14	83·5	13 27	63 13	83·3	13 20	62 11	83·1	13 13	61 10	82·8	13 05	60 09	82·6	195	345
16	164	14 35	65 09	83·3	14 28	64 07	83·1	14 21	63 06	82·8	14 13	62 04	82·6	14 05	61 03	82·3	13 57	60 02	82·1	196	344
17	163	15 29	65 02	82·9	15 22	64 00	82·6	15 14	62 59	82·4	15 06	61 57	82·1	14 58	60 56	81·8	14 49	59 54	81·6	197	343
18	162	16 24	64 55	82·5	16 16	63 53	82·2	16 08	62 51	81·9	15 59	61 49	81·6	15 50	60 47	81·3	15 41	59 46	81·0	198	342
19	161	17 18	64 47	82·0	17 10	63 45	81·7	17 01	62 43	81·4	16 52	61 41	81·1	16 42	60 39	80·8	16 33	59 37	80·5	199	341
20	160	18 12	64 39	81·6	18 03	63 36	81·3	17 54	62 34	80·9	17 45	61 32	80·6	17 35	60 30	80·3	17 24	59 28	80·0	200	340
21	159	19 07	64 30	81·1	18 57	63 28	80·8	18 47	62 25	80·4	18 37	61 23	80·1	18 27	60 20	79·8	18 16	59 18	79·5	201	339
22	158	20 01	64 21	80·7	19 51	63 18	80·3	19 41	62 15	80·0	19 30	61 13	79·6	19 19	60 10	79·3	19 08	59 08	78·9	202	338
23	157	20 55	64 11	80·2	20 44	63 08	79·8	20 34	62 05	79·5	20 22	61 02	79·1	20 11	59 59	78·7	19 59	58 57	78·4	203	337
24	156	21 49	64 01	79·7	21 38	62 58	79·3	21 27	61 54	79·0	21 15	60 51	78·6	21 03	59 48	78·2	20 50	58 45	77·8	204	336
25	155	22 43	63 50	79·3	22 31	62 46	78·9	22 19	61 43	78·4	22 07	60 39	78·0	21 55	59 36	77·7	21 42	58 33	77·3	205	335
26	154	23 36	63 39	78·8	23 25	62 35	78·4	23 12	61 31	77·9	22 59	60 27	77·5	22 46	59 24	77·1	22 33	58 20	76·7	206	334
27	153	24 30	63 27	78·3	24 18	62 22	77·8	24 05	61 18	77·4	23 52	60 14	77·0	23 38	59 10	76·5	23 24	58 07	76·1	207	333
28	152	25 24	63 14	77·8	25 11	62 10	77·3	24 57	61 05	76·9	24 44	60 01	76·4	24 29	58 57	76·0	24 15	57 53	75·5	208	332
29	151	26 17	63 01	77·3	26 04	61 56	76·8	25 50	60 51	76·3	25 36	59 47	75·9	25 21	58 42	75·4	25 05	57 38	75·0	209	331
30	150	27 11	62 48	76·8	26 57	61 42	76·3	26 42	60 37	75·8	26 27	59 32	75·3	26 12	58 27	74·8	25 56	57 23	74·4	210	330
31	149	28 04	62 33	76·3	27 50	61 27	75·8	27 35	60 22	75·2	27 19	59 16	74·7	27 03	58 11	74·2	26 46	57 07	73·8	211	329
32	148	28 57	62 18	75·7	28 42	61 12	75·2	28 27	60 06	74·7	28 10	59 00	74·2	27 54	57 55	73·7	27 37	56 50	73·1	212	328
33	147	29 50	62 02	75·2	29 35	60 56	74·7	29 19	59 49	74·1	29 02	58 43	73·6	28 45	57 38	73·0	28 27	56 32	72·5	213	327
34	146	30 43	61 46	74·7	30 27	60 39	74·1	30 10	59 32	73·5	29 53	58 26	73·0	29 35	57 20	72·4	29 17	56 14	71·9	214	326
35	145	31 36	61 28	74·1	31 19	60 21	73·5	31 02	59 14	72·9	30 44	58 07	72·4	30 26	57 01	71·8	30 07	55 55	71·2	215	325
36	144	32 29	61 10	73·5	32 11	60 02	72·9	31 53	58 55	72·3	31 35	57 48	71·7	31 16	56 41	71·2	30 56	55 35	70·6	216	324
37	143	33 21	60 52	73·0	33 03	59 43	72·3	32 45	58 35	71·7	32 26	57 28	71·1	32 06	56 21	70·5	31 46	55 14	69·9	217	323
38	142	34 13	60 32	72·4	33 55	59 23	71·7	33 36	58 15	71·1	33 16	57 07	70·5	32 56	55 59	69·9	32 35	54 53	69·3	218	322
39	141	35 06	60 11	71·8	34 47	59 02	71·1	34 27	57 53	70·5	34 06	56 45	69·8	33 45	55 37	69·2	33 24	54 30	68·6	219	321
40	140	35 58	59 50	71·2	35 38	58 40	70·5	35 17	57 31	69·8	34 56	56 22	69·1	34 35	55 14	68·5	34 12	54 07	67·9	220	320
41	139	36 49	59 28	70·5	36 29	58 17	69·8	36 08	57 08	69·1	35 46	55 59	68·5	35 24	54 50	67·8	35 01	53 42	67·1	221	319
42	138	37 41	59 04	69·9	37 20	57 54	69·2	36 58	56 43	68·5	36 36	55 34	67·8	36 13	54 25	67·1	35 49	53 17	66·4	222	318
43	137	38 32	58 40	69·2	38 11	57 29	68·5	37 48	56 18	67·8	37 25	55 08	67·1	37 02	53 59	66·4	36 37	52 50	65·7	223	317
44	136	39 23	58 15	68·6	39 01	57 03	67·8	38 38	55 52	67·1	38 14	54 41	66·3	37 50	53 32	65·6	37 25	52 23	64·9	224	316
45	135	40 14	57 48	67·9	39 51	56 36	67·1	39 28	55 24	66·3	39 03	54 13	65·6	38 38	53 04	64·9	38 12	51 54	64·1	225	315

Lat. / A		24°			25°			26°			27°			28°			29°			Lat. / A	
LHA/F		A/H	B/P	Z_1/Z_2	A/H	B/P	Z_1/Z_2	A/H	B/P	Z_1/Z_2	A/H	B/P	Z_1/Z_2	A/H	B/P	Z_1/Z_2	A/H	B/P	Z_1/Z_2	LHA	
°	°	° ′	° ′	°	° ′	° ′	°	° ′	° ′	°	° ′	° ′	°	° ′	° ′	°	° ′	° ′	°	°	°
45	135	40 14	57 48	67·9	39 51	56 36	67·1	39 28	55 24	66·3	39 03	54 13	65·6	38 38	53 04	64·9	38 12	51 54	64·1	225	315
46	134	41 05	57 21	67·2	40 41	56 08	66·4	40 17	54 56	65·6	39 52	53 44	64·8	39 26	52 34	64·1	38 59	51 25	63·3	226	314
47	133	41 55	56 52	66·4	41 31	55 38	65·6	41 06	54 26	64·8	40 40	53 14	64·0	40 13	52 04	63·3	39 46	50 54	62·5	227	313
48	132	42 45	56 22	65·7	42 20	55 08	64·9	41 54	53 55	64·0	41 28	52 43	63·2	41 00	51 32	62·5	40 32	50 22	61·7	228	312
49	131	43 35	55 50	64·9	43 09	54 36	64·1	42 43	53 22	63·2	42 15	52 10	62·4	41 47	50 59	61·6	41 18	49 48	60·9	229	311
50	130	44 25	55 17	64·1	43 58	54 02	63·3	43 31	52 49	62·4	43 03	51 36	61·6	42 34	50 24	60·8	42 04	49 14	60·0	230	310
51	129	45 14	54 43	63·3	44 47	53 28	62·4	44 18	52 13	61·6	43 49	51 00	60·7	43 20	49 48	59·9	42 49	48 38	59·1	231	309
52	128	46 03	54 08	62·5	45 35	52 52	61·6	45 06	51 37	60·7	44 36	50 23	59·8	44 05	49 11	59·0	43 34	48 00	58·2	232	308
53	127	46 51	53 30	61·6	46 22	52 14	60·7	45 52	50 59	59·8	45 22	49 45	58·9	44 51	48 32	58·1	44 18	47 21	57·2	233	307
54	126	47 39	52 51	60·8	47 09	51 34	59·8	46 39	50 19	58·9	46 07	49 05	58·0	45 35	47 52	57·1	45 02	46 41	56·3	234	306
55	125	48 27	52 11	59·8	47 56	50 53	58·9	47 25	49 37	58·0	46 53	48 23	57·0	46 19	47 10	56·2	45 46	45 59	55·3	235	305
56	124	49 14	51 28	58·9	48 43	50 11	57·9	48 10	48 54	57·0	47 37	47 40	56·1	47 03	46 27	55·2	46 29	45 15	54·3	236	304
57	123	50 01	50 44	57·9	49 28	49 26	56·9	48 55	48 09	56·0	48 21	46 54	55·0	47 46	45 41	54·1	47 11	44 30	53·3	237	303
58	122	50 47	49 58	56·9	50 14	48 39	55·9	49 40	47 22	54·9	49 05	46 07	54·0	48 29	44 54	53·1	47 53	43 43	52·2	238	302
59	121	51 33	49 09	55·9	50 58	47 51	54·9	50 23	46 34	53·9	49 48	45 18	52·9	49 11	44 05	52·0	48 34	42 54	51·1	239	301
60	120	52 18	48 19	54·8	51 43	47 00	53·8	51 07	45 43	52·8	50 30	44 28	51·8	49 53	43 14	50·9	49 14	42 03	50·0	240	300
61	119	53 02	47 26	53·7	52 26	46 07	52·7	51 49	44 50	51·7	51 12	43 35	50·7	50 33	42 22	49·7	49 54	41 10	48·8	241	299
62	118	53 46	46 31	52·6	53 09	45 12	51·5	52 31	43 54	50·5	51 53	42 39	49·5	51 13	41 27	48·6	50 33	40 16	47·6	242	298
63	117	54 29	45 33	51·4	53 51	44 14	50·3	53 13	42 57	49·3	52 33	41 42	48·3	51 53	40 30	47·3	51 12	39 19	46·4	243	297
64	116	55 12	44 33	50·2	54 33	43 14	49·1	53 53	41 57	48·1	53 13	40 42	47·1	52 31	39 30	46·1	51 49	38 20	45·2	244	296
65	115	55 53	43 30	48·9	55 13	42 11	47·8	54 33	40 55	46·8	53 51	39 40	45·8	53 09	38 29	44·8	52 26	37 19	43·9	245	295
66	114	56 34	42 25	47·6	55 53	41 06	46·5	55 12	39 50	45·4	54 29	38 36	44·4	53 46	37 25	43·5	53 02	36 16	42·6	246	294
67	113	57 14	41 16	46·2	56 32	39 58	45·1	55 50	38 42	44·1	55 06	37 29	43·1	54 22	36 19	42·1	53 37	35 11	41·2	247	293
68	112	57 53	40 05	44·8	57 10	38 47	43·7	56 27	37 32	42·7	55 42	36 19	41·7	54 57	35 10	40·7	54 11	34 03	39·8	248	292
69	111	58 32	38 50	43·3	57 47	37 33	42·2	57 03	36 18	41·2	56 17	35 07	40·2	55 31	33 59	39·3	54 44	32 53	38·4	249	291
70	110	59 09	37 32	41·8	58 24	36 16	40·7	57 38	35 02	39·7	56 51	33 52	38·7	56 04	32 45	37·8	55 16	31 41	36·9	250	290
71	109	59 45	36 11	40·2	58 58	34 55	39·2	58 12	33 43	38·1	57 24	32 35	37·2	56 36	31 29	36·3	55 47	30 26	35·4	251	289
72	108	60 19	34 46	38·6	59 32	33 32	37·6	58 44	32 21	36·5	57 56	31 14	35·6	57 07	30 10	34·7	56 17	29 08	33·8	252	288
73	107	60 53	33 18	36·9	60 05	32 05	35·9	59 16	30 56	34·9	58 26	29 51	34·0	57 36	28 48	33·1	56 46	27 49	32·2	253	287
74	106	61 25	31 46	35·2	60 36	30 35	34·2	59 46	29 28	33·2	58 55	28 25	32·3	58 05	27 24	31·4	57 13	26 26	30·6	254	286
75	105	61 56	30 10	33·4	61 06	29 02	32·4	60 15	27 57	31·4	59 23	26 56	30·5	58 31	25 57	29·7	57 39	25 02	28·9	255	285
76	104	62 26	28 31	31·5	61 34	27 25	30·5	60 42	26 23	29·6	59 50	25 24	28·8	58 57	24 28	28·0	58 04	23 35	27·2	256	284
77	103	62 53	26 48	29·6	62 01	25 45	28·6	61 08	24 46	27·8	60 15	23 49	27·0	59 21	22 56	26·2	58 27	22 05	25·5	257	283
78	102	63 20	25 02	27·6	62 26	24 02	26·7	61 32	23 05	25·9	60 38	22 12	25·1	59 44	21 21	24·4	58 49	20 34	23·7	258	282
79	101	63 44	23 12	25·5	62 50	22 15	24·7	61 55	21 22	23·9	61 00	20 32	23·2	60 05	19 44	22·5	59 09	19 00	21·8	259	281
80	100	64 07	21 18	23·4	63 12	20 25	22·6	62 16	19 36	21·9	61 20	18 49	21·2	60 24	18 05	20·6	59 28	17 24	20·0	260	280
81	99	64 28	19 22	21·3	63 32	18 33	20·5	62 35	17 47	19·9	61 39	17 04	19·2	60 42	16 24	18·6	59 45	15 46	18·1	261	279
82	98	64 47	17 22	19·1	63 50	16 37	18·4	62 53	15 56	17·8	61 56	15 17	17·2	60 58	14 40	16·7	60 01	14 06	16·2	262	278
83	97	65 03	15 18	16·8	64 06	14 39	16·2	63 08	14 02	15·6	62 10	13 27	15·1	61 12	12 55	14·7	60 14	12 24	14·2	263	277
84	96	65 18	13 13	14·5	64 20	12 38	14·0	63 22	12 06	13·5	62 23	11 36	13·0	61 25	11 07	12·6	60 26	10 41	12·2	264	276
85	95	65 31	11 05	12·1	64 32	10 35	11·7	63 33	10 08	11·3	62 35	9 42	10·9	61 36	9 19	10·6	60 37	8 56	10·2	265	275
86	94	65 41	8 54	9·8	64 42	8 30	9·4	63 43	8 08	9·1	62 44	7 48	8·8	61 44	7 28	8·5	60 45	7 10	8·2	266	274
87	93	65 49	6 42	7·3	64 50	6 24	7·1	63 50	6 07	6·8	62 51	5 52	6·6	61 51	5 37	6·4	60 52	5 24	6·2	267	273
88	92	65 55	4 29	4·9	64 56	4 17	4·7	63 56	4 06	4·6	62 56	3 55	4·4	61 56	3 45	4·3	60 56	3 36	4·1	268	272
89	91	65 59	2 15	2·5	64 59	2 09	2·4	63 59	2 03	2·3	62 59	1 58	2·2	61 59	1 53	2·1	60 59	1 48	2·1	269	271
90	90	66 00	0 00	0·0	65 00	0 00	0·0	64 00	0 00	0·0	63 00	0 00	0·0	62 00	0 00	0·0	61 00	0 00	0·0	270	270

N. Lat: for LHA > 180° … $Z_n = Z$
for LHA < 180° … $Z_n = 360° - Z$

S. Lat.: for LHA > 180° … $Z_n = 180° - Z$
for LHA < 180° … $Z_n = 180° + Z$

SIGHT REDUCTION TABLE

B: (−) for 90° < LHA < 270°
Dec:(−) for Lat. contrary name

Z_1: same sign as B
Z_2: (−) for F > 90°

Lat. / A		30°			31°			32°			33°			34°			35°			Lat. / A	
LHA/F		A/H	B/P	Z_1/Z_2	A/H	B/P	Z_1/Z_2	A/H	B/P	Z_1/Z_2	A/H	B/P	Z_1/Z_2	A/H	B/P	Z_1/Z_2	A/H	B/P	Z_1/Z_2	LHA	
°	°	° ′	° ′	°	° ′	° ′	°	° ′	° ′	°	° ′	° ′	°	° ′	° ′	°	° ′	° ′	°	°	°
0	180	0 00	60 00	90·0	0 00	59 00	90·0	0 00	58 00	90·0	0 00	57 00	90·0	0 00	56 00	90·0	0 00	55 00	90·0	180	360
1	179	0 52	60 00	89·5	0 51	59 00	89·5	0 51	58 00	89·5	0 50	57 00	89·5	0 50	56 00	89·4	0 49	55 00	89·4	181	359
2	178	1 44	59 59	89·0	1 43	58 59	89·0	1 42	57 59	88·9	1 41	56 59	88·9	1 39	55 59	88·9	1 38	54 59	88·9	182	358
3	177	2 36	59 58	88·5	2 34	58 58	88·5	2 33	57 58	88·4	2 31	56 58	88·4	2 29	55 58	88·3	2 27	54 58	88·3	183	357
4	176	3 28	59 56	88·0	3 26	58 56	87·9	3 23	57 56	87·9	3 21	56 56	87·8	3 19	55 56	87·8	3 17	54 56	87·7	184	356
5	175	4 20	59 54	87·5	4 17	58 54	87·4	4 14	57 54	87·3	4 12	56 54	87·3	4 09	55 54	87·2	4 06	54 54	87·1	185	355
6	174	5 12	59 52	87·0	5 08	58 52	86·9	5 05	57 52	86·8	5 02	56 51	86·7	4 58	55 51	86·6	4 55	54 51	86·6	186	354
7	173	6 04	59 49	86·5	6 00	58 49	86·4	5 56	57 48	86·3	5 52	56 48	86·2	5 48	55 48	86·1	5 44	54 48	86·0	187	353
8	172	6 55	59 45	86·0	6 51	58 45	85·9	6 47	57 45	85·7	6 42	56 45	85·6	6 38	55 44	85·5	6 33	54 44	85·4	188	352
9	171	7 47	59 42	85·5	7 42	58 41	85·3	7 37	57 41	85·2	7 32	56 40	85·1	7 27	55 40	84·9	7 22	54 40	84·8	189	351
10	170	8 39	59 37	85·0	8 34	58 37	84·8	8 28	57 36	84·7	8 22	56 36	84·5	8 17	55 36	84·4	8 11	54 35	84·2	190	350
11	169	9 31	59 32	84·4	9 25	58 32	84·3	9 19	57 31	84·1	9 13	56 31	84·0	9 06	55 30	83·8	9 00	54 30	83·6	191	349
12	168	10 22	59 27	83·9	10 16	58 26	83·8	10 09	57 26	83·6	10 03	56 25	83·4	9 56	55 25	83·2	9 48	54 24	83·0	192	348
13	167	11 14	59 21	83·4	11 07	58 20	83·2	11 00	57 20	83·0	10 52	56 19	82·8	10 45	55 18	82·6	10 37	54 18	82·5	193	347
14	166	12 06	59 15	82·9	11 58	58 14	82·7	11 50	57 13	82·5	11 42	56 12	82·3	11 34	55 12	82·1	11 26	54 11	81·9	194	346
15	165	12 57	59 08	82·4	12 49	58 07	82·1	12 41	57 06	81·9	12 32	56 05	81·7	12 23	55 04	81·5	12 14	54 04	81·3	195	345
16	164	13 49	59 01	81·8	13 40	57 59	81·6	13 31	56 58	81·4	13 22	55 57	81·1	13 13	54 57	80·9	13 03	53 56	80·7	196	344
17	163	14 40	58 53	81·3	14 31	57 51	81·1	14 21	56 50	80·8	14 12	55 49	80·5	14 02	54 48	80·3	13 51	53 47	80·1	197	343
18	162	15 31	58 44	80·8	15 22	57 43	80·5	15 12	56 42	80·2	15 01	55 40	80·0	14 51	54 39	79·7	14 40	53 38	79·4	198	342
19	161	16 23	58 35	80·2	16 12	57 34	79·9	16 02	56 32	79·7	15 51	55 31	79·4	15 40	54 30	79·1	15 28	53 29	78·8	199	341
20	160	17 14	58 26	79·7	17 03	57 24	79·4	16 52	56 23	79·1	16 40	55 21	78·8	16 28	54 20	78·5	16 16	53 19	78·2	200	340
21	159	18 05	58 16	79·1	17 53	57 14	78·8	17 42	56 12	78·5	17 29	55 11	78·2	17 17	54 09	77·9	17 04	53 08	77·6	201	339
22	158	18 56	58 05	78·6	18 44	57 03	78·2	18 31	56 01	77·9	18 19	55 00	77·6	18 06	53 58	77·3	17 52	52 56	77·0	202	338
23	157	19 47	57 54	78·0	19 34	56 52	77·7	19 21	55 50	77·3	19 08	54 48	77·0	18 54	53 46	76·6	18 40	52 44	76·3	203	337
24	156	20 37	57 42	77·4	20 24	56 40	77·1	20 11	55 38	76·7	19 57	54 36	76·4	19 42	53 34	76·0	19 28	52 32	75·7	204	336
25	155	21 28	57 30	76·9	21 14	56 27	76·5	21 00	55 25	76·1	20 46	54 23	75·7	20 31	53 21	75·4	20 15	52 19	75·0	205	335
26	154	22 19	57 17	76·3	22 04	56 14	75·9	21 49	55 12	75·5	21 34	54 09	75·1	21 19	53 07	74·7	21 03	52 05	74·4	206	334
27	153	23 09	57 03	75·7	22 54	56 00	75·3	22 39	54 57	74·9	22 23	53 55	74·5	22 07	52 52	74·1	21 50	51 50	73·7	207	333
28	152	23 59	56 49	75·1	23 44	55 46	74·7	23 28	54 43	74·3	23 11	53 40	73·8	22 54	52 37	73·4	22 37	51 35	73·0	208	332
29	151	24 50	56 34	74·5	24 33	55 31	74·1	24 17	54 27	73·6	23 59	53 24	73·2	23 42	52 22	72·8	23 24	51 19	72·4	209	331
30	150	25 40	56 19	73·9	25 23	55 15	73·4	25 05	54 11	73·0	24 48	53 08	72·5	24 29	52 05	72·1	24 11	51 03	71·7	210	330
31	149	26 29	56 02	73·3	26 12	54 58	72·8	25 54	53 54	72·3	25 35	52 51	71·9	25 17	51 48	71·4	24 57	50 45	71·0	211	329
32	148	27 19	55 45	72·6	27 01	54 41	72·2	26 42	53 37	71·7	26 23	52 33	71·2	26 04	51 30	70·7	25 44	50 27	70·3	212	328
33	147	28 09	55 27	72·0	27 50	54 23	71·5	27 31	53 19	71·0	27 11	52 15	70·5	26 50	51 12	70·0	26 30	50 08	69·6	213	327
34	146	28 58	55 09	71·4	28 38	54 04	70·8	28 19	53 00	70·3	27 58	51 56	69·8	27 37	50 52	69·3	27 16	49 49	68·8	214	326
35	145	29 47	54 49	70·7	29 27	53 44	70·2	29 06	52 40	69·6	28 45	51 36	69·1	28 24	50 32	68·6	28 01	49 29	68·1	215	325
36	144	30 36	54 29	70·0	30 15	53 24	69·5	29 54	52 19	68·9	29 32	51 15	68·4	29 10	50 11	67·9	28 47	49 07	67·4	216	324
37	143	31 25	54 08	69·4	31 03	53 03	68·8	30 41	51 58	68·2	30 19	50 53	67·7	29 56	49 49	67·2	29 32	48 45	66·6	217	323
38	142	32 13	53 46	68·7	31 51	52 40	68·1	31 28	51 35	67·5	31 05	50 30	66·9	30 41	49 26	66·4	30 17	48 23	65·9	218	322
39	141	33 02	53 23	68·0	32 39	52 17	67·4	32 15	51 12	66·8	31 51	50 07	66·2	31 27	49 03	65·6	31 02	47 59	65·1	219	321
40	140	33 50	53 00	67·2	33 26	51 53	66·6	33 02	50 48	66·0	32 37	49 43	65·4	32 12	48 38	64·9	31 46	47 34	64·3	220	320
41	139	34 37	52 35	66·5	34 13	51 29	65·9	33 48	50 23	65·3	33 23	49 17	64·7	32 57	48 13	64·1	32 30	47 09	63·5	221	319
42	138	35 25	52 09	65·8	35 00	51 03	65·1	34 34	49 56	64·5	34 08	48 51	63·9	33 42	47 46	63·3	33 14	46 42	62·7	222	318
43	137	36 12	51 43	65·0	35 46	50 36	64·3	35 20	49 29	63·7	34 53	48 24	63·1	34 26	47 19	62·5	33 58	46 15	61·9	223	317
44	136	36 59	51 15	64·2	36 33	50 08	63·6	36 06	49 01	62·9	35 38	47 55	62·3	35 10	46 51	61·6	34 41	45 46	61·0	224	316
45	135	37 46	50 46	63·4	37 19	49 39	62·7	36 51	48 32	62·1	36 22	47 26	61·4	35 53	46 21	60·8	35 24	45 17	60·2	225	315

Lat. / A		30°			31°			32°			33°			34°			35°			Lat. / A	
LHA/F		A/H	B/P	Z1/Z2	A/H	B/P	Z1/Z2	A/H	B/P	Z1/Z2	A/H	B/P	Z1/Z2	A/H	B/P	Z1/Z2	A/H	B/P	Z1/Z2	LHA	
°	°	° ′	° ′	°	° ′	° ′	°	° ′	° ′	°	° ′	° ′	°	° ′	° ′	°	° ′	° ′	°	°	°
45	135	37 46	50 46	63·4	37 19	49 39	62·7	36 51	48 32	62·1	36 22	47 26	61·4	35 53	46 21	60·8	35 24	45 17	60·2	225	315
46	134	38 32	50 16	62·6	38 04	49 08	61·9	37 36	48 02	61·2	37 06	46 56	60·6	36 37	45 51	59·9	36 06	44 46	59·3	226	314
47	133	39 18	49 45	61·8	38 49	48 37	61·1	38 20	47 30	60·4	37 50	46 24	59·7	37 19	45 19	59·1	36 48	44 15	58·4	227	313
48	132	40 04	49 13	61·0	39 34	48 05	60·2	39 04	46 58	59·5	38 33	45 51	58·8	38 02	44 46	58·2	37 30	43 42	57·5	228	312
49	131	40 49	48 39	60·1	40 19	47 31	59·4	39 48	46 24	58·6	39 16	45 18	57·9	38 44	44 12	57·2	38 11	43 08	56·6	229	311
50	130	41 34	48 04	59·2	41 03	46 56	58·5	40 31	45 49	57·7	39 59	44 42	57·0	39 26	43 37	56·3	38 52	42 33	55·6	230	310
51	129	42 18	47 28	58·3	41 46	46 20	57·5	41 14	45 12	56·8	40 41	44 06	56·1	40 07	43 01	55·4	39 32	41 57	54·7	231	309
52	128	43 02	46 50	57·4	42 29	45 42	56·6	41 56	44 34	55·9	41 22	43 28	55·1	40 47	42 23	54·4	40 12	41 19	53·7	232	308
53	127	43 46	46 11	56·4	43 12	45 03	55·6	42 38	43 55	54·9	42 03	42 49	54·1	41 28	41 44	53·4	40 52	40 41	52·7	233	307
54	126	44 29	45 31	55·5	43 54	44 22	54·7	43 19	43 15	53·9	42 44	42 09	53·1	42 07	41 04	52·4	41 30	40 01	51·7	234	306
55	125	45 11	44 49	54·5	44 36	43 40	53·7	44 00	42 33	52·9	43 24	41 27	52·1	42 46	40 23	51·4	42 09	39 19	50·7	235	305
56	124	45 53	44 05	53·5	45 17	42 57	52·6	44 40	41 50	51·8	44 03	40 44	51·1	43 25	39 40	50·3	42 46	38 37	49·6	236	304
57	123	46 35	43 20	52·4	45 58	42 11	51·6	45 20	41 05	50·8	44 42	39 59	50·0	44 03	38 55	49·3	43 24	37 53	48·5	237	303
58	122	47 16	42 33	51·3	46 38	41 25	50·5	45 59	40 18	49·7	45 20	39 13	48·9	44 40	38 09	48·2	44 00	37 07	47·5	238	302
59	121	47 56	41 44	50·2	47 17	40 36	49·4	46 38	39 30	48·6	45 58	38 25	47·8	45 17	37 22	47·1	44 36	36 20	46·3	239	301
60	120	48 35	40 54	49·1	47 56	39 46	48·3	47 16	38 40	47·5	46 35	37 36	46·7	45 53	36 33	45·9	45 11	35 32	45·2	240	300
61	119	49 14	40 01	47·9	48 34	38 54	47·1	47 53	37 48	46·3	47 11	36 45	45·5	46 29	35 42	44·7	45 46	34 42	44·0	241	299
62	118	49 53	39 07	46·8	49 11	38 00	45·9	48 29	36 55	45·1	47 46	35 52	44·3	47 03	34 50	43·6	46 19	33 50	42·8	242	298
63	117	50 30	38 11	45·5	49 48	37 04	44·7	49 05	36 00	43·9	48 21	34 57	43·1	47 37	33 57	42·3	46 53	32 57	41·6	243	297
64	116	51 07	37 13	44·3	50 23	36 07	43·4	49 40	35 03	42·6	48 55	34 01	41·8	48 10	33 01	41·1	47 25	32 03	40·4	244	296
65	115	51 43	36 12	43·0	50 58	35 07	42·2	50 14	34 04	41·3	49 28	33 03	40·6	48 43	32 04	39·8	47 56	31 07	39·1	245	295
66	114	52 18	35 10	41·7	51 33	34 06	40·8	50 47	33 04	40·0	50 01	32 04	39·3	49 14	31 05	38·5	48 27	30 09	37·8	246	294
67	113	52 52	34 05	40·3	52 06	33 02	39·5	51 19	32 01	38·7	50 32	31 02	37·9	49 44	30 05	37·2	48 56	29 10	36·5	247	293
68	112	53 25	32 59	38·9	52 38	31 56	38·1	51 50	30 57	37·3	51 02	29 59	36·6	50 14	29 03	35·8	49 25	28 09	35·2	248	292
69	111	53 57	31 50	37·5	53 09	30 49	36·7	52 21	29 50	35·9	51 32	28 53	35·2	50 43	27 59	34·5	49 53	27 06	33·8	249	291
70	110	54 28	30 39	36·1	53 39	29 39	35·2	52 50	28 42	34·5	52 00	27 46	33·8	51 10	26 53	33·1	50 20	26 02	32·4	250	290
71	109	54 58	29 25	34·6	54 08	28 27	33·8	53 18	27 31	33·0	52 28	26 38	32·3	51 37	25 46	31·6	50 46	24 56	31·0	251	289
72	108	55 27	28 09	33·0	54 37	27 13	32·2	53 46	26 19	31·5	52 54	25 27	30·8	52 03	24 37	30·2	51 10	23 49	29·5	252	288
73	107	55 55	26 51	31·4	55 03	25 57	30·7	54 12	25 04	30·0	53 19	24 14	29·3	52 27	23 26	28·7	51 34	22 40	28·1	253	287
74	106	56 21	25 31	29·8	55 29	24 39	29·1	54 36	23 48	28·4	53 43	23 00	27·8	52 50	22 14	27·1	51 57	21 29	26·6	254	286
75	105	56 46	24 09	28·2	55 53	23 18	27·5	55 00	22 30	26·8	54 06	21 44	26·2	53 12	21 00	25·6	52 18	20 17	25·0	255	285
76	104	57 10	22 44	26·5	56 16	21 56	25·8	55 22	21 10	25·2	54 28	20 26	24·6	53 33	19 44	24·0	52 38	19 04	23·5	256	284
77	103	57 33	21 17	24·8	56 38	20 31	24·1	55 43	19 48	23·5	54 48	19 06	23·0	53 53	18 27	22·4	52 57	17 49	21·9	257	283
78	102	57 54	19 48	23·0	56 59	19 05	22·4	56 03	18 24	21·9	55 07	17 45	21·3	54 11	17 08	20·8	53 15	16 32	20·3	258	282
79	101	58 13	18 17	21·2	57 17	17 37	20·7	56 21	16 59	20·1	55 25	16 22	19·6	54 28	15 48	19·2	53 31	15 15	18·7	259	281
80	100	58 32	16 44	19·4	57 35	16 07	18·9	56 38	15 32	18·4	55 41	14 58	17·9	54 44	14 26	17·5	53 47	13 56	17·1	260	280
81	99	58 48	15 10	17·6	57 51	14 36	17·1	56 53	14 03	16·6	55 56	13 33	16·2	54 58	13 03	15·8	54 00	12 36	15·4	261	279
82	98	59 03	13 33	15·7	58 05	13 02	15·3	57 07	12 33	14·9	56 09	12 06	14·5	55 11	11 40	14·1	54 13	11 14	13·8	262	278
83	97	59 16	11 55	13·8	58 18	11 28	13·4	57 19	11 02	13·0	56 21	10 38	12·7	55 22	10 14	12·4	54 24	9 52	12·1	263	277
84	96	59 28	10 16	11·9	58 29	9 52	11·5	57 30	9 30	11·2	56 31	9 09	10·9	55 32	8 49	10·6	54 33	8 29	10·4	264	276
85	95	59 37	8 35	9·9	58 38	8 15	9·6	57 39	7 56	9·4	56 40	7 39	9·1	55 41	7 22	8·9	54 41	7 06	8·7	265	275
86	94	59 46	6 53	8·0	58 46	6 37	7·7	57 47	6 22	7·5	56 47	6 08	7·3	55 48	5 54	7·1	54 48	5 41	7·0	266	274
87	93	59 52	5 11	6·0	58 52	4 59	5·8	57 52	4 47	5·6	56 53	4 36	5·5	55 53	4 26	5·4	54 53	4 16	5·2	267	273
88	92	59 56	3 28	4·0	58 57	3 19	3·9	57 57	3 12	3·8	56 57	3 05	3·7	55 57	2 58	3·6	54 57	2 51	3·5	268	272
89	91	59 59	1 44	2·0	58 59	1 40	1·9	57 59	1 36	1·9	56 59	1 32	1·8	55 59	1 29	1·8	54 59	1 26	1·7	269	271
90	90	60 00	0 00	0·0	59 00	0 00	0·0	58 00	0 00	0·0	57 00	0 00	0·0	56 00	0 00	0·0	55 00	0 00	0·0	270	270

N. Lat: for LHA > 180° … $Z_n = Z$
for LHA < 180° … $Z_n = 360° - Z$

S. Lat.: for LHA > 180° … $Z_n = 180° - Z$
for LHA < 180° … $Z_n = 180° + Z$

SIGHT REDUCTION TABLE

B: (−) for 90° < LHA < 270°
Dec:(−) for Lat. contrary name

Z_1: same sign as B
Z_2: (−) for F > 90°

Lat. / A		36°			37°			38°			39°			40°			41°			Lat. / A	
LHA/F		A/H	B/P	Z_1/Z_2	A/H	B/P	Z_1/Z_2	A/H	B/P	Z_1/Z_2	A/H	B/P	Z_1/Z_2	A/H	B/P	Z_1/Z_2	A/H	B/P	Z_1/Z_2	LHA	
°	°	° ′	° ′	°	° ′	° ′	°	° ′	° ′	°	° ′	° ′	°	° ′	° ′	°	° ′	° ′	°	°	°
0	180	0 00	54 00	90·0	0 00	53 00	90·0	0 00	52 00	90·0	0 00	51 00	90·0	0 00	50 00	90·0	0 00	49 00	90·0	180	360
1	179	0 49	54 00	89·4	0 48	53 00	89·4	0 47	52 00	89·4	0 47	51 00	89·4	0 46	50 00	89·4	0 45	49 00	89·3	181	359
2	178	1 37	53 59	88·8	1 36	52 59	88·8	1 35	51 59	88·8	1 33	50 59	88·7	1 32	49 59	88·7	1 31	48 59	88·7	182	358
3	177	2 26	53 58	88·2	2 24	52 58	88·2	2 22	51 58	88·2	2 20	50 58	88·1	2 18	49 58	88·1	2 16	48 58	88·0	183	357
4	176	3 14	53 56	87·6	3 12	52 56	87·6	3 09	51 56	87·5	3 06	50 56	87·5	3 04	49 56	87·4	3 01	48 56	87·4	184	356
5	175	4 03	53 54	87·1	3 59	52 54	87·0	3 56	51 54	86·9	3 53	50 54	86·8	3 50	49 54	86·8	3 46	48 54	86·7	185	355
6	174	4 51	53 51	86·5	4 47	52 51	86·4	4 43	51 51	86·3	4 40	50 51	86·2	4 36	49 51	86·1	4 31	48 51	86·1	186	354
7	173	5 39	53 48	85·9	5 35	52 48	85·8	5 31	51 48	85·7	5 26	50 47	85·6	5 21	49 47	85·5	5 17	48 47	85·4	187	353
8	172	6 28	53 44	85·3	6 23	52 44	85·2	6 18	51 44	85·1	6 13	50 44	84·9	6 07	49 43	84·8	6 02	48 43	84·7	188	352
9	171	7 16	53 40	84·7	7 11	52 39	84·6	7 05	51 39	84·4	6 59	50 39	84·3	6 53	49 39	84·2	6 47	48 39	84·1	189	351
10	170	8 05	53 35	84·1	7 58	52 35	83·9	7 52	51 34	83·8	7 45	50 34	83·7	7 39	49 34	83·5	7 32	48 34	83·4	190	350
11	169	8 53	53 30	83·5	8 46	52 29	83·3	8 39	51 29	83·2	8 32	50 29	83·0	8 24	49 29	82·9	8 17	48 28	82·7	191	349
12	168	9 41	53 24	82·9	9 33	52 23	82·7	9 26	51 23	82·5	9 18	50 23	82·4	9 10	49 23	82·2	9 02	48 22	82·1	192	348
13	167	10 29	53 17	82·3	10 21	52 17	82·1	10 13	51 17	81·9	10 04	50 16	81·7	9 55	49 16	81·6	9 46	48 16	81·4	193	347
14	166	11 17	53 10	81·7	11 08	52 10	81·5	10 59	51 10	81·3	10 50	50 09	81·1	10 41	49 09	80·9	10 31	48 09	80·7	194	346
15	165	12 05	53 03	81·0	11 56	52 02	80·8	11 46	51 02	80·6	11 36	50 02	80·4	11 26	49 01	80·2	11 16	48 01	80·0	195	345
16	164	12 53	52 55	80·4	12 43	51 54	80·2	12 33	50 54	80·0	12 22	49 53	79·8	12 11	48 53	79·6	12 00	47 53	79·3	196	344
17	163	13 41	52 46	79·8	13 30	51 46	79·6	13 19	50 45	79·3	13 08	49 45	79·1	12 57	48 44	78·9	12 45	47 44	78·7	197	343
18	162	14 29	52 37	79·2	14 17	51 37	78·9	14 06	50 36	78·7	13 54	49 35	78·4	13 42	48 35	78·2	13 29	47 34	78·0	198	342
19	161	15 16	52 28	78·6	15 04	51 27	78·3	14 52	50 26	78·0	14 39	49 25	77·8	14 27	48 25	77·5	14 13	47 24	77·3	199	341
20	160	16 04	52 17	77·9	15 51	51 16	77·6	15 38	50 16	77·4	15 25	49 15	77·1	15 11	48 14	76·8	14 58	47 14	76·6	200	340
21	159	16 51	52 07	77·3	16 38	51 05	77·0	16 24	50 05	76·7	16 10	49 04	76·4	15 56	48 03	76·1	15 42	47 03	75·9	201	339
22	158	17 39	51 55	76·6	17 24	50 54	76·3	17 10	49 53	76·0	16 56	48 52	75·7	16 41	47 51	75·4	16 25	46 51	75·2	202	338
23	157	18 26	51 43	76·0	18 11	50 42	75·7	17 56	49 41	75·4	17 41	48 40	75·0	17 25	47 39	74·7	17 09	46 38	74·4	203	337
24	156	19 13	51 30	75·3	18 57	50 29	75·0	18 42	49 28	74·7	18 26	48 27	74·3	18 09	47 26	74·0	17 53	46 25	73·7	204	336
25	155	20 00	51 17	74·7	19 44	50 15	74·3	19 27	49 14	74·0	19 10	48 13	73·6	18 53	47 12	73·3	18 36	46 12	73·0	205	335
26	154	20 46	51 03	74·0	20 30	50 01	73·6	20 13	49 00	73·3	19 55	47 59	72·9	19 37	46 58	72·6	19 19	45 57	72·3	206	334
27	153	21 33	50 48	73·3	21 15	49 47	73·0	20 58	48 45	72·6	20 40	47 44	72·2	20 21	46 43	71·9	20 02	45 42	71·5	207	333
28	152	22 19	50 33	72·6	22 01	49 31	72·3	21 43	48 30	71·9	21 24	47 28	71·5	21 05	46 28	71·1	20 45	45 27	70·8	208	332
29	151	23 06	50 17	72·0	22 47	49 15	71·6	22 28	48 14	71·2	22 08	47 12	70·8	21 48	46 11	70·4	21 28	45 11	70·0	209	331
30	150	23 52	50 00	71·3	23 32	48 58	70·8	23 12	47 57	70·4	22 52	46 55	70·0	22 31	45 54	69·6	22 10	44 54	69·3	210	330
31	149	24 37	49 43	70·5	24 17	48 41	70·1	23 57	47 39	69·7	23 36	46 38	69·3	23 14	45 37	68·9	22 52	44 36	68·5	211	329
32	148	25 23	49 25	69·8	25 02	48 23	69·4	24 41	47 21	69·0	24 19	46 19	68·5	23 57	45 18	68·1	23 34	44 17	67·7	212	328
33	147	26 09	49 06	69·1	25 47	48 04	68·7	25 25	47 02	68·2	25 02	46 00	67·8	24 40	44 59	67·3	24 16	43 58	66·9	213	327
34	146	26 54	48 46	68·4	26 32	47 44	67·9	26 09	46 42	67·4	25 45	45 40	67·0	25 22	44 39	66·6	24 58	43 39	66·1	214	326
35	145	27 39	48 26	67·6	27 16	47 23	67·1	26 52	46 21	66·7	26 28	45 20	66·2	26 04	44 19	65·8	25 39	43 18	65·3	215	325
36	144	28 24	48 04	66·9	28 00	47 02	66·4	27 36	46 00	65·9	27 11	44 58	65·4	26 46	43 57	65·0	26 20	42 57	64·5	216	324
37	143	29 08	47 42	66·1	28 44	46 40	65·6	28 19	45 38	65·1	27 53	44 36	64·6	27 27	43 35	64·2	27 01	42 34	63·7	217	323
38	142	29 52	47 19	65·3	29 27	46 17	64·8	29 01	45 15	64·3	28 35	44 13	63·8	28 08	43 12	63·3	27 41	42 12	62·9	218	322
39	141	30 36	46 56	64·5	30 10	45 53	64·0	29 44	44 51	63·5	29 17	43 49	63·0	28 49	42 48	62·5	28 21	41 48	62·0	219	321
40	140	31 20	46 31	63·7	30 53	45 28	63·2	30 26	44 26	62·7	29 58	43 25	62·2	29 30	42 24	61·7	29 01	41 23	61·2	220	320
41	139	32 03	46 05	62·9	31 36	45 03	62·4	31 08	44 01	61·8	30 39	42 59	61·3	30 10	41 58	60·8	29 41	40 58	60·3	221	319
42	138	32 46	45 39	62·1	32 18	44 36	61·5	31 49	43 34	61·0	31 20	42 33	60·5	30 50	41 32	59·9	30 20	40 32	59·4	222	318
43	137	33 29	45 11	61·3	33 00	44 09	60·7	32 30	43 07	60·1	32 00	42 05	59·6	31 30	41 05	59·1	30 59	40 04	58·5	223	317
44	136	34 12	44 43	60·4	33 42	43 40	59·8	33 11	42 38	59·3	32 40	41 37	58·7	32 09	40 36	58·2	31 37	39 36	57·6	224	316
45	135	34 54	44 13	59·6	34 23	43 11	59·0	33 52	42 09	58·4	33 20	41 08	57·8	32 48	40 07	57·3	32 15	39 08	56·7	225	315

Lat. / A		36°			37°			38°			39°			40°			41°			Lat. / A	
LHA/F		A/H	B/P	Z_1/Z_2	A/H	B/P	Z_1/Z_2	A/H	B/P	Z_1/Z_2	A/H	B/P	Z_1/Z_2	A/H	B/P	Z_1/Z_2	A/H	B/P	Z_1/Z_2	LHA	
°	°	° ′	° ′	°	° ′	° ′	°	° ′	° ′	°	° ′	° ′	°	° ′	° ′	°	° ′	° ′	°	°	°
45	135	34 54	44 13	59·6	34 23	43 11	59·0	33 52	42 09	58·4	33 20	41 08	57·8	32 48	40 07	57·3	32 15	39 08	56·7	225	315
46	134	35 35	43 43	58·7	35 04	42 40	58·1	34 32	41 38	57·5	33 59	40 37	56·9	33 26	39 37	56·4	32 53	38 38	55·8	226	314
47	133	36 17	43 11	57·8	35 44	42 09	57·2	35 12	41 07	56·6	34 38	40 06	56·0	34 04	39 06	55·4	33 30	38 07	54·9	227	313
48	132	36 57	42 39	56·9	36 24	41 36	56·2	35 51	40 35	55·6	35 17	39 34	55·0	34 42	38 34	54·5	34 07	37 35	53·9	228	312
49	131	37 38	42 05	55·9	37 04	41 03	55·3	36 30	40 01	54·7	35 55	39 01	54·1	35 19	38 01	53·5	34 43	37 03	53·0	229	311
50	130	38 18	41 30	55·0	37 43	40 28	54·4	37 08	39 27	53·7	36 32	38 27	53·1	35 56	37 27	52·5	35 19	36 29	52·0	230	310
51	129	38 57	40 54	54·0	38 22	39 52	53·4	37 46	38 51	52·8	37 09	37 51	52·1	36 32	36 52	51·6	35 55	35 54	51·0	231	309
52	128	39 36	40 17	53·0	39 00	39 15	52·4	38 23	38 14	51·8	37 46	37 15	51·1	37 08	36 16	50·6	36 30	35 18	50·0	232	308
53	127	40 15	39 38	52·0	39 38	38 37	51·4	39 00	37 36	50·8	38 22	36 37	50·1	37 43	35 39	49·5	37 04	34 42	49·0	233	307
54	126	40 53	38 58	51·0	40 15	37 57	50·4	39 36	36 57	49·7	38 57	35 58	49·1	38 18	35 01	48·5	37 38	34 04	47·9	234	306
55	125	41 30	38 17	50·0	40 52	37 17	49·3	40 12	36 17	48·7	39 32	35 19	48·1	38 52	34 21	47·4	38 11	33 25	46·9	235	305
56	124	42 07	37 35	48·9	41 28	36 35	48·3	40 47	35 36	47·6	40 07	34 38	47·0	39 26	33 41	46·4	38 44	32 45	45·8	236	304
57	123	42 44	36 51	47·9	42 03	35 51	47·2	41 22	34 53	46·5	40 41	33 55	45·9	39 59	32 59	45·3	39 16	32 04	44·7	237	303
58	122	43 19	36 06	46·8	42 38	35 07	46·1	41 56	34 09	45·4	41 14	33 12	44·8	40 31	32 16	44·2	39 48	31 22	43·6	238	302
59	121	43 54	35 20	45·6	43 12	34 21	45·0	42 29	33 24	44·3	41 46	32 27	43·7	41 03	31 32	43·1	40 19	30 39	42·5	239	301
60	120	44 29	34 32	44·5	43 46	33 34	43·8	43 02	32 37	43·2	42 18	31 42	42·5	41 34	30 47	41·9	40 49	29 54	41·3	240	300
61	119	45 02	33 43	43·3	44 18	32 45	42·6	43 34	31 49	42·0	42 49	30 55	41·4	42 04	30 01	40·8	41 18	29 09	40·2	241	299
62	118	45 35	32 52	42·1	44 51	31 55	41·5	44 05	31 00	40·8	43 20	30 06	40·2	42 34	29 14	39·6	41 47	28 22	39·0	242	298
63	117	46 07	32 00	40·9	45 22	31 04	40·3	44 36	30 10	39·6	43 49	29 17	39·0	43 03	28 25	38·4	42 15	27 35	37·8	243	297
64	116	46 39	31 06	39·7	45 52	30 11	39·0	45 06	29 18	38·4	44 18	28 26	37·8	43 31	27 35	37·2	42 43	26 46	36·6	244	296
65	115	47 09	30 11	38·4	46 22	29 17	37·8	45 35	28 25	37·1	44 47	27 34	36·5	43 58	26 44	36·0	43 09	25 56	35·4	245	295
66	114	47 39	29 14	37·1	46 51	28 21	36·5	46 03	27 30	35·9	45 14	26 40	35·3	44 25	25 52	34·7	43 35	25 04	34·2	246	294
67	113	48 08	28 16	35·8	47 19	27 24	35·2	46 30	26 34	34·6	45 40	25 45	34·0	44 50	24 58	33·4	44 00	24 12	32·9	247	293
68	112	48 36	27 17	34·5	47 46	26 26	33·9	46 56	25 37	33·3	46 06	24 50	32·7	45 15	24 03	32·2	44 24	23 19	31·6	248	292
69	111	49 03	26 15	33·1	48 13	25 26	32·5	47 22	24 38	31·9	46 31	23 52	31·4	45 39	23 08	30·8	44 48	22 24	30·3	249	291
70	110	49 29	25 13	31·8	48 38	24 25	31·2	47 46	23 39	30·6	46 55	22 54	30·0	46 03	22 11	29·5	45 10	21 29	29·0	250	290
71	109	49 54	24 08	30·4	49 02	23 22	29·8	48 10	22 37	29·2	47 17	21 54	28·7	46 25	21 12	28·2	45 32	20 32	27·7	251	289
72	108	50 18	23 02	28·9	49 25	22 18	28·4	48 33	21 35	27·8	47 39	20 53	27·3	46 46	20 13	26·8	45 52	19 34	26·3	252	288
73	107	50 41	21 55	27·5	49 48	21 12	26·9	48 54	20 31	26·4	48 00	19 51	25·9	47 06	19 13	25·4	46 12	18 35	25·0	253	287
74	106	51 03	20 47	26·0	50 09	20 06	25·5	49 15	19 26	25·0	48 20	18 48	24·5	47 25	18 11	24·0	46 30	17 36	23·6	254	286
75	105	51 24	19 36	24·5	50 29	18 57	24·0	49 34	18 20	23·5	48 39	17 43	23·1	47 44	17 09	22·6	46 48	16 35	22·2	255	285
76	104	51 43	18 25	23·0	50 48	17 48	22·5	49 52	17 12	22·0	48 57	16 38	21·6	48 01	16 05	21·2	47 05	15 33	20·8	256	284
77	103	52 02	17 12	21·4	51 06	16 37	21·0	50 09	16 04	20·6	49 13	15 31	20·1	48 17	15 00	19·8	47 20	14 31	19·4	257	283
78	102	52 19	15 58	19·9	51 22	15 25	19·5	50 25	14 54	19·0	49 29	14 24	18·7	48 32	13 55	18·3	47 35	13 27	18·0	258	282
79	101	52 35	14 43	18·3	51 37	14 13	17·9	50 40	13 43	17·5	49 43	13 16	17·2	48 46	12 49	16·8	47 48	12 23	16·5	259	281
80	100	52 49	13 27	16·7	51 52	12 59	16·3	50 54	12 32	16·0	49 56	12 06	15·7	48 58	11 42	15·3	48 01	11 18	15·0	260	280
81	99	53 02	12 09	15·1	52 04	11 44	14·7	51 06	11 19	14·4	50 08	10 56	14·1	49 10	10 34	13·8	48 12	10 12	13·6	261	279
82	98	53 14	10 51	13·4	52 16	10 28	13·1	51 18	10 06	12·9	50 19	9 45	12·6	49 20	9 25	12·3	48 22	9 06	12·1	262	278
83	97	53 25	9 31	11·8	52 26	9 11	11·5	51 27	8 52	11·3	50 29	8 34	11·0	49 30	8 16	10·8	48 31	7 59	10·6	263	277
84	96	53 34	8 11	10·1	52 35	7 54	9·9	51 36	7 37	9·7	50 37	7 21	9·5	49 38	7 06	9·3	48 38	6 51	9·1	264	276
85	95	53 42	6 50	8·5	52 43	6 36	8·3	51 43	6 22	8·1	50 44	6 09	7·9	49 44	5 56	7·8	48 45	5 44	7·6	265	275
86	94	53 49	5 29	6·8	52 49	5 17	6·6	51 49	5 06	6·5	50 50	4 55	6·3	49 50	4 45	6·2	48 50	4 35	6·1	266	274
87	93	53 54	4 07	5·1	52 54	3 58	5·0	51 54	3 50	4·9	50 54	3 42	4·8	49 54	3 34	4·7	48 55	3 27	4·6	267	273
88	92	53 57	2 45	3·4	52 57	2 39	3·3	51 57	2 33	3·2	50 57	2 28	3·2	49 58	2 23	3·1	48 58	2 18	3·0	268	272
89	91	53 59	1 23	1·7	52 59	1 20	1·7	51 59	1 17	1·6	50 59	1 14	1·6	49 59	1 11	1·6	48 59	1 09	1·5	269	271
90	90	54 00	0 00	0·0	53 00	0 00	0·0	52 00	0 00	0·0	51 00	0 00	0·0	50 00	0 00	0·0	49 00	0 00	0·0	270	270

N. Lat: for LHA > 180° … $Z_n = Z$
for LHA < 180° … $Z_n = 360° - Z$

S. Lat.: for LHA > 180° … $Z_n = 180° - Z$
for LHA < 180° … $Z_n = 180° + Z$

SIGHT REDUCTION TABLE

B: (−) for 90° < LHA < 270°
Dec:(−) for Lat. contrary name

Z_1: same sign as B
Z_2: (−) for F > 90°

Lat. / A		42°			43°			44°			45°			46°			47°			Lat. / A	
LHA/F		A/H	B/P	Z_1/Z_2	A/H	B/P	Z_1/Z_2	A/H	B/P	Z_1/Z_2	A/H	B/P	Z_1/Z_2	A/H	B/P	Z_1/Z_2	A/H	B/P	Z_1/Z_2	LHA	
°	°	° ′	° ′	°	° ′	° ′	°	° ′	° ′	°	° ′	° ′	°	° ′	° ′	°	° ′	° ′	°	°	°
0	180	0 00	48 00	90·0	0 00	47 00	90·0	0 00	46 00	90·0	0 00	45 00	90·0	0 00	44 00	90·0	0 00	43 00	90·0	180	360
1	179	0 45	48 00	89·3	0 44	47 00	89·3	0 43	46 00	89·3	0 42	45 00	89·3	0 42	44 00	89·3	0 41	43 00	89·3	181	359
2	178	1 29	47 59	88·7	1 28	46 59	88·6	1 26	45 59	88·6	1 25	44 59	88·6	1 23	43 59	88·6	1 22	42 59	88·5	182	358
3	177	2 14	47 58	88·0	2 12	46 58	88·0	2 09	45 58	87·9	2 07	44 58	87·9	2 05	43 58	87·8	2 03	42 58	87·8	183	357
4	176	2 58	47 56	87·3	2 55	46 56	87·3	2 53	45 56	87·2	2 50	44 56	87·2	2 47	43 56	87·1	2 44	42 56	87·1	184	356
5	175	3 43	47 53	86·6	3 39	46 53	86·6	3 36	45 53	86·5	3 32	44 53	86·5	3 28	43 53	86·4	3 24	42 53	86·3	185	355
6	174	4 27	47 51	86·0	4 23	46 51	85·9	4 19	45 51	85·8	4 14	44 51	85·7	4 10	43 51	85·7	4 05	42 51	85·6	186	354
7	173	5 12	47 47	85·3	5 07	46 47	85·2	5 02	45 47	85·1	4 57	44 47	85·0	4 51	43 47	85·0	4 46	42 47	84·9	187	353
8	172	5 56	47 43	84·6	5 51	46 43	84·5	5 45	45 43	84·4	5 39	44 43	84·3	5 33	43 43	84·2	5 27	42 43	84·1	188	352
9	171	6 41	47 39	84·0	6 34	46 39	83·8	6 28	45 39	83·7	6 21	44 39	83·6	6 14	43 39	83·5	6 07	42 39	83·4	189	351
10	170	7 25	47 34	83·3	7 18	46 34	83·1	7 11	45 34	83·0	7 03	44 34	82·9	6 56	43 34	82·8	6 48	42 34	82·7	190	350
11	169	8 09	47 28	82·6	8 01	46 28	82·4	7 53	45 28	82·3	7 45	44 28	82·2	7 37	43 28	82·0	7 29	42 28	81·9	191	349
12	168	8 53	47 22	81·9	8 45	46 22	81·8	8 36	45 22	81·6	8 27	44 22	81·5	8 18	43 22	81·3	8 09	42 22	81·2	192	348
13	167	9 37	47 16	81·2	9 28	46 15	81·1	9 19	45 15	80·9	9 09	44 15	80·7	8 59	43 15	80·6	8 49	42 16	80·4	193	347
14	166	10 21	47 08	80·5	10 11	46 08	80·3	10 01	45 08	80·2	9 51	44 08	80·0	9 40	43 08	79·8	9 30	42 08	79·7	194	346
15	165	11 05	47 01	79·8	10 55	46 00	79·6	10 44	45 00	79·5	10 33	44 00	79·3	10 21	43 00	79·1	10 10	42 01	78·9	195	345
16	164	11 49	46 52	79·1	11 38	45 52	78·9	11 26	44 52	78·7	11 14	43 52	78·5	11 02	42 52	78·3	10 50	41 52	78·2	196	344
17	163	12 33	46 43	78·4	12 21	45 43	78·2	12 08	44 43	78·0	11 56	43 43	77·8	11 43	42 43	77·6	11 30	41 44	77·4	197	343
18	162	13 17	46 34	77·7	13 04	45 34	77·5	12 51	44 34	77·3	12 37	43 34	77·1	12 24	42 34	76·8	12 10	41 34	76·6	198	342
19	161	14 00	46 24	77·0	13 46	45 24	76·8	13 33	44 24	76·5	13 19	43 24	76·3	13 04	42 24	76·1	12 50	41 24	75·9	199	341
20	160	14 43	46 13	76·3	14 29	45 13	76·1	14 15	44 13	75·8	14 00	43 13	75·6	13 45	42 13	75·3	13 29	41 14	75·1	200	340
21	159	15 27	46 02	75·6	15 12	45 02	75·3	14 56	44 02	75·1	14 41	43 02	74·8	14 25	42 02	74·6	14 09	41 03	74·3	201	339
22	158	16 10	45 50	74·9	15 54	44 50	74·6	15 38	43 50	74·3	15 22	42 50	74·1	15 05	41 50	73·8	14 48	40 51	73·5	202	338
23	157	16 53	45 38	74·1	16 36	44 38	73·9	16 19	43 38	73·6	16 02	42 38	73·3	15 45	41 38	73·0	15 27	40 39	72·8	203	337
24	156	17 36	45 25	73·4	17 18	44 25	73·1	17 01	43 25	72·8	16 43	42 25	72·5	16 25	41 25	72·2	16 06	40 26	72·0	204	336
25	155	18 18	45 11	72·7	18 00	44 11	72·4	17 42	43 11	72·1	17 23	42 11	71·8	17 04	41 12	71·5	16 45	40 12	71·2	205	335
26	154	19 01	44 57	71·9	18 42	43 57	71·6	18 23	42 57	71·3	18 03	41 57	71·0	17 44	40 57	70·7	17 24	39 58	70·4	206	334
27	153	19 43	44 42	71·2	19 24	43 42	70·8	19 04	42 42	70·5	18 43	41 42	70·2	18 23	40 43	69·9	18 02	39 43	69·6	207	333
28	152	20 25	44 26	70·4	20 05	43 26	70·1	19 44	42 26	69·7	19 23	41 27	69·4	19 02	40 27	69·1	18 40	39 28	68·8	208	332
29	151	21 07	44 10	69·6	20 46	43 10	69·3	20 25	42 10	68·9	20 03	41 10	68·6	19 41	40 11	68·3	19 18	39 12	67·9	209	331
30	150	21 49	43 53	68·9	21 27	42 53	68·5	21 05	41 53	68·1	20 42	40 54	67·8	20 19	39 54	67·4	19 56	38 55	67·1	210	330
31	149	22 30	43 35	68·1	22 08	42 35	67·7	21 45	41 36	67·3	21 21	40 36	67·0	20 58	39 37	66·6	20 34	38 38	66·3	211	329
32	148	23 11	43 17	67·3	22 48	42 17	66·9	22 24	41 17	66·5	22 00	40 18	66·2	21 36	39 19	65·8	21 11	38 20	65·4	212	328
33	147	23 53	42 58	66·5	23 28	41 58	66·1	23 04	40 58	65·7	22 39	39 59	65·3	22 14	39 00	65·0	21 48	38 02	64·6	213	327
34	146	24 33	42 38	65·7	24 08	41 38	65·3	23 43	40 39	64·9	23 17	39 40	64·5	22 51	38 41	64·1	22 25	37 42	63·7	214	326
35	145	25 14	42 18	64·9	24 48	41 18	64·5	24 22	40 18	64·1	23 56	39 19	63·7	23 29	38 21	63·3	23 02	37 23	62·9	215	325
36	144	25 54	41 56	64·1	25 28	40 57	63·6	25 01	39 57	63·2	24 34	38 58	62·8	24 06	38 00	62·4	23 38	37 02	62·0	216	324
37	143	26 34	41 34	63·2	26 07	40 35	62·8	25 39	39 35	62·4	25 11	38 37	61·9	24 43	37 38	61·5	24 14	36 41	61·1	217	323
38	142	27 14	41 11	62·4	26 46	40 12	61·9	26 17	39 13	61·5	25 48	38 14	61·1	25 19	37 16	60·7	24 50	36 19	60·3	218	322
39	141	27 53	40 48	61·5	27 24	39 48	61·1	26 55	38 50	60·6	26 25	37 51	60·2	25 55	36 53	59·8	25 25	35 56	59·4	219	321
40	140	28 32	40 23	60·7	28 02	39 24	60·2	27 32	38 25	59·8	27 02	37 27	59·3	26 31	36 30	58·9	26 00	35 32	58·5	220	320
41	139	29 11	39 58	59·8	28 40	38 59	59·3	28 10	38 01	58·9	27 38	37 03	58·4	27 07	36 05	58·0	26 35	35 08	57·6	221	319
42	138	29 49	39 32	58·9	29 18	38 33	58·4	28 46	37 35	58·0	28 14	36 37	57·5	27 42	35 40	57·1	27 09	34 43	56·6	222	318
43	137	30 27	39 05	58·0	29 55	38 06	57·5	29 23	37 08	57·1	28 50	36 11	56·6	28 17	35 14	56·1	27 43	34 18	55·7	223	317
44	136	31 05	38 37	57·1	30 32	37 39	56·6	29 59	36 41	56·1	29 25	35 44	55·7	28 51	34 47	55·2	28 17	33 51	54·8	224	316
45	135	31 42	38 09	56·2	31 08	37 10	55·7	30 34	36 13	55·2	30 00	35 16	54·7	29 25	34 20	54·3	28 50	33 24	53·8	225	315

Lat. / A		42°			43°			44°			45°			46°			47°			Lat. / A	
LHA/F		A/H	B/P	Z1/Z2	A/H	B/P	Z1/Z2	A/H	B/P	Z1/Z2	A/H	B/P	Z1/Z2	A/H	B/P	Z1/Z2	A/H	B/P	Z1/Z2	LHA	
°	°	° ′	° ′	°	° ′	° ′	°	° ′	° ′	°	° ′	° ′	°	° ′	° ′	°	° ′	° ′	°	°	°
45	135	31 42	38 09	56·2	31 08	37 10	55·7	30 34	36 13	55·2	30 00	35 16	54·7	29 25	34 20	54·3	28 50	33 24	53·8	225	315
46	134	32 19	37 39	55·3	31 45	36 41	54·8	31 10	35 44	54·3	30 34	34 47	53·8	29 59	33 51	53·3	29 23	32 56	52·9	226	314
47	133	32 55	37 08	54·3	32 20	36 11	53·8	31 45	35 14	53·3	31 08	34 18	52·8	30 32	33 22	52·4	29 55	32 27	51·9	227	313
48	132	33 31	36 37	53·4	32 55	35 40	52·9	32 19	34 43	52·3	31 42	33 47	51·9	31 05	32 52	51·4	30 27	31 58	50·9	228	312
49	131	34 07	36 05	52·4	33 30	35 08	51·9	32 53	34 11	51·4	32 15	33 16	50·9	31 37	32 21	50·4	30 59	31 27	49·9	229	311
50	130	34 42	35 31	51·4	34 04	34 35	50·9	33 26	33 39	50·4	32 48	32 44	49·9	32 09	31 50	49·4	31 30	30 56	48·9	230	310
51	129	35 17	34 57	50·4	34 38	34 01	49·9	33 59	33 05	49·4	33 20	32 11	48·9	32 40	31 17	48·4	32 00	30 24	47·9	231	309
52	128	35 51	34 22	49·4	35 12	33 26	48·9	34 32	32 31	48·4	33 52	31 37	47·9	33 11	30 44	47·4	32 30	29 52	46·9	232	308
53	127	36 24	33 45	48·4	35 44	32 50	47·9	35 04	31 56	47·3	34 23	31 02	46·8	33 42	30 10	46·3	33 00	29 18	45·9	233	307
54	126	36 57	33 08	47·4	36 17	32 13	46·8	35 35	31 20	46·3	34 54	30 27	45·8	34 12	29 35	45·3	33 29	28 44	44·8	234	306
55	125	37 30	32 30	46·3	36 48	31 36	45·8	36 06	30 43	45·2	35 24	29 50	44·7	34 41	28 59	44·2	33 58	28 08	43·8	235	305
56	124	38 02	31 51	45·2	37 19	30 57	44·7	36 37	30 04	44·2	35 53	29 13	43·6	35 10	28 22	43·2	34 26	27 32	42·7	236	304
57	123	38 33	31 10	44·1	37 50	30 17	43·6	37 06	29 25	43·1	36 22	28 34	42·6	35 38	27 45	42·1	34 53	26 56	41·6	237	303
58	122	39 04	30 29	43·0	38 20	29 36	42·5	37 36	28 45	42·0	36 51	27 55	41·5	36 06	27 06	41·0	35 20	26 18	40·5	238	302
59	121	39 34	29 46	41·9	38 49	28 55	41·4	38 04	28 04	40·9	37 19	27 15	40·4	36 33	26 27	39·9	35 46	25 39	39·4	239	301
60	120	40 04	29 03	40·8	39 18	28 12	40·2	38 32	27 22	39·7	37 46	26 34	39·2	36 59	25 46	38·8	36 12	25 00	38·3	240	300
61	119	40 32	28 18	39·6	39 46	27 28	39·1	38 59	26 39	38·6	38 12	25 52	38·1	37 25	25 05	37·6	36 37	24 20	37·2	241	299
62	118	41 00	27 32	38·5	40 13	26 43	37·9	39 26	25 56	37·4	38 38	25 09	36·9	37 50	24 23	36·5	37 02	23 39	36·0	242	298
63	117	41 28	26 45	37·3	40 40	25 58	36·8	39 52	25 11	36·3	39 03	24 25	35·8	38 14	23 40	35·3	37 25	22 57	34·9	243	297
64	116	41 54	25 58	36·1	41 06	25 11	35·6	40 17	24 25	35·1	39 28	23 40	34·6	38 38	22 57	34·1	37 48	22 14	33·7	244	296
65	115	42 20	25 09	34·9	41 31	24 23	34·4	40 41	23 38	33·9	39 51	22 55	33·4	39 01	22 12	33·0	38 11	21 31	32·5	245	295
66	114	42 45	24 19	33·6	41 55	23 34	33·1	41 05	22 50	32·7	40 14	22 08	32·2	39 23	21 27	31·8	38 32	20 46	31·3	246	294
67	113	43 10	23 28	32·4	42 19	22 44	31·9	41 28	22 02	31·4	40 37	21 21	31·0	39 45	20 40	30·5	38 53	20 01	30·1	247	293
68	112	43 33	22 35	31·1	42 42	21 53	30·6	41 50	21 12	30·2	40 58	20 32	29·7	40 06	19 53	29·3	39 13	19 15	28·9	248	292
69	111	43 56	21 42	29·8	43 04	21 01	29·4	42 11	20 22	28·9	41 19	19 43	28·5	40 26	19 05	28·1	39 33	18 29	27·7	249	291
70	110	44 18	20 48	28·5	43 25	20 08	28·1	42 32	19 30	27·7	41 38	18 53	27·2	40 45	18 17	26·8	39 51	17 41	26·5	250	290
71	109	44 38	19 53	27·2	43 45	19 15	26·8	42 51	18 38	26·4	41 57	18 02	26·0	41 03	17 27	25·6	40 09	16 53	25·2	251	289
72	108	44 58	18 57	25·9	44 04	18 20	25·5	43 10	17 45	25·1	42 16	17 10	24·7	41 21	16 37	24·3	40 26	16 05	24·0	252	288
73	107	45 17	17 59	24·6	44 23	17 24	24·1	43 28	16 51	23·8	42 33	16 18	23·4	41 38	15 46	23·0	40 42	15 15	22·7	253	287
74	106	45 35	17 01	23·2	44 40	16 28	22·8	43 45	15 56	22·4	42 49	15 25	22·1	41 54	14 54	21·7	40 58	14 25	21·4	254	286
75	105	45 53	16 02	21·8	44 57	15 31	21·4	44 01	15 00	21·1	43 05	14 31	20·8	42 09	14 02	20·4	41 12	13 34	20·1	255	285
76	104	46 09	15 02	20·4	45 12	14 33	20·1	44 16	14 04	19·7	43 19	13 36	19·4	42 23	13 09	19·1	41 26	12 43	18·8	256	284
77	103	46 24	14 02	19·0	45 27	13 34	18·7	44 30	13 07	18·4	43 33	12 41	18·1	42 36	12 15	17·8	41 39	11 51	17·5	257	283
78	102	46 38	13 00	17·6	45 40	12 34	17·3	44 43	12 09	17·0	43 46	11 45	16·7	42 48	11 21	16·5	41 51	10 58	16·2	258	282
79	101	46 51	11 58	16·2	45 53	11 34	15·9	44 55	11 11	15·6	43 57	10 48	15·4	43 00	10 26	15·1	42 02	10 05	14·9	259	281
80	100	47 03	10 55	14·8	46 04	10 33	14·5	45 06	10 12	14·2	44 08	9 51	14·0	43 10	9 31	13·8	42 12	9 12	13·6	260	280
81	99	47 13	9 51	13·3	46 15	9 31	13·1	45 16	9 12	12·8	44 18	8 53	12·6	43 19	8 35	12·4	42 21	8 18	12·2	261	279
82	98	47 23	8 47	11·9	46 24	8 29	11·6	45 26	8 12	11·4	44 27	7 55	11·2	43 28	7 39	11·1	42 29	7 24	10·9	262	278
83	97	47 32	7 42	10·4	46 33	7 27	10·2	45 34	7 12	10·0	44 34	6 57	9·9	43 35	6 43	9·7	42 36	6 29	9·5	263	277
84	96	47 39	6 37	8·9	46 40	6 24	8·8	45 41	6 11	8·6	44 41	5 58	8·5	43 42	5 46	8·3	42 42	5 34	8·2	264	276
85	95	47 46	5 32	7·4	46 46	5 20	7·3	45 46	5 09	7·2	44 47	4 59	7·1	43 47	4 49	6·9	42 48	4 39	6·8	265	275
86	94	47 51	4 26	6·0	46 51	4 17	5·9	45 51	4 08	5·7	44 52	3 59	5·6	43 52	3 51	5·6	42 52	3 43	5·5	266	274
87	93	47 55	3 20	4·5	46 55	3 13	4·4	45 55	3 06	4·3	44 55	3 00	4·2	43 55	2 54	4·2	42 56	2 48	4·1	267	273
88	92	47 58	2 13	3·0	46 58	2 09	2·9	45 58	2 04	2·9	44 58	2 00	2·8	43 58	1 56	2·8	42 58	1 52	2·7	268	272
89	91	47 59	1 07	1·5	46 59	1 04	1·5	45 59	1 02	1·4	44 59	1 00	1·4	43 59	0 58	1·4	43 00	0 56	1·4	269	271
90	90	48 00	0 00	0·0	47 00	0 00	0·0	46 00	0 00	0·0	45 00	0 00	0·0	44 00	0 00	0·0	43 00	0 00	0·0	270	270

N. Lat: for LHA > 180° … $Z_n = Z$
for LHA < 180° … $Z_n = 360° - Z$

S. Lat.: for LHA > 180° … $Z_n = 180° - Z$
for LHA < 180° … $Z_n = 180° + Z$

SIGHT REDUCTION TABLE

B: (−) for 90° < LHA < 270°
Dec:(−) for Lat. contrary name

Z_1: same sign as B
Z_2: (−) for F > 90°

Lat. / A		48°			49°			50°			51°			52°			53°			Lat. / A	
LHA/F		A/H	B/P	Z_1/Z_2	A/H	B/P	Z_1/Z_2	A/H	B/P	Z_1/Z_2	A/H	B/P	Z_1/Z_2	A/H	B/P	Z_1/Z_2	A/H	B/P	Z_1/Z_2	LHA	
°	°	° ′	° ′	°	° ′	° ′	°	° ′	° ′	°	° ′	° ′	°	° ′	° ′	°	° ′	° ′	°	°	°
0	180	0 00	42 00	90·0	0 00	41 00	90·0	0 00	40 00	90·0	0 00	39 00	90·0	0 00	38 00	90·0	0 00	37 00	90·0	180	360
1	179	0 40	42 00	89·3	0 39	41 00	89·2	0 39	40 00	89·2	0 38	39 00	89·2	0 37	38 00	89·2	0 36	37 00	89·2	181	359
2	178	1 20	41 59	88·5	1 19	40 59	88·5	1 17	39 59	88·5	1 16	38 59	88·4	1 14	37 59	88·4	1 12	36 59	88·4	182	358
3	177	2 00	41 58	87·8	1 58	40 58	87·7	1 56	39 58	87·7	1 53	38 58	87·7	1 51	37 58	87·6	1 48	36 58	87·6	183	357
4	176	2 41	41 56	87·0	2 37	40 56	87·0	2 34	39 56	86·9	2 31	38 56	86·9	2 28	37 56	86·8	2 24	36 56	86·8	184	356
5	175	3 21	41 53	86·3	3 17	40 54	86·2	3 13	39 54	86·2	3 09	38 54	86·1	3 05	37 54	86·1	3 00	36 54	86·0	185	355
6	174	4 01	41 51	85·5	3 56	40 51	85·5	3 51	39 51	85·4	3 46	38 51	85·3	3 41	37 51	85·3	3 36	36 51	85·2	186	354
7	173	4 41	41 47	84·8	4 35	40 47	84·7	4 30	39 47	84·6	4 24	38 47	84·5	4 18	37 48	84·5	4 12	36 48	84·4	187	353
8	172	5 21	41 43	84·0	5 14	40 43	83·9	5 08	39 43	83·9	5 01	38 44	83·8	4 55	37 44	83·7	4 48	36 44	83·6	188	352
9	171	6 01	41 39	83·3	5 53	40 39	83·2	5 46	39 39	83·1	5 39	38 39	83·0	5 32	37 39	82·9	5 24	36 40	82·8	189	351
10	170	6 40	41 34	82·5	6 32	40 34	82·4	6 25	39 34	82·3	6 16	38 34	82·2	6 08	37 35	82·1	6 00	36 35	82·0	190	350
11	169	7 20	41 28	81·8	7 11	40 28	81·7	7 03	39 29	81·5	6 54	38 29	81·4	6 45	37 29	81·3	6 36	36 29	81·2	191	349
12	168	8 00	41 22	81·0	7 50	40 22	80·9	7 41	39 23	80·8	7 31	38 23	80·6	7 21	37 23	80·5	7 11	36 24	80·4	192	348
13	167	8 39	41 16	80·3	8 29	40 16	80·1	8 19	39 16	80·0	8 08	38 16	79·8	7 58	37 17	79·7	7 47	36 17	79·6	193	347
14	166	9 19	41 09	79·5	9 08	40 09	79·3	8 57	39 09	79·2	8 45	38 09	79·0	8 34	37 10	78·9	8 22	36 10	78·7	194	346
15	165	9 58	41 01	78·7	9 47	40 01	78·6	9 35	39 02	78·4	9 22	38 02	78·2	9 10	37 02	78·1	8 58	36 03	77·9	195	345
16	164	10 38	40 53	78·0	10 25	39 53	77·8	10 12	38 53	77·6	9 59	37 54	77·4	9 46	36 54	77·3	9 33	35 55	77·1	196	344
17	163	11 17	40 44	77·2	11 04	39 44	77·0	10 50	38 45	76·8	10 36	37 45	76·6	10 22	36 46	76·5	10 08	35 47	76·3	197	343
18	162	11 56	40 34	76·4	11 42	39 35	76·2	11 27	38 35	76·0	11 13	37 36	75·8	10 58	36 37	75·6	10 43	35 38	75·5	198	342
19	161	12 35	40 25	75·6	12 20	39 25	75·4	12 05	38 26	75·2	11 49	37 26	75·0	11 34	36 27	74·8	11 18	35 28	74·6	199	341
20	160	13 14	40 14	74·9	12 58	39 15	74·6	12 42	38 15	74·4	12 26	37 16	74·2	12 09	36 17	74·0	11 53	35 18	73·8	200	340
21	159	13 52	40 03	74·1	13 36	39 04	73·8	13 19	38 04	73·6	13 02	37 05	73·4	12 45	36 06	73·2	12 27	35 08	73·0	201	339
22	158	14 31	39 51	73·3	14 14	38 52	73·0	13 56	37 53	72·8	13 38	36 54	72·6	13 20	35 55	72·3	13 02	34 56	72·1	202	338
23	157	15 09	39 39	72·5	14 51	38 40	72·2	14 33	37 41	72·0	14 14	36 42	71·7	13 55	35 43	71·5	13 36	34 45	71·3	203	337
24	156	15 48	39 26	71·7	15 29	38 27	71·4	15 09	37 28	71·2	14 50	36 30	70·9	14 30	35 31	70·7	14 10	34 33	70·4	204	336
25	155	16 26	39 13	70·9	16 06	38 14	70·6	15 46	37 15	70·3	15 25	36 17	70·1	15 05	35 18	69·8	14 44	34 20	69·6	205	335
26	154	17 03	38 59	70·1	16 43	38 00	69·8	16 22	37 01	69·5	16 01	36 03	69·2	15 39	35 05	69·0	15 18	34 07	68·7	206	334
27	153	17 41	38 44	69·3	17 20	37 46	69·0	16 58	36 47	68·7	16 36	35 49	68·4	16 14	34 51	68·1	15 51	33 53	67·9	207	333
28	152	18 19	38 29	68·4	17 56	37 30	68·1	17 34	36 32	67·8	17 11	35 34	67·5	16 48	34 36	67·3	16 25	33 38	67·0	208	332
29	151	18 56	38 13	67·6	18 33	37 15	67·3	18 09	36 16	67·0	17 46	35 18	66·7	17 22	34 21	66·4	16 58	33 23	66·1	209	331
30	150	19 33	37 57	66·8	19 09	36 58	66·5	18 45	36 00	66·1	18 20	35 03	65·8	17 56	34 05	65·5	17 31	33 08	65·2	210	330
31	149	20 10	37 40	65·9	19 45	36 41	65·6	19 20	35 44	65·3	18 55	34 46	65·0	18 29	33 49	64·7	18 03	32 52	64·4	211	329
32	148	20 46	37 22	65·1	20 21	36 24	64·8	19 55	35 26	64·4	19 29	34 29	64·1	19 02	33 32	63·8	18 36	32 35	63·5	212	328
33	147	21 22	37 03	64·2	20 56	36 06	63·9	20 30	35 08	63·6	20 03	34 11	63·2	19 35	33 14	62·9	19 08	32 18	62·6	213	327
34	146	21 58	36 44	63·4	21 31	35 47	63·0	21 04	34 49	62·7	20 36	33 53	62·3	20 08	32 56	62·0	19 40	32 00	61·7	214	326
35	145	22 34	36 25	62·5	22 06	35 27	62·1	21 38	34 30	61·8	21 10	33 33	61·4	20 41	32 37	61·1	20 12	31 41	60·8	215	325
36	144	23 10	36 04	61·6	22 41	35 07	61·3	22 12	34 10	60·9	21 43	33 14	60·5	21 13	32 18	60·2	20 43	31 22	59·9	216	324
37	143	23 45	35 43	60·8	23 15	34 46	60·4	22 45	33 50	60·0	22 15	32 53	59·6	21 45	31 58	59·3	21 14	31 02	59·0	217	323
38	142	24 20	35 21	59·9	23 49	34 25	59·5	23 19	33 28	59·1	22 48	32 33	58·7	22 16	31 37	58·4	21 45	30 42	58·0	218	322
39	141	24 54	34 59	59·0	24 23	34 02	58·6	23 52	33 07	58·2	23 20	32 11	57·8	22 48	31 16	57·5	22 15	30 21	57·1	219	321
40	140	25 28	34 36	58·1	24 57	33 40	57·7	24 24	32 44	57·3	23 52	31 49	56·9	23 19	30 54	56·5	22 45	30 00	56·2	220	320
41	139	26 02	34 12	57·1	25 30	33 16	56·7	24 57	32 21	56·3	24 23	31 26	56·0	23 49	30 32	55·6	23 15	29 38	55·2	221	319
42	138	26 36	33 47	56·2	26 02	32 52	55·8	25 28	31 57	55·4	24 54	31 02	55·0	24 20	30 08	54·6	23 45	29 15	54·3	222	318
43	137	27 09	33 22	55·3	26 35	32 27	54·9	26 00	31 32	54·5	25 25	30 38	54·1	24 50	29 45	53·7	24 14	28 52	53·3	223	317
44	136	27 42	32 56	54·3	27 07	32 01	53·9	26 31	31 07	53·5	25 55	30 13	53·1	25 19	29 20	52·7	24 43	28 28	52·4	224	316
45	135	28 14	32 29	53·4	27 38	31 35	53·0	27 02	30 41	52·5	26 25	29 48	52·1	25 48	28 55	51·8	25 11	28 03	51·4	225	315

Lat. / A		48°			49°			50°			51°			52°			53°			Lat. / A	
LHA/F		A/H	B/P	Z_1/Z_2	A/H	B/P	Z_1/Z_2	A/H	B/P	Z_1/Z_2	A/H	B/P	Z_1/Z_2	A/H	B/P	Z_1/Z_2	A/H	B/P	Z_1/Z_2	LHA	
°	°	° ′	° ′	°	° ′	° ′	°	° ′	° ′	°	° ′	° ′	°	° ′	° ′	°	° ′	° ′	°	°	°
45	135	28 14	32 29	53·4	27 38	31 35	53·0	27 02	30 41	52·5	26 25	29 48	52·1	25 48	28 55	51·8	25 11	28 03	51·4	225	315
46	134	28 46	32 01	52·4	28 10	31 08	52·0	27 32	30 14	51·6	26 55	29 22	51·2	26 17	28 29	50·8	25 39	27 38	50·4	226	314
47	133	29 18	31 33	51·4	28 40	30 40	51·0	28 02	29 47	50·6	27 24	28 55	50·2	26 46	28 03	49·8	26 07	27 12	49·4	227	313
48	132	29 49	31 04	50·5	29 11	30 11	50·0	28 32	29 19	49·6	27 53	28 27	49·2	27 14	27 36	48·8	26 34	26 46	48·4	228	312
49	131	30 20	30 34	49·5	29 41	29 42	49·0	29 01	28 50	48·6	28 21	27 59	48·2	27 41	27 08	47·8	27 01	26 18	47·4	229	311
50	130	30 50	30 04	48·5	30 10	29 12	48·0	29 30	28 20	47·6	28 49	27 30	47·2	28 08	26 40	46·8	27 27	25 51	46·4	230	310
51	129	31 20	29 32	47·5	30 39	28 41	47·0	29 58	27 50	46·6	29 17	27 00	46·2	28 35	26 11	45·8	27 53	25 22	45·4	231	309
52	128	31 49	29 00	46·4	31 08	28 09	46·0	30 26	27 19	45·6	29 44	26 30	45·2	29 01	25 41	44·8	28 19	24 53	44·4	232	308
53	127	32 18	28 27	45·4	31 36	27 37	45·0	30 53	26 48	44·5	30 10	25 59	44·1	29 27	25 11	43·7	28 44	24 24	43·3	233	307
54	126	32 46	27 53	44·4	32 03	27 04	43·9	31 20	26 15	43·5	30 36	25 27	43·1	29 52	24 40	42·7	29 08	23 53	42·3	234	306
55	125	33 14	27 19	43·3	32 30	26 30	42·9	31 46	25 42	42·4	31 02	24 55	42·0	30 17	24 08	41·6	29 32	23 23	41·2	235	305
56	124	33 42	26 44	42·2	32 57	25 55	41·8	32 12	25 08	41·4	31 27	24 22	41·0	30 41	23 36	40·6	29 56	22 51	40·2	236	304
57	123	34 08	26 07	41·1	33 23	25 20	40·7	32 37	24 34	40·3	31 51	23 48	39·9	31 05	23 03	39·5	30 19	22 19	39·1	237	303
58	122	34 34	25 30	40·1	33 48	24 44	39·6	33 02	23 58	39·2	32 15	23 14	38·8	31 28	22 29	38·4	30 41	21 46	38·0	238	302
59	121	35 00	24 53	39·0	34 13	24 07	38·5	33 26	23 22	38·1	32 39	22 38	37·7	31 51	21 55	37·3	31 03	21 13	37·0	239	301
60	120	35 25	24 14	37·8	34 37	23 30	37·4	33 50	22 46	37·0	33 02	22 03	36·6	32 13	21 20	36·2	31 25	20 39	35·9	240	300
61	119	35 49	23 35	36·7	35 01	22 51	36·3	34 12	22 08	35·9	33 24	21 26	35·5	32 35	20 45	35·1	31 46	20 04	34·8	241	299
62	118	36 13	22 55	35·6	35 24	22 12	35·2	34 35	21 30	34·8	33 45	20 49	34·4	32 56	20 09	34·0	32 06	19 29	33·7	242	298
63	117	36 36	22 14	34·4	35 46	21 32	34·0	34 56	20 51	33·6	34 06	20 11	33·3	33 16	19 32	32·9	32 26	18 53	32·5	243	297
64	116	36 58	21 32	33·3	36 08	20 52	32·9	35 17	20 12	32·5	34 27	19 33	32·1	33 36	18 54	31·8	32 45	18 17	31·4	244	296
65	115	37 20	20 50	32·1	36 29	20 10	31·7	35 38	19 32	31·3	34 47	18 54	31·0	33 55	18 16	30·6	33 03	17 40	30·3	245	295
66	114	37 41	20 07	30·9	36 49	19 28	30·5	35 58	18 51	30·2	35 06	18 14	29·8	34 13	17 38	29·5	33 21	17 02	29·1	246	294
67	113	38 01	19 23	29·7	37 09	18 46	29·4	36 17	18 09	29·0	35 24	17 33	28·6	34 31	16 59	28·3	33 38	16 24	28·0	247	293
68	112	38 21	18 38	28·5	37 28	18 02	28·2	36 35	17 27	27·8	35 42	16 53	27·5	34 48	16 19	27·1	33 55	15 46	26·8	248	292
69	111	38 40	17 53	27·3	37 46	17 18	27·0	36 53	16 44	26·6	35 59	16 11	26·3	35 05	15 38	26·0	34 11	15 07	25·7	249	291
70	110	38 58	17 07	26·1	38 04	16 33	25·7	37 10	16 01	25·4	36 15	15 29	25·1	35 21	14 58	24·8	34 26	14 27	24·5	250	290
71	109	39 15	16 20	24·9	38 20	15 48	24·5	37 26	15 17	24·2	36 31	14 46	23·9	35 36	14 16	23·6	34 41	13 47	23·3	251	289
72	108	39 31	15 33	23·6	38 36	15 02	23·3	37 41	14 32	23·0	36 46	14 03	22·7	35 50	13 34	22·4	34 55	13 07	22·1	252	288
73	107	39 47	14 45	22·4	38 51	14 16	22·1	37 56	13 47	21·8	37 00	13 19	21·5	36 04	12 52	21·2	35 08	12 25	20·9	253	287
74	106	40 02	13 56	21·1	39 06	13 28	20·8	38 10	13 01	20·5	37 13	12 35	20·3	36 17	12 09	20·0	35 21	11 44	19·8	254	286
75	105	40 16	13 07	19·8	39 19	12 41	19·5	38 23	12 15	19·3	37 26	11 50	19·0	36 29	11 26	18·8	35 33	11 02	18·5	255	285
76	104	40 29	12 17	18·5	39 32	11 53	18·3	38 35	11 28	18·0	37 38	11 05	17·8	36 41	10 42	17·6	35 44	10 20	17·3	256	284
77	103	40 41	11 27	17·3	39 44	11 04	17·0	38 47	10 41	16·8	37 49	10 19	16·5	36 52	9 58	16·3	35 54	9 37	16·1	257	283
78	102	40 53	10 36	16·0	39 55	10 15	15·7	38 57	9 54	15·5	38 00	9 33	15·3	37 02	9 14	15·1	36 04	8 54	14·9	258	282
79	101	41 04	9 45	14·7	40 05	9 25	14·4	39 07	9 06	14·2	38 09	8 47	14·0	37 11	8 29	13·9	36 13	8 11	13·7	259	281
80	100	41 13	8 53	13·3	40 15	8 35	13·2	39 16	8 17	13·0	38 18	8 00	12·8	37 19	7 44	12·6	36 21	7 27	12·5	260	280
81	99	41 22	8 01	12·0	40 23	7 45	11·9	39 25	7 29	11·7	38 26	7 13	11·5	37 27	6 58	11·4	36 28	6 43	11·2	261	279
82	98	41 30	7 09	10·7	40 31	6 54	10·5	39 32	6 40	10·4	38 33	6 26	10·3	37 34	6 12	10·1	36 35	5 59	10·0	262	278
83	97	41 37	6 16	9·4	40 38	6 03	9·2	39 39	5 50	9·1	38 39	5 38	9·0	37 40	5 26	8·9	36 41	5 15	8·7	263	277
84	96	41 43	5 23	8·1	40 44	5 12	7·9	39 44	5 01	7·8	38 45	4 50	7·7	37 45	4 40	7·6	36 46	4 30	7·5	264	276
85	95	41 48	4 29	6·7	40 49	4 20	6·6	39 49	4 11	6·5	38 49	4 02	6·4	37 50	3 54	6·3	36 50	3 45	6·3	265	275
86	94	41 52	3 36	5·4	40 53	3 28	5·3	39 53	3 21	5·2	38 53	3 14	5·1	37 53	3 07	5·1	36 54	3 01	5·0	266	274
87	93	41 56	2 42	4·0	40 56	2 36	4·0	39 56	2 31	3·9	38 56	2 26	3·9	37 56	2 20	3·8	36 56	2 16	3·8	267	273
88	92	41 58	1 48	2·7	40 58	1 44	2·6	39 58	1 41	2·6	38 58	1 37	2·6	37 58	1 34	2·5	36 58	1 30	2·5	268	272
89	91	42 00	0 54	1·3	41 00	0 52	1·3	40 00	0 50	1·3	39 00	0 49	1·3	38 00	0 47	1·3	37 00	0 45	1·3	269	271
90	90	42 00	0 00	0·0	41 00	0 00	0·0	40 00	0 00	0·0	39 00	0 00	0·0	38 00	0 00	0·0	37 00	0 00	0·0	270	270

N. Lat: for LHA > 180° … $Z_n = Z$
for LHA < 180° … $Z_n = 360° - Z$

S. Lat.: for LHA > 180° … $Z_n = 180° - Z$
for LHA < 180° … $Z_n = 180° + Z$

SIGHT REDUCTION TABLE

B: (−) for 90° < LHA < 270°
Dec:(−) for Lat. contrary name

Z_1: same sign as B
Z_2: (−) for F > 90°

Lat. / A		54°			55°			56°			57°			58°			59°			Lat. / A	
LHA/F		A/H	B/P	Z_1/Z_2	A/H	B/P	Z_1/Z_2	A/H	B/P	Z_1/Z_2	A/H	B/P	Z_1/Z_2	A/H	B/P	Z_1/Z_2	A/H	B/P	Z_1/Z_2	LHA	
°	°	° ′	° ′	°	° ′	° ′	°	° ′	° ′	°	° ′	° ′	°	° ′	° ′	°	° ′	° ′	°	°	°
0	180	0 00	36 00	90·0	0 00	35 00	90·0	0 00	34 00	90·0	0 00	33 00	90·0	0 00	32 00	90·0	0 00	31 00	90·0	180	360
1	179	0 35	36 00	89·2	0 34	35 00	89·2	0 34	34 00	89·2	0 33	33 00	89·2	0 32	32 00	89·2	0 31	31 00	89·1	181	359
2	178	1 11	35 59	88·4	1 09	34 59	88·4	1 07	33 59	88·3	1 05	32 59	88·3	1 04	31 59	88·3	1 02	30 59	88·3	182	358
3	177	1 46	35 58	87·6	1 43	34 58	87·5	1 41	33 58	87·5	1 38	32 58	87·5	1 35	31 58	87·5	1 33	30 58	87·4	183	357
4	176	2 21	35 56	86·8	2 18	34 56	86·7	2 14	33 56	86·7	2 11	32 56	86·6	2 07	31 56	86·6	2 04	30 56	86·6	184	356
5	175	2 56	35 54	86·0	2 52	34 54	85·9	2 48	33 54	85·9	2 43	32 54	85·8	2 39	31 54	85·8	2 34	30 54	85·7	185	355
6	174	3 31	35 51	85·1	3 26	34 51	85·1	3 21	33 51	85·0	3 16	32 51	85·0	3 11	31 52	84·9	3 05	30 52	84·9	186	354
7	173	4 06	35 48	84·3	4 00	34 48	84·3	3 54	33 48	84·2	3 48	32 48	84·1	3 42	31 48	84·1	3 36	30 49	84·0	187	353
8	172	4 42	35 44	83·5	4 35	34 44	83·4	4 28	33 44	83·4	4 21	32 45	83·3	4 14	31 45	83·2	4 07	30 45	83·1	188	352
9	171	5 17	35 40	82·7	5 09	34 40	82·6	5 01	33 40	82·5	4 53	32 41	82·4	4 45	31 41	82·3	4 37	30 41	82·3	189	351
10	170	5 51	35 35	81·9	5 43	34 35	81·8	5 34	33 36	81·7	5 26	32 36	81·6	5 17	31 36	81·5	5 08	30 37	81·4	190	350
11	169	6 26	35 30	81·1	6 17	34 30	81·0	6 08	33 31	80·8	5 58	32 31	80·7	5 48	31 31	80·6	5 38	30 32	80·5	191	349
12	168	7 01	35 24	80·2	6 51	34 24	80·1	6 41	33 25	80·0	6 30	32 25	79·9	6 20	31 26	79·8	6 09	30 27	79·7	192	348
13	167	7 36	35 18	79·4	7 25	34 18	79·3	7 14	33 19	79·2	7 02	32 19	79·0	6 51	31 20	78·9	6 39	30 21	78·8	193	347
14	166	8 11	35 11	78·6	7 59	34 12	78·5	7 46	33 12	78·3	7 34	32 13	78·2	7 22	31 14	78·1	7 09	30 15	77·9	194	346
15	165	8 45	35 04	77·8	8 32	34 04	77·6	8 19	33 05	77·5	8 06	32 06	77·3	7 53	31 07	77·2	7 40	30 08	77·1	195	345
16	164	9 19	34 56	76·9	9 06	33 57	76·8	8 52	32 58	76·6	8 38	31 58	76·5	8 24	31 00	76·3	8 10	30 01	76·2	196	344
17	163	9 54	34 47	76·1	9 39	33 48	75·9	9 25	32 49	75·8	9 10	31 50	75·6	8 55	30 52	75·5	8 40	29 53	75·3	197	343
18	162	10 28	34 39	75·3	10 13	33 40	75·1	9 57	32 41	74·9	9 41	31 42	74·8	9 25	30 43	74·6	9 09	29 45	74·4	198	342
19	161	11 02	34 29	74·4	10 46	33 30	74·2	10 29	32 32	74·1	10 13	31 33	73·9	9 56	30 35	73·7	9 39	29 36	73·6	199	341
20	160	11 36	34 19	73·6	11 19	33 21	73·4	11 02	32 22	73·2	10 44	31 24	73·0	10 27	30 25	72·8	10 09	29 27	72·7	200	340
21	159	12 10	34 09	72·7	11 52	33 10	72·5	11 34	32 12	72·3	11 15	31 14	72·2	10 57	30 15	72·0	10 38	29 17	71·8	201	339
22	158	12 43	33 58	71·9	12 24	33 00	71·7	12 06	32 01	71·5	11 46	31 03	71·3	11 27	30 05	71·1	11 07	29 07	70·9	202	338
23	157	13 17	33 46	71·0	12 57	32 48	70·8	12 37	31 50	70·6	12 17	30 52	70·4	11 57	29 54	70·2	11 37	28 57	70·0	203	337
24	156	13 50	33 34	70·2	13 29	32 36	70·0	13 09	31 38	69·7	12 48	30 41	69·5	12 27	29 43	69·3	12 06	28 46	69·1	204	336
25	155	14 23	33 22	69·3	14 02	32 24	69·1	13 40	31 26	68·9	13 18	30 29	68·6	12 56	29 31	68·4	12 34	28 34	68·2	205	335
26	154	14 56	33 09	68·5	14 34	32 11	68·2	14 11	31 14	68·0	13 49	30 16	67·8	13 26	29 19	67·5	13 03	28 22	67·3	206	334
27	153	15 29	32 55	67·6	15 06	31 58	67·3	14 42	31 00	67·1	14 19	30 03	66·9	13 55	29 06	66·6	13 31	28 10	66·4	207	333
28	152	16 01	32 41	66·7	15 37	31 44	66·5	15 13	30 47	66·2	14 49	29 50	66·0	14 24	28 53	65·7	14 00	27 57	65·5	208	332
29	151	16 33	32 26	65·8	16 09	31 29	65·6	15 44	30 32	65·3	15 19	29 36	65·1	14 53	28 39	64·8	14 28	27 43	64·6	209	331
30	150	17 05	32 11	65·0	16 40	31 14	64·7	16 14	30 17	64·4	15 48	29 21	64·2	15 22	28 25	63·9	14 55	27 29	63·7	210	330
31	149	17 37	31 55	64·1	17 11	30 58	63·8	16 44	30 02	63·5	16 17	29 06	63·3	15 50	28 10	63·0	15 23	27 15	62·7	211	329
32	148	18 09	31 38	63·2	17 42	30 42	62·9	17 14	29 46	62·6	16 47	28 51	62·3	16 19	27 55	62·1	15 50	27 00	61·8	212	328
33	147	18 40	31 21	62·3	18 12	30 25	62·0	17 44	29 30	61·7	17 15	28 34	61·4	16 47	27 39	61·2	16 17	26 45	60·9	213	327
34	146	19 11	31 04	61·4	18 42	30 08	61·1	18 13	29 13	60·8	17 44	28 18	60·5	17 14	27 23	60·2	16 44	26 29	60·0	214	326
35	145	19 42	30 46	60·5	19 12	29 50	60·2	18 42	28 55	59·9	18 12	28 01	59·6	17 42	27 06	59·3	17 11	26 12	59·0	215	325
36	144	20 13	30 27	59·6	19 42	29 32	59·2	19 11	28 37	58·9	18 40	27 43	58·6	18 09	26 49	58·4	17 37	25 55	58·1	216	324
37	143	20 43	30 07	58·6	20 12	29 13	58·3	19 40	28 19	58·0	19 08	27 25	57·7	18 36	26 31	57·4	18 03	25 38	57·1	217	323
38	142	21 13	29 48	57·7	20 41	28 53	57·4	20 08	27 59	57·1	19 35	27 06	56·8	19 02	26 13	56·5	18 29	25 20	56·2	218	322
39	141	21 43	29 27	56·8	21 10	28 33	56·4	20 36	27 40	56·1	20 03	26 47	55·8	19 29	25 54	55·5	18 55	25 02	55·2	219	321
40	140	22 12	29 06	55·8	21 38	28 13	55·5	21 04	27 20	55·2	20 30	26 27	54·9	19 55	25 35	54·6	19 20	24 43	54·3	220	320
41	139	22 41	28 44	54·9	22 06	27 51	54·5	21 31	26 59	54·2	20 56	26 07	53·9	20 21	25 15	53·6	19 45	24 24	53·3	221	319
42	138	23 10	28 22	53·9	22 34	27 29	53·6	21 58	26 37	53·3	21 22	25 46	52·9	20 46	24 55	52·6	20 10	24 04	52·3	222	318
43	137	23 38	27 59	53·0	23 02	27 07	52·6	22 25	26 15	52·3	21 48	25 24	52·0	21 11	24 34	51·7	20 34	23 43	51·4	223	317
44	136	24 06	27 36	52·0	23 29	26 44	51·7	22 51	25 53	51·3	22 14	25 02	51·0	21 36	24 12	50·7	20 58	23 23	50·4	224	316
45	135	24 34	27 11	51·0	23 56	26 20	50·7	23 17	25 30	50·3	22 39	24 40	50·0	22 00	23 50	49·7	21 21	23 01	49·4	225	315

Lat. / A		54°			55°			56°			57°			58°			59°			Lat. / A	
LHA/F		A/H	B/P	Z_1/Z_2	A/H	B/P	Z_1/Z_2	A/H	B/P	Z_1/Z_2	A/H	B/P	Z_1/Z_2	A/H	B/P	Z_1/Z_2	A/H	B/P	Z_1/Z_2	LHA	
°	°	° ′	° ′	°	° ′	° ′	°	° ′	° ′	°	° ′	° ′	°	° ′	° ′	°	° ′	° ′	°	°	°
45	135	24 34	27 11	51·0	23 56	26 20	50·7	23 17	25 30	50·3	22 39	24 40	50·0	22 00	23 50	49·7	21 21	23 01	49·4	225	315
46	134	25 01	26 47	50·0	24 22	25 56	49·7	23 43	25 06	49·4	23 04	24 17	49·0	22 24	23 28	48·7	21 45	22 39	48·4	226	314
47	133	25 28	26 22	49·1	24 48	25 32	48·7	24 08	24 42	48·4	23 28	23 53	48·0	22 48	23 05	47·7	22 08	22 17	47·4	227	313
48	132	25 54	25 56	48·1	25 14	25 06	47·7	24 33	24 17	47·4	23 53	23 29	47·0	23 11	22 41	46·7	22 30	21 54	46·4	228	312
49	131	26 20	25 29	47·1	25 39	24 40	46·7	24 58	23 52	46·4	24 16	23 05	46·0	23 34	22 17	45·7	22 52	21 31	45·4	229	311
50	130	26 46	25 02	46·0	26 04	24 14	45·7	25 22	23 26	45·3	24 40	22 39	45·0	23 57	21 53	44·7	23 14	21 07	44·4	230	310
51	129	27 11	24 34	45·0	26 28	23 47	44·7	25 45	23 00	44·3	25 02	22 14	44·0	24 19	21 28	43·7	23 36	20 43	43·4	231	309
52	128	27 36	24 06	44·0	26 52	23 19	43·6	26 09	22 33	43·3	25 25	21 48	43·0	24 41	21 03	42·7	23 57	20 18	42·3	232	308
53	127	28 00	23 37	43·0	27 16	22 51	42·6	26 32	22 06	42·3	25 47	21 21	41·9	25 02	20 37	41·6	24 17	19 53	41·3	233	307
54	126	28 24	23 07	41·9	27 39	22 22	41·6	26 54	21 38	41·2	26 09	20 54	40·9	25 23	20 10	40·6	24 37	19 27	40·3	234	306
55	125	28 47	22 37	40·9	28 01	21 53	40·5	27 16	21 09	40·2	26 30	20 26	39·9	25 44	19 43	39·5	24 57	19 01	39·2	235	305
56	124	29 10	22 07	39·8	28 24	21 23	39·5	27 37	20 40	39·1	26 50	19 57	38·8	26 04	19 16	38·5	25 17	18 34	38·2	236	304
57	123	29 32	21 35	38·8	28 45	20 52	38·4	27 58	20 10	38·1	27 11	19 29	37·8	26 23	18 48	37·4	25 35	18 07	37·1	237	303
58	122	29 54	21 03	37·7	29 06	20 21	37·3	28 19	19 40	37·0	27 31	18 59	36·7	26 42	18 19	36·4	25 54	17 40	36·1	238	302
59	121	30 15	20 31	36·6	29 27	19 50	36·3	28 38	19 09	35·9	27 50	18 30	35·6	27 01	17 50	35·3	26 12	17 12	35·0	239	301
60	120	30 36	19 58	35·5	29 47	19 18	35·2	28 58	18 38	34·9	28 09	17 59	34·5	27 19	17 21	34·2	26 29	16 43	34·0	240	300
61	119	30 56	19 24	34·4	30 07	18 45	34·1	29 17	18 06	33·8	28 27	17 29	33·5	27 37	16 51	33·2	26 46	16 14	32·9	241	299
62	118	31 16	18 50	33·3	30 26	18 12	33·0	29 35	17 34	32·7	28 45	16 57	32·4	27 54	16 21	32·1	27 03	15 45	31·8	242	298
63	117	31 35	18 15	32·2	30 44	17 38	31·9	29 53	17 02	31·6	29 02	16 26	31·3	28 10	15 50	31·0	27 19	15 15	30·7	243	297
64	116	31 53	17 40	31·1	31 02	17 04	30·8	30 10	16 28	30·5	29 19	15 53	30·2	28 27	15 19	29·9	27 35	14 45	29·6	244	296
65	115	32 11	17 04	30·0	31 19	16 29	29·7	30 27	15 55	29·4	29 35	15 21	29·1	28 42	14 48	28·8	27 50	14 15	28·5	245	295
66	114	32 29	16 28	28·8	31 36	15 54	28·5	30 43	15 20	28·2	29 50	14 48	28·0	28 57	14 16	27·7	28 04	13 44	27·4	246	294
67	113	32 45	15 51	27·7	31 52	15 18	27·4	30 59	14 46	27·1	30 05	14 14	26·8	29 12	13 43	26·6	28 18	13 13	26·3	247	293
68	112	33 01	15 14	26·5	32 08	14 42	26·3	31 14	14 11	26·0	30 20	13 40	25·7	29 26	13 10	25·5	28 31	12 41	25·2	248	292
69	111	33 17	14 36	25·4	32 23	14 05	25·1	31 28	13 35	24·8	30 34	13 06	24·6	29 39	12 37	24·4	28 44	12 09	24·1	249	291
70	110	33 32	13 57	24·2	32 37	13 28	24·0	31 42	12 59	23·7	30 47	12 31	23·5	29 52	12 04	23·2	28 57	11 37	23·0	250	290
71	109	33 46	13 18	23·1	32 51	12 51	22·8	31 55	12 23	22·6	31 00	11 56	22·3	30 04	11 30	22·1	29 09	11 04	21·9	251	289
72	108	33 59	12 39	21·9	33 04	12 13	21·6	32 08	11 46	21·4	31 12	11 21	21·2	30 16	10 56	21·0	29 20	10 31	20·8	252	288
73	107	34 12	12 00	20·7	33 16	11 34	20·5	32 20	11 09	20·2	31 23	10 45	20·0	30 27	10 21	19·8	29 30	9 58	19·6	253	287
74	106	34 24	11 19	19·5	33 28	10 55	19·3	32 31	10 32	19·1	31 34	10 09	18·9	30 37	9 46	18·7	29 41	9 24	18·5	254	286
75	105	34 36	10 39	18·3	33 39	10 16	18·1	32 42	9 54	17·9	31 44	9 32	17·7	30 47	9 11	17·5	29 50	8 50	17·4	255	285
76	104	34 46	9 58	17·1	33 49	9 37	16·9	32 52	9 16	16·7	31 54	8 56	16·6	30 57	8 36	16·4	29 59	8 16	16·2	256	284
77	103	34 56	9 17	15·9	33 59	8 57	15·7	33 01	8 38	15·6	32 03	8 19	15·4	31 05	8 00	15·2	30 07	7 42	15·1	257	283
78	102	35 06	8 35	14·7	34 08	8 17	14·5	33 10	7 59	14·4	32 11	7 41	14·2	31 13	7 24	14·1	30 15	7 07	13·9	258	282
79	101	35 14	7 54	13·5	34 16	7 37	13·3	33 18	7 20	13·2	32 19	7 04	13·0	31 21	6 48	12·9	30 22	6 32	12·8	259	281
80	100	35 22	7 11	12·3	34 24	6 56	12·1	33 25	6 41	12·0	32 26	6 26	11·9	31 27	6 12	11·7	30 29	5 57	11·6	260	280
81	99	35 29	6 29	11·1	34 30	6 15	10·9	33 32	6 01	10·8	32 33	5 48	10·7	31 34	5 35	10·6	30 35	5 22	10·5	261	279
82	98	35 36	5 46	9·9	34 37	5 34	9·7	33 37	5 22	9·6	32 38	5 10	9·5	31 39	4 58	9·4	30 40	4 47	9·3	262	278
83	97	35 41	5 04	8·6	34 42	4 53	8·5	33 43	4 42	8·4	32 43	4 32	8·3	31 44	4 21	8·2	30 45	4 11	8·2	263	277
84	96	35 46	4 21	7·4	34 47	4 11	7·3	33 47	4 02	7·2	32 48	3 53	7·1	31 48	3 44	7·1	30 49	3 36	7·0	264	276
85	95	35 51	3 37	6·2	34 51	3 30	6·1	33 51	3 22	6·0	32 52	3 14	6·0	31 52	3 07	5·9	30 52	3 00	5·8	265	275
86	94	35 54	2 54	4·9	34 54	2 48	4·9	33 54	2 42	4·8	32 55	2 36	4·8	31 55	2 30	4·7	30 55	2 24	4·7	266	274
87	93	35 57	2 11	3·7	34 57	2 06	3·7	33 57	2 01	3·6	32 57	1 57	3·6	31 57	1 52	3·5	30 57	1 48	3·5	267	273
88	92	35 58	1 27	2·5	34 59	1 24	2·4	33 59	1 21	2·4	32 59	1 18	2·4	31 59	1 15	2·4	30 59	1 12	2·3	268	272
89	91	36 00	0 44	1·2	35 00	0 42	1·2	34 00	0 40	1·2	33 00	0 39	1·2	32 00	0 37	1·2	31 00	0 36	1·2	269	271
90	90	36 00	0 00	0·0	35 00	0 00	0·0	34 00	0 00	0·0	33 00	0 00	0·0	32 00	0 00	0·0	31 00	0 00	0·0	270	270

N. Lat: for LHA > 180° … $Z_n = Z$
for LHA < 180° … $Z_n = 360° - Z$

S. Lat.: for LHA > 180° … $Z_n = 180° - Z$
for LHA < 180° … $Z_n = 180° + Z$

SIGHT REDUCTION TABLE

B: (−) for 90° < LHA < 270°
Dec:(−) for Lat. contrary name

Z_1: same sign as B
Z_2: (−) for F > 90°

Lat. / A		60°			61°			62°			63°			64°			65°			Lat. / A	
LHA/F		A/H	B/P	Z_1/Z_2	A/H	B/P	Z_1/Z_2	A/H	B/P	Z_1/Z_2	A/H	B/P	Z_1/Z_2	A/H	B/P	Z_1/Z_2	A/H	B/P	Z_1/Z_2	LHA	
°	°	° ′	° ′	°	° ′	° ′	°	° ′	° ′	°	° ′	° ′	°	° ′	° ′	°	° ′	° ′	°	°	°
0	180	0 00	30 00	90·0	0 00	29 00	90·0	0 00	28 00	90·0	0 00	27 00	90·0	0 00	26 00	90·0	0 00	25 00	90·0	180	360
1	179	0 30	30 00	89·1	0 29	29 00	89·1	0 28	28 00	89·1	0 27	27 00	89·1	0 26	26 00	89·1	0 25	25 00	89·1	181	359
2	178	1 00	29 59	88·3	0 58	28 59	88·3	0 56	27 59	88·2	0 54	26 59	88·2	0 53	25 59	88·2	0 51	24 59	88·2	182	358
3	177	1 30	29 58	87·4	1 27	28 58	87·4	1 24	27 58	87·4	1 22	26 58	87·3	1 19	25 58	87·3	1 16	24 58	87·3	183	357
4	176	2 00	29 56	86·5	1 56	28 56	86·5	1 53	27 57	86·5	1 49	26 57	86·4	1 45	25 57	86·4	1 41	24 57	86·4	184	356
5	175	2 30	29 54	85·7	2 25	28 54	85·6	2 21	27 55	85·6	2 16	26 55	85·5	2 11	25 55	85·5	2 07	24 55	85·5	185	355
6	174	3 00	29 52	84·8	2 54	28 52	84·7	2 49	27 52	84·7	2 43	26 52	84·6	2 38	25 53	84·6	2 32	24 53	84·6	186	354
7	173	3 30	29 49	83·9	3 23	28 49	83·9	3 17	27 49	83·8	3 10	26 50	83·8	3 04	25 50	83·7	2 57	24 50	83·7	187	353
8	172	3 59	29 45	83·1	3 52	28 46	83·0	3 45	27 46	82·9	3 37	26 46	82·9	3 30	25 47	82·8	3 22	24 47	82·7	188	352
9	171	4 29	29 42	82·2	4 21	28 42	82·1	4 13	27 42	82·0	4 04	26 43	82·0	3 56	25 43	81·9	3 47	24 44	81·8	189	351
10	170	4 59	29 37	81·3	4 50	28 38	81·2	4 41	27 38	81·2	4 31	26 39	81·1	4 22	25 39	81·0	4 13	24 40	80·9	190	350
11	169	5 28	29 33	80·4	5 18	28 33	80·4	5 08	27 34	80·3	4 58	26 34	80·2	4 48	25 35	80·1	4 38	24 36	80·0	191	349
12	168	5 58	29 27	79·6	5 47	28 28	79·5	5 36	27 29	79·4	5 25	26 29	79·3	5 14	25 30	79·2	5 02	24 31	79·1	192	348
13	167	6 27	29 22	78·7	6 16	28 22	78·6	6 04	27 23	78·5	5 52	26 24	78·4	5 40	25 25	78·3	5 27	24 26	78·2	193	347
14	166	6 57	29 15	77·8	6 44	28 16	77·7	6 31	27 17	77·6	6 18	26 18	77·5	6 05	25 20	77·4	5 52	24 21	77·3	194	346
15	165	7 26	29 09	76·9	7 13	28 10	76·8	6 59	27 11	76·7	6 45	26 12	76·6	6 31	25 14	76·5	6 17	24 15	76·4	195	345
16	164	7 55	29 02	76·1	7 41	28 03	75·9	7 26	27 04	75·8	7 11	26 06	75·7	6 56	25 07	75·5	6 41	24 09	75·4	196	344
17	163	8 24	28 54	75·2	8 09	27 56	75·0	7 53	26 57	74·9	7 38	25 59	74·8	7 22	25 00	74·6	7 06	24 02	74·5	197	343
18	162	8 53	28 46	74·3	8 37	27 48	74·1	8 20	26 50	74·0	8 04	25 51	73·9	7 47	24 53	73·7	7 30	23 55	73·6	198	342
19	161	9 22	28 38	73·4	9 05	27 40	73·2	8 48	26 41	73·1	8 30	25 43	72·9	8 12	24 45	72·8	7 55	23 48	72·7	199	341
20	160	9 51	28 29	72·5	9 33	27 31	72·3	9 14	26 33	72·2	8 56	25 35	72·0	8 37	24 37	71·9	8 19	23 40	71·7	200	340
21	159	10 19	28 19	71·6	10 00	27 22	71·4	9 41	26 24	71·3	9 22	25 26	71·1	9 02	24 29	71·0	8 43	23 32	70·8	201	339
22	158	10 48	28 10	70·7	10 28	27 12	70·5	10 08	26 15	70·4	9 48	25 17	70·2	9 27	24 20	70·0	9 07	23 23	69·9	202	338
23	157	11 16	27 59	69·8	10 55	27 02	69·6	10 34	26 05	69·5	10 13	25 08	69·3	9 52	24 11	69·1	9 30	23 14	69·0	203	337
24	156	11 44	27 49	68·9	11 22	26 51	68·7	11 00	25 54	68·5	10 38	24 58	68·4	10 16	24 01	68·2	9 54	23 04	68·0	204	336
25	155	12 12	27 37	68·0	11 49	26 40	67·8	11 27	25 44	67·6	11 04	24 47	67·4	10 41	23 51	67·3	10 17	22 55	67·1	205	335
26	154	12 40	27 26	67·1	12 16	26 29	66·9	11 53	25 33	66·7	11 29	24 36	66·5	11 05	23 40	66·3	10 41	22 44	66·2	206	334
27	153	13 07	27 13	66·2	12 43	26 17	66·0	12 18	25 21	65·8	11 54	24 25	65·6	11 29	23 29	65·4	11 04	22 34	65·2	207	333
28	152	13 35	27 01	65·3	13 09	26 05	65·1	12 44	25 09	64·9	12 18	24 13	64·7	11 53	23 18	64·5	11 27	22 23	64·3	208	332
29	151	14 02	26 48	64·4	13 36	25 52	64·1	13 09	24 56	63·9	12 43	24 01	63·7	12 16	23 06	63·5	11 49	22 11	63·3	209	331
30	150	14 29	26 34	63·4	14 02	25 39	63·2	13 35	24 43	63·0	13 07	23 49	62·8	12 40	22 54	62·6	12 12	21 59	62·4	210	330
31	149	14 55	26 20	62·5	14 28	25 25	62·3	14 00	24 30	62·1	13 31	23 36	61·8	13 03	22 41	61·6	12 34	21 47	61·4	211	329
32	148	15 22	26 05	61·6	14 53	25 11	61·3	14 24	24 16	61·1	13 55	23 22	60·9	13 26	22 28	60·7	12 56	21 35	60·5	212	328
33	147	15 48	25 50	60·6	15 19	24 56	60·4	14 49	24 02	60·2	14 19	23 08	59·9	13 49	22 15	59·7	13 18	21 22	59·5	213	327
34	146	16 14	25 35	59·7	15 44	24 41	59·5	15 13	23 47	59·2	14 42	22 54	59·0	14 11	22 01	58·8	13 40	21 08	58·6	214	326
35	145	16 40	25 19	58·8	16 09	24 25	58·5	15 37	23 32	58·3	15 06	22 39	58·0	14 34	21 47	57·8	14 02	20 54	57·6	215	325
36	144	17 05	25 02	57·8	16 33	24 09	57·6	16 01	23 17	57·3	15 29	22 24	57·1	14 56	21 32	56·9	14 23	20 40	56·6	216	324
37	143	17 31	24 45	56·9	16 58	23 53	56·6	16 25	23 00	56·4	15 51	22 09	56·1	15 18	21 17	55·9	14 44	20 26	55·7	217	323
38	142	17 56	24 28	55·9	17 22	23 36	55·7	16 48	22 44	55·4	16 14	21 53	55·2	15 39	21 01	54·9	15 05	20 11	54·7	218	322
39	141	18 20	24 10	55·0	17 46	23 18	54·7	17 11	22 27	54·4	16 36	21 36	54·2	16 01	20 46	54·0	15 25	19 55	53·7	219	321
40	140	18 45	23 52	54·0	18 09	23 00	53·7	17 34	22 10	53·5	16 58	21 19	53·2	16 22	20 29	53·0	15 46	19 39	52·7	220	320
41	139	19 09	23 33	53·0	18 33	22 42	52·8	17 56	21 52	52·5	17 20	21 02	52·2	16 43	20 13	52·0	16 06	19 23	51·8	221	319
42	138	19 33	23 13	52·1	18 56	22 23	51·8	18 19	21 34	51·5	17 41	20 44	51·3	17 03	19 55	51·0	16 26	19 07	50·8	222	318
43	137	19 56	22 54	51·1	19 18	22 04	50·8	18 40	21 15	50·5	18 02	20 26	50·3	17 24	19 38	50·0	16 45	18 50	49·8	223	317
44	136	20 19	22 33	50·1	19 41	21 44	49·8	19 02	20 56	49·5	18 23	20 08	49·3	17 44	19 20	49·0	17 04	18 33	48·8	224	316
45	135	20 42	22 12	49·1	20 03	21 24	48·8	19 23	20 36	48·6	18 43	19 49	48·3	18 03	19 02	48·1	17 23	18 15	47·8	225	315

Lat. / A		60°			61°			62°			63°			64°			65°			Lat. / A	
LHA/F		A/H	B/P	Z_1/Z_2	A/H	B/P	Z_1/Z_2	A/H	B/P	Z_1/Z_2	A/H	B/P	Z_1/Z_2	A/H	B/P	Z_1/Z_2	A/H	B/P	Z_1/Z_2	LHA	
°	°	° ′	° ′	°	° ′	° ′	°	° ′	° ′	°	° ′	° ′	°	° ′	° ′	°	° ′	° ′	°	°	°
45	135	20 42	22 12	49·1	20 03	21 24	48·8	19 23	20 36	48·6	18 43	19 49	48·3	18 03	19 02	48·1	17 23	18 15	47·8	225	315
46	134	21 05	21 51	48·1	20 25	21 04	47·8	19 44	20 16	47·6	19 04	19 29	47·3	18 23	18 43	47·1	17 42	17 57	46·8	226	314
47	133	21 27	21 30	47·1	20 46	20 43	46·8	20 05	19 56	46·6	19 24	19 10	46·3	18 42	18 24	46·1	18 00	17 39	45·8	227	313
48	132	21 49	21 07	46·1	21 07	20 21	45·8	20 25	19 35	45·6	19 43	18 50	45·3	19 01	18 04	45·1	18 18	17 20	44·8	228	312
49	131	22 10	20 45	45·1	21 28	19 59	44·8	20 45	19 14	44·6	20 02	18 29	44·3	19 19	17 45	44·0	18 36	17 01	43·8	229	311
50	130	22 31	20 22	44·1	21 48	19 37	43·8	21 05	18 52	43·5	20 21	18 08	43·3	19 37	17 24	43·0	18 53	16 41	42·8	230	310
51	129	22 52	19 58	43·1	22 08	19 14	42·8	21 24	18 30	42·5	20 40	17 47	42·3	19 55	17 04	42·0	19 10	16 21	41·8	231	309
52	128	23 12	19 34	42·1	22 28	18 51	41·8	21 43	18 08	41·5	20 58	17 25	41·2	20 13	16 43	41·0	19 27	16 01	40·8	232	308
53	127	23 32	19 10	41·0	22 47	18 27	40·7	22 01	17 45	40·5	21 15	17 03	40·2	20 30	16 21	40·0	19 44	15 41	39·7	233	307
54	126	23 52	18 45	40·0	23 06	18 03	39·7	22 19	17 21	39·4	21 33	16 40	39·2	20 46	16 00	39·0	20 00	15 20	38·7	234	306
55	125	24 11	18 19	39·0	23 24	17 38	38·7	22 37	16 58	38·4	21 50	16 17	38·2	21 03	15 38	37·9	20 15	14 58	37·7	235	305
56	124	24 29	17 54	37·9	23 42	17 13	37·6	22 54	16 34	37·4	22 07	15 54	37·1	21 19	15 15	36·9	20 31	14 37	36·7	236	304
57	123	24 48	17 27	36·9	23 59	16 48	36·6	23 11	16 09	36·3	22 23	15 31	36·1	21 34	14 53	35·8	20 46	14 15	35·6	237	303
58	122	25 05	17 01	35·8	24 17	16 22	35·5	23 28	15 44	35·3	22 39	15 07	35·0	21 49	14 29	34·8	21 00	13 53	34·6	238	302
59	121	25 23	16 34	34·8	24 33	15 56	34·5	23 44	15 19	34·2	22 54	14 42	34·0	22 04	14 06	33·8	21 14	13 30	33·5	239	301
60	120	25 40	16 06	33·7	24 50	15 29	33·4	23 59	14 53	33·2	23 09	14 18	32·9	22 19	13 42	32·7	21 28	13 07	32·5	240	300
61	119	25 56	15 38	32·6	25 05	15 03	32·4	24 15	14 27	32·1	23 24	13 53	31·9	22 33	13 18	31·7	21 42	12 44	31·5	241	299
62	118	26 12	15 10	31·5	25 21	14 35	31·3	24 29	14 01	31·1	23 38	13 27	30·8	22 46	12 54	30·6	21 55	12 21	30·4	242	298
63	117	26 27	14 41	30·5	25 36	14 08	30·2	24 44	13 34	30·0	23 52	13 01	29·8	22 59	12 29	29·5	22 07	11 57	29·3	243	297
64	116	26 42	14 12	29·4	25 50	13 39	29·1	24 57	13 07	28·9	24 05	12 35	28·7	23 12	12 04	28·5	22 19	11 33	28·3	244	296
65	115	26 57	13 43	28·3	26 04	13 11	28·1	25 11	12 40	27·8	24 18	12 09	27·6	23 25	11 39	27·4	22 31	11 09	27·2	245	295
66	114	27 11	13 13	27·2	26 17	12 42	27·0	25 24	12 12	26·8	24 30	11 43	26·6	23 36	11 13	26·4	22 43	10 44	26·2	246	294
67	113	27 24	12 43	26·1	26 30	12 13	25·9	25 36	11 44	25·7	24 42	11 16	25·5	23 48	10 47	25·3	22 54	10 20	25·1	247	293
68	112	27 37	12 12	25·0	26 43	11 44	24·8	25 48	11 16	24·6	24 54	10 48	24·4	23 59	10 21	24·2	23 04	9 55	24·0	248	292
69	111	27 50	11 41	23·9	26 55	11 14	23·7	26 00	10 47	23·5	25 05	10 21	23·3	24 09	9 55	23·1	23 14	9 29	23·0	249	291
70	110	28 01	11 10	22·8	27 06	10 44	22·6	26 11	10 18	22·4	25 15	9 53	22·2	24 20	9 28	22·0	23 24	9 04	21·9	250	290
71	109	28 13	10 39	21·7	27 17	10 14	21·5	26 21	9 49	21·3	25 25	9 25	21·1	24 29	9 01	21·0	23 33	8 38	20·8	251	289
72	108	28 24	10 07	20·6	27 27	9 43	20·4	26 31	9 20	20·2	25 35	8 57	20·0	24 38	8 34	19·9	23 42	8 12	19·7	252	288
73	107	28 34	9 35	19·4	27 37	9 12	19·3	26 41	8 50	19·1	25 44	8 28	18·9	24 47	8 07	18·8	23 50	7 46	18·6	253	287
74	106	28 44	9 03	18·3	27 47	8 41	18·2	26 50	8 20	18·0	25 52	8 00	17·8	24 55	7 39	17·7	23 58	7 19	17·6	254	286
75	105	28 53	8 30	17·2	27 55	8 10	17·0	26 58	7 50	16·9	26 01	7 31	16·7	25 03	7 12	16·6	24 06	6 53	16·5	255	285
76	104	29 01	7 57	16·1	28 04	7 38	15·9	27 06	7 20	15·8	26 08	7 02	15·6	25 10	6 44	15·5	24 13	6 26	15·4	256	284
77	103	29 09	7 24	14·9	28 11	7 06	14·8	27 13	6 49	14·7	26 15	6 32	14·5	25 17	6 16	14·4	24 19	5 59	14·3	257	283
78	102	29 17	6 51	13·8	28 18	6 34	13·7	27 20	6 19	13·5	26 22	6 03	13·4	25 23	5 47	13·3	24 25	5 32	13·2	258	282
79	101	29 24	6 17	12·7	28 25	6 02	12·5	27 27	5 48	12·4	26 28	5 33	12·3	25 29	5 19	12·2	24 31	5 05	12·1	259	281
80	100	29 30	5 44	11·5	28 31	5 30	11·4	27 32	5 17	11·3	26 33	5 03	11·2	25 35	4 50	11·1	24 36	4 38	11·0	260	280
81	99	29 36	5 10	10·4	28 37	4 57	10·3	27 38	4 45	10·2	26 38	4 33	10·1	25 39	4 22	10·0	24 40	4 10	9·9	261	279
82	98	29 41	4 36	9·2	28 41	4 25	9·1	27 42	4 14	9·0	26 43	4 03	9·0	25 44	3 53	8·9	24 44	3 43	8·8	262	278
83	97	29 45	4 01	8·1	28 46	3 52	8·0	27 46	3 42	7·9	26 47	3 33	7·8	25 48	3 24	7·8	24 48	3 15	7·7	263	277
84	96	29 49	3 27	6·9	28 50	3 19	6·9	27 50	3 11	6·8	26 50	3 03	6·7	25 51	2 55	6·7	24 51	2 47	6·6	264	276
85	95	29 52	2 53	5·8	28 53	2 46	5·7	27 53	2 39	5·7	26 53	2 33	5·6	25 54	2 26	5·6	24 54	2 20	5·5	265	275
86	94	29 55	2 18	4·6	28 55	2 13	4·6	27 56	2 07	4·5	26 56	2 02	4·5	25 56	1 57	4·4	24 56	1 52	4·4	266	274
87	93	29 57	1 44	3·5	28 57	1 40	3·4	27 57	1 36	3·4	26 58	1 32	3·4	25 58	1 28	3·3	24 58	1 24	3·3	267	273
88	92	29 59	1 09	2·3	28 59	1 06	2·3	27 59	1 04	2·3	26 59	1 01	2·2	25 59	0 59	2·2	24 59	0 56	2·2	268	272
89	91	30 00	0 35	1·2	29 00	0 33	1·1	28 00	0 32	1·1	27 00	0 31	1·1	26 00	0 29	1·1	25 00	0 28	1·1	269	271
90	90	30 00	0 00	0·0	29 00	0 00	0·0	28 00	0 00	0·0	27 00	0 00	0·0	26 00	0 00	0·0	25 00	0 00	0·0	270	270

N. Lat: for LHA > 180° … $Z_n = Z$
for LHA < 180° … $Z_n = 360° - Z$

S. Lat.: for LHA > 180° … $Z_n = 180° - Z$
for LHA < 180° … $Z_n = 180° + Z$

B: (–) for 90° < LHA < 270°
Dec:(–) for Lat. contrary name

SIGHT REDUCTION TABLE

Z_1: same sign as B
Z_2: (–) for F > 90°

Lat. / A		66°			67°			68°			69°			70°			71°			Lat. / A	
LHA/F		A/H	B/P	Z_1/Z_2	A/H	B/P	Z_1/Z_2	A/H	B/P	Z_1/Z_2	A/H	B/P	Z_1/Z_2	A/H	B/P	Z_1/Z_2	A/H	B/P	Z_1/Z_2	LHA	
°	°	° ′	° ′	°	° ′	° ′	°	° ′	° ′	°	° ′	° ′	°	° ′	° ′	°	° ′	° ′	°	°	°
0	180	0 00	24 00	90·0	0 00	23 00	90·0	0 00	22 00	90·0	0 00	21 00	90·0	0 00	20 00	90·0	0 00	19 00	90·0	180	360
1	179	0 24	24 00	89·1	0 23	23 00	89·1	0 22	22 00	89·1	0 22	21 00	89·1	0 21	20 00	89·1	0 20	19 00	89·1	181	359
2	178	0 49	23 59	88·2	0 47	22 59	88·2	0 45	21 59	88·1	0 43	20 59	88·1	0 41	19 59	88·1	0 39	18 59	88·1	182	358
3	177	1 13	23 58	87·3	1 10	22 58	87·2	1 07	21 58	87·2	1 04	20 58	87·2	1 02	19 58	87·2	0 59	18 59	87·2	183	357
4	176	1 38	23 57	86·3	1 34	22 57	86·3	1 30	21 57	86·3	1 26	20 57	86·3	1 22	19 57	86·2	1 18	18 57	86·2	184	356
5	175	2 02	23 55	85·4	1 57	22 55	85·4	1 52	21 55	85·4	1 47	20 56	85·3	1 42	19 56	85·3	1 38	18 56	85·3	185	355
6	174	2 26	23 53	84·5	2 20	22 53	84·5	2 15	21 53	84·4	2 09	20 54	84·4	2 03	19 54	84·4	1 57	18 54	84·3	186	354
7	173	2 50	23 50	83·6	2 44	22 51	83·6	2 37	21 51	83·5	2 30	20 51	83·5	2 23	19 52	83·4	2 16	18 52	83·4	187	353
8	172	3 15	23 48	82·7	3 07	22 48	82·6	2 59	21 48	82·6	2 52	20 49	82·5	2 44	19 49	82·5	2 36	18 50	82·4	188	352
9	171	3 39	23 44	81·8	3 30	22 45	81·7	3 22	21 45	81·6	3 13	20 46	81·6	3 04	19 46	81·5	2 55	18 47	81·5	189	351
10	170	4 03	23 41	80·8	3 53	22 41	80·8	3 44	21 42	80·7	3 34	20 42	80·7	3 24	19 43	80·6	3 14	18 44	80·5	190	350
11	169	4 27	23 36	79·9	4 17	22 37	79·9	4 06	21 38	79·8	3 55	20 39	79·7	3 45	19 40	79·6	3 34	18 41	79·6	191	349
12	168	4 51	23 32	79·0	4 40	22 33	78·9	4 28	21 34	78·9	4 16	20 35	78·8	4 05	19 36	78·7	3 53	18 37	78·6	192	348
13	167	5 15	23 27	78·1	5 03	22 28	78·0	4 50	21 29	77·9	4 37	20 30	77·8	4 25	19 32	77·8	4 12	18 33	77·7	193	347
14	166	5 39	23 22	77·2	5 25	22 23	77·1	5 12	21 24	77·0	4 58	20 26	76·9	4 45	19 27	76·8	4 31	18 28	76·7	194	346
15	165	6 03	23 16	76·2	5 48	22 18	76·1	5 34	21 19	76·0	5 19	20 21	76·0	5 05	19 22	75·9	4 50	18 24	75·8	195	345
16	164	6 26	23 10	75·3	6 11	22 12	75·2	5 56	21 13	75·1	5 40	20 15	75·0	5 25	19 17	74·9	5 09	18 19	74·8	196	344
17	163	6 50	23 04	74·4	6 34	22 06	74·3	6 17	21 08	74·2	6 01	20 09	74·1	5 44	19 11	74·0	5 28	18 14	73·9	197	343
18	162	7 13	22 57	73·5	6 56	21 59	73·3	6 39	21 01	73·2	6 21	20 03	73·1	6 04	19 06	73·0	5 46	18 08	72·9	198	342
19	161	7 37	22 50	72·5	7 19	21 52	72·4	7 00	20 54	72·3	6 42	19 57	72·2	6 24	18 59	72·1	6 05	18 02	72·0	199	341
20	160	8 00	22 42	71·6	7 41	21 45	71·5	7 22	20 47	71·4	7 02	19 50	71·2	6 43	18 53	71·1	6 24	17 56	71·0	200	340
21	159	8 23	22 34	70·7	8 03	21 37	70·5	7 43	20 40	70·4	7 23	19 43	70·3	7 02	18 46	70·2	6 42	17 49	70·1	201	339
22	158	8 46	22 26	69·7	8 25	21 29	69·6	8 04	20 32	69·5	7 43	19 35	69·3	7 22	18 39	69·2	7 00	17 42	69·1	202	338
23	157	9 09	22 17	68·8	8 47	21 21	68·7	8 25	20 24	68·5	8 03	19 28	68·4	7 41	18 31	68·3	7 19	17 35	68·1	203	337
24	156	9 31	22 08	67·9	9 09	21 12	67·7	8 46	20 16	67·6	8 23	19 19	67·4	8 00	18 24	67·3	7 37	17 28	67·2	204	336
25	155	9 54	21 58	66·9	9 30	21 03	66·8	9 07	20 07	66·6	8 43	19 11	66·5	8 19	18 15	66·3	7 55	17 20	66·2	205	335
26	154	10 16	21 49	66·0	9 52	20 53	65·8	9 27	19 57	65·7	9 02	19 02	65·5	8 37	18 07	65·4	8 12	17 12	65·2	206	334
27	153	10 38	21 38	65·0	10 13	20 43	64·9	9 48	19 48	64·7	9 22	18 53	64·6	8 56	17 58	64·4	8 30	17 03	64·3	207	333
28	152	11 00	21 28	64·1	10 34	20 33	63·9	10 08	19 38	63·8	9 41	18 43	63·6	9 14	17 49	63·5	8 48	16 55	63·3	208	332
29	151	11 22	21 17	63·1	10 55	20 22	63·0	10 28	19 28	62·8	10 00	18 34	62·6	9 33	17 39	62·5	9 05	16 46	62·3	209	331
30	150	11 44	21 05	62·2	11 16	20 11	62·0	10 48	19 17	61·8	10 19	18 23	61·7	9 51	17 30	61·5	9 22	16 36	61·4	210	330
31	149	12 06	20 53	61·2	11 37	20 00	61·1	11 07	19 06	60·9	10 38	18 13	60·7	10 09	17 20	60·5	9 39	16 27	60·4	211	329
32	148	12 27	20 41	60·3	11 57	19 48	60·1	11 27	18 55	59·9	10 57	18 02	59·7	10 27	17 09	59·6	9 56	16 17	59·4	212	328
33	147	12 48	20 29	59·3	12 17	19 36	59·1	11 46	18 43	58·9	11 15	17 51	58·8	10 44	16 58	58·6	10 13	16 06	58·4	213	327
34	146	13 09	20 16	58·4	12 37	19 23	58·2	12 06	18 31	58·0	11 34	17 39	57·8	11 02	16 47	57·6	10 29	15 56	57·5	214	326
35	145	13 29	20 02	57·4	12 57	19 10	57·2	12 24	18 19	57·0	11 52	17 27	56·8	11 19	16 36	56·7	10 46	15 45	56·5	215	325
36	144	13 50	19 49	56·4	13 17	18 57	56·2	12 43	18 06	56·0	12 10	17 15	55·9	11 36	16 24	55·7	11 02	15 34	55·5	216	324
37	143	14 10	19 34	55·5	13 36	18 44	55·3	13 02	17 53	55·1	12 27	17 03	54·9	11 53	16 12	54·7	11 18	15 23	54·5	217	323
38	142	14 30	19 20	54·5	13 55	18 30	54·3	13 20	17 40	54·1	12 45	16 50	53·9	12 09	16 00	53·7	11 34	15 11	53·5	218	322
39	141	14 50	19 05	53·5	14 14	18 15	53·3	13 38	17 26	53·1	13 02	16 37	52·9	12 26	15 48	52·7	11 49	14 59	52·6	219	321
40	140	15 09	18 50	52·5	14 33	18 01	52·3	13 56	17 12	52·1	13 19	16 23	51·9	12 42	15 35	51·7	12 05	14 47	51·6	220	320
41	139	15 29	18 34	51·5	14 51	17 46	51·3	14 14	16 57	51·1	13 36	16 09	50·9	12 58	15 22	50·8	12 20	14 34	50·6	221	319
42	138	15 48	18 18	50·6	15 09	17 30	50·3	14 31	16 43	50·1	13 52	15 55	49·9	13 14	15 08	49·8	12 35	14 21	49·6	222	318
43	137	16 06	18 02	49·6	15 27	17 15	49·4	14 48	16 28	49·2	14 09	15 41	49·0	13 29	14 54	48·8	12 50	14 08	48·6	223	317
44	136	16 25	17 46	48·6	15 45	16 59	48·4	15 05	16 12	48·2	14 25	15 26	48·0	13 45	14 40	47·8	13 04	13 55	47·6	224	316
45	135	16 43	17 29	47·6	16 02	16 42	47·4	15 22	15 57	47·2	14 41	15 11	47·0	14 00	14 26	46·8	13 19	13 41	46·6	225	315

Lat. / A		66°			67°			68°			69°			70°			71°			Lat. / A	
LHA/F		A/H	B/P	Z_1/Z_2	A/H	B/P	Z_1/Z_2	A/H	B/P	Z_1/Z_2	A/H	B/P	Z_1/Z_2	A/H	B/P	Z_1/Z_2	A/H	B/P	Z_1/Z_2	LHA	
°	°	° ′	° ′	°	° ′	° ′	°	° ′	° ′	°	° ′	° ′	°	° ′	° ′	°	° ′	° ′	°	°	°
45	135	16 43	17 29	47·6	16 02	16 42	47·4	15 22	15 57	47·2	14 41	15 11	47·0	14 00	14 26	46·8	13 19	13 41	46·6	225	315
46	134	17 01	17 11	46·6	16 19	16 26	46·4	15 38	15 41	46·2	14 56	14 56	46·0	14 15	14 11	45·8	13 33	13 27	45·6	226	314
47	133	17 18	16 53	45·6	16 36	16 09	45·4	15 54	15 24	45·2	15 12	14 40	45·0	14 29	13 56	44·8	13 46	13 13	44·6	227	313
48	132	17 36	16 35	44·6	16 53	15 51	44·4	16 10	15 08	44·2	15 27	14 24	44·0	14 43	13 41	43·8	14 00	12 58	43·6	228	312
49	131	17 53	16 17	43·6	17 09	15 34	43·4	16 25	14 51	43·2	15 42	14 08	43·0	14 58	13 26	42·8	14 13	12 44	42·6	229	311
50	130	18 09	15 58	42·6	17 25	15 16	42·4	16 41	14 33	42·1	15 56	13 52	41·9	15 11	13 10	41·8	14 27	12 29	41·6	230	310
51	129	18 26	15 39	41·6	17 41	14 57	41·3	16 56	14 16	41·1	16 10	13 35	40·9	15 25	12 54	40·8	14 39	12 14	40·6	231	309
52	128	18 42	15 20	40·5	17 56	14 39	40·3	17 10	13 58	40·1	16 24	13 18	39·9	15 38	12 38	39·7	14 52	11 58	39·6	232	308
53	127	18 57	15 00	39·5	18 11	14 20	39·3	17 24	13 40	39·1	16 38	13 00	38·9	15 51	12 21	38·7	15 04	11 42	38·6	233	307
54	126	19 13	14 40	38·5	18 26	14 01	38·3	17 39	13 22	38·1	16 51	12 43	37·9	16 04	12 05	37·7	15 16	11 26	37·5	234	306
55	125	19 28	14 20	37·5	18 40	13 41	37·3	17 52	13 03	37·1	17 04	12 25	36·9	16 16	11 48	36·7	15 28	11 10	36·5	235	305
56	124	19 42	13 59	36·4	18 54	13 21	36·2	18 06	12 44	36·0	17 17	12 07	35·8	16 28	11 30	35·7	15 40	10 54	35·5	236	304
57	123	19 57	13 38	35·4	19 08	13 01	35·2	18 19	12 25	35·0	17 29	11 49	34·8	16 40	11 13	34·6	15 51	10 37	34·5	237	303
58	122	20 11	13 17	34·4	19 21	12 41	34·2	18 31	12 05	34·0	17 42	11 30	33·8	16 52	10 55	33·6	16 02	10 20	33·5	238	302
59	121	20 24	12 55	33·3	19 34	12 20	33·1	18 44	11 45	32·9	17 53	11 11	32·8	17 03	10 37	32·6	16 12	10 03	32·4	239	301
60	120	20 37	12 33	32·3	19 47	11 59	32·1	18 56	11 25	31·9	18 05	10 52	31·7	17 14	10 19	31·6	16 23	9 46	31·4	240	300
61	119	20 50	12 11	31·2	19 59	11 38	31·1	19 08	11 05	30·9	18 16	10 33	30·7	17 24	10 00	30·5	16 33	9 29	30·4	241	299
62	118	21 03	11 48	30·2	20 11	11 16	30·0	19 19	10 44	29·8	18 27	10 13	29·7	17 35	9 42	29·5	16 42	9 11	29·4	242	298
63	117	21 15	11 26	29·2	20 22	10 54	29·0	19 30	10 24	28·8	18 37	9 53	28·6	17 45	9 23	28·5	16 52	8 53	28·3	243	297
64	116	21 27	11 03	28·1	20 34	10 32	27·9	19 41	10 03	27·7	18 47	9 33	27·6	17 54	9 04	27·4	17 01	8 35	27·3	244	296
65	115	21 38	10 39	27·0	20 44	10 10	26·9	19 51	9 41	26·7	18 57	9 13	26·5	18 03	8 45	26·4	17 10	8 17	26·3	245	295
66	114	21 49	10 16	26·0	20 55	9 48	25·8	20 01	9 20	25·7	19 07	8 52	25·5	18 12	8 25	25·4	17 18	7 58	25·2	246	294
67	113	21 59	9 52	24·9	21 05	9 25	24·8	20 10	8 58	24·6	19 16	8 32	24·5	18 21	8 06	24·3	17 26	7 40	24·2	247	293
68	112	22 09	9 28	23·9	21 14	9 02	23·7	20 19	8 36	23·5	19 24	8 11	23·4	18 29	7 46	23·3	17 34	7 21	23·1	248	292
69	111	22 19	9 04	22·8	21 24	8 39	22·6	20 28	8 14	22·5	19 33	7 50	22·4	18 37	7 26	22·2	17 42	7 02	22·1	249	291
70	110	22 28	8 39	21·7	21 32	8 16	21·6	20 37	7 52	21·4	19 41	7 29	21·3	18 45	7 06	21·2	17 49	6 43	21·1	250	290
71	109	22 37	8 15	20·7	21 41	7 52	20·5	20 45	7 30	20·4	19 48	7 07	20·2	18 52	6 45	20·1	17 56	6 24	20·0	251	289
72	108	22 45	7 50	19·6	21 49	7 28	19·4	20 52	7 07	19·3	19 56	6 46	19·2	18 59	6 25	19·1	18 02	6 04	19·0	252	288
73	107	22 53	7 25	18·5	21 56	7 04	18·4	21 00	6 44	18·2	20 03	6 24	18·1	19 05	6 04	18·0	18 08	5 45	17·9	253	287
74	106	23 01	7 00	17·4	22 04	6 40	17·3	21 06	6 21	17·2	20 09	6 02	17·1	19 12	5 44	17·0	18 14	5 25	16·9	254	286
75	105	23 08	6 34	16·3	22 10	6 16	16·2	21 13	5 58	16·1	20 15	5 40	16·0	19 17	5 23	15·9	18 20	5 06	15·8	255	285
76	104	23 15	6 09	15·3	22 17	5 52	15·2	21 19	5 35	15·1	20 21	5 18	15·0	19 23	5 02	14·9	18 25	4 46	14·8	256	284
77	103	23 21	5 43	14·2	22 23	5 27	14·1	21 24	5 12	14·0	20 26	4 56	13·9	19 28	4 41	13·8	18 30	4 26	13·7	257	283
78	102	23 27	5 17	13·1	22 28	5 03	13·0	21 30	4 48	12·9	20 31	4 34	12·8	19 33	4 20	12·7	18 34	4 06	12·7	258	282
79	101	23 32	4 51	12·0	22 33	4 38	11·9	21 35	4 24	11·8	20 36	4 11	11·8	19 37	3 58	11·7	18 38	3 46	11·6	259	281
80	100	23 37	4 25	10·9	22 38	4 13	10·8	21 39	4 01	10·8	20 40	3 49	10·7	19 41	3 37	10·6	18 42	3 25	10·6	260	280
81	99	23 41	3 59	9·8	22 42	3 48	9·8	21 43	3 37	9·7	20 44	3 26	9·6	19 45	3 16	9·6	18 45	3 05	9·5	261	279
82	98	23 45	3 33	8·7	22 46	3 23	8·7	21 46	3 13	8·6	20 47	3 03	8·6	19 48	2 54	8·5	18 48	2 45	8·5	262	278
83	97	23 49	3 06	7·7	22 49	2 58	7·6	21 50	2 49	7·5	20 50	2 41	7·5	19 51	2 32	7·4	18 51	2 24	7·4	263	277
84	96	23 52	2 40	6·6	22 52	2 32	6·5	21 52	2 25	6·5	20 53	2 18	6·4	19 53	2 11	6·4	18 54	2 04	6·3	264	276
85	95	23 54	2 13	5·5	22 54	2 07	5·4	21 55	2 01	5·4	20 55	1 55	5·4	19 55	1 49	5·3	18 55	1 43	5·3	265	275
86	94	23 56	1 47	4·4	22 56	1 42	4·3	21 57	1 37	4·3	20 57	1 32	4·3	19 57	1 27	4·3	18 57	1 23	4·2	266	274
87	93	23 58	1 20	3·3	22 58	1 16	3·3	21 58	1 13	3·2	20 58	1 09	3·2	19 58	1 05	3·2	18 58	1 02	3·2	267	273
88	92	23 59	0 53	2·2	22 59	0 51	2·2	21 59	0 48	2·2	20 59	0 46	2·1	19 59	0 44	2·1	18 59	0 41	2·1	268	272
89	91	24 00	0 27	1·1	23 00	0 25	1·1	22 00	0 24	1·1	21 00	0 23	1·1	20 00	0 22	1·1	19 00	0 21	1·1	269	271
90	90	24 00	0 00	0·0	23 00	0 00	0·0	22 00	0 00	0·0	21 00	0 00	0·0	20 00	0 00	0·0	19 00	0 00	0·0	270	270

N. Lat: for LHA > 180° … $Z_n = Z$
for LHA < 180° … $Z_n = 360° - Z$

S. Lat.: for LHA > 180° … $Z_n = 180° - Z$
for LHA < 180° … $Z_n = 180° + Z$

SIGHT REDUCTION TABLE

B: (–) for 90° < LHA < 270°
Dec: (–) for Lat. contrary name

Z_1: same sign as B
Z_2: (–) for F > 90°

Lat. / A		72°			73°			74°			75°			76°			77°			Lat. / A	
LHA/F		A/H	B/P	Z_1/Z_2	A/H	B/P	Z_1/Z_2	A/H	B/P	Z_1/Z_2	A/H	B/P	Z_1/Z_2	A/H	B/P	Z_1/Z_2	A/H	B/P	Z_1/Z_2	LHA	
°	°	° ′	° ′	°	° ′	° ′	°	° ′	° ′	°	° ′	° ′	°	° ′	° ′	°	° ′	° ′	°	°	°
0	180	0 00	18 00	90·0	0 00	17 00	90·0	0 00	16 00	90·0	0 00	15 00	90·0	0 00	14 00	90·0	0 00	13 00	90·0	180	360
1	179	0 19	18 00	89·0	0 18	17 00	89·0	0 17	16 00	89·0	0 16	15 00	89·0	0 15	14 00	89·0	0 13	13 00	89·0	181	359
2	178	0 37	17 59	88·1	0 35	16 59	88·1	0 33	15 59	88·1	0 31	14 59	88·1	0 29	14 00	88·1	0 27	13 00	88·1	182	358
3	177	0 56	17 59	87·1	0 53	16 59	87·1	0 50	15 59	87·1	0 47	14 59	87·1	0 44	13 59	87·1	0 40	12 59	87·1	183	357
4	176	1 14	17 58	86·2	1 10	16 58	86·2	1 06	15 58	86·2	1 02	14 58	86·1	0 58	13 58	86·1	0 54	12 58	86·1	184	356
5	175	1 33	17 56	85·2	1 28	16 56	85·2	1 23	15 57	85·2	1 18	14 57	85·2	1 12	13 57	85·1	1 07	12 57	85·1	185	355
6	174	1 51	17 54	84·3	1 45	16 55	84·3	1 39	15 55	84·2	1 33	14 55	84·2	1 27	13 56	84·2	1 21	12 56	84·2	186	354
7	173	2 09	17 52	83·3	2 03	16 53	83·3	1 56	15 53	83·3	1 48	14 54	83·2	1 41	13 54	83·2	1 34	12 54	83·2	187	353
8	172	2 28	17 50	82·4	2 20	16 51	82·3	2 12	15 51	82·3	2 04	14 52	82·3	1 56	13 52	82·2	1 48	12 53	82·2	188	352
9	171	2 46	17 48	81·4	2 37	16 48	81·4	2 28	15 49	81·3	2 19	14 49	81·3	2 10	13 50	81·3	2 01	12 51	81·2	189	351
10	170	3 05	17 45	80·5	2 55	16 45	80·4	2 45	15 46	80·4	2 35	14 47	80·3	2 24	13 48	80·3	2 14	12 49	80·3	190	350
11	169	3 23	17 41	79·5	3 12	16 42	79·5	3 01	15 43	79·4	2 50	14 44	79·4	2 39	13 45	79·3	2 28	12 46	79·3	191	349
12	168	3 41	17 38	78·6	3 29	16 39	78·5	3 17	15 40	78·5	3 05	14 41	78·4	2 53	13 42	78·3	2 41	12 44	78·3	192	348
13	167	3 59	17 34	77·6	3 46	16 35	77·5	3 33	15 37	77·5	3 20	14 38	77·4	3 07	13 39	77·4	2 54	12 41	77·3	193	347
14	166	4 17	17 30	76·7	4 03	16 31	76·6	3 49	15 33	76·5	3 35	14 34	76·5	3 21	13 36	76·4	3 07	12 38	76·3	194	346
15	165	4 35	17 25	75·7	4 20	16 27	75·6	4 05	15 29	75·6	3 50	14 31	75·5	3 35	13 32	75·4	3 20	12 34	75·4	195	345
16	164	4 53	17 21	74·7	4 37	16 23	74·7	4 21	15 25	74·6	4 05	14 27	74·5	3 49	13 29	74·5	3 33	12 31	74·4	196	344
17	163	5 11	17 16	73·8	4 54	16 18	73·7	4 37	15 20	73·6	4 20	14 22	73·5	4 03	13 25	73·5	3 46	12 27	73·4	197	343
18	162	5 29	17 10	72·8	5 11	16 13	72·7	4 53	15 15	72·7	4 35	14 18	72·6	4 17	13 20	72·5	3 59	12 23	72·4	198	342
19	161	5 46	17 05	71·9	5 28	16 07	71·8	5 09	15 10	71·7	4 50	14 13	71·6	4 31	13 16	71·5	4 12	12 19	71·5	199	341
20	160	6 04	16 59	70·9	5 44	16 02	70·8	5 25	15 05	70·7	5 05	14 08	70·6	4 45	13 11	70·5	4 25	12 14	70·5	200	340
21	159	6 21	16 52	69·9	6 01	15 56	69·8	5 40	14 59	69·7	5 19	14 03	69·7	4 58	13 06	69·6	4 37	12 10	69·5	201	339
22	158	6 39	16 46	69·0	6 17	15 50	68·9	5 56	14 53	68·8	5 34	13 57	68·7	5 12	13 01	68·6	4 50	12 05	68·5	202	338
23	157	6 56	16 39	68·0	6 34	15 43	67·9	6 11	14 47	67·8	5 48	13 51	67·7	5 25	12 56	67·6	5 03	12 00	67·5	203	337
24	156	7 13	16 32	67·1	6 50	15 36	66·9	6 26	14 41	66·8	6 03	13 45	66·7	5 39	12 50	66·6	5 15	11 55	66·5	204	336
25	155	7 30	16 25	66·1	7 06	15 29	66·0	6 41	14 34	65·9	6 17	13 39	65·8	5 52	12 44	65·7	5 27	11 49	65·6	205	335
26	154	7 47	16 17	65·1	7 22	15 22	65·0	6 56	14 27	64·9	6 31	13 32	64·8	6 05	12 38	64·7	5 40	11 43	64·6	206	334
27	153	8 04	16 09	64·1	7 38	15 14	64·0	7 11	14 20	63·9	6 45	13 26	63·8	6 18	12 32	63·7	5 52	11 37	63·6	207	333
28	152	8 20	16 00	63·2	7 53	15 06	63·0	7 26	14 12	62·9	6 59	13 19	62·8	6 31	12 25	62·7	6 04	11 31	62·6	208	332
29	151	8 37	15 52	62·2	8 09	14 58	62·1	7 41	14 05	61·9	7 13	13 11	61·8	6 44	12 18	61·7	6 16	11 25	61·6	209	331
30	150	8 53	15 43	61·2	8 24	14 50	61·1	7 55	13 57	61·0	7 26	13 04	60·9	6 57	12 11	60·7	6 27	11 18	60·6	210	330
31	149	9 09	15 34	60·3	8 40	14 41	60·1	8 10	13 49	60·0	7 40	12 56	59·9	7 09	12 04	59·8	6 39	11 12	59·7	211	329
32	148	9 25	15 24	59·3	8 55	14 32	59·1	8 24	13 40	59·0	7 53	12 48	58·9	7 22	11 56	58·8	6 51	11 05	58·7	212	328
33	147	9 41	15 15	58·3	9 10	14 23	58·2	8 38	13 31	58·0	8 06	12 40	57·9	7 34	11 49	57·8	7 02	10 57	57·7	213	327
34	146	9 57	15 05	57·3	9 25	14 13	57·2	8 52	13 22	57·0	8 19	12 31	56·9	7 46	11 41	56·8	7 14	10 50	56·7	214	326
35	145	10 13	14 54	56·3	9 39	14 04	56·2	9 06	13 13	56·1	8 32	12 23	55·9	7 59	11 33	55·8	7 25	10 43	55·7	215	325
36	144	10 28	14 44	55·4	9 54	13 54	55·2	9 19	13 04	55·1	8 45	12 14	54·9	8 11	11 24	54·8	7 36	10 35	54·7	216	324
37	143	10 43	14 33	54·4	10 08	13 43	54·2	9 33	12 54	54·1	8 58	12 05	53·9	8 22	11 16	53·8	7 47	10 27	53·7	217	323
38	142	10 58	14 22	53·4	10 22	13 33	53·2	9 46	12 44	53·1	9 10	11 55	53·0	8 34	11 07	52·8	7 58	10 19	52·7	218	322
39	141	11 13	14 10	52·4	10 36	13 22	52·2	9 59	12 34	52·1	9 22	11 46	52·0	8 45	10 58	51·8	8 08	10 10	51·7	219	321
40	140	11 27	13 59	51·4	10 50	13 11	51·3	10 12	12 23	51·1	9 35	11 36	51·0	8 57	10 49	50·8	8 19	10 02	50·7	220	320
41	139	11 42	13 47	50·4	11 04	13 00	50·3	10 25	12 13	50·1	9 47	11 26	50·0	9 08	10 39	49·9	8 29	9 53	49·7	221	319
42	138	11 56	13 34	49·4	11 17	12 48	49·3	10 38	12 02	49·1	9 58	11 16	49·0	9 19	10 30	48·9	8 39	9 44	48·7	222	318
43	137	12 10	13 22	48·4	11 30	12 36	48·3	10 50	11 51	48·1	10 10	11 05	48·0	9 30	10 20	47·9	8 49	9 35	47·7	223	317
44	136	12 24	13 09	47·4	11 43	12 24	47·3	11 02	11 39	47·1	10 21	10 55	47·0	9 40	10 10	46·9	8 59	9 26	46·7	224	316
45	135	12 37	12 56	46·4	11 56	12 12	46·3	11 14	11 28	46·1	10 33	10 44	46·0	9 51	10 00	45·9	9 09	9 16	45·7	225	315

Lat. / A		72°			73°			74°			75°			76°			77°			Lat. / A	
LHA/F		A/H	B/P	Z_1/Z_2	A/H	B/P	Z_1/Z_2	A/H	B/P	Z_1/Z_2	A/H	B/P	Z_1/Z_2	A/H	B/P	Z_1/Z_2	A/H	B/P	Z_1/Z_2	LHA	
°	°	° ′	° ′	°	° ′	° ′	°	° ′	° ′	°	° ′	° ′	°	° ′	° ′	°	° ′	° ′	°	°	°
45	135	12 37	12 56	46·4	11 56	12 12	46·3	11 14	11 28	46·1	10 33	10 44	46·0	9 51	10 00	45·9	9 09	9 16	45·7	225	315
46	134	12 51	12 43	45·4	12 08	11 59	45·3	11 26	11 16	45·1	10 44	10 33	45·0	10 01	9 50	44·9	9 19	9 07	44·7	226	314
47	133	13 04	12 30	44·4	12 21	11 47	44·3	11 38	11 04	44·1	10 55	10 21	44·0	10 11	9 39	43·9	9 28	8 57	43·7	227	313
48	132	13 17	12 16	43·4	12 33	11 34	43·3	11 49	10 52	43·1	11 05	10 10	43·0	10 21	9 28	42·9	9 37	8 47	42·7	228	312
49	131	13 29	12 02	42·4	12 45	11 21	42·3	12 00	10 39	42·1	11 16	9 58	42·0	10 31	9 17	41·9	9 46	8 37	41·7	229	311
50	130	13 42	11 48	41·4	12 57	11 07	41·3	12 11	10 27	41·1	11 26	9 46	41·0	10 41	9 06	40·9	9 55	8 26	40·7	230	310
51	129	13 54	11 33	40·4	13 08	10 53	40·3	12 22	10 14	40·1	11 36	9 34	40·0	10 50	8 55	39·8	10 04	8 16	39·7	231	309
52	128	14 06	11 19	39·4	13 19	10 40	39·2	12 33	10 01	39·1	11 46	9 22	39·0	10 59	8 44	38·8	10 13	8 05	38·7	232	308
53	127	14 17	11 04	38·4	13 30	10 26	38·2	12 43	9 47	38·1	11 56	9 10	38·0	11 08	8 32	37·8	10 21	7 55	37·7	233	307
54	126	14 29	10 49	37·4	13 41	10 11	37·2	12 53	9 34	37·1	12 05	8 57	36·9	11 17	8 20	36·8	10 29	7 44	36·7	234	306
55	125	14 40	10 33	36·4	13 51	9 57	36·2	13 03	9 20	36·1	12 14	8 44	35·9	11 26	8 08	35·8	10 37	7 33	35·7	235	305
56	124	14 51	10 18	35·3	14 02	9 42	35·2	13 13	9 07	35·1	12 23	8 31	34·9	11 34	7 56	34·8	10 45	7 21	34·7	236	304
57	123	15 01	10 02	34·3	14 12	9 27	34·2	13 22	8 53	34·0	12 32	8 18	33·9	11 42	7 44	33·8	10 52	7 10	33·7	237	303
58	122	15 12	9 46	33·3	14 21	9 12	33·2	13 31	8 38	33·0	12 41	8 05	32·9	11 50	7 32	32·8	11 00	6 58	32·7	238	302
59	121	15 22	9 30	32·3	14 31	8 57	32·1	13 40	8 24	32·0	12 49	7 51	31·9	11 58	7 19	31·8	11 07	6 47	31·7	239	301
60	120	15 31	9 14	31·3	14 40	8 41	31·1	13 49	8 10	31·0	12 57	7 38	30·9	12 06	7 06	30·8	11 14	6 35	30·6	240	300
61	119	15 41	8 57	30·2	14 49	8 26	30·1	13 57	7 55	30·0	13 05	7 24	29·8	12 13	6 54	29·7	11 21	6 23	29·6	241	299
62	118	15 50	8 40	29·2	14 58	8 10	29·1	14 05	7 40	28·9	13 13	7 10	28·8	12 20	6 41	28·7	11 27	6 11	28·6	242	298
63	117	15 59	8 23	28·2	15 06	7 54	28·0	14 13	7 25	27·9	13 20	6 56	27·8	12 27	6 27	27·7	11 34	5 59	27·6	243	297
64	116	16 08	8 06	27·2	15 14	7 38	27·0	14 21	7 10	26·9	13 27	6 42	26·8	12 34	6 14	26·7	11 40	5 47	26·6	244	296
65	115	16 16	7 49	26·1	15 22	7 22	26·0	14 28	6 55	25·9	13 34	6 28	25·8	12 40	6 01	25·7	11 46	5 34	25·6	245	295
66	114	16 24	7 32	25·1	15 29	7 05	25·0	14 35	6 39	24·9	13 41	6 13	24·7	12 46	5 47	24·6	11 52	5 22	24·6	246	294
67	113	16 32	7 14	24·1	15 37	6 49	23·9	14 42	6 24	23·8	13 47	5 59	23·7	12 52	5 34	23·6	11 57	5 09	23·5	247	293
68	112	16 39	6 56	23·0	15 44	6 32	22·9	14 48	6 08	22·8	13 53	5 44	22·7	12 58	5 20	22·6	12 02	4 57	22·5	248	292
69	111	16 46	6 38	22·0	15 50	6 15	21·9	14 55	5 52	21·8	13 59	5 29	21·7	13 03	5 06	21·6	12 07	4 44	21·5	249	291
70	110	16 53	6 20	20·9	15 57	5 58	20·8	15 01	5 36	20·7	14 05	5 14	20·6	13 08	4 52	20·6	12 12	4 31	20·5	250	290
71	109	16 59	6 02	19·9	16 03	5 41	19·8	15 06	5 20	19·7	14 10	4 59	19·6	13 13	4 38	19·5	12 17	4 18	19·5	251	289
72	108	17 05	5 44	18·9	16 09	5 24	18·8	15 12	5 04	18·7	14 15	4 44	18·6	13 18	4 24	18·5	12 21	4 05	18·4	252	288
73	107	17 11	5 26	17·8	16 14	5 06	17·7	15 17	4 48	17·6	14 20	4 29	17·6	13 23	4 10	17·5	12 25	3 52	17·4	253	287
74	106	17 17	5 07	16·8	16 19	4 49	16·7	15 22	4 31	16·6	14 24	4 13	16·5	13 27	3 56	16·5	12 29	3 38	16·4	254	286
75	105	17 22	4 48	15·7	16 24	4 31	15·7	15 26	4 15	15·6	14 29	3 58	15·5	13 31	3 42	15·4	12 33	3 25	15·4	255	285
76	104	17 27	4 30	14·7	16 29	4 14	14·6	15 31	3 58	14·5	14 33	3 43	14·5	13 35	3 27	14·4	12 36	3 12	14·4	256	284
77	103	17 31	4 11	13·6	16 33	3 56	13·6	15 35	3 41	13·5	14 36	3 27	13·4	13 38	3 13	13·4	12 40	2 58	13·3	257	283
78	102	17 36	3 52	12·6	16 37	3 38	12·5	15 38	3 25	12·5	14 40	3 11	12·4	13 41	2 58	12·4	12 43	2 45	12·3	258	282
79	101	17 39	3 33	11·6	16 41	3 20	11·5	15 42	3 08	11·4	14 43	2 56	11·4	13 44	2 43	11·3	12 45	2 31	11·3	259	281
80	100	17 43	3 14	10·5	16 44	3 02	10·4	15 45	2 51	10·4	14 46	2 40	10·3	13 47	2 29	10·3	12 48	2 18	10·3	260	280
81	99	17 46	2 55	9·5	16 47	2 44	9·4	15 48	2 34	9·4	14 49	2 24	9·3	13 49	2 14	9·3	12 50	2 04	9·2	261	279
82	98	17 49	2 35	8·4	16 50	2 26	8·4	15 50	2 17	8·3	14 51	2 08	8·3	13 52	1 59	8·2	12 52	1 50	8·2	262	278
83	97	17 52	2 16	7·4	16 52	2 08	7·3	15 53	2 00	7·3	14 53	1 52	7·2	13 54	1 44	7·2	12 54	1 37	7·2	263	277
84	96	17 54	1 57	6·3	16 54	1 50	6·3	15 55	1 43	6·2	14 55	1 36	6·2	13 55	1 30	6·2	12 56	1 23	6·2	264	276
85	95	17 56	1 37	5·3	16 56	1 32	5·2	15 56	1 26	5·2	14 56	1 20	5·2	13 57	1 15	5·2	12 57	1 09	5·1	265	275
86	94	17 57	1 18	4·2	16 57	1 13	4·2	15 58	1 09	4·2	14 58	1 04	4·1	13 58	1 00	4·1	12 58	0 55	4·1	266	274
87	93	17 58	0 58	3·2	16 59	0 55	3·1	15 59	0 52	3·1	14 59	0 48	3·1	13 59	0 45	3·1	12 59	0 42	3·1	267	273
88	92	17 59	0 39	2·1	16 59	0 37	2·1	15 59	0 34	2·1	14 59	0 32	2·1	13 59	0 30	2·1	13 00	0 28	2·1	268	272
89	91	18 00	0 19	1·1	17 00	0 18	1·0	16 00	0 17	1·0	15 00	0 16	1·0	14 00	0 15	1·0	13 00	0 14	1·0	269	271
90	90	18 00	0 00	0·0	17 00	0 00	0·0	16 00	0 00	0·0	15 00	0 00	0·0	14 00	0 00	0·0	13 00	0 00	0·0	270	270

N. Lat: for LHA > 180° ... $Z_n = Z$
for LHA < 180° ... $Z_n = 360° - Z$

S. Lat.: for LHA > 180° ... $Z_n = 180° - Z$
for LHA < 180° ... $Z_n = 180° + Z$

SIGHT REDUCTION TABLE

B: (−) for 90° < LHA < 270°
Dec:(−) for Lat. contrary name

Z_1: same sign as B
Z_2: (−) for F > 90°

Lat. / A		78°			79°			80°			81°			82°			83°			Lat. / A	
LHA/F		A/H	B/P	Z_1/Z_2	A/H	B/P	Z_1/Z_2	A/H	B/P	Z_1/Z_2	A/H	B/P	Z_1/Z_2	A/H	B/P	Z_1/Z_2	A/H	B/P	Z_1/Z_2	LHA	
°	°	° ′	° ′	°	° ′	° ′	°	° ′	° ′	°	° ′	° ′	°	° ′	° ′	°	° ′	° ′	°	°	°
0	180	0 00	12 00	90·0	0 00	11 00	90·0	0 00	10 00	90·0	0 00	9 00	90·0	0 00	8 00	90·0	0 00	7 00	90·0	180	360
1	179	0 12	12 00	89·0	0 11	11 00	89·0	0 10	10 00	89·0	0 09	9 00	89·0	0 08	8 00	89·0	0 07	7 00	89·0	181	359
2	178	0 25	12 00	88·0	0 23	11 00	88·0	0 21	10 00	88·0	0 19	9 00	88·0	0 17	8 00	88·0	0 15	7 00	88·0	182	358
3	177	0 37	11 59	87·1	0 34	10 59	87·1	0 31	9 59	87·0	0 28	8 59	87·0	0 25	7 59	87·0	0 22	6 59	87·0	183	357
4	176	0 50	11 58	86·1	0 46	10 58	86·1	0 42	9 59	86·1	0 38	8 59	86·0	0 33	7 59	86·0	0 29	6 59	86·0	184	356
5	175	1 02	11 57	85·1	0 57	10 58	85·1	0 52	9 58	85·1	0 47	8 58	85·1	0 42	7 58	85·0	0 37	6 58	85·0	185	355
6	174	1 15	11 56	84·1	1 09	10 56	84·1	1 02	9 57	84·1	0 56	8 57	84·1	0 50	7 57	84·1	0 44	6 58	84·0	186	354
7	173	1 27	11 55	83·2	1 20	10 55	83·1	1 13	9 56	83·1	1 06	8 56	83·1	0 58	7 56	83·1	0 51	6 57	83·1	187	353
8	172	1 39	11 53	82·2	1 31	10 54	82·1	1 23	9 54	82·1	1 15	8 55	82·1	1 07	7 55	82·1	0 58	6 56	82·1	188	352
9	171	1 52	11 51	81·2	1 43	10 52	81·2	1 33	9 53	81·1	1 24	8 53	81·1	1 15	7 54	81·1	1 06	6 55	81·1	189	351
10	170	2 04	11 49	80·2	1 54	10 50	80·2	1 44	9 51	80·1	1 33	8 52	80·1	1 23	7 53	80·1	1 13	6 54	80·1	190	350
11	169	2 16	11 47	79·2	2 05	10 48	79·2	1 54	9 49	79·2	1 43	8 50	79·1	1 31	7 51	79·1	1 20	6 52	79·1	191	349
12	168	2 29	11 45	78·3	2 16	10 46	78·2	2 04	9 47	78·2	1 52	8 48	78·1	1 39	7 50	78·1	1 27	6 51	78·1	192	348
13	167	2 41	11 42	77·3	2 28	10 43	77·2	2 14	9 45	77·2	2 01	8 46	77·2	1 48	7 48	77·1	1 34	6 49	77·1	193	347
14	166	2 53	11 39	76·3	2 39	10 41	76·2	2 24	9 43	76·2	2 10	8 44	76·2	1 56	7 46	76·1	1 41	6 48	76·1	194	346
15	165	3 05	11 36	75·3	2 50	10 38	75·3	2 35	9 40	75·2	2 19	8 42	75·2	2 04	7 44	75·1	1 48	6 46	75·1	195	345
16	164	3 17	11 33	74·3	3 01	10 35	74·3	2 45	9 37	74·2	2 28	8 39	74·2	2 12	7 42	74·1	1 56	6 44	74·1	196	344
17	163	3 29	11 29	73·4	3 12	10 32	73·3	2 55	9 34	73·2	2 37	8 37	73·2	2 20	7 39	73·2	2 03	6 42	73·1	197	343
18	162	3 41	11 26	72·4	3 23	10 28	72·3	3 05	9 31	72·3	2 46	8 34	72·2	2 28	7 37	72·2	2 09	6 40	72·1	198	342
19	161	3 53	11 22	71·4	3 34	10 25	71·3	3 14	9 28	71·3	2 55	8 31	71·2	2 36	7 34	71·2	2 16	6 37	71·1	199	341
20	160	4 05	11 18	70·4	3 45	10 21	70·3	3 24	9 24	70·3	3 04	8 28	70·2	2 44	7 31	70·2	2 23	6 35	70·1	200	340
21	159	4 16	11 13	69·4	3 55	10 17	69·4	3 34	9 21	69·3	3 13	8 25	69·2	2 52	7 28	69·2	2 30	6 32	69·1	201	339
22	158	4 28	11 09	68·4	4 06	10 13	68·4	3 44	9 17	68·3	3 22	8 21	68·2	2 59	7 25	68·2	2 37	6 30	68·1	202	338
23	157	4 40	11 04	67·5	4 17	10 09	67·4	3 53	9 13	67·3	3 30	8 18	67·3	3 07	7 22	67·2	2 44	6 27	67·2	203	337
24	156	4 51	10 59	66·5	4 27	10 04	66·4	4 03	9 09	66·3	3 39	8 14	66·3	3 15	7 19	66·2	2 50	6 24	66·2	204	336
25	155	5 02	10 54	65·5	4 38	9 59	65·4	4 13	9 05	65·3	3 47	8 10	65·3	3 22	7 16	65·2	2 57	6 21	65·2	205	335
26	154	5 14	10 49	64·5	4 48	9 55	64·4	4 22	9 00	64·3	3 56	8 06	64·3	3 30	7 12	64·2	3 04	6 18	64·2	206	334
27	153	5 25	10 43	63·5	4 58	9 50	63·4	4 31	8 56	63·4	4 04	8 02	63·3	3 37	7 08	63·2	3 10	6 15	63·2	207	333
28	152	5 36	10 38	62·5	5 08	9 44	62·4	4 41	8 51	62·4	4 13	7 58	62·3	3 45	7 04	62·2	3 17	6 11	62·2	208	332
29	151	5 47	10 32	61·5	5 18	9 39	61·4	4 50	8 46	61·4	4 21	7 53	61·3	3 52	7 00	61·2	3 23	6 08	61·2	209	331
30	150	5 58	10 26	60·5	5 28	9 33	60·5	4 59	8 41	60·4	4 29	7 49	60·3	3 59	6 56	60·2	3 30	6 04	60·2	210	330
31	149	6 09	10 20	59·6	5 38	9 28	59·5	5 08	8 36	59·4	4 37	7 44	59·3	4 07	6 52	59·2	3 36	6 00	59·2	211	329
32	148	6 20	10 13	58·6	5 48	9 22	58·5	5 17	8 30	58·4	4 45	7 39	58·3	4 14	6 48	58·3	3 42	5 57	58·2	212	328
33	147	6 30	10 06	57·6	5 58	9 16	57·5	5 26	8 25	57·4	4 53	7 34	57·3	4 21	6 43	57·3	3 48	5 53	57·2	213	327
34	146	6 41	10 00	56·6	6 08	9 09	56·5	5 34	8 19	56·4	5 01	7 29	56·3	4 28	6 39	56·3	3 54	5 49	56·2	214	326
35	145	6 51	9 53	55·6	6 17	9 03	55·5	5 43	8 13	55·4	5 09	7 24	55·3	4 35	6 34	55·3	4 00	5 45	55·2	215	325
36	144	7 01	9 45	54·6	6 26	8 56	54·5	5 51	8 07	54·4	5 17	7 18	54·3	4 42	6 29	54·3	4 06	5 40	54·2	216	324
37	143	7 11	9 38	53·6	6 36	8 49	53·5	6 00	8 01	53·4	5 24	7 13	53·3	4 48	6 24	53·3	4 12	5 36	53·2	217	323
38	142	7 21	9 31	52·6	6 45	8 43	52·5	6 08	7 55	52·4	5 32	7 07	52·3	4 55	6 19	52·3	4 18	5 32	52·2	218	322
39	141	7 31	9 23	51·6	6 54	8 35	51·5	6 16	7 48	51·4	5 39	7 01	51·3	5 01	6 14	51·3	4 24	5 27	51·2	219	321
40	140	7 41	9 15	50·6	7 03	8 28	50·5	6 25	7 42	50·4	5 46	6 55	50·3	5 08	6 09	50·3	4 30	5 22	50·2	220	320
41	139	7 50	9 07	49·6	7 11	8 21	49·5	6 32	7 35	49·4	5 53	6 49	49·4	5 14	6 03	49·3	4 35	5 18	49·2	221	319
42	138	8 00	8 59	48·6	7 20	8 13	48·5	6 40	7 28	48·4	6 01	6 43	48·4	5 21	5 58	48·3	4 41	5 13	48·2	222	318
43	137	8 09	8 50	47·6	7 29	8 05	47·5	6 48	7 21	47·4	6 07	6 36	47·4	5 27	5 52	47·3	4 46	5 08	47·2	223	317
44	136	8 18	8 42	46·6	7 37	7 58	46·5	6 56	7 14	46·4	6 14	6 30	46·4	5 33	5 46	46·3	4 51	5 03	46·2	224	316
45	135	8 27	8 33	45·6	7 45	7 50	45·5	7 03	7 06	45·4	6 21	6 23	45·4	5 39	5 41	45·3	4 57	4 58	45·2	225	315

Lat. / A		78°			79°			80°			81°			82°			83°			Lat. / A	
LHA/F		A/H	B/P	Z_1/Z_2	A/H	B/P	Z_1/Z_2	A/H	B/P	Z_1/Z_2	A/H	B/P	Z_1/Z_2	A/H	B/P	Z_1/Z_2	A/H	B/P	Z_1/Z_2	LHA	
°	°	° ′	° ′	°	° ′	° ′	°	° ′	° ′	°	° ′	° ′	°	° ′	° ′	°	° ′	° ′	°	°	°
45	135	8 27	8 33	45·6	7 45	7 50	45·5	7 03	7 06	45·4	6 21	6 23	45·4	5 39	5 41	45·3	4 57	4 58	45·2	225	315
46	134	8 36	8 24	44·6	7 53	7 41	44·5	7 11	6 59	44·4	6 28	6 17	44·4	5 45	5 35	44·3	5 02	4 53	44·2	226	314
47	133	8 45	8 15	43·6	8 01	7 33	43·5	7 18	6 51	43·4	6 34	6 10	43·4	5 51	5 28	43·3	5 07	4 47	43·2	227	313
48	132	8 53	8 06	42·6	8 09	7 25	42·5	7 25	6 44	42·4	6 41	6 03	42·4	5 56	5 22	42·3	5 12	4 42	42·2	228	312
49	131	9 02	7 56	41·6	8 17	7 16	41·5	7 32	6 36	41·4	6 47	5 56	41·4	6 02	5 16	41·3	5 17	4 36	41·2	229	311
50	130	9 10	7 47	40·6	8 24	7 07	40·5	7 39	6 28	40·4	6 53	5 49	40·3	6 07	5 10	40·3	5 21	4 31	40·2	230	310
51	129	9 18	7 37	39·6	8 32	6 58	39·5	7 45	6 20	39·4	6 59	5 42	39·3	6 13	5 03	39·3	5 26	4 25	39·2	231	309
52	128	9 26	7 27	38·6	8 39	6 49	38·5	7 52	6 12	38·4	7 05	5 34	38·3	6 18	4 57	38·3	5 31	4 19	38·2	232	308
53	127	9 33	7 17	37·6	8 46	6 40	37·5	7 58	6 03	37·4	7 11	5 27	37·3	6 23	4 50	37·3	5 35	4 14	37·2	233	307
54	126	9 41	7 07	36·6	8 53	6 31	36·5	8 05	5 55	36·4	7 16	5 19	36·3	6 28	4 43	36·3	5 39	4 08	36·2	234	306
55	125	9 48	6 57	35·6	9 00	6 22	35·5	8 11	5 47	35·4	7 22	5 11	35·3	6 33	4 37	35·3	5 44	4 02	35·2	235	305
56	124	9 56	6 47	34·6	9 06	6 12	34·5	8 17	5 38	34·4	7 27	5 04	34·3	6 38	4 30	34·3	5 48	3 56	34·2	236	304
57	123	10 03	6 36	33·6	9 13	6 03	33·5	8 22	5 29	33·4	7 32	4 56	33·3	6 42	4 23	33·3	5 52	3 50	33·2	237	303
58	122	10 09	6 26	32·6	9 19	5 53	32·5	8 28	5 20	32·4	7 37	4 48	32·3	6 47	4 16	32·3	5 56	3 43	32·2	238	302
59	121	10 16	6 15	31·6	9 25	5 43	31·5	8 34	5 11	31·4	7 42	4 40	31·3	6 51	4 08	31·2	6 00	3 37	31·2	239	301
60	120	10 22	6 04	30·6	9 31	5 33	30·5	8 39	5 02	30·4	7 47	4 32	30·3	6 55	4 01	30·2	6 04	3 31	30·2	240	300
61	119	10 29	5 53	29·5	9 36	5 23	29·5	8 44	4 53	29·4	7 52	4 23	29·3	6 59	3 54	29·2	6 07	3 24	29·2	241	299
62	118	10 35	5 42	28·5	9 42	5 13	28·4	8 49	4 44	28·4	7 56	4 15	28·3	7 04	3 46	28·2	6 11	3 18	28·2	242	298
63	117	10 41	5 31	27·5	9 47	5 03	27·4	8 54	4 35	27·4	8 01	4 07	27·3	7 07	3 39	27·2	6 14	3 11	27·2	243	297
64	116	10 46	5 19	26·5	9 52	4 52	26·4	8 59	4 25	26·3	8 05	3 58	26·3	7 11	3 32	26·2	6 17	3 05	26·2	244	296
65	115	10 52	5 08	25·5	9 57	4 42	25·4	9 03	4 16	25·3	8 09	3 50	25·3	7 15	3 24	25·2	6 20	2 58	25·2	245	295
66	114	10 57	4 56	24·5	10 02	4 31	24·4	9 08	4 06	24·3	8 13	3 41	24·3	7 18	3 16	24·2	6 24	2 52	24·2	246	294
67	113	11 02	4 45	23·5	10 07	4 21	23·4	9 12	3 56	23·3	8 17	3 32	23·3	7 22	3 09	23·2	6 26	2 45	23·2	247	293
68	112	11 07	4 33	22·4	10 11	4 10	22·4	9 16	3 47	22·3	8 20	3 24	22·2	7 25	3 01	22·2	6 29	2 38	22·1	248	292
69	111	11 12	4 21	21·4	10 16	3 59	21·4	9 20	3 37	21·3	8 24	3 15	21·2	7 28	2 53	21·2	6 32	2 31	21·1	249	291
70	110	11 16	4 09	20·4	10 20	3 48	20·3	9 23	3 27	20·3	8 27	3 06	20·2	7 31	2 45	20·2	6 35	2 24	20·1	250	290
71	109	11 20	3 58	19·4	10 24	3 37	19·3	9 27	3 17	19·3	8 30	2 57	19·2	7 34	2 37	19·2	6 37	2 17	19·1	251	289
72	108	11 24	3 45	18·4	10 27	3 26	18·3	9 30	3 07	18·3	8 33	2 48	18·2	7 36	2 29	18·2	6 39	2 10	18·1	252	288
73	107	11 28	3 33	17·4	10 31	3 15	17·3	9 34	2 57	17·2	8 36	2 39	17·2	7 39	2 21	17·2	6 42	2 03	17·1	253	287
74	106	11 32	3 21	16·3	10 34	3 04	16·3	9 37	2 47	16·2	8 39	2 30	16·2	7 41	2 13	16·1	6 44	1 56	16·1	254	286
75	105	11 35	3 09	15·3	10 37	2 53	15·3	9 39	2 37	15·2	8 41	2 21	15·2	7 44	2 05	15·1	6 46	1 49	15·1	255	285
76	104	11 38	2 57	14·3	10 40	2 42	14·3	9 42	2 27	14·2	8 44	2 12	14·2	7 46	1 57	14·1	6 47	1 42	14·1	256	284
77	103	11 41	2 44	13·3	10 43	2 30	13·2	9 44	2 16	13·2	8 46	2 02	13·2	7 48	1 49	13·1	6 49	1 35	13·1	257	283
78	102	11 44	2 32	12·3	10 45	2 19	12·2	9 47	2 06	12·2	8 48	1 53	12·1	7 49	1 40	12·1	6 51	1 28	12·1	258	282
79	101	11 47	2 19	11·2	10 48	2 07	11·2	9 49	1 56	11·2	8 50	1 44	11·1	7 51	1 32	11·1	6 52	1 21	11·1	259	281
80	100	11 49	2 07	10·2	10 50	1 56	10·2	9 51	1 45	10·2	8 52	1 35	10·1	7 53	1 24	10·1	6 54	1 13	10·1	260	280
81	99	11 51	1 54	9·2	10 52	1 45	9·2	9 53	1 35	9·1	8 53	1 25	9·1	7 54	1 16	9·1	6 55	1 06	9·1	261	279
82	98	11 53	1 42	8·2	10 53	1 33	8·1	9 54	1 24	8·1	8 55	1 16	8·1	7 55	1 07	8·1	6 56	0 59	8·1	262	278
83	97	11 55	1 29	7·2	10 55	1 21	7·1	9 55	1 14	7·1	8 56	1 06	7·1	7 56	0 59	7·1	6 57	0 51	7·1	263	277
84	96	11 56	1 16	6·1	10 56	1 10	6·1	9 57	1 03	6·1	8 57	0 57	6·1	7 57	0 50	6·1	6 58	0 44	6·0	264	276
85	95	11 57	1 04	5·1	10 57	0 58	5·1	9 58	0 53	5·1	8 58	0 47	5·1	7 58	0 42	5·0	6 58	0 37	5·0	265	275
86	94	11 58	0 51	4·1	10 58	0 47	4·1	9 59	0 42	4·1	8 59	0 38	4·0	7 59	0 34	4·0	6 59	0 29	4·0	266	274
87	93	11 59	0 38	3·1	10 59	0 35	3·1	9 59	0 32	3·0	8 59	0 28	3·0	7 59	0 25	3·0	6 59	0 22	3·0	267	273
88	92	12 00	0 26	2·0	11 00	0 23	2·0	10 00	0 21	2·0	9 00	0 19	2·0	8 00	0 17	2·0	7 00	0 15	2·0	268	272
89	91	12 00	0 13	1·0	11 00	0 12	1·0	10 00	0 11	1·0	9 00	0 10	1·0	8 00	0 08	1·0	7 00	0 07	1·0	269	271
90	90	12 00	0 00	0·0	11 00	0 00	0·0	10 00	0 00	0·0	9 00	0 00	0·0	8 00	0 00	0·0	7 00	0 00	0·0	270	270

N. Lat: for LHA > 180° … $Z_n = Z$
for LHA < 180° … $Z_n = 360° - Z$

S. Lat.: for LHA > 180° … $Z_n = 180° - Z$
for LHA < 180° … $Z_n = 180° + Z$

SIGHT REDUCTION TABLE

B: (−) for 90° < LHA < 270°
Dec:(−) for Lat. contrary name

Z_1: same sign as B
Z_2: (−) for F > 90°

Lat. / A		84°			85°			86°			87°			88°			89°			Lat. / A	
LHA/F		A/H	B/P	Z_1/Z_2	A/H	B/P	Z_1/Z_2	A/H	B/P	Z_1/Z_2	A/H	B/P	Z_1/Z_2	A/H	B/P	Z_1/Z_2	A/H	B/P	Z_1/Z_2	LHA	
°	°	° ′	° ′	°	° ′	° ′	°	° ′	° ′	°	° ′	° ′	°	° ′	° ′	°	° ′	° ′	°	°	°
0	180	0 00	6 00	90·0	0 00	5 00	90·0	0 00	4 00	90·0	0 00	3 00	90·0	0 00	2 00	90·0	0 00	1 00	90·0	180	360
1	179	0 06	6 00	89·0	0 05	5 00	89·0	0 04	4 00	89·0	0 03	3 00	89·0	0 02	2 00	89·0	0 01	1 00	89·0	181	359
2	178	0 13	6 00	88·0	0 10	5 00	88·0	0 08	4 00	88·0	0 06	3 00	88·0	0 04	2 00	88·0	0 02	1 00	88·0	182	358
3	177	0 19	6 00	87·0	0 16	5 00	87·0	0 13	4 00	87·0	0 09	3 00	87·0	0 06	2 00	87·0	0 03	1 00	87·0	183	357
4	176	0 25	5 59	86·0	0 21	4 59	86·0	0 17	3 59	86·0	0 13	3 00	86·0	0 08	2 00	86·0	0 04	1 00	86·0	184	356
5	175	0 31	5 59	85·0	0 26	4 59	85·0	0 21	3 59	85·0	0 16	2 59	85·0	0 10	2 00	85·0	0 05	1 00	85·0	185	355
6	174	0 38	5 58	84·0	0 31	4 58	84·0	0 25	3 59	84·0	0 19	2 59	84·0	0 13	1 59	84·0	0 06	1 00	84·0	186	354
7	173	0 44	5 57	83·0	0 37	4 58	83·0	0 29	3 58	83·0	0 22	2 59	83·0	0 15	1 59	83·0	0 07	1 00	83·0	187	353
8	172	0 50	5 57	82·0	0 42	4 57	82·0	0 33	3 58	82·0	0 25	2 58	82·0	0 17	1 59	82·0	0 08	0 59	82·0	188	352
9	171	0 56	5 56	81·0	0 47	4 56	81·0	0 38	3 57	81·0	0 28	2 58	81·0	0 19	1 59	81·0	0 09	0 59	81·0	189	351
10	170	1 02	5 55	80·1	0 52	4 55	80·0	0 42	3 56	80·0	0 31	2 57	80·0	0 21	1 58	80·0	0 10	0 59	80·0	190	350
11	169	1 09	5 53	79·1	0 57	4 55	79·0	0 46	3 56	79·0	0 34	2 57	79·0	0 23	1 58	79·0	0 11	0 59	79·0	191	349
12	168	1 15	5 52	78·1	1 02	4 53	78·0	0 50	3 55	78·0	0 37	2 56	78·0	0 25	1 57	78·0	0 12	0 59	78·0	192	348
13	167	1 21	5 51	77·1	1 07	4 52	77·0	0 54	3 54	77·0	0 40	2 55	77·0	0 27	1 57	77·0	0 13	0 58	77·0	193	347
14	166	1 27	5 49	76·1	1 12	4 51	76·1	0 58	3 53	76·0	0 44	2 55	76·0	0 29	1 56	76·0	0 15	0 58	76·0	194	346
15	165	1 33	5 48	75·1	1 18	4 50	75·1	1 02	3 52	75·0	0 47	2 54	75·0	0 31	1 56	75·0	0 16	0 58	75·0	195	345
16	164	1 39	5 46	74·1	1 23	4 48	74·1	1 06	3 51	74·0	0 50	2 53	74·0	0 33	1 55	74·0	0 17	0 58	74·0	196	344
17	163	1 45	5 44	73·1	1 28	4 47	73·1	1 10	3 50	73·0	0 53	2 52	73·0	0 35	1 55	73·0	0 18	0 57	73·0	197	343
18	162	1 51	5 42	72·1	1 33	4 45	72·1	1 14	3 48	72·0	0 56	2 51	72·0	0 37	1 54	72·0	0 19	0 57	72·0	198	342
19	161	1 57	5 41	71·1	1 38	4 44	71·1	1 18	3 47	71·0	0 59	2 50	71·0	0 39	1 53	71·0	0 20	0 57	71·0	199	341
20	160	2 03	5 38	70·1	1 42	4 42	70·1	1 22	3 46	70·0	1 02	2 49	70·0	0 41	1 53	70·0	0 21	0 56	70·0	200	340
21	159	2 09	5 36	69·1	1 47	4 40	69·1	1 26	3 44	69·0	1 04	2 48	69·0	0 43	1 52	69·0	0 22	0 56	69·0	201	339
22	158	2 15	5 34	68·1	1 52	4 38	68·1	1 30	3 43	68·0	1 07	2 47	68·0	0 45	1 51	68·0	0 22	0 56	68·0	202	338
23	157	2 20	5 32	67·1	1 57	4 36	67·1	1 34	3 41	67·1	1 10	2 46	67·0	0 47	1 50	67·0	0 23	0 55	67·0	203	337
24	156	2 26	5 29	66·1	2 02	4 34	66·1	1 38	3 39	66·1	1 13	2 44	66·0	0 49	1 50	66·0	0 24	0 55	66·0	204	336
25	155	2 32	5 26	65·1	2 07	4 32	65·1	1 41	3 38	65·1	1 16	2 43	65·0	0 51	1 49	65·0	0 25	0 54	65·0	205	335
26	154	2 38	5 24	64·1	2 11	4 30	64·1	1 45	3 36	64·1	1 19	2 42	64·0	0 53	1 48	64·0	0 26	0 54	64·0	206	334
27	153	2 43	5 21	63·1	2 16	4 27	63·1	1 49	3 34	63·1	1 22	2 40	63·0	0 54	1 47	63·0	0 27	0 53	63·0	207	333
28	152	2 49	5 18	62·1	2 21	4 25	62·1	1 53	3 32	62·1	1 24	2 39	62·0	0 56	1 46	62·0	0 28	0 53	62·0	208	332
29	151	2 54	5 15	61·1	2 25	4 23	61·1	1 56	3 30	61·1	1 27	2 37	61·0	0 58	1 45	61·0	0 29	0 52	61·0	209	331
30	150	3 00	5 12	60·1	2 30	4 20	60·1	2 00	3 28	60·1	1 30	2 36	60·0	1 00	1 44	60·0	0 30	0 52	60·0	210	330
31	149	3 05	5 09	59·1	2 34	4 17	59·1	2 04	3 26	59·1	1 33	2 34	59·0	1 02	1 43	59·0	0 31	0 51	59·0	211	329
32	148	3 11	5 06	58·1	2 39	4 15	58·1	2 07	3 24	58·1	1 35	2 33	58·0	1 04	1 42	58·0	0 32	0 51	58·0	212	328
33	147	3 16	5 02	57·1	2 43	4 12	57·1	2 11	3 21	57·1	1 38	2 31	57·0	1 05	1 41	57·0	0 33	0 50	57·0	213	327
34	146	3 21	4 59	56·1	2 48	4 09	56·1	2 14	3 19	56·1	1 41	2 29	56·0	1 07	1 39	56·0	0 34	0 50	56·0	214	326
35	145	3 26	4 55	55·1	2 52	4 06	55·1	2 18	3 17	55·1	1 43	2 27	55·0	1 09	1 38	55·0	0 34	0 49	55·0	215	325
36	144	3 31	4 52	54·1	2 56	4 03	54·1	2 21	3 14	54·1	1 46	2 26	54·0	1 11	1 37	54·0	0 35	0 49	54·0	216	324
37	143	3 36	4 48	53·2	3 00	4 00	53·1	2 24	3 12	53·1	1 48	2 24	53·0	1 12	1 36	53·0	0 36	0 48	53·0	217	323
38	142	3 41	4 44	52·2	3 05	3 57	52·1	2 28	3 09	52·1	1 51	2 22	52·0	1 14	1 35	52·0	0 37	0 47	52·0	218	322
39	141	3 46	4 40	51·2	3 09	3 53	51·1	2 31	3 07	51·1	1 53	2 20	51·0	1 16	1 33	51·0	0 38	0 47	51·0	219	321
40	140	3 51	4 36	50·2	3 13	3 50	50·1	2 34	3 04	50·1	1 56	2 18	50·0	1 17	1 32	50·0	0 39	0 46	50·0	220	320
41	139	3 56	4 32	49·2	3 17	3 47	49·1	2 37	3 01	49·1	1 58	2 16	49·0	1 19	1 31	49·0	0 39	0 45	49·0	221	319
42	138	4 01	4 28	48·2	3 21	3 43	48·1	2 41	2 58	48·1	2 00	2 14	48·0	1 20	1 29	48·0	0 40	0 45	48·0	222	318
43	137	4 05	4 24	47·2	3 24	3 40	47·1	2 44	2 56	47·1	2 03	2 12	47·0	1 22	1 28	47·0	0 41	0 44	47·0	223	317
44	136	4 10	4 19	46·2	3 28	3 36	46·1	2 47	2 53	46·1	2 05	2 10	46·0	1 23	1 26	46·0	0 42	0 43	46·0	224	316
45	135	4 14	4 15	45·2	3 32	3 32	45·1	2 50	2 50	45·1	2 07	2 07	45·0	1 25	1 25	45·0	0 42	0 42	45·0	225	315

Lat. / A		84°			85°			86°			87°			88°			89°			Lat. / A	
LHA/F		A/H	B/P	Z_1/Z_2	A/H	B/P	Z_1/Z_2	A/H	B/P	Z_1/Z_2	A/H	B/P	Z_1/Z_2	A/H	B/P	Z_1/Z_2	A/H	B/P	Z_1/Z_2	LHA	
°	°	° ′	° ′	°	° ′	° ′	°	° ′	° ′	°	° ′	° ′	°	° ′	° ′	°	° ′	° ′	°	°	°
45	135	4 14	4 15	45·2	3 32	3 32	45·1	2 50	2 50	45·1	2 07	2 07	45·0	1 25	1 25	45·0	0 42	0 42	45·0	225	315
46	134	4 19	4 11	44·2	3 36	3 29	44·1	2 53	2 47	44·1	2 09	2 05	44·0	1 26	1 23	44·0	0 43	0 42	44·0	226	314
47	133	4 23	4 06	43·2	3 39	3 25	43·1	2 55	2 44	43·1	2 12	2 03	43·0	1 28	1 22	43·0	0 44	0 41	43·0	227	313
48	132	4 27	4 01	42·2	3 43	3 21	42·1	2 58	2 41	42·1	2 14	2 01	42·0	1 29	1 20	42·0	0 45	0 40	42·0	228	312
49	131	4 31	3 57	41·2	3 46	3 17	41·1	3 01	2 38	41·1	2 16	1 58	41·0	1 31	1 19	41·0	0 45	0 39	41·0	229	311
50	130	4 36	3 52	40·2	3 50	3 13	40·1	3 04	2 34	40·1	2 18	1 56	40·0	1 32	1 17	40·0	0 46	0 39	40·0	230	310
51	129	4 40	3 47	39·2	3 53	3 09	39·1	3 06	2 31	39·1	2 20	1 53	39·0	1 33	1 16	39·0	0 47	0 38	39·0	231	309
52	128	4 43	3 42	38·2	3 56	3 05	38·1	3 09	2 28	38·1	2 22	1 51	38·0	1 35	1 14	38·0	0 47	0 37	38·0	232	308
53	127	4 47	3 37	37·2	3 59	3 01	37·1	3 12	2 25	37·1	2 24	1 48	37·0	1 36	1 12	37·0	0 48	0 36	37·0	233	307
54	126	4 51	3 32	36·1	4 03	2 57	36·1	3 14	2 21	36·1	2 26	1 46	36·0	1 37	1 11	36·0	0 49	0 35	36·0	234	306
55	125	4 55	3 27	35·1	4 06	2 52	35·1	3 17	2 18	35·1	2 27	1 43	35·0	1 38	1 09	35·0	0 49	0 34	35·0	235	305
56	124	4 58	3 22	34·1	4 09	2 48	34·1	3 19	2 14	34·1	2 29	1 41	34·0	1 39	1 07	34·0	0 50	0 34	34·0	236	304
57	123	5 02	3 17	33·1	4 12	2 44	33·1	3 21	2 11	33·1	2 31	1 38	33·0	1 41	1 05	33·0	0 50	0 33	33·0	237	303
58	122	5 05	3 11	32·1	4 14	2 39	32·1	3 23	2 07	32·1	2 33	1 35	32·0	1 42	1 04	32·0	0 51	0 32	32·0	238	302
59	121	5 08	3 06	31·1	4 17	2 35	31·1	3 26	2 04	31·1	2 34	1 33	31·0	1 43	1 02	31·0	0 51	0 31	31·0	239	301
60	120	5 12	3 00	30·1	4 20	2 30	30·1	3 28	2 00	30·1	2 36	1 30	30·0	1 44	1 00	30·0	0 52	0 30	30·0	240	300
61	119	5 15	2 55	29·1	4 22	2 26	29·1	3 30	1 56	29·1	2 37	1 27	29·0	1 45	0 58	29·0	0 52	0 29	29·0	241	299
62	118	5 18	2 49	28·1	4 25	2 21	28·1	3 32	1 53	28·1	2 39	1 25	28·0	1 46	0 56	28·0	0 53	0 28	28·0	242	298
63	117	5 21	2 44	27·1	4 27	2 16	27·1	3 34	1 49	27·1	2 40	1 22	27·0	1 47	0 54	27·0	0 53	0 27	27·0	243	297
64	116	5 23	2 38	26·1	4 30	2 12	26·1	3 36	1 45	26·1	2 42	1 19	26·0	1 48	0 53	26·0	0 54	0 26	26·0	244	296
65	115	5 26	2 33	25·1	4 32	2 07	25·1	3 37	1 42	25·1	2 43	1 16	25·0	1 49	0 51	25·0	0 54	0 25	25·0	245	295
66	114	5 29	2 27	24·1	4 34	2 02	24·1	3 39	1 38	24·1	2 44	1 13	24·0	1 50	0 49	24·0	0 55	0 24	24·0	246	294
67	113	5 31	2 21	23·1	4 36	1 57	23·1	3 41	1 34	23·1	2 46	1 10	23·0	1 50	0 47	23·0	0 55	0 23	23·0	247	293
68	112	5 34	2 15	22·1	4 38	1 53	22·1	3 42	1 30	22·0	2 47	1 07	22·0	1 51	0 45	22·0	0 56	0 22	22·0	248	292
69	111	5 36	2 09	21·1	4 40	1 48	21·1	3 44	1 26	21·0	2 48	1 05	21·0	1 52	0 43	21·0	0 56	0 22	21·0	249	291
70	110	5 38	2 04	20·1	4 42	1 43	20·1	3 46	1 22	20·0	2 49	1 02	20·0	1 53	0 41	20·0	0 56	0 21	20·0	250	290
71	109	5 40	1 58	19·1	4 44	1 38	19·1	3 47	1 18	19·0	2 50	0 59	19·0	1 53	0 39	19·0	0 57	0 20	19·0	251	289
72	108	5 42	1 52	18·1	4 45	1 33	18·1	3 48	1 14	18·0	2 51	0 56	18·0	1 54	0 37	18·0	0 57	0 19	18·0	252	288
73	107	5 44	1 46	17·1	4 47	1 28	17·1	3 49	1 10	17·0	2 52	0 53	17·0	1 55	0 35	17·0	0 57	0 18	17·0	253	287
74	106	5 46	1 40	16·1	4 48	1 23	16·1	3 51	1 06	16·0	2 53	0 50	16·0	1 55	0 33	16·0	0 58	0 17	16·0	254	286
75	105	5 48	1 33	15·1	4 50	1 18	15·1	3 52	1 02	15·0	2 54	0 47	15·0	1 56	0 31	15·0	0 58	0 16	15·0	255	285
76	104	5 49	1 27	14·1	4 51	1 13	14·1	3 53	0 58	14·0	2 55	0 44	14·0	1 56	0 29	14·0	0 58	0 15	14·0	256	284
77	103	5 51	1 21	13·1	4 52	1 08	13·0	3 54	0 54	13·0	2 55	0 41	13·0	1 57	0 27	13·0	0 58	0 13	13·0	257	283
78	102	5 52	1 15	12·1	4 53	1 03	12·0	3 55	0 50	12·0	2 56	0 37	12·0	1 57	0 25	12·0	0 59	0 12	12·0	258	282
79	101	5 53	1 09	11·1	4 54	0 57	11·0	3 56	0 46	11·0	2 57	0 34	11·0	1 58	0 23	11·0	0 59	0 11	11·0	259	281
80	100	5 55	1 03	10·1	4 55	0 52	10·0	3 56	0 42	10·0	2 57	0 31	10·0	1 58	0 21	10·0	0 59	0 10	10·0	260	280
81	99	5 56	0 57	9·0	4 56	0 47	9·0	3 57	0 38	9·0	2 58	0 28	9·0	1 59	0 19	9·0	0 59	0 09	9·0	261	279
82	98	5 56	0 50	8·0	4 57	0 42	8·0	3 58	0 33	8·0	2 58	0 25	8·0	1 59	0 17	8·0	0 59	0 08	8·0	262	278
83	97	5 57	0 44	7·0	4 58	0 37	7·0	3 58	0 29	7·0	2 59	0 22	7·0	1 59	0 15	7·0	1 00	0 07	7·0	263	277
84	96	5 58	0 38	6·0	4 58	0 31	6·0	3 59	0 25	6·0	2 59	0 19	6·0	1 59	0 13	6·0	1 00	0 06	6·0	264	276
85	95	5 59	0 31	5·0	4 59	0 26	5·0	3 59	0 21	5·0	2 59	0 16	5·0	2 00	0 10	5·0	1 00	0 05	5·0	265	275
86	94	5 59	0 25	4·0	4 59	0 21	4·0	3 59	0 17	4·0	3 00	0 13	4·0	2 00	0 08	4·0	1 00	0 04	4·0	266	274
87	93	6 00	0 19	3·0	5 00	0 16	3·0	4 00	0 13	3·0	3 00	0 09	3·0	2 00	0 06	3·0	1 00	0 03	3·0	267	273
88	92	6 00	0 13	2·0	5 00	0 10	2·0	4 00	0 08	2·0	3 00	0 06	2·0	2 00	0 04	2·0	1 00	0 02	2·0	268	272
89	91	6 00	0 06	1·0	5 00	0 05	1·0	4 00	0 04	1·0	3 00	0 03	1·0	2 00	0 02	1·0	1 00	0 01	1·0	269	271
90	90	6 00	0 00	0·0	5 00	0 00	0·0	4 00	0 00	0·0	3 00	0 00	0·0	2 00	0 00	0·0	1 00	0 00	0·0	270	270

N. Lat: for LHA > 180° … $Z_n = Z$
for LHA < 180° … $Z_n = 360° - Z$

S. Lat.: for LHA > 180° … $Z_n = 180° - Z$
for LHA < 180° … $Z_n = 180° + Z$

AUXILIARY TABLE

Sign of $corr_1$ for F′. *Reverse* sign if $F > 90°$. ↓

Sign for $corr_2$ for A′. ↓

F′ +/−	1	2	3	4	5	6	7	8	9	10	11	12	13	14	15	16	17	18	19	20	21	22	23	24	25	26	27	28	29	□	−/+ A′
	59	58	57	56	55	54	53	52	51	50	49	48	47	46	45	44	43	42	41	40	39	38	37	36	35	34	33	32	31	30	
P°	′	′	′	′	′	′	′	′	′	′	′	′	′	′	′	′	′	′	′	′	′	′	′	′	′	′	′	′	′	′	$Z_2°$
1	0	0	0	0	0	0	0	0	0	0	0	0	0	0	0	0	0	0	0	0	0	0	0	0	0	0	0	0	1	1	89
2	0	0	0	0	0	0	0	0	0	0	0	0	0	0	1	1	1	1	1	1	1	1	1	1	1	1	1	1	1	1	88
3	0	0	0	0	0	0	0	0	0	1	1	1	1	1	1	1	1	1	1	1	1	1	1	1	1	1	1	1	2	2	87
4	0	0	0	0	0	0	0	1	1	1	1	1	1	1	1	1	1	1	1	1	1	2	2	2	2	2	2	2	2	2	86
5	0	0	0	0	0	1	1	1	1	1	1	1	1	1	1	1	1	2	2	2	2	2	2	2	2	2	2	2	3	3	85
6	0	0	0	0	1	1	1	1	1	1	1	1	1	1	2	2	2	2	2	2	2	2	2	3	3	3	3	3	3	3	84
7	0	0	0	0	1	1	1	1	1	1	1	1	2	2	2	2	2	2	2	2	3	3	3	3	3	3	3	3	4	4	83
8	0	0	0	1	1	1	1	1	1	1	2	2	2	2	2	2	2	3	3	3	3	3	3	3	3	4	4	4	4	4	82
9	0	0	0	1	1	1	1	1	1	2	2	2	2	2	2	3	3	3	3	3	3	3	4	4	4	4	4	4	5	5	81
10	0	0	1	1	1	1	1	1	2	2	2	2	2	2	3	3	3	3	3	3	4	4	4	4	4	5	5	5	5	5	80
11	0	0	1	1	1	1	1	2	2	2	2	2	2	3	3	3	3	3	4	4	4	4	4	5	5	5	5	5	6	6	79
12	0	0	1	1	1	1	1	2	2	2	2	2	3	3	3	3	4	4	4	4	4	5	5	5	5	5	6	6	6	6	78
13	0	0	1	1	1	1	2	2	2	2	2	3	3	3	3	4	4	4	4	4	5	5	5	5	6	6	6	6	7	7	77
14	0	0	1	1	1	1	2	2	2	2	3	3	3	3	4	4	4	4	5	5	5	5	6	6	6	6	7	7	7	7	76
15	0	1	1	1	1	2	2	2	2	3	3	3	3	4	4	4	4	5	5	5	5	6	6	6	6	7	7	7	8	8	75
16	0	1	1	1	1	2	2	2	2	3	3	3	4	4	4	4	5	5	5	6	6	6	6	7	7	7	7	8	8	8	74
17	0	1	1	1	1	2	2	2	3	3	3	4	4	4	4	5	5	5	6	6	6	6	7	7	7	8	8	8	8	9	73
18	0	1	1	1	2	2	2	2	3	3	3	4	4	4	5	5	5	6	6	6	6	7	7	7	8	8	8	9	9	9	72
19	0	1	1	1	2	2	2	3	3	3	4	4	4	5	5	5	6	6	6	7	7	7	7	8	8	8	9	9	9	10	71
20	0	1	1	1	2	2	2	3	3	3	4	4	4	5	5	5	6	6	6	7	7	8	8	8	9	9	9	10	10	10	70
21	0	1	1	1	2	2	3	3	3	4	4	4	5	5	5	6	6	6	7	7	8	8	8	9	9	9	10	10	10	11	69
22	0	1	1	1	2	2	3	3	3	4	4	4	5	5	6	6	6	7	7	7	8	8	9	9	9	10	10	10	11	11	68
23	0	1	1	2	2	2	3	3	4	4	4	5	5	5	6	6	7	7	7	8	8	9	9	9	10	10	11	11	11	12	67
24	0	1	1	2	2	2	3	3	4	4	4	5	5	6	6	7	7	7	8	8	9	9	9	10	10	11	11	11	12	12	66
25	0	1	1	2	2	3	3	3	4	4	5	5	5	6	6	7	7	8	8	8	9	9	10	10	11	11	11	12	12	13	65
26	0	1	1	2	2	3	3	4	4	4	5	5	6	6	7	7	7	8	8	9	9	10	10	11	11	11	12	12	13	13	64
27	0	1	1	2	2	3	3	4	4	5	5	5	6	6	7	7	8	8	9	9	10	10	10	11	11	12	12	13	13	14	63
28	0	1	1	2	2	3	3	4	4	5	5	6	6	7	7	8	8	8	9	9	10	10	11	11	12	12	13	13	14	14	62
29	0	1	1	2	2	3	3	4	4	5	5	6	6	7	7	8	8	9	9	10	10	11	11	12	12	13	13	14	14	15	61
30	0	1	1	2	2	3	3	4	4	5	5	6	6	7	7	8	8	9	9	10	10	11	11	12	12	13	13	14	14	15	60
31	1	1	2	2	3	3	4	4	5	5	6	6	7	7	8	8	9	9	10	10	11	11	12	12	13	13	14	14	15	15	59
32	1	1	2	2	3	3	4	4	5	5	6	6	7	7	8	8	9	10	10	11	11	12	12	13	13	14	14	15	15	16	58
33	1	1	2	2	3	3	4	4	5	5	6	7	7	8	8	9	9	10	10	11	11	12	13	13	14	14	15	15	16	16	57
34	1	1	2	2	3	3	4	4	5	6	6	7	7	8	8	9	10	10	11	11	12	12	13	13	14	15	15	16	16	17	56
35	1	1	2	2	3	3	4	5	5	6	6	7	7	8	9	9	10	10	11	11	12	13	13	14	14	15	15	16	17	17	55
36	1	1	2	2	3	4	4	5	5	6	6	7	8	8	9	9	10	11	11	12	12	13	14	14	15	15	16	16	17	18	54
37	1	1	2	2	3	4	4	5	5	6	7	7	8	8	9	10	10	11	11	12	13	13	14	14	15	16	16	17	17	18	53
38	1	1	2	2	3	4	4	5	6	6	7	7	8	9	9	10	10	11	12	12	13	14	14	15	15	16	17	17	18	18	52
39	1	1	2	3	3	4	4	5	6	6	7	8	8	9	9	10	11	11	12	13	13	14	14	15	16	16	17	18	18	19	51
40	1	1	2	3	3	4	4	5	6	6	7	8	8	9	10	10	11	12	12	13	13	14	15	15	16	17	17	18	19	19	50

F′ +/−	1 59	2 58	3 57	4 56	5 55	6 54	7 53	8 52	9 51	10 50	11 49	12 48	13 47	14 46	15 45	16 44	17 43	18 42	19 41	20 40	21 39	22 38	23 37	24 36	25 35	26 34	27 33	28 32	29 31	□ 30	−/+ A′
P°	′	′	′	′	′	′	′	′	′	′	′	′	′	′	′	′	′	′	′	′	′	′	′	′	′	′	′	′	′	′	Z_2°
41	1	1	2	3	3	4	5	5	6	7	7	8	9	9	10	10	11	12	12	13	14	14	15	16	16	17	18	18	19	20	49
42	1	1	2	3	3	4	5	5	6	7	7	8	9	9	10	11	11	12	13	13	14	15	15	16	17	17	18	19	19	20	48
43	1	1	2	3	3	4	5	5	6	7	8	8	9	10	10	11	12	12	13	14	14	15	16	16	17	18	18	19	20	20	47
44	1	1	2	3	3	4	5	6	6	7	8	8	9	10	10	11	12	13	13	14	15	15	16	17	17	18	19	19	20	21	46
45	1	1	2	3	4	4	5	6	6	7	8	8	9	10	11	11	12	13	13	14	15	16	16	17	18	18	19	20	21	21	45
46	1	1	2	3	4	4	5	6	6	7	8	9	9	10	11	12	12	13	14	14	15	16	17	17	18	19	19	20	21	22	44
47	1	1	2	3	4	4	5	6	7	7	8	9	10	10	11	12	12	13	14	15	15	16	17	18	18	19	20	20	21	22	43
48	1	1	2	3	4	4	5	6	7	7	8	9	10	10	11	12	13	13	14	15	16	16	17	18	19	19	20	21	22	22	42
49	1	2	2	3	4	5	5	6	7	8	8	9	10	11	11	12	13	14	14	15	16	17	17	18	19	20	20	21	22	23	41
50	1	2	2	3	4	5	5	6	7	8	8	9	10	11	11	12	13	14	15	15	16	17	18	18	19	20	21	21	22	23	40
51	1	2	2	3	4	5	5	6	7	8	9	9	10	11	12	12	13	14	15	16	16	17	18	19	19	20	21	22	23	23	39
52	1	2	2	3	4	5	6	6	7	8	9	9	10	11	12	13	13	14	15	16	17	17	18	19	20	20	21	22	23	24	38
53	1	2	2	3	4	5	6	6	7	8	9	10	10	11	12	13	14	14	15	16	17	18	18	19	20	21	22	22	23	24	37
54	1	2	2	3	4	5	6	6	7	8	9	10	11	11	12	13	14	15	15	16	17	18	19	19	20	21	22	23	23	24	36
55	1	2	2	3	4	5	6	7	7	8	9	10	11	11	12	13	14	15	16	16	17	18	19	20	20	21	22	23	24	25	35
56	1	2	2	3	4	5	6	7	7	8	9	10	11	12	12	13	14	15	16	17	17	18	19	20	21	22	22	23	24	25	34
57	1	2	3	3	4	5	6	7	8	8	9	10	11	12	13	13	14	15	16	17	18	18	19	20	21	22	23	23	24	25	33
58	1	2	3	3	4	5	6	7	8	8	9	10	11	12	13	14	14	15	16	17	18	19	20	20	21	22	23	24	25	25	32
59	1	2	3	3	4	5	6	7	8	9	9	10	11	12	13	14	15	15	16	17	18	19	20	21	21	22	23	24	25	26	31
60	1	2	3	3	4	5	6	7	8	9	10	10	11	12	13	14	15	16	16	17	18	19	20	21	22	23	23	24	25	26	30
61	1	2	3	3	4	5	6	7	8	9	10	10	11	12	13	14	15	16	17	17	18	19	20	21	22	23	24	24	25	26	29
62	1	2	3	4	4	5	6	7	8	9	10	11	11	12	13	14	15	16	17	18	19	19	20	21	22	23	24	25	26	26	28
63	1	2	3	4	4	5	6	7	8	9	10	11	12	12	13	14	15	16	17	18	19	20	20	21	22	23	24	25	26	27	27
64	1	2	3	4	4	5	6	7	8	9	10	11	12	13	13	14	15	16	17	18	19	20	21	22	22	23	24	25	26	27	26
65	1	2	3	4	5	5	6	7	8	9	10	11	12	13	14	15	15	16	17	18	19	20	21	22	23	24	24	25	26	27	25
66	1	2	3	4	5	5	6	7	8	9	10	11	12	13	14	15	16	16	17	18	19	20	21	22	23	24	25	26	26	27	24
67	1	2	3	4	5	6	6	7	8	9	10	11	12	13	14	15	16	17	17	18	19	20	21	22	23	24	25	26	27	28	23
68	1	2	3	4	5	6	6	7	8	9	10	11	12	13	14	15	16	17	18	19	19	20	21	22	23	24	25	26	27	28	22
69	1	2	3	4	5	6	7	7	8	9	10	11	12	13	14	15	16	17	18	19	20	21	21	22	23	24	25	26	27	28	21
70	1	2	3	4	5	6	7	8	8	9	10	11	12	13	14	15	16	17	18	19	20	21	22	23	23	24	25	26	27	28	20
71	1	2	3	4	5	6	7	8	9	9	10	11	12	13	14	15	16	17	18	19	20	21	22	23	24	25	26	26	27	28	19
72	1	2	3	4	5	6	7	8	9	10	10	11	12	13	14	15	16	17	18	19	20	21	22	23	24	25	26	27	28	29	18
73	1	2	3	4	5	6	7	8	9	10	11	11	12	13	14	15	16	17	18	19	20	21	22	23	24	25	26	27	28	29	17
74	1	2	3	4	5	6	7	8	9	10	11	12	12	13	14	15	16	17	18	19	20	21	22	23	24	25	26	27	28	29	16
75	1	2	3	4	5	6	7	8	9	10	11	12	13	14	14	15	16	17	18	19	20	21	22	23	24	25	26	27	28	29	15
76	1	2	3	4	5	6	7	8	9	10	11	12	13	14	15	16	16	17	18	19	20	21	22	23	24	25	26	27	28	29	14
77	1	2	3	4	5	6	7	8	9	10	11	12	13	14	15	16	17	18	19	19	20	21	22	23	24	25	26	27	28	29	13
78	1	2	3	4	5	6	7	8	9	10	11	12	13	14	15	16	17	18	19	20	21	22	22	23	24	25	26	27	28	29	12
79	1	2	3	4	5	6	7	8	9	10	11	12	13	14	15	16	17	18	19	20	21	22	23	24	25	26	27	27	28	29	11
80	1	2	3	4	5	6	7	8	9	10	11	12	13	14	15	16	17	18	19	20	21	22	23	24	25	26	27	28	29	30	10

For P > 80°, use 80°

For $Z_2 < 10°$, use 10°

USE OF CONCISE SIGHT REDUCTION TABLES (continued)

4. *Example.* (b) Required the altitude and azimuth of *Vega* on 2016 July 29 at UT 04^h 50^m from the estimated position 152° west, 15° south.

1. Assumed latitude	$Lat =$	15° S		
From the almanac	$GHA =$	100° 24′		
Assumed longitude		152° 24′ W		
Local hour angle	$LHA =$	308		
2. Reduction table, 1st entry				
$(Lat, LHA) = (15, 308)$	$A =$	49 34	$A^\circ = 50$, $A' = 34$	
	$B =$	+66 29	$Z_1 = +71{\cdot}7$,	$LHA > 270°$
3. From the almanac	$Dec =$	−38 48		*Lat* and *Dec* contrary
Sum = $B + Dec$	$F =$	+27 41	$F^\circ = 28$, $F' = 41$	
4. Reduction table, 2nd entry				
$(A^\circ, F^\circ) = (50, 28)$	$H =$	17 34	$P^\circ = 37$	
			$Z_2 = 67{\cdot}8, Z_2{}^\circ = 68$	
5. Auxiliary table, 1st entry				
$(F', P^\circ) = (41, 37)$	$corr_1 =$	−11		$F < 90°$, $F' > 29'$
Sum		17 23		
6. Auxiliary table, 2nd entry				
$(A', Z_2{}^\circ) = (34, 68)$	$corr_2 =$	+10		$A' > 30'$
7. Sum = computed altitude	$H_C =$	+17° 33′		$F > 0°$
8. Azimuth, first component	$Z_1 =$	+71·7		same sign as *B*
second component	$Z_2 =$	+67·8		$F < 90°$, $F > 0°$
Sum = azimuth angle	$Z =$	139·5		
True azimuth	$Z_n =$	040°		S *Lat*, $LHA > 180°$

5. *Form for use with the Concise Sight Reduction Tables.* The form on the following page lays out the procedure explained on pages 284-285. Each step is shown, with notes and rules to ensure accuracy, rather than speed, throughout the calculation. The form is mainly intended for the calculation of star positions. It therefore includes the formation of the Greenwich hour of Aries (*GHA* Aries), and thus the Greenwich hour angle of the star (*GHA*) from its tabular sidereal hour angle (*SHA*). These calculations, included in step 1 of the form, can easily be replaced by the interpolation of *GHA* and *Dec* for the Sun, Moon or planets.

The form may be freely copied; however, acknowledgement of the source is requested.

Date & UT of observation h m s	**Body**	**Estimated Latitude & Longitude** ° ′ ° ′

Step	**Calculate Altitude & Azimuth**	**Summary of Rules & Notes**
Assumed latitude	$Lat =$ °	Nearest estimated latitude, integral number of degrees.
Assumed longitude	$Long =$ ° ′	Choose $Long$ so that LHA has integral number of degrees.
1. From the almanac:	$Dec =$ ° ′	Record the Dec for use in Step 3.
GHA Aries h	= ° ′	Needed if using SHA. Tabular value.
Increment m s	= ° ′	for minutes and seconds of time.
SHA	$SHA =$ ° ′	
$GHA = GHA\ Aries + SHA$	$GHA =$ ° ′	Remove multiples of 360°.
Assumed longitude	$Long =$ ° ′	West longitudes are negative.
$LHA = GHA + Long$	$LHA =$ °	Remove multiples of 360°.
2. Reduction table, 1st entry		
$(Lat, LHA) = (\quad °, \quad °)$	$A =$ ° ′ $A° =$ °	nearest whole degree of A.
record A, B and Z_1.	$A' =$ ′	minutes part of A.
	$B =$ ° ′	B is minus if $90° < LHA < 270°$.
	$Z_1 =$ °	Z_1 has the same sign as B.
3. From step 1	$Dec =$ ° ′	Dec is minus if contrary to Lat.
$F = B + Dec$	$F =$ ° ′	Regard F as positive until step 7.
	$F° =$ °	nearest whole degree of F.
	$F' =$ ′	minutes part of F.
4. Reduction table, 2nd entry		
$(A°, F°) = (\quad °, \quad °)$	$H =$ ° ′ $P° =$ °	nearest whole degree of P.
record H, P and Z_2.	$Z_2 =$ °	
5. Auxiliary table, 1st entry		
$(F', P°) = (\quad ′, \quad °)$	$corr_1 =$ ′	$corr_1$ is minus if $F < 90°$ & $F' > 29'$,
record $corr_1$		or if $F > 90°$ & $F' < 30'$.
6. Auxiliary table, 2nd entry		$Z_2°$ nearest whole degree of Z_2.
$(A', Z_2°) = (\quad ′, \quad °)$	$corr_2 =$ ′	$corr_2$ is minus if $A' < 30'$.
record $corr_2$		
7. Calculated altitude =	$Hc =$ ° ′	Hc is minus if F is negative, and
$Hc = H + corr_1 + corr_2$		object is below the horizon.
8. Azimuth, 1st component	$Z_1 =$ °	Z_1 has the same sign as B.
2nd component	$Z_2 =$ °	Z_2 is minus if $F > 90°$. If F is negative, $Z_2 = 180° - Z_2$
$Z = Z_1 + Z_2$	$Z =$ °	Ignore the sign of Z.
		N Lat: If $LHA > 180°$, $Z_n = Z$, or if $LHA < 180°$, $Z_n = 360° - Z$,
		S Lat: If $LHA > 180°$, $Z_n = 180° - Z$, or if $LHA < 180°$, $Z_n = 180° + Z$.
True azimuth	$Z_n =$ °	©HMNAO

For use with *The Nautical Almanac's* Concise Sight Reduction Tables pages 284-318.

POLAR PHENOMENA

EXPLANATION

1. *Introduction.* The graphs on pages 322-325 give data concerning the rising and setting of the Sun and Moon and the duration of civil twilight for high latitudes. Graphs are given instead of tables for high latitudes because they give a clearer picture of the phenomena and of the attainable accuracy in any given case. In the regions of the graph that are difficult to read accurately, the phenomenon itself is generally uncertain.

2. *Semiduration of sunlight.* The graphs for the semiduration of sunlight (page 322) give for latitudes north of N 65° the number of hours from sunrise to meridian passage or from meridian passage to sunset. There is continuous daylight in an area marked "Sun above horizon", and no direct sunlight in an area marked "Sun below horizon". The figures near the top indicate, for several convenient dates, the local mean times of meridian passage; with the aid of the intermediate dots the LMT on any given day may be obtained to the nearest minute. The LMT of sunrise may be found by subtracting the semiduration from the time of meridian passage, and the time of sunset by adding. The equation of time is given by subtracting the time of meridian passage from noon.

Examples. (a) Estimate the time of sunrise and sunset on 2016 March 10 at latitude N 78°. The semiduration of sunlight (page 322) is about $5^{h}00^{m}$. The time of meridian passage is $12^{h}10^{m}$, and hence the LMT of sunrise is $07^{h}10^{m}$, and of sunset $17^{h}10^{m}$. (b) Estimate the dates, for the first half of 2016, when the Sun is continuously below and above the horizon at latitude N 80°. The semiduration of sunlight graph (page 322) indicates the Sun is continuously below the horizon until about February 22, and is continuously above the horizon after April 14.

3. *Duration of civil twilight.* The graphs for the duration of twilight (page 322) give the interval from the beginning of morning civil twilight (Sun 6° below the horizon) to the time of sunrise or from the time of sunset to the end of evening civil twilight. In a region marked "No twilight or sunlight" the Sun is continuously below the horizon by more than 6°. In a region marked "Continuous twilight or sunlight" the Sun never goes lower than 6° below the horizon.

Adjacent to a region marked "No twilight or sunlight" is a region in which the Sun is continuously below the horizon, but so near to the horizon during a portion of the day that there is twilight. This area is the shaded region. The value given by the graph in this shaded region is the interval from the beginning of morning twilight to meridian passage of the Sun, or from meridian passage to the end of evening twilight, the total duration of twilight being twice the value given by the graph. The border between this shaded region and the remainder of the graph indicates that the Sun only just rises at meridian passage at the date and latitude shown. The remainder of the graph gives the total duration of civil twilight.

Examples. (a) Estimate the time of the beginning of morning civil twilight at latitude N 78° on 2016 March 10. The duration of twilight (page 322) is about $1^{h}40^{m}$. Applying this to the time of sunrise, $07^{h}10^{m}$, found in the preceding example, the beginning of morning civil twilight is $05^{h}30^{m}$ LMT. (b) Estimate, for the first half of 2016, the limiting dates of civil twilight and sunlight at latitude N 80°. The graphs (page 322) indicate there is no sunlight or twilight till about February 6, there is twilight but no sunlight from February 6 until February 22, sunlight and twilight till March 31, continuous twilight or sunlight till April 14, and then continuous sunlight. (c) Estimate the time of the beginning and end of civil twilight on 2016 February 14 at latitude N 80°. The graph (page 322) indicates there is no direct sunlight at this date and latitude, but three hours of twilight before and after meridian passage. Thus civil twilight begins at about 09^{h} and ends at about 15^{h} LMT.

4. *Semiduration of moonlight* The graphs, for each month, for the semiduration of moonlight give for the Moon the same data as the graphs for the semiduration of sunlight give for the Sun. The scale near the top gives the LMT of meridian passage. In addition, the phase symbols are placed on the graphs to show the day on which each phase occurs. Since the times of meridian passage and the semiduration change more rapidly from day to day for the Moon than for the Sun, special care will be required in reading the graphs accurately.

For most purposes in these high latitudes a rough idea of the time of moonrise or moonset is all that is required and this may be obtained by a glance at the graph.

Example. Estimate the moon phase and the time of moonrise and moonset on 2016 March 8 at latitude N 78°. The phase is found from pages 323-325 to be near new moon, and the Moon crosses the meridian at 12^h LMT. The semiduration of moonlight taken for the time of meridian passage is 4 hours, giving moonrise at 08^h LMT on March 8 and moonset at 16^h on March 8.

If greater accuracy is required it is necessary to read the graph for the UT of each phenomenon at the desired meridian. The dates indicated on the graph are for 00^h UT, and intermediate values of the UT may be located by estimation.

Example. Required to improve the results obtained in the preceding example, assuming the observer to be in longitude W 90° (6^h) west.

The values found previously were:

			d	h				d	h	
Time of meridian passage	2016	Mar.	8	12	LMT	=	Mar.	8	18	UT
Semiduration of moonlight				4						
Time of moonrise		Mar.	8	08	LMT	=	Mar.	8	14	UT
Time of moonset		Mar.	8	16	LMT	=	Mar.	8	22	UT

Returning to the graphs (pages 323-325) with these three values of the UT, the following results are obtained:

			d	h	m				d	h	m	
Time of meridian passage	2016	Mar.	8	12	10	LMT	=	Mar.	8	18	10	UT
Semiduration for moonrise				04	10							
Time of moonrise		Mar.	8	08	00	LMT	=	Mar.	8	14	00	UT
Semiduration for moonset				04	40							
Time of moonset		Mar.	8	16	50	LMT	=	Mar.	8	22	50	UT

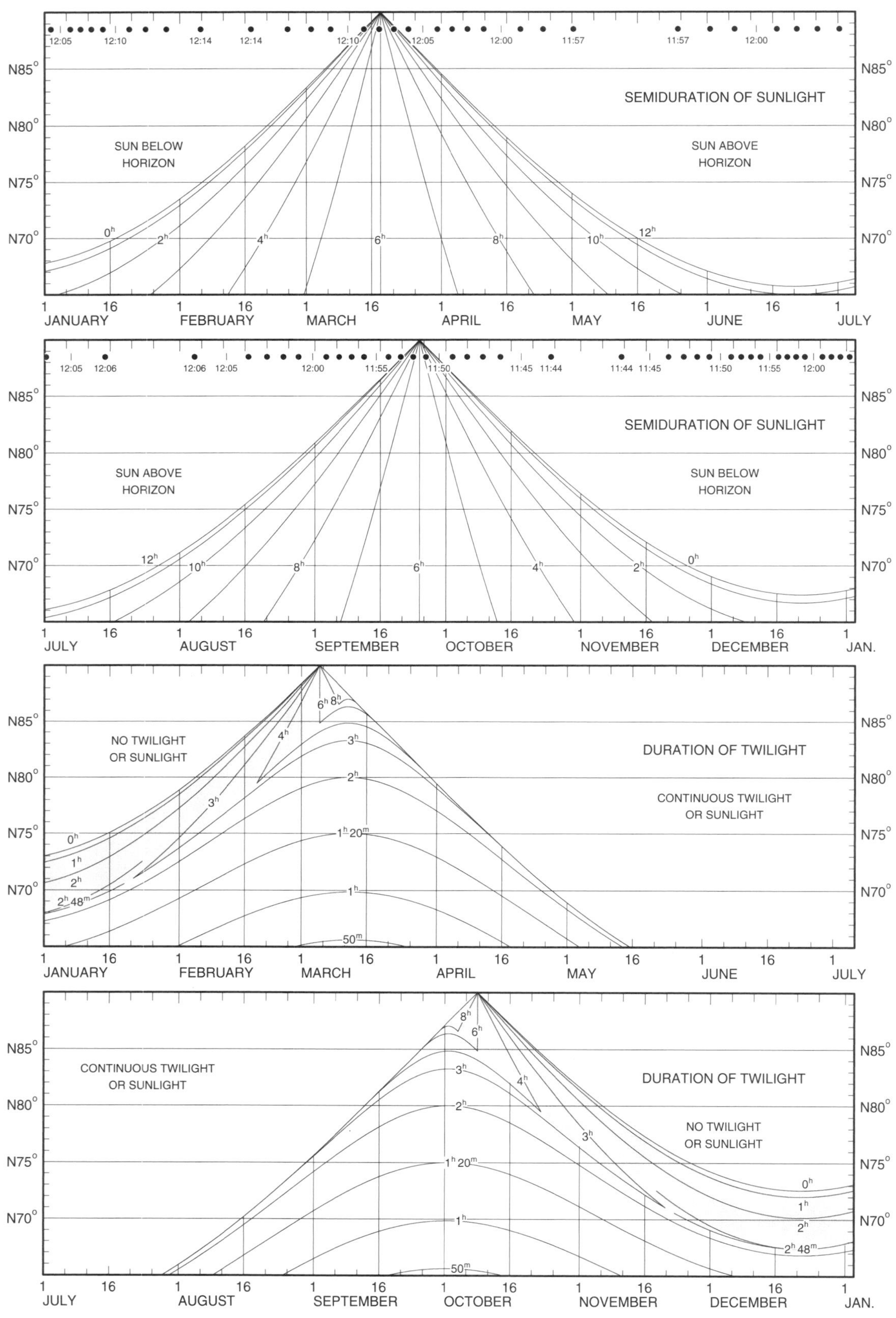
12:05
12:10
12:14
12:14
12:10
12:05
12:00
11:57
11:57
12:00
N85°
N80°
N75°
N70°
SEMIDURATION OF SUNLIGHT
SUN BELOW HORIZON
SUN ABOVE HORIZON
0h
2h
4h
6h
8h
10h
12h
JANUARY
FEBRUARY
MARCH
APRIL
MAY
JUNE
JULY
12:05
12:06
12:06
12:05
12:00
11:55
11:50
11:45
11:44
11:44
11:45
11:50
11:55
12:00
SEMIDURATION OF SUNLIGHT
SUN ABOVE HORIZON
SUN BELOW HORIZON
12h
10h
8h
6h
4h
2h
0h
JULY
AUGUST
SEPTEMBER
OCTOBER
NOVEMBER
DECEMBER
JAN.
NO TWILIGHT OR SUNLIGHT
DURATION OF TWILIGHT
CONTINUOUS TWILIGHT OR SUNLIGHT
6h
8h
4h
3h
2h
1h 20m
1h
50m
0h
2h 48m
JANUARY
FEBRUARY
MARCH
APRIL
MAY
JUNE
JULY
CONTINUOUS TWILIGHT OR SUNLIGHT
DURATION OF TWILIGHT
NO TWILIGHT OR SUNLIGHT
JULY
AUGUST
SEPTEMBER
OCTOBER
NOVEMBER
DECEMBER
JAN.

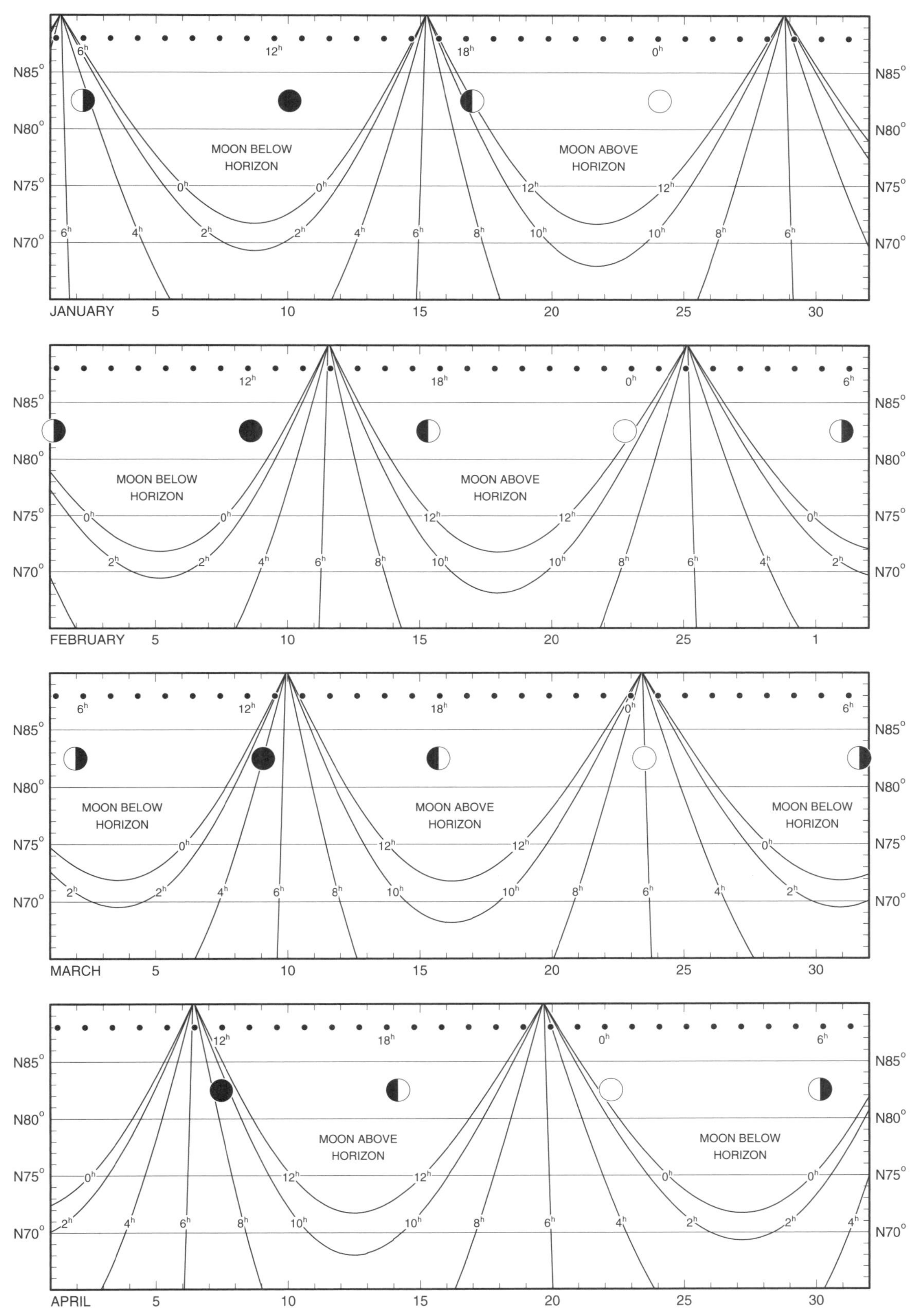
JANUARY
MOON BELOW HORIZON
MOON ABOVE HORIZON
FEBRUARY
MOON BELOW HORIZON
MOON ABOVE HORIZON
MARCH
MOON BELOW HORIZON
MOON ABOVE HORIZON
MOON BELOW HORIZON
APRIL
MOON ABOVE HORIZON
MOON BELOW HORIZON
N85°
N80°
N75°
N70°

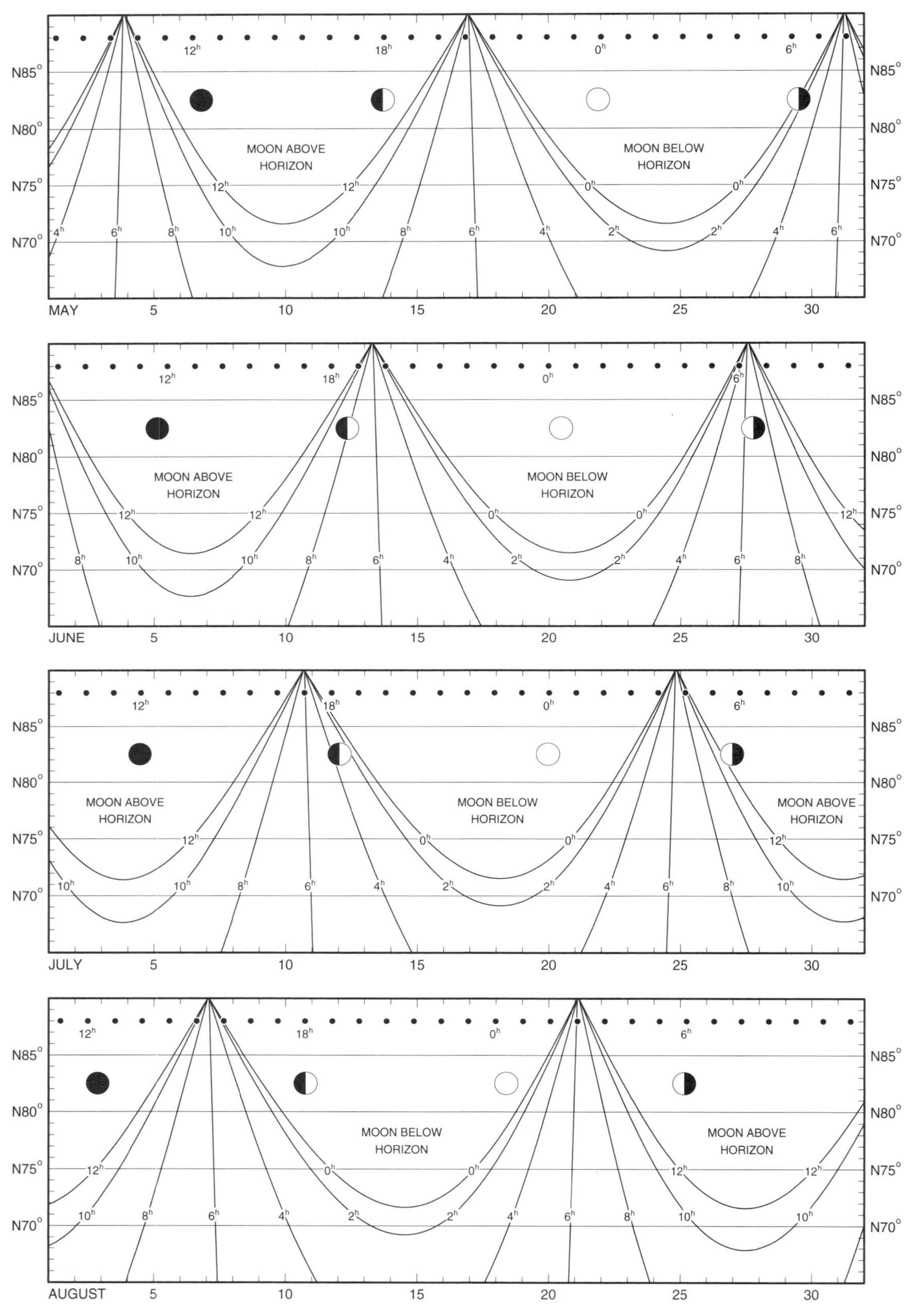
MAY
JUNE
JULY
AUGUST
MOON ABOVE HORIZON
MOON BELOW HORIZON
N85°
N80°
N75°
N70°
5
10
15
20
25
30

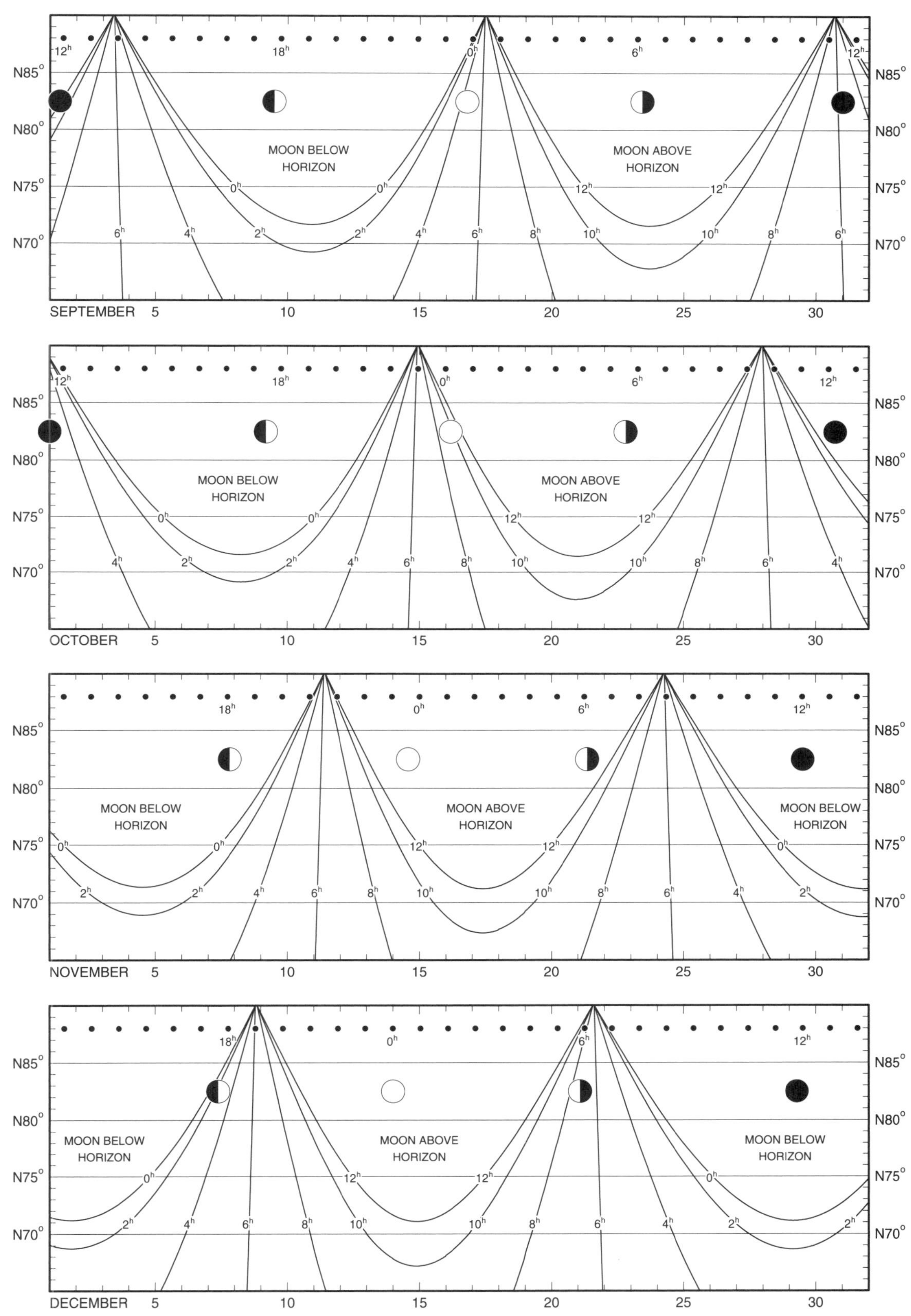

MOON BELOW HORIZON
MOON ABOVE HORIZON
N85°
N80°
N75°
N70°
SEPTEMBER 5 10 15 20 25 30
OCTOBER 5 10 15 20 25 30
NOVEMBER 5 10 15 20 25 30
DECEMBER 5 10 15 20 25 30

CONVERSION OF ARC TO TIME

0°–59°		60°–119°		120°–179°		180°–239°		240°–299°		300°–359°			0′.00	0′.25	0′.50	0′.75
°	h m	°	h m	°	h m	°	h m	°	h m	°	h m	′	m s	m s	m s	m s
0	0 00	**60**	4 00	**120**	8 00	**180**	12 00	**240**	16 00	**300**	20 00	**0**	0 00	0 01	0 02	0 03
1	0 04	**61**	4 04	**121**	8 04	**181**	12 04	**241**	16 04	**301**	20 04	**1**	0 04	0 05	0 06	0 07
2	0 08	**62**	4 08	**122**	8 08	**182**	12 08	**242**	16 08	**302**	20 08	**2**	0 08	0 09	0 10	0 11
3	0 12	**63**	4 12	**123**	8 12	**183**	12 12	**243**	16 12	**303**	20 12	**3**	0 12	0 13	0 14	0 15
4	0 16	**64**	4 16	**124**	8 16	**184**	12 16	**244**	16 16	**304**	20 16	**4**	0 16	0 17	0 18	0 19
5	0 20	**65**	4 20	**125**	8 20	**185**	12 20	**245**	16 20	**305**	20 20	**5**	0 20	0 21	0 22	0 23
6	0 24	**66**	4 24	**126**	8 24	**186**	12 24	**246**	16 24	**306**	20 24	**6**	0 24	0 25	0 26	0 27
7	0 28	**67**	4 28	**127**	8 28	**187**	12 28	**247**	16 28	**307**	20 28	**7**	0 28	0 29	0 30	0 31
8	0 32	**68**	4 32	**128**	8 32	**188**	12 32	**248**	16 32	**308**	20 32	**8**	0 32	0 33	0 34	0 35
9	0 36	**69**	4 36	**129**	8 36	**189**	12 36	**249**	16 36	**309**	20 36	**9**	0 36	0 37	0 38	0 39
10	0 40	**70**	4 40	**130**	8 40	**190**	12 40	**250**	16 40	**310**	20 40	**10**	0 40	0 41	0 42	0 43
11	0 44	**71**	4 44	**131**	8 44	**191**	12 44	**251**	16 44	**311**	20 44	**11**	0 44	0 45	0 46	0 47
12	0 48	**72**	4 48	**132**	8 48	**192**	12 48	**252**	16 48	**312**	20 48	**12**	0 48	0 49	0 50	0 51
13	0 52	**73**	4 52	**133**	8 52	**193**	12 52	**253**	16 52	**313**	20 52	**13**	0 52	0 53	0 54	0 55
14	0 56	**74**	4 56	**134**	8 56	**194**	12 56	**254**	16 56	**314**	20 56	**14**	0 56	0 57	0 58	0 59
15	1 00	**75**	5 00	**135**	9 00	**195**	13 00	**255**	17 00	**315**	21 00	**15**	1 00	1 01	1 02	1 03
16	1 04	**76**	5 04	**136**	9 04	**196**	13 04	**256**	17 04	**316**	21 04	**16**	1 04	1 05	1 06	1 07
17	1 08	**77**	5 08	**137**	9 08	**197**	13 08	**257**	17 08	**317**	21 08	**17**	1 08	1 09	1 10	1 11
18	1 12	**78**	5 12	**138**	9 12	**198**	13 12	**258**	17 12	**318**	21 12	**18**	1 12	1 13	1 14	1 15
19	1 16	**79**	5 16	**139**	9 16	**199**	13 16	**259**	17 16	**319**	21 16	**19**	1 16	1 17	1 18	1 19
20	1 20	**80**	5 20	**140**	9 20	**200**	13 20	**260**	17 20	**320**	21 20	**20**	1 20	1 21	1 22	1 23
21	1 24	**81**	5 24	**141**	9 24	**201**	13 24	**261**	17 24	**321**	21 24	**21**	1 24	1 25	1 26	1 27
22	1 28	**82**	5 28	**142**	9 28	**202**	13 28	**262**	17 28	**322**	21 28	**22**	1 28	1 29	1 30	1 31
23	1 32	**83**	5 32	**143**	9 32	**203**	13 32	**263**	17 32	**323**	21 32	**23**	1 32	1 33	1 34	1 35
24	1 36	**84**	5 36	**144**	9 36	**204**	13 36	**264**	17 36	**324**	21 36	**24**	1 36	1 37	1 38	1 39
25	1 40	**85**	5 40	**145**	9 40	**205**	13 40	**265**	17 40	**325**	21 40	**25**	1 40	1 41	1 42	1 43
26	1 44	**86**	5 44	**146**	9 44	**206**	13 44	**266**	17 44	**326**	21 44	**26**	1 44	1 45	1 46	1 47
27	1 48	**87**	5 48	**147**	9 48	**207**	13 48	**267**	17 48	**327**	21 48	**27**	1 48	1 49	1 50	1 51
28	1 52	**88**	5 52	**148**	9 52	**208**	13 52	**268**	17 52	**328**	21 52	**28**	1 52	1 53	1 54	1 55
29	1 56	**89**	5 56	**149**	9 56	**209**	13 56	**269**	17 56	**329**	21 56	**29**	1 56	1 57	1 58	1 59
30	2 00	**90**	6 00	**150**	10 00	**210**	14 00	**270**	18 00	**330**	22 00	**30**	2 00	2 01	2 02	2 03
31	2 04	**91**	6 04	**151**	10 04	**211**	14 04	**271**	18 04	**331**	22 04	**31**	2 04	2 05	2 06	2 07
32	2 08	**92**	6 08	**152**	10 08	**212**	14 08	**272**	18 08	**332**	22 08	**32**	2 08	2 09	2 10	2 11
33	2 12	**93**	6 12	**153**	10 12	**213**	14 12	**273**	18 12	**333**	22 12	**33**	2 12	2 13	2 14	2 15
34	2 16	**94**	6 16	**154**	10 16	**214**	14 16	**274**	18 16	**334**	22 16	**34**	2 16	2 17	2 18	2 19
35	2 20	**95**	6 20	**155**	10 20	**215**	14 20	**275**	18 20	**335**	22 20	**35**	2 20	2 21	2 22	2 23
36	2 24	**96**	6 24	**156**	10 24	**216**	14 24	**276**	18 24	**336**	22 24	**36**	2 24	2 25	2 26	2 27
37	2 28	**97**	6 28	**157**	10 28	**217**	14 28	**277**	18 28	**337**	22 28	**37**	2 28	2 29	2 30	2 31
38	2 32	**98**	6 32	**158**	10 32	**218**	14 32	**278**	18 32	**338**	22 32	**38**	2 32	2 33	2 34	2 35
39	2 36	**99**	6 36	**159**	10 36	**219**	14 36	**279**	18 36	**339**	22 36	**39**	2 36	2 37	2 38	2 39
40	2 40	**100**	6 40	**160**	10 40	**220**	14 40	**280**	18 40	**340**	22 40	**40**	2 40	2 41	2 42	2 43
41	2 44	**101**	6 44	**161**	10 44	**221**	14 44	**281**	18 44	**341**	22 44	**41**	2 44	2 45	2 46	2 47
42	2 48	**102**	6 48	**162**	10 48	**222**	14 48	**282**	18 48	**342**	22 48	**42**	2 48	2 49	2 50	2 51
43	2 52	**103**	6 52	**163**	10 52	**223**	14 52	**283**	18 52	**343**	22 52	**43**	2 52	2 53	2 54	2 55
44	2 56	**104**	6 56	**164**	10 56	**224**	14 56	**284**	18 56	**344**	22 56	**44**	2 56	2 57	2 58	2 59
45	3 00	**105**	7 00	**165**	11 00	**225**	15 00	**285**	19 00	**345**	23 00	**45**	3 00	3 01	3 02	3 03
46	3 04	**106**	7 04	**166**	11 04	**226**	15 04	**286**	19 04	**346**	23 04	**46**	3 04	3 05	3 06	3 07
47	3 08	**107**	7 08	**167**	11 08	**227**	15 08	**287**	19 08	**347**	23 08	**47**	3 08	3 09	3 10	3 11
48	3 12	**108**	7 12	**168**	11 12	**228**	15 12	**288**	19 12	**348**	23 12	**48**	3 12	3 13	3 14	3 15
49	3 16	**109**	7 16	**169**	11 16	**229**	15 16	**289**	19 16	**349**	23 16	**49**	3 16	3 17	3 18	3 19
50	3 20	**110**	7 20	**170**	11 20	**230**	15 20	**290**	19 20	**350**	23 20	**50**	3 20	3 21	3 22	3 23
51	3 24	**111**	7 24	**171**	11 24	**231**	15 24	**291**	19 24	**351**	23 24	**51**	3 24	3 25	3 26	3 27
52	3 28	**112**	7 28	**172**	11 28	**232**	15 28	**292**	19 28	**352**	23 28	**52**	3 28	3 29	3 30	3 31
53	3 32	**113**	7 32	**173**	11 32	**233**	15 32	**293**	19 32	**353**	23 32	**53**	3 32	3 33	3 34	3 35
54	3 36	**114**	7 36	**174**	11 36	**234**	15 36	**294**	19 36	**354**	23 36	**54**	3 36	3 37	3 38	3 39
55	3 40	**115**	7 40	**175**	11 40	**235**	15 40	**295**	19 40	**355**	23 40	**55**	3 40	3 41	3 42	3 43
56	3 44	**116**	7 44	**176**	11 44	**236**	15 44	**296**	19 44	**356**	23 44	**56**	3 44	3 45	3 46	3 47
57	3 48	**117**	7 48	**177**	11 48	**237**	15 48	**297**	19 48	**357**	23 48	**57**	3 48	3 49	3 50	3 51
58	3 52	**118**	7 52	**178**	11 52	**238**	15 52	**298**	19 52	**358**	23 52	**58**	3 52	3 53	3 54	3 55
59	3 56	**119**	7 56	**179**	11 56	**239**	15 56	**299**	19 56	**359**	23 56	**59**	3 56	3 57	3 58	3 59

The above table is for converting expressions in arc to their equivalent in time; its main use in this Almanac is for the conversion of longitude for application to LMT (*added* if *west*, *subtracted* if *east*) to give UT or vice versa, particularly in the case of sunrise, sunset, etc.

m 0 s	SUN PLANETS ° ′	ARIES ° ′	MOON ° ′	v or d ′	Corr^{n} ′	v or d ′	Corr^{n} ′	v or d ′	Corr^{n} ′
00	0 00·0	0 00·0	0 00·0	0·0	0·0	6·0	0·1	12·0	0·1
01	0 00·3	0 00·3	0 00·2	0·1	0·0	6·1	0·1	12·1	0·1
02	0 00·5	0 00·5	0 00·5	0·2	0·0	6·2	0·1	12·2	0·1
03	0 00·8	0 00·8	0 00·7	0·3	0·0	6·3	0·1	12·3	0·1
04	0 01·0	0 01·0	0 01·0	0·4	0·0	6·4	0·1	12·4	0·1
05	0 01·3	0 01·3	0 01·2	0·5	0·0	6·5	0·1	12·5	0·1
06	0 01·5	0 01·5	0 01·4	0·6	0·0	6·6	0·1	12·6	0·1
07	0 01·8	0 01·8	0 01·7	0·7	0·0	6·7	0·1	12·7	0·1
08	0 02·0	0 02·0	0 01·9	0·8	0·0	6·8	0·1	12·8	0·1
09	0 02·3	0 02·3	0 02·1	0·9	0·0	6·9	0·1	12·9	0·1
10	0 02·5	0 02·5	0 02·4	1·0	0·0	7·0	0·1	13·0	0·1
11	0 02·8	0 02·8	0 02·6	1·1	0·0	7·1	0·1	13·1	0·1
12	0 03·0	0 03·0	0 02·9	1·2	0·0	7·2	0·1	13·2	0·1
13	0 03·3	0 03·3	0 03·1	1·3	0·0	7·3	0·1	13·3	0·1
14	0 03·5	0 03·5	0 03·3	1·4	0·0	7·4	0·1	13·4	0·1
15	0 03·8	0 03·8	0 03·6	1·5	0·0	7·5	0·1	13·5	0·1
16	0 04·0	0 04·0	0 03·8	1·6	0·0	7·6	0·1	13·6	0·1
17	0 04·3	0 04·3	0 04·1	1·7	0·0	7·7	0·1	13·7	0·1
18	0 04·5	0 04·5	0 04·3	1·8	0·0	7·8	0·1	13·8	0·1
19	0 04·8	0 04·8	0 04·5	1·9	0·0	7·9	0·1	13·9	0·1
20	0 05·0	0 05·0	0 04·8	2·0	0·0	8·0	0·1	14·0	0·1
21	0 05·3	0 05·3	0 05·0	2·1	0·0	8·1	0·1	14·1	0·1
22	0 05·5	0 05·5	0 05·2	2·2	0·0	8·2	0·1	14·2	0·1
23	0 05·8	0 05·8	0 05·5	2·3	0·0	8·3	0·1	14·3	0·1
24	0 06·0	0 06·0	0 05·7	2·4	0·0	8·4	0·1	14·4	0·1
25	0 06·3	0 06·3	0 06·0	2·5	0·0	8·5	0·1	14·5	0·1
26	0 06·5	0 06·5	0 06·2	2·6	0·0	8·6	0·1	14·6	0·1
27	0 06·8	0 06·8	0 06·4	2·7	0·0	8·7	0·1	14·7	0·1
28	0 07·0	0 07·0	0 06·7	2·8	0·0	8·8	0·1	14·8	0·1
29	0 07·3	0 07·3	0 06·9	2·9	0·0	8·9	0·1	14·9	0·1
30	0 07·5	0 07·5	0 07·2	3·0	0·0	9·0	0·1	15·0	0·1
31	0 07·8	0 07·8	0 07·4	3·1	0·0	9·1	0·1	15·1	0·1
32	0 08·0	0 08·0	0 07·6	3·2	0·0	9·2	0·1	15·2	0·1
33	0 08·3	0 08·3	0 07·9	3·3	0·0	9·3	0·1	15·3	0·1
34	0 08·5	0 08·5	0 08·1	3·4	0·0	9·4	0·1	15·4	0·1
35	0 08·8	0 08·8	0 08·4	3·5	0·0	9·5	0·1	15·5	0·1
36	0 09·0	0 09·0	0 08·6	3·6	0·0	9·6	0·1	15·6	0·1
37	0 09·3	0 09·3	0 08·8	3·7	0·0	9·7	0·1	15·7	0·1
38	0 09·5	0 09·5	0 09·1	3·8	0·0	9·8	0·1	15·8	0·1
39	0 09·8	0 09·8	0 09·3	3·9	0·0	9·9	0·1	15·9	0·1
40	0 10·0	0 10·0	0 09·5	4·0	0·0	10·0	0·1	16·0	0·1
41	0 10·3	0 10·3	0 09·8	4·1	0·0	10·1	0·1	16·1	0·1
42	0 10·5	0 10·5	0 10·0	4·2	0·0	10·2	0·1	16·2	0·1
43	0 10·8	0 10·8	0 10·3	4·3	0·0	10·3	0·1	16·3	0·1
44	0 11·0	0 11·0	0 10·5	4·4	0·0	10·4	0·1	16·4	0·1
45	0 11·3	0 11·3	0 10·7	4·5	0·0	10·5	0·1	16·5	0·1
46	0 11·5	0 11·5	0 11·0	4·6	0·0	10·6	0·1	16·6	0·1
47	0 11·8	0 11·8	0 11·2	4·7	0·0	10·7	0·1	16·7	0·1
48	0 12·0	0 12·0	0 11·5	4·8	0·0	10·8	0·1	16·8	0·1
49	0 12·3	0 12·3	0 11·7	4·9	0·0	10·9	0·1	16·9	0·1
50	0 12·5	0 12·5	0 11·9	5·0	0·0	11·0	0·1	17·0	0·1
51	0 12·8	0 12·8	0 12·2	5·1	0·0	11·1	0·1	17·1	0·1
52	0 13·0	0 13·0	0 12·4	5·2	0·0	11·2	0·1	17·2	0·1
53	0 13·3	0 13·3	0 12·6	5·3	0·0	11·3	0·1	17·3	0·1
54	0 13·5	0 13·5	0 12·9	5·4	0·0	11·4	0·1	17·4	0·1
55	0 13·8	0 13·8	0 13·1	5·5	0·0	11·5	0·1	17·5	0·1
56	0 14·0	0 14·0	0 13·4	5·6	0·0	11·6	0·1	17·6	0·1
57	0 14·3	0 14·3	0 13·6	5·7	0·0	11·7	0·1	17·7	0·1
58	0 14·5	0 14·5	0 13·8	5·8	0·0	11·8	0·1	17·8	0·1
59	0 14·8	0 14·8	0 14·1	5·9	0·0	11·9	0·1	17·9	0·1
60	0 15·0	0 15·0	0 14·3	6·0	0·1	12·0	0·1	18·0	0·2

m 1 s	SUN PLANETS ° ′	ARIES ° ′	MOON ° ′	v or d ′	Corr^{n} ′	v or d ′	Corr^{n} ′	v or d ′	Corr^{n} ′
00	0 15·0	0 15·0	0 14·3	0·0	0·0	6·0	0·2	12·0	0·3
01	0 15·3	0 15·3	0 14·6	0·1	0·0	6·1	0·2	12·1	0·3
02	0 15·5	0 15·5	0 14·8	0·2	0·0	6·2	0·2	12·2	0·3
03	0 15·8	0 15·8	0 15·0	0·3	0·0	6·3	0·2	12·3	0·3
04	0 16·0	0 16·0	0 15·3	0·4	0·0	6·4	0·2	12·4	0·3
05	0 16·3	0 16·3	0 15·5	0·5	0·0	6·5	0·2	12·5	0·3
06	0 16·5	0 16·5	0 15·7	0·6	0·0	6·6	0·2	12·6	0·3
07	0 16·8	0 16·8	0 16·0	0·7	0·0	6·7	0·2	12·7	0·3
08	0 17·0	0 17·0	0 16·2	0·8	0·0	6·8	0·2	12·8	0·3
09	0 17·3	0 17·3	0 16·5	0·9	0·0	6·9	0·2	12·9	0·3
10	0 17·5	0 17·5	0 16·7	1·0	0·0	7·0	0·2	13·0	0·3
11	0 17·8	0 17·8	0 16·9	1·1	0·0	7·1	0·2	13·1	0·3
12	0 18·0	0 18·0	0 17·2	1·2	0·0	7·2	0·2	13·2	0·3
13	0 18·3	0 18·3	0 17·4	1·3	0·0	7·3	0·2	13·3	0·3
14	0 18·5	0 18·6	0 17·7	1·4	0·0	7·4	0·2	13·4	0·3
15	0 18·8	0 18·8	0 17·9	1·5	0·0	7·5	0·2	13·5	0·3
16	0 19·0	0 19·1	0 18·1	1·6	0·0	7·6	0·2	13·6	0·3
17	0 19·3	0 19·3	0 18·4	1·7	0·0	7·7	0·2	13·7	0·3
18	0 19·5	0 19·6	0 18·6	1·8	0·0	7·8	0·2	13·8	0·3
19	0 19·8	0 19·8	0 18·9	1·9	0·0	7·9	0·2	13·9	0·3
20	0 20·0	0 20·1	0 19·1	2·0	0·1	8·0	0·2	14·0	0·4
21	0 20·3	0 20·3	0 19·3	2·1	0·1	8·1	0·2	14·1	0·4
22	0 20·5	0 20·6	0 19·6	2·2	0·1	8·2	0·2	14·2	0·4
23	0 20·8	0 20·8	0 19·8	2·3	0·1	8·3	0·2	14·3	0·4
24	0 21·0	0 21·1	0 20·0	2·4	0·1	8·4	0·2	14·4	0·4
25	0 21·3	0 21·3	0 20·3	2·5	0·1	8·5	0·2	14·5	0·4
26	0 21·5	0 21·6	0 20·5	2·6	0·1	8·6	0·2	14·6	0·4
27	0 21·8	0 21·8	0 20·8	2·7	0·1	8·7	0·2	14·7	0·4
28	0 22·0	0 22·1	0 21·0	2·8	0·1	8·8	0·2	14·8	0·4
29	0 22·3	0 22·3	0 21·2	2·9	0·1	8·9	0·2	14·9	0·4
30	0 22·5	0 22·6	0 21·5	3·0	0·1	9·0	0·2	15·0	0·4
31	0 22·8	0 22·8	0 21·7	3·1	0·1	9·1	0·2	15·1	0·4
32	0 23·0	0 23·1	0 22·0	3·2	0·1	9·2	0·2	15·2	0·4
33	0 23·3	0 23·3	0 22·2	3·3	0·1	9·3	0·2	15·3	0·4
34	0 23·5	0 23·6	0 22·4	3·4	0·1	9·4	0·2	15·4	0·4
35	0 23·8	0 23·8	0 22·7	3·5	0·1	9·5	0·2	15·5	0·4
36	0 24·0	0 24·1	0 22·9	3·6	0·1	9·6	0·2	15·6	0·4
37	0 24·3	0 24·3	0 23·1	3·7	0·1	9·7	0·2	15·7	0·4
38	0 24·5	0 24·6	0 23·4	3·8	0·1	9·8	0·2	15·8	0·4
39	0 24·8	0 24·8	0 23·6	3·9	0·1	9·9	0·2	15·9	0·4
40	0 25·0	0 25·1	0 23·9	4·0	0·1	10·0	0·3	16·0	0·4
41	0 25·3	0 25·3	0 24·1	4·1	0·1	10·1	0·3	16·1	0·4
42	0 25·5	0 25·6	0 24·3	4·2	0·1	10·2	0·3	16·2	0·4
43	0 25·8	0 25·8	0 24·6	4·3	0·1	10·3	0·3	16·3	0·4
44	0 26·0	0 26·1	0 24·8	4·4	0·1	10·4	0·3	16·4	0·4
45	0 26·3	0 26·3	0 25·1	4·5	0·1	10·5	0·3	16·5	0·4
46	0 26·5	0 26·6	0 25·3	4·6	0·1	10·6	0·3	16·6	0·4
47	0 26·8	0 26·8	0 25·5	4·7	0·1	10·7	0·3	16·7	0·4
48	0 27·0	0 27·1	0 25·8	4·8	0·1	10·8	0·3	16·8	0·4
49	0 27·3	0 27·3	0 26·0	4·9	0·1	10·9	0·3	16·9	0·4
50	0 27·5	0 27·6	0 26·2	5·0	0·1	11·0	0·3	17·0	0·4
51	0 27·8	0 27·8	0 26·5	5·1	0·1	11·1	0·3	17·1	0·4
52	0 28·0	0 28·1	0 26·7	5·2	0·1	11·2	0·3	17·2	0·4
53	0 28·3	0 28·3	0 27·0	5·3	0·1	11·3	0·3	17·3	0·4
54	0 28·5	0 28·6	0 27·2	5·4	0·1	11·4	0·3	17·4	0·4
55	0 28·8	0 28·8	0 27·4	5·5	0·1	11·5	0·3	17·5	0·4
56	0 29·0	0 29·1	0 27·7	5·6	0·1	11·6	0·3	17·6	0·4
57	0 29·3	0 29·3	0 27·9	5·7	0·1	11·7	0·3	17·7	0·4
58	0 29·5	0 29·6	0 28·2	5·8	0·1	11·8	0·3	17·8	0·4
59	0 29·8	0 29·8	0 28·4	5·9	0·1	11·9	0·3	17·9	0·4
60	0 30·0	0 30·1	0 28·6	6·0	0·2	12·0	0·3	18·0	0·5

2m	SUN PLANETS	ARIES	MOON	v or d	Corr^{n}	v or d	Corr^{n}	v or d	Corr^{n}
s	° ′	° ′	° ′	′	′	′	′	′	′
00	0 30·0	0 30·1	0 28·6	0·0	0·0	6·0	0·3	12·0	0·5
01	0 30·3	0 30·3	0 28·9	0·1	0·0	6·1	0·3	12·1	0·5
02	0 30·5	0 30·6	0 29·1	0·2	0·0	6·2	0·3	12·2	0·5
03	0 30·8	0 30·8	0 29·3	0·3	0·0	6·3	0·3	12·3	0·5
04	0 31·0	0 31·1	0 29·6	0·4	0·0	6·4	0·3	12·4	0·5
05	0 31·3	0 31·3	0 29·8	0·5	0·0	6·5	0·3	12·5	0·5
06	0 31·5	0 31·6	0 30·1	0·6	0·0	6·6	0·3	12·6	0·5
07	0 31·8	0 31·8	0 30·3	0·7	0·0	6·7	0·3	12·7	0·5
08	0 32·0	0 32·1	0 30·5	0·8	0·0	6·8	0·3	12·8	0·5
09	0 32·3	0 32·3	0 30·8	0·9	0·0	6·9	0·3	12·9	0·5
10	0 32·5	0 32·6	0 31·0	1·0	0·0	7·0	0·3	13·0	0·5
11	0 32·8	0 32·8	0 31·3	1·1	0·0	7·1	0·3	13·1	0·5
12	0 33·0	0 33·1	0 31·5	1·2	0·1	7·2	0·3	13·2	0·6
13	0 33·3	0 33·3	0 31·7	1·3	0·1	7·3	0·3	13·3	0·6
14	0 33·5	0 33·6	0 32·0	1·4	0·1	7·4	0·3	13·4	0·6
15	0 33·8	0 33·8	0 32·2	1·5	0·1	7·5	0·3	13·5	0·6
16	0 34·0	0 34·1	0 32·5	1·6	0·1	7·6	0·3	13·6	0·6
17	0 34·3	0 34·3	0 32·7	1·7	0·1	7·7	0·3	13·7	0·6
18	0 34·5	0 34·6	0 32·9	1·8	0·1	7·8	0·3	13·8	0·6
19	0 34·8	0 34·8	0 33·2	1·9	0·1	7·9	0·3	13·9	0·6
20	0 35·0	0 35·1	0 33·4	2·0	0·1	8·0	0·3	14·0	0·6
21	0 35·3	0 35·3	0 33·6	2·1	0·1	8·1	0·3	14·1	0·6
22	0 35·5	0 35·6	0 33·9	2·2	0·1	8·2	0·3	14·2	0·6
23	0 35·8	0 35·8	0 34·1	2·3	0·1	8·3	0·3	14·3	0·6
24	0 36·0	0 36·1	0 34·4	2·4	0·1	8·4	0·4	14·4	0·6
25	0 36·3	0 36·3	0 34·6	2·5	0·1	8·5	0·4	14·5	0·6
26	0 36·5	0 36·6	0 34·8	2·6	0·1	8·6	0·4	14·6	0·6
27	0 36·8	0 36·9	0 35·1	2·7	0·1	8·7	0·4	14·7	0·6
28	0 37·0	0 37·1	0 35·3	2·8	0·1	8·8	0·4	14·8	0·6
29	0 37·3	0 37·4	0 35·6	2·9	0·1	8·9	0·4	14·9	0·6
30	0 37·5	0 37·6	0 35·8	3·0	0·1	9·0	0·4	15·0	0·6
31	0 37·8	0 37·9	0 36·0	3·1	0·1	9·1	0·4	15·1	0·6
32	0 38·0	0 38·1	0 36·3	3·2	0·1	9·2	0·4	15·2	0·6
33	0 38·3	0 38·4	0 36·5	3·3	0·1	9·3	0·4	15·3	0·6
34	0 38·5	0 38·6	0 36·7	3·4	0·1	9·4	0·4	15·4	0·6
35	0 38·8	0 38·9	0 37·0	3·5	0·1	9·5	0·4	15·5	0·6
36	0 39·0	0 39·1	0 37·2	3·6	0·2	9·6	0·4	15·6	0·7
37	0 39·3	0 39·4	0 37·5	3·7	0·2	9·7	0·4	15·7	0·7
38	0 39·5	0 39·6	0 37·7	3·8	0·2	9·8	0·4	15·8	0·7
39	0 39·8	0 39·9	0 37·9	3·9	0·2	9·9	0·4	15·9	0·7
40	0 40·0	0 40·1	0 38·2	4·0	0·2	10·0	0·4	16·0	0·7
41	0 40·3	0 40·4	0 38·4	4·1	0·2	10·1	0·4	16·1	0·7
42	0 40·5	0 40·6	0 38·7	4·2	0·2	10·2	0·4	16·2	0·7
43	0 40·8	0 40·9	0 38·9	4·3	0·2	10·3	0·4	16·3	0·7
44	0 41·0	0 41·1	0 39·1	4·4	0·2	10·4	0·4	16·4	0·7
45	0 41·3	0 41·4	0 39·4	4·5	0·2	10·5	0·4	16·5	0·7
46	0 41·5	0 41·6	0 39·6	4·6	0·2	10·6	0·4	16·6	0·7
47	0 41·8	0 41·9	0 39·8	4·7	0·2	10·7	0·4	16·7	0·7
48	0 42·0	0 42·1	0 40·1	4·8	0·2	10·8	0·5	16·8	0·7
49	0 42·3	0 42·4	0 40·3	4·9	0·2	10·9	0·5	16·9	0·7
50	0 42·5	0 42·6	0 40·6	5·0	0·2	11·0	0·5	17·0	0·7
51	0 42·8	0 42·9	0 40·8	5·1	0·2	11·1	0·5	17·1	0·7
52	0 43·0	0 43·1	0 41·0	5·2	0·2	11·2	0·5	17·2	0·7
53	0 43·3	0 43·4	0 41·3	5·3	0·2	11·3	0·5	17·3	0·7
54	0 43·5	0 43·6	0 41·5	5·4	0·2	11·4	0·5	17·4	0·7
55	0 43·8	0 43·9	0 41·8	5·5	0·2	11·5	0·5	17·5	0·7
56	0 44·0	0 44·1	0 42·0	5·6	0·2	11·6	0·5	17·6	0·7
57	0 44·3	0 44·4	0 42·2	5·7	0·2	11·7	0·5	17·7	0·7
58	0 44·5	0 44·6	0 42·5	5·8	0·2	11·8	0·5	17·8	0·7
59	0 44·8	0 44·9	0 42·7	5·9	0·2	11·9	0·5	17·9	0·7
60	0 45·0	0 45·1	0 43·0	6·0	0·3	12·0	0·5	18·0	0·8

3m	SUN PLANETS	ARIES	MOON	v or d	Corr^{n}	v or d	Corr^{n}	v or d	Corr^{n}
s	° ′	° ′	° ′	′	′	′	′	′	′
00	0 45·0	0 45·1	0 43·0	0·0	0·0	6·0	0·4	12·0	0·7
01	0 45·3	0 45·4	0 43·2	0·1	0·0	6·1	0·4	12·1	0·7
02	0 45·5	0 45·6	0 43·4	0·2	0·0	6·2	0·4	12·2	0·7
03	0 45·8	0 45·9	0 43·7	0·3	0·0	6·3	0·4	12·3	0·7
04	0 46·0	0 46·1	0 43·9	0·4	0·0	6·4	0·4	12·4	0·7
05	0 46·3	0 46·4	0 44·1	0·5	0·0	6·5	0·4	12·5	0·7
06	0 46·5	0 46·6	0 44·4	0·6	0·0	6·6	0·4	12·6	0·7
07	0 46·8	0 46·9	0 44·6	0·7	0·0	6·7	0·4	12·7	0·7
08	0 47·0	0 47·1	0 44·9	0·8	0·0	6·8	0·4	12·8	0·7
09	0 47·3	0 47·4	0 45·1	0·9	0·1	6·9	0·4	12·9	0·8
10	0 47·5	0 47·6	0 45·3	1·0	0·1	7·0	0·4	13·0	0·8
11	0 47·8	0 47·9	0 45·6	1·1	0·1	7·1	0·4	13·1	0·8
12	0 48·0	0 48·1	0 45·8	1·2	0·1	7·2	0·4	13·2	0·8
13	0 48·3	0 48·4	0 46·1	1·3	0·1	7·3	0·4	13·3	0·8
14	0 48·5	0 48·6	0 46·3	1·4	0·1	7·4	0·4	13·4	0·8
15	0 48·8	0 48·9	0 46·5	1·5	0·1	7·5	0·4	13·5	0·8
16	0 49·0	0 49·1	0 46·8	1·6	0·1	7·6	0·4	13·6	0·8
17	0 49·3	0 49·4	0 47·0	1·7	0·1	7·7	0·4	13·7	0·8
18	0 49·5	0 49·6	0 47·2	1·8	0·1	7·8	0·5	13·8	0·8
19	0 49·8	0 49·9	0 47·5	1·9	0·1	7·9	0·5	13·9	0·8
20	0 50·0	0 50·1	0 47·7	2·0	0·1	8·0	0·5	14·0	0·8
21	0 50·3	0 50·4	0 48·0	2·1	0·1	8·1	0·5	14·1	0·8
22	0 50·5	0 50·6	0 48·2	2·2	0·1	8·2	0·5	14·2	0·8
23	0 50·8	0 50·9	0 48·4	2·3	0·1	8·3	0·5	14·3	0·8
24	0 51·0	0 51·1	0 48·7	2·4	0·1	8·4	0·5	14·4	0·8
25	0 51·3	0 51·4	0 48·9	2·5	0·1	8·5	0·5	14·5	0·8
26	0 51·5	0 51·6	0 49·2	2·6	0·2	8·6	0·5	14·6	0·9
27	0 51·8	0 51·9	0 49·4	2·7	0·2	8·7	0·5	14·7	0·9
28	0 52·0	0 52·1	0 49·6	2·8	0·2	8·8	0·5	14·8	0·9
29	0 52·3	0 52·4	0 49·9	2·9	0·2	8·9	0·5	14·9	0·9
30	0 52·5	0 52·6	0 50·1	3·0	0·2	9·0	0·5	15·0	0·9
31	0 52·8	0 52·9	0 50·3	3·1	0·2	9·1	0·5	15·1	0·9
32	0 53·0	0 53·1	0 50·6	3·2	0·2	9·2	0·5	15·2	0·9
33	0 53·3	0 53·4	0 50·8	3·3	0·2	9·3	0·5	15·3	0·9
34	0 53·5	0 53·6	0 51·1	3·4	0·2	9·4	0·5	15·4	0·9
35	0 53·8	0 53·9	0 51·3	3·5	0·2	9·5	0·6	15·5	0·9
36	0 54·0	0 54·1	0 51·5	3·6	0·2	9·6	0·6	15·6	0·9
37	0 54·3	0 54·4	0 51·8	3·7	0·2	9·7	0·6	15·7	0·9
38	0 54·5	0 54·6	0 52·0	3·8	0·2	9·8	0·6	15·8	0·9
39	0 54·8	0 54·9	0 52·3	3·9	0·2	9·9	0·6	15·9	0·9
40	0 55·0	0 55·2	0 52·5	4·0	0·2	10·0	0·6	16·0	0·9
41	0 55·3	0 55·4	0 52·7	4·1	0·2	10·1	0·6	16·1	0·9
42	0 55·5	0 55·7	0 53·0	4·2	0·2	10·2	0·6	16·2	0·9
43	0 55·8	0 55·9	0 53·2	4·3	0·3	10·3	0·6	16·3	1·0
44	0 56·0	0 56·2	0 53·4	4·4	0·3	10·4	0·6	16·4	1·0
45	0 56·3	0 56·4	0 53·7	4·5	0·3	10·5	0·6	16·5	1·0
46	0 56·5	0 56·7	0 53·9	4·6	0·3	10·6	0·6	16·6	1·0
47	0 56·8	0 56·9	0 54·2	4·7	0·3	10·7	0·6	16·7	1·0
48	0 57·0	0 57·2	0 54·4	4·8	0·3	10·8	0·6	16·8	1·0
49	0 57·3	0 57·4	0 54·6	4·9	0·3	10·9	0·6	16·9	1·0
50	0 57·5	0 57·7	0 54·9	5·0	0·3	11·0	0·6	17·0	1·0
51	0 57·8	0 57·9	0 55·1	5·1	0·3	11·1	0·6	17·1	1·0
52	0 58·0	0 58·2	0 55·4	5·2	0·3	11·2	0·7	17·2	1·0
53	0 58·3	0 58·4	0 55·6	5·3	0·3	11·3	0·7	17·3	1·0
54	0 58·5	0 58·7	0 55·8	5·4	0·3	11·4	0·7	17·4	1·0
55	0 58·8	0 58·9	0 56·1	5·5	0·3	11·5	0·7	17·5	1·0
56	0 59·0	0 59·2	0 56·3	5·6	0·3	11·6	0·7	17·6	1·0
57	0 59·3	0 59·4	0 56·6	5·7	0·3	11·7	0·7	17·7	1·0
58	0 59·5	0 59·7	0 56·8	5·8	0·3	11·8	0·7	17·8	1·0
59	0 59·8	0 59·9	0 57·0	5·9	0·3	11·9	0·7	17·9	1·0
60	1 00·0	1 00·2	0 57·3	6·0	0·4	12·0	0·7	18·0	1·1

m 4 s	SUN PLANETS ° ′	ARIES ° ′	MOON ° ′	v or d ′	Corrn ′	v or d ′	Corrn ′	v or d ′	Corrn ′
00	1 00·0	1 00·2	0 57·3	0·0	0·0	6·0	0·5	12·0	0·9
01	1 00·3	1 00·4	0 57·5	0·1	0·0	6·1	0·5	12·1	0·9
02	1 00·5	1 00·7	0 57·7	0·2	0·0	6·2	0·5	12·2	0·9
03	1 00·8	1 00·9	0 58·0	0·3	0·0	6·3	0·5	12·3	0·9
04	1 01·0	1 01·2	0 58·2	0·4	0·0	6·4	0·5	12·4	0·9
05	1 01·3	1 01·4	0 58·5	0·5	0·0	6·5	0·5	12·5	0·9
06	1 01·5	1 01·7	0 58·7	0·6	0·0	6·6	0·5	12·6	0·9
07	1 01·8	1 01·9	0 58·9	0·7	0·1	6·7	0·5	12·7	1·0
08	1 02·0	1 02·2	0 59·2	0·8	0·1	6·8	0·5	12·8	1·0
09	1 02·3	1 02·4	0 59·4	0·9	0·1	6·9	0·5	12·9	1·0
10	1 02·5	1 02·7	0 59·7	1·0	0·1	7·0	0·5	13·0	1·0
11	1 02·8	1 02·9	0 59·9	1·1	0·1	7·1	0·5	13·1	1·0
12	1 03·0	1 03·2	1 00·1	1·2	0·1	7·2	0·5	13·2	1·0
13	1 03·3	1 03·4	1 00·4	1·3	0·1	7·3	0·5	13·3	1·0
14	1 03·5	1 03·7	1 00·6	1·4	0·1	7·4	0·6	13·4	1·0
15	1 03·8	1 03·9	1 00·8	1·5	0·1	7·5	0·6	13·5	1·0
16	1 04·0	1 04·2	1 01·1	1·6	0·1	7·6	0·6	13·6	1·0
17	1 04·3	1 04·4	1 01·3	1·7	0·1	7·7	0·6	13·7	1·0
18	1 04·5	1 04·7	1 01·6	1·8	0·1	7·8	0·6	13·8	1·0
19	1 04·8	1 04·9	1 01·8	1·9	0·1	7·9	0·6	13·9	1·0
20	1 05·0	1 05·2	1 02·0	2·0	0·2	8·0	0·6	14·0	1·1
21	1 05·3	1 05·4	1 02·3	2·1	0·2	8·1	0·6	14·1	1·1
22	1 05·5	1 05·7	1 02·5	2·2	0·2	8·2	0·6	14·2	1·1
23	1 05·8	1 05·9	1 02·8	2·3	0·2	8·3	0·6	14·3	1·1
24	1 06·0	1 06·2	1 03·0	2·4	0·2	8·4	0·6	14·4	1·1
25	1 06·3	1 06·4	1 03·2	2·5	0·2	8·5	0·6	14·5	1·1
26	1 06·5	1 06·7	1 03·5	2·6	0·2	8·6	0·6	14·6	1·1
27	1 06·8	1 06·9	1 03·7	2·7	0·2	8·7	0·7	14·7	1·1
28	1 07·0	1 07·2	1 03·9	2·8	0·2	8·8	0·7	14·8	1·1
29	1 07·3	1 07·4	1 04·2	2·9	0·2	8·9	0·7	14·9	1·1
30	1 07·5	1 07·7	1 04·4	3·0	0·2	9·0	0·7	15·0	1·1
31	1 07·8	1 07·9	1 04·7	3·1	0·2	9·1	0·7	15·1	1·1
32	1 08·0	1 08·2	1 04·9	3·2	0·2	9·2	0·7	15·2	1·1
33	1 08·3	1 08·4	1 05·1	3·3	0·2	9·3	0·7	15·3	1·1
34	1 08·5	1 08·7	1 05·4	3·4	0·3	9·4	0·7	15·4	1·2
35	1 08·8	1 08·9	1 05·6	3·5	0·3	9·5	0·7	15·5	1·2
36	1 09·0	1 09·2	1 05·9	3·6	0·3	9·6	0·7	15·6	1·2
37	1 09·3	1 09·4	1 06·1	3·7	0·3	9·7	0·7	15·7	1·2
38	1 09·5	1 09·7	1 06·3	3·8	0·3	9·8	0·7	15·8	1·2
39	1 09·8	1 09·9	1 06·6	3·9	0·3	9·9	0·7	15·9	1·2
40	1 10·0	1 10·2	1 06·8	4·0	0·3	10·0	0·8	16·0	1·2
41	1 10·3	1 10·4	1 07·0	4·1	0·3	10·1	0·8	16·1	1·2
42	1 10·5	1 10·7	1 07·3	4·2	0·3	10·2	0·8	16·2	1·2
43	1 10·8	1 10·9	1 07·5	4·3	0·3	10·3	0·8	16·3	1·2
44	1 11·0	1 11·2	1 07·8	4·4	0·3	10·4	0·8	16·4	1·2
45	1 11·3	1 11·4	1 08·0	4·5	0·3	10·5	0·8	16·5	1·2
46	1 11·5	1 11·7	1 08·2	4·6	0·3	10·6	0·8	16·6	1·2
47	1 11·8	1 11·9	1 08·5	4·7	0·4	10·7	0·8	16·7	1·3
48	1 12·0	1 12·2	1 08·7	4·8	0·4	10·8	0·8	16·8	1·3
49	1 12·3	1 12·4	1 09·0	4·9	0·4	10·9	0·8	16·9	1·3
50	1 12·5	1 12·7	1 09·2	5·0	0·4	11·0	0·8	17·0	1·3
51	1 12·8	1 12·9	1 09·4	5·1	0·4	11·1	0·8	17·1	1·3
52	1 13·0	1 13·2	1 09·7	5·2	0·4	11·2	0·8	17·2	1·3
53	1 13·3	1 13·5	1 09·9	5·3	0·4	11·3	0·8	17·3	1·3
54	1 13·5	1 13·7	1 10·2	5·4	0·4	11·4	0·9	17·4	1·3
55	1 13·8	1 14·0	1 10·4	5·5	0·4	11·5	0·9	17·5	1·3
56	1 14·0	1 14·2	1 10·6	5·6	0·4	11·6	0·9	17·6	1·3
57	1 14·3	1 14·5	1 10·9	5·7	0·4	11·7	0·9	17·7	1·3
58	1 14·5	1 14·7	1 11·1	5·8	0·4	11·8	0·9	17·8	1·3
59	1 14·8	1 15·0	1 11·3	5·9	0·4	11·9	0·9	17·9	1·3
60	1 15·0	1 15·2	1 11·6	6·0	0·5	12·0	0·9	18·0	1·4

m 5 s	SUN PLANETS ° ′	ARIES ° ′	MOON ° ′	v or d ′	Corrn ′	v or d ′	Corrn ′	v or d ′	Corrn ′
00	1 15·0	1 15·2	1 11·6	0·0	0·0	6·0	0·6	12·0	1·1
01	1 15·3	1 15·5	1 11·8	0·1	0·0	6·1	0·6	12·1	1·1
02	1 15·5	1 15·7	1 12·1	0·2	0·0	6·2	0·6	12·2	1·1
03	1 15·8	1 16·0	1 12·3	0·3	0·0	6·3	0·6	12·3	1·1
04	1 16·0	1 16·2	1 12·5	0·4	0·0	6·4	0·6	12·4	1·1
05	1 16·3	1 16·5	1 12·8	0·5	0·0	6·5	0·6	12·5	1·1
06	1 16·5	1 16·7	1 13·0	0·6	0·1	6·6	0·6	12·6	1·2
07	1 16·8	1 17·0	1 13·3	0·7	0·1	6·7	0·6	12·7	1·2
08	1 17·0	1 17·2	1 13·5	0·8	0·1	6·8	0·6	12·8	1·2
09	1 17·3	1 17·5	1 13·7	0·9	0·1	6·9	0·6	12·9	1·2
10	1 17·5	1 17·7	1 14·0	1·0	0·1	7·0	0·6	13·0	1·2
11	1 17·8	1 18·0	1 14·2	1·1	0·1	7·1	0·7	13·1	1·2
12	1 18·0	1 18·2	1 14·4	1·2	0·1	7·2	0·7	13·2	1·2
13	1 18·3	1 18·5	1 14·7	1·3	0·1	7·3	0·7	13·3	1·2
14	1 18·5	1 18·7	1 14·9	1·4	0·1	7·4	0·7	13·4	1·2
15	1 18·8	1 19·0	1 15·2	1·5	0·1	7·5	0·7	13·5	1·2
16	1 19·0	1 19·2	1 15·4	1·6	0·1	7·6	0·7	13·6	1·2
17	1 19·3	1 19·5	1 15·6	1·7	0·2	7·7	0·7	13·7	1·3
18	1 19·5	1 19·7	1 15·9	1·8	0·2	7·8	0·7	13·8	1·3
19	1 19·8	1 20·0	1 16·1	1·9	0·2	7·9	0·7	13·9	1·3
20	1 20·0	1 20·2	1 16·4	2·0	0·2	8·0	0·7	14·0	1·3
21	1 20·3	1 20·5	1 16·6	2·1	0·2	8·1	0·7	14·1	1·3
22	1 20·5	1 20·7	1 16·8	2·2	0·2	8·2	0·8	14·2	1·3
23	1 20·8	1 21·0	1 17·1	2·3	0·2	8·3	0·8	14·3	1·3
24	1 21·0	1 21·2	1 17·3	2·4	0·2	8·4	0·8	14·4	1·3
25	1 21·3	1 21·5	1 17·5	2·5	0·2	8·5	0·8	14·5	1·3
26	1 21·5	1 21·7	1 17·8	2·6	0·2	8·6	0·8	14·6	1·3
27	1 21·8	1 22·0	1 18·0	2·7	0·2	8·7	0·8	14·7	1·3
28	1 22·0	1 22·2	1 18·3	2·8	0·3	8·8	0·8	14·8	1·4
29	1 22·3	1 22·5	1 18·5	2·9	0·3	8·9	0·8	14·9	1·4
30	1 22·5	1 22·7	1 18·7	3·0	0·3	9·0	0·8	15·0	1·4
31	1 22·8	1 23·0	1 19·0	3·1	0·3	9·1	0·8	15·1	1·4
32	1 23·0	1 23·2	1 19·2	3·2	0·3	9·2	0·8	15·2	1·4
33	1 23·3	1 23·5	1 19·5	3·3	0·3	9·3	0·9	15·3	1·4
34	1 23·5	1 23·7	1 19·7	3·4	0·3	9·4	0·9	15·4	1·4
35	1 23·8	1 24·0	1 19·9	3·5	0·3	9·5	0·9	15·5	1·4
36	1 24·0	1 24·2	1 20·2	3·6	0·3	9·6	0·9	15·6	1·4
37	1 24·3	1 24·5	1 20·4	3·7	0·3	9·7	0·9	15·7	1·4
38	1 24·5	1 24·7	1 20·7	3·8	0·3	9·8	0·9	15·8	1·4
39	1 24·8	1 25·0	1 20·9	3·9	0·4	9·9	0·9	15·9	1·5
40	1 25·0	1 25·2	1 21·1	4·0	0·4	10·0	0·9	16·0	1·5
41	1 25·3	1 25·5	1 21·4	4·1	0·4	10·1	0·9	16·1	1·5
42	1 25·5	1 25·7	1 21·6	4·2	0·4	10·2	0·9	16·2	1·5
43	1 25·8	1 26·0	1 21·8	4·3	0·4	10·3	0·9	16·3	1·5
44	1 26·0	1 26·2	1 22·1	4·4	0·4	10·4	1·0	16·4	1·5
45	1 26·3	1 26·5	1 22·3	4·5	0·4	10·5	1·0	16·5	1·5
46	1 26·5	1 26·7	1 22·6	4·6	0·4	10·6	1·0	16·6	1·5
47	1 26·8	1 27·0	1 22·8	4·7	0·4	10·7	1·0	16·7	1·5
48	1 27·0	1 27·2	1 23·0	4·8	0·4	10·8	1·0	16·8	1·5
49	1 27·3	1 27·5	1 23·3	4·9	0·4	10·9	1·0	16·9	1·5
50	1 27·5	1 27·7	1 23·5	5·0	0·5	11·0	1·0	17·0	1·6
51	1 27·8	1 28·0	1 23·8	5·1	0·5	11·1	1·0	17·1	1·6
52	1 28·0	1 28·2	1 24·0	5·2	0·5	11·2	1·0	17·2	1·6
53	1 28·3	1 28·5	1 24·2	5·3	0·5	11·3	1·0	17·3	1·6
54	1 28·5	1 28·7	1 24·5	5·4	0·5	11·4	1·0	17·4	1·6
55	1 28·8	1 29·0	1 24·7	5·5	0·5	11·5	1·1	17·5	1·6
56	1 29·0	1 29·2	1 24·9	5·6	0·5	11·6	1·1	17·6	1·6
57	1 29·3	1 29·5	1 25·2	5·7	0·5	11·7	1·1	17·7	1·6
58	1 29·5	1 29·7	1 25·4	5·8	0·5	11·8	1·1	17·8	1·6
59	1 29·8	1 30·0	1 25·7	5·9	0·5	11·9	1·1	17·9	1·6
60	1 30·0	1 30·2	1 25·9	6·0	0·6	12·0	1·1	18·0	1·7

m 6 s	SUN PLANETS ° ′	ARIES ° ′	MOON ° ′	v or d ′	Corr^n ′	v or d ′	Corr^n ′	v or d ′	Corr^n ′
00	1 30·0	1 30·2	1 25·9	0·0	0·0	6·0	0·7	12·0	1·3
01	1 30·3	1 30·5	1 26·1	0·1	0·0	6·1	0·7	12·1	1·3
02	1 30·5	1 30·7	1 26·4	0·2	0·0	6·2	0·7	12·2	1·3
03	1 30·8	1 31·0	1 26·6	0·3	0·0	6·3	0·7	12·3	1·3
04	1 31·0	1 31·2	1 26·9	0·4	0·0	6·4	0·7	12·4	1·3
05	1 31·3	1 31·5	1 27·1	0·5	0·1	6·5	0·7	12·5	1·4
06	1 31·5	1 31·8	1 27·3	0·6	0·1	6·6	0·7	12·6	1·4
07	1 31·8	1 32·0	1 27·6	0·7	0·1	6·7	0·7	12·7	1·4
08	1 32·0	1 32·3	1 27·8	0·8	0·1	6·8	0·7	12·8	1·4
09	1 32·3	1 32·5	1 28·0	0·9	0·1	6·9	0·7	12·9	1·4
10	1 32·5	1 32·8	1 28·3	1·0	0·1	7·0	0·8	13·0	1·4
11	1 32·8	1 33·0	1 28·5	1·1	0·1	7·1	0·8	13·1	1·4
12	1 33·0	1 33·3	1 28·8	1·2	0·1	7·2	0·8	13·2	1·4
13	1 33·3	1 33·5	1 29·0	1·3	0·1	7·3	0·8	13·3	1·4
14	1 33·5	1 33·8	1 29·2	1·4	0·2	7·4	0·8	13·4	1·5
15	1 33·8	1 34·0	1 29·5	1·5	0·2	7·5	0·8	13·5	1·5
16	1 34·0	1 34·3	1 29·7	1·6	0·2	7·6	0·8	13·6	1·5
17	1 34·3	1 34·5	1 30·0	1·7	0·2	7·7	0·8	13·7	1·5
18	1 34·5	1 34·8	1 30·2	1·8	0·2	7·8	0·8	13·8	1·5
19	1 34·8	1 35·0	1 30·4	1·9	0·2	7·9	0·9	13·9	1·5
20	1 35·0	1 35·3	1 30·7	2·0	0·2	8·0	0·9	14·0	1·5
21	1 35·3	1 35·5	1 30·9	2·1	0·2	8·1	0·9	14·1	1·5
22	1 35·5	1 35·8	1 31·1	2·2	0·2	8·2	0·9	14·2	1·5
23	1 35·8	1 36·0	1 31·4	2·3	0·2	8·3	0·9	14·3	1·5
24	1 36·0	1 36·3	1 31·6	2·4	0·3	8·4	0·9	14·4	1·6
25	1 36·3	1 36·5	1 31·9	2·5	0·3	8·5	0·9	14·5	1·6
26	1 36·5	1 36·8	1 32·1	2·6	0·3	8·6	0·9	14·6	1·6
27	1 36·8	1 37·0	1 32·3	2·7	0·3	8·7	0·9	14·7	1·6
28	1 37·0	1 37·3	1 32·6	2·8	0·3	8·8	1·0	14·8	1·6
29	1 37·3	1 37·5	1 32·8	2·9	0·3	8·9	1·0	14·9	1·6
30	1 37·5	1 37·8	1 33·1	3·0	0·3	9·0	1·0	15·0	1·6
31	1 37·8	1 38·0	1 33·3	3·1	0·3	9·1	1·0	15·1	1·6
32	1 38·0	1 38·3	1 33·5	3·2	0·3	9·2	1·0	15·2	1·6
33	1 38·3	1 38·5	1 33·8	3·3	0·4	9·3	1·0	15·3	1·7
34	1 38·5	1 38·8	1 34·0	3·4	0·4	9·4	1·0	15·4	1·7
35	1 38·8	1 39·0	1 34·3	3·5	0·4	9·5	1·0	15·5	1·7
36	1 39·0	1 39·3	1 34·5	3·6	0·4	9·6	1·0	15·6	1·7
37	1 39·3	1 39·5	1 34·7	3·7	0·4	9·7	1·1	15·7	1·7
38	1 39·5	1 39·8	1 35·0	3·8	0·4	9·8	1·1	15·8	1·7
39	1 39·8	1 40·0	1 35·2	3·9	0·4	9·9	1·1	15·9	1·7
40	1 40·0	1 40·3	1 35·4	4·0	0·4	10·0	1·1	16·0	1·7
41	1 40·3	1 40·5	1 35·7	4·1	0·4	10·1	1·1	16·1	1·7
42	1 40·5	1 40·8	1 35·9	4·2	0·5	10·2	1·1	16·2	1·8
43	1 40·8	1 41·0	1 36·2	4·3	0·5	10·3	1·1	16·3	1·8
44	1 41·0	1 41·3	1 36·4	4·4	0·5	10·4	1·1	16·4	1·8
45	1 41·3	1 41·5	1 36·6	4·5	0·5	10·5	1·1	16·5	1·8
46	1 41·5	1 41·8	1 36·9	4·6	0·5	10·6	1·1	16·6	1·8
47	1 41·8	1 42·0	1 37·1	4·7	0·5	10·7	1·2	16·7	1·8
48	1 42·0	1 42·3	1 37·4	4·8	0·5	10·8	1·2	16·8	1·8
49	1 42·3	1 42·5	1 37·6	4·9	0·5	10·9	1·2	16·9	1·8
50	1 42·5	1 42·8	1 37·8	5·0	0·5	11·0	1·2	17·0	1·8
51	1 42·8	1 43·0	1 38·1	5·1	0·6	11·1	1·2	17·1	1·9
52	1 43·0	1 43·3	1 38·3	5·2	0·6	11·2	1·2	17·2	1·9
53	1 43·3	1 43·5	1 38·5	5·3	0·6	11·3	1·2	17·3	1·9
54	1 43·5	1 43·8	1 38·8	5·4	0·6	11·4	1·2	17·4	1·9
55	1 43·8	1 44·0	1 39·0	5·5	0·6	11·5	1·2	17·5	1·9
56	1 44·0	1 44·3	1 39·3	5·6	0·6	11·6	1·3	17·6	1·9
57	1 44·3	1 44·5	1 39·5	5·7	0·6	11·7	1·3	17·7	1·9
58	1 44·5	1 44·8	1 39·7	5·8	0·6	11·8	1·3	17·8	1·9
59	1 44·8	1 45·0	1 40·0	5·9	0·6	11·9	1·3	17·9	1·9
60	1 45·0	1 45·3	1 40·2	6·0	0·7	12·0	1·3	18·0	2·0

m 7 s	SUN PLANETS ° ′	ARIES ° ′	MOON ° ′	v or d ′	Corr^n ′	v or d ′	Corr^n ′	v or d ′	Corr^n ′
00	1 45·0	1 45·3	1 40·2	0·0	0·0	6·0	0·8	12·0	1·5
01	1 45·3	1 45·5	1 40·5	0·1	0·0	6·1	0·8	12·1	1·5
02	1 45·5	1 45·8	1 40·7	0·2	0·0	6·2	0·8	12·2	1·5
03	1 45·8	1 46·0	1 40·9	0·3	0·0	6·3	0·8	12·3	1·5
04	1 46·0	1 46·3	1 41·2	0·4	0·1	6·4	0·8	12·4	1·6
05	1 46·3	1 46·5	1 41·4	0·5	0·1	6·5	0·8	12·5	1·6
06	1 46·5	1 46·8	1 41·6	0·6	0·1	6·6	0·8	12·6	1·6
07	1 46·8	1 47·0	1 41·9	0·7	0·1	6·7	0·8	12·7	1·6
08	1 47·0	1 47·3	1 42·1	0·8	0·1	6·8	0·9	12·8	1·6
09	1 47·3	1 47·5	1 42·4	0·9	0·1	6·9	0·9	12·9	1·6
10	1 47·5	1 47·8	1 42·6	1·0	0·1	7·0	0·9	13·0	1·6
11	1 47·8	1 48·0	1 42·8	1·1	0·1	7·1	0·9	13·1	1·6
12	1 48·0	1 48·3	1 43·1	1·2	0·2	7·2	0·9	13·2	1·7
13	1 48·3	1 48·5	1 43·3	1·3	0·2	7·3	0·9	13·3	1·7
14	1 48·5	1 48·8	1 43·6	1·4	0·2	7·4	0·9	13·4	1·7
15	1 48·8	1 49·0	1 43·8	1·5	0·2	7·5	0·9	13·5	1·7
16	1 49·0	1 49·3	1 44·0	1·6	0·2	7·6	1·0	13·6	1·7
17	1 49·3	1 49·5	1 44·3	1·7	0·2	7·7	1·0	13·7	1·7
18	1 49·5	1 49·8	1 44·5	1·8	0·2	7·8	1·0	13·8	1·7
19	1 49·8	1 50·1	1 44·8	1·9	0·2	7·9	1·0	13·9	1·7
20	1 50·0	1 50·3	1 45·0	2·0	0·3	8·0	1·0	14·0	1·8
21	1 50·3	1 50·6	1 45·2	2·1	0·3	8·1	1·0	14·1	1·8
22	1 50·5	1 50·8	1 45·5	2·2	0·3	8·2	1·0	14·2	1·8
23	1 50·8	1 51·1	1 45·7	2·3	0·3	8·3	1·0	14·3	1·8
24	1 51·0	1 51·3	1 45·9	2·4	0·3	8·4	1·1	14·4	1·8
25	1 51·3	1 51·6	1 46·2	2·5	0·3	8·5	1·1	14·5	1·8
26	1 51·5	1 51·8	1 46·4	2·6	0·3	8·6	1·1	14·6	1·8
27	1 51·8	1 52·1	1 46·7	2·7	0·3	8·7	1·1	14·7	1·8
28	1 52·0	1 52·3	1 46·9	2·8	0·4	8·8	1·1	14·8	1·9
29	1 52·3	1 52·6	1 47·1	2·9	0·4	8·9	1·1	14·9	1·9
30	1 52·5	1 52·8	1 47·4	3·0	0·4	9·0	1·1	15·0	1·9
31	1 52·8	1 53·1	1 47·6	3·1	0·4	9·1	1·1	15·1	1·9
32	1 53·0	1 53·3	1 47·9	3·2	0·4	9·2	1·2	15·2	1·9
33	1 53·3	1 53·6	1 48·1	3·3	0·4	9·3	1·2	15·3	1·9
34	1 53·5	1 53·8	1 48·3	3·4	0·4	9·4	1·2	15·4	1·9
35	1 53·8	1 54·1	1 48·6	3·5	0·4	9·5	1·2	15·5	1·9
36	1 54·0	1 54·3	1 48·8	3·6	0·5	9·6	1·2	15·6	2·0
37	1 54·3	1 54·6	1 49·0	3·7	0·5	9·7	1·2	15·7	2·0
38	1 54·5	1 54·8	1 49·3	3·8	0·5	9·8	1·2	15·8	2·0
39	1 54·8	1 55·1	1 49·5	3·9	0·5	9·9	1·2	15·9	2·0
40	1 55·0	1 55·3	1 49·8	4·0	0·5	10·0	1·3	16·0	2·0
41	1 55·3	1 55·6	1 50·0	4·1	0·5	10·1	1·3	16·1	2·0
42	1 55·5	1 55·8	1 50·2	4·2	0·5	10·2	1·3	16·2	2·0
43	1 55·8	1 56·1	1 50·5	4·3	0·5	10·3	1·3	16·3	2·0
44	1 56·0	1 56·3	1 50·7	4·4	0·6	10·4	1·3	16·4	2·1
45	1 56·3	1 56·6	1 51·0	4·5	0·6	10·5	1·3	16·5	2·1
46	1 56·5	1 56·8	1 51·2	4·6	0·6	10·6	1·3	16·6	2·1
47	1 56·8	1 57·1	1 51·4	4·7	0·6	10·7	1·3	16·7	2·1
48	1 57·0	1 57·3	1 51·7	4·8	0·6	10·8	1·4	16·8	2·1
49	1 57·3	1 57·6	1 51·9	4·9	0·6	10·9	1·4	16·9	2·1
50	1 57·5	1 57·8	1 52·1	5·0	0·6	11·0	1·4	17·0	2·1
51	1 57·8	1 58·1	1 52·4	5·1	0·6	11·1	1·4	17·1	2·1
52	1 58·0	1 58·3	1 52·6	5·2	0·7	11·2	1·4	17·2	2·2
53	1 58·3	1 58·6	1 52·9	5·3	0·7	11·3	1·4	17·3	2·2
54	1 58·5	1 58·8	1 53·1	5·4	0·7	11·4	1·4	17·4	2·2
55	1 58·8	1 59·1	1 53·3	5·5	0·7	11·5	1·4	17·5	2·2
56	1 59·0	1 59·3	1 53·6	5·6	0·7	11·6	1·5	17·6	2·2
57	1 59·3	1 59·6	1 53·8	5·7	0·7	11·7	1·5	17·7	2·2
58	1 59·5	1 59·8	1 54·1	5·8	0·7	11·8	1·5	17·8	2·2
59	1 59·8	2 00·1	1 54·3	5·9	0·7	11·9	1·5	17·9	2·2
60	2 00·0	2 00·3	1 54·5	6·0	0·8	12·0	1·5	18·0	2·3

m 8	SUN PLANETS	ARIES	MOON	v or d	Corrⁿ	v or d	Corrⁿ	v or d	Corrⁿ
s	° ′	° ′	° ′	′	′	′	′	′	′
00	2 00·0	2 00·3	1 54·5	0·0	0·0	6·0	0·9	12·0	1·7
01	2 00·3	2 00·6	1 54·8	0·1	0·0	6·1	0·9	12·1	1·7
02	2 00·5	2 00·8	1 55·0	0·2	0·0	6·2	0·9	12·2	1·7
03	2 00·8	2 01·1	1 55·2	0·3	0·0	6·3	0·9	12·3	1·7
04	2 01·0	2 01·3	1 55·5	0·4	0·1	6·4	0·9	12·4	1·8
05	2 01·3	2 01·6	1 55·7	0·5	0·1	6·5	0·9	12·5	1·8
06	2 01·5	2 01·8	1 56·0	0·6	0·1	6·6	0·9	12·6	1·8
07	2 01·8	2 02·1	1 56·2	0·7	0·1	6·7	0·9	12·7	1·8
08	2 02·0	2 02·3	1 56·4	0·8	0·1	6·8	1·0	12·8	1·8
09	2 02·3	2 02·6	1 56·7	0·9	0·1	6·9	1·0	12·9	1·8
10	2 02·5	2 02·8	1 56·9	1·0	0·1	7·0	1·0	13·0	1·8
11	2 02·8	2 03·1	1 57·2	1·1	0·2	7·1	1·0	13·1	1·9
12	2 03·0	2 03·3	1 57·4	1·2	0·2	7·2	1·0	13·2	1·9
13	2 03·3	2 03·6	1 57·6	1·3	0·2	7·3	1·0	13·3	1·9
14	2 03·5	2 03·8	1 57·9	1·4	0·2	7·4	1·0	13·4	1·9
15	2 03·8	2 04·1	1 58·1	1·5	0·2	7·5	1·1	13·5	1·9
16	2 04·0	2 04·3	1 58·4	1·6	0·2	7·6	1·1	13·6	1·9
17	2 04·3	2 04·6	1 58·6	1·7	0·2	7·7	1·1	13·7	1·9
18	2 04·5	2 04·8	1 58·8	1·8	0·3	7·8	1·1	13·8	2·0
19	2 04·8	2 05·1	1 59·1	1·9	0·3	7·9	1·1	13·9	2·0
20	2 05·0	2 05·3	1 59·3	2·0	0·3	8·0	1·1	14·0	2·0
21	2 05·3	2 05·6	1 59·5	2·1	0·3	8·1	1·1	14·1	2·0
22	2 05·5	2 05·8	1 59·8	2·2	0·3	8·2	1·2	14·2	2·0
23	2 05·8	2 06·1	2 00·0	2·3	0·3	8·3	1·2	14·3	2·0
24	2 06·0	2 06·3	2 00·3	2·4	0·3	8·4	1·2	14·4	2·0
25	2 06·3	2 06·6	2 00·5	2·5	0·4	8·5	1·2	14·5	2·1
26	2 06·5	2 06·8	2 00·7	2·6	0·4	8·6	1·2	14·6	2·1
27	2 06·8	2 07·1	2 01·0	2·7	0·4	8·7	1·2	14·7	2·1
28	2 07·0	2 07·3	2 01·2	2·8	0·4	8·8	1·2	14·8	2·1
29	2 07·3	2 07·6	2 01·5	2·9	0·4	8·9	1·3	14·9	2·1
30	2 07·5	2 07·8	2 01·7	3·0	0·4	9·0	1·3	15·0	2·1
31	2 07·8	2 08·1	2 01·9	3·1	0·4	9·1	1·3	15·1	2·1
32	2 08·0	2 08·4	2 02·2	3·2	0·5	9·2	1·3	15·2	2·2
33	2 08·3	2 08·6	2 02·4	3·3	0·5	9·3	1·3	15·3	2·2
34	2 08·5	2 08·9	2 02·6	3·4	0·5	9·4	1·3	15·4	2·2
35	2 08·8	2 09·1	2 02·9	3·5	0·5	9·5	1·3	15·5	2·2
36	2 09·0	2 09·4	2 03·1	3·6	0·5	9·6	1·4	15·6	2·2
37	2 09·3	2 09·6	2 03·4	3·7	0·5	9·7	1·4	15·7	2·2
38	2 09·5	2 09·9	2 03·6	3·8	0·5	9·8	1·4	15·8	2·2
39	2 09·8	2 10·1	2 03·8	3·9	0·6	9·9	1·4	15·9	2·3
40	2 10·0	2 10·4	2 04·1	4·0	0·6	10·0	1·4	16·0	2·3
41	2 10·3	2 10·6	2 04·3	4·1	0·6	10·1	1·4	16·1	2·3
42	2 10·5	2 10·9	2 04·6	4·2	0·6	10·2	1·4	16·2	2·3
43	2 10·8	2 11·1	2 04·8	4·3	0·6	10·3	1·5	16·3	2·3
44	2 11·0	2 11·4	2 05·0	4·4	0·6	10·4	1·5	16·4	2·3
45	2 11·3	2 11·6	2 05·3	4·5	0·6	10·5	1·5	16·5	2·3
46	2 11·5	2 11·9	2 05·5	4·6	0·7	10·6	1·5	16·6	2·4
47	2 11·8	2 12·1	2 05·7	4·7	0·7	10·7	1·5	16·7	2·4
48	2 12·0	2 12·4	2 06·0	4·8	0·7	10·8	1·5	16·8	2·4
49	2 12·3	2 12·6	2 06·2	4·9	0·7	10·9	1·5	16·9	2·4
50	2 12·5	2 12·9	2 06·5	5·0	0·7	11·0	1·6	17·0	2·4
51	2 12·8	2 13·1	2 06·7	5·1	0·7	11·1	1·6	17·1	2·4
52	2 13·0	2 13·4	2 06·9	5·2	0·7	11·2	1·6	17·2	2·4
53	2 13·3	2 13·6	2 07·2	5·3	0·8	11·3	1·6	17·3	2·5
54	2 13·5	2 13·9	2 07·4	5·4	0·8	11·4	1·6	17·4	2·5
55	2 13·8	2 14·1	2 07·7	5·5	0·8	11·5	1·6	17·5	2·5
56	2 14·0	2 14·4	2 07·9	5·6	0·8	11·6	1·6	17·6	2·5
57	2 14·3	2 14·6	2 08·1	5·7	0·8	11·7	1·7	17·7	2·5
58	2 14·5	2 14·9	2 08·4	5·8	0·8	11·8	1·7	17·8	2·5
59	2 14·8	2 15·1	2 08·6	5·9	0·8	11·9	1·7	17·9	2·5
60	2 15·0	2 15·4	2 08·9	6·0	0·9	12·0	1·7	18·0	2·6

m 9	SUN PLANETS	ARIES	MOON	v or d	Corrⁿ	v or d	Corrⁿ	v or d	Corrⁿ
s	° ′	° ′	° ′	′	′	′	′	′	′
00	2 15·0	2 15·4	2 08·9	0·0	0·0	6·0	1·0	12·0	1·9
01	2 15·3	2 15·6	2 09·1	0·1	0·0	6·1	1·0	12·1	1·9
02	2 15·5	2 15·9	2 09·3	0·2	0·0	6·2	1·0	12·2	1·9
03	2 15·8	2 16·1	2 09·6	0·3	0·0	6·3	1·0	12·3	1·9
04	2 16·0	2 16·4	2 09·8	0·4	0·1	6·4	1·0	12·4	2·0
05	2 16·3	2 16·6	2 10·0	0·5	0·1	6·5	1·0	12·5	2·0
06	2 16·5	2 16·9	2 10·3	0·6	0·1	6·6	1·0	12·6	2·0
07	2 16·8	2 17·1	2 10·5	0·7	0·1	6·7	1·1	12·7	2·0
08	2 17·0	2 17·4	2 10·8	0·8	0·1	6·8	1·1	12·8	2·0
09	2 17·3	2 17·6	2 11·0	0·9	0·1	6·9	1·1	12·9	2·0
10	2 17·5	2 17·9	2 11·2	1·0	0·2	7·0	1·1	13·0	2·1
11	2 17·8	2 18·1	2 11·5	1·1	0·2	7·1	1·1	13·1	2·1
12	2 18·0	2 18·4	2 11·7	1·2	0·2	7·2	1·1	13·2	2·1
13	2 18·3	2 18·6	2 12·0	1·3	0·2	7·3	1·2	13·3	2·1
14	2 18·5	2 18·9	2 12·2	1·4	0·2	7·4	1·2	13·4	2·1
15	2 18·8	2 19·1	2 12·4	1·5	0·2	7·5	1·2	13·5	2·1
16	2 19·0	2 19·4	2 12·7	1·6	0·3	7·6	1·2	13·6	2·2
17	2 19·3	2 19·6	2 12·9	1·7	0·3	7·7	1·2	13·7	2·2
18	2 19·5	2 19·9	2 13·1	1·8	0·3	7·8	1·2	13·8	2·2
19	2 19·8	2 20·1	2 13·4	1·9	0·3	7·9	1·3	13·9	2·2
20	2 20·0	2 20·4	2 13·6	2·0	0·3	8·0	1·3	14·0	2·2
21	2 20·3	2 20·6	2 13·9	2·1	0·3	8·1	1·3	14·1	2·2
22	2 20·5	2 20·9	2 14·1	2·2	0·3	8·2	1·3	14·2	2·2
23	2 20·8	2 21·1	2 14·3	2·3	0·4	8·3	1·3	14·3	2·3
24	2 21·0	2 21·4	2 14·6	2·4	0·4	8·4	1·3	14·4	2·3
25	2 21·3	2 21·6	2 14·8	2·5	0·4	8·5	1·3	14·5	2·3
26	2 21·5	2 21·9	2 15·1	2·6	0·4	8·6	1·4	14·6	2·3
27	2 21·8	2 22·1	2 15·3	2·7	0·4	8·7	1·4	14·7	2·3
28	2 22·0	2 22·4	2 15·5	2·8	0·4	8·8	1·4	14·8	2·3
29	2 22·3	2 22·6	2 15·8	2·9	0·5	8·9	1·4	14·9	2·4
30	2 22·5	2 22·9	2 16·0	3·0	0·5	9·0	1·4	15·0	2·4
31	2 22·8	2 23·1	2 16·2	3·1	0·5	9·1	1·4	15·1	2·4
32	2 23·0	2 23·4	2 16·5	3·2	0·5	9·2	1·5	15·2	2·4
33	2 23·3	2 23·6	2 16·7	3·3	0·5	9·3	1·5	15·3	2·4
34	2 23·5	2 23·9	2 17·0	3·4	0·5	9·4	1·5	15·4	2·4
35	2 23·8	2 24·1	2 17·2	3·5	0·6	9·5	1·5	15·5	2·5
36	2 24·0	2 24·4	2 17·4	3·6	0·6	9·6	1·5	15·6	2·5
37	2 24·3	2 24·6	2 17·7	3·7	0·6	9·7	1·5	15·7	2·5
38	2 24·5	2 24·9	2 17·9	3·8	0·6	9·8	1·6	15·8	2·5
39	2 24·8	2 25·1	2 18·2	3·9	0·6	9·9	1·6	15·9	2·5
40	2 25·0	2 25·4	2 18·4	4·0	0·6	10·0	1·6	16·0	2·5
41	2 25·3	2 25·6	2 18·6	4·1	0·6	10·1	1·6	16·1	2·5
42	2 25·5	2 25·9	2 18·9	4·2	0·7	10·2	1·6	16·2	2·6
43	2 25·8	2 26·1	2 19·1	4·3	0·7	10·3	1·6	16·3	2·6
44	2 26·0	2 26·4	2 19·3	4·4	0·7	10·4	1·6	16·4	2·6
45	2 26·3	2 26·7	2 19·6	4·5	0·7	10·5	1·7	16·5	2·6
46	2 26·5	2 26·9	2 19·8	4·6	0·7	10·6	1·7	16·6	2·6
47	2 26·8	2 27·2	2 20·1	4·7	0·7	10·7	1·7	16·7	2·6
48	2 27·0	2 27·4	2 20·3	4·8	0·8	10·8	1·7	16·8	2·7
49	2 27·3	2 27·7	2 20·5	4·9	0·8	10·9	1·7	16·9	2·7
50	2 27·5	2 27·9	2 20·8	5·0	0·8	11·0	1·7	17·0	2·7
51	2 27·8	2 28·2	2 21·0	5·1	0·8	11·1	1·8	17·1	2·7
52	2 28·0	2 28·4	2 21·3	5·2	0·8	11·2	1·8	17·2	2·7
53	2 28·3	2 28·7	2 21·5	5·3	0·8	11·3	1·8	17·3	2·7
54	2 28·5	2 28·9	2 21·7	5·4	0·9	11·4	1·8	17·4	2·8
55	2 28·8	2 29·2	2 22·0	5·5	0·9	11·5	1·8	17·5	2·8
56	2 29·0	2 29·4	2 22·2	5·6	0·9	11·6	1·8	17·6	2·8
57	2 29·3	2 29·7	2 22·5	5·7	0·9	11·7	1·9	17·7	2·8
58	2 29·5	2 29·9	2 22·7	5·8	0·9	11·8	1·9	17·8	2·8
59	2 29·8	2 30·2	2 22·9	5·9	0·9	11·9	1·9	17·9	2·8
60	2 30·0	2 30·4	2 23·2	6·0	1·0	12·0	1·9	18·0	2·9

10^m	SUN PLANETS	ARIES	MOON	v or d	Corr^n	v or d	Corr^n	v or d	Corr^n
s	° ′	° ′	° ′	′	′	′	′	′	′
00	2 30·0	2 30·4	2 23·2	0·0	0·0	6·0	1·1	12·0	2·1
01	2 30·3	2 30·7	2 23·4	0·1	0·0	6·1	1·1	12·1	2·1
02	2 30·5	2 30·9	2 23·6	0·2	0·0	6·2	1·1	12·2	2·1
03	2 30·8	2 31·2	2 23·9	0·3	0·1	6·3	1·1	12·3	2·2
04	2 31·0	2 31·4	2 24·1	0·4	0·1	6·4	1·1	12·4	2·2
05	2 31·3	2 31·7	2 24·4	0·5	0·1	6·5	1·1	12·5	2·2
06	2 31·5	2 31·9	2 24·6	0·6	0·1	6·6	1·2	12·6	2·2
07	2 31·8	2 32·2	2 24·8	0·7	0·1	6·7	1·2	12·7	2·2
08	2 32·0	2 32·4	2 25·1	0·8	0·1	6·8	1·2	12·8	2·2
09	2 32·3	2 32·7	2 25·3	0·9	0·2	6·9	1·2	12·9	2·3
10	2 32·5	2 32·9	2 25·6	1·0	0·2	7·0	1·2	13·0	2·3
11	2 32·8	2 33·2	2 25·8	1·1	0·2	7·1	1·2	13·1	2·3
12	2 33·0	2 33·4	2 26·0	1·2	0·2	7·2	1·3	13·2	2·3
13	2 33·3	2 33·7	2 26·3	1·3	0·2	7·3	1·3	13·3	2·3
14	2 33·5	2 33·9	2 26·5	1·4	0·2	7·4	1·3	13·4	2·3
15	2 33·8	2 34·2	2 26·7	1·5	0·3	7·5	1·3	13·5	2·4
16	2 34·0	2 34·4	2 27·0	1·6	0·3	7·6	1·3	13·6	2·4
17	2 34·3	2 34·7	2 27·2	1·7	0·3	7·7	1·3	13·7	2·4
18	2 34·5	2 34·9	2 27·5	1·8	0·3	7·8	1·4	13·8	2·4
19	2 34·8	2 35·2	2 27·7	1·9	0·3	7·9	1·4	13·9	2·4
20	2 35·0	2 35·4	2 27·9	2·0	0·4	8·0	1·4	14·0	2·5
21	2 35·3	2 35·7	2 28·2	2·1	0·4	8·1	1·4	14·1	2·5
22	2 35·5	2 35·9	2 28·4	2·2	0·4	8·2	1·4	14·2	2·5
23	2 35·8	2 36·2	2 28·7	2·3	0·4	8·3	1·5	14·3	2·5
24	2 36·0	2 36·4	2 28·9	2·4	0·4	8·4	1·5	14·4	2·5
25	2 36·3	2 36·7	2 29·1	2·5	0·4	8·5	1·5	14·5	2·5
26	2 36·5	2 36·9	2 29·4	2·6	0·5	8·6	1·5	14·6	2·6
27	2 36·8	2 37·2	2 29·6	2·7	0·5	8·7	1·5	14·7	2·6
28	2 37·0	2 37·4	2 29·8	2·8	0·5	8·8	1·5	14·8	2·6
29	2 37·3	2 37·7	2 30·1	2·9	0·5	8·9	1·6	14·9	2·6
30	2 37·5	2 37·9	2 30·3	3·0	0·5	9·0	1·6	15·0	2·6
31	2 37·8	2 38·2	2 30·6	3·1	0·5	9·1	1·6	15·1	2·6
32	2 38·0	2 38·4	2 30·8	3·2	0·6	9·2	1·6	15·2	2·7
33	2 38·3	2 38·7	2 31·0	3·3	0·6	9·3	1·6	15·3	2·7
34	2 38·5	2 38·9	2 31·3	3·4	0·6	9·4	1·6	15·4	2·7
35	2 38·8	2 39·2	2 31·5	3·5	0·6	9·5	1·7	15·5	2·7
36	2 39·0	2 39·4	2 31·8	3·6	0·6	9·6	1·7	15·6	2·7
37	2 39·3	2 39·7	2 32·0	3·7	0·6	9·7	1·7	15·7	2·7
38	2 39·5	2 39·9	2 32·2	3·8	0·7	9·8	1·7	15·8	2·8
39	2 39·8	2 40·2	2 32·5	3·9	0·7	9·9	1·7	15·9	2·8
40	2 40·0	2 40·4	2 32·7	4·0	0·7	10·0	1·8	16·0	2·8
41	2 40·3	2 40·7	2 32·9	4·1	0·7	10·1	1·8	16·1	2·8
42	2 40·5	2 40·9	2 33·2	4·2	0·7	10·2	1·8	16·2	2·8
43	2 40·8	2 41·2	2 33·4	4·3	0·8	10·3	1·8	16·3	2·9
44	2 41·0	2 41·4	2 33·7	4·4	0·8	10·4	1·8	16·4	2·9
45	2 41·3	2 41·7	2 33·9	4·5	0·8	10·5	1·8	16·5	2·9
46	2 41·5	2 41·9	2 34·1	4·6	0·8	10·6	1·9	16·6	2·9
47	2 41·8	2 42·2	2 34·4	4·7	0·8	10·7	1·9	16·7	2·9
48	2 42·0	2 42·4	2 34·6	4·8	0·8	10·8	1·9	16·8	2·9
49	2 42·3	2 42·7	2 34·9	4·9	0·9	10·9	1·9	16·9	3·0
50	2 42·5	2 42·9	2 35·1	5·0	0·9	11·0	1·9	17·0	3·0
51	2 42·8	2 43·2	2 35·3	5·1	0·9	11·1	1·9	17·1	3·0
52	2 43·0	2 43·4	2 35·6	5·2	0·9	11·2	2·0	17·2	3·0
53	2 43·3	2 43·7	2 35·8	5·3	0·9	11·3	2·0	17·3	3·0
54	2 43·5	2 43·9	2 36·1	5·4	0·9	11·4	2·0	17·4	3·0
55	2 43·8	2 44·2	2 36·3	5·5	1·0	11·5	2·0	17·5	3·1
56	2 44·0	2 44·4	2 36·5	5·6	1·0	11·6	2·0	17·6	3·1
57	2 44·3	2 44·7	2 36·8	5·7	1·0	11·7	2·0	17·7	3·1
58	2 44·5	2 45·0	2 37·0	5·8	1·0	11·8	2·1	17·8	3·1
59	2 44·8	2 45·2	2 37·2	5·9	1·0	11·9	2·1	17·9	3·1
60	2 45·0	2 45·5	2 37·5	6·0	1·1	12·0	2·1	18·0	3·2

11^m	SUN PLANETS	ARIES	MOON	v or d	Corr^n	v or d	Corr^n	v or d	Corr^n
s	° ′	° ′	° ′	′	′	′	′	′	′
00	2 45·0	2 45·5	2 37·5	0·0	0·0	6·0	1·2	12·0	2·3
01	2 45·3	2 45·7	2 37·7	0·1	0·0	6·1	1·2	12·1	2·3
02	2 45·5	2 46·0	2 38·0	0·2	0·0	6·2	1·2	12·2	2·3
03	2 45·8	2 46·2	2 38·2	0·3	0·1	6·3	1·2	12·3	2·4
04	2 46·0	2 46·5	2 38·4	0·4	0·1	6·4	1·2	12·4	2·4
05	2 46·3	2 46·7	2 38·7	0·5	0·1	6·5	1·2	12·5	2·4
06	2 46·5	2 47·0	2 38·9	0·6	0·1	6·6	1·3	12·6	2·4
07	2 46·8	2 47·2	2 39·2	0·7	0·1	6·7	1·3	12·7	2·4
08	2 47·0	2 47·5	2 39·4	0·8	0·2	6·8	1·3	12·8	2·5
09	2 47·3	2 47·7	2 39·6	0·9	0·2	6·9	1·3	12·9	2·5
10	2 47·5	2 48·0	2 39·9	1·0	0·2	7·0	1·3	13·0	2·5
11	2 47·8	2 48·2	2 40·1	1·1	0·2	7·1	1·4	13·1	2·5
12	2 48·0	2 48·5	2 40·3	1·2	0·2	7·2	1·4	13·2	2·5
13	2 48·3	2 48·7	2 40·6	1·3	0·2	7·3	1·4	13·3	2·5
14	2 48·5	2 49·0	2 40·8	1·4	0·3	7·4	1·4	13·4	2·6
15	2 48·8	2 49·2	2 41·1	1·5	0·3	7·5	1·4	13·5	2·6
16	2 49·0	2 49·5	2 41·3	1·6	0·3	7·6	1·5	13·6	2·6
17	2 49·3	2 49·7	2 41·5	1·7	0·3	7·7	1·5	13·7	2·6
18	2 49·5	2 50·0	2 41·8	1·8	0·3	7·8	1·5	13·8	2·6
19	2 49·8	2 50·2	2 42·0	1·9	0·4	7·9	1·5	13·9	2·7
20	2 50·0	2 50·5	2 42·3	2·0	0·4	8·0	1·5	14·0	2·7
21	2 50·3	2 50·7	2 42·5	2·1	0·4	8·1	1·6	14·1	2·7
22	2 50·5	2 51·0	2 42·7	2·2	0·4	8·2	1·6	14·2	2·7
23	2 50·8	2 51·2	2 43·0	2·3	0·4	8·3	1·6	14·3	2·7
24	2 51·0	2 51·5	2 43·2	2·4	0·5	8·4	1·6	14·4	2·8
25	2 51·3	2 51·7	2 43·4	2·5	0·5	8·5	1·6	14·5	2·8
26	2 51·5	2 52·0	2 43·7	2·6	0·5	8·6	1·6	14·6	2·8
27	2 51·8	2 52·2	2 43·9	2·7	0·5	8·7	1·7	14·7	2·8
28	2 52·0	2 52·5	2 44·2	2·8	0·5	8·8	1·7	14·8	2·8
29	2 52·3	2 52·7	2 44·4	2·9	0·6	8·9	1·7	14·9	2·9
30	2 52·5	2 53·0	2 44·6	3·0	0·6	9·0	1·7	15·0	2·9
31	2 52·8	2 53·2	2 44·9	3·1	0·6	9·1	1·7	15·1	2·9
32	2 53·0	2 53·5	2 45·1	3·2	0·6	9·2	1·8	15·2	2·9
33	2 53·3	2 53·7	2 45·4	3·3	0·6	9·3	1·8	15·3	2·9
34	2 53·5	2 54·0	2 45·6	3·4	0·7	9·4	1·8	15·4	3·0
35	2 53·8	2 54·2	2 45·8	3·5	0·7	9·5	1·8	15·5	3·0
36	2 54·0	2 54·5	2 46·1	3·6	0·7	9·6	1·8	15·6	3·0
37	2 54·3	2 54·7	2 46·3	3·7	0·7	9·7	1·9	15·7	3·0
38	2 54·5	2 55·0	2 46·6	3·8	0·7	9·8	1·9	15·8	3·0
39	2 54·8	2 55·2	2 46·8	3·9	0·7	9·9	1·9	15·9	3·0
40	2 55·0	2 55·5	2 47·0	4·0	0·8	10·0	1·9	16·0	3·1
41	2 55·3	2 55·7	2 47·3	4·1	0·8	10·1	1·9	16·1	3·1
42	2 55·5	2 56·0	2 47·5	4·2	0·8	10·2	2·0	16·2	3·1
43	2 55·8	2 56·2	2 47·7	4·3	0·8	10·3	2·0	16·3	3·1
44	2 56·0	2 56·5	2 48·0	4·4	0·8	10·4	2·0	16·4	3·1
45	2 56·3	2 56·7	2 48·2	4·5	0·9	10·5	2·0	16·5	3·2
46	2 56·5	2 57·0	2 48·5	4·6	0·9	10·6	2·0	16·6	3·2
47	2 56·8	2 57·2	2 48·7	4·7	0·9	10·7	2·1	16·7	3·2
48	2 57·0	2 57·5	2 48·9	4·8	0·9	10·8	2·1	16·8	3·2
49	2 57·3	2 57·7	2 49·2	4·9	0·9	10·9	2·1	16·9	3·2
50	2 57·5	2 58·0	2 49·4	5·0	1·0	11·0	2·1	17·0	3·3
51	2 57·8	2 58·2	2 49·7	5·1	1·0	11·1	2·1	17·1	3·3
52	2 58·0	2 58·5	2 49·9	5·2	1·0	11·2	2·1	17·2	3·3
53	2 58·3	2 58·7	2 50·1	5·3	1·0	11·3	2·2	17·3	3·3
54	2 58·5	2 59·0	2 50·4	5·4	1·0	11·4	2·2	17·4	3·3
55	2 58·8	2 59·2	2 50·6	5·5	1·1	11·5	2·2	17·5	3·4
56	2 59·0	2 59·5	2 50·8	5·6	1·1	11·6	2·2	17·6	3·4
57	2 59·3	2 59·7	2 51·1	5·7	1·1	11·7	2·2	17·7	3·4
58	2 59·5	3 00·0	2 51·3	5·8	1·1	11·8	2·3	17·8	3·4
59	2 59·8	3 00·2	2 51·6	5·9	1·1	11·9	2·3	17·9	3·4
60	3 00·0	3 00·5	2 51·8	6·0	1·2	12·0	2·3	18·0	3·5

12m	SUN PLANETS	ARIES	MOON	v or d	Corrn	v or d	Corrn	v or d	Corrn
s	° ′	° ′	° ′	′	′	′	′	′	′
00	3 00·0	3 00·5	2 51·8	0·0	0·0	6·0	1·3	12·0	2·5
01	3 00·3	3 00·7	2 52·0	0·1	0·0	6·1	1·3	12·1	2·5
02	3 00·5	3 01·0	2 52·3	0·2	0·0	6·2	1·3	12·2	2·5
03	3 00·8	3 01·2	2 52·5	0·3	0·1	6·3	1·3	12·3	2·6
04	3 01·0	3 01·5	2 52·8	0·4	0·1	6·4	1·3	12·4	2·6
05	3 01·3	3 01·7	2 53·0	0·5	0·1	6·5	1·4	12·5	2·6
06	3 01·5	3 02·0	2 53·2	0·6	0·1	6·6	1·4	12·6	2·6
07	3 01·8	3 02·2	2 53·5	0·7	0·1	6·7	1·4	12·7	2·6
08	3 02·0	3 02·5	2 53·7	0·8	0·2	6·8	1·4	12·8	2·7
09	3 02·3	3 02·7	2 53·9	0·9	0·2	6·9	1·4	12·9	2·7
10	3 02·5	3 03·0	2 54·2	1·0	0·2	7·0	1·5	13·0	2·7
11	3 02·8	3 03·3	2 54·4	1·1	0·2	7·1	1·5	13·1	2·7
12	3 03·0	3 03·5	2 54·7	1·2	0·3	7·2	1·5	13·2	2·8
13	3 03·3	3 03·8	2 54·9	1·3	0·3	7·3	1·5	13·3	2·8
14	3 03·5	3 04·0	2 55·1	1·4	0·3	7·4	1·5	13·4	2·8
15	3 03·8	3 04·3	2 55·4	1·5	0·3	7·5	1·6	13·5	2·8
16	3 04·0	3 04·5	2 55·6	1·6	0·3	7·6	1·6	13·6	2·8
17	3 04·3	3 04·8	2 55·9	1·7	0·4	7·7	1·6	13·7	2·9
18	3 04·5	3 05·0	2 56·1	1·8	0·4	7·8	1·6	13·8	2·9
19	3 04·8	3 05·3	2 56·3	1·9	0·4	7·9	1·6	13·9	2·9
20	3 05·0	3 05·5	2 56·6	2·0	0·4	8·0	1·7	14·0	2·9
21	3 05·3	3 05·8	2 56·8	2·1	0·4	8·1	1·7	14·1	2·9
22	3 05·5	3 06·0	2 57·0	2·2	0·5	8·2	1·7	14·2	3·0
23	3 05·8	3 06·3	2 57·3	2·3	0·5	8·3	1·7	14·3	3·0
24	3 06·0	3 06·5	2 57·5	2·4	0·5	8·4	1·8	14·4	3·0
25	3 06·3	3 06·8	2 57·8	2·5	0·5	8·5	1·8	14·5	3·0
26	3 06·5	3 07·0	2 58·0	2·6	0·5	8·6	1·8	14·6	3·0
27	3 06·8	3 07·3	2 58·2	2·7	0·6	8·7	1·8	14·7	3·1
28	3 07·0	3 07·5	2 58·5	2·8	0·6	8·8	1·8	14·8	3·1
29	3 07·3	3 07·8	2 58·7	2·9	0·6	8·9	1·9	14·9	3·1
30	3 07·5	3 08·0	2 59·0	3·0	0·6	9·0	1·9	15·0	3·1
31	3 07·8	3 08·3	2 59·2	3·1	0·6	9·1	1·9	15·1	3·1
32	3 08·0	3 08·5	2 59·4	3·2	0·7	9·2	1·9	15·2	3·2
33	3 08·3	3 08·8	2 59·7	3·3	0·7	9·3	1·9	15·3	3·2
34	3 08·5	3 09·0	2 59·9	3·4	0·7	9·4	2·0	15·4	3·2
35	3 08·8	3 09·3	3 00·2	3·5	0·7	9·5	2·0	15·5	3·2
36	3 09·0	3 09·5	3 00·4	3·6	0·8	9·6	2·0	15·6	3·3
37	3 09·3	3 09·8	3 00·6	3·7	0·8	9·7	2·0	15·7	3·3
38	3 09·5	3 10·0	3 00·9	3·8	0·8	9·8	2·0	15·8	3·3
39	3 09·8	3 10·3	3 01·1	3·9	0·8	9·9	2·1	15·9	3·3
40	3 10·0	3 10·5	3 01·3	4·0	0·8	10·0	2·1	16·0	3·3
41	3 10·3	3 10·8	3 01·6	4·1	0·9	10·1	2·1	16·1	3·4
42	3 10·5	3 11·0	3 01·8	4·2	0·9	10·2	2·1	16·2	3·4
43	3 10·8	3 11·3	3 02·1	4·3	0·9	10·3	2·1	16·3	3·4
44	3 11·0	3 11·5	3 02·3	4·4	0·9	10·4	2·2	16·4	3·4
45	3 11·3	3 11·8	3 02·5	4·5	0·9	10·5	2·2	16·5	3·4
46	3 11·5	3 12·0	3 02·8	4·6	1·0	10·6	2·2	16·6	3·5
47	3 11·8	3 12·3	3 03·0	4·7	1·0	10·7	2·2	16·7	3·5
48	3 12·0	3 12·5	3 03·3	4·8	1·0	10·8	2·3	16·8	3·5
49	3 12·3	3 12·8	3 03·5	4·9	1·0	10·9	2·3	16·9	3·5
50	3 12·5	3 13·0	3 03·7	5·0	1·0	11·0	2·3	17·0	3·5
51	3 12·8	3 13·3	3 04·0	5·1	1·1	11·1	2·3	17·1	3·6
52	3 13·0	3 13·5	3 04·2	5·2	1·1	11·2	2·3	17·2	3·6
53	3 13·3	3 13·8	3 04·4	5·3	1·1	11·3	2·4	17·3	3·6
54	3 13·5	3 14·0	3 04·7	5·4	1·1	11·4	2·4	17·4	3·6
55	3 13·8	3 14·3	3 04·9	5·5	1·1	11·5	2·4	17·5	3·6
56	3 14·0	3 14·5	3 05·2	5·6	1·2	11·6	2·4	17·6	3·7
57	3 14·3	3 14·8	3 05·4	5·7	1·2	11·7	2·4	17·7	3·7
58	3 14·5	3 15·0	3 05·6	5·8	1·2	11·8	2·5	17·8	3·7
59	3 14·8	3 15·3	3 05·9	5·9	1·2	11·9	2·5	17·9	3·7
60	3 15·0	3 15·5	3 06·1	6·0	1·3	12·0	2·5	18·0	3·8

13m	SUN PLANETS	ARIES	MOON	v or d	Corrn	v or d	Corrn	v or d	Corrn
s	° ′	° ′	° ′	′	′	′	′	′	′
00	3 15·0	3 15·5	3 06·1	0·0	0·0	6·0	1·4	12·0	2·7
01	3 15·3	3 15·8	3 06·4	0·1	0·0	6·1	1·4	12·1	2·7
02	3 15·5	3 16·0	3 06·6	0·2	0·0	6·2	1·4	12·2	2·7
03	3 15·8	3 16·3	3 06·8	0·3	0·1	6·3	1·4	12·3	2·8
04	3 16·0	3 16·5	3 07·1	0·4	0·1	6·4	1·4	12·4	2·8
05	3 16·3	3 16·8	3 07·3	0·5	0·1	6·5	1·5	12·5	2·8
06	3 16·5	3 17·0	3 07·5	0·6	0·1	6·6	1·5	12·6	2·8
07	3 16·8	3 17·3	3 07·8	0·7	0·2	6·7	1·5	12·7	2·9
08	3 17·0	3 17·5	3 08·0	0·8	0·2	6·8	1·5	12·8	2·9
09	3 17·3	3 17·8	3 08·3	0·9	0·2	6·9	1·6	12·9	2·9
10	3 17·5	3 18·0	3 08·5	1·0	0·2	7·0	1·6	13·0	2·9
11	3 17·8	3 18·3	3 08·7	1·1	0·2	7·1	1·6	13·1	2·9
12	3 18·0	3 18·5	3 09·0	1·2	0·3	7·2	1·6	13·2	3·0
13	3 18·3	3 18·8	3 09·2	1·3	0·3	7·3	1·6	13·3	3·0
14	3 18·5	3 19·0	3 09·5	1·4	0·3	7·4	1·7	13·4	3·0
15	3 18·8	3 19·3	3 09·7	1·5	0·3	7·5	1·7	13·5	3·0
16	3 19·0	3 19·5	3 09·9	1·6	0·4	7·6	1·7	13·6	3·1
17	3 19·3	3 19·8	3 10·2	1·7	0·4	7·7	1·7	13·7	3·1
18	3 19·5	3 20·0	3 10·4	1·8	0·4	7·8	1·8	13·8	3·1
19	3 19·8	3 20·3	3 10·7	1·9	0·4	7·9	1·8	13·9	3·1
20	3 20·0	3 20·5	3 10·9	2·0	0·5	8·0	1·8	14·0	3·2
21	3 20·3	3 20·8	3 11·1	2·1	0·5	8·1	1·8	14·1	3·2
22	3 20·5	3 21·0	3 11·4	2·2	0·5	8·2	1·8	14·2	3·2
23	3 20·8	3 21·3	3 11·6	2·3	0·5	8·3	1·9	14·3	3·2
24	3 21·0	3 21·6	3 11·8	2·4	0·5	8·4	1·9	14·4	3·2
25	3 21·3	3 21·8	3 12·1	2·5	0·6	8·5	1·9	14·5	3·3
26	3 21·5	3 22·1	3 12·3	2·6	0·6	8·6	1·9	14·6	3·3
27	3 21·8	3 22·3	3 12·6	2·7	0·6	8·7	2·0	14·7	3·3
28	3 22·0	3 22·6	3 12·8	2·8	0·6	8·8	2·0	14·8	3·3
29	3 22·3	3 22·8	3 13·0	2·9	0·7	8·9	2·0	14·9	3·4
30	3 22·5	3 23·1	3 13·3	3·0	0·7	9·0	2·0	15·0	3·4
31	3 22·8	3 23·3	3 13·5	3·1	0·7	9·1	2·0	15·1	3·4
32	3 23·0	3 23·6	3 13·8	3·2	0·7	9·2	2·1	15·2	3·4
33	3 23·3	3 23·8	3 14·0	3·3	0·7	9·3	2·1	15·3	3·4
34	3 23·5	3 24·1	3 14·2	3·4	0·8	9·4	2·1	15·4	3·5
35	3 23·8	3 24·3	3 14·5	3·5	0·8	9·5	2·1	15·5	3·5
36	3 24·0	3 24·6	3 14·7	3·6	0·8	9·6	2·2	15·6	3·5
37	3 24·3	3 24·8	3 14·9	3·7	0·8	9·7	2·2	15·7	3·5
38	3 24·5	3 25·1	3 15·2	3·8	0·9	9·8	2·2	15·8	3·6
39	3 24·8	3 25·3	3 15·4	3·9	0·9	9·9	2·2	15·9	3·6
40	3 25·0	3 25·6	3 15·7	4·0	0·9	10·0	2·3	16·0	3·6
41	3 25·3	3 25·8	3 15·9	4·1	0·9	10·1	2·3	16·1	3·6
42	3 25·5	3 26·1	3 16·1	4·2	0·9	10·2	2·3	16·2	3·6
43	3 25·8	3 26·3	3 16·4	4·3	1·0	10·3	2·3	16·3	3·7
44	3 26·0	3 26·6	3 16·6	4·4	1·0	10·4	2·3	16·4	3·7
45	3 26·3	3 26·8	3 16·9	4·5	1·0	10·5	2·4	16·5	3·7
46	3 26·5	3 27·1	3 17·1	4·6	1·0	10·6	2·4	16·6	3·7
47	3 26·8	3 27·3	3 17·3	4·7	1·1	10·7	2·4	16·7	3·8
48	3 27·0	3 27·6	3 17·6	4·8	1·1	10·8	2·4	16·8	3·8
49	3 27·3	3 27·8	3 17·8	4·9	1·1	10·9	2·5	16·9	3·8
50	3 27·5	3 28·1	3 18·0	5·0	1·1	11·0	2·5	17·0	3·8
51	3 27·8	3 28·3	3 18·3	5·1	1·1	11·1	2·5	17·1	3·8
52	3 28·0	3 28·6	3 18·5	5·2	1·2	11·2	2·5	17·2	3·9
53	3 28·3	3 28·8	3 18·8	5·3	1·2	11·3	2·5	17·3	3·9
54	3 28·5	3 29·1	3 19·0	5·4	1·2	11·4	2·6	17·4	3·9
55	3 28·8	3 29·3	3 19·2	5·5	1·2	11·5	2·6	17·5	3·9
56	3 29·0	3 29·6	3 19·5	5·6	1·3	11·6	2·6	17·6	4·0
57	3 29·3	3 29·8	3 19·7	5·7	1·3	11·7	2·6	17·7	4·0
58	3 29·5	3 30·1	3 20·0	5·8	1·3	11·8	2·7	17·8	4·0
59	3 29·8	3 30·3	3 20·2	5·9	1·3	11·9	2·7	17·9	4·0
60	3 30·0	3 30·6	3 20·4	6·0	1·4	12·0	2·7	18·0	4·1

m 14	SUN PLANETS	ARIES	MOON	v or d	Corrn	v or d	Corrn	v or d	Corrn
s	° ′	° ′	° ′	′	′	′	′	′	′
00	3 30·0	3 30·6	3 20·4	0·0	0·0	6·0	1·5	12·0	2·9
01	3 30·3	3 30·8	3 20·7	0·1	0·0	6·1	1·5	12·1	2·9
02	3 30·5	3 31·1	3 20·9	0·2	0·0	6·2	1·5	12·2	2·9
03	3 30·8	3 31·3	3 21·1	0·3	0·1	6·3	1·5	12·3	3·0
04	3 31·0	3 31·6	3 21·4	0·4	0·1	6·4	1·5	12·4	3·0
05	3 31·3	3 31·8	3 21·6	0·5	0·1	6·5	1·6	12·5	3·0
06	3 31·5	3 32·1	3 21·9	0·6	0·1	6·6	1·6	12·6	3·0
07	3 31·8	3 32·3	3 22·1	0·7	0·2	6·7	1·6	12·7	3·1
08	3 32·0	3 32·6	3 22·3	0·8	0·2	6·8	1·6	12·8	3·1
09	3 32·3	3 32·8	3 22·6	0·9	0·2	6·9	1·7	12·9	3·1
10	3 32·5	3 33·1	3 22·8	1·0	0·2	7·0	1·7	13·0	3·1
11	3 32·8	3 33·3	3 23·1	1·1	0·3	7·1	1·7	13·1	3·2
12	3 33·0	3 33·6	3 23·3	1·2	0·3	7·2	1·7	13·2	3·2
13	3 33·3	3 33·8	3 23·5	1·3	0·3	7·3	1·8	13·3	3·2
14	3 33·5	3 34·1	3 23·8	1·4	0·3	7·4	1·8	13·4	3·2
15	3 33·8	3 34·3	3 24·0	1·5	0·4	7·5	1·8	13·5	3·3
16	3 34·0	3 34·6	3 24·3	1·6	0·4	7·6	1·8	13·6	3·3
17	3 34·3	3 34·8	3 24·5	1·7	0·4	7·7	1·9	13·7	3·3
18	3 34·5	3 35·1	3 24·7	1·8	0·4	7·8	1·9	13·8	3·3
19	3 34·8	3 35·3	3 25·0	1·9	0·5	7·9	1·9	13·9	3·4
20	3 35·0	3 35·6	3 25·2	2·0	0·5	8·0	1·9	14·0	3·4
21	3 35·3	3 35·8	3 25·4	2·1	0·5	8·1	2·0	14·1	3·4
22	3 35·5	3 36·1	3 25·7	2·2	0·5	8·2	2·0	14·2	3·4
23	3 35·8	3 36·3	3 25·9	2·3	0·6	8·3	2·0	14·3	3·5
24	3 36·0	3 36·6	3 26·2	2·4	0·6	8·4	2·0	14·4	3·5
25	3 36·3	3 36·8	3 26·4	2·5	0·6	8·5	2·1	14·5	3·5
26	3 36·5	3 37·1	3 26·6	2·6	0·6	8·6	2·1	14·6	3·5
27	3 36·8	3 37·3	3 26·9	2·7	0·7	8·7	2·1	14·7	3·6
28	3 37·0	3 37·6	3 27·1	2·8	0·7	8·8	2·1	14·8	3·6
29	3 37·3	3 37·8	3 27·4	2·9	0·7	8·9	2·2	14·9	3·6
30	3 37·5	3 38·1	3 27·6	3·0	0·7	9·0	2·2	15·0	3·6
31	3 37·8	3 38·3	3 27·8	3·1	0·7	9·1	2·2	15·1	3·6
32	3 38·0	3 38·6	3 28·1	3·2	0·8	9·2	2·2	15·2	3·7
33	3 38·3	3 38·8	3 28·3	3·3	0·8	9·3	2·2	15·3	3·7
34	3 38·5	3 39·1	3 28·5	3·4	0·8	9·4	2·3	15·4	3·7
35	3 38·8	3 39·3	3 28·8	3·5	0·8	9·5	2·3	15·5	3·7
36	3 39·0	3 39·6	3 29·0	3·6	0·9	9·6	2·3	15·6	3·8
37	3 39·3	3 39·9	3 29·3	3·7	0·9	9·7	2·3	15·7	3·8
38	3 39·5	3 40·1	3 29·5	3·8	0·9	9·8	2·4	15·8	3·8
39	3 39·8	3 40·4	3 29·7	3·9	0·9	9·9	2·4	15·9	3·8
40	3 40·0	3 40·6	3 30·0	4·0	1·0	10·0	2·4	16·0	3·9
41	3 40·3	3 40·9	3 30·2	4·1	1·0	10·1	2·4	16·1	3·9
42	3 40·5	3 41·1	3 30·5	4·2	1·0	10·2	2·5	16·2	3·9
43	3 40·8	3 41·4	3 30·7	4·3	1·0	10·3	2·5	16·3	3·9
44	3 41·0	3 41·6	3 30·9	4·4	1·1	10·4	2·5	16·4	4·0
45	3 41·3	3 41·9	3 31·2	4·5	1·1	10·5	2·5	16·5	4·0
46	3 41·5	3 42·1	3 31·4	4·6	1·1	10·6	2·6	16·6	4·0
47	3 41·8	3 42·4	3 31·6	4·7	1·1	10·7	2·6	16·7	4·0
48	3 42·0	3 42·6	3 31·9	4·8	1·2	10·8	2·6	16·8	4·1
49	3 42·3	3 42·9	3 32·1	4·9	1·2	10·9	2·6	16·9	4·1
50	3 42·5	3 43·1	3 32·4	5·0	1·2	11·0	2·7	17·0	4·1
51	3 42·8	3 43·4	3 32·6	5·1	1·2	11·1	2·7	17·1	4·1
52	3 43·0	3 43·6	3 32·8	5·2	1·3	11·2	2·7	17·2	4·2
53	3 43·3	3 43·9	3 33·1	5·3	1·3	11·3	2·7	17·3	4·2
54	3 43·5	3 44·1	3 33·3	5·4	1·3	11·4	2·8	17·4	4·2
55	3 43·8	3 44·4	3 33·6	5·5	1·3	11·5	2·8	17·5	4·2
56	3 44·0	3 44·6	3 33·8	5·6	1·4	11·6	2·8	17·6	4·3
57	3 44·3	3 44·9	3 34·0	5·7	1·4	11·7	2·8	17·7	4·3
58	3 44·5	3 45·1	3 34·3	5·8	1·4	11·8	2·9	17·8	4·3
59	3 44·8	3 45·4	3 34·5	5·9	1·4	11·9	2·9	17·9	4·3
60	3 45·0	3 45·6	3 34·8	6·0	1·5	12·0	2·9	18·0	4·4

m 15	SUN PLANETS	ARIES	MOON	v or d	Corrn	v or d	Corrn	v or d	Corrn
s	° ′	° ′	° ′	′	′	′	′	′	′
00	3 45·0	3 45·6	3 34·8	0·0	0·0	6·0	1·6	12·0	3·1
01	3 45·3	3 45·9	3 35·0	0·1	0·0	6·1	1·6	12·1	3·1
02	3 45·5	3 46·1	3 35·2	0·2	0·1	6·2	1·6	12·2	3·2
03	3 45·8	3 46·4	3 35·5	0·3	0·1	6·3	1·6	12·3	3·2
04	3 46·0	3 46·6	3 35·7	0·4	0·1	6·4	1·7	12·4	3·2
05	3 46·3	3 46·9	3 35·9	0·5	0·1	6·5	1·7	12·5	3·2
06	3 46·5	3 47·1	3 36·2	0·6	0·2	6·6	1·7	12·6	3·3
07	3 46·8	3 47·4	3 36·4	0·7	0·2	6·7	1·7	12·7	3·3
08	3 47·0	3 47·6	3 36·7	0·8	0·2	6·8	1·8	12·8	3·3
09	3 47·3	3 47·9	3 36·9	0·9	0·2	6·9	1·8	12·9	3·3
10	3 47·5	3 48·1	3 37·1	1·0	0·3	7·0	1·8	13·0	3·4
11	3 47·8	3 48·4	3 37·4	1·1	0·3	7·1	1·8	13·1	3·4
12	3 48·0	3 48·6	3 37·6	1·2	0·3	7·2	1·9	13·2	3·4
13	3 48·3	3 48·9	3 37·9	1·3	0·3	7·3	1·9	13·3	3·4
14	3 48·5	3 49·1	3 38·1	1·4	0·4	7·4	1·9	13·4	3·5
15	3 48·8	3 49·4	3 38·3	1·5	0·4	7·5	1·9	13·5	3·5
16	3 49·0	3 49·6	3 38·6	1·6	0·4	7·6	2·0	13·6	3·5
17	3 49·3	3 49·9	3 38·8	1·7	0·4	7·7	2·0	13·7	3·5
18	3 49·5	3 50·1	3 39·0	1·8	0·5	7·8	2·0	13·8	3·6
19	3 49·8	3 50·4	3 39·3	1·9	0·5	7·9	2·0	13·9	3·6
20	3 50·0	3 50·6	3 39·5	2·0	0·5	8·0	2·1	14·0	3·6
21	3 50·3	3 50·9	3 39·8	2·1	0·5	8·1	2·1	14·1	3·6
22	3 50·5	3 51·1	3 40·0	2·2	0·6	8·2	2·1	14·2	3·7
23	3 50·8	3 51·4	3 40·2	2·3	0·6	8·3	2·1	14·3	3·7
24	3 51·0	3 51·6	3 40·5	2·4	0·6	8·4	2·2	14·4	3·7
25	3 51·3	3 51·9	3 40·7	2·5	0·6	8·5	2·2	14·5	3·7
26	3 51·5	3 52·1	3 41·0	2·6	0·7	8·6	2·2	14·6	3·8
27	3 51·8	3 52·4	3 41·2	2·7	0·7	8·7	2·2	14·7	3·8
28	3 52·0	3 52·6	3 41·4	2·8	0·7	8·8	2·3	14·8	3·8
29	3 52·3	3 52·9	3 41·7	2·9	0·7	8·9	2·3	14·9	3·8
30	3 52·5	3 53·1	3 41·9	3·0	0·8	9·0	2·3	15·0	3·9
31	3 52·8	3 53·4	3 42·1	3·1	0·8	9·1	2·4	15·1	3·9
32	3 53·0	3 53·6	3 42·4	3·2	0·8	9·2	2·4	15·2	3·9
33	3 53·3	3 53·9	3 42·6	3·3	0·9	9·3	2·4	15·3	4·0
34	3 53·5	3 54·1	3 42·9	3·4	0·9	9·4	2·4	15·4	4·0
35	3 53·8	3 54·4	3 43·1	3·5	0·9	9·5	2·5	15·5	4·0
36	3 54·0	3 54·6	3 43·3	3·6	0·9	9·6	2·5	15·6	4·0
37	3 54·3	3 54·9	3 43·6	3·7	1·0	9·7	2·5	15·7	4·1
38	3 54·5	3 55·1	3 43·8	3·8	1·0	9·8	2·5	15·8	4·1
39	3 54·8	3 55·4	3 44·1	3·9	1·0	9·9	2·6	15·9	4·1
40	3 55·0	3 55·6	3 44·3	4·0	1·0	10·0	2·6	16·0	4·1
41	3 55·3	3 55·9	3 44·5	4·1	1·1	10·1	2·6	16·1	4·2
42	3 55·5	3 56·1	3 44·8	4·2	1·1	10·2	2·6	16·2	4·2
43	3 55·8	3 56·4	3 45·0	4·3	1·1	10·3	2·7	16·3	4·2
44	3 56·0	3 56·6	3 45·2	4·4	1·1	10·4	2·7	16·4	4·2
45	3 56·3	3 56·9	3 45·5	4·5	1·2	10·5	2·7	16·5	4·3
46	3 56·5	3 57·1	3 45·7	4·6	1·2	10·6	2·7	16·6	4·3
47	3 56·8	3 57·4	3 46·0	4·7	1·2	10·7	2·8	16·7	4·3
48	3 57·0	3 57·6	3 46·2	4·8	1·2	10·8	2·8	16·8	4·3
49	3 57·3	3 57·9	3 46·4	4·9	1·3	10·9	2·8	16·9	4·4
50	3 57·5	3 58·2	3 46·7	5·0	1·3	11·0	2·8	17·0	4·4
51	3 57·8	3 58·4	3 46·9	5·1	1·3	11·1	2·9	17·1	4·4
52	3 58·0	3 58·7	3 47·2	5·2	1·3	11·2	2·9	17·2	4·4
53	3 58·3	3 58·9	3 47·4	5·3	1·4	11·3	2·9	17·3	4·5
54	3 58·5	3 59·2	3 47·6	5·4	1·4	11·4	2·9	17·4	4·5
55	3 58·8	3 59·4	3 47·9	5·5	1·4	11·5	3·0	17·5	4·5
56	3 59·0	3 59·7	3 48·1	5·6	1·4	11·6	3·0	17·6	4·5
57	3 59·3	3 59·9	3 48·4	5·7	1·5	11·7	3·0	17·7	4·6
58	3 59·5	4 00·2	3 48·6	5·8	1·5	11·8	3·0	17·8	4·6
59	3 59·8	4 00·4	3 48·8	5·9	1·5	11·9	3·1	17·9	4·6
60	4 00·0	4 00·7	3 49·1	6·0	1·6	12·0	3·1	18·0	4·7

16^{m}	SUN PLANETS	ARIES	MOON	v or d	Corr^{n}	v or d	Corr^{n}	v or d	Corr^{n}
s	° ′	° ′	° ′	′	′	′	′	′	′
00	4 00·0	4 00·7	3 49·1	0·0	0·0	6·0	1·7	12·0	3·3
01	4 00·3	4 00·9	3 49·3	0·1	0·0	6·1	1·7	12·1	3·3
02	4 00·5	4 01·2	3 49·5	0·2	0·1	6·2	1·7	12·2	3·4
03	4 00·8	4 01·4	3 49·8	0·3	0·1	6·3	1·7	12·3	3·4
04	4 01·0	4 01·7	3 50·0	0·4	0·1	6·4	1·8	12·4	3·4
05	4 01·3	4 01·9	3 50·3	0·5	0·1	6·5	1·8	12·5	3·4
06	4 01·5	4 02·2	3 50·5	0·6	0·2	6·6	1·8	12·6	3·5
07	4 01·8	4 02·4	3 50·7	0·7	0·2	6·7	1·8	12·7	3·5
08	4 02·0	4 02·7	3 51·0	0·8	0·2	6·8	1·9	12·8	3·5
09	4 02·3	4 02·9	3 51·2	0·9	0·2	6·9	1·9	12·9	3·5
10	4 02·5	4 03·2	3 51·5	1·0	0·3	7·0	1·9	13·0	3·6
11	4 02·8	4 03·4	3 51·7	1·1	0·3	7·1	2·0	13·1	3·6
12	4 03·0	4 03·7	3 51·9	1·2	0·3	7·2	2·0	13·2	3·6
13	4 03·3	4 03·9	3 52·2	1·3	0·4	7·3	2·0	13·3	3·7
14	4 03·5	4 04·2	3 52·4	1·4	0·4	7·4	2·0	13·4	3·7
15	4 03·8	4 04·4	3 52·6	1·5	0·4	7·5	2·1	13·5	3·7
16	4 04·0	4 04·7	3 52·9	1·6	0·4	7·6	2·1	13·6	3·7
17	4 04·3	4 04·9	3 53·1	1·7	0·5	7·7	2·1	13·7	3·8
18	4 04·5	4 05·2	3 53·4	1·8	0·5	7·8	2·1	13·8	3·8
19	4 04·8	4 05·4	3 53·6	1·9	0·5	7·9	2·2	13·9	3·8
20	4 05·0	4 05·7	3 53·8	2·0	0·6	8·0	2·2	14·0	3·9
21	4 05·3	4 05·9	3 54·1	2·1	0·6	8·1	2·2	14·1	3·9
22	4 05·5	4 06·2	3 54·3	2·2	0·6	8·2	2·3	14·2	3·9
23	4 05·8	4 06·4	3 54·6	2·3	0·6	8·3	2·3	14·3	3·9
24	4 06·0	4 06·7	3 54·8	2·4	0·7	8·4	2·3	14·4	4·0
25	4 06·3	4 06·9	3 55·0	2·5	0·7	8·5	2·3	14·5	4·0
26	4 06·5	4 07·2	3 55·3	2·6	0·7	8·6	2·4	14·6	4·0
27	4 06·8	4 07·4	3 55·5	2·7	0·7	8·7	2·4	14·7	4·0
28	4 07·0	4 07·7	3 55·7	2·8	0·8	8·8	2·4	14·8	4·1
29	4 07·3	4 07·9	3 56·0	2·9	0·8	8·9	2·4	14·9	4·1
30	4 07·5	4 08·2	3 56·2	3·0	0·8	9·0	2·5	15·0	4·1
31	4 07·8	4 08·4	3 56·5	3·1	0·9	9·1	2·5	15·1	4·2
32	4 08·0	4 08·7	3 56·7	3·2	0·9	9·2	2·5	15·2	4·2
33	4 08·3	4 08·9	3 56·9	3·3	0·9	9·3	2·6	15·3	4·2
34	4 08·5	4 09·2	3 57·2	3·4	0·9	9·4	2·6	15·4	4·2
35	4 08·8	4 09·4	3 57·4	3·5	1·0	9·5	2·6	15·5	4·3
36	4 09·0	4 09·7	3 57·7	3·6	1·0	9·6	2·6	15·6	4·3
37	4 09·3	4 09·9	3 57·9	3·7	1·0	9·7	2·7	15·7	4·3
38	4 09·5	4 10·2	3 58·1	3·8	1·0	9·8	2·7	15·8	4·3
39	4 09·8	4 10·4	3 58·4	3·9	1·1	9·9	2·7	15·9	4·4
40	4 10·0	4 10·7	3 58·6	4·0	1·1	10·0	2·8	16·0	4·4
41	4 10·3	4 10·9	3 58·8	4·1	1·1	10·1	2·8	16·1	4·4
42	4 10·5	4 11·2	3 59·1	4·2	1·2	10·2	2·8	16·2	4·5
43	4 10·8	4 11·4	3 59·3	4·3	1·2	10·3	2·8	16·3	4·5
44	4 11·0	4 11·7	3 59·6	4·4	1·2	10·4	2·9	16·4	4·5
45	4 11·3	4 11·9	3 59·8	4·5	1·2	10·5	2·9	16·5	4·5
46	4 11·5	4 12·2	4 00·0	4·6	1·3	10·6	2·9	16·6	4·6
47	4 11·8	4 12·4	4 00·3	4·7	1·3	10·7	2·9	16·7	4·6
48	4 12·0	4 12·7	4 00·5	4·8	1·3	10·8	3·0	16·8	4·6
49	4 12·3	4 12·9	4 00·8	4·9	1·3	10·9	3·0	16·9	4·6
50	4 12·5	4 13·2	4 01·0	5·0	1·4	11·0	3·0	17·0	4·7
51	4 12·8	4 13·4	4 01·2	5·1	1·4	11·1	3·1	17·1	4·7
52	4 13·0	4 13·7	4 01·5	5·2	1·4	11·2	3·1	17·2	4·7
53	4 13·3	4 13·9	4 01·7	5·3	1·5	11·3	3·1	17·3	4·8
54	4 13·5	4 14·2	4 02·0	5·4	1·5	11·4	3·1	17·4	4·8
55	4 13·8	4 14·4	4 02·2	5·5	1·5	11·5	3·2	17·5	4·8
56	4 14·0	4 14·7	4 02·4	5·6	1·5	11·6	3·2	17·6	4·8
57	4 14·3	4 14·9	4 02·7	5·7	1·6	11·7	3·2	17·7	4·9
58	4 14·5	4 15·2	4 02·9	5·8	1·6	11·8	3·2	17·8	4·9
59	4 14·8	4 15·4	4 03·1	5·9	1·6	11·9	3·3	17·9	4·9
60	4 15·0	4 15·7	4 03·4	6·0	1·7	12·0	3·3	18·0	5·0

17^{m}	SUN PLANETS	ARIES	MOON	v or d	Corr^{n}	v or d	Corr^{n}	v or d	Corr^{n}
s	° ′	° ′	° ′	′	′	′	′	′	′
00	4 15·0	4 15·7	4 03·4	0·0	0·0	6·0	1·8	12·0	3·5
01	4 15·3	4 15·9	4 03·6	0·1	0·0	6·1	1·8	12·1	3·5
02	4 15·5	4 16·2	4 03·9	0·2	0·1	6·2	1·8	12·2	3·6
03	4 15·8	4 16·5	4 04·1	0·3	0·1	6·3	1·8	12·3	3·6
04	4 16·0	4 16·7	4 04·3	0·4	0·1	6·4	1·9	12·4	3·6
05	4 16·3	4 17·0	4 04·6	0·5	0·1	6·5	1·9	12·5	3·6
06	4 16·5	4 17·2	4 04·8	0·6	0·2	6·6	1·9	12·6	3·7
07	4 16·8	4 17·5	4 05·1	0·7	0·2	6·7	2·0	12·7	3·7
08	4 17·0	4 17·7	4 05·3	0·8	0·2	6·8	2·0	12·8	3·7
09	4 17·3	4 18·0	4 05·5	0·9	0·3	6·9	2·0	12·9	3·8
10	4 17·5	4 18·2	4 05·8	1·0	0·3	7·0	2·0	13·0	3·8
11	4 17·8	4 18·5	4 06·0	1·1	0·3	7·1	2·1	13·1	3·8
12	4 18·0	4 18·7	4 06·2	1·2	0·4	7·2	2·1	13·2	3·9
13	4 18·3	4 19·0	4 06·5	1·3	0·4	7·3	2·1	13·3	3·9
14	4 18·5	4 19·2	4 06·7	1·4	0·4	7·4	2·2	13·4	3·9
15	4 18·8	4 19·5	4 07·0	1·5	0·4	7·5	2·2	13·5	3·9
16	4 19·0	4 19·7	4 07·2	1·6	0·5	7·6	2·2	13·6	4·0
17	4 19·3	4 20·0	4 07·4	1·7	0·5	7·7	2·2	13·7	4·0
18	4 19·5	4 20·2	4 07·7	1·8	0·5	7·8	2·3	13·8	4·0
19	4 19·8	4 20·5	4 07·9	1·9	0·6	7·9	2·3	13·9	4·1
20	4 20·0	4 20·7	4 08·2	2·0	0·6	8·0	2·3	14·0	4·1
21	4 20·3	4 21·0	4 08·4	2·1	0·6	8·1	2·4	14·1	4·1
22	4 20·5	4 21·2	4 08·6	2·2	0·6	8·2	2·4	14·2	4·1
23	4 20·8	4 21·5	4 08·9	2·3	0·7	8·3	2·4	14·3	4·2
24	4 21·0	4 21·7	4 09·1	2·4	0·7	8·4	2·5	14·4	4·2
25	4 21·3	4 22·0	4 09·3	2·5	0·7	8·5	2·5	14·5	4·2
26	4 21·5	4 22·2	4 09·6	2·6	0·8	8·6	2·5	14·6	4·3
27	4 21·8	4 22·5	4 09·8	2·7	0·8	8·7	2·5	14·7	4·3
28	4 22·0	4 22·7	4 10·1	2·8	0·8	8·8	2·6	14·8	4·3
29	4 22·3	4 23·0	4 10·3	2·9	0·8	8·9	2·6	14·9	4·3
30	4 22·5	4 23·2	4 10·5	3·0	0·9	9·0	2·6	15·0	4·4
31	4 22·8	4 23·5	4 10·8	3·1	0·9	9·1	2·7	15·1	4·4
32	4 23·0	4 23·7	4 11·0	3·2	0·9	9·2	2·7	15·2	4·4
33	4 23·3	4 24·0	4 11·3	3·3	1·0	9·3	2·7	15·3	4·5
34	4 23·5	4 24·2	4 11·5	3·4	1·0	9·4	2·7	15·4	4·5
35	4 23·8	4 24·5	4 11·7	3·5	1·0	9·5	2·8	15·5	4·5
36	4 24·0	4 24·7	4 12·0	3·6	1·1	9·6	2·8	15·6	4·6
37	4 24·3	4 25·0	4 12·2	3·7	1·1	9·7	2·8	15·7	4·6
38	4 24·5	4 25·2	4 12·5	3·8	1·1	9·8	2·9	15·8	4·6
39	4 24·8	4 25·5	4 12·7	3·9	1·1	9·9	2·9	15·9	4·6
40	4 25·0	4 25·7	4 12·9	4·0	1·2	10·0	2·9	16·0	4·7
41	4 25·3	4 26·0	4 13·2	4·1	1·2	10·1	2·9	16·1	4·7
42	4 25·5	4 26·2	4 13·4	4·2	1·2	10·2	3·0	16·2	4·7
43	4 25·8	4 26·5	4 13·6	4·3	1·3	10·3	3·0	16·3	4·8
44	4 26·0	4 26·7	4 13·9	4·4	1·3	10·4	3·0	16·4	4·8
45	4 26·3	4 27·0	4 14·1	4·5	1·3	10·5	3·1	16·5	4·8
46	4 26·5	4 27·2	4 14·4	4·6	1·3	10·6	3·1	16·6	4·8
47	4 26·8	4 27·5	4 14·6	4·7	1·4	10·7	3·1	16·7	4·9
48	4 27·0	4 27·7	4 14·8	4·8	1·4	10·8	3·2	16·8	4·9
49	4 27·3	4 28·0	4 15·1	4·9	1·4	10·9	3·2	16·9	4·9
50	4 27·5	4 28·2	4 15·3	5·0	1·5	11·0	3·2	17·0	5·0
51	4 27·8	4 28·5	4 15·6	5·1	1·5	11·1	3·2	17·1	5·0
52	4 28·0	4 28·7	4 15·8	5·2	1·5	11·2	3·3	17·2	5·0
53	4 28·3	4 29·0	4 16·0	5·3	1·5	11·3	3·3	17·3	5·0
54	4 28·5	4 29·2	4 16·3	5·4	1·6	11·4	3·3	17·4	5·1
55	4 28·8	4 29·5	4 16·5	5·5	1·6	11·5	3·4	17·5	5·1
56	4 29·0	4 29·7	4 16·7	5·6	1·6	11·6	3·4	17·6	5·1
57	4 29·3	4 30·0	4 17·0	5·7	1·7	11·7	3·4	17·7	5·2
58	4 29·5	4 30·2	4 17·2	5·8	1·7	11·8	3·4	17·8	5·2
59	4 29·8	4 30·5	4 17·5	5·9	1·7	11·9	3·5	17·9	5·2
60	4 30·0	4 30·7	4 17·7	6·0	1·8	12·0	3·5	18·0	5·3

^{m} 18	SUN PLANETS	ARIES	MOON	v or d	Corr^n	v or d	Corr^n	v or d	Corr^n
s	° ′	° ′	° ′	′	′	′	′	′	′
00	4 30·0	4 30·7	4 17·7	0·0	0·0	6·0	1·9	12·0	3·7
01	4 30·3	4 31·0	4 17·9	0·1	0·0	6·1	1·9	12·1	3·7
02	4 30·5	4 31·2	4 18·2	0·2	0·1	6·2	1·9	12·2	3·8
03	4 30·8	4 31·5	4 18·4	0·3	0·1	6·3	1·9	12·3	3·8
04	4 31·0	4 31·7	4 18·7	0·4	0·1	6·4	2·0	12·4	3·8
05	4 31·3	4 32·0	4 18·9	0·5	0·2	6·5	2·0	12·5	3·9
06	4 31·5	4 32·2	4 19·1	0·6	0·2	6·6	2·0	12·6	3·9
07	4 31·8	4 32·5	4 19·4	0·7	0·2	6·7	2·1	12·7	3·9
08	4 32·0	4 32·7	4 19·6	0·8	0·2	6·8	2·1	12·8	3·9
09	4 32·3	4 33·0	4 19·8	0·9	0·3	6·9	2·1	12·9	4·0
10	4 32·5	4 33·2	4 20·1	1·0	0·3	7·0	2·2	13·0	4·0
11	4 32·8	4 33·5	4 20·3	1·1	0·3	7·1	2·2	13·1	4·0
12	4 33·0	4 33·7	4 20·6	1·2	0·4	7·2	2·2	13·2	4·1
13	4 33·3	4 34·0	4 20·8	1·3	0·4	7·3	2·3	13·3	4·1
14	4 33·5	4 34·2	4 21·0	1·4	0·4	7·4	2·3	13·4	4·1
15	4 33·8	4 34·5	4 21·3	1·5	0·5	7·5	2·3	13·5	4·2
16	4 34·0	4 34·8	4 21·5	1·6	0·5	7·6	2·3	13·6	4·2
17	4 34·3	4 35·0	4 21·8	1·7	0·5	7·7	2·4	13·7	4·2
18	4 34·5	4 35·3	4 22·0	1·8	0·6	7·8	2·4	13·8	4·3
19	4 34·8	4 35·5	4 22·2	1·9	0·6	7·9	2·4	13·9	4·3
20	4 35·0	4 35·8	4 22·5	2·0	0·6	8·0	2·5	14·0	4·3
21	4 35·3	4 36·0	4 22·7	2·1	0·6	8·1	2·5	14·1	4·3
22	4 35·5	4 36·3	4 22·9	2·2	0·7	8·2	2·5	14·2	4·4
23	4 35·8	4 36·5	4 23·2	2·3	0·7	8·3	2·6	14·3	4·4
24	4 36·0	4 36·8	4 23·4	2·4	0·7	8·4	2·6	14·4	4·4
25	4 36·3	4 37·0	4 23·7	2·5	0·8	8·5	2·6	14·5	4·5
26	4 36·5	4 37·3	4 23·9	2·6	0·8	8·6	2·7	14·6	4·5
27	4 36·8	4 37·5	4 24·1	2·7	0·8	8·7	2·7	14·7	4·5
28	4 37·0	4 37·8	4 24·4	2·8	0·9	8·8	2·7	14·8	4·6
29	4 37·3	4 38·0	4 24·6	2·9	0·9	8·9	2·7	14·9	4·6
30	4 37·5	4 38·3	4 24·9	3·0	0·9	9·0	2·8	15·0	4·6
31	4 37·8	4 38·5	4 25·1	3·1	1·0	9·1	2·8	15·1	4·7
32	4 38·0	4 38·8	4 25·3	3·2	1·0	9·2	2·8	15·2	4·7
33	4 38·3	4 39·0	4 25·6	3·3	1·0	9·3	2·9	15·3	4·7
34	4 38·5	4 39·3	4 25·8	3·4	1·0	9·4	2·9	15·4	4·7
35	4 38·8	4 39·5	4 26·1	3·5	1·1	9·5	2·9	15·5	4·8
36	4 39·0	4 39·8	4 26·3	3·6	1·1	9·6	3·0	15·6	4·8
37	4 39·3	4 40·0	4 26·5	3·7	1·1	9·7	3·0	15·7	4·8
38	4 39·5	4 40·3	4 26·8	3·8	1·2	9·8	3·0	15·8	4·9
39	4 39·8	4 40·5	4 27·0	3·9	1·2	9·9	3·1	15·9	4·9
40	4 40·0	4 40·8	4 27·2	4·0	1·2	10·0	3·1	16·0	4·9
41	4 40·3	4 41·0	4 27·5	4·1	1·3	10·1	3·1	16·1	5·0
42	4 40·5	4 41·3	4 27·7	4·2	1·3	10·2	3·1	16·2	5·0
43	4 40·8	4 41·5	4 28·0	4·3	1·3	10·3	3·2	16·3	5·0
44	4 41·0	4 41·8	4 28·2	4·4	1·4	10·4	3·2	16·4	5·1
45	4 41·3	4 42·0	4 28·4	4·5	1·4	10·5	3·2	16·5	5·1
46	4 41·5	4 42·3	4 28·7	4·6	1·4	10·6	3·3	16·6	5·1
47	4 41·8	4 42·5	4 28·9	4·7	1·4	10·7	3·3	16·7	5·1
48	4 42·0	4 42·8	4 29·2	4·8	1·5	10·8	3·3	16·8	5·2
49	4 42·3	4 43·0	4 29·4	4·9	1·5	10·9	3·4	16·9	5·2
50	4 42·5	4 43·3	4 29·6	5·0	1·5	11·0	3·4	17·0	5·2
51	4 42·8	4 43·5	4 29·9	5·1	1·6	11·1	3·4	17·1	5·3
52	4 43·0	4 43·8	4 30·1	5·2	1·6	11·2	3·5	17·2	5·3
53	4 43·3	4 44·0	4 30·3	5·3	1·6	11·3	3·5	17·3	5·3
54	4 43·5	4 44·3	4 30·6	5·4	1·7	11·4	3·5	17·4	5·4
55	4 43·8	4 44·5	4 30·8	5·5	1·7	11·5	3·5	17·5	5·4
56	4 44·0	4 44·8	4 31·1	5·6	1·7	11·6	3·6	17·6	5·4
57	4 44·3	4 45·0	4 31·3	5·7	1·8	11·7	3·6	17·7	5·5
58	4 44·5	4 45·3	4 31·5	5·8	1·8	11·8	3·6	17·8	5·5
59	4 44·8	4 45·5	4 31·8	5·9	1·8	11·9	3·7	17·9	5·5
60	4 45·0	4 45·8	4 32·0	6·0	1·9	12·0	3·7	18·0	5·6

^{m} 19	SUN PLANETS	ARIES	MOON	v or d	Corr^n	v or d	Corr^n	v or d	Corr^n
s	° ′	° ′	° ′	′	′	′	′	′	′
00	4 45·0	4 45·8	4 32·0	0·0	0·0	6·0	2·0	12·0	3·9
01	4 45·3	4 46·0	4 32·3	0·1	0·0	6·1	2·0	12·1	3·9
02	4 45·5	4 46·3	4 32·5	0·2	0·1	6·2	2·0	12·2	4·0
03	4 45·8	4 46·5	4 32·7	0·3	0·1	6·3	2·0	12·3	4·0
04	4 46·0	4 46·8	4 33·0	0·4	0·1	6·4	2·1	12·4	4·0
05	4 46·3	4 47·0	4 33·2	0·5	0·2	6·5	2·1	12·5	4·1
06	4 46·5	4 47·3	4 33·4	0·6	0·2	6·6	2·1	12·6	4·1
07	4 46·8	4 47·5	4 33·7	0·7	0·2	6·7	2·2	12·7	4·1
08	4 47·0	4 47·8	4 33·9	0·8	0·3	6·8	2·2	12·8	4·2
09	4 47·3	4 48·0	4 34·2	0·9	0·3	6·9	2·2	12·9	4·2
10	4 47·5	4 48·3	4 34·4	1·0	0·3	7·0	2·3	13·0	4·2
11	4 47·8	4 48·5	4 34·6	1·1	0·4	7·1	2·3	13·1	4·3
12	4 48·0	4 48·8	4 34·9	1·2	0·4	7·2	2·3	13·2	4·3
13	4 48·3	4 49·0	4 35·1	1·3	0·4	7·3	2·4	13·3	4·3
14	4 48·5	4 49·3	4 35·4	1·4	0·5	7·4	2·4	13·4	4·4
15	4 48·8	4 49·5	4 35·6	1·5	0·5	7·5	2·4	13·5	4·4
16	4 49·0	4 49·8	4 35·8	1·6	0·5	7·6	2·5	13·6	4·4
17	4 49·3	4 50·0	4 36·1	1·7	0·6	7·7	2·5	13·7	4·5
18	4 49·5	4 50·3	4 36·3	1·8	0·6	7·8	2·5	13·8	4·5
19	4 49·8	4 50·5	4 36·6	1·9	0·6	7·9	2·6	13·9	4·5
20	4 50·0	4 50·8	4 36·8	2·0	0·7	8·0	2·6	14·0	4·6
21	4 50·3	4 51·0	4 37·0	2·1	0·7	8·1	2·6	14·1	4·6
22	4 50·5	4 51·3	4 37·3	2·2	0·7	8·2	2·7	14·2	4·6
23	4 50·8	4 51·5	4 37·5	2·3	0·7	8·3	2·7	14·3	4·6
24	4 51·0	4 51·8	4 37·7	2·4	0·8	8·4	2·7	14·4	4·7
25	4 51·3	4 52·0	4 38·0	2·5	0·8	8·5	2·8	14·5	4·7
26	4 51·5	4 52·3	4 38·2	2·6	0·8	8·6	2·8	14·6	4·7
27	4 51·8	4 52·5	4 38·5	2·7	0·9	8·7	2·8	14·7	4·8
28	4 52·0	4 52·8	4 38·7	2·8	0·9	8·8	2·9	14·8	4·8
29	4 52·3	4 53·1	4 38·9	2·9	0·9	8·9	2·9	14·9	4·8
30	4 52·5	4 53·3	4 39·2	3·0	1·0	9·0	2·9	15·0	4·9
31	4 52·8	4 53·6	4 39·4	3·1	1·0	9·1	3·0	15·1	4·9
32	4 53·0	4 53·8	4 39·7	3·2	1·0	9·2	3·0	15·2	4·9
33	4 53·3	4 54·1	4 39·9	3·3	1·1	9·3	3·0	15·3	5·0
34	4 53·5	4 54·3	4 40·1	3·4	1·1	9·4	3·1	15·4	5·0
35	4 53·8	4 54·6	4 40·4	3·5	1·1	9·5	3·1	15·5	5·0
36	4 54·0	4 54·8	4 40·6	3·6	1·2	9·6	3·1	15·6	5·1
37	4 54·3	4 55·1	4 40·8	3·7	1·2	9·7	3·2	15·7	5·1
38	4 54·5	4 55·3	4 41·1	3·8	1·2	9·8	3·2	15·8	5·1
39	4 54·8	4 55·6	4 41·3	3·9	1·3	9·9	3·2	15·9	5·2
40	4 55·0	4 55·8	4 41·6	4·0	1·3	10·0	3·3	16·0	5·2
41	4 55·3	4 56·1	4 41·8	4·1	1·3	10·1	3·3	16·1	5·2
42	4 55·5	4 56·3	4 42·0	4·2	1·4	10·2	3·3	16·2	5·3
43	4 55·8	4 56·6	4 42·3	4·3	1·4	10·3	3·3	16·3	5·3
44	4 56·0	4 56·8	4 42·5	4·4	1·4	10·4	3·4	16·4	5·3
45	4 56·3	4 57·1	4 42·8	4·5	1·5	10·5	3·4	16·5	5·4
46	4 56·5	4 57·3	4 43·0	4·6	1·5	10·6	3·4	16·6	5·4
47	4 56·8	4 57·6	4 43·2	4·7	1·5	10·7	3·5	16·7	5·4
48	4 57·0	4 57·8	4 43·5	4·8	1·6	10·8	3·5	16·8	5·5
49	4 57·3	4 58·1	4 43·7	4·9	1·6	10·9	3·5	16·9	5·5
50	4 57·5	4 58·3	4 43·9	5·0	1·6	11·0	3·6	17·0	5·5
51	4 57·8	4 58·6	4 44·2	5·1	1·7	11·1	3·6	17·1	5·6
52	4 58·0	4 58·8	4 44·4	5·2	1·7	11·2	3·6	17·2	5·6
53	4 58·3	4 59·1	4 44·7	5·3	1·7	11·3	3·7	17·3	5·6
54	4 58·5	4 59·3	4 44·9	5·4	1·8	11·4	3·7	17·4	5·7
55	4 58·8	4 59·6	4 45·1	5·5	1·8	11·5	3·7	17·5	5·7
56	4 59·0	4 59·8	4 45·4	5·6	1·8	11·6	3·8	17·6	5·7
57	4 59·3	5 00·1	4 45·6	5·7	1·9	11·7	3·8	17·7	5·8
58	4 59·5	5 00·3	4 45·9	5·8	1·9	11·8	3·8	17·8	5·8
59	4 59·8	5 00·6	4 46·1	5·9	1·9	11·9	3·9	17·9	5·8
60	5 00·0	5 00·8	4 46·3	6·0	2·0	12·0	3·9	18·0	5·9

20^m	SUN PLANETS	ARIES	MOON	*v* or *d*	Corr^n	*v* or *d*	Corr^n	*v* or *d*	Corr^n
s	° ′	° ′	° ′	′	′	′	′	′	′
00	5 00·0	5 00·8	4 46·3	0·0	0·0	6·0	2·1	12·0	4·1
01	5 00·3	5 01·1	4 46·6	0·1	0·0	6·1	2·1	12·1	4·1
02	5 00·5	5 01·3	4 46·8	0·2	0·1	6·2	2·1	12·2	4·2
03	5 00·8	5 01·6	4 47·0	0·3	0·1	6·3	2·2	12·3	4·2
04	5 01·0	5 01·8	4 47·3	0·4	0·1	6·4	2·2	12·4	4·2
05	5 01·3	5 02·1	4 47·5	0·5	0·2	6·5	2·2	12·5	4·3
06	5 01·5	5 02·3	4 47·8	0·6	0·2	6·6	2·3	12·6	4·3
07	5 01·8	5 02·6	4 48·0	0·7	0·2	6·7	2·3	12·7	4·3
08	5 02·0	5 02·8	4 48·2	0·8	0·3	6·8	2·3	12·8	4·4
09	5 02·3	5 03·1	4 48·5	0·9	0·3	6·9	2·4	12·9	4·4
10	5 02·5	5 03·3	4 48·7	1·0	0·3	7·0	2·4	13·0	4·4
11	5 02·8	5 03·6	4 49·0	1·1	0·4	7·1	2·4	13·1	4·5
12	5 03·0	5 03·8	4 49·2	1·2	0·4	7·2	2·5	13·2	4·5
13	5 03·3	5 04·1	4 49·4	1·3	0·4	7·3	2·5	13·3	4·5
14	5 03·5	5 04·3	4 49·7	1·4	0·5	7·4	2·5	13·4	4·6
15	5 03·8	5 04·6	4 49·9	1·5	0·5	7·5	2·6	13·5	4·6
16	5 04·0	5 04·8	4 50·2	1·6	0·5	7·6	2·6	13·6	4·6
17	5 04·3	5 05·1	4 50·4	1·7	0·6	7·7	2·6	13·7	4·7
18	5 04·5	5 05·3	4 50·6	1·8	0·6	7·8	2·7	13·8	4·7
19	5 04·8	5 05·6	4 50·9	1·9	0·6	7·9	2·7	13·9	4·7
20	5 05·0	5 05·8	4 51·1	2·0	0·7	8·0	2·7	14·0	4·8
21	5 05·3	5 06·1	4 51·3	2·1	0·7	8·1	2·8	14·1	4·8
22	5 05·5	5 06·3	4 51·6	2·2	0·8	8·2	2·8	14·2	4·9
23	5 05·8	5 06·6	4 51·8	2·3	0·8	8·3	2·8	14·3	4·9
24	5 06·0	5 06·8	4 52·1	2·4	0·8	8·4	2·9	14·4	4·9
25	5 06·3	5 07·1	4 52·3	2·5	0·9	8·5	2·9	14·5	5·0
26	5 06·5	5 07·3	4 52·5	2·6	0·9	8·6	2·9	14·6	5·0
27	5 06·8	5 07·6	4 52·8	2·7	0·9	8·7	3·0	14·7	5·0
28	5 07·0	5 07·8	4 53·0	2·8	1·0	8·8	3·0	14·8	5·1
29	5 07·3	5 08·1	4 53·3	2·9	1·0	8·9	3·0	14·9	5·1
30	5 07·5	5 08·3	4 53·5	3·0	1·0	9·0	3·1	15·0	5·1
31	5 07·8	5 08·6	4 53·7	3·1	1·1	9·1	3·1	15·1	5·2
32	5 08·0	5 08·8	4 54·0	3·2	1·1	9·2	3·1	15·2	5·2
33	5 08·3	5 09·1	4 54·2	3·3	1·1	9·3	3·2	15·3	5·2
34	5 08·5	5 09·3	4 54·4	3·4	1·2	9·4	3·2	15·4	5·3
35	5 08·8	5 09·6	4 54·7	3·5	1·2	9·5	3·2	15·5	5·3
36	5 09·0	5 09·8	4 54·9	3·6	1·2	9·6	3·3	15·6	5·3
37	5 09·3	5 10·1	4 55·2	3·7	1·3	9·7	3·3	15·7	5·4
38	5 09·5	5 10·3	4 55·4	3·8	1·3	9·8	3·3	15·8	5·4
39	5 09·8	5 10·6	4 55·6	3·9	1·3	9·9	3·4	15·9	5·4
40	5 10·0	5 10·8	4 55·9	4·0	1·4	10·0	3·4	16·0	5·5
41	5 10·3	5 11·1	4 56·1	4·1	1·4	10·1	3·5	16·1	5·5
42	5 10·5	5 11·4	4 56·4	4·2	1·4	10·2	3·5	16·2	5·5
43	5 10·8	5 11·6	4 56·6	4·3	1·5	10·3	3·5	16·3	5·6
44	5 11·0	5 11·9	4 56·8	4·4	1·5	10·4	3·6	16·4	5·6
45	5 11·3	5 12·1	4 57·1	4·5	1·5	10·5	3·6	16·5	5·6
46	5 11·5	5 12·4	4 57·3	4·6	1·6	10·6	3·6	16·6	5·7
47	5 11·8	5 12·6	4 57·5	4·7	1·6	10·7	3·7	16·7	5·7
48	5 12·0	5 12·9	4 57·8	4·8	1·6	10·8	3·7	16·8	5·7
49	5 12·3	5 13·1	4 58·0	4·9	1·7	10·9	3·7	16·9	5·8
50	5 12·5	5 13·4	4 58·3	5·0	1·7	11·0	3·8	17·0	5·8
51	5 12·8	5 13·6	4 58·5	5·1	1·7	11·1	3·8	17·1	5·8
52	5 13·0	5 13·9	4 58·7	5·2	1·8	11·2	3·8	17·2	5·9
53	5 13·3	5 14·1	4 59·0	5·3	1·8	11·3	3·9	17·3	5·9
54	5 13·5	5 14·4	4 59·2	5·4	1·8	11·4	3·9	17·4	5·9
55	5 13·8	5 14·6	4 59·5	5·5	1·9	11·5	3·9	17·5	6·0
56	5 14·0	5 14·9	4 59·7	5·6	1·9	11·6	4·0	17·6	6·0
57	5 14·3	5 15·1	4 59·9	5·7	1·9	11·7	4·0	17·7	6·0
58	5 14·5	5 15·4	5 00·2	5·8	2·0	11·8	4·0	17·8	6·1
59	5 14·8	5 15·6	5 00·4	5·9	2·0	11·9	4·1	17·9	6·1
60	5 15·0	5 15·9	5 00·7	6·0	2·1	12·0	4·1	18·0	6·2

21^m	SUN PLANETS	ARIES	MOON	*v* or *d*	Corr^n	*v* or *d*	Corr^n	*v* or *d*	Corr^n
s	° ′	° ′	° ′	′	′	′	′	′	′
00	5 15·0	5 15·9	5 00·7	0·0	0·0	6·0	2·2	12·0	4·3
01	5 15·3	5 16·1	5 00·9	0·1	0·0	6·1	2·2	12·1	4·3
02	5 15·5	5 16·4	5 01·1	0·2	0·1	6·2	2·2	12·2	4·4
03	5 15·8	5 16·6	5 01·4	0·3	0·1	6·3	2·3	12·3	4·4
04	5 16·0	5 16·9	5 01·6	0·4	0·1	6·4	2·3	12·4	4·4
05	5 16·3	5 17·1	5 01·8	0·5	0·2	6·5	2·3	12·5	4·5
06	5 16·5	5 17·4	5 02·1	0·6	0·2	6·6	2·4	12·6	4·5
07	5 16·8	5 17·6	5 02·3	0·7	0·3	6·7	2·4	12·7	4·6
08	5 17·0	5 17·9	5 02·6	0·8	0·3	6·8	2·4	12·8	4·6
09	5 17·3	5 18·1	5 02·8	0·9	0·3	6·9	2·5	12·9	4·6
10	5 17·5	5 18·4	5 03·0	1·0	0·4	7·0	2·5	13·0	4·7
11	5 17·8	5 18·6	5 03·3	1·1	0·4	7·1	2·5	13·1	4·7
12	5 18·0	5 18·9	5 03·5	1·2	0·4	7·2	2·6	13·2	4·7
13	5 18·3	5 19·1	5 03·8	1·3	0·5	7·3	2·6	13·3	4·8
14	5 18·5	5 19·4	5 04·0	1·4	0·5	7·4	2·7	13·4	4·8
15	5 18·8	5 19·6	5 04·2	1·5	0·5	7·5	2·7	13·5	4·8
16	5 19·0	5 19·9	5 04·5	1·6	0·6	7·6	2·7	13·6	4·9
17	5 19·3	5 20·1	5 04·7	1·7	0·6	7·7	2·8	13·7	4·9
18	5 19·5	5 20·4	5 04·9	1·8	0·6	7·8	2·8	13·8	4·9
19	5 19·8	5 20·6	5 05·2	1·9	0·7	7·9	2·8	13·9	5·0
20	5 20·0	5 20·9	5 05·4	2·0	0·7	8·0	2·9	14·0	5·0
21	5 20·3	5 21·1	5 05·7	2·1	0·8	8·1	2·9	14·1	5·1
22	5 20·5	5 21·4	5 05·9	2·2	0·8	8·2	2·9	14·2	5·1
23	5 20·8	5 21·6	5 06·1	2·3	0·8	8·3	3·0	14·3	5·1
24	5 21·0	5 21·9	5 06·4	2·4	0·9	8·4	3·0	14·4	5·2
25	5 21·3	5 22·1	5 06·6	2·5	0·9	8·5	3·0	14·5	5·2
26	5 21·5	5 22·4	5 06·9	2·6	0·9	8·6	3·1	14·6	5·2
27	5 21·8	5 22·6	5 07·1	2·7	1·0	8·7	3·1	14·7	5·3
28	5 22·0	5 22·9	5 07·3	2·8	1·0	8·8	3·2	14·8	5·3
29	5 22·3	5 23·1	5 07·6	2·9	1·0	8·9	3·2	14·9	5·3
30	5 22·5	5 23·4	5 07·8	3·0	1·1	9·0	3·2	15·0	5·4
31	5 22·8	5 23·6	5 08·0	3·1	1·1	9·1	3·3	15·1	5·4
32	5 23·0	5 23·9	5 08·3	3·2	1·1	9·2	3·3	15·2	5·4
33	5 23·3	5 24·1	5 08·5	3·3	1·2	9·3	3·3	15·3	5·5
34	5 23·5	5 24·4	5 08·8	3·4	1·2	9·4	3·4	15·4	5·5
35	5 23·8	5 24·6	5 09·0	3·5	1·3	9·5	3·4	15·5	5·6
36	5 24·0	5 24·9	5 09·2	3·6	1·3	9·6	3·4	15·6	5·6
37	5 24·3	5 25·1	5 09·5	3·7	1·3	9·7	3·5	15·7	5·6
38	5 24·5	5 25·4	5 09·7	3·8	1·4	9·8	3·5	15·8	5·7
39	5 24·8	5 25·6	5 10·0	3·9	1·4	9·9	3·5	15·9	5·7
40	5 25·0	5 25·9	5 10·2	4·0	1·4	10·0	3·6	16·0	5·7
41	5 25·3	5 26·1	5 10·4	4·1	1·5	10·1	3·6	16·1	5·8
42	5 25·5	5 26·4	5 10·7	4·2	1·5	10·2	3·7	16·2	5·8
43	5 25·8	5 26·6	5 10·9	4·3	1·5	10·3	3·7	16·3	5·8
44	5 26·0	5 26·9	5 11·1	4·4	1·6	10·4	3·7	16·4	5·9
45	5 26·3	5 27·1	5 11·4	4·5	1·6	10·5	3·8	16·5	5·9
46	5 26·5	5 27·4	5 11·6	4·6	1·6	10·6	3·8	16·6	5·9
47	5 26·8	5 27·6	5 11·9	4·7	1·7	10·7	3·8	16·7	6·0
48	5 27·0	5 27·9	5 12·1	4·8	1·7	10·8	3·9	16·8	6·0
49	5 27·3	5 28·1	5 12·3	4·9	1·8	10·9	3·9	16·9	6·1
50	5 27·5	5 28·4	5 12·6	5·0	1·8	11·0	3·9	17·0	6·1
51	5 27·8	5 28·6	5 12·8	5·1	1·8	11·1	4·0	17·1	6·1
52	5 28·0	5 28·9	5 13·1	5·2	1·9	11·2	4·0	17·2	6·2
53	5 28·3	5 29·1	5 13·3	5·3	1·9	11·3	4·0	17·3	6·2
54	5 28·5	5 29·4	5 13·5	5·4	1·9	11·4	4·1	17·4	6·2
55	5 28·8	5 29·7	5 13·8	5·5	2·0	11·5	4·1	17·5	6·3
56	5 29·0	5 29·9	5 14·0	5·6	2·0	11·6	4·2	17·6	6·3
57	5 29·3	5 30·2	5 14·3	5·7	2·0	11·7	4·2	17·7	6·3
58	5 29·5	5 30·4	5 14·5	5·8	2·1	11·8	4·2	17·8	6·4
59	5 29·8	5 30·7	5 14·7	5·9	2·1	11·9	4·3	17·9	6·4
60	5 30·0	5 30·9	5 15·0	6·0	2·2	12·0	4·3	18·0	6·5

22m	SUN PLANETS	ARIES	MOON	v or d	Corrn	v or d	Corrn	v or d	Corrn
s	° ′	° ′	° ′	′	′	′	′	′	′
00	5 30·0	5 30·9	5 15·0	0·0	0·0	6·0	2·3	12·0	4·5
01	5 30·3	5 31·2	5 15·2	0·1	0·0	6·1	2·3	12·1	4·5
02	5 30·5	5 31·4	5 15·4	0·2	0·1	6·2	2·3	12·2	4·6
03	5 30·8	5 31·7	5 15·7	0·3	0·1	6·3	2·4	12·3	4·6
04	5 31·0	5 31·9	5 15·9	0·4	0·2	6·4	2·4	12·4	4·7
05	5 31·3	5 32·2	5 16·2	0·5	0·2	6·5	2·4	12·5	4·7
06	5 31·5	5 32·4	5 16·4	0·6	0·2	6·6	2·5	12·6	4·7
07	5 31·8	5 32·7	5 16·6	0·7	0·3	6·7	2·5	12·7	4·8
08	5 32·0	5 32·9	5 16·9	0·8	0·3	6·8	2·6	12·8	4·8
09	5 32·3	5 33·2	5 17·1	0·9	0·3	6·9	2·6	12·9	4·8
10	5 32·5	5 33·4	5 17·4	1·0	0·4	7·0	2·6	13·0	4·9
11	5 32·8	5 33·7	5 17·6	1·1	0·4	7·1	2·7	13·1	4·9
12	5 33·0	5 33·9	5 17·8	1·2	0·5	7·2	2·7	13·2	5·0
13	5 33·3	5 34·2	5 18·1	1·3	0·5	7·3	2·7	13·3	5·0
14	5 33·5	5 34·4	5 18·3	1·4	0·5	7·4	2·8	13·4	5·0
15	5 33·8	5 34·7	5 18·5	1·5	0·6	7·5	2·8	13·5	5·1
16	5 34·0	5 34·9	5 18·8	1·6	0·6	7·6	2·9	13·6	5·1
17	5 34·3	5 35·2	5 19·0	1·7	0·6	7·7	2·9	13·7	5·1
18	5 34·5	5 35·4	5 19·3	1·8	0·7	7·8	2·9	13·8	5·2
19	5 34·8	5 35·7	5 19·5	1·9	0·7	7·9	3·0	13·9	5·2
20	5 35·0	5 35·9	5 19·7	2·0	0·8	8·0	3·0	14·0	5·3
21	5 35·3	5 36·2	5 20·0	2·1	0·8	8·1	3·0	14·1	5·3
22	5 35·5	5 36·4	5 20·2	2·2	0·8	8·2	3·1	14·2	5·3
23	5 35·8	5 36·7	5 20·5	2·3	0·9	8·3	3·1	14·3	5·4
24	5 36·0	5 36·9	5 20·7	2·4	0·9	8·4	3·2	14·4	5·4
25	5 36·3	5 37·2	5 20·9	2·5	0·9	8·5	3·2	14·5	5·4
26	5 36·5	5 37·4	5 21·2	2·6	1·0	8·6	3·2	14·6	5·5
27	5 36·8	5 37·7	5 21·4	2·7	1·0	8·7	3·3	14·7	5·5
28	5 37·0	5 37·9	5 21·6	2·8	1·0	8·8	3·3	14·8	5·6
29	5 37·3	5 38·2	5 21·9	2·9	1·1	8·9	3·3	14·9	5·6
30	5 37·5	5 38·4	5 22·1	3·0	1·1	9·0	3·4	15·0	5·6
31	5 37·8	5 38·7	5 22·4	3·1	1·2	9·1	3·4	15·1	5·7
32	5 38·0	5 38·9	5 22·6	3·2	1·2	9·2	3·5	15·2	5·7
33	5 38·3	5 39·2	5 22·8	3·3	1·2	9·3	3·5	15·3	5·7
34	5 38·5	5 39·4	5 23·1	3·4	1·3	9·4	3·5	15·4	5·8
35	5 38·8	5 39·7	5 23·3	3·5	1·3	9·5	3·6	15·5	5·8
36	5 39·0	5 39·9	5 23·6	3·6	1·4	9·6	3·6	15·6	5·9
37	5 39·3	5 40·2	5 23·8	3·7	1·4	9·7	3·6	15·7	5·9
38	5 39·5	5 40·4	5 24·0	3·8	1·4	9·8	3·7	15·8	5·9
39	5 39·8	5 40·7	5 24·3	3·9	1·5	9·9	3·7	15·9	6·0
40	5 40·0	5 40·9	5 24·5	4·0	1·5	10·0	3·8	16·0	6·0
41	5 40·3	5 41·2	5 24·7	4·1	1·5	10·1	3·8	16·1	6·0
42	5 40·5	5 41·4	5 25·0	4·2	1·6	10·2	3·8	16·2	6·1
43	5 40·8	5 41·7	5 25·2	4·3	1·6	10·3	3·9	16·3	6·1
44	5 41·0	5 41·9	5 25·5	4·4	1·7	10·4	3·9	16·4	6·1
45	5 41·3	5 42·2	5 25·7	4·5	1·7	10·5	3·9	16·5	6·2
46	5 41·5	5 42·4	5 25·9	4·6	1·7	10·6	4·0	16·6	6·2
47	5 41·8	5 42·7	5 26·2	4·7	1·8	10·7	4·0	16·7	6·3
48	5 42·0	5 42·9	5 26·4	4·8	1·8	10·8	4·1	16·8	6·3
49	5 42·3	5 43·2	5 26·7	4·9	1·8	10·9	4·1	16·9	6·3
50	5 42·5	5 43·4	5 26·9	5·0	1·9	11·0	4·1	17·0	6·4
51	5 42·8	5 43·7	5 27·1	5·1	1·9	11·1	4·2	17·1	6·4
52	5 43·0	5 43·9	5 27·4	5·2	2·0	11·2	4·2	17·2	6·5
53	5 43·3	5 44·2	5 27·6	5·3	2·0	11·3	4·2	17·3	6·5
54	5 43·5	5 44·4	5 27·9	5·4	2·0	11·4	4·3	17·4	6·5
55	5 43·8	5 44·7	5 28·1	5·5	2·1	11·5	4·3	17·5	6·6
56	5 44·0	5 44·9	5 28·3	5·6	2·1	11·6	4·4	17·6	6·6
57	5 44·3	5 45·2	5 28·6	5·7	2·1	11·7	4·4	17·7	6·6
58	5 44·5	5 45·4	5 28·8	5·8	2·2	11·8	4·4	17·8	6·7
59	5 44·8	5 45·7	5 29·0	5·9	2·2	11·9	4·5	17·9	6·7
60	5 45·0	5 45·9	5 29·3	6·0	2·3	12·0	4·5	18·0	6·8

23m	SUN PLANETS	ARIES	MOON	v or d	Corrn	v or d	Corrn	v or d	Corrn
s	° ′	° ′	° ′	′	′	′	′	′	′
00	5 45·0	5 45·9	5 29·3	0·0	0·0	6·0	2·4	12·0	4·7
01	5 45·3	5 46·2	5 29·5	0·1	0·0	6·1	2·4	12·1	4·7
02	5 45·5	5 46·4	5 29·8	0·2	0·1	6·2	2·4	12·2	4·8
03	5 45·8	5 46·7	5 30·0	0·3	0·1	6·3	2·5	12·3	4·8
04	5 46·0	5 46·9	5 30·2	0·4	0·2	6·4	2·5	12·4	4·9
05	5 46·3	5 47·2	5 30·5	0·5	0·2	6·5	2·5	12·5	4·9
06	5 46·5	5 47·4	5 30·7	0·6	0·2	6·6	2·6	12·6	4·9
07	5 46·8	5 47·7	5 31·0	0·7	0·3	6·7	2·6	12·7	5·0
08	5 47·0	5 48·0	5 31·2	0·8	0·3	6·8	2·7	12·8	5·0
09	5 47·3	5 48·2	5 31·4	0·9	0·4	6·9	2·7	12·9	5·1
10	5 47·5	5 48·5	5 31·7	1·0	0·4	7·0	2·7	13·0	5·1
11	5 47·8	5 48·7	5 31·9	1·1	0·4	7·1	2·8	13·1	5·1
12	5 48·0	5 49·0	5 32·1	1·2	0·5	7·2	2·8	13·2	5·2
13	5 48·3	5 49·2	5 32·4	1·3	0·5	7·3	2·9	13·3	5·2
14	5 48·5	5 49·5	5 32·6	1·4	0·5	7·4	2·9	13·4	5·2
15	5 48·8	5 49·7	5 32·9	1·5	0·6	7·5	2·9	13·5	5·3
16	5 49·0	5 50·0	5 33·1	1·6	0·6	7·6	3·0	13·6	5·3
17	5 49·3	5 50·2	5 33·3	1·7	0·7	7·7	3·0	13·7	5·4
18	5 49·5	5 50·5	5 33·6	1·8	0·7	7·8	3·1	13·8	5·4
19	5 49·8	5 50·7	5 33·8	1·9	0·7	7·9	3·1	13·9	5·4
20	5 50·0	5 51·0	5 34·1	2·0	0·8	8·0	3·1	14·0	5·5
21	5 50·3	5 51·2	5 34·3	2·1	0·8	8·1	3·2	14·1	5·5
22	5 50·5	5 51·5	5 34·5	2·2	0·9	8·2	3·2	14·2	5·6
23	5 50·8	5 51·7	5 34·8	2·3	0·9	8·3	3·3	14·3	5·6
24	5 51·0	5 52·0	5 35·0	2·4	0·9	8·4	3·3	14·4	5·6
25	5 51·3	5 52·2	5 35·2	2·5	1·0	8·5	3·3	14·5	5·7
26	5 51·5	5 52·5	5 35·5	2·6	1·0	8·6	3·4	14·6	5·7
27	5 51·8	5 52·7	5 35·7	2·7	1·1	8·7	3·4	14·7	5·8
28	5 52·0	5 53·0	5 36·0	2·8	1·1	8·8	3·4	14·8	5·8
29	5 52·3	5 53·2	5 36·2	2·9	1·1	8·9	3·5	14·9	5·8
30	5 52·5	5 53·5	5 36·4	3·0	1·2	9·0	3·5	15·0	5·9
31	5 52·8	5 53·7	5 36·7	3·1	1·2	9·1	3·6	15·1	5·9
32	5 53·0	5 54·0	5 36·9	3·2	1·3	9·2	3·6	15·2	6·0
33	5 53·3	5 54·2	5 37·2	3·3	1·3	9·3	3·6	15·3	6·0
34	5 53·5	5 54·5	5 37·4	3·4	1·3	9·4	3·7	15·4	6·0
35	5 53·8	5 54·7	5 37·6	3·5	1·4	9·5	3·7	15·5	6·1
36	5 54·0	5 55·0	5 37·9	3·6	1·4	9·6	3·8	15·6	6·1
37	5 54·3	5 55·2	5 38·1	3·7	1·4	9·7	3·8	15·7	6·1
38	5 54·5	5 55·5	5 38·4	3·8	1·5	9·8	3·8	15·8	6·2
39	5 54·8	5 55·7	5 38·6	3·9	1·5	9·9	3·9	15·9	6·2
40	5 55·0	5 56·0	5 38·8	4·0	1·6	10·0	3·9	16·0	6·3
41	5 55·3	5 56·2	5 39·1	4·1	1·6	10·1	4·0	16·1	6·3
42	5 55·5	5 56·5	5 39·3	4·2	1·6	10·2	4·0	16·2	6·3
43	5 55·8	5 56·7	5 39·5	4·3	1·7	10·3	4·0	16·3	6·4
44	5 56·0	5 57·0	5 39·8	4·4	1·7	10·4	4·1	16·4	6·4
45	5 56·3	5 57·2	5 40·0	4·5	1·8	10·5	4·1	16·5	6·5
46	5 56·5	5 57·5	5 40·3	4·6	1·8	10·6	4·2	16·6	6·5
47	5 56·8	5 57·7	5 40·5	4·7	1·8	10·7	4·2	16·7	6·5
48	5 57·0	5 58·0	5 40·7	4·8	1·9	10·8	4·2	16·8	6·6
49	5 57·3	5 58·2	5 41·0	4·9	1·9	10·9	4·3	16·9	6·6
50	5 57·5	5 58·5	5 41·2	5·0	2·0	11·0	4·3	17·0	6·7
51	5 57·8	5 58·7	5 41·5	5·1	2·0	11·1	4·3	17·1	6·7
52	5 58·0	5 59·0	5 41·7	5·2	2·0	11·2	4·4	17·2	6·7
53	5 58·3	5 59·2	5 41·9	5·3	2·1	11·3	4·4	17·3	6·8
54	5 58·5	5 59·5	5 42·2	5·4	2·1	11·4	4·5	17·4	6·8
55	5 58·8	5 59·7	5 42·4	5·5	2·2	11·5	4·5	17·5	6·9
56	5 59·0	6 00·0	5 42·6	5·6	2·2	11·6	4·5	17·6	6·9
57	5 59·3	6 00·2	5 42·9	5·7	2·2	11·7	4·6	17·7	6·9
58	5 59·5	6 00·5	5 43·1	5·8	2·3	11·8	4·6	17·8	7·0
59	5 59·8	6 00·7	5 43·4	5·9	2·3	11·9	4·7	17·9	7·0
60	6 00·0	6 01·0	5 43·6	6·0	2·4	12·0	4·7	18·0	7·1

m 24 s	SUN PLANETS ° ′	ARIES ° ′	MOON ° ′	v or d ′	Corrⁿ ′	v or d ′	Corrⁿ ′	v or d ′	Corrⁿ ′
00	6 00·0	6 01·0	5 43·6	0·0	0·0	6·0	2·5	12·0	4·9
01	6 00·3	6 01·2	5 43·8	0·1	0·0	6·1	2·5	12·1	4·9
02	6 00·5	6 01·5	5 44·1	0·2	0·1	6·2	2·5	12·2	5·0
03	6 00·8	6 01·7	5 44·3	0·3	0·1	6·3	2·6	12·3	5·0
04	6 01·0	6 02·0	5 44·6	0·4	0·2	6·4	2·6	12·4	5·1
05	6 01·3	6 02·2	5 44·8	0·5	0·2	6·5	2·7	12·5	5·1
06	6 01·5	6 02·5	5 45·0	0·6	0·2	6·6	2·7	12·6	5·1
07	6 01·8	6 02·7	5 45·3	0·7	0·3	6·7	2·7	12·7	5·2
08	6 02·0	6 03·0	5 45·5	0·8	0·3	6·8	2·8	12·8	5·2
09	6 02·3	6 03·2	5 45·7	0·9	0·4	6·9	2·8	12·9	5·3
10	6 02·5	6 03·5	5 46·0	1·0	0·4	7·0	2·9	13·0	5·3
11	6 02·8	6 03·7	5 46·2	1·1	0·4	7·1	2·9	13·1	5·3
12	6 03·0	6 04·0	5 46·5	1·2	0·5	7·2	2·9	13·2	5·4
13	6 03·3	6 04·2	5 46·7	1·3	0·5	7·3	3·0	13·3	5·4
14	6 03·5	6 04·5	5 46·9	1·4	0·6	7·4	3·0	13·4	5·5
15	6 03·8	6 04·7	5 47·2	1·5	0·6	7·5	3·1	13·5	5·5
16	6 04·0	6 05·0	5 47·4	1·6	0·7	7·6	3·1	13·6	5·6
17	6 04·3	6 05·2	5 47·7	1·7	0·7	7·7	3·1	13·7	5·6
18	6 04·5	6 05·5	5 47·9	1·8	0·7	7·8	3·2	13·8	5·6
19	6 04·8	6 05·7	5 48·1	1·9	0·8	7·9	3·2	13·9	5·7
20	6 05·0	6 06·0	5 48·4	2·0	0·8	8·0	3·3	14·0	5·7
21	6 05·3	6 06·3	5 48·6	2·1	0·9	8·1	3·3	14·1	5·8
22	6 05·5	6 06·5	5 48·8	2·2	0·9	8·2	3·3	14·2	5·8
23	6 05·8	6 06·8	5 49·1	2·3	0·9	8·3	3·4	14·3	5·8
24	6 06·0	6 07·0	5 49·3	2·4	1·0	8·4	3·4	14·4	5·9
25	6 06·3	6 07·3	5 49·6	2·5	1·0	8·5	3·5	14·5	5·9
26	6 06·5	6 07·5	5 49·8	2·6	1·1	8·6	3·5	14·6	6·0
27	6 06·8	6 07·8	5 50·0	2·7	1·1	8·7	3·6	14·7	6·0
28	6 07·0	6 08·0	5 50·3	2·8	1·1	8·8	3·6	14·8	6·0
29	6 07·3	6 08·3	5 50·5	2·9	1·2	8·9	3·6	14·9	6·1
30	6 07·5	6 08·5	5 50·8	3·0	1·2	9·0	3·7	15·0	6·1
31	6 07·8	6 08·8	5 51·0	3·1	1·3	9·1	3·7	15·1	6·2
32	6 08·0	6 09·0	5 51·2	3·2	1·3	9·2	3·8	15·2	6·2
33	6 08·3	6 09·3	5 51·5	3·3	1·3	9·3	3·8	15·3	6·2
34	6 08·5	6 09·5	5 51·7	3·4	1·4	9·4	3·8	15·4	6·3
35	6 08·8	6 09·8	5 52·0	3·5	1·4	9·5	3·9	15·5	6·3
36	6 09·0	6 10·0	5 52·2	3·6	1·5	9·6	3·9	15·6	6·4
37	6 09·3	6 10·3	5 52·4	3·7	1·5	9·7	4·0	15·7	6·4
38	6 09·5	6 10·5	5 52·7	3·8	1·6	9·8	4·0	15·8	6·5
39	6 09·8	6 10·8	5 52·9	3·9	1·6	9·9	4·0	15·9	6·5
40	6 10·0	6 11·0	5 53·1	4·0	1·6	10·0	4·1	16·0	6·5
41	6 10·3	6 11·3	5 53·4	4·1	1·7	10·1	4·1	16·1	6·6
42	6 10·5	6 11·5	5 53·6	4·2	1·7	10·2	4·2	16·2	6·6
43	6 10·8	6 11·8	5 53·9	4·3	1·8	10·3	4·2	16·3	6·7
44	6 11·0	6 12·0	5 54·1	4·4	1·8	10·4	4·2	16·4	6·7
45	6 11·3	6 12·3	5 54·3	4·5	1·8	10·5	4·3	16·5	6·7
46	6 11·5	6 12·5	5 54·6	4·6	1·9	10·6	4·3	16·6	6·8
47	6 11·8	6 12·8	5 54·8	4·7	1·9	10·7	4·4	16·7	6·8
48	6 12·0	6 13·0	5 55·1	4·8	2·0	10·8	4·4	16·8	6·9
49	6 12·3	6 13·3	5 55·3	4·9	2·0	10·9	4·5	16·9	6·9
50	6 12·5	6 13·5	5 55·5	5·0	2·0	11·0	4·5	17·0	6·9
51	6 12·8	6 13·8	5 55·8	5·1	2·1	11·1	4·5	17·1	7·0
52	6 13·0	6 14·0	5 56·0	5·2	2·1	11·2	4·6	17·2	7·0
53	6 13·3	6 14·3	5 56·2	5·3	2·2	11·3	4·6	17·3	7·1
54	6 13·5	6 14·5	5 56·5	5·4	2·2	11·4	4·7	17·4	7·1
55	6 13·8	6 14·8	5 56·7	5·5	2·2	11·5	4·7	17·5	7·1
56	6 14·0	6 15·0	5 57·0	5·6	2·3	11·6	4·7	17·6	7·2
57	6 14·3	6 15·3	5 57·2	5·7	2·3	11·7	4·8	17·7	7·2
58	6 14·5	6 15·5	5 57·4	5·8	2·4	11·8	4·8	17·8	7·3
59	6 14·8	6 15·8	5 57·7	5·9	2·4	11·9	4·9	17·9	7·3
60	6 15·0	6 16·0	5 57·9	6·0	2·5	12·0	4·9	18·0	7·4

m 25 s	SUN PLANETS ° ′	ARIES ° ′	MOON ° ′	v or d ′	Corrⁿ ′	v or d ′	Corrⁿ ′	v or d ′	Corrⁿ ′
00	6 15·0	6 16·0	5 57·9	0·0	0·0	6·0	2·6	12·0	5·1
01	6 15·3	6 16·3	5 58·2	0·1	0·0	6·1	2·6	12·1	5·1
02	6 15·5	6 16·5	5 58·4	0·2	0·1	6·2	2·6	12·2	5·2
03	6 15·8	6 16·8	5 58·6	0·3	0·1	6·3	2·7	12·3	5·2
04	6 16·0	6 17·0	5 58·9	0·4	0·2	6·4	2·7	12·4	5·3
05	6 16·3	6 17·3	5 59·1	0·5	0·2	6·5	2·8	12·5	5·3
06	6 16·5	6 17·5	5 59·3	0·6	0·3	6·6	2·8	12·6	5·4
07	6 16·8	6 17·8	5 59·6	0·7	0·3	6·7	2·8	12·7	5·4
08	6 17·0	6 18·0	5 59·8	0·8	0·3	6·8	2·9	12·8	5·4
09	6 17·3	6 18·3	6 00·1	0·9	0·4	6·9	2·9	12·9	5·5
10	6 17·5	6 18·5	6 00·3	1·0	0·4	7·0	3·0	13·0	5·5
11	6 17·8	6 18·8	6 00·5	1·1	0·5	7·1	3·0	13·1	5·6
12	6 18·0	6 19·0	6 00·8	1·2	0·5	7·2	3·1	13·2	5·6
13	6 18·3	6 19·3	6 01·0	1·3	0·6	7·3	3·1	13·3	5·7
14	6 18·5	6 19·5	6 01·3	1·4	0·6	7·4	3·1	13·4	5·7
15	6 18·8	6 19·8	6 01·5	1·5	0·6	7·5	3·2	13·5	5·7
16	6 19·0	6 20·0	6 01·7	1·6	0·7	7·6	3·2	13·6	5·8
17	6 19·3	6 20·3	6 02·0	1·7	0·7	7·7	3·3	13·7	5·8
18	6 19·5	6 20·5	6 02·2	1·8	0·8	7·8	3·3	13·8	5·9
19	6 19·8	6 20·8	6 02·5	1·9	0·8	7·9	3·4	13·9	5·9
20	6 20·0	6 21·0	6 02·7	2·0	0·9	8·0	3·4	14·0	6·0
21	6 20·3	6 21·3	6 02·9	2·1	0·9	8·1	3·4	14·1	6·0
22	6 20·5	6 21·5	6 03·2	2·2	0·9	8·2	3·5	14·2	6·0
23	6 20·8	6 21·8	6 03·4	2·3	1·0	8·3	3·5	14·3	6·1
24	6 21·0	6 22·0	6 03·6	2·4	1·0	8·4	3·6	14·4	6·1
25	6 21·3	6 22·3	6 03·9	2·5	1·1	8·5	3·6	14·5	6·2
26	6 21·5	6 22·5	6 04·1	2·6	1·1	8·6	3·7	14·6	6·2
27	6 21·8	6 22·8	6 04·4	2·7	1·1	8·7	3·7	14·7	6·2
28	6 22·0	6 23·0	6 04·6	2·8	1·2	8·8	3·7	14·8	6·3
29	6 22·3	6 23·3	6 04·8	2·9	1·2	8·9	3·8	14·9	6·3
30	6 22·5	6 23·5	6 05·1	3·0	1·3	9·0	3·8	15·0	6·4
31	6 22·8	6 23·8	6 05·3	3·1	1·3	9·1	3·9	15·1	6·4
32	6 23·0	6 24·0	6 05·6	3·2	1·4	9·2	3·9	15·2	6·5
33	6 23·3	6 24·3	6 05·8	3·3	1·4	9·3	4·0	15·3	6·5
34	6 23·5	6 24·5	6 06·0	3·4	1·4	9·4	4·0	15·4	6·5
35	6 23·8	6 24·8	6 06·3	3·5	1·5	9·5	4·0	15·5	6·6
36	6 24·0	6 25·1	6 06·5	3·6	1·5	9·6	4·1	15·6	6·6
37	6 24·3	6 25·3	6 06·7	3·7	1·6	9·7	4·1	15·7	6·7
38	6 24·5	6 25·6	6 07·0	3·8	1·6	9·8	4·2	15·8	6·7
39	6 24·8	6 25·8	6 07·2	3·9	1·7	9·9	4·2	15·9	6·8
40	6 25·0	6 26·1	6 07·5	4·0	1·7	10·0	4·3	16·0	6·8
41	6 25·3	6 26·3	6 07·7	4·1	1·7	10·1	4·3	16·1	6·8
42	6 25·5	6 26·6	6 07·9	4·2	1·8	10·2	4·3	16·2	6·9
43	6 25·8	6 26·8	6 08·2	4·3	1·8	10·3	4·4	16·3	6·9
44	6 26·0	6 27·1	6 08·4	4·4	1·9	10·4	4·4	16·4	7·0
45	6 26·3	6 27·3	6 08·7	4·5	1·9	10·5	4·5	16·5	7·0
46	6 26·5	6 27·6	6 08·9	4·6	2·0	10·6	4·5	16·6	7·1
47	6 26·8	6 27·8	6 09·1	4·7	2·0	10·7	4·5	16·7	7·1
48	6 27·0	6 28·1	6 09·4	4·8	2·0	10·8	4·6	16·8	7·1
49	6 27·3	6 28·3	6 09·6	4·9	2·1	10·9	4·6	16·9	7·2
50	6 27·5	6 28·6	6 09·8	5·0	2·1	11·0	4·7	17·0	7·2
51	6 27·8	6 28·8	6 10·1	5·1	2·2	11·1	4·7	17·1	7·3
52	6 28·0	6 29·1	6 10·3	5·2	2·2	11·2	4·8	17·2	7·3
53	6 28·3	6 29·3	6 10·6	5·3	2·3	11·3	4·8	17·3	7·4
54	6 28·5	6 29·6	6 10·8	5·4	2·3	11·4	4·8	17·4	7·4
55	6 28·8	6 29·8	6 11·0	5·5	2·3	11·5	4·9	17·5	7·4
56	6 29·0	6 30·1	6 11·3	5·6	2·4	11·6	4·9	17·6	7·5
57	6 29·3	6 30·3	6 11·5	5·7	2·4	11·7	5·0	17·7	7·5
58	6 29·5	6 30·6	6 11·8	5·8	2·5	11·8	5·0	17·8	7·6
59	6 29·8	6 30·8	6 12·0	5·9	2·5	11·9	5·1	17·9	7·6
60	6 30·0	6 31·1	6 12·2	6·0	2·6	12·0	5·1	18·0	7·7

26m	SUN PLANETS	ARIES	MOON	v or d	Corrn	v or d	Corrn	v or d	Corrn
s	° ′	° ′	° ′	′	′	′	′	′	′
00	6 30·0	6 31·1	6 12·2	0·0	0·0	6·0	2·7	12·0	5·3
01	6 30·3	6 31·3	6 12·5	0·1	0·0	6·1	2·7	12·1	5·3
02	6 30·5	6 31·6	6 12·7	0·2	0·1	6·2	2·7	12·2	5·4
03	6 30·8	6 31·8	6 12·9	0·3	0·1	6·3	2·8	12·3	5·4
04	6 31·0	6 32·1	6 13·2	0·4	0·2	6·4	2·8	12·4	5·5
05	6 31·3	6 32·3	6 13·4	0·5	0·2	6·5	2·9	12·5	5·5
06	6 31·5	6 32·6	6 13·7	0·6	0·3	6·6	2·9	12·6	5·6
07	6 31·8	6 32·8	6 13·9	0·7	0·3	6·7	3·0	12·7	5·6
08	6 32·0	6 33·1	6 14·1	0·8	0·4	6·8	3·0	12·8	5·7
09	6 32·3	6 33·3	6 14·4	0·9	0·4	6·9	3·0	12·9	5·7
10	6 32·5	6 33·6	6 14·6	1·0	0·4	7·0	3·1	13·0	5·7
11	6 32·8	6 33·8	6 14·9	1·1	0·5	7·1	3·1	13·1	5·8
12	6 33·0	6 34·1	6 15·1	1·2	0·5	7·2	3·2	13·2	5·8
13	6 33·3	6 34·3	6 15·3	1·3	0·6	7·3	3·2	13·3	5·9
14	6 33·5	6 34·6	6 15·6	1·4	0·6	7·4	3·3	13·4	5·9
15	6 33·8	6 34·8	6 15·8	1·5	0·7	7·5	3·3	13·5	6·0
16	6 34·0	6 35·1	6 16·1	1·6	0·7	7·6	3·4	13·6	6·0
17	6 34·3	6 35·3	6 16·3	1·7	0·8	7·7	3·4	13·7	6·1
18	6 34·5	6 35·6	6 16·5	1·8	0·8	7·8	3·4	13·8	6·1
19	6 34·8	6 35·8	6 16·8	1·9	0·8	7·9	3·5	13·9	6·1
20	6 35·0	6 36·1	6 17·0	2·0	0·9	8·0	3·5	14·0	6·2
21	6 35·3	6 36·3	6 17·2	2·1	0·9	8·1	3·6	14·1	6·2
22	6 35·5	6 36·6	6 17·5	2·2	1·0	8·2	3·6	14·2	6·3
23	6 35·8	6 36·8	6 17·7	2·3	1·0	8·3	3·7	14·3	6·3
24	6 36·0	6 37·1	6 18·0	2·4	1·1	8·4	3·7	14·4	6·4
25	6 36·3	6 37·3	6 18·2	2·5	1·1	8·5	3·8	14·5	6·4
26	6 36·5	6 37·6	6 18·4	2·6	1·1	8·6	3·8	14·6	6·4
27	6 36·8	6 37·8	6 18·7	2·7	1·2	8·7	3·8	14·7	6·5
28	6 37·0	6 38·1	6 18·9	2·8	1·2	8·8	3·9	14·8	6·5
29	6 37·3	6 38·3	6 19·2	2·9	1·3	8·9	3·9	14·9	6·6
30	6 37·5	6 38·6	6 19·4	3·0	1·3	9·0	4·0	15·0	6·6
31	6 37·8	6 38·8	6 19·6	3·1	1·4	9·1	4·0	15·1	6·7
32	6 38·0	6 39·1	6 19·9	3·2	1·4	9·2	4·1	15·2	6·7
33	6 38·3	6 39·3	6 20·1	3·3	1·5	9·3	4·1	15·3	6·8
34	6 38·5	6 39·6	6 20·3	3·4	1·5	9·4	4·2	15·4	6·8
35	6 38·8	6 39·8	6 20·6	3·5	1·5	9·5	4·2	15·5	6·8
36	6 39·0	6 40·1	6 20·8	3·6	1·6	9·6	4·2	15·6	6·9
37	6 39·3	6 40·3	6 21·1	3·7	1·6	9·7	4·3	15·7	6·9
38	6 39·5	6 40·6	6 21·3	3·8	1·7	9·8	4·3	15·8	7·0
39	6 39·8	6 40·8	6 21·5	3·9	1·7	9·9	4·4	15·9	7·0
40	6 40·0	6 41·1	6 21·8	4·0	1·8	10·0	4·4	16·0	7·1
41	6 40·3	6 41·3	6 22·0	4·1	1·8	10·1	4·5	16·1	7·1
42	6 40·5	6 41·6	6 22·3	4·2	1·9	10·2	4·5	16·2	7·2
43	6 40·8	6 41·8	6 22·5	4·3	1·9	10·3	4·5	16·3	7·2
44	6 41·0	6 42·1	6 22·7	4·4	1·9	10·4	4·6	16·4	7·2
45	6 41·3	6 42·3	6 23·0	4·5	2·0	10·5	4·6	16·5	7·3
46	6 41·5	6 42·6	6 23·2	4·6	2·0	10·6	4·7	16·6	7·3
47	6 41·8	6 42·8	6 23·4	4·7	2·1	10·7	4·7	16·7	7·4
48	6 42·0	6 43·1	6 23·7	4·8	2·1	10·8	4·8	16·8	7·4
49	6 42·3	6 43·4	6 23·9	4·9	2·2	10·9	4·8	16·9	7·5
50	6 42·5	6 43·6	6 24·2	5·0	2·2	11·0	4·9	17·0	7·5
51	6 42·8	6 43·9	6 24·4	5·1	2·3	11·1	4·9	17·1	7·6
52	6 43·0	6 44·1	6 24·6	5·2	2·3	11·2	4·9	17·2	7·6
53	6 43·3	6 44·4	6 24·9	5·3	2·3	11·3	5·0	17·3	7·6
54	6 43·5	6 44·6	6 25·1	5·4	2·4	11·4	5·0	17·4	7·7
55	6 43·8	6 44·9	6 25·4	5·5	2·4	11·5	5·1	17·5	7·7
56	6 44·0	6 45·1	6 25·6	5·6	2·5	11·6	5·1	17·6	7·8
57	6 44·3	6 45·4	6 25·8	5·7	2·5	11·7	5·2	17·7	7·8
58	6 44·5	6 45·6	6 26·1	5·8	2·6	11·8	5·2	17·8	7·9
59	6 44·8	6 45·9	6 26·3	5·9	2·6	11·9	5·3	17·9	7·9
60	6 45·0	6 46·1	6 26·6	6·0	2·7	12·0	5·3	18·0	8·0

27m	SUN PLANETS	ARIES	MOON	v or d	Corrn	v or d	Corrn	v or d	Corrn
s	° ′	° ′	° ′	′	′	′	′	′	′
00	6 45·0	6 46·1	6 26·6	0·0	0·0	6·0	2·8	12·0	5·5
01	6 45·3	6 46·4	6 26·8	0·1	0·0	6·1	2·8	12·1	5·5
02	6 45·5	6 46·6	6 27·0	0·2	0·1	6·2	2·8	12·2	5·6
03	6 45·8	6 46·9	6 27·3	0·3	0·1	6·3	2·9	12·3	5·6
04	6 46·0	6 47·1	6 27·5	0·4	0·2	6·4	2·9	12·4	5·7
05	6 46·3	6 47·4	6 27·7	0·5	0·2	6·5	3·0	12·5	5·7
06	6 46·5	6 47·6	6 28·0	0·6	0·3	6·6	3·0	12·6	5·8
07	6 46·8	6 47·9	6 28·2	0·7	0·3	6·7	3·1	12·7	5·8
08	6 47·0	6 48·1	6 28·5	0·8	0·4	6·8	3·1	12·8	5·9
09	6 47·3	6 48·4	6 28·7	0·9	0·4	6·9	3·2	12·9	5·9
10	6 47·5	6 48·6	6 28·9	1·0	0·5	7·0	3·2	13·0	6·0
11	6 47·8	6 48·9	6 29·2	1·1	0·5	7·1	3·3	13·1	6·0
12	6 48·0	6 49·1	6 29·4	1·2	0·6	7·2	3·3	13·2	6·1
13	6 48·3	6 49·4	6 29·7	1·3	0·6	7·3	3·3	13·3	6·1
14	6 48·5	6 49·6	6 29·9	1·4	0·6	7·4	3·4	13·4	6·1
15	6 48·8	6 49·9	6 30·1	1·5	0·7	7·5	3·4	13·5	6·2
16	6 49·0	6 50·1	6 30·4	1·6	0·7	7·6	3·5	13·6	6·2
17	6 49·3	6 50·4	6 30·6	1·7	0·8	7·7	3·5	13·7	6·3
18	6 49·5	6 50·6	6 30·8	1·8	0·8	7·8	3·6	13·8	6·3
19	6 49·8	6 50·9	6 31·1	1·9	0·9	7·9	3·6	13·9	6·4
20	6 50·0	6 51·1	6 31·3	2·0	0·9	8·0	3·7	14·0	6·4
21	6 50·3	6 51·4	6 31·6	2·1	1·0	8·1	3·7	14·1	6·5
22	6 50·5	6 51·6	6 31·8	2·2	1·0	8·2	3·8	14·2	6·5
23	6 50·8	6 51·9	6 32·0	2·3	1·1	8·3	3·8	14·3	6·6
24	6 51·0	6 52·1	6 32·3	2·4	1·1	8·4	3·9	14·4	6·6
25	6 51·3	6 52·4	6 32·5	2·5	1·1	8·5	3·9	14·5	6·6
26	6 51·5	6 52·6	6 32·8	2·6	1·2	8·6	3·9	14·6	6·7
27	6 51·8	6 52·9	6 33·0	2·7	1·2	8·7	4·0	14·7	6·7
28	6 52·0	6 53·1	6 33·2	2·8	1·3	8·8	4·0	14·8	6·8
29	6 52·3	6 53·4	6 33·5	2·9	1·3	8·9	4·1	14·9	6·8
30	6 52·5	6 53·6	6 33·7	3·0	1·4	9·0	4·1	15·0	6·9
31	6 52·8	6 53·9	6 33·9	3·1	1·4	9·1	4·2	15·1	6·9
32	6 53·0	6 54·1	6 34·2	3·2	1·5	9·2	4·2	15·2	7·0
33	6 53·3	6 54·4	6 34·4	3·3	1·5	9·3	4·3	15·3	7·0
34	6 53·5	6 54·6	6 34·7	3·4	1·6	9·4	4·3	15·4	7·1
35	6 53·8	6 54·9	6 34·9	3·5	1·6	9·5	4·4	15·5	7·1
36	6 54·0	6 55·1	6 35·1	3·6	1·7	9·6	4·4	15·6	7·2
37	6 54·3	6 55·4	6 35·4	3·7	1·7	9·7	4·4	15·7	7·2
38	6 54·5	6 55·6	6 35·6	3·8	1·7	9·8	4·5	15·8	7·2
39	6 54·8	6 55·9	6 35·9	3·9	1·8	9·9	4·5	15·9	7·3
40	6 55·0	6 56·1	6 36·1	4·0	1·8	10·0	4·6	16·0	7·3
41	6 55·3	6 56·4	6 36·3	4·1	1·9	10·1	4·6	16·1	7·4
42	6 55·5	6 56·6	6 36·6	4·2	1·9	10·2	4·7	16·2	7·4
43	6 55·8	6 56·9	6 36·8	4·3	2·0	10·3	4·7	16·3	7·5
44	6 56·0	6 57·1	6 37·0	4·4	2·0	10·4	4·8	16·4	7·5
45	6 56·3	6 57·4	6 37·3	4·5	2·1	10·5	4·8	16·5	7·6
46	6 56·5	6 57·6	6 37·5	4·6	2·1	10·6	4·9	16·6	7·6
47	6 56·8	6 57·9	6 37·8	4·7	2·2	10·7	4·9	16·7	7·7
48	6 57·0	6 58·1	6 38·0	4·8	2·2	10·8	5·0	16·8	7·7
49	6 57·3	6 58·4	6 38·2	4·9	2·2	10·9	5·0	16·9	7·7
50	6 57·5	6 58·6	6 38·5	5·0	2·3	11·0	5·0	17·0	7·8
51	6 57·8	6 58·9	6 38·7	5·1	2·3	11·1	5·1	17·1	7·8
52	6 58·0	6 59·1	6 39·0	5·2	2·4	11·2	5·1	17·2	7·9
53	6 58·3	6 59·4	6 39·2	5·3	2·4	11·3	5·2	17·3	7·9
54	6 58·5	6 59·6	6 39·4	5·4	2·5	11·4	5·2	17·4	8·0
55	6 58·8	6 59·9	6 39·7	5·5	2·5	11·5	5·3	17·5	8·0
56	6 59·0	7 00·1	6 39·9	5·6	2·6	11·6	5·3	17·6	8·1
57	6 59·3	7 00·4	6 40·2	5·7	2·6	11·7	5·4	17·7	8·1
58	6 59·5	7 00·6	6 40·4	5·8	2·7	11·8	5·4	17·8	8·2
59	6 59·8	7 00·9	6 40·6	5·9	2·7	11·9	5·5	17·9	8·2
60	7 00·0	7 01·1	6 40·9	6·0	2·8	12·0	5·5	18·0	8·3

28m s	SUN PLANETS ° ′	ARIES ° ′	MOON ° ′	v or d ′	Corrn ′	v or d ′	Corrn ′	v or d ′	Corrn ′
00	7 00·0	7 01·1	6 40·9	0·0	0·0	6·0	2·9	12·0	5·7
01	7 00·3	7 01·4	6 41·1	0·1	0·0	6·1	2·9	12·1	5·7
02	7 00·5	7 01·7	6 41·3	0·2	0·1	6·2	2·9	12·2	5·8
03	7 00·8	7 01·9	6 41·6	0·3	0·1	6·3	3·0	12·3	5·8
04	7 01·0	7 02·2	6 41·8	0·4	0·2	6·4	3·0	12·4	5·9
05	7 01·3	7 02·4	6 42·1	0·5	0·2	6·5	3·1	12·5	5·9
06	7 01·5	7 02·7	6 42·3	0·6	0·3	6·6	3·1	12·6	6·0
07	7 01·8	7 02·9	6 42·5	0·7	0·3	6·7	3·2	12·7	6·0
08	7 02·0	7 03·2	6 42·8	0·8	0·4	6·8	3·2	12·8	6·1
09	7 02·3	7 03·4	6 43·0	0·9	0·4	6·9	3·3	12·9	6·1
10	7 02·5	7 03·7	6 43·3	1·0	0·5	7·0	3·3	13·0	6·2
11	7 02·8	7 03·9	6 43·5	1·1	0·5	7·1	3·4	13·1	6·2
12	7 03·0	7 04·2	6 43·7	1·2	0·6	7·2	3·4	13·2	6·3
13	7 03·3	7 04·4	6 44·0	1·3	0·6	7·3	3·5	13·3	6·3
14	7 03·5	7 04·7	6 44·2	1·4	0·7	7·4	3·5	13·4	6·4
15	7 03·8	7 04·9	6 44·4	1·5	0·7	7·5	3·6	13·5	6·4
16	7 04·0	7 05·2	6 44·7	1·6	0·8	7·6	3·6	13·6	6·5
17	7 04·3	7 05·4	6 44·9	1·7	0·8	7·7	3·7	13·7	6·5
18	7 04·5	7 05·7	6 45·2	1·8	0·9	7·8	3·7	13·8	6·6
19	7 04·8	7 05·9	6 45·4	1·9	0·9	7·9	3·8	13·9	6·6
20	7 05·0	7 06·2	6 45·6	2·0	1·0	8·0	3·8	14·0	6·7
21	7 05·3	7 06·4	6 45·9	2·1	1·0	8·1	3·8	14·1	6·7
22	7 05·5	7 06·7	6 46·1	2·2	1·0	8·2	3·9	14·2	6·7
23	7 05·8	7 06·9	6 46·4	2·3	1·1	8·3	3·9	14·3	6·8
24	7 06·0	7 07·2	6 46·6	2·4	1·1	8·4	4·0	14·4	6·8
25	7 06·3	7 07·4	6 46·8	2·5	1·2	8·5	4·0	14·5	6·9
26	7 06·5	7 07·7	6 47·1	2·6	1·2	8·6	4·1	14·6	6·9
27	7 06·8	7 07·9	6 47·3	2·7	1·3	8·7	4·1	14·7	7·0
28	7 07·0	7 08·2	6 47·5	2·8	1·3	8·8	4·2	14·8	7·0
29	7 07·3	7 08·4	6 47·8	2·9	1·4	8·9	4·2	14·9	7·1
30	7 07·5	7 08·7	6 48·0	3·0	1·4	9·0	4·3	15·0	7·1
31	7 07·8	7 08·9	6 48·3	3·1	1·5	9·1	4·3	15·1	7·2
32	7 08·0	7 09·2	6 48·5	3·2	1·5	9·2	4·4	15·2	7·2
33	7 08·3	7 09·4	6 48·7	3·3	1·6	9·3	4·4	15·3	7·3
34	7 08·5	7 09·7	6 49·0	3·4	1·6	9·4	4·5	15·4	7·3
35	7 08·8	7 09·9	6 49·2	3·5	1·7	9·5	4·5	15·5	7·4
36	7 09·0	7 10·2	6 49·5	3·6	1·7	9·6	4·6	15·6	7·4
37	7 09·3	7 10·4	6 49·7	3·7	1·8	9·7	4·6	15·7	7·5
38	7 09·5	7 10·7	6 49·9	3·8	1·8	9·8	4·7	15·8	7·5
39	7 09·8	7 10·9	6 50·2	3·9	1·9	9·9	4·7	15·9	7·6
40	7 10·0	7 11·2	6 50·4	4·0	1·9	10·0	4·8	16·0	7·6
41	7 10·3	7 11·4	6 50·6	4·1	1·9	10·1	4·8	16·1	7·6
42	7 10·5	7 11·7	6 50·9	4·2	2·0	10·2	4·8	16·2	7·7
43	7 10·8	7 11·9	6 51·1	4·3	2·0	10·3	4·9	16·3	7·7
44	7 11·0	7 12·2	6 51·4	4·4	2·1	10·4	4·9	16·4	7·8
45	7 11·3	7 12·4	6 51·6	4·5	2·1	10·5	5·0	16·5	7·8
46	7 11·5	7 12·7	6 51·8	4·6	2·2	10·6	5·0	16·6	7·9
47	7 11·8	7 12·9	6 52·1	4·7	2·2	10·7	5·1	16·7	7·9
48	7 12·0	7 13·2	6 52·3	4·8	2·3	10·8	5·1	16·8	8·0
49	7 12·3	7 13·4	6 52·6	4·9	2·3	10·9	5·2	16·9	8·0
50	7 12·5	7 13·7	6 52·8	5·0	2·4	11·0	5·2	17·0	8·1
51	7 12·8	7 13·9	6 53·0	5·1	2·4	11·1	5·3	17·1	8·1
52	7 13·0	7 14·2	6 53·3	5·2	2·5	11·2	5·3	17·2	8·2
53	7 13·3	7 14·4	6 53·5	5·3	2·5	11·3	5·4	17·3	8·2
54	7 13·5	7 14·7	6 53·8	5·4	2·6	11·4	5·4	17·4	8·3
55	7 13·8	7 14·9	6 54·0	5·5	2·6	11·5	5·5	17·5	8·3
56	7 14·0	7 15·2	6 54·2	5·6	2·7	11·6	5·5	17·6	8·4
57	7 14·3	7 15·4	6 54·5	5·7	2·7	11·7	5·6	17·7	8·4
58	7 14·5	7 15·7	6 54·7	5·8	2·8	11·8	5·6	17·8	8·5
59	7 14·8	7 15·9	6 54·9	5·9	2·8	11·9	5·7	17·9	8·5
60	7 15·0	7 16·2	6 55·2	6·0	2·9	12·0	5·7	18·0	8·6

29m s	SUN PLANETS ° ′	ARIES ° ′	MOON ° ′	v or d ′	Corrn ′	v or d ′	Corrn ′	v or d ′	Corrn ′
00	7 15·0	7 16·2	6 55·2	0·0	0·0	6·0	3·0	12·0	5·9
01	7 15·3	7 16·4	6 55·4	0·1	0·0	6·1	3·0	12·1	5·9
02	7 15·5	7 16·7	6 55·7	0·2	0·1	6·2	3·0	12·2	6·0
03	7 15·8	7 16·9	6 55·9	0·3	0·1	6·3	3·1	12·3	6·0
04	7 16·0	7 17·2	6 56·1	0·4	0·2	6·4	3·1	12·4	6·1
05	7 16·3	7 17·4	6 56·4	0·5	0·2	6·5	3·2	12·5	6·1
06	7 16·5	7 17·7	6 56·6	0·6	0·3	6·6	3·2	12·6	6·2
07	7 16·8	7 17·9	6 56·9	0·7	0·3	6·7	3·3	12·7	6·2
08	7 17·0	7 18·2	6 57·1	0·8	0·4	6·8	3·3	12·8	6·3
09	7 17·3	7 18·4	6 57·3	0·9	0·4	6·9	3·4	12·9	6·3
10	7 17·5	7 18·7	6 57·6	1·0	0·5	7·0	3·4	13·0	6·4
11	7 17·8	7 18·9	6 57·8	1·1	0·5	7·1	3·5	13·1	6·4
12	7 18·0	7 19·2	6 58·0	1·2	0·6	7·2	3·5	13·2	6·5
13	7 18·3	7 19·4	6 58·3	1·3	0·6	7·3	3·6	13·3	6·5
14	7 18·5	7 19·7	6 58·5	1·4	0·7	7·4	3·6	13·4	6·6
15	7 18·8	7 20·0	6 58·8	1·5	0·7	7·5	3·7	13·5	6·6
16	7 19·0	7 20·2	6 59·0	1·6	0·8	7·6	3·7	13·6	6·7
17	7 19·3	7 20·5	6 59·2	1·7	0·8	7·7	3·8	13·7	6·7
18	7 19·5	7 20·7	6 59·5	1·8	0·9	7·8	3·8	13·8	6·8
19	7 19·8	7 21·0	6 59·7	1·9	0·9	7·9	3·9	13·9	6·8
20	7 20·0	7 21·2	7 00·0	2·0	1·0	8·0	3·9	14·0	6·9
21	7 20·3	7 21·5	7 00·2	2·1	1·0	8·1	4·0	14·1	6·9
22	7 20·5	7 21·7	7 00·4	2·2	1·1	8·2	4·0	14·2	7·0
23	7 20·8	7 22·0	7 00·7	2·3	1·1	8·3	4·1	14·3	7·0
24	7 21·0	7 22·2	7 00·9	2·4	1·2	8·4	4·1	14·4	7·1
25	7 21·3	7 22·5	7 01·1	2·5	1·2	8·5	4·2	14·5	7·1
26	7 21·5	7 22·7	7 01·4	2·6	1·3	8·6	4·2	14·6	7·2
27	7 21·8	7 23·0	7 01·6	2·7	1·3	8·7	4·3	14·7	7·2
28	7 22·0	7 23·2	7 01·9	2·8	1·4	8·8	4·3	14·8	7·3
29	7 22·3	7 23·5	7 02·1	2·9	1·4	8·9	4·4	14·9	7·3
30	7 22·5	7 23·7	7 02·3	3·0	1·5	9·0	4·4	15·0	7·4
31	7 22·8	7 24·0	7 02·6	3·1	1·5	9·1	4·5	15·1	7·4
32	7 23·0	7 24·2	7 02·8	3·2	1·6	9·2	4·5	15·2	7·5
33	7 23·3	7 24·5	7 03·1	3·3	1·6	9·3	4·6	15·3	7·5
34	7 23·5	7 24·7	7 03·3	3·4	1·7	9·4	4·6	15·4	7·6
35	7 23·8	7 25·0	7 03·5	3·5	1·7	9·5	4·7	15·5	7·6
36	7 24·0	7 25·2	7 03·8	3·6	1·8	9·6	4·7	15·6	7·7
37	7 24·3	7 25·5	7 04·0	3·7	1·8	9·7	4·8	15·7	7·7
38	7 24·5	7 25·7	7 04·3	3·8	1·9	9·8	4·8	15·8	7·8
39	7 24·8	7 26·0	7 04·5	3·9	1·9	9·9	4·9	15·9	7·8
40	7 25·0	7 26·2	7 04·7	4·0	2·0	10·0	4·9	16·0	7·9
41	7 25·3	7 26·5	7 05·0	4·1	2·0	10·1	5·0	16·1	7·9
42	7 25·5	7 26·7	7 05·2	4·2	2·1	10·2	5·0	16·2	8·0
43	7 25·8	7 27·0	7 05·4	4·3	2·1	10·3	5·1	16·3	8·0
44	7 26·0	7 27·2	7 05·7	4·4	2·2	10·4	5·1	16·4	8·1
45	7 26·3	7 27·5	7 05·9	4·5	2·2	10·5	5·2	16·5	8·1
46	7 26·5	7 27·7	7 06·2	4·6	2·3	10·6	5·2	16·6	8·2
47	7 26·8	7 28·0	7 06·4	4·7	2·3	10·7	5·3	16·7	8·2
48	7 27·0	7 28·2	7 06·6	4·8	2·4	10·8	5·3	16·8	8·3
49	7 27·3	7 28·5	7 06·9	4·9	2·4	10·9	5·4	16·9	8·3
50	7 27·5	7 28·7	7 07·1	5·0	2·5	11·0	5·4	17·0	8·4
51	7 27·8	7 29·0	7 07·4	5·1	2·5	11·1	5·5	17·1	8·4
52	7 28·0	7 29·2	7 07·6	5·2	2·6	11·2	5·5	17·2	8·5
53	7 28·3	7 29·5	7 07·8	5·3	2·6	11·3	5·6	17·3	8·5
54	7 28·5	7 29·7	7 08·1	5·4	2·7	11·4	5·6	17·4	8·6
55	7 28·8	7 30·0	7 08·3	5·5	2·7	11·5	5·7	17·5	8·6
56	7 29·0	7 30·2	7 08·5	5·6	2·8	11·6	5·7	17·6	8·7
57	7 29·3	7 30·5	7 08·8	5·7	2·8	11·7	5·8	17·7	8·7
58	7 29·5	7 30·7	7 09·0	5·8	2·9	11·8	5·8	17·8	8·8
59	7 29·8	7 31·0	7 09·3	5·9	2·9	11·9	5·9	17·9	8·8
60	7 30·0	7 31·2	7 09·5	6·0	3·0	12·0	5·9	18·0	8·9

30ᵐ	SUN PLANETS	ARIES	MOON	v or d	Corrⁿ	v or d	Corrⁿ	v or d	Corrⁿ
s	° ′	° ′	° ′	′	′	′	′	′	′
00	7 30·0	7 31·2	7 09·5	0·0	0·0	6·0	3·1	12·0	6·1
01	7 30·3	7 31·5	7 09·7	0·1	0·1	6·1	3·1	12·1	6·2
02	7 30·5	7 31·7	7 10·0	0·2	0·1	6·2	3·2	12·2	6·2
03	7 30·8	7 32·0	7 10·2	0·3	0·2	6·3	3·2	12·3	6·3
04	7 31·0	7 32·2	7 10·5	0·4	0·2	6·4	3·3	12·4	6·3
05	7 31·3	7 32·5	7 10·7	0·5	0·3	6·5	3·3	12·5	6·4
06	7 31·5	7 32·7	7 10·9	0·6	0·3	6·6	3·4	12·6	6·4
07	7 31·8	7 33·0	7 11·2	0·7	0·4	6·7	3·4	12·7	6·5
08	7 32·0	7 33·2	7 11·4	0·8	0·4	6·8	3·5	12·8	6·5
09	7 32·3	7 33·5	7 11·6	0·9	0·5	6·9	3·5	12·9	6·6
10	7 32·5	7 33·7	7 11·9	1·0	0·5	7·0	3·6	13·0	6·6
11	7 32·8	7 34·0	7 12·1	1·1	0·6	7·1	3·6	13·1	6·7
12	7 33·0	7 34·2	7 12·4	1·2	0·6	7·2	3·7	13·2	6·7
13	7 33·3	7 34·5	7 12·6	1·3	0·7	7·3	3·7	13·3	6·8
14	7 33·5	7 34·7	7 12·8	1·4	0·7	7·4	3·8	13·4	6·8
15	7 33·8	7 35·0	7 13·1	1·5	0·8	7·5	3·8	13·5	6·9
16	7 34·0	7 35·2	7 13·3	1·6	0·8	7·6	3·9	13·6	6·9
17	7 34·3	7 35·5	7 13·6	1·7	0·9	7·7	3·9	13·7	7·0
18	7 34·5	7 35·7	7 13·8	1·8	0·9	7·8	4·0	13·8	7·0
19	7 34·8	7 36·0	7 14·0	1·9	1·0	7·9	4·0	13·9	7·1
20	7 35·0	7 36·2	7 14·3	2·0	1·0	8·0	4·1	14·0	7·1
21	7 35·3	7 36·5	7 14·5	2·1	1·1	8·1	4·1	14·1	7·2
22	7 35·5	7 36·7	7 14·7	2·2	1·1	8·2	4·2	14·2	7·2
23	7 35·8	7 37·0	7 15·0	2·3	1·2	8·3	4·2	14·3	7·3
24	7 36·0	7 37·2	7 15·2	2·4	1·2	8·4	4·3	14·4	7·3
25	7 36·3	7 37·5	7 15·5	2·5	1·3	8·5	4·3	14·5	7·4
26	7 36·5	7 37·7	7 15·7	2·6	1·3	8·6	4·4	14·6	7·4
27	7 36·8	7 38·0	7 15·9	2·7	1·4	8·7	4·4	14·7	7·5
28	7 37·0	7 38·3	7 16·2	2·8	1·4	8·8	4·5	14·8	7·5
29	7 37·3	7 38·5	7 16·4	2·9	1·5	8·9	4·5	14·9	7·6
30	7 37·5	7 38·8	7 16·7	3·0	1·5	9·0	4·6	15·0	7·6
31	7 37·8	7 39·0	7 16·9	3·1	1·6	9·1	4·6	15·1	7·7
32	7 38·0	7 39·3	7 17·1	3·2	1·6	9·2	4·7	15·2	7·7
33	7 38·3	7 39·5	7 17·4	3·3	1·7	9·3	4·7	15·3	7·8
34	7 38·5	7 39·8	7 17·6	3·4	1·7	9·4	4·8	15·4	7·8
35	7 38·8	7 40·0	7 17·9	3·5	1·8	9·5	4·8	15·5	7·9
36	7 39·0	7 40·3	7 18·1	3·6	1·8	9·6	4·9	15·6	7·9
37	7 39·3	7 40·5	7 18·3	3·7	1·9	9·7	4·9	15·7	8·0
38	7 39·5	7 40·8	7 18·6	3·8	1·9	9·8	5·0	15·8	8·0
39	7 39·8	7 41·0	7 18·8	3·9	2·0	9·9	5·0	15·9	8·1
40	7 40·0	7 41·3	7 19·0	4·0	2·0	10·0	5·1	16·0	8·1
41	7 40·3	7 41·5	7 19·3	4·1	2·1	10·1	5·1	16·1	8·2
42	7 40·5	7 41·8	7 19·5	4·2	2·1	10·2	5·2	16·2	8·2
43	7 40·8	7 42·0	7 19·8	4·3	2·2	10·3	5·2	16·3	8·3
44	7 41·0	7 42·3	7 20·0	4·4	2·2	10·4	5·3	16·4	8·3
45	7 41·3	7 42·5	7 20·2	4·5	2·3	10·5	5·3	16·5	8·4
46	7 41·5	7 42·8	7 20·5	4·6	2·3	10·6	5·4	16·6	8·4
47	7 41·8	7 43·0	7 20·7	4·7	2·4	10·7	5·4	16·7	8·5
48	7 42·0	7 43·3	7 21·0	4·8	2·4	10·8	5·5	16·8	8·5
49	7 42·3	7 43·5	7 21·2	4·9	2·5	10·9	5·5	16·9	8·6
50	7 42·5	7 43·8	7 21·4	5·0	2·5	11·0	5·6	17·0	8·6
51	7 42·8	7 44·0	7 21·7	5·1	2·6	11·1	5·6	17·1	8·7
52	7 43·0	7 44·3	7 21·9	5·2	2·6	11·2	5·7	17·2	8·7
53	7 43·3	7 44·5	7 22·1	5·3	2·7	11·3	5·7	17·3	8·8
54	7 43·5	7 44·8	7 22·4	5·4	2·7	11·4	5·8	17·4	8·8
55	7 43·8	7 45·0	7 22·6	5·5	2·8	11·5	5·8	17·5	8·9
56	7 44·0	7 45·3	7 22·9	5·6	2·8	11·6	5·9	17·6	8·9
57	7 44·3	7 45·5	7 23·1	5·7	2·9	11·7	5·9	17·7	9·0
58	7 44·5	7 45·8	7 23·3	5·8	2·9	11·8	6·0	17·8	9·0
59	7 44·8	7 46·0	7 23·6	5·9	3·0	11·9	6·0	17·9	9·1
60	7 45·0	7 46·3	7 23·8	6·0	3·1	12·0	6·1	18·0	9·2

31ᵐ	SUN PLANETS	ARIES	MOON	v or d	Corrⁿ	v or d	Corrⁿ	v or d	Corrⁿ
s	° ′	° ′	° ′	′	′	′	′	′	′
00	7 45·0	7 46·3	7 23·8	0·0	0·0	6·0	3·2	12·0	6·3
01	7 45·3	7 46·5	7 24·1	0·1	0·1	6·1	3·2	12·1	6·4
02	7 45·5	7 46·8	7 24·3	0·2	0·1	6·2	3·3	12·2	6·4
03	7 45·8	7 47·0	7 24·5	0·3	0·2	6·3	3·3	12·3	6·5
04	7 46·0	7 47·3	7 24·8	0·4	0·2	6·4	3·4	12·4	6·5
05	7 46·3	7 47·5	7 25·0	0·5	0·3	6·5	3·4	12·5	6·6
06	7 46·5	7 47·8	7 25·2	0·6	0·3	6·6	3·5	12·6	6·6
07	7 46·8	7 48·0	7 25·5	0·7	0·4	6·7	3·5	12·7	6·7
08	7 47·0	7 48·3	7 25·7	0·8	0·4	6·8	3·6	12·8	6·7
09	7 47·3	7 48·5	7 26·0	0·9	0·5	6·9	3·6	12·9	6·8
10	7 47·5	7 48·8	7 26·2	1·0	0·5	7·0	3·7	13·0	6·8
11	7 47·8	7 49·0	7 26·4	1·1	0·6	7·1	3·7	13·1	6·9
12	7 48·0	7 49·3	7 26·7	1·2	0·6	7·2	3·8	13·2	6·9
13	7 48·3	7 49·5	7 26·9	1·3	0·7	7·3	3·8	13·3	7·0
14	7 48·5	7 49·8	7 27·2	1·4	0·7	7·4	3·9	13·4	7·0
15	7 48·8	7 50·0	7 27·4	1·5	0·8	7·5	3·9	13·5	7·1
16	7 49·0	7 50·3	7 27·6	1·6	0·8	7·6	4·0	13·6	7·1
17	7 49·3	7 50·5	7 27·9	1·7	0·9	7·7	4·0	13·7	7·2
18	7 49·5	7 50·8	7 28·1	1·8	0·9	7·8	4·1	13·8	7·2
19	7 49·8	7 51·0	7 28·4	1·9	1·0	7·9	4·1	13·9	7·3
20	7 50·0	7 51·3	7 28·6	2·0	1·1	8·0	4·2	14·0	7·4
21	7 50·3	7 51·5	7 28·8	2·1	1·1	8·1	4·3	14·1	7·4
22	7 50·5	7 51·8	7 29·1	2·2	1·2	8·2	4·3	14·2	7·5
23	7 50·8	7 52·0	7 29·3	2·3	1·2	8·3	4·4	14·3	7·5
24	7 51·0	7 52·3	7 29·5	2·4	1·3	8·4	4·4	14·4	7·6
25	7 51·3	7 52·5	7 29·8	2·5	1·3	8·5	4·5	14·5	7·6
26	7 51·5	7 52·8	7 30·0	2·6	1·4	8·6	4·5	14·6	7·7
27	7 51·8	7 53·0	7 30·3	2·7	1·4	8·7	4·6	14·7	7·7
28	7 52·0	7 53·3	7 30·5	2·8	1·5	8·8	4·6	14·8	7·8
29	7 52·3	7 53·5	7 30·7	2·9	1·5	8·9	4·7	14·9	7·8
30	7 52·5	7 53·8	7 31·0	3·0	1·6	9·0	4·7	15·0	7·9
31	7 52·8	7 54·0	7 31·2	3·1	1·6	9·1	4·8	15·1	7·9
32	7 53·0	7 54·3	7 31·5	3·2	1·7	9·2	4·8	15·2	8·0
33	7 53·3	7 54·5	7 31·7	3·3	1·7	9·3	4·9	15·3	8·0
34	7 53·5	7 54·8	7 31·9	3·4	1·8	9·4	4·9	15·4	8·1
35	7 53·8	7 55·0	7 32·2	3·5	1·8	9·5	5·0	15·5	8·1
36	7 54·0	7 55·3	7 32·4	3·6	1·9	9·6	5·0	15·6	8·2
37	7 54·3	7 55·5	7 32·6	3·7	1·9	9·7	5·1	15·7	8·2
38	7 54·5	7 55·8	7 32·9	3·8	2·0	9·8	5·1	15·8	8·3
39	7 54·8	7 56·0	7 33·1	3·9	2·0	9·9	5·2	15·9	8·3
40	7 55·0	7 56·3	7 33·4	4·0	2·1	10·0	5·3	16·0	8·4
41	7 55·3	7 56·6	7 33·6	4·1	2·2	10·1	5·3	16·1	8·5
42	7 55·5	7 56·8	7 33·8	4·2	2·2	10·2	5·4	16·2	8·5
43	7 55·8	7 57·1	7 34·1	4·3	2·3	10·3	5·4	16·3	8·6
44	7 56·0	7 57·3	7 34·3	4·4	2·3	10·4	5·5	16·4	8·6
45	7 56·3	7 57·6	7 34·6	4·5	2·4	10·5	5·5	16·5	8·7
46	7 56·5	7 57·8	7 34·8	4·6	2·4	10·6	5·6	16·6	8·7
47	7 56·8	7 58·1	7 35·0	4·7	2·5	10·7	5·6	16·7	8·8
48	7 57·0	7 58·3	7 35·3	4·8	2·5	10·8	5·7	16·8	8·8
49	7 57·3	7 58·6	7 35·5	4·9	2·6	10·9	5·7	16·9	8·9
50	7 57·5	7 58·8	7 35·7	5·0	2·6	11·0	5·8	17·0	8·9
51	7 57·8	7 59·1	7 36·0	5·1	2·7	11·1	5·8	17·1	9·0
52	7 58·0	7 59·3	7 36·2	5·2	2·7	11·2	5·9	17·2	9·0
53	7 58·3	7 59·6	7 36·5	5·3	2·8	11·3	5·9	17·3	9·1
54	7 58·5	7 59·8	7 36·7	5·4	2·8	11·4	6·0	17·4	9·1
55	7 58·8	8 00·1	7 36·9	5·5	2·9	11·5	6·0	17·5	9·2
56	7 59·0	8 00·3	7 37·2	5·6	2·9	11·6	6·1	17·6	9·2
57	7 59·3	8 00·6	7 37·4	5·7	3·0	11·7	6·1	17·7	9·3
58	7 59·5	8 00·8	7 37·7	5·8	3·0	11·8	6·2	17·8	9·3
59	7 59·8	8 01·1	7 37·9	5·9	3·1	11·9	6·2	17·9	9·4
60	8 00·0	8 01·3	7 38·1	6·0	3·2	12·0	6·3	18·0	9·5

32ᵐ	SUN PLANETS	ARIES	MOON	v or d	Corrⁿ	v or d	Corrⁿ	v or d	Corrⁿ
s	° ′	° ′	° ′	′	′	′	′	′	′
00	8 00·0	8 01·3	7 38·1	0·0	0·0	6·0	3·3	12·0	6·5
01	8 00·3	8 01·6	7 38·4	0·1	0·1	6·1	3·3	12·1	6·6
02	8 00·5	8 01·8	7 38·6	0·2	0·1	6·2	3·4	12·2	6·6
03	8 00·8	8 02·1	7 38·8	0·3	0·2	6·3	3·4	12·3	6·7
04	8 01·0	8 02·3	7 39·1	0·4	0·2	6·4	3·5	12·4	6·7
05	8 01·3	8 02·6	7 39·3	0·5	0·3	6·5	3·5	12·5	6·8
06	8 01·5	8 02·8	7 39·6	0·6	0·3	6·6	3·6	12·6	6·8
07	8 01·8	8 03·1	7 39·8	0·7	0·4	6·7	3·6	12·7	6·9
08	8 02·0	8 03·3	7 40·0	0·8	0·4	6·8	3·7	12·8	6·9
09	8 02·3	8 03·6	7 40·3	0·9	0·5	6·9	3·7	12·9	7·0
10	8 02·5	8 03·8	7 40·5	1·0	0·5	7·0	3·8	13·0	7·0
11	8 02·8	8 04·1	7 40·8	1·1	0·6	7·1	3·8	13·1	7·1
12	8 03·0	8 04·3	7 41·0	1·2	0·7	7·2	3·9	13·2	7·2
13	8 03·3	8 04·6	7 41·2	1·3	0·7	7·3	4·0	13·3	7·2
14	8 03·5	8 04·8	7 41·5	1·4	0·8	7·4	4·0	13·4	7·3
15	8 03·8	8 05·1	7 41·7	1·5	0·8	7·5	4·1	13·5	7·3
16	8 04·0	8 05·3	7 42·0	1·6	0·9	7·6	4·1	13·6	7·4
17	8 04·3	8 05·6	7 42·2	1·7	0·9	7·7	4·2	13·7	7·4
18	8 04·5	8 05·8	7 42·4	1·8	1·0	7·8	4·2	13·8	7·5
19	8 04·8	8 06·1	7 42·7	1·9	1·0	7·9	4·3	13·9	7·5
20	8 05·0	8 06·3	7 42·9	2·0	1·1	8·0	4·3	14·0	7·6
21	8 05·3	8 06·6	7 43·1	2·1	1·1	8·1	4·4	14·1	7·6
22	8 05·5	8 06·8	7 43·4	2·2	1·2	8·2	4·4	14·2	7·7
23	8 05·8	8 07·1	7 43·6	2·3	1·2	8·3	4·5	14·3	7·7
24	8 06·0	8 07·3	7 43·9	2·4	1·3	8·4	4·6	14·4	7·8
25	8 06·3	8 07·6	7 44·1	2·5	1·4	8·5	4·6	14·5	7·9
26	8 06·5	8 07·8	7 44·3	2·6	1·4	8·6	4·7	14·6	7·9
27	8 06·8	8 08·1	7 44·6	2·7	1·5	8·7	4·7	14·7	8·0
28	8 07·0	8 08·3	7 44·8	2·8	1·5	8·8	4·8	14·8	8·0
29	8 07·3	8 08·6	7 45·1	2·9	1·6	8·9	4·8	14·9	8·1
30	8 07·5	8 08·8	7 45·3	3·0	1·6	9·0	4·9	15·0	8·1
31	8 07·8	8 09·1	7 45·5	3·1	1·7	9·1	4·9	15·1	8·2
32	8 08·0	8 09·3	7 45·8	3·2	1·7	9·2	5·0	15·2	8·2
33	8 08·3	8 09·6	7 46·0	3·3	1·8	9·3	5·0	15·3	8·3
34	8 08·5	8 09·8	7 46·2	3·4	1·8	9·4	5·1	15·4	8·3
35	8 08·8	8 10·1	7 46·5	3·5	1·9	9·5	5·1	15·5	8·4
36	8 09·0	8 10·3	7 46·7	3·6	2·0	9·6	5·2	15·6	8·5
37	8 09·3	8 10·6	7 47·0	3·7	2·0	9·7	5·3	15·7	8·5
38	8 09·5	8 10·8	7 47·2	3·8	2·1	9·8	5·3	15·8	8·6
39	8 09·8	8 11·1	7 47·4	3·9	2·1	9·9	5·4	15·9	8·6
40	8 10·0	8 11·3	7 47·7	4·0	2·2	10·0	5·4	16·0	8·7
41	8 10·3	8 11·6	7 47·9	4·1	2·2	10·1	5·5	16·1	8·7
42	8 10·5	8 11·8	7 48·2	4·2	2·3	10·2	5·5	16·2	8·8
43	8 10·8	8 12·1	7 48·4	4·3	2·3	10·3	5·6	16·3	8·8
44	8 11·0	8 12·3	7 48·6	4·4	2·4	10·4	5·6	16·4	8·9
45	8 11·3	8 12·6	7 48·9	4·5	2·4	10·5	5·7	16·5	8·9
46	8 11·5	8 12·8	7 49·1	4·6	2·5	10·6	5·7	16·6	9·0
47	8 11·8	8 13·1	7 49·3	4·7	2·5	10·7	5·8	16·7	9·0
48	8 12·0	8 13·3	7 49·6	4·8	2·6	10·8	5·9	16·8	9·1
49	8 12·3	8 13·6	7 49·8	4·9	2·7	10·9	5·9	16·9	9·2
50	8 12·5	8 13·8	7 50·1	5·0	2·7	11·0	6·0	17·0	9·2
51	8 12·8	8 14·1	7 50·3	5·1	2·8	11·1	6·0	17·1	9·3
52	8 13·0	8 14·3	7 50·5	5·2	2·8	11·2	6·1	17·2	9·3
53	8 13·3	8 14·6	7 50·8	5·3	2·9	11·3	6·1	17·3	9·4
54	8 13·5	8 14·9	7 51·0	5·4	2·9	11·4	6·2	17·4	9·4
55	8 13·8	8 15·1	7 51·3	5·5	3·0	11·5	6·2	17·5	9·5
56	8 14·0	8 15·4	7 51·5	5·6	3·0	11·6	6·3	17·6	9·5
57	8 14·3	8 15·6	7 51·7	5·7	3·1	11·7	6·3	17·7	9·6
58	8 14·5	8 15·9	7 52·0	5·8	3·1	11·8	6·4	17·8	9·6
59	8 14·8	8 16·1	7 52·2	5·9	3·2	11·9	6·4	17·9	9·7
60	8 15·0	8 16·4	7 52·5	6·0	3·3	12·0	6·5	18·0	9·8

33ᵐ	SUN PLANETS	ARIES	MOON	v or d	Corrⁿ	v or d	Corrⁿ	v or d	Corrⁿ
s	° ′	° ′	° ′	′	′	′	′	′	′
00	8 15·0	8 16·4	7 52·5	0·0	0·0	6·0	3·4	12·0	6·7
01	8 15·3	8 16·6	7 52·7	0·1	0·1	6·1	3·4	12·1	6·8
02	8 15·5	8 16·9	7 52·9	0·2	0·1	6·2	3·5	12·2	6·8
03	8 15·8	8 17·1	7 53·2	0·3	0·2	6·3	3·5	12·3	6·9
04	8 16·0	8 17·4	7 53·4	0·4	0·2	6·4	3·6	12·4	6·9
05	8 16·3	8 17·6	7 53·6	0·5	0·3	6·5	3·6	12·5	7·0
06	8 16·5	8 17·9	7 53·9	0·6	0·3	6·6	3·7	12·6	7·0
07	8 16·8	8 18·1	7 54·1	0·7	0·4	6·7	3·7	12·7	7·1
08	8 17·0	8 18·4	7 54·4	0·8	0·4	6·8	3·8	12·8	7·1
09	8 17·3	8 18·6	7 54·6	0·9	0·5	6·9	3·9	12·9	7·2
10	8 17·5	8 18·9	7 54·8	1·0	0·6	7·0	3·9	13·0	7·3
11	8 17·8	8 19·1	7 55·1	1·1	0·6	7·1	4·0	13·1	7·3
12	8 18·0	8 19·4	7 55·3	1·2	0·7	7·2	4·0	13·2	7·4
13	8 18·3	8 19·6	7 55·6	1·3	0·7	7·3	4·1	13·3	7·4
14	8 18·5	8 19·9	7 55·8	1·4	0·8	7·4	4·1	13·4	7·5
15	8 18·8	8 20·1	7 56·0	1·5	0·8	7·5	4·2	13·5	7·5
16	8 19·0	8 20·4	7 56·3	1·6	0·9	7·6	4·2	13·6	7·6
17	8 19·3	8 20·6	7 56·5	1·7	0·9	7·7	4·3	13·7	7·6
18	8 19·5	8 20·9	7 56·7	1·8	1·0	7·8	4·4	13·8	7·7
19	8 19·8	8 21·1	7 57·0	1·9	1·1	7·9	4·4	13·9	7·8
20	8 20·0	8 21·4	7 57·2	2·0	1·1	8·0	4·5	14·0	7·8
21	8 20·3	8 21·6	7 57·5	2·1	1·2	8·1	4·5	14·1	7·9
22	8 20·5	8 21·9	7 57·7	2·2	1·2	8·2	4·6	14·2	7·9
23	8 20·8	8 22·1	7 57·9	2·3	1·3	8·3	4·6	14·3	8·0
24	8 21·0	8 22·4	7 58·2	2·4	1·3	8·4	4·7	14·4	8·0
25	8 21·3	8 22·6	7 58·4	2·5	1·4	8·5	4·7	14·5	8·1
26	8 21·5	8 22·9	7 58·7	2·6	1·5	8·6	4·8	14·6	8·2
27	8 21·8	8 23·1	7 58·9	2·7	1·5	8·7	4·9	14·7	8·2
28	8 22·0	8 23·4	7 59·1	2·8	1·6	8·8	4·9	14·8	8·3
29	8 22·3	8 23·6	7 59·4	2·9	1·6	8·9	5·0	14·9	8·3
30	8 22·5	8 23·9	7 59·6	3·0	1·7	9·0	5·0	15·0	8·4
31	8 22·8	8 24·1	7 59·8	3·1	1·7	9·1	5·1	15·1	8·4
32	8 23·0	8 24·4	8 00·1	3·2	1·8	9·2	5·1	15·2	8·5
33	8 23·3	8 24·6	8 00·3	3·3	1·8	9·3	5·2	15·3	8·5
34	8 23·5	8 24·9	8 00·6	3·4	1·9	9·4	5·2	15·4	8·6
35	8 23·8	8 25·1	8 00·8	3·5	2·0	9·5	5·3	15·5	8·7
36	8 24·0	8 25·4	8 01·0	3·6	2·0	9·6	5·4	15·6	8·7
37	8 24·3	8 25·6	8 01·3	3·7	2·1	9·7	5·4	15·7	8·8
38	8 24·5	8 25·9	8 01·5	3·8	2·1	9·8	5·5	15·8	8·8
39	8 24·8	8 26·1	8 01·8	3·9	2·2	9·9	5·5	15·9	8·9
40	8 25·0	8 26·4	8 02·0	4·0	2·2	10·0	5·6	16·0	8·9
41	8 25·3	8 26·6	8 02·2	4·1	2·3	10·1	5·6	16·1	9·0
42	8 25·5	8 26·9	8 02·5	4·2	2·3	10·2	5·7	16·2	9·0
43	8 25·8	8 27·1	8 02·7	4·3	2·4	10·3	5·8	16·3	9·1
44	8 26·0	8 27·4	8 02·9	4·4	2·5	10·4	5·8	16·4	9·2
45	8 26·3	8 27·6	8 03·2	4·5	2·5	10·5	5·9	16·5	9·2
46	8 26·5	8 27·9	8 03·4	4·6	2·6	10·6	5·9	16·6	9·3
47	8 26·8	8 28·1	8 03·7	4·7	2·6	10·7	6·0	16·7	9·3
48	8 27·0	8 28·4	8 03·9	4·8	2·7	10·8	6·0	16·8	9·4
49	8 27·3	8 28·6	8 04·1	4·9	2·7	10·9	6·1	16·9	9·4
50	8 27·5	8 28·9	8 04·4	5·0	2·8	11·0	6·1	17·0	9·5
51	8 27·8	8 29·1	8 04·6	5·1	2·8	11·1	6·2	17·1	9·5
52	8 28·0	8 29·4	8 04·9	5·2	2·9	11·2	6·3	17·2	9·6
53	8 28·3	8 29·6	8 05·1	5·3	3·0	11·3	6·3	17·3	9·7
54	8 28·5	8 29·9	8 05·3	5·4	3·0	11·4	6·4	17·4	9·7
55	8 28·8	8 30·1	8 05·6	5·5	3·1	11·5	6·4	17·5	9·8
56	8 29·0	8 30·4	8 05·8	5·6	3·1	11·6	6·5	17·6	9·8
57	8 29·3	8 30·6	8 06·1	5·7	3·2	11·7	6·5	17·7	9·9
58	8 29·5	8 30·9	8 06·3	5·8	3·2	11·8	6·6	17·8	9·9
59	8 29·8	8 31·1	8 06·5	5·9	3·3	11·9	6·6	17·9	10·0
60	8 30·0	8 31·4	8 06·8	6·0	3·4	12·0	6·7	18·0	10·1

34m s	SUN PLANETS ° ′	ARIES ° ′	MOON ° ′	v or d ′	Corrn ′	v or d ′	Corrn ′	v or d ′	Corrn ′
00	8 30·0	8 31·4	8 06·8	0·0	0·0	6·0	3·5	12·0	6·9
01	8 30·3	8 31·6	8 07·0	0·1	0·1	6·1	3·5	12·1	7·0
02	8 30·5	8 31·9	8 07·2	0·2	0·1	6·2	3·6	12·2	7·0
03	8 30·8	8 32·1	8 07·5	0·3	0·2	6·3	3·6	12·3	7·1
04	8 31·0	8 32·4	8 07·7	0·4	0·2	6·4	3·7	12·4	7·1
05	8 31·3	8 32·6	8 08·0	0·5	0·3	6·5	3·7	12·5	7·2
06	8 31·5	8 32·9	8 08·2	0·6	0·3	6·6	3·8	12·6	7·2
07	8 31·8	8 33·2	8 08·4	0·7	0·4	6·7	3·9	12·7	7·3
08	8 32·0	8 33·4	8 08·7	0·8	0·5	6·8	3·9	12·8	7·4
09	8 32·3	8 33·7	8 08·9	0·9	0·5	6·9	4·0	12·9	7·4
10	8 32·5	8 33·9	8 09·2	1·0	0·6	7·0	4·0	13·0	7·5
11	8 32·8	8 34·2	8 09·4	1·1	0·6	7·1	4·1	13·1	7·5
12	8 33·0	8 34·4	8 09·6	1·2	0·7	7·2	4·1	13·2	7·6
13	8 33·3	8 34·7	8 09·9	1·3	0·7	7·3	4·2	13·3	7·6
14	8 33·5	8 34·9	8 10·1	1·4	0·8	7·4	4·3	13·4	7·7
15	8 33·8	8 35·2	8 10·3	1·5	0·9	7·5	4·3	13·5	7·8
16	8 34·0	8 35·4	8 10·6	1·6	0·9	7·6	4·4	13·6	7·8
17	8 34·3	8 35·7	8 10·8	1·7	1·0	7·7	4·4	13·7	7·9
18	8 34·5	8 35·9	8 11·1	1·8	1·0	7·8	4·5	13·8	7·9
19	8 34·8	8 36·2	8 11·3	1·9	1·1	7·9	4·5	13·9	8·0
20	8 35·0	8 36·4	8 11·5	2·0	1·2	8·0	4·6	14·0	8·1
21	8 35·3	8 36·7	8 11·8	2·1	1·2	8·1	4·7	14·1	8·1
22	8 35·5	8 36·9	8 12·0	2·2	1·3	8·2	4·7	14·2	8·2
23	8 35·8	8 37·2	8 12·3	2·3	1·3	8·3	4·8	14·3	8·2
24	8 36·0	8 37·4	8 12·5	2·4	1·4	8·4	4·8	14·4	8·3
25	8 36·3	8 37·7	8 12·7	2·5	1·4	8·5	4·9	14·5	8·3
26	8 36·5	8 37·9	8 13·0	2·6	1·5	8·6	4·9	14·6	8·4
27	8 36·8	8 38·2	8 13·2	2·7	1·6	8·7	5·0	14·7	8·5
28	8 37·0	8 38·4	8 13·4	2·8	1·6	8·8	5·1	14·8	8·5
29	8 37·3	8 38·7	8 13·7	2·9	1·7	8·9	5·1	14·9	8·6
30	8 37·5	8 38·9	8 13·9	3·0	1·7	9·0	5·2	15·0	8·6
31	8 37·8	8 39·2	8 14·2	3·1	1·8	9·1	5·2	15·1	8·7
32	8 38·0	8 39·4	8 14·4	3·2	1·8	9·2	5·3	15·2	8·7
33	8 38·3	8 39·7	8 14·6	3·3	1·9	9·3	5·3	15·3	8·8
34	8 38·5	8 39·9	8 14·9	3·4	2·0	9·4	5·4	15·4	8·9
35	8 38·8	8 40·2	8 15·1	3·5	2·0	9·5	5·5	15·5	8·9
36	8 39·0	8 40·4	8 15·4	3·6	2·1	9·6	5·5	15·6	9·0
37	8 39·3	8 40·7	8 15·6	3·7	2·1	9·7	5·6	15·7	9·0
38	8 39·5	8 40·9	8 15·8	3·8	2·2	9·8	5·6	15·8	9·1
39	8 39·8	8 41·2	8 16·1	3·9	2·2	9·9	5·7	15·9	9·1
40	8 40·0	8 41·4	8 16·3	4·0	2·3	10·0	5·8	16·0	9·2
41	8 40·3	8 41·7	8 16·5	4·1	2·4	10·1	5·8	16·1	9·3
42	8 40·5	8 41·9	8 16·8	4·2	2·4	10·2	5·9	16·2	9·3
43	8 40·8	8 42·2	8 17·0	4·3	2·5	10·3	5·9	16·3	9·4
44	8 41·0	8 42·4	8 17·3	4·4	2·5	10·4	6·0	16·4	9·4
45	8 41·3	8 42·7	8 17·5	4·5	2·6	10·5	6·0	16·5	9·5
46	8 41·5	8 42·9	8 17·7	4·6	2·6	10·6	6·1	16·6	9·5
47	8 41·8	8 43·2	8 18·0	4·7	2·7	10·7	6·2	16·7	9·6
48	8 42·0	8 43·4	8 18·2	4·8	2·8	10·8	6·2	16·8	9·7
49	8 42·3	8 43·7	8 18·5	4·9	2·8	10·9	6·3	16·9	9·7
50	8 42·5	8 43·9	8 18·7	5·0	2·9	11·0	6·3	17·0	9·8
51	8 42·8	8 44·2	8 18·9	5·1	2·9	11·1	6·4	17·1	9·8
52	8 43·0	8 44·4	8 19·2	5·2	3·0	11·2	6·4	17·2	9·9
53	8 43·3	8 44·7	8 19·4	5·3	3·0	11·3	6·5	17·3	9·9
54	8 43·5	8 44·9	8 19·7	5·4	3·1	11·4	6·6	17·4	10·0
55	8 43·8	8 45·2	8 19·9	5·5	3·2	11·5	6·6	17·5	10·1
56	8 44·0	8 45·4	8 20·1	5·6	3·2	11·6	6·7	17·6	10·1
57	8 44·3	8 45·7	8 20·4	5·7	3·3	11·7	6·7	17·7	10·2
58	8 44·5	8 45·9	8 20·6	5·8	3·3	11·8	6·8	17·8	10·2
59	8 44·8	8 46·2	8 20·8	5·9	3·4	11·9	6·8	17·9	10·3
60	8 45·0	8 46·4	8 21·1	6·0	3·5	12·0	6·9	18·0	10·4

35m s	SUN PLANETS ° ′	ARIES ° ′	MOON ° ′	v or d ′	Corrn ′	v or d ′	Corrn ′	v or d ′	Corrn ′
00	8 45·0	8 46·4	8 21·1	0·0	0·0	6·0	3·6	12·0	7·1
01	8 45·3	8 46·7	8 21·3	0·1	0·1	6·1	3·6	12·1	7·2
02	8 45·5	8 46·9	8 21·6	0·2	0·1	6·2	3·7	12·2	7·2
03	8 45·8	8 47·2	8 21·8	0·3	0·2	6·3	3·7	12·3	7·3
04	8 46·0	8 47·4	8 22·0	0·4	0·2	6·4	3·8	12·4	7·3
05	8 46·3	8 47·7	8 22·3	0·5	0·3	6·5	3·8	12·5	7·4
06	8 46·5	8 47·9	8 22·5	0·6	0·4	6·6	3·9	12·6	7·5
07	8 46·8	8 48·2	8 22·8	0·7	0·4	6·7	4·0	12·7	7·5
08	8 47·0	8 48·4	8 23·0	0·8	0·5	6·8	4·0	12·8	7·6
09	8 47·3	8 48·7	8 23·2	0·9	0·5	6·9	4·1	12·9	7·6
10	8 47·5	8 48·9	8 23·5	1·0	0·6	7·0	4·1	13·0	7·7
11	8 47·8	8 49·2	8 23·7	1·1	0·7	7·1	4·2	13·1	7·8
12	8 48·0	8 49·4	8 23·9	1·2	0·7	7·2	4·3	13·2	7·8
13	8 48·3	8 49·7	8 24·2	1·3	0·8	7·3	4·3	13·3	7·9
14	8 48·5	8 49·9	8 24·4	1·4	0·8	7·4	4·4	13·4	7·9
15	8 48·8	8 50·2	8 24·7	1·5	0·9	7·5	4·4	13·5	8·0
16	8 49·0	8 50·4	8 24·9	1·6	0·9	7·6	4·5	13·6	8·0
17	8 49·3	8 50·7	8 25·1	1·7	1·0	7·7	4·6	13·7	8·1
18	8 49·5	8 50·9	8 25·4	1·8	1·1	7·8	4·6	13·8	8·2
19	8 49·8	8 51·2	8 25·6	1·9	1·1	7·9	4·7	13·9	8·2
20	8 50·0	8 51·5	8 25·9	2·0	1·2	8·0	4·7	14·0	8·3
21	8 50·3	8 51·7	8 26·1	2·1	1·2	8·1	4·8	14·1	8·3
22	8 50·5	8 52·0	8 26·3	2·2	1·3	8·2	4·9	14·2	8·4
23	8 50·8	8 52·2	8 26·6	2·3	1·4	8·3	4·9	14·3	8·5
24	8 51·0	8 52·5	8 26·8	2·4	1·4	8·4	5·0	14·4	8·5
25	8 51·3	8 52·7	8 27·0	2·5	1·5	8·5	5·0	14·5	8·6
26	8 51·5	8 53·0	8 27·3	2·6	1·5	8·6	5·1	14·6	8·6
27	8 51·8	8 53·2	8 27·5	2·7	1·6	8·7	5·1	14·7	8·7
28	8 52·0	8 53·5	8 27·8	2·8	1·7	8·8	5·2	14·8	8·8
29	8 52·3	8 53·7	8 28·0	2·9	1·7	8·9	5·3	14·9	8·8
30	8 52·5	8 54·0	8 28·2	3·0	1·8	9·0	5·3	15·0	8·9
31	8 52·8	8 54·2	8 28·5	3·1	1·8	9·1	5·4	15·1	8·9
32	8 53·0	8 54·5	8 28·7	3·2	1·9	9·2	5·4	15·2	9·0
33	8 53·3	8 54·7	8 29·0	3·3	2·0	9·3	5·5	15·3	9·1
34	8 53·5	8 55·0	8 29·2	3·4	2·0	9·4	5·6	15·4	9·1
35	8 53·8	8 55·2	8 29·4	3·5	2·1	9·5	5·6	15·5	9·2
36	8 54·0	8 55·5	8 29·7	3·6	2·1	9·6	5·7	15·6	9·2
37	8 54·3	8 55·7	8 29·9	3·7	2·2	9·7	5·7	15·7	9·3
38	8 54·5	8 56·0	8 30·2	3·8	2·2	9·8	5·8	15·8	9·3
39	8 54·8	8 56·2	8 30·4	3·9	2·3	9·9	5·9	15·9	9·4
40	8 55·0	8 56·5	8 30·6	4·0	2·4	10·0	5·9	16·0	9·5
41	8 55·3	8 56·7	8 30·9	4·1	2·4	10·1	6·0	16·1	9·5
42	8 55·5	8 57·0	8 31·1	4·2	2·5	10·2	6·0	16·2	9·6
43	8 55·8	8 57·2	8 31·3	4·3	2·5	10·3	6·1	16·3	9·6
44	8 56·0	8 57·5	8 31·6	4·4	2·6	10·4	6·2	16·4	9·7
45	8 56·3	8 57·7	8 31·8	4·5	2·7	10·5	6·2	16·5	9·8
46	8 56·5	8 58·0	8 32·1	4·6	2·7	10·6	6·3	16·6	9·8
47	8 56·8	8 58·2	8 32·3	4·7	2·8	10·7	6·3	16·7	9·9
48	8 57·0	8 58·5	8 32·5	4·8	2·8	10·8	6·4	16·8	9·9
49	8 57·3	8 58·7	8 32·8	4·9	2·9	10·9	6·4	16·9	10·0
50	8 57·5	8 59·0	8 33·0	5·0	3·0	11·0	6·5	17·0	10·1
51	8 57·8	8 59·2	8 33·3	5·1	3·0	11·1	6·6	17·1	10·1
52	8 58·0	8 59·5	8 33·5	5·2	3·1	11·2	6·6	17·2	10·2
53	8 58·3	8 59·7	8 33·7	5·3	3·1	11·3	6·7	17·3	10·2
54	8 58·5	9 00·0	8 34·0	5·4	3·2	11·4	6·7	17·4	10·3
55	8 58·8	9 00·2	8 34·2	5·5	3·3	11·5	6·8	17·5	10·4
56	8 59·0	9 00·5	8 34·4	5·6	3·3	11·6	6·9	17·6	10·4
57	8 59·3	9 00·7	8 34·7	5·7	3·4	11·7	6·9	17·7	10·5
58	8 59·5	9 01·0	8 34·9	5·8	3·4	11·8	7·0	17·8	10·5
59	8 59·8	9 01·2	8 35·2	5·9	3·5	11·9	7·0	17·9	10·6
60	9 00·0	9 01·5	8 35·4	6·0	3·6	12·0	7·1	18·0	10·7

36^m	SUN PLANETS	ARIES	MOON	v or d	Corr^n	v or d	Corr^n	v or d	Corr^n
s	° ′	° ′	° ′	′	′	′	′	′	′
00	9 00·0	9 01·5	8 35·4	0·0	0·0	6·0	3·7	12·0	7·3
01	9 00·3	9 01·7	8 35·6	0·1	0·1	6·1	3·7	12·1	7·4
02	9 00·5	9 02·0	8 35·9	0·2	0·1	6·2	3·8	12·2	7·4
03	9 00·8	9 02·2	8 36·1	0·3	0·2	6·3	3·8	12·3	7·5
04	9 01·0	9 02·5	8 36·4	0·4	0·2	6·4	3·9	12·4	7·5
05	9 01·3	9 02·7	8 36·6	0·5	0·3	6·5	4·0	12·5	7·6
06	9 01·5	9 03·0	8 36·8	0·6	0·4	6·6	4·0	12·6	7·7
07	9 01·8	9 03·2	8 37·1	0·7	0·4	6·7	4·1	12·7	7·7
08	9 02·0	9 03·5	8 37·3	0·8	0·5	6·8	4·1	12·8	7·8
09	9 02·3	9 03·7	8 37·5	0·9	0·5	6·9	4·2	12·9	7·8
10	9 02·5	9 04·0	8 37·8	1·0	0·6	7·0	4·3	13·0	7·9
11	9 02·8	9 04·2	8 38·0	1·1	0·7	7·1	4·3	13·1	8·0
12	9 03·0	9 04·5	8 38·3	1·2	0·7	7·2	4·4	13·2	8·0
13	9 03·3	9 04·7	8 38·5	1·3	0·8	7·3	4·4	13·3	8·1
14	9 03·5	9 05·0	8 38·7	1·4	0·9	7·4	4·5	13·4	8·2
15	9 03·8	9 05·2	8 39·0	1·5	0·9	7·5	4·6	13·5	8·2
16	9 04·0	9 05·5	8 39·2	1·6	1·0	7·6	4·6	13·6	8·3
17	9 04·3	9 05·7	8 39·5	1·7	1·0	7·7	4·7	13·7	8·3
18	9 04·5	9 06·0	8 39·7	1·8	1·1	7·8	4·7	13·8	8·4
19	9 04·8	9 06·2	8 39·9	1·9	1·2	7·9	4·8	13·9	8·5
20	9 05·0	9 06·5	8 40·2	2·0	1·2	8·0	4·9	14·0	8·5
21	9 05·3	9 06·7	8 40·4	2·1	1·3	8·1	4·9	14·1	8·6
22	9 05·5	9 07·0	8 40·6	2·2	1·3	8·2	5·0	14·2	8·6
23	9 05·8	9 07·2	8 40·9	2·3	1·4	8·3	5·0	14·3	8·7
24	9 06·0	9 07·5	8 41·1	2·4	1·5	8·4	5·1	14·4	8·8
25	9 06·3	9 07·7	8 41·4	2·5	1·5	8·5	5·2	14·5	8·8
26	9 06·5	9 08·0	8 41·6	2·6	1·6	8·6	5·2	14·6	8·9
27	9 06·8	9 08·2	8 41·8	2·7	1·6	8·7	5·3	14·7	8·9
28	9 07·0	9 08·5	8 42·1	2·8	1·7	8·8	5·4	14·8	9·0
29	9 07·3	9 08·7	8 42·3	2·9	1·8	8·9	5·4	14·9	9·1
30	9 07·5	9 09·0	8 42·6	3·0	1·8	9·0	5·5	15·0	9·1
31	9 07·8	9 09·2	8 42·8	3·1	1·9	9·1	5·5	15·1	9·2
32	9 08·0	9 09·5	8 43·0	3·2	1·9	9·2	5·6	15·2	9·2
33	9 08·3	9 09·8	8 43·3	3·3	2·0	9·3	5·7	15·3	9·3
34	9 08·5	9 10·0	8 43·5	3·4	2·1	9·4	5·7	15·4	9·4
35	9 08·8	9 10·3	8 43·8	3·5	2·1	9·5	5·8	15·5	9·4
36	9 09·0	9 10·5	8 44·0	3·6	2·2	9·6	5·8	15·6	9·5
37	9 09·3	9 10·8	8 44·2	3·7	2·3	9·7	5·9	15·7	9·6
38	9 09·5	9 11·0	8 44·5	3·8	2·3	9·8	6·0	15·8	9·6
39	9 09·8	9 11·3	8 44·7	3·9	2·4	9·9	6·0	15·9	9·7
40	9 10·0	9 11·5	8 44·9	4·0	2·4	10·0	6·1	16·0	9·7
41	9 10·3	9 11·8	8 45·2	4·1	2·5	10·1	6·1	16·1	9·8
42	9 10·5	9 12·0	8 45·4	4·2	2·6	10·2	6·2	16·2	9·9
43	9 10·8	9 12·3	8 45·7	4·3	2·6	10·3	6·3	16·3	9·9
44	9 11·0	9 12·5	8 45·9	4·4	2·7	10·4	6·3	16·4	10·0
45	9 11·3	9 12·8	8 46·1	4·5	2·7	10·5	6·4	16·5	10·0
46	9 11·5	9 13·0	8 46·4	4·6	2·8	10·6	6·4	16·6	10·1
47	9 11·8	9 13·3	8 46·6	4·7	2·9	10·7	6·5	16·7	10·2
48	9 12·0	9 13·5	8 46·9	4·8	2·9	10·8	6·6	16·8	10·2
49	9 12·3	9 13·8	8 47·1	4·9	3·0	10·9	6·6	16·9	10·3
50	9 12·5	9 14·0	8 47·3	5·0	3·0	11·0	6·7	17·0	10·3
51	9 12·8	9 14·3	8 47·6	5·1	3·1	11·1	6·8	17·1	10·4
52	9 13·0	9 14·5	8 47·8	5·2	3·2	11·2	6·8	17·2	10·5
53	9 13·3	9 14·8	8 48·0	5·3	3·2	11·3	6·9	17·3	10·5
54	9 13·5	9 15·0	8 48·3	5·4	3·3	11·4	6·9	17·4	10·6
55	9 13·8	9 15·3	8 48·5	5·5	3·3	11·5	7·0	17·5	10·6
56	9 14·0	9 15·5	8 48·8	5·6	3·4	11·6	7·1	17·6	10·7
57	9 14·3	9 15·8	8 49·0	5·7	3·5	11·7	7·1	17·7	10·8
58	9 14·5	9 16·0	8 49·2	5·8	3·5	11·8	7·2	17·8	10·8
59	9 14·8	9 16·3	8 49·5	5·9	3·6	11·9	7·2	17·9	10·9
60	9 15·0	9 16·5	8 49·7	6·0	3·7	12·0	7·3	18·0	11·0

37^m	SUN PLANETS	ARIES	MOON	v or d	Corr^n	v or d	Corr^n	v or d	Corr^n
s	° ′	° ′	° ′	′	′	′	′	′	′
00	9 15·0	9 16·5	8 49·7	0·0	0·0	6·0	3·8	12·0	7·5
01	9 15·3	9 16·8	8 50·0	0·1	0·1	6·1	3·8	12·1	7·6
02	9 15·5	9 17·0	8 50·2	0·2	0·1	6·2	3·9	12·2	7·6
03	9 15·8	9 17·3	8 50·4	0·3	0·2	6·3	3·9	12·3	7·7
04	9 16·0	9 17·5	8 50·7	0·4	0·3	6·4	4·0	12·4	7·8
05	9 16·3	9 17·8	8 50·9	0·5	0·3	6·5	4·1	12·5	7·8
06	9 16·5	9 18·0	8 51·1	0·6	0·4	6·6	4·1	12·6	7·9
07	9 16·8	9 18·3	8 51·4	0·7	0·4	6·7	4·2	12·7	7·9
08	9 17·0	9 18·5	8 51·6	0·8	0·5	6·8	4·3	12·8	8·0
09	9 17·3	9 18·8	8 51·9	0·9	0·6	6·9	4·3	12·9	8·1
10	9 17·5	9 19·0	8 52·1	1·0	0·6	7·0	4·4	13·0	8·1
11	9 17·8	9 19·3	8 52·3	1·1	0·7	7·1	4·4	13·1	8·2
12	9 18·0	9 19·5	8 52·6	1·2	0·8	7·2	4·5	13·2	8·3
13	9 18·3	9 19·8	8 52·8	1·3	0·8	7·3	4·6	13·3	8·3
14	9 18·5	9 20·0	8 53·1	1·4	0·9	7·4	4·6	13·4	8·4
15	9 18·8	9 20·3	8 53·3	1·5	0·9	7·5	4·7	13·5	8·4
16	9 19·0	9 20·5	8 53·5	1·6	1·0	7·6	4·8	13·6	8·5
17	9 19·3	9 20·8	8 53·8	1·7	1·1	7·7	4·8	13·7	8·6
18	9 19·5	9 21·0	8 54·0	1·8	1·1	7·8	4·9	13·8	8·6
19	9 19·8	9 21·3	8 54·3	1·9	1·2	7·9	4·9	13·9	8·7
20	9 20·0	9 21·5	8 54·5	2·0	1·3	8·0	5·0	14·0	8·8
21	9 20·3	9 21·8	8 54·7	2·1	1·3	8·1	5·1	14·1	8·8
22	9 20·5	9 22·0	8 55·0	2·2	1·4	8·2	5·1	14·2	8·9
23	9 20·8	9 22·3	8 55·2	2·3	1·4	8·3	5·2	14·3	8·9
24	9 21·0	9 22·5	8 55·4	2·4	1·5	8·4	5·3	14·4	9·0
25	9 21·3	9 22·8	8 55·7	2·5	1·6	8·5	5·3	14·5	9·1
26	9 21·5	9 23·0	8 55·9	2·6	1·6	8·6	5·4	14·6	9·1
27	9 21·8	9 23·3	8 56·2	2·7	1·7	8·7	5·4	14·7	9·2
28	9 22·0	9 23·5	8 56·4	2·8	1·8	8·8	5·5	14·8	9·3
29	9 22·3	9 23·8	8 56·6	2·9	1·8	8·9	5·6	14·9	9·3
30	9 22·5	9 24·0	8 56·9	3·0	1·9	9·0	5·6	15·0	9·4
31	9 22·8	9 24·3	8 57·1	3·1	1·9	9·1	5·7	15·1	9·4
32	9 23·0	9 24·5	8 57·4	3·2	2·0	9·2	5·8	15·2	9·5
33	9 23·3	9 24·8	8 57·6	3·3	2·1	9·3	5·8	15·3	9·6
34	9 23·5	9 25·0	8 57·8	3·4	2·1	9·4	5·9	15·4	9·6
35	9 23·8	9 25·3	8 58·1	3·5	2·2	9·5	5·9	15·5	9·7
36	9 24·0	9 25·5	8 58·3	3·6	2·3	9·6	6·0	15·6	9·8
37	9 24·3	9 25·8	8 58·5	3·7	2·3	9·7	6·1	15·7	9·8
38	9 24·5	9 26·0	8 58·8	3·8	2·4	9·8	6·1	15·8	9·9
39	9 24·8	9 26·3	8 59·0	3·9	2·4	9·9	6·2	15·9	9·9
40	9 25·0	9 26·5	8 59·3	4·0	2·5	10·0	6·3	16·0	10·0
41	9 25·3	9 26·8	8 59·5	4·1	2·6	10·1	6·3	16·1	10·1
42	9 25·5	9 27·0	8 59·7	4·2	2·6	10·2	6·4	16·2	10·1
43	9 25·8	9 27·3	9 00·0	4·3	2·7	10·3	6·4	16·3	10·2
44	9 26·0	9 27·5	9 00·2	4·4	2·8	10·4	6·5	16·4	10·3
45	9 26·3	9 27·8	9 00·5	4·5	2·8	10·5	6·6	16·5	10·3
46	9 26·5	9 28·1	9 00·7	4·6	2·9	10·6	6·6	16·6	10·4
47	9 26·8	9 28·3	9 00·9	4·7	2·9	10·7	6·7	16·7	10·4
48	9 27·0	9 28·6	9 01·2	4·8	3·0	10·8	6·8	16·8	10·5
49	9 27·3	9 28·8	9 01·4	4·9	3·1	10·9	6·8	16·9	10·6
50	9 27·5	9 29·1	9 01·6	5·0	3·1	11·0	6·9	17·0	10·6
51	9 27·8	9 29·3	9 01·9	5·1	3·2	11·1	6·9	17·1	10·7
52	9 28·0	9 29·6	9 02·1	5·2	3·3	11·2	7·0	17·2	10·8
53	9 28·3	9 29·8	9 02·4	5·3	3·3	11·3	7·1	17·3	10·8
54	9 28·5	9 30·1	9 02·6	5·4	3·4	11·4	7·1	17·4	10·9
55	9 28·8	9 30·3	9 02·8	5·5	3·4	11·5	7·2	17·5	10·9
56	9 29·0	9 30·6	9 03·1	5·6	3·5	11·6	7·3	17·6	11·0
57	9 29·3	9 30·8	9 03·3	5·7	3·6	11·7	7·3	17·7	11·1
58	9 29·5	9 31·1	9 03·6	5·8	3·6	11·8	7·4	17·8	11·1
59	9 29·8	9 31·3	9 03·8	5·9	3·7	11·9	7·4	17·9	11·2
60	9 30·0	9 31·6	9 04·0	6·0	3·8	12·0	7·5	18·0	11·3

38^m	SUN PLANETS	ARIES	MOON	v or d	Corr^n	v or d	Corr^n	v or d	Corr^n
s	° ′	° ′	° ′	′	′	′	′	′	′
00	9 30·0	9 31·6	9 04·0	0·0	0·0	6·0	3·9	12·0	7·7
01	9 30·3	9 31·8	9 04·3	0·1	0·1	6·1	3·9	12·1	7·8
02	9 30·5	9 32·1	9 04·5	0·2	0·1	6·2	4·0	12·2	7·8
03	9 30·8	9 32·3	9 04·7	0·3	0·2	6·3	4·0	12·3	7·9
04	9 31·0	9 32·6	9 05·0	0·4	0·3	6·4	4·1	12·4	8·0
05	9 31·3	9 32·8	9 05·2	0·5	0·3	6·5	4·2	12·5	8·0
06	9 31·5	9 33·1	9 05·5	0·6	0·4	6·6	4·2	12·6	8·1
07	9 31·8	9 33·3	9 05·7	0·7	0·4	6·7	4·3	12·7	8·1
08	9 32·0	9 33·6	9 05·9	0·8	0·5	6·8	4·4	12·8	8·2
09	9 32·3	9 33·8	9 06·2	0·9	0·6	6·9	4·4	12·9	8·3
10	9 32·5	9 34·1	9 06·4	1·0	0·6	7·0	4·5	13·0	8·3
11	9 32·8	9 34·3	9 06·7	1·1	0·7	7·1	4·6	13·1	8·4
12	9 33·0	9 34·6	9 06·9	1·2	0·8	7·2	4·6	13·2	8·5
13	9 33·3	9 34·8	9 07·1	1·3	0·8	7·3	4·7	13·3	8·5
14	9 33·5	9 35·1	9 07·4	1·4	0·9	7·4	4·7	13·4	8·6
15	9 33·8	9 35·3	9 07·6	1·5	1·0	7·5	4·8	13·5	8·7
16	9 34·0	9 35·6	9 07·9	1·6	1·0	7·6	4·9	13·6	8·7
17	9 34·3	9 35·8	9 08·1	1·7	1·1	7·7	4·9	13·7	8·8
18	9 34·5	9 36·1	9 08·3	1·8	1·2	7·8	5·0	13·8	8·9
19	9 34·8	9 36·3	9 08·6	1·9	1·2	7·9	5·1	13·9	8·9
20	9 35·0	9 36·6	9 08·8	2·0	1·3	8·0	5·1	14·0	9·0
21	9 35·3	9 36·8	9 09·0	2·1	1·3	8·1	5·2	14·1	9·0
22	9 35·5	9 37·1	9 09·3	2·2	1·4	8·2	5·3	14·2	9·1
23	9 35·8	9 37·3	9 09·5	2·3	1·5	8·3	5·3	14·3	9·2
24	9 36·0	9 37·6	9 09·8	2·4	1·5	8·4	5·4	14·4	9·2
25	9 36·3	9 37·8	9 10·0	2·5	1·6	8·5	5·5	14·5	9·3
26	9 36·5	9 38·1	9 10·2	2·6	1·7	8·6	5·5	14·6	9·4
27	9 36·8	9 38·3	9 10·5	2·7	1·7	8·7	5·6	14·7	9·4
28	9 37·0	9 38·6	9 10·7	2·8	1·8	8·8	5·6	14·8	9·5
29	9 37·3	9 38·8	9 11·0	2·9	1·9	8·9	5·7	14·9	9·6
30	9 37·5	9 39·1	9 11·2	3·0	1·9	9·0	5·8	15·0	9·6
31	9 37·8	9 39·3	9 11·4	3·1	2·0	9·1	5·8	15·1	9·7
32	9 38·0	9 39·6	9 11·7	3·2	2·1	9·2	5·9	15·2	9·8
33	9 38·3	9 39·8	9 11·9	3·3	2·1	9·3	6·0	15·3	9·8
34	9 38·5	9 40·1	9 12·1	3·4	2·2	9·4	6·0	15·4	9·9
35	9 38·8	9 40·3	9 12·4	3·5	2·2	9·5	6·1	15·5	9·9
36	9 39·0	9 40·6	9 12·6	3·6	2·3	9·6	6·2	15·6	10·0
37	9 39·3	9 40·8	9 12·9	3·7	2·4	9·7	6·2	15·7	10·1
38	9 39·5	9 41·1	9 13·1	3·8	2·4	9·8	6·3	15·8	10·1
39	9 39·8	9 41·3	9 13·3	3·9	2·5	9·9	6·4	15·9	10·2
40	9 40·0	9 41·6	9 13·6	4·0	2·6	10·0	6·4	16·0	10·3
41	9 40·3	9 41·8	9 13·8	4·1	2·6	10·1	6·5	16·1	10·3
42	9 40·5	9 42·1	9 14·1	4·2	2·7	10·2	6·5	16·2	10·4
43	9 40·8	9 42·3	9 14·3	4·3	2·8	10·3	6·6	16·3	10·5
44	9 41·0	9 42·6	9 14·5	4·4	2·8	10·4	6·7	16·4	10·5
45	9 41·3	9 42·8	9 14·8	4·5	2·9	10·5	6·7	16·5	10·6
46	9 41·5	9 43·1	9 15·0	4·6	3·0	10·6	6·8	16·6	10·7
47	9 41·8	9 43·3	9 15·2	4·7	3·0	10·7	6·9	16·7	10·7
48	9 42·0	9 43·6	9 15·5	4·8	3·1	10·8	6·9	16·8	10·8
49	9 42·3	9 43·8	9 15·7	4·9	3·1	10·9	7·0	16·9	10·8
50	9 42·5	9 44·1	9 16·0	5·0	3·2	11·0	7·1	17·0	10·9
51	9 42·8	9 44·3	9 16·2	5·1	3·3	11·1	7·1	17·1	11·0
52	9 43·0	9 44·6	9 16·4	5·2	3·3	11·2	7·2	17·2	11·0
53	9 43·3	9 44·8	9 16·7	5·3	3·4	11·3	7·3	17·3	11·1
54	9 43·5	9 45·1	9 16·9	5·4	3·5	11·4	7·3	17·4	11·2
55	9 43·8	9 45·3	9 17·2	5·5	3·5	11·5	7·4	17·5	11·2
56	9 44·0	9 45·6	9 17·4	5·6	3·6	11·6	7·4	17·6	11·3
57	9 44·3	9 45·8	9 17·6	5·7	3·7	11·7	7·5	17·7	11·4
58	9 44·5	9 46·1	9 17·9	5·8	3·7	11·8	7·6	17·8	11·4
59	9 44·8	9 46·4	9 18·1	5·9	3·8	11·9	7·6	17·9	11·5
60	9 45·0	9 46·6	9 18·4	6·0	3·9	12·0	7·7	18·0	11·6

39^m	SUN PLANETS	ARIES	MOON	v or d	Corr^n	v or d	Corr^n	v or d	Corr^n
s	° ′	° ′	° ′	′	′	′	′	′	′
00	9 45·0	9 46·6	9 18·4	0·0	0·0	6·0	4·0	12·0	7·9
01	9 45·3	9 46·9	9 18·6	0·1	0·1	6·1	4·0	12·1	8·0
02	9 45·5	9 47·1	9 18·8	0·2	0·1	6·2	4·1	12·2	8·0
03	9 45·8	9 47·4	9 19·1	0·3	0·2	6·3	4·1	12·3	8·1
04	9 46·0	9 47·6	9 19·3	0·4	0·3	6·4	4·2	12·4	8·2
05	9 46·3	9 47·9	9 19·5	0·5	0·3	6·5	4·3	12·5	8·2
06	9 46·5	9 48·1	9 19·8	0·6	0·4	6·6	4·3	12·6	8·3
07	9 46·8	9 48·4	9 20·0	0·7	0·5	6·7	4·4	12·7	8·4
08	9 47·0	9 48·6	9 20·3	0·8	0·5	6·8	4·5	12·8	8·4
09	9 47·3	9 48·9	9 20·5	0·9	0·6	6·9	4·5	12·9	8·5
10	9 47·5	9 49·1	9 20·7	1·0	0·7	7·0	4·6	13·0	8·6
11	9 47·8	9 49·4	9 21·0	1·1	0·7	7·1	4·7	13·1	8·6
12	9 48·0	9 49·6	9 21·2	1·2	0·8	7·2	4·7	13·2	8·7
13	9 48·3	9 49·9	9 21·5	1·3	0·9	7·3	4·8	13·3	8·8
14	9 48·5	9 50·1	9 21·7	1·4	0·9	7·4	4·9	13·4	8·8
15	9 48·8	9 50·4	9 21·9	1·5	1·0	7·5	4·9	13·5	8·9
16	9 49·0	9 50·6	9 22·2	1·6	1·1	7·6	5·0	13·6	9·0
17	9 49·3	9 50·9	9 22·4	1·7	1·1	7·7	5·1	13·7	9·0
18	9 49·5	9 51·1	9 22·6	1·8	1·2	7·8	5·1	13·8	9·1
19	9 49·8	9 51·4	9 22·9	1·9	1·3	7·9	5·2	13·9	9·2
20	9 50·0	9 51·6	9 23·1	2·0	1·3	8·0	5·3	14·0	9·2
21	9 50·3	9 51·9	9 23·4	2·1	1·4	8·1	5·3	14·1	9·3
22	9 50·5	9 52·1	9 23·6	2·2	1·4	8·2	5·4	14·2	9·3
23	9 50·8	9 52·4	9 23·8	2·3	1·5	8·3	5·5	14·3	9·4
24	9 51·0	9 52·6	9 24·1	2·4	1·6	8·4	5·5	14·4	9·5
25	9 51·3	9 52·9	9 24·3	2·5	1·6	8·5	5·6	14·5	9·5
26	9 51·5	9 53·1	9 24·6	2·6	1·7	8·6	5·7	14·6	9·6
27	9 51·8	9 53·4	9 24·8	2·7	1·8	8·7	5·7	14·7	9·7
28	9 52·0	9 53·6	9 25·0	2·8	1·8	8·8	5·8	14·8	9·7
29	9 52·3	9 53·9	9 25·3	2·9	1·9	8·9	5·9	14·9	9·8
30	9 52·5	9 54·1	9 25·5	3·0	2·0	9·0	5·9	15·0	9·9
31	9 52·8	9 54·4	9 25·7	3·1	2·0	9·1	6·0	15·1	9·9
32	9 53·0	9 54·6	9 26·0	3·2	2·1	9·2	6·1	15·2	10·0
33	9 53·3	9 54·9	9 26·2	3·3	2·2	9·3	6·1	15·3	10·1
34	9 53·5	9 55·1	9 26·5	3·4	2·2	9·4	6·2	15·4	10·1
35	9 53·8	9 55·4	9 26·7	3·5	2·3	9·5	6·3	15·5	10·2
36	9 54·0	9 55·6	9 26·9	3·6	2·4	9·6	6·3	15·6	10·3
37	9 54·3	9 55·9	9 27·2	3·7	2·4	9·7	6·4	15·7	10·3
38	9 54·5	9 56·1	9 27·4	3·8	2·5	9·8	6·5	15·8	10·4
39	9 54·8	9 56·4	9 27·7	3·9	2·6	9·9	6·5	15·9	10·5
40	9 55·0	9 56·6	9 27·9	4·0	2·6	10·0	6·6	16·0	10·5
41	9 55·3	9 56·9	9 28·1	4·1	2·7	10·1	6·6	16·1	10·6
42	9 55·5	9 57·1	9 28·4	4·2	2·8	10·2	6·7	16·2	10·7
43	9 55·8	9 57·4	9 28·6	4·3	2·8	10·3	6·8	16·3	10·7
44	9 56·0	9 57·6	9 28·8	4·4	2·9	10·4	6·8	16·4	10·8
45	9 56·3	9 57·9	9 29·1	4·5	3·0	10·5	6·9	16·5	10·9
46	9 56·5	9 58·1	9 29·3	4·6	3·0	10·6	7·0	16·6	10·9
47	9 56·8	9 58·4	9 29·6	4·7	3·1	10·7	7·0	16·7	11·0
48	9 57·0	9 58·6	9 29·8	4·8	3·2	10·8	7·1	16·8	11·1
49	9 57·3	9 58·9	9 30·0	4·9	3·2	10·9	7·2	16·9	11·1
50	9 57·5	9 59·1	9 30·3	5·0	3·3	11·0	7·2	17·0	11·2
51	9 57·8	9 59·4	9 30·5	5·1	3·4	11·1	7·3	17·1	11·3
52	9 58·0	9 59·6	9 30·8	5·2	3·4	11·2	7·4	17·2	11·3
53	9 58·3	9 59·9	9 31·0	5·3	3·5	11·3	7·4	17·3	11·4
54	9 58·5	10 00·1	9 31·2	5·4	3·6	11·4	7·5	17·4	11·5
55	9 58·8	10 00·4	9 31·5	5·5	3·6	11·5	7·6	17·5	11·5
56	9 59·0	10 00·6	9 31·7	5·6	3·7	11·6	7·6	17·6	11·6
57	9 59·3	10 00·9	9 32·0	5·7	3·8	11·7	7·7	17·7	11·7
58	9 59·5	10 01·1	9 32·2	5·8	3·8	11·8	7·8	17·8	11·7
59	9 59·8	10 01·4	9 32·4	5·9	3·9	11·9	7·8	17·9	11·8
60	10 00·0	10 01·6	9 32·7	6·0	4·0	12·0	7·9	18·0	11·9

m 40	SUN PLANETS	ARIES	MOON	v or d	Corrⁿ	v or d	Corrⁿ	v or d	Corrⁿ
s	° ′	° ′	° ′	′	′	′	′	′	′
00	10 00·0	10 01·6	9 32·7	0·0	0·0	6·0	4·1	12·0	8·1
01	10 00·3	10 01·9	9 32·9	0·1	0·1	6·1	4·1	12·1	8·2
02	10 00·5	10 02·1	9 33·1	0·2	0·1	6·2	4·2	12·2	8·2
03	10 00·8	10 02·4	9 33·4	0·3	0·2	6·3	4·3	12·3	8·3
04	10 01·0	10 02·6	9 33·6	0·4	0·3	6·4	4·3	12·4	8·4
05	10 01·3	10 02·9	9 33·9	0·5	0·3	6·5	4·4	12·5	8·4
06	10 01·5	10 03·1	9 34·1	0·6	0·4	6·6	4·5	12·6	8·5
07	10 01·8	10 03·4	9 34·3	0·7	0·5	6·7	4·5	12·7	8·6
08	10 02·0	10 03·6	9 34·6	0·8	0·5	6·8	4·6	12·8	8·6
09	10 02·3	10 03·9	9 34·8	0·9	0·6	6·9	4·7	12·9	8·7
10	10 02·5	10 04·1	9 35·1	1·0	0·7	7·0	4·7	13·0	8·8
11	10 02·8	10 04·4	9 35·3	1·1	0·7	7·1	4·8	13·1	8·8
12	10 03·0	10 04·7	9 35·5	1·2	0·8	7·2	4·9	13·2	8·9
13	10 03·3	10 04·9	9 35·8	1·3	0·9	7·3	4·9	13·3	9·0
14	10 03·5	10 05·2	9 36·0	1·4	0·9	7·4	5·0	13·4	9·0
15	10 03·8	10 05·4	9 36·2	1·5	1·0	7·5	5·1	13·5	9·1
16	10 04·0	10 05·7	9 36·5	1·6	1·1	7·6	5·1	13·6	9·2
17	10 04·3	10 05·9	9 36·7	1·7	1·1	7·7	5·2	13·7	9·2
18	10 04·5	10 06·2	9 37·0	1·8	1·2	7·8	5·3	13·8	9·3
19	10 04·8	10 06·4	9 37·2	1·9	1·3	7·9	5·3	13·9	9·4
20	10 05·0	10 06·7	9 37·4	2·0	1·4	8·0	5·4	14·0	9·5
21	10 05·3	10 06·9	9 37·7	2·1	1·4	8·1	5·5	14·1	9·5
22	10 05·5	10 07·2	9 37·9	2·2	1·5	8·2	5·5	14·2	9·6
23	10 05·8	10 07·4	9 38·2	2·3	1·6	8·3	5·6	14·3	9·7
24	10 06·0	10 07·7	9 38·4	2·4	1·6	8·4	5·7	14·4	9·7
25	10 06·3	10 07·9	9 38·6	2·5	1·7	8·5	5·7	14·5	9·8
26	10 06·5	10 08·2	9 38·9	2·6	1·8	8·6	5·8	14·6	9·9
27	10 06·8	10 08·4	9 39·1	2·7	1·8	8·7	5·9	14·7	9·9
28	10 07·0	10 08·7	9 39·3	2·8	1·9	8·8	5·9	14·8	10·0
29	10 07·3	10 08·9	9 39·6	2·9	2·0	8·9	6·0	14·9	10·1
30	10 07·5	10 09·2	9 39·8	3·0	2·0	9·0	6·1	15·0	10·1
31	10 07·8	10 09·4	9 40·1	3·1	2·1	9·1	6·1	15·1	10·2
32	10 08·0	10 09·7	9 40·3	3·2	2·2	9·2	6·2	15·2	10·3
33	10 08·3	10 09·9	9 40·5	3·3	2·2	9·3	6·3	15·3	10·3
34	10 08·5	10 10·2	9 40·8	3·4	2·3	9·4	6·3	15·4	10·4
35	10 08·8	10 10·4	9 41·0	3·5	2·4	9·5	6·4	15·5	10·5
36	10 09·0	10 10·7	9 41·3	3·6	2·4	9·6	6·5	15·6	10·5
37	10 09·3	10 10·9	9 41·5	3·7	2·5	9·7	6·5	15·7	10·6
38	10 09·5	10 11·2	9 41·7	3·8	2·6	9·8	6·6	15·8	10·7
39	10 09·8	10 11·4	9 42·0	3·9	2·6	9·9	6·7	15·9	10·7
40	10 10·0	10 11·7	9 42·2	4·0	2·7	10·0	6·8	16·0	10·8
41	10 10·3	10 11·9	9 42·4	4·1	2·8	10·1	6·8	16·1	10·9
42	10 10·5	10 12·2	9 42·7	4·2	2·8	10·2	6·9	16·2	10·9
43	10 10·8	10 12·4	9 42·9	4·3	2·9	10·3	7·0	16·3	11·0
44	10 11·0	10 12·7	9 43·2	4·4	3·0	10·4	7·0	16·4	11·1
45	10 11·3	10 12·9	9 43·4	4·5	3·0	10·5	7·1	16·5	11·1
46	10 11·5	10 13·2	9 43·6	4·6	3·1	10·6	7·2	16·6	11·2
47	10 11·8	10 13·4	9 43·9	4·7	3·2	10·7	7·2	16·7	11·3
48	10 12·0	10 13·7	9 44·1	4·8	3·2	10·8	7·3	16·8	11·3
49	10 12·3	10 13·9	9 44·4	4·9	3·3	10·9	7·4	16·9	11·4
50	10 12·5	10 14·2	9 44·6	5·0	3·4	11·0	7·4	17·0	11·5
51	10 12·8	10 14·4	9 44·8	5·1	3·4	11·1	7·5	17·1	11·5
52	10 13·0	10 14·7	9 45·1	5·2	3·5	11·2	7·6	17·2	11·6
53	10 13·3	10 14·9	9 45·3	5·3	3·6	11·3	7·6	17·3	11·7
54	10 13·5	10 15·2	9 45·6	5·4	3·6	11·4	7·7	17·4	11·7
55	10 13·8	10 15·4	9 45·8	5·5	3·7	11·5	7·8	17·5	11·8
56	10 14·0	10 15·7	9 46·0	5·6	3·8	11·6	7·8	17·6	11·9
57	10 14·3	10 15·9	9 46·3	5·7	3·8	11·7	7·9	17·7	11·9
58	10 14·5	10 16·2	9 46·5	5·8	3·9	11·8	8·0	17·8	12·0
59	10 14·8	10 16·4	9 46·7	5·9	4·0	11·9	8·0	17·9	12·1
60	10 15·0	10 16·7	9 47·0	6·0	4·1	12·0	8·1	18·0	12·2

m 41	SUN PLANETS	ARIES	MOON	v or d	Corrⁿ	v or d	Corrⁿ	v or d	Corrⁿ
s	° ′	° ′	° ′	′	′	′	′	′	′
00	10 15·0	10 16·7	9 47·0	0·0	0·0	6·0	4·2	12·0	8·3
01	10 15·3	10 16·9	9 47·2	0·1	0·1	6·1	4·2	12·1	8·4
02	10 15·5	10 17·2	9 47·5	0·2	0·1	6·2	4·3	12·2	8·4
03	10 15·8	10 17·4	9 47·7	0·3	0·2	6·3	4·4	12·3	8·5
04	10 16·0	10 17·7	9 47·9	0·4	0·3	6·4	4·4	12·4	8·6
05	10 16·3	10 17·9	9 48·2	0·5	0·3	6·5	4·5	12·5	8·6
06	10 16·5	10 18·2	9 48·4	0·6	0·4	6·6	4·6	12·6	8·7
07	10 16·8	10 18·4	9 48·7	0·7	0·5	6·7	4·6	12·7	8·8
08	10 17·0	10 18·7	9 48·9	0·8	0·6	6·8	4·7	12·8	8·9
09	10 17·3	10 18·9	9 49·1	0·9	0·6	6·9	4·8	12·9	8·9
10	10 17·5	10 19·2	9 49·4	1·0	0·7	7·0	4·8	13·0	9·0
11	10 17·8	10 19·4	9 49·6	1·1	0·8	7·1	4·9	13·1	9·1
12	10 18·0	10 19·7	9 49·8	1·2	0·8	7·2	5·0	13·2	9·1
13	10 18·3	10 19·9	9 50·1	1·3	0·9	7·3	5·0	13·3	9·2
14	10 18·5	10 20·2	9 50·3	1·4	1·0	7·4	5·1	13·4	9·3
15	10 18·8	10 20·4	9 50·6	1·5	1·0	7·5	5·2	13·5	9·3
16	10 19·0	10 20·7	9 50·8	1·6	1·1	7·6	5·3	13·6	9·4
17	10 19·3	10 20·9	9 51·0	1·7	1·2	7·7	5·3	13·7	9·5
18	10 19·5	10 21·2	9 51·3	1·8	1·2	7·8	5·4	13·8	9·5
19	10 19·8	10 21·4	9 51·5	1·9	1·3	7·9	5·5	13·9	9·6
20	10 20·0	10 21·7	9 51·8	2·0	1·4	8·0	5·5	14·0	9·7
21	10 20·3	10 21·9	9 52·0	2·1	1·5	8·1	5·6	14·1	9·8
22	10 20·5	10 22·2	9 52·2	2·2	1·5	8·2	5·7	14·2	9·8
23	10 20·8	10 22·4	9 52·5	2·3	1·6	8·3	5·7	14·3	9·9
24	10 21·0	10 22·7	9 52·7	2·4	1·7	8·4	5·8	14·4	10·0
25	10 21·3	10 23·0	9 52·9	2·5	1·7	8·5	5·9	14·5	10·0
26	10 21·5	10 23·2	9 53·2	2·6	1·8	8·6	5·9	14·6	10·1
27	10 21·8	10 23·5	9 53·4	2·7	1·9	8·7	6·0	14·7	10·2
28	10 22·0	10 23·7	9 53·7	2·8	1·9	8·8	6·1	14·8	10·2
29	10 22·3	10 24·0	9 53·9	2·9	2·0	8·9	6·2	14·9	10·3
30	10 22·5	10 24·2	9 54·1	3·0	2·1	9·0	6·2	15·0	10·4
31	10 22·8	10 24·5	9 54·4	3·1	2·1	9·1	6·3	15·1	10·4
32	10 23·0	10 24·7	9 54·6	3·2	2·2	9·2	6·4	15·2	10·5
33	10 23·3	10 25·0	9 54·9	3·3	2·3	9·3	6·4	15·3	10·6
34	10 23·5	10 25·2	9 55·1	3·4	2·4	9·4	6·5	15·4	10·7
35	10 23·8	10 25·5	9 55·3	3·5	2·4	9·5	6·6	15·5	10·7
36	10 24·0	10 25·7	9 55·6	3·6	2·5	9·6	6·6	15·6	10·8
37	10 24·3	10 26·0	9 55·8	3·7	2·6	9·7	6·7	15·7	10·9
38	10 24·5	10 26·2	9 56·1	3·8	2·6	9·8	6·8	15·8	10·9
39	10 24·8	10 26·5	9 56·3	3·9	2·7	9·9	6·8	15·9	11·0
40	10 25·0	10 26·7	9 56·5	4·0	2·8	10·0	6·9	16·0	11·1
41	10 25·3	10 27·0	9 56·8	4·1	2·8	10·1	7·0	16·1	11·1
42	10 25·5	10 27·2	9 57·0	4·2	2·9	10·2	7·1	16·2	11·2
43	10 25·8	10 27·5	9 57·2	4·3	3·0	10·3	7·1	16·3	11·3
44	10 26·0	10 27·7	9 57·5	4·4	3·0	10·4	7·2	16·4	11·3
45	10 26·3	10 28·0	9 57·7	4·5	3·1	10·5	7·3	16·5	11·4
46	10 26·5	10 28·2	9 58·0	4·6	3·2	10·6	7·3	16·6	11·5
47	10 26·8	10 28·5	9 58·2	4·7	3·3	10·7	7·4	16·7	11·6
48	10 27·0	10 28·7	9 58·4	4·8	3·3	10·8	7·5	16·8	11·6
49	10 27·3	10 29·0	9 58·7	4·9	3·4	10·9	7·5	16·9	11·7
50	10 27·5	10 29·2	9 58·9	5·0	3·5	11·0	7·6	17·0	11·8
51	10 27·8	10 29·5	9 59·2	5·1	3·5	11·1	7·7	17·1	11·8
52	10 28·0	10 29·7	9 59·4	5·2	3·6	11·2	7·7	17·2	11·9
53	10 28·3	10 30·0	9 59·6	5·3	3·7	11·3	7·8	17·3	12·0
54	10 28·5	10 30·2	9 59·9	5·4	3·7	11·4	7·9	17·4	12·0
55	10 28·8	10 30·5	10 00·1	5·5	3·8	11·5	8·0	17·5	12·1
56	10 29·0	10 30·7	10 00·3	5·6	3·9	11·6	8·0	17·6	12·2
57	10 29·3	10 31·0	10 00·6	5·7	3·9	11·7	8·1	17·7	12·2
58	10 29·5	10 31·2	10 00·8	5·8	4·0	11·8	8·2	17·8	12·3
59	10 29·8	10 31·5	10 01·1	5·9	4·1	11·9	8·2	17·9	12·4
60	10 30·0	10 31·7	10 01·3	6·0	4·2	12·0	8·3	18·0	12·5

42^m	SUN PLANETS	ARIES	MOON	v or d	Corr^n	v or d	Corr^n	v or d	Corr^n
s	° ′	° ′	° ′	′	′	′	′	′	′
00	10 30·0	10 31·7	10 01·3	0·0	0·0	6·0	4·3	12·0	8·5
01	10 30·3	10 32·0	10 01·5	0·1	0·1	6·1	4·3	12·1	8·6
02	10 30·5	10 32·2	10 01·8	0·2	0·1	6·2	4·4	12·2	8·6
03	10 30·8	10 32·5	10 02·0	0·3	0·2	6·3	4·5	12·3	8·7
04	10 31·0	10 32·7	10 02·3	0·4	0·3	6·4	4·5	12·4	8·8
05	10 31·3	10 33·0	10 02·5	0·5	0·4	6·5	4·6	12·5	8·9
06	10 31·5	10 33·2	10 02·7	0·6	0·4	6·6	4·7	12·6	8·9
07	10 31·8	10 33·5	10 03·0	0·7	0·5	6·7	4·7	12·7	9·0
08	10 32·0	10 33·7	10 03·2	0·8	0·6	6·8	4·8	12·8	9·1
09	10 32·3	10 34·0	10 03·4	0·9	0·6	6·9	4·9	12·9	9·1
10	10 32·5	10 34·2	10 03·7	1·0	0·7	7·0	5·0	13·0	9·2
11	10 32·8	10 34·5	10 03·9	1·1	0·8	7·1	5·0	13·1	9·3
12	10 33·0	10 34·7	10 04·2	1·2	0·9	7·2	5·1	13·2	9·4
13	10 33·3	10 35·0	10 04·4	1·3	0·9	7·3	5·2	13·3	9·4
14	10 33·5	10 35·2	10 04·6	1·4	1·0	7·4	5·2	13·4	9·5
15	10 33·8	10 35·5	10 04·9	1·5	1·1	7·5	5·3	13·5	9·6
16	10 34·0	10 35·7	10 05·1	1·6	1·1	7·6	5·4	13·6	9·6
17	10 34·3	10 36·0	10 05·4	1·7	1·2	7·7	5·5	13·7	9·7
18	10 34·5	10 36·2	10 05·6	1·8	1·3	7·8	5·5	13·8	9·8
19	10 34·8	10 36·5	10 05·8	1·9	1·3	7·9	5·6	13·9	9·8
20	10 35·0	10 36·7	10 06·1	2·0	1·4	8·0	5·7	14·0	9·9
21	10 35·3	10 37·0	10 06·3	2·1	1·5	8·1	5·7	14·1	10·0
22	10 35·5	10 37·2	10 06·5	2·2	1·6	8·2	5·8	14·2	10·1
23	10 35·8	10 37·5	10 06·8	2·3	1·6	8·3	5·9	14·3	10·1
24	10 36·0	10 37·7	10 07·0	2·4	1·7	8·4	6·0	14·4	10·2
25	10 36·3	10 38·0	10 07·3	2·5	1·8	8·5	6·0	14·5	10·3
26	10 36·5	10 38·2	10 07·5	2·6	1·8	8·6	6·1	14·6	10·3
27	10 36·8	10 38·5	10 07·7	2·7	1·9	8·7	6·2	14·7	10·4
28	10 37·0	10 38·7	10 08·0	2·8	2·0	8·8	6·2	14·8	10·5
29	10 37·3	10 39·0	10 08·2	2·9	2·1	8·9	6·3	14·9	10·6
30	10 37·5	10 39·2	10 08·5	3·0	2·1	9·0	6·4	15·0	10·6
31	10 37·8	10 39·5	10 08·7	3·1	2·2	9·1	6·4	15·1	10·7
32	10 38·0	10 39·7	10 08·9	3·2	2·3	9·2	6·5	15·2	10·8
33	10 38·3	10 40·0	10 09·2	3·3	2·3	9·3	6·6	15·3	10·8
34	10 38·5	10 40·2	10 09·4	3·4	2·4	9·4	6·7	15·4	10·9
35	10 38·8	10 40·5	10 09·7	3·5	2·5	9·5	6·7	15·5	11·0
36	10 39·0	10 40·7	10 09·9	3·6	2·6	9·6	6·8	15·6	11·1
37	10 39·3	10 41·0	10 10·1	3·7	2·6	9·7	6·9	15·7	11·1
38	10 39·5	10 41·3	10 10·4	3·8	2·7	9·8	6·9	15·8	11·2
39	10 39·8	10 41·5	10 10·6	3·9	2·8	9·9	7·0	15·9	11·3
40	10 40·0	10 41·8	10 10·8	4·0	2·8	10·0	7·1	16·0	11·3
41	10 40·3	10 42·0	10 11·1	4·1	2·9	10·1	7·2	16·1	11·4
42	10 40·5	10 42·3	10 11·3	4·2	3·0	10·2	7·2	16·2	11·5
43	10 40·8	10 42·5	10 11·6	4·3	3·0	10·3	7·3	16·3	11·5
44	10 41·0	10 42·8	10 11·8	4·4	3·1	10·4	7·4	16·4	11·6
45	10 41·3	10 43·0	10 12·0	4·5	3·2	10·5	7·4	16·5	11·7
46	10 41·5	10 43·3	10 12·3	4·6	3·3	10·6	7·5	16·6	11·8
47	10 41·8	10 43·5	10 12·5	4·7	3·3	10·7	7·6	16·7	11·8
48	10 42·0	10 43·8	10 12·8	4·8	3·4	10·8	7·7	16·8	11·9
49	10 42·3	10 44·0	10 13·0	4·9	3·5	10·9	7·7	16·9	12·0
50	10 42·5	10 44·3	10 13·2	5·0	3·5	11·0	7·8	17·0	12·0
51	10 42·8	10 44·5	10 13·5	5·1	3·6	11·1	7·9	17·1	12·1
52	10 43·0	10 44·8	10 13·7	5·2	3·7	11·2	7·9	17·2	12·2
53	10 43·3	10 45·0	10 13·9	5·3	3·8	11·3	8·0	17·3	12·3
54	10 43·5	10 45·3	10 14·2	5·4	3·8	11·4	8·1	17·4	12·3
55	10 43·8	10 45·5	10 14·4	5·5	3·9	11·5	8·1	17·5	12·4
56	10 44·0	10 45·8	10 14·7	5·6	4·0	11·6	8·2	17·6	12·5
57	10 44·3	10 46·0	10 14·9	5·7	4·0	11·7	8·3	17·7	12·5
58	10 44·5	10 46·3	10 15·1	5·8	4·1	11·8	8·4	17·8	12·6
59	10 44·8	10 46·5	10 15·4	5·9	4·2	11·9	8·4	17·9	12·7
60	10 45·0	10 46·8	10 15·6	6·0	4·3	12·0	8·5	18·0	12·8

43^m	SUN PLANETS	ARIES	MOON	v or d	Corr^n	v or d	Corr^n	v or d	Corr^n
s	° ′	° ′	° ′	′	′	′	′	′	′
00	10 45·0	10 46·8	10 15·6	0·0	0·0	6·0	4·4	12·0	8·7
01	10 45·3	10 47·0	10 15·9	0·1	0·1	6·1	4·4	12·1	8·8
02	10 45·5	10 47·3	10 16·1	0·2	0·1	6·2	4·5	12·2	8·8
03	10 45·8	10 47·5	10 16·3	0·3	0·2	6·3	4·6	12·3	8·9
04	10 46·0	10 47·8	10 16·6	0·4	0·3	6·4	4·6	12·4	9·0
05	10 46·3	10 48·0	10 16·8	0·5	0·4	6·5	4·7	12·5	9·1
06	10 46·5	10 48·3	10 17·0	0·6	0·4	6·6	4·8	12·6	9·1
07	10 46·8	10 48·5	10 17·3	0·7	0·5	6·7	4·9	12·7	9·2
08	10 47·0	10 48·8	10 17·5	0·8	0·6	6·8	4·9	12·8	9·3
09	10 47·3	10 49·0	10 17·8	0·9	0·7	6·9	5·0	12·9	9·4
10	10 47·5	10 49·3	10 18·0	1·0	0·7	7·0	5·1	13·0	9·4
11	10 47·8	10 49·5	10 18·2	1·1	0·8	7·1	5·1	13·1	9·5
12	10 48·0	10 49·8	10 18·5	1·2	0·9	7·2	5·2	13·2	9·6
13	10 48·3	10 50·0	10 18·7	1·3	0·9	7·3	5·3	13·3	9·6
14	10 48·5	10 50·3	10 19·0	1·4	1·0	7·4	5·4	13·4	9·7
15	10 48·8	10 50·5	10 19·2	1·5	1·1	7·5	5·4	13·5	9·8
16	10 49·0	10 50·8	10 19·4	1·6	1·2	7·6	5·5	13·6	9·9
17	10 49·3	10 51·0	10 19·7	1·7	1·2	7·7	5·6	13·7	9·9
18	10 49·5	10 51·3	10 19·9	1·8	1·3	7·8	5·7	13·8	10·0
19	10 49·8	10 51·5	10 20·2	1·9	1·4	7·9	5·7	13·9	10·1
20	10 50·0	10 51·8	10 20·4	2·0	1·5	8·0	5·8	14·0	10·2
21	10 50·3	10 52·0	10 20·6	2·1	1·5	8·1	5·9	14·1	10·2
22	10 50·5	10 52·3	10 20·9	2·2	1·6	8·2	5·9	14·2	10·3
23	10 50·8	10 52·5	10 21·1	2·3	1·7	8·3	6·0	14·3	10·4
24	10 51·0	10 52·8	10 21·3	2·4	1·7	8·4	6·1	14·4	10·4
25	10 51·3	10 53·0	10 21·6	2·5	1·8	8·5	6·2	14·5	10·5
26	10 51·5	10 53·3	10 21·8	2·6	1·9	8·6	6·2	14·6	10·6
27	10 51·8	10 53·5	10 22·1	2·7	2·0	8·7	6·3	14·7	10·7
28	10 52·0	10 53·8	10 22·3	2·8	2·0	8·8	6·4	14·8	10·7
29	10 52·3	10 54·0	10 22·5	2·9	2·1	8·9	6·5	14·9	10·8
30	10 52·5	10 54·3	10 22·8	3·0	2·2	9·0	6·5	15·0	10·9
31	10 52·8	10 54·5	10 23·0	3·1	2·2	9·1	6·6	15·1	10·9
32	10 53·0	10 54·8	10 23·3	3·2	2·3	9·2	6·7	15·2	11·0
33	10 53·3	10 55·0	10 23·5	3·3	2·4	9·3	6·7	15·3	11·1
34	10 53·5	10 55·3	10 23·7	3·4	2·5	9·4	6·8	15·4	11·2
35	10 53·8	10 55·5	10 24·0	3·5	2·5	9·5	6·9	15·5	11·2
36	10 54·0	10 55·8	10 24·2	3·6	2·6	9·6	7·0	15·6	11·3
37	10 54·3	10 56·0	10 24·4	3·7	2·7	9·7	7·0	15·7	11·4
38	10 54·5	10 56·3	10 24·7	3·8	2·8	9·8	7·1	15·8	11·5
39	10 54·8	10 56·5	10 24·9	3·9	2·8	9·9	7·2	15·9	11·5
40	10 55·0	10 56·8	10 25·2	4·0	2·9	10·0	7·3	16·0	11·6
41	10 55·3	10 57·0	10 25·4	4·1	3·0	10·1	7·3	16·1	11·7
42	10 55·5	10 57·3	10 25·6	4·2	3·0	10·2	7·4	16·2	11·7
43	10 55·8	10 57·5	10 25·9	4·3	3·1	10·3	7·5	16·3	11·8
44	10 56·0	10 57·8	10 26·1	4·4	3·2	10·4	7·5	16·4	11·9
45	10 56·3	10 58·0	10 26·4	4·5	3·3	10·5	7·6	16·5	12·0
46	10 56·5	10 58·3	10 26·6	4·6	3·3	10·6	7·7	16·6	12·0
47	10 56·8	10 58·5	10 26·8	4·7	3·4	10·7	7·8	16·7	12·1
48	10 57·0	10 58·8	10 27·1	4·8	3·5	10·8	7·8	16·8	12·2
49	10 57·3	10 59·0	10 27·3	4·9	3·6	10·9	7·9	16·9	12·3
50	10 57·5	10 59·3	10 27·5	5·0	3·6	11·0	8·0	17·0	12·3
51	10 57·8	10 59·6	10 27·8	5·1	3·7	11·1	8·0	17·1	12·4
52	10 58·0	10 59·8	10 28·0	5·2	3·8	11·2	8·1	17·2	12·5
53	10 58·3	11 00·1	10 28·3	5·3	3·8	11·3	8·2	17·3	12·5
54	10 58·5	11 00·3	10 28·5	5·4	3·9	11·4	8·3	17·4	12·6
55	10 58·8	11 00·6	10 28·7	5·5	4·0	11·5	8·3	17·5	12·7
56	10 59·0	11 00·8	10 29·0	5·6	4·1	11·6	8·4	17·6	12·8
57	10 59·3	11 01·1	10 29·2	5·7	4·1	11·7	8·5	17·7	12·8
58	10 59·5	11 01·3	10 29·5	5·8	4·2	11·8	8·6	17·8	12·9
59	10 59·8	11 01·6	10 29·7	5·9	4·3	11·9	8·6	17·9	13·0
60	11 00·0	11 01·8	10 29·9	6·0	4·4	12·0	8·7	18·0	13·1

44m s	SUN PLANETS ° ′	ARIES ° ′	MOON ° ′	v or d ′	Corrⁿ ′	v or d ′	Corrⁿ ′	v or d ′	Corrⁿ ′
00	11 00·0	11 01·8	10 29·9	0·0	0·0	6·0	4·5	12·0	8·9
01	11 00·3	11 02·1	10 30·2	0·1	0·1	6·1	4·5	12·1	9·0
02	11 00·5	11 02·3	10 30·4	0·2	0·1	6·2	4·6	12·2	9·0
03	11 00·8	11 02·6	10 30·6	0·3	0·2	6·3	4·7	12·3	9·1
04	11 01·0	11 02·8	10 30·9	0·4	0·3	6·4	4·7	12·4	9·2
05	11 01·3	11 03·1	10 31·1	0·5	0·4	6·5	4·8	12·5	9·3
06	11 01·5	11 03·3	10 31·4	0·6	0·4	6·6	4·9	12·6	9·3
07	11 01·8	11 03·6	10 31·6	0·7	0·5	6·7	5·0	12·7	9·4
08	11 02·0	11 03·8	10 31·8	0·8	0·6	6·8	5·0	12·8	9·5
09	11 02·3	11 04·1	10 32·1	0·9	0·7	6·9	5·1	12·9	9·6
10	11 02·5	11 04·3	10 32·3	1·0	0·7	7·0	5·2	13·0	9·6
11	11 02·8	11 04·6	10 32·6	1·1	0·8	7·1	5·3	13·1	9·7
12	11 03·0	11 04·8	10 32·8	1·2	0·9	7·2	5·3	13·2	9·8
13	11 03·3	11 05·1	10 33·0	1·3	1·0	7·3	5·4	13·3	9·9
14	11 03·5	11 05·3	10 33·3	1·4	1·0	7·4	5·5	13·4	9·9
15	11 03·8	11 05·6	10 33·5	1·5	1·1	7·5	5·6	13·5	10·0
16	11 04·0	11 05·8	10 33·8	1·6	1·2	7·6	5·6	13·6	10·1
17	11 04·3	11 06·1	10 34·0	1·7	1·3	7·7	5·7	13·7	10·2
18	11 04·5	11 06·3	10 34·2	1·8	1·3	7·8	5·8	13·8	10·2
19	11 04·8	11 06·6	10 34·5	1·9	1·4	7·9	5·9	13·9	10·3
20	11 05·0	11 06·8	10 34·7	2·0	1·5	8·0	5·9	14·0	10·4
21	11 05·3	11 07·1	10 34·9	2·1	1·6	8·1	6·0	14·1	10·5
22	11 05·5	11 07·3	10 35·2	2·2	1·6	8·2	6·1	14·2	10·5
23	11 05·8	11 07·6	10 35·4	2·3	1·7	8·3	6·2	14·3	10·6
24	11 06·0	11 07·8	10 35·7	2·4	1·8	8·4	6·2	14·4	10·7
25	11 06·3	11 08·1	10 35·9	2·5	1·9	8·5	6·3	14·5	10·8
26	11 06·5	11 08·3	10 36·1	2·6	1·9	8·6	6·4	14·6	10·8
27	11 06·8	11 08·6	10 36·4	2·7	2·0	8·7	6·5	14·7	10·9
28	11 07·0	11 08·8	10 36·6	2·8	2·1	8·8	6·5	14·8	11·0
29	11 07·3	11 09·1	10 36·9	2·9	2·2	8·9	6·6	14·9	11·1
30	11 07·5	11 09·3	10 37·1	3·0	2·2	9·0	6·7	15·0	11·1
31	11 07·8	11 09·6	10 37·3	3·1	2·3	9·1	6·7	15·1	11·2
32	11 08·0	11 09·8	10 37·6	3·2	2·4	9·2	6·8	15·2	11·3
33	11 08·3	11 10·1	10 37·8	3·3	2·4	9·3	6·9	15·3	11·3
34	11 08·5	11 10·3	10 38·0	3·4	2·5	9·4	7·0	15·4	11·4
35	11 08·8	11 10·6	10 38·3	3·5	2·6	9·5	7·0	15·5	11·5
36	11 09·0	11 10·8	10 38·5	3·6	2·7	9·6	7·1	15·6	11·6
37	11 09·3	11 11·1	10 38·8	3·7	2·7	9·7	7·2	15·7	11·6
38	11 09·5	11 11·3	10 39·0	3·8	2·8	9·8	7·3	15·8	11·7
39	11 09·8	11 11·6	10 39·2	3·9	2·9	9·9	7·3	15·9	11·8
40	11 10·0	11 11·8	10 39·5	4·0	3·0	10·0	7·4	16·0	11·9
41	11 10·3	11 12·1	10 39·7	4·1	3·0	10·1	7·5	16·1	11·9
42	11 10·5	11 12·3	10 40·0	4·2	3·1	10·2	7·6	16·2	12·0
43	11 10·8	11 12·6	10 40·2	4·3	3·2	10·3	7·6	16·3	12·1
44	11 11·0	11 12·8	10 40·4	4·4	3·3	10·4	7·7	16·4	12·2
45	11 11·3	11 13·1	10 40·7	4·5	3·3	10·5	7·8	16·5	12·2
46	11 11·5	11 13·3	10 40·9	4·6	3·4	10·6	7·9	16·6	12·3
47	11 11·8	11 13·6	10 41·1	4·7	3·5	10·7	7·9	16·7	12·4
48	11 12·0	11 13·8	10 41·4	4·8	3·6	10·8	8·0	16·8	12·5
49	11 12·3	11 14·1	10 41·6	4·9	3·6	10·9	8·1	16·9	12·5
50	11 12·5	11 14·3	10 41·9	5·0	3·7	11·0	8·2	17·0	12·6
51	11 12·8	11 14·6	10 42·1	5·1	3·8	11·1	8·2	17·1	12·7
52	11 13·0	11 14·8	10 42·3	5·2	3·9	11·2	8·3	17·2	12·8
53	11 13·3	11 15·1	10 42·6	5·3	3·9	11·3	8·4	17·3	12·8
54	11 13·5	11 15·3	10 42·8	5·4	4·0	11·4	8·5	17·4	12·9
55	11 13·8	11 15·6	10 43·1	5·5	4·1	11·5	8·5	17·5	13·0
56	11 14·0	11 15·8	10 43·3	5·6	4·2	11·6	8·6	17·6	13·1
57	11 14·3	11 16·1	10 43·5	5·7	4·2	11·7	8·7	17·7	13·1
58	11 14·5	11 16·3	10 43·8	5·8	4·3	11·8	8·8	17·8	13·2
59	11 14·8	11 16·6	10 44·0	5·9	4·4	11·9	8·8	17·9	13·3
60	11 15·0	11 16·8	10 44·3	6·0	4·5	12·0	8·9	18·0	13·4

45m s	SUN PLANETS ° ′	ARIES ° ′	MOON ° ′	v or d ′	Corrⁿ ′	v or d ′	Corrⁿ ′	v or d ′	Corrⁿ ′
00	11 15·0	11 16·8	10 44·3	0·0	0·0	6·0	4·6	12·0	9·1
01	11 15·3	11 17·1	10 44·5	0·1	0·1	6·1	4·6	12·1	9·2
02	11 15·5	11 17·3	10 44·7	0·2	0·2	6·2	4·7	12·2	9·3
03	11 15·8	11 17·6	10 45·0	0·3	0·2	6·3	4·8	12·3	9·3
04	11 16·0	11 17·9	10 45·2	0·4	0·3	6·4	4·9	12·4	9·4
05	11 16·3	11 18·1	10 45·4	0·5	0·4	6·5	4·9	12·5	9·5
06	11 16·5	11 18·4	10 45·7	0·6	0·5	6·6	5·0	12·6	9·6
07	11 16·8	11 18·6	10 45·9	0·7	0·5	6·7	5·1	12·7	9·6
08	11 17·0	11 18·9	10 46·2	0·8	0·6	6·8	5·2	12·8	9·7
09	11 17·3	11 19·1	10 46·4	0·9	0·7	6·9	5·2	12·9	9·8
10	11 17·5	11 19·4	10 46·6	1·0	0·8	7·0	5·3	13·0	9·9
11	11 17·8	11 19·6	10 46·9	1·1	0·8	7·1	5·4	13·1	9·9
12	11 18·0	11 19·9	10 47·1	1·2	0·9	7·2	5·5	13·2	10·0
13	11 18·3	11 20·1	10 47·4	1·3	1·0	7·3	5·5	13·3	10·1
14	11 18·5	11 20·4	10 47·6	1·4	1·1	7·4	5·6	13·4	10·2
15	11 18·8	11 20·6	10 47·8	1·5	1·1	7·5	5·7	13·5	10·2
16	11 19·0	11 20·9	10 48·1	1·6	1·2	7·6	5·8	13·6	10·3
17	11 19·3	11 21·1	10 48·3	1·7	1·3	7·7	5·8	13·7	10·4
18	11 19·5	11 21·4	10 48·5	1·8	1·4	7·8	5·9	13·8	10·5
19	11 19·8	11 21·6	10 48·8	1·9	1·4	7·9	6·0	13·9	10·5
20	11 20·0	11 21·9	10 49·0	2·0	1·5	8·0	6·1	14·0	10·6
21	11 20·3	11 22·1	10 49·3	2·1	1·6	8·1	6·1	14·1	10·7
22	11 20·5	11 22·4	10 49·5	2·2	1·7	8·2	6·2	14·2	10·8
23	11 20·8	11 22·6	10 49·7	2·3	1·7	8·3	6·3	14·3	10·8
24	11 21·0	11 22·9	10 50·0	2·4	1·8	8·4	6·4	14·4	10·9
25	11 21·3	11 23·1	10 50·2	2·5	1·9	8·5	6·4	14·5	11·0
26	11 21·5	11 23·4	10 50·5	2·6	2·0	8·6	6·5	14·6	11·1
27	11 21·8	11 23·6	10 50·7	2·7	2·0	8·7	6·6	14·7	11·1
28	11 22·0	11 23·9	10 50·9	2·8	2·1	8·8	6·7	14·8	11·2
29	11 22·3	11 24·1	10 51·2	2·9	2·2	8·9	6·7	14·9	11·3
30	11 22·5	11 24·4	10 51·4	3·0	2·3	9·0	6·8	15·0	11·4
31	11 22·8	11 24·6	10 51·6	3·1	2·4	9·1	6·9	15·1	11·5
32	11 23·0	11 24·9	10 51·9	3·2	2·4	9·2	7·0	15·2	11·5
33	11 23·3	11 25·1	10 52·1	3·3	2·5	9·3	7·1	15·3	11·6
34	11 23·5	11 25·4	10 52·4	3·4	2·6	9·4	7·1	15·4	11·7
35	11 23·8	11 25·6	10 52·6	3·5	2·7	9·5	7·2	15·5	11·8
36	11 24·0	11 25·9	10 52·8	3·6	2·7	9·6	7·3	15·6	11·8
37	11 24·3	11 26·1	10 53·1	3·7	2·8	9·7	7·4	15·7	11·9
38	11 24·5	11 26·4	10 53·3	3·8	2·9	9·8	7·4	15·8	12·0
39	11 24·8	11 26·6	10 53·6	3·9	3·0	9·9	7·5	15·9	12·1
40	11 25·0	11 26·9	10 53·8	4·0	3·0	10·0	7·6	16·0	12·1
41	11 25·3	11 27·1	10 54·0	4·1	3·1	10·1	7·7	16·1	12·2
42	11 25·5	11 27·4	10 54·3	4·2	3·2	10·2	7·7	16·2	12·3
43	11 25·8	11 27·6	10 54·5	4·3	3·3	10·3	7·8	16·3	12·4
44	11 26·0	11 27·9	10 54·7	4·4	3·3	10·4	7·9	16·4	12·4
45	11 26·3	11 28·1	10 55·0	4·5	3·4	10·5	8·0	16·5	12·5
46	11 26·5	11 28·4	10 55·2	4·6	3·5	10·6	8·0	16·6	12·6
47	11 26·8	11 28·6	10 55·5	4·7	3·6	10·7	8·1	16·7	12·7
48	11 27·0	11 28·9	10 55·7	4·8	3·6	10·8	8·2	16·8	12·7
49	11 27·3	11 29·1	10 55·9	4·9	3·7	10·9	8·3	16·9	12·8
50	11 27·5	11 29·4	10 56·2	5·0	3·8	11·0	8·3	17·0	12·9
51	11 27·8	11 29·6	10 56·4	5·1	3·9	11·1	8·4	17·1	13·0
52	11 28·0	11 29·9	10 56·7	5·2	3·9	11·2	8·5	17·2	13·0
53	11 28·3	11 30·1	10 56·9	5·3	4·0	11·3	8·6	17·3	13·1
54	11 28·5	11 30·4	10 57·1	5·4	4·1	11·4	8·6	17·4	13·2
55	11 28·8	11 30·6	10 57·4	5·5	4·2	11·5	8·7	17·5	13·3
56	11 29·0	11 30·9	10 57·6	5·6	4·2	11·6	8·8	17·6	13·3
57	11 29·3	11 31·1	10 57·9	5·7	4·3	11·7	8·9	17·7	13·4
58	11 29·5	11 31·4	10 58·1	5·8	4·4	11·8	8·9	17·8	13·5
59	11 29·8	11 31·6	10 58·3	5·9	4·5	11·9	9·0	17·9	13·6
60	11 30·0	11 31·9	10 58·6	6·0	4·6	12·0	9·1	18·0	13·7

46ᵐ s	SUN PLANETS ° ′	ARIES ° ′	MOON ° ′	v or d ′	Corrⁿ ′	v or d ′	Corrⁿ ′	v or d ′	Corrⁿ ′
00	11 30·0	11 31·9	10 58·6	0·0	0·0	6·0	4·7	12·0	9·3
01	11 30·3	11 32·1	10 58·8	0·1	0·1	6·1	4·7	12·1	9·4
02	11 30·5	11 32·4	10 59·0	0·2	0·2	6·2	4·8	12·2	9·5
03	11 30·8	11 32·6	10 59·3	0·3	0·2	6·3	4·9	12·3	9·5
04	11 31·0	11 32·9	10 59·5	0·4	0·3	6·4	5·0	12·4	9·6
05	11 31·3	11 33·1	10 59·8	0·5	0·4	6·5	5·0	12·5	9·7
06	11 31·5	11 33·4	11 00·0	0·6	0·5	6·6	5·1	12·6	9·8
07	11 31·8	11 33·6	11 00·2	0·7	0·5	6·7	5·2	12·7	9·8
08	11 32·0	11 33·9	11 00·5	0·8	0·6	6·8	5·3	12·8	9·9
09	11 32·3	11 34·1	11 00·7	0·9	0·7	6·9	5·3	12·9	10·0
10	11 32·5	11 34·4	11 01·0	1·0	0·8	7·0	5·4	13·0	10·1
11	11 32·8	11 34·6	11 01·2	1·1	0·9	7·1	5·5	13·1	10·2
12	11 33·0	11 34·9	11 01·4	1·2	0·9	7·2	5·6	13·2	10·2
13	11 33·3	11 35·1	11 01·7	1·3	1·0	7·3	5·7	13·3	10·3
14	11 33·5	11 35·4	11 01·9	1·4	1·1	7·4	5·7	13·4	10·4
15	11 33·8	11 35·6	11 02·1	1·5	1·2	7·5	5·8	13·5	10·5
16	11 34·0	11 35·9	11 02·4	1·6	1·2	7·6	5·9	13·6	10·5
17	11 34·3	11 36·2	11 02·6	1·7	1·3	7·7	6·0	13·7	10·6
18	11 34·5	11 36·4	11 02·9	1·8	1·4	7·8	6·0	13·8	10·7
19	11 34·8	11 36·7	11 03·1	1·9	1·5	7·9	6·1	13·9	10·8
20	11 35·0	11 36·9	11 03·3	2·0	1·6	8·0	6·2	14·0	10·9
21	11 35·3	11 37·2	11 03·6	2·1	1·6	8·1	6·3	14·1	10·9
22	11 35·5	11 37·4	11 03·8	2·2	1·7	8·2	6·4	14·2	11·0
23	11 35·8	11 37·7	11 04·1	2·3	1·8	8·3	6·4	14·3	11·1
24	11 36·0	11 37·9	11 04·3	2·4	1·9	8·4	6·5	14·4	11·2
25	11 36·3	11 38·2	11 04·5	2·5	1·9	8·5	6·6	14·5	11·2
26	11 36·5	11 38·4	11 04·8	2·6	2·0	8·6	6·7	14·6	11·3
27	11 36·8	11 38·7	11 05·0	2·7	2·1	8·7	6·7	14·7	11·4
28	11 37·0	11 38·9	11 05·2	2·8	2·2	8·8	6·8	14·8	11·5
29	11 37·3	11 39·2	11 05·5	2·9	2·2	8·9	6·9	14·9	11·5
30	11 37·5	11 39·4	11 05·7	3·0	2·3	9·0	7·0	15·0	11·6
31	11 37·8	11 39·7	11 06·0	3·1	2·4	9·1	7·1	15·1	11·7
32	11 38·0	11 39·9	11 06·2	3·2	2·5	9·2	7·1	15·2	11·8
33	11 38·3	11 40·2	11 06·4	3·3	2·6	9·3	7·2	15·3	11·9
34	11 38·5	11 40·4	11 06·7	3·4	2·6	9·4	7·3	15·4	11·9
35	11 38·8	11 40·7	11 06·9	3·5	2·7	9·5	7·4	15·5	12·0
36	11 39·0	11 40·9	11 07·2	3·6	2·8	9·6	7·4	15·6	12·1
37	11 39·3	11 41·2	11 07·4	3·7	2·9	9·7	7·5	15·7	12·2
38	11 39·5	11 41·4	11 07·6	3·8	2·9	9·8	7·6	15·8	12·2
39	11 39·8	11 41·7	11 07·9	3·9	3·0	9·9	7·7	15·9	12·3
40	11 40·0	11 41·9	11 08·1	4·0	3·1	10·0	7·8	16·0	12·4
41	11 40·3	11 42·2	11 08·3	4·1	3·2	10·1	7·8	16·1	12·5
42	11 40·5	11 42·4	11 08·6	4·2	3·3	10·2	7·9	16·2	12·6
43	11 40·8	11 42·7	11 08·8	4·3	3·3	10·3	8·0	16·3	12·6
44	11 41·0	11 42·9	11 09·1	4·4	3·4	10·4	8·1	16·4	12·7
45	11 41·3	11 43·2	11 09·3	4·5	3·5	10·5	8·1	16·5	12·8
46	11 41·5	11 43·4	11 09·5	4·6	3·6	10·6	8·2	16·6	12·9
47	11 41·8	11 43·7	11 09·8	4·7	3·6	10·7	8·3	16·7	12·9
48	11 42·0	11 43·9	11 10·0	4·8	3·7	10·8	8·4	16·8	13·0
49	11 42·3	11 44·2	11 10·3	4·9	3·8	10·9	8·4	16·9	13·1
50	11 42·5	11 44·4	11 10·5	5·0	3·9	11·0	8·5	17·0	13·2
51	11 42·8	11 44·7	11 10·7	5·1	4·0	11·1	8·6	17·1	13·3
52	11 43·0	11 44·9	11 11·0	5·2	4·0	11·2	8·7	17·2	13·3
53	11 43·3	11 45·2	11 11·2	5·3	4·1	11·3	8·8	17·3	13·4
54	11 43·5	11 45·4	11 11·5	5·4	4·2	11·4	8·8	17·4	13·5
55	11 43·8	11 45·7	11 11·7	5·5	4·3	11·5	8·9	17·5	13·6
56	11 44·0	11 45·9	11 11·9	5·6	4·3	11·6	9·0	17·6	13·6
57	11 44·3	11 46·2	11 12·2	5·7	4·4	11·7	9·1	17·7	13·7
58	11 44·5	11 46·4	11 12·4	5·8	4·5	11·8	9·1	17·8	13·8
59	11 44·8	11 46·7	11 12·6	5·9	4·6	11·9	9·2	17·9	13·9
60	11 45·0	11 46·9	11 12·9	6·0	4·7	12·0	9·3	18·0	14·0

47ᵐ s	SUN PLANETS ° ′	ARIES ° ′	MOON ° ′	v or d ′	Corrⁿ ′	v or d ′	Corrⁿ ′	v or d ′	Corrⁿ ′
00	11 45·0	11 46·9	11 12·9	0·0	0·0	6·0	4·8	12·0	9·5
01	11 45·3	11 47·2	11 13·1	0·1	0·1	6·1	4·8	12·1	9·6
02	11 45·5	11 47·4	11 13·4	0·2	0·2	6·2	4·9	12·2	9·7
03	11 45·8	11 47·7	11 13·6	0·3	0·2	6·3	5·0	12·3	9·7
04	11 46·0	11 47·9	11 13·8	0·4	0·3	6·4	5·1	12·4	9·8
05	11 46·3	11 48·2	11 14·1	0·5	0·4	6·5	5·1	12·5	9·9
06	11 46·5	11 48·4	11 14·3	0·6	0·5	6·6	5·2	12·6	10·0
07	11 46·8	11 48·7	11 14·6	0·7	0·6	6·7	5·3	12·7	10·1
08	11 47·0	11 48·9	11 14·8	0·8	0·6	6·8	5·4	12·8	10·1
09	11 47·3	11 49·2	11 15·0	0·9	0·7	6·9	5·5	12·9	10·2
10	11 47·5	11 49·4	11 15·3	1·0	0·8	7·0	5·5	13·0	10·3
11	11 47·8	11 49·7	11 15·5	1·1	0·9	7·1	5·6	13·1	10·4
12	11 48·0	11 49·9	11 15·7	1·2	1·0	7·2	5·7	13·2	10·5
13	11 48·3	11 50·2	11 16·0	1·3	1·0	7·3	5·8	13·3	10·5
14	11 48·5	11 50·4	11 16·2	1·4	1·1	7·4	5·9	13·4	10·6
15	11 48·8	11 50·7	11 16·5	1·5	1·2	7·5	5·9	13·5	10·7
16	11 49·0	11 50·9	11 16·7	1·6	1·3	7·6	6·0	13·6	10·8
17	11 49·3	11 51·2	11 16·9	1·7	1·3	7·7	6·1	13·7	10·8
18	11 49·5	11 51·4	11 17·2	1·8	1·4	7·8	6·2	13·8	10·9
19	11 49·8	11 51·7	11 17·4	1·9	1·5	7·9	6·3	13·9	11·0
20	11 50·0	11 51·9	11 17·7	2·0	1·6	8·0	6·3	14·0	11·1
21	11 50·3	11 52·2	11 17·9	2·1	1·7	8·1	6·4	14·1	11·2
22	11 50·5	11 52·4	11 18·1	2·2	1·7	8·2	6·5	14·2	11·2
23	11 50·8	11 52·7	11 18·4	2·3	1·8	8·3	6·6	14·3	11·3
24	11 51·0	11 52·9	11 18·6	2·4	1·9	8·4	6·7	14·4	11·4
25	11 51·3	11 53·2	11 18·8	2·5	2·0	8·5	6·7	14·5	11·5
26	11 51·5	11 53·4	11 19·1	2·6	2·1	8·6	6·8	14·6	11·6
27	11 51·8	11 53·7	11 19·3	2·7	2·1	8·7	6·9	14·7	11·6
28	11 52·0	11 53·9	11 19·6	2·8	2·2	8·8	7·0	14·8	11·7
29	11 52·3	11 54·2	11 19·8	2·9	2·3	8·9	7·0	14·9	11·8
30	11 52·5	11 54·5	11 20·0	3·0	2·4	9·0	7·1	15·0	11·9
31	11 52·8	11 54·7	11 20·3	3·1	2·5	9·1	7·2	15·1	12·0
32	11 53·0	11 55·0	11 20·5	3·2	2·5	9·2	7·3	15·2	12·0
33	11 53·3	11 55·2	11 20·8	3·3	2·6	9·3	7·4	15·3	12·1
34	11 53·5	11 55·5	11 21·0	3·4	2·7	9·4	7·4	15·4	12·2
35	11 53·8	11 55·7	11 21·2	3·5	2·8	9·5	7·5	15·5	12·3
36	11 54·0	11 56·0	11 21·5	3·6	2·9	9·6	7·6	15·6	12·4
37	11 54·3	11 56·2	11 21·7	3·7	2·9	9·7	7·7	15·7	12·4
38	11 54·5	11 56·5	11 22·0	3·8	3·0	9·8	7·8	15·8	12·5
39	11 54·8	11 56·7	11 22·2	3·9	3·1	9·9	7·8	15·9	12·6
40	11 55·0	11 57·0	11 22·4	4·0	3·2	10·0	7·9	16·0	12·7
41	11 55·3	11 57·2	11 22·7	4·1	3·2	10·1	8·0	16·1	12·7
42	11 55·5	11 57·5	11 22·9	4·2	3·3	10·2	8·1	16·2	12·8
43	11 55·8	11 57·7	11 23·1	4·3	3·4	10·3	8·2	16·3	12·9
44	11 56·0	11 58·0	11 23·4	4·4	3·5	10·4	8·2	16·4	13·0
45	11 56·3	11 58·2	11 23·6	4·5	3·6	10·5	8·3	16·5	13·1
46	11 56·5	11 58·5	11 23·9	4·6	3·6	10·6	8·4	16·6	13·1
47	11 56·8	11 58·7	11 24·1	4·7	3·7	10·7	8·5	16·7	13·2
48	11 57·0	11 59·0	11 24·3	4·8	3·8	10·8	8·6	16·8	13·3
49	11 57·3	11 59·2	11 24·6	4·9	3·9	10·9	8·6	16·9	13·4
50	11 57·5	11 59·5	11 24·8	5·0	4·0	11·0	8·7	17·0	13·5
51	11 57·8	11 59·7	11 25·1	5·1	4·0	11·1	8·8	17·1	13·5
52	11 58·0	12 00·0	11 25·3	5·2	4·1	11·2	8·9	17·2	13·6
53	11 58·3	12 00·2	11 25·5	5·3	4·2	11·3	8·9	17·3	13·7
54	11 58·5	12 00·5	11 25·8	5·4	4·3	11·4	9·0	17·4	13·8
55	11 58·8	12 00·7	11 26·0	5·5	4·4	11·5	9·1	17·5	13·9
56	11 59·0	12 01·0	11 26·2	5·6	4·4	11·6	9·2	17·6	13·9
57	11 59·3	12 01·2	11 26·5	5·7	4·5	11·7	9·3	17·7	14·0
58	11 59·5	12 01·5	11 26·7	5·8	4·6	11·8	9·3	17·8	14·1
59	11 59·8	12 01·7	11 27·0	5·9	4·7	11·9	9·4	17·9	14·2
60	12 00·0	12 02·0	11 27·2	6·0	4·8	12·0	9·5	18·0	14·3

48ᵐ	SUN PLANETS	ARIES	MOON	v or d	Corrⁿ	v or d	Corrⁿ	v or d	Corrⁿ
s	° ′	° ′	° ′	′	′	′	′	′	′
00	12 00·0	12 02·0	11 27·2	0·0	0·0	6·0	4·9	12·0	9·7
01	12 00·3	12 02·2	11 27·4	0·1	0·1	6·1	4·9	12·1	9·8
02	12 00·5	12 02·5	11 27·7	0·2	0·2	6·2	5·0	12·2	9·9
03	12 00·8	12 02·7	11 27·9	0·3	0·2	6·3	5·1	12·3	9·9
04	12 01·0	12 03·0	11 28·2	0·4	0·3	6·4	5·2	12·4	10·0
05	12 01·3	12 03·2	11 28·4	0·5	0·4	6·5	5·3	12·5	10·1
06	12 01·5	12 03·5	11 28·6	0·6	0·5	6·6	5·3	12·6	10·2
07	12 01·8	12 03·7	11 28·9	0·7	0·6	6·7	5·4	12·7	10·3
08	12 02·0	12 04·0	11 29·1	0·8	0·6	6·8	5·5	12·8	10·3
09	12 02·3	12 04·2	11 29·3	0·9	0·7	6·9	5·6	12·9	10·4
10	12 02·5	12 04·5	11 29·6	1·0	0·8	7·0	5·7	13·0	10·5
11	12 02·8	12 04·7	11 29·8	1·1	0·9	7·1	5·7	13·1	10·6
12	12 03·0	12 05·0	11 30·1	1·2	1·0	7·2	5·8	13·2	10·7
13	12 03·3	12 05·2	11 30·3	1·3	1·1	7·3	5·9	13·3	10·8
14	12 03·5	12 05·5	11 30·5	1·4	1·1	7·4	6·0	13·4	10·8
15	12 03·8	12 05·7	11 30·8	1·5	1·2	7·5	6·1	13·5	10·9
16	12 04·0	12 06·0	11 31·0	1·6	1·3	7·6	6·1	13·6	11·0
17	12 04·3	12 06·2	11 31·3	1·7	1·4	7·7	6·2	13·7	11·1
18	12 04·5	12 06·5	11 31·5	1·8	1·5	7·8	6·3	13·8	11·2
19	12 04·8	12 06·7	11 31·7	1·9	1·5	7·9	6·4	13·9	11·2
20	12 05·0	12 07·0	11 32·0	2·0	1·6	8·0	6·5	14·0	11·3
21	12 05·3	12 07·2	11 32·2	2·1	1·7	8·1	6·5	14·1	11·4
22	12 05·5	12 07·5	11 32·4	2·2	1·8	8·2	6·6	14·2	11·5
23	12 05·8	12 07·7	11 32·7	2·3	1·9	8·3	6·7	14·3	11·6
24	12 06·0	12 08·0	11 32·9	2·4	1·9	8·4	6·8	14·4	11·6
25	12 06·3	12 08·2	11 33·2	2·5	2·0	8·5	6·9	14·5	11·7
26	12 06·5	12 08·5	11 33·4	2·6	2·1	8·6	7·0	14·6	11·8
27	12 06·8	12 08·7	11 33·6	2·7	2·2	8·7	7·0	14·7	11·9
28	12 07·0	12 09·0	11 33·9	2·8	2·3	8·8	7·1	14·8	12·0
29	12 07·3	12 09·2	11 34·1	2·9	2·3	8·9	7·2	14·9	12·0
30	12 07·5	12 09·5	11 34·4	3·0	2·4	9·0	7·3	15·0	12·1
31	12 07·8	12 09·7	11 34·6	3·1	2·5	9·1	7·4	15·1	12·2
32	12 08·0	12 10·0	11 34·8	3·2	2·6	9·2	7·4	15·2	12·3
33	12 08·3	12 10·2	11 35·1	3·3	2·7	9·3	7·5	15·3	12·4
34	12 08·5	12 10·5	11 35·3	3·4	2·7	9·4	7·6	15·4	12·4
35	12 08·8	12 10·7	11 35·6	3·5	2·8	9·5	7·7	15·5	12·5
36	12 09·0	12 11·0	11 35·8	3·6	2·9	9·6	7·8	15·6	12·6
37	12 09·3	12 11·2	11 36·0	3·7	3·0	9·7	7·8	15·7	12·7
38	12 09·5	12 11·5	11 36·3	3·8	3·1	9·8	7·9	15·8	12·8
39	12 09·8	12 11·7	11 36·5	3·9	3·2	9·9	8·0	15·9	12·9
40	12 10·0	12 12·0	11 36·7	4·0	3·2	10·0	8·1	16·0	12·9
41	12 10·3	12 12·2	11 37·0	4·1	3·3	10·1	8·2	16·1	13·0
42	12 10·5	12 12·5	11 37·2	4·2	3·4	10·2	8·2	16·2	13·1
43	12 10·8	12 12·8	11 37·5	4·3	3·5	10·3	8·3	16·3	13·2
44	12 11·0	12 13·0	11 37·7	4·4	3·6	10·4	8·4	16·4	13·3
45	12 11·3	12 13·3	11 37·9	4·5	3·6	10·5	8·5	16·5	13·3
46	12 11·5	12 13·5	11 38·2	4·6	3·7	10·6	8·6	16·6	13·4
47	12 11·8	12 13·8	11 38·4	4·7	3·8	10·7	8·6	16·7	13·5
48	12 12·0	12 14·0	11 38·7	4·8	3·9	10·8	8·7	16·8	13·6
49	12 12·3	12 14·3	11 38·9	4·9	4·0	10·9	8·8	16·9	13·7
50	12 12·5	12 14·5	11 39·1	5·0	4·0	11·0	8·9	17·0	13·7
51	12 12·8	12 14·8	11 39·4	5·1	4·1	11·1	9·0	17·1	13·8
52	12 13·0	12 15·0	11 39·6	5·2	4·2	11·2	9·1	17·2	13·9
53	12 13·3	12 15·3	11 39·8	5·3	4·3	11·3	9·1	17·3	14·0
54	12 13·5	12 15·5	11 40·1	5·4	4·4	11·4	9·2	17·4	14·1
55	12 13·8	12 15·8	11 40·3	5·5	4·4	11·5	9·3	17·5	14·1
56	12 14·0	12 16·0	11 40·6	5·6	4·5	11·6	9·4	17·6	14·2
57	12 14·3	12 16·3	11 40·8	5·7	4·6	11·7	9·5	17·7	14·3
58	12 14·5	12 16·5	11 41·0	5·8	4·7	11·8	9·5	17·8	14·4
59	12 14·8	12 16·8	11 41·3	5·9	4·8	11·9	9·6	17·9	14·5
60	12 15·0	12 17·0	11 41·5	6·0	4·9	12·0	9·7	18·0	14·6

49ᵐ	SUN PLANETS	ARIES	MOON	v or d	Corrⁿ	v or d	Corrⁿ	v or d	Corrⁿ
s	° ′	° ′	° ′	′	′	′	′	′	′
00	12 15·0	12 17·0	11 41·5	0·0	0·0	6·0	5·0	12·0	9·9
01	12 15·3	12 17·3	11 41·8	0·1	0·1	6·1	5·0	12·1	10·0
02	12 15·5	12 17·5	11 42·0	0·2	0·2	6·2	5·1	12·2	10·1
03	12 15·8	12 17·8	11 42·2	0·3	0·2	6·3	5·2	12·3	10·1
04	12 16·0	12 18·0	11 42·5	0·4	0·3	6·4	5·3	12·4	10·2
05	12 16·3	12 18·3	11 42·7	0·5	0·4	6·5	5·4	12·5	10·3
06	12 16·5	12 18·5	11 42·9	0·6	0·5	6·6	5·4	12·6	10·4
07	12 16·8	12 18·8	11 43·2	0·7	0·6	6·7	5·5	12·7	10·5
08	12 17·0	12 19·0	11 43·4	0·8	0·7	6·8	5·6	12·8	10·6
09	12 17·3	12 19·3	11 43·7	0·9	0·7	6·9	5·7	12·9	10·6
10	12 17·5	12 19·5	11 43·9	1·0	0·8	7·0	5·8	13·0	10·7
11	12 17·8	12 19·8	11 44·1	1·1	0·9	7·1	5·9	13·1	10·8
12	12 18·0	12 20·0	11 44·4	1·2	1·0	7·2	5·9	13·2	10·9
13	12 18·3	12 20·3	11 44·6	1·3	1·1	7·3	6·0	13·3	11·0
14	12 18·5	12 20·5	11 44·9	1·4	1·2	7·4	6·1	13·4	11·1
15	12 18·8	12 20·8	11 45·1	1·5	1·2	7·5	6·2	13·5	11·1
16	12 19·0	12 21·0	11 45·3	1·6	1·3	7·6	6·3	13·6	11·2
17	12 19·3	12 21·3	11 45·6	1·7	1·4	7·7	6·4	13·7	11·3
18	12 19·5	12 21·5	11 45·8	1·8	1·5	7·8	6·4	13·8	11·4
19	12 19·8	12 21·8	11 46·1	1·9	1·6	7·9	6·5	13·9	11·5
20	12 20·0	12 22·0	11 46·3	2·0	1·7	8·0	6·6	14·0	11·6
21	12 20·3	12 22·3	11 46·5	2·1	1·7	8·1	6·7	14·1	11·6
22	12 20·5	12 22·5	11 46·8	2·2	1·8	8·2	6·8	14·2	11·7
23	12 20·8	12 22·8	11 47·0	2·3	1·9	8·3	6·8	14·3	11·8
24	12 21·0	12 23·0	11 47·2	2·4	2·0	8·4	6·9	14·4	11·9
25	12 21·3	12 23·3	11 47·5	2·5	2·1	8·5	7·0	14·5	12·0
26	12 21·5	12 23·5	11 47·7	2·6	2·1	8·6	7·1	14·6	12·0
27	12 21·8	12 23·8	11 48·0	2·7	2·2	8·7	7·2	14·7	12·1
28	12 22·0	12 24·0	11 48·2	2·8	2·3	8·8	7·3	14·8	12·2
29	12 22·3	12 24·3	11 48·4	2·9	2·4	8·9	7·3	14·9	12·3
30	12 22·5	12 24·5	11 48·7	3·0	2·5	9·0	7·4	15·0	12·4
31	12 22·8	12 24·8	11 48·9	3·1	2·6	9·1	7·5	15·1	12·5
32	12 23·0	12 25·0	11 49·2	3·2	2·6	9·2	7·6	15·2	12·5
33	12 23·3	12 25·3	11 49·4	3·3	2·7	9·3	7·7	15·3	12·6
34	12 23·5	12 25·5	11 49·6	3·4	2·8	9·4	7·8	15·4	12·7
35	12 23·8	12 25·8	11 49·9	3·5	2·9	9·5	7·8	15·5	12·8
36	12 24·0	12 26·0	11 50·1	3·6	3·0	9·6	7·9	15·6	12·9
37	12 24·3	12 26·3	11 50·3	3·7	3·1	9·7	8·0	15·7	13·0
38	12 24·5	12 26·5	11 50·6	3·8	3·1	9·8	8·1	15·8	13·0
39	12 24·8	12 26·8	11 50·8	3·9	3·2	9·9	8·2	15·9	13·1
40	12 25·0	12 27·0	11 51·1	4·0	3·3	10·0	8·3	16·0	13·2
41	12 25·3	12 27·3	11 51·3	4·1	3·4	10·1	8·3	16·1	13·3
42	12 25·5	12 27·5	11 51·5	4·2	3·5	10·2	8·4	16·2	13·4
43	12 25·8	12 27·8	11 51·8	4·3	3·5	10·3	8·5	16·3	13·4
44	12 26·0	12 28·0	11 52·0	4·4	3·6	10·4	8·6	16·4	13·5
45	12 26·3	12 28·3	11 52·3	4·5	3·7	10·5	8·7	16·5	13·6
46	12 26·5	12 28·5	11 52·5	4·6	3·8	10·6	8·7	16·6	13·7
47	12 26·8	12 28·8	11 52·7	4·7	3·9	10·7	8·8	16·7	13·8
48	12 27·0	12 29·0	11 53·0	4·8	4·0	10·8	8·9	16·8	13·9
49	12 27·3	12 29·3	11 53·2	4·9	4·0	10·9	9·0	16·9	13·9
50	12 27·5	12 29·5	11 53·4	5·0	4·1	11·0	9·1	17·0	14·0
51	12 27·8	12 29·8	11 53·7	5·1	4·2	11·1	9·2	17·1	14·1
52	12 28·0	12 30·0	11 53·9	5·2	4·3	11·2	9·2	17·2	14·2
53	12 28·3	12 30·3	11 54·2	5·3	4·4	11·3	9·3	17·3	14·3
54	12 28·5	12 30·5	11 54·4	5·4	4·5	11·4	9·4	17·4	14·4
55	12 28·8	12 30·8	11 54·6	5·5	4·5	11·5	9·5	17·5	14·4
56	12 29·0	12 31·1	11 54·9	5·6	4·6	11·6	9·6	17·6	14·5
57	12 29·3	12 31·3	11 55·1	5·7	4·7	11·7	9·7	17·7	14·6
58	12 29·5	12 31·6	11 55·4	5·8	4·8	11·8	9·7	17·8	14·7
59	12 29·8	12 31·8	11 55·6	5·9	4·9	11·9	9·8	17·9	14·8
60	12 30·0	12 32·1	11 55·8	6·0	5·0	12·0	9·9	18·0	14·9

m 50	SUN PLANETS	ARIES	MOON	v or d	Corrn	v or d	Corrn	v or d	Corrn
s	° ′	° ′	° ′	′	′	′	′	′	′
00	12 30·0	12 32·1	11 55·8	0·0	0·0	6·0	5·1	12·0	10·1
01	12 30·3	12 32·3	11 56·1	0·1	0·1	6·1	5·1	12·1	10·2
02	12 30·5	12 32·6	11 56·3	0·2	0·2	6·2	5·2	12·2	10·3
03	12 30·8	12 32·8	11 56·5	0·3	0·3	6·3	5·3	12·3	10·4
04	12 31·0	12 33·1	11 56·8	0·4	0·3	6·4	5·4	12·4	10·4
05	12 31·3	12 33·3	11 57·0	0·5	0·4	6·5	5·5	12·5	10·5
06	12 31·5	12 33·6	11 57·3	0·6	0·5	6·6	5·6	12·6	10·6
07	12 31·8	12 33·8	11 57·5	0·7	0·6	6·7	5·6	12·7	10·7
08	12 32·0	12 34·1	11 57·7	0·8	0·7	6·8	5·7	12·8	10·8
09	12 32·3	12 34·3	11 58·0	0·9	0·8	6·9	5·8	12·9	10·9
10	12 32·5	12 34·6	11 58·2	1·0	0·8	7·0	5·9	13·0	10·9
11	12 32·8	12 34·8	11 58·5	1·1	0·9	7·1	6·0	13·1	11·0
12	12 33·0	12 35·1	11 58·7	1·2	1·0	7·2	6·1	13·2	11·1
13	12 33·3	12 35·3	11 58·9	1·3	1·1	7·3	6·1	13·3	11·2
14	12 33·5	12 35·6	11 59·2	1·4	1·2	7·4	6·2	13·4	11·3
15	12 33·8	12 35·8	11 59·4	1·5	1·3	7·5	6·3	13·5	11·4
16	12 34·0	12 36·1	11 59·7	1·6	1·3	7·6	6·4	13·6	11·4
17	12 34·3	12 36·3	11 59·9	1·7	1·4	7·7	6·5	13·7	11·5
18	12 34·5	12 36·6	12 00·1	1·8	1·5	7·8	6·6	13·8	11·6
19	12 34·8	12 36·8	12 00·4	1·9	1·6	7·9	6·6	13·9	11·7
20	12 35·0	12 37·1	12 00·6	2·0	1·7	8·0	6·7	14·0	11·8
21	12 35·3	12 37·3	12 00·8	2·1	1·8	8·1	6·8	14·1	11·9
22	12 35·5	12 37·6	12 01·1	2·2	1·9	8·2	6·9	14·2	12·0
23	12 35·8	12 37·8	12 01·3	2·3	1·9	8·3	7·0	14·3	12·0
24	12 36·0	12 38·1	12 01·6	2·4	2·0	8·4	7·1	14·4	12·1
25	12 36·3	12 38·3	12 01·8	2·5	2·1	8·5	7·2	14·5	12·2
26	12 36·5	12 38·6	12 02·0	2·6	2·2	8·6	7·2	14·6	12·3
27	12 36·8	12 38·8	12 02·3	2·7	2·3	8·7	7·3	14·7	12·4
28	12 37·0	12 39·1	12 02·5	2·8	2·4	8·8	7·4	14·8	12·5
29	12 37·3	12 39·3	12 02·8	2·9	2·4	8·9	7·5	14·9	12·5
30	12 37·5	12 39·6	12 03·0	3·0	2·5	9·0	7·6	15·0	12·6
31	12 37·8	12 39·8	12 03·2	3·1	2·6	9·1	7·7	15·1	12·7
32	12 38·0	12 40·1	12 03·5	3·2	2·7	9·2	7·7	15·2	12·8
33	12 38·3	12 40·3	12 03·7	3·3	2·8	9·3	7·8	15·3	12·9
34	12 38·5	12 40·6	12 03·9	3·4	2·9	9·4	7·9	15·4	13·0
35	12 38·8	12 40·8	12 04·2	3·5	2·9	9·5	8·0	15·5	13·0
36	12 39·0	12 41·1	12 04·4	3·6	3·0	9·6	8·1	15·6	13·1
37	12 39·3	12 41·3	12 04·7	3·7	3·1	9·7	8·2	15·7	13·2
38	12 39·5	12 41·6	12 04·9	3·8	3·2	9·8	8·2	15·8	13·3
39	12 39·8	12 41·8	12 05·1	3·9	3·3	9·9	8·3	15·9	13·4
40	12 40·0	12 42·1	12 05·4	4·0	3·4	10·0	8·4	16·0	13·5
41	12 40·3	12 42·3	12 05·6	4·1	3·5	10·1	8·5	16·1	13·6
42	12 40·5	12 42·6	12 05·9	4·2	3·5	10·2	8·6	16·2	13·6
43	12 40·8	12 42·8	12 06·1	4·3	3·6	10·3	8·7	16·3	13·7
44	12 41·0	12 43·1	12 06·3	4·4	3·7	10·4	8·8	16·4	13·8
45	12 41·3	12 43·3	12 06·6	4·5	3·8	10·5	8·8	16·5	13·9
46	12 41·5	12 43·6	12 06·8	4·6	3·9	10·6	8·9	16·6	14·0
47	12 41·8	12 43·8	12 07·0	4·7	4·0	10·7	9·0	16·7	14·1
48	12 42·0	12 44·1	12 07·3	4·8	4·0	10·8	9·1	16·8	14·1
49	12 42·3	12 44·3	12 07·5	4·9	4·1	10·9	9·2	16·9	14·2
50	12 42·5	12 44·6	12 07·8	5·0	4·2	11·0	9·3	17·0	14·3
51	12 42·8	12 44·8	12 08·0	5·1	4·3	11·1	9·3	17·1	14·4
52	12 43·0	12 45·1	12 08·2	5·2	4·4	11·2	9·4	17·2	14·5
53	12 43·3	12 45·3	12 08·5	5·3	4·5	11·3	9·5	17·3	14·6
54	12 43·5	12 45·6	12 08·7	5·4	4·5	11·4	9·6	17·4	14·6
55	12 43·8	12 45·8	12 09·0	5·5	4·6	11·5	9·7	17·5	14·7
56	12 44·0	12 46·1	12 09·2	5·6	4·7	11·6	9·8	17·6	14·8
57	12 44·3	12 46·3	12 09·4	5·7	4·8	11·7	9·8	17·7	14·9
58	12 44·5	12 46·6	12 09·7	5·8	4·9	11·8	9·9	17·8	15·0
59	12 44·8	12 46·8	12 09·9	5·9	5·0	11·9	10·0	17·9	15·1
60	12 45·0	12 47·1	12 10·2	6·0	5·1	12·0	10·1	18·0	15·2

m 51	SUN PLANETS	ARIES	MOON	v or d	Corrn	v or d	Corrn	v or d	Corrn
s	° ′	° ′	° ′	′	′	′	′	′	′
00	12 45·0	12 47·1	12 10·2	0·0	0·0	6·0	5·2	12·0	10·3
01	12 45·3	12 47·3	12 10·4	0·1	0·1	6·1	5·2	12·1	10·4
02	12 45·5	12 47·6	12 10·6	0·2	0·2	6·2	5·3	12·2	10·5
03	12 45·8	12 47·8	12 10·9	0·3	0·3	6·3	5·4	12·3	10·6
04	12 46·0	12 48·1	12 11·1	0·4	0·3	6·4	5·5	12·4	10·6
05	12 46·3	12 48·3	12 11·3	0·5	0·4	6·5	5·6	12·5	10·7
06	12 46·5	12 48·6	12 11·6	0·6	0·5	6·6	5·7	12·6	10·8
07	12 46·8	12 48·8	12 11·8	0·7	0·6	6·7	5·8	12·7	10·9
08	12 47·0	12 49·1	12 12·1	0·8	0·7	6·8	5·8	12·8	11·0
09	12 47·3	12 49·4	12 12·3	0·9	0·8	6·9	5·9	12·9	11·1
10	12 47·5	12 49·6	12 12·5	1·0	0·9	7·0	6·0	13·0	11·2
11	12 47·8	12 49·9	12 12·8	1·1	0·9	7·1	6·1	13·1	11·2
12	12 48·0	12 50·1	12 13·0	1·2	1·0	7·2	6·2	13·2	11·3
13	12 48·3	12 50·4	12 13·3	1·3	1·1	7·3	6·3	13·3	11·4
14	12 48·5	12 50·6	12 13·5	1·4	1·2	7·4	6·4	13·4	11·5
15	12 48·8	12 50·9	12 13·7	1·5	1·3	7·5	6·4	13·5	11·6
16	12 49·0	12 51·1	12 14·0	1·6	1·4	7·6	6·5	13·6	11·7
17	12 49·3	12 51·4	12 14·2	1·7	1·5	7·7	6·6	13·7	11·8
18	12 49·5	12 51·6	12 14·4	1·8	1·5	7·8	6·7	13·8	11·8
19	12 49·8	12 51·9	12 14·7	1·9	1·6	7·9	6·8	13·9	11·9
20	12 50·0	12 52·1	12 14·9	2·0	1·7	8·0	6·9	14·0	12·0
21	12 50·3	12 52·4	12 15·2	2·1	1·8	8·1	7·0	14·1	12·1
22	12 50·5	12 52·6	12 15·4	2·2	1·9	8·2	7·0	14·2	12·2
23	12 50·8	12 52·9	12 15·6	2·3	2·0	8·3	7·1	14·3	12·3
24	12 51·0	12 53·1	12 15·9	2·4	2·1	8·4	7·2	14·4	12·4
25	12 51·3	12 53·4	12 16·1	2·5	2·1	8·5	7·3	14·5	12·4
26	12 51·5	12 53·6	12 16·4	2·6	2·2	8·6	7·4	14·6	12·5
27	12 51·8	12 53·9	12 16·6	2·7	2·3	8·7	7·5	14·7	12·6
28	12 52·0	12 54·1	12 16·8	2·8	2·4	8·8	7·6	14·8	12·7
29	12 52·3	12 54·4	12 17·1	2·9	2·5	8·9	7·6	14·9	12·8
30	12 52·5	12 54·6	12 17·3	3·0	2·6	9·0	7·7	15·0	12·9
31	12 52·8	12 54·9	12 17·5	3·1	2·7	9·1	7·8	15·1	13·0
32	12 53·0	12 55·1	12 17·8	3·2	2·7	9·2	7·9	15·2	13·0
33	12 53·3	12 55·4	12 18·0	3·3	2·8	9·3	8·0	15·3	13·1
34	12 53·5	12 55·6	12 18·3	3·4	2·9	9·4	8·1	15·4	13·2
35	12 53·8	12 55·9	12 18·5	3·5	3·0	9·5	8·2	15·5	13·3
36	12 54·0	12 56·1	12 18·7	3·6	3·1	9·6	8·2	15·6	13·4
37	12 54·3	12 56·4	12 19·0	3·7	3·2	9·7	8·3	15·7	13·5
38	12 54·5	12 56·6	12 19·2	3·8	3·3	9·8	8·4	15·8	13·6
39	12 54·8	12 56·9	12 19·5	3·9	3·3	9·9	8·5	15·9	13·6
40	12 55·0	12 57·1	12 19·7	4·0	3·4	10·0	8·6	16·0	13·7
41	12 55·3	12 57·4	12 19·9	4·1	3·5	10·1	8·7	16·1	13·8
42	12 55·5	12 57·6	12 20·2	4·2	3·6	10·2	8·8	16·2	13·9
43	12 55·8	12 57·9	12 20·4	4·3	3·7	10·3	8·8	16·3	14·0
44	12 56·0	12 58·1	12 20·6	4·4	3·8	10·4	8·9	16·4	14·1
45	12 56·3	12 58·4	12 20·9	4·5	3·9	10·5	9·0	16·5	14·2
46	12 56·5	12 58·6	12 21·1	4·6	3·9	10·6	9·1	16·6	14·2
47	12 56·8	12 58·9	12 21·4	4·7	4·0	10·7	9·2	16·7	14·3
48	12 57·0	12 59·1	12 21·6	4·8	4·1	10·8	9·3	16·8	14·4
49	12 57·3	12 59·4	12 21·8	4·9	4·2	10·9	9·4	16·9	14·5
50	12 57·5	12 59·6	12 22·1	5·0	4·3	11·0	9·4	17·0	14·6
51	12 57·8	12 59·9	12 22·3	5·1	4·4	11·1	9·5	17·1	14·7
52	12 58·0	13 00·1	12 22·6	5·2	4·5	11·2	9·6	17·2	14·8
53	12 58·3	13 00·4	12 22·8	5·3	4·5	11·3	9·7	17·3	14·8
54	12 58·5	13 00·6	12 23·0	5·4	4·6	11·4	9·8	17·4	14·9
55	12 58·8	13 00·9	12 23·3	5·5	4·7	11·5	9·9	17·5	15·0
56	12 59·0	13 01·1	12 23·5	5·6	4·8	11·6	10·0	17·6	15·1
57	12 59·3	13 01·4	12 23·8	5·7	4·9	11·7	10·0	17·7	15·2
58	12 59·5	13 01·6	12 24·0	5·8	5·0	11·8	10·1	17·8	15·3
59	12 59·8	13 01·9	12 24·2	5·9	5·1	11·9	10·2	17·9	15·4
60	13 00·0	13 02·1	12 24·5	6·0	5·2	12·0	10·3	18·0	15·5

52m s	SUN PLANETS ° ′	ARIES ° ′	MOON ° ′	v or d ′	Corrⁿ ′	v or d ′	Corrⁿ ′	v or d ′	Corrⁿ ′
00	13 00·0	13 02·1	12 24·5	0·0	0·0	6·0	5·3	12·0	10·5
01	13 00·3	13 02·4	12 24·7	0·1	0·1	6·1	5·3	12·1	10·6
02	13 00·5	13 02·6	12 24·9	0·2	0·2	6·2	5·4	12·2	10·7
03	13 00·8	13 02·9	12 25·2	0·3	0·3	6·3	5·5	12·3	10·8
04	13 01·0	13 03·1	12 25·4	0·4	0·4	6·4	5·6	12·4	10·9
05	13 01·3	13 03·4	12 25·7	0·5	0·4	6·5	5·7	12·5	10·9
06	13 01·5	13 03·6	12 25·9	0·6	0·5	6·6	5·8	12·6	11·0
07	13 01·8	13 03·9	12 26·1	0·7	0·6	6·7	5·9	12·7	11·1
08	13 02·0	13 04·1	12 26·4	0·8	0·7	6·8	6·0	12·8	11·2
09	13 02·3	13 04·4	12 26·6	0·9	0·8	6·9	6·0	12·9	11·3
10	13 02·5	13 04·6	12 26·9	1·0	0·9	7·0	6·1	13·0	11·4
11	13 02·8	13 04·9	12 27·1	1·1	1·0	7·1	6·2	13·1	11·5
12	13 03·0	13 05·1	12 27·3	1·2	1·1	7·2	6·3	13·2	11·6
13	13 03·3	13 05·4	12 27·6	1·3	1·1	7·3	6·4	13·3	11·6
14	13 03·5	13 05·6	12 27·8	1·4	1·2	7·4	6·5	13·4	11·7
15	13 03·8	13 05·9	12 28·0	1·5	1·3	7·5	6·6	13·5	11·8
16	13 04·0	13 06·1	12 28·3	1·6	1·4	7·6	6·7	13·6	11·9
17	13 04·3	13 06·4	12 28·5	1·7	1·5	7·7	6·7	13·7	12·0
18	13 04·5	13 06·6	12 28·8	1·8	1·6	7·8	6·8	13·8	12·1
19	13 04·8	13 06·9	12 29·0	1·9	1·7	7·9	6·9	13·9	12·2
20	13 05·0	13 07·1	12 29·2	2·0	1·8	8·0	7·0	14·0	12·3
21	13 05·3	13 07·4	12 29·5	2·1	1·8	8·1	7·1	14·1	12·3
22	13 05·5	13 07·7	12 29·7	2·2	1·9	8·2	7·2	14·2	12·4
23	13 05·8	13 07·9	12 30·0	2·3	2·0	8·3	7·3	14·3	12·5
24	13 06·0	13 08·2	12 30·2	2·4	2·1	8·4	7·4	14·4	12·6
25	13 06·3	13 08·4	12 30·4	2·5	2·2	8·5	7·4	14·5	12·7
26	13 06·5	13 08·7	12 30·7	2·6	2·3	8·6	7·5	14·6	12·8
27	13 06·8	13 08·9	12 30·9	2·7	2·4	8·7	7·6	14·7	12·9
28	13 07·0	13 09·2	12 31·1	2·8	2·5	8·8	7·7	14·8	13·0
29	13 07·3	13 09·4	12 31·4	2·9	2·5	8·9	7·8	14·9	13·0
30	13 07·5	13 09·7	12 31·6	3·0	2·6	9·0	7·9	15·0	13·1
31	13 07·8	13 09·9	12 31·9	3·1	2·7	9·1	8·0	15·1	13·2
32	13 08·0	13 10·2	12 32·1	3·2	2·8	9·2	8·0	15·2	13·3
33	13 08·3	13 10·4	12 32·3	3·3	2·9	9·3	8·1	15·3	13·4
34	13 08·5	13 10·7	12 32·6	3·4	3·0	9·4	8·2	15·4	13·5
35	13 08·8	13 10·9	12 32·8	3·5	3·1	9·5	8·3	15·5	13·6
36	13 09·0	13 11·2	12 33·1	3·6	3·2	9·6	8·4	15·6	13·7
37	13 09·3	13 11·4	12 33·3	3·7	3·2	9·7	8·5	15·7	13·7
38	13 09·5	13 11·7	12 33·5	3·8	3·3	9·8	8·6	15·8	13·8
39	13 09·8	13 11·9	12 33·8	3·9	3·4	9·9	8·7	15·9	13·9
40	13 10·0	13 12·2	12 34·0	4·0	3·5	10·0	8·8	16·0	14·0
41	13 10·3	13 12·4	12 34·2	4·1	3·6	10·1	8·8	16·1	14·1
42	13 10·5	13 12·7	12 34·5	4·2	3·7	10·2	8·9	16·2	14·2
43	13 10·8	13 12·9	12 34·7	4·3	3·8	10·3	9·0	16·3	14·3
44	13 11·0	13 13·2	12 35·0	4·4	3·9	10·4	9·1	16·4	14·3
45	13 11·3	13 13·4	12 35·2	4·5	3·9	10·5	9·2	16·5	14·4
46	13 11·5	13 13·7	12 35·4	4·6	4·0	10·6	9·3	16·6	14·5
47	13 11·8	13 13·9	12 35·7	4·7	4·1	10·7	9·4	16·7	14·6
48	13 12·0	13 14·2	12 35·9	4·8	4·2	10·8	9·5	16·8	14·7
49	13 12·3	13 14·4	12 36·2	4·9	4·3	10·9	9·5	16·9	14·8
50	13 12·5	13 14·7	12 36·4	5·0	4·4	11·0	9·6	17·0	14·9
51	13 12·8	13 14·9	12 36·6	5·1	4·5	11·1	9·7	17·1	15·0
52	13 13·0	13 15·2	12 36·9	5·2	4·6	11·2	9·8	17·2	15·1
53	13 13·3	13 15·4	12 37·1	5·3	4·6	11·3	9·9	17·3	15·1
54	13 13·5	13 15·7	12 37·4	5·4	4·7	11·4	10·0	17·4	15·2
55	13 13·8	13 15·9	12 37·6	5·5	4·8	11·5	10·1	17·5	15·3
56	13 14·0	13 16·2	12 37·8	5·6	4·9	11·6	10·2	17·6	15·4
57	13 14·3	13 16·4	12 38·1	5·7	5·0	11·7	10·2	17·7	15·5
58	13 14·5	13 16·7	12 38·3	5·8	5·1	11·8	10·3	17·8	15·6
59	13 14·8	13 16·9	12 38·5	5·9	5·2	11·9	10·4	17·9	15·7
60	13 15·0	13 17·2	12 38·8	6·0	5·3	12·0	10·5	18·0	15·8

53m s	SUN PLANETS ° ′	ARIES ° ′	MOON ° ′	v or d ′	Corrⁿ ′	v or d ′	Corrⁿ ′	v or d ′	Corrⁿ ′
00	13 15·0	13 17·2	12 38·8	0·0	0·0	6·0	5·4	12·0	10·7
01	13 15·3	13 17·4	12 39·0	0·1	0·1	6·1	5·4	12·1	10·8
02	13 15·5	13 17·7	12 39·3	0·2	0·2	6·2	5·5	12·2	10·9
03	13 15·8	13 17·9	12 39·5	0·3	0·3	6·3	5·6	12·3	11·0
04	13 16·0	13 18·2	12 39·7	0·4	0·4	6·4	5·7	12·4	11·1
05	13 16·3	13 18·4	12 40·0	0·5	0·4	6·5	5·8	12·5	11·1
06	13 16·5	13 18·7	12 40·2	0·6	0·5	6·6	5·9	12·6	11·2
07	13 16·8	13 18·9	12 40·5	0·7	0·6	6·7	6·0	12·7	11·3
08	13 17·0	13 19·2	12 40·7	0·8	0·7	6·8	6·1	12·8	11·4
09	13 17·3	13 19·4	12 40·9	0·9	0·8	6·9	6·2	12·9	11·5
10	13 17·5	13 19·7	12 41·2	1·0	0·9	7·0	6·2	13·0	11·6
11	13 17·8	13 19·9	12 41·4	1·1	1·0	7·1	6·3	13·1	11·7
12	13 18·0	13 20·2	12 41·6	1·2	1·1	7·2	6·4	13·2	11·8
13	13 18·3	13 20·4	12 41·9	1·3	1·2	7·3	6·5	13·3	11·9
14	13 18·5	13 20·7	12 42·1	1·4	1·2	7·4	6·6	13·4	11·9
15	13 18·8	13 20·9	12 42·4	1·5	1·3	7·5	6·7	13·5	12·0
16	13 19·0	13 21·2	12 42·6	1·6	1·4	7·6	6·8	13·6	12·1
17	13 19·3	13 21·4	12 42·8	1·7	1·5	7·7	6·9	13·7	12·2
18	13 19·5	13 21·7	12 43·1	1·8	1·6	7·8	7·0	13·8	12·3
19	13 19·8	13 21·9	12 43·3	1·9	1·7	7·9	7·0	13·9	12·4
20	13 20·0	13 22·2	12 43·6	2·0	1·8	8·0	7·1	14·0	12·5
21	13 20·3	13 22·4	12 43·8	2·1	1·9	8·1	7·2	14·1	12·6
22	13 20·5	13 22·7	12 44·0	2·2	2·0	8·2	7·3	14·2	12·7
23	13 20·8	13 22·9	12 44·3	2·3	2·1	8·3	7·4	14·3	12·8
24	13 21·0	13 23·2	12 44·5	2·4	2·1	8·4	7·5	14·4	12·8
25	13 21·3	13 23·4	12 44·7	2·5	2·2	8·5	7·6	14·5	12·9
26	13 21·5	13 23·7	12 45·0	2·6	2·3	8·6	7·7	14·6	13·0
27	13 21·8	13 23·9	12 45·2	2·7	2·4	8·7	7·8	14·7	13·1
28	13 22·0	13 24·2	12 45·5	2·8	2·5	8·8	7·8	14·8	13·2
29	13 22·3	13 24·4	12 45·7	2·9	2·6	8·9	7·9	14·9	13·3
30	13 22·5	13 24·7	12 45·9	3·0	2·7	9·0	8·0	15·0	13·4
31	13 22·8	13 24·9	12 46·2	3·1	2·8	9·1	8·1	15·1	13·5
32	13 23·0	13 25·2	12 46·4	3·2	2·9	9·2	8·2	15·2	13·6
33	13 23·3	13 25·4	12 46·7	3·3	2·9	9·3	8·3	15·3	13·6
34	13 23·5	13 25·7	12 46·9	3·4	3·0	9·4	8·4	15·4	13·7
35	13 23·8	13 26·0	12 47·1	3·5	3·1	9·5	8·5	15·5	13·8
36	13 24·0	13 26·2	12 47·4	3·6	3·2	9·6	8·6	15·6	13·9
37	13 24·3	13 26·5	12 47·6	3·7	3·3	9·7	8·6	15·7	14·0
38	13 24·5	13 26·7	12 47·9	3·8	3·4	9·8	8·7	15·8	14·1
39	13 24·8	13 27·0	12 48·1	3·9	3·5	9·9	8·8	15·9	14·2
40	13 25·0	13 27·2	12 48·3	4·0	3·6	10·0	8·9	16·0	14·3
41	13 25·3	13 27·5	12 48·6	4·1	3·7	10·1	9·0	16·1	14·4
42	13 25·5	13 27·7	12 48·8	4·2	3·7	10·2	9·1	16·2	14·4
43	13 25·8	13 28·0	12 49·0	4·3	3·8	10·3	9·2	16·3	14·5
44	13 26·0	13 28·2	12 49·3	4·4	3·9	10·4	9·3	16·4	14·6
45	13 26·3	13 28·5	12 49·5	4·5	4·0	10·5	9·4	16·5	14·7
46	13 26·5	13 28·7	12 49·8	4·6	4·1	10·6	9·5	16·6	14·8
47	13 26·8	13 29·0	12 50·0	4·7	4·2	10·7	9·5	16·7	14·9
48	13 27·0	13 29·2	12 50·2	4·8	4·3	10·8	9·6	16·8	15·0
49	13 27·3	13 29·5	12 50·5	4·9	4·4	10·9	9·7	16·9	15·1
50	13 27·5	13 29·7	12 50·7	5·0	4·5	11·0	9·8	17·0	15·2
51	13 27·8	13 30·0	12 51·0	5·1	4·5	11·1	9·9	17·1	15·2
52	13 28·0	13 30·2	12 51·2	5·2	4·6	11·2	10·0	17·2	15·3
53	13 28·3	13 30·5	12 51·4	5·3	4·7	11·3	10·1	17·3	15·4
54	13 28·5	13 30·7	12 51·7	5·4	4·8	11·4	10·2	17·4	15·5
55	13 28·8	13 31·0	12 51·9	5·5	4·9	11·5	10·3	17·5	15·6
56	13 29·0	13 31·2	12 52·1	5·6	5·0	11·6	10·3	17·6	15·7
57	13 29·3	13 31·5	12 52·4	5·7	5·1	11·7	10·4	17·7	15·8
58	13 29·5	13 31·7	12 52·6	5·8	5·2	11·8	10·5	17·8	15·9
59	13 29·8	13 32·0	12 52·9	5·9	5·3	11·9	10·6	17·9	16·0
60	13 30·0	13 32·2	12 53·1	6·0	5·4	12·0	10·7	18·0	16·1

54m	SUN PLANETS	ARIES	MOON	v or d	Corrn	v or d	Corrn	v or d	Corrn
s	° ′	° ′	° ′	′	′	′	′	′	′
00	13 30·0	13 32·2	12 53·1	0·0	0·0	6·0	5·5	12·0	10·9
01	13 30·3	13 32·5	12 53·3	0·1	0·1	6·1	5·5	12·1	11·0
02	13 30·5	13 32·7	12 53·6	0·2	0·2	6·2	5·6	12·2	11·1
03	13 30·8	13 33·0	12 53·8	0·3	0·3	6·3	5·7	12·3	11·2
04	13 31·0	13 33·2	12 54·1	0·4	0·4	6·4	5·8	12·4	11·3
05	13 31·3	13 33·5	12 54·3	0·5	0·5	6·5	5·9	12·5	11·4
06	13 31·5	13 33·7	12 54·5	0·6	0·5	6·6	6·0	12·6	11·4
07	13 31·8	13 34·0	12 54·8	0·7	0·6	6·7	6·1	12·7	11·5
08	13 32·0	13 34·2	12 55·0	0·8	0·7	6·8	6·2	12·8	11·6
09	13 32·3	13 34·5	12 55·2	0·9	0·8	6·9	6·3	12·9	11·7
10	13 32·5	13 34·7	12 55·5	1·0	0·9	7·0	6·4	13·0	11·8
11	13 32·8	13 35·0	12 55·7	1·1	1·0	7·1	6·4	13·1	11·9
12	13 33·0	13 35·2	12 56·0	1·2	1·1	7·2	6·5	13·2	12·0
13	13 33·3	13 35·5	12 56·2	1·3	1·2	7·3	6·6	13·3	12·1
14	13 33·5	13 35·7	12 56·4	1·4	1·3	7·4	6·7	13·4	12·2
15	13 33·8	13 36·0	12 56·7	1·5	1·4	7·5	6·8	13·5	12·3
16	13 34·0	13 36·2	12 56·9	1·6	1·5	7·6	6·9	13·6	12·4
17	13 34·3	13 36·5	12 57·2	1·7	1·5	7·7	7·0	13·7	12·4
18	13 34·5	13 36·7	12 57·4	1·8	1·6	7·8	7·1	13·8	12·5
19	13 34·8	13 37·0	12 57·6	1·9	1·7	7·9	7·2	13·9	12·6
20	13 35·0	13 37·2	12 57·9	2·0	1·8	8·0	7·3	14·0	12·7
21	13 35·3	13 37·5	12 58·1	2·1	1·9	8·1	7·4	14·1	12·8
22	13 35·5	13 37·7	12 58·3	2·2	2·0	8·2	7·4	14·2	12·9
23	13 35·8	13 38·0	12 58·6	2·3	2·1	8·3	7·5	14·3	13·0
24	13 36·0	13 38·2	12 58·8	2·4	2·2	8·4	7·6	14·4	13·1
25	13 36·3	13 38·5	12 59·1	2·5	2·3	8·5	7·7	14·5	13·2
26	13 36·5	13 38·7	12 59·3	2·6	2·4	8·6	7·8	14·6	13·3
27	13 36·8	13 39·0	12 59·5	2·7	2·5	8·7	7·9	14·7	13·4
28	13 37·0	13 39·2	12 59·8	2·8	2·5	8·8	8·0	14·8	13·4
29	13 37·3	13 39·5	13 00·0	2·9	2·6	8·9	8·1	14·9	13·5
30	13 37·5	13 39·7	13 00·3	3·0	2·7	9·0	8·2	15·0	13·6
31	13 37·8	13 40·0	13 00·5	3·1	2·8	9·1	8·3	15·1	13·7
32	13 38·0	13 40·2	13 00·7	3·2	2·9	9·2	8·4	15·2	13·8
33	13 38·3	13 40·5	13 01·0	3·3	3·0	9·3	8·4	15·3	13·9
34	13 38·5	13 40·7	13 01·2	3·4	3·1	9·4	8·5	15·4	14·0
35	13 38·8	13 41·0	13 01·5	3·5	3·2	9·5	8·6	15·5	14·1
36	13 39·0	13 41·2	13 01·7	3·6	3·3	9·6	8·7	15·6	14·2
37	13 39·3	13 41·5	13 01·9	3·7	3·4	9·7	8·8	15·7	14·3
38	13 39·5	13 41·7	13 02·2	3·8	3·5	9·8	8·9	15·8	14·4
39	13 39·8	13 42·0	13 02·4	3·9	3·5	9·9	9·0	15·9	14·4
40	13 40·0	13 42·2	13 02·6	4·0	3·6	10·0	9·1	16·0	14·5
41	13 40·3	13 42·5	13 02·9	4·1	3·7	10·1	9·2	16·1	14·6
42	13 40·5	13 42·7	13 03·1	4·2	3·8	10·2	9·3	16·2	14·7
43	13 40·8	13 43·0	13 03·4	4·3	3·9	10·3	9·4	16·3	14·8
44	13 41·0	13 43·2	13 03·6	4·4	4·0	10·4	9·4	16·4	14·9
45	13 41·3	13 43·5	13 03·8	4·5	4·1	10·5	9·5	16·5	15·0
46	13 41·5	13 43·7	13 04·1	4·6	4·2	10·6	9·6	16·6	15·1
47	13 41·8	13 44·0	13 04·3	4·7	4·3	10·7	9·7	16·7	15·2
48	13 42·0	13 44·3	13 04·6	4·8	4·4	10·8	9·8	16·8	15·3
49	13 42·3	13 44·5	13 04·8	4·9	4·5	10·9	9·9	16·9	15·4
50	13 42·5	13 44·8	13 05·0	5·0	4·5	11·0	10·0	17·0	15·4
51	13 42·8	13 45·0	13 05·3	5·1	4·6	11·1	10·1	17·1	15·5
52	13 43·0	13 45·3	13 05·5	5·2	4·7	11·2	10·2	17·2	15·6
53	13 43·3	13 45·5	13 05·7	5·3	4·8	11·3	10·3	17·3	15·7
54	13 43·5	13 45·8	13 06·0	5·4	4·9	11·4	10·4	17·4	15·8
55	13 43·8	13 46·0	13 06·2	5·5	5·0	11·5	10·4	17·5	15·9
56	13 44·0	13 46·3	13 06·5	5·6	5·1	11·6	10·5	17·6	16·0
57	13 44·3	13 46·5	13 06·7	5·7	5·2	11·7	10·6	17·7	16·1
58	13 44·5	13 46·8	13 06·9	5·8	5·3	11·8	10·7	17·8	16·2
59	13 44·8	13 47·0	13 07·2	5·9	5·4	11·9	10·8	17·9	16·3
60	13 45·0	13 47·3	13 07·4	6·0	5·5	12·0	10·9	18·0	16·4

55m	SUN PLANETS	ARIES	MOON	v or d	Corrn	v or d	Corrn	v or d	Corrn
s	° ′	° ′	° ′	′	′	′	′	′	′
00	13 45·0	13 47·3	13 07·4	0·0	0·0	6·0	5·6	12·0	11·1
01	13 45·3	13 47·5	13 07·7	0·1	0·1	6·1	5·6	12·1	11·2
02	13 45·5	13 47·8	13 07·9	0·2	0·2	6·2	5·7	12·2	11·3
03	13 45·8	13 48·0	13 08·1	0·3	0·3	6·3	5·8	12·3	11·4
04	13 46·0	13 48·3	13 08·4	0·4	0·4	6·4	5·9	12·4	11·5
05	13 46·3	13 48·5	13 08·6	0·5	0·5	6·5	6·0	12·5	11·6
06	13 46·5	13 48·8	13 08·8	0·6	0·6	6·6	6·1	12·6	11·7
07	13 46·8	13 49·0	13 09·1	0·7	0·6	6·7	6·2	12·7	11·7
08	13 47·0	13 49·3	13 09·3	0·8	0·7	6·8	6·3	12·8	11·8
09	13 47·3	13 49·5	13 09·6	0·9	0·8	6·9	6·4	12·9	11·9
10	13 47·5	13 49·8	13 09·8	1·0	0·9	7·0	6·5	13·0	12·0
11	13 47·8	13 50·0	13 10·0	1·1	1·0	7·1	6·6	13·1	12·1
12	13 48·0	13 50·3	13 10·3	1·2	1·1	7·2	6·7	13·2	12·2
13	13 48·3	13 50·5	13 10·5	1·3	1·2	7·3	6·8	13·3	12·3
14	13 48·5	13 50·8	13 10·8	1·4	1·3	7·4	6·8	13·4	12·4
15	13 48·8	13 51·0	13 11·0	1·5	1·4	7·5	6·9	13·5	12·5
16	13 49·0	13 51·3	13 11·2	1·6	1·5	7·6	7·0	13·6	12·6
17	13 49·3	13 51·5	13 11·5	1·7	1·6	7·7	7·1	13·7	12·7
18	13 49·5	13 51·8	13 11·7	1·8	1·7	7·8	7·2	13·8	12·8
19	13 49·8	13 52·0	13 12·0	1·9	1·8	7·9	7·3	13·9	12·9
20	13 50·0	13 52·3	13 12·2	2·0	1·9	8·0	7·4	14·0	13·0
21	13 50·3	13 52·5	13 12·4	2·1	1·9	8·1	7·5	14·1	13·0
22	13 50·5	13 52·8	13 12·7	2·2	2·0	8·2	7·6	14·2	13·1
23	13 50·8	13 53·0	13 12·9	2·3	2·1	8·3	7·7	14·3	13·2
24	13 51·0	13 53·3	13 13·1	2·4	2·2	8·4	7·8	14·4	13·3
25	13 51·3	13 53·5	13 13·4	2·5	2·3	8·5	7·9	14·5	13·4
26	13 51·5	13 53·8	13 13·6	2·6	2·4	8·6	8·0	14·6	13·5
27	13 51·8	13 54·0	13 13·9	2·7	2·5	8·7	8·0	14·7	13·6
28	13 52·0	13 54·3	13 14·1	2·8	2·6	8·8	8·1	14·8	13·7
29	13 52·3	13 54·5	13 14·3	2·9	2·7	8·9	8·2	14·9	13·8
30	13 52·5	13 54·8	13 14·6	3·0	2·8	9·0	8·3	15·0	13·9
31	13 52·8	13 55·0	13 14·8	3·1	2·9	9·1	8·4	15·1	14·0
32	13 53·0	13 55·3	13 15·1	3·2	3·0	9·2	8·5	15·2	14·1
33	13 53·3	13 55·5	13 15·3	3·3	3·1	9·3	8·6	15·3	14·2
34	13 53·5	13 55·8	13 15·5	3·4	3·1	9·4	8·7	15·4	14·2
35	13 53·8	13 56·0	13 15·8	3·5	3·2	9·5	8·8	15·5	14·3
36	13 54·0	13 56·3	13 16·0	3·6	3·3	9·6	8·9	15·6	14·4
37	13 54·3	13 56·5	13 16·2	3·7	3·4	9·7	9·0	15·7	14·5
38	13 54·5	13 56·8	13 16·5	3·8	3·5	9·8	9·1	15·8	14·6
39	13 54·8	13 57·0	13 16·7	3·9	3·6	9·9	9·2	15·9	14·7
40	13 55·0	13 57·3	13 17·0	4·0	3·7	10·0	9·3	16·0	14·8
41	13 55·3	13 57·5	13 17·2	4·1	3·8	10·1	9·3	16·1	14·9
42	13 55·5	13 57·8	13 17·4	4·2	3·9	10·2	9·4	16·2	15·0
43	13 55·8	13 58·0	13 17·7	4·3	4·0	10·3	9·5	16·3	15·1
44	13 56·0	13 58·3	13 17·9	4·4	4·1	10·4	9·6	16·4	15·2
45	13 56·3	13 58·5	13 18·2	4·5	4·2	10·5	9·7	16·5	15·3
46	13 56·5	13 58·8	13 18·4	4·6	4·3	10·6	9·8	16·6	15·4
47	13 56·8	13 59·0	13 18·6	4·7	4·3	10·7	9·9	16·7	15·4
48	13 57·0	13 59·3	13 18·9	4·8	4·4	10·8	10·0	16·8	15·5
49	13 57·3	13 59·5	13 19·1	4·9	4·5	10·9	10·1	16·9	15·6
50	13 57·5	13 59·8	13 19·3	5·0	4·6	11·0	10·2	17·0	15·7
51	13 57·8	14 00·0	13 19·6	5·1	4·7	11·1	10·3	17·1	15·8
52	13 58·0	14 00·3	13 19·8	5·2	4·8	11·2	10·4	17·2	15·9
53	13 58·3	14 00·5	13 20·1	5·3	4·9	11·3	10·5	17·3	16·0
54	13 58·5	14 00·8	13 20·3	5·4	5·0	11·4	10·5	17·4	16·1
55	13 58·8	14 01·0	13 20·5	5·5	5·1	11·5	10·6	17·5	16·2
56	13 59·0	14 01·3	13 20·8	5·6	5·2	11·6	10·7	17·6	16·3
57	13 59·3	14 01·5	13 21·0	5·7	5·3	11·7	10·8	17·7	16·4
58	13 59·5	14 01·8	13 21·3	5·8	5·4	11·8	10·9	17·8	16·5
59	13 59·8	14 02·0	13 21·5	5·9	5·5	11·9	11·0	17·9	16·6
60	14 00·0	14 02·3	13 21·7	6·0	5·6	12·0	11·1	18·0	16·7

56m s	SUN PLANETS ° ′	ARIES ° ′	MOON ° ′	v or d ′	Corrn ′	v or d ′	Corrn ′	v or d ′	Corrn ′
00	14 00·0	14 02·3	13 21·7	0·0	0·0	6·0	5·7	12·0	11·3
01	14 00·3	14 02·6	13 22·0	0·1	0·1	6·1	5·7	12·1	11·4
02	14 00·5	14 02·8	13 22·2	0·2	0·2	6·2	5·8	12·2	11·5
03	14 00·8	14 03·1	13 22·4	0·3	0·3	6·3	5·9	12·3	11·6
04	14 01·0	14 03·3	13 22·7	0·4	0·4	6·4	6·0	12·4	11·7
05	14 01·3	14 03·6	13 22·9	0·5	0·5	6·5	6·1	12·5	11·8
06	14 01·5	14 03·8	13 23·2	0·6	0·6	6·6	6·2	12·6	11·9
07	14 01·8	14 04·1	13 23·4	0·7	0·7	6·7	6·3	12·7	12·0
08	14 02·0	14 04·3	13 23·6	0·8	0·8	6·8	6·4	12·8	12·1
09	14 02·3	14 04·6	13 23·9	0·9	0·8	6·9	6·5	12·9	12·1
10	14 02·5	14 04·8	13 24·1	1·0	0·9	7·0	6·6	13·0	12·2
11	14 02·8	14 05·1	13 24·4	1·1	1·0	7·1	6·7	13·1	12·3
12	14 03·0	14 05·3	13 24·6	1·2	1·1	7·2	6·8	13·2	12·4
13	14 03·3	14 05·6	13 24·8	1·3	1·2	7·3	6·9	13·3	12·5
14	14 03·5	14 05·8	13 25·1	1·4	1·3	7·4	7·0	13·4	12·6
15	14 03·8	14 06·1	13 25·3	1·5	1·4	7·5	7·1	13·5	12·7
16	14 04·0	14 06·3	13 25·6	1·6	1·5	7·6	7·2	13·6	12·8
17	14 04·3	14 06·6	13 25·8	1·7	1·6	7·7	7·3	13·7	12·9
18	14 04·5	14 06·8	13 26·0	1·8	1·7	7·8	7·3	13·8	13·0
19	14 04·8	14 07·1	13 26·3	1·9	1·8	7·9	7·4	13·9	13·1
20	14 05·0	14 07·3	13 26·5	2·0	1·9	8·0	7·5	14·0	13·2
21	14 05·3	14 07·6	13 26·7	2·1	2·0	8·1	7·6	14·1	13·3
22	14 05·5	14 07·8	13 27·0	2·2	2·1	8·2	7·7	14·2	13·4
23	14 05·8	14 08·1	13 27·2	2·3	2·2	8·3	7·8	14·3	13·5
24	14 06·0	14 08·3	13 27·5	2·4	2·3	8·4	7·9	14·4	13·6
25	14 06·3	14 08·6	13 27·7	2·5	2·4	8·5	8·0	14·5	13·7
26	14 06·5	14 08·8	13 27·9	2·6	2·4	8·6	8·1	14·6	13·7
27	14 06·8	14 09·1	13 28·2	2·7	2·5	8·7	8·2	14·7	13·8
28	14 07·0	14 09·3	13 28·4	2·8	2·6	8·8	8·3	14·8	13·9
29	14 07·3	14 09·6	13 28·7	2·9	2·7	8·9	8·4	14·9	14·0
30	14 07·5	14 09·8	13 28·9	3·0	2·8	9·0	8·5	15·0	14·1
31	14 07·8	14 10·1	13 29·1	3·1	2·9	9·1	8·6	15·1	14·2
32	14 08·0	14 10·3	13 29·4	3·2	3·0	9·2	8·7	15·2	14·3
33	14 08·3	14 10·6	13 29·6	3·3	3·1	9·3	8·8	15·3	14·4
34	14 08·5	14 10·8	13 29·8	3·4	3·2	9·4	8·9	15·4	14·5
35	14 08·8	14 11·1	13 30·1	3·5	3·3	9·5	8·9	15·5	14·6
36	14 09·0	14 11·3	13 30·3	3·6	3·4	9·6	9·0	15·6	14·7
37	14 09·3	14 11·6	13 30·6	3·7	3·5	9·7	9·1	15·7	14·8
38	14 09·5	14 11·8	13 30·8	3·8	3·6	9·8	9·2	15·8	14·9
39	14 09·8	14 12·1	13 31·0	3·9	3·7	9·9	9·3	15·9	15·0
40	14 10·0	14 12·3	13 31·3	4·0	3·8	10·0	9·4	16·0	15·1
41	14 10·3	14 12·6	13 31·5	4·1	3·9	10·1	9·5	16·1	15·2
42	14 10·5	14 12·8	13 31·8	4·2	4·0	10·2	9·6	16·2	15·3
43	14 10·8	14 13·1	13 32·0	4·3	4·0	10·3	9·7	16·3	15·3
44	14 11·0	14 13·3	13 32·2	4·4	4·1	10·4	9·8	16·4	15·4
45	14 11·3	14 13·6	13 32·5	4·5	4·2	10·5	9·9	16·5	15·5
46	14 11·5	14 13·8	13 32·7	4·6	4·3	10·6	10·0	16·6	15·6
47	14 11·8	14 14·1	13 32·9	4·7	4·4	10·7	10·1	16·7	15·7
48	14 12·0	14 14·3	13 33·2	4·8	4·5	10·8	10·2	16·8	15·8
49	14 12·3	14 14·6	13 33·4	4·9	4·6	10·9	10·3	16·9	15·9
50	14 12·5	14 14·8	13 33·7	5·0	4·7	11·0	10·4	17·0	16·0
51	14 12·8	14 15·1	13 33·9	5·1	4·8	11·1	10·5	17·1	16·1
52	14 13·0	14 15·3	13 34·1	5·2	4·9	11·2	10·5	17·2	16·2
53	14 13·3	14 15·6	13 34·4	5·3	5·0	11·3	10·6	17·3	16·3
54	14 13·5	14 15·8	13 34·6	5·4	5·1	11·4	10·7	17·4	16·4
55	14 13·8	14 16·1	13 34·9	5·5	5·2	11·5	10·8	17·5	16·5
56	14 14·0	14 16·3	13 35·1	5·6	5·3	11·6	10·9	17·6	16·6
57	14 14·3	14 16·6	13 35·3	5·7	5·4	11·7	11·0	17·7	16·7
58	14 14·5	14 16·8	13 35·6	5·8	5·5	11·8	11·1	17·8	16·8
59	14 14·8	14 17·1	13 35·8	5·9	5·6	11·9	11·2	17·9	16·9
60	14 15·0	14 17·3	13 36·1	6·0	5·7	12·0	11·3	18·0	17·0

57m s	SUN PLANETS ° ′	ARIES ° ′	MOON ° ′	v or d ′	Corrn ′	v or d ′	Corrn ′	v or d ′	Corrn ′
00	14 15·0	14 17·3	13 36·1	0·0	0·0	6·0	5·8	12·0	11·5
01	14 15·3	14 17·6	13 36·3	0·1	0·1	6·1	5·8	12·1	11·6
02	14 15·5	14 17·8	13 36·5	0·2	0·2	6·2	5·9	12·2	11·7
03	14 15·8	14 18·1	13 36·8	0·3	0·3	6·3	6·0	12·3	11·8
04	14 16·0	14 18·3	13 37·0	0·4	0·4	6·4	6·1	12·4	11·9
05	14 16·3	14 18·6	13 37·2	0·5	0·5	6·5	6·2	12·5	12·0
06	14 16·5	14 18·8	13 37·5	0·6	0·6	6·6	6·3	12·6	12·1
07	14 16·8	14 19·1	13 37·7	0·7	0·7	6·7	6·4	12·7	12·2
08	14 17·0	14 19·3	13 38·0	0·8	0·8	6·8	6·5	12·8	12·3
09	14 17·3	14 19·6	13 38·2	0·9	0·9	6·9	6·6	12·9	12·4
10	14 17·5	14 19·8	13 38·4	1·0	1·0	7·0	6·7	13·0	12·5
11	14 17·8	14 20·1	13 38·7	1·1	1·1	7·1	6·8	13·1	12·6
12	14 18·0	14 20·3	13 38·9	1·2	1·2	7·2	6·9	13·2	12·7
13	14 18·3	14 20·6	13 39·2	1·3	1·2	7·3	7·0	13·3	12·7
14	14 18·5	14 20·9	13 39·4	1·4	1·3	7·4	7·1	13·4	12·8
15	14 18·8	14 21·1	13 39·6	1·5	1·4	7·5	7·2	13·5	12·9
16	14 19·0	14 21·4	13 39·9	1·6	1·5	7·6	7·3	13·6	13·0
17	14 19·3	14 21·6	13 40·1	1·7	1·6	7·7	7·4	13·7	13·1
18	14 19·5	14 21·9	13 40·3	1·8	1·7	7·8	7·5	13·8	13·2
19	14 19·8	14 22·1	13 40·6	1·9	1·8	7·9	7·6	13·9	13·3
20	14 20·0	14 22·4	13 40·8	2·0	1·9	8·0	7·7	14·0	13·4
21	14 20·3	14 22·6	13 41·1	2·1	2·0	8·1	7·8	14·1	13·5
22	14 20·5	14 22·9	13 41·3	2·2	2·1	8·2	7·9	14·2	13·6
23	14 20·8	14 23·1	13 41·5	2·3	2·2	8·3	8·0	14·3	13·7
24	14 21·0	14 23·4	13 41·8	2·4	2·3	8·4	8·1	14·4	13·8
25	14 21·3	14 23·6	13 42·0	2·5	2·4	8·5	8·1	14·5	13·9
26	14 21·5	14 23·9	13 42·3	2·6	2·5	8·6	8·2	14·6	14·0
27	14 21·8	14 24·1	13 42·5	2·7	2·6	8·7	8·3	14·7	14·1
28	14 22·0	14 24·4	13 42·7	2·8	2·7	8·8	8·4	14·8	14·2
29	14 22·3	14 24·6	13 43·0	2·9	2·8	8·9	8·5	14·9	14·3
30	14 22·5	14 24·9	13 43·2	3·0	2·9	9·0	8·6	15·0	14·4
31	14 22·8	14 25·1	13 43·4	3·1	3·0	9·1	8·7	15·1	14·5
32	14 23·0	14 25·4	13 43·7	3·2	3·1	9·2	8·8	15·2	14·6
33	14 23·3	14 25·6	13 43·9	3·3	3·2	9·3	8·9	15·3	14·7
34	14 23·5	14 25·9	13 44·2	3·4	3·3	9·4	9·0	15·4	14·8
35	14 23·8	14 26·1	13 44·4	3·5	3·4	9·5	9·1	15·5	14·9
36	14 24·0	14 26·4	13 44·6	3·6	3·5	9·6	9·2	15·6	15·0
37	14 24·3	14 26·6	13 44·9	3·7	3·5	9·7	9·3	15·7	15·0
38	14 24·5	14 26·9	13 45·1	3·8	3·6	9·8	9·4	15·8	15·1
39	14 24·8	14 27·1	13 45·4	3·9	3·7	9·9	9·5	15·9	15·2
40	14 25·0	14 27·4	13 45·6	4·0	3·8	10·0	9·6	16·0	15·3
41	14 25·3	14 27·6	13 45·8	4·1	3·9	10·1	9·7	16·1	15·4
42	14 25·5	14 27·9	13 46·1	4·2	4·0	10·2	9·8	16·2	15·5
43	14 25·8	14 28·1	13 46·3	4·3	4·1	10·3	9·9	16·3	15·6
44	14 26·0	14 28·4	13 46·5	4·4	4·2	10·4	10·0	16·4	15·7
45	14 26·3	14 28·6	13 46·8	4·5	4·3	10·5	10·1	16·5	15·8
46	14 26·5	14 28·9	13 47·0	4·6	4·4	10·6	10·2	16·6	15·9
47	14 26·8	14 29·1	13 47·3	4·7	4·5	10·7	10·3	16·7	16·0
48	14 27·0	14 29·4	13 47·5	4·8	4·6	10·8	10·4	16·8	16·1
49	14 27·3	14 29·6	13 47·7	4·9	4·7	10·9	10·4	16·9	16·2
50	14 27·5	14 29·9	13 48·0	5·0	4·8	11·0	10·5	17·0	16·3
51	14 27·8	14 30·1	13 48·2	5·1	4·9	11·1	10·6	17·1	16·4
52	14 28·0	14 30·4	13 48·5	5·2	5·0	11·2	10·7	17·2	16·5
53	14 28·3	14 30·6	13 48·7	5·3	5·1	11·3	10·8	17·3	16·6
54	14 28·5	14 30·9	13 48·9	5·4	5·2	11·4	10·9	17·4	16·7
55	14 28·8	14 31·1	13 49·2	5·5	5·3	11·5	11·0	17·5	16·8
56	14 29·0	14 31·4	13 49·4	5·6	5·4	11·6	11·1	17·6	16·9
57	14 29·3	14 31·6	13 49·7	5·7	5·5	11·7	11·2	17·7	17·0
58	14 29·5	14 31·9	13 49·9	5·8	5·6	11·8	11·3	17·8	17·1
59	14 29·8	14 32·1	13 50·1	5·9	5·7	11·9	11·4	17·9	17·2
60	14 30·0	14 32·4	13 50·4	6·0	5·8	12·0	11·5	18·0	17·3

58m	SUN PLANETS	ARIES	MOON	v or d	Corrn	v or d	Corrn	v or d	Corrn
s	° ′	° ′	° ′	′	′	′	′	′	′
00	14 30·0	14 32·4	13 50·4	0·0	0·0	6·0	5·9	12·0	11·7
01	14 30·3	14 32·6	13 50·6	0·1	0·1	6·1	5·9	12·1	11·8
02	14 30·5	14 32·9	13 50·8	0·2	0·2	6·2	6·0	12·2	11·9
03	14 30·8	14 33·1	13 51·1	0·3	0·3	6·3	6·1	12·3	12·0
04	14 31·0	14 33·4	13 51·3	0·4	0·4	6·4	6·2	12·4	12·1
05	14 31·3	14 33·6	13 51·6	0·5	0·5	6·5	6·3	12·5	12·2
06	14 31·5	14 33·9	13 51·8	0·6	0·6	6·6	6·4	12·6	12·3
07	14 31·8	14 34·1	13 52·0	0·7	0·7	6·7	6·5	12·7	12·4
08	14 32·0	14 34·4	13 52·3	0·8	0·8	6·8	6·6	12·8	12·5
09	14 32·3	14 34·6	13 52·5	0·9	0·9	6·9	6·7	12·9	12·6
10	14 32·5	14 34·9	13 52·8	1·0	1·0	7·0	6·8	13·0	12·7
11	14 32·8	14 35·1	13 53·0	1·1	1·1	7·1	6·9	13·1	12·8
12	14 33·0	14 35·4	13 53·2	1·2	1·2	7·2	7·0	13·2	12·9
13	14 33·3	14 35·6	13 53·5	1·3	1·3	7·3	7·1	13·3	13·0
14	14 33·5	14 35·9	13 53·7	1·4	1·4	7·4	7·2	13·4	13·1
15	14 33·8	14 36·1	13 53·9	1·5	1·5	7·5	7·3	13·5	13·2
16	14 34·0	14 36·4	13 54·2	1·6	1·6	7·6	7·4	13·6	13·3
17	14 34·3	14 36·6	13 54·4	1·7	1·7	7·7	7·5	13·7	13·4
18	14 34·5	14 36·9	13 54·7	1·8	1·8	7·8	7·6	13·8	13·5
19	14 34·8	14 37·1	13 54·9	1·9	1·9	7·9	7·7	13·9	13·6
20	14 35·0	14 37·4	13 55·1	2·0	2·0	8·0	7·8	14·0	13·7
21	14 35·3	14 37·6	13 55·4	2·1	2·0	8·1	7·9	14·1	13·7
22	14 35·5	14 37·9	13 55·6	2·2	2·1	8·2	8·0	14·2	13·8
23	14 35·8	14 38·1	13 55·9	2·3	2·2	8·3	8·1	14·3	13·9
24	14 36·0	14 38·4	13 56·1	2·4	2·3	8·4	8·2	14·4	14·0
25	14 36·3	14 38·6	13 56·3	2·5	2·4	8·5	8·3	14·5	14·1
26	14 36·5	14 38·9	13 56·6	2·6	2·5	8·6	8·4	14·6	14·2
27	14 36·8	14 39·2	13 56·8	2·7	2·6	8·7	8·5	14·7	14·3
28	14 37·0	14 39·4	13 57·0	2·8	2·7	8·8	8·6	14·8	14·4
29	14 37·3	14 39·7	13 57·3	2·9	2·8	8·9	8·7	14·9	14·5
30	14 37·5	14 39·9	13 57·5	3·0	2·9	9·0	8·8	15·0	14·6
31	14 37·8	14 40·2	13 57·8	3·1	3·0	9·1	8·9	15·1	14·7
32	14 38·0	14 40·4	13 58·0	3·2	3·1	9·2	9·0	15·2	14·8
33	14 38·3	14 40·7	13 58·2	3·3	3·2	9·3	9·1	15·3	14·9
34	14 38·5	14 40·9	13 58·5	3·4	3·3	9·4	9·2	15·4	15·0
35	14 38·8	14 41·2	13 58·7	3·5	3·4	9·5	9·3	15·5	15·1
36	14 39·0	14 41·4	13 59·0	3·6	3·5	9·6	9·4	15·6	15·2
37	14 39·3	14 41·7	13 59·2	3·7	3·6	9·7	9·5	15·7	15·3
38	14 39·5	14 41·9	13 59·4	3·8	3·7	9·8	9·6	15·8	15·4
39	14 39·8	14 42·2	13 59·7	3·9	3·8	9·9	9·7	15·9	15·5
40	14 40·0	14 42·4	13 59·9	4·0	3·9	10·0	9·8	16·0	15·6
41	14 40·3	14 42·7	14 00·1	4·1	4·0	10·1	9·8	16·1	15·7
42	14 40·5	14 42·9	14 00·4	4·2	4·1	10·2	9·9	16·2	15·8
43	14 40·8	14 43·2	14 00·6	4·3	4·2	10·3	10·0	16·3	15·9
44	14 41·0	14 43·4	14 00·9	4·4	4·3	10·4	10·1	16·4	16·0
45	14 41·3	14 43·7	14 01·1	4·5	4·4	10·5	10·2	16·5	16·1
46	14 41·5	14 43·9	14 01·3	4·6	4·5	10·6	10·3	16·6	16·2
47	14 41·8	14 44·2	14 01·6	4·7	4·6	10·7	10·4	16·7	16·3
48	14 42·0	14 44·4	14 01·8	4·8	4·7	10·8	10·5	16·8	16·4
49	14 42·3	14 44·7	14 02·1	4·9	4·8	10·9	10·6	16·9	16·5
50	14 42·5	14 44·9	14 02·3	5·0	4·9	11·0	10·7	17·0	16·6
51	14 42·8	14 45·2	14 02·5	5·1	5·0	11·1	10·8	17·1	16·7
52	14 43·0	14 45·4	14 02·8	5·2	5·1	11·2	10·9	17·2	16·8
53	14 43·3	14 45·7	14 03·0	5·3	5·2	11·3	11·0	17·3	16·9
54	14 43·5	14 45·9	14 03·3	5·4	5·3	11·4	11·1	17·4	17·0
55	14 43·8	14 46·2	14 03·5	5·5	5·4	11·5	11·2	17·5	17·1
56	14 44·0	14 46·4	14 03·7	5·6	5·5	11·6	11·3	17·6	17·2
57	14 44·3	14 46·7	14 04·0	5·7	5·6	11·7	11·4	17·7	17·3
58	14 44·5	14 46·9	14 04·2	5·8	5·7	11·8	11·5	17·8	17·4
59	14 44·8	14 47·2	14 04·4	5·9	5·8	11·9	11·6	17·9	17·5
60	14 45·0	14 47·4	14 04·7	6·0	5·9	12·0	11·7	18·0	17·6

59m	SUN PLANETS	ARIES	MOON	v or d	Corrn	v or d	Corrn	v or d	Corrn
s	° ′	° ′	° ′	′	′	′	′	′	′
00	14 45·0	14 47·4	14 04·7	0·0	0·0	6·0	6·0	12·0	11·9
01	14 45·3	14 47·7	14 04·9	0·1	0·1	6·1	6·0	12·1	12·0
02	14 45·5	14 47·9	14 05·2	0·2	0·2	6·2	6·1	12·2	12·1
03	14 45·8	14 48·2	14 05·4	0·3	0·3	6·3	6·2	12·3	12·2
04	14 46·0	14 48·4	14 05·6	0·4	0·4	6·4	6·3	12·4	12·3
05	14 46·3	14 48·7	14 05·9	0·5	0·5	6·5	6·4	12·5	12·4
06	14 46·5	14 48·9	14 06·1	0·6	0·6	6·6	6·5	12·6	12·5
07	14 46·8	14 49·2	14 06·4	0·7	0·7	6·7	6·6	12·7	12·6
08	14 47·0	14 49·4	14 06·6	0·8	0·8	6·8	6·7	12·8	12·7
09	14 47·3	14 49·7	14 06·8	0·9	0·9	6·9	6·8	12·9	12·8
10	14 47·5	14 49·9	14 07·1	1·0	1·0	7·0	6·9	13·0	12·9
11	14 47·8	14 50·2	14 07·3	1·1	1·1	7·1	7·0	13·1	13·0
12	14 48·0	14 50·4	14 07·5	1·2	1·2	7·2	7·1	13·2	13·1
13	14 48·3	14 50·7	14 07·8	1·3	1·3	7·3	7·2	13·3	13·2
14	14 48·5	14 50·9	14 08·0	1·4	1·4	7·4	7·3	13·4	13·3
15	14 48·8	14 51·2	14 08·3	1·5	1·5	7·5	7·4	13·5	13·4
16	14 49·0	14 51·4	14 08·5	1·6	1·6	7·6	7·5	13·6	13·5
17	14 49·3	14 51·7	14 08·7	1·7	1·7	7·7	7·6	13·7	13·6
18	14 49·5	14 51·9	14 09·0	1·8	1·8	7·8	7·7	13·8	13·7
19	14 49·8	14 52·2	14 09·2	1·9	1·9	7·9	7·8	13·9	13·8
20	14 50·0	14 52·4	14 09·5	2·0	2·0	8·0	7·9	14·0	13·9
21	14 50·3	14 52·7	14 09·7	2·1	2·1	8·1	8·0	14·1	14·0
22	14 50·5	14 52·9	14 09·9	2·2	2·2	8·2	8·1	14·2	14·1
23	14 50·8	14 53·2	14 10·2	2·3	2·3	8·3	8·2	14·3	14·2
24	14 51·0	14 53·4	14 10·4	2·4	2·4	8·4	8·3	14·4	14·3
25	14 51·3	14 53·7	14 10·6	2·5	2·5	8·5	8·4	14·5	14·4
26	14 51·5	14 53·9	14 10·9	2·6	2·6	8·6	8·5	14·6	14·5
27	14 51·8	14 54·2	14 11·1	2·7	2·7	8·7	8·6	14·7	14·6
28	14 52·0	14 54·4	14 11·4	2·8	2·8	8·8	8·7	14·8	14·7
29	14 52·3	14 54·7	14 11·6	2·9	2·9	8·9	8·8	14·9	14·8
30	14 52·5	14 54·9	14 11·8	3·0	3·0	9·0	8·9	15·0	14·9
31	14 52·8	14 55·2	14 12·1	3·1	3·1	9·1	9·0	15·1	15·0
32	14 53·0	14 55·4	14 12·3	3·2	3·2	9·2	9·1	15·2	15·1
33	14 53·3	14 55·7	14 12·6	3·3	3·3	9·3	9·2	15·3	15·2
34	14 53·5	14 55·9	14 12·8	3·4	3·4	9·4	9·3	15·4	15·3
35	14 53·8	14 56·2	14 13·0	3·5	3·5	9·5	9·4	15·5	15·4
36	14 54·0	14 56·4	14 13·3	3·6	3·6	9·6	9·5	15·6	15·5
37	14 54·3	14 56·7	14 13·5	3·7	3·7	9·7	9·6	15·7	15·6
38	14 54·5	14 56·9	14 13·8	3·8	3·8	9·8	9·7	15·8	15·7
39	14 54·8	14 57·2	14 14·0	3·9	3·9	9·9	9·8	15·9	15·8
40	14 55·0	14 57·5	14 14·2	4·0	4·0	10·0	9·9	16·0	15·9
41	14 55·3	14 57·7	14 14·5	4·1	4·1	10·1	10·0	16·1	16·0
42	14 55·5	14 58·0	14 14·7	4·2	4·2	10·2	10·1	16·2	16·1
43	14 55·8	14 58·2	14 14·9	4·3	4·3	10·3	10·2	16·3	16·2
44	14 56·0	14 58·5	14 15·2	4·4	4·4	10·4	10·3	16·4	16·3
45	14 56·3	14 58·7	14 15·4	4·5	4·5	10·5	10·4	16·5	16·4
46	14 56·5	14 59·0	14 15·7	4·6	4·6	10·6	10·5	16·6	16·5
47	14 56·8	14 59·2	14 15·9	4·7	4·7	10·7	10·6	16·7	16·6
48	14 57·0	14 59·5	14 16·1	4·8	4·8	10·8	10·7	16·8	16·7
49	14 57·3	14 59·7	14 16·4	4·9	4·9	10·9	10·8	16·9	16·8
50	14 57·5	15 00·0	14 16·6	5·0	5·0	11·0	10·9	17·0	16·9
51	14 57·8	15 00·2	14 16·9	5·1	5·1	11·1	11·0	17·1	17·0
52	14 58·0	15 00·5	14 17·1	5·2	5·2	11·2	11·1	17·2	17·1
53	14 58·3	15 00·7	14 17·3	5·3	5·3	11·3	11·2	17·3	17·2
54	14 58·5	15 01·0	14 17·6	5·4	5·4	11·4	11·3	17·4	17·3
55	14 58·8	15 01·2	14 17·8	5·5	5·5	11·5	11·4	17·5	17·4
56	14 59·0	15 01·5	14 18·0	5·6	5·6	11·6	11·5	17·6	17·5
57	14 59·3	15 01·7	14 18·3	5·7	5·7	11·7	11·6	17·7	17·6
58	14 59·5	15 02·0	14 18·5	5·8	5·8	11·8	11·7	17·8	17·7
59	14 59·8	15 02·2	14 18·8	5·9	5·9	11·9	11·8	17·9	17·8
60	15 00·0	15 02·5	14 19·0	6·0	6·0	12·0	11·9	18·0	17·9

TABLES FOR INTERPOLATING SUNRISE, MOONRISE, ETC.

TABLE I—FOR LATITUDE

Tabular Interval 10°	5°	2°	5^m	10^m	15^m	20^m	25^m	30^m	35^m	40^m	45^m	50^m	55^m	60^m	1^h05^m	1^h10^m	1^h15^m	1^h20^m
° ′	° ′	° ′	m	m	m	m	m	m	m	m	m	m	m	m	h m	h m	h m	h m
0 30	**0 15**	**0 06**	0	0	1	1	1	1	1	2	2	2	2	2	0 02	0 02	0 02	0 02
1 00	**0 30**	**0 12**	0	1	1	2	2	3	3	3	4	4	4	5	05	05	05	05
1 30	**0 45**	**0 18**	1	1	2	3	3	4	4	5	5	6	7	7	07	07	07	07
2 00	**1 00**	**0 24**	1	2	3	4	5	5	6	7	7	8	9	10	10	10	10	10
2 30	**1 15**	**0 30**	1	2	4	5	6	7	8	9	9	10	11	12	12	13	13	13
3 00	**1 30**	**0 36**	1	3	4	6	7	8	9	10	11	12	13	14	0 15	0 15	0 16	0 16
3 30	**1 45**	**0 42**	2	3	5	7	8	10	11	12	13	14	16	17	18	18	19	19
4 00	**2 00**	**0 48**	2	4	6	8	9	11	13	14	15	16	18	19	20	21	22	22
4 30	**2 15**	**0 54**	2	4	7	9	11	13	15	16	18	19	21	22	23	24	25	26
5 00	**2 30**	**1 00**	2	5	7	10	12	14	16	18	20	22	23	25	26	27	28	29
5 30	**2 45**	**1 06**	3	5	8	11	13	16	18	20	22	24	26	28	0 29	0 30	0 31	0 32
6 00	**3 00**	**1 12**	3	6	9	12	14	17	20	22	24	26	29	31	32	33	34	36
6 30	**3 15**	**1 18**	3	6	10	13	16	19	22	24	26	29	31	34	36	37	38	40
7 00	**3 30**	**1 24**	3	7	10	14	17	20	23	26	29	31	34	37	39	41	42	44
7 30	**3 45**	**1 30**	4	7	11	15	18	22	25	28	31	34	37	40	43	44	46	48
8 00	**4 00**	**1 36**	4	8	12	16	20	23	27	30	34	37	41	44	0 47	0 48	0 51	0 53
8 30	**4 15**	**1 42**	4	8	13	17	21	25	29	33	36	40	44	48	0 51	0 53	0 56	0 58
9 00	**4 30**	**1 48**	4	9	13	18	22	27	31	35	39	43	47	52	0 55	0 58	1 01	1 04
9 30	**4 45**	**1 54**	5	9	14	19	24	28	33	38	42	47	51	56	1 00	1 04	1 08	1 12
10 00	**5 00**	**2 00**	5	10	15	20	25	30	35	40	45	50	55	60	1 05	1 10	1 15	1 20

(Column heading over the time columns: Difference between the times for consecutive latitudes)

Table I is for interpolating the LMT of sunrise, twilight, moonrise, etc., for latitude. It is to be entered, in the appropriate column on the left, with the difference between true latitude and the nearest tabular latitude which is *less* than the true latitude; and with the argument at the top which is the nearest value of the difference between the times for the tabular latitude and the next higher one; the correction so obtained is applied to the time for the tabular latitude; the sign of the correction can be seen by inspection. It is to be noted that the interpolation is not linear, so that when using this table it is essential to take out the tabular phenomenon for the latitude *less* than the true latitude.

TABLE II—FOR LONGITUDE

Long. East or West	10^m	20^m	30^m	40^m	50^m	60^m	1^h+10^m	1^h+20^m	1^h+30^m	1^h+40^m	1^h+50^m	1^h+60^m	2^h10^m	2^h20^m	2^h30^m	2^h40^m	2^h50^m	3^h00^m
°	m	m	m	m	m	m	m	m	m	m	m	m	h m	h m	h m	h m	h m	h m
0	0	0	0	0	0	0	0	0	0	0	0	0	0 00	0 00	0 00	0 00	0 00	0 00
10	0	1	1	1	1	2	2	2	2	3	3	3	04	04	04	04	05	05
20	1	1	2	2	3	3	4	4	5	6	6	7	07	08	08	09	09	10
30	1	2	2	3	4	5	6	7	7	8	9	10	11	12	12	13	14	15
40	1	2	3	4	6	7	8	9	10	11	12	13	14	16	17	18	19	20
50	1	3	4	6	7	8	10	11	12	14	15	17	0 18	0 19	0 21	0 22	0 24	0 25
60	2	3	5	7	8	10	12	13	15	17	18	20	22	23	25	27	28	30
70	2	4	6	8	10	12	14	16	17	19	21	23	25	27	29	31	33	35
80	2	4	7	9	11	13	16	18	20	22	24	27	29	31	33	36	38	40
90	2	5	7	10	12	15	17	20	22	25	27	30	32	35	37	40	42	45
100	3	6	8	11	14	17	19	22	25	28	31	33	0 36	0 39	0 42	0 44	0 47	0 50
110	3	6	9	12	15	18	21	24	27	31	34	37	40	43	46	49	0 52	0 55
120	3	7	10	13	17	20	23	27	30	33	37	40	43	47	50	53	0 57	1 00
130	4	7	11	14	18	22	25	29	32	36	40	43	47	51	54	0 58	1 01	1 05
140	4	8	12	16	19	23	27	31	35	39	43	47	51	54	0 58	1 02	1 06	1 10
150	4	8	13	17	21	25	29	33	38	42	46	50	0 54	0 58	1 03	1 07	1 11	1 15
160	4	9	13	18	22	27	31	36	40	44	49	53	0 58	1 02	1 07	1 11	1 16	1 20
170	5	9	14	19	24	28	33	38	42	47	52	57	1 01	1 06	1 11	1 16	1 20	1 25
180	5	10	15	20	25	30	35	40	45	50	55	60	1 05	1 10	1 15	1 20	1 25	1 30

(Column heading over the time columns: Difference between the times for given date and preceding date (for east longitude) or for given date and following date (for west longitude))

Table II is for interpolating the LMT of moonrise, moonset and the Moon's meridian passage for longitude. It is entered with longitude and with the difference between the times for the given date and for the preceding date (in east longitudes) or following date (in west longitudes). The correction is normally *added* for west longitudes and *subtracted* for east longitudes, but if, as occasionally happens, the times become earlier each day instead of later, the signs of the corrections must be reversed.

INDEX TO SELECTED STARS, 2016

Name	No	Mag	SHA	Dec
			°	°
Acamar	**7**	3·2	315	S 40
Achernar	**5**	0·5	335	S 57
Acrux	**30**	1·3	173	S 63
Adhara	**19**	1·5	255	S 29
Aldebaran	**10**	0·9	291	N 17
Alioth	**32**	1·8	166	N 56
Alkaid	**34**	1·9	153	N 49
Al Na'ir	**55**	1·7	28	S 47
Alnilam	**15**	1·7	276	S 1
Alphard	**25**	2·0	218	S 9
Alphecca	**41**	2·2	126	N 27
Alpheratz	**1**	2·1	358	N 29
Altair	**51**	0·8	62	N 9
Ankaa	**2**	2·4	353	S 42
Antares	**42**	1·0	112	S 26
Arcturus	**37**	0·0	146	N 19
Atria	**43**	1·9	107	S 69
Avior	**22**	1·9	234	S 60
Bellatrix	**13**	1·6	278	N 6
Betelgeuse	**16**	Var.*	271	N 7
Canopus	**17**	−0·7	264	S 53
Capella	**12**	0·1	281	N 46
Deneb	**53**	1·3	50	N 45
Denebola	**28**	2·1	183	N 14
Diphda	**4**	2·0	349	S 18
Dubhe	**27**	1·8	194	N 62
Elnath	**14**	1·7	278	N 29
Eltanin	**47**	2·2	91	N 51
Enif	**54**	2·4	34	N 10
Fomalhaut	**56**	1·2	15	S 30
Gacrux	**31**	1·6	172	S 57
Gienah	**29**	2·6	176	S 18
Hadar	**35**	0·6	149	S 60
Hamal	**6**	2·0	328	N 24
Kaus Australis	**48**	1·9	84	S 34
Kochab	**40**	2·1	137	N 74
Markab	**57**	2·5	14	N 15
Menkar	**8**	2·5	314	N 4
Menkent	**36**	2·1	148	S 36
Miaplacidus	**24**	1·7	222	S 70
Mirfak	**9**	1·8	309	N 50
Nunki	**50**	2·0	76	S 26
Peacock	**52**	1·9	53	S 57
Pollux	**21**	1·1	243	N 28
Procyon	**20**	0·4	245	N 5
Rasalhague	**46**	2·1	96	N 13
Regulus	**26**	1·4	208	N 12
Rigel	**11**	0·1	281	S 8
Rigil Kentaurus	**38**	−0·3	140	S 61
Sabik	**44**	2·4	102	S 16
Schedar	**3**	2·2	350	N 57
Shaula	**45**	1·6	96	S 37
Sirius	**18**	−1·5	259	S 17
Spica	**33**	1·0	158	S 11
Suhail	**23**	2·2	223	S 44
Vega	**49**	0·0	81	N 39
Zubenelgenubi	**39**	2·8	137	S 16

No	Name	Mag	SHA	Dec
			°	°
1	*Alpheratz*	2·1	358	N 29
2	*Ankaa*	2·4	353	S 42
3	*Schedar*	2·2	350	N 57
4	*Diphda*	2·0	349	S 18
5	*Achernar*	0·5	335	S 57
6	*Hamal*	2·0	328	N 24
7	*Acamar*	3·2	315	S 40
8	*Menkar*	2·5	314	N 4
9	*Mirfak*	1·8	309	N 50
10	*Aldebaran*	0·9	291	N 17
11	*Rigel*	0·1	281	S 8
12	*Capella*	0·1	281	N 46
13	*Bellatrix*	1·6	278	N 6
14	*Elnath*	1·7	278	N 29
15	*Alnilam*	1·7	276	S 1
16	*Betelgeuse*	Var.*	271	N 7
17	*Canopus*	−0·7	264	S 53
18	*Sirius*	−1·5	259	S 17
19	*Adhara*	1·5	255	S 29
20	*Procyon*	0·4	245	N 5
21	*Pollux*	1·1	243	N 28
22	*Avior*	1·9	234	S 60
23	*Suhail*	2·2	223	S 44
24	*Miaplacidus*	1·7	222	S 70
25	*Alphard*	2·0	218	S 9
26	*Regulus*	1·4	208	N 12
27	*Dubhe*	1·8	194	N 62
28	*Denebola*	2·1	183	N 14
29	*Gienah*	2·6	176	S 18
30	*Acrux*	1·3	173	S 63
31	*Gacrux*	1·6	172	S 57
32	*Alioth*	1·8	166	N 56
33	*Spica*	1·0	158	S 11
34	*Alkaid*	1·9	153	N 49
35	*Hadar*	0·6	149	S 60
36	*Menkent*	2·1	148	S 36
37	*Arcturus*	0·0	146	N 19
38	*Rigil Kentaurus*	−0·3	140	S 61
39	*Zubenelgenubi*	2·8	137	S 16
40	*Kochab*	2·1	137	N 74
41	*Alphecca*	2·2	126	N 27
42	*Antares*	1·0	112	S 26
43	*Atria*	1·9	107	S 69
44	*Sabik*	2·4	102	S 16
45	*Shaula*	1·6	96	S 37
46	*Rasalhague*	2·1	96	N 13
47	*Eltanin*	2·2	91	N 51
48	*Kaus Australis*	1·9	84	S 34
49	*Vega*	0·0	81	N 39
50	*Nunki*	2·0	76	S 26
51	*Altair*	0·8	62	N 9
52	*Peacock*	1·9	53	S 57
53	*Deneb*	1·3	50	N 45
54	*Enif*	2·4	34	N 10
55	*Al Na'ir*	1·7	28	S 47
56	*Fomalhaut*	1·2	15	S 30
57	*Markab*	2·5	14	N 15

*0·1 — 1·2

ALTITUDE CORRECTION TABLES 0°–35°— MOON

App. Alt.	0°–4° Corrⁿ	5°–9° Corrⁿ	10°–14° Corrⁿ	15°–19° Corrⁿ	20°–24° Corrⁿ	25°–29° Corrⁿ	30°–34° Corrⁿ	App. Alt.
′	°	°	°	°	°	°	°	′
00	0 34·5′	5 58·2′	10 62·1′	15 62·8′	20 62·2′	25 60·8′	30 58·9′	00
10	36·5	58·5	62·2	62·8	62·2	60·8	58·8	10
20	38·3	58·7	62·2	62·8	62·1	60·7	58·8	20
30	40·0	58·9	62·3	62·8	62·1	60·7	58·7	30
40	41·5	59·1	62·3	62·8	62·0	60·6	58·6	40
50	42·9	59·3	62·4	62·7	62·0	60·6	58·5	50
00	1 44·2	6 59·5	11 62·4	16 62·7	21 62·0	26 60·5	31 58·5	00
10	45·4	59·7	62·4	62·7	61·9	60·4	58·4	10
20	46·5	59·9	62·5	62·7	61·9	60·4	58·3	20
30	47·5	60·0	62·5	62·7	61·9	60·3	58·2	30
40	48·4	60·2	62·5	62·7	61·8	60·3	58·2	40
50	49·3	60·3	62·6	62·7	61·8	60·2	58·1	50
00	2 50·1	7 60·5	12 62·6	17 62·7	22 61·7	27 60·1	32 58·0	00
10	50·8	60·6	62·6	62·6	61·7	60·1	57·9	10
20	51·5	60·7	62·6	62·6	61·6	60·0	57·8	20
30	52·2	60·9	62·7	62·6	61·6	59·9	57·8	30
40	52·8	61·0	62·7	62·6	61·6	59·9	57·7	40
50	53·4	61·1	62·7	62·6	61·5	59·8	57·6	50
00	3 53·9	8 61·2	13 62·7	18 62·5	23 61·5	28 59·7	33 57·5	00
10	54·4	61·3	62·7	62·5	61·4	59·7	57·4	10
20	54·9	61·4	62·7	62·5	61·4	59·6	57·4	20
30	55·3	61·5	62·8	62·5	61·3	59·5	57·3	30
40	55·7	61·6	62·8	62·4	61·3	59·5	57·2	40
50	56·1	61·6	62·8	62·4	61·2	59·4	57·1	50
00	4 56·4	9 61·7	14 62·8	19 62·4	24 61·2	29 59·3	34 57·0	00
10	56·8	61·8	62·8	62·4	61·1	59·3	56·9	10
20	57·1	61·9	62·8	62·3	61·1	59·2	56·9	20
30	57·4	61·9	62·8	62·3	61·0	59·1	56·8	30
40	57·7	62·0	62·8	62·3	61·0	59·1	56·7	40
50	58·0	62·1	62·8	62·2	60·9	59·0	56·6	50

HP	L	U	L	U	L	U	L	U	L	U	L	U	L	U	HP
′	′	′	′	′	′	′	′	′	′	′	′	′	′	′	′
54·0	0·3	0·9	0·3	0·9	0·4	1·0	0·5	1·1	0·6	1·2	0·7	1·3	0·9	1·5	**54·0**
54·3	0·7	1·1	0·7	1·2	0·8	1·2	0·8	1·3	0·9	1·4	1·1	1·5	1·2	1·7	**54·3**
54·6	1·1	1·4	1·1	1·4	1·1	1·4	1·2	1·5	1·3	1·6	1·4	1·7	1·5	1·8	**54·6**
54·9	1·4	1·6	1·5	1·6	1·5	1·6	1·6	1·7	1·6	1·8	1·8	1·9	1·9	2·0	**54·9**
55·2	1·8	1·8	1·8	1·8	1·9	1·8	1·9	1·9	2·0	2·0	2·1	2·1	2·2	2·2	**55·2**
55·5	2·2	2·0	2·2	2·0	2·3	2·1	2·3	2·1	2·4	2·2	2·4	2·3	2·5	2·4	**55·5**
55·8	2·6	2·2	2·6	2·2	2·6	2·3	2·7	2·3	2·7	2·4	2·8	2·4	2·9	2·5	**55·8**
56·1	3·0	2·4	3·0	2·5	3·0	2·5	3·0	2·5	3·1	2·6	3·1	2·6	3·2	2·7	**56·1**
56·4	3·3	2·7	3·4	2·7	3·4	2·7	3·4	2·7	3·4	2·8	3·5	2·8	3·5	2·9	**56·4**
56·7	3·7	2·9	3·7	2·9	3·8	2·9	3·8	2·9	3·8	3·0	3·8	3·0	3·9	3·0	**56·7**
57·0	4·1	3·1	4·1	3·1	4·1	3·1	4·1	3·1	4·2	3·2	4·2	3·2	4·2	3·2	**57·0**
57·3	4·5	3·3	4·5	3·3	4·5	3·3	4·5	3·3	4·5	3·3	4·5	3·4	4·6	3·4	**57·3**
57·6	4·9	3·5	4·9	3·5	4·9	3·5	4·9	3·5	4·9	3·5	4·9	3·5	4·9	3·6	**57·6**
57·9	5·3	3·8	5·3	3·8	5·2	3·8	5·2	3·7	5·2	3·7	5·2	3·7	5·2	3·7	**57·9**
58·2	5·6	4·0	5·6	4·0	5·6	4·0	5·6	4·0	5·6	3·9	5·6	3·9	5·6	3·9	**58·2**
58·5	6·0	4·2	6·0	4·2	6·0	4·2	6·0	4·2	6·0	4·1	5·9	4·1	5·9	4·1	**58·5**
58·8	6·4	4·4	6·4	4·4	6·4	4·4	6·3	4·4	6·3	4·3	6·3	4·3	6·2	4·2	**58·8**
59·1	6·8	4·6	6·8	4·6	6·7	4·6	6·7	4·6	6·7	4·5	6·6	4·5	6·6	4·4	**59·1**
59·4	7·2	4·8	7·1	4·8	7·1	4·8	7·1	4·8	7·0	4·7	7·0	4·7	6·9	4·6	**59·4**
59·7	7·5	5·1	7·5	5·0	7·5	5·0	7·5	5·0	7·4	4·9	7·3	4·8	7·2	4·8	**59·7**
60·0	7·9	5·3	7·9	5·3	7·9	5·2	7·8	5·2	7·8	5·1	7·7	5·0	7·6	4·9	**60·0**
60·3	8·3	5·5	8·3	5·5	8·2	5·4	8·2	5·4	8·1	5·3	8·0	5·2	7·9	5·1	**60·3**
60·6	8·7	5·7	8·7	5·7	8·6	5·7	8·6	5·6	8·5	5·5	8·4	5·4	8·2	5·3	**60·6**
60·9	9·1	5·9	9·0	5·9	9·0	5·9	8·9	5·8	8·8	5·7	8·7	5·6	8·6	5·4	**60·9**
61·2	9·5	6·2	9·4	6·1	9·4	6·1	9·3	6·0	9·2	5·9	9·1	5·8	8·9	5·6	**61·2**
61·5	9·8	6·4	9·8	6·3	9·7	6·3	9·7	6·2	9·5	6·1	9·4	5·9	9·2	5·8	**61·5**

DIP

Ht. of Eye	Corrⁿ	Ht. of Eye	Ht. of Eye	Corrⁿ	Ht. of Eye
m		ft.	m		ft.
2·4		8·0	9·5		31·5
	−2·8′			−5·5′	
2·6		8·6	9·9		32·7
	−2·9			−5·6	
2·8		9·2	10·3		33·9
	−3·0			−5·7	
3·0		9·8	10·6		35·1
	−3·1			−5·8	
3·2		10·5	11·0		36·3
	−3·2			−5·9	
3·4		11·2	11·4		37·6
	−3·3			−6·0	
3·6		11·9	11·8		38·9
	−3·4			−6·1	
3·8		12·6	12·2		40·1
	−3·5			−6·2	
4·0		13·3	12·6		41·5
	−3·6			−6·3	
4·3		14·1	13·0		42·8
	−3·7			−6·4	
4·5		14·9	13·4		44·2
	−3·8			−6·5	
4·7		15·7	13·8		45·5
	−3·9			−6·6	
5·0		16·5	14·2		46·9
	−4·0			−6·7	
5·2		17·4	14·7		48·4
	−4·1			−6·8	
5·5		18·3	15·1		49·8
	−4·2			−6·9	
5·8		19·1	15·5		51·3
	−4·3			−7·0	
6·1		20·1	16·0		52·8
	−4·4			−7·1	
6·3		21·0	16·5		54·3
	−4·5			−7·2	
6·6		22·0	16·9		55·8
	−4·6			−7·3	
6·9		22·9	17·4		57·4
	−4·7			−7·4	
7·2		23·9	17·9		58·9
	−4·8			−7·5	
7·5		24·9	18·4		60·5
	−4·9			−7·6	
7·9		26·0	18·8		62·1
	−5·0			−7·7	
8·2		27·1	19·3		63·8
	−5·1			−7·8	
8·5		28·1	19·8		65·4
	−5·2			−7·9	
8·8		29·2	20·4		67·1
	−5·3			−8·0	
9·2		30·4	20·9		68·8
	−5·4			−8·1	
9·5		31·5	21·4		70·5

MOON CORRECTION TABLE

The correction is in two parts; the first correction is taken from the upper part of the table with argument apparent altitude, and the second from the lower part, with argument HP, in the same column as that from which the first correction was taken. Separate corrections are given in the lower part for lower (L) and upper(U) limbs. All corrections are to be **added** to apparent altitude, *but 30′ is to be subtracted from the altitude of the upper limb*.

For corrections for pressure and temperature see page A4.

For bubble sextant observations ignore dip, take the mean of upper and lower limb corrections and subtract 15′ from the altitude.

App. Alt. = Apparent altitude = Sextant altitude corrected for index error and dip.

ALTITUDE CORRECTION TABLES 35°–90°— MOON

App. Alt.	35°–39° Corrⁿ	40°–44° Corrⁿ	45°–49° Corrⁿ	50°–54° Corrⁿ	55°–59° Corrⁿ	60°–64° Corrⁿ	65°–69° Corrⁿ	70°–74° Corrⁿ	75°–79° Corrⁿ	80°–84° Corrⁿ	85°–89° Corrⁿ	App. Alt.
′	° ′	° ′	° ′	° ′	° ′	° ′	° ′	° ′	° ′	° ′	° ′	′
00	35 56·5	40 53·7	45 50·5	50 46·9	55 43·1	60 38·9	65 34·6	70 30·0	75 25·3	80 20·5	85 15·6	00
10	56·4	53·6	50·4	46·8	42·9	38·8	34·4	29·9	25·2	20·4	15·5	10
20	56·3	53·5	50·2	46·7	42·8	38·7	34·3	29·7	25·0	20·2	15·3	20
30	56·2	53·4	50·1	46·5	42·7	38·5	34·1	29·6	24·9	20·0	15·1	30
40	56·2	53·3	50·0	46·4	42·5	38·4	34·0	29·4	24·7	19·9	15·0	40
50	56·1	53·2	49·9	46·3	42·4	38·2	33·8	29·3	24·5	19·7	14·8	50
00	36 56·0	41 53·1	46 49·8	51 46·2	56 42·3	61 38·1	66 33·7	71 29·1	76 24·4	81 19·6	86 14·6	00
10	55·9	53·0	49·7	46·0	42·1	37·9	33·5	29·0	24·2	19·4	14·5	10
20	55·8	52·9	49·5	45·9	42·0	37·8	33·4	28·8	24·1	19·2	14·3	20
30	55·7	52·8	49·4	45·8	41·9	37·7	33·2	28·7	23·9	19·1	14·2	30
40	55·6	52·6	49·3	45·7	41·7	37·5	33·1	28·5	23·8	18·9	14·0	40
50	55·5	52·5	49·2	45·5	41·6	37·4	32·9	28·3	23·6	18·7	13·8	50
00	37 55·4	42 52·4	47 49·1	52 45·4	57 41·4	62 37·2	67 32·8	72 28·2	77 23·4	82 18·6	87 13·7	00
10	55·3	52·3	49·0	45·3	41·3	37·1	32·6	28·0	23·3	18·4	13·5	10
20	55·2	52·2	48·8	45·2	41·2	36·9	32·5	27·9	23·1	18·2	13·3	20
30	55·1	52·1	48·7	45·0	41·0	36·8	32·3	27·7	22·9	18·1	13·2	30
40	55·0	52·0	48·6	44·9	40·9	36·6	32·2	27·6	22·8	17·9	13·0	40
50	55·0	51·9	48·5	44·8	40·8	36·5	32·0	27·4	22·6	17·8	12·8	50
00	38 54·9	43 51·8	48 48·4	53 44·6	58 40·6	63 36·4	68 31·9	73 27·2	78 22·5	83 17·6	88 12·7	00
10	54·8	51·7	48·3	44·5	40·5	36·2	31·7	27·1	22·3	17·4	12·5	10
20	54·7	51·6	48·1	44·4	40·3	36·1	31·6	26·9	22·1	17·3	12·3	20
30	54·6	51·5	48·0	44·2	40·2	35·9	31·4	26·8	22·0	17·1	12·2	30
40	54·5	51·4	47·9	44·1	40·1	35·8	31·3	26·6	21·8	16·9	12·0	40
50	54·4	51·2	47·8	44·0	39·9	35·6	31·1	26·5	21·7	16·8	11·8	50
00	39 54·3	44 51·1	49 47·7	54 43·9	59 39·8	64 35·5	69 31·0	74 26·3	79 21·5	84 16·6	89 11·7	00
10	54·2	51·0	47·5	43·7	39·6	35·3	30·8	26·1	21·3	16·4	11·5	10
20	54·1	50·9	47·4	43·6	39·5	35·2	30·7	26·0	21·2	16·3	11·4	20
30	54·0	50·8	47·3	43·5	39·4	35·0	30·5	25·8	21·0	16·1	11·2	30
40	53·9	50·7	47·2	43·3	39·2	34·9	30·4	25·7	20·9	16·0	11·0	40
50	53·8	50·6	47·0	43·2	39·1	34·7	30·2	25·5	20·7	15·8	10·9	50

HP	L	U	L	U	L	U	L	U	L	U	L	U	L	U	L	U	L	U	L	U	L	U	HP
′	′	′	′	′	′	′	′	′	′	′	′	′	′	′	′	′	′	′	′	′	′	′	′
54·0	1·1	1·7	1·3	1·9	1·5	2·1	1·7	2·4	2·0	2·6	2·3	2·9	2·6	3·2	2·9	3·5	3·2	3·8	3·5	4·1	3·8	4·5	54·0
54·3	1·4	1·8	1·6	2·0	1·8	2·2	2·0	2·5	2·2	2·7	2·5	3·0	2·8	3·2	3·1	3·5	3·3	3·8	3·6	4·1	3·9	4·4	54·3
54·6	1·7	2·0	1·9	2·2	2·1	2·4	2·3	2·6	2·5	2·8	2·7	3·0	3·0	3·3	3·2	3·5	3·5	3·8	3·8	4·0	4·0	4·3	54·6
54·9	2·0	2·2	2·2	2·3	2·3	2·5	2·5	2·7	2·7	2·9	2·9	3·1	3·2	3·3	3·4	3·5	3·6	3·8	3·9	4·0	4·1	4·3	54·9
55·2	2·3	2·3	2·5	2·4	2·6	2·6	2·8	2·8	3·0	2·9	3·2	3·1	3·4	3·3	3·6	3·5	3·8	3·7	4·0	4·0	4·2	4·2	55·2
55·5	2·7	2·5	2·8	2·6	2·9	2·7	3·1	2·9	3·2	3·0	3·4	3·2	3·6	3·4	3·7	3·5	3·9	3·7	4·1	3·9	4·3	4·1	55·5
55·8	3·0	2·6	3·1	2·7	3·2	2·8	3·3	3·0	3·5	3·1	3·6	3·3	3·8	3·4	3·9	3·6	4·1	3·7	4·2	3·9	4·4	4·0	55·8
56·1	3·3	2·8	3·4	2·9	3·5	3·0	3·6	3·1	3·7	3·2	3·8	3·3	4·0	3·4	4·1	3·6	4·2	3·7	4·4	3·8	4·5	4·0	56·1
56·4	3·6	2·9	3·7	3·0	3·8	3·1	3·9	3·2	3·9	3·3	4·0	3·4	4·1	3·5	4·3	3·6	4·4	3·7	4·5	3·8	4·6	3·9	56·4
56·7	3·9	3·1	4·0	3·1	4·1	3·2	4·1	3·3	4·2	3·3	4·3	3·4	4·3	3·5	4·4	3·6	4·5	3·7	4·6	3·8	4·7	3·8	56·7
57·0	4·3	3·2	4·3	3·3	4·3	3·3	4·4	3·4	4·4	3·4	4·5	3·5	4·5	3·5	4·6	3·6	4·7	3·6	4·7	3·7	4·8	3·8	57·0
57·3	4·6	3·4	4·6	3·4	4·6	3·4	4·6	3·5	4·7	3·5	4·7	3·5	4·7	3·6	4·8	3·6	4·8	3·6	4·8	3·7	4·9	3·7	57·3
57·6	4·9	3·6	4·9	3·6	4·9	3·6	4·9	3·6	4·9	3·6	4·9	3·6	4·9	3·6	4·9	3·6	5·0	3·6	5·0	3·6	5·0	3·6	57·6
57·9	5·2	3·7	5·2	3·7	5·2	3·7	5·2	3·7	5·2	3·7	5·1	3·6	5·1	3·6	5·1	3·6	5·1	3·6	5·1	3·6	5·1	3·6	57·9
58·2	5·5	3·9	5·5	3·8	5·5	3·8	5·4	3·8	5·4	3·7	5·4	3·7	5·3	3·7	5·3	3·6	5·2	3·6	5·2	3·5	5·2	3·5	58·2
58·5	5·9	4·0	5·8	4·0	5·8	3·9	5·7	3·9	5·6	3·8	5·6	3·8	5·5	3·7	5·5	3·6	5·4	3·6	5·3	3·5	5·3	3·4	58·5
58·8	6·2	4·2	6·1	4·1	6·0	4·1	6·0	4·0	5·9	3·9	5·8	3·8	5·7	3·7	5·6	3·6	5·5	3·5	5·4	3·5	5·3	3·4	58·8
59·1	6·5	4·3	6·4	4·3	6·3	4·2	6·2	4·1	6·1	4·0	6·0	3·9	5·9	3·8	5·8	3·6	5·7	3·5	5·6	3·4	5·4	3·3	59·1
59·4	6·8	4·5	6·7	4·4	6·6	4·3	6·5	4·2	6·4	4·1	6·2	3·9	6·1	3·8	6·0	3·7	5·8	3·5	5·7	3·4	5·5	3·2	59·4
59·7	7·1	4·7	7·0	4·5	6·9	4·4	6·8	4·3	6·6	4·1	6·5	4·0	6·3	3·8	6·1	3·7	6·0	3·5	5·8	3·3	5·6	3·2	59·7
60·0	7·5	4·8	7·3	4·7	7·2	4·5	7·0	4·4	6·9	4·2	6·7	4·0	6·5	3·9	6·3	3·7	6·1	3·5	5·9	3·3	5·7	3·1	60·0
60·3	7·8	5·0	7·6	4·8	7·5	4·7	7·3	4·5	7·1	4·3	6·9	4·1	6·7	3·9	6·5	3·7	6·3	3·5	6·0	3·2	5·8	3·0	60·3
60·6	8·1	5·1	7·9	5·0	7·7	4·8	7·6	4·6	7·3	4·4	7·1	4·2	6·9	3·9	6·7	3·7	6·4	3·4	6·2	3·2	5·9	2·9	60·6
60·9	8·4	5·3	8·2	5·1	8·0	4·9	7·8	4·7	7·6	4·5	7·3	4·2	7·1	4·0	6·8	3·7	6·6	3·4	6·3	3·2	6·0	2·9	60·9
61·2	8·7	5·4	8·5	5·2	8·3	5·0	8·1	4·8	7·8	4·5	7·6	4·3	7·3	4·0	7·0	3·7	6·7	3·4	6·4	3·1	6·1	2·8	61·2
61·5	9·1	5·6	8·8	5·4	8·6	5·1	8·3	4·9	8·1	4·6	7·8	4·3	7·5	4·0	7·2	3·7	6·9	3·4	6·5	3·1	6·2	2·7	61·5

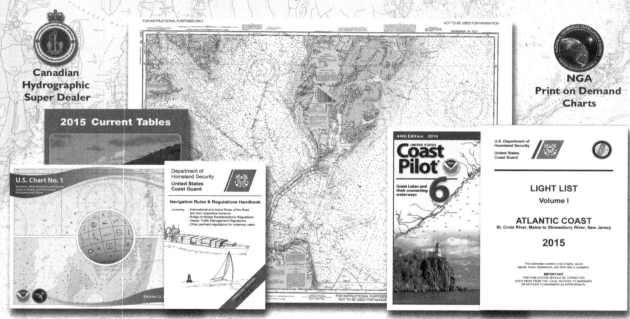

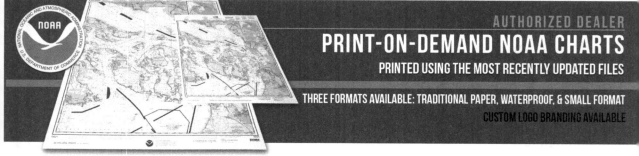

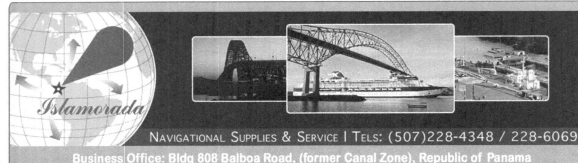

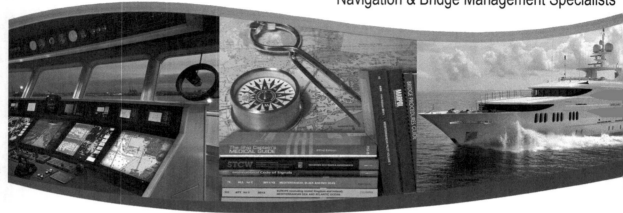